PRESENTED
TO

_____

BY

_____

ON

_____

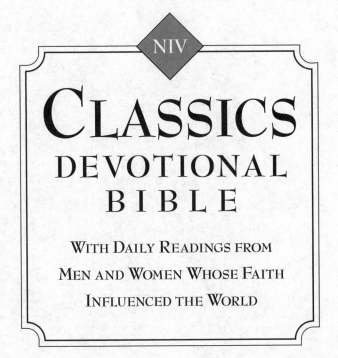

NIV

CLASSICS
DEVOTIONAL
BIBLE

WITH DAILY READINGS FROM
MEN AND WOMEN WHOSE FAITH
INFLUENCED THE WORLD

NIV

CLASSICS
DEVOTIONAL
BIBLE

WITH DAILY READINGS FROM
MEN AND WOMEN WHOSE FAITH
INFLUENCED THE WORLD

NEW INTERNATIONAL VERSION

Zondervan Publishing House
Grand Rapids, Michigan 49530, U.S.A.

TABLE OF CONTENTS

INTRODUCTION

elcome to the *NIV Classics Devotional Bible!* If you are like most people today, your life is full—perhaps even too full. With so many things to do and so many demands on your time, finding time to read and reflect on the Bible can be difficult at times. The *NIV Classics Devotional Bible* gives you a convenient Bible reading/devotional plan. Drawing from the writings of nearly 2000 years of church history, the *NIV Classics Devotional Bible* offers a wonderful selection of devotions that will take you into the thoughts of well-known Christian authors, thinkers, theologians, hymn writers, poets, and pastors. We earnestly hope these meditations will provide you with new perspective and inspiration.

Even though the Bible was written approximately 2000 years ago, it contains themes not unlike today—struggling between good and evil, dealing with suffering and loss, celebrating in laughter and joy, seeing God's promises fulfilled. As you read, you will discover how relevant God's Word is to your life today! Several features make the *NIV Classics Devotional Bible* an exceptional devotional guide:

THE BIBLE

The *NIV Classics Devotional Bible* features the complete text of the New International Version of the Bible. The NIV's accuracy and readability make it today's most popular modern translation.

THE DEVOTIONS

Your *NIV Classics Devotional Bible* contains devotions for Monday through Friday, plus special devotions for every weekend. This devotional Bible contains 312 devotions—one for every weekday and weekend of the year. Each devotion is placed close to the Scripture reading for that day, encouraging you to read the devotion and the related Bible verses. The top of each devotion provides both a "Verse" and a "Passage." The subject of each devotion is tied to the designated Scripture verse. And the passage provides the context, or Scripture that surrounds the verse.

Regardless of what day of the week you begin, simply turn to a devotion for that day. For the next day, look to the bottom of the devotion for the page number of the next day's devotion. For example, if you start on a Monday, you could turn to the first devotion in the book of Genesis. Glance at the bottom of Monday's devotion and you will see the page number for Tuesday's devotion—and so on as you keep reading on through Friday.

Friday's devotion will direct you to a "Weekend." The bottom of the "Weekend" will send you to the next Monday devotion. As you follow this format, you will find yourself well on your way—through a year of spending precious time in God's Word and growing closer to him.

THE BOOK INTRODUCTIONS

At the beginning of each book of the Bible, you will find an interesting and informative introduction. These introductions succinctly highlight the practical themes of each book. Each introduction also provides you with interesting facts and helpful background, as well as a practical application to encourage you as you read that particular book and the devotions within it.

READING PLANS

Do you need a structure to follow for reading your Bible in a disciplined way? Several reading plans (see page 1541) should provide just what you need, including ways to read the entire Bible.

Now that you've become acquainted with your *NIV Classics Devotional Bible*, open it and use it every day. You will never be sorry you took the time.

AUTHOR BIOGRAPHIES

You will very likely recognize many of the names of the people who contributed to the *NIV Classics Devotional Bible*. The detailed author biographies, found on page 1521, provide interesting and helpful information about each author, as well as a list of the pages where the author's devotion appears.

SUBJECT INDEX

At the back of your *NIV Classics Devotional Bible*, on page 1518, you'll find a guide for locating information within this Bible. If you're looking for Biblical perspectives on creation, or faith, or God's love, or prayer, or peace, or truth, or worship, or death, or any of over 175 other topics, this is the place to find it.

SUMMARY OF TIME ERAS

hen Jesus Christ gathered his disciples at Cesarea Phillipi, he spoke about an event of primary importance to the accomplishment of God's eternal purpose. There Jesus said, "I will build my church" (Matthew 16:18). During the brief period of Jesus' ministry on earth, he spoke of three essential prophecies. First, he spoke of his own death and resurrection. Second, he prophesied about his future return to earth with all of its tumult and glory. And third, he spoke of the building of the church. The first he fully accomplished with all of its profound effect on human history and individual lives. The second is yet to come. And the third is in process today, with each believer involved in some way with Christ in this work.

Of course, the building of the church has not been without its tumult as well. In fact, like all construction projects, the process of building the church has caused quite a disturbance. Church history can be read both as a document of this upheaval and as a record of the loving kindness and patience of the purposeful God. Scripture assures, however, that "Christ loved the church and gave himself up for her to make her holy, cleansing her by the washing with water through the word, and to present her to himself as a radiant church, without stain or wrinkle or any other blemish, but holy and blameless" (Ephesians 5:25–27). These verses richly describe the church's future.

The apostle Paul fully embraced the demanding work of building the church. "By the grace God has given me," he wrote, "I laid a foundation as an expert builder" (1 Corinthians 3:10). Then he seriously cautions those who would follow to build on the foundation "which is Jesus Christ" (1 Corinthians 3:11). His warning echoes through 1900 years of history: "Each one should be careful how he builds" (v. 10). And so the age of the church began. While some built with gold, silver, and costly stones, others built with wood, hay, and straw (v. 12). And when Christ returns, everyone's "work will be shown for what it is, because the Day will bring it to light" (v. 13).

In the meantime the church is the repository of the documents, writings, and records of some of the laborers who have gone before. The *Classics Devotional Bible* is a selection of these writings placed alongside the text of the Bible. This allows the reader to find the relevance of these works to the record of Scripture and enjoy both for the sake of the building up of the church.

While reading these selections, the reader can trace the path of church history through five main eras of the Christian church. The following briefly charts this path using authors and sources—most of which are included in this Bible—for milestones and landmarks along the way.

100   500

THE EARLY CHURCH ERA

Little but legend has remained of the history and fate of Christ's original disciples. After the Lord's crucifixion and resurrection, the defining event of the first century, as far as the church is concerned, was the destruction of Jerusalem by the Roman general Titus in A.D. 70. At that time the believers joined the Jews in their dispersal and the church at Jerusalem was no more. Any records or artifacts of the church's first years were burned by the Romans with the rest of the city. The surviving founders of that inaugural church were absorbed into the ancient world, and the single Christian church composed predominately of Jews disappeared. This was followed by 400 to 500 years of organizational, liturgical, and theological development.

The second generation of Christians immediately met opposition in various arenas. Written between A.D. 70 and 100, *The Epistle of Barnabas* attempts to show Christ in types and figures of the Old Testament. In its stridently polemical attack on Judaism, it succeeds in finding convincing testimonies for the Christian faith in the Old Testament. Ignatius of Antioch (d. c. 116) encountered a different source of conflict: Roman paganism. He was condemned to be devoured by wild beasts during the reign of the Roman emperor Trajan. While traveling to his death in Rome, Ignatius wrote seven letters that show he wanted nothing to stand in the way of his martyrdom. He is the prototypical martyr. His letters also show the development of early church structure, speak of the Virgin Birth of Jesus, emphasize the physical resurrection of Christ, and describe the church as *catholic* in reference to her universal quality. The first theological writer for the church was Irenaeus of Lyons (c. 175–195) who lived in southern France. The title of his primary work, *Against Heresies*, indicates his field of work. While refuting the gnostic heresies, Irenaeus cited the Old Testament, the four gospels, and other apostolic writings as the canon of Scripture. He also affirmed both creation and redemption as acts of God.

While wrestling with influences that threatened the young church, these and many other individuals developed the beliefs and practices that are still the structural constitution of the church today. Soon these began to be codified for the benefit of all the believers. The profession of faith called the *Athanasian Creed* was named after Athanasius (c. 295–373). This great defender of the faith strove against the teaching of Arius who advocated that Christ was not eternal but was created by the Father. This view threatened to turn the faith into a philosophy mixed with pagan thought. In A.D. 325 Emperor Constantine called the Council of Nicea to settle this issue. In *The Three Orations against the Arians* (c. 335), Athanasius emphasized the necessity for the Word to be as eternal as God if he was to form the divine image in man. The creed named for him is composed of two parts devoted respectively to the doctrines of the Trinity and Incarnation. Adherence to these, it declares, is necessary for salvation.

Other early documents include *The Didache*, a summary of moral principles, instructions on the organization of Christian communities, and rules on worship. It contains the oldest recorded eucharistic prayers, and orders on baptism, fasting, prayer, as well as the treatment of bishops, deacons, and prophets. *The Epistle to Diognetus,* a document from the second or third century, explains why paganism and Judaism cannot be accepted, describes Christians as the soul of the world, and declares that Christianity is the unique revelation of God and of God's love.

No event or precise date formally ends the church's early era, though one shining individual illuminates the transition to medieval times—Augustine of Hippo (354–430). This son of a pagan father and Christian mother in North Africa is a figure of major importance to the church. In his *Confessions* (c. 397) he presents a Biblical understanding of a person's life under grace. In his *City of God* (c. 413–26) he is the first to give a Biblical view of history, time, and the state. He established the doctrine of the church, gave a clear statement concerning the person of Christ, and made the grace of God a major theme of theology in the West.

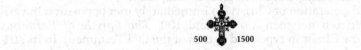

500 ✠ 1500

THE MEDIEVAL ERA

The centuries between approximately A.D. 500 and the commencement of the Protestant Reformation are frequently referred to as the Dark Ages. But for the church of God, they were anything but dark. In reality, some of the brightest minds of the day applied themselves to her theological and ecclesiastical advancement. And had it not been for the cache of documents protected within the walls of European and Middle Eastern monasteries, and the diligence of monastic scholars and copyists, the treasury of knowledge, art, and philosophy of the classical ages would have perished. It is difficult for Protestants to appreciate this era. Indeed the church's testimony did slowly dim as these centuries wore on and the ecclesiastical bushel basket of Romanism descended over her lamp. Yet we must not forget that it was at this time that the monk Anselm of Canterbury (c. 1033–1109) asked *and answered* the question posed by his most famous work: *Why Did God Become Man?* It was Benedict of Nursia (c. 480–c. 547) who wrote the *Benedictine Rule,* which not only established a balanced way of life for the monasteries that were to prove so vital to the preservation of human culture, it also became a basis of organizational thought until modern times. Another leading monk, Bernard of Clairvaux (1090–1153), made the act of loving God the foundation of his life and teaching. How precious it is still to find this tendency in a believer. It is he who wrote our beloved hymn "Jesus the very thought of thee with sweetness fills my soul." Bernard also challenged Christians to lead lives of true devotion to God and was a forerunner to our Reformers. The philosopher, theologian, and mystic Bonaventura (1221–1274) was more akin in thought to Augustine and the Protestant Reformers than he was to his contemporaries in Rome.

Not all Reformers were Protestant, but it was the Protestants who were most successful. The Spanish poet and monk John of the Cross (1542–1591) suffered greatly with his benefactor Teresa of Avila (1515–1582) for joining her in attempting to reform the monastic system. The result was some of the world's great poetic literature and the record of a true Christian mystic. The Dutch writer, scholar, and Renaissance intellectual Desiderius Erasmus

(c. 1466–1536) wrote, "It has long been my cherished wish to cleanse the Lord's temple of barbarous ignorance and to adorn it with treasures from afar, such as may kindle in generous hearts a warm love for the Scriptures." The great work of his life was an edition of the Greek New Testament text (1516) which became a touchstone for successive generations of scholars and a source for Bible translations in the common vernacular. These translations went far to fulfill the cherished wishes of Erasmus. Two women must also be mentioned: Julian of Norwich (c. 1342–c. 1413), whose *Sixteen Revelations of Divine Love* became the first book to be published in English by a female author; and Catherine of Siena (1347–1380), an illiterate Florentine nun who worked for ecclesiastical reform and became prominent among the church's mystics.

Readers of history know that the medieval era was a difficult time in the human drama. And it was at this time that the full weight of the hope of humanity was carried by the Christian church.

1500   1700

THE REFORMATION ERA

If the earth's gravity had shifted as much as the church's theology did during the Reformation, the globe may have spun off its axis. Combine this with the political, cultural, and social changes that were simultaneously operating in Europe and the result is a true revolution.

In fact the religious, political, cultural, and social realms were quite interconnected. This is seen clearly in the person of John Calvin (1509–1564), the French Protestant Reformer who labored in Geneva, Switzerland. His major work, *Institutes of the Christian Religion*, is considered one of the most influential in world literature. While laboring to organize evangelical churches, Calvin developed a highly adaptable model of church government. Meanwhile, social institutions were deteriorating. Many new institutions developed under the influence of Calvin's model and his "presbyterian" example even extended to influence modern democratic political theory. When John Calvin's contemporary, the Biblical translator, religious reformer, and writer William Tyndale (c. 1492–1536), left England to commence his work he said to a learned man, "If God spare my life, ere many years I will cause a boy that driveth the plough shall know more of the Scripture than thou dost." Considering that the Bible had been exclusively in a Latin translation for 1000 years and that Tyndale's proverbial ploughboy was an illiterate, the fact that Tyndale succeeded reveals not only his genius but also the harvest of cultural transformation caused by his English translation of the Bible. It is not commonly known that many of the finest passages of the King James Version of the Bible were taken unchanged from Tyndale's seminal work. These passages are treasures of the English language to this day.

These Reformers were struggling to free the human spirit from the bondage of religious darkness, but antiquated social systems and illiteracy were being overthrown as well. Simultaneously, the political world was in upheaval while emerging from its dominance by the church at Rome. Thomas Cranmer (1489–1556) was Archbishop of Canterbury and a leader of the English Reformation. As such he became embroiled in the maneuvers of Henry VIII to rid England of the influence of Rome. Cranmer himself renounced allegiance to the pope, directed that the pope's name be erased from every prayer book in England, and pronounced the king of England head of the English church. Cranmer was a brilliant editor, translator, and composer of prayers and formulae. His labor produced *The Book of Common Prayer* (1548), which is in use to this day in churches of the Anglican Communion. Political and religious shifts in England caused Cranmer to be condemned as a heretic; thus he joined the many martyrs of his time when he was burned at the stake in 1556.

An example of the quality of the people God enlisted to accomplish the Church's reformation is Blaise Pascal (1623–1662), one of the great minds in Western intellectual history. A Frenchman, Pascal was an eminent mathematician and physicist and one of the greatest mystical writers in Christian literature. At 19 he invented the first practical calculating machine. Later he verified the theory of atmospheric pressure and formulated the mathematical theory of probability, a fundamental element of modern theoretical physics. Pascal was an adherent of the Roman Catholic reform movement known as Jansenism. His *Provincial Letters* (1657), a classic in the literature of irony and satire, demanded a reemphasis on Augustine's doctrine of grace within the Catholic church. Yet God also gave the church John Bunyan (1628–1688), the impoverished son of a tinker who authored *The Pilgrim's Progress* while in prison. One of the most famous religious allegories in the English language, *The Pilgrim's Progress* became the most widely read book in English after the Bible.

Another descendant of peasants grew up to be perhaps the most crucial figure in modern European history—Martin Luther of Germany (1483–1546). We have noted that there were reform-minded individuals working in the church for centuries. But this German theologian appeared at the confluence of the flow of history to directly initiate the Protestant Reformation and thereby influence politics, economics, education, and language as well. Luther held the chair of Biblical theology at University of Wittenberg in 1512. This was his final station in his journey toward understanding that God's free grace is the unique source of salvation. On October 31, 1517, he published his Ninety-five Theses, which opposed certain beliefs and practices of the Catholic church. With Luther as its leader and innovator, the Reformation burst forth. Luther was a preacher, professor, theologian, linguist, educator, and political theorist. God places his treasure in earthen vessels and Martin Luther was the gifted and versatile man of the hour chosen to usher in a truly new era in human history.

1700   1900

THE POST-REFORMATION ERA

When the English mystic poet William Blake (1757–1827) wrote, "I will not cease from Mental Fight,/Nor shall my Sword sleep in my hand/Till we have built Jerusalem/In England's green and pleasant Land," he may indeed have been prophesying of the hopes of the post-Reformers. These individuals toiled to establish the truth of the gospel in their homelands and also to spread it to the entire world. They were preachers, missionaries, hymn writers, and revivalists. They included William Law (1688–1761), a preacher of the Church of England whose book *A Serious Call to a Devout and Holy Life* on Christian ethics and mysticism influenced John Wesley and George Whitefield; the iconoclast George Fox (1624–1691), founder of the Society of Friends who stressed the priesthood of all believers and advocated a simple life-style; and Jonathan Edwards (1703–1758), who presided over the revival known as the Great Awakening, which engulfed all New England.

Hymns like "Sweet Hour of Prayer" by Fanny Crosby (1820–1915), "When I Survey the Wondrous Cross" by Issac Watts (1674–1748), "For the Bread and For the Wine" by Horatius Bonar (1808–1889), and "In The Deep, Deep Winter" by Christina Rossetti (1830–1894), and the rich African-American spirituals still ring in our churches and feed our devotion to God. Native-Americans are indebted to the sacrifice of missionary David Brainerd (1718–1747). The faithful in China still stand on the foundation laid by James Hudson Taylor (1832–1905) and the China Inland Mission. And the world is a far better place for the labor of William Booth (1829–1912) and his Salvation Army. The Quaker John Woolman (1720–1772) and the former slaves Frederick Douglass (1817–1895) and Sojourner Truth (c. 1797–1883) insisted that the church heed her Scriptures and her conscience in the fight for the abolition of slavery.

The great lights of this era, like John Wesley (1703–1791), George Whitefield (1714–1770), and Charles H. Spurgeon (1834–1892), must share their place on history's pages with countless other saints. The sacrifices of these lesser-known servants of God salted and preserved the earth and its inhabitants by spreading and establishing the truth of the gospel of Jesus Christ as the unique source of salvation and the strengthening fiber of the human race.

1900   PRESENT

THE MODERN ERA

As we pass into the next millennium, we leave behind a century marked by two world wars, which all the world hopes never to repeat. Oswald Chambers (1874–1917), who labored for the Lord at the huge encampment of the Mediterranean Expeditionary Force at Zeitoun, Egypt, during World War I, sought to minister the hope of the message of Jesus Christ "in the full blaze of the intellectual problems and actual difficulties of the times in which we live." Modern times have posed this challenge to all Christians. This century has seen Karl Barth (1886–1968), the Swiss theologian teacher and writer who was driven to reconsider his liberal theological training when his teachers supported German militarism. He challenged German National Socialism with a series of pamphlets entitled *Theological Existence Today* and was forced to flee Germany in 1935. We witnessed the testimony of Dietrich Bonhoeffer (1906–1945), who refused to cooperate with Hitler's interference in church affairs. With Barth and others, he helped found the Confessing Church in Germany, began an illegal seminary, and early-on identified himself with the resistance against Nazism. As a result this German theologian was arrested and became a modern Christian martyr.

Peter Marshall (1902–1949), a Scottish emigrant to America, rose up to serve as chaplain to the United States Senate; and the Roman Catholic convert Thomas Merton (1915–1968) wrote eloquently about modern society from behind the walls of a Trappist monastery.

Our age has been filled with writers, preachers, and scholars, like F. F. Bruce (1910–990), the Scotsman who was the preeminent evangelical scholar of the post-World War II era; Francis Schaeffer (1912–1984), who together with his wife Edith founded an international study and ministry community in the Swiss Alps and wrote a total of 23 books; and Evelyn Underhill (1875–1941), whose classic evaluation of spirituality, *Mysticism: A Study in the Nature and Development of Man's Spiritual Consciousness*, examined the church from the first through the nineteenth centuries.

But our era has also witnessed the contributions of activists as well. Preeminent among these was Martin Luther King, Jr. (1929–1968), the son of a Baptist minister who was catapulted into national prominence as a leader for civil rights. He led a massive civil rights campaign, organized drives for black voter registration, desegregation, and better education and housing throughout the South. Dag Hammarskjöld (1905–61), the Swedish economist and diplomat, was elected secretary-general of the United Nations and was posthumously awarded the 1961 Nobel Peace Prize. His legacy to the church and the world is his book of meditations, *Markings*. And William Temple (1881–1944) effectively lead the Anglican Communion with a passionate concern for national and social righteousness.

The church of God is a steadfast presence in a capricious world. As this century marred by conflict closes, we hope for more than peace. We hope for Jesus Christ, the Prince of Peace, and pray that he will continue the cleansing of his church "by the washing with water through the word, and to present her to himself as a radiant church, without stain or wrinkle or any other blemish, but holy and blameless" (Ephesians 5:26–27).

PREFACE

HE NEW INTERNATIONAL VERSION is a completely new translation of the Holy Bible made by over a hundred scholars working directly from the best available Hebrew, Aramaic and Greek texts. It had its beginning in 1965 when, after several years of exploratory study by committees from the Christian Reformed Church and the National Association of Evangelicals, a group of scholars met at Palos Heights, Illinois, and concurred in the need for a new translation of the Bible in contemporary English. This group, though not made up of official church representatives, was transdenominational. Its conclusion was endorsed by a large number of leaders from many denominations who met in Chicago in 1966.

Responsibility for the new version was delegated by the Palos Heights group to a self-governing body of fifteen, the Committee on Bible Translation, composed for the most part of biblical scholars from colleges, universities and seminaries. In 1967 the New York Bible Society (now the International Bible Society) generously undertook the financial sponsorship of the project—a sponsorship that made it possible to enlist the help of many distinguished scholars. The fact that participants from the United States, Great Britain, Canada, Australia and New Zealand worked together gave the project its international scope. That they were from many denominations—including Anglican, Assemblies of God, Baptist, Brethren, Christian Reformed, Church of Christ, Evangelical Free, Lutheran, Mennonite, Methodist, Nazarene, Presbyterian, Wesleyan and other churches—helped to safeguard the translation from sectarian bias.

How it was made helps to give the New International Version its distinctiveness. The translation of each book was assigned to a team of scholars. Next, one of the Intermediate Editorial Committees revised the initial translation, with constant reference to the Hebrew, Aramaic or Greek. Their work then went to one of the General Editorial Committees, which checked it in detail and made another thorough revision. This revision in turn was carefully reviewed by the Committee on Bible Translation, which made further changes and then released the final version for publication. In this way the entire Bible underwent three revisions, during each of which the translation was examined for its faithfulness to the original languages and for its English style.

All this involved many thousands of hours of research and discussion regarding the meaning of the texts and the precise way of putting them into English. It may well be that no other translation has been made by a more thorough process of review and revision from committee to committee than this one.

From the beginning of the project, the Committee on Bible Translation held to certain goals for the New International Version: that it would be an accurate translation and one that would have clarity and literary quality and so prove suitable for public and private reading, teaching, preaching, memorizing and liturgical use. The Committee also sought to preserve some measure of continuity with the long tradition of translating the Scriptures into English.

In working toward these goals, the translators were united in their commitment to the authority and infallibility of the Bible as God's Word in written form. They believe that it contains the divine answer to the deepest needs of humanity, that it sheds unique light on our path in a dark world, and that it sets forth the way to our eternal well-being.

The first concern of the translators has been the accuracy of the translation and its fidelity to the thought of the biblical writers. They have weighed the significance of the lexical and grammatical details of the Hebrew, Aramaic and Greek texts. At the same time, they have striven for more than a word-for-word translation. Because thought patterns and syntax differ from language to language, faithful communication of the meaning of the writers of the Bible demands frequent modifications in sentence structure and constant regard for the contextual meanings of words.

A sensitive feeling for style does not always accompany scholarship. Accordingly the Committee on Bible Translation submitted the developing version to a number of stylistic consultants. Two of them read every book of both Old and New Testaments twice—once before and once after the last major revision—and made invaluable suggestions. Samples of the translation were tested for clarity and ease of reading by various kinds of people—young and old, highly educated and less well educated, ministers and laymen.

Concern for clear and natural English—that the New International Version should be idiomatic but not idiosyncratic, contemporary but not dated—motivated the translators and consultants. At the same time, they tried to reflect the differing styles of the biblical writers. In view of the international use of English, the translators sought to avoid obvious Americanisms on the one hand and obvious Anglicisms on the other. A British edition reflects the comparatively few differences of significant idiom and of spelling.

As for the traditional pronouns "thou," "thee" and "thine" in reference to the Deity, the translators judged that to use these archaisms (along with the old verb forms such as "doest," "wouldest" and "hadst") would violate accuracy in translation. Neither Hebrew, Aramaic nor Greek uses special pronouns for the persons of the Godhead. A present-day translation is not enhanced by forms that in the time of the King James Version were used in everyday speech, whether referring to God or man.

For the Old Testament the standard Hebrew text, the Masoretic Text as published in the latest editions of *Biblia Hebraica*, was used throughout. The Dead Sea Scrolls contain material bearing on an earlier stage of the Hebrew text. They were consulted, as were the Samaritan Pentateuch and the ancient scribal traditions relating to textual changes. Sometimes a variant Hebrew reading in the margin of the Masoretic Text was followed instead of the text itself. Such instances, being variants within the Masoretic tradition, are not specified by footnotes. In rare cases, words in the consonantal text were divided differently from the way they appear in the Masoretic Text. Footnotes indicate this. The translators also consulted the more important early versions—the Septuagint; Aquila, Symmachus and Theodotion; the Vulgate; the Syriac Peshitta; the Targums; and for the Psalms the *Juxta Hebraica* of Jerome. Readings from these versions were occasionally followed where the Masoretic Text seemed doubtful and where accepted principles of textual criticism showed that one or more of these textual witnesses appeared to provide the correct reading. Such instances are footnoted. Sometimes vowel letters and vowel signs did not, in the judgment of the translators, represent the correct vowels for the original consonantal text. Accordingly some words were read with a different set of vowels. These instances are usually not indicated by footnotes.

The Greek text used in translating the New Testament was an eclectic one. No other piece of ancient literature has such an abundance of manuscript witnesses as does the New Testament. Where existing manuscripts differ, the translators made their choice of readings according to accepted principles of New Testament textual criticism. Footnotes call attention to places where there was uncertainty about what the original text was. The best current printed texts of the Greek New Testament were used.

There is a sense in which the work of translation is never wholly finished. This applies to all great literature and uniquely so to the Bible. In 1973 the New Testament in the New International Version was published. Since then, suggestions for corrections and revisions have been received from various sources. The Committee on Bible Translation carefully considered the suggestions and adopted a number of them. These were incorporated in the first printing of the entire Bible in 1978. Additional revisions were made by the Committee on Bible Translation in 1983 and appear in printings after that date.

As in other ancient documents, the precise meaning of the biblical texts is sometimes uncertain. This is more often the case with the Hebrew and Aramaic texts than with the Greek text. Although archaeological and linguistic discoveries in this century aid in understanding difficult passages, some uncertainties remain. The more significant of these have been called to the reader's attention in the footnotes.

In regard to the divine name *YHWH*, commonly referred to as the *Tetragrammaton*, the translators adopted the device used in most English versions of rendering that name as "LORD" in capital letters to distinguish it from *Adonai*, another Hebrew word rendered "Lord," for which small letters are used. Wherever the two names stand together in the Old Testament as a compound name of God, they are rendered "Sovereign LORD."

Because for most readers today the phrases "the LORD of hosts" and "God of hosts" have little meaning, this version renders them "the LORD Almighty" and "God Almighty." These renderings convey the sense of the Hebrew, namely, "he who is sovereign over all the 'hosts' (powers) in heaven and on earth, especially over the 'hosts' (armies) of Israel." For readers unacquainted with Hebrew this does not make clear the distinction between *Sabaoth* ("hosts" or "Almighty") and *Shaddai* (which can also be translated "Almighty"), but the latter occurs infrequently and is always footnoted. When *Adonai* and *YHWH Sabaoth* occur together, they are rendered "the Lord, the LORD Almighty."

As for other proper nouns, the familiar spellings of the King James Version are generally retained. Names traditionally spelled with "ch," except where it is final, are usually spelled in this translation with "k" or "c," since the biblical languages do not have the sound that "ch" frequently indicates in English—for example, in *chant*. For well-known names such as Zechariah, however, the traditional spelling has been retained. Variation in the spelling of names in the original languages has usually not been indicated. Where a person or place has two or more different names in the Hebrew, Aramaic or Greek texts, the more familiar one has generally been used, with footnotes where needed.

To achieve clarity the translators sometimes supplied words not in the original texts but required by the context. If there was uncertainty about such material, it is enclosed in brackets. Also for the sake of clarity or style, nouns, including some proper nouns, are sometimes substituted for pronouns, and vice versa. And though the Hebrew writers often shifted back and forth between first, second and third personal pronouns without change of antecedent, this translation often makes them uniform, in accordance with English style and without the use of footnotes.

Poetical passages are printed as poetry, that is, with indentation of lines with separate stanzas. These are generally designed to reflect the structure of Hebrew poetry. This poetry is normally characterized by parallelism in balanced lines. Most of the poetry in the Bible is in the Old Testament, and scholars differ regarding the scansion of Hebrew lines. The translators determined the stanza divisions for the most part by analysis of the subject matter. The stanzas therefore serve as poetic paragraphs.

As an aid to the reader, italicized sectional headings are inserted in most of the books. They are not to be regarded as part of the NIV text, are not for oral reading, and are not intended to dictate the interpretation of the sections they head.

The footnotes in this version are of several kinds, most of which need no explanation. Those giving alternative translations begin with "Or" and generally introduce the alternative with the last word preceding it in the text, except when it is a single-word alternative; in poetry quoted in a footnote a slant mark indicates a line division. Footnotes introduced by "Or" do not have uniform significance. In some cases two possible translations were considered to have about equal validity. In other cases, though the translators were convinced that the translation in the text was correct, they judged that another interpretation was possible and of sufficient importance to be represented in a footnote.

In the New Testament, footnotes that refer to uncertainty regarding the original text are introduced by "Some manuscripts" or similar expressions. In the Old Testament, evidence for the reading chosen is given first and evidence for the alternative is added after a semicolon (for example: Septuagint; Hebrew *father*). In such notes the term "Hebrew" refers to the Masoretic Text.

It should be noted that minerals, flora and fauna, architectural details, articles of clothing and jewelry, musical instruments and other articles cannot always be identified with precision. Also measures of capacity in the biblical period are particularly uncertain (see the table of weights and measures following the text).

Like all translations of the Bible, made as they are by imperfect man, this one undoubtedly falls short of its goals. Yet we are grateful to God for the extent to which he has enabled us to realize these goals and for the strength he has given us and our colleagues to complete our task. We offer this version of the Bible to him in whose name and for whose glory it has been made. We pray that it will lead many into a better understanding of the Holy Scriptures and a fuller knowledge of Jesus Christ the incarnate Word, of whom the Scriptures so faithfully testify.

The Committee on Bible Translation

June 1978
(Revised August 1983)

Names of the translators and editors may be secured
from the International Bible Society,
translation sponsors of the New International Version,
1820 Jet Stream Drive, Colorado Springs, Colorado
80921-3696 U.S.A.

OLD
TESTAMENT

GENESIS

THE BOOK OF GENESIS IS ABOUT MANY BEGINNINGS—THE BEGINNING OF THE UNIVERSE, THE BEGINNING OF THE HUMAN RACE, THE BEGINNING OF SIN, AND THE BEGINNING OF GOD'S PROMISES AND PLAN FOR SALVATION. GENESIS IS MAINLY A STORY OF RELATIONSHIPS—BETWEEN GOD AND HIS PEOPLE, BETWEEN GOD AND NATURE, AND BETWEEN HIS PEOPLE AND OTHERS. GENESIS REMINDS US OF THE BEAUTIFUL WAYS IN WHICH GOD INITIATES AND ENTERS INTO COVENANTS WITH ALL OF HIS CHOSEN PEOPLE, AND HOW HE PLEDGES HIS LOVE AND FAITHFULNESS TO US.

The Beginning

1 In the beginning God created the heavens and the earth. ²Now the earth was*a* formless and empty, darkness was over the surface of the deep, and the Spirit of God was hovering over the waters.

³And God said, "Let there be light," and there was light. ⁴God saw that the light was good, and he separated the light from the darkness. ⁵God called the light "day," and the darkness he called "night." And there was evening, and there was morning—the first day.

⁶And God said, "Let there be an expanse between the waters to separate water from water." ⁷So God made the expanse and separated the water under the expanse from the water above it. And it was so. ⁸God called the expanse "sky." And there was evening, and there was morning—the second day.

⁹And God said, "Let the water under the sky be gathered to one place, and let dry ground appear." And it was so. ¹⁰God called the dry ground "land," and the gathered waters he called "seas." And God saw that it was good.

¹¹Then God said, "Let the land produce vegetation: seed-bearing plants and trees on the land that bear fruit with seed in it, according to their various kinds." And it was so. ¹²The land produced vegetation:

a 2 Or possibly *became*

plants bearing seed according to their kinds and trees bearing fruit with seed in it according to their kinds. And God saw that it was good. ¹³And there was evening, and there was morning—the third day.

¹⁴And God said, "Let there be lights in the expanse of the sky to separate the day from the night, and let them serve as signs to mark seasons and days and years, ¹⁵and let them be lights in the expanse of the sky to

MONDAY

EVOLUTION IS MISTAKEN FOR EXPLANATION
G. K. Chesterton

VERSE: Genesis 1:1   **PASSAGE:** Genesis 1:1—2:3

 have noticed that if you put a word like God into the same sentence with a word like dog, these abrupt and angular words affect people like pistol shots. Whether you say that God made the dog or the dog made God does not seem to matter; that is only one of the sterile disputations of the too subtle theologians. But so long as you begin with a long word like evolution the rest will roll harmlessly past . . .

Most modern histories of mankind begin with the word evolution, and with a rather wordy exposition of evolution, for much the same reason that operated in this case. There is something slow and soothing and gradual about the word and even about the idea. As a matter of fact, it is not, touching these primary things, a very practical word or a very profitable idea. Nobody can imagine how nothing could turn into something. Nobody can get an inch nearer to it by explaining how something could turn into something else. It is really far more logical to start by saying "In the beginning God created heaven and earth" even if you only mean "In the beginning some unthinkable power began some unthinkable process." For God is by its nature a name of mystery, and nobody ever supposed that man could imagine how a world was created any more than he could create one. But evolution really is mistaken for explanation. It has the fatal quality of leaving on many minds the impression that they do understand it and everything else; just as many of them live under a sort of illusion that they have read [The] Origin of Species.

ADDITIONAL SCRIPTURE READING:
Job 38:4–38; Psalm 104:1–26; John 1:1–10

Go to page 4 for your next devotional reading.

1900   Present

give light on the earth." And it was so. 16God made two great lights—the greater light to govern the day and the lesser light to govern the night. He also made the stars. 17God set them in the expanse of the sky to give light on the earth, 18to govern the day and the night, and to separate light from darkness. And God saw that it was good. 19And there was evening, and there was morning—the fourth day.

20And God said, "Let the water teem with living creatures, and let birds fly above the earth across the expanse of the sky." 21So God created the great creatures of the sea and every living and moving thing with which the water teems, according to their kinds, and every winged bird according to its kind. And God saw that it was good. 22God blessed them and said, "Be fruitful and increase in number and fill the water in the seas, and let the birds increase on the earth." 23And there was evening, and there was morning—the fifth day.

24And God said, "Let the land produce living creatures according to their kinds: livestock, creatures that move along the ground, and wild animals, each according to its kind." And it was so. 25God made the wild animals according to their kinds, the livestock according to their kinds, and all the creatures that move along the ground according to their kinds. And God saw that it was good.

26Then God said, "Let us make man in our image, in our likeness, and let them rule over the fish of the sea and the birds of the air, over the livestock, over all the earth,a and over all the creatures that move along the ground."

27So God created man in his own
    image,
in the image of God he created him;
male and female he created them.

28God blessed them and said to them, "Be fruitful and increase in number; fill the earth and subdue it. Rule over the fish of the sea and the birds of the air and over every living creature that moves on the ground."

29Then God said, "I give you every seed-bearing plant on the face of the whole earth and every tree that has fruit with seed in it. They will be yours for food. 30And to all the beasts of the earth and all the birds of the air and all the creatures that move on the ground—everything that has the breath of life in it—I give every green plant for food." And it was so.

31God saw all that he had made, and it was very good. And there was evening, and there was morning—the sixth day.

2 Thus the heavens and the earth were completed in all their vast array.

2By the seventh day God had finished the work he had been doing; so on the seventh day he restedb from all his work. 3And God blessed the seventh day and made it holy, because on it he rested from all the work of creating that he had done.

Adam and Eve

4This is the account of the heavens and the earth when they were created.

When the LORD God made the earth and the heavens— 5and no shrub of the field had yet appeared on the earthc and no plant of the field had yet sprung up, for the LORD God had not sent rain on the earthc and there was no man to work the ground, 6but streamsd came up from the earth and watered the whole surface of the ground— 7the LORD God

formed the mane from the dust of the ground and breathed into his nostrils the

---

a 26 Hebrew; Syriac *all the wild animals*   b 2 Or *ceased*; also in verse 3   c 5 Or *land*; also in verse 6
d 6 Or *mist*   e 7 The Hebrew for *man (adam)* sounds like and may be related to the Hebrew for *ground (adamah)*; it is also the name *Adam* (see Gen. 2:20).

breath of life, and the man became a living being.

⁸Now the LORD God had planted a garden in the east, in Eden; and there he put the man he had formed. ⁹And the LORD God made all kinds of trees grow out of the ground—trees that were pleasing to the eye and good for food. In the middle of the garden were the tree of life and the tree of the knowledge of good and evil.

¹⁰A river watering the garden flowed from Eden; from there it was separated into four headwaters. ¹¹The name of the first is the Pishon; it winds through the entire land of Havilah, where there is gold. ¹²(The gold of that land is good;

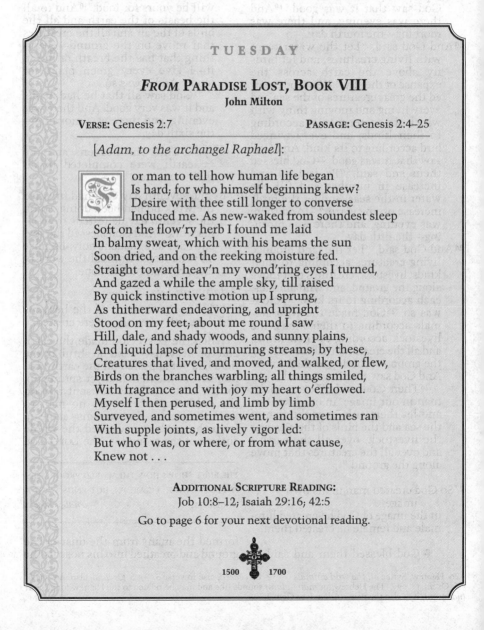

TUESDAY

FROM PARADISE LOST, BOOK VIII
John Milton

VERSE: Genesis 2:7   **PASSAGE:** Genesis 2:4–25

[Adam, to the archangel Raphael]:

or man to tell how human life began
Is hard; for who himself beginning knew?
Desire with thee still longer to converse
Induced me. As new-waked from soundest sleep
Soft on the flow'ry herb I found me laid
In balmy sweat, which with his beams the sun
Soon dried, and on the reeking moisture fed.
Straight toward heav'n my wond'ring eyes I turned,
And gazed a while the ample sky, till raised
By quick instinctive motion up I sprung,
As thitherward endeavoring, and upright
Stood on my feet; about me round I saw
Hill, dale, and shady woods, and sunny plains,
And liquid lapse of murmuring streams; by these,
Creatures that lived, and moved, and walked, or flew,
Birds on the branches warbling; all things smiled,
With fragrance and with joy my heart o'erflowed.
Myself I then perused, and limb by limb
Surveyed, and sometimes went, and sometimes ran
With supple joints, as lively vigor led:
But who I was, or where, or from what cause,
Knew not . . .

ADDITIONAL SCRIPTURE READING:
Job 10:8–12; Isaiah 29:16; 42:5

Go to page 6 for your next devotional reading.

1500   1700

aromatic resin[a] and onyx are also there.)
13The name of the second river is the Gihon; it winds through the entire land of Cush.[b] 14The name of the third river is the Tigris; it runs along the east side of Asshur. And the fourth river is the Euphrates.

15The LORD God took the man and put him in the Garden of Eden to work it and take care of it. 16And the LORD God commanded the man, "You are free to eat from any tree in the garden; 17but you must not eat from the tree of the knowledge of good and evil, for when you eat of it you will surely die."

18The LORD God said, "It is not good for the man to be alone. I will make a helper suitable for him."

19Now the LORD God had formed out of the ground all the beasts of the field and all the birds of the air. He brought them to the man to see what he would name them; and whatever the man called each living creature, that was its name. 20So the man gave names to all the livestock, the birds of the air and all the beasts of the field.

But for Adam[c] no suitable helper was found. 21So the LORD God caused the man to fall into a deep sleep; and while he was sleeping, he took one of the man's ribs[d] and closed up the place with flesh. 22Then the LORD God made a woman from the rib[e] he had taken out of the man, and he brought her to the man.

23The man said,

"This is now bone of my bones
    and flesh of my flesh;
she shall be called 'woman,[f]'
    for she was taken out of man."

24For this reason a man will leave his father and mother and be united to his wife, and they will become one flesh.

25The man and his wife were both naked, and they felt no shame.

The Fall of Man

3 Now the serpent was more crafty than any of the wild animals the LORD God had made. He said to the woman, "Did God really say, 'You must not eat from any tree in the garden'?"

2The woman said to the serpent, "We may eat fruit from the trees in the garden, 3but God did say, 'You must not eat fruit from the tree that is in the middle of the garden, and you must not touch it, or you will die.' "

4"You will not surely die," the serpent said to the woman. 5"For God knows that when you eat of it your eyes will be opened, and you will be like God, knowing good and evil."

6When the woman saw that the fruit of the tree was good for food and pleasing to the eye, and also desirable for gaining wisdom, she took some and ate it. She also gave some to her husband, who was with her, and he ate it. 7Then the eyes of both of them were opened, and they realized they were naked; so they sewed fig leaves together and made coverings for themselves.

8Then the man and his wife heard the sound of the LORD God as he was walking in the garden in the cool of the day, and they hid from the LORD God among the trees of the garden. 9But the LORD God called to the man, "Where are you?"

AS IN PARADISE, GOD WALKS IN THE HOLY SCRIPTURES, SEEKING MAN.   —Ambrose

---

10He answered, "I heard you in the garden, and I was afraid because I was naked; so I hid."

11And he said, "Who told you that you were naked? Have you eaten from the tree that I commanded you not to eat from?"

12The man said, "The woman you put here with me—she gave me some fruit from the tree, and I ate it."

13Then the LORD God said to the woman, "What is this you have done?"

The woman said, "The serpent deceived me, and I ate."

14So the LORD God said to the serpent, "Because you have done this,

"Cursed are you above all the
    livestock

---

a 12 Or good; pearls   b 13 Possibly southeast Mesopotamia   c 20 Or the man   d 21 Or took part of the man's side   e 22 Or part   f 23 The Hebrew for woman sounds like the Hebrew for man.

OF RESISTING TEMPTATION
Thomas à Kempis

VERSE: Genesis 3:1 **PASSAGE:** Genesis 3:1–9

o long as we live in this world we can not be without tribulation and temptation . . .

Every one therefore ought to be careful about his temptations, and to watch in prayer, lest the devil find an occasion to deceive him; who never sleepeth, but goeth about seeking whom he may devour (see 1 Peter 5:8).

No man is so perfect and holy, but he hath sometimes temptations; and altogether without them we can not be.

Nevertheless, temptations are often very profitable to us, though they be troublesome and grievous; for in them a man is humbled, purified, and instructed.

All saints passed through many tribulations and temptations, and profited thereby.

And they that could not bear temptations, became reprobate, and fell away.

There is no order so holy, nor place so secret, where there be not temptations, or adversities . . .

Some suffer great temptations in the beginning of their conversion; others at the end.

Others again are much troubled almost through the whole of their life.

Some are easily tempted, according to the wisdom and equity of the divine appointment, which weigheth the states and worth of men, and ordaineth all things for the welfare of his own chosen ones.

We ought not therefore to despair when we are tempted, but so much the more fervently to pray unto God, that he will grant us help in all tribulations; who, surely, according to the words of St. Paul, will give with the temptation a way of escape, that we may be able to bear it.

Let us therefore humble our souls under the hand of God in all temptations and tribulations, for he will save and exalt the humble in spirit.

ADDITIONAL SCRIPTURE READING:
Matthew 4:1–11; 1 Corinthians 10:13

Go to page 12 for your next devotional reading.

500 1500

and all the wild animals!
You will crawl on your belly
and you will eat dust
all the days of your life.
15 And I will put enmity
between you and the woman,
and between your offspring*a* and
hers;
he will crush*b* your head,
and you will strike his heel."

16 To the woman he said,

"I will greatly increase your pains in
childbearing;
with pain you will give birth to
children.
Your desire will be for your husband,
and he will rule over you."

17 To Adam he said, "Because you listened to your wife and ate from the tree about which I commanded you, 'You must not eat of it,'

"Cursed is the ground because of you;
through painful toil you will eat of
it
all the days of your life.
18 It will produce thorns and thistles for
you,
and you will eat the plants of the
field.
19 By the sweat of your brow
you will eat your food
until you return to the ground,
since from it you were taken;
for dust you are
and to dust you will return."

20 Adam*c* named his wife Eve,*d* because she would become the mother of all the living.
21 The LORD God made garments of skin for Adam and his wife and clothed them. 22 And the LORD God said, "The man has now become like one of us, knowing good and evil. He must not be allowed to reach out his hand and take also from the tree of life and eat, and live forever." 23 So the LORD God banished him from the Garden of Eden to work the ground from which he had been taken. 24 After he drove the man out, he placed on the east side*e* of the Garden of Eden cherubim and a flaming sword flashing back and forth to guard the way to the tree of life.

Cain and Abel

4 Adam*c* lay with his wife Eve, and she became pregnant and gave birth to Cain.*f* She said, "With the help of the LORD I have brought forth*g* a man." 2 Later she gave birth to his brother Abel.

Now Abel kept flocks, and Cain worked the soil. 3 In the course of time Cain brought some of the fruits of the soil as an offering to the LORD. 4 But Abel brought fat portions from some of the firstborn of his flock. The LORD looked with favor on Abel and his offering, 5 but on Cain and his offering he did not look with favor. So Cain was very angry, and his face was downcast.

6 Then the LORD said to Cain, "Why are you angry? Why is your face downcast? 7 If you do what is right, will you not be accepted? But if you do not do what is right, sin is crouching at your door; it desires to have you, but you must master it."

8 Now Cain said to his brother Abel, "Let's go out to the field."*h* And while they were in the field, Cain attacked his brother Abel and killed him.

9 Then the LORD said to Cain, "Where is your brother Abel?"

"I don't know," he replied. "Am I my brother's keeper?"

10 The LORD said, "What have you done? Listen! Your brother's blood cries out to me from the ground. 11 Now you are under a curse and driven from the ground, which opened its mouth to receive your brother's blood from your hand. 12 When you work the ground, it will no longer yield its crops for you. You will be a restless wanderer on the earth."

13 Cain said to the LORD, "My punishment is more than I can bear. 14 Today you are driving me from the land, and I will be hidden from your presence; I will

a 15 Or *seed*   *b 15* Or *strike*   *c 20,1* Or *The man*   *d 20 Eve* probably means *living.*   *e 24* Or *placed in front*   *f 1 Cain* sounds like the Hebrew for *brought forth* or *acquired.*   *g 1* Or *have acquired*   *h 8* Samaritan Pentateuch, Septuagint, Vulgate and Syriac; Masoretic Text does not have *"Let's go out to the field."*

be a restless wanderer on the earth, and whoever finds me will kill me."

15But the LORD said to him, "Not so*a*; if anyone kills Cain, he will suffer vengeance seven times over." Then the LORD put a mark on Cain so that no one who found him would kill him. 16So Cain went out from the LORD's presence and lived in the land of Nod,*b* east of Eden.

17Cain lay with his wife, and she became pregnant and gave birth to Enoch. Cain was then building a city, and he named it after his son Enoch. 18To Enoch was born Irad, and Irad was the father of Mehujael, and Mehujael was the father of Methushael, and Methushael was the father of Lamech.

19Lamech married two women, one named Adah and the other Zillah. 20Adah gave birth to Jabal; he was the father of those who live in tents and raise livestock. 21His brother's name was Jubal; he was the father of all who play the harp and flute. 22Zillah also had a son, Tubal-Cain, who forged all kinds of tools out of*c* bronze and iron. Tubal-Cain's sister was Naamah.

23Lamech said to his wives,

"Adah and Zillah, listen to me;
    wives of Lamech, hear my words.
I have killed*d* a man for wounding
    me,
    a young man for injuring me.
24If Cain is avenged seven times,
    then Lamech seventy-seven times."

25Adam lay with his wife again, and she gave birth to a son and named him Seth,*e* saying, "God has granted me another child in place of Abel, since Cain killed him." 26Seth also had a son, and he named him Enosh.

At that time men began to call on*f* the name of the LORD.

From Adam to Noah

 5 This is the written account of Adam's line.

When God created man, he made him in the likeness of God. 2He created them male and female and blessed them. And when they were created, he called them "man.*g* "

3When Adam had lived 130 years, he had a son in his own likeness, in his own image; and he named him Seth. 4After Seth was born, Adam lived 800 years and had other sons and daughters. 5Altogether, Adam lived 930 years, and then he died.

6When Seth had lived 105 years, he became the father*h* of Enosh. 7And after he became the father of Enosh, Seth lived 807 years and had other sons and daughters. 8Altogether, Seth lived 912 years, and then he died.

9When Enosh had lived 90 years, he became the father of Kenan. 10And after he became the father of Kenan, Enosh lived 815 years and had other sons and daughters. 11Altogether, Enosh lived 905 years, and then he died.

12When Kenan had lived 70 years, he became the father of Mahalalel. 13And after he became the father of Mahalalel, Kenan lived 840 years and had other sons and daughters. 14Altogether, Kenan lived 910 years, and then he died.

15When Mahalalel had lived 65 years, he became the father of Jared. 16And after he became the father of Jared, Mahalalel lived 830 years and had other sons and daughters. 17Altogether, Mahalalel lived 895 years, and then he died.

18When Jared had lived 162 years, he became the father of Enoch. 19And after he became the father of Enoch, Jared lived 800 years and had other sons and daughters. 20Altogether, Jared lived 962 years, and then he died.

21When Enoch had lived 65 years, he became the father of Methuselah. 22And after he became the father of Methuselah, Enoch walked with God 300 years and had other sons and daughters. 23Altogether, Enoch lived 365 years. 24Enoch walked with God; then he was no more, because God took him away.

25When Methuselah had lived 187 years, he became the father of Lamech. 26And after he became the father of Lamech, Methuselah lived 782 years

---

a 15 Septuagint, Vulgate and Syriac; Hebrew *Very well* 14).   *c* 22 Or *who instructed all who work in* granted.   *f* 26 Or *to proclaim*   *g* 2 Hebrew *adam* 7–26.   *b* 16 *Nod* means *wandering* (see verses 12 and   *d* 23 Or *I will kill*   *e* 25 *Seth* probably means   *h* 6 *Father* may mean *ancestor*; also in verses

and had other sons and daughters. ²⁷Altogether, Methuselah lived 969 years, and then he died.

²⁸When Lamech had lived 182 years, he had a son. ²⁹He named him Noah^a and said, "He will comfort us in the labor and painful toil of our hands caused by the ground the LORD has cursed." ³⁰After Noah was born, Lamech lived 595 years and had other sons and daughters. ³¹Altogether, Lamech lived 777 years, and then he died.

³²After Noah was 500 years old, he became the father of Shem, Ham and Japheth.

The Flood

6 When men began to increase in number on the earth and daughters were born to them, ²the sons of God saw that the daughters of men were beautiful, and they married any of them they chose. ³Then the LORD said, "My Spirit will not contend with^b man forever, for he is mortal^c; his days will be a hundred and twenty years."

⁴The Nephilim were on the earth in those days—and also afterward—when the sons of God went to the daughters of men and had children by them. They were the heroes of old, men of renown.

⁵The LORD saw how great man's wickedness on the earth had become, and that every inclination of the thoughts of his heart was only evil all the time. ⁶The LORD was grieved that he had made man on the earth, and his heart was filled with pain. ⁷So the LORD said, "I will wipe mankind, whom I have created, from the face of the earth—men and animals, and creatures that move along the ground, and birds of the air—for I am grieved that I have made them." ⁸But Noah found favor in the eyes of the LORD.

⁹This is the account of Noah.

Noah was a righteous man, blameless among the people of his time, and he walked with God. ¹⁰Noah had three sons: Shem, Ham and Japheth.

¹¹Now the earth was corrupt in God's sight and was full of violence. ¹²God saw how corrupt the earth had become, for all the people on earth had corrupted their ways. ¹³So God said to Noah, "I am going to put an end to all people, for the earth is filled with violence because of them. I am surely going to destroy both them and the earth. ¹⁴So make yourself an ark of cypress^d wood; make rooms in it and coat it with pitch inside and out. ¹⁵This is how you are to build it: The ark is to be 450 feet long, 75 feet wide and 45 feet high.^e ¹⁶Make a roof for it and finish^f the ark to within 18 inches^g of the top. Put a door in the side of the ark and make lower, middle and upper decks. ¹⁷I am going to bring floodwaters on the earth to destroy all life under the heavens, every creature that has the breath of life in it. Everything on earth will perish. ¹⁸But I will establish my covenant with you, and you will enter the ark—you and your sons and your wife and your sons' wives with you. ¹⁹You are to bring into the ark two of all living creatures, male and female, to keep them alive with you. ²⁰Two of every kind of bird, of every kind of animal and of every kind of creature that moves along the ground will come to you to be kept alive. ²¹You are to take every kind of food that is to be eaten and store it away as food for you and for them."

²²Noah did everything just as God commanded him.

7 The LORD then said to Noah, "Go into the ark, you and your whole family, because I have found you righteous in this generation. ²Take with you seven^h of every kind of clean animal, a male and its mate, and two of every kind of unclean animal, a male and its mate, ³and also seven of every kind of bird, male and female, to keep their various kinds alive throughout the earth. ⁴Seven days from now I will send rain on the earth for forty days and forty nights, and I will wipe from the face of the earth every living creature I have made."

⁵And Noah did all that the LORD commanded him.

---

^a 29 Noah sounds like the Hebrew for comfort.   ^b 3 Or My spirit will not remain in   ^c 3 Or corrupt   ^d 14 The meaning of the Hebrew for this word is uncertain.   ^e 15 Hebrew 300 cubits long, 50 cubits wide and 30 cubits high (about 140 meters long, 23 meters wide and 13.5 meters high)   ^f 16 Or Make an opening for light by finishing   ^g 16 Hebrew a cubit (about 0.5 meter)   ^h 2 Or seven pairs; also in verse 3

⁶Noah was six hundred years old when the floodwaters came on the earth. ⁷And Noah and his sons and his wife and his sons' wives entered the ark to escape the waters of the flood. ⁸Pairs of clean and unclean animals, of birds and of all creatures that move along the ground, ⁹male and female, came to Noah and entered the ark, as God had commanded Noah. ¹⁰And after the seven days the floodwaters came on the earth.

¹¹In the six hundredth year of Noah's life, on the seventeenth day of the second month—on that day all the springs of the great deep burst forth, and the floodgates of the heavens were opened. ¹²And rain fell on the earth forty days and forty nights.

¹³On that very day Noah and his sons, Shem, Ham and Japheth, together with his wife and the wives of his three sons, entered the ark. ¹⁴They had with them every wild animal according to its kind, all livestock according to their kinds, every creature that moves along the ground according to its kind and every bird according to its kind, everything with wings. ¹⁵Pairs of all creatures that have the breath of life in them came to Noah and entered the ark. ¹⁶The animals going in were male and female of every living thing, as God had commanded Noah. Then the LORD shut him in.

¹⁷For forty days the flood kept coming on the earth, and as the waters increased they lifted the ark high above the earth. ¹⁸The waters rose and increased greatly on the earth, and the ark floated on the surface of the water. ¹⁹They rose greatly on the earth, and all the high mountains under the entire heavens were covered. ²⁰The waters rose and covered the mountains to a depth of more than twenty feet.ᵃ,ᵇ ²¹Every living thing that moved on the earth perished—birds, livestock, wild animals, all the creatures that swarm over the earth, and all mankind. ²²Everything on dry land that had the breath of life in its nostrils died. ²³Every living thing on the face of the earth was wiped out; men and animals and the creatures that move along the ground and the birds of the air were wiped from the earth. Only Noah was left, and those with him in the ark.

²⁴The waters flooded the earth for a hundred and fifty days.

8 But God remembered Noah and all the wild animals and the livestock that were with him in the ark, and he sent a wind over the earth, and the waters receded. ²Now the springs of the deep and the floodgates of the heavens had been closed, and the rain had stopped falling from the sky. ³The water receded steadily from the earth. At the end of the hundred and fifty days the water had gone down, ⁴and on the seventeenth day of the seventh month the ark came to rest on the mountains of Ararat. ⁵The waters continued to recede until the tenth month, and on the first day of the tenth month the tops of the mountains became visible.

⁶After forty days Noah opened the window he had made in the ark ⁷and sent out a raven, and it kept flying back and forth until the water had dried up from the earth. ⁸Then he sent out a dove to see if the water had receded from the surface of the ground. ⁹But the dove could find no place to set its feet because there was water over all the surface of the earth; so it returned to Noah in the ark. He reached out his hand and took the dove and brought it back to himself in the ark. ¹⁰He waited seven more days and again sent out the dove from the ark. ¹¹When the dove returned to him in the evening, there in its beak was a freshly plucked olive leaf! Then Noah knew that the water had receded from the earth. ¹²He waited seven more days and sent the dove out again, but this time it did not return to him.

¹³By the first day of the first month of Noah's six hundred and first year, the water had dried up from the earth. Noah then removed the covering from the ark and saw that the surface of the ground was dry. ¹⁴By the twenty-seventh day of the second month the earth was completely dry.

¹⁵Then God said to Noah, ¹⁶"Come out of the ark, you and your wife and your sons and their wives. ¹⁷Bring out every kind of living creature that is with

---

ᵃ 20 Hebrew *fifteen cubits* (about 6.9 meters)   ᵇ 20 Or *rose more than twenty feet, and the mountains were covered*

you—the birds, the animals, and all the creatures that move along the ground—so they can multiply on the earth and be fruitful and increase in number upon it."

¹⁸So Noah came out, together with his sons and his wife and his sons' wives. ¹⁹All the animals and all the creatures that move along the ground and all the birds—everything that moves on the earth—came out of the ark, one kind after another.

²⁰Then Noah built an altar to the LORD and, taking some of all the clean animals and clean birds, he sacrificed burnt offerings on it. ²¹The LORD smelled the pleasing aroma and said in his heart: "Never again will I curse the ground because of man, even though*a* every inclination of his heart is evil from childhood. And never again will I destroy all living creatures, as I have done.

²² "As long as the earth endures,
    seedtime and harvest,
    cold and heat,
    summer and winter,
    day and night
    will never cease."

God's Covenant With Noah

9 Then God blessed Noah and his sons, saying to them, "Be fruitful and increase in number and fill the earth. ²The fear and dread of you will fall upon all the beasts of the earth and all the birds of the air, upon every creature that moves along the ground, and upon all the fish of the sea; they are given into your hands. ³Everything that lives and moves will be food for you. Just as I gave you the green plants, I now give you everything.

⁴"But you must not eat meat that has its lifeblood still in it. ⁵And for your lifeblood I will surely demand an accounting. I will demand an accounting from every animal. And from each man, too, I will demand an accounting for the life of his fellow man.

⁶ "Whoever sheds the blood of man,
    by man shall his blood be shed;
    for in the image of God
    has God made man.

⁷As for you, be fruitful and increase in number; multiply on the earth and increase upon it."

⁸Then God said to Noah and to his sons with him: ⁹"I now establish my covenant with you and with your descendants after you ¹⁰and with every living creature that was with you—the birds, the livestock and all the wild animals, all those that came out of the ark with you—every living creature on earth. ¹¹I establish my covenant with you: Never again will all life be cut off by the waters of a flood; never again will there be a flood to destroy the earth."

¹²And God said, "This is the sign of the covenant I am making between me and you and every living creature with you, a covenant for all generations to come: ¹³I have set my rainbow in the clouds, and it will be the sign of the covenant between me and the earth. ¹⁴Whenever I bring clouds over the earth and the rainbow appears in the clouds, ¹⁵I will remember my covenant between me and you and all living creatures of every kind. Never again will the waters become a flood to destroy all life. ¹⁶Whenever the rainbow appears in the clouds, I will see it and remember the everlasting covenant between God and all living creatures of every kind on the earth."

¹⁷So God said to Noah, "This is the sign of the covenant I have established between me and all life on the earth."

The Sons of Noah

¹⁸The sons of Noah who came out of the ark were Shem, Ham and Japheth. (Ham was the father of Canaan.) ¹⁹These were the three sons of Noah, and from them came the people who were scattered over the earth.

²⁰Noah, a man of the soil, proceeded*b* to plant a vineyard. ²¹When he drank some of its wine, he became drunk and lay uncovered inside his tent. ²²Ham, the father of Canaan, saw his father's nakedness and told his two brothers outside. ²³But Shem and Japheth took a garment and laid it across their shoulders; then they walked in backward and covered their father's nakedness. Their faces were turned the other way so that

a 21 Or man, for   b 20 Or soil, was the first

THE GLORY OF THE RAINBOW
Charles H. Spurgeon

VERSE: Genesis 9:13   **PASSAGE:** Genesis 9:12–17

 ooking from the little wooden bridge which passes over the brow of the beautiful waterfall of Handeck, on a bright day one will see a circular rainbow surrounding the fall like a coronet of gems. Every hue is there from the red to where the violet fades into the sky.

This fair vision reminded me of the mystic rainbow which the seer of Patmos beheld around the throne (see Revelation 4:3). It was seen by John as a *complete circle*; we see but half on earth. The upper arch of manifest glory we rejoice to gaze upon, but the lower and foundational arch of the eternal purpose, upon which the visible display of grace is founded, is reserved for our contemplation in another world.

I compared the little stream to the church of God, which in peaceful times flows on like a village brook, quiet and obscure, blessed and blessing others, but yet little known or considered by the sons of men. But when the church advances over the steeps of opposition and is dashed down the crags of persecution, then her glory is revealed. Then it is that the eternal God glorifies her with the rainbow of his everlasting grace, makes the beauty of her holiness to shine forth, and reveals a heavenly radiance, which all behold with astonishment.

The majestic rainbow of the divine presence encircles the chosen people when tribulation, affliction, and distress break them, as the stream is broken by the precipitous rocks on which it boldly casts itself, that its current may advance in its predestined channel. When forebodings foretell the coming of evil times for the church, remember that before the Spirit revealed to the beloved disciple the terrible beasts, the thundering trumpets, the falling stars, and the dreadful vials, he bade him mark with attention that the covenant rainbow was round about the throne. All is well, for God is true.

ADDITIONAL SCRIPTURE READING:
Ezekiel 1:28; Revelation 4:2–3; 10:1

Go to page 15 for your next devotional reading.

1700   1900

they would not see their father's nakedness. [24]When Noah awoke from his wine and found out what his youngest son had done to him, [25]he said,

"Cursed be Canaan!
    The lowest of slaves
    will he be to his brothers."

[26]He also said,

"Blessed be the LORD, the God of Shem!
    May Canaan be the slave of Shem.[a]
[27] May God extend the territory of Japheth[b];
    may Japheth live in the tents of Shem,
    and may Canaan be his[c] slave."

[28]After the flood Noah lived 350 years. [29]Altogether, Noah lived 950 years, and then he died.

The Table of Nations

10 This is the account of Shem, Ham and Japheth, Noah's sons, who themselves had sons after the flood.

The Japhethites

[2] The sons[d] of Japheth:
    Gomer, Magog, Madai, Javan, Tubal, Meshech and Tiras.
[3] The sons of Gomer:
    Ashkenaz, Riphath and Togarmah.
[4] The sons of Javan:
    Elishah, Tarshish, the Kittim and the Rodanim.[e] [5](From these the maritime peoples spread out into their territories by their clans within their nations, each with its own language.)

The Hamites

[6] The sons of Ham:
    Cush, Mizraim,[f] Put and Canaan.
[7] The sons of Cush:

Seba, Havilah, Sabtah, Raamah and Sabteca.
    The sons of Raamah:
    Sheba and Dedan.

[8]Cush was the father[g] of Nimrod, who grew to be a mighty warrior on the earth. [9]He was a mighty hunter before the LORD; that is why it is said, "Like Nimrod, a mighty hunter before the LORD." [10]The first centers of his kingdom were Babylon, Erech, Akkad and Calneh, in[h] Shinar.[i] [11]From that land he went to Assyria, where he built Nineveh, Rehoboth Ir,[i] Calah [12]and Resen, which is between Nineveh and Calah; that is the great city.

[13] Mizraim was the father of
    the Ludites, Anamites, Lehabites, Naphtuhites, [14]Pathrusites, Casluhites (from whom the Philistines came) and Caphtorites.
[15] Canaan was the father of
    Sidon his firstborn,[k] and of the Hittites, [16]Jebusites, Amorites, Girgashites, [17]Hivites, Arkites, Sinites, [18]Arvadites, Zemarites and Hamathites.

Later the Canaanite clans scattered [19]and the borders of Canaan reached from Sidon toward Gerar as far as Gaza, and then toward Sodom, Gomorrah, Admah and Zeboiim, as far as Lasha.
[20]These are the sons of Ham by their clans and languages, in their territories and nations.

The Semites

[21]Sons were also born to Shem, whose older brother was[l] Japheth; Shem was the ancestor of all the sons of Eber.

[22] The sons of Shem:
    Elam, Asshur, Arphaxad, Lud and Aram.
[23] The sons of Aram:
    Uz, Hul, Gether and Meshech.[m]
[24] Arphaxad was the father of[n] Shelah,
    and Shelah the father of Eber.

---

[a] 26 Or be his slave   [b] 27 Japheth sounds like the Hebrew for extend.   [c] 27 Or their   [d] 2 Sons may mean descendants or successors or nations; also in verses 3, 4, 6, 7, 20–23, 29 and 31.   [e] 4 Some manuscripts of the Masoretic Text and Samaritan Pentateuch (see also Septuagint and 1 Chron. 1:7); most manuscripts of the Masoretic Text Dodanim   [f] 6 That is, Egypt; also in verse 13   [g] 8 Father may mean ancestor or predecessor or founder; also in verses 13, 15, 24 and 26.   [h] 10 Or Erech and Akkad—all of them in   [i] 10 That is, Babylonia   [i] 11 Or Nineveh with its city squares   [k] 15 Or of the Sidonians, the foremost   [l] 21 Or Shem, the older brother of   [m] 23 See Septuagint and 1 Chron. 1:17; Hebrew Mash   [n] 24 Hebrew; Septuagint father of Cainan, and Cainan was the father of

25 Two sons were born to Eber:
One was named Peleg, *a* because
in his time the earth was divided;
his brother was named Joktan.
26 Joktan was the father of
Almodad, Sheleph, Hazarmaveth,
Jerah, 27 Hadoram, Uzal, Diklah,
28 Obal, Abimael, Sheba, 29 Ophir,
Havilah and Jobab. All these were
sons of Joktan.

30 The region where they lived stretched
from Mesha toward Sephar, in the eastern hill country.

31 These are the sons of Shem by their
clans and languages, in their territories
and nations.

32 These are the clans of Noah's sons,
according to their lines of descent, within their nations. From these the nations
spread out over the earth after the flood.

The Tower of Babel

11 Now the whole world had
one language and a common
speech. 2 As men moved eastward, *b* they
found a plain in Shinar *c* and settled
there.

3 They said to each other, "Come, let's
make bricks and bake them thoroughly." They used brick instead of stone,
and tar for mortar. 4 Then they said,
"Come, let us build ourselves a city,
with a tower that reaches to the heavens, so that we may make a name for
ourselves and not be scattered over the
face of the whole earth."

5 But the LORD came down to see the
city and the tower that the men were
building. 6 The LORD said, "If as one people speaking the same language they
have begun to do this, then nothing they
plan to do will be impossible for them.
7 Come, let us go down and confuse their
language so they will not understand
each other."

8 So the LORD scattered them from
there over all the earth, and they stopped
building the city. 9 That is why it was
called Babel *d*—because there the LORD

confused the language of the whole
world. From there the LORD scattered
them over the face of the whole earth.

From Shem to Abram

10 This is the account of Shem.

Two years after the flood, when Shem
was 100 years old, he became the father *e*
of Arphaxad. 11 And after he became the
father of Arphaxad, Shem lived 500
years and had other sons and daughters.

12 When Arphaxad had lived 35 years,
he became the father of Shelah. 13 And
after he became the father of Shelah,
Arphaxad lived 403 years and had other
sons and daughters. *f*

14 When Shelah had lived 30 years, he
became the father of Eber. 15 And after he
became the father of Eber, Shelah lived
403 years and had other sons and daughters.

16 When Eber had lived 34 years, he
became the father of Peleg. 17 And after he
became the father of Peleg, Eber lived 430
years and had other sons and daughters.

18 When Peleg had lived 30 years, he
became the father of Reu. 19 And after he
became the father of Reu, Peleg lived 209
years and had other sons and daughters.

20 When Reu had lived 32 years, he
became the father of Serug. 21 And after
he became the father of Serug, Reu lived
207 years and had other sons and daughters.

22 When Serug had lived 30 years, he
became the father of Nahor. 23 And after
he became the father of Nahor, Serug
lived 200 years and had other sons and
daughters.

24 When Nahor had lived 29 years, he
became the father of Terah. 25 And after
he became the father of Terah, Nahor
lived 119 years and had other sons and
daughters.

26 After Terah had lived 70 years, he
became the father of Abram, Nahor and
Haran.

27 This is the account of Terah.

Terah became the father of Abram,

---

a 25 Peleg means *division.*　　*b 2* Or *from the east;* or *in the east*　　*c 2* That is, Babylonia　　*d 9* That
is, Babylon; *Babel* sounds like the Hebrew for *confused.*　　*e 10 Father* may mean *ancestor;* also in verses
11–25.　　*f 12,13* Hebrew; Septuagint (see also Luke 3:35, 36 and note at Gen. 10:24) *35 years, he became
the father of Cainan. 13 And after he became the father of Cainan, Arphaxad lived 430 years and had
other sons and daughters, and then he died. When Cainan had lived 130 years, he became the father of
Shelah. And after he became the father of Shelah, Cainan lived 330 years and had other sons and
daughters*

Nahor and Haran. And Haran became the father of Lot. 28While his father Terah was still alive, Haran died in Ur of the Chaldeans, in the land of his birth. 29Abram and Nahor both married. The name of Abram's wife was Sarai, and the name of Nahor's wife was Milcah; she was the daughter of Haran, the father of both Milcah and Iscah. 30Now Sarai was barren; she had no children.

31Terah took his son Abram, his grandson Lot son of Haran, and his daughter-in-law Sarai, the wife of his son Abram, and together they set out from Ur of the

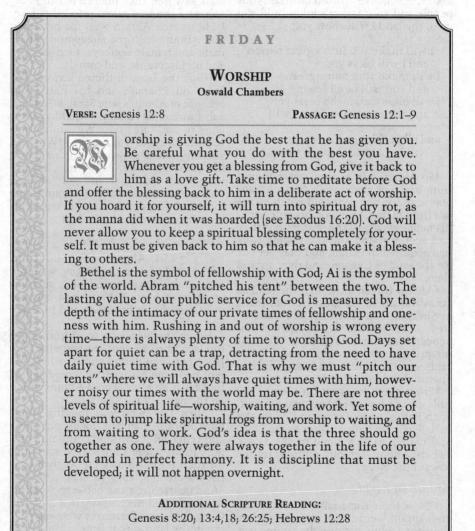

FRIDAY

WORSHIP
Oswald Chambers

VERSE: Genesis 12:8   **PASSAGE:** Genesis 12:1–9

orship is giving God the best that he has given you. Be careful what you do with the best you have. Whenever you get a blessing from God, give it back to him as a love gift. Take time to meditate before God and offer the blessing back to him in a deliberate act of worship. If you hoard it for yourself, it will turn into spiritual dry rot, as the manna did when it was hoarded (see Exodus 16:20). God will never allow you to keep a spiritual blessing completely for yourself. It must be given back to him so that he can make it a blessing to others.

Bethel is the symbol of fellowship with God; Ai is the symbol of the world. Abram "pitched his tent" between the two. The lasting value of our public service for God is measured by the depth of the intimacy of our private times of fellowship and oneness with him. Rushing in and out of worship is wrong every time—there is always plenty of time to worship God. Days set apart for quiet can be a trap, detracting from the need to have daily quiet time with God. That is why we must "pitch our tents" where we will always have quiet times with him, however noisy our times with the world may be. There are not three levels of spiritual life—worship, waiting, and work. Yet some of us seem to jump like spiritual frogs from worship to waiting, and from waiting to work. God's idea is that the three should go together as one. They were always together in the life of our Lord and in perfect harmony. It is a discipline that must be developed; it will not happen overnight.

ADDITIONAL SCRIPTURE READING:
Genesis 8:20; 13:4,18; 26:25; Hebrews 12:28

Go to page 17 for your next devotional reading.

1900   Present

Chaldeans to go to Canaan. But when they came to Haran, they settled there.

³²Terah lived 205 years, and he died in Haran.

The Call of Abram

12 The LORD had said to Abram, "Leave your country, your people and your father's household and go to the land I will show you.

2 "I will make you into a great nation
    and I will bless you;
I will make your name great,
    and you will be a blessing.
3 I will bless those who bless you,
    and whoever curses you I will
        curse;
and all peoples on earth
    will be blessed through you."

⁴So Abram left, as the LORD had told him; and Lot went with him. Abram was seventy-five years old when he set out from Haran. ⁵He took his wife Sarai, his nephew Lot, all the possessions they had accumulated and the people they had acquired in Haran, and they set out for the land of Canaan, and they arrived there.

⁶Abram traveled through the land as far as the site of the great tree of Moreh at Shechem. At that time the Canaanites were in the land. ⁷The LORD appeared to Abram and said, "To your offspring*a* I will give this land." So he built an altar there to the LORD, who had appeared to him.

⁸From there he went on toward the hills east of Bethel and pitched his tent, with Bethel on the west and Ai on the east. There he built an altar to the LORD and called on the name of the LORD. ⁹Then Abram set out and continued toward the Negev.

Abram in Egypt

¹⁰Now there was a famine in the land, and Abram went down to Egypt to live there for a while because the famine was severe. ¹¹As he was about to enter Egypt, he said to his wife Sarai, "I know what a beautiful woman you are. ¹²When the Egyptians see you, they will say, 'This is his wife.' Then they will

kill me but will let you live. ¹³Say you are my sister, so that I will be treated well for your sake and my life will be spared because of you."

¹⁴When Abram came to Egypt, the Egyptians saw that she was a very beautiful woman. ¹⁵And when Pharaoh's officials saw her, they praised her to Pharaoh, and she was taken into his palace. ¹⁶He treated Abram well for her sake, and Abram acquired sheep and cattle, male and female donkeys, menservants and maidservants, and camels.

¹⁷But the LORD inflicted serious diseases on Pharaoh and his household because of Abram's wife Sarai. ¹⁸So Pharaoh summoned Abram. "What have you done to me?" he said. "Why didn't you tell me she was your wife? ¹⁹Why did you say, 'She is my sister,' so that I took her to be my wife? Now then, here is your wife. Take her and go!" ²⁰Then Pharaoh gave orders about Abram to his men, and they sent him on his way, with his wife and everything he had.

Abram and Lot Separate

13 So Abram went up from Egypt to the Negev, with his wife and everything he had, and Lot went with him. ²Abram had become very wealthy in livestock and in silver and gold.

³From the Negev he went from place to place until he came to Bethel, to the place between Bethel and Ai where his tent had been earlier ⁴and where he had first built an altar. There Abram called on the name of the LORD.

⁵Now Lot, who was moving about with Abram, also had flocks and herds and tents. ⁶But the land could not support them while they stayed together, for their possessions were so great that they were not able to stay together. ⁷And quarreling arose between Abram's herdsmen and the herdsmen of Lot. The Canaanites and Perizzites were also living in the land at that time.

⁸So Abram said to Lot, "Let's not have any quarreling between you and me, or between your herdsmen and mine, for we are brothers. ⁹Is not the whole land before you? Let's part company. If you go

---

a 7 Or seed

WEEKEND

THE GOOD OR THE BEST?
Oswald Chambers

VERSE: Genesis 13:9   **PASSAGE:** Genesis 13:8–18

As soon as you begin to live the life of faith in God, fascinating and physically gratifying possibilities will open up before you. These things are yours by right, but if you are living the life of faith you will exercise your right to waive your rights, and let God make your choice for you. God sometimes allows you to get into a place of testing where your own welfare would be the appropriate thing to consider, if you were not living the life of faith. But if you are, you will joyfully waive your right and allow God to make your choice for you. This is the discipline God uses to transform the natural into the spiritual through obedience to his voice.

Whenever our *right* becomes the guiding factor of our lives, it dulls our spiritual insight. The greatest enemy of the life of faith in God is not sin, but good choices which are not quite good enough. The good is always the enemy of the best. In this passage, it would seem that the wisest thing in the world for Abram to do would be to choose. It was his right, and the people around him would consider him to be a fool for not choosing.

Many of us do not continue to grow spiritually because we prefer to choose on the basis of our rights, instead of relying on God to make the choice for us. We have to learn to walk according to the standard which has its eyes focused on God. And God says to us, as he did to Abram, "... *walk before me* ..." (Genesis 17:1).

ADDITIONAL SCRIPTURE READING:
Genesis 6:9; 17:1; 2 Kings 20:2–3

Go to page 26 for your next devotional reading.

1900   Present

to the left, I'll go to the right; if you go to the right, I'll go to the left."

¹⁰Lot looked up and saw that the whole plain of the Jordan was well watered, like the garden of the LORD, like the land of Egypt, toward Zoar. (This was before the LORD destroyed Sodom and Gomorrah.) ¹¹So Lot chose for himself the whole plain of the Jordan and set out toward the east. The two men parted company: ¹²Abram lived in the land of Canaan, while Lot lived among the cities of the plain and pitched his tents near Sodom. ¹³Now the men of Sodom were wicked and were sinning greatly against the LORD.

¹⁴The LORD said to Abram after Lot had parted from him, "Lift up your eyes from where you are and look north and south, east and west. ¹⁵All the land that you see I will give to you and your off-spring[a] forever. ¹⁶I will make your offspring like the dust of the earth, so that if anyone could count the dust, then your offspring could be counted. ¹⁷Go, walk through the length and breadth of the land, for I am giving it to you."

¹⁸So Abram moved his tents and went to live near the great trees of Mamre at Hebron, where he built an altar to the LORD.

Abram Rescues Lot

14 At this time Amraphel king of Shinar,[b] Arioch king of Ellasar, Kedorlaomer king of Elam and Tidal king of Goiim ²went to war against Bera king of Sodom, Birsha king of Gomorrah, Shinab king of Admah, Shemeber king of Zeboiim, and the king of Bela (that is, Zoar). ³All these latter kings joined forces in the Valley of Siddim (the Salt Sea[c]). ⁴For twelve years they had been subject to Kedorlaomer, but in the thirteenth year they rebelled.

⁵In the fourteenth year, Kedorlaomer and the kings allied with him went out and defeated the Rephaites in Ashteroth Karnaim, the Zuzites in Ham, the Emites in Shaveh Kiriathaim ⁶and the Horites in the hill country of Seir, as far as El Paran near the desert. ⁷Then they turned back and went to En Mishpat

(that is, Kadesh), and they conquered the whole territory of the Amalekites, as well as the Amorites who were living in Hazazon Tamar.

⁸Then the king of Sodom, the king of Gomorrah, the king of Admah, the king of Zeboiim and the king of Bela (that is, Zoar) marched out and drew up their battle lines in the Valley of Siddim ⁹against Kedorlaomer king of Elam, Tidal king of Goiim, Amraphel king of Shinar and Arioch king of Ellasar—four kings against five. ¹⁰Now the Valley of Siddim was full of tar pits, and when the kings of Sodom and Gomorrah fled, some of the men fell into them and the rest fled to the hills. ¹¹The four kings seized all the goods of Sodom and Gomorrah and all their food; then they went away. ¹²They also carried off Abram's nephew Lot and his posses-sions, since he was living in Sodom.

¹³One who had escaped came and reported this to Abram the Hebrew. Now Abram was living near the great trees of Mamre the Amorite, a brother[d] of Eshcol and Aner, all of whom were allied with Abram. ¹⁴When Abram heard that his relative had been taken captive, he called out the 318 trained men born in his household and went in pursuit as far as Dan. ¹⁵During the night Abram divided his men to attack them and he routed them, pursuing them as far as Hobah, north of Damascus. ¹⁶He recov-ered all the goods and brought back his relative Lot and his possessions, together with the women and the other people.

¹⁷After Abram returned from defeat-ing Kedorlaomer and the kings allied with him, the king of Sodom came out to meet him in the Valley of Shaveh (that is, the King's Valley).

¹⁸Then Melchizedek king of Salem[e] brought out bread and wine. He was priest of God Most High, ¹⁹and he blessed Abram, saying,

"Blessed be Abram by God Most
    High,
    Creator[f] of heaven and earth.
²⁰And blessed be[g] God Most High,

---

[a] 15 Or *seed;* also in verse 16   [b] 1 That is, Babylonia; also in verse 9   [c] 3 That is, the Dead Sea
[d] 13 Or *a relative;* or *an ally*   [e] 18 That is, Jerusalem   [f] 19 Or *Possessor;* also in verse 22   [g] 20 Or
And praise be to

who delivered your enemies into your hand."

Then Abram gave him a tenth of everything.

²¹The king of Sodom said to Abram, "Give me the people and keep the goods for yourself."

²²But Abram said to the king of Sodom, "I have raised my hand to the LORD, God Most High, Creator of heaven and earth, and have taken an oath ²³that I will accept nothing belonging to you, not even a thread or the thong of a sandal, so that you will never be able to say, 'I made Abram rich.' ²⁴I will accept nothing but what my men have eaten and the share that belongs to the men who went with me—to Aner, Eshcol and Mamre. Let them have their share."

God's Covenant With Abram

15 After this, the word of the LORD came to Abram in a vision:

"Do not be afraid, Abram.
  I am your shield,ᵃ
  your very great reward.ᵇ "

²But Abram said, "O Sovereign LORD, what can you give me since I remain childless and the one who will inheritᶜ my estate is Eliezer of Damascus?" ³And Abram said, "You have given me no children; so a servant in my household will be my heir."

⁴Then the word of the LORD came to him: "This man will not be your heir, but a son coming from your own body will be your heir." ⁵He took him outside and said, "Look up at the heavens and count the stars—if indeed you can count them." Then he said to him, "So shall your offspring be."

⁶Abram believed the LORD, and he credited it to him as righteousness.

⁷He also said to him, "I am the LORD, who brought you out of Ur of the Chaldeans to give you this land to take possession of it."

⁸But Abram said, "O Sovereign LORD, how can I know that I will gain possession of it?"

⁹So the LORD said to him, "Bring me a heifer, a goat and a ram, each three years old, along with a dove and a young pigeon."

¹⁰Abram brought all these to him, cut them in two and arranged the halves opposite each other; the birds, however, he did not cut in half. ¹¹Then birds of prey came down on the carcasses, but Abram drove them away.

¹²As the sun was setting, Abram fell into a deep sleep, and a thick and dreadful darkness came over him. ¹³Then the LORD said to him, "Know for certain that your descendants will be strangers in a country not their own, and they will be enslaved and mistreated four hundred years. ¹⁴But I will punish the nation they serve as slaves, and afterward they will come out with great possessions. ¹⁵You, however, will go to your fathers in peace and be buried at a good old age. ¹⁶In the fourth generation your descendants will come back here, for the sin of the Amorites has not yet reached its full measure."

¹⁷When the sun had set and darkness had fallen, a smoking firepot with a blazing torch appeared and passed between the pieces. ¹⁸On that day the LORD made a covenant with Abram and said, "To your descendants I give this land, from the riverᵈ of Egypt to the great river, the Euphrates— ¹⁹the land of the Kenites, Kenizzites, Kadmonites, ²⁰Hittites, Perizzites, Rephaites, ²¹Amorites, Canaanites, Girgashites and Jebusites."

Hagar and Ishmael

16 Now Sarai, Abram's wife, had borne him no children. But she had an Egyptian maidservant named Hagar; ²so she said to Abram, "The LORD has kept me from having children. Go, sleep with my maidservant; perhaps I can build a family through her."

Abram agreed to what Sarai said. ³So after Abram had been living in Canaan ten years, Sarai his wife took her Egyptian maidservant Hagar and gave her to her husband to be his wife. ⁴He slept with Hagar, and she conceived.

When she knew she was pregnant, she began to despise her mistress. ⁵Then

---

ᵃ 1 Or *sovereign*   ᵇ 1 Or *shield; / your reward will be very great*   ᶜ 2 The meaning of the Hebrew for this phrase is uncertain.   ᵈ 18 Or *Wadi*

Sarai said to Abram, "You are responsible for the wrong I am suffering. I put my servant in your arms, and now that she knows she is pregnant, she despises me. May the LORD judge between you and me."

6"Your servant is in your hands," Abram said. "Do with her whatever you think best." Then Sarai mistreated Hagar; so she fled from her.

7The angel of the LORD found Hagar near a spring in the desert; it was the spring that is beside the road to Shur. 8And he said, "Hagar, servant of Sarai, where have you come from, and where are you going?"

"I'm running away from my mistress Sarai," she answered.

9Then the angel of the LORD told her, "Go back to your mistress and submit to her." 10The angel added, "I will so increase your descendants that they will be too numerous to count."

11The angel of the LORD also said to her:

"You are now with child
    and you will have a son.
You shall name him Ishmael,*a*
    for the LORD has heard of your
        misery.
12He will be a wild donkey of a man;
    his hand will be against everyone
    and everyone's hand against him,
    and he will live in hostility
        toward*b* all his brothers."

13She gave this name to the LORD who spoke to her: "You are the God who sees me," for she said, "I have now seen*c* the One who sees me." 14That is why the well was called Beer Lahai Roi*d*; it is still there, between Kadesh and Bered.

15So Hagar bore Abram a son, and Abram gave the name Ishmael to the son she had borne. 16Abram was eighty-six years old when Hagar bore him Ishmael.

The Covenant of Circumcision

17 When Abram was ninety-nine years old, the LORD appeared to him and said, "I am God Almighty*e*; walk before me and be blameless. 2I will

confirm my covenant between me and you and will greatly increase your numbers."

3Abram fell facedown, and God said to him, 4"As for me, this is my covenant with you: You will be the father of many nations. 5No longer will you be called Abram*f*; your name will be Abraham,*g* for I have made you a father of many nations. 6I will make you very fruitful; I will make nations of you, and kings will come from you. 7I will establish my covenant as an everlasting covenant between me and you and your descendants after you for the generations to come, to be your God and the God of your descendants after you. 8The whole land of Canaan, where you are now an alien, I will give as an everlasting possession to you and your descendants after you; and I will be their God."

9Then God said to Abraham, "As for you, you must keep my covenant, you and your descendants after you for the generations to come. 10This is my covenant with you and your descendants after you, the covenant you are to keep: Every male among you shall be circumcised. 11You are to undergo circumcision, and it will be the sign of the covenant between me and you. 12For the generations to come every male among you who is eight days old must be circumcised, including those born in your household or bought with money from a foreigner—those who are not your offspring. 13Whether born in your household or bought with your money, they must be circumcised. My covenant in your flesh is to be an everlasting covenant. 14Any uncircumcised male, who has not been circumcised in the flesh, will be cut off from his people; he has broken my covenant."

15God also said to Abraham, "As for Sarai your wife, you are no longer to call her Sarai; her name will be Sarah. 16I will bless her and will surely give you a son by her. I will bless her so that she will be the mother of nations; kings of peoples will come from her."

17Abraham fell facedown; he laughed

---

a 11 Ishmael means *God hears.*   *b 12* Or *live to the east / of*   *c 13* Or *seen the back of*   *d 14 Beer Lahai Roi* means *well of the Living One who sees me.*   *e 1* Hebrew *El-Shaddai*   *f 5 Abram* means *exalted father.*   *g 5 Abraham* means *father of many.*

and said to himself, "Will a son be born to a man a hundred years old? Will Sarah bear a child at the age of ninety?" 18And Abraham said to God, "If only Ishmael might live under your blessing!"

19Then God said, "Yes, but your wife Sarah will bear you a son, and you will call him Isaac.*a* I will establish my covenant with him as an everlasting covenant for his descendants after him. 20And as for Ishmael, I have heard you: I will surely bless him; I will make him fruitful and will greatly increase his numbers. He will be the father of twelve rulers, and I will make him into a great nation. 21But my covenant I will establish with Isaac, whom Sarah will bear to you by this time next year." 22When he had finished speaking with Abraham, God went up from him.

23On that very day Abraham took his son Ishmael and all those born in his household or bought with his money, every male in his household, and circumcised them, as God told him. 24Abraham was ninety-nine years old when he was circumcised, 25and his son Ishmael was thirteen; 26Abraham and his son Ishmael were both circumcised on that same day. 27And every male in Abraham's household, including those born in his household or bought from a foreigner, was circumcised with him.

The Three Visitors

18 The LORD appeared to Abraham near the great trees of Mamre while he was sitting at the entrance to his tent in the heat of the day. 2Abraham looked up and saw three men standing nearby. When he saw them, he hurried from the entrance of his tent to meet them and bowed low to the ground.

3He said, "If I have found favor in your eyes, my lord,*b* do not pass your servant by. 4Let a little water be brought, and then you may all wash your feet and rest under this tree. 5Let me get you something to eat, so you can be refreshed and then go on your way—now that you have come to your servant."

"Very well," they answered, "do as you say."

6So Abraham hurried into the tent to Sarah. "Quick," he said, "get three seahs*c* of fine flour and knead it and bake some bread."

7Then he ran to the herd and selected a choice, tender calf and gave it to a servant, who hurried to prepare it. 8He then brought some curds and milk and the calf that had been prepared, and set these before them. While they ate, he stood near them under a tree.

9"Where is your wife Sarah?" they asked him.

"There, in the tent," he said.

10Then the LORD*d* said, "I will surely return to you about this time next year, and Sarah your wife will have a son."

Now Sarah was listening at the entrance to the tent, which was behind him. 11Abraham and Sarah were already old and well advanced in years, and Sarah was past the age of childbearing. 12So Sarah laughed to herself as she thought, "After I am worn out and my master*e* is old, will I now have this pleasure?"

13Then the LORD said to Abraham, "Why did Sarah laugh and say, 'Will I really have a child, now that I am old?' 14Is anything too hard for the LORD? I will return to you at the appointed time next year and Sarah will have a son."

15Sarah was afraid, so she lied and said, "I did not laugh."

But he said, "Yes, you did laugh."

Abraham Pleads for Sodom

16When the men got up to leave, they looked down toward Sodom, and Abraham walked along with them to see them on their way. 17Then the LORD said, "Shall I hide from Abraham what I am about to do? 18Abraham will surely become a great and powerful nation, and all nations on earth will be blessed through him. 19For I have chosen him, so that he will direct his children and his household after him to keep the way of the LORD by doing what is right and just, so that the LORD will bring about for Abraham what he has promised him."

20Then the LORD said, "The outcry against Sodom and Gomorrah is so great and their sin so grievous 21that I will go down and see if what they have done is

---

a 19 Isaac means *he laughs.*   *b 3* Or *O Lord*   *c 6* That is, probably about 20 quarts (about 22 liters)
d 10 Hebrew *Then he*   *e 12* Or *husband*

as bad as the outcry that has reached me. If not, I will know."

22The men turned away and went toward Sodom, but Abraham remained standing before the LORD.*a* 23Then Abraham approached him and said: "Will you sweep away the righteous with the wicked? 24What if there are fifty righteous people in the city? Will you really sweep it away and not spare*b* the place for the sake of the fifty righteous people in it? 25Far be it from you to do such a thing—to kill the righteous with the wicked, treating the righteous and the wicked alike. Far be it from you! Will not the Judge*c* of all the earth do right?"

26The LORD said, "If I find fifty righteous people in the city of Sodom, I will spare the whole place for their sake."

27Then Abraham spoke up again: "Now that I have been so bold as to speak to the Lord, though I am nothing but dust and ashes, 28what if the number of the righteous is five less than fifty? Will you destroy the whole city because of five people?"

"If I find forty-five there," he said, "I will not destroy it."

29Once again he spoke to him, "What if only forty are found there?"

He said, "For the sake of forty, I will not do it."

30Then he said, "May the Lord not be angry, but let me speak. What if only thirty can be found there?"

He answered, "I will not do it if I find thirty there."

31Abraham said, "Now that I have been so bold as to speak to the Lord, what if only twenty can be found there?"

He said, "For the sake of twenty, I will not destroy it."

32Then he said, "May the Lord not be angry, but let me speak just once more. What if only ten can be found there?"

He answered, "For the sake of ten, I will not destroy it."

33When the LORD had finished speaking with Abraham, he left, and Abraham returned home.

Sodom and Gomorrah Destroyed

19 The two angels arrived at Sodom in the evening, and Lot was sitting in the gateway of the city. When he saw them, he got up to meet them and bowed down with his face to the ground. 2"My lords," he said, "please turn aside to your servant's house. You can wash your feet and spend the night and then go on your way early in the morning."

"No," they answered, "we will spend the night in the square."

3But he insisted so strongly that they did go with him and entered his house. He prepared a meal for them, baking bread without yeast, and they ate. 4Before they had gone to bed, all the men from every part of the city of Sodom—both young and old—surrounded the house. 5They called to Lot, "Where are the men who came to you tonight? Bring them out to us so that we can have sex with them."

6Lot went outside to meet them and shut the door behind him 7and said, "No, my friends. Don't do this wicked thing. 8Look, I have two daughters who have never slept with a man. Let me bring them out to you, and you can do what you like with them. But don't do anything to these men, for they have come under the protection of my roof."

9"Get out of our way," they replied. And they said, "This fellow came here as an alien, and now he wants to play the judge! We'll treat you worse than them." They kept bringing pressure on Lot and moved forward to break down the door.

10But the men inside reached out and pulled Lot back into the house and shut the door. 11Then they struck the men who were at the door of the house, young and old, with blindness so that they could not find the door.

12The two men said to Lot, "Do you have anyone else here—sons-in-law, sons or daughters, or anyone else in the city who belongs to you? Get them out of here, 13because we are going to destroy this place. The outcry to the LORD against its people is so great that he has sent us to destroy it."

a 22 Masoretic Text; an ancient Hebrew scribal tradition *but the LORD remained standing before Abraham*   *b 24* Or *forgive;* also in verse 26   *c 25* Or *Ruler*

14So Lot went out and spoke to his sons-in-law, who were pledged to marry*a* his daughters. He said, "Hurry and get out of this place, because the LORD is about to destroy the city!" But his sons-in-law thought he was joking.

15With the coming of dawn, the angels urged Lot, saying, "Hurry! Take your wife and your two daughters who are here, or you will be swept away when the city is punished."

16When he hesitated, the men grasped his hand and the hands of his wife and of his two daughters and led them safely out of the city, for the LORD was merciful to them. 17As soon as they had brought them out, one of them said, "Flee for your lives! Don't look back, and don't stop anywhere in the plain! Flee to the mountains or you will be swept away!"

18But Lot said to them, "No, my lords,*b* please! 19Your*c* servant has found favor in your*c* eyes, and you*c* have shown great kindness to me in sparing my life. But I can't flee to the mountains; this disaster will overtake me, and I'll die. 20Look, here is a town near enough to run to, and it is small. Let me flee to it—it is very small, isn't it? Then my life will be spared."

21He said to him, "Very well, I will grant this request too; I will not overthrow the town you speak of. 22But flee there quickly, because I cannot do anything until you reach it." (That is why the town was called Zoar.*d*)

23By the time Lot reached Zoar, the sun had risen over the land. 24Then the LORD rained down burning sulfur on Sodom and Gomorrah—from the LORD out of the heavens. 25Thus he overthrew those cities and the entire plain, including all those living in the cities—and also the vegetation in the land. 26But Lot's wife looked back, and she became a pillar of salt.

27Early the next morning Abraham got up and returned to the place where he had stood before the LORD. 28He looked down toward Sodom and Gomorrah, toward all the land of the plain, and he saw dense smoke rising from the land, like smoke from a furnace.

29So when God destroyed the cities of the plain, he remembered Abraham, and he brought Lot out of the catastrophe that overthrew the cities where Lot had lived.

Lot and His Daughters

30Lot and his two daughters left Zoar and settled in the mountains, for he was afraid to stay in Zoar. He and his two daughters lived in a cave. 31One day the older daughter said to the younger, "Our father is old, and there is no man around here to lie with us, as is the custom all over the earth. 32Let's get our father to drink wine and then lie with him and preserve our family line through our father."

33That night they got their father to drink wine, and the older daughter went in and lay with him. He was not aware of it when she lay down or when she got up.

34The next day the older daughter said to the younger, "Last night I lay with my father. Let's get him to drink wine again tonight, and you go in and lie with him so we can preserve our family line through our father." 35So they got their father to drink wine that night also, and the younger daughter went and lay with him. Again he was not aware of it when she lay down or when she got up.

36So both of Lot's daughters became pregnant by their father. 37The older daughter had a son, and she named him Moab*e*; he is the father of the Moabites of today. 38The younger daughter also had a son, and she named him Ben-Ammi*f*; he is the father of the Ammonites of today.

Abraham and Abimelech

20 Now Abraham moved on from there into the region of the Negev and lived between Kadesh and Shur. For a while he stayed in Gerar, 2and there Abraham said of his wife Sarah, "She is my sister." Then Abimelech king of Gerar sent for Sarah and took her.

3But God came to Abimelech in a dream one night and said to him, "You are as good as dead because of the

---

a 14 Or *were married to*   *b* 18 Or *No, Lord;* or *No, my lord*   *c* 19 The Hebrew is singular.
d 22 *Zoar* means *small.*   *e* 37 *Moab* sounds like the Hebrew for *from father.*   *f* 38 *Ben-Ammi* means *son of my people.*

woman you have taken; she is a married woman."

⁴Now Abimelech had not gone near her, so he said, "Lord, will you destroy an innocent nation? ⁵Did he not say to me, 'She is my sister,' and didn't she also say, 'He is my brother'? I have done this with a clear conscience and clean hands."

⁶Then God said to him in the dream, "Yes, I know you did this with a clear conscience, and so I have kept you from sinning against me. That is why I did not let you touch her. ⁷Now return the man's wife, for he is a prophet, and he will pray for you and you will live. But if you do not return her, you may be sure that you and all yours will die."

⁸Early the next morning Abimelech summoned all his officials, and when he told them all that had happened, they were very much afraid. ⁹Then Abimelech called Abraham in and said, "What have you done to us? How have I wronged you that you have brought such great guilt upon me and my kingdom? You have done things to me that should not be done." ¹⁰And Abimelech asked Abraham, "What was your reason for doing this?"

¹¹Abraham replied, "I said to myself, 'There is surely no fear of God in this place, and they will kill me because of my wife.' ¹²Besides, she really is my sister, the daughter of my father though not of my mother; and she became my wife. ¹³And when God had me wander from my father's household, I said to her, 'This is how you can show your love to me: Everywhere we go, say of me, "He is my brother." ' "

¹⁴Then Abimelech brought sheep and cattle and male and female slaves and gave them to Abraham, and he returned Sarah his wife to him. ¹⁵And Abimelech said, "My land is before you; live wherever you like."

¹⁶To Sarah he said, "I am giving your brother a thousand shekels*a* of silver. This is to cover the offense against you before all who are with you; you are completely vindicated."

¹⁷Then Abraham prayed to God, and God healed Abimelech, his wife and his slave girls so they could have children again, ¹⁸for the LORD had closed up every womb in Abimelech's household because of Abraham's wife Sarah.

The Birth of Isaac

21 Now the LORD was gracious to Sarah as he had said, and the LORD did for Sarah what he had promised. ²Sarah became pregnant and bore a son to Abraham in his old age, at the very time God had promised him. ³Abraham gave the name Isaac*b* to the son Sarah bore him. ⁴When his son Isaac was eight days old, Abraham circumcised him, as God commanded him. ⁵Abraham was a hundred years old when his son Isaac was born to him.

⁶Sarah said, "God has brought me laughter, and everyone who hears about this will laugh with me." ⁷And she added, "Who would have said to Abraham that Sarah would nurse children? Yet I have borne him a son in his old age."

Hagar and Ishmael Sent Away

⁸The child grew and was weaned, and on the day Isaac was weaned Abraham held a great feast. ⁹But Sarah saw that the son whom Hagar the Egyptian had borne to Abraham was mocking, ¹⁰and she said to Abraham, "Get rid of that slave woman and her son, for that slave woman's son will never share in the inheritance with my son Isaac."

¹¹The matter distressed Abraham greatly because it concerned his son. ¹²But God said to him, "Do not be so distressed about the boy and your maidservant. Listen to whatever Sarah tells you, because it is through Isaac that your offspring*c* will be reckoned. ¹³I will make the son of the maidservant into a nation also, because he is your offspring."

¹⁴Early the next morning Abraham took some food and a skin of water and gave them to Hagar. He set them on her shoulders and then sent her off with the boy. She went on her way and wandered in the desert of Beersheba.

¹⁵When the water in the skin was gone, she put the boy under one of the bushes. ¹⁶Then she went off and sat down nearby, about a bowshot away, for she thought, "I cannot watch the boy

die." And as she sat there nearby, she[a] began to sob.

¹⁷God heard the boy crying, and the angel of God called to Hagar from heaven and said to her, "What is the matter, Hagar? Do not be afraid; God has heard the boy crying as he lies there. ¹⁸Lift the boy up and take him by the hand, for I will make him into a great nation."

¹⁹Then God opened her eyes and she saw a well of water. So she went and filled the skin with water and gave the boy a drink.

²⁰God was with the boy as he grew up. He lived in the desert and became an archer. ²¹While he was living in the Desert of Paran, his mother got a wife for him from Egypt.

The Treaty at Beersheba

²²At that time Abimelech and Phicol the commander of his forces said to Abraham, "God is with you in everything you do. ²³Now swear to me here before God that you will not deal falsely with me or my children or my descendants. Show to me and the country where you are living as an alien the same kindness I have shown to you."

²⁴Abraham said, "I swear it."

²⁵Then Abraham complained to Abimelech about a well of water that Abimelech's servants had seized. ²⁶But Abimelech said, "I don't know who has done this. You did not tell me, and I heard about it only today."

²⁷So Abraham brought sheep and cattle and gave them to Abimelech, and the two men made a treaty. ²⁸Abraham set apart seven ewe lambs from the flock, ²⁹and Abimelech asked Abraham, "What is the meaning of these seven ewe lambs you have set apart by themselves?"

³⁰He replied, "Accept these seven lambs from my hand as a witness that I dug this well."

³¹So that place was called Beersheba,[b] because the two men swore an oath there.

³²After the treaty had been made at Beersheba, Abimelech and Phicol the commander of his forces returned to the land of the Philistines. ³³Abraham planted a tamarisk tree in Beersheba, and there he called upon the name of the

LORD, the Eternal God. ³⁴And Abraham stayed in the land of the Philistines for a long time.

Abraham Tested

22 Some time later God tested Abraham. He said to him, "Abraham!"

"Here I am," he replied.

²Then God said, "Take your son, your only son, Isaac, whom you love, and go to the region of Moriah. Sacrifice him there as a burnt offering on one of the mountains I will tell you about."

³Early the next morning Abraham got up and saddled his donkey. He took with him two of his servants and his son Isaac. When he had cut enough wood for the burnt offering, he set out for the place God had told him about. ⁴On the third day Abraham looked up and saw the place in the distance. ⁵He said to his servants, "Stay here with the donkey while I and the boy go over there. We will worship and then we will come back to you."

⁶Abraham took the wood for the burnt offering and placed it on his son Isaac, and he himself carried the fire and the knife. As the two of them went on together, ⁷Isaac spoke up and said to his father Abraham, "Father?"

"Yes, my son?" Abraham replied.

"The fire and wood are here," Isaac said, "but where is the lamb for the burnt offering?"

⁸Abraham answered, "God himself will provide the lamb for the burnt offering, my son." And the two of them went on together.

⁹When they reached the place God had told him about, Abraham built an altar there and arranged the wood on it. He bound his son Isaac and laid him on the altar, on top of the wood. ¹⁰Then he reached out his hand and took the knife to slay his son. ¹¹But the angel of the LORD called out to him from heaven, "Abraham! Abraham!"

"Here I am," he replied.

¹²"Do not lay a hand on the boy," he said. "Do not do anything to him. Now I know that you fear God, because you have not withheld from me your son, your only son."

---

a 16 Hebrew; Septuagint *the child*   b 31 *Beersheba* can mean *well of seven* or *well of the oath.*

¹³Abraham looked up and there in a thicket he saw a ram*a* caught by its horns. He went over and took the ram and sacrificed it as a burnt offering instead of his son. ¹⁴So Abraham called that place The LORD Will Provide. And to this day it is said, "On the mountain of the LORD it will be provided."

¹⁵The angel of the LORD called to Abraham from heaven a second time ¹⁶and said, "I swear by myself, declares the LORD, that because you have done this and have not withheld your son, your only son, ¹⁷I will surely bless you and make your descendants as numerous as the stars in the sky and as the sand on the seashore. Your descendants will take possession of the cities of their enemies, ¹⁸and through your offspring*b* all nations on earth will be blessed, because you have obeyed me."

¹⁹Then Abraham returned to his ser-

a 13 Many manuscripts of the Masoretic Text, Samaritan Pentateuch, Septuagint and Syriac; most manuscripts of the Masoretic Text *a ram behind him,*   *b 18* Or *seed*

MONDAY

THE LOVE OF GOD
Dwight L. Moody

VERSE: Genesis 22:14   **PASSAGE:** Genesis 22:1–14

 remember that for the first few years after I was converted, I had a good deal more love for Christ than for God the Father. I looked upon God as the stern judge, while I regarded Christ as the mediator who had come between me and that stern judge to appease his wrath. But when I got a little better acquainted with my Bible, those views all fled.

After I became a father and woke up to the realization of what it cost God to have his Son die, I began to see that God was to be loved just as much as his Son was. Why, it took more love for God to give his Son to die than it would to die himself. You would a thousand times sooner die yourself in your son's place than have him taken away. If the executioner was about to take your son to the gallows, you would say, "Let me die in his stead; let my son be spared."

Oh, think of the love God must have had for this world that he gave his only begotten Son to die for it. And that is what I want you to understand. "The Father himself loves you because you have loved me . . ." (John 16:27). If a man has loved Christ, God will set his love upon him.

ADDITIONAL SCRIPTURE READING:
Deuteronomy 7:7–8; 1 John 4:19

Go to page 54 for your next devotional reading.

1900   Present

vants, and they set off together for Beersheba. And Abraham stayed in Beersheba.

Nahor's Sons

20Some time later Abraham was told, "Milcah is also a mother; she has borne sons to your brother Nahor: **21**Uz the firstborn, Buz his brother, Kemuel (the father of Aram), **22**Kesed, Hazo, Pildash, Jidlaph and Bethuel." **23**Bethuel became the father of Rebekah. Milcah bore these eight sons to Abraham's brother Nahor. **24**His concubine, whose name was Reumah, also had sons: Tebah, Gaham, Tahash and Maacah.

The Death of Sarah

23 Sarah lived to be a hundred and twenty-seven years old. **2**She died at Kiriath Arba (that is, Hebron) in the land of Canaan, and Abraham went to mourn for Sarah and to weep over her.

3Then Abraham rose from beside his dead wife and spoke to the Hittites.*a* He said, **4**"I am an alien and a stranger among you. Sell me some property for a burial site here so I can bury my dead."

5The Hittites replied to Abraham, **6**"Sir, listen to us. You are a mighty prince among us. Bury your dead in the choicest of our tombs. None of us will refuse you his tomb for burying your dead."

7Then Abraham rose and bowed down before the people of the land, the Hittites. **8**He said to them, "If you are willing to let me bury my dead, then listen to me and intercede with Ephron son of Zohar on my behalf **9**so he will sell me the cave of Machpelah, which belongs to him and is at the end of his field. Ask him to sell it to me for the full price as a burial site among you."

10Ephron the Hittite was sitting among his people and he replied to Abraham in the hearing of all the Hittites who had come to the gate of his city. **11**"No, my lord," he said. "Listen to me; I give*b* you the field, and I give*b* you the cave that is in it. I give*b* it to you in the presence of my people. Bury your dead."

12Again Abraham bowed down before the people of the land **13**and he said to Ephron in their hearing, "Listen to me, if you will. I will pay the price of the field. Accept it from me so I can bury my dead there."

14Ephron answered Abraham, **15**"Listen to me, my lord; the land is worth four hundred shekels*c* of silver, but what is that between me and you? Bury your dead."

16Abraham agreed to Ephron's terms and weighed out for him the price he had named in the hearing of the Hittites: four hundred shekels of silver, according to the weight current among the merchants.

17So Ephron's field in Machpelah near Mamre—both the field and the cave in it, and all the trees within the borders of the field—was deeded **18**to Abraham as his property in the presence of all the Hittites who had come to the gate of the city. **19**Afterward Abraham buried his wife Sarah in the cave in the field of Machpelah near Mamre (which is at Hebron) in the land of Canaan. **20**So the field and the cave in it were deeded to Abraham by the Hittites as a burial site.

Isaac and Rebekah

24 Abraham was now old and well advanced in years, and the LORD had blessed him in every way. **2**He said to the chief*d* servant in his household, the one in charge of all that he had, "Put your hand under my thigh. **3**I want you to swear by the LORD, the God of heaven and the God of earth, that you will not get a wife for my son from the daughters of the Canaanites, among whom I am living, **4**but will go to my country and my own relatives and get a wife for my son Isaac."

5The servant asked him, "What if the woman is unwilling to come back with

a 3 Or *the sons of Heth*; also in verses 5, 7, 10, 16, 18 and 20   *b* 11 Or *sell*   *c* 15 That is, about 10 pounds (about 4.5 kilograms)   *d* 2 Or *oldest*

me to this land? Shall I then take your son back to the country you came from?"

6"Make sure that you do not take my son back there," Abraham said. 7"The LORD, the God of heaven, who brought me out of my father's household and my native land and who spoke to me and promised me on oath, saying, 'To your offspring*a* I will give this land'—he will send his angel before you so that you can get a wife for my son from there. 8If the woman is unwilling to come back with you, then you will be released from this oath of mine. Only do not take my son back there." 9So the servant put his hand under the thigh of his master Abraham and swore an oath to him concerning this matter.

10Then the servant took ten of his master's camels and left, taking with him all kinds of good things from his master. He set out for Aram Naharaim*b* and made his way to the town of Nahor. 11He had the camels kneel down near the well outside the town; it was toward evening, the time the women go out to draw water.

12Then he prayed, "O LORD, God of my master Abraham, give me success today, and show kindness to my master Abraham. 13See, I am standing beside this spring, and the daughters of the townspeople are coming out to draw water. 14May it be that when I say to a girl, 'Please let down your jar that I may have a drink,' and she says, 'Drink, and I'll water your camels too'—let her be the one you have chosen for your servant Isaac. By this I will know that you have shown kindness to my master."

15Before he had finished praying, Rebekah came out with her jar on her shoulder. She was the daughter of Bethuel son of Milcah, who was the wife of Abraham's brother Nahor. 16The girl was very beautiful, a virgin; no man had ever lain with her. She went down to the spring, filled her jar and came up again.

17The servant hurried to meet her and said, "Please give me a little water from your jar."

18"Drink, my lord," she said, and quickly lowered the jar to her hands and gave him a drink.

19After she had given him a drink, she said, "I'll draw water for your camels too, until they have finished drinking." 20So she quickly emptied her jar into the trough, ran back to the well to draw more water, and drew enough for all his camels. 21Without saying a word, the man watched her closely to learn whether or not the LORD had made his journey successful.

22When the camels had finished drinking, the man took out a gold nose ring weighing a beka*c* and two gold bracelets weighing ten shekels.*d* 23Then he asked, "Whose daughter are you? Please tell me, is there room in your father's house for us to spend the night?"

24She answered him, "I am the daughter of Bethuel, the son that Milcah bore to Nahor." 25And she added, "We have plenty of straw and fodder, as well as room for you to spend the night."

26Then the man bowed down and worshiped the LORD, 27saying, "Praise be to the LORD, the God of my master Abraham, who has not abandoned his kindness and faithfulness to my master. As for me, the LORD has led me on the journey to the house of my master's relatives."

28The girl ran and told her mother's household about these things. 29Now Rebekah had a brother named Laban, and he hurried out to the man at the spring. 30As soon as he had seen the nose ring, and the bracelets on his sister's arms, and had heard Rebekah tell what the man said to her, he went out to the man and found him standing by the camels near the spring. 31"Come, you who are blessed by the LORD," he said. "Why are you standing out here? I have prepared the house and a place for the camels."

32So the man went to the house, and the camels were unloaded. Straw and fodder were brought for the camels, and water for him and his men to wash their feet. 33Then food was set before him, but he said, "I will not eat until I have told you what I have to say."

"Then tell us," ⌊Laban⌋ said.

34So he said, "I am Abraham's servant. 35The LORD has blessed my master abundantly, and he has become wealthy.

---

a 7 Or *seed*   *b* 10 That is, Northwest Mesopotamia   *c* 22 That is, about 1/5 ounce (about 5.5 grams)
d 22 That is, about 4 ounces (about 110 grams)

He has given him sheep and cattle, silver and gold, menservants and maidservants, and camels and donkeys. ³⁶My master's wife Sarah has borne him a son in her^a old age, and he has given him everything he owns. ³⁷And my master made me swear an oath, and said, 'You must not get a wife for my son from the daughters of the Canaanites, in whose land I live, ³⁸but go to my father's family and to my own clan, and get a wife for my son.'

³⁹"Then I asked my master, 'What if the woman will not come back with me?'

⁴⁰"He replied, 'The LORD, before whom I have walked, will send his angel with you and make your journey a success, so that you can get a wife for my son from my own clan and from my father's family. ⁴¹Then, when you go to my clan, you will be released from my oath even if they refuse to give her to you—you will be released from my oath.'

⁴²"When I came to the spring today, I said, 'O LORD, God of my master Abraham, if you will, please grant success to the journey on which I have come. ⁴³See, I am standing beside this spring; if a maiden comes out to draw water and I say to her, "Please let me drink a little water from your jar," ⁴⁴and if she says to me, "Drink, and I'll draw water for your camels too," let her be the one the LORD has chosen for my master's son.'

⁴⁵"Before I finished praying in my heart, Rebekah came out, with her jar on her shoulder. She went down to the spring and drew water, and I said to her, 'Please give me a drink.'

⁴⁶"She quickly lowered her jar from her shoulder and said, 'Drink, and I'll water your camels too.' So I drank, and she watered the camels also.

⁴⁷"I asked her, 'Whose daughter are you?'

"She said, 'The daughter of Bethuel son of Nahor, whom Milcah bore to him.'

"Then I put the ring in her nose and the bracelets on her arms, ⁴⁸and I bowed down and worshiped the LORD. I praised the LORD, the God of my master Abraham, who had led me on the right road to get the granddaughter of my master's brother for his son. ⁴⁹Now if you will

show kindness and faithfulness to my master, tell me; and if not, tell me, so I may know which way to turn."

⁵⁰Laban and Bethuel answered, "This is from the LORD; we can say nothing to you one way or the other. ⁵¹Here is Rebekah; take her and go, and let her become the wife of your master's son, as the LORD has directed."

⁵²When Abraham's servant heard what they said, he bowed down to the ground before the LORD. ⁵³Then the servant brought out gold and silver jewelry and articles of clothing and gave them to Rebekah; he also gave costly gifts to her brother and to her mother. ⁵⁴Then he and the men who were with him ate and drank and spent the night there.

When they got up the next morning, he said, "Send me on my way to my master."

⁵⁵But her brother and her mother replied, "Let the girl remain with us ten days or so; then you^b may go."

⁵⁶But he said to them, "Do not detain me, now that the LORD has granted success to my journey. Send me on my way so I may go to my master."

⁵⁷Then they said, "Let's call the girl and ask her about it." ⁵⁸So they called Rebekah and asked her, "Will you go with this man?"

"I will go," she said.

⁵⁹So they sent their sister Rebekah on her way, along with her nurse and Abraham's servant and his men. ⁶⁰And they blessed Rebekah and said to her,

"Our sister, may you increase
   to thousands upon thousands;
may your offspring possess
   the gates of their enemies."

⁶¹Then Rebekah and her maids got ready and mounted their camels and went back with the man. So the servant took Rebekah and left.

⁶²Now Isaac had come from Beer Lahai Roi, for he was living in the Negev. ⁶³He went out to the field one evening to meditate,^c and as he looked up, he saw camels approaching. ⁶⁴Rebekah also looked up and saw Isaac. She got down from her camel ⁶⁵and asked

the servant, "Who is that man in the field coming to meet us?"

"He is my master," the servant answered. So she took her veil and covered herself.

⁶⁶Then the servant told Isaac all he had done. ⁶⁷Isaac brought her into the tent of his mother Sarah, and he married Rebekah. So she became his wife, and he loved her; and Isaac was comforted after his mother's death.

GOD ALWAYS GIVES HIS VERY BEST TO THOSE WHO LEAVE THE CHOICE WITH HIM.

—*James Hudson Taylor*

The Death of Abraham

25 Abraham took[a] another wife, whose name was Keturah. ²She bore him Zimran, Jokshan, Medan, Midian, Ishbak and Shuah. ³Jokshan was the father of Sheba and Dedan; the descendants of Dedan were the Asshurites, the Letushites and the Leummites. ⁴The sons of Midian were Ephah, Epher, Hanoch, Abida and Eldaah. All these were descendants of Keturah.

⁵Abraham left everything he owned to Isaac. ⁶But while he was still living, he gave gifts to the sons of his concubines and sent them away from his son Isaac to the land of the east.

⁷Altogether, Abraham lived a hundred and seventy-five years. ⁸Then Abraham breathed his last and died at a good old age, an old man and full of years; and he was gathered to his people. ⁹His sons Isaac and Ishmael buried him in the cave of Machpelah near Mamre, in the field of Ephron son of Zohar the Hittite, ¹⁰the field Abraham had bought from the Hittites.[b] There Abraham was buried with his wife Sarah. ¹¹After Abraham's death, God blessed his son Isaac, who then lived near Beer Lahai Roi.

Ishmael's Sons

¹²This is the account of Abraham's son Ishmael, whom Sarah's maidservant, Hagar the Egyptian, bore to Abraham.

¹³These are the names of the sons of Ishmael, listed in the order of their birth: Nebaioth the firstborn of Ishmael, Kedar, Adbeel, Mibsam, ¹⁴Mishma, Dumah, Massa, ¹⁵Hadad, Tema, Jetur, Naphish and Kedemah. ¹⁶These were the sons of Ishmael, and these are the names of the twelve tribal rulers according to their settlements and camps. ¹⁷Altogether, Ishmael lived a hundred and thirty-seven years. He breathed his last and died, and he was gathered to his people. ¹⁸His descendants settled in the area from Havilah to Shur, near the border of Egypt, as you go toward Asshur. And they lived in hostility toward[c] all their brothers.

Jacob and Esau

¹⁹This is the account of Abraham's son Isaac.

Abraham became the father of Isaac, ²⁰and Isaac was forty years old when he married Rebekah daughter of Bethuel the Aramean from Paddan Aram[d] and sister of Laban the Aramean.

²¹Isaac prayed to the LORD on behalf of his wife, because she was barren. The LORD answered his prayer, and his wife Rebekah became pregnant. ²²The babies jostled each other within her, and she said, "Why is this happening to me?" So she went to inquire of the LORD.

²³The LORD said to her,

"Two nations are in your womb,
    and two peoples from within you
        will be separated;
one people will be stronger than the
        other,
    and the older will serve the
        younger."

²⁴When the time came for her to give birth, there were twin boys in her womb. ²⁵The first to come out was red, and his whole body was like a hairy garment; so they named him Esau.[e] ²⁶After this, his brother came out, with his hand grasping Esau's heel; so he was named Jacob.[f] Isaac was sixty years old when Rebekah gave birth to them.

²⁷The boys grew up, and Esau became

a 1 Or *had taken*   *b 10* Or *the sons of Heth*   *c 18* Or *lived to the east of*   *d 20* That is, Northwest Mesopotamia   *e 25* *Esau* may mean *hairy;* he was also called Edom, which means *red.*   *f 26* *Jacob* means *he grasps the heel* (figuratively, *he deceives*).

a skillful hunter, a man of the open country, while Jacob was a quiet man, staying among the tents. 28Isaac, who had a taste for wild game, loved Esau, but Rebekah loved Jacob.

29Once when Jacob was cooking some stew, Esau came in from the open country, famished. 30He said to Jacob, "Quick, let me have some of that red stew! I'm famished!" (That is why he was also called Edom.*a*)

31Jacob replied, "First sell me your birthright."

32"Look, I am about to die," Esau said. "What good is the birthright to me?"

33But Jacob said, "Swear to me first." So he swore an oath to him, selling his birthright to Jacob.

34Then Jacob gave Esau some bread and some lentil stew. He ate and drank, and then got up and left.

So Esau despised his birthright.

Isaac and Abimelech

26 Now there was a famine in the land—besides the earlier famine of Abraham's time—and Isaac went to Abimelech king of the Philistines in Gerar. 2The LORD appeared to Isaac and said, "Do not go down to Egypt; live in the land where I tell you to live. 3Stay in this land for a while, and I will be with you and will bless you. For to you and your descendants I will give all these lands and will confirm the oath I swore to your father Abraham. 4I will make your descendants as numerous as the stars in the sky and will give them all these lands, and through your offspring*b* all nations on earth will be blessed, 5because Abraham obeyed me and kept my requirements, my commands, my decrees and my laws." 6So Isaac stayed in Gerar.

7When the men of that place asked him about his wife, he said, "She is my sister," because he was afraid to say, "She is my wife." He thought, "The men of this place might kill me on account of Rebekah, because she is beautiful."

8When Isaac had been there a long time, Abimelech king of the Philistines looked down from a window and saw Isaac caressing his wife Rebekah. 9So

Abimelech summoned Isaac and said, "She is really your wife! Why did you say, 'She is my sister'?"

Isaac answered him, "Because I thought I might lose my life on account of her."

10Then Abimelech said, "What is this you have done to us? One of the men might well have slept with your wife, and you would have brought guilt upon us."

11So Abimelech gave orders to all the people: "Anyone who molests this man or his wife shall surely be put to death."

12Isaac planted crops in that land and the same year reaped a hundredfold, because the LORD blessed him. 13The man became rich, and his wealth continued to grow until he became very wealthy. 14He had so many flocks and herds and servants that the Philistines envied him. 15So all the wells that his father's servants had dug in the time of his father Abraham, the Philistines stopped up, filling them with earth.

16Then Abimelech said to Isaac, "Move away from us; you have become too powerful for us."

17So Isaac moved away from there and encamped in the Valley of Gerar and settled there. 18Isaac reopened the wells that had been dug in the time of his father Abraham, which the Philistines had stopped up after Abraham died, and he gave them the same names his father had given them.

19Isaac's servants dug in the valley and discovered a well of fresh water there. 20But the herdsmen of Gerar quarreled with Isaac's herdsmen and said, "The water is ours!" So he named the well Esek,*c* because they disputed with him. 21Then they dug another well, but they quarreled over that one also; so he named it Sitnah.*d* 22He moved on from there and dug another well, and no one quarreled over it. He named it Rehoboth,*e* saying, "Now the LORD has given us room and we will flourish in the land."

23From there he went up to Beersheba. 24That night the LORD appeared to him and said, "I am the God of your father Abraham. Do not be afraid, for I am with you; I will bless you and will increase

---

a 30 Edom means red.   b 4 Or seed   c 20 Esek means dispute.   d 21 Sitnah means opposition.
e 22 Rehoboth means room.

the number of your descendants for the sake of my servant Abraham."

25Isaac built an altar there and called on the name of the LORD. There he pitched his tent, and there his servants dug a well.

26Meanwhile, Abimelech had come to him from Gerar, with Ahuzzath his personal adviser and Phicol the commander of his forces. 27Isaac asked them, "Why have you come to me, since you were hostile to me and sent me away?"

28They answered, "We saw clearly that the LORD was with you; so we said, 'There ought to be a sworn agreement between us'—between us and you. Let us make a treaty with you 29that you will do us no harm, just as we did not molest you but always treated you well and sent you away in peace. And now you are blessed by the LORD."

30Isaac then made a feast for them, and they ate and drank. 31Early the next morning the men swore an oath to each other. Then Isaac sent them on their way, and they left him in peace.

32That day Isaac's servants came and told him about the well they had dug. They said, "We've found water!" 33He called it Shibah,a and to this day the name of the town has been Beersheba.b

34When Esau was forty years old, he married Judith daughter of Beeri the Hittite, and also Basemath daughter of Elon the Hittite. 35They were a source of grief to Isaac and Rebekah.

Jacob Gets Isaac's Blessing

27 When Isaac was old and his eyes were so weak that he could no longer see, he called for Esau his older son and said to him, "My son."

"Here I am," he answered.

2Isaac said, "I am now an old man and don't know the day of my death. 3Now then, get your weapons—your quiver and bow—and go out to the open country to hunt some wild game for me. 4Prepare me the kind of tasty food I like and bring it to me to eat, so that I may give you my blessing before I die."

5Now Rebekah was listening as Isaac spoke to his son Esau. When Esau left for the open country to hunt game and bring it back, 6Rebekah said to her son Jacob,

"Look, I overheard your father say to your brother Esau, 7'Bring me some game and prepare me some tasty food to eat, so that I may give you my blessing in the presence of the LORD before I die.' 8Now, my son, listen carefully and do what I tell you: 9Go out to the flock and bring me two choice young goats, so I can prepare some tasty food for your father, just the way he likes it. 10Then take it to your father to eat, so that he may give you his blessing before he dies."

11Jacob said to Rebekah his mother, "But my brother Esau is a hairy man, and I'm a man with smooth skin. 12What if my father touches me? I would appear to be tricking him and would bring down a curse on myself rather than a blessing."

13His mother said to him, "My son, let the curse fall on me. Just do what I say; go and get them for me."

14So he went and got them and brought them to his mother, and she prepared some tasty food, just the way his father liked it. 15Then Rebekah took the best clothes of Esau her older son, which she had in the house, and put them on her younger son Jacob. 16She also covered his hands and the smooth part of his neck with the goatskins. 17Then she handed to her son Jacob the tasty food and the bread she had made.

18He went to his father and said, "My father."

"Yes, my son," he answered. "Who is it?"

19Jacob said to his father, "I am Esau your firstborn. I have done as you told me. Please sit up and eat some of my game so that you may give me your blessing."

20Isaac asked his son, "How did you find it so quickly, my son?"

"The LORD your God gave me success," he replied.

21Then Isaac said to Jacob, "Come near so I can touch you, my son, to know whether you really are my son Esau or not."

22Jacob went close to his father Isaac, who touched him and said, "The voice is the voice of Jacob, but the hands are the hands of Esau." 23He did not recognize him, for his hands were hairy like

---

a 33 Shibah can mean oath or seven.   b 33 Beersheba can mean well of the oath or well of seven.

those of his brother Esau; so he blessed him. 24"Are you really my son Esau?" he asked.

"I am," he replied.

25Then he said, "My son, bring me some of your game to eat, so that I may give you my blessing."

Jacob brought it to him and he ate; and he brought some wine and he drank. 26Then his father Isaac said to him, "Come here, my son, and kiss me."

27So he went to him and kissed him. When Isaac caught the smell of his clothes, he blessed him and said,

"Ah, the smell of my son
  is like the smell of a field
  that the LORD has blessed.
28 May God give you of heaven's dew
  and of earth's richness—
  an abundance of grain and new
    wine.
29 May nations serve you
  and peoples bow down to you.
Be lord over your brothers,
  and may the sons of your mother
    bow down to you.
May those who curse you be cursed
  and those who bless you be
    blessed."

30After Isaac finished blessing him and Jacob had scarcely left his father's presence, his brother Esau came in from hunting. 31He too prepared some tasty food and brought it to his father. Then he said to him, "My father, sit up and eat some of my game, so that you may give me your blessing."

32His father Isaac asked him, "Who are you?"

"I am your son," he answered, "your firstborn, Esau."

33Isaac trembled violently and said, "Who was it, then, that hunted game and brought it to me? I ate it just before you came and I blessed him—and indeed he will be blessed!"

34When Esau heard his father's words, he burst out with a loud and bitter cry and said to his father, "Bless me—me too, my father!"

35But he said, "Your brother came deceitfully and took your blessing."

36Esau said, "Isn't he rightly named Jacob[a]? He has deceived me these two times: He took my birthright, and now he's taken my blessing!" Then he asked, "Haven't you reserved any blessing for me?"

37Isaac answered Esau, "I have made him lord over you and have made all his relatives his servants, and I have sustained him with grain and new wine. So what can I possibly do for you, my son?"

38Esau said to his father, "Do you have only one blessing, my father? Bless me too, my father!" Then Esau wept aloud.

39His father Isaac answered him,

"Your dwelling will be
  away from the earth's richness,
  away from the dew of heaven above.
40 You will live by the sword
  and you will serve your brother.
But when you grow restless,
  you will throw his yoke
  from off your neck."

Jacob Flees to Laban

41Esau held a grudge against Jacob because of the blessing his father had given him. He said to himself, "The days of mourning for my father are near; then I will kill my brother Jacob."

42When Rebekah was told what her older son Esau had said, she sent for her younger son Jacob and said to him, "Your brother Esau is consoling himself with the thought of killing you. 43Now then, my son, do what I say: Flee at once to my brother Laban in Haran. 44Stay with him for a while until your brother's fury subsides. 45When your brother is no longer angry with you and forgets what you did to him, I'll send word for you to come back from there. Why should I lose both of you in one day?"

46Then Rebekah said to Isaac, "I'm disgusted with living because of these Hittite women. If Jacob takes a wife from among the women of this land, from Hittite women like these, my life will not be worth living."

28 So Isaac called for Jacob and blessed[b] him and commanded him: "Do not marry a Canaanite woman. 2Go at once to Paddan Aram,[c]

---

a 36 Jacob means he grasps the heel (figuratively, he deceives).   b 1 Or greeted   c 2 That is,
Northwest Mesopotamia; also in verses 5, 6 and 7

to the house of your mother's father Bethuel. Take a wife for yourself there, from among the daughters of Laban, your mother's brother. ³May God Almighty*a* bless you and make you fruitful and increase your numbers until you become a community of peoples. ⁴May he give you and your descendants the blessing given to Abraham, so that you may take possession of the land where you now live as an alien, the land God gave to Abraham." ⁵Then Isaac sent Jacob on his way, and he went to Paddan Aram, to Laban son of Bethuel the Aramean, the brother of Rebekah, who was the mother of Jacob and Esau.

⁶Now Esau learned that Isaac had blessed Jacob and had sent him to Paddan Aram to take a wife from there, and that when he blessed him he commanded him, "Do not marry a Canaanite woman," ⁷and that Jacob had obeyed his father and mother and had gone to Paddan Aram. ⁸Esau then realized how displeasing the Canaanite women were to his father Isaac; ⁹so he went to Ishmael and married Mahalath, the sister of Nebaioth and daughter of Ishmael son of Abraham, in addition to the wives he already had.

Jacob's Dream at Bethel

¹⁰Jacob left Beersheba and set out for Haran. ¹¹When he reached a certain place, he stopped for the night because the sun had set. Taking one of the stones there, he put it under his head and lay down to sleep. ¹²He had a dream in which he saw a stairway*b* resting on the earth, with its top reaching to heaven, and the angels of God were ascending and descending on it. ¹³There above it*c* stood the LORD, and he said: "I am the LORD, the God of your father Abraham and the God of Isaac. I will give you and your descendants the land on which you are lying. ¹⁴Your descendants will be like the dust of the earth, and you will spread out to the west and to the east, to the north and to the south. All peoples on earth will be blessed through you and your offspring. ¹⁵I am with you and will watch over you wherever you go, and I

will bring you back to this land. I will not leave you until I have done what I have promised you."

¹⁶When Jacob awoke from his sleep, he thought, "Surely the LORD is in this place, and I was not aware of it." ¹⁷He was afraid and said, "How awesome is this place! This is none other than the house of God; this is the gate of heaven."

¹⁸Early the next morning Jacob took the stone he had placed under his head and set it up as a pillar and poured oil on top of it. ¹⁹He called that place Bethel,*d* though the city used to be called Luz.

²⁰Then Jacob made a vow, saying, "If God will be with me and will watch over me on this journey I am taking and will give me food to eat and clothes to wear ²¹so that I return safely to my father's house, then the LORD*e* will be my God ²²and*f* this stone that I have set up as a pillar will be God's house, and of all that you give me I will give you a tenth."

Jacob Arrives in Paddan Aram

29 Then Jacob continued on his journey and came to the land of the eastern peoples. ²There he saw a well in the field, with three flocks of sheep lying near it because the flocks were watered from that well. The stone over the mouth of the well was large. ³When all the flocks were gathered there, the shepherds would roll the stone away from the well's mouth and water the sheep. Then they would return the stone to its place over the mouth of the well.

⁴Jacob asked the shepherds, "My brothers, where are you from?"

"We're from Haran," they replied.

⁵He said to them, "Do you know Laban, Nahor's grandson?"

"Yes, we know him," they answered.

⁶Then Jacob asked them, "Is he well?"

"Yes, he is," they said, "and here comes his daughter Rachel with the sheep."

⁷"Look," he said, "the sun is still high; it is not time for the flocks to be gathered. Water the sheep and take them back to pasture."

⁸"We can't," they replied, "until all the flocks are gathered and the stone has

been rolled away from the mouth of the well. Then we will water the sheep."

⁹While he was still talking with them, Rachel came with her father's sheep, for she was a shepherdess. ¹⁰When Jacob saw Rachel daughter of Laban, his mother's brother, and Laban's sheep, he went over and rolled the stone away from the mouth of the well and watered his uncle's sheep. ¹¹Then Jacob kissed Rachel and began to weep aloud. ¹²He had told Rachel that he was a relative of her father and a son of Rebekah. So she ran and told her father.

¹³As soon as Laban heard the news about Jacob, his sister's son, he hurried to meet him. He embraced him and kissed him and brought him to his home, and there Jacob told him all these things. ¹⁴Then Laban said to him, "You are my own flesh and blood."

Jacob Marries Leah and Rachel

After Jacob had stayed with him for a whole month, ¹⁵Laban said to him, "Just because you are a relative of mine, should you work for me for nothing? Tell me what your wages should be."

¹⁶Now Laban had two daughters; the name of the older was Leah, and the name of the younger was Rachel. ¹⁷Leah had weakᵃ eyes, but Rachel was lovely in form, and beautiful. ¹⁸Jacob was in love with Rachel and said, "I'll work for you seven years in return for your younger daughter Rachel."

¹⁹Laban said, "It's better that I give her to you than to some other man. Stay here with me." ²⁰So Jacob served seven years to get Rachel, but they seemed like only a few days to him because of his love for her.

²¹Then Jacob said to Laban, "Give me my wife. My time is completed, and I want to lie with her."

²²So Laban brought together all the people of the place and gave a feast. ²³But when evening came, he took his daughter Leah and gave her to Jacob, and Jacob lay with her. ²⁴And Laban gave his servant girl Zilpah to his daughter as her maidservant.

²⁵When morning came, there was Leah! So Jacob said to Laban, "What is this you have done to me? I served you for Rachel, didn't I? Why have you deceived me?"

²⁶Laban replied, "It is not our custom here to give the younger daughter in marriage before the older one. ²⁷Finish this daughter's bridal week; then we will give you the younger one also, in return for another seven years of work."

²⁸And Jacob did so. He finished the week with Leah, and then Laban gave him his daughter Rachel to be his wife. ²⁹Laban gave his servant girl Bilhah to his daughter Rachel as her maidservant. ³⁰Jacob lay with Rachel also, and he loved Rachel more than Leah. And he worked for Laban another seven years.

Jacob's Children

³¹When the LORD saw that Leah was not loved, he opened her womb, but Rachel was barren. ³²Leah became pregnant and gave birth to a son. She named him Reuben,ᵇ for she said, "It is because the LORD has seen my misery. Surely my husband will love me now."

³³She conceived again, and when she gave birth to a son she said, "Because the LORD heard that I am not loved, he gave me this one too." So she named him Simeon.ᶜ

³⁴Again she conceived, and when she gave birth to a son she said, "Now at last my husband will become attached to me, because I have borne him three sons." So he was named Levi.ᵈ

³⁵She conceived again, and when she gave birth to a son she said, "This time I will praise the LORD." So she named him Judah.ᵉ Then she stopped having children.

30 When Rachel saw that she was not bearing Jacob any children, she became jealous of her sister. So she said to Jacob, "Give me children, or I'll die!"

²Jacob became angry with her and said, "Am I in the place of God, who has kept you from having children?"

³Then she said, "Here is Bilhah, my maidservant. Sleep with her so that she

---

ᵃ 17 Or delicate   ᵇ 32 Reuben sounds like the Hebrew for he has seen my misery; the name means see, a son.   ᶜ 33 Simeon probably means one who hears.   ᵈ 34 Levi sounds like and may be derived from the Hebrew for attached.   ᵉ 35 Judah sounds like and may be derived from the Hebrew for praise.

can bear children for me and that through her I too can build a family."

⁴So she gave him her servant Bilhah as a wife. Jacob slept with her, ⁵and she became pregnant and bore him a son. ⁶Then Rachel said, "God has vindicated me; he has listened to my plea and given me a son." Because of this she named him Dan.ᵃ

⁷Rachel's servant Bilhah conceived again and bore Jacob a second son. ⁸Then Rachel said, "I have had a great struggle with my sister, and I have won." So she named him Naphtali.ᵇ

⁹When Leah saw that she had stopped having children, she took her maidservant Zilpah and gave her to Jacob as a wife. ¹⁰Leah's servant Zilpah bore Jacob a son. ¹¹Then Leah said, "What good fortune!"ᶜ So she named him Gad.ᵈ

¹²Leah's servant Zilpah bore Jacob a second son. ¹³Then Leah said, "How happy I am! The women will call me happy." So she named him Asher.ᵉ

¹⁴During wheat harvest, Reuben went out into the fields and found some mandrake plants, which he brought to his mother Leah. Rachel said to Leah, "Please give me some of your son's mandrakes."

¹⁵But she said to her, "Wasn't it enough that you took away my husband? Will you take my son's mandrakes too?"

"Very well," Rachel said, "he can sleep with you tonight in return for your son's mandrakes."

¹⁶So when Jacob came in from the fields that evening, Leah went out to meet him. "You must sleep with me," she said. "I have hired you with my son's mandrakes." So he slept with her that night.

¹⁷God listened to Leah, and she became pregnant and bore Jacob a fifth son. ¹⁸Then Leah said, "God has rewarded me for giving my maidservant to my husband." So she named him Issachar.ᶠ

¹⁹Leah conceived again and bore Jacob a sixth son. ²⁰Then Leah said, "God has presented me with a precious gift. This time my husband will treat me with honor, because I have borne him six sons." So she named him Zebulun.ᵍ

²¹Some time later she gave birth to a daughter and named her Dinah.

²²Then God remembered Rachel; he listened to her and opened her womb. ²³She became pregnant and gave birth to a son and said, "God has taken away my disgrace." ²⁴She named him Joseph,ʰ and said, "May the LORD add to me another son."

Jacob's Flocks Increase

²⁵After Rachel gave birth to Joseph, Jacob said to Laban, "Send me on my way so I can go back to my own homeland. ²⁶Give me my wives and children, for whom I have served you, and I will be on my way. You know how much work I've done for you."

²⁷But Laban said to him, "If I have found favor in your eyes, please stay. I have learned by divination thatⁱ the LORD has blessed me because of you." ²⁸He added, "Name your wages, and I will pay them."

²⁹Jacob said to him, "You know how I have worked for you and how your livestock has fared under my care. ³⁰The little you had before I came has increased greatly, and the LORD has blessed you wherever I have been. But now, when may I do something for my own household?"

³¹"What shall I give you?" he asked.

"Don't give me anything," Jacob replied. "But if you will do this one thing for me, I will go on tending your flocks and watching over them: ³²Let me go through all your flocks today and remove from them every speckled or spotted sheep, every dark-colored lamb and every spotted or speckled goat. They will be my wages. ³³And my honesty will testify for me in the future, whenever you check on the wages you have paid me. Any goat in my possession that is not speckled or spotted, or any lamb that is not dark-colored, will be considered stolen."

³⁴"Agreed," said Laban. "Let it be as you have said." ³⁵That same day he removed all the male goats that were

---

ᵃ 6 Dan here means he has vindicated.   ᵇ 8 Naphtali means my struggle.   ᶜ 11 Or "A troop is coming!"   ᵈ 11 Gad can mean good fortune or a troop.   ᵉ 13 Asher means happy.   ᶠ 18 Issachar sounds like the Hebrew for reward.   ᵍ 20 Zebulun probably means honor.   ʰ 24 Joseph means may he add.   ⁱ 27 Or possibly have become rich and streaked or spotted, and all the speckled or spotted female goats (all that had white on them) and all the dark-colored lambs, and he placed them in the care of his sons. 36Then he put a three-day journey between himself and Jacob, while Jacob continued to tend the rest of Laban's flocks.

37Jacob, however, took fresh-cut branches from poplar, almond and plane trees and made white stripes on them by peeling the bark and exposing the white inner wood of the branches. 38Then he placed the peeled branches in all the watering troughs, so that they would be directly in front of the flocks when they came to drink. When the flocks were in heat and came to drink, 39they mated in front of the branches. And they bore young that were streaked or speckled or spotted. 40Jacob set apart the young of the flock by themselves, but made the rest face the streaked and dark-colored animals that belonged to Laban. Thus he made separate flocks for himself and did not put them with Laban's animals. 41Whenever the stronger females were in heat, Jacob would place the branches in the troughs in front of the animals so they would mate near the branches, 42but if the animals were weak, he would not place them there. So the weak animals went to Laban and the strong ones to Jacob. 43In this way the man grew exceedingly prosperous and came to own large flocks, and maidservants and menservants, and camels and donkeys.

Jacob Flees From Laban

31 Jacob heard that Laban's sons were saying, "Jacob has taken everything our father owned and has gained all this wealth from what belonged to our father." 2And Jacob noticed that Laban's attitude toward him was not what it had been.

3Then the LORD said to Jacob, "Go back to the land of your fathers and to your relatives, and I will be with you."

4So Jacob sent word to Rachel and Leah to come out to the fields where his flocks were. 5He said to them, "I see that your father's attitude toward me is not what it was before, but the God of my father has been with me. 6You know that I've worked for your father with all my strength, 7yet your father has cheated me by changing my wages ten times. However, God has not allowed him to harm me. 8If he said, 'The speckled ones will be your wages,' then all the flocks gave birth to speckled young; and if he said, 'The streaked ones will be your wages,' then all the flocks bore streaked young. 9So God has taken away your father's livestock and has given them to me.

10"In breeding season I once had a dream in which I looked up and saw that the male goats mating with the flock were streaked, speckled or spotted. 11The angel of God said to me in the dream, 'Jacob.' I answered, 'Here I am.' 12And he said, 'Look up and see that all the male goats mating with the flock are streaked, speckled or spotted, for I have seen all that Laban has been doing to you. 13I am the God of Bethel, where you anointed a pillar and where you made a vow to me. Now leave this land at once and go back to your native land.' "

14Then Rachel and Leah replied, "Do we still have any share in the inheritance of our father's estate? 15Does he not regard us as foreigners? Not only has he sold us, but he has used up what was paid for us. 16Surely all the wealth that God took away from our father belongs to us and our children. So do whatever God has told you."

17Then Jacob put his children and his wives on camels, 18and he drove all his livestock ahead of him, along with all the goods he had accumulated in Paddan Aram,ᵃ to go to his father Isaac in the land of Canaan.

19When Laban had gone to shear his sheep, Rachel stole her father's household gods. 20Moreover, Jacob deceived Laban the Aramean by not telling him he was running away. 21So he fled with all he had, and crossing the River,ᵇ he headed for the hill country of Gilead.

Laban Pursues Jacob

22On the third day Laban was told that Jacob had fled. 23Taking his relatives with him, he pursued Jacob for seven days and caught up with him in the hill

ᵃ 18 That is, Northwest Mesopotamia   ᵇ 21 That is, the Euphrates country of Gilead. 24Then God came to Laban the Aramean in a dream at night and said to him, "Be careful not to say anything to Jacob, either good or bad."

25Jacob had pitched his tent in the hill country of Gilead when Laban overtook him, and Laban and his relatives camped there too. 26Then Laban said to Jacob, "What have you done? You've deceived me, and you've carried off my daughters like captives in war. 27Why did you run off secretly and deceive me? Why didn't you tell me, so I could send you away with joy and singing to the music of tambourines and harps? 28You didn't even let me kiss my grandchildren and my daughters good-by. You have done a foolish thing. 29I have the power to harm you; but last night the God of your father said to me, 'Be careful not to say anything to Jacob, either good or bad.' 30Now you have gone off because you longed to return to your father's house. But why did you steal my gods?"

31Jacob answered Laban, "I was afraid, because I thought you would take your daughters away from me by force. 32But if you find anyone who has your gods, he shall not live. In the presence of our relatives, see for yourself whether there is anything of yours here with me; and if so, take it." Now Jacob did not know that Rachel had stolen the gods.

33So Laban went into Jacob's tent and into Leah's tent and into the tent of the two maidservants, but he found nothing. After he came out of Leah's tent, he entered Rachel's tent. 34Now Rachel had taken the household gods and put them inside her camel's saddle and was sitting on them. Laban searched through everything in the tent but found nothing.

35Rachel said to her father, "Don't be angry, my lord, that I cannot stand up in your presence; I'm having my period." So he searched but could not find the household gods.

36Jacob was angry and took Laban to task. "What is my crime?" he asked Laban. "What sin have I committed that you hunt me down? 37Now that you have searched through all my goods, what have you found that belongs to your household? Put it here in front of your relatives and mine, and let them judge between the two of us.

38"I have been with you for twenty years now. Your sheep and goats have not miscarried, nor have I eaten rams from your flocks. 39I did not bring you animals torn by wild beasts; I bore the loss myself. And you demanded payment from me for whatever was stolen by day or night. 40This was my situation: The heat consumed me in the daytime and the cold at night, and sleep fled from my eyes. 41It was like this for the twenty years I was in your household. I worked for you fourteen years for your two daughters and six years for your flocks, and you changed my wages ten times. 42If the God of my father, the God of Abraham and the Fear of Isaac, had not been with me, you would surely have sent me away empty-handed. But God has seen my hardship and the toil of my hands, and last night he rebuked you."

43Laban answered Jacob, "The women are my daughters, the children are my children, and the flocks are my flocks. All you see is mine. Yet what can I do today about these daughters of mine, or about the children they have borne? 44Come now, let's make a covenant, you and I, and let it serve as a witness between us."

45So Jacob took a stone and set it up as a pillar. 46He said to his relatives, "Gather some stones." So they took stones and piled them in a heap, and they ate there by the heap. 47Laban called it Jegar Sahadutha,a and Jacob called it Galeed.b

48Laban said, "This heap is a witness between you and me today." That is why it was called Galeed. 49It was also called Mizpah,c because he said, "May the LORD keep watch between you and me when we are away from each other. 50If you mistreat my daughters or if you take any wives besides my daughters, even though no one is with us, remember that God is a witness between you and me."

51Laban also said to Jacob, "Here is this heap, and here is this pillar I have set up between you and me. 52This heap is a witness, and this pillar is a witness, that I will not go past this heap to your side to harm you and that you will not

---

a 47 The Aramaic *Jegar Sahadutha* means *witness heap.*   b 47 The Hebrew *Galeed* means *witness heap.*   c 49 *Mizpah* means *watchtower.*

go past this heap and pillar to my side to harm me. ⁵³May the God of Abraham and the God of Nahor, the God of their father, judge between us."

So Jacob took an oath in the name of the Fear of his father Isaac. ⁵⁴He offered a sacrifice there in the hill country and invited his relatives to a meal. After they had eaten, they spent the night there.

⁵⁵Early the next morning Laban kissed his grandchildren and his daughters and blessed them. Then he left and returned home.

Jacob Prepares to Meet Esau

32 Jacob also went on his way, and the angels of God met him. ²When Jacob saw them, he said, "This is the camp of God!" So he named that place Mahanaim.^a

³Jacob sent messengers ahead of him to his brother Esau in the land of Seir, the country of Edom. ⁴He instructed them: "This is what you are to say to my master Esau: 'Your servant Jacob says, I have been staying with Laban and have remained there till now. ⁵I have cattle and donkeys, sheep and goats, menservants and maidservants. Now I am sending this message to my lord, that I may find favor in your eyes.' "

⁶When the messengers returned to Jacob, they said, "We went to your brother Esau, and now he is coming to meet you, and four hundred men are with him."

⁷In great fear and distress Jacob divided the people who were with him into two groups,^b and the flocks and herds and camels as well. ⁸He thought, "If Esau comes and attacks one group,^c the group^c that is left may escape."

⁹Then Jacob prayed, "O God of my father Abraham, God of my father Isaac, O LORD, who said to me, 'Go back to your country and your relatives, and I will make you prosper,' ¹⁰I am unworthy of all the kindness and faithfulness you have shown your servant. I had only my staff when I crossed this Jordan, but now I have become two groups. ¹¹Save me, I pray, from the hand of my brother Esau, for I am afraid he will come and attack me, and also the mothers with their children. ¹²But you have said, 'I will surely make you prosper and will make your descendants like the sand of the sea, which cannot be counted.' "

¹³He spent the night there, and from what he had with him he selected a gift for his brother Esau: ¹⁴two hundred female goats and twenty male goats, two hundred ewes and twenty rams, ¹⁵thirty female camels with their young, forty cows and ten bulls, and twenty female donkeys and ten male donkeys. ¹⁶He put them in the care of his servants, each herd by itself, and said to his servants, "Go ahead of me, and keep some space between the herds."

¹⁷He instructed the one in the lead: "When my brother Esau meets you and asks, 'To whom do you belong, and where are you going, and who owns all these animals in front of you?' ¹⁸then you are to say, 'They belong to your servant Jacob. They are a gift sent to my lord Esau, and he is coming behind us.' "

¹⁹He also instructed the second, the third and all the others who followed the herds: "You are to say the same thing to Esau when you meet him. ²⁰And be sure to say, 'Your servant Jacob is coming behind us.' " For he thought, "I will pacify him with these gifts I am sending on ahead; later, when I see him, perhaps he will receive me." ²¹So Jacob's gifts went on ahead of him, but he himself spent the night in the camp.

Jacob Wrestles With God

²²That night Jacob got up and took his two wives, his two maidservants and his eleven sons and crossed the ford of the Jabbok. ²³After he had sent them across the stream, he sent over all his possessions. ²⁴So Jacob was left alone, and a man wrestled with him till daybreak. ²⁵When the man saw that he could not overpower him, he touched the socket of Jacob's hip so that his hip was wrenched as he wrestled with the man. ²⁶Then the man said, "Let me go, for it is daybreak."

But Jacob replied, "I will not let you go unless you bless me."

²⁷The man asked him, "What is your name?"

"Jacob," he answered.

²⁸Then the man said, "Your name will

---

^a 2 *Mahanaim* means *two camps*.   ^b 7 Or *camps*; also in verse 10   ^c 8 Or *camp*

no longer be Jacob, but Israel,[a] because you have struggled with God and with men and have overcome."

29Jacob said, "Please tell me your name."

But he replied, "Why do you ask my name?" Then he blessed him there.

30So Jacob called the place Peniel,[b] saying, "It is because I saw God face to face, and yet my life was spared."

31The sun rose above him as he passed Peniel,[c] and he was limping because of his hip. 32Therefore to this day the Israelites do not eat the tendon attached to the socket of the hip, because the socket of Jacob's hip was touched near the tendon.

Jacob Meets Esau

33 Jacob looked up and there was Esau, coming with his four hundred men; so he divided the children among Leah, Rachel and the two maidservants. 2He put the maidservants and their children in front, Leah and her children next, and Rachel and Joseph in the rear. 3He himself went on ahead and bowed down to the ground seven times as he approached his brother.

4But Esau ran to meet Jacob and embraced him; he threw his arms around his neck and kissed him. And they wept. 5Then Esau looked up and saw the women and children. "Who are these with you?" he asked.

Jacob answered, "They are the children God has graciously given your servant."

6Then the maidservants and their children approached and bowed down. 7Next, Leah and her children came and bowed down. Last of all came Joseph and Rachel, and they too bowed down.

8Esau asked, "What do you mean by all these droves I met?"

"To find favor in your eyes, my lord," he said.

9But Esau said, "I already have plenty, my brother. Keep what you have for yourself."

10"No, please!" said Jacob. "If I have found favor in your eyes, accept this gift from me. For to see your face is like seeing the face of God, now that you have received me favorably. 11Please accept the present that was brought to you, for God has been gracious to me and I have all I need." And because Jacob insisted, Esau accepted it.

12Then Esau said, "Let us be on our way; I'll accompany you."

13But Jacob said to him, "My lord knows that the children are tender and that I must care for the ewes and cows that are nursing their young. If they are driven hard just one day, all the animals will die. 14So let my lord go on ahead of his servant, while I move along slowly at the pace of the droves before me and that of the children, until I come to my lord in Seir."

15Esau said, "Then let me leave some of my men with you."

"But why do that?" Jacob asked. "Just let me find favor in the eyes of my lord."

16So that day Esau started on his way back to Seir. 17Jacob, however, went to Succoth, where he built a place for himself and made shelters for his livestock. That is why the place is called Succoth.[d]

18After Jacob came from Paddan Aram,[e] he arrived safely at the[f] city of Shechem in Canaan and camped within sight of the city. 19For a hundred pieces of silver,[g] he bought from the sons of Hamor, the father of Shechem, the plot of ground where he pitched his tent. 20There he set up an altar and called it El Elohe Israel.[h]

Dinah and the Shechemites

34 Now Dinah, the daughter Leah had borne to Jacob, went out to visit the women of the land. 2When Shechem son of Hamor the Hivite, the ruler of that area, saw her, he took her and violated her. 3His heart was drawn to Dinah daughter of Jacob, and he loved the girl and spoke tenderly to her. 4And Shechem said to his father Hamor, "Get me this girl as my wife."

5When Jacob heard that his daughter Dinah had been defiled, his sons were in the fields with his livestock; so he kept quiet about it until they came home.

6Then Shechem's father Hamor went

---

[a] 28 *Israel* means *he struggles with God.*   [b] 30 *Peniel* means *face of God.*   [c] 31 Hebrew *Penuel*, a variant of *Peniel*   [d] 17 *Succoth* means *shelters.*   [e] 18 That is, Northwest Mesopotamia   [f] 18 Or *arrived at Shalem, a*   [g] 19 Hebrew *hundred kesitahs*; a kesitah was a unit of money of unknown weight and value.   [h] 20 *El Elohe Israel* can mean *God, the God of Israel* or *mighty is the God of Israel.*

out to talk with Jacob. [7]Now Jacob's sons had come in from the fields as soon as they heard what had happened. They were filled with grief and fury, because Shechem had done a disgraceful thing in[a] Israel by lying with Jacob's daughter—a thing that should not be done.

[8]But Hamor said to them, "My son Shechem has his heart set on your daughter. Please give her to him as his wife. [9]Intermarry with us; give us your daughters and take our daughters for yourselves. [10]You can settle among us; the land is open to you. Live in it, trade[b] in it, and acquire property in it."

[11]Then Shechem said to Dinah's father and brothers, "Let me find favor in your eyes, and I will give you whatever you ask. [12]Make the price for the bride and the gift I am to bring as great as you like, and I'll pay whatever you ask me. Only give me the girl as my wife."

[13]Because their sister Dinah had been defiled, Jacob's sons replied deceitfully as they spoke to Shechem and his father Hamor. [14]They said to them, "We can't do such a thing; we can't give our sister to a man who is not circumcised. That would be a disgrace to us. [15]We will give our consent to you on one condition only: that you become like us by circumcising all your males. [16]Then we will give you our daughters and take your daughters for ourselves. We'll settle among you and become one people with you. [17]But if you will not agree to be circumcised, we'll take our sister[c] and go."

[18]Their proposal seemed good to Hamor and his son Shechem. [19]The young man, who was the most honored of all his father's household, lost no time in doing what they said, because he was delighted with Jacob's daughter. [20]So Hamor and his son Shechem went to the gate of their city to speak to their fellow townsmen. [21]"These men are friendly toward us," they said. "Let them live in our land and trade in it; the land has plenty of room for them. We can marry their daughters and they can marry ours. [22]But the men will consent to live with us as one people only on the condition that our males be circumcised, as they

themselves are. [23]Won't their livestock, their property and all their other animals become ours? So let us give our consent to them, and they will settle among us."

[24]All the men who went out of the city gate agreed with Hamor and his son Shechem, and every male in the city was circumcised.

[25]Three days later, while all of them were still in pain, two of Jacob's sons, Simeon and Levi, Dinah's brothers, took their swords and attacked the unsuspecting city, killing every male. [26]They put Hamor and his son Shechem to the sword and took Dinah from Shechem's house and left. [27]The sons of Jacob came upon the dead bodies and looted the city where[d] their sister had been defiled. [28]They seized their flocks and herds and donkeys and everything else of theirs in the city and out in the fields. [29]They carried off all their wealth and all their women and children, taking as plunder everything in the houses.

[30]Then Jacob said to Simeon and Levi, "You have brought trouble on me by making me a stench to the Canaanites and Perizzites, the people living in this land. We are few in number, and if they join forces against me and attack me, I and my household will be destroyed."

[31]But they replied, "Should he have treated our sister like a prostitute?"

Jacob Returns to Bethel

35 Then God said to Jacob, "Go up to Bethel and settle there, and build an altar there to God, who appeared to you when you were fleeing from your brother Esau."

[2]So Jacob said to his household and to all who were with him, "Get rid of the foreign gods you have with you, and purify yourselves and change your clothes. [3]Then come, let us go up to Bethel, where I will build an altar to God, who answered me in the day of my distress and who has been with me wherever I have gone." [4]So they gave Jacob all the foreign gods they had and the rings in their ears, and Jacob buried them under the oak at Shechem. [5]Then they set out, and the terror of God fell

---

a 7 Or against   b 10 Or move about freely; also in verse 21   c 17 Hebrew daughter   d 27 Or because

upon the towns all around them so that no one pursued them.

⁶Jacob and all the people with him came to Luz (that is, Bethel) in the land of Canaan. ⁷There he built an altar, and he called the place El Bethel,ᵃ because it was there that God revealed himself to him when he was fleeing from his brother.

⁸Now Deborah, Rebekah's nurse, died and was buried under the oak below Bethel. So it was named Allon Bacuth.ᵇ

⁹After Jacob returned from Paddan Aram,ᶜ God appeared to him again and blessed him. ¹⁰God said to him, "Your name is Jacob,ᵈ but you will no longer be called Jacob; your name will be Israel.ᵉ " So he named him Israel.

¹¹And God said to him, "I am God Almightyᶠ; be fruitful and increase in number. A nation and a community of nations will come from you, and kings will come from your body. ¹²The land I gave to Abraham and Isaac I also give to you, and I will give this land to your descendants after you." ¹³Then God went up from him at the place where he had talked with him.

¹⁴Jacob set up a stone pillar at the place where God had talked with him, and he poured out a drink offering on it; he also poured oil on it. ¹⁵Jacob called the place where God had talked with him Bethel.ᵍ

The Deaths of Rachel and Isaac

¹⁶Then they moved on from Bethel. While they were still some distance from Ephrath, Rachel began to give birth and had great difficulty. ¹⁷And as she was having great difficulty in childbirth, the midwife said to her, "Don't be afraid, for you have another son." ¹⁸As she breathed her last—for she was dying—she named her son Ben-Oni.ʰ But his father named him Benjamin.ⁱ

¹⁹So Rachel died and was buried on the way to Ephrath (that is, Bethlehem). ²⁰Over her tomb Jacob set up a pillar, and to this day that pillar marks Rachel's tomb.

²¹Israel moved on again and pitched his tent beyond Migdal Eder. ²²While

Israel was living in that region, Reuben went in and slept with his father's concubine Bilhah, and Israel heard of it.

Jacob had twelve sons:

²³The sons of Leah:
  Reuben the firstborn of Jacob,
  Simeon, Levi, Judah, Issachar and
  Zebulun.
²⁴The sons of Rachel:
  Joseph and Benjamin.
²⁵The sons of Rachel's maidservant
  Bilhah:
  Dan and Naphtali.
²⁶The sons of Leah's maidservant Zil-
  pah:
  Gad and Asher.

These were the sons of Jacob, who were born to him in Paddan Aram.

²⁷Jacob came home to his father Isaac in Mamre, near Kiriath Arba (that is, Hebron), where Abraham and Isaac had stayed. ²⁸Isaac lived a hundred and eighty years. ²⁹Then he breathed his last and died and was gathered to his people, old and full of years. And his sons Esau and Jacob buried him.

Esau's Descendants

36 This is the account of Esau (that is, Edom).

²Esau took his wives from the women of Canaan: Adah daughter of Elon the Hittite, and Oholibamah daughter of Anah and granddaughter of Zibeon the Hivite— ³also Basemath daughter of Ishmael and sister of Nebaioth.

⁴Adah bore Eliphaz to Esau, Basemath bore Reuel, ⁵and Oholibamah bore Jeush, Jalam and Korah. These were the sons of Esau, who were born to him in Canaan.

⁶Esau took his wives and sons and daughters and all the members of his household, as well as his livestock and all his other animals and all the goods he had acquired in Canaan, and moved to a land some distance from his brother Jacob. ⁷Their possessions were too great for them to remain together; the land where

---

ᵃ 7 El Bethel means God of Bethel.   ᵇ 8 Allon Bacuth means oak of weeping.   ᶜ 9 That is, Northwest Mesopotamia; also in verse 26   ᵈ 10 Jacob means he grasps the heel (figuratively, he deceives).   ᵉ 10 Israel means he struggles with God.   ᶠ 11 Hebrew El-Shaddai   ᵍ 15 Bethel means house of God.   ʰ 18 Ben-Oni means son of my trouble.   ⁱ 18 Benjamin means son of my right hand.

they were staying could not support them both because of their livestock. [8]So Esau (that is, Edom) settled in the hill country of Seir.

[9]This is the account of Esau the father of the Edomites in the hill country of Seir.

[10]These are the names of Esau's sons:
Eliphaz, the son of Esau's wife Adah, and Reuel, the son of Esau's wife Basemath.
[11]The sons of Eliphaz:
Teman, Omar, Zepho, Gatam and Kenaz.
[12]Esau's son Eliphaz also had a concubine named Timna, who bore him Amalek. These were grandsons of Esau's wife Adah.
[13]The sons of Reuel:
Nahath, Zerah, Shammah and Mizzah. These were grandsons of Esau's wife Basemath.
[14]The sons of Esau's wife Oholibamah daughter of Anah and granddaughter of Zibeon, whom she bore to Esau:
Jeush, Jalam and Korah.

[15]These were the chiefs among Esau's descendants:
The sons of Eliphaz the firstborn of Esau:
Chiefs Teman, Omar, Zepho, Kenaz, [16]Korah,[a] Gatam and Amalek. These were the chiefs descended from Eliphaz in Edom; they were grandsons of Adah.
[17]The sons of Esau's son Reuel:
Chiefs Nahath, Zerah, Shammah and Mizzah. These were the chiefs descended from Reuel in Edom; they were grandsons of Esau's wife Basemath.
[18]The sons of Esau's wife Oholibamah:
Chiefs Jeush, Jalam and Korah. These were the chiefs descended from Esau's wife Oholibamah daughter of Anah.
[19]These were the sons of Esau (that is, Edom), and these were their chiefs.

[20]These were the sons of Seir the Horite, who were living in the region:

Lotan, Shobal, Zibeon, Anah, [21]Dishon, Ezer and Dishan. These sons of Seir in Edom were Horite chiefs.
[22]The sons of Lotan:
Hori and Homam.[b] Timna was Lotan's sister.
[23]The sons of Shobal:
Alvan, Manahath, Ebal, Shepho and Onam.
[24]The sons of Zibeon:
Aiah and Anah. This is the Anah who discovered the hot springs[c] in the desert while he was grazing the donkeys of his father Zibeon.
[25]The children of Anah:
Dishon and Oholibamah daughter of Anah.
[26]The sons of Dishon[d]:
Hemdan, Eshban, Ithran and Keran.
[27]The sons of Ezer:
Bilhan, Zaavan and Akan.
[28]The sons of Dishan:
Uz and Aran.
[29]These were the Horite chiefs:
Lotan, Shobal, Zibeon, Anah, [30]Dishon, Ezer and Dishan. These were the Horite chiefs, according to their divisions, in the land of Seir.

The Rulers of Edom

[31]These were the kings who reigned in Edom before any Israelite king reigned[e]:
[32]Bela son of Beor became king of Edom. His city was named Dinhabah.
[33]When Bela died, Jobab son of Zerah from Bozrah succeeded him as king.
[34]When Jobab died, Husham from the land of the Temanites succeeded him as king.
[35]When Husham died, Hadad son of Bedad, who defeated Midian in the country of Moab, succeeded him as king. His city was named Avith.
[36]When Hadad died, Samlah from Masrekah succeeded him as king.

---

[a] 16 Masoretic Text; Samaritan Pentateuch (see also Gen. 36:11 and 1 Chron. 1:36) does not have *Korah*.
[b] 22 Hebrew *Hemam*, a variant of *Homam* (see 1 Chron. 1:39)   [c] 24 Vulgate; Syriac *discovered water*; the meaning of the Hebrew for this word is uncertain.   [d] 26 Hebrew *Dishan*, a variant of *Dishon*
[e] 31 Or *before an Israelite king reigned over them*

37 When Samlah died, Shaul from Rehoboth on the river[a] succeeded him as king. 38 When Shaul died, Baal-Hanan son of Acbor succeeded him as king. 39 When Baal-Hanan son of Acbor died, Hadad[b] succeeded him as king. His city was named Pau, and his wife's name was Mehetabel daughter of Matred, the daughter of Me-Zahab.

40 These were the chiefs descended from Esau, by name, according to their clans and regions:

Timna, Alvah, Jetheth, 41 Oholibamah, Elah, Pinon, 42 Kenaz, Teman, Mibzar, 43 Magdiel and Iram. These were the chiefs of Edom, according to their settlements in the land they occupied.

This was Esau the father of the Edomites.

Joseph's Dreams

37 Jacob lived in the land where his father had stayed, the land of Canaan.

2 This is the account of Jacob.

Joseph, a young man of seventeen, was tending the flocks with his brothers, the sons of Bilhah and the sons of Zilpah, his father's wives, and he brought their father a bad report about them. 3 Now Israel loved Joseph more than any of his other sons, because he had been born to him in his old age; and he made a richly ornamented[c] robe for him. 4 When his brothers saw that their father loved him more than any of them, they hated him and could not speak a kind word to him.

CRUELTY IS A DETESTED SPORT THAT OWES ITS PLEASURES TO ANOTHER'S PAIN.

—*William Cowper*

---

5 Joseph had a dream, and when he told it to his brothers, they hated him all the more. 6 He said to them, "Listen to this dream I had: 7 We were binding sheaves of grain out in the field when suddenly my sheaf rose and stood upright, while your sheaves gathered around mine and bowed down to it."

8 His brothers said to him, "Do you intend to reign over us? Will you actually rule us?" And they hated him all the more because of his dream and what he had said.

9 Then he had another dream, and he told it to his brothers. "Listen," he said, "I had another dream, and this time the sun and moon and eleven stars were bowing down to me."

10 When he told his father as well as his brothers, his father rebuked him and said, "What is this dream you had? Will your mother and I and your brothers actually come and bow down to the ground before you?" 11 His brothers were jealous of him, but his father kept the matter in mind.

Joseph Sold by His Brothers

12 Now his brothers had gone to graze their father's flocks near Shechem, 13 and Israel said to Joseph, "As you know, your brothers are grazing the flocks near Shechem. Come, I am going to send you to them."

"Very well," he replied.

14 So he said to him, "Go and see if all is well with your brothers and with the flocks, and bring word back to me." Then he sent him off from the Valley of Hebron.

When Joseph arrived at Shechem, 15 a man found him wandering around in the fields and asked him, "What are you looking for?"

16 He replied, "I'm looking for my brothers. Can you tell me where they are grazing their flocks?"

17 "They have moved on from here," the man answered. "I heard them say, 'Let's go to Dothan.' "

So Joseph went after his brothers and found them near Dothan. 18 But they saw him in the distance, and before he reached them, they plotted to kill him.

19 "Here comes that dreamer!" they said to each other. 20 "Come now, let's

---

a 37 Possibly the Euphrates   *b 39* Many manuscripts of the Masoretic Text, Samaritan Pentateuch and Syriac (see also 1 Chron. 1:50); most manuscripts of the Masoretic Text *Hadar*   *c 3* The meaning of the Hebrew for *richly ornamented* is uncertain; also in verses 23 and 32.

kill him and throw him into one of these cisterns and say that a ferocious animal devoured him. Then we'll see what comes of his dreams."

²¹When Reuben heard this, he tried to rescue him from their hands. "Let's not take his life," he said. ²²"Don't shed any blood. Throw him into this cistern here in the desert, but don't lay a hand on him." Reuben said this to rescue him from them and take him back to his father.

²³So when Joseph came to his brothers, they stripped him of his robe—the richly ornamented robe he was wearing— ²⁴and they took him and threw him into the cistern. Now the cistern was empty; there was no water in it.

²⁵As they sat down to eat their meal, they looked up and saw a caravan of Ishmaelites coming from Gilead. Their camels were loaded with spices, balm and myrrh, and they were on their way to take them down to Egypt.

²⁶Judah said to his brothers, "What will we gain if we kill our brother and cover up his blood? ²⁷Come, let's sell him to the Ishmaelites and not lay our hands on him; after all, he is our brother, our own flesh and blood." His brothers agreed.

²⁸So when the Midianite merchants came by, his brothers pulled Joseph up out of the cistern and sold him for twenty shekels*ᵃ* of silver to the Ishmaelites, who took him to Egypt.

²⁹When Reuben returned to the cistern and saw that Joseph was not there, he tore his clothes. ³⁰He went back to his brothers and said, "The boy isn't there! Where can I turn now?"

³¹Then they got Joseph's robe, slaughtered a goat and dipped the robe in the blood. ³²They took the ornamented robe back to their father and said, "We found this. Examine it to see whether it is your son's robe."

³³He recognized it and said, "It is my son's robe! Some ferocious animal has devoured him. Joseph has surely been torn to pieces."

³⁴Then Jacob tore his clothes, put on sackcloth and mourned for his son many days. ³⁵All his sons and daughters came to comfort him, but he refused to be comforted. "No," he said, "in mourning will I go down to the grave*ᵇ* to my son." So his father wept for him.

³⁶Meanwhile, the Midianites*ᶜ* sold Joseph in Egypt to Potiphar, one of Pharaoh's officials, the captain of the guard.

Judah and Tamar

38 At that time, Judah left his brothers and went down to stay with a man of Adullam named Hirah. ²There Judah met the daughter of a Canaanite man named Shua. He married her and lay with her; ³she became pregnant and gave birth to a son, who was named Er. ⁴She conceived again and gave birth to a son and named him Onan. ⁵She gave birth to still another son and named him Shelah. It was at Kezib that she gave birth to him.

⁶Judah got a wife for Er, his firstborn, and her name was Tamar. ⁷But Er, Judah's firstborn, was wicked in the LORD's sight; so the LORD put him to death.

⁸Then Judah said to Onan, "Lie with your brother's wife and fulfill your duty to her as a brother-in-law to produce offspring for your brother." ⁹But Onan knew that the offspring would not be his; so whenever he lay with his brother's wife, he spilled his semen on the ground to keep from producing offspring for his brother. ¹⁰What he did was wicked in the LORD's sight; so he put him to death also.

¹¹Judah then said to his daughter-in-law Tamar, "Live as a widow in your father's house until my son Shelah grows up." For he thought, "He may die too, just like his brothers." So Tamar went to live in her father's house.

¹²After a long time Judah's wife, the daughter of Shua, died. When Judah had recovered from his grief, he went up to Timnah, to the men who were shearing his sheep, and his friend Hirah the Adullamite went with him.

¹³When Tamar was told, "Your father-in-law is on his way to Timnah to shear his sheep," ¹⁴she took off her widow's clothes, covered herself with a veil to disguise herself, and then sat down at the entrance to Enaim, which is on the

---

ᵃ 28 That is, about 8 ounces (about 0.2 kilogram)   *ᵇ 35* Hebrew *Sheol*   *ᶜ 36* Samaritan Pentateuch, Septuagint, Vulgate and Syriac (see also verse 28); Masoretic Text *Medanites*

road to Timnah. For she saw that, though Shelah had now grown up, she had not been given to him as his wife. ¹⁵When Judah saw her, he thought she was a prostitute, for she had covered her face. ¹⁶Not realizing that she was his daughter-in-law, he went over to her by the roadside and said, "Come now, let me sleep with you."

"And what will you give me to sleep with you?" she asked.

¹⁷"I'll send you a young goat from my flock," he said.

"Will you give me something as a pledge until you send it?" she asked.

¹⁸He said, "What pledge should I give you?"

"Your seal and its cord, and the staff in your hand," she answered. So he gave them to her and slept with her, and she became pregnant by him. ¹⁹After she left, she took off her veil and put on her widow's clothes again.

²⁰Meanwhile Judah sent the young goat by his friend the Adullamite in order to get his pledge back from the woman, but he did not find her. ²¹He asked the men who lived there, "Where is the shrine prostitute who was beside the road at Enaim?"

"There hasn't been any shrine prostitute here," they said.

²²So he went back to Judah and said, "I didn't find her. Besides, the men who lived there said, 'There hasn't been any shrine prostitute here.' "

²³Then Judah said, "Let her keep what she has, or we will become a laughing-stock. After all, I did send her this young goat, but you didn't find her."

²⁴About three months later Judah was told, "Your daughter-in-law Tamar is guilty of prostitution, and as a result she is now pregnant."

Judah said, "Bring her out and have her burned to death!"

²⁵As she was being brought out, she sent a message to her father-in-law. "I am pregnant by the man who owns these," she said. And she added, "See if you recognize whose seal and cord and staff these are."

²⁶Judah recognized them and said, "She is more righteous than I, since I

wouldn't give her to my son Shelah." And he did not sleep with her again.

²⁷When the time came for her to give birth, there were twin boys in her womb. ²⁸As she was giving birth, one of them put out his hand; so the midwife took a scarlet thread and tied it on his wrist and said, "This one came out first." ²⁹But when he drew back his hand, his brother came out, and she said, "So this is how you have broken out!" And he was named Perez.ᵃ ³⁰Then his brother, who had the scarlet thread on his wrist, came out and he was given the name Zerah.ᵇ

Joseph and Potiphar's Wife

39 Now Joseph had been taken down to Egypt. Potiphar, an Egyptian who was one of Pharaoh's officials, the captain of the guard, bought him from the Ishmaelites who had taken him there.

²The LORD was with Joseph and he prospered, and he lived in the house of his Egyptian master. ³When his master saw that the LORD was with him and that the LORD gave him success in everything he did, ⁴Joseph found favor in his eyes and became his attendant. Potiphar put him in charge of his household, and he entrusted to his care everything he owned. ⁵From the time he put him in charge of his household and of all that he owned, the LORD blessed the household of the Egyptian because of Joseph. The blessing of the LORD was on everything Potiphar had, both in the house and in the field. ⁶So he left in Joseph's care everything he had; with Joseph in charge, he did not concern himself with anything except the food he ate.

Now Joseph was well-built and handsome, ⁷and after a while his master's wife took notice of Joseph and said, "Come to bed with me!"

⁸But he refused. "With me in charge," he told her, "my master does not concern himself with anything in the house; everything he owns he has entrusted to my care. ⁹No one is greater in this house than I am. My master has withheld nothing from me except you, because you are his wife. How then could I do such a wicked thing and sin

---

ᵃ 29 *Perez* means *breaking out.*　　ᵇ 30 *Zerah* can mean *scarlet* or *brightness.*

against God?" ¹⁰And though she spoke to Joseph day after day, he refused to go to bed with her or even be with her.

¹¹One day he went into the house to attend to his duties, and none of the household servants was inside. ¹²She caught him by his cloak and said, "Come to bed with me!" But he left his cloak in her hand and ran out of the house.

¹³When she saw that he had left his cloak in her hand and had run out of the house, ¹⁴she called her household servants. "Look," she said to them, "this Hebrew has been brought to us to make sport of us! He came in here to sleep with me, but I screamed. ¹⁵When he heard me scream for help, he left his cloak beside me and ran out of the house."

¹⁶She kept his cloak beside her until his master came home. ¹⁷Then she told him this story: "That Hebrew slave you brought us came to me to make sport of me. ¹⁸But as soon as I screamed for help, he left his cloak beside me and ran out of the house."

¹⁹When his master heard the story his wife told him, saying, "This is how your slave treated me," he burned with anger. ²⁰Joseph's master took him and put him in prison, the place where the king's prisoners were confined.

But while Joseph was there in the prison, ²¹the Lord was with him; he showed him kindness and granted him favor in the eyes of the prison warden. ²²So the warden put Joseph in charge of all those held in the prison, and he was made responsible for all that was done there. ²³The warden paid no attention to anything under Joseph's care, because the Lord was with Joseph and gave him success in whatever he did.

The Cupbearer and the Baker

40 Some time later, the cupbearer and the baker of the king of Egypt offended their master, the king of Egypt. ²Pharaoh was angry with his two officials, the chief cupbearer and the chief baker, ³and put them in custody in the house of the captain of the guard, in the same prison where Joseph was confined. ⁴The captain of the guard assigned them to Joseph, and he attended them.

After they had been in custody for some time, ⁵each of the two men—the cupbearer and the baker of the king of Egypt, who were being held in prison—had a dream the same night, and each dream had a meaning of its own.

⁶When Joseph came to them the next morning, he saw that they were dejected. ⁷So he asked Pharaoh's officials who were in custody with him in his master's house, "Why are your faces so sad today?"

⁸"We both had dreams," they answered, "but there is no one to interpret them."

Then Joseph said to them, "Do not interpretations belong to God? Tell me your dreams."

⁹So the chief cupbearer told Joseph his dream. He said to him, "In my dream I saw a vine in front of me, ¹⁰and on the vine were three branches. As soon as it budded, it blossomed, and its clusters ripened into grapes. ¹¹Pharaoh's cup was in my hand, and I took the grapes, squeezed them into Pharaoh's cup and put the cup in his hand."

¹²"This is what it means," Joseph said to him. "The three branches are three days. ¹³Within three days Pharaoh will lift up your head and restore you to your position, and you will put Pharaoh's cup in his hand, just as you used to do when you were his cupbearer. ¹⁴But when all goes well with you, remember me and show me kindness; mention me to Pharaoh and get me out of this prison. ¹⁵For I was forcibly carried off from the land of the Hebrews, and even here I have done nothing to deserve being put in a dungeon."

¹⁶When the chief baker saw that Joseph had given a favorable interpretation, he said to Joseph, "I too had a dream: On my head were three baskets of bread.ᵃ ¹⁷In the top basket were all kinds of baked goods for Pharaoh, but the birds were eating them out of the basket on my head."

¹⁸"This is what it means," Joseph said. "The three baskets are three days. ¹⁹Within three days Pharaoh will lift off your head and hang you on a tree.ᵇ And the birds will eat away your flesh."

²⁰Now the third day was Pharaoh's birthday, and he gave a feast for all his

ᵃ 16 Or three wicker baskets   ᵇ 19 Or and impale you on a pole officials. He lifted up the heads of the chief cupbearer and the chief baker in the presence of his officials: 21He restored the chief cupbearer to his position, so that he once again put the cup into Pharaoh's hand, 22but he hanged*a* the chief baker, just as Joseph had said to them in his interpretation.

23The chief cupbearer, however, did not remember Joseph; he forgot him.

Pharaoh's Dreams

41 When two full years had passed, Pharaoh had a dream: He was standing by the Nile, 2when out of the river there came up seven cows, sleek and fat, and they grazed among the reeds. 3After them, seven other cows, ugly and gaunt, came up out of the Nile and stood beside those on the riverbank. 4And the cows that were ugly and gaunt ate up the seven sleek, fat cows. Then Pharaoh woke up.

5He fell asleep again and had a second dream: Seven heads of grain, healthy and good, were growing on a single stalk. 6After them, seven other heads of grain sprouted—thin and scorched by the east wind. 7The thin heads of grain swallowed up the seven healthy, full heads. Then Pharaoh woke up; it had been a dream.

8In the morning his mind was troubled, so he sent for all the magicians and wise men of Egypt. Pharaoh told them his dreams, but no one could interpret them for him.

9Then the chief cupbearer said to Pharaoh, "Today I am reminded of my shortcomings. 10Pharaoh was once angry with his servants, and he imprisoned me and the chief baker in the house of the captain of the guard. 11Each of us had a dream the same night, and each dream had a meaning of its own. 12Now a young Hebrew was there with us, a servant of the captain of the guard. We told him our dreams, and he interpreted them for us, giving each man the interpretation of his dream. 13And things turned out exactly as he interpreted them to us: I was restored to my position, and the other man was hanged.*a*"

14So Pharaoh sent for Joseph, and he was quickly brought from the dungeon. When he had shaved and changed his clothes, he came before Pharaoh.

15Pharaoh said to Joseph, "I had a dream, and no one can interpret it. But I have heard it said of you that when you hear a dream you can interpret it."

16"I cannot do it," Joseph replied to Pharaoh, "but God will give Pharaoh the answer he desires."

17Then Pharaoh said to Joseph, "In my dream I was standing on the bank of the Nile, 18when out of the river there came up seven cows, fat and sleek, and they grazed among the reeds. 19After them, seven other cows came up—scrawny and very ugly and lean. I had never seen such ugly cows in all the land of Egypt. 20The lean, ugly cows ate up the seven fat cows that came up first. 21But even after they ate them, no one could tell that they had done so; they looked just as ugly as before. Then I woke up.

22"In my dreams I also saw seven heads of grain, full and good, growing on a single stalk. 23After them, seven other heads sprouted—withered and thin and scorched by the east wind. 24The thin heads of grain swallowed up the seven good heads. I told this to the magicians, but none could explain it to me."

25Then Joseph said to Pharaoh, "The dreams of Pharaoh are one and the same. God has revealed to Pharaoh what he is about to do. 26The seven good cows are seven years, and the seven good heads of grain are seven years; it is one and the same dream. 27The seven lean, ugly cows that came up afterward are seven years, and so are the seven worthless heads of grain scorched by the east wind: They are seven years of famine.

28"It is just as I said to Pharaoh: God has shown Pharaoh what he is about to do. 29Seven years of great abundance are coming throughout the land of Egypt, 30but seven years of famine will follow them. Then all the abundance in Egypt will be forgotten, and the famine will ravage the land. 31The abundance in the land will not be remembered, because the famine that follows it will be so severe. 32The reason the dream was given to Pharaoh in two forms is that the matter has been firmly decided by God, and God will do it soon.

---

a 22,13 Or impaled

³³"And now let Pharaoh look for a discerning and wise man and put him in charge of the land of Egypt. ³⁴Let Pharaoh appoint commissioners over the land to take a fifth of the harvest of Egypt during the seven years of abundance. ³⁵They should collect all the food of these good years that are coming and store up the grain under the authority of Pharaoh, to be kept in the cities for food. ³⁶This food should be held in reserve for the country, to be used during the seven years of famine that will come upon Egypt, so that the country may not be ruined by the famine."

³⁷The plan seemed good to Pharaoh and to all his officials. ³⁸So Pharaoh asked them, "Can we find anyone like this man, one in whom is the spirit of God*a*?"

³⁹Then Pharaoh said to Joseph, "Since God has made all this known to you, there is no one so discerning and wise as you. ⁴⁰You shall be in charge of my palace, and all my people are to submit to your orders. Only with respect to the throne will I be greater than you."

Joseph in Charge of Egypt

⁴¹So Pharaoh said to Joseph, "I hereby put you in charge of the whole land of Egypt." ⁴²Then Pharaoh took his signet ring from his finger and put it on Joseph's finger. He dressed him in robes of fine linen and put a gold chain around his neck. ⁴³He had him ride in a chariot as his second-in-command,*b* and men shouted before him, "Make way*c*!" Thus he put him in charge of the whole land of Egypt.

⁴⁴Then Pharaoh said to Joseph, "I am Pharaoh, but without your word no one will lift hand or foot in all Egypt." ⁴⁵Pharaoh gave Joseph the name Zaphenath-Paneah and gave him Asenath daughter of Potiphera, priest of On,*d* to be his wife. And Joseph went throughout the land of Egypt.

⁴⁶Joseph was thirty years old when he entered the service of Pharaoh king of Egypt. And Joseph went out from Pharaoh's presence and traveled throughout Egypt. ⁴⁷During the seven years of abundance the land produced plentifully. ⁴⁸Joseph collected all the food produced in those seven years of abundance in Egypt and stored it in the cities. In each city he put the food grown in the fields surrounding it. ⁴⁹Joseph stored up huge quantities of grain, like the sand of the sea; it was so much that he stopped keeping records because it was beyond measure.

⁵⁰Before the years of famine came, two sons were born to Joseph by Asenath daughter of Potiphera, priest of On. ⁵¹Joseph named his firstborn Manasseh*e* and said, "It is because God has made me forget all my trouble and all my father's household." ⁵²The second son he named Ephraim*f* and said, "It is because God has made me fruitful in the land of my suffering."

⁵³The seven years of abundance in Egypt came to an end, ⁵⁴and the seven years of famine began, just as Joseph had said. There was famine in all the other lands, but in the whole land of Egypt there was food. ⁵⁵When all Egypt began to feel the famine, the people cried to Pharaoh for food. Then Pharaoh told all the Egyptians, "Go to Joseph and do what he tells you."

⁵⁶When the famine had spread over the whole country, Joseph opened the storehouses and sold grain to the Egyptians, for the famine was severe throughout Egypt. ⁵⁷And all the countries came to Egypt to buy grain from Joseph, because the famine was severe in all the world.

Joseph's Brothers Go to Egypt

42 When Jacob learned that there was grain in Egypt, he said to his sons, "Why do you just keep looking at each other?" ²He continued, "I have heard that there is grain in Egypt. Go down there and buy some for us, so that we may live and not die."

³Then ten of Joseph's brothers went down to buy grain from Egypt. ⁴But Jacob did not send Benjamin, Joseph's brother, with the others, because he was afraid that harm might come to him. ⁵So Israel's sons were among those who

---

a 38 Or *of the gods*   *b* 43 Or *in the chariot of his second-in-command;* or *in his second chariot*
c 43 Or *Bow down*   *d* 45 That is, Heliopolis; also in verse 50   *e* 51 *Manasseh* sounds like and may be derived from the Hebrew for *forget.*   *f* 52 *Ephraim* sounds like the Hebrew for *twice fruitful.*

went to buy grain, for the famine was in the land of Canaan also.

⁶Now Joseph was the governor of the land, the one who sold grain to all its people. So when Joseph's brothers arrived, they bowed down to him with their faces to the ground. ⁷As soon as Joseph saw his brothers, he recognized them, but he pretended to be a stranger and spoke harshly to them. "Where do you come from?" he asked.

"From the land of Canaan," they replied, "to buy food."

⁸Although Joseph recognized his brothers, they did not recognize him. ⁹Then he remembered his dreams about them and said to them, "You are spies! You have come to see where our land is unprotected."

¹⁰"No, my lord," they answered. "Your servants have come to buy food. ¹¹We are all the sons of one man. Your servants are honest men, not spies."

¹²"No!" he said to them. "You have come to see where our land is unprotected."

¹³But they replied, "Your servants were twelve brothers, the sons of one man, who lives in the land of Canaan. The youngest is now with our father, and one is no more."

¹⁴Joseph said to them, "It is just as I told you: You are spies! ¹⁵And this is how you will be tested: As surely as Pharaoh lives, you will not leave this place unless your youngest brother comes here. ¹⁶Send one of your number to get your brother; the rest of you will be kept in prison, so that your words may be tested to see if you are telling the truth. If you are not, then as surely as Pharaoh lives, you are spies!" ¹⁷And he put them all in custody for three days.

¹⁸On the third day, Joseph said to them, "Do this and you will live, for I fear God: ¹⁹If you are honest men, let one of your brothers stay here in prison, while the rest of you go and take grain back for your starving households. ²⁰But you must bring your youngest brother to me, so that your words may be verified and that you may not die." This they proceeded to do.

²¹They said to one another, "Surely we are being punished because of our brother. We saw how distressed he was when he pleaded with us for his life, but we would not listen; that's why this distress has come upon us."

²²Reuben replied, "Didn't I tell you not to sin against the boy? But you wouldn't listen! Now we must give an accounting for his blood." ²³They did not realize that Joseph could understand them, since he was using an interpreter.

²⁴He turned away from them and began to weep, but then turned back and spoke to them again. He had Simeon taken from them and bound before their eyes.

²⁵Joseph gave orders to fill their bags with grain, to put each man's silver back in his sack, and to give them provisions for their journey. After this was done for them, ²⁶they loaded their grain on their donkeys and left.

²⁷At the place where they stopped for the night one of them opened his sack to get feed for his donkey, and he saw his silver in the mouth of his sack. ²⁸"My silver has been returned," he said to his brothers. "Here it is in my sack."

Their hearts sank and they turned to each other trembling and said, "What is this that God has done to us?"

²⁹When they came to their father Jacob in the land of Canaan, they told him all that had happened to them. They said, ³⁰"The man who is lord over the land spoke harshly to us and treated us as though we were spying on the land. ³¹But we said to him, 'We are honest men; we are not spies. ³²We were twelve brothers, sons of one father. One is no more, and the youngest is now with our father in Canaan.'

³³"Then the man who is lord over the land said to us, 'This is how I will know whether you are honest men: Leave one of your brothers here with me, and take food for your starving households and go. ³⁴But bring your youngest brother to me so I will know that you are not spies but honest men. Then I will give your brother back to you, and you can trade*ᵃ* in the land.' "

³⁵As they were emptying their sacks, there in each man's sack was his pouch of silver! When they and their father saw the money pouches, they were

ᵃ 34 Or *move about freely*

frightened. 36Their father Jacob said to them, "You have deprived me of my children. Joseph is no more and Simeon is no more, and now you want to take Benjamin. Everything is against me!"

37Then Reuben said to his father, "You may put both of my sons to death if I do not bring him back to you. Entrust him to my care, and I will bring him back."

38But Jacob said, "My son will not go down there with you; his brother is dead and he is the only one left. If harm comes to him on the journey you are taking, you will bring my gray head down to the grave*a* in sorrow."

The Second Journey to Egypt

43 Now the famine was still severe in the land. 2So when they had eaten all the grain they had brought from Egypt, their father said to them, "Go back and buy us a little more food."

3But Judah said to him, "The man warned us solemnly, 'You will not see my face again unless your brother is with you.' 4If you will send our brother along with us, we will go down and buy food for you. 5But if you will not send him, we will not go down, because the man said to us, 'You will not see my face again unless your brother is with you.' "

6Israel asked, "Why did you bring this trouble on me by telling the man you had another brother?"

7They replied, "The man questioned us closely about ourselves and our family. 'Is your father still living?' he asked us. 'Do you have another brother?' We simply answered his questions. How were we to know he would say, 'Bring your brother down here'?"

8Then Judah said to Israel his father, "Send the boy along with me and we will go at once, so that we and you and our children may live and not die. 9I myself will guarantee his safety; you can hold me personally responsible for him. If I do not bring him back to you and set him here before you, I will bear the blame before you all my life. 10As it is, if we had not delayed, we could have gone and returned twice."

11Then their father Israel said to them, "If it must be, then do this: Put some of the best products of the land in your bags and take them down to the man as a gift—a little balm and a little honey, some spices and myrrh, some pistachio nuts and almonds. 12Take double the amount of silver with you, for you must return the silver that was put back into the mouths of your sacks. Perhaps it was a mistake. 13Take your brother also and go back to the man at once. 14And may God Almighty*b* grant you mercy before the man so that he will let your other brother and Benjamin come back with you. As for me, if I am bereaved, I am bereaved."

15So the men took the gifts and double the amount of silver, and Benjamin also. They hurried down to Egypt and presented themselves to Joseph. 16When Joseph saw Benjamin with them, he said to the steward of his house, "Take these men to my house, slaughter an animal and prepare dinner; they are to eat with me at noon."

17The man did as Joseph told him and took the men to Joseph's house. 18Now the men were frightened when they were taken to his house. They thought, "We were brought here because of the silver that was put back into our sacks the first time. He wants to attack us and overpower us and seize us as slaves and take our donkeys."

19So they went up to Joseph's steward and spoke to him at the entrance to the house. 20"Please, sir," they said, "we came down here the first time to buy food. 21But at the place where we stopped for the night we opened our sacks and each of us found his silver—the exact weight—in the mouth of his sack. So we have brought it back with us. 22We have also brought additional silver with us to buy food. We don't know who put our silver in our sacks."

23"It's all right," he said. "Don't be afraid. Your God, the God of your father, has given you treasure in your sacks; I received your silver." Then he brought Simeon out to them.

24The steward took the men into Joseph's house, gave them water to wash their feet and provided fodder for their donkeys. 25They prepared their gifts for

---

a 38 Hebrew *Sheol*   *b* 14 Hebrew *El-Shaddai*

Joseph's arrival at noon, because they had heard that they were to eat there.

²⁶When Joseph came home, they presented to him the gifts they had brought into the house, and they bowed down before him to the ground. ²⁷He asked them how they were, and then he said, "How is your aged father you told me about? Is he still living?"

²⁸They replied, "Your servant our father is still alive and well." And they bowed low to pay him honor.

²⁹As he looked about and saw his brother Benjamin, his own mother's son, he asked, "Is this your youngest brother, the one you told me about?" And he said, "God be gracious to you, my son." ³⁰Deeply moved at the sight of his brother, Joseph hurried out and looked for a place to weep. He went into his private room and wept there.

³¹After he had washed his face, he came out and, controlling himself, said, "Serve the food."

³²They served him by himself, the brothers by themselves, and the Egyptians who ate with him by themselves, because Egyptians could not eat with Hebrews, for that is detestable to Egyptians. ³³The men had been seated before him in the order of their ages, from the firstborn to the youngest; and they looked at each other in astonishment. ³⁴When portions were served to them from Joseph's table, Benjamin's portion was five times as much as anyone else's. So they feasted and drank freely with him.

A Silver Cup in a Sack

44 Now Joseph gave these instructions to the steward of his house: "Fill the men's sacks with as much food as they can carry, and put each man's silver in the mouth of his sack. ²Then put my cup, the silver one, in the mouth of the youngest one's sack, along with the silver for his grain." And he did as Joseph said.

³As morning dawned, the men were sent on their way with their donkeys. ⁴They had not gone far from the city when Joseph said to his steward, "Go after those men at once, and when you catch up with them, say to them, 'Why have you repaid good with evil? ⁵Isn't

this the cup my master drinks from and also uses for divination? This is a wicked thing you have done.' "

⁶When he caught up with them, he repeated these words to them. ⁷But they said to him, "Why does my lord say such things? Far be it from your servants to do anything like that! ⁸We even brought back to you from the land of Canaan the silver we found inside the mouths of our sacks. So why would we steal silver or gold from your master's house? ⁹If any of your servants is found to have it, he will die; and the rest of us will become my lord's slaves."

¹⁰"Very well, then," he said, "let it be as you say. Whoever is found to have it will become my slave; the rest of you will be free from blame."

¹¹Each of them quickly lowered his sack to the ground and opened it. ¹²Then the steward proceeded to search, beginning with the oldest and ending with the youngest. And the cup was found in Benjamin's sack. ¹³At this, they tore their clothes. Then they all loaded their donkeys and returned to the city.

¹⁴Joseph was still in the house when Judah and his brothers came in, and they threw themselves to the ground before him. ¹⁵Joseph said to them, "What is this you have done? Don't you know that a man like me can find things out by divination?"

¹⁶"What can we say to my lord?" Judah replied. "What can we say? How can we prove our innocence? God has uncovered your servants' guilt. We are now my lord's slaves—we ourselves and the one who was found to have the cup."

¹⁷But Joseph said, "Far be it from me to do such a thing! Only the man who was found to have the cup will become my slave. The rest of you, go back to your father in peace."

¹⁸Then Judah went up to him and said: "Please, my lord, let your servant speak a word to my lord. Do not be angry with your servant, though you are equal to Pharaoh himself. ¹⁹My lord asked his servants, 'Do you have a father or a brother?' ²⁰And we answered, 'We have an aged father, and there is a young son born to him in his old age. His brother is dead, and he is the only one of

his mother's sons left, and his father loves him.'

21"Then you said to your servants, 'Bring him down to me so I can see him for myself.' 22And we said to my lord, 'The boy cannot leave his father; if he leaves him, his father will die.' 23But you told your servants, 'Unless your youngest brother comes down with you, you will not see my face again.' 24When we went back to your servant my father, we told him what my lord had said.

25"Then our father said, 'Go back and buy a little more food.' 26But we said, 'We cannot go down. Only if our youngest brother is with us will we go. We cannot see the man's face unless our youngest brother is with us.'

27"Your servant my father said to us, 'You know that my wife bore me two sons. 28One of them went away from me, and I said, "He has surely been torn to pieces." And I have not seen him since. 29If you take this one from me too and harm comes to him, you will bring my gray head down to the grave*a* in misery.'

30"So now, if the boy is not with us when I go back to your servant my father and if my father, whose life is closely bound up with the boy's life, 31sees that the boy isn't there, he will die. Your servants will bring the gray head of our father down to the grave in sorrow. 32Your servant guaranteed the boy's safety to my father. I said, 'If I do not bring him back to you, I will bear the blame before you, my father, all my life!'

33"Now then, please let your servant remain here as my lord's slave in place of the boy, and let the boy return with his brothers. 34How can I go back to my father if the boy is not with me? No! Do not let me see the misery that would come upon my father."

Joseph Makes Himself Known

45 Then Joseph could no longer control himself before all his attendants, and he cried out, "Have everyone leave my presence!" So there was no one with Joseph when he made himself known to his brothers. 2And he wept so loudly that the Egyptians heard

him, and Pharaoh's household heard about it.

3Joseph said to his brothers, "I am Joseph! Is my father still living?" But his brothers were not able to answer him, because they were terrified at his presence.

4Then Joseph said to his brothers, "Come close to me." When they had done so, he said, "I am your brother Joseph, the one you sold into Egypt! 5And now, do not be distressed and do not be angry with yourselves for selling me here, because it was to save lives that God sent me ahead of you. 6For two years now there has been famine in the land, and for the next five years there will not be plowing and reaping. 7But God sent me ahead of you to preserve for you a remnant on earth and to save your lives by a great deliverance.*b*

8"So then, it was not you who sent me here, but God. He made me father to Pharaoh, lord of his entire household and ruler of all Egypt. 9Now hurry back to my father and say to him, 'This is what your son Joseph says: God has made me lord of all Egypt. Come down to me; don't delay. 10You shall live in the region of Goshen and be near me—you, your children and grandchildren, your flocks and herds, and all you have. 11I will provide for you there, because five years of famine are still to come. Otherwise you and your household and all who belong to you will become destitute.'

12"You can see for yourselves, and so can my brother Benjamin, that it is really I who am speaking to you. 13Tell my father about all the honor accorded me in Egypt and about everything you have seen. And bring my father down here quickly."

14Then he threw his arms around his brother Benjamin and wept, and Benjamin embraced him, weeping. 15And he kissed all his brothers and wept over them. Afterward his brothers talked with him.

16When the news reached Pharaoh's palace that Joseph's brothers had come, Pharaoh and all his officials were pleased. 17Pharaoh said to Joseph, "Tell your brothers, 'Do this: Load your animals and return to the land of Canaan,

a 29 Hebrew *Sheol*; also in verse 31   *b 7* Or *save you as a great band of survivors*

¹⁸and bring your father and your families back to me. I will give you the best of the land of Egypt and you can enjoy the fat of the land.'

¹⁹"You are also directed to tell them, 'Do this: Take some carts from Egypt for your children and your wives, and get your father and come. ²⁰Never mind about your belongings, because the best of all Egypt will be yours.' "

²¹So the sons of Israel did this. Joseph gave them carts, as Pharaoh had commanded, and he also gave them provisions for their journey. ²²To each of

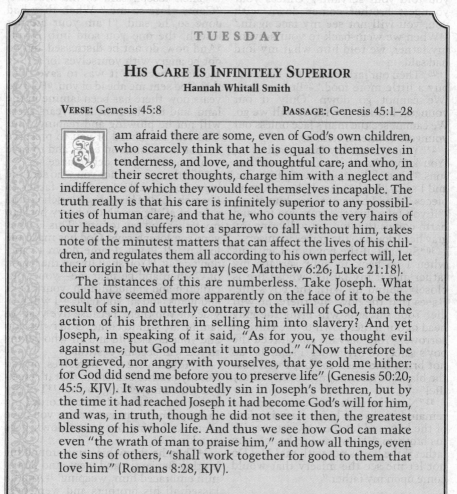

TUESDAY

HIS CARE IS INFINITELY SUPERIOR
Hannah Whitall Smith

VERSE: Genesis 45:8   **PASSAGE:** Genesis 45:1–28

I am afraid there are some, even of God's own children, who scarcely think that he is equal to themselves in tenderness, and love, and thoughtful care; and who, in their secret thoughts, charge him with a neglect and indifference of which they would feel themselves incapable. The truth really is that his care is infinitely superior to any possibilities of human care; and that he, who counts the very hairs of our heads, and suffers not a sparrow to fall without him, takes note of the minutest matters that can affect the lives of his children, and regulates them all according to his own perfect will, let their origin be what they may (see Matthew 6:26; Luke 21:18).

The instances of this are numberless. Take Joseph. What could have seemed more apparently on the face of it to be the result of sin, and utterly contrary to the will of God, than the action of his brethren in selling him into slavery? And yet Joseph, in speaking of it said, "As for you, ye thought evil against me; but God meant it unto good." "Now therefore be not grieved, nor angry with yourselves, that ye sold me hither: for God did send me before you to preserve life" (Genesis 50:20; 45:5, KJV). It was undoubtedly sin in Joseph's brethren, but by the time it had reached Joseph it had become God's will for him, and was, in truth, though he did not see it then, the greatest blessing of his whole life. And thus we see how God can make even "the wrath of man to praise him," and how all things, even the sins of others, "shall work together for good to them that love him" (Romans 8:28, KJV).

ADDITIONAL SCRIPTURE READING:
Genesis 50:20; Romans 8:28–39

Go to page 58 for your next devotional reading.

1700   1900

them he gave new clothing, but to Benjamin he gave three hundred shekels[a] of silver and five sets of clothes. 23And this is what he sent to his father: ten donkeys loaded with the best things of Egypt, and ten female donkeys loaded with grain and bread and other provisions for his journey. 24Then he sent his brothers away, and as they were leaving he said to them, "Don't quarrel on the way!"

25So they went up out of Egypt and came to their father Jacob in the land of Canaan. 26They told him, "Joseph is still alive! In fact, he is ruler of all Egypt." Jacob was stunned; he did not believe them. 27But when they told him everything Joseph had said to them, and when he saw the carts Joseph had sent to carry him back, the spirit of their father Jacob revived. 28And Israel said, "I'm convinced! My son Joseph is still alive. I will go and see him before I die."

Jacob Goes to Egypt

46 So Israel set out with all that was his, and when he reached Beersheba, he offered sacrifices to the God of his father Isaac.

2And God spoke to Israel in a vision at night and said, "Jacob! Jacob!"

"Here I am," he replied.

3"I am God, the God of your father," he said. "Do not be afraid to go down to Egypt, for I will make you into a great nation there. 4I will go down to Egypt with you, and I will surely bring you back again. And Joseph's own hand will close your eyes."

5Then Jacob left Beersheba, and Israel's sons took their father Jacob and their children and their wives in the carts that Pharaoh had sent to transport him. 6They also took with them their livestock and the possessions they had acquired in Canaan, and Jacob and all his offspring went to Egypt. 7He took with him to Egypt his sons and grandsons and his daughters and granddaughters—all his offspring.

8These are the names of the sons of Israel (Jacob and his descendants) who went to Egypt:

Reuben the firstborn of Jacob.
9The sons of Reuben:
Hanoch, Pallu, Hezron and Carmi.
10The sons of Simeon:
Jemuel, Jamin, Ohad, Jakin, Zohar and Shaul the son of a Canaanite woman.
11The sons of Levi:
Gershon, Kohath and Merari.
12The sons of Judah:
Er, Onan, Shelah, Perez and Zerah (but Er and Onan had died in the land of Canaan).
The sons of Perez:
Hezron and Hamul.
13The sons of Issachar:
Tola, Puah,[b] Jashub[c] and Shimron.
14The sons of Zebulun:
Sered, Elon and Jahleel.
15These were the sons Leah bore to Jacob in Paddan Aram,[d] besides his daughter Dinah. These sons and daughters of his were thirty-three in all.
16The sons of Gad:
Zephon,[e] Haggi, Shuni, Ezbon, Eri, Arodi and Areli.
17The sons of Asher:
Imnah, Ishvah, Ishvi and Beriah.
Their sister was Serah.
The sons of Beriah:
Heber and Malkiel.
18These were the children born to Jacob by Zilpah, whom Laban had given to his daughter Leah—sixteen in all.

19The sons of Jacob's wife Rachel:
Joseph and Benjamin. 20In Egypt, Manasseh and Ephraim were born to Joseph by Asenath daughter of Potiphera, priest of On.[f]
21The sons of Benjamin:
Bela, Beker, Ashbel, Gera, Naaman, Ehi, Rosh, Muppim, Huppim and Ard.
22These were the sons of Rachel who were born to Jacob—fourteen in all.

23The son of Dan:
Hushim.

---

[a] 22 That is, about 7 1/2 pounds (about 3.5 kilograms)   [b] 13 Samaritan Pentateuch and Syriac (see also 1 Chron. 7:1); Masoretic Text *Puvah*   [c] 13 Samaritan Pentateuch and some Septuagint manuscripts (see also Num. 26:24 and 1 Chron. 7:1); Masoretic Text *Iob*   [d] 15 That is, Northwest Mesopotamia   [e] 16 Samaritan Pentateuch and Septuagint (see also Num. 26:15); Masoretic Text *Ziphion*   [f] 20 That is, Heliopolis

24 The sons of Naphtali:
   Jahziel, Guni, Jezer and Shillem.
25 These were the sons born to Jacob by Bilhah, whom Laban had given to his daughter Rachel—seven in all.

26 All those who went to Egypt with Jacob—those who were his direct descendants, not counting his sons' wives—numbered sixty-six persons. 27 With the two sons[a] who had been born to Joseph in Egypt, the members of Jacob's family, which went to Egypt, were seventy[b] in all.

28 Now Jacob sent Judah ahead of him to Joseph to get directions to Goshen. When they arrived in the region of Goshen, 29 Joseph had his chariot made ready and went to Goshen to meet his father Israel. As soon as Joseph appeared before him, he threw his arms around his father[c] and wept for a long time.
30 Israel said to Joseph, "Now I am ready to die, since I have seen for myself that you are still alive."
31 Then Joseph said to his brothers and to his father's household, "I will go up and speak to Pharaoh and will say to him, 'My brothers and my father's household, who were living in the land of Canaan, have come to me. 32 The men are shepherds; they tend livestock, and they have brought along their flocks and herds and everything they own.' 33 When Pharaoh calls you in and asks, 'What is your occupation?' 34 you should answer, 'Your servants have tended livestock from our boyhood on, just as our fathers did.' Then you will be allowed to settle in the region of Goshen, for all shepherds are detestable to the Egyptians."

47 Joseph went and told Pharaoh, "My father and brothers, with their flocks and herds and everything they own, have come from the land of Canaan and are now in Goshen." 2 He chose five of his brothers and presented them before Pharaoh.
3 Pharaoh asked the brothers, "What is your occupation?"
   "Your servants are shepherds," they replied to Pharaoh, "just as our fathers were." 4 They also said to him, "We have come to live here awhile, because the famine is severe in Canaan and your servants' flocks have no pasture. So now, please let your servants settle in Goshen."

5 Pharaoh said to Joseph, "Your father and your brothers have come to you, 6 and the land of Egypt is before you; settle your father and your brothers in the best part of the land. Let them live in Goshen. And if you know of any among them with special ability, put them in charge of my own livestock."

7 Then Joseph brought his father Jacob in and presented him before Pharaoh. After Jacob blessed[d] Pharaoh, 8 Pharaoh asked him, "How old are you?"
9 And Jacob said to Pharaoh, "The years of my pilgrimage are a hundred and thirty. My years have been few and difficult, and they do not equal the years of the pilgrimage of my fathers." 10 Then Jacob blessed[e] Pharaoh and went out from his presence.

11 So Joseph settled his father and his brothers in Egypt and gave them property in the best part of the land, the district of Rameses, as Pharaoh directed. 12 Joseph also provided his father and his brothers and all his father's household with food, according to the number of their children.

Joseph and the Famine

13 There was no food, however, in the whole region because the famine was severe; both Egypt and Canaan wasted away because of the famine. 14 Joseph collected all the money that was to be found in Egypt and Canaan in payment for the grain they were buying, and he brought it to Pharaoh's palace. 15 When the money of the people of Egypt and Canaan was gone, all Egypt came to Joseph and said, "Give us food. Why should we die before your eyes? Our money is used up."

16 "Then bring your livestock," said Joseph. "I will sell you food in exchange for your livestock, since your money is gone." 17 So they brought their livestock to Joseph, and he gave them food in exchange for their horses, their sheep and goats, their cattle and donkeys. And

---

a 27 Hebrew; Septuagint *the nine children*   b 27 Hebrew (see also Exodus 1:5 and footnote); Septuagint (see also Acts 7:14) *seventy-five*   c 29 Hebrew *around him*   d 7 Or *greeted*   e 10 Or *said farewell to*

he brought them through that year with food in exchange for all their livestock.

18When that year was over, they came to him the following year and said, "We cannot hide from our lord the fact that since our money is gone and our livestock belongs to you, there is nothing left for our lord except our bodies and our land. 19Why should we perish before your eyes—we and our land as well? Buy us and our land in exchange for food, and we with our land will be in bondage to Pharaoh. Give us seed so that we may live and not die, and that the land may not become desolate."

20So Joseph bought all the land in Egypt for Pharaoh. The Egyptians, one and all, sold their fields, because the famine was too severe for them. The land became Pharaoh's, 21and Joseph reduced the people to servitude,*a* from one end of Egypt to the other. 22However, he did not buy the land of the priests, because they received a regular allotment from Pharaoh and had food enough from the allotment Pharaoh gave them. That is why they did not sell their land.

23Joseph said to the people, "Now that I have bought you and your land today for Pharaoh, here is seed for you so you can plant the ground. 24But when the crop comes in, give a fifth of it to Pharaoh. The other four-fifths you may keep as seed for the fields and as food for yourselves and your households and your children."

25"You have saved our lives," they said. "May we find favor in the eyes of our lord; we will be in bondage to Pharaoh."

26So Joseph established it as a law concerning land in Egypt—still in force today—that a fifth of the produce belongs to Pharaoh. It was only the land of the priests that did not become Pharaoh's.

27Now the Israelites settled in Egypt in the region of Goshen. They acquired property there and were fruitful and increased greatly in number.

28Jacob lived in Egypt seventeen years, and the years of his life were a hundred and forty-seven. 29When the time drew near for Israel to die, he called for his son Joseph and said to him, "If I have found favor in your eyes, put your hand under my thigh and promise that you will show me kindness and faithfulness. Do not bury me in Egypt, 30but when I rest with my fathers, carry me out of Egypt and bury me where they are buried."

"I will do as you say," he said.

31"Swear to me," he said. Then Joseph swore to him, and Israel worshiped as he leaned on the top of his staff.*b*

Manasseh and Ephraim

48 Some time later Joseph was told, "Your father is ill." So he took his two sons Manasseh and Ephraim along with him. 2When Jacob was told, "Your son Joseph has come to you," Israel rallied his strength and sat up on the bed.

3Jacob said to Joseph, "God Almighty*c* appeared to me at Luz in the land of Canaan, and there he blessed me 4and said to me, 'I am going to make you fruitful and will increase your numbers. I will make you a community of peoples, and I will give this land as an everlasting possession to your descendants after you.'

5"Now then, your two sons born to you in Egypt before I came to you here will be reckoned as mine; Ephraim and Manasseh will be mine, just as Reuben and Simeon are mine. 6Any children born to you after them will be yours; in the territory they inherit they will be reckoned under the names of their brothers. 7As I was returning from Paddan,*d* to my sorrow Rachel died in the land of Canaan while we were still on the way, a little distance from Ephrath. So I buried her there beside the road to Ephrath" (that is, Bethlehem).

8When Israel saw the sons of Joseph, he asked, "Who are these?"

9"They are the sons God has given me here," Joseph said to his father.

Then Israel said, "Bring them to me so I may bless them."

10Now Israel's eyes were failing because of old age, and he could hardly see. So Joseph brought his sons close to

---

a 21 Samaritan Pentateuch and Septuagint (see also Vulgate); Masoretic Text *and he moved the people into the cities*   *b 31* Or *Israel bowed down at the head of his bed*   *c 3* Hebrew *El-Shaddai*
d 7 That is, Northwest Mesopotamia

him, and his father kissed them and embraced them.

¹¹Israel said to Joseph, "I never expected to see your face again, and now God has allowed me to see your children too."

¹²Then Joseph removed them from Israel's knees and bowed down with his face to the ground. ¹³And Joseph took both of them, Ephraim on his right toward Israel's left hand and Manasseh on his left toward Israel's right hand, and brought them close to him. ¹⁴But Israel reached out his right hand and put it on Ephraim's head, though he was the younger, and crossing his arms, he put his left hand on Manasseh's head, even though Manasseh was the firstborn.

¹⁵Then he blessed Joseph and said,

"May the God before whom my
    fathers
  Abraham and Isaac walked,
the God who has been my shepherd
    all my life to this day,
¹⁶ the Angel who has delivered me from
    all harm
  —may he bless these boys.
May they be called by my name

WEDNESDAY

THE ANGELS WILL DELIVER US
Origen

VERSE: Genesis 48:16   **PASSAGE:** Genesis 48:8–16

hen anyone prays, the angels that minister to God and watch over mankind gather round about him and join with him in his prayer (see Hebrews 1:14). Nor is that all. Every Christian—each of the "little ones" who are in the church—has an angel of his own, who "always see the face of my Father in heaven" (see Matthew 18:10), and who looks upon the Godhead of the Creator. This angel prays with us and works with us, as far as he can, to obtain the things for which we ask.

"The angel of the Lord," so it is written, "encamps around those who fear him and he delivers them" (see Psalm 34:7), while Jacob speaks of "the angel who has delivered me from all harm" (see Genesis 48:16): and what he says is true not of himself only but of all those who set their trust in God. It would seem, then, that when a number of the faithful meet together genuinely for the glory of Christ, since they all fear the Lord, each of them will have, encamped beside him, his own angel whom God has appointed to guard him and care for him. So, when the saints are assembled, there will be a double church, one of men and one of angels.

ADDITIONAL SCRIPTURE READING:
Genesis 32:1; Psalm 34:7; Daniel 3:28

Go to page 64 for your next devotional reading.

100   500

and the names of my fathers
　　Abraham and Isaac,
and may they increase greatly
　　upon the earth."

17When Joseph saw his father placing his right hand on Ephraim's head he was displeased; so he took hold of his father's hand to move it from Ephraim's head to Manasseh's head. **18**Joseph said to him, "No, my father, this one is the firstborn; put your right hand on his head." **19**But his father refused and said, "I know, my son, I know. He too will become a people, and he too will become great. Nevertheless, his younger brother will be greater than he, and his descendants will become a group of nations." **20**He blessed them that day and said,

"In your*a* name will Israel pronounce
　　this blessing:
　　'May God make you like Ephraim
　　　and Manasseh.' "

So he put Ephraim ahead of Manasseh.

21Then Israel said to Joseph, "I am about to die, but God will be with you*b* and take you*b* back to the land of your*b* fathers. **22**And to you, as one who is over your brothers, I give the ridge of land*c* I took from the Amorites with my sword and my bow."

Jacob Blesses His Sons

49 Then Jacob called for his sons and said: "Gather around so I can tell you what will happen to you in days to come.

2 "Assemble and listen, sons of Jacob;
　　listen to your father Israel.

3 "Reuben, you are my firstborn,
　　my might, the first sign of my
　　　strength,
　　excelling in honor, excelling in
　　　power.
4 Turbulent as the waters, you will no
　　longer excel,

for you went up onto your father's
　　bed,
　　onto my couch and defiled it.

5 "Simeon and Levi are brothers—
　　their swords*d* are weapons of
　　　violence.
6 Let me not enter their council,
　　let me not join their assembly,
　　for they have killed men in their
　　　anger
　　and hamstrung oxen as they
　　　pleased.
7 Cursed be their anger, so fierce,
　　and their fury, so cruel!
　　I will scatter them in Jacob
　　and disperse them in Israel.

8 "Judah,*e* your brothers will praise
　　you;
　　your hand will be on the neck of
　　　your enemies;
　　your father's sons will bow down
　　　to you.
9 You are a lion's cub, O Judah;
　　you return from the prey, my son.
　　Like a lion he crouches and lies down,
　　like a lioness—who dares to rouse
　　　him?
10 The scepter will not depart from
　　Judah,
　　nor the ruler's staff from between
　　　his feet,
　　until he comes to whom it belongs*f*
　　and the obedience of the nations is
　　　his.
11 He will tether his donkey to a vine,
　　his colt to the choicest branch;
　　he will wash his garments in wine,
　　his robes in the blood of grapes.
12 His eyes will be darker than wine,
　　his teeth whiter than milk.*g*

13 "Zebulun will live by the seashore
　　and become a haven for ships;
　　his border will extend toward
　　　Sidon.

14 "Issachar is a rawboned*h* donkey
　　lying down between two
　　　saddlebags.*i*
15 When he sees how good is his resting
　　place
　　and how pleasant is his land,

---

a 20 The Hebrew is singular.　　*b 21* The Hebrew is plural.　　*c 22* Or *And to you I give one portion more than to your brothers—the portion*　　*d 5* The meaning of the Hebrew for this word is uncertain.　　*e 8 Judah* sounds like and may be derived from the Hebrew for *praise.*　　*f 10* Or *until Shiloh comes;* or *until he comes to whom tribute belongs*　　*g 12* Or *will be dull from wine, / his teeth white from milk*　　*h 14* Or *strong*　　*i 14* Or *campfires*

he will bend his shoulder to the
    burden
and submit to forced labor.

16 "Dan*a* will provide justice for his
    people
    as one of the tribes of Israel.
17 Dan will be a serpent by the roadside,
    a viper along the path,
that bites the horse's heels
    so that its rider tumbles backward.

18 "I look for your deliverance, O LORD.

19 "Gad*b* will be attacked by a band of
    raiders,
but he will attack them at their
    heels.

20 "Asher's food will be rich;
    he will provide delicacies fit for a
    king.

21 "Naphtali is a doe set free
    that bears beautiful fawns.*c*

22 "Joseph is a fruitful vine,
    a fruitful vine near a spring,
    whose branches climb over a wall.*d*
23 With bitterness archers attacked him;
    they shot at him with hostility.
24 But his bow remained steady,
    his strong arms stayed*e* limber,
because of the hand of the Mighty
    One of Jacob,
because of the Shepherd, the Rock
    of Israel,
25 because of your father's God, who
    helps you,
because of the Almighty,*f* who
    blesses you
with blessings of the heavens above,
    blessings of the deep that lies below,
    blessings of the breast and womb.
26 Your father's blessings are greater
    than the blessings of the ancient
    mountains,
    than*g* the bounty of the age-old
    hills.
Let all these rest on the head of
    Joseph,
on the brow of the prince among*h*
    his brothers.

27 "Benjamin is a ravenous wolf;

in the morning he devours the prey,
    in the evening he divides the
    plunder."

28 All these are the twelve tribes of
Israel, and this is what their father said
to them when he blessed them, giving
each the blessing appropriate to him.

The Death of Jacob

29 Then he gave them these instructions: "I am about to be gathered to my
people. Bury me with my fathers in the
cave in the field of Ephron the Hittite,
30 the cave in the field of Machpelah,
near Mamre in Canaan, which Abraham
bought as a burial place from Ephron the
Hittite, along with the field. 31 There
Abraham and his wife Sarah were
buried, there Isaac and his wife Rebekah
were buried, and there I buried Leah.
32 The field and the cave in it were
bought from the Hittites.*i* "

33 When Jacob had finished giving
instructions to his sons, he drew his feet
up into the bed, breathed his last and
was gathered to his people.

50 Joseph threw himself upon his
father and wept over him and
kissed him. 2 Then Joseph directed the
physicians in his service to embalm his
father Israel. So the physicians
embalmed him, 3 taking a full forty days,
for that was the time required for
embalming. And the Egyptians mourned
for him seventy days.

4 When the days of mourning had
passed, Joseph said to Pharaoh's court,
"If I have found favor in your eyes, speak
to Pharaoh for me. Tell him, 5 'My father
made me swear an oath and said, "I am
about to die; bury me in the tomb I dug
for myself in the land of Canaan." Now
let me go up and bury my father; then I
will return.' "

6 Pharaoh said, "Go up and bury your
father, as he made you swear to do."

7 So Joseph went up to bury his father.
All Pharaoh's officials accompanied
him—the dignitaries of his court and all
the dignitaries of Egypt— 8 besides all

---

a 16   Dan *here means* he provides justice.   *b 19*   Gad *can mean* attack *and* band of raiders.   *c 21*   Or
free; / he utters beautiful words   *d 22*   Or Joseph is a wild colt, / a wild colt near a spring, / a wild
donkey on a terraced hill   *e 23,24*   Or archers will attack . . . will shoot . . . will remain . . . will stay
f 25   Hebrew Shaddai   *g 26*   Or of my progenitors, / as great as   *h 26*   Or the one separated from
i 32   Or the sons of Heth

the members of Joseph's household and his brothers and those belonging to his father's household. Only their children and their flocks and herds were left in Goshen. ⁹Chariots and horsemen*a* also went up with him. It was a very large company.

¹⁰When they reached the threshing floor of Atad, near the Jordan, they lamented loudly and bitterly; and there Joseph observed a seven-day period of mourning for his father. ¹¹When the Canaanites who lived there saw the mourning at the threshing floor of Atad, they said, "The Egyptians are holding a solemn ceremony of mourning." That is why that place near the Jordan is called Abel Mizraim.*b*

¹²So Jacob's sons did as he had commanded them: ¹³They carried him to the land of Canaan and buried him in the cave in the field of Machpelah, near Mamre, which Abraham had bought as a burial place from Ephron the Hittite, along with the field. ¹⁴After burying his father, Joseph returned to Egypt, together with his brothers and all the others who had gone with him to bury his father.

Joseph Reassures His Brothers

¹⁵When Joseph's brothers saw that their father was dead, they said, "What if Joseph holds a grudge against us and pays us back for all the wrongs we did to him?" ¹⁶So they sent word to Joseph, saying, "Your father left these instructions before he died: ¹⁷'This is what you are to say to Joseph: I ask you to forgive your brothers the sins and the wrongs they committed in treating you so badly.' Now please forgive the sins of the servants of the God of your father." When their message came to him, Joseph wept.

¹⁸His brothers then came and threw themselves down before him. "We are your slaves," they said.

¹⁹But Joseph said to them, "Don't be afraid. Am I in the place of God? ²⁰You intended to harm me, but God intended it for good to accomplish what is now being done, the saving of many lives. ²¹So then, don't be afraid. I will provide for you and your children." And he reassured them and spoke kindly to them.

The Death of Joseph

²²Joseph stayed in Egypt, along with all his father's family. He lived a hundred and ten years ²³and saw the third generation of Ephraim's children. Also the children of Makir son of Manasseh were placed at birth on Joseph's knees.*c*

²⁴Then Joseph said to his brothers, "I am about to die. But God will surely come to your aid and take you up out of this land to the land he promised on oath to Abraham, Isaac and Jacob." ²⁵And Joseph made the sons of Israel swear an oath and said, "God will surely come to your aid, and then you must carry my bones up from this place."

²⁶So Joseph died at the age of a hundred and ten. And after they embalmed him, he was placed in a coffin in Egypt.

---

a 9 Or *charioteers*   *b 11* *Abel Mizraim* means *mourning of the Egyptians.*   *c 23* That is, were counted as his

EXODUS

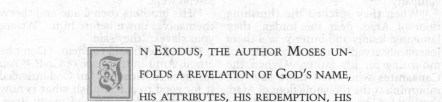

N EXODUS, THE AUTHOR MOSES UN-
FOLDS A REVELATION OF GOD'S NAME,
HIS ATTRIBUTES, HIS REDEMPTION, HIS
LAW AND HIS WORSHIP. HE TELLS THE EXCITING
STORIES OF HOW GOD DELIVERS HIS PEOPLE FROM
SLAVERY IN EGYPT AND HOW HE GIVES THEM THE
LAW AT MOUNT SINAI AND INSTRUCTS THEM TO
BUILD THE TABERNACLE. THE BOOK OF EXODUS
DEMONSTRATES THE DEPTH OF GOD'S SAVING
LOVE FOR HIS PEOPLE, AND YET HOW HIS HOLINESS
DEMANDS THEIR OBEDIENCE. THE TEN COM-
MANDMENTS EMBODY HIS CONCERN FOR OUR
WELFARE AND HOLINESS YET TODAY.

The Israelites Oppressed

1 These are the names of the sons of Israel who went to Egypt with Jacob, each with his family: ²Reuben, Simeon, Levi and Judah; ³Issachar, Zebulun and Benjamin; ⁴Dan and Naphtali; Gad and Asher. ⁵The descendants of Jacob numbered seventy*a* in all; Joseph was already in Egypt.

⁶Now Joseph and all his brothers and all that generation died, ⁷but the Israelites were fruitful and multiplied greatly and became exceedingly numerous, so that the land was filled with them.

⁸Then a new king, who did not know about Joseph, came to power in Egypt. ⁹"Look," he said to his people, "the Israelites have become much too numerous for us. ¹⁰Come, we must deal shrewdly with them or they will become even more numerous and, if war breaks out, will join our enemies, fight against us and leave the country."

¹¹So they put slave masters over them to oppress them with forced labor, and they built Pithom and Rameses as store cities for Pharaoh. ¹²But the more they were oppressed, the more they multiplied and spread; so the Egyptians came to dread the Israelites ¹³and worked them ruthlessly. ¹⁴They made their lives bitter with hard labor in brick and mortar and with all kinds of work in the fields; in all their hard labor the Egyptians used them ruthlessly.

¹⁵The king of Egypt said to the

---

a 5 Masoretic Text (see also Gen. 46:27); Dead Sea Scrolls and Septuagint (see also Acts 7:14 and note at Gen. 46:27) *seventy-five*

Hebrew midwives, whose names were Shiphrah and Puah, 16"When you help the Hebrew women in childbirth and observe them on the delivery stool, if it is a boy, kill him; but if it is a girl, let her live." 17The midwives, however, feared God and did not do what the king of Egypt had told them to do; they let the boys live. 18Then the king of Egypt summoned the midwives and asked them, "Why have you done this? Why have you let the boys live?"

19The midwives answered Pharaoh, "Hebrew women are not like Egyptian women; they are vigorous and give birth before the midwives arrive."

20So God was kind to the midwives and the people increased and became even more numerous. 21And because the midwives feared God, he gave them families of their own.

22Then Pharaoh gave this order to all his people: "Every boy that is born*a* you must throw into the Nile, but let every girl live."

The Birth of Moses

2 Now a man of the house of Levi married a Levite woman, 2and she became pregnant and gave birth to a son. When she saw that he was a fine child, she hid him for three months. 3But when she could hide him no longer, she got a papyrus basket for him and coated it with tar and pitch. Then she placed the child in it and put it among the reeds along the bank of the Nile. 4His sister stood at a distance to see what would happen to him.

5Then Pharaoh's daughter went down to the Nile to bathe, and her attendants were walking along the river bank. She saw the basket among the reeds and sent her slave girl to get it. 6She opened it and saw the baby. He was crying, and she felt sorry for him. "This is one of the Hebrew babies," she said.

7Then his sister asked Pharaoh's daughter, "Shall I go and get one of the Hebrew women to nurse the baby for you?"

8"Yes, go," she answered. And the girl went and got the baby's mother. 9Pharaoh's daughter said to her, "Take this baby and nurse him for me, and I will pay you." So the woman took the baby and nursed him. 10When the child grew older, she took him to Pharaoh's daughter and he became her son. She named him Moses,*b* saying, "I drew him out of the water."

Moses Flees to Midian

11One day, after Moses had grown up, he went out to where his own people were and watched them at their hard labor. He saw an Egyptian beating a Hebrew, one of his own people. 12Glancing this way and that and seeing no one, he killed the Egyptian and hid him in the sand. 13The next day he went out and saw two Hebrews fighting. He asked the one in the wrong, "Why are you hitting your fellow Hebrew?"

14The man said, "Who made you ruler and judge over us? Are you thinking of killing me as you killed the Egyptian?" Then Moses was afraid and thought, "What I did must have become known."

15When Pharaoh heard of this, he tried to kill Moses, but Moses fled from Pharaoh and went to live in Midian, where he sat down by a well. 16Now a priest of Midian had seven daughters, and they came to draw water and fill the troughs to water their father's flock. 17Some shepherds came along and drove them away, but Moses got up and came to their rescue and watered their flock.

18When the girls returned to Reuel their father, he asked them, "Why have you returned so early today?"

19They answered, "An Egyptian rescued us from the shepherds. He even drew water for us and watered the flock."

20"And where is he?" he asked his daughters. "Why did you leave him? Invite him to have something to eat."

21Moses agreed to stay with the man, who gave his daughter Zipporah to Moses in marriage. 22Zipporah gave birth to a son, and Moses named him Gershom,*c* saying, "I have become an alien in a foreign land."

23During that long period, the king of Egypt died. The Israelites groaned in their slavery and cried out, and their cry for help because of their slavery went up

---

a 22 Masoretic Text; Samaritan Pentateuch, Septuagint and Targums *born to the Hebrews*   *b 10 Moses* sounds like the Hebrew for *draw out.*   *c 22 Gershom* sounds like the Hebrew for *an alien there.*

FROM A LITANY OF ATLANTA
W. E. B. Du Bois

VERSE: Exodus 2:23   **PASSAGE:** Exodus 2:11–25

 city lay in travail, God our Lord, and from her loins sprang twin Murder and Black Hate. Red was the midnight; clang, crack and cry of death and fury filled the air and trembled underneath the stars when church spires pointed silently to thee. And all this was to sate the greed of greedy men who hide behind the veil of vengeance!

Bend us thine ear, O Lord!

In the pale, still morning we looked upon the deed. We stopped our ears and held our leaping hands, but they—did they not wag their heads and leer and cry with bloody jaws: *Cease from Crime!* The word was mockery, for thus they train a hundred crimes while we do cure one.

Turn again our captivity, O Lord!

Behold this maimed and broken thing; dear God, it was an humble black man who toiled and sweat to save a bit from the pittance paid him. They told him: *Work and Rise.* He worked. Did this man sin? Nay, but some one told how some one said another did—one whom he had never seen nor known. Yet for that man's crime this man lieth maimed and murdered, his wife naked to shame, his children, to poverty and evil.

Hear us, O heavenly Father!

Doth not this justice of hell stink in thy nostrils, O God? How long shall the mounting flood of innocent blood roar in thine ears and pound in our hearts for vengeance? Pile the pale frenzy of blood-crazed brutes who do such deeds high on thine altar, Jehovah Jireh, and burn it in hell forever and forever!

Forgive us, good Lord; we know not what we say!

Bewildered we are, and passion-tossed, mad with the madness of a mobbed and mocked and murdered people; straining at the armposts of thy throne, we raise our shackled hands and charge thee, God, by the bones of our stolen fathers, by the tears of our dead mothers, by the very blood of thy crucified Christ: *What meaneth this?* Tell us the plan; give us the sign!

Keep not thou silence, O God!

ADDITIONAL SCRIPTURE READING:
Exodus 1:14; Psalms 5:1–3; 22:19–24

Go to page 73 for your next devotional reading.

1900   Present

to God. 24God heard their groaning and he remembered his covenant with Abraham, with Isaac and with Jacob. 25So God looked on the Israelites and was concerned about them.

Moses and the Burning Bush

3 Now Moses was tending the flock of Jethro his father-in-law, the priest of Midian, and he led the flock to the far side of the desert and came to Horeb, the mountain of God. 2There the angel of the LORD appeared to him in flames of fire from within a bush. Moses saw that though the bush was on fire it did not burn up. 3So Moses thought, "I will go over and see this strange sight—why the bush does not burn up."

4When the LORD saw that he had gone over to look, God called to him from within the bush, "Moses! Moses!"

And Moses said, "Here I am."

5"Do not come any closer," God said. "Take off your sandals, for the place where you are standing is holy ground." 6Then he said, "I am the God of your father, the God of Abraham, the God of Isaac and the God of Jacob." At this, Moses hid his face, because he was afraid to look at God.

7The LORD said, "I have indeed seen the misery of my people in Egypt. I have heard them crying out because of their slave drivers, and I am concerned about their suffering. 8So I have come down to rescue them from the hand of the Egyptians and to bring them up out of that land into a good and spacious land, a land flowing with milk and honey—the home of the Canaanites, Hittites, Amorites, Perizzites, Hivites and Jebusites. 9And now the cry of the Israelites has reached me, and I have seen the way the Egyptians are oppressing them. 10So now, go. I am sending you to Pharaoh to bring my people the Israelites out of Egypt."

11But Moses said to God, "Who am I, that I should go to Pharaoh and bring the Israelites out of Egypt?"

12And God said, "I will be with you. And this will be the sign to you that it is I who have sent you: When you have brought the people out of Egypt, you*a* will worship God on this mountain."

13Moses said to God, "Suppose I go to the Israelites and say to them, 'The God of your fathers has sent me to you,' and they ask me, 'What is his name?' Then what shall I tell them?"

14God said to Moses, "I AM WHO I AM.*b* This is what you are to say to the Israelites: 'I AM has sent me to you.' "

15God also said to Moses, "Say to the Israelites, 'The LORD,*c* the God of your fathers—the God of Abraham, the God of Isaac and the God of Jacob—has sent me to you.' This is my name forever, the name by which I am to be remembered from generation to generation.

16"Go, assemble the elders of Israel and say to them, 'The LORD, the God of your fathers—the God of Abraham, Isaac and Jacob—appeared to me and said: I have watched over you and have seen what has been done to you in Egypt. 17And I have promised to bring you up out of your misery in Egypt into the land of the Canaanites, Hittites, Amorites, Perizzites, Hivites and Jebusites—a land flowing with milk and honey.'

18"The elders of Israel will listen to you. Then you and the elders are to go to the king of Egypt and say to him, 'The LORD, the God of the Hebrews, has met with us. Let us take a three-day journey into the desert to offer sacrifices to the LORD our God.' 19But I know that the king of Egypt will not let you go unless a mighty hand compels him. 20So I will stretch out my hand and strike the Egyptians with all the wonders that I will perform among them. After that, he will let you go.

21"And I will make the Egyptians favorably disposed toward this people, so that when you leave you will not go empty-handed. 22Every woman is to ask her neighbor and any woman living in her house for articles of silver and gold and for clothing, which you will put on your sons and daughters. And so you will plunder the Egyptians."

Signs for Moses

4 Moses answered, "What if they do not believe me or listen to me and say, 'The LORD did not appear to you'?"

---

a 12 The Hebrew is plural.   *b 14* Or *I WILL BE WHAT I WILL BE*   *c 15* The Hebrew for LORD sounds like and may be derived from the Hebrew for *I AM* in verse 14.

²Then the LORD said to him, "What is that in your hand?"

"A staff," he replied.

³The LORD said, "Throw it on the ground."

Moses threw it on the ground and it became a snake, and he ran from it. ⁴Then the LORD said to him, "Reach out your hand and take it by the tail." So Moses reached out and took hold of the snake and it turned back into a staff in his hand. ⁵"This," said the LORD, "is so that they may believe that the LORD, the God of their fathers—the God of Abraham, the God of Isaac and the God of Jacob—has appeared to you."

⁶Then the LORD said, "Put your hand inside your cloak." So Moses put his hand into his cloak, and when he took it out, it was leprous,ᵃ like snow.

⁷"Now put it back into your cloak," he said. So Moses put his hand back into his cloak, and when he took it out, it was restored, like the rest of his flesh.

⁸Then the LORD said, "If they do not believe you or pay attention to the first miraculous sign, they may believe the second. ⁹But if they do not believe these two signs or listen to you, take some water from the Nile and pour it on the dry ground. The water you take from the river will become blood on the ground."

¹⁰Moses said to the LORD, "O Lord, I have never been eloquent, neither in the past nor since you have spoken to your servant. I am slow of speech and tongue."

¹¹The LORD said to him, "Who gave man his mouth? Who makes him deaf or mute? Who gives him sight or makes him blind? Is it not I, the LORD? ¹²Now go; I will help you speak and will teach you what to say."

¹³But Moses said, "O Lord, please send someone else to do it."

¹⁴Then the LORD's anger burned against Moses and he said, "What about your brother, Aaron the Levite? I know he can speak well. He is already on his way to meet you, and his heart will be glad when he sees you. ¹⁵You shall speak to him and put words in his mouth; I will help both of you speak and will teach you what to do. ¹⁶He will speak to the people for you, and it will be as if he were your

mouth and as if you were God to him. ¹⁷But take this staff in your hand so you can perform miraculous signs with it."

Moses Returns to Egypt

¹⁸Then Moses went back to Jethro his father-in-law and said to him, "Let me go back to my own people in Egypt to see if any of them are still alive."

Jethro said, "Go, and I wish you well."

¹⁹Now the LORD had said to Moses in Midian, "Go back to Egypt, for all the men who wanted to kill you are dead." ²⁰So Moses took his wife and sons, put them on a donkey and started back to Egypt. And he took the staff of God in his hand.

²¹The LORD said to Moses, "When you return to Egypt, see that you perform before Pharaoh all the wonders I have given you the power to do. But I will harden his heart so that he will not let the people go. ²²Then say to Pharaoh, 'This is what the LORD says: Israel is my firstborn son, ²³and I told you, "Let my son go, so he may worship me." But you refused to let him go; so I will kill your firstborn son.' "

²⁴At a lodging place on the way, the LORD met ⌐Moses⌐ᵇ and was about to kill him. ²⁵But Zipporah took a flint knife, cut off her son's foreskin and touched ⌐Moses'⌐ feet with it.ᶜ "Surely you are a bridegroom of blood to me," she said. ²⁶So the LORD let him alone. (At that time she said "bridegroom of blood," referring to circumcision.)

²⁷The LORD said to Aaron, "Go into the desert to meet Moses." So he met Moses at the mountain of God and kissed him. ²⁸Then Moses told Aaron everything the LORD had sent him to say, and also about all the miraculous signs he had commanded him to perform.

²⁹Moses and Aaron brought together all the elders of the Israelites, ³⁰and Aaron told them everything the LORD had said to Moses. He also performed the signs before the people, ³¹and they believed. And when they heard that the LORD was concerned about them and had seen their misery, they bowed down and worshiped.

ᵃ 6 The Hebrew word was used for various diseases affecting the skin—not necessarily leprosy.
ᵇ 24 Or ⌐Moses' son⌐; Hebrew him   ᶜ 25 Or and drew near ⌐Moses'⌐ feet

Bricks Without Straw

5 Afterward Moses and Aaron went to Pharaoh and said, "This is what the LORD, the God of Israel, says: 'Let my people go, so that they may hold a festival to me in the desert.' "

²Pharaoh said, "Who is the LORD, that I should obey him and let Israel go? I do not know the LORD and I will not let Israel go."

³Then they said, "The God of the Hebrews has met with us. Now let us take a three-day journey into the desert to offer sacrifices to the LORD our God, or he may strike us with plagues or with the sword."

⁴But the king of Egypt said, "Moses and Aaron, why are you taking the people away from their labor? Get back to your work!" ⁵Then Pharaoh said, "Look, the people of the land are now numerous, and you are stopping them from working."

⁶That same day Pharaoh gave this order to the slave drivers and foremen in charge of the people: ⁷"You are no longer to supply the people with straw for making bricks; let them go and gather their own straw. ⁸But require them to make the same number of bricks as before; don't reduce the quota. They are lazy; that is why they are crying out, 'Let us go and sacrifice to our God.' ⁹Make the work harder for the men so that they keep working and pay no attention to lies."

¹⁰Then the slave drivers and the foremen went out and said to the people, "This is what Pharaoh says: 'I will not give you any more straw. ¹¹Go and get your own straw wherever you can find it, but your work will not be reduced at all.' " ¹²So the people scattered all over Egypt to gather stubble to use for straw. ¹³The slave drivers kept pressing them, saying, "Complete the work required of you for each day, just as when you had straw." ¹⁴The Israelite foremen appointed by Pharaoh's slave drivers were beaten and were asked, "Why didn't you meet your quota of bricks yesterday or today, as before?"

¹⁵Then the Israelite foremen went and appealed to Pharaoh: "Why have you treated your servants this way? ¹⁶Your servants are given no straw, yet we are told, 'Make bricks!' Your servants are being beaten, but the fault is with your own people."

¹⁷Pharaoh said, "Lazy, that's what you are—lazy! That is why you keep saying, 'Let us go and sacrifice to the LORD.' ¹⁸Now get to work. You will not be given any straw, yet you must produce your full quota of bricks."

¹⁹The Israelite foremen realized they were in trouble when they were told, "You are not to reduce the number of bricks required of you for each day." ²⁰When they left Pharaoh, they found Moses and Aaron waiting to meet them, ²¹and they said, "May the LORD look upon you and judge you! You have made us a stench to Pharaoh and his officials and have put a sword in their hand to kill us."

God Promises Deliverance

²²Moses returned to the LORD and said, "O Lord, why have you brought trouble upon this people? Is this why you sent me? ²³Ever since I went to Pharaoh to speak in your name, he has brought trouble upon this people, and you have not rescued your people at all."

6 Then the LORD said to Moses, "Now you will see what I will do to Pharaoh: Because of my mighty hand he will let them go; because of my mighty hand he will drive them out of his country."

²God also said to Moses, "I am the LORD. ³I appeared to Abraham, to Isaac and to Jacob as God Almighty,ᵃ but by my name the LORDᵇ I did not make myself known to them.ᶜ ⁴I also established my covenant with them to give them the land of Canaan, where they lived as aliens. ⁵Moreover, I have heard the groaning of the Israelites, whom the Egyptians are enslaving, and I have remembered my covenant.

⁶"Therefore, say to the Israelites: 'I am the LORD, and I will bring you out from under the yoke of the Egyptians. I will free you from being slaves to them, and I will redeem you with an outstretched arm and with mighty acts of

---

a 3 Hebrew *El-Shaddai*   *b 3* See note at Exodus 3:15.   *c 3* Or *Almighty, and by my name the LORD did I not let myself be known to them?*

judgment. ⁷I will take you as my own people, and I will be your God. Then you will know that I am the LORD your God, who brought you out from under the yoke of the Egyptians. ⁸And I will bring you to the land I swore with uplifted hand to give to Abraham, to Isaac and to Jacob. I will give it to you as a possession. I am the LORD.' "

⁹Moses reported this to the Israelites, but they did not listen to him because of their discouragement and cruel bondage.

¹⁰Then the LORD said to Moses, ¹¹"Go, tell Pharaoh king of Egypt to let the Israelites go out of his country."

¹²But Moses said to the LORD, "If the Israelites will not listen to me, why would Pharaoh listen to me, since I speak with faltering lips*a* ?"

Family Record of Moses and Aaron

¹³Now the LORD spoke to Moses and Aaron about the Israelites and Pharaoh king of Egypt, and he commanded them to bring the Israelites out of Egypt.

¹⁴These were the heads of their families*b*:

The sons of Reuben the firstborn son of Israel were Hanoch and Pallu, Hezron and Carmi. These were the clans of Reuben.

¹⁵The sons of Simeon were Jemuel, Jamin, Ohad, Jakin, Zohar and Shaul the son of a Canaanite woman. These were the clans of Simeon.

¹⁶These were the names of the sons of Levi according to their records: Gershon, Kohath and Merari. Levi lived 137 years.

¹⁷The sons of Gershon, by clans, were Libni and Shimei.

¹⁸The sons of Kohath were Amram, Izhar, Hebron and Uzziel. Kohath lived 133 years.

¹⁹The sons of Merari were Mahli and Mushi.

These were the clans of Levi according to their records.

²⁰Amram married his father's sister Jochebed, who bore him Aaron and Moses. Amram lived 137 years.

²¹The sons of Izhar were Korah, Nepheg and Zicri.

²²The sons of Uzziel were Mishael, Elzaphan and Sithri.

²³Aaron married Elisheba, daughter of Amminadab and sister of Nahshon, and she bore him Nadab and Abihu, Eleazar and Ithamar.

²⁴The sons of Korah were Assir, Elkanah and Abiasaph. These were the Korahite clans.

²⁵Eleazar son of Aaron married one of the daughters of Putiel, and she bore him Phinehas.

These were the heads of the Levite families, clan by clan.

²⁶It was this same Aaron and Moses to whom the LORD said, "Bring the Israelites out of Egypt by their divisions." ²⁷They were the ones who spoke to Pharaoh king of Egypt about bringing the Israelites out of Egypt. It was the same Moses and Aaron.

Aaron to Speak for Moses

²⁸Now when the LORD spoke to Moses in Egypt, ²⁹he said to him, "I am the LORD. Tell Pharaoh king of Egypt everything I tell you."

³⁰But Moses said to the LORD, "Since I speak with faltering lips, why would Pharaoh listen to me?"

7 Then the LORD said to Moses, "See, I have made you like God to Pharaoh, and your brother Aaron will be your prophet. ²You are to say everything I command you, and your brother Aaron is to tell Pharaoh to let the Israelites go out of his country. ³But I will harden Pharaoh's heart, and though I multiply my miraculous signs and wonders in Egypt, ⁴he will not listen to you. Then I will lay my hand on Egypt and with mighty acts of judgment I will bring out my divisions, my people the Israelites. ⁵And the Egyptians will know that I am the LORD when I stretch out my hand against Egypt and bring the Israelites out of it."

⁶Moses and Aaron did just as the LORD commanded them. ⁷Moses was eighty years old and Aaron eighty-three when they spoke to Pharaoh.

---

a 12 Hebrew *I am uncircumcised of lips*; also in verse 30   *b* 14 The Hebrew for *families* here and in verse 25 refers to units larger than clans.

Aaron's Staff Becomes a Snake

[8]The LORD said to Moses and Aaron, [9]"When Pharaoh says to you, 'Perform a miracle,' then say to Aaron, 'Take your staff and throw it down before Pharaoh,' and it will become a snake."

[10]So Moses and Aaron went to Pharaoh and did just as the LORD commanded. Aaron threw his staff down in front of Pharaoh and his officials, and it became a snake. [11]Pharaoh then summoned wise men and sorcerers, and the Egyptian magicians also did the same things by their secret arts: [12]Each one threw down his staff and it became a snake. But Aaron's staff swallowed up their staffs. [13]Yet Pharaoh's heart became hard and he would not listen to them, just as the LORD had said.

The Plague of Blood

[14]Then the LORD said to Moses, "Pharaoh's heart is unyielding; he refuses to let the people go. [15]Go to Pharaoh in the morning as he goes out to the water. Wait on the bank of the Nile to meet him, and take in your hand the staff that was changed into a snake. [16]Then say to him, 'The LORD, the God of the Hebrews, has sent me to say to you: Let my people go, so that they may worship me in the desert. But until now you have not listened. [17]This is what the LORD says: By this you will know that I am the LORD: With the staff that is in my hand I will strike the water of the Nile, and it will be changed into blood. [18]The fish in the Nile will die, and the river will stink; the Egyptians will not be able to drink its water.' "

[19]The LORD said to Moses, "Tell Aaron, 'Take your staff and stretch out your hand over the waters of Egypt— over the streams and canals, over the ponds and all the reservoirs'—and they will turn to blood. Blood will be everywhere in Egypt, even in the wooden buckets and stone jars."

[20]Moses and Aaron did just as the LORD had commanded. He raised his staff in the presence of Pharaoh and his officials and struck the water of the Nile, and all the water was changed into blood. [21]The fish in the Nile died, and the river smelled so bad that the Egyptians could not drink its water. Blood was everywhere in Egypt.

[22]But the Egyptian magicians did the same things by their secret arts, and Pharaoh's heart became hard; he would not listen to Moses and Aaron, just as the LORD had said. [23]Instead, he turned and went into his palace, and did not take even this to heart. [24]And all the Egyptians dug along the Nile to get drinking water, because they could not drink the water of the river.

The Plague of Frogs

[25]Seven days passed after the LORD struck the Nile. [8] [1]Then the LORD said to Moses, "Go to Pharaoh and say to him, 'This is what the LORD says: Let my people go, so that they may worship me. [2]If you refuse to let them go, I will plague your whole country with frogs. [3]The Nile will teem with frogs. They will come up into your palace and your bedroom and onto your bed, into the houses of your officials and on your people, and into your ovens and kneading troughs. [4]The frogs will go up on you and your people and all your officials.' "

[5]Then the LORD said to Moses, "Tell Aaron, 'Stretch out your hand with your staff over the streams and canals and ponds, and make frogs come up on the land of Egypt.' "

[6]So Aaron stretched out his hand over the waters of Egypt, and the frogs came up and covered the land. [7]But the magicians did the same things by their secret arts; they also made frogs come up on the land of Egypt.

[8]Pharaoh summoned Moses and Aaron and said, "Pray to the LORD to take the frogs away from me and my people, and I will let your people go to offer sacrifices to the LORD."

[9]Moses said to Pharaoh, "I leave to you the honor of setting the time for me to pray for you and your officials and your people that you and your houses may be rid of the frogs, except for those that remain in the Nile."

[10]"Tomorrow," Pharaoh said.

Moses replied, "It will be as you say, so that you may know there is no one like the LORD our God. [11]The frogs will leave you and your houses, your officials and your people; they will remain only in the Nile."

¹²After Moses and Aaron left Pharaoh, Moses cried out to the LORD about the frogs he had brought on Pharaoh. ¹³And the LORD did what Moses asked. The frogs died in the houses, in the courtyards and in the fields. ¹⁴They were piled into heaps, and the land reeked of them. ¹⁵But when Pharaoh saw that there was relief, he hardened his heart and would not listen to Moses and Aaron, just as the LORD had said.

The Plague of Gnats

¹⁶Then the LORD said to Moses, "Tell Aaron, 'Stretch out your staff and strike the dust of the ground,' and throughout the land of Egypt the dust will become gnats." ¹⁷They did this, and when Aaron stretched out his hand with the staff and struck the dust of the ground, gnats came upon men and animals. All the dust throughout the land of Egypt became gnats. ¹⁸But when the magicians tried to produce gnats by their secret arts, they could not. And the gnats were on men and animals.

¹⁹The magicians said to Pharaoh, "This is the finger of God." But Pharaoh's heart was hard and he would not listen, just as the LORD had said.

The Plague of Flies

²⁰Then the LORD said to Moses, "Get up early in the morning and confront Pharaoh as he goes to the water and say to him, 'This is what the LORD says: Let my people go, so that they may worship me. ²¹If you do not let my people go, I will send swarms of flies on you and your officials, on your people and into your houses. The houses of the Egyptians will be full of flies, and even the ground where they are.

²²" 'But on that day I will deal differently with the land of Goshen, where my people live; no swarms of flies will be there, so that you will know that I, the LORD, am in this land. ²³I will make a distinction[a] between my people and your people. This miraculous sign will occur tomorrow.' "

²⁴And the LORD did this. Dense swarms of flies poured into Pharaoh's palace and into the houses of his officials, and throughout Egypt the land was ruined by the flies.

²⁵Then Pharaoh summoned Moses and Aaron and said, "Go, sacrifice to your God here in the land."

²⁶But Moses said, "That would not be right. The sacrifices we offer the LORD our God would be detestable to the Egyptians. And if we offer sacrifices that are detestable in their eyes, will they not stone us? ²⁷We must take a three-day journey into the desert to offer sacrifices to the LORD our God, as he commands us."

²⁸Pharaoh said, "I will let you go to offer sacrifices to the LORD your God in the desert, but you must not go very far. Now pray for me."

²⁹Moses answered, "As soon as I leave you, I will pray to the LORD, and tomorrow the flies will leave Pharaoh and his officials and his people. Only be sure that Pharaoh does not act deceitfully again by not letting the people go to offer sacrifices to the LORD."

³⁰Then Moses left Pharaoh and prayed to the LORD, ³¹and the LORD did what Moses asked: The flies left Pharaoh and his officials and his people; not a fly remained. ³²But this time also Pharaoh hardened his heart and would not let the people go.

The Plague on Livestock

9 Then the LORD said to Moses, "Go to Pharaoh and say to him, 'This is what the LORD, the God of the Hebrews, says: "Let my people go, so that they may worship me." ²If you refuse to let them go and continue to hold them back, ³the hand of the LORD will bring a terrible plague on your livestock in the field—on your horses and donkeys and camels and on your cattle and sheep and goats. ⁴But the LORD will make a distinction between the livestock of Israel and that of Egypt, so that no animal belonging to the Israelites will die.' "

⁵The LORD set a time and said, "Tomorrow the LORD will do this in the land." ⁶And the next day the LORD did it: All the livestock of the Egyptians died, but not one animal belonging to

---

a 23 Septuagint and Vulgate; Hebrew *will put a deliverance*

the Israelites died. 7Pharaoh sent men to investigate and found that not even one of the animals of the Israelites had died. Yet his heart was unyielding and he would not let the people go.

The Plague of Boils

8Then the LORD said to Moses and Aaron, "Take handfuls of soot from a furnace and have Moses toss it into the air in the presence of Pharaoh. 9It will become fine dust over the whole land of Egypt, and festering boils will break out on men and animals throughout the land."

10So they took soot from a furnace and stood before Pharaoh. Moses tossed it into the air, and festering boils broke out on men and animals. 11The magicians could not stand before Moses because of the boils that were on them and on all the Egyptians. 12But the LORD hardened Pharaoh's heart and he would not listen to Moses and Aaron, just as the LORD had said to Moses.

The Plague of Hail

13Then the LORD said to Moses, "Get up early in the morning, confront Pharaoh and say to him, 'This is what the LORD, the God of the Hebrews, says: Let my people go, so that they may worship me, 14or this time I will send the full force of my plagues against you and against your officials and your people, so you may know that there is no one like me in all the earth. 15For by now I could have stretched out my hand and struck you and your people with a plague that would have wiped you off the earth. 16But I have raised you up*a* for this very purpose, that I might show you my power and that my name might be proclaimed in all the earth. 17You still set yourself against my people and will not let them go. 18Therefore, at this time tomorrow I will send the worst hailstorm that has ever fallen on Egypt, from the day it was founded till now. 19Give an order now to bring your livestock and everything you have in the field to a place of shelter, because the hail will fall on every man and animal that has not been brought in and is still out in the field, and they will die.' "

20Those officials of Pharaoh who feared the word of the LORD hurried to bring their slaves and their livestock inside. 21But those who ignored the word of the LORD left their slaves and livestock in the field.

22Then the LORD said to Moses, "Stretch out your hand toward the sky so that hail will fall all over Egypt—on men and animals and on everything growing in the fields of Egypt." 23When Moses stretched out his staff toward the sky, the LORD sent thunder and hail, and lightning flashed down to the ground. So the LORD rained hail on the land of Egypt; 24hail fell and lightning flashed back and forth. It was the worst storm in all the land of Egypt since it had become a nation. 25Throughout Egypt hail struck everything in the fields—both men and animals; it beat down everything growing in the fields and stripped every tree. 26The only place it did not hail was the land of Goshen, where the Israelites were.

27Then Pharaoh summoned Moses and Aaron. "This time I have sinned," he said to them. "The LORD is in the right, and I and my people are in the wrong. 28Pray to the LORD, for we have had enough thunder and hail. I will let you go; you don't have to stay any longer."

29Moses replied, "When I have gone out of the city, I will spread out my hands in prayer to the LORD. The thunder will stop and there will be no more hail, so you may know that the earth is the LORD's. 30But I know that you and your officials still do not fear the LORD God."

31(The flax and barley were destroyed, since the barley had headed and the flax was in bloom. 32The wheat and spelt, however, were not destroyed, because they ripen later.)

33Then Moses left Pharaoh and went out of the city. He spread out his hands toward the LORD; the thunder and hail stopped, and the rain no longer poured down on the land. 34When Pharaoh saw that the rain and hail and thunder had stopped, he sinned again: He and his officials hardened their hearts. 35So Pharaoh's heart was hard and he would not let the Israelites go, just as the LORD had said through Moses.

a 16 Or have spared you

The Plague of Locusts

10 Then the LORD said to Moses, "Go to Pharaoh, for I have hardened his heart and the hearts of his officials so that I may perform these miraculous signs of mine among them ²that you may tell your children and grandchildren how I dealt harshly with the Egyptians and how I performed my signs among them, and that you may know that I am the LORD."

³So Moses and Aaron went to Pharaoh and said to him, "This is what the LORD, the God of the Hebrews, says: 'How long will you refuse to humble yourself before me? Let my people go, so that they may worship me. ⁴If you refuse to let them go, I will bring locusts into your country tomorrow. ⁵They will cover the face of the ground so that it cannot be seen. They will devour what little you have left after the hail, including every tree that is growing in your fields. ⁶They will fill your houses and those of all your officials and all the Egyptians—something neither your fathers nor your forefathers have ever seen from the day they settled in this land till now.'" Then Moses turned and left Pharaoh.

⁷Pharaoh's officials said to him, "How long will this man be a snare to us? Let the people go, so that they may worship the LORD their God. Do you not yet realize that Egypt is ruined?"

⁸Then Moses and Aaron were brought back to Pharaoh. "Go, worship the LORD your God," he said. "But just who will be going?"

⁹Moses answered, "We will go with our young and old, with our sons and daughters, and with our flocks and herds, because we are to celebrate a festival to the LORD."

¹⁰Pharaoh said, "The LORD be with you—if I let you go, along with your women and children! Clearly you are bent on evil.ᵃ ¹¹No! Have only the men go; and worship the LORD, since that's what you have been asking for." Then Moses and Aaron were driven out of Pharaoh's presence.

¹²And the LORD said to Moses, "Stretch out your hand over Egypt so that locusts will swarm over the land and devour everything growing in the fields, everything left by the hail."

¹³So Moses stretched out his staff over Egypt, and the LORD made an east wind blow across the land all that day and all that night. By morning the wind had brought the locusts; ¹⁴they invaded all Egypt and settled down in every area of the country in great numbers. Never before had there been such a plague of locusts, nor will there ever be again. ¹⁵They covered all the ground until it was black. They devoured all that was left after the hail—everything growing in the fields and the fruit on the trees. Nothing green remained on tree or plant in all the land of Egypt.

¹⁶Pharaoh quickly summoned Moses and Aaron and said, "I have sinned against the LORD your God and against you. ¹⁷Now forgive my sin once more and pray to the LORD your God to take this deadly plague away from me."

¹⁸Moses then left Pharaoh and prayed to the LORD. ¹⁹And the LORD changed the wind to a very strong west wind, which caught up the locusts and carried them into the Red Sea.ᵇ Not a locust was left anywhere in Egypt. ²⁰But the LORD hardened Pharaoh's heart, and he would not let the Israelites go.

The Plague of Darkness

²¹Then the LORD said to Moses, "Stretch out your hand toward the sky so that darkness will spread over Egypt—darkness that can be felt." ²²So Moses stretched out his hand toward the sky, and total darkness covered all Egypt for three days. ²³No one could see anyone else or leave his place for three days. Yet all the Israelites had light in the places where they lived.

²⁴Then Pharaoh summoned Moses and said, "Go, worship the LORD. Even your women and children may go with you; only leave your flocks and herds behind."

²⁵But Moses said, "You must allow us to have sacrifices and burnt offerings to present to the LORD our God. ²⁶Our livestock too must go with us; not a hoof is to be left behind. We have to use some of them in worshiping the LORD our God, and until we get there we will not

ᵃ 10 Or Be careful, trouble is in store for you!   ᵇ 19 Hebrew Yam Suph; that is, Sea of Reeds

GO DOWN, MOSES

African-American Spiritual

VERSE: Exodus 10:3   **PASSAGE:** Exodus 10:1–20

hen Israel was in Egypt's land,
Let my people go,
Oppressed so hard they could not stand,
Let my people go.

Go down, Moses,
Way down in Egypt land,
Tell de Pharaoh
To let my people go.

Thus saith the Lord, bold Moses said,
Let my people go.
If not I'll smite your firstborn dead,
Let my people go.

No more shall they in bondage toil . . .
Let my people go.
Let them come out with Egypt's spoil . . .
Let my people go.

The Lord told Moses what to do . . .
Let my people go.
To lead the children of Israel through . . .
Let my people go.

As I stood by the waterside . . .
Let my people go.
At the command of God, it did divide . . .
Let my people go.

When they reached the other shore . . .
Let my people go.
They sang a song of triumph o'er . . .
Let my people go.

ADDITIONAL SCRIPTURE READING:
Exodus 4:21–23; James 4:10; 1 Peter 5:6

Go to page 75 for your next devotional reading.

1700   1900

know what we are to use to worship the LORD."

27But the LORD hardened Pharaoh's heart, and he was not willing to let them go. 28Pharaoh said to Moses, "Get out of my sight! Make sure you do not appear before me again! The day you see my face you will die."

29"Just as you say," Moses replied, "I will never appear before you again."

The Plague on the Firstborn

11 Now the LORD had said to Moses, "I will bring one more plague on Pharaoh and on Egypt. After that, he will let you go from here, and when he does, he will drive you out completely. 2Tell the people that men and women alike are to ask their neighbors for articles of silver and gold." 3(The LORD made the Egyptians favorably disposed toward the people, and Moses himself was highly regarded in Egypt by Pharaoh's officials and by the people.)

4So Moses said, "This is what the LORD says: 'About midnight I will go throughout Egypt. 5Every firstborn son in Egypt will die, from the firstborn son of Pharaoh, who sits on the throne, to the firstborn son of the slave girl, who is at her hand mill, and all the firstborn of the cattle as well. 6There will be loud wailing throughout Egypt—worse than there has ever been or ever will be again. 7But among the Israelites not a dog will bark at any man or animal.' Then you will know that the LORD makes a distinction between Egypt and Israel. 8All these officials of yours will come to me, bowing down before me and saying, 'Go, you and all the people who follow you!' After that I will leave." Then Moses, hot with anger, left Pharaoh.

9The LORD had said to Moses, "Pharaoh will refuse to listen to you—so that my wonders may be multiplied in Egypt." 10Moses and Aaron performed all these wonders before Pharaoh, but the LORD hardened Pharaoh's heart, and he would not let the Israelites go out of his country.

The Passover

12 The LORD said to Moses and Aaron in Egypt, 2"This month is to be for you the first month, the first month of your year. 3Tell the whole community of Israel that on the tenth day of this month each man is to take a lamb*a* for his family, one for each household. 4If any household is too small for a whole lamb, they must share one with their nearest neighbor, having taken into account the number of people there are. You are to determine the amount of lamb needed in accordance with what each person will eat. 5The animals you choose must be year-old males without defect, and you may take them from the sheep or the goats. 6Take care of them until the fourteenth day of the month, when all the people of the community of Israel must slaughter them at twilight. 7Then they are to take some of the blood and put it on the sides and tops of the doorframes of the houses where they eat the lambs. 8That same night they are to eat the meat roasted over the fire, along with bitter herbs, and bread made without yeast. 9Do not eat the meat raw or cooked in water, but roast it over the fire—head, legs and inner parts. 10Do not leave any of it till morning; if some is left till morning, you must burn it. 11This is how you are to eat it: with your cloak tucked into your belt, your sandals on your feet and your staff in your hand. Eat it in haste; it is the LORD's Passover.

12"On that same night I will pass through Egypt and strike down every firstborn—both men and animals—and I will bring judgment on all the gods of Egypt. I am the LORD. 13The blood will be a sign for you on the houses where you are; and when I see the blood, I will pass over you. No destructive plague will touch you when I strike Egypt.

14"This is a day you are to commemorate; for the generations to come you shall celebrate it as a festival to the LORD—a lasting ordinance. 15For seven days you are to eat bread made without yeast. On the first day remove the yeast from your houses, for whoever eats anything with yeast in it from the first day through the seventh must be cut off from Israel. 16On the first day hold a

a 3 The Hebrew word can mean *lamb* or *kid*; also in verse 4.

WEEKEND

EVIL'S COMPROMISE
G. Campbell Morgan

VERSE: Exodus 10:26   **PASSAGE:** Exodus 10:21–29

ot a hoof is to be left behind." This was the final word of Moses in a persistent conflict against anything in the nature of compromise. Pharaoh had attempted to bring this about since after the fourth plague. Note the stages of these attempts. At the beginning he had declared that these people should not go to sacrifice to Jehovah their God. After the plague of flies, the fourth, he suggested that they might sacrifice, but they could do it without going away from the land (Exodus 8:25). This Moses at once refused. Then Pharaoh suggested that if they must go, it should not be very far away (8:28). On this Moses entreated for him, and the plague was removed, but he would not let them go. He proposed later, after the eighth plague (that of locusts), that they should leave the women and children behind (10:8–11). Moses refused. After the ninth plague (that of the darkness), he suggested that the cattle be left (10:24). Then Moses spoke this final word: "Not a hoof is to be left behind."

That is the true attitude of the man of faith. Evil is always suggesting some compromise. To listen to it, is to remain enslaved. The only way into liberty is to leave the land of evil; to go accompanied by the women and the children; and to take all property also. It is when that attitude is assumed, that men pass out from all bondage, and find the liberty which is in the purpose of God for them.

ADDITIONAL SCRIPTURE READING:
Hosea 5:5–6; 1 Timothy 6:11

Go to page 76 for your next devotional reading.

1900   Present

sacred assembly, and another one on the seventh day. Do no work at all on these days, except to prepare food for everyone to eat—that is all you may do.

17 "Celebrate the Feast of Unleavened Bread, because it was on this very day that I brought your divisions out of Egypt. Celebrate this day as a lasting

MONDAY

JUST AS I AM
Charlotte Elliot

VERSE: Exodus 12:3   **PASSAGE:** Exodus 12:1–30

ust as I am, without one plea,
But that thy blood was shed for me,
And that thou bidd'st me come to thee,
O Lamb of God, I come, I come.

Just as I am, and waiting not
To rid my soul of one dark blot,
To thee whose blood can cleanse each spot,
O Lamb of God, I come, I come.

Just as I am, though tossed about
With many a conflict, many a doubt;
Fightings and fears within, without,
O Lamb of God, I come, I come.

Just as I am, poor, wretched, blind;
Sight, riches, healing of the mind,
Yea, all I need, in thee to find,
O Lamb of God, I come, I come.

Just as I am: thou wilt receive;
Wilt welcome, pardon, cleanse, relieve,
Because thy promise I believe,
O Lamb of God, I come, I come.

Just as I am, thy love unknown
Has broken every barrier down;
Now to be thine, yea, thine alone,
O Lamb of God, I come, I come.

ADDITIONAL SCRIPTURE READING:
Mark 14:12; John 1:29; 1 Corinthians 5:7

Go to page 80 for your next devotional reading.

1700   1900

ordinance for the generations to come. [18]In the first month you are to eat bread made without yeast, from the evening of the fourteenth day until the evening of the twenty-first day. [19]For seven days no yeast is to be found in your houses. And whoever eats anything with yeast in it must be cut off from the community of Israel, whether he is an alien or native-born. [20]Eat nothing made with yeast. Wherever you live, you must eat unleavened bread."

[21]Then Moses summoned all the elders of Israel and said to them, "Go at once and select the animals for your families and slaughter the Passover lamb. [22]Take a bunch of hyssop, dip it into the blood in the basin and put some of the blood on the top and on both sides of the doorframe. Not one of you shall go out the door of his house until morning. [23]When the LORD goes through the land to strike down the Egyptians, he will see the blood on the top and sides of the doorframe and will pass over that doorway, and he will not permit the destroyer to enter your houses and strike you down.

[24]"Obey these instructions as a lasting ordinance for you and your descendants. [25]When you enter the land that the LORD will give you as he promised, observe this ceremony. [26]And when your children ask you, 'What does this ceremony mean to you?' [27]then tell them, 'It is the Passover sacrifice to the LORD, who passed over the houses of the Israelites in Egypt and spared our homes when he struck down the Egyptians.' " Then the people bowed down and worshiped. [28]The Israelites did just what the LORD commanded Moses and Aaron.

[29]At midnight the LORD struck down all the firstborn in Egypt, from the firstborn of Pharaoh, who sat on the throne, to the firstborn of the prisoner, who was in the dungeon, and the firstborn of all the livestock as well. [30]Pharaoh and all his officials and all the Egyptians got up during the night, and there was loud wailing in Egypt, for there was not a house without someone dead.

The Exodus

[31]During the night Pharaoh summoned Moses and Aaron and said, "Up! Leave my people, you and the Israelites! Go, worship the LORD as you have requested. [32]Take your flocks and herds, as you have said, and go. And also bless me."

[33]The Egyptians urged the people to hurry and leave the country. "For otherwise," they said, "we will all die!" [34]So the people took their dough before the yeast was added, and carried it on their shoulders in kneading troughs wrapped in clothing. [35]The Israelites did as Moses instructed and asked the Egyptians for articles of silver and gold and for clothing. [36]The LORD had made the Egyptians favorably disposed toward the people, and they gave them what they asked for; so they plundered the Egyptians.

[37]The Israelites journeyed from Rameses to Succoth. There were about six hundred thousand men on foot, besides women and children. [38]Many other people went up with them, as well as large droves of livestock, both flocks and herds. [39]With the dough they had brought from Egypt, they baked cakes of unleavened bread. The dough was without yeast because they had been driven out of Egypt and did not have time to prepare food for themselves.

[40]Now the length of time the Israelite people lived in Egypt[a] was 430 years. [41]At the end of the 430 years, to the very day, all the LORD's divisions left Egypt. [42]Because the LORD kept vigil that night to bring them out of Egypt, on this night all the Israelites are to keep vigil to honor the LORD for the generations to come.

Passover Restrictions

[43]The LORD said to Moses and Aaron, "These are the regulations for the Passover:

"No foreigner is to eat of it. [44]Any slave you have bought may eat of it after you have circumcised him, [45]but a temporary resident and a hired worker may not eat of it.

[46]"It must be eaten inside one house; take none of the meat outside the house.

---

[a] 40 Masoretic Text; Samaritan Pentateuch and Septuagint *Egypt and Canaan*

Do not break any of the bones. ⁴⁷The whole community of Israel must celebrate it.

⁴⁸"An alien living among you who wants to celebrate the LORD's Passover must have all the males in his household circumcised; then he may take part like one born in the land. No uncircumcised male may eat of it. ⁴⁹The same law applies to the native-born and to the alien living among you."

⁵⁰All the Israelites did just what the LORD had commanded Moses and Aaron. ⁵¹And on that very day the LORD brought the Israelites out of Egypt by their divisions.

Consecration of the Firstborn

13 The LORD said to Moses, ²"Consecrate to me every firstborn male. The first offspring of every womb among the Israelites belongs to me, whether man or animal."

³Then Moses said to the people, "Commemorate this day, the day you came out of Egypt, out of the land of slavery, because the LORD brought you out of it with a mighty hand. Eat nothing containing yeast. ⁴Today, in the month of Abib, you are leaving. ⁵When the LORD brings you into the land of the Canaanites, Hittites, Amorites, Hivites and Jebusites—the land he swore to your forefathers to give you, a land flowing with milk and honey—you are to observe this ceremony in this month: ⁶For seven days eat bread made without yeast and on the seventh day hold a festival to the LORD. ⁷Eat unleavened bread during those seven days; nothing with yeast in it is to be seen among you, nor shall any yeast be seen anywhere within your borders. ⁸On that day tell your son, 'I do this because of what the LORD did for me when I came out of Egypt.' ⁹This observance will be for you like a sign on your hand and a reminder on your forehead that the law of the LORD is to be on your lips. For the LORD brought you out of Egypt with his mighty hand. ¹⁰You must keep this ordinance at the appointed time year after year.

¹¹"After the LORD brings you into the land of the Canaanites and gives it to you, as he promised on oath to you and your forefathers, ¹²you are to give over to the LORD the first offspring of every womb. All the firstborn males of your livestock belong to the LORD. ¹³Redeem with a lamb every firstborn donkey, but if you do not redeem it, break its neck. Redeem every firstborn among your sons.

¹⁴"In days to come, when your son asks you, 'What does this mean?' say to him, 'With a mighty hand the LORD brought us out of Egypt, out of the land of slavery. ¹⁵When Pharaoh stubbornly refused to let us go, the LORD killed every firstborn in Egypt, both man and animal. This is why I sacrifice to the LORD the first male offspring of every womb and redeem each of my firstborn sons.' ¹⁶And it will be like a sign on your hand and a symbol on your forehead that the LORD brought us out of Egypt with his mighty hand."

Crossing the Sea

¹⁷When Pharaoh let the people go, God did not lead them on the road through the Philistine country, though that was shorter. For God said, "If they face war, they might change their minds and return to Egypt." ¹⁸So God led the people around by the desert road toward the Red Sea.ᵃ The Israelites went up out of Egypt armed for battle.

¹⁹Moses took the bones of Joseph with him because Joseph had made the sons of Israel swear an oath. He had said, "God will surely come to your aid, and then you must carry my bones up with you from this place."ᵇ

²⁰After leaving Succoth they camped at Etham on the edge of the desert. ²¹By day the LORD went ahead of them in a pillar of cloud to guide them on their way and by night in a pillar of fire to give them light, so that they could travel by day or night. ²²Neither the pillar of cloud by day nor the pillar of fire by night left its place in front of the people.

14 Then the LORD said to Moses, ²"Tell the Israelites to turn back and encamp near Pi Hahiroth, between Migdol and the sea. They are to encamp by the sea, directly opposite

---

ᵃ 18 Hebrew *Yam Suph*; that is, Sea of Reeds   ᵇ 19 See Gen. 50:25.

Baal Zephon. ³Pharaoh will think, 'The Israelites are wandering around the land in confusion, hemmed in by the desert.' ⁴And I will harden Pharaoh's heart, and he will pursue them. But I will gain glory for myself through Pharaoh and all his army, and the Egyptians will know that I am the LORD." So the Israelites did this.

⁵When the king of Egypt was told that the people had fled, Pharaoh and his officials changed their minds about them and said, "What have we done? We have let the Israelites go and have lost their services!" ⁶So he had his chariot made ready and took his army with him. ⁷He took six hundred of the best chariots, along with all the other chariots of Egypt, with officers over all of them. ⁸The LORD hardened the heart of Pharaoh king of Egypt, so that he pursued the Israelites, who were marching out boldly. ⁹The Egyptians—all Pharaoh's horses and chariots, horsemenᵃ and troops—pursued the Israelites and overtook them as they camped by the sea near Pi Hahiroth, opposite Baal Zephon.

¹⁰As Pharaoh approached, the Israelites looked up, and there were the Egyptians, marching after them. They were terrified and cried out to the LORD. ¹¹They said to Moses, "Was it because there were no graves in Egypt that you brought us to the desert to die? What have you done to us by bringing us out of Egypt? ¹²Didn't we say to you in Egypt, 'Leave us alone; let us serve the Egyptians'? It would have been better for us to serve the Egyptians than to die in the desert!"

¹³Moses answered the people, "Do not be afraid. Stand firm and you will see the deliverance the LORD will bring you today. The Egyptians you see today you will never see again. ¹⁴The LORD will fight for you; you need only to be still."

¹⁵Then the LORD said to Moses, "Why are you crying out to me? Tell the Israelites to move on. ¹⁶Raise your staff and stretch out your hand over the sea to divide the water so that the Israelites can go through the sea on dry ground. ¹⁷I will harden the hearts of the Egyptians so that they will go in after them. And I

will gain glory through Pharaoh and all his army, through his chariots and his horsemen. ¹⁸The Egyptians will know that I am the LORD when I gain glory through Pharaoh, his chariots and his horsemen."

¹⁹Then the angel of God, who had been traveling in front of Israel's army, withdrew and went behind them. The pillar of cloud also moved from in front and stood behind them, ²⁰coming between the armies of Egypt and Israel. Throughout the night the cloud brought darkness to the one side and light to the other side; so neither went near the other all night long.

²¹Then Moses stretched out his hand over the sea, and all that night the LORD drove the sea back with a strong east wind and turned it into dry land. The waters were divided, ²²and the Israelites went through the sea on dry ground, with a wall of water on their right and on their left.

²³The Egyptians pursued them, and all Pharaoh's horses and chariots and horsemen followed them into the sea. ²⁴During the last watch of the night the LORD looked down from the pillar of fire and cloud at the Egyptian army and threw it into confusion. ²⁵He made the wheels of their chariots come offᵇ so that they had difficulty driving. And the Egyptians said, "Let's get away from the Israelites! The LORD is fighting for them against Egypt."

²⁶Then the LORD said to Moses, "Stretch out your hand over the sea so that the waters may flow back over the Egyptians and their chariots and horsemen." ²⁷Moses stretched out his hand over the sea, and at daybreak the sea went back to its place. The Egyptians were fleeing towardᶜ it, and the LORD swept them into the sea. ²⁸The water flowed back and covered the chariots and horsemen—the entire army of Pharaoh that had followed the Israelites into the sea. Not one of them survived.

²⁹But the Israelites went through the sea on dry ground, with a wall of water on their right and on their left. ³⁰That day the LORD saved Israel from the hands of the Egyptians, and Israel saw

---

ᵃ 9 Or charioteers; also in verses 17, 18, 23, 26 and 28   ᵇ 25 Or He jammed the wheels of their
chariots (see Samaritan Pentateuch, Septuagint and Syriac)   ᶜ 27 Or from

the Egyptians lying dead on the shore. ³¹And when the Israelites saw the great power the LORD displayed against the Egyptians, the people feared the LORD and put their trust in him and in Moses his servant.

TUESDAY

THE DEATH OF EVIL
Martin Luther King, Jr.

VERSE: Exodus 14:30   **PASSAGE:** Exodus 14:13–31

hen the children of Israel were held under the gripping yoke of Egyptian slavery, Egypt symbolized evil in the form of humiliating oppression, ungodly exploitation, and crushing domination, and the Israelites symbolized goodness in the form of devotion and dedication to the God of Abraham, Isaac, and Jacob. Egypt struggled to maintain her oppressive yoke, and Israel struggled to gain freedom. Pharaoh stubbornly refused to respond to the cry of Moses, even when plague after plague threatened his domain. This tells us something about evil that we must never forget, namely that evil is recalcitrant and determined, and never voluntarily relinquishes its hold short of a persistent, almost fanatical resistance. But there is a checkpoint in the universe: evil cannot permanently organize itself. So after a long and trying struggle, the Israelites, through the providence of God, crossed the Red Sea. But like the old guard that never surrenders, the Egyptians, in a desperate attempt to prevent the Israelites from escaping, had their armies go in the Red Sea behind them. As soon as the Egyptians got into the dried-up sea the parted waters swept back upon them, and the turbulence and momentum of the tidal waves soon drowned all of them. When the Israelites looked back, all they could see was here and there a poor drowned body beaten upon the seashore. For the Israelites, this was a great moment. It was the end of a frightful period in their history. It was a joyous daybreak that had come to end the long night of their captivity. The meaning of this story is not found in the drowning of Egyptian soldiers, for no one should rejoice at the death or defeat of a human being. Rather, this story symbolizes the death of evil and of inhuman oppression and unjust exploitation.

ADDITIONAL SCRIPTURE READING:
Joshua 3:14–17; Psalm 44:4–8

Go to page 94 for your next devotional reading.

1900   Present

The Song of Moses and Miriam

15 Then Moses and the Israelites sang this song to the LORD:

"I will sing to the LORD,
  for he is highly exalted.
The horse and its rider
  he has hurled into the sea.
2 The LORD is my strength and my
    song;
  he has become my salvation.
He is my God, and I will praise him,
  my father's God, and I will exalt
    him.
3 The LORD is a warrior;
  the LORD is his name.
4 Pharaoh's chariots and his army
  he has hurled into the sea.
The best of Pharaoh's officers
  are drowned in the Red Sea.*a*
5 The deep waters have covered them;
  they sank to the depths like a stone.

6 "Your right hand, O LORD,
  was majestic in power.
Your right hand, O LORD,
  shattered the enemy.
7 In the greatness of your majesty
  you threw down those who
    opposed you.
You unleashed your burning anger;
  it consumed them like stubble.
8 By the blast of your nostrils
  the waters piled up.
The surging waters stood firm like a
    wall;
  the deep waters congealed in the
    heart of the sea.
9 "The enemy boasted,
  'I will pursue, I will overtake them.
I will divide the spoils;
  I will gorge myself on them.
I will draw my sword
  and my hand will destroy them.'
10 But you blew with your breath,
  and the sea covered them.
They sank like lead
  in the mighty waters.

11 "Who among the gods is like you,
    O LORD?
Who is like you—
  majestic in holiness,
  awesome in glory,

working wonders?
12 You stretched out your right hand
  and the earth swallowed them.

13 "In your unfailing love you will lead
  the people you have redeemed.
In your strength you will guide them
  to your holy dwelling.
14 The nations will hear and tremble;
  anguish will grip the people of
    Philistia.
15 The chiefs of Edom will be terrified,
  the leaders of Moab will be seized
    with trembling,
the people*b* of Canaan will melt away;
16   terror and dread will fall upon them.
By the power of your arm
  they will be as still as a stone—
until your people pass by, O LORD,
  until the people you bought*c* pass
    by.
17 You will bring them in and plant
    them
  on the mountain of your
    inheritance—
the place, O LORD, you made for your
    dwelling,
  the sanctuary, O Lord, your hands
    established.
18 The LORD will reign
  for ever and ever."

19 When Pharaoh's horses, chariots and horsemen*d* went into the sea, the LORD brought the waters of the sea back over them, but the Israelites walked through the sea on dry ground. 20 Then Miriam the prophetess, Aaron's sister, took a tambourine in her hand, and all the women followed her, with tambourines and dancing. 21 Miriam sang to them:

"Sing to the LORD,
  for he is highly exalted.
The horse and its rider
  he has hurled into the sea."

The Waters of Marah and Elim

22 Then Moses led Israel from the Red Sea and they went into the Desert of Shur. For three days they traveled in the desert without finding water. 23 When they came to Marah, they could not drink its water because it was bitter. (That is why the place is called Marah.*e*)

---

a 4 Hebrew *Yam Suph;* that is, Sea of Reeds; also in verse 22   *b 15* Or *rulers*   *c 16* Or *created*
d 19 Or *charioteers*   *e 23 Marah* means *bitter.*

24So the people grumbled against Moses, saying, "What are we to drink?"

25Then Moses cried out to the LORD, and the LORD showed him a piece of wood. He threw it into the water, and the water became sweet.

There the LORD made a decree and a law for them, and there he tested them. 26He said, "If you listen carefully to the voice of the LORD your God and do what is right in his eyes, if you pay attention to his commands and keep all his decrees, I will not bring on you any of the diseases I brought on the Egyptians, for I am the LORD, who heals you."

27Then they came to Elim, where there were twelve springs and seventy palm trees, and they camped there near the water.

Manna and Quail

16 The whole Israelite community set out from Elim and came to the Desert of Sin, which is between Elim and Sinai, on the fifteenth day of the second month after they had come out of Egypt. 2In the desert the whole community grumbled against Moses and Aaron. 3The Israelites said to them, "If only we had died by the LORD's hand in Egypt! There we sat around pots of meat and ate all the food we wanted, but you have brought us out into this desert to starve this entire assembly to death."

4Then the LORD said to Moses, "I will rain down bread from heaven for you. The people are to go out each day and gather enough for that day. In this way I will test them and see whether they will follow my instructions. 5On the sixth day they are to prepare what they bring in, and that is to be twice as much as they gather on the other days."

6So Moses and Aaron said to all the Israelites, "In the evening you will know that it was the LORD who brought you out of Egypt, 7and in the morning you will see the glory of the LORD, because he has heard your grumbling against him. Who are we, that you should grumble against us?" 8Moses also said, "You will know that it was the LORD when he gives you meat to eat in the evening and all the bread you want

in the morning, because he has heard your grumbling against him. Who are we? You are not grumbling against us, but against the LORD."

9Then Moses told Aaron, "Say to the entire Israelite community, 'Come before the LORD, for he has heard your grumbling.' "

10While Aaron was speaking to the whole Israelite community, they looked toward the desert, and there was the glory of the LORD appearing in the cloud.

11The LORD said to Moses, 12"I have heard the grumbling of the Israelites. Tell them, 'At twilight you will eat meat, and in the morning you will be filled with bread. Then you will know that I am the LORD your God.' "

WHENEVER YOU FIND YOURSELF DISPOSED TO UNEASINESS OR MURMURING AT ANYTHING THAT IS THE EFFECT OF GOD'S PROVIDENCE, LOOK UPON YOURSELF AS DENYING EITHER THE WISDOM OR GOODNESS OF GOD.   —*William Law*

13That evening quail came and covered the camp, and in the morning there was a layer of dew around the camp. 14When the dew was gone, thin flakes like frost on the ground appeared on the desert floor. 15When the Israelites saw it, they said to each other, "What is it?" For they did not know what it was.

Moses said to them, "It is the bread the LORD has given you to eat. 16This is what the LORD has commanded: 'Each one is to gather as much as he needs. Take an omer*a* for each person you have in your tent.' "

17The Israelites did as they were told; some gathered much, some little. 18And when they measured it by the omer, he who gathered much did not have too much, and he who gathered little did not have too little. Each one gathered as much as he needed.

19Then Moses said to them, "No one is to keep any of it until morning."

20However, some of them paid no attention to Moses; they kept part of it until morning, but it was full of maggots

---

a 16 That is, probably about 2 quarts (about 2 liters); also in verses 18, 32, 33 and 36

and began to smell. So Moses was angry with them.

21Each morning everyone gathered as much as he needed, and when the sun grew hot, it melted away. 22On the sixth day, they gathered twice as much—two omers*a* for each person—and the leaders of the community came and reported this to Moses. 23He said to them, "This is what the LORD commanded: 'Tomorrow is to be a day of rest, a holy Sabbath to the LORD. So bake what you want to bake and boil what you want to boil. Save whatever is left and keep it until morning.' "

24So they saved it until morning, as Moses commanded, and it did not stink or get maggots in it. 25"Eat it today," Moses said, "because today is a Sabbath to the LORD. You will not find any of it on the ground today. 26Six days you are to gather it, but on the seventh day, the Sabbath, there will not be any."

27Nevertheless, some of the people went out on the seventh day to gather it, but they found none. 28Then the LORD said to Moses, "How long will you*b* refuse to keep my commands and my instructions? 29Bear in mind that the LORD has given you the Sabbath; that is why on the sixth day he gives you bread for two days. Everyone is to stay where he is on the seventh day; no one is to go out." 30So the people rested on the seventh day.

31The people of Israel called the bread manna.*c* It was white like coriander seed and tasted like wafers made with honey. 32Moses said, "This is what the LORD has commanded: 'Take an omer of manna and keep it for the generations to come, so they can see the bread I gave you to eat in the desert when I brought you out of Egypt.' "

33So Moses said to Aaron, "Take a jar and put an omer of manna in it. Then place it before the LORD to be kept for the generations to come."

34As the LORD commanded Moses, Aaron put the manna in front of the Testimony, that it might be kept. 35The Israelites ate manna forty years, until they came to a land that was settled;

they ate manna until they reached the border of Canaan.

36(An omer is one tenth of an ephah.)

Water From the Rock

17 The whole Israelite community set out from the Desert of Sin, traveling from place to place as the LORD commanded. They camped at Rephidim, but there was no water for the people to drink. 2So they quarreled with Moses and said, "Give us water to drink."

Moses replied, "Why do you quarrel with me? Why do you put the LORD to the test?"

3But the people were thirsty for water there, and they grumbled against Moses. They said, "Why did you bring us up out of Egypt to make us and our children and livestock die of thirst?"

4Then Moses cried out to the LORD, "What am I to do with these people? They are almost ready to stone me."

5The LORD answered Moses, "Walk on ahead of the people. Take with you some of the elders of Israel and take in your hand the staff with which you struck the Nile, and go. 6I will stand there before you by the rock at Horeb. Strike the rock, and water will come out of it for the people to drink." So Moses did this in the sight of the elders of Israel. 7And he called the place Massah*d* and Meribah*e* because the Israelites quarreled and because they tested the LORD saying, "Is the LORD among us or not?"

The Amalekites Defeated

8The Amalekites came and attacked the Israelites at Rephidim. 9Moses said to Joshua, "Choose some of our men and go out to fight the Amalekites. Tomorrow I will stand on top of the hill with the staff of God in my hands."

10So Joshua fought the Amalekites as Moses had ordered, and Moses, Aaron and Hur went to the top of the hill. 11As long as Moses held up his hands, the Israelites were winning, but whenever he lowered his hands, the Amalekites were winning. 12When Moses' hands grew tired, they took a stone and put it under him and he sat on it. Aaron and Hur held

a 22 That is, probably about 4 quarts (about 4.5 liters) means *What is it?* (see verse 15).   *b 28* The Hebrew is plural.   *c 31* Manna   *d 7* *Massah* means *testing.*   *e 7* *Meribah* means *quarreling.*

his hands up—one on one side, one on the other—so that his hands remained steady till sunset. ¹³So Joshua overcame the Amalekite army with the sword.

¹⁴Then the LORD said to Moses, "Write this on a scroll as something to be remembered and make sure that Joshua hears it, because I will completely blot out the memory of Amalek from under heaven."

¹⁵Moses built an altar and called it The LORD is my Banner. ¹⁶He said, "For hands were lifted up to the throne of the LORD. The^a LORD will be at war against the Amalekites from generation to generation."

Jethro Visits Moses

18 Now Jethro, the priest of Midian and father-in-law of Moses, heard of everything God had done for Moses and for his people Israel, and how the LORD had brought Israel out of Egypt.

²After Moses had sent away his wife Zipporah, his father-in-law Jethro received her ³and her two sons. One son was named Gershom,^b for Moses said, "I have become an alien in a foreign land"; ⁴and the other was named Eliezer,^c for he said, "My father's God was my helper; he saved me from the sword of Pharaoh."

⁵Jethro, Moses' father-in-law, together with Moses' sons and wife, came to him in the desert, where he was camped near the mountain of God. ⁶Jethro had sent word to him, "I, your father-in-law Jethro, am coming to you with your wife and her two sons."

⁷So Moses went out to meet his father-in-law and bowed down and kissed him. They greeted each other and then went into the tent. ⁸Moses told his father-in-law about everything the LORD had done to Pharaoh and the Egyptians for Israel's sake and about all the hardships they had met along the way and how the LORD had saved them.

⁹Jethro was delighted to hear about all the good things the LORD had done for Israel in rescuing them from the hand of the Egyptians. ¹⁰He said, "Praise be to the LORD, who rescued you from the

hand of the Egyptians and of Pharaoh, and who rescued the people from the hand of the Egyptians. ¹¹Now I know that the LORD is greater than all other gods, for he did this to those who had treated Israel arrogantly." ¹²Then Jethro, Moses' father-in-law, brought a burnt offering and other sacrifices to God, and Aaron came with all the elders of Israel to eat bread with Moses' father-in-law in the presence of God.

¹³The next day Moses took his seat to serve as judge for the people, and they stood around him from morning till evening. ¹⁴When his father-in-law saw all that Moses was doing for the people, he said, "What is this you are doing for the people? Why do you alone sit as judge, while all these people stand around you from morning till evening?"

¹⁵Moses answered him, "Because the people come to me to seek God's will. ¹⁶Whenever they have a dispute, it is brought to me, and I decide between the parties and inform them of God's decrees and laws."

¹⁷Moses' father-in-law replied, "What you are doing is not good. ¹⁸You and these people who come to you will only wear yourselves out. The work is too heavy for you; you cannot handle it alone. ¹⁹Listen now to me and I will give you some advice, and may God be with you. You must be the people's representative before God and bring their disputes to him. ²⁰Teach them the decrees and laws, and show them the way to live and the duties they are to perform. ²¹But select capable men from all the people—men who fear God, trustworthy men who hate dishonest gain—and appoint them as officials over thousands, hundreds, fifties and tens. ²²Have them serve as judges for the people at all times, but have them bring every difficult case to you; the simple cases they can decide themselves. That will make your load lighter, because they will share it with you. ²³If you do this and God so commands, you will be able to stand the strain, and all these people will go home satisfied."

²⁴Moses listened to his father-in-law and did everything he said. ²⁵He chose

a 16 Or *"Because a hand was against the throne of the LORD, the*   *b 3* Gershom sounds like the Hebrew for *an alien there.*   *c 4* Eliezer means *my God is helper.*

capable men from all Israel and made them leaders of the people, officials over thousands, hundreds, fifties and tens. ²⁶They served as judges for the people at all times. The difficult cases they brought to Moses, but the simple ones they decided themselves.

²⁷Then Moses sent his father-in-law on his way, and Jethro returned to his own country.

At Mount Sinai

19 In the third month after the Israelites left Egypt—on the very day—they came to the Desert of Sinai. ²After they set out from Rephidim, they entered the Desert of Sinai, and Israel camped there in the desert in front of the mountain.

³Then Moses went up to God, and the LORD called to him from the mountain and said, "This is what you are to say to the house of Jacob and what you are to tell the people of Israel: ⁴'You yourselves have seen what I did to Egypt, and how I carried you on eagles' wings and brought you to myself. ⁵Now if you obey me fully and keep my covenant, then out of all nations you will be my treasured possession. Although the whole earth is mine, ⁶you*a* will be for me a kingdom of priests and a holy nation.' These are the words you are to speak to the Israelites."

⁷So Moses went back and summoned the elders of the people and set before them all the words the LORD had commanded him to speak. ⁸The people all responded together, "We will do everything the LORD has said." So Moses brought their answer back to the LORD.

⁹The LORD said to Moses, "I am going to come to you in a dense cloud, so that the people will hear me speaking with you and will always put their trust in you." Then Moses told the LORD what the people had said.

¹⁰And the LORD said to Moses, "Go to the people and consecrate them today and tomorrow. Have them wash their clothes ¹¹and be ready by the third day, because on that day the LORD will come down on Mount Sinai in the sight of all the people. ¹²Put limits for the people around the mountain and tell them, 'Be careful that you do not go up the mountain or touch the foot of it. Whoever touches the mountain shall surely be put to death. ¹³He shall surely be stoned or shot with arrows; not a hand is to be laid on him. Whether man or animal, he shall not be permitted to live.' Only when the ram's horn sounds a long blast may they go up to the mountain."

¹⁴After Moses had gone down the mountain to the people, he consecrated them, and they washed their clothes. ¹⁵Then he said to the people, "Prepare yourselves for the third day. Abstain from sexual relations."

¹⁶On the morning of the third day there was thunder and lightning, with a thick cloud over the mountain, and a very loud trumpet blast. Everyone in the camp trembled. ¹⁷Then Moses led the people out of the camp to meet with God, and they stood at the foot of the mountain. ¹⁸Mount Sinai was covered with smoke, because the LORD descended on it in fire. The smoke billowed up from it like smoke from a furnace, the whole mountain*b* trembled violently, ¹⁹and the sound of the trumpet grew louder and louder. Then Moses spoke and the voice of God answered him.*c*

²⁰The LORD descended to the top of Mount Sinai and called Moses to the top of the mountain. So Moses went up ²¹and the LORD said to him, "Go down and warn the people so they do not force their way through to see the LORD and many of them perish. ²²Even the priests, who approach the LORD, must consecrate themselves, or the LORD will break out against them."

²³Moses said to the LORD, "The people cannot come up Mount Sinai, because you yourself warned us, 'Put limits around the mountain and set it apart as holy.'"

²⁴The LORD replied, "Go down and bring Aaron up with you. But the priests and the people must not force their way through to come up to the LORD, or he will break out against them."

²⁵So Moses went down to the people and told them.

---

a 5,6 Or *possession, for the whole earth is mine. 6You* manuscripts and Septuagint *all the people*   *c 19* Or *and God answered him with thunder*   *b 18* Most Hebrew manuscripts; a few Hebrew

The Ten Commandments

20 And God spoke all these words:

2 "I am the LORD your God, who brought you out of Egypt, out of the land of slavery.

3 "You shall have no other gods before[a] me.

4 "You shall not make for yourself an idol in the form of anything in heaven above or on the earth beneath or in the waters below. 5 You shall not bow down to them or worship them; for I, the LORD your God, am a jealous God, punishing the children for the sin of the fathers to the third and fourth generation of those who hate me, 6 but showing love

---

WHERE WOULD YOU BE IF GOD TOOK AWAY ALL YOUR CHRISTIAN WORK? TOO OFTEN IT IS OUR CHRISTIAN WORK THAT IS WORSHIPED AND NOT GOD. —Oswald Chambers

---

to a thousand ⌊generations⌋ of those who love me and keep my commandments.

7 "You shall not misuse the name of the LORD your God, for the LORD will not hold anyone guiltless who misuses his name.

8 "Remember the Sabbath day by keeping it holy. 9 Six days you shall labor and do all your work, 10 but the seventh day is a Sabbath to the LORD your God. On it you shall not do any work, neither you, nor your son or daughter, nor your manservant or maidservant, nor your animals, nor the alien within your gates. 11 For in six days the LORD made the heavens and the earth, the sea, and all that is in them, but he rested on the seventh day. Therefore the LORD blessed the Sabbath day and made it holy.

12 "Honor your father and your mother, so that you may live long in the land the LORD your God is giving you.

13 "You shall not murder.

14 "You shall not commit adultery.

15 "You shall not steal.

16 "You shall not give false testimony against your neighbor.

17 "You shall not covet your neighbor's house. You shall not covet your neighbor's wife, or his manservant or maidservant, his ox or donkey, or anything that belongs to your neighbor."

18 When the people saw the thunder and lightning and heard the trumpet and saw the mountain in smoke, they trembled with fear. They stayed at a distance 19 and said to Moses, "Speak to us yourself and we will listen. But do not have God speak to us or we will die."

20 Moses said to the people, "Do not be afraid. God has come to test you, so that the fear of God will be with you to keep you from sinning."

21 The people remained at a distance, while Moses approached the thick darkness where God was.

Idols and Altars

22 Then the LORD said to Moses, "Tell the Israelites this: 'You have seen for yourselves that I have spoken to you from heaven: 23 Do not make any gods to be alongside me; do not make for yourselves gods of silver or gods of gold.

24 " 'Make an altar of earth for me and sacrifice on it your burnt offerings and fellowship offerings,[b] your sheep and goats and your cattle. Wherever I cause my name to be honored, I will come to you and bless you. 25 If you make an altar of stones for me, do not build it with dressed stones, for you will defile it if you use a tool on it. 26 And do not go up to my altar on steps, lest your nakedness be exposed on it.'

21 "These are the laws you are to set before them:

Hebrew Servants

2 "If you buy a Hebrew servant, he is to serve you for six years. But in the seventh year, he shall go free, without

---

a 3 Or *besides*   *b 24* Traditionally *peace offerings* paying anything. ³If he comes alone, he is to go free alone; but if he has a wife when he comes, she is to go with him. ⁴If his master gives him a wife and she bears him sons or daughters, the woman and her children shall belong to her master, and only the man shall go free.

⁵"But if the servant declares, 'I love my master and my wife and children and do not want to go free,' ⁶then his master must take him before the judges.ᵃ He shall take him to the door or the doorpost and pierce his ear with an awl. Then he will be his servant for life.

⁷"If a man sells his daughter as a servant, she is not to go free as menservants do. ⁸If she does not please the master who has selected her for himself,ᵇ he must let her be redeemed. He has no right to sell her to foreigners, because he has broken faith with her. ⁹If he selects her for his son, he must grant her the rights of a daughter. ¹⁰If he marries another woman, he must not deprive the first one of her food, clothing and marital rights. ¹¹If he does not provide her with these three things, she is to go free, without any payment of money.

Personal Injuries

¹²"Anyone who strikes a man and kills him shall surely be put to death. ¹³However, if he does not do it intentionally, but God lets it happen, he is to flee to a place I will designate. ¹⁴But if a man schemes and kills another man deliberately, take him away from my altar and put him to death.

¹⁵"Anyone who attacksᶜ his father or his mother must be put to death.

¹⁶"Anyone who kidnaps another and either sells him or still has him when he is caught must be put to death.

¹⁷"Anyone who curses his father or mother must be put to death.

¹⁸"If men quarrel and one hits the other with a stone or with his fistᵈ and he does not die but is confined to bed, ¹⁹the one who struck the blow will not be held responsible if the other gets up and walks around outside with his staff; however, he must pay the injured man

for the loss of his time and see that he is completely healed.

²⁰"If a man beats his male or female slave with a rod and the slave dies as a direct result, he must be punished, ²¹but he is not to be punished if the slave gets up after a day or two, since the slave is his property.

²²"If men who are fighting hit a pregnant woman and she gives birth prematurelyᵉ but there is no serious injury, the offender must be fined whatever the woman's husband demands and the court allows. ²³But if there is serious

---

FOR US MURDER IS ONCE FOR ALL FORBIDDEN; SO EVEN THE CHILD IN THE WOMB . . . IS NOT LAWFUL FOR US TO DESTROY. TO FORBID BIRTH IS ONLY QUICKER MURDER . . . THE FRUIT IS ALWAYS PRESENT IN THE SEED.   —*Tertullian*

---

injury, you are to take life for life, ²⁴eye for eye, tooth for tooth, hand for hand, foot for foot, ²⁵burn for burn, wound for wound, bruise for bruise.

²⁶"If a man hits a manservant or maidservant in the eye and destroys it, he must let the servant go free to compensate for the eye. ²⁷And if he knocks out the tooth of a manservant or maidservant, he must let the servant go free to compensate for the tooth.

²⁸"If a bull gores a man or a woman to death, the bull must be stoned to death, and its meat must not be eaten. But the owner of the bull will not be held responsible. ²⁹If, however, the bull has had the habit of goring and the owner has been warned but has not kept it penned up and it kills a man or woman, the bull must be stoned and the owner also must be put to death. ³⁰However, if payment is demanded of him, he may redeem his life by paying whatever is demanded. ³¹This law also applies if the bull gores a son or daughter. ³²If the bull gores a male or female slave, the owner must pay thirty shekelsᶠ of silver to the master of the slave, and the bull must be stoned.

³³"If a man uncovers a pit or digs one and fails to cover it and an ox or a donkey falls into it, ³⁴the owner of the pit

---

ᵃ 6 Or *before God*   ᵇ 8 Or *master so that he does not choose her*   ᶜ 15 Or *kills*   ᵈ 18 Or *with a tool*   ᵉ 22 Or *she has a miscarriage*   ᶠ 32 That is, about 12 ounces (about 0.3 kilogram)

must pay for the loss; he must pay its owner, and the dead animal will be his.

³⁵"If a man's bull injures the bull of another and it dies, they are to sell the live one and divide both the money and the dead animal equally. ³⁶However, if it was known that the bull had the habit of goring, yet the owner did not keep it penned up, the owner must pay, animal for animal, and the dead animal will be his.

Protection of Property

22 "If a man steals an ox or a sheep and slaughters it or sells it, he must pay back five head of cattle for the ox and four sheep for the sheep.

²"If a thief is caught breaking in and is struck so that he dies, the defender is not guilty of bloodshed; ³but if it happens*a* after sunrise, he is guilty of bloodshed.

"A thief must certainly make restitution, but if he has nothing, he must be sold to pay for his theft.

⁴"If the stolen animal is found alive in his possession—whether ox or donkey or sheep—he must pay back double.

⁵"If a man grazes his livestock in a field or vineyard and lets them stray and they graze in another man's field, he must make restitution from the best of his own field or vineyard.

⁶"If a fire breaks out and spreads into thornbushes so that it burns shocks of grain or standing grain or the whole field, the one who started the fire must make restitution.

⁷"If a man gives his neighbor silver or goods for safekeeping and they are stolen from the neighbor's house, the thief, if he is caught, must pay back double. ⁸But if the thief is not found, the owner of the house must appear before the judges*b* to determine whether he has laid his hands on the other man's property. ⁹In all cases of illegal possession of an ox, a donkey, a sheep, a garment, or any other lost property about which somebody says, 'This is mine,' both parties are to bring their cases before the judges. The one whom the judges declare*c* guilty must pay back double to his neighbor.

¹⁰"If a man gives a donkey, an ox, a sheep or any other animal to his neighbor for safekeeping and it dies or is injured or is taken away while no one is looking, ¹¹the issue between them will be settled by the taking of an oath before the LORD that the neighbor did not lay hands on the other person's property. The owner is to accept this, and no restitution is required. ¹²But if the animal was stolen from the neighbor, he must make restitution to the owner. ¹³If it was torn to pieces by a wild animal, he shall bring in the remains as evidence and he will not be required to pay for the torn animal.

¹⁴"If a man borrows an animal from his neighbor and it is injured or dies while the owner is not present, he must make restitution. ¹⁵But if the owner is with the animal, the borrower will not have to pay. If the animal was hired, the money paid for the hire covers the loss.

Social Responsibility

¹⁶"If a man seduces a virgin who is not pledged to be married and sleeps with her, he must pay the bride-price, and she shall be his wife. ¹⁷If her father absolutely refuses to give her to him, he must still pay the bride-price for virgins.

¹⁸"Do not allow a sorceress to live.

¹⁹"Anyone who has sexual relations with an animal must be put to death.

²⁰"Whoever sacrifices to any god other than the LORD must be destroyed.*d*

²¹"Do not mistreat an alien or oppress him, for you were aliens in Egypt.

²²"Do not take advantage of a widow or an orphan. ²³If you do and they cry out to me, I will certainly hear their cry. ²⁴My anger will be aroused, and I will kill you with the sword; your wives will become widows and your children fatherless.

²⁵"If you lend money to one of my people among you who is needy, do not be like a moneylender; charge him no interest.*e* ²⁶If you take your neighbor's cloak as a pledge, return it to him by sunset, ²⁷because his cloak is the only covering he has for his body. What else will he sleep in? When he cries out to me, I will hear, for I am compassionate.

---

a 3 Or *if he strikes him*   *b 8* Or *before God;* also in verse 9   *c 9* Or *whom God declares*   *d 20* The Hebrew term refers to the irrevocable giving over of things or persons to the LORD, often by totally destroying them.   *e 25* Or *excessive interest*

²⁸"Do not blaspheme God*ᵃ* or curse the ruler of your people.

²⁹"Do not hold back offerings from your granaries or your vats.*ᵇ*

"You must give me the firstborn of your sons. ³⁰Do the same with your cattle and your sheep. Let them stay with their mothers for seven days, but give them to me on the eighth day.

³¹"You are to be my holy people. So do not eat the meat of an animal torn by wild beasts; throw it to the dogs.

Laws of Justice and Mercy

23 "Do not spread false reports. Do not help a wicked man by being a malicious witness.

²"Do not follow the crowd in doing wrong. When you give testimony in a lawsuit, do not pervert justice by siding with the crowd, ³and do not show favoritism to a poor man in his lawsuit.

⁴"If you come across your enemy's ox or donkey wandering off, be sure to take it back to him. ⁵If you see the donkey of someone who hates you fallen down under its load, do not leave it there; be sure you help him with it.

⁶"Do not deny justice to your poor people in their lawsuits. ⁷Have nothing to do with a false charge and do not put an innocent or honest person to death, for I will not acquit the guilty.

⁸"Do not accept a bribe, for a bribe blinds those who see and twists the words of the righteous.

⁹"Do not oppress an alien; you yourselves know how it feels to be aliens, because you were aliens in Egypt.

Sabbath Laws

¹⁰"For six years you are to sow your fields and harvest the crops, ¹¹but during the seventh year let the land lie unplowed and unused. Then the poor among your people may get food from it, and the wild animals may eat what they leave. Do the same with your vineyard and your olive grove.

¹²"Six days do your work, but on the seventh day do not work, so that your ox and your donkey may rest and the slave born in your household, and the alien as well, may be refreshed.

¹³"Be careful to do everything I have said to you. Do not invoke the names of other gods; do not let them be heard on your lips.

The Three Annual Festivals

¹⁴"Three times a year you are to celebrate a festival to me.

¹⁵"Celebrate the Feast of Unleavened Bread; for seven days eat bread made without yeast, as I commanded you. Do this at the appointed time in the month of Abib, for in that month you came out of Egypt.

"No one is to appear before me empty-handed.

¹⁶"Celebrate the Feast of Harvest with the firstfruits of the crops you sow in your field.

"Celebrate the Feast of Ingathering at the end of the year, when you gather in your crops from the field.

¹⁷"Three times a year all the men are to appear before the Sovereign LORD.

¹⁸"Do not offer the blood of a sacrifice to me along with anything containing yeast.

"The fat of my festival offerings must not be kept until morning.

¹⁹"Bring the best of the firstfruits of your soil to the house of the LORD your God.

"Do not cook a young goat in its mother's milk.

God's Angel to Prepare the Way

²⁰"See, I am sending an angel ahead of you to guard you along the way and to bring you to the place I have prepared. ²¹Pay attention to him and listen to what he says. Do not rebel against him; he will not forgive your rebellion, since my Name is in him. ²²If you listen carefully to what he says and do all that I say, I will be an enemy to your enemies and will oppose those who oppose you. ²³My angel will go ahead of you and bring you into the land of the Amorites, Hittites, Perizzites, Canaanites, Hivites and Jebusites, and I will wipe them out. ²⁴Do not bow down before their gods or worship them or follow their practices. You must demolish them and break their sacred stones to pieces. ²⁵Worship the LORD your God, and his blessing will be on your food and water. I will take

ᵃ 28 Or *Do not revile the judges*   *ᵇ 29* The meaning of the Hebrew for this phrase is uncertain.

away sickness from among you, 26and none will miscarry or be barren in your land. I will give you a full life span.

27"I will send my terror ahead of you and throw into confusion every nation you encounter. I will make all your enemies turn their backs and run. 28I will send the hornet ahead of you to drive the Hivites, Canaanites and Hittites out of your way. 29But I will not drive them out in a single year, because the land would become desolate and the wild animals too numerous for you. 30Little by little I will drive them out before you, until you have increased enough to take possession of the land.

31"I will establish your borders from the Red Sea*a* to the Sea of the Philistines,*b* and from the desert to the River.*c* I will hand over to you the people who live in the land and you will drive them out before you. 32Do not make a covenant with them or with their gods. 33Do not let them live in your land, or they will cause you to sin against me, because the worship of their gods will certainly be a snare to you."

The Covenant Confirmed

24 Then he said to Moses, "Come up to the LORD, you and Aaron, Nadab and Abihu, and seventy of the elders of Israel. You are to worship at a distance, 2but Moses alone is to approach the LORD; the others must not come near. And the people may not come up with him."

3When Moses went and told the people all the LORD's words and laws, they responded with one voice, "Everything the LORD has said we will do." 4Moses then wrote down everything the LORD had said.

He got up early the next morning and built an altar at the foot of the mountain and set up twelve stone pillars representing the twelve tribes of Israel. 5Then he sent young Israelite men, and they offered burnt offerings and sacrificed young bulls as fellowship offerings*d* to the LORD. 6Moses took half of the blood and put it in bowls, and the other half he sprinkled on the altar. 7Then he took the Book of the Covenant and read it to

the people. They responded, "We will do everything the LORD has said; we will obey."

8Moses then took the blood, sprinkled it on the people and said, "This is the blood of the covenant that the LORD has made with you in accordance with all these words."

9Moses and Aaron, Nadab and Abihu, and the seventy elders of Israel went up 10and saw the God of Israel. Under his feet was something like a pavement made of sapphire,*e* clear as the sky itself. 11But God did not raise his hand against these leaders of the Israelites; they saw God, and they ate and drank.

12The LORD said to Moses, "Come up to me on the mountain and stay here, and I will give you the tablets of stone, with the law and commands I have written for their instruction."

13Then Moses set out with Joshua his aide, and Moses went up on the mountain of God. 14He said to the elders, "Wait here for us until we come back to you. Aaron and Hur are with you, and anyone involved in a dispute can go to them."

15When Moses went up on the mountain, the cloud covered it, 16and the glory of the LORD settled on Mount Sinai. For six days the cloud covered the mountain, and on the seventh day the LORD called to Moses from within the cloud. 17To the Israelites the glory of the LORD looked like a consuming fire on top of the mountain. 18Then Moses entered the cloud as he went on up the mountain. And he stayed on the mountain forty days and forty nights.

Offerings for the Tabernacle

25 The LORD said to Moses, 2"Tell the Israelites to bring me an offering. You are to receive the offering for me from each man whose heart prompts him to give. 3These are the offerings you are to receive from them: gold, silver and bronze; 4blue, purple and scarlet yarn and fine linen; goat hair; 5ram skins dyed red and hides of sea cows*f*; acacia wood; 6olive oil for the light; spices for the anointing oil and for the fragrant incense; 7and onyx stones

---

a 31 Hebrew *Yam Suph;* that is, Sea of Reeds   *b 31* That is, the Mediterranean   *c 31* That is, the Euphrates   *d 5* Traditionally *peace offerings*   *e 10* Or *lapis lazuli*   *f 5* That is, dugongs

and other gems to be mounted on the ephod and breastpiece.

8"Then have them make a sanctuary for me, and I will dwell among them. 9Make this tabernacle and all its furnishings exactly like the pattern I will show you.

The Ark

10"Have them make a chest of acacia wood—two and a half cubits long, a cubit and a half wide, and a cubit and a half high.*a* 11Overlay it with pure gold, both inside and out, and make a gold molding around it. 12Cast four gold rings for it and fasten them to its four feet, with two rings on one side and two rings on the other. 13Then make poles of acacia wood and overlay them with gold. 14Insert the poles into the rings on the sides of the chest to carry it. 15The poles are to remain in the rings of this ark; they are not to be removed. 16Then put in the ark the Testimony, which I will give you.

17"Make an atonement cover*b* of pure gold—two and a half cubits long and a cubit and a half wide.*c* 18And make two cherubim out of hammered gold at the ends of the cover. 19Make one cherub on one end and the second cherub on the other; make the cherubim of one piece with the cover, at the two ends. 20The cherubim are to have their wings spread upward, overshadowing the cover with them. The cherubim are to face each other, looking toward the cover. 21Place the cover on top of the ark and put in the ark the Testimony, which I will give you. 22There, above the cover between the two cherubim that are over the ark of the Testimony, I will meet with you and give you all my commands for the Israelites.

The Table

23"Make a table of acacia wood—two cubits long, a cubit wide and a cubit and a half high.*d* 24Overlay it with pure gold and make a gold molding around it. 25Also make around it a rim a handbreadth*e* wide and put a gold molding on the rim. 26Make four gold rings for the table and fasten them to the four corners, where the four legs are. 27The rings are to be close to the rim to hold the poles used in carrying the table. 28Make the poles of acacia wood, overlay them with gold and carry the table with them. 29And make its plates and dishes of pure gold, as well as its pitchers and bowls for the pouring out of offerings. 30Put the bread of the Presence on this table to be before me at all times.

The Lampstand

31"Make a lampstand of pure gold and hammer it out, base and shaft; its flowerlike cups, buds and blossoms shall be of one piece with it. 32Six branches are to extend from the sides of the lampstand—three on one side and three on the other. 33Three cups shaped like almond flowers with buds and blossoms are to be on one branch, three on the next branch, and the same for all six branches extending from the lampstand. 34And on the lampstand there are to be four cups shaped like almond flowers with buds and blossoms. 35One bud shall be under the first pair of branches extending from the lampstand, a second bud under the second pair, and a third bud under the third pair—six branches in all. 36The buds and branches shall all be of one piece with the lampstand, hammered out of pure gold.

37"Then make its seven lamps and set them up on it so that they light the space in front of it. 38Its wick trimmers and trays are to be of pure gold. 39A talent*f* of pure gold is to be used for the lampstand and all these accessories. 40See that you make them according to the pattern shown you on the mountain.

The Tabernacle

26 "Make the tabernacle with ten curtains of finely twisted linen and blue, purple and scarlet yarn, with cherubim worked into them by a skilled craftsman. 2All the curtains are to be the same size—twenty-eight cubits long and four cubits wide.*g* 3Join

---

a 10 That is, about 3 3/4 feet (about 1.1 meters) long and 2 1/4 feet (about 0.7 meter) wide and high   *b 17* Traditionally *a mercy seat*   *c 17* That is, about 3 3/4 feet (about 1.1 meters) long and 2 1/4 feet (about 0.7 meter) wide   *d 23* That is, about 3 feet (about 0.9 meter) long and 1 1/2 feet (about 0.5 meter) wide and 2 1/4 feet (about 0.7 meter) high   *e 25* That is, about 3 inches (about 8 centimeters)   *f 39* That is, about 75 pounds (about 34 kilograms)   *g 2* That is, about 42 feet (about 12.5 meters) long and 6 feet (about 1.8 meters) wide

five of the curtains together, and do the same with the other five. ⁴Make loops of blue material along the edge of the end curtain in one set, and do the same with the end curtain in the other set. ⁵Make fifty loops on one curtain and fifty loops on the end curtain of the other set, with the loops opposite each other. ⁶Then make fifty gold clasps and use them to fasten the curtains together so that the tabernacle is a unit.

⁷"Make curtains of goat hair for the tent over the tabernacle—eleven altogether. ⁸All eleven curtains are to be the same size—thirty cubits long and four cubits wide.ᵃ ⁹Join five of the curtains together into one set and the other six into another set. Fold the sixth curtain double at the front of the tent. ¹⁰Make fifty loops along the edge of the end curtain in one set and also along the edge of the end curtain in the other set. ¹¹Then make fifty bronze clasps and put them in the loops to fasten the tent together as a unit. ¹²As for the additional length of the tent curtains, the half curtain that is left over is to hang down at the rear of the tabernacle. ¹³The tent curtains will be a cubitᵇ longer on both sides; what is left will hang over the sides of the tabernacle so as to cover it. ¹⁴Make for the tent a covering of ram skins dyed red, and over that a covering of hides of sea cows.ᶜ

¹⁵"Make upright frames of acacia wood for the tabernacle. ¹⁶Each frame is to be ten cubits long and a cubit and a half wide,ᵈ ¹⁷with two projections set parallel to each other. Make all the frames of the tabernacle in this way. ¹⁸Make twenty frames for the south side of the tabernacle ¹⁹and make forty silver bases to go under them—two bases for each frame, one under each projection. ²⁰For the other side, the north side of the tabernacle, make twenty frames ²¹and forty silver bases—two under each frame. ²²Make six frames for the far end, that is, the west end of the tabernacle, ²³and make two frames for the corners at the far end. ²⁴At these two corners they must be double from the bottom all the way to the top, and fitted into a single ring; both shall be like that. ²⁵So

there will be eight frames and sixteen silver bases—two under each frame.

²⁶"Also make crossbars of acacia wood: five for the frames on one side of the tabernacle, ²⁷five for those on the other side, and five for the frames on the west, at the far end of the tabernacle. ²⁸The center crossbar is to extend from end to end at the middle of the frames. ²⁹Overlay the frames with gold and make gold rings to hold the crossbars. Also overlay the crossbars with gold.

³⁰"Set up the tabernacle according to the plan shown you on the mountain.

³¹"Make a curtain of blue, purple and scarlet yarn and finely twisted linen, with cherubim worked into it by a skilled craftsman. ³²Hang it with gold hooks on four posts of acacia wood overlaid with gold and standing on four silver bases. ³³Hang the curtain from the clasps and place the ark of the Testimony behind the curtain. The curtain will separate the Holy Place from the Most Holy Place. ³⁴Put the atonement cover on the ark of the Testimony in the Most Holy Place. ³⁵Place the table outside the curtain on the north side of the tabernacle and put the lampstand opposite it on the south side.

³⁶"For the entrance to the tent make a curtain of blue, purple and scarlet yarn and finely twisted linen—the work of an embroiderer. ³⁷Make gold hooks for this curtain and five posts of acacia wood overlaid with gold. And cast five bronze bases for them.

The Altar of Burnt Offering

27 "Build an altar of acacia wood, three cubitsᵉ high; it is to be square, five cubits long and five cubits wide.ᶠ ²Make a horn at each of the four corners, so that the horns and the altar are of one piece, and overlay the altar with bronze. ³Make all its utensils of bronze—its pots to remove the ashes, and its shovels, sprinkling bowls, meat forks and firepans. ⁴Make a grating for it, a bronze network, and make a bronze ring at each of the four corners of the network. ⁵Put it under the ledge of the

ᵃ 8 That is, about 45 feet (about 13.5 meters) long and 6 feet (about 1.8 meters) wide   ᵇ 13 That is, about 1 1/2 feet (about 0.5 meter)   ᶜ 14 That is, dugongs   ᵈ 16 That is, about 15 feet (about 4.5 meters) long and 2 1/4 feet (about 0.7 meter) wide   ᵉ 1 That is, about 4 1/2 feet (about 1.3 meters) ᶠ 1 That is, about 7 1/2 feet (about 2.3 meters) long and wide

altar so that it is halfway up the altar. ⁶Make poles of acacia wood for the altar and overlay them with bronze. ⁷The poles are to be inserted into the rings so they will be on two sides of the altar when it is carried. ⁸Make the altar hollow, out of boards. It is to be made just as you were shown on the mountain.

The Courtyard

⁹"Make a courtyard for the tabernacle. The south side shall be a hundred cubits*a* long and is to have curtains of finely twisted linen, ¹⁰with twenty posts and twenty bronze bases and with silver hooks and bands on the posts. ¹¹The north side shall also be a hundred cubits long and is to have curtains, with twenty posts and twenty bronze bases and with silver hooks and bands on the posts.

¹²"The west end of the courtyard shall be fifty cubits*b* wide and have curtains, with ten posts and ten bases. ¹³On the east end, toward the sunrise, the courtyard shall also be fifty cubits wide. ¹⁴Curtains fifteen cubits*c* long are to be on one side of the entrance, with three posts and three bases, ¹⁵and curtains fifteen cubits long are to be on the other side, with three posts and three bases.

¹⁶"For the entrance to the courtyard, provide a curtain twenty cubits*d* long, of blue, purple and scarlet yarn and finely twisted linen—the work of an embroiderer—with four posts and four bases. ¹⁷All the posts around the courtyard are to have silver bands and hooks, and bronze bases. ¹⁸The courtyard shall be a hundred cubits long and fifty cubits wide,*e* with curtains of finely twisted linen five cubits*f* high, and with bronze bases. ¹⁹All the other articles used in the service of the tabernacle, whatever their function, including all the tent pegs for it and those for the courtyard, are to be of bronze.

Oil for the Lampstand

²⁰"Command the Israelites to bring you clear oil of pressed olives for the light so that the lamps may be kept burning. ²¹In the Tent of Meeting, outside the curtain that is in front of the Testimony, Aaron and his sons are to keep the lamps burning before the LORD from evening till morning. This is to be a lasting ordinance among the Israelites for the generations to come.

The Priestly Garments

28 "Have Aaron your brother brought to you from among the Israelites, along with his sons Nadab and Abihu, Eleazar and Ithamar, so they may serve me as priests. ²Make sacred garments for your brother Aaron, to give him dignity and honor. ³Tell all the skilled men to whom I have given wisdom in such matters that they are to make garments for Aaron, for his consecration, so he may serve me as priest. ⁴These are the garments they are to make: a breastpiece, an ephod, a robe, a woven tunic, a turban and a sash. They are to make these sacred garments for your brother Aaron and his sons, so they may serve me as priests. ⁵Have them use gold, and blue, purple and scarlet yarn, and fine linen.

The Ephod

⁶"Make the ephod of gold, and of blue, purple and scarlet yarn, and of finely twisted linen—the work of a skilled craftsman. ⁷It is to have two shoulder pieces attached to two of its corners, so it can be fastened. ⁸Its skillfully woven waistband is to be like it—of one piece with the ephod and made with gold, and with blue, purple and scarlet yarn, and with finely twisted linen.

⁹"Take two onyx stones and engrave on them the names of the sons of Israel ¹⁰in the order of their birth—six names on one stone and the remaining six on the other. ¹¹Engrave the names of the sons of Israel on the two stones the way a gem cutter engraves a seal. Then mount the stones in gold filigree settings ¹²and fasten them on the shoulder pieces of the ephod as memorial stones for the sons of Israel. Aaron is to bear the names on his shoulders as a memorial before the LORD. ¹³Make gold filigree settings ¹⁴and two braided chains of

a 9 That is, about 150 feet (about 46 meters); also in verse 11   *b 12* That is, about 75 feet (about 23 meters); also in verse 13   *c 14* That is, about 22 1/2 feet (about 6.9 meters); also in verse 15
d 16 That is, about 30 feet (about 9 meters)   *e 18* That is, about 150 feet (about 46 meters) long and 75 feet (about 23 meters) wide   *f 18* That is, about 7 1/2 feet (about 2.3 meters)

OIL AND THE LIGHT OF THE LAMPSTAND
A. B. Simpson

VERSE: Exodus 27:20   **PASSAGE:** Exodus 27:20–21

he two figures of light and oil are beautiful and interesting in their natural symbolism . . .

Light is that which makes the human face so full of loveliness. It is that which gives us everything beautiful in all the wonders of the natural world.

Nor have we only the light that comes from without. We have also the light that comes from within—the sense of sight and the power of insight that bring into our consciousness and perception the objects of nature around us.

We find this figure of light through all of God's Word. It was the most marked symbol of his presence. He appeared in the Garden of Eden in the light of the *shekinah*. He appeared to Abraham in the lamp that passed between the pieces of the sacrifice (see Genesis 15:17). He appeared to the migrating children of Israel in the pillar of fire (see Exodus 13:21). And he appeared to Moses in the burning bush (see Exodus 3:2).

Jesus uses this figure of himself. He claimed to be the light of the world, of his own children especially (see John 8:12). The Holy Spirit is also the source of light. And the vision of the Apocalypse closes with the light that is brighter than the sun and a rainbow gathering up all its beautiful effulgence around the throne forever.

Likewise the figure of oil expresses many interesting thoughts. It is the source of artificial light. It contains in itself the elements of life and healing and, in contact with fire, the elements of light.

We find it employed for many other purposes than light. It was used in connection with the consecration of the priesthood and in healing, but it was especially set apart for the lighting of God's sanctuary. And it was specifically prescribed by God himself and by the most awful sanctions guarded from being counterfeited. If anyone should endeavor to imitate or counterfeit it, he was to be cut off from among the people. Its ingredients were compounded together in some mysterious way for its sacred use, to light God's holy sanctuary.

ADDITIONAL SCRIPTURE READING:
Leviticus 24:1–3; Matthew 25:1–13

Go to page 99 for your next devotional reading.

1900   Present

pure gold, like a rope, and attach the chains to the settings.

The Breastpiece

15"Fashion a breastpiece for making decisions—the work of a skilled crafts-man. Make it like the ephod: of gold, and of blue, purple and scarlet yarn, and of finely twisted linen. 16It is to be square—a span*a* long and a span wide—and fold-ed double. 17Then mount four rows of precious stones on it. In the first row there shall be a ruby, a topaz and a beryl; 18in the second row a turquoise, a sap-phire*b* and an emerald; 19in the third row a jacinth, an agate and an amethyst; 20in the fourth row a chrysolite, an onyx and a jasper.*c* Mount them in gold filigree settings. 21There are to be twelve stones, one for each of the names of the sons of Israel, each engraved like a seal with the name of one of the twelve tribes.

22"For the breastpiece make braided chains of pure gold, like a rope. 23Make two gold rings for it and fasten them to two corners of the breastpiece. 24Fasten the two gold chains to the rings at the corners of the breastpiece, 25and the other ends of the chains to the two set-tings, attaching them to the shoulder pieces of the ephod at the front. 26Make two gold rings and attach them to the other two corners of the breastpiece on the inside edge next to the ephod. 27Make two more gold rings and attach them to the bottom of the shoulder pieces on the front of the ephod, close to the seam just above the waistband of the ephod. 28The rings of the breastpiece are to be tied to the rings of the ephod with blue cord, connecting it to the waist-band, so that the breastpiece will not swing out from the ephod.

29"Whenever Aaron enters the Holy Place, he will bear the names of the sons of Israel over his heart on the breast-piece of decision as a continuing memo-rial before the LORD. 30Also put the Urim and the Thummim in the breast-piece, so they may be over Aaron's heart whenever he enters the presence of the LORD. Thus Aaron will always bear the means of making decisions for the Isra-elites over his heart before the LORD.

Other Priestly Garments

31"Make the robe of the ephod entirely of blue cloth, 32with an opening for the head in its center. There shall be a woven edge like a collar*d* around this opening, so that it will not tear. 33Make pomegran-ates of blue, purple and scarlet yarn around the hem of the robe, with gold bells between them. 34The gold bells and the pomegranates are to alternate around the hem of the robe. 35Aaron must wear it when he ministers. The sound of the bells will be heard when he enters the Holy Place before the LORD and when he comes out, so that he will not die.

36"Make a plate of pure gold and engrave on it as on a seal: HOLY TO THE LORD. 37Fasten a blue cord to it to attach it to the turban; it is to be on the front of the turban. 38It will be on Aaron's fore-head, and he will bear the guilt involved in the sacred gifts the Israelites conse-crate, whatever their gifts may be. It will be on Aaron's forehead continually so that they will be acceptable to the LORD.

39"Weave the tunic of fine linen and make the turban of fine linen. The sash is to be the work of an embroiderer. 40Make tunics, sashes and headbands for Aaron's sons, to give them dignity and honor. 41After you put these clothes on your brother Aaron and his sons, anoint and ordain them. Consecrate them so they may serve me as priests.

42"Make linen undergarments as a covering for the body, reaching from the waist to the thigh. 43Aaron and his sons must wear them whenever they enter the Tent of Meeting or approach the altar to minister in the Holy Place, so that they will not incur guilt and die.

"This is to be a lasting ordinance for Aaron and his descendants.

Consecration of the Priests

29 "This is what you are to do to consecrate them, so they may serve me as priests: Take a young bull and two rams without defect. 2And from fine wheat flour, without yeast, make

---

a 16 That is, about 9 inches (about 22 centimeters)   *b 18* Or *lapis lazuli*   *c 20* The precise identification of some of these precious stones is uncertain.   *d 32* The meaning of the Hebrew for this word is uncertain.

bread, and cakes mixed with oil, and wafers spread with oil. ³Put them in a basket and present them in it—along with the bull and the two rams. ⁴Then bring Aaron and his sons to the entrance to the Tent of Meeting and wash them with water. ⁵Take the garments and dress Aaron with the tunic, the robe of the ephod, the ephod itself and the breastpiece. Fasten the ephod on him by its skillfully woven waistband. ⁶Put the turban on his head and attach the sacred diadem to the turban. ⁷Take the anointing oil and anoint him by pouring it on his head. ⁸Bring his sons and dress them in tunics ⁹and put headbands on them. Then tie sashes on Aaron and his sons.ᵃ The priesthood is theirs by a lasting ordinance. In this way you shall ordain Aaron and his sons.

¹⁰"Bring the bull to the front of the Tent of Meeting, and Aaron and his sons shall lay their hands on its head. ¹¹Slaughter it in the LORD's presence at the entrance to the Tent of Meeting. ¹²Take some of the bull's blood and put it on the horns of the altar with your finger, and pour out the rest of it at the base of the altar. ¹³Then take all the fat around the inner parts, the covering of the liver, and both kidneys with the fat on them, and burn them on the altar. ¹⁴But burn the bull's flesh and its hide and its offal outside the camp. It is a sin offering.

¹⁵"Take one of the rams, and Aaron and his sons shall lay their hands on its head. ¹⁶Slaughter it and take the blood and sprinkle it against the altar on all sides. ¹⁷Cut the ram into pieces and wash the inner parts and the legs, putting them with the head and the other pieces. ¹⁸Then burn the entire ram on the altar. It is a burnt offering to the LORD, a pleasing aroma, an offering made to the LORD by fire.

¹⁹"Take the other ram, and Aaron and his sons shall lay their hands on its head. ²⁰Slaughter it, take some of its blood and put it on the lobes of the right ears of Aaron and his sons, on the thumbs of their right hands, and on the big toes of their right feet. Then sprinkle blood against the altar on all sides. ²¹And take some of the blood on the altar and some of the anointing oil and sprinkle it on Aaron and his garments and on his sons and their garments. Then he and his sons and their garments will be consecrated.

²²"Take from this ram the fat, the fat tail, the fat around the inner parts, the covering of the liver, both kidneys with the fat on them, and the right thigh. (This is the ram for the ordination.) ²³From the basket of bread made without yeast, which is before the LORD, take a loaf, and a cake made with oil, and a wafer. ²⁴Put all these in the hands of Aaron and his sons and wave them before the LORD as a wave offering. ²⁵Then take them from their hands and burn them on the altar along with the burnt offering for a pleasing aroma to the LORD, an offering made to the LORD by fire. ²⁶After you take the breast of the ram for Aaron's ordination, wave it before the LORD as a wave offering, and it will be your share.

²⁷"Consecrate those parts of the ordination ram that belong to Aaron and his sons: the breast that was waved and the thigh that was presented. ²⁸This is always to be the regular share from the Israelites for Aaron and his sons. It is the contribution the Israelites are to make to the LORD from their fellowship offerings.ᵇ

²⁹"Aaron's sacred garments will belong to his descendants so that they can be anointed and ordained in them. ³⁰The son who succeeds him as priest and comes to the Tent of Meeting to minister in the Holy Place is to wear them seven days.

³¹"Take the ram for the ordination and cook the meat in a sacred place. ³²At the entrance to the Tent of Meeting, Aaron and his sons are to eat the meat of the ram and the bread that is in the basket. ³³They are to eat these offerings by which atonement was made for their ordination and consecration. But no one else may eat them, because they are sacred. ³⁴And if any of the meat of the ordination ram or any bread is left over till morning, burn it up. It must not be eaten, because it is sacred.

³⁵"Do for Aaron and his sons everything I have commanded you, taking seven days to ordain them. ³⁶Sacrifice a

ᵃ 9 Hebrew; Septuagint *on them*　　ᵇ 28 Traditionally *peace offerings* bull each day as a sin offering to make atonement. Purify the altar by making atonement for it, and anoint it to consecrate it. ³⁷For seven days make atonement for the altar and consecrate it. Then the altar will be most holy, and whatever touches it will be holy.

³⁸"This is what you are to offer on the altar regularly each day: two lambs a year old. ³⁹Offer one in the morning and the other at twilight. ⁴⁰With the first lamb offer a tenth of an ephah*a* of fine flour mixed with a quarter of a hin*b* of oil from pressed olives, and a quarter of a hin of wine as a drink offering. ⁴¹Sacrifice the other lamb at twilight with the same grain offering and its drink offering as in the morning—a pleasing aroma, an offering made to the LORD by fire.

⁴²"For the generations to come this burnt offering is to be made regularly at the entrance to the Tent of Meeting before the LORD. There I will meet you and speak to you; ⁴³there also I will meet with the Israelites, and the place will be consecrated by my glory.

⁴⁴"So I will consecrate the Tent of Meeting and the altar and will consecrate Aaron and his sons to serve me as priests. ⁴⁵Then I will dwell among the Israelites and be their God. ⁴⁶They will know that I am the LORD their God, who brought them out of Egypt so that I might dwell among them. I am the LORD their God.

The Altar of Incense

30 "Make an altar of acacia wood for burning incense. ²It is to be square, a cubit long and a cubit wide, and two cubits high*c*—its horns of one piece with it. ³Overlay the top and all the sides and the horns with pure gold, and make a gold molding around it. ⁴Make two gold rings for the altar below the molding—two on opposite sides—to hold the poles used to carry it. ⁵Make the poles of acacia wood and overlay them with gold. ⁶Put the altar in front of the curtain that is before the ark of the Testimony—before the atonement cover that is over the Testimony—where I will meet with you.

⁷"Aaron must burn fragrant incense on the altar every morning when he tends the lamps. ⁸He must burn incense again when he lights the lamps at twilight so incense will burn regularly before the LORD for the generations to come. ⁹Do not offer on this altar any other incense or any burnt offering or grain offering, and do not pour a drink offering on it. ¹⁰Once a year Aaron shall make atonement on its horns. This annual atonement must be made with the blood of the atoning sin offering for the generations to come. It is most holy to the LORD."

Atonement Money

¹¹Then the LORD said to Moses, ¹²"When you take a census of the Israelites to count them, each one must pay the LORD a ransom for his life at the time he is counted. Then no plague will come on them when you number them. ¹³Each one who crosses over to those already counted is to give a half shekel,*d* according to the sanctuary shekel, which weighs twenty gerahs. This half shekel is an offering to the LORD. ¹⁴All who cross over, those twenty years old or more, are to give an offering to the LORD. ¹⁵The rich are not to give more than a half shekel and the poor are not to give less when you make the offering to the LORD to atone for your lives. ¹⁶Receive the atonement money from the Israelites and use it for the service of the Tent of Meeting. It will be a memorial for the Israelites before the LORD, making atonement for your lives."

Basin for Washing

¹⁷Then the LORD said to Moses, ¹⁸"Make a bronze basin, with its bronze stand, for washing. Place it between the Tent of Meeting and the altar, and put water in it. ¹⁹Aaron and his sons are to wash their hands and feet with water from it. ²⁰Whenever they enter the Tent of Meeting, they shall wash with water so that they will not die. Also, when they approach the altar to minister by presenting an offering made to the LORD by fire, ²¹they shall wash their hands and feet so

---

a 40 That is, probably about 2 quarts (about 2 liters)   *b 40* That is, probably about 1 quart (about 1 liter)
c 2 That is, about 1 1/2 feet (about 0.5 meter) long and wide and about 3 feet (about 0.9 meter) high
d 13 That is, about 1/5 ounce (about 6 grams); also in verse 15

that they will not die. This is to be a lasting ordinance for Aaron and his descendants for the generations to come."

Anointing Oil

²²Then the LORD said to Moses, ²³"Take the following fine spices: 500 shekels*ᵃ* of liquid myrrh, half as much (that is, 250 shekels) of fragrant cinnamon, 250 shekels of fragrant cane, ²⁴500 shekels of cassia—all according to the sanctuary shekel—and a hin*ᵇ* of olive oil. ²⁵Make these into a sacred anointing oil, a fragrant blend, the work of a perfumer. It will be the sacred anointing oil. ²⁶Then use it to anoint the Tent of Meeting, the ark of the Testimony, ²⁷the table and all its articles, the lampstand and its accessories, the altar of incense, ²⁸the altar of burnt offering and all its utensils, and the basin with its stand. ²⁹You shall consecrate them so they will be most holy, and whatever touches them will be holy.

³⁰"Anoint Aaron and his sons and consecrate them so they may serve me as priests. ³¹Say to the Israelites, 'This is to be my sacred anointing oil for the generations to come. ³²Do not pour it on men's bodies and do not make any oil with the same formula. It is sacred, and you are to consider it sacred. ³³Whoever makes perfume like it and whoever puts it on anyone other than a priest must be cut off from his people.' "

Incense

³⁴Then the LORD said to Moses, "Take fragrant spices—gum resin, onycha and galbanum—and pure frankincense, all in equal amounts, ³⁵and make a fragrant blend of incense, the work of a perfumer. It is to be salted and pure and sacred. ³⁶Grind some of it to powder and place it in front of the Testimony in the Tent of Meeting, where I will meet with you. It shall be most holy to you. ³⁷Do not make any incense with this formula for yourselves; consider it holy to the LORD. ³⁸Whoever makes any like it to enjoy its fragrance must be cut off from his people."

Bezalel and Oholiab

31 Then the LORD said to Moses, ²"See, I have chosen Bezalel son of Uri, the son of Hur, of the tribe of Judah, ³and I have filled him with the Spirit of God, with skill, ability and knowledge in all kinds of crafts— ⁴to make artistic designs for work in gold, silver and bronze, ⁵to cut and set stones, to work in wood, and to engage in all kinds of craftsmanship. ⁶Moreover, I have appointed Oholiab son of Ahisamach, of the tribe of Dan, to help him. Also I have given skill to all the craftsmen to make everything I have commanded you: ⁷the Tent of Meeting, the ark of the Testimony with the atonement cover on it, and all the other furnishings of the tent— ⁸the table and its articles, the pure gold lampstand and all its accessories, the altar of incense, ⁹the altar of burnt offering and all its utensils, the basin with its stand— ¹⁰and also the woven garments, both the sacred garments for Aaron the priest and the garments for his sons when they serve as priests, ¹¹and the anointing oil and fragrant incense for the Holy Place. They are to make them just as I commanded you."

The Sabbath

¹²Then the LORD said to Moses, ¹³"Say to the Israelites, 'You must observe my Sabbaths. This will be a sign between me and you for the generations to come, so you may know that I am the LORD, who makes you holy.*ᶜ*

¹⁴" 'Observe the Sabbath, because it is holy to you. Anyone who desecrates it must be put to death; whoever does any work on that day must be cut off from his people. ¹⁵For six days, work is to be done, but the seventh day is a Sabbath of rest, holy to the LORD. Whoever does any work on the Sabbath day must be put to death. ¹⁶The Israelites are to observe the Sabbath, celebrating it for the generations to come as a lasting covenant. ¹⁷It will be a sign between me and the Israelites forever, for in six days the LORD made the heavens and the earth, and on the seventh day he abstained from work and rested.' "

ᵃ 23 That is, about 12 1/2 pounds (about 6 kilograms)   ᵇ 24 That is, probably about 4 quarts (about 4 liters)   ᶜ 13 Or who sanctifies you; or who sets you apart as holy

AN UNPRETENTIOUS AND GHASTLY ALTAR
A. B. Simpson

VERSE: Exodus 30:28　　　　　　　**PASSAGE:** Exodus 30:22–29

he altar of burnt offering in the ancient tabernacle court was the first object a person would notice upon entering the curtain that surrounded that ancient sanctuary. It stood just inside the entryway, accessible to all the people . . .

Its place at the entrance of the tabernacle teaches us that Christ's sacrifice, of which it is the type, stands at the very entrance of all our access to and communion with God.

Then again, the relation which it bore to the inner sections of the sanctuary, and that its blood was necessary in order to enter the inner shrine, shows us that Christ's blood is the only passport now to the presence of God, either on earth or in heaven. With it, we are accepted either on earth or in heaven to the very presence of God.

Further, it was accessible to the highest and the lowest, to every class of people. This indicates the fullness and graciousness of the great atonement that Christ has made for the sins of the whole world, sufficient for all, though effectual only for those who believe.

These are the chief lessons of the altar. There was nothing ornamental about it. It was unpretentious and ghastly looking. It was made of brass to bear the heaviest burdens and to sustain the streams of gore that bathed it and the ceaseless fires that burned upon it.

It was a place of suffering and blood, and it bore the constant mark of sin. So the cross of Calvary, the death of Christ and the whole doctrine of the atonement have nothing very sentimental about them. The culture of man does not like it; the philosophy of the world would get rid of it if it could. But God has made his people prize the precious blood of Jesus Christ above all price and honor and love.

ADDITIONAL SCRIPTURE READING:
Exodus 27:1–8; Hebrews 9:11–28

Go to page 103 for your next devotional reading.

1900　　Present

18When the LORD finished speaking to Moses on Mount Sinai, he gave him the two tablets of the Testimony, the tablets of stone inscribed by the finger of God.

The Golden Calf

32 When the people saw that Moses was so long in coming down from the mountain, they gathered around Aaron and said, "Come, make us gods*a* who will go before us. As for this fellow Moses who brought us up out of Egypt, we don't know what has happened to him."

2Aaron answered them, "Take off the gold earrings that your wives, your sons and your daughters are wearing, and bring them to me." 3So all the people took off their earrings and brought them to Aaron. 4He took what they handed him and made it into an idol cast in the shape of a calf, fashioning it with a tool. Then they said, "These are your gods,*b* O Israel, who brought you up out of Egypt."

5When Aaron saw this, he built an altar in front of the calf and announced, "Tomorrow there will be a festival to the LORD." 6So the next day the people rose early and sacrificed burnt offerings and presented fellowship offerings.*c* Afterward they sat down to eat and drink and got up to indulge in revelry.

7Then the LORD said to Moses, "Go down, because your people, whom you brought up out of Egypt, have become corrupt. 8They have been quick to turn away from what I commanded them and have made themselves an idol cast in the shape of a calf. They have bowed down to it and sacrificed to it and have said, 'These are your gods, O Israel, who brought you up out of Egypt.'

9"I have seen these people," the LORD said to Moses, "and they are a stiff-necked people. 10Now leave me alone so that my anger may burn against them and that I may destroy them. Then I will make you into a great nation."

11But Moses sought the favor of the LORD his God. "O LORD," he said, "why should your anger burn against your people, whom you brought out of Egypt

with great power and a mighty hand? 12Why should the Egyptians say, 'It was with evil intent that he brought them out, to kill them in the mountains and to wipe them off the face of the earth'? Turn from your fierce anger; relent and do not bring disaster on your people. 13Remember your servants Abraham, Isaac and Israel, to whom you swore by your own self: 'I will make your descendants as numerous as the stars in the sky and I will give your descendants all this land I promised them, and it will be their inheritance forever.' " 14Then the LORD relented and did not bring on his people the disaster he had threatened.

15Moses turned and went down the mountain with the two tablets of the Testimony in his hands. They were inscribed on both sides, front and back. 16The tablets were the work of God; the writing was the writing of God, engraved on the tablets.

17When Joshua heard the noise of the people shouting, he said to Moses, "There is the sound of war in the camp." 18Moses replied:

"It is not the sound of victory,
  it is not the sound of defeat;
  it is the sound of singing that I
    hear."

19When Moses approached the camp and saw the calf and the dancing, his anger burned and he threw the tablets out of his hands, breaking them to pieces at the foot of the mountain. 20And he took the calf they had made and burned it in the fire; then he ground it to powder, scattered it on the water and made the Israelites drink it.

21He said to Aaron, "What did these people do to you, that you led them into such great sin?"

22"Do not be angry, my lord," Aaron answered. "You know how prone these people are to evil. 23They said to me, 'Make us gods who will go before us. As for this fellow Moses who brought us up out of Egypt, we don't know what has happened to him.' 24So I told them, 'Whoever has any gold jewelry, take it

---

a 1 Or *a god;* also in verses 23 and 31   *b 4* Or *This is your god;* also in verse 8   *c 6* Traditionally *peace offerings*

off.' Then they gave me the gold, and I threw it into the fire, and out came this calf!"

25Moses saw that the people were running wild and that Aaron had let them get out of control and so become a laughingstock to their enemies. 26So he stood at the entrance to the camp and said, "Whoever is for the LORD, come to me." And all the Levites rallied to him.

27Then he said to them, "This is what the LORD, the God of Israel, says: 'Each man strap a sword to his side. Go back and forth through the camp from one end to the other, each killing his brother and friend and neighbor.' " 28The Levites did as Moses commanded, and that day about three thousand of the people died. 29Then Moses said, "You have been set apart to the LORD today, for you were against your own sons and brothers, and he has blessed you this day."

30The next day Moses said to the people, "You have committed a great sin. But now I will go up to the LORD; perhaps I can make atonement for your sin."

31So Moses went back to the LORD and said, "Oh, what a great sin these people have committed! They have made themselves gods of gold. 32But now, please forgive their sin—but if not, then blot me out of the book you have written."

33The LORD replied to Moses, "Whoever has sinned against me I will blot out of my book. 34Now go, lead the people to the place I spoke of, and my angel will go before you. However, when the time comes for me to punish, I will punish them for their sin."

35And the LORD struck the people with a plague because of what they did with the calf Aaron had made.

33 Then the LORD said to Moses, "Leave this place, you and the people you brought up out of Egypt, and go up to the land I promised on oath to Abraham, Isaac and Jacob, saying, 'I will give it to your descendants.' 2I will send an angel before you and drive out the Canaanites, Amorites, Hittites, Perizzites, Hivites and Jebusites. 3Go up to the land flowing with milk and honey. But I will not go with you, because you are a stiff-necked people and I might destroy you on the way."

4When the people heard these distressing words, they began to mourn and no one put on any ornaments. 5For the LORD had said to Moses, "Tell the Israelites, 'You are a stiff-necked people. If I were to go with you even for a moment, I might destroy you. Now take off your ornaments and I will decide what to do with you.' " 6So the Israelites stripped off their ornaments at Mount Horeb.

The Tent of Meeting

7Now Moses used to take a tent and pitch it outside the camp some distance away, calling it the "tent of meeting." Anyone inquiring of the LORD would go to the tent of meeting outside the camp. 8And whenever Moses went out to the tent, all the people rose and stood at the entrances to their tents, watching Moses until he entered the tent. 9As Moses went into the tent, the pillar of cloud would come down and stay at the entrance, while the LORD spoke with Moses. 10Whenever the people saw the pillar of cloud standing at the entrance to the tent, they all stood and worshiped, each at the entrance to his tent. 11The LORD would speak to Moses face to face, as a man speaks with his friend. Then Moses would return to the camp, but his young aide Joshua son of Nun did not leave the tent.

Moses and the Glory of the LORD

12Moses said to the LORD, "You have been telling me, 'Lead these people,' but you have not let me know whom you will send with me. You have said, 'I know you by name and you have found favor with me.' 13If you are pleased with me, teach me your ways so I may know you and continue to find favor with you. Remember that this nation is your people."

14The LORD replied, "My Presence will go with you, and I will give you rest."

15Then Moses said to him, "If your Presence does not go with us, do not send us up from here. 16How will anyone know that you are pleased with me and with your people unless you go with us? What else will distinguish me and your people from all the other people on the face of the earth?"

17And the LORD said to Moses, "I will

do the very thing you have asked, because I am pleased with you and I know you by name."

18 Then Moses said, "Now show me your glory."

19 And the LORD said, "I will cause all my goodness to pass in front of you, and I will proclaim my name, the LORD, in your presence. I will have mercy on whom I will have mercy, and I will have compassion on whom I will have compassion. 20 But," he said, "you cannot see my face, for no one may see me and live."

21 Then the LORD said, "There is a place near me where you may stand on a rock. 22 When my glory passes by, I will put you in a cleft in the rock and cover you with my hand until I have passed by. 23 Then I will remove my hand and you will see my back; but my face must not be seen."

The New Stone Tablets

34 The LORD said to Moses, "Chisel out two stone tablets like the first ones, and I will write on them the words that were on the first tablets, which you broke. 2 Be ready in the morning, and then come up on Mount Sinai. Present yourself to me there on top of the mountain. 3 No one is to come with you or be seen anywhere on the mountain; not even the flocks and herds may graze in front of the mountain."

4 So Moses chiseled out two stone tablets like the first ones and went up Mount Sinai early in the morning, as the LORD had commanded him; and he carried the two stone tablets in his hands. 5 Then the LORD came down in the cloud and stood there with him and proclaimed his name, the LORD. 6 And he passed in front of Moses, proclaiming, "The LORD, the LORD, the compassionate and gracious God, slow to anger, abounding in love and faithfulness, 7 maintaining love to thousands, and forgiving wickedness, rebellion and sin. Yet he does not leave the guilty unpunished; he punishes the children and their children for the sin of the fathers to the third and fourth generation."

8 Moses bowed to the ground at once and worshiped. 9 "O Lord, if I have found favor in your eyes," he said, "then let the Lord go with us. Although this is a stiff-necked people, forgive our wickedness and our sin, and take us as your inheritance."

10 Then the LORD said: "I am making a covenant with you. Before all your people I will do wonders never before done in any nation in all the world. The people you live among will see how awesome is the work that I, the LORD, will do for you. 11 Obey what I command you today. I will drive out before you the Amorites, Canaanites, Hittites, Perizzites, Hivites and Jebusites. 12 Be careful not to make a treaty with those who live in the land where you are going, or they will be a snare among you. 13 Break down their altars, smash their sacred stones and cut down their Asherah poles.ᵃ 14 Do not worship any other god, for the LORD, whose name is Jealous, is a jealous God.

15 "Be careful not to make a treaty with those who live in the land; for when they prostitute themselves to their gods and sacrifice to them, they will invite you and you will eat their sacrifices. 16 And when you choose some of their daughters as wives for your sons and those daughters prostitute themselves to their gods, they will lead your sons to do the same.

17 "Do not make cast idols.

18 "Celebrate the Feast of Unleavened Bread. For seven days eat bread made without yeast, as I commanded you. Do this at the appointed time in the month of Abib, for in that month you came out of Egypt.

19 "The first offspring of every womb belongs to me, including all the firstborn males of your livestock, whether from herd or flock. 20 Redeem the firstborn donkey with a lamb, but if you do not redeem it, break its neck. Redeem all your firstborn sons.

"No one is to appear before me empty-handed.

21 "Six days you shall labor, but on the seventh day you shall rest; even during the plowing season and harvest you must rest.

22 "Celebrate the Feast of Weeks with the firstfruits of the wheat harvest, and the Feast of Ingathering at the turn of

ᵃ 13 That is, symbols of the goddess Asherah

THE GLORY ON MOSES—THE GLORY IN US
George MacDonald

VERSE: Exodus 34:29   **PASSAGE:** Exodus 34:29–35

hen Moses came out from speaking with God, his face was radiant; its shining was a wonder to the people, and a power upon them. But the radiance began at once to diminish and die away, as was natural, for it was not indigenous in Moses. Therefore Moses put a veil upon his face that they might not see it fade. As to whether this was right or wise, opinion may differ: it is not my business to discuss the question. When he went again into the tabernacle, he took off his veil, talked with God with open face, and again put on the veil when he came out.

Paul says that the veil which obscured the face of Moses lies now upon the hearts of the Jews, so that they cannot understand him, but that when they turn to the Lord (go into the tabernacle with Moses) the veil shall be taken away, and they shall see God. Then will they understand that the glory is indeed faded upon the face of Moses, but by reason of the glory of Jesus that overshines it.

Paul says that the sight of the Lord will take that veil from their hearts (see 2 Corinthians 3:14–16). His light will burn it away. His presence gives liberty. Where he is, there is no more heaviness, no more bondage, no more wilderness or Mount Sinai. The Son makes free with sonship.

Paul's idea is, that when we take into our understanding, our heart, our conscience, our being, the glory of God—namely Jesus Christ as he shows himself to our eyes, our hearts, our consciences—he works upon us, and will keep working, till we are changed to the very likeness we have thus mirrored in us; for with his likeness he comes himself, and dwells in us. He will work until the same likeness is wrought out and perfected in us, the image, namely, of the humanity of God, in which image we were made at first, but which could never be developed in us except by the indwelling of the perfect likeness. By the power of Christ thus received and at home in us, we are changed—the glory in him becoming glory in us, his glory changing us to glory.

ADDITIONAL SCRIPTURE READING:
1 Corinthians 13:12; 2 Corinthians 3:7–18

Go to page 105 for your next devotional reading.

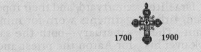

1700   1900

the year.*a* 23Three times a year all your men are to appear before the Sovereign LORD, the God of Israel. 24I will drive out nations before you and enlarge your territory, and no one will covet your land when you go up three times each year to appear before the LORD your God.

25"Do not offer the blood of a sacrifice to me along with anything containing yeast, and do not let any of the sacrifice from the Passover Feast remain until morning.

26"Bring the best of the firstfruits of your soil to the house of the LORD your God.

"Do not cook a young goat in its mother's milk."

27Then the LORD said to Moses, "Write down these words, for in accordance with these words I have made a covenant with you and with Israel." 28Moses was there with the LORD forty days and forty nights without eating bread or drinking water. And he wrote on the tablets the words of the covenant—the Ten Commandments.

The Radiant Face of Moses

29When Moses came down from Mount Sinai with the two tablets of the Testimony in his hands, he was not aware that his face was radiant because he had spoken with the LORD. 30When Aaron and all the Israelites saw Moses, his face was radiant, and they were afraid to come near him. 31But Moses called to them; so Aaron and all the leaders of the community came back to him, and he spoke to them. 32Afterward all the Israelites came near him, and he gave them all the commands the LORD had given him on Mount Sinai.

33When Moses finished speaking to them, he put a veil over his face. 34But whenever he entered the LORD's presence to speak with him, he removed the veil until he came out. And when he came out and told the Israelites what he had been commanded, 35they saw that his face was radiant. Then Moses would put the veil back over his face until he went in to speak with the LORD.

Sabbath Regulations

35 Moses assembled the whole Israelite community and said to them, "These are the things the LORD has commanded you to do: 2For six days, work is to be done, but the seventh day shall be your holy day, a Sabbath of rest to the LORD. Whoever does any work on it must be put to death. 3Do not light a fire in any of your dwellings on the Sabbath day."

Materials for the Tabernacle

4Moses said to the whole Israelite community, "This is what the LORD has commanded: 5From what you have, take an offering for the LORD. Everyone who is willing is to bring to the LORD an offering of gold, silver and bronze; 6blue, purple and scarlet yarn and fine linen; goat hair; 7ram skins dyed red and hides of sea cows*b*; acacia wood; 8olive oil for the light; spices for the anointing oil and for the fragrant incense; 9and onyx stones and other gems to be mounted on the ephod and breastpiece.

10"All who are skilled among you are to come and make everything the LORD has commanded: 11the tabernacle with its tent and its covering, clasps, frames, crossbars, posts and bases; 12the ark with its poles and the atonement cover and the curtain that shields it; 13the table with its poles and all its articles and the bread of the Presence; 14the lampstand that is for light with its accessories, lamps and oil for the light; 15the altar of incense with its poles, the anointing oil and the fragrant incense; the curtain for the doorway at the entrance to the tabernacle; 16the altar of burnt offering with its bronze grating, its poles and all its utensils; the bronze basin with its stand; 17the curtains of the courtyard with its posts and bases, and the curtain for the entrance to the courtyard; 18the tent pegs for the tabernacle and for the courtyard, and their ropes; 19the woven garments worn for ministering in the sanctuary—both the sacred garments for Aaron the priest and the garments for his sons when they serve as priests."

a 22 That is, in the fall   *b 7* That is, dugongs; also in verse 23

WEEKEND

THE ANOINTING OIL
Charles H. Spurgeon

VERSE: Exodus 35:8

PASSAGE: Exodus 35:4–29

uch use was made of this anointing oil under the law, and that which it represents is of primary importance under the gospel. The Holy Spirit, who anoints us for all holy service, is indispensable to us if we would serve the Lord acceptably. Without his aid our religious services are but a vain oblation, and our inward experience is a dead thing . . . To go before the Lord without anointing is as though some common Levite had thrust himself into the priest's office—his ministrations would have been sins rather than services. May we never venture into hallowed exercises without sacred anointings . . .

Choice spices were compounded with rarest art of the apothecary to form the anointing oil, to show forth to us how rich are all the influences of the Holy Spirit. All good things are found in the divine Comforter. Matchless consolation, infallible instruction, immortal quickening, spiritual energy, and divine sanctification all lie compounded with other excellencies in that sacred eye salve, the heavenly anointing oil of the Holy Spirit. It imparts a delightful fragrance to the character and person of the man on whom it is poured. Nothing like it can be found in all the treasuries of the rich, or the secrets of the wise. It is not to be imitated. It comes alone from God, and it is freely given, through Jesus Christ, to every waiting soul. Let us seek it, for we may have it, may have it this very evening. O Lord, anoint us, your servants.

ADDITIONAL SCRIPTURE READING:
Exodus 25:1–40; 30:23–25

Go to page 117 for your next devotional reading.

1700   1900

20Then the whole Israelite community withdrew from Moses' presence, 21and everyone who was willing and whose heart moved him came and brought an offering to the LORD for the work on the Tent of Meeting, for all its service, and for the sacred garments. 22All who were willing, men and women alike, came and brought gold jewelry of all kinds: brooches, earrings, rings and ornaments. They all presented their gold as a wave offering to the LORD. 23Everyone who had blue, purple or scarlet yarn or fine linen, or goat hair, ram skins dyed red or hides of sea cows brought them. 24Those presenting an offering of silver or bronze brought it as an offering to the LORD, and everyone who had acacia wood for any part of the work brought it. 25Every skilled woman spun with her hands and brought what she had spun—blue, purple or scarlet yarn or fine linen. 26And all the women who were willing and had the skill spun the goat hair. 27The leaders brought onyx stones and other gems to be mounted on the ephod and breastpiece. 28They also brought spices and olive oil for the light and for the anointing oil and for the fragrant incense. 29All the Israelite men and women who were willing brought to the LORD freewill offerings for all the work the LORD through Moses had commanded them to do.

Bezalel and Oholiab

30Then Moses said to the Israelites, "See, the LORD has chosen Bezalel son of Uri, the son of Hur, of the tribe of Judah, 31and he has filled him with the Spirit of God, with skill, ability and knowledge in all kinds of crafts— 32to make artistic designs for work in gold, silver and bronze, 33to cut and set stones, to work in wood and to engage in all kinds of artistic craftsmanship. 34And he has given both him and Oholiab son of Ahisamach, of the tribe of Dan, the ability to teach others. 35He has filled them with skill to do all kinds of work as craftsmen, designers, embroiderers in blue, purple and scarlet yarn and fine linen, and weavers—all of them master craftsmen and designers. 1So Bezalel, Oholiab and every skilled person to whom the LORD has given skill and ability to know how to carry out all the work of constructing the sanctuary are to do the work just as the Lord has commanded."

2Then Moses summoned Bezalel and Oholiab and every skilled person to whom the LORD had given ability and who was willing to come and do the work. 3They received from Moses all the offerings the Israelites had brought to carry out the work of constructing the sanctuary. And the people continued to bring freewill offerings morning after morning. 4So all the skilled craftsmen who were doing all the work on the sanctuary left their work 5and said to Moses, "The people are bringing more than enough for doing the work the LORD commanded to be done."

6Then Moses gave an order and they sent this word throughout the camp: "No man or woman is to make anything else as an offering for the sanctuary." And so the people were restrained from bringing more, 7because what they already had was more than enough to do all the work.

The Tabernacle

8All the skilled men among the workmen made the tabernacle with ten curtains of finely twisted linen and blue, purple and scarlet yarn, with cherubim worked into them by a skilled craftsman. 9All the curtains were the same size—twenty-eight cubits long and four cubits wide.a 10They joined five of the curtains together and did the same with the other five. 11Then they made loops of blue material along the edge of the end curtain in one set, and the same was done with the end curtain in the other set. 12They also made fifty loops on one curtain and fifty loops on the end curtain of the other set, with the loops opposite each other. 13Then they made fifty gold clasps and used them to fasten the two sets of curtains together so that the tabernacle was a unit.

14They made curtains of goat hair for the tent over the tabernacle—eleven altogether. 15All eleven curtains were the same size—thirty cubits long and

a 9 That is, about 42 feet (about 12.5 meters) long and 6 feet (about 1.8 meters) wide

four cubits wide.*a* 16They joined five of the curtains into one set and the other six into another set. 17Then they made fifty loops along the edge of the end curtain in one set and also along the edge of the end curtain in the other set. 18They made fifty bronze clasps to fasten the tent together as a unit. 19Then they made for the tent a covering of ram skins dyed red, and over that a covering of hides of sea cows.*b*

20They made upright frames of acacia wood for the tabernacle. 21Each frame was ten cubits long and a cubit and a half wide,*c* 22with two projections set parallel to each other. They made all the frames of the tabernacle in this way. 23They made twenty frames for the south side of the tabernacle 24and made forty silver bases to go under them—two bases for each frame, one under each projection. 25For the other side, the north side of the tabernacle, they made twenty frames 26and forty silver bases— two under each frame. 27They made six frames for the far end, that is, the west end of the tabernacle, 28and two frames were made for the corners of the tabernacle at the far end. 29At these two corners the frames were double from the bottom all the way to the top and fitted into a single ring; both were made alike. 30So there were eight frames and sixteen silver bases—two under each frame.

31They also made crossbars of acacia wood: five for the frames on one side of the tabernacle, 32five for those on the other side, and five for the frames on the west, at the far end of the tabernacle. 33They made the center crossbar so that it extended from end to end at the middle of the frames. 34They overlaid the frames with gold and made gold rings to hold the crossbars. They also overlaid the crossbars with gold.

35They made the curtain of blue, purple and scarlet yarn and finely twisted linen, with cherubim worked into it by a skilled craftsman. 36They made four posts of acacia wood for it and overlaid them with gold. They made gold hooks for them and cast their four silver bases. 37For the entrance to the tent they made a curtain of blue, purple and scarlet yarn and finely twisted linen—the work of an embroiderer; 38and they made five posts with hooks for them. They overlaid the tops of the posts and their bands with gold and made their five bases of bronze.

The Ark

37 Bezalel made the ark of acacia wood—two and a half cubits long, a cubit and a half wide, and a cubit and a half high.*d* 2He overlaid it with pure gold, both inside and out, and made a gold molding around it. 3He cast four gold rings for it and fastened them to its four feet, with two rings on one side and two rings on the other. 4Then he made poles of acacia wood and overlaid them with gold. 5And he inserted the poles into the rings on the sides of the ark to carry it.

6He made the atonement cover of pure gold—two and a half cubits long and a cubit and a half wide.*e* 7Then he made two cherubim out of hammered gold at the ends of the cover. 8He made one cherub on one end and the second cherub on the other; at the two ends he made them of one piece with the cover. 9The cherubim had their wings spread upward, overshadowing the cover with them. The cherubim faced each other, looking toward the cover.

The Table

10They*f* made the table of acacia wood—two cubits long, a cubit wide, and a cubit and a half high.*g* 11Then they overlaid it with pure gold and made a gold molding around it. 12They also made around it a rim a handbreadth*h* wide and put a gold molding on the rim. 13They cast four gold rings for the table and fastened them to the four corners, where the four legs were. 14The rings were put close to the rim to hold the poles used in carrying the table. 15The poles for carrying the table

---

a 15 That is, about 45 feet (about 13.5 meters) long and 6 feet (about 1.8 meters) wide   *b 19* That is, dugongs   *c 21* That is, about 15 feet (about 4.5 meters) long and 2 1/4 feet (about 0.7 meter) wide
d 1 That is, about 3 3/4 feet (about 1.1 meters) long and 2 1/4 feet (about 0.7 meter) wide and high
e 6 That is, about 3 3/4 feet (about 1.1 meters) long and 2 1/4 feet (about 0.7 meter) wide   *f 10* Or *He;* also in verses 11–29   *g 10* That is, about 3 feet (about 0.9 meter) long, 1 1/2 feet (about 0.5 meter) wide, and 2 1/4 feet (about 0.7 meter) high   *h 12* That is, about 3 inches (about 8 centimeters)

were made of acacia wood and were overlaid with gold. [16]And they made from pure gold the articles for the table—its plates and dishes and bowls and its pitchers for the pouring out of drink offerings.

The Lampstand

[17]They made the lampstand of pure gold and hammered it out, base and shaft; its flowerlike cups, buds and blossoms were of one piece with it. [18]Six branches extended from the sides of the lampstand—three on one side and three on the other. [19]Three cups shaped like almond flowers with buds and blossoms were on one branch, three on the next branch and the same for all six branches extending from the lampstand. [20]And on the lampstand were four cups shaped like almond flowers with buds and blossoms. [21]One bud was under the first pair of branches extending from the lampstand, a second bud under the second pair, and a third bud under the third pair—six branches in all. [22]The buds and the branches were all of one piece with the lampstand, hammered out of pure gold.

[23]They made its seven lamps, as well as its wick trimmers and trays, of pure gold. [24]They made the lampstand and all its accessories from one talent[a] of pure gold.

The Altar of Incense

[25]They made the altar of incense out of acacia wood. It was square, a cubit long and a cubit wide, and two cubits high[b]—its horns of one piece with it. [26]They overlaid the top and all the sides and the horns with pure gold, and made a gold molding around it. [27]They made two gold rings below the molding—two on opposite sides—to hold the poles used to carry it. [28]They made the poles of acacia wood and overlaid them with gold. [29]They also made the sacred anointing oil and the pure, fragrant incense—the work of a perfumer.

The Altar of Burnt Offering

38 They[c] built the altar of burnt offering of acacia wood, three cubits[d] high; it was square, five cubits long and five cubits wide.[e] [2]They made a horn at each of the four corners, so that the horns and the altar were of one piece, and they overlaid the altar with bronze. [3]They made all its utensils of bronze—its pots, shovels, sprinkling bowls, meat forks and firepans. [4]They made a grating for the altar, a bronze network, to be under its ledge, halfway up the altar. [5]They cast bronze rings to hold the poles for the four corners of the bronze grating. [6]They made the poles of acacia wood and overlaid them with bronze. [7]They inserted the poles into the rings so they would be on the sides of the altar for carrying it. They made it hollow, out of boards.

Basin for Washing

[8]They made the bronze basin and its bronze stand from the mirrors of the women who served at the entrance to the Tent of Meeting.

The Courtyard

[9]Next they made the courtyard. The south side was a hundred cubits[f] long and had curtains of finely twisted linen, [10]with twenty posts and twenty bronze bases, and with silver hooks and bands on the posts. [11]The north side was also a hundred cubits long and had twenty posts and twenty bronze bases, with silver hooks and bands on the posts.

[12]The west end was fifty cubits[g] wide and had curtains, with ten posts and ten bases, with silver hooks and bands on the posts. [13]The east end, toward the sunrise, was also fifty cubits wide. [14]Curtains fifteen cubits[h] long were on one side of the entrance, with three posts and three bases, [15]and curtains fifteen cubits long were on the other side of the entrance to the courtyard, with three posts and three bases. [16]All the curtains around the courtyard were of finely twisted linen. [17]The bases for the

---

[a] 24　That is, about 75 pounds (about 34 kilograms)　　[b] 25　That is, about 1 1/2 feet (about 0.5 meter)
long and wide, and about 3 feet (about 0.9 meter) high　　[c] 1　Or *He;* also in verses 2–9　　[d] 1　That is,
about 4 1/2 feet (about 1.3 meters)　　[e] 1　That is, about 7 1/2 feet (about 2.3 meters) long and wide
[f] 9　That is, about 150 feet (about 46 meters)　　[g] 12　That is, about 75 feet (about 23 meters)
[h] 14　That is, about 22 1/2 feet (about 6.9 meters)

posts were bronze. The hooks and bands on the posts were silver, and their tops were overlaid with silver; so all the posts of the courtyard had silver bands.

18The curtain for the entrance to the courtyard was of blue, purple and scarlet yarn and finely twisted linen—the work of an embroiderer. It was twenty cubits*a* long and, like the curtains of the courtyard, five cubits*b* high, 19with four posts and four bronze bases. Their hooks and bands were silver, and their tops were overlaid with silver. 20All the tent pegs of the tabernacle and of the surrounding courtyard were bronze.

The Materials Used

21These are the amounts of the materials used for the tabernacle, the tabernacle of the Testimony, which were recorded at Moses' command by the Levites under the direction of Ithamar son of Aaron, the priest. 22(Bezalel son of Uri, the son of Hur, of the tribe of Judah, made everything the LORD commanded Moses; 23with him was Oholiab son of Ahisamach, of the tribe of Dan—a craftsman and designer, and an embroiderer in blue, purple and scarlet yarn and fine linen.) 24The total amount of the gold from the wave offering used for all the work on the sanctuary was 29 talents and 730 shekels,*c* according to the sanctuary shekel.

25The silver obtained from those of the community who were counted in the census was 100 talents and 1,775 shekels,*d* according to the sanctuary shekel— 26one beka per person, that is, half a shekel,*e* according to the sanctuary shekel, from everyone who had crossed over to those counted, twenty years old or more, a total of 603,550 men. 27The 100 talents*f* of silver were used to cast the bases for the sanctuary and for the curtain—100 bases from the 100 talents, one talent for each base. 28They used the 1,775 shekels*g* to make the hooks for the posts, to overlay the tops of the posts, and to make their bands.

29The bronze from the wave offering was 70 talents and 2,400 shekels.*h* 30They used it to make the bases for the entrance to the Tent of Meeting, the bronze altar with its bronze grating and all its utensils, 31the bases for the surrounding courtyard and those for its entrance and all the tent pegs for the tabernacle and those for the surrounding courtyard.

The Priestly Garments

39 From the blue, purple and scarlet yarn they made woven garments for ministering in the sanctuary. They also made sacred garments for Aaron, as the LORD commanded Moses.

The Ephod

2They*i* made the ephod of gold, and of blue, purple and scarlet yarn, and of finely twisted linen. 3They hammered out thin sheets of gold and cut strands to be worked into the blue, purple and scarlet yarn and fine linen—the work of a skilled craftsman. 4They made shoulder pieces for the ephod, which were attached to two of its corners, so it could be fastened. 5Its skillfully woven waistband was like it—of one piece with the ephod and made with gold, and with blue, purple and scarlet yarn, and with finely twisted linen, as the LORD commanded Moses.

6They mounted the onyx stones in gold filigree settings and engraved them like a seal with the names of the sons of Israel. 7Then they fastened them on the shoulder pieces of the ephod as memorial stones for the sons of Israel, as the LORD commanded Moses.

The Breastpiece

8They fashioned the breastpiece—the work of a skilled craftsman. They made it like the ephod: of gold, and of blue, purple and scarlet yarn, and of finely twisted linen. 9It was square—a span*i* long and a span wide—and folded double. 10Then they mounted four rows of precious stones on it. In the first row there was a ruby, a topaz and a beryl; 11in the second

---

a 18 That is, about 30 feet (about 9 meters)   *b 18* That is, about 7 1/2 feet (about 2.3 meters)   *c 24* The weight of the gold was a little over one ton (about 1 metric ton).   *d 25* The weight of the silver was a little over 3 3/4 tons (about 3.4 metric tons).   *e 26* That is, about 1/5 ounce (about 5.5 grams)   *f 27* That is, about 3 3/4 tons (about 3.4 metric tons)   *g 28* That is, about 45 pounds (about 20 kilograms)   *h 29* The weight of the bronze was about 2 1/2 tons (about 2.4 metric tons).   *i 2* Or *He;* also in verses 7, 8 and 22   *i 9* That is, about 9 inches (about 22 centimeters)

row a turquoise, a sapphire[a] and an emerald; [12]in the third row a jacinth, an agate and an amethyst; [13]in the fourth row a chrysolite, an onyx and a jasper.[b] They were mounted in gold filigree settings. [14]There were twelve stones, one for each of the names of the sons of Israel, each engraved like a seal with the name of one of the twelve tribes.

[15]For the breastpiece they made braided chains of pure gold, like a rope. [16]They made two gold filigree settings and two gold rings, and fastened the rings to two of the corners of the breastpiece. [17]They fastened the two gold chains to the rings at the corners of the breastpiece, [18]and the other ends of the chains to the two settings, attaching them to the shoulder pieces of the ephod at the front. [19]They made two gold rings and attached them to the other two corners of the breastpiece on the inside edge next to the ephod. [20]Then they made two more gold rings and attached them to the bottom of the shoulder pieces on the front of the ephod, close to the seam just above the waistband of the ephod. [21]They tied the rings of the breastpiece to the rings of the ephod with blue cord, connecting it to the waistband so that the breastpiece would not swing out from the ephod—as the LORD commanded Moses.

Other Priestly Garments

[22]They made the robe of the ephod entirely of blue cloth—the work of a weaver— [23]with an opening in the center of the robe like the opening of a collar,[c] and a band around this opening, so that it would not tear. [24]They made pomegranates of blue, purple and scarlet yarn and finely twisted linen around the hem of the robe. [25]And they made bells of pure gold and attached them around the hem between the pomegranates. [26]The bells and pomegranates alternated around the hem of the robe to be worn for ministering, as the LORD commanded Moses.

[27]For Aaron and his sons, they made tunics of fine linen—the work of a weaver— [28]and the turban of fine linen, the linen headbands and the undergarments of finely twisted linen. [29]The sash was of finely twisted linen and blue, purple and scarlet yarn—the work of an embroiderer—as the LORD commanded Moses.

[30]They made the plate, the sacred diadem, out of pure gold and engraved on it, like an inscription on a seal: HOLY TO THE LORD. [31]Then they fastened a blue cord to it to attach it to the turban, as the LORD commanded Moses.

Moses Inspects the Tabernacle

[32]So all the work on the tabernacle, the Tent of Meeting, was completed. The Israelites did everything just as the LORD commanded Moses. [33]Then they brought the tabernacle to Moses: the tent and all its furnishings, its clasps, frames, crossbars, posts and bases; [34]the covering of ram skins dyed red, the covering of hides of sea cows[d] and the shielding curtain; [35]the ark of the Testimony with its poles and the atonement cover; [36]the table with all its articles and the bread of the Presence; [37]the pure gold lampstand with its row of lamps and all its accessories, and the oil for the light; [38]the gold altar, the anointing oil, the fragrant incense, and the curtain for the entrance to the tent; [39]the bronze altar with its bronze grating, its poles and all its utensils; the basin with its stand; [40]the curtains of the courtyard with its posts and bases, and the curtain for the entrance to the courtyard; the ropes and tent pegs for the courtyard; all the furnishings for the tabernacle, the Tent of Meeting; [41]and the woven garments worn for ministering in the sanctuary, both the sacred garments for Aaron the priest and the garments for his sons when serving as priests.

[42]The Israelites had done all the work just as the LORD had commanded Moses. [43]Moses inspected the work and saw that they had done it just as the LORD had commanded. So Moses blessed them.

Setting Up the Tabernacle

40 Then the LORD said to Moses: [2]"Set up the tabernacle, the Tent of Meeting, on the first day of the first month. [3]Place the ark of the Testimony in it and shield the ark with the

---

[a] 11 Or *lapis lazuli*   [b] 13 The precise identification of some of these precious stones is uncertain.
[c] 23 The meaning of the Hebrew for this word is uncertain.   [d] 34 That is, dugongs

curtain. 4Bring in the table and set out what belongs on it. Then bring in the lampstand and set up its lamps. 5Place the gold altar of incense in front of the ark of the Testimony and put the curtain at the entrance to the tabernacle.

6"Place the altar of burnt offering in front of the entrance to the tabernacle, the Tent of Meeting; 7place the basin between the Tent of Meeting and the altar and put water in it. 8Set up the courtyard around it and put the curtain at the entrance to the courtyard.

9"Take the anointing oil and anoint the tabernacle and everything in it; consecrate it and all its furnishings, and it will be holy. 10Then anoint the altar of burnt offering and all its utensils; consecrate the altar, and it will be most holy. 11Anoint the basin and its stand and consecrate them.

12"Bring Aaron and his sons to the entrance to the Tent of Meeting and wash them with water. 13Then dress Aaron in the sacred garments, anoint him and consecrate him so he may serve me as priest. 14Bring his sons and dress them in tunics. 15Anoint them just as you anointed their father, so they may serve me as priests. Their anointing will be to a priesthood that will continue for all generations to come." 16Moses did everything just as the LORD commanded him.

17So the tabernacle was set up on the first day of the first month in the second year. 18When Moses set up the tabernacle, he put the bases in place, erected the frames, inserted the crossbars and set up the posts. 19Then he spread the tent over the tabernacle and put the covering over the tent, as the LORD commanded him.

20He took the Testimony and placed it in the ark, attached the poles to the ark and put the atonement cover over it. 21Then he brought the ark into the tabernacle and hung the shielding curtain and shielded the ark of the Testimony, as the LORD commanded him.

22Moses placed the table in the Tent of Meeting on the north side of the tabernacle outside the curtain 23and set out the bread on it before the LORD, as the LORD commanded him.

24He placed the lampstand in the Tent of Meeting opposite the table on the south side of the tabernacle 25and set up the lamps before the LORD, as the LORD commanded him.

26Moses placed the gold altar in the Tent of Meeting in front of the curtain 27and burned fragrant incense on it, as the LORD commanded him. 28Then he put up the curtain at the entrance to the tabernacle.

29He set the altar of burnt offering near the entrance to the tabernacle, the Tent of Meeting, and offered on it burnt offerings and grain offerings, as the LORD commanded him.

30He placed the basin between the Tent of Meeting and the altar and put water in it for washing, 31and Moses and Aaron and his sons used it to wash their hands and feet. 32They washed whenever they entered the Tent of Meeting or approached the altar, as the LORD commanded Moses.

33Then Moses set up the courtyard around the tabernacle and altar and put up the curtain at the entrance to the courtyard. And so Moses finished the work.

The Glory of the LORD

34Then the cloud covered the Tent of Meeting, and the glory of the LORD filled the tabernacle. 35Moses could not enter the Tent of Meeting because the cloud had settled upon it, and the glory of the LORD filled the tabernacle.

36In all the travels of the Israelites, whenever the cloud lifted from above the tabernacle, they would set out; 37but if the cloud did not lift, they did not set out—until the day it lifted. 38So the cloud of the LORD was over the tabernacle by day, and fire was in the cloud by night, in the sight of all the house of Israel during all their travels.

LEVITICUS

OSES WRITES LEVITICUS WHILE THE ISRAELITES ARE IN THE DESERT, BEFORE THEY ENTER THE PROM-ISED LAND. THE BOOK'S KEY THOUGHT IS STATED IN 11:45—"BE HOLY, BECAUSE I AM HOLY." THE LAWS IN THE BOOK WERE GIVEN TO HELP THE ISRAELITES WORSHIP AND LIVE AS GOD'S HOLY PEOPLE. EVEN THOUGH THE NEW COVENANT HAS FREED US FROM THE INTRICACIES OF THE LEVITICAL LAW, LEVITI-CUS REMINDS US THAT EVERY PART OF OUR LIVES IS IMPORTANT TO GOD, AND THAT WE ARE TO LOVE AND SERVE HIM IN HOLINESS.

The Burnt Offering

1 The LORD called to Moses and spoke to him from the Tent of Meeting. He said, 2"Speak to the Israelites and say to them: 'When any of you brings an offering to the LORD, bring as your offering an animal from either the herd or the flock.

3" 'If the offering is a burnt offering from the herd, he is to offer a male without defect. He must present it at the entrance to the Tent of Meeting so that it*a* will be acceptable to the LORD. 4He is to lay his hand on the head of the burnt offering, and it will be accepted on his behalf to make atonement for him. 5He is to slaughter the young bull before the LORD, and then Aaron's sons the priests

shall bring the blood and sprinkle it against the altar on all sides at the entrance to the Tent of Meeting. 6He is to skin the burnt offering and cut it into pieces. 7The sons of Aaron the priest are to put fire on the altar and arrange wood on the fire. 8Then Aaron's sons the priests shall arrange the pieces, includ-ing the head and the fat, on the burning wood that is on the altar. 9He is to wash the inner parts and the legs with water, and the priest is to burn all of it on the altar. It is a burnt offering, an offering made by fire, an aroma pleasing to the LORD.

10" 'If the offering is a burnt offering from the flock, from either the sheep or the goats, he is to offer a male without defect. 11He is to slaughter it at the

a 3 Or he

north side of the altar before the LORD, and Aaron's sons the priests shall sprinkle its blood against the altar on all sides. ¹²He is to cut it into pieces, and the priest shall arrange them, including the head and the fat, on the burning wood that is on the altar. ¹³He is to wash the inner parts and the legs with water, and the priest is to bring all of it and burn it on the altar. It is a burnt offering, an offering made by fire, an aroma pleasing to the LORD.

¹⁴" 'If the offering to the LORD is a burnt offering of birds, he is to offer a dove or a young pigeon. ¹⁵The priest shall bring it to the altar, wring off the head and burn it on the altar; its blood shall be drained out on the side of the altar. ¹⁶He is to remove the crop with its contents*a* and throw it to the east side of the altar, where the ashes are. ¹⁷He shall tear it open by the wings, not severing it completely, and then the priest shall burn it on the wood that is on the fire on the altar. It is a burnt offering, an offering made by fire, an aroma pleasing to the LORD.

The Grain Offering

2 " 'When someone brings a grain offering to the LORD, his offering is to be of fine flour. He is to pour oil on it, put incense on it ²and take it to Aaron's sons the priests. The priest shall take a handful of the fine flour and oil, together with all the incense, and burn this as a memorial portion on the altar, an offering made by fire, an aroma pleasing to the LORD. ³The rest of the grain offering belongs to Aaron and his sons; it is a most holy part of the offerings made to the LORD by fire.

⁴" 'If you bring a grain offering baked in an oven, it is to consist of fine flour: cakes made without yeast and mixed with oil, or*b* wafers made without yeast and spread with oil. ⁵If your grain offering is prepared on a griddle, it is to be made of fine flour mixed with oil, and without yeast. ⁶Crumble it and pour oil on it; it is a grain offering. ⁷If your grain offering is cooked in a pan, it is to be made of fine flour and oil. ⁸Bring the grain offering made of these things to the LORD; present it to the priest, who shall take it to the altar. ⁹He shall take out the memorial portion from the grain offering and burn it on the altar as an offering made by fire, an aroma pleasing to the LORD. ¹⁰The rest of the grain offering belongs to Aaron and his sons; it is a most holy part of the offerings made to the LORD by fire.

¹¹" 'Every grain offering you bring to the LORD must be made without yeast, for you are not to burn any yeast or honey in an offering made to the LORD by fire. ¹²You may bring them to the LORD as an offering of the firstfruits, but they are not to be offered on the altar as a pleasing aroma. ¹³Season all your grain offerings with salt. Do not leave the salt of the covenant of your God out of your grain offerings; add salt to all your offerings.

¹⁴" 'If you bring a grain offering of firstfruits to the LORD, offer crushed heads of new grain roasted in the fire. ¹⁵Put oil and incense on it; it is a grain offering. ¹⁶The priest shall burn the memorial portion of the crushed grain and the oil, together with all the incense, as an offering made to the LORD by fire.

The Fellowship Offering

3 " 'If someone's offering is a fellowship offering,*c* and he offers an animal from the herd, whether male or female, he is to present before the LORD an animal without defect. ²He is to lay his hand on the head of his offering and slaughter it at the entrance to the Tent of Meeting. Then Aaron's sons the priests shall sprinkle the blood against the altar on all sides. ³From the fellowship offering he is to bring a sacrifice made to the LORD by fire: all the fat that covers the inner parts or is connected to them, ⁴both kidneys with the fat on them near the loins, and the covering of the liver, which he will remove with the kidneys. ⁵Then Aaron's sons are to burn it on the altar on top of the burnt offering that is on the burning wood, as an offering made by fire, an aroma pleasing to the LORD.

⁶" 'If he offers an animal from the flock as a fellowship offering to the LORD, he is to offer a male or female

---

a 16 Or *crop and the feathers;* the meaning of the Hebrew for this word is uncertain.   *b 4* Or *and*
c 1 Traditionally *peace offering;* also in verses 3, 6 and 9

without defect. 7If he offers a lamb, he is to present it before the LORD. 8He is to lay his hand on the head of his offering and slaughter it in front of the Tent of Meeting. Then Aaron's sons shall sprinkle its blood against the altar on all sides. 9From the fellowship offering he is to bring a sacrifice made to the LORD by fire: its fat, the entire fat tail cut off close to the backbone, all the fat that covers the inner parts or is connected to them, 10both kidneys with the fat on them near the loins, and the covering of the liver, which he will remove with the kidneys. 11The priest shall burn them on the altar as food, an offering made to the LORD by fire.

12" 'If his offering is a goat, he is to present it before the LORD. 13He is to lay his hand on its head and slaughter it in front of the Tent of Meeting. Then Aaron's sons shall sprinkle its blood against the altar on all sides. 14From what he offers he is to make this offering to the LORD by fire: all the fat that covers the inner parts or is connected to them, 15both kidneys with the fat on them near the loins, and the covering of the liver, which he will remove with the kidneys. 16The priest shall burn them on the altar as food, an offering made by fire, a pleasing aroma. All the fat is the LORD's.

17" 'This is a lasting ordinance for the generations to come, wherever you live: You must not eat any fat or any blood.' "

The Sin Offering

4 The LORD said to Moses, 2"Say to the Israelites: 'When anyone sins unintentionally and does what is forbidden in any of the LORD's commands—

3" 'If the anointed priest sins, bringing guilt on the people, he must bring to the LORD a young bull without defect as a sin offering for the sin he has committed. 4He is to present the bull at the entrance to the Tent of Meeting before the LORD. He is to lay his hand on its head and slaughter it before the LORD. 5Then the anointed priest shall take some of the bull's blood and carry it into the Tent of Meeting. 6He is to dip his finger into the blood and sprinkle some of it seven times before the LORD, in front of the curtain of the sanctuary. 7The priest shall then put some of the blood on the horns of the altar of fragrant incense that is before the LORD in the Tent of Meeting. The rest of the bull's blood he shall pour out at the base of the altar of burnt offering at the entrance to the Tent of Meeting. 8He shall remove all the fat from the bull of the sin offering—the fat that covers the inner parts or is connected to them, 9both kidneys with the fat on them near the loins, and the covering of the liver, which he will remove with the kidneys— 10just as the fat is removed from the ox*a* sacrificed as a fellowship offering.*b* Then the priest shall burn them on the altar of burnt offering. 11But the hide of the bull and all its flesh, as well as the head and legs, the inner parts and offal— 12that is, all the rest of the bull—he must take outside the camp to a place ceremonially clean, where the ashes are thrown, and burn it in a wood fire on the ash heap.

13" 'If the whole Israelite community sins unintentionally and does what is forbidden in any of the LORD's commands, even though the community is unaware of the matter, they are guilty. 14When they become aware of the sin they committed, the assembly must bring a young bull as a sin offering and present it before the Tent of Meeting. 15The elders of the community are to lay their hands on the bull's head before the LORD, and the bull shall be slaughtered before the LORD. 16Then the anointed priest is to take some of the bull's blood into the Tent of Meeting. 17He shall dip his finger into the blood and sprinkle it before the LORD seven times in front of the curtain. 18He is to put some of the blood on the horns of the altar that is before the LORD in the Tent of Meeting. The rest of the blood he shall pour out at the base of the altar of burnt offering at the entrance to the Tent of Meeting. 19He shall remove all the fat from it and burn it on the altar, 20and do with this bull just as he did with the bull for the sin offering. In this way the priest will make atonement for them, and they will be forgiven. 21Then he shall take the bull

---

a 10 The Hebrew word can include both male and female.   *b 10* Traditionally *peace offering;* also in verses 26, 31 and 35

outside the camp and burn it as he burned the first bull. This is the sin offering for the community.

22" 'When a leader sins unintentionally and does what is forbidden in any of the commands of the LORD his God, he is guilty. 23When he is made aware of the sin he committed, he must bring as his offering a male goat without defect. 24He is to lay his hand on the goat's head and slaughter it at the place where the burnt offering is slaughtered before the LORD. It is a sin offering. 25Then the priest shall take some of the blood of the sin offering with his finger and put it on the horns of the altar of burnt offering and pour out the rest of the blood at the base of the altar. 26He shall burn all the fat on the altar as he burned the fat of the fellowship offering. In this way the priest will make atonement for the man's sin, and he will be forgiven.

27" 'If a member of the community sins unintentionally and does what is forbidden in any of the LORD's commands, he is guilty. 28When he is made aware of the sin he committed, he must bring as his offering for the sin he committed a female goat without defect. 29He is to lay his hand on the head of the sin offering and slaughter it at the place of the burnt offering. 30Then the priest is to take some of the blood with his finger and put it on the horns of the altar of burnt offering and pour out the rest of the blood at the base of the altar. 31He shall remove all the fat, just as the fat is removed from the fellowship offering, and the priest shall burn it on the altar as an aroma pleasing to the LORD. In this way the priest will make atonement for him, and he will be forgiven.

32" 'If he brings a lamb as his sin offering, he is to bring a female without defect. 33He is to lay his hand on its head and slaughter it for a sin offering at the place where the burnt offering is slaughtered. 34Then the priest shall take some of the blood of the sin offering with his finger and put it on the horns of the altar of burnt offering and pour out the rest of the blood at the base of the altar. 35He shall remove all the fat, just as the fat is removed from the lamb of the fellowship offering, and the priest

shall burn it on the altar on top of the offerings made to the LORD by fire. In this way the priest will make atonement for him for the sin he has committed, and he will be forgiven.

5 " 'If a person sins because he does not speak up when he hears a public charge to testify regarding something he has seen or learned about, he will be held responsible.

2" 'Or if a person touches anything ceremonially unclean—whether the carcasses of unclean wild animals or of unclean livestock or of unclean creatures that move along the ground—even though he is unaware of it, he has become unclean and is guilty.

3" 'Or if he touches human uncleanness—anything that would make him unclean—even though he is unaware of it, when he learns of it he will be guilty.

4" 'Or if a person thoughtlessly takes an oath to do anything, whether good or evil—in any matter one might carelessly swear about—even though he is unaware of it, in any case when he learns of it he will be guilty.

5" 'When anyone is guilty in any of these ways, he must confess in what way he has sinned 6and, as a penalty for the sin he has committed, he must bring to the LORD a female lamb or goat from the flock as a sin offering; and the priest shall make atonement for him for his sin.

7" 'If he cannot afford a lamb, he is to bring two doves or two young pigeons to the LORD as a penalty for his sin—one for a sin offering and the other for a burnt offering. 8He is to bring them to the priest, who shall first offer the one for the sin offering. He is to wring its head from its neck, not severing it completely, 9and is to sprinkle some of the blood of the sin offering against the side of the altar; the rest of the blood must be drained out at the base of the altar. It is a sin offering. 10The priest shall then offer the other as a burnt offering in the prescribed way and make atonement for him for the sin he has committed, and he will be forgiven.

11" 'If, however, he cannot afford two doves or two young pigeons, he is to bring as an offering for his sin a tenth of an ephah*a* of fine flour for a sin offering. He must not put oil or incense on it, because it is a sin offering. ¹²He is to bring it to the priest, who shall take a handful of it as a memorial portion and burn it on the altar on top of the offerings made to the LORD by fire. It is a sin offering. ¹³In this way the priest will make atonement for him for any of these sins he has committed, and he will be forgiven. The rest of the offering will belong to the priest, as in the case of the grain offering.' "

The Guilt Offering

¹⁴The LORD said to Moses: ¹⁵"When a person commits a violation and sins unintentionally in regard to any of the LORD's holy things, he is to bring to the LORD as a penalty a ram from the flock, one without defect and of the proper value in silver, according to the sanctuary shekel.*b* It is a guilt offering. ¹⁶He must make restitution for what he has failed to do in regard to the holy things, add a fifth of the value to that and give it all to the priest, who will make atonement for him with the ram as a guilt offering, and he will be forgiven.

¹⁷"If a person sins and does what is forbidden in any of the LORD's commands, even though he does not know it, he is guilty and will be held responsible. ¹⁸He is to bring to the priest as a guilt offering a ram from the flock, one without defect and of the proper value. In this way the priest will make atonement for him for the wrong he has committed unintentionally, and he will be forgiven. ¹⁹It is a guilt offering; he has been guilty of*c* wrongdoing against the LORD."

6 The LORD said to Moses: ²"If anyone sins and is unfaithful to the LORD by deceiving his neighbor about something entrusted to him or left in his care or stolen, or if he cheats him, ³or if he finds lost property and lies about it, or if he swears falsely, or if he commits any such sin that people may do— ⁴when he thus sins and becomes guilty, he must return what he has stolen or taken by extortion, or what was entrusted to him, or the lost property he found, ⁵or whatever it was he

swore falsely about. He must make restitution in full, add a fifth of the value to it and give it all to the owner on the day he presents his guilt offering. ⁶And as a penalty he must bring to the priest, that is, to the LORD, his guilt offering, a ram from the flock, one without defect and of the proper value. ⁷In this way the priest will make atonement for him before the LORD, and he will be forgiven for any of these things he did that made him guilty."

The Burnt Offering

⁸The LORD said to Moses: ⁹"Give Aaron and his sons this command: 'These are the regulations for the burnt offering: The burnt offering is to remain on the altar hearth throughout the night, till morning, and the fire must be kept burning on the altar. ¹⁰The priest shall then put on his linen clothes, with linen undergarments next to his body, and shall remove the ashes of the burnt offering that the fire has consumed on the altar and place them beside the altar. ¹¹Then he is to take off these clothes and put on others, and carry the ashes outside the camp to a place that is ceremonially clean. ¹²The fire on the altar must be kept burning; it must not go out. Every morning the priest is to add firewood and arrange the burnt offering on the fire and burn the fat of the fellowship offerings*d* on it. ¹³The fire must be kept burning on the altar continuously; it must not go out.

The Grain Offering

¹⁴" 'These are the regulations for the grain offering: Aaron's sons are to bring it before the LORD, in front of the altar. ¹⁵The priest is to take a handful of fine flour and oil, together with all the incense on the grain offering, and burn the memorial portion on the altar as an aroma pleasing to the LORD. ¹⁶Aaron and his sons shall eat the rest of it, but it is to be eaten without yeast in a holy place; they are to eat it in the courtyard of the Tent of Meeting. ¹⁷It must not be baked with yeast; I have given it as their share of the offerings made to me by fire. Like the sin offering and the guilt offering, it

---

a 11 That is, probably about 2 quarts (about 2 liters)   *b 15* That is, about 2/5 ounce (about 11.5 grams)
c 19 Or *has made full expiation for his*   *d 12* Traditionally *peace offerings*

RESTITUTION AND SALVATION
William Booth

VERSE: Leviticus 6:4–5   **PASSAGE:** Leviticus 5:14—6:7

he entrance to the heavenly kingdom was closed against me by an evil act of the past which required restitution. In a boyish trading affair I had managed to make a profit out of my companions, whilst giving them to suppose that what I did was all in the way of a generous fellowship. As a testimonial of their gratitude they had given me a silver pencil case. Merely to return their gift would have been comparatively easy, but to confess the deception I had practiced upon them was a humiliation to which for some days I could not bring myself.

I remember, as if it were but yesterday, the spot in the corner of a room under the chapel, the hour, the resolution to end the matter, the rising up and rushing forth, the finding of the young fellow I had chiefly wronged, the acknowledgment of my sin, the return of the pencil case—the instant rolling away from my heart of the guilty burden, the peace that came in its place, and the going forth to serve my God and my generation from that hour.

It was in the open street that this great change passed over me, and if I could only have possessed the flagstone on which I stood at that happy moment, the sight of it occasionally might have been as useful to me as the stones carried up long ago from the bed of the Jordan were to the Israelites who had passed over them dry-shod.

Since that night, for it was near upon eleven o'clock when the happy change was realized, the business of my life has been not only to make a holy character but to live a life of loving activity in the service of God and man. I have ever felt that true religion consists not only in being holy myself, but in assisting my crucified Lord in his work of saving men and women, making them into his soldiers, keeping them faithful to death, and so getting them into heaven.

ADDITIONAL SCRIPTURE READING:
Exodus 22:3; Matthew 5:23–26; Philippians 4:7

Go to page 121 for your next devotional reading.

1700   1900

is most holy. [18]Any male descendant of Aaron may eat it. It is his regular share of the offerings made to the LORD by fire for the generations to come. Whatever touches them will become holy.[a'] "

[19]The LORD also said to Moses, [20]"This is the offering Aaron and his sons are to bring to the LORD on the day he[b] is anointed: a tenth of an ephah[c] of fine flour as a regular grain offering, half of it in the morning and half in the evening. [21]Prepare it with oil on a griddle; bring it well-mixed and present the grain offering broken[d] in pieces as an aroma pleasing to the LORD. [22]The son who is to succeed him as anointed priest shall prepare it. It is the LORD's regular share and is to be burned completely. [23]Every grain offering of a priest shall be burned completely; it must not be eaten."

The Sin Offering

[24]The LORD said to Moses, [25]"Say to Aaron and his sons: 'These are the regulations for the sin offering: The sin offering is to be slaughtered before the LORD in the place the burnt offering is slaughtered; it is most holy. [26]The priest who offers it shall eat it; it is to be eaten in a holy place, in the courtyard of the Tent of Meeting. [27]Whatever touches any of the flesh will become holy, and if any of the blood is spattered on a garment, you must wash it in a holy place. [28]The clay pot the meat is cooked in must be broken; but if it is cooked in a bronze pot, the pot is to be scoured and rinsed with water. [29]Any male in a priest's family may eat it; it is most holy. [30]But any sin offering whose blood is brought into the Tent of Meeting to make atonement in the Holy Place must not be eaten; it must be burned.

The Guilt Offering

7 " 'These are the regulations for the guilt offering, which is most holy: [2]The guilt offering is to be slaughtered in the place where the burnt offering is slaughtered, and its blood is to be sprinkled against the altar on all sides. [3]All its fat shall be offered: the fat tail and the fat that covers the inner parts,

[4]both kidneys with the fat on them near the loins, and the covering of the liver, which is to be removed with the kidneys. [5]The priest shall burn them on the altar as an offering made to the LORD by fire. It is a guilt offering. [6]Any male in a priest's family may eat it, but it must be eaten in a holy place; it is most holy.

[7]" 'The same law applies to both the sin offering and the guilt offering: They belong to the priest who makes atonement with them. [8]The priest who offers a burnt offering for anyone may keep its hide for himself. [9]Every grain offering baked in an oven or cooked in a pan or on a griddle belongs to the priest who offers it, [10]and every grain offering, whether mixed with oil or dry, belongs equally to all the sons of Aaron.

The Fellowship Offering

[11]" 'These are the regulations for the fellowship offering[e] a person may present to the LORD:

[12]" 'If he offers it as an expression of thankfulness, then along with this thank offering he is to offer cakes of bread made without yeast and mixed with oil, wafers made without yeast and spread with oil, and cakes of fine flour well-kneaded and mixed with oil. [13]Along with his fellowship offering of thanksgiving he is to present an offering with cakes of bread made with yeast. [14]He is to bring one of each kind as an offering, a contribution to the LORD; it belongs to the priest who sprinkles the blood of the fellowship offerings. [15]The meat of his fellowship offering of thanksgiving must be eaten on the day it is offered; he must leave none of it till morning.

[16]" 'If, however, his offering is the result of a vow or is a freewill offering, the sacrifice shall be eaten on the day he offers it, but anything left over may be eaten on the next day. [17]Any meat of the sacrifice left over till the third day must be burned up. [18]If any meat of the fellowship offering is eaten on the third day, it will not be accepted. It will not be credited to the one who offered it, for it is impure; the person who eats any of it will be held responsible.

---

[a] 18 Or *Whoever touches them must be holy*; similarly in verse 27   [b] 20 Or *each*   [c] 20 That is, probably about 2 quarts (about 2 liters)   [d] 21 The meaning of the Hebrew for this word is uncertain.   [e] 11 Traditionally *peace offering*; also in verses 13–37

19" 'Meat that touches anything ceremonially unclean must not be eaten; it must be burned up. As for other meat, anyone ceremonially clean may eat it. 20But if anyone who is unclean eats any meat of the fellowship offering belonging to the LORD, that person must be cut off from his people. 21If anyone touches something unclean—whether human uncleanness or an unclean animal or any unclean, detestable thing—and then eats any of the meat of the fellowship offering belonging to the LORD, that person must be cut off from his people.' "

Eating Fat and Blood Forbidden

22The LORD said to Moses, 23"Say to the Israelites: 'Do not eat any of the fat of cattle, sheep or goats. 24The fat of an animal found dead or torn by wild animals may be used for any other purpose, but you must not eat it. 25Anyone who eats the fat of an animal from which an offering by fire may be*a* made to the LORD must be cut off from his people. 26And wherever you live, you must not eat the blood of any bird or animal. 27If anyone eats blood, that person must be cut off from his people.' "

The Priests' Share

28The LORD said to Moses, 29"Say to the Israelites: 'Anyone who brings a fellowship offering to the LORD is to bring part of it as his sacrifice to the LORD. 30With his own hands he is to bring the offering made to the LORD by fire; he is to bring the fat, together with the breast, and wave the breast before the LORD as a wave offering. 31The priest shall burn the fat on the altar, but the breast belongs to Aaron and his sons. 32You are to give the right thigh of your fellowship offerings to the priest as a contribution. 33The son of Aaron who offers the blood and the fat of the fellowship offering shall have the right thigh as his share. 34From the fellowship offerings of the Israelites, I have taken the breast that is waved and the thigh that is presented and have given them to Aaron the priest and his sons as their regular share from the Israelites.' "

35This is the portion of the offerings made to the LORD by fire that were allotted to Aaron and his sons on the day

they were presented to serve the LORD as priests. 36On the day they were anointed, the LORD commanded that the Israelites give this to them as their regular share for the generations to come.

37These, then, are the regulations for the burnt offering, the grain offering, the sin offering, the guilt offering, the ordination offering and the fellowship offering, 38which the LORD gave Moses on Mount Sinai on the day he commanded the Israelites to bring their offerings to the LORD, in the Desert of Sinai.

The Ordination of Aaron and His Sons

8 The LORD said to Moses, 2"Bring Aaron and his sons, their garments, the anointing oil, the bull for the sin offering, the two rams and the basket containing bread made without yeast, 3and gather the entire assembly at the entrance to the Tent of Meeting." 4Moses did as the LORD commanded him, and the assembly gathered at the entrance to the Tent of Meeting.

5Moses said to the assembly, "This is what the LORD has commanded to be done." 6Then Moses brought Aaron and his sons forward and washed them with water. 7He put the tunic on Aaron, tied the sash around him, clothed him with the robe and put the ephod on him. He also tied the ephod to him by its skillfully woven waistband; so it was fastened on him. 8He placed the breastpiece on him and put the Urim and Thummim in the breastpiece. 9Then he placed the turban on Aaron's head and set the gold plate, the sacred diadem, on the front of it, as the LORD commanded Moses.

10Then Moses took the anointing oil and anointed the tabernacle and everything in it, and so consecrated them. 11He sprinkled some of the oil on the altar seven times, anointing the altar and all its utensils and the basin with its stand, to consecrate them. 12He poured some of the anointing oil on Aaron's head and anointed him to consecrate him. 13Then he brought Aaron's sons forward, put tunics on them, tied sashes around them and put headbands on them, as the LORD commanded Moses.

a 25 Or fire is

¹⁴He then presented the bull for the sin offering, and Aaron and his sons laid their hands on its head. ¹⁵Moses slaughtered the bull and took some of the blood, and with his finger he put it on all the horns of the altar to purify the altar. He poured out the rest of the blood at the base of the altar. So he consecrated it to make atonement for it. ¹⁶Moses also took all the fat around the inner parts, the covering of the liver, and both kidneys and their fat, and burned it on the altar. ¹⁷But the bull with its hide and its flesh and its offal he burned up outside the camp, as the LORD commanded Moses.

¹⁸He then presented the ram for the burnt offering, and Aaron and his sons laid their hands on its head. ¹⁹Then Moses slaughtered the ram and sprinkled the blood against the altar on all sides. ²⁰He cut the ram into pieces and burned the head, the pieces and the fat. ²¹He washed the inner parts and the legs with water and burned the whole ram on the altar as a burnt offering, a pleasing aroma, an offering made to the LORD by fire, as the LORD commanded Moses.

²²He then presented the other ram, the ram for the ordination, and Aaron and his sons laid their hands on its head. ²³Moses slaughtered the ram and took some of its blood and put it on the lobe of Aaron's right ear, on the thumb of his right hand and on the big toe of his right foot. ²⁴Moses also brought Aaron's sons forward and put some of the blood on the lobes of their right ears, on the thumbs of their right hands and on the big toes of their right feet. Then he sprinkled blood against the altar on all sides. ²⁵He took the fat, the fat tail, all the fat around the inner parts, the covering of the liver, both kidneys and their fat and the right thigh. ²⁶Then from the basket of bread made without yeast, which was before the LORD, he took a cake of bread, and one made with oil, and a wafer; he put these on the fat portions and on the right thigh. ²⁷He put all these in the hands of Aaron and his sons and waved them before the LORD as a wave offering. ²⁸Then Moses took them from their hands and burned them on the altar on top of the burnt offering as

an ordination offering, a pleasing aroma, an offering made to the LORD by fire. ²⁹He also took the breast—Moses' share of the ordination ram—and waved it before the LORD as a wave offering, as the LORD commanded Moses.

³⁰Then Moses took some of the anointing oil and some of the blood from the altar and sprinkled them on Aaron and his garments and on his sons and their garments. So he consecrated Aaron and his garments and his sons and their garments.

³¹Moses then said to Aaron and his sons, "Cook the meat at the entrance to the Tent of Meeting and eat it there with the bread from the basket of ordination offerings, as I commanded, saying,ᵃ 'Aaron and his sons are to eat it.' ³²Then burn up the rest of the meat and the bread. ³³Do not leave the entrance to the Tent of Meeting for seven days, until the days of your ordination are completed, for your ordination will last seven days. ³⁴What has been done today was commanded by the LORD to make atonement for you. ³⁵You must stay at the entrance to the Tent of Meeting day and night for seven days and do what the LORD requires, so you will not die; for that is what I have been commanded." ³⁶So Aaron and his sons did everything the LORD commanded through Moses.

The Priests Begin Their Ministry

9 On the eighth day Moses summoned Aaron and his sons and the elders of Israel. ²He said to Aaron, "Take a bull calf for your sin offering and a ram for your burnt offering, both without defect, and present them before the LORD. ³Then say to the Israelites: 'Take a male goat for a sin offering, a calf and a lamb—both a year old and without defect—for a burnt offering, ⁴and an oxᵇ and a ram for a fellowship offeringᶜ to sacrifice before the LORD, together with a grain offering mixed with oil. For today the LORD will appear to you.' "

⁵They took the things Moses commanded to the front of the Tent of Meeting, and the entire assembly came near and stood before the LORD. ⁶Then Moses said, "This is what the LORD has

---

ᵃ 31 Or I was commanded: ᵇ 4 The Hebrew word can include both male and female; also in verses 18 and 19.   ᶜ 4 Traditionally peace offering; also in verses 18 and 22

commanded you to do, so that the glory of the LORD may appear to you."

⁷Moses said to Aaron, "Come to the altar and sacrifice your sin offering and your burnt offering and make atonement for yourself and the people; sacrifice the offering that is for the people and make atonement for them, as the LORD has commanded."

⁸So Aaron came to the altar and

TUESDAY

SIN AND THE GLORY OF GOD
William Temple

VERSE: Leviticus 9:7, 22   PASSAGE: Leviticus 9:1–24

e tend to think of sin as consisting of acts which are done in defiance of conscience or are, whether we know it or not, contrary to God's command. Some people even say that so long as a man follows his conscience he cannot be committing sin. (The theologian would say that he is certainly not committing "formal sin" but he may be committing "material sin.") Certainly a man should follow his conscience; but that is not the whole of his duty. Still more important is it to enlighten conscience itself, lest "the light within you is darkness" (Matthew 6:23). The greatest crimes in history have been perpetrated at the bidding of conscience—such as the Spanish Inquisition. The disciples were warned to expect a time when *anyone who kills you will think he is offering a service to God* (John 16:2). A sin committed against the light is more wicked than another; the man who does it is more guilty. But sin is something much wider and deeper than guilt. Everything which is other than God would have it be is sin. "For all have sinned and fall short of the glory of God" (Romans 3:23); that is the definition of sin—to fall short of the glory of God! It is not enough that we should be as good as the people about us; nothing is enough except that we should be as good as God—"Be perfect, therefore, as your heavenly Father is perfect" (Matthew 5:48). But we shall not set ourselves that standard, to say nothing of attaining it, if we are left to our own resources. And we do not know what the perfection of God is until we have seen it in Christ. Unless we *believe on* him we are bound to be wrong in our whole idea about sin; for apart from that faith we have neither the stimulus nor the capacity to frame the true standard.

ADDITIONAL SCRIPTURE READING:
Leviticus 19:1–2; 1 Peter 1:14–16

Go to page 131 for your next devotional reading.

1900   Present

slaughtered the calf as a sin offering for himself. 9His sons brought the blood to him, and he dipped his finger into the blood and put it on the horns of the altar; the rest of the blood he poured out at the base of the altar. 10On the altar he burned the fat, the kidneys and the covering of the liver from the sin offering, as the LORD commanded Moses; 11the flesh and the hide he burned up outside the camp.

12Then he slaughtered the burnt offering. His sons handed him the blood, and he sprinkled it against the altar on all sides. 13They handed him the burnt offering piece by piece, including the head, and he burned them on the altar. 14He washed the inner parts and the legs and burned them on top of the burnt offering on the altar.

15Aaron then brought the offering that was for the people. He took the goat for the people's sin offering and slaughtered it and offered it for a sin offering as he did with the first one.

16He brought the burnt offering and offered it in the prescribed way. 17He also brought the grain offering, took a handful of it and burned it on the altar in addition to the morning's burnt offering.

18He slaughtered the ox and the ram as the fellowship offering for the people. His sons handed him the blood, and he sprinkled it against the altar on all sides. 19But the fat portions of the ox and the ram—the fat tail, the layer of fat, the kidneys and the covering of the liver— 20these they laid on the breasts, and then Aaron burned the fat on the altar. 21Aaron waved the breasts and the right thigh before the LORD as a wave offering, as Moses commanded.

22Then Aaron lifted his hands toward the people and blessed them. And having sacrificed the sin offering, the burnt offering and the fellowship offering, he stepped down.

23Moses and Aaron then went into the Tent of Meeting. When they came out, they blessed the people; and the glory of the LORD appeared to all the people. 24Fire came out from the presence of the LORD and consumed the burnt offering and the fat portions on the altar. And when all the people saw it, they shouted for joy and fell facedown.

The Death of Nadab and Abihu

10 Aaron's sons Nadab and Abihu took their censers, put fire in them and added incense; and they offered unauthorized fire before the LORD, contrary to his command. 2So fire came out from the presence of the LORD and consumed them, and they died before the LORD. 3Moses then said to Aaron, "This is what the LORD spoke of when he said:

" 'Among those who approach me
    I will show myself holy;
in the sight of all the people
    I will be honored.' "

Aaron remained silent.

4Moses summoned Mishael and Elzaphan, sons of Aaron's uncle Uzziel, and said to them, "Come here; carry your cousins outside the camp, away from the front of the sanctuary." 5So they came and carried them, still in their tunics, outside the camp, as Moses ordered.

6Then Moses said to Aaron and his sons Eleazar and Ithamar, "Do not let your hair become unkempt,a and do not tear your clothes, or you will die and the LORD will be angry with the whole community. But your relatives, all the house of Israel, may mourn for those the LORD has destroyed by fire. 7Do not leave the entrance to the Tent of Meeting or you will die, because the LORD's anointing oil is on you." So they did as Moses said.

8Then the LORD said to Aaron, 9"You and your sons are not to drink wine or other fermented drink whenever you go into the Tent of Meeting, or you will die. This is a lasting ordinance for the generations to come. 10You must distinguish between the holy and the common, between the unclean and the clean, 11and you must teach the Israelites all the decrees the LORD has given them through Moses."

12Moses said to Aaron and his remaining sons, Eleazar and Ithamar, "Take the grain offering left over from the offerings made to the LORD by fire and eat it prepared without yeast beside the altar, for it is most holy. 13Eat it in a holy place, because it is your share and your sons' share of the offerings made to the LORD

a 6 Or Do not uncover your heads

by fire; for so I have been commanded. [14]But you and your sons and your daughters may eat the breast that was waved and the thigh that was presented. Eat them in a ceremonially clean place; they have been given to you and your children as your share of the Israelites' fellowship offerings.[a] [15]The thigh that was presented and the breast that was waved must be brought with the fat portions of the offerings made by fire, to be waved before the LORD as a wave offering. This will be the regular share for you and your children, as the LORD has commanded."

[16]When Moses inquired about the goat of the sin offering and found that it had been burned up, he was angry with Eleazar and Ithamar, Aaron's remaining sons, and asked, [17]"Why didn't you eat the sin offering in the sanctuary area? It is most holy; it was given to you to take away the guilt of the community by making atonement for them before the LORD. [18]Since its blood was not taken into the Holy Place, you should have eaten the goat in the sanctuary area, as I commanded."

[19]Aaron replied to Moses, "Today they sacrificed their sin offering and their burnt offering before the LORD, but such things as this have happened to me. Would the LORD have been pleased if I had eaten the sin offering today?" [20]When Moses heard this, he was satisfied.

Clean and Unclean Food

11 The LORD said to Moses and Aaron, [2]"Say to the Israelites: 'Of all the animals that live on land, these are the ones you may eat: [3]You may eat any animal that has a split hoof completely divided and that chews the cud.

[4]" 'There are some that only chew the cud or only have a split hoof, but you must not eat them. The camel, though it chews the cud, does not have a split hoof; it is ceremonially unclean for you. [5]The coney,[b] though it chews the cud, does not have a split hoof; it is unclean for you. [6]The rabbit, though it chews the cud, does not have a split hoof; it is unclean for you. [7]And the pig, though it has a split hoof completely divided, does

not chew the cud; it is unclean for you. [8]You must not eat their meat or touch their carcasses; they are unclean for you.

[9]" 'Of all the creatures living in the water of the seas and the streams, you may eat any that have fins and scales. [10]But all creatures in the seas or streams that do not have fins and scales— whether among all the swarming things or among all the other living creatures in the water—you are to detest. [11]And since you are to detest them, you must not eat their meat and you must detest their carcasses. [12]Anything living in the water that does not have fins and scales is to be detestable to you.

[13]" 'These are the birds you are to detest and not eat because they are detestable: the eagle, the vulture, the black vulture, [14]the red kite, any kind of black kite, [15]any kind of raven, [16]the horned owl, the screech owl, the gull, any kind of hawk, [17]the little owl, the cormorant, the great owl, [18]the white owl, the desert owl, the osprey, [19]the stork, any kind of heron, the hoopoe and the bat.[c]

[20]" 'All flying insects that walk on all fours are to be detestable to you. [21]There are, however, some winged creatures that walk on all fours that you may eat: those that have jointed legs for hopping on the ground. [22]Of these you may eat any kind of locust, katydid, cricket or grasshopper. [23]But all other winged creatures that have four legs you are to detest.

[24]" 'You will make yourselves unclean by these; whoever touches their carcasses will be unclean till evening. [25]Whoever picks up one of their carcasses must wash his clothes, and he will be unclean till evening.

[26]" 'Every animal that has a split hoof not completely divided or that does not chew the cud is unclean for you; whoever touches ⌊the carcass of⌋ any of them will be unclean. [27]Of all the animals that walk on all fours, those that walk on their paws are unclean for you; whoever touches their carcasses will be unclean till evening. [28]Anyone who picks up their carcasses must wash his clothes, and he will be unclean till evening. They are unclean for you.

---

a 14 Traditionally *peace offerings*   *b 5* That is, the hyrax or rock badger   *c 19* The precise identification of some of the birds, insects and animals in this chapter is uncertain.

29" 'Of the animals that move about on the ground, these are unclean for you: the weasel, the rat, any kind of great lizard, 30the gecko, the monitor lizard, the wall lizard, the skink and the chameleon. 31Of all those that move along the ground, these are unclean for you. Whoever touches them when they are dead will be unclean till evening. 32When one of them dies and falls on something, that article, whatever its use, will be unclean, whether it is made of wood, cloth, hide or sackcloth. Put it in water; it will be unclean till evening, and then it will be clean. 33If one of them falls into a clay pot, everything in it will be unclean, and you must break the pot. 34Any food that could be eaten but has water on it from such a pot is unclean, and any liquid that could be drunk from it is unclean. 35Anything that one of their carcasses falls on becomes unclean; an oven or cooking pot must be broken up. They are unclean, and you are to regard them as unclean. 36A spring, however, or a cistern for collecting water remains clean, but anyone who touches one of these carcasses is unclean. 37If a carcass falls on any seeds that are to be planted, they remain clean. 38But if water has been put on the seed and a carcass falls on it, it is unclean for you.

39" 'If an animal that you are allowed to eat dies, anyone who touches the carcass will be unclean till evening. 40Anyone who eats some of the carcass must wash his clothes, and he will be unclean till evening. Anyone who picks up the carcass must wash his clothes, and he will be unclean till evening.

41" 'Every creature that moves about on the ground is detestable; it is not to be eaten. 42You are not to eat any creature that moves about on the ground, whether it moves on its belly or walks on all fours or on many feet; it is detestable. 43Do not defile yourselves by any of these creatures. Do not make yourselves unclean by means of them or be made unclean by them. 44I am the LORD your God; consecrate yourselves and be holy, because I am holy. Do not make yourselves unclean by any creature that moves about on the ground. 45I am the LORD who brought you up out of Egypt to be your God; therefore be holy, because I am holy.

46" 'These are the regulations concerning animals, birds, every living thing that moves in the water and every creature that moves about on the ground. 47You must distinguish between the unclean and the clean, between living creatures that may be eaten and those that may not be eaten.' "

Purification After Childbirth

12 The LORD said to Moses, 2"Say to the Israelites: 'A woman who becomes pregnant and gives birth to a son will be ceremonially unclean for seven days, just as she is unclean during her monthly period. 3On the eighth day the boy is to be circumcised. 4Then the woman must wait thirty-three days to be purified from her bleeding. She must not touch anything sacred or go to the sanctuary until the days of her purification are over. 5If she gives birth to a daughter, for two weeks the woman will be unclean, as during her period. Then she must wait sixty-six days to be purified from her bleeding.

6" 'When the days of her purification for a son or daughter are over, she is to bring to the priest at the entrance to the Tent of Meeting a year-old lamb for a burnt offering and a young pigeon or a dove for a sin offering. 7He shall offer them before the LORD to make atonement for her, and then she will be ceremonially clean from her flow of blood.

" 'These are the regulations for the woman who gives birth to a boy or a girl. 8If she cannot afford a lamb, she is to bring two doves or two young pigeons, one for a burnt offering and the other for a sin offering. In this way the priest will make atonement for her, and she will be clean.' "

Regulations About Infectious Skin Diseases

13 The LORD said to Moses and Aaron, 2"When anyone has a swelling or a rash or a bright spot on his skin that may become an infectious skin disease,*a* he must be brought to

---

a 2 Traditionally *leprosy;* the Hebrew word was used for various diseases affecting the skin—not necessarily leprosy; also elsewhere in this chapter.

Aaron the priest or to one of his sons*a*
who is a priest. ³The priest is to examine the sore on his skin, and if the hair
in the sore has turned white and the sore
appears to be more than skin deep,*b* it is
an infectious skin disease. When the
priest examines him, he shall pronounce
him ceremonially unclean. ⁴If the spot
on his skin is white but does not appear
to be more than skin deep and the hair
in it has not turned white, the priest is
to put the infected person in isolation
for seven days. ⁵On the seventh day the
priest is to examine him, and if he sees
that the sore is unchanged and has not
spread in the skin, he is to keep him in
isolation another seven days. ⁶On the
seventh day the priest is to examine him
again, and if the sore has faded and has
not spread in the skin, the priest shall
pronounce him clean; it is only a rash.
The man must wash his clothes, and he
will be clean. ⁷But if the rash does
spread in his skin after he has shown
himself to the priest to be pronounced
clean, he must appear before the priest
again. ⁸The priest is to examine him,
and if the rash has spread in the skin, he
shall pronounce him unclean; it is an
infectious disease.

⁹"When anyone has an infectious skin
disease, he must be brought to the
priest. ¹⁰The priest is to examine him,
and if there is a white swelling in the
skin that has turned the hair white and
if there is raw flesh in the swelling, ¹¹it
is a chronic skin disease and the priest
shall pronounce him unclean. He is not
to put him in isolation, because he is
already unclean.

¹²"If the disease breaks out all over his
skin and, so far as the priest can see, it
covers all the skin of the infected person
from head to foot, ¹³the priest is to
examine him, and if the disease has covered his whole body, he shall pronounce
that person clean. Since it has all turned
white, he is clean. ¹⁴But whenever raw
flesh appears on him, he will be unclean. ¹⁵When the priest sees the raw
flesh, he shall pronounce him unclean.
The raw flesh is unclean; he has an
infectious disease. ¹⁶Should the raw
flesh change and turn white, he must go
to the priest. ¹⁷The priest is to examine

him, and if the sores have turned white,
the priest shall pronounce the infected
person clean; then he will be clean.

¹⁸"When someone has a boil on his
skin and it heals, ¹⁹and in the place
where the boil was, a white swelling or
reddish-white spot appears, he must
present himself to the priest. ²⁰The
priest is to examine it, and if it appears to
be more than skin deep and the hair in it
has turned white, the priest shall pronounce him unclean. It is an infectious
skin disease that has broken out where
the boil was. ²¹But if, when the priest
examines it, there is no white hair in it
and it is not more than skin deep and has
faded, then the priest is to put him in isolation for seven days. ²²If it is spreading
in the skin, the priest shall pronounce
him unclean; it is infectious. ²³But if the
spot is unchanged and has not spread, it
is only a scar from the boil, and the priest
shall pronounce him clean.

²⁴"When someone has a burn on his
skin and a reddish-white or white spot
appears in the raw flesh of the burn,
²⁵the priest is to examine the spot, and if
the hair in it has turned white, and it
appears to be more than skin deep, it is
an infectious disease that has broken
out in the burn. The priest shall pronounce him unclean; it is an infectious
skin disease. ²⁶But if the priest examines
it and there is no white hair in the spot
and if it is not more than skin deep and
has faded, then the priest is to put him
in isolation for seven days. ²⁷On the seventh day the priest is to examine him,
and if it is spreading in the skin, the
priest shall pronounce him unclean; it is
an infectious skin disease. ²⁸If, however,
the spot is unchanged and has not
spread in the skin but has faded, it is a
swelling from the burn, and the priest
shall pronounce him clean; it is only a
scar from the burn.

²⁹"If a man or woman has a sore on
the head or on the chin, ³⁰the priest is
to examine the sore, and if it appears to
be more than skin deep and the hair in
it is yellow and thin, the priest shall
pronounce that person unclean; it is an
itch, an infectious disease of the head or
chin. ³¹But if, when the priest examines
this kind of sore, it does not seem to be

---

a 2 Or *descendants*   *b 3* Or *be lower than the rest of the skin;* also elsewhere in this chapter more than skin deep and there is no black hair in it, then the priest is to put the infected person in isolation for seven days. ³²On the seventh day the priest is to examine the sore, and if the itch has not spread and there is no yellow hair in it and it does not appear to be more than skin deep, ³³he must be shaved except for the diseased area, and the priest is to keep him in isolation another seven days. ³⁴On the seventh day the priest is to examine the itch, and if it has not spread in the skin and appears to be no more than skin deep, the priest shall pronounce him clean. He must wash his clothes, and he will be clean. ³⁵But if the itch does spread in the skin after he is pronounced clean, ³⁶the priest is to examine him, and if the itch has spread in the skin, the priest does not need to look for yellow hair; the person is unclean. ³⁷If, however, in his judgment it is unchanged and black hair has grown in it, the itch is healed. He is clean, and the priest shall pronounce him clean.

³⁸"When a man or woman has white spots on the skin, ³⁹the priest is to examine them, and if the spots are dull white, it is a harmless rash that has broken out on the skin; that person is clean.

⁴⁰"When a man has lost his hair and is bald, he is clean. ⁴¹If he has lost his hair from the front of his scalp and has a bald forehead, he is clean. ⁴²But if he has a reddish-white sore on his bald head or forehead, it is an infectious disease breaking out on his head or forehead. ⁴³The priest is to examine him, and if the swollen sore on his head or forehead is reddish-white like an infectious skin disease, ⁴⁴the man is diseased and is unclean. The priest shall pronounce him unclean because of the sore on his head.

⁴⁵"The person with such an infectious disease must wear torn clothes, let his hair be unkempt,ᵃ cover the lower part of his face and cry out, 'Unclean! Unclean!' ⁴⁶As long as he has the infection he remains unclean. He must live alone; he must live outside the camp.

Regulations About Mildew

⁴⁷"If any clothing is contaminated with mildew—any woolen or linen clothing, ⁴⁸any woven or knitted material of linen or wool, any leather or anything made of leather— ⁴⁹and if the contamination in the clothing, or leather, or woven or knitted material, or any leather article, is greenish or reddish, it is a spreading mildew and must be shown to the priest. ⁵⁰The priest is to examine the mildew and isolate the affected article for seven days. ⁵¹On the seventh day he is to examine it, and if the mildew has spread in the clothing, or the woven or knitted material, or the leather, whatever its use, it is a destructive mildew; the article is unclean. ⁵²He must burn up the clothing, or the woven or knitted material of wool or linen, or any leather article that has the contamination in it, because the mildew is destructive; the article must be burned up.

⁵³"But if, when the priest examines it, the mildew has not spread in the clothing, or the woven or knitted material, or the leather article, ⁵⁴he shall order that the contaminated article be washed. Then he is to isolate it for another seven days. ⁵⁵After the affected article has been washed, the priest is to examine it, and if the mildew has not changed its appearance, even though it has not spread, it is unclean. Burn it with fire, whether the mildew has affected one side or the other. ⁵⁶If, when the priest examines it, the mildew has faded after the article has been washed, he is to tear the contaminated part out of the clothing, or the leather, or the woven or knitted material. ⁵⁷But if it reappears in the clothing, or in the woven or knitted material, or in the leather article, it is spreading, and whatever has the mildew must be burned with fire. ⁵⁸The clothing, or the woven or knitted material, or any leather article that has been washed and is rid of the mildew, must be washed again, and it will be clean."

⁵⁹These are the regulations concerning contamination by mildew in woolen or linen clothing, woven or knitted material, or any leather article, for pronouncing them clean or unclean.

ᵃ 45 Or *clothes, uncover his head*

Cleansing From Infectious Skin Diseases

14 The LORD said to Moses, 2"These are the regulations for the diseased person at the time of his ceremonial cleansing, when he is brought to the priest: 3The priest is to go outside the camp and examine him. If the person has been healed of his infectious skin disease,*a* 4the priest shall order that two live clean birds and some cedar wood, scarlet yarn and hyssop be brought for the one to be cleansed. 5Then the priest shall order that one of the birds be killed over fresh water in a clay pot. 6He is then to take the live bird and dip it, together with the cedar wood, the scarlet yarn and the hyssop, into the blood of the bird that was killed over the fresh water. 7Seven times he shall sprinkle the one to be cleansed of the infectious disease and pronounce him clean. Then he is to release the live bird in the open fields.

8"The person to be cleansed must wash his clothes, shave off all his hair and bathe with water; then he will be ceremonially clean. After this he may come into the camp, but he must stay outside his tent for seven days. 9On the seventh day he must shave off all his hair; he must shave his head, his beard, his eyebrows and the rest of his hair. He must wash his clothes and bathe himself with water, and he will be clean.

10"On the eighth day he must bring two male lambs and one ewe lamb a year old, each without defect, along with three-tenths of an ephah*b* of fine flour mixed with oil for a grain offering, and one log*c* of oil. 11The priest who pronounces him clean shall present both the one to be cleansed and his offerings before the LORD at the entrance to the Tent of Meeting.

12"Then the priest is to take one of the male lambs and offer it as a guilt offering, along with the log of oil; he shall wave them before the LORD as a wave offering. 13He is to slaughter the lamb in the holy place where the sin offering and the burnt offering are slaughtered. Like the sin offering, the guilt offering belongs to the priest; it is most holy. 14The priest is to take some of the blood of the guilt offering and put it on the lobe of the right ear of the one to be cleansed, on the thumb of his right hand and on the big toe of his right foot. 15The priest shall then take some of the log of oil, pour it in the palm of his own left hand, 16dip his right forefinger into the oil in his palm, and with his finger sprinkle some of it before the LORD seven times. 17The priest is to put some of the oil remaining in his palm on the lobe of the right ear of the one to be cleansed, on the thumb of his right hand and on the big toe of his right foot, on top of the blood of the guilt offering. 18The rest of the oil in his palm the priest shall put on the head of the one to be cleansed and make atonement for him before the LORD.

19"Then the priest is to sacrifice the sin offering and make atonement for the one to be cleansed from his uncleanness. After that, the priest shall slaughter the burnt offering 20and offer it on the altar, together with the grain offering, and make atonement for him, and he will be clean.

21"If, however, he is poor and cannot afford these, he must take one male lamb as a guilt offering to be waved to make atonement for him, together with a tenth of an ephah*d* of fine flour mixed with oil for a grain offering, a log of oil, 22and two doves or two young pigeons, which he can afford, one for a sin offering and the other for a burnt offering.

23"On the eighth day he must bring them for his cleansing to the priest at the entrance to the Tent of Meeting, before the LORD. 24The priest is to take the lamb for the guilt offering, together with the log of oil, and wave them before the LORD as a wave offering. 25He shall slaughter the lamb for the guilt offering and take some of its blood and put it on the lobe of the right ear of the one to be cleansed, on the thumb of his right hand and on the big toe of his right foot. 26The priest is to pour some of the oil into the palm of his own left hand,

---

a 3 Traditionally *leprosy*; the Hebrew word was used for various diseases affecting the skin—not necessarily leprosy; also elsewhere in this chapter.   *b 10* That is, probably about 6 quarts (about 6.5 liters)   *c 10* That is, probably about 2/3 pint (about 0.3 liter); also in verses 12, 15, 21 and 24   *d 21* That is, probably about 2 quarts (about 2 liters)

27and with his right forefinger sprinkle some of the oil from his palm seven times before the LORD. 28Some of the oil in his palm he is to put on the same places he put the blood of the guilt offering—on the lobe of the right ear of the one to be cleansed, on the thumb of his right hand and on the big toe of his right foot. 29The rest of the oil in his palm the priest shall put on the head of the one to be cleansed, to make atonement for him before the LORD. 30Then he shall sacrifice the doves or the young pigeons, which the person can afford, 31one*a* as a sin offering and the other as a burnt offering, together with the grain offering. In this way the priest will make atonement before the LORD on behalf of the one to be cleansed."

32These are the regulations for anyone who has an infectious skin disease and who cannot afford the regular offerings for his cleansing.

Cleansing From Mildew

33The LORD said to Moses and Aaron, 34"When you enter the land of Canaan, which I am giving you as your possession, and I put a spreading mildew in a house in that land, 35the owner of the house must go and tell the priest, 'I have seen something that looks like mildew in my house.' 36The priest is to order the house to be emptied before he goes in to examine the mildew, so that nothing in the house will be pronounced unclean. After this the priest is to go in and inspect the house. 37He is to examine the mildew on the walls, and if it has greenish or reddish depressions that appear to be deeper than the surface of the wall, 38the priest shall go out the doorway of the house and close it up for seven days. 39On the seventh day the priest shall return to inspect the house. If the mildew has spread on the walls, 40he is to order that the contaminated stones be torn out and thrown into an unclean place outside the town. 41He must have all the inside walls of the house scraped and the material that is scraped off dumped into an unclean place outside the town. 42Then they are to take other stones to replace these and take new clay and plaster the house.

43"If the mildew reappears in the house after the stones have been torn out and the house scraped and plastered, 44the priest is to go and examine it and, if the mildew has spread in the house, it is a destructive mildew; the house is unclean. 45It must be torn down—its stones, timbers and all the plaster—and taken out of the town to an unclean place.

46"Anyone who goes into the house while it is closed up will be unclean till evening. 47Anyone who sleeps or eats in the house must wash his clothes.

48"But if the priest comes to examine it and the mildew has not spread after the house has been plastered, he shall pronounce the house clean, because the mildew is gone. 49To purify the house he is to take two birds and some cedar wood, scarlet yarn and hyssop. 50He shall kill one of the birds over fresh water in a clay pot. 51Then he is to take the cedar wood, the hyssop, the scarlet yarn and the live bird, dip them into the blood of the dead bird and the fresh water, and sprinkle the house seven times. 52He shall purify the house with the bird's blood, the fresh water, the live bird, the cedar wood, the hyssop and the scarlet yarn. 53Then he is to release the live bird in the open fields outside the town. In this way he will make atonement for the house, and it will be clean."

54These are the regulations for any infectious skin disease, for an itch, 55for mildew in clothing or in a house, 56and for a swelling, a rash or a bright spot, 57to determine when something is clean or unclean.

These are the regulations for infectious skin diseases and mildew.

Discharges Causing Uncleanness

15 The LORD said to Moses and Aaron, 2"Speak to the Israelites and say to them: 'When any man has a bodily discharge, the discharge is unclean. 3Whether it continues flowing from his body or is blocked, it will make him unclean. This is how his discharge will bring about uncleanness:

4" 'Any bed the man with a discharge lies on will be unclean, and anything he sits on will be unclean. 5Anyone who

---

a 31 Septuagint and Syriac; Hebrew *31such as the person can afford, one*

touches his bed must wash his clothes and bathe with water, and he will be unclean till evening. ⁶Whoever sits on anything that the man with a discharge sat on must wash his clothes and bathe with water, and he will be unclean till evening.

⁷" 'Whoever touches the man who has a discharge must wash his clothes and bathe with water, and he will be unclean till evening.

⁸" 'If the man with the discharge spits on someone who is clean, that person must wash his clothes and bathe with water, and he will be unclean till evening.

⁹" 'Everything the man sits on when riding will be unclean, ¹⁰and whoever touches any of the things that were under him will be unclean till evening; whoever picks up those things must wash his clothes and bathe with water, and he will be unclean till evening.

¹¹" 'Anyone the man with a discharge touches without rinsing his hands with water must wash his clothes and bathe with water, and he will be unclean till evening.

¹²" 'A clay pot that the man touches must be broken, and any wooden article is to be rinsed with water.

¹³" 'When a man is cleansed from his discharge, he is to count off seven days for his ceremonial cleansing; he must wash his clothes and bathe himself with fresh water, and he will be clean. ¹⁴On the eighth day he must take two doves or two young pigeons and come before the LORD to the entrance to the Tent of Meeting and give them to the priest. ¹⁵The priest is to sacrifice them, the one for a sin offering and the other for a burnt offering. In this way he will make atonement before the LORD for the man because of his discharge.

¹⁶" 'When a man has an emission of semen, he must bathe his whole body with water, and he will be unclean till evening. ¹⁷Any clothing or leather that has semen on it must be washed with water, and it will be unclean till evening. ¹⁸When a man lies with a woman and there is an emission of semen, both must bathe with water, and they will be unclean till evening.

¹⁹" 'When a woman has her regular flow of blood, the impurity of her monthly period will last seven days, and anyone who touches her will be unclean till evening.

²⁰" 'Anything she lies on during her period will be unclean, and anything she sits on will be unclean. ²¹Whoever touches her bed must wash his clothes and bathe with water, and he will be unclean till evening. ²²Whoever touches anything she sits on must wash his clothes and bathe with water, and he will be unclean till evening. ²³Whether it is the bed or anything she was sitting on, when anyone touches it, he will be unclean till evening.

²⁴" 'If a man lies with her and her monthly flow touches him, he will be unclean for seven days; any bed he lies on will be unclean.

²⁵" 'When a woman has a discharge of blood for many days at a time other than her monthly period or has a discharge that continues beyond her period, she will be unclean as long as she has the discharge, just as in the days of her period. ²⁶Any bed she lies on while her discharge continues will be unclean, as is her bed during her monthly period, and anything she sits on will be unclean, as during her period. ²⁷Whoever touches them will be unclean; he must wash his clothes and bathe with water, and he will be unclean till evening.

²⁸" 'When she is cleansed from her discharge, she must count off seven days, and after that she will be ceremonially clean. ²⁹On the eighth day she must take two doves or two young pigeons and bring them to the priest at the entrance to the Tent of Meeting. ³⁰The priest is to sacrifice one for a sin offering and the other for a burnt offering. In this way he will make atonement for her before the LORD for the uncleanness of her discharge.

³¹" 'You must keep the Israelites separate from things that make them unclean, so they will not die in their uncleanness for defiling my dwelling place,ᵃ which is among them.' "

³²These are the regulations for a man with a discharge, for anyone made unclean by an emission of semen, ³³for a

ᵃ 31 Or my tabernacle

woman in her monthly period, for a man or a woman with a discharge, and for a man who lies with a woman who is ceremonially unclean.

The Day of Atonement

16 The LORD spoke to Moses after the death of the two sons of Aaron who died when they approached the LORD. ²The LORD said to Moses: "Tell your brother Aaron not to come whenever he chooses into the Most Holy Place behind the curtain in front of the atonement cover on the ark, or else he will die, because I appear in the cloud over the atonement cover.

³"This is how Aaron is to enter the sanctuary area: with a young bull for a sin offering and a ram for a burnt offering. ⁴He is to put on the sacred linen tunic, with linen undergarments next to his body; he is to tie the linen sash around him and put on the linen turban. These are sacred garments; so he must bathe himself with water before he puts them on. ⁵From the Israelite community he is to take two male goats for a sin offering and a ram for a burnt offering.

⁶"Aaron is to offer the bull for his own sin offering to make atonement for himself and his household. ⁷Then he is to take the two goats and present them before the LORD at the entrance to the Tent of Meeting. ⁸He is to cast lots for the two goats—one lot for the LORD and the other for the scapegoat.ᵃ ⁹Aaron shall bring the goat whose lot falls to the LORD and sacrifice it for a sin offering. ¹⁰But the goat chosen by lot as the scapegoat shall be presented alive before the LORD to be used for making atonement by sending it into the desert as a scapegoat.

¹¹"Aaron shall bring the bull for his own sin offering to make atonement for himself and his household, and he is to slaughter the bull for his own sin offering. ¹²He is to take a censer full of burning coals from the altar before the LORD and two handfuls of finely ground fragrant incense and take them behind the curtain. ¹³He is to put the incense on the fire before the LORD, and the smoke of the incense will conceal the atonement cover above the Testimony, so that he will not die. ¹⁴He is to take some

of the bull's blood and with his finger sprinkle it on the front of the atonement cover; then he shall sprinkle some of it with his finger seven times before the atonement cover.

¹⁵"He shall then slaughter the goat for the sin offering for the people and take its blood behind the curtain and do with it as he did with the bull's blood: He shall sprinkle it on the atonement cover and in front of it. ¹⁶In this way he will make atonement for the Most Holy Place because of the uncleanness and rebellion of the Israelites, whatever their sins have been. He is to do the same for the Tent of Meeting, which is among them in the midst of their uncleanness. ¹⁷No one is to be in the Tent of Meeting from the time Aaron goes in to make atonement in the Most Holy Place until he comes out, having made atonement for himself, his household and the whole community of Israel.

¹⁸"Then he shall come out to the altar that is before the LORD and make atonement for it. He shall take some of the bull's blood and some of the goat's blood and put it on all the horns of the altar. ¹⁹He shall sprinkle some of the blood on it with his finger seven times to cleanse it and to consecrate it from the uncleanness of the Israelites.

²⁰"When Aaron has finished making atonement for the Most Holy Place, the Tent of Meeting and the altar, he shall bring forward the live goat. ²¹He is to lay both hands on the head of the live goat and confess over it all the wickedness and rebellion of the Israelites—all their sins—and put them on the goat's head. He shall send the goat away into the desert in the care of a man appointed for the task. ²²The goat will carry on itself all their sins to a solitary place; and the man shall release it in the desert.

²³"Then Aaron is to go into the Tent of Meeting and take off the linen garments he put on before he entered the Most Holy Place, and he is to leave them there. ²⁴He shall bathe himself with water in a holy place and put on his regular garments. Then he shall come out and sacrifice the burnt offering for himself and the burnt offering for the people, to make atonement for himself

---

ᵃ 8 That is, the goat of removal; Hebrew *azazel*; also in verses 10 and 26

and for the people. ²⁵He shall also burn the fat of the sin offering on the altar. ²⁶"The man who releases the goat as a scapegoat must wash his clothes and bathe himself with water; afterward he may come into the camp. ²⁷The bull and

OF THE SCAPEGOAT
Epistle of Barnabas

VERSE: Leviticus 16:8   PASSAGE: Leviticus 16:2–34

otice the directions he gave. *Take a couple of goats, unblemished and well-matched; bring them for an offering, and let the priest take one of them for a burnt-offering.* And what are they to do with the other? *The other,* he declares, *is accursed.* (Now see how plainly the type of Jesus appears.) *Spit on it, all of you; thrust your goads into it, wreathe its head with scarlet wool, and so let it be driven out into the desert.* This is done, and the goat-ward leads the animal into the desert, where he takes off the wool and leaves it there, on the bush we call a bramble (the plant we usually eat the berries of, if we come across it in the countryside; nothing has such tasty fruit as a bramble). Now what does that signify? Notice that the first goat is for the altar, and the other is accursed; and that it is the accursed one that wears the wreath. That is because they shall see him on that day clad to the ankles in his red woollen robe, and will say, "Is not this he whom we once crucified, and mocked and pierced and spat upon? Yes, this is the man who told us that he was the son of God." But how will he resemble the goat? The point of there being two similar goats, both of them fair and alike, is that when they see him coming on the day, they are going to be struck with terror at the manifest parallel between him and the goat. In this ordinance, then, you are to see typified the future sufferings of Jesus.

But why should they put the wool on the thorns? This too is a type of Jesus, meant for the church's instruction. For if one wanted to take the scarlet wool for himself, it would cost him much suffering, since the thorns were fearsome and could only be mastered with anguish. Similarly, says he, those who would behold me and possess my kingdom must go through affliction and suffering before they can reach me.

ADDITIONAL SCRIPTURE READING:
Numbers 29:7–11; Hebrews 9:1–14, 24–26

Go to page 133 for your next devotional reading.

100   500

the goat for the sin offerings, whose blood was brought into the Most Holy Place to make atonement, must be taken outside the camp; their hides, flesh and offal are to be burned up. ²⁸The man who burns them must wash his clothes and bathe himself with water; afterward he may come into the camp.

²⁹"This is to be a lasting ordinance for you: On the tenth day of the seventh month you must deny yourselves*ᵃ* and not do any work—whether native-born or an alien living among you— ³⁰because on this day atonement will be made for you, to cleanse you. Then, before the LORD, you will be clean from all your sins. ³¹It is a sabbath of rest, and you must deny yourselves; it is a lasting ordinance. ³²The priest who is anointed and ordained to succeed his father as high priest is to make atonement. He is to put on the sacred linen garments ³³and make atonement for the Most Holy Place, for the Tent of Meeting and the altar, and for the priests and all the people of the community.

³⁴"This is to be a lasting ordinance for you: Atonement is to be made once a year for all the sins of the Israelites."

And it was done, as the LORD commanded Moses.

Eating Blood Forbidden

17 The LORD said to Moses, ²"Speak to Aaron and his sons and to all the Israelites and say to them: 'This is what the LORD has commanded: ³Any Israelite who sacrifices an ox,*ᵇ* a lamb or a goat in the camp or outside of it ⁴instead of bringing it to the entrance to the Tent of Meeting to present it as an offering to the LORD in front of the tabernacle of the LORD—that man shall be considered guilty of bloodshed; he has shed blood and must be cut off from his people. ⁵This is so the Israelites will bring to the LORD the sacrifices they are now making in the open fields. They must bring them to the priest, that is, to the LORD, at the entrance to the Tent of Meeting and sacrifice them as fellowship offerings.*ᶜ* ⁶The priest is to sprinkle the blood against the altar of the LORD at the entrance to the Tent of Meeting and

burn the fat as an aroma pleasing to the LORD. ⁷They must no longer offer any of their sacrifices to the goat idols*ᵈ* to whom they prostitute themselves. This is to be a lasting ordinance for them and for the generations to come.'

⁸"Say to them: 'Any Israelite or any alien living among them who offers a burnt offering or sacrifice ⁹and does not bring it to the entrance to the Tent of Meeting to sacrifice it to the LORD—that man must be cut off from his people.

¹⁰" 'Any Israelite or any alien living among them who eats any blood—I will set my face against that person who eats blood and will cut him off from his people. ¹¹For the life of a creature is in the blood, and I have given it to you to make atonement for yourselves on the altar; it is the blood that makes atonement for one's life. ¹²Therefore I say to the Israelites, "None of you may eat blood, nor may an alien living among you eat blood."

¹³" 'Any Israelite or any alien living among you who hunts any animal or bird that may be eaten must drain out the blood and cover it with earth, ¹⁴because the life of every creature is its blood. That is why I have said to the Israelites, "You must not eat the blood of any creature, because the life of every creature is its blood; anyone who eats it must be cut off."

¹⁵" 'Anyone, whether native-born or alien, who eats anything found dead or torn by wild animals must wash his clothes and bathe with water, and he will be ceremonially unclean till evening; then he will be clean. ¹⁶But if he does not wash his clothes and bathe himself, he will be held responsible.' "

Unlawful Sexual Relations

18 The LORD said to Moses, ²"Speak to the Israelites and say to them: 'I am the LORD your God. ³You must not do as they do in Egypt, where you used to live, and you must not do as they do in the land of Canaan, where I am bringing you. Do not follow their practices. ⁴You must obey my laws and be careful to follow my decrees. I am the LORD your God. ⁵Keep my

ᵃ 29 Or *must fast;* also in verse 31   *ᵇ 3* The Hebrew word can include both male and female.
ᶜ 5 Traditionally *peace offerings*   *ᵈ 7* Or *demons*

decrees and laws, for the man who obeys them will live by them. I am the LORD.

⁶" 'No one is to approach any close relative to have sexual relations. I am the LORD.

⁷" 'Do not dishonor your father by having sexual relations with your mother. She is your mother; do not have relations with her.

⁸" 'Do not have sexual relations with your father's wife; that would dishonor your father.

⁹" 'Do not have sexual relations with your sister, either your father's daughter or your mother's daughter, whether she was born in the same home or elsewhere.

¹⁰" 'Do not have sexual relations with your son's daughter or your daughter's daughter; that would dishonor you.

THURSDAY

NOT WITHOUT BLOOD
Andrew Murray

VERSE: Leviticus 17:11   **PASSAGE:** Leviticus 17:10–12

od has made more than one covenant with man, but ever, not without blood! And why? . . . The life is in the blood. The blood shed is the token of death, life taken away . . . The shed blood sprinkled upon the altar, or the person, is the proof that death has been endured, that the penalty of the transgressions, for which atonement is being made, has been borne. In some cases the hands were laid upon the head of the sacrifice, confessing over it, and laying upon it, the sin to be atoned for. The shed blood upon the altar was the pledge that God accepted the death of the substitute: the sins were covered by the blood, and the guilty one restored to God's favor . . .

Not without blood! This is the wondrous note that rings through all Scripture, from Abel's sacrifice at the gate of paradise to the song of the ransomed in Revelation (see Genesis 4:4; Revelation 7:14). God is willing to receive fallen man back again to his fellowship, to admit him to his heart and his love, to make a covenant with him, to give full assurance of all this; but—not without blood. Even his own Son, the almighty and all-perfect One, the gift of his eternal love, even he could only redeem us, by the sacrifice of himself . . .

Not without blood! In earth and heaven, in each moment of our life, in each thought and act of worship, this word reigns supreme. There can be no fellowship with God, but in the blood, in the death, of his blessed Son.

ADDITIONAL SCRIPTURE READING:
Deuteronomy 12:23–27; Hebrews 9:18–22

Go to page 135 for your next devotional reading.

1700   1900

11 "'Do not have sexual relations with the daughter of your father's wife, born to your father; she is your sister.

12 "'Do not have sexual relations with your father's sister; she is your father's close relative.

13 "'Do not have sexual relations with your mother's sister, because she is your mother's close relative.

14 "'Do not dishonor your father's brother by approaching his wife to have sexual relations; she is your aunt.

15 "'Do not have sexual relations with your daughter-in-law. She is your son's wife; do not have relations with her.

16 "'Do not have sexual relations with your brother's wife; that would dishonor your brother.

17 "'Do not have sexual relations with both a woman and her daughter. Do not have sexual relations with either her son's daughter or her daughter's daughter; they are her close relatives. That is wickedness.

18 "'Do not take your wife's sister as a rival wife and have sexual relations with her while your wife is living.

19 "'Do not approach a woman to have sexual relations during the uncleanness of her monthly period.

20 "'Do not have sexual relations with your neighbor's wife and defile yourself with her.

21 "'Do not give any of your children to be sacrificed*a* to Molech, for you must not profane the name of your God. I am the LORD.

22 "'Do not lie with a man as one lies with a woman; that is detestable.

23 "'Do not have sexual relations with an animal and defile yourself with it. A woman must not present herself to an animal to have sexual relations with it; that is a perversion.

24 "'Do not defile yourselves in any of these ways, because this is how the nations that I am going to drive out before you became defiled. **25**Even the land was defiled; so I punished it for its sin, and the land vomited out its inhabitants. **26**But you must keep my decrees and my laws. The native-born and the aliens living among you must not do any of these detestable things, **27**for all these things were done by the people

who lived in the land before you, and the land became defiled. **28**And if you defile the land, it will vomit you out as it vomited out the nations that were before you.

29 "'Everyone who does any of these detestable things—such persons must be cut off from their people. **30**Keep my requirements and do not follow any of the detestable customs that were practiced before you came and do not defile yourselves with them. I am the LORD your God.' "

Various Laws

19 The LORD said to Moses, **2**"Speak to the entire assembly of Israel and say to them: 'Be holy because I, the LORD your God, am holy.

3 "'Each of you must respect his mother and father, and you must observe my Sabbaths. I am the LORD your God.

4 "'Do not turn to idols or make gods of cast metal for yourselves. I am the LORD your God.

5 "'When you sacrifice a fellowship offering*b* to the LORD, sacrifice it in such a way that it will be accepted on your behalf. **6**It shall be eaten on the day you sacrifice it or on the next day; anything left over until the third day must be burned up. **7**If any of it is eaten on the third day, it is impure and will not be accepted. **8**Whoever eats it will be held responsible because he has desecrated what is holy to the LORD; that person must be cut off from his people.

9 "'When you reap the harvest of your land, do not reap to the very edges of your field or gather the gleanings of your harvest. **10**Do not go over your vineyard a second time or pick up the grapes that have fallen. Leave them for the poor and the alien. I am the LORD your God.

11 "'Do not steal.

"'Do not lie.

"'Do not deceive one another.

12 "'Do not swear falsely by my name and so profane the name of your God. I am the LORD.

13 "'Do not defraud your neighbor or rob him.

"'Do not hold back the wages of a hired man overnight.

a 21 Or *to be passed through the fire*   *b 5* Traditionally *peace offering*

14" 'Do not curse the deaf or put a stumbling block in front of the blind, but fear your God. I am the LORD.

15" 'Do not pervert justice; do not show partiality to the poor or favoritism to the great, but judge your neighbor fairly.

FRIDAY

THE PROBLEM OF SELF-LOVE
François Fénelon

VERSE: Leviticus 19:18   **PASSAGE:** Leviticus 19:11–18

elf-love must be uprooted, and the love of God take its place in our hearts before we can see ourselves as we are. Then the same principle that enables us to see our imperfections will destroy them. When the light of truth has risen within us, then we see clearly what is there. Then we love ourselves without partiality, without flattery, as we love our neighbor. In the meantime, God spares us by revealing our weakness to us just in proportion as our strength to support the view of it increases. We discover our imperfections one by one as we are able to cure them. Without this merciful preparation that adapts our strength to the light within, we should be in despair. Those who correct others ought to watch the moment when God touches their hearts; they must bear a fault with patience till they perceive his spirit reproaching them within. Then they must follow his providence that gently reproaches them, so that they may feel that it is less God than their own hearts that condemns them. When we blame with impatience because we are displeased with the fault, it is a human censure and not the disapprobation of God. It is a sensitive self-love that cannot forgive the self-love of others. The more self-love we have, the more severe are our censures. There is nothing so vexatious as the collisions between one excessive self-love and another still more violent and sensitive. The passions of others are infinitely ridiculous to those who are under the dominion of their own. The ways of God are very different. He is ever full of kindness for us, he gives us strength, he regards us with pity and condescension, he remembers our weakness, he waits for us. The less we love ourselves, the more considerate we are of others. We wait for providence to give the occasion, and grace to open their hearts to receive it. If you would gather the fruit before its time, you lose it entirely.

ADDITIONAL SCRIPTURE READING:
Mark 12:31–34; Luke 10:27–37; Romans 13:9–10

Go to page 138 for your next devotional reading.

1500   1700

16" 'Do not go about spreading slander among your people.

" 'Do not do anything that endangers your neighbor's life. I am the LORD.

17" 'Do not hate your brother in your heart. Rebuke your neighbor frankly so you will not share in his guilt.

18" 'Do not seek revenge or bear a grudge against one of your people, but love your neighbor as yourself. I am the LORD.

HOW SELDOM WE WEIGH OUR NEIGHBOR IN THE SAME BALANCE WITH OURSELVES.

—*Thomas à Kempis*

19" 'Keep my decrees.

" 'Do not mate different kinds of animals.

" 'Do not plant your field with two kinds of seed.

" 'Do not wear clothing woven of two kinds of material.

20" 'If a man sleeps with a woman who is a slave girl promised to another man but who has not been ransomed or given her freedom, there must be due punishment. Yet they are not to be put to death, because she had not been freed. 21The man, however, must bring a ram to the entrance to the Tent of Meeting for a guilt offering to the LORD. 22With the ram of the guilt offering the priest is to make atonement for him before the LORD for the sin he has committed, and his sin will be forgiven.

23" 'When you enter the land and plant any kind of fruit tree, regard its fruit as forbidden.*a* For three years you are to consider it forbidden*a*; it must not be eaten. 24In the fourth year all its fruit will be holy, an offering of praise to the LORD. 25In the fifth year you may eat its fruit. In this way your harvest will be increased. I am the LORD your God.

26" 'Do not eat any meat with the blood still in it.

" 'Do not practice divination or sorcery.

27" 'Do not cut the hair at the sides of your head or clip off the edges of your beard.

28" 'Do not cut your bodies for the dead or put tattoo marks on yourselves. I am the LORD.

29" 'Do not degrade your daughter by making her a prostitute, or the land will turn to prostitution and be filled with wickedness.

30" 'Observe my Sabbaths and have reverence for my sanctuary. I am the LORD.

31" 'Do not turn to mediums or seek out spiritists, for you will be defiled by them. I am the LORD your God.

32" 'Rise in the presence of the aged, show respect for the elderly and revere your God. I am the LORD.

33" 'When an alien lives with you in your land, do not mistreat him. 34The alien living with you must be treated as one of your native-born. Love him as yourself, for you were aliens in Egypt. I am the LORD your God.

35" 'Do not use dishonest standards when measuring length, weight or quantity. 36Use honest scales and honest weights, an honest ephah*b* and an honest hin.*c* I am the LORD your God, who brought you out of Egypt.

37" 'Keep all my decrees and all my laws and follow them. I am the LORD.' "

Punishments for Sin

20 The LORD said to Moses, 2"Say to the Israelites: 'Any Israelite or any alien living in Israel who gives*d* any of his children to Molech must be put to death. The people of the community are to stone him. 3I will set my face against that man and I will cut him off from his people; for by giving his children to Molech, he has defiled my sanctuary and profaned my holy name. 4If the people of the community close their eyes when that man gives one of his children to Molech and they fail to put him to death, 5I will set my face against that man and his family and will cut off from their people both him and all who follow him in prostituting themselves to Molech.

6" 'I will set my face against the person who turns to mediums and spiritists to prostitute himself by following them, and I will cut him off from his people.

---

a 23 Hebrew *uncircumcised*   *b 36* An ephah was a dry measure.   *c 36* A hin was a liquid measure.
d 2 Or *sacrifices;* also in verses 3 and 4

⁷" 'Consecrate yourselves and be holy, because I am the LORD your God. ⁸Keep my decrees and follow them. I am the LORD, who makes you holy.ᵃ

⁹" 'If anyone curses his father or mother, he must be put to death. He has cursed his father or his mother, and his blood will be on his own head.

¹⁰" 'If a man commits adultery with another man's wife—with the wife of his neighbor—both the adulterer and the adulteress must be put to death.

¹¹" 'If a man sleeps with his father's wife, he has dishonored his father. Both the man and the woman must be put to death; their blood will be on their own heads.

¹²" 'If a man sleeps with his daughter-in-law, both of them must be put to death. What they have done is a perversion; their blood will be on their own heads.

¹³" 'If a man lies with a man as one lies with a woman, both of them have done what is detestable. They must be put to death; their blood will be on their own heads.

¹⁴" 'If a man marries both a woman and her mother, it is wicked. Both he and they must be burned in the fire, so that no wickedness will be among you.

¹⁵" 'If a man has sexual relations with an animal, he must be put to death, and you must kill the animal.

¹⁶" 'If a woman approaches an animal to have sexual relations with it, kill both the woman and the animal. They must be put to death; their blood will be on their own heads.

¹⁷" 'If a man marries his sister, the daughter of either his father or his mother, and they have sexual relations, it is a disgrace. They must be cut off before the eyes of their people. He has dishonored his sister and will be held responsible.

¹⁸" 'If a man lies with a woman during her monthly period and has sexual relations with her, he has exposed the source of her flow, and she has also uncovered it. Both of them must be cut off from their people.

¹⁹" 'Do not have sexual relations with the sister of either your mother or your father, for that would dishonor a close relative; both of you would be held responsible.

²⁰" 'If a man sleeps with his aunt, he has dishonored his uncle. They will be held responsible; they will die childless.

²¹" 'If a man marries his brother's wife, it is an act of impurity; he has dishonored his brother. They will be childless.

²²" 'Keep all my decrees and laws and follow them, so that the land where I am bringing you to live may not vomit you out. ²³You must not live according to the customs of the nations I am going to drive out before you. Because they did all these things, I abhorred them. ²⁴But I said to you, "You will possess their land; I will give it to you as an inheritance, a land flowing with milk and honey." I am the LORD your God, who has set you apart from the nations.

²⁵" 'You must therefore make a distinction between clean and unclean animals and between unclean and clean birds. Do not defile yourselves by any animal or bird or anything that moves along the ground—those which I have set apart as unclean for you. ²⁶You are to be holy to meᵇ because I, the LORD, am holy, and I have set you apart from the nations to be my own.

²⁷" 'A man or woman who is a medium or spiritist among you must be put to death. You are to stone them; their blood will be on their own heads.' "

Rules for Priests

21 The LORD said to Moses, "Speak to the priests, the sons of Aaron, and say to them: 'A priest must not make himself ceremonially unclean for any of his people who die, ²except for a close relative, such as his mother or father, his son or daughter, his brother, ³or an unmarried sister who is dependent on him since she has no husband—for her he may make himself unclean. ⁴He must not make himself unclean for people related to him by marriage,ᶜ and so defile himself.

⁵" 'Priests must not shave their heads or shave off the edges of their beards or cut their bodies. ⁶They must be holy to their God and must not profane the name of their God. Because they present

---

ᵃ 8 Or who sanctifies you; or who sets you apart as holy as a leader among his people   ᵇ 26 Or be my holy ones   ᶜ 4 Or unclean

WEEKEND

THE PILLAR OF THE CLOUD
Cardinal John Henry Newman

VERSE: Exodus 13:21   **PASSAGE:** Exodus 13:17–22

ead, kindly light, amid the circling gloom,
    Lead thou me on!
The night is dark, and I am far from home—
    Lead thou me on!
Keep thou my feet; I do not ask to see
The distant scene,—one step enough for me.

I was not ever thus, nor prayed that thou
    Shouldest lead me on!
I loved to choose and see my path; but now
    Lead thou me on!
I loved the garish day, and, spite of fears,
Pride ruled my will: remember not past years.

So long thy power hast blest me, sure it still
    Will lead me on,
O'er moor and fen, o'er crag and torrent, till
    The night is gone;
And with the morn those angel faces smile
Which I have loved long since, and lost awhile.

ADDITIONAL SCRIPTURE READING:
Exodus 14:19–24; Numbers 9:15–23; Psalm 105:39–45

Go to page 144 for your next devotional reading.

1700   1900

the offerings made to the Lord by fire, the food of their God, they are to be holy.

7" 'They must not marry women defiled by prostitution or divorced from their husbands, because priests are holy to their God. 8Regard them as holy, because they offer up the food of your God. Consider them holy, because I the Lord am holy—I who make you holy.*a*

9" 'If a priest's daughter defiles herself by becoming a prostitute, she disgraces her father; she must be burned in the fire.

10" 'The high priest, the one among his brothers who has had the anointing oil poured on his head and who has been ordained to wear the priestly garments, must not let his hair become unkempt*b* or tear his clothes. 11He must not enter a place where there is a dead body. He must not make himself unclean, even for his father or mother, 12nor leave the sanctuary of his God or desecrate it, because he has been dedicated by the anointing oil of his God. I am the Lord.

13" 'The woman he marries must be a virgin. 14He must not marry a widow, a divorced woman, or a woman defiled by prostitution, but only a virgin from his own people, 15so he will not defile his offspring among his people. I am the Lord, who makes him holy.*c* '"

16The Lord said to Moses, 17"Say to Aaron: 'For the generations to come none of your descendants who has a defect may come near to offer the food of his God. 18No man who has any defect may come near: no man who is blind or lame, disfigured or deformed; 19no man with a crippled foot or hand, 20or who is hunchbacked or dwarfed, or who has any eye defect, or who has festering or running sores or damaged testicles. 21No descendant of Aaron the priest who has any defect is to come near to present the offerings made to the Lord by fire. He has a defect; he must not come near to offer the food of his God. 22He may eat the most holy food of his God, as well as the holy food; 23yet because of his defect, he must not go near the curtain or approach the altar, and so desecrate my sanctuary. I am the Lord, who makes them holy.*d* '"

24So Moses told this to Aaron and his sons and to all the Israelites.

22 The Lord said to Moses, 2"Tell Aaron and his sons to treat with respect the sacred offerings the Israelites consecrate to me, so they will not profane my holy name. I am the Lord.

3"Say to them: 'For the generations to come, if any of your descendants is ceremonially unclean and yet comes near the sacred offerings that the Israelites consecrate to the Lord, that person must be cut off from my presence. I am the Lord.

4" 'If a descendant of Aaron has an infectious skin disease*e* or a bodily discharge, he may not eat the sacred offerings until he is cleansed. He will also be unclean if he touches something defiled by a corpse or by anyone who has an emission of semen, 5or if he touches any crawling thing that makes him unclean, or any person who makes him unclean, whatever the uncleanness may be. 6The one who touches any such thing will be unclean till evening. He must not eat any of the sacred offerings unless he has bathed himself with water. 7When the sun goes down, he will be clean, and after that he may eat the sacred offerings, for they are his food. 8He must not eat anything found dead or torn by wild animals, and so become unclean through it. I am the Lord.

9" 'The priests are to keep my requirements so that they do not become guilty and die for treating them with contempt. I am the Lord, who makes them holy.*f*

10" 'No one outside a priest's family may eat the sacred offering, nor may the guest of a priest or his hired worker eat it. 11But if a priest buys a slave with money, or if a slave is born in his household, that slave may eat his food. 12If a priest's daughter marries anyone other than a priest, she may not eat any of the sacred contributions. 13But if a priest's daughter becomes a widow or is divorced, yet has no children, and she returns to live in her father's house as in her youth, she may eat of her father's

---

a 8 Or *who sanctify you; or who set you apart as holy   b 10* Or *not uncover his head   c 15* Or *who sanctifies him; or who sets him apart as holy   d 23* Or *who sanctifies them; or who sets them apart as holy   e 4* Traditionally *leprosy;* the Hebrew word was used for various diseases affecting the skin—not necessarily leprosy.   *f 9* Or *who sanctifies them; or who sets them apart as holy;* also in verse 16

food. No unauthorized person, however, may eat any of it.

14" 'If anyone eats a sacred offering by mistake, he must make restitution to the priest for the offering and add a fifth of the value to it. 15The priests must not desecrate the sacred offerings the Israelites present to the LORD 16by allowing them to eat the sacred offerings and so bring upon them guilt requiring payment. I am the LORD, who makes them holy.' "

Unacceptable Sacrifices

17The LORD said to Moses, 18"Speak to Aaron and his sons and to all the Israelites and say to them: 'If any of you—either an Israelite or an alien living in Israel—presents a gift for a burnt offering to the LORD, either to fulfill a vow or as a freewill offering, 19you must present a male without defect from the cattle, sheep or goats in order that it may be accepted on your behalf. 20Do not bring anything with a defect, because it will not be accepted on your behalf. 21When anyone brings from the herd or flock a fellowship offering*a* to the LORD to fulfill a special vow or as a freewill offering, it must be without defect or blemish to be acceptable. 22Do not offer to the LORD the blind, the injured or the maimed, or anything with warts or festering or running sores. Do not place any of these on the altar as an offering made to the LORD by fire. 23You may, however, present as a freewill offering an ox*b* or a sheep that is deformed or stunted, but it will not be accepted in fulfillment of a vow. 24You must not offer to the LORD an animal whose testicles are bruised, crushed, torn or cut. You must not do this in your own land, 25and you must not accept such animals from the hand of a foreigner and offer them as the food of your God. They will not be accepted on your behalf, because they are deformed and have defects.' "

26The LORD said to Moses, 27"When a calf, a lamb or a goat is born, it is to remain with its mother for seven days. From the eighth day on, it will be acceptable as an offering made to the LORD by

fire. 28Do not slaughter a cow or a sheep and its young on the same day.

29"When you sacrifice a thank offering to the LORD, sacrifice it in such a way that it will be accepted on your behalf. 30It must be eaten that same day; leave none of it till morning. I am the LORD.

31"Keep my commands and follow them. I am the LORD. 32Do not profane my holy name. I must be acknowledged as holy by the Israelites. I am the LORD, who makes*c* you holy*d* 33and who brought you out of Egypt to be your God. I am the LORD."

23 The LORD said to Moses, 2"Speak to the Israelites and say to them: 'These are my appointed feasts, the appointed feasts of the LORD, which you are to proclaim as sacred assemblies.

The Sabbath

3" 'There are six days when you may work, but the seventh day is a Sabbath of rest, a day of sacred assembly. You are not to do any work; wherever you live, it is a Sabbath to the LORD.

The Passover and Unleavened Bread

4" 'These are the LORD's appointed feasts, the sacred assemblies you are to proclaim at their appointed times: 5The LORD's Passover begins at twilight on the fourteenth day of the first month. 6On the fifteenth day of that month the LORD's Feast of Unleavened Bread begins; for seven days you must eat bread made without yeast. 7On the first day hold a sacred assembly and do no regular work. 8For seven days present an offering made to the LORD by fire. And on the seventh day hold a sacred assembly and do no regular work.' "

Firstfruits

9The LORD said to Moses, 10"Speak to the Israelites and say to them: 'When you enter the land I am going to give you and you reap its harvest, bring to the priest a sheaf of the first grain you harvest. 11He is to wave the sheaf before the LORD so it will be accepted on your

---

a 21 Traditionally *peace offering*   *b 23* The Hebrew word can include both male and female.
c 32 Or *made*   *d 32* Or *who sanctifies you;* or *who sets you apart as holy*

behalf; the priest is to wave it on the day after the Sabbath. ¹²On the day you wave the sheaf, you must sacrifice as a burnt offering to the LORD a lamb a year old without defect, ¹³together with its grain offering of two-tenths of an ephah*a* of fine flour mixed with oil—an offering made to the LORD by fire, a pleasing aroma—and its drink offering of a quarter of a hin*b* of wine. ¹⁴You must not eat any bread, or roasted or new grain, until the very day you bring this offering to your God. This is to be a lasting ordinance for the generations to come, wherever you live.

Feast of Weeks

¹⁵" 'From the day after the Sabbath, the day you brought the sheaf of the wave offering, count off seven full weeks. ¹⁶Count off fifty days up to the day after the seventh Sabbath, and then present an offering of new grain to the LORD. ¹⁷From wherever you live, bring two loaves made of two-tenths of an ephah of fine flour, baked with yeast, as a wave offering of firstfruits to the LORD. ¹⁸Present with this bread seven male lambs, each a year old and without defect, one young bull and two rams. They will be a burnt offering to the LORD, together with their grain offerings and drink offerings—an offering made by fire, an aroma pleasing to the LORD. ¹⁹Then sacrifice one male goat for a sin offering and two lambs, each a year old, for a fellowship offering.*c* ²⁰The priest is to wave the two lambs before the LORD as a wave offering, together with the bread of the firstfruits. They are a sacred offering to the LORD for the priest. ²¹On that same day you are to proclaim a sacred assembly and do no regular work. This is to be a lasting ordinance for the generations to come, wherever you live.

²²" 'When you reap the harvest of your land, do not reap to the very edges of your field or gather the gleanings of your harvest. Leave them for the poor and the alien. I am the LORD your God.' "

Feast of Trumpets

²³The LORD said to Moses, ²⁴"Say to the Israelites: 'On the first day of the seventh month you are to have a day of rest, a sacred assembly commemorated with trumpet blasts. ²⁵Do no regular work, but present an offering made to the LORD by fire.' "

Day of Atonement

²⁶The LORD said to Moses, ²⁷"The tenth day of this seventh month is the Day of Atonement. Hold a sacred assembly and deny yourselves,*d* and present an offering made to the LORD by fire. ²⁸Do no work on that day, because it is the Day of Atonement, when atonement is made for you before the LORD your God. ²⁹Anyone who does not deny himself on that day must be cut off from his people. ³⁰I will destroy from among his people anyone who does any work on that day. ³¹You shall do no work at all. This is to be a lasting ordinance for the generations to come, wherever you live. ³²It is a sabbath of rest for you, and you must deny yourselves. From the evening of the ninth day of the month until the following evening you are to observe your sabbath."

Feast of Tabernacles

³³The LORD said to Moses, ³⁴"Say to the Israelites: 'On the fifteenth day of the seventh month the LORD's Feast of Tabernacles begins, and it lasts for seven days. ³⁵The first day is a sacred assembly; do no regular work. ³⁶For seven days present offerings made to the LORD by fire, and on the eighth day hold a sacred assembly and present an offering made to the LORD by fire. It is the closing assembly; do no regular work.

³⁷(" 'These are the LORD's appointed feasts, which you are to proclaim as sacred assemblies for bringing offerings made to the LORD by fire—the burnt offerings and grain offerings, sacrifices and drink offerings required for each day. ³⁸These offerings are in addition to those for the LORD's Sabbaths and*e* in addition to your gifts and whatever you

---

a 13 That is, probably about 4 quarts (about 4.5 liters); also in verse 17   *b 13* That is, probably about 1 quart (about 1 liter)   *c 19* Traditionally *peace offering*   *d 27* Or *and fast;* also in verses 29 and 32
e 38 Or *These feasts are in addition to the LORD's Sabbaths, and these offerings are*

have vowed and all the freewill offerings you give to the LORD.)

39" 'So beginning with the fifteenth day of the seventh month, after you have gathered the crops of the land, celebrate the festival to the LORD for seven days; the first day is a day of rest, and the eighth day also is a day of rest. 40On the first day you are to take choice fruit from the trees, and palm fronds, leafy branches and poplars, and rejoice before the LORD your God for seven days. 41Celebrate this as a festival to the LORD for seven days each year. This is to be a lasting ordinance for the generations to come; celebrate it in the seventh month. 42Live in booths for seven days: All native-born Israelites are to live in booths 43so your descendants will know that I had the Israelites live in booths when I brought them out of Egypt. I am the LORD your God.' "

44So Moses announced to the Israelites the appointed feasts of the LORD.

Oil and Bread Set Before the LORD

24 The LORD said to Moses, 2"Command the Israelites to bring you clear oil of pressed olives for the light so that the lamps may be kept burning continually. 3Outside the curtain of the Testimony in the Tent of Meeting, Aaron is to tend the lamps before the LORD from evening till morning, continually. This is to be a lasting ordinance for the generations to come. 4The lamps on the pure gold lampstand before the LORD must be tended continually.

5"Take fine flour and bake twelve loaves of bread, using two-tenths of an ephah*a* for each loaf. 6Set them in two rows, six in each row, on the table of pure gold before the LORD. 7Along each row put some pure incense as a memorial portion to represent the bread and to be an offering made to the LORD by fire. 8This bread is to be set out before the LORD regularly, Sabbath after Sabbath, on behalf of the Israelites, as a lasting covenant. 9It belongs to Aaron and his sons, who are to eat it in a holy place, because it is a most holy part of their regular share of the offerings made to the LORD by fire."

a 5 That is, probably about 4 quarts (about 4.5 liters)

A Blasphemer Stoned

10Now the son of an Israelite mother and an Egyptian father went out among the Israelites, and a fight broke out in the camp between him and an Israelite. 11The son of the Israelite woman blasphemed the Name with a curse; so they brought him to Moses. (His mother's name was Shelomith, the daughter of Dibri the Danite.) 12They put him in custody until the will of the LORD should be made clear to them.

13Then the LORD said to Moses: 14"Take the blasphemer outside the camp. All those who heard him are to lay their hands on his head, and the entire assembly is to stone him. 15Say to the Israelites: 'If anyone curses his God, he will be held responsible; 16anyone who blasphemes the name of the LORD must be put to death. The entire assembly must stone him. Whether an alien or native-born, when he blasphemes the Name, he must be put to death.

17" 'If anyone takes the life of a human being, he must be put to death. 18Anyone who takes the life of someone's animal must make restitution— life for life. 19If anyone injures his neighbor, whatever he has done must be done to him: 20fracture for fracture, eye for eye, tooth for tooth. As he has injured the other, so he is to be injured. 21Whoever kills an animal must make restitution, but whoever kills a man must be put to death. 22You are to have the same law for the alien and the native-born. I am the LORD your God.' "

23Then Moses spoke to the Israelites, and they took the blasphemer outside the camp and stoned him. The Israelites did as the LORD commanded Moses.

The Sabbath Year

25 The LORD said to Moses on Mount Sinai, 2"Speak to the Israelites and say to them: 'When you enter the land I am going to give you, the land itself must observe a sabbath to the LORD. 3For six years sow your fields, and for six years prune your vineyards and gather their crops. 4But in the seventh year the land is to have a sabbath of rest, a sabbath to the LORD. Do not sow

your fields or prune your vineyards. ⁵Do not reap what grows of itself or harvest the grapes of your untended vines. The land is to have a year of rest. ⁶Whatever the land yields during the sabbath year will be food for you—for yourself, your manservant and maidservant, and the hired worker and temporary resident who live among you, ⁷as well as for your livestock and the wild animals in your land. Whatever the land produces may be eaten.

The Year of Jubilee

⁸" 'Count off seven sabbaths of years—seven times seven years—so that the seven sabbaths of years amount to a period of forty-nine years. ⁹Then have the trumpet sounded everywhere on the tenth day of the seventh month; on the Day of Atonement sound the trumpet throughout your land. ¹⁰Consecrate the fiftieth year and proclaim liberty throughout the land to all its inhabitants. It shall be a jubilee for you; each one of you is to return to his family property and each to his own clan. ¹¹The fiftieth year shall be a jubilee for you; do not sow and do not reap what grows of itself or harvest the untended vines. ¹²For it is a jubilee and is to be holy for you; eat only what is taken directly from the fields.

¹³" 'In this Year of Jubilee everyone is to return to his own property.

¹⁴" 'If you sell land to one of your countrymen or buy any from him, do not take advantage of each other. ¹⁵You are to buy from your countryman on the basis of the number of years since the Jubilee. And he is to sell to you on the basis of the number of years left for harvesting crops. ¹⁶When the years are many, you are to increase the price, and when the years are few, you are to decrease the price, because what he is really selling you is the number of crops. ¹⁷Do not take advantage of each other, but fear your God. I am the LORD your God.

¹⁸" 'Follow my decrees and be careful to obey my laws, and you will live safely in the land. ¹⁹Then the land will yield its fruit, and you will eat your fill and live there in safety. ²⁰You may ask, "What will we eat in the seventh year if we do not plant or harvest our crops?"

²¹I will send you such a blessing in the sixth year that the land will yield enough for three years. ²²While you plant during the eighth year, you will eat from the old crop and will continue to eat from it until the harvest of the ninth year comes in.

²³" 'The land must not be sold permanently, because the land is mine and you are but aliens and my tenants. ²⁴Throughout the country that you hold as a possession, you must provide for the redemption of the land.

²⁵" 'If one of your countrymen becomes poor and sells some of his property, his nearest relative is to come and redeem what his countryman has sold. ²⁶If, however, a man has no one to redeem it for him but he himself prospers and acquires sufficient means to redeem it, ²⁷he is to determine the value for the years since he sold it and refund the balance to the man to whom he sold it; he can then go back to his own property. ²⁸But if he does not acquire the means to repay him, what he sold will remain in the possession of the buyer until the Year of Jubilee. It will be returned in the Jubilee, and he can then go back to his property.

²⁹" 'If a man sells a house in a walled city, he retains the right of redemption a full year after its sale. During that time he may redeem it. ³⁰If it is not redeemed before a full year has passed, the house in the walled city shall belong permanently to the buyer and his descendants. It is not to be returned in the Jubilee. ³¹But houses in villages without walls around them are to be considered as open country. They can be redeemed, and they are to be returned in the Jubilee.

³²" 'The Levites always have the right to redeem their houses in the Levitical towns, which they possess. ³³So the property of the Levites is redeemable—that is, a house sold in any town they hold—and is to be returned in the Jubilee, because the houses in the towns of the Levites are their property among the Israelites. ³⁴But the pastureland belonging to their towns must not be sold; it is their permanent possession.

³⁵" 'If one of your countrymen becomes poor and is unable to support himself among you, help him as you

UNCEASING DEPENDENCE—CONTINUAL PEACE
François Fénelon

VERSE: Leviticus 25:21   **PASSAGE:** Leviticus 25:18–22

 o not dwell upon remote events; this anxiety about the future is contrary to a religious state of mind. When God bestows any blessings upon you, look only to him in the comfort that you receive, and take every day of the manna that he sends you, as the Israelites did, without making yourself any provision for the morrow.

A life of faith produces two things. First, it enables us to see God in everything. Secondly, it holds the mind in a state of readiness for whatever may be his will. We must trust to God for whatever depends upon him, and only think of being faithful ourselves in the performance of our duties. This continual, unceasing dependence, this state of entire peace and acquiescence of the soul in whatever may happen, is the true, silent martyrdom of self. It is so slow, and gradual, and internal, that they who experience it are hardly conscious of it.

When God deprives you of any blessing, he can replace it either by other instruments or by himself. The very stones can in his hands become the children of Abraham. Sufficient for the day is the evil thereof; the morrow will take care of itself (see Matthew 6:34). He who has fed you today will take care of you tomorrow.

We shall sooner see the manna fall from heaven in the desert than the children of God shall want support.

Meditation

I sleep, but my heart waketh.

We sleep in peace in the arms of God when we yield ourselves up to his providence in a delightful consciousness of his tender mercies; no more restless uncertainties, no more anxious desires, no more impatience at the place we are in; for it is God who has put us there and who holds us in his arms. Can we be unsafe where he has placed us, and where he watches over us as a parent watches a child? This confiding repose, in which earthly care sleeps, is the true vigilance of the heart; yielding itself up to God, with no other support than him, it thus watches while we sleep. This is the love of him that will not sleep even in death. Amen.

ADDITIONAL SCRIPTURE READING:
Jeremiah 17:7–8; John 14:1; Philippians 4:6–7

Go to page 165 for your next devotional reading.

would an alien or a temporary resident, so he can continue to live among you. ³⁶Do not take interest of any kind*a* from him, but fear your God, so that your countryman may continue to live among you. ³⁷You must not lend him money at interest or sell him food at a profit. ³⁸I am the LORD your God, who brought you out of Egypt to give you the land of Canaan and to be your God.

³⁹" 'If one of your countrymen becomes poor among you and sells himself to you, do not make him work as a slave. ⁴⁰He is to be treated as a hired worker or a temporary resident among you; he is to work for you until the Year of Jubilee. ⁴¹Then he and his children are to be released, and he will go back to his own clan and to the property of his forefathers. ⁴²Because the Israelites are my servants, whom I brought out of Egypt, they must not be sold as slaves. ⁴³Do not rule over them ruthlessly, but fear your God.

⁴⁴" 'Your male and female slaves are to come from the nations around you; from them you may buy slaves. ⁴⁵You may also buy some of the temporary residents living among you and members of their clans born in your country, and they will become your property. ⁴⁶You can will them to your children as inherited property and can make them slaves for life, but you must not rule over your fellow Israelites ruthlessly.

⁴⁷" 'If an alien or a temporary resident among you becomes rich and one of your countrymen becomes poor and sells himself to the alien living among you or to a member of the alien's clan, ⁴⁸he retains the right of redemption after he has sold himself. One of his relatives may redeem him: ⁴⁹An uncle or a cousin or any blood relative in his clan may redeem him. Or if he prospers, he may redeem himself. ⁵⁰He and his buyer are to count the time from the year he sold himself up to the Year of Jubilee. The price for his release is to be based on the rate paid to a hired man for that number of years. ⁵¹If many years remain, he must pay for his redemption a larger share of the price paid for him. ⁵²If only a few years remain until the Year of Jubilee, he is to compute that and pay for his redemption accordingly. ⁵³He is to be treated as a man hired from year to year; you must see to it that his owner does not rule over him ruthlessly.

⁵⁴" 'Even if he is not redeemed in any of these ways, he and his children are to be released in the Year of Jubilee, ⁵⁵for the Israelites belong to me as servants. They are my servants, whom I brought out of Egypt. I am the LORD your God.

Reward for Obedience

26 " 'Do not make idols or set up an image or a sacred stone for yourselves, and do not place a carved stone in your land to bow down before it. I am the LORD your God.

²" 'Observe my Sabbaths and have reverence for my sanctuary. I am the LORD.

³" 'If you follow my decrees and are careful to obey my commands, ⁴I will send you rain in its season, and the ground will yield its crops and the trees of the field their fruit. ⁵Your threshing will continue until grape harvest and the grape harvest will continue until planting, and you will eat all the food you want and live in safety in your land.

⁶" 'I will grant peace in the land, and you will lie down and no one will make you afraid. I will remove savage beasts from the land, and the sword will not pass through your country. ⁷You will pursue your enemies, and they will fall by the sword before you. ⁸Five of you will chase a hundred, and a hundred of you will chase ten thousand, and your enemies will fall by the sword before you.

⁹" 'I will look on you with favor and make you fruitful and increase your numbers, and I will keep my covenant with you. ¹⁰You will still be eating last year's harvest when you will have to move it out to make room for the new. ¹¹I will put my dwelling place*b* among you, and I will not abhor you. ¹²I will walk among you and be your God, and you will be my people. ¹³I am the LORD your God, who brought you out of Egypt so that you would no longer be slaves to the Egyptians; I broke the bars of your yoke and enabled you to walk with heads held high.

---

a 36 Or *take excessive interest*; similarly in verse 37   *b* 11 Or *my tabernacle*

Punishment for Disobedience

14 " 'But if you will not listen to me and carry out all these commands, **15**and if you reject my decrees and abhor my laws and fail to carry out all my commands and so violate my covenant, **16**then I will do this to you: I will bring upon you sudden terror, wasting diseases and fever that will destroy your sight and drain away your life. You will plant seed in vain, because your enemies will eat it. **17**I will set my face against you so that you will be defeated by your enemies; those who hate you will rule over you, and you will flee even when no one is pursuing you.

18 " 'If after all this you will not listen to me, I will punish you for your sins seven times over. **19**I will break down your stubborn pride and make the sky above you like iron and the ground beneath you like bronze. **20**Your strength will be spent in vain, because your soil will not yield its crops, nor will the trees of the land yield their fruit.

21 " 'If you remain hostile toward me and refuse to listen to me, I will multiply your afflictions seven times over, as your sins deserve. **22**I will send wild animals against you, and they will rob you of your children, destroy your cattle and make you so few in number that your roads will be deserted.

23 " 'If in spite of these things you do not accept my correction but continue to be hostile toward me, **24**I myself will be hostile toward you and will afflict you for your sins seven times over. **25**And I will bring the sword upon you to avenge the breaking of the covenant. When you withdraw into your cities, I will send a plague among you, and you will be given into enemy hands. **26**When I cut off your supply of bread, ten women will be able to bake your bread in one oven, and they will dole out the bread by weight. You will eat, but you will not be satisfied.

27 " 'If in spite of this you still do not listen to me but continue to be hostile toward me, **28**then in my anger I will be hostile toward you, and I myself will punish you for your sins seven times over. **29**You will eat the flesh of your sons and the flesh of your daughters. **30**I will destroy your high places, cut down

your incense altars and pile your dead bodies on the lifeless forms of your idols, and I will abhor you. **31**I will turn your cities into ruins and lay waste your sanctuaries, and I will take no delight in the pleasing aroma of your offerings. **32**I will lay waste the land, so that your enemies who live there will be appalled. **33**I will scatter you among the nations and will draw out my sword and pursue you. Your land will be laid waste, and your cities will lie in ruins. **34**Then the land will enjoy its sabbath years all the time that it lies desolate and you are in the country of your enemies; then the land will rest and enjoy its sabbaths. **35**All the time that it lies desolate, the land will have the rest it did not have during the sabbaths you lived in it.

36 " 'As for those of you who are left, I will make their hearts so fearful in the lands of their enemies that the sound of a windblown leaf will put them to flight. They will run as though fleeing from the sword, and they will fall, even though no one is pursuing them. **37**They will stumble over one another as though fleeing from the sword, even though no one is pursuing them. So you will not be able to stand before your enemies. **38**You will perish among the nations; the land of your enemies will devour you. **39**Those of you who are left will waste away in the lands of their enemies because of their sins; also because of their fathers' sins they will waste away.

40 " 'But if they will confess their sins and the sins of their fathers—their treachery against me and their hostility toward me, **41**which made me hostile toward them so that I sent them into the land of their enemies—then when their uncircumcised hearts are humbled and they pay for their sin, **42**I will remember my covenant with Jacob and my covenant with Isaac and my covenant with Abraham, and I will remember the land. **43**For the land will be deserted by them and will enjoy its sabbaths while it lies desolate without them. They will pay for their sins because they rejected my laws and abhorred my decrees. **44**Yet in spite of this, when they are in the land of their enemies, I will not reject them or abhor them so as to destroy them completely, breaking my covenant with them. I am the LORD their God. ⁴⁵But for their sake I will remember the covenant with their ancestors whom I brought out of Egypt in the sight of the nations to be their God. I am the LORD.' "

⁴⁶These are the decrees, the laws and the regulations that the LORD established on Mount Sinai between himself and the Israelites through Moses.

Redeeming What Is the LORD's

27 The LORD said to Moses, ²"Speak to the Israelites and say to them: 'If anyone makes a special vow to dedicate persons to the LORD by giving equivalent values, ³set the value of a male between the ages of twenty and sixty at fifty shekels*a* of silver, according to the sanctuary shekel*b*; ⁴and if it is a female, set her value at thirty shekels.*c* ⁵If it is a person between the ages of five and twenty, set the value of a male at twenty shekels*d* and of a female at ten shekels.*e* ⁶If it is a person between one month and five years, set the value of a male at five shekels*f* of silver and that of a female at three shekels*g* of silver. ⁷If it is a person sixty years old or more, set the value of a male at fifteen shekels*h* and of a female at ten shekels. ⁸If anyone making the vow is too poor to pay the specified amount, he is to present the person to the priest, who will set the value for him according to what the man making the vow can afford.

⁹" 'If what he vowed is an animal that is acceptable as an offering to the LORD, such an animal given to the LORD becomes holy. ¹⁰He must not exchange it or substitute a good one for a bad one, or a bad one for a good one; if he should substitute one animal for another, both it and the substitute become holy. ¹¹If what he vowed is a ceremonially unclean animal—one that is not acceptable as an offering to the LORD—the animal must be presented to the priest, ¹²who will judge its quality as good or bad. Whatever value the priest then sets, that is what it will be. ¹³If the owner wishes

to redeem the animal, he must add a fifth to its value.

¹⁴" 'If a man dedicates his house as something holy to the LORD, the priest will judge its quality as good or bad. Whatever value the priest then sets, so it will remain. ¹⁵If the man who dedicates his house redeems it, he must add a fifth to its value, and the house will again become his.

¹⁶" 'If a man dedicates to the LORD part of his family land, its value is to be set according to the amount of seed required for it—fifty shekels of silver to a homer*i* of barley seed. ¹⁷If he dedicates his field during the Year of Jubilee, the value that has been set remains. ¹⁸But if he dedicates his field after the Jubilee, the priest will determine the value according to the number of years that remain until the next Year of Jubilee, and its set value will be reduced. ¹⁹If the man who dedicates the field wishes to redeem it, he must add a fifth to its value, and the field will again become his. ²⁰If, however, he does not redeem the field, or if he has sold it to someone else, it can never be redeemed. ²¹When the field is released in the Jubilee, it will become holy, like a field devoted to the LORD; it will become the property of the priests.*j*

²²" 'If a man dedicates to the LORD a field he has bought, which is not part of his family land, ²³the priest will determine its value up to the Year of Jubilee, and the man must pay its value on that day as something holy to the LORD. ²⁴In the Year of Jubilee the field will revert to the person from whom he bought it, the one whose land it was. ²⁵Every value is to be set according to the sanctuary shekel, twenty gerahs to the shekel.

²⁶" 'No one, however, may dedicate the firstborn of an animal, since the firstborn already belongs to the LORD; whether an ox*k* or a sheep, it is the LORD's. ²⁷If it is one of the unclean animals, he may buy it back at its set value, adding a fifth of the value to it. If he does not redeem it, it is to be sold at its set value.

---

a 3 That is, about 1 1/4 pounds (about 0.6 kilogram); also in verse 16   *b 3* That is, about 2/5 ounce (about 11.5 grams); also in verse 25   *c 4* That is, about 12 ounces (about 0.3 kilogram)   *d 5* That is, about 8 ounces (about 0.2 kilogram)   *e 5* That is, about 4 ounces (about 110 grams); also in verse 7   *f 6* That is, about 2 ounces (about 55 grams)   *g 6* That is, about 1 1/4 ounces (about 35 grams)   *h 7* That is, about 6 ounces (about 170 grams)   *i 16* That is, probably about 6 bushels (about 220 liters)   *j 21* Or *priest*   *k 26* The Hebrew word can include both male and female.

28" 'But nothing that a man owns and devotes[a] to the LORD—whether man or animal or family land—may be sold or redeemed; everything so devoted is most holy to the LORD.

29" 'No person devoted to destruction[b] may be ransomed; he must be put to death.

30" 'A tithe of everything from the land, whether grain from the soil or fruit from the trees, belongs to the LORD; it is holy to the LORD. ³¹If a man redeems any of his tithe, he must add a fifth of the value to it. ³²The entire tithe of the herd and flock—every tenth animal that passes under the shepherd's rod—will be holy to the LORD. ³³He must not pick out the good from the bad or make any substitution. If he does make a substitution, both the animal and its substitute become holy and cannot be redeemed.' "

³⁴These are the commands the LORD gave Moses on Mount Sinai for the Israelites.

NUMBERS

THE BOOK OF NUMBERS GETS ITS NAME FROM THE TWO NUMBERINGS, OR COUNTINGS, OF THE PEOPLE OF ISRAEL DURING THEIR YEARS OF WANDERING IN THE DESERT. NUMBERS PRESENTS AN ACCOUNT OF THAT WANDERING FOLLOWING THE ESTABLISHMENT OF THE COVENANT AT SINAI. IT TELLS OF THE MURMURING AND REBELLION OF GOD'S PEOPLE AND OF THEIR SUBSEQUENT JUDGMENT. THROUGHOUT THE YEARS IN THE DESERT ONE THING BECAME CLEAR TO ISRAEL—GOD'S CONSTANT CARE FOR THEM. NOT ONLY DID HE MEET THEIR NEEDS BUT HE ALSO LOVED AND CONTINUALLY FORGAVE HIS PEOPLE.

The Census

1 The LORD spoke to Moses in the Tent of Meeting in the Desert of Sinai on the first day of the second month of the second year after the Israelites came out of Egypt. He said: 2 "Take a census of the whole Israelite community by their clans and families, listing every man by name, one by one. 3 You and Aaron are to number by their divisions all the men in Israel twenty years old or more who are able to serve in the army. 4 One man from each tribe, each the head of his family, is to help you. 5 These are the names of the men who are to assist you:

from Reuben, Elizur son of Shedeur;
6 from Simeon, Shelumiel son of Zurishaddai;

7 from Judah, Nahshon son of Amminadab;
8 from Issachar, Nethanel son of Zuar;
9 from Zebulun, Eliab son of Helon;
10 from the sons of Joseph:
from Ephraim, Elishama son of Ammihud;
from Manasseh, Gamaliel son of Pedahzur;
11 from Benjamin, Abidan son of Gideoni;
12 from Dan, Ahiezer son of Ammishaddai;
13 from Asher, Pagiel son of Ocran;
14 from Gad, Eliasaph son of Deuel;
15 from Naphtali, Ahira son of Enan."

16 These were the men appointed from the community, the leaders of their ancestral tribes. They were the heads of the clans of Israel.

¹⁷Moses and Aaron took these men whose names had been given, ¹⁸and they called the whole community together on the first day of the second month. The people indicated their ancestry by their clans and families, and the men twenty years old or more were listed by name, one by one, ¹⁹as the LORD commanded Moses. And so he counted them in the Desert of Sinai:

²⁰From the descendants of Reuben the firstborn son of Israel:

All the men twenty years old or more who were able to serve in the army were listed by name, one by one, according to the records of their clans and families. ²¹The number from the tribe of Reuben was 46,500.

²²From the descendants of Simeon:

All the men twenty years old or more who were able to serve in the army were counted and listed by name, one by one, according to the records of their clans and families. ²³The number from the tribe of Simeon was 59,300.

²⁴From the descendants of Gad:

All the men twenty years old or more who were able to serve in the army were listed by name, according to the records of their clans and families. ²⁵The number from the tribe of Gad was 45,650.

²⁶From the descendants of Judah:

All the men twenty years old or more who were able to serve in the army were listed by name, according to the records of their clans and families. ²⁷The number from the tribe of Judah was 74,600.

²⁸From the descendants of Issachar:

All the men twenty years old or more who were able to serve in the army were listed by name, according to the records of their clans and families. ²⁹The number from the tribe of Issachar was 54,400.

³⁰From the descendants of Zebulun:

All the men twenty years old or more who were able to serve in the army were listed by name, according to the records of their clans and families. ³¹The number from the tribe of Zebulun was 57,400.

³²From the sons of Joseph:

From the descendants of Ephraim:

All the men twenty years old or more who were able to serve in the army were listed by name, according to the records of their clans and families. ³³The number from the tribe of Ephraim was 40,500.

³⁴From the descendants of Manasseh:

All the men twenty years old or more who were able to serve in the army were listed by name, according to the records of their clans and families. ³⁵The number from the tribe of Manasseh was 32,200.

³⁶From the descendants of Benjamin:

All the men twenty years old or more who were able to serve in the army were listed by name, according to the records of their clans and families. ³⁷The number from the tribe of Benjamin was 35,400.

³⁸From the descendants of Dan:

All the men twenty years old or more who were able to serve in the army were listed by name, according to the records of their clans and families. ³⁹The number from the tribe of Dan was 62,700.

⁴⁰From the descendants of Asher:

All the men twenty years old or more who were able to serve in the army were listed by name, according to the records of their clans and families. ⁴¹The number from the tribe of Asher was 41,500.

⁴²From the descendants of Naphtali:

All the men twenty years old or more who were able to serve in the army were listed by name, according to the records of their clans and families. ⁴³The number from the tribe of Naphtali was 53,400.

44These were the men counted by Moses and Aaron and the twelve leaders of Israel, each one representing his family. 45All the Israelites twenty years old or more who were able to serve in Israel's army were counted according to their families. 46The total number was 603,550.

47The families of the tribe of Levi, however, were not counted along with the others. 48The LORD had said to Moses: 49"You must not count the tribe of Levi or include them in the census of the other Israelites. 50Instead, appoint the Levites to be in charge of the tabernacle of the Testimony—over all its furnishings and everything belonging to it. They are to carry the tabernacle and all its furnishings; they are to take care of it and encamp around it. 51Whenever the tabernacle is to move, the Levites are to take it down, and whenever the tabernacle is to be set up, the Levites shall do it. Anyone else who goes near it shall be put to death. 52The Israelites are to set up their tents by divisions, each man in his own camp under his own standard. 53The Levites, however, are to set up their tents around the tabernacle of the Testimony so that wrath will not fall on the Israelite community. The Levites are to be responsible for the care of the tabernacle of the Testimony."

54The Israelites did all this just as the LORD commanded Moses.

The Arrangement of the Tribal Camps

2 The LORD said to Moses and Aaron: 2"The Israelites are to camp around the Tent of Meeting some distance from it, each man under his standard with the banners of his family."

3On the east, toward the sunrise, the divisions of the camp of Judah are to encamp under their standard. The leader of the people of Judah is Nahshon son of Amminadab. 4His division numbers 74,600.

5The tribe of Issachar will camp next to them. The leader of the people of Issachar is Nethanel son of Zuar. 6His division numbers 54,400. 7The tribe of Zebulun will be

next. The leader of the people of Zebulun is Eliab son of Helon. 8His division numbers 57,400.

9All the men assigned to the camp of Judah, according to their divisions, number 186,400. They will set out first.

10On the south will be the divisions of the camp of Reuben under their standard. The leader of the people of Reuben is Elizur son of Shedeur. 11His division numbers 46,500.

12The tribe of Simeon will camp next to them. The leader of the people of Simeon is Shelumiel son of Zurishaddai. 13His division numbers 59,300.

14The tribe of Gad will be next. The leader of the people of Gad is Eliasaph son of Deuel.a 15His division numbers 45,650.

16All the men assigned to the camp of Reuben, according to their divisions, number 151,450. They will set out second.

17Then the Tent of Meeting and the camp of the Levites will set out in the middle of the camps. They will set out in the same order as they encamp, each in his own place under his standard.

18On the west will be the divisions of the camp of Ephraim under their standard. The leader of the people of Ephraim is Elishama son of Ammihud. 19His division numbers 40,500.

20The tribe of Manasseh will be next to them. The leader of the people of Manasseh is Gamaliel son of Pedahzur. 21His division numbers 32,200.

22The tribe of Benjamin will be next. The leader of the people of Benjamin is Abidan son of Gideoni. 23His division numbers 35,400.

24All the men assigned to the camp of Ephraim, according to their divisions, number 108,100. They will set out third.

25On the north will be the divisions of the camp of Dan, under

a 14 Many manuscripts of the Masoretic Text, Samaritan Pentateuch and Vulgate (see also Num. 1:14); most manuscripts of the Masoretic Text Reuel

their standard. The leader of the people of Dan is Ahiezer son of Ammishaddai. 26His division numbers 62,700.

27The tribe of Asher will camp next to them. The leader of the people of Asher is Pagiel son of Ocran. 28His division numbers 41,500.

29The tribe of Naphtali will be next. The leader of the people of Naphtali is Ahira son of Enan. 30His division numbers 53,400.

31All the men assigned to the camp of Dan number 157,600. They will set out last, under their standards.

32These are the Israelites, counted according to their families. All those in the camps, by their divisions, number 603,550. 33The Levites, however, were not counted along with the other Israelites, as the LORD commanded Moses.

34So the Israelites did everything the LORD commanded Moses; that is the way they encamped under their standards, and that is the way they set out, each with his clan and family.

The Levites

3 This is the account of the family of Aaron and Moses at the time the LORD talked with Moses on Mount Sinai.

2The names of the sons of Aaron were Nadab the firstborn and Abihu, Eleazar and Ithamar. 3Those were the names of Aaron's sons, the anointed priests, who were ordained to serve as priests. 4Nadab and Abihu, however, fell dead before the LORD when they made an offering with unauthorized fire before him in the Desert of Sinai. They had no sons; so only Eleazar and Ithamar served as priests during the lifetime of their father Aaron.

5The LORD said to Moses, 6"Bring the tribe of Levi and present them to Aaron the priest to assist him. 7They are to perform duties for him and for the whole community at the Tent of Meeting by doing the work of the tabernacle. 8They are to take care of all the furnishings of the Tent of Meeting, fulfilling the obligations of the Israelites by doing the work of the tabernacle. 9Give the Levites to Aaron and his sons; they are the Israelites who are to be given wholly to him.*a* 10Appoint Aaron and his sons to serve as priests; anyone else who approaches the sanctuary must be put to death."

11The LORD also said to Moses, 12"I have taken the Levites from among the Israelites in place of the first male offspring of every Israelite woman. The Levites are mine, 13for all the firstborn are mine. When I struck down all the firstborn in Egypt, I set apart for myself every firstborn in Israel, whether man or animal. They are to be mine. I am the LORD."

14The LORD said to Moses in the Desert of Sinai, 15"Count the Levites by their families and clans. Count every male a month old or more." 16So Moses counted them, as he was commanded by the word of the LORD.

17These were the names of the sons of Levi:

    Gershon, Kohath and Merari.

18These were the names of the Gershonite clans:

    Libni and Shimei.

19The Kohathite clans:

    Amram, Izhar, Hebron and Uzziel.

20The Merarite clans:

    Mahli and Mushi.

These were the Levite clans, according to their families.

21To Gershon belonged the clans of the Libnites and Shimeites; these were the Gershonite clans. 22The number of all the males a month old or more who were counted was 7,500. 23The Gershonite clans were to camp on the west, behind the tabernacle. 24The leader of the families of the Gershonites was Eliasaph son of Lael. 25At the Tent of Meeting the Gershonites were responsible for the care of the tabernacle and tent, its coverings, the curtain at the entrance to the Tent of Meeting, 26the curtains of the courtyard, the curtain at the entrance to the courtyard surrounding the tabernacle and altar, and the ropes—and everything related to their use.

---

a 9 Most manuscripts of the Masoretic Text; some manuscripts of the Masoretic Text, Samaritan Pentateuch and Septuagint (see also Num. 8:16) *to me*

27To Kohath belonged the clans of the Amramites, Izharites, Hebronites and Uzzielites; these were the Kohathite clans. 28The number of all the males a month old or more was 8,600.a The Kohathites were responsible for the care of the sanctuary. 29The Kohathite clans were to camp on the south side of the tabernacle. 30The leader of the families of the Kohathite clans was Elizaphan son of Uzziel. 31They were responsible for the care of the ark, the table, the lampstand, the altars, the articles of the sanctuary used in ministering, the curtain, and everything related to their use. 32The chief leader of the Levites was Eleazar son of Aaron, the priest. He was appointed over those who were responsible for the care of the sanctuary.

33To Merari belonged the clans of the Mahlites and the Mushites; these were the Merarite clans. 34The number of all the males a month old or more who were counted was 6,200. 35The leader of the families of the Merarite clans was Zuriel son of Abihail; they were to camp on the north side of the tabernacle. 36The Merarites were appointed to take care of the frames of the tabernacle, its crossbars, posts, bases, all its equipment, and everything related to their use, 37as well as the posts of the surrounding courtyard with their bases, tent pegs and ropes.

38Moses and Aaron and his sons were to camp to the east of the tabernacle, toward the sunrise, in front of the Tent of Meeting. They were responsible for the care of the sanctuary on behalf of the Israelites. Anyone else who approached the sanctuary was to be put to death.

39The total number of Levites counted at the LORD's command by Moses and Aaron according to their clans, including every male a month old or more, was 22,000.

40The LORD said to Moses, "Count all the firstborn Israelite males who are a month old or more and make a list of their names. 41Take the Levites for me in place of all the firstborn of the Israelites, and the livestock of the Levites in place of all the firstborn of the livestock of the Israelites. I am the LORD."

42So Moses counted all the firstborn of the Israelites, as the LORD commanded him. 43The total number of firstborn males a month old or more, listed by name, was 22,273.

44The LORD also said to Moses, 45"Take the Levites in place of all the firstborn of Israel, and the livestock of the Levites in place of their livestock. The Levites are to be mine. I am the LORD. 46To redeem the 273 firstborn Israelites who exceed the number of the Levites, 47collect five shekelsb for each one, according to the sanctuary shekel, which weighs twenty gerahs. 48Give the money for the redemption of the additional Israelites to Aaron and his sons."

49So Moses collected the redemption money from those who exceeded the number redeemed by the Levites. 50From the firstborn of the Israelites he collected silver weighing 1,365 shekels,c according to the sanctuary shekel. 51Moses gave the redemption money to Aaron and his sons, as he was commanded by the word of the LORD.

The Kohathites

4 The LORD said to Moses and Aaron: 2"Take a census of the Kohathite branch of the Levites by their clans and families. 3Count all the men from thirty to fifty years of age who come to serve in the work in the Tent of Meeting.

4"This is the work of the Kohathites in the Tent of Meeting: the care of the most holy things. 5When the camp is to move, Aaron and his sons are to go in and take down the shielding curtain and cover the ark of the Testimony with it. 6Then they are to cover this with hides of sea cows,d spread a cloth of solid blue over that and put the poles in place.

7"Over the table of the Presence they are to spread a blue cloth and put on it the plates, dishes and bowls, and the jars for drink offerings; the bread that is

---

a 28 Hebrew; some Septuagint manuscripts 8,300
c 50 That is, about 35 pounds (about 15.5 kilograms)
14 and 25
b 47 That is, about 2 ounces (about 55 grams)
d 6 That is, dugongs; also in verses 8, 10, 11, 12,

continually there is to remain on it. 8Over these they are to spread a scarlet cloth, cover that with hides of sea cows and put its poles in place.

9"They are to take a blue cloth and cover the lampstand that is for light, together with its lamps, its wick trimmers and trays, and all its jars for the oil used to supply it. 10Then they are to wrap it and all its accessories in a covering of hides of sea cows and put it on a carrying frame.

11"Over the gold altar they are to spread a blue cloth and cover that with hides of sea cows and put its poles in place.

12"They are to take all the articles used for ministering in the sanctuary, wrap them in a blue cloth, cover that with hides of sea cows and put them on a carrying frame.

13"They are to remove the ashes from the bronze altar and spread a purple cloth over it. 14Then they are to place on it all the utensils used for ministering at the altar, including the firepans, meat forks, shovels and sprinkling bowls. Over it they are to spread a covering of hides of sea cows and put its poles in place.

15"After Aaron and his sons have finished covering the holy furnishings and all the holy articles, and when the camp is ready to move, the Kohathites are to come to do the carrying. But they must not touch the holy things or they will die. The Kohathites are to carry those things that are in the Tent of Meeting.

16"Eleazar son of Aaron, the priest, is to have charge of the oil for the light, the fragrant incense, the regular grain offering and the anointing oil. He is to be in charge of the entire tabernacle and everything in it, including its holy furnishings and articles."

17The LORD said to Moses and Aaron, 18"See that the Kohathite tribal clans are not cut off from the Levites. 19So that they may live and not die when they come near the most holy things, do this for them: Aaron and his sons are to go into the sanctuary and assign to each man his work and what he is to carry. 20But the Kohathites must not go in to look at the holy things, even for a moment, or they will die."

The Gershonites

21The LORD said to Moses, 22"Take a census also of the Gershonites by their families and clans. 23Count all the men from thirty to fifty years of age who come to serve in the work at the Tent of Meeting.

24"This is the service of the Gershonite clans as they work and carry burdens: 25They are to carry the curtains of the tabernacle, the Tent of Meeting, its covering and the outer covering of hides of sea cows, the curtains for the entrance to the Tent of Meeting, 26the curtains of the courtyard surrounding the tabernacle and altar, the curtain for the entrance, the ropes and all the equipment used in its service. The Gershonites are to do all that needs to be done with these things. 27All their service, whether carrying or doing other work, is to be done under the direction of Aaron and his sons. You shall assign to them as their responsibility all they are to carry. 28This is the service of the Gershonite clans at the Tent of Meeting. Their duties are to be under the direction of Ithamar son of Aaron, the priest.

The Merarites

29"Count the Merarites by their clans and families. 30Count all the men from thirty to fifty years of age who come to serve in the work at the Tent of Meeting. 31This is their duty as they perform service at the Tent of Meeting: to carry the frames of the tabernacle, its crossbars, posts and bases, 32as well as the posts of the surrounding courtyard with their bases, tent pegs, ropes, all their equipment and everything related to their use. Assign to each man the specific things he is to carry. 33This is the service of the Merarite clans as they work at the Tent of Meeting under the direction of Ithamar son of Aaron, the priest."

The Numbering of the Levite Clans

34Moses, Aaron and the leaders of the community counted the Kohathites by their clans and families. 35All the men from thirty to fifty years of age who came to serve in the work in the Tent of Meeting, 36counted by clans, were 2,750. 37This was the total of all those in the Kohathite clans who served in the

Tent of Meeting. Moses and Aaron counted them according to the LORD's command through Moses.

³⁸The Gershonites were counted by their clans and families. ³⁹All the men from thirty to fifty years of age who came to serve in the work at the Tent of Meeting, ⁴⁰counted by their clans and families, were 2,630. ⁴¹This was the total of those in the Gershonite clans who served at the Tent of Meeting. Moses and Aaron counted them according to the LORD's command.

⁴²The Merarites were counted by their clans and families. ⁴³All the men from thirty to fifty years of age who came to serve in the work at the Tent of Meeting, ⁴⁴counted by their clans, were 3,200. ⁴⁵This was the total of those in the Merarite clans. Moses and Aaron counted them according to the LORD's command through Moses.

⁴⁶So Moses, Aaron and the leaders of Israel counted all the Levites by their clans and families. ⁴⁷All the men from thirty to fifty years of age who came to do the work of serving and carrying the Tent of Meeting ⁴⁸numbered 8,580. ⁴⁹At the LORD's command through Moses, each was assigned his work and told what to carry.

Thus they were counted, as the LORD commanded Moses.

The Purity of the Camp

5 The LORD said to Moses, ²"Command the Israelites to send away from the camp anyone who has an infectious skin diseaseᵃ or a discharge of any kind, or who is ceremonially unclean because of a dead body. ³Send away male and female alike; send them outside the camp so they will not defile their camp, where I dwell among them." ⁴The Israelites did this; they sent them outside the camp. They did just as the LORD had instructed Moses.

Restitution for Wrongs

⁵The LORD said to Moses, ⁶"Say to the Israelites: 'When a man or woman wrongs another in any wayᵇ and so is unfaithful to the LORD, that person is guilty ⁷and must confess the sin he has committed. He must make full restitution for his wrong, add one fifth to it and give it all to the person he has wronged. ⁸But if that person has no close relative to whom restitution can be made for the wrong, the restitution belongs to the LORD and must be given to the priest, along with the ram with which atonement is made for him. ⁹All the sacred contributions the Israelites bring to a priest will belong to him. ¹⁰Each man's sacred gifts are his own, but what he gives to the priest will belong to the priest.' "

The Test for an Unfaithful Wife

¹¹Then the LORD said to Moses, ¹²"Speak to the Israelites and say to them: 'If a man's wife goes astray and is unfaithful to him ¹³by sleeping with another man, and this is hidden from her husband and her impurity is undetected (since there is no witness against her and she has not been caught in the act), ¹⁴and if feelings of jealousy come over her husband and he suspects his wife and she is impure—or if he is jealous and suspects her even though she is not impure— ¹⁵then he is to take his wife to the priest. He must also take an offering of a tenth of an ephahᶜ of barley flour on her behalf. He must not pour oil on it or put incense on it, because it is a grain offering for jealousy, a reminder offering to draw attention to guilt.

¹⁶" 'The priest shall bring her and have her stand before the LORD. ¹⁷Then he shall take some holy water in a clay jar and put some dust from the tabernacle floor into the water. ¹⁸After the priest has had the woman stand before the LORD, he shall loosen her hair and place in her hands the reminder offering, the grain offering for jealousy, while he himself holds the bitter water that brings a curse. ¹⁹Then the priest shall put the woman under oath and say to her, "If no other man has slept with you and you have not gone astray and become impure while married to your husband, may this bitter water that brings a curse not harm you. ²⁰But if you have gone astray while

---

ᵃ 2 Traditionally *leprosy*; the Hebrew word was used for various diseases affecting the skin—not necessarily leprosy.   ᵇ 6 Or *woman commits any wrong common to mankind*   ᶜ 15 That is, probably about 2 quarts (about 2 liters)

married to your husband and you have defiled yourself by sleeping with a man other than your husband"— 21here the priest is to put the woman under this curse of the oath—"may the LORD cause your people to curse and denounce you when he causes your thigh to waste away and your abdomen to swell.*a* 22May this water that brings a curse enter your body so that your abdomen swells and your thigh wastes away.*b* "

" 'Then the woman is to say, "Amen. So be it."

23" 'The priest is to write these curses on a scroll and then wash them off into the bitter water. 24He shall have the woman drink the bitter water that brings a curse, and this water will enter her and cause bitter suffering. 25The priest is to take from her hands the grain offering for jealousy, wave it before the LORD and bring it to the altar. 26The priest is then to take a handful of the grain offering as a memorial offering and burn it on the altar; after that, he is to have the woman drink the water. 27If she has defiled herself and been unfaithful to her husband, then when she is made to drink the water that brings a curse, it will go into her and cause bitter suffering; her abdomen will swell and her thigh waste away,*c* and she will become accursed among her people. 28If, however, the woman has not defiled herself and is free from impurity, she will be cleared of guilt and will be able to have children.

29" 'This, then, is the law of jealousy when a woman goes astray and defiles herself while married to her husband, 30or when feelings of jealousy come over a man because he suspects his wife. The priest is to have her stand before the LORD and is to apply this entire law to her. 31The husband will be innocent of any wrongdoing, but the woman will bear the consequences of her sin.' "

The Nazirite

6 The LORD said to Moses, 2"Speak to the Israelites and say to them: 'If a man or woman wants to make a special vow, a vow of separation to the LORD as a Nazirite, 3he must abstain from wine and other fermented drink and must not drink vinegar made from wine or from other fermented drink. He must not drink grape juice or eat grapes or raisins. 4As long as he is a Nazirite, he must not eat anything that comes from the grapevine, not even the seeds or skins.

5" 'During the entire period of his vow of separation no razor may be used on his head. He must be holy until the period of his separation to the LORD is over; he must let the hair of his head grow long. 6Throughout the period of his separation to the LORD he must not go near a dead body. 7Even if his own father or mother or brother or sister dies, he must not make himself ceremonially unclean on account of them, because the symbol of his separation to God is on his head. 8Throughout the period of his separation he is consecrated to the LORD.

9" 'If someone dies suddenly in his presence, thus defiling the hair he has dedicated, he must shave his head on the day of his cleansing—the seventh day. 10Then on the eighth day he must bring two doves or two young pigeons to the priest at the entrance to the Tent of Meeting. 11The priest is to offer one as a sin offering and the other as a burnt offering to make atonement for him because he sinned by being in the presence of the dead body. That same day he is to consecrate his head. 12He must dedicate himself to the LORD for the period of his separation and must bring a year-old male lamb as a guilt offering. The previous days do not count, because he became defiled during his separation.

13" 'Now this is the law for the Nazirite when the period of his separation is over. He is to be brought to the entrance to the Tent of Meeting. 14There he is to present his offerings to the LORD: a year-old male lamb without defect for a burnt offering, a year-old ewe lamb without defect for a sin offering, a ram without defect for a fellowship offering,*d* 15together with their grain offerings and drink offerings, and a basket of bread made without yeast—cakes made of fine

---

a 21 Or causes you to have a miscarrying womb and barrenness   b 22 Or body and cause you to be barren and have a miscarrying womb   c 27 Or suffering; she will have barrenness and a miscarrying womb   d 14 Traditionally peace offering; also in verses 17 and 18

flour mixed with oil, and wafers spread with oil.

16" 'The priest is to present them before the LORD and make the sin offering and the burnt offering. 17He is to present the basket of unleavened bread and is to sacrifice the ram as a fellowship offering to the LORD, together with its grain offering and drink offering.

18" 'Then at the entrance to the Tent of Meeting, the Nazirite must shave off the hair that he dedicated. He is to take the hair and put it in the fire that is under the sacrifice of the fellowship offering.

19" 'After the Nazirite has shaved off the hair of his dedication, the priest is to place in his hands a boiled shoulder of the ram, and a cake and a wafer from the basket, both made without yeast. 20The priest shall then wave them before the LORD as a wave offering; they are holy and belong to the priest, together with the breast that was waved and the thigh that was presented. After that, the Nazirite may drink wine.

21" 'This is the law of the Nazirite who vows his offering to the LORD in accordance with his separation, in addition to whatever else he can afford. He must fulfill the vow he has made, according to the law of the Nazirite.' "

The Priestly Blessing

22The LORD said to Moses, 23"Tell Aaron and his sons, 'This is how you are to bless the Israelites. Say to them:

24" ' "The LORD bless you
        and keep you;
25 the LORD make his face shine upon you
        and be gracious to you;
26 the LORD turn his face toward you
        and give you peace." '

27"So they will put my name on the Israelites, and I will bless them."

Offerings at the Dedication of the Tabernacle

7 When Moses finished setting up the tabernacle, he anointed it and consecrated it and all its furnishings.

He also anointed and consecrated the altar and all its utensils. 2Then the leaders of Israel, the heads of families who were the tribal leaders in charge of those who were counted, made offerings. 3They brought as their gifts before the LORD six covered carts and twelve oxen—an ox from each leader and a cart from every two. These they presented before the tabernacle.

4The LORD said to Moses, 5"Accept these from them, that they may be used in the work at the Tent of Meeting. Give them to the Levites as each man's work requires."

6So Moses took the carts and oxen and gave them to the Levites. 7He gave two carts and four oxen to the Gershonites, as their work required, 8and he gave four carts and eight oxen to the Merarites, as their work required. They were all under the direction of Ithamar son of Aaron, the priest. 9But Moses did not give any to the Kohathites, because they were to carry on their shoulders the holy things, for which they were responsible.

10When the altar was anointed, the leaders brought their offerings for its dedication and presented them before the altar. 11For the LORD had said to Moses, "Each day one leader is to bring his offering for the dedication of the altar."

12The one who brought his offering on the first day was Nahshon son of Amminadab of the tribe of Judah.

13His offering was one silver plate weighing a hundred and thirty shekels,a and one silver sprinkling bowl weighing seventy shekels,b both according to the sanctuary shekel, each filled with fine flour mixed with oil as a grain offering; 14one gold dish weighing ten shekels,c filled with incense; 15one young bull, one ram and one male lamb a year old, for a burnt offering; 16one male goat for a sin offering; 17and two oxen, five rams, five male goats and five male lambs a year old, to be sacrificed as a fellowship offering.d This was the offering of Nahshon son of Amminadab.

---

a 13 That is, about 3 1/4 pounds (about 1.5 kilograms); also elsewhere in this chapter   b 13 That is, about 1 3/4 pounds (about 0.8 kilogram); also elsewhere in this chapter   c 14 That is, about 4 ounces (about 110 grams); also elsewhere in this chapter   d 17 Traditionally *peace offering*; also elsewhere in this chapter

18On the second day Nethanel son of Zuar, the leader of Issachar, brought his offering. 19The offering he brought was one silver plate weighing a hundred and thirty shekels, and one silver sprinkling bowl weighing seventy shekels, both according to the sanctuary shekel, each filled with fine flour mixed with oil as a grain offering; 20one gold dish weighing ten shekels, filled with incense; 21one young bull, one ram and one male lamb a year old, for a burnt offering; 22one male goat for a sin offering; 23and two oxen, five rams, five male goats and five male lambs a year old, to be sacrificed as a fellowship offering. This was the offering of Nethanel son of Zuar.

24On the third day, Eliab son of Helon, the leader of the people of Zebulun, brought his offering. 25His offering was one silver plate weighing a hundred and thirty shekels, and one silver sprinkling bowl weighing seventy shekels, both according to the sanctuary shekel, each filled with fine flour mixed with oil as a grain offering; 26one gold dish weighing ten shekels, filled with incense; 27one young bull, one ram and one male lamb a year old, for a burnt offering; 28one male goat for a sin offering; 29and two oxen, five rams, five male goats and five male lambs a year old, to be sacrificed as a fellowship offering. This was the offering of Eliab son of Helon.

30On the fourth day Elizur son of Shedeur, the leader of the people of Reuben, brought his offering. 31His offering was one silver plate weighing a hundred and thirty shekels, and one silver sprinkling bowl weighing seventy shekels, both according to the sanctuary shekel, each filled with fine flour mixed with oil as a grain offering; 32one gold dish weighing ten shekels, filled with incense; 33one young bull, one ram and one male lamb a year old, for a burnt offering; 34one male goat for a sin offering; 35and two oxen, five rams, five male goats and five male lambs a year old, to be sacrificed as a fellowship offering. This was the offering of Elizur son of Shedeur.

36On the fifth day Shelumiel son of Zurishaddai, the leader of the people of Simeon, brought his offering. 37His offering was one silver plate weighing a hundred and thirty shekels, and one silver sprinkling bowl weighing seventy shekels, both according to the sanctuary shekel, each filled with fine flour mixed with oil as a grain offering; 38one gold dish weighing ten shekels, filled with incense; 39one young bull, one ram and one male lamb a year old, for a burnt offering; 40one male goat for a sin offering; 41and two oxen, five rams, five male goats and five male lambs a year old, to be sacrificed as a fellowship offering. This was the offering of Shelumiel son of Zurishaddai.

42On the sixth day Eliasaph son of Deuel, the leader of the people of Gad, brought his offering. 43His offering was one silver plate weighing a hundred and thirty shekels, and one silver sprinkling bowl weighing seventy shekels, both according to the sanctuary shekel, each filled with fine flour mixed with oil as a grain offering; 44one gold dish weighing ten shekels, filled with incense; 45one young bull, one ram and one male lamb a year old, for a burnt offering; 46one male goat for a sin offering; 47and two oxen, five rams, five male goats and five male lambs a year old, to be sacrificed as a fellowship offering. This was the offering of Eliasaph son of Deuel.

48On the seventh day Elishama son of Ammihud, the leader of the people of Ephraim, brought his offering. 49His offering was one silver plate weighing a hundred and thirty shekels, and one silver sprinkling bowl weighing seventy shekels, both according to the sanctuary shekel, each filled with fine flour mixed with oil as a grain offering;

⁵⁰one gold dish weighing ten shekels, filled with incense; ⁵¹one young bull, one ram and one male lamb a year old, for a burnt offering; ⁵²one male goat for a sin offering; ⁵³and two oxen, five rams, five male goats and five male lambs a year old, to be sacrificed as a fellowship offering. This was the offering of Elishama son of Ammihud.

⁵⁴On the eighth day Gamaliel son of Pedahzur, the leader of the people of Manasseh, brought his offering.

⁵⁵His offering was one silver plate weighing a hundred and thirty shekels, and one silver sprinkling bowl weighing seventy shekels, both according to the sanctuary shekel, each filled with fine flour mixed with oil as a grain offering; ⁵⁶one gold dish weighing ten shekels, filled with incense; ⁵⁷one young bull, one ram and one male lamb a year old, for a burnt offering; ⁵⁸one male goat for a sin offering; ⁵⁹and two oxen, five rams, five male goats and five male lambs a year old, to be sacrificed as a fellowship offering. This was the offering of Gamaliel son of Pedahzur.

⁶⁰On the ninth day Abidan son of Gideoni, the leader of the people of Benjamin, brought his offering.

⁶¹His offering was one silver plate weighing a hundred and thirty shekels, and one silver sprinkling bowl weighing seventy shekels, both according to the sanctuary shekel, each filled with fine flour mixed with oil as a grain offering; ⁶²one gold dish weighing ten shekels, filled with incense; ⁶³one young bull, one ram and one male lamb a year old, for a burnt offering; ⁶⁴one male goat for a sin offering; ⁶⁵and two oxen, five rams, five male goats and five male lambs a year old, to be sacrificed as a fellowship offering. This was the offering of Abidan son of Gideoni.

⁶⁶On the tenth day Ahiezer son of Ammishaddai, the leader of the people of Dan, brought his offering.

⁶⁷His offering was one silver plate weighing a hundred and thirty shekels, and one silver sprinkling bowl weighing seventy shekels, both according to the sanctuary shekel, each filled with fine flour mixed with oil as a grain offering; ⁶⁸one gold dish weighing ten shekels, filled with incense; ⁶⁹one young bull, one ram and one male lamb a year old, for a burnt offering; ⁷⁰one male goat for a sin offering; ⁷¹and two oxen, five rams, five male goats and five male lambs a year old, to be sacrificed as a fellowship offering. This was the offering of Ahiezer son of Ammishaddai.

⁷²On the eleventh day Pagiel son of Ocran, the leader of the people of Asher, brought his offering.

⁷³His offering was one silver plate weighing a hundred and thirty shekels, and one silver sprinkling bowl weighing seventy shekels, both according to the sanctuary shekel, each filled with fine flour mixed with oil as a grain offering; ⁷⁴one gold dish weighing ten shekels, filled with incense; ⁷⁵one young bull, one ram and one male lamb a year old, for a burnt offering; ⁷⁶one male goat for a sin offering; ⁷⁷and two oxen, five rams, five male goats and five male lambs a year old, to be sacrificed as a fellowship offering. This was the offering of Pagiel son of Ocran.

⁷⁸On the twelfth day Ahira son of Enan, the leader of the people of Naphtali, brought his offering.

⁷⁹His offering was one silver plate weighing a hundred and thirty shekels, and one silver sprinkling bowl weighing seventy shekels, both according to the sanctuary shekel, each filled with fine flour mixed with oil as a grain offering; ⁸⁰one gold dish weighing ten shekels, filled with incense; ⁸¹one young bull, one ram and one male lamb a year old, for a burnt offering; ⁸²one male goat for a sin offering; ⁸³and two oxen, five rams, five male goats and five male lambs a year old, to be sacrificed as a fellowship offering. This was the offering of Ahira son of Enan.

84These were the offerings of the Israelite leaders for the dedication of the altar when it was anointed: twelve silver plates, twelve silver sprinkling bowls and twelve gold dishes. 85Each silver plate weighed a hundred and thirty shekels, and each sprinkling bowl seventy shekels. Altogether, the silver dishes weighed two thousand four hundred shekels,a according to the sanctuary shekel. 86The twelve gold dishes filled with incense weighed ten shekels each, according to the sanctuary shekel. Altogether, the gold dishes weighed a hundred and twenty shekels.b 87The total number of animals for the burnt offering came to twelve young bulls, twelve rams and twelve male lambs a year old, together with their grain offering. Twelve male goats were used for the sin offering. 88The total number of animals for the sacrifice of the fellowship offering came to twenty-four oxen, sixty rams, sixty male goats and sixty male lambs a year old. These were the offerings for the dedication of the altar after it was anointed.

89When Moses entered the Tent of Meeting to speak with the LORD, he heard the voice speaking to him from between the two cherubim above the atonement cover on the ark of the Testimony. And he spoke with him.

Setting Up the Lamps

8 The LORD said to Moses, 2"Speak to Aaron and say to him, 'When you set up the seven lamps, they are to light the area in front of the lampstand.' "

3Aaron did so; he set up the lamps so that they faced forward on the lampstand, just as the LORD commanded Moses. 4This is how the lampstand was made: It was made of hammered gold—from its base to its blossoms. The lampstand was made exactly like the pattern the LORD had shown Moses.

The Setting Apart of the Levites

5The LORD said to Moses: 6"Take the Levites from among the other Israelites and make them ceremonially clean. 7To purify them, do this: Sprinkle the water of cleansing on them; then have them shave their whole bodies and wash their

clothes, and so purify themselves. 8Have them take a young bull with its grain offering of fine flour mixed with oil; then you are to take a second young bull for a sin offering. 9Bring the Levites to the front of the Tent of Meeting and assemble the whole Israelite community. 10You are to bring the Levites before the LORD, and the Israelites are to lay their hands on them. 11Aaron is to present the Levites before the LORD as a wave offering from the Israelites, so that they may be ready to do the work of the LORD.

12"After the Levites lay their hands on the heads of the bulls, use the one for a sin offering to the LORD and the other for a burnt offering, to make atonement for the Levites. 13Have the Levites stand in front of Aaron and his sons and then present them as a wave offering to the LORD. 14In this way you are to set the Levites apart from the other Israelites, and the Levites will be mine.

15"After you have purified the Levites and presented them as a wave offering, they are to come to do their work at the Tent of Meeting. 16They are the Israelites who are to be given wholly to me. I have taken them as my own in place of the firstborn, the first male offspring from every Israelite woman. 17Every firstborn male in Israel, whether man or animal, is mine. When I struck down all the firstborn in Egypt, I set them apart for myself. 18And I have taken the Levites in place of all the firstborn sons in Israel. 19Of all the Israelites, I have given the Levites as gifts to Aaron and his sons to do the work at the Tent of Meeting on behalf of the Israelites and to make atonement for them so that no plague will strike the Israelites when they go near the sanctuary."

20Moses, Aaron and the whole Israelite community did with the Levites just as the LORD commanded Moses. 21The Levites purified themselves and washed their clothes. Then Aaron presented them as a wave offering before the LORD and made atonement for them to purify them. 22After that, the Levites came to do their work at the Tent of Meeting under the supervision of Aaron and his sons. They did with the Levites just as the LORD commanded Moses.

---

a 85 That is, about 60 pounds (about 28 kilograms)   b 86 That is, about 3 pounds (about 1.4 kilograms)

23The LORD said to Moses, 24"This applies to the Levites: Men twenty-five years old or more shall come to take part in the work at the Tent of Meeting, 25but at the age of fifty, they must retire from their regular service and work no longer. 26They may assist their brothers in performing their duties at the Tent of Meeting, but they themselves must not do the work. This, then, is how you are to assign the responsibilities of the Levites."

The Passover

9 The LORD spoke to Moses in the Desert of Sinai in the first month of the second year after they came out of Egypt. He said, 2"Have the Israelites celebrate the Passover at the appointed time. 3Celebrate it at the appointed time, at twilight on the fourteenth day of this month, in accordance with all its rules and regulations."

4So Moses told the Israelites to celebrate the Passover, 5and they did so in the Desert of Sinai at twilight on the fourteenth day of the first month. The Israelites did everything just as the LORD commanded Moses.

6But some of them could not celebrate the Passover on that day because they were ceremonially unclean on account of a dead body. So they came to Moses and Aaron that same day 7and said to Moses, "We have become unclean because of a dead body, but why should we be kept from presenting the LORD's offering with the other Israelites at the appointed time?"

8Moses answered them, "Wait until I find out what the LORD commands concerning you."

9Then the LORD said to Moses, 10"Tell the Israelites: 'When any of you or your descendants are unclean because of a dead body or are away on a journey, they may still celebrate the LORD's Passover. 11They are to celebrate it on the fourteenth day of the second month at twilight. They are to eat the lamb, together with unleavened bread and bitter herbs. 12They must not leave any of it till morning or break any of its bones. When they celebrate the Passover, they must follow all the regulations. 13But if a man who is ceremonially clean and not on a journey fails to celebrate the Passover, that person must be cut off from his people because he did not present the LORD's offering at the appointed time. That man will bear the consequences of his sin.

14" 'An alien living among you who wants to celebrate the LORD's Passover must do so in accordance with its rules and regulations. You must have the same regulations for the alien and the native-born.' "

The Cloud Above the Tabernacle

15On the day the tabernacle, the Tent of the Testimony, was set up, the cloud covered it. From evening till morning the cloud above the tabernacle looked like fire. 16That is how it continued to be; the cloud covered it, and at night it looked like fire. 17Whenever the cloud lifted from above the Tent, the Israelites set out; wherever the cloud settled, the Israelites encamped. 18At the LORD's command the Israelites set out, and at his command they encamped. As long as the cloud stayed over the tabernacle, they remained in camp. 19When the cloud remained over the tabernacle a long time, the Israelites obeyed the LORD's order and did not set out. 20Sometimes the cloud was over the tabernacle only a few days; at the LORD's command they would encamp, and then at his command they would set out. 21Sometimes the cloud stayed only from evening till morning, and when it lifted in the morning, they set out. Whether by day or by night, whenever the cloud lifted, they set out. 22Whether the cloud stayed over the tabernacle for two days or a month or a year, the Israelites would remain in camp and not set out; but when it lifted, they would set out. 23At the LORD's command they encamped, and at the LORD's command they set out. They obeyed the LORD's order, in accordance with his command through Moses.

The Silver Trumpets

10 The LORD said to Moses: 2"Make two trumpets of hammered silver, and use them for calling the community together and for having the camps set out. 3When both are sounded, the whole community is to assemble before you at the entrance to the Tent of Meeting. 4If only one is

sounded, the leaders—the heads of the clans of Israel—are to assemble before you. 5When a trumpet blast is sounded, the tribes camping on the east are to set out. 6At the sounding of a second blast, the camps on the south are to set out. The blast will be the signal for setting out. 7To gather the assembly, blow the trumpets, but not with the same signal.

8"The sons of Aaron, the priests, are to blow the trumpets. This is to be a lasting ordinance for you and the generations to come. 9When you go into battle in your own land against an enemy who is oppressing you, sound a blast on the trumpets. Then you will be remembered by the LORD your God and rescued from your enemies. 10Also at your times of rejoicing—your appointed feasts and New Moon festivals—you are to sound the trumpets over your burnt offerings and fellowship offerings,a and they will be a memorial for you before your God. I am the LORD your God."

The Israelites Leave Sinai

11On the twentieth day of the second month of the second year, the cloud lifted from above the tabernacle of the Testimony. 12Then the Israelites set out from the Desert of Sinai and traveled from place to place until the cloud came to rest in the Desert of Paran. 13They set out, this first time, at the LORD's command through Moses.

14The divisions of the camp of Judah went first, under their standard. Nahshon son of Amminadab was in command. 15Nethanel son of Zuar was over the division of the tribe of Issachar, 16and Eliab son of Helon was over the division of the tribe of Zebulun. 17Then the tabernacle was taken down, and the Gershonites and Merarites, who carried it, set out.

18The divisions of the camp of Reuben went next, under their standard. Elizur son of Shedeur was in command. 19Shelumiel son of Zurishaddai was over the division of the tribe of Simeon, 20and Eliasaph son of Deuel was over the division of the tribe of Gad. 21Then the Kohathites set out, carrying the holy

things. The tabernacle was to be set up before they arrived.

22The divisions of the camp of Ephraim went next, under their standard. Elishama son of Ammihud was in command. 23Gamaliel son of Pedahzur was over the division of the tribe of Manasseh, 24and Abidan son of Gideoni was over the division of the tribe of Benjamin.

25Finally, as the rear guard for all the units, the divisions of the camp of Dan set out, under their standard. Ahiezer son of Ammishaddai was in command. 26Pagiel son of Ocran was over the division of the tribe of Asher, 27and Ahira son of Enan was over the division of the tribe of Naphtali. 28This was the order of march for the Israelite divisions as they set out.

29Now Moses said to Hobab son of Reuel the Midianite, Moses' father-in-law, "We are setting out for the place about which the LORD said, 'I will give it to you.' Come with us and we will treat you well, for the LORD has promised good things to Israel."

30He answered, "No, I will not go; I am going back to my own land and my own people."

31But Moses said, "Please do not leave us. You know where we should camp in the desert, and you can be our eyes. 32If you come with us, we will share with you whatever good things the LORD gives us."

33So they set out from the mountain of the LORD and traveled for three days. The ark of the covenant of the LORD went before them during those three days to find them a place to rest. 34The cloud of the LORD was over them by day when they set out from the camp.

35Whenever the ark set out, Moses said,

"Rise up, O LORD!
    May your enemies be scattered;
    may your foes flee before you."

36Whenever it came to rest, he said,

"Return, O LORD,
    to the countless thousands of
        Israel."

a 10 Traditionally peace offerings

Fire From the LORD

11 Now the people complained about their hardships in the hearing of the LORD, and when he heard them his anger was aroused. Then fire from the LORD burned among them and consumed some of the outskirts of the camp. ²When the people cried out to Moses, he prayed to the LORD and the fire died down. ³So that place was called Taberah,ᵃ because fire from the LORD had burned among them.

Quail From the LORD

⁴The rabble with them began to crave other food, and again the Israelites started wailing and said, "If only we had meat to eat! ⁵We remember the fish we ate in Egypt at no cost—also the cucumbers, melons, leeks, onions and garlic. ⁶But now we have lost our appetite; we never see anything but this manna!"

⁷The manna was like coriander seed and looked like resin. ⁸The people went around gathering it, and then ground it in a handmill or crushed it in a mortar. They cooked it in a pot or made it into cakes. And it tasted like something made with olive oil. ⁹When the dew settled on the camp at night, the manna also came down.

¹⁰Moses heard the people of every family wailing, each at the entrance to his tent. The LORD became exceedingly angry, and Moses was troubled. ¹¹He asked the LORD, "Why have you brought this trouble on your servant? What have I done to displease you that you put the burden of all these people on me? ¹²Did I conceive all these people? Did I give them birth? Why do you tell me to carry them in my arms, as a nurse carries an infant, to the land you promised on oath to their forefathers? ¹³Where can I get meat for all these people? They keep wailing to me, 'Give us meat to eat!' ¹⁴I cannot carry all these people by myself; the burden is too heavy for me. ¹⁵If this is how you are going to treat me, put me to death right now—if I have found favor in your eyes—and do not let me face my own ruin."

¹⁶The LORD said to Moses: "Bring me seventy of Israel's elders who are known to you as leaders and officials among the people. Have them come to the Tent of Meeting, that they may stand there with you. ¹⁷I will come down and speak with you there, and I will take of the Spirit that is on you and put the Spirit on them. They will help you carry the burden of the people so that you will not have to carry it alone.

¹⁸"Tell the people: 'Consecrate yourselves in preparation for tomorrow, when you will eat meat. The LORD heard you when you wailed, "If only we had meat to eat! We were better off in Egypt!" Now the LORD will give you meat, and you will eat it. ¹⁹You will not eat it for just one day, or two days, or five, ten or twenty days, ²⁰but for a whole month—until it comes out of your nostrils and you loathe it—because you have rejected the LORD, who is among you, and have wailed before him, saying, "Why did we ever leave Egypt?" ' "

²¹But Moses said, "Here I am among six hundred thousand men on foot, and you say, 'I will give them meat to eat for a whole month!' ²²Would they have enough if flocks and herds were slaughtered for them? Would they have enough if all the fish in the sea were caught for them?"

²³The LORD answered Moses, "Is the LORD's arm too short? You will now see whether or not what I say will come true for you."

²⁴So Moses went out and told the people what the LORD had said. He brought together seventy of their elders and had them stand around the Tent. ²⁵Then the LORD came down in the cloud and spoke with him, and he took of the Spirit that was on him and put the Spirit on the seventy elders. When the Spirit rested on them, they prophesied, but they did not do so again.ᵇ

²⁶However, two men, whose names were Eldad and Medad, had remained in the camp. They were listed among the elders, but did not go out to the Tent. Yet the Spirit also rested on them, and they prophesied in the camp. ²⁷A young man ran and told Moses, "Eldad and Medad are prophesying in the camp."

²⁸Joshua son of Nun, who had been

ᵃ *3 Taberah means burning.*   ᵇ *25 Or prophesied and continued to do so*

Moses' aide since youth, spoke up and said, "Moses, my lord, stop them!"

29But Moses replied, "Are you jealous for my sake? I wish that all the LORD's people were prophets and that the LORD would put his Spirit on them!" 30Then Moses and the elders of Israel returned to the camp.

31Now a wind went out from the LORD and drove quail in from the sea. It brought them*a* down all around the camp to about three feet*b* above the ground, as far as a day's walk in any direction. 32All that day and night and all the next day the people went out and gathered quail. No one gathered less than ten homers.*c* Then they spread them out all around the camp. 33But while the meat was still between their teeth and before it could be consumed, the anger of the LORD burned against the people, and he struck them with a severe plague. 34Therefore the place was named Kibroth Hattaavah,*d* because there they buried the people who had craved other food.

35From Kibroth Hattaavah the people traveled to Hazeroth and stayed there.

Miriam and Aaron Oppose Moses

12 Miriam and Aaron began to talk against Moses because of his Cushite wife, for he had married a Cushite. 2"Has the LORD spoken only through Moses?" they asked. "Hasn't he also spoken through us?" And the LORD heard this.

3(Now Moses was a very humble man, more humble than anyone else on the face of the earth.)

4At once the LORD said to Moses, Aaron and Miriam, "Come out to the Tent of Meeting, all three of you." So the three of them came out. 5Then the LORD came down in a pillar of cloud; he stood at the entrance to the Tent and summoned Aaron and Miriam. When both of them stepped forward, 6he said, "Listen to my words:

"When a prophet of the LORD is
    among you,
I reveal myself to him in visions,

I speak to him in dreams.
7But this is not true of my servant
    Moses;
he is faithful in all my house.
8With him I speak face to face,
    clearly and not in riddles;
he sees the form of the LORD.
Why then were you not afraid
    to speak against my servant
        Moses?"

9The anger of the LORD burned against them, and he left them.

10When the cloud lifted from above the Tent, there stood Miriam—leprous,*e* like snow. Aaron turned toward her and saw that she had leprosy; 11and he said to Moses, "Please, my lord, do not hold against us the sin we have so foolishly committed. 12Do not let her be like a stillborn infant coming from its mother's womb with its flesh half eaten away."

13So Moses cried out to the LORD, "O God, please heal her!"

14The LORD replied to Moses, "If her father had spit in her face, would she not have been in disgrace for seven days? Confine her outside the camp for seven days; after that she can be brought back." 15So Miriam was confined outside the camp for seven days, and the people did not move on till she was brought back.

16After that, the people left Hazeroth and encamped in the Desert of Paran.

Exploring Canaan

13 The LORD said to Moses, 2"Send some men to explore the land of Canaan, which I am giving to the Israelites. From each ancestral tribe send one of its leaders."

3So at the LORD's command Moses sent them out from the Desert of Paran. All of them were leaders of the Israelites. 4These are their names:

from the tribe of Reuben, Shammua
    son of Zaccur;
5from the tribe of Simeon, Shaphat
    son of Hori;
6from the tribe of Judah, Caleb son of
    Jephunneh;

---

a 31 Or *They flew*   *b 31* Hebrew *two cubits* (about 1 meter) (about 2.2 kiloliters)   *c 32* That is, probably about 60 bushels   *d 34 Kibroth Hattaavah* means *graves of craving.*   *e 10* The Hebrew word was used for various diseases affecting the skin—not necessarily leprosy.

TUESDAY

THOSE WHO MURMUR
Charles H. Spurgeon

VERSE: Numbers 12:1–2 **PASSAGE:** Numbers 12:1–16

 here are murmurers among Christians now, as there were in the camp of Israel. There are those who, when the rod falls, cry out against the afflictive dispensation. They ask, "Why am I afflicted? What have I done to be chastened like this?"

Allow me a word with you who murmur. Why should you murmur against the dispensations of your heavenly Father? Can he treat you more harshly than you deserve? Consider what a rebel you once were, but he pardoned you! Surely, if he in his wisdom sees fit to chasten you, you should not complain. Does not that proud, rebellious spirit of yours prove that your heart is not thoroughly sanctified? Those murmuring words are contrary to the holy, submissive nature of God's children. Is not the correction needed? But if you murmur against the chastening, take heed, for it will go hard with murmurers.

But know one thing—"He doth not afflict willingly, nor grieve the children of men" (Lamentations 3:33, KJV). All his corrections are sent in love, to purify you, and to draw you nearer to himself. Surely it must help you bear the chastening if you are able to recognize your Father's hand. For "whom the Lord loveth he chasteneth, and scourgeth every son whom he receiveth. If ye endure chastening, God dealeth with you as with sons" (Hebrews 12:6–7). "Neither murmur ye as some of them also murmured and were destroyed of the destroyer" (1 Corinthians 10:10).

ADDITIONAL SCRIPTURE READING:
Romans 8:12–14; 2 Corinthians 7:1

Go to page 167 for your next devotional reading.

1700   1900

7 from the tribe of Issachar, Igal son of Joseph;

8 from the tribe of Ephraim, Hoshea son of Nun;

9 from the tribe of Benjamin, Palti son of Raphu;

10 from the tribe of Zebulun, Gaddiel son of Sodi;

11 from the tribe of Manasseh (a tribe of Joseph), Gaddi son of Susi;

12 from the tribe of Dan, Ammiel son of Gemalli;

13 from the tribe of Asher, Sethur son of Michael;

14 from the tribe of Naphtali, Nahbi son of Vophsi;

15 from the tribe of Gad, Geuel son of Maki.

16 These are the names of the men Moses sent to explore the land. (Moses gave Hoshea son of Nun the name Joshua.)

17 When Moses sent them to explore Canaan, he said, "Go up through the Negev and on into the hill country. 18 See what the land is like and whether the people who live there are strong or weak, few or many. 19 What kind of land do they live in? Is it good or bad? What kind of towns do they live in? Are they unwalled or fortified? 20 How is the soil? Is it fertile or poor? Are there trees on it or not? Do your best to bring back some of the fruit of the land." (It was the season for the first ripe grapes.)

21 So they went up and explored the land from the Desert of Zin as far as Rehob, toward Lebo*a* Hamath. 22 They went up through the Negev and came to Hebron, where Ahiman, Sheshai and Talmai, the descendants of Anak, lived. (Hebron had been built seven years before Zoan in Egypt.) 23 When they reached the Valley of Eshcol,*b* they cut off a branch bearing a single cluster of grapes. Two of them carried it on a pole between them, along with some pomegranates and figs. 24 That place was called the Valley of Eshcol because of the cluster of grapes the Israelites cut off there. 25 At the end of forty days they returned from exploring the land.

Report on the Exploration

26 They came back to Moses and Aaron and the whole Israelite community at Kadesh in the Desert of Paran. There they reported to them and to the whole assembly and showed them the fruit of the land. 27 They gave Moses this account: "We went into the land to which you sent us, and it does flow with milk and honey! Here is its fruit. 28 But the people who live there are powerful, and the cities are fortified and very large. We even saw descendants of Anak there. 29 The Amalekites live in the Negev; the Hittites, Jebusites and Amorites live in the hill country; and the Canaanites live near the sea and along the Jordan."

30 Then Caleb silenced the people before Moses and said, "We should go up and take possession of the land, for we can certainly do it."

31 But the men who had gone up with him said, "We can't attack those people; they are stronger than we are." 32 And they spread among the Israelites a bad report about the land they had explored. They said, "The land we explored devours those living in it. All the people we saw there are of great size. 33 We saw the Nephilim there (the descendants of Anak come from the Nephilim). We seemed like grasshoppers in our own eyes, and we looked the same to them."

The People Rebel

14 That night all the people of the community raised their voices and wept aloud. 2 All the Israelites grumbled against Moses and Aaron, and the whole assembly said to them, "If only we had died in Egypt! Or in this desert! 3 Why is the LORD bringing us to this land only to let us fall by the sword? Our wives and children will be taken as plunder. Wouldn't it be better for us to go back to Egypt?" 4 And they said to each other, "We should choose a leader and go back to Egypt."

5 Then Moses and Aaron fell facedown in front of the whole Israelite assembly gathered there. 6 Joshua son of Nun and Caleb son of Jephunneh, who were among those who had explored the land, tore their clothes 7 and said to the entire Israelite assembly, "The land we passed through and explored is exceedingly good. 8 If the LORD is pleased with us, he

---

a 21 Or *toward the entrance to*　　*b* 23 *Eshcol* means *cluster;* also in verse 24.

will lead us into that land, a land flowing with milk and honey, and will give it to us. ⁹Only do not rebel against the LORD. And do not be afraid of the people of the land, because we will swallow them up. Their protection is gone, but the LORD is with us. Do not be afraid of them."

¹⁰But the whole assembly talked about stoning them. Then the glory of the LORD appeared at the Tent of Meeting to all the Israelites. ¹¹The LORD said to Moses, "How long will these people treat me with contempt? How long will they refuse to believe in me, in spite of all the miraculous signs I have performed among them? ¹²I will strike them down with a plague and destroy them, but I will make you into a nation greater and stronger than they."

¹³Moses said to the LORD, "Then the Egyptians will hear about it! By your power you brought these people up from among them. ¹⁴And they will tell the inhabitants of this land about it. They have already heard that you, O LORD, are with these people and that you, O LORD, have been seen face to face, that your cloud stays over them, and that you go before them in a pillar of cloud by day and a pillar of fire by night. ¹⁵If you put these people to death all at one time, the nations who have heard this report about you will say, ¹⁶'The LORD was not able to bring these people into the land he promised them on oath; so he slaughtered them in the desert.'

¹⁷"Now may the Lord's strength be displayed, just as you have declared: ¹⁸'The LORD is slow to anger, abounding in love and forgiving sin and rebellion. Yet he does not leave the guilty unpunished; he punishes the children for the sin of the fathers to the third and fourth generation.' ¹⁹In accordance with your

WEDNESDAY

TRUSTING HIM TO KEEP YOU
Andrew Murray

VERSE: Numbers 13:31   **PASSAGE:** Numbers 13:26–33

Dear souls! how little they know that the abiding in Christ is just meant for the weak, and so beautifully suited to their feebleness. It is not the doing of some great thing, and does not demand that we first lead a very holy and devoted life. No, it is simply weakness entrusting itself to a Mighty One to be kept—the unfaithful one casting self on One who is altogether trustworthy and true. Abiding in him is not a work that we have to do as the condition for enjoying his salvation, but a consenting to let him do all for us, and in us, and through us. It is a work he does for us—the fruit and the power of his redeeming love. Our part is simply to yield, to trust, and to wait for what he has engaged to perform.

ADDITIONAL SCRIPTURE READING:
Deuteronomy 1:27–32; John 15:1–7

Go to page 171 for your next devotional reading.

1700   1900

great love, forgive the sin of these people, just as you have pardoned them from the time they left Egypt until now."

²⁰The LORD replied, "I have forgiven them, as you asked. ²¹Nevertheless, as surely as I live and as surely as the glory of the LORD fills the whole earth, ²²not one of the men who saw my glory and the miraculous signs I performed in Egypt and in the desert but who disobeyed me and tested me ten times— ²³not one of them will ever see the land I promised on oath to their forefathers. No one who has treated me with contempt will ever see it. ²⁴But because my servant Caleb has a different spirit and follows me wholeheartedly, I will bring him into the land he went to, and his descendants will inherit it. ²⁵Since the Amalekites and Canaanites are living in the valleys, turn back tomorrow and set out toward the desert along the route to the Red Sea.ᵃ"

²⁶The LORD said to Moses and Aaron: ²⁷"How long will this wicked community grumble against me? I have heard the complaints of these grumbling Israelites. ²⁸So tell them, 'As surely as I live, declares the LORD, I will do to you the very things I heard you say: ²⁹In this desert your bodies will fall—every one of you twenty years old or more who was counted in the census and who has grumbled against me. ³⁰Not one of you will enter the land I swore with uplifted hand to make your home, except Caleb son of Jephunneh and Joshua son of Nun. ³¹As for your children that you said would be taken as plunder, I will bring them in to enjoy the land you have rejected. ³²But you— your bodies will fall in this desert. ³³Your children will be shepherds here for forty years, suffering for your unfaithfulness, until the last of your bodies lies in the desert. ³⁴For forty years—one year for each of the forty days you explored the land—you will suffer for your sins and know what it is like to have me against you.' ³⁵I, the LORD, have spoken, and I will surely do these things to this whole wicked community, which has banded together against me. They will meet their end in this desert; here they will die."

³⁶So the men Moses had sent to explore the land, who returned and made the whole community grumble against him by spreading a bad report

---

HE THAT COMPLAINS OR MURMURS IS NOT PERFECT, NOR IS HE EVEN A GOOD CHRISTIAN.

—*John of the Cross*

---

about it— ³⁷these men responsible for spreading the bad report about the land were struck down and died of a plague before the LORD. ³⁸Of the men who went to explore the land, only Joshua son of Nun and Caleb son of Jephunneh survived.

³⁹When Moses reported this to all the Israelites, they mourned bitterly. ⁴⁰Early the next morning they went up toward the high hill country. "We have sinned," they said. "We will go up to the place the LORD promised."

⁴¹But Moses said, "Why are you disobeying the LORD's command? This will not succeed! ⁴²Do not go up, because the LORD is not with you. You will be defeated by your enemies, ⁴³for the Amalekites and Canaanites will face you there. Because you have turned away from the LORD, he will not be with you and you will fall by the sword."

⁴⁴Nevertheless, in their presumption they went up toward the high hill country, though neither Moses nor the ark of the LORD's covenant moved from the camp. ⁴⁵Then the Amalekites and Canaanites who lived in that hill country came down and attacked them and beat them down all the way to Hormah.

Supplementary Offerings

15 The LORD said to Moses, ²"Speak to the Israelites and say to them: 'After you enter the land I am giving you as a home ³and you present to the LORD offerings made by fire, from the herd or the flock, as an aroma pleasing to the LORD—whether burnt offerings or sacrifices, for special vows or freewill offerings or festival offerings— ⁴then the one who brings his offering shall present to the LORD a grain offering of a tenth of an ephahᵇ of fine

---

ᵃ 25 Hebrew *Yam Suph*; that is, Sea of Reeds   ᵇ 4 That is, probably about 2 quarts (about 2 liters)

flour mixed with a quarter of a hin*a* of oil. 5With each lamb for the burnt offering or the sacrifice, prepare a quarter of a hin of wine as a drink offering.

6*" '*With a ram prepare a grain offering of two-tenths of an ephah*b* of fine flour mixed with a third of a hin*c* of oil, 7and a third of a hin of wine as a drink offering. Offer it as an aroma pleasing to the LORD.

8*" '*When you prepare a young bull as a burnt offering or sacrifice, for a special vow or a fellowship offering*d* to the LORD, 9bring with the bull a grain offering of three-tenths of an ephah*e* of fine flour mixed with half a hin*f* of oil. 10Also bring half a hin of wine as a drink offering. It will be an offering made by fire, an aroma pleasing to the LORD. 11Each bull or ram, each lamb or young goat, is to be prepared in this manner. 12Do this for each one, for as many as you prepare.

13*" '*Everyone who is native-born must do these things in this way when he brings an offering made by fire as an aroma pleasing to the LORD. 14For the generations to come, whenever an alien or anyone else living among you presents an offering made by fire as an aroma pleasing to the LORD, he must do exactly as you do. 15The community is to have the same rules for you and for the alien living among you; this is a lasting ordinance for the generations to come. You and the alien shall be the same before the LORD: 16The same laws and regulations will apply both to you and to the alien living among you.' "

17The LORD said to Moses, 18"Speak to the Israelites and say to them: 'When you enter the land to which I am taking you 19and you eat the food of the land, present a portion as an offering to the LORD. 20Present a cake from the first of your ground meal and present it as an offering from the threshing floor. 21Throughout the generations to come you are to give this offering to the LORD from the first of your ground meal.

Offerings for Unintentional Sins

22*" '*Now if you unintentionally fail to keep any of these commands the LORD gave Moses— 23any of the LORD's commands to you through him, from the day the LORD gave them and continuing through the generations to come— 24and if this is done unintentionally without the community being aware of it, then the whole community is to offer a young bull for a burnt offering as an aroma pleasing to the LORD, along with its prescribed grain offering and drink offering, and a male goat for a sin offering. 25The priest is to make atonement for the whole Israelite community, and they will be forgiven, for it was not intentional and they have brought to the LORD for their wrong an offering made by fire and a sin offering. 26The whole Israelite community and the aliens living among them will be forgiven, because all the people were involved in the unintentional wrong.

27*" '*But if just one person sins unintentionally, he must bring a year-old female goat for a sin offering. 28The priest is to make atonement before the LORD for the one who erred by sinning unintentionally, and when atonement has been made for him, he will be forgiven. 29One and the same law applies to everyone who sins unintentionally, whether he is a native-born Israelite or an alien.

30*" '*But anyone who sins defiantly, whether native-born or alien, blasphemes the LORD, and that person must be cut off from his people. 31Because he has despised the LORD's word and broken his commands, that person must surely be cut off; his guilt remains on him.' "

The Sabbath-Breaker Put to Death

32While the Israelites were in the desert, a man was found gathering wood on the Sabbath day. 33Those who found him gathering wood brought him to Moses and Aaron and the whole assembly, 34and they kept him in custody, because it was not clear what should be done to him. 35Then the LORD said to Moses, "The man must die. The whole assembly must stone him outside the camp." 36So the assembly took him outside the camp and stoned him to death, as the LORD commanded Moses.

---

a 4 That is, probably about 1 quart (about 1 liter); also in verse 5   *b 6* That is, probably about 4 quarts (about 4.5 liters)   *c 6* That is, probably about 1 1/4 quarts (about 1.2 liters); also in verse 7   *d 8* Traditionally *peace offering*   *e 9* That is, probably about 6 quarts (about 6.5 liters)   *f 9* That is, probably about 2 quarts (about 2 liters); also in verse 10

Tassels on Garments

37 The LORD said to Moses, **38** "Speak to the Israelites and say to them: 'Throughout the generations to come you are to make tassels on the corners of your garments, with a blue cord on each tassel. **39** You will have these tassels to look at and so you will remember all the commands of the LORD, that you may obey them and not prostitute yourselves by going after the lusts of your own hearts and eyes. **40** Then you will remember to obey all my commands and will be consecrated to your God. **41** I am the LORD your God, who brought you out of Egypt to be your God. I am the LORD your God.' "

Korah, Dathan and Abiram

16 Korah son of Izhar, the son of Kohath, the son of Levi, and certain Reubenites—Dathan and Abiram, sons of Eliab, and On son of Peleth—became insolent[a] **2** and rose up against Moses. With them were 250 Israelite men, well-known community leaders who had been appointed members of the council. **3** They came as a group to oppose Moses and Aaron and said to them, "You have gone too far! The whole community is holy, every one of them, and the LORD is with them. Why then do you set yourselves above the LORD's assembly?"

4 When Moses heard this, he fell facedown. **5** Then he said to Korah and all his followers: "In the morning the LORD will show who belongs to him and who is holy, and he will have that person come near him. The man he chooses he will cause to come near him. **6** You, Korah, and all your followers are to do this: Take censers **7** and tomorrow put fire and incense in them before the LORD. The man the LORD chooses will be the one who is holy. You Levites have gone too far!"

8 Moses also said to Korah, "Now listen, you Levites! **9** Isn't it enough for you that the God of Israel has separated you from the rest of the Israelite community and brought you near himself to do the work at the LORD's tabernacle and to stand before the community and

minister to them? **10** He has brought you and all your fellow Levites near himself, but now you are trying to get the priesthood too. **11** It is against the LORD that you and all your followers have banded together. Who is Aaron that you should grumble against him?"

12 Then Moses summoned Dathan and Abiram, the sons of Eliab. But they said, "We will not come! **13** Isn't it enough that you have brought us up out of a land flowing with milk and honey to kill us in the desert? And now you also want to lord it over us? **14** Moreover, you haven't brought us into a land flowing with milk and honey or given us an inheritance of fields and vineyards. Will you gouge out the eyes of[b] these men? No, we will not come!"

15 Then Moses became very angry and said to the LORD, "Do not accept their offering. I have not taken so much as a donkey from them, nor have I wronged any of them."

16 Moses said to Korah, "You and all your followers are to appear before the LORD tomorrow—you and they and Aaron. **17** Each man is to take his censer and put incense in it—250 censers in all—and present it before the LORD. You and Aaron are to present your censers also." **18** So each man took his censer, put fire and incense in it, and stood with Moses and Aaron at the entrance to the Tent of Meeting. **19** When Korah had gathered all his followers in opposition to them at the entrance to the Tent of Meeting, the glory of the LORD appeared to the entire assembly. **20** The LORD said to Moses and Aaron, **21** "Separate yourselves from this assembly so I can put an end to them at once."

22 But Moses and Aaron fell facedown and cried out, "O God, God of the spirits of all mankind, will you be angry with the entire assembly when only one man sins?"

23 Then the LORD said to Moses, **24** "Say to the assembly, 'Move away from the tents of Korah, Dathan and Abiram.' "

25 Moses got up and went to Dathan and Abiram, and the elders of Israel followed him. **26** He warned the assembly, "Move back from the tents of these wicked men! Do not touch anything

JEALOUSY AND THE GRACE OF REPENTANCE
Clement of Rome

VERSE: Numbers 16:1   **PASSAGE:** Numbers 16:1–3, 22–35

nd Cain said to Abel his brother, 'Let us go out to the field.' And it came to pass, while they were in the field, that Cain rose up against Abel his brother and killed him" (see Genesis 4:8). You see, brothers, jealousy and envy brought about a brother's murder. Because of jealousy our father Jacob ran away from the presence of Esau his brother. Jealousy caused Joseph to be persecuted nearly to death, and to be sold into slavery. Jealousy compelled Moses to flee from the presence of Pharaoh, king of Egypt, when he was asked by his own countryman, "Who made you a judge or ruler over us? Do you want to kill me, just as you killed the Egyptian yesterday?" (see Exodus 2:14). Because of jealousy Aaron and Miriam were excluded from the camp. Jealousy brought Dathan and Abiram down alive into *hades*, because they revolted against Moses, the servant of God. Because of jealousy David not only was envied by the Philistines, but also was persecuted by Saul, king of Israel.

But to pass from the examples of ancient times, let us come to those champions who lived nearest to our time. Let us set before us the noble examples which belong to our own generation. Because of jealousy and envy the greatest and most righteous pillars were persecuted, and fought to the death. Let us set before our eyes the good apostles . . .

We write these things, dear friends, not only to admonish you, but also to remind ourselves. For we are in the same arena, and the same contest awaits us. Therefore let us abandon empty and futile thoughts, and let us conform to the glorious and holy rule of our tradition; indeed, let us note what is good and what is pleasing and what is acceptable in the sight of him who made us. Let us fix our eyes on the blood of Christ and understand how precious it is to his Father, because, being poured out for our salvation, it won for the whole world the grace of repentance.

ADDITIONAL SCRIPTURE READING:
Job 5:2; Philippians 4:8–9; James 3:16

Go to page 185 for your next devotional reading.

belonging to them, or you will be swept away because of all their sins." 27So they moved away from the tents of Korah, Dathan and Abiram. Dathan and Abiram had come out and were standing with their wives, children and little ones at the entrances to their tents.

28Then Moses said, "This is how you will know that the LORD has sent me to do all these things and that it was not my idea: 29If these men die a natural death and experience only what usually happens to men, then the LORD has not sent me. 30But if the LORD brings about something totally new, and the earth opens its mouth and swallows them, with everything that belongs to them, and they go down alive into the grave,^a then you will know that these men have treated the LORD with contempt."

31As soon as he finished saying all this, the ground under them split apart 32and the earth opened its mouth and swallowed them, with their households and all Korah's men and all their possessions. 33They went down alive into the grave, with everything they owned; the earth closed over them, and they perished and were gone from the community. 34At their cries, all the Israelites around them fled, shouting, "The earth is going to swallow us too!"

35And fire came out from the LORD and consumed the 250 men who were offering the incense.

36The LORD said to Moses, 37"Tell Eleazar son of Aaron, the priest, to take the censers out of the smoldering remains and scatter the coals some distance away, for the censers are holy— 38the censers of the men who sinned at the cost of their lives. Hammer the censers into sheets to overlay the altar, for they were presented before the LORD and have become holy. Let them be a sign to the Israelites."

39So Eleazar the priest collected the bronze censers brought by those who had been burned up, and he had them hammered out to overlay the altar, 40as the LORD directed him through Moses. This was to remind the Israelites that no one except a descendant of Aaron should come to burn incense before the LORD, or he would become like Korah and his followers.

41The next day the whole Israelite community grumbled against Moses and Aaron. "You have killed the LORD's people," they said.

42But when the assembly gathered in opposition to Moses and Aaron and turned toward the Tent of Meeting, suddenly the cloud covered it and the glory of the LORD appeared. 43Then Moses and Aaron went to the front of the Tent of Meeting, 44and the LORD said to Moses, 45"Get away from this assembly so I can put an end to them at once." And they fell facedown.

46Then Moses said to Aaron, "Take your censer and put incense in it, along with fire from the altar, and hurry to the assembly to make atonement for them. Wrath has come out from the LORD; the plague has started." 47So Aaron did as Moses said, and ran into the midst of the assembly. The plague had already started among the people, but Aaron offered the incense and made atonement for them. 48He stood between the living and the dead, and the plague stopped. 49But 14,700 people died from the plague, in addition to those who had died because of Korah. 50Then Aaron returned to Moses at the entrance to the Tent of Meeting, for the plague had stopped.

The Budding of Aaron's Staff

17 The LORD said to Moses, 2"Speak to the Israelites and get twelve staffs from them, one from the leader of each of their ancestral tribes. Write the name of each man on his staff. 3On the staff of Levi write Aaron's name, for there must be one staff for the head of each ancestral tribe. 4Place them in the Tent of Meeting in front of the Testimony, where I meet with you. 5The staff belonging to the man I choose will sprout, and I will rid myself of this constant grumbling against you by the Israelites."

6So Moses spoke to the Israelites, and their leaders gave him twelve staffs, one for the leader of each of their ancestral tribes, and Aaron's staff was among them. 7Moses placed the staffs before the LORD in the Tent of the Testimony.

8The next day Moses entered the Tent of the Testimony and saw that Aaron's

^a 30 Hebrew *Sheol*; also in verse 33

staff, which represented the house of Levi, had not only sprouted but had budded, blossomed and produced almonds. ⁹Then Moses brought out all the staffs from the LORD's presence to all the Israelites. They looked at them, and each man took his own staff.

¹⁰The LORD said to Moses, "Put back Aaron's staff in front of the Testimony, to be kept as a sign to the rebellious. This will put an end to their grumbling against me, so that they will not die." ¹¹Moses did just as the LORD commanded him.

¹²The Israelites said to Moses, "We will die! We are lost, we are all lost! ¹³Anyone who even comes near the tabernacle of the LORD will die. Are we all going to die?"

Duties of Priests and Levites

18 The LORD said to Aaron, "You, your sons and your father's family are to bear the responsibility for offenses against the sanctuary, and you and your sons alone are to bear the responsibility for offenses against the priesthood. ²Bring your fellow Levites from your ancestral tribe to join you and assist you when you and your sons minister before the Tent of the Testimony. ³They are to be responsible to you and are to perform all the duties of the Tent, but they must not go near the furnishings of the sanctuary or the altar, or both they and you will die. ⁴They are to join you and be responsible for the care of the Tent of Meeting—all the work at the Tent—and no one else may come near where you are.

⁵"You are to be responsible for the care of the sanctuary and the altar, so that wrath will not fall on the Israelites again. ⁶I myself have selected your fellow Levites from among the Israelites as a gift to you, dedicated to the LORD to do the work at the Tent of Meeting. ⁷But only you and your sons may serve as priests in connection with everything at the altar and inside the curtain. I am giving you the service of the priesthood as a gift. Anyone else who comes near the sanctuary must be put to death."

Offerings for Priests and Levites

⁸Then the LORD said to Aaron, "I myself have put you in charge of the offerings presented to me; all the holy offerings the Israelites give me I give to you and your sons as your portion and regular share. ⁹You are to have the part of the most holy offerings that is kept from the fire. From all the gifts they bring me as most holy offerings, whether grain or sin or guilt offerings, that part belongs to you and your sons. ¹⁰Eat it as something most holy; every male shall eat it. You must regard it as holy.

¹¹"This also is yours: whatever is set aside from the gifts of all the wave offerings of the Israelites. I give this to you and your sons and daughters as your regular share. Everyone in your household who is ceremonially clean may eat it.

¹²"I give you all the finest olive oil and all the finest new wine and grain they give the LORD as the firstfruits of their harvest. ¹³All the land's firstfruits that they bring to the LORD will be yours. Everyone in your household who is ceremonially clean may eat it.

¹⁴"Everything in Israel that is devoted[a] to the LORD is yours. ¹⁵The first offspring of every womb, both man and animal, that is offered to the LORD is yours. But you must redeem every firstborn son and every firstborn male of unclean animals. ¹⁶When they are a month old, you must redeem them at the redemption price set at five shekels[b] of silver, according to the sanctuary shekel, which weighs twenty gerahs.

¹⁷"But you must not redeem the firstborn of an ox, a sheep or a goat; they are holy. Sprinkle their blood on the altar and burn their fat as an offering made by fire, an aroma pleasing to the LORD. ¹⁸Their meat is to be yours, just as the breast of the wave offering and the right thigh are yours. ¹⁹Whatever is set aside from the holy offerings the Israelites present to the LORD I give to you and your sons and daughters as your regular share. It is an everlasting covenant of salt before the LORD for both you and your offspring."

²⁰The LORD said to Aaron, "You will have no inheritance in their land, nor

---

a 14 The Hebrew term refers to the irrevocable giving over of things or persons to the LORD.   *b 16* That is, about 2 ounces (about 55 grams)

will you have any share among them; I am your share and your inheritance among the Israelites.

21 "I give to the Levites all the tithes in Israel as their inheritance in return for the work they do while serving at the Tent of Meeting. 22 From now on the Israelites must not go near the Tent of Meeting, or they will bear the consequences of their sin and will die. 23 It is the Levites who are to do the work at the Tent of Meeting and bear the responsibility for offenses against it. This is a lasting ordinance for the generations to come. They will receive no inheritance among the Israelites. 24 Instead, I give to the Levites as their inheritance the tithes that the Israelites present as an offering to the LORD. That is why I said concerning them: 'They will have no inheritance among the Israelites.' "

25 The LORD said to Moses, 26 "Speak to the Levites and say to them: 'When you receive from the Israelites the tithe I give you as your inheritance, you must present a tenth of that tithe as the LORD's offering. 27 Your offering will be reckoned to you as grain from the threshing floor or juice from the winepress. 28 In this way you also will present an offering to the LORD from all the tithes you receive from the Israelites. From these tithes you must give the LORD's portion to Aaron the priest. 29 You must present as the LORD's portion the best and holiest part of everything given to you.'

30 "Say to the Levites: 'When you present the best part, it will be reckoned to you as the product of the threshing floor or the winepress. 31 You and your households may eat the rest of it anywhere, for it is your wages for your work at the Tent of Meeting. 32 By presenting the best part of it you will not be guilty in this matter; then you will not defile the holy offerings of the Israelites, and you will not die.' "

The Water of Cleansing

19 The LORD said to Moses and Aaron: 2 "This is a requirement of the law that the LORD has commanded: Tell the Israelites to bring you a red heifer without defect or blemish and that has never been under a yoke. 3 Give it to Eleazar the priest; it is to be

taken outside the camp and slaughtered in his presence. 4 Then Eleazar the priest is to take some of its blood on his finger and sprinkle it seven times toward the front of the Tent of Meeting. 5 While he watches, the heifer is to be burned—its hide, flesh, blood and offal. 6 The priest is to take some cedar wood, hyssop and scarlet wool and throw them onto the burning heifer. 7 After that, the priest must wash his clothes and bathe himself with water. He may then come into the camp, but he will be ceremonially unclean till evening. 8 The man who burns it must also wash his clothes and bathe with water, and he too will be unclean till evening.

9 "A man who is clean shall gather up the ashes of the heifer and put them in a ceremonially clean place outside the camp. They shall be kept by the Israelite community for use in the water of cleansing; it is for purification from sin. 10 The man who gathers up the ashes of the heifer must also wash his clothes, and he too will be unclean till evening. This will be a lasting ordinance both for the Israelites and for the aliens living among them.

11 "Whoever touches the dead body of anyone will be unclean for seven days. 12 He must purify himself with the water on the third day and on the seventh day; then he will be clean. But if he does not purify himself on the third and seventh days, he will not be clean. 13 Whoever touches the dead body of anyone and fails to purify himself defiles the LORD's tabernacle. That person must be cut off from Israel. Because the water of cleansing has not been sprinkled on him, he is unclean; his uncleanness remains on him.

14 "This is the law that applies when a person dies in a tent: Anyone who enters the tent and anyone who is in it will be unclean for seven days, 15 and every open container without a lid fastened on it will be unclean.

16 "Anyone out in the open who touches someone who has been killed with a sword or someone who has died a natural death, or anyone who touches a human bone or a grave, will be unclean for seven days.

17 "For the unclean person, put some ashes from the burned purification

offering into a jar and pour fresh water over them. 18Then a man who is ceremonially clean is to take some hyssop, dip it in the water and sprinkle the tent and all the furnishings and the people who were there. He must also sprinkle anyone who has touched a human bone or a grave or someone who has been killed or someone who has died a natural death. 19The man who is clean is to sprinkle the unclean person on the third and seventh days, and on the seventh day he is to purify him. The person being cleansed must wash his clothes and bathe with water, and that evening he will be clean. 20But if a person who is unclean does not purify himself, he must be cut off from the community, because he has defiled the sanctuary of the LORD. The water of cleansing has not been sprinkled on him, and he is unclean. 21This is a lasting ordinance for them.

"The man who sprinkles the water of cleansing must also wash his clothes, and anyone who touches the water of cleansing will be unclean till evening. 22Anything that an unclean person touches becomes unclean, and anyone who touches it becomes unclean till evening."

Water From the Rock

20 In the first month the whole Israelite community arrived at the Desert of Zin, and they stayed at Kadesh. There Miriam died and was buried.

2Now there was no water for the community, and the people gathered in opposition to Moses and Aaron. 3They quarreled with Moses and said, "If only we had died when our brothers fell dead before the LORD! 4Why did you bring the LORD's community into this desert, that we and our livestock should die here? 5Why did you bring us up out of Egypt to this terrible place? It has no grain or figs, grapevines or pomegranates. And there is no water to drink!"

6Moses and Aaron went from the assembly to the entrance to the Tent of Meeting and fell facedown, and the glory of the LORD appeared to them. 7The LORD said to Moses, 8"Take the staff, and you and your brother Aaron

gather the assembly together. Speak to that rock before their eyes and it will pour out its water. You will bring water out of the rock for the community so they and their livestock can drink."

9So Moses took the staff from the LORD's presence, just as he commanded him. 10He and Aaron gathered the assembly together in front of the rock and Moses said to them, "Listen, you rebels, must we bring you water out of this rock?" 11Then Moses raised his arm and struck the rock twice with his staff. Water gushed out, and the community and their livestock drank.

12But the LORD said to Moses and Aaron, "Because you did not trust in me enough to honor me as holy in the sight of the Israelites, you will not bring this community into the land I give them."

13These were the waters of Meribah,a where the Israelites quarreled with the LORD and where he showed himself holy among them.

Edom Denies Israel Passage

14Moses sent messengers from Kadesh to the king of Edom, saying:

"This is what your brother Israel says: You know about all the hardships that have come upon us. 15Our forefathers went down into Egypt, and we lived there many years. The Egyptians mistreated us and our fathers, 16but when we cried out to the LORD, he heard our cry and sent an angel and brought us out of Egypt.

"Now we are here at Kadesh, a town on the edge of your territory. 17Please let us pass through your country. We will not go through any field or vineyard, or drink water from any well. We will travel along the king's highway and not turn to the right or to the left until we have passed through your territory."

18But Edom answered:

"You may not pass through here; if you try, we will march out and attack you with the sword."

19The Israelites replied:

"We will go along the main road,

a 13 Meribah means quarreling.

and if we or our livestock drink any of your water, we will pay for it. We only want to pass through on foot—nothing else."

20Again they answered:

"You may not pass through."

Then Edom came out against them with a large and powerful army. 21Since Edom refused to let them go through their territory, Israel turned away from them.

The Death of Aaron

22The whole Israelite community set out from Kadesh and came to Mount Hor. 23At Mount Hor, near the border of Edom, the LORD said to Moses and Aaron, 24"Aaron will be gathered to his people. He will not enter the land I give the Israelites, because both of you rebelled against my command at the waters of Meribah. 25Get Aaron and his son Eleazar and take them up Mount Hor. 26Remove Aaron's garments and put them on his son Eleazar, for Aaron will be gathered to his people; he will die there."

27Moses did as the LORD commanded: They went up Mount Hor in the sight of the whole community. 28Moses removed Aaron's garments and put them on his son Eleazar. And Aaron died there on top of the mountain. Then Moses and Eleazar came down from the mountain, 29and when the whole community learned that Aaron had died, the entire house of Israel mourned for him thirty days.

Arad Destroyed

21 When the Canaanite king of Arad, who lived in the Negev, heard that Israel was coming along the road to Atharim, he attacked the Israelites and captured some of them. 2Then Israel made this vow to the LORD: "If you will deliver these people into our hands, we will totally destroy*a* their cities." 3The LORD listened to Israel's plea and gave the Canaanites over to them. They completely destroyed them and

their towns; so the place was named Hormah.*b*

The Bronze Snake

4They traveled from Mount Hor along the route to the Red Sea,*c* to go around Edom. But the people grew impatient on the way; 5they spoke against God and against Moses, and said, "Why have you brought us up out of Egypt to die in the desert? There is no bread! There is no water! And we detest this miserable food!"

6Then the LORD sent venomous snakes among them; they bit the people and many Israelites died. 7The people came to Moses and said, "We sinned when we spoke against the LORD and against you. Pray that the LORD will take the snakes away from us." So Moses prayed for the people.

8The LORD said to Moses, "Make a snake and put it up on a pole; anyone who is bitten can look at it and live." 9So Moses made a bronze snake and put it up on a pole. Then when anyone was bitten by a snake and looked at the bronze snake, he lived.

The Journey to Moab

10The Israelites moved on and camped at Oboth. 11Then they set out from Oboth and camped in Iye Abarim, in the desert that faces Moab toward the sunrise. 12From there they moved on and camped in the Zered Valley. 13They set out from there and camped alongside the Arnon, which is in the desert extending into Amorite territory. The Arnon is the border of Moab, between Moab and the Amorites. 14That is why the Book of the Wars of the LORD says:

"... Waheb in Suphah*d* and the
    ravines,
  the Arnon 15and*e* the slopes of the
    ravines
that lead to the site of Ar
  and lie along the border of Moab."

16From there they continued on to Beer, the well where the LORD said to Moses,

---

a 2 The Hebrew term refers to the irrevocable giving over of things or persons to the LORD, often by totally destroying them; also in verse 3.　　*b 3* *Hormah* means *destruction.*　　*c 4* Hebrew *Yam Suph;* that is, Sea of Reeds　　*d 14* The meaning of the Hebrew for this phrase is uncertain.　　*e 14,15* Or "I have been given from Suphah and the ravines / of the Arnon* 15to*

"Gather the people together and I will give them water."

[17]Then Israel sang this song:

"Spring up, O well!
   Sing about it,
[18]about the well that the princes dug,
   that the nobles of the people sank—
   the nobles with scepters and staffs."

Then they went from the desert to Mattanah, [19]from Mattanah to Nahaliel, from Nahaliel to Bamoth, [20]and from Bamoth to the valley in Moab where the top of Pisgah overlooks the wasteland.

Defeat of Sihon and Og

[21]Israel sent messengers to say to Sihon king of the Amorites:

[22]"Let us pass through your country. We will not turn aside into any field or vineyard, or drink water from any well. We will travel along the king's highway until we have passed through your territory."

[23]But Sihon would not let Israel pass through his territory. He mustered his entire army and marched out into the desert against Israel. When he reached Jahaz, he fought with Israel. [24]Israel, however, put him to the sword and took over his land from the Arnon to the Jabbok, but only as far as the Ammonites, because their border was fortified. [25]Israel captured all the cities of the Amorites and occupied them, including Heshbon and all its surrounding settlements. [26]Heshbon was the city of Sihon king of the Amorites, who had fought against the former king of Moab and had taken from him all his land as far as the Arnon. [27]That is why the poets say:

"Come to Heshbon and let it be
   rebuilt;
   let Sihon's city be restored.

[28]"Fire went out from Heshbon,
   a blaze from the city of Sihon.
It consumed Ar of Moab,
   the citizens of Arnon's heights.
[29]Woe to you, O Moab!
   You are destroyed, O people of
   Chemosh!

He has given up his sons as fugitives
   and his daughters as captives
   to Sihon king of the Amorites.

[30]"But we have overthrown them;
   Heshbon is destroyed all the way
   to Dibon.
We have demolished them as far as
   Nophah,
   which extends to Medeba."

[31]So Israel settled in the land of the Amorites.

[32]After Moses had sent spies to Jazer, the Israelites captured its surrounding settlements and drove out the Amorites who were there. [33]Then they turned and went up along the road toward Bashan, and Og king of Bashan and his whole army marched out to meet them in battle at Edrei.

[34]The LORD said to Moses, "Do not be afraid of him, for I have handed him over to you, with his whole army and his land. Do to him what you did to Sihon king of the Amorites, who reigned in Heshbon."

[35]So they struck him down, together with his sons and his whole army, leaving them no survivors. And they took possession of his land.

Balak Summons Balaam

22 Then the Israelites traveled to the plains of Moab and camped along the Jordan across from Jericho.[a]

[2]Now Balak son of Zippor saw all that Israel had done to the Amorites, [3]and Moab was terrified because there were so many people. Indeed, Moab was filled with dread because of the Israelites.

[4]The Moabites said to the elders of Midian, "This horde is going to lick up everything around us, as an ox licks up the grass of the field."

So Balak son of Zippor, who was king of Moab at that time, [5]sent messengers to summon Balaam son of Beor, who was at Pethor, near the River,[b] in his native land. Balak said:

"A people has come out of Egypt;
   they cover the face of the land and
   have settled next to me. [6]Now come
   and put a curse on these people,

because they are too powerful for me. Perhaps then I will be able to defeat them and drive them out of the country. For I know that those you bless are blessed, and those you curse are cursed."

7The elders of Moab and Midian left, taking with them the fee for divination. When they came to Balaam, they told him what Balak had said.

8"Spend the night here," Balaam said to them, "and I will bring you back the answer the LORD gives me." So the Moabite princes stayed with him.

9God came to Balaam and asked, "Who are these men with you?"

10Balaam said to God, "Balak son of Zippor, king of Moab, sent me this message: 11'A people that has come out of Egypt covers the face of the land. Now come and put a curse on them for me. Perhaps then I will be able to fight them and drive them away.' "

12But God said to Balaam, "Do not go with them. You must not put a curse on those people, because they are blessed."

13The next morning Balaam got up and said to Balak's princes, "Go back to your own country, for the LORD has refused to let me go with you."

14So the Moabite princes returned to Balak and said, "Balaam refused to come with us."

15Then Balak sent other princes, more numerous and more distinguished than the first. 16They came to Balaam and said:

"This is what Balak son of Zippor says: Do not let anything keep you from coming to me, 17because I will reward you handsomely and do whatever you say. Come and put a curse on these people for me."

18But Balaam answered them, "Even if Balak gave me his palace filled with silver and gold, I could not do anything great or small to go beyond the command of the LORD my God. 19Now stay here tonight as the others did, and I will find out what else the LORD will tell me."

20That night God came to Balaam and said, "Since these men have come to summon you, go with them, but do only what I tell you."

Balaam's Donkey

21Balaam got up in the morning, saddled his donkey and went with the princes of Moab. 22But God was very angry when he went, and the angel of the LORD stood in the road to oppose him. Balaam was riding on his donkey, and his two servants were with him. 23When the donkey saw the angel of the LORD standing in the road with a drawn sword in his hand, she turned off the road into a field. Balaam beat her to get her back on the road.

24Then the angel of the LORD stood in a narrow path between two vineyards, with walls on both sides. 25When the donkey saw the angel of the LORD, she pressed close to the wall, crushing Balaam's foot against it. So he beat her again.

26Then the angel of the LORD moved on ahead and stood in a narrow place where there was no room to turn, either to the right or to the left. 27When the donkey saw the angel of the LORD, she lay down under Balaam, and he was angry and beat her with his staff. 28Then the LORD opened the donkey's mouth, and she said to Balaam, "What have I done to you to make you beat me these three times?"

29Balaam answered the donkey, "You have made a fool of me! If I had a sword in my hand, I would kill you right now."

30The donkey said to Balaam, "Am I not your own donkey, which you have always ridden, to this day? Have I been in the habit of doing this to you?"

"No," he said.

31Then the LORD opened Balaam's eyes, and he saw the angel of the LORD standing in the road with his sword drawn. So he bowed low and fell facedown.

32The angel of the LORD asked him, "Why have you beaten your donkey these three times? I have come here to oppose you because your path is a reckless one before me.a 33The donkey saw me and turned away from me these three times. If she had not turned away,

a 32 The meaning of the Hebrew for this clause is uncertain.

I would certainly have killed you by now, but I would have spared her."

34Balaam said to the angel of the LORD, "I have sinned. I did not realize you were standing in the road to oppose me. Now if you are displeased, I will go back."

35The angel of the LORD said to Balaam, "Go with the men, but speak only what I tell you." So Balaam went with the princes of Balak.

36When Balak heard that Balaam was coming, he went out to meet him at the Moabite town on the Arnon border, at the edge of his territory. 37Balak said to Balaam, "Did I not send you an urgent summons? Why didn't you come to me? Am I really not able to reward you?"

38"Well, I have come to you now," Balaam replied. "But can I say just anything? I must speak only what God puts in my mouth."

39Then Balaam went with Balak to Kiriath Huzoth. 40Balak sacrificed cattle and sheep, and gave some to Balaam and the princes who were with him. 41The next morning Balak took Balaam up to Bamoth Baal, and from there he saw part of the people.

Balaam's First Oracle

23 Balaam said, "Build me seven altars here, and prepare seven bulls and seven rams for me." 2Balak did as Balaam said, and the two of them offered a bull and a ram on each altar.

3Then Balaam said to Balak, "Stay here beside your offering while I go aside. Perhaps the LORD will come to meet with me. Whatever he reveals to me I will tell you." Then he went off to a barren height.

4God met with him, and Balaam said, "I have prepared seven altars, and on each altar I have offered a bull and a ram."

5The LORD put a message in Balaam's mouth and said, "Go back to Balak and give him this message."

6So he went back to him and found him standing beside his offering, with all the princes of Moab. 7Then Balaam uttered his oracle:

"Balak brought me from Aram,
    the king of Moab from the eastern
        mountains.
'Come,' he said, 'curse Jacob for me;
    come, denounce Israel.'
8How can I curse
    those whom God has not cursed?
How can I denounce
    those whom the LORD has not
        denounced?
9From the rocky peaks I see them,
    from the heights I view them.
I see a people who live apart
    and do not consider themselves
        one of the nations.
10Who can count the dust of Jacob
    or number the fourth part of Israel?
Let me die the death of the righteous,
    and may my end be like theirs!"

11Balak said to Balaam, "What have you done to me? I brought you to curse my enemies, but you have done nothing but bless them!"

12He answered, "Must I not speak what the LORD puts in my mouth?"

Balaam's Second Oracle

13Then Balak said to him, "Come with me to another place where you can see them; you will see only a part but not all of them. And from there, curse them for me." 14So he took him to the field of Zophim on the top of Pisgah, and there he built seven altars and offered a bull and a ram on each altar.

15Balaam said to Balak, "Stay here beside your offering while I meet with him over there."

16The LORD met with Balaam and put a message in his mouth and said, "Go back to Balak and give him this message."

17So he went to him and found him standing beside his offering, with the princes of Moab. Balak asked him, "What did the LORD say?"

18Then he uttered his oracle:

"Arise, Balak, and listen;
    hear me, son of Zippor.
19God is not a man, that he should lie,
    nor a son of man, that he should
        change his mind.
Does he speak and then not act?
Does he promise and not fulfill?
20I have received a command to bless;
    he has blessed, and I cannot change
        it.

21 "No misfortune is seen in Jacob,
  no misery observed in Israel.ᵃ
The LORD their God is with them;
  the shout of the King is among
    them.
22 God brought them out of Egypt;
  they have the strength of a wild ox.
23 There is no sorcery against Jacob,
  no divination against Israel.
It will now be said of Jacob
  and of Israel, 'See what God has
    done!'
24 The people rise like a lioness;
  they rouse themselves like a lion
that does not rest till he devours his
    prey
  and drinks the blood of his
    victims."

25 Then Balak said to Balaam, "Neither curse them at all nor bless them at all!"
26 Balaam answered, "Did I not tell you I must do whatever the LORD says?"

Balaam's Third Oracle

27 Then Balak said to Balaam, "Come, let me take you to another place. Perhaps it will please God to let you curse them for me from there." 28 And Balak took Balaam to the top of Peor, overlooking the wasteland.
29 Balaam said, "Build me seven altars here, and prepare seven bulls and seven rams for me." 30 Balak did as Balaam had said, and offered a bull and a ram on each altar.

24 Now when Balaam saw that it pleased the LORD to bless Israel, he did not resort to sorcery as at other times, but turned his face toward the desert. 2 When Balaam looked out and saw Israel encamped tribe by tribe, the Spirit of God came upon him 3 and he uttered his oracle:

"The oracle of Balaam son of Beor,
  the oracle of one whose eye sees
    clearly,
4 the oracle of one who hears the
    words of God,
  who sees a vision from the
    Almighty,ᵇ
who falls prostrate, and whose eyes
    are opened:

5 "How beautiful are your tents,
    O Jacob,
  your dwelling places, O Israel!

6 "Like valleys they spread out,
  like gardens beside a river,
like aloes planted by the LORD,
  like cedars beside the waters.
7 Water will flow from their buckets;
  their seed will have abundant
    water.

"Their king will be greater than Agag;
  their kingdom will be exalted.

8 "God brought them out of Egypt;
  they have the strength of a wild ox.
They devour hostile nations
  and break their bones in pieces;
  with their arrows they pierce them.
9 Like a lion they crouch and lie down,
  like a lioness—who dares to rouse
    them?

"May those who bless you be blessed
  and those who curse you be
    cursed!"

10 Then Balak's anger burned against Balaam. He struck his hands together and said to him, "I summoned you to curse my enemies, but you have blessed them these three times. 11 Now leave at once and go home! I said I would reward you handsomely, but the LORD has kept you from being rewarded."

12 Balaam answered Balak, "Did I not tell the messengers you sent me, 13 'Even if Balak gave me his palace filled with silver and gold, I could not do anything of my own accord, good or bad, to go beyond the command of the LORD—and I must say only what the LORD says'? 14 Now I am going back to my people, but come, let me warn you of what this people will do to your people in days to come."

Balaam's Fourth Oracle

15 Then he uttered his oracle:

"The oracle of Balaam son of Beor,
  the oracle of one whose eye sees
    clearly,
16 the oracle of one who hears the
    words of God,

ᵃ 21 Or He has not looked on Jacob's offenses / or on the wrongs found in Israel.   ᵇ 4 Hebrew Shaddai; also in verse 16

who has knowledge from the Most
   High,
who sees a vision from the Almighty,
   who falls prostrate, and whose eyes
   are opened:

17 "I see him, but not now;
   I behold him, but not near.
A star will come out of Jacob;
   a scepter will rise out of Israel.
He will crush the foreheads of Moab,
   the skulls*a* of*b* all the sons of
   Sheth.*c*
18 Edom will be conquered;
   Seir, his enemy, will be conquered,
   but Israel will grow strong.
19 A ruler will come out of Jacob
   and destroy the survivors of the
   city."

Balaam's Final Oracles

20 Then Balaam saw Amalek and
uttered his oracle:

"Amalek was first among the nations,
   but he will come to ruin at last."

21 Then he saw the Kenites and
uttered his oracle:

"Your dwelling place is secure,
   your nest is set in a rock;
22 yet you Kenites will be destroyed
   when Asshur takes you captive."

23 Then he uttered his oracle:

"Ah, who can live when God does
   this?*d*
24 Ships will come from the shores of
   Kittim;
they will subdue Asshur and Eber,
   but they too will come to ruin."

25 Then Balaam got up and returned
home and Balak went his own way.

Moab Seduces Israel

25 While Israel was staying in
Shittim, the men began to
indulge in sexual immorality with
Moabite women, 2who invited them to
the sacrifices to their gods. The people
ate and bowed down before these gods.

3 So Israel joined in worshiping the Baal
of Peor. And the LORD's anger burned
against them.

4 The LORD said to Moses, "Take all
the leaders of these people, kill them
and expose them in broad daylight
before the LORD, so that the LORD's
fierce anger may turn away from Israel."

5 So Moses said to Israel's judges,
"Each of you must put to death those of
your men who have joined in worshiping the Baal of Peor."

6 Then an Israelite man brought to his
family a Midianite woman right before
the eyes of Moses and the whole assembly of Israel while they were weeping at
the entrance to the Tent of Meeting.
7 When Phinehas son of Eleazar, the son
of Aaron, the priest, saw this, he left the
assembly, took a spear in his hand 8and
followed the Israelite into the tent. He
drove the spear through both of them—
through the Israelite and into the
woman's body. Then the plague against
the Israelites was stopped; 9but those
who died in the plague numbered 24,000.

10 The LORD said to Moses, 11 "Phinehas son of Eleazar, the son of Aaron, the
priest, has turned my anger away from
the Israelites; for he was as zealous as I
am for my honor among them, so that in
my zeal I did not put an end to them.
12 Therefore tell him I am making my
covenant of peace with him. 13 He and
his descendants will have a covenant of
a lasting priesthood, because he was
zealous for the honor of his God and
made atonement for the Israelites."

14 The name of the Israelite who was
killed with the Midianite woman was
Zimri son of Salu, the leader of a Sime-
onite family. 15 And the name of the
Midianite woman who was put to death
was Cozbi daughter of Zur, a tribal chief
of a Midianite family.

16 The LORD said to Moses, 17 "Treat
the Midianites as enemies and kill
them, 18because they treated you as enemies when they deceived you in the
affair of Peor and their sister Cozbi, the
daughter of a Midianite leader, the
woman who was killed when the plague
came as a result of Peor."

---

a 17 Samaritan Pentateuch (see also Jer. 48:45); the meaning of the word in the Masoretic Text is
uncertain.   *b* 17 Or possibly *Moab,* / *batter*   *c* 17 Or *all the noisy boasters*   *d* 23 Masoretic Text;
with a different word division of the Hebrew *A people will gather from the north.*

The Second Census

26 After the plague the LORD said to Moses and Eleazar son of Aaron, the priest, 2 "Take a census of the whole Israelite community by families—all those twenty years old or more who are able to serve in the army of Israel." 3 So on the plains of Moab by the Jordan across from Jericho,[a] Moses and Eleazar the priest spoke with them and said, 4 "Take a census of the men twenty years old or more, as the LORD commanded Moses."

These were the Israelites who came out of Egypt:

5 The descendants of Reuben, the first-born son of Israel, were:

through Hanoch, the Hanochite clan;

through Pallu, the Palluite clan;

6 through Hezron, the Hezronite clan;

through Carmi, the Carmite clan.

7 These were the clans of Reuben; those numbered were 43,730.

8 The son of Pallu was Eliab, 9 and the sons of Eliab were Nemuel, Dathan and Abiram. The same Dathan and Abiram were the community officials who rebelled against Moses and Aaron and were among Korah's followers when they rebelled against the LORD. 10 The earth opened its mouth and swallowed them along with Korah, whose followers died when the fire devoured the 250 men. And they served as a warning sign. 11 The line of Korah, however, did not die out.

12 The descendants of Simeon by their clans were:

through Nemuel, the Nemuelite clan;

through Jamin, the Jaminite clan;

through Jakin, the Jakinite clan;

13 through Zerah, the Zerahite clan;

through Shaul, the Shaulite clan.

14 These were the clans of Simeon; there were 22,200 men.

15 The descendants of Gad by their clans were:

through Zephon, the Zephonite clan;

through Haggi, the Haggite clan;

through Shuni, the Shunite clan;

16 through Ozni, the Oznite clan;

through Eri, the Erite clan;

17 through Arodi,[b] the Arodite clan;

through Areli, the Arelite clan.

18 These were the clans of Gad; those numbered were 40,500.

19 Er and Onan were sons of Judah, but they died in Canaan.

20 The descendants of Judah by their clans were:

through Shelah, the Shelanite clan;

through Perez, the Perezite clan;

through Zerah, the Zerahite clan.

21 The descendants of Perez were:

through Hezron, the Hezronite clan;

through Hamul, the Hamulite clan.

22 These were the clans of Judah; those numbered were 76,500.

23 The descendants of Issachar by their clans were:

through Tola, the Tolaite clan;

through Puah, the Puite[c] clan;

24 through Jashub, the Jashubite clan;

through Shimron, the Shimronite clan.

25 These were the clans of Issachar; those numbered were 64,300.

26 The descendants of Zebulun by their clans were:

through Sered, the Seredite clan;

through Elon, the Elonite clan;

through Jahleel, the Jahleelite clan.

27 These were the clans of Zebulun; those numbered were 60,500.

28 The descendants of Joseph by their clans through Manasseh and Ephraim were:

29 The descendants of Manasseh:

through Makir, the Makirite clan (Makir was the father of Gilead);

through Gilead, the Gileadite clan.

30 These were the descendants of Gilead:

through Iezer, the Iezerite clan;

---

a 3 Hebrew *Jordan of Jericho;* possibly an ancient name for the Jordan River; also in verse 63   *b 17* Samaritan Pentateuch and Syriac (see also Gen. 46:16); Masoretic Text *Arod*   *c 23* Samaritan Pentateuch, Septuagint, Vulgate and Syriac (see also 1 Chron. 7:1); Masoretic Text *through Puvah, the Punite*

through Helek, the Helekite clan;
31 through Asriel, the Asrielite clan;
through Shechem, the Shechemite clan;
32 through Shemida, the Shemidaite clan;
through Hepher, the Hepherite clan.
33 (Zelophehad son of Hepher had no sons; he had only daughters, whose names were Mahlah, Noah, Hoglah, Milcah and Tirzah.)
34 These were the clans of Manasseh; those numbered were 52,700.

35 These were the descendants of Ephraim by their clans:
through Shuthelah, the Shuthelahite clan;
through Beker, the Bekerite clan;
through Tahan, the Tahanite clan.
36 These were the descendants of Shuthelah:
through Eran, the Eranite clan.
37 These were the clans of Ephraim; those numbered were 32,500.

These were the descendants of Joseph by their clans.

38 The descendants of Benjamin by their clans were:
through Bela, the Belaite clan;
through Ashbel, the Ashbelite clan;
through Ahiram, the Ahiramite clan;
39 through Shupham,*a* the Shuphamite clan;
through Hupham, the Huphamite clan.
40 The descendants of Bela through Ard and Naaman were:
through Ard,*b* the Ardite clan;
through Naaman, the Naamite clan.
41 These were the clans of Benjamin; those numbered were 45,600.

42 These were the descendants of Dan by their clans:
through Shuham, the Shuhamite clan.
These were the clans of Dan: **43** All of them were Shuhamite clans; and those numbered were 64,400.

44 The descendants of Asher by their clans were:
through Imnah, the Imnite clan;
through Ishvi, the Ishvite clan;
through Beriah, the Beriite clan;
45 and through the descendants of Beriah:
through Heber, the Heberite clan;
through Malkiel, the Malkielite clan.
46 (Asher had a daughter named Serah.)
47 These were the clans of Asher; those numbered were 53,400.

48 The descendants of Naphtali by their clans were:
through Jahzeel, the Jahzeelite clan;
through Guni, the Gunite clan;
49 through Jezer, the Jezerite clan;
through Shillem, the Shillemite clan.
50 These were the clans of Naphtali; those numbered were 45,400.

51 The total number of the men of Israel was 601,730.

52 The LORD said to Moses, **53** "The land is to be allotted to them as an inheritance based on the number of names. **54** To a larger group give a larger inheritance, and to a smaller group a smaller one; each is to receive its inheritance according to the number of those listed. **55** Be sure that the land is distributed by lot. What each group inherits will be according to the names for its ancestral tribe. **56** Each inheritance is to be distributed by lot among the larger and smaller groups."

57 These were the Levites who were counted by their clans:
through Gershon, the Gershonite clan;
through Kohath, the Kohathite clan;
through Merari, the Merarite clan.
58 These also were Levite clans:
the Libnite clan,
the Hebronite clan,
the Mahlite clan,

---

a 39 A few manuscripts of the Masoretic Text, Samaritan Pentateuch, Vulgate and Syriac (see also Septuagint); most manuscripts of the Masoretic Text *Shephupham*   *b 40* Samaritan Pentateuch and Vulgate (see also Septuagint); Masoretic Text does not have *through Ard.*

the Mushite clan,
the Korahite clan.

(Kohath was the forefather of Amram; 59the name of Amram's wife was Jochebed, a descendant of Levi, who was born to the Levites*a* in Egypt. To Amram she bore Aaron, Moses and their sister Miriam. 60Aaron was the father of Nadab and Abihu, Eleazar and Ithamar. 61But Nadab and Abihu died when they made an offering before the LORD with unauthorized fire.)

62All the male Levites a month old or more numbered 23,000. They were not counted along with the other Israelites because they received no inheritance among them.

63These are the ones counted by Moses and Eleazar the priest when they counted the Israelites on the plains of Moab by the Jordan across from Jericho. 64Not one of them was among those counted by Moses and Aaron the priest when they counted the Israelites in the Desert of Sinai. 65For the LORD had told those Israelites they would surely die in the desert, and not one of them was left except Caleb son of Jephunneh and Joshua son of Nun.

Zelophehad's Daughters

27 The daughters of Zelophehad son of Hepher, the son of Gilead, the son of Makir, the son of Manasseh, belonged to the clans of Manasseh son of Joseph. The names of the daughters were Mahlah, Noah, Hoglah, Milcah and Tirzah. They approached 2the entrance to the Tent of Meeting and stood before Moses, Eleazar the priest, the leaders and the whole assembly, and said, 3"Our father died in the desert. He was not among Korah's followers, who banded together against the LORD, but he died for his own sin and left no sons. 4Why should our father's name disappear from his clan because he had no son? Give us property among our father's relatives."

5So Moses brought their case before the LORD 6and the LORD said to him, 7"What Zelophehad's daughters are saying is right. You must certainly give them property as an inheritance among their father's relatives and turn their father's inheritance over to them.

8"Say to the Israelites, 'If a man dies and leaves no son, turn his inheritance over to his daughter. 9If he has no daughter, give his inheritance to his brothers. 10If he has no brothers, give his inheritance to his father's brothers. 11If his father had no brothers, give his inheritance to the nearest relative in his clan, that he may possess it. This is to be a legal requirement for the Israelites, as the LORD commanded Moses.' "

Joshua to Succeed Moses

12Then the LORD said to Moses, "Go up this mountain in the Abarim range and see the land I have given the Israelites. 13After you have seen it, you too will be gathered to your people, as your brother Aaron was, 14for when the community rebelled at the waters in the Desert of Zin, both of you disobeyed my command to honor me as holy before their eyes." (These were the waters of Meribah Kadesh, in the Desert of Zin.)

15Moses said to the LORD, 16"May the LORD, the God of the spirits of all mankind, appoint a man over this community 17to go out and come in before them, one who will lead them out and bring them in, so the LORD's people will not be like sheep without a shepherd."

18So the LORD said to Moses, "Take Joshua son of Nun, a man in whom is the spirit,*b* and lay your hand on him. 19Have him stand before Eleazar the priest and the entire assembly and commission him in their presence. 20Give him some of your authority so the whole Israelite community will obey him. 21He is to stand before Eleazar the priest, who will obtain decisions for him by inquiring of the Urim before the LORD. At his command he and the entire community of the Israelites will go out, and at his command they will come in."

22Moses did as the LORD commanded him. He took Joshua and had him stand before Eleazar the priest and the whole assembly. 23Then he laid his hands on him and commissioned him, as the LORD instructed through Moses.

a 59 Or Jochebed, a daughter of Levi, who was born to Levi   b 18 Or Spirit

Daily Offerings

28 The LORD said to Moses, 2"Give this command to the Israelites and say to them: 'See that you present to me at the appointed time the food for my offerings made by fire, as an aroma pleasing to me.' 3Say to them: 'This is the offering made by fire that you are to present to the LORD: two lambs a year old without defect, as a regular

---

FRIDAY

OUR TIMES ARE AT HIS SOVEREIGN DISPOSAL
John Owen

VERSE: Numbers 27:13   **PASSAGE:** Numbers 27:12–23

Some desire to live that they may see more of that glorious work of God for his church, which they believe he will accomplish. So Moses prayed that he might not die in the wilderness, but go over Jordan, and see the good land, and that goodly mountain and Lebanon, the seat of the church and of the worship of God; which yet God thought meet to deny unto him. And this denial of the request of Moses, made on the highest consideration possible, is instructive unto all in the like case. Others may judge themselves to have some work to do in the world, wherein they suppose that the glory of God and good of the church are concerned; and therefore would be spared for a season. Paul knew not clearly whether it were not best for him to abide a while longer in the flesh on this account (see Philippians 1:21–25); and David often deprecates the present season of death because of the work which he had to do for God in the world. Others rise no higher than their own private interests or concerns with respect unto their persons, their families, their relations, and goods in this world. They would see these things in a better or more settled condition before they die, and then they shall be most willing so to do. But it is the love of life that lies at the bottom of all these desires in men; which of itself will never forsake them. But no man can die cheerfully or comfortably who lives not in a constant resignation of the time and season of his death unto the will of God, as well as himself with respect unto death itself. Our times are in his hand, at his sovereign disposal; and his will in all things must be complied withal. Without this resolution, without this resignation, no man can enjoy the least solid peace in this world.

ADDITIONAL SCRIPTURE READING:
Psalm 73:24–26; Luke 2:28–30; 2 Corinthians 5:8–9

Go to page 193 for your next devotional reading.

1500   1700

burnt offering each day. ⁴Prepare one lamb in the morning and the other at twilight, ⁵together with a grain offering of a tenth of an ephah*a* of fine flour mixed with a quarter of a hin*b* of oil from pressed olives. ⁶This is the regular burnt offering instituted at Mount Sinai as a pleasing aroma, an offering made to the LORD by fire. ⁷The accompanying drink offering is to be a quarter of a hin of fermented drink with each lamb. Pour out the drink offering to the LORD at the sanctuary. ⁸Prepare the second lamb at twilight, along with the same kind of grain offering and drink offering that you prepare in the morning. This is an offering made by fire, an aroma pleasing to the LORD.

Sabbath Offerings

⁹" 'On the Sabbath day, make an offering of two lambs a year old without defect, together with its drink offering and a grain offering of two-tenths of an ephah*c* of fine flour mixed with oil. ¹⁰This is the burnt offering for every Sabbath, in addition to the regular burnt offering and its drink offering.

Monthly Offerings

¹¹" 'On the first of every month, present to the LORD a burnt offering of two young bulls, one ram and seven male lambs a year old, all without defect. ¹²With each bull there is to be a grain offering of three-tenths of an ephah*d* of fine flour mixed with oil; with the ram, a grain offering of two-tenths of an ephah of fine flour mixed with oil; ¹³and with each lamb, a grain offering of a tenth of an ephah of fine flour mixed with oil. This is for a burnt offering, a pleasing aroma, an offering made to the LORD by fire. ¹⁴With each bull there is to be a drink offering of half a hin*e* of wine; with the ram, a third of a hin*f*; and with each lamb, a quarter of a hin. This is the monthly burnt offering to be made at each new moon during the year. ¹⁵Besides the regular burnt offering with its drink offering, one male goat is to be presented to the LORD as a sin offering.

The Passover

¹⁶" 'On the fourteenth day of the first month the LORD's Passover is to be held. ¹⁷On the fifteenth day of this month there is to be a festival; for seven days eat bread made without yeast. ¹⁸On the first day hold a sacred assembly and do no regular work. ¹⁹Present to the LORD an offering made by fire, a burnt offering of two young bulls, one ram and seven male lambs a year old, all without defect. ²⁰With each bull prepare a grain offering of three-tenths of an ephah of fine flour mixed with oil; with the ram, two-tenths; ²¹and with each of the seven lambs, one-tenth. ²²Include one male goat as a sin offering to make atonement for you. ²³Prepare these in addition to the regular morning burnt offering. ²⁴In this way prepare the food for the offering made by fire every day for seven days as an aroma pleasing to the LORD; it is to be prepared in addition to the regular burnt offering and its drink offering. ²⁵On the seventh day hold a sacred assembly and do no regular work.

Feast of Weeks

²⁶" 'On the day of firstfruits, when you present to the LORD an offering of new grain during the Feast of Weeks, hold a sacred assembly and do no regular work. ²⁷Present a burnt offering of two young bulls, one ram and seven male lambs a year old as an aroma pleasing to the LORD. ²⁸With each bull there is to be a grain offering of three-tenths of an ephah of fine flour mixed with oil; with the ram, two-tenths; ²⁹and with each of the seven lambs, one-tenth. ³⁰Include one male goat to make atonement for you. ³¹Prepare these together with their drink offerings, in addition to the regular burnt offering and its grain offering. Be sure the animals are without defect.

Feast of Trumpets

29 " 'On the first day of the seventh month hold a sacred assembly and do no regular work. It is a day for you to sound the trumpets. ²As

---

a 5 That is, probably about 2 quarts (about 2 liters); also in verses 13, 21 and 29   *b 5* That is, probably about 1 quart (about 1 liter); also in verses 7 and 14   *c 9* That is, probably about 4 quarts (about 4.5 liters); also in verses 12, 20 and 28   *d 12* That is, probably about 6 quarts (about 6.5 liters); also in verses 20 and 28   *e 14* That is, probably about 2 quarts (about 2 liters)   *f 14* That is, probably about 1 1/4 quarts (about 1.2 liters)

an aroma pleasing to the LORD, prepare a burnt offering of one young bull, one ram and seven male lambs a year old, all without defect. [3]With the bull prepare a grain offering of three-tenths of an ephah[a] of fine flour mixed with oil; with the ram, two-tenths[b]; [4]and with each of the seven lambs, one-tenth.[c] [5]Include one male goat as a sin offering to make atonement for you. [6]These are in addition to the monthly and daily burnt offerings with their grain offerings and drink offerings as specified. They are offerings made to the LORD by fire—a pleasing aroma.

Day of Atonement

[7]" 'On the tenth day of this seventh month hold a sacred assembly. You must deny yourselves[d] and do no work. [8]Present as an aroma pleasing to the LORD a burnt offering of one young bull, one ram and seven male lambs a year old, all without defect. [9]With the bull prepare a grain offering of three-tenths of an ephah of fine flour mixed with oil; with the ram, two-tenths; [10]and with each of the seven lambs, one-tenth. [11]Include one male goat as a sin offering, in addition to the sin offering for atonement and the regular burnt offering with its grain offering, and their drink offerings.

Feast of Tabernacles

[12]" 'On the fifteenth day of the seventh month, hold a sacred assembly and do no regular work. Celebrate a festival to the LORD for seven days. [13]Present an offering made by fire as an aroma pleasing to the LORD, a burnt offering of thirteen young bulls, two rams and fourteen male lambs a year old, all without defect. [14]With each of the thirteen bulls prepare a grain offering of three-tenths of an ephah of fine flour mixed with oil; with each of the two rams, two-tenths; [15]and with each of the fourteen lambs, one-tenth. [16]Include one male goat as a sin offering, in addition to the regular burnt offering with its grain offering and drink offering.

[17]" 'On the second day prepare twelve young bulls, two rams and fourteen male lambs a year old, all without defect. [18]With the bulls, rams and lambs, prepare their grain offerings and drink offerings according to the number specified. [19]Include one male goat as a sin offering, in addition to the regular burnt offering with its grain offering, and their drink offerings.

[20]" 'On the third day prepare eleven bulls, two rams and fourteen male lambs a year old, all without defect. [21]With the bulls, rams and lambs, prepare their grain offerings and drink offerings according to the number specified. [22]Include one male goat as a sin offering, in addition to the regular burnt offering with its grain offering and drink offering.

[23]" 'On the fourth day prepare ten bulls, two rams and fourteen male lambs a year old, all without defect. [24]With the bulls, rams and lambs, prepare their grain offerings and drink offerings according to the number specified. [25]Include one male goat as a sin offering, in addition to the regular burnt offering with its grain offering and drink offering.

[26]" 'On the fifth day prepare nine bulls, two rams and fourteen male lambs a year old, all without defect. [27]With the bulls, rams and lambs, prepare their grain offerings and drink offerings according to the number specified. [28]Include one male goat as a sin offering, in addition to the regular burnt offering with its grain offering and drink offering.

[29]" 'On the sixth day prepare eight bulls, two rams and fourteen male lambs a year old, all without defect. [30]With the bulls, rams and lambs, prepare their grain offerings and drink offerings according to the number specified. [31]Include one male goat as a sin offering, in addition to the regular burnt offering with its grain offering and drink offering.

[32]" 'On the seventh day prepare seven bulls, two rams and fourteen male lambs a year old, all without defect. [33]With the bulls, rams and lambs, prepare their grain offerings and drink offerings according to the number specified. [34]Include one male goat as a sin offering, in addition to the regular burnt offering with its grain offering and drink offering.

---

[a] 3 That is, probably about 6 quarts (about 6.5 liters); also in verses 9 and 14   [b] 3 That is, probably about 4 quarts (about 4.5 liters); also in verses 9 and 14   [c] 4 That is, probably about 2 quarts (about 2 liters); also in verses 10 and 15   [d] 7 Or must fast

35" 'On the eighth day hold an assembly and do no regular work. 36Present an offering made by fire as an aroma pleasing to the LORD, a burnt offering of one bull, one ram and seven male lambs a year old, all without defect. 37With the bull, the ram and the lambs, prepare their grain offerings and drink offerings according to the number specified. 38Include one male goat as a sin offering, in addition to the regular burnt offering with its grain offering and drink offering.

39" 'In addition to what you vow and your freewill offerings, prepare these for the LORD at your appointed feasts: your burnt offerings, grain offerings, drink offerings and fellowship offerings.*a' "*

40Moses told the Israelites all that the LORD commanded him.

Vows

30 Moses said to the heads of the tribes of Israel: "This is what the LORD commands: 2When a man makes a vow to the LORD or takes an oath to obligate himself by a pledge, he must not break his word but must do everything he said.

3"When a young woman still living in her father's house makes a vow to the LORD or obligates herself by a pledge 4and her father hears about her vow or pledge but says nothing to her, then all her vows and every pledge by which she obligated herself will stand. 5But if her father forbids her when he hears about it, none of her vows or the pledges by which she obligated herself will stand; the LORD will release her because her father has forbidden her.

6"If she marries after she makes a vow or after her lips utter a rash promise by which she obligates herself 7and her husband hears about it but says nothing to her, then her vows or the pledges by which she obligated herself will stand. 8But if her husband forbids her when he hears about it, he nullifies the vow that obligates her or the rash promise by which she obligates herself, and the LORD will release her.

9"Any vow or obligation taken by a widow or divorced woman will be binding on her.

10"If a woman living with her husband makes a vow or obligates herself by a pledge under oath 11and her husband hears about it but says nothing to her and does not forbid her, then all her vows or the pledges by which she obligated herself will stand. 12But if her husband nullifies them when he hears about them, then none of the vows or pledges that came from her lips will stand. Her husband has nullified them, and the LORD will release her. 13Her husband may confirm or nullify any vow she makes or any sworn pledge to deny herself. 14But if her husband says nothing to her about it from day to day, then he confirms all her vows or the pledges binding on her. He confirms them by saying nothing to her when he hears about them. 15If, however, he nullifies them some time after he hears about them, then he is responsible for her guilt."

16These are the regulations the LORD gave Moses concerning relationships between a man and his wife, and between a father and his young daughter still living in his house.

Vengeance on the Midianites

31 The LORD said to Moses, 2"Take vengeance on the Midianites for the Israelites. After that, you will be gathered to your people."

3So Moses said to the people, "Arm some of your men to go to war against the Midianites and to carry out the LORD's vengeance on them. 4Send into battle a thousand men from each of the tribes of Israel." 5So twelve thousand men armed for battle, a thousand from each tribe, were supplied from the clans of Israel. 6Moses sent them into battle, a thousand from each tribe, along with Phinehas son of Eleazar, the priest, who took with him articles from the sanctuary and the trumpets for signaling.

7They fought against Midian, as the LORD commanded Moses, and killed every man. 8Among their victims were Evi, Rekem, Zur, Hur and Reba—the five kings of Midian. They also killed Balaam son of Beor with the sword. 9The Israelites captured the Midianite women and children and took all the Midianite herds, flocks and goods as plunder. 10They burned all the towns where the

a 39 Traditionally peace offerings

Midianites had settled, as well as all their camps. **11**They took all the plunder and spoils, including the people and animals, **12**and brought the captives, spoils and plunder to Moses and Eleazar the priest and the Israelite assembly at their camp on the plains of Moab, by the Jordan across from Jericho.*ᵃ*

13Moses, Eleazar the priest and all the leaders of the community went to meet them outside the camp. **14**Moses was angry with the officers of the army—the commanders of thousands and commanders of hundreds—who returned from the battle.

15"Have you allowed all the women to live?" he asked them. **16**"They were the ones who followed Balaam's advice and were the means of turning the Israelites away from the LORD in what happened at Peor, so that a plague struck the LORD's people. **17**Now kill all the boys. And kill every woman who has slept with a man, **18**but save for yourselves every girl who has never slept with a man.

19"All of you who have killed anyone or touched anyone who was killed must stay outside the camp seven days. On the third and seventh days you must purify yourselves and your captives. **20**Purify every garment as well as everything made of leather, goat hair or wood."

21Then Eleazar the priest said to the soldiers who had gone into battle, "This is the requirement of the law that the LORD gave Moses: **22**Gold, silver, bronze, iron, tin, lead **23**and anything else that can withstand fire must be put through the fire, and then it will be clean. But it must also be purified with the water of cleansing. And whatever cannot withstand fire must be put through that water. **24**On the seventh day wash your clothes and you will be clean. Then you may come into the camp."

Dividing the Spoils

25The LORD said to Moses, **26**"You and Eleazar the priest and the family heads of the community are to count all the people and animals that were captured. **27**Divide the spoils between the soldiers who took part in the battle and the rest of the community. **28**From the soldiers

who fought in the battle, set apart as tribute for the LORD one out of every five hundred, whether persons, cattle, donkeys, sheep or goats. **29**Take this tribute from their half share and give it to Eleazar the priest as the LORD's part. **30**From the Israelites' half, select one out of every fifty, whether persons, cattle, donkeys, sheep, goats or other animals. Give them to the Levites, who are responsible for the care of the LORD's tabernacle." **31**So Moses and Eleazar the priest did as the LORD commanded Moses.

32The plunder remaining from the spoils that the soldiers took was 675,000 sheep, **33**72,000 cattle, **34**61,000 donkeys **35**and 32,000 women who had never slept with a man. **36**The half share of those who fought in the battle was:

    337,500 sheep, **37**of which the tribute for the LORD was 675;
3836,000 cattle, of which the tribute for the LORD was 72;
3930,500 donkeys, of which the tribute for the LORD was 61;
4016,000 people, of which the tribute for the LORD was 32.

41Moses gave the tribute to Eleazar the priest as the LORD's part, as the LORD commanded Moses.

42The half belonging to the Israelites, which Moses set apart from that of the fighting men— **43**the community's half—was 337,500 sheep, **44**36,000 cattle, **45**30,500 donkeys **46**and 16,000 people. **47**From the Israelites' half, Moses selected one out of every fifty persons and animals, as the LORD commanded him, and gave them to the Levites, who were responsible for the care of the LORD's tabernacle.

48Then the officers who were over the units of the army—the commanders of thousands and commanders of hundreds—went to Moses **49**and said to him, "Your servants have counted the soldiers under our command, and not one is missing. **50**So we have brought as an offering to the LORD the gold articles each of us acquired—armlets, bracelets, signet rings, earrings and necklaces—to make atonement for ourselves before the LORD."

ᵃ 12 Hebrew *Jordan of Jericho;* possibly an ancient name for the Jordan River

51Moses and Eleazar the priest accepted from them the gold—all the crafted articles. 52All the gold from the commanders of thousands and commanders of hundreds that Moses and Eleazar presented as a gift to the LORD weighed 16,750 shekels.*a* 53Each soldier had taken plunder for himself. 54Moses and Eleazar the priest accepted the gold from the commanders of thousands and commanders of hundreds and brought it into the Tent of Meeting as a memorial for the Israelites before the LORD.

The Transjordan Tribes

32 The Reubenites and Gadites, who had very large herds and flocks, saw that the lands of Jazer and Gilead were suitable for livestock. 2So they came to Moses and Eleazar the priest and to the leaders of the community, and said, 3"Ataroth, Dibon, Jazer, Nimrah, Heshbon, Elealeh, Sebam, Nebo and Beon— 4the land the LORD subdued before the people of Israel—are suitable for livestock, and your servants have livestock. 5If we have found favor in your eyes," they said, "let this land be given to your servants as our possession. Do not make us cross the Jordan."

6Moses said to the Gadites and Reubenites, "Shall your countrymen go to war while you sit here? 7Why do you discourage the Israelites from going over into the land the LORD has given them? 8This is what your fathers did when I sent them from Kadesh Barnea to look over the land. 9After they went up to the Valley of Eshcol and viewed the land, they discouraged the Israelites from entering the land the LORD had given them. 10The LORD's anger was aroused that day and he swore this oath: 11'Because they have not followed me wholeheartedly, not one of the men twenty years old or more who came up out of Egypt will see the land I promised on oath to Abraham, Isaac and Jacob— 12not one except Caleb son of Jephunneh the Kenizzite and Joshua son of Nun, for they followed the LORD wholeheartedly.' 13The LORD's anger burned against Israel and he made them wander in the desert forty years, until the whole generation of those who had done evil in his sight was gone.

14"And here you are, a brood of sinners, standing in the place of your fathers and making the LORD even more angry with Israel. 15If you turn away from following him, he will again leave all this people in the desert, and you will be the cause of their destruction."

16Then they came up to him and said, "We would like to build pens here for our livestock and cities for our women and children. 17But we are ready to arm ourselves and go ahead of the Israelites until we have brought them to their place. Meanwhile our women and children will live in fortified cities, for protection from the inhabitants of the land. 18We will not return to our homes until every Israelite has received his inheritance. 19We will not receive any inheritance with them on the other side of the Jordan, because our inheritance has come to us on the east side of the Jordan."

20Then Moses said to them, "If you will do this—if you will arm yourselves before the LORD for battle, 21and if all of you will go armed over the Jordan before the LORD until he has driven his enemies out before him— 22then when the land is subdued before the LORD, you may return and be free from your obligation to the LORD and to Israel. And this land will be your possession before the LORD.

23"But if you fail to do this, you will be sinning against the LORD; and you may be sure that your sin will find you out. 24Build cities for your women and children, and pens for your flocks, but do what you have promised."

25The Gadites and Reubenites said to Moses, "We your servants will do as our lord commands. 26Our children and wives, our flocks and herds will remain here in the cities of Gilead. 27But your servants, every man armed for battle, will cross over to fight before the LORD, just as our lord says."

28Then Moses gave orders about them to Eleazar the priest and Joshua son of Nun and to the family heads of the Israelite tribes. 29He said to them, "If the Gadites and Reubenites, every man armed for battle, cross over the Jordan with you before the LORD, then when

a 52 That is, about 420 pounds (about 190 kilograms)

the land is subdued before you, give them the land of Gilead as their possession. ³⁰But if they do not cross over with you armed, they must accept their possession with you in Canaan."

³¹The Gadites and Reubenites answered, "Your servants will do what the LORD has said. ³²We will cross over before the LORD into Canaan armed, but the property we inherit will be on this side of the Jordan."

³³Then Moses gave to the Gadites, the Reubenites and the half-tribe of Manasseh son of Joseph the kingdom of Sihon king of the Amorites and the kingdom of Og king of Bashan—the whole land with its cities and the territory around them.

³⁴The Gadites built up Dibon, Ataroth, Aroer, ³⁵Atroth Shophan, Jazer, Jogbehah, ³⁶Beth Nimrah and Beth Haran as fortified cities, and built pens for their flocks. ³⁷And the Reubenites rebuilt Heshbon, Elealeh and Kiriathaim, ³⁸as well as Nebo and Baal Meon (these names were changed) and Sibmah. They gave names to the cities they rebuilt.

³⁹The descendants of Makir son of Manasseh went to Gilead, captured it and drove out the Amorites who were there. ⁴⁰So Moses gave Gilead to the Makirites, the descendants of Manasseh, and they settled there. ⁴¹Jair, a descendant of Manasseh, captured their settlements and called them Havvoth Jair.ᵃ ⁴²And Nobah captured Kenath and its surrounding settlements and called it Nobah after himself.

Stages in Israel's Journey

33 Here are the stages in the journey of the Israelites when they came out of Egypt by divisions under the leadership of Moses and Aaron. ²At the LORD's command Moses recorded the stages in their journey. This is their journey by stages:

³The Israelites set out from Rameses on the fifteenth day of the first month, the day after the Passover. They marched out boldly in full view of all the Egyptians, ⁴who were burying all their firstborn, whom the LORD had struck down

among them; for the LORD had brought judgment on their gods.

⁵The Israelites left Rameses and camped at Succoth.

⁶They left Succoth and camped at Etham, on the edge of the desert.

⁷They left Etham, turned back to Pi Hahiroth, to the east of Baal Zephon, and camped near Migdol.

⁸They left Pi Hahirothᵇ and passed through the sea into the desert, and when they had traveled for three days in the Desert of Etham, they camped at Marah.

⁹They left Marah and went to Elim, where there were twelve springs and seventy palm trees, and they camped there.

¹⁰They left Elim and camped by the Red Sea.ᶜ

¹¹They left the Red Sea and camped in the Desert of Sin.

¹²They left the Desert of Sin and camped at Dophkah.

¹³They left Dophkah and camped at Alush.

¹⁴They left Alush and camped at Rephidim, where there was no water for the people to drink.

¹⁵They left Rephidim and camped in the Desert of Sinai.

¹⁶They left the Desert of Sinai and camped at Kibroth Hattaavah.

¹⁷They left Kibroth Hattaavah and camped at Hazeroth.

¹⁸They left Hazeroth and camped at Rithmah.

¹⁹They left Rithmah and camped at Rimmon Perez.

²⁰They left Rimmon Perez and camped at Libnah.

²¹They left Libnah and camped at Rissah.

²²They left Rissah and camped at Kehelathah.

²³They left Kehelathah and camped at Mount Shepher.

²⁴They left Mount Shepher and camped at Haradah.

²⁵They left Haradah and camped at Makheloth.

²⁶They left Makheloth and camped at Tahath.

ᵃ 41 Or them the settlements of Jair   ᵇ 8 Many manuscripts of the Masoretic Text, Samaritan Pentateuch and Vulgate; most manuscripts of the Masoretic Text left from before Hahiroth
ᶜ 10 Hebrew Yam Suph; that is, Sea of Reeds; also in verse 11

27They left Tahath and camped at Terah.

28They left Terah and camped at Mithcah.

29They left Mithcah and camped at Hashmonah.

30They left Hashmonah and camped at Moseroth.

31They left Moseroth and camped at Bene Jaakan.

32They left Bene Jaakan and camped at Hor Haggidgad.

33They left Hor Haggidgad and camped at Jotbathah.

34They left Jotbathah and camped at Abronah.

35They left Abronah and camped at Ezion Geber.

36They left Ezion Geber and camped at Kadesh, in the Desert of Zin.

37They left Kadesh and camped at Mount Hor, on the border of Edom. 38At the LORD's command Aaron the priest went up Mount Hor, where he died on the first day of the fifth month of the fortieth year after the Israelites came out of Egypt. 39Aaron was a hundred and twenty-three years old when he died on Mount Hor.

40The Canaanite king of Arad, who lived in the Negev of Canaan, heard that the Israelites were coming.

41They left Mount Hor and camped at Zalmonah.

42They left Zalmonah and camped at Punon.

43They left Punon and camped at Oboth.

44They left Oboth and camped at Iye Abarim, on the border of Moab.

45They left Iyim*a* and camped at Dibon Gad.

46They left Dibon Gad and camped at Almon Diblathaim.

47They left Almon Diblathaim and camped in the mountains of Abarim, near Nebo.

48They left the mountains of Abarim and camped on the plains of Moab by the Jordan across from Jericho.*b* 49There on the plains of Moab they camped along the Jordan from Beth Jeshimoth to Abel Shittim.

50On the plains of Moab by the Jordan across from Jericho the LORD said to Moses, 51"Speak to the Israelites and say to them: 'When you cross the Jordan into Canaan, 52drive out all the inhabitants of the land before you. Destroy all their carved images and their cast idols, and demolish all their high places. 53Take possession of the land and settle in it, for I have given you the land to possess. 54Distribute the land by lot, according to your clans. To a larger group give a larger inheritance, and to a smaller group a smaller one. Whatever falls to them by lot will be theirs. Distribute it according to your ancestral tribes.

55" 'But if you do not drive out the inhabitants of the land, those you allow to remain will become barbs in your eyes and thorns in your sides. They will give you trouble in the land where you will live. 56And then I will do to you what I plan to do to them.' "

Boundaries of Canaan

34 The LORD said to Moses, 2"Command the Israelites and say to them: 'When you enter Canaan, the land that will be allotted to you as an inheritance will have these boundaries:

3" 'Your southern side will include some of the Desert of Zin along the border of Edom. On the east, your southern boundary will start from the end of the Salt Sea,*c* 4cross south of Scorpion*d* Pass, continue on to Zin and go south of Kadesh Barnea. Then it will go to Hazar Addar and over to Azmon, 5where it will turn, join the Wadi of Egypt and end at the Sea.*e*

6" 'Your western boundary will be the coast of the Great Sea. This will be your boundary on the west.

7" 'For your northern boundary, run a line from the Great Sea to Mount Hor 8and from Mount Hor to Lebo*f* Hamath. Then the boundary will go to Zedad,

---

a 45 That is, Iye Abarim   *b 48* Hebrew *Jordan of Jericho;* possibly an ancient name for the Jordan River; also in verse 50   *c 3* That is, the Dead Sea; also in verse 12   *d 4* Hebrew *Akrabbim*
e 5 That is, the Mediterranean; also in verses 6 and 7   *f 8* Or *to the entrance to*

WEEKEND

ROCK MOUNT SINAI
African-American Spiritual

VERSE: Exodus 19:18   **PASSAGE:** Exodus 19:16–25

 rock, Mount Sinai,
Rock, Mount Sinai,
Rock, Mount Sinai, in that mornin'.
O, when you hear, my coffin soun',
Then you may know my body's boun'.
O, rock, Mount Sinai.

O, come on, Moses, don't you get los',
Smote the water an' come on the cross,
O, rock, Mount Sinai.

O, David, David, is a shepherd boy,
David killed Goliath and shouted for joy.
He killed Goliath, killed Goliath in that morning.
O, rock, Mount Sinai.

When I get to heaven, going to sit right down,
Going to ask my Lord for a starry crown.
O, rock, Mount Sinai.

O, Pilate's wife she dreamt a dream,
When the dream was over she said to Pilate:
O, give me a little water to wash my han',
So they won't be stained with the innocent man.

ADDITIONAL SCRIPTURE READING:
1 Samuel 17:1–46; Matthew 27:19–24

Go to page 202 for your next devotional reading.

1700   1900

9continue to Ziphron and end at Hazar Enan. This will be your boundary on the north.

10" 'For your eastern boundary, run a line from Hazar Enan to Shepham. 11The boundary will go down from Shepham to Riblah on the east side of Ain and continue along the slopes east of the Sea of Kinnereth.*a* 12Then the boundary will go down along the Jordan and end at the Salt Sea.

" 'This will be your land, with its boundaries on every side.' "

13Moses commanded the Israelites: "Assign this land by lot as an inheritance. The LORD has ordered that it be given to the nine and a half tribes, 14because the families of the tribe of Reuben, the tribe of Gad and the half-tribe of Manasseh have received their inheritance. 15These two and a half tribes have received their inheritance on the east side of the Jordan of Jericho,*b* toward the sunrise."

16The LORD said to Moses, 17"These are the names of the men who are to assign the land for you as an inheritance: Eleazar the priest and Joshua son of Nun. 18And appoint one leader from each tribe to help assign the land. 19These are their names:

Caleb son of Jephunneh,
   from the tribe of Judah;
20 Shemuel son of Ammihud,
   from the tribe of Simeon;
21 Elidad son of Kislon,
   from the tribe of Benjamin;
22 Bukki son of Jogli,
   the leader from the tribe of Dan;
23 Hanniel son of Ephod,
   the leader from the tribe of Manasseh son of Joseph;
24 Kemuel son of Shiphtan,
   the leader from the tribe of Ephraim son of Joseph;
25 Elizaphan son of Parnach,
   the leader from the tribe of Zebulun;
26 Paltiel son of Azzan,
   the leader from the tribe of Issachar;
27 Ahihud son of Shelomi,
   the leader from the tribe of Asher;

28 Pedahel son of Ammihud,
   the leader from the tribe of Naphtali."

29These are the men the LORD commanded to assign the inheritance to the Israelites in the land of Canaan.

Towns for the Levites

35 On the plains of Moab by the Jordan across from Jericho,*c* the LORD said to Moses, 2"Command the Israelites to give the Levites towns to live in from the inheritance the Israelites will possess. And give them pasturelands around the towns. 3Then they will have towns to live in and pasturelands for their cattle, flocks and all their other livestock.

4"The pasturelands around the towns that you give the Levites will extend out fifteen hundred feet*d* from the town wall. 5Outside the town, measure three thousand feet*e* on the east side, three thousand on the south side, three thousand on the west and three thousand on the north, with the town in the center. They will have this area as pastureland for the towns.

Cities of Refuge

6"Six of the towns you give the Levites will be cities of refuge, to which a person who has killed someone may flee. In addition, give them forty-two other towns. 7In all you must give the Levites forty-eight towns, together with their pasturelands. 8The towns you give the Levites from the land the Israelites possess are to be given in proportion to the inheritance of each tribe: Take many towns from a tribe that has many, but few from one that has few."

9Then the LORD said to Moses: 10"Speak to the Israelites and say to them: 'When you cross the Jordan into Canaan, 11select some towns to be your cities of refuge, to which a person who has killed someone accidentally may flee. 12They will be places of refuge from the avenger, so that a person accused of murder may not die before he stands trial before the assembly. 13These six

---

a 11 That is, Galilee   *b* 15 *Jordan of Jericho* was possibly an ancient name for the Jordan River.
c 1 Hebrew *Jordan of Jericho*; possibly an ancient name for the Jordan River   *d* 4 Hebrew *a thousand cubits* (about 450 meters)   *e* 5 Hebrew *two thousand cubits* (about 900 meters)

towns you give will be your cities of refuge. ¹⁴Give three on this side of the Jordan and three in Canaan as cities of refuge. ¹⁵These six towns will be a place of refuge for Israelites, aliens and any other people living among them, so that anyone who has killed another accidentally can flee there.

¹⁶" 'If a man strikes someone with an iron object so that he dies, he is a murderer; the murderer shall be put to death. ¹⁷Or if anyone has a stone in his hand that could kill, and he strikes someone so that he dies, he is a murderer; the murderer shall be put to death. ¹⁸Or if anyone has a wooden object in his hand that could kill, and he hits someone so that he dies, he is a murderer; the murderer shall be put to death. ¹⁹The avenger of blood shall put the murderer to death; when he meets him, he shall put him to death. ²⁰If anyone with malice aforethought shoves another or throws something at him intentionally so that he dies ²¹or if in hostility he hits him with his fist so that he dies, that person shall be put to death; he is a murderer. The avenger of blood shall put the murderer to death when he meets him.

²²" 'But if without hostility someone suddenly shoves another or throws something at him unintentionally ²³or, without seeing him, drops a stone on him that could kill him, and he dies, then since he was not his enemy and he did not intend to harm him, ²⁴the assembly must judge between him and the avenger of blood according to these regulations. ²⁵The assembly must protect the one accused of murder from the avenger of blood and send him back to the city of refuge to which he fled. He must stay there until the death of the high priest, who was anointed with the holy oil.

²⁶" 'But if the accused ever goes outside the limits of the city of refuge to which he has fled ²⁷and the avenger of blood finds him outside the city, the avenger of blood may kill the accused without being guilty of murder. ²⁸The accused must stay in his city of refuge until the death of the high priest; only after the death of the high priest may he return to his own property.

²⁹" 'These are to be legal requirements for you throughout the generations to come, wherever you live.

³⁰" 'Anyone who kills a person is to be put to death as a murderer only on the testimony of witnesses. But no one is to be put to death on the testimony of only one witness.

³¹" 'Do not accept a ransom for the life of a murderer, who deserves to die. He must surely be put to death.

³²" 'Do not accept a ransom for anyone who has fled to a city of refuge and so allow him to go back and live on his own land before the death of the high priest.

³³" 'Do not pollute the land where you are. Bloodshed pollutes the land, and atonement cannot be made for the land on which blood has been shed, except by the blood of the one who shed it. ³⁴Do not defile the land where you live and where I dwell, for I, the LORD, dwell among the Israelites.' "

Inheritance of Zelophehad's Daughters

36 The family heads of the clan of Gilead son of Makir, the son of Manasseh, who were from the clans of the descendants of Joseph, came and spoke before Moses and the leaders, the heads of the Israelite families. ²They said, "When the LORD commanded my lord to give the land as an inheritance to the Israelites by lot, he ordered you to give the inheritance of our brother Zelophehad to his daughters. ³Now suppose they marry men from other Israelite tribes; then their inheritance will be taken from our ancestral inheritance and added to that of the tribe they marry into. And so part of the inheritance allotted to us will be taken away. ⁴When the Year of Jubilee for the Israelites comes, their inheritance will be added to that of the tribe into which they marry, and their property will be taken from the tribal inheritance of our forefathers."

⁵Then at the LORD's command Moses gave this order to the Israelites: "What the tribe of the descendants of Joseph is saying is right. ⁶This is what the LORD commands for Zelophehad's daughters: They may marry anyone they please as long as they marry within the tribal clan

of their father. [7]No inheritance in Israel is to pass from tribe to tribe, for every Israelite shall keep the tribal land inherited from his forefathers. [8]Every daughter who inherits land in any Israelite tribe must marry someone in her father's tribal clan, so that every Israelite will possess the inheritance of his fathers. [9]No inheritance may pass from tribe to tribe, for each Israelite tribe is to keep the land it inherits."

[10]So Zelophehad's daughters did as the LORD commanded Moses. [11]Zelophehad's daughters—Mahlah, Tirzah, Hoglah, Milcah and Noah—married their cousins on their father's side. [12]They married within the clans of the descendants of Manasseh son of Joseph, and their inheritance remained in their father's clan and tribe.

[13]These are the commands and regulations the LORD gave through Moses to the Israelites on the plains of Moab by the Jordan across from Jericho.[a]

---

[a] 13 Hebrew *Jordan of Jericho*; possibly an ancient name for the Jordan River

DEUTERONOMY

FTER FORTY YEARS THE ISRAELITES
WERE ABOUT TO ENTER CANAAN.
BEFORE THEY DID, MOSES WANTED
TO REMIND THEM OF ALL THAT GOD HAD
DONE FOR THEM AND TO ENCOURAGE THEM
TO KEEP OBEYING THE LAWS GOD HAD GIVEN
THEM. MOSES REMINDED THE PEOPLE OF
GOD'S GOODNESS TO THEM THROUGH THEIR
JOURNEY AND HIS GIVING THEM THE LAND OF
CANAAN. ABOVE ALL, MOSES WANTED HIS
PEOPLE TO SEE HOW MUCH GOD LOVED THEM
AND HOW THEY WERE TO RETURN THAT LOVE
TO THEIR POWERFUL GOD.

The Command to Leave Horeb

1 These are the words Moses spoke to all Israel in the desert east of the Jordan—that is, in the Arabah—opposite Suph, between Paran and Tophel, Laban, Hazeroth and Dizahab. ²(It takes eleven days to go from Horeb to Kadesh Barnea by the Mount Seir road.)

³In the fortieth year, on the first day of the eleventh month, Moses proclaimed to the Israelites all that the LORD had commanded him concerning them. ⁴This was after he had defeated Sihon king of the Amorites, who reigned in Heshbon, and at Edrei had defeated Og king of Bashan, who reigned in Ashtaroth.

⁵East of the Jordan in the territory of Moab, Moses began to expound this law, saying:

⁶The LORD our God said to us at Horeb, "You have stayed long enough at this mountain. ⁷Break camp and advance into the hill country of the Amorites; go to all the neighboring peoples in the Arabah, in the mountains, in the western foothills, in the Negev and along the coast, to the land of the Canaanites and to Lebanon, as far as the great river, the Euphrates. ⁸See, I have given you this land. Go in and take possession of the land that the LORD swore he would give to your fathers—to Abraham, Isaac and Jacob—and to their descendants after them."

The Appointment of Leaders

⁹At that time I said to you, "You are too heavy a burden for me to carry alone. ¹⁰The LORD your God has increased your numbers so that today you are as many as

the stars in the sky. [11]May the LORD, the God of your fathers, increase you a thousand times and bless you as he has promised! [12]But how can I bear your problems and your burdens and your disputes all by myself? [13]Choose some wise, understanding and respected men from each of your tribes, and I will set them over you."

[14]You answered me, "What you propose to do is good."

[15]So I took the leading men of your tribes, wise and respected men, and appointed them to have authority over you—as commanders of thousands, of hundreds, of fifties and of tens and as tribal officials. [16]And I charged your judges at that time: Hear the disputes between your brothers and judge fairly, whether the case is between brother Israelites or between one of them and an alien. [17]Do not show partiality in judging; hear both small and great alike. Do not be afraid of any man, for judgment belongs to God. Bring me any case too hard for you, and I will hear it. [18]And at that time I told you everything you were to do.

Spies Sent Out

[19]Then, as the LORD our God commanded us, we set out from Horeb and went toward the hill country of the Amorites through all that vast and dreadful desert that you have seen, and so we reached Kadesh Barnea. [20]Then I said to you, "You have reached the hill country of the Amorites, which the LORD our God is giving us. [21]See, the LORD your God has given you the land. Go up and take possession of it as the LORD, the God of your fathers, told you. Do not be afraid; do not be discouraged."

[22]Then all of you came to me and said, "Let us send men ahead to spy out the land for us and bring back a report about the route we are to take and the towns we will come to."

[23]The idea seemed good to me; so I selected twelve of you, one man from each tribe. [24]They left and went up into the hill country, and came to the Valley of Eshcol and explored it. [25]Taking with them some of the fruit of the land, they brought it down to us and reported, "It is a good land that the LORD our God is giving us."

Rebellion Against the LORD

[26]But you were unwilling to go up; you rebelled against the command of the LORD your God. [27]You grumbled in your tents and said, "The LORD hates us; so he brought us out of Egypt to deliver us into the hands of the Amorites to destroy us. [28]Where can we go? Our brothers have made us lose heart. They say, 'The people are stronger and taller than we are; the cities are large, with walls up to the sky. We even saw the Anakites there.' "

[29]Then I said to you, "Do not be terrified; do not be afraid of them. [30]The LORD your God, who is going before you, will fight for you, as he did for you in Egypt, before your very eyes, [31]and in the desert. There you saw how the LORD your God carried you, as a father carries his son, all the way you went until you reached this place."

[32]In spite of this, you did not trust in the LORD your God, [33]who went ahead of you on your journey, in fire by night and in a cloud by day, to search out places for you to camp and to show you the way you should go.

[34]When the LORD heard what you said, he was angry and solemnly swore: [35]"Not a man of this evil generation shall see the good land I swore to give your forefathers, [36]except Caleb son of Jephunneh. He will see it, and I will give him and his descendants the land he set his feet on, because he followed the LORD wholeheartedly."

[37]Because of you the LORD became angry with me also and said, "You shall not enter it, either. [38]But your assistant, Joshua son of Nun, will enter it. Encourage him, because he will lead Israel to inherit it. [39]And the little ones that you said would be taken captive, your children who do not yet know good from bad—they will enter the land. I will give it to them and they will take possession of it. [40]But as for you, turn around and set out toward the desert along the route to the Red Sea.[a]"

[41]Then you replied, "We have sinned against the LORD. We will go up and fight, as the LORD our God commanded us." So every one of you put on his weapons, thinking it easy to go up into the hill country.

---

[a] 40 Hebrew *Yam Suph*; that is, Sea of Reeds

⁴²But the LORD said to me, "Tell them, 'Do not go up and fight, because I will not be with you. You will be defeated by your enemies.' "

⁴³So I told you, but you would not listen. You rebelled against the LORD's command and in your arrogance you marched up into the hill country. ⁴⁴The Amorites who lived in those hills came out against you; they chased you like a swarm of bees and beat you down from Seir all the way to Hormah. ⁴⁵You came back and wept before the LORD, but he paid no attention to your weeping and turned a deaf ear to you. ⁴⁶And so you stayed in Kadesh many days—all the time you spent there.

Wanderings in the Desert

2 Then we turned back and set out toward the desert along the route to the Red Sea,ᵃ as the LORD had directed me. For a long time we made our way around the hill country of Seir.

²Then the LORD said to me, ³"You have made your way around this hill country long enough; now turn north. ⁴Give the people these orders: 'You are about to pass through the territory of your brothers the descendants of Esau, who live in Seir. They will be afraid of you, but be very careful. ⁵Do not provoke them to war, for I will not give you any of their land, not even enough to put your foot on. I have given Esau the hill country of Seir as his own. ⁶You are to pay them in silver for the food you eat and the water you drink.' "

⁷The LORD your God has blessed you in all the work of your hands. He has watched over your journey through this vast desert. These forty years the LORD your God has been with you, and you have not lacked anything.

⁸So we went on past our brothers the descendants of Esau, who live in Seir. We turned from the Arabah road, which comes up from Elath and Ezion Geber, and traveled along the desert road of Moab.

⁹Then the LORD said to me, "Do not harass the Moabites or provoke them to war, for I will not give you any part of their land. I have given Ar to the descendants of Lot as a possession."

¹⁰(The Emites used to live there—a people strong and numerous, and as tall as the Anakites. ¹¹Like the Anakites, they too were considered Rephaites, but the Moabites called them Emites. ¹²Horites used to live in Seir, but the descendants of Esau drove them out. They destroyed the Horites from before them and settled in their place, just as Israel did in the land the LORD gave them as their possession.)

¹³And the LORD said, "Now get up and cross the Zered Valley." So we crossed the valley.

¹⁴Thirty-eight years passed from the time we left Kadesh Barnea until we crossed the Zered Valley. By then, that entire generation of fighting men had perished from the camp, as the LORD had sworn to them. ¹⁵The LORD's hand was against them until he had completely eliminated them from the camp.

¹⁶Now when the last of these fighting men among the people had died, ¹⁷the LORD said to me, ¹⁸"Today you are to pass by the region of Moab at Ar. ¹⁹When you come to the Ammonites, do not harass them or provoke them to war, for I will not give you possession of any land belonging to the Ammonites. I have given it as a possession to the descendants of Lot."

²⁰(That too was considered a land of the Rephaites, who used to live there; but the Ammonites called them Zamzummites. ²¹They were a people strong and numerous, and as tall as the Anakites. The LORD destroyed them from before the Ammonites, who drove them out and settled in their place. ²²The LORD had done the same for the descendants of Esau, who lived in Seir, when he destroyed the Horites from before them. They drove them out and have lived in their place to this day. ²³And as for the Avvites who lived in villages as far as Gaza, the Caphtorites coming out from Caphtorᵇ destroyed them and settled in their place.)

Defeat of Sihon King of Heshbon

²⁴"Set out now and cross the Arnon Gorge. See, I have given into your hand Sihon the Amorite, king of Heshbon, and his country. Begin to take possession of it and engage him in battle. ²⁵This very day I will begin to put the terror and fear of you on all the nations under heaven. They will

ᵃ 1 Hebrew *Yam Suph*; that is, Sea of Reeds   ᵇ 23 That is, Crete hear reports of you and will tremble and be in anguish because of you."

26From the desert of Kedemoth I sent messengers to Sihon king of Heshbon offering peace and saying, 27"Let us pass through your country. We will stay on the main road; we will not turn aside to the right or to the left. 28Sell us food to eat and water to drink for their price in silver. Only let us pass through on foot— 29as the descendants of Esau, who live in Seir, and the Moabites, who live in Ar, did for us—until we cross the Jordan into the land the LORD our God is giving us." 30But Sihon king of Heshbon refused to let us pass through. For the LORD your God had made his spirit stubborn and his heart obstinate in order to give him into your hands, as he has now done.

31The LORD said to me, "See, I have begun to deliver Sihon and his country over to you. Now begin to conquer and possess his land."

32When Sihon and all his army came out to meet us in battle at Jahaz, 33the LORD our God delivered him over to us and we struck him down, together with his sons and his whole army. 34At that time we took all his towns and completely destroyed*a* them—men, women and children. We left no survivors. 35But the livestock and the plunder from the towns we had captured we carried off for ourselves. 36From Aroer on the rim of the Arnon Gorge, and from the town in the gorge, even as far as Gilead, not one town was too strong for us. The LORD our God gave us all of them. 37But in accordance with the command of the LORD our God, you did not encroach on any of the land of the Ammonites, neither the land along the course of the Jabbok nor that around the towns in the hills.

Defeat of Og King of Bashan

3 Next we turned and went up along the road toward Bashan, and Og king of Bashan with his whole army marched out to meet us in battle at Edrei. 2The LORD said to me, "Do not be afraid of him, for I have handed him over to you with his whole army and his land. Do to him what you did to Sihon king of the Amorites, who reigned in Heshbon."

3So the LORD our God also gave into our hands Og king of Bashan and all his army. We struck them down, leaving no survivors. 4At that time we took all his cities. There was not one of the sixty cities that we did not take from them—the whole region of Argob, Og's kingdom in Bashan. 5All these cities were fortified with high walls and with gates and bars, and there were also a great many unwalled villages. 6We completely destroyed*a* them, as we had done with Sihon king of Heshbon, destroying*a* every city—men, women and children. 7But all the livestock and the plunder from their cities we carried off for ourselves.

8So at that time we took from these two kings of the Amorites the territory east of the Jordan, from the Arnon Gorge as far as Mount Hermon. 9(Hermon is called Sirion by the Sidonians; the Amorites call it Senir.) 10We took all the towns on the plateau, and all Gilead, and all Bashan as far as Salecah and Edrei, towns of Og's kingdom in Bashan. 11(Only Og king of Bashan was left of the remnant of the Rephaites. His bed*b* was made of iron and was more than thirteen feet long and six feet wide.*c* It is still in Rabbah of the Ammonites.)

Division of the Land

12Of the land that we took over at that time, I gave the Reubenites and the Gadites the territory north of Aroer by the Arnon Gorge, including half the hill country of Gilead, together with its towns. 13The rest of Gilead and also all of Bashan, the kingdom of Og, I gave to the half tribe of Manasseh. (The whole region of Argob in Bashan used to be known as a land of the Rephaites. 14Jair, a descendant of Manasseh, took the whole region of Argob as far as the border of the Geshurites and the Maacathites; it was named after him, so that to this day Bashan is called Havvoth Jair.*d*) 15And I gave Gilead to Makir. 16But to the Reubenites and the Gadites I gave the territory extending from Gilead down to the Arnon Gorge (the middle of the gorge being the border) and out to the Jabbok River, which is the border of the Ammonites. 17Its western border was the Jordan in the Arabah,

---

a 34,6 The Hebrew term refers to the irrevocable giving over of things or persons to the LORD, often by totally destroying them.   *b 11* Or *sarcophagus*   *c 11* Hebrew *nine cubits long and four cubits wide* (about 4 meters long and 1.8 meters wide)   *d 14* Or *called the settlements of Jair*

from Kinnereth to the Sea of the Arabah (the Salt Sea*a*), below the slopes of Pisgah.

18I commanded you at that time: "The LORD your God has given you this land to take possession of it. But all your able-bodied men, armed for battle, must cross over ahead of your brother Israelites. 19However, your wives, your children and your livestock (I know you have much livestock) may stay in the towns I have given you, 20until the LORD gives rest to your brothers as he has to you, and they too have taken over the land that the LORD your God is giving them, across the Jordan. After that, each of you may go back to the possession I have given you."

Moses Forbidden to Cross the Jordan

21At that time I commanded Joshua: "You have seen with your own eyes all that the LORD your God has done to these two kings. The LORD will do the same to all the kingdoms over there where you are going. 22Do not be afraid of them; the LORD your God himself will fight for you."

23At that time I pleaded with the LORD: 24"O Sovereign LORD, you have begun to show to your servant your greatness and your strong hand. For what god is there in heaven or on earth who can do the deeds and mighty works you do? 25Let me go over and see the good land beyond the Jordan—that fine hill country and Lebanon."

26But because of you the LORD was angry with me and would not listen to me. "That is enough," the LORD said. "Do not speak to me anymore about this matter. 27Go up to the top of Pisgah and look west and north and south and east. Look at the land with your own eyes, since you are not going to cross this Jordan. 28But commission Joshua, and encourage and strengthen him, for he will lead this people across and will cause them to inherit the land that you will see." 29So we stayed in the valley near Beth Peor.

Obedience Commanded

4 Hear now, O Israel, the decrees and laws I am about to teach you. Follow them so that you may live and may go in and take possession of the land that the LORD, the God of your fathers, is giving you. 2Do not add to what

I command you and do not subtract from it, but keep the commands of the LORD your God that I give you.

3You saw with your own eyes what the LORD did at Baal Peor. The LORD your God destroyed from among you everyone who followed the Baal of Peor, 4but all of you who held fast to the LORD your God are still alive today.

5See, I have taught you decrees and laws as the LORD my God commanded me, so that you may follow them in the land you are entering to take possession of it. 6Observe them carefully, for this will show your wisdom and understanding to the nations, who will hear about all these decrees and say, "Surely this great nation is a wise and understanding people." 7What other nation is so great as to have their gods near them the way the LORD our God is near us whenever we pray to him? 8And what other nation is so great as to have such righteous decrees and laws as this body of laws I am setting before you today?

9Only be careful, and watch yourselves closely so that you do not forget the things your eyes have seen or let them slip from your heart as long as you live. Teach them to your children and to their children after them. 10Remember the day you stood before the LORD your God at Horeb, when he said to me, "Assemble the people before me to hear my words so that they may learn to revere me as long as they live in the land and may teach them to their children." 11You came near and stood at the foot of the mountain while it blazed with fire to the very heavens, with black clouds and deep darkness. 12Then the LORD spoke to you out of the fire. You heard the sound of words but saw no form; there was only a voice. 13He declared to you his covenant, the Ten Commandments, which he commanded you to follow and then wrote them on two stone tablets. 14And the LORD directed me at that time to teach you the decrees and laws you are to follow in the land that you are crossing the Jordan to possess.

Idolatry Forbidden

15You saw no form of any kind the day the LORD spoke to you at Horeb out of

---

a 17 That is, the Dead Sea

the fire. Therefore watch yourselves very carefully, [16]so that you do not become corrupt and make for yourselves an idol, an image of any shape, whether formed like a man or a woman, [17]or like any animal on earth or any bird that flies in the air, [18]or like any creature that moves along the ground or any fish in the waters below. [19]And when you look up to the sky and see the sun, the moon and the stars—all the heavenly array—do not be enticed into bowing down to them and worshiping things the LORD your God has apportioned to all the nations under heaven. [20]But as for you, the LORD took you and brought you out of the iron-smelting furnace, out of Egypt, to be the people of his inheritance, as you now are.

[21]The LORD was angry with me because of you, and he solemnly swore

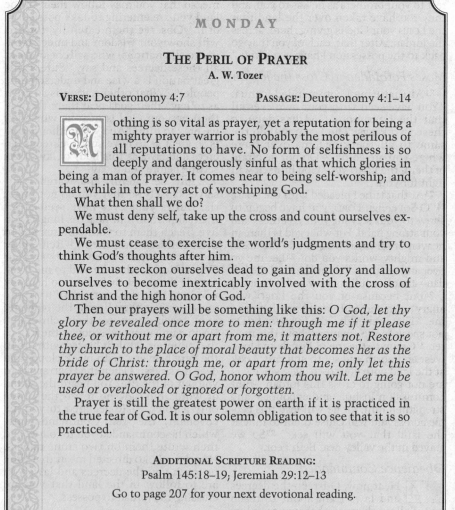

MONDAY

THE PERIL OF PRAYER
A. W. Tozer

VERSE: Deuteronomy 4:7   PASSAGE: Deuteronomy 4:1–14

Nothing is so vital as prayer, yet a reputation for being a mighty prayer warrior is probably the most perilous of all reputations to have. No form of selfishness is so deeply and dangerously sinful as that which glories in being a man of prayer. It comes near to being self-worship; and that while in the very act of worshiping God.

What then shall we do?

We must deny self, take up the cross and count ourselves expendable.

We must cease to exercise the world's judgments and try to think God's thoughts after him.

We must reckon ourselves dead to gain and glory and allow ourselves to become inextricably involved with the cross of Christ and the high honor of God.

Then our prayers will be something like this: *O God, let thy glory be revealed once more to men: through me if it please thee, or without me or apart from me, it matters not. Restore thy church to the place of moral beauty that becomes her as the bride of Christ: through me, or apart from me; only let this prayer be answered. O God, honor whom thou wilt. Let me be used or overlooked or ignored or forgotten.*

Prayer is still the greatest power on earth if it is practiced in the true fear of God. It is our solemn obligation to see that it is so practiced.

ADDITIONAL SCRIPTURE READING:
Psalm 145:18–19; Jeremiah 29:12–13

Go to page 207 for your next devotional reading.

1900   Present

that I would not cross the Jordan and enter the good land the LORD your God is giving you as your inheritance. 22I will die in this land; I will not cross the Jordan; but you are about to cross over and take possession of that good land. 23Be careful not to forget the covenant of the LORD your God that he made with you; do not make for yourselves an idol in the form of anything the LORD your God has forbidden. 24For the LORD your God is a consuming fire, a jealous God.

25After you have had children and grandchildren and have lived in the land a long time—if you then become corrupt and make any kind of idol, doing evil in the eyes of the LORD your God and provoking him to anger, 26I call heaven and earth as witnesses against you this day that you will quickly perish from the land that you are crossing the Jordan to possess. You will not live there long but will certainly be destroyed. 27The LORD will scatter you among the peoples, and only a few of you will survive among the nations to which the LORD will drive you. 28There you will worship man-made gods of wood and stone, which cannot see or hear or eat or smell. 29But if from there you seek the LORD your God, you will find him if you look for him with all your heart and with all your soul. 30When you are in distress and all these things have happened to you, then in later days you will return to the LORD your God and obey him. 31For the LORD your God is a merciful God; he will not abandon or destroy you or forget the covenant with your forefathers, which he confirmed to them by oath.

The LORD Is God

32Ask now about the former days, long before your time, from the day God created man on the earth; ask from one end of the heavens to the other. Has anything so great as this ever happened, or has anything like it ever been heard of? 33Has any other people heard the voice of God[a] speaking out of fire, as you have, and lived? 34Has any god ever tried to take for himself one nation out of another nation, by testings, by miraculous signs and wonders, by war, by a mighty hand and an outstretched arm, or by great and awesome deeds, like all the

things the LORD your God did for you in Egypt before your very eyes?

35You were shown these things so that you might know that the LORD is God; besides him there is no other. 36From heaven he made you hear his voice to discipline you. On earth he showed you his great fire, and you heard his words from out of the fire. 37Because he loved your forefathers and chose their descendants after them, he brought you out of Egypt by his Presence and his great strength, 38to drive out before you nations greater and stronger than you and to bring you into their land to give it to you for your inheritance, as it is today.

39Acknowledge and take to heart this day that the LORD is God in heaven above and on the earth below. There is no other. 40Keep his decrees and commands, which I am giving you today, so that it may go well with you and your children after you and that you may live long in the land the LORD your God gives you for all time.

Cities of Refuge

41Then Moses set aside three cities east of the Jordan, 42to which anyone who had killed a person could flee if he had unintentionally killed his neighbor without malice aforethought. He could flee into one of these cities and save his life. 43The cities were these: Bezer in the desert plateau, for the Reubenites; Ramoth in Gilead, for the Gadites; and Golan in Bashan, for the Manassites.

Introduction to the Law

44This is the law Moses set before the Israelites. 45These are the stipulations, decrees and laws Moses gave them when they came out of Egypt 46and were in the valley near Beth Peor east of the Jordan, in the land of Sihon king of the Amorites, who reigned in Heshbon and was defeated by Moses and the Israelites as they came out of Egypt. 47They took possession of his land and the land of Og king of Bashan, the two Amorite kings east of the Jordan. 48This land extended from Aroer on the rim of the Arnon Gorge to Mount Siyon[b] (that is, Hermon), 49and included all the Arabah east of the Jordan, as far as the Sea of the Arabah,[c] below the slopes of Pisgah.

a 33 Or *of a god*   *b 48* Hebrew; Syriac (see also Deut. 3:9) *Sirion*   *c 49* That is, the Dead Sea

The Ten Commandments

5 Moses summoned all Israel and said:

Hear, O Israel, the decrees and laws I declare in your hearing today. Learn them and be sure to follow them. ²The LORD our God made a covenant with us at Horeb. ³It was not with our fathers that the LORD made this covenant, but with us, with all of us who are alive here today. ⁴The LORD spoke to you face to face out of the fire on the mountain. ⁵(At that time I stood between the LORD and you to declare to you the word of the LORD, because you were afraid of the fire and did not go up the mountain.) And he said:

⁶ "I am the LORD your God, who brought you out of Egypt, out of the land of slavery.

⁷ "You shall have no other gods before*a* me.

⁸ "You shall not make for yourself an idol in the form of anything in heaven above or on the earth beneath or in the waters below. ⁹You shall not bow down to them or worship them; for I, the LORD your God, am a jealous God, punishing the children for the sin of the fathers to the third and fourth generation of those who hate me, ¹⁰but showing love to a thousand ∟generations⌟ of those who love me and keep my commandments.

¹¹ "You shall not misuse the name of the LORD your God, for the LORD will not hold anyone guiltless who misuses his name.

¹² "Observe the Sabbath day by keeping it holy, as the LORD your God has commanded you. ¹³Six days you shall labor and do all your work, ¹⁴but the seventh day is a Sabbath to the LORD your God. On it you shall not do any work, neither you, nor your son or daughter, nor your manservant or maidservant, nor your ox, your donkey or any of your animals, nor the alien within your gates, so that your manservant and maidservant may rest, as you do. ¹⁵Remem-

ber that you were slaves in Egypt and that the LORD your God brought you out of there with a mighty hand and an outstretched arm. Therefore the LORD your God has commanded you to observe the Sabbath day.

¹⁶ "Honor your father and your mother, as the LORD your God has commanded you, so that you may live long and that it may go well with you in the land the LORD your God is giving you.

¹⁷ "You shall not murder.

¹⁸ "You shall not commit adultery.

¹⁹ "You shall not steal.

²⁰ "You shall not give false testimony against your neighbor.

²¹ "You shall not covet your neighbor's wife. You shall not set your desire on your neighbor's house or land, his manservant or maidservant, his ox or donkey, or anything that belongs to your neighbor."

²²These are the commandments the LORD proclaimed in a loud voice to your whole assembly there on the mountain from out of the fire, the cloud and the deep darkness; and he added nothing more. Then he wrote them on two stone tablets and gave them to me.

²³When you heard the voice out of the darkness, while the mountain was ablaze with fire, all the leading men of your tribes and your elders came to me. ²⁴And you said, "The LORD our God has shown us his glory and his majesty, and we have heard his voice from the fire. Today we have seen that a man can live even if God speaks with him. ²⁵But now, why should we die? This great fire will consume us, and we will die if we hear the voice of the LORD our God any longer. ²⁶For what mortal man has ever heard the voice of the living God speaking out of fire, as we have, and survived? ²⁷Go near and listen to all that the LORD our God says. Then tell us whatever the LORD our God tells you. We will listen and obey."

²⁸The LORD heard you when you spoke to me and the LORD said to me, "I have heard what this people said to you. Everything they said was good. ²⁹Oh,

a 7 Or *besides*

that their hearts would be inclined to fear me and keep all my commands always, so that it might go well with them and their children forever!

30"Go, tell them to return to their tents. 31But you stay here with me so that I may give you all the commands, decrees and laws you are to teach them to follow in the land I am giving them to possess."

32So be careful to do what the LORD your God has commanded you; do not turn aside to the right or to the left. 33Walk in all the way that the LORD your God has commanded you, so that you may live and prosper and prolong your days in the land that you will possess.

Love the LORD Your God

6 These are the commands, decrees and laws the LORD your God directed me to teach you to observe in the land that you are crossing the Jordan to possess, 2so that you, your children and their children after them may fear the LORD your God as long as you live by keeping all his decrees and commands that I give you, and so that you may enjoy long life. 3Hear, O Israel, and be careful to obey so that it may go well with you and that you may increase greatly in a land flowing with milk and honey, just as the LORD, the God of your fathers, promised you.

4Hear, O Israel: The LORD our God, the LORD is one.a 5Love the LORD your God with all your heart and with all your soul and with all your strength. 6These commandments that I give you today are to be upon your hearts. 7Impress them on your children. Talk about them when you sit at home and when you walk along the road, when you lie down and when you get up. 8Tie them as symbols on your hands and bind them on your

foreheads. 9Write them on the doorframes of your houses and on your gates.

10When the LORD your God brings you into the land he swore to your fathers, to Abraham, Isaac and Jacob, to give you—a land with large, flourishing cities you did not build, 11houses filled with all kinds of good things you did not provide, wells you did not dig, and vineyards and olive groves you did not plant—then when you eat and are satisfied, 12be careful that you do not forget the LORD, who brought you out of Egypt, out of the land of slavery.

13Fear the LORD your God, serve him only and take your oaths in his name. 14Do not follow other gods, the gods of the peoples around you; 15for the LORD your God, who is among you, is a jealous God and his anger will burn against you, and he will destroy you from the face of the land. 16Do not test the LORD your God as you did at Massah. 17Be sure to keep the commands of the LORD your God and the stipulations and decrees he has given you. 18Do what is right and good in the LORD's sight, so that it may go well with you and you may go in and take over the good land that the LORD promised on oath to your forefathers, 19thrusting out all your enemies before you, as the LORD said.

20In the future, when your son asks you, "What is the meaning of the stipulations, decrees and laws the LORD our God has commanded you?" 21tell him: "We were slaves of Pharaoh in Egypt, but the LORD brought us out of Egypt with a mighty hand. 22Before our eyes the LORD sent miraculous signs and wonders—great and terrible—upon Egypt and Pharaoh and his whole household. 23But he brought us out from there to bring us in and give us the land that he promised on oath to our forefathers. 24The LORD commanded us to obey all these decrees and to fear the LORD our God, so that we might always prosper and be kept alive, as is the case today. 25And if we are careful to obey all this law before the LORD our God, as he has commanded us, that will be our righteousness."

Driving Out the Nations

7 When the LORD your God brings you into the land you are entering to possess and drives out before you many nations—the Hittites, Girgashites,

a 4 Or The LORD our God is one LORD; or The LORD is our God, the LORD is one; or The LORD is our God, the LORD alone

Amorites, Canaanites, Perizzites, Hivites and Jebusites, seven nations larger and stronger than you— ²and when the LORD your God has delivered them over to you and you have defeated them, then you must destroy them totally.ᵃ Make no treaty with them, and show them no mercy. ³Do not intermarry with them. Do not give your daughters to their sons or take their daughters for your sons, ⁴for they will turn your sons away from following me to serve other gods, and the LORD's anger will burn against you and will quickly destroy you. ⁵This is what you are to do to them: Break down their altars, smash their sacred stones, cut down their Asherah polesᵇ and burn their idols in the fire. ⁶For you are a people holy to the LORD your God. The LORD your God has chosen you out of all the peoples on the face of the earth to be his people, his treasured possession.

⁷The LORD did not set his affection on you and choose you because you were more numerous than other peoples, for you were the fewest of all peoples. ⁸But it was because the LORD loved you and kept the oath he swore to your forefathers that he brought you out with a mighty hand and redeemed you from the land of slavery, from the power of Pharaoh king of Egypt. ⁹Know therefore that the LORD your God is God; he is the faithful God, keeping his covenant of love to a thousand generations of those who love him and keep his commands. ¹⁰But

those who hate him he will repay to
   their face by destruction;
he will not be slow to repay to
   their face those who hate him.

¹¹Therefore, take care to follow the commands, decrees and laws I give you today.

¹²If you pay attention to these laws and are careful to follow them, then the LORD your God will keep his covenant of love with you, as he swore to your forefathers. ¹³He will love you and bless you and increase your numbers. He will bless the fruit of your womb, the crops of your land—your grain, new wine and oil—the calves of your herds and the lambs of your flocks in the land that he swore to your forefathers to give you. ¹⁴You will be blessed more than any other people; none of your men or women will be childless, nor any of your livestock without young. ¹⁵The LORD will keep you free from every disease. He will not inflict on you the horrible diseases you knew in Egypt, but he will inflict them on all who hate you. ¹⁶You must destroy all the peoples the LORD your God gives over to you. Do not look on them with pity and do not serve their gods, for that will be a snare to you.

¹⁷You may say to yourselves, "These nations are stronger than we are. How can we drive them out?" ¹⁸But do not be afraid of them; remember well what the LORD your God did to Pharaoh and to all Egypt. ¹⁹You saw with your own eyes the great trials, the miraculous signs and wonders, the mighty hand and outstretched arm, with which the LORD your God brought you out. The LORD your God will do the same to all the peoples you now fear. ²⁰Moreover, the LORD your God will send the hornet among them until even the survivors who hide from you have perished. ²¹Do not be terrified by them, for the LORD your God, who is among you, is a great and awesome God. ²²The LORD your God will drive out those nations before you, little by little. You will not be allowed to eliminate them all at once, or the wild animals will multiply around you. ²³But the LORD your God will deliver them over to you, throwing them into great confusion until they are destroyed. ²⁴He will give their kings into your hand, and you will wipe out their names from under heaven. No one will be able to stand up against you; you will destroy them. ²⁵The images of their gods you are to burn in the fire. Do not covet the silver and gold on them, and do not take it for yourselves, or you will be ensnared by it, for it is detestable to the LORD your God. ²⁶Do not bring a detestable thing into your house or you, like it, will be set apart for destruction. Utterly abhor and detest it, for it is set apart for destruction.

ᵃ 2 The Hebrew term refers to the irrevocable giving over of things or persons to the LORD, often by totally destroying them; also in verse 26.   ᵇ 5 That is, symbols of the goddess Asherah; here and elsewhere in Deuteronomy

GOD NEVER FORSAKES US
Martin Luther

VERSE: Deuteronomy 7:18   **PASSAGE:** Deuteronomy 7:17–24

 hen God . . . delivered the children of Israel out the long, wearisome, and heavy captivity in Egypt, and led them into the land of promise, he called Moses, to whom he afterwards gave his brother Aaron as an assistant. And though Pharaoh at first set himself hard against them, and plagued the people worse than before, yet he was forced in the end to let Israel go. And when he hunted after them with all his host, the Lord drowned Pharaoh with all his power in the Red Sea, and so delivered his people.

Again, in the time of Eli the priest, when matters stood very evil in Israel, the Philistines pressing hard upon them, and taking away the Ark of God into their land, and when Eli, in great sorrow of heart, fell backwards from his chair and broke his neck, and it seemed as if Israel were utterly undone. God raised up Samuel the prophet, and through him restored Israel, and the Philistines were overthrown.

Afterwards, when Saul was sore pressed by the Philistines, so that for anguish of heart he despaired and thrust himself through, three of his sons and many people dying with him, every man thought that now there was an end of Israel. But shortly after, when David was chosen king over all Israel, then came the golden time. For David, the chosen of God, not only saved Israel out of the enemies' hands, but also forced to obedience all kings and people that set themselves against him, and helped the kingdom up again in such manner, that in his and Solomon's time it was in full flourish, power, and glory.

Even so, when Judah was carried captive to Babylon, then God selected the prophets Ezekiel, Haggai, and Zechariah, who comforted men in their distress and captivity; making not only promise of their return into the land of Judah, but also that Christ should come in his due time.

Hence we may see that God never forsakes his people, nor even the wicked; though, by reason of their sins, he suffer them a long time to be severely punished and plagued as also, in this our time, he has graciously delivered us . . . God of his mercy grant we may thankfully acknowledge this.

ADDITIONAL SCRIPTURE READING:
Psalm 46:7–11; Isaiah 43:1–5; Matthew 28:20

Go to page 209 for your next devotional reading.

1500   1700

Do Not Forget the LORD

8 Be careful to follow every command I am giving you today, so that you may live and increase and may enter and possess the land that the LORD promised on oath to your forefathers. ²Remember how the LORD your God led you all the way in the desert these forty years, to humble you and to test you in order to know what was in your heart, whether or not you would keep his commands. ³He humbled you, causing you to hunger and then feeding you with manna, which neither you nor your fathers had known, to teach you that man does not live on bread alone but on every word that comes from the mouth of the LORD. ⁴Your clothes did not wear out and your feet did not swell during these forty years. ⁵Know then in your heart that as a man disciplines his son, so the LORD your God disciplines you.

⁶Observe the commands of the LORD your God, walking in his ways and revering him. ⁷For the LORD your God is bringing you into a good land—a land with streams and pools of water, with springs flowing in the valleys and hills; ⁸a land with wheat and barley, vines and fig trees, pomegranates, olive oil and honey; ⁹a land where bread will not be scarce and you will lack nothing; a land where the rocks are iron and you can dig copper out of the hills.

¹⁰When you have eaten and are satisfied, praise the LORD your God for the good land he has given you. ¹¹Be careful that you do not forget the LORD your God, failing to observe his commands, his laws and his decrees that I am giving you this day. ¹²Otherwise, when you eat and are satisfied, when you build fine houses and settle down, ¹³and when your herds and flocks grow large and your silver and gold increase and all you have is multiplied, ¹⁴then your heart will become proud and you will forget the LORD your God, who brought you out of Egypt, out of the land of slavery. ¹⁵He led you through the vast and dreadful desert, that thirsty and waterless land, with its venomous snakes and scorpions. He brought you water out of hard rock. ¹⁶He gave you manna to eat in the desert, something your fathers had never known, to humble and to test you so that in the end it might go well with you. ¹⁷You may say to yourself, "My power and the strength of my hands have produced this wealth for me." ¹⁸But remember the LORD your God, for it is he who gives you the ability to produce wealth, and so confirms his covenant, which he swore to your forefathers, as it is today.

¹⁹If you ever forget the LORD your God and follow other gods and worship and bow down to them, I testify against you today that you will surely be destroyed. ²⁰Like the nations the LORD destroyed before you, so you will be destroyed for not obeying the LORD your God.

Not Because of Israel's Righteousness

9 Hear, O Israel. You are now about to cross the Jordan to go in and dispossess nations greater and stronger than you, with large cities that have walls up to the sky. ²The people are strong and tall—Anakites! You know about them and have heard it said: "Who can stand up against the Anakites?" ³But be assured today that the LORD your God is the one who goes across ahead of you like a devouring fire. He will destroy them; he will subdue them before you. And you will drive them out and annihilate them quickly, as the LORD has promised you.

⁴After the LORD your God has driven them out before you, do not say to yourself, "The LORD has brought me here to take possession of this land because of my righteousness." No, it is on account of the wickedness of these nations that the LORD is going to drive them out before you. ⁵It is not because of your righteousness or your integrity that you are going in to take possession of their land; but on account of the wickedness of these nations, the LORD your God will drive them out before you, to accomplish what he swore to your fathers, to Abraham, Isaac and Jacob. ⁶Understand, then, that it is not because of your righteousness that the LORD your God is giving you this good land to possess, for you are a stiff-necked people.

The Golden Calf

⁷Remember this and never forget how you provoked the LORD your God to anger in the desert. From the day you left Egypt

until you arrived here, you have been rebellious against the LORD. 8At Horeb you aroused the LORD's wrath so that he was angry enough to destroy you. 9When I went up on the mountain to receive the tablets of stone, the tablets of the covenant that the LORD had made with you, I stayed on the mountain forty days and forty nights; I ate no bread and drank no water. 10The LORD gave me two stone tablets inscribed by the finger of God. On them were all the commandments the LORD proclaimed to you on the mountain out of the fire, on the day of the assembly.

11At the end of the forty days and forty nights, the LORD gave me the two stone tablets, the tablets of the covenant. 12Then the LORD told me, "Go down from here at once, because your people whom you brought out of Egypt have become corrupt. They have turned away quickly from what I commanded them and have made a cast idol for themselves."

13And the LORD said to me, "I have

NOT BY BREAD ALONE
F. B. Meyer

VERSE: Deuteronomy 8:3   **PASSAGE:** Deuteronomy 8:3

The Old Testament must be worth our study since it was our Savior's Bible, deeply pondered and often quoted. And the New [Testament] demands it, since it is so full of what he said and did, not only in his earthly life but through the medium of his holy apostles and prophets.

The advantages of a deep knowledge of the Bible are more than can be numbered here. It is the storehouse of the promises. It is the sword of the Spirit, before which temptation flees. It is the all-sufficient equipment of Christian usefulness. It is the believer's guidebook and directory in all possible circumstances. Words fail to tell how glad, how strong, how useful shall be the daily life of those who can say with the prophet: "Thy words were found, and I did eat them; and thy word was unto me the joy and rejoicing of mine heart" (Jeremiah 15:16, KJV).

But there is one thing, which may be said last, because it is most important and should linger in the memory and heart, though all the other exhortations of this chapter should pass away as a summer brook. It is this. It is useless to dream of making headway in the knowledge of Scripture unless we are prepared to practice each new and clearly-defined duty which looms out before our view.

ADDITIONAL SCRIPTURE READING:
Psalm 119:105; Jeremiah 15:16; Matthew 4:1–4

Go to page 230 for your next devotional reading.

1700   1900

seen this people, and they are a stiff-necked people indeed! ¹⁴Let me alone, so that I may destroy them and blot out their name from under heaven. And I will make you into a nation stronger and more numerous than they."

¹⁵So I turned and went down from the mountain while it was ablaze with fire. And the two tablets of the covenant were in my hands.ᵃ ¹⁶When I looked, I saw that you had sinned against the Lord your God; you had made for yourselves an idol cast in the shape of a calf. You had turned aside quickly from the way that the Lord had commanded you. ¹⁷So I took the two tablets and threw them out of my hands, breaking them to pieces before your eyes.

¹⁸Then once again I fell prostrate before the Lord for forty days and forty nights; I ate no bread and drank no water, because of all the sin you had committed, doing what was evil in the Lord's sight and so provoking him to anger. ¹⁹I feared the anger and wrath of the Lord, for he was angry enough with you to destroy you. But again the Lord listened to me. ²⁰And the Lord was angry enough with Aaron to destroy him, but at that time I prayed for Aaron too. ²¹Also I took that sinful thing of yours, the calf you had made, and burned it in the fire. Then I crushed it and ground it to powder as fine as dust and threw the dust into a stream that flowed down the mountain.

²²You also made the Lord angry at Taberah, at Massah and at Kibroth Hattaavah. ²³And when the Lord sent you out from Kadesh Barnea, he said, "Go up and take possession of the land I have given you." But you rebelled against the command of the Lord your God. You did not trust him or obey him. ²⁴You have been rebellious against the Lord ever since I have known you.

²⁵I lay prostrate before the Lord those forty days and forty nights because the Lord had said he would destroy you. ²⁶I prayed to the Lord and said, "O Sovereign Lord, do not destroy your people, your own inheritance that you redeemed by your great power and brought out of Egypt with a mighty hand. ²⁷Remember your servants Abraham, Isaac and Jacob. Overlook the stubbornness of this people, their wickedness and their sin.

²⁸Otherwise, the country from which you brought us will say, 'Because the Lord was not able to take them into the land he had promised them, and because he hated them, he brought them out to put them to death in the desert.' ²⁹But they are your people, your inheritance that you brought out by your great power and your outstretched arm."

Tablets Like the First Ones

10 At that time the Lord said to me, "Chisel out two stone tablets like the first ones and come up to me on the mountain. Also make a wooden chest.ᵇ ²I will write on the tablets the words that were on the first tablets, which you broke. Then you are to put them in the chest."

³So I made the ark out of acacia wood and chiseled out two stone tablets like the first ones, and I went up on the mountain with the two tablets in my hands. ⁴The Lord wrote on these tablets what he had written before, the Ten Commandments he had proclaimed to you on the mountain, out of the fire, on the day of the assembly. And the Lord gave them to me. ⁵Then I came back down the mountain and put the tablets in the ark I had made, as the Lord commanded me, and they are there now.

⁶(The Israelites traveled from the wells of the Jaakanites to Moserah. There Aaron died and was buried, and Eleazar his son succeeded him as priest. ⁷From there they traveled to Gudgodah and on to Jotbathah, a land with streams of water. ⁸At that time the Lord set apart the tribe of Levi to carry the ark of the covenant of the Lord, to stand before the Lord to minister and to pronounce blessings in his name, as they still do today. ⁹That is why the Levites have no share or inheritance among their brothers; the Lord is their inheritance, as the Lord your God told them.)

¹⁰Now I had stayed on the mountain forty days and nights, as I did the first time, and the Lord listened to me at this time also. It was not his will to destroy you. ¹¹"Go," the Lord said to me, "and lead the people on their way, so that they may enter and possess the land that I swore to their fathers to give them."

ᵃ 15 Or And I had the two tablets of the covenant with me, one in each hand   ᵇ 1 That is, an ark

Fear the LORD

12And now, O Israel, what does the LORD your God ask of you but to fear the LORD your God, to walk in all his ways, to love him, to serve the LORD your God with all your heart and with all your soul, **13**and to observe the LORD's commands and decrees that I am giving you today for your own good?

14To the LORD your God belong the heavens, even the highest heavens, the earth and everything in it. **15**Yet the LORD set his affection on your forefathers and loved them, and he chose you, their descendants, above all the nations, as it is today. **16**Circumcise your hearts, therefore, and do not be stiff-necked any longer. **17**For the LORD your God is God of gods and Lord of lords, the great God, mighty and awesome, who shows no partiality and accepts no bribes. **18**He defends the cause of the fatherless and the widow, and loves the alien, giving him food and clothing. **19**And you are to love those who are aliens, for you yourselves were aliens in Egypt. **20**Fear the LORD your God and serve him. Hold fast to him and take your oaths in his name. **21**He is your praise; he is your God, who performed for you those great and awesome wonders you saw with your own eyes. **22**Your forefathers who went down into Egypt were seventy in all, and now the LORD your God has made you as numerous as the stars in the sky.

Love and Obey the LORD

11 Love the LORD your God and keep his requirements, his decrees, his laws and his commands always. **2**Remember today that your children were not the ones who saw and experienced the discipline of the LORD your God: his majesty, his mighty hand, his outstretched arm; **3**the signs he performed and the things he did in the heart of Egypt, both to Pharaoh king of Egypt and to his whole country; **4**what he did to the Egyptian army, to its horses and chariots, how he overwhelmed them with the waters of the Red Sea[a] as they were pursuing you, and how the LORD brought lasting ruin on them. **5**It was not your children who saw what he did for you in the desert until you arrived at this place, **6**and what he did to Dathan and Abiram, sons of Eliab the Reubenite, when the earth opened its mouth right in the middle of all Israel and swallowed them up with their households, their tents and every living thing that belonged to them. **7**But it was your own eyes that saw all these great things the LORD has done.

8Observe therefore all the commands I am giving you today, so that you may have the strength to go in and take over the land that you are crossing the Jordan to possess, **9**and so that you may live long in the land that the LORD swore to your forefathers to give to them and their descendants, a land flowing with milk and honey. **10**The land you are entering to take over is not like the land of Egypt, from which you have come, where you planted your seed and irrigated it by foot as in a vegetable garden. **11**But the land you are crossing the Jordan to take possession of is a land of mountains and valleys that drinks rain from heaven. **12**It is a land the LORD your God cares for; the eyes of the LORD your God are continually on it from the beginning of the year to its end.

13So if you faithfully obey the commands I am giving you today—to love the LORD your God and to serve him with all your heart and with all your soul— **14**then I will send rain on your land in its season, both autumn and spring rains, so that you may gather in your grain, new wine and oil. **15**I will provide grass in the fields for your cattle, and you will eat and be satisfied.

16Be careful, or you will be enticed to turn away and worship other gods and bow down to them. **17**Then the LORD's anger will burn against you, and he will shut the heavens so that it will not rain and the ground will yield no produce, and you will soon perish from the good land the LORD is giving you. **18**Fix these words of mine in your hearts and minds; tie them as symbols on your hands and bind them on your foreheads. **19**Teach them to your children, talking about them when you sit at home and when you walk along the road, when you lie down and when you get up. **20**Write them on the doorframes of your houses and on your gates, **21**so that your days and the days of

---

a 4 Hebrew *Yam Suph;* that is, Sea of Reeds

your children may be many in the land that the LORD swore to give your forefathers, as many as the days that the heavens are above the earth.

22If you carefully observe all these commands I am giving you to follow—to love the LORD your God, to walk in all his ways and to hold fast to him— 23then the LORD will drive out all these nations before you, and you will dispossess nations larger and stronger than you. 24Every place where you set your foot will be yours: Your territory will extend from the desert to Lebanon, and from the Euphrates River to the western sea.*a* 25No man will be able to stand against you. The LORD your God, as he promised you, will put the terror and fear of you on the whole land, wherever you go.

26See, I am setting before you today a blessing and a curse— 27the blessing if you obey the commands of the LORD your God that I am giving you today; 28the curse if you disobey the commands of the LORD your God and turn from the way that I command you today by following other gods, which you have not known. 29When the LORD your God has brought you into the land you are entering to possess, you are to proclaim on Mount Gerizim the blessings, and on Mount Ebal the curses. 30As you know, these mountains are across the Jordan, west of the road,*b* toward the setting sun, near the great trees of Moreh, in the territory of those Canaanites living in the Arabah in the vicinity of Gilgal. 31You are about to cross the Jordan to enter and take possession of the land the LORD your God is giving you. When you have taken it over and are living there, 32be sure that you obey all the decrees and laws I am setting before you today.

The One Place of Worship

12 These are the decrees and laws you must be careful to follow in the land that the LORD, the God of your fathers, has given you to possess—as long as you live in the land. 2Destroy completely all the places on the high mountains and on the hills and under every spreading tree where the nations you are dispossessing worship their gods. 3Break down their altars, smash their sacred stones and burn their Asherah poles in the fire; cut down the idols of their gods and wipe out their names from those places.

4You must not worship the LORD your God in their way. 5But you are to seek the place the LORD your God will choose from among all your tribes to put his Name there for his dwelling. To that place you must go; 6there bring your burnt offerings and sacrifices, your tithes and special gifts, what you have vowed to give and your freewill offerings, and the firstborn of your herds and flocks. 7There, in the presence of the LORD your God, you and your families shall eat and shall rejoice in everything you have put your hand to, because the LORD your God has blessed you.

8You are not to do as we do here today, everyone as he sees fit, 9since you have not yet reached the resting place and the inheritance the LORD your God is giving you. 10But you will cross the Jordan and settle in the land the LORD your God is giving you as an inheritance, and he will give you rest from all your enemies around you so that you will live in safety. 11Then to the place the LORD your God will choose as a dwelling for his Name—there you are to bring everything I command you: your burnt offerings and sacrifices, your tithes and special gifts, and all the choice possessions you have vowed to the LORD. 12And there rejoice before the LORD your God, you, your sons and daughters, your menservants and maidservants, and the Levites from your towns, who have no allotment or inheritance of their own. 13Be careful not to sacrifice your burnt offerings anywhere you please. 14Offer them only at the place the LORD will choose in one of your tribes, and there observe everything I command you.

15Nevertheless, you may slaughter your animals in any of your towns and eat as much of the meat as you want, as if it were gazelle or deer, according to the blessing the LORD your God gives you. Both the ceremonially unclean and the clean may eat it. 16But you must not eat the blood; pour it out on the ground like water. 17You must not eat in your own towns the tithe of your grain and new

---

a 24 That is, the Mediterranean   b 30 Or Jordan, westward

wine and oil, or the firstborn of your herds and flocks, or whatever you have vowed to give, or your freewill offerings or special gifts. 18Instead, you are to eat them in the presence of the LORD your God at the place the LORD your God will choose—you, your sons and daughters, your menservants and maidservants, and the Levites from your towns—and you are to rejoice before the LORD your God in everything you put your hand to. 19Be careful not to neglect the Levites as long as you live in your land.

20When the LORD your God has enlarged your territory as he promised you, and you crave meat and say, "I would like some meat," then you may eat as much of it as you want. 21If the place where the LORD your God chooses to put his Name is too far away from you, you may slaughter animals from the herds and flocks the LORD has given you, as I have commanded you, and in your own towns you may eat as much of them as you want. 22Eat them as you would gazelle or deer. Both the ceremonially unclean and the clean may eat. 23But be sure you do not eat the blood, because the blood is the life, and you must not eat the life with the meat. 24You must not eat the blood; pour it out on the ground like water. 25Do not eat it, so that it may go well with you and your children after you, because you will be doing what is right in the eyes of the LORD.

26But take your consecrated things and whatever you have vowed to give, and go to the place the LORD will choose. 27Present your burnt offerings on the altar of the LORD your God, both the meat and the blood. The blood of your sacrifices must be poured beside the altar of the LORD your God, but you may eat the meat. 28Be careful to obey all these regulations I am giving you, so that it may always go well with you and your children after you, because you will be doing what is good and right in the eyes of the LORD your God.

29The LORD your God will cut off before you the nations you are about to invade and dispossess. But when you have driven them out and settled in their land, 30and after they have been destroyed before you, be careful not to be ensnared by inquiring about their gods, saying, "How do these nations serve their gods? We will do the same." 31You must not worship the LORD your God in their way, because in worshiping their gods, they do all kinds of detestable things the LORD hates. They even burn their sons and daughters in the fire as sacrifices to their gods.

32See that you do all I command you; do not add to it or take away from it.

Worshiping Other Gods

13 If a prophet, or one who foretells by dreams, appears among you and announces to you a miraculous sign or wonder, 2and if the sign or wonder of which he has spoken takes place, and he says, "Let us follow other gods" (gods you have not known) "and let us worship them," 3you must not listen to the words of that prophet or dreamer. The LORD your God is testing you to find out whether you love him with all your heart and with all your soul. 4It is the LORD your God you must follow, and him you must revere. Keep his commands and obey him; serve him and hold fast to him. 5That prophet or dreamer must be put to death, because he preached rebellion against the LORD your God, who brought you out of Egypt and redeemed you from the land of slavery; he has tried to turn you from the way the LORD your God commanded you to follow. You must purge the evil from among you.

6If your very own brother, or your son or daughter, or the wife you love, or your closest friend secretly entices you, saying, "Let us go and worship other gods" (gods that neither you nor your fathers have known, 7gods of the peoples around you, whether near or far, from one end of the land to the other), 8do not yield to him or listen to him. Show him no pity. Do not spare him or shield him. 9You must certainly put him to death. Your hand must be the first in putting him to death, and then the hands of all the people. 10Stone him to death, because he tried to turn you away from the LORD your God, who brought you out of Egypt, out of the land of slavery. 11Then all Israel will hear and be afraid, and no one among you will do such an evil thing again.

12If you hear it said about one of the towns the LORD your God is giving you to live in [13]that wicked men have arisen among you and have led the people of their town astray, saying, "Let us go and worship other gods" (gods you have not known), [14]then you must inquire, probe and investigate it thoroughly. And if it is true and it has been proved that this detestable thing has been done among you, [15]you must certainly put to the sword all who live in that town. Destroy it completely,[a] both its people and its livestock. [16]Gather all the plunder of the town into the middle of the public square and completely burn the town and all its plunder as a whole burnt offering to the LORD your God. It is to remain a ruin forever, never to be rebuilt. [17]None of those condemned things[a] shall be found in your hands, so that the LORD will turn from his fierce anger; he will show you mercy, have compassion on you, and increase your numbers, as he promised on oath to your forefathers, [18]because you obey the LORD your God, keeping all his commands that I am giving you today and doing what is right in his eyes.

Clean and Unclean Food

14 You are the children of the LORD your God. Do not cut yourselves or shave the front of your heads for the dead, [2]for you are a people holy to the LORD your God. Out of all the peoples on the face of the earth, the LORD has chosen you to be his treasured possession.

[3]Do not eat any detestable thing. [4]These are the animals you may eat: the ox, the sheep, the goat, [5]the deer, the gazelle, the roe deer, the wild goat, the ibex, the antelope and the mountain sheep.[b] [6]You may eat any animal that has a split hoof divided in two and that chews the cud. [7]However, of those that chew the cud or that have a split hoof completely divided you may not eat the camel, the rabbit or the coney.[c] Although they chew the cud, they do not have a split hoof; they are ceremonially unclean for you. [8]The pig is also unclean; although it has a split hoof, it does not chew the cud. You are not to eat their meat or touch their carcasses.

[9]Of all the creatures living in the water, you may eat any that has fins and scales. [10]But anything that does not have fins and scales you may not eat; for you it is unclean.

[11]You may eat any clean bird. [12]But these you may not eat: the eagle, the vulture, the black vulture, [13]the red kite, the black kite, any kind of falcon, [14]any kind of raven, [15]the horned owl, the screech owl, the gull, any kind of hawk, [16]the little owl, the great owl, the white owl, [17]the desert owl, the osprey, the cormorant, [18]the stork, any kind of heron, the hoopoe and the bat.

[19]All flying insects that swarm are unclean to you; do not eat them. [20]But any winged creature that is clean you may eat.

[21]Do not eat anything you find already dead. You may give it to an alien living in any of your towns, and he may eat it, or you may sell it to a foreigner. But you are a people holy to the LORD your God.

Do not cook a young goat in its mother's milk.

Tithes

[22]Be sure to set aside a tenth of all that your fields produce each year. [23]Eat the tithe of your grain, new wine and oil, and the firstborn of your herds and flocks in the presence of the LORD your God at the place he will choose as a dwelling for his Name, so that you may learn to revere the LORD your God always. [24]But if that place is too distant and you have been blessed by the LORD your God and cannot carry your tithe (because the place where the LORD will choose to put his Name is so far away), [25]then exchange your tithe for silver, and take the silver with you and go to the place the LORD your God will choose. [26]Use the silver to buy whatever you like: cattle, sheep, wine or other fermented drink, or anything you wish. Then you and your household shall eat there in the presence of the LORD your God and rejoice. [27]And do not neglect the Levites living in your towns, for they have no allotment or inheritance of their own.

[28]At the end of every three years, bring all the tithes of that year's produce and

---

[a] 15,17 The Hebrew term refers to the irrevocable giving over of things or persons to the LORD, often by totally destroying them.   [b] 5 The precise identification of some of the birds and animals in this chapter is uncertain.   [c] 7 That is, the hyrax or rock badger

store it in your towns, ²⁹so that the Levites (who have no allotment or inheritance of their own) and the aliens, the fatherless and the widows who live in your towns may come and eat and be satisfied, and so that the LORD your God may bless you in all the work of your hands.

The Year for Canceling Debts

15 At the end of every seven years you must cancel debts. ²This is how it is to be done: Every creditor shall cancel the loan he has made to his fellow Israelite. He shall not require payment from his fellow Israelite or brother, because the LORD's time for canceling debts has been proclaimed. ³You may require payment from a foreigner, but you must cancel any debt your brother owes you. ⁴However, there should be no poor among you, for in the land the LORD your God is giving you to possess as your inheritance, he will richly bless you, ⁵if only you fully obey the LORD your God and are careful to follow all these commands I am giving you today. ⁶For the LORD your God will bless you as he has promised, and you will lend to many nations but will borrow from none. You will rule over many nations but none will rule over you.

⁷If there is a poor man among your brothers in any of the towns of the land that the LORD your God is giving you, do not be hardhearted or tightfisted toward your poor brother. ⁸Rather be openhanded and freely lend him whatever he needs. ⁹Be careful not to harbor this wicked thought: "The seventh year, the year for canceling debts, is near," so that you do not show ill will toward your needy brother and give him nothing. He may then appeal to the LORD against

---

THE SAYING IS, THAT HE WHO GIVES TO THE POOR, LENDS TO THE LORD. BUT IT MAY BE SAID, NOT IMPROPERLY, THE LORD LENDS TO US TO GIVE TO THE POOR.   —*William Penn*

---

you, and you will be found guilty of sin. ¹⁰Give generously to him and do so without a grudging heart; then because of this the LORD your God will bless you in all your work and in everything you

put your hand to. ¹¹There will always be poor people in the land. Therefore I command you to be openhanded toward your brothers and toward the poor and needy in your land.

Freeing Servants

¹²If a fellow Hebrew, a man or a woman, sells himself to you and serves you six years, in the seventh year you must let him go free. ¹³And when you release him, do not send him away emptyhanded. ¹⁴Supply him liberally from your flock, your threshing floor and your winepress. Give to him as the LORD your God has blessed you. ¹⁵Remember that you were slaves in Egypt and the LORD your God redeemed you. That is why I give you this command today.

¹⁶But if your servant says to you, "I do not want to leave you," because he loves you and your family and is well off with you, ¹⁷then take an awl and push it through his ear lobe into the door, and he will become your servant for life. Do the same for your maidservant.

¹⁸Do not consider it a hardship to set your servant free, because his service to you these six years has been worth twice as much as that of a hired hand. And the LORD your God will bless you in everything you do.

The Firstborn Animals

¹⁹Set apart for the LORD your God every firstborn male of your herds and flocks. Do not put the firstborn of your oxen to work, and do not shear the firstborn of your sheep. ²⁰Each year you and your family are to eat them in the presence of the LORD your God at the place he will choose. ²¹If an animal has a defect, is lame or blind, or has any serious flaw, you must not sacrifice it to the LORD your God. ²²You are to eat it in your own towns. Both the ceremonially unclean and the clean may eat it, as if it were gazelle or deer. ²³But you must not eat the blood; pour it out on the ground like water.

Passover

16 Observe the month of Abib and celebrate the Passover of the LORD your God, because in the month of Abib he brought you out of

Egypt by night. ²Sacrifice as the Passover to the LORD your God an animal from your flock or herd at the place the LORD will choose as a dwelling for his Name. ³Do not eat it with bread made with yeast, but for seven days eat unleavened bread, the bread of affliction, because you left Egypt in haste—so that all the days of your life you may remember the time of your departure from Egypt. ⁴Let no yeast be found in your possession in all your land for seven days. Do not let any of the meat you sacrifice on the evening of the first day remain until morning.

⁵You must not sacrifice the Passover in any town the LORD your God gives you ⁶except in the place he will choose as a dwelling for his Name. There you must sacrifice the Passover in the evening, when the sun goes down, on the anniversary*a* of your departure from Egypt. ⁷Roast it and eat it at the place the LORD your God will choose. Then in the morning return to your tents. ⁸For six days eat unleavened bread and on the seventh day hold an assembly to the LORD your God and do no work.

Feast of Weeks

⁹Count off seven weeks from the time you begin to put the sickle to the standing grain. ¹⁰Then celebrate the Feast of Weeks to the LORD your God by giving a freewill offering in proportion to the blessings the LORD your God has given you. ¹¹And rejoice before the LORD your God at the place he will choose as a dwelling for his Name—you, your sons and daughters, your menservants and maidservants, the Levites in your towns, and the aliens, the fatherless and the widows living among you. ¹²Remember that you were slaves in Egypt, and follow carefully these decrees.

Feast of Tabernacles

¹³Celebrate the Feast of Tabernacles for seven days after you have gathered the produce of your threshing floor and your winepress. ¹⁴Be joyful at your Feast—you, your sons and daughters, your menservants and maidservants, and the Levites, the aliens, the fatherless and the widows who live in your towns. ¹⁵For seven days celebrate the Feast to

the LORD your God at the place the LORD will choose. For the LORD your God will bless you in all your harvest and in all the work of your hands, and your joy will be complete.

¹⁶Three times a year all your men must appear before the LORD your God at the place he will choose: at the Feast of Unleavened Bread, the Feast of Weeks and the Feast of Tabernacles. No man should appear before the LORD empty-handed: ¹⁷Each of you must bring a gift in proportion to the way the LORD your God has blessed you.

Judges

¹⁸Appoint judges and officials for each of your tribes in every town the LORD your God is giving you, and they shall judge the people fairly. ¹⁹Do not pervert justice or show partiality. Do not accept a bribe, for a bribe blinds the eyes of the wise and twists the words of the righteous. ²⁰Follow justice and justice alone, so that you may live and possess the land the LORD your God is giving you.

Worshiping Other Gods

²¹Do not set up any wooden Asherah pole*b* beside the altar you build to the LORD your God, ²²and do not erect a sacred stone, for these the LORD your God hates.

17 Do not sacrifice to the LORD your God an ox or a sheep that has any defect or flaw in it, for that would be detestable to him.

²If a man or woman living among you in one of the towns the LORD gives you is found doing evil in the eyes of the LORD your God in violation of his covenant, ³and contrary to my command has worshiped other gods, bowing down to them or to the sun or to the moon or the stars of the sky, ⁴and this has been brought to your attention, then you must investigate it thoroughly. If it is true and it has been proved that this detestable thing has been done in Israel, ⁵take the man or woman who has done this evil deed to your city gate and stone that person to death. ⁶On the testimony of two or three witnesses a man shall be put to death, but no one shall be put to death on the testimony of only one wit-

a 6 Or down, at the time of day   b 21 Or Do not plant any tree dedicated to Asherah ness. [7]The hands of the witnesses must be the first in putting him to death, and then the hands of all the people. You must purge the evil from among you.

Law Courts

[8]If cases come before your courts that are too difficult for you to judge—whether bloodshed, lawsuits or assaults—take them to the place the LORD your God will choose. [9]Go to the priests, who are Levites, and to the judge who is in office at that time. Inquire of them and they will give you the verdict. [10]You must act according to the decisions they give you at the place the LORD will choose. Be careful to do everything they direct you to do. [11]Act according to the law they teach you and the decisions they give you. Do not turn aside from what they tell you, to the right or to the left. [12]The man who shows contempt for the judge or for the priest who stands ministering there to the LORD your God must be put to death. You must purge the evil from Israel. [13]All the people will hear and be afraid, and will not be contemptuous again.

The King

[14]When you enter the land the LORD your God is giving you and have taken possession of it and settled in it, and you say, "Let us set a king over us like all the nations around us," [15]be sure to appoint over you the king the LORD your God chooses. He must be from among your own brothers. Do not place a foreigner over you, one who is not a brother Israelite. [16]The king, moreover, must not acquire great numbers of horses for himself or make the people return to Egypt to get more of them, for the LORD has told you, "You are not to go back that way again." [17]He must not take many wives, or his heart will be led astray. He must not accumulate large amounts of silver and gold.

[18]When he takes the throne of his kingdom, he is to write for himself on a scroll a copy of this law, taken from that of the priests, who are Levites. [19]It is to be with him, and he is to read it all the days of his life so that he may learn to revere the LORD his God and follow carefully all the words of this law and these decrees [20]and not consider himself better than his brothers and turn from the law to the right or to the left. Then he and his descendants will reign a long time over his kingdom in Israel.

Offerings for Priests and Levites

18 The priests, who are Levites—indeed the whole tribe of Levi—are to have no allotment or inheritance with Israel. They shall live on the offerings made to the LORD by fire, for that is their inheritance. [2]They shall have no inheritance among their brothers; the LORD is their inheritance, as he promised them.

[3]This is the share due the priests from the people who sacrifice a bull or a sheep: the shoulder, the jowls and the inner parts. [4]You are to give them the firstfruits of your grain, new wine and oil, and the first wool from the shearing of your sheep, [5]for the LORD your God has chosen them and their descendants out of all your tribes to stand and minister in the LORD's name always.

[6]If a Levite moves from one of your towns anywhere in Israel where he is living, and comes in all earnestness to the place the LORD will choose, [7]he may minister in the name of the LORD his God like all his fellow Levites who serve there in the presence of the LORD. [8]He is to share equally in their benefits, even though he has received money from the sale of family possessions.

Detestable Practices

[9]When you enter the land the LORD your God is giving you, do not learn to imitate the detestable ways of the nations there. [10]Let no one be found among you who sacrifices his son or daughter in[a] the fire, who practices divination or sorcery, interprets omens, engages in witchcraft, [11]or casts spells, or who is a medium or spiritist or who consults the dead. [12]Anyone who does these things is detestable to the LORD, and because of these detestable practices the LORD your God will drive out those nations before you. [13]You must be blameless before the LORD your God.

[a] 10 Or *who makes his son or daughter pass through*

The Prophet

14The nations you will dispossess listen to those who practice sorcery or divination. But as for you, the LORD your God has not permitted you to do so. **15**The LORD your God will raise up for you a prophet like me from among your own brothers. You must listen to him. **16**For this is what you asked of the LORD your God at Horeb on the day of the assembly when you said, "Let us not hear the voice of the LORD our God nor see this great fire anymore, or we will die."

17The LORD said to me: "What they say is good. **18**I will raise up for them a prophet like you from among their brothers; I will put my words in his mouth, and he will tell them everything I command him. **19**If anyone does not listen to my words that the prophet speaks in my name, I myself will call him to account. **20**But a prophet who presumes to speak in my name anything I have not commanded him to say, or a prophet who speaks in the name of other gods, must be put to death."

21You may say to yourselves, "How can we know when a message has not been spoken by the LORD?" **22**If what a prophet proclaims in the name of the LORD does not take place or come true, that is a message the LORD has not spoken. That prophet has spoken presumptuously. Do not be afraid of him.

Cities of Refuge

19 When the LORD your God has destroyed the nations whose land he is giving you, and when you have driven them out and settled in their towns and houses, **2**then set aside for yourselves three cities centrally located in the land the LORD your God is giving you to possess. **3**Build roads to them and divide into three parts the land the LORD your God is giving you as an inheritance, so that anyone who kills a man may flee there.

4This is the rule concerning the man who kills another and flees there to save his life—one who kills his neighbor unintentionally, without malice aforethought. **5**For instance, a man may go into the forest with his neighbor to cut wood, and as he swings his ax to fell a tree, the head may fly off and hit his neighbor and kill him. That man may flee to one of these cities and save his life. **6**Otherwise, the avenger of blood might pursue him in a rage, overtake him if the distance is too great, and kill him even though he is not deserving of death, since he did it to his neighbor without malice aforethought. **7**This is why I command you to set aside for yourselves three cities.

8If the LORD your God enlarges your territory, as he promised on oath to your forefathers, and gives you the whole land he promised them, **9**because you carefully follow all these laws I command you today—to love the LORD your God and to walk always in his ways— then you are to set aside three more cities. **10**Do this so that innocent blood will not be shed in your land, which the LORD your God is giving you as your inheritance, and so that you will not be guilty of bloodshed.

11But if a man hates his neighbor and lies in wait for him, assaults and kills him, and then flees to one of these cities, **12**the elders of his town shall send for him, bring him back from the city, and hand him over to the avenger of blood to die. **13**Show him no pity. You must purge from Israel the guilt of shedding innocent blood, so that it may go well with you.

14Do not move your neighbor's boundary stone set up by your predecessors in the inheritance you receive in the land the LORD your God is giving you to possess.

Witnesses

15One witness is not enough to convict a man accused of any crime or offense he may have committed. A matter must be established by the testimony of two or three witnesses.

16If a malicious witness takes the stand to accuse a man of a crime, **17**the two men involved in the dispute must stand in the presence of the LORD before the priests and the judges who are in office at the time. **18**The judges must make a thorough investigation, and if the witness proves to be a liar, giving false testimony against his brother, **19**then do to him as he intended to do to his brother. You must purge the evil from among you. 20The rest of the people will hear of this and be afraid, and never again will such an evil thing be done among you. 21Show no pity: life for life, eye for eye, tooth for tooth, hand for hand, foot for foot.

Going to War

20 When you go to war against your enemies and see horses and chariots and an army greater than yours, do not be afraid of them, because the LORD your God, who brought you up out of Egypt, will be with you. 2When you are about to go into battle, the priest shall come forward and address the army. 3He shall say: "Hear, O Israel, today you are going into battle against your enemies. Do not be fainthearted or afraid; do not be terrified or give way to panic before them. 4For the LORD your God is the one who goes with you to fight for you against your enemies to give you victory."

5The officers shall say to the army: "Has anyone built a new house and not dedicated it? Let him go home, or he may die in battle and someone else may dedicate it. 6Has anyone planted a vineyard and not begun to enjoy it? Let him go home, or he may die in battle and someone else enjoy it. 7Has anyone become pledged to a woman and not married her? Let him go home, or he may die in battle and someone else marry her." 8Then the officers shall add, "Is any man afraid or fainthearted? Let him go home so that his brothers will not become disheartened too." 9When the officers have finished speaking to the army, they shall appoint commanders over it.

10When you march up to attack a city, make its people an offer of peace. 11If they accept and open their gates, all the people in it shall be subject to forced labor and shall work for you. 12If they refuse to make peace and they engage you in battle, lay siege to that city. 13When the LORD your God delivers it into your hand, put to the sword all the men in it. 14As for the women, the children, the livestock and everything else in the city, you may take these as plunder for yourselves. And you may use the plunder the LORD your God gives you from your enemies. 15This is how you are to treat all the cities that are at a distance from you and do not belong to the nations nearby.

16However, in the cities of the nations the LORD your God is giving you as an inheritance, do not leave alive anything that breathes. 17Completely destroy[a] them—the Hittites, Amorites, Canaanites, Perizzites, Hivites and Jebusites—as the LORD your God has commanded you. 18Otherwise, they will teach you to follow all the detestable things they do in worshiping their gods, and you will sin against the LORD your God.

19When you lay siege to a city for a long time, fighting against it to capture it, do not destroy its trees by putting an ax to them, because you can eat their fruit. Do not cut them down. Are the trees of the field people, that you should besiege them?[b] 20However, you may cut down trees that you know are not fruit trees and use them to build siege works until the city at war with you falls.

Atonement for an Unsolved Murder

21 If a man is found slain, lying in a field in the land the LORD your God is giving you to possess, and it is not known who killed him, 2your elders and judges shall go out and measure the distance from the body to the neighboring towns. 3Then the elders of the town nearest the body shall take a heifer that has never been worked and has never worn a yoke 4and lead her down to a valley that has not been plowed or planted and where there is a flowing stream. There in the valley they are to break the heifer's neck. 5The priests, the sons of Levi, shall step forward, for the LORD your God has chosen them to minister and to pronounce blessings in the name of the LORD and to decide all cases of dispute and assault. 6Then all the elders of the town nearest the body shall wash their hands over the heifer whose neck was broken in the valley, 7and they shall declare: "Our hands did not shed this blood, nor did our eyes see it done. 8Accept this atonement for your people Israel, whom you have redeemed,

---

a 17 The Hebrew term refers to the irrevocable giving over of things or persons to the LORD, often by totally destroying them.   b 19 Or down to use in the siege, for the fruit trees are for the benefit of man.

O LORD, and do not hold your people guilty of the blood of an innocent man." And the bloodshed will be atoned for. [9]So you will purge from yourselves the guilt of shedding innocent blood, since you have done what is right in the eyes of the LORD.

Marrying a Captive Woman

[10]When you go to war against your enemies and the LORD your God delivers them into your hands and you take captives, [11]if you notice among the captives a beautiful woman and are attracted to her, you may take her as your wife. [12]Bring her into your home and have her shave her head, trim her nails [13]and put aside the clothes she was wearing when captured. After she has lived in your house and mourned her father and mother for a full month, then you may go to her and be her husband and she shall be your wife. [14]If you are not pleased with her, let her go wherever she wishes. You must not sell her or treat her as a slave, since you have dishonored her.

The Right of the Firstborn

[15]If a man has two wives, and he loves one but not the other, and both bear him sons but the firstborn is the son of the wife he does not love, [16]when he wills his property to his sons, he must not give the rights of the firstborn to the son of the wife he loves in preference to his actual firstborn, the son of the wife he does not love. [17]He must acknowledge the son of his unloved wife as the firstborn by giving him a double share of all he has. That son is the first sign of his father's strength. The right of the firstborn belongs to him.

A Rebellious Son

[18]If a man has a stubborn and rebellious son who does not obey his father and mother and will not listen to them when they discipline him, [19]his father and mother shall take hold of him and bring him to the elders at the gate of his town. [20]They shall say to the elders, "This son of ours is stubborn and rebellious. He will not obey us. He is a profligate and a drunkard." [21]Then all the men of his town shall stone him to death. You

must purge the evil from among you. All Israel will hear of it and be afraid.

Various Laws

[22]If a man guilty of a capital offense is put to death and his body is hung on a tree, [23]you must not leave his body on the tree overnight. Be sure to bury him that same day, because anyone who is hung on a tree is under God's curse. You must not desecrate the land the LORD your God is giving you as an inheritance.

22 If you see your brother's ox or sheep straying, do not ignore it but be sure to take it back to him. [2]If the brother does not live near you or if you do not know who he is, take it home with you and keep it until he comes looking for it. Then give it back to him. [3]Do the same if you find your brother's donkey or his cloak or anything he loses. Do not ignore it.

[4]If you see your brother's donkey or his ox fallen on the road, do not ignore it. Help him get it to its feet.

[5]A woman must not wear men's clothing, nor a man wear women's clothing, for the LORD your God detests anyone who does this.

[6]If you come across a bird's nest beside the road, either in a tree or on the ground, and the mother is sitting on the young or on the eggs, do not take the mother with the young. [7]You may take the young, but be sure to let the mother go, so that it may go well with you and you may have a long life.

[8]When you build a new house, make a parapet around your roof so that you may not bring the guilt of bloodshed on your house if someone falls from the roof.

[9]Do not plant two kinds of seed in your vineyard; if you do, not only the crops you plant but also the fruit of the vineyard will be defiled.[a]

[10]Do not plow with an ox and a donkey yoked together.

[11]Do not wear clothes of wool and linen woven together.

[12]Make tassels on the four corners of the cloak you wear.

Marriage Violations

[13]If a man takes a wife and, after lying with her, dislikes her [14]and slanders her

---

[a] 9 Or *be forfeited to the sanctuary*

and gives her a bad name, saying, "I married this woman, but when I approached her, I did not find proof of her virginity," ¹⁵then the girl's father and mother shall bring proof that she was a virgin to the town elders at the gate. ¹⁶The girl's father will say to the elders, "I gave my daughter in marriage to this man, but he dislikes her. ¹⁷Now he has slandered her and said, 'I did not find your daughter to be a virgin.' But here is the proof of my daughter's virginity." Then her parents shall display the cloth before the elders of the town, ¹⁸and the elders shall take the man and punish him. ¹⁹They shall fine him a hundred shekels of silver*ᵃ* and give them to the girl's father, because this man has given an Israelite virgin a bad name. She shall continue to be his wife; he must not divorce her as long as he lives.

²⁰If, however, the charge is true and no proof of the girl's virginity can be found, ²¹she shall be brought to the door of her father's house and there the men of her town shall stone her to death. She has done a disgraceful thing in Israel by being promiscuous while still in her father's house. You must purge the evil from among you.

²²If a man is found sleeping with another man's wife, both the man who slept with her and the woman must die. You must purge the evil from Israel.

²³If a man happens to meet in a town a virgin pledged to be married and he sleeps with her, ²⁴you shall take both of them to the gate of that town and stone them to death—the girl because she was in a town and did not scream for help, and the man because he violated another man's wife. You must purge the evil from among you.

²⁵But if out in the country a man happens to meet a girl pledged to be married and rapes her, only the man who has done this shall die. ²⁶Do nothing to the girl; she has committed no sin deserving death. This case is like that of someone who attacks and murders his neighbor, ²⁷for the man found the girl out in the country, and though the betrothed girl screamed, there was no one to rescue her.

²⁸If a man happens to meet a virgin who is not pledged to be married and rapes her and they are discovered, ²⁹he shall pay the girl's father fifty shekels of silver.*ᵇ* He must marry the girl, for he has violated her. He can never divorce her as long as he lives.

³⁰A man is not to marry his father's wife; he must not dishonor his father's bed.

Exclusion From the Assembly

23 No one who has been emasculated by crushing or cutting may enter the assembly of the LORD.

²No one born of a forbidden marriage*ᶜ* nor any of his descendants may enter the assembly of the LORD, even down to the tenth generation.

³No Ammonite or Moabite or any of his descendants may enter the assembly of the LORD, even down to the tenth generation. ⁴For they did not come to meet you with bread and water on your way when you came out of Egypt, and they hired Balaam son of Beor from Pethor in Aram Naharaim*ᵈ* to pronounce a curse on you. ⁵However, the LORD your God would not listen to Balaam but turned the curse into a blessing for you, because the LORD your God loves you. ⁶Do not seek a treaty of friendship with them as long as you live.

⁷Do not abhor an Edomite, for he is your brother. Do not abhor an Egyptian, because you lived as an alien in his country. ⁸The third generation of children born to them may enter the assembly of the LORD.

Uncleanness in the Camp

⁹When you are encamped against your enemies, keep away from everything impure. ¹⁰If one of your men is unclean because of a nocturnal emission, he is to go outside the camp and stay there. ¹¹But as evening approaches he is to wash himself, and at sunset he may return to the camp.

¹²Designate a place outside the camp where you can go to relieve yourself. ¹³As part of your equipment have something to dig with, and when you relieve yourself, dig a hole and cover up your excrement. ¹⁴For the LORD your God

---

ᵃ 19 That is, about 2 1/2 pounds (about 1 kilogram)
kilogram)   ᶜ 2 Or *one of illegitimate birth*   *ᵇ 29* That is, about 1 1/4 pounds (about 0.6
ᵈ 4 That is, Northwest Mesopotamia

moves about in your camp to protect you and to deliver your enemies to you. Your camp must be holy, so that he will not see among you anything indecent and turn away from you.

Miscellaneous Laws

¹⁵If a slave has taken refuge with you, do not hand him over to his master. ¹⁶Let him live among you wherever he likes and in whatever town he chooses. Do not oppress him.

¹⁷No Israelite man or woman is to become a shrine prostitute. ¹⁸You must not bring the earnings of a female prostitute or of a male prostitute*a* into the house of the LORD your God to pay any vow, because the LORD your God detests them both.

¹⁹Do not charge your brother interest, whether on money or food or anything else that may earn interest. ²⁰You may charge a foreigner interest, but not a brother Israelite, so that the LORD your God may bless you in everything you put your hand to in the land you are entering to possess.

²¹If you make a vow to the LORD your God, do not be slow to pay it, for the LORD your God will certainly demand it of you and you will be guilty of sin. ²²But if you refrain from making a vow, you will not be guilty. ²³Whatever your lips utter you must be sure to do, because you made your vow freely to the LORD your God with your own mouth.

²⁴If you enter your neighbor's vineyard, you may eat all the grapes you want, but do not put any in your basket. ²⁵If you enter your neighbor's grainfield, you may pick kernels with your hands, but you must not put a sickle to his standing grain.

24 If a man marries a woman who becomes displeasing to him because he finds something indecent about her, and he writes her a certificate of divorce, gives it to her and sends her from his house, ²and if after she leaves his house she becomes the wife of another man, ³and her second husband dislikes her and writes her a certificate of divorce, gives it to her and sends her from his house, or if he dies,

⁴then her first husband, who divorced her, is not allowed to marry her again after she has been defiled. That would be detestable in the eyes of the LORD. Do not bring sin upon the land the LORD your God is giving you as an inheritance.

⁵If a man has recently married, he must not be sent to war or have any other duty laid on him. For one year he is to be free to stay at home and bring happiness to the wife he has married.

⁶Do not take a pair of millstones—not even the upper one—as security for a debt, because that would be taking a man's livelihood as security.

⁷If a man is caught kidnapping one of his brother Israelites and treats him as a slave or sells him, the kidnapper must die. You must purge the evil from among you.

⁸In cases of leprous*b* diseases be very careful to do exactly as the priests, who are Levites, instruct you. You must follow carefully what I have commanded them. ⁹Remember what the LORD your God did to Miriam along the way after you came out of Egypt.

¹⁰When you make a loan of any kind to your neighbor, do not go into his house to get what he is offering as a pledge. ¹¹Stay outside and let the man to whom you are making the loan bring the pledge out to you. ¹²If the man is poor, do not go to sleep with his pledge in your possession. ¹³Return his cloak to him by sunset so that he may sleep in it. Then he will thank you, and it will be regarded as a righteous act in the sight of the LORD your God.

¹⁴Do not take advantage of a hired man who is poor and needy, whether he is a brother Israelite or an alien living in one of your towns. ¹⁵Pay him his wages each day before sunset, because he is poor and is counting on it. Otherwise he may cry to the LORD against you, and you will be guilty of sin.

¹⁶Fathers shall not be put to death for their children, nor children put to death for their fathers; each is to die for his own sin.

¹⁷Do not deprive the alien or the fatherless of justice, or take the cloak of the widow as a pledge. ¹⁸Remember that

---

a 18 Hebrew *of a dog*   *b* 8 The Hebrew word was used for various diseases affecting the skin—not necessarily leprosy.

you were slaves in Egypt and the LORD your God redeemed you from there. That is why I command you to do this.

19When you are harvesting in your field and you overlook a sheaf, do not go back to get it. Leave it for the alien, the fatherless and the widow, so that the LORD your God may bless you in all the work of your hands. 20When you beat the olives from your trees, do not go over the branches a second time. Leave what remains for the alien, the fatherless and the widow. 21When you harvest the grapes in your vineyard, do not go over the vines again. Leave what remains for the alien, the fatherless and the widow. 22Remember that you were slaves in Egypt. That is why I command you to do this.

25 When men have a dispute, they are to take it to court and the judges will decide the case, acquitting the innocent and condemning the guilty. 2If the guilty man deserves to be beaten, the judge shall make him lie down and have him flogged in his presence with the number of lashes his crime deserves, 3but he must not give him more than forty lashes. If he is flogged more than that, your brother will be degraded in your eyes.

4Do not muzzle an ox while it is treading out the grain.

5If brothers are living together and one of them dies without a son, his widow must not marry outside the family. Her husband's brother shall take her and marry her and fulfill the duty of a brother-in-law to her. 6The first son she bears shall carry on the name of the dead brother so that his name will not be blotted out from Israel.

7However, if a man does not want to marry his brother's wife, she shall go to the elders at the town gate and say, "My husband's brother refuses to carry on his brother's name in Israel. He will not fulfill the duty of a brother-in-law to me." 8Then the elders of his town shall summon him and talk to him. If he persists in saying, "I do not want to marry her," 9his brother's widow shall go up to him in the presence of the elders, take off one of his sandals, spit in his face and say, "This is what is done to the man who will not build up his brother's family line." 10That

man's line shall be known in Israel as The Family of the Unsandaled.

11If two men are fighting and the wife of one of them comes to rescue her husband from his assailant, and she reaches out and seizes him by his private parts, 12you shall cut off her hand. Show her no pity.

13Do not have two differing weights in your bag—one heavy, one light. 14Do not have two differing measures in your house—one large, one small. 15You must have accurate and honest weights and measures, so that you may live long in the land the LORD your God is giving you. 16For the LORD your God detests anyone who does these things, anyone who deals dishonestly.

17Remember what the Amalekites did to you along the way when you came out of Egypt. 18When you were weary and worn out, they met you on your journey and cut off all who were lagging behind; they had no fear of God. 19When the LORD your God gives you rest from all the enemies around you in the land he is giving you to possess as an inheritance, you shall blot out the memory of Amalek from under heaven. Do not forget!

Firstfruits and Tithes

26 When you have entered the land the LORD your God is giving you as an inheritance and have taken possession of it and settled in it, 2take some of the firstfruits of all that you produce from the soil of the land the LORD your God is giving you and put them in a basket. Then go to the place the LORD your God will choose as a dwelling for his Name 3and say to the priest in office at the time, "I declare today to the LORD your God that I have come to the land the LORD swore to our forefathers to give us." 4The priest shall take the basket from your hands and set it down in front of the altar of the LORD your God. 5Then you shall declare before the LORD your God: "My father was a wandering Aramean, and he went down into Egypt with a few people and lived there and became a great nation, powerful and numerous. 6But the Egyptians mistreated us and made us suffer, putting us to hard labor. 7Then we cried out to the LORD, the God of our fathers, and the LORD heard our

voice and saw our misery, toil and oppression. ⁸So the LORD brought us out of Egypt with a mighty hand and an outstretched arm, with great terror and with miraculous signs and wonders. ⁹He brought us to this place and gave us this land, a land flowing with milk and honey; ¹⁰and now I bring the firstfruits of the soil that you, O LORD, have given me." Place the basket before the LORD your God and bow down before him. ¹¹And you and the Levites and the aliens among you shall rejoice in all the good things the LORD your God has given to you and your household.

¹²When you have finished setting aside a tenth of all your produce in the third year, the year of the tithe, you shall give it to the Levite, the alien, the fatherless and the widow, so that they may eat in your towns and be satisfied. ¹³Then say to the LORD your God: "I have removed from my house the sacred portion and have given it to the Levite, the alien, the fatherless and the widow, according to all you commanded. I have not turned aside from your commands nor have I forgotten any of them. ¹⁴I have not eaten any of the sacred portion while I was in mourning, nor have I removed any of it while I was unclean, nor have I offered any of it to the dead. I have obeyed the LORD my God; I have done everything you commanded me. ¹⁵Look down from heaven, your holy dwelling place, and bless your people Israel and the land you have given us as you promised on oath to our forefathers, a land flowing with milk and honey."

Follow the LORD's Commands

¹⁶The LORD your God commands you this day to follow these decrees and laws; carefully observe them with all your heart and with all your soul. ¹⁷You have declared this day that the LORD is your God and that you will walk in his ways, that you will keep his decrees, commands and laws, and that you will obey him. ¹⁸And the LORD has declared this day that you are his people, his treasured possession as he promised, and that you are to keep all his commands. ¹⁹He has declared that he will set you in praise, fame and honor high above all

the nations he has made and that you will be a people holy to the LORD your God, as he promised.

The Altar on Mount Ebal

27 Moses and the elders of Israel commanded the people: "Keep all these commands that I give you today. ²When you have crossed the Jordan into the land the LORD your God is giving you, set up some large stones and coat them with plaster. ³Write on them all the words of this law when you have crossed over to enter the land the LORD your God is giving you, a land flowing with milk and honey, just as the LORD, the God of your fathers, promised you. ⁴And when you have crossed the Jordan, set up these stones on Mount Ebal, as I command you today, and coat them with plaster. ⁵Build there an altar to the LORD your God, an altar of stones. Do not use any iron tool upon them. ⁶Build the altar of the LORD your God with fieldstones and offer burnt offerings on it to the LORD your God. ⁷Sacrifice fellowship offerings[a] there, eating them and rejoicing in the presence of the LORD your God. ⁸And you shall write very clearly all the words of this law on these stones you have set up."

Curses From Mount Ebal

⁹Then Moses and the priests, who are Levites, said to all Israel, "Be silent, O Israel, and listen! You have now become the people of the LORD your God. ¹⁰Obey the LORD your God and follow his commands and decrees that I give you today."

¹¹On the same day Moses commanded the people:

¹²When you have crossed the Jordan, these tribes shall stand on Mount Gerizim to bless the people: Simeon, Levi, Judah, Issachar, Joseph and Benjamin. ¹³And these tribes shall stand on Mount Ebal to pronounce curses: Reuben, Gad, Asher, Zebulun, Dan and Naphtali.

¹⁴The Levites shall recite to all the people of Israel in a loud voice:

¹⁵"Cursed is the man who carves an image or casts an idol—a thing

---

ᵃ 7 Traditionally *peace offerings*

detestable to the LORD, the work of the craftsman's hands—and sets it up in secret."

Then all the people shall say, "Amen!"

16"Cursed is the man who dishonors his father or his mother."

Then all the people shall say, "Amen!"

17"Cursed is the man who moves his neighbor's boundary stone."

Then all the people shall say, "Amen!"

18"Cursed is the man who leads the blind astray on the road."

Then all the people shall say, "Amen!"

19"Cursed is the man who withholds justice from the alien, the fatherless or the widow."

Then all the people shall say, "Amen!"

20"Cursed is the man who sleeps with his father's wife, for he dishonors his father's bed."

Then all the people shall say, "Amen!"

21"Cursed is the man who has sexual relations with any animal."

Then all the people shall say, "Amen!"

22"Cursed is the man who sleeps with his sister, the daughter of his father or the daughter of his mother."

Then all the people shall say, "Amen!"

23"Cursed is the man who sleeps with his mother-in-law."

Then all the people shall say, "Amen!"

24"Cursed is the man who kills his neighbor secretly."

Then all the people shall say, "Amen!"

25"Cursed is the man who accepts a bribe to kill an innocent person."

Then all the people shall say, "Amen!"

26"Cursed is the man who does not uphold the words of this law by carrying them out."

Then all the people shall say, "Amen!"

Blessings for Obedience

28 If you fully obey the LORD your God and carefully follow all his commands I give you today, the LORD your God will set you high above all the nations on earth. 2All these blessings will come upon you and accompany you if you obey the LORD your God:

3You will be blessed in the city and blessed in the country.

4The fruit of your womb will be blessed, and the crops of your land and the young of your livestock—the calves of your herds and the lambs of your flocks.

5Your basket and your kneading trough will be blessed.

6You will be blessed when you come in and blessed when you go out.

7The LORD will grant that the enemies who rise up against you will be defeated before you. They will come at you from one direction but flee from you in seven.

8The LORD will send a blessing on your barns and on everything you put your hand to. The LORD your God will bless you in the land he is giving you.

9The LORD will establish you as his holy people, as he promised you on oath, if you keep the commands of the LORD your God and walk in his ways. 10Then all the peoples on earth will see that you are called by the name of the LORD, and they will fear you. 11The LORD will grant you abundant prosperity—in the fruit of your womb, the young of your livestock and the crops of your ground—in the land he swore to your forefathers to give you.

12The LORD will open the heavens, the storehouse of his bounty, to send rain on your land in season and to bless all the work of your hands. You will lend to many nations but will borrow from none. 13The LORD will make you the head, not the tail. If you pay attention to the commands of the LORD your God that I give you this day and carefully follow them, you will always be at the top, never at the bottom. 14Do not turn aside from any of the commands I give you today, to the right or to the left, following other gods and serving them.

Curses for Disobedience

15However, if you do not obey the LORD your God and do not carefully follow all his commands and decrees I am giving you today, all these curses will come upon you and overtake you:

16You will be cursed in the city and cursed in the country.

17Your basket and your kneading trough will be cursed.

18The fruit of your womb will be cursed, and the crops of your land, and the calves of your herds and the lambs of your flocks.

19You will be cursed when you come in and cursed when you go out.

20The LORD will send on you curses, confusion and rebuke in everything you put your hand to, until you are destroyed and come to sudden ruin because of the evil you have done in forsaking him.*a* 21The LORD will plague you with diseases until he has destroyed you from the land you are entering to possess. 22The LORD will strike you with wasting disease, with fever and inflammation, with scorching heat and drought, with blight and mildew, which will plague you until you perish. 23The sky over your head will be bronze, the ground beneath you iron. 24The LORD will turn the rain of your country into dust and powder; it will come down from the skies until you are destroyed.

25The LORD will cause you to be defeated before your enemies. You will come at them from one direction but flee from them in seven, and you will become a thing of horror to all the kingdoms on earth. 26Your carcasses will be food for all the birds of the air and the beasts of the earth, and there will be no one to frighten them away. 27The LORD will afflict you with the boils of Egypt and with tumors, festering sores and the itch, from which you cannot be cured. 28The LORD will afflict you with madness, blindness and confusion of mind. 29At midday you will grope about like a blind man in the dark. You will be unsuccessful in everything you do; day after day you will be oppressed and robbed, with no one to rescue you.

30You will be pledged to be married to a woman, but another will take her and ravish her. You will build a house, but you will not live in it. You will plant a vineyard, but you will not even begin to enjoy its fruit. 31Your ox will be slaughtered before your eyes, but you will eat none of it. Your donkey will be forcibly taken from you and will not be returned. Your sheep will be given to your enemies, and no one will rescue them. 32Your sons and daughters will be given to another nation, and you will wear out your eyes watching for them day after day, powerless to lift a hand. 33A people that you do not know will eat what your land and labor produce, and you will have nothing but cruel oppression all your days. 34The sights you see will drive you mad. 35The LORD will afflict your knees and legs with painful boils that cannot be cured, spreading from the soles of your feet to the top of your head.

36The LORD will drive you and the king you set over you to a nation unknown to you or your fathers. There you will worship other gods, gods of wood and stone. 37You will become a thing of horror and an object of scorn and ridicule to all the nations where the LORD will drive you.

38You will sow much seed in the field but you will harvest little, because locusts will devour it. 39You will plant vineyards and cultivate them but you will not drink the wine or gather the grapes, because worms will eat them. 40You will have olive trees throughout your country but you will not use the oil, because the olives will drop off. 41You will have sons and daughters but you will not keep them, because they will go into captivity. 42Swarms of locusts will take over all your trees and the crops of your land.

43The alien who lives among you will rise above you higher and higher, but you will sink lower and lower. 44He will lend to you, but you will not lend to him. He will be the head, but you will be the tail.

45All these curses will come upon you. They will pursue you and overtake you until you are destroyed, because you did not obey the LORD your God and observe the commands and decrees he gave you. 46They will be a sign and a wonder to you

a 20 Hebrew *me*

and your descendants forever. 47Because you did not serve the LORD your God joyfully and gladly in the time of prosperity, 48therefore in hunger and thirst, in nakedness and dire poverty, you will serve the enemies the LORD sends against you. He will put an iron yoke on your neck until he has destroyed you.

WE CAN STAND AFFLICTION BETTER THAN WE CAN PROSPERITY, FOR IN PROSPERITY WE FORGET GOD.   —Dwight L. Moody

---

49The LORD will bring a nation against you from far away, from the ends of the earth, like an eagle swooping down, a nation whose language you will not understand, 50a fierce-looking nation without respect for the old or pity for the young. 51They will devour the young of your livestock and the crops of your land until you are destroyed. They will leave you no grain, new wine or oil, nor any calves of your herds or lambs of your flocks until you are ruined. 52They will lay siege to all the cities throughout your land until the high fortified walls in which you trust fall down. They will besiege all the cities throughout the land the LORD your God is giving you.

53Because of the suffering that your enemy will inflict on you during the siege, you will eat the fruit of the womb, the flesh of the sons and daughters the LORD your God has given you. 54Even the most gentle and sensitive man among you will have no compassion on his own brother or the wife he loves or his surviving children, 55and he will not give to one of them any of the flesh of his children that he is eating. It will be all he has left because of the suffering your enemy will inflict on you during the siege of all your cities. 56The most gentle and sensitive woman among you—so sensitive and gentle that she would not venture to touch the ground with the sole of her foot—will begrudge the husband she loves and her own son or daughter 57the afterbirth from her womb and the children she bears. For she intends to eat them secretly during the siege and in the distress that your enemy will inflict on you in your cities. 58If you do not carefully follow all the words of this law, which are written in this book, and do not revere this glorious and awesome name—the LORD your God— 59the LORD will send fearful plagues on you and your descendants, harsh and prolonged disasters, and severe and lingering illnesses. 60He will bring upon you all the diseases of Egypt that you dreaded, and they will cling to you. 61The LORD will also bring on you every kind of sickness and disaster not recorded in this Book of the Law, until you are destroyed. 62You who were as numerous as the stars in the sky will be left but few in number, because you did not obey the LORD your God. 63Just as it pleased the LORD to make you prosper and increase in number, so it will please him to ruin and destroy you. You will be uprooted from the land you are entering to possess.

64Then the LORD will scatter you among all nations, from one end of the earth to the other. There you will worship other gods—gods of wood and stone, which neither you nor your fathers have known. 65Among those nations you will find no repose, no resting place for the sole of your foot. There the LORD will give you an anxious mind, eyes weary with longing, and a despairing heart. 66You will live in constant suspense, filled with dread both night and day, never sure of your life. 67In the morning you will say, "If only it were evening!" and in the evening, "If only it were morning!"—because of the terror that will fill your hearts and the sights that your eyes will see. 68The LORD will send you back in ships to Egypt on a journey I said you should never make again. There you will offer yourselves for sale to your enemies as male and female slaves, but no one will buy you.

Renewal of the Covenant

29 These are the terms of the covenant the LORD commanded Moses to make with the Israelites in Moab, in addition to the covenant he had made with them at Horeb.

2Moses summoned all the Israelites and said to them:

Your eyes have seen all that the LORD did in Egypt to Pharaoh, to all his officials and to all his land. 3With your own eyes you saw those great trials, those miraculous signs and great wonders. 4But to this day the LORD has not given you a mind that understands or eyes that see or ears that hear. 5During the forty years that I led you through the desert, your clothes did not wear out, nor did the sandals on your feet. 6You ate no bread and drank no wine or other fermented drink. I did this so that you might know that I am the LORD your God.

7When you reached this place, Sihon king of Heshbon and Og king of Bashan came out to fight against us, but we defeated them. 8We took their land and gave it as an inheritance to the Reubenites, the Gadites and the half-tribe of Manasseh.

9Carefully follow the terms of this covenant, so that you may prosper in everything you do. 10All of you are standing today in the presence of the LORD your God—your leaders and chief men, your elders and officials, and all the other men of Israel, 11together with your children and your wives, and the aliens living in your camps who chop your wood and carry your water. 12You are standing here in order to enter into a covenant with the LORD your God, a covenant the LORD is making with you this day and sealing with an oath, 13to confirm you this day as his people, that he may be your God as he promised you and as he swore to your fathers, Abraham, Isaac and Jacob. 14I am making this covenant, with its oath, not only with you 15who are standing here with us today in the presence of the LORD our God but also with those who are not here today.

16You yourselves know how we lived in Egypt and how we passed through the countries on the way here. 17You saw among them their detestable images and idols of wood and stone, of silver and gold. 18Make sure there is no man or woman, clan or tribe among you today whose heart turns away from the LORD our God to go and worship the gods of those nations; make sure there is no root among you that produces such bitter poison.

19When such a person hears the words of this oath, he invokes a blessing on himself and therefore thinks, "I will be safe, even though I persist in going my own way." This will bring disaster on the watered land as well as the dry.*a* 20The LORD will never be willing to forgive him; his wrath and zeal will burn against that man. All the curses written in this book will fall upon him, and the LORD will blot out his name from under heaven. 21The LORD will single him out from all the tribes of Israel for disaster, according to all the curses of the covenant written in this Book of the Law.

22Your children who follow you in later generations and foreigners who come from distant lands will see the calamities that have fallen on the land and the diseases with which the LORD has afflicted it. 23The whole land will be a burning waste of salt and sulfur—nothing planted, nothing sprouting, no vegetation growing on it. It will be like the destruction of Sodom and Gomorrah, Admah and Zeboiim, which the LORD overthrew in fierce anger. 24All the nations will ask: "Why has the LORD done this to this land? Why this fierce, burning anger?"

25And the answer will be: "It is because this people abandoned the covenant of the LORD, the God of their fathers, the covenant he made with them when he brought them out of Egypt. 26They went off and worshiped other gods and bowed down to them, gods they did not know, gods he had not given them. 27Therefore the LORD's anger burned against this land, so that he brought on it all the curses written in this book. 28In furious anger and in great wrath the LORD uprooted them from their land and thrust them into another land, as it is now."

29The secret things belong to the LORD our God, but the things revealed belong to us and to our children forever, that we may follow all the words of this law.

Prosperity After Turning to the LORD

30 When all these blessings and curses I have set before you come upon you and you take them to heart wherever the LORD your God disperses you among the nations, 2and when you and your children return to

---

a 19 Or way, in order to add drunkenness to thirst."

the LORD your God and obey him with all your heart and with all your soul according to everything I command you today, ³then the LORD your God will restore your fortunes*a* and have compassion on you and gather you again from all the nations where he scattered you. ⁴Even if you have been banished to the most distant land under the heavens, from there the LORD your God will gather you and bring you back. ⁵He will bring you to the land that belonged to your fathers, and you will take possession of it. He will make you more prosperous and numerous than your fathers. ⁶The LORD your God will circumcise your hearts and the hearts of your descendants, so that you may love him with all your heart and with all your soul, and live. ⁷The LORD your God will put all these curses on your enemies who hate and persecute you. ⁸You will again obey the LORD and follow all his commands I am giving you today. ⁹Then the LORD your God will make you most prosperous in all the work of your hands and in the fruit of your womb, the young of your livestock and the crops of your land. The LORD will again delight in you and make you prosperous, just as he delighted in your fathers, ¹⁰if you obey the LORD your God and keep his commands and decrees that are written in this Book of the Law and turn to the LORD your God with all your heart and with all your soul.

The Offer of Life or Death

¹¹Now what I am commanding you today is not too difficult for you or beyond your reach. ¹²It is not up in heaven, so that you have to ask, "Who will ascend into heaven to get it and proclaim it to us so we may obey it?" ¹³Nor is it beyond the sea, so that you have to ask, "Who will cross the sea to get it and proclaim it to us so we may obey it?" ¹⁴No, the word is very near you; it is in your mouth and in your heart so you may obey it.

¹⁵See, I set before you today life and prosperity, death and destruction. ¹⁶For I command you today to love the LORD your God, to walk in his ways, and to keep his commands, decrees and laws; then you will live and increase, and the

LORD your God will bless you in the land you are entering to possess.

¹⁷But if your heart turns away and you are not obedient, and if you are drawn away to bow down to other gods and worship them, ¹⁸I declare to you this day that you will certainly be destroyed. You will not live long in the land you are crossing the Jordan to enter and possess.

¹⁹This day I call heaven and earth as witnesses against you that I have set before you life and death, blessings and curses. Now choose life, so that you and your children may live ²⁰and that you may love the LORD your God, listen to his voice, and hold fast to him. For the LORD is your life, and he will give you many years in the land he swore to give to your fathers, Abraham, Isaac and Jacob.

Joshua to Succeed Moses

31 Then Moses went out and spoke these words to all Israel: ²"I am now a hundred and twenty years old and I am no longer able to lead you. The LORD has said to me, 'You shall not cross the Jordan.' ³The LORD your God himself will cross over ahead of you. He will destroy these nations before you, and you will take possession of their land. Joshua also will cross over ahead of you, as the LORD said. ⁴And the LORD will do to them what he did to Sihon and Og, the kings of the Amorites, whom he destroyed along with their land. ⁵The LORD will deliver them to you, and you must do to them all that I have commanded you. ⁶Be strong and courageous. Do not be afraid or terrified because of them, for the LORD your God goes with you; he will never leave you nor forsake you."

⁷Then Moses summoned Joshua and said to him in the presence of all Israel, "Be strong and courageous, for you must go with this people into the land that the LORD swore to their forefathers to give them, and you must divide it among them as their inheritance. ⁸The LORD himself goes before you and will be with you; he will never leave you nor forsake you. Do not be afraid; do not be discouraged."

a 3 Or will bring you back from captivity

The Reading of the Law

⁹So Moses wrote down this law and gave it to the priests, the sons of Levi, who carried the ark of the covenant of the LORD, and to all the elders of Israel. ¹⁰Then Moses commanded them: "At the end of every seven years, in the year for canceling debts, during the Feast of Tabernacles, ¹¹when all Israel comes to appear before the LORD your God at the

---

THURSDAY

THE BROOM OF THE LAW AND THE DUST OF SIN

John Bunyan

VERSE: Deuteronomy 30:14   **PASSAGE:** Deuteronomy 30:11–21

hen he took him by the hand, and led him into a very large parlor that was full of dust, because it was never swept; the which, after he had reviewed a little while, the Interpreter called for a man to sweep. Now when he began to sweep, the dust began so abundantly to fly about that Christian had almost therewith been choked. Then said the interpreter to a damsel that stood by, Bring hither the water and sprinkle the room; which when she had done, it was swept and cleansed with pleasure.

Then said Christian, What means this?

The Interpreter answered: This parlor is the heart of a man that was never sanctified by the sweet grace of the gospel: the dust is his original sin and inward corruptions that have defiled the whole man. He that began to sweep at first is the law; but she that brought water and did sprinkle it is the gospel. Now, whereas thou sawest that so soon as the first began to sweep, the dust did so fly about that the room by him could not be cleansed, but that thou wast almost choked therewith: this is to shew thee that the law, instead of cleansing the heart (by its working) from sin, doth revive, put strength into, and increase it in the soul, even as it doth discover and forbid it, but doth not give power to subdue.

Again, as thou sawest the damsel sprinkle the room with water, upon which it was cleansed with pleasure; this is to shew thee that when the gospel comes in the sweet and precious influences thereof to the heart, then, I say, even as thou sawest the damsel lay the dust by sprinkling the floor with water, so is sin vanquished and subdued, and the soul made clean, through the faith of it, and consequently fit for the King of glory to inhabit.

ADDITIONAL SCRIPTURE READING:
Psalm 51:2–10; Ezekiel 36:25–27; 1 John 1:6–10

Go to page 233 for your next devotional reading.

1500   1700

place he will choose, you shall read this law before them in their hearing. 12Assemble the people—men, women and children, and the aliens living in your towns—so they can listen and learn to fear the LORD your God and follow carefully all the words of this law. 13Their children, who do not know this law, must hear it and learn to fear the LORD your God as long as you live in the land you are crossing the Jordan to possess."

Israel's Rebellion Predicted

14The LORD said to Moses, "Now the day of your death is near. Call Joshua and present yourselves at the Tent of Meeting, where I will commission him." So Moses and Joshua came and presented themselves at the Tent of Meeting.

15Then the LORD appeared at the Tent in a pillar of cloud, and the cloud stood over the entrance to the Tent. 16And the LORD said to Moses: "You are going to rest with your fathers, and these people will soon prostitute themselves to the foreign gods of the land they are entering. They will forsake me and break the covenant I made with them. 17On that day I will become angry with them and forsake them; I will hide my face from them, and they will be destroyed. Many disasters and difficulties will come upon them, and on that day they will ask, 'Have not these disasters come upon us because our God is not with us?' 18And I will certainly hide my face on that day because of all their wickedness in turning to other gods.

19"Now write down for yourselves this song and teach it to the Israelites and have them sing it, so that it may be a witness for me against them. 20When I have brought them into the land flowing with milk and honey, the land I promised on oath to their forefathers, and when they eat their fill and thrive, they will turn to other gods and worship them, rejecting me and breaking my covenant. 21And when many disasters and difficulties come upon them, this song will testify against them, because it will not be forgotten by their descendants. I know what they are disposed to do, even before I bring them into the land I promised them on oath." 22So

Moses wrote down this song that day and taught it to the Israelites.

23The LORD gave this command to Joshua son of Nun: "Be strong and courageous, for you will bring the Israelites into the land I promised them on oath, and I myself will be with you."

24After Moses finished writing in a book the words of this law from beginning to end, 25he gave this command to the Levites who carried the ark of the covenant of the LORD: 26"Take this Book of the Law and place it beside the ark of the covenant of the LORD your God. There it will remain as a witness against you. 27For I know how rebellious and stiff-necked you are. If you have been rebellious against the LORD while I am still alive and with you, how much more will you rebel after I die! 28Assemble before me all the elders of your tribes and all your officials, so that I can speak these words in their hearing and call heaven and earth to testify against them. 29For I know that after my death you are sure to become utterly corrupt and to turn from the way I have commanded you. In days to come, disaster will fall upon you because you will do evil in the sight of the LORD and provoke him to anger by what your hands have made."

The Song of Moses

30And Moses recited the words of this song from beginning to end in the hearing of the whole assembly of Israel:

32 Listen, O heavens, and I will speak;
hear, O earth, the words of my
mouth.
2 Let my teaching fall like rain
and my words descend like dew,
like showers on new grass,
like abundant rain on tender plants.

3 I will proclaim the name of the LORD.
Oh, praise the greatness of our God!
4 He is the Rock, his works are perfect,
and all his ways are just.
A faithful God who does no wrong,
upright and just is he.

5 They have acted corruptly toward
him;
to their shame they are no longer
his children,

but a warped and crooked
generation.*a*

⁶ Is this the way you repay the Lord,
O foolish and unwise people?
Is he not your Father, your Creator,*b*
who made you and formed you?

⁷ Remember the days of old;
consider the generations long past.
Ask your father and he will tell you,
your elders, and they will explain
to you.

⁸ When the Most High gave the
nations their inheritance,
when he divided all mankind,
he set up boundaries for the peoples
according to the number of the
sons of Israel.*c*

⁹ For the Lord's portion is his people,
Jacob his allotted inheritance.

¹⁰ In a desert land he found him,
in a barren and howling waste.
He shielded him and cared for him;
he guarded him as the apple of his
eye,

¹¹ like an eagle that stirs up its nest
and hovers over its young,
that spreads its wings to catch them
and carries them on its pinions.

¹² The Lord alone led him;
no foreign god was with him.

¹³ He made him ride on the heights of
the land
and fed him with the fruit of the
fields.
He nourished him with honey from
the rock,
and with oil from the flinty crag,

¹⁴ with curds and milk from herd and
flock
and with fattened lambs and goats,
with choice rams of Bashan
and the finest kernels of wheat.
You drank the foaming blood of the
grape.

¹⁵ Jeshurun*d* grew fat and kicked;
filled with food, he became heavy
and sleek.
He abandoned the God who made him
and rejected the Rock his Savior.

¹⁶ They made him jealous with their
foreign gods

and angered him with their
detestable idols.

¹⁷ They sacrificed to demons, which are
not God—
gods they had not known,
gods that recently appeared,
gods your fathers did not fear.

¹⁸ You deserted the Rock, who fathered
you;
you forgot the God who gave you
birth.

¹⁹ The Lord saw this and rejected them
because he was angered by his sons
and daughters.

²⁰ "I will hide my face from them," he
said,
"and see what their end will be;
for they are a perverse generation,
children who are unfaithful.

²¹ They made me jealous by what is no
god
and angered me with their
worthless idols.
I will make them envious by those
who are not a people;
I will make them angry by a nation
that has no understanding.

²² For a fire has been kindled by my
wrath,
one that burns to the realm of
death*e* below.
It will devour the earth and its
harvests
and set afire the foundations of the
mountains.

²³ "I will heap calamities upon them
and spend my arrows against them.

²⁴ I will send wasting famine against
them,
consuming pestilence and deadly
plague;
I will send against them the fangs of
wild beasts,
the venom of vipers that glide in
the dust.

²⁵ In the street the sword will make
them childless;
in their homes terror will reign.
Young men and young women will
perish,
infants and gray-haired men.

²⁶ I said I would scatter them

---

a 5 Or *Corrupt are they and not his children, / a generation warped and twisted to their shame*
b 6 Or *Father, who bought you*   *c* 8 Masoretic Text; Dead Sea Scrolls (see also Septuagint) *sons of God*
d 15 *Jeshurun* means *the upright one,* that is, Israel.   *e* 22 Hebrew *to Sheol*

and blot out their memory from
   mankind,
27 but I dreaded the taunt of the enemy,
   lest the adversary misunderstand
and say, 'Our hand has triumphed;
   the LORD has not done all this.' "

28 They are a nation without sense,
   there is no discernment in them.
29 If only they were wise and would
   understand this
and discern what their end will be!
30 How could one man chase a thousand,

FRIDAY

FROM SINNERS IN THE HANDS OF AN ANGRY GOD
Jonathan Edwards

VERSE: Deuteronomy 32:35   **PASSAGE:** Deuteronomy 32:34–43

 ll wicked men's pains and *contrivance* which they use
to escape hell, while they continue to reject Christ,
and so remain wicked men, do not secure them from
hell one moment. Almost every natural man that
hears of hell, flatters himself that he shall escape it; he depends
upon himself for his own security; he flatters himself in what he
has done, in what he is now doing, or what he intends to do.
Every one lays out matters in his own mind how he shall avoid
damnation, and flatters himself that he contrives well for himself, and that his schemes will not fail. They hear indeed that
there are but few saved, and that the greater part of men that
have died heretofore are gone to hell; but each one imagines that
he lays out matters better for his own escape than others have
done. He does not intend to come to that place of torment; he
says within himself, that he intends to take effectual care, and to
order matters so for himself as not to fail . . .

   If we could speak with them and inquire of them, one by one,
whether they expected, when alive, and when they used to hear
about hell, ever to be the subjects of that misery: we doubtless,
should hear one and another reply, "No, I never intended to come
here: I had laid out matters otherwise in my mind; I thought my
scheme good. I intended to take effectual care; but it came upon
me unexpected; I did not look for it at that time, and in that manner; it came as a thief: Death outwitted me: God's wrath was too
quick for me. Oh, my cursed foolishness! I was flattering myself,
and pleasing myself with vain dreams of what I would do hereafter; and when I was saying, Peace and safety, then suddenly destruction came upon me" (see 1 Thessalonians 5:3).

ADDITIONAL SCRIPTURE READING:
Proverbs 16:9; Luke 12:19–21; 16:19–31

Go to page 239 for your next devotional reading.

1700   1900

or two put ten thousand to flight,
unless their Rock had sold them,
    unless the LORD had given them up?
31 For their rock is not like our Rock,
    as even our enemies concede.
32 Their vine comes from the vine of
        Sodom
    and from the fields of Gomorrah.
Their grapes are filled with poison,
    and their clusters with bitterness.
33 Their wine is the venom of serpents,
    the deadly poison of cobras.

34 "Have I not kept this in reserve
    and sealed it in my vaults?
35 It is mine to avenge; I will repay.
    In due time their foot will slip;
their day of disaster is near
    and their doom rushes upon them."

36 The LORD will judge his people
    and have compassion on his
        servants
when he sees their strength is gone
    and no one is left, slave or free.
37 He will say: "Now where are their
        gods,
    the rock they took refuge in,
38 the gods who ate the fat of their
        sacrifices
    and drank the wine of their drink
        offerings?
Let them rise up to help you!
    Let them give you shelter!

39 "See now that I myself am He!
    There is no god besides me.
I put to death and I bring to life,
    I have wounded and I will heal,
    and no one can deliver out of my
        hand.
40 I lift my hand to heaven and declare:
    As surely as I live forever,
41 when I sharpen my flashing sword
    and my hand grasps it in judgment,
I will take vengeance on my
        adversaries
    and repay those who hate me.
42 I will make my arrows drunk with
        blood,
    while my sword devours flesh:
the blood of the slain and the captives,
    the heads of the enemy leaders."

43 Rejoice, O nations, with his people,a,b

for he will avenge the blood of his
        servants;
he will take vengeance on his enemies
    and make atonement for his land
        and people.

44 Moses came with Joshuac son of Nun
and spoke all the words of this song in
the hearing of the people. 45 When Moses
finished reciting all these words to all Israel, 46 he said to them, "Take to heart all
the words I have solemnly declared to
you this day, so that you may command
your children to obey carefully all the
words of this law. 47 They are not just idle
words for you—they are your life. By
them you will live long in the land you
are crossing the Jordan to possess."

Moses to Die on Mount Nebo

48 On that same day the LORD told
Moses, 49 "Go up into the Abarim Range
to Mount Nebo in Moab, across from
Jericho, and view Canaan, the land I am
giving the Israelites as their own possession. 50 There on the mountain that you
have climbed you will die and be gathered to your people, just as your brother
Aaron died on Mount Hor and was gathered to his people. 51 This is because
both of you broke faith with me in the
presence of the Israelites at the waters
of Meribah Kadesh in the Desert of Zin
and because you did not uphold my holiness among the Israelites. 52 Therefore,
you will see the land only from a distance; you will not enter the land I am
giving to the people of Israel."

Moses Blesses the Tribes

33 This is the blessing that
Moses the man of God pro-
nounced on the Israelites before his
death. 2 He said:

"The LORD came from Sinai
    and dawned over them from Seir;
he shone forth from Mount Paran.
    He came withd myriads of holy ones
    from the south, from his mountain
        slopes.e
3 Surely it is you who love the people;
    all the holy ones are in your hand.

---

a 43 Or *Make his people rejoice, O nations*   b 43 Masoretic Text; Dead Sea Scrolls (see also Septuagint)
people, / and let all the angels worship him /   c 44 Hebrew *Hoshea,* a variant of *Joshua*   d 2 Or *from*
e 2 The meaning of the Hebrew for this phrase is uncertain.

At your feet they all bow down,
   and from you receive instruction,
4 the law that Moses gave us,
   the possession of the assembly of
   Jacob.
5 He was king over Jeshurun*a*
   when the leaders of the people
   assembled,
   along with the tribes of Israel.

6 "Let Reuben live and not die,
   nor*b* his men be few."

7 And this he said about Judah:

"Hear, O LORD, the cry of Judah;
   bring him to his people.
With his own hands he defends his
   cause.
   Oh, be his help against his foes!"

8 About Levi he said:

"Your Thummim and Urim belong
   to the man you favored.
You tested him at Massah;
   you contended with him at the
   waters of Meribah.
9 He said of his father and mother,
   'I have no regard for them.'
He did not recognize his brothers
   or acknowledge his own children,
but he watched over your word
   and guarded your covenant.
10 He teaches your precepts to Jacob
   and your law to Israel.
He offers incense before you
   and whole burnt offerings on your
   altar.
11 Bless all his skills, O LORD,
   and be pleased with the work of his
   hands.
Smite the loins of those who rise up
   against him;
   strike his foes till they rise no
   more."

12 About Benjamin he said:

"Let the beloved of the LORD rest
   secure in him,
   for he shields him all day long,
and the one the LORD loves rests
   between his shoulders."

13 About Joseph he said:

"May the LORD bless his land
   with the precious dew from heaven
   above
   and with the deep waters that lie
   below;
14 with the best the sun brings forth
   and the finest the moon can yield;
15 with the choicest gifts of the ancient
   mountains
   and the fruitfulness of the
   everlasting hills;
16 with the best gifts of the earth and its
   fullness
   and the favor of him who dwelt in
   the burning bush.
Let all these rest on the head of Joseph,
   on the brow of the prince among*c*
   his brothers.
17 In majesty he is like a firstborn bull;
   his horns are the horns of a wild ox.
With them he will gore the nations,
   even those at the ends of the earth.
Such are the ten thousands of
   Ephraim;
   such are the thousands of
   Manasseh."

18 About Zebulun he said:

"Rejoice, Zebulun, in your going out,
   and you, Issachar, in your tents.
19 They will summon peoples to the
   mountain
   and there offer sacrifices of
   righteousness;
they will feast on the abundance of
   the seas,
   on the treasures hidden in the
   sand."

20 About Gad he said:

"Blessed is he who enlarges Gad's
   domain!
Gad lives there like a lion,
   tearing at arm or head.
21 He chose the best land for himself;
   the leader's portion was kept for
   him.
When the heads of the people
   assembled,

---

a 5 *Jeshurun* means *the upright one,* that is, Israel; also in verse 26.   *b* 6 Or *but let*   *c* 16 Or *of the one separated from*

he carried out the LORD's righteous
   will,
and his judgments concerning
   Israel."

22About Dan he said:

"Dan is a lion's cub,
   springing out of Bashan."

23About Naphtali he said:

"Naphtali is abounding with the
   favor of the LORD
and is full of his blessing;
he will inherit southward to the
   lake."

24About Asher he said:

"Most blessed of sons is Asher;
   let him be favored by his brothers,
and let him bathe his feet in oil.
25The bolts of your gates will be iron
   and bronze,
and your strength will equal your
   days.

26"There is no one like the God of
   Jeshurun,
who rides on the heavens to help
   you
and on the clouds in his majesty.

NOR CAN WE FALL BELOW THE ARMS OF GOD,
HOW LOW SOEVER IT BE WE FALL.   —*William Penn*

27The eternal God is your refuge,
   and underneath are the everlasting
   arms.
He will drive out your enemy before
   you,
   saying, 'Destroy him!'
28So Israel will live in safety alone;
   Jacob's spring is secure
in a land of grain and new wine,
   where the heavens drop dew.
29Blessed are you, O Israel!

Who is like you,
   a people saved by the LORD?
He is your shield and helper
   and your glorious sword.
Your enemies will cower before you,
   and you will trample down their
     high places.*a*"

The Death of Moses

34 Then Moses climbed Mount
Nebo from the plains of Moab
to the top of Pisgah, across from Jericho.
There the LORD showed him the whole
land—from Gilead to Dan, 2all of Naphtali, the territory of Ephraim and Manasseh, all the land of Judah as far as the
western sea,*b* 3the Negev and the whole
region from the Valley of Jericho, the City
of Palms, as far as Zoar. 4Then the LORD
said to him, "This is the land I promised
on oath to Abraham, Isaac and Jacob
when I said, 'I will give it to your descendants.' I have let you see it with your
eyes, but you will not cross over into it."

5And Moses the servant of the LORD
died there in Moab, as the LORD had
said. 6He buried him*c* in Moab, in the
valley opposite Beth Peor, but to this
day no one knows where his grave is.
7Moses was a hundred and twenty years
old when he died, yet his eyes were not
weak nor his strength gone. 8The Israelites grieved for Moses in the plains of
Moab thirty days, until the time of
weeping and mourning was over.

9Now Joshua son of Nun was filled
with the spirit*d* of wisdom because
Moses had laid his hands on him. So the
Israelites listened to him and did what
the LORD had commanded Moses.

10Since then, no prophet has risen in
Israel like Moses, whom the LORD knew
face to face, 11who did all those miraculous signs and wonders the LORD sent
him to do in Egypt—to Pharaoh and to
all his officials and to his whole land.
12For no one has ever shown the mighty
power or performed the awesome deeds
that Moses did in the sight of all Israel.

---

a 29 Or *will tread upon their bodies*   *b* 2 That is, the Mediterranean   *c* 6 Or *He was buried*
d 9 Or *Spirit*

JOSHUA

AMED AFTER ITS LEADING CHAR-
ACTER, JOSHUA, WHOM GOD AP-
POINTED LEADER OF ISRAEL BEFORE
MOSES' DEATH, THE BOOK OF JOSHUA BEGINS
WITH THE TRIBES STILL CAMPED ON THE EAST
SIDE OF THE JORDAN RIVER. THIS BOOK
TELLS THE STORY OF HOW, WITH GOD'S HELP,
THE PEOPLE CROSSED THE JORDAN RIVER
AND TOOK POSSESSION OF THE PROMISED
LAND. JOSHUA REMINDS THE PEOPLE OF
GOD'S COVENANT PROMISES TO THEM AND
URGES THEM TO SERVE ONLY THE LORD.

The LORD Commands Joshua

1 After the death of Moses the servant of the LORD, the LORD said to Joshua son of Nun, Moses' aide: ²"Moses my servant is dead. Now then, you and all these people, get ready to cross the Jordan River into the land I am about to give to them—to the Israelites. ³I will give you every place where you set your foot, as I promised Moses. ⁴Your territory will extend from the desert to Lebanon, and from the great river, the Euphrates—all the Hittite country—to the Great Sea*a* on the west. ⁵No one will be able to stand up against you all the days of your life. As I was with Moses, so I will be with you; I will never leave you nor forsake you.

⁶"Be strong and courageous, because you will lead these people to inherit the land I swore to their forefathers to give them. ⁷Be strong and very courageous. Be careful to obey all the law my servant Moses gave you; do not turn from it to the right or to the left, that you may be successful wherever you go. ⁸Do not let this Book of the Law depart from your mouth; meditate on it day and night, so that you may be careful to do everything written in it. Then you will be prosperous and successful. ⁹Have I not commanded you? Be strong and courageous. Do not be terrified; do not be discouraged, for the LORD your God will be with you wherever you go."

¹⁰So Joshua ordered the officers of the people: ¹¹"Go through the camp and tell

a 4 That is, the Mediterranean

the people, 'Get your supplies ready. Three days from now you will cross the Jordan here to go in and take possession of the land the LORD your God is giving you for your own.' "

12But to the Reubenites, the Gadites and the half-tribe of Manasseh, Joshua said, 13"Remember the command that Moses the servant of the LORD gave you: 'The LORD your God is giving you rest and has granted you this land.' 14Your wives, your children and your livestock may stay in the land that Moses gave you east of the Jordan, but all your fighting men, fully armed, must cross over ahead of your brothers. You are to help your brothers 15until the LORD gives them rest, as he has done for you, and until they too have taken possession of the land that the LORD your God is giving them. After that, you may go back and occupy your own land, which Moses the servant of the LORD gave you east of the Jordan toward the sunrise."

16Then they answered Joshua, "Whatever you have commanded us we will do, and wherever you send us we will go. 17Just as we fully obeyed Moses, so we will obey you. Only may the LORD your God be with you as he was with Moses. 18Whoever rebels against your word and does not obey your words, whatever you may command them, will be put to death. Only be strong and courageous!"

Rahab and the Spies

2 Then Joshua son of Nun secretly sent two spies from Shittim. "Go, look over the land," he said, "especially Jericho." So they went and entered the house of a prostitute*a* named Rahab and stayed there.

2The king of Jericho was told, "Look! Some of the Israelites have come here tonight to spy out the land." 3So the king of Jericho sent this message to Rahab: "Bring out the men who came to you and entered your house, because they have come to spy out the whole land."

4But the woman had taken the two men and hidden them. She said, "Yes, the men came to me, but I did not know where they had come from. 5At dusk, when it was time to close the city gate, the men left. I don't know which way they went. Go after them quickly. You may catch up with them." 6(But she had taken them up to the roof and hidden them under the stalks of flax she had laid out on the roof.) 7So the men set out in pursuit of the spies on the road that leads to the fords of the Jordan, and as soon as the pursuers had gone out, the gate was shut.

8Before the spies lay down for the night, she went up on the roof 9and said to them, "I know that the LORD has given this land to you and that a great fear of you has fallen on us, so that all who live in this country are melting in fear because of you. 10We have heard how the LORD dried up the water of the Red Sea*b* for you when you came out of Egypt, and what you did to Sihon and Og, the two kings of the Amorites east of the Jordan, whom you completely destroyed.*c* 11When we heard of it, our hearts melted and everyone's courage failed because of you, for the LORD your God is God in heaven above and on the earth below. 12Now then, please swear to me by the LORD that you will show kindness to my family, because I have shown kindness to you. Give me a sure sign 13that you will spare the lives of my father and mother, my brothers and sisters, and all who belong to them, and that you will save us from death."

14"Our lives for your lives!" the men assured her. "If you don't tell what we are doing, we will treat you kindly and faithfully when the LORD gives us the land."

15So she let them down by a rope through the window, for the house she lived in was part of the city wall. 16Now she had said to them, "Go to the hills so the pursuers will not find you. Hide

---

a 1 Or possibly *an innkeeper*　*b 10* Hebrew *Yam Suph*; that is, Sea of Reeds　*c 10* The Hebrew term refers to the irrevocable giving over of things or persons to the LORD, often by totally destroying them.

WEEKEND

JEPHTHAH'S DAUGHTER
Lord George Gordon Noel Byron

VERSE: Judges 11:30–31   **PASSAGE:** Judges 11:30–38

ince our country, our God—Oh, my sire!
Demand that thy daughter expire;
Since thy triumph was bought by thy vow—
Strike the bosom that's bared for thee now!

And the voice of my mourning is o'er,
And the mountains behold me no more:
If the hand that I love lay me low,
There cannot be pain in the blow!

And of this, oh, my father! be sure—
That the blood of thy child is as pure
As the blessing I beg ere it flow,
And the last thought that soothes me below.

Though the virgins of Salem lament,
Be the judge and the hero unbent!
I have won the great battle for thee,
And my father and country are free!

When this blood of thy giving hath gushed,
When the voice that thou lovest is hushed,
Let my memory still be thy pride,
And forget not I smiled as I died!

ADDITIONAL SCRIPTURE READING:
Leviticus 27:28–29; Numbers 30:2–5; 1 Samuel 1:22–28

Go to page 241 for your next devotional reading.

1700   1900

yourselves there three days until they return, and then go on your way."

17The men said to her, "This oath you made us swear will not be binding on us 18unless, when we enter the land, you have tied this scarlet cord in the window through which you let us down, and unless you have brought your father and mother, your brothers and all your family into your house. 19If anyone goes outside your house into the street, his blood will be on his own head; we will not be responsible. As for anyone who is in the house with you, his blood will be on our head if a hand is laid on him. 20But if you tell what we are doing, we will be released from the oath you made us swear."

21"Agreed," she replied. "Let it be as you say." So she sent them away and they departed. And she tied the scarlet cord in the window.

22When they left, they went into the hills and stayed there three days, until the pursuers had searched all along the road and returned without finding them. 23Then the two men started back. They went down out of the hills, forded the river and came to Joshua son of Nun and told him everything that had happened to them. 24They said to Joshua, "The LORD has surely given the whole land into our hands; all the people are melting in fear because of us."

Crossing the Jordan

3 Early in the morning Joshua and all the Israelites set out from Shittim and went to the Jordan, where they camped before crossing over. 2After three days the officers went throughout the camp, 3giving orders to the people: "When you see the ark of the covenant of the LORD your God, and the priests, who are Levites, carrying it, you are to move out from your positions and follow it. 4Then you will know which way to go, since you have never been this way before. But keep a distance of about a thousand yards[a] between you and the ark; do not go near it."

5Joshua told the people, "Consecrate yourselves, for tomorrow the LORD will do amazing things among you."

6Joshua said to the priests, "Take up the ark of the covenant and pass on ahead of the people." So they took it up and went ahead of them.

7And the LORD said to Joshua, "Today I will begin to exalt you in the eyes of all Israel, so they may know that I am with you as I was with Moses. 8Tell the priests who carry the ark of the covenant: 'When you reach the edge of the Jordan's waters, go and stand in the river.' "

9Joshua said to the Israelites, "Come here and listen to the words of the LORD your God. 10This is how you will know that the living God is among you and that he will certainly drive out before you the Canaanites, Hittites, Hivites, Perizzites, Girgashites, Amorites and Jebusites. 11See, the ark of the covenant of the Lord of all the earth will go into the Jordan ahead of you. 12Now then, choose twelve men from the tribes of Israel, one from each tribe. 13And as soon as the priests who carry the ark of the LORD—the Lord of all the earth—set foot in the Jordan, its waters flowing downstream will be cut off and stand up in a heap."

14So when the people broke camp to cross the Jordan, the priests carrying the ark of the covenant went ahead of them. 15Now the Jordan is at flood stage all during harvest. Yet as soon as the priests who carried the ark reached the Jordan and their feet touched the water's edge, 16the water from upstream stopped flowing. It piled up in a heap a great distance away, at a town called Adam in the vicinity of Zarethan, while the water flowing down to the Sea of the Arabah (the Salt Sea[b]) was completely cut off. So the people crossed over opposite Jericho. 17The priests who carried the ark of the covenant of the LORD stood firm on dry ground in the middle of the Jordan, while all Israel passed by until the whole nation had completed the crossing on dry ground.

4 When the whole nation had finished crossing the Jordan, the LORD said to Joshua, 2"Choose twelve men from among the people, one from each tribe, 3and tell them to take up twelve stones from the middle of the Jordan from right where the priests

---

a 4 Hebrew *about two thousand cubits* (about 900 meters)   b 16 That is, the Dead Sea

stood and to carry them over with you and put them down at the place where you stay tonight."

⁴So Joshua called together the twelve men he had appointed from the Israelites, one from each tribe, ⁵and said to them, "Go over before the ark of the LORD your God into the middle of the Jordan. Each of you is to take up a stone on his shoulder, according to the number of the tribes of the Israelites, ⁶to serve as a sign among you. In the future, when your children ask you, 'What do these stones mean?' ⁷tell them that the flow of the Jordan was cut off before the ark of the covenant of the LORD. When it crossed the Jordan, the waters of the Jordan were cut off. These stones are to be a memorial to the people of Israel forever."

⁸So the Israelites did as Joshua commanded them. They took twelve stones from the middle of the Jordan, according to the number of the tribes of the Israelites, as the LORD had told Joshua; and they carried them over with them to their camp, where they put them down. ⁹Joshua set up the twelve stones that

MONDAY

STEP INTO THE WATERS
Hannah Whitall Smith

VERSE: Joshua 3:13   **PASSAGE:** Joshua 3:7–17

 man was obliged to descend into a deep well by sliding down a fixed rope which was supposed to be of ample length. But to his dismay he came to the end of it before his feet had touched the bottom. He had not the strength to climb up again, and to let go and drop seemed to him but to be dashed to pieces in the depths below. He held on until his strength was utterly exhausted, and then dropped, as he thought, to his death. He fell—just three inches—and found himself safe on the rock bottom.

Are you afraid to take this step? Does it seem too sudden, too much like a leap in the dark? Do you not know that the step of faith always "falls on the seeming void, but finds the rock beneath"? If ever you are to enter this glorious land, flowing with milk and honey, you must sooner or later step into the brimming waters, for there is no other path; and to do it now may save you months and even years of disappointment and grief. Hear the word of the Lord,—

"Have not I commanded thee? Be strong and of a good courage; be not afraid, neither be thou dismayed: for the Lord thy God is with thee, whithersoever thou goest" (Joshua 1:9, KJV).

ADDITIONAL SCRIPTURE READING:
Genesis 28:15; Joshua 1:6–7; Psalm 27:1

Go to page 253 for your next devotional reading.

1700   1900

had been*a* in the middle of the Jordan at the spot where the priests who carried the ark of the covenant had stood. And they are there to this day.

¹⁰Now the priests who carried the ark remained standing in the middle of the Jordan until everything the LORD had commanded Joshua was done by the people, just as Moses had directed Joshua. The people hurried over, ¹¹and as soon as all of them had crossed, the ark of the LORD and the priests came to the other side while the people watched. ¹²The men of Reuben, Gad and the half-tribe of Manasseh crossed over, armed, in front of the Israelites, as Moses had directed them. ¹³About forty thousand armed for battle crossed over before the LORD to the plains of Jericho for war.

¹⁴That day the LORD exalted Joshua in the sight of all Israel; and they revered him all the days of his life, just as they had revered Moses.

¹⁵Then the LORD said to Joshua, ¹⁶"Command the priests carrying the ark of the Testimony to come up out of the Jordan."

¹⁷So Joshua commanded the priests, "Come up out of the Jordan."

¹⁸And the priests came up out of the river carrying the ark of the covenant of the LORD. No sooner had they set their feet on the dry ground than the waters of the Jordan returned to their place and ran at flood stage as before.

¹⁹On the tenth day of the first month the people went up from the Jordan and camped at Gilgal on the eastern border of Jericho. ²⁰And Joshua set up at Gilgal the twelve stones they had taken out of the Jordan. ²¹He said to the Israelites, "In the future when your descendants ask their fathers, 'What do these stones mean?' ²²tell them, 'Israel crossed the Jordan on dry ground.' ²³For the LORD your God dried up the Jordan before you until you had crossed over. The LORD your God did to the Jordan just what he had done to the Red Sea*b* when he dried it up before us until we had crossed over. ²⁴He did this so that all the peoples of the earth might know that the hand of the LORD is powerful and so that you might always fear the LORD your God."

Circumcision at Gilgal

5 Now when all the Amorite kings west of the Jordan and all the Canaanite kings along the coast heard how the LORD had dried up the Jordan before the Israelites until we had crossed over, their hearts melted and they no longer had the courage to face the Israelites.

²At that time the LORD said to Joshua, "Make flint knives and circumcise the Israelites again." ³So Joshua made flint knives and circumcised the Israelites at Gibeath Haaraloth.*c*

⁴Now this is why he did so: All those who came out of Egypt—all the men of military age—died in the desert on the way after leaving Egypt. ⁵All the people that came out had been circumcised, but all the people born in the desert during the journey from Egypt had not. ⁶The Israelites had moved about in the desert forty years until all the men who were of military age when they left Egypt had died, since they had not obeyed the LORD. For the LORD had sworn to them that they would not see the land that he had solemnly promised their fathers to give us, a land flowing with milk and honey. ⁷So he raised up their sons in their place, and these were the ones Joshua circumcised. They were still uncircumcised because they had not been circumcised on the way. ⁸And after the whole nation had been circumcised, they remained where they were in camp until they were healed.

⁹Then the LORD said to Joshua, "Today I have rolled away the reproach of Egypt from you." So the place has been called Gilgal*d* to this day.

¹⁰On the evening of the fourteenth day of the month, while camped at Gilgal on the plains of Jericho, the Israelites celebrated the Passover. ¹¹The day after the Passover, that very day, they ate some of the produce of the land: unleavened bread and roasted grain. ¹²The manna stopped the day after*e* they ate this food from the land; there was no longer any manna for the Israelites, but that year they ate of the produce of Canaan.

a 9 Or Joshua also set up twelve stones   b 23 Hebrew Yam Suph; that is, Sea of Reeds   c 3 Gibeath Haaraloth means hill of foreskins.   d 9 Gilgal sounds like the Hebrew for roll.   e 12 Or the day

The Fall of Jericho

13Now when Joshua was near Jericho, he looked up and saw a man standing in front of him with a drawn sword in his hand. Joshua went up to him and asked, "Are you for us or for our enemies?"

14"Neither," he replied, "but as commander of the army of the LORD I have now come." Then Joshua fell facedown to the ground in reverence, and asked him, "What message does my Lord*a* have for his servant?"

15The commander of the LORD's army replied, "Take off your sandals, for the place where you are standing is holy." And Joshua did so.

6 Now Jericho was tightly shut up because of the Israelites. No one went out and no one came in.

2Then the LORD said to Joshua, "See, I have delivered Jericho into your hands, along with its king and its fighting men. **3**March around the city once with all the armed men. Do this for six days. **4**Have seven priests carry trumpets of rams' horns in front of the ark. On the seventh day, march around the city seven times, with the priests blowing the trumpets. **5**When you hear them sound a long blast on the trumpets, have all the people give a loud shout; then the wall of the city will collapse and the people will go up, every man straight in."

6So Joshua son of Nun called the priests and said to them, "Take up the ark of the covenant of the LORD and have seven priests carry trumpets in front of it." **7**And he ordered the people, "Advance! March around the city, with the armed guard going ahead of the ark of the LORD."

8When Joshua had spoken to the people, the seven priests carrying the seven trumpets before the LORD went forward, blowing their trumpets, and the ark of the LORD's covenant followed them. **9**The armed guard marched ahead of the priests who blew the trumpets, and the rear guard followed the ark. All this time the trumpets were sounding. **10**But Joshua had commanded the people, "Do not give a war cry, do not raise your voices, do not say a word until the day I tell you to shout. Then shout!" **11**So he had the ark of the LORD carried around the city, circling it once. Then the people returned to camp and spent the night there.

12Joshua got up early the next morning and the priests took up the ark of the LORD. **13**The seven priests carrying the seven trumpets went forward, marching before the ark of the LORD and blowing the trumpets. The armed men went ahead of them and the rear guard followed the ark of the LORD, while the trumpets kept sounding. **14**So on the second day they marched around the city once and returned to the camp. They did this for six days.

15On the seventh day, they got up at daybreak and marched around the city seven times in the same manner, except that on that day they circled the city seven times. **16**The seventh time around, when the priests sounded the trumpet blast, Joshua commanded the people, "Shout! For the LORD has given you the city! **17**The city and all that is in it are to be devoted*b* to the LORD. Only Rahab the prostitute*c* and all who are with her in her house shall be spared, because she hid the spies we sent. **18**But keep away from the devoted things, so that you will not bring about your own destruction by taking any of them. Otherwise you will make the camp of Israel liable to destruction and bring trouble on it. **19**All the silver and gold and the articles of bronze and iron are sacred to the LORD and must go into his treasury."

20When the trumpets sounded, the people shouted, and at the sound of the trumpet, when the people gave a loud shout, the wall collapsed; so every man charged straight in, and they took the city. **21**They devoted the city to the LORD and destroyed with the sword every living thing in it—men and women, young and old, cattle, sheep and donkeys.

22Joshua said to the two men who had spied out the land, "Go into the prostitute's house and bring her out and all who belong to her, in accordance with your oath to her." **23**So the young men who had done the spying went in and brought out Rahab, her father and

---

a 14 Or *lord*   *b 17* The Hebrew term refers to the irrevocable giving over of things or persons to the LORD, often by totally destroying them; also in verses 18 and 21.   *c 17* Or possibly *innkeeper*; also in verses 22 and 25

mother and brothers and all who belonged to her. They brought out her entire family and put them in a place outside the camp of Israel.

²⁴Then they burned the whole city and everything in it, but they put the silver and gold and the articles of bronze and iron into the treasury of the LORD's house. ²⁵But Joshua spared Rahab the prostitute, with her family and all who belonged to her, because she hid the men Joshua had sent as spies to Jericho—and she lives among the Israelites to this day.

²⁶At that time Joshua pronounced this solemn oath: "Cursed before the LORD is the man who undertakes to rebuild this city, Jericho:

"At the cost of his firstborn son
    will he lay its foundations;
at the cost of his youngest
    will he set up its gates."

²⁷So the LORD was with Joshua, and his fame spread throughout the land.

Achan's Sin

7 But the Israelites acted unfaithfully in regard to the devoted things*a*; Achan son of Carmi, the son of Zimri,*b* the son of Zerah, of the tribe of Judah, took some of them. So the LORD's anger burned against Israel.

²Now Joshua sent men from Jericho to Ai, which is near Beth Aven to the east of Bethel, and told them, "Go up and spy out the region." So the men went up and spied out Ai.

³When they returned to Joshua, they said, "Not all the people will have to go up against Ai. Send two or three thousand men to take it and do not weary all the people, for only a few men are there." ⁴So about three thousand men went up; but they were routed by the men of Ai, ⁵who killed about thirty-six of them. They chased the Israelites from the city gate as far as the stone quarries*c* and struck them down on the slopes. At this the hearts of the people melted and became like water.

⁶Then Joshua tore his clothes and fell facedown to the ground before the ark of the LORD, remaining there till evening. The elders of Israel did the same, and sprinkled dust on their heads. ⁷And Joshua said, "Ah, Sovereign LORD, why did you ever bring this people across the Jordan to deliver us into the hands of the Amorites to destroy us? If only we had been content to stay on the other side of the Jordan! ⁸O Lord, what can I say, now that Israel has been routed by its enemies? ⁹The Canaanites and the other people of the country will hear about this and they will surround us and wipe out our name from the earth. What then will you do for your own great name?"

¹⁰The LORD said to Joshua, "Stand up! What are you doing down on your face? ¹¹Israel has sinned; they have violated my covenant, which I commanded them to keep. They have taken some of the devoted things; they have stolen, they have lied, they have put them with their own possessions. ¹²That is why the Israelites cannot stand against their enemies; they turn their backs and run because they have been made liable to destruction. I will not be with you anymore unless you destroy whatever among you is devoted to destruction.

¹³"Go, consecrate the people. Tell them, 'Consecrate yourselves in preparation for tomorrow; for this is what the LORD, the God of Israel, says: That which is devoted is among you, O Israel. You cannot stand against your enemies until you remove it.

¹⁴" 'In the morning, present yourselves tribe by tribe. The tribe that the LORD takes shall come forward clan by clan; the clan that the LORD takes shall come forward family by family; and the family that the LORD takes shall come forward man by man. ¹⁵He who is caught with the devoted things shall be destroyed by fire, along with all that belongs to him. He has violated the covenant of the LORD and has done a disgraceful thing in Israel!' "

¹⁶Early the next morning Joshua had Israel come forward by tribes, and Judah was taken. ¹⁷The clans of Judah

---

a 1 The Hebrew term refers to the irrevocable giving over of things or persons to the LORD, often by totally destroying them; also in verses 11, 12, 13 and 15.   *b 1* See Septuagint and 1 Chron. 2:6; Hebrew *Zabdi;* also in verses 17 and 18.   *c 5* Or *as far as Shebarim*

came forward, and he took the Zera-hites. He had the clan of the Zerahites come forward by families, and Zimri was taken. ¹⁸Joshua had his family come forward man by man, and Achan son of Carmi, the son of Zimri, the son of Zerah, of the tribe of Judah, was taken.

¹⁹Then Joshua said to Achan, "My son, give glory to the LORD,^a the God of Israel, and give him the praise.^b Tell me what you have done; do not hide it from me."

²⁰Achan replied, "It is true! I have sinned against the LORD, the God of Israel. This is what I have done: ²¹When I saw in the plunder a beautiful robe from Babylonia,^c two hundred shekels^d of silver and a wedge of gold weighing fifty shekels,^e I coveted them and took them. They are hidden in the ground inside my tent, with the silver underneath."

RICHES HAVE MADE MORE COVETOUS MEN THAN COVETOUSNESS HATH MADE RICH MEN.

—Thomas Fuller

---

²²So Joshua sent messengers, and they ran to the tent, and there it was, hidden in his tent, with the silver underneath. ²³They took the things from the tent, brought them to Joshua and all the Israelites and spread them out before the LORD.

²⁴Then Joshua, together with all Israel, took Achan son of Zerah, the silver, the robe, the gold wedge, his sons and daughters, his cattle, donkeys and sheep, his tent and all that he had, to the Valley of Achor. ²⁵Joshua said, "Why have you brought this trouble on us? The LORD will bring trouble on you today."

Then all Israel stoned him, and after they had stoned the rest, they burned them. ²⁶Over Achan they heaped up a large pile of rocks, which remains to this day. Then the LORD turned from his fierce anger. Therefore that place has been called the Valley of Achor^f ever since.

Ai Destroyed

8 Then the LORD said to Joshua, "Do not be afraid; do not be dis-couraged. Take the whole army with you, and go up and attack Ai. For I have delivered into your hands the king of Ai, his people, his city and his land. ²You shall do to Ai and its king as you did to Jericho and its king, except that you may carry off their plunder and live-stock for yourselves. Set an ambush behind the city."

³So Joshua and the whole army moved out to attack Ai. He chose thirty thou-sand of his best fighting men and sent them out at night ⁴with these orders: "Listen carefully. You are to set an ambush behind the city. Don't go very far from it. All of you be on the alert. ⁵I and all those with me will advance on the city, and when the men come out against us, as they did before, we will flee from them. ⁶They will pursue us until we have lured them away from the city, for they will say, 'They are running away from us as they did before.' So when we flee from them, ⁷you are to rise up from ambush and take the city. The LORD your God will give it into your hand. ⁸When you have taken the city, set it on fire. Do what the LORD has commanded. See to it; you have my orders."

⁹Then Joshua sent them off, and they went to the place of ambush and lay in wait between Bethel and Ai, to the west of Ai—but Joshua spent that night with the people.

¹⁰Early the next morning Joshua mus-tered his men, and he and the leaders of Israel marched before them to Ai. ¹¹The entire force that was with him marched up and approached the city and arrived in front of it. They set up camp north of Ai, with the valley between them and the city. ¹²Joshua had taken about five thousand men and set them in ambush between Bethel and Ai, to the west of the city. ¹³They had the soldiers take up their positions—all those in the camp to the north of the city and the ambush to the west of it. That night Joshua went into the valley.

---

^a 19 A solemn charge to tell the truth   ^b 19 Or *and confess to him*   ^c 21 Hebrew *Shinar*
^d 21 That is, about 5 pounds (about 2.3 kilograms)   ^e 21 That is, about 1 1/4 pounds (about 0.6 kilogram)   ^f 26 *Achor* means *trouble*.

¹⁴When the king of Ai saw this, he and all the men of the city hurried out early in the morning to meet Israel in battle at a certain place overlooking the Arabah. But he did not know that an ambush had been set against him behind the city. ¹⁵Joshua and all Israel let themselves be driven back before them, and they fled toward the desert. ¹⁶All the men of Ai were called to pursue them, and they pursued Joshua and were lured away from the city. ¹⁷Not a man remained in Ai or Bethel who did not go after Israel. They left the city open and went in pursuit of Israel.

¹⁸Then the LORD said to Joshua, "Hold out toward Ai the javelin that is in your hand, for into your hand I will deliver the city." So Joshua held out his javelin toward Ai. ¹⁹As soon as he did this, the men in the ambush rose quickly from their position and rushed forward. They entered the city and captured it and quickly set it on fire.

²⁰The men of Ai looked back and saw the smoke of the city rising against the sky, but they had no chance to escape in any direction, for the Israelites who had been fleeing toward the desert had turned back against their pursuers. ²¹For when Joshua and all Israel saw that the ambush had taken the city and that smoke was going up from the city, they turned around and attacked the men of Ai. ²²The men of the ambush also came out of the city against them, so that they were caught in the middle, with Israelites on both sides. Israel cut them down, leaving them neither survivors nor fugitives. ²³But they took the king of Ai alive and brought him to Joshua.

²⁴When Israel had finished killing all the men of Ai in the fields and in the desert where they had chased them, and when every one of them had been put to the sword, all the Israelites returned to Ai and killed those who were in it. ²⁵Twelve thousand men and women fell that day—all the people of Ai. ²⁶For Joshua did not draw back the hand that held out his javelin until he had destroyed[a] all who lived in Ai. ²⁷But Israel did carry off for themselves the livestock and plunder of this city, as the LORD had instructed Joshua.

²⁸So Joshua burned Ai and made it a permanent heap of ruins, a desolate place to this day. ²⁹He hung the king of Ai on a tree and left him there until evening. At sunset, Joshua ordered them to take his body from the tree and throw it down at the entrance of the city gate. And they raised a large pile of rocks over it, which remains to this day.

The Covenant Renewed at Mount Ebal

³⁰Then Joshua built on Mount Ebal an altar to the LORD, the God of Israel, ³¹as Moses the servant of the LORD had commanded the Israelites. He built it according to what is written in the Book of the Law of Moses—an altar of uncut stones, on which no iron tool had been used. On it they offered to the LORD burnt offerings and sacrificed fellowship offerings.[b] ³²There, in the presence of the Israelites, Joshua copied on stones the law of Moses, which he had written. ³³All Israel, aliens and citizens alike, with their elders, officials and judges, were standing on both sides of the ark of the covenant of the LORD, facing those who carried it—the priests, who were Levites. Half of the people stood in front of Mount Gerizim and half of them in front of Mount Ebal, as Moses the servant of the LORD had formerly commanded when he gave instructions to bless the people of Israel.

³⁴Afterward, Joshua read all the words of the law—the blessings and the curses—just as it is written in the Book of the Law. ³⁵There was not a word of all that Moses had commanded that Joshua did not read to the whole assembly of Israel, including the women and children, and the aliens who lived among them.

The Gibeonite Deception

9 Now when all the kings west of the Jordan heard about these things—those in the hill country, in the western foothills, and along the entire coast of the Great Sea[c] as far as Lebanon (the kings of the Hittites, Amorites,

---

a 26 The Hebrew term refers to the irrevocable giving over of things or persons to the LORD, often by totally destroying them.   *b 31* Traditionally *peace offerings*   *c 1* That is, the Mediterranean

Canaanites, Perizzites, Hivites and Jebusites)— 2they came together to make war against Joshua and Israel.

3However, when the people of Gibeon heard what Joshua had done to Jericho and Ai, 4they resorted to a ruse: They went as a delegation whose donkeys were loaded*a* with worn-out sacks and old wineskins, cracked and mended. 5The men put worn and patched sandals on their feet and wore old clothes. All the bread of their food supply was dry and moldy. 6Then they went to Joshua in the camp at Gilgal and said to him and the men of Israel, "We have come from a distant country; make a treaty with us."

7The men of Israel said to the Hivites, "But perhaps you live near us. How then can we make a treaty with you?"

8"We are your servants," they said to Joshua.

But Joshua asked, "Who are you and where do you come from?"

9They answered: "Your servants have come from a very distant country because of the fame of the LORD your God. For we have heard reports of him: all that he did in Egypt, 10and all that he did to the two kings of the Amorites east of the Jordan—Sihon king of Heshbon, and Og king of Bashan, who reigned in Ashtaroth. 11And our elders and all those living in our country said to us, 'Take provisions for your journey; go and meet them and say to them, "We are your servants; make a treaty with us." ' 12This bread of ours was warm when we packed it at home on the day we left to come to you. But now see how dry and moldy it is. 13And these wineskins that we filled were new, but see how cracked they are. And our clothes and sandals are worn out by the very long journey."

14The men of Israel sampled their provisions but did not inquire of the LORD. 15Then Joshua made a treaty of peace with them to let them live, and the leaders of the assembly ratified it by oath.

16Three days after they made the treaty with the Gibeonites, the Israelites heard that they were neighbors, living near them. 17So the Israelites set out and on the third day came to their cities:

Gibeon, Kephirah, Beeroth and Kiriath Jearim. 18But the Israelites did not attack them, because the leaders of the assembly had sworn an oath to them by the LORD, the God of Israel.

The whole assembly grumbled against the leaders, 19but all the leaders answered, "We have given them our oath by the LORD, the God of Israel, and we cannot touch them now. 20This is what we will do to them: We will let them live, so that wrath will not fall on us for breaking the oath we swore to them." 21They continued, "Let them live, but let them be woodcutters and water carriers for the entire community." So the leaders' promise to them was kept.

22Then Joshua summoned the Gibeonites and said, "Why did you deceive us by saying, 'We live a long way from you,' while actually you live near us? 23You are now under a curse: You will never cease to serve as woodcutters and water carriers for the house of my God."

24They answered Joshua, "Your servants were clearly told how the LORD your God had commanded his servant Moses to give you the whole land and to wipe out all its inhabitants from before you. So we feared for our lives because of you, and that is why we did this. 25We are now in your hands. Do to us whatever seems good and right to you."

26So Joshua saved them from the Israelites, and they did not kill them. 27That day he made the Gibeonites woodcutters and water carriers for the community and for the altar of the LORD at the place the LORD would choose. And that is what they are to this day.

The Sun Stands Still

10 Now Adoni-Zedek king of Jerusalem heard that Joshua had taken Ai and totally destroyed*b* it, doing to Ai and its king as he had done to Jericho and its king, and that the people of Gibeon had made a treaty of peace with Israel and were living near them. 2He and his people were very much alarmed at this, because Gibeon was an important city, like one of the royal cities; it was larger than Ai, and all its men

---

a 4 Most Hebrew manuscripts; some Hebrew manuscripts, Vulgate and Syriac (see also Septuagint) *They prepared provisions and loaded their donkeys*   *b* 1 The Hebrew term refers to the irrevocable giving over of things or persons to the LORD, often by totally destroying them; also in verses 28, 35, 37, 39 and 40.

were good fighters. ³So Adoni-Zedek king of Jerusalem appealed to Hoham king of Hebron, Piram king of Jarmuth, Japhia king of Lachish and Debir king of Eglon. ⁴"Come up and help me attack Gibeon," he said, "because it has made peace with Joshua and the Israelites."

⁵Then the five kings of the Amorites—the kings of Jerusalem, Hebron, Jarmuth, Lachish and Eglon—joined forces. They moved up with all their troops and took up positions against Gibeon and attacked it.

⁶The Gibeonites then sent word to Joshua in the camp at Gilgal: "Do not abandon your servants. Come up to us quickly and save us! Help us, because all the Amorite kings from the hill country have joined forces against us."

⁷So Joshua marched up from Gilgal with his entire army, including all the best fighting men. ⁸The LORD said to Joshua, "Do not be afraid of them; I have given them into your hand. Not one of them will be able to withstand you."

⁹After an all-night march from Gilgal, Joshua took them by surprise. ¹⁰The LORD threw them into confusion before Israel, who defeated them in a great victory at Gibeon. Israel pursued them along the road going up to Beth Horon and cut them down all the way to Azekah and Makkedah. ¹¹As they fled before Israel on the road down from Beth Horon to Azekah, the LORD hurled large hailstones down on them from the sky, and more of them died from the hailstones than were killed by the swords of the Israelites.

¹²On the day the LORD gave the Amorites over to Israel, Joshua said to the LORD in the presence of Israel:

"O sun, stand still over Gibeon,
    O moon, over the Valley of
        Aijalon."
¹³So the sun stood still,
    and the moon stopped,
    till the nation avenged itself on*ª its
        enemies,

as it is written in the Book of Jashar.

The sun stopped in the middle of the sky and delayed going down about a full day. ¹⁴There has never been a day like it

before or since, a day when the LORD listened to a man. Surely the LORD was fighting for Israel!

¹⁵Then Joshua returned with all Israel to the camp at Gilgal.

Five Amorite Kings Killed

¹⁶Now the five kings had fled and hidden in the cave at Makkedah. ¹⁷When Joshua was told that the five kings had been found hiding in the cave at Makkedah, ¹⁸he said, "Roll large rocks up to the mouth of the cave, and post some men there to guard it. ¹⁹But don't stop! Pursue your enemies, attack them from the rear and don't let them reach their cities, for the LORD your God has given them into your hand."

²⁰So Joshua and the Israelites destroyed them completely—almost to a man—but the few who were left reached their fortified cities. ²¹The whole army then returned safely to Joshua in the camp at Makkedah, and no one uttered a word against the Israelites.

²²Joshua said, "Open the mouth of the cave and bring those five kings out to me." ²³So they brought the five kings out of the cave—the kings of Jerusalem, Hebron, Jarmuth, Lachish and Eglon. ²⁴When they had brought these kings to Joshua, he summoned all the men of Israel and said to the army commanders who had come with him, "Come here and put your feet on the necks of these kings." So they came forward and placed their feet on their necks.

²⁵Joshua said to them, "Do not be afraid; do not be discouraged. Be strong and courageous. This is what the LORD will do to all the enemies you are going to fight." ²⁶Then Joshua struck and killed the kings and hung them on five trees, and they were left hanging on the trees until evening.

²⁷At sunset Joshua gave the order and they took them down from the trees and threw them into the cave where they had been hiding. At the mouth of the cave they placed large rocks, which are there to this day.

²⁸That day Joshua took Makkedah. He put the city and its king to the sword and totally destroyed everyone in it. He left no survivors. And he did to the king

---

ª 13 Or *nation triumphed over*

of Makkedah as he had done to the king of Jericho.

Southern Cities Conquered

29Then Joshua and all Israel with him moved on from Makkedah to Libnah and attacked it. 30The LORD also gave that city and its king into Israel's hand. The city and everyone in it Joshua put to the sword. He left no survivors there. And he did to its king as he had done to the king of Jericho.

31Then Joshua and all Israel with him moved on from Libnah to Lachish; he took up positions against it and attacked it. 32The LORD handed Lachish over to Israel, and Joshua took it on the second day. The city and everyone in it he put to the sword, just as he had done to Libnah. 33Meanwhile, Horam king of Gezer had come up to help Lachish, but Joshua defeated him and his army—until no survivors were left.

34Then Joshua and all Israel with him moved on from Lachish to Eglon; they took up positions against it and attacked it. 35They captured it that same day and put it to the sword and totally destroyed everyone in it, just as they had done to Lachish.

36Then Joshua and all Israel with him went up from Eglon to Hebron and attacked it. 37They took the city and put it to the sword, together with its king, its villages and everyone in it. They left no survivors. Just as at Eglon, they totally destroyed it and everyone in it.

38Then Joshua and all Israel with him turned around and attacked Debir. 39They took the city, its king and its villages, and put them to the sword. Everyone in it they totally destroyed. They left no survivors. They did to Debir and its king as they had done to Libnah and its king and to Hebron.

40So Joshua subdued the whole region, including the hill country, the Negev, the western foothills and the mountain slopes, together with all their kings. He left no survivors. He totally destroyed all who breathed, just as the LORD, the God of Israel, had commanded. 41Joshua subdued them from Kadesh Barnea to Gaza and from the whole region of Goshen to Gibeon. 42All these kings and their lands Joshua conquered in one campaign, because the LORD, the God of Israel, fought for Israel.

43Then Joshua returned with all Israel to the camp at Gilgal.

Northern Kings Defeated

11 When Jabin king of Hazor heard of this, he sent word to Jobab king of Madon, to the kings of Shimron and Acshaph, 2and to the northern kings who were in the mountains, in the Arabah south of Kinnereth, in the western foothills and in Naphoth Dora on the west; 3to the Canaanites in the east and west; to the Amorites, Hittites, Perizzites and Jebusites in the hill country; and to the Hivites below Hermon in the region of Mizpah. 4They came out with all their troops and a large number of horses and chariots—a huge army, as numerous as the sand on the seashore. 5All these kings joined forces and made camp together at the Waters of Merom, to fight against Israel.

6The LORD said to Joshua, "Do not be afraid of them, because by this time tomorrow I will hand all of them over to Israel, slain. You are to hamstring their horses and burn their chariots."

7So Joshua and his whole army came against them suddenly at the Waters of Merom and attacked them, 8and the LORD gave them into the hand of Israel. They defeated them and pursued them all the way to Greater Sidon, to Misrephoth Maim, and to the Valley of Mizpah on the east, until no survivors were left. 9Joshua did to them as the LORD had directed: He hamstrung their horses and burned their chariots.

10At that time Joshua turned back and captured Hazor and put its king to the sword. (Hazor had been the head of all these kingdoms.) 11Everyone in it they put to the sword. They totally destroyedb them, not sparing anything that breathed, and he burned up Hazor itself.

12Joshua took all these royal cities and their kings and put them to the sword. He totally destroyed them, as Moses the servant of the LORD had commanded. 13Yet Israel did not burn any of the cities

---

a 2 Or *in the heights of Dor*   b 11 The Hebrew term refers to the irrevocable giving over of things or persons to the LORD, often by totally destroying them; also in verses 12, 20 and 21.

built on their mounds—except Hazor, which Joshua burned. **14**The Israelites carried off for themselves all the plunder and livestock of these cities, but all the people they put to the sword until they completely destroyed them, not sparing anyone that breathed. **15**As the LORD commanded his servant Moses, so Moses commanded Joshua, and Joshua did it; he left nothing undone of all that the LORD commanded Moses.

16So Joshua took this entire land: the hill country, all the Negev, the whole region of Goshen, the western foothills, the Arabah and the mountains of Israel with their foothills, **17**from Mount Halak, which rises toward Seir, to Baal Gad in the Valley of Lebanon below Mount Hermon. He captured all their kings and struck them down, putting them to death. **18**Joshua waged war against all these kings for a long time. **19**Except for the Hivites living in Gibeon, not one city made a treaty of peace with the Israelites, who took them all in battle. **20**For it was the LORD himself who hardened their hearts to wage war against Israel, so that he might destroy them totally, exterminating them without mercy, as the LORD had commanded Moses.

21At that time Joshua went and destroyed the Anakites from the hill country: from Hebron, Debir and Anab, from all the hill country of Judah, and from all the hill country of Israel. Joshua totally destroyed them and their towns. **22**No Anakites were left in Israelite territory; only in Gaza, Gath and Ashdod did any survive. **23**So Joshua took the entire land, just as the LORD had directed Moses, and he gave it as an inheritance to Israel according to their tribal divisions. Then the land had rest from war.

List of Defeated Kings

12 These are the kings of the land whom the Israelites had defeated and whose territory they took over east of the Jordan, from the Arnon Gorge to Mount Hermon, including all the eastern side of the Arabah:

2Sihon king of the Amorites,
who reigned in Heshbon. He ruled from Aroer on the rim of the Arnon Gorge—from the middle of the gorge—to the Jabbok River, which is the border of the Ammonites. This included half of Gilead. **3**He also ruled over the eastern Arabah from the Sea of Kinnereth*a* to the Sea of the Arabah (the Salt Sea*b*), to Beth Jeshimoth, and then southward below the slopes of Pisgah.

4And the territory of Og king of Bashan, one of the last of the Rephaites, who reigned in Ashtaroth and Edrei. **5**He ruled over Mount Hermon, Salecah, all of Bashan to the border of the people of Geshur and Maacah, and half of Gilead to the border of Sihon king of Heshbon.

6Moses, the servant of the LORD, and the Israelites conquered them. And Moses the servant of the LORD gave their land to the Reubenites, the Gadites and the half-tribe of Manasseh to be their possession.

7These are the kings of the land that Joshua and the Israelites conquered on the west side of the Jordan, from Baal Gad in the Valley of Lebanon to Mount Halak, which rises toward Seir (their lands Joshua gave as an inheritance to the tribes of Israel according to their tribal divisions— **8**the hill country, the western foothills, the Arabah, the mountain slopes, the desert and the Negev—the lands of the Hittites, Amorites, Canaanites, Perizzites, Hivites and Jebusites):

9the king of Jericho	one
the king of Ai (near Bethel)	one
10the king of Jerusalem	one
the king of Hebron	one
11the king of Jarmuth	one
the king of Lachish	one
12the king of Eglon	one
the king of Gezer	one
13the king of Debir	one
the king of Geder	one
14the king of Hormah	one
the king of Arad	one
15the king of Libnah	one
the king of Adullam	one
16the king of Makkedah	one
the king of Bethel	one
17the king of Tappuah	one
the king of Hepher	one

a 3 That is, Galilee   *b* 3 That is, the Dead Sea

<table>
<tr><td>18 the king of Aphek</td><td>one</td></tr>
<tr><td>the king of Lasharon</td><td>one</td></tr>
<tr><td>19 the king of Madon</td><td>one</td></tr>
<tr><td>the king of Hazor</td><td>one</td></tr>
<tr><td>20 the king of Shimron Meron</td><td>one</td></tr>
<tr><td>the king of Acshaph</td><td>one</td></tr>
<tr><td>21 the king of Taanach</td><td>one</td></tr>
<tr><td>the king of Megiddo</td><td>one</td></tr>
<tr><td>22 the king of Kedesh</td><td>one</td></tr>
<tr><td>the king of Jokneam in Carmel</td><td>one</td></tr>
<tr><td>23 the king of Dor (in Naphoth Dor^a)</td><td>one</td></tr>
<tr><td>the king of Goyim in Gilgal</td><td>one</td></tr>
<tr><td>24 the king of Tirzah</td><td>one</td></tr>
</table>

thirty-one kings in all.

Land Still to Be Taken

13 When Joshua was old and well advanced in years, the LORD said to him, "You are very old, and there are still very large areas of land to be taken over.

2 "This is the land that remains: all the regions of the Philistines and Geshurites: 3 from the Shihor River on the east of Egypt to the territory of Ekron on the north, all of it counted as Canaanite (the territory of the five Philistine rulers in Gaza, Ashdod, Ashkelon, Gath and Ekron—that of the Avvites); 4 from the south, all the land of the Canaanites, from Arah of the Sidonians as far as Aphek, the region of the Amorites, 5 the area of the Gebalites^b; and all Lebanon to the east, from Baal Gad below Mount Hermon to Lebo^c Hamath.

6 "As for all the inhabitants of the mountain regions from Lebanon to Misrephoth Maim, that is, all the Sidonians, I myself will drive them out before the Israelites. Be sure to allocate this land to Israel for an inheritance, as I have instructed you, 7 and divide it as an inheritance among the nine tribes and half of the tribe of Manasseh."

Division of the Land East of the Jordan

8 The other half of Manasseh,^d the Reubenites and the Gadites had received the inheritance that Moses had given them east of the Jordan, as he, the servant of the LORD, had assigned it to them.

9 It extended from Aroer on the rim of the Arnon Gorge, and from the town in the middle of the gorge, and included the whole plateau of Medeba as far as Dibon, 10 and all the towns of Sihon king of the Amorites, who ruled in Heshbon, out to the border of the Ammonites. 11 It also included Gilead, the territory of the people of Geshur and Maacah, all of Mount Hermon and all Bashan as far as Salecah— 12 that is, the whole kingdom of Og in Bashan, who had reigned in Ashtaroth and Edrei and had survived as one of the last of the Rephaites. Moses had defeated them and taken over their land. 13 But the Israelites did not drive out the people of Geshur and Maacah, so they continue to live among the Israelites to this day.

14 But to the tribe of Levi he gave no inheritance, since the offerings made by fire to the LORD, the God of Israel, are their inheritance, as he promised them.

15 This is what Moses had given to the tribe of Reuben, clan by clan:

16 The territory from Aroer on the rim of the Arnon Gorge, and from the town in the middle of the gorge, and the whole plateau past Medeba 17 to Heshbon and all its towns on the plateau, including Dibon, Bamoth Baal, Beth Baal Meon, 18 Jahaz, Kedemoth, Mephaath, 19 Kiriathaim, Sibmah, Zereth Shahar on the hill in the valley, 20 Beth Peor, the slopes of Pisgah, and Beth Jeshimoth 21 —all the towns on the plateau and the entire realm of Sihon king of the Amorites, who ruled at Heshbon. Moses had defeated him and the Midianite chiefs, Evi, Rekem, Zur, Hur and Reba—princes allied with Sihon— who lived in that country. 22 In addition to those slain in battle, the Israelites had put to the sword Balaam son of Beor, who practiced

---

^a 23 Or *in the heights of Dor*   ^b 5 That is, the area of Byblos   ^c 5 Or *to the entrance to*
^d 8 Hebrew *With it* (that is, with the other half of Manasseh)

divination. 23The boundary of the Reubenites was the bank of the Jordan. These towns and their villages were the inheritance of the Reubenites, clan by clan.

24This is what Moses had given to the tribe of Gad, clan by clan:

25The territory of Jazer, all the towns of Gilead and half the Ammonite country as far as Aroer, near Rabbah; 26and from Heshbon to Ramath Mizpah and Betonim, and from Mahanaim to the territory of Debir; 27and in the valley, Beth Haram, Beth Nimrah, Succoth and Zaphon with the rest of the realm of Sihon king of Heshbon (the east side of the Jordan, the territory up to the end of the Sea of Kinnereth*a*). 28These towns and their villages were the inheritance of the Gadites, clan by clan.

29This is what Moses had given to the half-tribe of Manasseh, that is, to half the family of the descendants of Manasseh, clan by clan:

30The territory extending from Mahanaim and including all of Bashan, the entire realm of Og king of Bashan—all the settlements of Jair in Bashan, sixty towns, 31half of Gilead, and Ashtaroth and Edrei (the royal cities of Og in Bashan). This was for the descendants of Makir son of Manasseh—for half of the sons of Makir, clan by clan.

32This is the inheritance Moses had given when he was in the plains of Moab across the Jordan east of Jericho. 33But to the tribe of Levi, Moses had given no inheritance; the LORD, the God of Israel, is their inheritance, as he promised them.

Division of the Land West of the Jordan

14 Now these are the areas the Israelites received as an inheritance in the land of Canaan, which Eleazar the priest, Joshua son of Nun and the heads of the tribal clans of Israel allotted to them. 2Their inheritances were assigned by lot to the nine-and-a-half tribes, as the LORD had commanded

through Moses. 3Moses had granted the two-and-a-half tribes their inheritance east of the Jordan but had not granted the Levites an inheritance among the rest, 4for the sons of Joseph had become two tribes—Manasseh and Ephraim. The Levites received no share of the land but only towns to live in, with pasturelands for their flocks and herds. 5So the Israelites divided the land, just as the LORD had commanded Moses.

Hebron Given to Caleb

6Now the men of Judah approached Joshua at Gilgal, and Caleb son of Jephunneh the Kenizzite said to him, "You know what the LORD said to Moses the man of God at Kadesh Barnea about you and me. 7I was forty years old when Moses the servant of the LORD sent me from Kadesh Barnea to explore the land. And I brought him back a report according to my convictions, 8but my brothers who went up with me made the hearts of the people melt with fear. I, however, followed the LORD my God wholeheartedly. 9So on that day Moses swore to me, 'The land on which your feet have walked will be your inheritance and that of your children forever, because you have followed the LORD my God wholeheartedly.'*b*

10"Now then, just as the LORD promised, he has kept me alive for forty-five years since the time he said this to Moses, while Israel moved about in the desert. So here I am today, eighty-five years old! 11I am still as strong today as the day Moses sent me out; I'm just as vigorous to go out to battle now as I was then. 12Now give me this hill country that the LORD promised me that day. You yourself heard then that the Anakites were there and their cities were large and fortified, but, the LORD helping me, I will drive them out just as he said."

13Then Joshua blessed Caleb son of Jephunneh and gave him Hebron as his inheritance. 14So Hebron has belonged to Caleb son of Jephunneh the Kenizzite ever since, because he followed the LORD, the God of Israel, wholeheartedly. 15(Hebron used to be called Kiriath Arba after Arba, who was the greatest man among the Anakites.)

Then the land had rest from war.

a 27 That is, Galilee   *b 9* Deut. 1:36

Allotment for Judah

 15 The allotment for the tribe of Judah, clan by clan, extended down to the territory of Edom, to the Desert of Zin in the extreme south.

²Their southern boundary started from the bay at the southern end of the Salt Sea,*ᵃ* ³crossed south of Scorpion*ᵇ* Pass, continued on to Zin and went over to the south of Kadesh Barnea. Then it ran past Hezron up to Addar and curved around to Karka. ⁴It then passed along to Azmon and joined the Wadi of Egypt, ending at the sea. This is their*ᶜ* southern boundary.

⁵The eastern boundary is the Salt Sea as far as the mouth of the Jordan.

The northern boundary started from the bay of the sea at the mouth of the Jordan, ⁶went up to Beth Hoglah and continued north of

---

ᵃ 2 That is, the Dead Sea; also in verse 5   *ᵇ 3* Hebrew *Akrabbim*   *ᶜ 4* Hebrew *your*

TUESDAY

"MORE TO FOLLOW"
Charles H. Spurgeon

VERSE: Joshua 14:9   **PASSAGE:** Joshua 14:6–12

A benevolent person gave Mr. Rowland Hill a hundred pounds to dispense to a poor minister a bit at a time, thinking it was too much to send him all at once. Mr. Hill forwarded five pounds in a letter, with only these words within the envelope, "More to follow." In a few days' time, the good man received another letter; this second messenger contained another five pounds, with the same motto, "And more to follow." A day or two after came a third and a fourth, and still the same promise, "And more to follow." Till the whole sum had been received, the astonished minister was made familiar with the cheering words, "And more to follow."

Every blessing that comes from God is sent with the same message, "And more to follow." "I forgive you your sins, but there's more to follow." "I justify you in the righteousness of Christ, but there's more to follow." "I adopt you into my family, but there's more to follow." "I educated you for heaven, but there's more to follow." "I give you grace upon grace, but there's more to follow." "I will uphold you in the hour of death, and as you are passing into the world of spirits, my mercy shall still continue with you, and when you land in the world to come there shall still be *more to follow*."

ADDITIONAL SCRIPTURE READING:
Matthew 7:11; 25:14–30; Revelation 2:26–28

Go to page 257 for your next devotional reading.

1700   1900

Beth Arabah to the Stone of Bohan son of Reuben. [7]The boundary then went up to Debir from the Valley of Achor and turned north to Gilgal, which faces the Pass of Adummim south of the gorge. It continued along to the waters of En Shemesh and came out at En Rogel. [8]Then it ran up the Valley of Ben Hinnom along the southern slope of the Jebusite city (that is, Jerusalem). From there it climbed to the top of the hill west of the Hinnom Valley at the northern end of the Valley of Rephaim. [9]From the hilltop the boundary headed toward the spring of the waters of Nephtoah, came out at the towns of Mount Ephron and went down toward Baalah (that is, Kiriath Jearim). [10]Then it curved westward from Baalah to Mount Seir, ran along the northern slope of Mount Jearim (that is, Kesalon), continued down to Beth Shemesh and crossed to Timnah. [11]It went to the northern slope of Ekron, turned toward Shikkeron, passed along to Mount Baalah and reached Jabneel. The boundary ended at the sea.

[12]The western boundary is the coastline of the Great Sea.[a] These are the boundaries around the people of Judah by their clans.

[13]In accordance with the LORD's command to him, Joshua gave to Caleb son of Jephunneh a portion in Judah—Kiriath Arba, that is, Hebron. (Arba was the forefather of Anak.) [14]From Hebron Caleb drove out the three Anakites—Sheshai, Ahiman and Talmai—descendants of Anak. [15]From there he marched against the people living in Debir (formerly called Kiriath Sepher). [16]And Caleb said, "I will give my daughter Acsah in marriage to the man who attacks and captures Kiriath Sepher." [17]Othniel son of Kenaz, Caleb's brother, took it; so Caleb gave his daughter Acsah to him in marriage.

[18]One day when she came to Othniel, she urged him[b] to ask her father for a field. When she got off her donkey, Caleb asked her, "What can I do for you?"

[19]She replied, "Do me a special favor. Since you have given me land in the Negev, give me also springs of water." So Caleb gave her the upper and lower springs.

[20]This is the inheritance of the tribe of Judah, clan by clan:

[21]The southernmost towns of the tribe of Judah in the Negev toward the boundary of Edom were:

Kabzeel, Eder, Jagur, [22]Kinah, Dimonah, Adadah, [23]Kedesh, Hazor, Ithnan, [24]Ziph, Telem, Bealoth, [25]Hazor Hadattah, Kerioth Hezron (that is, Hazor), [26]Amam, Shema, Moladah, [27]Hazar Gaddah, Heshmon, Beth Pelet, [28]Hazar Shual, Beersheba, Biziothiah, [29]Baalah, Iim, Ezem, [30]Eltolad, Kesil, Hormah, [31]Ziklag, Madmannah, Sansannah, [32]Lebaoth, Shilhim, Ain and Rimmon—a total of twenty-nine towns and their villages.

[33]In the western foothills:

Eshtaol, Zorah, Ashnah, [34]Zanoah, En Gannim, Tappuah, Enam, [35]Jarmuth, Adullam, Socoh, Azekah, [36]Shaaraim, Adithaim and Gederah (or Gederothaim)[c]—fourteen towns and their villages.

[37]Zenan, Hadashah, Migdal Gad, [38]Dilean, Mizpah, Joktheel, [39]Lachish, Bozkath, Eglon, [40]Cabbon, Lahmas, Kitlish, [41]Gederoth, Beth Dagon, Naamah and Makkedah—sixteen towns and their villages.

[42]Libnah, Ether, Ashan, [43]Iphtah, Ashnah, Nezib, [44]Keilah, Aczib and Mareshah—nine towns and their villages.

[45]Ekron, with its surrounding settlements and villages; [46]west of Ekron, all that were in the vicinity of Ashdod, together with their villages; [47]Ashdod, its surrounding settlements and villages; and Gaza, its settlements and villages, as far as the Wadi of Egypt and the coastline of the Great Sea.

[48]In the hill country:

Shamir, Jattir, Socoh, [49]Dannah,

---

[a] 12 That is, the Mediterranean; also in verse 47   [b] 18 Hebrew and some Septuagint manuscripts; other Septuagint manuscripts (see also note at Judges 1:14) *Othniel, he urged her*   [c] 36 Or *Gederah and Gederothaim*

Kiriath Sannah (that is, Debir),
50Anab, Eshtemoh, Anim, 51Goshen, Holon and Giloh—eleven towns and their villages.

52Arab, Dumah, Eshan, 53Janim, Beth Tappuah, Aphekah, 54Humtah, Kiriath Arba (that is, Hebron) and Zior—nine towns and their villages.

55Maon, Carmel, Ziph, Juttah, 56Jezreel, Jokdeam, Zanoah, 57Kain, Gibeah and Timnah—ten towns and their villages.

58Halhul, Beth Zur, Gedor, 59Maarath, Beth Anoth and Eltekon—six towns and their villages.

60Kiriath Baal (that is, Kiriath Jearim) and Rabbah—two towns and their villages.

61In the desert:
Beth Arabah, Middin, Secacah, 62Nibshan, the City of Salt and En Gedi—six towns and their villages.

63Judah could not dislodge the Jebusites, who were living in Jerusalem; to this day the Jebusites live there with the people of Judah.

Allotment for Ephraim and Manasseh

16 The allotment for Joseph began at the Jordan of Jericho,[a] east of the waters of Jericho, and went up from there through the desert into the hill country of Bethel. 2It went on from Bethel (that is, Luz),[b] crossed over to the territory of the Arkites in Ataroth, 3descended westward to the territory of the Japhletites as far as the region of Lower Beth Horon and on to Gezer, ending at the sea.

4So Manasseh and Ephraim, the descendants of Joseph, received their inheritance.

5This was the territory of Ephraim, clan by clan:

The boundary of their inheritance went from Ataroth Addar in the east to Upper Beth Horon 6and continued to the sea. From Micmethath on the north it curved eastward to Taanath Shiloh, passing by it to Janoah on the east. 7Then it

went down from Janoah to Ataroth and Naarah, touched Jericho and came out at the Jordan. 8From Tappuah the border went west to the Kanah Ravine and ended at the sea. This was the inheritance of the tribe of the Ephraimites, clan by clan. 9It also included all the towns and their villages that were set aside for the Ephraimites within the inheritance of the Manassites.

10They did not dislodge the Canaanites living in Gezer; to this day the Canaanites live among the people of Ephraim but are required to do forced labor.

17 This was the allotment for the tribe of Manasseh as Joseph's firstborn, that is, for Makir, Manasseh's firstborn. Makir was the ancestor of the Gileadites, who had received Gilead and Bashan because the Makirites were great soldiers. 2So this allotment was for the rest of the people of Manasseh—the clans of Abiezer, Helek, Asriel, Shechem, Hepher and Shemida. These are the other male descendants of Manasseh son of Joseph by their clans.

3Now Zelophehad son of Hepher, the son of Gilead, the son of Makir, the son of Manasseh, had no sons but only daughters, whose names were Mahlah, Noah, Hoglah, Milcah and Tirzah. 4They went to Eleazar the priest, Joshua son of Nun, and the leaders and said, "The LORD commanded Moses to give us an inheritance among our brothers." So Joshua gave them an inheritance along with the brothers of their father, according to the LORD's command. 5Manasseh's share consisted of ten tracts of land besides Gilead and Bashan east of the Jordan, 6because the daughters of the tribe of Manasseh received an inheritance among the sons. The land of Gilead belonged to the rest of the descendants of Manasseh.

7The territory of Manasseh extended from Asher to Micmethath east of Shechem. The boundary ran southward from there to include the people living at En Tappuah. 8(Manasseh had the land of Tappuah, but Tappuah itself, on the

---

a 1 Jordan of Jericho *was possibly an ancient name for the Jordan River.*   *b 2* Septuagint; Hebrew *Bethel to Luz*

boundary of Manasseh, belonged to the Ephraimites.) 9Then the boundary continued south to the Kanah Ravine. There were towns belonging to Ephraim lying among the towns of Manasseh, but the boundary of Manasseh was the northern side of the ravine and ended at the sea. 10On the south the land belonged to Ephraim, on the north to Manasseh. The territory of Manasseh reached the sea and bordered Asher on the north and Issachar on the east.

11Within Issachar and Asher, Manasseh also had Beth Shan, Ibleam and the people of Dor, Endor, Taanach and Megiddo, together with their surrounding settlements (the third in the list is Naphoth*a*).

12Yet the Manassites were not able to occupy these towns, for the Canaanites were determined to live in that region. 13However, when the Israelites grew stronger, they subjected the Canaanites to forced labor but did not drive them out completely.

14The people of Joseph said to Joshua, "Why have you given us only one allotment and one portion for an inheritance? We are a numerous people and the LORD has blessed us abundantly."

15"If you are so numerous," Joshua answered, "and if the hill country of Ephraim is too small for you, go up into the forest and clear land for yourselves there in the land of the Perizzites and Rephaites."

16The people of Joseph replied, "The hill country is not enough for us, and all the Canaanites who live in the plain have iron chariots, both those in Beth Shan and its settlements and those in the Valley of Jezreel."

17But Joshua said to the house of Joseph—to Ephraim and Manasseh— "You are numerous and very powerful. You will have not only one allotment 18but the forested hill country as well. Clear it, and its farthest limits will be yours; though the Canaanites have iron chariots and though they are strong, you can drive them out."

Division of the Rest of the Land

18 The whole assembly of the Israelites gathered at Shiloh and set up the Tent of Meeting there. The country was brought under their control, 2but there were still seven Israelite tribes who had not yet received their inheritance.

3So Joshua said to the Israelites: "How long will you wait before you begin to take possession of the land that the LORD, the God of your fathers, has given you? 4Appoint three men from each tribe. I will send them out to make a survey of the land and to write a description of it, according to the inheritance of each. Then they will return to me. 5You are to divide the land into seven parts. Judah is to remain in its territory on the south and the house of Joseph in its territory on the north. 6After you have written descriptions of the seven parts of the land, bring them here to me and I will cast lots for you in the presence of the LORD our God. 7The Levites, however, do not get a portion among you, because the priestly service of the LORD is their inheritance. And Gad, Reuben and the half-tribe of Manasseh have already received their inheritance on the east side of the Jordan. Moses the servant of the LORD gave it to them."

8As the men started on their way to map out the land, Joshua instructed them, "Go and make a survey of the land and write a description of it. Then return to me, and I will cast lots for you here at Shiloh in the presence of the LORD." 9So the men left and went through the land. They wrote its description on a scroll, town by town, in seven parts, and returned to Joshua in the camp at Shiloh. 10Joshua then cast lots for them in Shiloh in the presence of the LORD, and there he distributed the land to the Israelites according to their tribal divisions.

Allotment for Benjamin

11The lot came up for the tribe of Benjamin, clan by clan. Their allotted territory lay between the tribes of Judah and Joseph:

12On the north side their boundary began at the Jordan, passed the

---

a 11 That is, Naphoth Dor

northern slope of Jericho and headed west into the hill country, coming out at the desert of Beth Aven. 13From there it crossed to the south slope of Luz (that is, Bethel) and went down to Ataroth Addar on the hill south of Lower Beth Horon.

14From the hill facing Beth Horon on the south the boundary turned south along the western side and came out at Kiriath Baal (that is, Kiriath Jearim), a town of the people of Judah. This was the western side.

15The southern side began at the outskirts of Kiriath Jearim on the west, and the boundary came out at the spring of the waters of Nephtoah. 16The boundary went down to

---

WEDNESDAY

THE CONCLUSION OF THE TASK
F. B. Meyer

VERSE: Joshua 18:3   PASSAGE: Joshua 18:1–10

oshua rebuked the inertness of the people. He said to the children of Israel, "How long are ye slack to go in to possess the land, which the LORD God of your fathers hath given you?" (18:3, KJV). At that point the twenty-one commissioners arose to walk through the land and surveyed it . . . It may be that the account of what they had seen was the means under God of arousing the people from the apathy into which they had sunk.

Too long have we been slack to go in to possess that fullness of the Holy Spirit that might be in us as a living spring, making us perfectly satisfied. There is a knowledge of Jesus, a participation in his victory, a realization of blessedness, which are as much beyond the ordinary experience of Christians as Canaan was better than the wilderness. But how sad, that of all this we know so little.

How much we miss! The nomad life could not afford those seven tribes so much lasting enjoyment as their own freehold in Canaan. But the comparison is utterly inadequate to portray the loss to which we subject ourselves in refusing to appropriate and enjoy the blessedness that is laid up for us in Jesus. Let us come to our Joshua at Shiloh, and ask him to lead us into each of these.

ADDITIONAL SCRIPTURE READING:
Proverbs 2:2–6; Hosea 6:3; Philippians 3:13–14

Go to page 268 for your next devotional reading.

1700   1900

the foot of the hill facing the Valley of Ben Hinnom, north of the Valley of Rephaim. It continued down the Hinnom Valley along the southern slope of the Jebusite city and so to En Rogel. [17]It then curved north, went to En Shemesh, continued to Geliloth, which faces the Pass of Adummim, and ran down to the Stone of Bohan son of Reuben. [18]It continued to the northern slope of Beth Araba[a] and on down into the Arabah. [19]It then went to the northern slope of Beth Hoglah and came out at the northern bay of the Salt Sea,[b] at the mouth of the Jordan in the south. This was the southern boundary.

[20]The Jordan formed the boundary on the eastern side.

These were the boundaries that marked out the inheritance of the clans of Benjamin on all sides.

[21]The tribe of Benjamin, clan by clan, had the following cities:

Jericho, Beth Hoglah, Emek Keziz, [22]Beth Arabah, Zemaraim, Bethel, [23]Avvim, Parah, Ophrah, [24]Kephar Ammoni, Ophni and Geba—twelve towns and their villages.

[25]Gibeon, Ramah, Beeroth, [26]Mizpah, Kephirah, Mozah, [27]Rekem, Irpeel, Taralah, [28]Zelah, Haeleph, the Jebusite city (that is, Jerusalem), Gibeah and Kiriath—fourteen towns and their villages.

This was the inheritance of Benjamin for its clans.

Allotment for Simeon

19 The second lot came out for the tribe of Simeon, clan by clan. Their inheritance lay within the territory of Judah. [2]It included:

Beersheba (or Sheba),[c] Moladah, [3]Hazar Shual, Balah, Ezem, [4]Eltolad, Bethul, Hormah, [5]Ziklag, Beth Marcaboth, Hazar Susah, [6]Beth Lebaoth and Sharuhen—thirteen towns and their villages;

[7]Ain, Rimmon, Ether and Ashan—four towns and their villages— [8]and all the villages around these towns as far as Baalath Beer (Ramah in the Negev).

This was the inheritance of the tribe of the Simeonites, clan by clan. [9]The inheritance of the Simeonites was taken from the share of Judah, because Judah's portion was more than they needed. So the Simeonites received their inheritance within the territory of Judah.

Allotment for Zebulun

[10]The third lot came up for Zebulun, clan by clan:

The boundary of their inheritance went as far as Sarid. [11]Going west it ran to Maralah, touched Dabbesheth, and extended to the ravine near Jokneam. [12]It turned east from Sarid toward the sunrise to the territory of Kisloth Tabor and went on to Daberath and up to Japhia. [13]Then it continued eastward to Gath Hepher and Eth Kazin; it came out at Rimmon and turned toward Neah. [14]There the boundary went around on the north to Hannathon and ended at the Valley of Iphtah El. [15]Included were Kattath, Nahalal, Shimron, Idalah and Bethlehem. There were twelve towns and their villages.

[16]These towns and their villages were the inheritance of Zebulun, clan by clan.

Allotment for Issachar

[17]The fourth lot came out for Issachar, clan by clan. [18]Their territory included:

Jezreel, Kesulloth, Shunem, [19]Hapharaim, Shion, Anaharath, [20]Rabbith, Kishion, Ebez, [21]Remeth, En Gannim, En Haddah and Beth Pazzez. [22]The boundary touched Tabor, Shahazumah and Beth Shemesh, and ended at the Jordan. There were sixteen towns and their villages.

[23]These towns and their villages were the inheritance of the tribe of Issachar, clan by clan.

Allotment for Asher

[24]The fifth lot came out for the tribe of Asher, clan by clan. [25]Their territory included:

Helkath, Hali, Beten, Acshaph, [26]Allammelech, Amad and Mishal.

On the west the boundary touched Carmel and Shihor Libnath. 27It then turned east toward Beth Dagon, touched Zebulun and the Valley of Iphtah El, and went north to Beth Emek and Neiel, passing Cabul on the left. 28It went to Abdon,*a* Rehob, Hammon and Kanah, as far as Greater Sidon. 29The boundary then turned back toward Ramah and went to the fortified city of Tyre, turned toward Hosah and came out at the sea in the region of Aczib, 30Ummah, Aphek and Rehob. There were twenty-two towns and their villages.
31These towns and their villages were the inheritance of the tribe of Asher, clan by clan.

Allotment for Naphtali

32The sixth lot came out for Naphtali, clan by clan:
33Their boundary went from Heleph and the large tree in Zaanannim, passing Adami Nekeb and Jabneel to Lakkum and ending at the Jordan. 34The boundary ran west through Aznoth Tabor and came out at Hukkok. It touched Zebulun on the south, Asher on the west and the Jordan*b* on the east. 35The fortified cities were Ziddim, Zer, Hammath, Rakkath, Kinnereth, 36Adamah, Ramah, Hazor, 37Kedesh, Edrei, En Hazor, 38Iron, Migdal El, Horem, Beth Anath and Beth Shemesh. There were nineteen towns and their villages.
39These towns and their villages were the inheritance of the tribe of Naphtali, clan by clan.

Allotment for Dan

40The seventh lot came out for the tribe of Dan, clan by clan. 41The territory of their inheritance included:
Zorah, Eshtaol, Ir Shemesh, 42Shaalabbin, Aijalon, Ithlah, 43Elon, Timnah, Ekron, 44Eltekeh, Gibbethon, Baalath, 45Jehud, Bene Berak, Gath Rimmon, 46Me Jarkon and Rakkon, with the area facing Joppa.

47(But the Danites had difficulty taking possession of their territory, so they went up and attacked Leshem, took it, put it to the sword and occupied it. They settled in Leshem and named it Dan after their forefather.) 48These towns and their villages were the inheritance of the tribe of Dan, clan by clan.

Allotment for Joshua

49When they had finished dividing the land into its allotted portions, the Israelites gave Joshua son of Nun an inheritance among them, 50as the LORD had commanded. They gave him the town he asked for—Timnath Serah*c* in the hill country of Ephraim. And he built up the town and settled there.
51These are the territories that Eleazar the priest, Joshua son of Nun and the heads of the tribal clans of Israel assigned by lot at Shiloh in the presence of the LORD at the entrance to the Tent of Meeting. And so they finished dividing the land.

Cities of Refuge

20 Then the LORD said to Joshua: 2"Tell the Israelites to designate the cities of refuge, as I instructed you through Moses, 3so that anyone who kills a person accidentally and unintentionally may flee there and find protection from the avenger of blood.
4"When he flees to one of these cities, he is to stand in the entrance of the city gate and state his case before the elders of that city. Then they are to admit him into their city and give him a place to live with them. 5If the avenger of blood pursues him, they must not surrender the one accused, because he killed his neighbor unintentionally and without malice aforethought. 6He is to stay in that city until he has stood trial before the assembly and until the death of the high priest who is serving at that time. Then he may go back to his own home in the town from which he fled."
7So they set apart Kedesh in Galilee in the hill country of Naphtali, Shechem in the hill country of Ephraim, and Kiriath

a 28 Some Hebrew manuscripts (see also Joshua 21:30); most Hebrew manuscripts *Ebron*   *b 34* Septuagint; Hebrew *west, and Judah, the Jordan,*   *c 50* Also known as *Timnath Heres* (see Judges 2:9)

Arba (that is, Hebron) in the hill country of Judah. [8]On the east side of the Jordan of Jericho[a] they designated Bezer in the desert on the plateau in the tribe of Reuben, Ramoth in Gilead in the tribe of Gad, and Golan in Bashan in the tribe of Manasseh. [9]Any of the Israelites or any alien living among them who killed someone accidentally could flee to these designated cities and not be killed by the avenger of blood prior to standing trial before the assembly.

Towns for the Levites

21 Now the family heads of the Levites approached Eleazar the priest, Joshua son of Nun, and the heads of the other tribal families of Israel [2]at Shiloh in Canaan and said to them, "The LORD commanded through Moses that you give us towns to live in, with pasturelands for our livestock." [3]So, as the LORD had commanded, the Israelites gave the Levites the following towns and pasturelands out of their own inheritance:

[4]The first lot came out for the Kohathites, clan by clan. The Levites who were descendants of Aaron the priest were allotted thirteen towns from the tribes of Judah, Simeon and Benjamin. [5]The rest of Kohath's descendants were allotted ten towns from the clans of the tribes of Ephraim, Dan and half of Manasseh.

[6]The descendants of Gershon were allotted thirteen towns from the clans of the tribes of Issachar, Asher, Naphtali and the half-tribe of Manasseh in Bashan.

[7]The descendants of Merari, clan by clan, received twelve towns from the tribes of Reuben, Gad and Zebulun.

[8]So the Israelites allotted to the Levites these towns and their pasturelands, as the LORD had commanded through Moses.

[9]From the tribes of Judah and Simeon they allotted the following towns by name [10](these towns were assigned to the descendants of Aaron who were from the Kohathite clans of the Levites, because the first lot fell to them): [11]They gave them Kiriath Arba (that is, Hebron), with its surrounding pastureland, in the hill country of Judah. (Arba was the forefather of Anak.) [12]But the fields and villages around the city they had given to Caleb son of Jephunneh as his possession.

[13]So to the descendants of Aaron the priest they gave Hebron (a city of refuge for one accused of murder), Libnah, [14]Jattir, Eshtemoa, [15]Holon, Debir, [16]Ain, Juttah and Beth Shemesh, together with their pasturelands—nine towns from these two tribes.

[17]And from the tribe of Benjamin they gave them Gibeon, Geba, [18]Anathoth and Almon, together with their pasturelands—four towns.

[19]All the towns for the priests, the descendants of Aaron, were thirteen, together with their pasturelands.

[20]The rest of the Kohathite clans of the Levites were allotted towns from the tribe of Ephraim:

[21]In the hill country of Ephraim they were given Shechem (a city of refuge for one accused of murder) and Gezer, [22]Kibzaim and Beth Horon, together with their pasturelands—four towns.

[23]Also from the tribe of Dan they received Eltekeh, Gibbethon, [24]Aijalon and Gath Rimmon, together with their pasturelands—four towns.

[25]From half the tribe of Manasseh they received Taanach and Gath Rimmon, together with their pasturelands—two towns.

[26]All these ten towns and their pasturelands were given to the rest of the Kohathite clans.

[27]The Levite clans of the Gershonites were given:

from the half-tribe of Manasseh,
Golan in Bashan (a city of refuge for one accused of murder) and Be Eshtarah, together with their pasturelands—two towns;
[28]from the tribe of Issachar,
Kishion, Daberath, [29]Jarmuth and En Gannim, together with their pasturelands—four towns;
[30]from the tribe of Asher,

---

[a] 8 *Jordan of Jericho* was possibly an ancient name for the Jordan River.

Mishal, Abdon, 31Helkath and Rehob, together with their pasturelands—four towns;
32from the tribe of Naphtali,
    Kedesh in Galilee (a city of refuge for one accused of murder), Hammoth Dor and Kartan, together with their pasturelands—three towns.
33All the towns of the Gershonite clans were thirteen, together with their pasturelands.

34The Merarite clans (the rest of the Levites) were given:
    from the tribe of Zebulun,
    Jokneam, Kartah, 35Dimnah and Nahalal, together with their pasturelands—four towns;
36from the tribe of Reuben,
    Bezer, Jahaz, 37Kedemoth and Mephaath, together with their pasturelands—four towns;
38from the tribe of Gad,
    Ramoth in Gilead (a city of refuge for one accused of murder), Mahanaim, 39Heshbon and Jazer, together with their pasturelands—four towns in all.
40All the towns allotted to the Merarite clans, who were the rest of the Levites, were twelve.
41The towns of the Levites in the territory held by the Israelites were forty-eight in all, together with their pasturelands. 42Each of these towns had pasturelands surrounding it; this was true for all these towns.

43So the LORD gave Israel all the land he had sworn to give their forefathers, and they took possession of it and settled there. 44The LORD gave them rest on every side, just as he had sworn to their forefathers. Not one of their enemies withstood them; the LORD handed all their enemies over to them. 45Not one of all the LORD's good promises to the house of Israel failed; every one was fulfilled.

Eastern Tribes Return Home

22 Then Joshua summoned the Reubenites, the Gadites and the half-tribe of Manasseh 2and said to them, "You have done all that Moses the servant of the LORD commanded, and you have obeyed me in everything I commanded. 3For a long time now—to this very day—you have not deserted your brothers but have carried out the mission the LORD your God gave you. 4Now that the LORD your God has given your brothers rest as he promised, return to your homes in the land that Moses the servant of the LORD gave you on the other side of the Jordan. 5But be very careful to keep the commandment and the law that Moses the servant of the LORD gave you: to love the LORD your God, to walk in all his ways, to obey his commands, to hold fast to him and to serve him with all your heart and all your soul."

6Then Joshua blessed them and sent them away, and they went to their homes. 7(To the half-tribe of Manasseh Moses had given land in Bashan, and to the other half of the tribe Joshua gave land on the west side of the Jordan with their brothers.) When Joshua sent them home, he blessed them, 8saying, "Return to your homes with your great wealth—with large herds of livestock, with silver, gold, bronze and iron, and a great quantity of clothing—and divide with your brothers the plunder from your enemies."

9So the Reubenites, the Gadites and the half-tribe of Manasseh left the Israelites at Shiloh in Canaan to return to Gilead, their own land, which they had acquired in accordance with the command of the LORD through Moses.

10When they came to Geliloth near the Jordan in the land of Canaan, the Reubenites, the Gadites and the half-tribe of Manasseh built an imposing altar there by the Jordan. 11And when the Israelites heard that they had built the altar on the border of Canaan at Geliloth near the Jordan on the Israelite side, 12the whole assembly of Israel gathered at Shiloh to go to war against them.

13So the Israelites sent Phinehas son of Eleazar, the priest, to the land of Gilead—to Reuben, Gad and the half-tribe of Manasseh. 14With him they sent ten of the chief men, one for each of the tribes of Israel, each the head of a family division among the Israelite clans.

15When they went to Gilead—to Reuben, Gad and the half-tribe of Manasseh—they said to them: 16"The whole assembly of the LORD says: 'How could you break faith with the God of Israel like this? How could you turn away from the LORD and build yourselves an altar in rebellion against him now? ¹⁷Was not the sin of Peor enough for us? Up to this very day we have not cleansed ourselves from that sin, even though a plague fell on the community of the LORD! ¹⁸And are you now turning away from the LORD?

" 'If you rebel against the LORD today, tomorrow he will be angry with the whole community of Israel. ¹⁹If the land you possess is defiled, come over to the LORD's land, where the LORD's tabernacle stands, and share the land with us. But do not rebel against the LORD or against us by building an altar for yourselves, other than the altar of the LORD our God. ²⁰When Achan son of Zerah acted unfaithfully regarding the devoted things,ᵃ did not wrath come upon the whole community of Israel? He was not the only one who died for his sin.' "

²¹Then Reuben, Gad and the half-tribe of Manasseh replied to the heads of the clans of Israel: ²²"The Mighty One, God, the LORD! The Mighty One, God, the LORD! He knows! And let Israel know! If this has been in rebellion or disobedience to the LORD, do not spare us this day. ²³If we have built our own altar to turn away from the LORD and to offer burnt offerings and grain offerings, or to sacrifice fellowship offeringsᵇ on it, may the LORD himself call us to account.

²⁴"No! We did it for fear that some day your descendants might say to ours, 'What do you have to do with the LORD, the God of Israel? ²⁵The LORD has made the Jordan a boundary between us and you—you Reubenites and Gadites! You have no share in the LORD.' So your descendants might cause ours to stop fearing the LORD.

²⁶"That is why we said, 'Let us get ready and build an altar—but not for burnt offerings or sacrifices.' ²⁷On the contrary, it is to be a witness between us and you and the generations that follow, that we will worship the LORD at his sanctuary with our burnt offerings, sacrifices and fellowship offerings. Then in the future your descendants will not be able to say to ours, 'You have no share in the LORD.'

²⁸"And we said, 'If they ever say this to us, or to our descendants, we will answer: Look at the replica of the LORD's altar, which our fathers built, not for burnt offerings and sacrifices, but as a witness between us and you.'

²⁹"Far be it from us to rebel against the LORD and turn away from him today by building an altar for burnt offerings, grain offerings and sacrifices, other than the altar of the LORD our God that stands before his tabernacle."

³⁰When Phinehas the priest and the leaders of the community—the heads of the clans of the Israelites—heard what Reuben, Gad and Manasseh had to say, they were pleased. ³¹And Phinehas son of Eleazar, the priest, said to Reuben, Gad and Manasseh, "Today we know that the LORD is with us, because you have not acted unfaithfully toward the LORD in this matter. Now you have rescued the Israelites from the LORD's hand."

³²Then Phinehas son of Eleazar, the priest, and the leaders returned to Canaan from their meeting with the Reubenites and Gadites in Gilead and reported to the Israelites. ³³They were glad to hear the report and praised God. And they talked no more about going to war against them to devastate the country where the Reubenites and the Gadites lived.

³⁴And the Reubenites and the Gadites gave the altar this name: A Witness Between Us that the LORD is God.

Joshua's Farewell to the Leaders

23 After a long time had passed and the LORD had given Israel rest from all their enemies around them, Joshua, by then old and well advanced in years, ²summoned all Israel—their elders, leaders, judges and officials—and said to them: "I am old and well advanced in years. ³You yourselves have seen everything the LORD your God has done to all these nations for your sake; it was the LORD your God who fought for you. ⁴Remember how I have allotted as an inheritance for your tribes all the

---

ᵃ 20 The Hebrew term refers to the irrevocable giving over of things or persons to the LORD, often by totally destroying them.   ᵇ 23 Traditionally *peace offerings*; also in verse 27

land of the nations that remain—the nations I conquered—between the Jordan and the Great Sea*a* in the west. 5The LORD your God himself will drive them out of your way. He will push them out before you, and you will take possession of their land, as the LORD your God promised you.

6"Be very strong; be careful to obey all that is written in the Book of the Law of Moses, without turning aside to the right or to the left. 7Do not associate with these nations that remain among you; do not invoke the names of their gods or swear by them. You must not serve them or bow down to them. 8But you are to hold fast to the LORD your God, as you have until now.

9"The LORD has driven out before you great and powerful nations; to this day no one has been able to withstand you. 10One of you routs a thousand, because the LORD your God fights for you, just as he promised. 11So be very careful to love the LORD your God.

12"But if you turn away and ally yourselves with the survivors of these nations that remain among you and if you intermarry with them and associate with them, 13then you may be sure that the LORD your God will no longer drive out these nations before you. Instead, they will become snares and traps for you, whips on your backs and thorns in your eyes, until you perish from this good land, which the LORD your God has given you.

14"Now I am about to go the way of all the earth. You know with all your heart and soul that not one of all the good promises the LORD your God gave you has failed. Every promise has been fulfilled; not one has failed. 15But just as every good promise of the LORD your God has come true, so the LORD will bring on you all the evil he has threatened, until he has destroyed you from this good land he has given you. 16If you violate the covenant of the LORD your God, which he commanded you, and go and serve other gods and bow down to them, the LORD's anger will burn against you, and you will quickly perish from the good land he has given you."

The Covenant Renewed at Shechem

24 Then Joshua assembled all the tribes of Israel at Shechem. He summoned the elders, leaders, judges and officials of Israel, and they presented themselves before God.

2Joshua said to all the people, "This is what the LORD, the God of Israel, says: 'Long ago your forefathers, including Terah the father of Abraham and Nahor, lived beyond the River*b* and worshiped other gods. 3But I took your father Abraham from the land beyond the River and led him throughout Canaan and gave him many descendants. I gave him Isaac, 4and to Isaac I gave Jacob and Esau. I assigned the hill country of Seir to Esau, but Jacob and his sons went down to Egypt.

5" 'Then I sent Moses and Aaron, and I afflicted the Egyptians by what I did there, and I brought you out. 6When I brought your fathers out of Egypt, you came to the sea, and the Egyptians pursued them with chariots and horsemen*c* as far as the Red Sea.*d* 7But they cried to the LORD for help, and he put darkness between you and the Egyptians; he brought the sea over them and covered them. You saw with your own eyes what I did to the Egyptians. Then you lived in the desert for a long time.

8" 'I brought you to the land of the Amorites who lived east of the Jordan. They fought against you, but I gave them into your hands. I destroyed them from before you, and you took possession of their land. 9When Balak son of Zippor, the king of Moab, prepared to fight against Israel, he sent for Balaam son of Beor to put a curse on you. 10But I would not listen to Balaam, so he blessed you again and again, and I delivered you out of his hand.

11" 'Then you crossed the Jordan and came to Jericho. The citizens of Jericho fought against you, as did also the Amorites, Perizzites, Canaanites, Hittites, Girgashites, Hivites and Jebusites, but I gave them into your hands. 12I sent the hornet ahead of you, which drove them out before you—also the two Amorite kings. You did not do it with your own sword and bow. 13So I gave you a land on

---

a 4 That is, the Mediterranean   *b 2* That is, the Euphrates; also in verses 3, 14 and 15
c 6 Or *charioteers*   *d 6* Hebrew *Yam Suph*; that is, Sea of Reeds

which you did not toil and cities you did not build; and you live in them and eat from vineyards and olive groves that you did not plant.'

¹⁴"Now fear the LORD and serve him with all faithfulness. Throw away the gods your forefathers worshiped beyond the River and in Egypt, and serve the LORD. ¹⁵But if serving the LORD seems undesirable to you, then choose for yourselves this day whom you will serve, whether the gods your forefathers served beyond the River, or the gods of the Amorites, in whose land you are living. But as for me and my household, we will serve the LORD."

¹⁶Then the people answered, "Far be it from us to forsake the LORD to serve other gods! ¹⁷It was the LORD our God himself who brought us and our fathers up out of Egypt, from that land of slavery, and performed those great signs before our eyes. He protected us on our entire journey and among all the nations through which we traveled. ¹⁸And the LORD drove out before us all the nations, including the Amorites, who lived in the land. We too will serve the LORD, because he is our God."

¹⁹Joshua said to the people, "You are not able to serve the LORD. He is a holy God; he is a jealous God. He will not forgive your rebellion and your sins. ²⁰If you forsake the LORD and serve foreign gods, he will turn and bring disaster on you and make an end of you, after he has been good to you."

²¹But the people said to Joshua, "No! We will serve the LORD."

²²Then Joshua said, "You are witnesses against yourselves that you have chosen to serve the LORD."

"Yes, we are witnesses," they replied.

²³"Now then," said Joshua, "throw away the foreign gods that are among you and yield your hearts to the LORD, the God of Israel."

²⁴And the people said to Joshua, "We will serve the LORD our God and obey him."

²⁵On that day Joshua made a covenant for the people, and there at Shechem he drew up for them decrees and laws. ²⁶And Joshua recorded these things in the Book of the Law of God. Then he took a large stone and set it up there under the oak near the holy place of the LORD.

²⁷"See!" he said to all the people. "This stone will be a witness against us. It has heard all the words the LORD has said to us. It will be a witness against you if you are untrue to your God."

Buried in the Promised Land

²⁸Then Joshua sent the people away, each to his own inheritance.

²⁹After these things, Joshua son of Nun, the servant of the LORD, died at the age of a hundred and ten. ³⁰And they buried him in the land of his inheritance, at Timnath Serah*a* in the hill country of Ephraim, north of Mount Gaash.

³¹Israel served the LORD throughout the lifetime of Joshua and of the elders who outlived him and who had experienced everything the LORD had done for Israel.

³²And Joseph's bones, which the Israelites had brought up from Egypt, were buried at Shechem in the tract of land that Jacob bought for a hundred pieces of silver*b* from the sons of Hamor, the father of Shechem. This became the inheritance of Joseph's descendants.

³³And Eleazar son of Aaron died and was buried at Gibeah, which had been allotted to his son Phinehas in the hill country of Ephraim.

---

a 30 Also known as *Timnath Heres* (see Judges 2:9) unit of money of unknown weight and value.   *b 32* Hebrew *hundred kesitahs;* a kesitah was a

JUDGES

HE BOOK OF JUDGES TELLS THE ACCOUNT OF ISRAEL'S FREQUENT FAILURES AND APOSTASY, WHICH IN TURN PROVOKES GOD'S CHASTENING. IT ALSO TELLS OF THE PEOPLE'S URGENT APPEALS TO GOD IN TIMES OF CRISIS, MOVING HIM TO RAISE UP LEADERS (JUDGES) THROUGH WHOM HE THROWS OFF OPPRESSION AND RESTORES THE LAND TO PEACE. JUDGES REMINDS US TO LET GO OF OUR REBELLION AND FIND JOY IN GOD'S FIRM BUT LOVING AND FORGIVING PRESENCE.

Israel Fights the Remaining Canaanites

1 After the death of Joshua, the Israelites asked the LORD, "Who will be the first to go up and fight for us against the Canaanites?"

²The LORD answered, "Judah is to go; I have given the land into their hands."

³Then the men of Judah said to the Simeonites their brothers, "Come up with us into the territory allotted to us, to fight against the Canaanites. We in turn will go with you into yours." So the Simeonites went with them.

⁴When Judah attacked, the LORD gave the Canaanites and Perizzites into their hands and they struck down ten thousand men at Bezek. ⁵It was there that they found Adoni-Bezek and fought against him, putting to rout the Canaan-ites and Perizzites. ⁶Adoni-Bezek fled, but they chased him and caught him, and cut off his thumbs and big toes.

⁷Then Adoni-Bezek said, "Seventy kings with their thumbs and big toes cut off have picked up scraps under my table. Now God has paid me back for what I did to them." They brought him to Jerusalem, and he died there.

⁸The men of Judah attacked Jerusalem also and took it. They put the city to the sword and set it on fire.

⁹After that, the men of Judah went down to fight against the Canaanites living in the hill country, the Negev and the western foothills. ¹⁰They advanced against the Canaanites living in Hebron (formerly called Kiriath Arba) and defeated Sheshai, Ahiman and Talmai. ¹¹From there they advanced against

the people living in Debir (formerly called Kiriath Sepher). 12And Caleb said, "I will give my daughter Acsah in marriage to the man who attacks and captures Kiriath Sepher." 13Othniel son of Kenaz, Caleb's younger brother, took it; so Caleb gave his daughter Acsah to him in marriage.

14One day when she came to Othniel, she urged him*a* to ask her father for a field. When she got off her donkey, Caleb asked her, "What can I do for you?"

15She replied, "Do me a special favor. Since you have given me land in the Negev, give me also springs of water." Then Caleb gave her the upper and lower springs.

16The descendants of Moses' father-in-law, the Kenite, went up from the City of Palms*b* with the men of Judah to live among the people of the Desert of Judah in the Negev near Arad.

17Then the men of Judah went with the Simeonites their brothers and attacked the Canaanites living in Zephath, and they totally destroyed*c* the city. Therefore it was called Hormah.*d* 18The men of Judah also took*e* Gaza, Ashkelon and Ekron—each city with its territory.

19The LORD was with the men of Judah. They took possession of the hill country, but they were unable to drive the people from the plains, because they had iron chariots. 20As Moses had promised, Hebron was given to Caleb, who drove from it the three sons of Anak. 21The Benjamites, however, failed to dislodge the Jebusites, who were living in Jerusalem; to this day the Jebusites live there with the Benjamites.

22Now the house of Joseph attacked Bethel, and the LORD was with them. 23When they sent men to spy out Bethel (formerly called Luz), 24the spies saw a man coming out of the city and they said to him, "Show us how to get into the city and we will see that you are treated well." 25So he showed them, and they put the city to the sword but spared the man and his whole family. 26He then went to the land of the Hittites,

where he built a city and called it Luz, which is its name to this day.

27But Manasseh did not drive out the people of Beth Shan or Taanach or Dor or Ibleam or Megiddo and their surrounding settlements, for the Canaanites were determined to live in that land. 28When Israel became strong, they pressed the Canaanites into forced labor but never drove them out completely. 29Nor did Ephraim drive out the Canaanites living in Gezer, but the Canaanites continued to live there among them. 30Neither did Zebulun drive out the Canaanites living in Kitron or Nahalol, who remained among them; but they did subject them to forced labor. 31Nor did Asher drive out those living in Acco or Sidon or Ahlab or Aczib or Helbah or Aphek or Rehob, 32and because of this the people of Asher lived among the Canaanite inhabitants of the land. 33Neither did Naphtali drive out those living in Beth Shemesh or Beth Anath; but the Naphtalites too lived among the Canaanite inhabitants of the land, and those living in Beth Shemesh and Beth Anath became forced laborers for them. 34The Amorites confined the Danites to the hill country, not allowing them to come down into the plain. 35And the Amorites were determined also to hold out in Mount Heres, Aijalon and Shaalbim, but when the power of the house of Joseph increased, they too were pressed into forced labor. 36The boundary of the Amorites was from Scorpion*f* Pass to Sela and beyond.

The Angel of the LORD at Bokim

2 The angel of the LORD went up from Gilgal to Bokim and said, "I brought you up out of Egypt and led you into the land that I swore to give to your forefathers. I said, 'I will never break my covenant with you, 2and you shall not make a covenant with the people of this land, but you shall break down their altars.' Yet you have disobeyed me. Why have you done this? 3Now therefore I tell you that I will not

---

a 14 Hebrew; Septuagint and Vulgate *Othniel, he urged her*   *b 16* That is, Jericho   *c 17* The Hebrew term refers to the irrevocable giving over of things or persons to the LORD, often by totally destroying them.   *d 17 Hormah* means *destruction.*   *e 18* Hebrew; Septuagint *Judah did not take*
f 36 Hebrew *Akrabbim*

drive them out before you; they will be ⌊thorns⌋ in your sides and their gods will be a snare to you."

⁴When the angel of the LORD had spoken these things to all the Israelites, the people wept aloud, ⁵and they called that place Bokim.ᵃ There they offered sacrifices to the LORD.

Disobedience and Defeat

⁶After Joshua had dismissed the Israelites, they went to take possession of the land, each to his own inheritance. ⁷The people served the LORD throughout the lifetime of Joshua and of the elders who outlived him and who had seen all the great things the LORD had done for Israel.

⁸Joshua son of Nun, the servant of the LORD, died at the age of a hundred and ten. ⁹And they buried him in the land of his inheritance, at Timnath Heresᵇ in the hill country of Ephraim, north of Mount Gaash.

¹⁰After that whole generation had been gathered to their fathers, another generation grew up, who knew neither the LORD nor what he had done for Israel. ¹¹Then the Israelites did evil in the eyes of the LORD and served the Baals. ¹²They forsook the LORD, the God of their fathers, who had brought them out of Egypt. They followed and worshiped various gods of the peoples around them. They provoked the LORD to anger ¹³because they forsook him and served Baal and the Ashtoreths. ¹⁴In his anger against Israel the LORD handed them over to raiders who plundered them. He sold them to their enemies all around, whom they were no longer able to resist. ¹⁵Whenever Israel went out to fight, the hand of the LORD was against them to defeat them, just as he had sworn to them. They were in great distress.

¹⁶Then the LORD raised up judges,ᶜ who saved them out of the hands of these raiders. ¹⁷Yet they would not listen to their judges but prostituted themselves to other gods and worshiped them. Unlike their fathers, they quickly turned from the way in which their fathers had walked, the way of obedience to the LORD's commands. ¹⁸Whenever

the LORD raised up a judge for them, he was with the judge and saved them out of the hands of their enemies as long as the judge lived; for the LORD had compassion on them as they groaned under those who oppressed and afflicted them. ¹⁹But when the judge died, the people returned to ways even more corrupt than those of their fathers, following other gods and serving and worshiping them. They refused to give up their evil practices and stubborn ways.

²⁰Therefore the LORD was very angry with Israel and said, "Because this nation has violated the covenant that I laid down for their forefathers and has not listened to me, ²¹I will no longer drive out before them any of the nations Joshua left when he died. ²²I will use them to test Israel and see whether they will keep the way of the LORD and walk in it as their forefathers did." ²³The LORD had allowed those nations to remain; he did not drive them out at once by giving them into the hands of Joshua.

3 These are the nations the LORD left to test all those Israelites who had not experienced any of the wars in Canaan ²(he did this only to teach warfare to the descendants of the Israelites who had not had previous battle experience): ³the five rulers of the Philistines, all the Canaanites, the Sidonians, and the Hivites living in the Lebanon mountains from Mount Baal Hermon to Leboᵈ Hamath. ⁴They were left to test the Israelites to see whether they would obey the LORD's commands, which he had given their forefathers through Moses.

⁵The Israelites lived among the Canaanites, Hittites, Amorites, Perizzites, Hivites and Jebusites. ⁶They took their daughters in marriage and gave their own daughters to their sons, and served their gods.

Othniel

⁷The Israelites did evil in the eyes of the LORD; they forgot the LORD their God and served the Baals and the Asherahs. ⁸The anger of the LORD burned against Israel so that he sold them into

---

ᵃ 5 *Bokim* means *weepers.*   ᵇ 9 Also known as *Timnath Serah* (see Joshua 19:50 and 24:30)
ᶜ 16 Or *leaders;* similarly in verses 17–19   ᵈ 3 Or *to the entrance to*

the hands of Cushan-Rishathaim king of Aram Naharaim,[a] to whom the Israelites were subject for eight years. 9But when they cried out to the LORD, he raised up for them a deliverer, Othniel son of Kenaz, Caleb's younger brother, who saved them. 10The Spirit of the LORD came upon him, so that he became

[a] 8 That is, Northwest Mesopotamia

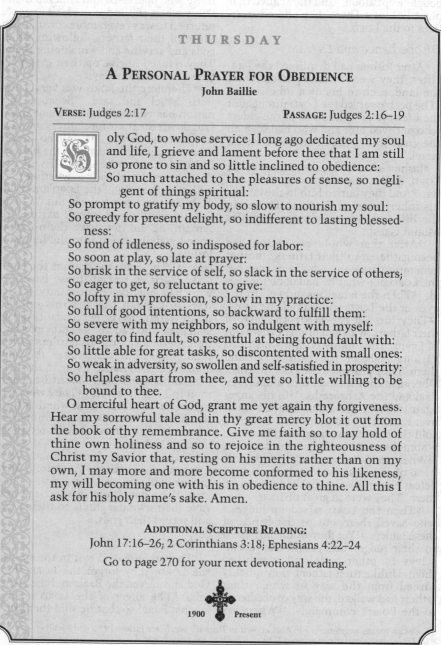

THURSDAY

A PERSONAL PRAYER FOR OBEDIENCE
John Baillie

VERSE: Judges 2:17   **PASSAGE:** Judges 2:16–19

oly God, to whose service I long ago dedicated my soul and life, I grieve and lament before thee that I am still so prone to sin and so little inclined to obedience:
So much attached to the pleasures of sense, so negligent of things spiritual:
So prompt to gratify my body, so slow to nourish my soul:
So greedy for present delight, so indifferent to lasting blessedness:
So fond of idleness, so indisposed for labor:
So soon at play, so late at prayer:
So brisk in the service of self, so slack in the service of others;
So eager to get, so reluctant to give:
So lofty in my profession, so low in my practice:
So full of good intentions, so backward to fulfill them:
So severe with my neighbors, so indulgent with myself:
So eager to find fault, so resentful at being found fault with:
So little able for great tasks, so discontented with small ones:
So weak in adversity, so swollen and self-satisfied in prosperity:
So helpless apart from thee, and yet so little willing to be bound to thee.
O merciful heart of God, grant me yet again thy forgiveness. Hear my sorrowful tale and in thy great mercy blot it out from the book of thy remembrance. Give me faith so to lay hold of thine own holiness and so to rejoice in the righteousness of Christ my Savior that, resting on his merits rather than on my own, I may more and more become conformed to his likeness, my will becoming one with his in obedience to thine. All this I ask for his holy name's sake. Amen.

ADDITIONAL SCRIPTURE READING:
John 17:16–26; 2 Corinthians 3:18; Ephesians 4:22–24

Go to page 270 for your next devotional reading.

1900   Present

Israel's judge[a] and went to war. The LORD gave Cushan-Rishathaim king of Aram into the hands of Othniel, who overpowered him. [11]So the land had peace for forty years, until Othniel son of Kenaz died.

Ehud

[12]Once again the Israelites did evil in the eyes of the LORD, and because they did this evil the LORD gave Eglon king of Moab power over Israel. [13]Getting the Ammonites and Amalekites to join him, Eglon came and attacked Israel, and they took possession of the City of Palms.[b] [14]The Israelites were subject to Eglon king of Moab for eighteen years.

[15]Again the Israelites cried out to the LORD, and he gave them a deliverer— Ehud, a left-handed man, the son of Gera the Benjamite. The Israelites sent him with tribute to Eglon king of Moab. [16]Now Ehud had made a double-edged sword about a foot and a half[c] long, which he strapped to his right thigh under his clothing. [17]He presented the tribute to Eglon king of Moab, who was a very fat man. [18]After Ehud had presented the tribute, he sent on their way the men who had carried it. [19]At the idols[d] near Gilgal he himself turned back and said, "I have a secret message for you, O king."

The king said, "Quiet!" And all his attendants left him.

[20]Ehud then approached him while he was sitting alone in the upper room of his summer palace[e] and said, "I have a message from God for you." As the king rose from his seat, [21]Ehud reached with his left hand, drew the sword from his right thigh and plunged it into the king's belly. [22]Even the handle sank in after the blade, which came out his back. Ehud did not pull the sword out, and the fat closed in over it. [23]Then Ehud went out to the porch[f]; he shut the doors of the upper room behind him and locked them.

[24]After he had gone, the servants came and found the doors of the upper room locked. They said, "He must be relieving himself in the inner room of the house." [25]They waited to the point of embarrassment, but when he did not open the doors of the room, they took a key and unlocked them. There they saw their lord fallen to the floor, dead.

[26]While they waited, Ehud got away. He passed by the idols and escaped to Seirah. [27]When he arrived there, he blew a trumpet in the hill country of Ephraim, and the Israelites went down with him from the hills, with him leading them.

[28]"Follow me," he ordered, "for the LORD has given Moab, your enemy, into your hands." So they followed him down and, taking possession of the fords of the Jordan that led to Moab, they allowed no one to cross over. [29]At that time they struck down about ten thousand Moabites, all vigorous and strong; not a man escaped. [30]That day Moab was made subject to Israel, and the land had peace for eighty years.

Shamgar

[31]After Ehud came Shamgar son of Anath, who struck down six hundred Philistines with an oxgoad. He too saved Israel.

Deborah

4 After Ehud died, the Israelites once again did evil in the eyes of the LORD. [2]So the LORD sold them into the hands of Jabin, a king of Canaan, who reigned in Hazor. The commander of his army was Sisera, who lived in Harosheth Haggoyim. [3]Because he had nine hundred iron chariots and had cruelly oppressed the Israelites for twenty years, they cried to the LORD for help.

[4]Deborah, a prophetess, the wife of Lappidoth, was leading[g] Israel at that time. [5]She held court under the Palm of Deborah between Ramah and Bethel in the hill country of Ephraim, and the Israelites came to her to have their disputes decided. [6]She sent for Barak son of Abinoam from Kedesh in Naphtali and said to him, "The LORD, the God of Israel, commands you: 'Go, take with you ten thousand men of Naphtali and Zebulun and lead the way to Mount Tabor. [7]I will lure Sisera, the commander of Jabin's army, with his chariots and his

---

[a] 10 Or leader   [b] 13 That is, Jericho   [c] 16 Hebrew a cubit (about 0.5 meter)   [d] 19 Or the stone quarries; also in verse 26   [e] 20 The meaning of the Hebrew for this phrase is uncertain.   [f] 23 The meaning of the Hebrew for this word is uncertain.   [g] 4 Traditionally judging

troops to the Kishon River and give him into your hands.' "

⁸Barak said to her, "If you go with me, I will go; but if you don't go with me, I won't go."

⁹"Very well," Deborah said, "I will go with you. But because of the way you are going about this,ᵃ the honor will not be yours, for the LORD will hand Sisera over to a woman." So Deborah went

with Barak to Kedesh, ¹⁰where he summoned Zebulun and Naphtali. Ten thousand men followed him, and Deborah also went with him.

¹¹Now Heber the Kenite had left the other Kenites, the descendants of Hobab, Moses' brother-in-law,ᵇ and pitched his tent by the great tree in Zaanannim near Kedesh.

¹²When they told Sisera that Barak

ᵃ 9 Or But on the expedition you are undertaking   ᵇ 11 Or father-in-law

---

FRIDAY

GOD'S IMPARTIALITY
G. Campbell Morgan

VERSE: Judges 4:4   **PASSAGE:** Judges 4:1–10

n the light of subsequent Jewish prejudice against women as leaders, the story of Deborah is full of interest, as it reveals the fact that there never was any such prejudice in the mind of God. Whereas motherhood in all the sanctity and beauty of that great word, is the special function and glory of womanhood, yet when a woman is specially gifted for the exercise of prophetic and administrative work, she is not barred by any Divine law from such work. Deborah was a prophetess in the full sense of that word; that is, she was the inspired mouthpiece of the Word of God to her people. She also judged Israel, and whatever that meant in the case of the men who exercised that office, it also meant in her case. She was a savior, a deliverer; she administered the affairs of the people, and led them out of the circumstances of difficulty into which their sin had brought them . . . Ever and anon in the long history of God's patient dealing with men, we find him raising up some woman to lead, to guide, to inspire; and always there is this same element of enthusiasm and force. The one great message of the story seems to be that it warns us to take heed that we do not imagine ourselves to be wiser than God. When he calls and equips a woman to high service, let us beware lest we dishonor him by refusing to recognize her, or cooperate with her.

ADDITIONAL SCRIPTURE READING:
Judges 5:12–15; 2 Kings 22:14–20; Luke 2:36–38

Go to page 275 for your next devotional reading.

1900   Present

son of Abinoam had gone up to Mount Tabor, 13Sisera gathered together his nine hundred iron chariots and all the men with him, from Harosheth Haggoyim to the Kishon River.

14Then Deborah said to Barak, "Go! This is the day the LORD has given Sisera into your hands. Has not the LORD gone ahead of you?" So Barak went down Mount Tabor, followed by ten thousand men. 15At Barak's advance, the LORD routed Sisera and all his chariots and army by the sword, and Sisera abandoned his chariot and fled on foot. 16But Barak pursued the chariots and army as far as Harosheth Haggoyim. All the troops of Sisera fell by the sword; not a man was left.

17Sisera, however, fled on foot to the tent of Jael, the wife of Heber the Kenite, because there were friendly relations between Jabin king of Hazor and the clan of Heber the Kenite.

18Jael went out to meet Sisera and said to him, "Come, my lord, come right in. Don't be afraid." So he entered her tent, and she put a covering over him.

19"I'm thirsty," he said. "Please give me some water." She opened a skin of milk, gave him a drink, and covered him up.

20"Stand in the doorway of the tent," he told her. "If someone comes by and asks you, 'Is anyone here?' say 'No.' "

21But Jael, Heber's wife, picked up a tent peg and a hammer and went quietly to him while he lay fast asleep, exhausted. She drove the peg through his temple into the ground, and he died.

22Barak came by in pursuit of Sisera, and Jael went out to meet him. "Come," she said, "I will show you the man you're looking for." So he went in with her, and there lay Sisera with the tent peg through his temple—dead.

23On that day God subdued Jabin, the Canaanite king, before the Israelites. 24And the hand of the Israelites grew stronger and stronger against Jabin, the Canaanite king, until they destroyed him.

The Song of Deborah

5 On that day Deborah and Barak son of Abinoam sang this song:

2 "When the princes in Israel take the
    lead,
  when the people willingly offer
    themselves—
  praise the LORD!

3 "Hear this, you kings! Listen, you
    rulers!
  I will sing to*a* the LORD, I will sing;
  I will make music to*b* the LORD,
    the God of Israel.

4 "O LORD, when you went out from
    Seir,
  when you marched from the land
    of Edom,
  the earth shook, the heavens poured,
    the clouds poured down water.
5 The mountains quaked before the
    LORD, the One of Sinai,
  before the LORD, the God of Israel.

6 "In the days of Shamgar son of Anath,
  in the days of Jael, the roads were
    abandoned;
  travelers took to winding paths.
7 Village life*c* in Israel ceased,
  ceased until I,*d* Deborah, arose,
  arose a mother in Israel.
8 When they chose new gods,
  war came to the city gates,
  and not a shield or spear was seen
    among forty thousand in Israel.
9 My heart is with Israel's princes,
  with the willing volunteers among
    the people.
  Praise the LORD!

10 "You who ride on white donkeys,
  sitting on your saddle blankets,
  and you who walk along the road,
  consider 11the voice of the singers*e* at
    the watering places.
  They recite the righteous acts of
    the LORD,
  the righteous acts of his warriors*f*
    in Israel.

  "Then the people of the LORD
    went down to the city gates.
12 'Wake up, wake up, Deborah!

---

a 3 Or *of*   *b 3* Or */ with song I will praise*   *c 7* Or *Warriors*   *d 7* Or *you*   *e 11* Or *archers;* the meaning of the Hebrew for this word is uncertain.   *f 11* Or *villagers*

Wake up, wake up, break out in
    song!
Arise, O Barak!
    Take captive your captives, O son
      of Abinoam.'

13 "Then the men who were left
    came down to the nobles;
the people of the LORD
    came to me with the mighty.
14 Some came from Ephraim, whose
    roots were in Amalek;
Benjamin was with the people who
    followed you.
From Makir captains came down,
    from Zebulun those who bear a
      commander's staff.
15 The princes of Issachar were with
    Deborah;
yes, Issachar was with Barak,
    rushing after him into the valley.
In the districts of Reuben
    there was much searching of heart.
16 Why did you stay among the
    campfires[a]
to hear the whistling for the flocks?
In the districts of Reuben
    there was much searching of heart.
17 Gilead stayed beyond the Jordan.
    And Dan, why did he linger by the
      ships?
Asher remained on the coast
    and stayed in his coves.
18 The people of Zebulun risked their
    very lives;
so did Naphtali on the heights of
    the field.

19 "Kings came, they fought;
    the kings of Canaan fought
at Taanach by the waters of Megiddo,
    but they carried off no silver, no
      plunder.
20 From the heavens the stars fought,
    from their courses they fought
      against Sisera.
21 The river Kishon swept them away,
    the age-old river, the river Kishon.
March on, my soul; be strong!
22 Then thundered the horses' hoofs—
    galloping, galloping go his mighty
      steeds.
23 'Curse Meroz,' said the angel of the
    LORD.
    'Curse its people bitterly,

because they did not come to help
    the LORD,
to help the LORD against the
    mighty.'

24 "Most blessed of women be Jael,
    the wife of Heber the Kenite,
most blessed of tent-dwelling
    women.
25 He asked for water, and she gave him
    milk;
in a bowl fit for nobles she brought
    him curdled milk.
26 Her hand reached for the tent peg,
    her right hand for the workman's
      hammer.
She struck Sisera, she crushed his
    head,
    she shattered and pierced his
      temple.
27 At her feet he sank,
    he fell; there he lay.
At her feet he sank, he fell;
    where he sank, there he fell—dead.

28 "Through the window peered Sisera's
    mother;
    behind the lattice she cried out,
'Why is his chariot so long in coming?
Why is the clatter of his chariots
    delayed?'
29 The wisest of her ladies answer her;
    indeed, she keeps saying to herself,
30 'Are they not finding and dividing the
    spoils:
a girl or two for each man,
colorful garments as plunder for
    Sisera,
colorful garments embroidered,
highly embroidered garments for
    my neck—
all this as plunder?'

31 "So may all your enemies perish,
    O LORD!
But may they who love you be like
    the sun
    when it rises in its strength."

Then the land had peace forty years.

Gideon

6 Again the Israelites did evil in the eyes of the LORD, and for seven years he gave them into the hands

---

[a] 16 Or *saddlebags*

of the Midianites. ²Because the power of Midian was so oppressive, the Israelites prepared shelters for themselves in mountain clefts, caves and strongholds. ³Whenever the Israelites planted their crops, the Midianites, Amalekites and other eastern peoples invaded the country. ⁴They camped on the land and ruined the crops all the way to Gaza and did not spare a living thing for Israel, neither sheep nor cattle nor donkeys. ⁵They came up with their livestock and their tents like swarms of locusts. It was impossible to count the men and their camels; they invaded the land to ravage it. ⁶Midian so impoverished the Israelites that they cried out to the LORD for help.

⁷When the Israelites cried to the LORD because of Midian, ⁸he sent them a prophet, who said, "This is what the LORD, the God of Israel, says: I brought you up out of Egypt, out of the land of slavery. ⁹I snatched you from the power of Egypt and from the hand of all your oppressors. I drove them from before you and gave you their land. ¹⁰I said to you, 'I am the LORD your God; do not worship the gods of the Amorites, in whose land you live.' But you have not listened to me."

¹¹The angel of the LORD came and sat down under the oak in Ophrah that belonged to Joash the Abiezrite, where his son Gideon was threshing wheat in a winepress to keep it from the Midianites. ¹²When the angel of the LORD appeared to Gideon, he said, "The LORD is with you, mighty warrior."

¹³"But sir," Gideon replied, "if the LORD is with us, why has all this happened to us? Where are all his wonders that our fathers told us about when they said, 'Did not the LORD bring us up out of Egypt?' But now the LORD has abandoned us and put us into the hand of Midian."

¹⁴The LORD turned to him and said, "Go in the strength you have and save Israel out of Midian's hand. Am I not sending you?"

¹⁵"But Lord,ᵃ " Gideon asked, "how can I save Israel? My clan is the weakest in Manasseh, and I am the least in my family."

¹⁶The LORD answered, "I will be with you, and you will strike down all the Midianites together."

¹⁷Gideon replied, "If now I have found favor in your eyes, give me a sign that it is really you talking to me. ¹⁸Please do not go away until I come back and bring my offering and set it before you."

And the LORD said, "I will wait until you return."

¹⁹Gideon went in, prepared a young goat, and from an ephahᵇ of flour he made bread without yeast. Putting the meat in a basket and its broth in a pot, he brought them out and offered them to him under the oak.

²⁰The angel of God said to him, "Take the meat and the unleavened bread, place them on this rock, and pour out the broth." And Gideon did so. ²¹With the tip of the staff that was in his hand, the angel of the LORD touched the meat and the unleavened bread. Fire flared from the rock, consuming the meat and the bread. And the angel of the LORD disappeared. ²²When Gideon realized that it was the angel of the LORD, he exclaimed, "Ah, Sovereign LORD! I have seen the angel of the LORD face to face!"

²³But the LORD said to him, "Peace! Do not be afraid. You are not going to die."

²⁴So Gideon built an altar to the LORD there and called it The LORD is Peace. To this day it stands in Ophrah of the Abiezrites.

²⁵That same night the LORD said to him, "Take the second bull from your father's herd, the one seven years old.ᶜ Tear down your father's altar to Baal and cut down the Asherah poleᵈ beside it. ²⁶Then build a proper kind ofᵉ altar to the LORD your God on the top of this height. Using the wood of the Asherah pole that you cut down, offer the secondᶠ bull as a burnt offering."

²⁷So Gideon took ten of his servants and did as the LORD told him. But because he was afraid of his family and the men of the town, he did it at night rather than in the daytime.

²⁸In the morning when the men of the town got up, there was Baal's altar, demolished, with the Asherah pole

---

ᵃ 15 Or sir   ᵇ 19 That is, probably about 3/5 bushel (about 22 liters)   ᶜ 25 Or Take a full-grown, mature bull from your father's herd   ᵈ 25 That is, a symbol of the goddess Asherah; here and elsewhere in Judges   ᵉ 26 Or build with layers of stone an   ᶠ 26 Or full-grown; also in verse 28

beside it cut down and the second bull sacrificed on the newly built altar!

²⁹They asked each other, "Who did this?"

When they carefully investigated, they were told, "Gideon son of Joash did it."

³⁰The men of the town demanded of Joash, "Bring out your son. He must die, because he has broken down Baal's altar and cut down the Asherah pole beside it."

³¹But Joash replied to the hostile crowd around him, "Are you going to plead Baal's cause? Are you trying to save him? Whoever fights for him shall be put to death by morning! If Baal really is a god, he can defend himself when someone breaks down his altar." ³²So that day they called Gideon "Jerub-Baal,ᵃ" saying, "Let Baal contend with him," because he broke down Baal's altar.

³³Now all the Midianites, Amalekites and other eastern peoples joined forces and crossed over the Jordan and camped in the Valley of Jezreel. ³⁴Then the Spirit of the LORD came upon Gideon, and he blew a trumpet, summoning the Abiezrites to follow him. ³⁵He sent messengers throughout Manasseh, calling them to arms, and also into Asher, Zebulun and Naphtali, so that they too went up to meet them.

³⁶Gideon said to God, "If you will save Israel by my hand as you have promised— ³⁷look, I will place a wool fleece on the threshing floor. If there is dew only on the fleece and all the ground is dry, then I will know that you will save Israel by my hand, as you said." ³⁸And that is what happened. Gideon rose early the next day; he squeezed the fleece and wrung out the dew—a bowlful of water.

³⁹Then Gideon said to God, "Do not be angry with me. Let me make just one more request. Allow me one more test with the fleece. This time make the fleece dry and the ground covered with dew." ⁴⁰That night God did so. Only the fleece was dry; all the ground was covered with dew.

Gideon Defeats the Midianites

7 Early in the morning, Jerub-Baal (that is, Gideon) and all his men camped at the spring of Harod. The camp of Midian was north of them in the valley near the hill of Moreh. ²The LORD said to Gideon, "You have too many men for me to deliver Midian into their hands. In order that Israel may not boast against me that her own strength has saved her, ³announce now to the people, 'Anyone who trembles with fear may turn back and leave Mount Gilead.' " So twenty-two thousand men left, while ten thousand remained.

⁴But the LORD said to Gideon, "There are still too many men. Take them down to the water, and I will sift them for you there. If I say, 'This one shall go with you,' he shall go; but if I say, 'This one shall not go with you,' he shall not go."

⁵So Gideon took the men down to the water. There the LORD told him, "Separate those who lap the water with their tongues like a dog from those who kneel down to drink." ⁶Three hundred men lapped with their hands to their mouths. All the rest got down on their knees to drink.

⁷The LORD said to Gideon, "With the three hundred men that lapped I will save you and give the Midianites into your hands. Let all the other men go, each to his own place." ⁸So Gideon sent the rest of the Israelites to their tents but kept the three hundred, who took over the provisions and trumpets of the others.

Now the camp of Midian lay below him in the valley. ⁹During that night the LORD said to Gideon, "Get up, go down against the camp, because I am going to give it into your hands. ¹⁰If you are afraid to attack, go down to the camp with your servant Purah ¹¹and listen to what they are saying. Afterward, you will be encouraged to attack the camp." So he and Purah his servant went down to the outposts of the camp. ¹²The Midianites, the Amalekites and all the other eastern peoples had settled in the valley, thick as locusts. Their camels could no more be counted than the sand on the seashore.

¹³Gideon arrived just as a man was telling a friend his dream. "I had a dream," he was saying. "A round loaf of

---

ᵃ 32 *Jerub-Baal* means *let Baal contend*.

WEEKEND

FOR GOD'S GRACE IN OUR HELPLESSNESS
Peter Marshall

VERSE: Judges 7:2 **PASSAGE:** Judges 7:1–8, 20–21

 e know, our Father, that at this desperate hour in world affairs, we need thee. We need thy strength, thy guidance, thy wisdom.

There are problems far greater than any wisdom of man can solve. What shall our leaders do in such an hour?

May thy wisdom and thy power come upon the President of these United States, the Senators and Congressmen, to whom have been entrusted leadership. May the responsibility lie heavily on their hearts, until they are ready to acknowledge their helplessness and turn to thee. Give to them the honesty, the courage, and the moral integrity to confess that they don't know what to do. Only then can they lead us as a nation beyond human wisdom to thee, who alone hast the answer.

Lead us to this high adventure. Remind us that a "mighty fortress is our God"—not a hiding place where we can escape for an easy life, but rather an arsenal of courage and strength—the mightiest of all, who will march beside us into the battle for righteousness and world brotherhood.

O our God, may we never recover from our feeling of helplessness and our need of thee! In the strong name of Jesus, our Lord, we pray. Amen.

ADDITIONAL SCRIPTURE READING:
2 Chronicles 14:11; Zechariah 4:6; 2 Corinthians 4:6–7

Go to page 294 for your next devotional reading.

1900 Present

barley bread came tumbling into the Midianite camp. It struck the tent with such force that the tent overturned and collapsed."

14His friend responded, "This can be nothing other than the sword of Gideon son of Joash, the Israelite. God has given the Midianites and the whole camp into his hands."

15When Gideon heard the dream and its interpretation, he worshiped God. He returned to the camp of Israel and called out, "Get up! The LORD has given the Midianite camp into your hands." 16Dividing the three hundred men into three companies, he placed trumpets and empty jars in the hands of all of them, with torches inside.

17"Watch me," he told them. "Follow my lead. When I get to the edge of the camp, do exactly as I do. 18When I and all who are with me blow our trumpets, then from all around the camp blow yours and shout, 'For the LORD and for Gideon.' "

19Gideon and the hundred men with him reached the edge of the camp at the beginning of the middle watch, just after they had changed the guard. They blew their trumpets and broke the jars that were in their hands. 20The three companies blew the trumpets and smashed the jars. Grasping the torches in their left hands and holding in their right hands the trumpets they were to blow, they shouted, "A sword for the LORD and for Gideon!" 21While each man held his position around the camp, all the Midianites ran, crying out as they fled.

22When the three hundred trumpets sounded, the LORD caused the men throughout the camp to turn on each other with their swords. The army fled to Beth Shittah toward Zererah as far as the border of Abel Meholah near Tabbath. 23Israelites from Naphtali, Asher and all Manasseh were called out, and they pursued the Midianites. 24Gideon sent messengers throughout the hill country of Ephraim, saying, "Come down against the Midianites and seize the waters of the Jordan ahead of them as far as Beth Barah."

So all the men of Ephraim were called out and they took the waters of the Jordan as far as Beth Barah. 25They also captured two of the Midianite leaders, Oreb and Zeeb. They killed Oreb at the rock of Oreb, and Zeeb at the winepress of Zeeb. They pursued the Midianites and brought the heads of Oreb and Zeeb to Gideon, who was by the Jordan.

Zebah and Zalmunna

8 Now the Ephraimites asked Gideon, "Why have you treated us like this? Why didn't you call us when you went to fight Midian?" And they criticized him sharply.

2But he answered them, "What have I accomplished compared to you? Aren't the gleanings of Ephraim's grapes better than the full grape harvest of Abiezer? 3God gave Oreb and Zeeb, the Midianite leaders, into your hands. What was I able to do compared to you?" At this, their resentment against him subsided.

4Gideon and his three hundred men, exhausted yet keeping up the pursuit, came to the Jordan and crossed it. 5He said to the men of Succoth, "Give my troops some bread; they are worn out, and I am still pursuing Zebah and Zalmunna, the kings of Midian."

6But the officials of Succoth said, "Do you already have the hands of Zebah and Zalmunna in your possession? Why should we give bread to your troops?"

7Then Gideon replied, "Just for that, when the LORD has given Zebah and Zalmunna into my hand, I will tear your flesh with desert thorns and briers."

8From there he went up to Peniel[a] and made the same request of them, but they answered as the men of Succoth had. 9So he said to the men of Peniel, "When I return in triumph, I will tear down this tower."

10Now Zebah and Zalmunna were in Karkor with a force of about fifteen thousand men, all that were left of the armies of the eastern peoples; a hundred and twenty thousand swordsmen had fallen. 11Gideon went up by the route of the nomads east of Nobah and Jogbehah and fell upon the unsuspecting army. 12Zebah and Zalmunna, the two kings of Midian, fled, but he pursued them and captured them, routing their entire army.

a 8 Hebrew *Penuel*, a variant of *Peniel*; also in verses 9 and 17

¹³Gideon son of Joash then returned from the battle by the Pass of Heres. ¹⁴He caught a young man of Succoth and questioned him, and the young man wrote down for him the names of the seventy-seven officials of Succoth, the elders of the town. ¹⁵Then Gideon came and said to the men of Succoth, "Here are Zebah and Zalmunna, about whom you taunted me by saying, 'Do you already have the hands of Zebah and Zalmunna in your possession? Why should we give bread to your exhausted men?' " ¹⁶He took the elders of the town and taught the men of Succoth a lesson by punishing them with desert thorns and briers. ¹⁷He also pulled down the tower of Peniel and killed the men of the town.

¹⁸Then he asked Zebah and Zalmunna, "What kind of men did you kill at Tabor?"

"Men like you," they answered, "each one with the bearing of a prince."

¹⁹Gideon replied, "Those were my brothers, the sons of my own mother. As surely as the LORD lives, if you had spared their lives, I would not kill you." ²⁰Turning to Jether, his oldest son, he said, "Kill them!" But Jether did not draw his sword, because he was only a boy and was afraid.

²¹Zebah and Zalmunna said, "Come, do it yourself. 'As is the man, so is his strength.' " So Gideon stepped forward and killed them, and took the ornaments off their camels' necks.

Gideon's Ephod

²²The Israelites said to Gideon, "Rule over us—you, your son and your grandson—because you have saved us out of the hand of Midian."

²³But Gideon told them, "I will not rule over you, nor will my son rule over you. The LORD will rule over you." ²⁴And he said, "I do have one request, that each of you give me an earring from your share of the plunder." (It was the custom of the Ishmaelites to wear gold earrings.)

²⁵They answered, "We'll be glad to give them." So they spread out a garment, and each man threw a ring from his plunder onto it. ²⁶The weight of the gold rings he asked for came to seventeen hundred shekels,ᵃ not counting the ornaments, the pendants and the purple garments worn by the kings of Midian or the chains that were on their camels' necks. ²⁷Gideon made the gold into an ephod, which he placed in Ophrah, his town. All Israel prostituted themselves by worshiping it there, and it became a snare to Gideon and his family.

Gideon's Death

²⁸Thus Midian was subdued before the Israelites and did not raise its head again. During Gideon's lifetime, the land enjoyed peace forty years.

²⁹Jerub-Baal son of Joash went back home to live. ³⁰He had seventy sons of his own, for he had many wives. ³¹His concubine, who lived in Shechem, also bore him a son, whom he named Abimelech. ³²Gideon son of Joash died at a good old age and was buried in the tomb of his father Joash in Ophrah of the Abiezrites.

³³No sooner had Gideon died than the Israelites again prostituted themselves to the Baals. They set up Baal-Berith as their god and ³⁴did not remember the LORD their God, who had rescued them from the hands of all their enemies on every side. ³⁵They also failed to show kindness to the family of Jerub-Baal (that is, Gideon) for all the good things he had done for them.

Abimelech

9 Abimelech son of Jerub-Baal went to his mother's brothers in Shechem and said to them and to all his mother's clan, ²"Ask all the citizens of Shechem, 'Which is better for you: to have all seventy of Jerub-Baal's sons rule over you, or just one man?' Remember, I am your flesh and blood."

³When the brothers repeated all this to the citizens of Shechem, they were inclined to follow Abimelech, for they said, "He is our brother." ⁴They gave him seventy shekelsᵇ of silver from the temple of Baal-Berith, and Abimelech used it to hire reckless adventurers, who became his followers. ⁵He went to his father's home in Ophrah and on one stone murdered his seventy brothers,

ᵃ 26 That is, about 43 pounds (about 19.5 kilograms)   ᵇ 4 That is, about 1 3/4 pounds (about 0.8 kilogram)

the sons of Jerub-Baal. But Jotham, the youngest son of Jerub-Baal, escaped by hiding. 6Then all the citizens of Shechem and Beth Millo gathered beside the great tree at the pillar in Shechem to crown Abimelech king.

7When Jotham was told about this, he climbed up on the top of Mount Gerizim and shouted to them, "Listen to me, citizens of Shechem, so that God may listen to you. 8One day the trees went out to anoint a king for themselves. They said to the olive tree, 'Be our king.'

9"But the olive tree answered, 'Should I give up my oil, by which both gods and men are honored, to hold sway over the trees?'

10"Next, the trees said to the fig tree, 'Come and be our king.'

11"But the fig tree replied, 'Should I give up my fruit, so good and sweet, to hold sway over the trees?'

12"Then the trees said to the vine, 'Come and be our king.'

13"But the vine answered, 'Should I give up my wine, which cheers both gods and men, to hold sway over the trees?'

14"Finally all the trees said to the thornbush, 'Come and be our king.'

15"The thornbush said to the trees, 'If you really want to anoint me king over you, come and take refuge in my shade; but if not, then let fire come out of the thornbush and consume the cedars of Lebanon!'

16"Now if you have acted honorably and in good faith when you made Abimelech king, and if you have been fair to Jerub-Baal and his family, and if you have treated him as he deserves— 17and to think that my father fought for you, risked his life to rescue you from the hand of Midian 18(but today you have revolted against my father's family, murdered his seventy sons on a single stone, and made Abimelech, the son of his slave girl, king over the citizens of Shechem because he is your brother)— 19if then you have acted honorably and in good faith toward Jerub-Baal and his family today, may Abimelech be your joy, and may you be his, too! 20But if you have not, let fire come out from Abimelech and consume you, citizens of Shechem and Beth Millo, and let fire come out from you, citizens of Shechem and Beth Millo, and consume Abimelech!"

21Then Jotham fled, escaping to Beer, and he lived there because he was afraid of his brother Abimelech.

22After Abimelech had governed Israel three years, 23God sent an evil spirit between Abimelech and the citizens of Shechem, who acted treacherously against Abimelech. 24God did this in order that the crime against Jerub-Baal's seventy sons, the shedding of their blood, might be avenged on their brother Abimelech and on the citizens of Shechem, who had helped him murder his brothers. 25In opposition to him these citizens of Shechem set men on the hilltops to ambush and rob everyone who passed by, and this was reported to Abimelech.

26Now Gaal son of Ebed moved with his brothers into Shechem, and its citizens put their confidence in him. 27After they had gone out into the fields and gathered the grapes and trodden them, they held a festival in the temple of their god. While they were eating and drinking, they cursed Abimelech. 28Then Gaal son of Ebed said, "Who is Abimelech, and who is Shechem, that we should be subject to him? Isn't he Jerub-Baal's son, and isn't Zebul his deputy? Serve the men of Hamor, Shechem's father! Why should we serve Abimelech? 29If only this people were under my command! Then I would get rid of him. I would say to Abimelech, 'Call out your whole army!' "a

30When Zebul the governor of the city heard what Gaal son of Ebed said, he was very angry. 31Under cover he sent messengers to Abimelech, saying, "Gaal son of Ebed and his brothers have come to Shechem and are stirring up the city against you. 32Now then, during the night you and your men should come and lie in wait in the fields. 33In the morning at sunrise, advance against the city. When Gaal and his men come out against you, do whatever your hand finds to do."

34So Abimelech and all his troops set out by night and took up concealed positions near Shechem in four companies. 35Now Gaal son of Ebed had gone out and was standing at the entrance to the

---

a 29 Septuagint; Hebrew him." Then he said to Abimelech, "Call out your whole army!"

city gate just as Abimelech and his soldiers came out from their hiding place.

36When Gaal saw them, he said to Zebul, "Look, people are coming down from the tops of the mountains!"

Zebul replied, "You mistake the shadows of the mountains for men."

37But Gaal spoke up again: "Look, people are coming down from the center of the land, and a company is coming from the direction of the soothsayers' tree."

38Then Zebul said to him, "Where is your big talk now, you who said, 'Who is Abimelech that we should be subject to him?' Aren't these the men you ridiculed? Go out and fight them!"

39So Gaal led out*a* the citizens of Shechem and fought Abimelech. 40Abimelech chased him, and many fell wounded in the flight—all the way to the entrance to the gate. 41Abimelech stayed in Arumah, and Zebul drove Gaal and his brothers out of Shechem.

42The next day the people of Shechem went out to the fields, and this was reported to Abimelech. 43So he took his men, divided them into three companies and set an ambush in the fields. When he saw the people coming out of the city, he rose to attack them. 44Abimelech and the companies with him rushed forward to a position at the entrance to the city gate. Then two companies rushed upon those in the fields and struck them down. 45All that day Abimelech pressed his attack against the city until he had captured it and killed its people. Then he destroyed the city and scattered salt over it.

46On hearing this, the citizens in the tower of Shechem went into the stronghold of the temple of El-Berith. 47When Abimelech heard that they had assembled there, 48he and all his men went up Mount Zalmon. He took an ax and cut off some branches, which he lifted to his shoulders. He ordered the men with him, "Quick! Do what you have seen me do!" 49So all the men cut branches and followed Abimelech. They piled them against the stronghold and set it on fire over the people inside. So all the people in the tower of Shechem, about a thousand men and women, also died.

50Next Abimelech went to Thebez and besieged it and captured it. 51Inside the city, however, was a strong tower, to which all the men and women—all the people of the city—fled. They locked themselves in and climbed up on the tower roof. 52Abimelech went to the tower and stormed it. But as he approached the entrance to the tower to set it on fire, 53a woman dropped an upper millstone on his head and cracked his skull.

54Hurriedly he called to his armor-bearer, "Draw your sword and kill me, so that they can't say, 'A woman killed him.'" So his servant ran him through, and he died. 55When the Israelites saw that Abimelech was dead, they went home.

56Thus God repaid the wickedness that Abimelech had done to his father by murdering his seventy brothers. 57God also made the men of Shechem pay for all their wickedness. The curse of Jotham son of Jerub-Baal came on them.

Tola

10 After the time of Abimelech a man of Issachar, Tola son of Puah, the son of Dodo, rose to save Israel. He lived in Shamir, in the hill country of Ephraim. 2He led*b* Israel twenty-three years; then he died, and was buried in Shamir.

Jair

3He was followed by Jair of Gilead, who led Israel twenty-two years. 4He had thirty sons, who rode thirty donkeys. They controlled thirty towns in Gilead, which to this day are called Havvoth Jair.*c* 5When Jair died, he was buried in Kamon.

Jephthah

6Again the Israelites did evil in the eyes of the LORD. They served the Baals and the Ashtoreths, and the gods of Aram, the gods of Sidon, the gods of Moab, the gods of the Ammonites and the gods of the Philistines. And because the Israelites forsook the LORD and no longer served him, 7he became angry with them. He sold them into the hands

a 39 Or *Gaal went out in the sight of*   *b 2* Traditionally *judged;* also in verse 3   *c 4* Or *called the settlements of Jair*

of the Philistines and the Ammonites, ⁸who that year shattered and crushed them. For eighteen years they oppressed all the Israelites on the east side of the Jordan in Gilead, the land of the Amorites. ⁹The Ammonites also crossed the Jordan to fight against Judah, Benjamin and the house of Ephraim; and Israel was in great distress. ¹⁰Then the Israelites cried out to the LORD, "We have sinned against you, forsaking our God and serving the Baals."

¹¹The LORD replied, "When the Egyptians, the Amorites, the Ammonites, the Philistines, ¹²the Sidonians, the Amalekites and the Maonites*ᵃ* oppressed you and you cried to me for help, did I not save you from their hands? ¹³But you have forsaken me and served other gods, so I will no longer save you. ¹⁴Go and cry out to the gods you have chosen. Let them save you when you are in trouble!"

¹⁵But the Israelites said to the LORD, "We have sinned. Do with us whatever you think best, but please rescue us now." ¹⁶Then they got rid of the foreign gods among them and served the LORD. And he could bear Israel's misery no longer.

¹⁷When the Ammonites were called to arms and camped in Gilead, the Israelites assembled and camped at Mizpah. ¹⁸The leaders of the people of Gilead said to each other, "Whoever will launch the attack against the Ammonites will be the head of all those living in Gilead."

11 Jephthah the Gileadite was a mighty warrior. His father was Gilead; his mother was a prostitute. ²Gilead's wife also bore him sons, and when they were grown up, they drove Jephthah away. "You are not going to get any inheritance in our family," they said, "because you are the son of another woman." ³So Jephthah fled from his brothers and settled in the land of Tob, where a group of adventurers gathered around him and followed him.

⁴Some time later, when the Ammonites made war on Israel, ⁵the elders of Gilead went to get Jephthah from the land of Tob. ⁶"Come," they said, "be our commander, so we can fight the Ammonites."

⁷Jephthah said to them, "Didn't you hate me and drive me from my father's house? Why do you come to me now, when you're in trouble?"

⁸The elders of Gilead said to him, "Nevertheless, we are turning to you now; come with us to fight the Ammonites, and you will be our head over all who live in Gilead."

⁹Jephthah answered, "Suppose you take me back to fight the Ammonites and the LORD gives them to me—will I really be your head?"

¹⁰The elders of Gilead replied, "The LORD is our witness; we will certainly do as you say." ¹¹So Jephthah went with the elders of Gilead, and the people made him head and commander over them. And he repeated all his words before the LORD in Mizpah.

¹²Then Jephthah sent messengers to the Ammonite king with the question: "What do you have against us that you have attacked our country?"

¹³The king of the Ammonites answered Jephthah's messengers, "When Israel came up out of Egypt, they took away my land from the Arnon to the Jabbok, all the way to the Jordan. Now give it back peaceably."

¹⁴Jephthah sent back messengers to the Ammonite king, ¹⁵saying:

"This is what Jephthah says: Israel did not take the land of Moab or the land of the Ammonites. ¹⁶But when they came up out of Egypt, Israel went through the desert to the Red Sea*ᵇ* and on to Kadesh. ¹⁷Then Israel sent messengers to the king of Edom, saying, 'Give us permission to go through your country,' but the king of Edom would not listen. They sent also to the king of Moab, and he refused. So Israel stayed at Kadesh.

¹⁸"Next they traveled through the desert, skirted the lands of Edom and Moab, passed along the eastern side of the country of Moab, and camped on the other side of the Arnon. They did not enter the territory of Moab, for the Arnon was its border.

¹⁹"Then Israel sent messengers to Sihon king of the Amorites, who ruled in Heshbon, and said to him,

---

ᵃ 12 Hebrew; some Septuagint manuscripts *Midianites*   *ᵇ* 16 Hebrew *Yam Suph*; that is, Sea of Reeds

'Let us pass through your country to our own place.' 20Sihon, however, did not trust Israel*a* to pass through his territory. He mustered all his men and encamped at Jahaz and fought with Israel.

21"Then the LORD, the God of Israel, gave Sihon and all his men into Israel's hands, and they defeated them. Israel took over all the land of the Amorites who lived in that country, 22capturing all of it from the Arnon to the Jabbok and from the desert to the Jordan.

23"Now since the LORD, the God of Israel, has driven the Amorites out before his people Israel, what right have you to take it over? 24Will you not take what your god Chemosh gives you? Likewise, whatever the LORD our God has given us, we will possess. 25Are you better than Balak son of Zippor, king of Moab? Did he ever quarrel with Israel or fight with them? 26For three hundred years Israel occupied Heshbon, Aroer, the surrounding settlements and all the towns along the Arnon. Why didn't you retake them during that time? 27I have not wronged you, but you are doing me wrong by waging war against me. Let the LORD, the Judge,*b* decide the dispute this day between the Israelites and the Ammonites."

28The king of Ammon, however, paid no attention to the message Jephthah sent him.

29Then the Spirit of the LORD came upon Jephthah. He crossed Gilead and Manasseh, passed through Mizpah of Gilead, and from there he advanced against the Ammonites. 30And Jephthah made a vow to the LORD: "If you give the Ammonites into my hands, 31whatever comes out of the door of my house to meet me when I return in triumph from the Ammonites will be the LORD's, and I will sacrifice it as a burnt offering."

32Then Jephthah went over to fight the Ammonites, and the LORD gave them into his hands. 33He devastated twenty towns from Aroer to the vicinity of Minnith, as far as Abel Keramim. Thus Israel subdued Ammon.

34When Jephthah returned to his home in Mizpah, who should come out to meet him but his daughter, dancing to the sound of tambourines! She was an only child. Except for her he had neither son nor daughter. 35When he saw her, he tore his clothes and cried, "Oh! My daughter! You have made me miserable and wretched, because I have made a vow to the LORD that I cannot break."

36"My father," she replied, "you have given your word to the LORD. Do to me just as you promised, now that the LORD has avenged you of your enemies, the Ammonites. 37But grant me this one request," she said. "Give me two months to roam the hills and weep with my friends, because I will never marry."

38"You may go," he said. And he let her go for two months. She and the girls went into the hills and wept because she would never marry. 39After the two months, she returned to her father and he did to her as he had vowed. And she was a virgin.

From this comes the Israelite custom 40that each year the young women of Israel go out for four days to commemorate the daughter of Jephthah the Gileadite.

Jephthah and Ephraim

12 The men of Ephraim called out their forces, crossed over to Zaphon and said to Jephthah, "Why did you go to fight the Ammonites without calling us to go with you? We're going to burn down your house over your head."

2Jephthah answered, "I and my people were engaged in a great struggle with the Ammonites, and although I called, you didn't save me out of their hands. 3When I saw that you wouldn't help, I took my life in my hands and crossed over to fight the Ammonites, and the LORD gave me the victory over them. Now why have you come up today to fight me?"

4Jephthah then called together the men of Gilead and fought against Ephraim. The Gileadites struck them down because the Ephraimites had said, "You Gileadites are renegades from

---

a 20 Or however, would not make an agreement for Israel   *b 27 Or Ruler*

Ephraim and Manasseh." ⁵The Gileadites captured the fords of the Jordan leading to Ephraim, and whenever a survivor of Ephraim said, "Let me cross over," the men of Gilead asked him, "Are you an Ephraimite?" If he replied, "No," ⁶they said, "All right, say 'Shibboleth.'" If he said, "Sibboleth," because he could not pronounce the word correctly, they seized him and killed him at the fords of the Jordan. Forty-two thousand Ephraimites were killed at that time.

⁷Jephthah led*a* Israel six years. Then Jephthah the Gileadite died, and was buried in a town in Gilead.

Ibzan, Elon and Abdon

⁸After him, Ibzan of Bethlehem led Israel. ⁹He had thirty sons and thirty daughters. He gave his daughters away in marriage to those outside his clan, and for his sons he brought in thirty young women as wives from outside his clan. Ibzan led Israel seven years. ¹⁰Then Ibzan died, and was buried in Bethlehem.

¹¹After him, Elon the Zebulunite led Israel ten years. ¹²Then Elon died, and was buried in Aijalon in the land of Zebulun.

¹³After him, Abdon son of Hillel, from Pirathon, led Israel. ¹⁴He had forty sons and thirty grandsons, who rode on seventy donkeys. He led Israel eight years. ¹⁵Then Abdon son of Hillel died, and was buried at Pirathon in Ephraim, in the hill country of the Amalekites.

The Birth of Samson

13 Again the Israelites did evil in the eyes of the LORD, so the LORD delivered them into the hands of the Philistines for forty years.

²A certain man of Zorah, named Manoah, from the clan of the Danites, had a wife who was sterile and remained childless. ³The angel of the LORD appeared to her and said, "You are sterile and childless, but you are going to conceive and have a son. ⁴Now see to it that you drink no wine or other fermented drink and that you do not eat anything unclean, ⁵because you will conceive and give birth to a son. No razor may be used on his head, because the boy is to be a Nazirite, set apart to God from birth, and he will begin the deliverance of Israel from the hands of the Philistines."

⁶Then the woman went to her husband and told him, "A man of God came to me. He looked like an angel of God, very awesome. I didn't ask him where he came from, and he didn't tell me his name. ⁷But he said to me, 'You will conceive and give birth to a son. Now then, drink no wine or other fermented drink and do not eat anything unclean, because the boy will be a Nazirite of God from birth until the day of his death.'"

⁸Then Manoah prayed to the LORD: "O Lord, I beg you, let the man of God you sent to us come again to teach us how to bring up the boy who is to be born."

⁹God heard Manoah, and the angel of God came again to the woman while she was out in the field; but her husband Manoah was not with her. ¹⁰The woman hurried to tell her husband, "He's here! The man who appeared to me the other day!"

¹¹Manoah got up and followed his wife. When he came to the man, he said, "Are you the one who talked to my wife?"

"I am," he said.

¹²So Manoah asked him, "When your words are fulfilled, what is to be the rule for the boy's life and work?"

¹³The angel of the LORD answered, "Your wife must do all that I have told her. ¹⁴She must not eat anything that comes from the grapevine, nor drink any wine or other fermented drink nor eat anything unclean. She must do everything I have commanded her."

¹⁵Manoah said to the angel of the LORD, "We would like you to stay until we prepare a young goat for you."

¹⁶The angel of the LORD replied, "Even though you detain me, I will not eat any of your food. But if you prepare a burnt offering, offer it to the LORD." (Manoah did not realize that it was the angel of the LORD.)

¹⁷Then Manoah inquired of the angel of the LORD, "What is your name, so that we may honor you when your word comes true?"

¹⁸He replied, "Why do you ask my

---

a 7 Traditionally *judged;* also in verses 8–14

name? It is beyond understanding.*a* "
¹⁹Then Manoah took a young goat, together with the grain offering, and sacrificed it on a rock to the LORD. And the LORD did an amazing thing while Manoah and his wife watched: ²⁰As the flame blazed up from the altar toward heaven, the angel of the LORD ascended in the flame. Seeing this, Manoah and his wife fell with their faces to the ground. ²¹When the angel of the LORD did not show himself again to Manoah and his wife, Manoah realized that it was the angel of the LORD.

²²"We are doomed to die!" he said to his wife. "We have seen God!"

²³But his wife answered, "If the LORD had meant to kill us, he would not have accepted a burnt offering and grain offering from our hands, nor shown us all these things or now told us this."

²⁴The woman gave birth to a boy and named him Samson. He grew and the LORD blessed him, ²⁵and the Spirit of the LORD began to stir him while he was in Mahaneh Dan, between Zorah and Eshtaol.

Samson's Marriage

14 Samson went down to Timnah and saw there a young Philistine woman. ²When he returned, he said to his father and mother, "I have seen a Philistine woman in Timnah; now get her for me as my wife."

³His father and mother replied, "Isn't there an acceptable woman among your relatives or among all our people? Must you go to the uncircumcised Philistines to get a wife?"

But Samson said to his father, "Get her for me. She's the right one for me." ⁴(His parents did not know that this was from the LORD, who was seeking an occasion to confront the Philistines; for at that time they were ruling over Israel.) ⁵Samson went down to Timnah together with his father and mother. As they approached the vineyards of Timnah, suddenly a young lion came roaring toward him. ⁶The Spirit of the LORD came upon him in power so that he tore the lion apart with his bare hands as he might have torn a young goat. But he told neither his father nor his mother

what he had done. ⁷Then he went down and talked with the woman, and he liked her.

⁸Some time later, when he went back to marry her, he turned aside to look at the lion's carcass. In it was a swarm of bees and some honey, ⁹which he scooped out with his hands and ate as he went along. When he rejoined his parents, he gave them some, and they too ate it. But he did not tell them that he had taken the honey from the lion's carcass.

¹⁰Now his father went down to see the woman. And Samson made a feast there, as was customary for bridegrooms. ¹¹When he appeared, he was given thirty companions.

¹²"Let me tell you a riddle," Samson said to them. "If you can give me the answer within the seven days of the feast, I will give you thirty linen garments and thirty sets of clothes. ¹³If you can't tell me the answer, you must give me thirty linen garments and thirty sets of clothes."

"Tell us your riddle," they said. "Let's hear it."

¹⁴He replied,

"Out of the eater, something to eat;
  out of the strong, something
    sweet."

For three days they could not give the answer.

¹⁵On the fourth*b* day, they said to Samson's wife, "Coax your husband into explaining the riddle for us, or we will burn you and your father's household to death. Did you invite us here to rob us?"

¹⁶Then Samson's wife threw herself on him, sobbing, "You hate me! You don't really love me. You've given my people a riddle, but you haven't told me the answer."

"I haven't even explained it to my father or mother," he replied, "so why should I explain it to you?" ¹⁷She cried the whole seven days of the feast. So on the seventh day he finally told her, because she continued to press him. She in turn explained the riddle to her people.

¹⁸Before sunset on the seventh day the men of the town said to him,

---

a 18 Or *is wonderful*   *b* 15 Some Septuagint manuscripts and Syriac; Hebrew *seventh*

"What is sweeter than honey?
  What is stronger than a lion?"

Samson said to them,

"If you had not plowed with my
    heifer,
  you would not have solved my
    riddle."

¹⁹Then the Spirit of the LORD came upon him in power. He went down to Ashkelon, struck down thirty of their men, stripped them of their belongings and gave their clothes to those who had explained the riddle. Burning with anger, he went up to his father's house. ²⁰And Samson's wife was given to the friend who had attended him at his wedding.

Samson's Vengeance on the Philistines

15 Later on, at the time of wheat harvest, Samson took a young goat and went to visit his wife. He said, "I'm going to my wife's room." But her father would not let him go in.

²"I was so sure you thoroughly hated her," he said, "that I gave her to your friend. Isn't her younger sister more attractive? Take her instead."

³Samson said to them, "This time I have a right to get even with the Philistines; I will really harm them." ⁴So he went out and caught three hundred foxes and tied them tail to tail in pairs. He then fastened a torch to every pair of tails, ⁵lit the torches and let the foxes loose in the standing grain of the Philistines. He burned up the shocks and standing grain, together with the vineyards and olive groves.

⁶When the Philistines asked, "Who did this?" they were told, "Samson, the Timnite's son-in-law, because his wife was given to his friend."

So the Philistines went up and burned her and her father to death. ⁷Samson said to them, "Since you've acted like this, I won't stop until I get my revenge on you." ⁸He attacked them viciously and slaughtered many of them. Then he went down and stayed in a cave in the rock of Etam.

⁹The Philistines went up and camped in Judah, spreading out near Lehi. ¹⁰The men of Judah asked, "Why have you come to fight us?"

"We have come to take Samson prisoner," they answered, "to do to him as he did to us."

¹¹Then three thousand men from Judah went down to the cave in the rock of Etam and said to Samson, "Don't you realize that the Philistines are rulers over us? What have you done to us?"

He answered, "I merely did to them what they did to me."

¹²They said to him, "We've come to tie you up and hand you over to the Philistines."

Samson said, "Swear to me that you won't kill me yourselves."

¹³"Agreed," they answered. "We will only tie you up and hand you over to them. We will not kill you." So they bound him with two new ropes and led him up from the rock. ¹⁴As he approached Lehi, the Philistines came toward him shouting. The Spirit of the LORD came upon him in power. The ropes on his arms became like charred flax, and the bindings dropped from his hands. ¹⁵Finding a fresh jawbone of a donkey, he grabbed it and struck down a thousand men.

¹⁶Then Samson said,

"With a donkey's jawbone
  I have made donkeys of them.ᵃ
With a donkey's jawbone
  I have killed a thousand men."

¹⁷When he finished speaking, he threw away the jawbone; and the place was called Ramath Lehi.ᵇ

¹⁸Because he was very thirsty, he cried out to the LORD, "You have given your servant this great victory. Must I now die of thirst and fall into the hands of the uncircumcised?" ¹⁹Then God opened up the hollow place in Lehi, and water came out of it. When Samson drank, his strength returned and he revived. So the spring was called En Hakkore,ᶜ and it is still there in Lehi.

²⁰Samson ledᵈ Israel for twenty years in the days of the Philistines.

ᵃ 16 Or made a heap or two; the Hebrew for donkey sounds like the Hebrew for heap.   ᵇ 17 Ramath Lehi means jawbone hill.   ᶜ 19 En Hakkore means caller's spring.   ᵈ 20 Traditionally judged

Samson and Delilah

16 One day Samson went to Gaza, where he saw a prostitute. He went in to spend the night with her. ²The people of Gaza were told, "Samson is here!" So they surrounded the place and lay in wait for him all night at the city gate. They made no move during the night, saying, "At dawn we'll kill him."

³But Samson lay there only until the middle of the night. Then he got up and took hold of the doors of the city gate, together with the two posts, and tore them loose, bar and all. He lifted them to his shoulders and carried them to the top of the hill that faces Hebron.

⁴Some time later, he fell in love with a woman in the Valley of Sorek whose name was Delilah. ⁵The rulers of the Philistines went to her and said, "See if you can lure him into showing you the secret of his great strength and how we can overpower him so we may tie him up and subdue him. Each one of us will give you eleven hundred shekels*a* of silver."

⁶So Delilah said to Samson, "Tell me the secret of your great strength and how you can be tied up and subdued."

⁷Samson answered her, "If anyone ties me with seven fresh thongs*b* that have not been dried, I'll become as weak as any other man."

⁸Then the rulers of the Philistines brought her seven fresh thongs that had not been dried, and she tied him with them. ⁹With men hidden in the room, she called to him, "Samson, the Philistines are upon you!" But he snapped the thongs as easily as a piece of string snaps when it comes close to a flame. So the secret of his strength was not discovered.

¹⁰Then Delilah said to Samson, "You have made a fool of me; you lied to me. Come now, tell me how you can be tied."

¹¹He said, "If anyone ties me securely with new ropes that have never been used, I'll become as weak as any other man."

¹²So Delilah took new ropes and tied him with them. Then, with men hidden in the room, she called to him, "Samson, the Philistines are upon you!" But he snapped the ropes off his arms as if they were threads.

¹³Delilah then said to Samson, "Until now, you have been making a fool of me and lying to me. Tell me how you can be tied."

He replied, "If you weave the seven braids of my head into the fabric on the loom and tighten it with the pin, I'll become as weak as any other man." So while he was sleeping, Delilah took the seven braids of his head, wove them into the fabric ¹⁴and*c* tightened it with the pin.

Again she called to him, "Samson, the Philistines are upon you!" He awoke from his sleep and pulled up the pin and the loom, with the fabric.

¹⁵Then she said to him, "How can you say, 'I love you,' when you won't confide in me? This is the third time you have made a fool of me and haven't told me the secret of your great strength." ¹⁶With such nagging she prodded him day after day until he was tired to death.

¹⁷So he told her everything. "No razor has ever been used on my head," he said, "because I have been a Nazirite set apart to God since birth. If my head were shaved, my strength would leave me, and I would become as weak as any other man."

¹⁸When Delilah saw that he had told her everything, she sent word to the rulers of the Philistines, "Come back once more; he has told me everything." So the rulers of the Philistines returned with the silver in their hands. ¹⁹Having put him to sleep on her lap, she called a man to shave off the seven braids of his hair, and so began to subdue him.*d* And his strength left him.

TO KEEP YOUR SECRET IS WISDOM; BUT TO EXPECT OTHERS TO KEEP IT IS FOOLISH.

—*Samuel Johnson*

---

²⁰Then she called, "Samson, the Philistines are upon you!"

---

a 5 That is, about 28 pounds (about 13 kilograms)   *b 7* Or *bowstrings*; also in verses 8 and 9
c 13,14 Some Septuagint manuscripts; Hebrew *"I can, if you weave the seven braids of my head into the fabric on the loom."* *¹⁴So she*   *d 19* Hebrew; some Septuagint manuscripts *and he began to weaken*

He awoke from his sleep and thought, "I'll go out as before and shake myself free." But he did not know that the LORD had left him.

²¹Then the Philistines seized him, gouged out his eyes and took him down to Gaza. Binding him with bronze shackles, they set him to grinding in the prison. ²²But the hair on his head began to grow again after it had been shaved.

The Death of Samson

²³Now the rulers of the Philistines assembled to offer a great sacrifice to Dagon their god and to celebrate, saying, "Our god has delivered Samson, our enemy, into our hands."

²⁴When the people saw him, they praised their god, saying,

"Our god has delivered our enemy
    into our hands,
the one who laid waste our land
    and multiplied our slain."

²⁵While they were in high spirits, they shouted, "Bring out Samson to entertain us." So they called Samson out of the prison, and he performed for them.

When they stood him among the pillars, ²⁶Samson said to the servant who held his hand, "Put me where I can feel the pillars that support the temple, so that I may lean against them." ²⁷Now the temple was crowded with men and women; all the rulers of the Philistines were there, and on the roof were about three thousand men and women watching Samson perform. ²⁸Then Samson prayed to the LORD, "O Sovereign LORD, remember me. O God, please strengthen me just once more, and let me with one blow get revenge on the Philistines for my two eyes." ²⁹Then Samson reached toward the two central pillars on which the temple stood. Bracing himself against them, his right hand on the one and his left hand on the other, ³⁰Samson said, "Let me die with the Philistines!" Then he pushed with all his might, and down came the temple on the rulers and all the people in it. Thus he killed many more when he died than while he lived.

³¹Then his brothers and his father's whole family went down to get him. They brought him back and buried him between Zorah and Eshtaol in the tomb of Manoah his father. He had led*a* Israel twenty years.

Micah's Idols

17 Now a man named Micah from the hill country of Ephraim ²said to his mother, "The eleven hundred shekels*b* of silver that were taken from you and about which I heard you utter a curse—I have that silver with me; I took it."

Then his mother said, "The LORD bless you, my son!"

³When he returned the eleven hundred shekels of silver to his mother, she said, "I solemnly consecrate my silver to the LORD for my son to make a carved image and a cast idol. I will give it back to you."

⁴So he returned the silver to his mother, and she took two hundred shekels*c* of silver and gave them to a silversmith, who made them into the image and the idol. And they were put in Micah's house.

⁵Now this man Micah had a shrine, and he made an ephod and some idols and installed one of his sons as his priest. ⁶In those days Israel had no king; everyone did as he saw fit.

⁷A young Levite from Bethlehem in Judah, who had been living within the clan of Judah, ⁸left that town in search of some other place to stay. On his way*d* he came to Micah's house in the hill country of Ephraim.

⁹Micah asked him, "Where are you from?"

"I'm a Levite from Bethlehem in Judah," he said, "and I'm looking for a place to stay."

¹⁰Then Micah said to him, "Live with me and be my father and priest, and I'll give you ten shekels*e* of silver a year, your clothes and your food." ¹¹So the Levite agreed to live with him, and the young man was to him like one of his sons. ¹²Then Micah installed the Levite, and the young man became his priest

and lived in his house. 13And Micah said, "Now I know that the LORD will be good to me, since this Levite has become my priest."

Danites Settle in Laish

18 In those days Israel had no king.

And in those days the tribe of the Danites was seeking a place of their own where they might settle, because they had not yet come into an inheritance among the tribes of Israel. 2So the Danites sent five warriors from Zorah and Eshtaol to spy out the land and explore it. These men represented all their clans. They told them, "Go, explore the land."

The men entered the hill country of Ephraim and came to the house of Micah, where they spent the night. 3When they were near Micah's house, they recognized the voice of the young Levite; so they turned in there and asked him, "Who brought you here? What are you doing in this place? Why are you here?"

4He told them what Micah had done for him, and said, "He has hired me and I am his priest."

5Then they said to him, "Please inquire of God to learn whether our journey will be successful."

6The priest answered them, "Go in peace. Your journey has the LORD's approval."

7So the five men left and came to Laish, where they saw that the people were living in safety, like the Sidonians, unsuspecting and secure. And since their land lacked nothing, they were prosperous.a Also, they lived a long way from the Sidonians and had no relationship with anyone else.b

8When they returned to Zorah and Eshtaol, their brothers asked them, "How did you find things?"

9They answered, "Come on, let's attack them! We have seen that the land is very good. Aren't you going to do something? Don't hesitate to go there and take it over. 10When you get there, you will find an unsuspecting people and a spacious land that God has put into your hands, a land that lacks nothing whatever."

11Then six hundred men from the clan of the Danites, armed for battle, set out from Zorah and Eshtaol. 12On their way they set up camp near Kiriath Jearim in Judah. This is why the place west of Kiriath Jearim is called Mahaneh Danc to this day. 13From there they went on to the hill country of Ephraim and came to Micah's house.

14Then the five men who had spied out the land of Laish said to their brothers, "Do you know that one of these houses has an ephod, other household gods, a carved image and a cast idol? Now you know what to do." 15So they turned in there and went to the house of the young Levite at Micah's place and greeted him. 16The six hundred Danites, armed for battle, stood at the entrance to the gate. 17The five men who had spied out the land went inside and took the carved image, the ephod, the other household gods and the cast idol while the priest and the six hundred armed men stood at the entrance to the gate.

18When these men went into Micah's house and took the carved image, the ephod, the other household gods and the cast idol, the priest said to them, "What are you doing?"

19They answered him, "Be quiet! Don't say a word. Come with us, and be our father and priest. Isn't it better that you serve a tribe and clan in Israel as priest rather than just one man's household?" 20Then the priest was glad. He took the ephod, the other household gods and the carved image and went along with the people. 21Putting their little children, their livestock and their possessions in front of them, they turned away and left.

22When they had gone some distance from Micah's house, the men who lived near Micah were called together and overtook the Danites. 23As they shouted after them, the Danites turned and said to Micah, "What's the matter with you that you called out your men to fight?"

24He replied, "You took the gods I made, and my priest, and went away. What else do I have? How can you ask, 'What's the matter with you?'"

---

a 7 The meaning of the Hebrew for this clause is uncertain.   b 7 Hebrew; some Septuagint manuscripts with the Arameans   c 12 Mahaneh Dan means Dan's camp.

25The Danites answered, "Don't argue with us, or some hot-tempered men will attack you, and you and your family will lose your lives." 26So the Danites went their way, and Micah, seeing that they were too strong for him, turned around and went back home.

27Then they took what Micah had made, and his priest, and went on to Laish, against a peaceful and unsuspecting people. They attacked them with the sword and burned down their city. 28There was no one to rescue them because they lived a long way from Sidon and had no relationship with anyone else. The city was in a valley near Beth Rehob.

The Danites rebuilt the city and settled there. 29They named it Dan after their forefather Dan, who was born to Israel—though the city used to be called Laish. 30There the Danites set up for themselves the idols, and Jonathan son of Gershom, the son of Moses,a and his sons were priests for the tribe of Dan until the time of the captivity of the land. 31They continued to use the idols Micah had made, all the time the house of God was in Shiloh.

A Levite and His Concubine

19 In those days Israel had no king.

Now a Levite who lived in a remote area in the hill country of Ephraim took a concubine from Bethlehem in Judah. 2But she was unfaithful to him. She left him and went back to her father's house in Bethlehem, Judah. After she had been there four months, 3her husband went to her to persuade her to return. He had with him his servant and two donkeys. She took him into her father's house, and when her father saw him, he gladly welcomed him. 4His father-in-law, the girl's father, prevailed upon him to stay; so he remained with him three days, eating and drinking, and sleeping there.

5On the fourth day they got up early and he prepared to leave, but the girl's father said to his son-in-law, "Refresh yourself with something to eat; then you can go." 6So the two of them sat down to eat and drink together. Afterward the girl's father said, "Please stay tonight and enjoy yourself." 7And when the man got up to go, his father-in-law persuaded him, so he stayed there that night. 8On the morning of the fifth day, when he rose to go, the girl's father said, "Refresh yourself. Wait till afternoon!" So the two of them ate together.

9Then when the man, with his concubine and his servant, got up to leave, his father-in-law, the girl's father, said, "Now look, it's almost evening. Spend the night here; the day is nearly over. Stay and enjoy yourself. Early tomorrow morning you can get up and be on your way home." 10But, unwilling to stay another night, the man left and went toward Jebus (that is, Jerusalem), with his two saddled donkeys and his concubine.

11When they were near Jebus and the day was almost gone, the servant said to his master, "Come, let's stop at this city of the Jebusites and spend the night."

12His master replied, "No. We won't go into an alien city, whose people are not Israelites. We will go on to Gibeah." 13He added, "Come, let's try to reach Gibeah or Ramah and spend the night in one of those places." 14So they went on, and the sun set as they neared Gibeah in Benjamin. 15There they stopped to spend the night. They went and sat in the city square, but no one took them into his home for the night.

16That evening an old man from the hill country of Ephraim, who was living in Gibeah (the men of the place were Benjamites), came in from his work in the fields. 17When he looked and saw the traveler in the city square, the old man asked, "Where are you going? Where did you come from?"

18He answered, "We are on our way from Bethlehem in Judah to a remote area in the hill country of Ephraim where I live. I have been to Bethlehem in Judah and now I am going to the house of the LORD. No one has taken me into his house. 19We have both straw and fodder for our donkeys and bread and wine for ourselves your servants— me, your maidservant, and the young man with us. We don't need anything."

20"You are welcome at my house," the old man said. "Let me supply what-

---

a 30 An ancient Hebrew scribal tradition, some Septuagint manuscripts and Vulgate; Masoretic Text Manasseh ever you need. Only don't spend the night in the square." ²¹So he took him into his house and fed his donkeys. After they had washed their feet, they had something to eat and drink.

²²While they were enjoying themselves, some of the wicked men of the city surrounded the house. Pounding on the door, they shouted to the old man who owned the house, "Bring out the man who came to your house so we can have sex with him."

²³The owner of the house went outside and said to them, "No, my friends, don't be so vile. Since this man is my guest, don't do this disgraceful thing. ²⁴Look, here is my virgin daughter, and his concubine. I will bring them out to you now, and you can use them and do to them whatever you wish. But to this man, don't do such a disgraceful thing."

²⁵But the men would not listen to him. So the man took his concubine and sent her outside to them, and they raped her and abused her throughout the night, and at dawn they let her go. ²⁶At daybreak the woman went back to the house where her master was staying, fell down at the door and lay there until daylight.

²⁷When her master got up in the morning and opened the door of the house and stepped out to continue on his way, there lay his concubine, fallen in the doorway of the house, with her hands on the threshold. ²⁸He said to her, "Get up; let's go." But there was no answer. Then the man put her on his donkey and set out for home.

²⁹When he reached home, he took a knife and cut up his concubine, limb by limb, into twelve parts and sent them into all the areas of Israel. ³⁰Everyone who saw it said, "Such a thing has never been seen or done, not since the day the Israelites came up out of Egypt. Think about it! Consider it! Tell us what to do!"

Israelites Fight the Benjamites

20 Then all the Israelites from Dan to Beersheba and from the land of Gilead came out as one man and assembled before the LORD in Mizpah. ²The leaders of all the people of the tribes of Israel took their places in the assembly of the people of God,

four hundred thousand soldiers armed with swords. ³(The Benjamites heard that the Israelites had gone up to Mizpah.) Then the Israelites said, "Tell us how this awful thing happened."

⁴So the Levite, the husband of the murdered woman, said, "I and my concubine came to Gibeah in Benjamin to spend the night. ⁵During the night the men of Gibeah came after me and surrounded the house, intending to kill me. They raped my concubine, and she died. ⁶I took my concubine, cut her into pieces and sent one piece to each region of Israel's inheritance, because they committed this lewd and disgraceful act in Israel. ⁷Now, all you Israelites, speak up and give your verdict."

⁸All the people rose as one man, saying, "None of us will go home. No, not one of us will return to his house. ⁹But now this is what we'll do to Gibeah: We'll go up against it as the lot directs. ¹⁰We'll take ten men out of every hundred from all the tribes of Israel, and a hundred from a thousand, and a thousand from ten thousand, to get provisions for the army. Then, when the army arrives at Gibeah*a* in Benjamin, it can give them what they deserve for all this vileness done in Israel." ¹¹So all the men of Israel got together and united as one man against the city.

¹²The tribes of Israel sent men throughout the tribe of Benjamin, saying, "What about this awful crime that was committed among you? ¹³Now surrender those wicked men of Gibeah so that we may put them to death and purge the evil from Israel."

But the Benjamites would not listen to their fellow Israelites. ¹⁴From their towns they came together at Gibeah to fight against the Israelites. ¹⁵At once the Benjamites mobilized twenty-six thousand swordsmen from their towns, in addition to seven hundred chosen men from those living in Gibeah. ¹⁶Among all these soldiers there were seven hundred chosen men who were left-handed, each of whom could sling a stone at a hair and not miss.

¹⁷Israel, apart from Benjamin, mustered four hundred thousand swordsmen, all of them fighting men.

a 10 One Hebrew manuscript; most Hebrew manuscripts *Geba,* a variant of *Gibeah*

18The Israelites went up to Bethel*a* and inquired of God. They said, "Who of us shall go first to fight against the Benjamites?"

The LORD replied, "Judah shall go first."

19The next morning the Israelites got up and pitched camp near Gibeah. 20The men of Israel went out to fight the Benjamites and took up battle positions against them at Gibeah. 21The Benjamites came out of Gibeah and cut down twenty-two thousand Israelites on the battlefield that day. 22But the men of Israel encouraged one another and again took up their positions where they had stationed themselves the first day. 23The Israelites went up and wept before the LORD until evening, and they inquired of the LORD. They said, "Shall we go up again to battle against the Benjamites, our brothers?"

The LORD answered, "Go up against them."

24Then the Israelites drew near to Benjamin the second day. 25This time, when the Benjamites came out from Gibeah to oppose them, they cut down another eighteen thousand Israelites, all of them armed with swords.

26Then the Israelites, all the people, went up to Bethel, and there they sat weeping before the LORD. They fasted that day until evening and presented burnt offerings and fellowship offerings*b* to the LORD. 27And the Israelites inquired of the LORD. (In those days the ark of the covenant of God was there, 28with Phinehas son of Eleazar, the son of Aaron, ministering before it.) They asked, "Shall we go up again to battle with Benjamin our brother, or not?"

The LORD responded, "Go, for tomorrow I will give them into your hands."

29Then Israel set an ambush around Gibeah. 30They went up against the Benjamites on the third day and took up positions against Gibeah as they had done before. 31The Benjamites came out to meet them and were drawn away from the city. They began to inflict casualties on the Israelites as before, so that about thirty men fell in the open field and on the roads—the one leading to Bethel and the other to Gibeah.

32While the Benjamites were saying, "We are defeating them as before," the Israelites were saying, "Let's retreat and draw them away from the city to the roads."

33All the men of Israel moved from their places and took up positions at Baal Tamar, and the Israelite ambush charged out of its place on the west*c* of Gibeah.*d* 34Then ten thousand of Israel's finest men made a frontal attack on Gibeah. The fighting was so heavy that the Benjamites did not realize how near disaster was. 35The LORD defeated Benjamin before Israel, and on that day the Israelites struck down 25,100 Benjamites, all armed with swords. 36Then the Benjamites saw that they were beaten.

Now the men of Israel had given way before Benjamin, because they relied on the ambush they had set near Gibeah. 37The men who had been in ambush made a sudden dash into Gibeah, spread out and put the whole city to the sword. 38The men of Israel had arranged with the ambush that they should send up a great cloud of smoke from the city, 39and then the men of Israel would turn in the battle.

The Benjamites had begun to inflict casualties on the men of Israel (about thirty), and they said, "We are defeating them as in the first battle." 40But when the column of smoke began to rise from the city, the Benjamites turned and saw the smoke of the whole city going up into the sky. 41Then the men of Israel turned on them, and the men of Benjamin were terrified, because they realized that disaster had come upon them. 42So they fled before the Israelites in the direction of the desert, but they could not escape the battle. And the men of Israel who came out of the towns cut them down there. 43They surrounded the Benjamites, chased them and easily*e* overran them in the vicinity of Gibeah on the east. 44Eighteen thousand Benjamites fell, all of them valiant fighters. 45As they turned and fled toward the desert to the rock of Rimmon, the Isra-

---

a 18 Or *to the house of God;* also in verse 26   *b 26* Traditionally *peace offerings*   *c 33* Some Septuagint manuscripts and Vulgate; the meaning of the Hebrew for this word is uncertain.   *d 33* Hebrew *Geba,* a variant of *Gibeah*   *e 43* The meaning of the Hebrew for this word is uncertain.

elites cut down five thousand men along the roads. They kept pressing after the Benjamites as far as Gidom and struck down two thousand more.

46On that day twenty-five thousand Benjamite swordsmen fell, all of them valiant fighters. 47But six hundred men turned and fled into the desert to the rock of Rimmon, where they stayed four months. 48The men of Israel went back to Benjamin and put all the towns to the sword, including the animals and everything else they found. All the towns they came across they set on fire.

Wives for the Benjamites

21 The men of Israel had taken an oath at Mizpah: "Not one of us will give his daughter in marriage to a Benjamite."

2The people went to Bethel,a where they sat before God until evening, raising their voices and weeping bitterly. 3"O LORD, the God of Israel," they cried, "why has this happened to Israel? Why should one tribe be missing from Israel today?"

4Early the next day the people built an altar and presented burnt offerings and fellowship offerings.b

5Then the Israelites asked, "Who from all the tribes of Israel has failed to assemble before the LORD?" For they had taken a solemn oath that anyone who failed to assemble before the LORD at Mizpah should certainly be put to death.

6Now the Israelites grieved for their brothers, the Benjamites. "Today one tribe is cut off from Israel," they said. 7"How can we provide wives for those who are left, since we have taken an oath by the LORD not to give them any of our daughters in marriage?" 8Then they asked, "Which one of the tribes of Israel failed to assemble before the LORD at Mizpah?" They discovered that no one from Jabesh Gilead had come to the camp for the assembly. 9For when they counted the people, they found that none of the people of Jabesh Gilead were there.

10So the assembly sent twelve thousand fighting men with instructions to go to Jabesh Gilead and put to the sword those living there, including the women and children. 11"This is what you are to do," they said. "Kill every male and every woman who is not a virgin." 12They found among the people living in Jabesh Gilead four hundred young women who had never slept with a man, and they took them to the camp at Shiloh in Canaan.

13Then the whole assembly sent an offer of peace to the Benjamites at the rock of Rimmon. 14So the Benjamites returned at that time and were given the women of Jabesh Gilead who had been spared. But there were not enough for all of them.

15The people grieved for Benjamin, because the LORD had made a gap in the tribes of Israel. 16And the elders of the assembly said, "With the women of Benjamin destroyed, how shall we provide wives for the men who are left? 17The Benjamite survivors must have heirs," they said, "so that a tribe of Israel will not be wiped out. 18We can't give them our daughters as wives, since we Israelites have taken this oath: 'Cursed be anyone who gives a wife to a Benjamite.' 19But look, there is the annual festival of the LORD in Shiloh, to the north of Bethel, and east of the road that goes from Bethel to Shechem, and to the south of Lebonah."

20So they instructed the Benjamites, saying, "Go and hide in the vineyards 21and watch. When the girls of Shiloh come out to join in the dancing, then rush from the vineyards and each of you seize a wife from the girls of Shiloh and go to the land of Benjamin. 22When their fathers or brothers complain to us, we will say to them, 'Do us a kindness by helping them, because we did not get wives for them during the war, and you are innocent, since you did not give your daughters to them.' "

23So that is what the Benjamites did. While the girls were dancing, each man caught one and carried her off to be his wife. Then they returned to their inheritance and rebuilt the towns and settled in them.

24At that time the Israelites left that place and went home to their tribes and clans, each to his own inheritance.

25In those days Israel had no king; everyone did as he saw fit.

a 2 Or to the house of God   b 4 Traditionally peace offerings

RUTH

HIS BOOK TELLS THE STORY OF RUTH, A YOUNG MOABITE WOMAN AND GREAT-GRANDMOTHER OF KING DAVID. SET IN THE TIME OF THE JUDGES, THE BOOK OF RUTH GIVES A SERIES OF INTIMATE GLANCES INTO THE PRIVATE LIVES OF THE MEMBERS OF AN ISRAELITE FAMILY AND PRESENTS A DELIGHTFUL ACCOUNT OF TRUE FAITH AND PIETY. IN THIS POWERFUL STORY OF LOVE AND DEVOTION, LOOK FOR GOD AT WORK TO BRING FULLNESS IN THE LIVES OF THOSE WHO FEEL EMPTY.

Naomi and Ruth

1 In the days when the judges ruled,*a* there was a famine in the land, and a man from Bethlehem in Judah, together with his wife and two sons, went to live for a while in the country of Moab. ²The man's name was Elimelech, his wife's name Naomi, and the names of his two sons were Mahlon and Kilion. They were Ephrathites from Bethlehem, Judah. And they went to Moab and lived there.

³Now Elimelech, Naomi's husband, died, and she was left with her two sons. ⁴They married Moabite women, one named Orpah and the other Ruth. After they had lived there about ten years, ⁵both Mahlon and Kilion also died, and Naomi was left without her two sons and her husband.

⁶When she heard in Moab that the LORD had come to the aid of his people by providing food for them, Naomi and her daughters-in-law prepared to return home from there. ⁷With her two daughters-in-law she left the place where she had been living and set out on the road that would take them back to the land of Judah.

⁸Then Naomi said to her two daughters-in-law, "Go back, each of you, to your mother's home. May the LORD show kindness to you, as you have shown to your dead and to me. ⁹May the LORD grant that each of you will find rest in the home of another husband."

Then she kissed them and they wept

a 1 Traditionally *judged*

aloud [10]and said to her, "We will go back with you to your people."

[11]But Naomi said, "Return home, my daughters. Why would you come with me? Am I going to have any more sons, who could become your husbands? [12]Return home, my daughters; I am too old to have another husband. Even if I thought there was still hope for me— even if I had a husband tonight and then gave birth to sons— [13]would you wait until they grew up? Would you remain unmarried for them? No, my daughters. It is more bitter for me than for you, because the LORD's hand has gone out against me!"

[14]At this they wept again. Then Orpah kissed her mother-in-law goodby, but Ruth clung to her.

[15]"Look," said Naomi, "your sister-in-law is going back to her people and her gods. Go back with her."

[16]But Ruth replied, "Don't urge me to leave you or to turn back from you. Where you go I will go, and where you stay I will stay. Your people will be my people and your God my God. [17]Where you die I will die, and there I will be buried. May the LORD deal with me, be it ever so severely, if anything but death separates you and me." [18]When Naomi realized that Ruth was determined to go with her, she stopped urging her.

[19]So the two women went on until they came to Bethlehem. When they arrived in Bethlehem, the whole town was stirred because of them, and the women exclaimed, "Can this be Naomi?"

[20]"Don't call me Naomi,[a]" she told them. "Call me Mara,[b] because the Almighty[c] has made my life very bitter. [21]I went away full, but the LORD has brought me back empty. Why call me Naomi? The LORD has afflicted[d] me; the Almighty has brought misfortune upon me."

[22]So Naomi returned from Moab accompanied by Ruth the Moabitess, her daughter-in-law, arriving in Bethlehem as the barley harvest was beginning.

Ruth Meets Boaz

[2] Now Naomi had a relative on her husband's side, from the clan of Elimelech, a man of standing, whose name was Boaz.

[2]And Ruth the Moabitess said to Naomi, "Let me go to the fields and pick up the leftover grain behind anyone in whose eyes I find favor."

Naomi said to her, "Go ahead, my daughter." [3]So she went out and began to glean in the fields behind the harvesters. As it turned out, she found herself working in a field belonging to Boaz, who was from the clan of Elimelech.

[4]Just then Boaz arrived from Bethlehem and greeted the harvesters, "The LORD be with you!"

"The LORD bless you!" they called back.

[5]Boaz asked the foreman of his harvesters, "Whose young woman is that?"

[6]The foreman replied, "She is the Moabitess who came back from Moab with Naomi. [7]She said, 'Please let me glean and gather among the sheaves behind the harvesters.' She went into the field and has worked steadily from morning till now, except for a short rest in the shelter."

[8]So Boaz said to Ruth, "My daughter, listen to me. Don't go and glean in another field and don't go away from here. Stay here with my servant girls. [9]Watch the field where the men are harvesting, and follow along after the girls. I have told the men not to touch you. And whenever you are thirsty, go and get a drink from the water jars the men have filled."

[10]At this, she bowed down with her face to the ground. She exclaimed, "Why have I found such favor in your eyes that you notice me—a foreigner?"

[11]Boaz replied, "I've been told all about what you have done for your mother-in-law since the death of your husband—how you left your father and mother and your homeland and came to live with a people you did not know before. [12]May the LORD repay you for what you have done. May you be richly rewarded by the LORD, the God of Israel, under whose wings you have come to take refuge."

a 20 Naomi means *pleasant;* also in verse 21.   *b 20 Mara* means *bitter.*   *c 20* Hebrew *Shaddai;* also in verse 21   *d 21* Or *has testified against*

13"May I continue to find favor in your eyes, my lord," she said. "You have given me comfort and have spoken kindly to your servant—though I do not have the standing of one of your servant girls."

14At mealtime Boaz said to her, "Come over here. Have some bread and dip it in the wine vinegar."

When she sat down with the harvesters, he offered her some roasted grain. She ate all she wanted and had some left over. 15As she got up to glean, Boaz gave orders to his men, "Even if she gathers among the sheaves, don't embarrass her. 16Rather, pull out some stalks for her from the bundles and leave them for her to pick up, and don't rebuke her."

17So Ruth gleaned in the field until evening. Then she threshed the barley she had gathered, and it amounted to about an ephah. *a* 18She carried it back to town, and her mother-in-law saw how

a 17 That is, probably about 3/5 bushel (about 22 liters)

MONDAY

HAPPENSTANCE
Charles H. Spurgeon

VERSE: Ruth 2:3   **PASSAGE: Ruth 2:2–20**

 t seemed nothing but an accidental happenstance, but how divinely was it planned! Ruth had gone forth with her [mother-in-law's] blessing under the care of her [mother-in-law's] God to humble but honorable toil, and the providence of God was guiding her every step. Little did she know that amid the sheaves she would find a husband, that he would make her the joint owner of all those broad acres, and that she, a poor foreigner, would become one of the progenitors of the great Messiah. God is very good to those who trust in him and often surprises them with unlooked for blessings. Little do we know what may happen to us tomorrow, but this sweet fact may cheer us, that no good thing shall be withheld. Chance is banished from the faith of Christians, for they see the hand of God in everything. The trivial events of today or tomorrow may involve consequences of the highest importance. O Lord, deal as graciously with your servants as you did with Ruth.

How blessed would it be, if, in wandering in the field of meditation tonight, our [happenstance] should be to "light" on the place where our next Kinsman will reveal himself to us! O Spirit of God, guide us to him. We would sooner glean in his field than bear away the whole harvest from any other.

ADDITIONAL SCRIPTURE READING:
2 Kings 8:5–6; Matthew 10:29; Luke 10:30–33

Go to page 298 for your next devotional reading.

1700   1900

much she had gathered. Ruth also brought out and gave her what she had left over after she had eaten enough.

¹⁹Her mother-in-law asked her, "Where did you glean today? Where did you work? Blessed be the man who took notice of you!"

Then Ruth told her mother-in-law about the one at whose place she had been working. "The name of the man I worked with today is Boaz," she said.

²⁰"The LORD bless him!" Naomi said to her daughter-in-law. "He has not stopped showing his kindness to the living and the dead." She added, "That man is our close relative; he is one of our kinsman-redeemers."

²¹Then Ruth the Moabitess said, "He even said to me, 'Stay with my workers until they finish harvesting all my grain.' "

²²Naomi said to Ruth her daughter-in-law, "It will be good for you, my daughter, to go with his girls, because in someone else's field you might be harmed."

²³So Ruth stayed close to the servant girls of Boaz to glean until the barley and wheat harvests were finished. And she lived with her mother-in-law.

Ruth and Boaz at the Threshing Floor

3 One day Naomi her mother-in-law said to her, "My daughter, should I not try to find a home*a* for you, where you will be well provided for? ²Is not Boaz, with whose servant girls you have been, a kinsman of ours? Tonight he will be winnowing barley on the threshing floor. ³Wash and perfume yourself, and put on your best clothes. Then go down to the threshing floor, but don't let him know you are there until he has finished eating and drinking. ⁴When he lies down, note the place where he is lying. Then go and uncover his feet and lie down. He will tell you what to do."

⁵"I will do whatever you say," Ruth answered. ⁶So she went down to the threshing floor and did everything her mother-in-law told her to do.

⁷When Boaz had finished eating and drinking and was in good spirits, he went over to lie down at the far end of the grain pile. Ruth approached quietly, uncovered his feet and lay down. ⁸In the middle of the night something startled the man, and he turned and discovered a woman lying at his feet.

⁹"Who are you?" he asked.

"I am your servant Ruth," she said. "Spread the corner of your garment over me, since you are a kinsman-redeemer."

¹⁰"The LORD bless you, my daughter," he replied. "This kindness is greater than that which you showed earlier: You have not run after the younger men, whether rich or poor. ¹¹And now, my daughter, don't be afraid. I will do for you all you ask. All my fellow townsmen know that you are a woman of noble character. ¹²Although it is true that I am near of kin, there is a kinsman-redeemer nearer than I. ¹³Stay here for the night, and in the morning if he wants to redeem, good; let him redeem. But if he is not willing, as surely as the LORD lives I will do it. Lie here until morning."

¹⁴So she lay at his feet until morning, but got up before anyone could be recognized; and he said, "Don't let it be known that a woman came to the threshing floor."

¹⁵He also said, "Bring me the shawl you are wearing and hold it out." When she did so, he poured into it six measures of barley and put it on her. Then he*b* went back to town.

¹⁶When Ruth came to her mother-in-law, Naomi asked, "How did it go, my daughter?"

Then she told her everything Boaz had done for her ¹⁷and added, "He gave me these six measures of barley, saying, 'Don't go back to your mother-in-law empty-handed.' "

¹⁸Then Naomi said, "Wait, my daughter, until you find out what happens. For the man will not rest until the matter is settled today."

Boaz Marries Ruth

4 Meanwhile Boaz went up to the town gate and sat there. When the kinsman-redeemer he had mentioned came along, Boaz said, "Come over here, my friend, and sit down." So he went over and sat down.

---

a 1 Hebrew *find rest* (see Ruth 1:9)   *b* 15 Most Hebrew manuscripts; many Hebrew manuscripts, Vulgate and Syriac *she*

²Boaz took ten of the elders of the town and said, "Sit here," and they did so. ³Then he said to the kinsman-redeemer, "Naomi, who has come back from Moab, is selling the piece of land that belonged to our brother Elimelech. ⁴I thought I should bring the matter to your attention and suggest that you buy it in the presence of these seated here and in the presence of the elders of my people. If you will redeem it, do so. But if you*a* will not, tell me, so I will know. For no one has the right to do it except you, and I am next in line."

"I will redeem it," he said.

---

⁵Then Boaz said, "On the day you buy the land from Naomi and from Ruth the Moabitess, you acquire*b* the dead man's widow, in order to maintain the name of the dead with his property."

⁶At this, the kinsman-redeemer said, "Then I cannot redeem it because I might endanger my own estate. You redeem it yourself. I cannot do it."

⁷(Now in earlier times in Israel, for the redemption and transfer of property to become final, one party took off his sandal and gave it to the other. This was the method of legalizing transactions in Israel.)

⁸So the kinsman-redeemer said to Boaz, "Buy it yourself." And he removed his sandal.

⁹Then Boaz announced to the elders and all the people, "Today you are witnesses that I have bought from Naomi all the property of Elimelech, Kilion and Mahlon. ¹⁰I have also acquired Ruth the Moabitess, Mahlon's widow, as my wife, in order to maintain the name of the dead with his property, so that his name will not disappear from among his family or from the town records. Today you are witnesses!"

¹¹Then the elders and all those at the gate said, "We are witnesses. May the LORD make the woman who is coming into your home like Rachel and Leah, who together built up the house of Israel. May you have standing in Ephrathah and be famous in Bethlehem. ¹²Through the offspring the LORD gives you by this young woman, may your family be like that of Perez, whom Tamar bore to Judah."

The Genealogy of David

¹³So Boaz took Ruth and she became his wife. Then he went to her, and the LORD enabled her to conceive, and she gave birth to a son. ¹⁴The women said to Naomi: "Praise be to the LORD, who this day has not left you without a kinsman-redeemer. May he become famous throughout Israel! ¹⁵He will renew your life and sustain you in your old age. For your daughter-in-law, who loves you and who is better to you than seven sons, has given him birth." ¹⁶Then Naomi took the child, laid him in her lap and cared for him. ¹⁷The women living there said, "Naomi has a son." And they named him Obed. He was the father of Jesse, the father of David.

¹⁸This, then, is the family line of Perez:

Perez was the father of Hezron,
¹⁹Hezron the father of Ram,
   Ram the father of Amminadab,
²⁰Amminadab the father of Nahshon,
   Nahshon the father of Salmon,*c*
²¹Salmon the father of Boaz,
   Boaz the father of Obed,
²²Obed the father of Jesse,
   and Jesse the father of David.

---

a 4 Many Hebrew manuscripts, Septuagint, Vulgate and Syriac; most Hebrew manuscripts *he*
b 5 Hebrew; Vulgate and Syriac *Naomi, you acquire Ruth the Moabitess,*   *c 20* A few Hebrew manuscripts, some Septuagint manuscripts and Vulgate (see also verse 21 and Septuagint of 1 Chron. 2:11); most Hebrew manuscripts *Salma*

1 SAMUEL

HE BOOK OF 1 SAMUEL RECORDS THE LIVES OF SAMUEL AND SAUL, AND MUCH OF THE LIFE OF DAVID. HERE YOU WILL FIND THE STORY OF ISRAEL'S FIRST KING, SAUL. BUT SAUL DISOBEYED GOD, WHO IN TURN REJECTED HIM AS KING. THE PROPHET SAMUEL SECRETLY ANOINTED DAVID TO TAKE SAUL'S PLACE. THE REST OF THE BOOK RECORDS THE STRUGGLES BETWEEN SAUL AND DAVID. AS YOU READ THIS BOOK, NOTE HOW GOD PROTECTS AND BLESSES THOSE WHO FOLLOW HIM OBEDI-ENTLY, AND HOW THOSE WHO DISREGARD HIM INEVITABLY FACE DIFFICULTIES.

The Birth of Samuel

1 There was a certain man from Ramathaim, a Zuphite*a* from the hill country of Ephraim, whose name was Elkanah son of Jeroham, the son of Elihu, the son of Tohu, the son of Zuph, an Ephraimite. ²He had two wives; one was called Hannah and the other Peninnah. Peninnah had children, but Hannah had none.

³Year after year this man went up from his town to worship and sacrifice to the LORD Almighty at Shiloh, where Hophni and Phinehas, the two sons of Eli, were priests of the LORD. ⁴Whenever the day came for Elkanah to sacrifice, he would give portions of the meat to his wife Peninnah and to all her sons and daugh-ters. ⁵But to Hannah he gave a double portion because he loved her, and the LORD had closed her womb. ⁶And because the LORD had closed her womb, her rival kept provoking her in order to irritate her. ⁷This went on year after year. Whenever Hannah went up to the house of the LORD, her rival provoked her till she wept and would not eat. ⁸Elkanah her husband would say to her, "Hannah, why are you weeping? Why don't you eat? Why are you downhearted? Don't I mean more to you than ten sons?"

⁹Once when they had finished eating and drinking in Shiloh, Hannah stood up. Now Eli the priest was sitting on a chair by the doorpost of the LORD's temple.*b* ¹⁰In bitterness of soul Hannah wept much and prayed to the LORD. ¹¹And she

---

a 1 Or *from Ramathaim Zuphim*   *b* 9 That is, tabernacle

made a vow, saying, "O LORD Almighty, if you will only look upon your servant's misery and remember me, and not forget your servant but give her a son, then I will give him to the LORD for all the days of his life, and no razor will ever be used on his head."

¹²As she kept on praying to the LORD, Eli observed her mouth. ¹³Hannah was praying in her heart, and her lips were moving but her voice was not heard. Eli thought she was drunk ¹⁴and said to her, "How long will you keep on getting drunk? Get rid of your wine."

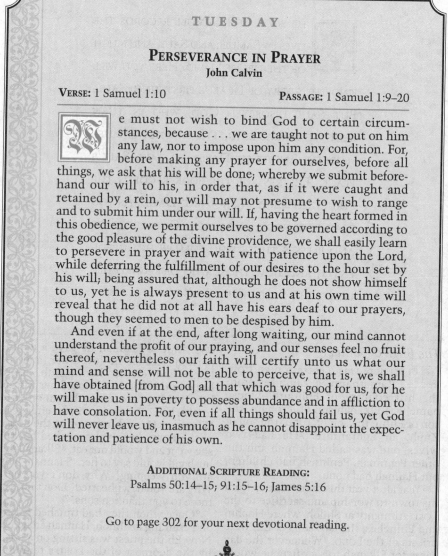

TUESDAY

PERSEVERANCE IN PRAYER
John Calvin

VERSE: 1 Samuel 1:10   **PASSAGE:** 1 Samuel 1:9–20

We must not wish to bind God to certain circumstances, because . . . we are taught not to put on him any law, nor to impose upon him any condition. For, before making any prayer for ourselves, before all things, we ask that his will be done; whereby we submit beforehand our will to his, in order that, as if it were caught and retained by a rein, our will may not presume to wish to range and to submit him under our will. If, having the heart formed in this obedience, we permit ourselves to be governed according to the good pleasure of the divine providence, we shall easily learn to persevere in prayer and wait with patience upon the Lord, while deferring the fulfillment of our desires to the hour set by his will; being assured that, although he does not show himself to us, yet he is always present to us and at his own time will reveal that he did not at all have his ears deaf to our prayers, though they seemed to men to be despised by him.

And even if at the end, after long waiting, our mind cannot understand the profit of our praying, and our senses feel no fruit thereof, nevertheless our faith will certify unto us what our mind and sense will not be able to perceive, that is, we shall have obtained [from God] all that which was good for us, for he will make us in poverty to possess abundance and in affliction to have consolation. For, even if all things should fail us, yet God will never leave us, inasmuch as he cannot disappoint the expectation and patience of his own.

ADDITIONAL SCRIPTURE READING:
Psalms 50:14–15; 91:15–16; James 5:16

Go to page 302 for your next devotional reading.

1500   1700

¹⁵"Not so, my lord," Hannah replied, "I am a woman who is deeply troubled. I have not been drinking wine or beer; I was pouring out my soul to the LORD. ¹⁶Do not take your servant for a wicked woman; I have been praying here out of my great anguish and grief."

¹⁷Eli answered, "Go in peace, and may the God of Israel grant you what you have asked of him."

¹⁸She said, "May your servant find favor in your eyes." Then she went her way and ate something, and her face was no longer downcast.

¹⁹Early the next morning they arose and worshiped before the LORD and then went back to their home at Ramah. Elkanah lay with Hannah his wife, and the LORD remembered her. ²⁰So in the course of time Hannah conceived and gave birth to a son. She named him Samuel,ᵃ saying, "Because I asked the LORD for him."

Hannah Dedicates Samuel

²¹When the man Elkanah went up with all his family to offer the annual sacrifice to the LORD and to fulfill his vow, ²²Hannah did not go. She said to her husband, "After the boy is weaned, I will take him and present him before the LORD, and he will live there always."

²³"Do what seems best to you," Elkanah her husband told her. "Stay here until you have weaned him; only may the LORD make good hisᵇ word." So the woman stayed at home and nursed her son until she had weaned him. ²⁴After he was weaned, she took the boy with her, young as he was, along with a three-year-old bull,ᶜ an ephahᵈ of flour and a skin of wine, and brought him to the house of the LORD at Shiloh. ²⁵When they had slaughtered the bull, they brought the boy to Eli, ²⁶and she said to him, "As surely as you live, my lord, I am the woman who stood here beside you praying to the LORD. ²⁷I prayed for this child, and the LORD has granted me what I asked of him. ²⁸So now I give him to the LORD. For his whole life he will be given over to the LORD." And he worshiped the LORD there.

Hannah's Prayer

2 Then Hannah prayed and said:

"My heart rejoices in the LORD;
    in the LORD my hornᵉ is lifted high.
My mouth boasts over my enemies,
    for I delight in your deliverance.

² "There is no one holyᶠ like the LORD;
    there is no one besides you;
    there is no Rock like our God.

³ "Do not keep talking so proudly
    or let your mouth speak such arrogance,
for the LORD is a God who knows,
    and by him deeds are weighed.

⁴ "The bows of the warriors are broken,
    but those who stumbled are armed with strength.
⁵ Those who were full hire themselves out for food,
    but those who were hungry hunger no more.
She who was barren has borne seven children,
    but she who has had many sons pines away.

⁶ "The LORD brings death and makes alive;
    he brings down to the graveᵍ and raises up.
⁷ The LORD sends poverty and wealth;
    he humbles and he exalts.
⁸ He raises the poor from the dust
    and lifts the needy from the ash heap;
he seats them with princes
    and has them inherit a throne of honor.

"For the foundations of the earth are the LORD's;
    upon them he has set the world.
⁹ He will guard the feet of his saints,
    but the wicked will be silenced in darkness.

"It is not by strength that one prevails;
¹⁰   those who oppose the LORD will be shattered.
He will thunder against them from heaven;

ᵃ 20 *Samuel* sounds like the Hebrew for *heard of God.*   ᵇ 23 Masoretic Text; Dead Sea Scrolls, Septuagint and Syriac *your*   ᶜ 24 Dead Sea Scrolls, Septuagint and Syriac; Masoretic Text *with three bulls*   ᵈ 24 That is, probably about 3/5 bushel (about 22 liters)   ᵉ 1 *Horn* here symbolizes strength; also in verse 10.   ᶠ 2 Or *no Holy One*   ᵍ 6 Hebrew *Sheol*

the LORD will judge the ends of the
earth.

"He will give strength to his king
and exalt the horn of his anointed."

¹¹Then Elkanah went home to Ramah, but the boy ministered before the
LORD under Eli the priest.

Eli's Wicked Sons

¹²Eli's sons were wicked men; they had
no regard for the LORD. ¹³Now it was the
practice of the priests with the people
that whenever anyone offered a sacrifice
and while the meat was being boiled, the
servant of the priest would come with a
three-pronged fork in his hand. ¹⁴He
would plunge it into the pan or kettle or
caldron or pot, and the priest would take
for himself whatever the fork brought up.
This is how they treated all the Israelites
who came to Shiloh. ¹⁵But even before
the fat was burned, the servant of the
priest would come and say to the man
who was sacrificing, "Give the priest
some meat to roast; he won't accept
boiled meat from you, but only raw."

¹⁶If the man said to him, "Let the fat
be burned up first, and then take whatever you want," the servant would then
answer, "No, hand it over now; if you
don't, I'll take it by force."

¹⁷This sin of the young men was very
great in the LORD's sight, for they*a* were
treating the LORD's offering with contempt.

¹⁸But Samuel was ministering before
the LORD—a boy wearing a linen ephod.
¹⁹Each year his mother made him a little robe and took it to him when she
went up with her husband to offer the
annual sacrifice. ²⁰Eli would bless Elkanah and his wife, saying, "May the LORD
give you children by this woman to take
the place of the one she prayed for and
gave to the LORD." Then they would go
home. ²¹And the LORD was gracious to
Hannah; she conceived and gave birth to
three sons and two daughters. Meanwhile, the boy Samuel grew up in the
presence of the LORD.

²²Now Eli, who was very old, heard
about everything his sons were doing to
all Israel and how they slept with the
women who served at the entrance to
the Tent of Meeting. ²³So he said to
them, "Why do you do such things? I
hear from all the people about these
wicked deeds of yours. ²⁴No, my sons; it
is not a good report that I hear spreading
among the LORD's people. ²⁵If a man sins
against another man, God*b* may mediate
for him; but if a man sins against the
LORD, who will intercede for him?" His
sons, however, did not listen to their
father's rebuke, for it was the LORD's
will to put them to death.

²⁶And the boy Samuel continued to
grow in stature and in favor with the
LORD and with men.

Prophecy Against the House of Eli

²⁷Now a man of God came to Eli and
said to him, "This is what the LORD
says: 'Did I not clearly reveal myself to
your father's house when they were in
Egypt under Pharaoh? ²⁸I chose your
father out of all the tribes of Israel to be
my priest, to go up to my altar, to burn
incense, and to wear an ephod in my
presence. I also gave your father's house
all the offerings made with fire by the
Israelites. ²⁹Why do you*c* scorn my sacrifice and offering that I prescribed for
my dwelling? Why do you honor your
sons more than me by fattening yourselves on the choice parts of every offering made by my people Israel?'

³⁰"Therefore the LORD, the God of
Israel, declares: 'I promised that your
house and your father's house would
minister before me forever.' But now the
LORD declares: 'Far be it from me! Those
who honor me I will honor, but those
who despise me will be disdained. ³¹The
time is coming when I will cut short
your strength and the strength of your
father's house, so that there will not
be an old man in your family line ³²and
you will see distress in my dwelling.
Although good will be done to Israel, in
your family line there will never be an
old man. ³³Every one of you that I do not
cut off from my altar will be spared only
to blind your eyes with tears and to
grieve your heart, and all your descendants will die in the prime of life.

³⁴" 'And what happens to your two
sons, Hophni and Phinehas, will be a

---

a 17 Or *men*   *b 25* Or *the judges*   *c 29* The Hebrew is plural.

sign to you—they will both die on the same day. 35I will raise up for myself a faithful priest, who will do according to what is in my heart and mind. I will firmly establish his house, and he will minister before my anointed one always. 36Then everyone left in your family line will come and bow down before him for a piece of silver and a crust of bread and plead, "Appoint me to some priestly office so I can have food to eat." ' "

The Lord Calls Samuel

3 The boy Samuel ministered before the LORD under Eli. In those days the word of the LORD was rare; there were not many visions.

2One night Eli, whose eyes were becoming so weak that he could barely see, was lying down in his usual place. 3The lamp of God had not yet gone out, and Samuel was lying down in the temple*a* of the LORD, where the ark of God was. 4Then the LORD called Samuel.

Samuel answered, "Here I am." 5And he ran to Eli and said, "Here I am; you called me."

IF YOU SAY THAT MAN IS TOO LITTLE FOR GOD TO SPEAK TO HIM, YOU MUST BE VERY BIG TO BE ABLE TO JUDGE.   —*Blaise Pascal*

But Eli said, "I did not call; go back and lie down." So he went and lay down.

6Again the LORD called, "Samuel!" And Samuel got up and went to Eli and said, "Here I am; you called me."

"My son," Eli said, "I did not call; go back and lie down."

7Now Samuel did not yet know the LORD: The word of the LORD had not yet been revealed to him.

8The LORD called Samuel a third time, and Samuel got up and went to Eli and said, "Here I am; you called me."

Then Eli realized that the LORD was calling the boy. 9So Eli told Samuel, "Go and lie down, and if he calls you, say, 'Speak, LORD, for your servant is listening.' " So Samuel went and lay down in his place.

10The LORD came and stood there, calling as at the other times, "Samuel! Samuel!"

Then Samuel said, "Speak, for your servant is listening."

11And the LORD said to Samuel: "See, I am about to do something in Israel that will make the ears of everyone who hears of it tingle. 12At that time I will carry out against Eli everything I spoke against his family—from beginning to end. 13For I told him that I would judge his family forever because of the sin he knew about; his sons made themselves contemptible,*b* and he failed to restrain them. 14Therefore, I swore to the house of Eli, 'The guilt of Eli's house will never be atoned for by sacrifice or offering.' "

15Samuel lay down until morning and then opened the doors of the house of the LORD. He was afraid to tell Eli the vision, 16but Eli called him and said, "Samuel, my son."

Samuel answered, "Here I am."

17"What was it he said to you?" Eli asked. "Do not hide it from me. May God deal with you, be it ever so severely, if you hide from me anything he told you." 18So Samuel told him everything, hiding nothing from him. Then Eli said, "He is the LORD; let him do what is good in his eyes."

19The LORD was with Samuel as he grew up, and he let none of his words fall to the ground. 20And all Israel from Dan to Beersheba recognized that Samuel was attested as a prophet of the LORD. 21The LORD continued to appear at Shiloh, and there he revealed himself to Samuel through his word.

4 And Samuel's word came to all Israel.

The Philistines Capture the Ark

Now the Israelites went out to fight against the Philistines. The Israelites camped at Ebenezer, and the Philistines at Aphek. 2The Philistines deployed their forces to meet Israel, and as the battle spread, Israel was defeated by the Philistines, who killed about four thousand of them on the battlefield. 3When the soldiers returned to camp, the elders of Israel asked, "Why did the LORD bring defeat upon us today before

---

a 3 That is, tabernacle   *b* 13 Masoretic Text; an ancient Hebrew scribal tradition and Septuagint *sons blasphemed God*

the Philistines? Let us bring the ark of the LORD's covenant from Shiloh, so that it*a* may go with us and save us from the hand of our enemies."

4So the people sent men to Shiloh, and they brought back the ark of the covenant of the LORD Almighty, who is enthroned between the cherubim. And Eli's two sons, Hophni and Phinehas, were there with the ark of the covenant of God.

5When the ark of the LORD's covenant came into the camp, all Israel raised such a great shout that the ground shook. 6Hearing the uproar, the Philistines asked, "What's all this shouting in the Hebrew camp?"

When they learned that the ark of the LORD had come into the camp, 7the Philistines were afraid. "A god has come into the camp," they said. "We're in trouble!

a 3 Or *he*

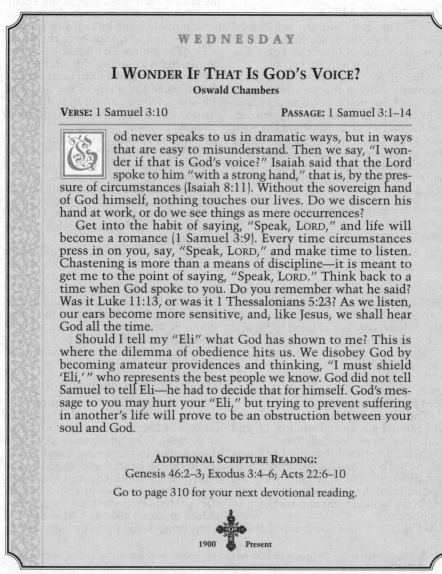

WEDNESDAY

I WONDER IF THAT IS GOD'S VOICE?
Oswald Chambers

VERSE: 1 Samuel 3:10   **PASSAGE:** 1 Samuel 3:1–14

od never speaks to us in dramatic ways, but in ways that are easy to misunderstand. Then we say, "I wonder if that is God's voice?" Isaiah said that the Lord spoke to him "with a strong hand," that is, by the pressure of circumstances (Isaiah 8:11). Without the sovereign hand of God himself, nothing touches our lives. Do we discern his hand at work, or do we see things as mere occurrences?

Get into the habit of saying, "Speak, LORD," and life will become a romance (1 Samuel 3:9). Every time circumstances press in on you, say, "Speak, LORD," and make time to listen. Chastening is more than a means of discipline—it is meant to get me to the point of saying, "Speak, LORD." Think back to a time when God spoke to you. Do you remember what he said? Was it Luke 11:13, or was it 1 Thessalonians 5:23? As we listen, our ears become more sensitive, and, like Jesus, we shall hear God all the time.

Should I tell my "Eli" what God has shown to me? This is where the dilemma of obedience hits us. We disobey God by becoming amateur providences and thinking, "I must shield 'Eli,'" who represents the best people we know. God did not tell Samuel to tell Eli—he had to decide that for himself. God's message to you may hurt your "Eli," but trying to prevent suffering in another's life will prove to be an obstruction between your soul and God.

ADDITIONAL SCRIPTURE READING:
Genesis 46:2–3; Exodus 3:4–6; Acts 22:6–10

Go to page 310 for your next devotional reading.

1900   Present

Nothing like this has happened before. ⁸Woe to us! Who will deliver us from the hand of these mighty gods? They are the gods who struck the Egyptians with all kinds of plagues in the desert. ⁹Be strong, Philistines! Be men, or you will be subject to the Hebrews, as they have been to you. Be men, and fight!"

¹⁰So the Philistines fought, and the Israelites were defeated and every man fled to his tent. The slaughter was very great; Israel lost thirty thousand foot soldiers. ¹¹The ark of God was captured, and Eli's two sons, Hophni and Phinehas, died.

Death of Eli

¹²That same day a Benjamite ran from the battle line and went to Shiloh, his clothes torn and dust on his head. ¹³When he arrived, there was Eli sitting on his chair by the side of the road, watching, because his heart feared for the ark of God. When the man entered the town and told what had happened, the whole town sent up a cry.

¹⁴Eli heard the outcry and asked, "What is the meaning of this uproar?"

The man hurried over to Eli, ¹⁵who was ninety-eight years old and whose eyes were set so that he could not see. ¹⁶He told Eli, "I have just come from the battle line; I fled from it this very day."

Eli asked, "What happened, my son?"

¹⁷The man who brought the news replied, "Israel fled before the Philistines, and the army has suffered heavy losses. Also your two sons, Hophni and Phinehas, are dead, and the ark of God has been captured."

¹⁸When he mentioned the ark of God, Eli fell backward off his chair by the side of the gate. His neck was broken and he died, for he was an old man and heavy. He had led*ᵃ* Israel forty years.

¹⁹His daughter-in-law, the wife of Phinehas, was pregnant and near the time of delivery. When she heard the news that the ark of God had been captured and that her father-in-law and her husband were dead, she went into labor and gave birth, but was overcome by her labor pains. ²⁰As she was dying, the women attending her said, "Don't despair; you have given birth to a son." But she did not respond or pay any attention.

²¹She named the boy Ichabod,ᵇ saying, "The glory has departed from Israel"—because of the capture of the ark of God and the deaths of her father-in-law and her husband. ²²She said, "The glory has departed from Israel, for the ark of God has been captured."

The Ark in Ashdod and Ekron

5 After the Philistines had captured the ark of God, they took it from Ebenezer to Ashdod. ²Then they carried the ark into Dagon's temple and set it beside Dagon. ³When the people of Ashdod rose early the next day, there was Dagon, fallen on his face on the ground before the ark of the LORD! They took Dagon and put him back in his place. ⁴But the following morning when they rose, there was Dagon, fallen on his face on the ground before the ark of the LORD! His head and hands had been broken off and were lying on the threshold; only his body remained. ⁵That is why to this day neither the priests of Dagon nor any others who enter Dagon's temple at Ashdod step on the threshold.

⁶The LORD's hand was heavy upon the people of Ashdod and its vicinity; he brought devastation upon them and afflicted them with tumors.ᶜ ⁷When the men of Ashdod saw what was happening, they said, "The ark of the god of Israel must not stay here with us, because his hand is heavy upon us and upon Dagon our god." ⁸So they called together all the rulers of the Philistines and asked them, "What shall we do with the ark of the god of Israel?"

They answered, "Have the ark of the god of Israel moved to Gath." So they moved the ark of the God of Israel.

⁹But after they had moved it, the LORD's hand was against that city, throwing it into a great panic. He afflicted the people of the city, both young and old, with an outbreak of tumors.ᵈ ¹⁰So they sent the ark of God to Ekron.

As the ark of God was entering Ekron, the people of Ekron cried out, "They

---

ᵃ 18 Traditionally *judged*   ᵇ 21 *Ichabod* means *no glory.*   ᶜ 6 Hebrew; Septuagint and Vulgate *tumors. And rats appeared in their land, and death and destruction were throughout the city*   ᵈ 9 Or *with tumors in the groin* (see Septuagint)

have brought the ark of the god of Israel around to us to kill us and our people." ¹¹So they called together all the rulers of the Philistines and said, "Send the ark of the god of Israel away; let it go back to its own place, or it*a* will kill us and our people." For death had filled the city with panic; God's hand was very heavy upon it. ¹²Those who did not die were afflicted with tumors, and the outcry of the city went up to heaven.

The Ark Returned to Israel

6 When the ark of the LORD had been in Philistine territory seven months, ²the Philistines called for the priests and the diviners and said, "What shall we do with the ark of the LORD? Tell us how we should send it back to its place."

³They answered, "If you return the ark of the god of Israel, do not send it away empty, but by all means send a guilt offering to him. Then you will be healed, and you will know why his hand has not been lifted from you."

⁴The Philistines asked, "What guilt offering should we send to him?"

They replied, "Five gold tumors and five gold rats, according to the number of the Philistine rulers, because the same plague has struck both you and your rulers. ⁵Make models of the tumors and of the rats that are destroying the country, and pay honor to Israel's god. Perhaps he will lift his hand from you and your gods and your land. ⁶Why do you harden your hearts as the Egyptians and Pharaoh did? When he*b* treated them harshly, did they not send the Israelites out so they could go on their way?

⁷"Now then, get a new cart ready, with two cows that have calved and have never been yoked. Hitch the cows to the cart, but take their calves away and pen them up. ⁸Take the ark of the LORD and put it on the cart, and in a chest beside it put the gold objects you are sending back to him as a guilt offering. Send it on its way, ⁹but keep watching it. If it goes up to its own territory, toward Beth Shemesh, then the LORD has brought this great disaster on us. But

if it does not, then we will know that it was not his hand that struck us and that it happened to us by chance."

¹⁰So they did this. They took two such cows and hitched them to the cart and penned up their calves. ¹¹They placed the ark of the LORD on the cart and along with it the chest containing the gold rats and the models of the tumors. ¹²Then the cows went straight up toward Beth Shemesh, keeping on the road and lowing all the way; they did not turn to the right or to the left. The rulers of the Philistines followed them as far as the border of Beth Shemesh.

¹³Now the people of Beth Shemesh were harvesting their wheat in the valley, and when they looked up and saw the ark, they rejoiced at the sight. ¹⁴The cart came to the field of Joshua of Beth Shemesh, and there it stopped beside a large rock. The people chopped up the wood of the cart and sacrificed the cows as a burnt offering to the LORD. ¹⁵The Levites took down the ark of the LORD, together with the chest containing the gold objects, and placed them on the large rock. On that day the people of Beth Shemesh offered burnt offerings and made sacrifices to the LORD. ¹⁶The five rulers of the Philistines saw all this and then returned that same day to Ekron.

¹⁷These are the gold tumors the Philistines sent as a guilt offering to the LORD—one each for Ashdod, Gaza, Ashkelon, Gath and Ekron. ¹⁸And the number of the gold rats was according to the number of Philistine towns belonging to the five rulers—the fortified towns with their country villages. The large rock, on which*c* they set the ark of the LORD, is a witness to this day in the field of Joshua of Beth Shemesh.

¹⁹But God struck down some of the men of Beth Shemesh, putting seventy*d* of them to death because they had looked into the ark of the LORD. The people mourned because of the heavy blow the LORD had dealt them, ²⁰and the men of Beth Shemesh asked, "Who can stand in the presence of the LORD, this holy God? To whom will the ark go up from here?" ²¹Then they sent messengers to the

---

a 11 Or *he*   *b 6* That is, God   *c 18* A few Hebrew manuscripts (see also Septuagint); most Hebrew manuscripts *villages as far as Greater Abel, where*   *d 19* A few Hebrew manuscripts; most Hebrew manuscripts and Septuagint *50,070*

people of Kiriath Jearim, saying, "The Philistines have returned the ark of the LORD. Come down and take it up to your

7 place." ¹So the men of Kiriath Jearim came and took up the ark of the LORD. They took it to Abinadab's house on the hill and consecrated Eleazar his son to guard the ark of the LORD.

Samuel Subdues the Philistines at Mizpah

²It was a long time, twenty years in all, that the ark remained at Kiriath Jearim, and all the people of Israel mourned and sought after the LORD. ³And Samuel said to the whole house of Israel, "If you are returning to the LORD with all your hearts, then rid yourselves of the foreign gods and the Ashtoreths and commit yourselves to the LORD and serve him only, and he will deliver you out of the hand of the Philistines." ⁴So the Israelites put away their Baals and Ashtoreths, and served the LORD only.

⁵Then Samuel said, "Assemble all Israel at Mizpah and I will intercede with the LORD for you." ⁶When they had assembled at Mizpah, they drew water and poured it out before the LORD. On that day they fasted and there they confessed, "We have sinned against the LORD." And Samuel was leader*a* of Israel at Mizpah.

⁷When the Philistines heard that Israel had assembled at Mizpah, the rulers of the Philistines came up to attack them. And when the Israelites heard of it, they were afraid because of the Philistines. ⁸They said to Samuel, "Do not stop crying out to the LORD our God for us, that he may rescue us from the hand of the Philistines." ⁹Then Samuel took a suckling lamb and offered it up as a whole burnt offering to the LORD. He cried out to the LORD on Israel's behalf, and the LORD answered him. ¹⁰While Samuel was sacrificing the burnt offering, the Philistines drew near to engage Israel in battle. But that day the LORD thundered with loud thunder against the Philistines and threw them into such a panic that they were routed before the Israelites. ¹¹The men of Israel rushed out of Mizpah and pursued the

Philistines, slaughtering them along the way to a point below Beth Car.

¹²Then Samuel took a stone and set it up between Mizpah and Shen. He named it Ebenezer,*b* saying, "Thus far has the LORD helped us." ¹³So the Philistines were subdued and did not invade Israelite territory again.

Throughout Samuel's lifetime, the hand of the LORD was against the Philistines. ¹⁴The towns from Ekron to Gath that the Philistines had captured from Israel were restored to her, and Israel delivered the neighboring territory from the power of the Philistines. And there was peace between Israel and the Amorites.

¹⁵Samuel continued as judge over Israel all the days of his life. ¹⁶From year to year he went on a circuit from Bethel to Gilgal to Mizpah, judging Israel in all those places. ¹⁷But he always went back to Ramah, where his home was, and there he also judged Israel. And he built an altar there to the LORD.

Israel Asks for a King

8 When Samuel grew old, he appointed his sons as judges for Israel. ²The name of his firstborn was Joel and the name of his second was Abijah, and they served at Beersheba. ³But his sons did not walk in his ways. They turned aside after dishonest gain and accepted bribes and perverted justice.

⁴So all the elders of Israel gathered together and came to Samuel at Ramah. ⁵They said to him, "You are old, and your sons do not walk in your ways; now appoint a king to lead*c* us, such as all the other nations have."

⁶But when they said, "Give us a king to lead us," this displeased Samuel; so he prayed to the LORD. ⁷And the LORD told him: "Listen to all that the people are saying to you; it is not you they have rejected, but they have rejected me as their king. ⁸As they have done from the day I brought them up out of Egypt until this day, forsaking me and serving other gods, so they are doing to you. ⁹Now listen to them; but warn them solemnly and let them know what the king who will reign over them will do."

---

a 6 Traditionally *judge*   *b* 12 *Ebenezer* means *stone of help*.   *c* 5 Traditionally *judge;* also in verses 6 and 20

¹⁰Samuel told all the words of the LORD to the people who were asking him for a king. ¹¹He said, "This is what the king who will reign over you will do: He will take your sons and make them serve with his chariots and horses, and they will run in front of his chariots. ¹²Some he will assign to be commanders of thousands and commanders of fifties, and others to plow his ground and reap his harvest, and still others to make weapons of war and equipment for his chariots. ¹³He will take your daughters to be perfumers and cooks and bakers. ¹⁴He will take the best of your fields and vineyards and olive groves and give them to his attendants. ¹⁵He will take a tenth of your grain and of your vintage and give it to his officials and attendants. ¹⁶Your menservants and maidservants and the best of your cattleᵃ and donkeys he will take for his own use. ¹⁷He will take a tenth of your flocks, and you yourselves will become his slaves. ¹⁸When that day comes, you will cry out for relief from the king you have chosen, and the LORD will not answer you in that day."

¹⁹But the people refused to listen to Samuel. "No!" they said. "We want a king over us. ²⁰Then we will be like all the other nations, with a king to lead us and to go out before us and fight our battles."

²¹When Samuel heard all that the people said, he repeated it before the LORD. ²²The LORD answered, "Listen to them and give them a king."

Then Samuel said to the men of Israel, "Everyone go back to his town."

Samuel Anoints Saul

9 There was a Benjamite, a man of standing, whose name was Kish son of Abiel, the son of Zeror, the son of Becorath, the son of Aphiah of Benjamin. ²He had a son named Saul, an impressive young man without equal among the Israelites—a head taller than any of the others.

³Now the donkeys belonging to Saul's father Kish were lost, and Kish said to his son Saul, "Take one of the servants with you and go and look for the donkeys." ⁴So he passed through the hill country of Ephraim and through the area around Shalisha, but they did not find them. They went on into the district of Shaalim, but the donkeys were not there. Then he passed through the territory of Benjamin, but they did not find them.

⁵When they reached the district of Zuph, Saul said to the servant who was with him, "Come, let's go back, or my father will stop thinking about the donkeys and start worrying about us."

⁶But the servant replied, "Look, in this town there is a man of God; he is highly respected, and everything he says comes true. Let's go there now. Perhaps he will tell us what way to take."

⁷Saul said to his servant, "If we go, what can we give the man? The food in our sacks is gone. We have no gift to take to the man of God. What do we have?"

⁸The servant answered him again. "Look," he said, "I have a quarter of a shekelᵇ of silver. I will give it to the man of God so that he will tell us what way to take." ⁹(Formerly in Israel, if a man went to inquire of God, he would say, "Come, let us go to the seer," because the prophet of today used to be called a seer.)

¹⁰"Good," Saul said to his servant. "Come, let's go." So they set out for the town where the man of God was.

¹¹As they were going up the hill to the town, they met some girls coming out to draw water, and they asked them, "Is the seer here?"

¹²"He is," they answered. "He's ahead of you. Hurry now; he has just come to our town today, for the people have a sacrifice at the high place. ¹³As soon as you enter the town, you will find him before he goes up to the high place to eat. The people will not begin eating until he comes, because he must bless the sacrifice; afterward, those who are invited will eat. Go up now; you should find him about this time."

¹⁴They went up to the town, and as they were entering it, there was Samuel, coming toward them on his way up to the high place.

¹⁵Now the day before Saul came, the LORD had revealed this to Samuel: ¹⁶"About this time tomorrow I will send you a man from the land of Benjamin. Anoint him leader over my people Israel;

ᵃ 16 Septuagint; Hebrew *young men*   ᵇ 8 That is, about 1/10 ounce (about 3 grams)

he will deliver my people from the hand of the Philistines. I have looked upon my people, for their cry has reached me."

¹⁷When Samuel caught sight of Saul, the LORD said to him, "This is the man I spoke to you about; he will govern my people."

¹⁸Saul approached Samuel in the gateway and asked, "Would you please tell me where the seer's house is?"

¹⁹"I am the seer," Samuel replied. "Go up ahead of me to the high place, for today you are to eat with me, and in the morning I will let you go and will tell you all that is in your heart. ²⁰As for the donkeys you lost three days ago, do not worry about them; they have been found. And to whom is all the desire of Israel turned, if not to you and all your father's family?"

²¹Saul answered, "But am I not a Benjamite, from the smallest tribe of Israel, and is not my clan the least of all the clans of the tribe of Benjamin? Why do you say such a thing to me?"

²²Then Samuel brought Saul and his servant into the hall and seated them at the head of those who were invited—about thirty in number. ²³Samuel said to the cook, "Bring the piece of meat I gave you, the one I told you to lay aside."

²⁴So the cook took up the leg with what was on it and set it in front of Saul. Samuel said, "Here is what has been kept for you. Eat, because it was set aside for you for this occasion, from the time I said, 'I have invited guests.' " And Saul dined with Samuel that day.

²⁵After they came down from the high place to the town, Samuel talked with Saul on the roof of his house. ²⁶They rose about daybreak and Samuel called to Saul on the roof, "Get ready, and I will send you on your way." When Saul got ready, he and Samuel went outside together. ²⁷As they were going down to the edge of the town, Samuel said to Saul, "Tell the servant to go on ahead of us"—and the servant did so—"but you stay here awhile, so that I may give you a message from God."

10 Then Samuel took a flask of oil and poured it on Saul's head and kissed him, saying, "Has not the LORD anointed you leader over his inheritance?ᵃ ²When you leave me today, you will meet two men near Rachel's tomb, at Zelzah on the border of Benjamin. They will say to you, 'The donkeys you set out to look for have been found. And now your father has stopped thinking about them and is worried about you. He is asking, "What shall I do about my son?" '

³"Then you will go on from there until you reach the great tree of Tabor. Three men going up to God at Bethel will meet you there. One will be carrying three young goats, another three loaves of bread, and another a skin of wine. ⁴They will greet you and offer you two loaves of bread, which you will accept from them.

⁵"After that you will go to Gibeah of God, where there is a Philistine outpost. As you approach the town, you will meet a procession of prophets coming down from the high place with lyres, tambourines, flutes and harps being played before them, and they will be prophesying. ⁶The Spirit of the LORD will come upon you in power, and you will prophesy with them; and you will be changed into a different person. ⁷Once these signs are fulfilled, do whatever your hand finds to do, for God is with you.

⁸"Go down ahead of me to Gilgal. I will surely come down to you to sacrifice burnt offerings and fellowship offerings,ᵇ but you must wait seven days until I come to you and tell you what you are to do."

Saul Made King

⁹As Saul turned to leave Samuel, God changed Saul's heart, and all these signs were fulfilled that day. ¹⁰When they arrived at Gibeah, a procession of prophets met him; the Spirit of God came upon him in power, and he joined in their prophesying. ¹¹When all those who had formerly known him saw him prophesying with the prophets, they asked each other, "What is this that has

---

ᵃ 1 Hebrew; Septuagint and Vulgate *over his people Israel? You will reign over the* LORD's *people and save them from the power of their enemies round about. And this will be a sign to you that the* LORD *has anointed you leader over his inheritance:*   ᵇ 8 Traditionally *peace offerings*

happened to the son of Kish? Is Saul also among the prophets?"

12A man who lived there answered, "And who is their father?" So it became a saying: "Is Saul also among the prophets?" 13After Saul stopped prophesying, he went to the high place.

14Now Saul's uncle asked him and his servant, "Where have you been?"

"Looking for the donkeys," he said. "But when we saw they were not to be found, we went to Samuel."

15Saul's uncle said, "Tell me what Samuel said to you."

16Saul replied, "He assured us that the donkeys had been found." But he did not tell his uncle what Samuel had said about the kingship.

17Samuel summoned the people of Israel to the LORD at Mizpah 18and said to them, "This is what the LORD, the God of Israel, says: 'I brought Israel up out of Egypt, and I delivered you from the power of Egypt and all the kingdoms that oppressed you.' 19But you have now rejected your God, who saves you out of all your calamities and distresses. And you have said, 'No, set a king over us.' So now present yourselves before the LORD by your tribes and clans."

20When Samuel brought all the tribes of Israel near, the tribe of Benjamin was chosen. 21Then he brought forward the tribe of Benjamin, clan by clan, and Matri's clan was chosen. Finally Saul son of Kish was chosen. But when they looked for him, he was not to be found. 22So they inquired further of the LORD, "Has the man come here yet?"

And the LORD said, "Yes, he has hidden himself among the baggage."

23They ran and brought him out, and as he stood among the people he was a head taller than any of the others. 24Samuel said to all the people, "Do you see the man the LORD has chosen? There is no one like him among all the people."

Then the people shouted, "Long live the king!"

25Samuel explained to the people the regulations of the kingship. He wrote them down on a scroll and deposited it before the LORD. Then Samuel dismissed the people, each to his own home.

26Saul also went to his home in Gibeah, accompanied by valiant men whose hearts God had touched. 27But some troublemakers said, "How can this fellow save us?" They despised him and brought him no gifts. But Saul kept silent.

Saul Rescues the City of Jabesh

11 Nahash the Ammonite went up and besieged Jabesh Gilead. And all the men of Jabesh said to him, "Make a treaty with us, and we will be subject to you."

2But Nahash the Ammonite replied, "I will make a treaty with you only on the condition that I gouge out the right eye of every one of you and so bring disgrace on all Israel."

3The elders of Jabesh said to him, "Give us seven days so we can send messengers throughout Israel; if no one comes to rescue us, we will surrender to you."

4When the messengers came to Gibeah of Saul and reported these terms to the people, they all wept aloud. 5Just then Saul was returning from the fields, behind his oxen, and he asked, "What is wrong with the people? Why are they weeping?" Then they repeated to him what the men of Jabesh had said.

6When Saul heard their words, the Spirit of God came upon him in power, and he burned with anger. 7He took a pair of oxen, cut them into pieces, and sent the pieces by messengers throughout Israel, proclaiming, "This is what will be done to the oxen of anyone who does not follow Saul and Samuel." Then the terror of the LORD fell on the people, and they turned out as one man. 8When Saul mustered them at Bezek, the men of Israel numbered three hundred thousand and the men of Judah thirty thousand.

9They told the messengers who had come, "Say to the men of Jabesh Gilead, 'By the time the sun is hot tomorrow, you will be delivered.' " When the messengers went and reported this to the men of Jabesh, they were elated. 10They said to the Ammonites, "Tomorrow we will surrender to you, and you can do to us whatever seems good to you."

11The next day Saul separated his men into three divisions; during the last watch of the night they broke into the camp of the Ammonites and slaughtered them until the heat of the day. Those who survived were scattered, so that no two of them were left together.

Saul Confirmed as King

12The people then said to Samuel, "Who was it that asked, 'Shall Saul reign over us?' Bring these men to us and we will put them to death."

13But Saul said, "No one shall be put to death today, for this day the LORD has rescued Israel."

14Then Samuel said to the people, "Come, let us go to Gilgal and there reaffirm the kingship." 15So all the people went to Gilgal and confirmed Saul as king in the presence of the LORD. There they sacrificed fellowship offerings*a* before the LORD, and Saul and all the Israelites held a great celebration.

Samuel's Farewell Speech

12 Samuel said to all Israel, "I have listened to everything you said to me and have set a king over you. 2Now you have a king as your leader. As for me, I am old and gray, and my sons are here with you. I have been your leader from my youth until this day. 3Here I stand. Testify against me in the presence of the LORD and his anointed. Whose ox have I taken? Whose donkey have I taken? Whom have I cheated? Whom have I oppressed? From whose hand have I accepted a bribe to make me shut my eyes? If I have done any of these, I will make it right."

4"You have not cheated or oppressed us," they replied. "You have not taken anything from anyone's hand."

5Samuel said to them, "The LORD is witness against you, and also his anointed is witness this day, that you have not found anything in my hand."

"He is witness," they said.

6Then Samuel said to the people, "It is the LORD who appointed Moses and Aaron and brought your forefathers up out of Egypt. 7Now then, stand here, because I am going to confront you with evidence before the LORD as to all the righteous acts performed by the LORD for you and your fathers.

8"After Jacob entered Egypt, they cried to the LORD for help, and the LORD sent Moses and Aaron, who brought your forefathers out of Egypt and settled them in this place.

9"But they forgot the LORD their God; so he sold them into the hand of Sisera, the commander of the army of Hazor, and into the hands of the Philistines and the king of Moab, who fought against them. 10They cried out to the LORD and said, 'We have sinned; we have forsaken the LORD and served the Baals and the Ashtoreths. But now deliver us from the hands of our enemies, and we will serve you.' 11Then the LORD sent Jerub-Baal,*b* Barak,*c* Jephthah and Samuel,*d* and he delivered you from the hands of your enemies on every side, so that you lived securely.

12"But when you saw that Nahash king of the Ammonites was moving against you, you said to me, 'No, we want a king to rule over us'—even though the LORD your God was your king. 13Now here is the king you have chosen, the one you asked for; see, the LORD has set a king over you. 14If you fear the LORD and serve and obey him and do not rebel against his commands, and if both you and the king who reigns over you follow the LORD your God—good! 15But if you do not obey the LORD, and if you rebel against his commands, his hand will be against you, as it was against your fathers.

16"Now then, stand still and see this great thing the LORD is about to do before your eyes! 17Is it not wheat harvest now? I will call upon the LORD to send thunder and rain. And you will realize what an evil thing you did in the eyes of the LORD when you asked for a king."

18Then Samuel called upon the LORD, and that same day the LORD sent thunder and rain. So all the people stood in awe of the LORD and of Samuel.

19The people all said to Samuel, "Pray to the LORD your God for your servants so that we will not die, for we have added to all our other sins the evil of asking for a king."

20"Do not be afraid," Samuel replied. "You have done all this evil; yet do not

---

a 15 Traditionally *peace offerings*   *b 11* Also called *Gideon*   *c 11* Some Septuagint manuscripts and Syriac; Hebrew *Bedan*   *d 11* Hebrew; some Septuagint manuscripts and Syriac *Samson*

turn away from the LORD, but serve the LORD with all your heart. ²¹Do not turn away after useless idols. They can do you no good, nor can they rescue you, because they are useless. ²²For the sake of his great name the LORD will not

---

THURSDAY

THE ONLY REAL APOSTOLIC LIFE
Evelyn Underhill

VERSE: 1 Samuel 12:19   **PASSAGE:** 1 Samuel 12:19–25

hat then is a real man of prayer? He is one who deliberately wills and steadily desires that his intercourse with God and other souls shall be controlled and actuated at every point by God himself; one who has so far developed and educated his spiritual sense, that his supernatural environment is more real and solid to him than his natural environment. A man of prayer is not necessarily a person who says a number of offices, or abounds in detailed intercessions; but he is a child of God, who is and knows himself to be in the deeps of his soul attached to God, and is wholly and entirely guided by the creative Spirit in his prayer and his work. This is not merely a bit of pious language. It is a description, as real and concrete as I can make it, of the only really apostolic life. Every Christian starts with a chance of it; but only a few develop it. The laity distinguish in a moment the clergy who have it from the clergy who have it not: there is nothing that you can do for God or for the souls of men, which exceeds in importance the achievement of that spiritual temper and attitude.

It is only through adoration and attention that we make our personal discoveries about him . . . I think that if you have only as little as half an hour to give each morning to your private prayer, it is not too much to make up your minds to spend half that time in such adoration. For it is the central service asked by God of human souls; and its neglect is responsible for much lack of spiritual depth and power.

In the flood tide of such adoring prayer, the soul is released from the strife and confusions of temporal life; it is lifted far beyond all petty controversies, petty worries and vanities—and none of us escapes these things. It is carried into God, hidden in him.

ADDITIONAL SCRIPTURE READING:
Psalm 19:12–14; Luke 11:1–4; Romans 8:26–27

Go to page 315 for your next devotional reading.

1900   Present

reject his people, because the LORD was pleased to make you his own. [23]As for me, far be it from me that I should sin against the LORD by failing to pray for you. And I will teach you the way that is good and right. [24]But be sure to fear the LORD and serve him faithfully with all your heart; consider what great things he has done for you. [25]Yet if you persist in doing evil, both you and your king will be swept away."

Samuel Rebukes Saul

13 Saul was ⌊thirty⌋[a] years old when he became king, and he reigned over Israel ⌊forty-⌋[b] two years. [2]Saul[c] chose three thousand men from Israel; two thousand were with him at Micmash and in the hill country of Bethel, and a thousand were with Jonathan at Gibeah in Benjamin. The rest of the men he sent back to their homes.

[3]Jonathan attacked the Philistine outpost at Geba, and the Philistines heard about it. Then Saul had the trumpet blown throughout the land and said, "Let the Hebrews hear!" [4]So all Israel heard the news: "Saul has attacked the Philistine outpost, and now Israel has become a stench to the Philistines." And the people were summoned to join Saul at Gilgal.

[5]The Philistines assembled to fight Israel, with three thousand[d] chariots, six thousand charioteers, and soldiers as numerous as the sand on the seashore. They went up and camped at Micmash, east of Beth Aven. [6]When the men of Israel saw that their situation was critical and that their army was hard pressed, they hid in caves and thickets, among the rocks, and in pits and cisterns. [7]Some Hebrews even crossed the Jordan to the land of Gad and Gilead.

Saul remained at Gilgal, and all the troops with him were quaking with fear. [8]He waited seven days, the time set by Samuel; but Samuel did not come to Gilgal, and Saul's men began to scatter. [9]So he said, "Bring me the burnt offering and the fellowship offerings.[e]" And Saul offered up the burnt offering. [10]Just as he finished making the offering, Samuel arrived, and Saul went out to greet him.

[11]"What have you done?" asked Samuel.

Saul replied, "When I saw that the men were scattering, and that you did not come at the set time, and that the Philistines were assembling at Micmash, [12]I thought, 'Now the Philistines will come down against me at Gilgal, and I have not sought the LORD's favor.' So I felt compelled to offer the burnt offering."

[13]"You acted foolishly," Samuel said. "You have not kept the command the LORD your God gave you; if you had, he would have established your kingdom over Israel for all time. [14]But now your kingdom will not endure; the LORD has sought out a man after his own heart and appointed him leader of his people, because you have not kept the LORD's command."

[15]Then Samuel left Gilgal[f] and went up to Gibeah in Benjamin, and Saul counted the men who were with him. They numbered about six hundred.

Israel Without Weapons

[16]Saul and his son Jonathan and the men with them were staying in Gibeah[g] in Benjamin, while the Philistines camped at Micmash. [17]Raiding parties went out from the Philistine camp in three detachments. One turned toward Ophrah in the vicinity of Shual, [18]another toward Beth Horon, and the third toward the borderland overlooking the Valley of Zeboim facing the desert.

[19]Not a blacksmith could be found in the whole land of Israel, because the Philistines had said, "Otherwise the Hebrews will make swords or spears!" [20]So all Israel went down to the Philistines to have their plowshares, mattocks, axes and sickles[h] sharpened. [21]The price was two thirds of a shekel[i]

---

[a] 1 A few late manuscripts of the Septuagint; Hebrew does not have *thirty*.   [b] 1 See the round number in Acts 13:21; Hebrew does not have *forty-*.   [c] 1,2 Or *and when he had reigned over Israel two years,* [2]*he*   [d] 5 Some Septuagint manuscripts and Syriac; Hebrew *thirty thousand*   [e] 9 Traditionally *peace offerings*   [f] 15 Hebrew; Septuagint *Gilgal and went his way; the rest of the people went after Saul to meet the army, and they went out of Gilgal*   [g] 16 Two Hebrew manuscripts; most Hebrew manuscripts *Geba*, a variant of *Gibeah*   [h] 20 Septuagint; Hebrew *plowshares*   [i] 21 Hebrew *pim*; that is, about 1/4 ounce (about 8 grams)

for sharpening plowshares and mattocks, and a third of a shekel*a* for sharpening forks and axes and for repointing goads.

22So on the day of the battle not a soldier with Saul and Jonathan had a sword or spear in his hand; only Saul and his son Jonathan had them.

Jonathan Attacks the Philistines

23Now a detachment of Philistines had gone out to the pass at Micmash.

14 1One day Jonathan son of Saul said to the young man bearing his armor, "Come, let's go over to the Philistine outpost on the other side." But he did not tell his father.

2Saul was staying on the outskirts of Gibeah under a pomegranate tree in Migron. With him were about six hundred men, 3among whom was Ahijah, who was wearing an ephod. He was a son of Ichabod's brother Ahitub son of Phinehas, the son of Eli, the LORD's priest in Shiloh. No one was aware that Jonathan had left.

4On each side of the pass that Jonathan intended to cross to reach the Philistine outpost was a cliff; one was called Bozez, and the other Seneh. 5One cliff stood to the north toward Micmash, the other to the south toward Geba.

6Jonathan said to his young armor-bearer, "Come, let's go over to the outpost of those uncircumcised fellows. Perhaps the LORD will act in our behalf. Nothing can hinder the LORD from saving, whether by many or by few."

7"Do all that you have in mind," his armor-bearer said. "Go ahead; I am with you heart and soul."

8Jonathan said, "Come, then; we will cross over toward the men and let them see us. 9If they say to us, 'Wait there until we come to you,' we will stay where we are and not go up to them. 10But if they say, 'Come up to us,' we will climb up, because that will be our sign that the LORD has given them into our hands."

11So both of them showed themselves to the Philistine outpost. "Look!" said the Philistines. "The Hebrews are crawling out of the holes they were hiding in." 12The men of the outpost shouted to Jonathan and his armor-bearer, "Come up to us and we'll teach you a lesson."

So Jonathan said to his armor-bearer, "Climb up after me; the LORD has given them into the hand of Israel."

13Jonathan climbed up, using his hands and feet, with his armor-bearer right behind him. The Philistines fell before Jonathan, and his armor-bearer followed and killed behind him. 14In that first attack Jonathan and his armor-bearer killed some twenty men in an area of about half an acre.*b*

Israel Routs the Philistines

15Then panic struck the whole army—those in the camp and field, and those in the outposts and raiding parties—and the ground shook. It was a panic sent by God.*c*

16Saul's lookouts at Gibeah in Benjamin saw the army melting away in all directions. 17Then Saul said to the men who were with him, "Muster the forces and see who has left us." When they did, it was Jonathan and his armor-bearer who were not there.

18Saul said to Ahijah, "Bring the ark of God." (At that time it was with the Israelites.)*d* 19While Saul was talking to the priest, the tumult in the Philistine camp increased more and more. So Saul said to the priest, "Withdraw your hand."

20Then Saul and all his men assembled and went to the battle. They found the Philistines in total confusion, striking each other with their swords. 21Those Hebrews who had previously been with the Philistines and had gone up with them to their camp went over to the Israelites who were with Saul and Jonathan. 22When all the Israelites who had hidden in the hill country of Ephraim heard that the Philistines were on the run, they joined the battle in hot pursuit. 23So the LORD rescued Israel that day, and the battle moved on beyond Beth Aven.

Jonathan Eats Honey

24Now the men of Israel were in distress that day, because Saul had bound the people under an oath, saying,

---

a 21 That is, about 1/8 ounce (about 4 grams) by a yoke of oxen in one day.   *b 14* Hebrew *half a yoke;* a "yoke" was the land plowed   *c 15* Or *a terrible panic*   *d 18* Hebrew; Septuagint *"Bring the ephod."* (At that time he wore the ephod before the Israelites.)

"Cursed be any man who eats food before evening comes, before I have avenged myself on my enemies!" So none of the troops tasted food.

25The entire army*a* entered the woods, and there was honey on the ground. 26When they went into the woods, they saw the honey oozing out, yet no one put his hand to his mouth, because they feared the oath. 27But Jonathan had not heard that his father had bound the people with the oath, so he reached out the end of the staff that was in his hand and dipped it into the honeycomb. He raised his hand to his mouth, and his eyes brightened.*b* 28Then one of the soldiers told him, "Your father bound the army under a strict oath, saying, 'Cursed be any man who eats food today!' That is why the men are faint."

29Jonathan said, "My father has made trouble for the country. See how my eyes brightened*c* when I tasted a little of this honey. 30How much better it would have been if the men had eaten today some of the plunder they took from their enemies. Would not the slaughter of the Philistines have been even greater?"

31That day, after the Israelites had struck down the Philistines from Micmash to Aijalon, they were exhausted. 32They pounced on the plunder and, taking sheep, cattle and calves, they butchered them on the ground and ate them, together with the blood. 33Then someone said to Saul, "Look, the men are sinning against the LORD by eating meat that has blood in it."

"You have broken faith," he said. "Roll a large stone over here at once." 34Then he said, "Go out among the men and tell them, 'Each of you bring me your cattle and sheep, and slaughter them here and eat them. Do not sin against the LORD by eating meat with blood still in it.' "

So everyone brought his ox that night and slaughtered it there. 35Then Saul built an altar to the LORD; it was the first time he had done this.

36Saul said, "Let us go down after the Philistines by night and plunder them till dawn, and let us not leave one of them alive."

"Do whatever seems best to you," they replied.

But the priest said, "Let us inquire of God here."

37So Saul asked God, "Shall I go down after the Philistines? Will you give them into Israel's hand?" But God did not answer him that day.

38Saul therefore said, "Come here, all you who are leaders of the army, and let us find out what sin has been committed today. 39As surely as the LORD who rescues Israel lives, even if it lies with my son Jonathan, he must die." But not one of the men said a word.

40Saul then said to all the Israelites, "You stand over there; I and Jonathan my son will stand over here."

"Do what seems best to you," the men replied.

41Then Saul prayed to the LORD, the God of Israel, "Give me the right answer."*d* And Jonathan and Saul were taken by lot, and the men were cleared. 42Saul said, "Cast the lot between me and Jonathan my son." And Jonathan was taken.

43Then Saul said to Jonathan, "Tell me what you have done."

So Jonathan told him, "I merely tasted a little honey with the end of my staff. And now must I die?"

44Saul said, "May God deal with me, be it ever so severely, if you do not die, Jonathan."

45But the men said to Saul, "Should Jonathan die—he who has brought about this great deliverance in Israel? Never! As surely as the LORD lives, not a hair of his head will fall to the ground, for he did this today with God's help." So the men rescued Jonathan, and he was not put to death.

46Then Saul stopped pursuing the Philistines, and they withdrew to their own land.

47After Saul had assumed rule over Israel, he fought against their enemies on every side: Moab, the Ammonites, Edom, the kings*e* of Zobah, and the Philistines. Wherever he turned, he inflicted

---

a 25 Or *Now all the people of the land*   *b 27* Or *his strength was renewed*   *c 29* Or *my strength was renewed*   *d 41* Hebrew; Septuagint *"Why have you not answered your servant today? If the fault is in me or my son Jonathan, respond with Urim, but if the men of Israel are at fault, respond with Thummim."*   *e 47* Masoretic Text; Dead Sea Scrolls and Septuagint *king*

punishment on them.*a* **48**He fought valiantly and defeated the Amalekites, delivering Israel from the hands of those who had plundered them.

Saul's Family

49Saul's sons were Jonathan, Ishvi and Malki-Shua. The name of his older daughter was Merab, and that of the younger was Michal. **50**His wife's name was Ahinoam daughter of Ahimaaz. The name of the commander of Saul's army was Abner son of Ner, and Ner was Saul's uncle. **51**Saul's father Kish and Abner's father Ner were sons of Abiel.

52All the days of Saul there was bitter war with the Philistines, and whenever Saul saw a mighty or brave man, he took him into his service.

The LORD Rejects Saul as King

15 Samuel said to Saul, "I am the one the LORD sent to anoint you king over his people Israel; so listen now to the message from the LORD. **2**This is what the LORD Almighty says: 'I will punish the Amalekites for what they did to Israel when they waylaid them as they came up from Egypt. **3**Now go, attack the Amalekites and totally destroy*b* everything that belongs to them. Do not spare them; put to death men and women, children and infants, cattle and sheep, camels and donkeys.' "

4So Saul summoned the men and mustered them at Telaim—two hundred thousand foot soldiers and ten thousand men from Judah. **5**Saul went to the city of Amalek and set an ambush in the ravine. **6**Then he said to the Kenites, "Go away, leave the Amalekites so that I do not destroy you along with them; for you showed kindness to all the Israelites when they came up out of Egypt." So the Kenites moved away from the Amalekites.

7Then Saul attacked the Amalekites all the way from Havilah to Shur, to the east of Egypt. **8**He took Agag king of the Amalekites alive, and all his people he totally destroyed with the sword. **9**But Saul and the army spared Agag and the

best of the sheep and cattle, the fat calves*c* and lambs—everything that was good. These they were unwilling to destroy completely, but everything that was despised and weak they totally destroyed.

10Then the word of the LORD came to Samuel: **11**"I am grieved that I have made Saul king, because he has turned away from me and has not carried out my instructions." Samuel was troubled, and he cried out to the LORD all that night.

12Early in the morning Samuel got up and went to meet Saul, but he was told, "Saul has gone to Carmel. There he has set up a monument in his own honor and has turned and gone on down to Gilgal."

13When Samuel reached him, Saul said, "The LORD bless you! I have carried out the LORD's instructions."

14But Samuel said, "What then is this bleating of sheep in my ears? What is this lowing of cattle that I hear?"

15Saul answered, "The soldiers brought them from the Amalekites; they spared the best of the sheep and cattle to sacrifice to the LORD your God, but we totally destroyed the rest."

16"Stop!" Samuel said to Saul. "Let me tell you what the LORD said to me last night."

"Tell me," Saul replied.

17Samuel said, "Although you were once small in your own eyes, did you not become the head of the tribes of Israel? The LORD anointed you king over Israel. **18**And he sent you on a mission, saying, 'Go and completely destroy those wicked people, the Amalekites; make war on them until you have wiped them out.' **19**Why did you not obey the LORD? Why did you pounce on the plunder and do evil in the eyes of the LORD?"

20"But I did obey the LORD," Saul said. "I went on the mission the LORD assigned me. I completely destroyed the Amalekites and brought back Agag their king. **21**The soldiers took sheep and cattle from the plunder, the best of what was devoted to God, in order to sacrifice them to the LORD your God at Gilgal."

a 47 Hebrew; Septuagint *he was victorious*   *b 3* The Hebrew term refers to the irrevocable giving over of things or persons to the LORD, often by totally destroying them; also in verses 8, 9, 15, 18, 20 and 21.
c 9 Or *the grown bulls*; the meaning of the Hebrew for this phrase is uncertain.

22But Samuel replied:

"Does the LORD delight in burnt
    offerings and sacrifices
  as much as in obeying the voice of
    the LORD?
To obey is better than sacrifice,
  and to heed is better than the fat of
    rams.
23 For rebellion is like the sin of
    divination,
  and arrogance like the evil of
    idolatry.
Because you have rejected the word
    of the LORD,
  he has rejected you as king."

24Then Saul said to Samuel, "I have
sinned. I violated the LORD's command
and your instructions. I was afraid of the

JUSTICE IS THE INSURANCE WE HAVE ON OUR
LIVES, AND OBEDIENCE IS THE PREMIUM WE
PAY FOR IT.   —*William Penn*

---

people and so I gave in to them. 25Now I
beg you, forgive my sin and come back
with me, so that I may worship the
LORD."

26But Samuel said to him, "I will not
go back with you. You have rejected the

FRIDAY

GOD'S GREAT DELIGHT
Matthew Henry

VERSE: 1 Samuel 15:22   **PASSAGE:** 1 Samuel 15:10–23

ere we are plainly told . . . that humble, sincere, and
conscientious obedience to the will of God is more
pleasing and acceptable to him than *all burnt offerings
and sacrifices*. A careful conformity to moral precepts
recommends us to God more than all ceremonial observances
(see Micah 6:6–8; Hosea 6:6). Obedience was the law of innocen-
cy, but sacrifice supposes sin come into the world and is but a
feeble attempt to take that away which obedience would have
prevented. It is much easier to bring a bullock or lamb to be
burnt upon the altar than to bring *every high thought into obedience* to God and the will subject to his will. Nothing is so provoking to God as disobedience, setting up our wills in competi-
tion with his. This is here called *rebellion* and *stubbornness*,
and is said to be as bad as *witchcraft* and *idolatry* (v. 23, KJV). It
is as bad to set up other gods as to live in disobedience to the true
God . . . Those are unfit and unworthy to rule over men who are
not willing that God should rule over them.

ADDITIONAL SCRIPTURE READING:
Jeremiah 7:23; Hosea 6:6

Go to page 319 for your next devotional reading.

1700   1900

word of the LORD, and the LORD has rejected you as king over Israel!"

27As Samuel turned to leave, Saul caught hold of the hem of his robe, and it tore. 28Samuel said to him, "The LORD has torn the kingdom of Israel from you today and has given it to one of your neighbors—to one better than you. 29He who is the Glory of Israel does not lie or change his mind; for he is not a man, that he should change his mind."

30Saul replied, "I have sinned. But please honor me before the elders of my people and before Israel; come back with me, so that I may worship the LORD your God." 31So Samuel went back with Saul, and Saul worshiped the LORD.

32Then Samuel said, "Bring me Agag king of the Amalekites."

Agag came to him confidently,*a* thinking, "Surely the bitterness of death is past."

33But Samuel said,

"As your sword has made women
     childless,
   so will your mother be childless
     among women."

And Samuel put Agag to death before the LORD at Gilgal.

34Then Samuel left for Ramah, but Saul went up to his home in Gibeah of Saul. 35Until the day Samuel died, he did not go to see Saul again, though Samuel mourned for him. And the LORD was grieved that he had made Saul king over Israel.

Samuel Anoints David

16 The LORD said to Samuel, "How long will you mourn for Saul, since I have rejected him as king over Israel? Fill your horn with oil and be on your way; I am sending you to Jesse of Bethlehem. I have chosen one of his sons to be king."

2But Samuel said, "How can I go? Saul will hear about it and kill me."

The LORD said, "Take a heifer with you and say, 'I have come to sacrifice to the LORD.' 3Invite Jesse to the sacrifice, and I will show you what to do. You are to anoint for me the one I indicate."

4Samuel did what the LORD said. When he arrived at Bethlehem, the elders of the town trembled when they met him. They asked, "Do you come in peace?"

5Samuel replied, "Yes, in peace; I have come to sacrifice to the LORD. Consecrate yourselves and come to the sacrifice with me." Then he consecrated Jesse and his sons and invited them to the sacrifice.

6When they arrived, Samuel saw Eliab and thought, "Surely the LORD's anointed stands here before the LORD."

7But the LORD said to Samuel, "Do not consider his appearance or his height, for I have rejected him. The LORD does not look at the things man looks at. Man looks at the outward appearance, but the LORD looks at the heart."

8Then Jesse called Abinadab and had him pass in front of Samuel. But Samuel said, "The LORD has not chosen this one either." 9Jesse then had Shammah pass by, but Samuel said, "Nor has the LORD chosen this one." 10Jesse had seven of his sons pass before Samuel, but Samuel said to him, "The LORD has not chosen these." 11So he asked Jesse, "Are these all the sons you have?"

"There is still the youngest," Jesse answered, "but he is tending the sheep."

Samuel said, "Send for him; we will not sit down*b* until he arrives."

12So he sent and had him brought in. He was ruddy, with a fine appearance and handsome features.

Then the LORD said, "Rise and anoint him; he is the one."

13So Samuel took the horn of oil and anointed him in the presence of his brothers, and from that day on the Spirit of the LORD came upon David in power. Samuel then went to Ramah.

David in Saul's Service

14Now the Spirit of the LORD had departed from Saul, and an evil*c* spirit from the LORD tormented him.

15Saul's attendants said to him, "See, an evil spirit from God is tormenting you. 16Let our lord command his servants here to search for someone who can play the harp. He will play when the

---

a 32 Or *him trembling, yet*   *b 11* Some Septuagint manuscripts; Hebrew *not gather around*
c 14 Or *injurious;* also in verses 15, 16 and 23

evil spirit from God comes upon you, and you will feel better."

¹⁷So Saul said to his attendants, "Find someone who plays well and bring him to me."

¹⁸One of the servants answered, "I have seen a son of Jesse of Bethlehem who knows how to play the harp. He is a brave man and a warrior. He speaks well and is a fine-looking man. And the LORD is with him."

¹⁹Then Saul sent messengers to Jesse and said, "Send me your son David, who is with the sheep." ²⁰So Jesse took a donkey loaded with bread, a skin of wine and a young goat and sent them with his son David to Saul.

²¹David came to Saul and entered his service. Saul liked him very much, and David became one of his armor-bearers. ²²Then Saul sent word to Jesse, saying, "Allow David to remain in my service, for I am pleased with him."

²³Whenever the spirit from God came upon Saul, David would take his harp and play. Then relief would come to Saul; he would feel better, and the evil spirit would leave him.

David and Goliath

17 Now the Philistines gathered their forces for war and assembled at Socoh in Judah. They pitched camp at Ephes Dammim, between Socoh and Azekah. ²Saul and the Israelites assembled and camped in the Valley of Elah and drew up their battle line to meet the Philistines. ³The Philistines occupied one hill and the Israelites another, with the valley between them.

⁴A champion named Goliath, who was from Gath, came out of the Philistine camp. He was over nine feet*a* tall. ⁵He had a bronze helmet on his head and wore a coat of scale armor of bronze weighing five thousand shekels*b*; ⁶on his legs he wore bronze greaves, and a bronze javelin was slung on his back. ⁷His spear shaft was like a weaver's rod, and its iron point weighed six hundred shekels.*c* His shield bearer went ahead of him.

⁸Goliath stood and shouted to the ranks of Israel, "Why do you come out

and line up for battle? Am I not a Philistine, and are you not the servants of Saul? Choose a man and have him come down to me. ⁹If he is able to fight and kill me, we will become your subjects; but if I overcome him and kill him, you will become our subjects and serve us." ¹⁰Then the Philistine said, "This day I defy the ranks of Israel! Give me a man and let us fight each other." ¹¹On hearing the Philistine's words, Saul and all the Israelites were dismayed and terrified.

¹²Now David was the son of an Ephrathite named Jesse, who was from Bethlehem in Judah. Jesse had eight sons, and in Saul's time he was old and well advanced in years. ¹³Jesse's three oldest sons had followed Saul to the war: The firstborn was Eliab; the second, Abinadab; and the third, Shammah. ¹⁴David was the youngest. The three oldest followed Saul, ¹⁵but David went back and forth from Saul to tend his father's sheep at Bethlehem.

¹⁶For forty days the Philistine came forward every morning and evening and took his stand.

¹⁷Now Jesse said to his son David, "Take this ephah*d* of roasted grain and these ten loaves of bread for your brothers and hurry to their camp. ¹⁸Take along these ten cheeses to the commander of their unit.*e* See how your brothers are and bring back some assurance*f* from them. ¹⁹They are with Saul and all the men of Israel in the Valley of Elah, fighting against the Philistines."

²⁰Early in the morning David left the flock with a shepherd, loaded up and set out, as Jesse had directed. He reached the camp as the army was going out to its battle positions, shouting the war cry. ²¹Israel and the Philistines were drawing up their lines facing each other. ²²David left his things with the keeper of supplies, ran to the battle lines and greeted his brothers. ²³As he was talking with them, Goliath, the Philistine champion from Gath, stepped out from his lines and shouted his usual defiance, and David heard it. ²⁴When the Israelites saw the man, they all ran from him in great fear.

---

a 4 Hebrew *was six cubits and a span* (about 3 meters)   *b 5* That is, about 125 pounds (about 57 kilograms)   *c 7* That is, about 15 pounds (about 7 kilograms)   *d 17* That is, probably about 3/5 bushel (about 22 liters)   *e 18* Hebrew *thousand*   *f 18* Or *some token; or some pledge of spoils*

25Now the Israelites had been saying, "Do you see how this man keeps coming out? He comes out to defy Israel. The king will give great wealth to the man who kills him. He will also give him his daughter in marriage and will exempt his father's family from taxes in Israel."

26David asked the men standing near him, "What will be done for the man who kills this Philistine and removes this disgrace from Israel? Who is this uncircumcised Philistine that he should defy the armies of the living God?"

27They repeated to him what they had been saying and told him, "This is what will be done for the man who kills him."

28When Eliab, David's oldest brother, heard him speaking with the men, he burned with anger at him and asked, "Why have you come down here? And with whom did you leave those few sheep in the desert? I know how conceited you are and how wicked your heart is; you came down only to watch the battle."

29"Now what have I done?" said David. "Can't I even speak?" 30He then turned away to someone else and brought up the same matter, and the men answered him as before. 31What David said was overheard and reported to Saul, and Saul sent for him.

32David said to Saul, "Let no one lose heart on account of this Philistine; your servant will go and fight him."

33Saul replied, "You are not able to go out against this Philistine and fight him; you are only a boy, and he has been a fighting man from his youth."

34But David said to Saul, "Your servant has been keeping his father's sheep. When a lion or a bear came and carried off a sheep from the flock, 35I went after it, struck it and rescued the sheep from its mouth. When it turned on me, I seized it by its hair, struck it and killed it. 36Your servant has killed both the lion and the bear; this uncircumcised Philistine will be like one of them, because he has defied the armies of the living God. 37The LORD who delivered me from the paw of the lion and the paw of the bear will deliver me from the hand of this Philistine."

Saul said to David, "Go, and the LORD be with you."

38Then Saul dressed David in his own tunic. He put a coat of armor on him and a bronze helmet on his head. 39David fastened on his sword over the tunic and tried walking around, because he was not used to them.

"I cannot go in these," he said to Saul, "because I am not used to them." So he took them off. 40Then he took his staff in his hand, chose five smooth stones from the stream, put them in the pouch of his shepherd's bag and, with his sling in his hand, approached the Philistine.

41Meanwhile, the Philistine, with his shield bearer in front of him, kept coming closer to David. 42He looked David over and saw that he was only a boy, ruddy and handsome, and he despised him. 43He said to David, "Am I a dog, that you come at me with sticks?" And the Philistine cursed David by his gods. 44"Come here," he said, "and I'll give your flesh to the birds of the air and the beasts of the field!"

45David said to the Philistine, "You come against me with sword and spear and javelin, but I come against you in the name of the LORD Almighty, the God of the armies of Israel, whom you have defied. 46This day the LORD will hand you over to me, and I'll strike you down and cut off your head. Today I will give the carcasses of the Philistine army to the birds of the air and the beasts of the earth, and the whole world will know that there is a God in Israel. 47All those gathered here will know that it is not by sword or spear that the LORD saves; for the battle is the LORD's, and he will give all of you into our hands."

48As the Philistine moved closer to attack him, David ran quickly toward the battle line to meet him. 49Reaching into his bag and taking out a stone, he slung it and struck the Philistine on the forehead. The stone sank into his forehead, and he fell facedown on the ground.

50So David triumphed over the Philistine with a sling and a stone; without a sword in his hand he struck down the Philistine and killed him.

51David ran and stood over him. He took hold of the Philistine's sword and drew it from the scabbard. After he killed him, he cut off his head with the sword.

WEEKEND

GOD'S OPPORTUNITY IN DISGUISE
C. H. Parkhurst

VERSE: 1 Samuel 17:34   **PASSAGE:** 1 Samuel 17:12–50

t is a source of inspiration and strength to come in touch with the youthful David, trusting God. Through faith in God he conquered a lion and a bear, and afterwards overthrew the mighty Goliath. When that lion came to despoil that flock, it came as a wondrous *opportunity* to David. If he had failed or faltered he would have missed God's opportunity for him and probably would never have come to be God's chosen king of Israel.

One would not think that a lion was a special blessing from God; one would think that only an occasion of alarm. The lion was *God's opportunity in disguise.* Every difficulty that presents itself to us, if we receive it in the right way, is God's opportunity. Every temptation that comes is God's opportunity.

When the "lion" comes, recognize it as God's opportunity no matter how rough the exterior . . . May God open our eyes to see him, whether in temptations, trials, dangers, or misfortunes.

ADDITIONAL SCRIPTURE READING:
Matthew 26:41; Luke 11:4; 1 Corinthians 10:13

Go to page 327 for your next devotional reading.

1700   1900

When the Philistines saw that their hero was dead, they turned and ran. 52Then the men of Israel and Judah surged forward with a shout and pursued the Philistines to the entrance of Gath*a* and to the gates of Ekron. Their dead were strewn along the Shaaraim road to Gath and Ekron. 53When the Israelites returned from chasing the Philistines, they plundered their camp. 54David took the Philistine's head and brought it to Jerusalem, and he put the Philistine's weapons in his own tent.

55As Saul watched David going out to meet the Philistine, he said to Abner, commander of the army, "Abner, whose son is that young man?"

Abner replied, "As surely as you live, O king, I don't know."

56The king said, "Find out whose son this young man is."

57As soon as David returned from killing the Philistine, Abner took him and brought him before Saul, with David still holding the Philistine's head.

58"Whose son are you, young man?" Saul asked him.

David said, "I am the son of your servant Jesse of Bethlehem."

Saul's Jealousy of David

18 After David had finished talking with Saul, Jonathan became one in spirit with David, and he loved him as himself. 2From that day Saul kept David with him and did not let him return to his father's house. 3And Jonathan made a covenant with David because he loved him as himself. 4Jonathan took off the robe he was wearing and gave it to David, along with his tunic, and even his sword, his bow and his belt.

5Whatever Saul sent him to do, David did it so successfully*b* that Saul gave him a high rank in the army. This pleased all the people, and Saul's officers as well.

6When the men were returning home after David had killed the Philistine, the women came out from all the towns of Israel to meet King Saul with singing and dancing, with joyful songs and with tambourines and lutes. 7As they danced, they sang:

"Saul has slain his thousands, and David his tens of thousands."

8Saul was very angry; this refrain galled him. "They have credited David with tens of thousands," he thought, "but me with only thousands. What more can he get but the kingdom?" 9And from that time on Saul kept a jealous eye on David.

10The next day an evil*c* spirit from God came forcefully upon Saul. He was prophesying in his house, while David was playing the harp, as he usually did. Saul had a spear in his hand 11and he hurled it, saying to himself, "I'll pin David to the wall." But David eluded him twice.

12Saul was afraid of David, because the LORD was with David but had left Saul. 13So he sent David away from him and gave him command over a thousand men, and David led the troops in their campaigns. 14In everything he did he had great success,*d* because the LORD was with him. 15When Saul saw how successful*e* he was, he was afraid of him. 16But all Israel and Judah loved David, because he led them in their campaigns.

17Saul said to David, "Here is my older daughter Merab. I will give her to you in marriage; only serve me bravely and fight the battles of the LORD." For Saul said to himself, "I will not raise a hand against him. Let the Philistines do that!"

18But David said to Saul, "Who am I, and what is my family or my father's clan in Israel, that I should become the king's son-in-law?" 19So*f* when the time came for Merab, Saul's daughter, to be given to David, she was given in marriage to Adriel of Meholah.

20Now Saul's daughter Michal was in love with David, and when they told Saul about it, he was pleased. 21"I will give her to him," he thought, "so that she may be a snare to him and so that the hand of the Philistines may be against him." So Saul said to David, "Now you have a second opportunity to become my son-in-law."

22Then Saul ordered his attendants: "Speak to David privately and say,

a 52 Some Septuagint manuscripts; Hebrew *a valley was very wise*   *e* 15 Or *wise*   *f* 19 Or *However,*   *b* 5 Or *wisely*   *c* 10 Or *injurious*   *d* 14 Or *he*

'Look, the king is pleased with you, and his attendants all like you; now become his son-in-law.' "

23They repeated these words to David. But David said, "Do you think it is a small matter to become the king's son-in-law? I'm only a poor man and little known."

24When Saul's servants told him what David had said, 25Saul replied, "Say to David, 'The king wants no other price for the bride than a hundred Philistine foreskins, to take revenge on his enemies.' " Saul's plan was to have David fall by the hands of the Philistines.

26When the attendants told David these things, he was pleased to become the king's son-in-law. So before the allotted time elapsed, 27David and his men went out and killed two hundred Philistines. He brought their foreskins and presented the full number to the king so that he might become the king's son-in-law. Then Saul gave him his daughter Michal in marriage.

28When Saul realized that the LORD was with David and that his daughter Michal loved David, 29Saul became still more afraid of him, and he remained his enemy the rest of his days.

30The Philistine commanders continued to go out to battle, and as often as they did, David met with more success*a* than the rest of Saul's officers, and his name became well known.

Saul Tries to Kill David

19 Saul told his son Jonathan and all the attendants to kill David. But Jonathan was very fond of David 2and warned him, "My father Saul is looking for a chance to kill you. Be on your guard tomorrow morning; go into hiding and stay there. 3I will go out and stand with my father in the field where you are. I'll speak to him about you and will tell you what I find out."

4Jonathan spoke well of David to Saul his father and said to him, "Let not the king do wrong to his servant David; he has not wronged you, and what he has done has benefited you greatly. 5He took his life in his hands when he killed the Philistine. The LORD won a great victory for all Israel, and you saw it and were

glad. Why then would you do wrong to an innocent man like David by killing him for no reason?"

6Saul listened to Jonathan and took this oath: "As surely as the LORD lives, David will not be put to death."

7So Jonathan called David and told him the whole conversation. He brought him to Saul, and David was with Saul as before.

8Once more war broke out, and David went out and fought the Philistines. He struck them with such force that they fled before him.

9But an evil*b* spirit from the LORD came upon Saul as he was sitting in his house with his spear in his hand. While David was playing the harp, 10Saul tried to pin him to the wall with his spear, but David eluded him as Saul drove the spear into the wall. That night David made good his escape.

11Saul sent men to David's house to watch it and to kill him in the morning. But Michal, David's wife, warned him, "If you don't run for your life tonight, tomorrow you'll be killed." 12So Michal let David down through a window, and he fled and escaped. 13Then Michal took an idol*c* and laid it on the bed, covering it with a garment and putting some goats' hair at the head.

14When Saul sent the men to capture David, Michal said, "He is ill."

15Then Saul sent the men back to see David and told them, "Bring him up to me in his bed so that I may kill him." 16But when the men entered, there was the idol in the bed, and at the head was some goats' hair.

17Saul said to Michal, "Why did you deceive me like this and send my enemy away so that he escaped?"

Michal told him, "He said to me, 'Let me get away. Why should I kill you?' "

18When David had fled and made his escape, he went to Samuel at Ramah and told him all that Saul had done to him. Then he and Samuel went to Naioth and stayed there. 19Word came to Saul: "David is in Naioth at Ramah"; 20so he sent men to capture him. But when they saw a group of prophets prophesying, with Samuel standing there as their leader, the Spirit of God

---

a 30 Or *David acted more wisely*   *b 9* Or *injurious*   *c 13* Hebrew *teraphim*; also in verse 16

came upon Saul's men and they also prophesied. 21Saul was told about it, and he sent more men, and they prophesied too. Saul sent men a third time, and they also prophesied. 22Finally, he himself left for Ramah and went to the great cistern at Secu. And he asked, "Where are Samuel and David?"

"Over in Naioth at Ramah," they said.

23So Saul went to Naioth at Ramah. But the Spirit of God came even upon him, and he walked along prophesying until he came to Naioth. 24He stripped off his robes and also prophesied in Samuel's presence. He lay that way all that day and night. This is why people say, "Is Saul also among the prophets?"

David and Jonathan

20 Then David fled from Naioth at Ramah and went to Jonathan and asked, "What have I done? What is my crime? How have I wronged your father, that he is trying to take my life?"

2"Never!" Jonathan replied. "You are not going to die! Look, my father doesn't do anything, great or small, without confiding in me. Why would he hide this from me? It's not so!"

3But David took an oath and said, "Your father knows very well that I have found favor in your eyes, and he has said to himself, 'Jonathan must not know this or he will be grieved.' Yet as surely as the LORD lives and as you live, there is only a step between me and death."

4Jonathan said to David, "Whatever you want me to do, I'll do for you."

5So David said, "Look, tomorrow is the New Moon festival, and I am supposed to dine with the king; but let me go and hide in the field until the evening of the day after tomorrow. 6If your father misses me at all, tell him, 'David earnestly asked my permission to hurry to Bethlehem, his hometown, because an annual sacrifice is being made there for his whole clan.' 7If he says, 'Very well,' then your servant is safe. But if he loses his temper, you can be sure that he is determined to harm me. 8As for you, show kindness to your servant, for you have brought him into a covenant with you before the LORD. If

I am guilty, then kill me yourself! Why hand me over to your father?"

9"Never!" Jonathan said. "If I had the least inkling that my father was determined to harm you, wouldn't I tell you?"

10David asked, "Who will tell me if your father answers you harshly?"

11"Come," Jonathan said, "let's go out into the field." So they went there together.

12Then Jonathan said to David: "By the LORD, the God of Israel, I will surely sound out my father by this time the day after tomorrow! If he is favorably disposed toward you, will I not send you word and let you know? 13But if my father is inclined to harm you, may the LORD deal with me, be it ever so severely, if I do not let you know and send you away safely. May the LORD be with you as he has been with my father. 14But show me unfailing kindness like that of the LORD as long as I live, so that I may not be killed, 15and do not ever cut off your kindness from my family—not even when the LORD has cut off every one of David's enemies from the face of the earth."

16So Jonathan made a covenant with the house of David, saying, "May the LORD call David's enemies to account." 17And Jonathan had David reaffirm his oath out of love for him, because he loved him as he loved himself.

18Then Jonathan said to David: "Tomorrow is the New Moon festival. You will be missed, because your seat will be empty. 19The day after tomorrow, toward evening, go to the place where you hid when this trouble began, and wait by the stone Ezel. 20I will shoot three arrows to the side of it, as though I were shooting at a target. 21Then I will send a boy and say, 'Go, find the arrows.' If I say to him, 'Look, the arrows are on this side of you; bring them here,' then come, because, as surely as the LORD lives, you are safe; there is no danger. 22But if I say to the boy, 'Look, the arrows are beyond you,' then you must go, because the LORD has sent you away. 23And about the matter you and I discussed—remember, the LORD is witness between you and me forever."

24So David hid in the field, and when the New Moon festival came, the king sat down to eat. 25He sat in his customary place by the wall, opposite Jonathan,ᵃ and Abner sat next to Saul, but David's place was empty. 26Saul said nothing that day, for he thought, "Something must have happened to David to make him ceremonially unclean—surely he is unclean." 27But the next day, the second day of the month, David's place was empty again. Then Saul said to his son Jonathan, "Why hasn't the son of Jesse come to the meal, either yesterday or today?"

28Jonathan answered, "David earnestly asked me for permission to go to Bethlehem. 29He said, 'Let me go, because our family is observing a sacrifice in the town and my brother has ordered me to be there. If I have found favor in your eyes, let me get away to see my brothers.' That is why he has not come to the king's table."

30Saul's anger flared up at Jonathan and he said to him, "You son of a perverse and rebellious woman! Don't I know that you have sided with the son of Jesse to your own shame and to the shame of the mother who bore you? 31As long as the son of Jesse lives on this earth, neither you nor your kingdom will be established. Now send and bring him to me, for he must die!"

32"Why should he be put to death? What has he done?" Jonathan asked his father. 33But Saul hurled his spear at him to kill him. Then Jonathan knew that his father intended to kill David.

34Jonathan got up from the table in fierce anger; on that second day of the month he did not eat, because he was grieved at his father's shameful treatment of David.

35In the morning Jonathan went out to the field for his meeting with David. He had a small boy with him, 36and he said to the boy, "Run and find the arrows I shoot." As the boy ran, he shot an arrow beyond him. 37When the boy came to the place where Jonathan's arrow had fallen, Jonathan called out after him, "Isn't the arrow beyond you?" 38Then he shouted, "Hurry! Go quickly! Don't stop!" The boy picked up the arrow and returned to his master. 39(The boy knew nothing of all this; only Jonathan and David knew.) 40Then Jonathan gave his weapons to the boy and said, "Go, carry them back to town."

41After the boy had gone, David got up from the south side ⌞of the stone⌟ and bowed down before Jonathan three times, with his face to the ground. Then they kissed each other and wept together—but David wept the most.

42Jonathan said to David, "Go in peace, for we have sworn friendship with each other in the name of the LORD, saying, 'The LORD is witness between you and me, and between your descendants and my descendants forever.'" Then David left, and Jonathan went back to the town.

David at Nob

21 David went to Nob, to Ahimelech the priest. Ahimelech trembled when he met him, and asked, "Why are you alone? Why is no one with you?"

2David answered Ahimelech the priest, "The king charged me with a certain matter and said to me, 'No one is to know anything about your mission and your instructions.' As for my men, I have told them to meet me at a certain place. 3Now then, what do you have on hand? Give me five loaves of bread, or whatever you can find."

4But the priest answered David, "I don't have any ordinary bread on hand; however, there is some consecrated bread here—provided the men have kept themselves from women."

5David replied, "Indeed women have been kept from us, as usual wheneverᵇ I set out. The men's thingsᶜ are holy even on missions that are not holy. How much more so today!" 6So the priest gave him the consecrated bread, since there was no bread there except the bread of the Presence that had been removed from before the LORD and replaced by hot bread on the day it was taken away.

7Now one of Saul's servants was there that day, detained before the LORD; he was Doeg the Edomite, Saul's head shepherd.

ᵃ 25 Septuagint; Hebrew *wall. Jonathan arose*   ᵇ 5 Or *from us in the past few days since*
ᶜ 5 Or *bodies*

8David asked Ahimelech, "Don't you have a spear or a sword here? I haven't brought my sword or any other weapon, because the king's business was urgent."

9The priest replied, "The sword of Goliath the Philistine, whom you killed in the Valley of Elah, is here; it is wrapped in a cloth behind the ephod. If you want it, take it; there is no sword here but that one."

David said, "There is none like it; give it to me."

David at Gath

10That day David fled from Saul and went to Achish king of Gath. 11But the servants of Achish said to him, "Isn't this David, the king of the land? Isn't he the one they sing about in their dances:

" 'Saul has slain his thousands,
    and David his tens of thousands'?"

12David took these words to heart and was very much afraid of Achish king of Gath. 13So he pretended to be insane in their presence; and while he was in their hands he acted like a madman, making marks on the doors of the gate and letting saliva run down his beard.

14Achish said to his servants, "Look at the man! He is insane! Why bring him to me? 15Am I so short of madmen that you have to bring this fellow here to carry on like this in front of me? Must this man come into my house?"

David at Adullam and Mizpah

22 David left Gath and escaped to the cave of Adullam. When his brothers and his father's household heard about it, they went down to him there. 2All those who were in distress or in debt or discontented gathered around him, and he became their leader. About four hundred men were with him.

3From there David went to Mizpah in Moab and said to the king of Moab, "Would you let my father and mother come and stay with you until I learn what God will do for me?" 4So he left them with the king of Moab, and they stayed with him as long as David was in the stronghold.

5But the prophet Gad said to David, "Do not stay in the stronghold. Go into the land of Judah." So David left and went to the forest of Hereth.

Saul Kills the Priests of Nob

6Now Saul heard that David and his men had been discovered. And Saul, spear in hand, was seated under the tamarisk tree on the hill at Gibeah, with all his officials standing around him. 7Saul said to them, "Listen, men of Benjamin! Will the son of Jesse give all of you fields and vineyards? Will he make all of you commanders of thousands and commanders of hundreds? 8Is that why you have all conspired against me? No one tells me when my son makes a covenant with the son of Jesse. None of you is concerned about me or tells me that my son has incited my servant to lie in wait for me, as he does today."

9But Doeg the Edomite, who was standing with Saul's officials, said, "I saw the son of Jesse come to Ahimelech son of Ahitub at Nob. 10Ahimelech inquired of the LORD for him; he also gave him provisions and the sword of Goliath the Philistine."

11Then the king sent for the priest Ahimelech son of Ahitub and his father's whole family, who were the priests at Nob, and they all came to the king. 12Saul said, "Listen now, son of Ahitub."

"Yes, my lord," he answered.

13Saul said to him, "Why have you conspired against me, you and the son of Jesse, giving him bread and a sword and inquiring of God for him, so that he has rebelled against me and lies in wait for me, as he does today?"

14Ahimelech answered the king, "Who of all your servants is as loyal as David, the king's son-in-law, captain of your bodyguard and highly respected in your household? 15Was that day the first time I inquired of God for him? Of course not! Let not the king accuse your servant or any of his father's family, for your servant knows nothing at all about this whole affair."

16But the king said, "You will surely die, Ahimelech, you and your father's whole family."

17Then the king ordered the guards at his side: "Turn and kill the priests of the LORD, because they too have sided with

David. They knew he was fleeing, yet they did not tell me."

But the king's officials were not willing to raise a hand to strike the priests of the LORD.

18The king then ordered Doeg, "You turn and strike down the priests." So Doeg the Edomite turned and struck them down. That day he killed eighty-five men who wore the linen ephod. 19He also put to the sword Nob, the town of the priests, with its men and women, its children and infants, and its cattle, donkeys and sheep.

20But Abiathar, a son of Ahimelech son of Ahitub, escaped and fled to join David. 21He told David that Saul had killed the priests of the LORD. 22Then David said to Abiathar: "That day, when Doeg the Edomite was there, I knew he would be sure to tell Saul. I am responsible for the death of your father's whole family. 23Stay with me; don't be afraid; the man who is seeking your life is seeking mine also. You will be safe with me."

David Saves Keilah

23 When David was told, "Look, the Philistines are fighting against Keilah and are looting the threshing floors," 2he inquired of the LORD, saying, "Shall I go and attack these Philistines?"

The LORD answered him, "Go, attack the Philistines and save Keilah."

3But David's men said to him, "Here in Judah we are afraid. How much more, then, if we go to Keilah against the Philistine forces!"

4Once again David inquired of the LORD, and the LORD answered him, "Go down to Keilah, for I am going to give the Philistines into your hand." 5So David and his men went to Keilah, fought the Philistines and carried off their livestock. He inflicted heavy losses on the Philistines and saved the people of Keilah. 6(Now Abiathar son of Ahimelech had brought the ephod down with him when he fled to David at Keilah.)

Saul Pursues David

7Saul was told that David had gone to Keilah, and he said, "God has handed him over to me, for David has imprisoned himself by entering a town with gates and bars." 8And Saul called up all his forces for battle, to go down to Keilah to besiege David and his men.

9When David learned that Saul was plotting against him, he said to Abiathar the priest, "Bring the ephod." 10David said, "O LORD, God of Israel, your servant has heard definitely that Saul plans to come to Keilah and destroy the town on account of me. 11Will the citizens of Keilah surrender me to him? Will Saul come down, as your servant has heard? O LORD, God of Israel, tell your servant."

And the LORD said, "He will."

12Again David asked, "Will the citizens of Keilah surrender me and my men to Saul?"

And the LORD said, "They will."

13So David and his men, about six hundred in number, left Keilah and kept moving from place to place. When Saul was told that David had escaped from Keilah, he did not go there.

14David stayed in the desert strongholds and in the hills of the Desert of Ziph. Day after day Saul searched for him, but God did not give David into his hands.

15While David was at Horesh in the Desert of Ziph, he learned that Saul had come out to take his life. 16And Saul's son Jonathan went to David at Horesh and helped him find strength in God. 17"Don't be afraid," he said. "My father Saul will not lay a hand on you. You will be king over Israel, and I will be second to you. Even my father Saul knows this." 18The two of them made a covenant before the LORD. Then Jonathan went home, but David remained at Horesh.

19The Ziphites went up to Saul at Gibeah and said, "Is not David hiding among us in the strongholds at Horesh, on the hill of Hakilah, south of Jeshimon? 20Now, O king, come down whenever it pleases you to do so, and we will be responsible for handing him over to the king."

21Saul replied, "The LORD bless you for your concern for me. 22Go and make further preparation. Find out where David usually goes and who has seen him there. They tell me he is very crafty. 23Find out about all the hiding places he uses and come back to me with definite information.*a* Then I will go with you; if he is in the area, I will track him down among all the clans of Judah."

²⁴So they set out and went to Ziph ahead of Saul. Now David and his men were in the Desert of Maon, in the Arabah south of Jeshimon. ²⁵Saul and his men began the search, and when David was told about it, he went down to the rock and stayed in the Desert of Maon. When Saul heard this, he went into the Desert of Maon in pursuit of David.

²⁶Saul was going along one side of the mountain, and David and his men were on the other side, hurrying to get away from Saul. As Saul and his forces were closing in on David and his men to capture them, ²⁷a messenger came to Saul, saying, "Come quickly! The Philistines are raiding the land." ²⁸Then Saul broke off his pursuit of David and went to meet the Philistines. That is why they call this place Sela Hammahlekoth.*b* ²⁹And David went up from there and lived in the strongholds of En Gedi.

David Spares Saul's Life

24 After Saul returned from pursuing the Philistines, he was told, "David is in the Desert of En Gedi." ²So Saul took three thousand chosen men from all Israel and set out to look for David and his men near the Crags of the Wild Goats.

³He came to the sheep pens along the way; a cave was there, and Saul went in to relieve himself. David and his men were far back in the cave. ⁴The men said, "This is the day the LORD spoke of when he said*c* to you, 'I will give your enemy into your hands for you to deal with as you wish.'" Then David crept up unnoticed and cut off a corner of Saul's robe.

⁵Afterward, David was conscience-stricken for having cut off a corner of his robe. ⁶He said to his men, "The LORD forbid that I should do such a thing to my master, the LORD's anointed, or lift my hand against him; for he is the anointed of the LORD." ⁷With these words David rebuked his men and did not allow them to attack Saul. And Saul left the cave and went his way.

⁸Then David went out of the cave and called out to Saul, "My lord the king!" When Saul looked behind him, David bowed down and prostrated himself with his face to the ground. ⁹He said to Saul, "Why do you listen when men say, 'David is bent on harming you'? ¹⁰This day you have seen with your own eyes how the LORD delivered you into my hands in the cave. Some urged me to kill you, but I spared you; I said, 'I will not lift my hand against my master, because he is the LORD's anointed.' ¹¹See, my father, look at this piece of your robe in my hand! I cut off the corner of your robe but did not kill you. Now understand and recognize that I am not guilty of wrongdoing or rebellion. I have not wronged you, but you are hunting me down to take my life. ¹²May the LORD judge between you and me. And may the LORD avenge the wrongs you have done to me, but my hand will not touch you. ¹³As the old saying goes, 'From evildoers come evil deeds,' so my hand will not touch you.

¹⁴"Against whom has the king of Israel come out? Whom are you pursuing? A dead dog? A flea? ¹⁵May the LORD be our judge and decide between us. May he consider my cause and uphold it; may he vindicate me by delivering me from your hand."

¹⁶When David finished saying this, Saul asked, "Is that your voice, David my son?" And he wept aloud. ¹⁷"You are more righteous than I," he said. "You have treated me well, but I have treated you badly. ¹⁸You have just now told me of the good you did to me; the LORD delivered me into your hands, but you did not kill me. ¹⁹When a man finds his enemy, does he let him get away unharmed? May the LORD reward you well for the way you treated me today. ²⁰I know that you will surely be king and that the kingdom of Israel will be established in your hands. ²¹Now swear to me by the LORD that you will not cut off my descendants or wipe out my name from my father's family."

²²So David gave his oath to Saul. Then Saul returned home, but David and his men went up to the stronghold.

---

a 23 Or *me at Nacon*   *b 28 Sela Hammahlekoth* means *rock of parting.*   *c 4* Or *"Today the LORD is saying*

David, Nabal and Abigail

25 Now Samuel died, and all Israel assembled and mourned for him; and they buried him at his home in Ramah.

Then David moved down into the Desert of Maon.*a* **2**A certain man in Maon, who had property there at Carmel, was very wealthy. He had a thousand goats and three thousand sheep, which he was shearing in Carmel. **3**His name was Nabal and his wife's name was Abigail. She was an intelligent and beautiful woman, but her husband, a Calebite, was surly and mean in his dealings.

4While David was in the desert, he heard that Nabal was shearing sheep. **5**So he sent ten young men and said to them, "Go up to Nabal at Carmel and greet him in my name. **6**Say to him: 'Long life to you! Good health to you and your household! And good health to all that is yours!

7" 'Now I hear that it is sheep-shearing time. When your shepherds were with us, we did not mistreat them, and the whole time they were at Carmel nothing of theirs was missing. **8**Ask your own servants and they will tell you. Therefore be favorable toward my young men, since we come at a festive time. Please give your servants and your son David whatever you can find for them.' "

a 1 Some Septuagint manuscripts; Hebrew *Paran*

MONDAY

GOD'S SURE WORD
Martin Luther

VERSE: 1 Samuel 24:11   **PASSAGE:** 1 Samuel 24:1–19

any strange things, according to human sense and reason, are written in the books of the kings; they seem to be slight and simple books, but in the spirit they are of great weight. David endured much; Saul persecuted and plagued him ten whole years; yet David remained constant in faith, and believed that the kingdom pertained unto him. I should have gone my way, and said: Lord! thou hast deceived me; wilt thou make me a king, and sufferest me in this sort to be tormented, persecuted, and plagued? But David was like a strong wall. He was also a good and a godly man; he refused to lay hands on the king when he had fit opportunity; for he had God's word, and that made him remain so steadfast; he was sure that God's word and promise never would or could fail him . . .

So it often happens, that the good are punished for the sake of the wicked and ungodly. The Son of God himself was not spared.

ADDITIONAL SCRIPTURE READING:
1 Samuel 26:17–25; Psalm 25:20–21

Go to page 342 for your next devotional reading.

1500   1700

⁹When David's men arrived, they gave Nabal this message in David's name. Then they waited.

¹⁰Nabal answered David's servants, "Who is this David? Who is this son of Jesse? Many servants are breaking away from their masters these days. ¹¹Why should I take my bread and water, and the meat I have slaughtered for my shearers, and give it to men coming from who knows where?"

¹²David's men turned around and went back. When they arrived, they reported every word. ¹³David said to his men, "Put on your swords!" So they put on their swords, and David put on his. About four hundred men went up with David, while two hundred stayed with the supplies.

¹⁴One of the servants told Nabal's wife Abigail: "David sent messengers from the desert to give our master his greetings, but he hurled insults at them. ¹⁵Yet these men were very good to us. They did not mistreat us, and the whole time we were out in the fields near them nothing was missing. ¹⁶Night and day they were a wall around us all the time we were herding our sheep near them. ¹⁷Now think it over and see what you can do, because disaster is hanging over our master and his whole household. He is such a wicked man that no one can talk to him."

¹⁸Abigail lost no time. She took two hundred loaves of bread, two skins of wine, five dressed sheep, five seahs*ᵃ* of roasted grain, a hundred cakes of raisins and two hundred cakes of pressed figs, and loaded them on donkeys. ¹⁹Then she told her servants, "Go on ahead; I'll follow you." But she did not tell her husband Nabal.

²⁰As she came riding her donkey into a mountain ravine, there were David and his men descending toward her, and she met them. ²¹David had just said, "It's been useless—all my watching over this fellow's property in the desert so that nothing of his was missing. He has paid me back evil for good. ²²May God deal with David,*ᵇ* be it ever so severely, if by morning I leave alive one male of all who belong to him!"

²³When Abigail saw David, she quickly got off her donkey and bowed down before David with her face to the ground. ²⁴She fell at his feet and said: "My lord, let the blame be on me alone. Please let your servant speak to you; hear what your servant has to say. ²⁵May my lord pay no attention to that wicked man Nabal. He is just like his name—his name is Fool, and folly goes with him. But as for me, your servant, I did not see the men my master sent.

²⁶"Now since the LORD has kept you, my master, from bloodshed and from avenging yourself with your own hands, as surely as the LORD lives and as you live, may your enemies and all who intend to harm my master be like Nabal. ²⁷And let this gift, which your servant has brought to my master, be given to the men who follow you. ²⁸Please forgive your servant's offense, for the LORD will certainly make a lasting dynasty for my master, because he fights the LORD's battles. Let no wrongdoing be found in you as long as you live. ²⁹Even though someone is pursuing you to take your life, the life of my master will be bound securely in the bundle of the living by the LORD your God. But the lives of your enemies he will hurl away as from the pocket of a sling. ³⁰When the LORD has done for my master every good thing he promised concerning him and has appointed him leader over Israel, ³¹my master will not have on his conscience the staggering burden of needless bloodshed or of having avenged himself. And when the LORD has brought my master success, remember your servant."

³²David said to Abigail, "Praise be to the LORD, the God of Israel, who has sent you today to meet me. ³³May you be blessed for your good judgment and for keeping me from bloodshed this day and from avenging myself with my own hands. ³⁴Otherwise, as surely as the LORD, the God of Israel, lives, who has kept me from harming you, if you had not come quickly to meet me, not one male belonging to Nabal would have been left alive by daybreak."

³⁵Then David accepted from her hand

ᵃ 18 That is, probably about a bushel (about 37 liters)
with *David's enemies*

ᵇ 22 Some Septuagint manuscripts; Hebrew

what she had brought him and said, "Go home in peace. I have heard your words and granted your request."

³⁶When Abigail went to Nabal, he was in the house holding a banquet like that of a king. He was in high spirits and very drunk. So she told him nothing until daybreak. ³⁷Then in the morning, when Nabal was sober, his wife told him all these things, and his heart failed him and he became like a stone. ³⁸About ten days later, the LORD struck Nabal and he died.

³⁹When David heard that Nabal was dead, he said, "Praise be to the LORD, who has upheld my cause against Nabal for treating me with contempt. He has kept his servant from doing wrong and has brought Nabal's wrongdoing down on his own head."

Then David sent word to Abigail, asking her to become his wife. ⁴⁰His servants went to Carmel and said to Abigail, "David has sent us to you to take you to become his wife."

⁴¹She bowed down with her face to the ground and said, "Here is your maidservant, ready to serve you and wash the feet of my master's servants." ⁴²Abigail quickly got on a donkey and, attended by her five maids, went with David's messengers and became his wife. ⁴³David had also married Ahinoam of Jezreel, and they both were his wives. ⁴⁴But Saul had given his daughter Michal, David's wife, to Paltiel[a] son of Laish, who was from Gallim.

David Again Spares Saul's Life

26 The Ziphites went to Saul at Gibeah and said, "Is not David hiding on the hill of Hakilah, which faces Jeshimon?"

²So Saul went down to the Desert of Ziph, with his three thousand chosen men of Israel, to search there for David. ³Saul made his camp beside the road on the hill of Hakilah facing Jeshimon, but David stayed in the desert. When he saw that Saul had followed him there, ⁴he sent out scouts and learned that Saul had definitely arrived.[b]

⁵Then David set out and went to the place where Saul had camped. He saw

where Saul and Abner son of Ner, the commander of the army, had lain down. Saul was lying inside the camp, with the army encamped around him.

⁶David then asked Ahimelech the Hittite and Abishai son of Zeruiah, Joab's brother, "Who will go down into the camp with me to Saul?"

"I'll go with you," said Abishai.

⁷So David and Abishai went to the army by night, and there was Saul, lying asleep inside the camp with his spear stuck in the ground near his head. Abner and the soldiers were lying around him.

⁸Abishai said to David, "Today God has delivered your enemy into your hands. Now let me pin him to the ground with one thrust of my spear; I won't strike him twice."

⁹But David said to Abishai, "Don't destroy him! Who can lay a hand on the LORD's anointed and be guiltless? ¹⁰As surely as the LORD lives," he said, "the LORD himself will strike him; either his time will come and he will die, or he will go into battle and perish. ¹¹But the LORD forbid that I should lay a hand on the LORD's anointed. Now get the spear and water jug that are near his head, and let's go."

PLENTEOUS GRACE WITH THEE IS FOUND,
GRACE TO COVER ALL MY SIN;
LET THE HEALING STREAMS ABOUND,
MAKE AND KEEP ME PURE WITHIN.
—*Charles Wesley*

---

¹²So David took the spear and water jug near Saul's head, and they left. No one saw or knew about it, nor did anyone wake up. They were all sleeping, because the LORD had put them into a deep sleep.

¹³Then David crossed over to the other side and stood on top of the hill some distance away; there was a wide space between them. ¹⁴He called out to the army and to Abner son of Ner, "Aren't you going to answer me, Abner?"

Abner replied, "Who are you who calls to the king?"

¹⁵David said, "You're a man, aren't you? And who is like you in Israel? Why

---

a 44 Hebrew *Palti*, a variant of *Paltiel*   *b 4* Or *had come to Nacon* didn't you guard your lord the king? Someone came to destroy your lord the king. ¹⁶What you have done is not good. As surely as the LORD lives, you and your men deserve to die, because you did not guard your master, the LORD's anointed. Look around you. Where are the king's spear and water jug that were near his head?"

¹⁷Saul recognized David's voice and said, "Is that your voice, David my son?"

David replied, "Yes it is, my lord the king." ¹⁸And he added, "Why is my lord pursuing his servant? What have I done, and what wrong am I guilty of? ¹⁹Now let my lord the king listen to his servant's words. If the LORD has incited you against me, then may he accept an offering. If, however, men have done it, may they be cursed before the LORD! They have now driven me from my share in the LORD's inheritance and have said, 'Go, serve other gods.' ²⁰Now do not let my blood fall to the ground far from the presence of the LORD. The king of Israel has come out to look for a flea—as one hunts a partridge in the mountains."

²¹Then Saul said, "I have sinned. Come back, David my son. Because you considered my life precious today, I will not try to harm you again. Surely I have acted like a fool and have erred greatly."

²²"Here is the king's spear," David answered. "Let one of your young men come over and get it. ²³The LORD rewards every man for his righteousness and faithfulness. The LORD delivered you into my hands today, but I would not lay a hand on the LORD's anointed. ²⁴As surely as I valued your life today, so may the LORD value my life and deliver me from all trouble."

²⁵Then Saul said to David, "May you be blessed, my son David; you will do great things and surely triumph."

So David went on his way, and Saul returned home.

David Among the Philistines

27 But David thought to himself, "One of these days I will be destroyed by the hand of Saul. The best thing I can do is to escape to the land of the Philistines. Then Saul will give up searching for me anywhere in Israel, and I will slip out of his hand."

²So David and the six hundred men with him left and went over to Achish son of Maoch king of Gath. ³David and his men settled in Gath with Achish. Each man had his family with him, and David had his two wives: Ahinoam of Jezreel and Abigail of Carmel, the widow of Nabal. ⁴When Saul was told that David had fled to Gath, he no longer searched for him.

⁵Then David said to Achish, "If I have found favor in your eyes, let a place be assigned to me in one of the country towns, that I may live there. Why should your servant live in the royal city with you?"

⁶So on that day Achish gave him Ziklag, and it has belonged to the kings of Judah ever since. ⁷David lived in Philistine territory a year and four months.

⁸Now David and his men went up and raided the Geshurites, the Girzites and the Amalekites. (From ancient times these peoples had lived in the land extending to Shur and Egypt.) ⁹Whenever David attacked an area, he did not leave a man or woman alive, but took sheep and cattle, donkeys and camels, and clothes. Then he returned to Achish.

¹⁰When Achish asked, "Where did you go raiding today?" David would say, "Against the Negev of Judah" or "Against the Negev of Jerahmeel" or "Against the Negev of the Kenites." ¹¹He did not leave a man or woman alive to be brought to Gath, for he thought, "They might inform on us and say, 'This is what David did.' " And such was his practice as long as he lived in Philistine territory. ¹²Achish trusted David and said to himself, "He has become so odious to his people, the Israelites, that he will be my servant forever."

Saul and the Witch of Endor

28 In those days the Philistines gathered their forces to fight against Israel. Achish said to David, "You must understand that you and your men will accompany me in the army."

²David said, "Then you will see for yourself what your servant can do."

Achish replied, "Very well, I will make you my bodyguard for life."

³Now Samuel was dead, and all Israel had mourned for him and buried him in

his own town of Ramah. Saul had expelled the mediums and spiritists from the land.

4The Philistines assembled and came and set up camp at Shunem, while Saul gathered all the Israelites and set up camp at Gilboa. 5When Saul saw the Philistine army, he was afraid; terror filled his heart. 6He inquired of the LORD, but the LORD did not answer him by dreams or Urim or prophets. 7Saul then said to his attendants, "Find me a woman who is a medium, so I may go and inquire of her."

"There is one in Endor," they said.

8So Saul disguised himself, putting on other clothes, and at night he and two men went to the woman. "Consult a spirit for me," he said, "and bring up for me the one I name."

9But the woman said to him, "Surely you know what Saul has done. He has cut off the mediums and spiritists from the land. Why have you set a trap for my life to bring about my death?"

10Saul swore to her by the LORD, "As surely as the LORD lives, you will not be punished for this."

11Then the woman asked, "Whom shall I bring up for you?"

"Bring up Samuel," he said.

12When the woman saw Samuel, she cried out at the top of her voice and said to Saul, "Why have you deceived me? You are Saul!"

13The king said to her, "Don't be afraid. What do you see?"

The woman said, "I see a spirit*a* coming up out of the ground."

14"What does he look like?" he asked.

"An old man wearing a robe is coming up," she said.

Then Saul knew it was Samuel, and he bowed down and prostrated himself with his face to the ground.

15Samuel said to Saul, "Why have you disturbed me by bringing me up?"

"I am in great distress," Saul said. "The Philistines are fighting against me, and God has turned away from me. He no longer answers me, either by prophets or by dreams. So I have called on you to tell me what to do."

16Samuel said, "Why do you consult me, now that the LORD has turned away

from you and become your enemy? 17The LORD has done what he predicted through me. The LORD has torn the kingdom out of your hands and given it to one of your neighbors—to David. 18Because you did not obey the LORD or carry out his fierce wrath against the Amalekites, the LORD has done this to you today. 19The LORD will hand over both Israel and you to the Philistines, and tomorrow you and your sons will be with me. The LORD will also hand over the army of Israel to the Philistines."

20Immediately Saul fell full length on the ground, filled with fear because of Samuel's words. His strength was gone, for he had eaten nothing all that day and night.

21When the woman came to Saul and saw that he was greatly shaken, she said, "Look, your maidservant has obeyed you. I took my life in my hands and did what you told me to do. 22Now please listen to your servant and let me give you some food so you may eat and have the strength to go on your way."

23He refused and said, "I will not eat."

But his men joined the woman in urging him, and he listened to them. He got up from the ground and sat on the couch.

24The woman had a fattened calf at the house, which she butchered at once. She took some flour, kneaded it and baked bread without yeast. 25Then she set it before Saul and his men, and they ate. That same night they got up and left.

Achish Sends David Back to Ziklag

29 The Philistines gathered all their forces at Aphek, and Israel camped by the spring in Jezreel. 2As the Philistine rulers marched with their units of hundreds and thousands, David and his men were marching at the rear with Achish. 3The commanders of the Philistines asked, "What about these Hebrews?"

Achish replied, "Is this not David, who was an officer of Saul king of Israel? He has already been with me for over a year, and from the day he left Saul until now, I have found no fault in him."

4But the Philistine commanders were angry with him and said, "Send the man back, that he may return to the place

a 13 Or *see spirits;* or *see gods*

you assigned him. He must not go with us into battle, or he will turn against us during the fighting. How better could he regain his master's favor than by taking the heads of our own men? ⁵Isn't this the David they sang about in their dances:

" 'Saul has slain his thousands,
    and David his tens of thousands'?"

⁶So Achish called David and said to him, "As surely as the LORD lives, you have been reliable, and I would be pleased to have you serve with me in the army. From the day you came to me until now, I have found no fault in you, but the rulers don't approve of you. ⁷Turn back and go in peace; do nothing to displease the Philistine rulers."

⁸"But what have I done?" asked David. "What have you found against your servant from the day I came to you until now? Why can't I go and fight against the enemies of my lord the king?"

⁹Achish answered, "I know that you have been as pleasing in my eyes as an angel of God; nevertheless, the Philistine commanders have said, 'He must not go up with us into battle.' ¹⁰Now get up early, along with your master's servants who have come with you, and leave in the morning as soon as it is light."

¹¹So David and his men got up early in the morning to go back to the land of the Philistines, and the Philistines went up to Jezreel.

David Destroys the Amalekites

30 David and his men reached Ziklag on the third day. Now the Amalekites had raided the Negev and Ziklag. They had attacked Ziklag and burned it, ²and had taken captive the women and all who were in it, both young and old. They killed none of them, but carried them off as they went on their way.

³When David and his men came to Ziklag, they found it destroyed by fire and their wives and sons and daughters taken captive. ⁴So David and his men wept aloud until they had no strength left to weep. ⁵David's two wives had been captured—Ahinoam of Jezreel and Abigail, the widow of Nabal of Carmel. ⁶David was greatly distressed because

the men were talking of stoning him; each one was bitter in spirit because of his sons and daughters. But David found strength in the LORD his God.

⁷Then David said to Abiathar the priest, the son of Ahimelech, "Bring me the ephod." Abiathar brought it to him, ⁸and David inquired of the LORD, "Shall I pursue this raiding party? Will I overtake them?"

"Pursue them," he answered. "You will certainly overtake them and succeed in the rescue."

⁹David and the six hundred men with him came to the Besor Ravine, where some stayed behind, ¹⁰for two hundred men were too exhausted to cross the ravine. But David and four hundred men continued the pursuit.

¹¹They found an Egyptian in a field and brought him to David. They gave him water to drink and food to eat— ¹²part of a cake of pressed figs and two cakes of raisins. He ate and was revived, for he had not eaten any food or drunk any water for three days and three nights.

¹³David asked him, "To whom do you belong, and where do you come from?"

He said, "I am an Egyptian, the slave of an Amalekite. My master abandoned me when I became ill three days ago. ¹⁴We raided the Negev of the Kerethites and the territory belonging to Judah and the Negev of Caleb. And we burned Ziklag."

¹⁵David asked him, "Can you lead me down to this raiding party?"

He answered, "Swear to me before God that you will not kill me or hand me over to my master, and I will take you down to them."

¹⁶He led David down, and there they were, scattered over the countryside, eating, drinking and reveling because of the great amount of plunder they had taken from the land of the Philistines and from Judah. ¹⁷David fought them from dusk until the evening of the next day, and none of them got away, except four hundred young men who rode off on camels and fled. ¹⁸David recovered everything the Amalekites had taken, including his two wives. ¹⁹Nothing was missing: young or old, boy or girl, plunder or anything else they had taken. David brought everything back. ²⁰He

took all the flocks and herds, and his men drove them ahead of the other livestock, saying, "This is David's plunder."

21Then David came to the two hundred men who had been too exhausted to follow him and who were left behind at the Besor Ravine. They came out to meet David and the people with him. As David and his men approached, he greeted them. 22But all the evil men and troublemakers among David's followers said, "Because they did not go out with us, we will not share with them the plunder we recovered. However, each man may take his wife and children and go."

23David replied, "No, my brothers, you must not do that with what the LORD has given us. He has protected us and handed over to us the forces that came against us. 24Who will listen to what you say? The share of the man who stayed with the supplies is to be the same as that of him who went down to the battle. All will share alike." 25David made this a statute and ordinance for Israel from that day to this.

26When David arrived in Ziklag, he sent some of the plunder to the elders of Judah, who were his friends, saying, "Here is a present for you from the plunder of the LORD's enemies."

27He sent it to those who were in Bethel, Ramoth Negev and Jattir; 28to those in Aroer, Siphmoth, Eshtemoa 29and Racal; to those in the towns of the Jerahmeelites and the Kenites; 30to those in Hormah, Bor Ashan, Athach 31and Hebron; and to those in all the other places where David and his men had roamed.

Saul Takes His Life

31 Now the Philistines fought against Israel; the Israelites fled before them, and many fell slain on Mount Gilboa. 2The Philistines pressed hard after Saul and his sons, and they killed his sons Jonathan, Abinadab and Malki-Shua. 3The fighting grew fierce around Saul, and when the archers overtook him, they wounded him critically.

4Saul said to his armor-bearer, "Draw your sword and run me through, or these uncircumcised fellows will come and run me through and abuse me."

But his armor-bearer was terrified and would not do it; so Saul took his own sword and fell on it. 5When the armor-bearer saw that Saul was dead, he too fell on his sword and died with him. 6So Saul and his three sons and his armor-bearer and all his men died together that same day.

7When the Israelites along the valley and those across the Jordan saw that the Israelite army had fled and that Saul and his sons had died, they abandoned their towns and fled. And the Philistines came and occupied them.

8The next day, when the Philistines came to strip the dead, they found Saul and his three sons fallen on Mount Gilboa. 9They cut off his head and stripped off his armor, and they sent messengers throughout the land of the Philistines to proclaim the news in the temple of their idols and among their people. 10They put his armor in the temple of the Ashtoreths and fastened his body to the wall of Beth Shan.

11When the people of Jabesh Gilead heard of what the Philistines had done to Saul, 12all their valiant men journeyed through the night to Beth Shan. They took down the bodies of Saul and his sons from the wall of Beth Shan and went to Jabesh, where they burned them. 13Then they took their bones and buried them under a tamarisk tree at Jabesh, and they fasted seven days.

2 SAMUEL

THIS BOOK TELLS THE STORY OF
DAVID'S REIGN OVER ISRAEL. AL-
THOUGH GOD CALLED DAVID A
MAN AFTER HIS OWN HEART (ACTS 13:22),
DAVID KNEW SIN AND FAILURE. THE BOOK OF
2 SAMUEL TELLS THE STORY OF DAVID'S
ADULTERY AND TESTIFIES TO THE POWER OF
GOD'S FAITHFULNESS AND FORGIVING LOVE.
LOOK FOR GOD'S HAND AT WORK AS THE
NATION PROSPERS UNDER DAVID'S RULE.
AND TAKE COMFORT THAT AS YOU LAY YOUR
SINS BEFORE GOD, HE WILL FORGIVE YOU AND
USE YOU ONCE AGAIN IN HIS SERVICE.

David Hears of Saul's Death

1 After the death of Saul, David returned from defeating the Amalekites and stayed in Ziklag two days. ²On the third day a man arrived from Saul's camp, with his clothes torn and with dust on his head. When he came to David, he fell to the ground to pay him honor.

³"Where have you come from?" David asked him.

He answered, "I have escaped from the Israelite camp."

⁴"What happened?" David asked. "Tell me."

He said, "The men fled from the battle. Many of them fell and died. And Saul and his son Jonathan are dead."

⁵Then David said to the young man who brought him the report, "How do you know that Saul and his son Jonathan are dead?"

⁶"I happened to be on Mount Gilboa," the young man said, "and there was Saul, leaning on his spear, with the chariots and riders almost upon him. ⁷When he turned around and saw me, he called out to me, and I said, 'What can I do?'

⁸"He asked me, 'Who are you?'

" 'An Amalekite,' I answered.

⁹"Then he said to me, 'Stand over me and kill me! I am in the throes of death, but I'm still alive.'

¹⁰"So I stood over him and killed him, because I knew that after he had fallen he could not survive. And I took the crown that was on his head and the band on his arm and have brought them here to my lord."

¹¹Then David and all the men with

him took hold of their clothes and tore them. 12They mourned and wept and fasted till evening for Saul and his son Jonathan, and for the army of the LORD and the house of Israel, because they had fallen by the sword.

13David said to the young man who brought him the report, "Where are you from?"

"I am the son of an alien, an Amalekite," he answered.

14David asked him, "Why were you not afraid to lift your hand to destroy the LORD's anointed?"

15Then David called one of his men and said, "Go, strike him down!" So he struck him down, and he died. 16For David had said to him, "Your blood be on your own head. Your own mouth testified against you when you said, 'I killed the LORD's anointed.'"

David's Lament for Saul and Jonathan

17David took up this lament concerning Saul and his son Jonathan, 18and ordered that the men of Judah be taught this lament of the bow (it is written in the Book of Jashar):

19 "Your glory, O Israel, lies slain on
  your heights.
  How the mighty have fallen!

20 "Tell it not in Gath,
  proclaim it not in the streets of
    Ashkelon,
  lest the daughters of the Philistines
    be glad,
  lest the daughters of the
    uncircumcised rejoice.

21 "O mountains of Gilboa,
  may you have neither dew nor rain,
  nor fields that yield offerings
    ⌊of grain⌋.
  For there the shield of the mighty
    was defiled,
  the shield of Saul—no longer
    rubbed with oil.

22 From the blood of the slain,
  from the flesh of the mighty,
  the bow of Jonathan did not turn back,
  the sword of Saul did not return
    unsatisfied.

23 "Saul and Jonathan—
  in life they were loved and gracious,

and in death they were not parted.
  They were swifter than eagles,
  they were stronger than lions.

24 "O daughters of Israel,
  weep for Saul,
  who clothed you in scarlet and finery,
  who adorned your garments with
    ornaments of gold.

25 "How the mighty have fallen in
    battle!
  Jonathan lies slain on your heights.
26 I grieve for you, Jonathan my brother;
  you were very dear to me.
  Your love for me was wonderful,
  more wonderful than that of
    women.

27 "How the mighty have fallen!
  The weapons of war have perished!"

David Anointed King Over Judah

2 In the course of time, David inquired of the LORD. "Shall I go up to one of the towns of Judah?" he asked.

The LORD said, "Go up."

David asked, "Where shall I go?"

"To Hebron," the LORD answered.

2So David went up there with his two wives, Ahinoam of Jezreel and Abigail, the widow of Nabal of Carmel. 3David also took the men who were with him, each with his family, and they settled in Hebron and its towns. 4Then the men of Judah came to Hebron and there they anointed David king over the house of Judah.

When David was told that it was the men of Jabesh Gilead who had buried Saul, 5he sent messengers to the men of Jabesh Gilead to say to them, "The LORD bless you for showing this kindness to Saul your master by burying him. 6May the LORD now show you kindness and faithfulness, and I too will show you the same favor because you have done this. 7Now then, be strong and brave, for Saul your master is dead, and the house of Judah has anointed me king over them."

War Between the Houses of David and Saul

8Meanwhile, Abner son of Ner, the commander of Saul's army, had taken Ish-Bosheth son of Saul and brought him over to Mahanaim. 9He made him king over Gilead, Ashuri[a] and Jezreel, and also over Ephraim, Benjamin and all Israel.

¹⁰Ish-Bosheth son of Saul was forty years old when he became king over Israel, and he reigned two years. The house of Judah, however, followed David. ¹¹The length of time David was king in Hebron over the house of Judah was seven years and six months.

¹²Abner son of Ner, together with the men of Ish-Bosheth son of Saul, left Mahanaim and went to Gibeon. ¹³Joab son of Zeruiah and David's men went out and met them at the pool of Gibeon. One group sat down on one side of the pool and one group on the other side.

¹⁴Then Abner said to Joab, "Let's have some of the young men get up and fight hand to hand in front of us."

"All right, let them do it," Joab said.

¹⁵So they stood up and were counted off—twelve men for Benjamin and Ish-Bosheth son of Saul, and twelve for David. ¹⁶Then each man grabbed his opponent by the head and thrust his dagger into his opponent's side, and they fell down together. So that place in Gibeon was called Helkath Hazzurim.[b]

¹⁷The battle that day was very fierce, and Abner and the men of Israel were defeated by David's men.

¹⁸The three sons of Zeruiah were there: Joab, Abishai and Asahel. Now Asahel was as fleet-footed as a wild gazelle. ¹⁹He chased Abner, turning neither to the right nor to the left as he pursued him. ²⁰Abner looked behind him and asked, "Is that you, Asahel?"

"It is," he answered.

²¹Then Abner said to him, "Turn aside to the right or to the left; take on one of the young men and strip him of his weapons." But Asahel would not stop chasing him.

²²Again Abner warned Asahel, "Stop chasing me! Why should I strike you down? How could I look your brother Joab in the face?"

²³But Asahel refused to give up the pursuit; so Abner thrust the butt of his spear into Asahel's stomach, and the spear came out through his back. He fell there and died on the spot. And every man stopped when he came to the place where Asahel had fallen and died.

²⁴But Joab and Abishai pursued Abner, and as the sun was setting, they came to the hill of Ammah, near Giah on the way to the wasteland of Gibeon. ²⁵Then the men of Benjamin rallied behind Abner. They formed themselves into a group and took their stand on top of a hill.

²⁶Abner called out to Joab, "Must the sword devour forever? Don't you realize that this will end in bitterness? How long before you order your men to stop pursuing their brothers?"

²⁷Joab answered, "As surely as God lives, if you had not spoken, the men would have continued the pursuit of their brothers until morning.[c] "

²⁸So Joab blew the trumpet, and all the men came to a halt; they no longer pursued Israel, nor did they fight anymore.

²⁹All that night Abner and his men marched through the Arabah. They crossed the Jordan, continued through the whole Bithron[d] and came to Mahanaim.

³⁰Then Joab returned from pursuing Abner and assembled all his men. Besides Asahel, nineteen of David's men were found missing. ³¹But David's men had killed three hundred and sixty Benjamites who were with Abner. ³²They took Asahel and buried him in his father's tomb at Bethlehem. Then Joab and his men marched all night and arrived at Hebron by daybreak.

3 The war between the house of Saul and the house of David lasted a long time. David grew stronger and stronger, while the house of Saul grew weaker and weaker.

²Sons were born to David in Hebron:

His firstborn was Amnon the son of Ahinoam of Jezreel;

³his second, Kileab the son of Abigail the widow of Nabal of Carmel;

the third, Absalom the son of Maacah daughter of Talmai king of Geshur;

⁴the fourth, Adonijah the son of Haggith;

---

[a] 9 Or *Asher*   [b] 16 *Helkath Hazzurim* means *field of daggers* or *field of hostilities.*   [c] 27 Or *spoken this morning, the men would not have taken up the pursuit of their brothers; or spoken, the men would have given up the pursuit of their brothers by morning*   [d] 29 Or *morning; or ravine;* the meaning of the Hebrew for this word is uncertain.

the fifth, Shephatiah the son of Abital;

5 and the sixth, Ithream the son of David's wife Eglah.

These were born to David in Hebron.

Abner Goes Over to David

6 During the war between the house of Saul and the house of David, Abner had been strengthening his own position in the house of Saul. 7 Now Saul had had a concubine named Rizpah daughter of Aiah. And Ish-Bosheth said to Abner, "Why did you sleep with my father's concubine?"

8 Abner was very angry because of what Ish-Bosheth said and he answered, "Am I a dog's head—on Judah's side? This very day I am loyal to the house of your father Saul and to his family and friends. I haven't handed you over to David. Yet now you accuse me of an offense involving this woman! 9 May God deal with Abner, be it ever so severely, if I do not do for David what the LORD promised him on oath 10 and transfer the kingdom from the house of Saul and establish David's throne over Israel and Judah from Dan to Beersheba." 11 Ish-Bosheth did not dare to say another word to Abner, because he was afraid of him.

12 Then Abner sent messengers on his behalf to say to David, "Whose land is it? Make an agreement with me, and I will help you bring all Israel over to you."

13 "Good," said David. "I will make an agreement with you. But I demand one thing of you: Do not come into my presence unless you bring Michal daughter of Saul when you come to see me." 14 Then David sent messengers to Ish-Bosheth son of Saul, demanding, "Give me my wife Michal, whom I betrothed to myself for the price of a hundred Philistine foreskins."

15 So Ish-Bosheth gave orders and had her taken away from her husband Paltiel son of Laish. 16 Her husband, however, went with her, weeping behind her all the way to Bahurim. Then Abner said to him, "Go back home!" So he went back.

17 Abner conferred with the elders of Israel and said, "For some time you have wanted to make David your king. 18 Now do it! For the LORD promised David, 'By my servant David I will rescue my people Israel from the hand of the Philistines and from the hand of all their enemies.' "

19 Abner also spoke to the Benjamites in person. Then he went to Hebron to tell David everything that Israel and the whole house of Benjamin wanted to do. 20 When Abner, who had twenty men with him, came to David at Hebron, David prepared a feast for him and his men. 21 Then Abner said to David, "Let me go at once and assemble all Israel for my lord the king, so that they may make a compact with you, and that you may rule over all that your heart desires." So David sent Abner away, and he went in peace.

Joab Murders Abner

22 Just then David's men and Joab returned from a raid and brought with them a great deal of plunder. But Abner was no longer with David in Hebron, because David had sent him away, and he had gone in peace. 23 When Joab and all the soldiers with him arrived, he was told that Abner son of Ner had come to the king and that the king had sent him away and that he had gone in peace.

24 So Joab went to the king and said, "What have you done? Look, Abner came to you. Why did you let him go? Now he is gone! 25 You know Abner son of Ner; he came to deceive you and observe your movements and find out everything you are doing."

26 Joab then left David and sent messengers after Abner, and they brought him back from the well of Sirah. But David did not know it. 27 Now when Abner returned to Hebron, Joab took him aside into the gateway, as though to speak with him privately. And there, to avenge the blood of his brother Asahel, Joab stabbed him in the stomach, and he died.

28 Later, when David heard about this, he said, "I and my kingdom are forever innocent before the LORD concerning the blood of Abner son of Ner. 29 May his blood fall upon the head of Joab and upon all his father's house! May Joab's house never be without someone who

has a running sore or leprosy[a] or who leans on a crutch or who falls by the sword or who lacks food."

[30](Joab and his brother Abishai murdered Abner because he had killed their brother Asahel in the battle at Gibeon.)

[31]Then David said to Joab and all the people with him, "Tear your clothes and put on sackcloth and walk in mourning in front of Abner." King David himself walked behind the bier. [32]They buried Abner in Hebron, and the king wept aloud at Abner's tomb. All the people wept also.

[33]The king sang this lament for Abner:

"Should Abner have died as the
　　lawless die?
[34]　Your hands were not bound,
　　your feet were not fettered.
You fell as one falls before wicked
　　men."

And all the people wept over him again.

[35]Then they all came and urged David to eat something while it was still day; but David took an oath, saying, "May God deal with me, be it ever so severely, if I taste bread or anything else before the sun sets!"

[36]All the people took note and were pleased; indeed, everything the king did pleased them. [37]So on that day all the people and all Israel knew that the king had no part in the murder of Abner son of Ner.

[38]Then the king said to his men, "Do you not realize that a prince and a great man has fallen in Israel this day? [39]And today, though I am the anointed king, I am weak, and these sons of Zeruiah are too strong for me. May the LORD repay the evildoer according to his evil deeds!"

Ish-Bosheth Murdered

4 When Ish-Bosheth son of Saul heard that Abner had died in Hebron, he lost courage, and all Israel became alarmed. [2]Now Saul's son had two men who were leaders of raiding bands. One was named Baanah and the other Recab; they were sons of Rimmon the Beerothite from the tribe of Benjamin—Beeroth is considered part of Benjamin, [3]because the people of Beeroth fled to Gittaim and have lived there as aliens to this day.

[4](Jonathan son of Saul had a son who was lame in both feet. He was five years old when the news about Saul and Jonathan came from Jezreel. His nurse picked him up and fled, but as she hurried to leave, he fell and became crippled. His name was Mephibosheth.)

[5]Now Recab and Baanah, the sons of Rimmon the Beerothite, set out for the house of Ish-Bosheth, and they arrived there in the heat of the day while he was taking his noonday rest. [6]They went into the inner part of the house as if to get some wheat, and they stabbed him in the stomach. Then Recab and his brother Baanah slipped away.

[7]They had gone into the house while he was lying on the bed in his bedroom. After they stabbed and killed him, they cut off his head. Taking it with them, they traveled all night by way of the Arabah. [8]They brought the head of Ish-Bosheth to David at Hebron and said to the king, "Here is the head of Ish-Bosheth son of Saul, your enemy, who tried to take your life. This day the LORD has avenged my lord the king against Saul and his offspring."

[9]David answered Recab and his brother Baanah, the sons of Rimmon the Beerothite, "As surely as the LORD lives, who has delivered me out of all trouble, [10]when a man told me, 'Saul is dead,' and thought he was bringing good news, I seized him and put him to death in Ziklag. That was the reward I gave him for his news! [11]How much more—when wicked men have killed an innocent man in his own house and on his own bed—should I not now demand his blood from your hand and rid the earth of you!"

[12]So David gave an order to his men, and they killed them. They cut off their hands and feet and hung the bodies by the pool in Hebron. But they took the head of Ish-Bosheth and buried it in Abner's tomb at Hebron.

David Becomes King Over Israel

5 All the tribes of Israel came to David at Hebron and said, "We are your own flesh and blood. [2]In the

---

[a] 29 The Hebrew word was used for various diseases affecting the skin—not necessarily leprosy.

past, while Saul was king over us, you were the one who led Israel on their military campaigns. And the LORD said to you, 'You will shepherd my people Israel, and you will become their ruler.' "

³When all the elders of Israel had come to King David at Hebron, the king made a compact with them at Hebron before the LORD, and they anointed David king over Israel.

⁴David was thirty years old when he became king, and he reigned forty years. ⁵In Hebron he reigned over Judah seven years and six months, and in Jerusalem he reigned over all Israel and Judah thirty-three years.

David Conquers Jerusalem

⁶The king and his men marched to Jerusalem to attack the Jebusites, who lived there. The Jebusites said to David, "You will not get in here; even the blind and the lame can ward you off." They thought, "David cannot get in here." ⁷Nevertheless, David captured the fortress of Zion, the City of David.

⁸On that day, David said, "Anyone who conquers the Jebusites will have to use the water shaft*a* to reach those 'lame and blind' who are David's enemies.*b* " That is why they say, "The 'blind and lame' will not enter the palace."

⁹David then took up residence in the fortress and called it the City of David. He built up the area around it, from the supporting terraces*c* inward. ¹⁰And he became more and more powerful, because the LORD God Almighty was with him.

¹¹Now Hiram king of Tyre sent messengers to David, along with cedar logs and carpenters and stonemasons, and they built a palace for David. ¹²And David knew that the LORD had established him as king over Israel and had exalted his kingdom for the sake of his people Israel.

¹³After he left Hebron, David took more concubines and wives in Jerusalem, and more sons and daughters were born to him. ¹⁴These are the names of the children born to him there:

Shammua, Shobab, Nathan, Solomon, ¹⁵Ibhar, Elishua, Nepheg, Japhia, ¹⁶Elishama, Eliada and Eliphelet.

David Defeats the Philistines

¹⁷When the Philistines heard that David had been anointed king over Israel, they went up in full force to search for him, but David heard about it and went down to the stronghold. ¹⁸Now the Philistines had come and spread out in the Valley of Rephaim; ¹⁹so David inquired of the LORD, "Shall I go and attack the Philistines? Will you hand them over to me?"

The LORD answered him, "Go, for I will surely hand the Philistines over to you."

²⁰So David went to Baal Perazim, and there he defeated them. He said, "As waters break out, the LORD has broken out against my enemies before me." So that place was called Baal Perazim.*d* ²¹The Philistines abandoned their idols there, and David and his men carried them off.

²²Once more the Philistines came up and spread out in the Valley of Rephaim; ²³so David inquired of the LORD, and he answered, "Do not go straight up, but circle around behind them and attack them in front of the balsam trees. ²⁴As soon as you hear the sound of marching in the tops of the balsam trees, move quickly, because that will mean the LORD has gone out in front of you to strike the Philistine army." ²⁵So David did as the LORD commanded him, and he struck down the Philistines all the way from Gibeon*e* to Gezer.

The Ark Brought to Jerusalem

6 David again brought together out of Israel chosen men, thirty thousand in all. ²He and all his men set out from Baalah of Judah*f* to bring up from there the ark of God, which is called by the Name,*g* the name of the LORD Almighty, who is enthroned between the cherubim that are on the ark. ³They set the ark of God on a new cart and brought it from the house of

---

a 8 Or *use scaling hooks*   *b 8* Or *are hated by David*   *c 9* Or *the Millo*   *d 20 Baal Perazim* means *the lord who breaks out.*   *e 25* Septuagint (see also 1 Chron. 14:16); Hebrew *Geba*   *f 2* That is, Kiriath Jearim; Hebrew *Baale Judah*, a variant of *Baalah of Judah*   *g 2* Hebrew; Septuagint and Vulgate do not have *the Name.*

Abinadab, which was on the hill. Uzzah and Ahio, sons of Abinadab, were guiding the new cart [4]with the ark of God on it,[a] and Ahio was walking in front of it. [5]David and the whole house of Israel were celebrating with all their might before the LORD, with songs[b] and with harps, lyres, tambourines, sistrums and cymbals.

[6]When they came to the threshing floor of Nacon, Uzzah reached out and took hold of the ark of God, because the oxen stumbled. [7]The LORD's anger burned against Uzzah because of his irreverent act; therefore God struck him down and he died there beside the ark of God.

[8]Then David was angry because the LORD's wrath had broken out against Uzzah, and to this day that place is called Perez Uzzah.[c]

[9]David was afraid of the LORD that day and said, "How can the ark of the LORD ever come to me?" [10]He was not willing to take the ark of the LORD to be with him in the City of David. Instead, he took it aside to the house of Obed-Edom the Gittite. [11]The ark of the LORD remained in the house of Obed-Edom the Gittite for three months, and the LORD blessed him and his entire household.

[12]Now King David was told, "The LORD has blessed the household of Obed-Edom and everything he has, because of the ark of God." So David went down and brought up the ark of God from the house of Obed-Edom to the City of David with rejoicing. [13]When those who were carrying the ark of the LORD had taken six steps, he sacrificed a bull and a fattened calf. [14]David, wearing a linen ephod, danced before the LORD with all his might, [15]while he and the entire house of Israel brought up the ark of the LORD with shouts and the sound of trumpets.

[16]As the ark of the LORD was entering the City of David, Michal daughter of Saul watched from a window. And when she saw King David leaping and dancing before the LORD, she despised him in her heart.

[17]They brought the ark of the LORD and set it in its place inside the tent that David had pitched for it, and David sacrificed burnt offerings and fellowship offerings[d] before the LORD. [18]After he had finished sacrificing the burnt offerings and fellowship offerings, he blessed the people in the name of the LORD Almighty. [19]Then he gave a loaf of bread, a cake of dates and a cake of raisins to each person in the whole crowd of Israelites, both men and women. And all the people went to their homes.

[20]When David returned home to bless his household, Michal daughter of Saul came out to meet him and said, "How the king of Israel has distinguished himself today, disrobing in the sight of the slave girls of his servants as any vulgar fellow would!"

[21]David said to Michal, "It was before the LORD, who chose me rather than your father or anyone from his house when he appointed me ruler over the LORD's people Israel—I will celebrate before the LORD. [22]I will become even more undignified than this, and I will be humiliated in my own eyes. But by these slave girls you spoke of, I will be held in honor."

[23]And Michal daughter of Saul had no children to the day of her death.

God's Promise to David

7 After the king was settled in his palace and the LORD had given him rest from all his enemies around him, [2]he said to Nathan the prophet, "Here I am, living in a palace of cedar, while the ark of God remains in a tent."

[3]Nathan replied to the king, "Whatever you have in mind, go ahead and do it, for the LORD is with you."

[4]That night the word of the LORD came to Nathan, saying:

[5]"Go and tell my servant David, 'This is what the LORD says: Are you the one to build me a house to dwell in? [6]I have not dwelt in a house from the day I brought the Israelites up out of Egypt to this

---

[a] 3,4 Dead Sea Scrolls and some Septuagint manuscripts; Masoretic Text *cart* [4]*and they brought it with the ark of God from the house of Abinadab, which was on the hill*　　　[b] 5 See Dead Sea Scrolls, Septuagint and 1 Chronicles 13:8; Masoretic Text *celebrating before the LORD with all kinds of instruments made of pine.*　　　[c] 8 *Perez Uzzah* means *outbreak against Uzzah.*　　　[d] 17 Traditionally *peace offerings*; also in verse 18

day. I have been moving from place to place with a tent as my dwelling. ⁷Wherever I have moved with all the Israelites, did I ever say to any of their rulers whom I commanded to shepherd my people Israel, "Why have you not built me a house of cedar?" '

⁸"Now then, tell my servant David, 'This is what the LORD Almighty says: I took you from the pasture and from following the flock to be ruler over my people Israel. ⁹I have been with you wherever you have gone, and I have cut off all your enemies from before you. Now I will make your name great, like the names of the greatest men of the earth. ¹⁰And I will provide a place for my people Israel and will plant them so that they can have a home of their own and no longer be disturbed. Wicked people will not oppress them anymore, as they did at the beginning ¹¹and have done ever since the time I appointed leaders*a* over my people Israel. I will also give you rest from all your enemies.

" 'The LORD declares to you that the LORD himself will establish a house for you: ¹²When your days are over and you rest with your fathers, I will raise up your offspring to succeed you, who will come from your own body, and I will establish his kingdom. ¹³He is the one who will build a house for my Name, and I will establish the throne of his kingdom forever. ¹⁴I will be his father, and he will be my son. When he does wrong, I will punish him with the rod of men, with floggings inflicted by men. ¹⁵But my love will never be taken away from him, as I took it away from Saul, whom I removed from before you. ¹⁶Your house and your kingdom will endure forever before me*b*; your throne will be established forever.' "

¹⁷Nathan reported to David all the words of this entire revelation.

David's Prayer

¹⁸Then King David went in and sat before the LORD, and he said:

"Who am I, O Sovereign LORD, and what is my family, that you have brought me this far? ¹⁹And as if this were not enough in your sight, O Sovereign LORD, you have also spoken about the future of the house of your servant. Is this your usual way of dealing with man, O Sovereign LORD?

²⁰"What more can David say to you? For you know your servant, O Sovereign LORD. ²¹For the sake of your word and according to your will, you have done this great thing and made it known to your servant.

²²"How great you are, O Sovereign LORD! There is no one like you, and there is no God but you, as we have heard with our own ears. ²³And who is like your people Israel—the one nation on earth that God went out to redeem as a people for himself, and to make a name for himself, and to perform great and awesome wonders by driving out nations and their gods from before your people, whom you redeemed from Egypt?*c* ²⁴You have established your people Israel as your very own forever, and you, O LORD, have become their God.

²⁵"And now, LORD God, keep forever the promise you have made concerning your servant and his house. Do as you promised, ²⁶so that your name will be great forever. Then men will say, 'The LORD Almighty is God over Israel!' And the house of your servant David will be established before you.

²⁷"O LORD Almighty, God of Israel, you have revealed this to your servant, saying, 'I will build a house for you.' So your servant has found courage to offer you this prayer. ²⁸O Sovereign LORD, you are God! Your words are trustworthy, and you have promised these good things to your servant. ²⁹Now be

---

a 11 Traditionally *judges*   *b* 16 Some Hebrew manuscripts and Septuagint; most Hebrew manuscripts *you*   *c* 23 See Septuagint and 1 Chron. 17:21; Hebrew *wonders for your land and before your people, whom you redeemed from Egypt, from the nations and their gods.*

pleased to bless the house of your servant, that it may continue forever in your sight; for you, O Sovereign LORD, have spoken, and with your blessing the house of your servant will be blessed forever."

THE BLESSINGS OF HIS COVENANT
Oswald Chambers

VERSE: 2 Samuel 7:28   **PASSAGE:** 2 Samuel 7:18–29

t is the will of God that human beings should get into a right-standing relationship with him, and his covenants are designed for this purpose. Why doesn't God save me? He has accomplished and provided for my salvation, but I have not yet entered into a relationship with him. Why doesn't God do everything we ask? He has done it. The point is—will I step into that covenant relationship? All the great blessings of God are finished and complete, but they are not mine until I enter into a relationship with him on the basis of his covenant.

Waiting for God to act is fleshly unbelief. It means that I have no faith in him. I wait for him to do something in me so I may trust in that. But God won't do it, because that is not the basis of the God-and-man relationship. Man must go beyond the physical body and feelings in his covenant with God, just as God goes beyond himself in reaching out with his covenant to man. It is a question of faith in God—a very rare thing. We only have faith in our feelings. I don't believe God until he puts something tangible in my hand, so that I know I have it. Then I say, "Now I believe." There is no faith exhibited in that. God says, "Look to me, and be saved . . . " (Isaiah 45:22).

When I have really transacted business with God on the basis of his covenant, letting everything else go, there is no sense of personal achievement—no human ingredient in it at all. Instead, there is a complete overwhelming sense of being brought into union with God, and my life is transformed and radiates peace and joy.

ADDITIONAL SCRIPTURE READING:
Jeremiah 31:31–34; Hebrews 8

Go to page 345 for your next devotional reading.

1900   Present

David's Victories

8 In the course of time, David defeated the Philistines and subdued them, and he took Metheg Ammah from the control of the Philistines.

2David also defeated the Moabites. He made them lie down on the ground and measured them off with a length of cord. Every two lengths of them were put to death, and the third length was allowed to live. So the Moabites became subject to David and brought tribute.

3Moreover, David fought Hadadezer son of Rehob, king of Zobah, when he went to restore his control along the Euphrates River. 4David captured a thousand of his chariots, seven thousand charioteers*a* and twenty thousand foot soldiers. He hamstrung all but a hundred of the chariot horses.

5When the Arameans of Damascus came to help Hadadezer king of Zobah, David struck down twenty-two thousand of them. 6He put garrisons in the Aramean kingdom of Damascus, and the Arameans became subject to him and brought tribute. The LORD gave David victory wherever he went.

7David took the gold shields that belonged to the officers of Hadadezer and brought them to Jerusalem. 8From Tebah*b* and Berothai, towns that belonged to Hadadezer, King David took a great quantity of bronze.

9When Tou*c* king of Hamath heard that David had defeated the entire army of Hadadezer, 10he sent his son Joram*d* to King David to greet him and congratulate him on his victory in battle over Hadadezer, who had been at war with Tou. Joram brought with him articles of silver and gold and bronze.

11King David dedicated these articles to the LORD, as he had done with the silver and gold from all the nations he had subdued: 12Edom*e* and Moab, the Ammonites and the Philistines, and Amalek. He also dedicated the plunder taken from Hadadezer son of Rehob, king of Zobah.

13And David became famous after he returned from striking down eighteen thousand Edomites*f* in the Valley of Salt.

14He put garrisons throughout Edom, and all the Edomites became subject to David. The LORD gave David victory wherever he went.

David's Officials

15David reigned over all Israel, doing what was just and right for all his people. 16Joab son of Zeruiah was over the army; Jehoshaphat son of Ahilud was recorder; 17Zadok son of Ahitub and Ahimelech son of Abiathar were priests; Seraiah was secretary; 18Benaiah son of Jehoiada was over the Kerethites and Pelethites; and David's sons were royal advisers.*g*

David and Mephibosheth

9 David asked, "Is there anyone still left of the house of Saul to whom I can show kindness for Jonathan's sake?"

2Now there was a servant of Saul's household named Ziba. They called him to appear before David, and the king said to him, "Are you Ziba?"

"Your servant," he replied.

3The king asked, "Is there no one still left of the house of Saul to whom I can show God's kindness?"

Ziba answered the king, "There is still a son of Jonathan; he is crippled in both feet."

4"Where is he?" the king asked.

Ziba answered, "He is at the house of Makir son of Ammiel in Lo Debar."

5So King David had him brought from Lo Debar, from the house of Makir son of Ammiel.

6When Mephibosheth son of Jonathan, the son of Saul, came to David, he bowed down to pay him honor.

David said, "Mephibosheth!"

"Your servant," he replied.

7"Don't be afraid," David said to him, "for I will surely show you kindness for the sake of your father Jonathan. I will restore to you all the land that belonged to your grandfather Saul, and you will always eat at my table."

---

a 4 Septuagint (see also Dead Sea Scrolls and 1 Chron. 18:4); Masoretic Text *captured seventeen hundred of his charioteers*   *b 8* See some Septuagint manuscripts (see also 1 Chron. 18:8); Hebrew *Betah.*   *c 9* Hebrew *Toi,* a variant of *Tou;* also in verse 10   *d 10* A variant of *Hadoram*   *e 12* Some Hebrew manuscripts, Septuagint and Syriac (see also 1 Chron. 18:11); most Hebrew manuscripts *Aram*   *f 13* A few Hebrew manuscripts, Septuagint and Syriac (see also 1 Chron. 18:12); most Hebrew manuscripts *Aram* (that is, Arameans)   *g 18* Or *were priests*

8Mephibosheth bowed down and said, "What is your servant, that you should notice a dead dog like me?"

9Then the king summoned Ziba, Saul's servant, and said to him, "I have given your master's grandson everything that belonged to Saul and his family. 10You and your sons and your servants are to farm the land for him and bring in the crops, so that your master's grandson may be provided for. And Mephibosheth, grandson of your master, will always eat at my table." (Now Ziba had fifteen sons and twenty servants.)

11Then Ziba said to the king, "Your servant will do whatever my lord the king commands his servant to do." So Mephibosheth ate at David's*a* table like one of the king's sons.

12Mephibosheth had a young son named Mica, and all the members of Ziba's household were servants of Mephibosheth. 13And Mephibosheth lived in Jerusalem, because he always ate at the king's table, and he was crippled in both feet.

David Defeats the Ammonites

10 In the course of time, the king of the Ammonites died, and his son Hanun succeeded him as king. 2David thought, "I will show kindness to Hanun son of Nahash, just as his father showed kindness to me." So David sent a delegation to express his sympathy to Hanun concerning his father.

When David's men came to the land of the Ammonites, 3the Ammonite nobles said to Hanun their lord, "Do you think David is honoring your father by sending men to you to express sympathy? Hasn't David sent them to you to explore the city and spy it out and overthrow it?" 4So Hanun seized David's men, shaved off half of each man's beard, cut off their garments in the middle at the buttocks, and sent them away.

5When David was told about this, he sent messengers to meet the men, for they were greatly humiliated. The king said, "Stay at Jericho till your beards have grown, and then come back."

6When the Ammonites realized that they had become a stench in David's nostrils, they hired twenty thousand Aramean foot soldiers from Beth Rehob and Zobah, as well as the king of Maacah with a thousand men, and also twelve thousand men from Tob.

7On hearing this, David sent Joab out with the entire army of fighting men. 8The Ammonites came out and drew up in battle formation at the entrance to their city gate, while the Arameans of Zobah and Rehob and the men of Tob and Maacah were by themselves in the open country.

9Joab saw that there were battle lines in front of him and behind him; so he selected some of the best troops in Israel and deployed them against the Arameans. 10He put the rest of the men under the command of Abishai his brother and deployed them against the Ammonites. 11Joab said, "If the Arameans are too strong for me, then you are to come to my rescue; but if the Ammonites are too strong for you, then I will come to rescue you. 12Be strong and let us fight bravely for our people and the cities of our God. The LORD will do what is good in his sight."

13Then Joab and the troops with him advanced to fight the Arameans, and they fled before him. 14When the Ammonites saw that the Arameans were fleeing, they fled before Abishai and went inside the city. So Joab returned from fighting the Ammonites and came to Jerusalem.

15After the Arameans saw that they had been routed by Israel, they regrouped. 16Hadadezer had Arameans brought from beyond the River*b*; they went to Helam, with Shobach the commander of Hadadezer's army leading them.

17When David was told of this, he gathered all Israel, crossed the Jordan and went to Helam. The Arameans formed their battle lines to meet David and fought against him. 18But they fled before Israel, and David killed seven hundred of their charioteers and forty thousand of their foot soldiers.*c* He also struck down Shobach the commander of their army, and he died there. 19When all the kings who were vassals of Hadadezer saw that they had been defeated by Israel, they

---

a 11 Septuagint; Hebrew *my*   *b* 16 That is, the Euphrates   *c* 18 Some Septuagint manuscripts (see also 1 Chron. 19:18); Hebrew *horsemen*

made peace with the Israelites and became subject to them.

So the Arameans were afraid to help the Ammonites anymore.

David and Bathsheba

 11 In the spring, at the time when kings go off to war, David sent Joab out with the king's men and the whole Israelite army. They destroyed the Ammonites and besieged Rabbah. But David remained in Jerusalem.

[2] One evening David got up from his bed and walked around on the roof of the palace. From the roof he saw a woman bathing. The woman was very beautiful, [3] and David sent someone to find out about her. The man said, "Isn't this Bathsheba, the daughter of Eliam and the wife of Uriah the Hittite?" [4] Then David sent messengers to get her. She came to him, and he slept with her. (She had purified herself from her uncleanness.) Then[a] she went back

[a] 4 Or *with her. When she purified herself from her uncleanness,*

WEDNESDAY

TEMPTATION'S REACH
Charles H. Spurgeon

VERSE: 2 Samuel 11:2   **PASSAGE:** 2 Samuel 11:1–27

We are never out of the reach of temptation. Both at home and abroad we are liable to meet with allurements to evil; the morning opens with peril, and the shades of evening find us still in jeopardy . . . Those who think themselves secure are more exposed to danger than any others. The armor-bearer of sin is self-confidence . . . When I see the King of Israel sluggishly leaving his couch at the close of the day, and falling at once into temptation, let me take warning, and set holy watchfulness to guard the door.

Is it possible that the king had climbed to his housetop for retirement and devotion? If so, what a caution is given us to count no place, however secret, a sanctuary from sin! Since our hearts are so like a tinderbox and sparks so plentiful, we had better use all diligence in all places to prevent a blaze. Satan can climb housetops and enter closets, and even if we could shut out that foul fiend, our own corruptions are enough to work our ruin unless grace prevents. Reader, beware of evening temptations. Do not be secure. The sun is down but sin is up. We need a watchman for the night as well as a guardian for the day. O blessed Spirit, keep us from all evil this night. Amen.

ADDITIONAL SCRIPTURE READING:
Psalm 32:1–5; Mark 14:38

Go to page 356 for your next devotional reading.

1700   1900

home. ⁵The woman conceived and sent word to David, saying, "I am pregnant."

⁶So David sent this word to Joab: "Send me Uriah the Hittite." And Joab sent him to David. ⁷When Uriah came to him, David asked him how Joab was, how the soldiers were and how the war was going. ⁸Then David said to Uriah, "Go down to your house and wash your feet." So Uriah left the palace, and a gift from the king was sent after him. ⁹But Uriah slept at the entrance to the palace with all his master's servants and did not go down to his house.

¹⁰When David was told, "Uriah did not go home," he asked him, "Haven't you just come from a distance? Why didn't you go home?"

¹¹Uriah said to David, "The ark and Israel and Judah are staying in tents, and my master Joab and my lord's men are camped in the open fields. How could I go to my house to eat and drink and lie with my wife? As surely as you live, I will not do such a thing!"

¹²Then David said to him, "Stay here one more day, and tomorrow I will send you back." So Uriah remained in Jerusalem that day and the next. ¹³At David's invitation, he ate and drank with him, and David made him drunk. But in the evening Uriah went out to sleep on his mat among his master's servants; he did not go home.

¹⁴In the morning David wrote a letter to Joab and sent it with Uriah. ¹⁵In it he wrote, "Put Uriah in the front line where the fighting is fiercest. Then withdraw from him so he will be struck down and die."

¹⁶So while Joab had the city under siege, he put Uriah at a place where he knew the strongest defenders were. ¹⁷When the men of the city came out and fought against Joab, some of the men in David's army fell; moreover, Uriah the Hittite died.

¹⁸Joab sent David a full account of the battle. ¹⁹He instructed the messenger: "When you have finished giving the king this account of the battle, ²⁰the king's anger may flare up, and he may ask you, 'Why did you get so close to the city to fight? Didn't you know they would shoot arrows from the wall?

²¹Who killed Abimelech son of Jerub-Besheth*a*? Didn't a woman throw an upper millstone on him from the wall, so that he died in Thebez? Why did you get so close to the wall?' If he asks you this, then say to him, 'Also, your servant Uriah the Hittite is dead.' "

²²The messenger set out, and when he arrived he told David everything Joab had sent him to say. ²³The messenger said to David, "The men overpowered us and came out against us in the open, but we drove them back to the entrance to the city gate. ²⁴Then the archers shot arrows at your servants from the wall, and some of the king's men died. Moreover, your servant Uriah the Hittite is dead."

²⁵David told the messenger, "Say this to Joab: 'Don't let this upset you; the sword devours one as well as another. Press the attack against the city and destroy it.' Say this to encourage Joab."

²⁶When Uriah's wife heard that her husband was dead, she mourned for him. ²⁷After the time of mourning was over, David had her brought to his house, and she became his wife and bore him a son. But the thing David had done displeased the LORD.

Nathan Rebukes David

12 The LORD sent Nathan to David. When he came to him, he said, "There were two men in a certain town, one rich and the other poor. ²The rich man had a very large number of sheep and cattle, ³but the poor man had nothing except one little ewe lamb he had bought. He raised it, and it grew up with him and his children. It shared his food, drank from his cup and even slept in his arms. It was like a daughter to him.

⁴"Now a traveler came to the rich man, but the rich man refrained from taking one of his own sheep or cattle to prepare a meal for the traveler who had come to him. Instead, he took the ewe lamb that belonged to the poor man and prepared it for the one who had come to him."

⁵David burned with anger against the man and said to Nathan, "As surely as the LORD lives, the man who did this deserves to die! ⁶He must pay for that

a 21 Also known as *Jerub-Baal* (that is, Gideon)

lamb four times over, because he did such a thing and had no pity."

7Then Nathan said to David, "You are the man! This is what the LORD, the God of Israel, says: 'I anointed you king over Israel, and I delivered you from the hand of Saul. 8I gave your master's house to you, and your master's wives into your arms. I gave you the house of Israel and Judah. And if all this had been too little, I would have given you even more. 9Why did you despise the word of the LORD by doing what is evil in his eyes? You struck down Uriah the Hittite with the sword and took his wife to be your own. You killed him with the sword of the Ammonites. 10Now, therefore, the sword will never depart from your house, because you despised me and took the wife of Uriah the Hittite to be your own.'

11"This is what the LORD says: 'Out of your own household I am going to bring calamity upon you. Before your very eyes I will take your wives and give them to one who is close to you, and he will lie with your wives in broad daylight. 12You did it in secret, but I will do this thing in broad daylight before all Israel.' "

13Then David said to Nathan, "I have sinned against the LORD."

Nathan replied, "The LORD has taken away your sin. You are not going to die. 14But because by doing this you have made the enemies of the LORD show utter contempt,a the son born to you will die."

15After Nathan had gone home, the LORD struck the child that Uriah's wife had borne to David, and he became ill. 16David pleaded with God for the child. He fasted and went into his house and spent the nights lying on the ground. 17The elders of his household stood beside him to get him up from the ground, but he refused, and he would not eat any food with them.

18On the seventh day the child died. David's servants were afraid to tell him that the child was dead, for they thought, "While the child was still living, we spoke to David but he would not listen to us. How can we tell him the child is dead? He may do something desperate."

19David noticed that his servants were whispering among themselves and he realized the child was dead. "Is the child dead?" he asked.

"Yes," they replied, "he is dead."

20Then David got up from the ground. After he had washed, put on lotions and changed his clothes, he went into the house of the LORD and worshiped. Then he went to his own house, and at his request they served him food, and he ate.

21His servants asked him, "Why are you acting this way? While the child was alive, you fasted and wept, but now that the child is dead, you get up and eat!"

22He answered, "While the child was still alive, I fasted and wept. I thought, 'Who knows? The LORD may be gracious to me and let the child live.' 23But now that he is dead, why should I fast? Can I bring him back again? I will go to him, but he will not return to me."

24Then David comforted his wife Bathsheba, and he went to her and lay with her. She gave birth to a son, and they named him Solomon. The LORD loved him; 25and because the LORD loved him, he sent word through Nathan the prophet to name him Jedidiah.b

26Meanwhile Joab fought against Rabbah of the Ammonites and captured the royal citadel. 27Joab then sent messengers to David, saying, "I have fought against Rabbah and taken its water supply. 28Now muster the rest of the troops and besiege the city and capture it. Otherwise I will take the city, and it will be named after me."

29So David mustered the entire army and went to Rabbah, and attacked and captured it. 30He took the crown from the head of their kingc—its weight was a talentd of gold, and it was set with precious stones—and it was placed on David's head. He took a great quantity of plunder from the city 31and brought out the people who were there, consigning them to labor with saws and with iron picks and axes, and he made them work at brickmaking.e He did this to all the Ammonite towns. Then David and his entire army returned to Jerusalem.

---

a 14 Masoretic Text; an ancient Hebrew scribal tradition *this you have shown utter contempt for the LORD*   b 25 *Jedidiah* means *loved by the LORD.*   c 30 Or *of Milcom* (that is, Molech)   d 30 That is, about 75 pounds (about 34 kilograms)   e 31 The meaning of the Hebrew for this clause is uncertain.

Amnon and Tamar

13 In the course of time, Amnon son of David fell in love with Tamar, the beautiful sister of Absalom son of David.

2 Amnon became frustrated to the point of illness on account of his sister Tamar, for she was a virgin, and it seemed impossible for him to do anything to her.

3 Now Amnon had a friend named Jonadab son of Shimeah, David's brother. Jonadab was a very shrewd man. 4 He asked Amnon, "Why do you, the king's son, look so haggard morning after morning? Won't you tell me?"

Amnon said to him, "I'm in love with Tamar, my brother Absalom's sister."

5 "Go to bed and pretend to be ill," Jonadab said. "When your father comes to see you, say to him, 'I would like my sister Tamar to come and give me something to eat. Let her prepare the food in my sight so I may watch her and then eat it from her hand.'"

6 So Amnon lay down and pretended to be ill. When the king came to see him, Amnon said to him, "I would like my sister Tamar to come and make some special bread in my sight, so I may eat from her hand."

7 David sent word to Tamar at the palace: "Go to the house of your brother Amnon and prepare some food for him." 8 So Tamar went to the house of her brother Amnon, who was lying down. She took some dough, kneaded it, made the bread in his sight and baked it. 9 Then she took the pan and served him the bread, but he refused to eat.

"Send everyone out of here," Amnon said. So everyone left him. 10 Then Amnon said to Tamar, "Bring the food here into my bedroom so I may eat from your hand." And Tamar took the bread she had prepared and brought it to her brother Amnon in his bedroom. 11 But when she took it to him to eat, he grabbed her and said, "Come to bed with me, my sister."

12 "Don't, my brother!" she said to him. "Don't force me. Such a thing should not be done in Israel! Don't do this wicked thing. 13 What about me?

Where could I get rid of my disgrace? And what about you? You would be like one of the wicked fools in Israel. Please speak to the king; he will not keep me from being married to you." 14 But he refused to listen to her, and since he was stronger than she, he raped her.

15 Then Amnon hated her with intense hatred. In fact, he hated her more than he had loved her. Amnon said to her, "Get up and get out!"

16 "No!" she said to him. "Sending me away would be a greater wrong than what you have already done to me."

But he refused to listen to her. 17 He called his personal servant and said, "Get this woman out of here and bolt the door after her." 18 So his servant put her out and bolted the door after her. She was wearing a richly ornamented^a robe, for this was the kind of garment the virgin daughters of the king wore. 19 Tamar put ashes on her head and tore the ornamented^b robe she was wearing. She put her hand on her head and went away, weeping aloud as she went.

20 Her brother Absalom said to her, "Has that Amnon, your brother, been with you? Be quiet now, my sister; he is your brother. Don't take this thing to heart." And Tamar lived in her brother Absalom's house, a desolate woman.

21 When King David heard all this, he was furious. 22 Absalom never said a word to Amnon, either good or bad; he hated Amnon because he had disgraced his sister Tamar.

Absalom Kills Amnon

23 Two years later, when Absalom's sheepshearers were at Baal Hazor near the border of Ephraim, he invited all the king's sons to come there. 24 Absalom went to the king and said, "Your servant has had shearers come. Will the king and his officials please join me?"

25 "No, my son," the king replied. "All of us should not go; we would only be a burden to you." Although Absalom urged him, he still refused to go, but gave him his blessing.

26 Then Absalom said, "If not, please let my brother Amnon come with us."

---

^a 18 The meaning of the Hebrew for this phrase is uncertain.   ^b 19 The meaning of the Hebrew for this word is uncertain.

The king asked him, "Why should he go with you?" ²⁷But Absalom urged him, so he sent with him Amnon and the rest of the king's sons.

²⁸Absalom ordered his men, "Listen! When Amnon is in high spirits from drinking wine and I say to you, 'Strike Amnon down,' then kill him. Don't be afraid. Have not I given you this order? Be strong and brave." ²⁹So Absalom's men did to Amnon what Absalom had ordered. Then all the king's sons got up, mounted their mules and fled.

³⁰While they were on their way, the report came to David: "Absalom has struck down all the king's sons; not one of them is left." ³¹The king stood up, tore his clothes and lay down on the ground; and all his servants stood by with their clothes torn.

³²But Jonadab son of Shimeah, David's brother, said, "My lord should not think that they killed all the princes; only Amnon is dead. This has been Absalom's expressed intention ever since the day Amnon raped his sister Tamar. ³³My lord the king should not be concerned about the report that all the king's sons are dead. Only Amnon is dead."

³⁴Meanwhile, Absalom had fled.

Now the man standing watch looked up and saw many people on the road west of him, coming down the side of the hill. The watchman went and told the king, "I see men in the direction of Horonaim, on the side of the hill."^a

³⁵Jonadab said to the king, "See, the king's sons are here; it has happened just as your servant said."

³⁶As he finished speaking, the king's sons came in, wailing loudly. The king, too, and all his servants wept very bitterly.

³⁷Absalom fled and went to Talmai son of Ammihud, the king of Geshur. But King David mourned for his son every day.

³⁸After Absalom fled and went to Geshur, he stayed there three years. ³⁹And the spirit of the king^b longed to go to Absalom, for he was consoled concerning Amnon's death.

Absalom Returns to Jerusalem

14 Joab son of Zeruiah knew that the king's heart longed for Absalom. ²So Joab sent someone to Tekoa and had a wise woman brought from there. He said to her, "Pretend you are in mourning. Dress in mourning clothes, and don't use any cosmetic lotions. Act like a woman who has spent many days grieving for the dead. ³Then go to the king and speak these words to him." And Joab put the words in her mouth.

⁴When the woman from Tekoa went^c to the king, she fell with her face to the ground to pay him honor, and she said, "Help me, O king!"

⁵The king asked her, "What is troubling you?"

She said, "I am indeed a widow; my husband is dead. ⁶I your servant had two sons. They got into a fight with each other in the field, and no one was there to separate them. One struck the other and killed him. ⁷Now the whole clan has risen up against your servant; they say, 'Hand over the one who struck his brother down, so that we may put him to death for the life of his brother whom he killed; then we will get rid of the heir as well.' They would put out the only burning coal I have left, leaving my husband neither name nor descendant on the face of the earth."

⁸The king said to the woman, "Go home, and I will issue an order in your behalf."

⁹But the woman from Tekoa said to him, "My lord the king, let the blame rest on me and on my father's family, and let the king and his throne be without guilt."

¹⁰The king replied, "If anyone says anything to you, bring him to me, and he will not bother you again."

¹¹She said, "Then let the king invoke the LORD his God to prevent the avenger of blood from adding to the destruction, so that my son will not be destroyed."

"As surely as the LORD lives," he said, "not one hair of your son's head will fall to the ground."

^a 34 Septuagint; Hebrew does not have this sentence.
^b 39 Dead Sea Scrolls and some Septuagint manuscripts; Masoretic Text *But the spirit of David the king* ^c 4 Many Hebrew manuscripts, Septuagint, Vulgate and Syriac; most Hebrew manuscripts *spoke*

12Then the woman said, "Let your servant speak a word to my lord the king."

"Speak," he replied.

13The woman said, "Why then have you devised a thing like this against the people of God? When the king says this, does he not convict himself, for the king has not brought back his banished son? 14Like water spilled on the ground, which cannot be recovered, so we must die. But God does not take away life; instead, he devises ways so that a banished person may not remain estranged from him.

15"And now I have come to say this to my lord the king because the people have made me afraid. Your servant thought, 'I will speak to the king; perhaps he will do what his servant asks. 16Perhaps the king will agree to deliver his servant from the hand of the man who is trying to cut off both me and my son from the inheritance God gave us.'

17"And now your servant says, 'May the word of my lord the king bring me rest, for my lord the king is like an angel of God in discerning good and evil. May the LORD your God be with you.' "

18Then the king said to the woman, "Do not keep from me the answer to what I am going to ask you."

"Let my lord the king speak," the woman said.

19The king asked, "Isn't the hand of Joab with you in all this?"

The woman answered, "As surely as you live, my lord the king, no one can turn to the right or to the left from anything my lord the king says. Yes, it was your servant Joab who instructed me to do this and who put all these words into the mouth of your servant. 20Your servant Joab did this to change the present situation. My lord has wisdom like that of an angel of God—he knows everything that happens in the land."

21The king said to Joab, "Very well, I will do it. Go, bring back the young man Absalom."

22Joab fell with his face to the ground to pay him honor, and he blessed the king. Joab said, "Today your servant knows that he has found favor in your eyes, my lord the king, because the king has granted his servant's request."

23Then Joab went to Geshur and brought Absalom back to Jerusalem. 24But the king said, "He must go to his own house; he must not see my face." So Absalom went to his own house and did not see the face of the king.

25In all Israel there was not a man so highly praised for his handsome appearance as Absalom. From the top of his head to the sole of his foot there was no blemish in him. 26Whenever he cut the hair of his head—he used to cut his hair from time to time when it became too heavy for him—he would weigh it, and its weight was two hundred shekels*a* by the royal standard.

27Three sons and a daughter were born to Absalom. The daughter's name was Tamar, and she became a beautiful woman.

28Absalom lived two years in Jerusalem without seeing the king's face. 29Then Absalom sent for Joab in order to send him to the king, but Joab refused to come to him. So he sent a second time, but he refused to come. 30Then he said to his servants, "Look, Joab's field is next to mine, and he has barley there. Go and set it on fire." So Absalom's servants set the field on fire.

31Then Joab did go to Absalom's house and he said to him, "Why have your servants set my field on fire?"

32Absalom said to Joab, "Look, I sent word to you and said, 'Come here so I can send you to the king to ask, "Why have I come from Geshur? It would be better for me if I were still there!" ' Now then, I want to see the king's face, and if I am guilty of anything, let him put me to death."

33So Joab went to the king and told him this. Then the king summoned Absalom, and he came in and bowed down with his face to the ground before the king. And the king kissed Absalom.

Absalom's Conspiracy

15 In the course of time, Absalom provided himself with a chariot and horses and with fifty men to run ahead of him. 2He would get up early and stand by the side of the road leading to the city gate. Whenever anyone came with a complaint to be placed before the king for a decision, Absalom

---

a 26 That is, about 5 pounds (about 2.3 kilograms)

would call out to him, "What town are you from?" He would answer, "Your servant is from one of the tribes of Israel." ³Then Absalom would say to him, "Look, your claims are valid and proper, but there is no representative of the king to hear you." ⁴And Absalom would add, "If only I were appointed judge in the land! Then everyone who has a complaint or case could come to me and I would see that he gets justice."

⁵Also, whenever anyone approached him to bow down before him, Absalom would reach out his hand, take hold of him and kiss him. ⁶Absalom behaved in this way toward all the Israelites who came to the king asking for justice, and so he stole the hearts of the men of Israel.

⁷At the end of four*a* years, Absalom said to the king, "Let me go to Hebron and fulfill a vow I made to the LORD. ⁸While your servant was living at Geshur in Aram, I made this vow: 'If the LORD takes me back to Jerusalem, I will worship the LORD in Hebron.*b* ' "

⁹The king said to him, "Go in peace." So he went to Hebron.

¹⁰Then Absalom sent secret messengers throughout the tribes of Israel to say, "As soon as you hear the sound of the trumpets, then say, 'Absalom is king in Hebron.' " ¹¹Two hundred men from Jerusalem had accompanied Absalom. They had been invited as guests and went quite innocently, knowing nothing about the matter. ¹²While Absalom was offering sacrifices, he also sent for Ahithophel the Gilonite, David's counselor, to come from Giloh, his hometown. And so the conspiracy gained strength, and Absalom's following kept on increasing.

David Flees

¹³A messenger came and told David, "The hearts of the men of Israel are with Absalom."

¹⁴Then David said to all his officials who were with him in Jerusalem, "Come! We must flee, or none of us will escape from Absalom. We must leave immediately, or he will move quickly to overtake us and bring ruin upon us and put the city to the sword."

¹⁵The king's officials answered him, "Your servants are ready to do whatever our lord the king chooses."

¹⁶The king set out, with his entire household following him; but he left ten concubines to take care of the palace. ¹⁷So the king set out, with all the people following him, and they halted at a place some distance away. ¹⁸All his men marched past him, along with all the Kerethites and Pelethites; and all the six hundred Gittites who had accompanied him from Gath marched before the king.

¹⁹The king said to Ittai the Gittite, "Why should you come along with us? Go back and stay with King Absalom. You are a foreigner, an exile from your homeland. ²⁰You came only yesterday. And today shall I make you wander about with us, when I do not know where I am going? Go back, and take your countrymen. May kindness and faithfulness be with you."

²¹But Ittai replied to the king, "As surely as the LORD lives, and as my lord the king lives, wherever my lord the king may be, whether it means life or death, there will your servant be."

²²David said to Ittai, "Go ahead, march on." So Ittai the Gittite marched on with all his men and the families that were with him. ²³The whole countryside wept aloud as all the people passed by. The king also crossed the Kidron Valley, and all the people moved on toward the desert.

²⁴Zadok was there, too, and all the Levites who were with him were carrying the ark of the covenant of God. They set down the ark of God, and Abiathar offered sacrifices*c* until all the people had finished leaving the city. ²⁵Then the king said to Zadok, "Take the ark of God back into the city. If I find favor in the LORD's eyes, he will bring me back and let me see it and his dwelling place again. ²⁶But if he says, 'I am not pleased with you,' then I am ready; let him do to me whatever seems good to him."

²⁷The king also said to Zadok the priest, "Aren't you a seer? Go back to the city in peace, with your son Ahimaaz and Jonathan son of Abiathar. You and Abiathar take your two sons with

---

a 7 Some Septuagint manuscripts, Syriac and Josephus; Hebrew *forty*   *b* 8 Some Septuagint manuscripts; Hebrew does not have *in Hebron.*   *c* 24 Or *Abiathar went up*

you. 28I will wait at the fords in the desert until word comes from you to inform me." 29So Zadok and Abiathar took the ark of God back to Jerusalem and stayed there.

30But David continued up the Mount of Olives, weeping as he went; his head was covered and he was barefoot. All the people with him covered their heads too and were weeping as they went up. 31Now David had been told, "Ahithophel is among the conspirators with Absalom." So David prayed, "O LORD, turn Ahithophel's counsel into foolishness."

32When David arrived at the summit, where people used to worship God, Hushai the Arkite was there to meet him, his robe torn and dust on his head. 33David said to him, "If you go with me, you will be a burden to me. 34But if you return to the city and say to Absalom, 'I will be your servant, O king; I was your father's servant in the past, but now I will be your servant,' then you can help me by frustrating Ahithophel's advice. 35Won't the priests Zadok and Abiathar be there with you? Tell them anything you hear in the king's palace. 36Their two sons, Ahimaaz son of Zadok and Jonathan son of Abiathar, are there with them. Send them to me with anything you hear."

37So David's friend Hushai arrived at Jerusalem as Absalom was entering the city.

David and Ziba

16 When David had gone a short distance beyond the summit, there was Ziba, the steward of Mephibosheth, waiting to meet him. He had a string of donkeys saddled and loaded with two hundred loaves of bread, a hundred cakes of raisins, a hundred cakes of figs and a skin of wine.

2The king asked Ziba, "Why have you brought these?"

Ziba answered, "The donkeys are for the king's household to ride on, the bread and fruit are for the men to eat, and the wine is to refresh those who become exhausted in the desert."

3The king then asked, "Where is your master's grandson?"

Ziba said to him, "He is staying in Jerusalem, because he thinks, 'Today the house of Israel will give me back my grandfather's kingdom.'"

4Then the king said to Ziba, "All that belonged to Mephibosheth is now yours."

"I humbly bow," Ziba said. "May I find favor in your eyes, my lord the king."

Shimei Curses David

5As King David approached Bahurim, a man from the same clan as Saul's family came out from there. His name was Shimei son of Gera, and he cursed as he came out. 6He pelted David and all the king's officials with stones, though all the troops and the special guard were on David's right and left. 7As he cursed, Shimei said, "Get out, get out, you man of blood, you scoundrel! 8The LORD has repaid you for all the blood you shed in the household of Saul, in whose place you have reigned. The LORD has handed the kingdom over to your son Absalom. You have come to ruin because you are a man of blood!"

9Then Abishai son of Zeruiah said to the king, "Why should this dead dog curse my lord the king? Let me go over and cut off his head."

10But the king said, "What do you and I have in common, you sons of Zeruiah? If he is cursing because the LORD said to him, 'Curse David,' who can ask, 'Why do you do this?'"

11David then said to Abishai and all his officials, "My son, who is of my own flesh, is trying to take my life. How much more, then, this Benjamite! Leave him alone; let him curse, for the LORD has told him to. 12It may be that the LORD will see my distress and repay me with good for the cursing I am receiving today."

13So David and his men continued along the road while Shimei was going along the hillside opposite him, cursing as he went and throwing stones at him and showering him with dirt. 14The king and all the people with him arrived at their destination exhausted. And there he refreshed himself.

The Advice of Hushai and Ahithophel

15Meanwhile, Absalom and all the men of Israel came to Jerusalem, and

Ahithophel was with him. 16Then Hushai the Arkite, David's friend, went to Absalom and said to him, "Long live the king! Long live the king!"

17Absalom asked Hushai, "Is this the love you show your friend? Why didn't you go with your friend?"

18Hushai said to Absalom, "No, the one chosen by the LORD, by these people, and by all the men of Israel—his I will be, and I will remain with him. 19Furthermore, whom should I serve? Should I not serve the son? Just as I served your father, so I will serve you."

20Absalom said to Ahithophel, "Give us your advice. What should we do?"

21Ahithophel answered, "Lie with your father's concubines whom he left to take care of the palace. Then all Israel will hear that you have made yourself a stench in your father's nostrils, and the hands of everyone with you will be strengthened." 22So they pitched a tent for Absalom on the roof, and he lay with his father's concubines in the sight of all Israel.

23Now in those days the advice Ahithophel gave was like that of one who inquires of God. That was how both David and Absalom regarded all of Ahithophel's advice.

17 Ahithophel said to Absalom, "I would*a* choose twelve thousand men and set out tonight in pursuit of David. 2I would*b* attack him while he is weary and weak. I would*b* strike him with terror, and then all the people with him will flee. I would*b* strike down only the king 3and bring all the people back to you. The death of the man you seek will mean the return of all; all the people will be unharmed." 4This plan seemed good to Absalom and to all the elders of Israel.

5But Absalom said, "Summon also Hushai the Arkite, so we can hear what he has to say." 6When Hushai came to him, Absalom said, "Ahithophel has given this advice. Should we do what he says? If not, give us your opinion."

7Hushai replied to Absalom, "The advice Ahithophel has given is not good this time. 8You know your father and his men; they are fighters, and as fierce as a wild bear robbed of her cubs. Be-

sides, your father is an experienced fighter; he will not spend the night with the troops. 9Even now, he is hidden in a cave or some other place. If he should attack your troops first,*c* whoever hears about it will say, 'There has been a slaughter among the troops who follow Absalom.' 10Then even the bravest soldier, whose heart is like the heart of a lion, will melt with fear, for all Israel knows that your father is a fighter and that those with him are brave.

11"So I advise you: Let all Israel, from Dan to Beersheba—as numerous as the sand on the seashore—be gathered to you, with you yourself leading them into battle. 12Then we will attack him wherever he may be found, and we will fall on him as dew settles on the ground. Neither he nor any of his men will be left alive. 13If he withdraws into a city, then all Israel will bring ropes to that city, and we will drag it down to the valley until not even a piece of it can be found."

14Absalom and all the men of Israel said, "The advice of Hushai the Arkite is better than that of Ahithophel." For the LORD had determined to frustrate the good advice of Ahithophel in order to bring disaster on Absalom.

15Hushai told Zadok and Abiathar, the priests, "Ahithophel has advised Absalom and the elders of Israel to do such and such, but I have advised them to do so and so. 16Now send a message immediately and tell David, 'Do not spend the night at the fords in the desert; cross over without fail, or the king and all the people with him will be swallowed up.' "

17Jonathan and Ahimaaz were staying at En Rogel. A servant girl was to go and inform them, and they were to go and tell King David, for they could not risk being seen entering the city. 18But a young man saw them and told Absalom. So the two of them left quickly and went to the house of a man in Bahurim. He had a well in his courtyard, and they climbed down into it. 19His wife took a covering and spread it out over the opening of the well and scattered grain over it. No one knew anything about it.

20When Absalom's men came to the woman at the house, they asked, "Where are Ahimaaz and Jonathan?"

a 1 Or Let me   b 2 Or will   c 9 Or When some of the men fall at the first attack

The woman answered them, "They crossed over the brook."[a] The men searched but found no one, so they returned to Jerusalem.

²¹After the men had gone, the two climbed out of the well and went to inform King David. They said to him, "Set out and cross the river at once; Ahithophel has advised such and such against you." ²²So David and all the people with him set out and crossed the Jordan. By daybreak, no one was left who had not crossed the Jordan.

²³When Ahithophel saw that his advice had not been followed, he saddled his donkey and set out for his house in his hometown. He put his house in order and then hanged himself. So he died and was buried in his father's tomb.

²⁴David went to Mahanaim, and Absalom crossed the Jordan with all the men of Israel. ²⁵Absalom had appointed Amasa over the army in place of Joab. Amasa was the son of a man named Jether,[b] an Israelite[c] who had married Abigail,[d] the daughter of Nahash and sister of Zeruiah the mother of Joab. ²⁶The Israelites and Absalom camped in the land of Gilead.

²⁷When David came to Mahanaim, Shobi son of Nahash from Rabbah of the Ammonites, and Makir son of Ammiel from Lo Debar, and Barzillai the Gileadite from Rogelim ²⁸brought bedding and bowls and articles of pottery. They also brought wheat and barley, flour and roasted grain, beans and lentils,[e] ²⁹honey and curds, sheep, and cheese from cows' milk for David and his people to eat. For they said, "The people have become hungry and tired and thirsty in the desert."

Absalom's Death

18 David mustered the men who were with him and appointed over them commanders of thousands and commanders of hundreds. ²David sent the troops out—a third under the command of Joab, a third under Joab's brother Abishai son of Zeruiah, and a third under Ittai the Gittite. The king told the troops, "I myself will surely march out with you."

³But the men said, "You must not go out; if we are forced to flee, they won't care about us. Even if half of us die, they won't care; but you are worth ten thousand of us.[f] It would be better now for you to give us support from the city."

⁴The king answered, "I will do whatever seems best to you."

So the king stood beside the gate while all the men marched out in units of hundreds and of thousands. ⁵The king commanded Joab, Abishai and Ittai, "Be gentle with the young man Absalom for my sake." And all the troops heard the king giving orders concerning Absalom to each of the commanders.

⁶The army marched into the field to fight Israel, and the battle took place in the forest of Ephraim. ⁷There the army of Israel was defeated by David's men, and the casualties that day were great—twenty thousand men. ⁸The battle spread out over the whole countryside, and the forest claimed more lives that day than the sword.

⁹Now Absalom happened to meet David's men. He was riding his mule, and as the mule went under the thick branches of a large oak, Absalom's head got caught in the tree. He was left hanging in midair, while the mule he was riding kept on going.

¹⁰When one of the men saw this, he told Joab, "I just saw Absalom hanging in an oak tree."

¹¹Joab said to the man who had told him this, "What! You saw him? Why didn't you strike him to the ground right there? Then I would have had to give you ten shekels[g] of silver and a warrior's belt."

¹²But the man replied, "Even if a thousand shekels[h] were weighed out into my hands, I would not lift my hand against the king's son. In our hearing the king commanded you and Abishai and Ittai, 'Protect the young man Absalom

---

[a] 20 Or *"They passed by the sheep pen toward the water."*   [b] 25 Hebrew *Ithra,* a variant of *Jether*
[c] 25 Hebrew and some Septuagint manuscripts; other Septuagint manuscripts (see also 1 Chron. 2:17) *Ishmaelite* or *Jezreelite*   [d] 25 Hebrew *Abigal,* a variant of *Abigail*   [e] 28 Most Septuagint manuscripts and Syriac; Hebrew *lentils, and roasted grain*   [f] 3 Two Hebrew manuscripts, some Septuagint manuscripts and Vulgate; most Hebrew manuscripts *care; for now there are ten thousand like us*
[g] 11 That is, about 4 ounces (about 115 grams)   [h] 12 That is, about 25 pounds (about 11 kilograms)

for my sake.ᵃ ' ¹³And if I had put my life in jeopardyᵇ—and nothing is hidden from the king—you would have kept your distance from me."

¹⁴Joab said, "I'm not going to wait like this for you." So he took three javelins in his hand and plunged them into Absalom's heart while Absalom was still alive in the oak tree. ¹⁵And ten of Joab's armor-bearers surrounded Absalom, struck him and killed him.

¹⁶Then Joab sounded the trumpet, and the troops stopped pursuing Israel, for Joab halted them. ¹⁷They took Absalom, threw him into a big pit in the forest and piled up a large heap of rocks over him. Meanwhile, all the Israelites fled to their homes.

¹⁸During his lifetime Absalom had taken a pillar and erected it in the King's Valley as a monument to himself, for he thought, "I have no son to carry on the memory of my name." He named the pillar after himself, and it is called Absalom's Monument to this day.

David Mourns

¹⁹Now Ahimaaz son of Zadok said, "Let me run and take the news to the king that the LORD has delivered him from the hand of his enemies."

²⁰"You are not the one to take the news today," Joab told him. "You may take the news another time, but you must not do so today, because the king's son is dead."

²¹Then Joab said to a Cushite, "Go, tell the king what you have seen." The Cushite bowed down before Joab and ran off.

²²Ahimaaz son of Zadok again said to Joab, "Come what may, please let me run behind the Cushite."

But Joab replied, "My son, why do you want to go? You don't have any news that will bring you a reward."

²³He said, "Come what may, I want to run."

So Joab said, "Run!" Then Ahimaaz ran by way of the plainᶜ and outran the Cushite.

²⁴While David was sitting between the inner and outer gates, the watchman went up to the roof of the gateway by the wall. As he looked out, he saw a man running alone. ²⁵The watchman called out to the king and reported it.

The king said, "If he is alone, he must have good news." And the man came closer and closer.

²⁶Then the watchman saw another man running, and he called down to the gatekeeper, "Look, another man running alone!"

The king said, "He must be bringing good news, too."

²⁷The watchman said, "It seems to me that the first one runs like Ahimaaz son of Zadok."

"He's a good man," the king said. "He comes with good news."

²⁸Then Ahimaaz called out to the king, "All is well!" He bowed down before the king with his face to the ground and said, "Praise be to the LORD your God! He has delivered up the men who lifted their hands against my lord the king."

²⁹The king asked, "Is the young man Absalom safe?"

Ahimaaz answered, "I saw great confusion just as Joab was about to send the king's servant and me, your servant, but I don't know what it was."

³⁰The king said, "Stand aside and wait here." So he stepped aside and stood there.

³¹Then the Cushite arrived and said, "My lord the king, hear the good news! The LORD has delivered you today from all who rose up against you."

³²The king asked the Cushite, "Is the young man Absalom safe?"

The Cushite replied, "May the enemies of my lord the king and all who rise up to harm you be like that young man."

³³The king was shaken. He went up to the room over the gateway and wept. As he went, he said: "O my son Absalom! My son, my son Absalom! If only I had died instead of you—O Absalom, my son, my son!"

19 Joab was told, "The king is weeping and mourning for Absalom." ²And for the whole army the victory that day was turned into mourning, because on that day the troops

---

ᵃ 12 A few Hebrew manuscripts, Septuagint, Vulgate and Syriac; most Hebrew manuscripts may be translated *Absalom, whoever you may be.*   ᵇ 13 Or *Otherwise, if I had acted treacherously toward him*   ᶜ 23 That is, the plain of the Jordan

heard it said, "The king is grieving for his son." ³The men stole into the city that day as men steal in who are ashamed when they flee from battle. ⁴The king covered his face and cried aloud, "O my son Absalom! O Absalom, my son, my son!"

⁵Then Joab went into the house to the king and said, "Today you have humiliated all your men, who have just saved your life and the lives of your sons and daughters and the lives of your wives and concubines. ⁶You love those who hate you and hate those who love you. You have made it clear today that the commanders and their men mean nothing to you. I see that you would be pleased if Absalom were alive today and all of us were dead. ⁷Now go out and encourage your men. I swear by the LORD that if you don't go out, not a man will be left with you by nightfall. This will be worse for you than all the calamities that have come upon you from your youth till now."

⁸So the king got up and took his seat in the gateway. When the men were told, "The king is sitting in the gateway," they all came before him.

David Returns to Jerusalem

Meanwhile, the Israelites had fled to their homes. ⁹Throughout the tribes of Israel, the people were all arguing with each other, saying, "The king delivered us from the hand of our enemies; he is the one who rescued us from the hand of the Philistines. But now he has fled the

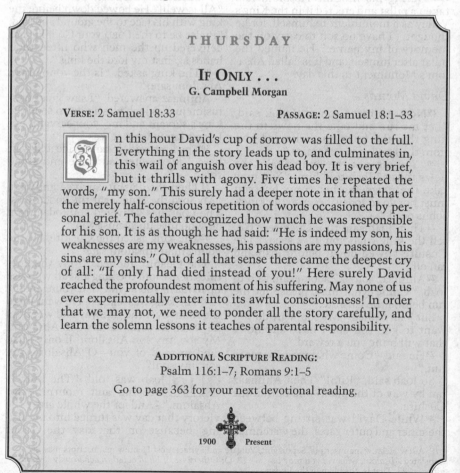

THURSDAY

IF ONLY . . .
G. Campbell Morgan

VERSE: 2 Samuel 18:33   **PASSAGE:** 2 Samuel 18:1–33

I n this hour David's cup of sorrow was filled to the full. Everything in the story leads up to, and culminates in, this wail of anguish over his dead boy. It is very brief, but it thrills with agony. Five times he repeated the words, "my son." This surely had a deeper note in it than that of the merely half-conscious repetition of words occasioned by personal grief. The father recognized how much he was responsible for his son. It is as though he had said: "He is indeed my son, his weaknesses are my weaknesses, his passions are my passions, his sins are my sins." Out of all that sense there came the deepest cry of all: "If only I had died instead of you!" Here surely David reached the profoundest moment of his suffering. May none of us ever experimentally enter into its awful consciousness! In order that we may not, we need to ponder all the story carefully, and learn the solemn lessons it teaches of parental responsibility.

ADDITIONAL SCRIPTURE READING:
Psalm 116:1–7; Romans 9:1–5

Go to page 363 for your next devotional reading.

1900   Present

country because of Absalom; 10and Absalom, whom we anointed to rule over us, has died in battle. So why do you say nothing about bringing the king back?"

11King David sent this message to Zadok and Abiathar, the priests: "Ask the elders of Judah, 'Why should you be the last to bring the king back to his palace, since what is being said throughout Israel has reached the king at his quarters? 12You are my brothers, my own flesh and blood. So why should you be the last to bring back the king?' 13And say to Amasa, 'Are you not my own flesh and blood? May God deal with me, be it ever so severely, if from now on you are not the commander of my army in place of Joab.' "

14He won over the hearts of all the men of Judah as though they were one man. They sent word to the king, "Return, you and all your men." 15Then the king returned and went as far as the Jordan.

Now the men of Judah had come to Gilgal to go out and meet the king and bring him across the Jordan. 16Shimei son of Gera, the Benjamite from Bahurim, hurried down with the men of Judah to meet King David. 17With him were a thousand Benjamites, along with Ziba, the steward of Saul's household, and his fifteen sons and twenty servants. They rushed to the Jordan, where the king was. 18They crossed at the ford to take the king's household over and to do whatever he wished.

When Shimei son of Gera crossed the Jordan, he fell prostrate before the king 19and said to him, "May my lord not hold me guilty. Do not remember how your servant did wrong on the day my lord the king left Jerusalem. May the king put it out of his mind. 20For I your servant know that I have sinned, but today I have come here as the first of the whole house of Joseph to come down and meet my lord the king."

21Then Abishai son of Zeruiah said, "Shouldn't Shimei be put to death for this? He cursed the LORD's anointed."

22David replied, "What do you and I have in common, you sons of Zeruiah? This day you have become my adversaries! Should anyone be put to death in Israel today? Do I not know that today I

am king over Israel?" 23So the king said to Shimei, "You shall not die." And the king promised him on oath.

24Mephibosheth, Saul's grandson, also went down to meet the king. He had not taken care of his feet or trimmed his mustache or washed his clothes from the day the king left until the day he returned safely. 25When he came from Jerusalem to meet the king, the king asked him, "Why didn't you go with me, Mephibosheth?"

26He said, "My lord the king, since I your servant am lame, I said, 'I will have my donkey saddled and will ride on it, so I can go with the king.' But Ziba my servant betrayed me. 27And he has slandered your servant to my lord the king. My lord the king is like an angel of God; so do whatever pleases you. 28All my grandfather's descendants deserved nothing but death from my lord the king, but you gave your servant a place among those who eat at your table. So what right do I have to make any more appeals to the king?"

29The king said to him, "Why say more? I order you and Ziba to divide the fields."

30Mephibosheth said to the king, "Let him take everything, now that my lord the king has arrived home safely."

31Barzillai the Gileadite also came down from Rogelim to cross the Jordan with the king and to send him on his way from there. 32Now Barzillai was a very old man, eighty years of age. He had provided for the king during his stay in Mahanaim, for he was a very wealthy man. 33The king said to Barzillai, "Cross over with me and stay with me in Jerusalem, and I will provide for you."

34But Barzillai answered the king, "How many more years will I live, that I should go up to Jerusalem with the king? 35I am now eighty years old. Can I tell the difference between what is good and what is not? Can your servant taste what he eats and drinks? Can I still hear the voices of men and women singers? Why should your servant be an added burden to my lord the king? 36Your servant will cross over the Jordan with the king for a short distance, but why should the king reward me in this way? 37Let your servant return, that I may die in my own town near the tomb of my father and mother. But here is your servant Kimham. Let him cross over with my lord the king. Do for him whatever pleases you."

38The king said, "Kimham shall cross over with me, and I will do for him whatever pleases you. And anything you desire from me I will do for you."

39So all the people crossed the Jordan, and then the king crossed over. The king kissed Barzillai and gave him his blessing, and Barzillai returned to his home.

40When the king crossed over to Gilgal, Kimham crossed with him. All the troops of Judah and half the troops of Israel had taken the king over.

41Soon all the men of Israel were coming to the king and saying to him, "Why did our brothers, the men of Judah, steal the king away and bring him and his household across the Jordan, together with all his men?"

42All the men of Judah answered the men of Israel, "We did this because the king is closely related to us. Why are you angry about it? Have we eaten any of the king's provisions? Have we taken anything for ourselves?"

43Then the men of Israel answered the men of Judah, "We have ten shares in the king; and besides, we have a greater claim on David than you have. So why do you treat us with contempt? Were we not the first to speak of bringing back our king?"

But the men of Judah responded even more harshly than the men of Israel.

Sheba Rebels Against David

20 Now a troublemaker named Sheba son of Bicri, a Benjamite, happened to be there. He sounded the trumpet and shouted,

"We have no share in David,
　no part in Jesse's son!
Every man to his tent, O Israel!"

2So all the men of Israel deserted David to follow Sheba son of Bicri. But the men of Judah stayed by their king all the way from the Jordan to Jerusalem.

3When David returned to his palace in Jerusalem, he took the ten concubines he had left to take care of the palace and put them in a house under guard. He provided for them, but did not lie with them. They were kept in confinement till the day of their death, living as widows.

4Then the king said to Amasa, "Summon the men of Judah to come to me within three days, and be here yourself." 5But when Amasa went to summon Judah, he took longer than the time the king had set for him.

6David said to Abishai, "Now Sheba son of Bicri will do us more harm than Absalom did. Take your master's men and pursue him, or he will find fortified cities and escape from us." 7So Joab's men and the Kerethites and Pelethites and all the mighty warriors went out under the command of Abishai. They marched out from Jerusalem to pursue Sheba son of Bicri.

8While they were at the great rock in Gibeon, Amasa came to meet them. Joab was wearing his military tunic, and strapped over it at his waist was a belt with a dagger in its sheath. As he stepped forward, it dropped out of its sheath.

9Joab said to Amasa, "How are you, my brother?" Then Joab took Amasa by the beard with his right hand to kiss him. 10Amasa was not on his guard against the dagger in Joab's hand, and Joab plunged it into his belly, and his intestines spilled out on the ground. Without being stabbed again, Amasa died. Then Joab and his brother Abishai pursued Sheba son of Bicri.

11One of Joab's men stood beside Amasa and said, "Whoever favors Joab, and whoever is for David, let him follow Joab!" 12Amasa lay wallowing in his blood in the middle of the road, and the man saw that all the troops came to a halt there. When he realized that everyone who came up to Amasa stopped, he dragged him from the road into a field and threw a garment over him. 13After Amasa had been removed from the road, all the men went on with Joab to pursue Sheba son of Bicri.

14Sheba passed through all the tribes of Israel to Abel Beth Maacah*a* and through the entire region of the Berites, who gathered together and followed him. 15All the troops with Joab came

a 14 Or Abel, even Beth Maacah; also in verse 15

and besieged Sheba in Abel Beth Maacah. They built a siege ramp up to the city, and it stood against the outer fortifications. While they were battering the wall to bring it down, **16**a wise woman called from the city, "Listen! Listen! Tell Joab to come here so I can speak to him." **17**He went toward her, and she asked, "Are you Joab?"

"I am," he answered.

She said, "Listen to what your servant has to say."

"I'm listening," he said.

18She continued, "Long ago they used to say, 'Get your answer at Abel,' and that settled it. **19**We are the peaceful and faithful in Israel. You are trying to destroy a city that is a mother in Israel. Why do you want to swallow up the LORD's inheritance?"

20"Far be it from me!" Joab replied, "Far be it from me to swallow up or destroy! **21**That is not the case. A man named Sheba son of Bicri, from the hill country of Ephraim, has lifted up his hand against the king, against David. Hand over this one man, and I'll withdraw from the city."

The woman said to Joab, "His head will be thrown to you from the wall."

22Then the woman went to all the people with her wise advice, and they cut off the head of Sheba son of Bicri and threw it to Joab. So he sounded the trumpet, and his men dispersed from the city, each returning to his home. And Joab went back to the king in Jerusalem.

23Joab was over Israel's entire army; Benaiah son of Jehoiada was over the Kerethites and Pelethites; **24**Adoniram*a* was in charge of forced labor; Jehoshaphat son of Ahilud was recorder; **25**Sheva was secretary; Zadok and Abiathar were priests; **26**and Ira the Jairite was David's priest.

The Gibeonites Avenged

21 During the reign of David, there was a famine for three successive years; so David sought the face of the LORD. The LORD said, "It is on account of Saul and his blood-stained house; it is because he put the Gibeonites to death."

2The king summoned the Gibeonites and spoke to them. (Now the Gibeonites were not a part of Israel but were survivors of the Amorites; the Israelites had sworn to ⌊spare⌋ them, but Saul in his zeal for Israel and Judah had tried to annihilate them.) **3**David asked the Gibeonites, "What shall I do for you? How shall I make amends so that you will bless the LORD's inheritance?"

4The Gibeonites answered him, "We have no right to demand silver or gold from Saul or his family, nor do we have the right to put anyone in Israel to death."

"What do you want me to do for you?" David asked.

5They answered the king, "As for the man who destroyed us and plotted against us so that we have been decimated and have no place anywhere in Israel, **6**let seven of his male descendants be given to us to be killed and exposed before the LORD at Gibeah of Saul—the LORD's chosen one."

So the king said, "I will give them to you."

7The king spared Mephibosheth son of Jonathan, the son of Saul, because of the oath before the LORD between David and Jonathan son of Saul. **8**But the king took Armoni and Mephibosheth, the two sons of Aiah's daughter Rizpah, whom she had borne to Saul, together with the five sons of Saul's daughter Merab,*b* whom she had borne to Adriel son of Barzillai the Meholathite. **9**He handed them over to the Gibeonites, who killed and exposed them on a hill before the LORD. All seven of them fell together; they were put to death during the first days of the harvest, just as the barley harvest was beginning.

10Rizpah daughter of Aiah took sackcloth and spread it out for herself on a rock. From the beginning of the harvest till the rain poured down from the heavens on the bodies, she did not let the birds of the air touch them by day or the wild animals by night. **11**When David was told what Aiah's daughter Rizpah, Saul's concubine, had done, **12**he went and took the bones of Saul and his son

---

a 24 Some Septuagint manuscripts (see also 1 Kings 4:6 and 5:14); Hebrew *Adoram*   *b 8* Two Hebrew manuscripts, some Septuagint manuscripts and Syriac (see also 1 Samuel 18:19); most Hebrew and Septuagint manuscripts *Michal*

Jonathan from the citizens of Jabesh Gilead. (They had taken them secretly from the public square at Beth Shan, where the Philistines had hung them after they struck Saul down on Gilboa.) ¹³David brought the bones of Saul and his son Jonathan from there, and the bones of those who had been killed and exposed were gathered up.

¹⁴They buried the bones of Saul and his son Jonathan in the tomb of Saul's father Kish, at Zela in Benjamin, and did everything the king commanded. After that, God answered prayer in behalf of the land.

Wars Against the Philistines

¹⁵Once again there was a battle between the Philistines and Israel. David went down with his men to fight against the Philistines, and he became exhausted. ¹⁶And Ishbi-Benob, one of the descendants of Rapha, whose bronze spearhead weighed three hundred shekels[a] and who was armed with a new sword, said he would kill David. ¹⁷But Abishai son of Zeruiah came to David's rescue; he struck the Philistine down and killed him. Then David's men swore to him, saying, "Never again will you go out with us to battle, so that the lamp of Israel will not be extinguished."

¹⁸In the course of time, there was another battle with the Philistines, at Gob. At that time Sibbecai the Hushathite killed Saph, one of the descendants of Rapha.

¹⁹In another battle with the Philistines at Gob, Elhanan son of Jaare-Oregim[b] the Bethlehemite killed Goliath[c] the Gittite, who had a spear with a shaft like a weaver's rod.

²⁰In still another battle, which took place at Gath, there was a huge man with six fingers on each hand and six toes on each foot—twenty-four in all. He also was descended from Rapha. ²¹When he taunted Israel, Jonathan son of Shimeah, David's brother, killed him.

²²These four were descendants of Rapha in Gath, and they fell at the hands of David and his men.

David's Song of Praise

22 David sang to the LORD the words of this song when the LORD delivered him from the hand of all his enemies and from the hand of Saul. ²He said:

"The LORD is my rock, my fortress
    and my deliverer;
³ my God is my rock, in whom I
    take refuge,
my shield and the horn[d] of my
    salvation.
He is my stronghold, my refuge and
    my savior—
    from violent men you save me.
⁴I call to the LORD, who is worthy of
    praise,
    and I am saved from my enemies.
⁵ "The waves of death swirled about
    me;
    the torrents of destruction
    overwhelmed me.
⁶ The cords of the grave[e] coiled around
    me;
    the snares of death confronted me.
⁷ In my distress I called to the LORD;
    I called out to my God.
From his temple he heard my voice;
    my cry came to his ears.
⁸ "The earth trembled and quaked,
    the foundations of the heavens[f]
    shook;
    they trembled because he was
    angry.
⁹ Smoke rose from his nostrils;
    consuming fire came from his
    mouth,
    burning coals blazed out of it.
¹⁰ He parted the heavens and came
    down;
    dark clouds were under his feet.
¹¹ He mounted the cherubim and flew;
    he soared[g] on the wings of the
    wind.
¹² He made darkness his canopy around
    him—
    the dark[h] rain clouds of the sky.
¹³ Out of the brightness of his presence
    bolts of lightning blazed forth.

---

^a 16 That is, about 7 1/2 pounds (about 3.5 kilograms)   ^b 19 Or *son of Jair the weaver*   ^c 19 Hebrew and Septuagint; 1 Chron. 20:5 *son of Jair killed Lahmi the brother of Goliath*   ^d 3 *Horn* here symbolizes strength.   ^e 6 Hebrew *Sheol*   ^f 8 Hebrew; Vulgate and Syriac (see also Psalm 18:7) *mountains*   ^g 11 Many Hebrew manuscripts (see also Psalm 18:10); most Hebrew manuscripts *appeared*   ^h 12 Septuagint and Vulgate (see also Psalm 18:11); Hebrew *massed*

¹⁴ The LORD thundered from heaven;
  the voice of the Most High
    resounded.
¹⁵ He shot arrows and scattered ⌊the
    enemies⌋,
  bolts of lightning and routed them.
¹⁶ The valleys of the sea were exposed
    and the foundations of the earth
      laid bare
  at the rebuke of the LORD,
    at the blast of breath from his
      nostrils.

¹⁷ "He reached down from on high and
      took hold of me;
  he drew me out of deep waters.
¹⁸ He rescued me from my powerful
      enemy,
  from my foes, who were too strong
      for me.
¹⁹ They confronted me in the day of my
      disaster,
  but the LORD was my support.
²⁰ He brought me out into a spacious
      place;
  he rescued me because he
      delighted in me.

²¹ "The LORD has dealt with me
      according to my righteousness;
  according to the cleanness of my
      hands he has rewarded me.
²² For I have kept the ways of the LORD;
  I have not done evil by turning
      from my God.
²³ All his laws are before me;
  I have not turned away from his
      decrees.
²⁴ I have been blameless before him
  and have kept myself from sin.
²⁵ The LORD has rewarded me according
      to my righteousness,
  according to my cleanness*a* in his
      sight.

²⁶ "To the faithful you show yourself
      faithful,
  to the blameless you show yourself
      blameless,
²⁷ to the pure you show yourself pure,
  but to the crooked you show
      yourself shrewd.
²⁸ You save the humble,
  but your eyes are on the haughty to
      bring them low.

²⁹ You are my lamp, O LORD;
  the LORD turns my darkness into
      light.
³⁰ With your help I can advance against
      a troop*b*;
  with my God I can scale a wall.

³¹ "As for God, his way is perfect;
  the word of the LORD is flawless.
He is a shield
  for all who take refuge in him.
³² For who is God besides the LORD?
  And who is the Rock except our
      God?
³³ It is God who arms me with strength*c*
  and makes my way perfect.
³⁴ He makes my feet like the feet of a
      deer;
  he enables me to stand on the
      heights.
³⁵ He trains my hands for battle;
  my arms can bend a bow of bronze.
³⁶ You give me your shield of victory;
  you stoop down to make me great.
³⁷ You broaden the path beneath me,
  so that my ankles do not turn.

³⁸ "I pursued my enemies and crushed
      them;
  I did not turn back till they were
      destroyed.
³⁹ I crushed them completely, and they
      could not rise;
  they fell beneath my feet.
⁴⁰ You armed me with strength for
      battle;
  you made my adversaries bow at
      my feet.
⁴¹ You made my enemies turn their
      backs in flight,
  and I destroyed my foes.
⁴² They cried for help, but there was no
      one to save them—
  to the LORD, but he did not answer.
⁴³ I beat them as fine as the dust of the
      earth;
  I pounded and trampled them like
      mud in the streets.

⁴⁴ "You have delivered me from the
      attacks of my people;
  you have preserved me as the head
      of nations.
People I did not know are subject to
      me,

---

a 25 Hebrew; Septuagint and Vulgate (see also Psalm 18:24) *to the cleanness of my hands*   *b 30* Or *can run through a barricade*   *c 33* Dead Sea Scrolls, some Septuagint manuscripts, Vulgate and Syriac (see also Psalm 18:32); Masoretic Text *who is my strong refuge*

45 and foreigners come cringing to
      me;
   as soon as they hear me, they obey
      me.
46 They all lose heart;
   they come trembling*a* from their
      strongholds.
47 "The LORD lives! Praise be to my
      Rock!
   Exalted be God, the Rock, my
      Savior!
48 He is the God who avenges me,
   who puts the nations under me,
49 who sets me free from my
      enemies.
   You exalted me above my foes;
      from violent men you rescued me.
50 Therefore I will praise you, O LORD,
      among the nations;
   I will sing praises to your name.
51 He gives his king great victories;
   he shows unfailing kindness to his
      anointed,
   to David and his descendants
      forever."

THE FETTERS OF MY TONGUE DO THOU UNBIND,
THAT I MAY HAVE THE POWER TO SING OF THEE,
AND SOUND THY PRAISES EVERLASTINGLY.

—*William Wordsworth*

The Last Words of David

23 These are the last words of
     David:

"The oracle of David son of Jesse,
   the oracle of the man exalted by
      the Most High,
the man anointed by the God of
      Jacob,
   Israel's singer of songs*b*:

2 "The Spirit of the LORD spoke
      through me;
   his word was on my tongue.
3 The God of Israel spoke,
   the Rock of Israel said to me:
   'When one rules over men in
      righteousness,

when he rules in the fear of God,
4 he is like the light of morning at
      sunrise
   on a cloudless morning,
   like the brightness after rain
      that brings the grass from the
      earth.'

5 "Is not my house right with God?
   Has he not made with me an
      everlasting covenant,
   arranged and secured in every part?
   Will he not bring to fruition my
      salvation
   and grant me my every desire?
6 But evil men are all to be cast aside
      like thorns,
   which are not gathered with the
      hand.
7 Whoever touches thorns
   uses a tool of iron or the shaft of a
      spear;
   they are burned up where they lie."

David's Mighty Men

8 These are the names of David's
mighty men:

Josheb-Basshebeth,*c* a Tahkemonite,*d*
was chief of the Three; he raised his
spear against eight hundred men, whom
he killed*e* in one encounter.
9 Next to him was Eleazar son of
Dodai the Ahohite. As one of the three
mighty men, he was with David when
they taunted the Philistines gathered
ᴸat Pas Dammim,*f* for battle. Then the
men of Israel retreated, **10** but he stood
his ground and struck down the Philistines till his hand grew tired and froze
to the sword. The LORD brought about
a great victory that day. The troops
returned to Eleazar, but only to strip
the dead.
11 Next to him was Shammah son of
Agee the Hararite. When the Philistines
banded together at a place where there
was a field full of lentils, Israel's troops
fled from them. **12** But Shammah took
his stand in the middle of the field. He

*a 46 Some Septuagint manuscripts and Vulgate (see also Psalm 18:45); Masoretic Text they arm
themselves.   b 1 Or Israel's beloved singer   c 8 Hebrew; some Septuagint manuscripts suggest Ish-
Bosheth, that is, Esh-Baal (see also 1 Chron. 11:11) Jashobeam).   d 8 Probably a variant of Hacmonite
(see 1 Chron. 11:11)   e 8 Some Septuagint manuscripts (see also 1 Chron. 11:11); Hebrew and other
Septuagint manuscripts Three; it was Adino the Eznite who killed eight hundred men   f 9 See
1 Chron. 11:13; Hebrew gathered there.*

defended it and struck the Philistines down, and the LORD brought about a great victory.

¹³During harvest time, three of the thirty chief men came down to David at the cave of Adullam, while a band of Philistines was encamped in the Valley of Rephaim. ¹⁴At that time David was in the stronghold, and the Philistine garrison was at Bethlehem. ¹⁵David longed for water and said, "Oh, that someone would get me a drink of water from the well near the gate of Bethle-hem!" ¹⁶So the three mighty men broke through the Philistine lines, drew water from the well near the gate of Bethlehem and carried it back to David. But he refused to drink it; instead, he poured it out before the LORD. ¹⁷"Far be it from me, O LORD, to do this!" he said. "Is it not the blood of men who went at the risk of their lives?" And David would not drink it.

Such were the exploits of the three mighty men.

¹⁸Abishai the brother of Joab son of

FRIDAY

POURED-OUT SATISFACTION
Oswald Chambers

VERSE: 2 Samuel 23:16   **PASSAGE:** 2 Samuel 23:13–17

 can never sanctify to God that with which I long to satisfy myself. If I am going to satisfy myself with the blessings of God, they will corrupt me; I have to sacrifice them, pour them out, do with them what any commonsense man would say is an absurd waste. Take it in the case of friendship, or of blessing, or of spiritual experiences; as soon as I long to hold any of these for myself I cannot sanctify them to the Lord. David had the right idea when he poured out the water before the Lord.

What has been like water from the well of Bethlehem to you recently? Love, friendship, spiritual blessing? Then at the peril of your soul, you take it to satisfy yourself. If you do, you cannot pour out before the Lord. How am I to pour out spiritual gifts, or natural friendship, or love? How can I give them to the Lord? In one way only—in the determination of my mind, and that takes about two seconds. If I hold spiritual blessings or friendship for myself they will corrupt me, no matter how beautiful they are. I have to pour them out before the Lord, give them to him in my mind, though it looks as if I am wasting them; even as when David poured the water out on the sand, to be instantly sucked up.

ADDITIONAL SCRIPTURE READING:
Numbers 28:7; Philippians 2:17–18; 2 Timothy 4:6–7

Go to page 369 for your next devotional reading.

1900   Present

Zeruiah was chief of the Three.*a* He raised his spear against three hundred men, whom he killed, and so he became as famous as the Three. **19**Was he not held in greater honor than the Three? He became their commander, even though he was not included among them.

20Benaiah son of Jehoiada was a valiant fighter from Kabzeel, who performed great exploits. He struck down two of Moab's best men. He also went down into a pit on a snowy day and killed a lion. **21**And he struck down a huge Egyptian. Although the Egyptian had a spear in his hand, Benaiah went against him with a club. He snatched the spear from the Egyptian's hand and killed him with his own spear. **22**Such were the exploits of Benaiah son of Jehoiada; he too was as famous as the three mighty men. **23**He was held in greater honor than any of the Thirty, but he was not included among the Three. And David put him in charge of his bodyguard.

24Among the Thirty were:
Asahel the brother of Joab,
Elhanan son of Dodo from Bethlehem,
25Shammah the Harodite,
Elika the Harodite,
26Helez the Paltite,
Ira son of Ikkesh from Tekoa,
27Abiezer from Anathoth,
Mebunnai*b* the Hushathite,
28Zalmon the Ahohite,
Maharai the Netophathite,
29Heled*c* son of Baanah the Netophathite,
Ithai son of Ribai from Gibeah in Benjamin,
30Benaiah the Pirathonite,
Hiddai*d* from the ravines of Gaash,
31Abi-Albon the Arbathite,
Azmaveth the Barhumite,
32Eliahba the Shaalbonite,
the sons of Jashen,
Jonathan **33**son of*e* Shammah the Hararite,

Ahiam son of Sharar*f* the Hararite,
34Eliphelet son of Ahasbai the Maacathite,
Eliam son of Ahithophel the Gilonite,
35Hezro the Carmelite,
Paarai the Arbite,
36Igal son of Nathan from Zobah,
the son of Hagri,*g*
37Zelek the Ammonite,
Naharai the Beerothite, the armorbearer of Joab son of Zeruiah,
38Ira the Ithrite,
Gareb the Ithrite
39and Uriah the Hittite.
There were thirty-seven in all.

David Counts the Fighting Men

24 Again the anger of the Lord burned against Israel, and he incited David against them, saying, "Go and take a census of Israel and Judah."

2So the king said to Joab and the army commanders*h* with him, "Go throughout the tribes of Israel from Dan to Beersheba and enroll the fighting men, so that I may know how many there are."

3But Joab replied to the king, "May the Lord your God multiply the troops a hundred times over, and may the eyes of my lord the king see it. But why does my lord the king want to do such a thing?"

4The king's word, however, overruled Joab and the army commanders; so they left the presence of the king to enroll the fighting men of Israel.

5After crossing the Jordan, they camped near Aroer, south of the town in the gorge, and then went through Gad and on to Jazer. **6**They went to Gilead and the region of Tahtim Hodshi, and on to Dan Jaan and around toward Sidon. **7**Then they went toward the fortress of Tyre and all the towns of the Hivites and Canaanites. Finally, they went on to Beersheba in the Negev of Judah.

8After they had gone through the entire land, they came back to Jerusalem

---

a 18 Most Hebrew manuscripts (see also 1 Chron. 11:20); two Hebrew manuscripts and Syriac *Thirty*   *b 27* Hebrew; some Septuagint manuscripts (see also 1 Chron. 11:29) *Sibbecai*   *c 29* Some Hebrew manuscripts and Vulgate (see also 1 Chron. 11:30); most Hebrew manuscripts *Heleb*   *d 30* Hebrew; some Septuagint manuscripts (see also 1 Chron. 11:32) *Hurai*   *e 33* Some Septuagint manuscripts (see also 1 Chron. 11:34); Hebrew does not have *son of.*   *f 33* Hebrew; some Septuagint manuscripts (see also 1 Chron. 11:35) *Sacar*   *g 36* Some Septuagint manuscripts (see also 1 Chron. 11:38); Hebrew *Haggadi*   *h 2* Septuagint (see also verse 4 and 1 Chron. 21:2); Hebrew *Joab the army commander*

at the end of nine months and twenty days.

⁹Joab reported the number of the fighting men to the king: In Israel there were eight hundred thousand able-bodied men who could handle a sword, and in Judah five hundred thousand.

¹⁰David was conscience-stricken after he had counted the fighting men, and he said to the LORD, "I have sinned greatly in what I have done. Now, O LORD, I beg you, take away the guilt of your servant. I have done a very foolish thing."

¹¹Before David got up the next morning, the word of the LORD had come to Gad the prophet, David's seer: ¹²"Go and tell David, 'This is what the LORD says: I am giving you three options. Choose one of them for me to carry out against you.'"

¹³So Gad went to David and said to him, "Shall there come upon you three*a* years of famine in your land? Or three months of fleeing from your enemies while they pursue you? Or three days of plague in your land? Now then, think it over and decide how I should answer the one who sent me."

¹⁴David said to Gad, "I am in deep distress. Let us fall into the hands of the LORD, for his mercy is great; but do not let me fall into the hands of men."

¹⁵So the LORD sent a plague on Israel from that morning until the end of the time designated, and seventy thousand of the people from Dan to Beersheba died. ¹⁶When the angel stretched out his hand to destroy Jerusalem, the LORD was grieved because of the calamity and said to the angel who was afflicting the people, "Enough! Withdraw your hand." The angel of the LORD was then at the threshing floor of Araunah the Jebusite.

¹⁷When David saw the angel who was striking down the people, he said to the LORD, "I am the one who has sinned and done wrong. These are but sheep. What have they done? Let your hand fall upon me and my family."

David Builds an Altar

¹⁸On that day Gad went to David and said to him, "Go up and build an altar to the LORD on the threshing floor of Araunah the Jebusite." ¹⁹So David went up, as the LORD had commanded through Gad. ²⁰When Araunah looked and saw the king and his men coming toward him, he went out and bowed down before the king with his face to the ground.

²¹Araunah said, "Why has my lord the king come to his servant?"

"To buy your threshing floor," David answered, "so I can build an altar to the LORD, that the plague on the people may be stopped."

²²Araunah said to David, "Let my lord the king take whatever pleases him and offer it up. Here are oxen for the burnt offering, and here are threshing sledges and ox yokes for the wood. ²³O king, Araunah gives all this to the king." Araunah also said to him, "May the LORD your God accept you."

²⁴But the king replied to Araunah, "No, I insist on paying you for it. I will not sacrifice to the LORD my God burnt offerings that cost me nothing."

So David bought the threshing floor and the oxen and paid fifty shekels*b* of silver for them. ²⁵David built an altar to the LORD there and sacrificed burnt offerings and fellowship offerings.*c* Then the LORD answered prayer in behalf of the land, and the plague on Israel was stopped.

---

a 13 Septuagint (see also 1 Chron. 21:12); Hebrew *seven*   *b* 24 That is, about 1 1/4 pounds (about 0.6 kilogram)   *c* 25 Traditionally *peace offerings*

1 KINGS

 HE BOOKS OF 1 AND 2 KINGS WERE ORIGINALLY ONE LITERARY WORK, CALLED "KINGS." BEGINNING WITH SOLOMON'S REIGN, 1 KINGS RECORDS THE HISTORY OF ISRAEL THROUGH THE DIVIDED KINGDOM TO THE DEATH OF KING AHAZ. IN GENERAL, 1 AND 2 KINGS DESCRIBES THE HISTORY OF THE KINGS OF ISRAEL AND JUDAH IN THE LIGHT OF GOD'S COVENANTS. AS YOU READ THE ACCOUNTS, NOTE THE POSITIVE EXAMPLES TO FOLLOW AND THE MISTAKES TO AVOID AS YOU SEEK TO SERVE GOD IN YOUR LIFE.

Adonijah Sets Himself Up as King

1 When King David was old and well advanced in years, he could not keep warm even when they put covers over him. ²So his servants said to him, "Let us look for a young virgin to attend the king and take care of him. She can lie beside him so that our lord the king may keep warm."

³Then they searched throughout Israel for a beautiful girl and found Abishag, a Shunammite, and brought her to the king. ⁴The girl was very beautiful; she took care of the king and waited on him, but the king had no intimate relations with her.

⁵Now Adonijah, whose mother was Haggith, put himself forward and said, "I will be king." So he got chariots and horses*a* ready, with fifty men to run ahead of him. ⁶(His father had never interfered with him by asking, "Why do you behave as you do?" He was also very handsome and was born next after Absalom.)

⁷Adonijah conferred with Joab son of Zeruiah and with Abiathar the priest, and they gave him their support. ⁸But Zadok the priest, Benaiah son of Jehoiada, Nathan the prophet, Shimei and Rei*b* and David's special guard did not join Adonijah.

⁹Adonijah then sacrificed sheep, cattle and fattened calves at the Stone of Zoheleth near En Rogel. He invited all his brothers, the king's sons, and all the men of Judah who were royal officials,

a 5 Or *charioteers*   *b 8* Or *and his friends*

¹⁰but he did not invite Nathan the prophet or Benaiah or the special guard or his brother Solomon.

¹¹Then Nathan asked Bathsheba, Solomon's mother, "Have you not heard that Adonijah, the son of Haggith, has become king without our lord David's knowing it? ¹²Now then, let me advise you how you can save your own life and the life of your son Solomon. ¹³Go in to King David and say to him, 'My lord the king, did you not swear to me your servant: "Surely Solomon your son shall be king after me, and he will sit on my throne"? Why then has Adonijah become king?' ¹⁴While you are still there talking to the king, I will come in and confirm what you have said."

¹⁵So Bathsheba went to see the aged king in his room, where Abishag the Shunammite was attending him. ¹⁶Bathsheba bowed low and knelt before the king. "What is it you want?" the king asked.

¹⁷She said to him, "My lord, you yourself swore to me your servant by the LORD your God: 'Solomon your son shall be king after me, and he will sit on my throne.' ¹⁸But now Adonijah has become king, and you, my lord the king, do not know about it. ¹⁹He has sacrificed great numbers of cattle, fattened calves, and sheep, and has invited all the king's sons, Abiathar the priest and Joab the commander of the army, but he has not invited Solomon your servant. ²⁰My lord the king, the eyes of all Israel are on you, to learn from you who will sit on the throne of my lord the king after him. ²¹Otherwise, as soon as my lord the king is laid to rest with his fathers, I and my son Solomon will be treated as criminals."

²²While she was still speaking with the king, Nathan the prophet arrived. ²³And they told the king, "Nathan the prophet is here." So he went before the king and bowed with his face to the ground.

²⁴Nathan said, "Have you, my lord the king, declared that Adonijah shall be king after you, and that he will sit on your throne? ²⁵Today he has gone down and sacrificed great numbers of cattle, fattened calves, and sheep. He has invited all the king's sons, the commanders of the army and Abiathar the priest. Right now they are eating and drinking with him and saying, 'Long live King Adonijah!' ²⁶But me your servant, and Zadok the priest, and Benaiah son of Jehoiada, and your servant Solomon he did not invite. ²⁷Is this something my lord the king has done without letting his servants know who should sit on the throne of my lord the king after him?"

David Makes Solomon King

²⁸Then King David said, "Call in Bathsheba." So she came into the king's presence and stood before him.

²⁹The king then took an oath: "As surely as the LORD lives, who has delivered me out of every trouble, ³⁰I will surely carry out today what I swore to you by the LORD, the God of Israel: Solomon your son shall be king after me, and he will sit on my throne in my place."

³¹Then Bathsheba bowed low with her face to the ground and, kneeling before the king, said, "May my lord King David live forever!"

³²King David said, "Call in Zadok the priest, Nathan the prophet and Benaiah son of Jehoiada." When they came before the king, ³³he said to them: "Take your lord's servants with you and set Solomon my son on my own mule and take him down to Gihon. ³⁴There have Zadok the priest and Nathan the prophet anoint him king over Israel. Blow the trumpet and shout, 'Long live King Solomon!' ³⁵Then you are to go up with him, and he is to come and sit on my throne and reign in my place. I have appointed him ruler over Israel and Judah."

³⁶Benaiah son of Jehoiada answered the king, "Amen! May the LORD, the God of my lord the king, so declare it. ³⁷As the LORD was with my lord the king, so may he be with Solomon to make his throne even greater than the throne of my lord King David!"

³⁸So Zadok the priest, Nathan the prophet, Benaiah son of Jehoiada, the Kerethites and the Pelethites went down and put Solomon on King David's mule and escorted him to Gihon. ³⁹Zadok the priest took the horn of oil from the sacred tent and anointed Solomon. Then they sounded the trumpet and all the people shouted, "Long live King Solomon!" ⁴⁰And all the people went up after him, playing flutes and

rejoicing greatly, so that the ground shook with the sound.

⁴¹Adonijah and all the guests who were with him heard it as they were finishing their feast. On hearing the sound of the trumpet, Joab asked, "What's the meaning of all the noise in the city?"

⁴²Even as he was speaking, Jonathan son of Abiathar the priest arrived. Adonijah said, "Come in. A worthy man like you must be bringing good news."

⁴³"Not at all!" Jonathan answered. "Our lord King David has made Solomon king. ⁴⁴The king has sent with him Zadok the priest, Nathan the prophet, Benaiah son of Jehoiada, the Kerethites and the Pelethites, and they have put him on the king's mule, ⁴⁵and Zadok the priest and Nathan the prophet have anointed him king at Gihon. From there they have gone up cheering, and the city resounds with it. That's the noise you hear. ⁴⁶Moreover, Solomon has taken his seat on the royal throne. ⁴⁷Also, the royal officials have come to congratulate our lord King David, saying, 'May your God make Solomon's name more famous than yours and his throne greater than yours!' And the king bowed in worship on his bed ⁴⁸and said, 'Praise be to the LORD, the God of Israel, who has allowed my eyes to see a successor on my throne today.' "

⁴⁹At this, all Adonijah's guests rose in alarm and dispersed. ⁵⁰But Adonijah, in fear of Solomon, went and took hold of the horns of the altar. ⁵¹Then Solomon was told, "Adonijah is afraid of King Solomon and is clinging to the horns of the altar. He says, 'Let King Solomon swear to me today that he will not put his servant to death with the sword.' "

⁵²Solomon replied, "If he shows himself to be a worthy man, not a hair of his head will fall to the ground; but if evil is found in him, he will die." ⁵³Then King Solomon sent men, and they brought him down from the altar. And Adonijah came and bowed down to King Solomon, and Solomon said, "Go to your home."

David's Charge to Solomon

2 When the time drew near for David to die, he gave a charge to Solomon his son.

²"I am about to go the way of all the earth," he said. "So be strong, show yourself a man, ³and observe what the LORD your God requires: Walk in his ways, and keep his decrees and commands, his laws and requirements, as written in the Law of Moses, so that you may prosper in all you do and wherever you go, ⁴and that the LORD may keep his promise to me: 'If your descendants watch how they live, and if they walk faithfully before me with all their heart and soul, you will never fail to have a man on the throne of Israel.'

⁵"Now you yourself know what Joab son of Zeruiah did to me—what he did to the two commanders of Israel's armies, Abner son of Ner and Amasa son of Jether. He killed them, shedding their blood in peacetime as if in battle, and with that blood stained the belt around his waist and the sandals on his feet. ⁶Deal with him according to your wisdom, but do not let his gray head go down to the graveᵃ in peace.

⁷"But show kindness to the sons of Barzillai of Gilead and let them be among those who eat at your table. They stood by me when I fled from your brother Absalom.

⁸"And remember, you have with you Shimei son of Gera, the Benjamite from Bahurim, who called down bitter curses on me the day I went to Mahanaim. When he came down to meet me at the Jordan, I swore to him by the LORD: 'I will not put you to death by the sword.' ⁹But now, do not consider him innocent. You are a man of wisdom; you will know what to do to him. Bring his gray head down to the grave in blood."

¹⁰Then David rested with his fathers and was buried in the City of David. ¹¹He had reigned forty years over Israel—seven years in Hebron and thirty-three in Jerusalem. ¹²So Solomon sat on the throne of his father David, and his rule was firmly established.

Solomon's Throne Established

¹³Now Adonijah, the son of Haggith, went to Bathsheba, Solomon's mother. Bathsheba asked him, "Do you come peacefully?"

He answered, "Yes, peacefully." ¹⁴Then

ᵃ 6 Hebrew *Sheol*; also in verse 9

WEEKEND

CROSSING THE BAR
Alfred, Lord Tennyson

VERSE: 1 Kings 2:10   **PASSAGE:** 1 Kings 2:10–12

 unset and evening star,
       And one clear call for me!
And may there be no moaning of the bar,
       When I put out to sea,

But such a tide as moving seems asleep,
       Too full for sound and foam,
When that which drew from out the boundless deep
       Turns again home.

Twilight and evening bell,
       And after that the dark!
And may there be no sadness of farewell,
       When I embark;

For though from out our bourn of time and place
       The flood may bear me far,
I hope to see my Pilot face to face
       When I have crossed the bar.

ADDITIONAL SCRIPTURE READING:
Luke 12:35–40; 1 Corinthians 13:12; 1 John 3:2

Go to page 375 for your next devotional reading.

1700   1900

he added, "I have something to say to you."

"You may say it," she replied.

15"As you know," he said, "the kingdom was mine. All Israel looked to me as their king. But things changed, and the kingdom has gone to my brother; for it has come to him from the LORD. 16Now I have one request to make of you. Do not refuse me."

"You may make it," she said.

17So he continued, "Please ask King Solomon—he will not refuse you—to give me Abishag the Shunammite as my wife."

18"Very well," Bathsheba replied, "I will speak to the king for you."

19When Bathsheba went to King Solomon to speak to him for Adonijah, the king stood up to meet her, bowed down to her and sat down on his throne. He had a throne brought for the king's mother, and she sat down at his right hand.

20"I have one small request to make of you," she said. "Do not refuse me."

The king replied, "Make it, my mother; I will not refuse you."

21So she said, "Let Abishag the Shunammite be given in marriage to your brother Adonijah."

22King Solomon answered his mother, "Why do you request Abishag the Shunammite for Adonijah? You might as well request the kingdom for him—after all, he is my older brother—yes, for him and for Abiathar the priest and Joab son of Zeruiah!"

23Then King Solomon swore by the LORD: "May God deal with me, be it ever so severely, if Adonijah does not pay with his life for this request! 24And now, as surely as the LORD lives—he who has established me securely on the throne of my father David and has founded a dynasty for me as he promised—Adonijah shall be put to death today!" 25So King Solomon gave orders to Benaiah son of Jehoiada, and he struck down Adonijah and he died.

26To Abiathar the priest the king said, "Go back to your fields in Anathoth. You deserve to die, but I will not put you to death now, because you carried the ark of the Sovereign LORD before my father David and shared all my father's hardships." 27So Solomon removed Abiathar from the priesthood of the LORD, fulfilling the word the LORD had spoken at Shiloh about the house of Eli.

28When the news reached Joab, who had conspired with Adonijah though not with Absalom, he fled to the tent of the LORD and took hold of the horns of the altar. 29King Solomon was told that Joab had fled to the tent of the LORD and was beside the altar. Then Solomon ordered Benaiah son of Jehoiada, "Go, strike him down!"

30So Benaiah entered the tent of the LORD and said to Joab, "The king says, 'Come out!'"

But he answered, "No, I will die here."

Benaiah reported to the king, "This is how Joab answered me."

31Then the king commanded Benaiah, "Do as he says. Strike him down and bury him, and so clear me and my father's house of the guilt of the innocent blood that Joab shed. 32The LORD will repay him for the blood he shed, because without the knowledge of my father David he attacked two men and killed them with the sword. Both of them—Abner son of Ner, commander of Israel's army, and Amasa son of Jether, commander of Judah's army—were better men and more upright than he. 33May the guilt of their blood rest on the head of Joab and his descendants forever. But on David and his descendants, his house and his throne, may there be the LORD's peace forever."

34So Benaiah son of Jehoiada went up and struck down Joab and killed him, and he was buried on his own land*a* in the desert. 35The king put Benaiah son of Jehoiada over the army in Joab's position and replaced Abiathar with Zadok the priest.

36Then the king sent for Shimei and said to him, "Build yourself a house in Jerusalem and live there, but do not go anywhere else. 37The day you leave and cross the Kidron Valley, you can be sure you will die; your blood will be on your own head."

38Shimei answered the king, "What you say is good. Your servant will do as

---

a 34 Or buried in his tomb

my lord the king has said." And Shimei stayed in Jerusalem for a long time.

³⁹But three years later, two of Shimei's slaves ran off to Achish son of Maacah, king of Gath, and Shimei was told, "Your slaves are in Gath." ⁴⁰At this, he saddled his donkey and went to Achish at Gath in search of his slaves. So Shimei went away and brought the slaves back from Gath.

⁴¹When Solomon was told that Shimei had gone from Jerusalem to Gath and had returned, ⁴²the king summoned Shimei and said to him, "Did I not make you swear by the LORD and warn you, 'On the day you leave to go anywhere else, you can be sure you will die'? At that time you said to me, 'What you say is good. I will obey.' ⁴³Why then did you not keep your oath to the LORD and obey the command I gave you?"

⁴⁴The king also said to Shimei, "You know in your heart all the wrong you did to my father David. Now the LORD will repay you for your wrongdoing. ⁴⁵But King Solomon will be blessed, and David's throne will remain secure before the LORD forever."

⁴⁶Then the king gave the order to Benaiah son of Jehoiada, and he went out and struck Shimei down and killed him.

The kingdom was now firmly established in Solomon's hands.

Solomon Asks for Wisdom

3 Solomon made an alliance with Pharaoh king of Egypt and married his daughter. He brought her to the City of David until he finished building his palace and the temple of the LORD, and the wall around Jerusalem. ²The people, however, were still sacrificing at the high places, because a temple had not yet been built for the Name of the LORD. ³Solomon showed his love for the LORD by walking according to the statutes of his father David, except that he offered sacrifices and burned incense on the high places.

⁴The king went to Gibeon to offer sacrifices, for that was the most important high place, and Solomon offered a thousand burnt offerings on that altar. ⁵At Gibeon the LORD appeared to Solomon during the night in a dream, and God

said, "Ask for whatever you want me to give you."

⁶Solomon answered, "You have shown great kindness to your servant, my father David, because he was faithful to you and righteous and upright in heart. You have continued this great kindness to him and have given him a son to sit on his throne this very day.

⁷"Now, O LORD my God, you have made your servant king in place of my father David. But I am only a little child and do not know how to carry out my duties. ⁸Your servant is here among the people you have chosen, a great people, too numerous to count or number. ⁹So give your servant a discerning heart to govern your people and to distinguish between right and wrong. For who is able to govern this great people of yours?"

¹⁰The Lord was pleased that Solomon had asked for this. ¹¹So God said to him, "Since you have asked for this and not for long life or wealth for yourself, nor have asked for the death of your enemies but for discernment in administering justice, ¹²I will do what you have asked. I will give you a wise and discerning heart, so that there will never have been anyone like you, nor will there ever be. ¹³Moreover, I will give you what you have not asked for—both riches and honor—so that in your lifetime you will have no equal among kings. ¹⁴And if you walk in my ways and obey my statutes and commands as David your father did, I will give you a long life." ¹⁵Then Solomon awoke—and he realized it had been a dream.

He returned to Jerusalem, stood before the ark of the Lord's covenant and sacrificed burnt offerings and fellowship offerings.ᵃ Then he gave a feast for all his court.

A Wise Ruling

¹⁶Now two prostitutes came to the king and stood before him. ¹⁷One of them said, "My lord, this woman and I live in the same house. I had a baby while she was there with me. ¹⁸The third day after my child was born, this woman also had a baby. We were alone; there was no one in the house but the two of us.

¹⁹"During the night this woman's son died because she lay on him. ²⁰So she got up in the middle of the night and took my son from my side while I your servant was asleep. She put him by her breast and put her dead son by my breast. ²¹The next morning, I got up to nurse my son—and he was dead! But when I looked at him closely in the morning light, I saw that it wasn't the son I had borne."

²²The other woman said, "No! The living one is my son; the dead one is yours."

But the first one insisted, "No! The dead one is yours; the living one is mine." And so they argued before the king.

²³The king said, "This one says, 'My son is alive and your son is dead,' while that one says, 'No! Your son is dead and mine is alive.' "

²⁴Then the king said, "Bring me a sword." So they brought a sword for the king. ²⁵He then gave an order: "Cut the living child in two and give half to one and half to the other."

²⁶The woman whose son was alive was filled with compassion for her son and said to the king, "Please, my lord, give her the living baby! Don't kill him!"

But the other said, "Neither I nor you shall have him. Cut him in two!"

²⁷Then the king gave his ruling: "Give the living baby to the first woman. Do not kill him; she is his mother."

²⁸When all Israel heard the verdict the king had given, they held the king in awe, because they saw that he had wisdom from God to administer justice.

Solomon's Officials and Governors

4 So King Solomon ruled over all Israel. ²And these were his chief officials:

Azariah son of Zadok—the priest;
³Elihoreph and Ahijah, sons of Shisha—secretaries;
Jehoshaphat son of Ahilud—recorder;
⁴Benaiah son of Jehoiada—commander in chief;
Zadok and Abiathar—priests;
⁵Azariah son of Nathan—in charge of the district officers;

Zabud son of Nathan—a priest and personal adviser to the king;
⁶Ahishar—in charge of the palace;
Adoniram son of Abda—in charge of forced labor.

⁷Solomon also had twelve district governors over all Israel, who supplied provisions for the king and the royal household. Each one had to provide supplies for one month in the year. ⁸These are their names:

Ben-Hur—in the hill country of Ephraim;
⁹Ben-Deker—in Makaz, Shaalbim, Beth Shemesh and Elon Bethhanan;
¹⁰Ben-Hesed—in Arubboth (Socoh and all the land of Hepher were his);
¹¹Ben-Abinadab—in Naphoth Dorᵃ (he was married to Taphath daughter of Solomon);
¹²Baana son of Ahilud—in Taanach and Megiddo, and in all of Beth Shan next to Zarethan below Jezreel, from Beth Shan to Abel Meholah across to Jokmeam;
¹³Ben-Geber—in Ramoth Gilead (the settlements of Jair son of Manasseh in Gilead were his, as well as the district of Argob in Bashan and its sixty large walled cities with bronze gate bars);
¹⁴Ahinadab son of Iddo—in Mahanaim;
¹⁵Ahimaaz—in Naphtali (he had married Basemath daughter of Solomon);
¹⁶Baana son of Hushai—in Asher and in Aloth;
¹⁷Jehoshaphat son of Paruah—in Issachar;
¹⁸Shimei son of Ela—in Benjamin;
¹⁹Geber son of Uri—in Gilead (the country of Sihon king of the Amorites and the country of Og king of Bashan). He was the only governor over the district.

Solomon's Daily Provisions

²⁰The people of Judah and Israel were as numerous as the sand on the seashore; they ate, they drank and they were happy. ²¹And Solomon ruled over

ᵃ 11 Or in the heights of Dor

all the kingdoms from the River[a] to the land of the Philistines, as far as the border of Egypt. These countries brought tribute and were Solomon's subjects all his life.

22Solomon's daily provisions were thirty cors[b] of fine flour and sixty cors[c] of meal, 23ten head of stall-fed cattle, twenty of pasture-fed cattle and a hundred sheep and goats, as well as deer, gazelles, roebucks and choice fowl. 24For he ruled over all the kingdoms west of the River, from Tiphsah to Gaza, and had peace on all sides. 25During Solomon's lifetime Judah and Israel, from Dan to Beersheba, lived in safety, each man under his own vine and fig tree.

26Solomon had four[d] thousand stalls for chariot horses, and twelve thousand horses.[e]

27The district officers, each in his month, supplied provisions for King Solomon and all who came to the king's table. They saw to it that nothing was lacking. 28They also brought to the proper place their quotas of barley and straw for the chariot horses and the other horses.

Solomon's Wisdom

29God gave Solomon wisdom and very great insight, and a breadth of understanding as measureless as the sand on the seashore. 30Solomon's wisdom was greater than the wisdom of all the men of the East, and greater than all the wisdom of Egypt. 31He was wiser than any other man, including Ethan the Ezrahite—wiser than Heman, Calcol and Darda, the sons of Mahol. And his fame spread to all the surrounding nations. 32He spoke three thousand proverbs and his songs numbered a thousand and five. 33He described plant life, from the cedar of Lebanon to the hyssop that grows out of walls. He also taught about animals and birds, reptiles and fish. 34Men of all nations came to listen to Solomon's wisdom, sent by all the kings of the world, who had heard of his wisdom.

Preparations for Building the Temple

5 When Hiram king of Tyre heard that Solomon had been anointed king to succeed his father David, he sent his envoys to Solomon, because he had always been on friendly terms with David. 2Solomon sent back this message to Hiram:

3"You know that because of the wars waged against my father David from all sides, he could not build a temple for the Name of the LORD his God until the LORD put his enemies under his feet. 4But now the LORD my God has given me rest on every side, and there is no adversary or disaster. 5I intend, therefore, to build a temple for the Name of the LORD my God, as the LORD told my father David, when he said, 'Your son whom I will put on the throne in your place will build the temple for my Name.'

6"So give orders that cedars of Lebanon be cut for me. My men will work with yours, and I will pay you for your men whatever wages you set. You know that we have no one so skilled in felling timber as the Sidonians."

7When Hiram heard Solomon's message, he was greatly pleased and said, "Praise be to the LORD today, for he has given David a wise son to rule over this great nation."

8So Hiram sent word to Solomon:

"I have received the message you sent me and will do all you want in providing the cedar and pine logs. 9My men will haul them down from Lebanon to the sea, and I will float them in rafts by sea to the place you specify. There I will separate them and you can take them away. And you are to grant my wish by providing food for my royal household."

10In this way Hiram kept Solomon supplied with all the cedar and pine logs he wanted, 11and Solomon gave Hiram

---

a 21 That is, the Euphrates; also in verse 24   b 22 That is, probably about 185 bushels (about 6.6 kiloliters)   c 22 That is, probably about 375 bushels (about 13.2 kiloliters)   d 26 Some Septuagint manuscripts (see also 2 Chron. 9:25); Hebrew forty   e 26 Or charioteers

twenty thousand cors*a* of wheat as food for his household, in addition to twenty thousand baths*b,c* of pressed olive oil. Solomon continued to do this for Hiram year after year. 12The LORD gave Solomon wisdom, just as he had promised him. There were peaceful relations between Hiram and Solomon, and the two of them made a treaty.

13King Solomon conscripted laborers from all Israel—thirty thousand men. 14He sent them off to Lebanon in shifts of ten thousand a month, so that they spent one month in Lebanon and two months at home. Adoniram was in charge of the forced labor. 15Solomon had seventy thousand carriers and eighty thousand stonecutters in the hills, 16as well as thirty-three hundred*d* foremen who supervised the project and directed the workmen. 17At the king's command they removed from the quarry large blocks of quality stone to provide a foundation of dressed stone for the temple. 18The craftsmen of Solomon and Hiram and the men of Gebal*e* cut and prepared the timber and stone for the building of the temple.

Solomon Builds the Temple

6 In the four hundred and eightieth*f* year after the Israelites had come out of Egypt, in the fourth year of Solomon's reign over Israel, in the month of Ziv, the second month, he began to build the temple of the LORD.

2The temple that King Solomon built for the LORD was sixty cubits long, twenty wide and thirty high.*g* 3The portico at the front of the main hall of the temple extended the width of the temple, that is twenty cubits,*h* and projected ten cubits*i* from the front of the temple. 4He made narrow clerestory windows in the temple. 5Against the walls of the main hall and inner sanctuary he built a structure around the building, in which there were side rooms. 6The lowest floor was five cubits*i* wide, the middle floor

six cubits*k* and the third floor seven.*l* He made offset ledges around the outside of the temple so that nothing would be inserted into the temple walls.

7In building the temple, only blocks dressed at the quarry were used, and no hammer, chisel or any other iron tool was heard at the temple site while it was being built.

8The entrance to the lowest*m* floor was on the south side of the temple; a stairway led up to the middle level and from there to the third. 9So he built the temple and completed it, roofing it with beams and cedar planks. 10And he built the side rooms all along the temple. The height of each was five cubits, and they were attached to the temple by beams of cedar.

11The word of the LORD came to Solomon: 12"As for this temple you are building, if you follow my decrees, carry out my regulations and keep all my commands and obey them, I will fulfill through you the promise I gave to David your father. 13And I will live among the Israelites and will not abandon my people Israel."

14So Solomon built the temple and completed it. 15He lined its interior walls with cedar boards, paneling them from the floor of the temple to the ceiling, and covered the floor of the temple with planks of pine. 16He partitioned off twenty cubits*h* at the rear of the temple with cedar boards from floor to ceiling to form within the temple an inner sanctuary, the Most Holy Place. 17The main hall in front of this room was forty cubits*n* long. 18The inside of the temple was cedar, carved with gourds and open flowers. Everything was cedar; no stone was to be seen.

19He prepared the inner sanctuary within the temple to set the ark of the covenant of the LORD there. 20The inner sanctuary was twenty cubits long, twenty wide and twenty high.*o* He overlaid the inside with pure gold, and he also overlaid the altar of cedar. 21Solomon

---

a 11 That is, probably about 125,000 bushels (about 4,400 kiloliters)   *b 11* Septuagint (see also 2 Chron. 2:10); Hebrew *twenty cors*   *c 11* That is, about 115,000 gallons (about 440 kiloliters)   *d 16* Hebrew; some Septuagint manuscripts (see also 2 Chron. 2:2, 18) *thirty-six hundred*   *e 18* That is, Byblos   *f 1* Hebrew; Septuagint *four hundred and fortieth*   *g 2* That is, about 90 feet (about 27 meters) long and 30 feet (about 9 meters) wide and 45 feet (about 13.5 meters) high   *h 3,16* That is, about 30 feet (about 9 meters)   *i 3* That is, about 15 feet (about 4.5 meters)   *i 6* That is, about 7 1/2 feet (about 2.3 meters); also in verses 10 and 24   *k 6* That is, about 9 feet (about 2.7 meters)   *l 6* That is, about 10 1/2 feet (about 3.1 meters)   *m 8* Septuagint; Hebrew *middle*   *n 17* That is, about 60 feet (about 18 meters)   *o 20* That is, about 30 feet (about 9 meters) long, wide and high

covered the inside of the temple with pure gold, and he extended gold chains across the front of the inner sanctuary, which was overlaid with gold. 22So he overlaid the whole interior with gold. He also overlaid with gold the altar that belonged to the inner sanctuary.

23In the inner sanctuary he made a pair of cherubim of olive wood, each ten cubits[a] high. 24One wing of the first cherub was five cubits long, and the other wing five cubits—ten cubits from wing tip to wing tip. 25The second cherub also measured ten cubits, for the two cherubim were identical in size and shape. 26The height of each cherub was ten cubits. 27He placed the cherubim inside the innermost room of the temple, with their wings spread out. The wing of one cherub touched one wall, while the wing of the other touched the other wall, and their wings touched each other in the middle of the room. 28He overlaid the cherubim with gold.

29On the walls all around the temple, in both the inner and outer rooms, he carved cherubim, palm trees and open flowers. 30He also covered the floors of both the inner and outer rooms of the temple with gold.

31For the entrance of the inner sanctuary he made doors of olive wood with five-sided jambs. 32And on the two olive wood doors he carved cherubim, palm trees and open flowers, and overlaid the cherubim and palm trees with beaten

a 23 That is, about 15 feet (about 4.5 meters)

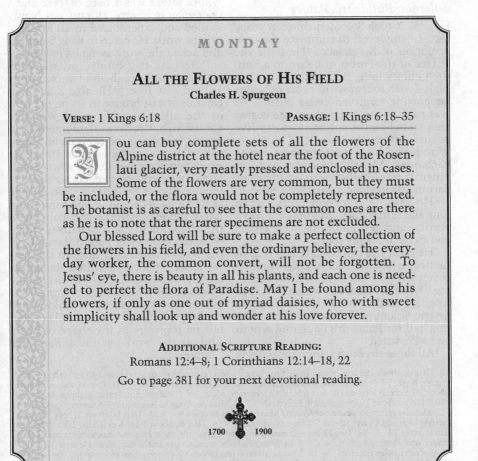

MONDAY

ALL THE FLOWERS OF HIS FIELD
Charles H. Spurgeon

VERSE: 1 Kings 6:18   PASSAGE: 1 Kings 6:18–35

Y ou can buy complete sets of all the flowers of the Alpine district at the hotel near the foot of the Rosenlaui glacier, very neatly pressed and enclosed in cases. Some of the flowers are very common, but they must be included, or the flora would not be completely represented. The botanist is as careful to see that the common ones are there as he is to note that the rarer specimens are not excluded.

Our blessed Lord will be sure to make a perfect collection of the flowers in his field, and even the ordinary believer, the everyday worker, the common convert, will not be forgotten. To Jesus' eye, there is beauty in all his plants, and each one is needed to perfect the flora of Paradise. May I be found among his flowers, if only as one out of myriad daisies, who with sweet simplicity shall look up and wonder at his love forever.

ADDITIONAL SCRIPTURE READING:
Romans 12:4–8; 1 Corinthians 12:14–18, 22

Go to page 381 for your next devotional reading.

1700   1900

gold. ³³In the same way he made four-sided jambs of olive wood for the entrance to the main hall. ³⁴He also made two pine doors, each having two leaves that turned in sockets. ³⁵He carved cherubim, palm trees and open flowers on them and overlaid them with gold hammered evenly over the carvings.

³⁶And he built the inner courtyard of three courses of dressed stone and one course of trimmed cedar beams.

³⁷The foundation of the temple of the LORD was laid in the fourth year, in the month of Ziv. ³⁸In the eleventh year in the month of Bul, the eighth month, the temple was finished in all its details according to its specifications. He had spent seven years building it.

Solomon Builds His Palace

7 It took Solomon thirteen years, however, to complete the construction of his palace. ²He built the Palace of the Forest of Lebanon a hundred cubits long, fifty wide and thirty high,ᵃ with four rows of cedar columns supporting trimmed cedar beams. ³It was roofed with cedar above the beams that rested on the columns—forty-five beams, fifteen to a row. ⁴Its windows were placed high in sets of three, facing each other. ⁵All the doorways had rectangular frames; they were in the front part in sets of three, facing each other.ᵇ

⁶He made a colonnade fifty cubits long and thirty wide.ᶜ In front of it was a portico, and in front of that were pillars and an overhanging roof.

⁷He built the throne hall, the Hall of Justice, where he was to judge, and he covered it with cedar from floor to ceiling.ᵈ ⁸And the palace in which he was to live, set farther back, was similar in design. Solomon also made a palace like this hall for Pharaoh's daughter, whom he had married.

⁹All these structures, from the outside to the great courtyard and from foundation to eaves, were made of blocks of high-grade stone cut to size and trimmed with a saw on their inner and outer faces. ¹⁰The foundations were laid with large stones of good quality, some measuring ten cubitsᵉ and some eight.ᶠ ¹¹Above were high-grade stones, cut to size, and cedar beams. ¹²The great courtyard was surrounded by a wall of three courses of dressed stone and one course of trimmed cedar beams, as was the inner courtyard of the temple of the LORD with its portico.

The Temple's Furnishings

¹³King Solomon sent to Tyre and brought Huram,ᵍ ¹⁴whose mother was a widow from the tribe of Naphtali and whose father was a man of Tyre and a craftsman in bronze. Huram was highly skilled and experienced in all kinds of bronze work. He came to King Solomon and did all the work assigned to him.

¹⁵He cast two bronze pillars, each eighteen cubits high and twelve cubits around,ʰ by line. ¹⁶He also made two capitals of cast bronze to set on the tops of the pillars; each capital was five cubitsⁱ high. ¹⁷A network of interwoven chains festooned the capitals on top of the pillars, seven for each capital. ¹⁸He made pomegranates in two rowsʲ encircling each network to decorate the capitals on top of the pillars.ᵏ He did the same for each capital. ¹⁹The capitals on top of the pillars in the portico were in the shape of lilies, four cubitsˡ high. ²⁰On the capitals of both pillars, above the bowl-shaped part next to the network, were the two hundred pomegranates in rows all around. ²¹He erected the pillars at the portico of the temple. The pillar to the south he named Jakinᵐ and the one to the north Boaz.ⁿ ²²The capitals on top were in the shape of lilies. And so the work on the pillars was completed.

ᵃ 2 That is, about 150 feet (about 46 meters) long, 75 feet (about 23 meters) wide and 45 feet (about 13.5 meters) high   ᵇ 5 The meaning of the Hebrew for this verse is uncertain.   ᶜ 6 That is, about 75 feet (about 23 meters) long and 45 feet (about 13.5 meters) wide   ᵈ 7 Vulgate and Syriac; Hebrew *floor*   ᵉ 10 That is, about 15 feet (about 4.5 meters)   ᶠ 10 That is, about 12 feet (about 3.6 meters)   ᵍ 13 Hebrew *Hiram*, a variant of *Huram*; also in verses 40 and 45   ʰ 15 That is, about 27 feet (about 8.1 meters) high and 18 feet (about 5.4 meters) around   ⁱ 16 That is, about 7 1/2 feet (about 2.3 meters); also in verse 23   ʲ 18 Two Hebrew manuscripts and Septuagint; most Hebrew manuscripts *made the pillars, and there were two rows*   ᵏ 18 Many Hebrew manuscripts and Syriac; most Hebrew manuscripts *pomegranates*   ˡ 19 That is, about 6 feet (about 1.8 meters); also in verse 38   ᵐ 21 *Jakin* probably means *he establishes*.   ⁿ 21 *Boaz* probably means *in him is strength*.

23He made the Sea of cast metal, circular in shape, measuring ten cubits*a* from rim to rim and five cubits high. It took a line of thirty cubits*b* to measure around it. **24**Below the rim, gourds encircled it—ten to a cubit. The gourds were cast in two rows in one piece with the Sea.

25The Sea stood on twelve bulls, three facing north, three facing west, three facing south and three facing east. The Sea rested on top of them, and their hindquarters were toward the center. **26**It was a handbreadth*c* in thickness, and its rim was like the rim of a cup, like a lily blossom. It held two thousand baths.*d*

27He also made ten movable stands of bronze; each was four cubits long, four wide and three high.*e* **28**This is how the stands were made: They had side panels attached to uprights. **29**On the panels between the uprights were lions, bulls and cherubim—and on the uprights as well. Above and below the lions and bulls were wreaths of hammered work. **30**Each stand had four bronze wheels with bronze axles, and each had a basin resting on four supports, cast with wreaths on each side. **31**On the inside of the stand there was an opening that had a circular frame one cubit*f* deep. This opening was round, and with its basework it measured a cubit and a half.*g* Around its opening there was engraving. The panels of the stands were square, not round. **32**The four wheels were under the panels, and the axles of the wheels were attached to the stand. The diameter of each wheel was a cubit and a half. **33**The wheels were made like chariot wheels; the axles, rims, spokes and hubs were all of cast metal.

34Each stand had four handles, one on each corner, projecting from the stand. **35**At the top of the stand there was a circular band half a cubit*h* deep. The supports and panels were attached to the top of the stand. **36**He engraved cherubim, lions and palm trees on the surfaces of the supports and on the panels, in every available space, with wreaths all around. **37**This is the way he made the ten stands.

They were all cast in the same molds and were identical in size and shape.

38He then made ten bronze basins, each holding forty baths*i* and measuring four cubits across, one basin to go on each of the ten stands. **39**He placed five of the stands on the south side of the temple and five on the north. He placed the Sea on the south side, at the southeast corner of the temple. **40**He also made the basins and shovels and sprinkling bowls.

So Huram finished all the work he had undertaken for King Solomon in the temple of the LORD:

41the two pillars;
the two bowl-shaped capitals on top of the pillars;
the two sets of network decorating the two bowl-shaped capitals on top of the pillars;
42the four hundred pomegranates for the two sets of network (two rows of pomegranates for each network, decorating the bowl-shaped capitals on top of the pillars);
43the ten stands with their ten basins;
44the Sea and the twelve bulls under it;
45the pots, shovels and sprinkling bowls.

All these objects that Huram made for King Solomon for the temple of the LORD were of burnished bronze. **46**The king had them cast in clay molds in the plain of the Jordan between Succoth and Zarethan. **47**Solomon left all these things unweighed, because there were so many; the weight of the bronze was not determined.

48Solomon also made all the furnishings that were in the LORD's temple:

the golden altar;
the golden table on which was the bread of the Presence;
49the lampstands of pure gold (five on the right and five on the left, in front of the inner sanctuary);
the gold floral work and lamps and tongs;

a 23 That is, about 15 feet (about 4.5 meters) *b 23* That is, about 45 feet (about 13.5 meters)
c 26 That is, about 3 inches (about 8 centimeters) *d 26* That is, probably about 11,500 gallons (about
44 kiloliters); the Septuagint does not have this sentence. *e 27* That is, about 6 feet (about 1.8 meters)
long and wide and about 4 1/2 feet (about 1.3 meters) high *f 31* That is, about 1 1/2 feet (about 0.5
meter) *g 31* That is, about 2 1/4 feet (about 0.7 meter); also in verse 32 *h 35* That is, about 3/4 foot
(about 0.2 meter) *i 38* That is, about 230 gallons (about 880 liters)

⁵⁰the pure gold basins, wick trimmers, sprinkling bowls, dishes and censers;

and the gold sockets for the doors of the innermost room, the Most Holy Place, and also for the doors of the main hall of the temple.

⁵¹When all the work King Solomon had done for the temple of the LORD was finished, he brought in the things his father David had dedicated—the silver and gold and the furnishings—and he placed them in the treasuries of the LORD's temple.

The Ark Brought to the Temple

8 Then King Solomon summoned into his presence at Jerusalem the elders of Israel, all the heads of the tribes and the chiefs of the Israelite families, to bring up the ark of the LORD's covenant from Zion, the City of David. ²All the men of Israel came together to King Solomon at the time of the festival in the month of Ethanim, the seventh month.

³When all the elders of Israel had arrived, the priests took up the ark, ⁴and they brought up the ark of the LORD and the Tent of Meeting and all the sacred furnishings in it. The priests and Levites carried them up, ⁵and King Solomon and the entire assembly of Israel that had gathered about him were before the ark, sacrificing so many sheep and cattle that they could not be recorded or counted.

⁶The priests then brought the ark of the LORD's covenant to its place in the inner sanctuary of the temple, the Most Holy Place, and put it beneath the wings of the cherubim. ⁷The cherubim spread their wings over the place of the ark and overshadowed the ark and its carrying poles. ⁸These poles were so long that their ends could be seen from the Holy Place in front of the inner sanctuary, but not from outside the Holy Place; and they are still there today. ⁹There was nothing in the ark except the two stone tablets that Moses had placed in it at Horeb, where the LORD made a covenant with the Israelites after they came out of Egypt.

¹⁰When the priests withdrew from the Holy Place, the cloud filled the temple of the LORD. ¹¹And the priests could not perform their service because of the cloud, for the glory of the LORD filled his temple.

¹²Then Solomon said, "The LORD has said that he would dwell in a dark cloud; ¹³I have indeed built a magnificent temple for you, a place for you to dwell forever."

¹⁴While the whole assembly of Israel was standing there, the king turned around and blessed them. ¹⁵Then he said:

"Praise be to the LORD, the God of Israel, who with his own hand has fulfilled what he promised with his own mouth to my father David. For he said, ¹⁶'Since the day I brought my people Israel out of Egypt, I have not chosen a city in any tribe of Israel to have a temple built for my Name to be there, but I have chosen David to rule my people Israel.'

¹⁷"My father David had it in his heart to build a temple for the Name of the LORD, the God of Israel. ¹⁸But the LORD said to my father David, 'Because it was in your heart to build a temple for my Name, you did well to have this in your heart. ¹⁹Nevertheless, you are not the one to build the temple, but your son, who is your own flesh and blood—he is the one who will build the temple for my Name.'

²⁰"The LORD has kept the promise he made: I have succeeded David my father and now I sit on the throne of Israel, just as the LORD promised, and I have built the temple for the Name of the LORD, the God of Israel. ²¹I have provided a place there for the ark, in which is the covenant of the LORD that he made with our fathers when he brought them out of Egypt."

Solomon's Prayer of Dedication

²²Then Solomon stood before the altar of the LORD in front of the whole assembly of Israel, spread out his hands toward heaven ²³and said:

"O LORD, God of Israel, there is no God like you in heaven above or on earth below—you who keep your covenant of love with your servants who continue wholeheartedly in your way. 24You have kept your promise to your servant David my father; with your mouth you have promised and with your hand you have fulfilled it—as it is today.

25"Now LORD, God of Israel, keep for your servant David my father the promises you made to him when you said, 'You shall never fail to have a man to sit before me on the throne of Israel, if only your sons are careful in all they do to walk before me as you have done.' 26And now, O God of Israel, let your word that you promised your servant David my father come true.

27"But will God really dwell on earth? The heavens, even the highest heaven, cannot contain you. How much less this temple I have built! 28Yet give attention to your servant's prayer and his plea for mercy, O LORD my God. Hear the cry and the prayer that your servant is praying in your presence this day. 29May your eyes be open toward this temple night and day, this place of which you said, 'My Name shall be there,' so that you will hear the prayer your servant prays toward this place. 30Hear the supplication of your servant and of your people Israel when they pray toward this place. Hear from heaven, your dwelling place, and when you hear, forgive.

31"When a man wrongs his neighbor and is required to take an oath and he comes and swears the oath before your altar in this temple, 32then hear from heaven and act. Judge between your servants, condemning the guilty and bringing down on his own head what he has done. Declare the innocent not guilty, and so establish his innocence.

33"When your people Israel have been defeated by an enemy because they have sinned against you, and when they turn back to you and confess your name, praying and making supplication to you in this temple, 34then hear from heaven and forgive the sin of your people Israel and bring them back to the land you gave to their fathers.

35"When the heavens are shut up and there is no rain because your people have sinned against you, and when they pray toward this place and confess your name and turn from their sin because you have afflicted them, 36then hear from heaven and forgive the sin of your servants, your people Israel. Teach them the right way to live, and send rain on the land you gave your people for an inheritance.

37"When famine or plague comes to the land, or blight or mildew, locusts or grasshoppers, or when an enemy besieges them in any of their cities, whatever disaster or disease may come, 38and when a prayer or plea is made by any of your people Israel—each one aware of the afflictions of his own heart, and spreading out his hands toward this temple— 39then hear from heaven, your dwelling place. Forgive and act; deal with each man according to all he does, since you know his heart (for you alone know the hearts of all men), 40so that they will fear you all the time they live in the land you gave our fathers.

41"As for the foreigner who does not belong to your people Israel but has come from a distant land because of your name— 42for men will hear of your great name and your mighty hand and your outstretched arm—when he comes and prays toward this temple, 43then hear from heaven, your dwelling place, and do whatever the foreigner asks of you, so that all the peoples of the earth may know your name and fear you, as do your own people Israel, and may know that this house I have built bears your Name.

44"When your people go to war against their enemies, wherever you send them, and when they pray to the LORD toward the city you have chosen and the temple I have built for your Name, 45then hear from heaven their prayer and their plea, and uphold their cause.

46"When they sin against you—for there is no one who does not sin—and you become angry with them and give them over to the enemy, who takes them captive to his own land, far away or near; 47and if they have a change of heart in the land where they are held captive, and repent and plead with you in the land of their conquerors and say, 'We have sinned, we have done wrong, we have acted wickedly'; 48and if they turn back to you with all their heart and soul in the land of their enemies who took them captive, and pray to you toward the land you gave their fathers, toward the city you have chosen and the temple I have built for your Name; 49then from heaven, your dwelling place, hear their prayer and their plea, and uphold their cause. 50And forgive your people, who have sinned against you; forgive all the offenses they have committed against you, and cause their conquerors to show them mercy; 51for they are your people and your inheritance, whom you brought out of Egypt, out of that iron-smelting furnace.

52"May your eyes be open to your servant's plea and to the plea of your people Israel, and may you listen to them whenever they cry out to you. 53For you singled them out from all the nations of the world to be your own inheritance, just as you declared through your servant Moses when you, O Sovereign LORD, brought our fathers out of Egypt."

54When Solomon had finished all these prayers and supplications to the LORD, he rose from before the altar of the LORD, where he had been kneeling with his hands spread out toward heaven. 55He stood and blessed the whole assembly of Israel in a loud voice, saying:

56"Praise be to the LORD, who has given rest to his people Israel just as he promised. Not one word has failed of all the good promises he gave through his servant Moses. 57May the LORD our God be with us as he was with our fathers; may he never leave us nor forsake us. 58May he turn our hearts to him, to walk in all his ways and to keep the commands, decrees and regulations he gave our fathers. 59And may these words of mine, which I have prayed before the LORD, be near to the LORD our God day and night, that he may uphold the cause of his servant and the cause of his people Israel according to each day's need, 60so that all the peoples of the earth may know that the LORD is God and that there is no other. 61But your hearts must be fully committed to the LORD our God, to live by his decrees and obey his commands, as at this time."

The Dedication of the Temple

62Then the king and all Israel with him offered sacrifices before the LORD. 63Solomon offered a sacrifice of fellowship offerings*a* to the LORD: twenty-two thousand cattle and a hundred and twenty thousand sheep and goats. So the king and all the Israelites dedicated the temple of the LORD.

64On that same day the king consecrated the middle part of the courtyard in front of the temple of the LORD, and there he offered burnt offerings, grain offerings and the fat of the fellowship offerings, because the bronze altar before the LORD was too small to hold the burnt offerings, the grain offerings and the fat of the fellowship offerings.

65So Solomon observed the festival at that time, and all Israel with him— a vast assembly, people from Lebo*b* Hamath to the Wadi of Egypt. They celebrated it before the LORD our God for seven days and seven days more, fourteen days in all. 66On the following day he sent the people away. They blessed the king and then went home, joyful and glad in heart for all the good things the LORD had done for his servant David and his people Israel.

The LORD Appears to Solomon

9 When Solomon had finished building the temple of the LORD and the royal palace, and had achieved all he had desired to do, 2the LORD appeared to him a second time, as he had appeared to him at Gibeon. 3The LORD said to him:

a 63 Traditionally *peace offerings;* also in verse 64   *b 65* Or *from the entrance to*

"I have heard the prayer and plea you have made before me; I have consecrated this temple, which you have built, by putting my Name there forever. My eyes and my heart will always be there.

⁴ "As for you, if you walk before me in integrity of heart and

TUESDAY

PRAYERS
Book of Common Prayer

VERSE: 1 Kings 8:54   PASSAGE: 1 Kings 8:54–61

A Collect for Peace

 ost holy God, the source of all good desires, all right judgments, and all just works: Give to us, your servants, that peace which the world cannot give, so that our minds may be fixed on the doing of your will, and that we, being delivered from the fear of all enemies, may live in peace and quietness; through the mercies of Christ Jesus our Savior. *Amen.*

A Collect for Aid Against Perils

Be our light in the darkness, O Lord, and in your great mercy defend us from all perils and dangers of this night; for the love of your only Son, our Savior Jesus Christ. *Amen.*

A Collect for Protection

O God, the life of all who live, the light of the faithful, the strength of those who labor, and the repose of the dead: We thank you for the blessings of the day that is past, and humbly ask for your protection through the coming night. Bring us in safety to the morning hours; through him who died and rose again for us, your Son our Savior Jesus Christ. *Amen.*

A Collect for the Presence of Christ

Lord Jesus, stay with us, for evening is at hand and the day is past; be our companion in the way, kindle our hearts, and awaken hope, that we may know you as you are revealed in Scripture and the breaking of bread. Grant this for the sake of your love. *Amen.*

ADDITIONAL SCRIPTURE READING:
Matthew 6:6–8; Luke 11:1–4; Romans 8:26–27

Go to page 383 for your next devotional reading.

1500   1700

uprightness, as David your father did, and do all I command and observe my decrees and laws, 5I will establish your royal throne over Israel forever, as I promised David your father when I said, 'You shall never fail to have a man on the throne of Israel.'

6"But if you*a* or your sons turn away from me and do not observe the commands and decrees I have given you*a* and go off to serve other gods and worship them, 7then I will cut off Israel from the land I have given them and will reject this temple I have consecrated for my Name. Israel will then become a byword and an object of ridicule among all peoples. 8And though this temple is now imposing, all who pass by will be appalled and will scoff and say, 'Why has the LORD done such a thing to this land and to this temple?' 9People will answer, 'Because they have forsaken the LORD their God, who brought their fathers out of Egypt, and have embraced other gods, worshiping and serving them—that is why the LORD brought all this disaster on them.' "

Solomon's Other Activities

10At the end of twenty years, during which Solomon built these two buildings—the temple of the LORD and the royal palace— 11King Solomon gave twenty towns in Galilee to Hiram king of Tyre, because Hiram had supplied him with all the cedar and pine and gold he wanted. 12But when Hiram went from Tyre to see the towns that Solomon had given him, he was not pleased with them. 13"What kind of towns are these you have given me, my brother?" he asked. And he called them the Land of Cabul,*b* a name they have to this day. 14Now Hiram had sent to the king 120 talents*c* of gold.

15Here is the account of the forced labor King Solomon conscripted to build the LORD's temple, his own pal-ace, the supporting terraces,*d* the wall of Jerusalem, and Hazor, Megiddo and Gezer. 16(Pharaoh king of Egypt had attacked and captured Gezer. He had set it on fire. He killed its Canaanite inhabitants and then gave it as a wedding gift to his daughter, Solomon's wife. 17And Solomon rebuilt Gezer.) He built up Lower Beth Horon, 18Baalath, and Tadmor*e* in the desert, within his land, 19as well as all his store cities and the towns for his chariots and for his horses*f*—whatever he desired to build in Jerusalem, in Lebanon and throughout all the territory he ruled.

20All the people left from the Amorites, Hittites, Perizzites, Hivites and Jebusites (these peoples were not Israelites), 21that is, their descendants remaining in the land, whom the Israelites could not exterminate*g*—these Solomon conscripted for his slave labor force, as it is to this day. 22But Solomon did not make slaves of any of the Israelites; they were his fighting men, his government officials, his officers, his captains, and the commanders of his chariots and charioteers. 23They were also the chief officials in charge of Solomon's projects—550 officials supervising the men who did the work.

24After Pharaoh's daughter had come up from the City of David to the palace Solomon had built for her, he constructed the supporting terraces.

25Three times a year Solomon sacrificed burnt offerings and fellowship offerings*h* on the altar he had built for the LORD, burning incense before the LORD along with them, and so fulfilled the temple obligations.

26King Solomon also built ships at Ezion Geber, which is near Elath in Edom, on the shore of the Red Sea.*i* 27And Hiram sent his men—sailors who knew the sea—to serve in the fleet with Solomon's men. 28They sailed to Ophir and brought back 420 talents*j* of gold, which they delivered to King Solomon.

---

a 6 The Hebrew is plural.   *b* 13 *Cabul* sounds like the Hebrew for *good-for-nothing.*   *c* 14 That is, about 4 1/2 tons (about 4 metric tons)   *d* 15 Or *the Millo;* also in verse 24   *e* 18 The Hebrew may also be read *Tamar.*   *f* 19 Or *charioteers*   *g* 21 The Hebrew term refers to the irrevocable giving over of things or persons to the LORD, often by totally destroying them.   *h* 25 Traditionally *peace offerings* *i* 26 Hebrew *Yam Suph;* that is, Sea of Reeds   *j* 28 That is, about 16 tons (about 14.5 metric tons)

The Queen of Sheba Visits Solomon

10 When the queen of Sheba heard about the fame of Solomon and his relation to the name of the LORD, she came to test him with hard questions. ²Arriving at Jerusalem with a very great caravan—with camels carrying spices, large quantities of gold, and precious stones—she came to Solomon and talked with him about all that she had on her mind. ³Solomon answered all her questions; nothing was too hard for the king to explain to her. ⁴When the queen of Sheba saw all the wisdom of Solomon and the palace he had built, ⁵the food on his table, the seating of his officials, the attending servants in their robes, his cupbearers, and the burnt offerings he made at*ᵃ* the temple of the LORD, she was overwhelmed.

⁶She said to the king, "The report I heard in my own country about your achievements and your wisdom is true. ⁷But I did not believe these things until I came and saw with my own eyes. Indeed, not even half was told me; in wisdom and wealth you have far exceeded the report I heard. ⁸How happy your men must be! How happy your officials, who continually stand before you and hear your wisdom! ⁹Praise be to the LORD your God, who has delighted in you and placed you on the throne of Israel. Because of the LORD's eternal love for

---

ᵃ 5 Or the ascent by which he went up to

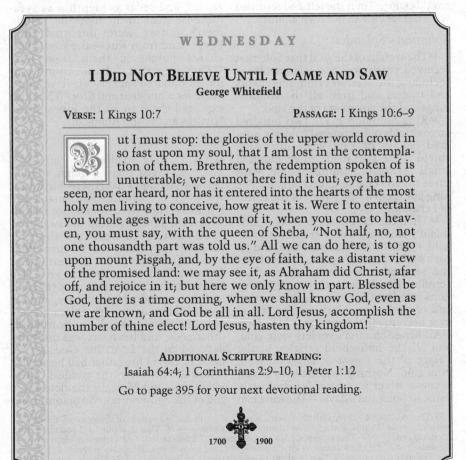

WEDNESDAY

I DID NOT BELIEVE UNTIL I CAME AND SAW
George Whitefield

VERSE: 1 Kings 10:7   **PASSAGE:** 1 Kings 10:6–9

ut I must stop: the glories of the upper world crowd in so fast upon my soul, that I am lost in the contemplation of them. Brethren, the redemption spoken of is unutterable; we cannot here find it out; eye hath not seen, nor ear heard, nor has it entered into the hearts of the most holy men living to conceive, how great it is. Were I to entertain you whole ages with an account of it, when you come to heaven, you must say, with the queen of Sheba, "Not half, no, not one thousandth part was told us." All we can do here, is to go upon mount Pisgah, and, by the eye of faith, take a distant view of the promised land: we may see it, as Abraham did Christ, afar off, and rejoice in it; but here we only know in part. Blessed be God, there is a time coming, when we shall know God, even as we are known, and God be all in all. Lord Jesus, accomplish the number of thine elect! Lord Jesus, hasten thy kingdom!

ADDITIONAL SCRIPTURE READING:
Isaiah 64:4; 1 Corinthians 2:9–10; 1 Peter 1:12

Go to page 395 for your next devotional reading.

1700   1900

Israel, he has made you king, to maintain justice and righteousness."

¹⁰And she gave the king 120 talents*ᵃ* of gold, large quantities of spices, and precious stones. Never again were so many spices brought in as those the queen of Sheba gave to King Solomon.

¹¹(Hiram's ships brought gold from Ophir; and from there they brought great cargoes of almugwood*ᵇ* and precious stones. ¹²The king used the almugwood to make supports for the temple of the LORD and for the royal palace, and to make harps and lyres for the musicians. So much almugwood has never been imported or seen since that day.)

¹³King Solomon gave the queen of Sheba all she desired and asked for, besides what he had given her out of his royal bounty. Then she left and returned with her retinue to her own country.

Solomon's Splendor

¹⁴The weight of the gold that Solomon received yearly was 666 talents,*ᶜ* ¹⁵not including the revenues from merchants and traders and from all the Arabian kings and the governors of the land.

¹⁶King Solomon made two hundred large shields of hammered gold; six hundred bekas*ᵈ* of gold went into each shield. ¹⁷He also made three hundred small shields of hammered gold, with three minas*ᵉ* of gold in each shield. The king put them in the Palace of the Forest of Lebanon.

¹⁸Then the king made a great throne inlaid with ivory and overlaid with fine gold. ¹⁹The throne had six steps, and its back had a rounded top. On both sides of the seat were armrests, with a lion standing beside each of them. ²⁰Twelve lions stood on the six steps, one at either end of each step. Nothing like it had ever been made for any other kingdom. ²¹All King Solomon's goblets were gold, and all the household articles in the Palace of the Forest of Lebanon were pure gold. Nothing was made of silver, because silver was considered of little value in Solomon's days. ²²The king had a fleet of trading ships*ᶠ* at sea along with the ships of Hiram. Once every three years it returned, carrying gold, silver and ivory, and apes and baboons.

²³King Solomon was greater in riches and wisdom than all the other kings of the earth. ²⁴The whole world sought audience with Solomon to hear the wisdom God had put in his heart. ²⁵Year after year, everyone who came brought a gift—articles of silver and gold, robes, weapons and spices, and horses and mules.

²⁶Solomon accumulated chariots and horses; he had fourteen hundred chariots and twelve thousand horses,*ᵍ* which he kept in the chariot cities and also with him in Jerusalem. ²⁷The king made silver as common in Jerusalem as stones, and cedar as plentiful as sycamore-fig trees in the foothills. ²⁸Solomon's horses were imported from Egypt*ʰ* and from Kue*ⁱ*—the royal merchants purchased them from Kue. ²⁹They imported a chariot from Egypt for six hundred shekels*ʲ* of silver, and a horse for a hundred and fifty.*ᵏ* They also exported them to all the kings of the Hittites and of the Arameans.

Solomon's Wives

11 King Solomon, however, loved many foreign women besides Pharaoh's daughter—Moabites, Ammonites, Edomites, Sidonians and Hittites. ²They were from nations about which the LORD had told the Israelites, "You must not intermarry with them, because they will surely turn your hearts after their gods." Nevertheless, Solomon held fast to them in love. ³He had seven hundred wives of royal birth and three hundred concubines, and his wives led him astray. ⁴As Solomon grew old, his wives turned his heart after other gods, and his heart was not fully devoted to the LORD his God, as the heart of David his father had been. ⁵He followed Ashtoreth the goddess of the Sidonians, and Molech*ˡ* the detestable god of the Ammonites. ⁶So Solomon did

---

ᵃ 10 That is, about 4 1/2 tons (about 4 metric tons)
ᵇ 11 Probably a variant of *algumwood*; also in verse 12   *ᶜ 14* That is, about 25 tons (about 23 metric tons)   *ᵈ 16* That is, about 7 1/2 pounds (about 3.5 kilograms)   *ᵉ 17* That is, about 3 3/4 pounds (about 1.7 kilograms)   *ᶠ 22* Hebrew *of ships of Tarshish*   *ᵍ 26* Or *charioteers*   *ʰ 28* Or possibly *Muzur,* a region in Cilicia; also in verse 29   *ⁱ 28* Probably *Cilicia*   *ʲ 29* That is, about 15 pounds (about 7 kilograms)   *ᵏ 29* That is, about 3 3/4 pounds (about 1.7 kilograms)   *ˡ 5* Hebrew *Milcom*; also in verse 33

evil in the eyes of the LORD; he did not follow the LORD completely, as David his father had done.

⁷On a hill east of Jerusalem, Solomon built a high place for Chemosh the detestable god of Moab, and for Molech the detestable god of the Ammonites. ⁸He did the same for all his foreign wives, who burned incense and offered sacrifices to their gods.

⁹The LORD became angry with Solomon because his heart had turned away from the LORD, the God of Israel, who had appeared to him twice. ¹⁰Although he had forbidden Solomon to follow other gods, Solomon did not keep the LORD's command. ¹¹So the LORD said to Solomon, "Since this is your attitude and you have not kept my covenant and my decrees, which I commanded you, I will most certainly tear the kingdom away from you and give it to one of your subordinates. ¹²Nevertheless, for the sake of David your father, I will not do it during your lifetime. I will tear it out of the hand of your son. ¹³Yet I will not tear the whole kingdom from him, but will give him one tribe for the sake of David my servant and for the sake of Jerusalem, which I have chosen."

Solomon's Adversaries

¹⁴Then the LORD raised up against Solomon an adversary, Hadad the Edomite, from the royal line of Edom. ¹⁵Earlier when David was fighting with Edom, Joab the commander of the army, who had gone up to bury the dead, had struck down all the men in Edom. ¹⁶Joab and all the Israelites stayed there for six months, until they had destroyed all the men in Edom. ¹⁷But Hadad, still only a boy, fled to Egypt with some Edomite officials who had served his father. ¹⁸They set out from Midian and went to Paran. Then taking men from Paran with them, they went to Egypt, to Pharaoh king of Egypt, who gave Hadad a house and land and provided him with food.

¹⁹Pharaoh was so pleased with Hadad that he gave him a sister of his own wife, Queen Tahpenes, in marriage. ²⁰The sister of Tahpenes bore him a son named Genubath, whom Tahpenes brought up in the royal palace. There Genubath lived with Pharaoh's own children.

²¹While he was in Egypt, Hadad heard that David rested with his fathers and that Joab the commander of the army was also dead. Then Hadad said to Pharaoh, "Let me go, that I may return to my own country."

²²"What have you lacked here that you want to go back to your own country?" Pharaoh asked.

"Nothing," Hadad replied, "but do let me go!"

²³And God raised up against Solomon another adversary, Rezon son of Eliada, who had fled from his master, Hadadezer king of Zobah. ²⁴He gathered men around him and became the leader of a band of rebels when David destroyed the forces[a] ⌊of Zobah⌋; the rebels went to Damascus, where they settled and took control. ²⁵Rezon was Israel's adversary as long as Solomon lived, adding to the trouble caused by Hadad. So Rezon ruled in Aram and was hostile toward Israel.

Jeroboam Rebels Against Solomon

²⁶Also, Jeroboam son of Nebat rebelled against the king. He was one of Solomon's officials, an Ephraimite from Zeredah, and his mother was a widow named Zeruah.

²⁷Here is the account of how he rebelled against the king: Solomon had built the supporting terraces[b] and had filled in the gap in the wall of the city of David his father. ²⁸Now Jeroboam was a man of standing, and when Solomon saw how well the young man did his work, he put him in charge of the whole labor force of the house of Joseph.

²⁹About that time Jeroboam was going out of Jerusalem, and Ahijah the prophet of Shiloh met him on the way, wearing a new cloak. The two of them were alone out in the country, ³⁰and Ahijah took hold of the new cloak he was wearing and tore it into twelve pieces. ³¹Then he said to Jeroboam, "Take ten pieces for yourself, for this is what the LORD, the God of Israel, says: 'See, I am going to tear the kingdom out of Solomon's hand and give you ten tribes. ³²But for the sake of my servant David and the city of Jerusalem, which I have chosen out of

---

a 24 Hebrew *destroyed them*   *b 27* Or *the Millo*

all the tribes of Israel, he will have one tribe. 33I will do this because they have*a* forsaken me and worshiped Ashtoreth the goddess of the Sidonians, Chemosh the god of the Moabites, and Molech the god of the Ammonites, and have not walked in my ways, nor done what is right in my eyes, nor kept my statutes and laws as David, Solomon's father, did.

34" 'But I will not take the whole kingdom out of Solomon's hand; I have made him ruler all the days of his life for the sake of David my servant, whom I chose and who observed my commands and statutes. 35I will take the kingdom from his son's hands and give you ten tribes. 36I will give one tribe to his son so that David my servant may always have a lamp before me in Jerusalem, the city where I chose to put my Name. 37However, as for you, I will take you, and you will rule over all that your heart desires; you will be king over Israel. 38If you do whatever I command you and walk in my ways and do what is right in my eyes by keeping my statutes and commands, as David my servant did, I will be with you. I will build you a dynasty as enduring as the one I built for David and will give Israel to you. 39I will humble David's descendants because of this, but not forever.' "

40Solomon tried to kill Jeroboam, but Jeroboam fled to Egypt, to Shishak the king, and stayed there until Solomon's death.

Solomon's Death

41As for the other events of Solomon's reign—all he did and the wisdom he displayed—are they not written in the book of the annals of Solomon? 42Solomon reigned in Jerusalem over all Israel forty years. 43Then he rested with his fathers and was buried in the city of David his father. And Rehoboam his son succeeded him as king.

Israel Rebels Against Rehoboam

12 Rehoboam went to Shechem, for all the Israelites had gone there to make him king. 2When Jeroboam son of Nebat heard this (he was still in Egypt, where he had fled from King Solomon), he returned from*b* Egypt. 3So

they sent for Jeroboam, and he and the whole assembly of Israel went to Rehoboam and said to him: 4"Your father put a heavy yoke on us, but now lighten the harsh labor and the heavy yoke he put on us, and we will serve you."

5Rehoboam answered, "Go away for three days and then come back to me." So the people went away.

6Then King Rehoboam consulted the elders who had served his father Solomon during his lifetime. "How would you advise me to answer these people?" he asked.

7They replied, "If today you will be a servant to these people and serve them and give them a favorable answer, they will always be your servants."

8But Rehoboam rejected the advice the elders gave him and consulted the young men who had grown up with him and were serving him. 9He asked them, "What is your advice? How should we answer these people who say to me, 'Lighten the yoke your father put on us'?"

10The young men who had grown up with him replied, "Tell these people who have said to you, 'Your father put a heavy yoke on us, but make our yoke lighter'—tell them, 'My little finger is thicker than my father's waist. 11My father laid on you a heavy yoke; I will make it even heavier. My father scourged you with whips; I will scourge you with scorpions.' "

12Three days later Jeroboam and all the people returned to Rehoboam, as the king had said, "Come back to me in three days." 13The king answered the people harshly. Rejecting the advice given him by the elders, 14he followed the advice of the young men and said, "My father made your yoke heavy; I will make it even heavier. My father scourged you with whips; I will scourge you with scorpions." 15So the king did not listen to the people, for this turn of events was from the LORD, to fulfill the word the LORD had spoken to Jeroboam son of Nebat through Ahijah the Shilonite.

16When all Israel saw that the king refused to listen to them, they answered the king:

a 33 Hebrew; Septuagint, Vulgate and Syriac because he has   *b 2 Or he remained in*

"What share do we have in David,
  what part in Jesse's son?
To your tents, O Israel!
  Look after your own house,
    O David!"

So the Israelites went home. ¹⁷But as for the Israelites who were living in the towns of Judah, Rehoboam still ruled over them.

¹⁸King Rehoboam sent out Adoniram,ᵃ who was in charge of forced labor, but all Israel stoned him to death. King Rehoboam, however, managed to get into his chariot and escape to Jerusalem. ¹⁹So Israel has been in rebellion against the house of David to this day.

²⁰When all the Israelites heard that Jeroboam had returned, they sent and called him to the assembly and made him king over all Israel. Only the tribe of Judah remained loyal to the house of David.

²¹When Rehoboam arrived in Jerusalem, he mustered the whole house of Judah and the tribe of Benjamin—a hundred and eighty thousand fighting men—to make war against the house of Israel and to regain the kingdom for Rehoboam son of Solomon.

²²But this word of God came to Shemaiah the man of God: ²³"Say to Rehoboam son of Solomon king of Judah, to the whole house of Judah and Benjamin, and to the rest of the people, ²⁴'This is what the LORD says: Do not go up to fight against your brothers, the Israelites. Go home, every one of you, for this is my doing.'" So they obeyed the word of the LORD and went home again, as the LORD had ordered.

Golden Calves at Bethel and Dan

²⁵Then Jeroboam fortified Shechem in the hill country of Ephraim and lived there. From there he went out and built up Peniel.ᵇ

²⁶Jeroboam thought to himself, "The kingdom will now likely revert to the house of David. ²⁷If these people go up to offer sacrifices at the temple of the LORD in Jerusalem, they will again give their allegiance to their lord, Rehoboam

king of Judah. They will kill me and return to King Rehoboam."

²⁸After seeking advice, the king made two golden calves. He said to the people, "It is too much for you to go up to Jerusalem. Here are your gods, O Israel, who brought you up out of Egypt." ²⁹One he set up in Bethel, and the other in Dan. ³⁰And this thing became a sin; the people went even as far as Dan to worship the one there.

³¹Jeroboam built shrines on high places and appointed priests from all sorts of people, even though they were not Levites. ³²He instituted a festival on the fifteenth day of the eighth month, like the festival held in Judah, and offered sacrifices on the altar. This he did in Bethel, sacrificing to the calves he had made. And at Bethel he also installed priests at the high places he had made. ³³On the fifteenth day of the eighth month, a month of his own choosing, he offered sacrifices on the altar he had built at Bethel. So he instituted the festival for the Israelites and went up to the altar to make offerings.

The Man of God From Judah

13 By the word of the LORD a man of God came from Judah to Bethel, as Jeroboam was standing by the altar to make an offering. ²He cried out against the altar by the word of the LORD: "O altar, altar! This is what the LORD says: 'A son named Josiah will be born to the house of David. On you he will sacrifice the priests of the high places who now make offerings here, and human bones will be burned on you.'" ³That same day the man of God gave a sign: "This is the sign the LORD has declared: The altar will be split apart and the ashes on it will be poured out."

⁴When King Jeroboam heard what the man of God cried out against the altar at Bethel, he stretched out his hand from the altar and said, "Seize him!" But the hand he stretched out toward the man shriveled up, so that he could not pull it back. ⁵Also, the altar was split apart and its ashes poured out according to the sign given by the man of God by the word of the LORD.

ᵃ 18 Some Septuagint manuscripts and Syriac (see also 1 Kings 4:6 and 5:14); Hebrew Adoram
ᵇ 25 Hebrew Penuel, a variant of Peniel

⁶Then the king said to the man of God, "Intercede with the LORD your God and pray for me that my hand may be restored." So the man of God interceded with the LORD, and the king's hand was restored and became as it was before.

WE OUGHT TO ACT WITH GOD IN THE GREATEST SIMPLICITY, SPEAKING TO HIM FRANKLY AND PLAINLY, AND IMPLORING HIS ASSISTANCE IN OUR AFFAIRS, JUST AS THEY HAPPEN.

—*Brother Lawrence*

---

⁷The king said to the man of God, "Come home with me and have something to eat, and I will give you a gift."

⁸But the man of God answered the king, "Even if you were to give me half your possessions, I would not go with you, nor would I eat bread or drink water here. ⁹For I was commanded by the word of the LORD: 'You must not eat bread or drink water or return by the way you came.' " ¹⁰So he took another road and did not return by the way he had come to Bethel.

¹¹Now there was a certain old prophet living in Bethel, whose sons came and told him all that the man of God had done there that day. They also told their father what he had said to the king. ¹²Their father asked them, "Which way did he go?" And his sons showed him which road the man of God from Judah had taken. ¹³So he said to his sons, "Saddle the donkey for me." And when they had saddled the donkey for him, he mounted it ¹⁴and rode after the man of God. He found him sitting under an oak tree and asked, "Are you the man of God who came from Judah?"

"I am," he replied.

¹⁵So the prophet said to him, "Come home with me and eat."

¹⁶The man of God said, "I cannot turn back and go with you, nor can I eat bread or drink water with you in this place. ¹⁷I have been told by the word of the LORD: 'You must not eat bread or drink water there or return by the way you came.' "

¹⁸The old prophet answered, "I too am a prophet, as you are. And an angel said to me by the word of the LORD: 'Bring him back with you to your house so that

he may eat bread and drink water.' " (But he was lying to him.) ¹⁹So the man of God returned with him and ate and drank in his house.

²⁰While they were sitting at the table, the word of the LORD came to the old prophet who had brought him back. ²¹He cried out to the man of God who had come from Judah, "This is what the LORD says: 'You have defied the word of the LORD and have not kept the command the LORD your God gave you. ²²You came back and ate bread and drank water in the place where he told you not to eat or drink. Therefore your body will not be buried in the tomb of your fathers.' "

²³When the man of God had finished eating and drinking, the prophet who had brought him back saddled his donkey for him. ²⁴As he went on his way, a lion met him on the road and killed him, and his body was thrown down on the road, with both the donkey and the lion standing beside it. ²⁵Some people who passed by saw the body thrown down there, with the lion standing beside the body, and they went and reported it in the city where the old prophet lived.

²⁶When the prophet who had brought him back from his journey heard of it, he said, "It is the man of God who defied the word of the LORD. The LORD has given him over to the lion, which has mauled him and killed him, as the word of the LORD had warned him."

²⁷The prophet said to his sons, "Saddle the donkey for me," and they did so. ²⁸Then he went out and found the body thrown down on the road, with the donkey and the lion standing beside it. The lion had neither eaten the body nor mauled the donkey. ²⁹So the prophet picked up the body of the man of God, laid it on the donkey, and brought it back to his own city to mourn for him and bury him. ³⁰Then he laid the body in his own tomb, and they mourned over him and said, "Oh, my brother!"

³¹After burying him, he said to his sons, "When I die, bury me in the grave where the man of God is buried; lay my bones beside his bones. ³²For the message he declared by the word of the LORD against the altar in Bethel and against all the shrines on the high places in the towns of Samaria will certainly come true."

³³Even after this, Jeroboam did not change his evil ways, but once more appointed priests for the high places from all sorts of people. Anyone who wanted to become a priest he consecrated for the high places. ³⁴This was the sin of the house of Jeroboam that led to its downfall and to its destruction from the face of the earth.

Ahijah's Prophecy Against Jeroboam

14 At that time Abijah son of Jeroboam became ill, ²and Jeroboam said to his wife, "Go, disguise yourself, so you won't be recognized as the wife of Jeroboam. Then go to Shiloh. Ahijah the prophet is there—the one who told me I would be king over this people. ³Take ten loaves of bread with you, some cakes and a jar of honey, and go to him. He will tell you what will happen to the boy." ⁴So Jeroboam's wife did what he said and went to Ahijah's house in Shiloh.

Now Ahijah could not see; his sight was gone because of his age. ⁵But the LORD had told Ahijah, "Jeroboam's wife is coming to ask you about her son, for he is ill, and you are to give her such and such an answer. When she arrives, she will pretend to be someone else."

⁶So when Ahijah heard the sound of her footsteps at the door, he said, "Come in, wife of Jeroboam. Why this pretense? I have been sent to you with bad news. ⁷Go, tell Jeroboam that this is what the LORD, the God of Israel, says: 'I raised you up from among the people and made you a leader over my people Israel. ⁸I tore the kingdom away from the house of David and gave it to you, but you have not been like my servant David, who kept my commands and followed me with all his heart, doing only what was right in my eyes. ⁹You have done more evil than all who lived before you. You have made for yourself other gods, idols made of metal; you have provoked me to anger and thrust me behind your back.

¹⁰"'Because of this, I am going to bring disaster on the house of Jeroboam. I will cut off from Jeroboam every last male in Israel—slave or free. I will burn up the house of Jeroboam as one burns dung, until it is all gone. ¹¹Dogs will eat those belonging to Jeroboam who die in the city, and the birds of the air will feed on those who die in the country. The LORD has spoken!'

¹²"As for you, go back home. When you set foot in your city, the boy will die. ¹³All Israel will mourn for him and bury him. He is the only one belonging to Jeroboam who will be buried, because he is the only one in the house of Jeroboam in whom the LORD, the God of Israel, has found anything good.

¹⁴"The LORD will raise up for himself a king over Israel who will cut off the family of Jeroboam. This is the day! What? Yes, even now.^a ¹⁵And the LORD will strike Israel, so that it will be like a reed swaying in the water. He will uproot Israel from this good land that he gave to their forefathers and scatter them beyond the River,^b because they provoked the LORD to anger by making Asherah poles.^c ¹⁶And he will give Israel up because of the sins Jeroboam has committed and has caused Israel to commit."

¹⁷Then Jeroboam's wife got up and left and went to Tirzah. As soon as she stepped over the threshold of the house, the boy died. ¹⁸They buried him, and all Israel mourned for him, as the LORD had said through his servant the prophet Ahijah.

¹⁹The other events of Jeroboam's reign, his wars and how he ruled, are written in the book of the annals of the kings of Israel. ²⁰He reigned for twenty-two years and then rested with his fathers. And Nadab his son succeeded him as king.

Rehoboam King of Judah

²¹Rehoboam son of Solomon was king in Judah. He was forty-one years old when he became king, and he reigned seventeen years in Jerusalem, the city the LORD had chosen out of all the tribes of Israel in which to put his Name. His mother's name was Naamah; she was an Ammonite.

²²Judah did evil in the eyes of the LORD. By the sins they committed they stirred up his jealous anger more than

^a 14 The meaning of the Hebrew for this sentence is uncertain.   ^b 15 That is, the Euphrates
^c 15 That is, symbols of the goddess Asherah; here and elsewhere in 1 Kings

their fathers had done. 23They also set up for themselves high places, sacred stones and Asherah poles on every high hill and under every spreading tree. 24There were even male shrine prostitutes in the land; the people engaged in all the detestable practices of the nations the LORD had driven out before the Israelites.

25In the fifth year of King Rehoboam, Shishak king of Egypt attacked Jerusalem. 26He carried off the treasures of the temple of the LORD and the treasures of the royal palace. He took everything, including all the gold shields Solomon had made. 27So King Rehoboam made bronze shields to replace them and assigned these to the commanders of the guard on duty at the entrance to the royal palace. 28Whenever the king went to the LORD's temple, the guards bore the shields, and afterward they returned them to the guardroom.

29As for the other events of Rehoboam's reign, and all he did, are they not written in the book of the annals of the kings of Judah? 30There was continual warfare between Rehoboam and Jeroboam. 31And Rehoboam rested with his fathers and was buried with them in the City of David. His mother's name was Naamah; she was an Ammonite. And Abijah*a* his son succeeded him as king.

Abijah King of Judah

15 In the eighteenth year of the reign of Jeroboam son of Nebat, Abijah*b* became king of Judah, 2and he reigned in Jerusalem three years. His mother's name was Maacah daughter of Abishalom.*c*

3He committed all the sins his father had done before him; his heart was not fully devoted to the LORD his God, as the heart of David his forefather had been. 4Nevertheless, for David's sake the LORD his God gave him a lamp in Jerusalem by raising up a son to succeed him and by making Jerusalem strong. 5For David had done what was right in the eyes of the LORD and had not failed to keep any of the LORD's commands all

the days of his life—except in the case of Uriah the Hittite.

6There was war between Rehoboam*d* and Jeroboam throughout ⌊Abijah's⌋ lifetime. 7As for the other events of Abijah's reign, and all he did, are they not written in the book of the annals of the kings of Judah? There was war between Abijah and Jeroboam. 8And Abijah rested with his fathers and was buried in the City of David. And Asa his son succeeded him as king.

Asa King of Judah

9In the twentieth year of Jeroboam king of Israel, Asa became king of Judah, 10and he reigned in Jerusalem forty-one years. His grandmother's name was Maacah daughter of Abishalom.

11Asa did what was right in the eyes of the LORD, as his father David had done. 12He expelled the male shrine prostitutes from the land and got rid of all the idols his fathers had made. 13He even deposed his grandmother Maacah from her position as queen mother, because she had made a repulsive Asherah pole. Asa cut the pole down and burned it in the Kidron Valley. 14Although he did not remove the high places, Asa's heart was fully committed to the LORD all his life. 15He brought into the temple of the LORD the silver and gold and the articles that he and his father had dedicated.

16There was war between Asa and Baasha king of Israel throughout their reigns. 17Baasha king of Israel went up against Judah and fortified Ramah to prevent anyone from leaving or entering the territory of Asa king of Judah.

18Asa then took all the silver and gold that was left in the treasuries of the LORD's temple and of his own palace. He entrusted it to his officials and sent them to Ben-Hadad son of Tabrimmon, the son of Hezion, the king of Aram, who was ruling in Damascus. 19"Let there be a treaty between me and you," he said, "as there was between my father and your father. See, I am sending you a gift of silver and gold. Now break

---

a 31 Some Hebrew manuscripts and Septuagint (see also 2 Chron. 12:16); most Hebrew manuscripts *Abijam*   *b 1* Some Hebrew manuscripts and Septuagint (see also 2 Chron. 12:16); most Hebrew manuscripts *Abijam*; also in verses 7 and 8   *c 2* A variant of *Absalom*; also in verse 10   *d 6* Most Hebrew manuscripts; some Hebrew manuscripts and Syriac *Abijam* (that is, Abijah)

your treaty with Baasha king of Israel so he will withdraw from me."

20Ben-Hadad agreed with King Asa and sent the commanders of his forces against the towns of Israel. He conquered Ijon, Dan, Abel Beth Maacah and all Kinnereth in addition to Naphtali. 21When Baasha heard this, he stopped building Ramah and withdrew to Tirzah. 22Then King Asa issued an order to all Judah—no one was exempt—and they carried away from Ramah the stones and timber Baasha had been using there. With them King Asa built up Geba in Benjamin, and also Mizpah.

23As for all the other events of Asa's reign, all his achievements, all he did and the cities he built, are they not written in the book of the annals of the kings of Judah? In his old age, however, his feet became diseased. 24Then Asa rested with his fathers and was buried with them in the city of his father David. And Jehoshaphat his son succeeded him as king.

Nadab King of Israel

25Nadab son of Jeroboam became king of Israel in the second year of Asa king of Judah, and he reigned over Israel two years. 26He did evil in the eyes of the LORD, walking in the ways of his father and in his sin, which he had caused Israel to commit.

27Baasha son of Ahijah of the house of Issachar plotted against him, and he struck him down at Gibbethon, a Philistine town, while Nadab and all Israel were besieging it. 28Baasha killed Nadab in the third year of Asa king of Judah and succeeded him as king.

29As soon as he began to reign, he killed Jeroboam's whole family. He did not leave Jeroboam anyone that breathed, but destroyed them all, according to the word of the LORD given through his servant Ahijah the Shilonite— 30because of the sins Jeroboam had committed and had caused Israel to commit, and because he provoked the LORD, the God of Israel, to anger. 31As for the other events of Nadab's reign, and all he did, are they not written in the book of the annals of the kings of Israel? 32There was war between Asa

and Baasha king of Israel throughout their reigns.

Baasha King of Israel

33In the third year of Asa king of Judah, Baasha son of Ahijah became king of all Israel in Tirzah, and he reigned twenty-four years. 34He did evil in the eyes of the LORD, walking in the ways of Jeroboam and in his sin, which he had caused Israel to commit.

16 Then the word of the LORD came to Jehu son of Hanani against Baasha: 2"I lifted you up from the dust and made you leader of my people Israel, but you walked in the ways of Jeroboam and caused my people Israel to sin and to provoke me to anger by their sins. 3So I am about to consume Baasha and his house, and I will make your house like that of Jeroboam son of Nebat. 4Dogs will eat those belonging to Baasha who die in the city, and the birds of the air will feed on those who die in the country."

5As for the other events of Baasha's reign, what he did and his achievements, are they not written in the book of the annals of the kings of Israel? 6Baasha rested with his fathers and was buried in Tirzah. And Elah his son succeeded him as king.

7Moreover, the word of the LORD came through the prophet Jehu son of Hanani to Baasha and his house, because of all the evil he had done in the eyes of the LORD, provoking him to anger by the things he did, and becoming like the house of Jeroboam—and also because he destroyed it.

Elah King of Israel

8In the twenty-sixth year of Asa king of Judah, Elah son of Baasha became king of Israel, and he reigned in Tirzah two years. 9Zimri, one of his officials, who had command of half his chariots, plotted against him. Elah was in Tirzah at the time, getting drunk in the home of Arza, the man in charge of the palace at Tirzah. 10Zimri came in, struck him down and killed him in the twenty-seventh year of Asa king of Judah. Then he succeeded him as king.

11As soon as he began to reign and was seated on the throne, he killed off

Baasha's whole family. He did not spare a single male, whether relative or friend. ¹²So Zimri destroyed the whole family of Baasha, in accordance with the word of the LORD spoken against Baasha through the prophet Jehu— ¹³because of all the sins Baasha and his son Elah had committed and had caused Israel to commit, so that they provoked the LORD, the God of Israel, to anger by their worthless idols.

¹⁴As for the other events of Elah's reign, and all he did, are they not written in the book of the annals of the kings of Israel?

Zimri King of Israel

¹⁵In the twenty-seventh year of Asa king of Judah, Zimri reigned in Tirzah seven days. The army was encamped near Gibbethon, a Philistine town. ¹⁶When the Israelites in the camp heard that Zimri had plotted against the king and murdered him, they proclaimed Omri, the commander of the army, king over Israel that very day there in the camp. ¹⁷Then Omri and all the Israelites with him withdrew from Gibbethon and laid siege to Tirzah. ¹⁸When Zimri saw that the city was taken, he went into the citadel of the royal palace and set the palace on fire around him. So he died, ¹⁹because of the sins he had committed, doing evil in the eyes of the LORD and walking in the ways of Jeroboam and in the sin he had committed and had caused Israel to commit.

²⁰As for the other events of Zimri's reign, and the rebellion he carried out, are they not written in the book of the annals of the kings of Israel?

Omri King of Israel

²¹Then the people of Israel were split into two factions; half supported Tibni son of Ginath for king, and the other half supported Omri. ²²But Omri's followers proved stronger than those of Tibni son of Ginath. So Tibni died and Omri became king.

²³In the thirty-first year of Asa king of Judah, Omri became king of Israel, and he reigned twelve years, six of them in Tirzah. ²⁴He bought the hill of Samaria from Shemer for two talents[a] of silver and built a city on the hill, calling it Samaria, after Shemer, the name of the former owner of the hill.

²⁵But Omri did evil in the eyes of the LORD and sinned more than all those before him. ²⁶He walked in all the ways of Jeroboam son of Nebat and in his sin, which he had caused Israel to commit, so that they provoked the LORD, the God of Israel, to anger by their worthless idols.

²⁷As for the other events of Omri's reign, what he did and the things he achieved, are they not written in the book of the annals of the kings of Israel? ²⁸Omri rested with his fathers and was buried in Samaria. And Ahab his son succeeded him as king.

Ahab Becomes King of Israel

²⁹In the thirty-eighth year of Asa king of Judah, Ahab son of Omri became king of Israel, and he reigned in Samaria over Israel twenty-two years. ³⁰Ahab son of Omri did more evil in the eyes of the LORD than any of those before him. ³¹He not only considered it trivial to commit the sins of Jeroboam son of Nebat, but he also married Jezebel daughter of Ethbaal king of the Sidonians, and began to serve Baal and worship him. ³²He set up an altar for Baal in the temple of Baal that he built in Samaria. ³³Ahab also made an Asherah pole and did more to provoke the LORD, the God of Israel, to anger than did all the kings of Israel before him.

³⁴In Ahab's time, Hiel of Bethel rebuilt Jericho. He laid its foundations at the cost of his firstborn son Abiram, and he set up its gates at the cost of his youngest son Segub, in accordance with the word of the LORD spoken by Joshua son of Nun.

Elijah Fed by Ravens

17 Now Elijah the Tishbite, from Tishbe[b] in Gilead, said to Ahab, "As the LORD, the God of Israel, lives, whom I serve, there will be neither dew nor rain in the next few years except at my word."

²Then the word of the LORD came to Elijah: ³"Leave here, turn eastward and hide in the Kerith Ravine, east of the Jordan. ⁴You will drink from the brook, and

---

a 24 That is, about 150 pounds (about 70 kilograms)   b 1 Or *Tishbite, of the settlers*

I have ordered the ravens to feed you there."

⁵So he did what the LORD had told him. He went to the Kerith Ravine, east of the Jordan, and stayed there. ⁶The ravens brought him bread and meat in the morning and bread and meat in the evening, and he drank from the brook.

The Widow at Zarephath

⁷Some time later the brook dried up because there had been no rain in the land. ⁸Then the word of the LORD came to him: ⁹"Go at once to Zarephath of Sidon and stay there. I have commanded a widow in that place to supply you with food." ¹⁰So he went to Zarephath. When he came to the town gate, a widow was there gathering sticks. He called to her and asked, "Would you bring me a little water in a jar so I may have a drink?" ¹¹As she was going to get it, he called, "And bring me, please, a piece of bread."

¹²"As surely as the LORD your God lives," she replied, "I don't have any bread—only a handful of flour in a jar and a little oil in a jug. I am gathering a few sticks to take home and make a meal for myself and my son, that we may eat it—and die."

¹³Elijah said to her, "Don't be afraid. Go home and do as you have said. But first make a small cake of bread for me from what you have and bring it to me, and then make something for yourself and your son. ¹⁴For this is what the LORD, the God of Israel, says: 'The jar of flour will not be used up and the jug of oil will not run dry until the day the LORD gives rain on the land.' "

¹⁵She went away and did as Elijah had told her. So there was food every day for Elijah and for the woman and her family. ¹⁶For the jar of flour was not used up and the jug of oil did not run dry, in keeping with the word of the LORD spoken by Elijah.

¹⁷Some time later the son of the woman who owned the house became ill. He grew worse and worse, and finally stopped breathing. ¹⁸She said to Elijah, "What do you have against me, man of God? Did you come to remind me of my sin and kill my son?"

¹⁹"Give me your son," Elijah replied. He took him from her arms, carried him to the upper room where he was staying, and laid him on his bed. ²⁰Then he cried out to the LORD, "O LORD my God, have you brought tragedy also upon this widow I am staying with, by causing her son to die?" ²¹Then he stretched himself out on the boy three times and cried to the LORD, "O LORD my God, let this boy's life return to him!"

²²The LORD heard Elijah's cry, and the boy's life returned to him, and he lived. ²³Elijah picked up the child and carried him down from the room into the house. He gave him to his mother and said, "Look, your son is alive!"

²⁴Then the woman said to Elijah, "Now I know that you are a man of God and that the word of the LORD from your mouth is the truth."

Elijah and Obadiah

18 After a long time, in the third year, the word of the LORD came to Elijah: "Go and present yourself to Ahab, and I will send rain on the land." ²So Elijah went to present himself to Ahab.

Now the famine was severe in Samaria, ³and Ahab had summoned Obadiah, who was in charge of his palace. (Obadiah was a devout believer in the LORD. ⁴While Jezebel was killing off the LORD's prophets, Obadiah had taken a hundred prophets and hidden them in two caves, fifty in each, and had supplied them with food and water.) ⁵Ahab had said to Obadiah, "Go through the land to all the springs and valleys. Maybe we can find some grass to keep the horses and mules alive so we will not have to kill any of our animals." ⁶So they divided the land they were to cover, Ahab going in one direction and Obadiah in another.

⁷As Obadiah was walking along, Elijah met him. Obadiah recognized him, bowed down to the ground, and said, "Is it really you, my lord Elijah?"

⁸"Yes," he replied. "Go tell your master, 'Elijah is here.' "

⁹"What have I done wrong," asked Obadiah, "that you are handing your servant over to Ahab to be put to death? ¹⁰As surely as the LORD your God lives, there is not a nation or kingdom where my master has not sent someone to look for you. And whenever a nation or king-

dom claimed you were not there, he made them swear they could not find you. [11]But now you tell me to go to my master and say, 'Elijah is here.' [12]I don't know where the Spirit of the LORD may carry you when I leave you. If I go and tell Ahab and he doesn't find you, he will kill me. Yet I your servant have worshiped the LORD since my youth. [13]Haven't you heard, my lord, what I did while Jezebel was killing the prophets of the LORD? I hid a hundred of the LORD's prophets in two caves, fifty in each, and supplied them with food and water. [14]And now you tell me to go to my master and say, 'Elijah is here.' He will kill me!"

[15]Elijah said, "As the LORD Almighty lives, whom I serve, I will surely present myself to Ahab today."

Elijah on Mount Carmel

[16]So Obadiah went to meet Ahab and told him, and Ahab went to meet Elijah. [17]When he saw Elijah, he said to him, "Is that you, you troubler of Israel?"

[18]"I have not made trouble for Israel," Elijah replied. "But you and your father's family have. You have abandoned the LORD's commands and have followed the Baals. [19]Now summon the people from all over Israel to meet me on Mount Carmel. And bring the four hundred and fifty prophets of Baal and the four hundred prophets of Asherah, who eat at Jezebel's table."

[20]So Ahab sent word throughout all Israel and assembled the prophets on Mount Carmel. [21]Elijah went before the people and said, "How long will you waver between two opinions? If the LORD is God, follow him; but if Baal is God, follow him."

But the people said nothing. [22]Then Elijah said to them, "I am the only one of the LORD's prophets left, but Baal has four hundred and fifty prophets. [23]Get two bulls for us. Let them choose one for themselves, and let them cut it into pieces and put it on the wood but not set fire to it. I will prepare the other bull and put it on the wood but not set fire to it. [24]Then you call on the name of your god, and I will call on the name of the LORD. The god who answers by fire—he is God."

Then all the people said, "What you say is good."

[25]Elijah said to the prophets of Baal, "Choose one of the bulls and prepare it first, since there are so many of you. Call on the name of your god, but do not light the fire." [26]So they took the bull given them and prepared it.

Then they called on the name of Baal from morning till noon. "O Baal, answer us!" they shouted. But there was no response; no one answered. And they danced around the altar they had made.

[27]At noon Elijah began to taunt them. "Shout louder!" he said. "Surely he is a god! Perhaps he is deep in thought, or busy, or traveling. Maybe he is sleeping and must be awakened." [28]So they shouted louder and slashed themselves with swords and spears, as was their custom, until their blood flowed. [29]Midday passed, and they continued their frantic prophesying until the time for the evening sacrifice. But there was no response, no one answered, no one paid attention.

[30]Then Elijah said to all the people, "Come here to me." They came to him, and he repaired the altar of the LORD, which was in ruins. [31]Elijah took twelve stones, one for each of the tribes descended from Jacob, to whom the word of the LORD had come, saying, "Your name shall be Israel." [32]With the stones he built an altar in the name of the LORD, and he dug a trench around it large enough to hold two seahs[a] of seed. [33]He arranged the wood, cut the bull into pieces and laid it on the wood. Then he said to them, "Fill four large jars with water and pour it on the offering and on the wood."

[34]"Do it again," he said, and they did it again.

"Do it a third time," he ordered, and they did it the third time. [35]The water ran down around the altar and even filled the trench.

[36]At the time of sacrifice, the prophet Elijah stepped forward and prayed: "O LORD, God of Abraham, Isaac and Israel, let it be known today that you are God in Israel and that I am your servant and have done all these things at your command. [37]Answer me, O LORD,

---

[a] 32 That is, probably about 13 quarts (about 15 liters)

answer me, so these people will know that you, O LORD, are God, and that you are turning their hearts back again."

38Then the fire of the LORD fell and burned up the sacrifice, the wood, the stones and the soil, and also licked up the water in the trench.

39When all the people saw this, they fell prostrate and cried, "The LORD—he is God! The LORD—he is God!"

40Then Elijah commanded them, "Seize the prophets of Baal. Don't let anyone get away!" They seized them, and Elijah had them brought down to the Kishon Valley and slaughtered there.

41And Elijah said to Ahab, "Go, eat

THURSDAY

THE COURAGE OF OBEDIENCE
James Hudson Taylor

VERSE: 1 Kings 18:24   PASSAGE: 1 Kings 18:19–39

 ant of trust is at the root of almost all our sins and all our weaknesses; and how shall we escape it but by looking to him and observing his faithfulness? The man who holds God's faithfulness will not be foolhardy or reckless, but he will be ready for every emergency. The man who holds God's faithfulness will dare to obey him, however impolitic it may appear. Abraham held God's faithfulness and offered up Isaac, "accounting that God was able to raise him . . . from the dead" (Hebrews 11:19, KJV). Moses held God's faithfulness and led the millions of Israel into the waste, howling wilderness. "And what shall I more say? for the time would fail me to tell" of those who, holding God's faithfulness, had faith, and by it "subdued kingdoms, wrought righteousness, obtained promises . . . out of weakness were made strong, waxed valiant in fight, turned to flight the armies of the aliens" (11:33–34).

Satan, too, has his creed: Doubt God's faithfulness. "Hath God said? Are you not mistaken as to his commands? He could not really mean just that. You take an extreme view, give too literal a meaning to the words." How constantly, and alas, how successfully are such arguments used to prevent wholehearted trust in God, wholehearted consecration to God! How many estimate difficulties in the light of their own resources, and thus attempt little and often fail in the little they attempt! All God's giants have been weak men, who did great things for God because they reckoned on his being with them.

ADDITIONAL SCRIPTURE READING:
Genesis 3:1–5; Matthew 4:1–10; Mark 11:22–24

Go to page 406 for your next devotional reading.

1700   1900

and drink, for there is the sound of a heavy rain." ⁴²So Ahab went off to eat and drink, but Elijah climbed to the top of Carmel, bent down to the ground and put his face between his knees.

⁴³"Go and look toward the sea," he told his servant. And he went up and looked.

"There is nothing there," he said.

Seven times Elijah said, "Go back."

⁴⁴The seventh time the servant reported, "A cloud as small as a man's hand is rising from the sea."

So Elijah said, "Go and tell Ahab, 'Hitch up your chariot and go down before the rain stops you.' "

⁴⁵Meanwhile, the sky grew black with clouds, the wind rose, a heavy rain came on and Ahab rode off to Jezreel. ⁴⁶The power of the LORD came upon Elijah and, tucking his cloak into his belt, he ran ahead of Ahab all the way to Jezreel.

Elijah Flees to Horeb

19 Now Ahab told Jezebel everything Elijah had done and how he had killed all the prophets with the sword. ²So Jezebel sent a messenger to Elijah to say, "May the gods deal with me, be it ever so severely, if by this time tomorrow I do not make your life like that of one of them."

³Elijah was afraid*ᵃ* and ran for his life. When he came to Beersheba in Judah, he left his servant there, ⁴while he himself went a day's journey into the desert. He came to a broom tree, sat down under it and prayed that he might die. "I have had enough, LORD," he said. "Take my life; I am no better than my ancestors."

⁵Then he lay down under the tree and fell asleep.

All at once an angel touched him and said, "Get up and eat." ⁶He looked around, and there by his head was a cake of bread baked over hot coals, and a jar of water. He ate and drank and then lay down again.

⁷The angel of the LORD came back a second time and touched him and said, "Get up and eat, for the journey is too much for you." ⁸So he got up and ate and drank. Strengthened by that food, he traveled forty days and forty nights until he reached Horeb, the mountain of God. ⁹There he went into a cave and spent the night.

The LORD Appears to Elijah

And the word of the LORD came to him: "What are you doing here, Elijah?"

¹⁰He replied, "I have been very zealous for the LORD God Almighty. The Israelites have rejected your covenant, broken down your altars, and put your prophets to death with the sword. I am the only one left, and now they are trying to kill me too."

¹¹The LORD said, "Go out and stand on the mountain in the presence of the LORD, for the LORD is about to pass by."

Then a great and powerful wind tore the mountains apart and shattered the rocks before the LORD, but the LORD was not in the wind. After the wind there was an earthquake, but the LORD was not in the earthquake. ¹²After the earthquake came a fire, but the LORD was not in the fire. And after the fire came a gentle whisper. ¹³When Elijah heard it, he pulled his cloak over his face and went out and stood at the mouth of the cave.

Then a voice said to him, "What are you doing here, Elijah?"

¹⁴He replied, "I have been very zealous for the LORD God Almighty. The Israelites have rejected your covenant, broken down your altars, and put your prophets to death with the sword. I am the only one left, and now they are trying to kill me too."

¹⁵The LORD said to him, "Go back the way you came, and go to the Desert of Damascus. When you get there, anoint Hazael king over Aram. ¹⁶Also, anoint Jehu son of Nimshi king over Israel, and anoint Elisha son of Shaphat from Abel Meholah to succeed you as prophet. ¹⁷Jehu will put to death any who escape the sword of Hazael, and Elisha will put to death any who escape the sword of Jehu. ¹⁸Yet I reserve seven thousand in Israel—all whose knees have not bowed down to Baal and all whose mouths have not kissed him."

The Call of Elisha

¹⁹So Elijah went from there and found

Elisha son of Shaphat. He was plowing with twelve yoke of oxen, and he himself was driving the twelfth pair. Elijah went up to him and threw his cloak around him. 20Elisha then left his oxen and ran after Elijah. "Let me kiss my father and mother good-by," he said, "and then I will come with you."

"Go back," Elijah replied. "What have I done to you?"

21So Elisha left him and went back. He took his yoke of oxen and slaughtered them. He burned the plowing equipment to cook the meat and gave it to the people, and they ate. Then he set out to follow Elijah and became his attendant.

Ben-Hadad Attacks Samaria

20 Now Ben-Hadad king of Aram mustered his entire army. Accompanied by thirty-two kings with their horses and chariots, he went up and besieged Samaria and attacked it. 2He sent messengers into the city to Ahab king of Israel, saying, "This is what Ben-Hadad says: 3'Your silver and gold are mine, and the best of your wives and children are mine.' "

4The king of Israel answered, "Just as you say, my lord the king. I and all I have are yours."

5The messengers came again and said, "This is what Ben-Hadad says: 'I sent to demand your silver and gold, your wives and your children. 6But about this time tomorrow I am going to send my officials to search your palace and the houses of your officials. They will seize everything you value and carry it away.' "

7The king of Israel summoned all the elders of the land and said to them, "See how this man is looking for trouble! When he sent for my wives and my children, my silver and my gold, I did not refuse him."

8The elders and the people all answered, "Don't listen to him or agree to his demands."

9So he replied to Ben-Hadad's messengers, "Tell my lord the king, 'Your servant will do all you demanded the first time, but this demand I cannot meet.' " They left and took the answer back to Ben-Hadad.

10Then Ben-Hadad sent another message to Ahab: "May the gods deal with me, be it ever so severely, if enough dust remains in Samaria to give each of my men a handful."

11The king of Israel answered, "Tell him: 'One who puts on his armor should not boast like one who takes it off.' "

12Ben-Hadad heard this message while he and the kings were drinking in their tents,*a* and he ordered his men: "Prepare to attack." So they prepared to attack the city.

Ahab Defeats Ben-Hadad

13Meanwhile a prophet came to Ahab king of Israel and announced, "This is what the LORD says: 'Do you see this vast army? I will give it into your hand today, and then you will know that I am the LORD.' "

14"But who will do this?" asked Ahab.

The prophet replied, "This is what the LORD says: 'The young officers of the provincial commanders will do it.' "

"And who will start the battle?" he asked.

The prophet answered, "You will."

15So Ahab summoned the young officers of the provincial commanders, 232 men. Then he assembled the rest of the Israelites, 7,000 in all. 16They set out at noon while Ben-Hadad and the 32 kings allied with him were in their tents getting drunk. 17The young officers of the provincial commanders went out first.

Now Ben-Hadad had dispatched scouts, who reported, "Men are advancing from Samaria."

18He said, "If they have come out for peace, take them alive; if they have come out for war, take them alive."

19The young officers of the provincial commanders marched out of the city with the army behind them 20and each one struck down his opponent. At that, the Arameans fled, with the Israelites in pursuit. But Ben-Hadad king of Aram escaped on horseback with some of his horsemen. 21The king of Israel advanced and overpowered the horses and chariots and inflicted heavy losses on the Arameans.

22Afterward, the prophet came to the king of Israel and said, "Strengthen your position and see what must be done,

a 12 Or *in Succoth;* also in verse 16

because next spring the king of Aram will attack you again."

23 Meanwhile, the officials of the king of Aram advised him, "Their gods are gods of the hills. That is why they were too strong for us. But if we fight them on the plains, surely we will be stronger than they. 24 Do this: Remove all the kings from their commands and replace them with other officers. 25 You must also raise an army like the one you lost—horse for horse and chariot for chariot—so we can fight Israel on the plains. Then surely we will be stronger than they." He agreed with them and acted accordingly.

26 The next spring Ben-Hadad mustered the Arameans and went up to Aphek to fight against Israel. 27 When the Israelites were also mustered and given provisions, they marched out to meet them. The Israelites camped opposite them like two small flocks of goats, while the Arameans covered the countryside.

28 The man of God came up and told the king of Israel, "This is what the LORD says: 'Because the Arameans think the LORD is a god of the hills and not a god of the valleys, I will deliver this vast army into your hands, and you will know that I am the LORD.' "

29 For seven days they camped opposite each other, and on the seventh day the battle was joined. The Israelites inflicted a hundred thousand casualties on the Aramean foot soldiers in one day. 30 The rest of them escaped to the city of Aphek, where the wall collapsed on twenty-seven thousand of them. And Ben-Hadad fled to the city and hid in an inner room.

31 His officials said to him, "Look, we have heard that the kings of the house of Israel are merciful. Let us go to the king of Israel with sackcloth around our waists and ropes around our heads. Perhaps he will spare your life."

32 Wearing sackcloth around their waists and ropes around their heads, they went to the king of Israel and said, "Your servant Ben-Hadad says: 'Please let me live.' "

The king answered, "Is he still alive? He is my brother."

33 The men took this as a good sign and were quick to pick up his word. "Yes, your brother Ben-Hadad!" they said.

"Go and get him," the king said. When Ben-Hadad came out, Ahab had him come up into his chariot.

34 "I will return the cities my father took from your father," Ben-Hadad offered. "You may set up your own market areas in Damascus, as my father did in Samaria."

⌐Ahab said,⌐ "On the basis of a treaty I will set you free." So he made a treaty with him, and let him go.

A Prophet Condemns Ahab

35 By the word of the LORD one of the sons of the prophets said to his companion, "Strike me with your weapon," but the man refused.

36 So the prophet said, "Because you have not obeyed the LORD, as soon as you leave me a lion will kill you." And after the man went away, a lion found him and killed him.

37 The prophet found another man and said, "Strike me, please." So the man struck him and wounded him. 38 Then the prophet went and stood by the road waiting for the king. He disguised himself with his headband down over his eyes. 39 As the king passed by, the prophet called out to him, "Your servant went into the thick of the battle, and someone came to me with a captive and said, 'Guard this man. If he is missing, it will be your life for his life, or you must pay a talent[a] of silver.' 40 While your servant was busy here and there, the man disappeared."

"That is your sentence," the king of Israel said. "You have pronounced it yourself."

41 Then the prophet quickly removed the headband from his eyes, and the king of Israel recognized him as one of the prophets. 42 He said to the king, "This is what the LORD says: 'You have set free a man I had determined should die.[b] Therefore it is your life for his life, your people for his people.' " 43 Sullen and angry, the king of Israel went to his palace in Samaria.

---

a 39 That is, about 75 pounds (about 34 kilograms)   b 42 The Hebrew term refers to the irrevocable giving over of things or persons to the LORD, often by totally destroying them.

Naboth's Vineyard

21 Some time later there was an incident involving a vineyard belonging to Naboth the Jezreelite. The vineyard was in Jezreel, close to the palace of Ahab king of Samaria. ²Ahab said to Naboth, "Let me have your vineyard to use for a vegetable garden, since it is close to my palace. In exchange I will give you a better vineyard or, if you prefer, I will pay you whatever it is worth."

³But Naboth replied, "The LORD forbid that I should give you the inheritance of my fathers."

⁴So Ahab went home, sullen and angry because Naboth the Jezreelite had said, "I will not give you the inheritance of my fathers." He lay on his bed sulking and refused to eat.

⁵His wife Jezebel came in and asked him, "Why are you so sullen? Why won't you eat?"

⁶He answered her, "Because I said to Naboth the Jezreelite, 'Sell me your vineyard; or if you prefer, I will give you another vineyard in its place.' But he said, 'I will not give you my vineyard.'"

⁷Jezebel his wife said, "Is this how you act as king over Israel? Get up and eat! Cheer up. I'll get you the vineyard of Naboth the Jezreelite."

⁸So she wrote letters in Ahab's name, placed his seal on them, and sent them to the elders and nobles who lived in Naboth's city with him. ⁹In those letters she wrote:

"Proclaim a day of fasting and seat Naboth in a prominent place among the people. ¹⁰But seat two scoundrels opposite him and have them testify that he has cursed both God and the king. Then take him out and stone him to death."

¹¹So the elders and nobles who lived in Naboth's city did as Jezebel directed in the letters she had written to them. ¹²They proclaimed a fast and seated Naboth in a prominent place among the people. ¹³Then two scoundrels came and sat opposite him and brought charges against Naboth before the people, saying, "Naboth has cursed both God and the king." So they took him

outside the city and stoned him to death. ¹⁴Then they sent word to Jezebel: "Naboth has been stoned and is dead."

¹⁵As soon as Jezebel heard that Naboth had been stoned to death, she said to Ahab, "Get up and take possession of the vineyard of Naboth the Jezreelite that he refused to sell you. He is no longer alive, but dead." ¹⁶When Ahab heard that Naboth was dead, he got up and went down to take possession of Naboth's vineyard.

¹⁷Then the word of the LORD came to Elijah the Tishbite: ¹⁸"Go down to meet Ahab king of Israel, who rules in Samaria. He is now in Naboth's vineyard, where he has gone to take possession of it. ¹⁹Say to him, 'This is what the LORD says: Have you not murdered a man and seized his property?' Then say to him, 'This is what the LORD says: In the place where dogs licked up Naboth's blood, dogs will lick up your blood—yes, yours!'"

²⁰Ahab said to Elijah, "So you have found me, my enemy!"

"I have found you," he answered, "because you have sold yourself to do evil in the eyes of the LORD. ²¹I am going to bring disaster on you. I will consume your descendants and cut off from Ahab every last male in Israel—slave or free. ²²I will make your house like that of Jeroboam son of Nebat and that of Baasha son of Ahijah, because you have provoked me to anger and have caused Israel to sin.'

²³"And also concerning Jezebel the LORD says: 'Dogs will devour Jezebel by the wall ofᵃ Jezreel.'

²⁴"Dogs will eat those belonging to Ahab who die in the city, and the birds of the air will feed on those who die in the country."

²⁵(There was never a man like Ahab, who sold himself to do evil in the eyes of the LORD, urged on by Jezebel his wife. ²⁶He behaved in the vilest manner by going after idols, like the Amorites the LORD drove out before Israel.)

²⁷When Ahab heard these words, he tore his clothes, put on sackcloth and fasted. He lay in sackcloth and went around meekly.

²⁸Then the word of the LORD came to Elijah the Tishbite: ²⁹"Have you noticed

---

ᵃ 23 Most Hebrew manuscripts; a few Hebrew manuscripts, Vulgate and Syriac (see also 2 Kings 9:26) *the plot of ground at* how Ahab has humbled himself before me? Because he has humbled himself, I will not bring this disaster in his day, but I will bring it on his house in the days of his son."

Micaiah Prophesies Against Ahab

22 For three years there was no war between Aram and Israel. ²But in the third year Jehoshaphat king of Judah went down to see the king of Israel. ³The king of Israel had said to his officials, "Don't you know that Ramoth Gilead belongs to us and yet we are doing nothing to retake it from the king of Aram?"

⁴So he asked Jehoshaphat, "Will you go with me to fight against Ramoth Gilead?"

Jehoshaphat replied to the king of Israel, "I am as you are, my people as your people, my horses as your horses." ⁵But Jehoshaphat also said to the king of Israel, "First seek the counsel of the LORD."

⁶So the king of Israel brought together the prophets—about four hundred men—and asked them, "Shall I go to war against Ramoth Gilead, or shall I refrain?"

"Go," they answered, "for the Lord will give it into the king's hand."

⁷But Jehoshaphat asked, "Is there not a prophet of the LORD here whom we can inquire of?"

⁸The king of Israel answered Jehoshaphat, "There is still one man through whom we can inquire of the LORD, but I hate him because he never prophesies anything good about me, but always bad. He is Micaiah son of Imlah."

"The king should not say that," Jehoshaphat replied.

⁹So the king of Israel called one of his officials and said, "Bring Micaiah son of Imlah at once."

¹⁰Dressed in their royal robes, the king of Israel and Jehoshaphat king of Judah were sitting on their thrones at the threshing floor by the entrance of the gate of Samaria, with all the prophets prophesying before them. ¹¹Now Zedekiah son of Kenaanah had made iron horns and he declared, "This is what the LORD says: 'With these you will gore the Arameans until they are destroyed.'"

¹²All the other prophets were prophe-sying the same thing. "Attack Ramoth Gilead and be victorious," they said, "for the LORD will give it into the king's hand."

¹³The messenger who had gone to summon Micaiah said to him, "Look, as one man the other prophets are predict-ing success for the king. Let your word agree with theirs, and speak favorably."

¹⁴But Micaiah said, "As surely as the LORD lives, I can tell him only what the LORD tells me."

¹⁵When he arrived, the king asked him, "Micaiah, shall we go to war against Ramoth Gilead, or shall I refrain?"

"Attack and be victorious," he answered, "for the LORD will give it into the king's hand."

¹⁶The king said to him, "How many times must I make you swear to tell me nothing but the truth in the name of the LORD?"

¹⁷Then Micaiah answered, "I saw all Israel scattered on the hills like sheep without a shepherd, and the LORD said, 'These people have no master. Let each one go home in peace.'"

¹⁸The king of Israel said to Jehosha-phat, "Didn't I tell you that he never prophesies anything good about me, but only bad?"

¹⁹Micaiah continued, "Therefore hear the word of the LORD: I saw the LORD sit-ting on his throne with all the host of heaven standing around him on his right and on his left. ²⁰And the LORD said, 'Who will entice Ahab into attacking Ramoth Gilead and going to his death there?'

"One suggested this, and another that. ²¹Finally, a spirit came forward, stood before the LORD and said, 'I will entice him.'

²²" 'By what means?' the LORD asked.

" 'I will go out and be a lying spirit in the mouths of all his prophets,' he said.

" 'You will succeed in enticing him,' said the LORD. 'Go and do it.'

²³"So now the LORD has put a lying spirit in the mouths of all these prophets of yours. The LORD has decreed disaster for you."

²⁴Then Zedekiah son of Kenaanah went up and slapped Micaiah in the face. "Which way did the spirit from*ᵃ*

ᵃ 24 Or *Spirit of*

the LORD go when he went from me to speak to you?" he asked.

25Micaiah replied, "You will find out on the day you go to hide in an inner room."

26The king of Israel then ordered, "Take Micaiah and send him back to Amon the ruler of the city and to Joash the king's son 27and say, 'This is what the king says: Put this fellow in prison and give him nothing but bread and water until I return safely.' "

28Micaiah declared, "If you ever return safely, the LORD has not spoken through me." Then he added, "Mark my words, all you people!"

Ahab Killed at Ramoth Gilead

29So the king of Israel and Jehoshaphat king of Judah went up to Ramoth Gilead. 30The king of Israel said to Jehoshaphat, "I will enter the battle in disguise, but you wear your royal robes." So the king of Israel disguised himself and went into battle.

31Now the king of Aram had ordered his thirty-two chariot commanders, "Do not fight with anyone, small or great, except the king of Israel." 32When the chariot commanders saw Jehoshaphat, they thought, "Surely this is the king of Israel." So they turned to attack him, but when Jehoshaphat cried out, 33the chariot commanders saw that he was not the king of Israel and stopped pursuing him.

34But someone drew his bow at random and hit the king of Israel between the sections of his armor. The king told his chariot driver, "Wheel around and get me out of the fighting. I've been wounded." 35All day long the battle raged, and the king was propped up in his chariot facing the Arameans. The blood from his wound ran onto the floor of the chariot, and that evening he died. 36As the sun was setting, a cry spread through the army: "Every man to his town; everyone to his land!"

37So the king died and was brought to Samaria, and they buried him there. 38They washed the chariot at a pool in Samaria (where the prostitutes bathed),a and the dogs licked up his blood, as the word of the LORD had declared.

39As for the other events of Ahab's reign, including all he did, the palace he built and inlaid with ivory, and the cities he fortified, are they not written in the book of the annals of the kings of Israel? 40Ahab rested with his fathers. And Ahaziah his son succeeded him as king.

Jehoshaphat King of Judah

41Jehoshaphat son of Asa became king of Judah in the fourth year of Ahab king of Israel. 42Jehoshaphat was thirty-five years old when he became king, and he reigned in Jerusalem twenty-five years. His mother's name was Azubah daughter of Shilhi. 43In everything he walked in the ways of his father Asa and did not stray from them; he did what was right in the eyes of the LORD. The high places, however, were not removed, and the people continued to offer sacrifices and burn incense there. 44Jehoshaphat was also at peace with the king of Israel.

45As for the other events of Jehoshaphat's reign, the things he achieved and his military exploits, are they not written in the book of the annals of the kings of Judah? 46He rid the land of the rest of the male shrine prostitutes who remained there even after the reign of his father Asa. 47There was then no king in Edom; a deputy ruled.

48Now Jehoshaphat built a fleet of trading shipsb to go to Ophir for gold, but they never set sail—they were wrecked at Ezion Geber. 49At that time Ahaziah son of Ahab said to Jehoshaphat, "Let my men sail with your men," but Jehoshaphat refused.

50Then Jehoshaphat rested with his fathers and was buried with them in the city of David his father. And Jehoram his son succeeded him.

Ahaziah King of Israel

51Ahaziah son of Ahab became king of Israel in Samaria in the seventeenth year of Jehoshaphat king of Judah, and he reigned over Israel two years. 52He did evil in the eyes of the LORD, because he walked in the ways of his father and mother and in the ways of Jeroboam son of Nebat, who caused Israel to sin. 53He served and worshiped Baal and provoked the LORD, the God of Israel, to anger, just as his father had done.

---

a 38 Or Samaria and cleaned the weapons   b 48 Hebrew of ships of Tarshish

2 KINGS

THE BOOK OF 2 KINGS CONTINUES THE HISTORY OF ISRAEL AND JUDAH BEGUN IN 1 KINGS. IT INCLUDES THE FASCINATING STORIES OF THE GREAT PROPHETS ELIJAH AND ELISHA. LOOK FOR THE PROPHET'S WARNINGS THAT GOD WOULD PUNISH THE PEOPLE IF THEY DID NOT REPENT OF THEIR SINS, AND NOTE THE TERRIBLE LOSSES GOD'S PEOPLE ENDURED BECAUSE OF THEIR SIN.

The LORD's Judgment on Ahaziah

1 After Ahab's death, Moab rebelled against Israel. ²Now Ahaziah had fallen through the lattice of his upper room in Samaria and injured himself. So he sent messengers, saying to them, "Go and consult Baal-Zebub, the god of Ekron, to see if I will recover from this injury."

³But the angel of the LORD said to Elijah the Tishbite, "Go up and meet the messengers of the king of Samaria and ask them, 'Is it because there is no God in Israel that you are going off to consult Baal-Zebub, the god of Ekron?' ⁴Therefore this is what the LORD says: 'You will not leave the bed you are lying on. You will certainly die!'" So Elijah went.

⁵When the messengers returned to the king, he asked them, "Why have you come back?"

⁶"A man came to meet us," they replied. "And he said to us, 'Go back to the king who sent you and tell him, "This is what the LORD says: Is it because there is no God in Israel that you are sending men to consult Baal-Zebub, the god of Ekron? Therefore you will not leave the bed you are lying on. You will certainly die!"'"

⁷The king asked them, "What kind of man was it who came to meet you and told you this?"

⁸They replied, "He was a man with a garment of hair and with a leather belt around his waist."

The king said, "That was Elijah the Tishbite."

⁹Then he sent to Elijah a captain with

his company of fifty men. The captain went up to Elijah, who was sitting on the top of a hill, and said to him, "Man of God, the king says, 'Come down!' "

¹⁰Elijah answered the captain, "If I am a man of God, may fire come down from heaven and consume you and your fifty men!" Then fire fell from heaven and consumed the captain and his men.

¹¹At this the king sent to Elijah another captain with his fifty men. The captain said to him, "Man of God, this is what the king says, 'Come down at once!' "

¹²"If I am a man of God," Elijah replied, "may fire come down from heaven and consume you and your fifty men!" Then the fire of God fell from heaven and consumed him and his fifty men.

¹³So the king sent a third captain with his fifty men. This third captain went up and fell on his knees before Elijah. "Man of God," he begged, "please have respect for my life and the lives of these fifty men, your servants! ¹⁴See, fire has fallen from heaven and consumed the first two captains and all their men. But now have respect for my life!"

¹⁵The angel of the LORD said to Elijah, "Go down with him; do not be afraid of him." So Elijah got up and went down with him to the king.

¹⁶He told the king, "This is what the LORD says: Is it because there is no God in Israel for you to consult that you have sent messengers to consult Baal-Zebub, the god of Ekron? Because you have done this, you will never leave the bed you are lying on. You will certainly die!" ¹⁷So he died, according to the word of the LORD that Elijah had spoken.

Because Ahaziah had no son, Joramᵃ succeeded him as king in the second year of Jehoram son of Jehoshaphat king of Judah. ¹⁸As for all the other events of Ahaziah's reign, and what he did, are they not written in the book of the annals of the kings of Israel?

Elijah Taken Up to Heaven

2 When the LORD was about to take Elijah up to heaven in a whirlwind, Elijah and Elisha were on their way from Gilgal. ²Elijah said to Elisha, "Stay here; the LORD has sent me to Bethel."

But Elisha said, "As surely as the LORD lives and as you live, I will not leave you." So they went down to Bethel.

³The company of the prophets at Bethel came out to Elisha and asked, "Do you know that the LORD is going to take your master from you today?"

"Yes, I know," Elisha replied, "but do not speak of it."

⁴Then Elijah said to him, "Stay here, Elisha; the LORD has sent me to Jericho."

And he replied, "As surely as the LORD lives and as you live, I will not leave you." So they went to Jericho.

⁵The company of the prophets at Jericho went up to Elisha and asked him, "Do you know that the LORD is going to take your master from you today?"

"Yes, I know," he replied, "but do not speak of it."

⁶Then Elijah said to him, "Stay here; the LORD has sent me to the Jordan."

And he replied, "As surely as the LORD lives and as you live, I will not leave you." So the two of them walked on.

⁷Fifty men of the company of the prophets went and stood at a distance, facing the place where Elijah and Elisha had stopped at the Jordan. ⁸Elijah took his cloak, rolled it up and struck the water with it. The water divided to the right and to the left, and the two of them crossed over on dry ground.

⁹When they had crossed, Elijah said to Elisha, "Tell me, what can I do for you before I am taken from you?"

"Let me inherit a double portion of your spirit," Elisha replied.

¹⁰"You have asked a difficult thing," Elijah said, "yet if you see me when I am taken from you, it will be yours—otherwise not."

¹¹As they were walking along and talking together, suddenly a chariot of fire and horses of fire appeared and separated the two of them, and Elijah went up to heaven in a whirlwind. ¹²Elisha saw this and cried out, "My father! My father! The chariots and horsemen of Israel!" And Elisha saw him no more. Then he took hold of his own clothes and tore them apart.

¹³He picked up the cloak that had

ᵃ 17 Hebrew *Jehoram,* a variant of *Joram*

fallen from Elijah and went back and stood on the bank of the Jordan. 14Then he took the cloak that had fallen from him and struck the water with it. "Where now is the LORD, the God of Elijah?" he asked. When he struck the water, it divided to the right and to the left, and he crossed over.

15The company of the prophets from Jericho, who were watching, said, "The spirit of Elijah is resting on Elisha." And they went to meet him and bowed to the ground before him. 16"Look," they said, "we your servants have fifty able men. Let them go and look for your master. Perhaps the Spirit of the LORD has picked him up and set him down on some mountain or in some valley."

"No," Elisha replied, "do not send them."

17But they persisted until he was too ashamed to refuse. So he said, "Send them." And they sent fifty men, who searched for three days but did not find him. 18When they returned to Elisha, who was staying in Jericho, he said to them, "Didn't I tell you not to go?"

Healing of the Water

19The men of the city said to Elisha, "Look, our lord, this town is well situated, as you can see, but the water is bad and the land is unproductive."

20"Bring me a new bowl," he said, "and put salt in it." So they brought it to him.

21Then he went out to the spring and threw the salt into it, saying, "This is what the LORD says: 'I have healed this water. Never again will it cause death or make the land unproductive.' " 22And the water has remained wholesome to this day, according to the word Elisha had spoken.

Elisha Is Jeered

23From there Elisha went up to Bethel. As he was walking along the road, some youths came out of the town and jeered at him. "Go on up, you baldhead!" they said. "Go on up, you baldhead!" 24He turned around, looked at them and called down a curse on them in the name of the LORD. Then two bears came out of the woods and mauled forty-two of the youths. 25And he went

on to Mount Carmel and from there returned to Samaria.

Moab Revolts

3 Jorama son of Ahab became king of Israel in Samaria in the eighteenth year of Jehoshaphat king of Judah, and he reigned twelve years. 2He did evil in the eyes of the LORD, but not as his father and mother had done. He got rid of the sacred stone of Baal that his father had made. 3Nevertheless he clung to the sins of Jeroboam son of Nebat, which he had caused Israel to commit; he did not turn away from them.

4Now Mesha king of Moab raised sheep, and he had to supply the king of Israel with a hundred thousand lambs and with the wool of a hundred thousand rams. 5But after Ahab died, the king of Moab rebelled against the king of Israel. 6So at that time King Joram set out from Samaria and mobilized all Israel. 7He also sent this message to Jehoshaphat king of Judah: "The king of Moab has rebelled against me. Will you go with me to fight against Moab?"

"I will go with you," he replied. "I am as you are, my people as your people, my horses as your horses."

8"By what route shall we attack?" he asked.

"Through the Desert of Edom," he answered.

9So the king of Israel set out with the king of Judah and the king of Edom. After a roundabout march of seven days, the army had no more water for themselves or for the animals with them.

10"What!" exclaimed the king of Israel. "Has the LORD called us three kings together only to hand us over to Moab?"

11But Jehoshaphat asked, "Is there no prophet of the LORD here, that we may inquire of the LORD through him?"

An officer of the king of Israel answered, "Elisha son of Shaphat is here. He used to pour water on the hands of Elijah.b"

12Jehoshaphat said, "The word of the LORD is with him." So the king of Israel and Jehoshaphat and the king of Edom went down to him.

13Elisha said to the king of Israel, "What do we have to do with each

other? Go to the prophets of your father
and the prophets of your mother."

"No," the king of Israel answered,
"because it was the LORD who called us
three kings together to hand us over to
Moab."

¹⁴Elisha said, "As surely as the LORD
Almighty lives, whom I serve, if I did
not have respect for the presence of
Jehoshaphat king of Judah, I would not
look at you or even notice you. ¹⁵But
now bring me a harpist."

While the harpist was playing, the
hand of the LORD came upon Elisha ¹⁶and
he said, "This is what the LORD says:
Make this valley full of ditches. ¹⁷For
this is what the LORD says: You will see
neither wind nor rain, yet this valley will
be filled with water, and you, your cattle
and your other animals will drink. ¹⁸This
is an easy thing in the eyes of the LORD;
he will also hand Moab over to you.
¹⁹You will overthrow every fortified city
and every major town. You will cut down
every good tree, stop up all the springs,
and ruin every good field with stones."

²⁰The next morning, about the time for
offering the sacrifice, there it was—water
flowing from the direction of Edom! And
the land was filled with water.

²¹Now all the Moabites had heard
that the kings had come to fight against
them; so every man, young and old, who
could bear arms was called up and stationed on the border. ²²When they got
up early in the morning, the sun was
shining on the water. To the Moabites
across the way, the water looked red—
like blood. ²³"That's blood!" they said.
"Those kings must have fought and
slaughtered each other. Now to the
plunder, Moab!"

²⁴But when the Moabites came to the
camp of Israel, the Israelites rose up and
fought them until they fled. And the
Israelites invaded the land and slaughtered the Moabites. ²⁵They destroyed
the towns, and each man threw a stone
on every good field until it was covered.
They stopped up all the springs and cut
down every good tree. Only Kir Hare-
seth was left with its stones in place, but
men armed with slings surrounded it
and attacked it as well.

²⁶When the king of Moab saw that the
battle had gone against him, he took with
him seven hundred swordsmen to break
through to the king of Edom, but they
failed. ²⁷Then he took his firstborn son,
who was to succeed him as king, and
offered him as a sacrifice on the city wall.
The fury against Israel was great; they
withdrew and returned to their own land.

The Widow's Oil

4 The wife of a man from the
company of the prophets cried
out to Elisha, "Your servant my husband
is dead, and you know that he revered
the LORD. But now his creditor is coming
to take my two boys as his slaves."

²Elisha replied to her, "How can I help
you? Tell me, what do you have in your
house?"

"Your servant has nothing there at
all," she said, "except a little oil."

³Elisha said, "Go around and ask all
your neighbors for empty jars. Don't ask
for just a few. ⁴Then go inside and shut
the door behind you and your sons. Pour
oil into all the jars, and as each is filled,
put it to one side."

⁵She left him and afterward shut the
door behind her and her sons. They
brought the jars to her and she kept
pouring. ⁶When all the jars were full, she
said to her son, "Bring me another one."

But he replied, "There is not a jar
left." Then the oil stopped flowing.

⁷She went and told the man of God,
and he said, "Go, sell the oil and pay
your debts. You and your sons can live
on what is left."

The Shunammite's Son Restored
to Life

⁸One day Elisha went to Shunem. And
a well-to-do woman was there, who
urged him to stay for a meal. So whenever he came by, he stopped there to eat.
⁹She said to her husband, "I know that
this man who often comes our way is a
holy man of God. ¹⁰Let's make a small
room on the roof and put in it a bed and a
table, a chair and a lamp for him. Then he
can stay there whenever he comes to us."

¹¹One day when Elisha came, he went
up to his room and lay down there. ¹²He
said to his servant Gehazi, "Call the
Shunammite." So he called her, and she
stood before him. ¹³Elisha said to him,
"Tell her, 'You have gone to all this trou-

ble for us. Now what can be done for you? Can we speak on your behalf to the king or the commander of the army?' "

She replied, "I have a home among my own people."

¹⁴"What can be done for her?" Elisha asked.

Gehazi said, "Well, she has no son and her husband is old."

¹⁵Then Elisha said, "Call her." So he called her, and she stood in the doorway. ¹⁶"About this time next year," Elisha said, "you will hold a son in your arms."

"No, my lord," she objected. "Don't mislead your servant, O man of God!"

¹⁷But the woman became pregnant, and the next year about that same time she gave birth to a son, just as Elisha had told her.

¹⁸The child grew, and one day he went out to his father, who was with the reapers. ¹⁹"My head! My head!" he said to his father.

His father told a servant, "Carry him to his mother." ²⁰After the servant had lifted him up and carried him to his mother, the boy sat on her lap until noon, and then he died. ²¹She went up and laid him on the bed of the man of God, then shut the door and went out.

²²She called her husband and said, "Please send me one of the servants and a donkey so I can go to the man of God quickly and return."

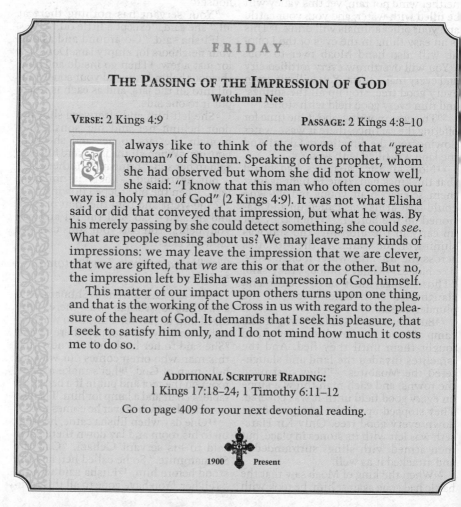

FRIDAY

THE PASSING OF THE IMPRESSION OF GOD
Watchman Nee

VERSE: 2 Kings 4:9　　　　　　　　　　**PASSAGE:** 2 Kings 4:8–10

I always like to think of the words of that "great woman" of Shunem. Speaking of the prophet, whom she had observed but whom she did not know well, she said: "I know that this man who often comes our way is a holy man of God" (2 Kings 4:9). It was not what Elisha said or did that conveyed that impression, but what he was. By his merely passing by she could detect something; she could *see*. What are people sensing about us? We may leave many kinds of impressions: we may leave the impression that we are clever, that we are gifted, that *we* are this or that or the other. But no, the impression left by Elisha was an impression of God himself.

This matter of our impact upon others turns upon one thing, and that is the working of the Cross in us with regard to the pleasure of the heart of God. It demands that I seek his pleasure, that I seek to satisfy him only, and I do not mind how much it costs me to do so.

ADDITIONAL SCRIPTURE READING:
1 Kings 17:18–24; 1 Timothy 6:11–12

Go to page 409 for your next devotional reading.

1900　　Present

23"Why go to him today?" he asked. "It's not the New Moon or the Sabbath."

"It's all right," she said.

24She saddled the donkey and said to her servant, "Lead on; don't slow down for me unless I tell you." 25So she set out and came to the man of God at Mount Carmel.

When he saw her in the distance, the man of God said to his servant Gehazi, "Look! There's the Shunammite! 26Run to meet her and ask her, 'Are you all right? Is your husband all right? Is your child all right?' "

"Everything is all right," she said.

27When she reached the man of God at the mountain, she took hold of his feet. Gehazi came over to push her away, but the man of God said, "Leave her alone! She is in bitter distress, but the LORD has hidden it from me and has not told me why."

28"Did I ask you for a son, my lord?" she said. "Didn't I tell you, 'Don't raise my hopes'?"

29Elisha said to Gehazi, "Tuck your cloak into your belt, take my staff in your hand and run. If you meet anyone, do not greet him, and if anyone greets you, do not answer. Lay my staff on the boy's face."

30But the child's mother said, "As surely as the LORD lives and as you live, I will not leave you." So he got up and followed her.

31Gehazi went on ahead and laid the staff on the boy's face, but there was no sound or response. So Gehazi went back to meet Elisha and told him, "The boy has not awakened."

32When Elisha reached the house, there was the boy lying dead on his couch. 33He went in, shut the door on the two of them and prayed to the LORD. 34Then he got on the bed and lay upon the boy, mouth to mouth, eyes to eyes, hands to hands. As he stretched himself out upon him, the boy's body grew warm. 35Elisha turned away and walked back and forth in the room and then got on the bed and stretched out upon him once more. The boy sneezed seven times and opened his eyes.

36Elisha summoned Gehazi and said, "Call the Shunammite." And he did. When she came, he said, "Take your son." 37She came in, fell at his feet and bowed to the ground. Then she took her son and went out.

Death in the Pot

38Elisha returned to Gilgal and there was a famine in that region. While the company of the prophets was meeting with him, he said to his servant, "Put on the large pot and cook some stew for these men."

39One of them went out into the fields to gather herbs and found a wild vine. He gathered some of its gourds and filled the fold of his cloak. When he returned, he cut them up into the pot of stew, though no one knew what they were. 40The stew was poured out for the men, but as they began to eat it, they cried out, "O man of God, there is death in the pot!" And they could not eat it.

41Elisha said, "Get some flour." He put it into the pot and said, "Serve it to the people to eat." And there was nothing harmful in the pot.

Feeding of a Hundred

42A man came from Baal Shalishah, bringing the man of God twenty loaves of barley bread baked from the first ripe grain, along with some heads of new grain. "Give it to the people to eat," Elisha said.

43"How can I set this before a hundred men?" his servant asked.

But Elisha answered, "Give it to the people to eat. For this is what the LORD says: 'They will eat and have some left over.' " 44Then he set it before them, and they ate and had some left over, according to the word of the LORD.

Naaman Healed of Leprosy

5 Now Naaman was commander of the army of the king of Aram. He was a great man in the sight of his master and highly regarded, because through him the LORD had given victory to Aram. He was a valiant soldier, but he had leprosy.[a]

---

[a] 1 The Hebrew word was used for various diseases affecting the skin—not necessarily leprosy; also in verses 3, 6, 7, 11 and 27.

²Now bands from Aram had gone out and had taken captive a young girl from Israel, and she served Naaman's wife. ³She said to her mistress, "If only my master would see the prophet who is in Samaria! He would cure him of his leprosy."

⁴Naaman went to his master and told him what the girl from Israel had said. ⁵"By all means, go," the king of Aram replied. "I will send a letter to the king of Israel." So Naaman left, taking with him ten talents*a* of silver, six thousand shekels*b* of gold and ten sets of clothing. ⁶The letter that he took to the king of Israel read: "With this letter I am sending my servant Naaman to you so that you may cure him of his leprosy."

⁷As soon as the king of Israel read the letter, he tore his robes and said, "Am I God? Can I kill and bring back to life? Why does this fellow send someone to me to be cured of his leprosy? See how he is trying to pick a quarrel with me!"

⁸When Elisha the man of God heard that the king of Israel had torn his robes, he sent him this message: "Why have you torn your robes? Have the man come to me and he will know that there is a prophet in Israel." ⁹So Naaman went with his horses and chariots and stopped at the door of Elisha's house. ¹⁰Elisha sent a messenger to say to him, "Go, wash yourself seven times in the Jordan, and your flesh will be restored and you will be cleansed."

¹¹But Naaman went away angry and said, "I thought that he would surely come out to me and stand and call on the name of the LORD his God, wave his hand over the spot and cure me of my leprosy. ¹²Are not Abana and Pharpar, the rivers of Damascus, better than any of the waters of Israel? Couldn't I wash in them and be cleansed?" So he turned and went off in a rage.

¹³Naaman's servants went to him and said, "My father, if the prophet had told you to do some great thing, would you not have done it? How much more, then, when he tells you, 'Wash and be cleansed'!" ¹⁴So he went down and dipped himself in the Jordan seven times, as the man of God had told him,

and his flesh was restored and became clean like that of a young boy.

¹⁵Then Naaman and all his attendants went back to the man of God. He stood before him and said, "Now I know that there is no God in all the world except in Israel. Please accept now a gift from your servant."

¹⁶The prophet answered, "As surely as the LORD lives, whom I serve, I will not accept a thing." And even though Naaman urged him, he refused.

¹⁷"If you will not," said Naaman, "please let me, your servant, be given as much earth as a pair of mules can carry, for your servant will never again make burnt offerings and sacrifices to any other god but the LORD. ¹⁸But may the LORD forgive your servant for this one thing: When my master enters the temple of Rimmon to bow down and he is leaning on my arm and I bow there also—when I bow down in the temple of Rimmon, may the LORD forgive your servant for this."

¹⁹"Go in peace," Elisha said.

After Naaman had traveled some distance, ²⁰Gehazi, the servant of Elisha the man of God, said to himself, "My master was too easy on Naaman, this Aramean, by not accepting from him what he brought. As surely as the LORD lives, I will run after him and get something from him."

²¹So Gehazi hurried after Naaman. When Naaman saw him running toward him, he got down from the chariot to meet him. "Is everything all right?" he asked.

²²"Everything is all right," Gehazi answered. "My master sent me to say, 'Two young men from the company of the prophets have just come to me from the hill country of Ephraim. Please give them a talent*c* of silver and two sets of clothing.'"

²³"By all means, take two talents," said Naaman. He urged Gehazi to accept them, and then tied up the two talents of silver in two bags, with two sets of clothing. He gave them to two of his servants, and they carried them ahead of Gehazi. ²⁴When Gehazi came to the hill, he took the things from the servants and put

---

a 5 That is, about 750 pounds (about 340 kilograms)   *b 5* That is, about 150 pounds (about 70 kilograms)   *c 22* That is, about 75 pounds (about 34 kilograms)

WEEKEND

UNCONDITIONAL SURRENDER
Dwight L. Moody

VERSE: 2 Kings 5:15   **PASSAGE:** 2 Kings 5:1–15

he history of Naaman in 2 Kings 5:15 shows what Naaman's faith led him to believe. "Then Naaman and all his attendants went back to the man of God. He stood before him and said, 'Now I know that there is no God in all the world except in Israel . . . ' " I want particularly to call your attention to the words "I know."

There is no hesitation about it, no qualifying the expression. Naaman doesn't now say, "I think"; no, he says, "I know there is a God who has power to forgive sins and to cleanse the leprosy."

Then there is another thought. Naaman left only one thing in Samaria, and that was his sin, his leprosy. The only thing God wishes you to leave with him is your sin; and yet it is the only thing you seem not to care about giving up . . .

How long did it take Naaman to be cured? The seventh time he went down, away went the leprosy! Read the great conversions recorded in the Bible—Saul of Tarsus, Zacchaeus, and a host of others; how long did it take the Lord to bring them about (see Acts 9:1–36; Luke 9:1–8)? They were effected in a minute. We are born in iniquity, shaped in it, dead in trespasses and sin; but when spiritual life comes it comes in a moment, and we are freed both from sin and death.

ADDITIONAL SCRIPTURE READING:
Isaiah 43:10–11; Daniel 6:26–27

Go to page 420 for your next devotional reading.

1900   Present

them away in the house. He sent the men away and they left. 25Then he went in and stood before his master Elisha.

"Where have you been, Gehazi?" Elisha asked.

"Your servant didn't go anywhere," Gehazi answered.

26But Elisha said to him, "Was not my spirit with you when the man got down from his chariot to meet you? Is this the time to take money, or to accept clothes, olive groves, vineyards, flocks, herds, or menservants and maidservants? 27Naaman's leprosy will cling to you and to your descendants forever." Then Gehazi went from Elisha's presence and he was leprous, as white as snow.

An Axhead Floats

6 The company of the prophets said to Elisha, "Look, the place where we meet with you is too small for us. 2Let us go to the Jordan, where each of us can get a pole; and let us build a place there for us to live."

And he said, "Go."

3Then one of them said, "Won't you please come with your servants?"

"I will," Elisha replied. 4And he went with them.

They went to the Jordan and began to cut down trees. 5As one of them was cutting down a tree, the iron axhead fell into the water. "Oh, my lord," he cried out, "it was borrowed!"

6The man of God asked, "Where did it fall?" When he showed him the place, Elisha cut a stick and threw it there, and made the iron float. 7"Lift it out," he said. Then the man reached out his hand and took it.

Elisha Traps Blinded Arameans

8Now the king of Aram was at war with Israel. After conferring with his officers, he said, "I will set up my camp in such and such a place."

9The man of God sent word to the king of Israel: "Beware of passing that place, because the Arameans are going down there." 10So the king of Israel checked on the place indicated by the man of God. Time and again Elisha warned the king, so that he was on his guard in such places.

11This enraged the king of Aram. He summoned his officers and demanded of them, "Will you not tell me which of us is on the side of the king of Israel?"

12"None of us, my lord the king," said one of his officers, "but Elisha, the prophet who is in Israel, tells the king of Israel the very words you speak in your bedroom."

13"Go, find out where he is," the king ordered, "so I can send men and capture him." The report came back: "He is in Dothan." 14Then he sent horses and chariots and a strong force there. They went by night and surrounded the city.

15When the servant of the man of God got up and went out early the next morning, an army with horses and chariots had surrounded the city. "Oh, my lord, what shall we do?" the servant asked.

16"Don't be afraid," the prophet answered. "Those who are with us are more than those who are with them."

17And Elisha prayed, "O LORD, open his eyes so he may see." Then the LORD opened the servant's eyes, and he looked and saw the hills full of horses and chariots of fire all around Elisha.

18As the enemy came down toward him, Elisha prayed to the LORD, "Strike these people with blindness." So he struck them with blindness, as Elisha had asked.

19Elisha told them, "This is not the road and this is not the city. Follow me, and I will lead you to the man you are looking for." And he led them to Samaria.

20After they entered the city, Elisha said, "LORD, open the eyes of these men so they can see." Then the LORD opened their eyes and they looked, and there they were, inside Samaria.

21When the king of Israel saw them, he asked Elisha, "Shall I kill them, my father? Shall I kill them?"

22"Do not kill them," he answered. "Would you kill men you have captured with your own sword or bow? Set food and water before them so that they may eat and drink and then go back to their master." 23So he prepared a great feast for them, and after they had finished eating and drinking, he sent them away, and they returned to their master. So the bands from Aram stopped raiding Israel's territory.

Famine in Besieged Samaria

²⁴Some time later, Ben-Hadad king of Aram mobilized his entire army and marched up and laid siege to Samaria. ²⁵There was a great famine in the city; the siege lasted so long that a donkey's head sold for eighty shekels[a] of silver, and a quarter of a cab[b] of seed pods[c] for five shekels.[d]

²⁶As the king of Israel was passing by on the wall, a woman cried to him, "Help me, my lord the king!"

²⁷The king replied, "If the LORD does not help you, where can I get help for you? From the threshing floor? From the winepress?" ²⁸Then he asked her, "What's the matter?"

She answered, "This woman said to me, 'Give up your son so we may eat him today, and tomorrow we'll eat my son.' ²⁹So we cooked my son and ate him. The next day I said to her, 'Give up your son so we may eat him,' but she had hidden him."

³⁰When the king heard the woman's words, he tore his robes. As he went along the wall, the people looked, and there, underneath, he had sackcloth on his body. ³¹He said, "May God deal with me, be it ever so severely, if the head of Elisha son of Shaphat remains on his shoulders today!"

³²Now Elisha was sitting in his house, and the elders were sitting with him. The king sent a messenger ahead, but before he arrived, Elisha said to the elders, "Don't you see how this murderer is sending someone to cut off my head? Look, when the messenger comes, shut the door and hold it shut against him. Is not the sound of his master's footsteps behind him?" ³³While he was still talking to them, the messenger came down to him. And ₜthe kingⱼ said, "This disaster is from the LORD. Why should I wait for the LORD any longer?"

7 Elisha said, "Hear the word of the LORD. This is what the LORD says: About this time tomorrow, a seah[e] of flour will sell for a shekel[f] and two seahs[g] of barley for a shekel at the gate of Samaria."

²The officer on whose arm the king was leaning said to the man of God, "Look, even if the LORD should open the floodgates of the heavens, could this happen?"

"You will see it with your own eyes," answered Elisha, "but you will not eat any of it!"

The Siege Lifted

³Now there were four men with leprosy[h] at the entrance of the city gate. They said to each other, "Why stay here until we die? ⁴If we say, 'We'll go into the city'—the famine is there, and we will die. And if we stay here, we will die. So let's go over to the camp of the Arameans and surrender. If they spare us, we live; if they kill us, then we die."

⁵At dusk they got up and went to the camp of the Arameans. When they reached the edge of the camp, not a man was there, ⁶for the Lord had caused the Arameans to hear the sound of chariots and horses and a great army, so that they said to one another, "Look, the king of Israel has hired the Hittite and Egyptian kings to attack us!" ⁷So they got up and fled in the dusk and abandoned their tents and their horses and donkeys. They left the camp as it was and ran for their lives.

⁸The men who had leprosy reached the edge of the camp and entered one of the tents. They ate and drank, and carried away silver, gold and clothes, and went off and hid them. They returned and entered another tent and took some things from it and hid them also.

⁹Then they said to each other, "We're not doing right. This is a day of good news and we are keeping it to ourselves. If we wait until daylight, punishment will overtake us. Let's go at once and report this to the royal palace."

¹⁰So they went and called out to the city gatekeepers and told them, "We went into the Aramean camp and not a man was there—not a sound of anyone—only tethered horses and donkeys,

---

a 25 That is, about 2 pounds (about 1 kilogram)   *b 25* That is, probably about 1/2 pint (about 0.3 liter)   *c 25* Or *of dove's dung*   *d 25* That is, about 2 ounces (about 55 grams)   *e 1* That is, probably about 7 quarts (about 7.3 liters); also in verses 16 and 18   *f 1* That is, about 2/5 ounce (about 11 grams); also in verses 16 and 18   *g 1* That is, probably about 13 quarts (about 15 liters); also in verses 16 and 18   *h 3* The Hebrew word is used for various diseases affecting the skin—not necessarily leprosy; also in verse 8.

and the tents left just as they were."
11The gatekeepers shouted the news, and it was reported within the palace.

12The king got up in the night and said to his officers, "I will tell you what the Arameans have done to us. They know we are starving; so they have left the camp to hide in the countryside, thinking, 'They will surely come out, and then we will take them alive and get into the city.' "

13One of his officers answered, "Have some men take five of the horses that are left in the city. Their plight will be like that of all the Israelites left here—yes, they will only be like all these Israelites who are doomed. So let us send them to find out what happened."

14So they selected two chariots with their horses, and the king sent them after the Aramean army. He commanded the drivers, "Go and find out what has happened." 15They followed them as far as the Jordan, and they found the whole road strewn with the clothing and equipment the Arameans had thrown away in their headlong flight. So the messengers returned and reported to the king. 16Then the people went out and plundered the camp of the Arameans. So a seah of flour sold for a shekel, and two seahs of barley sold for a shekel, as the LORD had said.

17Now the king had put the officer on whose arm he leaned in charge of the gate, and the people trampled him in the gateway, and he died, just as the man of God had foretold when the king came down to his house. 18It happened as the man of God had said to the king: "About this time tomorrow, a seah of flour will sell for a shekel and two seahs of barley for a shekel at the gate of Samaria."

19The officer had said to the man of God, "Look, even if the LORD should open the floodgates of the heavens, could this happen?" The man of God had replied, "You will see it with your own eyes, but you will not eat any of it!" 20And that is exactly what happened to him, for the people trampled him in the gateway, and he died.

The Shunammite's Land Restored

8 Now Elisha had said to the woman whose son he had restored to life, "Go away with your family and stay for a while wherever you can, because the LORD has decreed a famine in the land that will last seven years." 2The woman proceeded to do as the man of God said. She and her family went away and stayed in the land of the Philistines seven years.

3At the end of the seven years she came back from the land of the Philistines and went to the king to beg for her house and land. 4The king was talking to Gehazi, the servant of the man of God, and had said, "Tell me about all the great things Elisha has done." 5Just as Gehazi was telling the king how Elisha had restored the dead to life, the woman whose son Elisha had brought back to life came to beg the king for her house and land.

Gehazi said, "This is the woman, my lord the king, and this is her son whom Elisha restored to life." 6The king asked the woman about it, and she told him.

Then he assigned an official to her case and said to him, "Give back everything that belonged to her, including all the income from her land from the day she left the country until now."

Hazael Murders Ben-Hadad

7Elisha went to Damascus, and Ben-Hadad king of Aram was ill. When the king was told, "The man of God has come all the way up here," 8he said to Hazael, "Take a gift with you and go to meet the man of God. Consult the LORD through him; ask him, 'Will I recover from this illness?' "

9Hazael went to meet Elisha, taking with him as a gift forty camel-loads of all the finest wares of Damascus. He went in and stood before him, and said, "Your son Ben-Hadad king of Aram has sent me to ask, 'Will I recover from this illness?' "

10Elisha answered, "Go and say to him, 'You will certainly recover'; but*a* the LORD has revealed to me that he will in fact die." 11He stared at him with a

a 10 The Hebrew may also be read *Go and say, 'You will certainly not recover,' for.*

fixed gaze until Hazael felt ashamed. Then the man of God began to weep.

¹²"Why is my lord weeping?" asked Hazael.

"Because I know the harm you will do to the Israelites," he answered. "You will set fire to their fortified places, kill their young men with the sword, dash their little children to the ground, and rip open their pregnant women."

¹³Hazael said, "How could your servant, a mere dog, accomplish such a feat?"

"The LORD has shown me that you will become king of Aram," answered Elisha.

¹⁴Then Hazael left Elisha and returned to his master. When Ben-Hadad asked, "What did Elisha say to you?" Hazael replied, "He told me that you would certainly recover." ¹⁵But the next day he took a thick cloth, soaked it in water and spread it over the king's face, so that he died. Then Hazael succeeded him as king.

Jehoram King of Judah

¹⁶In the fifth year of Joram son of Ahab king of Israel, when Jehoshaphat was king of Judah, Jehoram son of Jehoshaphat began his reign as king of Judah. ¹⁷He was thirty-two years old when he became king, and he reigned in Jerusalem eight years. ¹⁸He walked in the ways of the kings of Israel, as the house of Ahab had done, for he married a daughter of Ahab. He did evil in the eyes of the LORD. ¹⁹Nevertheless, for the sake of his servant David, the LORD was not willing to destroy Judah. He had promised to maintain a lamp for David and his descendants forever.

²⁰In the time of Jehoram, Edom rebelled against Judah and set up its own king. ²¹So Jehoramª went to Zair with all his chariots. The Edomites surrounded him and his chariot commanders, but he rose up and broke through by night; his army, however, fled back home. ²²To this day Edom has been in rebellion against Judah. Libnah revolted at the same time.

²³As for the other events of Jehoram's reign, and all he did, are they not written in the book of the annals of the kings of Judah? ²⁴Jehoram rested with his fathers and was buried with them in the City of David. And Ahaziah his son succeeded him as king.

Ahaziah King of Judah

²⁵In the twelfth year of Joram son of Ahab king of Israel, Ahaziah son of Jehoram king of Judah began to reign. ²⁶Ahaziah was twenty-two years old when he became king, and he reigned in Jerusalem one year. His mother's name was Athaliah, a granddaughter of Omri king of Israel. ²⁷He walked in the ways of the house of Ahab and did evil in the eyes of the LORD, as the house of Ahab had done, for he was related by marriage to Ahab's family.

²⁸Ahaziah went with Joram son of Ahab to war against Hazael king of Aram at Ramoth Gilead. The Arameans wounded Joram; ²⁹so King Joram returned to Jezreel to recover from the wounds the Arameans had inflicted on him at Ramothᵇ in his battle with Hazael king of Aram.

Then Ahaziah son of Jehoram king of Judah went down to Jezreel to see Joram son of Ahab, because he had been wounded.

Jehu Anointed King of Israel

9 The prophet Elisha summoned a man from the company of the prophets and said to him, "Tuck your cloak into your belt, take this flask of oil with you and go to Ramoth Gilead. ²When you get there, look for Jehu son of Jehoshaphat, the son of Nimshi. Go to him, get him away from his companions and take him into an inner room. ³Then take the flask and pour the oil on his head and declare, 'This is what the LORD says: I anoint you king over Israel.' Then open the door and run; don't delay!"

⁴So the young man, the prophet, went to Ramoth Gilead. ⁵When he arrived, he found the army officers sitting together. "I have a message for you, commander," he said.

"For which of us?" asked Jehu.

"For you, commander," he replied.

⁶Jehu got up and went into the house. Then the prophet poured the oil on Jehu's

---

ª 21 Hebrew *Joram*, a variant of *Jehoram*; also in verses 23 and 24   ᵇ 29 Hebrew *Ramah*, a variant of *Ramoth*

head and declared, "This is what the LORD, the God of Israel, says: 'I anoint you king over the LORD's people Israel. [7] You are to destroy the house of Ahab your master, and I will avenge the blood of my servants the prophets and the blood of all the LORD's servants shed by Jezebel. [8] The whole house of Ahab will perish. I will cut off from Ahab every last male in Israel—slave or free. [9] I will make the house of Ahab like the house of Jeroboam son of Nebat and like the house of Baasha son of Ahijah. [10] As for Jezebel, dogs will devour her on the plot of ground at Jezreel, and no one will bury her.' " Then he opened the door and ran.

[11] When Jehu went out to his fellow officers, one of them asked him, "Is everything all right? Why did this madman come to you?"

"You know the man and the sort of things he says," Jehu replied.

[12] "That's not true!" they said. "Tell us."

Jehu said, "Here is what he told me: 'This is what the LORD says: I anoint you king over Israel.' "

[13] They hurried and took their cloaks and spread them under him on the bare steps. Then they blew the trumpet and shouted, "Jehu is king!"

Jehu Kills Joram and Ahaziah

[14] So Jehu son of Jehoshaphat, the son of Nimshi, conspired against Joram. (Now Joram and all Israel had been defending Ramoth Gilead against Hazael king of Aram, [15] but King Joram[a] had returned to Jezreel to recover from the wounds the Arameans had inflicted on him in the battle with Hazael king of Aram.) Jehu said, "If this is the way you feel, don't let anyone slip out of the city to go and tell the news in Jezreel." [16] Then he got into his chariot and rode to Jezreel, because Joram was resting there and Ahaziah king of Judah had gone down to see him.

[17] When the lookout standing on the tower in Jezreel saw Jehu's troops approaching, he called out, "I see some troops coming."

"Get a horseman," Joram ordered.

"Send him to meet them and ask, 'Do you come in peace?' "

[18] The horseman rode off to meet Jehu and said, "This is what the king says: 'Do you come in peace?' "

"What do you have to do with peace?" Jehu replied. "Fall in behind me."

The lookout reported, "The messenger has reached them, but he isn't coming back."

[19] So the king sent out a second horseman. When he came to them he said, "This is what the king says: 'Do you come in peace?' "

Jehu replied, "What do you have to do with peace? Fall in behind me."

[20] The lookout reported, "He has reached them, but he isn't coming back either. The driving is like that of Jehu son of Nimshi—he drives like a madman."

[21] "Hitch up my chariot," Joram ordered. And when it was hitched up, Joram king of Israel and Ahaziah king of Judah rode out, each in his own chariot, to meet Jehu. They met him at the plot of ground that had belonged to Naboth the Jezreelite. [22] When Joram saw Jehu he asked, "Have you come in peace, Jehu?"

"How can there be peace," Jehu replied, "as long as all the idolatry and witchcraft of your mother Jezebel abound?"

[23] Joram turned about and fled, calling out to Ahaziah, "Treachery, Ahaziah!"

[24] Then Jehu drew his bow and shot Joram between the shoulders. The arrow pierced his heart and he slumped down in his chariot. [25] Jehu said to Bidkar, his chariot officer, "Pick him up and throw him on the field that belonged to Naboth the Jezreelite. Remember how you and I were riding together in chariots behind Ahab his father when the LORD made this prophecy about him: [26] 'Yesterday I saw the blood of Naboth and the blood of his sons, declares the LORD, and I will surely make you pay for it on this plot of ground, declares the LORD.'[b] Now then, pick him up and throw him on that plot, in accordance with the word of the LORD."

[27] When Ahaziah king of Judah saw what had happened, he fled up the road to Beth Haggan.[c] Jehu chased him,

---

[a] 15 Hebrew *Jehoram*, a variant of *Joram*; also in verses 17 and 21–24   [b] 26 See 1 Kings 21:19.
[c] 27 Or *fled by way of the garden house*

shouting, "Kill him too!" They wounded him in his chariot on the way up to Gur near Ibleam, but he escaped to Megiddo and died there. ²⁸His servants took him by chariot to Jerusalem and buried him with his fathers in his tomb in the City of David. ²⁹(In the eleventh year of Joram son of Ahab, Ahaziah had become king of Judah.)

Jezebel Killed

³⁰Then Jehu went to Jezreel. When Jezebel heard about it, she painted her eyes, arranged her hair and looked out of a window. ³¹As Jehu entered the gate, she asked, "Have you come in peace, Zimri, you murderer of your master?"ᵃ

³²He looked up at the window and called out, "Who is on my side? Who?" Two or three eunuchs looked down at him. ³³"Throw her down!" Jehu said. So they threw her down, and some of her blood spattered the wall and the horses as they trampled her underfoot.

³⁴Jehu went in and ate and drank. "Take care of that cursed woman," he said, "and bury her, for she was a king's daughter." ³⁵But when they went out to bury her, they found nothing except her skull, her feet and her hands. ³⁶They went back and told Jehu, who said, "This is the word of the LORD that he spoke through his servant Elijah the Tishbite: On the plot of ground at Jezreel dogs will devour Jezebel's flesh.ᵇ ³⁷Jezebel's body will be like refuse on the ground in the plot at Jezreel, so that no one will be able to say, 'This is Jezebel.' "

Ahab's Family Killed

10 Now there were in Samaria seventy sons of the house of Ahab. So Jehu wrote letters and sent them to Samaria: to the officials of Jezreel,ᶜ to the elders and to the guardians of Ahab's children. He said, ²"As soon as this letter reaches you, since your master's sons are with you and you have chariots and horses, a fortified city and weapons, ³choose the best and most worthy of your master's sons and set him on his father's throne. Then fight for your master's house."

⁴But they were terrified and said, "If two kings could not resist him, how can we?"

⁵So the palace administrator, the city governor, the elders and the guardians sent this message to Jehu: "We are your servants and we will do anything you say. We will not appoint anyone as king; you do whatever you think best."

⁶Then Jehu wrote them a second letter, saying, "If you are on my side and will obey me, take the heads of your master's sons and come to me in Jezreel by this time tomorrow."

Now the royal princes, seventy of them, were with the leading men of the city, who were rearing them. ⁷When the letter arrived, these men took the princes and slaughtered all seventy of them. They put their heads in baskets and sent them to Jehu in Jezreel. ⁸When the messenger arrived, he told Jehu, "They have brought the heads of the princes."

Then Jehu ordered, "Put them in two piles at the entrance of the city gate until morning."

⁹The next morning Jehu went out. He stood before all the people and said, "You are innocent. It was I who conspired against my master and killed him, but who killed all these? ¹⁰Know then, that not a word the LORD has spoken against the house of Ahab will fail. The LORD has done what he promised through his servant Elijah." ¹¹So Jehu killed everyone in Jezreel who remained of the house of Ahab, as well as all his chief men, his close friends and his priests, leaving him no survivor.

¹²Jehu then set out and went toward Samaria. At Beth Eked of the Shepherds, ¹³he met some relatives of Ahaziah king of Judah and asked, "Who are you?"

They said, "We are relatives of Ahaziah, and we have come down to greet the families of the king and of the queen mother."

¹⁴"Take them alive!" he ordered. So they took them alive and slaughtered them by the well of Beth Eked—forty-two men. He left no survivor.

¹⁵After he left there, he came upon Jehonadab son of Recab, who was on his way to meet him. Jehu greeted him and

---

ᵃ 31 Or "Did Zimri have peace, who murdered his master?" ᵇ 36 See 1 Kings 21:23. ᶜ 1 Hebrew; some Septuagint manuscripts and Vulgate of the city

said, "Are you in accord with me, as I am with you?"

"I am," Jehonadab answered.

"If so," said Jehu, "give me your hand." So he did, and Jehu helped him up into the chariot. [16]Jehu said, "Come with me and see my zeal for the LORD." Then he had him ride along in his chariot.

[17]When Jehu came to Samaria, he killed all who were left there of Ahab's family; he destroyed them, according to the word of the LORD spoken to Elijah.

Ministers of Baal Killed

[18]Then Jehu brought all the people together and said to them, "Ahab served Baal a little; Jehu will serve him much. [19]Now summon all the prophets of Baal, all his ministers and all his priests. See that no one is missing, because I am going to hold a great sacrifice for Baal. Anyone who fails to come will no longer live." But Jehu was acting deceptively in order to destroy the ministers of Baal.

[20]Jehu said, "Call an assembly in honor of Baal." So they proclaimed it. [21]Then he sent word throughout Israel, and all the ministers of Baal came; not one stayed away. They crowded into the temple of Baal until it was full from one end to the other. [22]And Jehu said to the keeper of the wardrobe, "Bring robes for all the ministers of Baal." So he brought out robes for them.

[23]Then Jehu and Jehonadab son of Recab went into the temple of Baal. Jehu said to the ministers of Baal, "Look around and see that no servants of the LORD are here with you—only ministers of Baal." [24]So they went in to make sacrifices and burnt offerings. Now Jehu had posted eighty men outside with this warning: "If one of you lets any of the men I am placing in your hands escape, it will be your life for his life."

[25]As soon as Jehu had finished making the burnt offering, he ordered the guards and officers: "Go in and kill them; let no one escape." So they cut them down with the sword. The guards and officers threw the bodies out and then entered the inner shrine of the temple of Baal. [26]They brought the sacred stone out of the temple of Baal and burned it. [27]They demolished the sacred stone of Baal and

tore down the temple of Baal, and people have used it for a latrine to this day.

[28]So Jehu destroyed Baal worship in Israel. [29]However, he did not turn away from the sins of Jeroboam son of Nebat, which he had caused Israel to commit—the worship of the golden calves at Bethel and Dan.

[30]The LORD said to Jehu, "Because you have done well in accomplishing what is right in my eyes and have done to the house of Ahab all I had in mind to do, your descendants will sit on the throne of Israel to the fourth generation." [31]Yet Jehu was not careful to keep the law of the LORD, the God of Israel, with all his heart. He did not turn away from the sins of Jeroboam, which he had caused Israel to commit.

[32]In those days the LORD began to reduce the size of Israel. Hazael overpowered the Israelites throughout their territory [33]east of the Jordan in all the land of Gilead (the region of Gad, Reuben and Manasseh), from Aroer by the Arnon Gorge through Gilead to Bashan.

[34]As for the other events of Jehu's reign, all he did, and all his achievements, are they not written in the book of the annals of the kings of Israel?

[35]Jehu rested with his fathers and was buried in Samaria. And Jehoahaz his son succeeded him as king. [36]The time that Jehu reigned over Israel in Samaria was twenty-eight years.

Athaliah and Joash

11 When Athaliah the mother of Ahaziah saw that her son was dead, she proceeded to destroy the whole royal family. [2]But Jehosheba, the daughter of King Jehoram[a] and sister of Ahaziah, took Joash son of Ahaziah and stole him away from among the royal princes, who were about to be murdered. She put him and his nurse in a bedroom to hide him from Athaliah; so he was not killed. [3]He remained hidden with his nurse at the temple of the LORD for six years while Athaliah ruled the land.

[4]In the seventh year Jehoiada sent for the commanders of units of a hundred, the Carites and the guards and had them brought to him at the temple of the LORD. He made a covenant with them and put

<hr>

[a] 2 Hebrew *Joram*, a variant of *Jehoram*

them under oath at the temple of the LORD. Then he showed them the king's son. ⁵He commanded them, saying, "This is what you are to do: You who are in the three companies that are going on duty on the Sabbath—a third of you guarding the royal palace, ⁶a third at the Sur Gate, and a third at the gate behind the guard, who take turns guarding the temple— ⁷and you who are in the other two companies that normally go off Sabbath duty are all to guard the temple for the king. ⁸Station yourselves around the king, each man with his weapon in his hand. Anyone who approaches your ranksᵃ must be put to death. Stay close to the king wherever he goes."

⁹The commanders of units of a hundred did just as Jehoiada the priest ordered. Each one took his men—those who were going on duty on the Sabbath and those who were going off duty—and came to Jehoiada the priest. ¹⁰Then he gave the commanders the spears and shields that had belonged to King David and that were in the temple of the LORD. ¹¹The guards, each with his weapon in his hand, stationed themselves around the king—near the altar and the temple, from the south side to the north side of the temple.

¹²Jehoiada brought out the king's son and put the crown on him; he presented him with a copy of the covenant and proclaimed him king. They anointed him, and the people clapped their hands and shouted, "Long live the king!"

¹³When Athaliah heard the noise made by the guards and the people, she went to the people at the temple of the LORD. ¹⁴She looked and there was the king, standing by the pillar, as the custom was. The officers and the trumpeters were beside the king, and all the people of the land were rejoicing and blowing trumpets. Then Athaliah tore her robes and called out, "Treason! Treason!"

¹⁵Jehoiada the priest ordered the commanders of units of a hundred, who were in charge of the troops: "Bring her out between the ranksᵇ and put to the sword anyone who follows her." For the priest had said, "She must not be put to death in the temple of the LORD." ¹⁶So

they seized her as she reached the place where the horses enter the palace grounds, and there she was put to death.

¹⁷Jehoiada then made a covenant between the LORD and the king and people that they would be the LORD's people. He also made a covenant between the king and the people. ¹⁸All the people of the land went to the temple of Baal and tore it down. They smashed the altars and idols to pieces and killed Mattan the priest of Baal in front of the altars.

Then Jehoiada the priest posted guards at the temple of the LORD. ¹⁹He took with him the commanders of hundreds, the Carites, the guards and all the people of the land, and together they brought the king down from the temple of the LORD and went into the palace, entering by way of the gate of the guards. The king then took his place on the royal throne, ²⁰and all the people of the land rejoiced. And the city was quiet, because Athaliah had been slain with the sword at the palace.

²¹Joashᶜ was seven years old when he began to reign.

Joash Repairs the Temple

12 In the seventh year of Jehu, Joashᵈ became king, and he reigned in Jerusalem forty years. His mother's name was Zibiah; she was from Beersheba. ²Joash did what was right in the eyes of the LORD all the years Jehoiada the priest instructed him. ³The high places, however, were not removed; the people continued to offer sacrifices and burn incense there.

⁴Joash said to the priests, "Collect all the money that is brought as sacred offerings to the temple of the LORD— the money collected in the census, the money received from personal vows and the money brought voluntarily to the temple. ⁵Let every priest receive the money from one of the treasurers, and let it be used to repair whatever damage is found in the temple."

⁶But by the twenty-third year of King Joash the priests still had not repaired the temple. ⁷Therefore King Joash summoned Jehoiada the priest and the other priests and asked them, "Why aren't you

ᵃ 8 Or *approaches the precincts*   ᵇ 15 Or *out from the precincts*   ᶜ 21 Hebrew *Jehoash,* a variant of *Joash*   ᵈ 1 Hebrew *Jehoash,* a variant of *Joash;* also in verses 2, 4, 6, 7 and 18

repairing the damage done to the temple? Take no more money from your treasurers, but hand it over for repairing the temple." 8The priests agreed that they would not collect any more money from the people and that they would not repair the temple themselves.

9Jehoiada the priest took a chest and bored a hole in its lid. He placed it beside the altar, on the right side as one enters the temple of the LORD. The priests who guarded the entrance put into the chest all the money that was brought to the temple of the LORD. 10Whenever they saw that there was a large amount of money in the chest, the royal secretary and the high priest came, counted the money that had been brought into the temple of the LORD and put it into bags. 11When the amount had been determined, they gave the money to the men appointed to supervise the work on the temple. With it they paid those who worked on the temple of the LORD—the carpenters and builders, 12the masons and stonecutters. They purchased timber and dressed stone for the repair of the temple of the LORD, and met all the other expenses of restoring the temple.

13The money brought into the temple was not spent for making silver basins, wick trimmers, sprinkling bowls, trumpets or any other articles of gold or silver for the temple of the LORD; 14it was paid to the workmen, who used it to repair the temple. 15They did not require an accounting from those to whom they gave the money to pay the workers, because they acted with complete honesty. 16The money from the guilt offerings and sin offerings was not brought into the temple of the LORD; it belonged to the priests.

17About this time Hazael king of Aram went up and attacked Gath and captured it. Then he turned to attack Jerusalem. 18But Joash king of Judah took all the sacred objects dedicated by his fathers—Jehoshaphat, Jehoram and Ahaziah, the kings of Judah—and the gifts he himself had dedicated and all the gold found in the treasuries of the temple of the LORD and of the royal palace, and he

sent them to Hazael king of Aram, who then withdrew from Jerusalem.

19As for the other events of the reign of Joash, and all he did, are they not written in the book of the annals of the kings of Judah? 20His officials conspired against him and assassinated him at Beth Millo, on the road down to Silla. 21The officials who murdered him were Jozabad son of Shimeath and Jehozabad son of Shomer. He died and was buried with his fathers in the City of David. And Amaziah his son succeeded him as king.

Jehoahaz King of Israel

13 In the twenty-third year of Joash son of Ahaziah king of Judah, Jehoahaz son of Jehu became king of Israel in Samaria, and he reigned seventeen years. 2He did evil in the eyes of the LORD by following the sins of Jeroboam son of Nebat, which he had caused Israel to commit, and he did not turn away from them. 3So the LORD's anger burned against Israel, and for a long time he kept them under the power of Hazael king of Aram and Ben-Hadad his son.

4Then Jehoahaz sought the LORD's favor, and the LORD listened to him, for he saw how severely the king of Aram was oppressing Israel. 5The LORD provided a deliverer for Israel, and they escaped from the power of Aram. So the Israelites lived in their own homes as they had before. 6But they did not turn away from the sins of the house of Jeroboam, which he had caused Israel to commit; they continued in them. Also, the Asherah pole[a] remained standing in Samaria.

7Nothing had been left of the army of Jehoahaz except fifty horsemen, ten chariots and ten thousand foot soldiers, for the king of Aram had destroyed the rest and made them like the dust at threshing time.

8As for the other events of the reign of Jehoahaz, all he did and his achievements, are they not written in the book of the annals of the kings of Israel? 9Jehoahaz rested with his fathers and was buried in Samaria. And Jehoash[b] his son succeeded him as king.

---

a 6 That is, a symbol of the goddess Asherah; here and elsewhere in 2 Kings   b 9 Hebrew Joash, a variant of Jehoash; also in verses 12–14 and 25

Jehoash King of Israel

¹⁰In the thirty-seventh year of Joash king of Judah, Jehoash son of Jehoahaz became king of Israel in Samaria, and he reigned sixteen years. ¹¹He did evil in the eyes of the LORD and did not turn away from any of the sins of Jeroboam son of Nebat, which he had caused Israel to commit; he continued in them.

¹²As for the other events of the reign of Jehoash, all he did and his achievements, including his war against Amaziah king of Judah, are they not written in the book of the annals of the kings of Israel? ¹³Jehoash rested with his fathers, and Jeroboam succeeded him on the throne. Jehoash was buried in Samaria with the kings of Israel.

¹⁴Now Elisha was suffering from the illness from which he died. Jehoash king of Israel went down to see him and wept over him. "My father! My father!" he cried. "The chariots and horsemen of Israel!"

¹⁵Elisha said, "Get a bow and some arrows," and he did so. ¹⁶"Take the bow in your hands," he said to the king of Israel. When he had taken it, Elisha put his hands on the king's hands.

¹⁷"Open the east window," he said, and he opened it. "Shoot!" Elisha said, and he shot. "The LORD's arrow of victory, the arrow of victory over Aram!" Elisha declared. "You will completely destroy the Arameans at Aphek."

¹⁸Then he said, "Take the arrows," and the king took them. Elisha told him, "Strike the ground." He struck it three times and stopped. ¹⁹The man of God was angry with him and said, "You should have struck the ground five or six times; then you would have defeated Aram and completely destroyed it. But now you will defeat it only three times."

²⁰Elisha died and was buried.

Now Moabite raiders used to enter the country every spring. ²¹Once while some Israelites were burying a man, suddenly they saw a band of raiders; so they threw the man's body into Elisha's tomb. When the body touched Elisha's bones, the man came to life and stood up on his feet.

²²Hazael king of Aram oppressed Israel throughout the reign of Jehoahaz. ²³But the LORD was gracious to them and had compassion and showed concern for them because of his covenant with Abraham, Isaac and Jacob. To this day he has been unwilling to destroy them or banish them from his presence.

THE DEW OF COMPASSION IS A TEAR.
—*Lord George Gordon Noel Byron*

---

²⁴Hazael king of Aram died, and Ben-Hadad his son succeeded him as king. ²⁵Then Jehoash son of Jehoahaz recaptured from Ben-Hadad son of Hazael the towns he had taken in battle from his father Jehoahaz. Three times Jehoash defeated him, and so he recovered the Israelite towns.

Amaziah King of Judah

14 In the second year of Jehoash[a] son of Jehoahaz king of Israel, Amaziah son of Joash king of Judah began to reign. ²He was twenty-five years old when he became king, and he reigned in Jerusalem twenty-nine years. His mother's name was Jehoaddin; she was from Jerusalem. ³He did what was right in the eyes of the LORD, but not as his father David had done. In everything he followed the example of his father Joash. ⁴The high places, however, were not removed; the people continued to offer sacrifices and burn incense there.

⁵After the kingdom was firmly in his grasp, he executed the officials who had murdered his father the king. ⁶Yet he did not put the sons of the assassins to death, in accordance with what is written in the Book of the Law of Moses where the LORD commanded: "Fathers shall not be put to death for their children, nor children put to death for their fathers; each is to die for his own sins."[b]

⁷He was the one who defeated ten thousand Edomites in the Valley of Salt and captured Sela in battle, calling it Joktheel, the name it has to this day.

⁸Then Amaziah sent messengers to Jehoash son of Jehoahaz, the son of Jehu, king of Israel, with the challenge: "Come, meet me face to face."

---

a 1 Hebrew *Joash,* a variant of *Jehoash;* also in verses 13, 23 and 27   *b 6* Deut. 24:16

⁹But Jehoash king of Israel replied to Amaziah king of Judah: "A thistle in Lebanon sent a message to a cedar in Lebanon, 'Give your daughter to my son in marriage.' Then a wild beast in Lebanon came along and trampled the thistle underfoot. ¹⁰You have indeed defeated Edom and now you are arrogant. Glory in your victory, but stay at home! Why ask for trouble and cause your own downfall and that of Judah also?"

¹¹Amaziah, however, would not listen, so Jehoash king of Israel attacked. He and Amaziah king of Judah faced each other at Beth Shemesh in Judah. ¹²Judah was routed by Israel, and every man fled to his home. ¹³Jehoash king of Israel captured Amaziah king of Judah, the son of Joash, the son of Ahaziah, at Beth Shemesh. Then Jehoash went to Jerusalem and broke down the wall of Jerusalem from the Ephraim Gate to the Corner Gate—a section about six hundred feet long.ᵃ ¹⁴He took all the gold and silver and all the articles found in the temple of the LORD and in the treasuries of the royal palace. He also took hostages and returned to Samaria.

ᵃ 13 Hebrew *four hundred cubits* (about 180 meters)

MONDAY

COMPLETE OBEDIENCE
Charles G. Finney

VERSE: 2 Kings 14:4   **PASSAGE:** 2 Kings 14:1–7

hosoever keeps the whole law yet offends at one point is guilty of all (see James 2:10). He is rightly subject to the whole penalty. If he habitually disobeys God in one thing, then he doesn't obey him in anything, because obedience to God consists in an attitude of the heart. It is willingness to obey God, to let him rule everything. So if a person habitually disobeys God in one thing, his state of heart renders obedience in anything else impossible, because a person can't in one area obey God out of respect for his authority while in another area refuse obedience.

Obedience to God is an obedient state of heart, a preference for God's authority and commandments over everything else. If a person therefore appears to obey in some areas yet he knowingly disobeys in others, he is deceived. He offends in one point, and this proves he is guilty of all; in other words, he doesn't obey from the heart at all . . . If a person refuses to obey God's law, even a single duty, he . . . has no true faith, and his outwardly spiritual acts are loathsome.

ADDITIONAL SCRIPTURE READING:
2 Chronicles 25:1–2; Zechariah 1:4–6

Go to page 426 for your next devotional reading.

1700   1900

15As for the other events of the reign of Jehoash, what he did and his achievements, including his war against Amaziah king of Judah, are they not written in the book of the annals of the kings of Israel? 16Jehoash rested with his fathers and was buried in Samaria with the kings of Israel. And Jeroboam his son succeeded him as king.

17Amaziah son of Joash king of Judah lived for fifteen years after the death of Jehoash son of Jehoahaz king of Israel. 18As for the other events of Amaziah's reign, are they not written in the book of the annals of the kings of Judah?

19They conspired against him in Jerusalem, and he fled to Lachish, but they sent men after him to Lachish and killed him there. 20He was brought back by horse and was buried in Jerusalem with his fathers, in the City of David.

21Then all the people of Judah took Azariah,a who was sixteen years old, and made him king in place of his father Amaziah. 22He was the one who rebuilt Elath and restored it to Judah after Amaziah rested with his fathers.

Jeroboam II King of Israel

23In the fifteenth year of Amaziah son of Joash king of Judah, Jeroboam son of Jehoash king of Israel became king in Samaria, and he reigned forty-one years. 24He did evil in the eyes of the LORD and did not turn away from any of the sins of Jeroboam son of Nebat, which he had caused Israel to commit. 25He was the one who restored the boundaries of Israel from Lebob Hamath to the Sea of the Arabah,c in accordance with the word of the LORD, the God of Israel, spoken through his servant Jonah son of Amittai, the prophet from Gath Hepher.

26The LORD had seen how bitterly everyone in Israel, whether slave or free, was suffering; there was no one to help them. 27And since the LORD had not said he would blot out the name of Israel from under heaven, he saved them by the hand of Jeroboam son of Jehoash.

28As for the other events of Jeroboam's reign, all he did, and his military achieve-

ments, including how he recovered for Israel both Damascus and Hamath, which had belonged to Yaudi,d are they not written in the book of the annals of the kings of Israel? 29Jeroboam rested with his fathers, the kings of Israel. And Zechariah his son succeeded him as king.

Azariah King of Judah

15 In the twenty-seventh year of Jeroboam king of Israel, Azariah son of Amaziah king of Judah began to reign. 2He was sixteen years old when he became king, and he reigned in Jerusalem fifty-two years. His mother's name was Jecoliah; she was from Jerusalem. 3He did what was right in the eyes of the LORD, just as his father Amaziah had done. 4The high places, however, were not removed; the people continued to offer sacrifices and burn incense there.

5The LORD afflicted the king with leprosye until the day he died, and he lived in a separate house.f Jotham the king's son had charge of the palace and governed the people of the land.

6As for the other events of Azariah's reign, and all he did, are they not written in the book of the annals of the kings of Judah? 7Azariah rested with his fathers and was buried near them in the City of David. And Jotham his son succeeded him as king.

Zechariah King of Israel

8In the thirty-eighth year of Azariah king of Judah, Zechariah son of Jeroboam became king of Israel in Samaria, and he reigned six months. 9He did evil in the eyes of the LORD, as his fathers had done. He did not turn away from the sins of Jeroboam son of Nebat, which he had caused Israel to commit.

10Shallum son of Jabesh conspired against Zechariah. He attacked him in front of the people,g assassinated him and succeeded him as king. 11The other events of Zechariah's reign are written in the book of the annals of the kings of Israel. 12So the word of the LORD spoken to Jehu was fulfilled: "Your descendants

a 21 Also called Uzziah   b 25 Or from the entrance to   c 25 That is, the Dead Sea   d 28 Or Judah   e 5 The Hebrew word was used for various diseases affecting the skin—not necessarily leprosy.   f 5 Or in a house where he was relieved of responsibility   g 10 Hebrew; some Septuagint manuscripts in Ibleam

will sit on the throne of Israel to the fourth generation."[a]

Shallum King of Israel

[13]Shallum son of Jabesh became king in the thirty-ninth year of Uzziah king of Judah, and he reigned in Samaria one month. [14]Then Menahem son of Gadi went from Tirzah up to Samaria. He attacked Shallum son of Jabesh in Samaria, assassinated him and succeeded him as king.

[15]The other events of Shallum's reign, and the conspiracy he led, are written in the book of the annals of the kings of Israel.

[16]At that time Menahem, starting out from Tirzah, attacked Tiphsah and everyone in the city and its vicinity, because they refused to open their gates. He sacked Tiphsah and ripped open all the pregnant women.

Menahem King of Israel

[17]In the thirty-ninth year of Azariah king of Judah, Menahem son of Gadi became king of Israel, and he reigned in Samaria ten years. [18]He did evil in the eyes of the LORD. During his entire reign he did not turn away from the sins of Jeroboam son of Nebat, which he had caused Israel to commit.

[19]Then Pul[b] king of Assyria invaded the land, and Menahem gave him a thousand talents[c] of silver to gain his support and strengthen his own hold on the kingdom. [20]Menahem exacted this money from Israel. Every wealthy man had to contribute fifty shekels[d] of silver to be given to the king of Assyria. So the king of Assyria withdrew and stayed in the land no longer.

[21]As for the other events of Menahem's reign, and all he did, are they not written in the book of the annals of the kings of Israel? [22]Menahem rested with his fathers. And Pekahiah his son succeeded him as king.

Pekahiah King of Israel

[23]In the fiftieth year of Azariah king of Judah, Pekahiah son of Menahem became king of Israel in Samaria, and he reigned two years. [24]Pekahiah did evil in the eyes of the LORD. He did not turn away from the sins of Jeroboam son of Nebat, which he had caused Israel to commit. [25]One of his chief officers, Pekah son of Remaliah, conspired against him. Taking fifty men of Gilead with him, he assassinated Pekahiah, along with Argob and Arieh, in the citadel of the royal palace at Samaria. So Pekah killed Pekahiah and succeeded him as king.

[26]The other events of Pekahiah's reign, and all he did, are written in the book of the annals of the kings of Israel.

Pekah King of Israel

[27]In the fifty-second year of Azariah king of Judah, Pekah son of Remaliah became king of Israel in Samaria, and he reigned twenty years. [28]He did evil in the eyes of the LORD. He did not turn away from the sins of Jeroboam son of Nebat, which he had caused Israel to commit.

[29]In the time of Pekah king of Israel, Tiglath-Pileser king of Assyria came and took Ijon, Abel Beth Maacah, Janoah, Kedesh and Hazor. He took Gilead and Galilee, including all the land of Naphtali, and deported the people to Assyria. [30]Then Hoshea son of Elah conspired against Pekah son of Remaliah. He attacked and assassinated him, and then succeeded him as king in the twentieth year of Jotham son of Uzziah.

[31]As for the other events of Pekah's reign, and all he did, are they not written in the book of the annals of the kings of Israel?

Jotham King of Judah

[32]In the second year of Pekah son of Remaliah king of Israel, Jotham son of Uzziah king of Judah began to reign. [33]He was twenty-five years old when he became king, and he reigned in Jerusalem sixteen years. His mother's name was Jerusha daughter of Zadok. [34]He did what was right in the eyes of the LORD, just as his father Uzziah had done. [35]The high places, however, were not removed; the people continued to offer sacrifices and burn incense there. Jotham rebuilt the Upper Gate of the temple of the LORD.

[36]As for the other events of Jotham's

---

[a] 12 2 Kings 10:30　　[b] 19 Also called *Tiglath-Pileser*　　[c] 19 That is, about 37 tons (about 34 metric tons)　　[d] 20 That is, about 1 1/4 pounds (about 0.6 kilogram)

reign, and what he did, are they not written in the book of the annals of the kings of Judah? ³⁷(In those days the LORD began to send Rezin king of Aram and Pekah son of Remaliah against Judah.) ³⁸Jotham rested with his fathers and was buried with them in the City of David, the city of his father. And Ahaz his son succeeded him as king.

Ahaz King of Judah

16 In the seventeenth year of Pekah son of Remaliah, Ahaz son of Jotham king of Judah began to reign. ²Ahaz was twenty years old when he became king, and he reigned in Jerusalem sixteen years. Unlike David his father, he did not do what was right in the eyes of the LORD his God. ³He walked in the ways of the kings of Israel and even sacrificed his son in*a* the fire, following the detestable ways of the nations the LORD had driven out before the Israelites. ⁴He offered sacrifices and burned incense at the high places, on the hilltops and under every spreading tree.

⁵Then Rezin king of Aram and Pekah son of Remaliah king of Israel marched up to fight against Jerusalem and besieged Ahaz, but they could not overpower him. ⁶At that time, Rezin king of Aram recovered Elath for Aram by driving out the men of Judah. Edomites then moved into Elath and have lived there to this day.

⁷Ahaz sent messengers to say to Tiglath-Pileser king of Assyria, "I am your servant and vassal. Come up and save me out of the hand of the king of Aram and of the king of Israel, who are attacking me." ⁸And Ahaz took the silver and gold found in the temple of the LORD and in the treasuries of the royal palace and sent it as a gift to the king of Assyria. ⁹The king of Assyria complied by attacking Damascus and capturing it. He deported its inhabitants to Kir and put Rezin to death.

¹⁰Then King Ahaz went to Damascus to meet Tiglath-Pileser king of Assyria. He saw an altar in Damascus and sent to Uriah the priest a sketch of the altar, with detailed plans for its construction. ¹¹So Uriah the priest built an altar in accordance with all the plans that King Ahaz had sent from Damascus and finished it before King Ahaz returned. ¹²When the king came back from Damascus and saw the altar, he approached it and presented offerings*b* on it. ¹³He offered up his burnt offering and grain offering, poured out his drink offering, and sprinkled the blood of his fellowship offerings*c* on the altar. ¹⁴The bronze altar that stood before the LORD he brought from the front of the temple—from between the new altar and the temple of the LORD—and put it on the north side of the new altar.

¹⁵King Ahaz then gave these orders to Uriah the priest: "On the large new altar, offer the morning burnt offering and the evening grain offering, the king's burnt offering and his grain offering, and the burnt offering of all the people of the land, and their grain offering and their drink offering. Sprinkle on the altar all the blood of the burnt offerings and sacrifices. But I will use the bronze altar for seeking guidance." ¹⁶And Uriah the priest did just as King Ahaz had ordered.

¹⁷King Ahaz took away the side panels and removed the basins from the movable stands. He removed the Sea from the bronze bulls that supported it and set it on a stone base. ¹⁸He took away the Sabbath canopy*d* that had been built at the temple and removed the royal entryway outside the temple of the LORD, in deference to the king of Assyria.

¹⁹As for the other events of the reign of Ahaz, and what he did, are they not written in the book of the annals of the kings of Judah? ²⁰Ahaz rested with his fathers and was buried with them in the City of David. And Hezekiah his son succeeded him as king.

Hoshea Last King of Israel

17 In the twelfth year of Ahaz king of Judah, Hoshea son of Elah became king of Israel in Samaria, and he reigned nine years. ²He did evil in the eyes of the LORD, but not like the kings of Israel who preceded him.

³Shalmaneser king of Assyria came up to attack Hoshea, who had been Shalmaneser's vassal and had paid him trib-

---

a 3 Or *even made his son pass through*   *b 12* Or *and went up*   *c 13* Traditionally *peace offerings*
d 18 Or *the dais of his throne* (see Septuagint)

ute. **4**But the king of Assyria discovered that Hoshea was a traitor, for he had sent envoys to So[a] king of Egypt, and he no longer paid tribute to the king of Assyria, as he had done year by year. Therefore Shalmaneser seized him and put him in prison. **5**The king of Assyria invaded the entire land, marched against Samaria and laid siege to it for three years. **6**In the ninth year of Hoshea, the king of Assyria captured Samaria and deported the Israelites to Assyria. He settled them in Halah, in Gozan on the Habor River and in the towns of the Medes.

Israel Exiled Because of Sin

7All this took place because the Israelites had sinned against the LORD their God, who had brought them up out of Egypt from under the power of Pharaoh king of Egypt. They worshiped other gods **8**and followed the practices of the nations the LORD had driven out before them, as well as the practices that the kings of Israel had introduced. **9**The Israelites secretly did things against the LORD their God that were not right. From watchtower to fortified city they built themselves high places in all their towns. **10**They set up sacred stones and Asherah poles on every high hill and under every spreading tree. **11**At every high place they burned incense, as the nations whom the LORD had driven out before them had done. They did wicked things that provoked the LORD to anger. **12**They worshiped idols, though the LORD had said, "You shall not do this."[b] **13**The LORD warned Israel and Judah through all his prophets and seers: "Turn from your evil ways. Observe my commands and decrees, in accordance with the entire Law that I commanded your fathers to obey and that I delivered to you through my servants the prophets."

14But they would not listen and were as stiff-necked as their fathers, who did not trust in the LORD their God. **15**They rejected his decrees and the covenant he had made with their fathers and the warnings he had given them. They followed worthless idols and themselves became worthless. They imitated the nations around them although the LORD

had ordered them, "Do not do as they do," and they did the things the LORD had forbidden them to do.

16They forsook all the commands of the LORD their God and made for themselves two idols cast in the shape of calves, and an Asherah pole. They bowed down to all the starry hosts, and they worshiped Baal. **17**They sacrificed their sons and daughters in[c] the fire. They practiced divination and sorcery and sold themselves to do evil in the eyes of the LORD, provoking him to anger.

18So the LORD was very angry with Israel and removed them from his presence. Only the tribe of Judah was left, **19**and even Judah did not keep the commands of the LORD their God. They followed the practices Israel had introduced. **20**Therefore the LORD rejected all the people of Israel; he afflicted them and gave them into the hands of plunderers, until he thrust them from his presence.

21When he tore Israel away from the house of David, they made Jeroboam son of Nebat their king. Jeroboam enticed Israel away from following the LORD and caused them to commit a great sin. **22**The Israelites persisted in all the sins of Jeroboam and did not turn away from them **23**until the LORD removed them from his presence, as he had warned through all his servants the prophets. So the people of Israel were taken from their homeland into exile in Assyria, and they are still there.

Samaria Resettled

24The king of Assyria brought people from Babylon, Cuthah, Avva, Hamath and Sepharvaim and settled them in the towns of Samaria to replace the Israelites. They took over Samaria and lived in its towns. **25**When they first lived there, they did not worship the LORD; so he sent lions among them and they killed some of the people. **26**It was reported to the king of Assyria: "The people you deported and resettled in the towns of Samaria do not know what the god of that country requires. He has sent lions among them, which are killing them off, because the people do not know what he requires."

a 4 Or *to Sais, to the; So* is possibly an abbreviation for *Osorkon.*   *b 12* Exodus 20:4, 5   *c 17* Or *They made their sons and daughters pass through*

²⁷Then the king of Assyria gave this order: "Have one of the priests you took captive from Samaria go back to live there and teach the people what the god of the land requires." ²⁸So one of the priests who had been exiled from Samaria came to live in Bethel and taught them how to worship the LORD.

²⁹Nevertheless, each national group made its own gods in the several towns where they settled, and set them up in the shrines the people of Samaria had made at the high places. ³⁰The men from Babylon made Succoth Benoth, the men from Cuthah made Nergal, and the men from Hamath made Ashima; ³¹the Avvites made Nibhaz and Tartak, and the Sepharvites burned their children in the fire as sacrifices to Adrammelech and Anammelech, the gods of Sepharvaim. ³²They worshiped the LORD, but they also appointed all sorts of their own people to officiate for them as priests in the shrines at the high places. ³³They worshiped the LORD, but they also served their own gods in accordance with the customs of the nations from which they had been brought.

³⁴To this day they persist in their former practices. They neither worship the LORD nor adhere to the decrees and ordinances, the laws and commands that the LORD gave the descendants of Jacob, whom he named Israel. ³⁵When the LORD made a covenant with the Israelites, he commanded them: "Do not worship any other gods or bow down to them, serve them or sacrifice to them. ³⁶But the LORD, who brought you up out of Egypt with mighty power and outstretched arm, is the one you must worship. To him you shall bow down and to him offer sacrifices. ³⁷You must always be careful to keep the decrees and ordinances, the laws and commands he wrote for you. Do not worship other gods. ³⁸Do not forget the covenant I have made with you, and do not worship other gods. ³⁹Rather, worship the LORD your God; it is he who will deliver you from the hand of all your enemies."

⁴⁰They would not listen, however, but persisted in their former practices. ⁴¹Even while these people were worshiping the LORD, they were serving their idols. To this day their children and grandchildren continue to do as their fathers did.

Hezekiah King of Judah

18 In the third year of Hoshea son of Elah king of Israel, Hezekiah son of Ahaz king of Judah began to reign. ²He was twenty-five years old when he became king, and he reigned in Jerusalem twenty-nine years. His mother's name was Abijah[a] daughter of Zechariah. ³He did what was right in the eyes of the LORD, just as his father David had done. ⁴He removed the high places, smashed the sacred stones and cut down the Asherah poles. He broke into pieces the bronze snake Moses had made, for up to that time the Israelites had been burning incense to it. (It was called[b] Nehushtan.[c])

⁵Hezekiah trusted in the LORD, the God of Israel. There was no one like him among all the kings of Judah, either before him or after him. ⁶He held fast to the LORD and did not cease to follow him; he kept the commands the LORD had given Moses. ⁷And the LORD was with him; he was successful in whatever he undertook. He rebelled against the king of Assyria and did not serve him. ⁸From watchtower to fortified city, he defeated the Philistines, as far as Gaza and its territory.

⁹In King Hezekiah's fourth year, which was the seventh year of Hoshea son of Elah king of Israel, Shalmaneser king of Assyria marched against Samaria and laid siege to it. ¹⁰At the end of three years the Assyrians took it. So Samaria was captured in Hezekiah's sixth year, which was the ninth year of Hoshea king of Israel. ¹¹The king of Assyria deported Israel to Assyria and settled them in Halah, in Gozan on the Habor River and in towns of the Medes. ¹²This happened because they had not obeyed the LORD their God, but had violated his covenant—all that Moses the servant of the LORD commanded. They neither listened to the commands nor carried them out.

¹³In the fourteenth year of King Hezekiah's reign, Sennacherib king of Assyria

---

a 2 Hebrew *Abi,* a variant of *Abijah*   *b 4* Or *He called it*   *c 4* *Nehushtan* sounds like the Hebrew for *bronze* and *snake* and *unclean thing.*

attacked all the fortified cities of Judah and captured them. 14So Hezekiah king of Judah sent this message to the king of Assyria at Lachish: "I have done wrong. Withdraw from me, and I will pay whatever you demand of me." The king of Assyria exacted from Hezekiah king of Judah three hundred talents*a* of silver and thirty talents*b* of gold. 15So Hezekiah gave him all the silver that was found in the temple of the LORD and in the treasuries of the royal palace.

16At this time Hezekiah king of Judah stripped off the gold with which he had covered the doors and doorposts of the temple of the LORD, and gave it to the king of Assyria.

Sennacherib Threatens Jerusalem

17The king of Assyria sent his supreme commander, his chief officer and his field commander with a large army, from Lachish to King Hezekiah at Jerusalem. They came up to Jerusalem and stopped

---

a 14 That is, about 11 tons (about 10 metric tons)   *b 14* That is, about 1 ton (about 1 metric ton)

TUESDAY

THE ROD, THE SERPENT AND HOLINESS
Horatius Bonar

VERSE: 2 Kings 18:4   **PASSAGE:** 2 Kings 18:1–7

gainst evil, divine truth is quick and powerful. It acts like some chemical ingredient that precipitates all impurities and leaves the water clear. It works like a spell of disenchantment against the evil one, casting him out, and casting him down. It is "the sword of the Spirit," with whose keen edge we cut our way through hostile thousands. It is the rod of Moses, by which we divide the Red Sea, and defeat Amalek, and bring water from the desert rock (see Exodus 14:16; 17:6). What evil, what enemy, within or without, is there that can withstand this unconquered and unconquerable Word? Satan's object at present is to undermine that Word and to disparage its perfection. Let us the more magnify it, and the more make constant use of it. It is indeed only a fragment of man's language, made up of human letters and syllables; but it is furnished with superhuman virtue.

That rod in the hand of Moses, what was it? A piece of common wood. Yet it cut the Red Sea in two. That serpent on the pole, what was it? A bit of brass. Yet it healed thousands (see Numbers 21:9). Why all this? Because that wood and that brass were connected with omnipotence, conductors of the heavenly electricity.

ADDITIONAL SCRIPTURE READING:
Numbers 21:8–9; John 3:14–15

Go to page 456 for your next devotional reading.

1700   1900

at the aqueduct of the Upper Pool, on the road to the Washerman's Field. ¹⁸They called for the king; and Eliakim son of Hilkiah the palace administrator, Shebna the secretary, and Joah son of Asaph the recorder went out to them.

¹⁹The field commander said to them, "Tell Hezekiah:

" 'This is what the great king, the king of Assyria, says: On what are you basing this confidence of yours? ²⁰You say you have strategy and military strength—but you speak only empty words. On whom are you depending, that you rebel against me? ²¹Look now, you are depending on Egypt, that splintered reed of a staff, which pierces a man's hand and wounds him if he leans on it! Such is Pharaoh king of Egypt to all who depend on him. ²²And if you say to me, "We are depending on the LORD our God"—isn't he the one whose high places and altars Hezekiah removed, saying to Judah and Jerusalem, "You must worship before this altar in Jerusalem"?

²³" 'Come now, make a bargain with my master, the king of Assyria: I will give you two thousand horses—if you can put riders on them! ²⁴How can you repulse one officer of the least of my master's officials, even though you are depending on Egypt for chariots and horsemen*a*? ²⁵Furthermore, have I come to attack and destroy this place without word from the LORD? The LORD himself told me to march against this country and destroy it.' "

²⁶Then Eliakim son of Hilkiah, and Shebna and Joah said to the field commander, "Please speak to your servants in Aramaic, since we understand it. Don't speak to us in Hebrew in the hearing of the people on the wall."

²⁷But the commander replied, "Was it only to your master and you that my master sent me to say these things, and not to the men sitting on the wall—who, like you, will have to eat their own filth and drink their own urine?"

²⁸Then the commander stood and called out in Hebrew: "Hear the word of the great king, the king of Assyria! ²⁹This is what the king says: Do not let Hezekiah deceive you. He cannot deliver you from my hand. ³⁰Do not let Hezekiah persuade you to trust in the LORD when he says, 'The LORD will surely deliver us; this city will not be given into the hand of the king of Assyria.'

³¹"Do not listen to Hezekiah. This is what the king of Assyria says: Make peace with me and come out to me. Then every one of you will eat from his own vine and fig tree and drink water from his own cistern, ³²until I come and take you to a land like your own, a land of grain and new wine, a land of bread and vineyards, a land of olive trees and honey. Choose life and not death!

"Do not listen to Hezekiah, for he is misleading you when he says, 'The LORD will deliver us.' ³³Has the god of any nation ever delivered his land from the hand of the king of Assyria? ³⁴Where are the gods of Hamath and Arpad? Where are the gods of Sepharvaim, Hena and Ivvah? Have they rescued Samaria from my hand? ³⁵Who of all the gods of these countries has been able to save his land from me? How then can the LORD deliver Jerusalem from my hand?"

³⁶But the people remained silent and said nothing in reply, because the king had commanded, "Do not answer him."

³⁷Then Eliakim son of Hilkiah the palace administrator, Shebna the secretary and Joah son of Asaph the recorder went to Hezekiah, with their clothes torn, and told him what the field commander had said.

Jerusalem's Deliverance Foretold

19 When King Hezekiah heard this, he tore his clothes and put on sackcloth and went into the temple of the LORD. ²He sent Eliakim the palace administrator, Shebna the secretary and the leading priests, all wearing sackcloth, to the prophet Isaiah son of Amoz. ³They told him, "This is what Hezekiah says: This day is a day of distress and rebuke and disgrace, as when children come to the point of birth and there is no strength to deliver them. ⁴It may be that the LORD your God will hear

a 24 Or charioteers

all the words of the field commander, whom his master, the king of Assyria, has sent to ridicule the living God, and that he will rebuke him for the words the LORD your God has heard. Therefore pray for the remnant that still survives."

⁵When King Hezekiah's officials came to Isaiah, ⁶Isaiah said to them, "Tell your master, 'This is what the LORD says: Do not be afraid of what you have heard—those words with which the underlings of the king of Assyria have blasphemed me. ⁷Listen! I am going to put such a spirit in him that when he hears a certain report, he will return to his own country, and there I will have him cut down with the sword.' "

⁸When the field commander heard that the king of Assyria had left Lachish, he withdrew and found the king fighting against Libnah.

⁹Now Sennacherib received a report that Tirhakah, the Cushite*ᵃ* king ⸳of Egypt⸴, was marching out to fight against him. So he again sent messengers to Hezekiah with this word: ¹⁰"Say to Hezekiah king of Judah: Do not let the god you depend on deceive you when he says, 'Jerusalem will not be handed over to the king of Assyria.' ¹¹Surely you have heard what the kings of Assyria have done to all the countries, destroying them completely. And will you be delivered? ¹²Did the gods of the nations that were destroyed by my forefathers deliver them: the gods of Gozan, Haran, Rezeph and the people of Eden who were in Tel Assar? ¹³Where is the king of Hamath, the king of Arpad, the king of the city of Sepharvaim, or of Hena or Ivvah?"

Hezekiah's Prayer

¹⁴Hezekiah received the letter from the messengers and read it. Then he went up to the temple of the LORD and spread it out before the LORD. ¹⁵And Hezekiah prayed to the LORD: "O LORD, God of Israel, enthroned between the cherubim, you alone are God over all the kingdoms of the earth. You have made heaven and earth. ¹⁶Give ear, O LORD, and hear; open your eyes, O LORD, and see; listen to the words Sennacherib has sent to insult the living God.

¹⁷"It is true, O LORD, that the Assyrian

kings have laid waste these nations and their lands. ¹⁸They have thrown their gods into the fire and destroyed them, for they were not gods but only wood and stone, fashioned by men's hands. ¹⁹Now, O LORD our God, deliver us from his hand, so that all kingdoms on earth may know that you alone, O LORD, are God."

Isaiah Prophesies Sennacherib's Fall

²⁰Then Isaiah son of Amoz sent a message to Hezekiah: "This is what the LORD, the God of Israel, says: I have heard your prayer concerning Sennacherib king of Assyria. ²¹This is the word that the LORD has spoken against him:

" 'The Virgin Daughter of Zion
   despises you and mocks you.
The Daughter of Jerusalem
   tosses her head as you flee.
²²Who is it you have insulted and
      blasphemed?
   Against whom have you raised
      your voice
and lifted your eyes in pride?
   Against the Holy One of Israel!
²³By your messengers
   you have heaped insults on the
      Lord.
And you have said,
   "With my many chariots
I have ascended the heights of the
      mountains,
   the utmost heights of Lebanon.
I have cut down its tallest cedars,
   the choicest of its pines.
I have reached its remotest parts,
   the finest of its forests.
²⁴I have dug wells in foreign lands
   and drunk the water there.
With the soles of my feet
   I have dried up all the streams of
      Egypt."
²⁵" 'Have you not heard?
   Long ago I ordained it.
In days of old I planned it;
   now I have brought it to pass,
that you have turned fortified cities
   into piles of stone.
²⁶Their people, drained of power,
   are dismayed and put to shame.
They are like plants in the field,

ᵃ 9 That is, from the upper Nile region

like tender green shoots,
like grass sprouting on the roof,
scorched before it grows up.

27 " 'But I know where you stay
and when you come and go
and how you rage against me.
28 Because you rage against me
and your insolence has reached my
ears,
I will put my hook in your nose
and my bit in your mouth,
and I will make you return
by the way you came.'

29 "This will be the sign for you,
O Hezekiah:

"This year you will eat what grows
by itself,
and the second year what springs
from that.
But in the third year sow and reap,
plant vineyards and eat their fruit.
30 Once more a remnant of the house of
Judah
will take root below and bear fruit
above.
31 For out of Jerusalem will come a
remnant,
and out of Mount Zion a band of
survivors.

The zeal of the LORD Almighty will
accomplish this.

32 "Therefore this is what the LORD
says concerning the king of Assyria:

"He will not enter this city
or shoot an arrow here.
He will not come before it with
shield
or build a siege ramp against it.
33 By the way that he came he will
return;
he will not enter this city,
declares the LORD.
34 I will defend this city and save it,
for my sake and for the sake of
David my servant."

35 That night the angel of the LORD
went out and put to death a hundred and
eighty-five thousand men in the Assyrian camp. When the people got up the
next morning—there were all the dead
bodies! 36 So Sennacherib king of Assyria
broke camp and withdrew. He returned
to Nineveh and stayed there.

37 One day, while he was worshiping in
the temple of his god Nisroch, his sons
Adrammelech and Sharezer cut him
down with the sword, and they escaped
to the land of Ararat. And Esarhaddon
his son succeeded him as king.

Hezekiah's Illness

20 In those days Hezekiah
became ill and was at the
point of death. The prophet Isaiah son of
Amoz went to him and said, "This is
what the LORD says: Put your house in
order, because you are going to die; you
will not recover."

2 Hezekiah turned his face to the wall
and prayed to the LORD, 3 "Remember,
O LORD, how I have walked before you
faithfully and with wholehearted devotion and have done what is good in your
eyes." And Hezekiah wept bitterly.

4 Before Isaiah had left the middle
court, the word of the LORD came to
him: 5 "Go back and tell Hezekiah, the
leader of my people, 'This is what the
LORD, the God of your father David, says:
I have heard your prayer and seen your
tears; I will heal you. On the third day
from now you will go up to the temple of
the LORD. 6 I will add fifteen years to your
life. And I will deliver you and this city
from the hand of the king of Assyria. I
will defend this city for my sake and for
the sake of my servant David.' "

7 Then Isaiah said, "Prepare a poultice
of figs." They did so and applied it to the
boil, and he recovered.

8 Hezekiah had asked Isaiah, "What
will be the sign that the LORD will heal
me and that I will go up to the temple of
the LORD on the third day from now?"

9 Isaiah answered, "This is the LORD's
sign to you that the LORD will do what
he has promised: Shall the shadow go
forward ten steps, or shall it go back ten
steps?"

10 "It is a simple matter for the shadow
to go forward ten steps," said Hezekiah.
"Rather, have it go back ten steps."

11 Then the prophet Isaiah called upon
the LORD, and the LORD made the shadow go back the ten steps it had gone
down on the stairway of Ahaz.

Envoys From Babylon

12At that time Merodach-Baladan son of Baladan king of Babylon sent Hezekiah letters and a gift, because he had heard of Hezekiah's illness. **13**Hezekiah received the messengers and showed them all that was in his storehouses—the silver, the gold, the spices and the fine oil—his armory and everything found among his treasures. There was nothing in his palace or in all his kingdom that Hezekiah did not show them.

14Then Isaiah the prophet went to King Hezekiah and asked, "What did those men say, and where did they come from?"

"From a distant land," Hezekiah replied. "They came from Babylon."

15The prophet asked, "What did they see in your palace?"

"They saw everything in my palace," Hezekiah said. "There is nothing among my treasures that I did not show them."

16Then Isaiah said to Hezekiah, "Hear the word of the LORD: **17**The time will surely come when everything in your palace, and all that your fathers have stored up until this day, will be carried off to Babylon. Nothing will be left, says the LORD. **18**And some of your descendants, your own flesh and blood, that will be born to you, will be taken away, and they will become eunuchs in the palace of the king of Babylon."

19"The word of the LORD you have spoken is good," Hezekiah replied. For he thought, "Will there not be peace and security in my lifetime?"

20As for the other events of Hezekiah's reign, all his achievements and how he made the pool and the tunnel by which he brought water into the city, are they not written in the book of the annals of the kings of Judah? **21**Hezekiah rested with his fathers. And Manasseh his son succeeded him as king.

Manasseh King of Judah

21 Manasseh was twelve years old when he became king, and he reigned in Jerusalem fifty-five years. His mother's name was Hephzibah. **2**He did evil in the eyes of the LORD, following the detestable practices of the nations the LORD had driven out before the Israelites. **3**He rebuilt the high places his father Hezekiah had destroyed; he also erected altars to Baal and made an Asherah pole, as Ahab king of Israel had done. He bowed down to all the starry hosts and worshiped them. **4**He built altars in the temple of the LORD, of which the LORD had said, "In Jerusalem I will put my Name." **5**In both courts of the temple of the LORD, he built altars to all the starry hosts. **6**He sacrificed his own son in*a* the fire, practiced sorcery and divination, and consulted mediums and spiritists. He did much evil in the eyes of the LORD, provoking him to anger.

7He took the carved Asherah pole he had made and put it in the temple, of which the LORD had said to David and to his son Solomon, "In this temple and in Jerusalem, which I have chosen out of all the tribes of Israel, I will put my Name forever. **8**I will not again make the feet of the Israelites wander from the land I gave their forefathers, if only they will be careful to do everything I commanded them and will keep the whole Law that my servant Moses gave them." **9**But the people did not listen. Manasseh led them astray, so that they did more evil than the nations the LORD had destroyed before the Israelites.

10The LORD said through his servants the prophets: **11**"Manasseh king of Judah has committed these detestable sins. He has done more evil than the Amorites who preceded him and has led Judah into sin with his idols. **12**Therefore this is what the LORD, the God of Israel, says: I am going to bring such disaster on Jerusalem and Judah that the ears of everyone who hears of it will tingle. **13**I will stretch out over Jerusalem the measuring line used against Samaria and the plumb line used against the house of Ahab. I will wipe out Jerusalem as one wipes a dish, wiping it and turning it upside down. **14**I will forsake the remnant of my inheritance and hand them over to their enemies. They will be looted and plundered by all their foes, **15**because they have done evil in my eyes and have provoked me to anger from the day their forefathers came out of Egypt until this day.'"

---

a 6 Or *He made his own son pass through*

16Moreover, Manasseh also shed so much innocent blood that he filled Jerusalem from end to end—besides the sin that he had caused Judah to commit, so that they did evil in the eyes of the LORD.

17As for the other events of Manasseh's reign, and all he did, including the sin he committed, are they not written in the book of the annals of the kings of Judah? 18Manasseh rested with his fathers and was buried in his palace garden, the garden of Uzza. And Amon his son succeeded him as king.

Amon King of Judah

19Amon was twenty-two years old when he became king, and he reigned in Jerusalem two years. His mother's name was Meshullemeth daughter of Haruz; she was from Jotbah. 20He did evil in the eyes of the LORD, as his father Manasseh had done. 21He walked in all the ways of his father; he worshiped the idols his father had worshiped, and bowed down to them. 22He forsook the LORD, the God of his fathers, and did not walk in the way of the LORD.

23Amon's officials conspired against him and assassinated the king in his palace. 24Then the people of the land killed all who had plotted against King Amon, and they made Josiah his son king in his place.

25As for the other events of Amon's reign, and what he did, are they not written in the book of the annals of the kings of Judah? 26He was buried in his grave in the garden of Uzza. And Josiah his son succeeded him as king.

The Book of the Law Found

22 Josiah was eight years old when he became king, and he reigned in Jerusalem thirty-one years. His mother's name was Jedidah daughter of Adaiah; she was from Bozkath. 2He did what was right in the eyes of the LORD and walked in all the ways of his father David, not turning aside to the right or to the left.

3In the eighteenth year of his reign, King Josiah sent the secretary, Shaphan son of Azaliah, the son of Meshullam, to the temple of the LORD. He said: 4"Go up to Hilkiah the high priest and have him get ready the money that has been brought into the temple of the LORD, which the doorkeepers have collected from the people. 5Have them entrust it to the men appointed to supervise the work on the temple. And have these men pay the workers who repair the temple of the LORD— 6the carpenters, the builders and the masons. Also have them purchase timber and dressed stone to repair the temple. 7But they need not account for the money entrusted to them, because they are acting faithfully."

8Hilkiah the high priest said to Shaphan the secretary, "I have found the Book of the Law in the temple of the LORD." He gave it to Shaphan, who read it. 9Then Shaphan the secretary went to the king and reported to him: "Your officials have paid out the money that was in the temple of the LORD and have entrusted it to the workers and supervisors at the temple." 10Then Shaphan the secretary informed the king, "Hilkiah the priest has given me a book." And Shaphan read from it in the presence of the king.

11When the king heard the words of the Book of the Law, he tore his robes. 12He gave these orders to Hilkiah the priest, Ahikam son of Shaphan, Acbor son of Micaiah, Shaphan the secretary and Asaiah the king's attendant: 13"Go and inquire of the LORD for me and for the people and for all Judah about what is written in this book that has been found. Great is the LORD's anger that burns against us because our fathers have not obeyed the words of this book; they have not acted in accordance with all that is written there concerning us."

14Hilkiah the priest, Ahikam, Acbor, Shaphan and Asaiah went to speak to the prophetess Huldah, who was the wife of Shallum son of Tikvah, the son of Harhas, keeper of the wardrobe. She lived in Jerusalem, in the Second District.

15She said to them, "This is what the LORD, the God of Israel, says: Tell the man who sent you to me, 16'This is what the LORD says: I am going to bring disaster on this place and its people, according to everything written in the book the king of Judah has read. 17Because they have forsaken me and burned incense to other gods and provoked me to anger by all the idols their hands have made,ᵃ my anger will burn against this place and will not be quenched.' ¹⁸Tell the king of Judah, who sent you to inquire of the LORD, 'This is what the LORD, the God of Israel, says concerning the words you heard: ¹⁹Because your heart was responsive and you humbled yourself before the LORD when you heard what I have spoken against this place and its people, that they would become accursed and laid waste, and because you tore your robes and wept in my presence, I have heard you, declares the LORD. ²⁰Therefore I will gather you to your fathers, and you will be buried in peace. Your eyes will not see all the disaster I am going to bring on this place.' "

So they took her answer back to the king.

Josiah Renews the Covenant

23 Then the king called together all the elders of Judah and Jerusalem. ²He went up to the temple of the LORD with the men of Judah, the people of Jerusalem, the priests and the prophets—all the people from the least to the greatest. He read in their hearing all the words of the Book of the Covenant, which had been found in the temple of the LORD. ³The king stood by the pillar and renewed the covenant in the presence of the LORD—to follow the LORD and keep his commands, regulations and decrees with all his heart and all his soul, thus confirming the words of the covenant written in this book. Then all the people pledged themselves to the covenant.

⁴The king ordered Hilkiah the high priest, the priests next in rank and the doorkeepers to remove from the temple of the LORD all the articles made for Baal and Asherah and all the starry hosts. He burned them outside Jerusalem in the fields of the Kidron Valley and took the ashes to Bethel. ⁵He did away with the pagan priests appointed by the kings of Judah to burn incense on the high places of the towns of Judah and on those around Jerusalem—those who burned incense to Baal, to the sun and moon, to the constellations and to all the starry

hosts. ⁶He took the Asherah pole from the temple of the LORD to the Kidron Valley outside Jerusalem and burned it there. He ground it to powder and scattered the dust over the graves of the common people. ⁷He also tore down the quarters of the male shrine prostitutes, which were in the temple of the LORD and where women did weaving for Asherah.

⁸Josiah brought all the priests from the towns of Judah and desecrated the high places, from Geba to Beersheba, where the priests had burned incense. He broke down the shrinesᵇ at the gates—at the entrance to the Gate of Joshua, the city governor, which is on the left of the city gate. ⁹Although the priests of the high places did not serve at the altar of the LORD in Jerusalem, they ate unleavened bread with their fellow priests.

¹⁰He desecrated Topheth, which was in the Valley of Ben Hinnom, so no one could use it to sacrifice his son or daughter in the fire to Molech. ¹¹He removed from the entrance to the temple of the LORD the horses that the kings of Judah had dedicated to the sun. They were in the court near the room of an official named Nathan-Melech. Josiah then burned the chariots dedicated to the sun.

¹²He pulled down the altars the kings of Judah had erected on the roof near the upper room of Ahaz, and the altars Manasseh had built in the two courts of the temple of the LORD. He removed them from there, smashed them to pieces and threw the rubble into the Kidron Valley. ¹³The king also desecrated the high places that were east of Jerusalem on the south of the Hill of Corruption—the ones Solomon king of Israel had built for Ashtoreth the vile goddess of the Sidonians, for Chemosh the vile god of Moab, and for Molechᵈ the detestable god of the people of Ammon. ¹⁴Josiah smashed the sacred stones and cut down the Asherah poles and covered the sites with human bones.

¹⁵Even the altar at Bethel, the high place made by Jeroboam son of Nebat, who had caused Israel to sin—even that altar and high place he demolished. He burned the high place and ground it to powder, and burned the Asherah pole

also. ¹⁶Then Josiah looked around, and when he saw the tombs that were there on the hillside, he had the bones removed from them and burned on the altar to defile it, in accordance with the word of the LORD proclaimed by the man of God who foretold these things.

¹⁷The king asked, "What is that tombstone I see?"

The men of the city said, "It marks the tomb of the man of God who came from Judah and pronounced against the altar of Bethel the very things you have done to it."

¹⁸"Leave it alone," he said. "Don't let anyone disturb his bones." So they spared his bones and those of the prophet who had come from Samaria.

¹⁹Just as he had done at Bethel, Josiah removed and defiled all the shrines at the high places that the kings of Israel had built in the towns of Samaria that had provoked the LORD to anger. ²⁰Josiah slaughtered all the priests of those high places on the altars and burned human bones on them. Then he went back to Jerusalem.

²¹The king gave this order to all the people: "Celebrate the Passover to the LORD your God, as it is written in this Book of the Covenant." ²²Not since the days of the judges who led Israel, nor throughout the days of the kings of Israel and the kings of Judah, had any such Passover been observed. ²³But in the eighteenth year of King Josiah, this Passover was celebrated to the LORD in Jerusalem.

²⁴Furthermore, Josiah got rid of the mediums and spiritists, the household gods, the idols and all the other detestable things seen in Judah and Jerusalem. This he did to fulfill the requirements of the law written in the book that Hilkiah the priest had discovered in the temple of the LORD. ²⁵Neither before nor after Josiah was there a king like him who turned to the LORD as he did—with all his heart and with all his soul and with all his strength, in accordance with all the Law of Moses.

²⁶Nevertheless, the LORD did not turn away from the heat of his fierce anger, which burned against Judah because of all that Manasseh had done to provoke him to anger. ²⁷So the LORD said, "I will remove Judah also from my presence as I removed Israel, and I will reject Jerusalem, the city I chose, and this temple, about which I said, 'There shall my Name be.'ᵃ "

²⁸As for the other events of Josiah's reign, and all he did, are they not written in the book of the annals of the kings of Judah?

²⁹While Josiah was king, Pharaoh Neco king of Egypt went up to the Euphrates River to help the king of Assyria. King Josiah marched out to meet him in battle, but Neco faced him and killed him at Megiddo. ³⁰Josiah's servants brought his body in a chariot from Megiddo to Jerusalem and buried him in his own tomb. And the people of the land took Jehoahaz son of Josiah and anointed him and made him king in place of his father.

Jehoahaz King of Judah

³¹Jehoahaz was twenty-three years old when he became king, and he reigned in Jerusalem three months. His mother's name was Hamutal daughter of Jeremiah; she was from Libnah. ³²He did evil in the eyes of the LORD, just as his fathers had done. ³³Pharaoh Neco put him in chains at Riblah in the land of Hamathᵇ so that he might not reign in Jerusalem, and he imposed on Judah a levy of a hundred talentsᶜ of silver and a talentᵈ of gold. ³⁴Pharaoh Neco made Eliakim son of Josiah king in place of his father Josiah and changed Eliakim's name to Jehoiakim. But he took Jehoahaz and carried him off to Egypt, and there he died. ³⁵Jehoiakim paid Pharaoh Neco the silver and gold he demanded. In order to do so, he taxed the land and exacted the silver and gold from the people of the land according to their assessments.

Jehoiakim King of Judah

³⁶Jehoiakim was twenty-five years old when he became king, and he reigned in Jerusalem eleven years. His mother's name was Zebidah daughter of Pedaiah;

ᵃ 27 1 Kings 8:29   ᵇ 33 Hebrew; Septuagint (see also 2 Chron. 36:3) *Neco at Riblah in Hamath removed him*   ᶜ 33 That is, about 3 3/4 tons (about 3.4 metric tons)   ᵈ 33 That is, about 75 pounds (about 34 kilograms)

she was from Rumah. [37]And he did evil in the eyes of the LORD, just as his fathers had done.

24 During Jehoiakim's reign, Nebuchadnezzar king of Babylon invaded the land, and Jehoiakim became his vassal for three years. But then he changed his mind and rebelled against Nebuchadnezzar. [2]The LORD sent Babylonian,[a] Aramean, Moabite and Ammonite raiders against him. He sent them to destroy Judah, in accordance with the word of the LORD proclaimed by his servants the prophets. [3]Surely these things happened to Judah according to the LORD's command, in order to remove them from his presence because of the sins of Manasseh and all he had done, [4]including the shedding of innocent blood. For he had filled Jerusalem with innocent blood, and the LORD was not willing to forgive.

[5]As for the other events of Jehoiakim's reign, and all he did, are they not written in the book of the annals of the kings of Judah? [6]Jehoiakim rested with his fathers. And Jehoiachin his son succeeded him as king.

[7]The king of Egypt did not march out from his own country again, because the king of Babylon had taken all his territory, from the Wadi of Egypt to the Euphrates River.

Jehoiachin King of Judah

[8]Jehoiachin was eighteen years old when he became king, and he reigned in Jerusalem three months. His mother's name was Nehushta daughter of Elnathan; she was from Jerusalem. [9]He did evil in the eyes of the LORD, just as his father had done.

[10]At that time the officers of Nebuchadnezzar king of Babylon advanced on Jerusalem and laid siege to it, [11]and Nebuchadnezzar himself came up to the city while his officers were besieging it. [12]Jehoiachin king of Judah, his mother, his attendants, his nobles and his officials all surrendered to him.

In the eighth year of the reign of the king of Babylon, he took Jehoiachin prisoner. [13]As the LORD had declared, Nebuchadnezzar removed all the treasures from the temple of the LORD and from the royal palace, and took away all the gold articles that Solomon king of Israel had made for the temple of the LORD. [14]He carried into exile all Jerusalem: all the officers and fighting men, and all the craftsmen and artisans—a total of ten thousand. Only the poorest people of the land were left.

[15]Nebuchadnezzar took Jehoiachin captive to Babylon. He also took from Jerusalem to Babylon the king's mother, his wives, his officials and the leading men of the land. [16]The king of Babylon also deported to Babylon the entire force of seven thousand fighting men, strong and fit for war, and a thousand craftsmen and artisans. [17]He made Mattaniah, Jehoiachin's uncle, king in his place and changed his name to Zedekiah.

Zedekiah King of Judah

[18]Zedekiah was twenty-one years old when he became king, and he reigned in Jerusalem eleven years. His mother's name was Hamutal daughter of Jeremiah; she was from Libnah. [19]He did evil in the eyes of the LORD, just as Jehoiakim had done. [20]It was because of the LORD's anger that all this happened to Jerusalem and Judah, and in the end he thrust them from his presence.

The Fall of Jerusalem

Now Zedekiah rebelled against the king of Babylon.

25 So in the ninth year of Zedekiah's reign, on the tenth day of the tenth month, Nebuchadnezzar king of Babylon marched against Jerusalem with his whole army. He encamped outside the city and built siege works all around it. [2]The city was kept under siege until the eleventh year of King Zedekiah. [3]By the ninth day of the ⌊fourth⌋[b] month the famine in the city had become so severe that there was no food for the people to eat. [4]Then the city wall was broken through, and the whole army fled at night through the gate between the two walls near the king's garden, though the Babylonians[c] were surrounding the city. They fled toward the Arabah,[d] [5]but the Babylonian[e] army pursued the king and

---

[a] 2 Or *Chaldean*   [b] 3 See Jer. 52:6.   [c] 4 Or *Chaldeans*; also in verses 13, 25 and 26   [d] 4 Or *the Jordan Valley*   [e] 5 Or *Chaldean*; also in verses 10 and 24

overtook him in the plains of Jericho. All his soldiers were separated from him and scattered, 6and he was captured. He was taken to the king of Babylon at Riblah, where sentence was pronounced on him. 7They killed the sons of Zedekiah before his eyes. Then they put out his eyes, bound him with bronze shackles and took him to Babylon.

8On the seventh day of the fifth month, in the nineteenth year of Nebuchadnezzar king of Babylon, Nebuzaradan commander of the imperial guard, an official of the king of Babylon, came to Jerusalem. 9He set fire to the temple of the LORD, the royal palace and all the houses of Jerusalem. Every important building he burned down. 10The whole Babylonian army, under the commander of the imperial guard, broke down the walls around Jerusalem. 11Nebuzaradan the commander of the guard carried into exile the people who remained in the city, along with the rest of the populace and those who had gone over to the king of Babylon. 12But the commander left behind some of the poorest people of the land to work the vineyards and fields.

13The Babylonians broke up the bronze pillars, the movable stands and the bronze Sea that were at the temple of the LORD and they carried the bronze to Babylon. 14They also took away the pots, shovels, wick trimmers, dishes and all the bronze articles used in the temple service. 15The commander of the imperial guard took away the censers and sprinkling bowls—all that were made of pure gold or silver.

16The bronze from the two pillars, the Sea and the movable stands, which Solomon had made for the temple of the LORD, was more than could be weighed. 17Each pillar was twenty-seven feet[a] high. The bronze capital on top of one pillar was four and a half feet[b] high and was decorated with a network and pomegranates of bronze all around. The other pillar, with its network, was similar.

18The commander of the guard took as prisoners Seraiah the chief priest, Zephaniah the priest next in rank and the three doorkeepers. 19Of those still in the city, he took the officer in charge of the fighting men and five royal advisers. He also took the secretary who was chief officer in charge of conscripting the people of the land and sixty of his men who were found in the city. 20Nebuzaradan the commander took them all and brought them to the king of Babylon at Riblah. 21There at Riblah, in the land of Hamath, the king had them executed.

So Judah went into captivity, away from her land.

22Nebuchadnezzar king of Babylon appointed Gedaliah son of Ahikam, the son of Shaphan, to be over the people he had left behind in Judah. 23When all the army officers and their men heard that the king of Babylon had appointed Gedaliah as governor, they came to Gedaliah at Mizpah—Ishmael son of Nethaniah, Johanan son of Kareah, Seraiah son of Tanhumeth the Netophathite, Jaazaniah the son of the Maacathite, and their men. 24Gedaliah took an oath to reassure them and their men. "Do not be afraid of the Babylonian officials," he said. "Settle down in the land and serve the king of Babylon, and it will go well with you."

25In the seventh month, however, Ishmael son of Nethaniah, the son of Elishama, who was of royal blood, came with ten men and assassinated Gedaliah and also the men of Judah and the Babylonians who were with him at Mizpah. 26At this, all the people from the least to the greatest, together with the army officers, fled to Egypt for fear of the Babylonians.

Jehoiachin Released

27In the thirty-seventh year of the exile of Jehoiachin king of Judah, in the year Evil-Merodach[c] became king of Babylon, he released Jehoiachin from prison on the twenty-seventh day of the twelfth month. 28He spoke kindly to him and gave him a seat of honor higher than those of the other kings who were with him in Babylon. 29So Jehoiachin put aside his prison clothes and for the rest of his life ate regularly at the king's table. 30Day by day the king gave Jehoiachin a regular allowance as long as he lived.

---

a 17 Hebrew *eighteen cubits* (about 8.1 meters)   b 17 Hebrew *three cubits* (about 1.3 meters)
c 27 Also called *Amel-Marduk*

1 CHRONICLES

 HE BOOK OF 1 CHRONICLES WAS
WRITTEN FOR THE EXILES WHO
HAD RETURNED TO ISRAEL AFTER
THE BABYLONIAN CAPTIVITY TO REMIND
THEM THAT THEY WERE STILL GOD'S CHOSEN
PEOPLE. THE BURNING ISSUE WAS THE QUES-
TION OF CONTINUITY WITH THE PAST: IS
GOD STILL INTERESTED IN US? ARE HIS COV-
ENANTS STILL IN FORCE? DO WE STILL FIT
INTO HIS PLAN? BE ENCOURAGED BY GOD'S
AFFIRMATION THAT HIS PEOPLE BELONG TO
HIM, AND THEN RESPOND TO HIM WITH
WORSHIP AND THANKSGIVING.

Historical Records From Adam to Abraham

To Noah's Sons

1 Adam, Seth, Enosh, ²Kenan, Mahalalel, Jared, ³Enoch, Methuselah, Lamech, Noah.

⁴The sons of Noah:ᵃ
Shem, Ham and Japheth.

The Japhethites

⁵The sonsᵇ of Japheth:
Gomer, Magog, Madai, Javan, Tubal, Meshech and Tiras.
⁶The sons of Gomer:
Ashkenaz, Riphathᶜ and Togarmah.
⁷The sons of Javan:
Elishah, Tarshish, the Kittim and the Rodanim.

The Hamites

⁸The sons of Ham:
Cush, Mizraim,ᵈ Put and Canaan.
⁹The sons of Cush:
Seba, Havilah, Sabta, Raamah and Sabteca.
The sons of Raamah:
Sheba and Dedan.
¹⁰Cush was the fatherᵉ of

ᵃ 4 Septuagint; Hebrew does not have *The sons of Noah*:   ᵇ 5 *Sons* may mean *descendants* or
successors or *nations*; also in verses 6–10, 17 and 20.   ᶜ 6 Many Hebrew manuscripts and Vulgate (see
also Septuagint and Gen. 10:3); most Hebrew manuscripts *Diphath*   ᵈ 8 That is, Egypt; also in verse 11
ᵉ 10 *Father* may mean *ancestor* or *predecessor* or *founder*; also in verses 11, 13, 18 and 20.

Nimrod, who grew to be a mighty warrior on earth.

11 Mizraim was the father of
the Ludites, Anamites, Lehabites, Naphtuhites, 12 Pathrusites, Casluhites (from whom the Philistines came) and Caphtorites.

13 Canaan was the father of
Sidon his firstborn,*a* and of the Hittites, 14 Jebusites, Amorites, Girgashites, 15 Hivites, Arkites, Sinites, 16 Arvadites, Zemarites and Hamathites.

The Semites

17 The sons of Shem:
Elam, Asshur, Arphaxad, Lud and Aram.
The sons of Aram*b*:
Uz, Hul, Gether and Meshech.

18 Arphaxad was the father of Shelah, and Shelah the father of Eber.

19 Two sons were born to Eber:
One was named Peleg,*c* because in his time the earth was divided; his brother was named Joktan.

20 Joktan was the father of
Almodad, Sheleph, Hazarmaveth, Jerah, 21 Hadoram, Uzal, Diklah, 22 Obal,*d* Abimael, Sheba, 23 Ophir, Havilah and Jobab. All these were sons of Joktan.

24 Shem, Arphaxad,*e* Shelah,
25 Eber, Peleg, Reu,
26 Serug, Nahor, Terah
27 and Abram (that is, Abraham).

The Family of Abraham

28 The sons of Abraham:
Isaac and Ishmael.

Descendants of Hagar

29 These were their descendants:
Nebaioth the firstborn of Ishmael, Kedar, Adbeel, Mibsam, 30 Mishma, Dumah, Massa, Hadad, Tema, 31 Jetur, Naphish and Kedemah. These were the sons of Ishmael.

Descendants of Keturah

32 The sons born to Keturah, Abraham's concubine:
Zimran, Jokshan, Medan, Midian, Ishbak and Shuah.
The sons of Jokshan:
Sheba and Dedan.

33 The sons of Midian:
Ephah, Epher, Hanoch, Abida and Eldaah.
All these were descendants of Keturah.

Descendants of Sarah

34 Abraham was the father of Isaac.
The sons of Isaac:
Esau and Israel.

Esau's Sons

35 The sons of Esau:
Eliphaz, Reuel, Jeush, Jalam and Korah.

36 The sons of Eliphaz:
Teman, Omar, Zepho,*f* Gatam and Kenaz;
by Timna: Amalek.*g*

37 The sons of Reuel:
Nahath, Zerah, Shammah and Mizzah.

The People of Seir in Edom

38 The sons of Seir:
Lotan, Shobal, Zibeon, Anah, Dishon, Ezer and Dishan.

39 The sons of Lotan:
Hori and Homam. Timna was Lotan's sister.

40 The sons of Shobal:
Alvan,*h* Manahath, Ebal, Shepho and Onam.
The sons of Zibeon:
Aiah and Anah.

41 The son of Anah:
Dishon.
The sons of Dishon:
Hemdan,*i* Eshban, Ithran and Keran.

42 The sons of Ezer:

a 13 Or *of the Sidonians, the foremost*   *b 17* One Hebrew manuscript and some Septuagint manuscripts (see also Gen. 10:23); most Hebrew manuscripts do not have this line.   *c 19 Peleg* means *division.*   *d 22* Some Hebrew manuscripts and Syriac (see also Gen. 10:28); most Hebrew manuscripts *Ebal*   *e 24* Hebrew; some Septuagint manuscripts *Arphaxad, Cainan* (see also note at Gen. 11:10)   *f 36* Many Hebrew manuscripts, some Septuagint manuscripts and Syriac (see also Gen. 36:11); most Hebrew manuscripts *Zephi*   *g 36* Some Septuagint manuscripts (see also Gen. 36:12); Hebrew *Gatam, Kenaz, Timna and Amalek*   *h 40* Many Hebrew manuscripts and some Septuagint manuscripts (see also Gen. 36:23); most Hebrew manuscripts *Alian*   *i 41* Many Hebrew manuscripts and some Septuagint manuscripts (see also Gen. 36:26); most Hebrew manuscripts *Hamran*

Bilhan, Zaavan and Akan.*a*
The sons of Dishan*b*:
Uz and Aran.

The Rulers of Edom

43 These were the kings who reigned in Edom before any Israelite king reigned*c*:
Bela son of Beor, whose city was named Dinhabah.
44 When Bela died, Jobab son of Zerah from Bozrah succeeded him as king.
45 When Jobab died, Husham from the land of the Temanites succeeded him as king.
46 When Husham died, Hadad son of Bedad, who defeated Midian in the country of Moab, succeeded him as king. His city was named Avith.
47 When Hadad died, Samlah from Masrekah succeeded him as king.
48 When Samlah died, Shaul from Rehoboth on the river*d* succeeded him as king.
49 When Shaul died, Baal-Hanan son of Acbor succeeded him as king.
50 When Baal-Hanan died, Hadad succeeded him as king. His city was named Pau,*e* and his wife's name was Mehetabel daughter of Matred, the daughter of Me-Zahab. **51** Hadad also died.

The chiefs of Edom were:
Timna, Alvah, Jetheth, **52** Oholi-bamah, Elah, Pinon, **53** Kenaz, Teman, Mibzar, **54** Magdiel and Iram. These were the chiefs of Edom.

Israel's Sons

2 These were the sons of Israel:
Reuben, Simeon, Levi, Judah, Issachar, Zebulun, **2** Dan, Joseph, Benjamin, Naphtali, Gad and Asher.

Judah

To Hezron's Sons

3 The sons of Judah:
Er, Onan and Shelah. These three were born to him by a Canaanite woman, the daughter of Shua. Er, Judah's firstborn, was wicked in the LORD's sight; so the LORD put him to death. **4** Tamar, Judah's daughter-in-law, bore him Perez and Zerah. Judah had five sons in all.

5 The sons of Perez:
Hezron and Hamul.
6 The sons of Zerah:
Zimri, Ethan, Heman, Calcol and Darda*f*—five in all.
7 The son of Carmi:
Achar,*g* who brought trouble on Israel by violating the ban on taking devoted things.*h*
8 The son of Ethan:
Azariah.
9 The sons born to Hezron were:
Jerahmeel, Ram and Caleb.*i*

From Ram Son of Hezron

10 Ram was the father of
Amminadab, and Amminadab the father of Nahshon, the leader of the people of Judah. **11** Nahshon was the father of Salmon,*j* Salmon the father of Boaz, **12** Boaz the father of Obed and Obed the father of Jesse.
13 Jesse was the father of
Eliab his firstborn; the second son was Abinadab, the third Shimea, **14** the fourth Nethanel, the fifth Raddai, **15** the sixth Ozem and the seventh David. **16** Their sisters were Zeruiah and Abigail. Zeruiah's three sons were Abishai, Joab and Asahel. **17** Abigail was the mother of Amasa, whose father was Jether the Ishmaelite.

---

a 42 Many Hebrew and Septuagint manuscripts (see also Gen. 36:27); most Hebrew manuscripts *Zaavan, Jaakan*   *b 42* Hebrew *Dishon,* a variant of *Dishan*   *c 43* Or *before an Israelite king reigned over them*   *d 48* Possibly the Euphrates   *e 50* Many Hebrew manuscripts, some Septuagint manuscripts, Vulgate and Syriac (see also Gen. 36:39); most Hebrew manuscripts *Pai*   *f 6* Many Hebrew manuscripts, some Septuagint manuscripts and Syriac (see also 1 Kings 4:31); most Hebrew manuscripts *Dara*   *g 7 Achar* means *trouble; Achar* is called *Achan* in Joshua.   *h 7* The Hebrew term refers to the irrevocable giving over of things or persons to the LORD, often by totally destroying them.   *i 9* Hebrew *Kelubai,* a variant of *Caleb*   *j 11* Septuagint (see also Ruth 4:21); Hebrew *Salma*

Caleb Son of Hezron

18 Caleb son of Hezron had children by his wife Azubah (and by Jerioth). These were her sons: Jesher, Shobab and Ardon. **19** When Azubah died, Caleb married Ephrath, who bore him Hur. **20** Hur was the father of Uri, and Uri the father of Bezalel.

21 Later, Hezron lay with the daughter of Makir the father of Gilead (he had married her when he was sixty years old), and she bore him Segub. **22** Segub was the father of Jair, who controlled twenty-three towns in Gilead. **23** (But Geshur and Aram captured Havvoth Jair,*a* as well as Kenath with its surrounding settlements—sixty towns.) All these were descendants of Makir the father of Gilead.

24 After Hezron died in Caleb Ephrathah, Abijah the wife of Hezron bore him Ashhur the father*b* of Tekoa.

Jerahmeel Son of Hezron

25 The sons of Jerahmeel the firstborn of Hezron:
Ram his firstborn, Bunah, Oren, Ozem and*c* Ahijah. **26** Jerahmeel had another wife, whose name was Atarah; she was the mother of Onam.
27 The sons of Ram the firstborn of Jerahmeel:
Maaz, Jamin and Eker.
28 The sons of Onam:
Shammai and Jada.
The sons of Shammai:
Nadab and Abishur.
29 Abishur's wife was named Abihail, who bore him Ahban and Molid.
30 The sons of Nadab:
Seled and Appaim. Seled died without children.
31 The son of Appaim:
Ishi, who was the father of Sheshan.
Sheshan was the father of Ahlai.
32 The sons of Jada, Shammai's brother:
Jether and Jonathan. Jether died without children.
33 The sons of Jonathan:
Peleth and Zaza.
These were the descendants of Jerahmeel.
34 Sheshan had no sons—only daughters.
He had an Egyptian servant named Jarha. **35** Sheshan gave his daughter in marriage to his servant Jarha, and she bore him Attai.
36 Attai was the father of Nathan, Nathan the father of Zabad,
37 Zabad the father of Ephlal, Ephlal the father of Obed,
38 Obed the father of Jehu, Jehu the father of Azariah,
39 Azariah the father of Helez, Helez the father of Eleasah,
40 Eleasah the father of Sismai, Sismai the father of Shallum,
41 Shallum the father of Jekamiah, and Jekamiah the father of Elishama.

The Clans of Caleb

42 The sons of Caleb the brother of Jerahmeel:
Mesha his firstborn, who was the father of Ziph, and his son Mareshah,*d* who was the father of Hebron.
43 The sons of Hebron:
Korah, Tappuah, Rekem and Shema. **44** Shema was the father of Raham, and Raham the father of Jorkeam. Rekem was the father of Shammai. **45** The son of Shammai was Maon, and Maon was the father of Beth Zur.
46 Caleb's concubine Ephah was the mother of Haran, Moza and Gazez. Haran was the father of Gazez.
47 The sons of Jahdai:
Regem, Jotham, Geshan, Pelet, Ephah and Shaaph.
48 Caleb's concubine Maacah was the mother of Sheber and Tirhanah. **49** She also gave birth to Shaaph the father of Madmannah and to Sheva the father of Macbenah and

a 23 Or *captured the settlements of Jair*   *b 24* *Father* may mean *civic leader* or *military leader;* also in verses 42, 45, 49–52 and possibly elsewhere.   *c 25* Or *Oren and Ozem, by*   *d 42* The meaning of the Hebrew for this phrase is uncertain.

Gibea. Caleb's daughter was Acsah. [50]These were the descendants of Caleb.

The sons of Hur the firstborn of Ephrathah:
Shobal the father of Kiriath Jearim, [51]Salma the father of Bethlehem, and Hareph the father of Beth Gader.

[52]The descendants of Shobal the father of Kiriath Jearim were:
Haroeh, half the Manahathites, [53]and the clans of Kiriath Jearim: the Ithrites, Puthites, Shumathites and Mishraites. From these descended the Zorathites and Eshtaolites.

[54]The descendants of Salma:
Bethlehem, the Netophathites, Atroth Beth Joab, half the Manahathites, the Zorites, [55]and the clans of scribes[a] who lived at Jabez: the Tirathites, Shimeathites and Sucathites. These are the Kenites who came from Hammath, the father of the house of Recab.[b]

The Sons of David

3 These were the sons of David born to him in Hebron:
The firstborn was Amnon the son of Ahinoam of Jezreel;
the second, Daniel the son of Abigail of Carmel;
[2]the third, Absalom the son of Maacah daughter of Talmai king of Geshur;
the fourth, Adonijah the son of Haggith;
[3]the fifth, Shephatiah the son of Abital;
and the sixth, Ithream, by his wife Eglah.

[4]These six were born to David in Hebron, where he reigned seven years and six months.

David reigned in Jerusalem thirty-three years, [5]and these were the children born to him there:
Shammua,[c] Shobab, Nathan and

Solomon. These four were by Bathsheba[d] daughter of Ammiel.
[6]There were also Ibhar, Elishua,[e] Eliphelet, [7]Nogah, Nepheg, Japhia, [8]Elishama, Eliada and Eliphelet—nine in all. [9]All these were the sons of David, besides his sons by his concubines. And Tamar was their sister.

The Kings of Judah

[10]Solomon's son was Rehoboam,
Abijah his son,
Asa his son,
Jehoshaphat his son,
[11]Jehoram[f] his son,
Ahaziah his son,
Joash his son,
[12]Amaziah his son,
Azariah his son,
Jotham his son,
[13]Ahaz his son,
Hezekiah his son,
Manasseh his son,
[14]Amon his son,
Josiah his son.
[15]The sons of Josiah:
Johanan the firstborn,
Jehoiakim the second son,
Zedekiah the third,
Shallum the fourth.
[16]The successors of Jehoiakim:
Jehoiachin[g] his son,
and Zedekiah.

The Royal Line After the Exile

[17]The descendants of Jehoiachin the captive:
Shealtiel his son, [18]Malkiram, Pedaiah, Shenazzar, Jekamiah, Hoshama and Nedabiah.
[19]The sons of Pedaiah:
Zerubbabel and Shimei.
The sons of Zerubbabel:
Meshullam and Hananiah.
Shelomith was their sister.
[20]There were also five others:
Hashubah, Ohel, Berekiah, Hasadiah and Jushab-Hesed.
[21]The descendants of Hananiah:
Pelatiah and Jeshaiah, and the

a 55 Or of the Sopherites   b 55 Or father of Beth Recab   c 5 Hebrew Shimea, a variant of Shammua   d 5 One Hebrew manuscript and Vulgate (see also Septuagint and 2 Samuel 11:3); most Hebrew manuscripts Bathshua   e 6 Two Hebrew manuscripts (see also 2 Samuel 5:15 and 1 Chron. 14:5); most Hebrew manuscripts Elishama   f 11 Hebrew Joram, a variant of Jehoram   g 16 Hebrew Jeconiah, a variant of Jehoiachin; also in verse 17

sons of Rephaiah, of Arnan, of Obadiah and of Shecaniah.

²² The descendants of Shecaniah:
Shemaiah and his sons:
Hattush, Igal, Bariah, Neariah and Shaphat—six in all.

²³ The sons of Neariah:
Elioenai, Hizkiah and Azrikam—three in all.

²⁴ The sons of Elioenai:
Hodaviah, Eliashib, Pelaiah, Akkub, Johanan, Delaiah and Anani—seven in all.

Other Clans of Judah

4 The descendants of Judah:
Perez, Hezron, Carmi, Hur and Shobal.

² Reaiah son of Shobal was the father of Jahath, and Jahath the father of Ahumai and Lahad. These were the clans of the Zorathites.

³ These were the sons[a] of Etam:
Jezreel, Ishma and Idbash. Their sister was named Hazzelelponi. ⁴ Penuel was the father of Gedor, and Ezer the father of Hushah.

These were the descendants of Hur, the firstborn of Ephrathah and father[b] of Bethlehem.

⁵ Ashhur the father of Tekoa had two wives, Helah and Naarah.

⁶ Naarah bore him Ahuzzam, Hepher, Temeni and Haahashtari. These were the descendants of Naarah.

⁷ The sons of Helah:
Zereth, Zohar, Ethnan, ⁸ and Koz, who was the father of Anub and Hazzobebah and of the clans of Aharhel son of Harum.

⁹ Jabez was more honorable than his brothers. His mother had named him Jabez,[c] saying, "I gave birth to him in pain." ¹⁰ Jabez cried out to the God of Israel, "Oh, that you would bless me and enlarge my territory! Let your hand be with me, and keep me from harm so that I will be free from pain." And God granted his request.

¹¹ Kelub, Shuhah's brother, was the father of Mehir, who was the father of Eshton. ¹² Eshton was the father of Beth Rapha, Paseah and Tehinnah the father of Ir Nahash.[d] These were the men of Recah.

¹³ The sons of Kenaz:
Othniel and Seraiah.
The sons of Othniel:
Hathath and Meonothai.[e] ¹⁴ Meonothai was the father of Ophrah.

Seraiah was the father of Joab, the father of Ge Harashim.[f] It was called this because its people were craftsmen.

¹⁵ The sons of Caleb son of Jephunneh:
Iru, Elah and Naam.
The son of Elah:
Kenaz.

¹⁶ The sons of Jehallelel:
Ziph, Ziphah, Tiria and Asarel.

¹⁷ The sons of Ezrah:
Jether, Mered, Epher and Jalon. One of Mered's wives gave birth to Miriam, Shammai and Ishbah the father of Eshtemoa. ¹⁸ (His Judean wife gave birth to Jered the father of Gedor, Heber the father of Soco, and Jekuthiel the father of Zanoah.) These were the children of Pharaoh's daughter Bithiah, whom Mered had married.

¹⁹ The sons of Hodiah's wife, the sister of Naham:
the father of Keilah the Garmite, and Eshtemoa the Maacathite.

²⁰ The sons of Shimon:
Amnon, Rinnah, Ben-Hanan and Tilon.
The descendants of Ishi:
Zoheth and Ben-Zoheth.

²¹ The sons of Shelah son of Judah:
Er the father of Lecah, Laadah the father of Mareshah and the clans of the linen workers at Beth Ashbea, ²² Jokim, the men of Cozeba, and Joash and Saraph, who ruled in Moab and Jashubi Lehem. (These records are from ancient times.) ²³ They were the potters who lived at Netaim and Gederah; they stayed there and worked for the king.

---

^a 3 Some Septuagint manuscripts (see also Vulgate); Hebrew *father*   ^b 4 *Father* may mean *civic leader* or *military leader*; also in verses 12, 14, 17, 18 and possibly elsewhere.   ^c 9 *Jabez* sounds like the Hebrew for *pain*.   ^d 12 Or *of the city of Nahash*   ^e 13 Some Septuagint manuscripts and Vulgate; Hebrew does not have *and Meonothai*.   ^f 14 *Ge Harashim* means *valley of craftsmen*.

Simeon

24 The descendants of Simeon:
    Nemuel, Jamin, Jarib, Zerah and
    Shaul;
    25 Shallum was Shaul's son, Mib-
    sam his son and Mishma his son.
26 The descendants of Mishma:
    Hammuel his son, Zaccur his son
    and Shimei his son.

27 Shimei had sixteen sons and six
daughters, but his brothers did not have
many children; so their entire clan did
not become as numerous as the people
of Judah. 28 They lived in Beersheba,
Moladah, Hazar Shual, 29 Bilhah, Ezem,
Tolad, 30 Bethuel, Hormah, Ziklag,
31 Beth Marcaboth, Hazar Susim, Beth
Biri and Shaaraim. These were their
towns until the reign of David. 32 Their
surrounding villages were Etam, Ain,
Rimmon, Token and Ashan—five
towns— 33 and all the villages around
these towns as far as Baalath.ᵃ These
were their settlements. And they kept a
genealogical record.

34 Meshobab, Jamlech, Joshah son
of Amaziah, 35 Joel, Jehu son of
Joshibiah, the son of Seraiah, the
son of Asiel, 36 also Elioenai, Jaako-
bah, Jeshohaiah, Asaiah, Adiel,
Jesimiel, Benaiah, 37 and Ziza son of
Shiphi, the son of Allon, the son of
Jedaiah, the son of Shimri, the son
of Shemaiah.

38 The men listed above by name were
leaders of their clans. Their families
increased greatly, 39 and they went to the
outskirts of Gedor to the east of the valley in search of pasture for their flocks.
40 They found rich, good pasture, and the
land was spacious, peaceful and quiet.
Some Hamites had lived there formerly.
41 The men whose names were listed
came in the days of Hezekiah king of
Judah. They attacked the Hamites in
their dwellings and also the Meunites
who were there and completely de-
stroyedᵇ them, as is evident to this day.
Then they settled in their place, because
there was pasture for their flocks. 42 And
five hundred of these Simeonites, led by
Pelatiah, Neariah, Rephaiah and Uzziel,
the sons of Ishi, invaded the hill country
of Seir. 43 They killed the remaining
Amalekites who had escaped, and they
have lived there to this day.

Reuben

5 The sons of Reuben the firstborn of Israel (he was the firstborn, but when he defiled his father's
marriage bed, his rights as firstborn were
given to the sons of Joseph son of Israel;
so he could not be listed in the genealogical record in accordance with his
birthright, 2 and though Judah was the
strongest of his brothers and a ruler
came from him, the rights of the firstborn belonged to Joseph)— 3 the sons of
Reuben the firstborn of Israel:
    Hanoch, Pallu, Hezron and Carmi.
4 The descendants of Joel:
    Shemaiah his son, Gog his son,
    Shimei his son, 5 Micah his son,
    Reaiah his son, Baal his son,
6 and Beerah his son, whom Tig-
    lath-Pileserᶜ king of Assyria took
    into exile. Beerah was a leader of
    the Reubenites.
7 Their relatives by clans, listed
    according to their genealogical
    records:
    Jeiel the chief, Zechariah, 8 and
    Bela son of Azaz, the son of
    Shema, the son of Joel. They set-
    tled in the area from Aroer to
    Nebo and Baal Meon. 9 To the east
    they occupied the land up to the
    edge of the desert that extends to
    the Euphrates River, because their
    livestock had increased in Gilead.
10 During Saul's reign they waged
    war against the Hagrites, who were
    defeated at their hands; they occu-
    pied the dwellings of the Hagrites
    throughout the entire region east of
    Gilead.

Gad

11 The Gadites lived next to them in
    Bashan, as far as Salecah:
    12 Joel was the chief, Shapham the
    second, then Janai and Shaphat,
    in Bashan.
13 Their relatives, by families, were:

ᵃ 33 Some Septuagint manuscripts (see also Joshua 19:8); Hebrew Baal   ᵇ 41 The Hebrew term refers
to the irrevocable giving over of things or persons to the LORD, often by totally destroying them.
ᶜ 6 Hebrew Tilgath-Pilneser, a variant of Tiglath-Pileser; also in verse 26

Michael, Meshullam, Sheba, Jorai, Jacan, Zia and Eber—seven in all.

14 These were the sons of Abihail son of Huri, the son of Jaroah, the son of Gilead, the son of Michael, the son of Jeshishai, the son of Jahdo, the son of Buz.

15 Ahi son of Abdiel, the son of Guni, was head of their family.

16 The Gadites lived in Gilead, in Bashan and its outlying villages, and on all the pasturelands of Sharon as far as they extended.

17 All these were entered in the genealogical records during the reigns of Jotham king of Judah and Jeroboam king of Israel.

18 The Reubenites, the Gadites and the half-tribe of Manasseh had 44,760 men ready for military service—able-bodied men who could handle shield and sword, who could use a bow, and who were trained for battle. 19 They waged war against the Hagrites, Jetur, Naphish and Nodab. 20 They were helped in fighting them, and God handed the Hagrites and all their allies over to them, because they cried out to him during the battle. He answered their prayers, because they trusted in him. 21 They seized the livestock of the Hagrites—fifty thousand camels, two hundred fifty thousand sheep and two thousand donkeys. They also took one hundred thousand people captive, 22 and many others fell slain, because the battle was God's. And they occupied the land until the exile.

The Half-Tribe of Manasseh

23 The people of the half-tribe of Manasseh were numerous; they settled in the land from Bashan to Baal Hermon, that is, to Senir (Mount Hermon). 24 These were the heads of their families: Epher, Ishi, Eliel, Azriel, Jeremiah, Hodaviah and Jahdiel. They were brave warriors, famous men, and heads of their families. 25 But they were unfaithful to the God of their fathers and prostituted themselves to the gods of the peoples of the land, whom God had destroyed before them. 26 So the God of Israel stirred up the spirit of Pul king of

Assyria (that is, Tiglath-Pileser king of Assyria), who took the Reubenites, the Gadites and the half-tribe of Manasseh into exile. He took them to Halah, Habor, Hara and the river of Gozan, where they are to this day.

Levi

6 The sons of Levi:
Gershon, Kohath and Merari.
2 The sons of Kohath:
Amram, Izhar, Hebron and Uzziel.
3 The children of Amram:
Aaron, Moses and Miriam.
The sons of Aaron:
Nadab, Abihu, Eleazar and Ithamar.
4 Eleazar was the father of Phinehas,
Phinehas the father of Abishua,
5 Abishua the father of Bukki,
Bukki the father of Uzzi,
6 Uzzi the father of Zerahiah,
Zerahiah the father of Meraioth,
7 Meraioth the father of Amariah,
Amariah the father of Ahitub,
8 Ahitub the father of Zadok,
Zadok the father of Ahimaaz,
9 Ahimaaz the father of Azariah,
Azariah the father of Johanan,
10 Johanan the father of Azariah (it was he who served as priest in the temple Solomon built in Jerusalem),
11 Azariah the father of Amariah,
Amariah the father of Ahitub,
12 Ahitub the father of Zadok,
Zadok the father of Shallum,
13 Shallum the father of Hilkiah,
Hilkiah the father of Azariah,
14 Azariah the father of Seraiah,
and Seraiah the father of Jehozadak.

15 Jehozadak was deported when the LORD sent Judah and Jerusalem into exile by the hand of Nebuchadnezzar.

16 The sons of Levi:
Gershon,[a] Kohath and Merari.
17 These are the names of the sons of Gershon:
Libni and Shimei.
18 The sons of Kohath:

---

a 16 Hebrew *Gershom*, a variant of *Gershon*; also in verses 17, 20, 43, 62 and 71

Amram, Izhar, Hebron and Uzziel.
19 The sons of Merari:
Mahli and Mushi.

These are the clans of the Levites
listed according to their fathers:
20 Of Gershon:
Libni his son, Jehath his son,
Zimmah his son, 21 Joah his son,
Iddo his son, Zerah his son
and Jeatherai his son.
22 The descendants of Kohath:
Amminadab his son, Korah his
son,
Assir his son, 23 Elkanah his son,
Ebiasaph his son, Assir his son,
24 Tahath his son, Uriel his son,
Uzziah his son and Shaul his son.
25 The descendants of Elkanah:
Amasai, Ahimoth,
26 Elkanah his son,a Zophai his son,
Nahath his son, 27 Eliab his son,
Jeroham his son, Elkanah his son
and Samuel his son.b
28 The sons of Samuel:
Joelc the firstborn
and Abijah the second son.
29 The descendants of Merari:
Mahli, Libni his son,
Shimei his son, Uzzah his son,
30 Shimea his son, Haggiah his son
and Asaiah his son.

The Temple Musicians

31 These are the men David put in
charge of the music in the house of the
LORD after the ark came to rest there.
32 They ministered with music before
the tabernacle, the Tent of Meeting,
until Solomon built the temple of the
LORD in Jerusalem. They performed
their duties according to the regulations
laid down for them.
33 Here are the men who served,
together with their sons:
From the Kohathites:
Heman, the musician,
the son of Joel, the son of Samuel,
34 the son of Elkanah, the son of
Jeroham,
the son of Eliel, the son of Toah,

35 the son of Zuph, the son of Elkanah,
the son of Mahath, the son of
Amasai,
36 the son of Elkanah, the son of Joel,
the son of Azariah, the son of
Zephaniah,
37 the son of Tahath, the son of Assir,
the son of Ebiasaph, the son of
Korah,
38 the son of Izhar, the son of
Kohath,
the son of Levi, the son of Israel;
39 and Heman's associate Asaph, who
served at his right hand:
Asaph son of Berekiah, the son of
Shimea,
40 the son of Michael, the son of
Baaseiah,d
the son of Malkijah, 41 the son of
Ethni,
the son of Zerah, the son of Adaiah,
42 the son of Ethan, the son of Zimmah,
the son of Shimei, 43 the son of
Jahath,
the son of Gershon, the son of
Levi;
44 and from their associates, the Merarites, at his left hand:
Ethan son of Kishi, the son of
Abdi,
the son of Malluch, 45 the son of
Hashabiah,
the son of Amaziah, the son of
Hilkiah,
46 the son of Amzi, the son of Bani,
the son of Shemer, 47 the son of
Mahli,
the son of Mushi, the son of
Merari,
the son of Levi.

48 Their fellow Levites were assigned
to all the other duties of the tabernacle,
the house of God. 49 But Aaron and his
descendants were the ones who presented offerings on the altar of burnt offering
and on the altar of incense in connection
with all that was done in the Most Holy
Place, making atonement for Israel, in

---

a 26 Some Hebrew manuscripts, Septuagint and Syriac; most Hebrew manuscripts *Ahimoth* 26*and
Elkanah. The sons of Elkanah:* b 27 Some Septuagint manuscripts (see also 1 Samuel 1:19,20 and
1 Chron. 6:33,34); Hebrew does not have *and Samuel his son.* c 28 Some Septuagint manuscripts and
Syriac (see also 1 Samuel 8:2 and 1 Chron. 6:33); Hebrew does not have *Joel.* d 40 Most Hebrew
manuscripts; some Hebrew manuscripts, one Septuagint manuscript and Syriac *Maaseiah*

accordance with all that Moses the servant of God had commanded.

50 These were the descendants of Aaron:
Eleazar his son, Phinehas his son, Abishua his son, 51Bukki his son, Uzzi his son, Zerahiah his son, 52Meraioth his son, Amariah his son,
Ahitub his son, 53Zadok his son and Ahimaaz his son.

54These were the locations of their settlements allotted as their territory (they were assigned to the descendants of Aaron who were from the Kohathite clan, because the first lot was for them): 55They were given Hebron in Judah with its surrounding pasturelands. 56But the fields and villages around the city were given to Caleb son of Jephunneh. 57So the descendants of Aaron were given Hebron (a city of refuge), and Libnah,ᵃ Jattir, Eshtemoa, 58Hilen, Debir, 59Ashan, Juttahᵇ and Beth Shemesh, together with their pasturelands. 60And from the tribe of Benjamin they were given Gibeon,ᶜ Geba, Alemeth and Anathoth, together with their pasturelands.
These towns, which were distributed among the Kohathite clans, were thirteen in all.
61The rest of Kohath's descendants were allotted ten towns from the clans of half the tribe of Manasseh.
62The descendants of Gershon, clan by clan, were allotted thirteen towns from the tribes of Issachar, Asher and Naphtali, and from the part of the tribe of Manasseh that is in Bashan.
63The descendants of Merari, clan by clan, were allotted twelve towns from the tribes of Reuben, Gad and Zebulun.
64So the Israelites gave the Levites these towns and their pasturelands. 65From the tribes of Judah, Simeon and Benjamin they allotted the previously named towns.
66Some of the Kohathite clans were given as their territory towns from the tribe of Ephraim.

67In the hill country of Ephraim they were given Shechem (a city of refuge), and Gezer,ᵈ 68Jokmeam, Beth Horon, 69Aijalon and Gath Rimmon, together with their pasturelands.
70And from half the tribe of Manasseh the Israelites gave Aner and Bileam, together with their pasturelands, to the rest of the Kohathite clans.

71The Gershonites received the following:
From the clan of the half-tribe of Manasseh
they received Golan in Bashan and also Ashtaroth, together with their pasturelands;
72from the tribe of Issachar
they received Kedesh, Daberath, 73Ramoth and Anem, together with their pasturelands;
74from the tribe of Asher
they received Mashal, Abdon, 75Hukok and Rehob, together with their pasturelands;
76and from the tribe of Naphtali
they received Kedesh in Galilee, Hammon and Kiriathaim, together with their pasturelands.

77The Merarites (the rest of the Levites) received the following:
From the tribe of Zebulun
they received Jokneam, Kartah,ᵉ Rimmono and Tabor, together with their pasturelands;
78from the tribe of Reuben across the Jordan east of Jericho
they received Bezer in the desert, Jahzah, 79Kedemoth and Mephaath, together with their pasturelands;
80and from the tribe of Gad
they received Ramoth in Gilead, Mahanaim, 81Heshbon and Jazer, together with their pasturelands.

Issachar

7 The sons of Issachar:
Tola, Puah, Jashub and Shimron—four in all.

ᵃ 57 See Joshua 21:13; Hebrew *given the cities of refuge: Hebron, Libnah.*   ᵇ 59 Syriac (see also Septuagint and Joshua 21:16); Hebrew does not have *Juttah.*   ᶜ 60 See Joshua 21:17; Hebrew does not have *Gibeon.*   ᵈ 67 See Joshua 21:21; Hebrew *given the cities of refuge: Shechem, Gezer.*   ᵉ 77 See Septuagint and Joshua 21:34; Hebrew does not have *Jokneam, Kartah.*

2 The sons of Tola:

Uzzi, Rephaiah, Jeriel, Jahmai, Ibsam and Samuel—heads of their families. During the reign of David, the descendants of Tola listed as fighting men in their genealogy numbered 22,600. **3** The son of Uzzi:

Izrahiah.

The sons of Izrahiah:

Michael, Obadiah, Joel and Isshiah. All five of them were chiefs. **4** According to their family genealogy, they had 36,000 men ready for battle, for they had many wives and children. **5** The relatives who were fighting men belonging to all the clans of Issachar, as listed in their genealogy, were 87,000 in all.

Benjamin

6 Three sons of Benjamin:

Bela, Beker and Jediael. **7** The sons of Bela:

Ezbon, Uzzi, Uzziel, Jerimoth and Iri, heads of families—five in all. Their genealogical record listed 22,034 fighting men. **8** The sons of Beker:

Zemirah, Joash, Eliezer, Elioenai, Omri, Jeremoth, Abijah, Anathoth and Alemeth. All these were the sons of Beker. **9** Their genealogical record listed the heads of families and 20,200 fighting men. **10** The son of Jediael:

Bilhan.

The sons of Bilhan:

Jeush, Benjamin, Ehud, Kenaanah, Zethan, Tarshish and Ahishahar. **11** All these sons of Jediael were heads of families. There were 17,200 fighting men ready to go out to war. **12** The Shuppites and Huppites were the descendants of Ir, and the Hushites the descendants of Aher.

Naphtali

13 The sons of Naphtali:

Jahziel, Guni, Jezer and Shillem[a]—the descendants of Bilhah.

Manasseh

14 The descendants of Manasseh:

Asriel was his descendant through his Aramean concubine. She gave birth to Makir the father of Gilead. **15** Makir took a wife from among the Huppites and Shuppites. His sister's name was Maacah.

Another descendant was named Zelophehad, who had only daughters.

16 Makir's wife Maacah gave birth to a son and named him Peresh. His brother was named Sheresh, and his sons were Ulam and Rakem. **17** The son of Ulam:

Bedan.

These were the sons of Gilead son of Makir, the son of Manasseh. **18** His sister Hammoleketh gave birth to Ishhod, Abiezer and Mahlah. **19** The sons of Shemida were:

Ahian, Shechem, Likhi and Aniam.

Ephraim

20 The descendants of Ephraim:

Shuthelah, Bered his son,
Tahath his son, Eleadah his son,
Tahath his son, **21** Zabad his son
and Shuthelah his son.

Ezer and Elead were killed by the native-born men of Gath, when they went down to seize their livestock. **22** Their father Ephraim mourned for them many days, and his relatives came to comfort him. **23** Then he lay with his wife again, and she became pregnant and gave birth to a son. He named him Beriah,[b] because there had been misfortune in his family. **24** His daughter was Sheerah, who built Lower and Upper Beth Horon as well as Uzzen Sheerah. **25** Rephah was his son, Resheph his son,[c]

Telah his son, Tahan his son,
26 Ladan his son, Ammihud his son,
Elishama his son, **27** Nun his son
and Joshua his son.

---

[a] 13 Some Hebrew and Septuagint manuscripts (see also Gen. 46:24 and Num. 26:49); most Hebrew manuscripts *Shallum*   [b] 23 *Beriah* sounds like the Hebrew for *misfortune.*   [c] 25 Some Septuagint manuscripts; Hebrew does not have *his son.*

28 Their lands and settlements included Bethel and its surrounding villages, Naaran to the east, Gezer and its villages to the west, and Shechem and its villages all the way to Ayyah and its villages. 29 Along the borders of Manasseh were Beth Shan, Taanach, Megiddo and Dor, together with their villages. The descendants of Joseph son of Israel lived in these towns.

Asher

30 The sons of Asher:

Imnah, Ishvah, Ishvi and Beriah. Their sister was Serah.

31 The sons of Beriah:

Heber and Malkiel, who was the father of Birzaith.

32 Heber was the father of Japhlet, Shomer and Hotham and of their sister Shua.

33 The sons of Japhlet:

Pasach, Bimhal and Ashvath. These were Japhlet's sons.

34 The sons of Shomer:

Ahi, Rohgah,ᵃ Hubbah and Aram.

35 The sons of his brother Helem:

Zophah, Imna, Shelesh and Amal.

36 The sons of Zophah:

Suah, Harnepher, Shual, Beri, Imrah, 37 Bezer, Hod, Shamma, Shilshah, Ithranᵇ and Beera.

38 The sons of Jether:

Jephunneh, Pispah and Ara.

39 The sons of Ulla:

Arah, Hanniel and Rizia.

40 All these were descendants of Asher—heads of families, choice men, brave warriors and outstanding leaders. The number of men ready for battle, as listed in their genealogy, was 26,000.

The Genealogy of Saul the Benjamite

8 Benjamin was the father of Bela his firstborn,

Ashbel the second son, Aharah the third,

2 Nohah the fourth and Rapha the fifth.

3 The sons of Bela were:

Addar, Gera, Abihud,ᶜ 4 Abishua, Naaman, Ahoah, 5 Gera, Shephuphan and Huram.

6 These were the descendants of Ehud, who were heads of families of those living in Geba and were deported to Manahath:

7 Naaman, Ahijah, and Gera, who deported them and who was the father of Uzza and Ahihud.

8 Sons were born to Shaharaim in Moab after he had divorced his wives Hushim and Baara. 9 By his wife Hodesh he had Jobab, Zibia, Mesha, Malcam, 10 Jeuz, Sakia and Mirmah. These were his sons, heads of families. 11 By Hushim he had Abitub and Elpaal.

12 The sons of Elpaal:

Eber, Misham, Shemed (who built Ono and Lod with its surrounding villages), 13 and Beriah and Shema, who were heads of families of those living in Aijalon and who drove out the inhabitants of Gath.

14 Ahio, Shashak, Jeremoth, 15 Zebadiah, Arad, Eder, 16 Michael, Ishpah and Joha were the sons of Beriah.

17 Zebadiah, Meshullam, Hizki, Heber, 18 Ishmerai, Izliah and Jobab were the sons of Elpaal.

19 Jakim, Zicri, Zabdi, 20 Elienai, Zillethai, Eliel, 21 Adaiah, Beraiah and Shimrath were the sons of Shimei.

22 Ishpan, Eber, Eliel, 23 Abdon, Zicri, Hanan, 24 Hananiah, Elam, Anthothijah, 25 Iphdeiah and Penuel were the sons of Shashak.

26 Shamsherai, Shehariah, Athaliah, 27 Jaareshiah, Elijah and Zicri were the sons of Jeroham.

28 All these were heads of families, chiefs as listed in their genealogy, and they lived in Jerusalem.

29 Jeielᵈ the fatherᵉ of Gibeon lived in Gibeon.

His wife's name was Maacah, 30 and his firstborn son was Abdon, followed by Zur, Kish, Baal, Ner,ᶠ Nadab, 31 Gedor, Ahio, Zeker 32 and Mikloth, who was the father

---

ᵃ 34 Or *of his brother Shomer: Rohgah*　　ᵇ 37 Possibly a variant of *Jether*　　ᶜ 3 Or *Gera the father of Ehud*　　ᵈ 29 Some Septuagint manuscripts (see also 1 Chron. 9:35); Hebrew does not have *Jeiel*.　　ᵉ 29 *Father* may mean *civic leader* or *military leader.*　　ᶠ 30 Some Septuagint manuscripts (see also 1 Chron. 9:36); Hebrew does not have *Ner.*

of Shimeah. They too lived near their relatives in Jerusalem.

33 Ner was the father of Kish, Kish the father of Saul, and Saul the father of Jonathan, Malki-Shua, Abinadab and Esh-Baal.*a*

34 The son of Jonathan:
Merib-Baal,*b* who was the father of Micah.

35 The sons of Micah:
Pithon, Melech, Tarea and Ahaz.

36 Ahaz was the father of Jehoaddah, Jehoaddah was the father of Alemeth, Azmaveth and Zimri, and Zimri was the father of Moza.

37 Moza was the father of Binea; Raphah was his son, Eleasah his son and Azel his son.

38 Azel had six sons, and these were their names:
Azrikam, Bokeru, Ishmael, Sheariah, Obadiah and Hanan. All these were the sons of Azel.

39 The sons of his brother Eshek:
Ulam his firstborn, Jeush the second son and Eliphelet the third.

40 The sons of Ulam were brave warriors who could handle the bow. They had many sons and grandsons—150 in all.

All these were the descendants of Benjamin.

9 All Israel was listed in the genealogies recorded in the book of the kings of Israel.

The People in Jerusalem

The people of Judah were taken captive to Babylon because of their unfaithfulness. 2 Now the first to resettle on their own property in their own towns were some Israelites, priests, Levites and temple servants.

3 Those from Judah, from Benjamin, and from Ephraim and Manasseh who lived in Jerusalem were:

4 Uthai son of Ammihud, the son of Omri, the son of Imri, the son of Bani, a descendant of Perez son of Judah.

5 Of the Shilonites:
Asaiah the firstborn and his sons.

6 Of the Zerahites:
Jeuel.

The people from Judah numbered 690.

7 Of the Benjamites:
Sallu son of Meshullam, the son of Hodaviah, the son of Hassenuah;

8 Ibneiah son of Jeroham; Elah son of Uzzi, the son of Micri; and Meshullam son of Shephatiah, the son of Reuel, the son of Ibnijah.

9 The people from Benjamin, as listed in their genealogy, numbered 956. All these men were heads of their families.

10 Of the priests:
Jedaiah; Jehoiarib; Jakin;

11 Azariah son of Hilkiah, the son of Meshullam, the son of Zadok, the son of Meraioth, the son of Ahitub, the official in charge of the house of God;

12 Adaiah son of Jeroham, the son of Pashhur, the son of Malkijah; and Maasai son of Adiel, the son of Jahzerah, the son of Meshullam, the son of Meshillemith, the son of Immer.

13 The priests, who were heads of families, numbered 1,760. They were able men, responsible for ministering in the house of God.

14 Of the Levites:
Shemaiah son of Hasshub, the son of Azrikam, the son of Hashabiah, a Merarite; 15 Bakbakkar, Heresh, Galal and Mattaniah son of Mica, the son of Zicri, the son of Asaph; 16 Obadiah son of Shemaiah, the son of Galal, the son of Jeduthun; and Berekiah son of Asa, the son of Elkanah, who lived in the villages of the Netophathites.

17 The gatekeepers:
Shallum, Akkub, Talmon, Ahiman and their brothers, Shallum their chief 18 being stationed at the King's Gate on the east, up to the present time. These were the gatekeepers belonging to the camp of the Levites. 19 Shallum son of Kore, the son of Ebiasaph, the son of Korah, and his fellow gatekeepers from his family (the Korahites) were responsible for guarding the thresholds of the

---

a 33 Also known as *Ish-Bosheth*   *b* 34 Also known as *Mephibosheth*

Tent[a] just as their fathers had been responsible for guarding the entrance to the dwelling of the LORD. [20]In earlier times Phinehas son of Eleazar was in charge of the gatekeepers, and the LORD was with him. [21]Zechariah son of Meshelemiah was the gatekeeper at the entrance to the Tent of Meeting.

[22]Altogether, those chosen to be gatekeepers at the thresholds numbered 212. They were registered by genealogy in their villages. The gatekeepers had been assigned to their positions of trust by David and Samuel the seer. [23]They and their descendants were in charge of guarding the gates of the house of the LORD—the house called the Tent. [24]The gatekeepers were on the four sides: east, west, north and south. [25]Their brothers in their villages had to come from time to time and share their duties for seven-day periods. [26]But the four principal gatekeepers, who were Levites, were entrusted with the responsibility for the rooms and treasuries in the house of God. [27]They would spend the night stationed around the house of God, because they had to guard it; and they had charge of the key for opening it each morning.

[28]Some of them were in charge of the articles used in the temple service; they counted them when they were brought in and when they were taken out. [29]Others were assigned to take care of the furnishings and all the other articles of the sanctuary, as well as the flour and wine, and the oil, incense and spices. [30]But some of the priests took care of mixing the spices. [31]A Levite named Mattithiah, the firstborn son of Shallum the Korahite, was entrusted with the responsibility for baking the offering bread. [32]Some of their Kohathite brothers were in charge of preparing for every Sabbath the bread set out on the table.

[33]Those who were musicians, heads of Levite families, stayed in the rooms of the temple and were exempt from other duties because they were responsible for the work day and night.

[34]All these were heads of Levite families, chiefs as listed in their genealogy, and they lived in Jerusalem.

The Genealogy of Saul

[35]Jeiel the father[b] of Gibeon lived in Gibeon.

His wife's name was Maacah, [36]and his firstborn son was Abdon, followed by Zur, Kish, Baal, Ner, Nadab, [37]Gedor, Ahio, Zechariah and Mikloth. [38]Mikloth was the father of Shimeam. They too lived near their relatives in Jerusalem.

[39]Ner was the father of Kish, Kish the father of Saul, and Saul the father of Jonathan, Malki-Shua, Abinadab and Esh-Baal.[c]

[40]The son of Jonathan:

Merib-Baal,[d] who was the father of Micah.

[41]The sons of Micah:

Pithon, Melech, Tahrea and Ahaz.[e]

[42]Ahaz was the father of Jadah, Jadah[f] was the father of Alemeth, Azmaveth and Zimri, and Zimri was the father of Moza. [43]Moza was the father of Binea; Rephaiah was his son, Eleasah his son and Azel his son.

[44]Azel had six sons, and these were their names:

Azrikam, Bokeru, Ishmael, Sheariah, Obadiah and Hanan. These were the sons of Azel.

Saul Takes His Life

10 Now the Philistines fought against Israel; the Israelites fled before them, and many fell slain on Mount Gilboa. [2]The Philistines pressed hard after Saul and his sons, and they killed his sons Jonathan, Abinadab and Malki-Shua. [3]The fighting grew fierce around Saul, and when the archers overtook him, they wounded him.

[4]Saul said to his armor-bearer, "Draw your sword and run me through, or these uncircumcised fellows will come and abuse me."

---

[a] 19 That is, the temple; also in verses 21 and 23   [b] 35 Father may mean civic leader or military leader.   [c] 39 Also known as Ish-Bosheth   [d] 40 Also known as Mephibosheth   [e] 41 Vulgate and Syriac (see also Septuagint and 1 Chron. 8:35); Hebrew does not have and Ahaz.   [f] 42 Some Hebrew manuscripts and Septuagint (see also 1 Chron. 8:36); most Hebrew manuscripts Jarah, Jarah

But his armor-bearer was terrified and would not do it; so Saul took his own sword and fell on it. ⁵When the armor-bearer saw that Saul was dead, he too fell on his sword and died. ⁶So Saul and his three sons died, and all his house died together.

⁷When all the Israelites in the valley saw that the army had fled and that Saul and his sons had died, they abandoned their towns and fled. And the Philistines came and occupied them.

⁸The next day, when the Philistines came to strip the dead, they found Saul and his sons fallen on Mount Gilboa. ⁹They stripped him and took his head and his armor, and sent messengers throughout the land of the Philistines to proclaim the news among their idols and their people. ¹⁰They put his armor in the temple of their gods and hung up his head in the temple of Dagon.

¹¹When all the inhabitants of Jabesh Gilead heard of everything the Philistines had done to Saul, ¹²all their valiant men went and took the bodies of Saul and his sons and brought them to Jabesh. Then they buried their bones under the great tree in Jabesh, and they fasted seven days.

¹³Saul died because he was unfaithful to the LORD; he did not keep the word of the LORD and even consulted a medium for guidance, ¹⁴and did not inquire of the LORD. So the LORD put him to death and turned the kingdom over to David son of Jesse.

David Becomes King Over Israel

11 All Israel came together to David at Hebron and said, "We are your own flesh and blood. ²In the past, even while Saul was king, you were the one who led Israel on their military campaigns. And the LORD your God said to you, 'You will shepherd my people Israel, and you will become their ruler.'"

³When all the elders of Israel had come to King David at Hebron, he made a compact with them at Hebron before the LORD, and they anointed David king over Israel, as the LORD had promised through Samuel.

David Conquers Jerusalem

⁴David and all the Israelites marched to Jerusalem (that is, Jebus). The Jebusites who lived there ⁵said to David, "You will not get in here." Nevertheless, David captured the fortress of Zion, the City of David.

⁶David had said, "Whoever leads the attack on the Jebusites will become commander-in-chief." Joab son of Zeruiah went up first, and so he received the command.

⁷David then took up residence in the fortress, and so it was called the City of David. ⁸He built up the city around it, from the supporting terraces^a to the surrounding wall, while Joab restored the rest of the city. ⁹And David became more and more powerful, because the LORD Almighty was with him.

David's Mighty Men

¹⁰These were the chiefs of David's mighty men—they, together with all Israel, gave his kingship strong support to extend it over the whole land, as the LORD had promised— ¹¹this is the list of David's mighty men:

Jashobeam,^b a Hacmonite, was chief of the officers^c; he raised his spear against three hundred men, whom he killed in one encounter.

¹²Next to him was Eleazar son of Dodai the Ahohite, one of the three mighty men. ¹³He was with David at Pas Dammim when the Philistines gathered there for battle. At a place where there was a field full of barley, the troops fled from the Philistines. ¹⁴But they took their stand in the middle of the field. They defended it and struck the Philistines down, and the LORD brought about a great victory.

¹⁵Three of the thirty chiefs came down to David to the rock at the cave of Adullam, while a band of Philistines was encamped in the Valley of Rephaim. ¹⁶At that time David was in the stronghold, and the Philistine garrison was at Bethlehem. ¹⁷David longed for water and said, "Oh, that someone would get me a drink of water from the well near the gate of Bethlehem!" ¹⁸So the Three broke through the Philistine lines, drew

^a 8 Or the Millo   ^b 11 Possibly a variant of Jashob-Baal   ^c 11 Or Thirty; some Septuagint manuscripts Three (see also 2 Samuel 23:8)

water from the well near the gate of Bethlehem and carried it back to David. But he refused to drink it; instead, he poured it out before the LORD. **19** "God forbid that I should do this!" he said. "Should I drink the blood of these men who went at the risk of their lives?" Because they risked their lives to bring it back, David would not drink it.

Such were the exploits of the three mighty men.

20 Abishai the brother of Joab was chief of the Three. He raised his spear against three hundred men, whom he killed, and so he became as famous as the Three. **21** He was doubly honored above the Three and became their commander, even though he was not included among them.

22 Benaiah son of Jehoiada was a valiant fighter from Kabzeel, who performed great exploits. He struck down two of Moab's best men. He also went down into a pit on a snowy day and killed a lion. **23** And he struck down an Egyptian who was seven and a half feet*a* tall. Although the Egyptian had a spear like a weaver's rod in his hand, Benaiah went against him with a club. He snatched the spear from the Egyptian's hand and killed him with his own spear. **24** Such were the exploits of Benaiah son of Jehoiada; he too was as famous as the three mighty men. **25** He was held in greater honor than any of the Thirty, but he was not included among the Three. And David put him in charge of his bodyguard.

26 The mighty men were:
> Asahel the brother of Joab,
> Elhanan son of Dodo from Bethlehem,
> **27** Shammoth the Harorite,
> Helez the Pelonite,
> **28** Ira son of Ikkesh from Tekoa,
> Abiezer from Anathoth,
> **29** Sibbecai the Hushathite,
> Ilai the Ahohite,
> **30** Maharai the Netophathite,
> Heled son of Baanah the Netophathite,
> **31** Ithai son of Ribai from Gibeah in Benjamin,
> Benaiah the Pirathonite,

> **32** Hurai from the ravines of Gaash,
> Abiel the Arbathite,
> **33** Azmaveth the Baharumite,
> Eliahba the Shaalbonite,
> **34** the sons of Hashem the Gizonite,
> Jonathan son of Shagee the Hararite,
> **35** Ahiam son of Sacar the Hararite,
> Eliphal son of Ur,
> **36** Hepher the Mekerathite,
> Ahijah the Pelonite,
> **37** Hezro the Carmelite,
> Naarai son of Ezbai,
> **38** Joel the brother of Nathan,
> Mibhar son of Hagri,
> **39** Zelek the Ammonite,
> Naharai the Berothite, the armorbearer of Joab son of Zeruiah,
> **40** Ira the Ithrite,
> Gareb the Ithrite,
> **41** Uriah the Hittite,
> Zabad son of Ahlai,
> **42** Adina son of Shiza the Reubenite, who was chief of the Reubenites, and the thirty with him,
> **43** Hanan son of Maacah,
> Joshaphat the Mithnite,
> **44** Uzzia the Ashterathite,
> Shama and Jeiel the sons of Hotham the Aroerite,
> **45** Jediael son of Shimri,
> his brother Joha the Tizite,
> **46** Eliel the Mahavite,
> Jeribai and Joshaviah the sons of Elnaam,
> Ithmah the Moabite,
> **47** Eliel, Obed and Jaasiel the Mezobaite.

Warriors Join David

12 These were the men who came to David at Ziklag, while he was banished from the presence of Saul son of Kish (they were among the warriors who helped him in battle; **2** they were armed with bows and were able to shoot arrows or to sling stones right-handed or left-handed; they were kinsmen of Saul from the tribe of Benjamin):

3 Ahiezer their chief and Joash the sons of Shemaah the Gibeathite; Jeziel and Pelet the sons of Azmaveth; Beracah, Jehu the Anathothite, **4** and Ishmaiah the Gibeonite, a

---

a 23 Hebrew *five cubits* (about 2.3 meters)

mighty man among the Thirty, who was a leader of the Thirty; Jeremiah, Jahaziel, Johanan, Jozabad the Gederathite, [5]Eluzai, Jerimoth, Bealiah, Shemariah and Shephatiah the Haruphite; [6]Elkanah, Isshiah, Azarel, Joezer and Jashobeam the Korahites; [7]and Joelah and Zebadiah the sons of Jeroham from Gedor.

[8]Some Gadites defected to David at his stronghold in the desert. They were brave warriors, ready for battle and able to handle the shield and spear. Their faces were the faces of lions, and they were as swift as gazelles in the mountains.

[9]Ezer was the chief,
　Obadiah the second in command,
　　Eliab the third,
[10]Mishmannah the fourth, Jeremiah
　　the fifth,
[11]Attai the sixth, Eliel the seventh,
[12]Johanan the eighth, Elzabad the
　　ninth,
[13]Jeremiah the tenth and Macbannai
　　the eleventh.

[14]These Gadites were army commanders; the least was a match for a hundred, and the greatest for a thousand. [15]It was they who crossed the Jordan in the first month when it was overflowing all its banks, and they put to flight everyone living in the valleys, to the east and to the west.

[16]Other Benjamites and some men from Judah also came to David in his stronghold. [17]David went out to meet them and said to them, "If you have come to me in peace, to help me, I am ready to have you unite with me. But if you have come to betray me to my enemies when my hands are free from violence, may the God of our fathers see it and judge you."

[18]Then the Spirit came upon Amasai, chief of the Thirty, and he said:

"We are yours, O David!
　We are with you, O son of Jesse!
Success, success to you,
　and success to those who help you,
　　for your God will help you."

So David received them and made them leaders of his raiding bands.

[19]Some of the men of Manasseh defected to David when he went with the Philistines to fight against Saul. (He and his men did not help the Philistines because, after consultation, their rulers sent him away. They said, "It will cost us our heads if he deserts to his master Saul.") [20]When David went to Ziklag, these were the men of Manasseh who defected to him: Adnah, Jozabad, Jediael, Michael, Jozabad, Elihu and Zillethai, leaders of units of a thousand in Manasseh. [21]They helped David against raiding bands, for all of them were brave warriors, and they were commanders in his army. [22]Day after day men came to help David, until he had a great army, like the army of God.[a]

Others Join David at Hebron

[23]These are the numbers of the men armed for battle who came to David at Hebron to turn Saul's kingdom over to him, as the LORD had said:

[24]men of Judah, carrying shield and
　spear—6,800 armed for battle;
[25]men of Simeon, warriors ready for
　battle—7,100;
[26]men of Levi—4,600, [27]including
　Jehoiada, leader of the family of
　Aaron, with 3,700 men, [28]and
　Zadok, a brave young warrior,
　with 22 officers from his family;
[29]men of Benjamin, Saul's kinsmen—
　3,000, most of whom had remained loyal to Saul's house
　until then;
[30]men of Ephraim, brave warriors,
　famous in their own clans—
　20,800;
[31]men of half the tribe of Manasseh,
　designated by name to come and
　make David king—18,000;
[32]men of Issachar, who understood
　the times and knew what Israel
　should do—200 chiefs, with all
　their relatives under their command;
[33]men of Zebulun, experienced soldiers prepared for battle with
　every type of weapon, to help
　David with undivided loyalty—
　50,000;
[34]men of Naphtali—1,000 officers,

[a] 22 Or *a great and mighty army*

together with 37,000 men carrying shields and spears;

35 men of Dan, ready for battle—28,600;

36 men of Asher, experienced soldiers prepared for battle—40,000;

37 and from east of the Jordan, men of Reuben, Gad and the half-tribe of Manasseh, armed with every type of weapon—120,000.

38 All these were fighting men who volunteered to serve in the ranks. They came to Hebron fully determined to make David king over all Israel. All the rest of the Israelites were also of one mind to make David king. 39 The men spent three days there with David, eating and drinking, for their families had supplied provisions for them. 40 Also, their neighbors from as far away as Issachar, Zebulun and Naphtali came bringing food on donkeys, camels, mules and oxen. There were plentiful supplies of flour, fig cakes, raisin cakes, wine, oil, cattle and sheep, for there was joy in Israel.

Bringing Back the Ark

13 David conferred with each of his officers, the commanders of thousands and commanders of hundreds. 2 He then said to the whole assembly of Israel, "If it seems good to you and if it is the will of the LORD our God, let us send word far and wide to the rest of our brothers throughout the territories of Israel, and also to the priests and Levites who are with them in their towns and pasturelands, to come and join us. 3 Let us bring the ark of our God back to us, for we did not inquire of*a* it*b* during the reign of Saul." 4 The whole assembly agreed to do this, because it seemed right to all the people.

5 So David assembled all the Israelites, from the Shihor River in Egypt to Lebo*c* Hamath, to bring the ark of God from Kiriath Jearim. 6 David and all the Israelites with him went to Baalah of Judah (Kiriath Jearim) to bring up from there the ark of God the LORD, who is enthroned between the cherubim—the ark that is called by the Name.

7 They moved the ark of God from Abinadab's house on a new cart, with Uzzah and Ahio guiding it. 8 David and all the Israelites were celebrating with all their might before God, with songs and with harps, lyres, tambourines, cymbals and trumpets.

9 When they came to the threshing floor of Kidon, Uzzah reached out his hand to steady the ark, because the oxen stumbled. 10 The LORD's anger burned against Uzzah, and he struck him down because he had put his hand on the ark. So he died there before God.

11 Then David was angry because the LORD's wrath had broken out against Uzzah, and to this day that place is called Perez Uzzah.*d*

12 David was afraid of God that day and asked, "How can I ever bring the ark of God to me?" 13 He did not take the ark to be with him in the City of David. Instead, he took it aside to the house of Obed-Edom the Gittite. 14 The ark of God remained with the family of Obed-Edom in his house for three months, and the LORD blessed his household and everything he had.

David's House and Family

14 Now Hiram king of Tyre sent messengers to David, along with cedar logs, stonemasons and carpenters to build a palace for him. 2 And David knew that the LORD had established him as king over Israel and that his kingdom had been highly exalted for the sake of his people Israel.

3 In Jerusalem David took more wives and became the father of more sons and daughters. 4 These are the names of the children born to him there: Shammua, Shobab, Nathan, Solomon, 5 Ibhar, Elishua, Elpelet, 6 Nogah, Nepheg, Japhia, 7 Elishama, Beeliada*e* and Eliphelet.

David Defeats the Philistines

8 When the Philistines heard that David had been anointed king over all Israel, they went up in full force to search for him, but David heard about it and went out to meet them. 9 Now the Philistines had come and raided the Valley of Rephaim; 10 so David inquired of

---

a 3 Or *we neglected*   *b 3* Or *him*   *c 5* Or *to the entrance to*   *d 11* *Perez Uzzah* means *outbreak against Uzzah.*   *e 7* A variant of *Eliada*

God: "Shall I go and attack the Philistines? Will you hand them over to me?"

The LORD answered him, "Go, I will hand them over to you."

¹¹So David and his men went up to Baal Perazim, and there he defeated them. He said, "As waters break out, God has broken out against my enemies by my hand." So that place was called Baal Perazim.ᵃ ¹²The Philistines had abandoned their gods there, and David gave orders to burn them in the fire.

¹³Once more the Philistines raided the valley; ¹⁴so David inquired of God again, and God answered him, "Do not go straight up, but circle around them and attack them in front of the balsam trees. ¹⁵As soon as you hear the sound of marching in the tops of the balsam trees, move out to battle, because that will mean God has gone out in front of you to strike the Philistine army." ¹⁶So David did as God commanded him, and they struck down the Philistine army, all the way from Gibeon to Gezer.

¹⁷So David's fame spread throughout every land, and the LORD made all the nations fear him.

The Ark Brought to Jerusalem

15 After David had constructed buildings for himself in the City of David, he prepared a place for the ark of God and pitched a tent for it. ²Then David said, "No one but the Levites may carry the ark of God, because the LORD chose them to carry the ark of the LORD and to minister before him forever."

³David assembled all Israel in Jerusalem to bring up the ark of the LORD to the place he had prepared for it. ⁴He called together the descendants of Aaron and the Levites:

⁵From the descendants of Kohath,
Uriel the leader and 120 relatives;
⁶from the descendants of Merari,
Asaiah the leader and 220 relatives;
⁷from the descendants of Gershon,ᵇ
Joel the leader and 130 relatives;
⁸from the descendants of Elizaphan,

Shemaiah the leader and 200 relatives;
⁹from the descendants of Hebron,
Eliel the leader and 80 relatives;
¹⁰from the descendants of Uzziel,
Amminadab the leader and 112 relatives.

¹¹Then David summoned Zadok and Abiathar the priests, and Uriel, Asaiah, Joel, Shemaiah, Eliel and Amminadab the Levites. ¹²He said to them, "You are the heads of the Levitical families; you and your fellow Levites are to consecrate yourselves and bring up the ark of the LORD, the God of Israel, to the place I have prepared for it. ¹³It was because you, the Levites, did not bring it up the first time that the LORD our God broke out in anger against us. We did not inquire of him about how to do it in the prescribed way." ¹⁴So the priests and Levites consecrated themselves in order to bring up the ark of the LORD, the God of Israel. ¹⁵And the Levites carried the ark of God with the poles on their shoulders, as Moses had commanded in accordance with the word of the LORD.

¹⁶David told the leaders of the Levites to appoint their brothers as singers to sing joyful songs, accompanied by musical instruments: lyres, harps and cymbals.

¹⁷So the Levites appointed Heman son of Joel; from his brothers, Asaph son of Berekiah; and from their brothers the Merarites, Ethan son of Kushaiah; ¹⁸and with them their brothers next in rank: Zechariah,ᶜ Jaaziel, Shemiramoth, Jehiel, Unni, Eliab, Benaiah, Maaseiah, Mattithiah, Eliphelehu, Mikneiah, Obed-Edom and Jeiel,ᵈ the gatekeepers.

¹⁹The musicians Heman, Asaph and Ethan were to sound the bronze cymbals; ²⁰Zechariah, Aziel, Shemiramoth, Jehiel, Unni, Eliab, Maaseiah and Benaiah were to play the lyres according to alamoth,ᵉ ²¹and Mattithiah, Eliphelehu, Mikneiah, Obed-Edom, Jeiel and Azaziah were to play the harps, directing according to sheminith.ᵉ ²²Kenaniah the head Levite was in charge of the singing; that was his responsibility because he was skillful at it.

ᵃ 11 Baal Perazim means the lord who breaks out.   ᵇ 7 Hebrew Gershom, a variant of Gershon
ᶜ 18 Three Hebrew manuscripts and most Septuagint manuscripts (see also verse 20 and 1 Chron. 16:5); most Hebrew manuscripts Zechariah son and or Zechariah, Ben and   ᵈ 18 Hebrew; Septuagint (see also verse 21) Jeiel and Azaziah   ᵉ 20,21 Probably a musical term

23Berekiah and Elkanah were to be doorkeepers for the ark. 24Shebaniah, Joshaphat, Nethanel, Amasai, Zechariah, Benaiah and Eliezer the priests were to blow trumpets before the ark of God. Obed-Edom and Jehiah were also to be doorkeepers for the ark.

25So David and the elders of Israel and the commanders of units of a thousand went to bring up the ark of the covenant of the LORD from the house of Obed-Edom, with rejoicing. 26Because God had helped the Levites who were carrying the ark of the covenant of the LORD, seven bulls and seven rams were sacrificed. 27Now David was clothed in a robe of fine linen, as were all the Levites who were carrying the ark, and as were the singers, and Kenaniah, who was in charge of the singing of the choirs. David also wore a linen ephod. 28So all Israel brought up the ark of the covenant of the LORD with shouts, with the sounding of rams' horns and trumpets, and of cymbals, and the playing of lyres and harps.

29As the ark of the covenant of the LORD was entering the City of David, Michal daughter of Saul watched from a window. And when she saw King David dancing and celebrating, she despised him in her heart.

16 They brought the ark of God and set it inside the tent that David had pitched for it, and they presented burnt offerings and fellowship offerings[a] before God. 2After David had finished sacrificing the burnt offerings and fellowship offerings, he blessed the people in the name of the LORD. 3Then he gave a loaf of bread, a cake of dates and a cake of raisins to each Israelite man and woman.

4He appointed some of the Levites to minister before the ark of the LORD, to make petition, to give thanks, and to praise the LORD, the God of Israel: 5Asaph was the chief, Zechariah second, then Jeiel, Shemiramoth, Jehiel, Mattithiah, Eliab, Benaiah, Obed-Edom and Jeiel. They were to play the lyres and harps, Asaph was to sound the cymbals, 6and Benaiah and Jahaziel the priests were to blow the trumpets regularly before the ark of the covenant of God.

David's Psalm of Thanks

7That day David first committed to Asaph and his associates this psalm of thanks to the LORD:

8Give thanks to the LORD, call on his
    name;
  make known among the nations
    what he has done.
9Sing to him, sing praise to him;
  tell of all his wonderful acts.
10Glory in his holy name;
  let the hearts of those who seek
    the LORD rejoice.
11Look to the LORD and his strength;
  seek his face always.

12Remember the wonders he has done,
  his miracles, and the judgments he
    pronounced,
13O descendants of Israel his servant,
  O sons of Jacob, his chosen ones.

14He is the LORD our God;
  his judgments are in all the earth.
15He remembers[b] his covenant forever,
  the word he commanded, for a
    thousand generations,
16the covenant he made with Abraham,
  the oath he swore to Isaac.
17He confirmed it to Jacob as a decree,
  to Israel as an everlasting covenant:
18"To you I will give the land of Canaan
  as the portion you will inherit."

19When they were but few in number,
  few indeed, and strangers in it,
20they[c] wandered from nation to nation,
  from one kingdom to another.
21He allowed no man to oppress them;
  for their sake he rebuked kings:
22"Do not touch my anointed ones;
  do my prophets no harm."

23Sing to the LORD, all the earth;
  proclaim his salvation day after day.
24Declare his glory among the nations,
  his marvelous deeds among all
    peoples.
25For great is the LORD and most
    worthy of praise;
  he is to be feared above all gods.

a 1 Traditionally *peace offerings*; also in verse 2   b 15 Some Septuagint manuscripts (see also Psalm 105:8); Hebrew *Remember*   c 18–20 One Hebrew manuscript, Septuagint and Vulgate (see also Psalm 105:12); most Hebrew manuscripts *inherit,* / 19*though you are but few in number,* / *few indeed, and strangers in it."* / 20*They*

THE FOUNDATION OF A PREVIOUS RELIGION
Blaise Pascal

VERSE: 1 Chronicles 16:8   **PASSAGE:** 1 Chronicles 16:7–36

 see Christianity founded on a previous religion, in which I find the following facts.

(I am not speaking here of the miracles of Moses, Christ and the apostles, because they do not at first appear convincing, and I want here only to bring as evidence all those foundations of Christianity which are beyond doubt and cannot be called in doubt by anyone whatever.)

It is certain that in certain parts of the world we can see a peculiar people, separated from the other peoples of the world, and this is called the Jewish people.

I see then makers of religions in several parts of the world and throughout the ages, but their morality fails to satisfy me and their proofs fail to give me pause. Thus I should have refused alike the Moslem religion, that of China, of the ancient Romans, and of the Egyptians solely because, none of them bearing the stamp of truth more than another, nor anything which forces me to choose it, reason cannot incline towards one rather than another.

But as I consider this shifting and odd variety of customs and beliefs in different ages, I find in one corner of the world a peculiar people, separated from all the other peoples of the earth, who are the most ancient of all and whose history is earlier by several centuries than the oldest histories we have.

I find then this great and numerous people, descended from one man, worshiping one God, and living according to a law which they claim to have received from his hand. They maintain that they are the only people in the world to whom God has revealed his mysteries; that all men are corrupt and in disgrace with God, that they have all been abandoned to their senses and their own minds; and that this is the reason for the strange aberrations and continual changes of religions and customs among them, whereas these people remain unshakable in their conduct; but that God will not leave the other peoples for ever in darkness, that a redeemer will come, for all; that they are in the world to proclaim him to men; that they have been expressly created to be the forerunners and heralds of this great coming, and to call all peoples to unite with them in looking forward to this redeemer.

ADDITIONAL SCRIPTURE READING:
Deuteronomy 14:2; Titus 2:11–14; 1 Peter 2:9–12

Go to page 470 for your next devotional reading.

1500   1700

26 For all the gods of the nations are
      idols,
   but the LORD made the heavens.
27 Splendor and majesty are before him;
   strength and joy in his dwelling
      place.
28 Ascribe to the LORD, O families of
      nations,
   ascribe to the LORD glory and
      strength,
29   ascribe to the LORD the glory due
      his name.
   Bring an offering and come before
      him;
   worship the LORD in the splendor
      of his*a* holiness.
30 Tremble before him, all the earth!
   The world is firmly established; it
      cannot be moved.
31 Let the heavens rejoice, let the earth
      be glad;
   let them say among the nations,
      "The LORD reigns!"
32 Let the sea resound, and all that is in
      it;
   let the fields be jubilant, and
      everything in them!
33 Then the trees of the forest will sing,
   they will sing for joy before the
      LORD,
   for he comes to judge the earth.

34 Give thanks to the LORD, for he is
      good;
   his love endures forever.
35 Cry out, "Save us, O God our Savior;
   gather us and deliver us from the
      nations,
   that we may give thanks to your holy
      name,
   that we may glory in your praise."

THE CRY OF A YOUNG RAVEN IS NOTHING BUT
THE NATURAL CRY OF A CREATURE, BUT YOUR
CRY, IF IT BE SINCERE, IS THE RESULT OF A WORK
OF GRACE IN YOUR HEART.   —*C. H. Spurgeon*

---

36 Praise be to the LORD, the God of
      Israel,
   from everlasting to everlasting.

Then all the people said "Amen" and
"Praise the LORD."

37 David left Asaph and his associates
before the ark of the covenant of the
LORD to minister there regularly, according to each day's requirements. 38 He
also left Obed-Edom and his sixty-eight
associates to minister with them. Obed-
Edom son of Jeduthun, and also Hosah,
were gatekeepers.

39 David left Zadok the priest and his
fellow priests before the tabernacle of
the LORD at the high place in Gibeon
40 to present burnt offerings to the LORD
on the altar of burnt offering regularly,
morning and evening, in accordance
with everything written in the Law of
the LORD, which he had given Israel.
41 With them were Heman and Jeduthun
and the rest of those chosen and designated by name to give thanks to the
LORD, "for his love endures forever."
42 Heman and Jeduthun were responsible
for the sounding of the trumpets and
cymbals and for the playing of the other
instruments for sacred song. The sons of
Jeduthun were stationed at the gate.

43 Then all the people left, each for his
own home, and David returned home to
bless his family.

God's Promise to David

17 After David was settled in his
palace, he said to Nathan the
prophet, "Here I am, living in a palace of
cedar, while the ark of the covenant of
the LORD is under a tent."

2 Nathan replied to David, "Whatever
you have in mind, do it, for God is with
you."

3 That night the word of God came to
Nathan, saying:

4 "Go and tell my servant David,
'This is what the LORD says: You are
not the one to build me a house to
dwell in. 5 I have not dwelt in a house
from the day I brought Israel up out
of Egypt to this day. I have moved
from one tent site to another, from
one dwelling place to another.
6 Wherever I have moved with all the
Israelites, did I ever say to any of
their leaders*b* whom I commanded
to shepherd my people, "Why have
you not built me a house of cedar?" '

---

a 29 Or LORD *with the splendor of*   *b 6* Traditionally *judges;* also in verse 10

7"Now then, tell my servant David, 'This is what the LORD Almighty says: I took you from the pasture and from following the flock, to be ruler over my people Israel. 8I have been with you wherever you have gone, and I have cut off all your enemies from before you. Now I will make your name like the names of the greatest men of the earth. 9And I will provide a place for my people Israel and will plant them so that they can have a home of their own and no longer be disturbed. Wicked people will not oppress them anymore, as they did at the beginning 10and have done ever since the time I appointed leaders over my people Israel. I will also subdue all your enemies.

" 'I declare to you that the LORD will build a house for you: 11When your days are over and you go to be with your fathers, I will raise up your offspring to succeed you, one of your own sons, and I will establish his kingdom. 12He is the one who will build a house for me, and I will establish his throne forever. 13I will be his father, and he will be my son. I will never take my love away from him, as I took it away from your predecessor. 14I will set him over my house and my kingdom forever; his throne will be established forever.' "

15Nathan reported to David all the words of this entire revelation.

David's Prayer

16Then King David went in and sat before the LORD, and he said:

"Who am I, O LORD God, and what is my family, that you have brought me this far? 17And as if this were not enough in your sight, O God, you have spoken about the future of the house of your servant. You have looked on me as though I were the most exalted of men, O LORD God.

18"What more can David say to you for honoring your servant? For you know your servant, 19O LORD. For the sake of your servant and according to your will, you have done this great thing and made known all these great promises.

20"There is no one like you, O LORD, and there is no God but you, as we have heard with our own ears. 21And who is like your people Israel—the one nation on earth whose God went out to redeem a people for himself, and to make a name for yourself, and to perform great and awesome wonders by driving out nations from before your people, whom you redeemed from Egypt? 22You made your people Israel your very own forever, and you, O LORD, have become their God.

23"And now, LORD, let the promise you have made concerning your servant and his house be established forever. Do as you promised, 24so that it will be established and that your name will be great forever. Then men will say, 'The LORD Almighty, the God over Israel, is Israel's God!' And the house of your servant David will be established before you.

25"You, my God, have revealed to your servant that you will build a house for him. So your servant has found courage to pray to you. 26O LORD, you are God! You have promised these good things to your servant. 27Now you have been pleased to bless the house of your servant, that it may continue forever in your sight; for you, O LORD, have blessed it, and it will be blessed forever."

David's Victories

18 In the course of time, David defeated the Philistines and subdued them, and he took Gath and its surrounding villages from the control of the Philistines.

2David also defeated the Moabites, and they became subject to him and brought tribute.

3Moreover, David fought Hadadezer king of Zobah, as far as Hamath, when he went to establish his control along the Euphrates River. 4David captured a thousand of his chariots, seven thousand charioteers and twenty thousand foot soldiers. He hamstrung all but a hundred of the chariot horses.

⁵When the Arameans of Damascus came to help Hadadezer king of Zobah, David struck down twenty-two thousand of them. ⁶He put garrisons in the Aramean kingdom of Damascus, and the Arameans became subject to him and brought tribute. The LORD gave David victory everywhere he went.

⁷David took the gold shields carried by the officers of Hadadezer and brought them to Jerusalem. ⁸From Tebahᵃ and Cun, towns that belonged to Hadadezer, David took a great quantity of bronze, which Solomon used to make the bronze Sea, the pillars and various bronze articles.

⁹When Tou king of Hamath heard that David had defeated the entire army of Hadadezer king of Zobah, ¹⁰he sent his son Hadoram to King David to greet him and congratulate him on his victory in battle over Hadadezer, who had been at war with Tou. Hadoram brought all kinds of articles of gold and silver and bronze.

¹¹King David dedicated these articles to the LORD, as he had done with the silver and gold he had taken from all these nations: Edom and Moab, the Ammonites and the Philistines, and Amalek.

¹²Abishai son of Zeruiah struck down eighteen thousand Edomites in the Valley of Salt. ¹³He put garrisons in Edom, and all the Edomites became subject to David. The LORD gave David victory everywhere he went.

David's Officials

¹⁴David reigned over all Israel, doing what was just and right for all his people. ¹⁵Joab son of Zeruiah was over the army; Jehoshaphat son of Ahilud was recorder; ¹⁶Zadok son of Ahitub and Ahimelechᵇ son of Abiathar were priests; Shavsha was secretary; ¹⁷Benaiah son of Jehoiada was over the Kerethites and Pelethites; and David's sons were chief officials at the king's side.

The Battle Against the Ammonites

19 In the course of time, Nahash king of the Ammonites died, and his son succeeded him as king. ²David thought, "I will show kindness to Hanun son of Nahash, because his father showed kindness to me." So David sent a delegation to express his sympathy to Hanun concerning his father.

When David's men came to Hanun in the land of the Ammonites to express sympathy to him, ³the Ammonite nobles said to Hanun, "Do you think David is honoring your father by sending men to you to express sympathy? Haven't his men come to you to explore and spy out the country and overthrow it?" ⁴So Hanun seized David's men, shaved them, cut off their garments in the middle at the buttocks, and sent them away.

⁵When someone came and told David about the men, he sent messengers to meet them, for they were greatly humiliated. The king said, "Stay at Jericho till your beards have grown, and then come back."

⁶When the Ammonites realized that they had become a stench in David's nostrils, Hanun and the Ammonites sent a thousand talentsᶜ of silver to hire chariots and charioteers from Aram Naharaim,ᵈ Aram Maacah and Zobah. ⁷They hired thirty-two thousand chariots and charioteers, as well as the king of Maacah with his troops, who came and camped near Medeba, while the Ammonites were mustered from their towns and moved out for battle.

⁸On hearing this, David sent Joab out with the entire army of fighting men. ⁹The Ammonites came out and drew up in battle formation at the entrance to their city, while the kings who had come were by themselves in the open country.

¹⁰Joab saw that there were battle lines in front of him and behind him; so he selected some of the best troops in Israel and deployed them against the Arameans. ¹¹He put the rest of the men under the command of Abishai his brother, and they were deployed against the Ammonites. ¹²Joab said, "If the Arameans are too strong for me, then you

---

ᵃ 8 Hebrew *Tibhath*, a variant of *Tebah*   ᵇ 16 Some Hebrew manuscripts, Vulgate and Syriac (see also 2 Samuel 8:17); most Hebrew manuscripts *Abimelech*   ᶜ 6 That is, about 37 tons (about 34 metric tons)   ᵈ 6 That is, Northwest Mesopotamia

are to rescue me; but if the Ammonites are too strong for you, then I will rescue you. ¹³Be strong and let us fight bravely for our people and the cities of our God. The LORD will do what is good in his sight."

¹⁴Then Joab and the troops with him advanced to fight the Arameans, and they fled before him. ¹⁵When the Ammonites saw that the Arameans were fleeing, they too fled before his brother Abishai and went inside the city. So Joab went back to Jerusalem.

¹⁶After the Arameans saw that they had been routed by Israel, they sent messengers and had Arameans brought from beyond the River,ᵃ with Shophach the commander of Hadadezer's army leading them.

¹⁷When David was told of this, he gathered all Israel and crossed the Jordan; he advanced against them and formed his battle lines opposite them. David formed his lines to meet the Arameans in battle, and they fought against him. ¹⁸But they fled before Israel, and David killed seven thousand of their charioteers and forty thousand of their foot soldiers. He also killed Shophach the commander of their army.

¹⁹When the vassals of Hadadezer saw that they had been defeated by Israel, they made peace with David and became subject to him.

So the Arameans were not willing to help the Ammonites anymore.

The Capture of Rabbah

20 In the spring, at the time when kings go off to war, Joab led out the armed forces. He laid waste the land of the Ammonites and went to Rabbah and besieged it, but David remained in Jerusalem. Joab attacked Rabbah and left it in ruins. ²David took the crown from the head of their kingᵇ— its weight was found to be a talentᶜ of gold, and it was set with precious stones—and it was placed on David's head. He took a great quantity of plunder from the city ³and brought out the people who were there, consigning them to labor with saws and with iron picks and axes. David did this to all the Ammonite

towns. Then David and his entire army returned to Jerusalem.

War With the Philistines

⁴In the course of time, war broke out with the Philistines, at Gezer. At that time Sibbecai the Hushathite killed Sippai, one of the descendants of the Rephaites, and the Philistines were subjugated.

⁵In another battle with the Philistines, Elhanan son of Jair killed Lahmi the brother of Goliath the Gittite, who had a spear with a shaft like a weaver's rod.

⁶In still another battle, which took place at Gath, there was a huge man with six fingers on each hand and six toes on each foot—twenty-four in all. He also was descended from Rapha. ⁷When he taunted Israel, Jonathan son of Shimea, David's brother, killed him.

⁸These were descendants of Rapha in Gath, and they fell at the hands of David and his men.

David Numbers the Fighting Men

21 Satan rose up against Israel and incited David to take a census of Israel. ²So David said to Joab and the commanders of the troops, "Go and count the Israelites from Beersheba to Dan. Then report back to me so that I may know how many there are."

³But Joab replied, "May the LORD multiply his troops a hundred times over. My lord the king, are they not all my lord's subjects? Why does my lord want to do this? Why should he bring guilt on Israel?"

⁴The king's word, however, overruled Joab; so Joab left and went throughout Israel and then came back to Jerusalem. ⁵Joab reported the number of the fighting men to David: In all Israel there were one million one hundred thousand men who could handle a sword, including four hundred and seventy thousand in Judah.

⁶But Joab did not include Levi and Benjamin in the numbering, because the king's command was repulsive to him. ⁷This command was also evil in the sight of God; so he punished Israel.

⁸Then David said to God, "I have sinned greatly by doing this. Now, I beg

---

ᵃ 16 That is, the Euphrates   ᵇ 2 Or of Milcom, that is, Molech   ᶜ 2 That is, about 75 pounds (about 34 kilograms)

you, take away the guilt of your servant. I have done a very foolish thing."

⁹The LORD said to Gad, David's seer, ¹⁰"Go and tell David, 'This is what the LORD says: I am giving you three options. Choose one of them for me to carry out against you.' "

¹¹So Gad went to David and said to him, "This is what the LORD says: 'Take your choice: ¹²three years of famine, three months of being swept away*a* before your enemies, with their swords overtaking you, or three days of the sword of the LORD—days of plague in the land, with the angel of the LORD ravaging every part of Israel.' Now then, decide how I should answer the one who sent me."

¹³David said to Gad, "I am in deep distress. Let me fall into the hands of the LORD, for his mercy is very great; but do not let me fall into the hands of men."

¹⁴So the LORD sent a plague on Israel, and seventy thousand men of Israel fell dead. ¹⁵And God sent an angel to destroy Jerusalem. But as the angel was doing so, the LORD saw it and was grieved because of the calamity and said to the angel who was destroying the people, "Enough! Withdraw your hand." The angel of the LORD was then standing at the threshing floor of Araunah*b* the Jebusite.

¹⁶David looked up and saw the angel of the LORD standing between heaven and earth, with a drawn sword in his hand extended over Jerusalem. Then David and the elders, clothed in sackcloth, fell facedown.

¹⁷David said to God, "Was it not I who ordered the fighting men to be counted? I am the one who has sinned and done wrong. These are but sheep. What have they done? O LORD my God, let your hand fall upon me and my family, but do not let this plague remain on your people."

¹⁸Then the angel of the LORD ordered Gad to tell David to go up and build an altar to the LORD on the threshing floor of Araunah the Jebusite. ¹⁹So David went up in obedience to the word that Gad had spoken in the name of the LORD.

²⁰While Araunah was threshing wheat, he turned and saw the angel; his four sons who were with him hid themselves. ²¹Then David approached, and when Araunah looked and saw him, he left the threshing floor and bowed down before David with his face to the ground.

²²David said to him, "Let me have the site of your threshing floor so I can build an altar to the LORD, that the plague on the people may be stopped. Sell it to me at the full price."

²³Araunah said to David, "Take it! Let my lord the king do whatever pleases him. Look, I will give the oxen for the burnt offerings, the threshing sledges for the wood, and the wheat for the grain offering. I will give all this."

²⁴But King David replied to Araunah, "No, I insist on paying the full price. I will not take for the LORD what is yours, or sacrifice a burnt offering that costs me nothing."

²⁵So David paid Araunah six hundred shekels*c* of gold for the site. ²⁶David built an altar to the LORD there and sacrificed burnt offerings and fellowship offerings.*d* He called on the LORD, and the LORD answered him with fire from heaven on the altar of burnt offering.

²⁷Then the LORD spoke to the angel, and he put his sword back into its sheath. ²⁸At that time, when David saw that the LORD had answered him on the threshing floor of Araunah the Jebusite, he offered sacrifices there. ²⁹The tabernacle of the LORD, which Moses had made in the desert, and the altar of burnt offering were at that time on the high place at Gibeon. ³⁰But David could not go before it to inquire of God, because he was afraid of the sword of the angel of the LORD.

22 Then David said, "The house of the LORD God is to be here, and also the altar of burnt offering for Israel."

Preparations for the Temple

²So David gave orders to assemble the aliens living in Israel, and from among them he appointed stonecutters to prepare dressed stone for building the house of God. ³He provided a large amount of

---

a 12 Hebrew; Septuagint and Vulgate (see also 2 Samuel 24:13) *of fleeing*   *b 15* Hebrew *Ornan,* a variant of *Araunah;* also in verses 18–28   *c 25* That is, about 15 pounds (about 7 kilograms)
d 26 Traditionally *peace offerings*

iron to make nails for the doors of the gateways and for the fittings, and more bronze than could be weighed. ⁴He also provided more cedar logs than could be counted, for the Sidonians and Tyrians had brought large numbers of them to David.

⁵David said, "My son Solomon is young and inexperienced, and the house to be built for the LORD should be of great magnificence and fame and splendor in the sight of all the nations. Therefore I will make preparations for it." So David made extensive preparations before his death.

⁶Then he called for his son Solomon and charged him to build a house for the LORD, the God of Israel. ⁷David said to Solomon: "My son, I had it in my heart to build a house for the Name of the LORD my God. ⁸But this word of the LORD came to me: 'You have shed much blood and have fought many wars. You are not to build a house for my Name, because you have shed much blood on the earth in my sight. ⁹But you will have a son who will be a man of peace and rest, and I will give him rest from all his enemies on every side. His name will be Solomon,ᵃ and I will grant Israel peace and quiet during his reign. ¹⁰He is the one who will build a house for my Name. He will be my son, and I will be his father. And I will establish the throne of his kingdom over Israel forever.'

¹¹"Now, my son, the LORD be with you, and may you have success and build the house of the LORD your God, as he said you would. ¹²May the LORD give you discretion and understanding when he puts you in command over Israel, so that you may keep the law of the LORD your God. ¹³Then you will have success if you are careful to observe the decrees and laws that the LORD gave Moses for Israel. Be strong and courageous. Do not be afraid or discouraged.

¹⁴"I have taken great pains to provide for the temple of the LORD a hundred thousand talentsᵇ of gold, a million talentsᶜ of silver, quantities of bronze and iron too great to be weighed, and wood and stone. And you may add to them. ¹⁵You have many

workmen: stonecutters, masons and carpenters, as well as men skilled in every kind of work ¹⁶in gold and silver, bronze and iron—craftsmen beyond number. Now begin the work, and the LORD be with you."

¹⁷Then David ordered all the leaders of Israel to help his son Solomon. ¹⁸He said to them, "Is not the LORD your God with you? And has he not granted you rest on every side? For he has handed the inhabitants of the land over to me, and the land is subject to the LORD and to his people. ¹⁹Now devote your heart and soul to seeking the LORD your God. Begin to build the sanctuary of the LORD God, so that you may bring the ark of the covenant of the LORD and the sacred articles belonging to God into the temple that will be built for the Name of the LORD."

The Levites

23 When David was old and full of years, he made his son Solomon king over Israel.

²He also gathered together all the leaders of Israel, as well as the priests and Levites. ³The Levites thirty years old or more were counted, and the total number of men was thirty-eight thousand. ⁴David said, "Of these, twenty-four thousand are to supervise the work of the temple of the LORD and six thousand are to be officials and judges. ⁵Four thousand are to be gatekeepers and four thousand are to praise the LORD with the musical instruments I have provided for that purpose."

⁶David divided the Levites into groups corresponding to the sons of Levi: Gershon, Kohath and Merari.

Gershonites

⁷Belonging to the Gershonites:
Ladan and Shimei.
⁸The sons of Ladan:
Jehiel the first, Zetham and Joel—three in all.
⁹The sons of Shimei:
Shelomoth, Haziel and Haran—three in all.
These were the heads of the families of Ladan.

ᵃ 9 *Solomon* sounds like and may be derived from the Hebrew for *peace*.   ᵇ 14 That is, about 3,750 tons (about 3,450 metric tons)   ᶜ 14 That is, about 37,500 tons (about 34,500 metric tons)

10 And the sons of Shimei:
Jahath, Ziza,ᵃ Jeush and Beriah.
These were the sons of Shimei—
four in all.

11 Jahath was the first and Ziza the
second, but Jeush and Beriah did
not have many sons; so they were
counted as one family with one
assignment.

Kohathites

12 The sons of Kohath:
Amram, Izhar, Hebron and Uzziel—four in all.

13 The sons of Amram:
Aaron and Moses.
Aaron was set apart, he and his
descendants forever, to consecrate the most holy things, to
offer sacrifices before the LORD, to
minister before him and to pronounce blessings in his name forever. 14 The sons of Moses the
man of God were counted as part
of the tribe of Levi.

15 The sons of Moses:
Gershom and Eliezer.

16 The descendants of Gershom:
Shubael was the first.

17 The descendants of Eliezer:
Rehabiah was the first.
Eliezer had no other sons, but the
sons of Rehabiah were very numerous.

18 The sons of Izhar:
Shelomith was the first.

19 The sons of Hebron:
Jeriah the first, Amariah the second, Jahaziel the third and Jekameam the fourth.

20 The sons of Uzziel:
Micah the first and Isshiah the
second.

Merarites

21 The sons of Merari:
Mahli and Mushi.
The sons of Mahli:
Eleazar and Kish.

22 Eleazar died without having sons:
he had only daughters. Their
cousins, the sons of Kish, married
them.

23 The sons of Mushi:
Mahli, Eder and Jerimoth—three
in all.

24 These were the descendants of Levi
by their families—the heads of families
as they were registered under their
names and counted individually, that is,
the workers twenty years old or more
who served in the temple of the LORD.
25 For David had said, "Since the LORD,
the God of Israel, has granted rest to his
people and has come to dwell in Jerusalem forever, 26 the Levites no longer
need to carry the tabernacle or any of
the articles used in its service."
27 According to the last instructions of
David, the Levites were counted from
those twenty years old or more.

28 The duty of the Levites was to help
Aaron's descendants in the service of the
temple of the LORD: to be in charge of
the courtyards, the side rooms, the
purification of all sacred things and the
performance of other duties at the house
of God. 29 They were in charge of the
bread set out on the table, the flour for
the grain offerings, the unleavened
wafers, the baking and the mixing, and
all measurements of quantity and size.
30 They were also to stand every morning to thank and praise the LORD. They
were to do the same in the evening
31 and whenever burnt offerings were
presented to the LORD on Sabbaths and
at New Moon festivals and at appointed
feasts. They were to serve before the
LORD regularly in the proper number
and in the way prescribed for them.

32 And so the Levites carried out their
responsibilities for the Tent of Meeting,
for the Holy Place and, under their
brothers the descendants of Aaron, for
the service of the temple of the LORD.

The Divisions of Priests

24 These were the divisions of
the sons of Aaron:

The sons of Aaron were Nadab, Abihu,
Eleazar and Ithamar. 2 But Nadab and
Abihu died before their father did, and
they had no sons; so Eleazar and Ithamar
served as the priests. 3 With the help of
Zadok a descendant of Eleazar and Ahimelech a descendant of Ithamar, David separated them into divisions for their

---

ᵃ 10 One Hebrew manuscript, Septuagint and Vulgate (see also verse 11); most Hebrew manuscripts *Zina*

appointed order of ministering. [4] A larger number of leaders were found among Eleazar's descendants than among Ithamar's, and they were divided accordingly: sixteen heads of families from Eleazar's descendants and eight heads of families from Ithamar's descendants. [5] They divided them impartially by drawing lots, for there were officials of the sanctuary and officials of God among the descendants of both Eleazar and Ithamar.

[6] The scribe Shemaiah son of Nethanel, a Levite, recorded their names in the presence of the king and of the officials: Zadok the priest, Ahimelech son of Abiathar and the heads of families of the priests and of the Levites—one family being taken from Eleazar and then one from Ithamar.

[7] The first lot fell to Jehoiarib,
　　the second to Jedaiah,
[8] the third to Harim,
　　the fourth to Seorim,
[9] the fifth to Malkijah,
　　the sixth to Mijamin,
[10] the seventh to Hakkoz,
　　the eighth to Abijah,
[11] the ninth to Jeshua,
　　the tenth to Shecaniah,
[12] the eleventh to Eliashib,
　　the twelfth to Jakim,
[13] the thirteenth to Huppah,
　　the fourteenth to Jeshebeab,
[14] the fifteenth to Bilgah,
　　the sixteenth to Immer,
[15] the seventeenth to Hezir,
　　the eighteenth to Happizzez,
[16] the nineteenth to Pethahiah,
　　the twentieth to Jehezkel,
[17] the twenty-first to Jakin,
　　the twenty-second to Gamul,
[18] the twenty-third to Delaiah
　　and the twenty-fourth to Maaziah.

[19] This was their appointed order of ministering when they entered the temple of the LORD, according to the regulations prescribed for them by their forefather Aaron, as the LORD, the God of Israel, had commanded him.

The Rest of the Levites

[20] As for the rest of the descendants of Levi:

from the sons of Amram: Shubael;
　　from the sons of Shubael: Jehdeiah.
[21] As for Rehabiah, from his sons:
　　Isshiah was the first.
[22] From the Izharites: Shelomoth;
　　from the sons of Shelomoth:
　　Jahath.
[23] The sons of Hebron: Jeriah the first,[a] Amariah the second, Jahaziel the third and Jekameam the fourth.
[24] The son of Uzziel: Micah;
　　from the sons of Micah: Shamir.
[25] The brother of Micah: Isshiah;
　　from the sons of Isshiah: Zechariah.
[26] The sons of Merari: Mahli and Mushi.
　　The son of Jaaziah: Beno.
[27] The sons of Merari:
　　from Jaaziah: Beno, Shoham, Zaccur and Ibri.
[28] From Mahli: Eleazar, who had no sons.
[29] From Kish: the son of Kish: Jerahmeel.
[30] And the sons of Mushi: Mahli, Eder and Jerimoth.

These were the Levites, according to their families. [31] They also cast lots, just as their brothers the descendants of Aaron did, in the presence of King David and of Zadok, Ahimelech, and the heads of families of the priests and of the Levites. The families of the oldest brother were treated the same as those of the youngest.

The Singers

25 David, together with the commanders of the army, set apart some of the sons of Asaph, Heman and Jeduthun for the ministry of prophesying, accompanied by harps, lyres and cymbals. Here is the list of the men who performed this service:

[2] From the sons of Asaph:
Zaccur, Joseph, Nethaniah and Asarelah. The sons of Asaph were under the supervision of Asaph, who prophesied under the king's supervision.

---

a 23 Two Hebrew manuscripts and some Septuagint manuscripts (see also 1 Chron. 23:19); most Hebrew manuscripts *The sons of Jeriah:*

the half-tribe of Manasseh for every matter pertaining to God and for the affairs of the king.

Army Divisions

27 This is the list of the Israelites—heads of families, commanders of thousands and commanders of hundreds, and their officers, who served the king in all that concerned the army divisions that were on duty month by month throughout the year. Each division consisted of 24,000 men.

2 In charge of the first division, for the first month, was Jashobeam son of Zabdiel. There were 24,000 men in his division. 3 He was a descendant of Perez and chief of all the army officers for the first month.

4 In charge of the division for the second month was Dodai the Ahohite; Mikloth was the leader of his division. There were 24,000 men in his division.

5 The third army commander, for the third month, was Benaiah son of Jehoiada the priest. He was chief and there were 24,000 men in his division. 6 This was the Benaiah who was a mighty man among the Thirty and was over the Thirty. His son Ammizabad was in charge of his division.

7 The fourth, for the fourth month, was Asahel the brother of Joab; his son Zebadiah was his successor. There were 24,000 men in his division.

8 The fifth, for the fifth month, was the commander Shamhuth the Izrahite. There were 24,000 men in his division.

9 The sixth, for the sixth month, was Ira the son of Ikkesh the Tekoite. There were 24,000 men in his division.

10 The seventh, for the seventh month, was Helez the Pelonite, an Ephraimite. There were 24,000 men in his division.

11 The eighth, for the eighth month, was Sibbecai the Hushathite, a Zerahite. There were 24,000 men in his division.

12 The ninth, for the ninth month, was Abiezer the Anathothite, a Benjamite. There were 24,000 men in his division.

13 The tenth, for the tenth month, was Maharai the Netophathite, a Zerahite. There were 24,000 men in his division.

14 The eleventh, for the eleventh month, was Benaiah the Pirathonite, an Ephraimite. There were 24,000 men in his division.

15 The twelfth, for the twelfth month, was Heldai the Netophathite, from the family of Othniel. There were 24,000 men in his division.

Officers of the Tribes

16 The officers over the tribes of Israel:

over the Reubenites: Eliezer son of Zicri;

over the Simeonites: Shephatiah son of Maacah;

17 over Levi: Hashabiah son of Kemuel;

over Aaron: Zadok;

18 over Judah: Elihu, a brother of David;

over Issachar: Omri son of Michael;

19 over Zebulun: Ishmaiah son of Obadiah;

over Naphtali: Jerimoth son of Azriel;

20 over the Ephraimites: Hoshea son of Azaziah;

over half the tribe of Manasseh: Joel son of Pedaiah;

21 over the half-tribe of Manasseh in Gilead: Iddo son of Zechariah;

over Benjamin: Jaasiel son of Abner;

22 over Dan: Azarel son of Jeroham.

These were the officers over the tribes of Israel.

23 David did not take the number of the men twenty years old or less, because the LORD had promised to make Israel as numerous as the stars in the sky. 24 Joab son of Zeruiah began to count the men but did not finish. Wrath came on Israel on account of this numbering, and the number was not entered in the book[a] of the annals of King David.

The King's Overseers

25 Azmaveth son of Adiel was in charge of the royal storehouses.

Jonathan son of Uzziah was in charge

---

a 24 Septuagint; Hebrew *number*

of the storehouses in the outlying districts, in the towns, the villages and the watchtowers.

26Ezri son of Kelub was in charge of the field workers who farmed the land.

27Shimei the Ramathite was in charge of the vineyards.

Zabdi the Shiphmite was in charge of the produce of the vineyards for the wine vats.

28Baal-Hanan the Gederite was in charge of the olive and sycamore-fig trees in the western foothills.

Joash was in charge of the supplies of olive oil.

29Shitrai the Sharonite was in charge of the herds grazing in Sharon.

Shaphat son of Adlai was in charge of the herds in the valleys.

30Obil the Ishmaelite was in charge of the camels.

Jehdeiah the Meronothite was in charge of the donkeys.

31Jaziz the Hagrite was in charge of the flocks.

All these were the officials in charge of King David's property.

32Jonathan, David's uncle, was a counselor, a man of insight and a scribe. Jehiel son of Hacmoni took care of the king's sons.

33Ahithophel was the king's counselor. Hushai the Arkite was the king's friend. 34Ahithophel was succeeded by Jehoiada son of Benaiah and by Abiathar.

Joab was the commander of the royal army.

David's Plans for the Temple

28 David summoned all the officials of Israel to assemble at Jerusalem: the officers over the tribes, the commanders of the divisions in the service of the king, the commanders of thousands and commanders of hundreds, and the officials in charge of all the property and livestock belonging to the king and his sons, together with the palace officials, the mighty men and all the brave warriors.

2King David rose to his feet and said: "Listen to me, my brothers and my people. I had it in my heart to build a house as a place of rest for the ark of the covenant of the LORD, for the footstool of our God, and I made plans to build it.

3But God said to me, 'You are not to build a house for my Name, because you are a warrior and have shed blood.'

4"Yet the LORD, the God of Israel, chose me from my whole family to be king over Israel forever. He chose Judah as leader, and from the house of Judah he chose my family, and from my father's sons he was pleased to make me king over all Israel. 5Of all my sons—and the LORD has given me many—he has chosen my son Solomon to sit on the throne of the kingdom of the LORD over Israel. 6He said to me: 'Solomon your son is the one who will build my house and my courts, for I have chosen him to be my son, and I will be his father. 7I will establish his kingdom forever if he is unswerving in carrying out my commands and laws, as is being done at this time.'

8"So now I charge you in the sight of all Israel and of the assembly of the LORD, and in the hearing of our God: Be careful to follow all the commands of the LORD your God, that you may possess this good land and pass it on as an inheritance to your descendants forever.

9"And you, my son Solomon, acknowledge the God of your father, and serve him with wholehearted devotion and with a willing mind, for the LORD searches every heart and understands every motive behind the thoughts. If you seek him, he will be found by you; but if you forsake him, he will reject you forever. 10Consider now, for the LORD has chosen you to build a temple as a sanctuary. Be strong and do the work."

11Then David gave his son Solomon the plans for the portico of the temple, its buildings, its storerooms, its upper parts, its inner rooms and the place of atonement. 12He gave him the plans of all that the Spirit had put in his mind for the courts of the temple of the LORD and all the surrounding rooms, for the treasuries of the temple of God and for the treasuries for the dedicated things. 13He gave him instructions for the divisions of the priests and Levites, and for all the work of serving in the temple of the LORD, as well as for all the articles to be used in its service. 14He designated the weight of gold for all the gold articles to be used in various kinds of service, and the weight of silver for all the silver articles to be used in various kinds of service: **15**the weight of gold for the gold lampstands and their lamps, with the weight for each lampstand and its lamps; and the weight of silver for each silver lampstand and its lamps, according to the use of each lampstand; **16**the weight of gold for each table for consecrated bread; the weight of silver for the silver tables; **17**the weight of pure gold for the forks, sprinkling bowls and pitchers; the weight of gold for each gold dish; the weight of silver for each silver dish; **18**and the weight of the refined gold for the altar of incense. He also gave him the plan for the chariot, that is, the cherubim of gold that spread their wings and shelter the ark of the covenant of the LORD.

19"All this," David said, "I have in writing from the hand of the LORD upon me, and he gave me understanding in all the details of the plan."

20David also said to Solomon his son, "Be strong and courageous, and do the work. Do not be afraid or discouraged, for the LORD God, my God, is with you. He will not fail you or forsake you until all the work for the service of the temple of the LORD is finished. **21**The divisions of the priests and Levites are ready for all the work on the temple of God, and every willing man skilled in any craft will help you in all the work. The officials and all the people will obey your every command."

Gifts for Building the Temple

29 Then King David said to the whole assembly: "My son Solomon, the one whom God has chosen, is young and inexperienced. The task is great, because this palatial structure is not for man but for the LORD God. **2**With all my resources I have provided for the temple of my God—gold for the gold work, silver for the silver, bronze for the bronze, iron for the iron and wood for the wood, as well as onyx for the settings, turquoise,*a* stones of various colors, and all kinds of fine stone and marble—all of these in large quantities. **3**Besides, in my devotion to

the temple of my God I now give my personal treasures of gold and silver for the temple of my God, over and above everything I have provided for this holy temple: **4**three thousand talents*b* of gold (gold of Ophir) and seven thousand talents*c* of refined silver, for the overlaying of the walls of the buildings, **5**for the gold work and the silver work, and for all the work to be done by the craftsmen. Now, who is willing to consecrate himself today to the LORD?"

6Then the leaders of families, the officers of the tribes of Israel, the commanders of thousands and commanders of hundreds, and the officials in charge of the king's work gave willingly. **7**They gave toward the work on the temple of God five thousand talents*d* and ten thousand darics*e* of gold, ten thousand talents*f* of silver, eighteen thousand talents*g* of bronze and a hundred thousand talents*h* of iron. **8**Any who had precious stones gave them to the treasury of the temple of the LORD in the custody of Jehiel the Gershonite. **9**The people rejoiced at the willing response of their leaders, for they had given freely and wholeheartedly to the LORD. David the king also rejoiced greatly.

David's Prayer

10David praised the LORD in the presence of the whole assembly, saying,

"Praise be to you, O LORD,
  God of our father Israel,
  from everlasting to everlasting.
11Yours, O LORD, is the greatness and
    the power
  and the glory and the majesty and
    the splendor,
  for everything in heaven and earth
    is yours.
Yours, O LORD, is the kingdom;
  you are exalted as head over all.
12Wealth and honor come from you;
  you are the ruler of all things.
In your hands are strength and power
  to exalt and give strength to all.
13Now, our God, we give you thanks,
  and praise your glorious name.

---

a 2 The meaning of the Hebrew for this word is uncertain.   *b* 4 That is, about 110 tons (about 100 metric tons)   *c* 4 That is, about 260 tons (about 240 metric tons)   *d* 7 That is, about 190 tons (about 170 metric tons)   *e* 7 That is, about 185 pounds (about 84 kilograms)   *f* 7 That is, about 375 tons (about 345 metric tons)   *g* 7 That is, about 675 tons (about 610 metric tons)   *h* 7 That is, about 3,750 tons (about 3,450 metric tons)

¹⁴"But who am I, and who are my people, that we should be able to give as generously as this? Everything comes from you, and we have given you only what comes from your hand. ¹⁵We are aliens and strangers in your sight, as were all our forefathers. Our days on earth are like a shadow, without hope. ¹⁶O LORD our God, as for all this abundance that we have provided for building you a temple for your Holy Name, it comes from your hand, and all of it belongs to you. ¹⁷I know, my God, that you test the heart and are pleased with integrity. All these things have I given willingly and with honest intent. And now I have seen with joy how willingly your people who are here have given to you. ¹⁸O LORD, God of our fathers Abraham, Isaac and Israel, keep this desire in

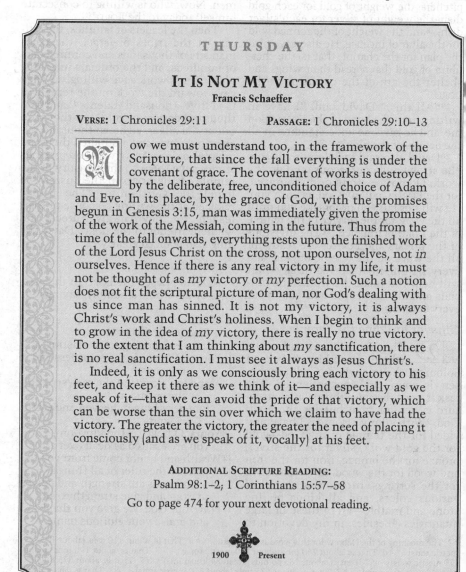

THURSDAY

IT IS NOT MY VICTORY
Francis Schaeffer

VERSE: 1 Chronicles 29:11　　　**PASSAGE:** 1 Chronicles 29:10–13

Now we must understand too, in the framework of the Scripture, that since the fall everything is under the covenant of grace. The covenant of works is destroyed by the deliberate, free, unconditioned choice of Adam and Eve. In its place, by the grace of God, with the promises begun in Genesis 3:15, man was immediately given the promise of the work of the Messiah, coming in the future. Thus from the time of the fall onwards, everything rests upon the finished work of the Lord Jesus Christ on the cross, not upon ourselves, not *in* ourselves. Hence if there is any real victory in my life, it must not be thought of as *my* victory or *my* perfection. Such a notion does not fit the scriptural picture of man, nor God's dealing with us since man has sinned. It is not my victory, it is always Christ's work and Christ's holiness. When I begin to think and to grow in the idea of *my* victory, there is really no true victory. To the extent that I am thinking about *my* sanctification, there is no real sanctification. I must see it always as Jesus Christ's.

Indeed, it is only as we consciously bring each victory to his feet, and keep it there as we think of it—and especially as we speak of it—that we can avoid the pride of that victory, which can be worse than the sin over which we claim to have had the victory. The greater the victory, the greater the need of placing it consciously (and as we speak of it, vocally) at his feet.

ADDITIONAL SCRIPTURE READING:
Psalm 98:1–2; 1 Corinthians 15:57–58

Go to page 474 for your next devotional reading.

1900　　　Present

the hearts of your people forever, and keep their hearts loyal to you. ¹⁹And give my son Solomon the wholehearted devotion to keep your commands, requirements and decrees and to do everything to build the palatial structure for which I have provided."

²⁰Then David said to the whole assembly, "Praise the LORD your God." So they all praised the LORD, the God of their fathers; they bowed low and fell prostrate before the LORD and the king.

Solomon Acknowledged as King

²¹The next day they made sacrifices to the LORD and presented burnt offerings to him: a thousand bulls, a thousand rams and a thousand male lambs, together with their drink offerings, and other sacrifices in abundance for all Israel. ²²They ate and drank with great joy in the presence of the LORD that day.

Then they acknowledged Solomon son of David as king a second time, anointing him before the LORD to be ruler and Zadok to be priest. ²³So Solomon sat on the throne of the LORD as king in place of his father David. He prospered and all Israel obeyed him. ²⁴All the officers and mighty men, as well as all of King David's sons, pledged their submission to King Solomon.

²⁵The LORD highly exalted Solomon in the sight of all Israel and bestowed on him royal splendor such as no king over Israel ever had before.

The Death of David

²⁶David son of Jesse was king over all Israel. ²⁷He ruled over Israel forty years—seven in Hebron and thirty-three in Jerusalem. ²⁸He died at a good old age, having enjoyed long life, wealth and honor. His son Solomon succeeded him as king.

²⁹As for the events of King David's reign, from beginning to end, they are written in the records of Samuel the seer, the records of Nathan the prophet and the records of Gad the seer, ³⁰together with the details of his reign and power, and the circumstances that surrounded him and Israel and the kingdoms of all the other lands.

2 CHRONICLES

HE BOOK OF 2 CHRONICLES CONTINUES THE HISTORY OF DAVID'S ROYAL LINE. THIS BOOK, LIKE 1 CHRONICLES, TEACHES THAT THE PEOPLE'S RELATIONSHIP TO GOD WAS CRUCIAL TO THEIR DAILY LIVING. NOTICE HOW WHEN THE AUTHOR WRITES ABOUT THE KINGS, HE MEASURES THEM ON THE BASIS OF THEIR FAITHFULNESS TO GOD. THE REIGNS OF EVIL KINGS ARE REPORTED BY THE AUTHOR BRIEFLY, WHILE THE REIGNS OF GOOD KINGS ARE DESCRIBED IN MORE DETAIL.

Solomon Asks for Wisdom

1 Solomon son of David established himself firmly over his kingdom, for the LORD his God was with him and made him exceedingly great.

²Then Solomon spoke to all Israel—to the commanders of thousands and commanders of hundreds, to the judges and to all the leaders in Israel, the heads of families— ³and Solomon and the whole assembly went to the high place at Gibeon, for God's Tent of Meeting was there, which Moses the LORD's servant had made in the desert. ⁴Now David had brought up the ark of God from Kiriath Jearim to the place he had prepared for it, because he had pitched a tent for it in Jerusalem. ⁵But the bronze altar that Bezalel son of Uri, the son of Hur, had made was in Gibeon in front of the tabernacle of the LORD; so Solomon and the assembly inquired of him there. ⁶Solomon went up to the bronze altar before the LORD in the Tent of Meeting and offered a thousand burnt offerings on it.

⁷That night God appeared to Solomon and said to him, "Ask for whatever you want me to give you."

⁸Solomon answered God, "You have shown great kindness to David my father and have made me king in his place. ⁹Now, LORD God, let your promise to my father David be confirmed, for you have made me king over a people who are as numerous as the dust of the earth. ¹⁰Give me wisdom and knowledge, that I may lead this people, for who is able to govern this great people of yours?"

¹¹God said to Solomon, "Since this is your heart's desire and you have not

asked for wealth, riches or honor, nor for the death of your enemies, and since you have not asked for a long life but for wisdom and knowledge to govern my people over whom I have made you king, 12therefore wisdom and knowledge will be given you. And I will also give you wealth, riches and honor, such as no king who was before you ever had and none after you will have."

13Then Solomon went to Jerusalem from the high place at Gibeon, from before the Tent of Meeting. And he reigned over Israel.

14Solomon accumulated chariots and horses; he had fourteen hundred chariots and twelve thousand horses,*a* which he kept in the chariot cities and also with him in Jerusalem. 15The king made silver and gold as common in Jerusalem as stones, and cedar as plentiful as sycamore-fig trees in the foothills. 16Solomon's horses were imported from Egypt*b* and from Kue*c*—the royal merchants purchased them from Kue. 17They imported a chariot from Egypt for six hundred shekels*d* of silver, and a horse for a hundred and fifty.*e* They also exported them to all the kings of the Hittites and of the Arameans.

Preparations for Building the Temple

2 Solomon gave orders to build a temple for the Name of the LORD and a royal palace for himself. 2He conscripted seventy thousand men as carriers and eighty thousand as stonecutters in the hills and thirty-six hundred as foremen over them.

3Solomon sent this message to Hiram*f* king of Tyre:

"Send me cedar logs as you did for my father David when you sent him cedar to build a palace to live in. 4Now I am about to build a temple for the Name of the LORD my God and to dedicate it to him for burning fragrant incense before him, for setting out the consecrated bread regularly, and for making

burnt offerings every morning and evening and on Sabbaths and New Moons and at the appointed feasts of the LORD our God. This is a lasting ordinance for Israel.

5"The temple I am going to build will be great, because our God is greater than all other gods. 6But who is able to build a temple for him, since the heavens, even the highest heavens, cannot contain him? Who then am I to build a temple for him, except as a place to burn sacrifices before him?

7"Send me, therefore, a man skilled to work in gold and silver, bronze and iron, and in purple, crimson and blue yarn, and experienced in the art of engraving, to work in Judah and Jerusalem with my skilled craftsmen, whom my father David provided.

8"Send me also cedar, pine and algum*g* logs from Lebanon, for I know that your men are skilled in cutting timber there. My men will work with yours 9to provide me with plenty of lumber, because the temple I build must be large and magnificent. 10I will give your servants, the woodsmen who cut the timber, twenty thousand cors*h* of ground wheat, twenty thousand cors of barley, twenty thousand baths*i* of wine and twenty thousand baths of olive oil."

11Hiram king of Tyre replied by letter to Solomon:

"Because the LORD loves his people, he has made you their king."

12And Hiram added:

"Praise be to the LORD, the God of Israel, who made heaven and earth! He has given King David a wise son, endowed with intelligence and discernment, who will build a temple for the LORD and a palace for himself.

13"I am sending you Huram-Abi, a man of great skill, 14whose mother

---

a 14 Or *charioteers*   *b 16* Or possibly *Muzur,* a region in Cilicia; also in verse 17   *c 16* Probably Cilicia   *d 17* That is, about 15 pounds (about 7 kilograms)   *e 17* That is, about 3 3/4 pounds (about 1.7 kilograms)   *f 3* Hebrew *Huram,* a variant of *Hiram;* also in verses 11 and 12   *g 8* Probably a variant of *almug;* possibly juniper   *h 10* That is, probably about 125,000 bushels (about 4,400 kiloliters)   *i 10* That is, probably about 115,000 gallons (about 440 kiloliters)

was from Dan and whose father was from Tyre. He is trained to work in gold and silver, bronze and iron, stone and wood, and with purple and blue and crimson yarn and fine linen. He is experienced in all kinds of engraving and can execute any design given to him. He will work with your craftsmen and with those of my lord, David your father.

15 "Now let my lord send his servants the wheat and barley and the

FRIDAY

THE TEMPLE HE HAD SPOKEN OF WAS HIS BODY
Evelyn Underhill

VERSE: 2 Chronicles 2:7   **PASSAGE:** 2 Chronicles 2:1–10

It sometimes happens that one goes to see a cathedral which is famous for the splendor of its glass; only to discover that, seen from outside, the windows give us no hint whatever of that which awaits us within. They all look alike; dull, thick, and grubby . . . Then we open the door, and go inside . . . and at once we are surrounded by a radiance, a beauty, that lie beyond the fringe of speech. The universal light of God in which we live and move, and yet which in its reality always escapes us, pours through those windows . . . and shows us things of which we never dreamed before.

In the same way, the deep mysteries of the being of God . . . cannot be seen by us, until they have passed through a human medium, a human life. Nor can that life, and all that it means as a revelation of God, his eternal truth and beauty, be realized by us from the outside . . . It is only within the place of prayer, recollection, worship and love . . . that we can cleanse our vision . . . and fully and truly receive the revelation of reality which is made to us in Christ . . .

For here, a light we can bear to look at . . . comes to us from a light we cannot bear to look at even whilst we worship it . . . What we see is not very sensational . . . First we see a baby, and a long hidden growth; and then the unmeasured outpouring and self spending of an other-worldly love and mercy, teaching, healing, rescuing and transforming, but never trying to get anything for itself . . . consummated at last in the most generous and lonely of deaths, issuing in a victory which has given life ever since to men's souls.

ADDITIONAL SCRIPTURE READING:
1 Corinthians 6:19–20; Ephesians 2:19–22; 1 Peter 2:5

Go to page 480 for your next devotional reading.

1900   Present

olive oil and wine he promised, [16]and we will cut all the logs from Lebanon that you need and will float them in rafts by sea down to Joppa. You can then take them up to Jerusalem."

[17]Solomon took a census of all the aliens who were in Israel, after the census his father David had taken; and they were found to be 153,600. [18]He assigned 70,000 of them to be carriers and 80,000 to be stonecutters in the hills, with 3,600 foremen over them to keep the people working.

Solomon Builds the Temple

3 Then Solomon began to build the temple of the LORD in Jerusalem on Mount Moriah, where the LORD had appeared to his father David. It was on the threshing floor of Araunah[a] the Jebusite, the place provided by David. [2]He began building on the second day of the second month in the fourth year of his reign.

[3]The foundation Solomon laid for building the temple of God was sixty cubits long and twenty cubits wide[b] (using the cubit of the old standard). [4]The portico at the front of the temple was twenty cubits[c] long across the width of the building and twenty cubits[d] high.

He overlaid the inside with pure gold. [5]He paneled the main hall with pine and covered it with fine gold and decorated it with palm tree and chain designs. [6]He adorned the temple with precious stones. And the gold he used was gold of Parvaim. [7]He overlaid the ceiling beams, doorframes, walls and doors of the temple with gold, and he carved cherubim on the walls.

[8]He built the Most Holy Place, its length corresponding to the width of the temple—twenty cubits long and twenty cubits wide. He overlaid the inside with six hundred talents[e] of fine gold. [9]The

gold nails weighed fifty shekels.[f] He also overlaid the upper parts with gold.

[10]In the Most Holy Place he made a pair of sculptured cherubim and overlaid them with gold. [11]The total wingspan of the cherubim was twenty cubits. One wing of the first cherub was five cubits[g] long and touched the temple wall, while its other wing, also five cubits long, touched the wing of the other cherub. [12]Similarly one wing of the second cherub was five cubits long and touched the other temple wall, and its other wing, also five cubits long, touched the wing of the first cherub. [13]The wings of these cherubim extended twenty cubits. They stood on their feet, facing the main hall.[h]

[14]He made the curtain of blue, purple and crimson yarn and fine linen, with cherubim worked into it.

[15]In the front of the temple he made two pillars, which together, were thirty-five cubits[i] long, each with a capital on top measuring five cubits. [16]He made interwoven chains[j] and put them on top of the pillars. He also made a hundred pomegranates and attached them to the chains. [17]He erected the pillars in the front of the temple, one to the south and one to the north. The one to the south he named Jakin[k] and the one to the north Boaz.[l]

The Temple's Furnishings

4 He made a bronze altar twenty cubits long, twenty cubits wide and ten cubits high.[m] [2]He made the Sea of cast metal, circular in shape, measuring ten cubits from rim to rim and five cubits[n] high. It took a line of thirty cubits[o] to measure around it. [3]Below the rim, figures of bulls encircled it—ten to a cubit.[p] The bulls were cast in two rows in one piece with the Sea.

[4]The Sea stood on twelve bulls, three facing north, three facing west, three facing south and three facing east. The Sea rested on top of them, and their

---

a 1 Hebrew *Ornan,* a variant of *Araunah*   *b 3* That is, about 90 feet (about 27 meters) long and 30 feet (about 9 meters) wide   *c 4* That is, about 30 feet (about 9 meters); also in verses 8, 11 and 13   *d 4* Some Septuagint and Syriac manuscripts; Hebrew *and a hundred and twenty*   *e 8* That is, about 23 tons (about 21 metric tons)   *f 9* That is, about 1 1/4 pounds (about 0.6 kilogram)   *g 11* That is, about 7 1/2 feet (about 2.3 meters); also in verse 15   *h 13* Or *facing inward*   *i 15* That is, about 52 feet (about 16 meters)   *j 16* Or possibly *made chains in the inner sanctuary;* the meaning of the Hebrew for this phrase is uncertain.   *k 17* *Jakin* probably means *he establishes.*   *l 17* *Boaz* probably means *in him is strength.*   *m 1* That is, about 30 feet (about 9 meters) long and wide, and about 15 feet (about 4.5 meters) high   *n 2* That is, about 7 1/2 feet (about 2.3 meters)   *o 2* That is, about 45 feet (about 13.5 meters)   *p 3* That is, about 1 1/2 feet (about 0.5 meter)

hindquarters were toward the center. [5]It was a handbreadth[a] in thickness, and its rim was like the rim of a cup, like a lily blossom. It held three thousand baths.[b]

[6]He then made ten basins for washing and placed five on the south side and five on the north. In them the things to be used for the burnt offerings were rinsed, but the Sea was to be used by the priests for washing.

[7]He made ten gold lampstands according to the specifications for them and placed them in the temple, five on the south side and five on the north.

[8]He made ten tables and placed them in the temple, five on the south side and five on the north. He also made a hundred gold sprinkling bowls.

[9]He made the courtyard of the priests, and the large court and the doors for the court, and overlaid the doors with bronze. [10]He placed the Sea on the south side, at the southeast corner.

[11]He also made the pots and shovels and sprinkling bowls.

So Huram finished the work he had undertaken for King Solomon in the temple of God:

[12] the two pillars;

the two bowl-shaped capitals on top of the pillars;

the two sets of network decorating the two bowl-shaped capitals on top of the pillars;

[13] the four hundred pomegranates for the two sets of network (two rows of pomegranates for each network, decorating the bowl-shaped capitals on top of the pillars);

[14] the stands with their basins;

[15] the Sea and the twelve bulls under it;

[16] the pots, shovels, meat forks and all related articles.

All the objects that Huram-Abi made for King Solomon for the temple of the LORD were of polished bronze. [17]The king had them cast in clay molds in the plain of the Jordan between Succoth and Zarethan.[c] [18]All these things that Solomon made amounted to so much that the weight of the bronze was not determined.

[19]Solomon also made all the furnishings that were in God's temple:

the golden altar;

the tables on which was the bread of the Presence;

[20] the lampstands of pure gold with their lamps, to burn in front of the inner sanctuary as prescribed;

[21] the gold floral work and lamps and tongs (they were solid gold);

[22] the pure gold wick trimmers, sprinkling bowls, dishes and censers; and the gold doors of the temple: the inner doors to the Most Holy Place and the doors of the main hall.

5 When all the work Solomon had done for the temple of the LORD was finished, he brought in the things his father David had dedicated—the silver and gold and all the furnishings—and he placed them in the treasuries of God's temple.

The Ark Brought to the Temple

[2]Then Solomon summoned to Jerusalem the elders of Israel, all the heads of the tribes and the chiefs of the Israelite families, to bring up the ark of the LORD's covenant from Zion, the City of David. [3]And all the men of Israel came together to the king at the time of the festival in the seventh month.

[4]When all the elders of Israel had arrived, the Levites took up the ark, [5]and they brought up the ark and the Tent of Meeting and all the sacred furnishings in it. The priests, who were Levites, carried them up; [6]and King Solomon and the entire assembly of Israel that had gathered about him were before the ark, sacrificing so many sheep and cattle that they could not be recorded or counted.

[7]The priests then brought the ark of the LORD's covenant to its place in the inner sanctuary of the temple, the Most Holy Place, and put it beneath the wings of the cherubim. [8]The cherubim spread their wings over the place of the ark and covered the ark and its carrying poles. [9]These poles were so long that their ends, extending from the ark, could be seen from in front of the inner sanctuary, but not from outside the Holy Place; and they are still there today. [10]There

---

[a] 5 That is, about 3 inches (about 8 centimeters)   [b] 5 That is, about 17,500 gallons (about 66 kiloliters)
[c] 17 Hebrew *Zeredatha*, a variant of *Zarethan*

was nothing in the ark except the two tablets that Moses had placed in it at Horeb, where the LORD made a covenant with the Israelites after they came out of Egypt.

¹¹The priests then withdrew from the Holy Place. All the priests who were there had consecrated themselves, regardless of their divisions. ¹²All the Levites who were musicians—Asaph, Heman, Jeduthun and their sons and relatives—stood on the east side of the altar, dressed in fine linen and playing cymbals, harps and lyres. They were accompanied by 120 priests sounding trumpets. ¹³The trumpeters and singers joined in unison, as with one voice, to give praise and thanks to the LORD. Accompanied by trumpets, cymbals and other instruments, they raised their voices in praise to the LORD and sang:

"He is good;
  his love endures forever."

Then the temple of the LORD was filled with a cloud, ¹⁴and the priests could not perform their service because of the cloud, for the glory of the LORD filled the temple of God.

6 Then Solomon said, "The LORD has said that he would dwell in a dark cloud; ²I have built a magnificent temple for you, a place for you to dwell forever."

³While the whole assembly of Israel was standing there, the king turned around and blessed them. ⁴Then he said:

"Praise be to the LORD, the God of Israel, who with his hands has fulfilled what he promised with his mouth to my father David. For he said, ⁵'Since the day I brought my people out of Egypt, I have not chosen a city in any tribe of Israel to have a temple built for my Name to be there, nor have I chosen anyone to be the leader over my people Israel. ⁶But now I have chosen Jerusalem for my Name to be there, and I have chosen David to rule my people Israel.'

⁷"My father David had it in his heart to build a temple for the Name of the LORD, the God of Israel. ⁸But the LORD said to my father David, 'Because it was in your heart to build a temple for my Name, you did well to have this in your heart. ⁹Nevertheless, you are not the one to build the temple, but your son, who is your own flesh and blood— he is the one who will build the temple for my Name.'

¹⁰"The LORD has kept the promise he made. I have succeeded David my father and now I sit on the throne of Israel, just as the LORD promised, and I have built the temple for the Name of the LORD, the God of Israel. ¹¹There I have placed the ark, in which is the covenant of the LORD that he made with the people of Israel."

Solomon's Prayer of Dedication

¹²Then Solomon stood before the altar of the LORD in front of the whole assembly of Israel and spread out his hands. ¹³Now he had made a bronze platform, five cubits*ᵃ* long, five cubits wide and three cubits*ᵇ* high, and had placed it in the center of the outer court. He stood on the platform and then knelt down before the whole assembly of Israel and spread out his hands toward heaven. ¹⁴He said:

"O LORD, God of Israel, there is no God like you in heaven or on earth—you who keep your covenant of love with your servants who continue wholeheartedly in your way. ¹⁵You have kept your promise to your servant David my father; with your mouth you have promised and with your hand you have fulfilled it—as it is today. ¹⁶"Now LORD, God of Israel, keep for your servant David my father the promises you made to him when you said, 'You shall never fail to have a man to sit before me on the throne of Israel, if only your sons are careful in all they do to walk before me according to my law, as you have done.' ¹⁷And now, O LORD, God of Israel, let your word

---

ᵃ 13 That is, about 7 1/2 feet (about 2.3 meters)   *ᵇ 13* That is, about 4 1/2 feet (about 1.3 meters)

that you promised your servant David come true.

18"But will God really dwell on earth with men? The heavens, even the highest heavens, cannot contain you. How much less this temple I have built! 19Yet give attention to your servant's prayer and his plea for mercy, O LORD my God. Hear the cry and the prayer that your servant is praying in your presence. 20May your eyes be open toward this temple day and night, this place of which you said you would put your Name there. May you hear the prayer your servant prays toward this place. 21Hear the supplications of your servant and of your people Israel when they pray toward this place. Hear from heaven, your dwelling place; and when you hear, forgive.

22"When a man wrongs his neighbor and is required to take an oath and he comes and swears the oath before your altar in this temple, 23then hear from heaven and act. Judge between your servants, repaying the guilty by bringing down on his own head what he has done. Declare the innocent not guilty and so establish his innocence.

24"When your people Israel have been defeated by an enemy because they have sinned against you and when they turn back and confess your name, praying and making supplication before you in this temple, 25then hear from heaven and forgive the sin of your people Israel and bring them back to the land you gave to them and their fathers.

AFFLICTIONS ARE BUT THE SHADOW OF GOD'S
WINGS.   —George MacDonald

26"When the heavens are shut up and there is no rain because your people have sinned against you, and when they pray toward this place and confess your name and turn from their sin because you have afflicted them, 27then hear from heaven and forgive the sin of your servants, your people Israel. Teach them the right way to live, and send rain on the land you gave your people for an inheritance.

28"When famine or plague comes to the land, or blight or mildew, locusts or grasshoppers, or when enemies besiege them in any of their cities, whatever disaster or disease may come, 29and when a prayer or plea is made by any of your people Israel—each one aware of his afflictions and pains, and spreading out his hands toward this temple— 30then hear from heaven, your dwelling place. Forgive, and deal with each man according to all he does, since you know his heart (for you alone know the hearts of men), 31so that they will fear you and walk in your ways all the time they live in the land you gave our fathers.

32"As for the foreigner who does not belong to your people Israel but has come from a distant land because of your great name and your mighty hand and your outstretched arm—when he comes and prays toward this temple, 33then hear from heaven, your dwelling place, and do whatever the foreigner asks of you, so that all the peoples of the earth may know your name and fear you, as do your own people Israel, and may know that this house I have built bears your Name.

34"When your people go to war against their enemies, wherever you send them, and when they pray to you toward this city you have chosen and the temple I have built for your Name, 35then hear from heaven their prayer and their plea, and uphold their cause.

36"When they sin against you— for there is no one who does not sin—and you become angry with them and give them over to the enemy, who takes them captive to a land far away or near; 37and if they have a change of heart in the land where they are held captive, and repent and plead with you in the land of their captivity and say, 'We have sinned, we have done wrong and acted wickedly'; 38and if they turn back to you with all their heart and soul in the land of their captivity where they were taken, and pray toward the land you gave their fathers, toward the city you have chosen and toward the temple I have built for your Name; ³⁹then from heaven, your dwelling place, hear their prayer and their pleas, and uphold their cause. And forgive your people, who have sinned against you.

⁴⁰"Now, my God, may your eyes be open and your ears attentive to the prayers offered in this place.

⁴¹ "Now arise, O LORD God, and
    come to your resting place,
    you and the ark of your might.
May your priests, O LORD God,
    be clothed with salvation,
    may your saints rejoice in your
    goodness.
⁴² O LORD God, do not reject your
    anointed one.
    Remember the great love
    promised to David your
    servant."

The Dedication of the Temple

7 When Solomon finished praying, fire came down from heaven and consumed the burnt offering and the sacrifices, and the glory of the LORD filled the temple. ²The priests could not enter the temple of the LORD because the glory of the LORD filled it. ³When all the Israelites saw the fire coming down and the glory of the LORD above the temple, they knelt on the pavement with their faces to the ground, and they worshiped and gave thanks to the LORD, saying,

"He is good;
    his love endures forever."

⁴Then the king and all the people offered sacrifices before the LORD. ⁵And King Solomon offered a sacrifice of twenty-two thousand head of cattle and a hundred and twenty thousand sheep and goats. So the king and all the people dedicated the temple of God. ⁶The priests took their positions, as did the Levites with the LORD's musical instruments, which King David had made for praising the LORD and which were used when he gave thanks, saying, "His love endures forever." Opposite the Levites, the priests blew their trumpets, and all the Israelites were standing.

⁷Solomon consecrated the middle part of the courtyard in front of the temple of the LORD, and there he offered burnt offerings and the fat of the fellowship offerings,ᵃ because the bronze altar he had made could not hold the burnt offerings, the grain offerings and the fat portions.

⁸So Solomon observed the festival at that time for seven days, and all Israel with him—a vast assembly, people from Leboᵇ Hamath to the Wadi of Egypt. ⁹On the eighth day they held an assembly, for they had celebrated the dedication of the altar for seven days and the festival for seven days more. ¹⁰On the twenty-third day of the seventh month he sent the people to their homes, joyful and glad in heart for the good things the LORD had done for David and Solomon and for his people Israel.

The LORD Appears to Solomon

¹¹When Solomon had finished the temple of the LORD and the royal palace, and had succeeded in carrying out all he had in mind to do in the temple of the LORD and in his own palace, ¹²the LORD appeared to him at night and said:

"I have heard your prayer and have chosen this place for myself as a temple for sacrifices.

¹³"When I shut up the heavens so that there is no rain, or command locusts to devour the land or send a plague among my people, ¹⁴if my people, who are called by my name, will humble themselves and pray and seek my face and turn from their wicked ways, then will I hear from heaven and will forgive their sin and will heal their land. ¹⁵Now my eyes will be open and my ears attentive to the prayers offered in this place. ¹⁶I have chosen and consecrated this temple so that my Name may be there forever. My eyes and my heart will always be there.

¹⁷"As for you, if you walk before

ᵃ 7 Traditionally *peace offerings*   ᵇ 8 Or *from the entrance to*

WEEKEND

A MORNING WATCH
Jacob Boehme

VERSE: 2 Chronicles 7:14   **PASSAGE:** 2 Chronicles 7:11–22

On Waking

iving Lord, you have watched over me, and put your hand on my head, during the long, dark hours of night. Your holy angels have protected me from all harm and pain. To you, Lord, I owe life itself. Continue to watch over me and bless me during the hours of day.

On Rising

Rule over me this day, O God, leading me on the path of righteousness. Put your Word in my mind and your truth in my heart, that this day I neither think nor feel anything except what is good and honest. Protect me from all lies and falsehood, helping me to discern deception wherever I meet it. Let my eyes always look straight ahead on the road you wish me to tread, that I might not be tempted by any distraction. And make my eyes pure, that no false desires may be awakened within me.

On Going to Work

Give me, dear Lord, a pure heart and a wise mind, that I may carry out my work according to your will. Save me from all false desires, from pride, greed, envy and anger, and let me accept joyfully every task you set before me. Let me seek to serve the poor, the sad and those unable to work. Help me to discern honestly my own gifts that I may do the things of which I am capable, and happily and humbly leave the rest to others. Above all, remind me constantly that I have nothing except what you give me, and can do nothing except what you enable me to do.

ADDITIONAL SCRIPTURE READING:
2 Chronicles 6:29–30; Psalm 139:23–24; Lamentations 3:40–41

Go to page 496 for your next devotional reading.

1500   1700

me as David your father did, and do all I command, and observe my decrees and laws, **18**I will establish your royal throne, as I covenanted with David your father when I said, 'You shall never fail to have a man to rule over Israel.'

19"But if you*a* turn away and forsake the decrees and commands I have given you*a* and go off to serve other gods and worship them, **20**then I will uproot Israel from my land, which I have given them, and will reject this temple I have consecrated for my Name. I will make it a byword and an object of ridicule among all peoples. **21**And though this temple is now so imposing, all who pass by will be appalled and say, 'Why has the LORD done such a thing to this land and to this temple?' **22**People will answer, 'Because they have forsaken the LORD, the God of their fathers, who brought them out of Egypt, and have embraced other gods, worshiping and serving them—that is why he brought all this disaster on them.' "

Solomon's Other Activities

8 At the end of twenty years, during which Solomon built the temple of the LORD and his own palace, **2**Solomon rebuilt the villages that Hiram*b* had given him, and settled Israelites in them. **3**Solomon then went to Hamath Zobah and captured it. **4**He also built up Tadmor in the desert and all the store cities he had built in Hamath. **5**He rebuilt Upper Beth Horon and Lower Beth Horon as fortified cities, with walls and with gates and bars, **6**as well as Baalath and all his store cities, and all the cities for his chariots and for his horses*c*—whatever he desired to build in Jerusalem, in Lebanon and throughout all the territory he ruled.

7All the people left from the Hittites, Amorites, Perizzites, Hivites and Jebusites (these peoples were not Israelites), **8**that is, their descendants remaining in the land, whom the Israelites had not destroyed—these Solomon conscripted for his slave labor force, as it is to this day. **9**But Solomon did not make slaves of the Israelites for his work; they were his fighting men, commanders of his captains, and commanders of his chariots and charioteers. **10**They were also King Solomon's chief officials—two hundred and fifty officials supervising the men.

11Solomon brought Pharaoh's daughter up from the City of David to the palace he had built for her, for he said, "My wife must not live in the palace of David king of Israel, because the places the ark of the LORD has entered are holy."

12On the altar of the LORD that he had built in front of the portico, Solomon sacrificed burnt offerings to the LORD, **13**according to the daily requirement for offerings commanded by Moses for Sabbaths, New Moons and the three annual feasts—the Feast of Unleavened Bread, the Feast of Weeks and the Feast of Tabernacles. **14**In keeping with the ordinance of his father David, he appointed the divisions of the priests for their duties, and the Levites to lead the praise and to assist the priests according to each day's requirement. He also appointed the gatekeepers by divisions for the various gates, because this was what David the man of God had ordered. **15**They did not deviate from the king's commands to the priests or to the Levites in any matter, including that of the treasuries.

16All Solomon's work was carried out, from the day the foundation of the temple of the LORD was laid until its completion. So the temple of the LORD was finished.

17Then Solomon went to Ezion Geber and Elath on the coast of Edom. **18**And Hiram sent him ships commanded by his own officers, men who knew the sea. These, with Solomon's men, sailed to Ophir and brought back four hundred and fifty talents*d* of gold, which they delivered to King Solomon.

The Queen of Sheba Visits Solomon

9 When the queen of Sheba heard of Solomon's fame, she came to Jerusalem to test him with hard questions. Arriving with a very great caravan—with camels carrying spices, large quantities of gold, and precious stones—

---

a 19 The Hebrew is plural.   *b 2* Hebrew *Huram,* a variant of *Hiram;* also in verse 18   *c 6* Or *charioteers*   *d 18* That is, about 17 tons (about 16 metric tons)

she came to Solomon and talked with him about all she had on her mind. ²Solomon answered all her questions; nothing was too hard for him to explain to her. ³When the queen of Sheba saw the wisdom of Solomon, as well as the palace he had built, ⁴the food on his table, the seating of his officials, the attending servants in their robes, the cupbearers in their robes and the burnt offerings he made at*a* the temple of the LORD, she was overwhelmed.

⁵She said to the king, "The report I heard in my own country about your achievements and your wisdom is true. ⁶But I did not believe what they said until I came and saw with my own eyes. Indeed, not even half the greatness of your wisdom was told me; you have far exceeded the report I heard. ⁷How happy your men must be! How happy your officials, who continually stand before you and hear your wisdom! ⁸Praise be to the LORD your God, who has delighted in you and placed you on his throne as king to rule for the LORD your God. Because of the love of your God for Israel and his desire to uphold them forever, he has made you king over them, to maintain justice and righteousness."

⁹Then she gave the king 120 talents*b* of gold, large quantities of spices, and precious stones. There had never been such spices as those the queen of Sheba gave to King Solomon.

¹⁰(The men of Hiram and the men of Solomon brought gold from Ophir; they also brought algumwood*c* and precious stones. ¹¹The king used the algumwood to make steps for the temple of the LORD and for the royal palace, and to make harps and lyres for the musicians. Nothing like them had ever been seen in Judah.)

¹²King Solomon gave the queen of Sheba all she desired and asked for; he gave her more than she had brought to him. Then she left and returned with her retinue to her own country.

Solomon's Splendor

¹³The weight of the gold that Solomon received yearly was 666 talents,*d* ¹⁴not including the revenues brought in by merchants and traders. Also all the kings of Arabia and the governors of the land brought gold and silver to Solomon.

¹⁵King Solomon made two hundred large shields of hammered gold; six hundred bekas*e* of hammered gold went into each shield. ¹⁶He also made three hundred small shields of hammered gold, with three hundred bekas*f* of gold in each shield. The king put them in the Palace of the Forest of Lebanon.

¹⁷Then the king made a great throne inlaid with ivory and overlaid with pure gold. ¹⁸The throne had six steps, and a footstool of gold was attached to it. On both sides of the seat were armrests, with a lion standing beside each of them. ¹⁹Twelve lions stood on the six steps, one at either end of each step. Nothing like it had ever been made for any other kingdom. ²⁰All King Solomon's goblets were gold, and all the household articles in the Palace of the Forest of Lebanon were pure gold. Nothing was made of silver, because silver was considered of little value in Solomon's day. ²¹The king had a fleet of trading ships*g* manned by Hiram's*h* men. Once every three years it returned, carrying gold, silver and ivory, and apes and baboons.

²²King Solomon was greater in riches and wisdom than all the other kings of the earth. ²³All the kings of the earth sought audience with Solomon to hear the wisdom God had put in his heart. ²⁴Year after year, everyone who came brought a gift—articles of silver and gold, and robes, weapons and spices, and horses and mules.

²⁵Solomon had four thousand stalls for horses and chariots, and twelve thousand horses,*i* which he kept in the chariot cities and also with him in Jerusalem. ²⁶He ruled over all the kings from the River*j* to the land of the Philistines, as far as the border of Egypt. ²⁷The king made silver as common in Jerusalem as stones, and cedar as plentiful as sycamore-fig trees in the foothills.

---

a 4 Or *the ascent by which he went up to*   *b 9* That is, about 4 1/2 tons (about 4 metric tons)
c 10 Probably a variant of *almugwood*   *d 13* That is, about 25 tons (about 23 metric tons)   *e 15* That is, about 7 1/2 pounds (about 3.5 kilograms)   *f 16* That is, about 3 3/4 pounds (about 1.7 kilograms)
g 21 Hebrew *of ships that could go to Tarshish*   *h 21* Hebrew *Huram,* a variant of *Hiram*   *i 25* Or *charioteers*   *j 26* That is, the Euphrates

[28]Solomon's horses were imported from Egypt[a] and from all other countries.

Solomon's Death

[29]As for the other events of Solomon's reign, from beginning to end, are they not written in the records of Nathan the prophet, in the prophecy of Ahijah the Shilonite and in the visions of Iddo the seer concerning Jeroboam son of Nebat? [30]Solomon reigned in Jerusalem over all Israel forty years. [31]Then he rested with his fathers and was buried in the city of David his father. And Rehoboam his son succeeded him as king.

Israel Rebels Against Rehoboam

10 Rehoboam went to Shechem, for all the Israelites had gone there to make him king. [2]When Jeroboam son of Nebat heard this (he was in Egypt, where he had fled from King Solomon), he returned from Egypt. [3]So they sent for Jeroboam, and he and all Israel went to Rehoboam and said to him: [4]"Your father put a heavy yoke on us, but now lighten the harsh labor and the heavy yoke he put on us, and we will serve you."

[5]Rehoboam answered, "Come back to me in three days." So the people went away.

[6]Then King Rehoboam consulted the elders who had served his father Solomon during his lifetime. "How would you advise me to answer these people?" he asked.

[7]They replied, "If you will be kind to these people and please them and give them a favorable answer, they will always be your servants."

[8]But Rehoboam rejected the advice the elders gave him and consulted the young men who had grown up with him and were serving him. [9]He asked them, "What is your advice? How should we answer these people who say to me, 'Lighten the yoke your father put on us'?"

[10]The young men who had grown up with him replied, "Tell the people who have said to you, 'Your father put a heavy yoke on us, but make our yoke lighter'—tell them, 'My little finger is thicker than my father's waist. [11]My father laid on you a heavy yoke; I will make it even heavier. My father scourged you with whips; I will scourge you with scorpions.' "

[12]Three days later Jeroboam and all the people returned to Rehoboam, as the king had said, "Come back to me in three days." [13]The king answered them harshly. Rejecting the advice of the elders, [14]he followed the advice of the young men and said, "My father made your yoke heavy; I will make it even heavier. My father scourged you with whips; I will scourge you with scorpions." [15]So the king did not listen to the people, for this turn of events was from God, to fulfill the word the LORD had spoken to Jeroboam son of Nebat through Ahijah the Shilonite.

[16]When all Israel saw that the king refused to listen to them, they answered the king:

> "What share do we have in David,
>   what part in Jesse's son?
> To your tents, O Israel!
>   Look after your own house,
>   O David!"

So all the Israelites went home. [17]But as for the Israelites who were living in the towns of Judah, Rehoboam still ruled over them.

[18]King Rehoboam sent out Adoniram,[b] who was in charge of forced labor, but the Israelites stoned him to death. King Rehoboam, however, managed to get into his chariot and escape to Jerusalem. [19]So Israel has been in rebellion against the house of David to this day.

11 When Rehoboam arrived in Jerusalem, he mustered the house of Judah and Benjamin—a hundred and eighty thousand fighting men—to make war against Israel and to regain the kingdom for Rehoboam.

[2]But this word of the LORD came to Shemaiah the man of God: [3]"Say to Rehoboam son of Solomon king of Judah and to all the Israelites in Judah and Benjamin, [4]'This is what the LORD says: Do not go up to fight against your brothers. Go home, every one of you, for this is my doing.' " So they obeyed

---

[a] 28 Or possibly *Muzur*, a region in Cilicia   [b] 18 Hebrew *Hadoram*, a variant of *Adoniram*

the words of the LORD and turned back from marching against Jeroboam.

Rehoboam Fortifies Judah

5Rehoboam lived in Jerusalem and built up towns for defense in Judah: 6Bethlehem, Etam, Tekoa, 7Beth Zur, Soco, Adullam, 8Gath, Mareshah, Ziph, 9Adoraim, Lachish, Azekah, 10Zorah, Aijalon and Hebron. These were fortified cities in Judah and Benjamin. 11He strengthened their defenses and put commanders in them, with supplies of food, olive oil and wine. 12He put shields and spears in all the cities, and made them very strong. So Judah and Benjamin were his.

13The priests and Levites from all their districts throughout Israel sided with him. 14The Levites even abandoned their pasturelands and property, and came to Judah and Jerusalem because Jeroboam and his sons had rejected them as priests of the LORD. 15And he appointed his own priests for the high places and for the goat and calf idols he had made. 16Those from every tribe of Israel who set their hearts on seeking the LORD, the God of Israel, followed the Levites to Jerusalem to offer sacrifices to the LORD, the God of their fathers. 17They strengthened the kingdom of Judah and supported Rehoboam son of Solomon three years, walking in the ways of David and Solomon during this time.

Rehoboam's Family

18Rehoboam married Mahalath, who was the daughter of David's son Jerimoth and of Abihail, the daughter of Jesse's son Eliab. 19She bore him sons: Jeush, Shemariah and Zaham. 20Then he married Maacah daughter of Absalom, who bore him Abijah, Attai, Ziza and Shelomith. 21Rehoboam loved Maacah daughter of Absalom more than any of his other wives and concubines. In all, he had eighteen wives and sixty concubines, twenty-eight sons and sixty daughters. 22Rehoboam appointed Abijah son of Maacah to be the chief prince among his brothers, in order to make him king. 23He acted wisely, dispersing some of his sons throughout the districts of Judah and Benjamin, and to all the fortified cities.

He gave them abundant provisions and took many wives for them.

Shishak Attacks Jerusalem

12 After Rehoboam's position as king was established and he had become strong, he and all Israel*a* with him abandoned the law of the LORD. 2Because they had been unfaithful to the LORD, Shishak king of Egypt attacked Jerusalem in the fifth year of King Rehoboam. 3With twelve hundred chariots and sixty thousand horsemen and the innumerable troops of Libyans, Sukkites and Cushites*b* that came with him from Egypt, 4he captured the fortified cities of Judah and came as far as Jerusalem.

5Then the prophet Shemaiah came to Rehoboam and to the leaders of Judah who had assembled in Jerusalem for fear of Shishak, and he said to them, "This is what the LORD says, 'You have abandoned me; therefore, I now abandon you to Shishak.' "

6The leaders of Israel and the king humbled themselves and said, "The LORD is just."

7When the LORD saw that they humbled themselves, this word of the LORD came to Shemaiah: "Since they have humbled themselves, I will not destroy them but will soon give them deliverance. My wrath will not be poured out on Jerusalem through Shishak. 8They will, however, become subject to him, so that they may learn the difference between serving me and serving the kings of other lands."

9When Shishak king of Egypt attacked Jerusalem, he carried off the treasures of the temple of the LORD and the treasures of the royal palace. He took everything, including the gold shields Solomon had made. 10So King Rehoboam made bronze shields to replace them and assigned these to the commanders of the guard on duty at the entrance to the royal palace. 11Whenever the king went to the LORD's temple, the guards went with him, bearing the shields, and afterward they returned them to the guardroom. 12Because Rehoboam humbled himself, the LORD's anger turned from him,

---

a 1 That is, Judah, as frequently in 2 Chronicles   *b* 3 That is, people from the upper Nile region

and he was not totally destroyed. Indeed, there was some good in Judah.

¹³King Rehoboam established himself firmly in Jerusalem and continued as king. He was forty-one years old when he became king, and he reigned seventeen years in Jerusalem, the city the LORD had chosen out of all the tribes of Israel in which to put his Name. His mother's name was Naamah; she was an Ammonite. ¹⁴He did evil because he had not set his heart on seeking the LORD.

¹⁵As for the events of Rehoboam's reign, from beginning to end, are they not written in the records of Shemaiah the prophet and of Iddo the seer that deal with genealogies? There was continual warfare between Rehoboam and Jeroboam. ¹⁶Rehoboam rested with his fathers and was buried in the City of David. And Abijah his son succeeded him as king.

Abijah King of Judah

13 In the eighteenth year of the reign of Jeroboam, Abijah became king of Judah, ²and he reigned in Jerusalem three years. His mother's name was Maacah,ᵃ a daughterᵇ of Uriel of Gibeah.

There was war between Abijah and Jeroboam. ³Abijah went into battle with a force of four hundred thousand able fighting men, and Jeroboam drew up a battle line against him with eight hundred thousand able troops.

⁴Abijah stood on Mount Zemaraim, in the hill country of Ephraim, and said, "Jeroboam and all Israel, listen to me! ⁵Don't you know that the LORD, the God of Israel, has given the kingship of Israel to David and his descendants forever by a covenant of salt? ⁶Yet Jeroboam son of Nebat, an official of Solomon son of David, rebelled against his master. ⁷Some worthless scoundrels gathered around him and opposed Rehoboam son of Solomon when he was young and indecisive and not strong enough to resist them.

⁸"And now you plan to resist the kingdom of the LORD, which is in the hands of David's descendants. You are indeed a vast army and have with you the golden calves that Jeroboam made to be your gods. ⁹But didn't you drive out the priests of the LORD, the sons of Aaron, and the Levites, and make priests of your own as the peoples of other lands do? Whoever comes to consecrate himself with a young bull and seven rams may become a priest of what are not gods.

¹⁰"As for us, the LORD is our God, and we have not forsaken him. The priests who serve the LORD are sons of Aaron, and the Levites assist them. ¹¹Every morning and evening they present burnt offerings and fragrant incense to the LORD. They set out the bread on the ceremonially clean table and light the lamps on the gold lampstand every evening. We are observing the requirements of the LORD our God. But you have forsaken him. ¹²God is with us; he is our leader. His priests with their trumpets will sound the battle cry against you. Men of Israel, do not fight against the LORD, the God of your fathers, for you will not succeed."

¹³Now Jeroboam had sent troops around to the rear, so that while he was in front of Judah the ambush was behind them. ¹⁴Judah turned and saw that they were being attacked at both front and rear. Then they cried out to the LORD. The priests blew their trumpets ¹⁵and the men of Judah raised the battle cry. At the sound of their battle cry, God routed Jeroboam and all Israel before Abijah and Judah. ¹⁶The Israelites fled before Judah, and God delivered them into their hands. ¹⁷Abijah and his men inflicted heavy losses on them, so that there were five hundred thousand casualties among Israel's able men. ¹⁸The men of Israel were subdued on that occasion, and the men of Judah were victorious because they relied on the LORD, the God of their fathers.

¹⁹Abijah pursued Jeroboam and took from him the towns of Bethel, Jeshanah and Ephron, with their surrounding villages. ²⁰Jeroboam did not regain power during the time of Abijah. And the LORD struck him down and he died.

²¹But Abijah grew in strength. He married fourteen wives and had twenty-two sons and sixteen daughters.

²²The other events of Abijah's reign,

ᵃ 2 Most Septuagint manuscripts and Syriac (see also 2 Chron. 11:20 and 1 Kings 15:2); Hebrew *Micaiah*
ᵇ 2 Or *granddaughter*

what he did and what he said, are written in the annotations of the prophet Iddo.

| 14 | And Abijah rested with his fathers and was buried in the City of David. Asa his son succeeded him as king, and in his days the country was at peace for ten years.

Asa King of Judah

²Asa did what was good and right in the eyes of the LORD his God. ³He removed the foreign altars and the high places, smashed the sacred stones and cut down the Asherah poles.ᵃ ⁴He commanded Judah to seek the LORD, the God of their fathers, and to obey his laws and commands. ⁵He removed the high places and incense altars in every town in Judah, and the kingdom was at peace under him. ⁶He built up the fortified cities of Judah, since the land was at peace. No one was at war with him during those years, for the LORD gave him rest.

⁷"Let us build up these towns," he said to Judah, "and put walls around them, with towers, gates and bars. The land is still ours, because we have sought the LORD our God; we sought him and he has given us rest on every side." So they built and prospered.

⁸Asa had an army of three hundred thousand men from Judah, equipped with large shields and with spears, and two hundred and eighty thousand from Benjamin, armed with small shields and with bows. All these were brave fighting men.

⁹Zerah the Cushite marched out against them with a vast armyᵇ and three hundred chariots, and came as far as Mareshah. ¹⁰Asa went out to meet him, and they took up battle positions in the Valley of Zephathah near Mareshah.

¹¹Then Asa called to the LORD his God and said, "LORD, there is no one like you to help the powerless against the mighty. Help us, O LORD our God, for we rely on you, and in your name we have come against this vast army. O LORD, you are our God; do not let man prevail against you."

¹²The LORD struck down the Cushites before Asa and Judah. The Cushites fled, ¹³and Asa and his army pursued them as far as Gerar. Such a great number of Cushites fell that they could not recover; they were crushed before the LORD and his forces. The men of Judah carried off a large amount of plunder. ¹⁴They destroyed all the villages around Gerar, for the terror of the LORD had fallen upon them. They plundered all these villages, since there was much booty there. ¹⁵They also attacked the camps of the herdsmen and carried off droves of sheep and goats and camels. Then they returned to Jerusalem.

Asa's Reform

| 15 | The Spirit of God came upon Azariah son of Oded. ²He went out to meet Asa and said to him, "Listen to me, Asa and all Judah and Benjamin. The LORD is with you when you are with him. If you seek him, he will be found by you, but if you forsake him, he will forsake you. ³For a long time Israel was without the true God, without a priest to teach and without the law. ⁴But in their distress they turned to the LORD, the God of Israel, and sought him, and he was found by them. ⁵In those days it was not safe to travel about, for all the inhabitants of the lands were in great turmoil. ⁶One nation was being crushed by another and one city by another, because God was troubling them with every kind of distress. ⁷But as for you, be strong and do not give up, for your work will be rewarded."

⁸When Asa heard these words and the prophecy of Azariah son ofᶜ Oded the prophet, he took courage. He removed the detestable idols from the whole land of Judah and Benjamin and from the towns he had captured in the hills of Ephraim. He repaired the altar of the LORD that was in front of the portico of the LORD's temple.

⁹Then he assembled all Judah and Benjamin and the people from Ephraim, Manasseh and Simeon who had settled among them, for large numbers had come over to him from Israel when they saw that the LORD his God was with him.

¹⁰They assembled at Jerusalem in the third month of the fifteenth year of

---

ᵃ 3 That is, symbols of the goddess Asherah; here and elsewhere in 2 Chronicles   ᵇ 9 Hebrew *with an army of a thousand thousands* or *with an army of thousands upon thousands*   ᶜ 8 Vulgate and Syriac (see also Septuagint and verse 1); Hebrew does not have *Azariah son of*.

Asa's reign. ¹¹At that time they sacrificed to the LORD seven hundred head of cattle and seven thousand sheep and goats from the plunder they had brought back. ¹²They entered into a covenant to seek the LORD, the God of their fathers, with all their heart and soul. ¹³All who would not seek the LORD, the God of Israel, were to be put to death, whether small or great, man or woman. ¹⁴They took an oath to the LORD with loud acclamation, with shouting and with trumpets and horns. ¹⁵All Judah rejoiced about the oath because they had sworn it wholeheartedly. They sought God eagerly, and he was found by them. So the LORD gave them rest on every side.

¹⁶King Asa also deposed his grandmother Maacah from her position as queen mother, because she had made a repulsive Asherah pole. Asa cut the pole down, broke it up and burned it in the Kidron Valley. ¹⁷Although he did not remove the high places from Israel, Asa's heart was fully committed ₁to the LORDⱼ all his life. ¹⁸He brought into the temple of God the silver and gold and the articles that he and his father had dedicated.

¹⁹There was no more war until the thirty-fifth year of Asa's reign.

Asa's Last Years

16 In the thirty-sixth year of Asa's reign Baasha king of Israel went up against Judah and fortified Ramah to prevent anyone from leaving or entering the territory of Asa king of Judah.

²Asa then took the silver and gold out of the treasuries of the LORD's temple and of his own palace and sent it to Ben-Hadad king of Aram, who was ruling in Damascus. ³"Let there be a treaty between me and you," he said, "as there was between my father and your father. See, I am sending you silver and gold. Now break your treaty with Baasha king of Israel so he will withdraw from me."

⁴Ben-Hadad agreed with King Asa and sent the commanders of his forces against the towns of Israel. They conquered Ijon, Dan, Abel Maim*a* and all the store cities of Naphtali. ⁵When Baasha heard this, he stopped building Ramah and abandoned his work. ⁶Then King Asa brought all the men of Judah, and they carried away from Ramah the stones and timber Baasha had been using. With them he built up Geba and Mizpah.

⁷At that time Hanani the seer came to Asa king of Judah and said to him: "Because you relied on the king of Aram and not on the LORD your God, the army of the king of Aram has escaped from your hand. ⁸Were not the Cushites*b* and Libyans a mighty army with great numbers of chariots and horsemen*c*? Yet when you relied on the LORD, he delivered them into your hand. ⁹For the eyes of the LORD range throughout the earth to strengthen those whose hearts are fully committed to him. You have done a foolish thing, and from now on you will be at war."

¹⁰Asa was angry with the seer because of this; he was so enraged that he put him in prison. At the same time Asa brutally oppressed some of the people.

¹¹The events of Asa's reign, from beginning to end, are written in the book of the kings of Judah and Israel. ¹²In the thirty-ninth year of his reign Asa was afflicted with a disease in his feet. Though his disease was severe, even in his illness he did not seek help from the LORD, but only from the physicians. ¹³Then in the forty-first year of his reign Asa died and rested with his fathers. ¹⁴They buried him in the tomb that he had cut out for himself in the City of David. They laid him on a bier covered with spices and various blended perfumes, and they made a huge fire in his honor.

Jehoshaphat King of Judah

17 Jehoshaphat his son succeeded him as king and strengthened himself against Israel. ²He stationed troops in all the fortified cities of Judah and put garrisons in Judah and in the towns of Ephraim that his father Asa had captured.

³The LORD was with Jehoshaphat because in his early years he walked in the ways his father David had followed. He did not consult the Baals ⁴but sought the God of his father and followed his

---

a 4 Also known as *Abel Beth Maacah*   *b 8* That is, people from the upper Nile region   *c 8* Or *charioteers*

commands rather than the practices of Israel. 5The LORD established the kingdom under his control; and all Judah brought gifts to Jehoshaphat, so that he had great wealth and honor. 6His heart was devoted to the ways of the LORD; furthermore, he removed the high places and the Asherah poles from Judah.

7In the third year of his reign he sent his officials Ben-Hail, Obadiah, Zechariah, Nethanel and Micaiah to teach in the towns of Judah. 8With them were certain Levites—Shemaiah, Nethaniah, Zebadiah, Asahel, Shemiramoth, Jehonathan, Adonijah, Tobijah and Tob-Adonijah—and the priests Elishama and Jehoram. 9They taught throughout Judah, taking with them the Book of the Law of the LORD; they went around to all the towns of Judah and taught the people.

10The fear of the LORD fell on all the kingdoms of the lands surrounding Judah, so that they did not make war with Jehoshaphat. 11Some Philistines brought Jehoshaphat gifts and silver as tribute, and the Arabs brought him flocks: seven thousand seven hundred rams and seven thousand seven hundred goats.

12Jehoshaphat became more and more powerful; he built forts and store cities in Judah 13and had large supplies in the towns of Judah. He also kept experienced fighting men in Jerusalem. 14Their enrollment by families was as follows:

From Judah, commanders of units of 1,000:

Adnah the commander, with 300,000 fighting men;

15next, Jehohanan the commander, with 280,000;

16next, Amasiah son of Zicri, who volunteered himself for the service of the LORD, with 200,000.

17From Benjamin:

Eliada, a valiant soldier, with 200,000 men armed with bows and shields;

18next, Jehozabad, with 180,000 men armed for battle.

19These were the men who served the king, besides those he stationed in the fortified cities throughout Judah.

Micaiah Prophesies Against Ahab

18 Now Jehoshaphat had great wealth and honor, and he allied himself with Ahab by marriage. 2Some years later he went down to visit Ahab in Samaria. Ahab slaughtered many sheep and cattle for him and the people with him and urged him to attack Ramoth Gilead. 3Ahab king of Israel asked Jehoshaphat king of Judah, "Will you go with me against Ramoth Gilead?"

Jehoshaphat replied, "I am as you are, and my people as your people; we will join you in the war." 4But Jehoshaphat also said to the king of Israel, "First seek the counsel of the LORD."

5So the king of Israel brought together the prophets—four hundred men—and asked them, "Shall we go to war against Ramoth Gilead, or shall I refrain?"

"Go," they answered, "for God will give it into the king's hand."

6But Jehoshaphat asked, "Is there not a prophet of the LORD here whom we can inquire of?"

7The king of Israel answered Jehoshaphat, "There is still one man through whom we can inquire of the LORD, but I hate him because he never prophesies anything good about me, but always bad. He is Micaiah son of Imlah."

"The king should not say that," Jehoshaphat replied.

8So the king of Israel called one of his officials and said, "Bring Micaiah son of Imlah at once."

9Dressed in their royal robes, the king of Israel and Jehoshaphat king of Judah were sitting on their thrones at the threshing floor by the entrance to the gate of Samaria, with all the prophets prophesying before them. 10Now Zedekiah son of Kenaanah had made iron horns, and he declared, "This is what the LORD says: 'With these you will gore the Arameans until they are destroyed.' "

11All the other prophets were prophesying the same thing. "Attack Ramoth Gilead and be victorious," they said, "for the LORD will give it into the king's hand."

12The messenger who had gone to summon Micaiah said to him, "Look, as one man the other prophets are predicting success for the king. Let your word agree with theirs, and speak favorably."

13But Micaiah said, "As surely as the LORD lives, I can tell him only what my God says."

14When he arrived, the king asked him, "Micaiah, shall we go to war against Ramoth Gilead, or shall I refrain?"

"Attack and be victorious," he answered, "for they will be given into your hand."

15The king said to him, "How many times must I make you swear to tell me nothing but the truth in the name of the LORD?"

16Then Micaiah answered, "I saw all Israel scattered on the hills like sheep without a shepherd, and the LORD said, 'These people have no master. Let each one go home in peace.' "

17The king of Israel said to Jehoshaphat, "Didn't I tell you that he never prophesies anything good about me, but only bad?"

18Micaiah continued, "Therefore hear the word of the LORD: I saw the LORD sitting on his throne with all the host of heaven standing on his right and on his left. 19And the LORD said, 'Who will entice Ahab king of Israel into attacking Ramoth Gilead and going to his death there?'

"One suggested this, and another that. 20Finally, a spirit came forward, stood before the LORD and said, 'I will entice him.'

" 'By what means?' the LORD asked.

21" 'I will go and be a lying spirit in the mouths of all his prophets,' he said.

" 'You will succeed in enticing him,' said the LORD. 'Go and do it.'

22"So now the LORD has put a lying spirit in the mouths of these prophets of yours. The LORD has decreed disaster for you."

23Then Zedekiah son of Kenaanah went up and slapped Micaiah in the face. "Which way did the spirit from[a] the LORD go when he went from me to speak to you?" he asked.

24Micaiah replied, "You will find out on the day you go to hide in an inner room."

25The king of Israel then ordered, "Take Micaiah and send him back to Amon the ruler of the city and to Joash the king's son, 26and say, 'This is what

the king says: Put this fellow in prison and give him nothing but bread and water until I return safely.' "

27Micaiah declared, "If you ever return safely, the LORD has not spoken through me." Then he added, "Mark my words, all you people!"

Ahab Killed at Ramoth Gilead

28So the king of Israel and Jehoshaphat king of Judah went up to Ramoth Gilead. 29The king of Israel said to Jehoshaphat, "I will enter the battle in disguise, but you wear your royal robes." So the king of Israel disguised himself and went into battle.

30Now the king of Aram had ordered his chariot commanders, "Do not fight with anyone, small or great, except the king of Israel." 31When the chariot commanders saw Jehoshaphat, they thought, "This is the king of Israel." So they turned to attack him, but Jehoshaphat cried out, and the LORD helped him. God drew them away from him, 32for when the chariot commanders saw that he was not the king of Israel, they stopped pursuing him.

33But someone drew his bow at random and hit the king of Israel between the sections of his armor. The king told the chariot driver, "Wheel around and get me out of the fighting. I've been wounded." 34All day long the battle raged, and the king of Israel propped himself up in his chariot facing the Arameans until evening. Then at sunset he died.

19 When Jehoshaphat king of Judah returned safely to his palace in Jerusalem, 2Jehu the seer, the son of Hanani, went out to meet him and said to the king, "Should you help the wicked and love[b] those who hate the LORD? Because of this, the wrath of the LORD is upon you. 3There is, however, some good in you, for you have rid the land of the Asherah poles and have set your heart on seeking God."

Jehoshaphat Appoints Judges

4Jehoshaphat lived in Jerusalem, and he went out again among the people from Beersheba to the hill country of Ephraim and turned them back to the LORD, the God of their fathers. 5He

---

a 23 Or *Spirit of*   b 2 Or *and make alliances with*

appointed judges in the land, in each of the fortified cities of Judah. ⁶He told them, "Consider carefully what you do, because you are not judging for man but for the LORD, who is with you whenever you give a verdict. ⁷Now let the fear of the LORD be upon you. Judge carefully, for with the LORD our God there is no injustice or partiality or bribery."

⁸In Jerusalem also, Jehoshaphat appointed some of the Levites, priests and heads of Israelite families to administer the law of the LORD and to settle disputes. And they lived in Jerusalem. ⁹He gave them these orders: "You must serve faithfully and wholeheartedly in the fear of the LORD. ¹⁰In every case that comes before you from your fellow countrymen who live in the cities—whether bloodshed or other concerns of the law, commands, decrees or ordinances—you are to warn them not to sin against the LORD; otherwise his wrath will come on you and your brothers. Do this, and you will not sin.

¹¹"Amariah the chief priest will be over you in any matter concerning the LORD, and Zebadiah son of Ishmael, the leader of the tribe of Judah, will be over you in any matter concerning the king, and the Levites will serve as officials before you. Act with courage, and may the LORD be with those who do well."

Jehoshaphat Defeats Moab and Ammon

20 After this, the Moabites and Ammonites with some of the Meunites*ᵃ* came to make war on Jehoshaphat.

²Some men came and told Jehoshaphat, "A vast army is coming against you from Edom,*ᵇ* from the other side of the Sea.*ᶜ* It is already in Hazazon Tamar" (that is, En Gedi). ³Alarmed, Jehoshaphat resolved to inquire of the LORD, and he proclaimed a fast for all Judah. ⁴The people of Judah came together to seek help from the LORD; indeed, they came from every town in Judah to seek him.

⁵Then Jehoshaphat stood up in the assembly of Judah and Jerusalem at the temple of the LORD in the front of the new courtyard ⁶and said:

"O LORD, God of our fathers, are you not the God who is in heaven? You rule over all the kingdoms of the nations. Power and might are in your hand, and no one can withstand you. ⁷O our God, did you not drive out the inhabitants of this land before your people Israel and give it forever to the descendants of Abraham your friend? ⁸They have lived in it and have built in it a sanctuary for your Name, saying, ⁹'If calamity comes upon us, whether the sword of judgment, or plague or famine, we will stand in your presence before this temple that bears your Name and will cry out to you in our distress, and you will hear us and save us.'

¹⁰"But now here are men from Ammon, Moab and Mount Seir, whose territory you would not allow Israel to invade when they came from Egypt; so they turned away from them and did not destroy them. ¹¹See how they are repaying us by coming to drive us out of the possession you gave us as an inheritance. ¹²O our God, will you not judge them? For we have no power to face this vast army that is attacking us. We do not know what to do, but our eyes are upon you."

¹³All the men of Judah, with their wives and children and little ones, stood there before the LORD.

¹⁴Then the Spirit of the LORD came upon Jahaziel son of Zechariah, the son of Benaiah, the son of Jeiel, the son of Mattaniah, a Levite and descendant of Asaph, as he stood in the assembly.

¹⁵He said: "Listen, King Jehoshaphat and all who live in Judah and Jerusalem! This is what the LORD says to you: 'Do not be afraid or discouraged because of this vast army. For the battle is not yours, but God's. ¹⁶Tomorrow march down against them. They will be climbing up by the Pass of Ziz, and you will find them at the end of the gorge in the Desert of Jeruel. ¹⁷You will not have to

---

ᵃ 1 Some Septuagint manuscripts; Hebrew *Ammonites*　　*ᵇ* 2 One Hebrew manuscript; most Hebrew manuscripts, Septuagint and Vulgate *Aram*　　*ᶜ* 2 That is, the Dead Sea

fight this battle. Take up your positions; stand firm and see the deliverance the LORD will give you, O Judah and Jerusalem. Do not be afraid; do not be discouraged. Go out to face them tomorrow, and the LORD will be with you.' "

¹⁸Jehoshaphat bowed with his face to the ground, and all the people of Judah and Jerusalem fell down in worship before the LORD. ¹⁹Then some Levites from the Kohathites and Korahites stood up and praised the LORD, the God of Israel, with very loud voice.

²⁰Early in the morning they left for the Desert of Tekoa. As they set out, Jehoshaphat stood and said, "Listen to me, Judah and people of Jerusalem! Have faith in the LORD your God and you will be upheld; have faith in his prophets and you will be successful." ²¹After consulting the people, Jehoshaphat appointed men to sing to the LORD and to praise him for the splendor of his[a] holiness as they went out at the head of the army, saying:

"Give thanks to the LORD,
    for his love endures forever."

²²As they began to sing and praise, the LORD set ambushes against the men of Ammon and Moab and Mount Seir who were invading Judah, and they were defeated. ²³The men of Ammon and Moab rose up against the men from Mount Seir to destroy and annihilate them. After they finished slaughtering the men from Seir, they helped to destroy one another.

²⁴When the men of Judah came to the place that overlooks the desert and looked toward the vast army, they saw only dead bodies lying on the ground; no one had escaped. ²⁵So Jehoshaphat and his men went to carry off their plunder, and they found among them a great amount of equipment and clothing[b] and also articles of value—more than they could take away. There was so much plunder that it took three days to collect it. ²⁶On the fourth day they assembled in the Valley of Beracah, where they praised the LORD. This is why it is called the Valley of Beracah[c] to this day.

²⁷Then, led by Jehoshaphat, all the men of Judah and Jerusalem returned joyfully to Jerusalem, for the LORD had given them cause to rejoice over their enemies. ²⁸They entered Jerusalem and went to the temple of the LORD with harps and lutes and trumpets.

²⁹The fear of God came upon all the kingdoms of the countries when they heard how the LORD had fought against the enemies of Israel. ³⁰And the kingdom of Jehoshaphat was at peace, for his God had given him rest on every side.

The End of Jehoshaphat's Reign

³¹So Jehoshaphat reigned over Judah. He was thirty-five years old when he became king of Judah, and he reigned in Jerusalem twenty-five years. His mother's name was Azubah daughter of Shilhi. ³²He walked in the ways of his father Asa and did not stray from them; he did what was right in the eyes of the LORD. ³³The high places, however, were not removed, and the people still had not set their hearts on the God of their fathers.

³⁴The other events of Jehoshaphat's reign, from beginning to end, are written in the annals of Jehu son of Hanani, which are recorded in the book of the kings of Israel.

³⁵Later, Jehoshaphat king of Judah made an alliance with Ahaziah king of Israel, who was guilty of wickedness. ³⁶He agreed with him to construct a fleet of trading ships.[d] After these were built at Ezion Geber, ³⁷Eliezer son of Dodavahu of Mareshah prophesied against Jehoshaphat, saying, "Because you have made an alliance with Ahaziah, the LORD will destroy what you have made." The ships were wrecked and were not able to set sail to trade.[e]

21 Then Jehoshaphat rested with his fathers and was buried with them in the City of David. And Jehoram his son succeeded him as king. ²Jehoram's brothers, the sons of Jehoshaphat, were Azariah, Jehiel, Zechariah, Azariahu, Michael and Shephatiah. All these were sons of Jehoshaphat king of

---

a 21 Or *him with the splendor of*   b 25 Some Hebrew manuscripts and Vulgate; most Hebrew manuscripts *corpses*   c 26 *Beracah* means *praise.*   d 36 Hebrew *of ships that could go to Tarshish*
e 37 Hebrew *sail for Tarshish*

Israel.*a* ³Their father had given them many gifts of silver and gold and articles of value, as well as fortified cities in Judah, but he had given the kingdom to Jehoram because he was his firstborn son.

Jehoram King of Judah

⁴When Jehoram established himself firmly over his father's kingdom, he put all his brothers to the sword along with some of the princes of Israel. ⁵Jehoram was thirty-two years old when he became king, and he reigned in Jerusalem eight years. ⁶He walked in the ways of the kings of Israel, as the house of Ahab had done, for he married a daughter of Ahab. He did evil in the eyes of the LORD. ⁷Nevertheless, because of the covenant the LORD had made with David, the LORD was not willing to destroy the house of David. He had promised to maintain a lamp for him and his descendants forever.

⁸In the time of Jehoram, Edom rebelled against Judah and set up its own king. ⁹So Jehoram went there with his officers and all his chariots. The Edomites surrounded him and his chariot commanders, but he rose up and broke through by night. ¹⁰To this day Edom has been in rebellion against Judah.

Libnah revolted at the same time, because Jehoram had forsaken the LORD, the God of his fathers. ¹¹He had also built high places on the hills of Judah and had caused the people of Jerusalem to prostitute themselves and had led Judah astray.

¹²Jehoram received a letter from Elijah the prophet, which said:

"This is what the LORD, the God of your father David, says: 'You have not walked in the ways of your father Jehoshaphat or of Asa king of Judah. ¹³But you have walked in the ways of the kings of Israel, and you have led Judah and the people of Jerusalem to prostitute themselves, just as the house of Ahab did. You have also murdered your own brothers, members of your father's house, men who were better than

you. ¹⁴So now the LORD is about to strike your people, your sons, your wives and everything that is yours, with a heavy blow. ¹⁵You yourself will be very ill with a lingering disease of the bowels, until the disease causes your bowels to come out.' "

¹⁶The LORD aroused against Jehoram the hostility of the Philistines and of the Arabs who lived near the Cushites. ¹⁷They attacked Judah, invaded it and carried off all the goods found in the king's palace, together with his sons and wives. Not a son was left to him except Ahaziah,*b* the youngest.

¹⁸After all this, the LORD afflicted Jehoram with an incurable disease of the bowels. ¹⁹In the course of time, at the end of the second year, his bowels came out because of the disease, and he died in great pain. His people made no fire in his honor, as they had for his fathers.

²⁰Jehoram was thirty-two years old when he became king, and he reigned in Jerusalem eight years. He passed away, to no one's regret, and was buried in the City of David, but not in the tombs of the kings.

Ahaziah King of Judah

22 The people of Jerusalem made Ahaziah, Jehoram's youngest son, king in his place, since the raiders, who came with the Arabs into the camp, had killed all the older sons. So Ahaziah son of Jehoram king of Judah began to reign.

²Ahaziah was twenty-two*c* years old when he became king, and he reigned in Jerusalem one year. His mother's name was Athaliah, a granddaughter of Omri.

³He too walked in the ways of the house of Ahab, for his mother encouraged him in doing wrong. ⁴He did evil in the eyes of the LORD, as the house of Ahab had done, for after his father's death they became his advisers, to his undoing. ⁵He also followed their counsel when he went with Joram*d* son of Ahab king of Israel to war against Hazael king of Aram at Ramoth Gilead. The Arameans wounded Joram; ⁶so he returned to Jezreel to recover from the

---

a 2 That is, Judah, as frequently in 2 Chronicles   *b* 17 Hebrew *Jehoahaz*, a variant of *Ahaziah*
c 2 Some Septuagint manuscripts and Syriac (see also 2 Kings 8:26); Hebrew *forty-two*   *d* 5 Hebrew *Jehoram*, a variant of *Joram*; also in verses 6 and 7

wounds they had inflicted on him at Ramoth[a] in his battle with Hazael king of Aram.

Then Ahaziah[b] son of Jehoram king of Judah went down to Jezreel to see Joram son of Ahab because he had been wounded.

[7]Through Ahaziah's visit to Joram, God brought about Ahaziah's downfall. When Ahaziah arrived, he went out with Joram to meet Jehu son of Nimshi, whom the LORD had anointed to destroy the house of Ahab. [8]While Jehu was executing judgment on the house of Ahab, he found the princes of Judah and the sons of Ahaziah's relatives, who had been attending Ahaziah, and he killed them. [9]He then went in search of Ahaziah, and his men captured him while he was hiding in Samaria. He was brought to Jehu and put to death. They buried him, for they said, "He was a son of Jehoshaphat, who sought the LORD with all his heart." So there was no one in the house of Ahaziah powerful enough to retain the kingdom.

Athaliah and Joash

[10]When Athaliah the mother of Ahaziah saw that her son was dead, she proceeded to destroy the whole royal family of the house of Judah. [11]But Jehosheba,[c] the daughter of King Jehoram, took Joash son of Ahaziah and stole him away from among the royal princes who were about to be murdered and put him and his nurse in a bedroom. Because Jehosheba,[c] the daughter of King Jehoram and wife of the priest Jehoiada, was Ahaziah's sister, she hid the child from Athaliah so she could not kill him. [12]He remained hidden with them at the temple of God for six years while Athaliah ruled the land.

23 In the seventh year Jehoiada showed his strength. He made a covenant with the commanders of units of a hundred: Azariah son of Jeroham, Ishmael son of Jehohanan, Azariah son of Obed, Maaseiah son of Adaiah, and Elishaphat son of Zicri. [2]They went throughout Judah and gathered the Levites and the heads of Israelite families from all the towns. When they came

to Jerusalem, [3]the whole assembly made a covenant with the king at the temple of God.

Jehoiada said to them, "The king's son shall reign, as the LORD promised concerning the descendants of David. [4]Now this is what you are to do: A third of you priests and Levites who are going on duty on the Sabbath are to keep watch at the doors, [5]a third of you at the royal palace and a third at the Foundation Gate, and all the other men are to be in the courtyards of the temple of the LORD. [6]No one is to enter the temple of the LORD except the priests and Levites on duty; they may enter because they are consecrated, but all the other men are to guard what the LORD has assigned to them.[d] [7]The Levites are to station themselves around the king, each man with his weapons in his hand. Anyone who enters the temple must be put to death. Stay close to the king wherever he goes."

[8]The Levites and all the men of Judah did just as Jehoiada the priest ordered. Each one took his men—those who were going on duty on the Sabbath and those who were going off duty—for Jehoiada the priest had not released any of the divisions. [9]Then he gave the commanders of units of a hundred the spears and the large and small shields that had belonged to King David and that were in the temple of God. [10]He stationed all the men, each with his weapon in his hand, around the king—near the altar and the temple, from the south side to the north side of the temple.

[11]Jehoiada and his sons brought out the king's son and put the crown on him; they presented him with a copy of the covenant and proclaimed him king. They anointed him and shouted, "Long live the king!"

[12]When Athaliah heard the noise of the people running and cheering the king, she went to them at the temple of the LORD. [13]She looked, and there was the king, standing by his pillar at the entrance. The officers and the trumpeters were beside the king, and all the people of the land were rejoicing and

---

a 6 Hebrew *Ramah,* a variant of *Ramoth*   *b 6* Some Hebrew manuscripts, Septuagint, Vulgate and Syriac (see also 2 Kings 8:29); most Hebrew manuscripts *Azariah*   *c 11* Hebrew *Jehoshabeath,* a variant of *Jehosheba*   *d 6* Or *to observe the LORD's command not to enter*

blowing trumpets, and singers with musical instruments were leading the praises. Then Athaliah tore her robes and shouted, "Treason! Treason!"

¹⁴Jehoiada the priest sent out the commanders of units of a hundred, who were in charge of the troops, and said to them: "Bring her out between the ranks*a* and put to the sword anyone who follows her." For the priest had said, "Do not put her to death at the temple of the LORD." ¹⁵So they seized her as she reached the entrance of the Horse Gate on the palace grounds, and there they put her to death.

¹⁶Jehoiada then made a covenant that he and the people and the king*b* would be the LORD's people. ¹⁷All the people went to the temple of Baal and tore it down. They smashed the altars and idols and killed Mattan the priest of Baal in front of the altars.

¹⁸Then Jehoiada placed the oversight of the temple of the LORD in the hands of the priests, who were Levites, to whom David had made assignments in the temple, to present the burnt offerings of the LORD as written in the Law of Moses, with rejoicing and singing, as David had ordered. ¹⁹He also stationed doorkeepers at the gates of the LORD's temple so that no one who was in any way unclean might enter.

²⁰He took with him the commanders of hundreds, the nobles, the rulers of the people and all the people of the land and brought the king down from the temple of the LORD. They went into the palace through the Upper Gate and seated the king on the royal throne, ²¹and all the people of the land rejoiced. And the city was quiet, because Athaliah had been slain with the sword.

Joash Repairs the Temple

24 Joash was seven years old when he became king, and he reigned in Jerusalem forty years. His mother's name was Zibiah; she was from Beersheba. ²Joash did what was right in the eyes of the LORD all the years of Jehoiada the priest. ³Jehoiada chose two wives for him, and he had sons and daughters.

⁴Some time later Joash decided to restore the temple of the LORD. ⁵He called together the priests and Levites and said to them, "Go to the towns of Judah and collect the money due annually from all Israel, to repair the temple of your God. Do it now." But the Levites did not act at once.

⁶Therefore the king summoned Jehoiada the chief priest and said to him, "Why haven't you required the Levites to bring in from Judah and Jerusalem the tax imposed by Moses the servant of the LORD and by the assembly of Israel for the Tent of the Testimony?"

⁷Now the sons of that wicked woman Athaliah had broken into the temple of God and had used even its sacred objects for the Baals.

⁸At the king's command, a chest was made and placed outside, at the gate of the temple of the LORD. ⁹A proclamation was then issued in Judah and Jerusalem that they should bring to the LORD the tax that Moses the servant of God had required of Israel in the desert. ¹⁰All the officials and all the people brought their contributions gladly, dropping them into the chest until it was full. ¹¹Whenever the chest was brought in by the Levites to the king's officials and they saw that there was a large amount of money, the royal secretary and the officer of the chief priest would come and empty the chest and carry it back to its place. They did this regularly and collected a great amount of money. ¹²The king and Jehoiada gave it to the men who carried out the work required for the temple of the LORD. They hired masons and carpenters to restore the LORD's temple, and also workers in iron and bronze to repair the temple.

¹³The men in charge of the work were diligent, and the repairs progressed under them. They rebuilt the temple of God according to its original design and reinforced it. ¹⁴When they had finished, they brought the rest of the money to the king and Jehoiada, and with it were made articles for the LORD's temple: articles for the service and for the burnt offerings, and also dishes and other objects of gold and silver. As long as Jehoiada lived,

---

a 14 Or *out from the precincts*   *b* 16 Or *covenant between ⸤the LORD⸥ and the people and the king that they* (see 2 Kings 11:17)

burnt offerings were presented continually in the temple of the LORD.

¹⁵Now Jehoiada was old and full of years, and he died at the age of a hundred and thirty. ¹⁶He was buried with the kings in the City of David, because of the good he had done in Israel for God and his temple.

The Wickedness of Joash

¹⁷After the death of Jehoiada, the officials of Judah came and paid homage to the king, and he listened to them. ¹⁸They abandoned the temple of the LORD, the God of their fathers, and worshiped Asherah poles and idols. Because of their guilt, God's anger came upon Judah and Jerusalem. ¹⁹Although the LORD sent prophets to the people to bring them back to him, and though they testified against them, they would not listen.

²⁰Then the Spirit of God came upon Zechariah son of Jehoiada the priest. He stood before the people and said, "This is what God says: 'Why do you disobey the LORD's commands? You will not prosper. Because you have forsaken the LORD, he has forsaken you.' "

²¹But they plotted against him, and by order of the king they stoned him to death in the courtyard of the LORD's temple. ²²King Joash did not remember the kindness Zechariah's father Jehoiada had shown him but killed his son, who said as he lay dying, "May the LORD see this and call you to account."

²³At the turn of the year,ᵃ the army of Aram marched against Joash; it invaded Judah and Jerusalem and killed all the leaders of the people. They sent all the plunder to their king in Damascus. ²⁴Although the Aramean army had come with only a few men, the LORD delivered into their hands a much larger army. Because Judah had forsaken the LORD, the God of their fathers, judgment was executed on Joash. ²⁵When the Arameans withdrew, they left Joash severely wounded. His officials conspired against him for murdering the son of Jehoiada the priest, and they killed him in his bed. So he died and was buried in the City of David, but not in the tombs of the kings.

²⁶Those who conspired against him were Zabad,ᵇ son of Shimeath an Ammonite woman, and Jehozabad, son of Shimrithᶜ a Moabite woman. ²⁷The account of his sons, the many prophecies about him, and the record of the restoration of the temple of God are written in the annotations on the book of the kings. And Amaziah his son succeeded him as king.

Amaziah King of Judah

25 Amaziah was twenty-five years old when he became king, and he reigned in Jerusalem twenty-nine years. His mother's name was Jehoaddin,ᵈ; she was from Jerusalem. ²He did what was right in the eyes of the LORD, but not wholeheartedly. ³After the kingdom was firmly in his control, he executed the officials who had murdered his father the king. ⁴Yet he did not put their sons to death, but acted in accordance with what is written in the Law, in the Book of Moses, where the LORD commanded: "Fathers shall not be put to death for their children, nor children put to death for their fathers; each is to die for his own sins."ᵉ

⁵Amaziah called the people of Judah together and assigned them according to their families to commanders of thousands and commanders of hundreds for all Judah and Benjamin. He then mustered those twenty years old or more and found that there were three hundred thousand men ready for military service, able to handle the spear and shield. ⁶He also hired a hundred thousand fighting men from Israel for a hundred talentsᶠ of silver.

⁷But a man of God came to him and said, "O king, these troops from Israel must not march with you, for the LORD is not with Israel—not with any of the people of Ephraim. ⁸Even if you go and fight courageously in battle, God will overthrow you before the enemy, for God has the power to help or to overthrow."

⁹Amaziah asked the man of God, "But what about the hundred talents I paid for these Israelite troops?"

ᵃ 23 Probably in the spring   ᵇ 26 A variant of *Jozabad*   ᶜ 26 A variant of *Shomer*   ᵈ 1 Hebrew *Jehoaddan*, a variant of *Jehoaddin*   ᵉ 4 Deut. 24:16   ᶠ 6 That is, about 3 3/4 tons (about 3.4 metric tons); also in verse 9

THE MARTYRDOM OF JOHN HUSS
John Foxe

VERSE: 2 Chronicles 24:21   **PASSAGE:** 2 Chronicles 24:17–22

ohn Huss was summoned . . . arrested, and committed prisoner . . . While Huss was in confinement, the Council acted the part of inquisitors . . .

John Huss's answer was this: "I did appeal unto the pope; who being dead, and the cause of my matter remaining undetermined, I appealed likewise unto his successor John XXIII: before whom when, by the space of two years, I could not be admitted by my advocates to defend my cause, I appealed unto the high judge Christ."

When John Huss had spoken these words, it was demanded of him whether he had received absolution of the pope or no? He answered, "No." Then again, whether it were lawful for him to appeal unto Christ or no? Whereunto John Huss answered: "Verily I do affirm here before you all, that there is no more just or effectual appeal, than that appeal which is made unto Christ, forasmuch as the law doth determine, that to appeal is no other thing than in a cause of grief or wrong done by an inferior judge, to implore and require aid at a higher Judge's hand. Who is then a higher Judge than Christ? Who, I say, can know or judge the matter more justly, or with more equity? when in him there is found no deceit, neither can he be deceived; or, who can better help the miserable and oppressed than he?" While John Huss, with a devout and sober countenance, was speaking and pronouncing those words, he was derided and mocked by all the whole council.

These excellent sentences were esteemed as so many expressions of treason, and tended to inflame his adversaries. Accordingly, the bishops appointed by the council stripped him of his priestly garments, degraded him, put a paper miter on his head, on which was painted devils, with this inscription, "A ringleader of heretics." Which when he saw, he said: "My Lord Jesus Christ, for my sake, did wear a crown of thorns; why should not I then, for his sake, again wear this light crown, be it ever so ignominious? Truly I will do it, and that willingly."

ADDITIONAL SCRIPTURE READING:
Jeremiah 38:3–6; Acts 5:34–40

Go to page 502 for your next devotional reading.

1500   1700

The man of God replied, "The LORD can give you much more than that."

¹⁰So Amaziah dismissed the troops who had come to him from Ephraim and sent them home. They were furious with Judah and left for home in a great rage.

¹¹Amaziah then marshaled his strength and led his army to the Valley of Salt, where he killed ten thousand men of Seir. ¹²The army of Judah also captured ten thousand men alive, took them to the top of a cliff and threw them down so that all were dashed to pieces.

¹³Meanwhile the troops that Amaziah had sent back and had not allowed to take part in the war raided Judean towns from Samaria to Beth Horon. They killed three thousand people and carried off great quantities of plunder.

¹⁴When Amaziah returned from slaughtering the Edomites, he brought back the gods of the people of Seir. He set them up as his own gods, bowed down to them and burned sacrifices to them. ¹⁵The anger of the LORD burned against Amaziah, and he sent a prophet to him, who said, "Why do you consult this people's gods, which could not save their own people from your hand?"

¹⁶While he was still speaking, the king said to him, "Have we appointed you an adviser to the king? Stop! Why be struck down?"

So the prophet stopped but said, "I know that God has determined to destroy you, because you have done this and have not listened to my counsel."

¹⁷After Amaziah king of Judah consulted his advisers, he sent this challenge to Jehoash[a] son of Jehoahaz, the son of Jehu, king of Israel: "Come, meet me face to face."

¹⁸But Jehoash king of Israel replied to Amaziah king of Judah: "A thistle in Lebanon sent a message to a cedar in Lebanon, 'Give your daughter to my son in marriage.' Then a wild beast in Lebanon came along and trampled the thistle underfoot. ¹⁹You say to yourself that you have defeated Edom, and now you are arrogant and proud. But stay at home! Why ask for trouble and cause your own downfall and that of Judah also?"

²⁰Amaziah, however, would not listen, for God so worked that he might hand them over to Jehoash, because they sought the gods of Edom. ²¹So Jehoash king of Israel attacked. He and Amaziah king of Judah faced each other at Beth Shemesh in Judah. ²²Judah was routed by Israel, and every man fled to his home. ²³Jehoash king of Israel captured Amaziah king of Judah, the son of Joash, the son of Ahaziah,[b] at Beth Shemesh. Then Jehoash brought him to Jerusalem and broke down the wall of Jerusalem from the Ephraim Gate to the Corner Gate—a section about six hundred feet[c] long. ²⁴He took all the gold and silver and all the articles found in the temple of God that had been in the care of Obed-Edom, together with the palace treasures and the hostages, and returned to Samaria.

²⁵Amaziah son of Joash king of Judah lived for fifteen years after the death of Jehoash son of Jehoahaz king of Israel. ²⁶As for the other events of Amaziah's reign, from beginning to end, are they not written in the book of the kings of Judah and Israel? ²⁷From the time that Amaziah turned away from following the LORD, they conspired against him in Jerusalem and he fled to Lachish, but they sent men after him to Lachish and killed him there. ²⁸He was brought back by horse and was buried with his fathers in the City of Judah.

Uzziah King of Judah

26 Then all the people of Judah took Uzziah,[d] who was sixteen years old, and made him king in place of his father Amaziah. ²He was the one who rebuilt Elath and restored it to Judah after Amaziah rested with his fathers.

³Uzziah was sixteen years old when he became king, and he reigned in Jerusalem fifty-two years. His mother's name was Jecoliah; she was from Jerusalem. ⁴He did what was right in the eyes of the LORD, just as his father Amaziah had done. ⁵He sought God during the days of Zechariah, who instructed him in the fear[e] of God. As long as he sought the LORD, God gave him success.

a 17 Hebrew *Joash*, a variant of *Jehoash*; also in verses 18, 21, 23 and 25   *b 23* Hebrew *Jehoahaz*, a variant of *Ahaziah*   *c 23* Hebrew *four hundred cubits* (about 180 meters)   *d 1* Also called *Azariah*   *e 5* Many Hebrew manuscripts, Septuagint and Syriac; other Hebrew manuscripts *vision*

⁶He went to war against the Philistines and broke down the walls of Gath, Jabneh and Ashdod. He then rebuilt towns near Ashdod and elsewhere among the Philistines. ⁷God helped him against the Philistines and against the Arabs who lived in Gur Baal and against the Meunites. ⁸The Ammonites brought tribute to Uzziah, and his fame spread as far as the border of Egypt, because he had become very powerful.

⁹Uzziah built towers in Jerusalem at the Corner Gate, at the Valley Gate and at the angle of the wall, and he fortified them. ¹⁰He also built towers in the desert and dug many cisterns, because he had much livestock in the foothills and in the plain. He had people working his fields and vineyards in the hills and in the fertile lands, for he loved the soil.

¹¹Uzziah had a well-trained army, ready to go out by divisions according to their numbers as mustered by Jeiel the secretary and Maaseiah the officer under the direction of Hananiah, one of the royal officials. ¹²The total number of family leaders over the fighting men was 2,600. ¹³Under their command was an army of 307,500 men trained for war, a powerful force to support the king against his enemies. ¹⁴Uzziah provided shields, spears, helmets, coats of armor, bows and slingstones for the entire army. ¹⁵In Jerusalem he made machines designed by skillful men for use on the towers and on the corner defenses to shoot arrows and hurl large stones. His fame spread far and wide, for he was greatly helped until he became powerful.

¹⁶But after Uzziah became powerful, his pride led to his downfall. He was unfaithful to the LORD his God, and entered the temple of the LORD to burn incense on the altar of incense. ¹⁷Azariah the priest with eighty other courageous priests of the LORD followed him in. ¹⁸They confronted him and said, "It is not right for you, Uzziah, to burn incense to the LORD. That is for the priests, the descendants of Aaron, who have been consecrated to burn incense. Leave the sanctuary, for you have been

unfaithful; and you will not be honored by the LORD God."

¹⁹Uzziah, who had a censer in his hand ready to burn incense, became angry. While he was raging at the priests in their presence before the incense altar in the LORD's temple, leprosy*a* broke out on his forehead. ²⁰When Azariah the chief priest and all the other priests looked at him, they saw that he had leprosy on his forehead, so they hurried him out. Indeed, he himself was eager to leave, because the LORD had afflicted him.

²¹King Uzziah had leprosy until the day he died. He lived in a separate house*b*—leprous, and excluded from the temple of the LORD. Jotham his son had charge of the palace and governed the people of the land.

²²The other events of Uzziah's reign, from beginning to end, are recorded by the prophet Isaiah son of Amoz. ²³Uzziah rested with his fathers and was buried near them in a field for burial that belonged to the kings, for people said, "He had leprosy." And Jotham his son succeeded him as king.

Jotham King of Judah

27 Jotham was twenty-five years old when he became king, and he reigned in Jerusalem sixteen years. His mother's name was Jerusha daughter of Zadok. ²He did what was right in the eyes of the LORD, just as his father Uzziah had done, but unlike him he did not enter the temple of the LORD. The people, however, continued their corrupt practices. ³Jotham rebuilt the Upper Gate of the temple of the LORD and did extensive work on the wall at the hill of Ophel. ⁴He built towns in the Judean hills and forts and towers in wooded areas.

⁵Jotham made war on the king of the Ammonites and conquered them. That year the Ammonites paid him a hundred talents*c* of silver, ten thousand cors*d* of wheat and ten thousand cors of barley. The Ammonites brought him the same amount also in the second and third years.

⁶Jotham grew powerful because he

---

a 19 The Hebrew word was used for various diseases affecting the skin—not necessarily leprosy; also in verses 20, 21 and 23.   *b 21* Or *in a house where he was relieved of responsibilities*   *c 5* That is, about 3 3/4 tons (about 3.4 metric tons)   *d 5* That is, probably about 62,000 bushels (about 2,200 kiloliters)

walked steadfastly before the LORD his God.

7The other events in Jotham's reign, including all his wars and the other things he did, are written in the book of the kings of Israel and Judah. 8He was twenty-five years old when he became king, and he reigned in Jerusalem sixteen years. 9Jotham rested with his fathers and was buried in the City of David. And Ahaz his son succeeded him as king.

Ahaz King of Judah

28 Ahaz was twenty years old when he became king, and he reigned in Jerusalem sixteen years. Unlike David his father, he did not do what was right in the eyes of the LORD. 2He walked in the ways of the kings of Israel and also made cast idols for worshiping the Baals. 3He burned sacrifices in the Valley of Ben Hinnom and sacrificed his sons in the fire, following the detestable ways of the nations the LORD had driven out before the Israelites. 4He offered sacrifices and burned incense at the high places, on the hilltops and under every spreading tree.

5Therefore the LORD his God handed him over to the king of Aram. The Arameans defeated him and took many of his people as prisoners and brought them to Damascus.

He was also given into the hands of the king of Israel, who inflicted heavy casualties on him. 6In one day Pekah son of Remaliah killed a hundred and twenty thousand soldiers in Judah—because Judah had forsaken the LORD, the God of their fathers. 7Zicri, an Ephraimite warrior, killed Maaseiah the king's son, Azrikam the officer in charge of the palace, and Elkanah, second to the king. 8The Israelites took captive from their kinsmen two hundred thousand wives, sons and daughters. They also took a great deal of plunder, which they carried back to Samaria.

9But a prophet of the LORD named Oded was there, and he went out to meet the army when it returned to Samaria. He said to them, "Because the LORD, the God of your fathers, was angry with Judah, he gave them into your hand. But you have slaughtered them in a rage that reaches to heaven. 10And now you intend to make the men and women of Judah and Jerusalem your slaves. But aren't you also guilty of sins against the LORD your God? 11Now listen to me! Send back your fellow countrymen you have taken as prisoners, for the LORD's fierce anger rests on you."

12Then some of the leaders in Ephraim—Azariah son of Jehohanan, Berekiah son of Meshillemoth, Jehizkiah son of Shallum, and Amasa son of Hadlai—confronted those who were arriving from the war. 13"You must not bring those prisoners here," they said, "or we will be guilty before the LORD. Do you intend to add to our sin and guilt? For our guilt is already great, and his fierce anger rests on Israel."

14So the soldiers gave up the prisoners and plunder in the presence of the officials and all the assembly. 15The men designated by name took the prisoners, and from the plunder they clothed all who were naked. They provided them with clothes and sandals, food and drink, and healing balm. All those who were weak they put on donkeys. So they took them back to their fellow countrymen at Jericho, the City of Palms, and returned to Samaria.

16At that time King Ahaz sent to the kinga of Assyria for help. 17The Edomites had again come and attacked Judah and carried away prisoners, 18while the Philistines had raided towns in the foothills and in the Negev of Judah. They captured and occupied Beth Shemesh, Aijalon and Gederoth, as well as Soco, Timnah and Gimzo, with their surrounding villages. 19The LORD had humbled Judah because of Ahaz king of Israel,b for he had promoted wickedness in Judah and had been most unfaithful to the LORD. 20Tiglath-Pileserc king of Assyria came to him, but he gave him trouble instead of help. 21Ahaz took some of the things from the temple of the LORD and from the royal palace and from the princes and presented them to the king of Assyria, but that did not help him.

---

a 16 One Hebrew manuscript, Septuagint and Vulgate (see also 2 Kings 16:7); most Hebrew manuscripts kings   b 19 That is, Judah, as frequently in 2 Chronicles   c 20 Hebrew Tilgath-Pilneser, a variant of Tiglath-Pileser

²²In his time of trouble King Ahaz became even more unfaithful to the LORD. ²³He offered sacrifices to the gods of Damascus, who had defeated him; for he thought, "Since the gods of the kings of Aram have helped them, I will sacrifice to them so they will help me." But they were his downfall and the downfall of all Israel.

²⁴Ahaz gathered together the furnishings from the temple of God and took them away.ᵃ He shut the doors of the LORD's temple and set up altars at every street corner in Jerusalem. ²⁵In every town in Judah he built high places to burn sacrifices to other gods and provoked the LORD, the God of his fathers, to anger.

²⁶The other events of his reign and all his ways, from beginning to end, are written in the book of the kings of Judah and Israel. ²⁷Ahaz rested with his fathers and was buried in the city of Jerusalem, but he was not placed in the tombs of the kings of Israel. And Hezekiah his son succeeded him as king.

Hezekiah Purifies the Temple

29 Hezekiah was twenty-five years old when he became king, and he reigned in Jerusalem twenty-nine years. His mother's name was Abijah daughter of Zechariah. ²He did what was right in the eyes of the LORD, just as his father David had done.

³In the first month of the first year of his reign, he opened the doors of the temple of the LORD and repaired them. ⁴He brought in the priests and the Levites, assembled them in the square on the east side ⁵and said: "Listen to me, Levites! Consecrate yourselves now and consecrate the temple of the LORD, the God of your fathers. Remove all defilement from the sanctuary. ⁶Our fathers were unfaithful; they did evil in the eyes of the LORD our God and forsook him. They turned their faces away from the LORD's dwelling place and turned their backs on him. ⁷They also shut the doors of the portico and put out the lamps. They did not burn incense or present any burnt offerings at the sanctuary to the God of Israel. ⁸Therefore, the anger of the LORD has fallen on Judah and Jerusalem; he has made

them an object of dread and horror and scorn, as you can see with your own eyes. ⁹This is why our fathers have fallen by the sword and why our sons and daughters and our wives are in captivity. ¹⁰Now I intend to make a covenant with the LORD, the God of Israel, so that his fierce anger will turn away from us. ¹¹My sons, do not be negligent now, for the LORD has chosen you to stand before him and serve him, to minister before him and to burn incense."

¹²Then these Levites set to work:
from the Kohathites,
　Mahath son of Amasai and Joel
　　son of Azariah;
from the Merarites,
　Kish son of Abdi and Azariah son
　　of Jehallelel;
from the Gershonites,
　Joah son of Zimmah and Eden
　　son of Joah;
¹³from the descendants of Elizaphan,
　Shimri and Jeiel;
from the descendants of Asaph,
　Zechariah and Mattaniah;
¹⁴from the descendants of Heman,
　Jehiel and Shimei;
from the descendants of Jeduthun,
　Shemaiah and Uzziel.

¹⁵When they had assembled their brothers and consecrated themselves, they went in to purify the temple of the LORD, as the king had ordered, following the word of the LORD. ¹⁶The priests went into the sanctuary of the LORD to purify it. They brought out to the courtyard of the LORD's temple everything unclean that they found in the temple of the LORD. The Levites took it and carried it out to the Kidron Valley. ¹⁷They began the consecration on the first day of the first month, and by the eighth day of the month they reached the portico of the LORD. For eight more days they consecrated the temple of the LORD itself, finishing on the sixteenth day of the first month.

¹⁸Then they went in to King Hezekiah and reported: "We have purified the entire temple of the LORD, the altar of burnt offering with all its utensils, and the table for setting out the consecrated bread, with all its articles. ¹⁹We have prepared and consecrated all the articles

---

ᵃ 24 Or *and cut them up*

that King Ahaz removed in his unfaithfulness while he was king. They are now in front of the LORD's altar."

²⁰Early the next morning King Hezekiah gathered the city officials together and went up to the temple of the LORD. ²¹They brought seven bulls, seven rams, seven male lambs and seven male goats as a sin offering for the kingdom, for the sanctuary and for Judah. The king commanded the priests, the descendants of Aaron, to offer these on the altar of the LORD. ²²So they slaughtered the bulls, and the priests took the blood and sprinkled it on the altar; next they slaughtered the rams and sprinkled their blood on the altar; then they slaughtered the lambs and sprinkled their blood on the altar. ²³The goats for the sin offering were brought before the king and the assembly, and they laid their hands on them. ²⁴The priests then slaughtered the goats and presented their blood on the altar for a sin offering to atone for all Israel, because the king had ordered the burnt offering and the sin offering for all Israel.

²⁵He stationed the Levites in the temple of the LORD with cymbals, harps and lyres in the way prescribed by David and Gad the king's seer and Nathan the prophet; this was commanded by the LORD through his prophets. ²⁶So the Levites stood ready with David's instruments, and the priests with their trumpets.

²⁷Hezekiah gave the order to sacrifice the burnt offering on the altar. As the offering began, singing to the LORD began also, accompanied by trumpets and the instruments of David king of Israel. ²⁸The whole assembly bowed in worship, while the singers sang and the trumpeters played. All this continued until the sacrifice of the burnt offering was completed.

²⁹When the offerings were finished, the king and everyone present with him knelt down and worshiped. ³⁰King Hezekiah and his officials ordered the Levites to praise the LORD with the words of David and of Asaph the seer. So they sang praises with gladness and bowed their heads and worshiped.

³¹Then Hezekiah said, "You have now dedicated yourselves to the LORD. Come and bring sacrifices and thank offerings to the temple of the LORD." So the assembly brought sacrifices and thank offerings, and all whose hearts were willing brought burnt offerings.

³²The number of burnt offerings the assembly brought was seventy bulls, a hundred rams and two hundred male lambs—all of them for burnt offerings to the LORD. ³³The animals consecrated as sacrifices amounted to six hundred bulls and three thousand sheep and goats. ³⁴The priests, however, were too few to skin all the burnt offerings; so their kinsmen the Levites helped them until the task was finished and until other priests had been consecrated, for the Levites had been more conscientious in consecrating themselves than the priests had been. ³⁵There were burnt offerings in abundance, together with the fat of the fellowship offerings*a* and the drink offerings that accompanied the burnt offerings.

So the service of the temple of the LORD was reestablished. ³⁶Hezekiah and all the people rejoiced at what God had brought about for his people, because it was done so quickly.

Hezekiah Celebrates the Passover

30 Hezekiah sent word to all Israel and Judah and also wrote letters to Ephraim and Manasseh, inviting them to come to the temple of the LORD in Jerusalem and celebrate the Passover to the LORD, the God of Israel. ²The king and his officials and the whole assembly in Jerusalem decided to celebrate the Passover in the second month. ³They had not been able to celebrate it at the regular time because not enough priests had consecrated themselves and the people had not assembled in Jerusalem. ⁴The plan seemed right both to the king and to the whole assembly. ⁵They decided to send a proclamation throughout Israel, from Beersheba to Dan, calling the people to come to Jerusalem and celebrate the Passover to the LORD, the God of Israel. It had not been celebrated in large numbers according to what was written.

⁶At the king's command, couriers went throughout Israel and Judah with

a 35 Traditionally *peace offerings*

letters from the king and from his officials, which read:

"People of Israel, return to the LORD, the God of Abraham, Isaac and Israel, that he may return to you who are left, who have escaped from the hand of the kings of Assyria. ⁷Do not be like your fathers and brothers, who were unfaithful to the LORD, the God of their fathers, so that he made them an object of horror, as you see. ⁸Do not be stiffnecked, as your fathers were; submit to the LORD. Come to the sanctuary, which he has consecrated forever. Serve the LORD your God, so that his fierce anger will turn away from you. ⁹If you return to the LORD, then your brothers and your children will be shown compassion by their captors and will come back to this land, for the LORD your God

TUESDAY

THE SEEKER'S COVENANT
Matthew Henry

VERSE: 2 Chronicles 30:6   **PASSAGE:** 2 Chronicles 30:1–20

ield yourselves unto the Lord" (2 Chronicles 30:8, KJV). Before you can come into communion with him you must come into covenant with him. *Give the hand to the Lord* (so the word is), that is, "Consent to take him for your God." "The doors of the sanctuary are now opened, and you have liberty to enter; the temple service is now revived, and you are welcome to join in it. You are children of Israel. The God you are called to return to is the God of Abraham, Isaac, and Jacob, a God in covenant with your first fathers. Your late fathers that forsook him and trespassed against him have been given up to desolation; their apostasy and idolatry have been their ruin, as you see (v. 7). You yourselves are but a *remnant* narrowly *escaped out of the hands of the kings of Assyria.* If you return to God in a way of duty, he will return to you in a way of mercy."

. . . Could anything be expressed more pathetically, more movingly? Could there be a better cause, or could it be better pleaded? . . . In the worst of times God has had a remnant; so he had here . . . A command was given to the men of Judah to attend this solemnity; and they universally obeyed it. They did it with one heart, were all of a mind in it, and *the hand of God gave* them that *one heart* (v. 12, KJV) . . . For this is the one thing needful, that we seek God, his favor, his honor, and that we set our hearts to do it.

ADDITIONAL SCRIPTURE READING:
Isaiah 55:6–7; Joel 2:12–14; James 4:8

Go to page 508 for your next devotional reading.

1700   1900

is gracious and compassionate. He will not turn his face from you if you return to him."

¹⁰The couriers went from town to town in Ephraim and Manasseh, as far as Zebulun, but the people scorned and ridiculed them. ¹¹Nevertheless, some men of Asher, Manasseh and Zebulun humbled themselves and went to Jerusalem. ¹²Also in Judah the hand of God was on the people to give them unity of mind to carry out what the king and his officials had ordered, following the word of the LORD.

¹³A very large crowd of people assembled in Jerusalem to celebrate the Feast of Unleavened Bread in the second month. ¹⁴They removed the altars in Jerusalem and cleared away the incense altars and threw them into the Kidron Valley.

¹⁵They slaughtered the Passover lamb on the fourteenth day of the second month. The priests and the Levites were ashamed and consecrated themselves and brought burnt offerings to the temple of the LORD. ¹⁶Then they took up their regular positions as prescribed in the Law of Moses the man of God. The priests sprinkled the blood handed to them by the Levites. ¹⁷Since many in the crowd had not consecrated themselves, the Levites had to kill the Passover lambs for all those who were not ceremonially clean and could not consecrate ʟtheir lambsʜ to the LORD. ¹⁸Although most of the many people who came from Ephraim, Manasseh, Issachar and Zebulun had not purified themselves, yet they ate the Passover, contrary to what was written. But Hezekiah prayed for them, saying, "May the LORD, who is good, pardon everyone ¹⁹who sets his heart on seeking God— the LORD, the God of his fathers—even if he is not clean according to the rules of the sanctuary." ²⁰And the LORD heard Hezekiah and healed the people.

²¹The Israelites who were present in Jerusalem celebrated the Feast of Unleavened Bread for seven days with great rejoicing, while the Levites and priests sang to the LORD every day, accompanied by the LORD's instruments of praise.ᵃ

²²Hezekiah spoke encouragingly to all the Levites, who showed good understanding of the service of the LORD. For the seven days they ate their assigned portion and offered fellowship offeringsᵇ and praised the LORD, the God of their fathers.

²³The whole assembly then agreed to celebrate the festival seven more days; so for another seven days they celebrated joyfully. ²⁴Hezekiah king of Judah provided a thousand bulls and seven thousand sheep and goats for the assembly, and the officials provided them with a thousand bulls and ten thousand sheep and goats. A great number of priests consecrated themselves. ²⁵The entire assembly of Judah rejoiced, along with the priests and Levites and all who had assembled from Israel, including the aliens who had come from Israel and those who lived in Judah. ²⁶There was great joy in Jerusalem, for since the days of Solomon son of David king of Israel there had been nothing like this in Jerusalem. ²⁷The priests and the Levites stood to bless the people, and God heard them, for their prayer reached heaven, his holy dwelling place.

31 When all this had ended, the Israelites who were there went out to the towns of Judah, smashed the sacred stones and cut down the Asherah poles. They destroyed the high places and the altars throughout Judah and Benjamin and in Ephraim and Manasseh. After they had destroyed all of them, the Israelites returned to their own towns and to their own property.

Contributions for Worship

²Hezekiah assigned the priests and Levites to divisions—each of them according to their duties as priests or Levites—to offer burnt offerings and fellowship offerings,ᵇ to minister, to give thanks and to sing praises at the gates of the LORD's dwelling. ³The king contributed from his own possessions for the morning and evening burnt offerings and for the burnt offerings on the Sabbaths, New Moons and appointed feasts as written in the Law of the LORD. ⁴He ordered the people living in Jerusalem to give the portion due the priests and Levites so

ᵃ 21 Or *priests praised the LORD every day with resounding instruments belonging to the LORD*
ᵇ 22,2 Traditionally *peace offerings*

they could devote themselves to the Law of the LORD. 5As soon as the order went out, the Israelites generously gave the firstfruits of their grain, new wine, oil and honey and all that the fields produced. They brought a great amount, a tithe of everything. 6The men of Israel and Judah who lived in the towns of Judah also brought a tithe of their herds and flocks and a tithe of the holy things dedicated to the LORD their God, and they piled them in heaps. 7They began doing this in the third month and finished in the seventh month. 8When Hezekiah and his officials came and saw the heaps, they praised the LORD and blessed his people Israel.

9Hezekiah asked the priests and Levites about the heaps; 10and Azariah the chief priest, from the family of Zadok, answered, "Since the people began to bring their contributions to the temple of the LORD, we have had enough to eat and plenty to spare, because the LORD has blessed his people, and this great amount is left over."

11Hezekiah gave orders to prepare storerooms in the temple of the LORD, and this was done. 12Then they faithfully brought in the contributions, tithes and dedicated gifts. Conaniah, a Levite, was in charge of these things, and his brother Shimei was next in rank. 13Jehiel, Azaziah, Nahath, Asahel, Jerimoth, Jozabad, Eliel, Ismakiah, Mahath and Benaiah were supervisors under Conaniah and Shimei his brother, by appointment of King Hezekiah and Azariah the official in charge of the temple of God.

14Kore son of Imnah the Levite, keeper of the East Gate, was in charge of the freewill offerings given to God, distributing the contributions made to the LORD and also the consecrated gifts. 15Eden, Miniamin, Jeshua, Shemaiah, Amariah and Shecaniah assisted him faithfully in the towns of the priests, distributing to their fellow priests according to their divisions, old and young alike.

16In addition, they distributed to the males three years old or more whose names were in the genealogical records—all who would enter the temple of the LORD to perform the daily duties of their various tasks, according to their responsibilities and their divisions. 17And they distributed to the priests enrolled by their families in the genealogical records and likewise to the Levites twenty years old or more, according to their responsibilities and their divisions. 18They included all the little ones, the wives, and the sons and daughters of the whole community listed in these genealogical records. For they were faithful in consecrating themselves.

19As for the priests, the descendants of Aaron, who lived on the farm lands around their towns or in any other towns, men were designated by name to distribute portions to every male among them and to all who were recorded in the genealogies of the Levites.

20This is what Hezekiah did throughout Judah, doing what was good and right and faithful before the LORD his God. 21In everything that he undertook in the service of God's temple and in obedience to the law and the commands, he sought his God and worked wholeheartedly. And so he prospered.

Sennacherib Threatens Jerusalem

32 After all that Hezekiah had so faithfully done, Sennacherib king of Assyria came and invaded Judah. He laid siege to the fortified cities, thinking to conquer them for himself. 2When Hezekiah saw that Sennacherib had come and that he intended to make war on Jerusalem, 3he consulted with his officials and military staff about blocking off the water from the springs outside the city, and they helped him. 4A large force of men assembled, and they blocked all the springs and the stream that flowed through the land. "Why should the kingsa of Assyria come and find plenty of water?" they said. 5Then he worked hard repairing all the broken sections of the wall and building towers on it. He built another wall outside that one and reinforced the supporting terracesb of the City of David. He also made large numbers of weapons and shields.

6He appointed military officers over the people and assembled them before him in the square at the city gate and encouraged them with these words: 7"Be strong and courageous. Do not be

---

a 4 Hebrew; Septuagint and Syriac king   b 5 Or the Millo

afraid or discouraged because of the king of Assyria and the vast army with him, for there is a greater power with us than with him. ⁸With him is only the arm of flesh, but with us is the LORD our God to help us and to fight our battles." And the people gained confidence from what Hezekiah the king of Judah said.

⁹Later, when Sennacherib king of Assyria and all his forces were laying siege to Lachish, he sent his officers to Jerusalem with this message for Hezekiah king of Judah and for all the people of Judah who were there:

¹⁰"This is what Sennacherib king of Assyria says: On what are you basing your confidence, that you remain in Jerusalem under siege? ¹¹When Hezekiah says, 'The LORD our God will save us from the hand of the king of Assyria,' he is misleading you, to let you die of hunger and thirst. ¹²Did not Hezekiah himself remove this god's high places and altars, saying to Judah and Jerusalem, 'You must worship before one altar and burn sacrifices on it'?

¹³"Do you not know what I and my fathers have done to all the peoples of the other lands? Were the gods of those nations ever able to deliver their land from my hand? ¹⁴Who of all the gods of these nations that my fathers destroyed has been able to save his people from me? How then can your god deliver you from my hand? ¹⁵Now do not let Hezekiah deceive you and mislead you like this. Do not believe him, for no god of any nation or kingdom has been able to deliver his people from my hand or the hand of my fathers. How much less will your god deliver you from my hand!"

¹⁶Sennacherib's officers spoke further against the LORD God and against his servant Hezekiah. ¹⁷The king also wrote letters insulting the LORD, the God of Israel, and saying this against him: "Just as the gods of the peoples of the other lands did not rescue their people from my hand, so the god of Hezekiah will not rescue his people from my hand." ¹⁸Then they called out in Hebrew to the people of Jerusalem who were on the wall, to terrify them and make them afraid in order to capture the city. ¹⁹They spoke about the God of Jerusalem as they did about the gods of the other peoples of the world—the work of men's hands.

²⁰King Hezekiah and the prophet Isaiah son of Amoz cried out in prayer to heaven about this. ²¹And the LORD sent an angel, who annihilated all the fighting men and the leaders and officers in the camp of the Assyrian king. So he withdrew to his own land in disgrace. And when he went into the temple of his god, some of his sons cut him down with the sword.

²²So the LORD saved Hezekiah and the people of Jerusalem from the hand of Sennacherib king of Assyria and from the hand of all others. He took care of them*a* on every side. ²³Many brought offerings to Jerusalem for the LORD and valuable gifts for Hezekiah king of Judah. From then on he was highly regarded by all the nations.

Hezekiah's Pride, Success and Death

²⁴In those days Hezekiah became ill and was at the point of death. He prayed to the LORD, who answered him and gave him a miraculous sign. ²⁵But Hezekiah's heart was proud and he did not respond to the kindness shown him; therefore the LORD's wrath was on him and on Judah and Jerusalem. ²⁶Then Hezekiah repented of the pride of his heart, as did the people of Jerusalem; therefore the LORD's wrath did not come upon them during the days of Hezekiah.

²⁷Hezekiah had very great riches and honor, and he made treasuries for his silver and gold and for his precious stones, spices, shields and all kinds of valuables. ²⁸He also made buildings to store the harvest of grain, new wine and oil; and he made stalls for various kinds of cattle, and pens for the flocks. ²⁹He built villages and acquired great numbers of flocks and herds, for God had given him very great riches.

³⁰It was Hezekiah who blocked the upper outlet of the Gihon spring and channeled the water down to the west

---

a 22 Hebrew; Septuagint and Vulgate *He gave them rest*

side of the City of David. He succeeded in everything he undertook. ³¹But when envoys were sent by the rulers of Babylon to ask him about the miraculous sign that had occurred in the land, God left him to test him and to know everything that was in his heart.

³²The other events of Hezekiah's reign and his acts of devotion are written in the vision of the prophet Isaiah son of Amoz in the book of the kings of Judah and Israel. ³³Hezekiah rested with his fathers and was buried on the hill where the tombs of David's descendants are. All Judah and the people of Jerusalem honored him when he died. And Manasseh his son succeeded him as king.

Manasseh King of Judah

33 Manasseh was twelve years old when he became king, and he reigned in Jerusalem fifty-five years. ²He did evil in the eyes of the LORD, following the detestable practices of the nations the LORD had driven out before the Israelites. ³He rebuilt the high places his father Hezekiah had demolished; he also erected altars to the Baals and made Asherah poles. He bowed down to all the starry hosts and worshiped them. ⁴He built altars in the temple of the LORD, of which the LORD had said, "My Name will remain in Jerusalem forever." ⁵In both courts of the temple of the LORD, he built altars to all the starry hosts. ⁶He sacrificed his sons in ⁿ the fire in the Valley of Ben Hinnom, practiced sorcery, divination and witchcraft, and consulted mediums and spiritists. He did much evil in the eyes of the LORD, provoking him to anger.

⁷He took the carved image he had made and put it in God's temple, of which God had said to David and to his son Solomon, "In this temple and in Jerusalem, which I have chosen out of all the tribes of Israel, I will put my Name forever. ⁸I will not again make the feet of the Israelites leave the land I assigned to your forefathers, if only they will be careful to do everything I commanded them concerning all the laws, decrees and ordinances given through

Moses." ⁹But Manasseh led Judah and the people of Jerusalem astray, so that they did more evil than the nations the LORD had destroyed before the Israelites.

¹⁰The LORD spoke to Manasseh and his people, but they paid no attention. ¹¹So the LORD brought against them the army commanders of the king of Assyria, who took Manasseh prisoner, put a hook in his nose, bound him with bronze shackles and took him to Babylon. ¹²In his distress he sought the favor of the LORD his God and humbled himself greatly before the God of his fathers. ¹³And when he prayed to him, the LORD was moved by his entreaty and listened to his plea; so he brought him back to Jerusalem and to his kingdom. Then Manasseh knew that the LORD is God.

¹⁴Afterward he rebuilt the outer wall of the City of David, west of the Gihon spring in the valley, as far as the entrance of the Fish Gate and encircling the hill of Ophel; he also made it much higher. He stationed military commanders in all the fortified cities in Judah.

¹⁵He got rid of the foreign gods and removed the image from the temple of the LORD, as well as all the altars he had built on the temple hill and in Jerusalem; and he threw them out of the city. ¹⁶Then he restored the altar of the LORD and sacrificed fellowship offerings ᵇ and thank offerings on it, and told Judah to serve the LORD, the God of Israel. ¹⁷The people, however, continued to sacrifice at the high places, but only to the LORD their God.

¹⁸The other events of Manasseh's reign, including his prayer to his God and the words the seers spoke to him in the name of the LORD, the God of Israel, are written in the annals of the kings of Israel. ᶜ ¹⁹His prayer and how God was moved by his entreaty, as well as all his sins and unfaithfulness, and the sites where he built high places and set up Asherah poles and idols before he humbled himself—all are written in the records of the seers. ᵈ ²⁰Manasseh rested with his fathers and was buried in his palace. And Amon his son succeeded him as king.

ᵃ 6 Or *He made his sons pass through*   ᵇ 16 Traditionally *peace offerings*   ᶜ 18 That is, Judah, as frequently in 2 Chronicles   ᵈ 19 One Hebrew manuscript and Septuagint; most Hebrew manuscripts of *Hozai*

Amon King of Judah

21Amon was twenty-two years old when he became king, and he reigned in Jerusalem two years. 22He did evil in the eyes of the LORD, as his father Manasseh had done. Amon worshiped and offered sacrifices to all the idols Manasseh had made. 23But unlike his father Manasseh, he did not humble himself before the LORD; Amon increased his guilt.

24Amon's officials conspired against him and assassinated him in his palace. 25Then the people of the land killed all who had plotted against King Amon, and they made Josiah his son king in his place.

Josiah's Reforms

34 Josiah was eight years old when he became king, and he reigned in Jerusalem thirty-one years. 2He did what was right in the eyes of the LORD and walked in the ways of his father David, not turning aside to the right or to the left.

3In the eighth year of his reign, while he was still young, he began to seek the God of his father David. In his twelfth year he began to purge Judah and Jerusalem of high places, Asherah poles, carved idols and cast images. 4Under his direction the altars of the Baals were torn down; he cut to pieces the incense altars that were above them, and smashed the Asherah poles, the idols and the images. These he broke to pieces and scattered over the graves of those who had sacrificed to them. 5He burned the bones of the priests on their altars, and so he purged Judah and Jerusalem. 6In the towns of Manasseh, Ephraim and Simeon, as far as Naphtali, and in the ruins around them, 7he tore down the altars and the Asherah poles and crushed the idols to powder and cut to pieces all the incense altars throughout Israel. Then he went back to Jerusalem.

8In the eighteenth year of Josiah's reign, to purify the land and the temple, he sent Shaphan son of Azaliah and Maaseiah the ruler of the city, with Joah son of Joahaz, the recorder, to repair the temple of the LORD his God.

9They went to Hilkiah the high priest and gave him the money that had been brought into the temple of God, which the Levites who were the doorkeepers had collected from the people of Manasseh, Ephraim and the entire remnant of Israel and from all the people of Judah and Benjamin and the inhabitants of Jerusalem. 10Then they entrusted it to the men appointed to supervise the work on the LORD's temple. These men paid the workers who repaired and restored the temple. 11They also gave money to the carpenters and builders to purchase dressed stone, and timber for joists and beams for the buildings that the kings of Judah had allowed to fall into ruin.

12The men did the work faithfully. Over them to direct them were Jahath and Obadiah, Levites descended from Merari, and Zechariah and Meshullam, descended from Kohath. The Levites— all who were skilled in playing musical instruments— 13had charge of the laborers and supervised all the workers from job to job. Some of the Levites were secretaries, scribes and doorkeepers.

The Book of the Law Found

14While they were bringing out the money that had been taken into the temple of the LORD, Hilkiah the priest found the Book of the Law of the LORD that had been given through Moses. 15Hilkiah said to Shaphan the secretary, "I have found the Book of the Law in the temple of the LORD." He gave it to Shaphan.

16Then Shaphan took the book to the king and reported to him: "Your officials are doing everything that has been committed to them. 17They have paid out the money that was in the temple of the LORD and have entrusted it to the supervisors and workers." 18Then Shaphan the secretary informed the king, "Hilkiah the priest has given me a book." And Shaphan read from it in the presence of the king.

19When the king heard the words of the Law, he tore his robes. 20He gave these orders to Hilkiah, Ahikam son of Shaphan, Abdon son of Micah,a Shaphan the secretary and Asaiah the king's attendant: 21"Go and inquire of the LORD for me and for the remnant in Israel and Judah about what is written in

---

a 20 Also called Acbor son of Micaiah

THE TERRIFYING OF THE CONSCIENCE AND THE PREACHING OF THE LAW

Martin Luther

VERSE: 2 Chronicles 34:21   **PASSAGE:** 2 Chronicles 34:14–21

 e must preach the law for the sake of the evil and wicked, but for the most part it lights upon the good and godly who, although they need it not, except so far as may concern the old Adam, yet accept it. The preaching of the gospel we must have for the sake of the good and godly, yet it falls among the wicked and ungodly, who take it to themselves, whereas it profits them not; for they abuse it, and are thereby made confident. It is even as when it rains in the water or on a desert wilderness, while meantime the good pastures and grounds are parched and dried up. The ungodly suck only a fleshly liberty out of the gospel, and become worse thereby; therefore not the gospel but the law belongs to them. Even as when my little son John offends, if then I should not whip him but call him to the table to me and give him sugarplums, I should thereby make him worse, yea, quite spoil him.

The gospel is like a fresh, mild, and cool air in the extreme heat of summer, a solace and comfort in the anguish of the conscience. But as this heat proceeds from the rays of the sun, so likewise the terrifying of the conscience must proceed from the preaching of the law, to the end that we may know we have offended against the laws of God.

Now, when the mind is refreshed and quickened again by the cool air of the gospel, we must not then be idle, or lie down and sleep. That is, when our consciences are settled in peace, quieted and comforted through God's Spirit, we must prove our faith by such good works as God has commanded. But so long as we live in this vale of misery, we shall be plagued and vexed with flies, with beetles, and with vermin, that is, with the devil, the world, and our own flesh. Yet we must press through, and not suffer ourselves to recoil.

ADDITIONAL SCRIPTURE READING:
Job 27:6; Acts 24:16; Hebrews 10:22–24

Go to page 522 for your next devotional reading.

1500   1700

this book that has been found. Great is the LORD's anger that is poured out on us because our fathers have not kept the word of the LORD; they have not acted in accordance with all that is written in this book."

22Hilkiah and those the king had sent with him*a* went to speak to the prophetess Huldah, who was the wife of Shallum son of Tokhath,*b* the son of Hasrah,*c* keeper of the wardrobe. She lived in Jerusalem, in the Second District.

23She said to them, "This is what the LORD, the God of Israel, says: Tell the man who sent you to me, 24'This is what the LORD says: I am going to bring disaster on this place and its people—all the curses written in the book that has been read in the presence of the king of Judah. 25Because they have forsaken me and burned incense to other gods and provoked me to anger by all that their hands have made,*d* my anger will be poured out on this place and will not be quenched.' 26Tell the king of Judah, who sent you to inquire of the LORD, 'This is what the LORD, the God of Israel, says concerning the words you heard: 27Because your heart was responsive and you humbled yourself before God when you heard what he spoke against this place and its people, and because you humbled yourself before me and tore your robes and wept in my presence, I have heard you, declares the LORD. 28Now I will gather you to your fathers, and you will be buried in peace. Your eyes will not see all the disaster I am going to bring on this place and on those who live here.' "

So they took her answer back to the king.

29Then the king called together all the elders of Judah and Jerusalem. 30He went up to the temple of the LORD with the men of Judah, the people of Jerusalem, the priests and the Levites—all the people from the least to the greatest. He read in their hearing all the words of the Book of the Covenant, which had been found in the temple of the LORD. 31The king stood by his pillar and renewed the covenant in the presence of the LORD—to follow the LORD and keep his commands, regulations and decrees with all his heart and all his soul, and to obey the words of the covenant written in this book.

32Then he had everyone in Jerusalem and Benjamin pledge themselves to it; the people of Jerusalem did this in accordance with the covenant of God, the God of their fathers.

33Josiah removed all the detestable idols from all the territory belonging to the Israelites, and he had all who were present in Israel serve the LORD their God. As long as he lived, they did not fail to follow the LORD, the God of their fathers.

Josiah Celebrates the Passover

35 Josiah celebrated the Passover to the LORD in Jerusalem, and the Passover lamb was slaughtered on the fourteenth day of the first month. 2He appointed the priests to their duties and encouraged them in the service of the LORD's temple. 3He said to the Levites, who instructed all Israel and who had been consecrated to the LORD: "Put the sacred ark in the temple that Solomon son of David king of Israel built. It is not to be carried about on your shoulders. Now serve the LORD your God and his people Israel. 4Prepare yourselves by families in your divisions, according to the directions written by David king of Israel and by his son Solomon.

5"Stand in the holy place with a group of Levites for each subdivision of the families of your fellow countrymen, the lay people. 6Slaughter the Passover lambs, consecrate yourselves and prepare ⌐the lambs⌐ for your fellow countrymen, doing what the LORD commanded through Moses."

7Josiah provided for all the lay people who were there a total of thirty thousand sheep and goats for the Passover offerings, and also three thousand cattle—all from the king's own possessions.

8His officials also contributed voluntarily to the people and the priests and Levites. Hilkiah, Zechariah and Jehiel, the administrators of God's temple, gave the priests twenty-six hundred Passover offerings and three hundred cattle. 9Also

---

a 22 One Hebrew manuscript, Vulgate and Syriac; most Hebrew manuscripts do not have *had sent with him.*   *b 22* Also called *Tikvah*   *c 22* Also called *Harhas*   *d 25* Or *by everything they have done*

Conaniah along with Shemaiah and Nethanel, his brothers, and Hashabiah, Jeiel and Jozabad, the leaders of the Levites, provided five thousand Passover offerings and five hundred head of cattle for the Levites.

10The service was arranged and the priests stood in their places with the Levites in their divisions as the king had ordered. 11The Passover lambs were slaughtered, and the priests sprinkled the blood handed to them, while the Levites skinned the animals. 12They set aside the burnt offerings to give them to the subdivisions of the families of the people to offer to the LORD, as is written in the Book of Moses. They did the same with the cattle. 13They roasted the Passover animals over the fire as prescribed, and boiled the holy offerings in pots, caldrons and pans and served them quickly to all the people. 14After this, they made preparations for themselves and for the priests, because the priests, the descendants of Aaron, were sacrificing the burnt offerings and the fat portions until nightfall. So the Levites made preparations for themselves and for the Aaronic priests.

15The musicians, the descendants of Asaph, were in the places prescribed by David, Asaph, Heman and Jeduthun the king's seer. The gatekeepers at each gate did not need to leave their posts, because their fellow Levites made the preparations for them.

16So at that time the entire service of the LORD was carried out for the celebration of the Passover and the offering of burnt offerings on the altar of the LORD, as King Josiah had ordered. 17The Israelites who were present celebrated the Passover at that time and observed the Feast of Unleavened Bread for seven days. 18The Passover had not been observed like this in Israel since the days of the prophet Samuel; and none of the kings of Israel ever celebrated such a Passover as did Josiah, with the priests, the Levites and all Judah and Israel who were there with the people of Jerusalem. 19This Passover was celebrated in the eighteenth year of Josiah's reign.

The Death of Josiah

20After all this, when Josiah had set the temple in order, Neco king of Egypt went up to fight at Carchemish on the Euphrates, and Josiah marched out to meet him in battle. 21But Neco sent messengers to him, saying, "What quarrel is there between you and me, O king of Judah? It is not you I am attacking at this time, but the house with which I am at war. God has told me to hurry; so stop opposing God, who is with me, or he will destroy you."

22Josiah, however, would not turn away from him, but disguised himself to engage him in battle. He would not listen to what Neco had said at God's command but went to fight him on the plain of Megiddo.

23Archers shot King Josiah, and he told his officers, "Take me away; I am badly wounded." 24So they took him out of his chariot, put him in the other chariot he had and brought him to Jerusalem, where he died. He was buried in the tombs of his fathers, and all Judah and Jerusalem mourned for him.

25Jeremiah composed laments for Josiah, and to this day all the men and women singers commemorate Josiah in the laments. These became a tradition in Israel and are written in the Laments.

26The other events of Josiah's reign and his acts of devotion, according to what is written in the Law of the LORD— 27all the events, from beginning to end, are written in the book of the kings of Israel and Judah. **36** 1And the people of the land took Jehoahaz son of Josiah and made him king in Jerusalem in place of his father.

Jehoahaz King of Judah

2Jehoahaz[a] was twenty-three years old when he became king, and he reigned in Jerusalem three months. 3The king of Egypt dethroned him in Jerusalem and imposed on Judah a levy of a hundred talents[b] of silver and a talent[c] of gold. 4The king of Egypt made Eliakim, a brother of Jehoahaz, king over Judah and Jerusalem and changed Eliakim's name to Jehoiakim. But Neco took Eliakim's

---

a 2 Hebrew *Joahaz*, a variant of *Jehoahaz*; also in verse 4   b 3 That is, about 3 3/4 tons (about 3.4 metric tons)   c 3 That is, about 75 pounds (about 34 kilograms)

brother Jehoahaz and carried him off to Egypt.

Jehoiakim King of Judah

5Jehoiakim was twenty-five years old when he became king, and he reigned in Jerusalem eleven years. He did evil in the eyes of the LORD his God. 6Nebuchadnezzar king of Babylon attacked him and bound him with bronze shackles to take him to Babylon. 7Nebuchadnezzar also took to Babylon articles from the temple of the LORD and put them in his temple*a* there.

8The other events of Jehoiakim's reign, the detestable things he did and all that was found against him, are written in the book of the kings of Israel and Judah. And Jehoiachin his son succeeded him as king.

Jehoiachin King of Judah

9Jehoiachin was eighteen*b* years old when he became king, and he reigned in Jerusalem three months and ten days. He did evil in the eyes of the LORD. 10In the spring, King Nebuchadnezzar sent for him and brought him to Babylon, together with articles of value from the temple of the LORD, and he made Jehoiachin's uncle,*c* Zedekiah, king over Judah and Jerusalem.

Zedekiah King of Judah

11Zedekiah was twenty-one years old when he became king, and he reigned in Jerusalem eleven years. 12He did evil in the eyes of the LORD his God and did not humble himself before Jeremiah the prophet, who spoke the word of the LORD. 13He also rebelled against King Nebuchadnezzar, who had made him take an oath in God's name. He became stiff-necked and hardened his heart and would not turn to the LORD, the God of Israel. 14Furthermore, all the leaders of the priests and the people became more and more unfaithful, following all the detestable practices of the nations and defiling the temple of the LORD, which he had consecrated in Jerusalem.

The Fall of Jerusalem

15The LORD, the God of their fathers, sent word to them through his messengers again and again, because he had pity on his people and on his dwelling place. 16But they mocked God's messengers, despised his words and scoffed at his prophets until the wrath of the LORD was aroused against his people and there was no remedy. 17He brought up against them the king of the Babylonians,*d* who killed their young men with the sword in the sanctuary, and spared neither young man nor young woman, old man or aged. God handed all of them over to Nebuchadnezzar. 18He carried to Babylon all the articles from the temple of God, both large and small, and the treasures of the LORD's temple and the treasures of the king and his officials. 19They set fire to God's temple and broke down the wall of Jerusalem; they burned all the palaces and destroyed everything of value there.

20He carried into exile to Babylon the remnant, who escaped from the sword, and they became servants to him and his sons until the kingdom of Persia came to power. 21The land enjoyed its sabbath rests; all the time of its desolation it rested, until the seventy years were completed in fulfillment of the word of the LORD spoken by Jeremiah.

22In the first year of Cyrus king of Persia, in order to fulfill the word of the LORD spoken by Jeremiah, the LORD moved the heart of Cyrus king of Persia to make a proclamation throughout his realm and to put it in writing:

23"This is what Cyrus king of Persia says:

" 'The LORD, the God of heaven, has given me all the kingdoms of the earth and he has appointed me to build a temple for him at Jerusalem in Judah. Anyone of his people among you—may the LORD his God be with him, and let him go up.' "

---

a 7 Or *palace*   *b 9* One Hebrew manuscript, some Septuagint manuscripts and Syriac (see also 2 Kings 24:8); most Hebrew manuscripts *eight*   *c 10* Hebrew *brother*, that is, relative (see 2 Kings 24:17)
d 17 Or *Chaldeans*

EZRA

ZRA TELLS OF THE RETURN OF THE JEWS FROM EXILE IN BABYLON AND ALSO OF THE REBUILDING OF THE TEMPLE. THE PEOPLE COMPLETED AND DEDICATED THE TEMPLE IN 516 B.C. AFTER BEING DELAYED FOR 18 YEARS BY THEIR ENEMIES FROM THE NORTH. AS YOU READ THIS BOOK, TAKE COMFORT IN THE STORY OF ORDINARY PEOPLE RESTORED BY GOD, AND REJOICE IN THE GOD WHO ALWAYS GIVES YOU A SECOND CHANCE TO TRUST AND FOLLOW HIM.

Cyrus Helps the Exiles to Return

1 In the first year of Cyrus king of Persia, in order to fulfill the word of the LORD spoken by Jeremiah, the LORD moved the heart of Cyrus king of Persia to make a proclamation throughout his realm and to put it in writing:

2"This is what Cyrus king of Persia says:

" 'The LORD, the God of heaven, has given me all the kingdoms of the earth and he has appointed me to build a temple for him at Jerusalem in Judah. 3Anyone of his people among you—may his God be with him, and let him go up to Jerusalem in Judah and build the temple of the LORD, the God of Israel, the God who is in Jerusalem. 4And the people of any place where survivors may now be living are to provide him with silver and gold, with goods and livestock, and with freewill offerings for the temple of God in Jerusalem.' "

5Then the family heads of Judah and Benjamin, and the priests and Levites—everyone whose heart God had moved—prepared to go up and build the house of the LORD in Jerusalem. 6All their neighbors assisted them with articles of silver and gold, with goods and livestock, and with valuable gifts, in addition to all the freewill offerings. 7Moreover, King Cyrus brought out the articles belonging to the temple of the LORD, which Nebuchadnezzar had carried away from Jerusalem and had placed in the temple of his god.*a* **8**Cyrus king of Persia had them brought by Mithredath the treasurer, who counted them out to Sheshbazzar the prince of Judah.

9This was the inventory:

gold dishes	30
silver dishes	1,000
silver pans*b*	29
10gold bowls	30
matching silver bowls	410
other articles	1,000

11In all, there were 5,400 articles of gold and of silver. Sheshbazzar brought all these along when the exiles came up from Babylon to Jerusalem.

The List of the Exiles Who Returned

2 Now these are the people of the province who came up from the captivity of the exiles, whom Nebuchadnezzar king of Babylon had taken captive to Babylon (they returned to Jerusalem and Judah, each to his own town, **2**in company with Zerubbabel, Jeshua, Nehemiah, Seraiah, Reelaiah, Mordecai, Bilshan, Mispar, Bigvai, Rehum and Baanah):

The list of the men of the people of Israel:

3the descendants of Parosh	2,172
4of Shephatiah	372
5of Arah	775
6of Pahath-Moab (through the line of Jeshua and Joab)	2,812
7of Elam	1,254
8of Zattu	945
9of Zaccai	760
10of Bani	642
11of Bebai	623
12of Azgad	1,222
13of Adonikam	666
14of Bigvai	2,056
15of Adin	454
16of Ater (through Hezekiah)	98
17of Bezai	323
18of Jorah	112
19of Hashum	223
20of Gibbar	95
21the men of Bethlehem	123
22of Netophah	56
23of Anathoth	128

24of Azmaveth	42
25of Kiriath Jearim,*c* Kephirah and Beeroth	743
26of Ramah and Geba	621
27of Micmash	122
28of Bethel and Ai	223
29of Nebo	52
30of Magbish	156
31of the other Elam	1,254
32of Harim	320
33of Lod, Hadid and Ono	725
34of Jericho	345
35of Senaah	3,630

36The priests:

the descendants of Jedaiah (through the family of Jeshua)	973
37of Immer	1,052
38of Pashhur	1,247
39of Harim	1,017

40The Levites:

the descendants of Jeshua and Kadmiel (through the line of Hodaviah)	74

41The singers:

the descendants of Asaph	128

42The gatekeepers of the temple:

the descendants of Shallum, Ater, Talmon, Akkub, Hatita and Shobai	139

43The temple servants:

the descendants of
Ziha, Hasupha, Tabbaoth,
44Keros, Siaha, Padon,
45Lebanah, Hagabah, Akkub,
46Hagab, Shalmai, Hanan,
47Giddel, Gahar, Reaiah,
48Rezin, Nekoda, Gazzam,
49Uzza, Paseah, Besai,
50Asnah, Meunim, Nephussim,
51Bakbuk, Hakupha, Harhur,
52Bazluth, Mehida, Harsha,
53Barkos, Sisera, Temah,
54Neziah and Hatipha

55The descendants of the servants of Solomon:

the descendants of
Sotai, Hassophereth, Peruda,

---

a 7 Or *gods*   *b* 9 The meaning of the Hebrew for this word is uncertain.   *c* 25 See Septuagint (see also Neh. 7:29); Hebrew *Kiriath Arim*.

56 Jaala, Darkon, Giddel,
57 Shephatiah, Hattil,
    Pokereth-Hazzebaim and Ami

58 The temple servants and the
    descendants of the servants
    of Solomon　392

59 The following came up from
the towns of Tel Melah, Tel Harsha,
Kerub, Addon and Immer, but they
could not show that their families
were descended from Israel:

60 The descendants of
    Delaiah, Tobiah and
    Nekoda　652

61 And from among the priests:

The descendants of
    Hobaiah, Hakkoz and Barzillai
    (a man who had married a
    daughter of Barzillai the Gile-
    adite and was called by that
    name).
62 These searched for their family
records, but they could not find
them and so were excluded from
the priesthood as unclean. 63 The
governor ordered them not to eat
any of the most sacred food until
there was a priest ministering with
the Urim and Thummim.

64 The whole company numbered
42,360, 65 besides their 7,337 menservants and maidservants; and
they also had 200 men and women
singers. 66 They had 736 horses, 245
mules, 67 435 camels and 6,720 donkeys.

68 When they arrived at the house of
the LORD in Jerusalem, some of the heads
of the families gave freewill offerings
toward the rebuilding of the house of
God on its site. 69 According to their ability they gave to the treasury for this work
61,000 drachmas[a] of gold, 5,000 minas[b]
of silver and 100 priestly garments.

70 The priests, the Levites, the singers,
the gatekeepers and the temple servants
settled in their own towns, along with
some of the other people, and the rest of
the Israelites settled in their towns.

Rebuilding the Altar

3 When the seventh month came
and the Israelites had settled in
their towns, the people assembled as one
man in Jerusalem. 2 Then Jeshua son of
Jozadak and his fellow priests and Zerubbabel son of Shealtiel and his associates
began to build the altar of the God of
Israel to sacrifice burnt offerings on it, in
accordance with what is written in the
Law of Moses the man of God. 3 Despite
their fear of the peoples around them,
they built the altar on its foundation and
sacrificed burnt offerings on it to the
LORD, both the morning and evening sacrifices. 4 Then in accordance with what is
written, they celebrated the Feast of
Tabernacles with the required number of
burnt offerings prescribed for each day.
5 After that, they presented the regular
burnt offerings, the New Moon sacrifices
and the sacrifices for all the appointed
sacred feasts of the LORD, as well as those
brought as freewill offerings to the LORD.
6 On the first day of the seventh month
they began to offer burnt offerings to the
LORD, though the foundation of the
LORD's temple had not yet been laid.

Rebuilding the Temple

7 Then they gave money to the masons
and carpenters, and gave food and drink
and oil to the people of Sidon and Tyre,
so that they would bring cedar logs by
sea from Lebanon to Joppa, as authorized
by Cyrus king of Persia.

8 In the second month of the second
year after their arrival at the house of
God in Jerusalem, Zerubbabel son of
Shealtiel, Jeshua son of Jozadak and the
rest of their brothers (the priests and the
Levites and all who had returned from
the captivity to Jerusalem) began the
work, appointing Levites twenty years of
age and older to supervise the building
of the house of the LORD. 9 Jeshua and his
sons and brothers and Kadmiel and
his sons (descendants of Hodaviah[c])
and the sons of Henadad and their sons
and brothers—all Levites—joined together in supervising those working on
the house of God.

10 When the builders laid the foundation of the temple of the LORD, the

---

[a] 69 That is, about 1,100 pounds (about 500 kilograms)　[b] 69 That is, about 3 tons (about 2.9 metric
tons)　[c] 9 Hebrew *Yehudah*, probably a variant of *Hodaviah*

priests in their vestments and with trumpets, and the Levites (the sons of Asaph) with cymbals, took their places to praise the LORD, as prescribed by David king of Israel. 11With praise and thanksgiving they sang to the LORD:

"He is good;
   his love to Israel endures forever."

And all the people gave a great shout of praise to the LORD, because the foundation of the house of the LORD was laid. 12But many of the older priests and Levites and family heads, who had seen the former temple, wept aloud when they saw the foundation of this temple being laid, while many others shouted for joy. 13No one could distinguish the sound of the shouts of joy from the sound of weeping, because the people made so much noise. And the sound was heard far away.

Opposition to the Rebuilding

4 When the enemies of Judah and Benjamin heard that the exiles were building a temple for the LORD, the God of Israel, 2they came to Zerubbabel and to the heads of the families and said, "Let us help you build because, like you, we seek your God and have been sacrificing to him since the time of Esarhaddon king of Assyria, who brought us here." 3But Zerubbabel, Jeshua and the rest of the heads of the families of Israel answered, "You have no part with us in building a temple to our God. We alone will build it for the LORD, the God of Israel, as King Cyrus, the king of Persia, commanded us."

WHEREVER SOULS ARE BEING TRIED AND RIPENED, IN WHATEVER COMMONPLACE AND HOMELY WAY, THERE GOD IS HEWING OUT THE PILLARS FOR HIS TEMPLE.   —*Phillips Brooks*

4Then the peoples around them set out to discourage the people of Judah and make them afraid to go on building.*a* 5They hired counselors to work

against them and frustrate their plans during the entire reign of Cyrus king of Persia and down to the reign of Darius king of Persia.

Later Opposition Under Xerxes and Artaxerxes

6At the beginning of the reign of Xerxes,*b* they lodged an accusation against the people of Judah and Jerusalem.

7And in the days of Artaxerxes king of Persia, Bishlam, Mithredath, Tabeel and the rest of his associates wrote a letter to Artaxerxes. The letter was written in Aramaic script and in the Aramaic language.*c,d*

8Rehum the commanding officer and Shimshai the secretary wrote a letter against Jerusalem to Artaxerxes the king as follows:

9Rehum the commanding officer and Shimshai the secretary, together with the rest of their associates— the judges and officials over the men from Tripolis, Persia,*e* Erech and Babylon, the Elamites of Susa, 10and the other people whom the great and honorable Ashurbanipal*f* deported and settled in the city of Samaria and elsewhere in Trans-Euphrates.

11(This is a copy of the letter they sent him.)

To King Artaxerxes,

From your servants, the men of Trans-Euphrates:

12The king should know that the Jews who came up to us from you have gone to Jerusalem and are rebuilding that rebellious and wicked city. They are restoring the walls and repairing the foundations.

13Furthermore, the king should know that if this city is built and its walls are restored, no more taxes, tribute or duty will be paid, and the royal revenues will suffer. 14Now since we are under obligation to the palace and it is not proper for us to see the king dishonored, we are

---

a 4 Or *and troubled them as they built*   *b 6* Hebrew *Ahasuerus,* a variant of Xerxes' Persian name   *c 7* Or *written in Aramaic and translated*   *d 7* The text of Ezra 4:8—6:18 is in Aramaic.   *e 9* Or *officials, magistrates and governors over the men from*   *f 10* Aramaic *Osnappar,* a variant of *Ashurbanipal*

sending this message to inform the king, [15]so that a search may be made in the archives of your predecessors. In these records you will find that this city is a rebellious city, troublesome to kings and provinces, a place of rebellion from ancient times. That is why this city was destroyed. [16]We inform the king that if this city is built and its walls are restored, you will be left with nothing in Trans-Euphrates.

[17]The king sent this reply:

To Rehum the commanding officer, Shimshai the secretary and the rest of their associates living in Samaria and elsewhere in Trans-Euphrates:

Greetings.

[18]The letter you sent us has been read and translated in my presence. [19]I issued an order and a search was made, and it was found that this city has a long history of revolt against kings and has been a place of rebellion and sedition. [20]Jerusalem has had powerful kings ruling over the whole of Trans-Euphrates, and taxes, tribute and duty were paid to them. [21]Now issue an order to these men to stop work, so that this city will not be rebuilt until I so order. [22]Be careful not to neglect this matter. Why let this threat grow, to the detriment of the royal interests?

[23]As soon as the copy of the letter of King Artaxerxes was read to Rehum and Shimshai the secretary and their associates, they went immediately to the Jews in Jerusalem and compelled them by force to stop.

[24]Thus the work on the house of God in Jerusalem came to a standstill until the second year of the reign of Darius king of Persia.

Tattenai's Letter to Darius

5 Now Haggai the prophet and Zechariah the prophet, a descendant of Iddo, prophesied to the Jews in Judah and Jerusalem in the name of the God of Israel, who was over them.

[2]Then Zerubbabel son of Shealtiel and Jeshua son of Jozadak set to work to rebuild the house of God in Jerusalem. And the prophets of God were with them, helping them.

[3]At that time Tattenai, governor of Trans-Euphrates, and Shethar-Bozenai and their associates went to them and asked, "Who authorized you to rebuild this temple and restore this structure?" [4]They also asked, "What are the names of the men constructing this building?"[a] [5]But the eye of their God was watching over the elders of the Jews, and they were not stopped until a report could go to Darius and his written reply be received.

[6]This is a copy of the letter that Tattenai, governor of Trans-Euphrates, and Shethar-Bozenai and their associates, the officials of Trans-Euphrates, sent to King Darius. [7]The report they sent him read as follows:

To King Darius:

Cordial greetings.

[8]The king should know that we went to the district of Judah, to the temple of the great God. The people are building it with large stones and placing the timbers in the walls. The work is being carried on with diligence and is making rapid progress under their direction.

[9]We questioned the elders and asked them, "Who authorized you to rebuild this temple and restore this structure?" [10]We also asked them their names, so that we could write down the names of their leaders for your information.

[11]This is the answer they gave us:

"We are the servants of the God of heaven and earth, and we are rebuilding the temple that was built many years ago, one that a great king of Israel built and finished. [12]But because our fathers angered the God of heaven, he handed them over to Nebuchadnezzar the Chaldean, king of Babylon, who destroyed this temple and deported the people to Babylon.

[13]"However, in the first year of Cyrus king of Babylon, King Cyrus

<hr/>

a 4 See Septuagint; Aramaic *We told them the names of the men constructing this building.*

issued a decree to rebuild this house of God. [14]He even removed from the temple[a] of Babylon the gold and silver articles of the house of God, which Nebuchadnezzar had taken from the temple in Jerusalem and brought to the temple[a] in Babylon.

"Then King Cyrus gave them to a man named Sheshbazzar, whom he had appointed governor, [15]and he told him, 'Take these articles and go and deposit them in the temple in Jerusalem. And rebuild the house of God on its site.' [16]So this Sheshbazzar came and laid the foundations of the house of God in Jerusalem. From that day to the present it has been under construction but is not yet finished."

[17]Now if it pleases the king, let a search be made in the royal archives of Babylon to see if King Cyrus did in fact issue a decree to rebuild this house of God in Jerusalem. Then let the king send us his decision in this matter.

The Decree of Darius

6 King Darius then issued an order, and they searched in the archives stored in the treasury at Babylon. [2]A scroll was found in the citadel of Ecbatana in the province of Media, and this was written on it:

Memorandum:

[3]In the first year of King Cyrus, the king issued a decree concerning the temple of God in Jerusalem:

Let the temple be rebuilt as a place to present sacrifices, and let its foundations be laid. It is to be ninety feet[b] high and ninety feet wide, [4]with three courses of large stones and one of timbers. The costs are to be paid by the royal treasury. [5]Also, the gold and silver articles of the house of God, which Nebuchadnezzar took from the temple in Jerusalem and brought to Babylon, are to be returned to their places in the temple in Jerusalem; they are to be deposited in the house of God.

[6]Now then, Tattenai, governor of Trans-Euphrates, and Shethar-Bozenai and you, their fellow officials of that province, stay away from there. [7]Do not interfere with the work on this temple of God. Let the governor of the Jews and the Jewish elders rebuild this house of God on its site.

[8]Moreover, I hereby decree what you are to do for these elders of the Jews in the construction of this house of God:

The expenses of these men are to be fully paid out of the royal treasury, from the revenues of Trans-Euphrates, so that the work will not stop. [9]Whatever is needed—young bulls, rams, male lambs for burnt offerings to the God of heaven, and wheat, salt, wine and oil, as requested by the priests in Jerusalem—must be given them daily without fail, [10]so that they may offer sacrifices pleasing to the God of heaven and pray for the well-being of the king and his sons.

[11]Furthermore, I decree that if anyone changes this edict, a beam is to be pulled from his house and he is to be lifted up and impaled on it. And for this crime his house is to be made a pile of rubble. [12]May God, who has caused his Name to dwell there, overthrow any king or people who lifts a hand to change this decree or to destroy this temple in Jerusalem.

I Darius have decreed it. Let it be carried out with diligence.

Completion and Dedication of the Temple

[13]Then, because of the decree King Darius had sent, Tattenai, governor of Trans-Euphrates, and Shethar-Bozenai and their associates carried it out with diligence. [14]So the elders of the Jews continued to build and prosper under the preaching of Haggai the prophet and Zechariah, a descendant of Iddo. They finished building the temple according to the command of the God of Israel and the decrees of Cyrus, Darius and Artaxerxes, kings of Persia. [15]The temple was

---

a 14 Or palace   b 3 Aramaic sixty cubits (about 27 meters)

completed on the third day of the month Adar, in the sixth year of the reign of King Darius.

16Then the people of Israel—the priests, the Levites and the rest of the exiles—celebrated the dedication of the house of God with joy. 17For the dedication of this house of God they offered a hundred bulls, two hundred rams, four hundred male lambs and, as a sin offering for all Israel, twelve male goats, one for each of the tribes of Israel. 18And they installed the priests in their divisions and the Levites in their groups for the service of God at Jerusalem, according to what is written in the Book of Moses.

The Passover

19On the fourteenth day of the first month, the exiles celebrated the Passover. 20The priests and Levites had purified themselves and were all ceremonially clean. The Levites slaughtered the Passover lamb for all the exiles, for their brothers the priests and for themselves. 21So the Israelites who had returned from the exile ate it, together with all who had separated themselves from the unclean practices of their Gentile neighbors in order to seek the LORD, the God of Israel. 22For seven days they celebrated with joy the Feast of Unleavened Bread, because the LORD had filled them with joy by changing the attitude of the king of Assyria, so that he assisted them in the work on the house of God, the God of Israel.

Ezra Comes to Jerusalem

7 After these things, during the reign of Artaxerxes king of Persia, Ezra son of Seraiah, the son of Azariah, the son of Hilkiah, 2the son of Shallum, the son of Zadok, the son of Ahitub, 3the son of Amariah, the son of Azariah, the son of Meraioth, 4the son of Zerahiah, the son of Uzzi, the son of Bukki, 5the son of Abishua, the son of Phinehas, the son of Eleazar, the son of Aaron the chief priest— 6this Ezra came up from Babylon. He was a teacher well versed in the Law of Moses, which the LORD, the God of Israel, had given. The king had granted him everything he asked, for the hand of the

LORD his God was on him. 7Some of the Israelites, including priests, Levites, singers, gatekeepers and temple servants, also came up to Jerusalem in the seventh year of King Artaxerxes.

8Ezra arrived in Jerusalem in the fifth month of the seventh year of the king. 9He had begun his journey from Babylon on the first day of the first month, and he arrived in Jerusalem on the first day of the fifth month, for the gracious hand of his God was on him. 10For Ezra had devoted himself to the study and observance of the Law of the LORD, and to teaching its decrees and laws in Israel.

King Artaxerxes' Letter to Ezra

11This is a copy of the letter King Artaxerxes had given to Ezra the priest and teacher, a man learned in matters concerning the commands and decrees of the LORD for Israel:

12*a* Artaxerxes, king of kings,

To Ezra the priest, a teacher of the Law of the God of heaven:

Greetings.

13Now I decree that any of the Israelites in my kingdom, including priests and Levites, who wish to go to Jerusalem with you, may go. 14You are sent by the king and his seven advisers to inquire about Judah and Jerusalem with regard to the Law of your God, which is in your hand. 15Moreover, you are to take with you the silver and gold that the king and his advisers have freely given to the God of Israel, whose dwelling is in Jerusalem, 16together with all the silver and gold you may obtain from the province of Babylon, as well as the freewill offerings of the people and priests for the temple of their God in Jerusalem. 17With this money be sure to buy bulls, rams and male lambs, together with their grain offerings and drink offerings, and sacrifice them on the altar of the temple of your God in Jerusalem.

18You and your brother Jews may then do whatever seems best with the rest of the silver and gold, in

---

a 12 The text of Ezra 7:12–26 is in Aramaic.

accordance with the will of your God. ¹⁹Deliver to the God of Jerusalem all the articles entrusted to you for worship in the temple of your God. ²⁰And anything else needed for the temple of your God that you may have occasion to supply, you may provide from the royal treasury.

²¹Now I, King Artaxerxes, order all the treasurers of Trans-Euphrates to provide with diligence whatever Ezra the priest, a teacher of the Law of the God of heaven, may ask of you— ²²up to a hundred talents*a* of silver, a hundred cors*b* of wheat, a hundred baths*c* of wine, a hundred baths*c* of olive oil, and salt without limit. ²³Whatever the God of heaven has prescribed, let it be done with diligence for the temple of the God of heaven. Why should there be wrath against the realm of the king and of his sons? ²⁴You are also to know that you have no authority to impose taxes, tribute or duty on any of the priests, Levites, singers, gatekeepers, temple servants or other workers at this house of God.

²⁵And you, Ezra, in accordance with the wisdom of your God, which you possess, appoint magistrates and judges to administer justice to all the people of Trans-Euphrates—all who know the laws of your God. And you are to teach any who do not know them. ²⁶Whoever does not obey the law of your God and the law of the king must surely be punished by death, banishment, confiscation of property, or imprisonment.

²⁷Praise be to the LORD, the God of our fathers, who has put it into the king's heart to bring honor to the house of the LORD in Jerusalem in this way ²⁸and who has extended his good favor to me before the king and his advisers and all the king's powerful officials. Because the hand of the LORD my God was on me, I took courage and gathered leading men from Israel to go up with me.

List of the Family Heads Returning With Ezra

8 These are the family heads and those registered with them who came up with me from Babylon during the reign of King Artaxerxes:

²of the descendants of Phinehas, Gershom;

of the descendants of Ithamar, Daniel;

of the descendants of David, Hattush ³of the descendants of Shecaniah;

of the descendants of Parosh, Zechariah, and with him were registered 150 men;

⁴of the descendants of Pahath-Moab, Eliehoenai son of Zerahiah, and with him 200 men;

⁵of the descendants of Zattu,*d* Shecaniah son of Jahaziel, and with him 300 men;

⁶of the descendants of Adin, Ebed son of Jonathan, and with him 50 men;

⁷of the descendants of Elam, Jeshaiah son of Athaliah, and with him 70 men;

⁸of the descendants of Shephatiah, Zebadiah son of Michael, and with him 80 men;

⁹of the descendants of Joab, Obadiah son of Jehiel, and with him 218 men;

¹⁰of the descendants of Bani,*e* Shelomith son of Josiphiah, and with him 160 men;

¹¹of the descendants of Bebai, Zechariah son of Bebai, and with him 28 men;

¹²of the descendants of Azgad, Johanan son of Hakkatan, and with him 110 men;

¹³of the descendants of Adonikam, the last ones, whose names were Eliphelet, Jeuel and Shemaiah, and with them 60 men;

¹⁴of the descendants of Bigvai, Uthai and Zaccur, and with them 70 men.

---

a 22 That is, about 3 3/4 tons (about 3.4 metric tons)   *b 22* That is, probably about 600 bushels (about 22 kiloliters)   *c 22* That is, probably about 600 gallons (about 2.2 kiloliters)   *d 5* Some Septuagint manuscripts (also 1 Esdras 8:32); Hebrew does not have *Zattu.*   *e 10* Some Septuagint manuscripts (also 1 Esdras 8:36); Hebrew does not have *Bani.*

The Return to Jerusalem

15I assembled them at the canal that flows toward Ahava, and we camped there three days. When I checked among the people and the priests, I found no Levites there. 16So I summoned Eliezer, Ariel, Shemaiah, Elnathan, Jarib, Elnathan, Nathan, Zechariah and Meshullam, who were leaders, and Joiarib and Elnathan, who were men of learning, 17and I sent them to Iddo, the leader in Casiphia. I told them what to say to Iddo and his kinsmen, the temple servants in Casiphia, so that they might bring attendants to us for the house of our God. 18Because the gracious hand of our God was on us, they brought us Sherebiah, a capable man, from the descendants of Mahli son of Levi, the son of Israel, and Sherebiah's sons and brothers, 18 men; 19and Hashabiah, together with Jeshaiah from the descendants of Merari, and his brothers and nephews, 20 men. 20They also brought 220 of the temple servants—a body that David and the officials had established to assist the Levites. All were registered by name.

21There, by the Ahava Canal, I proclaimed a fast, so that we might humble ourselves before our God and ask him for a safe journey for us and our children, with all our possessions. 22I was ashamed to ask the king for soldiers and horsemen to protect us from enemies on the road, because we had told the king, "The gracious hand of our God is on everyone who looks to him, but his great anger is against all who forsake him." 23So we fasted and petitioned our God about this, and he answered our prayer.

24Then I set apart twelve of the leading priests, together with Sherebiah, Hashabiah and ten of their brothers, 25and I weighed out to them the offering of silver and gold and the articles that the king, his advisers, his officials and all Israel present there had donated for the house of our God. 26I weighed out to them 650 talents*a* of silver, silver articles weighing 100 talents,*b* 100 talents*b* of gold, 2720 bowls of gold valued at 1,000 darics,*c* and two fine articles of polished bronze, as precious as gold.

28I said to them, "You as well as these articles are consecrated to the LORD. The silver and gold are a freewill offering to the LORD, the God of your fathers. 29Guard them carefully until you weigh them out in the chambers of the house of the LORD in Jerusalem before the leading priests and the Levites and the family heads of Israel." 30Then the priests and Levites received the silver and gold and sacred articles that had been weighed out to be taken to the house of our God in Jerusalem.

31On the twelfth day of the first month we set out from the Ahava Canal to go to Jerusalem. The hand of our God was on us, and he protected us from enemies and bandits along the way. 32So we arrived in Jerusalem, where we rested three days.

33On the fourth day, in the house of our God, we weighed out the silver and gold and the sacred articles into the hands of Meremoth son of Uriah, the priest. Eleazar son of Phinehas was with him, and so were the Levites Jozabad son of Jeshua and Noadiah son of Binnui. 34Everything was accounted for by number and weight, and the entire weight was recorded at that time.

35Then the exiles who had returned from captivity sacrificed burnt offerings to the God of Israel: twelve bulls for all Israel, ninety-six rams, seventy-seven male lambs and, as a sin offering, twelve male goats. All this was a burnt offering to the LORD. 36They also delivered the king's orders to the royal satraps and to the governors of Trans-Euphrates, who then gave assistance to the people and to the house of God.

Ezra's Prayer About Intermarriage

9 After these things had been done, the leaders came to me and said, "The people of Israel, including the priests and the Levites, have not kept themselves separate from the neighboring peoples with their detestable practices, like those of the Canaanites, Hittites, Perizzites, Jebusites, Ammonites, Moabites, Egyptians and Amorites. 2They have taken some of their daughters as wives for themselves and their

a 26 That is, about 25 tons (about 22 metric tons)   *b 26* That is, about 3 3/4 tons (about 3.4 metric tons)   *c 27* That is, about 19 pounds (about 8.5 kilograms)

sons, and have mingled the holy race with the peoples around them. And the leaders and officials have led the way in this unfaithfulness."

³When I heard this, I tore my tunic and cloak, pulled hair from my head and beard and sat down appalled. ⁴Then everyone who trembled at the words of the God of Israel gathered around me because of this unfaithfulness of the exiles. And I sat there appalled until the evening sacrifice.

⁵Then, at the evening sacrifice, I rose from my self-abasement, with my tunic and cloak torn, and fell on my knees with my hands spread out to the LORD my God ⁶and prayed:

"O my God, I am too ashamed and disgraced to lift up my face to you, my God, because our sins are higher than our heads and our guilt has reached to the heavens. ⁷From the days of our forefathers until now, our guilt has been great. Because of our sins, we and our kings and our priests have been subjected to the sword and captivity, to pillage and humiliation at the hand of foreign kings, as it is today.

⁸"But now, for a brief moment, the LORD our God has been gracious in leaving us a remnant and giving us a firm place in his sanctuary, and so our God gives light to our eyes and a little relief in our bondage. ⁹Though we are slaves, our God has not deserted us in our bondage. He has shown us kindness in the sight of the kings of Persia: He has granted us new life to rebuild the house of our God and repair its ruins, and he has given us a wall of protection in Judah and Jerusalem.

¹⁰"But now, O our God, what can we say after this? For we have disregarded the commands ¹¹you gave through your servants the prophets when you said: 'The land you are entering to possess is a land polluted by the corruption of its peoples. By their detestable practices they have filled it with their impurity from one end to the other. ¹²Therefore, do not give your daughters in marriage to their sons or take their daughters for your sons. Do not

seek a treaty of friendship with them at any time, that you may be strong and eat the good things of the land and leave it to your children as an everlasting inheritance.'

¹³"What has happened to us is a result of our evil deeds and our great guilt, and yet, our God, you have punished us less than our sins have deserved and have given us a remnant like this. ¹⁴Shall we again break your commands and intermarry with the peoples who commit such detestable practices? Would you not be angry enough with us to destroy us, leaving us no remnant or survivor? ¹⁵O LORD, God of Israel, you are righteous! We are left this day as a remnant. Here we are before you in our guilt, though because of it not one of us can stand in your presence."

The People's Confession of Sin

10 While Ezra was praying and confessing, weeping and throwing himself down before the house of God, a large crowd of Israelites—men, women and children—gathered around him. They too wept bitterly. ²Then Shecaniah son of Jehiel, one of the descendants of Elam, said to Ezra, "We have been unfaithful to our God by marrying foreign women from the peoples around us. But in spite of this, there is still hope for Israel. ³Now let us make a covenant before our God to send away all these women and their children, in accordance with the counsel of my lord and of those who fear the commands of our God. Let it be done according to the Law. ⁴Rise up; this matter is in your hands. We will support you, so take courage and do it."

⁵So Ezra rose up and put the leading priests and Levites and all Israel under oath to do what had been suggested. And they took the oath. ⁶Then Ezra withdrew from before the house of God and went to the room of Jehohanan son of Eliashib. While he was there, he ate no food and drank no water, because he continued to mourn over the unfaithfulness of the exiles.

⁷A proclamation was then issued throughout Judah and Jerusalem for all

the exiles to assemble in Jerusalem. ⁸Anyone who failed to appear within three days would forfeit all his property, in accordance with the decision of the officials and elders, and would himself be expelled from the assembly of the exiles.

⁹Within the three days, all the men of Judah and Benjamin had gathered in Jerusalem. And on the twentieth day of the ninth month, all the people were sitting in the square before the house of God, greatly distressed by the occasion and because of the rain. ¹⁰Then Ezra the priest stood up and said to them, "You

have been unfaithful; you have married foreign women, adding to Israel's guilt. ¹¹Now make confession to the LORD, the God of your fathers, and do his will. Separate yourselves from the peoples around you and from your foreign wives."

¹²The whole assembly responded with a loud voice: "You are right! We must do as you say. ¹³But there are many people here and it is the rainy season; so we cannot stand outside. Besides, this matter cannot be taken care of in a day or two, because we have sinned greatly in this thing. ¹⁴Let our officials act for the whole assembly.

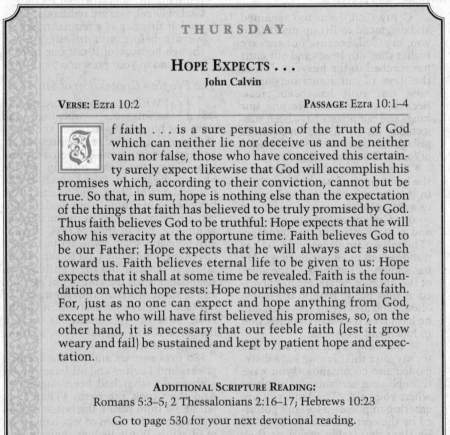

THURSDAY

HOPE EXPECTS . . .
John Calvin

VERSE: Ezra 10:2   **PASSAGE: Ezra 10:1–4**

f faith . . . is a sure persuasion of the truth of God which can neither lie nor deceive us and be neither vain nor false, those who have conceived this certainty surely expect likewise that God will accomplish his promises which, according to their conviction, cannot but be true. So that, in sum, hope is nothing else than the expectation of the things that faith has believed to be truly promised by God. Thus faith believes God to be truthful: Hope expects that he will show his veracity at the opportune time. Faith believes God to be our Father: Hope expects that he will always act as such toward us. Faith believes eternal life to be given to us: Hope expects that it shall at some time be revealed. Faith is the foundation on which hope rests: Hope nourishes and maintains faith. For, just as no one can expect and hope anything from God, except he who will have first believed his promises, so, on the other hand, it is necessary that our feeble faith (lest it grow weary and fail) be sustained and kept by patient hope and expectation.

ADDITIONAL SCRIPTURE READING:
Romans 5:3–5; 2 Thessalonians 2:16–17; Hebrews 10:23

Go to page 530 for your next devotional reading.

1500   1700

Then let everyone in our towns who has married a foreign woman come at a set time, along with the elders and judges of each town, until the fierce anger of our God in this matter is turned away from us." [15]Only Jonathan son of Asahel and Jahzeiah son of Tikvah, supported by Meshullam and Shabbethai the Levite, opposed this.

[16]So the exiles did as was proposed. Ezra the priest selected men who were family heads, one from each family division, and all of them designated by name. On the first day of the tenth month they sat down to investigate the cases, [17]and by the first day of the first month they finished dealing with all the men who had married foreign women.

Those Guilty of Intermarriage

[18]Among the descendants of the priests, the following had married foreign women:

From the descendants of Jeshua son of Jozadak, and his brothers: Maaseiah, Eliezer, Jarib and Gedaliah. [19](They all gave their hands in pledge to put away their wives, and for their guilt they each presented a ram from the flock as a guilt offering.)

[20]From the descendants of Immer:
Hanani and Zebadiah.

[21]From the descendants of Harim:
Maaseiah, Elijah, Shemaiah, Jehiel and Uzziah.

[22]From the descendants of Pashhur:
Elioenai, Maaseiah, Ishmael, Nethanel, Jozabad and Elasah.

[23]Among the Levites:

Jozabad, Shimei, Kelaiah (that is, Kelita), Pethahiah, Judah and Eliezer.

[24]From the singers:
Eliashib.

From the gatekeepers:
Shallum, Telem and Uri.

[25]And among the other Israelites:

From the descendants of Parosh:
Ramiah, Izziah, Malkijah, Mijamin, Eleazar, Malkijah and Benaiah.

[26]From the descendants of Elam:
Mattaniah, Zechariah, Jehiel, Abdi, Jeremoth and Elijah.

[27]From the descendants of Zattu:
Elioenai, Eliashib, Mattaniah, Jeremoth, Zabad and Aziza.

[28]From the descendants of Bebai:
Jehohanan, Hananiah, Zabbai and Athlai.

[29]From the descendants of Bani:
Meshullam, Malluch, Adaiah, Jashub, Sheal and Jeremoth.

[30]From the descendants of Pahath-Moab:
Adna, Kelal, Benaiah, Maaseiah, Mattaniah, Bezalel, Binnui and Manasseh.

[31]From the descendants of Harim:
Eliezer, Ishijah, Malkijah, Shemaiah, Shimeon, [32]Benjamin, Malluch and Shemariah.

[33]From the descendants of Hashum:
Mattenai, Mattattah, Zabad, Eliphelet, Jeremai, Manasseh and Shimei.

[34]From the descendants of Bani:
Maadai, Amram, Uel, [35]Benaiah, Bedeiah, Keluhi, [36]Vaniah, Meremoth, Eliashib, [37]Mattaniah, Mattenai and Jaasu.

[38]From the descendants of Binnui:[a]
Shimei, [39]Shelemiah, Nathan, Adaiah, [40]Macnadebai, Shashai, Sharai, [41]Azarel, Shelemiah, Shemariah, [42]Shallum, Amariah and Joseph.

[43]From the descendants of Nebo:
Jeiel, Mattithiah, Zabad, Zebina, Jaddai, Joel and Benaiah.

[44]All these had married foreign women, and some of them had children by these wives.[b]

---

[a] 37,38 See Septuagint (also 1 Esdras 9:34); Hebrew Jaasu [38]and Bani and Binnui.   [b] 44 Or and they sent them away with their children

NEHEMIAH

The Book of Nehemiah continues the history of the Jews
who returned from exile in
Babylon. Nehemiah went to Jerusalem
in 445 b.c. and led the people in repairing the walls. With Ezra he provided
leadership for the people. A recurring
theme of this book is the description
of the importance of prayer to Nehemiah. As you read this book, learn
from Nehemiah's example of balanc-
ing spirituality with down-to-earth
action.

Nehemiah's Prayer

1 The words of Nehemiah son of
Hacaliah:

In the month of Kislev in the twentieth year, while I was in the citadel of
Susa, ²Hanani, one of my brothers, came
from Judah with some other men, and I
questioned them about the Jewish remnant that survived the exile, and also
about Jerusalem.

³They said to me, "Those who survived the exile and are back in the province are in great trouble and disgrace. The
wall of Jerusalem is broken down, and its
gates have been burned with fire."

⁴When I heard these things, I sat down
and wept. For some days I mourned and
fasted and prayed before the God of
heaven. ⁵Then I said:

"O Lord, God of heaven, the
great and awesome God, who keeps
his covenant of love with those who
love him and obey his commands,
⁶let your ear be attentive and your
eyes open to hear the prayer your
servant is praying before you day
and night for your servants, the people of Israel. I confess the sins we
Israelites, including myself and my
father's house, have committed
against you. ⁷We have acted very
wickedly toward you. We have not
obeyed the commands, decrees and
laws you gave your servant Moses.

⁸"Remember the instruction
you gave your servant Moses, saying, 'If you are unfaithful, I will
scatter you among the nations,
⁹but if you return to me and obey

my commands, then even if your exiled people are at the farthest horizon, I will gather them from there and bring them to the place I have chosen as a dwelling for my Name.'

10"They are your servants and your people, whom you redeemed by your great strength and your mighty hand. 11O Lord, let your ear be attentive to the prayer of this your servant and to the prayer of your servants who delight in revering your name. Give your servant success today by granting him favor in the presence of this man."

I was cupbearer to the king.

MORE THINGS ARE WROUGHT BY PRAYER THAN THIS WORLD DREAMS OF. —Alfred, Lord Tennyson

---

Artaxerxes Sends Nehemiah to Jerusalem

2 In the month of Nisan in the twentieth year of King Artaxerxes, when wine was brought for him, I took the wine and gave it to the king. I had not been sad in his presence before; 2so the king asked me, "Why does your face look so sad when you are not ill? This can be nothing but sadness of heart."

I was very much afraid, 3but I said to the king, "May the king live forever! Why should my face not look sad when the city where my fathers are buried lies in ruins, and its gates have been destroyed by fire?"

4The king said to me, "What is it you want?"

Then I prayed to the God of heaven, 5and I answered the king, "If it pleases the king and if your servant has found favor in his sight, let him send me to the city in Judah where my fathers are buried so that I can rebuild it."

6Then the king, with the queen sitting beside him, asked me, "How long will your journey take, and when will you get back?" It pleased the king to send me; so I set a time.

7I also said to him, "If it pleases the king, may I have letters to the governors of Trans-Euphrates, so that they will provide me safe-conduct until I arrive in Judah? 8And may I have a letter to Asaph, keeper of the king's forest, so he will give me timber to make beams for the gates of the citadel by the temple and for the city wall and for the residence I will occupy?" And because the gracious hand of my God was upon me, the king granted my requests. 9So I went to the governors of Trans-Euphrates and gave them the king's letters. The king had also sent army officers and cavalry with me.

10When Sanballat the Horonite and Tobiah the Ammonite official heard about this, they were very much disturbed that someone had come to promote the welfare of the Israelites.

Nehemiah Inspects Jerusalem's Walls

11I went to Jerusalem, and after staying there three days 12I set out during the night with a few men. I had not told anyone what my God had put in my heart to do for Jerusalem. There were no mounts with me except the one I was riding on.

13By night I went out through the Valley Gate toward the Jackal[a] Well and the Dung Gate, examining the walls of Jerusalem, which had been broken down, and its gates, which had been destroyed by fire. 14Then I moved on toward the Fountain Gate and the King's Pool, but there was not enough room for my mount to get through; 15so I went up the valley by night, examining the wall. Finally, I turned back and reentered through the Valley Gate. 16The officials did not know where I had gone or what I was doing, because as yet I had said nothing to the Jews or the priests or nobles or officials or any others who would be doing the work.

17Then I said to them, "You see the trouble we are in: Jerusalem lies in ruins, and its gates have been burned with fire. Come, let us rebuild the wall of Jerusalem, and we will no longer be in

---

a 13 Or Serpent or Fig

disgrace." ¹⁸I also told them about the gracious hand of my God upon me and what the king had said to me.

They replied, "Let us start rebuilding." So they began this good work.

¹⁹But when Sanballat the Horonite, Tobiah the Ammonite official and Geshem the Arab heard about it, they mocked and ridiculed us. "What is this you are doing?" they asked. "Are you rebelling against the king?"

²⁰I answered them by saying, "The God of heaven will give us success. We his servants will start rebuilding, but as for you, you have no share in Jerusalem or any claim or historic right to it."

Builders of the Wall

3 Eliashib the high priest and his fellow priests went to work and rebuilt the Sheep Gate. They dedicated it and set its doors in place, building as far as the Tower of the Hundred, which they dedicated, and as far as the Tower of Hananel. ²The men of Jericho built the adjoining section, and Zaccur son of Imri built next to them.

³The Fish Gate was rebuilt by the sons of Hassenaah. They laid its beams and put its doors and bolts and bars in place. ⁴Meremoth son of Uriah, the son of Hakkoz, repaired the next section. Next to him Meshullam son of Berekiah, the son of Meshezabel, made repairs, and next to him Zadok son of Baana also made repairs. ⁵The next section was repaired by the men of Tekoa, but their nobles would not put their shoulders to the work under their supervisors.ᵃ

⁶The Jeshanahᵇ Gate was repaired by Joiada son of Paseah and Meshullam son of Besodeiah. They laid its beams and put its doors and bolts and bars in place. ⁷Next to them, repairs were made by men from Gibeon and Mizpah—Melatiah of Gibeon and Jadon of Meronoth—places under the authority of the governor of Trans-Euphrates. ⁸Uzziel son of Harhaiah, one of the goldsmiths, repaired the next section;

and Hananiah, one of the perfume-makers, made repairs next to that. They restoredᶜ Jerusalem as far as the Broad Wall. ⁹Rephaiah son of Hur, ruler of a half-district of Jerusalem, repaired the next section. ¹⁰Adjoining this, Jedaiah son of Harumaph made repairs opposite his house, and Hattush son of Hashabneiah made repairs next to him. ¹¹Malkijah son of Harim and Hasshub son of Pahath-Moab repaired another section and the Tower of the Ovens. ¹²Shallum son of Hallohesh, ruler of a half-district of Jerusalem, repaired the next section with the help of his daughters.

¹³The Valley Gate was repaired by Hanun and the residents of Zanoah. They rebuilt it and put its doors and bolts and bars in place. They also repaired five hundred yardsᵈ of the wall as far as the Dung Gate.

¹⁴The Dung Gate was repaired by Malkijah son of Recab, ruler of the district of Beth Hakkerem. He rebuilt it and put its doors and bolts and bars in place.

¹⁵The Fountain Gate was repaired by Shallun son of Col-Hozeh, ruler of the district of Mizpah. He rebuilt it, roofing it over and putting its doors and bolts and bars in place. He also repaired the wall of the Pool of Siloam,ᵉ by the King's Garden, as far as the steps going down from the City of David. ¹⁶Beyond him, Nehemiah son of Azbuk, ruler of a half-district of Beth Zur, made repairs up to a point opposite the tombsᶠ of David, as far as the artificial pool and the House of the Heroes.

¹⁷Next to him, the repairs were made by the Levites under Rehum son of Bani. Beside him, Hashabiah, ruler of half the district of Keilah, carried out repairs for his district. ¹⁸Next to him, the repairs were made by their countrymen under Binnuiᵍ son of Henadad, ruler of the other half-district of Keilah. ¹⁹Next to him, Ezer son of Jeshua, ruler of Mizpah, repaired another section, from a point facing the ascent to the armory as far as

ᵃ 5 Or *their Lord* or *the governor*   ᵇ 6 Or *Old*   ᶜ 8 Or *They left out part of*   ᵈ 13 Hebrew *a thousand cubits* (about 450 meters)   ᵉ 15 Hebrew *Shelah*, a variant of *Shiloah*, that is, Siloam   ᶠ 16 Hebrew; Septuagint, some Vulgate manuscripts and Syriac *tomb*   ᵍ 18 Two Hebrew manuscripts and Syriac (see also Septuagint and verse 24); most Hebrew manuscripts *Bavvai*

the angle. 20Next to him, Baruch son of Zabbai zealously repaired another section, from the angle to the entrance of the house of Eliashib the high priest. 21Next to him, Meremoth son of Uriah, the son of Hakkoz, repaired another section, from the entrance of Eliashib's house to the end of it.

22The repairs next to him were made by the priests from the surrounding region. 23Beyond them, Benjamin and Hasshub made repairs in front of their house; and next to them, Azariah son of Maaseiah, the son of Ananiah, made repairs beside his house. 24Next to him, Binnui son of Henadad repaired another section, from Azariah's house to the angle and the corner, 25and Palal son of Uzai worked opposite the angle and the tower projecting from the upper palace near the court of the guard. Next to him, Pedaiah son of Parosh 26and the temple servants living on the hill of Ophel made repairs up to a point opposite the Water Gate toward the east and the projecting tower. 27Next to them, the men of Tekoa repaired another section, from the great projecting tower to the wall of Ophel.

28Above the Horse Gate, the priests made repairs, each in front of his own house. 29Next to them, Zadok son of Immer made repairs opposite his house. Next to him, Shemaiah son of Shecaniah, the guard at the East Gate, made repairs. 30Next to him, Hananiah son of Shelemiah, and Hanun, the sixth son of Zalaph, repaired another section. Next to them, Meshullam son of Berekiah made repairs opposite his living quarters. 31Next to him, Malkijah, one of the goldsmiths, made repairs as far as the house of the temple servants and the merchants, opposite the Inspection Gate, and as far as the room above the corner; 32and between the room above the corner and the Sheep Gate the goldsmiths and merchants made repairs.

Opposition to the Rebuilding

4 When Sanballat heard that we were rebuilding the wall, he became angry and was greatly incensed.

He ridiculed the Jews, 2and in the presence of his associates and the army of Samaria, he said, "What are those feeble Jews doing? Will they restore their wall? Will they offer sacrifices? Will they finish in a day? Can they bring the stones back to life from those heaps of rubble—burned as they are?"

3Tobiah the Ammonite, who was at his side, said, "What they are building—if even a fox climbed up on it, he would break down their wall of stones!"

4Hear us, O our God, for we are despised. Turn their insults back on their own heads. Give them over as plunder in a land of captivity. 5Do not cover up their guilt or blot out their sins from your sight, for they have thrown insults in the face of*a* the builders.

6So we rebuilt the wall till all of it reached half its height, for the people worked with all their heart.

7But when Sanballat, Tobiah, the Arabs, the Ammonites and the men of Ashdod heard that the repairs to Jerusalem's walls had gone ahead and that the gaps were being closed, they were very angry. 8They all plotted together to come and fight against Jerusalem and stir up trouble against it. 9But we prayed to our God and posted a guard day and night to meet this threat.

10Meanwhile, the people in Judah said, "The strength of the laborers is giving out, and there is so much rubble that we cannot rebuild the wall."

11Also our enemies said, "Before they know it or see us, we will be right there among them and will kill them and put an end to the work."

12Then the Jews who lived near them came and told us ten times over, "Wherever you turn, they will attack us."

13Therefore I stationed some of the people behind the lowest points of the wall at the exposed places, posting them by families, with their swords, spears and bows. 14After I looked things over, I stood up and said to the nobles, the officials and the rest of the people, "Don't be afraid of them. Remember the Lord, who is great and awesome, and fight for

a 5 Or have provoked you to anger before

your brothers, your sons and your daughters, your wives and your homes."

¹⁵When our enemies heard that we were aware of their plot and that God had frustrated it, we all returned to the wall, each to his own work.

¹⁶From that day on, half of my men did the work, while the other half were equipped with spears, shields, bows and armor. The officers posted themselves behind all the people of Judah ¹⁷who were building the wall. Those who carried materials did their work with one hand and held a weapon in the other, ¹⁸and each of the builders wore his sword at his side as he worked. But the man who sounded the trumpet stayed with me.

¹⁹Then I said to the nobles, the officials and the rest of the people, "The work is extensive and spread out, and we are widely separated from each other along the wall. ²⁰Wherever you hear the sound of the trumpet, join us there. Our God will fight for us!"

²¹So we continued the work with half the men holding spears, from the first light of dawn till the stars came out. ²²At that time I also said to the people, "Have every man and his helper stay inside Jerusalem at night, so they can serve us as guards by night and workmen by day." ²³Neither I nor my brothers nor my men nor the guards with me took off our clothes; each had his weapon, even when he went for water.[a]

Nehemiah Helps the Poor

5 Now the men and their wives raised a great outcry against their Jewish brothers. ²Some were saying, "We and our sons and daughters are numerous; in order for us to eat and stay alive, we must get grain."

³Others were saying, "We are mortgaging our fields, our vineyards and our homes to get grain during the famine."

⁴Still others were saying, "We have had to borrow money to pay the king's tax on our fields and vineyards. ⁵Although we are of the same flesh and blood as our countrymen and though our sons are as good as theirs,

yet we have to subject our sons and daughters to slavery. Some of our daughters have already been enslaved, but we are powerless, because our fields and our vineyards belong to others."

⁶When I heard their outcry and these charges, I was very angry. ⁷I pondered them in my mind and then accused the nobles and officials. I told them, "You are exacting usury from your own countrymen!" So I called together a large meeting to deal with them ⁸and said: "As far as possible, we have bought back our Jewish brothers who were sold to the Gentiles. Now you are selling your brothers, only for them to be sold back to us!" They kept quiet, because they could find nothing to say.

⁹So I continued, "What you are doing is not right. Shouldn't you walk in the fear of our God to avoid the reproach of our Gentile enemies? ¹⁰I and my brothers and my men are also lending the people money and grain. But let the exacting of usury stop! ¹¹Give back to them immediately their fields, vineyards, olive groves and houses, and also the usury you are charging them—the hundredth part of the money, grain, new wine and oil."

¹²"We will give it back," they said. "And we will not demand anything more from them. We will do as you say."

Then I summoned the priests and made the nobles and officials take an oath to do what they had promised. ¹³I also shook out the folds of my robe and said, "In this way may God shake out of his house and possessions every man who does not keep this promise. So may such a man be shaken out and emptied!"

At this the whole assembly said, "Amen," and praised the LORD. And the people did as they had promised.

¹⁴Moreover, from the twentieth year of King Artaxerxes, when I was appointed to be their governor in the land of Judah, until his thirty-second year—twelve years—neither I nor my brothers ate the food allotted to the governor. ¹⁵But the earlier governors—those preceding me—placed a heavy burden on

---

a 23 The meaning of the Hebrew for this clause is uncertain.

the people and took forty shekels*a* of silver from them in addition to food and wine. Their assistants also lorded it over the people. But out of reverence for God I did not act like that. 16Instead, I devoted myself to the work on this wall. All my men were assembled there for the work; we*b* did not acquire any land.

17Furthermore, a hundred and fifty Jews and officials ate at my table, as well as those who came to us from the surrounding nations. 18Each day one ox, six choice sheep and some poultry were prepared for me, and every ten days an abundant supply of wine of all kinds. In spite of all this, I never demanded the food allotted to the governor, because the demands were heavy on these people.

19Remember me with favor, O my God, for all I have done for these people.

Further Opposition to the Rebuilding

6 When word came to Sanballat, Tobiah, Geshem the Arab and the rest of our enemies that I had rebuilt the wall and not a gap was left in it—though up to that time I had not set the doors in the gates— 2Sanballat and Geshem sent me this message: "Come, let us meet together in one of the villages*c* on the plain of Ono."

But they were scheming to harm me; 3so I sent messengers to them with this reply: "I am carrying on a great project and cannot go down. Why should the work stop while I leave it and go down to you?" 4Four times they sent me the same message, and each time I gave them the same answer.

5Then, the fifth time, Sanballat sent his aide to me with the same message, and in his hand was an unsealed letter 6in which was written:

"It is reported among the nations—and Geshem*d* says it is true—that you and the Jews are plotting to revolt, and therefore you are building the wall. Moreover, according to these reports you are about to become their king 7and have even appointed prophets to make this proclamation about you

in Jerusalem: 'There is a king in Judah!' Now this report will get back to the king; so come, let us confer together."

8I sent him this reply: "Nothing like what you are saying is happening; you are just making it up out of your head."

9They were all trying to frighten us, thinking, "Their hands will get too weak for the work, and it will not be completed."

˻But I prayed,˼ "Now strengthen my hands."

10One day I went to the house of Shemaiah son of Delaiah, the son of Mehetabel, who was shut in at his home. He said, "Let us meet in the house of God, inside the temple, and let us close the temple doors, because men are coming to kill you—by night they are coming to kill you."

11But I said, "Should a man like me run away? Or should one like me go into the temple to save his life? I will not go!" 12I realized that God had not sent him, but that he had prophesied against me because Tobiah and Sanballat had hired him. 13He had been hired to intimidate me so that I would commit a sin by doing this, and then they would give me a bad name to discredit me.

14Remember Tobiah and Sanballat, O my God, because of what they have done; remember also the prophetess Noadiah and the rest of the prophets who have been trying to intimidate me.

The Completion of the Wall

15So the wall was completed on the twenty-fifth of Elul, in fifty-two days. 16When all our enemies heard about this, all the surrounding nations were afraid and lost their self-confidence, because they realized that this work had been done with the help of our God.

17Also, in those days the nobles of Judah were sending many letters to Tobiah, and replies from Tobiah kept coming to them. 18For many in Judah were under oath to him, since he was

---

a 15 That is, about 1 pound (about 0.5 kilogram)   *b* 16 Most Hebrew manuscripts; some Hebrew manuscripts, Septuagint, Vulgate and Syriac *I*   *c* 2 Or *in Kephirim*   *d* 6 Hebrew *Gashmu,* a variant of *Geshem*

son-in-law to Shecaniah son of Arah, and his son Jehohanan had married the daughter of Meshullam son of Berekiah. [19]Moreover, they kept reporting to me his good deeds and then telling him what I said. And Tobiah sent letters to intimidate me.

7 After the wall had been rebuilt and I had set the doors in place, the gatekeepers and the singers and the Levites were appointed. [2]I put in charge of Jerusalem my brother Hanani, along with[a] Hananiah the commander of the citadel, because he was a man of integri-

ty and feared God more than most men do. [3]I said to them, "The gates of Jerusalem are not to be opened until the sun is hot. While the gatekeepers are still on duty, have them shut the doors and bar them. Also appoint residents of Jerusalem as guards, some at their posts and some near their own houses."

The List of the Exiles Who Returned

[4]Now the city was large and spacious, but there were few people in it, and the houses had not yet been rebuilt. [5]So my God put it into my heart to assemble

[a] 2 Or *Hanani, that is,*

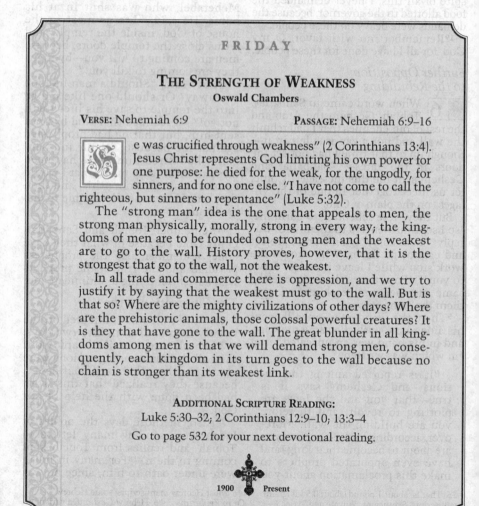

FRIDAY

THE STRENGTH OF WEAKNESS
Oswald Chambers

VERSE: Nehemiah 6:9   PASSAGE: Nehemiah 6:9–16

"e was crucified through weakness" (2 Corinthians 13:4). Jesus Christ represents God limiting his own power for one purpose: he died for the weak, for the ungodly, for sinners, and for no one else. "I have not come to call the righteous, but sinners to repentance" (Luke 5:32).

The "strong man" idea is the one that appeals to men, the strong man physically, morally, strong in every way; the kingdoms of men are to be founded on strong men and the weakest are to go to the wall. History proves, however, that it is the strongest that go to the wall, not the weakest.

In all trade and commerce there is oppression, and we try to justify it by saying that the weakest must go to the wall. But is that so? Where are the mighty civilizations of other days? Where are the prehistoric animals, those colossal powerful creatures? It is they that have gone to the wall. The great blunder in all kingdoms among men is that we will demand strong men, consequently, each kingdom in its turn goes to the wall because no chain is stronger than its weakest link.

ADDITIONAL SCRIPTURE READING:
Luke 5:30–32; 2 Corinthians 12:9–10; 13:3–4

Go to page 532 for your next devotional reading.

1900   Present

the nobles, the officials and the common people for registration by families. I found the genealogical record of those who had been the first to return. This is what I found written there:

⁶These are the people of the province who came up from the captivity of the exiles whom Nebuchadnezzar king of Babylon had taken captive (they returned to Jerusalem and Judah, each to his own town, ⁷in company with Zerubbabel, Jeshua, Nehemiah, Azariah, Raamiah, Nahamani, Mordecai, Bilshan, Mispereth, Bigvai, Nehum and Baanah):

The list of the men of Israel:

⁸ the descendants of Parosh	2,172
⁹ of Shephatiah	372
¹⁰ of Arah	652
¹¹ of Pahath-Moab (through the line of Jeshua and Joab)	2,818
¹² of Elam	1,254
¹³ of Zattu	845
¹⁴ of Zaccai	760
¹⁵ of Binnui	648
¹⁶ of Bebai	628
¹⁷ of Azgad	2,322
¹⁸ of Adonikam	667
¹⁹ of Bigvai	2,067
²⁰ of Adin	655
²¹ of Ater (through Hezekiah)	98
²² of Hashum	328
²³ of Bezai	324
²⁴ of Hariph	112
²⁵ of Gibeon	95
²⁶ the men of Bethlehem and Netophah	188
²⁷ of Anathoth	128
²⁸ of Beth Azmaveth	42
²⁹ of Kiriath Jearim, Kephirah and Beeroth	743
³⁰ of Ramah and Geba	621
³¹ of Micmash	122
³² of Bethel and Ai	123
³³ of the other Nebo	52
³⁴ of the other Elam	1,254
³⁵ of Harim	320
³⁶ of Jericho	345
³⁷ of Lod, Hadid and Ono	721
³⁸ of Senaah	3,930

³⁹The priests:

the descendants of Jedaiah

(through the family of Jeshua)	973
⁴⁰ of Immer	1,052
⁴¹ of Pashhur	1,247
⁴² of Harim	1,017

⁴³The Levites:

the descendants of Jeshua (through Kadmiel through the line of Hodaviah)	74

⁴⁴The singers:

the descendants of Asaph	148

⁴⁵The gatekeepers:

the descendants of Shallum, Ater, Talmon, Akkub, Hatita and Shobai	138

⁴⁶The temple servants:

the descendants of Ziha, Hasupha, Tabbaoth, ⁴⁷Keros, Sia, Padon, ⁴⁸Lebana, Hagaba, Shalmai, ⁴⁹Hanan, Giddel, Gahar, ⁵⁰Reaiah, Rezin, Nekoda, ⁵¹Gazzam, Uzza, Paseah, ⁵²Besai, Meunim, Nephussim, ⁵³Bakbuk, Hakupha, Harhur, ⁵⁴Bazluth, Mehida, Harsha, ⁵⁵Barkos, Sisera, Temah, ⁵⁶Neziah and Hatipha

⁵⁷The descendants of the servants of Solomon:

the descendants of Sotai, Sophereth, Perida, ⁵⁸Jaala, Darkon, Giddel, ⁵⁹Shephatiah, Hattil, Pokereth-Hazzebaim and Amon

⁶⁰ The temple servants and the descendants of the servants of Solomon	392

⁶¹The following came up from the towns of Tel Melah, Tel Harsha, Kerub, Addon and Immer, but they could not show that their families were descended from Israel:

⁶² the descendants of Delaiah, Tobiah and Nekoda	642

⁶³And from among the priests:

the descendants of Hobaiah, Hakkoz and Barzillai

WEEKEND

O FOR A THOUSAND TONGUES TO SING!

Charles Wesley

VERSE: Psalm 19:1   **PASSAGE:** Psalm 19:1–4

 for a thousand tongues to sing
My dear Redeemer's praise,
The glories of my God and King,
The triumphs of his grace!

My gracious Master and my God,
Assist me to proclaim
And spread through all the earth abroad
The honors of thy name.

Jesus! the name that charms our fears
And bids our sorrows cease;
'Tis music in the sinner's ears,
'Tis life and health and peace.

ADDITIONAL SCRIPTURE READING:
Psalms 35:28; 104:33–34

Go to page 534 for your next devotional reading.

1700   1900

(a man who had married a daughter of Barzillai the Gileadite and was called by that name).

64 These searched for their family records, but they could not find them and so were excluded from the priesthood as unclean. 65 The governor, therefore, ordered them not to eat any of the most sacred food until there should be a priest ministering with the Urim and Thummim.

66 The whole company numbered 42,360, 67 besides their 7,337 menservants and maidservants; and they also had 245 men and women singers. 68 There were 736 horses, 245 mules, *a* 69 435 camels and 6,720 donkeys.

70 Some of the heads of the families contributed to the work. The governor gave to the treasury 1,000 drachmas *b* of gold, 50 bowls and 530 garments for priests. 71 Some of the heads of the families gave to the treasury for the work 20,000 drachmas *c* of gold and 2,200 minas *d* of silver. 72 The total given by the rest of the people was 20,000 drachmas of gold, 2,000 minas *e* of silver and 67 garments for priests.

73 The priests, the Levites, the gatekeepers, the singers and the temple servants, along with certain of the people and the rest of the Israelites, settled in their own towns.

Ezra Reads the Law

When the seventh month came and the Israelites had settled in their towns,

8 1 all the people assembled as one man in the square before the Water Gate. They told Ezra the scribe to bring out the Book of the Law of Moses, which the LORD had commanded for Israel.

2 So on the first day of the seventh month Ezra the priest brought the Law before the assembly, which was made up of men and women and all who were able to understand. 3 He read it aloud from daybreak till noon as he faced the square before the Water Gate in the presence of the men, women and others who could understand. And all the people listened attentively to the Book of the Law.

THE BIBLE WAS NEVER INTENDED TO BE A BOOK FOR SCHOLARS AND SPECIALISTS ONLY. FROM THE VERY BEGINNING IT WAS INTENDED TO BE EVERYBODY'S BOOK, AND THAT IS WHAT IT CONTINUES TO BE.   —F. F. Bruce

---

4 Ezra the scribe stood on a high wooden platform built for the occasion. Beside him on his right stood Mattithiah, Shema, Anaiah, Uriah, Hilkiah and Maaseiah; and on his left were Pedaiah, Mishael, Malkijah, Hashum, Hashbaddanah, Zechariah and Meshullam.

5 Ezra opened the book. All the people could see him because he was standing above them; and as he opened it, the people all stood up. 6 Ezra praised the LORD, the great God; and all the people lifted their hands and responded, "Amen! Amen!" Then they bowed down and worshiped the LORD with their faces to the ground.

7 The Levites—Jeshua, Bani, Sherebiah, Jamin, Akkub, Shabbethai, Hodiah, Maaseiah, Kelita, Azariah, Jozabad, Hanan and Pelaiah—instructed the people in the Law while the people were standing there. 8 They read from the Book of the Law of God, making it clear *f* and giving the meaning so that the people could understand what was being read.

9 Then Nehemiah the governor, Ezra the priest and scribe, and the Levites who were instructing the people said to them all, "This day is sacred to the LORD your God. Do not mourn or weep." For all the people had been weeping as they listened to the words of the Law.

10 Nehemiah said, "Go and enjoy choice food and sweet drinks, and send some to those who have nothing prepared. This day is sacred to our Lord. Do not grieve, for the joy of the LORD is your strength."

---

a 68 Some Hebrew manuscripts (see also Ezra 2:66); most Hebrew manuscripts do not have this verse.   *b 70* That is, about 19 pounds (about 8.5 kilograms)   *c 71* That is, about 375 pounds (about 170 kilograms); also in verse 72   *d 71* That is, about 1 1/3 tons (about 1.2 metric tons)   *e 72* That is, about 1 1/4 tons (about 1.1 metric tons)   *f 8* Or *God, translating it*

¹¹The Levites calmed all the people, saying, "Be still, for this is a sacred day. Do not grieve."

¹²Then all the people went away to eat and drink, to send portions of food and to celebrate with great joy, because they now understood the words that had been made known to them.

¹³On the second day of the month, the heads of all the families, along with the priests and the Levites, gathered around Ezra the scribe to give attention to the words of the Law. ¹⁴They found written in the Law, which the LORD had commanded through Moses, that the Israelites were to live in booths during the feast of the seventh month ¹⁵and that

they should proclaim this word and spread it throughout their towns and in Jerusalem: "Go out into the hill country and bring back branches from olive and wild olive trees, and from myrtles, palms and shade trees, to make booths"—as it is written.ᵃ

¹⁶So the people went out and brought back branches and built themselves booths on their own roofs, in their courtyards, in the courts of the house of God and in the square by the Water Gate and the one by the Gate of Ephraim. ¹⁷The whole company that had returned from exile built booths and lived in them. From the days of Joshua son of Nun until that day, the Israelites had

ᵃ 15 See Lev. 23:37–40.

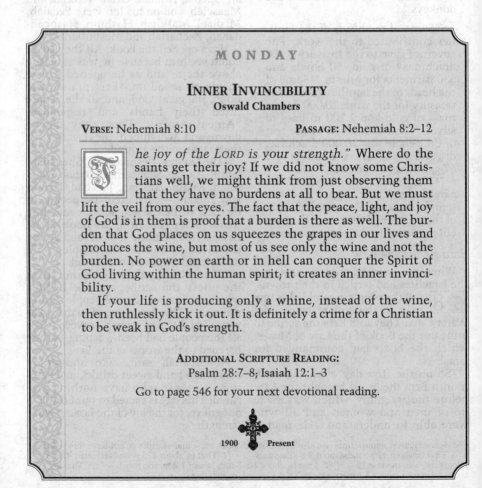

MONDAY

INNER INVINCIBILITY
Oswald Chambers

VERSE: Nehemiah 8:10　　　　　　　**PASSAGE:** Nehemiah 8:2–12

*T*he joy of the LORD is your strength." Where do the saints get their joy? If we did not know some Christians well, we might think from just observing them that they have no burdens at all to bear. But we must lift the veil from our eyes. The fact that the peace, light, and joy of God is in them is proof that a burden is there as well. The burden that God places on us squeezes the grapes in our lives and produces the wine, but most of us see only the wine and not the burden. No power on earth or in hell can conquer the Spirit of God living within the human spirit; it creates an inner invincibility.

If your life is producing only a whine, instead of the wine, then ruthlessly kick it out. It is definitely a crime for a Christian to be weak in God's strength.

ADDITIONAL SCRIPTURE READING:
Psalm 28:7–8; Isaiah 12:1–3

Go to page 546 for your next devotional reading.

1900　✠　Present

not celebrated it like this. And their joy was very great.

18Day after day, from the first day to the last, Ezra read from the Book of the Law of God. They celebrated the feast for seven days, and on the eighth day, in accordance with the regulation, there was an assembly.

The Israelites Confess Their Sins

9 On the twenty-fourth day of the same month, the Israelites gathered together, fasting and wearing sackcloth and having dust on their heads. 2Those of Israelite descent had separated themselves from all foreigners. They stood in their places and confessed their sins and the wickedness of their fathers. 3They stood where they were and read from the Book of the Law of the LORD their God for a quarter of the day, and spent another quarter in confession and in worshiping the LORD their God. 4Standing on the stairs were the Levites—Jeshua, Bani, Kadmiel, Shebaniah, Bunni, Sherebiah, Bani and Kenani—who called with loud voices to the LORD their God. 5And the Levites—Jeshua, Kadmiel, Bani, Hashabneiah, Sherebiah, Hodiah, Shebaniah and Pethahiah—said: "Stand up and praise the LORD your God, who is from everlasting to everlasting.a "

"Blessed be your glorious name, and may it be exalted above all blessing and praise. 6You alone are the LORD. You made the heavens, even the highest heavens, and all their starry host, the earth and all that is on it, the seas and all that is in them. You give life to everything, and the multitudes of heaven worship you.

7"You are the LORD God, who chose Abram and brought him out of Ur of the Chaldeans and named him Abraham. 8You found his heart faithful to you, and you made a covenant with him to give to his descendants the land of the Canaanites, Hittites, Amorites, Perizzites, Jebusites and Girgashites. You have kept your promise because you are righteous.

9"You saw the suffering of our forefathers in Egypt; you heard their cry at the Red Sea.b 10You sent miraculous signs and wonders against Pharaoh, against all his officials and all the people of his land, for you knew how arrogantly the Egyptians treated them. You made a name for yourself, which remains to this day. 11You divided the sea before them, so that they passed through it on dry ground, but you hurled their pursuers into the depths, like a stone into mighty waters. 12By day you led them with a pillar of cloud, and by night with a pillar of fire to give them light on the way they were to take.

13"You came down on Mount Sinai; you spoke to them from heaven. You gave them regulations and laws that are just and right, and decrees and commands that are good. 14You made known to them your holy Sabbath and gave them commands, decrees and laws through your servant Moses. 15In their hunger you gave them bread from heaven and in their thirst you brought them water from the rock; you told them to go in and take possession of the land you had sworn with uplifted hand to give them.

16"But they, our forefathers, became arrogant and stiff-necked, and did not obey your commands. 17They refused to listen and failed to remember the miracles you performed among them. They became stiff-necked and in their rebellion appointed a leader in order to return to their slavery. But you are a forgiving God, gracious and compassionate, slow to anger and abounding in love. Therefore you did not desert them, 18even when they cast for themselves an image of a calf and said, 'This is your god, who brought you up out of Egypt,' or when they committed awful blasphemies.

19"Because of your great compassion you did not abandon them in the desert. By day the pillar of cloud did not cease to guide them on their

a 5 Or God for ever and ever   b 9 Hebrew Yam Suph; that is, Sea of Reeds

path, nor the pillar of fire by night to shine on the way they were to take. 20You gave your good Spirit to instruct them. You did not withhold your manna from their mouths, and you gave them water for their thirst. 21For forty years you sustained them in the desert; they lacked nothing, their clothes did not wear out nor did their feet become swollen.

22"You gave them kingdoms and nations, allotting to them even the remotest frontiers. They took over the country of Sihon*a* king of Heshbon and the country of Og king of Bashan. 23You made their sons as numerous as the stars in the sky, and you brought them into the land that you told their fathers to enter and possess. 24Their sons went in and took possession of the land. You subdued before them the Canaanites, who lived in the land; you handed the Canaanites over to them, along with their kings and the peoples of the land, to deal with them as they pleased. 25They captured fortified cities and fertile land; they took possession of houses filled with all kinds of good things, wells already dug, vineyards, olive groves and fruit trees in abundance. They ate to the full and were well-nourished; they reveled in your great goodness.

26"But they were disobedient and rebelled against you; they put your law behind their backs. They killed your prophets, who had admonished them in order to turn them back to you; they committed awful blasphemies. 27So you handed them over to their enemies, who oppressed them. But when they were oppressed they cried out to you. From heaven you heard them, and in your great compassion you gave them deliverers, who rescued them from the hand of their enemies.

28"But as soon as they were at rest, they again did what was evil in your sight. Then you abandoned them to the hand of their enemies so that they ruled over them. And when they cried out to you again, you heard from heaven, and in your compassion you delivered them time after time.

29"You warned them to return to your law, but they became arrogant and disobeyed your commands. They sinned against your ordinances, by which a man will live if he obeys them. Stubbornly they turned their backs on you, became stiff-necked and refused to listen. 30For many years you were patient with them. By your Spirit you admonished them through your prophets. Yet they paid no attention, so you handed them over to the neighboring peoples. 31But in your great mercy you did not put an end to them or abandon them, for you are a gracious and merciful God.

32"Now therefore, O our God, the great, mighty and awesome God, who keeps his covenant of love, do not let all this hardship seem trifling in your eyes—the hardship that has come upon us, upon our kings and leaders, upon our priests and prophets, upon our fathers and all your people, from the days of the kings of Assyria until today. 33In all that has happened to us, you have been just; you have acted faithfully, while we did wrong. 34Our kings, our leaders, our priests and our fathers did not follow your law; they did not pay attention to your commands or the warnings you gave them. 35Even while they were in their kingdom, enjoying your great goodness to them in the spacious and fertile land you gave them, they did not serve you or turn from their evil ways.

36"But see, we are slaves today, slaves in the land you gave our forefathers so they could eat its fruit and the other good things it produces. 37Because of our sins, its abundant harvest goes to the kings you have placed over us. They rule over our bodies and our cattle as they please. We are in great distress.

a 22 One Hebrew manuscript and Septuagint; most Hebrew manuscripts *Sihon, that is, the country of the*

The Agreement of the People

38 "In view of all this, we are making a binding agreement, putting it in writing, and our leaders, our Levites and our priests are affixing their seals to it."

10 Those who sealed it were:

Nehemiah the governor, the son of Hacaliah.

Zedekiah, 2Seraiah, Azariah, Jeremiah,
3 Pashhur, Amariah, Malkijah,
4 Hattush, Shebaniah, Malluch,
5 Harim, Meremoth, Obadiah,
6 Daniel, Ginnethon, Baruch,
7 Meshullam, Abijah, Mijamin,
8 Maaziah, Bilgai and Shemaiah.

These were the priests.

9 The Levites:

Jeshua son of Azaniah, Binnui of the sons of Henadad, Kadmiel,
10 and their associates: Shebaniah, Hodiah, Kelita, Pelaiah, Hanan,
11 Mica, Rehob, Hashabiah,
12 Zaccur, Sherebiah, Shebaniah,
13 Hodiah, Bani and Beninu.

14 The leaders of the people:

Parosh, Pahath-Moab, Elam, Zattu, Bani,
15 Bunni, Azgad, Bebai,
16 Adonijah, Bigvai, Adin,
17 Ater, Hezekiah, Azzur,
18 Hodiah, Hashum, Bezai,
19 Hariph, Anathoth, Nebai,
20 Magpiash, Meshullam, Hezir,
21 Meshezabel, Zadok, Jaddua,
22 Pelatiah, Hanan, Anaiah,
23 Hoshea, Hananiah, Hasshub,
24 Hallohesh, Pilha, Shobek,
25 Rehum, Hashabnah, Maaseiah,
26 Ahiah, Hanan, Anan,
27 Malluch, Harim and Baanah.

28 "The rest of the people—priests, Levites, gatekeepers, singers, temple servants and all who separated themselves from the neighboring peoples for the sake of the Law of God, together with their wives and all their sons and daughters who are able to understand— 29all these now join their brothers the nobles, and bind themselves with a curse and an oath to follow the Law of God given through Moses the servant of God and to obey carefully all the commands, regulations and decrees of the LORD our Lord.

30 "We promise not to give our daughters in marriage to the peoples around us or take their daughters for our sons.

31 "When the neighboring peoples bring merchandise or grain to sell on the Sabbath, we will not buy from them on the Sabbath or on any holy day. Every seventh year we will forgo working the land and will cancel all debts.

32 "We assume the responsibility for carrying out the commands to give a third of a shekel*a* each year for the service of the house of our God: 33for the bread set out on the table; for the regular grain offerings and burnt offerings; for the offerings on the Sabbaths, New Moon festivals and appointed feasts; for the holy offerings; for sin offerings to make atonement for Israel; and for all the duties of the house of our God.

34 "We—the priests, the Levites and the people—have cast lots to determine when each of our families is to bring to the house of our God at set times each year a contribution of wood to burn on the altar of the LORD our God, as it is written in the Law.

35 "We also assume responsibility for bringing to the house of the LORD each year the firstfruits of our crops and of every fruit tree.

36 "As it is also written in the Law, we will bring the firstborn of our sons and of our cattle, of our herds and of our flocks to the house of our God, to the priests ministering there.

37 "Moreover, we will bring to the storerooms of the house of our God, to the priests, the first of our ground meal, of our ⌞grain⌟ offerings, of the fruit of all our trees and of our new wine and oil. And we will bring a tithe of our crops to the

a 32 That is, about 1/8 ounce (about 4 grams)

Levites, for it is the Levites who collect the tithes in all the towns where we work. 38A priest descended from Aaron is to accompany the Levites when they receive the tithes, and the Levites are to bring a tenth of the tithes up to the house of our God, to the storerooms of the treasury. 39The people of Israel, including the Levites, are to bring their contributions of grain, new wine and oil to the storerooms where the articles for the sanctuary are kept and where the ministering priests, the gatekeepers and the singers stay.

"We will not neglect the house of our God."

The New Residents of Jerusalem

11 Now the leaders of the people settled in Jerusalem, and the rest of the people cast lots to bring one out of every ten to live in Jerusalem, the holy city, while the remaining nine were to stay in their own towns. 2The people commended all the men who volunteered to live in Jerusalem.

3These are the provincial leaders who settled in Jerusalem (now some Israelites, priests, Levites, temple servants and descendants of Solomon's servants lived in the towns of Judah, each on his own property in the various towns, 4while other people from both Judah and Benjamin lived in Jerusalem):

From the descendants of Judah:

Athaiah son of Uzziah, the son of Zechariah, the son of Amariah, the son of Shephatiah, the son of Mahalalel, a descendant of Perez; 5and Maaseiah son of Baruch, the son of Col-Hozeh, the son of Hazaiah, the son of Adaiah, the son of Joiarib, the son of Zechariah, a descendant of Shelah. 6The descendants of Perez who lived in Jerusalem totaled 468 able men.

7From the descendants of Benjamin:

Sallu son of Meshullam, the son of Joed, the son of Pedaiah, the son of Kolaiah, the son of Maaseiah, the son of Ithiel, the son of Jeshaiah,

8and his followers, Gabbai and Sallai—928 men. 9Joel son of Zicri was their chief officer, and Judah son of Hassenuah was over the Second District of the city.

10From the priests:

Jedaiah; the son of Joiarib; Jakin; 11Seraiah son of Hilkiah, the son of Meshullam, the son of Zadok, the son of Meraioth, the son of Ahitub, supervisor in the house of God, 12and their associates, who carried on work for the temple—822 men; Adaiah son of Jeroham, the son of Pelaliah, the son of Amzi, the son of Zechariah, the son of Pashhur, the son of Malkijah, 13and his associates, who were heads of families—242 men; Amashsai son of Azarel, the son of Ahzai, the son of Meshillemoth, the son of Immer, 14and hisa associates, who were able men—128. Their chief officer was Zabdiel son of Haggedolim.

15From the Levites:

Shemaiah son of Hasshub, the son of Azrikam, the son of Hashabiah, the son of Bunni; 16Shabbethai and Jozabad, two of the heads of the Levites, who had charge of the outside work of the house of God; 17Mattaniah son of Mica, the son of Zabdi, the son of Asaph, the director who led in thanksgiving and prayer; Bakbukiah, second among his associates; and Abda son of Shammua, the son of Galal, the son of Jeduthun. 18The Levites in the holy city totaled 284.

19The gatekeepers:

Akkub, Talmon and their associates, who kept watch at the gates—172 men.

20The rest of the Israelites, with the priests and Levites, were in all the towns of Judah, each on his ancestral property.
21The temple servants lived on the hill of Ophel, and Ziha and Gishpa were in charge of them.
22The chief officer of the Levites in

---

a 14 Most Septuagint manuscripts; Hebrew *their*

Jerusalem was Uzzi son of Bani, the son of Hashabiah, the son of Mattaniah, the son of Mica. Uzzi was one of Asaph's descendants, who were the singers responsible for the service of the house of God. 23The singers were under the king's orders, which regulated their daily activity.

24Pethahiah son of Meshezabel, one of the descendants of Zerah son of Judah, was the king's agent in all affairs relating to the people.

25As for the villages with their fields, some of the people of Judah lived in Kiriath Arba and its surrounding settlements, in Dibon and its settlements, in Jekabzeel and its villages, 26in Jeshua, in Moladah, in Beth Pelet, 27in Hazar Shual, in Beersheba and its settlements, 28in Ziklag, in Meconah and its settlements, 29in En Rimmon, in Zorah, in Jarmuth, 30Zanoah, Adullam and their villages, in Lachish and its fields, and in Azekah and its settlements. So they were living all the way from Beersheba to the Valley of Hinnom.

31The descendants of the Benjamites from Geba lived in Micmash, Aija, Bethel and its settlements, 32in Anathoth, Nob and Ananiah, 33in Hazor, Ramah and Gittaim, 34in Hadid, Zeboim and Neballat, 35in Lod and Ono, and in the Valley of the Craftsmen.

36Some of the divisions of the Levites of Judah settled in Benjamin.

Priests and Levites

12 These were the priests and Levites who returned with Zerubbabel son of Shealtiel and with Jeshua:

Seraiah, Jeremiah, Ezra,
2Amariah, Malluch, Hattush,
3Shecaniah, Rehum, Meremoth,
4Iddo, Ginnethon,*a* Abijah,
5Mijamin,*b* Moadiah, Bilgah,
6Shemaiah, Joiarib, Jedaiah,
7Sallu, Amok, Hilkiah and Jedaiah.

These were the leaders of the priests and their associates in the days of Jeshua.

8The Levites were Jeshua, Binnui, Kadmiel, Sherebiah, Judah, and also Mattaniah, who, together with his associates, was in charge of the songs of thanksgiving. 9Bakbukiah and Unni, their associates, stood opposite them in the services.

10Jeshua was the father of Joiakim, Joiakim the father of Eliashib, Eliashib the father of Joiada, 11Joiada the father of Jonathan, and Jonathan the father of Jaddua.

12In the days of Joiakim, these were the heads of the priestly families:
of Seraiah's family, Meraiah;
of Jeremiah's, Hananiah;
13of Ezra's, Meshullam;
of Amariah's, Jehohanan;
14of Malluch's, Jonathan;
of Shecaniah's,*c* Joseph;
15of Harim's, Adna;
of Meremoth's,*d* Helkai;
16of Iddo's, Zechariah;
of Ginnethon's, Meshullam;
17of Abijah's, Zicri;
of Miniamin's and of Moadiah's, Piltai;
18of Bilgah's, Shammua;
of Shemaiah's, Jehonathan;
19of Joiarib's, Mattenai;
of Jedaiah's, Uzzi;
20of Sallu's, Kallai;
of Amok's, Eber;
21of Hilkiah's, Hashabiah;
of Jedaiah's, Nethanel.

22The family heads of the Levites in the days of Eliashib, Joiada, Johanan and Jaddua, as well as those of the priests, were recorded in the reign of Darius the Persian. 23The family heads among the descendants of Levi up to the time of Johanan son of Eliashib were recorded in the book of the annals. 24And the leaders of the Levites were Hashabiah, Sherebiah, Jeshua son of Kadmiel, and their associates, who stood opposite them to give praise and thanksgiving, one section responding to the other, as prescribed by David the man of God.

25Mattaniah, Bakbukiah, Obadiah, Meshullam, Talmon and Akkub were gatekeepers who guarded the storerooms at the gates. 26They served in the days of Joiakim son of Jeshua, the son of Jozadak, and in the days of Nehemiah

---

a 4 Many Hebrew manuscripts and Vulgate (see also Neh. 12:16); most Hebrew manuscripts *Ginnethoi*   *b 5* A variant of *Miniamin*   *c 14* Very many Hebrew manuscripts, some Septuagint manuscripts and Syriac (see also Neh. 12:3); most Hebrew manuscripts *Shebaniah's*   *d 15* Some Septuagint manuscripts (see also Neh. 12:3); Hebrew *Meraioth's*

the governor and of Ezra the priest and scribe.

Dedication of the Wall of Jerusalem

27 At the dedication of the wall of Jerusalem, the Levites were sought out from where they lived and were brought to Jerusalem to celebrate joyfully the dedication with songs of thanksgiving and with the music of cymbals, harps and lyres. 28 The singers also were brought together from the region around Jerusalem—from the villages of the Netophathites, 29 from Beth Gilgal, and from the area of Geba and Azmaveth, for the singers had built villages for themselves around Jerusalem. 30 When the priests and Levites had purified themselves ceremonially, they purified the people, the gates and the wall.

31 I had the leaders of Judah go up on top*a* of the wall. I also assigned two large choirs to give thanks. One was to proceed on top*b* of the wall to the right, toward the Dung Gate. 32 Hoshaiah and half the leaders of Judah followed them, 33 along with Azariah, Ezra, Meshullam, 34 Judah, Benjamin, Shemaiah, Jeremiah, 35 as well as some priests with trumpets, and also Zechariah son of Jonathan, the son of Shemaiah, the son of Mattaniah, the son of Micaiah, the son of Zaccur, the son of Asaph, 36 and his associates— Shemaiah, Azarel, Milalai, Gilalai, Maai, Nethanel, Judah and Hanani— with musical instruments ⌐prescribed by⌐ David the man of God. Ezra the scribe led the procession. 37 At the Fountain Gate they continued directly up the steps of the City of David on the ascent to the wall and passed above the house of David to the Water Gate on the east.

38 The second choir proceeded in the opposite direction. I followed them on top*c* of the wall, together with half the people—past the Tower of the Ovens to the Broad Wall, 39 over the Gate of Ephraim, the Jeshanah*d* Gate, the Fish Gate, the Tower of Hananel and the Tower of the Hundred, as far as the Sheep Gate. At the Gate of the Guard they stopped.

40 The two choirs that gave thanks then took their places in the house of God; so did I, together with half the officials, 41 as well as the priests—Eliakim, Maaseiah, Miniamin, Micaiah, Elioenai, Zechariah and Hananiah with their trumpets— 42 and also Maaseiah, Shemaiah, Eleazar, Uzzi, Jehohanan, Malkijah, Elam and Ezer. The choirs sang under the direction of Jezrahiah. 43 And on that day they offered great sacrifices, rejoicing because God had given them great joy. The women and children also rejoiced. The sound of rejoicing in Jerusalem could be heard far away.

44 At that time men were appointed to be in charge of the storerooms for the contributions, firstfruits and tithes. From the fields around the towns they were to bring into the storerooms the portions required by the Law for the priests and the Levites, for Judah was pleased with the ministering priests and Levites. 45 They performed the service of their God and the service of purification, as did also the singers and gatekeepers, according to the commands of David and his son Solomon. 46 For long ago, in the days of David and Asaph, there had been directors for the singers and for the songs of praise and thanksgiving to God. 47 So in the days of Zerubbabel and of Nehemiah, all Israel contributed the daily portions for the singers and gatekeepers. They also set aside the portion for the other Levites, and the Levites set aside the portion for the descendants of Aaron.

Nehemiah's Final Reforms

13 On that day the Book of Moses was read aloud in the hearing of the people and there it was found written that no Ammonite or Moabite should ever be admitted into the assembly of God, 2 because they had not met the Israelites with food and water but had hired Balaam to call a curse down on them. (Our God, however, turned the curse into a blessing.) 3 When the people heard this law, they excluded from Israel all who were of foreign descent.

4 Before this, Eliashib the priest had been put in charge of the storerooms of

---

a 31 Or go alongside   *b* 31 Or proceed alongside   *c* 38 Or them alongside   *d* 39 Or Old

the house of our God. He was closely associated with Tobiah, ⁵and he had provided him with a large room formerly used to store the grain offerings and incense and temple articles, and also the tithes of grain, new wine and oil prescribed for the Levites, singers and gatekeepers, as well as the contributions for the priests.

⁶But while all this was going on, I was not in Jerusalem, for in the thirty-second year of Artaxerxes king of Babylon I had returned to the king. Some time later I asked his permission ⁷and came back to Jerusalem. Here I learned about the evil thing Eliashib had done in providing Tobiah a room in the courts of the house of God. ⁸I was greatly displeased and threw all Tobiah's household goods out of the room. ⁹I gave orders to purify the rooms, and then I put back into them the equipment of the house of God, with the grain offerings and the incense.

¹⁰I also learned that the portions assigned to the Levites had not been given to them, and that all the Levites and singers responsible for the service had gone back to their own fields. ¹¹So I rebuked the officials and asked them, "Why is the house of God neglected?" Then I called them together and stationed them at their posts.

¹²All Judah brought the tithes of grain, new wine and oil into the storerooms. ¹³I put Shelemiah the priest, Zadok the scribe, and a Levite named Pedaiah in charge of the storerooms and made Hanan son of Zaccur, the son of Mattaniah, their assistant, because these men were considered trustworthy. They were made responsible for distributing the supplies to their brothers.

¹⁴Remember me for this, O my God, and do not blot out what I have so faithfully done for the house of my God and its services.

¹⁵In those days I saw men in Judah treading winepresses on the Sabbath and bringing in grain and loading it on donkeys, together with wine, grapes, figs and all other kinds of loads. And they were bringing all this into Jerusalem on the Sabbath. Therefore I warned them against selling food on that day. ¹⁶Men

from Tyre who lived in Jerusalem were bringing in fish and all kinds of merchandise and selling them in Jerusalem on the Sabbath to the people of Judah. ¹⁷I rebuked the nobles of Judah and said to them, "What is this wicked thing you are doing—desecrating the Sabbath day? ¹⁸Didn't your forefathers do the same things, so that our God brought all this calamity upon us and upon this city? Now you are stirring up more wrath against Israel by desecrating the Sabbath."

¹⁹When evening shadows fell on the gates of Jerusalem before the Sabbath, I ordered the doors to be shut and not opened until the Sabbath was over. I stationed some of my own men at the gates so that no load could be brought in on the Sabbath day. ²⁰Once or twice the merchants and sellers of all kinds of goods spent the night outside Jerusalem. ²¹But I warned them and said, "Why do you spend the night by the wall? If you do this again, I will lay hands on you." From that time on they no longer came on the Sabbath. ²²Then I commanded the Levites to purify themselves and go and guard the gates in order to keep the Sabbath day holy.

Remember me for this also, O my God, and show mercy to me according to your great love.

²³Moreover, in those days I saw men of Judah who had married women from Ashdod, Ammon and Moab. ²⁴Half of their children spoke the language of Ashdod or the language of one of the other peoples, and did not know how to speak the language of Judah. ²⁵I rebuked them and called curses down on them. I beat some of the men and pulled out their hair. I made them take an oath in God's name and said: "You are not to give your daughters in marriage to their sons, nor are you to take their daughters in marriage for your sons or for yourselves. ²⁶Was it not because of marriages like these that Solomon king of Israel sinned? Among the many nations there was no king like him. He was loved by his God, and God made him king over all Israel, but even he was led into sin by foreign women. ²⁷Must we hear now that you too are doing all this

terrible wickedness and are being unfaithful to our God by marrying foreign women?"

28One of the sons of Joiada son of Eliashib the high priest was son-in-law to Sanballat the Horonite. And I drove him away from me.

29Remember them, O my God, because they defiled the priestly office and the covenant of the priesthood and of the Levites.

30So I purified the priests and the Levites of everything foreign, and assigned them duties, each to his own task. **31**I also made provision for contributions of wood at designated times, and for the firstfruits.

Remember me with favor, O my God.

ESTHER

HIS BOOK, NAMED AFTER ITS
LEADING CHARACTER, A BEAUTI-
FUL JEWISH GIRL WHOM KING
XERXES OF PERSIA CHOSE TO BE HIS
QUEEN, REMEMBERS THE GREAT DELIVER-
ANCE OF THE JEWISH PEOPLE DURING THE
REIGN OF XERXES. ALTHOUGH THE NAME
OF GOD DOES NOT APPEAR IN THE BOOK,
HIS CARE FOR HIS CHOSEN PEOPLE IS CLEAR-
LY SHOWN. BE ASSURED THAT HE IS AT
WORK IN YOUR LIFE TODAY AS WELL.

Queen Vashti Deposed

1 This is what happened during the time of Xerxes,*a* the Xerxes who ruled over 127 provinces stretching from India to Cush*b*: ²At that time King Xerxes reigned from his royal throne in the citadel of Susa, ³and in the third year of his reign he gave a banquet for all his nobles and officials. The military leaders of Persia and Media, the princes, and the nobles of the provinces were present.

⁴For a full 180 days he displayed the vast wealth of his kingdom and the splendor and glory of his majesty. ⁵When these days were over, the king gave a banquet, lasting seven days, in the enclosed garden of the king's palace, for all the people from the least to the greatest, who were in the citadel of Susa. ⁶The garden had hangings of white and blue linen, fastened with cords of white linen and purple material to silver rings on marble pillars. There were couches of gold and silver on a mosaic pavement of porphyry, marble, mother-of-pearl and other costly stones. ⁷Wine was served in goblets of gold, each one different from the other, and the royal wine was abundant, in keeping with the king's liberality. ⁸By the king's command each guest was allowed to drink in his own way, for the king instructed all the wine stewards to serve each man what he wished.

⁹Queen Vashti also gave a banquet for the women in the royal palace of King Xerxes.

a 1 Hebrew *Ahasuerus,* a variant of Xerxes' Persian name; here and throughout Esther   *b 1* That is, the upper Nile region

10On the seventh day, when King Xerxes was in high spirits from wine, he commanded the seven eunuchs who served him—Mehuman, Biztha, Harbona, Bigtha, Abagtha, Zethar and Carcas— 11to bring before him Queen Vashti, wearing her royal crown, in order to display her beauty to the people and nobles, for she was lovely to look at. 12But when the attendants delivered the king's command, Queen Vashti refused to come. Then the king became furious and burned with anger.

13Since it was customary for the king to consult experts in matters of law and justice, he spoke with the wise men who understood the times 14and were closest to the king—Carshena, Shethar, Admatha, Tarshish, Meres, Marsena and Memucan, the seven nobles of Persia and Media who had special access to the king and were highest in the kingdom.

15"According to law, what must be done to Queen Vashti?" he asked. "She has not obeyed the command of King Xerxes that the eunuchs have taken to her."

16Then Memucan replied in the presence of the king and the nobles, "Queen Vashti has done wrong, not only against the king but also against all the nobles and the peoples of all the provinces of King Xerxes. 17For the queen's conduct will become known to all the women, and so they will despise their husbands and say, 'King Xerxes commanded Queen Vashti to be brought before him, but she would not come.' 18This very day the Persian and Median women of the nobility who have heard about the queen's conduct will respond to all the king's nobles in the same way. There will be no end of disrespect and discord.

19"Therefore, if it pleases the king, let him issue a royal decree and let it be written in the laws of Persia and Media, which cannot be repealed, that Vashti is never again to enter the presence of King Xerxes. Also let the king give her royal position to someone else who is better than she. 20Then when the king's edict is proclaimed throughout all his vast realm, all the women will respect their husbands, from the least to the greatest."

21The king and his nobles were pleased with this advice, so the king did as Memucan proposed. 22He sent dispatches to all parts of the kingdom, to each province in its own script and to each people in its own language, proclaiming in each people's tongue that every man should be ruler over his own household.

Esther Made Queen

2 Later when the anger of King Xerxes had subsided, he remembered Vashti and what she had done and what he had decreed about her. 2Then the king's personal attendants proposed, "Let a search be made for beautiful young virgins for the king. 3Let the king appoint commissioners in every province of his realm to bring all these beautiful girls into the harem at the citadel of Susa. Let them be placed under the care of Hegai, the king's eunuch, who is in charge of the women; and let beauty treatments be given to them. 4Then let the girl who pleases the king be queen instead of Vashti." This advice appealed to the king, and he followed it.

5Now there was in the citadel of Susa a Jew of the tribe of Benjamin, named Mordecai son of Jair, the son of Shimei, the son of Kish, 6who had been carried into exile from Jerusalem by Nebuchadnezzar king of Babylon, among those taken captive with Jehoiachin[a] king of Judah. 7Mordecai had a cousin named Hadassah, whom he had brought up because she had neither father nor mother. This girl, who was also known as Esther, was lovely in form and features, and Mordecai had taken her as his own daughter when her father and mother died.

8When the king's order and edict had been proclaimed, many girls were brought to the citadel of Susa and put under the care of Hegai. Esther also was taken to the king's palace and entrusted to Hegai, who had charge of the harem. 9The girl pleased him and won his favor. Immediately he provided her with her beauty treatments and special food. He assigned to her seven maids selected from the king's palace and moved her and her maids into the best place in the harem.

---

a 6 Hebrew *Jeconiah*, a variant of *Jehoiachin*

10Esther had not revealed her nationality and family background, because Mordecai had forbidden her to do so. 11Every day he walked back and forth near the courtyard of the harem to find out how Esther was and what was happening to her.

12Before a girl's turn came to go in to King Xerxes, she had to complete twelve months of beauty treatments prescribed for the women, six months with oil of myrrh and six with perfumes and cosmetics. 13And this is how she would go to the king: Anything she wanted was given her to take with her from the harem to the king's palace. 14In the evening she would go there and in the morning return to another part of the harem to the care of Shaashgaz, the king's eunuch who was in charge of the concubines. She would not return to the king unless he was pleased with her and summoned her by name.

15When the turn came for Esther (the girl Mordecai had adopted, the daughter of his uncle Abihail) to go to the king, she asked for nothing other than what Hegai, the king's eunuch who was in charge of the harem, suggested. And Esther won the favor of everyone who saw her. 16She was taken to King Xerxes in the royal residence in the tenth month, the month of Tebeth, in the seventh year of his reign.

17Now the king was attracted to Esther more than to any of the other women, and she won his favor and approval more than any of the other virgins. So he set a royal crown on her head and made her queen instead of Vashti. 18And the king gave a great banquet, Esther's banquet, for all his nobles and officials. He proclaimed a holiday throughout the provinces and distributed gifts with royal liberality.

Mordecai Uncovers a Conspiracy

19When the virgins were assembled a second time, Mordecai was sitting at the king's gate. 20But Esther had kept secret her family background and nationality just as Mordecai had told her to do, for she continued to follow Mordecai's instructions as she had done when he was bringing her up.

21During the time Mordecai was sitting at the king's gate, Bigthana[a] and Teresh, two of the king's officers who guarded the doorway, became angry and conspired to assassinate King Xerxes. 22But Mordecai found out about the plot and told Queen Esther, who in turn reported it to the king, giving credit to Mordecai. 23And when the report was investigated and found to be true, the two officials were hanged on a gallows.[b] All this was recorded in the book of the annals in the presence of the king.

Haman's Plot to Destroy the Jews

3 After these events, King Xerxes honored Haman son of Hammedatha, the Agagite, elevating him and giving him a seat of honor higher than that of all the other nobles. 2All the royal officials at the king's gate knelt down and paid honor to Haman, for the king had commanded this concerning him. But Mordecai would not kneel down or pay him honor.

3Then the royal officials at the king's gate asked Mordecai, "Why do you disobey the king's command?" 4Day after day they spoke to him but he refused to comply. Therefore they told Haman about it to see whether Mordecai's behavior would be tolerated, for he had told them he was a Jew.

5When Haman saw that Mordecai would not kneel down or pay him honor, he was enraged. 6Yet having learned who Mordecai's people were, he scorned the idea of killing only Mordecai. Instead Haman looked for a way to destroy all Mordecai's people, the Jews, throughout the whole kingdom of Xerxes.

7In the twelfth year of King Xerxes, in the first month, the month of Nisan, they cast the *pur* (that is, the lot) in the presence of Haman to select a day and month. And the lot fell on[c] the twelfth month, the month of Adar.

8Then Haman said to King Xerxes, "There is a certain people dispersed and scattered among the peoples in all the provinces of your kingdom whose customs are different from those of all other

PRIDE MEANS ENMITY

C. S. Lewis

VERSE: Esther 3:5–6   **PASSAGE:** Esther 3:1–15

reed will certainly make a man want money, for the sake of a better house, better holidays, better things to eat and drink. But only up to a point. What is it that makes a man with £10,000 a year anxious to get £20,000 a year? It is not the greed for more pleasure. £10,000 will give all the luxuries that any man can really enjoy. It is pride—the wish to be richer than some other rich man, and (still more) the wish for power. For, of course, power is what pride really enjoys: there is nothing makes a man feel so superior to others as being able to move them about like toy soldiers. What makes a pretty girl spread misery wherever she goes by collecting admirers? Certainly not her sexual instinct: that kind of girl is quite often sexually frigid. It is pride. What is it that makes a political leader or a whole nation go on and on, demanding more and more? Pride again. Pride is competitive by its very nature: that is why it goes on and on. If I am a proud man, then, as long as there is one man in the whole world more powerful, or richer, or cleverer than I, he is my rival and my enemy.

The Christians are right: it is pride which has been the chief cause of misery in every nation and every family since the world began. Other vices may sometimes bring people together: you may find good fellowship and jokes and friendliness among drunken people or unchaste people. But pride always means enmity—it *is* enmity. And not only enmity between man and man, but enmity to God.

In God you come up against something which is in every respect immeasurably superior to yourself. Unless you know God as that—and, therefore, know yourself as nothing in comparison—you do not know God at all. As long as you are proud you cannot know God. A proud man is always looking down on things and people: and, of course, as long as you are looking down, you cannot see something that is above you.

ADDITIONAL SCRIPTURE READING:
Proverbs 11:2; Mark 9:33–37; James 4:1–3

Go to page 548 for your next devotional reading.

1900   Present

people and who do not obey the king's laws; it is not in the king's best interest to tolerate them. 9If it pleases the king, let a decree be issued to destroy them, and I will put ten thousand talents*a* of silver into the royal treasury for the men who carry out this business."

10So the king took his signet ring from his finger and gave it to Haman son of Hammedatha, the Agagite, the enemy of the Jews. 11"Keep the money," the king said to Haman, "and do with the people as you please."

12Then on the thirteenth day of the first month the royal secretaries were summoned. They wrote out in the script of each province and in the language of each people all Haman's orders to the king's satraps, the governors of the various provinces and the nobles of the various peoples. These were written in the name of King Xerxes himself and sealed with his own ring. 13Dispatches were sent by couriers to all the king's provinces with the order to destroy, kill and annihilate all the Jews—young and old, women and little children—on a single day, the thirteenth day of the twelfth month, the month of Adar, and to plunder their goods. 14A copy of the text of the edict was to be issued as law in every province and made known to the people of every nationality so they would be ready for that day.

15Spurred on by the king's command, the couriers went out, and the edict was issued in the citadel of Susa. The king and Haman sat down to drink, but the city of Susa was bewildered.

Mordecai Persuades Esther to Help

4 When Mordecai learned of all that had been done, he tore his clothes, put on sackcloth and ashes, and went out into the city, wailing loudly and bitterly. 2But he went only as far as the king's gate, because no one clothed in sackcloth was allowed to enter it. 3In every province to which the edict and order of the king came, there was great mourning among the Jews, with fasting, weeping and wailing. Many lay in sackcloth and ashes.

4When Esther's maids and eunuchs came and told her about Mordecai, she was in great distress. She sent clothes for him to put on instead of his sackcloth, but he would not accept them. 5Then Esther summoned Hathach, one of the king's eunuchs assigned to attend her, and ordered him to find out what was troubling Mordecai and why.

6So Hathach went out to Mordecai in the open square of the city in front of the king's gate. 7Mordecai told him everything that had happened to him, including the exact amount of money Haman had promised to pay into the royal treasury for the destruction of the Jews. 8He also gave him a copy of the text of the edict for their annihilation, which had been published in Susa, to show to Esther and explain it to her, and he told him to urge her to go into the king's presence to beg for mercy and plead with him for her people.

9Hathach went back and reported to Esther what Mordecai had said. 10Then she instructed him to say to Mordecai, 11"All the king's officials and the people of the royal provinces know that for any man or woman who approaches the king in the inner court without being summoned the king has but one law: that he be put to death. The only exception to this is for the king to extend the gold scepter to him and spare his life. But thirty days have passed since I was called to go to the king."

12When Esther's words were reported to Mordecai, 13he sent back this answer: "Do not think that because you are in the king's house you alone of all the Jews will escape. 14For if you remain silent at this time, relief and deliverance for the Jews will arise from another place, but you and your father's family will perish. And who knows but that you have come to royal position for such a time as this?"

15Then Esther sent this reply to Mordecai: 16"Go, gather together all the Jews who are in Susa, and fast for me. Do not eat or drink for three days, night or day. I and my maids will fast as you do. When this is done, I will go to the king, even though it is against the law. And if I perish, I perish."

17So Mordecai went away and carried out all of Esther's instructions.

a 9 That is, about 375 tons (about 345 metric tons)

Esther's Request to the King

5 On the third day Esther put on her royal robes and stood in the inner court of the palace, in front of the king's hall. The king was sitting on his royal throne in the hall, facing the entrance. ²When he saw Queen Esther standing in the court, he was pleased with her and held out to her the gold scepter that was in his hand. So Esther approached and touched the tip of the scepter.

³Then the king asked, "What is it, Queen Esther? What is your request?

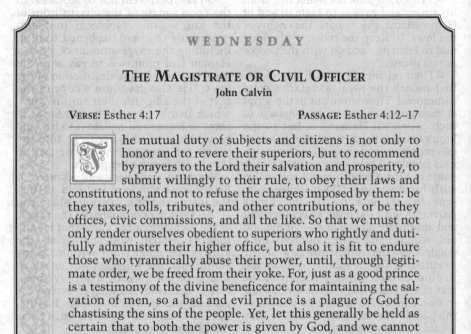

WEDNESDAY

THE MAGISTRATE OR CIVIL OFFICER
John Calvin

VERSE: Esther 4:17   **PASSAGE:** Esther 4:12–17

The mutual duty of subjects and citizens is not only to honor and to revere their superiors, but to recommend by prayers to the Lord their salvation and prosperity, to submit willingly to their rule, to obey their laws and constitutions, and not to refuse the charges imposed by them: be they taxes, tolls, tributes, and other contributions, or be they offices, civic commissions, and all the like. So that we must not only render ourselves obedient to superiors who rightly and dutifully administer their higher office, but also it is fit to endure those who tyrannically abuse their power, until, through legitimate order, we be freed from their yoke. For, just as a good prince is a testimony of the divine beneficence for maintaining the salvation of men, so a bad and evil prince is a plague of God for chastising the sins of the people. Yet, let this generally be held as certain that to both the power is given by God, and we cannot resist them without our resisting the ordinance of God.

But from obedience to superiors we must always except one thing: that it does not draw us away from obedience to him to whose edicts the commands of all kings must yield. The Lord, therefore, is the king of kings, and, once he has opened his sacred mouth, he must be listened to by all and above all. Only after that, we are subject to men who are constituted over us, but not otherwise than in him. If men command us to do something against him, we must do nothing, nor keep any account of such an order. On the contrary, let rather this sentence take place: that it is necessary to "obey God rather than men!" (Acts 5:29).

ADDITIONAL SCRIPTURE READING:
Romans 13:1–5; Titus 3:1; 1 Peter 2:13–17

Go to page 555 for your next devotional reading.

1500   1700

Even up to half the kingdom, it will be given you."

⁴"If it pleases the king," replied Esther, "let the king, together with Haman, come today to a banquet I have prepared for him."

⁵"Bring Haman at once," the king said, "so that we may do what Esther asks."

So the king and Haman went to the banquet Esther had prepared. ⁶As they were drinking wine, the king again asked Esther, "Now what is your petition? It will be given you. And what is your request? Even up to half the kingdom, it will be granted."

⁷Esther replied, "My petition and my request is this: ⁸If the king regards me with favor and if it pleases the king to grant my petition and fulfill my request, let the king and Haman come tomorrow to the banquet I will prepare for them. Then I will answer the king's question."

Haman's Rage Against Mordecai

⁹Haman went out that day happy and in high spirits. But when he saw Mordecai at the king's gate and observed that he neither rose nor showed fear in his presence, he was filled with rage against Mordecai. ¹⁰Nevertheless, Haman restrained himself and went home.

Calling together his friends and Zeresh, his wife, ¹¹Haman boasted to them about his vast wealth, his many sons, and all the ways the king had honored him and how he had elevated him above the other nobles and officials. ¹²"And that's not all," Haman added. "I'm the only person Queen Esther invited to accompany the king to the banquet she gave. And she has invited me along with the king tomorrow. ¹³But all this gives me no satisfaction as long as I see that Jew Mordecai sitting at the king's gate."

¹⁴His wife Zeresh and all his friends said to him, "Have a gallows built, seventy-five feet[a] high, and ask the king in the morning to have Mordecai hanged on it. Then go with the king to the dinner and be happy." This suggestion delighted Haman, and he had the gallows built.

Mordecai Honored

6 That night the king could not sleep; so he ordered the book of the chronicles, the record of his reign, to be brought in and read to him. ²It was found recorded there that Mordecai had exposed Bigthana and Teresh, two of the king's officers who guarded the doorway, who had conspired to assassinate King Xerxes.

³"What honor and recognition has Mordecai received for this?" the king asked.

"Nothing has been done for him," his attendants answered.

⁴The king said, "Who is in the court?" Now Haman had just entered the outer court of the palace to speak to the king about hanging Mordecai on the gallows he had erected for him.

⁵His attendants answered, "Haman is standing in the court."

"Bring him in," the king ordered.

⁶When Haman entered, the king asked him, "What should be done for the man the king delights to honor?"

Now Haman thought to himself, "Who is there that the king would rather honor than me?" ⁷So he answered the king, "For the man the king delights to honor, ⁸have them bring a royal robe the king has worn and a horse the king has ridden, one with a royal crest placed on its head. ⁹Then let the robe and horse be entrusted to one of the king's most noble princes. Let them robe the man the king delights to honor, and lead him on the horse through the city streets, proclaiming before him, 'This is what is done for the man the king delights to honor!' "

¹⁰"Go at once," the king commanded Haman. "Get the robe and the horse and do just as you have suggested for Mordecai the Jew, who sits at the king's gate. Do not neglect anything you have recommended."

¹¹So Haman got the robe and the horse. He robed Mordecai, and led him on horseback through the city streets, proclaiming before him, "This is what is done for the man the king delights to honor!"

¹²Afterward Mordecai returned to the king's gate. But Haman rushed home, with his head covered in grief, ¹³and told

---

a 14 Hebrew *fifty cubits* (about 23 meters)

Zeresh his wife and all his friends every-thing that had happened to him.

His advisers and his wife Zeresh said to him, "Since Mordecai, before whom your downfall has started, is of Jewish origin, you cannot stand against him—you will surely come to ruin!" [14]While they were still talking with him, the king's eunuchs arrived and hurried Haman away to the banquet Esther had prepared.

Haman Hanged

7 So the king and Haman went to dine with Queen Esther, [2]and as they were drinking wine on that second day, the king again asked, "Queen Esther, what is your petition? It will be given you. What is your request? Even up to half the kingdom, it will be granted."

[3]Then Queen Esther answered, "If I have found favor with you, O king, and if it pleases your majesty, grant me my life—this is my petition. And spare my people—this is my request. [4]For I and my people have been sold for destruc-tion and slaughter and annihilation. If we had merely been sold as male and female slaves, I would have kept quiet, because no such distress would justify disturbing the king.[a] "

[5]King Xerxes asked Queen Esther, "Who is he? Where is the man who has dared to do such a thing?"

[6]Esther said, "The adversary and enemy is this vile Haman."

Then Haman was terrified before the king and queen. [7]The king got up in a rage, left his wine and went out into the palace garden. But Haman, realizing that the king had already decided his fate, stayed behind to beg Queen Esther for his life.

[8]Just as the king returned from the palace garden to the banquet hall, Haman was falling on the couch where Esther was reclining.

The king exclaimed, "Will he even molest the queen while she is with me in the house?"

As soon as the word left the king's mouth, they covered Haman's face. [9]Then Harbona, one of the eunuchs attending the king, said, "A gallows sev-enty-five feet[b] high stands by Haman's house. He had it made for Mordecai, who spoke up to help the king."

The king said, "Hang him on it!" [10]So they hanged Haman on the gallows he had prepared for Mordecai. Then the king's fury subsided.

The King's Edict in Behalf of the Jews

8 That same day King Xerxes gave Queen Esther the estate of Haman, the enemy of the Jews. And Mordecai came into the presence of the king, for Esther had told how he was related to her. [2]The king took off his signet ring, which he had reclaimed from Haman, and presented it to Morde-cai. And Esther appointed him over Haman's estate.

[3]Esther again pleaded with the king, falling at his feet and weeping. She begged him to put an end to the evil plan of Haman the Agagite, which he had devised against the Jews. [4]Then the king extended the gold scepter to Esther and she arose and stood before him.

[5]"If it pleases the king," she said, "and if he regards me with favor and thinks it the right thing to do, and if he is pleased with me, let an order be writ-ten overruling the dispatches that Haman son of Hammedatha, the Agag-ite, devised and wrote to destroy the Jews in all the king's provinces. [6]For how can I bear to see disaster fall on my people? How can I bear to see the destruction of my family?"

[7]King Xerxes replied to Queen Esther and to Mordecai the Jew, "Because Haman attacked the Jews, I have given his estate to Esther, and they have hanged him on the gallows. [8]Now write another decree in the king's name in behalf of the Jews as seems best to you, and seal it with the king's signet ring—for no document written in the king's name and sealed with his ring can be revoked."

[9]At once the royal secretaries were summoned—on the twenty-third day of the third month, the month of Sivan. They wrote out all Mordecai's orders to the Jews, and to the satraps, governors and nobles of the 127

---

a 4 Or quiet, but the compensation our adversary offers cannot be compared with the loss the king would suffer   b 9 Hebrew fifty cubits (about 23 meters)

provinces stretching from India to Cush.ᵃ These orders were written in the script of each province and the language of each people and also to the Jews in their own script and language. ¹⁰Mordecai wrote in the name of King Xerxes, sealed the dispatches with the king's signet ring, and sent them by mounted couriers, who rode fast horses especially bred for the king.

¹¹The king's edict granted the Jews in every city the right to assemble and protect themselves; to destroy, kill and annihilate any armed force of any nationality or province that might attack them and their women and children; and to plunder the property of their enemies. ¹²The day appointed for the Jews to do this in all the provinces of King Xerxes was the thirteenth day of the twelfth month, the month of Adar. ¹³A copy of the text of the edict was to be issued as law in every province and made known to the people of every nationality so that the Jews would be ready on that day to avenge themselves on their enemies.

¹⁴The couriers, riding the royal horses, raced out, spurred on by the king's command. And the edict was also issued in the citadel of Susa.

¹⁵Mordecai left the king's presence wearing royal garments of blue and white, a large crown of gold and a purple robe of fine linen. And the city of Susa held a joyous celebration. ¹⁶For the Jews it was a time of happiness and joy, gladness and honor. ¹⁷In every province and in every city, wherever the edict of the king went, there was joy and gladness among the Jews, with feasting and celebrating. And many people of other nationalities became Jews because fear of the Jews had seized them.

Triumph of the Jews

9 On the thirteenth day of the twelfth month, the month of Adar, the edict commanded by the king was to be carried out. On this day the enemies of the Jews had hoped to overpower them, but now the tables were turned and the Jews got the upper hand over those who hated them. ²The Jews assembled in their cities in all the provinces of King Xerxes to attack those seeking their destruction. No one could stand against them, because the people of all the other nationalities were afraid of them. ³And all the nobles of the provinces, the satraps, the governors and the king's administrators helped the Jews, because fear of Mordecai had seized them. ⁴Mordecai was prominent in the palace; his reputation spread throughout the provinces, and he became more and more powerful.

⁵The Jews struck down all their enemies with the sword, killing and destroying them, and they did what they pleased to those who hated them. ⁶In the citadel of Susa, the Jews killed and destroyed five hundred men. ⁷They also killed Parshandatha, Dalphon, Aspatha, ⁸Poratha, Adalia, Aridatha, ⁹Parmashta, Arisai, Aridai and Vaizatha, ¹⁰the ten sons of Haman son of Hammedatha, the enemy of the Jews. But they did not lay their hands on the plunder.

¹¹The number of those slain in the citadel of Susa was reported to the king that same day. ¹²The king said to Queen Esther, "The Jews have killed and destroyed five hundred men and the ten sons of Haman in the citadel of Susa. What have they done in the rest of the king's provinces? Now what is your petition? It will be given you. What is your request? It will also be granted."

¹³"If it pleases the king," Esther answered, "give the Jews in Susa permission to carry out this day's edict tomorrow also, and let Haman's ten sons be hanged on gallows."

¹⁴So the king commanded that this be done. An edict was issued in Susa, and they hanged the ten sons of Haman. ¹⁵The Jews in Susa came together on the fourteenth day of the month of Adar, and they put to death in Susa three hundred men, but they did not lay their hands on the plunder.

¹⁶Meanwhile, the remainder of the Jews who were in the king's provinces also assembled to protect themselves and get relief from their enemies. They killed seventy-five thousand of them but did not lay their hands on the plunder. ¹⁷This happened on the thirteenth day of the month of Adar, and on the

ᵃ 9 That is, the upper Nile region

fourteenth they rested and made it a day of feasting and joy.

Purim Celebrated

18The Jews in Susa, however, had assembled on the thirteenth and fourteenth, and then on the fifteenth they rested and made it a day of feasting and joy.

19That is why rural Jews—those living in villages—observe the fourteenth of the month of Adar as a day of joy and feasting, a day for giving presents to each other.

20Mordecai recorded these events, and he sent letters to all the Jews throughout the provinces of King Xerxes, near and far, 21to have them celebrate annually the fourteenth and fifteenth days of the month of Adar 22as the time when the Jews got relief from their enemies, and as the month when their sorrow was turned into joy and their mourning into a day of celebration. He wrote them to observe the days as days of feasting and joy and giving presents of food to one another and gifts to the poor.

23So the Jews agreed to continue the celebration they had begun, doing what Mordecai had written to them. 24For Haman son of Hammedatha, the Agagite, the enemy of all the Jews, had plotted against the Jews to destroy them and had cast the *pur* (that is, the lot) for their ruin and destruction. 25But when the plot came to the king's attention,*a* he issued written orders that the evil scheme Haman had devised against the Jews should come back onto his own head, and that he and his sons should be hanged on the gallows. 26(Therefore these days were called Purim, from the word *pur*.) Because of everything written in this letter and because of what they had seen and what had happened to them,

27the Jews took it upon themselves to establish the custom that they and their descendants and all who join them should without fail observe these two days every year, in the way prescribed and at the time appointed. 28These days should be remembered and observed in every generation by every family, and in every province and in every city. And these days of Purim should never cease to be celebrated by the Jews, nor should the memory of them die out among their descendants.

29So Queen Esther, daughter of Abihail, along with Mordecai the Jew, wrote with full authority to confirm this second letter concerning Purim. 30And Mordecai sent letters to all the Jews in the 127 provinces of the kingdom of Xerxes—words of goodwill and assurance— 31to establish these days of Purim at their designated times, as Mordecai the Jew and Queen Esther had decreed for them, and as they had established for themselves and their descendants in regard to their times of fasting and lamentation. 32Esther's decree confirmed these regulations about Purim, and it was written down in the records.

The Greatness of Mordecai

10 King Xerxes imposed tribute throughout the empire, to its distant shores. 2And all his acts of power and might, together with a full account of the greatness of Mordecai to which the king had raised him, are they not written in the book of the annals of the kings of Media and Persia? 3Mordecai the Jew was second in rank to King Xerxes, preeminent among the Jews, and held in high esteem by his many fellow Jews, because he worked for the good of his people and spoke up for the welfare of all the Jews.

a 25 Or when Esther came before the king

JOB

THE BOOK OF JOB IS NAMED FOR ITS MAIN CHARACTER, A RIGHTEOUS MAN WHO WAS VERY RICH. EVEN AFTER LOSING EVERYTHING HE OWNED AND SUFFERING FROM A TERRIBLE SICKNESS, JOB STILL CONFESSED HIS TRUST IN GOD. THE BOOK PROVIDES A PROFOUND STATEMENT ON GOD'S JUSTICE IN LIGHT OF HUMAN SUFFERING. HOW CAN THE JUSTICE OF AN ALMIGHTY GOD BE DEFENDED IN THE FACE OF EVIL, ESPECIALLY HUMAN SUFFERING, AND EVEN MORE POIGNANTLY, THE SUFFERING OF THE INNOCENT? AS YOU READ THIS BOOK, REMEMBER THAT EVEN THOUGH YOU DON'T HAVE ALL THE ANSWERS TO QUESTIONS ABOUT SUFFERING, GOD IS STILL IN CONTROL.

Prologue

1 In the land of Uz there lived a man whose name was Job. This man was blameless and upright; he feared God and shunned evil. ²He had seven sons and three daughters, ³and he owned seven thousand sheep, three thousand camels, five hundred yoke of oxen and five hundred donkeys, and had a large number of servants. He was the greatest man among all the people of the East.

⁴His sons used to take turns holding feasts in their homes, and they would invite their three sisters to eat and drink with them. ⁵When a period of feasting had run its course, Job would send and have them purified. Early in the morning he would sacrifice a burnt offering for each of them, thinking, "Perhaps my children have sinned and cursed God in their hearts." This was Job's regular custom.

Job's First Test

⁶One day the angels*a* came to present themselves before the LORD, and Satan*b* also came with them. ⁷The LORD said to Satan, "Where have you come from?"

Satan answered the LORD, "From roaming through the earth and going back and forth in it."

⁸Then the LORD said to Satan, "Have you considered my servant Job? There is no one on earth like him; he is blameless and upright, a man who fears God and shuns evil."

---

a 6 Hebrew *the sons of God*   *b* 6 *Satan* means *accuser.*

9"Does Job fear God for nothing?" Satan replied. 10"Have you not put a hedge around him and his household and everything he has? You have blessed the work of his hands, so that his flocks and herds are spread throughout the land. 11But stretch out your hand and strike everything he has, and he will surely curse you to your face."

12The LORD said to Satan, "Very well, then, everything he has is in your hands, but on the man himself do not lay a finger."

Then Satan went out from the presence of the LORD.

13One day when Job's sons and daughters were feasting and drinking wine at the oldest brother's house, 14a messenger came to Job and said, "The oxen were plowing and the donkeys were grazing nearby, 15and the Sabeans attacked and carried them off. They put the servants to the sword, and I am the only one who has escaped to tell you!"

16While he was still speaking, another messenger came and said, "The fire of God fell from the sky and burned up the sheep and the servants, and I am the only one who has escaped to tell you!"

17While he was still speaking, another messenger came and said, "The Chaldeans formed three raiding parties and swept down on your camels and carried them off. They put the servants to the sword, and I am the only one who has escaped to tell you!"

18While he was still speaking, yet another messenger came and said, "Your sons and daughters were feasting and drinking wine at the oldest brother's house, 19when suddenly a mighty wind swept in from the desert and struck the four corners of the house. It collapsed on them and they are dead, and I am the only one who has escaped to tell you!"

20At this, Job got up and tore his robe and shaved his head. Then he fell to the ground in worship 21and said:

"Naked I came from my mother's
    womb,
and naked I will depart.a
The LORD gave and the LORD has
    taken away;

may the name of the LORD be
    praised."

22In all this, Job did not sin by charging God with wrongdoing.

Job's Second Test

2 On another day the angelsb came to present themselves before the LORD, and Satan also came with them to present himself before him. 2And the LORD said to Satan, "Where have you come from?"

Satan answered the LORD, "From roaming through the earth and going back and forth in it."

3Then the LORD said to Satan, "Have you considered my servant Job? There is no one on earth like him; he is blameless and upright, a man who fears God and shuns evil. And he still maintains his integrity, though you incited me against him to ruin him without any reason."

4"Skin for skin!" Satan replied. "A man will give all he has for his own life. 5But stretch out your hand and strike his flesh and bones, and he will surely curse you to your face."

6The LORD said to Satan, "Very well, then, he is in your hands; but you must spare his life."

7So Satan went out from the presence of the LORD and afflicted Job with painful sores from the soles of his feet to the top of his head. 8Then Job took a piece of broken pottery and scraped himself with it as he sat among the ashes.

9His wife said to him, "Are you still holding on to your integrity? Curse God and die!"

10He replied, "You are talking like a foolishc woman. Shall we accept good from God, and not trouble?"

In all this, Job did not sin in what he said.

Job's Three Friends

11When Job's three friends, Eliphaz the Temanite, Bildad the Shuhite and Zophar the Naamathite, heard about all the troubles that had come upon him, they set out from their homes and met together by agreement to go and

a 21 Or will return there   b 1 Hebrew the sons of God   c 10 The Hebrew word rendered foolish denotes moral deficiency.

sympathize with him and comfort him. ¹²When they saw him from a distance, they could hardly recognize him; they began to weep aloud, and they tore their robes and sprinkled dust on their heads. ¹³Then they sat on the ground with him for seven days and seven nights. No one said a word to him, because they saw how great his suffering was.

Job Speaks

3 After this, Job opened his mouth and cursed the day of his birth. ²He said:

³ "May the day of my birth perish,
    and the night it was said, 'A boy is
        born!'
⁴ That day—may it turn to darkness;
    may God above not care about it;

THURSDAY

ABUNDANT LIVING "IN SPITE OF"
E. Stanley Jones

VERSE: Job 1:21   **PASSAGE:** Job 1:13–22

bundant living is sometimes on account of, but more often, perhaps, in spite of. When circumstances are against us, we must be able to set the sails of our souls and use even adverse winds. The Christian faith does not offer exemption from sorrow and pain and frustration—it offers the power, not merely to bear, but to use these adversities. The secret of using pain and suffering and frustration is in many ways life's greatest secret. When you have learned that, you are unbeatable and unbreakable . . .

The Christian "can take it," because he can take hold of adversity and use it . . . [Christ] bore the cross, for he could use the cross. You cannot bear the cross long—it will break your spirit, unless you can take that cross and make it serve higher purposes. The stoic bears the cross; the Christian makes the cross bear fruit.

Any movement that has learned the secret of making the bitterest tree—the cross—bear the sweet fruit has learned the secret of abundant living.

O Christ, we begin to see thy secret. Thou didst lay hold of life when life was speaking its cruelest word and didst turn that very word into God's most redemptive word. Thou didst not bear the cross—thou didst use it. Give me power to do just that. Then, in thee, I am invincible. Amen.

ADDITIONAL SCRIPTURE READING:
Job 2:10; 1 Thessalonians 5:18; James 1:12

Go to page 569 for your next devotional reading.

1900   Present

may no light shine upon it.
5 May darkness and deep shadow*a*
    claim it once more;
    may a cloud settle over it;
    may blackness overwhelm its light.
6 That night—may thick darkness
        seize it;
    may it not be included among the
        days of the year
    nor be entered in any of the
        months.
7 May that night be barren;
    may no shout of joy be heard in it.
8 May those who curse days*b* curse
        that day,
    those who are ready to rouse
        Leviathan.
9 May its morning stars become dark;
    may it wait for daylight in vain
    and not see the first rays of dawn,
10 for it did not shut the doors of the
        womb on me
    to hide trouble from my eyes.

11 "Why did I not perish at birth,
    and die as I came from the womb?
12 Why were there knees to receive me
    and breasts that I might be nursed?
13 For now I would be lying down in
        peace;
    I would be asleep and at rest
14 with kings and counselors of the
        earth,
    who built for themselves places
        now lying in ruins,
15 with rulers who had gold,
    who filled their houses with silver.
16 Or why was I not hidden in the
        ground like a stillborn child,
    like an infant who never saw the
        light of day?
17 There the wicked cease from
        turmoil,
    and there the weary are at rest.
18 Captives also enjoy their ease;
    they no longer hear the slave
        driver's shout.
19 The small and the great are there,
    and the slave is freed from his
        master.

20 "Why is light given to those in
        misery,
    and life to the bitter of soul,
21 to those who long for death that does
        not come,

who search for it more than for
        hidden treasure,
22 who are filled with gladness
    and rejoice when they reach the
        grave?
23 Why is life given to a man
    whose way is hidden,
    whom God has hedged in?
24 For sighing comes to me instead of
        food;
    my groans pour out like water.
25 What I feared has come upon me;
    what I dreaded has happened to
        me.
26 I have no peace, no quietness;
    I have no rest, but only turmoil."

Eliphaz

4 Then Eliphaz the Temanite
    replied:

2 "If someone ventures a word with
        you, will you be impatient?
    But who can keep from speaking?
3 Think how you have instructed
        many,
    how you have strengthened feeble
        hands.
4 Your words have supported those
        who stumbled;
    you have strengthened faltering
        knees.
5 But now trouble comes to you, and
        you are discouraged;
    it strikes you, and you are
        dismayed.
6 Should not your piety be your
        confidence
    and your blameless ways your
        hope?

7 "Consider now: Who, being
        innocent, has ever perished?
    Where were the upright ever
        destroyed?
8 As I have observed, those who plow
        evil
    and those who sow trouble reap it.
9 At the breath of God they are
        destroyed;
    at the blast of his anger they
        perish.
10 The lions may roar and growl,
    yet the teeth of the great lions are
        broken.

a 5 Or and the shadow of death   b 8 Or the sea

11 The lion perishes for lack of prey,
  and the cubs of the lioness are
    scattered.

12 "A word was secretly brought to me,
  my ears caught a whisper of it.
13 Amid disquieting dreams in the night,
  when deep sleep falls on men,
14 fear and trembling seized me
  and made all my bones shake.
15 A spirit glided past my face,
  and the hair on my body stood on
    end.
16 It stopped,
  but I could not tell what it was.
  A form stood before my eyes,
  and I heard a hushed voice:
17 'Can a mortal be more righteous than
    God?
  Can a man be more pure than his
    Maker?
18 If God places no trust in his servants,
  if he charges his angels with error,
19 how much more those who live in
    houses of clay,
  whose foundations are in the dust,
  who are crushed more readily than
    a moth!
20 Between dawn and dusk they are
    broken to pieces;
  unnoticed, they perish forever.
21 Are not the cords of their tent pulled
    up,
  so that they die without wisdom?'a

5 "Call if you will, but who will
    answer you?
  To which of the holy ones will you
    turn?
2 Resentment kills a fool,
  and envy slays the simple.
3 I myself have seen a fool taking root,
  but suddenly his house was cursed.
4 His children are far from safety,
  crushed in court without a
    defender.
5 The hungry consume his harvest,
  taking it even from among thorns,
  and the thirsty pant after his
    wealth.
6 For hardship does not spring from the
    soil,
  nor does trouble sprout from the
    ground.
7 Yet man is born to trouble
  as surely as sparks fly upward.

8 "But if it were I, I would appeal to
    God;
  I would lay my cause before him.
9 He performs wonders that cannot be
    fathomed,
  miracles that cannot be counted.
10 He bestows rain on the earth;
  he sends water upon the
    countryside.
11 The lowly he sets on high,
  and those who mourn are lifted to
    safety.
12 He thwarts the plans of the crafty,
  so that their hands achieve no
    success.
13 He catches the wise in their
    craftiness,
  and the schemes of the wily are
    swept away.
14 Darkness comes upon them in the
    daytime;
  at noon they grope as in the night.
15 He saves the needy from the sword in
    their mouth;
  he saves them from the clutches of
    the powerful.
16 So the poor have hope,
  and injustice shuts its mouth.

17 "Blessed is the man whom God
    corrects;
  so do not despise the discipline of
    the Almighty.b
18 For he wounds, but he also binds up;
  he injures, but his hands also heal.
19 From six calamities he will rescue
    you;
  in seven no harm will befall you.
20 In famine he will ransom you from
    death,
  and in battle from the stroke of the
    sword.
21 You will be protected from the lash
    of the tongue,
  and need not fear when destruction
    comes.
22 You will laugh at destruction and
    famine,
  and need not fear the beasts of the
    earth.
23 For you will have a covenant with
    the stones of the field,
  and the wild animals will be at
    peace with you.

a 21 Some interpreters end the quotation after verse 17.   b 17 Hebrew Shaddai; here and throughout Job

²⁴You will know that your tent is
      secure;
   you will take stock of your
      property and find nothing
      missing.
²⁵You will know that your children
      will be many,
   and your descendants like the grass
      of the earth.
²⁶You will come to the grave in full
      vigor,
   like sheaves gathered in season.
²⁷"We have examined this, and it is
      true.
   So hear it and apply it to yourself."

Job

6 Then Job replied:

²"If only my anguish could be
      weighed
   and all my misery be placed on the
      scales!
³It would surely outweigh the sand of
      the seas—
   no wonder my words have been
      impetuous.
⁴The arrows of the Almighty are in me,
   my spirit drinks in their poison;
   God's terrors are marshaled against
      me.
⁵Does a wild donkey bray when it has
      grass,
   or an ox bellow when it has fodder?
⁶Is tasteless food eaten without salt,
   or is there flavor in the white of an
      egg*a*?
⁷I refuse to touch it;
   such food makes me ill.

⁸"Oh, that I might have my request,
   that God would grant what I hope
      for,
⁹that God would be willing to crush
      me,
   to let loose his hand and cut me
      off!
¹⁰Then I would still have this
      consolation—
   my joy in unrelenting pain—
   that I had not denied the words of
      the Holy One.

¹¹"What strength do I have, that I
      should still hope?

What prospects, that I should be
      patient?
¹²Do I have the strength of stone?
   Is my flesh bronze?
¹³Do I have any power to help myself,
   now that success has been driven
      from me?

¹⁴"A despairing man should have the
      devotion of his friends,
   even though he forsakes the fear of
      the Almighty.
¹⁵But my brothers are as undependable
      as intermittent streams,
   as the streams that overflow
¹⁶when darkened by thawing ice
   and swollen with melting snow,
¹⁷but that cease to flow in the dry
      season,
   and in the heat vanish from their
      channels.
¹⁸Caravans turn aside from their
      routes;
   they go up into the wasteland and
      perish.
¹⁹The caravans of Tema look for water,
   the traveling merchants of Sheba
      look in hope.
²⁰They are distressed, because they had
      been confident;
   they arrive there, only to be
      disappointed.
²¹Now you too have proved to be of no
      help;
   you see something dreadful and are
      afraid.
²²Have I ever said, 'Give something on
      my behalf,
   pay a ransom for me from your
      wealth,
²³deliver me from the hand of the
      enemy,
   ransom me from the clutches of
      the ruthless'?

²⁴"Teach me, and I will be quiet;
   show me where I have been wrong.
²⁵How painful are honest words!
   But what do your arguments
      prove?
²⁶Do you mean to correct what I say,
   and treat the words of a despairing
      man as wind?
²⁷You would even cast lots for the
      fatherless
   and barter away your friend.

---

a 6 The meaning of the Hebrew for this phrase is uncertain.

28 "But now be so kind as to look at me.
   Would I lie to your face?
29 Relent, do not be unjust;
   reconsider, for my integrity is at
   stake.*a*
30 Is there any wickedness on my lips?
   Can my mouth not discern malice?

7 "Does not man have hard
   service on earth?
   Are not his days like those of a
   hired man?
2 Like a slave longing for the evening
   shadows,
   or a hired man waiting eagerly for
   his wages,
3 so I have been allotted months of
   futility,
   and nights of misery have been
   assigned to me.
4 When I lie down I think, 'How long
   before I get up?'
   The night drags on, and I toss till
   dawn.
5 My body is clothed with worms and
   scabs,
   my skin is broken and festering.

6 "My days are swifter than a weaver's
   shuttle,
   and they come to an end without
   hope.
7 Remember, O God, that my life is
   but a breath;
   my eyes will never see happiness
   again.
8 The eye that now sees me will see
   me no longer;
   you will look for me, but I will be
   no more.
9 As a cloud vanishes and is gone,
   so he who goes down to the grave*b*
   does not return.
10 He will never come to his house
   again;
   his place will know him no more.

11 "Therefore I will not keep silent;
   I will speak out in the anguish of
   my spirit,
   I will complain in the bitterness of
   my soul.
12 Am I the sea, or the monster of the
   deep,
   that you put me under guard?

13 When I think my bed will comfort
   me
   and my couch will ease my
   complaint,
14 even then you frighten me with
   dreams
   and terrify me with visions,
15 so that I prefer strangling and death,
   rather than this body of mine.
16 I despise my life; I would not live
   forever.
   Let me alone; my days have no
   meaning.

17 "What is man that you make so
   much of him,
   that you give him so much
   attention,
18 that you examine him every morning
   and test him every moment?
19 Will you never look away from me,
   or let me alone even for an instant?
20 If I have sinned, what have I done to
   you,
   O watcher of men?
   Why have you made me your target?
   Have I become a burden to you?*c*
21 Why do you not pardon my offenses
   and forgive my sins?
   For I will soon lie down in the dust;
   you will search for me, but I will
   be no more."

Bildad

8 Then Bildad the Shuhite replied:

2 "How long will you say such things?
   Your words are a blustering wind.
3 Does God pervert justice?
   Does the Almighty pervert what is
   right?
4 When your children sinned against
   him,
   he gave them over to the penalty of
   their sin.
5 But if you will look to God
   and plead with the Almighty,
6 if you are pure and upright,
   even now he will rouse himself on
   your behalf
   and restore you to your rightful
   place.
7 Your beginnings will seem humble,
   so prosperous will your future be.

a 29 Or *my righteousness still stands*   *b 9* Hebrew *Sheol*   *c 20* A few manuscripts of the Masoretic
Text, an ancient Hebrew scribal tradition and Septuagint; most manuscripts of the Masoretic Text *I have
become a burden to myself.*

8 "Ask the former generations
　and find out what their fathers
　　learned,
9 for we were born only yesterday and
　　know nothing,
　and our days on earth are but a
　　shadow.
10 Will they not instruct you and tell
　　you?
　Will they not bring forth words
　　from their understanding?
11 Can papyrus grow tall where there is
　　no marsh?
　Can reeds thrive without water?
12 While still growing and uncut,
　they wither more quickly than
　　grass.
13 Such is the destiny of all who forget
　　God;
　so perishes the hope of the godless.
14 What he trusts in is fragile[a];
　what he relies on is a spider's
　　web.
15 He leans on his web, but it gives way;
　he clings to it, but it does not
　　hold.
16 He is like a well-watered plant in the
　　sunshine,
　spreading its shoots over the
　　garden;
17 it entwines its roots around a pile of
　　rocks
　and looks for a place among the
　　stones.
18 But when it is torn from its spot,
　that place disowns it and says, 'I
　　never saw you.'
19 Surely its life withers away,
　and[b] from the soil other plants
　　grow.

20 "Surely God does not reject a
　　blameless man
　or strengthen the hands of
　　evildoers.
21 He will yet fill your mouth with
　　laughter
　and your lips with shouts of joy.
22 Your enemies will be clothed in
　　shame,
　and the tents of the wicked will be
　　no more."

Job

9 Then Job replied:

2 "Indeed, I know that this is true.
　But how can a mortal be righteous
　　before God?
3 Though one wished to dispute with
　　him,
　he could not answer him one time
　　out of a thousand.
4 His wisdom is profound, his power is
　　vast.
　Who has resisted him and come
　　out unscathed?
5 He moves mountains without their
　　knowing it
　and overturns them in his anger.
6 He shakes the earth from its place
　and makes its pillars tremble.
7 He speaks to the sun and it does not
　　shine;
　he seals off the light of the stars.
8 He alone stretches out the heavens
　and treads on the waves of the sea.
9 He is the Maker of the Bear and
　　Orion,
　the Pleiades and the constellations
　　of the south.
10 He performs wonders that cannot be
　　fathomed,
　miracles that cannot be counted.
11 When he passes me, I cannot see
　　him;
　when he goes by, I cannot perceive
　　him.
12 If he snatches away, who can stop
　　him?
　Who can say to him, 'What are you
　　doing?'
13 God does not restrain his anger;
　even the cohorts of Rahab cowered
　　at his feet.

14 "How then can I dispute with him?
　How can I find words to argue with
　　him?
15 Though I were innocent, I could not
　　answer him;
　I could only plead with my Judge
　　for mercy.
16 Even if I summoned him and he
　　responded,
　I do not believe he would give me a
　　hearing.
17 He would crush me with a storm

---

[a] 14 The meaning of the Hebrew for this word is uncertain.　　[b] 19 Or *Surely all the joy it has / is that*

and multiply my wounds for no reason.

¹⁸ He would not let me regain my breath
but would overwhelm me with misery.

¹⁹ If it is a matter of strength, he is mighty!
And if it is a matter of justice, who will summon him*?

²⁰ Even if I were innocent, my mouth would condemn me;
if I were blameless, it would pronounce me guilty.

²¹ "Although I am blameless,
I have no concern for myself;
I despise my own life.

²² It is all the same; that is why I say,
'He destroys both the blameless and the wicked.'

²³ When a scourge brings sudden death,
he mocks the despair of the innocent.

²⁴ When a land falls into the hands of the wicked,
he blindfolds its judges.
If it is not he, then who is it?

²⁵ "My days are swifter than a runner;
they fly away without a glimpse of joy.

²⁶ They skim past like boats of papyrus,
like eagles swooping down on their prey.

²⁷ If I say, 'I will forget my complaint,
I will change my expression, and smile,'

²⁸ I still dread all my sufferings,
for I know you will not hold me innocent.

²⁹ Since I am already found guilty,
why should I struggle in vain?

³⁰ Even if I washed myself with soap*ᵇ*
and my hands with washing soda,

³¹ you would plunge me into a slime pit
so that even my clothes would detest me.

³² "He is not a man like me that I might answer him,
that we might confront each other in court.

³³ If only there were someone to arbitrate between us,
to lay his hand upon us both,

³⁴ someone to remove God's rod from me,
so that his terror would frighten me no more.

³⁵ Then I would speak up without fear of him,
but as it now stands with me, I cannot.

10 "I loathe my very life;
therefore I will give free rein to my complaint
and speak out in the bitterness of my soul.

² I will say to God: Do not condemn me,
but tell me what charges you have against me.

³ Does it please you to oppress me,
to spurn the work of your hands,
while you smile on the schemes of the wicked?

⁴ Do you have eyes of flesh?
Do you see as a mortal sees?

⁵ Are your days like those of a mortal
or your years like those of a man,

⁶ that you must search out my faults
and probe after my sin—

⁷ though you know that I am not guilty
and that no one can rescue me from your hand?

⁸ "Your hands shaped me and made me.
Will you now turn and destroy me?

⁹ Remember that you molded me like clay.
Will you now turn me to dust again?

¹⁰ Did you not pour me out like milk
and curdle me like cheese,

¹¹ clothe me with skin and flesh
and knit me together with bones and sinews?

¹² You gave me life and showed me kindness,
and in your providence watched over my spirit.

¹³ "But this is what you concealed in your heart,
and I know that this was in your mind:

¹⁴ If I sinned, you would be watching me
and would not let my offense go unpunished.

---

a 19 See Septuagint; Hebrew *me.*   *b 30* Or *snow*

15 If I am guilty—woe to me!
Even if I am innocent, I cannot lift
my head,
for I am full of shame
and drowned in*a* my affliction.
16 If I hold my head high, you stalk me
like a lion
and again display your awesome
power against me.
17 You bring new witnesses against me
and increase your anger toward
me;
your forces come against me wave
upon wave.
18 "Why then did you bring me out of
the womb?
I wish I had died before any eye
saw me.
19 If only I had never come into being,
or had been carried straight from
the womb to the grave!
20 Are not my few days almost over?
Turn away from me so I can have a
moment's joy
21 before I go to the place of no return,
to the land of gloom and deep
shadow,*b*
22 to the land of deepest night,
of deep shadow and disorder,
where even the light is like
darkness."

Zophar

11 Then Zophar the Naamathite
replied:

2 "Are all these words to go
unanswered?
Is this talker to be vindicated?
3 Will your idle talk reduce men to
silence?
Will no one rebuke you when you
mock?
4 You say to God, 'My beliefs are
flawless
and I am pure in your sight.'
5 Oh, how I wish that God would
speak,
that he would open his lips against
you
6 and disclose to you the secrets of
wisdom,
for true wisdom has two sides.

Know this: God has even forgotten
some of your sin.
7 "Can you fathom the mysteries of
God?
Can you probe the limits of the
Almighty?
8 They are higher than the heavens—
what can you do?
They are deeper than the depths of
the grave*c*—what can you
know?
9 Their measure is longer than the
earth
and wider than the sea.
10 "If he comes along and confines you
in prison
and convenes a court, who can
oppose him?
11 Surely he recognizes deceitful men;
and when he sees evil, does he not
take note?
12 But a witless man can no more
become wise
than a wild donkey's colt can be
born a man.*d*
13 "Yet if you devote your heart to him
and stretch out your hands to him,
14 if you put away the sin that is in your
hand
and allow no evil to dwell in your
tent,
15 then you will lift up your face
without shame;
you will stand firm and without
fear.
16 You will surely forget your trouble,
recalling it only as waters gone by.
17 Life will be brighter than noonday,
and darkness will become like
morning.
18 You will be secure, because there is
hope;
you will look about you and take
your rest in safety.
19 You will lie down, with no one to
make you afraid,
and many will court your favor.
20 But the eyes of the wicked will fail,
and escape will elude them;
their hope will become a dying
gasp."

---

a 15 Or *and aware of*   *b* 21 Or *and the shadow of death;* also in verse 22   *c* 8 Hebrew *than Sheol*
d 12 Or *wild donkey can be born tame*

Job

12

Then Job replied:

2 "Doubtless you are the people,
    and wisdom will die with you!
3 But I have a mind as well as you;
    I am not inferior to you.
    Who does not know all these
        things?

4 "I have become a laughingstock to
        my friends,
    though I called upon God and he
        answered—
    a mere laughingstock, though
        righteous and blameless!
5 Men at ease have contempt for
        misfortune
    as the fate of those whose feet are
        slipping.
6 The tents of marauders are
        undisturbed,
    and those who provoke God are
        secure—
    those who carry their god in their
        hands.*a*

7 "But ask the animals, and they will
        teach you,
    or the birds of the air, and they will
        tell you;
8 or speak to the earth, and it will
        teach you,
    or let the fish of the sea inform
        you.
9 Which of all these does not know
    that the hand of the LORD has done
        this?
10 In his hand is the life of every
        creature
    and the breath of all mankind.
11 Does not the ear test words
    as the tongue tastes food?
12 Is not wisdom found among the aged?
    Does not long life bring
        understanding?

13 "To God belong wisdom and power;
    counsel and understanding are his.
14 What he tears down cannot be
        rebuilt;
    the man he imprisons cannot be
        released.
15 If he holds back the waters, there is
        drought;

if he lets them loose, they
    devastate the land.
16 To him belong strength and victory;
    both deceived and deceiver are his.
17 He leads counselors away stripped
    and makes fools of judges.
18 He takes off the shackles put on by
        kings
    and ties a loincloth*b* around their
        waist.
19 He leads priests away stripped
    and overthrows men long
        established.
20 He silences the lips of trusted
        advisers
    and takes away the discernment of
        elders.
21 He pours contempt on nobles
    and disarms the mighty.
22 He reveals the deep things of
        darkness
    and brings deep shadows into the
        light.
23 He makes nations great, and destroys
        them;
    he enlarges nations, and disperses
        them.
24 He deprives the leaders of the earth
        of their reason;
    he sends them wandering through
        a trackless waste.

ATHEISTS PUT ON A FALSE COURAGE AND
ALACRITY IN THE MIDST OF THEIR DARKNESS
AND APPREHENSIONS, LIKE CHILDREN WHO,
WHEN THEY FEAR TO GO INTO THE DARK, WILL
SING OR WHISTLE TO KEEP UP THEIR COURAGE.

—*Alexander Pope*

---

25 They grope in darkness with no light;
    he makes them stagger like
        drunkards.

13

"My eyes have seen all this,
    my ears have heard and
        understood it.
2 What you know, I also know;
    I am not inferior to you.
3 But I desire to speak to the Almighty
    and to argue my case with God.
4 You, however, smear me with lies;
    you are worthless physicians, all of
        you!

---

a 6 Or *secure / in what God's hand brings them*   *b 18* Or *shackles of kings / and ties a belt*

⁵ If only you would be altogether silent!
  For you, that would be wisdom.
⁶ Hear now my argument;
  listen to the plea of my lips.
⁷ Will you speak wickedly on God's
    behalf?
  Will you speak deceitfully for him?
⁸ Will you show him partiality?
  Will you argue the case for God?
⁹ Would it turn out well if he
    examined you?
  Could you deceive him as you
    might deceive men?
¹⁰ He would surely rebuke you
  if you secretly showed partiality.
¹¹ Would not his splendor terrify you?
  Would not the dread of him fall on
    you?
¹² Your maxims are proverbs of ashes;
  your defenses are defenses of clay.

¹³ "Keep silent and let me speak;
  then let come to me what may.
¹⁴ Why do I put myself in jeopardy
  and take my life in my hands?
¹⁵ Though he slay me, yet will I hope in
    him;
  I will surely ᵃ defend my ways to
    his face.
¹⁶ Indeed, this will turn out for my
    deliverance,
  for no godless man would dare
    come before him!
¹⁷ Listen carefully to my words;
  let your ears take in what I say.
¹⁸ Now that I have prepared my case,
  I know I will be vindicated.
¹⁹ Can anyone bring charges against me?
  If so, I will be silent and die.

²⁰ "Only grant me these two things,
    O God,
  and then I will not hide from you:
²¹ Withdraw your hand far from me,
  and stop frightening me with your
    terrors.
²² Then summon me and I will answer,
  or let me speak, and you reply.
²³ How many wrongs and sins have I
    committed?
  Show me my offense and my sin.
²⁴ Why do you hide your face
  and consider me your enemy?
²⁵ Will you torment a windblown leaf?
  Will you chase after dry chaff?

²⁶ For you write down bitter things
    against me
  and make me inherit the sins of
    my youth.
²⁷ You fasten my feet in shackles;
  you keep close watch on all my
    paths
  by putting marks on the soles of
    my feet.

²⁸ "So man wastes away like something
    rotten,
  like a garment eaten by moths.

14 "Man born of woman
  is of few days and full of
    trouble.
² He springs up like a flower and
    withers away;
  like a fleeting shadow, he does not
    endure.
³ Do you fix your eye on such a one?
  Will you bring him ᵇ before you for
    judgment?
⁴ Who can bring what is pure from the
    impure?
  No one!
⁵ Man's days are determined;
  you have decreed the number of
    his months
  and have set limits he cannot
    exceed.
⁶ So look away from him and let him
    alone,
  till he has put in his time like a
    hired man.

⁷ "At least there is hope for a tree:
  If it is cut down, it will sprout
    again,
  and its new shoots will not fail.
⁸ Its roots may grow old in the
    ground
  and its stump die in the soil,
⁹ yet at the scent of water it will bud
  and put forth shoots like a plant.
¹⁰ But man dies and is laid low;
  he breathes his last and is no more.
¹¹ As water disappears from the sea
  or a riverbed becomes parched and
    dry,
¹² so man lies down and does not rise;
  till the heavens are no more, men
    will not awake
  or be roused from their sleep.

ᵃ 15 Or *He will surely slay me; I have no hope — / yet I will* ᵇ 3 Septuagint, Vulgate and Syriac;
Hebrew *me*

13 "If only you would hide me in the
      grave^a
   and conceal me till your anger has
      passed!
   If only you would set me a time
      and then remember me!
14 If a man dies, will he live again?
   All the days of my hard service
   I will wait for my renewal^b to
      come.
15 You will call and I will answer you;
   you will long for the creature your
      hands have made.
16 Surely then you will count my steps
   but not keep track of my sin.
17 My offenses will be sealed up in a bag;
   you will cover over my sin.

18 "But as a mountain erodes and
      crumbles
   and as a rock is moved from its
      place,
19 as water wears away stones
   and torrents wash away the soil,
   so you destroy man's hope.
20 You overpower him once for all, and
      he is gone;
   you change his countenance and
      send him away.
21 If his sons are honored, he does not
      know it;
   if they are brought low, he does not
      see it.
22 He feels but the pain of his own body
   and mourns only for himself."

Eliphaz

15 Then Eliphaz the Temanite
replied:

2 "Would a wise man answer with
      empty notions
   or fill his belly with the hot east
      wind?
3 Would he argue with useless words,
   with speeches that have no value?
4 But you even undermine piety
   and hinder devotion to God.
5 Your sin prompts your mouth;
   you adopt the tongue of the crafty.
6 Your own mouth condemns you, not
      mine;
   your own lips testify against you.

7 "Are you the first man ever born?

Were you brought forth before the
      hills?
8 Do you listen in on God's council?
   Do you limit wisdom to yourself?
9 What do you know that we do not
      know?
   What insights do you have that we
      do not have?
10 The gray-haired and the aged are on
      our side,
   men even older than your father.
11 Are God's consolations not enough
      for you,
   words spoken gently to you?
12 Why has your heart carried you away,
   and why do your eyes flash,
13 so that you vent your rage against
      God
   and pour out such words from your
      mouth?

14 "What is man, that he could be pure,
   or one born of woman, that he
      could be righteous?
15 If God places no trust in his holy ones,
   if even the heavens are not pure in
      his eyes,
16 how much less man, who is vile and
      corrupt,
   who drinks up evil like water!

17 "Listen to me and I will explain to
      you;
   let me tell you what I have seen,
18 what wise men have declared,
   hiding nothing received from their
      fathers
19 (to whom alone the land was given
   when no alien passed among
      them):
20 All his days the wicked man suffers
      torment,
   the ruthless through all the years
      stored up for him.
21 Terrifying sounds fill his ears;
   when all seems well, marauders
      attack him.
22 He despairs of escaping the darkness;
   he is marked for the sword.
23 He wanders about—food for
      vultures^c;
   he knows the day of darkness is at
      hand.
24 Distress and anguish fill him with
      terror;

^a 13 Hebrew *Sheol*   ^b 14 Or *release*   ^c 23 Or *about, looking for food*

they overwhelm him, like a king
poised to attack,

25 because he shakes his fist at God
and vaunts himself against the
Almighty,

26 defiantly charging against him
with a thick, strong shield.

27 "Though his face is covered with fat
and his waist bulges with flesh,

28 he will inhabit ruined towns
and houses where no one lives,
houses crumbling to rubble.

29 He will no longer be rich and his
wealth will not endure,
nor will his possessions spread
over the land.

30 He will not escape the darkness;
a flame will wither his shoots,
and the breath of God's mouth will
carry him away.

31 Let him not deceive himself by
trusting what is worthless,
for he will get nothing in return.

32 Before his time he will be paid in full,
and his branches will not flourish.

33 He will be like a vine stripped of its
unripe grapes,
like an olive tree shedding its
blossoms.

34 For the company of the godless will
be barren,
and fire will consume the tents of
those who love bribes.

35 They conceive trouble and give birth
to evil;
their womb fashions deceit."

Job

16 Then Job replied:

2 "I have heard many things like these;
miserable comforters are you all!

3 Will your long-winded speeches
never end?
What ails you that you keep on
arguing?

4 I also could speak like you,
if you were in my place;
I could make fine speeches against
you
and shake my head at you.

5 But my mouth would encourage you;
comfort from my lips would bring
you relief.

6 "Yet if I speak, my pain is not
relieved;
and if I refrain, it does not go away.

7 Surely, O God, you have worn me
out;
you have devastated my entire
household.

8 You have bound me—and it has
become a witness;
my gauntness rises up and testifies
against me.

9 God assails me and tears me in his
anger
and gnashes his teeth at me;
my opponent fastens on me his
piercing eyes.

10 Men open their mouths to jeer at me;
they strike my cheek in scorn
and unite together against me.

11 God has turned me over to evil men
and thrown me into the clutches of
the wicked.

12 All was well with me, but he
shattered me;
he seized me by the neck and
crushed me.
He has made me his target;

13   his archers surround me.
Without pity, he pierces my kidneys
and spills my gall on the ground.

14 Again and again he bursts upon me;
he rushes at me like a warrior.

15 "I have sewed sackcloth over my
skin
and buried my brow in the dust.

16 My face is red with weeping,
deep shadows ring my eyes;

17 yet my hands have been free of
violence
and my prayer is pure.

18 "O earth, do not cover my blood;
may my cry never be laid to rest!

19 Even now my witness is in heaven;
my advocate is on high.

20 My intercessor is my friend[a]
as my eyes pour out tears to God;

21 on behalf of a man he pleads with
God
as a man pleads for his friend.

22 "Only a few years will pass
before I go on the journey of no
return.

a 20 Or *My friends treat me with scorn*

17

¹ My spirit is broken,
  my days are cut short,
  the grave awaits me.
² Surely mockers surround me;
  my eyes must dwell on their
    hostility.

³ "Give me, O God, the pledge you
    demand.
  Who else will put up security for
    me?
⁴ You have closed their minds to
    understanding;
  therefore you will not let them
    triumph.
⁵ If a man denounces his friends for
    reward,
  the eyes of his children will fail.

⁶ "God has made me a byword to
    everyone,
  a man in whose face people spit.
⁷ My eyes have grown dim with grief;
  my whole frame is but a shadow.
⁸ Upright men are appalled at this;
  the innocent are aroused against
    the ungodly.
⁹ Nevertheless, the righteous will hold
    to their ways,
  and those with clean hands will
    grow stronger.

¹⁰ "But come on, all of you, try again!
  I will not find a wise man among
    you.
¹¹ My days have passed, my plans are
    shattered,
  and so are the desires of my heart.
¹² These men turn night into day;
  in the face of darkness they say,
    'Light is near.'
¹³ If the only home I hope for is the
    grave,[a]
  if I spread out my bed in darkness,
¹⁴ if I say to corruption, 'You are my
    father,'
  and to the worm, 'My mother' or
    'My sister,'
¹⁵ where then is my hope?
  Who can see any hope for me?
¹⁶ Will it go down to the gates of
    death[a]?
  Will we descend together into the
    dust?"

Bildad

18

Then Bildad the Shuhite
replied:

² "When will you end these speeches?
  Be sensible, and then we can talk.
³ Why are we regarded as cattle
  and considered stupid in your
    sight?
⁴ You who tear yourself to pieces in
    your anger,
  is the earth to be abandoned for
    your sake?
  Or must the rocks be moved from
    their place?

⁵ "The lamp of the wicked is snuffed
    out;
  the flame of his fire stops burning.
⁶ The light in his tent becomes dark;
  the lamp beside him goes out.
⁷ The vigor of his step is weakened;
  his own schemes throw him down.
⁸ His feet thrust him into a net
  and he wanders into its mesh.
⁹ A trap seizes him by the heel;
  a snare holds him fast.
¹⁰ A noose is hidden for him on the
    ground;
  a trap lies in his path.
¹¹ Terrors startle him on every side
  and dog his every step.
¹² Calamity is hungry for him;
  disaster is ready for him when he
    falls.
¹³ It eats away parts of his skin;
  death's firstborn devours his limbs.
¹⁴ He is torn from the security of his
    tent
  and marched off to the king of
    terrors.
¹⁵ Fire resides[b] in his tent;
  burning sulfur is scattered over his
    dwelling.
¹⁶ His roots dry up below
  and his branches wither above.
¹⁷ The memory of him perishes from
    the earth;
  he has no name in the land.
¹⁸ He is driven from light into darkness
  and is banished from the world.
¹⁹ He has no offspring or descendants
    among his people,
  no survivor where once he lived.

---

a 13,16 Hebrew *Sheol*   *b 15* Or *Nothing he had remains*

20 Men of the west are appalled at his
fate;
men of the east are seized with
horror.
21 Surely such is the dwelling of an evil
man;
such is the place of one who knows
not God."

Job

19 Then Job replied:

2 "How long will you torment me
and crush me with words?
3 Ten times now you have reproached
me;
shamelessly you attack me.
4 If it is true that I have gone astray,
my error remains my concern
alone.
5 If indeed you would exalt yourselves
above me
and use my humiliation against me,
6 then know that God has wronged me
and drawn his net around me.

7 "Though I cry, 'I've been wronged!' I
get no response;
though I call for help, there is no
justice.
8 He has blocked my way so I cannot
pass;
he has shrouded my paths in
darkness.
9 He has stripped me of my honor
and removed the crown from my
head.
10 He tears me down on every side till I
am gone;
he uproots my hope like a tree.
11 His anger burns against me;
he counts me among his enemies.
12 His troops advance in force;
they build a siege ramp against me
and encamp around my tent.

13 "He has alienated my brothers from
me;
my acquaintances are completely
estranged from me.
14 My kinsmen have gone away;
my friends have forgotten me.

15 My guests and my maidservants
count me a stranger;
they look upon me as an alien.
16 I summon my servant, but he does
not answer,
though I beg him with my own
mouth.
17 My breath is offensive to my wife;
I am loathsome to my own
brothers.
18 Even the little boys scorn me;
when I appear, they ridicule me.
19 All my intimate friends detest me;
those I love have turned against
me.
20 I am nothing but skin and bones;
I have escaped with only the skin
of my teeth.[a]

21 "Have pity on me, my friends, have
pity,
for the hand of God has struck me.
22 Why do you pursue me as God
does?
Will you never get enough of my
flesh?

23 "Oh, that my words were recorded,
that they were written on a scroll,
24 that they were inscribed with an iron
tool on[b] lead,
or engraved in rock forever!
25 I know that my Redeemer[c] lives,
and that in the end he will stand
upon the earth.[d]
26 And after my skin has been
destroyed,
yet[e] in[f] my flesh I will see God;
27 I myself will see him
with my own eyes—I, and not
another.
How my heart yearns within me!

28 "If you say, 'How we will hound him,
since the root of the trouble lies in
him,[g] '
29 you should fear the sword
yourselves;
for wrath will bring punishment by
the sword,
and then you will know that there
is judgment.[h] "

---

a 20 Or *only my gums*   *b 24* Or *and*   *c 25* Or *defender*   *d 25* Or *upon my grave*   *e 26* Or *And*
after I awake, / though this body has been destroyed, / then   *f 26* Or */ apart from*   *g 28* Many
Hebrew manuscripts, Septuagint and Vulgate; most Hebrew manuscripts *me*   *h 29* Or */ that you may*
come to know the Almighty

Zophar

20 Then Zophar the Naamathite replied:

2 "My troubled thoughts prompt me to
answer
because I am greatly disturbed.

3 I hear a rebuke that dishonors me,
and my understanding inspires me
to reply.

4 "Surely you know how it has been
from of old,
ever since man*a* was placed on the
earth,

a 4 Or Adam

FRIDAY

LET US KNIT FAST OUR SOULS TO HIM
Clement of Rome

VERSE: Job 19:25   **PASSAGE:** Job 19:25–27

eed we find it such a great wonder that he has a resurrection in store for those who have served him in holiness and in the confidence of a sound faith? For in
Scripture we read, *You will raise me up, and I will
praise you;* and also, *After I had lain down and fallen asleep, I
rose up again; for you are with me.* Job too, says, *You will raise
up this flesh of mine which has had all these trials to endure.*

Seeing then that we have this hope, let us knit fast our souls
to him who is ever true to his word and righteous in his judgments. He who has forbidden us to use any deception can much
less be a deceiver himself; untruth is the only thing that is impossible to God. So let us rekindle the ardor of our belief in him,
and also remind ourselves that there is nothing in the world
with which he is not in close touch. With the word of his greatness has he assembled all that exists, and with a word he is able
to overturn it again; for *who can say to him, What have you
done? or who shall withstand the power of his might?* He will
act at all times, as, and when, he chooses; and not one of his decrees shall fail. The entire universe lies open before him; and
there is nothing that is hidden from his counsel; for *the heavens
are a proclamation of God's glory, and the firmament a declaration of his handiwork. Day utters the message to day, and night
proclaims the knowledge though there are no words or speeches
and their voices are inaudible* (see Psalm 19:1–3).

ADDITIONAL SCRIPTURE READING:
Numbers 23:19; John 5:24–29

Go to page 573 for your next devotional reading.

100   500

5 that the mirth of the wicked is brief,
　　the joy of the godless lasts but a
　　moment.
6 Though his pride reaches to the
　　heavens
　　and his head touches the clouds,
7 he will perish forever, like his own
　　dung;
　　those who have seen him will say,
　　'Where is he?'
8 Like a dream he flies away, no more
　　to be found,
　　banished like a vision of the night.
9 The eye that saw him will not see
　　him again;
　　his place will look on him no
　　more.
10 His children must make amends to
　　the poor;
　　his own hands must give back his
　　wealth.
11 The youthful vigor that fills his
　　bones
　　will lie with him in the dust.

12 "Though evil is sweet in his mouth
　　and he hides it under his tongue,
13 though he cannot bear to let it go
　　and keeps it in his mouth,
14 yet his food will turn sour in his
　　stomach;
　　it will become the venom of
　　serpents within him.
15 He will spit out the riches he
　　swallowed;
　　God will make his stomach vomit
　　them up.
16 He will suck the poison of serpents;
　　the fangs of an adder will kill him.
17 He will not enjoy the streams,
　　the rivers flowing with honey and
　　cream.
18 What he toiled for he must give back
　　uneaten;
　　he will not enjoy the profit from
　　his trading.
19 For he has oppressed the poor and left
　　them destitute;
　　he has seized houses he did not
　　build.
20 "Surely he will have no respite from
　　his craving;
　　he cannot save himself by his
　　treasure.
21 Nothing is left for him to devour;

　　his prosperity will not endure.
22 In the midst of his plenty, distress
　　will overtake him;
　　the full force of misery will come
　　upon him.
23 When he has filled his belly,
　　God will vent his burning anger
　　against him
　　and rain down his blows upon him.
24 Though he flees from an iron weapon,
　　a bronze-tipped arrow pierces him.
25 He pulls it out of his back,
　　the gleaming point out of his liver.
　　Terrors will come over him;
26 　total darkness lies in wait for his
　　treasures.
　　A fire unfanned will consume him
　　and devour what is left in his tent.
27 The heavens will expose his guilt;
　　the earth will rise up against him.
28 A flood will carry off his house,
　　rushing waters*a* on the day of
　　God's wrath.
29 Such is the fate God allots the wicked,
　　the heritage appointed for them by
　　God."

Job

21 Then Job replied:

2 "Listen carefully to my words;
　　let this be the consolation you give
　　me.
3 Bear with me while I speak,
　　and after I have spoken, mock on.

4 "Is my complaint directed to man?
　　Why should I not be impatient?
5 Look at me and be astonished;
　　clap your hand over your mouth.
6 When I think about this, I am
　　terrified;
　　trembling seizes my body.
7 Why do the wicked live on,
　　growing old and increasing in
　　power?
8 They see their children established
　　around them,
　　their offspring before their eyes.
9 Their homes are safe and free from
　　fear;
　　the rod of God is not upon them.
10 Their bulls never fail to breed;
　　their cows calve and do not
　　miscarry.

a 28 Or *The possessions in his house will be carried off, / washed away*

11 They send forth their children as a
    flock;
    their little ones dance about.
12 They sing to the music of
    tambourine and harp;
    they make merry to the sound of
    the flute.
13 They spend their years in prosperity
    and go down to the grave*a* in
    peace.*b*
14 Yet they say to God, 'Leave us alone!
    We have no desire to know your
    ways.
15 Who is the Almighty, that we should
    serve him?
    What would we gain by praying to
    him?'
16 But their prosperity is not in their
    own hands,
    so I stand aloof from the counsel of
    the wicked.

17 "Yet how often is the lamp of the
    wicked snuffed out?
    How often does calamity come
    upon them,
    the fate God allots in his anger?
18 How often are they like straw before
    the wind,
    like chaff swept away by a gale?
19 ⌊It is said,⌋ 'God stores up a man's
    punishment for his sons.'
    Let him repay the man himself, so
    that he will know it!
20 Let his own eyes see his destruction;
    let him drink of the wrath of the
    Almighty.*c*
21 For what does he care about the
    family he leaves behind
    when his allotted months come to
    an end?

22 "Can anyone teach knowledge to
    God,
    since he judges even the highest?
23 One man dies in full vigor,
    completely secure and at ease,
24 his body*d* well nourished,
    his bones rich with marrow.
25 Another man dies in bitterness of
    soul,
    never having enjoyed anything
    good.
26 Side by side they lie in the dust,

and worms cover them both.

27 "I know full well what you are
    thinking,
    the schemes by which you would
    wrong me.
28 You say, 'Where now is the great
    man's house,
    the tents where wicked men
    lived?'
29 Have you never questioned those
    who travel?
    Have you paid no regard to their
    accounts—
30 that the evil man is spared from the
    day of calamity,
    that he is delivered from*e* the day
    of wrath?
31 Who denounces his conduct to his
    face?
    Who repays him for what he has
    done?
32 He is carried to the grave,
    and watch is kept over his tomb.
33 The soil in the valley is sweet to
    him;
    all men follow after him,
    and a countless throng goes*f* before
    him.

34 "So how can you console me with
    your nonsense?
    Nothing is left of your answers but
    falsehood!"

Eliphaz

22 Then Eliphaz the Temanite
    replied:

2 "Can a man be of benefit to God?
    Can even a wise man benefit him?
3 What pleasure would it give the
    Almighty if you were
    righteous?
    What would he gain if your ways
    were blameless?

4 "Is it for your piety that he rebukes
    you
    and brings charges against you?
5 Is not your wickedness great?
    Are not your sins endless?
6 You demanded security from your
    brothers for no reason;

---

a 13 Hebrew *Sheol*   *b 13* Or *in an instant*   *c 17–20* Verses 17 and 18 may be taken as exclamations and
19 and 20 as declarations.   *d 24* The meaning of the Hebrew for this word is uncertain.   *e 30* Or *man is
reserved for the day of calamity, / that he is brought forth to*   *f 33* Or / *as a countless throng went*

you stripped men of their clothing,
    leaving them naked.
7 You gave no water to the weary
    and you withheld food from the
        hungry,
8 though you were a powerful man,
        owning land—
    an honored man, living on it.
9 And you sent widows away empty-
        handed
    and broke the strength of the
        fatherless.
10 That is why snares are all around
        you,
    why sudden peril terrifies you,
11 why it is so dark you cannot see,
    and why a flood of water covers
        you.

12 "Is not God in the heights of heaven?
    And see how lofty are the highest
        stars!
13 Yet you say, 'What does God know?
    Does he judge through such
        darkness?
14 Thick clouds veil him, so he does not
        see us
    as he goes about in the vaulted
        heavens.'
15 Will you keep to the old path
    that evil men have trod?
16 They were carried off before their
        time,
    their foundations washed away by
        a flood.
17 They said to God, 'Leave us alone!
    What can the Almighty do to us?'
18 Yet it was he who filled their houses
        with good things,
    so I stand aloof from the counsel of
        the wicked.

19 "The righteous see their ruin and
        rejoice;
    the innocent mock them, saying,
20 'Surely our foes are destroyed,
    and fire devours their wealth.'

21 "Submit to God and be at peace with
        him;
    in this way prosperity will come to
        you.
22 Accept instruction from his mouth
    and lay up his words in your heart.
23 If you return to the Almighty, you
        will be restored:

If you remove wickedness far from
        your tent
24 and assign your nuggets to the dust,
    your gold of Ophir to the rocks in
        the ravines,
25 then the Almighty will be your gold,
    the choicest silver for you.
26 Surely then you will find delight in
        the Almighty
    and will lift up your face to God.
27 You will pray to him, and he will
        hear you,
    and you will fulfill your vows.
28 What you decide on will be done,
    and light will shine on your ways.
29 When men are brought low and you
        say, 'Lift them up!'
    then he will save the downcast.
30 He will deliver even one who is not
        innocent,
    who will be delivered through the
        cleanness of your hands."

Job

23 Then Job replied:

2 "Even today my complaint is bitter;
    his hand*a* is heavy in spite of*b* my
        groaning.
3 If only I knew where to find him;
    if only I could go to his dwelling!
4 I would state my case before him
    and fill my mouth with arguments.
5 I would find out what he would
        answer me,
    and consider what he would say.
6 Would he oppose me with great
        power?
    No, he would not press charges
        against me.
7 There an upright man could present
        his case before him,
    and I would be delivered forever
        from my judge.

8 "But if I go to the east, he is not
        there;
    if I go to the west, I do not find
        him.
9 When he is at work in the north, I do
        not see him;
    when he turns to the south, I catch
        no glimpse of him.
10 But he knows the way that I take;

a 2 Septuagint and Syriac; Hebrew / *the hand on me*   *b 2* Or *heavy on me in*

WEEKEND

BATTER MY HEART
John Donne

VERSE: Job 23:10   **PASSAGE:** Job 23:8–12

atter my heart, three-personed God, for you
As yet but knock, breathe, shine, and seek to
   mend;
That I may rise and stand, o'erthrow me, and
   bend
Your force to break, blow, burn and make me new.
I, like an usurped town, to another due,
Labour to admit you, but oh, to no end;
Reason your viceroy in me, me should defend,
But is captived, and proves weak or untrue.
Yet dearly I love you, and would be loved fain,
But am betrothed unto your enemy:
Divorce me, untie, or break that knot again,
Take me to you, imprison me, for I
Except you enthrall me, never shall be free,
Nor ever chaste, except you ravish me.

ADDITIONAL SCRIPTURE READING:
Job 1:11–12; Zechariah 13:9; James 1:2–4

Go to page 576 for your next devotional reading.

1500   1700

when he has tested me, I will come forth as gold.

11 My feet have closely followed his steps;
I have kept to his way without turning aside.

12 I have not departed from the commands of his lips;
I have treasured the words of his mouth more than my daily bread.

13 "But he stands alone, and who can oppose him?
He does whatever he pleases.

14 He carries out his decree against me,
and many such plans he still has in store.

15 That is why I am terrified before him;
when I think of all this, I fear him.

16 God has made my heart faint;
the Almighty has terrified me.

17 Yet I am not silenced by the darkness,
by the thick darkness that covers my face.

24

"Why does the Almighty not set times for judgment?
Why must those who know him look in vain for such days?

2 Men move boundary stones;
they pasture flocks they have stolen.

3 They drive away the orphan's donkey
and take the widow's ox in pledge.

4 They thrust the needy from the path
and force all the poor of the land into hiding.

5 Like wild donkeys in the desert,
the poor go about their labor of foraging food;
the wasteland provides food for their children.

6 They gather fodder in the fields
and glean in the vineyards of the wicked.

7 Lacking clothes, they spend the night naked;
they have nothing to cover themselves in the cold.

8 They are drenched by mountain rains
and hug the rocks for lack of shelter.

9 The fatherless child is snatched from the breast;
the infant of the poor is seized for a debt.

10 Lacking clothes, they go about naked;
they carry the sheaves, but still go hungry.

11 They crush olives among the terraces[a];
they tread the winepresses, yet suffer thirst.

12 The groans of the dying rise from the city,
and the souls of the wounded cry out for help.
But God charges no one with wrongdoing.

13 "There are those who rebel against the light,
who do not know its ways or stay in its paths.

14 When daylight is gone, the murderer rises up
and kills the poor and needy;
in the night he steals forth like a thief.

15 The eye of the adulterer watches for dusk;
he thinks, 'No eye will see me,'
and he keeps his face concealed.

16 In the dark, men break into houses,
but by day they shut themselves in;
they want nothing to do with the light.

17 For all of them, deep darkness is their morning[b];
they make friends with the terrors of darkness.[c]

18 "Yet they are foam on the surface of the water;
their portion of the land is cursed,
so that no one goes to the vineyards.

19 As heat and drought snatch away the melted snow,
so the grave[d] snatches away those who have sinned.

20 The womb forgets them,
the worm feasts on them;
evil men are no longer remembered
but are broken like a tree.

21 They prey on the barren and childless woman,

---

a 11 Or olives between the millstones; the meaning of the Hebrew for this word is uncertain.   b 17 Or them, their morning is like the shadow of death   c 17 Or of the shadow of death   d 19 Hebrew Sheol

and to the widow show no
   kindness.
22 But God drags away the mighty by
   his power;
   though they become established,
     they have no assurance of life.
23 He may let them rest in a feeling of
   security,
   but his eyes are on their ways.
24 For a little while they are exalted,
    and then they are gone;
   they are brought low and gathered
    up like all others;
   they are cut off like heads of grain.

25 "If this is not so, who can prove me
   false
   and reduce my words to nothing?"

Bildad

25 Then Bildad the Shuhite
replied:

2 "Dominion and awe belong to God;
   he establishes order in the heights
    of heaven.
3 Can his forces be numbered?
   Upon whom does his light not rise?
4 How then can a man be righteous
    before God?
   How can one born of woman be
    pure?
5 If even the moon is not bright
   and the stars are not pure in his
    eyes,
6 how much less man, who is but a
    maggot—
   a son of man, who is only a worm!"

Job

26 Then Job replied:

2 "How you have helped the
    powerless!
   How you have saved the arm that
    is feeble!
3 What advice you have offered to one
    without wisdom!
   And what great insight you have
    displayed!
4 Who has helped you utter these
    words?
   And whose spirit spoke from your
    mouth?

5 "The dead are in deep anguish,

those beneath the waters and all
   that live in them.
6 Death[a] is naked before God;
   Destruction[b] lies uncovered.
7 He spreads out the northern ⌞skies⌟
   over empty space;
   he suspends the earth over
    nothing.
8 He wraps up the waters in his clouds,
   yet the clouds do not burst under
    their weight.
9 He covers the face of the full moon,
   spreading his clouds over it.
10 He marks out the horizon on the face
    of the waters
   for a boundary between light and
    darkness.
11 The pillars of the heavens quake,
   aghast at his rebuke.
12 By his power he churned up the sea;
   by his wisdom he cut Rahab to
    pieces.
13 By his breath the skies became fair;
   his hand pierced the gliding
    serpent.
14 And these are but the outer fringe of
    his works;
   how faint the whisper we hear of
    him!
   Who then can understand the
    thunder of his power?"

27 And Job continued his discourse:

2 "As surely as God lives, who has
    denied me justice,
   the Almighty, who has made me
    taste bitterness of soul,
3 as long as I have life within me,
   the breath of God in my nostrils,
4 my lips will not speak wickedness,
   and my tongue will utter no deceit.
5 I will never admit you are in the right;
   till I die, I will not deny my
    integrity.
6 I will maintain my righteousness and
    never let go of it;
   my conscience will not reproach
    me as long as I live.

7 "May my enemies be like the
    wicked,
   my adversaries like the unjust!
8 For what hope has the godless when
    he is cut off,

---

a 6 Hebrew *Sheol*   *b 6* Hebrew *Abaddon*

when God takes away his life?
⁹Does God listen to his cry
   when distress comes upon him?
¹⁰Will he find delight in the Almighty?
   Will he call upon God at all times?

¹¹"I will teach you about the power of
   God;
   the ways of the Almighty I will not
    conceal.
¹²You have all seen this yourselves.
   Why then this meaningless talk?

¹³"Here is the fate God allots to the
   wicked,

the heritage a ruthless man
   receives from the Almighty:
¹⁴However many his children, their
   fate is the sword;
   his offspring will never have
    enough to eat.
¹⁵The plague will bury those who
   survive him,
   and their widows will not weep for
   them.
¹⁶Though he heaps up silver like dust
   and clothes like piles of clay,
¹⁷what he lays up the righteous will
   wear,

MONDAY

THE TRIBULATIONS OF JOB
Martin Luther

VERSE: Job 27:5   **PASSAGE:** Job 27:1–6

 ob had many tribulations; he was also plagued of his own friends, who fiercely assaulted him. The text says, that his friends fell upon him, and were full of wrath against him; they tormented him thoroughly, but he held his peace, suffered them to talk their talk, as if he should say, you know not what you prate about. Job is an example of God's goodness and mercy; for how upright and holy soever he was, yet he sorely fell into temptation; but he was not forsaken, he was again delivered and redeemed through God's grace and mercy . . .

When Satan will not leave off tempting thee, then bear with patience, hold on hand and foot, nor faint, as if there would be no end thereof, but stand courageously, and attend God's leisure, knowing that what the devil cannot accomplish by his sudden and powerful assaults, he thinks to gain by craft, by persevering to vex and tempt thee, thereby to make thee faint and weary . . . But be fully assured, that in this sport with the devil, God, with all his holy angels, takes delight and joy; and assure thyself, also, that the end thereof will be blessed and happy.

ADDITIONAL SCRIPTURE READING:
Job 13:15; 2 Corinthians 1:12

Go to page 582 for your next devotional reading.

1500   1700

and the innocent will divide his
silver.
18 The house he builds is like a moth's
cocoon,
like a hut made by a watchman.
19 He lies down wealthy, but will do so
no more;
when he opens his eyes, all is
gone.
20 Terrors overtake him like a flood;
a tempest snatches him away in
the night.
21 The east wind carries him off, and he
is gone;
it sweeps him out of his place.
22 It hurls itself against him without
mercy
as he flees headlong from its
power.
23 It claps its hands in derision
and hisses him out of his place.

28 "There is a mine for silver
and a place where gold is
refined.
2 Iron is taken from the earth,
and copper is smelted from ore.
3 Man puts an end to the darkness;
he searches the farthest recesses
for ore in the blackest darkness.
4 Far from where people dwell he cuts
a shaft,
in places forgotten by the foot of
man;
far from men he dangles and
sways.
5 The earth, from which food comes,
is transformed below as by fire;
6 sapphires[a] come from its rocks,
and its dust contains nuggets of
gold.
7 No bird of prey knows that hidden
path,
no falcon's eye has seen it.
8 Proud beasts do not set foot on it,
and no lion prowls there.
9 Man's hand assaults the flinty rock
and lays bare the roots of the
mountains.
10 He tunnels through the rock;
his eyes see all its treasures.
11 He searches[b] the sources of the rivers
and brings hidden things to light.

12 "But where can wisdom be found?

Where does understanding dwell?
13 Man does not comprehend its
worth;
it cannot be found in the land of
the living.
14 The deep says, 'It is not in me';
the sea says, 'It is not with me.'
15 It cannot be bought with the finest
gold,
nor can its price be weighed in
silver.
16 It cannot be bought with the gold of
Ophir,
with precious onyx or sapphires.
17 Neither gold nor crystal can compare
with it,
nor can it be had for jewels of gold.
18 Coral and jasper are not worthy of
mention;
the price of wisdom is beyond
rubies.
19 The topaz of Cush cannot compare
with it;
it cannot be bought with pure gold.

20 "Where then does wisdom come
from?
Where does understanding dwell?
21 It is hidden from the eyes of every
living thing,
concealed even from the birds of
the air.
22 Destruction[c] and Death say,
'Only a rumor of it has reached our
ears.'
23 God understands the way to it
and he alone knows where it
dwells,
24 for he views the ends of the earth
and sees everything under the
heavens.
25 When he established the force of the
wind
and measured out the waters,
26 when he made a decree for the rain
and a path for the thunderstorm,
27 then he looked at wisdom and
appraised it;
he confirmed it and tested it.
28 And he said to man,
'The fear of the Lord—that is
wisdom,
and to shun evil is
understanding.' "

---

a 6 Or lapis lazuli; also in verse 16   b 11 Septuagint, Aquila and Vulgate; Hebrew He dams up
c 22 Hebrew Abaddon

29

Job continued his discourse:

2 "How I long for the months gone by,
 for the days when God watched
 over me,
3 when his lamp shone upon my head
 and by his light I walked through
 darkness!
4 Oh, for the days when I was in my
 prime,
 when God's intimate friendship
 blessed my house,
5 when the Almighty was still with me
 and my children were around me,
6 when my path was drenched with
 cream
 and the rock poured out for me
 streams of olive oil.

7 "When I went to the gate of the city
 and took my seat in the public
 square,
8 the young men saw me and stepped
 aside
 and the old men rose to their feet;
9 the chief men refrained from
 speaking
 and covered their mouths with
 their hands;
10 the voices of the nobles were hushed,
 and their tongues stuck to the roof
 of their mouths.
11 Whoever heard me spoke well of me,
 and those who saw me
 commended me,
12 because I rescued the poor who cried
 for help,
 and the fatherless who had none to
 assist him.
13 The man who was dying blessed me;
 I made the widow's heart sing.
14 I put on righteousness as my
 clothing;
 justice was my robe and my
 turban.
15 I was eyes to the blind
 and feet to the lame.
16 I was a father to the needy;
 I took up the case of the stranger.
17 I broke the fangs of the wicked
 and snatched the victims from
 their teeth.

18 "I thought, 'I will die in my own
 house,

my days as numerous as the grains
 of sand.
19 My roots will reach to the water,
 and the dew will lie all night on
 my branches.
20 My glory will remain fresh in me,
 the bow ever new in my hand.'

21 "Men listened to me expectantly,
 waiting in silence for my counsel.
22 After I had spoken, they spoke no
 more;
 my words fell gently on their ears.
23 They waited for me as for showers
 and drank in my words as the
 spring rain.
24 When I smiled at them, they scarcely
 believed it;
 the light of my face was precious to
 them.^a
25 I chose the way for them and sat as
 their chief;
 I dwelt as a king among his troops;
 I was like one who comforts
 mourners.

30

"But now they mock me,
 men younger than I,
 whose fathers I would have disdained
 to put with my sheep dogs.
2 Of what use was the strength of their
 hands to me,
 since their vigor had gone from
 them?
3 Haggard from want and hunger,
 they roamed^b the parched land
 in desolate wastelands at night.
4 In the brush they gathered salt herbs,
 and their food^c was the root of the
 broom tree.
5 They were banished from their
 fellow men,
 shouted at as if they were thieves.
6 They were forced to live in the dry
 stream beds,
 among the rocks and in holes in
 the ground.
7 They brayed among the bushes
 and huddled in the undergrowth.
8 A base and nameless brood,
 they were driven out of the land.

9 "And now their sons mock me in
 song;
 I have become a byword among
 them.

10 They detest me and keep their
distance;
they do not hesitate to spit in my
face.
11 Now that God has unstrung my bow
and afflicted me,
they throw off restraint in my
presence.
12 On my right the tribe*a* attacks;
they lay snares for my feet,
they build their siege ramps
against me.
13 They break up my road;
they succeed in destroying me—
without anyone's helping them.*b*
14 They advance as through a gaping
breach;
amid the ruins they come rolling
in.
15 Terrors overwhelm me;
my dignity is driven away as by the
wind,
my safety vanishes like a cloud.

16 "And now my life ebbs away;
days of suffering grip me.
17 Night pierces my bones;
my gnawing pains never rest.
18 In his great power ˌGodˌ becomes like
clothing to me*c*;
he binds me like the neck of my
garment.
19 He throws me into the mud,
and I am reduced to dust and ashes.

20 "I cry out to you, O God, but you do
not answer;
I stand up, but you merely look at
me.
21 You turn on me ruthlessly;
with the might of your hand you
attack me.
22 You snatch me up and drive me
before the wind;
you toss me about in the storm.
23 I know you will bring me down to
death,
to the place appointed for all the
living.

24 "Surely no one lays a hand on a
broken man
when he cries for help in his
distress.
25 Have I not wept for those in trouble?

Has not my soul grieved for the
poor?
26 Yet when I hoped for good, evil came;
when I looked for light, then came
darkness.
27 The churning inside me never stops;
days of suffering confront me.
28 I go about blackened, but not by the
sun;
I stand up in the assembly and cry
for help.
29 I have become a brother of jackals,
a companion of owls.
30 My skin grows black and peels;
my body burns with fever.
31 My harp is tuned to mourning,
and my flute to the sound of
wailing.

31 "I made a covenant with my
eyes
not to look lustfully at a girl.
2 For what is man's lot from God
above,
his heritage from the Almighty on
high?
3 Is it not ruin for the wicked,
disaster for those who do wrong?
4 Does he not see my ways
and count my every step?

5 "If I have walked in falsehood
or my foot has hurried after
deceit—
6 let God weigh me in honest scales
and he will know that I am
blameless—
7 if my steps have turned from the
path,
if my heart has been led by my
eyes,
or if my hands have been defiled,
8 then may others eat what I have
sown,
and may my crops be uprooted.

9 "If my heart has been enticed by a
woman,
or if I have lurked at my neighbor's
door,
10 then may my wife grind another
man's grain,
and may other men sleep with her.
11 For that would have been shameful,
a sin to be judged.
12 It is a fire that burns to Destruction*d*;

---

a 12 The meaning of the Hebrew for this word is uncertain.   *b 13* Or *me. / 'No one can help him,'*
ˌ*they say*ˌ.   *c 18* Hebrew; Septuagint ˌ*God*ˌ *grasps my clothing*   *d 12* Hebrew *Abaddon*

it would have uprooted my
　　harvest.

13 "If I have denied justice to my
　　menservants and maidservants
　　when they had a grievance against
　　me,
14 what will I do when God confronts
　　me?
　　What will I answer when called to
　　account?
15 Did not he who made me in the
　　womb make them?
　　Did not the same one form us both
　　within our mothers?

16 "If I have denied the desires of the
　　poor
　　or let the eyes of the widow grow
　　weary,
17 if I have kept my bread to myself,
　　not sharing it with the fatherless—
18 but from my youth I reared him as
　　would a father,
　　and from my birth I guided the
　　widow—
19 if I have seen anyone perishing for
　　lack of clothing,
　　or a needy man without a garment,
20 and his heart did not bless me
　　for warming him with the fleece
　　from my sheep,
21 if I have raised my hand against the
　　fatherless,
　　knowing that I had influence in
　　court,
22 then let my arm fall from the
　　shoulder,
　　let it be broken off at the joint.
23 For I dreaded destruction from God,
　　and for fear of his splendor I could
　　not do such things.

24 "If I have put my trust in gold
　　or said to pure gold, 'You are my
　　security,'
25 if I have rejoiced over my great
　　wealth,
　　the fortune my hands had gained,
26 if I have regarded the sun in its
　　radiance
　　or the moon moving in splendor,
27 so that my heart was secretly
　　enticed
　　and my hand offered them a kiss of
　　homage,

28 then these also would be sins to be
　　judged,
　　for I would have been unfaithful to
　　God on high.

29 "If I have rejoiced at my enemy's
　　misfortune
　　or gloated over the trouble that
　　came to him—
30 I have not allowed my mouth to sin
　　by invoking a curse against his
　　life—
31 if the men of my household have
　　never said,
　　'Who has not had his fill of Job's
　　meat?'—
32 but no stranger had to spend the
　　night in the street,
　　for my door was always open to
　　the traveler—
33 if I have concealed my sin as men
　　do,^a
　　by hiding my guilt in my heart
34 because I so feared the crowd
　　and so dreaded the contempt of the
　　clans
　　that I kept silent and would not go
　　outside

35 ("Oh, that I had someone to hear
　　me!
　　I sign now my defense—let the
　　Almighty answer me;
　　let my accuser put his indictment
　　in writing.
36 Surely I would wear it on my
　　shoulder,
　　I would put it on like a crown.
37 I would give him an account of my
　　every step;
　　like a prince I would approach
　　him.)—

38 "if my land cries out against me
　　and all its furrows are wet with
　　tears,
39 if I have devoured its yield without
　　payment
　　or broken the spirit of its tenants,
40 then let briers come up instead of
　　wheat
　　and weeds instead of barley."

The words of Job are ended.

^a 33 Or *as Adam did*

Elihu

32 So these three men stopped answering Job, because he was righteous in his own eyes. ²But Elihu son of Barakel the Buzite, of the family of Ram, became very angry with Job for justifying himself rather than God. ³He was also angry with the three friends, because they had found no way to refute Job, and yet had condemned him.ᵃ ⁴Now Elihu had waited before speaking to Job because they were older than he. ⁵But when he saw that the three men had nothing more to say, his anger was aroused.

⁶So Elihu son of Barakel the Buzite said:

"I am young in years,
    and you are old;
that is why I was fearful,
    not daring to tell you what I know.
⁷I thought, 'Age should speak;
    advanced years should teach
        wisdom.'
⁸But it is the spiritᵇ in a man,
    the breath of the Almighty, that
        gives him understanding.
⁹It is not only the oldᶜ who are wise,
    not only the aged who understand
        what is right.

¹⁰"Therefore I say: Listen to me;
    I too will tell you what I know.
¹¹I waited while you spoke,
    I listened to your reasoning;
while you were searching for words,
¹²   I gave you my full attention.
But not one of you has proved Job
        wrong;
    none of you has answered his
        arguments.
¹³Do not say, 'We have found wisdom;
    let God refute him, not man.'
¹⁴But Job has not marshaled his words
        against me,
    and I will not answer him with
        your arguments.

¹⁵"They are dismayed and have no
        more to say;
    words have failed them.
¹⁶Must I wait, now that they are silent,
    now that they stand there with no
        reply?

¹⁷I too will have my say;
    I too will tell what I know.
¹⁸For I am full of words,
    and the spirit within me compels
        me;
¹⁹inside I am like bottled-up wine,
    like new wineskins ready to burst.
²⁰I must speak and find relief;
    I must open my lips and reply.
²¹I will show partiality to no one,
    nor will I flatter any man;
²²for if I were skilled in flattery,
    my Maker would soon take me
        away.

33 "But now, Job, listen to my
        words;
    pay attention to everything I say.
²I am about to open my mouth;
    my words are on the tip of my
        tongue.
³My words come from an upright
        heart;
    my lips sincerely speak what I
        know.
⁴The Spirit of God has made me;
    the breath of the Almighty gives
        me life.
⁵Answer me then, if you can;
    prepare yourself and confront me.
⁶I am just like you before God;
    I too have been taken from clay.
⁷No fear of me should alarm you,
    nor should my hand be heavy upon
        you.

⁸"But you have said in my hearing—
    I heard the very words—
⁹'I am pure and without sin;
    I am clean and free from guilt.
¹⁰Yet God has found fault with me;
    he considers me his enemy.
¹¹He fastens my feet in shackles;
    he keeps close watch on all my
        paths.'

¹²"But I tell you, in this you are not
        right,
    for God is greater than man.
¹³Why do you complain to him
    that he answers none of man's
        wordsᵈ?
¹⁴For God does speak—now one way,
        now another—
    though man may not perceive it.
¹⁵In a dream, in a vision of the night,

ᵃ 3 Masoretic Text; an ancient Hebrew scribal tradition *Job, and so had condemned God*   ᵇ 8 Or *Spirit;* also in verse 18   ᶜ 9 Or *many;* or *great*   ᵈ 13 Or *that he does not answer for any of his actions*

when deep sleep falls on men
   as they slumber in their beds,
¹⁶ he may speak in their ears

and terrify them with warnings,
¹⁷ to turn man from wrongdoing
   and keep him from pride,

TUESDAY

RANSOMED TO BE ONE WITH CHRIST
James Hudson Taylor

VERSE: Job 33:24   **PASSAGE:** Job 33:22–28

 am no better than before (may I not say, in a sense, I do not wish to be, nor am I striving to be); but I am dead and buried with Christ—aye, and risen too and ascended; and now Christ lives in me, and "the life that I now live in the flesh, I live by the faith of the Son of God, who loved me, and gave himself for me" (Galatians 2:20, KJV). I now *believe* I am dead to sin. God reckons me so, and tells me to reckon myself so. He knows best. All my past experience may have shown that it *was* not so; but I dare not say it *is* not now, when he says it is. I feel and know that old things have passed away. I am as capable of sinning as ever, but Christ is realized as present as never before. He cannot sin; and he can keep me from sinning. I cannot say (I am sorry to have to confess it) that since I have seen this light I have not sinned; but I do feel there was no need to have done so. And further—walking more in the light, my conscience has been more tender; sin has been instantly seen, confessed, pardoned; and peace and joy (with humility) instantly restored; with one exception, when for several hours peace and joy did not return—from want, as I had to learn, of full confession, and from some attempt to justify self . . .

And now I must close, I have not said half I would, nor *as* I would had I more time. May God give you to lay hold on these blessed truths. Do not let us continue to say, in *effect*, "Who shall ascend into heaven? that is, to bring Christ down from above" (Romans 10:6, KJV). In other words, do not let us consider him as afar off, when God has made us *one with him*, members of his very body. Nor should we look upon this experience, these truths, as for the few. They are the birthright of every child of God, and no one can dispense with them without dishonor to our Lord. The only power for deliverance from sin or for true service is Christ.

ADDITIONAL SCRIPTURE READING:
Romans 10:5–10; 2 Corinthians 5:7; Galatians 2:20

Go to page 585 for your next devotional reading.

1700 ✚ 1900

18 to preserve his soul from the pit,*a*
   his life from perishing by the
   sword.*b*
19 Or a man may be chastened on a bed
   of pain
   with constant distress in his bones,
20 so that his very being finds food
   repulsive
   and his soul loathes the choicest
   meal.
21 His flesh wastes away to nothing,
   and his bones, once hidden, now
   stick out.
22 His soul draws near to the pit,*c*
   and his life to the messengers of
   death.*d*

23 "Yet if there is an angel on his side
   as a mediator, one out of a
   thousand,
   to tell a man what is right for him,
24 to be gracious to him and say,
   'Spare him from going down to the
   pit*e*;
   I have found a ransom for him'—
25 then his flesh is renewed like a child's;
   it is restored as in the days of his
   youth.
26 He prays to God and finds favor with
   him,
   he sees God's face and shouts for
   joy;
   he is restored by God to his
   righteous state.
27 Then he comes to men and says,
   'I sinned, and perverted what was
   right,
   but I did not get what I deserved.
28 He redeemed my soul from going
   down to the pit,*f*
   and I will live to enjoy the light.'

29 "God does all these things to a man—
   twice, even three times—
30 to turn back his soul from the pit,*g*
   that the light of life may shine on
   him.

31 "Pay attention, Job, and listen to me;
   be silent, and I will speak.
32 If you have anything to say, answer
   me;
   speak up, for I want you to be
   cleared.
33 But if not, then listen to me;

be silent, and I will teach you
wisdom."

34 Then Elihu said:

2 "Hear my words, you wise men;
   listen to me, you men of learning.
3 For the ear tests words
   as the tongue tastes food.
4 Let us discern for ourselves what is
   right;
   let us learn together what is good.

5 "Job says, 'I am innocent,
   but God denies me justice.
6 Although I am right,
   I am considered a liar;
   although I am guiltless,
   his arrow inflicts an incurable
   wound.'
7 What man is like Job,
   who drinks scorn like water?
8 He keeps company with evildoers;
   he associates with wicked men.
9 For he says, 'It profits a man nothing
   when he tries to please God.'

10 "So listen to me, you men of
   understanding.
   Far be it from God to do evil,
   from the Almighty to do wrong.
11 He repays a man for what he has done;
   he brings upon him what his
   conduct deserves.
12 It is unthinkable that God would do
   wrong,
   that the Almighty would pervert
   justice.
13 Who appointed him over the earth?
   Who put him in charge of the
   whole world?
14 If it were his intention
   and he withdrew his spirit*h* and
   breath,
15 all mankind would perish together
   and man would return to the dust.

16 "If you have understanding, hear this;
   listen to what I say.
17 Can he who hates justice govern?
   Will you condemn the just and
   mighty One?
18 Is he not the One who says to kings,
   'You are worthless,'
   and to nobles, 'You are wicked,'

---

a 18 Or *preserve him from the grave*   *b 18* Or *from crossing the River*   *c 22* Or *He draws near to the grave*   *d 22* Or *to the dead*   *e 24* Or *grave*   *f 28* Or *redeemed me from going down to the grave*   *g 30* Or *turn him back from the grave*   *h 14* Or *Spirit*

¹⁹who shows no partiality to princes
    and does not favor the rich over the
        poor,
    for they are all the work of his
        hands?
²⁰They die in an instant, in the middle
    of the night;
    the people are shaken and they
        pass away;
    the mighty are removed without
        human hand.

²¹"His eyes are on the ways of men;
    he sees their every step.
²²There is no dark place, no deep
        shadow,
    where evildoers can hide.
²³God has no need to examine men
        further,
    that they should come before him
        for judgment.
²⁴Without inquiry he shatters the
        mighty
    and sets up others in their place.
²⁵Because he takes note of their deeds,
    he overthrows them in the night
        and they are crushed.
²⁶He punishes them for their
        wickedness
    where everyone can see them,
²⁷because they turned from following
        him
    and had no regard for any of his
        ways.
²⁸They caused the cry of the poor to
        come before him,
    so that he heard the cry of the
        needy.
²⁹But if he remains silent, who can
        condemn him?
    If he hides his face, who can see
        him?
    Yet he is over man and nation alike,
³⁰   to keep a godless man from ruling,
    from laying snares for the people.

³¹"Suppose a man says to God,
    'I am guilty but will offend no more.
³²Teach me what I cannot see;
    if I have done wrong, I will not do
        so again.'
³³Should God then reward you on your
        terms,
    when you refuse to repent?
    You must decide, not I;
    so tell me what you know.

³⁴"Men of understanding declare,
    wise men who hear me say to me,
³⁵'Job speaks without knowledge;
    his words lack insight.'
³⁶Oh, that Job might be tested to the
        utmost
    for answering like a wicked man!
³⁷To his sin he adds rebellion;
    scornfully he claps his hands
        among us
    and multiplies his words against
        God."

35   Then Elihu said:

²"Do you think this is just?
    You say, 'I will be cleared by
        God.^a'
³Yet you ask him, 'What profit is it to
        me,^b
    and what do I gain by not sinning?'

⁴"I would like to reply to you
    and to your friends with you.
⁵Look up at the heavens and see;
    gaze at the clouds so high above
        you.
⁶If you sin, how does that affect him?
    If your sins are many, what does
        that do to him?
⁷If you are righteous, what do you give
        to him,
    or what does he receive from your
        hand?
⁸Your wickedness affects only a man
        like yourself,
    and your righteousness only the
        sons of men.

⁹"Men cry out under a load of
        oppression;
    they plead for relief from the arm
        of the powerful.
¹⁰But no one says, 'Where is God my
        Maker,
    who gives songs in the night,
¹¹who teaches more to us than to^c the
        beasts of the earth
    and makes us wiser than^d the birds
        of the air?'
¹²He does not answer when men cry
        out
    because of the arrogance of the
        wicked.
¹³Indeed, God does not listen to their
        empty plea;

---

^a 2 Or *My righteousness is more than God's*   ^b 3 Or *you*   ^c 11 Or *teaches us by*   ^d 11 Or *us wise by*

the Almighty pays no attention to it.

14 How much less, then, will he listen
when you say that you do not see
him,
that your case is before him
and you must wait for him,
15 and further, that his anger never
punishes
and he does not take the least
notice of wickedness.[a]
16 So Job opens his mouth with empty
talk;

without knowledge he multiplies
words."

 36 Elihu continued:

2 "Bear with me a little longer and I
will show you
that there is more to be said in
God's behalf.
3 I get my knowledge from afar;
I will ascribe justice to my Maker.
4 Be assured that my words are not
false;

---

[a] 15 Symmachus, Theodotion and Vulgate; the meaning of the Hebrew for this word is uncertain.

WEDNESDAY

SONGS IN THE NIGHT
Charles H. Spurgeon

VERSE: Job 35:10   **PASSAGE:** Job 35:4–16

Any man can sing in the day. When the cup is full, man draws inspiration from it. When wealth rolls in abundance around him, any man can praise the God who gives a plenteous harvest or sends home a loaded argosy . . .

It is easy to sing when we can read the notes by daylight; but he is skillful who sings when there is not a ray of light to read by, who sings from his heart. No man can make a song in the night of himself; he may attempt it, but he will find that a song in the night must be divinely inspired. Let all things go well, I can weave songs, fashioning them wherever I go out of the flowers that grow on my path; but put me in a desert, where no green thing grows, and wherewith shall I frame a hymn of praise to God? . . .

No, it is not in man's power to sing when all is adverse . . . Since our Maker gives *songs in the night*, let us wait on him for the music . . . Let us not remain songless because affliction is upon us, but tune our lips to the melody of thanksgiving.

ADDITIONAL SCRIPTURE READING:
Psalms 42:8; 77:5–7; Acts 16:25

Go to page 588 for your next devotional reading.

1700   1900

one perfect in knowledge is with
  you.

5 "God is mighty, but does not despise
  men;
  he is mighty, and firm in his
  purpose.
6 He does not keep the wicked alive
  but gives the afflicted their rights.
7 He does not take his eyes off the
  righteous;
  he enthrones them with kings
  and exalts them forever.
8 But if men are bound in chains,
  held fast by cords of affliction,
9 he tells them what they have done—
  that they have sinned arrogantly.
10 He makes them listen to correction
  and commands them to repent of
  their evil.
11 If they obey and serve him,
  they will spend the rest of their
  days in prosperity
  and their years in contentment.
12 But if they do not listen,
  they will perish by the sword*a*
  and die without knowledge.

13 "The godless in heart harbor
  resentment;
  even when he fetters them, they do
  not cry for help.
14 They die in their youth,
  among male prostitutes of the
  shrines.
15 But those who suffer he delivers in
  their suffering;
  he speaks to them in their affliction.

AFFLICTION IS ABLE TO DROWN OUT EVERY
EARTHLY VOICE . . . BUT THE VOICE OF ETERNITY
WITHIN A MAN IT CANNOT DROWN. WHEN BY
THE AID OF AFFLICTION ALL IRRELEVANT VOICES
ARE BROUGHT TO SILENCE, IT CAN BE HEARD,
THIS VOICE WITHIN.   —*Søren Kierkegaard*

---

16 "He is wooing you from the jaws of
  distress
  to a spacious place free from
  restriction,
  to the comfort of your table laden
  with choice food.

17 But now you are laden with the
  judgment due the wicked;
  judgment and justice have taken
  hold of you.
18 Be careful that no one entices you by
  riches;
  do not let a large bribe turn you
  aside.
19 Would your wealth
  or even all your mighty efforts
  sustain you so you would not be in
  distress?
20 Do not long for the night,
  to drag people away from their
  homes.*b*
21 Beware of turning to evil,
  which you seem to prefer to
  affliction.

22 "God is exalted in his power.
  Who is a teacher like him?
23 Who has prescribed his ways for him,
  or said to him, 'You have done
  wrong'?
24 Remember to extol his work,
  which men have praised in song.
25 All mankind has seen it;
  men gaze on it from afar.
26 How great is God—beyond our
  understanding!
  The number of his years is past
  finding out.

27 "He draws up the drops of water,
  which distill as rain to the streams*c*;
28 the clouds pour down their moisture
  and abundant showers fall on
  mankind.
29 Who can understand how he spreads
  out the clouds,
  how he thunders from his
  pavilion?
30 See how he scatters his lightning
  about him,
  bathing the depths of the sea.
31 This is the way he governs*d* the
  nations
  and provides food in abundance.
32 He fills his hands with lightning
  and commands it to strike its mark.
33 His thunder announces the coming
  storm;
  even the cattle make known its
  approach.*e*

---

a 12 Or *will cross the River*   *b* 20 The meaning of the Hebrew for verses 18–20 is uncertain.   *c* 27 Or
distill from the mist as rain   *d* 31 Or *nourishes*   *e* 33 Or *announces his coming— / the One zealous*
against evil

37 "At this my heart pounds
and leaps from its place.
2 Listen! Listen to the roar of his voice,
to the rumbling that comes from
his mouth.
3 He unleashes his lightning beneath
the whole heaven
and sends it to the ends of the earth.
4 After that comes the sound of his
roar;
he thunders with his majestic voice.
When his voice resounds,
he holds nothing back.
5 God's voice thunders in marvelous
ways;
he does great things beyond our
understanding.
6 He says to the snow, 'Fall on the
earth,'
and to the rain shower, 'Be a
mighty downpour.'
7 So that all men he has made may
know his work,
he stops every man from his labor.*a*
8 The animals take cover;
they remain in their dens.
9 The tempest comes out from its
chamber,
the cold from the driving winds.
10 The breath of God produces ice,
and the broad waters become
frozen.
11 He loads the clouds with moisture;
he scatters his lightning through
them.
12 At his direction they swirl around
over the face of the whole earth
to do whatever he commands
them.
13 He brings the clouds to punish men,
or to water his earth*b* and show his
love.

14 "Listen to this, Job;
stop and consider God's wonders.
15 Do you know how God controls the
clouds
and makes his lightning flash?
16 Do you know how the clouds hang
poised,
those wonders of him who is
perfect in knowledge?
17 You who swelter in your clothes
when the land lies hushed under
the south wind,

18 can you join him in spreading out the
skies,
hard as a mirror of cast bronze?

19 "Tell us what we should say to him;
we cannot draw up our case
because of our darkness.
20 Should he be told that I want to
speak?
Would any man ask to be
swallowed up?
21 Now no one can look at the sun,
bright as it is in the skies
after the wind has swept them
clean.
22 Out of the north he comes in golden
splendor;
God comes in awesome majesty.
23 The Almighty is beyond our reach
and exalted in power;
in his justice and great
righteousness, he does not
oppress.
24 Therefore, men revere him,
for does he not have regard for all
the wise in heart?*c* "

The Lord Speaks

38 Then the Lord answered Job
out of the storm. He said:

2 "Who is this that darkens my
counsel
with words without knowledge?
3 Brace yourself like a man;
I will question you,
and you shall answer me.

4 "Where were you when I laid the
earth's foundation?
Tell me, if you understand.
5 Who marked off its dimensions?
Surely you know!
Who stretched a measuring line
across it?
6 On what were its footings set,
or who laid its cornerstone—
7 while the morning stars sang
together
and all the angels*d* shouted for joy?

8 "Who shut up the sea behind doors
when it burst forth from the
womb,
9 when I made the clouds its garment
and wrapped it in thick darkness,

---

a 7 Or / *he fills all men with fear by his power*   *b 13* Or *to favor them*   *c 24* Or *for he does not have
regard for any who think they are wise.*   *d 7* Hebrew *the sons of God*

10 when I fixed limits for it
and set its doors and bars in place,
11 when I said, 'This far you may come
and no farther;
here is where your proud waves
halt'?

12 "Have you ever given orders to the
morning,
or shown the dawn its place,
13 that it might take the earth by the
edges
and shake the wicked out of it?

THURSDAY

THE RAYS OF THE NATURE OF GOD
Origen

VERSE: Job 38:12   **PASSAGE:** Job 38

 aving refuted, then, as well as we could, every notion which might suggest that we were to think of God as in any degree corporeal, we go on to say that, according to strict truth, God is incomprehensible, and incapable of being measured. For whatever be the knowledge which we are able to obtain of God, either by perception or reflection, we must of necessity believe that he is by many degrees far better than what we perceive him to be . . . But among all intelligent, that is, incorporeal beings, what is so superior to all others—so unspeakably and incalculably superior—as God, whose nature cannot be grasped or seen by the power of any human understanding, even the purest and brightest?

. . . Our eyes frequently cannot look upon the nature of the light itself—that is, upon the substance of the sun; but when we behold his splendor or his rays pouring in, perhaps, through windows or some small openings to admit the light, we can reflect how great is the supply and source of the light of the body. So, in like manner, the works of divine Providence and the plan of this whole world are a sort of rays, as it were, of the nature of God, in comparison with his real substance and being. As, therefore, our understanding is unable of itself to behold God himself as he is, it knows the Father of the world from the beauty of his works and the comeliness of his creatures. God, therefore, is not to be thought of as being either a body or as existing in a body, but as an uncompounded intellectual nature, admitting within himself no addition of any kind.

ADDITIONAL SCRIPTURE READING:
Isaiah 9:2; John 8:12; Acts 13:47

Go to page 593 for your next devotional reading.

100   500

14 The earth takes shape like clay under
    a seal;
  its features stand out like those of
    a garment.
15 The wicked are denied their light,
  and their upraised arm is broken.

16 "Have you journeyed to the springs
    of the sea
  or walked in the recesses of the
    deep?
17 Have the gates of death been shown
    to you?
  Have you seen the gates of the
    shadow of death*a*?
18 Have you comprehended the vast
    expanses of the earth?
  Tell me, if you know all this.

19 "What is the way to the abode of
    light?
  And where does darkness reside?
20 Can you take them to their places?
  Do you know the paths to their
    dwellings?
21 Surely you know, for you were
    already born!
  You have lived so many years!

22 "Have you entered the storehouses of
    the snow
  or seen the storehouses of the hail,
23 which I reserve for times of trouble,
  for days of war and battle?
24 What is the way to the place where
    the lightning is dispersed,
  or the place where the east winds
    are scattered over the earth?
25 Who cuts a channel for the torrents
    of rain,
  and a path for the thunderstorm,
26 to water a land where no man lives,
  a desert with no one in it,
27 to satisfy a desolate wasteland
  and make it sprout with grass?
28 Does the rain have a father?
  Who fathers the drops of dew?
29 From whose womb comes the ice?
  Who gives birth to the frost from
    the heavens
30 when the waters become hard as
    stone,
  when the surface of the deep is
    frozen?

31 "Can you bind the beautiful*b*
    Pleiades?
  Can you loose the cords of Orion?
32 Can you bring forth the
    constellations in their seasons*c*
  or lead out the Bear*d* with its cubs?
33 Do you know the laws of the
    heavens?
  Can you set up ˻God's*e*˼ dominion
    over the earth?

34 "Can you raise your voice to the
    clouds
  and cover yourself with a flood of
    water?
35 Do you send the lightning bolts on
    their way?
  Do they report to you, 'Here we
    are'?
36 Who endowed the heart*f* with
    wisdom
  or gave understanding to the
    mind*f*?
37 Who has the wisdom to count the
    clouds?
  Who can tip over the water jars of
    the heavens
38 when the dust becomes hard
  and the clods of earth stick
    together?

39 "Do you hunt the prey for the lioness
  and satisfy the hunger of the lions
40 when they crouch in their dens
  or lie in wait in a thicket?
41 Who provides food for the raven
  when its young cry out to God
  and wander about for lack of food?

39 "Do you know when the
    mountain goats give birth?
  Do you watch when the doe bears
    her fawn?
2 Do you count the months till they
    bear?
  Do you know the time they give
    birth?
3 They crouch down and bring forth
    their young;
  their labor pains are ended.
4 Their young thrive and grow strong
    in the wilds;
  they leave and do not return.

5 "Who let the wild donkey go free?

---

a 17 Or *gates of deep shadows*   *b 31* Or *the twinkling;* or *the chains of the*   *c 32* Or *the morning
star in its season*   *d 32* Or *out Leo*   *e 33* Or *his;* or *their*   *f 36* The meaning of the Hebrew for this
word is uncertain.

Who untied his ropes?
6 I gave him the wasteland as his
home,
the salt flats as his habitat.
7 He laughs at the commotion in the
town;
he does not hear a driver's shout.
8 He ranges the hills for his pasture
and searches for any green thing.

9 "Will the wild ox consent to serve
you?
Will he stay by your manger at
night?
10 Can you hold him to the furrow with
a harness?
Will he till the valleys behind you?
11 Will you rely on him for his great
strength?
Will you leave your heavy work to
him?
12 Can you trust him to bring in your
grain
and gather it to your threshing
floor?

13 "The wings of the ostrich flap
joyfully,
but they cannot compare with the
pinions and feathers of the
stork.
14 She lays her eggs on the ground
and lets them warm in the sand,
15 unmindful that a foot may crush
them,
that some wild animal may
trample them.
16 She treats her young harshly, as if
they were not hers;
she cares not that her labor was in
vain,
17 for God did not endow her with
wisdom
or give her a share of good sense.
18 Yet when she spreads her feathers to
run,
she laughs at horse and rider.

19 "Do you give the horse his strength
or clothe his neck with a flowing
mane?
20 Do you make him leap like a locust,
striking terror with his proud
snorting?
21 He paws fiercely, rejoicing in his
strength,
and charges into the fray.
22 He laughs at fear, afraid of nothing;

he does not shy away from the
sword.
23 The quiver rattles against his side,
along with the flashing spear and
lance.
24 In frenzied excitement he eats up the
ground;
he cannot stand still when the
trumpet sounds.
25 At the blast of the trumpet he snorts,
'Aha!'
He catches the scent of battle from
afar,
the shout of commanders and the
battle cry.

26 "Does the hawk take flight by your
wisdom
and spread his wings toward the
south?
27 Does the eagle soar at your command
and build his nest on high?
28 He dwells on a cliff and stays there at
night;
a rocky crag is his stronghold.
29 From there he seeks out his food;
his eyes detect it from afar.
30 His young ones feast on blood,
and where the slain are, there is
he."

40 The LORD said to Job:

2 "Will the one who contends with the
Almighty correct him?
Let him who accuses God answer
him!"

3 Then Job answered the LORD:

4 "I am unworthy—how can I reply to
you?
I put my hand over my mouth.
5 I spoke once, but I have no answer—
twice, but I will say no more."

6 Then the LORD spoke to Job out of
the storm:

7 "Brace yourself like a man;
I will question you,
and you shall answer me.

8 "Would you discredit my justice?
Would you condemn me to justify
yourself?
9 Do you have an arm like God's,

and can your voice thunder like his?

10 Then adorn yourself with glory and splendor,
   and clothe yourself in honor and majesty.
11 Unleash the fury of your wrath,
   look at every proud man and bring him low,
12 look at every proud man and humble him,
   crush the wicked where they stand.
13 Bury them all in the dust together;
   shroud their faces in the grave.
14 Then I myself will admit to you
   that your own right hand can save you.

15 "Look at the behemoth,[a]
   which I made along with you
   and which feeds on grass like an ox.
16 What strength he has in his loins,
   what power in the muscles of his belly!
17 His tail[b] sways like a cedar;
   the sinews of his thighs are close-knit.
18 His bones are tubes of bronze,
   his limbs like rods of iron.
19 He ranks first among the works of God,
   yet his Maker can approach him with his sword.
20 The hills bring him their produce,
   and all the wild animals play nearby.
21 Under the lotus plants he lies,
   hidden among the reeds in the marsh.
22 The lotuses conceal him in their shadow;
   the poplars by the stream surround him.
23 When the river rages, he is not alarmed;
   he is secure, though the Jordan should surge against his mouth.
24 Can anyone capture him by the eyes,[c]
   or trap him and pierce his nose?

41 "Can you pull in the leviathan[d] with a fishhook
   or tie down his tongue with a rope?
2 Can you put a cord through his nose
   or pierce his jaw with a hook?
3 Will he keep begging you for mercy?
   Will he speak to you with gentle words?
4 Will he make an agreement with you
   for you to take him as your slave for life?
5 Can you make a pet of him like a bird
   or put him on a leash for your girls?
6 Will traders barter for him?
   Will they divide him up among the merchants?
7 Can you fill his hide with harpoons
   or his head with fishing spears?
8 If you lay a hand on him,
   you will remember the struggle and never do it again!
9 Any hope of subduing him is false;
   the mere sight of him is overpowering.
10 No one is fierce enough to rouse him.
   Who then is able to stand against me?
11 Who has a claim against me that I must pay?
   Everything under heaven belongs to me.

12 "I will not fail to speak of his limbs,
   his strength and his graceful form.
13 Who can strip off his outer coat?
   Who would approach him with a bridle?
14 Who dares open the doors of his mouth,
   ringed about with his fearsome teeth?
15 His back has[e] rows of shields
   tightly sealed together;
16 each is so close to the next
   that no air can pass between.
17 They are joined fast to one another;
   they cling together and cannot be parted.
18 His snorting throws out flashes of light;
   his eyes are like the rays of dawn.

---

a 15 Possibly the hippopotamus or the elephant   b 17 Possibly trunk   c 24 Or by a water hole
d 1 Possibly the crocodile   e 15 Or His pride is his

19 Firebrands stream from his mouth;
    sparks of fire shoot out.
20 Smoke pours from his nostrils
    as from a boiling pot over a fire of
    reeds.
21 His breath sets coals ablaze,
    and flames dart from his mouth.
22 Strength resides in his neck;
    dismay goes before him.
23 The folds of his flesh are tightly
    joined;
    they are firm and immovable.
24 His chest is hard as rock,
    hard as a lower millstone.
25 When he rises up, the mighty are
    terrified;
    they retreat before his thrashing.
26 The sword that reaches him has no
    effect,
    nor does the spear or the dart or the
    javelin.
27 Iron he treats like straw
    and bronze like rotten wood.
28 Arrows do not make him flee;
    slingstones are like chaff to him.
29 A club seems to him but a piece of
    straw;
    he laughs at the rattling of the
    lance.
30 His undersides are jagged potsherds,
    leaving a trail in the mud like a
    threshing sledge.
31 He makes the depths churn like a
    boiling caldron
    and stirs up the sea like a pot of
    ointment.
32 Behind him he leaves a glistening
    wake;
    one would think the deep had
    white hair.
33 Nothing on earth is his equal—
    a creature without fear.
34 He looks down on all that are
    haughty;
    he is king over all that are proud."

Job

42 Then Job replied to the LORD:

2 "I know that you can do all things;
    no plan of yours can be thwarted.
3 ˪You asked,˩ 'Who is this that
    obscures my counsel without
    knowledge?'

Surely I spoke of things I did not
    understand,
    things too wonderful for me to
    know.

4 ˪"You said,˩ 'Listen now, and I will
    speak;
    I will question you,
    and you shall answer me.'
5 My ears had heard of you
    but now my eyes have seen you.
6 Therefore I despise myself
    and repent in dust and ashes."

SEEING GOD, JOB FORGETS ALL HE WANTED TO
SAY, ALL HE THOUGHT HE WOULD SAY IF HE
COULD BUT SEE HIM.   —George MacDonald

Epilogue

7 After the LORD had said these things
to Job, he said to Eliphaz the Temanite,
"I am angry with you and your two
friends, because you have not spoken of
me what is right, as my servant Job has.
8 So now take seven bulls and seven
rams and go to my servant Job and sacrifice a burnt offering for yourselves. My
servant Job will pray for you, and I will
accept his prayer and not deal with you
according to your folly. You have not
spoken of me what is right, as my servant Job has." 9 So Eliphaz the Temanite,
Bildad the Shuhite and Zophar the Naamathite did what the LORD told them;
and the LORD accepted Job's prayer.

10 After Job had prayed for his friends,
the LORD made him prosperous again
and gave him twice as much as he had
before. 11 All his brothers and sisters and
everyone who had known him before
came and ate with him in his house.
They comforted and consoled him over
all the trouble the LORD had brought
upon him, and each one gave him a
piece of silver*a* and a gold ring.

12 The LORD blessed the latter part of
Job's life more than the first. He had
fourteen thousand sheep, six thousand
camels, a thousand yoke of oxen and a
thousand donkeys. 13 And he also had
seven sons and three daughters. 14 The
first daughter he named Jemimah, the
second Keziah and the third Keren-Hap-

---

a 11 Hebrew him a kesitah; a kesitah was a unit of money of unknown weight and value.

puch. ¹⁵Nowhere in all the land were there found women as beautiful as Job's daughters, and their father granted them an inheritance along with their brothers.

¹⁶After this, Job lived a hundred and forty years; he saw his children and their children to the fourth generation. ¹⁷And so he died, old and full of years.

FRIDAY

THE GREAT MYSTERY OF HUMAN LIFE
Fyodor Dostoyevsky

VERSE: Job 42:10   **PASSAGE:** Job 42:10–16

hat a book it is, and what lessons there are in it! What a book the Bible is, what a miracle, what strength is given with it to man. It is like a mold cast of the world and man and human nature, everything is there, and a law for everything for all the ages. And what mysteries are solved and revealed; God raises Job again, gives him wealth again. Many years pass by, and he has other children and loves them. But how could he love those new ones when those first children are no more, when he has lost them? Remembering them, how could he be fully happy with those new ones, however dear the new ones might be? But he could, he could. It's the great mystery of human life that old grief passes gradually into quiet, tender joy. The mild serenity of age takes the place of the riotous blood of youth. I bless the rising sun each day, and as before, my heart sings to meet it, but now I love even more its setting, its long slanting rays and the soft, tender, gentle memories that come with them, the dear images from the whole of my long happy life—and over all the divine truth, softening, reconciling, forgiving! My life is ending, I know that well, but every day that is left me I feel how my earthly life is in touch with a new, infinite, unknown, but approaching life, the nearness of which sets my soul quivering with rapture, my mind glowing and my heart weeping with joy.

ADDITIONAL SCRIPTURE READING:
Isaiah 61:7–8; 1 Timothy 6:17; James 5:11

Go to page 595 for your next devotional reading.

1700   1900

PSALMS

THE BOOK OF PSALMS GIVES VOICE TO HUMAN EMOTION. THIS IS NOT A BOOK OF CATECHISM OR DOCTRINE; IT IS FOR THE MOST PART A BOOK OF PRAYER AND PRAISE. IT SPEAKS TO GOD IN PRAYER AND OF GOD IN PRAISE AND IN PROFESSIONS OF FAITH AND TRUST. THINK OF THE PSALMS AS ENTRIES IN A DIARY, REFLECTING PEOPLE'S MOST INTIMATE DEALINGS WITH GOD. YOU'LL FIND COMFORT AND STRENGTH HERE WHEN YOU IDENTIFY WITH THE OLD TESTAMENT SAINTS WHO WROTE THESE PRAYERS AND SONGS.

BOOK I
Psalms 1–41

Psalm

 1

¹ Blessed is the man
  who does not walk in the counsel
    of the wicked
  or stand in the way of sinners
    or sit in the seat of mockers.
² But his delight is in the law of the
    LORD,
  and on his law he meditates day
    and night.
³ He is like a tree planted by streams of
    water,
  which yields its fruit in season

and whose leaf does not wither.
  Whatever he does prospers.

⁴ Not so the wicked!
  They are like chaff
    that the wind blows away.
⁵ Therefore the wicked will not stand
    in the judgment,
  nor sinners in the assembly of the
    righteous.

THE PSALMS ARE THE ANATOMY OF THE SOUL.

—John Calvin

---

⁶ For the LORD watches over the way of
    the righteous,
  but the way of the wicked will
    perish.

4 The One enthroned in heaven
    laughs;
    the Lord scoffs at them.
5 Then he rebukes them in his anger
    and terrifies them in his wrath,
    saying,
6 "I have installed my King*a*
    on Zion, my holy hill."

7 I will proclaim the decree of the
LORD:

He said to me, "You are my Son*b*;
    today I have become your Father.*c*
8 Ask of me,
    and I will make the nations your
        inheritance,
    the ends of the earth your
        possession.
9 You will rule them with an iron
        scepter*d*;
    you will dash them to pieces like
        pottery."

10 Therefore, you kings, be wise;
    be warned, you rulers of the earth.
11 Serve the LORD with fear
    and rejoice with trembling.
12 Kiss the Son, lest he be angry
    and you be destroyed in your way,
    for his wrath can flare up in a
        moment.
    Blessed are all who take refuge in
        him.

Psalm

A psalm of David. When he fled from
his son Absalom.

1 O LORD, how many are my foes!
    How many rise up against me!
2 Many are saying of me,
    "God will not deliver him." *Selah*e

3 But you are a shield around me,
    O LORD;
    you bestow glory on me and lift*f* up
        my head.
4 To the LORD I cry aloud,
    and he answers me from his holy
        hill.   *Selah*

5 I lie down and sleep;
    I wake again, because the LORD
        sustains me.
6 I will not fear the tens of thousands
    drawn up against me on every side.

7 Arise, O LORD!
    Deliver me, O my God!
    Strike all my enemies on the jaw;
    break the teeth of the wicked.

8 From the LORD comes deliverance.
    May your blessing be on your
        people.   *Selah*

Psalm

For the director of music. With stringed
instruments. A psalm of David.

1 Answer me when I call to you,
    O my righteous God.
    Give me relief from my distress;
    be merciful to me and hear my
        prayer.

2 How long, O men, will you turn my
        glory into shame*g*?
    How long will you love delusions
        and seek false gods*h*?   *Selah*
3 Know that the LORD has set apart the
        godly for himself;
    the LORD will hear when I call to
        him.

4 In your anger do not sin;
    when you are on your beds,
    search your hearts and be silent.
                                    Selah
5 Offer right sacrifices
    and trust in the LORD.

6 Many are asking, "Who can show us
        any good?"
    Let the light of your face shine
        upon us, O LORD.
7 You have filled my heart with greater
        joy
    than when their grain and new
        wine abound.
8 I will lie down and sleep in peace,
    for you alone, O LORD,
    make me dwell in safety.

a 6 Or *king*   *b* 7 Or *son*; also in verse 12   *c* 7 Or *have begotten you*   *d* 9 Or *will break them with a rod of iron*   *e* 2 A word of uncertain meaning, occurring frequently in the Psalms; possibly a musical term   *f* 3 Or LORD, / *my Glorious One, who lifts*   *g* 2 Or *you dishonor my Glorious One*   *h* 2 Or *seek lies*

IN THE SILENCE
Dag Hammarskjold

VERSE: Psalm 4:4   **PASSAGE:** Psalm 4:4–8

ave mercy
Upon us.
Have mercy
Upon our efforts,
That we
Before thee,
In love and in faith,
Righteousness and humility,
May follow thee,
With self-denial, steadfastness, and courage,
And meet thee
In the silence.

Give us
A pure heart
That we may see thee,
A humble heart
That we may hear thee,
A heart of love
That we may serve thee,
A heart of faith
That we may live thee,

Thou
Whom I do not know
But whose I am.

Thou
Whom I do not comprehend
But who hast dedicated me
To my fate.
Thou—

ADDITIONAL SCRIPTURE READING:
Exodus 34:5–8; 1 Kings 19:11–12

Go to page 599 for your next devotional reading.

1900   Present

Psalm

For the director of music. For flutes.
A psalm of David.

¹Give ear to my words, O LORD,
consider my sighing.
²Listen to my cry for help,
my King and my God,
for to you I pray.
³In the morning, O LORD, you hear my
voice;
in the morning I lay my requests
before you
and wait in expectation.

⁴You are not a God who takes pleasure
in evil;

WEDNESDAY

HOW TO BEGIN MORNING DEVOTIONS
William Law

VERSE: Psalm 5:3   **PASSAGE:** Psalm 5:1–3

 he first thing that you are to do, when you are upon your knees, is to shut your eyes, and with a short silence let your soul place itself in the presence of God; that is, you are to use this, or some other better method, to separate yourself from all common thoughts, and make your heart as sensible as you can of the divine presence.

Now if this recollection of spirit is necessary—as who can say it is not?—then how poorly must they perform their devotions, who are always in a hurry; who begin them in haste, and hardly allow themselves time to repeat their very form, with any gravity or attention! Theirs is properly saying prayers, instead of praying . . .

When you begin your petitions, use such various expressions of the attributes of God, as may make you most sensible of the greatness and power of the divine nature.

Begin, therefore, in words like these: O Being of all beings, Fountain of all light and glory, gracious Father of men and angels, whose universal Spirit is everywhere present, giving life, and light, and joy, to all angels in heaven, and all creatures upon earth . . .

For these representations of the divine attributes, which show us in some degree the majesty and greatness of God, are an excellent means of raising our hearts into lively acts of worship and adoration.

ADDITIONAL SCRIPTURE READING:
Psalms 88:13; 130:6; Mark 1:35

Go to page 601 for your next devotional reading.

1700   1900

with you the wicked cannot dwell.
5 The arrogant cannot stand in your
   presence;
   you hate all who do wrong.
6 You destroy those who tell lies;
   bloodthirsty and deceitful men
   the LORD abhors.

7 But I, by your great mercy,
   will come into your house;
   in reverence will I bow down
   toward your holy temple.
8 Lead me, O LORD, in your
   righteousness
   because of my enemies—
   make straight your way before
   me.

9 Not a word from their mouth can be
   trusted;
   their heart is filled with
   destruction.
   Their throat is an open grave;
   with their tongue they speak
   deceit.
10 Declare them guilty, O God!
   Let their intrigues be their
   downfall.
   Banish them for their many sins,
   for they have rebelled against you.

11 But let all who take refuge in you be
   glad;
   let them ever sing for joy.
   Spread your protection over them,
   that those who love your name
   may rejoice in you.
12 For surely, O LORD, you bless the
   righteous;
   you surround them with your favor
   as with a shield.

Psalm

6

For the director of music. With stringed
instruments. According to *sheminith.*[a]
A psalm of David.

1 O LORD, do not rebuke me in your
   anger
   or discipline me in your wrath.
2 Be merciful to me, LORD, for I am
   faint;
   O LORD, heal me, for my bones are
   in agony.

3 My soul is in anguish.
   How long, O LORD, how long?

4 Turn, O LORD, and deliver me;
   save me because of your unfailing
   love.
5 No one remembers you when he is
   dead.
   Who praises you from the grave[b]?

6 I am worn out from groaning;
   all night long I flood my bed with
   weeping
   and drench my couch with tears.
7 My eyes grow weak with sorrow;
   they fail because of all my foes.

8 Away from me, all you who do evil,
   for the LORD has heard my
   weeping.
9 The LORD has heard my cry for
   mercy;
   the LORD accepts my prayer.
10 All my enemies will be ashamed and
   dismayed;
   they will turn back in sudden
   disgrace.

Psalm

7

A *shiggaion*[c] of David, which he sang to the
LORD concerning Cush, a Benjamite.

1 O LORD my God, I take refuge in you;
   save and deliver me from all who
   pursue me,
2 or they will tear me like a lion
   and rip me to pieces with no one to
   rescue me.

3 O LORD my God, if I have done this
   and there is guilt on my hands—
4 if I have done evil to him who is at
   peace with me
   or without cause have robbed my
   foe—
5 then let my enemy pursue and
   overtake me;
   let him trample my life to the
   ground
   and make me sleep in the dust.
                                      Selah

6 Arise, O LORD, in your anger;
   rise up against the rage of my
   enemies.

---

[a] Title: Probably a musical term   [b] 5 Hebrew *Sheol*   [c] Title: Probably a literary or musical term

Awake, my God; decree justice.
7 Let the assembled peoples gather
   around you.
Rule over them from on high;
8   let the LORD judge the peoples.
Judge me, O LORD, according to my
   righteousness,
   according to my integrity, O Most
   High.
9 O righteous God,
   who searches minds and hearts,
bring to an end the violence of the
   wicked
   and make the righteous secure.

10 My shield[a] is God Most High,
   who saves the upright in heart.
11 God is a righteous judge,
   a God who expresses his wrath
      every day.
12 If he does not relent,
   he[b] will sharpen his sword;
   he will bend and string his bow.
13 He has prepared his deadly weapons;
   he makes ready his flaming arrows.

14 He who is pregnant with evil
   and conceives trouble gives birth
      to disillusionment.
15 He who digs a hole and scoops it out

a 10 Or *sovereign*   b 12 Or *If a man does not repent, / God*

THURSDAY

GOD'S WATER
Teresa of Avila

VERSE: Psalm 6:6   **PASSAGE:** Psalm 6:6–10

et's not think that everything is accomplished through much weeping but set our hands to the task of hard work and virtue. These are what we must pay attention to; let the tears come when God sends them and without any effort on our part to induce them. These tears from God will irrigate this dry earth, and they are a great help in producing fruit. The less attention we pay to them the more there are, for they are the water that falls from heaven. The tears we draw out by tiring ourselves in digging cannot compare with the tears that come from God, for often in digging we shall get worn out and not find even a puddle of water, much less a flowing well. Therefore, sisters, I consider it better for us to place ourselves in the presence of the Lord and look at his mercy and grandeur and at our own lowliness, and let him give us what he wants, whether water or dryness. He knows best what is suitable for us. With such an attitude we shall go about refreshed, and the devil will not have so much chance to play tricks on us.

ADDITIONAL SCRIPTURE READING:
2 Kings 20:5; Psalms 56:8; 126:5–6

Go to page 603 for your next devotional reading.

1500   1700

falls into the pit he has made.
¹⁶ The trouble he causes recoils on
   himself;
   his violence comes down on his
      own head.

¹⁷ I will give thanks to the LORD
      because of his righteousness
   and will sing praise to the name of
      the LORD Most High.

Psalm

8

For the director of music. According to
   gittith. ᵃ A psalm of David.

¹ O LORD, our Lord,
   how majestic is your name in all
      the earth!

You have set your glory
   above the heavens.
² From the lips of children and infants
   you have ordained praise ᵇ
because of your enemies,
   to silence the foe and the avenger.

³ When I consider your heavens,
   the work of your fingers,
the moon and the stars,
   which you have set in place,
⁴ what is man that you are mindful of
      him,
   the son of man that you care for
      him?
⁵ You made him a little lower than the
      heavenly beings ᶜ
   and crowned him with glory and
      honor.

⁶ You made him ruler over the works
      of your hands;
   you put everything under his feet:
⁷ all flocks and herds,
   and the beasts of the field,
⁸ the birds of the air,
   and the fish of the sea,
   all that swim the paths of the seas.

⁹ O LORD, our Lord,
   how majestic is your name in all
      the earth!

Psalm

9 ᵈ

For the director of music. To the tune of
"The Death of the Son." A psalm of David.

¹ I will praise you, O LORD, with all my
      heart;
   I will tell of all your wonders.
² I will be glad and rejoice in you;
   I will sing praise to your name,
      O Most High.

³ My enemies turn back;
   they stumble and perish before
      you.
⁴ For you have upheld my right and my
      cause;
   you have sat on your throne,
      judging righteously.
⁵ You have rebuked the nations and
      destroyed the wicked;
   you have blotted out their name
      for ever and ever.
⁶ Endless ruin has overtaken the
      enemy,
   you have uprooted their cities;
   even the memory of them has
      perished.

⁷ The LORD reigns forever;
   he has established his throne for
      judgment.
⁸ He will judge the world in
      righteousness;
   he will govern the peoples with
      justice.
⁹ The LORD is a refuge for the
      oppressed,
   a stronghold in times of trouble.
¹⁰ Those who know your name will
      trust in you,
   for you, LORD, have never forsaken
      those who seek you.

¹¹ Sing praises to the LORD, enthroned
      in Zion;
   proclaim among the nations what
      he has done.
¹² For he who avenges blood
      remembers;
   he does not ignore the cry of the
      afflicted.

ᵃ Title: Probably a musical term   ᵇ 2 Or *strength*   ᶜ 5 Or *than God*   ᵈ Psalms 9 and 10 may have
been originally a single acrostic poem, the stanzas of which begin with the successive letters of the
Hebrew alphabet. In the Septuagint they constitute one psalm.

A PRAYER OF THANKSGIVING
South Africa, National Service of Thanksgiving

VERSE: Psalm 9:1   PASSAGE: Psalm 9:1–10

 God our loving eternal Parent, we praise you with a great shout of joy! Your ruling power has provided victorious! For centuries our land seemed too dark for sunrise, too bloody for healing, too sick for recovery, too hateful for reconciliation. But you have brought us into the daylight of liberation; you have healed us with new hope; you have stirred us to believe our nation can be reborn; we see the eyes of our sisters and brothers shining with resolve to build a new South Africa. Accept our prayers of praise and thanksgiving.

We thank you for our grandmothers and grandfathers who taught us to believe in liberation. We thank you for those who are great names to all our country now: Luthuli, Sobukwe, Biko, Visser, Joseph, Ngoyi, Hani, Tambo, and a thousand others. Many are named with our own names, treasured in our hearts, honored in our memories. Many rest in graves in other lands so that South African love embraces the world. We remember those thousands of people overseas who gave themselves in solidarity that our nation might be changed.

For all of these we thank and praise you. We thank you that democracy has come, and for the wonder of a government of national unity. We thank you for the commitment among all people to seek justice and peace, homes and jobs, education and health, reconciliation and reconstruction. We thank you that because apartheid has gone we can turn from the days of destruction to the work of reconstruction together. For our rich variety, our rich vision and our rich land, we thank you.

We thank you for the spiritual power which gives us new birth. You have given us the courage to change our minds, to open our hearts to those we despised, and to discover we can disagree without being enemies. We are not winners and losers, but citizens who push and pull together to move the nation forward. We thank you for the good news that you will always be with us, and will always overcome: that love will conquer hatred; that tolerance will conquer antagonism; that cooperation will conquer conflict; that your Holy Spirit can empower our spirits; through Jesus Christ our Lord.

ADDITIONAL SCRIPTURE READING:
Psalms 107:15–16; 117

Go to page 609 for your next devotional reading.

1900   Present

¹³O LORD, see how my enemies
　persecute me!
　Have mercy and lift me up from
　　the gates of death,
¹⁴that I may declare your praises
　in the gates of the Daughter of
　　Zion
　and there rejoice in your
　　salvation.
¹⁵The nations have fallen into the pit
　they have dug;
　their feet are caught in the net they
　　have hidden.
¹⁶The LORD is known by his justice;
　the wicked are ensnared by the
　　work of their hands.
　　　　　　　Higgaion.ᵃ Selah
¹⁷The wicked return to the grave,ᵇ
　all the nations that forget God.
¹⁸But the needy will not always be
　　forgotten,
　nor the hope of the afflicted ever
　　perish.

¹⁹Arise, O LORD, let not man triumph;
　let the nations be judged in your
　　presence.
²⁰Strike them with terror, O LORD;
　let the nations know they are but
　　men.　　　　　　　Selah

Psalm

10 ᶜ

¹Why, O LORD, do you stand far off?
　Why do you hide yourself in times
　　of trouble?

²In his arrogance the wicked man
　　hunts down the weak,
　who are caught in the schemes he
　　devises.
³He boasts of the cravings of his
　　heart;
　he blesses the greedy and reviles
　　the LORD.
⁴In his pride the wicked does not seek
　　him;
　in all his thoughts there is no room
　　for God.
⁵His ways are always prosperous;
　he is haughty and your laws are far
　　from him;

　he sneers at all his enemies.
⁶He says to himself, "Nothing will
　　shake me;
　I'll always be happy and never have
　　trouble."
⁷His mouth is full of curses and lies
　　and threats;
　trouble and evil are under his
　　tongue.
⁸He lies in wait near the villages;
　from ambush he murders the
　　innocent,
　watching in secret for his victims.
⁹He lies in wait like a lion in cover;
　he lies in wait to catch the
　　helpless;
　he catches the helpless and drags
　　them off in his net.
¹⁰His victims are crushed, they
　　collapse;
　they fall under his strength.
¹¹He says to himself, "God has
　　forgotten;
　he covers his face and never sees."

¹²Arise, LORD! Lift up your hand,
　O God.
　Do not forget the helpless.
¹³Why does the wicked man revile
　　God?
　Why does he say to himself,
　"He won't call me to account"?
¹⁴But you, O God, do see trouble and
　　grief;
　you consider it to take it in hand.
　The victim commits himself to you;
　you are the helper of the
　　fatherless.
¹⁵Break the arm of the wicked and evil
　　man;
　call him to account for his
　　wickedness
　that would not be found out.

¹⁶The LORD is King for ever and ever;
　the nations will perish from his
　　land.
¹⁷You hear, O LORD, the desire of the
　　afflicted;
　you encourage them, and you
　　listen to their cry,
¹⁸defending the fatherless and the
　　oppressed,

ᵃ 16 Or *Meditation*; possibly a musical notation　　ᵇ 17 Hebrew *Sheol*　　ᶜ Psalms 9 and 10 may have
been originally a single acrostic poem, the stanzas of which begin with the successive letters of the
Hebrew alphabet. In the Septuagint they constitute one psalm.

in order that man, who is of the
earth, may terrify no more.

Psalm

 11

For the director of music. Of David.

1 In the LORD I take refuge.
　　How then can you say to me:
　　"Flee like a bird to your
　　　mountain.
2 For look, the wicked bend their
　　　bows;
　　they set their arrows against the
　　　strings
　　to shoot from the shadows
　　at the upright in heart.
3 When the foundations are being
　　　destroyed,
　　what can the righteous do[a]?"

4 The LORD is in his holy temple;
　　the LORD is on his heavenly
　　　throne.
　　He observes the sons of men;
　　his eyes examine them.
5 The LORD examines the righteous,
　　but the wicked[b] and those who
　　　love violence
　　his soul hates.
6 On the wicked he will rain
　　fiery coals and burning sulfur;
　　a scorching wind will be their lot.

7 For the LORD is righteous,
　　he loves justice;
　　upright men will see his face.

Psalm

 12

For the director of music. According to
　sheminith.[c] A psalm of David.

1 Help, LORD, for the godly are no
　　　more;
　　the faithful have vanished from
　　　among men.
2 Everyone lies to his neighbor;
　　their flattering lips speak with
　　　deception.

3 May the LORD cut off all flattering
　　lips

and every boastful tongue
4 that says, "We will triumph with our
　　　tongues;
　　we own our lips[d]—who is our
　　　master?"

5 "Because of the oppression of the
　　　weak
　　and the groaning of the needy,
　　I will now arise," says the LORD.
　　"I will protect them from those
　　who malign them."
6 And the words of the LORD are
　　　flawless,
　　like silver refined in a furnace of
　　　clay,
　　purified seven times.

7 O LORD, you will keep us safe
　　and protect us from such people
　　　forever.
8 The wicked freely strut about
　　when what is vile is honored
　　　among men.

Psalm

 13

For the director of music. A psalm of David.

1 How long, O LORD? Will you forget
　　me forever?
　　How long will you hide your face
　　from me?
2 How long must I wrestle with my
　　　thoughts
　　and every day have sorrow in my
　　　heart?
　　How long will my enemy triumph
　　over me?

3 Look on me and answer, O LORD my
　　　God.
　　Give light to my eyes, or I will
　　　sleep in death;
4 my enemy will say, "I have overcome
　　　him,"
　　and my foes will rejoice when I
　　　fall.

5 But I trust in your unfailing love;
　　my heart rejoices in your
　　　salvation.
6 I will sing to the LORD,
　　for he has been good to me.

---

a 3 Or what is the Righteous One doing　　b 5 Or The LORD, the Righteous One, examines the wicked, /
c Title: Probably a musical term　　d 4 Or / our lips are our plowshares

Psalm 14

For the director of music. Of David.

1 The fool[a] says in his heart,
    "There is no God."
They are corrupt, their deeds are vile;
    there is no one who does good.

I WAS . . . LIVING, LIKE SO MANY ATHEISTS OR
ANTITHEISTS, IN A WHIRL OF CONTRADICTIONS. I
MAINTAINED THAT GOD DID NOT EXIST. I WAS
ALSO VERY ANGRY WITH GOD FOR NOT EXISTING.
I WAS EQUALLY ANGRY WITH HIM FOR CREATING
A WORLD.
                                              —C. S. Lewis

---

2 The LORD looks down from heaven
    on the sons of men
to see if there are any who understand,
    any who seek God.
3 All have turned aside,
    they have together become
        corrupt;
there is no one who does good,
    not even one.

4 Will evildoers never learn—
    those who devour my people as
        men eat bread
    and who do not call on the LORD?
5 There they are, overwhelmed with
        dread,
    for God is present in the company
        of the righteous.
6 You evildoers frustrate the plans of
        the poor,
    but the LORD is their refuge.

7 Oh, that salvation for Israel would
        come out of Zion!
When the LORD restores the
        fortunes of his people,
    let Jacob rejoice and Israel be glad!

Psalm 15

A psalm of David.

1 LORD, who may dwell in your
        sanctuary?
Who may live on your holy hill?

2 He whose walk is blameless
    and who does what is righteous,
    who speaks the truth from his heart
3   and has no slander on his tongue,
    who does his neighbor no wrong
    and casts no slur on his fellowman,
4 who despises a vile man
    but honors those who fear the
        LORD,
    who keeps his oath
        even when it hurts,
5 who lends his money without usury
    and does not accept a bribe against
        the innocent.

He who does these things
    will never be shaken.

Psalm 16

A miktam[b] of David.

1 Keep me safe, O God,
    for in you I take refuge.

2 I said to the LORD, "You are my Lord;
    apart from you I have no good
        thing."
3 As for the saints who are in the land,
    they are the glorious ones in whom
        is all my delight.[c]
4 The sorrows of those will increase
    who run after other gods.
I will not pour out their libations of
        blood
    or take up their names on my lips.

5 LORD, you have assigned me my
        portion and my cup;
    you have made my lot secure.
6 The boundary lines have fallen for
        me in pleasant places;
    surely I have a delightful
        inheritance.

7 I will praise the LORD, who counsels
        me;
    even at night my heart instructs
        me.
8 I have set the LORD always before me.
    Because he is at my right hand,
    I will not be shaken.

---

a 1 The Hebrew words rendered *fool* in Psalms denote one who is morally deficient.   b Title: Probably a
literary or musical term   c 3 Or *As for the pagan priests who are in the land / and the nobles in whom
all delight, I said:*

9 Therefore my heart is glad and my
tongue rejoices;
my body also will rest secure,
10 because you will not abandon me to
the grave,[a]
nor will you let your Holy One[b]
see decay.
11 You have made[c] known to me the
path of life;
you will fill me with joy in your
presence,
with eternal pleasures at your right
hand.

Psalm 17

A prayer of David.

1 Hear, O LORD, my righteous plea;
listen to my cry.
Give ear to my prayer—
it does not rise from deceitful lips.
2 May my vindication come from
you;
may your eyes see what is right.

3 Though you probe my heart and
examine me at night,
though you test me, you will find
nothing;
I have resolved that my mouth will
not sin.
4 As for the deeds of men—
by the word of your lips
I have kept myself
from the ways of the violent.
5 My steps have held to your paths;
my feet have not slipped.

6 I call on you, O God, for you will
answer me;
give ear to me and hear my prayer.
7 Show the wonder of your great love,
you who save by your right hand
those who take refuge in you from
their foes.
8 Keep me as the apple of your eye;
hide me in the shadow of your
wings
9 from the wicked who assail me,
from my mortal enemies who
surround me.

10 They close up their callous hearts,
and their mouths speak with
arrogance.
11 They have tracked me down, they
now surround me,
with eyes alert, to throw me to the
ground.
12 They are like a lion hungry for prey,
like a great lion crouching in cover.

13 Rise up, O LORD, confront them,
bring them down;
rescue me from the wicked by your
sword.
14 O LORD, by your hand save me from
such men,
from men of this world whose
reward is in this life.

You still the hunger of those you
cherish;
their sons have plenty,
and they store up wealth for their
children.
15 And I—in righteousness I will see
your face;
when I awake, I will be satisfied
with seeing your likeness.

Psalm 18

For the director of music. Of David the
servant of the LORD. He sang to the LORD the
words of this song when the LORD delivered
him from the hand of all his enemies and
from the hand of Saul. He said:

1 I love you, O LORD, my strength.

2 The LORD is my rock, my fortress and
my deliverer;
my God is my rock, in whom I
take refuge.
He is my shield and the horn[d] of
my salvation, my stronghold.
3 I call to the LORD, who is worthy of
praise,
and I am saved from my enemies.

4 The cords of death entangled me;
the torrents of destruction
overwhelmed me.
5 The cords of the grave[a] coiled around
me;
the snares of death confronted me.
6 In my distress I called to the LORD;

---

[a] 10,5 Hebrew Sheol
symbolizes strength.
[b] 10 Or your faithful one
[c] 11 Or You will make
[d] 2 Horn here

I cried to my God for help.
From his temple he heard my voice;
my cry came before him, into his
ears.

7 The earth trembled and quaked,
and the foundations of the
mountains shook;
they trembled because he was
angry.
8 Smoke rose from his nostrils;
consuming fire came from his
mouth,
burning coals blazed out of it.
9 He parted the heavens and came
down;
dark clouds were under his feet.
10 He mounted the cherubim and flew;
he soared on the wings of the wind.
11 He made darkness his covering, his
canopy around him—
the dark rain clouds of the sky.
12 Out of the brightness of his presence
clouds advanced,
with hailstones and bolts of
lightning.
13 The Lord thundered from heaven;
the voice of the Most High
resounded.*a*
14 He shot his arrows and scattered ₁the
enemies₁,
great bolts of lightning and routed
them.
15 The valleys of the sea were exposed
and the foundations of the earth
laid bare
at your rebuke, O Lord,
at the blast of breath from your
nostrils.

16 He reached down from on high and
took hold of me;
he drew me out of deep waters.
17 He rescued me from my powerful
enemy,
from my foes, who were too strong
for me.
18 They confronted me in the day of my
disaster,
but the Lord was my support.
19 He brought me out into a spacious
place;
he rescued me because he
delighted in me.

20 The Lord has dealt with me
according to my righteousness;
according to the cleanness of my
hands he has rewarded me.
21 For I have kept the ways of the Lord;
I have not done evil by turning
from my God.
22 All his laws are before me;
I have not turned away from his
decrees.
23 I have been blameless before him
and have kept myself from sin.
24 The Lord has rewarded me according
to my righteousness,
according to the cleanness of my
hands in his sight.

25 To the faithful you show yourself
faithful,
to the blameless you show yourself
blameless,
26 to the pure you show yourself pure,
but to the crooked you show
yourself shrewd.
27 You save the humble
but bring low those whose eyes are
haughty.
28 You, O Lord, keep my lamp burning;
my God turns my darkness into
light.
29 With your help I can advance against
a troop*b*;
with my God I can scale a wall.

30 As for God, his way is perfect;
the word of the Lord is flawless.
He is a shield
for all who take refuge in him.
31 For who is God besides the Lord?
And who is the Rock except our
God?
32 It is God who arms me with strength
and makes my way perfect.
33 He makes my feet like the feet of a
deer;
he enables me to stand on the
heights.
34 He trains my hands for battle;
my arms can bend a bow of bronze.
35 You give me your shield of victory,
and your right hand sustains me;
you stoop down to make me great.
36 You broaden the path beneath me,
so that my ankles do not turn.

---

a 13 Some Hebrew manuscripts and Septuagint (see also 2 Samuel 22:14); most Hebrew manuscripts
resounded, / amid hailstones and bolts of lightning   *b 29* Or *can run through a barricade*

WEEKEND

A SONG OF ASCENTS
Charles Wesley

VERSE: Psalm 133:1   **PASSAGE:** Psalm 133

 ehold how good a thing
It is to dwell in peace;
How pleasing to our king,
This fruit of righteousness;
When brethren all in one agree,
They know the joy of unity!
They know the joy of unity!

When all are sweetly joined
(True followers of the Lamb),
They're one in heart and mind,
They think and speak the same;
When all in love together dwell;
The comfort is unspeakable!
The comfort is unspeakable!

Where unity takes place,
The joys of heav'n we prove;
This is the gospel grace,
The unction from above;
The Spirit on all saints is shed,
Descending swift from Christ the head.
Descending swift from Christ the head.

Where unity is found,
The sweet anointing grace
Extends to all around,
And shines from every face;
To every praising saint it comes,
And fills him with divine perfumes.
And fills him with divine perfumes.

ADDITIONAL SCRIPTURE READING:
Ephesians 4:3–7; Philippians 2:2–5; 1 Peter 3:8

Go to page 615 for your next devotional reading.

1700   1900

37 I pursued my enemies and overtook
    them;
  I did not turn back till they were
    destroyed.
38 I crushed them so that they could not
    rise;
  they fell beneath my feet.
39 You armed me with strength for
    battle;
  you made my adversaries bow at
    my feet.
40 You made my enemies turn their
    backs in flight,
  and I destroyed my foes.
41 They cried for help, but there was no
    one to save them—
  to the LORD, but he did not answer.
42 I beat them as fine as dust borne on
    the wind;
  I poured them out like mud in the
    streets.

43 You have delivered me from the
    attacks of the people;
  you have made me the head of
    nations;
  people I did not know are subject
    to me.
44 As soon as they hear me, they obey
    me;
  foreigners cringe before me.
45 They all lose heart;
  they come trembling from their
    strongholds.

46 The LORD lives! Praise be to my
    Rock!
  Exalted be God my Savior!
47 He is the God who avenges me,
  who subdues nations under me,
48   who saves me from my enemies.
  You exalted me above my foes;
  from violent men you rescued
    me.
49 Therefore I will praise you among the
    nations, O LORD;
  I will sing praises to your name.
50 He gives his king great victories;
  he shows unfailing kindness to his
    anointed,
  to David and his descendants
    forever.

Psalm 19

For the director of music. A psalm of David.

1 The heavens declare the glory of
    God;
  the skies proclaim the work of his
    hands.
2 Day after day they pour forth
    speech;
  night after night they display
    knowledge.
3 There is no speech or language
  where their voice is not heard.[a]
4 Their voice[b] goes out into all the
    earth,
  their words to the ends of the
    world.

In the heavens he has pitched a tent
    for the sun,
5   which is like a bridegroom coming
    forth from his pavilion,
  like a champion rejoicing to run
    his course.
6 It rises at one end of the heavens
  and makes its circuit to the
    other;
  nothing is hidden from its heat.

7 The law of the LORD is perfect,
  reviving the soul.
The statutes of the LORD are
    trustworthy,
  making wise the simple.
8 The precepts of the LORD are right,
  giving joy to the heart.
The commands of the LORD are
    radiant,
  giving light to the eyes.
9 The fear of the LORD is pure,
  enduring forever.
The ordinances of the LORD are sure
  and altogether righteous.
10 They are more precious than gold,
  than much pure gold;
  they are sweeter than honey,
  than honey from the comb.
11 By them is your servant warned;
  in keeping them there is great
    reward.

12 Who can discern his errors?
  Forgive my hidden faults.

---

[a] 3 Or *They have no speech, there are no words; / no sound is heard from them*   [b] 4 Septuagint,
Jerome and Syriac; Hebrew *line*

13 Keep your servant also from willful
    sins;
  may they not rule over me.
Then will I be blameless,
  innocent of great transgression.

14 May the words of my mouth and the
    meditation of my heart
  be pleasing in your sight,
  O LORD, my Rock and my
    Redeemer.

Psalm

 20

For the director of music. A psalm of David.

1 May the LORD answer you when you
    are in distress;
  may the name of the God of Jacob
    protect you.
2 May he send you help from the
    sanctuary
  and grant you support from Zion.
3 May he remember all your
    sacrifices
  and accept your burnt offerings.
                                    Selah
4 May he give you the desire of your
    heart
  and make all your plans succeed.
5 We will shout for joy when you are
    victorious
  and will lift up our banners in the
    name of our God.
  May the LORD grant all your requests.

6 Now I know that the LORD saves his
    anointed;
  he answers him from his holy
    heaven
  with the saving power of his right
    hand.
7 Some trust in chariots and some in
    horses,
  but we trust in the name of the
    LORD our God.
8 They are brought to their knees and
    fall,
  but we rise up and stand firm.

9 O LORD, save the king!
  Answer^a us when we call!

Psalm

21

For the director of music. A psalm of David.

1 O LORD, the king rejoices in your
    strength.
  How great is his joy in the victories
    you give!
2 You have granted him the desire of
    his heart
  and have not withheld the request
    of his lips.   *Selah*
3 You welcomed him with rich
    blessings
  and placed a crown of pure gold on
    his head.
4 He asked you for life, and you gave it
    to him—
  length of days, for ever and ever.
5 Through the victories you gave, his
    glory is great;
  you have bestowed on him
    splendor and majesty.
6 Surely you have granted him eternal
    blessings
  and made him glad with the joy of
    your presence.
7 For the king trusts in the LORD;
  through the unfailing love of the
    Most High
  he will not be shaken.

8 Your hand will lay hold on all your
    enemies;
  your right hand will seize your
    foes.
9 At the time of your appearing
  you will make them like a fiery
    furnace.
In his wrath the LORD will swallow
    them up,
  and his fire will consume them.
10 You will destroy their descendants
    from the earth,
  their posterity from mankind.
11 Though they plot evil against you
  and devise wicked schemes, they
    cannot succeed;
12 for you will make them turn their
    backs
  when you aim at them with drawn
    bow.

^{a} 9 Or *save! / O King, answer*

13 Be exalted, O Lord, in your
strength;
we will sing and praise your might.

Psalm 22

For the director of music. To ʟthe tune ofʟ
"The Doe of the Morning." A psalm
of David.

1 My God, my God, why have you
forsaken me?
Why are you so far from saving me,
so far from the words of my
groaning?
2 O my God, I cry out by day, but you
do not answer,
by night, and am not silent.

3 Yet you are enthroned as the Holy
One;
you are the praise of Israel.ᵃ
4 In you our fathers put their trust;
they trusted and you delivered
them.
5 They cried to you and were saved;
in you they trusted and were not
disappointed.

6 But I am a worm and not a man,
scorned by men and despised by
the people.
7 All who see me mock me;
they hurl insults, shaking their
heads:
8 "He trusts in the Lord;
let the Lord rescue him.
Let him deliver him,
since he delights in him."

9 Yet you brought me out of the womb;
you made me trust in you
even at my mother's breast.
10 From birth I was cast upon you;
from my mother's womb you have
been my God.
11 Do not be far from me,
for trouble is near
and there is no one to help.

12 Many bulls surround me;
strong bulls of Bashan encircle me.
13 Roaring lions tearing their prey

open their mouths wide against
me.
14 I am poured out like water,
and all my bones are out of joint.
My heart has turned to wax;
it has melted away within me.
15 My strength is dried up like a
potsherd,
and my tongue sticks to the roof of
my mouth;
you lay meᵇ in the dust of death.
16 Dogs have surrounded me;
a band of evil men has encircled
me,
they have piercedᶜ my hands and
my feet.
17 I can count all my bones;
people stare and gloat over me.
18 They divide my garments among
them
and cast lots for my clothing.

19 But you, O Lord, be not far off;
O my Strength, come quickly to
help me.
20 Deliver my life from the sword,
my precious life from the power of
the dogs.
21 Rescue me from the mouth of the
lions;
saveᵈ me from the horns of the
wild oxen.

22 I will declare your name to my
brothers;
in the congregation I will praise
you.
23 You who fear the Lord, praise him!
All you descendants of Jacob,
honor him!
Revere him, all you descendants of
Israel!
24 For he has not despised or disdained
the suffering of the afflicted one;
he has not hidden his face from him
but has listened to his cry for help.

25 From you comes the theme of my
praise in the great assembly;
before those who fear youᵉ will I
fulfill my vows.
26 The poor will eat and be satisfied;
they who seek the Lord will praise
him—
may your hearts live forever!

ᵃ 3 Or Yet you are holy, / enthroned on the praises of Israel   ᵇ 15 Or / I am laid   ᶜ 16 Some Hebrew
manuscripts, Septuagint and Syriac; most Hebrew manuscripts / like the lion,   ᵈ 21 Or / you have
heard   ᵉ 25 Hebrew him

27 All the ends of the earth
will remember and turn to the
L ORD,
and all the families of the nations
will bow down before him,
28 for dominion belongs to the L ORD
and he rules over the nations.

29 All the rich of the earth will feast and
worship;
all who go down to the dust will
kneel before him—
those who cannot keep themselves
alive.
30 Posterity will serve him;
future generations will be told
about the Lord.
31 They will proclaim his
righteousness
to a people yet unborn—
for he has done it.

Psalm

 23

A psalm of David.

1 The L ORD is my shepherd, I shall not
be in want.
2   He makes me lie down in green
pastures,
he leads me beside quiet waters,
3   he restores my soul.
He guides me in paths of
righteousness
for his name's sake.

THE TWENTY-THIRD PSALM IS THE NIGHTINGALE
OF THE PSALMS. IT IS SMALL, OF A HOMELY FEATH-
ER, SINGING SHYLY OUT OF OBSCURITY; BUT IT
HAS FILLED THE AIR OF THE WHOLE WORLD WITH
MELODIOUS JOY.   —*Henry Ward Beecher*

---

4 Even though I walk
through the valley of the shadow of
death,*a*
I will fear no evil,
for you are with me;
your rod and your staff,
they comfort me.
5 You prepare a table before me
in the presence of my enemies.

You anoint my head with oil;
my cup overflows.
6 Surely goodness and love will follow
me
all the days of my life,
and I will dwell in the house of the
L ORD
forever.

Psalm

 24

Of David. A psalm.

1 The earth is the L ORD's, and
everything in it,
the world, and all who live in it;
2 for he founded it upon the seas
and established it upon the
waters.

3 Who may ascend the hill of the
L ORD?
Who may stand in his holy place?
4 He who has clean hands and a pure
heart,
who does not lift up his soul to an
idol
or swear by what is false.*b*
5 He will receive blessing from the
L ORD
and vindication from God his
Savior.
6 Such is the generation of those who
seek him,
who seek your face, O God of
Jacob.*c*   *Selah*

7 Lift up your heads, O you gates;
be lifted up, you ancient doors,
that the King of glory may come
in.
8 Who is this King of glory?
The L ORD strong and mighty,
the L ORD mighty in battle.
9 Lift up your heads, O you gates;
lift them up, you ancient doors,
that the King of glory may come
in.
10 Who is he, this King of glory?
The L ORD Almighty—
he is the King of glory.   *Selah*

---

a 4 Or *through the darkest valley*   *b 4* Or *swear falsely*   *c 6* Two Hebrew manuscripts and Syriac
(see also Septuagint); most Hebrew manuscripts *face, Jacob*

Psalm

25 [a]

Of David.

1 To you, O LORD, I lift up my soul;
2   in you I trust, O my God.
  Do not let me be put to shame,
    nor let my enemies triumph over
      me.
3 No one whose hope is in you
    will ever be put to shame,
  but they will be put to shame
    who are treacherous without
      excuse.

4 Show me your ways, O LORD,
    teach me your paths;
5 guide me in your truth and teach me,
    for you are God my Savior,
    and my hope is in you all day long.
6 Remember, O LORD, your great
      mercy and love,
    for they are from of old.
7 Remember not the sins of my youth
    and my rebellious ways;
  according to your love remember me,
    for you are good, O LORD.

8 Good and upright is the LORD;
    therefore he instructs sinners in
      his ways.
9 He guides the humble in what is
      right
    and teaches them his way.
10 All the ways of the LORD are loving
      and faithful
    for those who keep the demands of
      his covenant.
11 For the sake of your name, O LORD,
    forgive my iniquity, though it is
      great.
12 Who, then, is the man that fears the
      LORD?
  He will instruct him in the way
    chosen for him.
13 He will spend his days in prosperity,
    and his descendants will inherit
      the land.
14 The LORD confides in those who fear
      him;
  he makes his covenant known to
    them.
15 My eyes are ever on the LORD,

for only he will release my feet
    from the snare.
16 Turn to me and be gracious to me,
    for I am lonely and afflicted.
17 The troubles of my heart have
      multiplied;
    free me from my anguish.
18 Look upon my affliction and my
      distress
    and take away all my sins.
19 See how my enemies have increased
    and how fiercely they hate me!
20 Guard my life and rescue me;
    let me not be put to shame,
    for I take refuge in you.
21 May integrity and uprightness
      protect me,
    because my hope is in you.

22 Redeem Israel, O God,
    from all their troubles!

Psalm

26

Of David.

1 Vindicate me, O LORD,
    for I have led a blameless life;
  I have trusted in the LORD
    without wavering.
2 Test me, O LORD, and try me,
    examine my heart and my mind;
3 for your love is ever before me,
    and I walk continually in your
      truth.
4 I do not sit with deceitful men,
    nor do I consort with hypocrites;
5 I abhor the assembly of evildoers
    and refuse to sit with the wicked.
6 I wash my hands in innocence,
    and go about your altar, O LORD,
7 proclaiming aloud your praise
    and telling of all your wonderful
      deeds.
8 I love the house where you live,
      O LORD,
    the place where your glory dwells.

9 Do not take away my soul along with
      sinners,
    my life with bloodthirsty men,
10 in whose hands are wicked schemes,
    whose right hands are full of bribes.

a This psalm is an acrostic poem, the verses of which begin with the successive letters of the Hebrew
alphabet.

11 But I lead a blameless life;
    redeem me and be merciful to me.

12 My feet stand on level ground;
    in the great assembly I will praise
       the LORD.

Psalm

Of David.

1 The LORD is my light and my
    salvation—
  whom shall I fear?

The LORD is the stronghold of my
    life—
  of whom shall I be afraid?
2 When evil men advance against me
    to devour my flesh,[a]
  when my enemies and my foes
       attack me,
  they will stumble and fall.
3 Though an army besiege me,
    my heart will not fear;
  though war break out against me,
    even then will I be confident.

4 One thing I ask of the LORD,
    this is what I seek:

[a] 2 Or *to slander me*

MONDAY

THE SECRETS OF PROVIDENCE
A. B. Simpson

VERSE: Psalm 25:14   PASSAGE: Psalm 25

 here are secrets of providence which God's dear children may learn. His dealings with them often seem, to
the outward eye, dark and terrible. Faith looks deeper
and says, "This is God's secret. You look only on the
outside; I can look deeper and see the hidden meaning."

Sometimes diamonds are done up in rough packages, so that
their value cannot be seen. When the tabernacle was built in the
wilderness there was nothing rich in its outside appearance. The
costly things were all within, and its outward covering of rough
badger skin gave no hint of the valuable things which it contained.

God may send you, dear friends, some costly packages. Do
not worry if they are done up in rough wrappings. You may be
sure there are treasures of love, and kindness, and wisdom hidden within. If we take what he sends, *and trust him* for the goodness in it, even in the dark, we shall learn the meaning of the
secrets of providence.

ADDITIONAL SCRIPTURE READING:
Genesis 18:17–19; Proverbs 3:32; Matthew 13:11–12

Go to page 618 for your next devotional reading.

1900   Present

that I may dwell in the house of the
  LORD
all the days of my life,
to gaze upon the beauty of the LORD
  and to seek him in his temple.
⁵ For in the day of trouble
  he will keep me safe in his
    dwelling;
he will hide me in the shelter of his
  tabernacle
  and set me high upon a rock.
⁶ Then my head will be exalted
  above the enemies who surround
    me;
at his tabernacle will I sacrifice with
  shouts of joy;
  I will sing and make music to the
    LORD.

⁷ Hear my voice when I call, O LORD;
  be merciful to me and answer me.
⁸ My heart says of you, "Seek his*ᵃ* face!"
  Your face, LORD, I will seek.
⁹ Do not hide your face from me,
  do not turn your servant away in
    anger;
  you have been my helper.
Do not reject me or forsake me,
  O God my Savior.
¹⁰ Though my father and mother
    forsake me,
  the LORD will receive me.
¹¹ Teach me your way, O LORD;
  lead me in a straight path
  because of my oppressors.
¹² Do not turn me over to the desire of
    my foes,
  for false witnesses rise up against
    me,
  breathing out violence.

¹³ I am still confident of this:
  I will see the goodness of the LORD
  in the land of the living.
¹⁴ Wait for the LORD;
  be strong and take heart
  and wait for the LORD.

Psalm

Of David.

¹ To you I call, O LORD my Rock;
  do not turn a deaf ear to me.

For if you remain silent,
  I will be like those who have gone
    down to the pit.
² Hear my cry for mercy
  as I call to you for help,
  as I lift up my hands
  toward your Most Holy Place.

³ Do not drag me away with the
    wicked,
  with those who do evil,
who speak cordially with their
  neighbors
  but harbor malice in their hearts.
⁴ Repay them for their deeds
  and for their evil work;
repay them for what their hands have
    done
  and bring back upon them what
    they deserve.
⁵ Since they show no regard for the
    works of the LORD
  and what his hands have done,
he will tear them down
  and never build them up again.

⁶ Praise be to the LORD,
  for he has heard my cry for mercy.
⁷ The LORD is my strength and my
    shield;
  my heart trusts in him, and I am
    helped.
My heart leaps for joy
  and I will give thanks to him in
    song.

⁸ The LORD is the strength of his
    people,
  a fortress of salvation for his
    anointed one.
⁹ Save your people and bless your
    inheritance;
  be their shepherd and carry them
    forever.

Psalm
29

A psalm of David.

¹ Ascribe to the LORD, O mighty ones,
  ascribe to the LORD glory and
    strength.
² Ascribe to the LORD the glory due his
    name;

ᵃ 8 Or *To you, O my heart, he has said, "Seek my*

worship the LORD in the splendor of his*a* holiness.

3 The voice of the LORD is over the waters;
the God of glory thunders,
the LORD thunders over the mighty waters.
4 The voice of the LORD is powerful;
the voice of the LORD is majestic.
5 The voice of the LORD breaks the cedars;
the LORD breaks in pieces the cedars of Lebanon.
6 He makes Lebanon skip like a calf,
Sirion*b* like a young wild ox.
7 The voice of the LORD strikes with flashes of lightning.
8 The voice of the LORD shakes the desert;
the LORD shakes the Desert of Kadesh.
9 The voice of the LORD twists the oaks*c*
and strips the forests bare.
And in his temple all cry, "Glory!"

10 The LORD sits*d* enthroned over the flood;
the LORD is enthroned as King forever.
11 The LORD gives strength to his people;
the LORD blesses his people with peace.

Psalm 30

A psalm. A song. For the dedication of the temple.*e* Of David.

1 I will exalt you, O LORD,
for you lifted me out of the depths
and did not let my enemies gloat over me.
2 O LORD my God, I called to you for help
and you healed me.
3 O LORD, you brought me up from the grave*f*;
you spared me from going down into the pit.

4 Sing to the LORD, you saints of his;
praise his holy name.
5 For his anger lasts only a moment,
but his favor lasts a lifetime;
weeping may remain for a night,
but rejoicing comes in the morning.

6 When I felt secure, I said,
"I will never be shaken."
7 O LORD, when you favored me,
you made my mountain*g* stand firm;
but when you hid your face,
I was dismayed.

8 To you, O LORD, I called;
to the Lord I cried for mercy:
9 "What gain is there in my destruction,*h*
in my going down into the pit?
Will the dust praise you?
Will it proclaim your faithfulness?
10 Hear, O LORD, and be merciful to me;
O LORD, be my help."

11 You turned my wailing into dancing;
you removed my sackcloth and clothed me with joy,
12 that my heart may sing to you and not be silent.
O LORD my God, I will give you thanks forever.

Psalm 31

For the director of music. A psalm of David.

1 In you, O LORD, I have taken refuge;
let me never be put to shame;
deliver me in your righteousness.
2 Turn your ear to me,
come quickly to my rescue;
be my rock of refuge,
a strong fortress to save me.
3 Since you are my rock and my fortress,
for the sake of your name lead and guide me.
4 Free me from the trap that is set for me,
for you are my refuge.
5 Into your hands I commit my spirit;

a 2 Or LORD with the splendor of   b 6 That is, Mount Hermon   c 9 Or LORD makes the deer give birth   d 10 Or sat   e Title: Or palace   f 3 Hebrew Sheol   g 7 Or hill country   h 9 Or there if I am silenced

THE DAWN WILL COME
Martin Luther King, Jr.

VERSE: Psalm 30:5   **PASSAGE:** Psalm 30:1–5

 t the beginning of the bus boycott in Montgomery, Alabama, we set up a voluntary car pool to get the people to and from their jobs. For eleven long months our car pool functioned extraordinarily well. Then Mayor Gayle introduced a resolution instructing the city's legal department to file such proceedings as it might deem proper to stop the operation of the car pool or any transportation system growing out of the bus boycott. A hearing was set for Tuesday, November 13, 1956.

At our regular weekly mass meeting, scheduled the night before the hearing, . . . I [said] "We have moved all of these months . . . in the daring faith that God is with us in our struggle. The many experiences of days gone by have vindicated that faith in a marvelous way. Tonight we must believe that a way will be made out of no way." Yet I could feel the cold breeze of pessimism pass over the audience. The night was darker than a thousand midnights. The light of hope was about to fade and the lamp of faith to flicker . . .

At noon, during a brief recess, I noticed an unusual commotion in the courtroom. Mayor Gayle was called to the back room. Several reporters moved excitedly in and out of the room. Momentarily a reporter came to the table where, as chief defendant, I sat with the lawyers. "Here is the decision that you have been waiting for," he said. "Read this release."

In anxiety and hope, I read these words: "The United States Supreme Court today unanimously ruled bus segregation unconstitutional in Montgomery, Alabama." My heart throbbed with an inexpressible joy. The darkest hour of our struggle had become the first hour of victory. Someone shouted from the back of the courtroom, "God Almighty has spoken from Washington!"

The dawn will come. Disappointment, sorrow, and despair are born at midnight, but morning follows. "Weeping may remain for a night," says the psalmist, "but rejoicing comes in the morning."

ADDITIONAL SCRIPTURE READING:
Psalms 6:6–9; 125:5–6

Go to page 623 for your next devotional reading.

1900   Present

redeem me, O LORD, the God of
truth.

⁶ I hate those who cling to worthless
idols;
I trust in the LORD.
⁷ I will be glad and rejoice in your love,
for you saw my affliction
and knew the anguish of my soul.
⁸ You have not handed me over to the
enemy
but have set my feet in a spacious
place.

⁹ Be merciful to me, O LORD, for I am
in distress;
my eyes grow weak with sorrow,
my soul and my body with grief.
¹⁰ My life is consumed by anguish
and my years by groaning;
my strength fails because of my
affliction,ᵃ
and my bones grow weak.
¹¹ Because of all my enemies,
I am the utter contempt of my
neighbors;
I am a dread to my friends—
those who see me on the street flee
from me.
¹² I am forgotten by them as though I
were dead;
I have become like broken pottery.
¹³ For I hear the slander of many;
there is terror on every side;
they conspire against me
and plot to take my life.

¹⁴ But I trust in you, O LORD;
I say, "You are my God."
¹⁵ My times are in your hands;
deliver me from my enemies
and from those who pursue me.
¹⁶ Let your face shine on your servant;
save me in your unfailing love.
¹⁷ Let me not be put to shame, O LORD,
for I have cried out to you;
but let the wicked be put to shame
and lie silent in the grave.ᵇ
¹⁸ Let their lying lips be silenced,
for with pride and contempt
they speak arrogantly against the
righteous.

¹⁹ How great is your goodness,
which you have stored up for those
who fear you,

which you bestow in the sight of
men
on those who take refuge in you.
²⁰ In the shelter of your presence you
hide them
from the intrigues of men;
in your dwelling you keep them safe
from accusing tongues.

²¹ Praise be to the LORD,
for he showed his wonderful love
to me
when I was in a besieged city.
²² In my alarm I said,
"I am cut off from your sight!"
Yet you heard my cry for mercy
when I called to you for help.

²³ Love the LORD, all his saints!
The LORD preserves the faithful,
but the proud he pays back in full.
²⁴ Be strong and take heart,
all you who hope in the LORD.

Psalm

32

Of David. A *maskil*.ᶜ

¹ Blessed is he
whose transgressions are forgiven,
whose sins are covered.
² Blessed is the man
whose sin the LORD does not count
against him
and in whose spirit is no deceit.

³ When I kept silent,
my bones wasted away
through my groaning all day long.
⁴ For day and night
your hand was heavy upon me;
my strength was sapped
as in the heat of summer.   *Selah*
⁵ Then I acknowledged my sin to you
and did not cover up my iniquity.
I said, "I will confess
my transgressions to the LORD"—
and you forgave
the guilt of my sin.   *Selah*

⁶ Therefore let everyone who is godly
pray to you
while you may be found;
surely when the mighty waters rise,
they will not reach him.

ᵃ 10 Or *guilt*   ᵇ 17 Hebrew *Sheol*   ᶜ Title: Probably a literary or musical term

7 You are my hiding place;
   you will protect me from trouble
   and surround me with songs of
      deliverance.   *Selah*

8 I will instruct you and teach you in
   the way you should go;
   I will counsel you and watch over
      you.
9 Do not be like the horse or the mule,
   which have no understanding
but must be controlled by bit and
      bridle
or they will not come to you.
10 Many are the woes of the wicked,
   but the LORD's unfailing love
   surrounds the man who trusts in
      him.

11 Rejoice in the LORD and be glad, you
      righteous;
   sing, all you who are upright in
      heart!

Psalm 33

1 Sing joyfully to the LORD, you
      righteous;
   it is fitting for the upright to praise
      him.
2 Praise the LORD with the harp;
   make music to him on the ten-
      stringed lyre.
3 Sing to him a new song;
   play skillfully, and shout for joy.

4 For the word of the LORD is right and
      true;
   he is faithful in all he does.
5 The LORD loves righteousness and
      justice;
   the earth is full of his unfailing
      love.

6 By the word of the LORD were the
      heavens made,
   their starry host by the breath of
      his mouth.
7 He gathers the waters of the sea into
      jars*a*;
   he puts the deep into storehouses.
8 Let all the earth fear the LORD;
   let all the people of the world
      revere him.

9 For he spoke, and it came to be;
   he commanded, and it stood firm.
10 The LORD foils the plans of the
      nations;
   he thwarts the purposes of the
      peoples.
11 But the plans of the LORD stand firm
      forever,
   the purposes of his heart through
      all generations.

12 Blessed is the nation whose God is
      the LORD,
   the people he chose for his
      inheritance.
13 From heaven the LORD looks down
   and sees all mankind;
14 from his dwelling place he watches
   all who live on earth—
15 he who forms the hearts of all,
   who considers everything they do.
16 No king is saved by the size of his
      army;
   no warrior escapes by his great
      strength.
17 A horse is a vain hope for
      deliverance;
   despite all its great strength it
      cannot save.
18 But the eyes of the LORD are on those
   who fear him,
   on those whose hope is in his
      unfailing love,
19 to deliver them from death
   and keep them alive in famine.

20 We wait in hope for the LORD;
   he is our help and our shield.
21 In him our hearts rejoice,
   for we trust in his holy name.
22 May your unfailing love rest upon us,
      O LORD,
   even as we put our hope in you.

Psalm 34 *b*

Of David. When he pretended to be insane
before Abimelech, who drove him away,
and he left.

1 I will extol the LORD at all times;
   his praise will always be on my lips.
2 My soul will boast in the LORD;
   let the afflicted hear and rejoice.

---

a 7 Or *sea as into a heap*   *b* This psalm is an acrostic poem, the verses of which begin with the
successive letters of the Hebrew alphabet.

3 Glorify the LORD with me;
  let us exalt his name together.

4 I sought the LORD, and he answered
    me;
  he delivered me from all my fears.

5 Those who look to him are radiant;
  their faces are never covered with
    shame.

6 This poor man called, and the LORD
    heard him;
  he saved him out of all his
    troubles.

7 The angel of the LORD encamps
    around those who fear him,
  and he delivers them.

8 Taste and see that the LORD is good;
  blessed is the man who takes
    refuge in him.

9 Fear the LORD, you his saints,
  for those who fear him lack
    nothing.

10 The lions may grow weak and
    hungry,
   but those who seek the LORD lack
    no good thing.

11 Come, my children, listen to me;
   I will teach you the fear of the
    LORD.

12 Whoever of you loves life
   and desires to see many good days,

13 keep your tongue from evil
   and your lips from speaking lies.

14 Turn from evil and do good;
   seek peace and pursue it.

15 The eyes of the LORD are on the
    righteous
   and his ears are attentive to their
    cry;

16 the face of the LORD is against those
    who do evil,
   to cut off the memory of them
    from the earth.

17 The righteous cry out, and the LORD
    hears them;
   he delivers them from all their
    troubles.

18 The LORD is close to the
    brokenhearted
   and saves those who are crushed in
    spirit.

19 A righteous man may have many
    troubles,

but the LORD delivers him from
    them all;

20 he protects all his bones,
   not one of them will be broken.

21 Evil will slay the wicked;
   the foes of the righteous will be
    condemned.

22 The LORD redeems his servants;
   no one will be condemned who
    takes refuge in him.

Psalm

35

Of David.

1 Contend, O LORD, with those who
    contend with me;
  fight against those who fight
    against me.

2 Take up shield and buckler;
  arise and come to my aid.

3 Brandish spear and javelin[a]
  against those who pursue me.
  Say to my soul,
  "I am your salvation."

4 May those who seek my life
    be disgraced and put to shame;
  may those who plot my ruin
    be turned back in dismay.

5 May they be like chaff before the
    wind,
  with the angel of the LORD driving
    them away;

6 may their path be dark and slippery,
  with the angel of the LORD
    pursuing them.

7 Since they hid their net for me
    without cause
  and without cause dug a pit for me,

8 may ruin overtake them by
    surprise—
  may the net they hid entangle
    them,
  may they fall into the pit, to their
    ruin.

9 Then my soul will rejoice in the
    LORD
  and delight in his salvation.

10 My whole being will exclaim,
   "Who is like you, O LORD?
  You rescue the poor from those too
    strong for them,

a 3 Or *and block the way*

the poor and needy from those who rob them."

11 Ruthless witnesses come forward;
   they question me on things I know
      nothing about.
12 They repay me evil for good
   and leave my soul forlorn.
13 Yet when they were ill, I put on
      sackcloth
   and humbled myself with fasting.
When my prayers returned to me
      unanswered,
14   I went about mourning
   as though for my friend or brother.
I bowed my head in grief
   as though weeping for my mother.
15 But when I stumbled, they gathered
      in glee;
   attackers gathered against me
      when I was unaware.
They slandered me without
      ceasing.
16 Like the ungodly they maliciously
      mocked*a*;
   they gnashed their teeth at me.
17 O Lord, how long will you look on?
   Rescue my life from their ravages,
   my precious life from these lions.
18 I will give you thanks in the great
      assembly;
   among throngs of people I will
      praise you.

19 Let not those gloat over me
   who are my enemies without
      cause;
   let not those who hate me without
      reason
   maliciously wink the eye.
20 They do not speak peaceably,
   but devise false accusations
   against those who live quietly in
      the land.
21 They gape at me and say, "Aha! Aha!
   With our own eyes we have seen
      it."

22 O Lord, you have seen this; be not
      silent.
   Do not be far from me, O Lord.
23 Awake, and rise to my defense!
   Contend for me, my God and Lord.
24 Vindicate me in your righteousness,
      O Lord my God;
   do not let them gloat over me.

25 Do not let them think, "Aha, just
      what we wanted!"
   or say, "We have swallowed him
      up."
26 May all who gloat over my distress
   be put to shame and confusion;
   may all who exalt themselves over
      me
   be clothed with shame and
      disgrace.
27 May those who delight in my
      vindication
   shout for joy and gladness;
   may they always say, "The Lord be
      exalted,
   who delights in the well-being of
      his servant."
28 My tongue will speak of your
      righteousness
   and of your praises all day long.

Psalm
 36

For the director of music. Of David the
servant of the Lord.

1 An oracle is within my heart
   concerning the sinfulness of the
      wicked:*b*
There is no fear of God
   before his eyes.
2 For in his own eyes he flatters himself
   too much to detect or hate his sin.
3 The words of his mouth are wicked
      and deceitful;
   he has ceased to be wise and to do
      good.
4 Even on his bed he plots evil;
   he commits himself to a sinful
      course
   and does not reject what is wrong.

5 Your love, O Lord, reaches to the
      heavens,
   your faithfulness to the skies.
6 Your righteousness is like the mighty
      mountains,
   your justice like the great deep.
O Lord, you preserve both man and
      beast.
7   How priceless is your unfailing
      love!
Both high and low among men

a 16 Septuagint; Hebrew may mean *ungodly circle of mockers*.   *b* 1 Or *heart: / Sin proceeds from the wicked*.

find*a* refuge in the shadow of your
wings.
8 They feast on the abundance of your
house;
you give them drink from your
river of delights.
9 For with you is the fountain of life;
in your light we see light.

10 Continue your love to those who
know you,
your righteousness to the upright
in heart.
11 May the foot of the proud not come
against me,
nor the hand of the wicked drive
me away.

a 7 Or *love, O God!* / *Men find;* or *love!* / *Both heavenly beings and men* / *find*

WEDNESDAY

SEA, LIGHT, FIRE
Catherine of Siena

VERSE: Psalm 36:9   **PASSAGE:** Psalm 36:5–10

 ternal Trinity, you are like a deep sea, in which the
more I seek, the more I find; and the more I find, the
more eagerly I seek. You fill the soul, yet never fully
satisfy it; the soul continues to hunger and thirst for
you, desiring you, longing to see you who are the source of all
light.

In your light, eternal Trinity, I have seen into the deep ocean
of your love, and have rejoiced in the beauty of your creation.
Then looking at myself in you, I have recognized that you have
made me in your image. This is the most precious gift which I
receive from you in your power and in your wisdom.

Eternal Trinity, you are the creator and I the creature. I have
come to know you because you have created me anew in your
Son Jesus Christ. You are in love with me out of your love for
him. You have given yourself to me. What more could I ask?

You are a fire, ever burning and never consumed. You consume in your heart all the self-love within my soul, taking away
all coldness. You are a light, ever shining and never fading. You
drive away all the darkness within my heart, enabling me to see
your glorious truth.

You are goodness beyond all goodness, beauty beyond all
beauty, wisdom beyond all wisdom.

You are the garment that covers all nakedness. You are the
food that satisfies all hunger.

ADDITIONAL SCRIPTURE READING:
Psalm 27:1; Colossians 1:16–17

Go to page 629 for your next devotional reading.

500   1500

12 See how the evildoers lie fallen—
　thrown down, not able to rise!

Psalm

 37 [a]

Of David.

1 Do not fret because of evil men
　or be envious of those who do
　　wrong;
2 for like the grass they will soon
　　wither,
　like green plants they will soon die
　　away.

3 Trust in the LORD and do good;
　dwell in the land and enjoy safe
　　pasture.
4 Delight yourself in the LORD
　and he will give you the desires of
　　your heart.

5 Commit your way to the LORD;
　trust in him and he will do this:
6 He will make your righteousness
　　shine like the dawn,
　the justice of your cause like the
　　noonday sun.

7 Be still before the LORD and wait
　　patiently for him;
　do not fret when men succeed in
　　their ways,
　when they carry out their wicked
　　schemes.

8 Refrain from anger and turn from
　　wrath;
　do not fret—it leads only to evil.

FRETFULNESS SPRINGS FROM A DETERMINATION
TO GET MY OWN WAY.　　　—*Oswald Chambers*

---

9 For evil men will be cut off,
　but those who hope in the LORD
　　will inherit the land.

10 A little while, and the wicked will be
　　no more;
　though you look for them, they
　　will not be found.
11 But the meek will inherit the land
　and enjoy great peace.

12 The wicked plot against the righteous
　and gnash their teeth at them;
13 but the Lord laughs at the wicked,
　for he knows their day is coming.

14 The wicked draw the sword
　and bend the bow
　to bring down the poor and needy,
　to slay those whose ways are
　　upright.
15 But their swords will pierce their
　　own hearts,
　and their bows will be broken.

16 Better the little that the righteous
　　have
　than the wealth of many wicked;
17 for the power of the wicked will be
　　broken,
　but the LORD upholds the
　　righteous.

18 The days of the blameless are known
　　to the LORD,
　and their inheritance will endure
　　forever.
19 In times of disaster they will not
　　wither;
　in days of famine they will enjoy
　　plenty.

20 But the wicked will perish:
　The LORD's enemies will be like
　　the beauty of the fields,
　they will vanish—vanish like
　　smoke.

21 The wicked borrow and do not repay,
　but the righteous give generously;
22 those the LORD blesses will inherit
　　the land,
　but those he curses will be cut off.

23 If the LORD delights in a man's way,
　he makes his steps firm;
24 though he stumble, he will not fall,
　for the LORD upholds him with his
　　hand.

25 I was young and now I am old,
　yet I have never seen the righteous
　　forsaken
　or their children begging bread.
26 They are always generous and lend
　　freely;
　their children will be blessed.

27 Turn from evil and do good;

---

a This psalm is an acrostic poem, the stanzas of which begin with the successive letters of the Hebrew
alphabet.

then you will dwell in the land
	forever.
28 For the LORD loves the just
	and will not forsake his faithful
		ones.

They will be protected forever,
	but the offspring of the wicked will
		be cut off;
29 the righteous will inherit the land
	and dwell in it forever.

30 The mouth of the righteous man
		utters wisdom,
	and his tongue speaks what is just.
31 The law of his God is in his heart;
	his feet do not slip.

32 The wicked lie in wait for the
		righteous,
	seeking their very lives;
33 but the LORD will not leave them in
		their power
	or let them be condemned when
		brought to trial.

34 Wait for the LORD
	and keep his way.
He will exalt you to inherit the land;
	when the wicked are cut off, you
		will see it.

35 I have seen a wicked and ruthless
		man
	flourishing like a green tree in its
		native soil,
36 but he soon passed away and was no
		more;
	though I looked for him, he could
		not be found.

37 Consider the blameless, observe the
		upright;
	there is a future*a* for the man of
		peace.
38 But all sinners will be destroyed;
	the future*b* of the wicked will be
		cut off.

39 The salvation of the righteous comes
		from the LORD;
	he is their stronghold in time of
		trouble.
40 The LORD helps them and delivers
		them;
	he delivers them from the wicked
		and saves them,
	because they take refuge in him.

Psalm 38

A psalm of David. A petition.

1 O LORD, do not rebuke me in your
		anger
	or discipline me in your wrath.
2 For your arrows have pierced me,
	and your hand has come down
		upon me.
3 Because of your wrath there is no
		health in my body;
	my bones have no soundness
		because of my sin.
4 My guilt has overwhelmed me
	like a burden too heavy to bear.

5 My wounds fester and are loathsome
	because of my sinful folly.
6 I am bowed down and brought very
		low;
	all day long I go about mourning.
7 My back is filled with searing pain;
	there is no health in my body.
8 I am feeble and utterly crushed;
	I groan in anguish of heart.

9 All my longings lie open before you,
		O Lord;
	my sighing is not hidden from you.
10 My heart pounds, my strength fails
		me;
	even the light has gone from my
		eyes.
11 My friends and companions avoid me
		because of my wounds;
	my neighbors stay far away.
12 Those who seek my life set their
		traps,
	those who would harm me talk of
		my ruin;
	all day long they plot deception.

13 I am like a deaf man, who cannot
		hear,
	like a mute, who cannot open his
		mouth;
14 I have become like a man who does
		not hear,
	whose mouth can offer no reply.
15 I wait for you, O LORD;
	you will answer, O Lord my God.
16 For I said, "Do not let them gloat
	or exalt themselves over me when
		my foot slips."

a 37 Or *there will be posterity*   *b 38* Or *posterity*

17 For I am about to fall,
   and my pain is ever with me.
18 I confess my iniquity;
   I am troubled by my sin.
19 Many are those who are my vigorous
      enemies;
   those who hate me without reason
      are numerous.
20 Those who repay my good with evil
   slander me when I pursue what is
      good.
21 O LORD, do not forsake me;
   be not far from me, O my God.
22 Come quickly to help me,
   O Lord my Savior.

Psalm 39

For the director of music. For Jeduthun.
A psalm of David.

1 I said, "I will watch my ways
   and keep my tongue from sin;
I will put a muzzle on my mouth
   as long as the wicked are in my
      presence."
2 But when I was silent and still,
   not even saying anything good,
   my anguish increased.
3 My heart grew hot within me,
   and as I meditated, the fire burned;
   then I spoke with my tongue:

4 "Show me, O LORD, my life's end
   and the number of my days;
   let me know how fleeting is my
      life.
5 You have made my days a mere
      handbreadth;
   the span of my years is as nothing
      before you.
Each man's life is but a breath.
                              Selah
6 Man is a mere phantom as he goes to
      and fro:
He bustles about, but only in vain;
he heaps up wealth, not knowing
   who will get it.

7 "But now, Lord, what do I look for?
   My hope is in you.
8 Save me from all my transgressions;
   do not make me the scorn of fools.

9 I was silent; I would not open my
      mouth,
   for you are the one who has done
      this.
10 Remove your scourge from me;
   I am overcome by the blow of your
      hand.
11 You rebuke and discipline men for
      their sin;
   you consume their wealth like a
      moth—
   each man is but a breath.   *Selah*

12 "Hear my prayer, O LORD,
   listen to my cry for help;
   be not deaf to my weeping.
For I dwell with you as an alien,
   a stranger, as all my fathers were.
13 Look away from me, that I may
      rejoice again
   before I depart and am no more."

Psalm 40

For the director of music. Of David. A psalm.

1 I waited patiently for the LORD;
   he turned to me and heard my cry.
2 He lifted me out of the slimy pit,
   out of the mud and mire;
   he set my feet on a rock
   and gave me a firm place to stand.

STARS MAY BE SEEN FROM THE BOTTOM OF A DEEP
WELL WHEN THEY CANNOT BE DISCERNED FROM
THE TOP OF A MOUNTAIN.   —*C. H. Spurgeon*

---

3 He put a new song in my mouth,
   a hymn of praise to our God.
Many will see and fear
   and put their trust in the LORD.

4 Blessed is the man
   who makes the LORD his trust,
who does not look to the proud,
   to those who turn aside to false
      gods.*a*
5 Many, O LORD my God,
   are the wonders you have done.
The things you planned for us
   no one can recount to you;
were I to speak and tell of them,

a 4 Or *to falsehood*

they would be too many to declare.

6 Sacrifice and offering you did not
  desire,
 but my ears you have pierced^{a, b};
 burnt offerings and sin offerings
  you did not require.
7 Then I said, "Here I am, I have
  come—
 it is written about me in the
  scroll.^c
8 I desire to do your will, O my God;
 your law is within my heart."

9 I proclaim righteousness in the great
  assembly;
 I do not seal my lips,
 as you know, O LORD.
10 I do not hide your righteousness in
  my heart;
 I speak of your faithfulness and
  salvation.
 I do not conceal your love and your
  truth
 from the great assembly.

11 Do not withhold your mercy from
  me, O LORD;
 may your love and your truth
  always protect me.
12 For troubles without number
  surround me;
 my sins have overtaken me, and I
  cannot see.
 They are more than the hairs of my
  head,
 and my heart fails within me.

13 Be pleased, O LORD, to save me;
 O LORD, come quickly to help me.
14 May all who seek to take my life
 be put to shame and confusion;
 may all who desire my ruin
 be turned back in disgrace.
15 May those who say to me, "Aha!
  Aha!"
 be appalled at their own shame.
16 But may all who seek you
 rejoice and be glad in you;
 may those who love your salvation
  always say,
 "The LORD be exalted!"

17 Yet I am poor and needy;
 may the Lord think of me.
 You are my help and my deliverer;
 O my God, do not delay.

Psalm 41

For the director of music. A psalm of David.

1 Blessed is he who has regard for the
  weak;
 the LORD delivers him in times of
  trouble.
2 The LORD will protect him and
  preserve his life;
 he will bless him in the land
 and not surrender him to the desire
  of his foes.
3 The LORD will sustain him on his
  sickbed
 and restore him from his bed of
  illness.

4 I said, "O LORD, have mercy on me;
 heal me, for I have sinned against
  you."
5 My enemies say of me in malice,
 "When will he die and his name
  perish?"
6 Whenever one comes to see me,
 he speaks falsely, while his heart
  gathers slander;
 then he goes out and spreads it
  abroad.

7 All my enemies whisper together
  against me;
 they imagine the worst for me,
  saying,
8 "A vile disease has beset him;
 he will never get up from the place
  where he lies."
9 Even my close friend, whom I trusted,
 he who shared my bread,
 has lifted up his heel against me.

10 But you, O LORD, have mercy on me;
 raise me up, that I may repay them.
11 I know that you are pleased with me,
 for my enemy does not triumph
  over me.
12 In my integrity you uphold me
 and set me in your presence
  forever.

13 Praise be to the LORD, the God of
  Israel,
 from everlasting to everlasting.
  Amen and Amen.

^a 6 Hebrew; Septuagint *but a body you have prepared for me* (see also Symmachus and Theodotion)
^b 6 Or *opened* ^c 7 Or *come / with the scroll written for me*

BOOK II
Psalms 42–72

Psalm

42[a]

For the director of music. A *maskil*[b] of the
Sons of Korah.

1 As the deer pants for streams of
    water,
  so my soul pants for you, O God.
2 My soul thirsts for God, for the living
    God.
  When can I go and meet with God?
3 My tears have been my food
    day and night,
  while men say to me all day long,
    "Where is your God?"
4 These things I remember
    as I pour out my soul:
  how I used to go with the multitude,
    leading the procession to the house
      of God,
  with shouts of joy and thanksgiving
    among the festive throng.

5 Why are you downcast, O my soul?
    Why so disturbed within me?
  Put your hope in God,
    for I will yet praise him,
    my Savior and 6 my God.

  My[c] soul is downcast within me;
    therefore I will remember you
  from the land of the Jordan,
    the heights of Hermon—from
      Mount Mizar.
7 Deep calls to deep
    in the roar of your waterfalls;
  all your waves and breakers
    have swept over me.

8 By day the LORD directs his love,
    at night his song is with me—
  a prayer to the God of my life.

9 I say to God my Rock,
    "Why have you forgotten me?
  Why must I go about mourning,
    oppressed by the enemy?"
10 My bones suffer mortal agony
    as my foes taunt me,
  saying to me all day long,
    "Where is your God?"

11 Why are you downcast, O my soul?
    Why so disturbed within me?
  Put your hope in God,
    for I will yet praise him,
    my Savior and my God.

Psalm

43[a]

1 Vindicate me, O God,
    and plead my cause against an
      ungodly nation;
  rescue me from deceitful and
    wicked men.
2 You are God my stronghold.
    Why have you rejected me?
  Why must I go about mourning,
    oppressed by the enemy?
3 Send forth your light and your truth,
    let them guide me;
  let them bring me to your holy
    mountain,
  to the place where you dwell.
4 Then will I go to the altar of God,
    to God, my joy and my delight.
  I will praise you with the harp,
    O God, my God.

5 Why are you downcast, O my soul?
    Why so disturbed within me?
  Put your hope in God,
    for I will yet praise him,
    my Savior and my God.

Psalm

44

For the director of music. Of the Sons of
Korah. A *maskil.*[b]

1 We have heard with our ears, O God;
    our fathers have told us
  what you did in their days,
    in days long ago.
2 With your hand you drove out the
      nations
    and planted our fathers;
  you crushed the peoples
    and made our fathers flourish.
3 It was not by their sword that they
      won the land,

---

a In many Hebrew manuscripts Psalms 42 and 43 constitute one psalm.   *b* Title: Probably a literary or
musical term   *c* 5,6 A few Hebrew manuscripts, Septuagint and Syriac; most Hebrew manuscripts
praise him for his saving help. / 6 O my God, my

PANTING AFTER GOD
A. W. Tozer

VERSE: Psalm 42:1   **PASSAGE:** Psalm 42

 ithin the hearts of a growing number of evangelicals in recent days has arisen a new yearning after an above-average spiritual experience. Yet the greater number still shy away from it and raise objections that evidence misunderstanding or fear or plain unbelief. They point to the neurotic, the psychotic, the pseudo-Christian cultist and the intemperate fanatic, and lump them all together without discrimination as followers of the "deeper life."

While this is of course completely preposterous, the fact that such confusion exists obliges those who advocate the Spirit-filled life to define their terms and explain their position. Just what, then, do we mean? And what are we advocating?

For myself, I am reverently concerned that I teach nothing but Christ crucified. For me to accept a teaching or even an emphasis, I must be persuaded that it is scriptural and altogether apostolic in spirit and temper. And it must be in full harmony with the best in the historic church and in the tradition marked by the finest devotional works, the sweetest and most radiant hymnody and the loftiest experiences revealed in Christian biography . . .

To speak of the "deeper life" is . . . to insist that believers explore the depth of the Christian evangel for those riches it surely contains but which we are as surely missing. The "deeper life" is deeper only because the average Christian life is tragically shallow.

They who advocate the deeper life today might compare unfavorably with almost any of the Christians that surrounded Paul or Peter in early times. While they may not as yet have made much progress, their faces are toward the light and they are beckoning us on. It is hard to see how we can justify our refusal to heed their call.

What the deeper life advocates are telling us is that we should press on to enjoy in personal inward experience the exalted privileges that are ours in Christ Jesus; that we should insist upon tasting the sweetness of internal worship in spirit as well as in truth; that to reach this ideal we should if necessary push beyond our contented brethren and bring upon ourselves whatever opposition may follow as a result.

ADDITIONAL SCRIPTURE READING:
Jeremiah 9:23–24; Ephesians 1:17–18; Colossians 1:9–12

Go to page 632 for your next devotional reading.

1900   Present

nor did their arm bring them
victory;
it was your right hand, your arm,
and the light of your face, for you
loved them.

4 You are my King and my God,
who decrees[a] victories for Jacob.
5 Through you we push back our
enemies;
through your name we trample our
foes.
6 I do not trust in my bow,
my sword does not bring me
victory;
7 but you give us victory over our
enemies,
you put our adversaries to shame.
8 In God we make our boast all day
long,
and we will praise your name
forever.   *Selah*

9 But now you have rejected and
humbled us;
you no longer go out with our
armies.
10 You made us retreat before the
enemy,
and our adversaries have plundered
us.
11 You gave us up to be devoured like
sheep
and have scattered us among the
nations.
12 You sold your people for a pittance,
gaining nothing from their sale.

13 You have made us a reproach to our
neighbors,
the scorn and derision of those
around us.
14 You have made us a byword among
the nations;
the peoples shake their heads at us.
15 My disgrace is before me all day long,
and my face is covered with shame
16 at the taunts of those who reproach
and revile me,
because of the enemy, who is bent
on revenge.

17 All this happened to us,
though we had not forgotten you
or been false to your covenant.
18 Our hearts had not turned back;

our feet had not strayed from your
path.
19 But you crushed us and made us a
haunt for jackals
and covered us over with deep
darkness.
20 If we had forgotten the name of our
God
or spread out our hands to a foreign
god,
21 would not God have discovered it,
since he knows the secrets of the
heart?
22 Yet for your sake we face death all
day long;
we are considered as sheep to be
slaughtered.

23 Awake, O Lord! Why do you sleep?
Rouse yourself! Do not reject us
forever.
24 Why do you hide your face
and forget our misery and
oppression?

25 We are brought down to the dust;
our bodies cling to the ground.
26 Rise up and help us;
redeem us because of your
unfailing love.

Psalm

45

For the director of music. To ⸤the tune of⸥
"Lilies." Of the Sons of Korah. A *maskil*.[b]
A wedding song.

1 My heart is stirred by a noble theme
as I recite my verses for the king;
my tongue is the pen of a skillful
writer.

2 You are the most excellent of men
and your lips have been anointed
with grace,
since God has blessed you forever.
3 Gird your sword upon your side,
O mighty one;
clothe yourself with splendor and
majesty.
4 In your majesty ride forth
victoriously
in behalf of truth, humility and
righteousness;

---

a 4 Septuagint, Aquila and Syriac; Hebrew *King, O God; / command*   *b* Title: Probably a literary or
musical term

let your right hand display
    awesome deeds.
5 Let your sharp arrows pierce the
    hearts of the king's enemies;
  let the nations fall beneath your
    feet.
6 Your throne, O God, will last for ever
    and ever;
  a scepter of justice will be the
    scepter of your kingdom.
7 You love righteousness and hate
    wickedness;
  therefore God, your God, has set
    you above your companions
  by anointing you with the oil of
    joy.
8 All your robes are fragrant with
    myrrh and aloes and cassia;
  from palaces adorned with ivory
  the music of the strings makes you
    glad.
9 Daughters of kings are among your
    honored women;
  at your right hand is the royal bride
    in gold of Ophir.

10 Listen, O daughter, consider and give
    ear:
  Forget your people and your
    father's house.
11 The king is enthralled by your
    beauty;
  honor him, for he is your lord.
12 The Daughter of Tyre will come with
    a gift,[a]
  men of wealth will seek your favor.

13 All glorious is the princess within
    ⌊her chamber⌋;
  her gown is interwoven with
    gold.
14 In embroidered garments she is led to
    the king;
  her virgin companions follow her
  and are brought to you.
15 They are led in with joy and gladness;
  they enter the palace of the king.

16 Your sons will take the place of your
    fathers;
  you will make them princes
    throughout the land.
17 I will perpetuate your memory
    through all generations;
  therefore the nations will praise
    you for ever and ever.

Psalm 46

For the director of music. Of the Sons of
Korah. According to *alamoth*.[b] A song.

1 God is our refuge and strength,
  an ever-present help in trouble.
2 Therefore we will not fear, though
    the earth give way
  and the mountains fall into the
    heart of the sea,
3 though its waters roar and foam
  and the mountains quake with
    their surging.   *Selah*

4 There is a river whose streams make
    glad the city of God,
  the holy place where the Most
    High dwells.
5 God is within her, she will not fall;
  God will help her at break of day.
6 Nations are in uproar, kingdoms fall;
  he lifts his voice, the earth melts.

7 The LORD Almighty is with us;
  the God of Jacob is our fortress.
                   Selah

8 Come and see the works of the LORD,
  the desolations he has brought on
    the earth.
9 He makes wars cease to the ends of
    the earth;
  he breaks the bow and shatters the
    spear,
  he burns the shields[c] with fire.
10 "Be still, and know that I am God;
  I will be exalted among the
    nations,
  I will be exalted in the earth."

11 The LORD Almighty is with us;
  the God of Jacob is our fortress.
                   Selah

Psalm 47

For the director of music. Of the Sons of
Korah. A psalm.

1 Clap your hands, all you nations;
  shout to God with cries of joy.
2 How awesome is the LORD Most
    High,

---

a 12 Or *A Tyrian robe is among the gifts*   *b* Title: Probably a musical term   *c 9* Or *chariots*

the great King over all the earth!
³ He subdued nations under us,
peoples under our feet.
⁴ He chose our inheritance for us,
the pride of Jacob, whom he loved.
Selah

⁵ God has ascended amid shouts of joy,

a 7 Or *a maskil* (probably a literary or musical term)

the LORD amid the sounding of
trumpets.
⁶ Sing praises to God, sing praises;
sing praises to our King, sing praises.
⁷ For God is the King of all the earth;
sing to him a psalm*a* of praise.
⁸ God reigns over the nations;

THE CITY OF GLORIOUS WORKS
Augustine

VERSE: Psalm 46:4   **PASSAGE:** Psalm 46:4–7

e give the name of the city of God unto that society whereof that Scripture bears witness, which has got the most excellent authority and preeminence of all the other works whatsoever, by the disposing of the divine providence, not the affectation of men's judgments. For there it is said: "Glorious things are said of you, O city of God" and in another place, "Great is the LORD, and most worthy of praise, in the city of our God, his holy mountain. It is beautiful in its loftiness, the joy of the whole earth." And by and by in the same psalm: "As we have heard, so have we seen in the city of the LORD Almighty, in the city of our God: God makes her secure forever." And in another: "There is a river whose streams make glad the city of God, the holy place where the Most High dwells. God is within her, she will not fall." These testimonies, and thousands more, teach us that there is a city of God, whereof his inspired love makes us desire to be members. The earthly citizens prefer their gods before this heavenly city's holy founder, knowing not that he is the God of gods, not of those false, wicked, and proud ones (which wanting his light so universal and unchangeable, and being thereby cast into an extreme needy power, each one follows his own state, as it were, and begs peculiar honors of his servants), but of the godly and holy ones, who select their own submission to him, rather than the world's to them, and love rather to worship him, their God, than to be worshiped for gods themselves.

ADDITIONAL SCRIPTURE READING:
Psalm 48:1–3; Revelation 21:10–22

Go to page 634 for your next devotional reading.

100   500

God is seated on his holy throne.
9 The nobles of the nations assemble
  as the people of the God of
    Abraham,
for the kings*a* of the earth belong to
    God;
  he is greatly exalted.

Psalm

A song. A psalm of the Sons of Korah.

1 Great is the LORD, and most worthy
    of praise,
  in the city of our God, his holy
    mountain.
2 It is beautiful in its loftiness,
    the joy of the whole earth.
  Like the utmost heights of Zaphon*b*
    is Mount Zion,
    the*c* city of the Great King.
3 God is in her citadels;
  he has shown himself to be her
    fortress.

4 When the kings joined forces,
  when they advanced together,
5 they saw ⌊her⌋ and were astounded;
  they fled in terror.
6 Trembling seized them there,
  pain like that of a woman in labor.
7 You destroyed them like ships of
    Tarshish
  shattered by an east wind.

8 As we have heard,
  so have we seen
in the city of the LORD Almighty,
  in the city of our God:
  God makes her secure forever.
                              Selah

9 Within your temple, O God,
  we meditate on your unfailing
    love.
10 Like your name, O God,
  your praise reaches to the ends of
    the earth;
  your right hand is filled with
    righteousness.
11 Mount Zion rejoices,
  the villages of Judah are glad
  because of your judgments.

12 Walk about Zion, go around her,
    count her towers,
13 consider well her ramparts,
    view her citadels,
    that you may tell of them to the
      next generation.
14 For this God is our God for ever and
      ever;
    he will be our guide even to the
      end.

Psalm

49

For the director of music. Of the Sons of
    Korah. A psalm.

1 Hear this, all you peoples;
    listen, all who live in this world,
2 both low and high,
    rich and poor alike:
3 My mouth will speak words of
      wisdom;
    the utterance from my heart will
      give understanding.
4 I will turn my ear to a proverb;
    with the harp I will expound my
      riddle:

5 Why should I fear when evil days
      come,
    when wicked deceivers surround
      me—
6 those who trust in their wealth
    and boast of their great riches?
7 No man can redeem the life of
      another
    or give to God a ransom for him—
8 the ransom for a life is costly,
    no payment is ever enough—
9 that he should live on forever
    and not see decay.

10 For all can see that wise men die;
    the foolish and the senseless alike
      perish
    and leave their wealth to others.
11 Their tombs will remain their
      houses*d* forever,
    their dwellings for endless
      generations,
    though they had*e* named lands
      after themselves.

---

a 9 Or *shields* *b 2* Zaphon can refer to a sacred mountain or the direction north. *c 2* Or *earth, /
Mount Zion, on the northern side / of the* *d 11* Septuagint and Syriac; Hebrew *In their thoughts their
houses will remain* *e 11* Or / *for they have*

WEEKEND

BROTHER SUN, SISTER MOON
Francis of Assisi

VERSE: Psalm 50:1   **PASSAGE:** Psalm 50:1–15

 ost high, omnipotent, righteous Lord, to you be all praise, glory, honor and blessing. To you alone are they due, and no man is worthy to mention you.

Praise be to you, my Lord, for all your creatures, above all Brother Sun, who gives us the light of day. He is beautiful and radiant with great splendor, and so is like you most high Lord.

Praise be to you, my Lord, for Sister Moon and the stars. In heaven you fashioned them, clear and precious and beautiful.

Praise be to you, my Lord, for Brother Wind, and for every kind of weather, cloudy or fair, stormy or serene, by which you cherish all that you have made.

Praise be to you, my Lord, for Sister Water, which is useful and humble and precious and pure.

Praise be to you, my Lord, for Brother Fire, by whom you lighten the night, for he is beautiful and playful and robust and strong.

Praise be to you, my Lord, for our Sister Earth, who sustains and governs us, and produces varied fruits with colored flowers and herbs.

Praise be to you, my Lord, for those who forgive sins in your love, and for those who bear sickness and tribulation. Blessed are those who endure in peace, for by you, most high Lord, they shall be crowned.

Praise and bless my Lord, giving him thanks and serving him with great humility.

ADDITIONAL SCRIPTURE READING:
Job 11:7–8; Psalm 108:4–5; Acts 17:24

Go to page 637 for your next devotional reading.

12 But man, despite his riches, does not
  endure;
  he is*a* like the beasts that perish.

13 This is the fate of those who trust in
  themselves,
  and of their followers, who approve
  their sayings.   *Selah*
14 Like sheep they are destined for the
  grave,*b*
  and death will feed on them.
  The upright will rule over them in
  the morning;
  their forms will decay in the
  grave,*b*
  far from their princely mansions.
15 But God will redeem my life*c* from
  the grave;
  he will surely take me to himself.
                Selah

16 Do not be overawed when a man
  grows rich,
  when the splendor of his house
  increases;
17 for he will take nothing with him
  when he dies,
  his splendor will not descend with
  him.
18 Though while he lived he counted
  himself blessed—
  and men praise you when you
  prosper—
19 he will join the generation of his
  fathers,
  who will never see the light ⌞of
  life⌟.

20 A man who has riches without
  understanding
  is like the beasts that perish.

Psalm

 50

A psalm of Asaph.

1 The Mighty One, God, the LORD,
  speaks and summons the earth
  from the rising of the sun to the
  place where it sets.
2 From Zion, perfect in beauty,
  God shines forth.
3 Our God comes and will not be
  silent;

a fire devours before him,
  and around him a tempest rages.
4 He summons the heavens above,
  and the earth, that he may judge
  his people:
5 "Gather to me my consecrated ones,
  who made a covenant with me by
  sacrifice."
6 And the heavens proclaim his
  righteousness,
  for God himself is judge.   *Selah*

7 "Hear, O my people, and I will speak,
  O Israel, and I will testify against
  you:
  I am God, your God.
8 I do not rebuke you for your
  sacrifices
  or your burnt offerings, which are
  ever before me.
9 I have no need of a bull from your
  stall
  or of goats from your pens,
10 for every animal of the forest is mine,
  and the cattle on a thousand hills.
11 I know every bird in the mountains,
  and the creatures of the field are
  mine.
12 If I were hungry I would not tell you,
  for the world is mine, and all that
  is in it.
13 Do I eat the flesh of bulls
  or drink the blood of goats?
14 Sacrifice thank offerings to God,
  fulfill your vows to the Most High,
15 and call upon me in the day of
  trouble;
  I will deliver you, and you will
  honor me."

16 But to the wicked, God says:

"What right have you to recite my
  laws
  or take my covenant on your lips?
17 You hate my instruction
  and cast my words behind you.
18 When you see a thief, you join with
  him;
  you throw in your lot with
  adulterers.
19 You use your mouth for evil
  and harness your tongue to deceit.
20 You speak continually against your
  brother

---

a 12 Hebrew; Septuagint and Syriac read verse 12 the same as verse 20.   *b 14* Hebrew *Sheol*; also in
verse 15   *c 15* Or *soul*

and slander your own mother's
    son.
21 These things you have done and I
    kept silent;
    you thought I was altogether[a] like
      you.
But I will rebuke you
    and accuse you to your face.

22 "Consider this, you who forget God,
    or I will tear you to pieces, with
      none to rescue:
23 He who sacrifices thank offerings
      honors me,
    and he prepares the way
    so that I may show him[b] the
      salvation of God."

Psalm 51

For the director of music. A psalm of David.
When the prophet Nathan came to him after
   David had committed adultery with
      Bathsheba.

1 Have mercy on me, O God,
    according to your unfailing love;
 according to your great compassion
    blot out my transgressions.
2 Wash away all my iniquity
    and cleanse me from my sin.

3 For I know my transgressions,
    and my sin is always before me.
4 Against you, you only, have I sinned
    and done what is evil in your sight,
so that you are proved right when
      you speak
    and justified when you judge.
5 Surely I was sinful at birth,
    sinful from the time my mother
      conceived me.
6 Surely you desire truth in the inner
      parts[c];
    you teach[d] me wisdom in the
      inmost place.

7 Cleanse me with hyssop, and I will
      be clean;
    wash me, and I will be whiter than
      snow.
8 Let me hear joy and gladness;
    let the bones you have crushed
      rejoice.

9 Hide your face from my sins
    and blot out all my iniquity.
10 Create in me a pure heart, O God,
    and renew a steadfast spirit within
      me.
11 Do not cast me from your presence
    or take your Holy Spirit from me.
12 Restore to me the joy of your
      salvation
    and grant me a willing spirit, to
      sustain me.

13 Then I will teach transgressors your
      ways,
    and sinners will turn back to you.
14 Save me from bloodguilt, O God,
    the God who saves me,
    and my tongue will sing of your
      righteousness.
15 O Lord, open my lips,
    and my mouth will declare your
      praise.
16 You do not delight in sacrifice, or I
      would bring it;
    you do not take pleasure in burnt
      offerings.
17 The sacrifices of God are[e] a broken
      spirit;
    a broken and contrite heart,
    O God, you will not despise.

18 In your good pleasure make Zion
      prosper;
    build up the walls of Jerusalem.
19 Then there will be righteous
      sacrifices,
    whole burnt offerings to delight
      you;
    then bulls will be offered on your
      altar.

Psalm 52

For the director of music. A maskil[f] of David.
When Doeg the Edomite had gone to Saul and
  told him: "David has gone to the house of
      Ahimelech."

1 Why do you boast of evil, you mighty
      man?
    Why do you boast all day long,
    you who are a disgrace in the eyes
      of God?

---

a 21 Or thought the 'I AM' was   b 23 Or and to him who considers his way / I will show   c 6 The
meaning of the Hebrew for this phrase is uncertain.   d 6 Or you desired . . . ; / you taught   e 17 Or
My sacrifice, O God, is   f Title: Probably a literary or musical term

JESUS CHRIST—THE MIDDLE WAY

Blaise Pascal

VERSE: Psalm 51:1   **PASSAGE:** Psalm 51:1–10

he God of Christians is not a God who is simply the author of mathematical truths, or of the order of the elements, as is the god of the pagans and of Epicureans. Nor is he merely a God who providentially disposes the life and fortunes of men, to crown his worshipers with length of happy years. Such was the portion of the Jews. But the God of Abraham, the God of Isaac, the God of Jacob, the God of Christians, is a God of love and consolation, a God who fills the souls and hearts of his own, a God who makes them feel their inward wretchedness and his infinite mercy, who unites himself to their inmost spirit, filling it with humility and joy, with confidence and love, rendering them incapable of any end other than himself.

All who seek God apart from Jesus Christ, and who rest in nature, either find no light to satisfy them, or form for themselves a means of knowing God and serving him without a mediator. Thus they fall either into atheism or into deism, two things which the Christian religion almost equally abhors.

The God of Christians is a God who makes the soul perceive that he is her only good, that her only rest is in him, her only joy in loving him; who makes her at the same time abhor the obstacles which withhold her from loving him with all her strength. Her two hindrances, self-love and lust, are insupportable to her. This God makes her perceive that the root of self-love destroys her, and that he alone can heal.

The knowledge of God without that of our wretchedness creates pride. The knowledge of our wretchedness without that of God creates despair. The knowledge of Jesus Christ is the middle way, because in him we find both God and our wretchedness.

ADDITIONAL SCRIPTURE READING:

Exodus 34:6–7; Micah 7:18–20; Romans 7:24–25

Go to page 644 for your next devotional reading.

1500   1700

2 Your tongue plots destruction;
   it is like a sharpened razor,
   you who practice deceit.
3 You love evil rather than good,
   falsehood rather than speaking the
      truth.   *Selah*
4 You love every harmful word,
   O you deceitful tongue!

5 Surely God will bring you down to
      everlasting ruin:
   He will snatch you up and tear you
      from your tent;
   he will uproot you from the land of
      the living.   *Selah*
6 The righteous will see and fear;
   they will laugh at him, saying,
7 "Here now is the man
   who did not make God his
      stronghold
   but trusted in his great wealth
   and grew strong by destroying
      others!"

8 But I am like an olive tree
   flourishing in the house of God;
   I trust in God's unfailing love
   for ever and ever.
9 I will praise you forever for what you
      have done;
   in your name I will hope, for your
      name is good.
   I will praise you in the presence of
      your saints.

Psalm 53

For the director of music. According to
mahalath.[a] A *maskil*[b] of David.

1 The fool says in his heart,
   "There is no God."
   They are corrupt, and their ways are
      vile;
   there is no one who does good.
2 God looks down from heaven
   on the sons of men
   to see if there are any who
      understand,
   any who seek God.
3 Everyone has turned away,
   they have together become
      corrupt;

there is no one who does good,
   not even one.

4 Will the evildoers never learn—
   those who devour my people as
      men eat bread
   and who do not call on God?
5 There they were, overwhelmed with
      dread,
   where there was nothing to dread.
   God scattered the bones of those who
      attacked you;
   you put them to shame, for God
      despised them.

6 Oh, that salvation for Israel would
      come out of Zion!
   When God restores the fortunes of
      his people,
   let Jacob rejoice and Israel be glad!

Psalm 54

For the director of music. With stringed
instruments. A *maskil*[b] of David. When the
Ziphites had gone to Saul and said, "Is not
David hiding among us?"

1 Save me, O God, by your name;
   vindicate me by your might.
2 Hear my prayer, O God;
   listen to the words of my mouth.

3 Strangers are attacking me;
   ruthless men seek my life—
   men without regard for God.
                              Selah

4 Surely God is my help;
   the Lord is the one who sustains
      me.

5 Let evil recoil on those who slander
      me;
   in your faithfulness destroy them.

6 I will sacrifice a freewill offering to
      you;
   I will praise your name, O LORD,
   for it is good.
7 For he has delivered me from all my
      troubles,
   and my eyes have looked in
      triumph on my foes.

---

a Title: Probably a musical term   *b* Title: Probably a literary or musical term

Psalm

 55

For the director of music. With stringed instruments. A *maskil*[a] of David.

1 Listen to my prayer, O God,
  do not ignore my plea;
2 hear me and answer me.
My thoughts trouble me and I am distraught
3 at the voice of the enemy,
  at the stares of the wicked;
for they bring down suffering upon me
  and revile me in their anger.

4 My heart is in anguish within me;
  the terrors of death assail me.
5 Fear and trembling have beset me;
  horror has overwhelmed me.
6 I said, "Oh, that I had the wings of a dove!
  I would fly away and be at rest—
7 I would flee far away
  and stay in the desert;   *Selah*
8 I would hurry to my place of shelter,
  far from the tempest and storm."

9 Confuse the wicked, O Lord,
  confound their speech,
  for I see violence and strife in the city.
10 Day and night they prowl about on its walls;
  malice and abuse are within it.
11 Destructive forces are at work in the city;
  threats and lies never leave its streets.

12 If an enemy were insulting me,
  I could endure it;
if a foe were raising himself against me,
  I could hide from him.
13 But it is you, a man like myself,
  my companion, my close friend,
14 with whom I once enjoyed sweet fellowship
  as we walked with the throng at the house of God.
15 Let death take my enemies by surprise;

let them go down alive to the grave,[b]
  for evil finds lodging among them.

16 But I call to God,
  and the LORD saves me.
17 Evening, morning and noon
  I cry out in distress,
  and he hears my voice.
18 He ransoms me unharmed
  from the battle waged against me,
  even though many oppose me.
19 God, who is enthroned forever,
  will hear them and afflict them—
                         Selah
  men who never change their ways
  and have no fear of God.

20 My companion attacks his friends;
  he violates his covenant.
21 His speech is smooth as butter,
  yet war is in his heart;
his words are more soothing than oil,
  yet they are drawn swords.

22 Cast your cares on the LORD
  and he will sustain you;
  he will never let the righteous fall.
23 But you, O God, will bring down the wicked
  into the pit of corruption;
bloodthirsty and deceitful men
  will not live out half their days.

But as for me, I trust in you.

Psalm

56

For the director of music. To the tune of "A Dove on Distant Oaks." Of David. A *miktam.*[a] When the Philistines had seized him in Gath.

1 Be merciful to me, O God, for men hotly pursue me;
  all day long they press their attack.
2 My slanderers pursue me all day long;
  many are attacking me in their pride.
3 When I am afraid,
  I will trust in you.
4 In God, whose word I praise,
  in God I trust; I will not be afraid.

---

a Title: Probably a literary or musical term   b 15 Hebrew *Sheol*

What can mortal man do to me?

5 All day long they twist my words;
    they are always plotting to harm
        me.
6 They conspire, they lurk,
    they watch my steps,
    eager to take my life.

7 On no account let them escape;
    in your anger, O God, bring down
        the nations.
8 Record my lament;
    list my tears on your scroll*a*—
    are they not in your record?

9 Then my enemies will turn back
    when I call for help.
    By this I will know that God is for
        me.
10 In God, whose word I praise,
    in the LORD, whose word I praise—
11 in God I trust; I will not be afraid.
    What can man do to me?

12 I am under vows to you, O God;
    I will present my thank offerings to
        you.
13 For you have delivered me*b* from
        death
    and my feet from stumbling,
    that I may walk before God
    in the light of life.*c*

Psalm 57

For the director of music. ⌊To the tune of⌋
"Do Not Destroy." Of David. A *miktam*.*d*
When he had fled from Saul into the cave.

1 Have mercy on me, O God, have
        mercy on me,
    for in you my soul takes refuge.
    I will take refuge in the shadow of
        your wings
    until the disaster has passed.

2 I cry out to God Most High,
    to God, who fulfills ⌊his purpose⌋
        for me.
3 He sends from heaven and saves me,
    rebuking those who hotly pursue
        me;   *Selah*
    God sends his love and his
        faithfulness.

4 I am in the midst of lions;
    I lie among ravenous beasts—
    men whose teeth are spears and
        arrows,
    whose tongues are sharp swords.

5 Be exalted, O God, above the
        heavens;
    let your glory be over all the earth.

6 They spread a net for my feet—
    I was bowed down in distress.
    They dug a pit in my path—
    but they have fallen into it
        themselves.   *Selah*

7 My heart is steadfast, O God,
    my heart is steadfast;
    I will sing and make music.
8 Awake, my soul!
    Awake, harp and lyre!
    I will awaken the dawn.

9 I will praise you, O Lord, among the
        nations;
    I will sing of you among the
        peoples.
10 For great is your love, reaching to the
        heavens;
    your faithfulness reaches to the
        skies.

11 Be exalted, O God, above the
        heavens;
    let your glory be over all the earth.

Psalm 58

For the director of music. ⌊To the tune of⌋
"Do Not Destroy." Of David. A *miktam*.*d*

1 Do you rulers indeed speak justly?
    Do you judge uprightly among
        men?
2 No, in your heart you devise
        injustice,
    and your hands mete out violence
        on the earth.
3 Even from birth the wicked go astray;
    from the womb they are wayward
        and speak lies.
4 Their venom is like the venom of a
        snake,
    like that of a cobra that has
        stopped its ears,

---

a 8 Or / *put my tears in your wineskin*   *b 13* Or *my soul*   *c 13* Or *the land of the living*   *d* Title:
Probably a literary or musical term

⁵ that will not heed the tune of the
　charmer,
　however skillful the enchanter
　may be.

⁶ Break the teeth in their mouths,
　O God;
　tear out, O LORD, the fangs of the
　lions!
⁷ Let them vanish like water that flows
　away;
　when they draw the bow, let their
　arrows be blunted.
⁸ Like a slug melting away as it moves
　along,
　like a stillborn child, may they not
　see the sun.

⁹ Before your pots can feel ⌊the heat of⌋
　the thorns—
　whether they be green or dry—the
　wicked will be swept away.ᵃ
¹⁰ The righteous will be glad when they
　are avenged,
　when they bathe their feet in the
　blood of the wicked.
¹¹ Then men will say,
　"Surely the righteous still are
　rewarded;
　surely there is a God who judges
　the earth."

Psalm

For the director of music. ⌊To the tune of⌋
"Do Not Destroy." Of David. A *miktam.* ᵇ
When Saul had sent men to watch David's
house in order to kill him.

¹ Deliver me from my enemies,
　O God;
　protect me from those who rise up
　against me.
² Deliver me from evildoers
　and save me from bloodthirsty
　men.

³ See how they lie in wait for me!
　Fierce men conspire against me
　for no offense or sin of mine,
　O LORD.
⁴ I have done no wrong, yet they are
　ready to attack me.
　Arise to help me; look on my plight!

⁵ O LORD God Almighty, the God of
　Israel,
　rouse yourself to punish all the
　nations;
　show no mercy to wicked traitors.
　　　　　　　　　　Selah

⁶ They return at evening,
　snarling like dogs,
　and prowl about the city.
⁷ See what they spew from their
　mouths—
　they spew out swords from their
　lips,
　and they say, "Who can hear us?"
⁸ But you, O LORD, laugh at them;
　you scoff at all those nations.

⁹ O my Strength, I watch for you;
　you, O God, are my fortress, ¹⁰my
　loving God.

　God will go before me
　and will let me gloat over those
　who slander me.
¹¹ But do not kill them, O Lord our
　shield,ᶜ
　or my people will forget.
　In your might make them wander
　about,
　and bring them down.
¹² For the sins of their mouths,
　for the words of their lips,
　let them be caught in their pride.
　For the curses and lies they utter,
¹³　consume them in wrath,
　consume them till they are no
　more.
　Then it will be known to the ends of
　the earth
　that God rules over Jacob.   *Selah*

¹⁴ They return at evening,
　snarling like dogs,
　and prowl about the city.
¹⁵ They wander about for food
　and howl if not satisfied.
¹⁶ But I will sing of your strength,
　in the morning I will sing of your
　love;
　for you are my fortress,
　my refuge in times of trouble.

¹⁷ O my Strength, I sing praise to you;
　you, O God, are my fortress, my
　loving God.

ᵃ 9 The meaning of the Hebrew for this verse is uncertain.　ᵇ Title: Probably a literary or musical term
ᶜ 11 Or *sovereign*

Psalm

For the director of music. To ⌊the tune of⌋ "The Lily of the Covenant." A *miktam*[a] of David. For teaching. When he fought Aram Naharaim[b] and Aram Zobah,[c] and when Joab returned and struck down twelve thousand Edomites in the Valley of Salt.

¹ You have rejected us, O God, and
   burst forth upon us;
   you have been angry—now restore
      us!
² You have shaken the land and torn it
      open;
   mend its fractures, for it is
      quaking.
³ You have shown your people
      desperate times;
   you have given us wine that makes
      us stagger.

⁴ But for those who fear you, you have
      raised a banner
   to be unfurled against the bow.
                              Selah

⁵ Save us and help us with your right
      hand,
   that those you love may be
      delivered.
⁶ God has spoken from his sanctuary:
   "In triumph I will parcel out
      Shechem
   and measure off the Valley of
      Succoth.
⁷ Gilead is mine, and Manasseh is
      mine;
   Ephraim is my helmet,
   Judah my scepter.
⁸ Moab is my washbasin,
   upon Edom I toss my sandal;
   over Philistia I shout in
      triumph."

⁹ Who will bring me to the fortified
      city?
   Who will lead me to Edom?
¹⁰ Is it not you, O God, you who have
      rejected us
   and no longer go out with our
      armies?
¹¹ Give us aid against the enemy,
   for the help of man is worthless.

¹² With God we will gain the victory,
   and he will trample down our
      enemies.

Psalm

For the director of music. With stringed instruments. Of David.

¹ Hear my cry, O God;
   listen to my prayer.
² From the ends of the earth I call to
      you,
   I call as my heart grows faint;
   lead me to the rock that is higher
      than I.
³ For you have been my refuge,
   a strong tower against the foe.

⁴ I long to dwell in your tent forever
   and take refuge in the shelter of
      your wings.   *Selah*
⁵ For you have heard my vows, O God;
   you have given me the heritage of
      those who fear your name.

⁶ Increase the days of the king's life,
   his years for many generations.
⁷ May he be enthroned in God's
      presence forever;
   appoint your love and faithfulness
      to protect him.

⁸ Then will I ever sing praise to your
      name
   and fulfill my vows day after day.

Psalm

For the director of music. For Jeduthun. A psalm of David.

¹ My soul finds rest in God alone;
   my salvation comes from him.
² He alone is my rock and my
      salvation;
   he is my fortress, I will never be
      shaken.

³ How long will you assault a man?
   Would all of you throw him down—
   this leaning wall, this tottering
      fence?

---

a Title: Probably a literary or musical term   *b* Title: That is, Arameans of Northwest Mesopotamia
c Title: That is, Arameans of central Syria

4 They fully intend to topple him
    from his lofty place;
    they take delight in lies.
With their mouths they bless,
    but in their hearts they curse. *Selah*

5 Find rest, O my soul, in God alone;
    my hope comes from him.
6 He alone is my rock and my
      salvation;
    he is my fortress, I will not be
      shaken.
7 My salvation and my honor depend
      on God[a];
    he is my mighty rock, my refuge.
8 Trust in him at all times, O people;
    pour out your hearts to him,
    for God is our refuge.   *Selah*

9 Lowborn men are but a breath,
    the highborn are but a lie;
if weighed on a balance, they are
      nothing;
    together they are only a breath.
10 Do not trust in extortion
    or take pride in stolen goods;
though your riches increase,
    do not set your heart on them.

11 One thing God has spoken,
    two things have I heard:
that you, O God, are strong,
12   and that you, O Lord, are loving.
    Surely you will reward each person
    according to what he has done.

Psalm

A psalm of David. When he was in the Desert
of Judah.

1 O God, you are my God,
    earnestly I seek you;
my soul thirsts for you,
    my body longs for you,
in a dry and weary land
    where there is no water.

2 I have seen you in the sanctuary
    and beheld your power and your
      glory.
3 Because your love is better than life,
    my lips will glorify you.
4 I will praise you as long as I live,

and in your name I will lift up my
      hands.
5 My soul will be satisfied as with the
      richest of foods;
    with singing lips my mouth will
      praise you.

6 On my bed I remember you;
    I think of you through the watches
      of the night.
7 Because you are my help,
    I sing in the shadow of your wings.
8 My soul clings to you;
    your right hand upholds me.

9 They who seek my life will be
      destroyed;
    they will go down to the depths of
      the earth.
10 They will be given over to the sword
    and become food for jackals.

11 But the king will rejoice in God;
    all who swear by God's name will
      praise him,
    while the mouths of liars will be
      silenced.

Psalm

64

For the director of music. A psalm of David.

1 Hear me, O God, as I voice my
      complaint;
    protect my life from the threat of
      the enemy.
2 Hide me from the conspiracy of the
      wicked,
    from that noisy crowd of evildoers.

3 They sharpen their tongues like
      swords
    and aim their words like deadly
      arrows.
4 They shoot from ambush at the
      innocent man;
    they shoot at him suddenly,
      without fear.

5 They encourage each other in evil
      plans,
    they talk about hiding their snares;
    they say, "Who will see them[b]?"
6 They plot injustice and say,
    "We have devised a perfect plan!"

a 7 Or | *God Most High is my salvation and my honor*   *b 5* Or *us*

Surely the mind and heart of man
　　are cunning.

⁷But God will shoot them with arrows;
　　suddenly they will be struck down.
⁸He will turn their own tongues
　　against them
　and bring them to ruin;
　all who see them will shake their
　　heads in scorn.

⁹All mankind will fear;
　they will proclaim the works of God
　and ponder what he has done.

¹⁰Let the righteous rejoice in the LORD
　　and take refuge in him;
　let all the upright in heart praise
　　him!

Psalm

For the director of music. A psalm of David.
A song.

¹Praise awaits*ᵃ* you, O God, in Zion;
　to you our vows will be fulfilled.

ᵃ 1 Or *befits;* the meaning of the Hebrew for this word is uncertain.

TUESDAY

PERSONAL PRAYER AT NIGHT
Gregory of Nazianzus

VERSE: Psalm 63:6　　　　　　　　　　　　**PASSAGE:** Psalm 63

ord Jesus, you are light from eternal lights.
You have dissolved all spiritual darkness
And my soul is filled with your brightness.
Your light makes all things beautiful.

You lit the skies with the sun and the moon.
You ordered night and day to follow each other peaceably.
And so you made the sun and the moon friends.
May I be friends with all whom I meet.

At night you give rest to our bodies.
By day you spur us on to work.
May I work with diligence and devotion,
That at night my conscience is at peace.

As I lay down on my bed at night,
May your fingers draw down my eyelids.
Lay your hand of blessing on my head
That righteous sleep may descend upon me.

ADDITIONAL SCRIPTURE READING:
Psalms 42:8; 119:147–148; 139:17–18

Go to page 649 for your next devotional reading.

100　　500

² O you who hear prayer,
   to you all men will come.
³ When we were overwhelmed by
      sins,
   you forgave*a* our transgressions.
⁴ Blessed are those you choose
   and bring near to live in your
      courts!
   We are filled with the good things of
      your house,
   of your holy temple.

⁵ You answer us with awesome deeds
      of righteousness,
   O God our Savior,
   the hope of all the ends of the earth
   and of the farthest seas,
⁶ who formed the mountains by your
      power,
   having armed yourself with
      strength,
⁷ who stilled the roaring of the seas,
   the roaring of their waves,
   and the turmoil of the nations.
⁸ Those living far away fear your
      wonders;
   where morning dawns and evening
      fades
   you call forth songs of joy.

⁹ You care for the land and water it;
   you enrich it abundantly.
   The streams of God are filled with
      water
   to provide the people with grain,
   for so you have ordained it.*b*
¹⁰ You drench its furrows
   and level its ridges;
   you soften it with showers
   and bless its crops.
¹¹ You crown the year with your
      bounty,
   and your carts overflow with
      abundance.
¹² The grasslands of the desert
      overflow;
   the hills are clothed with gladness.
¹³ The meadows are covered with
      flocks
   and the valleys are mantled with
      grain;
   they shout for joy and sing.

Psalm 66

For the director of music. A song. A psalm.

¹ Shout with joy to God, all the earth!
²   Sing the glory of his name;
   make his praise glorious!
³ Say to God, "How awesome are your
      deeds!
   So great is your power
   that your enemies cringe before
      you.
⁴ All the earth bows down to you;
   they sing praise to you,
   they sing praise to your name."
                                    Selah

⁵ Come and see what God has done,
   how awesome his works in man's
      behalf!
⁶ He turned the sea into dry land,
   they passed through the waters on
      foot—
   come, let us rejoice in him.
⁷ He rules forever by his power,
   his eyes watch the nations—
   let not the rebellious rise up
      against him.   *Selah*

⁸ Praise our God, O peoples,
   let the sound of his praise be heard;
⁹ he has preserved our lives
   and kept our feet from slipping.
¹⁰ For you, O God, tested us;
   you refined us like silver.
¹¹ You brought us into prison
   and laid burdens on our backs.
¹² You let men ride over our heads;
   we went through fire and water,
   but you brought us to a place of
      abundance.

¹³ I will come to your temple with
      burnt offerings
   and fulfill my vows to you—
¹⁴ vows my lips promised and my
      mouth spoke
   when I was in trouble.
¹⁵ I will sacrifice fat animals to you
   and an offering of rams;
   I will offer bulls and goats.   *Selah*

¹⁶ Come and listen, all you who fear
      God;

---

a 3 Or *made atonement for*   *b* 9 Or *for that is how you prepare the land*

let me tell you what he has done
  for me.
17 I cried out to him with my mouth;
  his praise was on my tongue.
18 If I had cherished sin in my heart,
  the Lord would not have listened;
19 but God has surely listened
  and heard my voice in prayer.
20 Praise be to God,
  who has not rejected my prayer
  or withheld his love from me!

Psalm 67

For the director of music. With stringed
  instruments. A psalm. A song.

1 May God be gracious to us and bless
  us
  and make his face shine upon us,
                                    Selah
2 that your ways may be known on
  earth,
  your salvation among all nations.

3 May the peoples praise you, O God;
  may all the peoples praise you.
4 May the nations be glad and sing for
  joy,
  for you rule the peoples justly
  and guide the nations of the earth.
                                    Selah
5 May the peoples praise you, O God;
  may all the peoples praise you.

6 Then the land will yield its harvest,
  and God, our God, will bless us.
7 God will bless us,
  and all the ends of the earth will
  fear him.

Psalm 68

For the director of music. Of David. A psalm.
  A song.

1 May God arise, may his enemies be
  scattered;
  may his foes flee before him.
2 As smoke is blown away by the
  wind,
  may you blow them away;

as wax melts before the fire,
  may the wicked perish before God.
3 But may the righteous be glad
  and rejoice before God;
  may they be happy and joyful.

4 Sing to God, sing praise to his name,
  extol him who rides on the
  clouds*a*—
  his name is the LORD—
  and rejoice before him.
5 A father to the fatherless, a defender
  of widows,
  is God in his holy dwelling.
6 God sets the lonely in families,*b*
  he leads forth the prisoners with
  singing;
  but the rebellious live in a sun-
  scorched land.

7 When you went out before your
  people, O God,
  when you marched through the
  wasteland,   *Selah*
8 the earth shook,
  the heavens poured down rain,
  before God, the One of Sinai,
  before God, the God of Israel.
9 You gave abundant showers, O God;
  you refreshed your weary
  inheritance.
10 Your people settled in it,
  and from your bounty, O God, you
  provided for the poor.

11 The Lord announced the word,
  and great was the company of
  those who proclaimed it:
12 "Kings and armies flee in haste;
  in the camps men divide the
  plunder.
13 Even while you sleep among the
  campfires,*c*
  the wings of ˻my˼ dove are
  sheathed with silver,
  its feathers with shining gold."
14 When the Almighty*d* scattered the
  kings in the land,
  it was like snow fallen on Zalmon.

15 The mountains of Bashan are
  majestic mountains;
  rugged are the mountains of
  Bashan.
16 Why gaze in envy, O rugged
  mountains,

a 4 Or / *prepare the way for him who rides through the deserts*   *b 6* Or *the desolate in a homeland*
c 13 Or *saddlebags*   *d 14* Hebrew *Shaddai*

at the mountain where God
  chooses to reign,
where the LORD himself will dwell
  forever?
17 The chariots of God are tens of
    thousands
  and thousands of thousands;
  the Lord ⌊has come⌋ from Sinai into
    his sanctuary.
18 When you ascended on high,
  you led captives in your train;
  you received gifts from men,
  even from*a* the rebellious—
  that you,*b* O LORD God, might
    dwell there.

19 Praise be to the Lord, to God our
    Savior,
  who daily bears our burdens. *Selah*
20 Our God is a God who saves;
  from the Sovereign LORD comes
    escape from death.

21 Surely God will crush the heads of
    his enemies,
  the hairy crowns of those who go
    on in their sins.
22 The Lord says, "I will bring them
    from Bashan;
  I will bring them from the depths
    of the sea,
23 that you may plunge your feet in the
    blood of your foes,
  while the tongues of your dogs
    have their share."

24 Your procession has come into view,
    O God,
  the procession of my God and King
    into the sanctuary.
25 In front are the singers, after them
    the musicians;
  with them are the maidens playing
    tambourines.
26 Praise God in the great congregation;
  praise the LORD in the assembly of
    Israel.
27 There is the little tribe of Benjamin,
    leading them,
  there the great throng of Judah's
    princes,
  and there the princes of Zebulun
    and of Naphtali.

28 Summon your power, O God*c*;

show us your strength, O God, as
  you have done before.
29 Because of your temple at Jerusalem
  kings will bring you gifts.
30 Rebuke the beast among the reeds,
  the herd of bulls among the calves
    of the nations.
  Humbled, may it bring bars of silver.
  Scatter the nations who delight in
    war.
31 Envoys will come from Egypt;
  Cush*d* will submit herself to God.

32 Sing to God, O kingdoms of the
    earth,
  sing praise to the Lord,   *Selah*
33 to him who rides the ancient skies
    above,
  who thunders with mighty voice.
34 Proclaim the power of God,
  whose majesty is over Israel,
  whose power is in the skies.
35 You are awesome, O God, in your
    sanctuary;
  the God of Israel gives power and
    strength to his people.

Praise be to God!

Psalm

 69

For the director of music. To ⌊the tune of⌋
  "Lilies." Of David.

1 Save me, O God,
  for the waters have come up to my
    neck.
2 I sink in the miry depths,
  where there is no foothold.
  I have come into the deep waters;
  the floods engulf me.
3 I am worn out calling for help;
  my throat is parched.
  My eyes fail,
  looking for my God.
4 Those who hate me without reason
  outnumber the hairs of my head;
  many are my enemies without cause,
  those who seek to destroy me.
  I am forced to restore
  what I did not steal.

5 You know my folly, O God;
  my guilt is not hidden from you.

---

a 18 Or *gifts for men, / even*   *b 18* Or *they*   *c 28* Many Hebrew manuscripts, Septuagint and Syriac;
most Hebrew manuscripts *Your God has summoned power for you*   *d 31* That is, the upper Nile region

⁶ May those who hope in you
        not be disgraced because of me,
    O Lord, the LORD Almighty;
    may those who seek you
        not be put to shame because of me,
    O God of Israel.
⁷ For I endure scorn for your sake,
        and shame covers my face.
⁸ I am a stranger to my brothers,
        an alien to my own mother's
            sons;
⁹ for zeal for your house consumes
            me,
    and the insults of those who insult
        you fall on me.
¹⁰ When I weep and fast,
        I must endure scorn;
¹¹ when I put on sackcloth,
        people make sport of me.
¹² Those who sit at the gate mock me,
        and I am the song of the drunkards.

¹³ But I pray to you, O LORD,
        in the time of your favor;
    in your great love, O God,
        answer me with your sure
            salvation.
¹⁴ Rescue me from the mire,
        do not let me sink;
    deliver me from those who hate me,
        from the deep waters.
¹⁵ Do not let the floodwaters engulf
            me
    or the depths swallow me up
    or the pit close its mouth over me.
¹⁶ Answer me, O LORD, out of the
            goodness of your love;
    in your great mercy turn to me.
¹⁷ Do not hide your face from your
            servant;
    answer me quickly, for I am in
            trouble.
¹⁸ Come near and rescue me;
        redeem me because of my foes.

¹⁹ You know how I am scorned,
            disgraced and shamed;
    all my enemies are before you.
²⁰ Scorn has broken my heart
        and has left me helpless;
    I looked for sympathy, but there was
            none,
        for comforters, but I found none.
²¹ They put gall in my food
        and gave me vinegar for my
            thirst.

²² May the table set before them
            become a snare;
    may it become retribution and*ᵃ* a
            trap.
²³ May their eyes be darkened so they
            cannot see,
    and their backs be bent forever.
²⁴ Pour out your wrath on them;
        let your fierce anger overtake
            them.
²⁵ May their place be deserted;
        let there be no one to dwell in their
            tents.
²⁶ For they persecute those you
            wound
    and talk about the pain of those
            you hurt.
²⁷ Charge them with crime upon crime;
        do not let them share in your
            salvation.
²⁸ May they be blotted out of the book
            of life
    and not be listed with the
            righteous.

²⁹ I am in pain and distress;
        may your salvation, O God, protect
            me.
³⁰ I will praise God's name in song
        and glorify him with
            thanksgiving.
³¹ This will please the LORD more than
            an ox,
    more than a bull with its horns and
            hoofs.
³² The poor will see and be glad—
        you who seek God, may your
            hearts live!
³³ The LORD hears the needy
        and does not despise his captive
            people.

³⁴ Let heaven and earth praise him,
        the seas and all that move in
            them,
³⁵ for God will save Zion
        and rebuild the cities of Judah.
    Then people will settle there and
            possess it;
³⁶   the children of his servants will
            inherit it,
        and those who love his name will
            dwell there.

ᵃ 22 Or snare / and their fellowship become

Psalm

70

For the director of music. Of David.
A petition.

¹ Hasten, O God, to save me;
   O LORD, come quickly to help
   me.
² May those who seek my life
   be put to shame and confusion;
may all who desire my ruin
   be turned back in disgrace.
³ May those who say to me, "Aha!
   Aha!"
   turn back because of their shame.
⁴ But may all who seek you
   rejoice and be glad in you;

may those who love your salvation
   always say,
   "Let God be exalted!"

⁵ Yet I am poor and needy;
   come quickly to me, O God.
You are my help and my deliverer;
   O LORD, do not delay.

Psalm

71

¹ In you, O LORD, I have taken refuge;
   let me never be put to shame.
² Rescue me and deliver me in your
   righteousness;
   turn your ear to me and save me.
³ Be my rock of refuge,

WEDNESDAY

A MEDITATION OF IMMORTALITY
John Calvin

VERSE: Psalm 70:4   **PASSAGE:** Psalm 70:1–4

s no man is found, however barbarous and even savage
he may be, who is not touched by some idea of religion, it is clear that we all are created in order that we
may know the majesty of our Creator, that having
known it, we may esteem it above all and honor it with all awe,
love, and reverence.

But, leaving aside the unbelievers, who seek nothing but to
efface from their memory that idea of God which is planted in
their hearts, we, who make profession of personal religion, must
reflect that this decrepit life of ours, which will soon end, must
be nothing else but a meditation of immortality. Now, nowhere
can eternal and immortal life be found except in God. It is necessary, therefore, that the principal care and solicitude of our life
be to seek God, to aspire to him with all the affection of our
heart, and to repose nowhere else but in him alone.

ADDITIONAL SCRIPTURE READING:
Ecclesiastes 3:11; Romans 1:18–23

Go to page 652 for your next devotional reading.

1500   1700

to which I can always go;
give the command to save me,
    for you are my rock and my
        fortress.
4 Deliver me, O my God, from the
        hand of the wicked,
    from the grasp of evil and cruel
        men.

5 For you have been my hope,
        O Sovereign LORD,
    my confidence since my youth.
6 From birth I have relied on you;
    you brought me forth from my
        mother's womb.
    I will ever praise you.
7 I have become like a portent to many,
    but you are my strong refuge.
8 My mouth is filled with your praise,
    declaring your splendor all day
        long.

9 Do not cast me away when I am old;
    do not forsake me when my
        strength is gone.
10 For my enemies speak against me;
    those who wait to kill me conspire
        together.
11 They say, "God has forsaken him;
    pursue him and seize him,
    for no one will rescue him."
12 Be not far from me, O God;
    come quickly, O my God, to help
        me.
13 May my accusers perish in shame;
    may those who want to harm me
    be covered with scorn and disgrace.

14 But as for me, I will always have
        hope;
    I will praise you more and more.
15 My mouth will tell of your
        righteousness,
    of your salvation all day long,
    though I know not its measure.
16 I will come and proclaim your
        mighty acts, O Sovereign
        LORD;
    I will proclaim your righteousness,
        yours alone.
17 Since my youth, O God, you have
        taught me,
    and to this day I declare your
        marvelous deeds.
18 Even when I am old and gray,
    do not forsake me, O God,

till I declare your power to the next
        generation,
    your might to all who are to come.

19 Your righteousness reaches to the
        skies, O God,
    you who have done great things.
    Who, O God, is like you?
20 Though you have made me see
        troubles, many and bitter,
    you will restore my life again;
    from the depths of the earth
    you will again bring me up.
21 You will increase my honor
    and comfort me once again.

22 I will praise you with the harp
    for your faithfulness, O my God;
    I will sing praise to you with the lyre,
        O Holy One of Israel.
23 My lips will shout for joy
    when I sing praise to you—
    I, whom you have redeemed.
24 My tongue will tell of your righteous
        acts
    all day long,
    for those who wanted to harm me
    have been put to shame and
        confusion.

Psalm

 72

Of Solomon.

1 Endow the king with your justice,
        O God,
    the royal son with your
        righteousness.
2 He will[a] judge your people in
        righteousness,
    your afflicted ones with justice.
3 The mountains will bring prosperity
        to the people,
    the hills the fruit of righteousness.
4 He will defend the afflicted among
        the people
    and save the children of the needy;
    he will crush the oppressor.
5 He will endure[b] as long as the sun,
    as long as the moon, through all
        generations.
6 He will be like rain falling on a
        mown field,
    like showers watering the earth.

a 2 Or May he; similarly in verses 3–11 and 17   b 5 Septuagint; Hebrew You will be feared

7 In his days the righteous will flourish;
   prosperity will abound till the
      moon is no more.

8 He will rule from sea to sea
   and from the River*a* to the ends of
      the earth.*b*
9 The desert tribes will bow before him
   and his enemies will lick the dust.
10 The kings of Tarshish and of distant
      shores
   will bring tribute to him;
   the kings of Sheba and Seba
   will present him gifts.
11 All kings will bow down to him
   and all nations will serve him.

12 For he will deliver the needy who cry
      out,
   the afflicted who have no one to
      help.
13 He will take pity on the weak and
      the needy
   and save the needy from death.
14 He will rescue them from oppression
      and violence,
   for precious is their blood in his
      sight.

15 Long may he live!
   May gold from Sheba be given him.
   May people ever pray for him
   and bless him all day long.
16 Let grain abound throughout the land;
   on the tops of the hills may it sway.
   Let its fruit flourish like Lebanon;
   let it thrive like the grass of the
      field.
17 May his name endure forever;
   may it continue as long as the sun.

   All nations will be blessed through
      him,
   and they will call him blessed.

18 Praise be to the LORD God, the God of
      Israel,
   who alone does marvelous deeds.
19 Praise be to his glorious name forever;
   may the whole earth be filled with
      his glory.
         Amen and Amen.

20 This concludes the prayers of David
      son of Jesse.

BOOK III
Psalms 73–89

Psalm

73

A psalm of Asaph.

1 Surely God is good to Israel,
   to those who are pure in heart.

2 But as for me, my feet had almost
      slipped;
   I had nearly lost my foothold.
3 For I envied the arrogant
   when I saw the prosperity of the
      wicked.

4 They have no struggles;
   their bodies are healthy and
      strong.*c*
5 They are free from the burdens
      common to man;
   they are not plagued by human ills.
6 Therefore pride is their necklace;
   they clothe themselves with
      violence.
7 From their callous hearts comes
      iniquity*d*;
   the evil conceits of their minds
      know no limits.
8 They scoff, and speak with malice;
   in their arrogance they threaten
      oppression.
9 Their mouths lay claim to heaven,
   and their tongues take possession
      of the earth.
10 Therefore their people turn to them
   and drink up waters in abundance.*e*
11 They say, "How can God know?
   Does the Most High have
      knowledge?"

12 This is what the wicked are like—
   always carefree, they increase in
      wealth.

13 Surely in vain have I kept my heart
      pure;
   in vain have I washed my hands in
      innocence.
14 All day long I have been plagued;
   I have been punished every
      morning.

---

a 8 That is, the Euphrates   *b* 8 Or *the end of the land*   *c* 4 With a different word division of the Hebrew; Masoretic Text *struggles at their death; / their bodies are healthy*   *d* 7 Syriac (see also Septuagint); Hebrew *Their eyes bulge with fat*   *e* 10 The meaning of the Hebrew for this verse is uncertain.

15 If I had said, "I will speak thus,"
   I would have betrayed your
      children.
16 When I tried to understand all this,
   it was oppressive to me
17 till I entered the sanctuary of God;
   then I understood their final
      destiny.

18 Surely you place them on slippery
      ground;
   you cast them down to ruin.
19 How suddenly are they destroyed,
   completely swept away by terrors!
20 As a dream when one awakes,

so when you arise, O Lord,
   you will despise them as fantasies.

21 When my heart was grieved
   and my spirit embittered,
22 I was senseless and ignorant;
   I was a brute beast before you.

23 Yet I am always with you;
   you hold me by my right hand.
24 You guide me with your counsel,
   and afterward you will take me
      into glory.
25 Whom have I in heaven but you?
   And earth has nothing I desire
      besides you.

THURSDAY

GOD'S CONTINUAL PRESENCE
Martin Luther

VERSE: Psalm 73:23   **PASSAGE:** Psalm 73

f for the sake of God's Word hardship, sorrow, and persecution come to us, all which follow in the train of the holy cross, the following thoughts should, with God's help, comfort and console us, and should make us determine to be of good cheer, full of courage and confidence, and lead us to surrender the cause trustfully into God's gracious and fatherly will.

First, that our cause is in the hands of him who says so clearly, "No man shall pluck them from my hand" (see John 10:28). It would not be wise to take our cause into our own hands, for we could and should lose it by our loose ways. Likewise all the comfortable words are true and do not lie, which say, "God is our refuge and strength" (Psalm 46:1). Has any man who puts his trust in God ever been put to shame? All who trust in God will be saved, and again: "Thou Lord hast not forsaken them that seek thee" (Psalm 9:10, KJV). Thus it is really true that God gave his only-begotten Son for our salvation. If God gave his own Son for us, how could he ever bring himself to desert us in small things?

ADDITIONAL SCRIPTURE READING:
Psalms 16:8; 139:1–12; Matthew 28:20

Go to page 665 for your next devotional reading.

1500　　1700

26 My flesh and my heart may fail,
  but God is the strength of my heart
    and my portion forever.

27 Those who are far from you will
    perish;
  you destroy all who are unfaithful
    to you.
28 But as for me, it is good to be near
    God.
  I have made the Sovereign LORD
    my refuge;
  I will tell of all your deeds.

Psalm

 74

A *maskil*[a] of Asaph.

1 Why have you rejected us forever,
    O God?
  Why does your anger smolder
    against the sheep of your
      pasture?
2 Remember the people you purchased
    of old,
  the tribe of your inheritance,
    whom you redeemed—
  Mount Zion, where you dwelt.
3 Turn your steps toward these
    everlasting ruins,
  all this destruction the enemy has
    brought on the sanctuary.

4 Your foes roared in the place where
    you met with us;
  they set up their standards as signs.
5 They behaved like men wielding axes
    to cut through a thicket of trees.
6 They smashed all the carved paneling
    with their axes and hatchets.
7 They burned your sanctuary to the
    ground;
  they defiled the dwelling place of
    your Name.
8 They said in their hearts, "We will
    crush them completely!"
  They burned every place where
    God was worshiped in the
      land.
9 We are given no miraculous signs;
  no prophets are left,
  and none of us knows how long
    this will be.

10 How long will the enemy mock you,
    O God?
  Will the foe revile your name
    forever?
11 Why do you hold back your hand,
    your right hand?
  Take it from the folds of your
    garment and destroy them!

12 But you, O God, are my king from of
    old;
  you bring salvation upon the earth.
13 It was you who split open the sea by
    your power;
  you broke the heads of the monster
    in the waters.
14 It was you who crushed the heads of
    Leviathan
  and gave him as food to the
    creatures of the desert.
15 It was you who opened up springs
    and streams;
  you dried up the ever flowing
    rivers.
16 The day is yours, and yours also the
    night;
  you established the sun and moon.
17 It was you who set all the boundaries
    of the earth;
  you made both summer and
    winter.

18 Remember how the enemy has
    mocked you, O LORD,
  how foolish people have reviled
    your name.
19 Do not hand over the life of your
    dove to wild beasts;
  do not forget the lives of your
    afflicted people forever.
20 Have regard for your covenant,
  because haunts of violence fill the
    dark places of the land.
21 Do not let the oppressed retreat in
    disgrace;
  may the poor and needy praise
    your name.

22 Rise up, O God, and defend your
    cause;
  remember how fools mock you all
    day long.
23 Do not ignore the clamor of your
    adversaries,
  the uproar of your enemies, which
    rises continually.

---

a Title: Probably a literary or musical term

Psalm

For the director of music. To the tune of "Do Not Destroy." A psalm of Asaph. A song.

1 We give thanks to you, O God,
   we give thanks, for your Name is
      near;
   men tell of your wonderful deeds.

2 You say, "I choose the appointed
      time;
   it is I who judge uprightly.
3 When the earth and all its people
      quake,
   it is I who hold its pillars firm.
                              Selah

4 To the arrogant I say, 'Boast no more,'
   and to the wicked, 'Do not lift up
      your horns.
5 Do not lift your horns against
      heaven;
   do not speak with outstretched
      neck.' "

6 No one from the east or the west
   or from the desert can exalt a man.
7 But it is God who judges:
   He brings one down, he exalts
      another.
8 In the hand of the LORD is a cup
   full of foaming wine mixed with
      spices;
   he pours it out, and all the wicked of
      the earth
   drink it down to its very dregs.

9 As for me, I will declare this forever;
   I will sing praise to the God of
      Jacob.
10 I will cut off the horns of all the
      wicked,
   but the horns of the righteous will
      be lifted up.

Psalm

For the director of music. With stringed instruments. A psalm of Asaph. A song.

1 In Judah God is known;
   his name is great in Israel.
2 His tent is in Salem,
   his dwelling place in Zion.
3 There he broke the flashing arrows,
   the shields and the swords, the
      weapons of war.   *Selah*

4 You are resplendent with light,
   more majestic than mountains rich
      with game.
5 Valiant men lie plundered,
   they sleep their last sleep;
   not one of the warriors
   can lift his hands.
6 At your rebuke, O God of Jacob,
   both horse and chariot lie still.
7 You alone are to be feared.
   Who can stand before you when
      you are angry?
8 From heaven you pronounced
      judgment,
   and the land feared and was
      quiet—
9 when you, O God, rose up to judge,
   to save all the afflicted of the land.
                              Selah
10 Surely your wrath against men brings
      you praise,
   and the survivors of your wrath are
      restrained.*a*

11 Make vows to the LORD your God
      and fulfill them;
   let all the neighboring lands
   bring gifts to the One to be feared.
12 He breaks the spirit of rulers;
   he is feared by the kings of the
      earth.

Psalm

77

For the director of music. For Jeduthun. Of Asaph. A psalm.

1 I cried out to God for help;
   I cried out to God to hear me.
2 When I was in distress, I sought the
      Lord;
   at night I stretched out untiring
      hands
   and my soul refused to be
      comforted.

3 I remembered you, O God, and I
      groaned;
   I mused, and my spirit grew faint.
                              Selah

a 10 Or Surely the wrath of men brings you praise, / and with the remainder of wrath you arm yourself

4 You kept my eyes from closing;
   I was too troubled to speak.
5 I thought about the former days,
   the years of long ago;
6 I remembered my songs in the night.
   My heart mused and my spirit
      inquired:

7 "Will the Lord reject forever?
   Will he never show his favor again?
8 Has his unfailing love vanished
      forever?
   Has his promise failed for all time?
9 Has God forgotten to be merciful?
   Has he in anger withheld his
      compassion?"   *Selah*

10 Then I thought, "To this I will
      appeal:
   the years of the right hand of the
      Most High."
11 I will remember the deeds of the
      LORD;
   yes, I will remember your miracles
      of long ago.
12 I will meditate on all your works
   and consider all your mighty deeds.

13 Your ways, O God, are holy.
   What god is so great as our God?
14 You are the God who performs
      miracles;
   you display your power among the
      peoples.
15 With your mighty arm you redeemed
      your people,
   the descendants of Jacob and
      Joseph.   *Selah*

16 The waters saw you, O God,
   the waters saw you and writhed;
   the very depths were convulsed.
17 The clouds poured down water,
   the skies resounded with thunder;
   your arrows flashed back and forth.
18 Your thunder was heard in the
      whirlwind,
   your lightning lit up the world;
   the earth trembled and quaked.
19 Your path led through the sea,
   your way through the mighty
      waters,
   though your footprints were not
      seen.
20 You led your people like a flock
   by the hand of Moses and Aaron.

a Title: Probably a literary or musical term

Psalm

 78

A *maskil*[a] of Asaph.

1 O my people, hear my teaching;
   listen to the words of my mouth.
2 I will open my mouth in parables,
   I will utter hidden things, things
      from of old—
3 what we have heard and known,
   what our fathers have told us.
4 We will not hide them from their
      children;
   we will tell the next generation
   the praiseworthy deeds of the LORD,
   his power, and the wonders he has
      done.
5 He decreed statutes for Jacob
   and established the law in Israel,
   which he commanded our forefathers
   to teach their children,
6 so the next generation would know
      them,
   even the children yet to be born,
   and they in turn would tell their
      children.
7 Then they would put their trust in
      God
   and would not forget his deeds
   but would keep his commands.
8 They would not be like their
      forefathers—
   a stubborn and rebellious
      generation,
   whose hearts were not loyal to God,
   whose spirits were not faithful to
      him.

9 The men of Ephraim, though armed
      with bows,
   turned back on the day of battle;
10 they did not keep God's covenant
   and refused to live by his law.
11 They forgot what he had done,
   the wonders he had shown them.
12 He did miracles in the sight of their
      fathers
   in the land of Egypt, in the region
      of Zoan.
13 He divided the sea and led them
      through;
   he made the water stand firm like
      a wall.

14 He guided them with the cloud by
       day
     and with light from the fire all
       night.
15 He split the rocks in the desert
     and gave them water as abundant
       as the seas;
16 he brought streams out of a rocky
       crag
     and made water flow down like
       rivers.

17 But they continued to sin against
       him,
     rebelling in the desert against the
       Most High.
18 They willfully put God to the test
     by demanding the food they
       craved.
19 They spoke against God, saying,
     "Can God spread a table in the
       desert?
20 When he struck the rock, water
       gushed out,
     and streams flowed abundantly.
   But can he also give us food?
     Can he supply meat for his
       people?"
21 When the LORD heard them, he was
       very angry;
     his fire broke out against Jacob,
     and his wrath rose against Israel,
22 for they did not believe in God
     or trust in his deliverance.
23 Yet he gave a command to the skies
       above
     and opened the doors of the
       heavens;
24 he rained down manna for the people
       to eat,
     he gave them the grain of heaven.
25 Men ate the bread of angels;
     he sent them all the food they
       could eat.
26 He let loose the east wind from the
       heavens
     and led forth the south wind by his
       power.
27 He rained meat down on them like
       dust,
     flying birds like sand on the
       seashore.
28 He made them come down inside
       their camp,
     all around their tents.
29 They ate till they had more than
       enough,

for he had given them what they
       craved.
30 But before they turned from the food
       they craved,
     even while it was still in their
       mouths,
31 God's anger rose against them;
     he put to death the sturdiest
       among them,
     cutting down the young men of
       Israel.

32 In spite of all this, they kept on
       sinning;
     in spite of his wonders, they did
       not believe.
33 So he ended their days in futility
     and their years in terror.
34 Whenever God slew them, they
       would seek him;
     they eagerly turned to him again.
35 They remembered that God was their
       Rock,
     that God Most High was their
       Redeemer.
36 But then they would flatter him with
       their mouths,
     lying to him with their tongues;
37 their hearts were not loyal to him,
     they were not faithful to his
       covenant.
38 Yet he was merciful;
     he forgave their iniquities
     and did not destroy them.
   Time after time he restrained his
       anger
     and did not stir up his full wrath.
39 He remembered that they were but
       flesh,
     a passing breeze that does not
       return.

40 How often they rebelled against him
       in the desert
     and grieved him in the wasteland!
41 Again and again they put God to the
       test;
     they vexed the Holy One of Israel.
42 They did not remember his power—
     the day he redeemed them from
       the oppressor,
43 the day he displayed his miraculous
       signs in Egypt,
     his wonders in the region of Zoan.
44 He turned their rivers to blood;
     they could not drink from their
       streams.

45 He sent swarms of flies that
    devoured them,
    and frogs that devastated them.
46 He gave their crops to the
    grasshopper,
    their produce to the locust.
47 He destroyed their vines with hail
    and their sycamore-figs with sleet.
48 He gave over their cattle to the hail,
    their livestock to bolts of lightning.
49 He unleashed against them his hot
    anger,
    his wrath, indignation and
    hostility—
    a band of destroying angels.
50 He prepared a path for his anger;
    he did not spare them from death
    but gave them over to the plague.
51 He struck down all the firstborn of
    Egypt,
    the firstfruits of manhood in the
    tents of Ham.
52 But he brought his people out like a
    flock;
    he led them like sheep through the
    desert.
53 He guided them safely, so they were
    unafraid;
    but the sea engulfed their enemies.
54 Thus he brought them to the border
    of his holy land,
    to the hill country his right hand
    had taken.
55 He drove out nations before them
    and allotted their lands to them as
    an inheritance;
    he settled the tribes of Israel in
    their homes.

56 But they put God to the test
    and rebelled against the Most
    High;
    they did not keep his statutes.
57 Like their fathers they were disloyal
    and faithless,
    as unreliable as a faulty bow.
58 They angered him with their high
    places;
    they aroused his jealousy with
    their idols.
59 When God heard them, he was very
    angry;
    he rejected Israel completely.
60 He abandoned the tabernacle of
    Shiloh,
    the tent he had set up among men.

61 He sent the ark of his might into
    captivity,
    his splendor into the hands of the
    enemy.
62 He gave his people over to the sword;
    he was very angry with his
    inheritance.
63 Fire consumed their young men,
    and their maidens had no wedding
    songs;
64 their priests were put to the sword,
    and their widows could not weep.
65 Then the Lord awoke as from sleep,
    as a man wakes from the stupor of
    wine.
66 He beat back his enemies;
    he put them to everlasting shame.
67 Then he rejected the tents of Joseph,
    he did not choose the tribe of
    Ephraim;
68 but he chose the tribe of Judah,
    Mount Zion, which he loved.
69 He built his sanctuary like the
    heights,
    like the earth that he established
    forever.
70 He chose David his servant
    and took him from the sheep pens;
71 from tending the sheep he brought
    him
    to be the shepherd of his people
    Jacob,
    of Israel his inheritance.
72 And David shepherded them with
    integrity of heart;
    with skillful hands he led them.

Psalm

A psalm of Asaph.

1 O God, the nations have invaded
    your inheritance;
    they have defiled your holy temple,
    they have reduced Jerusalem to
    rubble.
2 They have given the dead bodies of
    your servants
    as food to the birds of the air,
    the flesh of your saints to the
    beasts of the earth.
3 They have poured out blood like
    water
    all around Jerusalem,

and there is no one to bury the dead.
4 We are objects of reproach to our
    neighbors,
  of scorn and derision to those
    around us.

5 How long, O LORD? Will you be
    angry forever?
  How long will your jealousy burn
    like fire?
6 Pour out your wrath on the nations
    that do not acknowledge you,
  on the kingdoms
    that do not call on your name;
7 for they have devoured Jacob
  and destroyed his homeland.
8 Do not hold against us the sins of the
    fathers;
  may your mercy come quickly to
    meet us,
  for we are in desperate need.

9 Help us, O God our Savior,
    for the glory of your name;
  deliver us and forgive our sins
    for your name's sake.
10 Why should the nations say,
    "Where is their God?"
  Before our eyes, make known among
    the nations
  that you avenge the outpoured
    blood of your servants.
11 May the groans of the prisoners come
    before you;
  by the strength of your arm
  preserve those condemned to die.

12 Pay back into the laps of our
    neighbors seven times
  the reproach they have hurled at
    you, O Lord.
13 Then we your people, the sheep of
    your pasture,
  will praise you forever;
  from generation to generation
    we will recount your praise.

Psalm
80

For the director of music. To the tune of
"The Lilies of the Covenant." Of Asaph.
A psalm.

1 Hear us, O Shepherd of Israel,
  you who lead Joseph like a flock;
  you who sit enthroned between the
    cherubim, shine forth
2 before Ephraim, Benjamin and
    Manasseh.
  Awaken your might;
    come and save us.

3 Restore us, O God;
  make your face shine upon us,
  that we may be saved.

4 O LORD God Almighty,
  how long will your anger smolder
    against the prayers of your people?
5 You have fed them with the bread of
    tears;
  you have made them drink tears by
    the bowlful.
6 You have made us a source of
    contention to our neighbors,
  and our enemies mock us.

7 Restore us, O God Almighty;
  make your face shine upon us,
  that we may be saved.

8 You brought a vine out of Egypt;
  you drove out the nations and
    planted it.
9 You cleared the ground for it,
  and it took root and filled the land.
10 The mountains were covered with its
    shade,
  the mighty cedars with its
    branches.
11 It sent out its boughs to the Sea, *a*
  its shoots as far as the River. *b*

12 Why have you broken down its walls
  so that all who pass by pick its
    grapes?
13 Boars from the forest ravage it
  and the creatures of the field feed
    on it.
14 Return to us, O God Almighty!
  Look down from heaven and see!
  Watch over this vine,
15 the root your right hand has
    planted,
  the son *c* you have raised up for
    yourself.

16 Your vine is cut down, it is burned
    with fire;
  at your rebuke your people perish.
17 Let your hand rest on the man at
    your right hand,

a 11 Probably the Mediterranean   *b 11* That is, the Euphrates   *c 15* Or *branch*

the son of man you have raised up
    for yourself.
¹⁸ Then we will not turn away from you;
    revive us, and we will call on your
    name.
¹⁹ Restore us, O LORD God Almighty;
    make your face shine upon us,
    that we may be saved.

Psalm

For the director of music. According to
    gittith.ᵃ Of Asaph.

¹ Sing for joy to God our strength;
    shout aloud to the God of Jacob!
² Begin the music, strike the
        tambourine,
    play the melodious harp and lyre.
³ Sound the ram's horn at the New
        Moon,
    and when the moon is full, on the
        day of our Feast;
⁴ this is a decree for Israel,
    an ordinance of the God of Jacob.
⁵ He established it as a statute for
        Joseph
    when he went out against Egypt,
    where we heard a language we did
        not understand.ᵇ

⁶ He says, "I removed the burden from
    their shoulders;
    their hands were set free from the
        basket.
⁷ In your distress you called and I
        rescued you,
    I answered you out of a
        thundercloud;
    I tested you at the waters of
        Meribah.   *Selah*

⁸ "Hear, O my people, and I will warn
        you—
    if you would but listen to me,
        O Israel!
⁹ You shall have no foreign god among
        you;
    you shall not bow down to an alien
        god.
¹⁰ I am the LORD your God,
    who brought you up out of Egypt.

Open wide your mouth and I will
    fill it.
¹¹ "But my people would not listen to
        me;
    Israel would not submit to me.
¹² So I gave them over to their stubborn
        hearts
    to follow their own devices.

¹³ "If my people would but listen to me,
    if Israel would follow my ways,
¹⁴ how quickly would I subdue their
        enemies
    and turn my hand against their
        foes!
¹⁵ Those who hate the LORD would
        cringe before him,
    and their punishment would last
        forever.
¹⁶ But you would be fed with the finest
        of wheat;
    with honey from the rock I would
        satisfy you."

Psalm

A psalm of Asaph.

¹ God presides in the great assembly;
    he gives judgment among the
    "gods":

² "How long will youᶜ defend the
        unjust
    and show partiality to the wicked?
                        Selah
³ Defend the cause of the weak and
        fatherless;
    maintain the rights of the poor and
        oppressed.
⁴ Rescue the weak and needy;
    deliver them from the hand of the
        wicked.

⁵ "They know nothing, they
        understand nothing.
    They walk about in darkness;
    all the foundations of the earth are
        shaken.

⁶ "I said, 'You are "gods";
    you are all sons of the Most High.'
⁷ But you will die like mere men;
    you will fall like every other ruler."

ᵃ Title: Probably a musical term   ᵇ 5 Or / *and we heard a voice we had not known*   ᶜ 2 The Hebrew
is plural.

8 Rise up, O God, judge the earth,
for all the nations are your
inheritance.

Psalm 83

A song. A psalm of Asaph.

1 O God, do not keep silent;
be not quiet, O God, be not still.
2 See how your enemies are astir,
how your foes rear their heads.
3 With cunning they conspire against
your people;
they plot against those you
cherish.
4 "Come," they say, "let us destroy
them as a nation,
that the name of Israel be
remembered no more."

5 With one mind they plot together;
they form an alliance against
you—
6 the tents of Edom and the
Ishmaelites,
of Moab and the Hagrites,
7 Gebal,[a] Ammon and Amalek,
Philistia, with the people of Tyre.
8 Even Assyria has joined them
to lend strength to the descendants
of Lot.   Selah

9 Do to them as you did to Midian,
as you did to Sisera and Jabin at the
river Kishon,
10 who perished at Endor
and became like refuse on the
ground.
11 Make their nobles like Oreb and
Zeeb,
all their princes like Zebah and
Zalmunna,
12 who said, "Let us take possession
of the pasturelands of God."

13 Make them like tumbleweed, O my
God,
like chaff before the wind.
14 As fire consumes the forest
or a flame sets the mountains
ablaze,
15 so pursue them with your tempest
and terrify them with your storm.
16 Cover their faces with shame

so that men will seek your name,
O LORD.

17 May they ever be ashamed and
dismayed;
may they perish in disgrace.
18 Let them know that you, whose
name is the LORD—
that you alone are the Most High
over all the earth.

Psalm 84

For the director of music. According to
gittith.[b] Of the Sons of Korah. A psalm.

1 How lovely is your dwelling place,
O LORD Almighty!
2 My soul yearns, even faints,
for the courts of the LORD;
my heart and my flesh cry out
for the living God.

3 Even the sparrow has found a home,
and the swallow a nest for herself,
where she may have her young—
a place near your altar,
O LORD Almighty, my King and
my God.
4 Blessed are those who dwell in your
house;
they are ever praising you.   Selah

5 Blessed are those whose strength is in
you,
who have set their hearts on
pilgrimage.
6 As they pass through the Valley of
Baca,
they make it a place of springs;
the autumn rains also cover it with
pools.[c]
7 They go from strength to strength,
till each appears before God in
Zion.

8 Hear my prayer, O LORD God
Almighty;
listen to me, O God of Jacob.   Selah
9 Look upon our shield,[d] O God;
look with favor on your anointed
one.

10 Better is one day in your courts
than a thousand elsewhere;

---

[a] 7 That is, Byblos   [b] Title: Probably a musical term   [c] 6 Or *blessings*   [d] 9 Or *sovereign*

I would rather be a doorkeeper in the
   house of my God
   than dwell in the tents of the
      wicked.
¹¹ For the LORD God is a sun and shield;
   the LORD bestows favor and honor;
   no good thing does he withhold
      from those whose walk is
      blameless.

¹² O LORD Almighty,
   blessed is the man who trusts in
      you.

Psalm

 85

For the director of music. Of the Sons of
   Korah. A psalm.

¹ You showed favor to your land,
   O LORD;
   you restored the fortunes of Jacob.
² You forgave the iniquity of your
   people
   and covered all their sins.   *Selah*
³ You set aside all your wrath
   and turned from your fierce anger.

⁴ Restore us again, O God our Savior,
   and put away your displeasure
      toward us.
⁵ Will you be angry with us forever?
   Will you prolong your anger
      through all generations?
⁶ Will you not revive us again,
   that your people may rejoice in
      you?
⁷ Show us your unfailing love, O LORD,
   and grant us your salvation.

⁸ I will listen to what God the LORD
   will say;
   he promises peace to his people,
      his saints—
   but let them not return to folly.
⁹ Surely his salvation is near those
   who fear him,
   that his glory may dwell in our
      land.

¹⁰ Love and faithfulness meet together;
   righteousness and peace kiss each
      other.
¹¹ Faithfulness springs forth from the
   earth,

and righteousness looks down from
   heaven.
¹² The LORD will indeed give what is
   good,
   and our land will yield its harvest.
¹³ Righteousness goes before him
   and prepares the way for his steps.

Psalm

 86

A prayer of David.

¹ Hear, O LORD, and answer me,
   for I am poor and needy.
² Guard my life, for I am devoted to
   you.
   You are my God; save your servant
      who trusts in you.
³ Have mercy on me, O Lord,
   for I call to you all day long.
⁴ Bring joy to your servant,
   for to you, O Lord,
   I lift up my soul.

⁵ You are forgiving and good, O Lord,
   abounding in love to all who call to
      you.
⁶ Hear my prayer, O LORD;
   listen to my cry for mercy.
⁷ In the day of my trouble I will call to
   you,
   for you will answer me.

⁸ Among the gods there is none like
   you, O Lord;
   no deeds can compare with yours.
⁹ All the nations you have made
   will come and worship before you,
      O Lord;
   they will bring glory to your name.
¹⁰ For you are great and do marvelous
   deeds;
   you alone are God.

¹¹ Teach me your way, O LORD,
   and I will walk in your truth;
   give me an undivided heart,
      that I may fear your name.
¹² I will praise you, O Lord my God,
   with all my heart;
   I will glorify your name forever.
¹³ For great is your love toward me;
   you have delivered me from the
      depths of the grave.ᵃ

ᵃ 13 Hebrew *Sheol*

14 The arrogant are attacking me,
  O God;
  a band of ruthless men seeks my
    life—
  men without regard for you.
15 But you, O Lord, are a compassionate
    and gracious God,
  slow to anger, abounding in love
    and faithfulness.
16 Turn to me and have mercy on me;
  grant your strength to your
    servant
  and save the son of your
    maidservant.ᵃ
17 Give me a sign of your goodness,
  that my enemies may see it and be
    put to shame,
  for you, O Lord, have helped me
    and comforted me.

Psalm 87

Of the Sons of Korah. A psalm. A song.

1 He has set his foundation on the holy
    mountain;
2   the Lord loves the gates of Zion
  more than all the dwellings of
    Jacob.
3 Glorious things are said of you,
  O city of God: Selah
4 "I will record Rahabᵇ and Babylon
  among those who acknowledge
    me—
  Philistia too, and Tyre, along with
    Cushᶜ—
  and will say, 'Thisᵈ one was born
    in Zion.' "
5 Indeed, of Zion it will be said,
  "This one and that one were born
    in her,
  and the Most High himself will
    establish her."
6 The Lord will write in the register of
    the peoples:
  "This one was born in Zion."
                            Selah
7 As they make music they will sing,
  "All my fountains are in you."

Psalm 88

A song. A psalm of the Sons of Korah. For the
director of music. According to mahalath
leannoth.ᵉ A maskilᶠ of Heman the Ezrahite.

1 O Lord, the God who saves me,
  day and night I cry out before you.
2 May my prayer come before you;
  turn your ear to my cry.

3 For my soul is full of trouble
  and my life draws near the grave.ᵍ
4 I am counted among those who go
    down to the pit;
  I am like a man without strength.
5 I am set apart with the dead,
  like the slain who lie in the grave,
  whom you remember no more,
  who are cut off from your care.

6 You have put me in the lowest pit,
  in the darkest depths.
7 Your wrath lies heavily upon me;
  you have overwhelmed me with all
    your waves.   Selah
8 You have taken from me my closest
    friends
  and have made me repulsive to
    them.
  I am confined and cannot escape;
9   my eyes are dim with grief.

  I call to you, O Lord, every day;
  I spread out my hands to you.
10 Do you show your wonders to the
    dead?
  Do those who are dead rise up and
    praise you?   Selah
11 Is your love declared in the grave,
  your faithfulness in Destructionʰ?
12 Are your wonders known in the place
    of darkness,
  or your righteous deeds in the land
    of oblivion?

13 But I cry to you for help, O Lord;
  in the morning my prayer comes
    before you.
14 Why, O Lord, do you reject me
  and hide your face from me?
15 From my youth I have been afflicted
    and close to death;

ᵃ 16 Or save your faithful son   ᵇ 4 A poetic name for Egypt   ᶜ 4 That is, the upper Nile region
ᵈ 4 Or "O Rahab and Babylon, / Philistia, Tyre and Cush, / I will record concerning those who
acknowledge me: / 'This   ᵉ Title: Possibly a tune, "The Suffering of Affliction"   ᶠ Title: Probably a
literary or musical term   ᵍ 3 Hebrew Sheol   ʰ 11 Hebrew Abaddon

I have suffered your terrors and am
in despair.
16 Your wrath has swept over me;
your terrors have destroyed me.
17 All day long they surround me like a
flood;
they have completely engulfed me.
18 You have taken my companions and
loved ones from me;
the darkness is my closest friend.

Psalm

 89

A *maskil*[a] of Ethan the Ezrahite.

1 I will sing of the LORD's great love
forever;
with my mouth I will make your
faithfulness known through all
generations.
2 I will declare that your love stands
firm forever,
that you established your
faithfulness in heaven itself.

3 You said, "I have made a covenant
with my chosen one,
I have sworn to David my servant,
4 'I will establish your line forever
and make your throne firm
through all generations.' "
Selah

5 The heavens praise your wonders,
O LORD,
your faithfulness too, in the
assembly of the holy ones.
6 For who in the skies above can
compare with the LORD?
Who is like the LORD among the
heavenly beings?
7 In the council of the holy ones God is
greatly feared;
he is more awesome than all who
surround him.
8 O LORD God Almighty, who is like
you?
You are mighty, O LORD, and your
faithfulness surrounds you.

9 You rule over the surging sea;
when its waves mount up, you still
them.

10 You crushed Rahab like one of the
slain;
with your strong arm you scattered
your enemies.
11 The heavens are yours, and yours
also the earth;
you founded the world and all that
is in it.
12 You created the north and the south;
Tabor and Hermon sing for joy at
your name.
13 Your arm is endued with power;
your hand is strong, your right
hand exalted.

14 Righteousness and justice are the
foundation of your throne;
love and faithfulness go before you.
15 Blessed are those who have learned
to acclaim you,
who walk in the light of your
presence, O LORD.
16 They rejoice in your name all day
long;
they exult in your righteousness.
17 For you are their glory and strength,
and by your favor you exalt our
horn.[b]
18 Indeed, our shield[c] belongs to the
LORD,
our king to the Holy One of Israel.

19 Once you spoke in a vision,
to your faithful people you said:
"I have bestowed strength on a
warrior;
I have exalted a young man from
among the people.
20 I have found David my servant;
with my sacred oil I have anointed
him.
21 My hand will sustain him;
surely my arm will strengthen
him.
22 No enemy will subject him to
tribute;
no wicked man will oppress him.
23 I will crush his foes before him
and strike down his adversaries.
24 My faithful love will be with him,
and through my name his horn[d]
will be exalted.
25 I will set his hand over the sea,
his right hand over the rivers.

---

a Title: Probably a literary or musical term   *b 17 Horn* here symbolizes strong one.   *c 18* Or
sovereign   *d 24 Horn* here symbolizes strength.

26 He will call out to me, 'You are my
    Father,
  my God, the Rock my Savior.'
27 I will also appoint him my firstborn,
  the most exalted of the kings of the
    earth.
28 I will maintain my love to him
    forever,
  and my covenant with him will
    never fail.
29 I will establish his line forever,
  his throne as long as the heavens
    endure.

30 "If his sons forsake my law
  and do not follow my statutes,
31 if they violate my decrees
  and fail to keep my commands,
32 I will punish their sin with the rod,
  their iniquity with flogging;
33 but I will not take my love from
    him,
  nor will I ever betray my
    faithfulness.
34 I will not violate my covenant
  or alter what my lips have uttered.
35 Once for all, I have sworn by my
    holiness—
  and I will not lie to David—
36 that his line will continue forever
  and his throne endure before me
    like the sun;
37 it will be established forever like the
    moon,
  the faithful witness in the sky."
                      Selah

38 But you have rejected, you have
    spurned,
  you have been very angry with
    your anointed one.
39 You have renounced the covenant
    with your servant
  and have defiled his crown in the
    dust.
40 You have broken through all his
    walls
  and reduced his strongholds to
    ruins.
41 All who pass by have plundered him;
  he has become the scorn of his
    neighbors.
42 You have exalted the right hand of
    his foes;
  you have made all his enemies
    rejoice.

43 You have turned back the edge of his
    sword
  and have not supported him in
    battle.
44 You have put an end to his splendor
  and cast his throne to the ground.
45 You have cut short the days of his
    youth;
  you have covered him with a
    mantle of shame.   *Selah*

46 How long, O LORD? Will you hide
    yourself forever?
  How long will your wrath burn
    like fire?
47 Remember how fleeting is my life.
  For what futility you have created
    all men!
48 What man can live and not see
    death,
  or save himself from the power of
    the grave*a*?   *Selah*
49 O Lord, where is your former great
    love,
  which in your faithfulness you
    swore to David?
50 Remember, Lord, how your servant
  has*b* been mocked,
  how I bear in my heart the taunts
    of all the nations,
51 the taunts with which your enemies
    have mocked, O LORD,
  with which they have mocked
    every step of your anointed
    one.

52 Praise be to the LORD forever!
  Amen and Amen.

BOOK IV
Psalms 90–106

Psalm

A prayer of Moses the man of God.

1 Lord, you have been our dwelling
    place
  throughout all generations.
2 Before the mountains were born
  or you brought forth the earth and
    the world,

---

a 48 Hebrew *Sheol*   *b 50* Or *your servants have*

THE FIRST SIX VERSES OF THE NINETIETH PSALM
Robert Burns

VERSE: Psalm 90:1   **PASSAGE:** Psalm 90:1–6

 thou, the first, the greatest friend
    Of all the human race!
Whose strong right hand has ever been
    Their stay and dwelling place!

Before the mountains heaved their heads
    Beneath thy forming hand,
Before this ponderous globe itself
    Arose at thy command:

That power which raised and still upholds
    This universal frame,
From countless, unbeginning time
    Was ever still the same.

Those mighty periods of years
    Which seem to us so vast,
Appear no more before thy sight
    Than yesterday that's past.

Thou giv'st the word; thy creature, man,
    Is to existence brought;
Again thou sayst, 'Ye sons of men,
    'Return ye into nought!'

Thou layest them with all their cares
    In everlasting sleep;
As with a flood thou tak'st them off
    With overwhelming sweep.

They flourish like the morning flower
    In beauty's pride arrayed;
But long ere night cut down it lies
    All withered and decayed.

ADDITIONAL SCRIPTURE READING:
Deuteronomy 33:27; Psalm 91:1

Go to page 675 for your next devotional reading.

1700   1900

from everlasting to everlasting you
are God.

³ You turn men back to dust,
saying, "Return to dust, O sons of
men."
⁴ For a thousand years in your sight
are like a day that has just gone by,
or like a watch in the night.
⁵ You sweep men away in the sleep of
death;
they are like the new grass of the
morning—
⁶ though in the morning it springs up
new,
by evening it is dry and withered.

⁷ We are consumed by your anger
and terrified by your indignation.
⁸ You have set our iniquities before
you,
our secret sins in the light of your
presence.
⁹ All our days pass away under your
wrath;
we finish our years with a moan.
¹⁰ The length of our days is seventy
years—
or eighty, if we have the strength;
yet their span ᵃ is but trouble and
sorrow,
for they quickly pass, and we fly
away.
¹¹ Who knows the power of your anger?
For your wrath is as great as the
fear that is due you.
¹² Teach us to number our days aright,
that we may gain a heart of
wisdom.

¹³ Relent, O LORD! How long will it be?
Have compassion on your servants.
¹⁴ Satisfy us in the morning with your
unfailing love,
that we may sing for joy and be
glad all our days.
¹⁵ Make us glad for as many days as you
have afflicted us,
for as many years as we have seen
trouble.
¹⁶ May your deeds be shown to your
servants,
your splendor to their children.

¹⁷ May the favor ᵇ of the Lord our God
rest upon us;

establish the work of our hands for
us—
yes, establish the work of our
hands.

Psalm

91

¹ He who dwells in the shelter of the
Most High
will rest in the shadow of the
Almighty. ᶜ
² I will say ᵈ of the LORD, "He is my
refuge and my fortress,
my God, in whom I trust."

³ Surely he will save you from the
fowler's snare
and from the deadly pestilence.
⁴ He will cover you with his feathers,
and under his wings you will find
refuge;
his faithfulness will be your shield
and rampart.
⁵ You will not fear the terror of night,
nor the arrow that flies by day,
⁶ nor the pestilence that stalks in the
darkness,
nor the plague that destroys at
midday.
⁷ A thousand may fall at your side,
ten thousand at your right hand,
but it will not come near you.
⁸ You will only observe with your
eyes
and see the punishment of the
wicked.

⁹ If you make the Most High your
dwelling—
even the LORD, who is my refuge—
¹⁰ then no harm will befall you,
no disaster will come near your
tent.
¹¹ For he will command his angels
concerning you
to guard you in all your ways;
¹² they will lift you up in their hands,
so that you will not strike your
foot against a stone.
¹³ You will tread upon the lion and the
cobra;
you will trample the great lion and
the serpent.

ᵃ 10 Or *yet the best of them*   ᵇ 17 Or *beauty*   ᶜ 1 Hebrew *Shaddai*   ᵈ 2 Or *He says*

14 "Because he loves me," says the
   LORD, "I will rescue him;
   I will protect him, for he
      acknowledges my name.
15 He will call upon me, and I will
      answer him;
   I will be with him in trouble,
   I will deliver him and honor him.
16 With long life will I satisfy him
   and show him my salvation."

Psalm

 92

A psalm. A song. For the Sabbath day.

1 It is good to praise the LORD
   and make music to your name,
      O Most High,
2 to proclaim your love in the
      morning
   and your faithfulness at night,
3 to the music of the ten-stringed lyre
   and the melody of the harp.

4 For you make me glad by your deeds,
      O LORD;
   I sing for joy at the works of your
      hands.
5 How great are your works, O LORD,
   how profound your thoughts!
6 The senseless man does not know,
   fools do not understand,
7 that though the wicked spring up like
      grass
   and all evildoers flourish,
   they will be forever destroyed.

8 But you, O LORD, are exalted forever.

9 For surely your enemies, O LORD,
   surely your enemies will perish;
   all evildoers will be scattered.
10 You have exalted my horn[a] like that
      of a wild ox;
   fine oils have been poured upon
      me.
11 My eyes have seen the defeat of my
      adversaries;
   my ears have heard the rout of my
      wicked foes.

12 The righteous will flourish like a
      palm tree,
   they will grow like a cedar of
      Lebanon;

13 planted in the house of the LORD,
   they will flourish in the courts of
      our God.
14 They will still bear fruit in old age,
   they will stay fresh and green,
15 proclaiming, "The LORD is upright;
   he is my Rock, and there is no
      wickedness in him."

Psalm

 93

1 The LORD reigns, he is robed in
      majesty;
   the LORD is robed in majesty
   and is armed with strength.
   The world is firmly established;
   it cannot be moved.
2 Your throne was established long ago;
   you are from all eternity.

3 The seas have lifted up, O LORD,
   the seas have lifted up their voice;
   the seas have lifted up their
      pounding waves.
4 Mightier than the thunder of the
      great waters,
   mightier than the breakers of the
      sea—
   the LORD on high is mighty.

5 Your statutes stand firm;
   holiness adorns your house
   for endless days, O LORD.

Psalm

94

1 O LORD, the God who avenges,
   O God who avenges, shine forth.
2 Rise up, O Judge of the earth;
   pay back to the proud what they
      deserve.
3 How long will the wicked, O LORD,
   how long will the wicked be
      jubilant?

4 They pour out arrogant words;
   all the evildoers are full of
      boasting.
5 They crush your people, O LORD;
   they oppress your inheritance.
6 They slay the widow and the alien;
   they murder the fatherless.

---

a 10 Horn here symbolizes strength.

7 They say, "The LORD does not see;
　the God of Jacob pays no heed."

8 Take heed, you senseless ones among
　　the people;
　you fools, when will you become
　　wise?
9 Does he who implanted the ear not
　　hear?
　Does he who formed the eye not
　　see?
10 Does he who disciplines nations not
　　punish?
　Does he who teaches man lack
　　knowledge?
11 The LORD knows the thoughts of
　　man;
　he knows that they are futile.

12 Blessed is the man you discipline,
　　O LORD,
　the man you teach from your law;
13 you grant him relief from days of
　　trouble,
　till a pit is dug for the wicked.
14 For the LORD will not reject his
　　people;
　he will never forsake his
　　inheritance.
15 Judgment will again be founded on
　　righteousness,
　and all the upright in heart will
　　follow it.

16 Who will rise up for me against the
　　wicked?
　Who will take a stand for me
　　against evildoers?
17 Unless the LORD had given me help,
　I would soon have dwelt in the
　　silence of death.
18 When I said, "My foot is slipping,"
　your love, O LORD, supported me.
19 When anxiety was great within me,
　your consolation brought joy to my
　　soul.

20 Can a corrupt throne be allied with
　　you—
　one that brings on misery by its
　　decrees?
21 They band together against the
　　righteous
　and condemn the innocent to
　　death.
22 But the LORD has become my
　　fortress,

and my God the rock in whom I
　　take refuge.
23 He will repay them for their sins
　and destroy them for their
　　wickedness;
　the LORD our God will destroy
　　them.

Psalm

1 Come, let us sing for joy to the LORD;
　let us shout aloud to the Rock of
　　our salvation.
2 Let us come before him with
　　thanksgiving
　and extol him with music and
　　song.

3 For the LORD is the great God,
　the great King above all gods.
4 In his hand are the depths of the
　　earth,
　and the mountain peaks belong to
　　him.
5 The sea is his, for he made it,
　and his hands formed the dry
　　land.

6 Come, let us bow down in worship,
　let us kneel before the LORD our
　　Maker;
7 for he is our God
　and we are the people of his
　　pasture,
　the flock under his care.

　Today, if you hear his voice,
8 　do not harden your hearts as you
　　did at Meribah,a
　as you did that day at Massahb in
　　the desert,
9 where your fathers tested and tried
　　me,
　though they had seen what I did.
10 For forty years I was angry with that
　　generation;
　I said, "They are a people whose
　　hearts go astray,
　and they have not known my
　　ways."
11 So I declared on oath in my anger,
　"They shall never enter my rest."

---

a 8 *Meribah* means *quarreling*.　　b 8 *Massah* means *testing*.

Psalm

96

1 Sing to the LORD a new song;
  sing to the LORD, all the earth.
2 Sing to the LORD, praise his name;
  proclaim his salvation day after
  day.
3 Declare his glory among the nations,
  his marvelous deeds among all
  peoples.

4 For great is the LORD and most
  worthy of praise;
  he is to be feared above all gods.
5 For all the gods of the nations are
  idols,
  but the LORD made the heavens.
6 Splendor and majesty are before him;
  strength and glory are in his
  sanctuary.

7 Ascribe to the LORD, O families of
  nations,
  ascribe to the LORD glory and
  strength.
8 Ascribe to the LORD the glory due his
  name;
  bring an offering and come into his
  courts.
9 Worship the LORD in the splendor of
  his*a* holiness;
  tremble before him, all the earth.

10 Say among the nations, "The LORD
   reigns."
   The world is firmly established, it
   cannot be moved;
   he will judge the peoples with
   equity.
11 Let the heavens rejoice, let the earth
   be glad;
   let the sea resound, and all that is
   in it;
12 let the fields be jubilant, and
   everything in them.
   Then all the trees of the forest will
   sing for joy;
13 they will sing before the LORD, for
   he comes,
   he comes to judge the earth.
   He will judge the world in
   righteousness
   and the peoples in his truth.

a 9 Or LORD with the splendor of

Psalm

97

1 The LORD reigns, let the earth be glad;
  let the distant shores rejoice.

2 Clouds and thick darkness surround
  him;
  righteousness and justice are the
  foundation of his throne.
3 Fire goes before him
  and consumes his foes on every
  side.
4 His lightning lights up the world;
  the earth sees and trembles.
5 The mountains melt like wax before
  the LORD,
  before the Lord of all the earth.
6 The heavens proclaim his
  righteousness,
  and all the peoples see his glory.

7 All who worship images are put to
  shame,
  those who boast in idols—
  worship him, all you gods!

8 Zion hears and rejoices
  and the villages of Judah are glad
  because of your judgments,
  O LORD.
9 For you, O LORD, are the Most High
  over all the earth;
  you are exalted far above all gods.

10 Let those who love the LORD hate evil,
   for he guards the lives of his
   faithful ones
   and delivers them from the hand of
   the wicked.
11 Light is shed upon the righteous
   and joy on the upright in heart.
12 Rejoice in the LORD, you who are
   righteous,
   and praise his holy name.

Psalm

98

A psalm.

1 Sing to the LORD a new song,
  for he has done marvelous things;
  his right hand and his holy arm
  have worked salvation for him.

2 The LORD has made his salvation known
    and revealed his righteousness to the nations.
3 He has remembered his love
    and his faithfulness to the house of Israel;
  all the ends of the earth have seen
    the salvation of our God.

4 Shout for joy to the LORD, all the earth,
    burst into jubilant song with music;
5 make music to the LORD with the harp,
    with the harp and the sound of singing,
6 with trumpets and the blast of the ram's horn—
    shout for joy before the LORD, the King.

7 Let the sea resound, and everything in it,
    the world, and all who live in it.
8 Let the rivers clap their hands,
    let the mountains sing together for joy;
9 let them sing before the LORD,
    for he comes to judge the earth.
  He will judge the world in righteousness
    and the peoples with equity.

Psalm 99

1 The LORD reigns,
    let the nations tremble;
  he sits enthroned between the cherubim,
    let the earth shake.
2 Great is the LORD in Zion;
    he is exalted over all the nations.
3 Let them praise your great and awesome name—
    he is holy.

4 The King is mighty, he loves justice—
    you have established equity;
  in Jacob you have done
    what is just and right.
5 Exalt the LORD our God
    and worship at his footstool;
    he is holy.

6 Moses and Aaron were among his priests,
    Samuel was among those who called on his name;
  they called on the LORD
    and he answered them.
7 He spoke to them from the pillar of cloud;
    they kept his statutes and the decrees he gave them.

8 O LORD our God,
    you answered them;
  you were to Israel[a] a forgiving God,
    though you punished their misdeeds.[b]
9 Exalt the LORD our God
    and worship at his holy mountain,
    for the LORD our God is holy.

Psalm 100

A psalm. For giving thanks.

1 Shout for joy to the LORD, all the earth.
2   Worship the LORD with gladness;
    come before him with joyful songs.
3 Know that the LORD is God.
    It is he who made us, and we are his[c];
  we are his people, the sheep of his pasture.

4 Enter his gates with thanksgiving
    and his courts with praise;
  give thanks to him and praise his name.
5 For the LORD is good and his love endures forever;
    his faithfulness continues through all generations.

Psalm 101

Of David. A psalm.

1 I will sing of your love and justice;
    to you, O LORD, I will sing praise.
2 I will be careful to lead a blameless life—
    when will you come to me?

---

a 8 Hebrew *them*   b 8 Or / *an avenger of the wrongs done to them*   c 3 Or *and not we ourselves*

I will walk in my house
    with blameless heart.
³ I will set before my eyes
    no vile thing.

The deeds of faithless men I hate;
    they will not cling to me.
⁴ Men of perverse heart shall be far
      from me;
    I will have nothing to do with evil.

⁵ Whoever slanders his neighbor in
      secret,
    him will I put to silence;
whoever has haughty eyes and a
      proud heart,
    him will I not endure.

⁶ My eyes will be on the faithful in the
      land,
    that they may dwell with me;
he whose walk is blameless
    will minister to me.

⁷ No one who practices deceit
    will dwell in my house;
no one who speaks falsely
    will stand in my presence.

⁸ Every morning I will put to silence
    all the wicked in the land;
I will cut off every evildoer
    from the city of the LORD.

Psalm

102

A prayer of an afflicted man. When he is faint
and pours out his lament before the LORD.

¹ Hear my prayer, O LORD;
    let my cry for help come to you.
² Do not hide your face from me
    when I am in distress.
Turn your ear to me;
    when I call, answer me quickly.

³ For my days vanish like smoke;
    my bones burn like glowing
      embers.
⁴ My heart is blighted and withered
    like grass;
    I forget to eat my food.
⁵ Because of my loud groaning
    I am reduced to skin and bones.
⁶ I am like a desert owl,
    like an owl among the ruins.

⁷ I lie awake; I have become
    like a bird alone on a roof.
⁸ All day long my enemies taunt me;
    those who rail against me use my
      name as a curse.
⁹ For I eat ashes as my food
    and mingle my drink with tears
¹⁰ because of your great wrath,
    for you have taken me up and
      thrown me aside.
¹¹ My days are like the evening shadow;
    I wither away like grass.

¹² But you, O LORD, sit enthroned
      forever;
    your renown endures through all
      generations.
¹³ You will arise and have compassion
      on Zion,
    for it is time to show favor to her;
    the appointed time has come.
¹⁴ For her stones are dear to your
      servants;
    her very dust moves them to pity.
¹⁵ The nations will fear the name of the
      LORD,
    all the kings of the earth will
      revere your glory.
¹⁶ For the LORD will rebuild Zion
    and appear in his glory.
¹⁷ He will respond to the prayer of the
      destitute;
    he will not despise their plea.

¹⁸ Let this be written for a future
      generation,
    that a people not yet created may
      praise the LORD:
¹⁹ "The LORD looked down from his
      sanctuary on high,
    from heaven he viewed the earth,
²⁰ to hear the groans of the prisoners
    and release those condemned to
      death."
²¹ So the name of the LORD will be
      declared in Zion
    and his praise in Jerusalem
²² when the peoples and the kingdoms
    assemble to worship the LORD.

²³ In the course of my life*ᵃ* he broke my
      strength;
    he cut short my days.
²⁴ So I said:
    "Do not take me away, O my God,
      in the midst of my days;

ᵃ 23 Or *By his power*

your years go on through all
   generations.
25 In the beginning you laid the
   foundations of the earth,
   and the heavens are the work of
   your hands.
26 They will perish, but you remain;
   they will all wear out like a
   garment.
Like clothing you will change them
   and they will be discarded.
27 But you remain the same,
   and your years will never end.
28 The children of your servants will
   live in your presence;
   their descendants will be
   established before you."

Psalm

103

Of David.

1 Praise the LORD, O my soul;
   all my inmost being, praise his
   holy name.
2 Praise the LORD, O my soul,
   and forget not all his benefits—
3 who forgives all your sins
   and heals all your diseases,
4 who redeems your life from the pit
   and crowns you with love and
   compassion,
5 who satisfies your desires with good
   things
   so that your youth is renewed like
   the eagle's.

6 The LORD works righteousness
   and justice for all the oppressed.

7 He made known his ways to Moses,
   his deeds to the people of Israel:
8 The LORD is compassionate and
   gracious,
   slow to anger, abounding in love.
9 He will not always accuse,
   nor will he harbor his anger
   forever;
10 he does not treat us as our sins
   deserve
   or repay us according to our
   iniquities.
11 For as high as the heavens are above
   the earth,
   so great is his love for those who
   fear him;

12 as far as the east is from the west,
   so far has he removed our
   transgressions from us.
13 As a father has compassion on his
   children,
   so the LORD has compassion on
   those who fear him;
14 for he knows how we are formed,
   he remembers that we are dust.
15 As for man, his days are like grass,
   he flourishes like a flower of the
   field;
16 the wind blows over it and it is gone,
   and its place remembers it no
   more.
17 But from everlasting to everlasting
   the LORD's love is with those who
   fear him,
   and his righteousness with their
   children's children—
18 with those who keep his covenant
   and remember to obey his precepts.

19 The LORD has established his throne
   in heaven,
   and his kingdom rules over all.

20 Praise the LORD, you his angels,
   you mighty ones who do his
   bidding,
   who obey his word.
21 Praise the LORD, all his heavenly
   hosts,
   you his servants who do his will.
22 Praise the LORD, all his works
   everywhere in his dominion.

Praise the LORD, O my soul.

Psalm
104

1 Praise the LORD, O my soul.

O LORD my God, you are very great;
   you are clothed with splendor and
   majesty.
2 He wraps himself in light as with a
   garment;
   he stretches out the heavens like a
   tent
3   and lays the beams of his upper
   chambers on their waters.
He makes the clouds his chariot
   and rides on the wings of the wind.

4 He makes winds his messengers,[a]
  flames of fire his servants.

5 He set the earth on its foundations;
  it can never be moved.
6 You covered it with the deep as with
    a garment;
  the waters stood above the
    mountains.
7 But at your rebuke the waters fled,
  at the sound of your thunder they
    took to flight;
8 they flowed over the mountains,
  they went down into the valleys,
  to the place you assigned for them.
9 You set a boundary they cannot cross;
  never again will they cover the
    earth.

10 He makes springs pour water into the
    ravines;
  it flows between the mountains.
11 They give water to all the beasts of
    the field;
  the wild donkeys quench their
    thirst.
12 The birds of the air nest by the waters;
  they sing among the branches.
13 He waters the mountains from his
    upper chambers;
  the earth is satisfied by the fruit of
    his work.
14 He makes grass grow for the cattle,
  and plants for man to cultivate—
  bringing forth food from the earth:
15 wine that gladdens the heart of man,
  oil to make his face shine,
  and bread that sustains his heart.
16 The trees of the LORD are well
    watered,
  the cedars of Lebanon that he
    planted.
17 There the birds make their nests;
  the stork has its home in the pine
    trees.
18 The high mountains belong to the
    wild goats;
  the crags are a refuge for the
    coneys.[b]
19 The moon marks off the seasons,
  and the sun knows when to go
    down.
20 You bring darkness, it becomes night,
  and all the beasts of the forest
    prowl.

21 The lions roar for their prey
  and seek their food from God.
22 The sun rises, and they steal away;
  they return and lie down in their
    dens.
23 Then man goes out to his work,
  to his labor until evening.

24 How many are your works, O LORD!
  In wisdom you made them all;
  the earth is full of your creatures.
25 There is the sea, vast and spacious,
  teeming with creatures beyond
    number—
  living things both large and small.
26 There the ships go to and fro,
  and the leviathan, which you
    formed to frolic there.

27 These all look to you
  to give them their food at the
    proper time.
28 When you give it to them,
  they gather it up;
  when you open your hand,
  they are satisfied with good things.
29 When you hide your face,
  they are terrified;
  when you take away their breath,
  they die and return to the dust.
30 When you send your Spirit,
  they are created,
  and you renew the face of the earth.

31 May the glory of the LORD endure
    forever;
  may the LORD rejoice in his works—
32 he who looks at the earth, and it
    trembles,
  who touches the mountains, and
    they smoke.

33 I will sing to the LORD all my life;
  I will sing praise to my God as long
    as I live.

CONTEMPLATION IS LIKE SLEEP IN THE ARMS OF
GOD.   —*Bernard of Clairvaux*

---

34 May my meditation be pleasing to
    him,
  as I rejoice in the LORD.
35 But may sinners vanish from the
    earth
  and the wicked be no more.

---

a 4 Or *angels*   b 18 That is, the hyrax or rock badger

Praise the LORD, O my soul.
Praise the LORD.[a]

Psalm

105

¹ Give thanks to the LORD, call on his
name;
make known among the nations
what he has done.
² Sing to him, sing praise to him;
tell of all his wonderful acts.
³ Glory in his holy name;
let the hearts of those who seek
the LORD rejoice.
⁴ Look to the LORD and his strength;
seek his face always.

⁵ Remember the wonders he has done,
his miracles, and the judgments he
pronounced,
⁶ O descendants of Abraham his
servant,
O sons of Jacob, his chosen ones.
⁷ He is the LORD our God;
his judgments are in all the earth.

⁸ He remembers his covenant forever,
the word he commanded, for a
thousand generations,
⁹ the covenant he made with
Abraham,
the oath he swore to Isaac.
¹⁰ He confirmed it to Jacob as a decree,
to Israel as an everlasting covenant:
¹¹ "To you I will give the land of
Canaan
as the portion you will inherit."

¹² When they were but few in number,
few indeed, and strangers in it,
¹³ they wandered from nation to nation,
from one kingdom to another.
¹⁴ He allowed no one to oppress them;
for their sake he rebuked kings:
¹⁵ "Do not touch my anointed ones;
do my prophets no harm."

¹⁶ He called down famine on the land
and destroyed all their supplies of
food;
¹⁷ and he sent a man before them—
Joseph, sold as a slave.
¹⁸ They bruised his feet with shackles,
his neck was put in irons,

¹⁹ till what he foretold came to pass,
till the word of the LORD proved
him true.
²⁰ The king sent and released him,
the ruler of peoples set him free.
²¹ He made him master of his
household,
ruler over all he possessed,
²² to instruct his princes as he pleased
and teach his elders wisdom.

²³ Then Israel entered Egypt;
Jacob lived as an alien in the land
of Ham.
²⁴ The LORD made his people very
fruitful;
he made them too numerous for
their foes,
²⁵ whose hearts he turned to hate his
people,
to conspire against his servants.
²⁶ He sent Moses his servant,
and Aaron, whom he had chosen.
²⁷ They performed his miraculous signs
among them,
his wonders in the land of Ham.
²⁸ He sent darkness and made the land
dark—
for had they not rebelled against
his words?
²⁹ He turned their waters into blood,
causing their fish to die.
³⁰ Their land teemed with frogs,
which went up into the bedrooms
of their rulers.
³¹ He spoke, and there came swarms of
flies,
and gnats throughout their
country.
³² He turned their rain into hail,
with lightning throughout their
land;
³³ he struck down their vines and fig
trees
and shattered the trees of their
country.
³⁴ He spoke, and the locusts came,
grasshoppers without number;
³⁵ they ate up every green thing in their
land,
ate up the produce of their soil.
³⁶ Then he struck down all the firstborn
in their land,
the firstfruits of all their manhood.

a 35 Hebrew *Hallelu Yah*; in the Septuagint this line stands at the beginning of Psalm 105.

WEEKEND

DOST THOU NOT CARE?
Christina Rossetti

VERSE: Psalm 95:7 **PASSAGE:** Psalm 95:1–7

 love and love not: Lord, it breaks my heart
　　To love and not to love.
Thou veiled within thy glory, gone apart
　　Into thy shrine which is above,
Dost thou not love me, Lord, or care
　　For this mine ill?—
I love thee here or there
　　I will accept thy broken heart, lie still.

Lord, it was well with me in time gone by
　　That cometh not again,
When I was fresh and cheerful, who but I?
　　I fresh, I cheerful: worn with pain
Now, out of sight and out of heart;
　　O Lord, how long?—
I watch thee as thou art,
　　I will accept thy fainting heart, be strong.

'Lie still,' 'be strong,' today: but, Lord, to-morrow,
　　What of to-morrow, Lord?
Shall there be rest from toil, be truce from sorrow,
　　Be living green upon the sward
Now but a barren grave to me,
　　Be joy for sorrow?—
Did I not die for thee?
　　Do I not live for thee? Leave Me to-morrow.

ADDITIONAL SCRIPTURE READING:
Psalm 42:1–2; Romans 7:15,19–25

Go to page 685 for your next devotional reading.

1700　1900

37 He brought out Israel, laden with
    silver and gold,
  and from among their tribes no one
    faltered.
38 Egypt was glad when they left,
  because dread of Israel had fallen
    on them.
39 He spread out a cloud as a covering,
  and a fire to give light at night.
40 They asked, and he brought them
    quail
  and satisfied them with the bread
    of heaven.
41 He opened the rock, and water
    gushed out;
  like a river it flowed in the desert.

42 For he remembered his holy promise
  given to his servant Abraham.
43 He brought out his people with
    rejoicing,
  his chosen ones with shouts of joy;
44 he gave them the lands of the
    nations,
  and they fell heir to what others
    had toiled for—
45 that they might keep his precepts
  and observe his laws.

Praise the LORD.[a]

Psalm

106

1 Praise the LORD.[b]

Give thanks to the LORD, for he is
    good;
  his love endures forever.
2 Who can proclaim the mighty acts of
    the LORD
  or fully declare his praise?
3 Blessed are they who maintain
    justice,
  who constantly do what is right.
4 Remember me, O LORD, when you
    show favor to your people,
  come to my aid when you save
    them,
5 that I may enjoy the prosperity of
    your chosen ones,
  that I may share in the joy of your
    nation
  and join your inheritance in giving
    praise.

6 We have sinned, even as our fathers
    did;
  we have done wrong and acted
    wickedly.
7 When our fathers were in Egypt,
  they gave no thought to your
    miracles;
  they did not remember your many
    kindnesses,
  and they rebelled by the sea, the
    Red Sea.[c]
8 Yet he saved them for his name's
    sake,
  to make his mighty power known.
9 He rebuked the Red Sea, and it dried
    up;
  he led them through the depths as
    through a desert.
10 He saved them from the hand of the
    foe;
  from the hand of the enemy he
    redeemed them.
11 The waters covered their adversaries;
  not one of them survived.
12 Then they believed his promises
  and sang his praise.

13 But they soon forgot what he had
    done
  and did not wait for his counsel.
14 In the desert they gave in to their
    craving;
  in the wasteland they put God to
    the test.
15 So he gave them what they asked
    for,
  but sent a wasting disease upon
    them.

16 In the camp they grew envious of
    Moses
  and of Aaron, who was consecrated
    to the LORD.
17 The earth opened up and swallowed
    Dathan;
  it buried the company of Abiram.
18 Fire blazed among their followers;
  a flame consumed the wicked.

19 At Horeb they made a calf
  and worshiped an idol cast from
    metal.
20 They exchanged their Glory
  for an image of a bull, which eats
    grass.

---

a 45 Hebrew *Hallelu Yah*   *b* 1 Hebrew *Hallelu Yah;* also in verse 48   *c* 7 Hebrew *Yam Suph;* that is,
Sea of Reeds; also in verses 9 and 22

21 They forgot the God who saved
        them,
    who had done great things in
        Egypt,
22 miracles in the land of Ham
    and awesome deeds by the Red Sea.
23 So he said he would destroy them—
    had not Moses, his chosen one,
    stood in the breach before him
        to keep his wrath from destroying
        them.

24 Then they despised the pleasant land;
    they did not believe his promise.
25 They grumbled in their tents
    and did not obey the LORD.
26 So he swore to them with uplifted
        hand
    that he would make them fall in
        the desert,
27 make their descendants fall among
        the nations
    and scatter them throughout the
        lands.

28 They yoked themselves to the Baal of
        Peor
    and ate sacrifices offered to lifeless
        gods;
29 they provoked the LORD to anger by
        their wicked deeds,
    and a plague broke out among
        them.
30 But Phinehas stood up and
        intervened,
    and the plague was checked.
31 This was credited to him as
        righteousness
    for endless generations to come.

32 By the waters of Meribah they
        angered the LORD,
    and trouble came to Moses because
        of them;
33 for they rebelled against the Spirit of
        God,
    and rash words came from Moses'
        lips.ᵃ

34 They did not destroy the peoples
    as the LORD had commanded them,
35 but they mingled with the nations
    and adopted their customs.
36 They worshiped their idols,
    which became a snare to them.
37 They sacrificed their sons
    and their daughters to demons.

38 They shed innocent blood,
    the blood of their sons and
        daughters,
    whom they sacrificed to the idols of
        Canaan,
    and the land was desecrated by
        their blood.
39 They defiled themselves by what
        they did;
    by their deeds they prostituted
        themselves.

40 Therefore the LORD was angry with
        his people
    and abhorred his inheritance.
41 He handed them over to the nations,
    and their foes ruled over them.
42 Their enemies oppressed them
    and subjected them to their power.
43 Many times he delivered them,
    but they were bent on rebellion
    and they wasted away in their sin.

44 But he took note of their distress
    when he heard their cry;
45 for their sake he remembered his
        covenant
    and out of his great love he relented.
46 He caused them to be pitied
    by all who held them captive.

47 Save us, O LORD our God,
    and gather us from the nations,
    that we may give thanks to your holy
        name
    and glory in your praise.

48 Praise be to the LORD, the God of
        Israel,
    from everlasting to everlasting.
    Let all the people say, "Amen!"

Praise the LORD.

BOOK V
Psalms 107–150
Psalm

107

1 Give thanks to the LORD, for he is
        good;
    his love endures forever.
2 Let the redeemed of the LORD say
        this—

ᵃ 33 Or *against his spirit, / and rash words came from his lips*

those he redeemed from the hand
of the foe,
3 those he gathered from the lands,
from east and west, from north and
south.a

4 Some wandered in desert wastelands,
finding no way to a city where they
could settle.
5 They were hungry and thirsty,
and their lives ebbed away.
6 Then they cried out to the LORD in
their trouble,
and he delivered them from their
distress.
7 He led them by a straight way
to a city where they could settle.
8 Let them give thanks to the LORD for
his unfailing love
and his wonderful deeds for men,
9 for he satisfies the thirsty
and fills the hungry with good
things.

10 Some sat in darkness and the deepest
gloom,
prisoners suffering in iron chains,
11 for they had rebelled against the
words of God
and despised the counsel of the
Most High.
12 So he subjected them to bitter labor;
they stumbled, and there was no
one to help.
13 Then they cried to the LORD in their
trouble,
and he saved them from their
distress.
14 He brought them out of darkness and
the deepest gloom
and broke away their chains.
15 Let them give thanks to the LORD for
his unfailing love
and his wonderful deeds for men,
16 for he breaks down gates of bronze
and cuts through bars of iron.

17 Some became fools through their
rebellious ways
and suffered affliction because of
their iniquities.
18 They loathed all food
and drew near the gates of death.
19 Then they cried to the LORD in their
trouble,

and he saved them from their
distress.
20 He sent forth his word and healed
them;
he rescued them from the grave.
21 Let them give thanks to the LORD for
his unfailing love
and his wonderful deeds for men.
22 Let them sacrifice thank offerings
and tell of his works with songs of
joy.

23 Others went out on the sea in ships;
they were merchants on the
mighty waters.
24 They saw the works of the LORD,
his wonderful deeds in the deep.
25 For he spoke and stirred up a tempest
that lifted high the waves.
26 They mounted up to the heavens and
went down to the depths;
in their peril their courage melted
away.
27 They reeled and staggered like
drunken men;
they were at their wits' end.
28 Then they cried out to the LORD in
their trouble,
and he brought them out of their
distress.
29 He stilled the storm to a whisper;
the waves of the sea were hushed.
30 They were glad when it grew calm,
and he guided them to their desired
haven.
31 Let them give thanks to the LORD for
his unfailing love
and his wonderful deeds for men.
32 Let them exalt him in the assembly
of the people
and praise him in the council of
the elders.

33 He turned rivers into a desert,
flowing springs into thirsty ground,
34 and fruitful land into a salt waste,
because of the wickedness of those
who lived there.
35 He turned the desert into pools of
water
and the parched ground into
flowing springs;
36 there he brought the hungry to live,
and they founded a city where they
could settle.

a 3 Hebrew north and the sea

37 They sowed fields and planted
   vineyards
   that yielded a fruitful harvest;
38 he blessed them, and their numbers
   greatly increased,
   and he did not let their herds
   diminish.
39 Then their numbers decreased, and
   they were humbled
   by oppression, calamity and
   sorrow;
40 he who pours contempt on nobles
   made them wander in a trackless
   waste.
41 But he lifted the needy out of their
   affliction
   and increased their families like
   flocks.
42 The upright see and rejoice,
   but all the wicked shut their
   mouths.

43 Whoever is wise, let him heed these
   things
   and consider the great love of the
   LORD.

Psalm

108

A song. A psalm of David.

1 My heart is steadfast, O God;
   I will sing and make music with all
   my soul.
2 Awake, harp and lyre!
   I will awaken the dawn.
3 I will praise you, O LORD, among the
   nations;
   I will sing of you among the
   peoples.
4 For great is your love, higher than the
   heavens;
   your faithfulness reaches to the
   skies.
5 Be exalted, O God, above the
   heavens,
   and let your glory be over all the
   earth.

6 Save us and help us with your right
   hand,
   that those you love may be
   delivered.

7 God has spoken from his sanctuary:
   "In triumph I will parcel out
   Shechem
   and measure off the Valley of
   Succoth.
8 Gilead is mine, Manasseh is mine;
   Ephraim is my helmet,
   Judah my scepter.
9 Moab is my washbasin,
   upon Edom I toss my sandal;
   over Philistia I shout in triumph."
10 Who will bring me to the fortified
   city?
   Who will lead me to Edom?
11 Is it not you, O God, you who have
   rejected us
   and no longer go out with our
   armies?
12 Give us aid against the enemy,
   for the help of man is worthless.
13 With God we will gain the victory,
   and he will trample down our
   enemies.

Psalm

 109

For the director of music. Of David. A psalm.

1 O God, whom I praise,
   do not remain silent,
2 for wicked and deceitful men
   have opened their mouths against
   me;
   they have spoken against me with
   lying tongues.
3 With words of hatred they surround
   me;
   they attack me without cause.
4 In return for my friendship they
   accuse me,
   but I am a man of prayer.
5 They repay me evil for good,
   and hatred for my friendship.

6 Appoint[a] an evil man[b] to oppose him;
   let an accuser[c] stand at his right
   hand.
7 When he is tried, let him be found
   guilty,
   and may his prayers condemn him.
8 May his days be few;
   may another take his place of
   leadership.

---

a 6 Or ⌐They say:⌐ "Appoint (with quotation marks at the end of verse 19)   b 6 Or the Evil One
c 6 Or let Satan

⁹ May his children be fatherless
and his wife a widow.
¹⁰ May his children be wandering
beggars;
may they be driven*a* from their
ruined homes.
¹¹ May a creditor seize all he has;
may strangers plunder the fruits of
his labor.
¹² May no one extend kindness to him
or take pity on his fatherless
children.
¹³ May his descendants be cut off,
their names blotted out from the
next generation.
¹⁴ May the iniquity of his fathers be
remembered before the Lord;
may the sin of his mother never be
blotted out.
¹⁵ May their sins always remain before
the Lord,
that he may cut off the memory of
them from the earth.

¹⁶ For he never thought of doing a
kindness,
but hounded to death the poor
and the needy and the
brokenhearted.
¹⁷ He loved to pronounce a curse—
may it*b* come on him;
he found no pleasure in blessing—
may it be*c* far from him.
¹⁸ He wore cursing as his garment;
it entered into his body like
water,
into his bones like oil.
¹⁹ May it be like a cloak wrapped about
him,
like a belt tied forever around
him.
²⁰ May this be the Lord's payment to
my accusers,
to those who speak evil of me.

²¹ But you, O Sovereign Lord,
deal well with me for your name's
sake;
out of the goodness of your love,
deliver me.
²² For I am poor and needy,
and my heart is wounded within
me.
²³ I fade away like an evening shadow;
I am shaken off like a locust.

²⁴ My knees give way from fasting;
my body is thin and gaunt.
²⁵ I am an object of scorn to my
accusers;
when they see me, they shake their
heads.

²⁶ Help me, O Lord my God;
save me in accordance with your
love.
²⁷ Let them know that it is your hand,
that you, O Lord, have done it.
²⁸ They may curse, but you will bless;
when they attack they will be put
to shame,
but your servant will rejoice.
²⁹ My accusers will be clothed with
disgrace
and wrapped in shame as in a
cloak.

³⁰ With my mouth I will greatly extol
the Lord;
in the great throng I will praise
him.
³¹ For he stands at the right hand of the
needy one,
to save his life from those who
condemn him.

Psalm

Of David. A psalm.

¹ The Lord says to my Lord:
"Sit at my right hand
until I make your enemies
a footstool for your feet."

² The Lord will extend your mighty
scepter from Zion;
you will rule in the midst of your
enemies.
³ Your troops will be willing
on your day of battle.
Arrayed in holy majesty,
from the womb of the dawn
you will receive the dew of your
youth.*d*

⁴ The Lord has sworn
and will not change his mind:
"You are a priest forever,
in the order of Melchizedek."

---

a 10 Septuagint; Hebrew *sought*   *b* 17 Or *curse, / and it has*   *c* 17 Or *blessing, / and it is*
d 3 Or / *your young men will come to you like the dew*

5 The Lord is at your right hand;
  he will crush kings on the day of
    his wrath.
6 He will judge the nations, heaping up
    the dead
  and crushing the rulers of the
    whole earth.
7 He will drink from a brook beside the
    way*a*;
  therefore he will lift up his head.

Psalm
 111*b*

1 Praise the LORD.*c*

I will extol the LORD with all my
    heart
  in the council of the upright and in
    the assembly.

2 Great are the works of the LORD;
  they are pondered by all who
    delight in them.
3 Glorious and majestic are his deeds,
  and his righteousness endures
    forever.
4 He has caused his wonders to be
    remembered;
  the LORD is gracious and
    compassionate.
5 He provides food for those who fear
    him;
  he remembers his covenant
    forever.
6 He has shown his people the power
    of his works,
  giving them the lands of other
    nations.
7 The works of his hands are faithful
    and just;
  all his precepts are trustworthy.
8 They are steadfast for ever and ever,
  done in faithfulness and
    uprightness.
9 He provided redemption for his
    people;
  he ordained his covenant forever—
  holy and awesome is his name.

10 The fear of the LORD is the beginning
    of wisdom;

all who follow his precepts have
    good understanding.
To him belongs eternal praise.

Psalm
112*b*

1 Praise the LORD.*c*

Blessed is the man who fears the
    LORD,
  who finds great delight in his
    commands.

2 His children will be mighty in the
    land;
  the generation of the upright will
    be blessed.
3 Wealth and riches are in his house,
  and his righteousness endures
    forever.
4 Even in darkness light dawns for the
    upright,
  for the gracious and compassionate
    and righteous man.*d*
5 Good will come to him who is
    generous and lends freely,
  who conducts his affairs with
    justice.
6 Surely he will never be shaken;
  a righteous man will be
    remembered forever.
7 He will have no fear of bad news;
  his heart is steadfast, trusting in
    the LORD.
8 His heart is secure, he will have no
    fear;
  in the end he will look in triumph
    on his foes.
9 He has scattered abroad his gifts to
    the poor,
  his righteousness endures forever;
  his horn*e* will be lifted high in
    honor.

10 The wicked man will see and be
    vexed,
  he will gnash his teeth and waste
    away;
  the longings of the wicked will
    come to nothing.

---

a 7 Or / *The One who grants succession will set him in authority*   *b* This psalm is an acrostic poem,
the lines of which begin with the successive letters of the Hebrew alphabet.   *c* 1 Hebrew *Hallelu Yah*
d 4 Or / *for the* LORD *is gracious and compassionate and righteous*   *e* 9 *Horn* here symbolizes dignity.

Psalm

113

[1] Praise the LORD.[a]

Praise, O servants of the LORD,
  praise the name of the LORD.
[2] Let the name of the LORD be praised,
  both now and forevermore.
[3] From the rising of the sun to the
    place where it sets,
  the name of the LORD is to be
    praised.

[4] The LORD is exalted over all the
    nations,
  his glory above the heavens.
[5] Who is like the LORD our God,
  the One who sits enthroned on
    high,
[6] who stoops down to look
  on the heavens and the earth?

[7] He raises the poor from the dust
  and lifts the needy from the ash
    heap;
[8] he seats them with princes,
  with the princes of their people.
[9] He settles the barren woman in her
    home
  as a happy mother of children.

Praise the LORD.

Psalm

114

[1] When Israel came out of Egypt,
  the house of Jacob from a people of
    foreign tongue,
[2] Judah became God's sanctuary,
  Israel his dominion.

[3] The sea looked and fled,
  the Jordan turned back;
[4] the mountains skipped like rams,
  the hills like lambs.

[5] Why was it, O sea, that you fled,
  O Jordan, that you turned back,
[6] you mountains, that you skipped like
    rams,
  you hills, like lambs?

[7] Tremble, O earth, at the presence of
    the Lord,

at the presence of the God of Jacob,
[8] who turned the rock into a pool,
  the hard rock into springs of water.

Psalm

115

[1] Not to us, O LORD, not to us
  but to your name be the glory,
  because of your love and
    faithfulness.

[2] Why do the nations say,
  "Where is their God?"
[3] Our God is in heaven;
  he does whatever pleases him.
[4] But their idols are silver and gold,
  made by the hands of men.
[5] They have mouths, but cannot speak,
  eyes, but they cannot see;
[6] they have ears, but cannot hear,
  noses, but they cannot smell;
[7] they have hands, but cannot feel,
  feet, but they cannot walk;
  nor can they utter a sound with
    their throats.
[8] Those who make them will be like
    them,
  and so will all who trust in them.

[9] O house of Israel, trust in the LORD—
  he is their help and shield.
[10] O house of Aaron, trust in the
    LORD—
  he is their help and shield.
[11] You who fear him, trust in the
    LORD—
  he is their help and shield.

[12] The LORD remembers us and will
    bless us:
  He will bless the house of Israel,
  he will bless the house of Aaron,
[13] he will bless those who fear the
    LORD—
  small and great alike.

[14] May the LORD make you increase,
  both you and your children.
[15] May you be blessed by the LORD,
  the Maker of heaven and earth.

[16] The highest heavens belong to the
    LORD,
  but the earth he has given to man.

---

[a] 1 Hebrew *Hallelu Yah*; also in verse 9

17 It is not the dead who praise the
  LORD,
  those who go down to silence;
18 it is we who extol the LORD,
  both now and forevermore.

Praise the LORD. *a*

Psalm

116

1 I love the LORD, for he heard my
    voice;
  he heard my cry for mercy.
2 Because he turned his ear to me,
  I will call on him as long as I live.

3 The cords of death entangled me,
  the anguish of the grave *b* came
    upon me;
  I was overcome by trouble and
    sorrow.
4 Then I called on the name of the
  LORD:
  "O LORD, save me!"

5 The LORD is gracious and righteous;
  our God is full of compassion.
6 The LORD protects the simplehearted;
  when I was in great need, he saved
    me.

7 Be at rest once more, O my soul,
  for the LORD has been good to you.

8 For you, O LORD, have delivered my
    soul from death,
  my eyes from tears,
  my feet from stumbling,
9 that I may walk before the LORD
  in the land of the living.
10 I believed; therefore *c* I said,
  "I am greatly afflicted."
11 And in my dismay I said,
  "All men are liars."

12 How can I repay the LORD
  for all his goodness to me?
13 I will lift up the cup of salvation
  and call on the name of the LORD.
14 I will fulfill my vows to the LORD
  in the presence of all his people.

15 Precious in the sight of the LORD
  is the death of his saints.
16 O LORD, truly I am your servant;

I am your servant, the son of your
  maidservant *d*;
  you have freed me from my chains.

17 I will sacrifice a thank offering to you
  and call on the name of the LORD.
18 I will fulfill my vows to the LORD
  in the presence of all his people,
19 in the courts of the house of the
  LORD—
  in your midst, O Jerusalem.

Praise the LORD. *a*

Psalm

117

1 Praise the LORD, all you nations;
  extol him, all you peoples.
2 For great is his love toward us,
  and the faithfulness of the LORD
    endures forever.

Praise the LORD. *a*

Psalm

118

1 Give thanks to the LORD, for he is
    good;
  his love endures forever.

2 Let Israel say:
  "His love endures forever."
3 Let the house of Aaron say:
  "His love endures forever."
4 Let those who fear the LORD say:
  "His love endures forever."

5 In my anguish I cried to the LORD,
  and he answered by setting me
    free.
6 The LORD is with me; I will not be
    afraid.
  What can man do to me?
7 The LORD is with me; he is my
    helper.
  I will look in triumph on my
    enemies.

8 It is better to take refuge in the LORD
  than to trust in man.
9 It is better to take refuge in the LORD
  than to trust in princes.

a 18,19, 2 Hebrew *Hallelu Yah*   *b 3* Hebrew *Sheol*   *c 10* Or *believed even when*   *d 16* Or *servant,*
your faithful son

¹⁰All the nations surrounded me,
    but in the name of the LORD I cut
        them off.
¹¹They surrounded me on every side,
    but in the name of the LORD I cut
        them off.
¹²They swarmed around me like bees,
    but they died out as quickly as
        burning thorns;
    in the name of the LORD I cut them
        off.
¹³I was pushed back and about to fall,
    but the LORD helped me.
¹⁴The LORD is my strength and my
        song;
    he has become my salvation.

¹⁵Shouts of joy and victory
    resound in the tents of the
        righteous:
  "The LORD's right hand has done
        mighty things!
¹⁶   The LORD's right hand is lifted
        high;
    the LORD's right hand has done
        mighty things!"

¹⁷I will not die but live,
    and will proclaim what the LORD
        has done.
¹⁸The LORD has chastened me severely,
    but he has not given me over to
        death.

¹⁹Open for me the gates of
        righteousness;
    I will enter and give thanks to the
        LORD.
²⁰This is the gate of the LORD
    through which the righteous may
        enter.
²¹I will give you thanks, for you
        answered me;
    you have become my salvation.

²²The stone the builders rejected
    has become the capstone;
²³the LORD has done this,
    and it is marvelous in our eyes.
²⁴This is the day the LORD has made;
    let us rejoice and be glad in it.

²⁵O LORD, save us;
    O LORD, grant us success.
²⁶Blessed is he who comes in the name
    of the LORD.

From the house of the LORD we
        bless you.ᵃ
²⁷The LORD is God,
    and he has made his light shine
        upon us.
With boughs in hand, join in the
        festal procession
    upᵇ to the horns of the altar.

²⁸You are my God, and I will give you
        thanks;
    you are my God, and I will exalt
        you.

²⁹Give thanks to the LORD, for he is
        good;
    his love endures forever.

Psalm

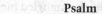

119ᶜ

א Aleph

¹Blessed are they whose ways are
        blameless,
    who walk according to the law of
        the LORD.
²Blessed are they who keep his
        statutes
    and seek him with all their heart.
³They do nothing wrong;
    they walk in his ways.
⁴You have laid down precepts
    that are to be fully obeyed.
⁵Oh, that my ways were steadfast
    in obeying your decrees!
⁶Then I would not be put to shame
    when I consider all your
        commands.
⁷I will praise you with an upright
        heart
    as I learn your righteous laws.
⁸I will obey your decrees;
    do not utterly forsake me.

ב Beth

⁹How can a young man keep his way
        pure?
    By living according to your word.
¹⁰I seek you with all my heart;
    do not let me stray from your
        commands.
¹¹I have hidden your word in my heart

ᵃ 26 The Hebrew is plural.   ᵇ 27 Or *Bind the festal sacrifice with ropes / and take it*   ᶜ This psalm is
an acrostic poem; the verses of each stanza begin with the same letter of the Hebrew alphabet.

that I might not sin against you.

12 Praise be to you, O LORD;
   teach me your decrees.

13 With my lips I recount
    all the laws that come from your
    mouth.

MONDAY

HYMN 15
Christopher Smart

VERSE: Psalm 119:11   **PASSAGE:** Psalm 119:9–16

guide my judgment and my taste,
    Sweet Spirit, author of the book
Of wonders, told in language chaste
    And plainness, not to be mistook.

O let me muse, and yet at sight
    The page admire, the page believe;
"Let there be light, and there was light,
    Let there be Paradise and Eve!"

Who his soul's rapture can refrain?
    At Joseph's ever-pleasing tale
Of marvels, the prodigious train,
    To Sinai's hill from Goshen's vale.

The psalmist and proverbial seer,
    And all the prophets sons of song,
Make all things precious, all things dear,
    And bear the brilliant word along.

O take the book from off the shelf,
    And con it meekly on thy knees;
Best panegyric on itself,
    And self-avouch'd to teach and please.

Respect, adore it heart and mind.
    How greatly sweet, how sweetly grand,
Who reads the most, is most refin'd,
    And polish'd by the Master's hand.

ADDITIONAL SCRIPTURE READING:
2 Timothy 3:16–17; Hebrews 4:12; 2 Peter 1:19–21

Go to page 691 for your next devotional reading.

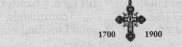

1700   1900

14 I rejoice in following your statutes
    as one rejoices in great riches.
15 I meditate on your precepts
    and consider your ways.
16 I delight in your decrees;
    I will not neglect your word.

ג Gimel

17 Do good to your servant, and I will
    live;
    I will obey your word.
18 Open my eyes that I may see
    wonderful things in your law.
19 I am a stranger on earth;
    do not hide your commands from
    me.
20 My soul is consumed with longing
    for your laws at all times.
21 You rebuke the arrogant, who are
    cursed
    and who stray from your
    commands.
22 Remove from me scorn and
    contempt,
    for I keep your statutes.
23 Though rulers sit together and
    slander me,
    your servant will meditate on your
    decrees.
24 Your statutes are my delight;
    they are my counselors.

ד Daleth

25 I am laid low in the dust;
    preserve my life according to your
    word.
26 I recounted my ways and you
    answered me;
    teach me your decrees.
27 Let me understand the teaching of
    your precepts;
    then I will meditate on your
    wonders.
28 My soul is weary with sorrow;
    strengthen me according to your
    word.
29 Keep me from deceitful ways;
    be gracious to me through your
    law.
30 I have chosen the way of truth;
    I have set my heart on your laws.
31 I hold fast to your statutes, O LORD;
    do not let me be put to shame.

32 I run in the path of your commands,
    for you have set my heart free.

ה He

33 Teach me, O LORD, to follow your
    decrees;
    then I will keep them to the end.
34 Give me understanding, and I will
    keep your law
    and obey it with all my heart.
35 Direct me in the path of your
    commands,
    for there I find delight.
36 Turn my heart toward your statutes
    and not toward selfish gain.
37 Turn my eyes away from worthless
    things;
    preserve my life according to your
    word.*a*
38 Fulfill your promise to your servant,
    so that you may be feared.
39 Take away the disgrace I dread,
    for your laws are good.
40 How I long for your precepts!
    Preserve my life in your
    righteousness.

ו Waw

41 May your unfailing love come to me,
    O LORD,
    your salvation according to your
    promise;
42 then I will answer the one who
    taunts me,
    for I trust in your word.
43 Do not snatch the word of truth from
    my mouth,
    for I have put my hope in your
    laws.
44 I will always obey your law,
    for ever and ever.
45 I will walk about in freedom,
    for I have sought out your precepts.
46 I will speak of your statutes before
    kings
    and will not be put to shame,
47 for I delight in your commands
    because I love them.
48 I lift up my hands to*b* your
    commands, which I love,
    and I meditate on your decrees.

a 37 Two manuscripts of the Masoretic Text and Dead Sea Scrolls; most manuscripts of the Masoretic
Text *life in your way*   *b* 48 Or *for*

ז Zayin

49 Remember your word to your
        servant,
    for you have given me hope.
50 My comfort in my suffering is this:
    Your promise preserves my life.
51 The arrogant mock me without
        restraint,
    but I do not turn from your law.
52 I remember your ancient laws,
        O LORD,
    and I find comfort in them.
53 Indignation grips me because of the
        wicked,
    who have forsaken your law.
54 Your decrees are the theme of my
        song
    wherever I lodge.
55 In the night I remember your name,
        O LORD,
    and I will keep your law.
56 This has been my practice:
    I obey your precepts.

ח Heth

57 You are my portion, O LORD;
    I have promised to obey your
        words.
58 I have sought your face with all my
        heart;
    be gracious to me according to
        your promise.
59 I have considered my ways
    and have turned my steps to your
        statutes.
60 I will hasten and not delay
    to obey your commands.
61 Though the wicked bind me with
        ropes,
    I will not forget your law.
62 At midnight I rise to give you thanks
    for your righteous laws.
63 I am a friend to all who fear you,
    to all who follow your precepts.
64 The earth is filled with your love,
        O LORD;
    teach me your decrees.

ט Teth

65 Do good to your servant
    according to your word, O LORD.
66 Teach me knowledge and good
        judgment,
    for I believe in your commands.
67 Before I was afflicted I went astray,

but now I obey your word.
68 You are good, and what you do is
        good;
    teach me your decrees.
69 Though the arrogant have smeared
        me with lies,
    I keep your precepts with all my
        heart.
70 Their hearts are callous and
        unfeeling,
    but I delight in your law.
71 It was good for me to be afflicted
    so that I might learn your decrees.
72 The law from your mouth is more
        precious to me
    than thousands of pieces of silver
        and gold.

י Yodh

73 Your hands made me and formed me;
    give me understanding to learn
        your commands.
74 May those who fear you rejoice when
        they see me,
    for I have put my hope in your
        word.
75 I know, O LORD, that your laws are
        righteous,
    and in faithfulness you have
        afflicted me.
76 May your unfailing love be my
        comfort,
    according to your promise to your
        servant.
77 Let your compassion come to me
        that I may live,
    for your law is my delight.
78 May the arrogant be put to shame for
        wronging me without cause;
    but I will meditate on your
        precepts.
79 May those who fear you turn to me,
    those who understand your
        statutes.
80 May my heart be blameless toward
        your decrees,
    that I may not be put to shame.

כ Kaph

81 My soul faints with longing for your
        salvation,
    but I have put my hope in your
        word.
82 My eyes fail, looking for your
        promise;

I say, "When will you comfort
　me?"
83 Though I am like a wineskin in the
　　smoke,
　I do not forget your decrees.
84 How long must your servant wait?
　When will you punish my
　　persecutors?
85 The arrogant dig pitfalls for me,
　contrary to your law.
86 All your commands are trustworthy;
　help me, for men persecute me
　　without cause.
87 They almost wiped me from the
　　earth,
　but I have not forsaken your
　　precepts.
88 Preserve my life according to your
　　love,
　and I will obey the statutes of your
　　mouth.

ל Lamedh

89 Your word, O LORD, is eternal;
　it stands firm in the heavens.
90 Your faithfulness continues through
　　all generations;
　you established the earth, and it
　　endures.
91 Your laws endure to this day,
　for all things serve you.
92 If your law had not been my delight,
　I would have perished in my
　　affliction.
93 I will never forget your precepts,
　for by them you have preserved my
　　life.
94 Save me, for I am yours;
　I have sought out your precepts.
95 The wicked are waiting to destroy
　　me,
　but I will ponder your statutes.
96 To all perfection I see a limit;
　but your commands are boundless.

מ Mem

97 Oh, how I love your law!
　I meditate on it all day long.
98 Your commands make me wiser
　　than my enemies,
　for they are ever with me.
99 I have more insight than all my
　　teachers,
　for I meditate on your statutes.
100 I have more understanding than the
　　elders,

for I obey your precepts.
101 I have kept my feet from every evil
　　path
　so that I might obey your word.
102 I have not departed from your laws,
　for you yourself have taught me.
103 How sweet are your words to my
　　taste,
　sweeter than honey to my mouth!
104 I gain understanding from your
　　precepts;
　therefore I hate every wrong path.

נ Nun

105 Your word is a lamp to my feet
　and a light for my path.

THE BIBLE IS GOD'S CHART FOR YOU TO STEER BY,
TO KEEP YOU FROM THE BOTTOM OF THE SEA,
AND TO SHOW YOU WHERE THE HARBOR IS, AND
HOW TO REACH IT WITHOUT RUNNING ON ROCKS
AND BARS.　　　　　—*Henry Ward Beecher*

---

106 I have taken an oath and
　　confirmed it,
　that I will follow your righteous
　　laws.
107 I have suffered much;
　preserve my life, O LORD,
　　according to your word.
108 Accept, O LORD, the willing praise
　　of my mouth,
　and teach me your laws.
109 Though I constantly take my life in
　　my hands,
　I will not forget your law.
110 The wicked have set a snare for me,
　but I have not strayed from your
　　precepts.
111 Your statutes are my heritage
　　forever;
　they are the joy of my heart.
112 My heart is set on keeping your
　　decrees
　to the very end.

ס Samekh

113 I hate double-minded men,
　but I love your law.
114 You are my refuge and my shield;
　I have put my hope in your word.
115 Away from me, you evildoers,
　that I may keep the commands of
　　my God!

116 Sustain me according to your
      promise, and I will live;
    do not let my hopes be dashed.
117 Uphold me, and I will be delivered;
    I will always have regard for your
      decrees.
118 You reject all who stray from your
      decrees,
    for their deceitfulness is in vain.
119 All the wicked of the earth you
      discard like dross;
    therefore I love your statutes.
120 My flesh trembles in fear of you;
    I stand in awe of your laws.

ע Ayin

121 I have done what is righteous and
      just;
    do not leave me to my oppressors.
122 Ensure your servant's well-being;
    let not the arrogant oppress me.
123 My eyes fail, looking for your
      salvation,
    looking for your righteous promise.
124 Deal with your servant according to
      your love
    and teach me your decrees.
125 I am your servant; give me
      discernment
    that I may understand your
      statutes.
126 It is time for you to act, O LORD;
    your law is being broken.
127 Because I love your commands
      more than gold, more than pure
      gold,
128 and because I consider all your
      precepts right,
    I hate every wrong path.

פ Pe

129 Your statutes are wonderful;
    therefore I obey them.
130 The unfolding of your words gives
      light;
    it gives understanding to the
      simple.
131 I open my mouth and pant,
    longing for your commands.
132 Turn to me and have mercy on me,
    as you always do to those who love
      your name.
133 Direct my footsteps according to
      your word;
    let no sin rule over me.

134 Redeem me from the oppression of
      men,
    that I may obey your precepts.
135 Make your face shine upon your
      servant
    and teach me your decrees.
136 Streams of tears flow from my eyes,
    for your law is not obeyed.

צ Tsadhe

137 Righteous are you, O LORD,
    and your laws are right.
138 The statutes you have laid down are
      righteous;
    they are fully trustworthy.
139 My zeal wears me out,
    for my enemies ignore your words.
140 Your promises have been thoroughly
      tested,
    and your servant loves them.
141 Though I am lowly and despised,
    I do not forget your precepts.
142 Your righteousness is everlasting
    and your law is true.
143 Trouble and distress have come
      upon me,
    but your commands are my delight.
144 Your statutes are forever right;
    give me understanding that I may
      live.

ק Qoph

145 I call with all my heart; answer me,
      O LORD,
    and I will obey your decrees.
146 I call out to you; save me
    and I will keep your statutes.
147 I rise before dawn and cry for help;
    I have put my hope in your word.
148 My eyes stay open through the
      watches of the night,
    that I may meditate on your
      promises.
149 Hear my voice in accordance with
      your love;
    preserve my life, O LORD,
      according to your laws.
150 Those who devise wicked schemes
      are near,
    but they are far from your law.
151 Yet you are near, O LORD,
    and all your commands are true.
152 Long ago I learned from your
      statutes
    that you established them to last
      forever.

ר Resh

153 Look upon my suffering and
    deliver me,
  for I have not forgotten your law.
154 Defend my cause and redeem me;
  preserve my life according to your
    promise.
155 Salvation is far from the wicked,
  for they do not seek out your
    decrees.
156 Your compassion is great, O Lord;
  preserve my life according to your
    laws.
157 Many are the foes who
    persecute me,
  but I have not turned from your
    statutes.
158 I look on the faithless with loathing,
  for they do not obey your word.
159 See how I love your precepts;
  preserve my life, O Lord,
    according to your love.
160 All your words are true;
  all your righteous laws are eternal.

שׂ Sin and Shin

161 Rulers persecute me without cause,
  but my heart trembles at your word.
162 I rejoice in your promise
  like one who finds great spoil.
163 I hate and abhor falsehood
  but I love your law.
164 Seven times a day I praise you
  for your righteous laws.
165 Great peace have they who love
    your law,
  and nothing can make them
    stumble.
166 I wait for your salvation, O Lord,
  and I follow your commands.
167 I obey your statutes,
  for I love them greatly.
168 I obey your precepts and your
    statutes,
  for all my ways are known to you.

ת Taw

169 May my cry come before you,
    O Lord;
  give me understanding according
    to your word.
170 May my supplication come before
    you;
  deliver me according to your
    promise.

171 May my lips overflow with praise,
  for you teach me your decrees.
172 May my tongue sing of your word,
  for all your commands are
    righteous.
173 May your hand be ready to help me,
  for I have chosen your precepts.
174 I long for your salvation, O Lord,
  and your law is my delight.
175 Let me live that I may praise you,
  and may your laws sustain me.
176 I have strayed like a lost sheep.
  Seek your servant,
  for I have not forgotten your
    commands.

Psalm

A song of ascents.

1 I call on the Lord in my distress,
  and he answers me.
2 Save me, O Lord, from lying lips
  and from deceitful tongues.

3 What will he do to you,
  and what more besides, O deceitful
    tongue?
4 He will punish you with a warrior's
    sharp arrows,
  with burning coals of the broom
    tree.

5 Woe to me that I dwell in Meshech,
  that I live among the tents of
    Kedar!
6 Too long have I lived
  among those who hate peace.
7 I am a man of peace;
  but when I speak, they are for war.

BELLIGERENTS ARE NOT RELUCTANT TO HAVE
PEACE, BUT THEY WANT A PEACE TO THEIR OWN
LIKING.   *—Augustine*

Psalm

A song of ascents.

1 I lift up my eyes to the hills—
  where does my help come from?

I FELT MY HEART STRANGELY WARMED
John Wesley

VERSE: Psalm 119:165   PASSAGE: Psalm 119:165–168

Wed. May 24, 1738

n the evening I went very unwillingly to a society in Aldersgate-street, where one was reading Luther's preface to the epistle to the Romans. About a quarter before nine, while he was describing the change which God works in the heart through faith in Christ, I felt my heart strangely warmed. I felt I did trust in Christ, Christ alone, for salvation; and an assurance was given me that he had taken away my sins, even mine, and saved me from the law of sin and death.

I began to pray with all my might for those who had in a more especial manner despitefully used me and persecuted me. I then testified openly to all there what I now first felt in my heart. But it was not long before the enemy suggested, "This cannot be faith; for where is thy joy?" Then was I taught that peace and victory over sin are essential to faith in the captain of our salvation; but that, as to the transports of joy that usually attend the beginning of it, especially in those who have mourned deeply, God sometimes giveth, sometimes withholdeth them, according to the counsels of his own will . . .

Thurs. May 25, 1738

The moment I awaked, "Jesus, Master," was in my heart and in my mouth; and I found all my strength lay in keeping my eye fixed upon him, and my soul waiting on him continually. Being again at St. Paul's in the afternoon, I could taste the good word of God in the anthem, which began, "My song shall be always of the lovingkindness of the Lord: with my mouth will I ever be showing forth thy truth from one generation to another." Yet the enemy injected a fear, "If thou dost believe, why is there not a more sensible change?" I answered (yet not I), "That I know not. But this I know, I have 'now peace with God.' And I sin not today, and Jesus my Master has forbid me to take thought for the morrow."

ADDITIONAL SCRIPTURE READING:
Isaiah 32:17; Romans 5:1–2; Ephesians 2:14–17

Go to page 699 for your next devotional reading.

1700   1900

2 My help comes from the LORD,
  the Maker of heaven and earth.

3 He will not let your foot slip—
  he who watches over you will not
    slumber;
4 indeed, he who watches over Israel
  will neither slumber nor sleep.

5 The LORD watches over you—
  the LORD is your shade at your
    right hand;
6 the sun will not harm you by day,
  nor the moon by night.

7 The LORD will keep you from all
    harm—
  he will watch over your life;
8 the LORD will watch over your
    coming and going
  both now and forevermore.

Psalm

A song of ascents. Of David.

1 I rejoiced with those who said to me,
  "Let us go to the house of the
    LORD."
2 Our feet are standing
  in your gates, O Jerusalem.

3 Jerusalem is built like a city
  that is closely compacted together.
4 That is where the tribes go up,
  the tribes of the LORD,
  to praise the name of the LORD
  according to the statute given to
    Israel.
5 There the thrones for judgment
    stand,
  the thrones of the house of David.

6 Pray for the peace of Jerusalem:
  "May those who love you be
    secure.
7 May there be peace within your walls
  and security within your citadels."
8 For the sake of my brothers and
    friends,
  I will say, "Peace be within you."
9 For the sake of the house of the LORD
  our God,
  I will seek your prosperity.

Psalm

A song of ascents.

1 I lift up my eyes to you,
  to you whose throne is in heaven.
2 As the eyes of slaves look to the hand
  of their master,
  as the eyes of a maid look to the
    hand of her mistress,
  so our eyes look to the LORD our
    God,
  till he shows us his mercy.

3 Have mercy on us, O LORD, have
    mercy on us,
  for we have endured much
    contempt.
4 We have endured much ridicule from
  the proud,
  much contempt from the
    arrogant.

Psalm

A song of ascents. Of David.

1 If the LORD had not been on our
    side—
  let Israel say—
2 if the LORD had not been on our
    side
  when men attacked us,
3 when their anger flared against us,
  they would have swallowed us
    alive;
4 the flood would have engulfed us,
  the torrent would have swept over
    us,
5 the raging waters
  would have swept us away.

6 Praise be to the LORD,
  who has not let us be torn by their
    teeth.
7 We have escaped like a bird
  out of the fowler's snare;
  the snare has been broken,
  and we have escaped.
8 Our help is in the name of the
    LORD,
  the Maker of heaven and earth.

Psalm

A song of ascents.

¹ Those who trust in the LORD are like
  Mount Zion,
  which cannot be shaken but
   endures forever.
² As the mountains surround
   Jerusalem,
  so the LORD surrounds his people
   both now and forevermore.
³ The scepter of the wicked will not
   remain
  over the land allotted to the
   righteous,
  for then the righteous might use
   their hands to do evil.
⁴ Do good, O LORD, to those who are
   good,
  to those who are upright in heart.
⁵ But those who turn to crooked ways
  the LORD will banish with the
   evildoers.

Peace be upon Israel.

Psalm

A song of ascents.

¹ When the LORD brought back the
   captives toᵃ Zion,
  we were like men who dreamed.ᵇ
² Our mouths were filled with
   laughter,
  our tongues with songs of joy.
  Then it was said among the nations,
   "The LORD has done great things
    for them."
³ The LORD has done great things for us,
  and we are filled with joy.

⁴ Restore our fortunes,ᶜ O LORD,
  like streams in the Negev.
⁵ Those who sow in tears
  will reap with songs of joy.
⁶ He who goes out weeping,
   carrying seed to sow,
  will return with songs of joy,
   carrying sheaves with him.

Psalm

A song of ascents. Of Solomon.

¹ Unless the LORD builds the house,
  its builders labor in vain.
  Unless the LORD watches over the
   city,
  the watchmen stand guard in
   vain.
² In vain you rise early
  and stay up late,
  toiling for food to eat—
  for he grants sleep toᵈ those he
   loves.

³ Sons are a heritage from the LORD,
  children a reward from him.
⁴ Like arrows in the hands of a
   warrior
  are sons born in one's youth.
⁵ Blessed is the man
  whose quiver is full of them.
  They will not be put to shame
  when they contend with their
   enemies in the gate.

Psalm

A song of ascents.

¹ Blessed are all who fear the LORD,
  who walk in his ways.
² You will eat the fruit of your labor;
  blessings and prosperity will be
   yours.
³ Your wife will be like a fruitful vine
  within your house;
  your sons will be like olive shoots
   around your table.
⁴ Thus is the man blessed
  who fears the LORD.

⁵ May the LORD bless you from Zion
  all the days of your life;
  may you see the prosperity of
   Jerusalem,
⁶   and may you live to see your
   children's children.

Peace be upon Israel.

ᵃ 1 Or LORD restored the fortunes of   ᵇ 1 Or men restored to health   ᶜ 4 Or Bring back our captives
ᵈ 2 Or eat— / for while they sleep he provides for

Psalm

A song of ascents.

1 They have greatly oppressed me from
    my youth—
    let Israel say—
2 they have greatly oppressed me from
    my youth,
    but they have not gained the
    victory over me.
3 Plowmen have plowed my back
    and made their furrows long.
4 But the LORD is righteous;
    he has cut me free from the cords
    of the wicked.

5 May all who hate Zion
    be turned back in shame.
6 May they be like grass on the roof,
    which withers before it can grow;
7 with it the reaper cannot fill his
    hands,
    nor the one who gathers fill his
    arms.
8 May those who pass by not say,
    "The blessing of the LORD be upon
    you;
    we bless you in the name of the
    LORD."

Psalm

A song of ascents.

1 Out of the depths I cry to you,
    O LORD;
2   O Lord, hear my voice.
Let your ears be attentive
    to my cry for mercy.

3 If you, O LORD, kept a record of sins,
    O Lord, who could stand?
4 But with you there is forgiveness;
    therefore you are feared.

5 I wait for the LORD, my soul waits,
    and in his word I put my hope.
6 My soul waits for the Lord
    more than watchmen wait for the
    morning,

more than watchmen wait for the
    morning.
7 O Israel, put your hope in the LORD,
    for with the LORD is unfailing love
    and with him is full redemption.
8 He himself will redeem Israel
    from all their sins.

Psalm

A song of ascents. Of David.

1 My heart is not proud, O LORD,
    my eyes are not haughty;
I do not concern myself with great
    matters
    or things too wonderful for me.
2 But I have stilled and quieted my soul;
    like a weaned child with its
    mother,
    like a weaned child is my soul
    within me.

3 O Israel, put your hope in the LORD
    both now and forevermore.

Psalm

A song of ascents.

1 O LORD, remember David
    and all the hardships he endured.

2 He swore an oath to the LORD
    and made a vow to the Mighty One
    of Jacob:
3 "I will not enter my house
    or go to my bed—
4 I will allow no sleep to my eyes,
    no slumber to my eyelids,
5 till I find a place for the LORD,
    a dwelling for the Mighty One of
    Jacob."

6 We heard it in Ephrathah,
    we came upon it in the fields of
    Jaar^{a;b}
7 "Let us go to his dwelling place;
    let us worship at his footstool—
8 arise, O LORD, and come to your
    resting place,
    you and the ark of your might.

a 6 That is, Kiriath Jearim   *b 6* Or *heard of it in Ephrathah, / we found it in the fields of Jaar.* (And no
quotes around verses 7–9)

9 May your priests be clothed with
   righteousness;
      may your saints sing for joy."

10 For the sake of David your servant,
      do not reject your anointed one.

11 The LORD swore an oath to David,
      a sure oath that he will not revoke:
   "One of your own descendants
   I will place on your throne—
12 if your sons keep my covenant
      and the statutes I teach them,
   then their sons will sit
      on your throne for ever and ever."

13 For the LORD has chosen Zion,
      he has desired it for his dwelling:
14 "This is my resting place for ever and
      ever;
      here I will sit enthroned, for I have
         desired it—
15 I will bless her with abundant
         provisions;
      her poor will I satisfy with food.
16 I will clothe her priests with
         salvation,
      and her saints will ever sing for joy.

17 "Here I will make a horn*a* grow for
      David
      and set up a lamp for my anointed
         one.
18 I will clothe his enemies with
         shame,
      but the crown on his head will be
         resplendent."

Psalm

133

A song of ascents. Of David.

1 How good and pleasant it is
      when brothers live together in
         unity!
2 It is like precious oil poured on the
      head,
      running down on the beard,
   running down on Aaron's beard,
      down upon the collar of his robes.
3 It is as if the dew of Hermon
      were falling on Mount Zion.
   For there the LORD bestows his
         blessing,
      even life forevermore.

Psalm

134

A song of ascents.

1 Praise the LORD, all you servants of
      the LORD
   who minister by night in the house
      of the LORD.
2 Lift up your hands in the sanctuary
      and praise the LORD.

3 May the LORD, the Maker of heaven
      and earth,
      bless you from Zion.

Psalm

135

1 Praise the LORD.*b*

   Praise the name of the LORD;
      praise him, you servants of the
         LORD,
2 you who minister in the house of the
      LORD,
      in the courts of the house of our
         God.

3 Praise the LORD, for the LORD is good;
      sing praise to his name, for that is
         pleasant.
4 For the LORD has chosen Jacob to be
      his own,
      Israel to be his treasured
         possession.

5 I know that the LORD is great,
      that our Lord is greater than all
         gods.
6 The LORD does whatever pleases him,
      in the heavens and on the earth,
      in the seas and all their depths.
7 He makes clouds rise from the ends
      of the earth;
   he sends lightning with the rain
      and brings out the wind from his
         storehouses.

8 He struck down the firstborn of
      Egypt,
      the firstborn of men and animals.
9 He sent his signs and wonders into
      your midst, O Egypt,
      against Pharaoh and all his
         servants.

---

a 17 *Horn* here symbolizes strong one, that is, king.   *b* 1 Hebrew *Hallelu Yah*; also in verses 3 and 21

10 He struck down many nations
    and killed mighty kings—
11 Sihon king of the Amorites,
    Og king of Bashan
    and all the kings of Canaan—
12 and he gave their land as an
        inheritance,
    an inheritance to his people Israel.

13 Your name, O LORD, endures forever,
    your renown, O LORD, through all
        generations.
14 For the LORD will vindicate his
        people
    and have compassion on his
        servants.

15 The idols of the nations are silver and
        gold,
    made by the hands of men.
16 They have mouths, but cannot speak,
    eyes, but they cannot see;
17 they have ears, but cannot hear,
    nor is there breath in their
        mouths.
18 Those who make them will be like
        them,
    and so will all who trust in them.

19 O house of Israel, praise the LORD;
    O house of Aaron, praise the LORD;
20 O house of Levi, praise the LORD;
    you who fear him, praise the
        LORD.
21 Praise be to the LORD from Zion,
    to him who dwells in Jerusalem.

    Praise the LORD.

Psalm
136

1 Give thanks to the LORD, for he is
        good.
        His love endures forever.
2 Give thanks to the God of gods.
        His love endures forever.
3 Give thanks to the Lord of lords:
        His love endures forever.

4 to him who alone does great
        wonders,
        His love endures forever.
5 who by his understanding made the
        heavens,
        His love endures forever.

6 who spread out the earth upon the
        waters,
        His love endures forever.
7 who made the great lights—
        His love endures forever.
8 the sun to govern the day,
        His love endures forever.
9 the moon and stars to govern the
        night;
        His love endures forever.

10 to him who struck down the
        firstborn of Egypt
        His love endures forever.
11 and brought Israel out from among
        them
        His love endures forever.
12 with a mighty hand and outstretched
        arm;
        His love endures forever.

13 to him who divided the Red Sea[a]
        asunder
        His love endures forever.
14 and brought Israel through the midst
        of it,
        His love endures forever.
15 but swept Pharaoh and his army into
        the Red Sea;
        His love endures forever.

16 to him who led his people through
        the desert,
        His love endures forever.
17 who struck down great kings,
        His love endures forever.
18 and killed mighty kings—
        His love endures forever.
19 Sihon king of the Amorites
        His love endures forever.
20 and Og king of Bashan—
        His love endures forever.
21 and gave their land as an inheritance,
        His love endures forever.
22 an inheritance to his servant Israel;
        His love endures forever.

23 to the One who remembered us in
        our low estate
        His love endures forever.
24 and freed us from our enemies,
        His love endures forever.
25 and who gives food to every creature.
        His love endures forever.
26 Give thanks to the God of heaven.
        His love endures forever.

a 13 Hebrew *Yam Suph*; that is, Sea of Reeds; also in verse 15

Psalm 137

¹ By the rivers of Babylon we sat and
wept
when we remembered Zion.
² There on the poplars
we hung our harps,
³ for there our captors asked us for
songs,
our tormentors demanded songs of
joy;
they said, "Sing us one of the songs
of Zion!"

⁴ How can we sing the songs of the
LORD
while in a foreign land?
⁵ If I forget you, O Jerusalem,
may my right hand forget its skill.
⁶ May my tongue cling to the roof of
my mouth
if I do not remember you,
if I do not consider Jerusalem
my highest joy.

⁷ Remember, O LORD, what the
Edomites did
on the day Jerusalem fell.
"Tear it down," they cried,
"tear it down to its foundations!"

⁸ O Daughter of Babylon, doomed to
destruction,
happy is he who repays you
for what you have done to us—
⁹ he who seizes your infants
and dashes them against the rocks.

Psalm 138

Of David.

¹ I will praise you, O LORD, with all my
heart;
before the "gods" I will sing your
praise.
² I will bow down toward your holy
temple
and will praise your name
for your love and your faithfulness,
for you have exalted above all things
your name and your word.
³ When I called, you answered me;

a 8 Hebrew *Sheol*

you made me bold and
stouthearted.
⁴ May all the kings of the earth praise
you, O LORD,
when they hear the words of your
mouth.
⁵ May they sing of the ways of the
LORD,
for the glory of the LORD is great.
⁶ Though the LORD is on high, he looks
upon the lowly,
but the proud he knows from afar.
⁷ Though I walk in the midst of
trouble,
you preserve my life;
you stretch out your hand against the
anger of my foes,
with your right hand you save me.
⁸ The LORD will fulfill his purpose for
me;
your love, O LORD, endures
forever—
do not abandon the works of your
hands.

Psalm 139

For the director of music. Of David. A psalm.

¹ O LORD, you have searched me
and you know me.
² You know when I sit and when I rise;
you perceive my thoughts from
afar.
³ You discern my going out and my
lying down;
you are familiar with all my ways.
⁴ Before a word is on my tongue
you know it completely, O LORD.
⁵ You hem me in—behind and before;
you have laid your hand upon me.
⁶ Such knowledge is too wonderful for
me,
too lofty for me to attain.

⁷ Where can I go from your Spirit?
Where can I flee from your
presence?
⁸ If I go up to the heavens, you are
there;
if I make my bed in the depths,ᵃ
you are there.

9 If I rise on the wings of the dawn,
   if I settle on the far side of the sea,
10 even there your hand will guide me,
   your right hand will hold me fast.

---

11 If I say, "Surely the darkness will
      hide me
   and the light become night around
      me,"
12 even the darkness will not be dark to
      you;
   the night will shine like the day,
   for darkness is as light to you.

13 For you created my inmost being;
   you knit me together in my
      mother's womb.
14 I praise you because I am fearfully
      and wonderfully made;
   your works are wonderful,
   I know that full well.
15 My frame was not hidden from you
   when I was made in the secret
      place.
   When I was woven together in the
      depths of the earth,
16   your eyes saw my unformed body.
   All the days ordained for me
      were written in your book
   before one of them came to be.

17 How precious to*a* me are your
      thoughts, O God!
   How vast is the sum of them!
18 Were I to count them,
   they would outnumber the grains
      of sand.
   When I awake,
   I am still with you.

19 If only you would slay the wicked,
      O God!
   Away from me, you bloodthirsty
      men!
20 They speak of you with evil intent;
   your adversaries misuse your name.

21 Do I not hate those who hate you,
      O LORD,
   and abhor those who rise up
      against you?
22 I have nothing but hatred for them;
   I count them my enemies.

23 Search me, O God, and know my
      heart;
   test me and know my anxious
      thoughts.
24 See if there is any offensive way in
      me,
   and lead me in the way everlasting.

Psalm

140

For the director of music. A psalm of David.

1 Rescue me, O LORD, from evil men;
   protect me from men of violence,
2 who devise evil plans in their hearts
   and stir up war every day.
3 They make their tongues as sharp as
      a serpent's;
   the poison of vipers is on their lips.
                              Selah

4 Keep me, O LORD, from the hands of
      the wicked;
   protect me from men of violence
   who plan to trip my feet.
5 Proud men have hidden a snare for
      me;
   they have spread out the cords of
      their net
   and have set traps for me along my
      path.   *Selah*

6 O LORD, I say to you, "You are my
      God."
   Hear, O LORD, my cry for mercy.
7 O Sovereign LORD, my strong
      deliverer,
   who shields my head in the day of
      battle—
8 do not grant the wicked their desires,
      O LORD;
   do not let their plans succeed,
   or they will become proud.   *Selah*

9 Let the heads of those who surround
      me
   be covered with the trouble their
      lips have caused.

---

a 17 Or *concerning*

SEARCH ME, O GOD

A. W. Tozer

VERSE: Psalm 139:23   **PASSAGE:** Psalm 139:1–7,23–24

he author of the celebrated devotional work, *The Cloud of Unknowing*, begins his little book with a prayer that expresses the spirit of the deeper life teaching: "God, unto whom all hearts be open . . . and unto whom no secret thing is hid, I beseech thee so for to cleanse the intent of mine heart with the unspeakable gift of thy grace, that I may perfectly love thee and worthily praise thee. Amen."

Who that is truly born of the Spirit, unless he has been prejudiced by wrong teaching, can object to such a thorough cleansing of the heart as will enable him perfectly to love God and worthily to praise him? Yet this is exactly what we mean when we speak about the "deeper life" experience. Only we mean that it should be literally fulfilled within the heart, not merely accepted by the head.

Nicephorus, a father of the Eastern Church, in a little treatise on the Spirit-filled life, begins with a call that sounds strange to us only because we have been for so long accustomed to following Jesus afar off and to living among a people that follow him afar off. "You, who desire to capture the wondrous divine illumination of our Savior Jesus Christ—who seek to feel the divine fire in your heart—who strive to sense and experience the feeling of reconciliation with God—who, in order to unearth the treasure buried in the field of your heart and to gain possession of it, have renounced everything worldly—who desire the candles of our souls to burn brightly even now, and who for this purpose have renounced all the world—who wish by conscious experience to know and to receive the kingdom of heaven existing within you–come and I will impart to you the science of eternal heavenly life—"

Such quotations as these might easily be multiplied till they filled half a dozen volumes. This yearning after God has never completely died in any generation. Always there were some who scorned the low paths and insisted upon walking the high road of spiritual perfection. Yet, strangely enough, that word perfection never meant a spiritual terminal point nor a state of purity that made watchfulness and prayer unnecessary. Exactly the opposite was true.

ADDITIONAL SCRIPTURE READING:
Psalm 26:2; Hebrews 4:13

1900   Present

10 Let burning coals fall upon them;
　　may they be thrown into the fire,
　　into miry pits, never to rise.
11 Let slanderers not be established in
　　　the land;
　　may disaster hunt down men of
　　　violence.

12 I know that the LORD secures justice
　　　for the poor
　　and upholds the cause of the needy.
13 Surely the righteous will praise your
　　　name
　　and the upright will live before you.

Psalm

A psalm of David.

1 O LORD, I call to you; come quickly
　　　to me.
　　Hear my voice when I call to you.
2 May my prayer be set before you like
　　　incense;
　　may the lifting up of my hands be
　　　like the evening sacrifice.

3 Set a guard over my mouth, O LORD;
　　keep watch over the door of my
　　　lips.
4 Let not my heart be drawn to what is
　　　evil,
　　to take part in wicked deeds
with men who are evildoers;
　　let me not eat of their delicacies.

5 Let a righteous man*a* strike me—it is
　　　a kindness;
　　let him rebuke me—it is oil on my
　　　head.
　　My head will not refuse it.

Yet my prayer is ever against the
　　　deeds of evildoers;
6 　their rulers will be thrown down
　　　from the cliffs,
　　and the wicked will learn that my
　　　words were well spoken.
7 ⌊They will say,⌋ "As one plows and
　　　breaks up the earth,
　　so our bones have been scattered at
　　　the mouth of the grave.*b* "

8 But my eyes are fixed on you,
　　O Sovereign LORD;

in you I take refuge—do not give
　　me over to death.
9 Keep me from the snares they have
　　　laid for me,
　　from the traps set by evildoers.
10 Let the wicked fall into their own
　　　nets,
　　while I pass by in safety.

Psalm

A *maskil*c of David. When he was in the
cave. A prayer.

1 I cry aloud to the LORD;
　　I lift up my voice to the LORD for
　　　mercy.
2 I pour out my complaint before him;
　　before him I tell my trouble.

3 When my spirit grows faint within
　　　me,
　　it is you who know my way.
　In the path where I walk
　　men have hidden a snare for me.
4 Look to my right and see;
　　no one is concerned for me.
　I have no refuge;
　　no one cares for my life.

5 I cry to you, O LORD;
　　I say, "You are my refuge,
　　my portion in the land of the
　　　living."
6 Listen to my cry,
　　for I am in desperate need;
　　rescue me from those who pursue me,
　　for they are too strong for me.
7 Set me free from my prison,
　　that I may praise your name.

Then the righteous will gather about
　　me
　　because of your goodness to me.

Psalm

A psalm of David.

1 O LORD, hear my prayer,
　　listen to my cry for mercy;
　in your faithfulness and
　　righteousness

---

a 5 Or *Let the Righteous One*　　*b* 7 Hebrew *Sheol*　　*c* Title: Probably a literary or musical term

come to my relief.
² Do not bring your servant into
  judgment,
  for no one living is righteous before
    you.

³ The enemy pursues me,
  he crushes me to the ground;
  he makes me dwell in darkness
  like those long dead.
⁴ So my spirit grows faint within me;
  my heart within me is dismayed.

⁵ I remember the days of long ago;
  I meditate on all your works
  and consider what your hands have
    done.
⁶ I spread out my hands to you;
  my soul thirsts for you like a
    parched land.   *Selah*

⁷ Answer me quickly, O Lord;
  my spirit fails.
  Do not hide your face from me
  or I will be like those who go down
    to the pit.
⁸ Let the morning bring me word of
    your unfailing love,
  for I have put my trust in you.
  Show me the way I should go,
  for to you I lift up my soul.
⁹ Rescue me from my enemies, O Lord,
  for I hide myself in you.
¹⁰ Teach me to do your will,
  for you are my God;
  may your good Spirit
  lead me on level ground.

¹¹ For your name's sake, O Lord,
    preserve my life;
  in your righteousness, bring me
    out of trouble.
¹² In your unfailing love, silence my
    enemies;
  destroy all my foes,
  for I am your servant.

Psalm

144

Of David.

¹ Praise be to the Lord my Rock,
  who trains my hands for war,
  my fingers for battle.

² He is my loving God and my fortress,
  my stronghold and my deliverer,
  my shield, in whom I take refuge,
  who subdues peoples*ᵃ* under me.

³ O Lord, what is man that you care
    for him,
  the son of man that you think of
    him?
⁴ Man is like a breath;
  his days are like a fleeting shadow.

⁵ Part your heavens, O Lord, and come
    down;
  touch the mountains, so that they
    smoke.
⁶ Send forth lightning and scatter ∟the
    enemies⌐;
  shoot your arrows and rout them.
⁷ Reach down your hand from on high;
  deliver me and rescue me
  from the mighty waters,
  from the hands of foreigners
⁸ whose mouths are full of lies,
  whose right hands are deceitful.

⁹ I will sing a new song to you, O God;
  on the ten-stringed lyre I will make
    music to you,
¹⁰ to the One who gives victory to
    kings,
  who delivers his servant David
  from the deadly sword.

¹¹ Deliver me and rescue me
  from the hands of foreigners
  whose mouths are full of lies,
  whose right hands are deceitful.

¹² Then our sons in their youth
  will be like well-nurtured plants,
  and our daughters will be like pillars
  carved to adorn a palace.
¹³ Our barns will be filled
  with every kind of provision.
  Our sheep will increase by thousands,
  by tens of thousands in our fields;
¹⁴   our oxen will draw heavy loads.*ᵇ*
  There will be no breaching of walls,
  no going into captivity,
  no cry of distress in our streets.

¹⁵ Blessed are the people of whom this
    is true;
  blessed are the people whose God
  is the Lord.

ᵃ 2 Many manuscripts of the Masoretic Text, Dead Sea Scrolls, Aquila, Jerome and Syriac; most
manuscripts of the Masoretic Text *subdues my people*   *ᵇ 14* Or *our chieftains will be firmly
established*

Psalm

145 [a]

A psalm of praise. Of David.

1 I will exalt you, my God the King;
   I will praise your name for ever and
      ever.
2 Every day I will praise you
   and extol your name for ever and
      ever.

3 Great is the LORD and most worthy
      of praise;
   his greatness no one can fathom.
4 One generation will commend your
      works to another;
   they will tell of your mighty acts.
5 They will speak of the glorious
      splendor of your majesty,
   and I will meditate on your
      wonderful works. [b]
6 They will tell of the power of your
      awesome works,
   and I will proclaim your great
      deeds.
7 They will celebrate your abundant
      goodness
   and joyfully sing of your
      righteousness.

8 The LORD is gracious and
      compassionate,
   slow to anger and rich in love.
9 The LORD is good to all;
   he has compassion on all he has
      made.
10 All you have made will praise you,
      O LORD;
   your saints will extol you.
11 They will tell of the glory of your
      kingdom
   and speak of your might,
12 so that all men may know of your
      mighty acts
   and the glorious splendor of your
      kingdom.
13 Your kingdom is an everlasting
      kingdom,
   and your dominion endures
      through all generations.

The LORD is faithful to all his
      promises
   and loving toward all he has
      made. [c]
14 The LORD upholds all those who fall
   and lifts up all who are bowed
      down.
15 The eyes of all look to you,
   and you give them their food at the
      proper time.
16 You open your hand
   and satisfy the desires of every
      living thing.

17 The LORD is righteous in all his ways
   and loving toward all he has made.
18 The LORD is near to all who call on
      him,
   to all who call on him in truth.
19 He fulfills the desires of those who
      fear him;
   he hears their cry and saves them.
20 The LORD watches over all who love
      him,
   but all the wicked he will destroy.

21 My mouth will speak in praise of the
      LORD.
   Let every creature praise his holy
      name
   for ever and ever.

Psalm

146

1 Praise the LORD. [d]

Praise the LORD, O my soul.
2   I will praise the LORD all my life;
   I will sing praise to my God as long
      as I live.

3 Do not put your trust in princes,
   in mortal men, who cannot save.
4 When their spirit departs, they return
      to the ground;
   on that very day their plans come
      to nothing.

5 Blessed is he whose help is the God
      of Jacob,
   whose hope is in the LORD his God,
6 the Maker of heaven and earth,

---

[a] This psalm is an acrostic poem, the verses of which (including verse 13b) begin with the successive letters of the Hebrew alphabet.   [b] 5 Dead Sea Scrolls and Syriac (see also Septuagint); Masoretic Text *On the glorious splendor of your majesty / and on your wonderful works I will meditate*   [c] 13 One manuscript of the Masoretic Text, Dead Sea Scrolls and Syriac (see also Septuagint); most manuscripts of the Masoretic Text do not have the last two lines of verse 13.   [d] 1 Hebrew *Hallelu Yah*; also in verse 10

the sea, and everything in them—
the LORD, who remains faithful
forever.
⁷He upholds the cause of the
oppressed
and gives food to the hungry.
The LORD sets prisoners free,
⁸ the LORD gives sight to the blind,
the LORD lifts up those who are
bowed down,
the LORD loves the righteous.
⁹The LORD watches over the alien
and sustains the fatherless and the
widow,
but he frustrates the ways of the
wicked.

¹⁰The LORD reigns forever,
your God, O Zion, for all
generations.

Praise the LORD.

Psalm

¹Praise the LORD.ᵃ

How good it is to sing praises to our
God,
how pleasant and fitting to praise
him!

²The LORD builds up Jerusalem;
he gathers the exiles of Israel.
³He heals the brokenhearted
and binds up their wounds.

⁴He determines the number of the
stars
and calls them each by name.
⁵Great is our Lord and mighty in
power;
his understanding has no limit.
⁶The LORD sustains the humble
but casts the wicked to the ground.

⁷Sing to the LORD with thanksgiving;
make music to our God on the
harp.
⁸He covers the sky with clouds;
he supplies the earth with rain
and makes grass grow on the hills.
⁹He provides food for the cattle
and for the young ravens when
they call.

¹⁰His pleasure is not in the strength of
the horse,
nor his delight in the legs of a man;
¹¹the LORD delights in those who fear
him,
who put their hope in his unfailing
love.

¹²Extol the LORD, O Jerusalem;
praise your God, O Zion,
¹³for he strengthens the bars of your
gates
and blesses your people within
you.
¹⁴He grants peace to your borders
and satisfies you with the finest of
wheat.

¹⁵He sends his command to the earth;
his word runs swiftly.
¹⁶He spreads the snow like wool
and scatters the frost like ashes.
¹⁷He hurls down his hail like pebbles.
Who can withstand his icy blast?
¹⁸He sends his word and melts them;
he stirs up his breezes, and the
waters flow.

¹⁹He has revealed his word to Jacob,
his laws and decrees to Israel.
²⁰He has done this for no other nation;
they do not know his laws.

Praise the LORD.

Psalm
148

¹Praise the LORD.ᵇ

Praise the LORD from the heavens,
praise him in the heights above.
²Praise him, all his angels,
praise him, all his heavenly hosts.
³Praise him, sun and moon,
praise him, all you shining stars.
⁴Praise him, you highest heavens
and you waters above the skies.
⁵Let them praise the name of the
LORD,
for he commanded and they were
created.
⁶He set them in place for ever and
ever;
he gave a decree that will never
pass away.

ᵃ 1 Hebrew *Hallelu Yah*; also in verse 20   ᵇ 1 Hebrew *Hallelu Yah*; also in verse 14

7 Praise the LORD from the earth,
   you great sea creatures and all
      ocean depths,
8 lightning and hail, snow and clouds,
   stormy winds that do his bidding,
9 you mountains and all hills,
   fruit trees and all cedars,
10 wild animals and all cattle,
   small creatures and flying birds,

11 kings of the earth and all nations,
   you princes and all rulers on earth,
12 young men and maidens,
   old men and children.

13 Let them praise the name of the
      LORD,
   for his name alone is exalted;
   his splendor is above the earth and
      the heavens.

THURSDAY

BROKEN HEARTS AND NUMBERED STARS

J. Stuart Holden

VERSE: Psalm 147:3–4   PASSAGE: Psalm 147:1–6

 e healeth the broken in heart . . . He telleth the number of the stars" (KJV). What a surprising conjunction is found in this twin attribute of God—active pity in the small circles of human experience and unmeasured power in the great realms of creation! Here is God manifesting himself in both the remotest and the nearest things of which we have any knowledge—the universal and the personal.

At first sight, it seems incongruous to suggest that these two things have anything in common. Surely there can be little, if any, connection between the starry heavens above and the suffering hearts below; between that which is so infinitely great and that which is so infinitely little; between that of which no man knows much and that of which all men know a great deal; between that which transcends in its greatness all our thoughts, and that which in its bitterness touches all our lives.

But in this declaration of the majesty and mercy of God, the psalmist is not indulging in mere flights of fancy. Nor is he doing violence to the separate revelations of God's power and love, as though these could ever be in contrast.

Instead, he is pointing to an underlying relationship between stars and sorrows—one that unerringly points to the overruling care of God. If we can understand this truth as we should, it will direct our hearts into the safe anchor of his love as nothing else could do.

ADDITIONAL SCRIPTURE READING:
Job 5:17–18; Hosea 6:1; Romans 11:33

Go to page 709 for your next devotional reading.

1700   1900

14 He has raised up for his people a
   horn,*a*
   the praise of all his saints,
   of Israel, the people close to his
      heart.

Praise the LORD.

Psalm

149

1 Praise the LORD.*b*

Sing to the LORD a new song,
   his praise in the assembly of the
      saints.
2 Let Israel rejoice in their Maker;
   let the people of Zion be glad in
      their King.
3 Let them praise his name with
      dancing
   and make music to him with
      tambourine and harp.
4 For the LORD takes delight in his
      people;
   he crowns the humble with
      salvation.
5 Let the saints rejoice in this honor
   and sing for joy on their beds.
6 May the praise of God be in their
      mouths
   and a double-edged sword in their
      hands,

7 to inflict vengeance on the nations
   and punishment on the peoples,
8 to bind their kings with fetters,
   their nobles with shackles of iron,
9 to carry out the sentence written
      against them.
   This is the glory of all his saints.

Praise the LORD.

Psalm
150

1 Praise the LORD.*c*

Praise God in his sanctuary;
   praise him in his mighty heavens.
2 Praise him for his acts of power;
   praise him for his surpassing
      greatness.
3 Praise him with the sounding of the
      trumpet,
   praise him with the harp and lyre,
4 praise him with tambourine and
      dancing,
   praise him with the strings and
      flute,
5 praise him with the clash of cymbals,
   praise him with resounding
      cymbals.
6 Let everything that has breath praise
      the LORD.

Praise the LORD.

---

a 14 *Horn* here symbolizes strong one, that is, king.   *b* 1 Hebrew *Hallelu Yah;* also in verse 9
c 1 Hebrew *Hallelu Yah;* also in verse 6

PROVERBS

CCORDING TO THE PROLOGUE,
PROVERBS WAS WRITTEN TO GIVE
"PRUDENCE TO THE SIMPLE,
KNOWLEDGE AND DISCRETION TO THE
YOUNG" (1:4), AND TO MAKE THE WISE WISER
(1:5). ACQUIRING WISDOM AND KNOWING
HOW TO AVOID THE PITFALLS OF FOLLY WILL
LEAD TO HEALTH AND SUCCESS. ALTHOUGH
PROVERBS IS A PRACTICAL BOOK DEALING
WITH THE ART OF LIVING, IT BASES WISDOM
SOLIDLY ON THE FEAR OF THE LORD (1:7).
HERE YOU WILL FIND WISDOM THAT WORKS
AND INSIGHTS THAT WON'T WEAR OUT.

Prologue: Purpose and Theme

1 The proverbs of Solomon son of David, king of Israel:

2 for attaining wisdom and discipline;
  for understanding words of insight;
3 for acquiring a disciplined and
    prudent life,
  doing what is right and just and
    fair;
4 for giving prudence to the simple,
  knowledge and discretion to the
    young—
5 let the wise listen and add to their
    learning,
  and let the discerning get
    guidance—
6 for understanding proverbs and
    parables,
  the sayings and riddles of the wise.

7 The fear of the LORD is the beginning
    of knowledge,
  but fools*a* despise wisdom and
    discipline.

Exhortations to Embrace Wisdom

Warning Against Enticement

8 Listen, my son, to your father's
    instruction
  and do not forsake your mother's
    teaching.
9 They will be a garland to grace your
    head

---

a 7 The Hebrew words rendered *fool* in Proverbs, and often elsewhere in the Old Testament, denote one who is morally deficient.

and a chain to adorn your neck.

10 My son, if sinners entice you,
   do not give in to them.
11 If they say, "Come along with us;
   let's lie in wait for someone's
      blood,
   let's waylay some harmless soul;
12 let's swallow them alive, like the
      grave,[a]
   and whole, like those who go down
      to the pit;
13 we will get all sorts of valuable
      things
   and fill our houses with plunder;
14 throw in your lot with us,
   and we will share a common
      purse"—
15 my son, do not go along with them,
   do not set foot on their paths;
16 for their feet rush into sin,
   they are swift to shed blood.
17 How useless to spread a net
   in full view of all the birds!
18 These men lie in wait for their own
      blood;
   they waylay only themselves!
19 Such is the end of all who go after ill-
      gotten gain;
   it takes away the lives of those
      who get it.

Warning Against Rejecting Wisdom

20 Wisdom calls aloud in the street,
   she raises her voice in the public
      squares;
21 at the head of the noisy streets[b] she
      cries out,
   in the gateways of the city she
      makes her speech:

22 "How long will you simple ones[c]
      love your simple ways?
   How long will mockers delight in
      mockery
   and fools hate knowledge?
23 If you had responded to my rebuke,
   I would have poured out my heart
      to you
   and made my thoughts known to
      you.
24 But since you rejected me when I
      called
   and no one gave heed when I
      stretched out my hand,

25 since you ignored all my advice
   and would not accept my rebuke,
26 I in turn will laugh at your disaster;
   I will mock when calamity
      overtakes you—
27 when calamity overtakes you like a
      storm,
   when disaster sweeps over you like
      a whirlwind,
   when distress and trouble
      overwhelm you.

28 "Then they will call to me but I will
      not answer;
   they will look for me but will not
      find me.
29 Since they hated knowledge
   and did not choose to fear the LORD,
30 since they would not accept my
      advice
   and spurned my rebuke,
31 they will eat the fruit of their ways
   and be filled with the fruit of their
      schemes.
32 For the waywardness of the simple
      will kill them,
   and the complacency of fools will
      destroy them;
33 but whoever listens to me will live in
      safety
   and be at ease, without fear of
      harm."

MOCK ON, MOCK ON, VOLTAIRE, ROUSSEAU;
MOCK ON, MOCK ON; 'TIS ALL IN VAIN!
YOU THROW THE SAND AGAINST THE WIND,
AND THE WIND BLOWS IT BACK AGAIN.

—*William Blake*

Moral Benefits of Wisdom

2 My son, if you accept my
      words
   and store up my commands within
      you,
2 turning your ear to wisdom
   and applying your heart to
      understanding,
3 and if you call out for insight
   and cry aloud for understanding,
4 and if you look for it as for silver
   and search for it as for hidden
      treasure,

---

a 12 Hebrew *Sheol*   *b 21* Hebrew; Septuagint / *on the tops of the walls*   *c 22* The Hebrew word
rendered *simple* in Proverbs generally denotes one without moral direction and inclined to evil.

5 then you will understand the fear of
    the LORD
  and find the knowledge of God.
6 For the LORD gives wisdom,
    and from his mouth come
      knowledge and understanding.
7 He holds victory in store for the
    upright,
  he is a shield to those whose walk
    is blameless,
8 for he guards the course of the just
    and protects the way of his faithful
      ones.

9 Then you will understand what is
    right and just
  and fair—every good path.
10 For wisdom will enter your heart,
    and knowledge will be pleasant to
      your soul.
11 Discretion will protect you,
    and understanding will guard you.

12 Wisdom will save you from the ways
    of wicked men,
  from men whose words are
    perverse,
13 who leave the straight paths
    to walk in dark ways,
14 who delight in doing wrong
    and rejoice in the perverseness of
      evil,
15 whose paths are crooked
    and who are devious in their ways.

16 It will save you also from the
    adulteress,
  from the wayward wife with her
    seductive words,
17 who has left the partner of her youth
    and ignored the covenant she made
      before God.ᵃ
18 For her house leads down to death
    and her paths to the spirits of the
      dead.
19 None who go to her return
    or attain the paths of life.

20 Thus you will walk in the ways of
    good men
  and keep to the paths of the
    righteous.
21 For the upright will live in the land,
    and the blameless will remain in it;
22 but the wicked will be cut off from
    the land,

and the unfaithful will be torn
    from it.

Further Benefits of Wisdom

3 My son, do not forget my
    teaching,
  but keep my commands in your
    heart,
2 for they will prolong your life many
    years
  and bring you prosperity.

3 Let love and faithfulness never leave
    you;
  bind them around your neck,
  write them on the tablet of your
    heart.
4 Then you will win favor and a good
    name
  in the sight of God and man.

5 Trust in the LORD with all your heart
    and lean not on your own
      understanding;
6 in all your ways acknowledge him,
    and he will make your paths
      straight.ᵇ

7 Do not be wise in your own eyes;
    fear the LORD and shun evil.
8 This will bring health to your body
    and nourishment to your bones.

9 Honor the LORD with your wealth,
    with the firstfruits of all your crops;
10 then your barns will be filled to
    overflowing,
  and your vats will brim over with
    new wine.

11 My son, do not despise the LORD's
    discipline
  and do not resent his rebuke,
12 because the LORD disciplines those
    he loves,
  as a fatherᶜ the son he delights in.

13 Blessed is the man who finds
    wisdom,
  the man who gains understanding,
14 for she is more profitable than silver
    and yields better returns than gold.
15 She is more precious than rubies;
    nothing you desire can compare
      with her.
16 Long life is in her right hand;

ᵃ 17 Or covenant of her God   ᵇ 6 Or will direct your paths   ᶜ 12 Hebrew; Septuagint / and he
punishes

in her left hand are riches and
   honor.
17 Her ways are pleasant ways,
   and all her paths are peace.
18 She is a tree of life to those who
   embrace her;
   those who lay hold of her will be
   blessed.

19 By wisdom the LORD laid the earth's
   foundations,

by understanding he set the
   heavens in place;
20 by his knowledge the deeps were
   divided,
   and the clouds let drop the dew.

21 My son, preserve sound judgment
   and discernment,
   do not let them out of your sight;
22 they will be life for you,
   an ornament to grace your neck.

FRIDAY

FOLLOW THIS PATH

G. Campbell Morgan

VERSE: Proverbs 3:5   **PASSAGE:** Proverbs 3:5–7

o simple and so clear is the statement, that interpretation is unnecessary. The reader, then, will be patient if for this once the writer becomes reminiscent, and so a witness rather than an advocate. I distinctly remember the day when I left home to face life, amid its crowded ways, for myself. My father, whose philosophy was certainly that of the Hebrew wisdom, gave me these verses as providing a complete guide to life. Looking back over the intervening years I know he was right. In them there has been much of failure, many turnings aside from the straight highway, many devious and sorrowful wanderings from the true paths of life. All such failure, such turnings aside, such wanderings, have resulted from leaning to one's own understanding. The measure in which I have trusted Jehovah, and acknowledged him, has been the measure of walking in the paths of real life. Doubt of God, pride of intellect, and independence in volition, these are the things which blight and blast. Paths chosen for us by God all lead onward and upward, even when they seem to us to turn about in inextricable confusion, and to move downward to the valleys of humiliation and suffering. He is the All-Wise, and to him, wisdom is the way by which Love gains his victory.

ADDITIONAL SCRIPTURE READING:
Proverbs 28:26; Jeremiah 9:23–24; 1 Corinthians 8:2–3

Go to page 712 for your next devotional reading.

1900   Present

²³ Then you will go on your way in
  safety,
    and your foot will not stumble;
²⁴ when you lie down, you will not be
  afraid;
    when you lie down, your sleep will
    be sweet.
²⁵ Have no fear of sudden disaster
    or of the ruin that overtakes the
    wicked,
²⁶ for the LORD will be your confidence
    and will keep your foot from being
    snared.

²⁷ Do not withhold good from those
  who deserve it,
    when it is in your power to act.
²⁸ Do not say to your neighbor,
    "Come back later; I'll give it
    tomorrow"—
    when you now have it with you.

²⁹ Do not plot harm against your
  neighbor,
    who lives trustfully near you.
³⁰ Do not accuse a man for no reason—
    when he has done you no harm.

³¹ Do not envy a violent man
    or choose any of his ways,
³² for the LORD detests a perverse man
    but takes the upright into his
    confidence.

³³ The LORD's curse is on the house of
  the wicked,
    but he blesses the home of the
    righteous.
³⁴ He mocks proud mockers
    but gives grace to the humble.
³⁵ The wise inherit honor,
    but fools he holds up to shame.

Wisdom Is Supreme

4 Listen, my sons, to a father's
  instruction;
    pay attention and gain
    understanding.
² I give you sound learning,
    so do not forsake my teaching.
³ When I was a boy in my father's
  house,
    still tender, and an only child of
    my mother,
⁴ he taught me and said,
    "Lay hold of my words with all
    your heart;

keep my commands and you will
  live.
⁵ Get wisdom, get understanding;
    do not forget my words or swerve
    from them.
⁶ Do not forsake wisdom, and she will
    protect you;
    love her, and she will watch over
    you.
⁷ Wisdom is supreme; therefore get
    wisdom.
    Though it cost all you have,ᵃ get
    understanding.
⁸ Esteem her, and she will exalt you;
    embrace her, and she will honor
    you.
⁹ She will set a garland of grace on
    your head
    and present you with a crown of
    splendor."

¹⁰ Listen, my son, accept what I say,
    and the years of your life will be
    many.
¹¹ I guide you in the way of wisdom
    and lead you along straight paths.
¹² When you walk, your steps will not
    be hampered;
    when you run, you will not
    stumble.
¹³ Hold on to instruction, do not let it
    go;
    guard it well, for it is your life.
¹⁴ Do not set foot on the path of the
    wicked
    or walk in the way of evil men.
¹⁵ Avoid it, do not travel on it;
    turn from it and go on your way.
¹⁶ For they cannot sleep till they do
    evil;
    they are robbed of slumber till they
    make someone fall.
¹⁷ They eat the bread of wickedness
    and drink the wine of violence.

¹⁸ The path of the righteous is like the
    first gleam of dawn,
    shining ever brighter till the full
    light of day.
¹⁹ But the way of the wicked is like
    deep darkness;
    they do not know what makes
    them stumble.

²⁰ My son, pay attention to what I say;
    listen closely to my words.

ᵃ 7 Or *Whatever else you get*

²¹ Do not let them out of your sight,
 keep them within your heart;
²² for they are life to those who find
 them
 and health to a man's whole body.
²³ Above all else, guard your heart,
 for it is the wellspring of life.
²⁴ Put away perversity from your mouth;
 keep corrupt talk far from your lips.
²⁵ Let your eyes look straight ahead,
 fix your gaze directly before you.
²⁶ Make level^a paths for your feet
 and take only ways that are firm.
²⁷ Do not swerve to the right or the left;
 keep your foot from evil.

Warning Against Adultery

5 My son, pay attention to my
 wisdom,
 listen well to my words of insight,
² that you may maintain discretion
 and your lips may preserve
 knowledge.
³ For the lips of an adulteress drip
 honey,
 and her speech is smoother than oil;
⁴ but in the end she is bitter as gall,
 sharp as a double-edged sword.
⁵ Her feet go down to death;
 her steps lead straight to the
 grave.^b
⁶ She gives no thought to the way of
 life;
 her paths are crooked, but she
 knows it not.

⁷ Now then, my sons, listen to me;
 do not turn aside from what I say.
⁸ Keep to a path far from her,
 do not go near the door of her
 house,
⁹ lest you give your best strength to
 others
 and your years to one who is cruel,
¹⁰ lest strangers feast on your wealth
 and your toil enrich another man's
 house.
¹¹ At the end of your life you will groan,
 when your flesh and body are
 spent.
¹² You will say, "How I hated discipline!
 How my heart spurned correction!
¹³ I would not obey my teachers
 or listen to my instructors.
¹⁴ I have come to the brink of utter ruin

in the midst of the whole
 assembly."

¹⁵ Drink water from your own cistern,
 running water from your own well.
¹⁶ Should your springs overflow in the
 streets,
 your streams of water in the public
 squares?
¹⁷ Let them be yours alone,
 never to be shared with strangers.
¹⁸ May your fountain be blessed,
 and may you rejoice in the wife of
 your youth.
¹⁹ A loving doe, a graceful deer—
 may her breasts satisfy you always,
 may you ever be captivated by her
 love.
²⁰ Why be captivated, my son, by an
 adulteress?
 Why embrace the bosom of
 another man's wife?

²¹ For a man's ways are in full view of
 the LORD,
 and he examines all his paths.
²² The evil deeds of a wicked man
 ensnare him;
 the cords of his sin hold him fast.
²³ He will die for lack of discipline,
 led astray by his own great folly.

Warnings Against Folly

6 My son, if you have put up
 security for your neighbor,
 if you have struck hands in pledge
 for another,
² if you have been trapped by what you
 said,
 ensnared by the words of your
 mouth,
³ then do this, my son, to free yourself,
 since you have fallen into your
 neighbor's hands:
 Go and humble yourself;
 press your plea with your neighbor!
⁴ Allow no sleep to your eyes,
 no slumber to your eyelids.
⁵ Free yourself, like a gazelle from the
 hand of the hunter,
 like a bird from the snare of the
 fowler.

⁶ Go to the ant, you sluggard;
 consider its ways and be wise!
⁷ It has no commander,

^a 26 Or *Consider the* ^b 5 Hebrew *Sheol*

WEEKEND

JESUS, THE VERY THOUGHT OF THEE
Bernard of Clairvaux

VERSE: Isaiah 26:3   **PASSAGE:** Isaiah 26:1–10

 esus, the very thought of thee
With sweetness fills the breast;
But sweeter far thy face to see,
And in thy presence rest.

No voice can sing, no heart can frame,
Nor can the memory find,
A sweeter sound than Jesus' name,
The Savior of mankind.

O hope of every contrite heart,
O joy of all the meek,
To those who fall, how kind thou art:
How good to those who seek!

But what to those who find? Ah, this
Nor tongue nor pen can show;
The love of Jesus, what it is,
None but who love him know.

Jesus, our only joy be thou,
As thou our prize wilt be;
In thee be all our glory now,
And through eternity.

ADDITIONAL SCRIPTURE READING:
Isaiah 12:2; Matthew 1:21–23; Luke 1:31–33

Go to page 716 for your next devotional reading.

no overseer or ruler,
8 yet it stores its provisions in summer
  and gathers its food at harvest.

9 How long will you lie there, you
     sluggard?
  When will you get up from your
     sleep?
10 A little sleep, a little slumber,
   a little folding of the hands to
     rest—
11 and poverty will come on you like a
     bandit
   and scarcity like an armed man.ᵃ

12 A scoundrel and villain,
   who goes about with a corrupt
     mouth,
13   who winks with his eye,
     signals with his feet
     and motions with his fingers,
14   who plots evil with deceit in his
       heart—
     he always stirs up dissension.
15 Therefore disaster will overtake him
     in an instant;
   he will suddenly be destroyed—
     without remedy.

16 There are six things the LORD hates,
   seven that are detestable to him:
17   haughty eyes,
     a lying tongue,
     hands that shed innocent blood,
18   a heart that devises wicked
       schemes,
     feet that are quick to rush into
       evil,
19   a false witness who pours out lies
     and a man who stirs up
       dissension among brothers.

Warning Against Adultery

20 My son, keep your father's
     commands
   and do not forsake your mother's
     teaching.
21 Bind them upon your heart forever;
   fasten them around your neck.
22 When you walk, they will guide you;
   when you sleep, they will watch
     over you;
   when you awake, they will speak
     to you.
23 For these commands are a lamp,
   this teaching is a light,

and the corrections of discipline
   are the way to life,
24 keeping you from the immoral
     woman,
   from the smooth tongue of the
     wayward wife.
25 Do not lust in your heart after her
     beauty
   or let her captivate you with her
     eyes,
26 for the prostitute reduces you to a
     loaf of bread,
   and the adulteress preys upon your
     very life.
27 Can a man scoop fire into his lap
   without his clothes being burned?
28 Can a man walk on hot coals
   without his feet being scorched?
29 So is he who sleeps with another
     man's wife;
   no one who touches her will go
     unpunished.

30 Men do not despise a thief if he steals
   to satisfy his hunger when he is
     starving.
31 Yet if he is caught, he must pay
     sevenfold,
   though it costs him all the wealth
     of his house.
32 But a man who commits adultery
     lacks judgment;
   whoever does so destroys himself.
33 Blows and disgrace are his lot,
   and his shame will never be wiped
     away;
34 for jealousy arouses a husband's fury,
   and he will show no mercy when
     he takes revenge.
35 He will not accept any
     compensation;
   he will refuse the bribe, however
     great it is.

Warning Against the Adulteress

7 My son, keep my words
   and store up my commands
     within you.
2 Keep my commands and you will
     live;
   guard my teachings as the apple of
     your eye.
3 Bind them on your fingers;
   write them on the tablet of your
     heart.

ᵃ 11 Or like a vagrant / and scarcity like a beggar

⁴ Say to wisdom, "You are my sister,"
    and call understanding your
       kinsman;
⁵ they will keep you from the
       adulteress,
    from the wayward wife with her
       seductive words.

⁶ At the window of my house
    I looked out through the lattice.
⁷ I saw among the simple,
    I noticed among the young men,
    a youth who lacked judgment.
⁸ He was going down the street near
       her corner,
    walking along in the direction of
       her house
⁹ at twilight, as the day was fading,
    as the dark of night set in.

¹⁰ Then out came a woman to meet
       him,
    dressed like a prostitute and with
       crafty intent.
¹¹ (She is loud and defiant,
    her feet never stay at home;
¹² now in the street, now in the squares,
    at every corner she lurks.)
¹³ She took hold of him and kissed him
    and with a brazen face she said:

¹⁴ "I have fellowship offerings[a] at home;
    today I fulfilled my vows.
¹⁵ So I came out to meet you;
    I looked for you and have found
       you!
¹⁶ I have covered my bed
    with colored linens from Egypt.
¹⁷ I have perfumed my bed
    with myrrh, aloes and cinnamon.
¹⁸ Come, let's drink deep of love till
       morning;
    let's enjoy ourselves with love!
¹⁹ My husband is not at home;
    he has gone on a long journey.
²⁰ He took his purse filled with money
    and will not be home till full
       moon."

²¹ With persuasive words she led him
       astray;
    she seduced him with her smooth
       talk.
²² All at once he followed her
    like an ox going to the slaughter,
    like a deer[b] stepping into a noose[c]

²³   till an arrow pierces his liver,
    like a bird darting into a snare,
    little knowing it will cost him his
       life.
²⁴ Now then, my sons, listen to me;
    pay attention to what I say.
²⁵ Do not let your heart turn to her
       ways
    or stray into her paths.
²⁶ Many are the victims she has
       brought down;
    her slain are a mighty throng.
²⁷ Her house is a highway to the grave,[d]
    leading down to the chambers of
       death.

Wisdom's Call

8 Does not wisdom call out?
    Does not understanding raise
       her voice?
² On the heights along the way,
    where the paths meet, she takes
       her stand;
³ beside the gates leading into the city,
    at the entrances, she cries aloud:
⁴ "To you, O men, I call out;
    I raise my voice to all mankind.
⁵ You who are simple, gain prudence;
    you who are foolish, gain
       understanding.
⁶ Listen, for I have worthy things to
       say;
    I open my lips to speak what is
       right.
⁷ My mouth speaks what is true,
    for my lips detest wickedness.
⁸ All the words of my mouth are just;
    none of them is crooked or
       perverse.
⁹ To the discerning all of them are
       right;
    they are faultless to those who
       have knowledge.
¹⁰ Choose my instruction instead of
       silver,
    knowledge rather than choice gold,
¹¹ for wisdom is more precious than
       rubies,
    and nothing you desire can
       compare with her.

¹² "I, wisdom, dwell together with
       prudence;
    I possess knowledge and discretion.

---

a 14 Traditionally *peace offerings*   *b 22* Syriac (see also Septuagint); Hebrew *fool*   *c 22* The meaning of the Hebrew for this line is uncertain.   *d 27* Hebrew *Sheol*

¹³ To fear the LORD is to hate evil;
   I hate pride and arrogance,
   evil behavior and perverse speech.
¹⁴ Counsel and sound judgment are
   mine;
   I have understanding and power.
¹⁵ By me kings reign
   and rulers make laws that are just;
¹⁶ by me princes govern,
   and all nobles who rule on earth.ᵃ
¹⁷ I love those who love me,
   and those who seek me find me.

O LORD OUR GOD, GRANT US GRACE TO DESIRE
THEE WITH OUR WHOLE HEART; THAT SO DESIR-
ING, WE MAY SEEK, AND SEEKING, FIND THEE; AND
SO FINDING THEE, MAY LOVE THEE; AND LOVING
THEE, MAY HATE THOSE SINS FROM WHICH THOU
HAST REDEEMED US. AMEN.   —Anselm

---

¹⁸ With me are riches and honor,
   enduring wealth and prosperity.
¹⁹ My fruit is better than fine gold;
   what I yield surpasses choice
   silver.
²⁰ I walk in the way of righteousness,
   along the paths of justice,
²¹ bestowing wealth on those who love
   me
   and making their treasuries full.

²² "The LORD brought me forth as the
   first of his works,ᵇ,ᶜ
   before his deeds of old;
²³ I was appointedᵈ from eternity,
   from the beginning, before the
   world began.
²⁴ When there were no oceans, I was
   given birth,
   when there were no springs
   abounding with water;
²⁵ before the mountains were settled in
   place,
   before the hills, I was given birth,
²⁶ before he made the earth or its fields
   or any of the dust of the world.
²⁷ I was there when he set the heavens
   in place,
   when he marked out the horizon
   on the face of the deep,
²⁸ when he established the clouds
   above

and fixed securely the fountains of
   the deep,
²⁹ when he gave the sea its boundary
   so the waters would not overstep
   his command,
   and when he marked out the
   foundations of the earth.
³⁰   Then I was the craftsman at his
   side.
   I was filled with delight day after day,
   rejoicing always in his presence,
³¹ rejoicing in his whole world
   and delighting in mankind.

³² "Now then, my sons, listen to me;
   blessed are those who keep my
   ways.
³³ Listen to my instruction and be wise;
   do not ignore it.
³⁴ Blessed is the man who listens to me,
   watching daily at my doors,
   waiting at my doorway.
³⁵ For whoever finds me finds life
   and receives favor from the LORD.

I NEVER KNEW ALL THERE WAS IN THE BIBLE UNTIL
I SPENT THOSE YEARS IN JAIL. I WAS CONSTANTLY
FINDING NEW TREASURES.   —John Bunyan

---

³⁶ But whoever fails to find me harms
   himself;
   all who hate me love death."

Invitations of Wisdom and of Folly

9 Wisdom has built her house;
   she has hewn out its seven
   pillars.
² She has prepared her meat and mixed
   her wine;
   she has also set her table.
³ She has sent out her maids, and she
   calls
   from the highest point of the city.
⁴ "Let all who are simple come in
   here!"
   she says to those who lack
   judgment.
⁵ "Come, eat my food
   and drink the wine I have mixed.
⁶ Leave your simple ways and you will
   live;
   walk in the way of understanding.

ᵃ 16 Many Hebrew manuscripts and Septuagint; most Hebrew manuscripts *and nobles—all righteous
rulers*   ᵇ 22 Or *way*; or *dominion*   ᶜ 22 Or *The LORD possessed me at the beginning of his work*; or
The LORD brought me forth at the beginning of his work   ᵈ 23 Or *fashioned*

7 "Whoever corrects a mocker invites
    insult;
  whoever rebukes a wicked man
    incurs abuse.
8 Do not rebuke a mocker or he will
    hate you;
  rebuke a wise man and he will love
    you.
9 Instruct a wise man and he will be
    wiser still;
  teach a righteous man and he will
    add to his learning.

10 "The fear of the LORD is the
    beginning of wisdom,
  and knowledge of the Holy One is
    understanding.
11 For through me your days will be
    many,

and years will be added to your life.
12 If you are wise, your wisdom will
    reward you;
  if you are a mocker, you alone will
    suffer."

13 The woman Folly is loud;
  she is undisciplined and without
    knowledge.
14 She sits at the door of her house,
  on a seat at the highest point of the
    city,
15 calling out to those who pass by,
  who go straight on their way.
16 "Let all who are simple come in
    here!"
  she says to those who lack
    judgment.
17 "Stolen water is sweet;

MONDAY

CONTINUE IN HIS PRESENCE
Brother Lawrence

VERSE: Proverbs 8:30   PASSAGE: Proverbs 8:27–31

here is no sweeter manner of living in the world than
continuous communion with God . . .
    If I were a preacher, I would preach nothing but prac-
ticing the presence of God. If I were to be responsible
for guiding souls in the right direction, I would urge everyone to
be aware of God's constant presence, if for no other reason than
because his presence is a delight to our souls and spirits.
    It is, however, also necessary. If we only knew how much we
need God's grace, we would never lose touch with him. Believe
me. Make a commitment never to deliberately stray from him,
to live the rest of your life in his holy presence. Don't do this in
expectation of receiving heavenly comforts; simply do it out of
love for him.
    Put your hand to the task! If you do it right, you will soon see
the results.

ADDITIONAL SCRIPTURE READING:
Joshua 18:6–10; 2 Chronicles 34:31; Romans 8:38–39

Go to page 720 for your next devotional reading.

1500   1700

food eaten in secret is delicious!"
18 But little do they know that the dead
   are there,
   that her guests are in the depths of
   the grave.*a*

CHARACTER IS WHAT YOU ARE IN THE DARK.
—*Dwight L. Moody*

Proverbs of Solomon

10 The proverbs of Solomon:

A wise son brings joy to his father,
   but a foolish son grief to his
   mother.

2 Ill-gotten treasures are of no value,
   but righteousness delivers from
   death.

3 The LORD does not let the righteous
   go hungry
   but he thwarts the craving of the
   wicked.

4 Lazy hands make a man poor,
   but diligent hands bring wealth.

5 He who gathers crops in summer is a
   wise son,
   but he who sleeps during harvest is
   a disgraceful son.

6 Blessings crown the head of the
   righteous,
   but violence overwhelms the
   mouth of the wicked.*b*

7 The memory of the righteous will be
   a blessing,
   but the name of the wicked will
   rot.

8 The wise in heart accept commands,
   but a chattering fool comes to ruin.

9 The man of integrity walks securely,
   but he who takes crooked paths
   will be found out.

10 He who winks maliciously causes
   grief,
   and a chattering fool comes to
   ruin.

11 The mouth of the righteous is a
   fountain of life,

but violence overwhelms the
   mouth of the wicked.

12 Hatred stirs up dissension,
   but love covers over all wrongs.

13 Wisdom is found on the lips of the
   discerning,
   but a rod is for the back of him
   who lacks judgment.

14 Wise men store up knowledge,
   but the mouth of a fool invites
   ruin.

15 The wealth of the rich is their
   fortified city,
   but poverty is the ruin of the poor.

16 The wages of the righteous bring
   them life,
   but the income of the wicked
   brings them punishment.

17 He who heeds discipline shows the
   way to life,
   but whoever ignores correction
   leads others astray.

18 He who conceals his hatred has lying
   lips,
   and whoever spreads slander is a
   fool.

19 When words are many, sin is not
   absent,
   but he who holds his tongue is
   wise.

20 The tongue of the righteous is choice
   silver,
   but the heart of the wicked is of
   little value.

21 The lips of the righteous nourish
   many,
   but fools die for lack of judgment.

22 The blessing of the LORD brings
   wealth,
   and he adds no trouble to it.

23 A fool finds pleasure in evil conduct,
   but a man of understanding
   delights in wisdom.

24 What the wicked dreads will
   overtake him;
   what the righteous desire will be
   granted.

---

a 18 Hebrew *Sheol*   *b* 6 Or *but the mouth of the wicked conceals violence;* also in verse 11

25 When the storm has swept by, the
      wicked are gone,
   but the righteous stand firm forever.

26 As vinegar to the teeth and smoke to
      the eyes,
   so is a sluggard to those who send
      him.

27 The fear of the LORD adds length to
      life,
   but the years of the wicked are cut
      short.

28 The prospect of the righteous is joy,
   but the hopes of the wicked come
      to nothing.

29 The way of the LORD is a refuge for
      the righteous,
   but it is the ruin of those who do
      evil.

30 The righteous will never be uprooted,
   but the wicked will not remain in
      the land.

31 The mouth of the righteous brings
      forth wisdom,
   but a perverse tongue will be cut
      out.

32 The lips of the righteous know what
      is fitting,
   but the mouth of the wicked only
      what is perverse.

11 The LORD abhors dishonest
      scales,
   but accurate weights are his
      delight.

2 When pride comes, then comes
      disgrace,
   but with humility comes wisdom.

3 The integrity of the upright guides
      them,
   but the unfaithful are destroyed by
      their duplicity.

4 Wealth is worthless in the day of
      wrath,
   but righteousness delivers from
      death.

5 The righteousness of the blameless
      makes a straight way for them,
   but the wicked are brought down
      by their own wickedness.

6 The righteousness of the upright
      delivers them,

but the unfaithful are trapped by
      evil desires.

7 When a wicked man dies, his hope
      perishes;
   all he expected from his power
      comes to nothing.

8 The righteous man is rescued from
      trouble,
   and it comes on the wicked instead.

9 With his mouth the godless destroys
      his neighbor,
   but through knowledge the
      righteous escape.

10 When the righteous prosper, the city
      rejoices;
   when the wicked perish, there are
      shouts of joy.

11 Through the blessing of the upright a
      city is exalted,
   but by the mouth of the wicked it
      is destroyed.

12 A man who lacks judgment derides
      his neighbor,
   but a man of understanding holds
      his tongue.

13 A gossip betrays a confidence,
   but a trustworthy man keeps a
      secret.

14 For lack of guidance a nation falls,
   but many advisers make victory
      sure.

15 He who puts up security for another
      will surely suffer,
   but whoever refuses to strike
      hands in pledge is safe.

16 A kindhearted woman gains respect,
   but ruthless men gain only wealth.

17 A kind man benefits himself,
   but a cruel man brings trouble on
      himself.

18 The wicked man earns deceptive
      wages,
   but he who sows righteousness
      reaps a sure reward.

19 The truly righteous man attains life,
   but he who pursues evil goes to his
      death.

20 The LORD detests men of perverse
      heart

but he delights in those whose
ways are blameless.

21 Be sure of this: The wicked will not
go unpunished,
but those who are righteous will go
free.

22 Like a gold ring in a pig's snout
is a beautiful woman who shows
no discretion.

23 The desire of the righteous ends only
in good,
but the hope of the wicked only in
wrath.

24 One man gives freely, yet gains even
more;
another withholds unduly, but
comes to poverty.

25 A generous man will prosper;
he who refreshes others will
himself be refreshed.

26 People curse the man who hoards
grain,
but blessing crowns him who is
willing to sell.

27 He who seeks good finds goodwill,
but evil comes to him who
searches for it.

28 Whoever trusts in his riches will fall,
but the righteous will thrive like a
green leaf.

29 He who brings trouble on his family
will inherit only wind,
and the fool will be servant to the
wise.

30 The fruit of the righteous is a tree of
life,
and he who wins souls is wise.

31 If the righteous receive their due on
earth,
how much more the ungodly and
the sinner!

12 Whoever loves discipline
loves knowledge,
but he who hates correction is
stupid.

2 A good man obtains favor from the
LORD,
but the LORD condemns a crafty
man.

3 A man cannot be established through
wickedness,
but the righteous cannot be
uprooted.

4 A wife of noble character is her
husband's crown,
but a disgraceful wife is like decay
in his bones.

5 The plans of the righteous are just,
but the advice of the wicked is
deceitful.

6 The words of the wicked lie in wait
for blood,
but the speech of the upright
rescues them.

7 Wicked men are overthrown and are
no more,
but the house of the righteous
stands firm.

8 A man is praised according to his
wisdom,
but men with warped minds are
despised.

9 Better to be a nobody and yet have a
servant
than pretend to be somebody and
have no food.

10 A righteous man cares for the needs
of his animal,
but the kindest acts of the wicked
are cruel.

11 He who works his land will have
abundant food,
but he who chases fantasies lacks
judgment.

12 The wicked desire the plunder of evil
men,
but the root of the righteous
flourishes.

13 An evil man is trapped by his sinful
talk,
but a righteous man escapes
trouble.

14 From the fruit of his lips a man is
filled with good things
as surely as the work of his hands
rewards him.

15 The way of a fool seems right to him,
but a wise man listens to advice.

16 A fool shows his annoyance at once,
but a prudent man overlooks an
insult.

AN INSULT IS EITHER SUSTAINED OR DESTROYED,
NOT BY THE DISPOSITION OF THOSE WHO INSULT,
BUT IN THE DISPOSITION OF THOSE WHO BEAR IT.
—*John Chrysostom*

17 A truthful witness gives honest
testimony,
but a false witness tells lies.

18 Reckless words pierce like a sword,
but the tongue of the wise brings
healing.

19 Truthful lips endure forever,
but a lying tongue lasts only a
moment.

TUESDAY

WHAT IS THE VIRTUE OF A HORSE?
Chrysostom

VERSE: Proverbs 11:28   **PASSAGE:** Proverbs 11:27–31

hat then is the virtue of a horse? is it to have a bridle
studded with gold and girths to match, and a band of
silken threads to fasten the housing, and clothes
wrought in divers colors and gold tissue, and head
gear studded with jewels, and locks of hair plaited with gold
cord? or is it to be swift and strong in its legs, and even in its
paces, and to have hoofs suitable to a well bred horse, and
courage fitted for long journeys and warfare, and to be able to
behave with calmness in the battlefield, and if a rout takes place
to save its rider? Is it not manifest that these are the things
which constitute the virtue of the horse, not the others? . . .
Well, let us act in the same way in the case of human beings
also: let us determine what is the virtue of man, and let us regard
that alone as an injury, which is destructive to it. What then is
the virtue of man? not riches that thou shouldest fear poverty:
nor health of body that thou shouldest dread sickness, nor the
opinion of the public, that thou shouldest view an evil reputation with alarm, nor life simply for its own sake, that death
should be terrible to thee: nor liberty that thou shouldest avoid
servitude: but carefulness in holding true doctrine, and rectitude
in life. Of these things not even the devil himself will be able to
rob a man, if he who possesses them guards them with the needful carefulness.

ADDITIONAL SCRIPTURE READING:
Psalms 20:7; 33:16–17; Jeremiah 17:5–7

Go to page 723 for your next devotional reading.

100   500

20 There is deceit in the hearts of those
   who plot evil,
      but joy for those who promote
      peace.

21 No harm befalls the righteous,
      but the wicked have their fill of
      trouble.

22 The LORD detests lying lips,
      but he delights in men who are
      truthful.

23 A prudent man keeps his knowledge
   to himself,
      but the heart of fools blurts out
      folly.

24 Diligent hands will rule,
      but laziness ends in slave labor.

25 An anxious heart weighs a man
   down,
      but a kind word cheers him up.

26 A righteous man is cautious in
   friendship,*a*
   but the way of the wicked leads
      them astray.

27 The lazy man does not roast*b* his
   game,
      but the diligent man prizes his
      possessions.

28 In the way of righteousness there is
   life;
      along that path is immortality.

13 A wise son heeds his father's
   instruction,
      but a mocker does not listen to
      rebuke.

2 From the fruit of his lips a man
   enjoys good things,
      but the unfaithful have a craving
      for violence.

3 He who guards his lips guards his
   life,
      but he who speaks rashly will
      come to ruin.

4 The sluggard craves and gets nothing,
      but the desires of the diligent are
      fully satisfied.

5 The righteous hate what is false,
      but the wicked bring shame and
      disgrace.

6 Righteousness guards the man of
   integrity,
      but wickedness overthrows the
      sinner.

7 One man pretends to be rich, yet has
   nothing;
      another pretends to be poor, yet
      has great wealth.

8 A man's riches may ransom his life,
      but a poor man hears no threat.

9 The light of the righteous shines
   brightly,
      but the lamp of the wicked is
      snuffed out.

10 Pride only breeds quarrels,
      but wisdom is found in those who
      take advice.

11 Dishonest money dwindles away,
      but he who gathers money little by
      little makes it grow.

12 Hope deferred makes the heart sick,
      but a longing fulfilled is a tree of
      life.

13 He who scorns instruction will pay
   for it,
      but he who respects a command is
      rewarded.

14 The teaching of the wise is a fountain
   of life,
      turning a man from the snares of
      death.

15 Good understanding wins favor,
      but the way of the unfaithful is
      hard.*c*

16 Every prudent man acts out of
   knowledge,
      but a fool exposes his folly.

17 A wicked messenger falls into
   trouble,
      but a trustworthy envoy brings
      healing.

18 He who ignores discipline comes to
   poverty and shame,
      but whoever heeds correction is
      honored.

19 A longing fulfilled is sweet to the
   soul,
      but fools detest turning from evil.

---

a 26 Or *man is a guide to his neighbor*   *b* 27 The meaning of the Hebrew for this word is uncertain.
c 15 Or *unfaithful does not endure*

20 He who walks with the wise grows
    wise,
  but a companion of fools suffers
    harm.

21 Misfortune pursues the sinner,
  but prosperity is the reward of the
    righteous.

22 A good man leaves an inheritance for
    his children's children,
  but a sinner's wealth is stored up
    for the righteous.

23 A poor man's field may produce
    abundant food,
  but injustice sweeps it away.

24 He who spares the rod hates his son,
  but he who loves him is careful to
    discipline him.

25 The righteous eat to their hearts'
    content,
  but the stomach of the wicked goes
    hungry.

14 The wise woman builds her
  house,
  but with her own hands the foolish
    one tears hers down.

2 He whose walk is upright fears the
    LORD,
  but he whose ways are devious
    despises him.

3 A fool's talk brings a rod to his back,
  but the lips of the wise protect
    them.

4 Where there are no oxen, the manger
    is empty,
  but from the strength of an ox
    comes an abundant harvest.

5 A truthful witness does not deceive,
  but a false witness pours out lies.

6 The mocker seeks wisdom and finds
    none,
  but knowledge comes easily to the
    discerning.

7 Stay away from a foolish man,
  for you will not find knowledge on
    his lips.

8 The wisdom of the prudent is to give
    thought to their ways,
  but the folly of fools is deception.

9 Fools mock at making amends for
    sin,
  but goodwill is found among the
    upright.

10 Each heart knows its own bitterness,
  and no one else can share its joy.

11 The house of the wicked will be
    destroyed,
  but the tent of the upright will
    flourish.

12 There is a way that seems right to a
    man,
  but in the end it leads to death.

13 Even in laughter the heart may ache,
  and joy may end in grief.

14 The faithless will be fully repaid for
    their ways,
  and the good man rewarded for his.

15 A simple man believes anything,
  but a prudent man gives thought to
    his steps.

16 A wise man fears the LORD and shuns
    evil,
  but a fool is hotheaded and
    reckless.

17 A quick-tempered man does foolish
    things,
  and a crafty man is hated.

18 The simple inherit folly,
  but the prudent are crowned with
    knowledge.

19 Evil men will bow down in the
    presence of the good,
  and the wicked at the gates of the
    righteous.

20 The poor are shunned even by their
    neighbors,
  but the rich have many friends.

21 He who despises his neighbor sins,
  but blessed is he who is kind to the
    needy.

22 Do not those who plot evil go astray?
  But those who plan what is good
    find^a love and faithfulness.

23 All hard work brings a profit,
  but mere talk leads only to
    poverty.

^{a} 22 Or *show*

²⁴ The wealth of the wise is their crown,
but the folly of fools yields folly.

²⁵ A truthful witness saves lives,
but a false witness is deceitful.

²⁶ He who fears the LORD has a secure
fortress,
and for his children it will be a
refuge.

²⁷ The fear of the LORD is a fountain of
life,
turning a man from the snares of
death.

WEDNESDAY

A BETTER RESURRECTION
Christina Rossetti

VERSE: Proverbs 14:10   **PASSAGE:** Proverbs 14:10, 13

I have no wit, no words, no tears;
    My heart within me like a stone
Is numbed too much for hopes or fears;
    Look right, look left, I dwell alone;
I lift mine eyes, but dimmed with grief
    No everlasting hills I see;
My life is in the falling leaf:
    O Jesus, quicken me.

My life is like a faded leaf,
    My harvest dwindled to a husk;
Truly my life is void and brief
    And tedious in the barren dusk;
My life is like a frozen thing,
    No bud nor greenness can I see:
Yet rise it shall—the sap of spring;
    O Jesus, rise in me.

My life is like a broken bowl,
    A broken bowl that cannot hold
One drop of water for my soul
    Or cordial in the searching cold;
Cast in the fire the perished thing,
    Melt and remold it, till it be
A royal cup for him my king:
    O Jesus, drink of me.

ADDITIONAL SCRIPTURE READING:
Job 23:10; Proverbs 17:3; Isaiah 64:8

Go to page 725 for your next devotional reading.

1700   1900

28 A large population is a king's glory,
   but without subjects a prince is
      ruined.

29 A patient man has great
      understanding,
   but a quick-tempered man displays
      folly.

30 A heart at peace gives life to the
      body,
   but envy rots the bones.

31 He who oppresses the poor shows
      contempt for their Maker,
   but whoever is kind to the needy
      honors God.

32 When calamity comes, the wicked
      are brought down,
   but even in death the righteous
      have a refuge.

33 Wisdom reposes in the heart of the
      discerning
   and even among fools she lets
      herself be known.*a*

34 Righteousness exalts a nation,
   but sin is a disgrace to any people.

35 A king delights in a wise servant,
   but a shameful servant incurs his
      wrath.

15 A gentle answer turns away
      wrath,
   but a harsh word stirs up anger.

2 The tongue of the wise commends
      knowledge,
   but the mouth of the fool gushes
      folly.

3 The eyes of the LORD are everywhere,
   keeping watch on the wicked and
      the good.

4 The tongue that brings healing is a
      tree of life,
   but a deceitful tongue crushes the
      spirit.

5 A fool spurns his father's discipline,
   but whoever heeds correction
      shows prudence.

6 The house of the righteous contains
      great treasure,
   but the income of the wicked
      brings them trouble.

7 The lips of the wise spread
      knowledge,
   not so the hearts of fools.

8 The LORD detests the sacrifice of the
      wicked,
   but the prayer of the upright
      pleases him.

9 The LORD detests the way of the
      wicked
   but he loves those who pursue
      righteousness.

10 Stern discipline awaits him who
      leaves the path,
   he who hates correction will die.

11 Death and Destruction*b* lie open
      before the LORD—
   how much more the hearts
      of men!

12 A mocker resents correction,
   he will not consult the wise.

13 A happy heart makes the face
      cheerful,
   but heartache crushes the spirit.

14 The discerning heart seeks
      knowledge,
   but the mouth of a fool feeds on
      folly.

15 All the days of the oppressed are
      wretched,
   but the cheerful heart has a
      continual feast.

CHEERFULNESS IS NO SIN, NOR IS THERE ANY
GRACE IN A SOLEMN CAST OF COUNTENANCE.

—John Newton

---

16 Better a little with the fear of the
      LORD
   than great wealth with turmoil.

17 Better a meal of vegetables where
      there is love
   than a fattened calf with hatred.

18 A hot-tempered man stirs up
      dissension,
   but a patient man calms a quarrel.

19 The way of the sluggard is blocked
      with thorns,

---

a 33 Hebrew; Septuagint and Syriac / *but in the heart of fools she is not known*   *b 11* Hebrew *Sheol and Abaddon*

but the path of the upright is a
    highway.

20 A wise son brings joy to his father,
    but a foolish man despises his
    mother.

21 Folly delights a man who lacks
    judgment,
    but a man of understanding keeps a
    straight course.

22 Plans fail for lack of counsel,

THURSDAY

TOUCHING HEAVEN IN PRAYER
A. W. Tozer

VERSE: Proverbs 15:8   **PASSAGE:** Proverbs 15:6–9

Too many praying persons seek to use prayer as a means to ends that are not wholly pure. Prayer is often conceived to be little more than a technique for self-advancement, a heavenly method of achieving earthly success.

Every kind of personal religious project these days is being made the object of prayer. Some of these projects are unscriptural, or at least extrascriptural, and many of them have no higher motive than to relieve the promoter of the unpleasant task of earning an honest living . . .

The Scriptures are very clear about the place of prayer in the economy of God . . . "The prayer of a righteous man is powerful and effective," wrote the inspired James (James 5:16) . . . With this the whole Bible and Christian experience agree: *Prayer is effective.* When it is not answered something is wrong.

The same apostle who affirmed the effective power of prayer admitted also that prayer is sometimes ineffective: "When you ask, you do not receive, because you ask with wrong motives, that you may spend what you get on your pleasures" (James 4:3).

Prayer that slavishly follows the day-by-day development of world news may quite easily be wasted. Most world events as reported by various news media are like ping-pong balls being batted back and forth. They are lively enough, they make an attention-getting racket, but they lack significance.

Surely the God who presides over history knows how few things matter. But he knows also what things do matter; and if we are spiritual enough to hear his voice he will lead us to engage in the kind of praying that will be effective.

ADDITIONAL SCRIPTURE READING:
1 Chronicles 29:17; Psalm 17:1; Proverbs 15:29

Go to page 729 for your next devotional reading.

1900   Present

but with many advisers they
   succeed.

23 A man finds joy in giving an apt
   reply—
   and how good is a timely word!

24 The path of life leads upward for the
   wise
   to keep him from going down to
   the grave.*a*

25 The Lord tears down the proud
   man's house
   but he keeps the widow's
   boundaries intact.

26 The Lord detests the thoughts of the
   wicked,
   but those of the pure are pleasing
   to him.

27 A greedy man brings trouble to his
   family,
   but he who hates bribes will live.

28 The heart of the righteous weighs its
   answers,
   but the mouth of the wicked
   gushes evil.

29 The Lord is far from the wicked
   but he hears the prayer of the
   righteous.

30 A cheerful look brings joy to the heart,
   and good news gives health to the
   bones.

31 He who listens to a life-giving rebuke
   will be at home among the wise.

32 He who ignores discipline despises
   himself,
   but whoever heeds correction gains
   understanding.

33 The fear of the Lord teaches a man
   wisdom,*b*
   and humility comes before honor.

16 To man belong the plans of
   the heart,
   but from the Lord comes the reply
   of the tongue.

2 All a man's ways seem innocent to
   him,
   but motives are weighed by the
   Lord.

3 Commit to the Lord whatever you
   do,
   and your plans will succeed.

4 The Lord works out everything for
   his own ends—
   even the wicked for a day of
   disaster.

5 The Lord detests all the proud of
   heart.
   Be sure of this: They will not go
   unpunished.

6 Through love and faithfulness sin is
   atoned for;
   through the fear of the Lord a man
   avoids evil.

7 When a man's ways are pleasing to
   the Lord,
   he makes even his enemies live at
   peace with him.

WE MUST LEARN TO LIVE TOGETHER AS BROTH-
ERS OR PERISH TOGETHER AS FOOLS.

—*Martin Luther King, Jr.*

---

8 Better a little with righteousness
   than much gain with injustice.

9 In his heart a man plans his course,
   but the Lord determines his steps.

10 The lips of a king speak as an
   oracle,
   and his mouth should not betray
   justice.

11 Honest scales and balances are from
   the Lord;
   all the weights in the bag are of his
   making.

12 Kings detest wrongdoing,
   for a throne is established through
   righteousness.

13 Kings take pleasure in honest lips;
   they value a man who speaks the
   truth.

14 A king's wrath is a messenger of
   death,
   but a wise man will appease it.

15 When a king's face brightens, it
   means life;

---

a 24 Hebrew *Sheol*   *b 33* Or *Wisdom teaches the fear of the Lord*

his favor is like a rain cloud in
    spring.

16 How much better to get wisdom than
    gold,
  to choose understanding rather
    than silver!

17 The highway of the upright avoids
    evil;
  he who guards his way guards his
    life.

18 Pride goes before destruction,
  a haughty spirit before a fall.

19 Better to be lowly in spirit and
    among the oppressed
  than to share plunder with the
    proud.

20 Whoever gives heed to instruction
    prospers,
  and blessed is he who trusts in the
    Lord.

21 The wise in heart are called
    discerning,
  and pleasant words promote
    instruction.[a]

22 Understanding is a fountain of life to
    those who have it,
  but folly brings punishment to
    fools.

23 A wise man's heart guides his mouth,
  and his lips promote instruction.[b]

24 Pleasant words are a honeycomb,
  sweet to the soul and healing to
    the bones.

25 There is a way that seems right to a
    man,
  but in the end it leads to death.

26 The laborer's appetite works for him;
  his hunger drives him on.

27 A scoundrel plots evil,
  and his speech is like a scorching
    fire.

28 A perverse man stirs up dissension,
  and a gossip separates close friends.

29 A violent man entices his neighbor
  and leads him down a path that is
    not good.

30 He who winks with his eye is
    plotting perversity;
  he who purses his lips is bent on
    evil.

31 Gray hair is a crown of splendor;
  it is attained by a righteous life.

32 Better a patient man than a warrior,
  a man who controls his temper
    than one who takes a city.

33 The lot is cast into the lap,
  but its every decision is from the
    Lord.

17 Better a dry crust with peace
  and quiet
than a house full of feasting,[c] with
    strife.

2 A wise servant will rule over a
    disgraceful son,
  and will share the inheritance as
    one of the brothers.

3 The crucible for silver and the
    furnace for gold,
  but the Lord tests the heart.

4 A wicked man listens to evil lips;
  a liar pays attention to a malicious
    tongue.

5 He who mocks the poor shows
    contempt for their Maker;
  whoever gloats over disaster will
    not go unpunished.

6 Children's children are a crown to
    the aged,
  and parents are the pride of their
    children.

7 Arrogant[d] lips are unsuited to a
    fool—
  how much worse lying lips to a
    ruler!

8 A bribe is a charm to the one who
    gives it;
  wherever he turns, he succeeds.

9 He who covers over an offense
    promotes love,
  but whoever repeats the matter
    separates close friends.

10 A rebuke impresses a man of
    discernment
  more than a hundred lashes a fool.

---

a 21 Or words make a man persuasive   *b 23 Or mouth / and makes his lips persuasive*   *c 1 Hebrew
sacrifices*   *d 7 Or Eloquent*

¹¹An evil man is bent only on
rebellion;
a merciless official will be sent
against him.

¹²Better to meet a bear robbed of her
cubs
than a fool in his folly.

¹³If a man pays back evil for good,
evil will never leave his house.

¹⁴Starting a quarrel is like breaching a
dam;
so drop the matter before a dispute
breaks out.

¹⁵Acquitting the guilty and
condemning the innocent—
the Lord detests them both.

¹⁶Of what use is money in the hand of
a fool,
since he has no desire to get
wisdom?

¹⁷A friend loves at all times,
and a brother is born for adversity.

¹⁸A man lacking in judgment strikes
hands in pledge
and puts up security for his
neighbor.

¹⁹He who loves a quarrel loves sin;
he who builds a high gate invites
destruction.

²⁰A man of perverse heart does not
prosper;
he whose tongue is deceitful falls
into trouble.

²¹To have a fool for a son brings grief;
there is no joy for the father of a
fool.

²²A cheerful heart is good medicine,
but a crushed spirit dries up the
bones.

²³A wicked man accepts a bribe in
secret
to pervert the course of justice.

²⁴A discerning man keeps wisdom in
view,
but a fool's eyes wander to the ends
of the earth.

²⁵A foolish son brings grief to his father
and bitterness to the one who bore
him.

²⁶It is not good to punish an innocent
man,
or to flog officials for their
integrity.

²⁷A man of knowledge uses words with
restraint,
and a man of understanding is
even-tempered.

²⁸Even a fool is thought wise if he
keeps silent,
and discerning if he holds his
tongue.

18 An unfriendly man pursues
selfish ends;
he defies all sound judgment.

²A fool finds no pleasure in
understanding
but delights in airing his own
opinions.

³When wickedness comes, so does
contempt,
and with shame comes disgrace.

⁴The words of a man's mouth are deep
waters,
but the fountain of wisdom is a
bubbling brook.

⁵It is not good to be partial to the
wicked
or to deprive the innocent of
justice.

⁶A fool's lips bring him strife,
and his mouth invites a beating.

⁷A fool's mouth is his undoing,
and his lips are a snare to his soul.

⁸The words of a gossip are like choice
morsels;
they go down to a man's inmost
parts.

⁹One who is slack in his work
is brother to one who destroys.

¹⁰The name of the Lord is a strong
tower;
the righteous run to it and are safe.

¹¹The wealth of the rich is their
fortified city;
they imagine it an unscalable wall.

¹²Before his downfall a man's heart is
proud,
but humility comes before honor.

13 He who answers before listening—
  that is his folly and his shame.

14 A man's spirit sustains him in
  sickness,
  but a crushed spirit who can bear?

15 The heart of the discerning acquires
  knowledge;
  the ears of the wise seek it out.

16 A gift opens the way for the giver
  and ushers him into the presence
  of the great.

17 The first to present his case seems
  right,
  till another comes forward and
  questions him.

18 Casting the lot settles disputes
  and keeps strong opponents apart.

19 An offended brother is more
  unyielding than a fortified
  city,
  and disputes are like the barred
  gates of a citadel.

20 From the fruit of his mouth a man's
  stomach is filled;
  with the harvest from his lips he is
  satisfied.

FRIDAY

TRUSTWORTHY FRIENDSHIP

Charles Kingsley

VERSE: Proverbs 18:24   **PASSAGE:** Proverbs 18

 blessed thing it is for any man or woman to have a friend; one human soul whom we can trust utterly; who knows the best and the worst of us, and who loves us, in spite of our faults: who will speak the honest truth to us, while the world flatters us to our faces, and laughs at us behind our backs; who will give us counsel and reproof in the day of prosperity and self conceit; but who, again will comfort and encourage us in the day of difficulty and sorrow, when the world leaves us alone to fight our own battles as we can.

If we have had the good fortune to win such a friend, let us do anything rather than lose him. We must give and forgive; live and let live. If our friends have faults we must bear with them. We must hope all things, believe all things, endure all things rather than lose that most precious of all earthly possessions—a trusty friend. And a friend once won, need never be lost, if we will only be trusty and true ourselves.

ADDITIONAL SCRIPTURE READING:
2 Samuel 9:1–13; Proverbs 17:17; John 15:14–15

Go to page 732 for your next devotional reading.

1700   1900

21 The tongue has the power of life and
death,
  and those who love it will eat its
  fruit.

22 He who finds a wife finds what is good
  and receives favor from the LORD.

23 A poor man pleads for mercy,
  but a rich man answers harshly.

24 A man of many companions may
come to ruin,
  but there is a friend who sticks
  closer than a brother.

19 Better a poor man whose
walk is blameless
  than a fool whose lips are perverse.

2 It is not good to have zeal without
knowledge,
  nor to be hasty and miss the way.

3 A man's own folly ruins his life,
  yet his heart rages against the LORD.

4 Wealth brings many friends,
  but a poor man's friend deserts him.

5 A false witness will not go
unpunished,
  and he who pours out lies will not
  go free.

6 Many curry favor with a ruler,
  and everyone is the friend of a man
  who gives gifts.

7 A poor man is shunned by all his
relatives—
  how much more do his friends
  avoid him!
Though he pursues them with
  pleading,
  they are nowhere to be found.a

8 He who gets wisdom loves his own
soul;
  he who cherishes understanding
  prospers.

9 A false witness will not go
unpunished,
  and he who pours out lies will
  perish.

10 It is not fitting for a fool to live in
luxury—
  how much worse for a slave to rule
  over princes!

11 A man's wisdom gives him patience;
  it is to his glory to overlook an
  offense.

12 A king's rage is like the roar of a lion,
  but his favor is like dew on the
  grass.

13 A foolish son is his father's ruin,
  and a quarrelsome wife is like a
  constant dripping.

14 Houses and wealth are inherited
from parents,
  but a prudent wife is from the
  LORD.

15 Laziness brings on deep sleep,
  and the shiftless man goes hungry.

16 He who obeys instructions guards his
life,
  but he who is contemptuous of his
  ways will die.

17 He who is kind to the poor lends to
the LORD,
  and he will reward him for what he
  has done.

18 Discipline your son, for in that there
is hope;
  do not be a willing party to his
  death.

19 A hot-tempered man must pay the
penalty;
  if you rescue him, you will have to
  do it again.

20 Listen to advice and accept
instruction,
  and in the end you will be wise.

21 Many are the plans in a man's heart,
  but it is the LORD's purpose that
  prevails.

MAN PROPOSES BUT GOD DISPOSES.
  —*Thomas à Kempis*

---

22 What a man desires is unfailing
loveb;
  better to be poor than a liar.

23 The fear of the LORD leads to life:
  Then one rests content, untouched
  by trouble.

---

a 7 The meaning of the Hebrew for this sentence is uncertain.   b 22 Or *A man's greed is his shame*

²⁴The sluggard buries his hand in the
    dish;
  he will not even bring it back to
    his mouth!

²⁵Flog a mocker, and the simple will
    learn prudence;
  rebuke a discerning man, and he
    will gain knowledge.

²⁶He who robs his father and drives out
    his mother
  is a son who brings shame and
    disgrace.

²⁷Stop listening to instruction, my son,
  and you will stray from the words
    of knowledge.

²⁸A corrupt witness mocks at justice,
  and the mouth of the wicked gulps
    down evil.

²⁹Penalties are prepared for mockers,
  and beatings for the backs of fools.

20 Wine is a mocker and beer a
    brawler;
  whoever is led astray by them is
    not wise.

²A king's wrath is like the roar of a
    lion;
  he who angers him forfeits his life.

³It is to a man's honor to avoid strife,
  but every fool is quick to quarrel.

⁴A sluggard does not plow in season;
  so at harvest time he looks but
    finds nothing.

⁵The purposes of a man's heart are
    deep waters,
  but a man of understanding draws
    them out.

⁶Many a man claims to have unfailing
    love,
  but a faithful man who can find?

⁷The righteous man leads a blameless
    life;
  blessed are his children after him.

⁸When a king sits on his throne to
    judge,
  he winnows out all evil with his
    eyes.

⁹Who can say, "I have kept my heart
    pure;
  I am clean and without sin"?

¹⁰Differing weights and differing
    measures—
  the LORD detests them both.

¹¹Even a child is known by his actions,
  by whether his conduct is pure and
    right.

¹²Ears that hear and eyes that see—
  the LORD has made them both.

¹³Do not love sleep or you will grow
    poor;
  stay awake and you will have food
    to spare.

¹⁴"It's no good, it's no good!" says the
    buyer;
  then off he goes and boasts about
    his purchase.

¹⁵Gold there is, and rubies in
    abundance,
  but lips that speak knowledge are a
    rare jewel.

¹⁶Take the garment of one who puts up
    security for a stranger;
  hold it in pledge if he does it for a
    wayward woman.

¹⁷Food gained by fraud tastes sweet to a
    man,
  but he ends up with a mouth full of
    gravel.

¹⁸Make plans by seeking advice;
  if you wage war, obtain guidance.

¹⁹A gossip betrays a confidence;
  so avoid a man who talks too
    much.

²⁰If a man curses his father or mother,
  his lamp will be snuffed out in
    pitch darkness.

²¹An inheritance quickly gained at the
    beginning
  will not be blessed at the end.

²²Do not say, "I'll pay you back for this
    wrong!"
  Wait for the LORD, and he will
    deliver you.

²³The LORD detests differing weights,
  and dishonest scales do not please
    him.

The Loom of Time
Author Unknown

Verse: Proverbs 20:24   **Passage:** Proverbs 20

an's life is laid in the loom of time
    To a pattern he does not see,
While the weavers work and the shuttles fly
    Till the dawn of eternity.

Some shuttles are filled with silver threads
    And some with threads of gold,
While often but the darker hues
    Are all that they may hold.

But the weaver watches with skillful eye
    Each shuttle fly to and fro,
And sees the pattern so deftly wrought
    As the loom moves sure and slow.

God surely planned the pattern:
    Each thread, the dark and fair,
Is chosen by his master skill
    And placed in the web with care.

He only knows its beauty,
    And guides the shuttles which hold
The threads so unattractive,
    As well as the threads of gold.

Not till each loom is silent
    And the shuttles cease to fly,
Shall God reveal the pattern
    And explain the reason why

The dark threads were as needful
    In the weaver's skillful hand
As the threads of gold and silver
    For the pattern which he planned.

Additional Scripture Reading:
Psalm 37:23; Jeremiah 10:23; Acts 17:28

Go to page 736 for your next devotional reading.

24 A man's steps are directed by the
LORD.
How then can anyone understand
his own way?

25 It is a trap for a man to dedicate
something rashly
and only later to consider his vows.

26 A wise king winnows out the
wicked;
he drives the threshing wheel over
them.

27 The lamp of the LORD searches the
spirit of a man*a*;
it searches out his inmost being.

28 Love and faithfulness keep a king
safe;
through love his throne is made
secure.

29 The glory of young men is their
strength,
gray hair the splendor of the old.

30 Blows and wounds cleanse away evil,
and beatings purge the inmost
being.

21 The king's heart is in the
hand of the LORD;
he directs it like a watercourse
wherever he pleases.

2 All a man's ways seem right to him,
but the LORD weighs the heart.

3 To do what is right and just
is more acceptable to the LORD
than sacrifice.

4 Haughty eyes and a proud heart,
the lamp of the wicked, are sin!

5 The plans of the diligent lead to
profit
as surely as haste leads to poverty.

6 A fortune made by a lying tongue
is a fleeting vapor and a deadly
snare.*b*

7 The violence of the wicked will drag
them away,
for they refuse to do what is right.

8 The way of the guilty is devious,

but the conduct of the innocent is
upright.

9 Better to live on a corner of the roof
than share a house with a
quarrelsome wife.

10 The wicked man craves evil;
his neighbor gets no mercy from
him.

11 When a mocker is punished, the
simple gain wisdom;
when a wise man is instructed, he
gets knowledge.

12 The Righteous One*c* takes note of the
house of the wicked
and brings the wicked to ruin.

13 If a man shuts his ears to the cry of
the poor,
he too will cry out and not be
answered.

14 A gift given in secret soothes anger,
and a bribe concealed in the cloak
pacifies great wrath.

15 When justice is done, it brings joy to
the righteous
but terror to evildoers.

16 A man who strays from the path of
understanding
comes to rest in the company of
the dead.

17 He who loves pleasure will become
poor;
whoever loves wine and oil will
never be rich.

18 The wicked become a ransom for the
righteous,
and the unfaithful for the upright.

19 Better to live in a desert
than with a quarrelsome and ill-
tempered wife.

20 In the house of the wise are stores of
choice food and oil,
but a foolish man devours all he
has.

21 He who pursues righteousness and
love
finds life, prosperity*d* and honor.

a 27 Or *The spirit of man is the* LORD's *lamp*   *b 6* Some Hebrew manuscripts, Septuagint and Vulgate;
most Hebrew manuscripts *vapor for those who seek death*   *c 12* Or *The righteous man*   *d 21* Or
righteousness

22 A wise man attacks the city of the
mighty
and pulls down the stronghold in
which they trust.

23 He who guards his mouth and his
tongue
keeps himself from calamity.

24 The proud and arrogant man—
"Mocker" is his name;
he behaves with overweening
pride.

25 The sluggard's craving will be the
death of him,
because his hands refuse to work.

26 All day long he craves for more,
but the righteous give without
sparing.

27 The sacrifice of the wicked is
detestable—
how much more so when brought
with evil intent!

28 A false witness will perish,
and whoever listens to him will be
destroyed forever.[a]

29 A wicked man puts up a bold front,
but an upright man gives thought
to his ways.

30 There is no wisdom, no insight, no
plan
that can succeed against the LORD.

31 The horse is made ready for the day
of battle,
but victory rests with the LORD.

22 A good name is more
desirable than great riches;
to be esteemed is better than silver
or gold.

IT IS NOT THE BRAINS THAT MATTER MOST, BUT
THAT WHICH GUIDES THEM—THE CHARACTER,
THE HEART, GENEROUS QUALITIES, PROGRESSIVE
IDEAS.   —*Fyodor Dostoyevsky*

---

2 Rich and poor have this in common:
The LORD is the Maker of them all.

3 A prudent man sees danger and takes
refuge,

but the simple keep going and
suffer for it.

4 Humility and the fear of the LORD
bring wealth and honor and life.

5 In the paths of the wicked lie thorns
and snares,
but he who guards his soul stays
far from them.

6 Train[b] a child in the way he should
go,
and when he is old he will not turn
from it.

7 The rich rule over the poor,
and the borrower is servant to the
lender.

8 He who sows wickedness reaps
trouble,
and the rod of his fury will be
destroyed.

9 A generous man will himself be
blessed,
for he shares his food with the
poor.

10 Drive out the mocker, and out goes
strife;
quarrels and insults are ended.

11 He who loves a pure heart and whose
speech is gracious
will have the king for his friend.

12 The eyes of the LORD keep watch
over knowledge,
but he frustrates the words of the
unfaithful.

13 The sluggard says, "There is a lion
outside!"
or, "I will be murdered in the
streets!"

14 The mouth of an adulteress is a deep
pit;
he who is under the LORD's wrath
will fall into it.

15 Folly is bound up in the heart of a
child,
but the rod of discipline will drive
it far from him.

16 He who oppresses the poor to
increase his wealth

---

a 28 Or / *but the words of an obedient man will live on*   *b 6* Or *Start*

and he who gives gifts to the rich—
    both come to poverty.

Sayings of the Wise

17 Pay attention and listen to the
    sayings of the wise;
  apply your heart to what I teach,
18 for it is pleasing when you keep them
    in your heart
  and have all of them ready on your
    lips.
19 So that your trust may be in the
    Lord,
  I teach you today, even you.
20 Have I not written thirty*a* sayings for
    you,
  sayings of counsel and knowledge,
21 teaching you true and reliable words,
  so that you can give sound answers
    to him who sent you?

22 Do not exploit the poor because they
    are poor
  and do not crush the needy in
    court,
23 for the Lord will take up their case
  and will plunder those who
    plunder them.

24 Do not make friends with a hot-
    tempered man,
  do not associate with one easily
    angered,
25 or you may learn his ways
  and get yourself ensnared.

26 Do not be a man who strikes hands
    in pledge
  or puts up security for debts;
27 if you lack the means to pay,
  your very bed will be snatched
    from under you.

28 Do not move an ancient boundary
    stone
  set up by your forefathers.

29 Do you see a man skilled in his work?
  He will serve before kings;
  he will not serve before obscure
    men.

23 When you sit to dine with a
    ruler,
  note well what*b* is before you,
2 and put a knife to your throat
  if you are given to gluttony.

3 Do not crave his delicacies,
  for that food is deceptive.

4 Do not wear yourself out to get rich;
  have the wisdom to show restraint.
5 Cast but a glance at riches, and they
    are gone,
  for they will surely sprout wings
  and fly off to the sky like an eagle.

6 Do not eat the food of a stingy man,
  do not crave his delicacies;
7 for he is the kind of man
  who is always thinking about the
    cost.*c*
  "Eat and drink," he says to you,
  but his heart is not with you.
8 You will vomit up the little you have
    eaten
  and will have wasted your
    compliments.

9 Do not speak to a fool,
  for he will scorn the wisdom of
    your words.

10 Do not move an ancient boundary
    stone
  or encroach on the fields of the
    fatherless,
11 for their Defender is strong;
  he will take up their case against
    you.

12 Apply your heart to instruction
  and your ears to words of
    knowledge.

13 Do not withhold discipline from a
    child;
  if you punish him with the rod, he
    will not die.
14 Punish him with the rod
  and save his soul from death.*d*

15 My son, if your heart is wise,
  then my heart will be glad;
16 my inmost being will rejoice
  when your lips speak what is right.

17 Do not let your heart envy sinners,
  but always be zealous for the fear
    of the Lord.
18 There is surely a future hope for you,
  and your hope will not be cut off.

19 Listen, my son, and be wise,
  and keep your heart on the right
    path.

---

a 20 Or *not formerly written; or not written excellent
himself, / so he is; or for as he puts on a feast, / so he is*
    b 1 Or *who*   *c 7* Or *for as he thinks within
d 14* Hebrew *Sheol*

20 Do not join those who drink too much wine
or gorge themselves on meat,
21 for drunkards and gluttons become poor,
and drowsiness clothes them in rags.

22 Listen to your father, who gave you life,
and do not despise your mother when she is old.
23 Buy the truth and do not sell it;
get wisdom, discipline and understanding.

MONDAY

THE HERB CALLED "HEARTS-EASE"
John Bunyan

VERSE: Proverbs 22:4   **Passages**: Proverbs 15:33; 18:12

ow as they were going along and talking, they espied a boy feeding his father's sheep. The boy was in very mean clothes, but of a very fresh and well-favored countenance, and as he sat by himself he sang. Hark, said Mr. Greatheart, to what the shepherd's boy saith. So they hearkened, and he said:

He that is down needs fear no fall,
     He that is low no pride:
He that is humble ever shall
     Have God to be his guide.

I am content with what I have,
     Little be it or much:
And, Lord, contentment still I crave,
     Because thou savest such.

Fullness to such a burden is
     That go on pilgrimage:
Here little, and hereafter bliss,
     Is best from age to age.

Then said their guide, Do you hear him? I will dare to say that this boy lives a merrier life, and wears more of that herb called hearts-ease in his bosom, than he that is clad in silk and velvet.

ADDITIONAL SCRIPTURE READING:
Philippians 4:11–13; 1 Timothy 6:6–8

Go to page 742 for your next devotional reading.

1500   1700

24 The father of a righteous man has
     great joy;
   he who has a wise son delights in
     him.
25 May your father and mother be glad;
   may she who gave you birth rejoice!

26 My son, give me your heart
   and let your eyes keep to my ways,
27 for a prostitute is a deep pit
   and a wayward wife is a narrow
     well.
28 Like a bandit she lies in wait,
   and multiplies the unfaithful
     among men.

29 Who has woe? Who has sorrow?
   Who has strife? Who has
     complaints?
   Who has needless bruises? Who
     has bloodshot eyes?
30 Those who linger over wine,
   who go to sample bowls of mixed
     wine.
31 Do not gaze at wine when it is red,
   when it sparkles in the cup,
   when it goes down smoothly!
32 In the end it bites like a snake
   and poisons like a viper.
33 Your eyes will see strange sights
   and your mind imagine confusing
     things.
34 You will be like one sleeping on the
     high seas,
   lying on top of the rigging.
35 "They hit me," you will say, "but I'm
     not hurt!
   They beat me, but I don't feel it!
   When will I wake up
     so I can find another drink?"

24 Do not envy wicked men,
   do not desire their company;
2 for their hearts plot violence,
   and their lips talk about making
     trouble.

3 By wisdom a house is built,
   and through understanding it is
     established;
4 through knowledge its rooms are
     filled
   with rare and beautiful treasures.

5 A wise man has great power,
   and a man of knowledge increases
     strength;
6 for waging war you need guidance,
   and for victory many advisers.

7 Wisdom is too high for a fool;
   in the assembly at the gate he has
     nothing to say.

8 He who plots evil
   will be known as a schemer.
9 The schemes of folly are sin,
   and men detest a mocker.

10 If you falter in times of trouble,
   how small is your strength!

11 Rescue those being led away to death;
   hold back those staggering toward
     slaughter.
12 If you say, "But we knew nothing
     about this,"
   does not he who weighs the heart
     perceive it?
   Does not he who guards your life
     know it?
   Will he not repay each person
     according to what he has done?

13 Eat honey, my son, for it is good;
   honey from the comb is sweet to
     your taste.
14 Know also that wisdom is sweet to
     your soul;
   if you find it, there is a future hope
     for you,
   and your hope will not be cut off.

15 Do not lie in wait like an outlaw
   against a righteous man's
     house,
   do not raid his dwelling place;
16 for though a righteous man falls
     seven times, he rises again,
   but the wicked are brought down
     by calamity.

17 Do not gloat when your enemy falls;
   when he stumbles, do not let your
     heart rejoice,
18 or the LORD will see and disapprove
   and turn his wrath away from him.

19 Do not fret because of evil men
   or be envious of the wicked,
20 for the evil man has no future hope,
   and the lamp of the wicked will be
     snuffed out.

21 Fear the LORD and the king, my son,
   and do not join with the rebellious,
22 for those two will send sudden
     destruction upon them,
   and who knows what calamities
     they can bring?

Further Sayings of the Wise

23 These also are sayings of the wise:

To show partiality in judging is not
    good:
24 Whoever says to the guilty, "You are
    innocent"—
    peoples will curse him and nations
    denounce him.
25 But it will go well with those who
    convict the guilty,
    and rich blessing will come upon
    them.

26 An honest answer
    is like a kiss on the lips.

27 Finish your outdoor work
    and get your fields ready;
    after that, build your house.

28 Do not testify against your neighbor
    without cause,
    or use your lips to deceive.
29 Do not say, "I'll do to him as he has
    done to me;
    I'll pay that man back for what he
    did."

30 I went past the field of the sluggard,
    past the vineyard of the man who
    lacks judgment;
31 thorns had come up everywhere,
    the ground was covered with weeds,
    and the stone wall was in ruins.
32 I applied my heart to what I observed
    and learned a lesson from what I
    saw:
33 A little sleep, a little slumber,
    a little folding of the hands to rest—
34 and poverty will come on you like a
    bandit
    and scarcity like an armed man. a

More Proverbs of Solomon

25 These are more proverbs of
Solomon, copied by the men
of Hezekiah king of Judah:

2 It is the glory of God to conceal a
    matter;
    to search out a matter is the glory
    of kings.

3 As the heavens are high and the earth
    is deep,

so the hearts of kings are
    unsearchable.

4 Remove the dross from the silver,
    and out comes material for b the
    silversmith;
5 remove the wicked from the king's
    presence,
    and his throne will be established
    through righteousness.

6 Do not exalt yourself in the king's
    presence,
    and do not claim a place among
    great men;
7 it is better for him to say to you,
    "Come up here,"
    than for him to humiliate you
    before a nobleman.

What you have seen with your eyes
8   do not bring c hastily to court,
    for what will you do in the end
    if your neighbor puts you to
    shame?

9 If you argue your case with a
    neighbor,
    do not betray another man's
    confidence,
10 or he who hears it may shame you
    and you will never lose your bad
    reputation.

11 A word aptly spoken
    is like apples of gold in settings of
    silver.

12 Like an earring of gold or an
    ornament of fine gold
    is a wise man's rebuke to a
    listening ear.

13 Like the coolness of snow at harvest
    time
    is a trustworthy messenger to
    those who send him;
    he refreshes the spirit of his
    masters.

14 Like clouds and wind without rain
    is a man who boasts of gifts he
    does not give.

15 Through patience a ruler can be
    persuaded,
    and a gentle tongue can break a
    bone.

a 34 Or like a vagrant / and scarcity like a beggar
on whom you had set your eyes. / 8Do not go   b 4 Or comes a vessel from   c 7,8 Or nobleman /

16 If you find honey, eat just enough—
   too much of it, and you will vomit.
17 Seldom set foot in your neighbor's
      house—
   too much of you, and he will hate
      you.
18 Like a club or a sword or a sharp
      arrow
   is the man who gives false
      testimony against his neighbor.
19 Like a bad tooth or a lame foot
   is reliance on the unfaithful in
      times of trouble.
20 Like one who takes away a garment
      on a cold day,
   or like vinegar poured on soda,
   is one who sings songs to a heavy
      heart.
21 If your enemy is hungry, give him
      food to eat;
   if he is thirsty, give him water to
      drink.
22 In doing this, you will heap burning
      coals on his head,
   and the LORD will reward you.

23 As a north wind brings rain,
   so a sly tongue brings angry looks.

24 Better to live on a corner of the roof
   than share a house with a
      quarrelsome wife.

25 Like cold water to a weary soul
   is good news from a distant land.

26 Like a muddied spring or a polluted
      well
   is a righteous man who gives way
      to the wicked.

27 It is not good to eat too much honey,
   nor is it honorable to seek one's
      own honor.

28 Like a city whose walls are broken
      down
   is a man who lacks self-control.

26 Like snow in summer or rain
      in harvest,
   honor is not fitting for a fool.

2 Like a fluttering sparrow or a darting
      swallow,
   an undeserved curse does not come
      to rest.

3 A whip for the horse, a halter for the
      donkey,
   and a rod for the backs of fools!

4 Do not answer a fool according to his
      folly,
   or you will be like him yourself.

5 Answer a fool according to his folly,
   or he will be wise in his own eyes.

6 Like cutting off one's feet or drinking
      violence
   is the sending of a message by the
      hand of a fool.

7 Like a lame man's legs that hang
      limp
   is a proverb in the mouth of a fool.

8 Like tying a stone in a sling
   is the giving of honor to a fool.

9 Like a thornbush in a drunkard's
      hand
   is a proverb in the mouth of a fool.

10 Like an archer who wounds at
      random
   is he who hires a fool or any passer-
      by.

11 As a dog returns to its vomit,
   so a fool repeats his folly.

12 Do you see a man wise in his own
      eyes?
   There is more hope for a fool than
      for him.

13 The sluggard says, "There is a lion in
      the road,
   a fierce lion roaming the streets!"

14 As a door turns on its hinges,
   so a sluggard turns on his bed.

15 The sluggard buries his hand in the
      dish;
   he is too lazy to bring it back to his
      mouth.

16 The sluggard is wiser in his own eyes
   than seven men who answer
      discreetly.

17 Like one who seizes a dog by the ears
   is a passer-by who meddles in a
      quarrel not his own.

18 Like a madman shooting
      firebrands or deadly arrows
19 is a man who deceives his neighbor
   and says, "I was only joking!"

20 Without wood a fire goes out;
   without gossip a quarrel dies down.

21 As charcoal to embers and as wood to
   fire,
   so is a quarrelsome man for
   kindling strife.

22 The words of a gossip are like choice
   morsels;
   they go down to a man's inmost
   parts.

23 Like a coating of glaze[a] over
   earthenware
   are fervent lips with an evil heart.

24 A malicious man disguises himself
   with his lips,
   but in his heart he harbors deceit.
25 Though his speech is charming, do
   not believe him,
   for seven abominations fill his
   heart.
26 His malice may be concealed by
   deception,

SOME PEOPLE ARE CONTENT NOT TO DO MEAN
ACTIONS; I WANT TO BECOME INCAPABLE OF A
MEAN THOUGHT OR FEELING.

—George MacDonald

---

   but his wickedness will be exposed
   in the assembly.
27 If a man digs a pit, he will fall into it;
   if a man rolls a stone, it will roll
   back on him.
28 A lying tongue hates those it hurts,
   and a flattering mouth works ruin.

27 Do not boast about
   tomorrow,
   for you do not know what a day
   may bring forth.

2 Let another praise you, and not your
   own mouth;
   someone else, and not your own
   lips.

3 Stone is heavy and sand a burden,
   but provocation by a fool is heavier
   than both.

4 Anger is cruel and fury overwhelming,
   but who can stand before jealousy?

5 Better is open rebuke
   than hidden love.

6 Wounds from a friend can be trusted,
   but an enemy multiplies kisses.

7 He who is full loathes honey,
   but to the hungry even what is
   bitter tastes sweet.

8 Like a bird that strays from its nest
   is a man who strays from his
   home.

9 Perfume and incense bring joy to the
   heart,
   and the pleasantness of one's friend
   springs from his earnest
   counsel.

10 Do not forsake your friend and the
   friend of your father,
   and do not go to your brother's
   house when disaster strikes
   you—
   better a neighbor nearby than a
   brother far away.

11 Be wise, my son, and bring joy to my
   heart;
   then I can answer anyone who
   treats me with contempt.

12 The prudent see danger and take
   refuge,
   but the simple keep going and
   suffer for it.

13 Take the garment of one who puts up
   security for a stranger;
   hold it in pledge if he does it for a
   wayward woman.

14 If a man loudly blesses his neighbor
   early in the morning,
   it will be taken as a curse.

15 A quarrelsome wife is like
   a constant dripping on a rainy day;
16 restraining her is like restraining the
   wind
   or grasping oil with the hand.

17 As iron sharpens iron,
   so one man sharpens another.

18 He who tends a fig tree will eat its
   fruit,
   and he who looks after his master
   will be honored.

---

a 23 With a different word division of the Hebrew; Masoretic Text *of silver dross*

19 As water reflects a face,
  so a man's heart reflects the man.

20 Death and Destruction[a] are never
    satisfied,
  and neither are the eyes of man.

21 The crucible for silver and the
    furnace for gold,
  but man is tested by the praise he
    receives.

22 Though you grind a fool in a mortar,
    grinding him like grain with a
    pestle,
  you will not remove his folly from
    him.

23 Be sure you know the condition of
    your flocks,
  give careful attention to your
    herds;

24 for riches do not endure forever,
  and a crown is not secure for all
    generations.

25 When the hay is removed and new
    growth appears
  and the grass from the hills is
    gathered in,

26 the lambs will provide you with
    clothing,
  and the goats with the price of a
    field.

27 You will have plenty of goats' milk
    to feed you and your family
  and to nourish your servant girls.

28 The wicked man flees
    though no one pursues,
  but the righteous are as bold as a
    lion.

2 When a country is rebellious, it has
    many rulers,
  but a man of understanding and
    knowledge maintains order.

3 A ruler[b] who oppresses the poor
  is like a driving rain that leaves no
    crops.

4 Those who forsake the law praise the
    wicked,
  but those who keep the law resist
    them.

5 Evil men do not understand justice,
  but those who seek the LORD
    understand it fully.

6 Better a poor man whose walk is
    blameless
  than a rich man whose ways are
    perverse.

7 He who keeps the law is a discerning
    son,
  but a companion of gluttons
    disgraces his father.

8 He who increases his wealth by
    exorbitant interest
  amasses it for another, who will be
    kind to the poor.

9 If anyone turns a deaf ear to the
    law,
  even his prayers are detestable.

10 He who leads the upright along an
    evil path
  will fall into his own trap,
  but the blameless will receive a
    good inheritance.

11 A rich man may be wise in his own
    eyes,
  but a poor man who has
    discernment sees through
    him.

12 When the righteous triumph, there is
    great elation;
  but when the wicked rise to power,
    men go into hiding.

13 He who conceals his sins does not
    prosper,
  but whoever confesses and
    renounces them finds mercy.

14 Blessed is the man who always fears
    the LORD,
  but he who hardens his heart falls
    into trouble.

15 Like a roaring lion or a charging
    bear
  is a wicked man ruling over a
    helpless people.

16 A tyrannical ruler lacks judgment,
  but he who hates ill-gotten gain
    will enjoy a long life.

17 A man tormented by the guilt of
    murder
  will be a fugitive till death;
  let no one support him.

---

a 20 Hebrew *Sheol and Abaddon*   b 3 Or *A poor man*

18 He whose walk is blameless is kept
safe,
but he whose ways are perverse
will suddenly fall.

19 He who works his land will have
abundant food,

but the one who chases fantasies
will have his fill of poverty.

20 A faithful man will be richly
blessed,
but one eager to get rich will not go
unpunished.

TUESDAY

HOLY BOLDNESS
Charles H. Spurgeon

VERSE: Proverbs 28:1   PASSAGE: Proverbs 28

oly boldness honors the gospel. In the olden times, when Oriental despots had things pretty much their own way, they expected all ambassadors from the West to lay their mouths in the dust if permitted to appear before . . . the [Emperor]. Money-loving traders agreed to all this and ate dust as readily as reptiles, but when England sent her ambassadors abroad, the daring islanders stood bolt upright. They were told that they could not be indulged with a vision of the [Emperor] without going down on their hands and knees. "Very well," said the Englishmen, " . . . But tell his Celestial Splendor that it is very likely that his serenity will hear our cannon at his palace gates before long, and that their booming is not quite so harmless as the cooing of his sublimity's doves." The ambassadors of the British Crown were no cringing petitioners; [and] the British empire rose in the respect of the Oriental nations.

Our cowardice has subjected the gospel to contempt. Jesus was humble, and his servants must not be proud, but Jesus was never mean or cowardly, nor must his servants be. There was no braver man than Christ. He could stoop to save a soul, but he would stoop to nothing by which his character might be compromised, or truth and righteousness insulted. To preach the gospel boldly is to deliver it as such a message ought to be delivered. Blush to preach of a dying Savior? Apologize for talking about the Son of God condescending to be made man, that he might redeem us from all iniquity? *Never!* Oh, by the grace of God let us purpose with Paul "to be yet more bold," that the gospel may be yet more fully preached throughout all ranks of mankind.

ADDITIONAL SCRIPTURE READING:
Psalms 27:1–2; 46:2–3; Acts 4:13

Go to page 748 for your next devotional reading.

1700   1900

21 To show partiality is not good—
    yet a man will do wrong for a piece
        of bread.

22 A stingy man is eager to get rich
    and is unaware that poverty awaits
        him.

23 He who rebukes a man will in the
        end gain more favor
    than he who has a flattering
        tongue.

24 He who robs his father or mother
    and says, "It's not wrong"—
    he is partner to him who destroys.

25 A greedy man stirs up dissension,
    but he who trusts in the LORD will
        prosper.

26 He who trusts in himself is a fool,
    but he who walks in wisdom is
        kept safe.

27 He who gives to the poor will lack
        nothing,
    but he who closes his eyes to them
        receives many curses.

28 When the wicked rise to power,
        people go into hiding;
    but when the wicked perish, the
        righteous thrive.

29 A man who remains stiff-
    necked after many rebukes
    will suddenly be destroyed—
        without remedy.

2 When the righteous thrive, the
        people rejoice;
    when the wicked rule, the people
        groan.

3 A man who loves wisdom brings joy
        to his father,
    but a companion of prostitutes
        squanders his wealth.

4 By justice a king gives a country
        stability,
    but one who is greedy for bribes
        tears it down.

5 Whoever flatters his neighbor
    is spreading a net for his feet.

6 An evil man is snared by his own sin,
    but a righteous one can sing and be
        glad.

7 The righteous care about justice for
        the poor,
    but the wicked have no such
        concern.

8 Mockers stir up a city,
    but wise men turn away anger.

9 If a wise man goes to court with a fool,
    the fool rages and scoffs, and there
        is no peace.

10 Bloodthirsty men hate a man of
        integrity
    and seek to kill the upright.

11 A fool gives full vent to his anger,
    but a wise man keeps himself
        under control.

12 If a ruler listens to lies,
    all his officials become wicked.

13 The poor man and the oppressor have
        this in common:
    The LORD gives sight to the eyes of
        both.

14 If a king judges the poor with fairness,
    his throne will always be secure.

15 The rod of correction imparts
        wisdom,
    but a child left to himself disgraces
        his mother.

16 When the wicked thrive, so does sin,
    but the righteous will see their
        downfall.

17 Discipline your son, and he will give
        you peace;
    he will bring delight to your soul.

18 Where there is no revelation, the
        people cast off restraint;
    but blessed is he who keeps the
        law.

19 A servant cannot be corrected by
        mere words;
    though he understands, he will not
        respond.

20 Do you see a man who speaks in
        haste?
    There is more hope for a fool than
        for him.

21 If a man pampers his servant from
        youth,
    he will bring grief[a] in the end.

a 21 The meaning of the Hebrew for this word is uncertain.

22 An angry man stirs up dissension,
  and a hot-tempered one commits
    many sins.

23 A man's pride brings him low,
  but a man of lowly spirit gains
    honor.

24 The accomplice of a thief is his own
    enemy;
  he is put under oath and dare not
    testify.

25 Fear of man will prove to be a snare,
  but whoever trusts in the LORD is
    kept safe.

26 Many seek an audience with a ruler,
  but it is from the LORD that man
    gets justice.

27 The righteous detest the dishonest;
  the wicked detest the upright.

Sayings of Agur

30 The sayings of Agur son of
  Jakeh—an oracle[a]:

This man declared to Ithiel,
  to Ithiel and to Ucal:[b]

2 "I am the most ignorant of men;
  I do not have a man's
    understanding.
3 I have not learned wisdom,
  nor have I knowledge of the Holy
    One.
4 Who has gone up to heaven and come
    down?
  Who has gathered up the wind in
    the hollow of his hands?
  Who has wrapped up the waters in
    his cloak?
  Who has established all the ends of
    the earth?
  What is his name, and the name of
    his son?
  Tell me if you know!

5 "Every word of God is flawless;
  he is a shield to those who take
    refuge in him.
6 Do not add to his words,
  or he will rebuke you and prove
    you a liar.

7 "Two things I ask of you, O LORD;
  do not refuse me before I die:

8 Keep falsehood and lies far from me;
  give me neither poverty nor
    riches,
  but give me only my daily bread.
9 Otherwise, I may have too much and
    disown you
  and say, 'Who is the LORD?'
  Or I may become poor and steal,
    and so dishonor the name of my
      God.

10 "Do not slander a servant to his
    master,
  or he will curse you, and you will
    pay for it.

11 "There are those who curse their
    fathers
  and do not bless their mothers;
12 those who are pure in their own eyes
  and yet are not cleansed of their
    filth;
13 those whose eyes are ever so
    haughty,
  whose glances are so disdainful;
14 those whose teeth are swords
  and whose jaws are set with knives
  to devour the poor from the earth,
    the needy from among mankind.

15 "The leech has two daughters.
  'Give! Give!' they cry.

"There are three things that are never
    satisfied,
  four that never say, 'Enough!':
16 the grave,[c] the barren womb,
  land, which is never satisfied with
    water,
  and fire, which never says,
    'Enough!'

17 "The eye that mocks a father,
  that scorns obedience to a mother,
  will be pecked out by the ravens of
    the valley,
  will be eaten by the vultures.

18 "There are three things that are too
    amazing for me,
  four that I do not understand:
19 the way of an eagle in the sky,
  the way of a snake on a rock,
  the way of a ship on the high seas,
    and the way of a man with a
      maiden.

---

a 1 Or *Jakeh of Massa*   b 1 Masoretic Text; with a different word division of the Hebrew *declared,* "I
am weary, O God; / I am weary, O God, and faint.   c 16 Hebrew *Sheol*

20 "This is the way of an adulteress:
    She eats and wipes her mouth
    and says, 'I've done nothing
        wrong.'

21 "Under three things the earth
        trembles,
    under four it cannot bear up:
22 a servant who becomes king,
    a fool who is full of food,
23 an unloved woman who is married,
    and a maidservant who displaces
        her mistress.

24 "Four things on earth are small,
    yet they are extremely wise:
25 Ants are creatures of little strength,
    yet they store up their food in the
        summer;
26 coneys*a* are creatures of little power,
    yet they make their home in the
        crags;
27 locusts have no king,
    yet they advance together in ranks;
28 a lizard can be caught with the hand,
    yet it is found in kings' palaces.

29 "There are three things that are
        stately in their stride,
    four that move with stately
        bearing:
30 a lion, mighty among beasts,
    who retreats before nothing;
31 a strutting rooster, a he-goat,
    and a king with his army around
        him.*b*

32 "If you have played the fool and
        exalted yourself,
    or if you have planned evil,
    clap your hand over your mouth!
33 For as churning the milk produces
        butter,
    and as twisting the nose produces
        blood,
    so stirring up anger produces
        strife."

Sayings of King Lemuel

31 The sayings of King Lemuel—
    an oracle*c* his mother taught
him:

2 "O my son, O son of my womb,
    O son of my vows,*d*

3 do not spend your strength on
        women,
    your vigor on those who ruin kings.

4 "It is not for kings, O Lemuel—
    not for kings to drink wine,
    not for rulers to crave beer,
5 lest they drink and forget what the
        law decrees,
    and deprive all the oppressed of
        their rights.
6 Give beer to those who are perishing,
    wine to those who are in anguish;
7 let them drink and forget their
        poverty
    and remember their misery no
        more.

8 "Speak up for those who cannot
        speak for themselves,
    for the rights of all who are
        destitute.
9 Speak up and judge fairly;
    defend the rights of the poor and
        needy."

Epilogue: The Wife of Noble Character

10 *e* A wife of noble character who can
        find?
    She is worth far more than rubies.
11 Her husband has full confidence in
        her
    and lacks nothing of value.
12 She brings him good, not harm,
    all the days of her life.
13 She selects wool and flax
    and works with eager hands.
14 She is like the merchant ships,
    bringing her food from afar.
15 She gets up while it is still dark;
    she provides food for her family
    and portions for her servant girls.
16 She considers a field and buys it;
    out of her earnings she plants a
        vineyard.
17 She sets about her work vigorously;
    her arms are strong for her tasks.
18 She sees that her trading is profitable,
    and her lamp does not go out at
        night.
19 In her hand she holds the distaff
    and grasps the spindle with her
        fingers.

a 26 That is, the hyrax or rock badger   *b 31* Or *king secure against revolt*   *c 1* Or *of Lemuel king of Massa, which*   *d 2* Or */ the answer to my prayers*   *e 10* Verses 10–31 are an acrostic, each verse beginning with a successive letter of the Hebrew alphabet.

20 She opens her arms to the poor
  and extends her hands to the needy.
21 When it snows, she has no fear for
    her household;
  for all of them are clothed in
    scarlet.
22 She makes coverings for her bed;
  she is clothed in fine linen and
    purple.
23 Her husband is respected at the city
    gate,
  where he takes his seat among the
    elders of the land.
24 She makes linen garments and sells
    them,
  and supplies the merchants with
    sashes.
25 She is clothed with strength and
    dignity;
  she can laugh at the days to come.

26 She speaks with wisdom,
  and faithful instruction is on her
    tongue.
27 She watches over the affairs of her
    household
  and does not eat the bread of
    idleness.
28 Her children arise and call her
    blessed;
  her husband also, and he praises
    her:
29 "Many women do noble things,
  but you surpass them all."
30 Charm is deceptive, and beauty is
    fleeting;
  but a woman who fears the LORD is
    to be praised.
31 Give her the reward she has earned,
  and let her works bring her praise
    at the city gate.

ECCLESIASTES

THIS BOOK TEACHES THAT LIFE NOT CENTERED ON GOD IS PURPOSELESS AND MEANINGLESS. WITHOUT GOD, NOTHING CAN SATISFY (2:25). WITH HIM, ALL OF LIFE AND HIS GOOD GIFTS ARE TO BE GRATEFULLY RECEIVED AND USED AND ENJOYED TO THE FULL (2:26; 11:8). AS YOU READ THIS BOOK, YOU WILL CONFRONT HONEST CONFESSIONS OF DOUBTS AND STRUGGLES WITH DISILLUSIONMENT. THINK ABOUT YOUR OWN SENSE OF PURPOSE AS YOU SEEK TO CULTIVATE A GOD-FEARING ATTITUDE TOWARD LIFE.

Everything Is Meaningless

1 The words of the Teacher,*a* son of David, king in Jerusalem:

2 "Meaningless! Meaningless!"
    says the Teacher.
"Utterly meaningless!
    Everything is meaningless."

3 What does man gain from all his labor
    at which he toils under the sun?
4 Generations come and generations go,
    but the earth remains forever.
5 The sun rises and the sun sets,
    and hurries back to where it rises.
6 The wind blows to the south
    and turns to the north;
round and round it goes,
    ever returning on its course.
7 All streams flow into the sea,
    yet the sea is never full.
To the place the streams come from,
    there they return again.
8 All things are wearisome,
    more than one can say.
The eye never has enough of seeing,
    nor the ear its fill of hearing.
9 What has been will be again,
    what has been done will be done again;
    there is nothing new under the sun.
10 Is there anything of which one can say,
    "Look! This is something new"?
It was here already, long ago;
    it was here before our time.

a 1 Or leader of the assembly; also in verses 2 and 12

THE CONSECRATION OF TIME
Thomas Merton

VERSE: Ecclesiastes 1:9   **PASSAGE:** Ecclesiastes 1:1–11

he fundamental theme of Ecclesiastes is the paradox that, although there is "nothing new under the sun," each new generation of mankind is condemned by nature to wear itself out in the pursuit of "novelties" that do not exist. This concept . . . . contains in itself the one great enigma of paganism. Only Christ, only the incarnation, by which God emerged from his eternity to enter into time and consecrate it to himself, could save time from being an endless circle of frustrations. Only Christianity can, in Saint Paul's phrase, "redeem the times." Other religions can break out of the wheel of time as though from a prison: but they can make nothing of time itself.

Saint Gregory of Nyssa, pursuing his meditations on the psychology of attachment and illusion, vision and detachment, which constitute his commentary on Ecclesiastes, observes how time weaves about us this web of illusion. It is not enough to say that the man who is attached to this world has bound himself to it, once and for all, by a wrong choice. No: he spins a whole net of falsities around his spirit by the repeated consecration of his whole self to values that do not exist. He exhausts himself in the pursuit of mirages that ever fade and are renewed as fast as they have faded, drawing him further and further into the wilderness where he must die of thirst . . .

And so, that "utter meaninglessness" which so exercised the ancient preacher of Ecclesiastes and his commentator is a life not merely of deluded thoughts and aspirations, but above all a life of ceaseless and sterile activity. What is more, in such a life the measure of illusion is the very intensity of activity itself. The less you have, the more you do. The final delusion is movement, change, and variety for their own sakes alone.

ADDITIONAL SCRIPTURE READING:
Psalm 39:5–6; Ecclesiastes 6:10

Go to page 751 for your next devotional reading.

1900   Present

11 There is no remembrance of men of
old,
   and even those who are yet to come
will not be remembered
   by those who follow.

Wisdom Is Meaningless

12 I, the Teacher, was king over Israel
in Jerusalem. **13** I devoted myself to study
and to explore by wisdom all that is
done under heaven. What a heavy burden God has laid on men! **14** I have seen
all the things that are done under the
sun; all of them are meaningless, a chasing after the wind.

15 What is twisted cannot be
straightened;
   what is lacking cannot be counted.

16 I thought to myself, "Look, I have
grown and increased in wisdom more
than anyone who has ruled over Jerusalem before me; I have experienced
much of wisdom and knowledge."
17 Then I applied myself to the understanding of wisdom, and also of madness and folly, but I learned that this,
too, is a chasing after the wind.

18 For with much wisdom comes much
sorrow;
   the more knowledge, the more
grief.

Pleasures Are Meaningless

2 I thought in my heart, "Come
now, I will test you with pleasure to find out what is good." But that
also proved to be meaningless. **2** "Laughter," I said, "is foolish. And what does
pleasure accomplish?" **3** I tried cheering
myself with wine, and embracing
folly—my mind still guiding me with
wisdom. I wanted to see what was
worthwhile for men to do under heaven
during the few days of their lives.

4 I undertook great projects: I built
houses for myself and planted vineyards.
5 I made gardens and parks and planted all
kinds of fruit trees in them. **6** I made
reservoirs to water groves of flourishing
trees. **7** I bought male and female slaves
and had other slaves who were born in
my house. I also owned more herds and
flocks than anyone in Jerusalem before
me. **8** I amassed silver and gold for myself,
and the treasure of kings and provinces. I
acquired men and women singers, and a
harem*a* as well—the delights of the heart
of man. **9** I became greater by far than anyone in Jerusalem before me. In all this my
wisdom stayed with me.

10 I denied myself nothing my eyes
desired;
   I refused my heart no pleasure.
My heart took delight in all my
work,
   and this was the reward for all my
labor.
11 Yet when I surveyed all that my
hands had done
   and what I had toiled to achieve,
everything was meaningless, a
chasing after the wind;
   nothing was gained under the sun.

Wisdom and Folly Are Meaningless

12 Then I turned my thoughts to
consider wisdom,
   and also madness and folly.
What more can the king's successor
do
   than what has already been done?
13 I saw that wisdom is better than
folly,
   just as light is better than darkness.
14 The wise man has eyes in his head,
   while the fool walks in the
darkness;
but I came to realize
   that the same fate overtakes them
both.

15 Then I thought in my heart,

"The fate of the fool will overtake
me also.
   What then do I gain by being
wise?"
I said in my heart,
   "This too is meaningless."
16 For the wise man, like the fool, will
not be long remembered;
   in days to come both will be
forgotten.
Like the fool, the wise man too must
die!

---

a 8 The meaning of the Hebrew for this phrase is uncertain.

Toil Is Meaningless

17So I hated life, because the work that is done under the sun was grievous to me. All of it is meaningless, a chasing after the wind. **18**I hated all the things I had toiled for under the sun, because I must leave them to the one who comes after me. **19**And who knows whether he will be a wise man or a fool? Yet he will have control over all the work into which I have poured my effort and skill under the sun. This too is meaningless. **20**So my heart began to despair over all my toilsome labor under the sun. **21**For a man may do his work with wisdom, knowledge and skill, and then he must leave all he owns to someone who has not worked for it. This too is meaningless and a great misfortune. **22**What does a man get for all the toil and anxious striving with which he labors under the sun? **23**All his days his work is pain and grief; even at night his mind does not rest. This too is meaningless.

24A man can do nothing better than to eat and drink and find satisfaction in his work. This too, I see, is from the hand of God, **25**for without him, who can eat or find enjoyment? **26**To the man who pleases him, God gives wisdom, knowledge and happiness, but to the sinner he gives the task of gathering and storing up wealth to hand it over to the one who pleases God. This too is meaningless, a chasing after the wind.

A Time for Everything

 3 There is a time for everything,
and a season for every activity
　　under heaven:

2 a time to be born and a time to die,
　a time to plant and a time to
　　uproot,
3 a time to kill and a time to heal,
　a time to tear down and a time to
　　build,
4 a time to weep and a time to laugh,
　a time to mourn and a time to
　　dance,
5 a time to scatter stones and a time
　　to gather them,
　a time to embrace and a time to
　　refrain,

6 a time to search and a time to give
　　up,
　a time to keep and a time to throw
　　away,
7 a time to tear and a time to mend,
　a time to be silent and a time to
　　speak,
8 a time to love and a time to hate,
　a time for war and a time for peace.

9What does the worker gain from his toil? **10**I have seen the burden God has laid on men. **11**He has made everything beautiful in its time. He has also set eternity in the hearts of men; yet they cannot fathom what God has done from beginning to end. **12**I know that there is nothing better for men than to be happy and do good while they live. **13**That everyone may eat and drink, and find satisfaction in all his toil—this is the gift of God. **14**I know that everything God does will endure forever; nothing can be added to it and nothing taken from it. God does it so that men will revere him.

15Whatever is has already been,
　and what will be has been before;
　and God will call the past to
　　account.*a*

16And I saw something else under the sun:

In the place of judgment—
　　wickedness was there,
　in the place of justice—wickedness
　　was there.

17I thought in my heart,

"God will bring to judgment
　both the righteous and the wicked,
for there will be a time for every
　　activity,
　a time for every deed."

18I also thought, "As for men, God tests them so that they may see that they are like the animals. **19**Man's fate is like that of the animals; the same fate awaits them both: As one dies, so dies the other. All have the same breath*b*; man has no advantage over the animal. Everything is

a 15 Or *God calls back the past*　　*b 19* Or *spirit*

PREFACES FOR SEASONS
Book of Common Prayer

VERSE: Ecclesiastes 3:1   PASSAGE: Ecclesiastes 3:1–8

Advent

 ecause thou didst send thy beloved Son to redeem us from sin and death, and to make us heirs in him of everlasting life; that when he shall come again in power and great triumph to judge the world, we may without shame or fear rejoice to behold his appearing.

Incarnation

Because thou didst give Jesus Christ, thine only Son, to be born for us; who, by the mighty power of the Holy Ghost, was made very man of the substance of the Virgin Mary his mother; that we might be delivered from the bondage of sin, and receive power to become thy children.

Easter

But chiefly are we bound to praise thee for the glorious resurrection of thy Son Jesus Christ our Lord; for he is the very paschal lamb, who was sacrificed for us, and hath taken away the sin of the world; who by his death hath destroyed death, and by his rising to life again hath won for us everlasting life.

Ascension

Through thy dearly beloved son Jesus Christ our Lord; who after his glorious resurrection manifestly appeared to his disciples; and in their sight ascended into heaven, to prepare a place for us; that where he is, there we might also be, and reign with him in glory.

Pentecost

Through Jesus Christ our Lord; according to whose true promise the Holy Ghost came down [on this day] from heaven, lighting upon the disciples, to teach them and to lead them into all truth; uniting peoples of many tongues in the confession of one faith, and giving to thy church the power to serve thee as a royal priesthood, and to preach the Gospel to all nations.

ADDITIONAL SCRIPTURE READING:
Ecclesiastes 8:5–6; Song of Songs 2:12

Go to page 755 for your next devotional reading.

1700   1900

meaningless. **20**All go to the same place; all come from dust, and to dust all return. **21**Who knows if the spirit of man rises upward and if the spirit of the animal*ᵃ* goes down into the earth?"

22So I saw that there is nothing better for a man than to enjoy his work, because that is his lot. For who can bring him to see what will happen after him?

Oppression, Toil, Friendlessness

4 Again I looked and saw all the oppression that was taking place under the sun:

> I saw the tears of the oppressed—
> and they have no comforter;
> power was on the side of their
> oppressors—
> and they have no comforter.
> **2** And I declared that the dead,
> who had already died,
> are happier than the living,
> who are still alive.
> **3** But better than both
> is he who has not yet been,
> who has not seen the evil
> that is done under the sun.

4And I saw that all labor and all achievement spring from man's envy of his neighbor. This too is meaningless, a chasing after the wind.

> **5** The fool folds his hands
> and ruins himself.
> **6** Better one handful with tranquillity
> than two handfuls with toil
> and chasing after the wind.

7Again I saw something meaningless under the sun:

> **8** There was a man all alone;
> he had neither son nor brother.
> There was no end to his toil,
> yet his eyes were not content with
> his wealth.
> "For whom am I toiling," he asked,
> "and why am I depriving myself of
> enjoyment?"
> This too is meaningless—
> a miserable business!

> **9** Two are better than one,

because they have a good return for their work:
> **10** If one falls down,
> his friend can help him up.
> But pity the man who falls
> and has no one to help him up!
> **11** Also, if two lie down together, they
> will keep warm.
> But how can one keep warm alone?
> **12** Though one may be overpowered,
> two can defend themselves.
> A cord of three strands is not quickly
> broken.

Advancement Is Meaningless

13Better a poor but wise youth than an old but foolish king who no longer knows how to take warning. **14**The youth may have come from prison to the kingship, or he may have been born in poverty within his kingdom. **15**I saw that all who lived and walked under the sun followed the youth, the king's successor. **16**There was no end to all the people who were before them. But those who came later were not pleased with the successor. This too is meaningless, a chasing after the wind.

Stand in Awe of God

5 Guard your steps when you go to the house of God. Go near to listen rather than to offer the sacrifice of fools, who do not know that they do wrong.

> **2** Do not be quick with your mouth,
> do not be hasty in your heart
> to utter anything before God.
> God is in heaven
> and you are on earth,
> so let your words be few.
> **3** As a dream comes when there are
> many cares,
> so the speech of a fool when there
> are many words.

4When you make a vow to God, do not delay in fulfilling it. He has no pleasure in fools; fulfill your vow. **5**It is better not to vow than to make a vow and not fulfill it. **6**Do not let your mouth lead you into sin. And do not protest to the ⌊temple⌋ messenger, "My vow was a mistake." Why should God be angry at

---

ᵃ 21 Or Who knows the spirit of man, which rises upward, or the spirit of the animal, which

what you say and destroy the work of your hands? [7]Much dreaming and many words are meaningless. Therefore stand in awe of God.

Riches Are Meaningless

[8]If you see the poor oppressed in a district, and justice and rights denied, do not be surprised at such things; for one official is eyed by a higher one, and over them both are others higher still. [9]The increase from the land is taken by all; the king himself profits from the fields.

[10]Whoever loves money never has
    money enough;
  whoever loves wealth is never
    satisfied with his income.
  This too is meaningless.

[11]As goods increase,
  so do those who consume them.
And what benefit are they to the
    owner
  except to feast his eyes on them?

[12]The sleep of a laborer is sweet,
  whether he eats little or much,
but the abundance of a rich man
  permits him no sleep.

[13]I have seen a grievous evil under the sun:

  wealth hoarded to the harm of its
    owner,
[14] or wealth lost through some
    misfortune,
so that when he has a son
  there is nothing left for him.
[15]Naked a man comes from his
    mother's womb,
  and as he comes, so he departs.
He takes nothing from his labor
  that he can carry in his hand.

[16]This too is a grievous evil:

As a man comes, so he departs,
  and what does he gain,
  since he toils for the wind?
[17]All his days he eats in darkness,
  with great frustration, affliction
    and anger.

[18]Then I realized that it is good and proper for a man to eat and drink, and to find satisfaction in his toilsome labor under the sun during the few days of life God has given him—for this is his lot. [19]Moreover, when God gives any man wealth and possessions, and enables him to enjoy them, to accept his lot and be happy in his work—this is a gift of God. [20]He seldom reflects on the days of his life, because God keeps him occupied with gladness of heart.

[6]I have seen another evil under the sun, and it weighs heavily on men: [2]God gives a man wealth, possessions and honor, so that he lacks nothing his heart desires, but God does not enable him to enjoy them, and a stranger enjoys them instead. This is meaningless, a grievous evil.

[3]A man may have a hundred children and live many years; yet no matter how long he lives, if he cannot enjoy his prosperity and does not receive proper burial, I say that a stillborn child is better off than he. [4]It comes without meaning, it departs in darkness, and in darkness its name is shrouded. [5]Though it never saw the sun or knew anything, it has more rest than does that man— [6]even if he lives a thousand years twice over but fails to enjoy his prosperity. Do not all go to the same place?

[7]All man's efforts are for his mouth,
  yet his appetite is never satisfied.
[8]What advantage has a wise man
    over a fool?
What does a poor man gain
  by knowing how to conduct
    himself before others?
[9]Better what the eye sees
  than the roving of the appetite.
This too is meaningless,
  a chasing after the wind.

[10]Whatever exists has already been
    named,
  and what man is has been known;
no man can contend
  with one who is stronger than he.
[11]The more the words,
  the less the meaning,
  and how does that profit anyone?

[12]For who knows what is good for a man in life, during the few and meaningless days he passes through like a

shadow? Who can tell him what will happen under the sun after he is gone?

Wisdom

7 A good name is better than fine perfume,
 and the day of death better than the day of birth.
2 It is better to go to a house of mourning
 than to go to a house of feasting,
for death is the destiny of every man;
 the living should take this to heart.
3 Sorrow is better than laughter,
 because a sad face is good for the heart.
4 The heart of the wise is in the house of mourning,
 but the heart of fools is in the house of pleasure.
5 It is better to heed a wise man's rebuke
 than to listen to the song of fools.
6 Like the crackling of thorns under the pot,
 so is the laughter of fools.
 This too is meaningless.

7 Extortion turns a wise man into a fool,
 and a bribe corrupts the heart.

8 The end of a matter is better than its beginning,
 and patience is better than pride.
9 Do not be quickly provoked in your spirit,
 for anger resides in the lap of fools.

10 Do not say, "Why were the old days better than these?"
 For it is not wise to ask such questions.

11 Wisdom, like an inheritance, is a good thing
 and benefits those who see the sun.
12 Wisdom is a shelter
 as money is a shelter,
 but the advantage of knowledge is this:
 that wisdom preserves the life of its possessor.

13 Consider what God has done:

Who can straighten
 what he has made crooked?

14 When times are good, be happy;
 but when times are bad, consider:
God has made the one
 as well as the other.
Therefore, a man cannot discover
 anything about his future.

15 In this meaningless life of mine I have seen both of these:

a righteous man perishing in his righteousness,
 and a wicked man living long in his wickedness.
16 Do not be overrighteous,
 neither be overwise—
 why destroy yourself?
17 Do not be overwicked,
 and do not be a fool—
 why die before your time?
18 It is good to grasp the one
 and not let go of the other.
 The man who fears God will avoid all ⌊extremes⌋.*a*

19 Wisdom makes one wise man more powerful
 than ten rulers in a city.

20 There is not a righteous man on earth
 who does what is right and never sins.

21 Do not pay attention to every word people say,
 or you may hear your servant cursing you—
22 for you know in your heart
 that many times you yourself have cursed others.

23 All this I tested by wisdom and I said,

"I am determined to be wise"—
 but this was beyond me.
24 Whatever wisdom may be,
 it is far off and most profound—
 who can discover it?
25 So I turned my mind to understand,
 to investigate and to search out wisdom and the scheme of things
and to understand the stupidity of wickedness
 and the madness of folly.

26 I find more bitter than death

a 18 Or will follow them both

the woman who is a snare,
whose heart is a trap
and whose hands are chains.
The man who pleases God will
escape her,
but the sinner she will ensnare.

[a] 27 Or *leader of the assembly*

27 "Look," says the Teacher,[a] "this is what I have discovered:

"Adding one thing to another to
discover the scheme of
things—

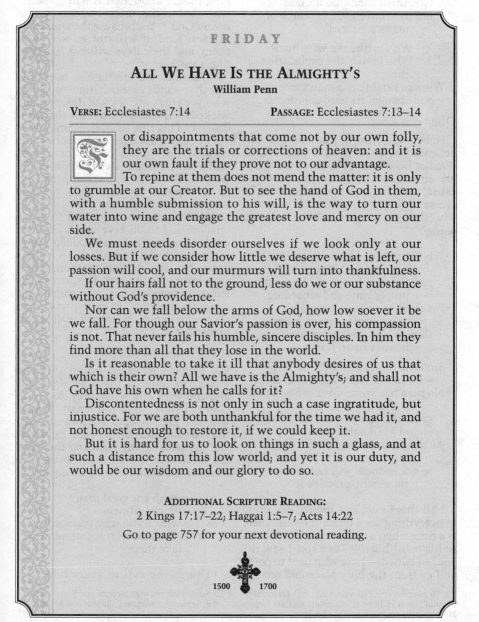

FRIDAY

ALL WE HAVE IS THE ALMIGHTY'S
William Penn

VERSE: Ecclesiastes 7:14   **PASSAGE:** Ecclesiastes 7:13–14

or disappointments that come not by our own folly, they are the trials or corrections of heaven: and it is our own fault if they prove not to our advantage.

To repine at them does not mend the matter: it is only to grumble at our Creator. But to see the hand of God in them, with a humble submission to his will, is the way to turn our water into wine and engage the greatest love and mercy on our side.

We must needs disorder ourselves if we look only at our losses. But if we consider how little we deserve what is left, our passion will cool, and our murmurs will turn into thankfulness.

If our hairs fall not to the ground, less do we or our substance without God's providence.

Nor can we fall below the arms of God, how low soever it be we fall. For though our Savior's passion is over, his compassion is not. That never fails his humble, sincere disciples. In him they find more than all that they lose in the world.

Is it reasonable to take it ill that anybody desires of us that which is their own? All we have is the Almighty's; and shall not God have his own when he calls for it?

Discontentedness is not only in such a case ingratitude, but injustice. For we are both unthankful for the time we had it, and not honest enough to restore it, if we could keep it.

But it is hard for us to look on things in such a glass, and at such a distance from this low world; and yet it is our duty, and would be our wisdom and our glory to do so.

ADDITIONAL SCRIPTURE READING:
2 Kings 17:17–22; Haggai 1:5–7; Acts 14:22

Go to page 757 for your next devotional reading.

1500   1700

28 while I was still searching
    but not finding—
I found one ⌊upright⌋ man among a
    thousand,
    but not one ⌊upright⌋ woman
    among them all.
29 This only have I found:
    God made mankind upright,
    but men have gone in search of
    many schemes."

8 Who is like the wise man?
    Who knows the explanation of
    things?
Wisdom brightens a man's face
    and changes its hard appearance.

Obey the King

2 Obey the king's command, I say, because you took an oath before God. 3 Do not be in a hurry to leave the king's presence. Do not stand up for a bad cause, for he will do whatever he pleases. 4 Since a king's word is supreme, who can say to him, "What are you doing?"

5 Whoever obeys his command will
    come to no harm,
and the wise heart will know the
    proper time and procedure.
6 For there is a proper time and
    procedure for every matter,
though a man's misery weighs
    heavily upon him.

7 Since no man knows the future,
    who can tell him what is to come?
8 No man has power over the wind to
    contain it[a];
so no one has power over the day
    of his death.
As no one is discharged in time of
    war,
so wickedness will not release
    those who practice it.

9 All this I saw, as I applied my mind to everything done under the sun. There is a time when a man lords it over others to his own[b] hurt. 10 Then too, I saw the wicked buried—those who used to come and go from the holy place and receive praise[c] in the city where they did this. This too is meaningless.

11 When the sentence for a crime is not quickly carried out, the hearts of the people are filled with schemes to do wrong. 12 Although a wicked man commits a hundred crimes and still lives a long time, I know that it will go better with God-fearing men, who are reverent before God. 13 Yet because the wicked do not fear God, it will not go well with them, and their days will not lengthen like a shadow.

14 There is something else meaningless that occurs on earth: righteous men who get what the wicked deserve, and wicked men who get what the righteous deserve. This too, I say, is meaningless. 15 So I commend the enjoyment of life, because nothing is better for a man under the sun than to eat and drink and be glad. Then joy will accompany him in his work all the days of the life God has given him under the sun.

16 When I applied my mind to know wisdom and to observe man's labor on earth—his eyes not seeing sleep day or night— 17 then I saw all that God has done. No one can comprehend what goes on under the sun. Despite all his efforts to search it out, man cannot discover its meaning. Even if a wise man claims he knows, he cannot really comprehend it.

A Common Destiny for All

9 So I reflected on all this and concluded that the righteous and the wise and what they do are in God's hands, but no man knows whether love or hate awaits him. 2 All share a common destiny—the righteous and the wicked, the good and the bad,[d] the clean and the unclean, those who offer sacrifices and those who do not.

As it is with the good man,
    so with the sinner;
as it is with those who take oaths,
    so with those who are afraid to
    take them.

3 This is the evil in everything that

---

[a] 8 Or *over his spirit to retain it*   [b] 9 Or *to their* (Aquila); most Hebrew manuscripts *and are forgotten*   [c] 10 Some Hebrew manuscripts and Septuagint Hebrew does not have *and the bad.*   [d] 2 Septuagint (Aquila), Vulgate and Syriac;

WEEKEND

JESUS THE LORD, OUR RIGHTEOUSNESS
Count Nikolaus Ludwig von Zinzendorf

VERSE: Isaiah 61:10 **PASSAGE:** Isaiah 61:10–11

 esus, thy blood and righteousness,
My beauty are, my glorious dress;
Midst flaming worlds, in these arrayed,
With joy shall I lift up my head.

Lord, I believe thy precious blood,
Which, at the mercy seat of God,
Forever doth for sinners plead,
For me, e'en for my soul, was shed.

Lord, I believe were sinners more
Than sands upon the ocean shore,
Thou hast for all a ransom paid,
For all a full redemption made.

Bold shall I stand in that great day,
For who aught to my charge shall lay?
Fully, by thee, absolved I am
From sin and fear, from guilt and shame.

This spotless robe the same appears,
When ruined nature sinks in years;
No age can change its glorious hue,
Its glory is forever new.

Thou God of power, thou God of love,
Let many more, thy mercy prove;
Their beauty this, their glorious dress,
Jesus the Lord, our righteousness.

ADDITIONAL SCRIPTURE READING:
Psalm 132:9; Romans 13:14; Revelation 7:9–14

Go to page 759 for your next devotional reading.

1700   1900

happens under the sun: The same destiny overtakes all. The hearts of men, moreover, are full of evil and there is madness in their hearts while they live, and afterward they join the dead. ⁴Anyone who is among the living has hope[a]—even a live dog is better off than a dead lion!

⁵For the living know that they will die,
  but the dead know nothing;
they have no further reward,
  and even the memory of them is
    forgotten.
⁶Their love, their hate
  and their jealousy have long since
    vanished;
never again will they have a part
  in anything that happens under the
    sun.

⁷Go, eat your food with gladness, and drink your wine with a joyful heart, for it is now that God favors what you do. ⁸Always be clothed in white, and always anoint your head with oil. ⁹Enjoy life with your wife, whom you love, all the days of this meaningless life that God has given you under the sun— all your meaningless days. For this is your lot in life and in your toilsome labor under the sun. ¹⁰Whatever your hand finds to do, do it with all your might, for in the grave,[b] where you are going, there is neither working nor planning nor knowledge nor wisdom.

¹¹I have seen something else under the sun:

The race is not to the swift
  or the battle to the strong,
nor does food come to the wise
  or wealth to the brilliant
  or favor to the learned;
but time and chance happen to them
  all.

¹²Moreover, no man knows when his hour will come:

As fish are caught in a cruel net,
  or birds are taken in a snare,
so men are trapped by evil times
  that fall unexpectedly upon them.

Wisdom Better Than Folly

¹³I also saw under the sun this example of wisdom that greatly impressed me: ¹⁴There was once a small city with only a few people in it. And a powerful king came against it, surrounded it and built huge siegeworks against it. ¹⁵Now there lived in that city a man poor but wise, and he saved the city by his wisdom. But nobody remembered that poor man. ¹⁶So I said, "Wisdom is better than strength." But the poor man's wisdom is despised, and his words are no longer heeded.

¹⁷The quiet words of the wise are more
    to be heeded
than the shouts of a ruler of fools.
¹⁸Wisdom is better than weapons of
    war,
  but one sinner destroys much
    good.

10 As dead flies give perfume a
    bad smell,
so a little folly outweighs wisdom
    and honor.
²The heart of the wise inclines to the
    right,
  but the heart of the fool to the left.
³Even as he walks along the road,
  the fool lacks sense
  and shows everyone how stupid he
    is.
⁴If a ruler's anger rises against you,
  do not leave your post;
  calmness can lay great errors to rest.
⁵There is an evil I have seen under the
    sun,
  the sort of error that arises from a
    ruler:
⁶Fools are put in many high positions,
  while the rich occupy the low
    ones.
⁷I have seen slaves on horseback,
  while princes go on foot like slaves.
⁸Whoever digs a pit may fall into it;
  whoever breaks through a wall
    may be bitten by a snake.
⁹Whoever quarries stones may be
    injured by them;
  whoever splits logs may be
    endangered by them.
¹⁰If the ax is dull
  and its edge unsharpened,

---

[a] 4 Or *What then is to be chosen? With all who live, there is hope*   [b] 10 Hebrew *Sheol*

more strength is needed
but skill will bring success.

11 If a snake bites before it is charmed,
there is no profit for the charmer.

12 Words from a wise man's mouth are
gracious,
but a fool is consumed by his own
lips.

13 At the beginning his words are folly;

MONDAY

IN FORESIGHT OF THE GRAVE
Christina Rossetti

VERSE: Ecclesiastes 9:10   **PASSAGE:** Ecclesiastes 9:7–10

 ears ago a small party of us crossed the Alps into Italy by the Pass of Mount St. Gotthard . . .

At a certain point of the ascent the mountain bloomed into an actual garden of forget-me-nots.

Unforgotten and never to be forgotten that lovely lavish efflorescence which made earth cerulean as the sky.

Thus I remember the mountain. But without that flower of memory could I have forgotten it?

Surely not: yet there, not elsewhere, a countless multitude of forget-me-nots made their home.

Such oftentimes seems the principle of allotment (if reverently I may term it so) among the human family. Many persons whose chief gifts taken one by one would suffice to memorialize them, engross not those only but along with them the winning graces which endear. Forget-me-nots enamel the height.

And what shall they do who display neither loftiness nor loveliness? If "one member be honored, all the members rejoice with it" (1 Corinthians 12:26, KJV).

Or, if this standard appears too exalted for frail flesh and blood to attain, then send thought onwards.

The crowning summit of Mount St. Gotthard abides invested, not with flowers, but with perpetual snow: not with life, but with lifelessness.

In foresight of the grave, whither we all are hastening, is it worthwhile to envy any? "There is no work, nor device, nor knowledge, nor wisdom, in the grave whither thou goest" (Ecclesiastes 9:10, KJV). "Grudge not one against another, brethren, lest ye be condemned: behold the judge standeth before the door" (James 5:9, KJV).

ADDITIONAL SCRIPTURE READING:
Job 14:7–12; James 5:9

Go to page 764 for your next devotional reading.

1700   1900

at the end they are wicked
madness—
14 and the fool multiplies words.

No one knows what is coming—
who can tell him what will happen
after him?

15 A fool's work wearies him;
he does not know the way to town.

16 Woe to you, O land whose king was a
servant[a]
and whose princes feast in the
morning.
17 Blessed are you, O land whose king is
of noble birth
and whose princes eat at a proper
time—
for strength and not for
drunkenness.

18 If a man is lazy, the rafters sag;
if his hands are idle, the house
leaks.

19 A feast is made for laughter,
and wine makes life merry,
but money is the answer for
everything.

20 Do not revile the king even in your
thoughts,
or curse the rich in your bedroom,
because a bird of the air may carry
your words,
and a bird on the wing may report
what you say.

Bread Upon the Waters

11 Cast your bread upon the
waters,
for after many days you will find it
again.
2 Give portions to seven, yes to eight,
for you do not know what disaster
may come upon the land.

3 If clouds are full of water,
they pour rain upon the earth.
Whether a tree falls to the south or to
the north,
in the place where it falls, there
will it lie.
4 Whoever watches the wind will not
plant;
whoever looks at the clouds will
not reap.

5 As you do not know the path of the
wind,
or how the body is formed[b] in a
mother's womb,
so you cannot understand the work
of God,
the Maker of all things.

6 Sow your seed in the morning,
and at evening let not your hands
be idle,
for you do not know which will
succeed,
whether this or that,
or whether both will do equally
well.

Remember Your Creator While Young

7 Light is sweet,
and it pleases the eyes to see the
sun.
8 However many years a man may live,
let him enjoy them all.
But let him remember the days of
darkness,
for they will be many.
Everything to come is meaningless.

9 Be happy, young man, while you are
young,
and let your heart give you joy in
the days of your youth.
Follow the ways of your heart
and whatever your eyes see,
but know that for all these things
God will bring you to judgment.
10 So then, banish anxiety from your
heart
and cast off the troubles of your
body,
for youth and vigor are meaningless.

12 Remember your Creator
in the days of your youth,
before the days of trouble come
and the years approach when you
will say,
"I find no pleasure in them"—
2 before the sun and the light
and the moon and the stars grow
dark,
and the clouds return after the rain;
3 when the keepers of the house
tremble,
and the strong men stoop,

when the grinders cease because they
are few,
and those looking through the
windows grow dim;
4 when the doors to the street are
closed
and the sound of grinding fades;
when men rise up at the sound of
birds,
but all their songs grow faint;
5 when men are afraid of heights
and of dangers in the streets;
when the almond tree blossoms
and the grasshopper drags himself
along
and desire no longer is stirred.
Then man goes to his eternal home
and mourners go about the streets.

6 Remember him—before the silver
cord is severed,
or the golden bowl is broken;
before the pitcher is shattered at the
spring,
or the wheel broken at the well,
7 and the dust returns to the ground it
came from,
and the spirit returns to God who
gave it.

8 "Meaningless! Meaningless!" says
the Teacher.*a*
"Everything is meaningless!"

The Conclusion of the Matter

9 Not only was the Teacher wise, but
also he imparted knowledge to the people. He pondered and searched out and
set in order many proverbs. 10 The
Teacher searched to find just the right
words, and what he wrote was upright
and true.

11 The words of the wise are like
goads, their collected sayings like firmly
embedded nails—given by one Shepherd. 12 Be warned, my son, of anything
in addition to them.

Of making many books there is no
end, and much study wearies the body.

13 Now all has been heard;
here is the conclusion of the matter:
Fear God and keep his
commandments,
for this is the whole ⌊duty⌋ of man.

GIVE ME A PERSON WHO SAYS, "THIS ONE THING I
DO," AND NOT, "THESE FIFTY THINGS I DABBLE
IN."
—*Dwight L. Moody*

---

14 For God will bring every deed into
judgment,
including every hidden thing,
whether it is good or evil.

a 8 Or the leader of the assembly; also in verses 9 and 10

SONG OF SONGS

I N ANCIENT ISRAEL EVERYTHING
HUMAN CAME TO EXPRESSION IN
WORDS. IN THE SONG, LOVE FINDS
WORDS—INSPIRED WORDS THAT DISCLOSE ITS
EXQUISITE CHARM AND BEAUTY AS ONE OF
GOD'S CHOICEST GIFTS. IT ILLUMINATES THE
SPONTANEOUS AND EXCLUSIVE LOVE BETWEEN
A LOVER AND HIS BELOVED, DEMONSTRATING
AT THE SAME TIME THE KIND OF LOVE CHRIST
HAS FOR HIS CHURCH. REJOICE IN THE GIFT OF
LOVE, AS YOU READ THIS TIMELESS EXPRES-
SION OF THE JOY AND INTIMACY OF LOVE, THE
GIFT OF OUR CREATOR.

---

1 Solomon's Song of Songs.

Beloved[a]

2 Let him kiss me with the kisses of
    his mouth—
  for your love is more delightful
    than wine.
3 Pleasing is the fragrance of your
    perfumes;
  your name is like perfume poured
    out.
  No wonder the maidens love you!
4 Take me away with you—let us
    hurry!

Let the king bring me into his
  chambers.

JOB—HOW TO SUFFER;
PSALMS—HOW TO PRAY;
PROVERBS—HOW TO ACT;
ECCLESIASTES—HOW TO ENJOY;
SONG OF [SONGS]—HOW TO LOVE.
    —*Oswald Chambers*

Friends

  We rejoice and delight in you[b];
    we will praise your love more than
      wine.

---

a Primarily on the basis of the gender of the Hebrew pronouns used, male and female speakers are
indicated in the margins by the captions *Lover* and *Beloved* respectively. The words of others are marked
Friends. In some instances the divisions and their captions are debatable.   *b 4* The Hebrew is
masculine singular.

Beloved

How right they are to adore you!

⁵Dark am I, yet lovely,
   O daughters of Jerusalem,
   dark like the tents of Kedar,
   like the tent curtains of Solomon.*ᵃ*
⁶Do not stare at me because I am dark,
   because I am darkened by the sun.
My mother's sons were angry with me
   and made me take care of the
      vineyards;
   my own vineyard I have neglected.
⁷Tell me, you whom I love, where you
      graze your flock
   and where you rest your sheep at
      midday.
Why should I be like a veiled woman
   beside the flocks of your friends?

Friends

⁸If you do not know, most beautiful of
      women,
   follow the tracks of the sheep
and graze your young goats
   by the tents of the shepherds.

Lover

⁹I liken you, my darling, to a mare
      harnessed to one of the chariots of
      Pharaoh.
¹⁰Your cheeks are beautiful with
      earrings,
   your neck with strings of jewels.
¹¹We will make you earrings of gold,
   studded with silver.

Beloved

¹²While the king was at his table,
   my perfume spread its fragrance.
¹³My lover is to me a sachet of myrrh
   resting between my breasts.
¹⁴My lover is to me a cluster of henna
      blossoms
   from the vineyards of En Gedi.

Lover

¹⁵How beautiful you are, my darling!
   Oh, how beautiful!
   Your eyes are doves.

Beloved

¹⁶How handsome you are, my lover!
   Oh, how charming!
   And our bed is verdant.

Lover

¹⁷The beams of our house are cedars;
   our rafters are firs.

*Beloved*ᵇ

2 I am a rose*ᶜ* of Sharon,
   a lily of the valleys.

Lover

²Like a lily among thorns
   is my darling among the maidens.

Beloved

³Like an apple tree among the trees of
      the forest
   is my lover among the young men.
I delight to sit in his shade,
   and his fruit is sweet to my taste.
⁴He has taken me to the banquet hall,
   and his banner over me is love.
⁵Strengthen me with raisins,
   refresh me with apples,
   for I am faint with love.
⁶His left arm is under my head,
   and his right arm embraces me.
⁷Daughters of Jerusalem, I charge
      you
   by the gazelles and by the does of
      the field:
Do not arouse or awaken love
   until it so desires.

⁸Listen! My lover!
   Look! Here he comes,
leaping across the mountains,
   bounding over the hills.
⁹My lover is like a gazelle or a young
      stag.
   Look! There he stands behind our
      wall,
gazing through the windows,
   peering through the lattice.
¹⁰My lover spoke and said to me,
   "Arise, my darling,
   my beautiful one, and come with
      me.
¹¹See! The winter is past;
   the rains are over and gone.
¹²Flowers appear on the earth;
   the season of singing has come,
the cooing of doves
   is heard in our land.
¹³The fig tree forms its early fruit;
   the blossoming vines spread their
      fragrance.

ᵃ 5 Or *Salma*   *ᵇ 1* Or *Lover*   *ᶜ 1* Possibly a member of the crocus family

Arise, come, my darling;
  my beautiful one, come with me."

Lover

14 My dove in the clefts of the rock,
  in the hiding places on the
    mountainside,
show me your face,
  let me hear your voice;
for your voice is sweet,
  and your face is lovely.

15 Catch for us the foxes,
  the little foxes
that ruin the vineyards,
  our vineyards that are in bloom.

Beloved

16 My lover is mine and I am his;
  he browses among the lilies.
17 Until the day breaks
  and the shadows flee,
  turn, my lover,

TUESDAY

LATE HAVE I LOVED THEE
Augustine

VERSE: Song of Songs 2:5   **PASSAGE:** Song of Songs 2:3–13

Late Have I Loved Thee

ate have I love thee, O Beauty so ancient and so new;
late have I loved thee: for behold thou wert within me,
and I outside; and I sought thee outside and in my
unloveliness fell upon those lovely things that thou
hast made. Thou wert with me, and I was not with thee. I was
kept from thee by those things, yet had they not been in thee,
they would not have been at all. Thou didst call and cry to me to
break open my deafness: and thou didst send forth thy beams
and shine upon me and chase away my blindness: thou didst
breathe fragrance upon me, and I drew in my breath and do now
pant for thee: I tasted thee, and now hunger and thirst for thee:
thou didst touch me, and I have burned for thy peace.

Now I Love Thee Alone

Now I love thee alone.
Thee alone do I follow.
Thee alone do I seek.
Thee alone am I ready to serve.
For thou alone hast just dominion.
Under thy sway I long to be.

ADDITIONAL SCRIPTURE READING:
Psalms 42:1–3; 63:1–3; 119:130–131

Go to page 767 for your next devotional reading.

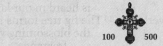

100   500

and be like a gazelle
or like a young stag
   on the rugged hills.*a*

 3 All night long on my bed
   I looked for the one my heart
    loves;
I looked for him but did not find
   him.
2 I will get up now and go about the
   city,
   through its streets and squares;
I will search for the one my heart
   loves.
   So I looked for him but did not find
   him.
3 The watchmen found me
   as they made their rounds in the
    city.
"Have you seen the one my heart
   loves?"
4 Scarcely had I passed them
   when I found the one my heart
    loves.
I held him and would not let him go
   till I had brought him to my
    mother's house,
   to the room of the one who
    conceived me.
5 Daughters of Jerusalem, I charge you
   by the gazelles and by the does of
    the field:
Do not arouse or awaken love
   until it so desires.

6 Who is this coming up from the
   desert
   like a column of smoke,
perfumed with myrrh and incense
   made from all the spices of the
    merchant?
7 Look! It is Solomon's carriage,
   escorted by sixty warriors,
   the noblest of Israel,
8 all of them wearing the sword,
   all experienced in battle,
each with his sword at his side,
   prepared for the terrors of the
    night.
9 King Solomon made for himself the
   carriage;
   he made it of wood from Lebanon.
10 Its posts he made of silver,
   its base of gold.
Its seat was upholstered with purple,

   its interior lovingly inlaid
   by*b* the daughters of Jerusalem.
11 Come out, you daughters of Zion,
   and look at King Solomon wearing
    the crown,
   the crown with which his mother
    crowned him
on the day of his wedding,
   the day his heart rejoiced.

Lover

 4 How beautiful you are, my
   darling!
   Oh, how beautiful!
   Your eyes behind your veil are
    doves.
Your hair is like a flock of goats
   descending from Mount Gilead.
2 Your teeth are like a flock of sheep
   just shorn,
   coming up from the washing.
Each has its twin;
   not one of them is alone.
3 Your lips are like a scarlet ribbon;
   your mouth is lovely.
Your temples behind your veil
   are like the halves of a
    pomegranate.
4 Your neck is like the tower of David,
   built with elegance*c*;
on it hang a thousand shields,
   all of them shields of warriors.
5 Your two breasts are like two fawns,
   like twin fawns of a gazelle
   that browse among the lilies.
6 Until the day breaks
   and the shadows flee,
I will go to the mountain of myrrh
   and to the hill of incense.
7 All beautiful you are, my darling;
   there is no flaw in you.

8 Come with me from Lebanon, my
   bride,
   come with me from Lebanon.
Descend from the crest of Amana,
   from the top of Senir, the summit
    of Hermon,
from the lions' dens
   and the mountain haunts of the
    leopards.
9 You have stolen my heart, my sister,
   my bride;
   you have stolen my heart
with one glance of your eyes,

---

a 17 Or *the hills of Bether*   *b 10* Or *its inlaid interior a gift of love / from*   *c 4* The meaning of the
Hebrew for this word is uncertain.

with one jewel of your necklace.

10 How delightful is your love, my
    sister, my bride!
How much more pleasing is your
    love than wine,
and the fragrance of your perfume
    than any spice!

11 Your lips drop sweetness as the
    honeycomb, my bride;
milk and honey are under your
    tongue.
The fragrance of your garments is
    like that of Lebanon.

12 You are a garden locked up, my sister,
    my bride;
you are a spring enclosed, a sealed
    fountain.

13 Your plants are an orchard of
    pomegranates
with choice fruits,
with henna and nard,

14   nard and saffron,
calamus and cinnamon,
with every kind of incense tree,
with myrrh and aloes
and all the finest spices.

15 You are*a* a garden fountain,
a well of flowing water
streaming down from Lebanon.

Beloved

16 Awake, north wind,
and come, south wind!
Blow on my garden,
that its fragrance may spread
    abroad.
Let my lover come into his garden
and taste its choice fruits.

Lover

5 I have come into my garden,
my sister, my bride;
I have gathered my myrrh with my
    spice.
I have eaten my honeycomb and my
    honey;
I have drunk my wine and my milk.

Friends

Eat, O friends, and drink;
    drink your fill, O lovers.

Beloved

2 I slept but my heart was awake.
Listen! My lover is knocking:

"Open to me, my sister, my darling,
    my dove, my flawless one.
My head is drenched with dew,
    my hair with the dampness of the
    night."

3 I have taken off my robe—
    must I put it on again?
I have washed my feet—
    must I soil them again?

4 My lover thrust his hand through the
    latch-opening;
my heart began to pound for him.

5 I arose to open for my lover,
and my hands dripped with myrrh,
my fingers with flowing myrrh,
    on the handles of the lock.

6 I opened for my lover,
    but my lover had left; he was gone.
My heart sank at his departure.*b*
I looked for him but did not find him.
I called him but he did not answer.

7 The watchmen found me
as they made their rounds in the
    city.
They beat me, they bruised me;
    they took away my cloak,
those watchmen of the walls!

8 O daughters of Jerusalem, I charge
    you—
if you find my lover,
what will you tell him?
Tell him I am faint with love.

Friends

9 How is your beloved better than
    others,
    most beautiful of women?
How is your beloved better than
    others,
    that you charge us so?

Beloved

10 My lover is radiant and ruddy,
    outstanding among ten thousand.

11 His head is purest gold;
    his hair is wavy
    and black as a raven.

12 His eyes are like doves
    by the water streams,
washed in milk,
    mounted like jewels.

13 His cheeks are like beds of spice
    yielding perfume.
His lips are like lilies
    dripping with myrrh.

---

a 15 Or *I am* (spoken by the *Beloved*)   *b* 6 Or *heart had gone out to him when he spoke*

[14] His arms are rods of gold
set with chrysolite.
His body is like polished ivory
decorated with sapphires.[a]
[15] His legs are pillars of marble
set on bases of pure gold.
His appearance is like Lebanon,
choice as its cedars.
[16] His mouth is sweetness itself;
he is altogether lovely.
This is my lover, this my friend,
O daughters of Jerusalem.

Friends

6 Where has your lover gone,
most beautiful of women?
Which way did your lover turn,
that we may look for him with you?

Beloved

[2] My lover has gone down to his garden,
to the beds of spices,
to browse in the gardens

[a] 14 Or *lapis lazuli*

WEDNESDAY

Faint With Love for Him

Francis of Assisi

Verse: Song of Songs 5:8 **Passage:** Song of Songs 5:2–8

Let us all love with all our heart, with all our soul, with all our mind, with all our strength and fortitude, with all our understanding and with all our powers, with our whole might and whole affection, with our innermost parts, our whole desires, and wills, the Lord God, who has given and gives to us all, the whole body, the whole soul, and our life; who has created and redeemed us, and by his mercy alone will save us; who has done and does all good to us, miserable and wretched, vile, unclean, ungrateful, and evil.

Let us therefore desire nothing else, wish for nothing else, and let nothing please and delight us except our Creator and Redeemer, and Savior, the only true God, who is full of good, all good, entire good, the true and supreme good, who alone is good, merciful and kind, gentle and sweet, who alone is holy, just, true, and upright, who alone is benign, pure, and clean, from whom, and through whom, and in whom is all mercy, all grace, all glory of all penitents and of the just, and of all the blessed rejoicing in heaven. Let nothing therefore hinder us, let nothing separate us, let nothing come between us.

Additional Scripture Reading:
Psalm 42:1–3; Jude 24–25

Go to page 772 for your next devotional reading.

500 1500

and to gather lilies.
³ I am my lover's and my lover is mine;
  he browses among the lilies.

Lover

⁴ You are beautiful, my darling, as
    Tirzah,
  lovely as Jerusalem,
  majestic as troops with banners.
⁵ Turn your eyes from me;
  they overwhelm me.
  Your hair is like a flock of goats
  descending from Gilead.
⁶ Your teeth are like a flock of sheep
  coming up from the washing.
  Each has its twin,
  not one of them is alone.
⁷ Your temples behind your veil
  are like the halves of a
    pomegranate.
⁸ Sixty queens there may be,
  and eighty concubines,
  and virgins beyond number;
⁹ but my dove, my perfect one, is
    unique,
  the only daughter of her mother,
  the favorite of the one who bore her.
  The maidens saw her and called her
    blessed;
  the queens and concubines praised
    her.

Friends

¹⁰ Who is this that appears like the
    dawn,
  fair as the moon, bright as the sun,
  majestic as the stars in procession?

Lover

¹¹ I went down to the grove of nut trees
  to look at the new growth in the
    valley,
  to see if the vines had budded
  or the pomegranates were in
    bloom.
¹² Before I realized it,
  my desire set me among the royal
    chariots of my people.ᵃ

Friends

¹³ Come back, come back,
  O Shulammite;
  come back, come back, that we
    may gaze on you!

Lover

Why would you gaze on the
    Shulammite
  as on the dance of Mahanaim?

7 How beautiful your sandaled
    feet,
  O prince's daughter!
  Your graceful legs are like jewels,
  the work of a craftsman's hands.
² Your navel is a rounded goblet
  that never lacks blended wine.
  Your waist is a mound of wheat
  encircled by lilies.
³ Your breasts are like two fawns,
  twins of a gazelle.
⁴ Your neck is like an ivory tower.
  Your eyes are the pools of Heshbon
  by the gate of Bath Rabbim.
  Your nose is like the tower of
    Lebanon
  looking toward Damascus.
⁵ Your head crowns you like Mount
    Carmel.
  Your hair is like royal tapestry;
  the king is held captive by its
    tresses.
⁶ How beautiful you are and how
    pleasing,
  O love, with your delights!
⁷ Your stature is like that of the palm,
  and your breasts like clusters of
    fruit.
⁸ I said, "I will climb the palm tree;
  I will take hold of its fruit."
  May your breasts be like the clusters
    of the vine,
  the fragrance of your breath like
    apples,
⁹ and your mouth like the best wine.

Beloved

May the wine go straight to my lover,
  flowing gently over lips and teeth.ᵇ
¹⁰ I belong to my lover,
  and his desire is for me.
¹¹ Come, my lover, let us go to the
    countryside,
  let us spend the night in the
    villages.ᶜ
¹² Let us go early to the vineyards
  to see if the vines have budded,
  if their blossoms have opened,

ᵃ 12 Or *among the chariots of Amminadab;* or *among the chariots of the people of the prince*
ᵇ 9 Septuagint, Aquila, Vulgate and Syriac; Hebrew *lips of sleepers*   ᶜ 11 Or *henna bushes*

and if the pomegranates are in
  bloom—
there I will give you my love.
¹³ The mandrakes send out their
  fragrance,
and at our door is every delicacy,
both new and old,
  that I have stored up for you, my
  lover.

8 If only you were to me like a
  brother,
who was nursed at my mother's
  breasts!
Then, if I found you outside,
  I would kiss you,
and no one would despise me.
² I would lead you
  and bring you to my mother's
  house—
  she who has taught me.
I would give you spiced wine to
  drink,
the nectar of my pomegranates.
³ His left arm is under my head
  and his right arm embraces me.
⁴ Daughters of Jerusalem, I charge you:
  Do not arouse or awaken love
  until it so desires.

Friends

⁵ Who is this coming up from the
  desert
  leaning on her lover?

Beloved

Under the apple tree I roused you;
  there your mother conceived you,
  there she who was in labor gave
  you birth.
⁶ Place me like a seal over your heart,
  like a seal on your arm;
for love is as strong as death,
  its jealousy*a* unyielding as the
  grave.*b*
It burns like blazing fire,

like a mighty flame.*c*
⁷ Many waters cannot quench love;
  rivers cannot wash it away.
If one were to give
  all the wealth of his house for love,
  it*d* would be utterly scorned.

Friends

⁸ We have a young sister,
  and her breasts are not yet grown.
What shall we do for our sister
  for the day she is spoken for?
⁹ If she is a wall,
  we will build towers of silver on
  her.
If she is a door,
  we will enclose her with panels of
  cedar.

Beloved

¹⁰ I am a wall,
  and my breasts are like towers.
Thus I have become in his eyes
  like one bringing contentment.
¹¹ Solomon had a vineyard in Baal
  Hamon;
he let out his vineyard to tenants.
Each was to bring for its fruit
  a thousand shekels*e* of silver.
¹² But my own vineyard is mine to give;
  the thousand shekels are for you,
    O Solomon,
and two hundred*f* are for those who
  tend its fruit.

Lover

¹³ You who dwell in the gardens
  with friends in attendance,
  let me hear your voice!

Beloved

¹⁴ Come away, my lover,
  and be like a gazelle
or like a young stag
  on the spice-laden mountains.

---

a 6 Or *ardor*   *b* 6 Hebrew *Sheol*   *c* 6 Or / *like the very flame of the LORD*   *d* 7 Or *he*   *e* 11 That
is, about 25 pounds (about 11.5 kilograms); also in verse 12   *f* 12 That is, about 5 pounds (about 2.3
kilograms)

ISAIAH

SAIAH WROTE DURING THE STORMY PERIOD MARKING THE EXPANSION OF THE ASSYRIAN EMPIRE AND THE DECLINE OF ISRAEL. ISAIAH UNVEILS THE FULL DIMENSIONS OF GOD'S JUDGMENT, WARNING JUDAH THAT HER SIN WOULD BRING CAPTIVITY AT THE HANDS OF BABYLON. YET, FOLLOWING ROUND AFTER ROUND OF WARNING, ISAIAH TURNS TO THE PROMISE OF GOD'S COMFORT, FORGIVENESS AND RESTORATION. THE RESTORED EARTH AND THE RESTORED PEOPLE WILL THEN CONFORM TO THE DIVINE IDEAL, AND ALL WILL RESULT IN THE PRAISE AND GLORY OF THE HOLY GOD OF ISRAEL.

1 The vision concerning Judah and Jerusalem that Isaiah son of Amoz saw during the reigns of Uzziah, Jotham, Ahaz and Hezekiah, kings of Judah.

A Rebellious Nation

2 Hear, O heavens! Listen, O earth!
For the LORD has spoken:
"I reared children and brought them up,
but they have rebelled against me.
3 The ox knows his master,
the donkey his owner's manger,
but Israel does not know,
my people do not understand."

4 Ah, sinful nation,
a people loaded with guilt,
a brood of evildoers,
children given to corruption!
They have forsaken the LORD;
they have spurned the Holy One of Israel
and turned their backs on him.

5 Why should you be beaten anymore?
Why do you persist in rebellion?
Your whole head is injured,
your whole heart afflicted.
6 From the sole of your foot to the top of your head
there is no soundness—
only wounds and welts
and open sores,
not cleansed or bandaged
or soothed with oil.

7 Your country is desolate,
your cities burned with fire;

your fields are being stripped by
    foreigners
    right before you,
    laid waste as when overthrown by
      strangers.
⁸ The Daughter of Zion is left
    like a shelter in a vineyard,
    like a hut in a field of melons,
    like a city under siege.
⁹ Unless the LORD Almighty
    had left us some survivors,
    we would have become like Sodom,
    we would have been like
      Gomorrah.

¹⁰ Hear the word of the LORD,
    you rulers of Sodom;
    listen to the law of our God,
    you people of Gomorrah!
¹¹ "The multitude of your sacrifices—
    what are they to me?" says the
      LORD.
    "I have more than enough of burnt
      offerings,
    of rams and the fat of fattened
      animals;
    I have no pleasure
    in the blood of bulls and lambs and
      goats.
¹² When you come to appear before me,
    who has asked this of you,
    this trampling of my courts?
¹³ Stop bringing meaningless offerings!
    Your incense is detestable to me.
New Moons, Sabbaths and
      convocations—
    I cannot bear your evil assemblies.
¹⁴ Your New Moon festivals and your
      appointed feasts
    my soul hates.
They have become a burden to me;
    I am weary of bearing them.
¹⁵ When you spread out your hands in
      prayer,
    I will hide my eyes from you;
    even if you offer many prayers,
    I will not listen.
Your hands are full of blood;
¹⁶   wash and make yourselves clean.
Take your evil deeds
    out of my sight!
Stop doing wrong,
¹⁷   learn to do right!
Seek justice,
    encourage the oppressed.ᵃ

Defend the cause of the fatherless,
    plead the case of the widow.

¹⁸ "Come now, let us reason together,"
    says the LORD.
    "Though your sins are like scarlet,
    they shall be as white as snow;
    though they are red as crimson,
    they shall be like wool.
¹⁹ If you are willing and obedient,
    you will eat the best from the land;
²⁰ but if you resist and rebel,
    you will be devoured by the sword."
      For the mouth of the LORD
        has spoken.

²¹ See how the faithful city
    has become a harlot!
She once was full of justice;
    righteousness used to dwell in
      her—
    but now murderers!
²² Your silver has become dross,
    your choice wine is diluted with
      water.
²³ Your rulers are rebels,
    companions of thieves;
they all love bribes
    and chase after gifts.
They do not defend the cause of the
      fatherless;
    the widow's case does not come
      before them.
²⁴ Therefore the Lord, the LORD
      Almighty,
    the Mighty One of Israel, declares:
    "Ah, I will get relief from my foes
    and avenge myself on my enemies.
²⁵ I will turn my hand against you;
    I will thoroughly purge away your
      dross
    and remove all your impurities.
²⁶ I will restore your judges as in days of
      old,
    your counselors as at the
      beginning.
Afterward you will be called
    the City of Righteousness,
    the Faithful City."

²⁷ Zion will be redeemed with justice,
    her penitent ones with
      righteousness.
²⁸ But rebels and sinners will both be
      broken,

ᵃ 17 Or / rebuke the oppressor

THAT IN WHICH OUR RELIGION LIES
George Fox

VERSE: Isaiah 1:17   **PASSAGE:** Isaiah 1:14–17

hen the priests and professors raged exceedingly against us and printed books against us; and said that our religion lay in not wearing fine clothes, and lace, and ribands, and in not eating good cheer, when we could not make feasts for the priests or professors as we used to do, nor feasts for companies in the cities; but if they would join with us, when they made feasts, to feast such as could not feast them again, we would make a feast for all the poor of the parish that could not feast us and them again. And this was according to Christ's command, but in this their selfish principle would never join with us.

We told them that when they went to their sports, and games, and plays, and the like, they had better serve God than spend their time so vainly. And that costly apparel, with the lace that we formally had hung upon our backs that kept us not warm, with that we could maintain a company of poor people that had no clothes.

And so our religion lay not in meats, nor drinks, nor clothes, nor thee nor thou, nor putting off hats nor making curtseys (at which they were greatly offended because we thee'd and thou'd them and could not put off our hats nor bow to them), and therefore they said our religion lay in such things. But our answer was, "Nay; for though the Spirit of God led into that which was comely and decent, and from chambering and wantonness, and from sporting and pastimes and feasting as in the day of slaughter, and from wearing costly apparel, as the apostle commands, and from the world's honor, fashions and customs—our religion lies in that which brings to visit the poor, and fatherless, and widows, and keeps from the spots of the world (which religion is pure and undefiled before God [see James 1:27]). This is our religion which we own, which the apostles were in above 1600 years since; and we do deny all vain religions got up since, which are not only spotted with the world, but plead for a body of sin and death to the grave; and their widows and fatherless lie begging up and down the streets and countries."

ADDITIONAL SCRIPTURE READING:
Deuteronomy 10:12–13; Micah 6:8; James 1:27

Go to page 776 for your next devotional reading.

1700   1900

and those who forsake the LORD
  will perish.

29 "You will be ashamed because of the
    sacred oaks
  in which you have delighted;
you will be disgraced because of the
    gardens
  that you have chosen.
30 You will be like an oak with fading
    leaves,
  like a garden without water.
31 The mighty man will become tinder
  and his work a spark;
both will burn together,
  with no one to quench the fire."

The Mountain of the LORD

2 This is what Isaiah son of Amoz
    saw concerning Judah and Jeru-
salem:

2 In the last days

the mountain of the LORD's temple
    will be established
  as chief among the mountains;
it will be raised above the hills,
  and all nations will stream to it.

3 Many peoples will come and say,

"Come, let us go up to the mountain
    of the LORD,
  to the house of the God of Jacob.
He will teach us his ways,
  so that we may walk in his paths."
The law will go out from Zion,
  the word of the LORD from
    Jerusalem.
4 He will judge between the nations
  and will settle disputes for many
    peoples.
They will beat their swords into
    plowshares
  and their spears into pruning
    hooks.
Nation will not take up sword
    against nation,
  nor will they train for war
    anymore.
5 Come, O house of Jacob,
  let us walk in the light of the LORD.

The Day of the LORD

6 You have abandoned your people,
    the house of Jacob.
They are full of superstitions from
    the East;
  they practice divination like the
    Philistines
  and clasp hands with pagans.
7 Their land is full of silver and gold;
  there is no end to their treasures.
Their land is full of horses;
  there is no end to their chariots.
8 Their land is full of idols;
  they bow down to the work of
    their hands,
  to what their fingers have made.
9 So man will be brought low
  and mankind humbled—
  do not forgive them.[a]

10 Go into the rocks,
  hide in the ground
from dread of the LORD
  and the splendor of his majesty!
11 The eyes of the arrogant man will be
    humbled
  and the pride of men brought low;
  the LORD alone will be exalted in that
    day.

12 The LORD Almighty has a day in
    store
  for all the proud and lofty,
  for all that is exalted
    (and they will be humbled),
13 for all the cedars of Lebanon, tall and
    lofty,
  and all the oaks of Bashan,
14 for all the towering mountains
  and all the high hills,
15 for every lofty tower
  and every fortified wall,
16 for every trading ship[b]
  and every stately vessel.
17 The arrogance of man will be brought
    low
  and the pride of men humbled;
  the LORD alone will be exalted in that
    day,
18   and the idols will totally disappear.

19 Men will flee to caves in the rocks
  and to holes in the ground
from dread of the LORD
  and the splendor of his majesty,
  when he rises to shake the earth.

---

a 9 Or not raise them up   b 16 Hebrew every ship of Tarshish

20 In that day men will throw away
　　to the rodents and bats
　　their idols of silver and idols of gold,
　　which they made to worship.
21 They will flee to caverns in the rocks
　　and to the overhanging crags
　from dread of the LORD
　　and the splendor of his majesty,
　　when he rises to shake the earth.

22 Stop trusting in man,
　　who has but a breath in his
　　　nostrils.
　Of what account is he?

Judgment on Jerusalem and Judah

3 See now, the Lord,
　　the LORD Almighty,
　is about to take from Jerusalem and
　　Judah
　　both supply and support:
　all supplies of food and all supplies of
　　water,
2 　the hero and warrior,
　the judge and prophet,
　　the soothsayer and elder,
3 the captain of fifty and man of rank,
　　the counselor, skilled craftsman
　　and clever enchanter.

4 I will make boys their officials;
　　mere children will govern them.
5 People will oppress each other—
　　man against man, neighbor against
　　neighbor.
　The young will rise up against the
　　old,
　　the base against the honorable.

6 A man will seize one of his brothers
　　at his father's home, and say,
　"You have a cloak, you be our leader;
　　take charge of this heap of ruins!"
7 But in that day he will cry out,
　　"I have no remedy.
　I have no food or clothing in my
　　house;
　　do not make me the leader of the
　　people."

8 Jerusalem staggers,
　　Judah is falling;
　their words and deeds are against the
　　LORD,
　　defying his glorious presence.
9 The look on their faces testifies
　　against them;
　　they parade their sin like Sodom;

they do not hide it.
Woe to them!
　They have brought disaster upon
　　themselves.

10 Tell the righteous it will be well with
　　them,
　　for they will enjoy the fruit of their
　　deeds.
11 Woe to the wicked! Disaster is upon
　　them!
　They will be paid back for what their
　　hands have done.

12 Youths oppress my people,
　　women rule over them.
　O my people, your guides lead you
　　astray;
　　they turn you from the path.

13 The LORD takes his place in court;
　　he rises to judge the people.
14 The LORD enters into judgment
　　against the elders and leaders of his
　　people:
　"It is you who have ruined my
　　vineyard;
　　the plunder from the poor is in
　　your houses.
15 What do you mean by crushing my
　　people
　　and grinding the faces of the poor?"
　　　　　declares the Lord,
　　　　the LORD Almighty.

16 The LORD says,
　　"The women of Zion are haughty,
　walking along with outstretched
　　necks,
　　flirting with their eyes,
　tripping along with mincing steps,
　　with ornaments jingling on their
　　ankles.
17 Therefore the Lord will bring sores
　　on the heads of the women of
　　Zion;
　　the LORD will make their scalps
　　bald."

18 In that day the Lord will snatch
away their finery: the bangles and headbands and crescent necklaces, 19 the earrings and bracelets and veils, 20 the head-
dresses and ankle chains and sashes, the
perfume bottles and charms, 21 the
signet rings and nose rings, 22 the fine
robes and the capes and cloaks, the

purses ²³and mirrors, and the linen garments and tiaras and shawls.

²⁴Instead of fragrance there will be a
    stench;
    instead of a sash, a rope;
    instead of well-dressed hair, baldness;
    instead of fine clothing, sackcloth;
    instead of beauty, branding.
²⁵Your men will fall by the sword,
    your warriors in battle.
²⁶The gates of Zion will lament and
    mourn;
    destitute, she will sit on the
    ground.

4 In that day seven women
    will take hold of one man
and say, "We will eat our own food
and provide our own clothes;
only let us be called by your name.
Take away our disgrace!"

The Branch of the LORD

²In that day the Branch of the LORD will be beautiful and glorious, and the fruit of the land will be the pride and glory of the survivors in Israel. ³Those who are left in Zion, who remain in Jerusalem, will be called holy, all who are recorded among the living in Jerusalem. ⁴The Lord will wash away the filth of the women of Zion; he will cleanse the bloodstains from Jerusalem by a spirit[a] of judgment and a spirit[a] of fire. ⁵Then the LORD will create over all of Mount Zion and over those who assemble there a cloud of smoke by day and a glow of flaming fire by night; over all the glory will be a canopy. ⁶It will be a shelter and shade from the heat of the day, and a refuge and hiding place from the storm and rain.

The Song of the Vineyard

5 I will sing for the one I love
    a song about his vineyard:
My loved one had a vineyard
    on a fertile hillside.
²He dug it up and cleared it of stones
    and planted it with the choicest
    vines.
He built a watchtower in it
    and cut out a winepress as well.

Then he looked for a crop of good
    grapes,
    but it yielded only bad fruit.

³"Now you dwellers in Jerusalem and
    men of Judah,
    judge between me and my
    vineyard.
⁴What more could have been done for
    my vineyard
    than I have done for it?
When I looked for good grapes,
    why did it yield only bad?
⁵Now I will tell you
    what I am going to do to my
    vineyard:
I will take away its hedge,
    and it will be destroyed;
I will break down its wall,
    and it will be trampled.
⁶I will make it a wasteland,
    neither pruned nor cultivated,
    and briers and thorns will grow
    there.
I will command the clouds
    not to rain on it."

⁷The vineyard of the LORD Almighty
    is the house of Israel,
and the men of Judah
    are the garden of his delight.
And he looked for justice, but saw
    bloodshed;
    for righteousness, but heard cries of
    distress.

Woes and Judgments

⁸Woe to you who add house to house
    and join field to field
till no space is left
    and you live alone in the land.

⁹The LORD Almighty has declared in
my hearing:

"Surely the great houses will become
    desolate,
    the fine mansions left without
    occupants.
¹⁰A ten-acre[b] vineyard will produce
    only a bath[c] of wine,
    a homer[d] of seed only an ephah[e] of
    grain."

---

a 4 Or *the Spirit*   *b 10* Hebrew *ten-yoke,* that is, the land plowed by 10 yoke of oxen in one day
c 10 That is, probably about 6 gallons (about 22 liters)   *d 10* That is, probably about 6 bushels (about 220 liters)   *e 10* That is, probably about 3/5 bushel (about 22 liters)

11 Woe to those who rise early in the
   morning
   to run after their drinks,
who stay up late at night
   till they are inflamed with wine.
12 They have harps and lyres at their
   banquets,
   tambourines and flutes and wine,
but they have no regard for the deeds
   of the LORD,
   no respect for the work of his hands.
13 Therefore my people will go into exile
   for lack of understanding;
   their men of rank will die of hunger
   and their masses will be parched
   with thirst.

FRIDAY

PERSONAL LIFE AND SOCIAL JUSTICE
Harry Emerson Fosdick

VERSE: Isaiah 5:7   **PASSAGE:** Isaiah 5:1–7

Anyone who cares about character must care about social conditions, for every unfair economic situation, every social evil left to run its course means ruin to character. And the God of the Bible, because he cares supremely for personal life at its best, is zealously in earnest about social justice; his prophets blazed with indignation at all inequity, and his Son made the coming kingdom, when God's will would be done on earth, the center of his message. To fellowship with this earnest purpose of God we all are summoned; God believes in the glorious possibilities of life on earth; he is counting on us to put away the sins that hold the kingdom back and to fight the abuses that crush character in men. To believe in God, therefore—the God who is fighting his way with his children up through ignorance, brutality, and selfishness to a "new heaven and a new earth, the home of righteousness"—is no weakly comfortable blessing (see 2 Peter 3:13). It means joining a moral war; it means devotion, sacrifice; its spirit is the Cross and its motive an undiscourageable faith. And our underlying assurance that this war for a better world can be won is not simply our belief that it can be done, but *our faith that God is, and that he believes that it can be done.* When we pray we say, "your kingdom come," and we are full of hope about the long, sacrificial struggle, for the purpose behind and through it all is first of all God's. Our earnestness is but an echo of his.

ADDITIONAL SCRIPTURE READING:
Isaiah 58:6–8; Zechariah 7:9–14; Matthew 3:8

Go to page 778 for your next devotional reading.

1900   Present

14 Therefore the grave[a] enlarges its
     appetite
  and opens its mouth without limit;
  into it will descend their nobles and
     masses
  with all their brawlers and revelers.
15 So man will be brought low
  and mankind humbled,
  the eyes of the arrogant humbled.
16 But the LORD Almighty will be
     exalted by his justice,
  and the holy God will show
     himself holy by his
     righteousness.
17 Then sheep will graze as in their own
     pasture;
  lambs will feed[b] among the ruins
     of the rich.

18 Woe to those who draw sin along
     with cords of deceit,
  and wickedness as with cart ropes,
19 to those who say, "Let God hurry,
  let him hasten his work
     so we may see it.
  Let it approach,
  let the plan of the Holy One of
     Israel come,
     so we may know it."

20 Woe to those who call evil good
     and good evil,
  who put darkness for light
     and light for darkness,
  who put bitter for sweet
     and sweet for bitter.

21 Woe to those who are wise in their
     own eyes
  and clever in their own sight.

22 Woe to those who are heroes at
     drinking wine
  and champions at mixing drinks,
23 who acquit the guilty for a bribe,
  but deny justice to the innocent.
24 Therefore, as tongues of fire lick up
     straw
  and as dry grass sinks down in the
     flames,
  so their roots will decay
  and their flowers blow away like
     dust;
  for they have rejected the law of the
     LORD Almighty
  and spurned the word of the Holy
     One of Israel.

25 Therefore the LORD's anger burns
     against his people;
  his hand is raised and he strikes
     them down.
  The mountains shake,
  and the dead bodies are like refuse
     in the streets.

  Yet for all this, his anger is not
     turned away,
  his hand is still upraised.

26 He lifts up a banner for the distant
     nations,
  he whistles for those at the ends of
     the earth.
  Here they come,
     swiftly and speedily!
27 Not one of them grows tired or
     stumbles,
  not one slumbers or sleeps;
  not a belt is loosened at the waist,
  not a sandal thong is broken.
28 Their arrows are sharp,
  all their bows are strung;
  their horses' hoofs seem like flint,
  their chariot wheels like a
     whirlwind.
29 Their roar is like that of the lion,
  they roar like young lions;
  they growl as they seize their prey
  and carry it off with no one to
     rescue.
30 In that day they will roar over it
  like the roaring of the sea.
  And if one looks at the land,
  he will see darkness and distress;
  even the light will be darkened by
     the clouds.

Isaiah's Commission

6 In the year that King Uzziah
  died, I saw the Lord seated on a
throne, high and exalted, and the train of
his robe filled the temple. 2 Above him
were seraphs, each with six wings: With
two wings they covered their faces, with
two they covered their feet, and with two
they were flying. 3 And they were calling
to one another:

  "Holy, holy, holy is the LORD
     Almighty;
  the whole earth is full of his glory."

4 At the sound of their voices the

---

[a] 14 Hebrew *Sheol*   [b] 17 Septuagint; Hebrew / *strangers will eat*

WEEKEND

LORD, SPEAK TO ME, THAT I MAY SPEAK
Frances Ridley Havergal

VERSE: Isaiah 6:8   **PASSAGE:** Isaiah 6:1–8

ord, speak to me, that I may speak
  In living echoes of thy tone;
As thou hast sought, so let me seek
  Thy erring children lost and lone.

O teach me, Lord, that I may teach
  The precious things thou dost impart;
And wing my words, that they may reach
  The hidden depths of many a heart.

O fill me with thy fullness, Lord,
  Until my very heart o'erflow
In kindling thought and glowing word,
  Thy love to tell, thy praise to show.

O use me, Lord, use even me,
  Just as thou wilt, and when and where;
Until thy blessed face I see,
  Thy rest, thy joy, thy glory share.

ADDITIONAL SCRIPTURE READING:
Exodus 4:10–13; Acts 26:16–18

Go to page 780 for your next devotional reading.

1700   1900

doorposts and thresholds shook and the temple was filled with smoke.

5"Woe to me!" I cried. "I am ruined! For I am a man of unclean lips, and I live among a people of unclean lips, and my eyes have seen the King, the LORD Almighty."

6Then one of the seraphs flew to me with a live coal in his hand, which he had taken with tongs from the altar. 7With it he touched my mouth and said, "See, this has touched your lips; your guilt is taken away and your sin atoned for."

8Then I heard the voice of the Lord saying, "Whom shall I send? And who will go for us?"

And I said, "Here am I. Send me!"

9He said, "Go and tell this people:

" 'Be ever hearing, but never
      understanding;
   be ever seeing, but never
      perceiving.'
10Make the heart of this people
      calloused;
   make their ears dull
   and close their eyes.*a*
Otherwise they might see with their
      eyes,
   hear with their ears,
   understand with their hearts,
and turn and be healed."

11Then I said, "For how long, O Lord?"

And he answered:

"Until the cities lie ruined
   and without inhabitant,
until the houses are left deserted
   and the fields ruined and ravaged,
12until the LORD has sent everyone far
      away
   and the land is utterly forsaken.
13And though a tenth remains in the
      land,
   it will again be laid waste.
But as the terebinth and oak
   leave stumps when they are cut
      down,
so the holy seed will be the stump
   in the land."

The Sign of Immanuel

7 When Ahaz son of Jotham, the son of Uzziah, was king of Judah, King Rezin of Aram and Pekah son of Remaliah king of Israel marched up to fight against Jerusalem, but they could not overpower it.

2Now the house of David was told, "Aram has allied itself with*b* Ephraim"; so the hearts of Ahaz and his people were shaken, as the trees of the forest are shaken by the wind.

3Then the LORD said to Isaiah, "Go out, you and your son Shear-Jashub,*c* to meet Ahaz at the end of the aqueduct of the Upper Pool, on the road to the Washerman's Field. 4Say to him, 'Be careful, keep calm and don't be afraid. Do not lose heart because of these two smoldering stubs of firewood—because of the fierce anger of Rezin and Aram and of the son of Remaliah. 5Aram, Ephraim and Remaliah's son have plotted your ruin, saying, 6"Let us invade Judah; let us tear it apart and divide it among ourselves, and make the son of Tabeel king over it." 7Yet this is what the Sovereign LORD says:

" 'It will not take place,
   it will not happen,
8for the head of Aram is Damascus,
   and the head of Damascus is only
      Rezin.
Within sixty-five years
   Ephraim will be too shattered to be
      a people.
9The head of Ephraim is Samaria,
   and the head of Samaria is only
      Remaliah's son.
If you do not stand firm in your faith,
   you will not stand at all.' "

10Again the LORD spoke to Ahaz, 11"Ask the LORD your God for a sign, whether in the deepest depths or in the highest heights."

12But Ahaz said, "I will not ask; I will not put the LORD to the test."

13Then Isaiah said, "Hear now, you house of David! Is it not enough to try the patience of men? Will you try the

---

a 9,10 Hebrew; Septuagint *'You will be ever hearing, but never understanding; / you will be ever seeing, but never perceiving.' / 10This people's heart has become calloused; / they hardly hear with their ears, / and they have closed their eyes   b 2* Or *has set up camp in   c 3 Shear-Jashub* means *a remnant will return.*

patience of my God also? [14]Therefore the Lord himself will give you[a] a sign: The virgin will be with child and will give birth to a son, and[b] will call him Immanuel.[c] [15]He will eat curds and honey when he knows enough to reject the wrong and choose the right. [16]But before the boy knows enough to reject the wrong and choose the right, the land of the two kings you dread will be laid waste. [17]The LORD will bring on you and on your people and on the house of your

a 14 The Hebrew is plural.   *b 14* Masoretic Text; Dead Sea Scrolls *and he* or *and they*
c 14 *Immanuel* means *God with us.*

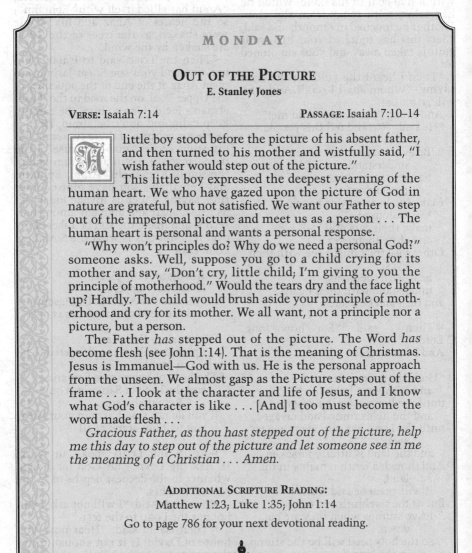

MONDAY

OUT OF THE PICTURE
E. Stanley Jones

VERSE: Isaiah 7:14   **PASSAGE:** Isaiah 7:10–14

A little boy stood before the picture of his absent father, and then turned to his mother and wistfully said, "I wish father would step out of the picture."

This little boy expressed the deepest yearning of the human heart. We who have gazed upon the picture of God in nature are grateful, but not satisfied. We want our Father to step out of the impersonal picture and meet us as a person . . . The human heart is personal and wants a personal response.

"Why won't principles do? Why do we need a personal God?" someone asks. Well, suppose you go to a child crying for its mother and say, "Don't cry, little child; I'm giving to you the principle of motherhood." Would the tears dry and the face light up? Hardly. The child would brush aside your principle of motherhood and cry for its mother. We all want, not a principle nor a picture, but a person.

The Father *has* stepped out of the picture. The Word *has* become flesh (see John 1:14). That is the meaning of Christmas. Jesus is Immanuel—God with us. He is the personal approach from the unseen. We almost gasp as the Picture steps out of the frame . . . I look at the character and life of Jesus, and I know what God's character is like . . . [And] I too must become the word made flesh . . .

Gracious Father, as thou hast stepped out of the picture, help me this day to step out of the picture and let someone see in me the meaning of a Christian . . . Amen.

ADDITIONAL SCRIPTURE READING:
Matthew 1:23; Luke 1:35; John 1:14

Go to page 786 for your next devotional reading.

1900   Present

father a time unlike any since Ephraim broke away from Judah—he will bring the king of Assyria."

18In that day the LORD will whistle for flies from the distant streams of Egypt and for bees from the land of Assyria. 19They will all come and settle in the steep ravines and in the crevices in the rocks, on all the thornbushes and at all the water holes. 20In that day the Lord will use a razor hired from beyond the River*a*—the king of Assyria—to shave your head and the hair of your legs, and to take off your beards also. 21In that day, a man will keep alive a young cow and two goats. 22And because of the abundance of the milk they give, he will have curds to eat. All who remain in the land will eat curds and honey. 23In that day, in every place where there were a thousand vines worth a thousand silver shekels,*b* there will be only briers and thorns. 24Men will go there with bow and arrow, for the land will be covered with briers and thorns. 25As for all the hills once cultivated by the hoe, you will no longer go there for fear of the briers and thorns; they will become places where cattle are turned loose and where sheep run.

Assyria, the LORD's Instrument

8 The LORD said to me, "Take a large scroll and write on it with an ordinary pen: Maher-Shalal-Hash-Baz.*c* 2And I will call in Uriah the priest and Zechariah son of Jeberekiah as reliable witnesses for me."

3Then I went to the prophetess, and she conceived and gave birth to a son. And the LORD said to me, "Name him Maher-Shalal-Hash-Baz. 4Before the boy knows how to say 'My father' or 'My mother,' the wealth of Damascus and the plunder of Samaria will be carried off by the king of Assyria."

5The LORD spoke to me again:

6 "Because this people has rejected
    the gently flowing waters of
      Shiloah
  and rejoices over Rezin

and the son of Remaliah,
7 therefore the Lord is about to bring
    against them
  the mighty floodwaters of the
      River*a*—
  the king of Assyria with all his
      pomp.
It will overflow all its channels,
  run over all its banks
8 and sweep on into Judah, swirling
    over it,
  passing through it and reaching up
    to the neck.
Its outspread wings will cover the
    breadth of your land,
  O Immanuel*d* !"

9 Raise the war cry,*e* you nations, and
    be shattered!
  Listen, all you distant lands.
  Prepare for battle, and be shattered!
  Prepare for battle, and be shattered!
10 Devise your strategy, but it will be
    thwarted;
  propose your plan, but it will not
    stand,
  for God is with us.*f*

Fear God

11The LORD spoke to me with his strong hand upon me, warning me not to follow the way of this people. He said:

12 "Do not call conspiracy
    everything that these people call
      conspiracy*g*;
  do not fear what they fear,
    and do not dread it.
13 The LORD Almighty is the one you
    are to regard as holy,
  he is the one you are to fear,
  he is the one you are to dread,
14 and he will be a sanctuary;
    but for both houses of Israel he will
      be
a stone that causes men to stumble
  and a rock that makes them fall.
And for the people of Jerusalem he
    will be
  a trap and a snare.
15 Many of them will stumble;
  they will fall and be broken,
  they will be snared and captured."

---

a 20,7 That is, the Euphrates   *b 23* That is, about 25 pounds (about 11.5 kilograms)   *c 1 Maher-Shalal-Hash-Baz* means *quick to the plunder, swift to the spoil;* also in verse 3.   *d 8 Immanuel* means *God with us.*   *e 9* Or *Do your worst*   *f 10* Hebrew *Immanuel*   *g 12* Or *Do not call for a treaty / every time these people call for a treaty*

16Bind up the testimony
and seal up the law among my
disciples.
17I will wait for the LORD,
who is hiding his face from the
house of Jacob.
I will put my trust in him.

18Here am I, and the children the
LORD has given me. We are signs and
symbols in Israel from the LORD
Almighty, who dwells on Mount Zion.
19When men tell you to consult mediums and spiritists, who whisper and
mutter, should not a people inquire of
their God? Why consult the dead on
behalf of the living? 20To the law and to
the testimony! If they do not speak
according to this word, they have no light
of dawn. 21Distressed and hungry, they
will roam through the land; when they
are famished, they will become enraged
and, looking upward, will curse their
king and their God. 22Then they will
look toward the earth and see only distress and darkness and fearful gloom, and
they will be thrust into utter darkness.

To Us a Child Is Born

9 Nevertheless, there will be no
more gloom for those who were
in distress. In the past he humbled the
land of Zebulun and the land of Naphtali, but in the future he will honor Galilee of the Gentiles, by the way of the
sea, along the Jordan—

2The people walking in darkness
have seen a great light;
on those living in the land of the
shadow of death*a*
a light has dawned.
3You have enlarged the nation
and increased their joy;
they rejoice before you
as people rejoice at the harvest,
as men rejoice
when dividing the plunder.
4For as in the day of Midian's defeat,
you have shattered
the yoke that burdens them,
the bar across their shoulders,
the rod of their oppressor.
5Every warrior's boot used in battle
and every garment rolled in blood

will be destined for burning,
will be fuel for the fire.
6For to us a child is born,
to us a son is given,
and the government will be on his
shoulders.
And he will be called
Wonderful Counselor,*b* Mighty
God,
Everlasting Father, Prince of Peace.
7Of the increase of his government
and peace
there will be no end.
He will reign on David's throne
and over his kingdom,
establishing and upholding it
with justice and righteousness
from that time on and forever.
The zeal of the LORD Almighty
will accomplish this.

The LORD's Anger Against Israel

8The Lord has sent a message against
Jacob;
it will fall on Israel.
9All the people will know it—
Ephraim and the inhabitants of
Samaria—
who say with pride
and arrogance of heart,
10"The bricks have fallen down,
but we will rebuild with dressed
stone;
the fig trees have been felled,
but we will replace them with
cedars."
11But the LORD has strengthened
Rezin's foes against them
and has spurred their enemies on.
12Arameans from the east and
Philistines from the west
have devoured Israel with open
mouth.

Yet for all this, his anger is not
turned away,
his hand is still upraised.

13But the people have not returned to
him who struck them,
nor have they sought the LORD
Almighty.
14So the LORD will cut off from Israel
both head and tail,
both palm branch and reed in a
single day;

a 2 Or *land of darkness*   *b 6* Or *Wonderful, Counselor*

15 the elders and prominent men are the
      head,
   the prophets who teach lies are the
      tail.
16 Those who guide this people mislead
      them,
   and those who are guided are led
      astray.
17 Therefore the Lord will take no
      pleasure in the young men,
   nor will he pity the fatherless and
      widows,
for everyone is ungodly and wicked,
   every mouth speaks vileness.

Yet for all this, his anger is not
      turned away,
   his hand is still upraised.

18 Surely wickedness burns like a fire;
   it consumes briers and thorns,
   it sets the forest thickets ablaze,
   so that it rolls upward in a column
      of smoke.
19 By the wrath of the LORD Almighty
   the land will be scorched
and the people will be fuel for the fire;
   no one will spare his brother.
20 On the right they will devour,
   but still be hungry;
on the left they will eat,
   but not be satisfied.
Each will feed on the flesh of his own
      offspring*a*:
21   Manasseh will feed on Ephraim,
      and Ephraim on Manasseh;
   together they will turn against
      Judah.

Yet for all this, his anger is not
      turned away,
   his hand is still upraised.

10 Woe to those who make
      unjust laws,
   to those who issue oppressive
      decrees,
2 to deprive the poor of their rights
   and withhold justice from the
      oppressed of my people,
making widows their prey
   and robbing the fatherless.
3 What will you do on the day of
      reckoning,
   when disaster comes from afar?
To whom will you run for help?

Where will you leave your riches?
4 Nothing will remain but to cringe
      among the captives
   or fall among the slain.

Yet for all this, his anger is not
      turned away,
   his hand is still upraised.

God's Judgment on Assyria

5 "Woe to the Assyrian, the rod of my
      anger,
   in whose hand is the club of my
      wrath!
6 I send him against a godless nation,
   I dispatch him against a people
      who anger me,
to seize loot and snatch plunder,
   and to trample them down like
      mud in the streets.
7 But this is not what he intends,
   this is not what he has in mind;
his purpose is to destroy,
   to put an end to many nations.
8 'Are not my commanders all kings?'
   he says.
9   'Has not Calno fared like
      Carchemish?
Is not Hamath like Arpad,
   and Samaria like Damascus?
10 As my hand seized the kingdoms of
      the idols,
   kingdoms whose images excelled
      those of Jerusalem and
      Samaria—
11 shall I not deal with Jerusalem and
      her images
   as I dealt with Samaria and her
      idols?' "

12 When the Lord has finished all his
work against Mount Zion and Jerusalem, he will say, "I will punish the
king of Assyria for the willful pride of
his heart and the haughty look in his
eyes. 13 For he says:

" 'By the strength of my hand I have
      done this,
   and by my wisdom, because I have
      understanding.
I removed the boundaries of nations,
   I plundered their treasures;
   like a mighty one I subdued*b* their
      kings.

a 20 Or *arm*   *b 13* Or / *I subdued the mighty,*

14 As one reaches into a nest,
  so my hand reached for the wealth
    of the nations;
as men gather abandoned eggs,
  so I gathered all the countries;
not one flapped a wing,
  or opened its mouth to chirp.' "

15 Does the ax raise itself above him
    who swings it,
  or the saw boast against him who
    uses it?
As if a rod were to wield him who
    lifts it up,
  or a club brandish him who is not
    wood!

16 Therefore, the Lord, the LORD
    Almighty,
  will send a wasting disease upon
    his sturdy warriors;
under his pomp a fire will be kindled
  like a blazing flame.

17 The Light of Israel will become a fire,
    their Holy One a flame;
in a single day it will burn and
    consume
  his thorns and his briers.

18 The splendor of his forests and fertile
    fields
  it will completely destroy,
    as when a sick man wastes away.

19 And the remaining trees of his forests
    will be so few
  that a child could write them
    down.

The Remnant of Israel

20 In that day the remnant of Israel,
    the survivors of the house of Jacob,
  will no longer rely on him
    who struck them down
  but will truly rely on the LORD,
    the Holy One of Israel.

21 A remnant will return,[a] a remnant of
    Jacob
  will return to the Mighty God.

22 Though your people, O Israel, be like
    the sand by the sea,
  only a remnant will return.
Destruction has been decreed,
  overwhelming and righteous.

23 The Lord, the LORD Almighty, will
    carry out
  the destruction decreed upon the
    whole land.

24 Therefore, this is what the Lord, the
LORD Almighty, says:

"O my people who live in Zion,
  do not be afraid of the Assyrians,
who beat you with a rod
  and lift up a club against you, as
    Egypt did.

25 Very soon my anger against you will
    end
  and my wrath will be directed to
    their destruction."

26 The LORD Almighty will lash them
    with a whip,
  as when he struck down Midian at
    the rock of Oreb;
and he will raise his staff over the
    waters,
  as he did in Egypt.

27 In that day their burden will be lifted
    from your shoulders,
  their yoke from your neck;
the yoke will be broken
  because you have grown so fat.[b]

28 They enter Aiath;
  they pass through Migron;
    they store supplies at Micmash.

29 They go over the pass, and say,
  "We will camp overnight at Geba."
Ramah trembles;
  Gibeah of Saul flees.

30 Cry out, O Daughter of Gallim!
  Listen, O Laishah!
    Poor Anathoth!

31 Madmenah is in flight;
  the people of Gebim take cover.

32 This day they will halt at Nob;
  they will shake their fist
at the mount of the Daughter of
    Zion,
  at the hill of Jerusalem.

33 See, the Lord, the LORD Almighty,
  will lop off the boughs with great
    power.
The lofty trees will be felled,
  the tall ones will be brought low.

34 He will cut down the forest thickets
    with an ax;
  Lebanon will fall before the Mighty
    One.

a 21 Hebrew shear-jashub; also in verse 22   b 27 Hebrew; Septuagint broken / from your shoulders

The Branch From Jesse

11 A shoot will come up from
the stump of Jesse;
from his roots a Branch will bear
fruit.
2 The Spirit of the LORD will rest on
him—
the Spirit of wisdom and of
understanding,
the Spirit of counsel and of power,
the Spirit of knowledge and of the
fear of the LORD—
3 and he will delight in the fear of the
LORD.

He will not judge by what he sees
with his eyes,
or decide by what he hears with his
ears;
4 but with righteousness he will judge
the needy,
with justice he will give decisions
for the poor of the earth.
He will strike the earth with the rod
of his mouth;
with the breath of his lips he will
slay the wicked.
5 Righteousness will be his belt
and faithfulness the sash around
his waist.

6 The wolf will live with the lamb,
the leopard will lie down with the
goat,
the calf and the lion and the yearling*a*
together;
and a little child will lead them.
7 The cow will feed with the bear,
their young will lie down together,
and the lion will eat straw like the
ox.
8 The infant will play near the hole of
the cobra,
and the young child put his hand
into the viper's nest.
9 They will neither harm nor destroy
on all my holy mountain,
for the earth will be full of the
knowledge of the LORD
as the waters cover the sea.

10 In that day the Root of Jesse will
stand as a banner for the peoples; the
nations will rally to him, and his place
of rest will be glorious. 11 In that day the
Lord will reach out his hand a second
time to reclaim the remnant that is left
of his people from Assyria, from Lower
Egypt, from Upper Egypt,*b* from Cush,*c*
from Elam, from Babylonia,*d* from
Hamath and from the islands of the sea.

12 He will raise a banner for the nations
and gather the exiles of Israel;
he will assemble the scattered people
of Judah
from the four quarters of the earth.
13 Ephraim's jealousy will vanish,
and Judah's enemies*e* will be cut
off;
Ephraim will not be jealous of Judah,
nor Judah hostile toward Ephraim.
14 They will swoop down on the slopes
of Philistia to the west;
together they will plunder the
people to the east.
They will lay hands on Edom and
Moab,
and the Ammonites will be subject
to them.
15 The LORD will dry up
the gulf of the Egyptian sea;
with a scorching wind he will sweep
his hand
over the Euphrates River.*f*
He will break it up into seven
streams
so that men can cross over in
sandals.
16 There will be a highway for the
remnant of his people
that is left from Assyria,
as there was for Israel
when they came up from Egypt.

Songs of Praise

12 In that day you will say:

"I will praise you, O LORD.
Although you were angry with me,
your anger has turned away
and you have comforted me.
2 Surely God is my salvation;
I will trust and not be afraid.
The LORD, the LORD, is my strength
and my song;
he has become my salvation."
3 With joy you will draw water
from the wells of salvation.

---

a 6 Hebrew; Septuagint *lion will feed*   *b 11* Hebrew *from Pathros*   *c 11* That is, the upper Nile
region   *d 11* Hebrew *Shinar*   *e 13* Or *hostility*   *f 15* Hebrew *the River*

⁴In that day you will say:

"Give thanks to the LORD, call on his
    name;
make known among the nations
    what he has done,
and proclaim that his name is
    exalted.
⁵Sing to the LORD, for he has done
    glorious things;
let this be known to all the world.
⁶Shout aloud and sing for joy, people
    of Zion,

for great is the Holy One of Israel
    among you."

A Prophecy Against Babylon

 13 An oracle concerning Babylon that Isaiah son of Amoz
saw:

²Raise a banner on a bare hilltop,
    shout to them;
beckon to them
    to enter the gates of the nobles.
³I have commanded my holy ones;

TUESDAY

THE WELLS OF SALVATION
J. H. Jowett

VERSE: Isaiah 12:3   **PASSAGE:** Isaiah 12:1–3

he wells of the Lord are to be found where most I need
them. The Lord of the way knows the pilgrim life, and
the wells have been unsealed just where the soul is
prone to become dry and faint. At the foot of the hill
Difficulty was found a spring! Yes, these health-springs are lifting their crystal flood in the cheerless wastes of evil antago-
nisms and exhausting grief.

Sometimes I am foolish, and in my need I assume that the
well is far away. I knew a farmer who for a generation had carried
every pail of water from a distant well to meet the needs of his
homestead. And one day he sunk a shaft by his own house door,
and to his great joy he found that the water was waiting at his
own gate! My soul, thy well is near, even here! Go not in search
of him! Thy pilgrimage is ended, the waters are at thy feet!

But I must *"draw* the water out of the wells of salvation."
The hand of faith must lift the gracious gift to the parched lips,
and so refresh the panting soul. "I will *take* the cup of salvation." Stretch out thy "lame hand of faith," and take the holy,
hallowing energy offered by the Lord.

ADDITIONAL SCRIPTURE READING:
Isaiah 55:1–3; John 4:10–14; 7:37–39

Go to page 798 for your next devotional reading.

1700   1900

I have summoned my warriors to
　　carry out my wrath—
　　those who rejoice in my triumph.

4 Listen, a noise on the mountains,
　　like that of a great multitude!
　Listen, an uproar among the
　　kingdoms,
　　like nations massing together!
　The LORD Almighty is mustering
　　an army for war.
5 They come from faraway lands,
　　from the ends of the heavens—
　the LORD and the weapons of his
　　wrath—
　　to destroy the whole country.

6 Wail, for the day of the LORD is near;
　　it will come like destruction from
　　the Almighty.*a*
7 Because of this, all hands will go limp,
　　every man's heart will melt.
8 Terror will seize them,
　　pain and anguish will grip them;
　　they will writhe like a woman in
　　labor.
　They will look aghast at each other,
　　their faces aflame.

9 See, the day of the LORD is coming
　　—a cruel day, with wrath and
　　fierce anger—
　to make the land desolate
　　and destroy the sinners within it.
10 The stars of heaven and their
　　constellations
　　will not show their light.
　The rising sun will be darkened
　　and the moon will not give its light.
11 I will punish the world for its evil,
　　the wicked for their sins.
　I will put an end to the arrogance of
　　the haughty
　　and will humble the pride of the
　　ruthless.
12 I will make man scarcer than pure
　　gold,
　　more rare than the gold of Ophir.
13 Therefore I will make the heavens
　　tremble;
　　and the earth will shake from its
　　place
　at the wrath of the LORD Almighty,
　　in the day of his burning anger.

14 Like a hunted gazelle,
　　like sheep without a shepherd,

each will return to his own people,
　　each will flee to his native land.
15 Whoever is captured will be thrust
　　through;
　all who are caught will fall by the
　　sword.
16 Their infants will be dashed to pieces
　　before their eyes;
　　their houses will be looted and
　　their wives ravished.

17 See, I will stir up against them the
　　Medes,
　　who do not care for silver
　　and have no delight in gold.
18 Their bows will strike down the
　　young men;
　　they will have no mercy on infants
　　nor will they look with
　　compassion on children.
19 Babylon, the jewel of kingdoms,
　　the glory of the Babylonians'*b* pride,
　will be overthrown by God
　　like Sodom and Gomorrah.
20 She will never be inhabited
　　or lived in through all generations;
　no Arab will pitch his tent there,
　　no shepherd will rest his flocks
　　there.
21 But desert creatures will lie there,
　　jackals will fill her houses;
　there the owls will dwell,
　　and there the wild goats will leap
　　about.
22 Hyenas will howl in her strongholds,
　　jackals in her luxurious palaces.
　Her time is at hand,
　　and her days will not be prolonged.

14 The LORD will have
　　compassion on Jacob;
　once again he will choose Israel
　　and will settle them in their own
　　land.
　Aliens will join them
　　and unite with the house of Jacob.
2 Nations will take them
　　and bring them to their own place.
　And the house of Israel will possess
　　the nations
　　as menservants and maidservants
　　in the LORD's land.
　They will make captives of their
　　captors
　　and rule over their oppressors.

---

a 6 Hebrew *Shaddai*　　*b* 19 Or *Chaldeans'*

³On the day the LORD gives you relief from suffering and turmoil and cruel bondage, ⁴you will take up this taunt against the king of Babylon:

How the oppressor has come to an
end!
How his fury*a* has ended!
⁵ The LORD has broken the rod of the
wicked,
the scepter of the rulers,
⁶ which in anger struck down peoples
with unceasing blows,
and in fury subdued nations
with relentless aggression.
⁷ All the lands are at rest and at peace;
they break into singing.
⁸ Even the pine trees and the cedars of
Lebanon
exult over you and say,
"Now that you have been laid low,
no woodsman comes to cut us
down."

⁹ The grave*b* below is all astir
to meet you at your coming;
it rouses the spirits of the departed to
greet you—
all those who were leaders in the
world;
it makes them rise from their
thrones—
all those who were kings over the
nations.
¹⁰ They will all respond,
they will say to you,
"You also have become weak, as we
are;
you have become like us."
¹¹ All your pomp has been brought
down to the grave,
along with the noise of your harps;
maggots are spread out beneath you
and worms cover you.

¹² How you have fallen from heaven,
O morning star, son of the dawn!
You have been cast down to the
earth,
you who once laid low the nations!
¹³ You said in your heart,
"I will ascend to heaven;
I will raise my throne
above the stars of God;

I will sit enthroned on the mount of
assembly,
on the utmost heights of the sacred
mountain.*c*
¹⁴ I will ascend above the tops of the
clouds;
I will make myself like the Most
High."
¹⁵ But you are brought down to the
grave,
to the depths of the pit.

¹⁶ Those who see you stare at you,
they ponder your fate:
"Is this the man who shook the earth
and made kingdoms tremble,
¹⁷ the man who made the world a
desert,
who overthrew its cities
and would not let his captives go
home?"

¹⁸ All the kings of the nations lie in
state,
each in his own tomb.
¹⁹ But you are cast out of your tomb
like a rejected branch;
you are covered with the slain,
with those pierced by the sword,
those who descend to the stones of
the pit.
Like a corpse trampled underfoot,
20   you will not join them in burial,
for you have destroyed your land
and killed your people.

The offspring of the wicked
will never be mentioned again.
²¹ Prepare a place to slaughter his sons
for the sins of their forefathers;
they are not to rise to inherit the land
and cover the earth with their
cities.

²² "I will rise up against them,"
declares the LORD Almighty.
"I will cut off from Babylon her name
and survivors,
her offspring and descendants,"
declares the LORD.
²³ "I will turn her into a place for owls
and into swampland;
I will sweep her with the broom of
destruction,"
declares the LORD Almighty.

a 4 Dead Sea Scrolls, Septuagint and Syriac; the meaning of the word in the Masoretic Text is uncertain.
b 9 Hebrew *Sheol*; also in verses 11 and 15   *c 13* Or *the north*; Hebrew *Zaphon*

A Prophecy Against Assyria

24 The LORD Almighty has sworn,

"Surely, as I have planned, so it will
    be,
and as I have purposed, so it will
    stand.
25 I will crush the Assyrian in my land;
    on my mountains I will trample
        him down.
His yoke will be taken from my
        people,
    and his burden removed from their
        shoulders."

26 This is the plan determined for the
        whole world;
    this is the hand stretched out over
        all nations.
27 For the LORD Almighty has purposed,
        and who can thwart him?
    His hand is stretched out, and who
        can turn it back?

A Prophecy Against the Philistines

28 This oracle came in the year King
Ahaz died:

29 Do not rejoice, all you Philistines,
    that the rod that struck you is
        broken;
from the root of that snake will
        spring up a viper,
    its fruit will be a darting,
        venomous serpent.
30 The poorest of the poor will find
        pasture,
    and the needy will lie down in
        safety.
But your root I will destroy by
        famine;
    it will slay your survivors.

31 Wail, O gate! Howl, O city!
    Melt away, all you Philistines!
A cloud of smoke comes from the
        north,
    and there is not a straggler in its
        ranks.
32 What answer shall be given
        to the envoys of that nation?
    "The LORD has established Zion,
        and in her his afflicted people will
            find refuge."

A Prophecy Against Moab

15 An oracle concerning Moab:

Ar in Moab is ruined,
    destroyed in a night!
Kir in Moab is ruined,
    destroyed in a night!
2 Dibon goes up to its temple,
    to its high places to weep;
Moab wails over Nebo and
        Medeba.
Every head is shaved
    and every beard cut off.
3 In the streets they wear sackcloth;
    on the roofs and in the public
        squares
they all wail,
    prostrate with weeping.
4 Heshbon and Elealeh cry out,
    their voices are heard all the way
        to Jahaz.
Therefore the armed men of Moab
        cry out,
    and their hearts are faint.

5 My heart cries out over Moab;
    her fugitives flee as far as Zoar,
    as far as Eglath Shelishiyah.
They go up the way to Luhith,
    weeping as they go;
on the road to Horonaim
    they lament their destruction.
6 The waters of Nimrim are dried up
    and the grass is withered;
the vegetation is gone
    and nothing green is left.
7 So the wealth they have acquired and
        stored up
    they carry away over the Ravine of
        the Poplars.
8 Their outcry echoes along the border
        of Moab;
    their wailing reaches as far as
        Eglaim,
    their lamentation as far as Beer
        Elim.
9 Dimon's[a] waters are full of blood,
    but I will bring still more upon
        Dimon[a]—
a lion upon the fugitives of Moab
    and upon those who remain in the
        land.

---

a 9 Masoretic Text; Dead Sea Scrolls, some Septuagint manuscripts and Vulgate Dibon

16 Send lambs as tribute
        to the ruler of the land,
from Sela, across the desert,
    to the mount of the Daughter of
        Zion.
2 Like fluttering birds
    pushed from the nest,
so are the women of Moab
    at the fords of the Arnon.

3 "Give us counsel,
    render a decision.
Make your shadow like night—
    at high noon.
Hide the fugitives,
    do not betray the refugees.
4 Let the Moabite fugitives stay with
        you;
    be their shelter from the
        destroyer."

The oppressor will come to an end,
    and destruction will cease;
    the aggressor will vanish from the
        land.
5 In love a throne will be established;
    in faithfulness a man will sit on
        it—
    one from the house*a* of David—
one who in judging seeks justice
    and speeds the cause of
        righteousness.

6 We have heard of Moab's pride—
    her overweening pride and conceit,
her pride and her insolence—
    but her boasts are empty.
7 Therefore the Moabites wail,
    they wail together for Moab.
Lament and grieve
    for the men*b* of Kir Hareseth.
8 The fields of Heshbon wither,
    the vines of Sibmah also.
The rulers of the nations
    have trampled down the choicest
        vines,
which once reached Jazer
    and spread toward the desert.
Their shoots spread out
    and went as far as the sea.
9 So I weep, as Jazer weeps,
    for the vines of Sibmah.
O Heshbon, O Elealeh,
    I drench you with tears!
The shouts of joy over your ripened
        fruit

and over your harvests have been
        stilled.
10 Joy and gladness are taken away from
        the orchards;
    no one sings or shouts in the
        vineyards;
    no one treads out wine at the presses,
        for I have put an end to the
        shouting.
11 My heart laments for Moab like a
        harp,
    my inmost being for Kir Hareseth.
12 When Moab appears at her high
        place,
    she only wears herself out;
    when she goes to her shrine to pray,
        it is to no avail.

13 This is the word the LORD has
already spoken concerning Moab. 14 But
now the LORD says: "Within three years,
as a servant bound by contract would
count them, Moab's splendor and all her
many people will be despised, and her
survivors will be very few and feeble."

An Oracle Against Damascus

17 An oracle concerning Damas-
        cus:

"See, Damascus will no longer be a
        city
    but will become a heap of ruins.
2 The cities of Aroer will be deserted
    and left to flocks, which will lie
        down,
    with no one to make them afraid.
3 The fortified city will disappear from
        Ephraim,
    and royal power from Damascus;
    the remnant of Aram will be
        like the glory of the Israelites,"
            declares the LORD Almighty.

4 "In that day the glory of Jacob will
        fade;
    the fat of his body will waste away.
5 It will be as when a reaper gathers
        the standing grain
    and harvests the grain with his
        arm—
as when a man gleans heads of grain
    in the Valley of Rephaim.
6 Yet some gleanings will remain,
    as when an olive tree is beaten,

---

a 5 Hebrew *tent*   *b 7* Or *"raisin cakes,"* a wordplay

leaving two or three olives on the
topmost branches,
    four or five on the fruitful boughs,"
        declares the LORD,
        the God of Israel.

7 In that day men will look to their
Maker
    and turn their eyes to the Holy
One of Israel.
8 They will not look to the altars,
    the work of their hands,
and they will have no regard for the
Asherah poles*a*
    and the incense altars their fingers
have made.

9 In that day their strong cities, which
they left because of the Israelites, will be
like places abandoned to thickets and
undergrowth. And all will be desolation.

10 You have forgotten God your Savior;
    you have not remembered the
Rock, your fortress.
Therefore, though you set out the
finest plants
    and plant imported vines,
11 though on the day you set them out,
    you make them grow,
and on the morning when you
plant them, you bring them to
bud,
    yet the harvest will be as nothing
in the day of disease and incurable
pain.

12 Oh, the raging of many nations—
    they rage like the raging sea!
Oh, the uproar of the peoples—
    they roar like the roaring of great
waters!
13 Although the peoples roar like the
roar of surging waters,
    when he rebukes them they flee far
away,
driven before the wind like chaff on
the hills,
    like tumbleweed before a gale.
14 In the evening, sudden terror!
    Before the morning, they are gone!
This is the portion of those who loot
us,
    the lot of those who plunder us.

A Prophecy Against Cush

18 Woe to the land of whirring
wings*b*
along the rivers of Cush,*c*
2 which sends envoys by sea
    in papyrus boats over the water.

Go, swift messengers,
to a people tall and smooth-skinned,
to a people feared far and wide,
an aggressive nation of strange
speech,
    whose land is divided by rivers.

3 All you people of the world,
    you who live on the earth,
when a banner is raised on the
mountains,
    you will see it,
and when a trumpet sounds,
    you will hear it.
4 This is what the LORD says to me:
"I will remain quiet and will look
on from my dwelling place,
like shimmering heat in the
sunshine,
like a cloud of dew in the heat of
harvest."
5 For, before the harvest, when the
blossom is gone
    and the flower becomes a ripening
grape,
he will cut off the shoots with
pruning knives,
    and cut down and take away the
spreading branches.
6 They will all be left to the mountain
birds of prey
    and to the wild animals;
the birds will feed on them all
summer,
    the wild animals all winter.

7 At that time gifts will be brought to
the LORD Almighty

from a people tall and smooth-
skinned,
    from a people feared far and wide,
an aggressive nation of strange
speech,
    whose land is divided by rivers—

the gifts will be brought to Mount Zion,
the place of the Name of the LORD
Almighty.

---

a 8 That is, symbols of the goddess Asherah   *b* 1 Or *of locusts*   *c* 1 That is, the upper Nile region

A Prophecy About Egypt

19 An oracle concerning Egypt:

See, the LORD rides on a swift cloud
and is coming to Egypt.
The idols of Egypt tremble before
him,
and the hearts of the Egyptians
melt within them.

2 "I will stir up Egyptian against
Egyptian—
brother will fight against brother,
neighbor against neighbor,
city against city,
kingdom against kingdom.
3 The Egyptians will lose heart,
and I will bring their plans to
nothing;
they will consult the idols and the
spirits of the dead,
the mediums and the spiritists.
4 I will hand the Egyptians over
to the power of a cruel master,
and a fierce king will rule over
them,"
declares the Lord, the LORD
Almighty.

5 The waters of the river will dry up,
and the riverbed will be parched
and dry.
6 The canals will stink;
the streams of Egypt will dwindle
and dry up.
The reeds and rushes will wither,
7   also the plants along the Nile,
at the mouth of the river.
Every sown field along the Nile
will become parched, will blow
away and be no more.
8 The fishermen will groan and
lament,
all who cast hooks into the Nile;
those who throw nets on the water
will pine away.
9 Those who work with combed flax
will despair,
the weavers of fine linen will lose
hope.
10 The workers in cloth will be
dejected,
and all the wage earners will be
sick at heart.

11 The officials of Zoan are nothing but
fools;
the wise counselors of Pharaoh
give senseless advice.
How can you say to Pharaoh,
"I am one of the wise men,
a disciple of the ancient kings"?
12 Where are your wise men now?
Let them show you and make
known
what the LORD Almighty
has planned against Egypt.
13 The officials of Zoan have become
fools,
the leaders of Memphis[a] are
deceived;
the cornerstones of her peoples
have led Egypt astray.
14 The LORD has poured into them
a spirit of dizziness;
they make Egypt stagger in all that
she does,
as a drunkard staggers around in
his vomit.
15 There is nothing Egypt can do—
head or tail, palm branch or reed.

16In that day the Egyptians will be like women. They will shudder with fear at the uplifted hand that the LORD Almighty raises against them. 17And the land of Judah will bring terror to the Egyptians; everyone to whom Judah is mentioned will be terrified, because of what the LORD Almighty is planning against them.

18In that day five cities in Egypt will speak the language of Canaan and swear allegiance to the LORD Almighty. One of them will be called the City of Destruction.[b]

19In that day there will be an altar to the LORD in the heart of Egypt, and a monument to the LORD at its border. 20It will be a sign and witness to the LORD Almighty in the land of Egypt. When they cry out to the LORD because of their oppressors, he will send them a savior and defender, and he will rescue them. 21So the LORD will make himself known to the Egyptians, and in that day they will acknowledge the LORD. They will worship with sacrifices and grain offerings; they will make vows to the LORD

---

a 13 Hebrew *Noph*   *b 18* Most manuscripts of the Masoretic Text; some manuscripts of the Masoretic Text, Dead Sea Scrolls and Vulgate *City of the Sun* (that is, Heliopolis)

and keep them. ²²The LORD will strike Egypt with a plague; he will strike them and heal them. They will turn to the LORD, and he will respond to their pleas and heal them.

²³In that day there will be a highway from Egypt to Assyria. The Assyrians will go to Egypt and the Egyptians to Assyria. The Egyptians and Assyrians will worship together. ²⁴In that day Israel will be the third, along with Egypt and Assyria, a blessing on the earth. ²⁵The LORD Almighty will bless them, saying, "Blessed be Egypt my people, Assyria my handiwork, and Israel my inheritance."

A Prophecy Against Egypt and Cush

20 In the year that the supreme commander, sent by Sargon king of Assyria, came to Ashdod and attacked and captured it— ²at that time the LORD spoke through Isaiah son of Amoz. He said to him, "Take off the sackcloth from your body and the sandals from your feet." And he did so, going around stripped and barefoot.

³Then the LORD said, "Just as my servant Isaiah has gone stripped and barefoot for three years, as a sign and portent against Egypt and Cush,ᵃ ⁴so the king of Assyria will lead away stripped and barefoot the Egyptian captives and Cushite exiles, young and old, with buttocks bared—to Egypt's shame. ⁵Those who trusted in Cush and boasted in Egypt will be afraid and put to shame. ⁶In that day the people who live on this coast will say, 'See what has happened to those we relied on, those we fled to for help and deliverance from the king of Assyria! How then can we escape?' "

A Prophecy Against Babylon

21 An oracle concerning the Desert by the Sea:

Like whirlwinds sweeping through
the southland,
an invader comes from the desert,
from a land of terror.

² A dire vision has been shown to me:
The traitor betrays, the looter
takes loot.
Elam, attack! Media, lay siege!

I will bring to an end all the
groaning she caused.

³ At this my body is racked with pain,
pangs seize me, like those of a
woman in labor;
I am staggered by what I hear,
I am bewildered by what I see.
⁴ My heart falters,
fear makes me tremble;
the twilight I longed for
has become a horror to me.

⁵ They set the tables,
they spread the rugs,
they eat, they drink!
Get up, you officers,
oil the shields!

⁶ This is what the Lord says to me:

"Go, post a lookout
and have him report what he sees.
⁷ When he sees chariots
with teams of horses,
riders on donkeys
or riders on camels,
let him be alert,
fully alert."

⁸ And the lookoutᵇ shouted,

"Day after day, my lord, I stand on
the watchtower;
every night I stay at my post.
⁹ Look, here comes a man in a chariot
with a team of horses.
And he gives back the answer:
'Babylon has fallen, has fallen!
All the images of its gods
lie shattered on the ground!' "

¹⁰ O my people, crushed on the
threshing floor,
I tell you what I have heard
from the LORD Almighty,
from the God of Israel.

A Prophecy Against Edom

¹¹ An oracle concerning Dumahᶜ:

Someone calls to me from Seir,
"Watchman, what is left of the
night?
Watchman, what is left of the
night?"

ᵃ 3 That is, the upper Nile region; also in verse 5   ᵇ 8 Dead Sea Scrolls and Syriac; Masoretic Text
A lion   ᶜ 11 Dumah means silence or stillness, a wordplay on Edom.

¹²The watchman replies,
    "Morning is coming, but also the
        night.
  If you would ask, then ask;
    and come back yet again."

A Prophecy Against Arabia

¹³An oracle concerning Arabia:

You caravans of Dedanites,
    who camp in the thickets of
        Arabia,
¹⁴ bring water for the thirsty;
  you who live in Tema,
    bring food for the fugitives.
¹⁵They flee from the sword,
    from the drawn sword,
  from the bent bow
    and from the heat of battle.

¹⁶This is what the Lord says to me:
"Within one year, as a servant bound by
contract would count it, all the pomp of
Kedar will come to an end. ¹⁷The survivors of the bowmen, the warriors of
Kedar, will be few." The LORD, the God
of Israel, has spoken.

A Prophecy About Jerusalem

22 An oracle concerning the Valley of Vision:

What troubles you now,
    that you have all gone up on the
        roofs,
²O town full of commotion,
  O city of tumult and revelry?
  Your slain were not killed by the
        sword,
    nor did they die in battle.
³All your leaders have fled together;
    they have been captured without
        using the bow.
  All you who were caught were taken
        prisoner together,
    having fled while the enemy was
        still far away.
⁴Therefore I said, "Turn away from
        me;
    let me weep bitterly.
  Do not try to console me
    over the destruction of my people."

⁵The Lord, the LORD Almighty, has a
        day
    of tumult and trampling and terror
  in the Valley of Vision,

a day of battering down walls
    and of crying out to the mountains.
⁶Elam takes up the quiver,
    with her charioteers and horses;
  Kir uncovers the shield.
⁷Your choicest valleys are full of
        chariots,
    and horsemen are posted at the
        city gates;
⁸ the defenses of Judah are stripped
        away.

And you looked in that day
    to the weapons in the Palace of the
        Forest;
⁹you saw that the City of David
    had many breaches in its defenses;
  you stored up water
    in the Lower Pool.
¹⁰You counted the buildings in
        Jerusalem
    and tore down houses to
        strengthen the wall.
¹¹You built a reservoir between the two
        walls
    for the water of the Old Pool,
  but you did not look to the One who
        made it,
    or have regard for the One who
        planned it long ago.

¹²The Lord, the LORD Almighty,
        called you on that day
  to weep and to wail,
    to tear out your hair and put on
        sackcloth.
¹³But see, there is joy and revelry,
    slaughtering of cattle and killing of
        sheep,
    eating of meat and drinking of
        wine!
  "Let us eat and drink," you say,
    "for tomorrow we die!"

¹⁴The LORD Almighty has revealed
this in my hearing: "Till your dying day
this sin will not be atoned for," says the
Lord, the LORD Almighty.

¹⁵This is what the Lord, the LORD
Almighty, says:

"Go, say to this steward,
    to Shebna, who is in charge of the
        palace:
¹⁶What are you doing here and who
        gave you permission
    to cut out a grave for yourself here,

hewing your grave on the height
  and chiseling your resting place in
    the rock?
17 "Beware, the LORD is about to take
    firm hold of you
  and hurl you away, O you mighty
    man.
18 He will roll you up tightly like a ball
    and throw you into a large country.
  There you will die
    and there your splendid chariots
      will remain—
  you disgrace to your master's
    house!
19 I will depose you from your office,
    and you will be ousted from your
      position.

20 "In that day I will summon my servant, Eliakim son of Hilkiah. 21 I will clothe him with your robe and fasten your sash around him and hand your authority over to him. He will be a father to those who live in Jerusalem and to the house of Judah. 22 I will place on his shoulder the key to the house of David; what he opens no one can shut, and what he shuts no one can open. 23 I will drive him like a peg into a firm place; he will be a seat*a* of honor for the house of his father. 24 All the glory of his family will hang on him: its offspring and offshoots—all its lesser vessels, from the bowls to all the jars.

25 "In that day," declares the LORD Almighty, "the peg driven into the firm place will give way; it will be sheared off and will fall, and the load hanging on it will be cut down." The LORD has spoken.

A Prophecy About Tyre

23 An oracle concerning Tyre:

Wail, O ships of Tarshish!
  For Tyre is destroyed
    and left without house or harbor.
From the land of Cyprus*b*
  word has come to them.

2 Be silent, you people of the island
  and you merchants of Sidon,

whom the seafarers have enriched.
3 On the great waters
  came the grain of the Shihor;
the harvest of the Nile*c* was the
    revenue of Tyre,
  and she became the marketplace of
    the nations.

4 Be ashamed, O Sidon, and you,
    O fortress of the sea,
  for the sea has spoken:
"I have neither been in labor nor
    given birth;
  I have neither reared sons nor
    brought up daughters."
5 When word comes to Egypt,
  they will be in anguish at the
    report from Tyre.

6 Cross over to Tarshish;
  wail, you people of the island.
7 Is this your city of revelry,
    the old, old city,
  whose feet have taken her
    to settle in far-off lands?
8 Who planned this against Tyre,
    the bestower of crowns,
  whose merchants are princes,
    whose traders are renowned in the
      earth?
9 The LORD Almighty planned it,
    to bring low the pride of all glory
  and to humble all who are
    renowned on the earth.

10 Till*d* your land as along the Nile,
    O Daughter of Tarshish,
  for you no longer have a harbor.
11 The LORD has stretched out his hand
    over the sea
  and made its kingdoms tremble.
He has given an order concerning
    Phoenicia*e*
  that her fortresses be destroyed.
12 He said, "No more of your reveling,
    O Virgin Daughter of Sidon, now
      crushed!

"Up, cross over to Cyprus*b*;
  even there you will find no rest."
13 Look at the land of the Babylonians,*f*
    this people that is now of no
      account!
The Assyrians have made it
  a place for desert creatures;

---

a 23 Or *throne*   *b 1,12* Hebrew *Kittim*   *c 2,3* Masoretic Text; one Dead Sea Scroll *Sidon, / who cross over the sea; / your envoys 3are on the great waters. / The grain of the Shihor, / the harvest of the Nile,*   *d 10* Dead Sea Scrolls and some Septuagint manuscripts; Masoretic Text *Go through*   *e 11* Hebrew *Canaan*   *f 13* Or *Chaldeans*

they raised up their siege towers,
　　they stripped its fortresses bare
　　and turned it into a ruin.
14 Wail, you ships of Tarshish;
　　your fortress is destroyed!

15 At that time Tyre will be forgotten for seventy years, the span of a king's life. But at the end of these seventy years, it will happen to Tyre as in the song of the prostitute:

16 "Take up a harp, walk through the
　　city,
　　O prostitute forgotten;
play the harp well, sing many a song,
　　so that you will be remembered."

17 At the end of seventy years, the LORD will deal with Tyre. She will return to her hire as a prostitute and will ply her trade with all the kingdoms on the face of the earth. 18 Yet her profit and her earnings will be set apart for the LORD; they will not be stored up or hoarded. Her profits will go to those who live before the LORD, for abundant food and fine clothes.

The LORD's Devastation of the Earth

24 See, the LORD is going to lay
　　waste the earth
　　and devastate it;
　　he will ruin its face
　　and scatter its inhabitants—
2 it will be the same
　　for priest as for people,
　　for master as for servant,
　　for mistress as for maid,
　　for seller as for buyer,
　　for borrower as for lender,
　　for debtor as for creditor.
3 The earth will be completely laid
　　waste
　　and totally plundered.
　　　　　The LORD has spoken
　　　　　　　　this word.

4 The earth dries up and withers,
　　the world languishes and withers,
　　the exalted of the earth languish.
5 The earth is defiled by its people;
　　they have disobeyed the laws,
　violated the statutes
　　and broken the everlasting
　　　covenant.

6 Therefore a curse consumes the
　　earth;
　　its people must bear their guilt.
Therefore earth's inhabitants are
　　burned up,
　　and very few are left.
7 The new wine dries up and the vine
　　withers;
　　all the merrymakers groan.
8 The gaiety of the tambourines is
　　stilled,
　　the noise of the revelers has
　　　stopped,
　　the joyful harp is silent.
9 No longer do they drink wine with a
　　song;
　　the beer is bitter to its drinkers.
10 The ruined city lies desolate;
　　the entrance to every house is
　　　barred.
11 In the streets they cry out for wine;
　　all joy turns to gloom,
　　all gaiety is banished from the
　　　earth.
12 The city is left in ruins,
　　its gate is battered to pieces.
13 So will it be on the earth
　　and among the nations,
　as when an olive tree is beaten,
　　or as when gleanings are left after
　　　the grape harvest.

14 They raise their voices, they shout
　　for joy;
　　from the west they acclaim the
　　　LORD's majesty.
15 Therefore in the east give glory to the
　　LORD;
　　exalt the name of the LORD, the
　　　God of Israel,
　　in the islands of the sea.
16 From the ends of the earth we hear
　　singing:
　　"Glory to the Righteous One."

But I said, "I waste away, I waste
　　away!
　　Woe to me!
　　The treacherous betray!
　　With treachery the treacherous
　　　betray!"
17 Terror and pit and snare await you,
　　O people of the earth.
18 Whoever flees at the sound of terror
　　will fall into a pit;
　　whoever climbs out of the pit
　　will be caught in a snare.

The floodgates of the heavens are
 opened,
  the foundations of the earth shake.
19 The earth is broken up,
  the earth is split asunder,
  the earth is thoroughly shaken.
20 The earth reels like a drunkard,
  it sways like a hut in the wind;
 so heavy upon it is the guilt of its
  rebellion
  that it falls—never to rise again.

21 In that day the LORD will punish
  the powers in the heavens above
  and the kings on the earth below.
22 They will be herded together
  like prisoners bound in a dungeon;
 they will be shut up in prison
  and be punished*a* after many days.
23 The moon will be abashed, the sun
  ashamed;
  for the LORD Almighty will reign
 on Mount Zion and in Jerusalem,
  and before its elders, gloriously.

Praise to the LORD

25 O LORD, you are my God;
  I will exalt you and praise
   your name,
 for in perfect faithfulness
  you have done marvelous things,
  things planned long ago.
2 You have made the city a heap of
   rubble,
  the fortified town a ruin,
 the foreigners' stronghold a city no
   more;
  it will never be rebuilt.
3 Therefore strong peoples will honor
   you;
  cities of ruthless nations will
   revere you.
4 You have been a refuge for the poor,
  a refuge for the needy in his
   distress,
 a shelter from the storm
  and a shade from the heat.
 For the breath of the ruthless
  is like a storm driving against a
   wall
5 and like the heat of the desert.
 You silence the uproar of foreigners;
  as heat is reduced by the shadow of
   a cloud,
  so the song of the ruthless is stilled.

6 On this mountain the LORD
   Almighty will prepare
  a feast of rich food for all peoples,
 a banquet of aged wine—
  the best of meats and the finest of
   wines.
7 On this mountain he will destroy
  the shroud that enfolds all peoples,
 the sheet that covers all nations;
8   he will swallow up death forever.
 The Sovereign LORD will wipe away
   the tears
  from all faces;
 he will remove the disgrace of his
   people
  from all the earth.
          The LORD has spoken.

9 In that day they will say,

 "Surely this is our God;
  we trusted in him, and he saved us.
 This is the LORD, we trusted in him;
  let us rejoice and be glad in his
   salvation."

10 The hand of the LORD will rest on
   this mountain;
  but Moab will be trampled under
   him
  as straw is trampled down in the
   manure.
11 They will spread out their hands in
   it,
  as a swimmer spreads out his
   hands to swim.
 God will bring down their pride
  despite the cleverness*b* of their
   hands.
12 He will bring down your high
   fortified walls
  and lay them low;
 he will bring them down to the
   ground,
  to the very dust.

A Song of Praise

26 In that day this song will be
  sung in the land of Judah:

 We have a strong city;
  God makes salvation
   its walls and ramparts.
2 Open the gates
  that the righteous nation may enter,

---

a 22 Or *released*   *b 11* The meaning of the Hebrew for this word is uncertain.

the nation that keeps faith.
3 You will keep in perfect peace
    him whose mind is steadfast,
  because he trusts in you.
4 Trust in the LORD forever,
    for the LORD, the LORD, is the Rock
      eternal.
5 He humbles those who dwell on high,
    he lays the lofty city low;
  he levels it to the ground
    and casts it down to the dust.

6 Feet trample it down—
    the feet of the oppressed,
    the footsteps of the poor.
7 The path of the righteous is level;
    O upright One, you make the way
      of the righteous smooth.
8 Yes, LORD, walking in the way of
      your laws, *a*
    we wait for you;
  your name and renown
    are the desire of our hearts.

a 8 Or judgments

WEDNESDAY

IS YOUR MIND STAYED ON GOD?
Oswald Chambers

VERSE: Isaiah 26:3   **PASSAGE:** Isaiah 26:1–6

s your mind stayed on God or is it starved? Starvation of the mind, caused by neglect, is one of the chief sources of exhaustion and weakness in a servant's life. If you have never used your mind to place yourself before God, begin to do it now. There is no reason to wait for God to come to you. You must turn your thoughts and your eyes away from the face of idols and look to him and be saved (see Isaiah 45:22).

Your mind is the greatest gift God has given you and it ought to be devoted entirely to him . . . When you have thoughts and ideas that are worthy of credit to God, learn to compare and associate them with all that happens in nature—the rising and the setting of the sun, the shining of the moon and the stars, and the changing of the seasons. You will begin to see that your thoughts are from God as well, and your mind will no longer be at the mercy of your impulsive thinking, but will always be used in service to God . . .

Remember whose you are and whom you serve. Encourage yourself to remember, and your affection for God will increase tenfold. Your mind will no longer be starved, but will be quick and enthusiastic, and your hope will be inexpressibly bright.

ADDITIONAL SCRIPTURE READING:
Isaiah 48:2; Jeremiah 17:7–8; Romans 4:18–21

Go to page 804 for your next devotional reading.

1900   Present

⁹My soul yearns for you in the night;
  in the morning my spirit longs for
    you.
When your judgments come upon the
    earth,
  the people of the world learn
    righteousness.
¹⁰Though grace is shown to the
    wicked,
  they do not learn righteousness;
even in a land of uprightness they go
    on doing evil
  and regard not the majesty of the
    LORD.
¹¹O LORD, your hand is lifted high,
  but they do not see it.
Let them see your zeal for your
    people and be put to shame;
  let the fire reserved for your
    enemies consume them.

¹²LORD, you establish peace for us;
  all that we have accomplished you
    have done for us.
¹³O LORD, our God, other lords besides
    you have ruled over us,
  but your name alone do we honor.
¹⁴They are now dead, they live no
    more;
  those departed spirits do not rise.
You punished them and brought
    them to ruin;
  you wiped out all memory of them.
¹⁵You have enlarged the nation,
    O LORD;
  you have enlarged the nation.
You have gained glory for yourself;
  you have extended all the borders
    of the land.

¹⁶LORD, they came to you in their
    distress;
  when you disciplined them,
  they could barely whisper a
    prayer.ᵃ
¹⁷As a woman with child and about to
    give birth
  writhes and cries out in her pain,
so were we in your presence,
    O LORD.
¹⁸We were with child, we writhed in
    pain,
  but we gave birth to wind.
We have not brought salvation to the
    earth;

we have not given birth to people
    of the world.

¹⁹But your dead will live;
  their bodies will rise.
You who dwell in the dust,
  wake up and shout for joy.
Your dew is like the dew of the
    morning;
  the earth will give birth to her
    dead.

²⁰Go, my people, enter your rooms
  and shut the doors behind you;
hide yourselves for a little while
  until his wrath has passed by.
²¹See, the LORD is coming out of his
    dwelling
  to punish the people of the earth
    for their sins.
The earth will disclose the blood
    shed upon her;
  she will conceal her slain no
    longer.

Deliverance of Israel

27 In that day,

the LORD will punish with his sword,
  his fierce, great and powerful
    sword,
Leviathan the gliding serpent,
  Leviathan the coiling serpent;
he will slay the monster of the sea.

²In that day—

"Sing about a fruitful vineyard:
³ I, the LORD, watch over it;
    I water it continually.
I guard it day and night
  so that no one may harm it.
⁴ I am not angry.
If only there were briers and thorns
    confronting me!
  I would march against them in
    battle;
  I would set them all on fire.
⁵Or else let them come to me for
    refuge;
  let them make peace with me,
  yes, let them make peace with
    me."

⁶In days to come Jacob will take root,
  Israel will bud and blossom

ᵃ 16 The meaning of the Hebrew for this clause is uncertain.

and fill all the world with fruit.
7 Has ⌊the LORD⌋ struck her
  as he struck down those who
    struck her?
Has she been killed
  as those were killed who killed
    her?
8 By warfare*a* and exile you contend
    with her—
  with his fierce blast he drives her
    out,
  as on a day the east wind blows.
9 By this, then, will Jacob's guilt be
    atoned for,
  and this will be the full fruitage of
    the removal of his sin:
When he makes all the altar stones
  to be like chalk stones crushed to
    pieces,
no Asherah poles*b* or incense altars
  will be left standing.
10 The fortified city stands desolate,
  an abandoned settlement, forsaken
    like the desert;
  there the calves graze,
    there they lie down;
  they strip its branches bare.
11 When its twigs are dry, they are
    broken off
  and women come and make fires
    with them.
For this is a people without
    understanding;
  so their Maker has no compassion
    on them,
  and their Creator shows them no
    favor.

12 In that day the LORD will thresh
from the flowing Euphrates*c* to the Wadi
of Egypt, and you, O Israelites, will be
gathered up one by one. 13 And in that
day a great trumpet will sound. Those
who were perishing in Assyria and those
who were exiled in Egypt will come and
worship the LORD on the holy mountain
in Jerusalem.

Woe to Ephraim

28 Woe to that wreath, the pride
  of Ephraim's drunkards,
to the fading flower, his glorious
    beauty,

set on the head of a fertile valley—
to that city, the pride of those laid
    low by wine!
2 See, the Lord has one who is
    powerful and strong.
Like a hailstorm and a destructive
    wind,
like a driving rain and a flooding
    downpour,
  he will throw it forcefully to the
    ground.
3 That wreath, the pride of Ephraim's
    drunkards,
  will be trampled underfoot.
4 That fading flower, his glorious
    beauty,
  set on the head of a fertile valley,
will be like a fig ripe before harvest—
  as soon as someone sees it and
    takes it in his hand,
  he swallows it.

5 In that day the LORD Almighty
  will be a glorious crown,
  a beautiful wreath
  for the remnant of his people.
6 He will be a spirit of justice
  to him who sits in judgment,
  a source of strength
  to those who turn back the battle
    at the gate.

7 And these also stagger from wine
  and reel from beer:
Priests and prophets stagger from
    beer
  and are befuddled with wine;
they reel from beer,
  they stagger when seeing visions,
  they stumble when rendering
    decisions.
8 All the tables are covered with vomit
  and there is not a spot without
    filth.

9 "Who is it he is trying to teach?
  To whom is he explaining his
    message?
To children weaned from their milk,
  to those just taken from the breast?
10 For it is:
Do and do, do and do,
  rule on rule, rule on rule*d*;
  a little here, a little there."

a 8 See Septuagint; the meaning of the Hebrew for this word is uncertain.   *b 9* That is, symbols of the
goddess Asherah   *c 12* Hebrew *River*   *d 10* Hebrew / *sav lasav sav lasav* / *kav lakav kav lakav*
(possibly meaningless sounds; perhaps a mimicking of the prophet's words); also in verse 13

11 Very well then, with foreign lips and
strange tongues
God will speak to this people,
12 to whom he said,
"This is the resting place, let the
weary rest";
and, "This is the place of repose"—
but they would not listen.
13 So then, the word of the LORD to
them will become:
Do and do, do and do,
rule on rule, rule on rule;
a little here, a little there—
so that they will go and fall
backward,
be injured and snared and captured.

14 Therefore hear the word of the LORD,
you scoffers
who rule this people in Jerusalem.
15 You boast, "We have entered into a
covenant with death,
with the grave*a* we have made an
agreement.
When an overwhelming scourge
sweeps by,
it cannot touch us,
for we have made a lie our refuge
and falsehood*b* our hiding place."

16 So this is what the Sovereign LORD
says:

"See, I lay a stone in Zion,
a tested stone,
a precious cornerstone for a sure
foundation;
the one who trusts will never be
dismayed.
17 I will make justice the measuring
line
and righteousness the plumb line;
hail will sweep away your refuge, the
lie,
and water will overflow your
hiding place.
18 Your covenant with death will be
annulled;
your agreement with the grave will
not stand.
When the overwhelming scourge
sweeps by,
you will be beaten down by it.
19 As often as it comes it will carry you
away;

morning after morning, by day and
by night,
it will sweep through."

The understanding of this message
will bring sheer terror.
20 The bed is too short to stretch out
on,
the blanket too narrow to wrap
around you.
21 The LORD will rise up as he did at
Mount Perazim,
he will rouse himself as in the
Valley of Gibeon—
to do his work, his strange work,
and perform his task, his alien
task.
22 Now stop your mocking,
or your chains will become
heavier;
the Lord, the LORD Almighty, has
told me
of the destruction decreed against
the whole land.

23 Listen and hear my voice;
pay attention and hear what I say.
24 When a farmer plows for planting,
does he plow continually?
Does he keep on breaking up and
harrowing the soil?
25 When he has leveled the surface,
does he not sow caraway and
scatter cummin?
Does he not plant wheat in its place,*c*
barley in its plot,*c*
and spelt in its field?
26 His God instructs him
and teaches him the right way.

27 Caraway is not threshed with a
sledge,
nor is a cartwheel rolled over
cummin;
caraway is beaten out with a rod,
and cummin with a stick.
28 Grain must be ground to make bread;
so one does not go on threshing it
forever.
Though he drives the wheels of his
threshing cart over it,
his horses do not grind it.
29 All this also comes from the LORD
Almighty,
wonderful in counsel and
magnificent in wisdom.

---

a 15 Hebrew *Sheol;* also in verse 18   *b 15* Or *false gods*   *c 25* The meaning of the Hebrew for this
word is uncertain.

Woe to David's City

29 Woe to you, Ariel, Ariel,
the city where David settled!
Add year to year
and let your cycle of festivals go
on.
² Yet I will besiege Ariel;
she will mourn and lament,
she will be to me like an altar
hearth.ᵃ
³ I will encamp against you all around;
I will encircle you with towers
and set up my siege works against
you.
⁴ Brought low, you will speak from the
ground;
your speech will mumble out of
the dust.
Your voice will come ghostlike from
the earth;
out of the dust your speech will
whisper.

⁵ But your many enemies will become
like fine dust,
the ruthless hordes like blown
chaff.
Suddenly, in an instant,
⁶　the LORD Almighty will come
with thunder and earthquake and
great noise,
with windstorm and tempest and
flames of a devouring fire.
⁷ Then the hordes of all the nations
that fight against Ariel,
that attack her and her fortress and
besiege her,
will be as it is with a dream,
with a vision in the night—
⁸ as when a hungry man dreams that
he is eating,
but he awakens, and his hunger
remains;
as when a thirsty man dreams that he
is drinking,
but he awakens faint, with his
thirst unquenched.
So will it be with the hordes of all the
nations
that fight against Mount Zion.

⁹ Be stunned and amazed,
blind yourselves and be sightless;
be drunk, but not from wine,
stagger, but not from beer.

¹⁰ The LORD has brought over you a
deep sleep:
He has sealed your eyes (the
prophets);
he has covered your heads (the
seers).

¹¹ For you this whole vision is nothing
but words sealed in a scroll. And if you
give the scroll to someone who can read,
and say to him, "Read this, please," he
will answer, "I can't; it is sealed." ¹² Or if
you give the scroll to someone who cannot read, and say, "Read this, please," he
will answer, "I don't know how to
read."

¹³ The Lord says:

"These people come near to me with
their mouth
and honor me with their lips,
but their hearts are far from me.
Their worship of me
is made up only of rules taught by
men.ᵇ
¹⁴ Therefore once more I will astound
these people
with wonder upon wonder;
the wisdom of the wise will perish,
the intelligence of the intelligent
will vanish."
¹⁵ Woe to those who go to great depths
to hide their plans from the LORD,
who do their work in darkness and
think,
"Who sees us? Who will know?"
¹⁶ You turn things upside down,
as if the potter were thought to be
like the clay!
Shall what is formed say to him who
formed it,
"He did not make me"?
Can the pot say of the potter,
"He knows nothing"?

¹⁷ In a very short time, will not
Lebanon be turned into a
fertile field
and the fertile field seem like a
forest?
¹⁸ In that day the deaf will hear the
words of the scroll,
and out of gloom and darkness
the eyes of the blind will see.

ᵃ 2 The Hebrew for *altar hearth* sounds like the Hebrew for *Ariel.*　ᵇ 13 Hebrew; Septuagint *They
worship me in vain; / their teachings are but rules taught by men*

19 Once more the humble will rejoice in
      the LORD;
   the needy will rejoice in the Holy
      One of Israel.
20 The ruthless will vanish,
   the mockers will disappear,
   and all who have an eye for evil
      will be cut down—
21 those who with a word make a man
      out to be guilty,
   who ensnare the defender in court
   and with false testimony deprive
      the innocent of justice.

22 Therefore this is what the LORD,
who redeemed Abraham, says to the
house of Jacob:

   "No longer will Jacob be ashamed;
      no longer will their faces grow
         pale.
23 When they see among them their
      children,
      the work of my hands,
   they will keep my name holy;
      they will acknowledge the holiness
         of the Holy One of Jacob,
      and will stand in awe of the God of
         Israel.
24 Those who are wayward in spirit will
      gain understanding;
      those who complain will accept
         instruction."

Woe to the Obstinate Nation

30 "Woe to the obstinate
      children,"
   declares the LORD,
   "to those who carry out plans that
      are not mine,
      forming an alliance, but not by my
         Spirit,
   heaping sin upon sin;
2 who go down to Egypt
      without consulting me;
   who look for help to Pharaoh's
      protection,
   to Egypt's shade for refuge.
3 But Pharaoh's protection will be to
      your shame,
   Egypt's shade will bring you
      disgrace.
4 Though they have officials in Zoan
   and their envoys have arrived in
      Hanes,
5 everyone will be put to shame

because of a people useless to
      them,
   who bring neither help nor
      advantage,
      but only shame and disgrace."

6 An oracle concerning the animals of
the Negev:

Through a land of hardship and
      distress,
   of lions and lionesses,
   of adders and darting snakes,
   the envoys carry their riches on
      donkeys' backs,
      their treasures on the humps of
         camels,
   to that unprofitable nation,
7   to Egypt, whose help is utterly
         useless.
   Therefore I call her
      Rahab the Do-Nothing.

8 Go now, write it on a tablet for them,
      inscribe it on a scroll,
   that for the days to come
      it may be an everlasting witness.
9 These are rebellious people, deceitful
      children,
   children unwilling to listen to the
      LORD's instruction.
10 They say to the seers,
      "See no more visions!"
   and to the prophets,
      "Give us no more visions of what
         is right!
   Tell us pleasant things,
      prophesy illusions.
11 Leave this way,
      get off this path,
   and stop confronting us
      with the Holy One of Israel!"

12 Therefore, this is what the Holy
One of Israel says:

   "Because you have rejected this
      message,
      relied on oppression
      and depended on deceit,
13 this sin will become for you
      like a high wall, cracked and
         bulging,
      that collapses suddenly, in an
         instant.
14 It will break in pieces like pottery,
      shattered so mercilessly

that among its pieces not a fragment
will be found
  for taking coals from a hearth
  or scooping water out of a cistern."

[15]This is what the Sovereign LORD,
the Holy One of Israel, says:

"In repentance and rest is your
  salvation,
  in quietness and trust is your
  strength,
but you would have none of it.
[16]You said, 'No, we will flee on horses.'
  Therefore you will flee!

You said, 'We will ride off on swift
  horses.'
  Therefore your pursuers will be
  swift!
[17]A thousand will flee
  at the threat of one;
at the threat of five
  you will all flee away,
till you are left
  like a flagstaff on a mountaintop,
  like a banner on a hill."

[18]Yet the LORD longs to be gracious to
  you;
  he rises to show you compassion.

THURSDAY

POURING OUT YOUR COMPLAINT
Martin Luther

VERSE: Isaiah 30:19   **PASSAGE:** Isaiah 30:15–19

ou must learn to pray and not sit alone or lie about, hanging your head and shaking it, brooding over your thoughts, worrying about how you can escape and looking at nothing but yourself and your sad and painful condition. Get up, you lazy villain, then fall upon your knees, lift your eyes and hands towards heaven, take a Psalm or the Lord's Prayer, and pour out your trouble with tears before God, lamenting and calling upon him . . .

The lifting up of hands, prayer, and the mentioning of trouble are sacrifices most pleasing to God. He desires it, and it is his will, that you should pour out your trouble before him, and not let it lie upon yourself, dragging it about with you and being chafed and tortured by it, so that in the end you make two, or even ten or a hundred calamities out of one. He wills that you should be too weak to bear and overcome such trouble, in order that you may learn to find strength in him, and that he may be praised through his strength in you. Behold, this is how Christians are made!

ADDITIONAL SCRIPTURE READING:
Isaiah 65:24; Jeremiah 29:11–13; 1 John 5:14–15

Go to page 807 for your next devotional reading.

1500   1700

For the LORD is a God of justice.
Blessed are all who wait for him!

19O people of Zion, who live in Jerusalem, you will weep no more. How gracious he will be when you cry for help!
As soon as he hears, he will answer you.
20Although the Lord gives you the bread
of adversity and the water of affliction,
your teachers will be hidden no more;
with your own eyes you will see them.
21Whether you turn to the right or to the
left, your ears will hear a voice behind
you, saying, "This is the way; walk in
it." 22Then you will defile your idols
overlaid with silver and your images
covered with gold; you will throw them
away like a menstrual cloth and say to
them, "Away with you!"

23He will also send you rain for the
seed you sow in the ground, and the food
that comes from the land will be rich and
plentiful. In that day your cattle will
graze in broad meadows. 24The oxen and
donkeys that work the soil will eat fodder
and mash, spread out with fork and shov-
el. 25In the day of great slaughter, when
the towers fall, streams of water will flow
on every high mountain and every lofty
hill. 26The moon will shine like the sun,
and the sunlight will be seven times
brighter, like the light of seven full days,
when the LORD binds up the bruises of his
people and heals the wounds he inflicted.

27 See, the Name of the LORD comes
        from afar,
    with burning anger and dense
        clouds of smoke;
  his lips are full of wrath,
    and his tongue is a consuming fire.
28 His breath is like a rushing torrent,
    rising up to the neck.
  He shakes the nations in the sieve of
        destruction;
    he places in the jaws of the peoples
    a bit that leads them astray.
29 And you will sing
      as on the night you celebrate a holy
        festival;
    your hearts will rejoice
      as when people go up with flutes
    to the mountain of the LORD,
    to the Rock of Israel.
30 The LORD will cause men to hear his
        majestic voice

and will make them see his arm
    coming down
  with raging anger and consuming
      fire,
    with cloudburst, thunderstorm and
        hail.
31 The voice of the LORD will shatter
      Assyria;
    with his scepter he will strike
        them down.
32 Every stroke the LORD lays on them
    with his punishing rod
  will be to the music of tambourines
      and harps,
    as he fights them in battle with the
        blows of his arm.
33 Topheth has long been prepared;
    it has been made ready for the
        king.
  Its fire pit has been made deep and
      wide,
    with an abundance of fire and wood;
  the breath of the LORD,
    like a stream of burning sulfur,
    sets it ablaze.

Woe to Those Who Rely on Egypt

31 Woe to those who go down to
      Egypt for help,
  who rely on horses,
who trust in the multitude of their
      chariots
  and in the great strength of their
      horsemen,
but do not look to the Holy One of
      Israel,
  or seek help from the LORD.
2 Yet he too is wise and can bring
      disaster;
  he does not take back his words.
He will rise up against the house of
      the wicked,
  against those who help evildoers.
3 But the Egyptians are men and not
      God;
  their horses are flesh and not spirit.
When the LORD stretches out his
      hand,
  he who helps will stumble,
  he who is helped will fall;
    both will perish together.

4This is what the LORD says to me:

"As a lion growls,
    a great lion over his prey—

and though a whole band of
shepherds
is called together against him,
he is not frightened by their shouts
or disturbed by their clamor—
so the LORD Almighty will come
down
to do battle on Mount Zion and on
its heights.
5 Like birds hovering overhead,
the LORD Almighty will shield
Jerusalem;
he will shield it and deliver it,
he will 'pass over' it and will
rescue it."

6 Return to him you have so greatly
revolted against, O Israelites. 7 For in
that day every one of you will reject the
idols of silver and gold your sinful hands
have made.

8 "Assyria will fall by a sword that is
not of man;
a sword, not of mortals, will
devour them.
They will flee before the sword
and their young men will be put to
forced labor.
9 Their stronghold will fall because of
terror;
at sight of the battle standard their
commanders will panic,"
declares the LORD,
whose fire is in Zion,
whose furnace is in Jerusalem.

The Kingdom of Righteousness

32 See, a king will reign in
righteousness
and rulers will rule with justice.
2 Each man will be like a shelter from
the wind
and a refuge from the storm,
like streams of water in the desert
and the shadow of a great rock in a
thirsty land.

3 Then the eyes of those who see will
no longer be closed,
and the ears of those who hear will
listen.
4 The mind of the rash will know and
understand,
and the stammering tongue will be
fluent and clear.

5 No longer will the fool be called
noble
nor the scoundrel be highly
respected.
6 For the fool speaks folly,
his mind is busy with evil:
He practices ungodliness
and spreads error concerning the
LORD;
the hungry he leaves empty
and from the thirsty he withholds
water.
7 The scoundrel's methods are wicked,
he makes up evil schemes
to destroy the poor with lies,
even when the plea of the needy is
just.
8 But the noble man makes noble
plans,
and by noble deeds he stands.

The Women of Jerusalem

9 You women who are so complacent,
rise up and listen to me;
you daughters who feel secure,
hear what I have to say!
10 In little more than a year
you who feel secure will tremble;
the grape harvest will fail,
and the harvest of fruit will not
come.
11 Tremble, you complacent women;
shudder, you daughters who feel
secure!
Strip off your clothes,
put sackcloth around your waists.
12 Beat your breasts for the pleasant
fields,
for the fruitful vines
13 and for the land of my people,
a land overgrown with thorns and
briers—
yes, mourn for all houses of
merriment
and for this city of revelry.
14 The fortress will be abandoned,
the noisy city deserted;
citadel and watchtower will become
a wasteland forever,
the delight of donkeys, a pasture
for flocks,
15 till the Spirit is poured upon us from
on high,
and the desert becomes a fertile
field,

I Have Loved the Doctrines of the Gospel
Jonathan Edwards

VERSE: Isaiah 32:2   **PASSAGE:** Isaiah 32:1–8

 n January 12, 1723, I made a solemn dedication of myself to God, and wrote it down; giving up myself, and all that I had to God; to be for the future, in no respect, my own; to act as one that had no right to himself, in any respect. And solemnly vowed, to take God for my whole portion and felicity; looking on nothing else, as any part of my happiness, nor acting as if it were; and his law for the constant rule of my obedience: engaging to fight, with all my might, against the world, the flesh, and the devil, to the end of my life. But I have reason to be infinitely humbled, when I consider, how much I have failed, of answering my obligation . . .

I have loved the doctrines of the gospel; they have been to my soul like green pastures. The gospel has seemed to me the richest treasure; the treasure that I have most desired, and longed that it might dwell richly in me. The way of salvation by Christ, has appeared, in a general way, glorious and excellent, most pleasant and most beautiful. It has often seemed to me, that it would, in a great measure, spoil heaven, to receive it in any other way. That text has often been affecting and delightful to me, Isaiah 32:2 (KJV), *A man shall be as an hiding place from the wind, and a covert from the tempest . . .*

Though it seems to me, that in some respects, I was a far better Christian, for two or three years after my first conversion, than I am now; and lived in a more constant delight and pleasure; yet of late years, I have had a more full and constant sense of the absolute sovereignty of God, and a delight in that sovereignty; and have had more of a sense of the glory of Christ, as a mediator revealed in the gospel. On one Saturday night, in particular, I had such a discovery of the excellency of the gospel above all other doctrines, that I could not but say to myself, "This is my chosen light, my chosen doctrine," and of Christ, "This is my chosen prophet." It appeared sweet, beyond all expression, to follow Christ, and to be taught, and enlightened, and instructed by him; to learn of him, and live to him.

ADDITIONAL SCRIPTURE READING:
Psalm 32:7; Isaiah 25:4

Go to page 811 for your next devotional reading.

1700   1900

and the fertile field seems like a
forest.

16 Justice will dwell in the desert
and righteousness live in the fertile
field.
17 The fruit of righteousness will be
peace;
the effect of righteousness will be
quietness and confidence
forever.
18 My people will live in peaceful
dwelling places,
in secure homes,
in undisturbed places of rest.
19 Though hail flattens the forest
and the city is leveled completely,
20 how blessed you will be,
sowing your seed by every stream,
and letting your cattle and donkeys
range free.

Distress and Help

33 Woe to you, O destroyer,
you who have not been
destroyed!
Woe to you, O traitor,
you who have not been betrayed!
When you stop destroying,
you will be destroyed;
when you stop betraying,
you will be betrayed.

2 O LORD, be gracious to us;
we long for you.
Be our strength every morning,
our salvation in time of distress.
3 At the thunder of your voice, the
peoples flee;
when you rise up, the nations
scatter.
4 Your plunder, O nations, is harvested
as by young locusts;
like a swarm of locusts men
pounce on it.

5 The LORD is exalted, for he dwells on
high;
he will fill Zion with justice and
righteousness.
6 He will be the sure foundation for
your times,
a rich store of salvation and
wisdom and knowledge;
the fear of the LORD is the key to
this treasure.*a*

7 Look, their brave men cry aloud in
the streets;
the envoys of peace weep bitterly.
8 The highways are deserted,
no travelers are on the roads.
The treaty is broken,
its witnesses*b* are despised,
no one is respected.
9 The land mourns*c* and wastes away,
Lebanon is ashamed and withers;
Sharon is like the Arabah,
and Bashan and Carmel drop their
leaves.

10 "Now will I arise," says the LORD.
"Now will I be exalted;
now will I be lifted up.
11 You conceive chaff,
you give birth to straw;
your breath is a fire that consumes
you.
12 The peoples will be burned as if to
lime;
like cut thornbushes they will be
set ablaze."

13 You who are far away, hear what I
have done;
you who are near, acknowledge my
power!
14 The sinners in Zion are terrified;
trembling grips the godless:
"Who of us can dwell with the
consuming fire?
Who of us can dwell with
everlasting burning?"
15 He who walks righteously
and speaks what is right,
who rejects gain from extortion
and keeps his hand from accepting
bribes,
who stops his ears against plots of
murder
and shuts his eyes against
contemplating evil—
16 this is the man who will dwell on the
heights,
whose refuge will be the mountain
fortress.
His bread will be supplied,
and water will not fail him.

17 Your eyes will see the king in his
beauty
and view a land that stretches afar.

a 6 Or is a treasure from him   b 8 Dead Sea Scrolls; Masoretic Text / the cities   c 9 Or dries up

18 In your thoughts you will ponder the
    former terror:
  "Where is that chief officer?
  Where is the one who took the
    revenue?
  Where is the officer in charge of
    the towers?"
19 You will see those arrogant people no
    more,
  those people of an obscure speech,
  with their strange,
    incomprehensible tongue.

20 Look upon Zion, the city of our
    festivals;
  your eyes will see Jerusalem,
  a peaceful abode, a tent that will
    not be moved;
  its stakes will never be pulled up,
  nor any of its ropes broken.
21 There the LORD will be our Mighty
    One.
  It will be like a place of broad
    rivers and streams.
  No galley with oars will ride them,
  no mighty ship will sail them.
22 For the LORD is our judge,
  the LORD is our lawgiver,
  the LORD is our king;
  it is he who will save us.

23 Your rigging hangs loose:
  The mast is not held secure,
  the sail is not spread.
  Then an abundance of spoils will be
    divided
  and even the lame will carry off
    plunder.
24 No one living in Zion will say, "I am
    ill";
  and the sins of those who dwell
    there will be forgiven.

Judgment Against the Nations

34 Come near, you nations, and
listen;
  pay attention, you peoples!
  Let the earth hear, and all that is in
    it,
  the world, and all that comes out
    of it!
2 The LORD is angry with all nations;
  his wrath is upon all their armies.
  He will totally destroy[a] them,
  he will give them over to slaughter.

3 Their slain will be thrown out,
  their dead bodies will send up a
    stench;
  the mountains will be soaked with
    their blood.
4 All the stars of the heavens will be
    dissolved
  and the sky rolled up like a scroll;
  all the starry host will fall
  like withered leaves from the vine,
  like shriveled figs from the fig tree.

5 My sword has drunk its fill in the
    heavens;
  see, it descends in judgment on
    Edom,
  the people I have totally destroyed.
6 The sword of the LORD is bathed in
    blood,
  it is covered with fat—
  the blood of lambs and goats,
  fat from the kidneys of rams.
  For the LORD has a sacrifice in Bozrah
  and a great slaughter in Edom.
7 And the wild oxen will fall with
    them,
  the bull calves and the great bulls.
  Their land will be drenched with
    blood,
  and the dust will be soaked with
    fat.

8 For the LORD has a day of vengeance,
  a year of retribution, to uphold
    Zion's cause.
9 Edom's streams will be turned into
    pitch,
  her dust into burning sulfur;
  her land will become blazing pitch!
10 It will not be quenched night and
    day;
  its smoke will rise forever.
  From generation to generation it will
    lie desolate;
  no one will ever pass through it
    again.
11 The desert owl[b] and screech owl[b]
    will possess it;
  the great owl[b] and the raven will
    nest there.
  God will stretch out over Edom
  the measuring line of chaos
  and the plumb line of desolation.
12 Her nobles will have nothing there to
    be called a kingdom,

---

a 2 The Hebrew term refers to the irrevocable giving over of things or persons to the LORD, often by totally destroying them; also in verse 5.   *b 11* The precise identification of these birds is uncertain.

all her princes will vanish away.
13 Thorns will overrun her citadels,
     nettles and brambles her
         strongholds.
   She will become a haunt for jackals,
     a home for owls.
14 Desert creatures will meet with
         hyenas,
     and wild goats will bleat to each
         other;
   there the night creatures will also
         repose
     and find for themselves places of
         rest.
15 The owl will nest there and lay eggs,
     she will hatch them, and care for
         her young under the shadow of
         her wings;
   there also the falcons will gather,
     each with its mate.

16 Look in the scroll of the LORD and
read:

None of these will be missing,
     not one will lack her mate.
For it is his mouth that has given the
         order,
     and his Spirit will gather them
         together.
17 He allots their portions;
     his hand distributes them by
         measure.
They will possess it forever
     and dwell there from generation to
         generation.

Joy of the Redeemed

35 The desert and the parched
land will be glad;
   the wilderness will rejoice and
         blossom.
Like the crocus, 2 it will burst into
         bloom;
   it will rejoice greatly and shout for
         joy.
The glory of Lebanon will be given to
         it,
   the splendor of Carmel and Sharon;
they will see the glory of the LORD,
     the splendor of our God.

3 Strengthen the feeble hands,
     steady the knees that give way;
4 say to those with fearful hearts,

"Be strong, do not fear;
your God will come,
     he will come with vengeance;
with divine retribution
     he will come to save you."

5 Then will the eyes of the blind be
         opened
     and the ears of the deaf unstopped.
6 Then will the lame leap like a deer,
     and the mute tongue shout for joy.
Water will gush forth in the
         wilderness
     and streams in the desert.
7 The burning sand will become a pool,
     the thirsty ground bubbling
         springs.
In the haunts where jackals once lay,
     grass and reeds and papyrus will
         grow.

8 And a highway will be there;
     it will be called the Way of
         Holiness.
The unclean will not journey on it;
     it will be for those who walk in
         that Way;
       wicked fools will not go about on
         it.[a]
9 No lion will be there,
     nor will any ferocious beast get up
         on it;
     they will not be found there.
But only the redeemed will walk
         there,
10   and the ransomed of the LORD will
         return.
They will enter Zion with singing;
     everlasting joy will crown their
         heads.
Gladness and joy will overtake them,
     and sorrow and sighing will flee
         away.

Sennacherib Threatens Jerusalem

36 In the fourteenth year of King
Hezekiah's reign, Sennacherib
king of Assyria attacked all the fortified
cities of Judah and captured them. 2 Then the king of Assyria sent his field
commander with a large army from
Lachish to King Hezekiah at Jerusalem.
When the commander stopped at the
aqueduct of the Upper Pool, on the road
to the Washerman's Field, 3 Eliakim son
of Hilkiah the palace administrator,

---

[a] 8 Or / the simple will not stray from it

NATIVITY
John Donne

VERSE: Matthew 1:18   **PASSAGE:** Matthew 1:18–25

Immensity cloistered in thy dear womb,
Now leaves his well-beloved imprisonment,
There he hath made himself to his intent
Weak enough, now into our world to come;
But Oh, for thee, for him, hath th' inn no room?
Yet lay him in this stall, and from the Orient,
Stars, and wisemen will travel to prevent
Th' effect of Herod's jealous general doom.
Seest thou, my soul, with thy faith's eyes, how he
Which fills all place, yet none holds him, doth lie?
Was not his pity towards thee wondrous high,
That would have need to be pitied by thee?
Kiss him, and with him into Egypt go,
With his kind mother, who partakes thy woe.

ADDITIONAL SCRIPTURE READING:
Luke 1:27–80; Galatians 4:4

Go to page 816 for your next devotional reading.

1500   1700

Shebna the secretary, and Joah son of Asaph the recorder went out to him. ⁴The field commander said to them, "Tell Hezekiah,

" 'This is what the great king, the king of Assyria, says: On what are you basing this confidence of yours? ⁵You say you have strategy and military strength—but you speak only empty words. On whom are you depending, that you rebel against me? ⁶Look now, you are depending on Egypt, that splintered reed of a staff, which pierces a man's hand and wounds him if he leans on it! Such is Pharaoh king of Egypt to all who depend on him. ⁷And if you say to me, "We are depending on the LORD our God"—isn't he the one whose high places and altars Hezekiah removed, saying to Judah and Jerusalem, "You must worship before this altar"?

⁸" 'Come now, make a bargain with my master, the king of Assyria: I will give you two thousand horses—if you can put riders on them! ⁹How then can you repulse one officer of the least of my master's officials, even though you are depending on Egypt for chariots and horsemen? ¹⁰Furthermore, have I come to attack and destroy this land without the LORD? The LORD himself told me to march against this country and destroy it.' "

¹¹Then Eliakim, Shebna and Joah said to the field commander, "Please speak to your servants in Aramaic, since we understand it. Don't speak to us in Hebrew in the hearing of the people on the wall."

¹²But the commander replied, "Was it only to your master and you that my master sent me to say these things, and not to the men sitting on the wall—who, like you, will have to eat their own filth and drink their own urine?"

¹³Then the commander stood and called out in Hebrew, "Hear the words of the great king, the king of Assyria! ¹⁴This is what the king says: Do not let Hezekiah deceive you. He cannot deliver you! ¹⁵Do not let Hezekiah persuade you to trust in the LORD when he says,

'The LORD will surely deliver us; this city will not be given into the hand of the king of Assyria.'

¹⁶"Do not listen to Hezekiah. This is what the king of Assyria says: Make peace with me and come out to me. Then every one of you will eat from his own vine and fig tree and drink water from his own cistern, ¹⁷until I come and take you to a land like your own—a land of grain and new wine, a land of bread and vineyards.

¹⁸"Do not let Hezekiah mislead you when he says, 'The LORD will deliver us.' Has the god of any nation ever delivered his land from the hand of the king of Assyria? ¹⁹Where are the gods of Hamath and Arpad? Where are the gods of Sepharvaim? Have they rescued Samaria from my hand? ²⁰Who of all the gods of these countries has been able to save his land from me? How then can the LORD deliver Jerusalem from my hand?"

²¹But the people remained silent and said nothing in reply, because the king had commanded, "Do not answer him."

²²Then Eliakim son of Hilkiah the palace administrator, Shebna the secretary, and Joah son of Asaph the recorder went to Hezekiah, with their clothes torn, and told him what the field commander had said.

Jerusalem's Deliverance Foretold

37 When King Hezekiah heard this, he tore his clothes and put on sackcloth and went into the temple of the LORD. ²He sent Eliakim the palace administrator, Shebna the secretary, and the leading priests, all wearing sackcloth, to the prophet Isaiah son of Amoz. ³They told him, "This is what Hezekiah says: This day is a day of distress and rebuke and disgrace, as when children come to the point of birth and there is no strength to deliver them. ⁴It may be that the LORD your God will hear the words of the field commander, whom his master, the king of Assyria, has sent to ridicule the living God, and that he will rebuke him for the words the LORD your God has heard. Therefore pray for the remnant that still survives."

⁵When King Hezekiah's officials came to Isaiah, ⁶Isaiah said to them, "Tell your master, 'This is what the LORD

says: Do not be afraid of what you have heard—those words with which the underlings of the king of Assyria have blasphemed me. ⁷Listen! I am going to put a spirit in him so that when he hears a certain report, he will return to his own country, and there I will have him cut down with the sword.' "

⁸When the field commander heard that the king of Assyria had left Lachish, he withdrew and found the king fighting against Libnah.

⁹Now Sennacherib received a report that Tirhakah, the Cushite*ᵃ* king ₁of Egypt₁, was marching out to fight against him. When he heard it, he sent messengers to Hezekiah with this word: ¹⁰"Say to Hezekiah king of Judah: Do not let the god you depend on deceive you when he says, 'Jerusalem will not be handed over to the king of Assyria.' ¹¹Surely you have heard what the kings of Assyria have done to all the countries, destroying them completely. And will you be delivered? ¹²Did the gods of the nations that were destroyed by my forefathers deliver them—the gods of Gozan, Haran, Rezeph and the people of Eden who were in Tel Assar? ¹³Where is the king of Hamath, the king of Arpad, the king of the city of Sepharvaim, or of Hena or Ivvah?"

Hezekiah's Prayer

¹⁴Hezekiah received the letter from the messengers and read it. Then he went up to the temple of the LORD and spread it out before the LORD. ¹⁵And Hezekiah prayed to the LORD: ¹⁶"O LORD Almighty, God of Israel, enthroned between the cherubim, you alone are God over all the kingdoms of the earth. You have made heaven and earth. ¹⁷Give ear, O LORD, and hear; open your eyes, O LORD, and see; listen to all the words Sennacherib has sent to insult the living God.

¹⁸"It is true, O LORD, that the Assyrian kings have laid waste all these peoples and their lands. ¹⁹They have thrown their gods into the fire and destroyed them, for they were not gods but only wood and stone, fashioned by

human hands. ²⁰Now, O LORD our God, deliver us from his hand, so that all kingdoms on earth may know that you alone, O LORD, are God.*ᵇ*"

Sennacherib's Fall

²¹Then Isaiah son of Amoz sent a message to Hezekiah: "This is what the LORD, the God of Israel, says: Because you have prayed to me concerning Sennacherib king of Assyria, ²²this is the word the LORD has spoken against him:

"The Virgin Daughter of Zion
    despises and mocks you.
The Daughter of Jerusalem
    tosses her head as you flee.
²³ Who is it you have insulted and
        blasphemed?
    Against whom have you raised
        your voice
and lifted your eyes in pride?
    Against the Holy One of Israel!
²⁴ By your messengers
    you have heaped insults on the
        Lord.
And you have said,
    'With my many chariots
I have ascended the heights of the
        mountains,
    the utmost heights of Lebanon.
I have cut down its tallest cedars,
    the choicest of its pines.
I have reached its remotest heights,
    the finest of its forests.
²⁵ I have dug wells in foreign lands*ᶜ*
    and drunk the water there.
With the soles of my feet
    I have dried up all the streams of
        Egypt.'

²⁶ "Have you not heard?
    Long ago I ordained it.
In days of old I planned it;
    now I have brought it to pass,
that you have turned fortified cities
    into piles of stone.
²⁷ Their people, drained of power,
    are dismayed and put to shame.
They are like plants in the field,
    like tender green shoots,
like grass sprouting on the roof,
    scorched*ᵈ* before it grows up.

ᵃ 9 That is, from the upper Nile region   *ᵇ 20* Dead Sea Scrolls (see also 2 Kings 19:19); Masoretic Text *alone are the LORD*   *ᶜ 25* Dead Sea Scrolls (see also 2 Kings 19:24); Masoretic Text does not have *in foreign lands.*   *ᵈ 27* Some manuscripts of the Masoretic Text, Dead Sea Scrolls and some Septuagint manuscripts (see also 2 Kings 19:26); most manuscripts of the Masoretic Text *roof / and terraced fields*

28 "But I know where you stay
and when you come and go
and how you rage against me.
29 Because you rage against me
and because your insolence has
reached my ears,
I will put my hook in your nose
and my bit in your mouth,
and I will make you return
by the way you came.

30 "This will be the sign for you,
O Hezekiah:

"This year you will eat what grows
by itself,
and the second year what springs
from that.
But in the third year sow and reap,
plant vineyards and eat their fruit.
31 Once more a remnant of the house of
Judah
will take root below and bear fruit
above.
32 For out of Jerusalem will come a
remnant,
and out of Mount Zion a band of
survivors.
The zeal of the LORD Almighty
will accomplish this.

33 "Therefore this is what the LORD
says concerning the king of Assyria:

"He will not enter this city
or shoot an arrow here.
He will not come before it with
shield
or build a siege ramp against it.
34 By the way that he came he will
return;
he will not enter this city,"
declares the LORD.
35 "I will defend this city and save it,
for my sake and for the sake of
David my servant!"

36 Then the angel of the LORD went
out and put to death a hundred and
eighty-five thousand men in the Assyrian camp. When the people got up the
next morning—there were all the dead
bodies! **37** So Sennacherib king of Assyria

broke camp and withdrew. He returned
to Nineveh and stayed there.
38 One day, while he was worshiping in
the temple of his god Nisroch, his sons
Adrammelech and Sharezer cut him
down with the sword, and they escaped
to the land of Ararat. And Esarhaddon
his son succeeded him as king.

Hezekiah's Illness

38 In those days Hezekiah became ill and was at the point
of death. The prophet Isaiah son of
Amoz went to him and said, "This is
what the LORD says: Put your house in
order, because you are going to die; you
will not recover."

2 Hezekiah turned his face to the wall
and prayed to the LORD, **3** "Remember,
O LORD, how I have walked before you
faithfully and with wholehearted devotion and have done what is good in your
eyes." And Hezekiah wept bitterly.

4 Then the word of the LORD came to
Isaiah: **5** "Go and tell Hezekiah, 'This is
what the LORD, the God of your father
David, says: I have heard your prayer
and seen your tears; I will add fifteen
years to your life. **6** And I will deliver you
and this city from the hand of the king
of Assyria. I will defend this city.

7 " 'This is the LORD's sign to you that
the LORD will do what he has promised:
8 I will make the shadow cast by the sun
go back the ten steps it has gone down
on the stairway of Ahaz.' " So the sunlight went back the ten steps it had gone
down.

9 A writing of Hezekiah king of Judah
after his illness and recovery:

10 I said, "In the prime of my life
must I go through the gates of
death[a]
and be robbed of the rest of my
years?"
11 I said, "I will not again see the LORD,
the LORD, in the land of the living;
no longer will I look on mankind,
or be with those who now dwell in
this world.[b]
12 Like a shepherd's tent my house
has been pulled down and taken
from me.

---

a 10 Hebrew *Sheol*   *b 11* A few Hebrew manuscripts; most Hebrew manuscripts *in the place of
cessation*

Like a weaver I have rolled up my
　　life,
　　and he has cut me off from the
　　　　loom;
　　day and night you made an end of
　　　　me.
13 I waited patiently till dawn,
　　but like a lion he broke all my
　　　　bones;
　　day and night you made an end of
　　　　me.
14 I cried like a swift or thrush,
　　I moaned like a mourning dove.
　My eyes grew weak as I looked to the
　　heavens.
　　I am troubled; O Lord, come to my
　　　　aid!"
15 But what can I say?
　　He has spoken to me, and he
　　　　himself has done this.
　I will walk humbly all my years
　　because of this anguish of my soul.
16 Lord, by such things men live;
　　and my spirit finds life in them too.
　You restored me to health
　　and let me live.
17 Surely it was for my benefit
　　that I suffered such anguish.
　In your love you kept me
　　from the pit of destruction;
　you have put all my sins
　　behind your back.
18 For the grave[a] cannot praise you,
　　death cannot sing your praise;
　those who go down to the pit
　　cannot hope for your faithfulness.
19 The living, the living—they praise
　　you,
　　as I am doing today;
　fathers tell their children
　　about your faithfulness.

20 The LORD will save me,
　　and we will sing with stringed
　　　　instruments
　all the days of our lives
　　in the temple of the LORD.

21 Isaiah had said, "Prepare a poultice
of figs and apply it to the boil, and he
will recover." 22 Hezekiah had asked, "What will be
the sign that I will go up to the temple of
the LORD?"

a 18 Hebrew *Sheol*

Envoys From Babylon

39 At that time Merodach-Baladan son of Baladan king of Babylon sent Hezekiah letters and a gift, because he had heard of his illness and recovery. 2 Hezekiah received the envoys gladly and showed them what was in his storehouses—the silver, the gold, the spices, the fine oil, his entire armory and everything found among his treasures. There was nothing in his palace or in all his kingdom that Hezekiah did not show them.

3 Then Isaiah the prophet went to King Hezekiah and asked, "What did those men say, and where did they come from?"

"From a distant land," Hezekiah replied. "They came to me from Babylon."

4 The prophet asked, "What did they see in your palace?"

"They saw everything in my palace," Hezekiah said. "There is nothing among my treasures that I did not show them."

5 Then Isaiah said to Hezekiah, "Hear the word of the LORD Almighty: 6 The time will surely come when everything in your palace, and all that your fathers have stored up until this day, will be carried off to Babylon. Nothing will be left, says the LORD. 7 And some of your descendants, your own flesh and blood who will be born to you, will be taken away, and they will become eunuchs in the palace of the king of Babylon."

8 "The word of the LORD you have spoken is good," Hezekiah replied. For he thought, "There will be peace and security in my lifetime."

Comfort for God's People

40 Comfort, comfort my people,
　　says your God.
2 Speak tenderly to Jerusalem,
　　and proclaim to her
　that her hard service has been
　　completed,
　that her sin has been paid for,
　that she has received from the LORD's
　　hand
　double for all her sins.

3 A voice of one calling:
　"In the desert prepare

THE COMFORT OF THE SOVEREIGN PHYSICIAN
Brother Lawrence

VERSE: Isaiah 38:16   **PASSAGE:** Isaiah 38:12–17

I do not pray that you may be delivered from your pains, but I pray God earnestly that he would give you strength and patience to bear them as long as he pleases. Comfort yourself with him who holds you fastened to the cross. He will loose you when he thinks fit. Happy those who suffer with him. Accustom yourself to suffer in that manner, and seek from him the strength to endure as much, and as long, as he shall judge to be necessary for you. The men of the world do not comprehend these truths, nor is it to be wondered at, since they suffer like what they are, and not like Christians. They consider sickness as a pain to nature, and not as a favor from God; and seeing it only in that light, they find nothing in it but grief and distress. But those who consider sickness as coming from the hand of God, as the effect of his mercy, and the means which he employs for their salvation—such commonly find in it great sweetness and sensible consolation.

I wish you could convince yourself that God is often (in some sense) nearer to us, and more effectually present with us, in sickness than in health. Rely upon no other physician; for, according to my apprehension, he reserves your cure to himself. Put, then, all your trust in him, and you will soon find the effects of it in your recovery, which we often retard by putting greater confidence in physic than in God.

Whatever remedies you make use of, they will succeed only so far as he permits. When pains come from God, he only can cure them. He often sends diseases of the body to cure those of the soul. Comfort yourself with the sovereign Physician both of the soul and body.

Be satisfied with the condition in which God places you . . . Continue, then, always with God; it is the only support and comfort for your affliction. I shall beseech him to be with you. I present my service. I am,

Yours . . .

ADDITIONAL SCRIPTURE READING:
Psalm 71:20; Lamentations 3:25–26

Go to page 821 for your next devotional reading.

1500   1700

the way for the Lord*a*;
make straight in the wilderness
a highway for our God. *b*
4 Every valley shall be raised up,
every mountain and hill made low;
the rough ground shall become level,
the rugged places a plain.
5 And the glory of the Lord will be
revealed,
and all mankind together will see
it.
For the mouth of the Lord
has spoken."

6 A voice says, "Cry out."
And I said, "What shall I cry?"

"All men are like grass,
and all their glory is like the
flowers of the field.
7 The grass withers and the flowers
fall,
because the breath of the Lord
blows on them.
Surely the people are grass.
8 The grass withers and the flowers
fall,
but the word of our God stands
forever."

9 You who bring good tidings to Zion,
go up on a high mountain.
You who bring good tidings to
Jerusalem,*c*
lift up your voice with a shout,
lift it up, do not be afraid;
say to the towns of Judah,
"Here is your God!"
10 See, the Sovereign Lord comes with
power,
and his arm rules for him.
See, his reward is with him,
and his recompense accompanies
him.
11 He tends his flock like a shepherd:
He gathers the lambs in his arms
and carries them close to his heart;
he gently leads those that have
young.

12 Who has measured the waters in the
hollow of his hand,
or with the breadth of his hand
marked off the heavens?

Who has held the dust of the earth in
a basket,
or weighed the mountains on the
scales
and the hills in a balance?
13 Who has understood the mind*d* of the
Lord,
or instructed him as his counselor?
14 Whom did the Lord consult to
enlighten him,
and who taught him the right way?
Who was it that taught him
knowledge
or showed him the path of
understanding?

15 Surely the nations are like a drop in a
bucket;
they are regarded as dust on the
scales;
he weighs the islands as though
they were fine dust.
16 Lebanon is not sufficient for altar
fires,
nor its animals enough for burnt
offerings.
17 Before him all the nations are as
nothing;
they are regarded by him as
worthless
and less than nothing.

18 To whom, then, will you compare
God?
What image will you compare him
to?
19 As for an idol, a craftsman casts it,
and a goldsmith overlays it with
gold
and fashions silver chains for it.
20 A man too poor to present such an
offering
selects wood that will not rot.
He looks for a skilled craftsman
to set up an idol that will not
topple.

21 Do you not know?
Have you not heard?
Has it not been told you from the
beginning?
Have you not understood since the
earth was founded?
22 He sits enthroned above the circle of
the earth,

a 3 Or *A voice of one calling in the desert:* / *"Prepare the way for the Lord*   *b 3* Hebrew; Septuagint
make straight the paths of our God   *c 9* Or *O Zion, bringer of good tidings,* / *go up on a high
mountain.* / *O Jerusalem, bringer of good tidings*   *d 13* Or *Spirit;* or *spirit*

and its people are like
   grasshoppers.
He stretches out the heavens like a
      canopy,
   and spreads them out like a tent to
      live in.
²³ He brings princes to naught
   and reduces the rulers of this world
      to nothing.
²⁴ No sooner are they planted,
   no sooner are they sown,
   no sooner do they take root in the
      ground,
than he blows on them and they
      wither,
   and a whirlwind sweeps them
      away like chaff.

²⁵ "To whom will you compare me?
   Or who is my equal?" says the
      Holy One.
²⁶ Lift your eyes and look to the
      heavens:
   Who created all these?
He who brings out the starry host
      one by one,
   and calls them each by name.
Because of his great power and
      mighty strength,
   not one of them is missing.

²⁷ Why do you say, O Jacob,
   and complain, O Israel,
"My way is hidden from the LORD;
   my cause is disregarded by my
      God"?
²⁸ Do you not know?
   Have you not heard?
The LORD is the everlasting God,
   the Creator of the ends of the
      earth.
He will not grow tired or weary,
   and his understanding no one can
      fathom.
²⁹ He gives strength to the weary
   and increases the power of the
      weak.
³⁰ Even youths grow tired and weary,
   and young men stumble and fall;
³¹ but those who hope in the LORD
   will renew their strength.
They will soar on wings like eagles;
   they will run and not grow weary,
   they will walk and not be faint.

The Helper of Israel

41 "Be silent before me, you
      islands!
   Let the nations renew their
      strength!
Let them come forward and speak;
   let us meet together at the place of
      judgment.

² "Who has stirred up one from the
      east,
   calling him in righteousness to his
      service*a*?
He hands nations over to him
   and subdues kings before him.
He turns them to dust with his
      sword,
   to windblown chaff with his bow.
³ He pursues them and moves on
      unscathed,
   by a path his feet have not traveled
      before.
⁴ Who has done this and carried it
      through,
   calling forth the generations from
      the beginning?
I, the LORD—with the first of them
   and with the last—I am he."

⁵ The islands have seen it and fear;
   the ends of the earth tremble.
They approach and come forward;
⁶   each helps the other
   and says to his brother, "Be
      strong!"
⁷ The craftsman encourages the
      goldsmith,
   and he who smooths with the
      hammer
   spurs on him who strikes the anvil.
He says of the welding, "It is good."
   He nails down the idol so it will
      not topple.

⁸ "But you, O Israel, my servant,
   Jacob, whom I have chosen,
   you descendants of Abraham my
      friend,
⁹ I took you from the ends of the earth,
   from its farthest corners I called
      you.
I said, 'You are my servant';
   I have chosen you and have not
      rejected you.
¹⁰ So do not fear, for I am with you;

do not be dismayed, for I am your
    God.
I will strengthen you and help you;
    I will uphold you with my
        righteous right hand.

11 "All who rage against you
    will surely be ashamed and
        disgraced;
those who oppose you
    will be as nothing and perish.
12 Though you search for your enemies,
    you will not find them.
Those who wage war against you
    will be as nothing at all.
13 For I am the LORD, your God,
    who takes hold of your right hand
and says to you, Do not fear;
    I will help you.
14 Do not be afraid, O worm Jacob,
    O little Israel,
for I myself will help you," declares
    the LORD,
    your Redeemer, the Holy One of
        Israel.
15 "See, I will make you into a
        threshing sledge,
    new and sharp, with many teeth.
You will thresh the mountains and
        crush them,
    and reduce the hills to chaff.
16 You will winnow them, the wind
        will pick them up,
    and a gale will blow them away.
But you will rejoice in the LORD
    and glory in the Holy One of Israel.

17 "The poor and needy search for
        water,
    but there is none;
    their tongues are parched with
        thirst.
But I the LORD will answer them;
    I, the God of Israel, will not forsake
        them.
18 I will make rivers flow on barren
        heights,
    and springs within the valleys.
I will turn the desert into pools of
        water,
    and the parched ground into
        springs.
19 I will put in the desert
    the cedar and the acacia, the
        myrtle and the olive.
I will set pines in the wasteland,
    the fir and the cypress together,

20 so that people may see and know,
    may consider and understand,
that the hand of the LORD has done
    this,
    that the Holy One of Israel has
        created it.

21 "Present your case," says the LORD.
    "Set forth your arguments," says
        Jacob's King.
22 "Bring in ˻your idols˼ to tell us
    what is going to happen.
Tell us what the former things
        were,
    so that we may consider them
    and know their final outcome.
Or declare to us the things to come,
23   tell us what the future holds,
    so we may know that you are
        gods.
Do something, whether good or bad,
    so that we will be dismayed and
        filled with fear.
24 But you are less than nothing
    and your works are utterly
        worthless;
he who chooses you is detestable.

25 "I have stirred up one from the north,
        and he comes—
    one from the rising sun who calls
        on my name.
He treads on rulers as if they were
        mortar,
    as if he were a potter treading the
        clay.
26 Who told of this from the beginning,
    so we could know,
    or beforehand, so we could say, 'He
        was right'?
No one told of this,
    no one foretold it,
    no one heard any words from
        you.
27 I was the first to tell Zion, 'Look,
    here they are!'
    I gave to Jerusalem a messenger of
        good tidings.
28 I look but there is no one—
    no one among them to give
        counsel,
    no one to give answer when I ask
        them.
29 See, they are all false!
    Their deeds amount to nothing;
    their images are but wind and
        confusion.

The Servant of the LORD

42 "Here is my servant, whom I uphold,
my chosen one in whom I delight;
I will put my Spirit on him
and he will bring justice to the
nations.
2 He will not shout or cry out,
or raise his voice in the streets.
3 A bruised reed he will not break,
and a smoldering wick he will not
snuff out.
In faithfulness he will bring forth
justice;
4 he will not falter or be discouraged
till he establishes justice on earth.
In his law the islands will put their
hope."

5 This is what God the LORD says—
he who created the heavens and
stretched them out,
who spread out the earth and all
that comes out of it,
who gives breath to its people,
and life to those who walk on it:
6 "I, the LORD, have called you in
righteousness;
I will take hold of your hand.
I will keep you and will make you
to be a covenant for the people
and a light for the Gentiles,
7 to open eyes that are blind,
to free captives from prison
and to release from the dungeon
those who sit in darkness.

8 "I am the LORD; that is my name!
I will not give my glory to another
or my praise to idols.
9 See, the former things have taken
place,
and new things I declare;
before they spring into being
I announce them to you."

Song of Praise to the LORD

10 Sing to the LORD a new song,
his praise from the ends of the
earth,
you who go down to the sea, and all
that is in it,
you islands, and all who live in
them.
11 Let the desert and its towns raise
their voices;

let the settlements where Kedar
lives rejoice.
Let the people of Sela sing for joy;
let them shout from the
mountaintops.
12 Let them give glory to the LORD
and proclaim his praise in the
islands.
13 The LORD will march out like a
mighty man,
like a warrior he will stir up his
zeal;
with a shout he will raise the battle
cry
and will triumph over his enemies.

14 "For a long time I have kept silent,
I have been quiet and held myself
back.
But now, like a woman in childbirth,
I cry out, I gasp and pant.
15 I will lay waste the mountains and
hills
and dry up all their vegetation;
I will turn rivers into islands
and dry up the pools.
16 I will lead the blind by ways they
have not known,
along unfamiliar paths I will guide
them;
I will turn the darkness into light
before them
and make the rough places smooth.
These are the things I will do;
I will not forsake them.
17 But those who trust in idols,
who say to images, 'You are our
gods,'
will be turned back in utter shame.

Israel Blind and Deaf

18 "Hear, you deaf;
look, you blind, and see!
19 Who is blind but my servant,
and deaf like the messenger I send?
Who is blind like the one committed
to me,
blind like the servant of the LORD?
20 You have seen many things, but have
paid no attention;
your ears are open, but you hear
nothing."
21 It pleased the LORD
for the sake of his righteousness
to make his law great and glorious.
22 But this is a people plundered and
looted,

all of them trapped in pits
or hidden away in prisons.
They have become plunder,
with no one to rescue them;
they have been made loot,
with no one to say, "Send them
back."

23 Which of you will listen to this
or pay close attention in time to
come?
24 Who handed Jacob over to become
loot,
and Israel to the plunderers?
Was it not the LORD,
against whom we have sinned?
For they would not follow his ways;
they did not obey his law.

TUESDAY

GOD'S TERRIBLENESS AND GENTLENESS
Joseph Parker

VERSE: Isaiah 42:14   **PASSAGE:** Isaiah 42:14–16

The combination of great power and great restraint—indeed, the combination of opposite qualities and uses generally—is well-known in civilized life and in the laws of nature. The fire that warms the room when properly regulated, will, if abused, reduce the proudest palaces to ashes. The river, which softens and refreshes the landscape, if allowed to escape its banks, can devastate the most fruitful fields . . .

In our text in Isaiah we are confronted with the highest expression of the same truth: The mighty God is the everlasting Father; the terrible One is more gentle than the gentlest friend; he who rides in the chariot of thunder stoops to lead the blind by a way that they know not and to gather the lambs in his bosom.

In pointing out the terribleness of God, I do not appeal to fear . . . We do not say, "Be good, or God will crush you." That is not virtue, that is not liberty—it is vice put on its good behavior. It is iniquity with a sword suspended over its head . . .

The great truth to be learned is that all the terribleness of God is the good man's security. When the good man sees God wasting the mountains and the hills, and drying up the rivers, he does not say, "I must worship him or he will destroy me." He says, "The beneficent side of that power is all mine. Because of that power I am safe. The very lightning is my guardian, and in the whirlwind I hear a pledge of benediction."

ADDITIONAL SCRIPTURE READING:
Psalms 107:33–34; 114:3–8; Nahum 1:5–8

Go to page 830 for your next devotional reading.

1700   1900

²⁵ So he poured out on them his
          burning anger,
    the violence of war.
  It enveloped them in flames, yet they
          did not understand;
    it consumed them, but they did
          not take it to heart.

Israel's Only Savior

43 But now, this is what the
          LORD says—
    he who created you, O Jacob,
    he who formed you, O Israel:
  "Fear not, for I have redeemed you;
    I have summoned you by name;
          you are mine.
² When you pass through the waters,
    I will be with you;
  and when you pass through the
          rivers,
    they will not sweep over you.
  When you walk through the fire,
    you will not be burned;
    the flames will not set you ablaze.
³ For I am the LORD, your God,
    the Holy One of Israel, your Savior;
  I give Egypt for your ransom,
    Cush*ᵃ* and Seba in your stead.
⁴ Since you are precious and honored
          in my sight,
    and because I love you,
  I will give men in exchange for you,
    and people in exchange for your
          life.
⁵ Do not be afraid, for I am with you;
    I will bring your children from the
          east
    and gather you from the west.
⁶ I will say to the north, 'Give them
          up!'
    and to the south, 'Do not hold
          them back.'
  Bring my sons from afar
    and my daughters from the ends of
          the earth—
⁷ everyone who is called by my name,
    whom I created for my glory,
    whom I formed and made."

⁸ Lead out those who have eyes but are
          blind,
    who have ears but are deaf.
⁹ All the nations gather together
    and the peoples assemble.
  Which of them foretold this

and proclaimed to us the former
          things?
  Let them bring in their witnesses to
          prove they were right,
    so that others may hear and say, "It
          is true."
¹⁰ "You are my witnesses," declares the
          LORD,
    "and my servant whom I have
          chosen,
  so that you may know and believe
          me
    and understand that I am he.
  Before me no god was formed,
    nor will there be one after me.
¹¹ I, even I, am the LORD,
    and apart from me there is no
          savior.
¹² I have revealed and saved and
          proclaimed—
    I, and not some foreign god among
          you.
  You are my witnesses," declares the
          LORD, "that I am God.
¹³   Yes, and from ancient days I am he.
  No one can deliver out of my hand.
    When I act, who can reverse it?"

God's Mercy and Israel's Unfaithfulness

¹⁴ This is what the LORD says—
    your Redeemer, the Holy One of
          Israel:
  "For your sake I will send to Babylon
    and bring down as fugitives all the
          Babylonians,*ᵇ*
    in the ships in which they took
          pride.
¹⁵ I am the LORD, your Holy One,
    Israel's Creator, your King."

¹⁶ This is what the LORD says—
    he who made a way through the
          sea,
    a path through the mighty waters,
¹⁷ who drew out the chariots and
          horses,
    the army and reinforcements
          together,
  and they lay there, never to rise
          again,
    extinguished, snuffed out like a
          wick:
¹⁸ "Forget the former things;
    do not dwell on the past.

ᵃ 3 That is, the upper Nile region   *ᵇ 14* Or *Chaldeans*

¹⁹See, I am doing a new thing!
    Now it springs up; do you not
        perceive it?
I am making a way in the desert
    and streams in the wasteland.
²⁰The wild animals honor me,
    the jackals and the owls,
because I provide water in the desert
    and streams in the wasteland,
to give drink to my people, my
    chosen,
²¹ the people I formed for myself
    that they may proclaim my praise.

²²"Yet you have not called upon me,
    O Jacob,
you have not wearied yourselves
    for me, O Israel.
²³You have not brought me sheep for
    burnt offerings,
    nor honored me with your
        sacrifices.
I have not burdened you with grain
    offerings
    nor wearied you with demands for
        incense.
²⁴You have not bought any fragrant
    calamus for me,
    or lavished on me the fat of your
        sacrifices.
But you have burdened me with your
    sins
    and wearied me with your offenses.

²⁵"I, even I, am he who blots out
    your transgressions, for my own
        sake,
    and remembers your sins no more.
²⁶Review the past for me,
    let us argue the matter together;
    state the case for your innocence.
²⁷Your first father sinned;
    your spokesmen rebelled against
        me.
²⁸So I will disgrace the dignitaries of
    your temple,
    and I will consign Jacob to
        destruction*a*
    and Israel to scorn.

Israel the Chosen

44 "But now listen, O Jacob, my
    servant,
Israel, whom I have chosen.
²This is what the LORD says—

he who made you, who formed you
    in the womb,
    and who will help you:
Do not be afraid, O Jacob, my
    servant,
    Jeshurun, whom I have chosen.
³For I will pour water on the thirsty
    land,
    and streams on the dry ground;
I will pour out my Spirit on your
    offspring,
    and my blessing on your
        descendants.
⁴They will spring up like grass in a
    meadow,
    like poplar trees by flowing
        streams.
⁵One will say, 'I belong to the LORD';
    another will call himself by the
        name of Jacob;
still another will write on his hand,
    'The LORD's,'
    and will take the name Israel.

The LORD, Not Idols

⁶"This is what the LORD says—
    Israel's King and Redeemer, the
        LORD Almighty:
I am the first and I am the last;
    apart from me there is no God.
⁷Who then is like me? Let him
    proclaim it.
    Let him declare and lay out before
        me
what has happened since I
    established my ancient people,
    and what is yet to come—
    yes, let him foretell what will
        come.
⁸Do not tremble, do not be afraid.
    Did I not proclaim this and foretell
        it long ago?
You are my witnesses. Is there any
    God besides me?
    No, there is no other Rock; I know
        not one."

⁹All who make idols are nothing,
    and the things they treasure are
        worthless.
Those who would speak up for them
    are blind;
    they are ignorant, to their own
        shame.
¹⁰Who shapes a god and casts an idol,

which can profit him nothing?
11 He and his kind will be put to shame;
craftsmen are nothing but men.
Let them all come together and take
their stand;
they will be brought down to terror
and infamy.

12 The blacksmith takes a tool
and works with it in the coals;
he shapes an idol with hammers,
he forges it with the might of his
arm.
He gets hungry and loses his
strength;
he drinks no water and grows faint.
13 The carpenter measures with a line
and makes an outline with a
marker;
he roughs it out with chisels
and marks it with compasses.
He shapes it in the form of man,
of man in all his glory,
that it may dwell in a shrine.
14 He cut down cedars,
or perhaps took a cypress or oak.
He let it grow among the trees of the
forest,
or planted a pine, and the rain
made it grow.
15 It is man's fuel for burning;
some of it he takes and warms
himself,
he kindles a fire and bakes bread.
But he also fashions a god and
worships it;
he makes an idol and bows down
to it.
16 Half of the wood he burns in the fire;
over it he prepares his meal,
he roasts his meat and eats his fill.
He also warms himself and says,
"Ah! I am warm; I see the fire."
17 From the rest he makes a god, his
idol;
he bows down to it and worships.
He prays to it and says,
"Save me; you are my god."
18 They know nothing, they understand
nothing;
their eyes are plastered over so
they cannot see,
and their minds closed so they
cannot understand.
19 No one stops to think,
no one has the knowledge or
understanding to say,

"Half of it I used for fuel;
I even baked bread over its coals,
I roasted meat and I ate.
Shall I make a detestable thing from
what is left?
Shall I bow down to a block of
wood?"
20 He feeds on ashes, a deluded heart
misleads him;
he cannot save himself, or say,
"Is not this thing in my right hand
a lie?"

21 "Remember these things, O Jacob,
for you are my servant, O Israel.
I have made you, you are my servant;
O Israel, I will not forget you.
22 I have swept away your offenses like
a cloud,
your sins like the morning mist.
Return to me,
for I have redeemed you."

23 Sing for joy, O heavens, for the LORD
has done this;
shout aloud, O earth beneath.
Burst into song, you mountains,
you forests and all your trees,
for the LORD has redeemed Jacob,
he displays his glory in Israel.

Jerusalem to Be Inhabited

24 "This is what the LORD says—
your Redeemer, who formed you in
the womb:

I am the LORD,
who has made all things,
who alone stretched out the heavens,
who spread out the earth by myself,

25 who foils the signs of false prophets
and makes fools of diviners,
who overthrows the learning of the
wise
and turns it into nonsense,
26 who carries out the words of his
servants
and fulfills the predictions of his
messengers,

who says of Jerusalem, 'It shall be
inhabited,'
of the towns of Judah, 'They shall
be built,'
and of their ruins, 'I will restore
them,'
27 who says to the watery deep, 'Be dry,
and I will dry up your streams,'

²⁸ who says of Cyrus, 'He is my
shepherd
and will accomplish all that I
please;
he will say of Jerusalem, "Let it be
rebuilt,"
and of the temple, "Let its
foundations be laid." '

45 "This is what the LORD says
to his anointed,
to Cyrus, whose right hand I take
hold of
to subdue nations before him
and to strip kings of their armor,
to open doors before him
so that gates will not be shut:
² I will go before you
and will level the mountains[a];
I will break down gates of bronze
and cut through bars of iron.
³ I will give you the treasures of
darkness,
riches stored in secret places,
so that you may know that I am the
LORD,
the God of Israel, who summons
you by name.
⁴ For the sake of Jacob my servant,
of Israel my chosen,
I summon you by name
and bestow on you a title of honor,
though you do not acknowledge
me.
⁵ I am the LORD, and there is no other;
apart from me there is no God.
I will strengthen you,
though you have not
acknowledged me,
⁶ so that from the rising of the sun
to the place of its setting
men may know there is none besides
me.
I am the LORD, and there is no
other.
⁷ I form the light and create darkness,
I bring prosperity and create
disaster;
I, the LORD, do all these things.

⁸ "You heavens above, rain down
righteousness;
let the clouds shower it down.
Let the earth open wide,
let salvation spring up,

let righteousness grow with it;
I, the LORD, have created it.

⁹ "Woe to him who quarrels with his
Maker,
to him who is but a potsherd
among the potsherds on the
ground.
Does the clay say to the potter,
'What are you making?'
Does your work say,
'He has no hands'?
¹⁰ Woe to him who says to his father,
'What have you begotten?'
or to his mother,
'What have you brought to birth?'

¹¹ "This is what the LORD says—
the Holy One of Israel, and its
Maker:
Concerning things to come,
do you question me about my
children,
or give me orders about the work
of my hands?
¹² It is I who made the earth
and created mankind upon it.
My own hands stretched out the
heavens;
I marshaled their starry hosts.
¹³ I will raise up Cyrus[b] in my
righteousness:
I will make all his ways straight.
He will rebuild my city
and set my exiles free,
but not for a price or reward,
says the LORD Almighty."

¹⁴ This is what the LORD says:

"The products of Egypt and the
merchandise of Cush,[c]
and those tall Sabeans—
they will come over to you
and will be yours;
they will trudge behind you,
coming over to you in chains.
They will bow down before you
and plead with you, saying,
'Surely God is with you, and there is
no other;
there is no other god.' "

¹⁵ Truly you are a God who hides
himself,
O God and Savior of Israel.

^a 2 Dead Sea Scrolls and Septuagint; the meaning of the word in the Masoretic Text is uncertain.
^b 13 Hebrew *him*   ^c 14 That is, the upper Nile region

16 All the makers of idols will be put to
shame and disgraced;
they will go off into disgrace
together.
17 But Israel will be saved by the LORD
with an everlasting salvation;
you will never be put to shame or
disgraced,
to ages everlasting.

18 For this is what the LORD says—
he who created the heavens,
he is God;
he who fashioned and made the
earth,
he founded it;
he did not create it to be empty,
but formed it to be inhabited—
he says:
"I am the LORD,
and there is no other.
19 I have not spoken in secret,
from somewhere in a land of
darkness;
I have not said to Jacob's
descendants,
'Seek me in vain.'
I, the LORD, speak the truth;
I declare what is right.

20 "Gather together and come;
assemble, you fugitives from the
nations.
Ignorant are those who carry about
idols of wood,
who pray to gods that cannot save.
21 Declare what is to be, present it—
let them take counsel together.
Who foretold this long ago,
who declared it from the distant
past?
Was it not I, the LORD?
And there is no God apart from
me,
a righteous God and a Savior;
there is none but me.

22 "Turn to me and be saved,
all you ends of the earth;
for I am God, and there is no other.
23 By myself I have sworn,
my mouth has uttered in all
integrity
a word that will not be revoked:
Before me every knee will bow;
by me every tongue will swear.

24 They will say of me, 'In the LORD
alone
are righteousness and strength.' "
All who have raged against him
will come to him and be put to
shame.
25 But in the LORD all the descendants
of Israel
will be found righteous and will
exult.

Gods of Babylon

46 Bel bows down, Nebo stoops
low;
their idols are borne by beasts of
burden.[a]
The images that are carried about are
burdensome,
a burden for the weary.
2 They stoop and bow down together;
unable to rescue the burden,
they themselves go off into
captivity.

3 "Listen to me, O house of Jacob,
all you who remain of the house of
Israel,
you whom I have upheld since you
were conceived,
and have carried since your birth.
4 Even to your old age and gray hairs
I am he, I am he who will sustain
you.
I have made you and I will carry you;
I will sustain you and I will rescue
you.

5 "To whom will you compare me or
count me equal?
To whom will you liken me that
we may be compared?
6 Some pour out gold from their bags
and weigh out silver on the
scales;
they hire a goldsmith to make it into
a god,
and they bow down and worship it.
7 They lift it to their shoulders and
carry it;
they set it up in its place, and there
it stands.
From that spot it cannot move.
Though one cries out to it, it does
not answer;
it cannot save him from his
troubles.

a 1 Or are but beasts and cattle

8 "Remember this, fix it in mind,
  take it to heart, you rebels.
9 Remember the former things, those
    of long ago;
  I am God, and there is no other;
  I am God, and there is none like
    me.
10 I make known the end from the
    beginning,
  from ancient times, what is still to
    come.
  I say: My purpose will stand,
    and I will do all that I please.
11 From the east I summon a bird of
    prey;
  from a far-off land, a man to fulfill
    my purpose.
  What I have said, that will I bring
    about;
  what I have planned, that will I do.
12 Listen to me, you stubborn-hearted,
  you who are far from
    righteousness.
13 I am bringing my righteousness near,
    it is not far away;
  and my salvation will not be
    delayed.
  I will grant salvation to Zion,
    my splendor to Israel.

The Fall of Babylon

47 "Go down, sit in the dust,
    Virgin Daughter of Babylon;
  sit on the ground without a throne,
    Daughter of the Babylonians.*a*
  No more will you be called
    tender or delicate.
2 Take millstones and grind flour;
    take off your veil.
  Lift up your skirts, bare your legs,
    and wade through the streams.
3 Your nakedness will be exposed
    and your shame uncovered.
  I will take vengeance;
    I will spare no one."

4 Our Redeemer—the LORD Almighty
    is his name—
  is the Holy One of Israel.

5 "Sit in silence, go into darkness,
    Daughter of the Babylonians;
  no more will you be called
    queen of kingdoms.
6 I was angry with my people
    and desecrated my inheritance;

I gave them into your hand,
    and you showed them no mercy.
  Even on the aged
    you laid a very heavy yoke.
7 You said, 'I will continue forever—
    the eternal queen!'
  But you did not consider these things
    or reflect on what might happen.

8 "Now then, listen, you wanton
    creature,
  lounging in your security
  and saying to yourself,
    'I am, and there is none besides me.
  I will never be a widow
    or suffer the loss of children.'
9 Both of these will overtake you
    in a moment, on a single day:
  loss of children and widowhood.
  They will come upon you in full
    measure,
  in spite of your many sorceries
    and all your potent spells.
10 You have trusted in your wickedness
    and have said, 'No one sees me.'
  Your wisdom and knowledge mislead
    you
  when you say to yourself,
    'I am, and there is none besides
      me.'
11 Disaster will come upon you,
    and you will not know how to
      conjure it away.
  A calamity will fall upon you
    that you cannot ward off with a
      ransom;
  a catastrophe you cannot foresee
    will suddenly come upon you.

12 "Keep on, then, with your magic
    spells
  and with your many sorceries,
    which you have labored at since
      childhood.
  Perhaps you will succeed,
    perhaps you will cause terror.
13 All the counsel you have received has
    only worn you out!
  Let your astrologers come forward,
  those stargazers who make
    predictions month by month,
  let them save you from what is
    coming upon you.
14 Surely they are like stubble;
    the fire will burn them up.
  They cannot even save themselves

a 1 Or *Chaldeans*; also in verse 5

from the power of the flame.
Here are no coals to warm anyone;
here is no fire to sit by.
15 That is all they can do for you—
these you have labored with
and trafficked with since
childhood.
Each of them goes on in his error;
there is not one that can save you.

Stubborn Israel

48 "Listen to this, O house of
Jacob,
you who are called by the name of
Israel
and come from the line of Judah,
you who take oaths in the name of
the LORD
and invoke the God of Israel—
but not in truth or righteousness—
2 you who call yourselves citizens of
the holy city
and rely on the God of Israel—
the LORD Almighty is his name:
3 I foretold the former things long ago,
my mouth announced them and I
made them known;
then suddenly I acted, and they
came to pass.
4 For I knew how stubborn you were;
the sinews of your neck were iron,
your forehead was bronze.
5 Therefore I told you these things long
ago;
before they happened I announced
them to you
so that you could not say,
'My idols did them;
my wooden image and metal god
ordained them.'
6 You have heard these things; look at
them all.
Will you not admit them?

"From now on I will tell you of new
things,
of hidden things unknown to you.
7 They are created now, and not long
ago;
you have not heard of them before
today.
So you cannot say,
'Yes, I knew of them.'
8 You have neither heard nor
understood;

from of old your ear has not been
open.
Well do I know how treacherous you
are;
you were called a rebel from birth.
9 For my own name's sake I delay my
wrath;
for the sake of my praise I hold it
back from you,
so as not to cut you off.
10 See, I have refined you, though not as
silver;
I have tested you in the furnace of
affliction.
11 For my own sake, for my own sake, I
do this.
How can I let myself be defamed?
I will not yield my glory to
another.

Israel Freed

12 "Listen to me, O Jacob,
Israel, whom I have called:
I am he;
I am the first and I am the last.
13 My own hand laid the foundations of
the earth,
and my right hand spread out the
heavens;
when I summon them,
they all stand up together.

14 "Come together, all of you, and
listen:
Which of ⌊the idols⌋ has foretold
these things?
The LORD's chosen ally
will carry out his purpose against
Babylon;
his arm will be against the
Babylonians.*a*
15 I, even I, have spoken;
yes, I have called him.
I will bring him,
and he will succeed in his
mission.

16 "Come near me and listen to this:

"From the first announcement I have
not spoken in secret;
at the time it happens, I am there."

And now the Sovereign LORD has
sent me,
with his Spirit.

---

a 14 Or Chaldeans; also in verse 20

17 This is what the LORD says—
  your Redeemer, the Holy One of
    Israel:
  "I am the LORD your God,
    who teaches you what is best for
      you,
    who directs you in the way you
      should go.
18 If only you had paid attention to my
      commands,
    your peace would have been like a
      river,
    your righteousness like the waves
      of the sea.
19 Your descendants would have been
      like the sand,
    your children like its numberless
      grains;
  their name would never be cut off
    nor destroyed from before me."

20 Leave Babylon,
    flee from the Babylonians!
  Announce this with shouts of joy
    and proclaim it.
  Send it out to the ends of the earth;
    say, "The LORD has redeemed his
      servant Jacob."
21 They did not thirst when he led them
      through the deserts;
    he made water flow for them from
      the rock;
  he split the rock
    and water gushed out.

22 "There is no peace," says the LORD,
    "for the wicked."

The Servant of the LORD

49 Listen to me, you islands;
    hear this, you distant
      nations:
  Before I was born the LORD called me;
    from my birth he has made
      mention of my name.
2 He made my mouth like a sharpened
    sword,
    in the shadow of his hand he hid
      me;
  he made me into a polished arrow
    and concealed me in his quiver.
3 He said to me, "You are my servant,
  Israel, in whom I will display my
    splendor."
4 But I said, "I have labored to no
    purpose;

  I have spent my strength in vain
    and for nothing.
  Yet what is due me is in the LORD's
    hand,
    and my reward is with my God."

5 And now the LORD says—
  he who formed me in the womb to
    be his servant
  to bring Jacob back to him
    and gather Israel to himself,
  for I am honored in the eyes of the
    LORD
    and my God has been my
      strength—
6 he says:
  "It is too small a thing for you to be
    my servant
  to restore the tribes of Jacob
    and bring back those of Israel I
      have kept.
  I will also make you a light for the
    Gentiles,
    that you may bring my salvation to
      the ends of the earth."

7 This is what the LORD says—
  the Redeemer and Holy One of
    Israel—
  to him who was despised and
    abhorred by the nation,
    to the servant of rulers:
  "Kings will see you and rise up,
    princes will see and bow down,
  because of the LORD, who is faithful,
    the Holy One of Israel, who has
      chosen you."

Restoration of Israel

8 This is what the LORD says:

  "In the time of my favor I will
    answer you,
    and in the day of salvation I will
      help you;
  I will keep you and will make you
    to be a covenant for the people,
  to restore the land
    and to reassign its desolate
      inheritances,
9 to say to the captives, 'Come out,'
    and to those in darkness, 'Be free!'

  "They will feed beside the roads
    and find pasture on every barren
      hill.
10 They will neither hunger nor thirst,

nor will the desert heat or the sun
  beat upon them.
He who has compassion on them
  will guide them
and lead them beside springs of
  water.
11 I will turn all my mountains into
  roads,
and my highways will be raised up.
12 See, they will come from afar—
some from the north, some from
  the west,
some from the region of Aswan.*a*"

13 Shout for joy, O heavens;
  rejoice, O earth;
burst into song, O mountains!
For the LORD comforts his people
  and will have compassion on his
  afflicted ones.

a 12 Dead Sea Scrolls; Masoretic Text *Sinim*

WEDNESDAY

BEFORE HIS DEATH AT THE STAKE
Thomas Cranmer

VERSE: Isaiah 49:7   **PASSAGE:** Isaiah 49:1–13

Father of heaven; O Son of God, Redeemer of the world; O Holy Ghost, proceeding from them both; three persons, and one God; have mercy upon me, most wretched caitiff and miserable sinner. I have offended both heaven and earth, more grievously than any tongue can express. Whither then may I go, or wither should I flee for succor? To heaven I may be ashamed to lift up mine eyes, and in earth I find no refuge or succor. What shall I then do? Shall I despair? God forbid. O good God, thou art merciful, and refusest none that cometh unto thee for succor. To thee, therefore, do I run; to thee do I humble myself; saying, O Lord God, my sins be great, but yet have mercy upon me for thy great mercy. O God the Son, this great mystery was not wrought (that God became man) for few or small offenses; nor thou didst not give thy Son unto death, O God the Father, for our little and small sins only, but for all the greatest sins of the world, so that the sinner return unto thee with a penitent heart, as I do here at this present. Wherefore have mercy upon me, O Lord, whose property is always to have mercy; for although my sins be great, yet thy mercy is greater. And I crave nothing, O Lord, for mine own merits, but for thy name's sake, that it may be glorified thereby.

ADDITIONAL SCRIPTURE READING:
Psalms 51:1; 86:3; Mark 10:47

Go to page 835 for your next devotional reading.

1500   1700

14 But Zion said, "The LORD has
forsaken me,
the Lord has forgotten me."

15 "Can a mother forget the baby at her
breast
and have no compassion on the
child she has borne?
Though she may forget,
I will not forget you!
16 See, I have engraved you on the
palms of my hands;
your walls are ever before me.
17 Your sons hasten back,
and those who laid you waste
depart from you.
18 Lift up your eyes and look around;
all your sons gather and come to
you.
As surely as I live," declares the LORD,
"you will wear them all as
ornaments;
you will put them on, like a bride.

19 "Though you were ruined and made
desolate
and your land laid waste,
now you will be too small for your
people,
and those who devoured you will
be far away.
20 The children born during your
bereavement
will yet say in your hearing,
'This place is too small for us;
give us more space to live in.'
21 Then you will say in your heart,
'Who bore me these?
I was bereaved and barren;
I was exiled and rejected.
Who brought these up?
I was left all alone,
but these—where have they come
from?' "

22 This is what the Sovereign LORD
says:

"See, I will beckon to the Gentiles,
I will lift up my banner to the
peoples;
they will bring your sons in their arms
and carry your daughters on their
shoulders.
23 Kings will be your foster fathers,

and their queens your nursing
mothers.
They will bow down before you with
their faces to the ground;
they will lick the dust at your feet.
Then you will know that I am the
LORD;
those who hope in me will not be
disappointed."

24 Can plunder be taken from warriors,
or captives rescued from the
fierce*a* ?

25 But this is what the LORD says:

"Yes, captives will be taken from
warriors,
and plunder retrieved from the
fierce;
I will contend with those who
contend with you,
and your children I will save.
26 I will make your oppressors eat their
own flesh;
they will be drunk on their own
blood, as with wine.
Then all mankind will know
that I, the LORD, am your Savior,
your Redeemer, the Mighty One of
Jacob."

Israel's Sin and the Servant's Obedience

50 This is what the LORD says:

"Where is your mother's certificate
of divorce
with which I sent her away?
Or to which of my creditors
did I sell you?
Because of your sins you were sold;
because of your transgressions your
mother was sent away.
2 When I came, why was there no one?
When I called, why was there no
one to answer?
Was my arm too short to ransom
you?
Do I lack the strength to rescue
you?
By a mere rebuke I dry up the sea,
I turn rivers into a desert;
their fish rot for lack of water
and die of thirst.

a 24 Dead Sea Scrolls, Vulgate and Syriac (see also Septuagint and verse 25); Masoretic Text *righteous*

³ I clothe the sky with darkness
and make sackcloth its covering."

⁴ The Sovereign LORD has given me an
instructed tongue,
to know the word that sustains the
weary.
He wakens me morning by morning,
wakens my ear to listen like one
being taught.
⁵ The Sovereign LORD has opened my
ears,
and I have not been rebellious;
I have not drawn back.
⁶ I offered my back to those who beat
me,
my cheeks to those who pulled out
my beard;
I did not hide my face
from mocking and spitting.
⁷ Because the Sovereign LORD helps
me,
I will not be disgraced.
Therefore have I set my face like
flint,
and I know I will not be put to
shame.
⁸ He who vindicates me is near.
Who then will bring charges
against me?
Let us face each other!
Who is my accuser?
Let him confront me!
⁹ It is the Sovereign LORD who helps
me.
Who is he that will condemn me?
They will all wear out like a
garment;
the moths will eat them up.

¹⁰ Who among you fears the LORD
and obeys the word of his servant?
Let him who walks in the dark,
who has no light,
trust in the name of the LORD
and rely on his God.
¹¹ But now, all you who light fires
and provide yourselves with
flaming torches,
go, walk in the light of your fires
and of the torches you have set
ablaze.
This is what you shall receive from
my hand:
You will lie down in torment.

Everlasting Salvation for Zion

51 "Listen to me, you who
pursue righteousness
and who seek the LORD:
Look to the rock from which you
were cut
and to the quarry from which you
were hewn;
² look to Abraham, your father,
and to Sarah, who gave you birth.
When I called him he was but one,
and I blessed him and made him
many.
³ The LORD will surely comfort Zion
and will look with compassion on
all her ruins;
he will make her deserts like Eden,
her wastelands like the garden of
the LORD.
Joy and gladness will be found in her,
thanksgiving and the sound of
singing.

⁴ "Listen to me, my people;
hear me, my nation:
The law will go out from me;
my justice will become a light to
the nations.
⁵ My righteousness draws near
speedily,
my salvation is on the way,
and my arm will bring justice to
the nations.
The islands will look to me
and wait in hope for my arm.
⁶ Lift up your eyes to the heavens,
look at the earth beneath;
the heavens will vanish like smoke,
the earth will wear out like a
garment
and its inhabitants die like flies.
But my salvation will last forever,
my righteousness will never fail.

⁷ "Hear me, you who know what is
right,
you people who have my law in
your hearts:
Do not fear the reproach of men
or be terrified by their insults.
⁸ For the moth will eat them up like a
garment;
the worm will devour them like
wool.
But my righteousness will last
forever,

my salvation through all generations."

⁹Awake, awake! Clothe yourself with strength,
O arm of the LORD;
awake, as in days gone by,
as in generations of old.
Was it not you who cut Rahab to pieces,
who pierced that monster through?
¹⁰Was it not you who dried up the sea,
the waters of the great deep,
who made a road in the depths of the sea
so that the redeemed might cross over?
¹¹The ransomed of the LORD will return.
They will enter Zion with singing;
everlasting joy will crown their heads.
Gladness and joy will overtake them,
and sorrow and sighing will flee away.

¹²"I, even I, am he who comforts you.
Who are you that you fear mortal men,
the sons of men, who are but grass,
¹³that you forget the LORD your Maker,
who stretched out the heavens
and laid the foundations of the earth,
that you live in constant terror every day
because of the wrath of the oppressor,
who is bent on destruction?
For where is the wrath of the oppressor?
¹⁴   The cowering prisoners will soon be set free;
they will not die in their dungeon,
nor will they lack bread.
¹⁵For I am the LORD your God,
who churns up the sea so that its waves roar—
the LORD Almighty is his name.
¹⁶I have put my words in your mouth
and covered you with the shadow of my hand—
I who set the heavens in place,
who laid the foundations of the earth,

and who say to Zion, 'You are my people.' "

The Cup of the LORD's Wrath

¹⁷Awake, awake!
Rise up, O Jerusalem,
you who have drunk from the hand of the LORD
the cup of his wrath,
you who have drained to its dregs
the goblet that makes men stagger.
¹⁸Of all the sons she bore
there was none to guide her;
of all the sons she reared
there was none to take her by the hand.
¹⁹These double calamities have come upon you—
who can comfort you?—
ruin and destruction, famine and sword—
who can[a] console you?
²⁰Your sons have fainted;
they lie at the head of every street,
like antelope caught in a net.
They are filled with the wrath of the LORD
and the rebuke of your God.
²¹Therefore hear this, you afflicted one,
made drunk, but not with wine.
²²This is what your Sovereign LORD says,
your God, who defends his people:
"See, I have taken out of your hand
the cup that made you stagger;
from that cup, the goblet of my wrath,
you will never drink again.
²³I will put it into the hands of your tormentors,
who said to you,
'Fall prostrate that we may walk over you.'
And you made your back like the ground,
like a street to be walked over."

52 Awake, awake, O Zion,
clothe yourself with strength.
Put on your garments of splendor,
O Jerusalem, the holy city.
The uncircumcised and defiled
will not enter you again.
²Shake off your dust;

---

a 19 Dead Sea Scrolls, Septuagint, Vulgate and Syriac; Masoretic Text / *how can I*

rise up, sit enthroned, O Jerusalem.
Free yourself from the chains on your
    neck,
  O captive Daughter of Zion.

3For this is what the LORD says:

"You were sold for nothing,
  and without money you will be
    redeemed."

4For this is what the Sovereign LORD
says:

"At first my people went down to
    Egypt to live;
  lately, Assyria has oppressed them.

5"And now what do I have here?"
declares the LORD.

"For my people have been taken
    away for nothing,
  and those who rule them mock,a "
                    declares the LORD.
"And all day long
  my name is constantly
    blasphemed.
6Therefore my people will know my
    name;
  therefore in that day they will
    know
that it is I who foretold it.
  Yes, it is I."

7How beautiful on the mountains
  are the feet of those who bring
    good news,
who proclaim peace,
  who bring good tidings,
  who proclaim salvation,
who say to Zion,
  "Your God reigns!"
8Listen! Your watchmen lift up their
    voices;
  together they shout for joy.
When the LORD returns to Zion,
  they will see it with their own
    eyes.
9Burst into songs of joy together,
  you ruins of Jerusalem,
for the LORD has comforted his
    people,
  he has redeemed Jerusalem.
10The LORD will lay bare his holy arm

in the sight of all the nations,
  and all the ends of the earth will see
    the salvation of our God.

11Depart, depart, go out from there!
  Touch no unclean thing!
Come out from it and be pure,
  you who carry the vessels of the
    LORD.
12But you will not leave in haste
  or go in flight;
for the LORD will go before you,
  the God of Israel will be your rear
    guard.

The Suffering and Glory of the Servant

13See, my servant will act wiselyb;
  he will be raised and lifted up and
    highly exalted.
14Just as there were many who were
    appalled at himc—
  his appearance was so disfigured
    beyond that of any man
  and his form marred beyond
    human likeness—
15so will he sprinkle many nations,d
  and kings will shut their mouths
    because of him.
For what they were not told, they
    will see,
  and what they have not heard, they
    will understand.

53 Who has believed our
    message
and to whom has the arm of the
    LORD been revealed?
2He grew up before him like a tender
    shoot,
  and like a root out of dry ground.
He had no beauty or majesty to
    attract us to him,
  nothing in his appearance that we
    should desire him.
3He was despised and rejected by men,
  a man of sorrows, and familiar
    with suffering.
Like one from whom men hide their
    faces
  he was despised, and we esteemed
    him not.

4Surely he took up our infirmities
  and carried our sorrows,

a 5 Dead Sea Scrolls and Vulgate; Masoretic Text wail   b 13 Or will prosper   c 14 Hebrew you
d 15 Hebrew; Septuagint so will many nations marvel at him

yet we considered him stricken by
    God,
  smitten by him, and afflicted.
⁵ But he was pierced for our
    transgressions,
  he was crushed for our iniquities;
  the punishment that brought us
    peace was upon him,
  and by his wounds we are healed.
⁶ We all, like sheep, have gone astray,

each of us has turned to his own
    way;
  and the Lord has laid on him
    the iniquity of us all.

⁷ He was oppressed and afflicted,
  yet he did not open his mouth;
  he was led like a lamb to the
    slaughter,
  and as a sheep before her shearers
    is silent,

THURSDAY

HE HATH BORNE OUR GRIEFS
Martin Luther

VERSE: Isaiah 53:4   **PASSAGE:** Isaiah 53:1–6

 hese are clear and powerful words. The sufferings of
this king are our griefs and sorrows. He carries the burden which ought to be ours for ever. The stripes and
bruises which we have merited, namely, that we
should suffer thirst and hunger, and die eternally, all this is laid
on him. His suffering avails for me, and for you, and for us all; for
it was undertaken for our good. But we esteemed him to be the
one who was afflicted and smitten of God.

And that is true. For Moses himself says, "Cursed be the man
that hangeth on the tree" (Deuteronomy 21:23, KJV). That is
why he was railed at as one condemned and cursed. He cannot
even help himself, how then can he heal others (see Matthew
27:42–43)? But they did not see properly. For lo, he is carrying
our sorrows. According to the outward appearance he seems to
be cursed, but according to the spirit he carries my sorrows and
yours, and the sorrows of us all. "The chastisement of our peace
was upon him, and with his stripes we are healed" (Isaiah 53:5,
KJV). He is chastised, we are in peace. I and you, and all men
have called forth God's wrath; he has atoned, that we, redeemed
from sin, may rest in peace. He must suffer, we are set free.

We ought not so shamefully to forget such great love and
mercy.

ADDITIONAL SCRIPTURE READING:
Isaiah 53:11–12; Matthew 8:17; Galatians 3:13

Go to page 846 for your next devotional reading.

1500   1700

so he did not open his mouth.
⁸ By oppression*a* and judgment he was
    taken away.
And who can speak of his
    descendants?
For he was cut off from the land of
    the living;
for the transgression of my people
    he was stricken.*b*
⁹ He was assigned a grave with the
    wicked,
and with the rich in his death,
though he had done no violence,
    nor was any deceit in his mouth.

¹⁰ Yet it was the LORD's will to crush
    him and cause him to suffer,
and though the LORD makes*c* his
    life a guilt offering,
he will see his offspring and prolong
    his days,
and the will of the LORD will
    prosper in his hand.
¹¹ After the suffering of his soul,
    he will see the light ₁of life₁*d* and be
    satisfied*e*;
by his knowledge*f* my righteous
    servant will justify many,
and he will bear their iniquities.
¹² Therefore I will give him a portion
    among the great,*g*
and he will divide the spoils with
    the strong,*h*
because he poured out his life unto
    death,
and was numbered with the
    transgressors.
For he bore the sin of many,
    and made intercession for the
    transgressors.

The Future Glory of Zion

54 "Sing, O barren woman,
    you who never bore a child;
burst into song, shout for joy,
    you who were never in labor;
because more are the children of the
    desolate woman
than of her who has a husband,"
    says the LORD.
² "Enlarge the place of your tent,
    stretch your tent curtains wide,

do not hold back;
lengthen your cords,
    strengthen your stakes.
³ For you will spread out to the right
    and to the left;
your descendants will dispossess
    nations
    and settle in their desolate cities.

⁴ "Do not be afraid; you will not suffer
    shame.
Do not fear disgrace; you will not
    be humiliated.
You will forget the shame of your
    youth
and remember no more the
    reproach of your widowhood.
⁵ For your Maker is your husband—
    the LORD Almighty is his name—
the Holy One of Israel is your
    Redeemer;
he is called the God of all the
    earth.
⁶ The LORD will call you back
    as if you were a wife deserted and
    distressed in spirit—
a wife who married young,
    only to be rejected," says your
    God.
⁷ "For a brief moment I abandoned
    you,
but with deep compassion I will
    bring you back.
⁸ In a surge of anger
    I hid my face from you for a
    moment,
but with everlasting kindness
    I will have compassion on you,"
    says the LORD your Redeemer.

⁹ "To me this is like the days of Noah,
    when I swore that the waters of
    Noah would never again cover
    the earth.
So now I have sworn not to be angry
    with you,
    never to rebuke you again.
¹⁰ Though the mountains be shaken
    and the hills be removed,
yet my unfailing love for you will not
    be shaken
nor my covenant of peace be
    removed,"

a 8 Or *From arrest*   *b* 8 Or *away. / Yet who of his generation considered / that he was cut off from the land of the living / for the transgression of my people, / to whom the blow was due*   *c* 10 Hebrew *though you make*   *d* 11 Dead Sea Scrolls (see also Septuagint); Masoretic Text does not have *the light ₁of life₁*.   *e* 11 Or (with Masoretic Text) *¹¹He will see the result of the suffering of his soul / and be satisfied*   *f* 11 Or *by knowledge of him*   *g* 12 Or *many*   *h* 12 Or *numerous*

says the LORD, who has
   compassion on you.

11 "O afflicted city, lashed by storms
      and not comforted,
   I will build you with stones of
      turquoise,[a]
   your foundations with sapphires.[b]
12 I will make your battlements of
      rubies,
   your gates of sparkling jewels,
   and all your walls of precious
      stones.
13 All your sons will be taught by the
      LORD,
   and great will be your children's
      peace.
14 In righteousness you will be
      established:
   Tyranny will be far from you;
      you will have nothing to fear.
   Terror will be far removed;
      it will not come near you.
15 If anyone does attack you, it will not
      be my doing;
   whoever attacks you will surrender
      to you.

16 "See, it is I who created the
      blacksmith
   who fans the coals into flame
   and forges a weapon fit for its work.
   And it is I who have created the
      destroyer to work havoc;
17   no weapon forged against you will
      prevail,
   and you will refute every tongue
      that accuses you.
   This is the heritage of the servants of
      the LORD,
   and this is their vindication from
      me,"
                        declares the LORD.

Invitation to the Thirsty

55 "Come, all you who are
      thirsty,
   come to the waters;
   and you who have no money,
      come, buy and eat!
   Come, buy wine and milk
      without money and without cost.
2 Why spend money on what is not
      bread,
   and your labor on what does not
      satisfy?

Listen, listen to me, and eat what is
      good,
   and your soul will delight in the
      richest of fare.
3 Give ear and come to me;
   hear me, that your soul may live.
   I will make an everlasting covenant
      with you,
   my faithful love promised to
      David.
4 See, I have made him a witness to the
      peoples,
   a leader and commander of the
      peoples.
5 Surely you will summon nations you
      know not,
   and nations that do not know you
      will hasten to you,
   because of the LORD your God,
      the Holy One of Israel,
   for he has endowed you with
      splendor."

6 Seek the LORD while he may be
      found;
   call on him while he is near.
7 Let the wicked forsake his way
   and the evil man his thoughts.
   Let him turn to the LORD, and he will
      have mercy on him,
   and to our God, for he will freely
      pardon.

8 "For my thoughts are not your
      thoughts,
   neither are your ways my ways,"
                        declares the LORD.
9 "As the heavens are higher than the
      earth,
   so are my ways higher than your
      ways
   and my thoughts than your
      thoughts.
10 As the rain and the snow
   come down from heaven,
   and do not return to it
   without watering the earth
   and making it bud and flourish,
   so that it yields seed for the sower
      and bread for the eater,
11 so is my word that goes out from my
      mouth:
   It will not return to me empty,
   but will accomplish what I desire
   and achieve the purpose for which
      I sent it.

---

[a] 11 The meaning of the Hebrew for this word is uncertain.   [b] 11 Or *lapis lazuli*

12 You will go out in joy
  and be led forth in peace;
the mountains and hills
  will burst into song before you,
and all the trees of the field
  will clap their hands.
13 Instead of the thornbush will grow
    the pine tree,
  and instead of briers the myrtle
    will grow.
  This will be for the LORD's renown,
  for an everlasting sign,
  which will not be destroyed."

Salvation for Others

56 This is what the LORD says:

"Maintain justice
  and do what is right,
for my salvation is close at hand
  and my righteousness will soon be
    revealed.
2 Blessed is the man who does this,
  the man who holds it fast,
who keeps the Sabbath without
    desecrating it,
  and keeps his hand from doing any
    evil."

3 Let no foreigner who has bound
    himself to the LORD say,
  "The LORD will surely exclude me
    from his people."
And let not any eunuch complain,
  "I am only a dry tree."

4 For this is what the LORD says:

"To the eunuchs who keep my
    Sabbaths,
  who choose what pleases me
    and hold fast to my covenant—
5 to them I will give within my temple
    and its walls
  a memorial and a name
    better than sons and daughters;
I will give them an everlasting name
  that will not be cut off.
6 And foreigners who bind themselves
    to the LORD
  to serve him,
to love the name of the LORD,
  and to worship him,
all who keep the Sabbath without
    desecrating it
  and who hold fast to my
    covenant—

7 these I will bring to my holy
    mountain
  and give them joy in my house of
    prayer.
Their burnt offerings and sacrifices
  will be accepted on my altar;
for my house will be called
  a house of prayer for all nations."
8 The Sovereign LORD declares—
  he who gathers the exiles of Israel:
"I will gather still others to them
  besides those already gathered."

God's Accusation Against the Wicked

9 Come, all you beasts of the field,
  come and devour, all you beasts of
    the forest!
10 Israel's watchmen are blind,
  they all lack knowledge;
they are all mute dogs,
  they cannot bark;
they lie around and dream,
  they love to sleep.
11 They are dogs with mighty appetites;
  they never have enough.
They are shepherds who lack
    understanding;
  they all turn to their own way,
  each seeks his own gain.
12 "Come," each one cries, "let me get
    wine!
  Let us drink our fill of beer!
And tomorrow will be like today,
  or even far better."

57 The righteous perish,
    and no one ponders it in his
      heart;
devout men are taken away,
  and no one understands
that the righteous are taken away
  to be spared from evil.

A GREAT MANY PEOPLE ARE TRYING TO MAKE
PEACE, BUT THAT HAS ALREADY BEEN DONE. GOD
HAS NOT LEFT IT FOR US TO DO; ALL WE HAVE TO
DO IS TO ENTER INTO IT.   —*Dwight L. Moody*

2 Those who walk uprightly
    enter into peace;
  they find rest as they lie in death.

3 "But you—come here, you sons of a
    sorceress,

you offspring of adulterers and
    prostitutes!
⁴Whom are you mocking?
    At whom do you sneer
    and stick out your tongue?
Are you not a brood of rebels,
    the offspring of liars?
⁵You burn with lust among the oaks
    and under every spreading tree;
you sacrifice your children in the
    ravines
    and under the overhanging crags.
⁶The idols, among the smooth stones
    of the ravines are your portion;
they, they are your lot.
Yes, to them you have poured out
    drink offerings
    and offered grain offerings.
In the light of these things, should
    I relent?
⁷You have made your bed on a high
    and lofty hill;
    there you went up to offer your
    sacrifices.
⁸Behind your doors and your
    doorposts
    you have put your pagan symbols.
Forsaking me, you uncovered your
    bed,
    you climbed into it and opened it
    wide;
you made a pact with those whose
    beds you love,
    and you looked on their nakedness.
⁹You went to Molech*a* with olive oil
    and increased your perfumes.
You sent your ambassadors*b* far
    away;
    you descended to the grave*c* itself!
¹⁰You were wearied by all your ways,
    but you would not say, 'It is
    hopeless.'
You found renewal of your strength,
    and so you did not faint.

¹¹"Whom have you so dreaded and
    feared
    that you have been false to me,
and have neither remembered me
    nor pondered this in your hearts?
Is it not because I have long been
    silent
    that you do not fear me?
¹²I will expose your righteousness and
    your works,

and they will not benefit you.
¹³When you cry out for help,
    let your collection ⌞of idols⌟ save
    you!
The wind will carry all of them off,
    a mere breath will blow them
    away.
But the man who makes me his
    refuge
    will inherit the land
    and possess my holy mountain."

Comfort for the Contrite

¹⁴And it will be said:

"Build up, build up, prepare the road!
    Remove the obstacles out of the
    way of my people."
¹⁵For this is what the high and lofty
    One says—
    he who lives forever, whose name
    is holy:
"I live in a high and holy place,
    but also with him who is contrite
    and lowly in spirit,
to revive the spirit of the lowly
    and to revive the heart of the
    contrite.
¹⁶I will not accuse forever,
    nor will I always be angry,
for then the spirit of man would grow
    faint before me—
    the breath of man that I have
    created.
¹⁷I was enraged by his sinful greed;
    I punished him, and hid my face in
    anger,
    yet he kept on in his willful ways.
¹⁸I have seen his ways, but I will heal
    him;
    I will guide him and restore
    comfort to him,
¹⁹   creating praise on the lips of the
    mourners in Israel.
Peace, peace, to those far and near,"
    says the LORD. "And I will heal
    them."
²⁰But the wicked are like the tossing
    sea,
    which cannot rest,
    whose waves cast up mire and
    mud.
²¹"There is no peace," says my God,
    "for the wicked."

---

a 9 Or *to the king*   *b 9* Or *idols*   *c 9* Hebrew *Sheol*

True Fasting

58 "Shout it aloud, do not hold back.
　Raise your voice like a trumpet.
Declare to my people their rebellion
　and to the house of Jacob their sins.
2 For day after day they seek me out;
　they seem eager to know my ways,
as if they were a nation that does
　　what is right
　and has not forsaken the
　　commands of its God.
They ask me for just decisions
　and seem eager for God to come
　　near them.
3 'Why have we fasted,' they say,
　'and you have not seen it?
Why have we humbled ourselves,
　and you have not noticed?'

"Yet on the day of your fasting, you
　　do as you please
　and exploit all your workers.
4 Your fasting ends in quarreling and
　　strife,
　and in striking each other with
　　wicked fists.
You cannot fast as you do today
　and expect your voice to be heard
　　on high.
5 Is this the kind of fast I have chosen,
　only a day for a man to humble
　　himself?
Is it only for bowing one's head like a
　　reed
　and for lying on sackcloth and
　　ashes?
Is that what you call a fast,
　a day acceptable to the LORD?

---

6 "Is not this the kind of fasting I have
　　chosen:
to loose the chains of injustice
　and untie the cords of the yoke,
to set the oppressed free
　and break every yoke?
7 Is it not to share your food with the
　　hungry

and to provide the poor wanderer
　　with shelter—
when you see the naked, to clothe
　　him,
　and not to turn away from your
　　own flesh and blood?
8 Then your light will break forth like
　　the dawn,
　and your healing will quickly
　　appear;
then your righteousness[a] will go
　　before you,
　and the glory of the LORD will be
　　your rear guard.
9 Then you will call, and the LORD will
　　answer;
　you will cry for help, and he will
　　say: Here am I.

"If you do away with the yoke of
　　oppression,
　with the pointing finger and
　　malicious talk,
10 and if you spend yourselves in behalf
　　of the hungry
　and satisfy the needs of the
　　oppressed,
then your light will rise in the
　　darkness,
　and your night will become like
　　the noonday.
11 The LORD will guide you always;
　he will satisfy your needs in a sun-
　　scorched land
　and will strengthen your frame.
You will be like a well-watered
　　garden,
　like a spring whose waters never
　　fail.
12 Your people will rebuild the ancient
　　ruins
　and will raise up the age-old
　　foundations;
you will be called Repairer of Broken
　　Walls,
　Restorer of Streets with Dwellings.

13 "If you keep your feet from breaking
　　the Sabbath
　and from doing as you please on
　　my holy day,
if you call the Sabbath a delight
　and the LORD's holy day honorable,
and if you honor it by not going your
　　own way

---

a 8 Or your righteous One

and not doing as you please or
speaking idle words,
14 then you will find your joy in the
LORD,
and I will cause you to ride on the
heights of the land
and to feast on the inheritance of
your father Jacob."
The mouth of the LORD
has spoken.

Sin, Confession and Redemption

59 Surely the arm of the LORD is
not too short to save,
nor his ear too dull to hear.
2 But your iniquities have separated
you from your God;
your sins have hidden his face from
you,
so that he will not hear.
3 For your hands are stained with
blood,
your fingers with guilt.
Your lips have spoken lies,
and your tongue mutters wicked
things.
4 No one calls for justice;
no one pleads his case with
integrity.
They rely on empty arguments and
speak lies;
they conceive trouble and give
birth to evil.
5 They hatch the eggs of vipers
and spin a spider's web.
Whoever eats their eggs will die,
and when one is broken, an adder
is hatched.
6 Their cobwebs are useless for
clothing;
they cannot cover themselves with
what they make.
Their deeds are evil deeds,
and acts of violence are in their
hands.
7 Their feet rush into sin;
they are swift to shed innocent
blood.
Their thoughts are evil thoughts;
ruin and destruction mark their
ways.
8 The way of peace they do not know;
there is no justice in their paths.
They have turned them into crooked
roads;

no one who walks in them will
know peace.

9 So justice is far from us,
and righteousness does not reach
us.
We look for light, but all is darkness;
for brightness, but we walk in deep
shadows.
10 Like the blind we grope along the
wall,
feeling our way like men without
eyes.
At midday we stumble as if it were
twilight;
among the strong, we are like the
dead.
11 We all growl like bears;
we moan mournfully like doves.
We look for justice, but find none;
for deliverance, but it is far away.

12 For our offenses are many in your
sight,
and our sins testify against us.
Our offenses are ever with us,
and we acknowledge our iniquities:
13 rebellion and treachery against the
LORD,
turning our backs on our God,
fomenting oppression and revolt,
uttering lies our hearts have
conceived.
14 So justice is driven back,
and righteousness stands at a
distance;
truth has stumbled in the streets,
honesty cannot enter.
15 Truth is nowhere to be found,
and whoever shuns evil becomes a
prey.

The LORD looked and was displeased
that there was no justice.
16 He saw that there was no one,
he was appalled that there was no
one to intervene;
so his own arm worked salvation for
him,
and his own righteousness
sustained him.
17 He put on righteousness as his
breastplate,
and the helmet of salvation on his
head;
he put on the garments of vengeance
and wrapped himself in zeal as in a
cloak.

18 According to what they have done,
so will he repay
wrath to his enemies
and retribution to his foes;
he will repay the islands their due.
19 From the west, men will fear the
name of the LORD,
and from the rising of the sun, they
will revere his glory.
For he will come like a pent-up flood
that the breath of the LORD drives
along.[a]
20 "The Redeemer will come to Zion,
to those in Jacob who repent of
their sins,"
declares the LORD.

21 "As for me, this is my covenant
with them," says the LORD. "My Spirit,
who is on you, and my words that I have
put in your mouth will not depart from
your mouth, or from the mouths of your
children, or from the mouths of their
descendants from this time on and forever," says the LORD.

The Glory of Zion

60 "Arise, shine, for your light
has come,
and the glory of the LORD rises
upon you.
2 See, darkness covers the earth
and thick darkness is over the
peoples,
but the LORD rises upon you
and his glory appears over you.
3 Nations will come to your light,
and kings to the brightness of your
dawn.

4 "Lift up your eyes and look about
you:
All assemble and come to you;
your sons come from afar,
and your daughters are carried on
the arm.
5 Then you will look and be radiant,
your heart will throb and swell
with joy;
the wealth on the seas will be
brought to you,
to you the riches of the nations
will come.
6 Herds of camels will cover your land,

young camels of Midian and
Ephah.
And all from Sheba will come,
bearing gold and incense
and proclaiming the praise of the
LORD.
7 All Kedar's flocks will be gathered to
you,
the rams of Nebaioth will serve
you;
they will be accepted as offerings on
my altar,
and I will adorn my glorious
temple.

8 "Who are these that fly along like
clouds,
like doves to their nests?
9 Surely the islands look to me;
in the lead are the ships of
Tarshish,[b]
bringing your sons from afar,
with their silver and gold,
to the honor of the LORD your God,
the Holy One of Israel,
for he has endowed you with
splendor.

10 "Foreigners will rebuild your walls,
and their kings will serve you.
Though in anger I struck you,
in favor I will show you
compassion.
11 Your gates will always stand open,
they will never be shut, day or
night,
so that men may bring you the
wealth of the nations—
their kings led in triumphal
procession.
12 For the nation or kingdom that will
not serve you will perish;
it will be utterly ruined.

13 "The glory of Lebanon will come to
you,
the pine, the fir and the cypress
together,
to adorn the place of my sanctuary;
and I will glorify the place of my
feet.
14 The sons of your oppressors will
come bowing before you;
all who despise you will bow down
at your feet

---

a 19 Or When the enemy comes in like a flood, / the Spirit of the LORD will put him to flight   b 9 Or
the trading ships

and will call you the City of the
  LORD,
    Zion of the Holy One of Israel.

15 "Although you have been forsaken
    and hated,
    with no one traveling through,
  I will make you the everlasting pride
    and the joy of all generations.
16 You will drink the milk of nations
    and be nursed at royal breasts.
  Then you will know that I, the LORD,
    am your Savior,
    your Redeemer, the Mighty One of
    Jacob.
17 Instead of bronze I will bring you
    gold,
    and silver in place of iron.
  Instead of wood I will bring you
    bronze,
    and iron in place of stones.
  I will make peace your governor
    and righteousness your ruler.
18 No longer will violence be heard in
    your land,
    nor ruin or destruction within your
    borders,
  but you will call your walls Salvation
    and your gates Praise.
19 The sun will no more be your light
    by day,
    nor will the brightness of the moon
    shine on you,
  for the LORD will be your everlasting
    light,
    and your God will be your glory.
20 Your sun will never set again,
    and your moon will wane no more;
  the LORD will be your everlasting
    light,
    and your days of sorrow will end.
21 Then will all your people be
    righteous
    and they will possess the land
    forever.
  They are the shoot I have planted,
    the work of my hands,
    for the display of my splendor.
22 The least of you will become a
    thousand,
    the smallest a mighty nation.
  I am the LORD;
    in its time I will do this swiftly."

a 1 Hebrew; Septuagint *the blind*

The Year of the LORD's Favor

61 The Spirit of the Sovereign
    LORD is on me,
  because the LORD has anointed me
    to preach good news to the poor.
  He has sent me to bind up the
    brokenhearted,
    to proclaim freedom for the
    captives
    and release from darkness for the
    prisoners,*a*
2 to proclaim the year of the LORD's
    favor
    and the day of vengeance of our
    God,
  to comfort all who mourn,
3   and provide for those who grieve in
    Zion—
  to bestow on them a crown of
    beauty
    instead of ashes,
  the oil of gladness
    instead of mourning,
  and a garment of praise
    instead of a spirit of despair.
  They will be called oaks of
    righteousness,
    a planting of the LORD
    for the display of his splendor.

4 They will rebuild the ancient ruins
    and restore the places long
    devastated;
  they will renew the ruined cities
    that have been devastated for
    generations.
5 Aliens will shepherd your flocks;
    foreigners will work your fields
    and vineyards.
6 And you will be called priests of the
    LORD,
    you will be named ministers of our
    God.
  You will feed on the wealth of
    nations,
    and in their riches you will boast.

7 Instead of their shame
    my people will receive a double
    portion,
  and instead of disgrace
    they will rejoice in their
    inheritance;
  and so they will inherit a double
    portion in their land,
    and everlasting joy will be theirs.

8 "For I, the LORD, love justice;
　I hate robbery and iniquity.
In my faithfulness I will reward them
　and make an everlasting covenant
　with them.
9 Their descendants will be known
　among the nations
　and their offspring among the
　peoples.
All who see them will acknowledge
　that they are a people the LORD has
　blessed."

10 I delight greatly in the LORD;
　my soul rejoices in my God.
For he has clothed me with garments
　of salvation
　and arrayed me in a robe of
　righteousness,
as a bridegroom adorns his head like
　a priest,
　and as a bride adorns herself with
　her jewels.
11 For as the soil makes the sprout
　come up
　and a garden causes seeds to grow,
so the Sovereign LORD will make
　righteousness and praise
　spring up before all nations.

Zion's New Name

62 For Zion's sake I will not
　keep silent,
for Jerusalem's sake I will not
　remain quiet,
till her righteousness shines out like
　the dawn,
　her salvation like a blazing torch.
2 The nations will see your
　righteousness,
　and all kings your glory;
you will be called by a new name
　that the mouth of the LORD will
　bestow.
3 You will be a crown of splendor in
　the LORD's hand,
　a royal diadem in the hand of your
　God.
4 No longer will they call you
　Deserted,
　or name your land Desolate.
But you will be called Hephzibah,[a]
　and your land Beulah;[b]
for the LORD will take delight in you,
　and your land will be married.

5 As a young man marries a maiden,
　so will your sons[c] marry you;
as a bridegroom rejoices over his
　bride,
　so will your God rejoice over you.

6 I have posted watchmen on your
　walls, O Jerusalem;
　they will never be silent day or
　night.
You who call on the LORD,
　give yourselves no rest,
7 and give him no rest till he
　establishes Jerusalem
　and makes her the praise of the
　earth.

8 The LORD has sworn by his right
　hand
　and by his mighty arm:
"Never again will I give your grain
　as food for your enemies,
　and never again will foreigners drink
　the new wine
for which you have toiled;
9 but those who harvest it will eat it
　and praise the LORD,
　and those who gather the grapes will
　drink it
　in the courts of my sanctuary."

10 Pass through, pass through the gates!
　Prepare the way for the people.
Build up, build up the highway!
　Remove the stones.
Raise a banner for the nations.

11 The LORD has made proclamation
　to the ends of the earth:
"Say to the Daughter of Zion,
　'See, your Savior comes!
See, his reward is with him,
　and his recompense accompanies
　him.' "
12 They will be called the Holy People,
　the Redeemed of the LORD;
and you will be called Sought After,
　the City No Longer Deserted.

God's Day of Vengeance and Redemption

63 Who is this coming from
　Edom,
from Bozrah, with his garments
　stained crimson?
Who is this, robed in splendor,

---

a 4 *Hephzibah* means *my delight is in her.*　b 4 *Beulah* means *married.*　c 5 Or *Builder*

striding forward in the greatness of
his strength?

"It is I, speaking in righteousness,
mighty to save."

2 Why are your garments red,
like those of one treading the
winepress?

3 "I have trodden the winepress alone;
from the nations no one was with
me.
I trampled them in my anger
and trod them down in my wrath;
their blood spattered my garments,
and I stained all my clothing.
4 For the day of vengeance was in my
heart,
and the year of my redemption has
come.
5 I looked, but there was no one to help,
I was appalled that no one gave
support;
so my own arm worked salvation for
me,
and my own wrath sustained me.
6 I trampled the nations in my anger;
in my wrath I made them drunk
and poured their blood on the
ground."

Praise and Prayer

7 I will tell of the kindnesses of the
LORD,
the deeds for which he is to be
praised,
according to all the LORD has done
for us—
yes, the many good things he has
done
for the house of Israel,
according to his compassion and
many kindnesses.
8 He said, "Surely they are my people,
sons who will not be false to me";
and so he became their Savior.
9 In all their distress he too was
distressed,
and the angel of his presence saved
them.
In his love and mercy he redeemed
them;
he lifted them up and carried them
all the days of old.
10 Yet they rebelled

and grieved his Holy Spirit.
So he turned and became their
enemy
and he himself fought against them.

11 Then his people recalled*a* the days of
old,
the days of Moses and his people—
where is he who brought them
through the sea,
with the shepherd of his flock?
Where is he who set
his Holy Spirit among them,
12 who sent his glorious arm of power
to be at Moses' right hand,
who divided the waters before them,
to gain for himself everlasting
renown,
13 who led them through the depths?
Like a horse in open country,
they did not stumble;
14 like cattle that go down to the plain,
they were given rest by the Spirit
of the LORD.
This is how you guided your people
to make for yourself a glorious
name.

15 Look down from heaven and see
from your lofty throne, holy and
glorious.
Where are your zeal and your might?
Your tenderness and compassion
are withheld from us.
16 But you are our Father,
though Abraham does not know us
or Israel acknowledge us;
you, O LORD, are our Father,
our Redeemer from of old is your
name.
17 Why, O LORD, do you make us
wander from your ways
and harden our hearts so we do not
revere you?
Return for the sake of your servants,
the tribes that are your
inheritance.
18 For a little while your people
possessed your holy place,
but now our enemies have trampled
down your sanctuary.
19 We are yours from of old;
but you have not ruled over them,
they have not been called by your
name.*b*

a 11 Or *But may he recall*   *b 19* Or *We are like those you have never ruled, / like those never called
by your name*

64 Oh, that you would rend the
heavens and come down,
that the mountains would tremble
before you!
2 As when fire sets twigs ablaze
and causes water to boil,
come down to make your name
known to your enemies
and cause the nations to quake
before you!
3 For when you did awesome things
that we did not expect,

you came down, and the mountains
trembled before you.
4 Since ancient times no one has heard,
no ear has perceived,
no eye has seen any God besides you,
who acts on behalf of those who
wait for him.
5 You come to the help of those who
gladly do right,
who remember your ways.
But when we continued to sin
against them,

FRIDAY

THE OVERRIDING FUNCTION OF THE FATHER
Hannah Whitall Smith

VERSE: Isaiah 64:8   **PASSAGE:** Isaiah 64:8–12

ut you may say what about the other names of God . . .
This blessed name of Father . . . must underlie every
other name by which he has ever been known. Has he
been called a judge? Yes, but he is a father judge, one
who judges as a loving father would. Is he a king? Yes, but he is
a king who is at the same time the father of his subjects, and
who rules them with a father's tenderness. Is he a lawgiver? Yes,
but he is a lawgiver who gives laws as a father would, remembering the weakness and ignorance of his helpless children.
"Like as a father pitieth his children, so the Lord pitieth them
that fear him. For he knoweth our frame; he remembereth that
we are dust" (Psalm 103:13–14, KJV). It is not "as a judge judges,
so the Lord judges"; not "as a taskmaster controls, so the Lord
controls"; not "as a lawgiver imposes laws, so the Lord imposes
laws"; but, "as a father pitieth, so the Lord pitieth."

Never, never must we think of God in any other way than as
"our Father." All other attributes with which we endow him in
our conceptions must be based upon and limited by this one of
"our Father." What a good father could not do, God, who is our
Father, cannot do either; and what a good father ought to do,
God, who is our Father, is absolutely sure to do.

ADDITIONAL SCRIPTURE READING:
Deuteronomy 32:6; Isaiah 63:16; Galatians 3:26

Go to page 848 for your next devotional reading.

1700   1900

you were angry.
How then can we be saved?
6 All of us have become like one who
is unclean,
and all our righteous acts are like
filthy rags;
we all shrivel up like a leaf,
and like the wind our sins sweep
us away.
7 No one calls on your name
or strives to lay hold of you;
for you have hidden your face from
us
and made us waste away because
of our sins.

8 Yet, O LORD, you are our Father.
We are the clay, you are the potter;
we are all the work of your hand.
9 Do not be angry beyond measure,
O LORD;
do not remember our sins forever.
Oh, look upon us, we pray,
for we are all your people.
10 Your sacred cities have become a
desert;
even Zion is a desert, Jerusalem a
desolation.
11 Our holy and glorious temple, where
our fathers praised you,
has been burned with fire,
and all that we treasured lies in
ruins.
12 After all this, O LORD, will you hold
yourself back?
Will you keep silent and punish us
beyond measure?

Judgment and Salvation

65 "I revealed myself to those
who did not ask for me;
I was found by those who did not
seek me.
To a nation that did not call on my
name,
I said, 'Here am I, here am I.'
2 All day long I have held out my
hands
to an obstinate people,
who walk in ways not good,
pursuing their own imaginations—
3 a people who continually provoke me
to my very face,
offering sacrifices in gardens
and burning incense on altars of
brick;
4 who sit among the graves

and spend their nights keeping
secret vigil;
who eat the flesh of pigs,
and whose pots hold broth of
unclean meat;
5 who say, 'Keep away; don't come
near me,
for I am too sacred for you!'
Such people are smoke in my
nostrils,
a fire that keeps burning all day.

6 "See, it stands written before me:
I will not keep silent but will pay
back in full;
I will pay it back into their laps—
7 both your sins and the sins of your
fathers,"
says the LORD.
"Because they burned sacrifices on
the mountains
and defied me on the hills,
I will measure into their laps
the full payment for their former
deeds."

8 This is what the LORD says:

"As when juice is still found in a
cluster of grapes
and men say, 'Don't destroy it,
there is yet some good in it,'
so will I do in behalf of my servants;
I will not destroy them all.
9 I will bring forth descendants from
Jacob,
and from Judah those who will
possess my mountains;
my chosen people will inherit them,
and there will my servants live.
10 Sharon will become a pasture for
flocks,
and the Valley of Achor a resting
place for herds,
for my people who seek me.

11 "But as for you who forsake the LORD
and forget my holy mountain,
who spread a table for Fortune
and fill bowls of mixed wine for
Destiny,
12 I will destine you for the sword,
and you will all bend down for the
slaughter;
for I called but you did not answer,
I spoke but you did not listen.
You did evil in my sight

WEEKEND

I Arise Today
Patrick of Ireland

Verse: Psalm 23:4   **Passage:** Psalm 23

I arise today
Through God's strength to pilot me;
God's might to uphold me,
God's wisdom to guide me,
God's eye to look before me,
God's ear to hear me,
God's word to speak for me,
God's hand to guard me,
God's way to lie before me,
God's shield to protect me,
God's hosts to save me
From snares of the devil,
From temptations of vices,
From every one who desires me ill,
Afar or anear,
Alone or in a multitude.

ADDITIONAL SCRIPTURE READING:
Psalm 72:3–7; Daniel 6:26–27; Malachi 3:18

Go to page 851 for your next devotional reading.

100   500

and chose what displeases me."

13 Therefore this is what the Sovereign
LORD says:

"My servants will eat,
    but you will go hungry;
my servants will drink,
    but you will go thirsty;
my servants will rejoice,
    but you will be put to shame.
14 My servants will sing
    out of the joy of their hearts,
but you will cry out
    from anguish of heart
    and wail in brokenness of spirit.
15 You will leave your name
    to my chosen ones as a curse;
the Sovereign LORD will put you to
        death,
    but to his servants he will give
        another name.
16 Whoever invokes a blessing in the
        land
    will do so by the God of truth;
he who takes an oath in the land
    will swear by the God of truth.
For the past troubles will be forgotten
    and hidden from my eyes.

New Heavens and a New Earth

17 "Behold, I will create
    new heavens and a new earth.
The former things will not be
        remembered,
    nor will they come to mind.
18 But be glad and rejoice forever
    in what I will create,
for I will create Jerusalem to be a
        delight
    and its people a joy.
19 I will rejoice over Jerusalem
    and take delight in my people;
the sound of weeping and of crying
    will be heard in it no more.

20 "Never again will there be in it
    an infant who lives but a few days,
    or an old man who does not live
        out his years;
he who dies at a hundred
    will be thought a mere youth;
he who fails to reach[a] a hundred
    will be considered accursed.

21 They will build houses and dwell in
        them;
    they will plant vineyards and eat
        their fruit.
22 No longer will they build houses and
        others live in them,
    or plant and others eat.
For as the days of a tree,
    so will be the days of my people;
my chosen ones will long enjoy
    the works of their hands.
23 They will not toil in vain
    or bear children doomed to
        misfortune;
for they will be a people blessed by
    the LORD,
    they and their descendants with
        them.
24 Before they call I will answer;
    while they are still speaking I will
        hear.
25 The wolf and the lamb will feed
        together,
    and the lion will eat straw like the
        ox,
    but dust will be the serpent's food.
They will neither harm nor destroy
    on all my holy mountain,"
                    says the LORD.

Judgment and Hope

66 This is what the LORD says:

"Heaven is my throne,
    and the earth is my footstool.
Where is the house you will build for
        me?
    Where will my resting place be?
2 Has not my hand made all these
        things,
    and so they came into being?"
                    declares the LORD.

"This is the one I esteem:
    he who is humble and contrite in
        spirit,
    and trembles at my word.
3 But whoever sacrifices a bull
    is like one who kills a man,
and whoever offers a lamb,
    like one who breaks a dog's neck;
whoever makes a grain offering
    is like one who presents pig's
        blood,

---

a 20 Or / the sinner who reaches

and whoever burns memorial
incense,
　like one who worships an idol.
They have chosen their own ways,
　and their souls delight in their
　　abominations;
4 so I also will choose harsh treatment
　　for them
　and will bring upon them what
　　they dread.
For when I called, no one answered,
　when I spoke, no one listened.
They did evil in my sight
　and chose what displeases me."

5 Hear the word of the LORD,
　you who tremble at his word:
"Your brothers who hate you,
　and exclude you because of my
　　name, have said,
'Let the LORD be glorified,
　that we may see your joy!'
Yet they will be put to shame.
6 Hear that uproar from the city,
　hear that noise from the temple!
It is the sound of the LORD
　repaying his enemies all they
　　deserve.

7 "Before she goes into labor,
　she gives birth;
before the pains come upon her,
　she delivers a son.
8 Who has ever heard of such a thing?
　Who has ever seen such things?
Can a country be born in a day
　or a nation be brought forth in a
　　moment?
Yet no sooner is Zion in labor
　than she gives birth to her
　　children.
9 Do I bring to the moment of birth
　and not give delivery?" says the
　　LORD.
"Do I close up the womb
　when I bring to delivery?" says
　　your God.
10 "Rejoice with Jerusalem and be glad
　　for her,
　all you who love her;
rejoice greatly with her,
　all you who mourn over her.
11 For you will nurse and be satisfied
　　at her comforting breasts;
　you will drink deeply

and delight in her overflowing
　abundance."

12 For this is what the LORD says:

"I will extend peace to her like a
　river,
　and the wealth of nations like a
　　flooding stream;
you will nurse and be carried on her
　arm
　and dandled on her knees.
13 As a mother comforts her child,
　so will I comfort you;
　and you will be comforted over
　　Jerusalem."

14 When you see this, your heart will
　rejoice
　and you will flourish like grass;
the hand of the LORD will be made
　　known to his servants,
　but his fury will be shown to his
　　foes.
15 See, the LORD is coming with fire,
　and his chariots are like a
　　whirlwind;
he will bring down his anger with
　　fury,
　and his rebuke with flames of fire.
16 For with fire and with his sword
　the LORD will execute judgment
　　upon all men,
　and many will be those slain by
　　the LORD.

17 "Those who consecrate and purify
themselves to go into the gardens, following the one in the midst of[a] those
who eat the flesh of pigs and rats and
other abominable things—they will meet
their end together," declares the LORD.

18 "And I, because of their actions and
their imaginations, am about to come[b]
and gather all nations and tongues, and
they will come and see my glory.

19 "I will set a sign among them, and I
will send some of those who survive to
the nations—to Tarshish, to the Libyans[c]
and Lydians (famous as archers), to Tubal
and Greece, and to the distant islands
that have not heard of my fame or seen
my glory. They will proclaim my glory
among the nations. 20 And they will bring
all your brothers, from all the nations, to

a 17 Or gardens behind one of your temples, and
uncertain.　　c 19 Some Septuagint manuscripts Put (Libyans); Hebrew Pul
　　　　　　　　b 18 The meaning of the Hebrew for this clause is

THE HOPE OF FINDING THE GOD OF COMFORT
Henry Ward Beecher

VERSE: Isaiah 66:13   **PASSAGE:** Isaiah 66:10–13

h! What need there is that up out of this darkness and trouble and sadness, out of these calamities, there should be exalted, somewhere, an image that writes upon itself, "I am the God of comfort." That brings God right home to man's need. The world would die if it had no hope of finding such a God.

He penetrates and pervades the universe with his nature and with his disposition. My flagging faith has need of some such assurance. I have walked very much in thought with those old philosophers who believe that there was a God of evil, as well as one of good. I am more willingly a disciple, therefore, of that inspired teaching which declared that evil is not a personage. It is not even an empire.

Like the emery and sand with which we scour off rude surfaces, evil and trouble in this world are but instruments. And they are in the hands of God. If they bite with sharp attrition, it is because we need more scouring. It is because men's troubles need ruder handling and chiseling, that evils float in the air, swim in the sea, and spring up from out of the ground.

But all is under the control of *the God of consolation*, as it is said elsewhere; *the God of comfort* (see 2 Corinthians 1:3–4), *and the Father of mercies*, as it is said here. More are the tender thoughts, the inspired potential actions, in God, than in the stars in the heavens. Innumerable are the sweet influences that he sends down from his realm above. More and purer are his blessings than the drops of dew that night shakes down on the flowers and grass.

He penetrates and pervades the world with more saving mercies than does the sun with particles of light and heat. He declares that his nature in himself is boundless—that his heart of mercy is inexhaustible—that his work of comfort is endless.

ADDITIONAL SCRIPTURE READING:
Romans 15:5; 2 Corinthians 1:3–5; 2 Thessalonians 2:16–17

Go to page 865 for your next devotional reading.

1700   1900

my holy mountain in Jerusalem as an offering to the LORD—on horses, in chariots and wagons, and on mules and camels," says the LORD. "They will bring them, as the Israelites bring their grain offerings, to the temple of the LORD in ceremonially clean vessels. 21And I will select some of them also to be priests and Levites," says the LORD.

22"As the new heavens and the new earth that I make will endure before me," declares the LORD, "so will your name and descendants endure. 23From one New Moon to another and from one Sabbath to another, all mankind will come and bow down before me," says the LORD. 24"And they will go out and look upon the dead bodies of those who rebelled against me; their worm will not die, nor will their fire be quenched, and they will be loathsome to all mankind."

JEREMIAH

EREMIAH PROPHESIED IN JUDAH DURING A PERIOD WHEN THE DOOM OF ENTIRE NATIONS—INCLUDING JUDAH ITSELF—WAS BEING SEALED. JEREMIAH'S PERSONAL LIFE AND STRUGGLES ARE KNOWN TO US IN GREATER DETAIL THAN THOSE OF ANY OTHER OLD TESTA-MENT PROPHET. JUDGMENT IS ONE OF THE PERVA-SIVE THEMES IN HIS WRITINGS, ALTHOUGH, LIKE ISAIAH, HE WRITES STIRRING WORDS OF HOPE ABOUT JUDAH'S FUTURE REDEMPTION. WATCH FOR JEREMIAH'S ENCOURAGEMENT—PROPHECIES THAT ARE BEING FULFILLED TODAY WHENEVER SINFUL HEARTS ARE TRANSFORMED BY GOD.

1 The words of Jeremiah son of Hilkiah, one of the priests at Anathoth in the territory of Benjamin. ²The word of the LORD came to him in the thirteenth year of the reign of Josiah son of Amon king of Judah, ³and through the reign of Jehoiakim son of Josiah king of Judah, down to the fifth month of the eleventh year of Zedekiah son of Josiah king of Judah, when the people of Jerusalem went into exile.

The Call of Jeremiah

⁴The word of the LORD came to me, saying,

⁵ "Before I formed you in the womb I
    knew*a* you,

before you were born I set you
    apart;
I appointed you as a prophet to the
    nations."

⁶"Ah, Sovereign LORD," I said, "I do not know how to speak; I am only a child."

⁷But the LORD said to me, "Do not say, 'I am only a child.' You must go to everyone I send you to and say whatever I command you. ⁸Do not be afraid of them, for I am with you and will rescue you," declares the LORD.

⁹Then the LORD reached out his hand and touched my mouth and said to me, "Now, I have put my words in your mouth. ¹⁰See, today I appoint you over nations and kingdoms to uproot and tear

a 5 Or chose

down, to destroy and overthrow, to build and to plant."

¹¹The word of the LORD came to me: "What do you see, Jeremiah?"

"I see the branch of an almond tree," I replied.

¹²The LORD said to me, "You have seen correctly, for I am watching*a* to see that my word is fulfilled."

¹³The word of the LORD came to me again: "What do you see?"

"I see a boiling pot, tilting away from the north," I answered.

¹⁴The LORD said to me, "From the north disaster will be poured out on all who live in the land. ¹⁵I am about to summon all the peoples of the northern kingdoms," declares the LORD.

"Their kings will come and set up
    their thrones
  in the entrance of the gates of
    Jerusalem;
they will come against all her
    surrounding walls
and against all the towns of Judah.
¹⁶I will pronounce my judgments on
    my people
  because of their wickedness in
    forsaking me,
in burning incense to other gods
  and in worshiping what their
    hands have made.

¹⁷"Get yourself ready! Stand up and say to them whatever I command you. Do not be terrified by them, or I will terrify you before them. ¹⁸Today I have made you a fortified city, an iron pillar and a bronze wall to stand against the whole land—against the kings of Judah, its officials, its priests and the people of the land. ¹⁹They will fight against you but will not overcome you, for I am with you and will rescue you," declares the LORD.

Israel Forsakes God

2 The word of the LORD came to me: ²"Go and proclaim in the hearing of Jerusalem:

" 'I remember the devotion of your
    youth,

how as a bride you loved me
  and followed me through the desert,
    through a land not sown.
³Israel was holy to the LORD,
  the firstfruits of his harvest;
all who devoured her were held
    guilty,
  and disaster overtook them,' "
                 declares the LORD.

⁴Hear the word of the LORD, O house
    of Jacob,
  all you clans of the house of Israel.

⁵This is what the LORD says:

"What fault did your fathers find in
    me,
  that they strayed so far from me?
They followed worthless idols
  and became worthless themselves.
⁶They did not ask, 'Where is the LORD,
  who brought us up out of Egypt
and led us through the barren
    wilderness,
  through a land of deserts and rifts,
a land of drought and darkness,*b*
  a land where no one travels and no
    one lives?'
⁷I brought you into a fertile land
  to eat its fruit and rich produce.
But you came and defiled my land
  and made my inheritance
    detestable.
⁸The priests did not ask,
  'Where is the LORD?'
Those who deal with the law did not
    know me;
  the leaders rebelled against me.
The prophets prophesied by Baal,
  following worthless idols.

⁹"Therefore I bring charges against
    you again,"
                 declares the LORD.
"And I will bring charges against
    your children's children.
¹⁰Cross over to the coasts of Kittim*c*
    and look,
  send to Kedar*d* and observe closely;
  see if there has ever been anything
    like this:
¹¹Has a nation ever changed its gods?
  (Yet they are not gods at all.)

---

a 12 The Hebrew for *watching* sounds like the Hebrew for *almond tree.*   *b* 6 Or *and the shadow of death*
c 10 That is, Cyprus and western coastlands   *d* 10 The home of Bedouin tribes in the Syro-Arabian desert

But my people have exchanged their[a]
    Glory
  for worthless idols.
12 Be appalled at this, O heavens,
    and shudder with great horror,"
                declares the LORD.
13 "My people have committed two sins:
  They have forsaken me,
    the spring of living water,
  and have dug their own cisterns,
    broken cisterns that cannot hold
    water.
14 Is Israel a servant, a slave by birth?
  Why then has he become plunder?
15 Lions have roared;
  they have growled at him.
They have laid waste his land;
  his towns are burned and deserted.
16 Also, the men of Memphis[b] and
    Tahpanhes
  have shaved the crown of your
    head.[c]
17 Have you not brought this on
    yourselves
  by forsaking the LORD your God
    when he led you in the way?
18 Now why go to Egypt
  to drink water from the Shihor[d]?
And why go to Assyria
  to drink water from the River[e]?
19 Your wickedness will punish you;
  your backsliding will rebuke you.
Consider then and realize
  how evil and bitter it is for you
when you forsake the LORD your God
  and have no awe of me,"
             declares the Lord,
        the LORD Almighty.

20 "Long ago you broke off your yoke
  and tore off your bonds;
  you said, 'I will not serve you!'
Indeed, on every high hill
  and under every spreading tree
  you lay down as a prostitute.
21 I had planted you like a choice vine
  of sound and reliable stock.
How then did you turn against me
  into a corrupt, wild vine?
22 Although you wash yourself with
    soda
  and use an abundance of soap,
  the stain of your guilt is still before
    me,"
        declares the Sovereign LORD.

23 "How can you say, 'I am not defiled;
  I have not run after the Baals'?
See how you behaved in the valley;
  consider what you have done.
You are a swift she-camel
  running here and there,
24 a wild donkey accustomed to the
    desert,
  sniffing the wind in her craving—
  in her heat who can restrain her?
Any males that pursue her need not
    tire themselves;
  at mating time they will find her.
25 Do not run until your feet are bare
  and your throat is dry.
But you said, 'It's no use!
  I love foreign gods,
  and I must go after them.'

26 "As a thief is disgraced when he is
    caught,
  so the house of Israel is disgraced—
they, their kings and their officials,
  their priests and their prophets.
27 They say to wood, 'You are my
    father,'
  and to stone, 'You gave me birth.'
They have turned their backs to me
  and not their faces;
yet when they are in trouble, they
    say,
  'Come and save us!'
28 Where then are the gods you made
    for yourselves?
Let them come if they can save
    you
  when you are in trouble!
For you have as many gods
  as you have towns, O Judah.

29 "Why do you bring charges against
    me?
You have all rebelled against me,"
             declares the LORD.
30 "In vain I punished your people;
  they did not respond to correction.
Your sword has devoured your
    prophets
  like a ravening lion.

31 "You of this generation, consider
the word of the LORD:

"Have I been a desert to Israel
  or a land of great darkness?

---

[a] 11 Masoretic Text; an ancient Hebrew scribal tradition *my*   [b] 16 Hebrew *Noph*   [c] 16 Or *have cracked your skull*   [d] 18 That is, a branch of the Nile   [e] 18 That is, the Euphrates

Why do my people say, 'We are free
   to roam;
  we will come to you no more'?
³²Does a maiden forget her jewelry,
   a bride her wedding ornaments?
Yet my people have forgotten me,
   days without number.
³³How skilled you are at pursuing love!
  Even the worst of women can learn
   from your ways.
³⁴On your clothes men find
   the lifeblood of the innocent poor,
   though you did not catch them
   breaking in.
Yet in spite of all this
³⁵   you say, 'I am innocent;
   he is not angry with me.'
But I will pass judgment on you
  because you say, 'I have not sinned.'
³⁶Why do you go about so much,
   changing your ways?
You will be disappointed by Egypt
  as you were by Assyria.
³⁷You will also leave that place
   with your hands on your head,
for the LORD has rejected those you
   trust;
   you will not be helped by them.

3 "If a man divorces his wife
  and she leaves him and marries
   another man,
should he return to her again?
  Would not the land be completely
   defiled?
But you have lived as a prostitute
   with many lovers—
  would you now return to me?"
            declares the LORD.
²"Look up to the barren heights and
   see.
Is there any place where you have
   not been ravished?
By the roadside you sat waiting for
   lovers,
sat like a nomadᵃ in the desert.
You have defiled the land
   with your prostitution and
   wickedness.
³Therefore the showers have been
   withheld,
  and no spring rains have fallen.
Yet you have the brazen look of a
   prostitute;
  you refuse to blush with shame.

⁴Have you not just called to me:
  'My Father, my friend from my
   youth,
⁵will you always be angry?
  Will your wrath continue forever?'
This is how you talk,
  but you do all the evil you can."

Unfaithful Israel

⁶During the reign of King Josiah, the
LORD said to me, "Have you seen what
faithless Israel has done? She has gone
up on every high hill and under every
spreading tree and has committed adultery there. ⁷I thought that after she had
done all this she would return to me but
she did not, and her unfaithful sister
Judah saw it. ⁸I gave faithless Israel her
certificate of divorce and sent her away
because of all her adulteries. Yet I saw
that her unfaithful sister Judah had no
fear; she also went out and committed
adultery. ⁹Because Israel's immorality
mattered so little to her, she defiled the
land and committed adultery with stone
and wood. ¹⁰In spite of all this, her
unfaithful sister Judah did not return to
me with all her heart, but only in pre-
tense," declares the LORD.

¹¹The LORD said to me, "Faithless
Israel is more righteous than unfaithful
Judah. ¹²Go, proclaim this message
toward the north:

" 'Return, faithless Israel,' declares
   the LORD,
'I will frown on you no longer,
for I am merciful,' declares the LORD,
  'I will not be angry forever.
¹³Only acknowledge your guilt—
  you have rebelled against the LORD
   your God,
you have scattered your favors to
   foreign gods
  under every spreading tree,
  and have not obeyed me,' "
            declares the LORD.

¹⁴"Return, faithless people," declares
the LORD, "for I am your husband. I will
choose you—one from a town and two
from a clan—and bring you to Zion.
¹⁵Then I will give you shepherds after
my own heart, who will lead you with
knowledge and understanding. ¹⁶In those

ᵃ 2 Or *an Arab*

days, when your numbers have increased greatly in the land," declares the LORD, "men will no longer say, 'The ark of the covenant of the LORD.' It will never enter their minds or be remembered; it will not be missed, nor will another one be made. ¹⁷ At that time they will call Jerusalem The Throne of the LORD, and all nations will gather in Jerusalem to honor the name of the LORD. No longer will they follow the stubbornness of their evil hearts. ¹⁸ In those days the house of Judah will join the house of Israel, and together they will come from a northern land to the land I gave your forefathers as an inheritance.

¹⁹ "I myself said,

" 'How gladly would I treat you like
    sons
  and give you a desirable land,
    the most beautiful inheritance of
    any nation.'
I thought you would call me 'Father'
  and not turn away from following
  me.
²⁰ But like a woman unfaithful to her
    husband,
  so you have been unfaithful to me,
    O house of Israel,"
                    declares the LORD.

²¹ A cry is heard on the barren heights,
  the weeping and pleading of the
    people of Israel,
because they have perverted their
    ways
  and have forgotten the LORD their
    God.

²² "Return, faithless people;
  I will cure you of backsliding."

"Yes, we will come to you,
  for you are the LORD our God.
²³ Surely the ⌞idolatrous⌟ commotion on
    the hills
  and mountains is a deception;
surely in the LORD our God
  is the salvation of Israel.
²⁴ From our youth shameful gods have
    consumed
  the fruits of our fathers' labor—
    their flocks and herds,
    their sons and daughters.
²⁵ Let us lie down in our shame,
  and let our disgrace cover us.

We have sinned against the LORD our
    God,
  both we and our fathers;
from our youth till this day
  we have not obeyed the LORD our
    God."

4 "If you will return, O Israel,
    return to me,"
                    declares the LORD.
"If you put your detestable idols out
    of my sight
  and no longer go astray,
² and if in a truthful, just and righteous
    way
  you swear, 'As surely as the LORD
    lives,'
then the nations will be blessed by
    him
  and in him they will glory."

³ This is what the LORD says to the men of Judah and to Jerusalem:

"Break up your unplowed ground
  and do not sow among thorns.
⁴ Circumcise yourselves to the LORD,
  circumcise your hearts,
  you men of Judah and people of
    Jerusalem,
or my wrath will break out and burn
    like fire
  because of the evil you have done—
  burn with no one to quench it.

Disaster From the North

⁵ "Announce in Judah and proclaim in
    Jerusalem and say:
  'Sound the trumpet throughout the
    land!'
Cry aloud and say:
  'Gather together!
  Let us flee to the fortified cities!'
⁶ Raise the signal to go to Zion!
  Flee for safety without delay!
For I am bringing disaster from the
    north,
  even terrible destruction."

⁷ A lion has come out of his lair;
  a destroyer of nations has set out.
He has left his place
  to lay waste your land.
Your towns will lie in ruins
  without inhabitant.
⁸ So put on sackcloth,
  lament and wail,

for the fierce anger of the LORD
    has not turned away from us.

9 "In that day," declares the LORD,
    "the king and the officials will lose
        heart,
  the priests will be horrified,
    and the prophets will be appalled."

10 Then I said, "Ah, Sovereign LORD,
how completely you have deceived this
people and Jerusalem by saying, 'You
will have peace,' when the sword is at
our throats."

11 At that time this people and Jerusalem will be told, "A scorching wind
from the barren heights in the desert
blows toward my people, but not to winnow or cleanse; 12 a wind too strong for
that comes from me.[a] Now I pronounce
my judgments against them."

13 Look! He advances like the clouds,
    his chariots come like a whirlwind,
  his horses are swifter than eagles.
    Woe to us! We are ruined!
14 O Jerusalem, wash the evil from your
    heart and be saved.
  How long will you harbor wicked
    thoughts?
15 A voice is announcing from Dan,
    proclaiming disaster from the hills
      of Ephraim.
16 "Tell this to the nations,
    proclaim it to Jerusalem:
 'A besieging army is coming from a
    distant land,
  raising a war cry against the cities
    of Judah.
17 They surround her like men guarding
    a field,
  because she has rebelled against
    me,' "
                declares the LORD.
18 "Your own conduct and actions
    have brought this upon you.
  This is your punishment.
    How bitter it is!
    How it pierces to the heart!"

19 Oh, my anguish, my anguish!
    I writhe in pain.
  Oh, the agony of my heart!
    My heart pounds within me,
    I cannot keep silent.

For I have heard the sound of the
    trumpet;
    I have heard the battle cry.
20 Disaster follows disaster;
    the whole land lies in ruins.
In an instant my tents are destroyed,
    my shelter in a moment.
21 How long must I see the battle
    standard
    and hear the sound of the trumpet?

22 "My people are fools;
    they do not know me.
They are senseless children;
    they have no understanding.
They are skilled in doing evil;
    they know not how to do good."

23 I looked at the earth,
    and it was formless and empty;
  and at the heavens,
    and their light was gone.
24 I looked at the mountains,
    and they were quaking;
    all the hills were swaying.
25 I looked, and there were no people;
    every bird in the sky had flown
      away.
26 I looked, and the fruitful land was a
    desert;
  all its towns lay in ruins
    before the LORD, before his fierce
      anger.

27 This is what the LORD says:

"The whole land will be ruined,
    though I will not destroy it
      completely.
28 Therefore the earth will mourn
  and the heavens above grow dark,
  because I have spoken and will not
    relent,
    I have decided and will not turn
      back."

29 At the sound of horsemen and
    archers
    every town takes to flight.
Some go into the thickets;
    some climb up among the rocks.
All the towns are deserted;
    no one lives in them.

30 What are you doing, O devastated
    one?
  Why dress yourself in scarlet

---

a 12 Or comes at my command

and put on jewels of gold?
Why shade your eyes with paint?
You adorn yourself in vain.
Your lovers despise you;
they seek your life.

31 I hear a cry as of a woman in labor,
a groan as of one bearing her first
child—
the cry of the Daughter of Zion
gasping for breath,
stretching out her hands and
saying,
"Alas! I am fainting;
my life is given over to murderers."

Not One Is Upright

5 "Go up and down the streets of
Jerusalem,
look around and consider,
search through her squares.
If you can find but one person
who deals honestly and seeks the
truth,
I will forgive this city.
2 Although they say, 'As surely as the
LORD lives,'
still they are swearing falsely."

3 O LORD, do not your eyes look for
truth?
You struck them, but they felt no
pain;
you crushed them, but they refused
correction.
They made their faces harder than
stone
and refused to repent.
4 I thought, "These are only the poor;
they are foolish,
for they do not know the way of the
LORD,
the requirements of their God.
5 So I will go to the leaders
and speak to them;
surely they know the way of the
LORD,
the requirements of their God."
But with one accord they too had
broken off the yoke
and torn off the bonds.
6 Therefore a lion from the forest will
attack them,
a wolf from the desert will ravage
them,
a leopard will lie in wait near their
towns

to tear to pieces any who venture
out,
for their rebellion is great
and their backslidings many.

7 "Why should I forgive you?
Your children have forsaken me
and sworn by gods that are not
gods.
I supplied all their needs,
yet they committed adultery
and thronged to the houses of
prostitutes.
8 They are well-fed, lusty stallions,
each neighing for another man's
wife.
9 Should I not punish them for this?"
declares the LORD.
"Should I not avenge myself
on such a nation as this?

10 "Go through her vineyards and
ravage them,
but do not destroy them
completely.
Strip off her branches,
for these people do not belong to
the LORD.
11 The house of Israel and the house of
Judah
have been utterly unfaithful to me,"
declares the LORD.

12 They have lied about the LORD;
they said, "He will do nothing!
No harm will come to us;
we will never see sword or famine.
13 The prophets are but wind
and the word is not in them;
so let what they say be done to
them."

14 Therefore this is what the LORD God
Almighty says:

"Because the people have spoken
these words,
I will make my words in your
mouth a fire
and these people the wood it
consumes.
15 O house of Israel," declares the LORD,
"I am bringing a distant nation
against you—
an ancient and enduring nation,
a people whose language you do
not know,

whose speech you do not
  understand.
16 Their quivers are like an open grave;
  all of them are mighty warriors.
17 They will devour your harvests and
    food,
  devour your sons and daughters;
  they will devour your flocks and
    herds,
  devour your vines and fig trees.
  With the sword they will destroy
    the fortified cities in which you
      trust.

18 "Yet even in those days," declares
the LORD, "I will not destroy you completely. 19 And when the people ask,
'Why has the LORD our God done all this
to us?' you will tell them, 'As you have
forsaken me and served foreign gods in
your own land, so now you will serve
foreigners in a land not your own.'

20 "Announce this to the house of Jacob
  and proclaim it in Judah:
21 Hear this, you foolish and senseless
    people,
  who have eyes but do not see,
  who have ears but do not hear:
22 Should you not fear me?" declares
    the LORD.
  "Should you not tremble in my
    presence?
  I made the sand a boundary for the
    sea,
  an everlasting barrier it cannot
    cross.
  The waves may roll, but they cannot
    prevail;
  they may roar, but they cannot
    cross it.
23 But these people have stubborn and
    rebellious hearts;
  they have turned aside and gone
    away.
24 They do not say to themselves,
  'Let us fear the LORD our God,
  who gives autumn and spring rains in
    season,
  who assures us of the regular
    weeks of harvest.'
25 Your wrongdoings have kept these
    away;
  your sins have deprived you of
    good.
26 "Among my people are wicked men

who lie in wait like men who snare
    birds
  and like those who set traps to
    catch men.
27 Like cages full of birds,
  their houses are full of deceit;
  they have become rich and powerful
28   and have grown fat and sleek.
  Their evil deeds have no limit;
  they do not plead the case of the
    fatherless to win it,
  they do not defend the rights of the
    poor.
29 Should I not punish them for this?"
    declares the LORD.
  "Should I not avenge myself
    on such a nation as this?

30 "A horrible and shocking thing
  has happened in the land:
31 The prophets prophesy lies,
  the priests rule by their own
    authority,
  and my people love it this way.
  But what will you do in the end?

Jerusalem Under Siege

6 "Flee for safety, people of
    Benjamin!
  Flee from Jerusalem!
  Sound the trumpet in Tekoa!
  Raise the signal over Beth
    Hakkerem!
  For disaster looms out of the north,
    even terrible destruction.
2 I will destroy the Daughter of Zion,
  so beautiful and delicate.
3 Shepherds with their flocks will
    come against her;
  they will pitch their tents around
    her,
  each tending his own portion."

4 "Prepare for battle against her!
  Arise, let us attack at noon!
  But, alas, the daylight is fading,
    and the shadows of evening grow
      long.
5 So arise, let us attack at night
  and destroy her fortresses!"

6 This is what the LORD Almighty
says:

"Cut down the trees
  and build siege ramps against
    Jerusalem.

This city must be punished;
    it is filled with oppression.
⁷ As a well pours out its water,
    so she pours out her wickedness.
Violence and destruction resound in
    her;
    her sickness and wounds are ever
      before me.
⁸ Take warning, O Jerusalem,
    or I will turn away from you
and make your land desolate
    so no one can live in it."

⁹ This is what the LORD Almighty
says:

"Let them glean the remnant of Israel
    as thoroughly as a vine;
pass your hand over the branches
    again,
    like one gathering grapes."

¹⁰ To whom can I speak and give
    warning?
    Who will listen to me?
Their ears are closed[a]
    so they cannot hear.
The word of the LORD is offensive to
    them;
    they find no pleasure in it.
¹¹ But I am full of the wrath of the LORD,
    and I cannot hold it in.

"Pour it out on the children in the
    street
    and on the young men gathered
      together;
both husband and wife will be caught
    in it,
    and the old, those weighed down
      with years.
¹² Their houses will be turned over to
    others,
    together with their fields and their
      wives,
when I stretch out my hand
    against those who live in the land,"
                declares the LORD.
¹³ "From the least to the greatest,
    all are greedy for gain;
prophets and priests alike,
    all practice deceit.
¹⁴ They dress the wound of my people
    as though it were not serious.
'Peace, peace,' they say,
    when there is no peace.

¹⁵ Are they ashamed of their loathsome
    conduct?
No, they have no shame at all;
    they do not even know how to
      blush.
So they will fall among the fallen;
    they will be brought down when I
      punish them,"
                says the LORD.

¹⁶ This is what the LORD says:

"Stand at the crossroads and look;
    ask for the ancient paths,
ask where the good way is, and walk
    in it,
    and you will find rest for your
      souls.
But you said, 'We will not walk in
    it.'
¹⁷ I appointed watchmen over you and
    said,
    'Listen to the sound of the
      trumpet!'
But you said, 'We will not listen.'
¹⁸ Therefore hear, O nations;
    observe, O witnesses,
    what will happen to them.
¹⁹ Hear, O earth:
I am bringing disaster on this people,
    the fruit of their schemes,
because they have not listened to my
    words
    and have rejected my law.
²⁰ What do I care about incense from
    Sheba
    or sweet calamus from a distant
      land?
Your burnt offerings are not
    acceptable;
    your sacrifices do not please me."

²¹ Therefore this is what the LORD
says:

"I will put obstacles before this
    people.
Fathers and sons alike will stumble
    over them;
neighbors and friends will perish."

²² This is what the LORD says:

"Look, an army is coming
    from the land of the north;

---

a great nation is being stirred up
from the ends of the earth.
23 They are armed with bow and spear;
they are cruel and show no mercy.
They sound like the roaring sea
as they ride on their horses;
they come like men in battle
formation
to attack you, O Daughter of Zion."

24 We have heard reports about them,
and our hands hang limp.
Anguish has gripped us,
pain like that of a woman in labor.
25 Do not go out to the fields
or walk on the roads,
for the enemy has a sword,
and there is terror on every side.
26 O my people, put on sackcloth
and roll in ashes;
mourn with bitter wailing
as for an only son,
for suddenly the destroyer
will come upon us.

27 "I have made you a tester of metals
and my people the ore,
that you may observe
and test their ways.
28 They are all hardened rebels,
going about to slander.
They are bronze and iron;
they all act corruptly.
29 The bellows blow fiercely
to burn away the lead with fire,
but the refining goes on in vain;
the wicked are not purged out.
30 They are called rejected silver,
because the LORD has rejected
them."

False Religion Worthless

7 This is the word that came to
Jeremiah from the LORD:
2 "Stand at the gate of the LORD's house
and there proclaim this message:

" 'Hear the word of the LORD, all you
people of Judah who come through these
gates to worship the LORD. 3 This is what
the LORD Almighty, the God of Israel,
says: Reform your ways and your
actions, and I will let you live in this
place. 4 Do not trust in deceptive words
and say, "This is the temple of the LORD,
the temple of the LORD, the temple of
the LORD!" 5 If you really change your

ways and your actions and deal with
each other justly, 6 if you do not oppress
the alien, the fatherless or the widow
and do not shed innocent blood in this
place, and if you do not follow other
gods to your own harm, 7 then I will let
you live in this place, in the land I gave
your forefathers for ever and ever. 8 But
look, you are trusting in deceptive
words that are worthless.

9 " 'Will you steal and murder, commit adultery and perjury,[a] burn incense
to Baal and follow other gods you have
not known, 10 and then come and stand
before me in this house, which bears my
Name, and say, "We are safe"—safe to
do all these detestable things? 11 Has this
house, which bears my Name, become a
den of robbers to you? But I have been
watching! declares the LORD.

12 " 'Go now to the place in Shiloh
where I first made a dwelling for my
Name, and see what I did to it because
of the wickedness of my people Israel.
13 While you were doing all these things,
declares the LORD, I spoke to you again
and again, but you did not listen; I called
you, but you did not answer. 14 Therefore, what I did to Shiloh I will now do
to the house that bears my Name, the
temple you trust in, the place I gave to
you and your fathers. 15 I will thrust you
from my presence, just as I did all your
brothers, the people of Ephraim.'

16 "So do not pray for this people nor
offer any plea or petition for them; do
not plead with me, for I will not listen to
you. 17 Do you not see what they are
doing in the towns of Judah and in the
streets of Jerusalem? 18 The children
gather wood, the fathers light the fire,
and the women knead the dough and
make cakes of bread for the Queen of
Heaven. They pour out drink offerings
to other gods to provoke me to anger.
19 But am I the one they are provoking?
declares the LORD. Are they not rather
harming themselves, to their own
shame?

20 " 'Therefore this is what the Sovereign LORD says: My anger and my wrath
will be poured out on this place, on man
and beast, on the trees of the field and
on the fruit of the ground, and it will
burn and not be quenched.

---

[a] 9 Or and swear by false gods

21 " 'This is what the LORD Almighty, the God of Israel, says: Go ahead, add your burnt offerings to your other sacrifices and eat the meat yourselves! 22For when I brought your forefathers out of Egypt and spoke to them, I did not just give them commands about burnt offerings and sacrifices, 23but I gave them this command: Obey me, and I will be your God and you will be my people. Walk in all the ways I command you, that it may go well with you. 24But they did not listen or pay attention; instead, they followed the stubborn inclinations of their evil hearts. They went backward and not forward. 25From the time your forefathers left Egypt until now, day after day, again and again I sent you my servants the prophets. 26But they did not listen to me or pay attention. They were stiff-necked and did more evil than their forefathers.'

27 "When you tell them all this, they will not listen to you; when you call to them, they will not answer. 28Therefore say to them, 'This is the nation that has not obeyed the LORD its God or responded to correction. Truth has perished; it has vanished from their lips. 29Cut off your hair and throw it away; take up a lament on the barren heights, for the LORD has rejected and abandoned this generation that is under his wrath.

The Valley of Slaughter

30 " 'The people of Judah have done evil in my eyes, declares the LORD. They have set up their detestable idols in the house that bears my Name and have defiled it. 31They have built the high places of Topheth in the Valley of Ben Hinnom to burn their sons and daughters in the fire—something I did not command, nor did it enter my mind. 32So beware, the days are coming, declares the LORD, when people will no longer call it Topheth or the Valley of Ben Hinnom, but the Valley of Slaughter, for they will bury the dead in Topheth until there is no more room. 33Then the carcasses of this people will become food for the birds of the air and the beasts of the earth, and there will be no one to frighten them away. 34I will bring an end to the sounds of joy and gladness and to the voices of bride and bridegroom in the towns of Judah and the streets of Jerusalem, for the land will become desolate.

8 " 'At that time, declares the LORD, the bones of the kings and officials of Judah, the bones of the priests and prophets, and the bones of the people of Jerusalem will be removed from their graves. 2They will be exposed to the sun and the moon and all the stars of the heavens, which they have loved and served and which they have followed and consulted and worshiped. They will not be gathered up or buried, but will be like refuse lying on the ground. 3Wherever I banish them, all the survivors of this evil nation will prefer death to life, declares the LORD Almighty.'

Sin and Punishment

4 "Say to them, 'This is what the LORD says:

" 'When men fall down, do they not
      get up?
   When a man turns away, does he
      not return?
5 Why then have these people turned
      away?
   Why does Jerusalem always turn
      away?
   They cling to deceit;
      they refuse to return.
6 I have listened attentively,
      but they do not say what is right.
   No one repents of his wickedness,
      saying, "What have I done?"
   Each pursues his own course
      like a horse charging into battle.
7 Even the stork in the sky
      knows her appointed seasons,
   and the dove, the swift and the thrush
      observe the time of their migration.
   But my people do not know
      the requirements of the LORD.

8 " 'How can you say, "We are wise,
      for we have the law of the LORD,"
   when actually the lying pen of the
         scribes
      has handled it falsely?
9 The wise will be put to shame;
      they will be dismayed and trapped.
   Since they have rejected the word of
         the LORD,
      what kind of wisdom do they have?
10 Therefore I will give their wives to
         other men

and their fields to new owners.
From the least to the greatest,
    all are greedy for gain;
prophets and priests alike,
    all practice deceit.
11 They dress the wound of my people
    as though it were not serious.
"Peace, peace," they say,
    when there is no peace.
12 Are they ashamed of their loathsome
        conduct?
    No, they have no shame at all;
    they do not even know how to
        blush.
So they will fall among the fallen;
    they will be brought down when
        they are punished,
                            says the LORD.

13 " 'I will take away their harvest,
                    declares the LORD.
    There will be no grapes on the
        vine.
There will be no figs on the tree,
    and their leaves will wither.
What I have given them
    will be taken from them.*a' "

14 "Why are we sitting here?
    Gather together!
Let us flee to the fortified cities
    and perish there!
For the LORD our God has doomed us
        to perish
    and given us poisoned water to
        drink,
    because we have sinned against
        him.
15 We hoped for peace
    but no good has come,
for a time of healing
    but there was only terror.
16 The snorting of the enemy's horses
    is heard from Dan;
at the neighing of their stallions
    the whole land trembles.
They have come to devour
    the land and everything in it,
    the city and all who live there."

17 "See, I will send venomous snakes
        among you,
    vipers that cannot be charmed,
    and they will bite you,"
                    declares the LORD.

18 O my Comforter*b in sorrow,
    my heart is faint within me.
19 Listen to the cry of my people
    from a land far away:
"Is the LORD not in Zion?
    Is her King no longer there?"

"Why have they provoked me to
        anger with their images,
    with their worthless foreign
        idols?"

20 "The harvest is past,
    the summer has ended,
    and we are not saved."

21 Since my people are crushed, I am
        crushed;
    I mourn, and horror grips me.
22 Is there no balm in Gilead?
    Is there no physician there?
Why then is there no healing
    for the wound of my people?

9 1 Oh, that my head were a
        spring of water
    and my eyes a fountain of tears!
I would weep day and night
    for the slain of my people.
2 Oh, that I had in the desert
    a lodging place for travelers,
so that I might leave my people
    and go away from them;
for they are all adulterers,
    a crowd of unfaithful people.

3 "They make ready their tongue
    like a bow, to shoot lies;
it is not by truth
    that they triumph*c in the land.
They go from one sin to another;
    they do not acknowledge me,"
                    declares the LORD.
4 "Beware of your friends;
    do not trust your brothers.
For every brother is a deceiver,*d
    and every friend a slanderer.
5 Friend deceives friend,
    and no one speaks the truth.
They have taught their tongues to lie;
    they weary themselves with
        sinning.
6 You*e live in the midst of deception;
    in their deceit they refuse to
        acknowledge me,"
                    declares the LORD.

---

a 13 The meaning of the Hebrew for this sentence is uncertain.   *b 18* The meaning of the Hebrew for
this word is uncertain.   *c 3* Or *lies; / they are not valiant for truth*   *d 4* Or *a deceiving Jacob*
e 6 That is, Jeremiah (the Hebrew is singular)

7Therefore this is what the LORD Almighty says:

"See, I will refine and test them,
  for what else can I do
  because of the sin of my people?
8Their tongue is a deadly arrow;
  it speaks with deceit.
With his mouth each speaks cordially
    to his neighbor,
  but in his heart he sets a trap for
    him.
9Should I not punish them for this?"
  declares the LORD.
"Should I not avenge myself
  on such a nation as this?"

10I will weep and wail for the
  mountains

and take up a lament concerning
  the desert pastures.
They are desolate and untraveled,
  and the lowing of cattle is not
    heard.
The birds of the air have fled
  and the animals are gone.

11"I will make Jerusalem a heap of
    ruins,
  a haunt of jackals;
and I will lay waste the towns of
    Judah
  so no one can live there."

12What man is wise enough to understand this? Who has been instructed by the LORD and can explain it? Why has the land been ruined and laid waste like a desert that no one can cross?

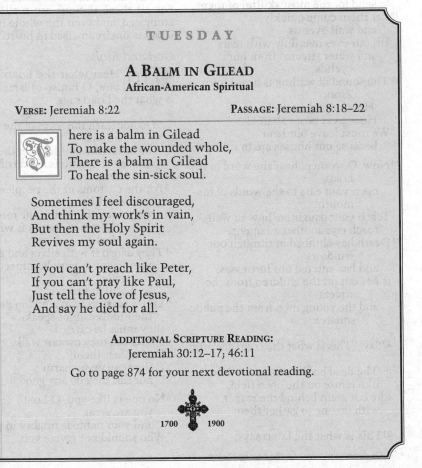

TUESDAY

A BALM IN GILEAD
African-American Spiritual

VERSE: Jeremiah 8:22   PASSAGE: Jeremiah 8:18–22

here is a balm in Gilead
To make the wounded whole,
There is a balm in Gilead
To heal the sin-sick soul.

Sometimes I feel discouraged,
And think my work's in vain,
But then the Holy Spirit
Revives my soul again.

If you can't preach like Peter,
If you can't pray like Paul,
Just tell the love of Jesus,
And say he died for all.

ADDITIONAL SCRIPTURE READING:
Jeremiah 30:12–17; 46:11

Go to page 874 for your next devotional reading.

1700   1900

13The LORD said, "It is because they have forsaken my law, which I set before them; they have not obeyed me or followed my law. 14Instead, they have followed the stubbornness of their hearts; they have followed the Baals, as their fathers taught them." 15Therefore, this is what the LORD Almighty, the God of Israel, says: "See, I will make this people eat bitter food and drink poisoned water. 16I will scatter them among nations that neither they nor their fathers have known, and I will pursue them with the sword until I have destroyed them."

17This is what the LORD Almighty says:

"Consider now! Call for the wailing
 women to come;
 send for the most skillful of them.
18Let them come quickly
 and wail over us
 till our eyes overflow with tears
 and water streams from our
 eyelids.
19The sound of wailing is heard from
 Zion:
 'How ruined we are!
 How great is our shame!
 We must leave our land
 because our houses are in ruins.' "

20Now, O women, hear the word of the
 LORD;
 open your ears to the words of his
 mouth.
 Teach your daughters how to wail;
 teach one another a lament.
21Death has climbed in through our
 windows
 and has entered our fortresses;
 it has cut off the children from the
 streets
 and the young men from the public
 squares.

22Say, "This is what the LORD declares:

" 'The dead bodies of men will lie
 like refuse on the open field,
 like cut grain behind the reaper,
 with no one to gather them.' "

23This is what the LORD says:

"Let not the wise man boast of his
 wisdom
 or the strong man boast of his
 strength
 or the rich man boast of his riches,
24but let him who boasts boast about
 this:
 that he understands and knows
 me,
 that I am the LORD, who exercises
 kindness,
 justice and righteousness on earth,
 for in these I delight,"
                      declares the LORD.

25"The days are coming," declares the LORD, "when I will punish all who are circumcised only in the flesh— 26Egypt, Judah, Edom, Ammon, Moab and all who live in the desert in distant places.*a* For all these nations are really uncircumcised, and even the whole house of Israel is uncircumcised in heart."

God and Idols

10 Hear what the LORD says to you, O house of Israel. 2This is what the LORD says:

"Do not learn the ways of the
 nations
 or be terrified by signs in the sky,
 though the nations are terrified by
 them.
3For the customs of the peoples are
 worthless;
 they cut a tree out of the forest,
 and a craftsman shapes it with his
 chisel.
4They adorn it with silver and gold;
 they fasten it with hammer and
 nails
 so it will not totter.
5Like a scarecrow in a melon patch,
 their idols cannot speak;
 they must be carried
 because they cannot walk.
 Do not fear them;
 they can do no harm
 nor can they do any good."

6No one is like you, O LORD;
 you are great,
 and your name is mighty in power.
7Who should not revere you,

a 26 Or desert and who clip the hair by their foreheads

O King of the nations?
This is your due.
Among all the wise men of the
nations
and in all their kingdoms,
there is no one like you.
⁸They are all senseless and foolish;
they are taught by worthless
wooden idols.
⁹Hammered silver is brought from
Tarshish
and gold from Uphaz.
What the craftsman and goldsmith
have made
is then dressed in blue and purple—
all made by skilled workers.
¹⁰But the LORD is the true God;
he is the living God, the eternal
King.
When he is angry, the earth trembles;
the nations cannot endure his
wrath.

¹¹"Tell them this: 'These gods, who did not make the heavens and the earth, will perish from the earth and from under the heavens.' "*ᵃ*

¹²But God made the earth by his
power;
he founded the world by his
wisdom
and stretched out the heavens by
his understanding.
¹³When he thunders, the waters in the
heavens roar;
he makes clouds rise from the ends
of the earth.
He sends lightning with the rain
and brings out the wind from his
storehouses.
¹⁴Everyone is senseless and without
knowledge;
every goldsmith is shamed by his
idols.
His images are a fraud;
they have no breath in them.
¹⁵They are worthless, the objects of
mockery;
when their judgment comes, they
will perish.
¹⁶He who is the Portion of Jacob is not
like these,
for he is the Maker of all things,

including Israel, the tribe of his
inheritance—
the LORD Almighty is his name.

Coming Destruction

¹⁷Gather up your belongings to leave
the land,
you who live under siege.
¹⁸For this is what the LORD says:
"At this time I will hurl out
those who live in this land;
I will bring distress on them
so that they may be captured."

¹⁹Woe to me because of my injury!
My wound is incurable!
Yet I said to myself,
"This is my sickness, and I must
endure it."
²⁰My tent is destroyed;
all its ropes are snapped.
My sons are gone from me and are no
more;
no one is left now to pitch my tent
or to set up my shelter.
²¹The shepherds are senseless
and do not inquire of the LORD;
so they do not prosper
and all their flock is scattered.
²²Listen! The report is coming—
a great commotion from the land
of the north!
It will make the towns of Judah
desolate,
a haunt of jackals.

Jeremiah's Prayer

²³I know, O LORD, that a man's life is
not his own;
it is not for man to direct his steps.
²⁴Correct me, LORD, but only with
justice—
not in your anger,
lest you reduce me to nothing.
²⁵Pour out your wrath on the nations
that do not acknowledge you,
on the peoples who do not call on
your name.
For they have devoured Jacob;
they have devoured him
completely
and destroyed his homeland.

ᵃ 11 The text of this verse is in Aramaic.

The Covenant Is Broken

11 This is the word that came to Jeremiah from the LORD: 2 "Listen to the terms of this covenant and tell them to the people of Judah and to those who live in Jerusalem. 3 Tell them that this is what the LORD, the God of Israel, says: 'Cursed is the man who does not obey the terms of this covenant— 4 the terms I commanded your forefathers when I brought them out of Egypt, out of the iron-smelting furnace.' I said, 'Obey me and do everything I command you, and you will be my people, and I will be your God. 5 Then I will fulfill the oath I swore to your forefathers, to give them a land flowing with milk and honey'—the land you possess today."

I answered, "Amen, LORD."

6 The LORD said to me, "Proclaim all these words in the towns of Judah and in the streets of Jerusalem: 'Listen to the terms of this covenant and follow them. 7 From the time I brought your forefathers up from Egypt until today, I warned them again and again, saying, "Obey me." 8 But they did not listen or pay attention; instead, they followed the stubbornness of their evil hearts. So I brought on them all the curses of the covenant I had commanded them to follow but that they did not keep.' "

9 Then the LORD said to me, "There is a conspiracy among the people of Judah and those who live in Jerusalem. 10 They have returned to the sins of their forefathers, who refused to listen to my words. They have followed other gods to serve them. Both the house of Israel and the house of Judah have broken the covenant I made with their forefathers. 11 Therefore this is what the LORD says: 'I will bring on them a disaster they cannot escape. Although they cry out to me, I will not listen to them. 12 The towns of Judah and the people of Jerusalem will go and cry out to the gods to whom they burn incense, but they will not help them at all when disaster strikes. 13 You have as many gods as you have towns, O Judah; and the altars you have set up to burn incense to that shameful god Baal are as many as the streets of Jerusalem.'

14 "Do not pray for this people nor offer any plea or petition for them, because I will not listen when they call to me in the time of their distress.

15 "What is my beloved doing in my temple
    as she works out her evil schemes with many?
    Can consecrated meat avert ˩your punishment˩?
When you engage in your wickedness,
    then you rejoice. *a* "

16 The LORD called you a thriving olive tree
    with fruit beautiful in form.
But with the roar of a mighty storm
    he will set it on fire,
    and its branches will be broken.

17 The LORD Almighty, who planted you, has decreed disaster for you, because the house of Israel and the house of Judah have done evil and provoked me to anger by burning incense to Baal.

Plot Against Jeremiah

18 Because the LORD revealed their plot to me, I knew it, for at that time he showed me what they were doing. 19 I had been like a gentle lamb led to the slaughter; I did not realize that they had plotted against me, saying,

"Let us destroy the tree and its fruit;
    let us cut him off from the land of the living,
    that his name be remembered no more."
20 But, O LORD Almighty, you who judge righteously
    and test the heart and mind,
let me see your vengeance upon them,
    for to you I have committed my cause.

21 "Therefore this is what the LORD says about the men of Anathoth who are seeking your life and saying, 'Do not prophesy in the name of the LORD or you will die by our hands'— 22 therefore this is what the LORD Almighty says: 'I will punish them. Their young men will die

---

a 15 Or *Could consecrated meat avert your punishment!* / *Then you would rejoice*

by the sword, their sons and daughters by famine. ²³Not even a remnant will be left to them, because I will bring disaster on the men of Anathoth in the year of their punishment.' "

Jeremiah's Complaint

12 You are always righteous, O LORD,
    when I bring a case before you.
Yet I would speak with you about
        your justice:
    Why does the way of the wicked
        prosper?
    Why do all the faithless live at
        ease?
² You have planted them, and they
        have taken root;
    they grow and bear fruit.
    You are always on their lips
    but far from their hearts.
³ Yet you know me, O LORD;
    you see me and test my thoughts
        about you.
    Drag them off like sheep to be
        butchered!
    Set them apart for the day of
        slaughter!
⁴ How long will the land lie parched*a*
    and the grass in every field be
        withered?
    Because those who live in it are
        wicked,
    the animals and birds have
        perished.
    Moreover, the people are saying,
    "He will not see what happens to
        us."

God's Answer

⁵ "If you have raced with men on foot
    and they have worn you out,
    how can you compete with horses?
    If you stumble in safe country,*b*
    how will you manage in the
        thickets by*c* the Jordan?
⁶ Your brothers, your own family—
    even they have betrayed you;
    they have raised a loud cry against
        you.
    Do not trust them,
    though they speak well of you.

⁷ "I will forsake my house,
    abandon my inheritance;

I will give the one I love
    into the hands of her enemies.
⁸ My inheritance has become to me
    like a lion in the forest.
    She roars at me;
    therefore I hate her.
⁹ Has not my inheritance become to
        me
    like a speckled bird of prey
    that other birds of prey surround
        and attack?
    Go and gather all the wild beasts;
    bring them to devour.
¹⁰ Many shepherds will ruin my
        vineyard
    and trample down my field;
    they will turn my pleasant field
    into a desolate wasteland.
¹¹ It will be made a wasteland,
    parched and desolate before me;
    the whole land will be laid waste
    because there is no one who cares.
¹² Over all the barren heights in the
        desert
    destroyers will swarm,
    for the sword of the LORD will devour
    from one end of the land to the
        other;
    no one will be safe.
¹³ They will sow wheat but reap thorns;
    they will wear themselves out but
        gain nothing.
    So bear the shame of your harvest
    because of the LORD's fierce anger."

¹⁴This is what the LORD says: "As for all my wicked neighbors who seize the inheritance I gave my people Israel, I will uproot them from their lands and I will uproot the house of Judah from among them. ¹⁵But after I uproot them, I will again have compassion and will bring each of them back to his own inheritance and his own country. ¹⁶And if they learn well the ways of my people and swear by my name, saying, 'As surely as the LORD lives'—even as they once taught my people to swear by Baal—then they will be established among my people. ¹⁷But if any nation does not listen, I will completely uproot and destroy it," declares the LORD.

a 4 Or *land mourn*   *b 5* Or *If you put your trust in a land of safety*   *c 5* Or *the flooding of*

A Linen Belt

13 This is what the LORD said to me: "Go and buy a linen belt and put it around your waist, but do not let it touch water." ²So I bought a belt, as the LORD directed, and put it around my waist.

³Then the word of the LORD came to me a second time: ⁴"Take the belt you bought and are wearing around your waist, and go now to Perath*a* and hide it there in a crevice in the rocks." ⁵So I went and hid it at Perath, as the LORD told me.

⁶Many days later the LORD said to me, "Go now to Perath and get the belt I told you to hide there." ⁷So I went to Perath and dug up the belt and took it from the place where I had hidden it, but now it was ruined and completely useless.

⁸Then the word of the LORD came to me: ⁹"This is what the LORD says: 'In the same way I will ruin the pride of Judah and the great pride of Jerusalem. ¹⁰These wicked people, who refuse to listen to my words, who follow the stubbornness of their hearts and go after other gods to serve and worship them, will be like this belt—completely useless! ¹¹For as a belt is bound around a man's waist, so I bound the whole house of Israel and the whole house of Judah to me,' declares the LORD, 'to be my people for my renown and praise and honor. But they have not listened.'

Wineskins

¹²"Say to them: 'This is what the LORD, the God of Israel, says: Every wineskin should be filled with wine.' And if they say to you, 'Don't we know that every wineskin should be filled with wine?' ¹³then tell them, 'This is what the LORD says: I am going to fill with drunkenness all who live in this land, including the kings who sit on David's throne, the priests, the prophets and all those living in Jerusalem. ¹⁴I will smash them one against the other, fathers and sons alike, declares the LORD. I will allow no pity or mercy or compassion to keep me from destroying them.' "

Threat of Captivity

¹⁵Hear and pay attention,
  do not be arrogant,
  for the LORD has spoken.
¹⁶Give glory to the LORD your God
  before he brings the darkness,
before your feet stumble
  on the darkening hills.
You hope for light,
  but he will turn it to thick
    darkness
  and change it to deep gloom.
¹⁷But if you do not listen,
  I will weep in secret
  because of your pride;
my eyes will weep bitterly,
  overflowing with tears,
  because the LORD's flock will be
    taken captive.

¹⁸Say to the king and to the queen
    mother,
  "Come down from your thrones,
for your glorious crowns
  will fall from your heads."
¹⁹The cities in the Negev will be shut
    up,
  and there will be no one to open
    them.
All Judah will be carried into exile,
  carried completely away.

²⁰Lift up your eyes and see
  those who are coming from the
    north.
Where is the flock that was entrusted
    to you,
  the sheep of which you boasted?
²¹What will you say when ⌊the LORD⌋
    sets over you
  those you cultivated as your
    special allies?
Will not pain grip you
  like that of a woman in labor?
²²And if you ask yourself,
  "Why has this happened to me?"—
it is because of your many sins
  that your skirts have been torn off
  and your body mistreated.
²³Can the Ethiopian*b* change his skin
  or the leopard its spots?
Neither can you do good
  who are accustomed to doing evil.

²⁴"I will scatter you like chaff

---

a 4 Or possibly *the Euphrates*; also in verses 5–7   *b* 23 Hebrew *Cushite* (probably a person from the upper Nile region)

driven by the desert wind.
²⁵ This is your lot,
    the portion I have decreed for you,"
           declares the LORD,
"because you have forgotten me
    and trusted in false gods.
²⁶ I will pull up your skirts over your
       face
    that your shame may be seen—
²⁷ your adulteries and lustful neighings,
    your shameless prostitution!
I have seen your detestable acts
    on the hills and in the fields.
Woe to you, O Jerusalem!
    How long will you be unclean?"

Drought, Famine, Sword

14 This is the word of the LORD to Jeremiah concerning the drought:

² "Judah mourns,
    her cities languish;
they wail for the land,
    and a cry goes up from Jerusalem.
³ The nobles send their servants for
       water;
    they go to the cisterns
    but find no water.
They return with their jars unfilled;
    dismayed and despairing,
    they cover their heads.
⁴ The ground is cracked
    because there is no rain in the land;
the farmers are dismayed
    and cover their heads.
⁵ Even the doe in the field
    deserts her newborn fawn
    because there is no grass.
⁶ Wild donkeys stand on the barren
       heights
    and pant like jackals;
their eyesight fails
    for lack of pasture."

⁷ Although our sins testify against us,
    O LORD, do something for the sake
       of your name.
For our backsliding is great;
    we have sinned against you.
⁸ O Hope of Israel,
    its Savior in times of distress,
why are you like a stranger in the
       land,

like a traveler who stays only a
       night?
⁹ Why are you like a man taken by
       surprise,
    like a warrior powerless to save?
You are among us, O LORD,
    and we bear your name;
    do not forsake us!

¹⁰ This is what the LORD says about this people:

"They greatly love to wander;
    they do not restrain their feet.
So the LORD does not accept them;
    he will now remember their
       wickedness
    and punish them for their sins."

¹¹ Then the LORD said to me, "Do not pray for the well-being of this people. ¹² Although they fast, I will not listen to their cry; though they offer burnt offerings and grain offerings, I will not accept them. Instead, I will destroy them with the sword, famine and plague."

¹³ But I said, "Ah, Sovereign LORD, the prophets keep telling them, 'You will not see the sword or suffer famine. Indeed, I will give you lasting peace in this place.' "

¹⁴ Then the LORD said to me, "The prophets are prophesying lies in my name. I have not sent them or appointed them or spoken to them. They are prophesying to you false visions, divinations, idolatries*a* and the delusions of their own minds. ¹⁵ Therefore, this is what the LORD says about the prophets who are prophesying in my name: I did not send them, yet they are saying, 'No sword or famine will touch this land.' Those same prophets will perish by sword and famine. ¹⁶ And the people they are prophesying to will be thrown out into the streets of Jerusalem because of the famine and sword. There will be no one to bury them or their wives, their sons or their daughters. I will pour out on them the calamity they deserve.

¹⁷ "Speak this word to them:

" 'Let my eyes overflow with tears
    night and day without ceasing;

---

a 14 Or *visions, worthless divinations*

for my virgin daughter—my people—
　　has suffered a grievous wound,
　　a crushing blow.
18 If I go into the country,
　　I see those slain by the sword;
　if I go into the city,
　　I see the ravages of famine.
　Both prophet and priest
　　have gone to a land they know
　　　not.' "

19 Have you rejected Judah completely?
　　Do you despise Zion?
　Why have you afflicted us
　　so that we cannot be healed?
　We hoped for peace
　　but no good has come,
　for a time of healing
　　but there is only terror.
20 O LORD, we acknowledge our
　　　wickedness
　　and the guilt of our fathers;
　we have indeed sinned against you.
21 For the sake of your name do not
　　　despise us;
　　do not dishonor your glorious
　　　throne.
　Remember your covenant with us
　　and do not break it.
22 Do any of the worthless idols of the
　　　nations bring rain?
　Do the skies themselves send
　　　down showers?
　No, it is you, O LORD our God.
　Therefore our hope is in you,
　　for you are the one who does all
　　　this.

15 Then the LORD said to me:
"Even if Moses and Samuel
were to stand before me, my heart
would not go out to this people. Send
them away from my presence! Let them
go! 2 And if they ask you, 'Where shall
we go?' tell them, 'This is what the
LORD says:

　" 'Those destined for death, to death;
　those for the sword, to the sword;
　those for starvation, to starvation;
　those for captivity, to captivity.'

3 "I will send four kinds of destroyers
against them," declares the LORD, "the
sword to kill and the dogs to drag away
and the birds of the air and the beasts of
the earth to devour and destroy. 4 I will

make them abhorrent to all the kingdoms of the earth because of what
Manasseh son of Hezekiah king of Judah
did in Jerusalem.

5 "Who will have pity on you,
　　O Jerusalem?
　Who will mourn for you?
　Who will stop to ask how you are?
6 You have rejected me," declares the
　　LORD.
　"You keep on backsliding.
　So I will lay hands on you and
　　destroy you;
　　I can no longer show compassion.
7 I will winnow them with a
　　winnowing fork
　　at the city gates of the land.
　I will bring bereavement and
　　destruction on my people,
　for they have not changed their
　　ways.
8 I will make their widows more
　　numerous
　　than the sand of the sea.
　At midday I will bring a destroyer
　　against the mothers of their young
　　men;
　suddenly I will bring down on them
　　anguish and terror.
9 The mother of seven will grow faint
　　and breathe her last.
　Her sun will set while it is still day;
　　she will be disgraced and
　　　humiliated.
　I will put the survivors to the sword
　　before their enemies,"
　　　　　　　　　declares the LORD.

10 Alas, my mother, that you gave me
　　　birth,
　　a man with whom the whole land
　　　strives and contends!
　I have neither lent nor borrowed,
　　yet everyone curses me.

11 The LORD said,

"Surely I will deliver you for a good
　　purpose;
　surely I will make your enemies
　　plead with you
　in times of disaster and times of
　　distress.

12 "Can a man break iron—
　　iron from the north—or bronze?

13 Your wealth and your treasures
  I will give as plunder, without
      charge,
  because of all your sins
    throughout your country.
14 I will enslave you to your enemies
  in^a a land you do not know,
  for my anger will kindle a fire
    that will burn against you."

15 You understand, O LORD;
  remember me and care for me.
  Avenge me on my persecutors.
  You are long-suffering—do not take
      me away;
    think of how I suffer reproach for
      your sake.
16 When your words came, I ate them;
  they were my joy and my heart's
      delight,
  for I bear your name,
    O LORD God Almighty.
17 I never sat in the company of
      revelers,
    never made merry with them;
  I sat alone because your hand was on
      me
    and you had filled me with
      indignation.
18 Why is my pain unending
  and my wound grievous and
      incurable?
  Will you be to me like a deceptive
      brook,
    like a spring that fails?

19 Therefore this is what the LORD
says:

  "If you repent, I will restore you
    that you may serve me;
  if you utter worthy, not worthless,
      words,
    you will be my spokesman.
  Let this people turn to you,
    but you must not turn to them.
20 I will make you a wall to this people,
    a fortified wall of bronze;
  they will fight against you
    but will not overcome you,
  for I am with you
    to rescue and save you,"
              declares the LORD.
21 "I will save you from the hands of
    the wicked

and redeem you from the grasp of
    the cruel."

Day of Disaster

16 Then the word of the LORD came to me: 2 "You must not marry and have sons or daughters in this place." 3 For this is what the LORD says about the sons and daughters born in this land and about the women who are their mothers and the men who are their fathers: 4 "They will die of deadly diseases. They will not be mourned or buried but will be like refuse lying on the ground. They will perish by sword and famine, and their dead bodies will become food for the birds of the air and the beasts of the earth."

5 For this is what the LORD says: "Do not enter a house where there is a funeral meal; do not go to mourn or show sympathy, because I have withdrawn my blessing, my love and my pity from this people," declares the LORD. 6 "Both high and low will die in this land. They will not be buried or mourned, and no one will cut himself or shave his head for them. 7 No one will offer food to comfort those who mourn for the dead—not even for a father or a mother—nor will anyone give them a drink to console them.

8 "And do not enter a house where there is feasting and sit down to eat and drink. 9 For this is what the LORD Almighty, the God of Israel, says: Before your eyes and in your days I will bring an end to the sounds of joy and gladness and to the voices of bride and bridegroom in this place.

10 "When you tell these people all this and they ask you, 'Why has the LORD decreed such a great disaster against us? What wrong have we done? What sin have we committed against the LORD our God?' 11 then say to them, 'It is because your fathers forsook me,' declares the LORD, 'and followed other gods and served and worshiped them. They forsook me and did not keep my law. 12 But you have behaved more wickedly than your fathers. See how each of you is following the stubbornness of his evil heart instead of obeying

a 14 Some Hebrew manuscripts, Septuagint and Syriac (see also Jer. 17:4); most Hebrew manuscripts
I will cause your enemies to bring you / into

me. ¹³So I will throw you out of this land into a land neither you nor your fathers have known, and there you will serve other gods day and night, for I will show you no favor.'

¹⁴"However, the days are coming," declares the LORD, "when men will no longer say, 'As surely as the LORD lives, who brought the Israelites up out of Egypt,' ¹⁵but they will say, 'As surely as the LORD lives, who brought the Israelites up out of the land of the north and out of all the countries where he had banished them.' For I will restore them to the land I gave their forefathers.

¹⁶"But now I will send for many fishermen," declares the LORD, "and they will catch them. After that I will send

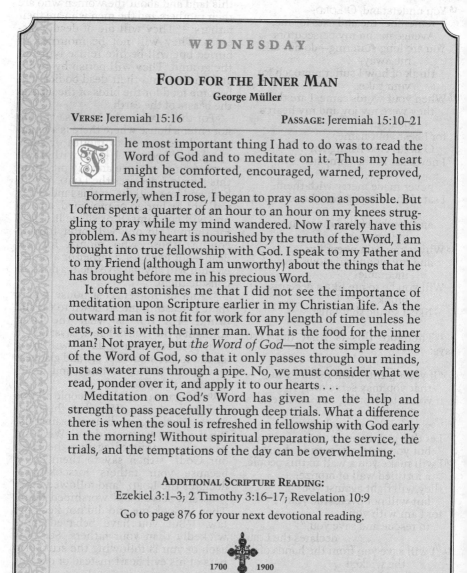

WEDNESDAY

FOOD FOR THE INNER MAN
George Müller

VERSE: Jeremiah 15:16   **PASSAGE:** Jeremiah 15:10–21

he most important thing I had to do was to read the Word of God and to meditate on it. Thus my heart might be comforted, encouraged, warned, reproved, and instructed.

Formerly, when I rose, I began to pray as soon as possible. But I often spent a quarter of an hour to an hour on my knees struggling to pray while my mind wandered. Now I rarely have this problem. As my heart is nourished by the truth of the Word, I am brought into true fellowship with God. I speak to my Father and to my Friend (although I am unworthy) about the things that he has brought before me in his precious Word.

It often astonishes me that I did not see the importance of meditation upon Scripture earlier in my Christian life. As the outward man is not fit for work for any length of time unless he eats, so it is with the inner man. What is the food for the inner man? Not prayer, but *the Word of God*—not the simple reading of the Word of God, so that it only passes through our minds, just as water runs through a pipe. No, we must consider what we read, ponder over it, and apply it to our hearts . . .

Meditation on God's Word has given me the help and strength to pass peacefully through deep trials. What a difference there is when the soul is refreshed in fellowship with God early in the morning! Without spiritual preparation, the service, the trials, and the temptations of the day can be overwhelming.

ADDITIONAL SCRIPTURE READING:
Ezekiel 3:1–3; 2 Timothy 3:16–17; Revelation 10:9

Go to page 876 for your next devotional reading.

1700   1900

for many hunters, and they will hunt them down on every mountain and hill and from the crevices of the rocks. ¹⁷My eyes are on all their ways; they are not hidden from me, nor is their sin concealed from my eyes. ¹⁸I will repay them double for their wickedness and their sin, because they have defiled my land with the lifeless forms of their vile images and have filled my inheritance with their detestable idols."

¹⁹O Lord, my strength and my fortress,
    my refuge in time of distress,
to you the nations will come
    from the ends of the earth and say,
"Our fathers possessed nothing but
        false gods,
    worthless idols that did them no
        good.
²⁰Do men make their own gods?
    Yes, but they are not gods!"

²¹"Therefore I will teach them—
    this time I will teach them
    my power and might.
Then they will know
    that my name is the Lord.

17 "Judah's sin is engraved with an iron tool,
    inscribed with a flint point,
on the tablets of their hearts
    and on the horns of their altars.
²Even their children remember
    their altars and Asherah poles*a*
beside the spreading trees
    and on the high hills.
³My mountain in the land
    and your*b* wealth and all your
        treasures
I will give away as plunder,
    together with your high places,
    because of sin throughout your
        country.
⁴Through your own fault you will lose
    the inheritance I gave you.
I will enslave you to your enemies
    in a land you do not know,
for you have kindled my anger,
    and it will burn forever."

⁵This is what the Lord says:

"Cursed is the one who trusts in man,

who depends on flesh for his
        strength
    and whose heart turns away from
        the Lord.
⁶He will be like a bush in the
        wastelands;
    he will not see prosperity when it
        comes.
He will dwell in the parched places of
        the desert,
    in a salt land where no one lives.

⁷"But blessed is the man who trusts in
        the Lord,
    whose confidence is in him.

---

⁸He will be like a tree planted by the
        water
    that sends out its roots by the
        stream.
It does not fear when heat comes;
    its leaves are always green.
It has no worries in a year of drought
    and never fails to bear fruit."

⁹The heart is deceitful above all things
    and beyond cure.
    Who can understand it?

¹⁰"I the Lord search the heart
    and examine the mind,
to reward a man according to his
        conduct,
    according to what his deeds
        deserve."

¹¹Like a partridge that hatches eggs it
        did not lay
    is the man who gains riches by
        unjust means.
When his life is half gone, they will
        desert him,
    and in the end he will prove to be a
        fool.

¹²A glorious throne, exalted from the
        beginning,
    is the place of our sanctuary.

---

a 2 That is, symbols of the goddess Asherah   *b* 2,3 Or *hills* / *³and the mountains of the land.* / *Your*

13 O LORD, the hope of Israel,
   all who forsake you will be put to
      shame.
Those who turn away from you will
   be written in the dust
because they have forsaken the
   LORD,

the spring of living water.
14 Heal me, O LORD, and I will be healed;
   save me and I will be saved,
   for you are the one I praise.
15 They keep saying to me,
   "Where is the word of the LORD?
   Let it now be fulfilled!"

THURSDAY

PERPETUAL PROSPERITY?
Charles H. Spurgeon

VERSE: Jeremiah 17:11   PASSAGE: Jeremiah 17:11–18

The path of the Christian is not always bright with sunshine; he has his seasons of darkness and of storm. True, ... religion is calculated to give a man happiness below as well as bliss above; but experience tells us that if the course of the just be "As the shining light that shineth more and more unto the perfect day," then sometimes *that* light is eclipsed (see Proverbs 4:18). At certain periods clouds cover the believer's sun, and he walks in darkness and sees no light.

There are many who have rejoiced in the presence of God for a season; they have basked in the sunshine in the earlier stages of their Christian career; they have walked along the "green pastures" by the side of the "still waters," but suddenly they find the glorious sky is clouded. Instead of the Land of Goshen, they have to tread the sandy desert: in the place of sweet waters, they find troubled streams, bitter to the taste, and they say, "Surely, if I were a child of God, this would not happen."

Oh! say not this, you who are walking in darkness ... No Christian has enjoyed perpetual prosperity; no believer can always keep his harp from the willows. Perhaps the Lord allotted you at first a smooth and unclouded path because you were weak and timid. He tempered the wind to the shorn lamb, but now that you are stronger in the spiritual life, you must enter the riper and rougher experience of God's full-grown children. We need winds and tempests to exercise our faith, to tear off the rotten bough of self-dependence, and to root us more firmly in Christ. The day of evil reveals to us the value of our glorious hope.

ADDITIONAL SCRIPTURE READING:
Psalm 41:1; Jeremiah 16:19; Nahum 1:7

Go to page 890 for your next devotional reading.

1700   1900

16I have not run away from being your
    shepherd;
  you know I have not desired the
    day of despair.
  What passes my lips is open before
    you.
17Do not be a terror to me;
  you are my refuge in the day of
    disaster.
18Let my persecutors be put to shame,
    but keep me from shame;
  let them be terrified,
    but keep me from terror.
  Bring on them the day of disaster;
    destroy them with double
      destruction.

Keeping the Sabbath Holy

19This is what the LORD said to me:
"Go and stand at the gate of the people,
through which the kings of Judah go in
and out; stand also at all the other gates
of Jerusalem. 20Say to them, 'Hear the
word of the LORD, O kings of Judah and
all people of Judah and everyone living
in Jerusalem who come through these
gates. 21This is what the LORD says: Be
careful not to carry a load on the Sabbath day or bring it through the gates of
Jerusalem. 22Do not bring a load out of
your houses or do any work on the Sabbath, but keep the Sabbath day holy, as
I commanded your forefathers. 23Yet
they did not listen or pay attention;
they were stiff-necked and would not
listen or respond to discipline. 24But if
you are careful to obey me, declares the
LORD, and bring no load through the
gates of this city on the Sabbath, but
keep the Sabbath day holy by not doing
any work on it, 25then kings who sit on
David's throne will come through the
gates of this city with their officials.
They and their officials will come riding in chariots and on horses, accompanied by the men of Judah and those living in Jerusalem, and this city will be
inhabited forever. 26People will come
from the towns of Judah and the villages around Jerusalem, from the territory of Benjamin and the western
foothills, from the hill country and the
Negev, bringing burnt offerings and
sacrifices, grain offerings, incense and
thank offerings to the house of the
LORD. 27But if you do not obey me to

keep the Sabbath day holy by not carrying any load as you come through the
gates of Jerusalem on the Sabbath day,
then I will kindle an unquenchable fire
in the gates of Jerusalem that will consume her fortresses.' "

At the Potter's House

18 This is the word that came to
Jeremiah from the LORD:
2"Go down to the potter's house, and
there I will give you my message." 3So I
went down to the potter's house, and I
saw him working at the wheel. 4But the
pot he was shaping from the clay was
marred in his hands; so the potter
formed it into another pot, shaping it as
seemed best to him.

5Then the word of the LORD came to
me: 6"O house of Israel, can I not do
with you as this potter does?" declares
the LORD. "Like clay in the hand of the
potter, so are you in my hand, O house
of Israel. 7If at any time I announce that
a nation or kingdom is to be uprooted,
torn down and destroyed, 8and if that
nation I warned repents of its evil, then I
will relent and not inflict on it the disaster I had planned. 9And if at another
time I announce that a nation or kingdom is to be built up and planted, 10and
if it does evil in my sight and does not
obey me, then I will reconsider the good
I had intended to do for it.

11"Now therefore say to the people of
Judah and those living in Jerusalem,
'This is what the LORD says: Look! I am
preparing a disaster for you and devising
a plan against you. So turn from your
evil ways, each one of you, and reform
your ways and your actions.' 12But they
will reply, 'It's no use. We will continue
with our own plans; each of us will follow the stubbornness of his evil heart.' "

13Therefore this is what the LORD says:

"Inquire among the nations:
  Who has ever heard anything like
    this?
A most horrible thing has been done
  by Virgin Israel.
14Does the snow of Lebanon
  ever vanish from its rocky slopes?
Do its cool waters from distant
  sources

ever cease to flow?*a*
15 Yet my people have forgotten me;
they burn incense to worthless
idols,
which made them stumble in their
ways
and in the ancient paths.
They made them walk in bypaths
and on roads not built up.
16 Their land will be laid waste,
an object of lasting scorn;
all who pass by will be appalled
and will shake their heads.
17 Like a wind from the east,
I will scatter them before their
enemies;
I will show them my back and not
my face
in the day of their disaster."

18 They said, "Come, let's make plans
against Jeremiah; for the teaching of the
law by the priest will not be lost, nor
will counsel from the wise, nor the word
from the prophets. So come, let's attack
him with our tongues and pay no attention to anything he says."

19 Listen to me, O LORD;
hear what my accusers are saying!
20 Should good be repaid with evil?
Yet they have dug a pit for me.
Remember that I stood before you
and spoke in their behalf
to turn your wrath away from
them.
21 So give their children over to famine;
hand them over to the power of the
sword.
Let their wives be made childless and
widows;
let their men be put to death,
their young men slain by the sword
in battle.
22 Let a cry be heard from their houses
when you suddenly bring invaders
against them,
for they have dug a pit to capture me
and have hidden snares for my feet.
23 But you know, O LORD,
all their plots to kill me.
Do not forgive their crimes
or blot out their sins from your
sight.

Let them be overthrown before you;
deal with them in the time of your
anger.

19 This is what the LORD says:
"Go and buy a clay jar from a
potter. Take along some of the elders of
the people and of the priests 2 and go
out to the Valley of Ben Hinnom, near
the entrance of the Potsherd Gate.
There proclaim the words I tell you,
3 and say, 'Hear the word of the LORD,
O kings of Judah and people of Jerusalem. This is what the LORD Almighty, the God of Israel, says: Listen!
I am going to bring a disaster on this
place that will make the ears of everyone who hears of it tingle. 4 For they
have forsaken me and made this a place
of foreign gods; they have burned sacrifices in it to gods that neither they nor
their fathers nor the kings of Judah ever
knew, and they have filled this place
with the blood of the innocent. 5 They
have built the high places of Baal to
burn their sons in the fire as offerings
to Baal—something I did not command
or mention, nor did it enter my mind.
6 So beware, the days are coming,
declares the LORD, when people will no
longer call this place Topheth or the
Valley of Ben Hinnom, but the Valley
of Slaughter.

7 " 'In this place I will ruin*b* the plans
of Judah and Jerusalem. I will make
them fall by the sword before their enemies, at the hands of those who seek
their lives, and I will give their carcasses
as food to the birds of the air and the
beasts of the earth. 8 I will devastate this
city and make it an object of scorn; all
who pass by will be appalled and will
scoff because of all its wounds. 9 I will
make them eat the flesh of their sons
and daughters, and they will eat one
another's flesh during the stress of the
siege imposed on them by the enemies
who seek their lives.'

10 "Then break the jar while those
who go with you are watching, 11 and say
to them, 'This is what the LORD
Almighty says: I will smash this nation
and this city just as this potter's jar is
smashed and cannot be repaired. They

---

a 14 The meaning of the Hebrew for this sentence is uncertain.   *b* 7 The Hebrew for *ruin* sounds like
the Hebrew for *jar* (see verses 1 and 10).

will bury the dead in Topheth until there is no more room. ¹²This is what I will do to this place and to those who live here, declares the LORD. I will make this city like Topheth. ¹³The houses in Jerusalem and those of the kings of Judah will be defiled like this place, Topheth—all the houses where they burned incense on the roofs to all the starry hosts and poured out drink offerings to other gods.' "

¹⁴Jeremiah then returned from Topheth, where the LORD had sent him to prophesy, and stood in the court of the LORD's temple and said to all the people, ¹⁵"This is what the LORD Almighty, the God of Israel, says: 'Listen! I am going to bring on this city and the villages around it every disaster I pronounced against them, because they were stiff-necked and would not listen to my words.' "

Jeremiah and Pashhur

20 When the priest Pashhur son of Immer, the chief officer in the temple of the LORD, heard Jeremiah prophesying these things, ²he had Jeremiah the prophet beaten and put in the stocks at the Upper Gate of Benjamin at the LORD's temple. ³The next day, when Pashhur released him from the stocks, Jeremiah said to him, "The LORD's name for you is not Pashhur, but Magor-Missabib.ᵃ ⁴For this is what the LORD says: 'I will make you a terror to yourself and to all your friends; with your own eyes you will see them fall by the sword of their enemies. I will hand all Judah over to the king of Babylon, who will carry them away to Babylon or put them to the sword. ⁵I will hand over to their enemies all the wealth of this city—all its products, all its valuables and all the treasures of the kings of Judah. They will take it away as plunder and carry it off to Babylon. ⁶And you, Pashhur, and all who live in your house will go into exile to Babylon. There you will die and be buried, you and all your friends to whom you have prophesied lies.' "

Jeremiah's Complaint

⁷O LORD, you deceivedᵇ me, and I was
   deceivedᵇ;
   you overpowered me and prevailed.

I am ridiculed all day long;
   everyone mocks me.
⁸Whenever I speak, I cry out
   proclaiming violence and
     destruction.
So the word of the LORD has brought
   me
   insult and reproach all day long.
⁹But if I say, "I will not mention him
   or speak any more in his name,"
his word is in my heart like a fire,
   a fire shut up in my bones.
I am weary of holding it in;
   indeed, I cannot.
¹⁰I hear many whispering,
   "Terror on every side!
   Report him! Let's report him!"
All my friends
   are waiting for me to slip, saying,
"Perhaps he will be deceived;
   then we will prevail over him
   and take our revenge on him."

¹¹But the LORD is with me like a
   mighty warrior;
so my persecutors will stumble
   and not prevail.
They will fail and be thoroughly
   disgraced;
   their dishonor will never be
     forgotten.
¹²O LORD Almighty, you who examine
   the righteous
   and probe the heart and mind,
let me see your vengeance upon
   them,
   for to you I have committed my
     cause.

¹³Sing to the LORD!
   Give praise to the LORD!
He rescues the life of the needy
   from the hands of the wicked.

¹⁴Cursed be the day I was born!
   May the day my mother bore me
     not be blessed!
¹⁵Cursed be the man who brought my
   father the news,
   who made him very glad, saying,
"A child is born to you—a son!"
¹⁶May that man be like the towns
   the LORD overthrew without pity.
May he hear wailing in the morning,
   a battle cry at noon.
¹⁷For he did not kill me in the womb,

ᵃ 3 *Magor-Missabib* means *terror on every side.*   ᵇ 7 Or *persuaded*

with my mother as my grave,
　her womb enlarged forever.
18 Why did I ever come out of the womb
　to see trouble and sorrow
　and to end my days in shame?

God Rejects Zedekiah's Request

21 The word came to Jeremiah from the LORD when King Zedekiah sent to him Pashhur son of Malkijah and the priest Zephaniah son of Maaseiah. They said: 2 "Inquire now of the LORD for us because Nebuchadnezzar[a] king of Babylon is attacking us. Perhaps the LORD will perform wonders for us as in times past so that he will withdraw from us."

3 But Jeremiah answered them, "Tell Zedekiah, 4 'This is what the LORD, the God of Israel, says: I am about to turn against you the weapons of war that are in your hands, which you are using to fight the king of Babylon and the Babylonians[b] who are outside the wall besieging you. And I will gather them inside this city. 5 I myself will fight against you with an outstretched hand and a mighty arm in anger and fury and great wrath. 6 I will strike down those who live in this city—both men and animals—and they will die of a terrible plague. 7 After that, declares the LORD, I will hand over Zedekiah king of Judah, his officials and the people in this city who survive the plague, sword and famine, to Nebuchadnezzar king of Babylon and to their enemies who seek their lives. He will put them to the sword; he will show them no mercy or pity or compassion.'

8 "Furthermore, tell the people, 'This is what the LORD says: See, I am setting before you the way of life and the way of death. 9 Whoever stays in this city will die by the sword, famine or plague. But whoever goes out and surrenders to the Babylonians who are besieging you will live; he will escape with his life. 10 I have determined to do this city harm and not good, declares the LORD. It will be given into the hands of the king of Babylon, and he will destroy it with fire.'

11 "Moreover, say to the royal house of Judah, 'Hear the word of the LORD;

12 O house of David, this is what the LORD says:

" 'Administer justice every morning;
　rescue from the hand of his
　　oppressor
the one who has been robbed,
or my wrath will break out and burn
　like fire
because of the evil you have
　done—
burn with no one to quench it.
13 I am against you, ⌐Jerusalem,⌐
you who live above this valley
　on the rocky plateau,
　　　　　declares the LORD—
you who say, "Who can come against
　us?
Who can enter our refuge?"
14 I will punish you as your deeds
　deserve,
　　　　　declares the LORD.
I will kindle a fire in your forests
　that will consume everything
　around you.' "

Judgment Against Evil Kings

22 This is what the LORD says: "Go down to the palace of the king of Judah and proclaim this message there: 2 'Hear the word of the LORD, O king of Judah, you who sit on David's throne—you, your officials and your people who come through these gates. 3 This is what the LORD says: Do what is just and right. Rescue from the hand of his oppressor the one who has been robbed. Do no wrong or violence to the alien, the fatherless or the widow, and do not shed innocent blood in this place. 4 For if you are careful to carry out these commands, then kings who sit on David's throne will come through the gates of this palace, riding in chariots and on horses, accompanied by their officials and their people. 5 But if you do not obey these commands, declares the LORD, I swear by myself that this palace will become a ruin.' "

6 For this is what the LORD says about the palace of the king of Judah:

"Though you are like Gilead to me,
　like the summit of Lebanon,

---

a 2 Hebrew *Nebuchadrezzar*, of which *Nebuchadnezzar* is a variant; here and often in Jeremiah and Ezekiel   b 4 Or *Chaldeans*; also in verse 9

I will surely make you like a desert,
  like towns not inhabited.
⁷ I will send destroyers against you,
  each man with his weapons,
and they will cut up your fine cedar
    beams
  and throw them into the fire.

⁸ "People from many nations will pass
by this city and will ask one another,
'Why has the LORD done such a thing to
this great city?' ⁹ And the answer will be:
'Because they have forsaken the covenant of the LORD their God and have
worshiped and served other gods.' "

¹⁰ Do not weep for the dead ˌkingˌ or
    mourn his loss;
  rather, weep bitterly for him who
    is exiled,
because he will never return
  nor see his native land again.

¹¹ For this is what the LORD says about
Shallumᵃ son of Josiah, who succeeded
his father as king of Judah but has gone
from this place: "He will never return.
¹²He will die in the place where they
have led him captive; he will not see
this land again."

¹³ "Woe to him who builds his palace
    by unrighteousness,
  his upper rooms by injustice,
making his countrymen work for
    nothing,
  not paying them for their labor.
¹⁴ He says, 'I will build myself a great
    palace
  with spacious upper rooms.'
So he makes large windows in it,
  panels it with cedar
  and decorates it in red.

¹⁵ "Does it make you a king
  to have more and more cedar?
Did not your father have food and
    drink?
  He did what was right and just,
  so all went well with him.
¹⁶ He defended the cause of the poor
    and needy,
  and so all went well.
Is that not what it means to know
    me?"

declares the LORD.
¹⁷ "But your eyes and your heart
  are set only on dishonest gain,
on shedding innocent blood
  and on oppression and extortion."

¹⁸ Therefore this is what the LORD says
about Jehoiakim son of Josiah king of
Judah:

"They will not mourn for him:
  'Alas, my brother! Alas, my sister!'
They will not mourn for him:
  'Alas, my master! Alas, his
    splendor!'
¹⁹ He will have the burial of a donkey—
  dragged away and thrown
  outside the gates of Jerusalem."

²⁰ "Go up to Lebanon and cry out,
  let your voice be heard in Bashan,
cry out from Abarim,
  for all your allies are crushed.
²¹ I warned you when you felt secure,
  but you said, 'I will not listen!'
This has been your way from your
    youth;
  you have not obeyed me.
²² The wind will drive all your
    shepherds away,
  and your allies will go into exile.
Then you will be ashamed and
    disgraced
  because of all your wickedness.
²³ You who live in 'Lebanon,ᵇ'
  who are nestled in cedar buildings,
how you will groan when pangs
    come upon you,
  pain like that of a woman in labor!

²⁴ "As surely as I live," declares the
LORD, "even if you, Jehoiachinᶜ son of
Jehoiakim king of Judah, were a signet
ring on my right hand, I would still pull
you off. ²⁵ I will hand you over to those
who seek your life, those you fear—to
Nebuchadnezzar king of Babylon and to
the Babylonians.ᵈ ²⁶ I will hurl you and
the mother who gave you birth into
another country, where neither of you
was born, and there you both will die.
²⁷ You will never come back to the land
you long to return to."

ᵃ 11 Also called Jehoahaz   ᵇ 23 That is, the palace in Jerusalem (see 1 Kings 7:2)   ᶜ 24 Hebrew
Coniah, a variant of Jehoiachin; also in verse 28   ᵈ 25 Or Chaldeans

²⁸Is this man Jehoiachin a despised,
   broken pot,
an object no one wants?
Why will he and his children be
   hurled out,
   cast into a land they do not know?
²⁹O land, land, land,
   hear the word of the LORD!
³⁰This is what the LORD says:
"Record this man as if childless,
   a man who will not prosper in his
      lifetime,
for none of his offspring will prosper,
   none will sit on the throne of David
   or rule anymore in Judah."

The Righteous Branch

23 "Woe to the shepherds who are destroying and scattering the sheep of my pasture!" declares the LORD. ²Therefore this is what the LORD, the God of Israel, says to the shepherds who tend my people: "Because you have scattered my flock and driven them away and have not bestowed care on them, I will bestow punishment on you for the evil you have done," declares the LORD. ³"I myself will gather the remnant of my flock out of all the countries where I have driven them and will bring them back to their pasture, where they will be fruitful and increase in number. ⁴I will place shepherds over them who will tend them, and they will no longer be afraid or terrified, nor will any be missing," declares the LORD.

⁵"The days are coming," declares the
   LORD,
"when I will raise up to David^a a
   righteous Branch,
a King who will reign wisely
   and do what is just and right in the
      land.
⁶In his days Judah will be saved
   and Israel will live in safety.
This is the name by which he will be
   called:
   The LORD Our Righteousness.

⁷"So then, the days are coming," declares the LORD, "when people will no longer say, 'As surely as the LORD lives, who brought the Israelites up out of Egypt,' ⁸but they will say, 'As surely as

the LORD lives, who brought the descendants of Israel up out of the land of the north and out of all the countries where he had banished them.' Then they will live in their own land."

Lying Prophets

⁹Concerning the prophets:

My heart is broken within me;
   all my bones tremble.
I am like a drunken man,
   like a man overcome by wine,
because of the LORD
   and his holy words.
¹⁰The land is full of adulterers;
   because of the curse^b the land lies
      parched^c
   and the pastures in the desert are
      withered.
The ʟprophetsʟ follow an evil course
   and use their power unjustly.

¹¹"Both prophet and priest are godless;
   even in my temple I find their
      wickedness,"
                  declares the LORD.
¹²"Therefore their path will become
      slippery;
   they will be banished to darkness
   and there they will fall.
I will bring disaster on them
   in the year they are punished,"
                  declares the LORD.

¹³"Among the prophets of Samaria
   I saw this repulsive thing:
They prophesied by Baal
   and led my people Israel astray.
¹⁴And among the prophets of Jerusalem
   I have seen something horrible:
They commit adultery and live a
   lie.
They strengthen the hands of
      evildoers,
   so that no one turns from his
      wickedness.
They are all like Sodom to me;
   the people of Jerusalem are like
      Gomorrah."

¹⁵Therefore, this is what the LORD Almighty says concerning the prophets:

"I will make them eat bitter food
   and drink poisoned water,

because from the prophets of
  Jerusalem
ungodliness has spread throughout
  the land."

¹⁶This is what the LORD Almighty
says:

"Do not listen to what the prophets
  are prophesying to you;
they fill you with false hopes.
They speak visions from their own
  minds,
  not from the mouth of the LORD.
¹⁷They keep saying to those who
  despise me,
  'The LORD says: You will have
  peace.'
And to all who follow the
  stubbornness of their hearts
they say, 'No harm will come to
  you.'
¹⁸But which of them has stood in the
  council of the LORD
to see or to hear his word?
Who has listened and heard his
  word?
¹⁹See, the storm of the LORD
  will burst out in wrath,
a whirlwind swirling down
  on the heads of the wicked.
²⁰The anger of the LORD will not turn
  back
  until he fully accomplishes
  the purposes of his heart.
In days to come
  you will understand it clearly.
²¹I did not send these prophets,
  yet they have run with their
  message;
I did not speak to them,
  yet they have prophesied.
²²But if they had stood in my council,
  they would have proclaimed my
  words to my people
and would have turned them from
  their evil ways
  and from their evil deeds.

²³"Am I only a God nearby,"
                  declares the LORD,
  "and not a God far away?
²⁴Can anyone hide in secret places
  so that I cannot see him?"
                  declares the LORD.

"Do not I fill heaven and earth?"
                  declares the LORD.

²⁵"I have heard what the prophets say
who prophesy lies in my name. They
say, 'I had a dream! I had a dream!'
²⁶How long will this continue in the
hearts of these lying prophets, who
prophesy the delusions of their own
minds? ²⁷They think the dreams they
tell one another will make my people
forget my name, just as their fathers forgot my name through Baal worship.
²⁸Let the prophet who has a dream tell
his dream, but let the one who has my
word speak it faithfully. For what has
straw to do with grain?" declares the
LORD. ²⁹"Is not my word like fire,"
declares the LORD, "and like a hammer
that breaks a rock in pieces?

³⁰"Therefore," declares the LORD, "I
am against the prophets who steal from
one another words supposedly from me.
³¹Yes," declares the LORD, "I am against
the prophets who wag their own
tongues and yet declare, 'The LORD
declares.' ³²Indeed, I am against those
who prophesy false dreams," declares
the LORD. "They tell them and lead my
people astray with their reckless lies,
yet I did not send or appoint them. They
do not benefit these people in the least,"
declares the LORD.

False Oracles and False Prophets

³³"When these people, or a prophet or
a priest, ask you, 'What is the oracle*a* of
the LORD?' say to them, 'What oracle?*b* I
will forsake you, declares the LORD.' ³⁴If
a prophet or a priest or anyone else
claims, 'This is the oracle of the LORD,' I
will punish that man and his household.
³⁵This is what each of you keeps on saying to his friend or relative: 'What is the
LORD's answer?' or 'What has the LORD
spoken?' ³⁶But you must not mention
'the oracle of the LORD' again, because
every man's own word becomes his oracle and so you distort the words of the
living God, the LORD Almighty, our God.
³⁷This is what you keep saying to a
prophet: 'What is the LORD's answer to
you?' or 'What has the LORD spoken?'
³⁸Although you claim, 'This is the oracle

---

a 33 Or *burden* (see Septuagint and Vulgate)   *b 33* Hebrew; Septuagint and Vulgate *'You are the*
burden. (The Hebrew for *oracle* and *burden* is the same.)

of the LORD,' this is what the LORD says: You used the words, 'This is the oracle of the LORD,' even though I told you that you must not claim, 'This is the oracle of the LORD.' ³⁹Therefore, I will surely forget you and cast you out of my presence along with the city I gave to you and your fathers. ⁴⁰I will bring upon you everlasting disgrace—everlasting shame that will not be forgotten."

Two Baskets of Figs

24 After Jehoiachin[a] son of Jehoiakim king of Judah and the officials, the craftsmen and the artisans of Judah were carried into exile from Jerusalem to Babylon by Nebuchadnezzar king of Babylon, the LORD showed me two baskets of figs placed in front of the temple of the LORD. ²One basket had very good figs, like those that ripen early; the other basket had very poor figs, so bad they could not be eaten. ³Then the LORD asked me, "What do you see, Jeremiah?"

"Figs," I answered. "The good ones are very good, but the poor ones are so bad they cannot be eaten."

⁴Then the word of the LORD came to me: ⁵"This is what the LORD, the God of Israel, says: 'Like these good figs, I regard as good the exiles from Judah, whom I sent away from this place to the land of the Babylonians.[b] ⁶My eyes will watch over them for their good, and I will bring them back to this land. I will build them up and not tear them down; I will plant them and not uproot them. ⁷I will give them a heart to know me, that I am the LORD. They will be my people, and I will be their God, for they will return to me with all their heart.

⁸" 'But like the poor figs, which are so bad they cannot be eaten,' says the LORD, 'so will I deal with Zedekiah king of Judah, his officials and the survivors from Jerusalem, whether they remain in this land or live in Egypt. ⁹I will make them abhorrent and an offense to all the kingdoms of the earth, a reproach and a byword, an object of ridicule and cursing, wherever I banish them. ¹⁰I will send the sword, famine and plague against them until they are destroyed from the land I gave to them and their fathers.' "

Seventy Years of Captivity

25 The word came to Jeremiah concerning all the people of Judah in the fourth year of Jehoiakim son of Josiah king of Judah, which was the first year of Nebuchadnezzar king of Babylon. ²So Jeremiah the prophet said to all the people of Judah and to all those living in Jerusalem: ³For twenty-three years—from the thirteenth year of Josiah son of Amon king of Judah until this very day—the word of the LORD has come to me and I have spoken to you again and again, but you have not listened.

⁴And though the LORD has sent all his servants the prophets to you again and again, you have not listened or paid any attention. ⁵They said, "Turn now, each of you, from your evil ways and your evil practices, and you can stay in the land the LORD gave to you and your fathers for ever and ever. ⁶Do not follow other gods to serve and worship them; do not provoke me to anger with what your hands have made. Then I will not harm you."

⁷"But you did not listen to me," declares the LORD, "and you have provoked me with what your hands have made, and you have brought harm to yourselves."

⁸Therefore the LORD Almighty says this: "Because you have not listened to my words, ⁹I will summon all the peoples of the north and my servant Nebuchadnezzar king of Babylon," declares the LORD, "and I will bring them against this land and its inhabitants and against all the surrounding nations. I will completely destroy[c] them and make them an object of horror and scorn, and an everlasting ruin. ¹⁰I will banish from them the sounds of joy and gladness, the voices of bride and bridegroom, the sound of millstones and the light of the lamp. ¹¹This whole country will become a desolate wasteland, and these nations will serve the king of Babylon seventy years. ¹²"But when the seventy years are fulfilled, I will punish the king of Babylon

---

a 1 Hebrew *Jeconiah,* a variant of *Jehoiachin*   *b 5* Or *Chaldeans*   *c 9* The Hebrew term refers to the irrevocable giving over of things or persons to the LORD, often by totally destroying them.

and his nation, the land of the Babylonians,^{a} for their guilt," declares the LORD, "and will make it desolate forever. ¹³I will bring upon that land all the things I have spoken against it, all that are written in this book and prophesied by Jeremiah against all the nations. ¹⁴They themselves will be enslaved by many nations and great kings; I will repay them according to their deeds and the work of their hands."

The Cup of God's Wrath

¹⁵This is what the LORD, the God of Israel, said to me: "Take from my hand this cup filled with the wine of my wrath and make all the nations to whom I send you drink it. ¹⁶When they drink it, they will stagger and go mad because of the sword I will send among them."

¹⁷So I took the cup from the LORD's hand and made all the nations to whom he sent me drink it: ¹⁸Jerusalem and the towns of Judah, its kings and officials, to make them a ruin and an object of horror and scorn and cursing, as they are today; ¹⁹Pharaoh king of Egypt, his attendants, his officials and all his people, ²⁰and all the foreign people there; all the kings of Uz; all the kings of the Philistines (those of Ashkelon, Gaza, Ekron, and the people left at Ashdod); ²¹Edom, Moab and Ammon; ²²all the kings of Tyre and Sidon; the kings of the coastlands across the sea; ²³Dedan, Tema, Buz and all who are in distant places^b; ²⁴all the kings of Arabia and all the kings of the foreign people who live in the desert; ²⁵all the kings of Zimri, Elam and Media; ²⁶and all the kings of the north, near and far, one after the other— all the kingdoms on the face of the earth. And after all of them, the king of Sheshach^c will drink it too.

²⁷"Then tell them, 'This is what the LORD Almighty, the God of Israel, says: Drink, get drunk and vomit, and fall to rise no more because of the sword I will send among you.' ²⁸But if they refuse to take the cup from your hand and drink, tell them, 'This is what the LORD Almighty says: You must drink it! ²⁹See, I am beginning to bring disaster on the city that bears my Name, and will you

indeed go unpunished? You will not go unpunished, for I am calling down a sword upon all who live on the earth, declares the LORD Almighty.'

³⁰"Now prophesy all these words against them and say to them:

" 'The LORD will roar from on high;
   he will thunder from his holy
      dwelling
   and roar mightily against his land.
He will shout like those who tread
      the grapes,
   shout against all who live on the
      earth.
³¹ The tumult will resound to the ends
      of the earth,
   for the LORD will bring charges
      against the nations;
he will bring judgment on all
      mankind
   and put the wicked to the sword,' "
                        declares the LORD.

³²This is what the LORD Almighty says:

"Look! Disaster is spreading
   from nation to nation;
a mighty storm is rising
   from the ends of the earth."

³³At that time those slain by the LORD will be everywhere—from one end of the earth to the other. They will not be mourned or gathered up or buried, but will be like refuse lying on the ground.

³⁴ Weep and wail, you shepherds;
   roll in the dust, you leaders of the
      flock.
For your time to be slaughtered has
      come;
   you will fall and be shattered like
      fine pottery.
³⁵ The shepherds will have nowhere to
      flee,
   the leaders of the flock no place to
      escape.
³⁶ Hear the cry of the shepherds,
   the wailing of the leaders of the
      flock,
   for the LORD is destroying their
      pasture.

---

^{a} 12 Or *Chaldeans* ^{b} 23 Or *who clip the hair by their foreheads* ^{c} 26 *Sheshach* is a cryptogram for Babylon.

37 The peaceful meadows will be laid
waste
　　because of the fierce anger of the
　　LORD.
38 Like a lion he will leave his lair,
　　and their land will become desolate
　　because of the sword*a* of the oppressor
　　and because of the LORD's fierce
　　anger.

Jeremiah Threatened With Death

26 Early in the reign of Jehoiakim son of Josiah king of Judah, this word came from the LORD: 2 "This is what the LORD says: Stand in the courtyard of the LORD's house and speak to all the people of the towns of Judah who come to worship in the house of the LORD. Tell them everything I command you; do not omit a word. 3 Perhaps they will listen and each will turn from his evil way. Then I will relent and not bring on them the disaster I was planning because of the evil they have done. 4 Say to them, 'This is what the LORD says: If you do not listen to me and follow my law, which I have set before you, 5 and if you do not listen to the words of my servants the prophets, whom I have sent to you again and again (though you have not listened), 6 then I will make this house like Shiloh and this city an object of cursing among all the nations of the earth.' "

7 The priests, the prophets and all the people heard Jeremiah speak these words in the house of the LORD. 8 But as soon as Jeremiah finished telling all the people everything the LORD had commanded him to say, the priests, the prophets and all the people seized him and said, "You must die! 9 Why do you prophesy in the LORD's name that this house will be like Shiloh and this city will be desolate and deserted?" And all the people crowded around Jeremiah in the house of the LORD.

10 When the officials of Judah heard about these things, they went up from the royal palace to the house of the LORD and took their places at the entrance of the New Gate of the LORD's house. 11 Then the priests and the prophets said to the officials and all the people, "This man should be sentenced to death because he has prophesied against this city. You have heard it with your own ears!"

12 Then Jeremiah said to all the officials and all the people: "The LORD sent me to prophesy against this house and this city all the things you have heard. 13 Now reform your ways and your actions and obey the LORD your God. Then the LORD will relent and not bring the disaster he has pronounced against you. 14 As for me, I am in your hands; do with me whatever you think is good and right. 15 Be assured, however, that if you put me to death, you will bring the guilt of innocent blood on yourselves and on this city and on those who live in it, for in truth the LORD has sent me to you to speak all these words in your hearing."

16 Then the officials and all the people said to the priests and the prophets, "This man should not be sentenced to death! He has spoken to us in the name of the LORD our God."

17 Some of the elders of the land stepped forward and said to the entire assembly of people, 18 "Micah of Moresheth prophesied in the days of Hezekiah king of Judah. He told all the people of Judah, 'This is what the LORD Almighty says:

　" 'Zion will be plowed like a field,
　　Jerusalem will become a heap of
　　　rubble,
　　the temple hill a mound overgrown
　　　with thickets.'*b*

19 "Did Hezekiah king of Judah or anyone else in Judah put him to death? Did not Hezekiah fear the LORD and seek his favor? And did not the LORD relent, so that he did not bring the disaster he pronounced against them? We are about to bring a terrible disaster on ourselves!"

20 (Now Uriah son of Shemaiah from Kiriath Jearim was another man who prophesied in the name of the LORD; he prophesied the same things against this city and this land as Jeremiah did. 21 When King Jehoiakim and all his officers and officials heard his words, the king sought to put him to death. But

---

a 38 Some Hebrew manuscripts and Septuagint (see also Jer. 46:16 and 50:16); most Hebrew manuscripts *anger*　　*b 18* Micah 3:12

Uriah heard of it and fled in fear to Egypt. ²²King Jehoiakim, however, sent Elnathan son of Acbor to Egypt, along with some other men. ²³They brought Uriah out of Egypt and took him to King Jehoiakim, who had him struck down with a sword and his body thrown into the burial place of the common people.)

²⁴Furthermore, Ahikam son of Shaphan supported Jeremiah, and so he was not handed over to the people to be put to death.

Judah to Serve Nebuchadnezzar

27 Early in the reign of Zedekiah[a] son of Josiah king of Judah, this word came to Jeremiah from the Lord: ²This is what the Lord said to me: "Make a yoke out of straps and crossbars and put it on your neck. ³Then send word to the kings of Edom, Moab, Ammon, Tyre and Sidon through the envoys who have come to Jerusalem to Zedekiah king of Judah. ⁴Give them a message for their masters and say, 'This is what the Lord Almighty, the God of Israel, says: "Tell this to your masters: ⁵With my great power and outstretched arm I made the earth and its people and the animals that are on it, and I give it to anyone I please. ⁶Now I will hand all your countries over to my servant Nebuchadnezzar king of Babylon; I will make even the wild animals subject to him. ⁷All nations will serve him and his son and his grandson until the time for his land comes; then many nations and great kings will subjugate him.

⁸" ' "If, however, any nation or kingdom will not serve Nebuchadnezzar king of Babylon or bow its neck under his yoke, I will punish that nation with the sword, famine and plague, declares the Lord, until I destroy it by his hand. ⁹So do not listen to your prophets, your diviners, your interpreters of dreams, your mediums or your sorcerers who tell you, 'You will not serve the king of Babylon.' ¹⁰They prophesy lies to you that will only serve to remove you far from your lands; I will banish you and you will perish. ¹¹But if any nation will bow its neck under the yoke of the king of Babylon and serve him, I will let that nation remain in its own land to till it and to live there, declares the Lord." ' "

¹²I gave the same message to Zedekiah king of Judah. I said, "Bow your neck under the yoke of the king of Babylon; serve him and his people, and you will live. ¹³Why will you and your people die by the sword, famine and plague with which the Lord has threatened any nation that will not serve the king of Babylon? ¹⁴Do not listen to the words of the prophets who say to you, 'You will not serve the king of Babylon,' for they are prophesying lies to you. ¹⁵'I have not sent them,' declares the Lord. 'They are prophesying lies in my name. Therefore, I will banish you and you will perish, both you and the prophets who prophesy to you.' "

¹⁶Then I said to the priests and all these people, "This is what the Lord says: Do not listen to the prophets who say, 'Very soon now the articles from the Lord's house will be brought back from Babylon.' They are prophesying lies to you. ¹⁷Do not listen to them. Serve the king of Babylon, and you will live. Why should this city become a ruin? ¹⁸If they are prophets and have the word of the Lord, let them plead with the Lord Almighty that the furnishings remaining in the house of the Lord and in the palace of the king of Judah and in Jerusalem not be taken to Babylon. ¹⁹For this is what the Lord Almighty says about the pillars, the Sea, the movable stands and the other furnishings that are left in this city, ²⁰which Nebuchadnezzar king of Babylon did not take away when he carried Jehoiachin[b] son of Jehoiakim king of Judah into exile from Jerusalem to Babylon, along with all the nobles of Judah and Jerusalem— ²¹yes, this is what the Lord Almighty, the God of Israel, says about the things that are left in the house of the Lord and in the palace of the king of Judah and in Jerusalem: ²²'They will be taken to Babylon and there they will remain until the day I come for them,' declares the Lord. 'Then I will bring them back and restore them to this place.' "

---

[a] 1 A few Hebrew manuscripts and Syriac (see also Jer. 27:3, 12 and 28:1); most Hebrew manuscripts *Jehoiakim* (Most Septuagint manuscripts do not have this verse.)   [b] 20 Hebrew *Jeconiah,* a variant of *Jehoiachin*

The False Prophet Hananiah

28 In the fifth month of that same year, the fourth year, early in the reign of Zedekiah king of Judah, the prophet Hananiah son of Azzur, who was from Gibeon, said to me in the house of the LORD in the presence of the priests and all the people: 2"This is what the LORD Almighty, the God of Israel, says: 'I will break the yoke of the king of Babylon. 3Within two years I will bring back to this place all the articles of the LORD's house that Nebuchadnezzar king of Babylon removed from here and took to Babylon. 4I will also bring back to this place Jehoiachin*a* son of Jehoiakim king of Judah and all the other exiles from Judah who went to Babylon,' declares the LORD, 'for I will break the yoke of the king of Babylon.'"

5Then the prophet Jeremiah replied to the prophet Hananiah before the priests and all the people who were standing in the house of the LORD. 6He said, "Amen! May the LORD do so! May the LORD fulfill the words you have prophesied by bringing the articles of the LORD's house and all the exiles back to this place from Babylon. 7Nevertheless, listen to what I have to say in your hearing and in the hearing of all the people: 8From early times the prophets who preceded you and me have prophesied war, disaster and plague against many countries and great kingdoms. 9But the prophet who prophesies peace will be recognized as one truly sent by the LORD only if his prediction comes true."

10Then the prophet Hananiah took the yoke off the neck of the prophet Jeremiah and broke it, 11and he said before all the people, "This is what the LORD says: 'In the same way will I break the yoke of Nebuchadnezzar king of Babylon off the neck of all the nations within two years.'" At this, the prophet Jeremiah went on his way.

12Shortly after the prophet Hananiah had broken the yoke off the neck of the prophet Jeremiah, the word of the LORD came to Jeremiah: 13"Go and tell Hananiah, 'This is what the LORD says: You have broken a wooden yoke, but in its place you will get a yoke of iron. 14This is what the LORD Almighty, the God of Israel, says: I will put an iron yoke on the necks of all these nations to make them serve Nebuchadnezzar king of Babylon, and they will serve him. I will even give him control over the wild animals.'"

15Then the prophet Jeremiah said to Hananiah the prophet, "Listen, Hananiah! The LORD has not sent you, yet you have persuaded this nation to trust in lies. 16Therefore, this is what the LORD says: 'I am about to remove you from the face of the earth. This very year you are going to die, because you have preached rebellion against the LORD.'"

17In the seventh month of that same year, Hananiah the prophet died.

A Letter to the Exiles

29 This is the text of the letter that the prophet Jeremiah sent from Jerusalem to the surviving elders among the exiles and to the priests, the prophets and all the other people Nebuchadnezzar had carried into exile from Jerusalem to Babylon. 2(This was after King Jehoiachin*a* and the queen mother, the court officials and the leaders of Judah and Jerusalem, the craftsmen and the artisans had gone into exile from Jerusalem.) 3He entrusted the letter to Elasah son of Shaphan and to Gemariah son of Hilkiah, whom Zedekiah king of Judah sent to King Nebuchadnezzar in Babylon. It said:

4This is what the LORD Almighty, the God of Israel, says to all those I carried into exile from Jerusalem to Babylon: 5"Build houses and settle down; plant gardens and eat what they produce. 6Marry and have sons and daughters; find wives for your sons and give your daughters in marriage, so that they too may have sons and daughters. Increase in number there; do not decrease. 7Also, seek the peace and prosperity of the city to which I have carried you into exile. Pray to the LORD for it, because if it prospers, you too will prosper." 8Yes, this is what the LORD Almighty, the God of Israel, says: "Do not let the prophets and diviners among you deceive you. Do not

a 4,2 Hebrew Jeconiah, a variant of Jehoiachin

listen to the dreams you encourage them to have. ⁹They are prophesying lies to you in my name. I have not sent them," declares the LORD.

¹⁰This is what the LORD says: "When seventy years are completed for Babylon, I will come to you and fulfill my gracious promise to bring you back to this place. ¹¹For I know the plans I have for you," declares the LORD, "plans to prosper you and not to harm you, plans to give you hope and a future. ¹²Then you will call upon me and come and pray to me, and I will listen to you. ¹³You will seek me and find me when you seek me with all your heart. ¹⁴I will be found by you," declares the LORD, "and will bring you back from captivity.ᵃ I will gather you from all the nations and places where I have banished you," declares the LORD, "and will bring you back to the place from which I carried you into exile."

¹⁵You may say, "The LORD has raised up prophets for us in Babylon," ¹⁶but this is what the LORD says about the king who sits on David's throne and all the people who remain in this city, your countrymen who did not go with you into exile— ¹⁷yes, this is what the LORD Almighty says: "I will send the sword, famine and plague against them and I will make them like poor figs that are so bad they cannot be eaten. ¹⁸I will pursue them with the sword, famine and plague and will make them abhorrent to all the kingdoms of the earth and an object of cursing and horror, of scorn and reproach, among all the nations where I drive them. ¹⁹For they have not listened to my words," declares the LORD, "words that I sent to them again and again by my servants the prophets. And you exiles have not listened either," declares the LORD.

²⁰Therefore, hear the word of the LORD, all you exiles whom I have sent away from Jerusalem to Babylon. ²¹This is what the LORD Almighty, the God of Israel, says

about Ahab son of Kolaiah and Zedekiah son of Maaseiah, who are prophesying lies to you in my name: "I will hand them over to Nebuchadnezzar king of Babylon, and he will put them to death before your very eyes. ²²Because of them, all the exiles from Judah who are in Babylon will use this curse: 'The LORD treat you like Zedekiah and Ahab, whom the king of Babylon burned in the fire.' ²³For they have done outrageous things in Israel; they have committed adultery with their neighbors' wives and in my name have spoken lies, which I did not tell them to do. I know it and am a witness to it," declares the LORD.

Message to Shemaiah

²⁴Tell Shemaiah the Nehelamite, ²⁵"This is what the LORD Almighty, the God of Israel, says: You sent letters in your own name to all the people in Jerusalem, to Zephaniah son of Maaseiah the priest, and to all the other priests. You said to Zephaniah, ²⁶'The LORD has appointed you priest in place of Jehoiada to be in charge of the house of the LORD; you should put any madman who acts like a prophet into the stocks and neckirons. ²⁷So why have you not reprimanded Jeremiah from Anathoth, who poses as a prophet among you? ²⁸He has sent this message to us in Babylon: It will be a long time. Therefore build houses and settle down; plant gardens and eat what they produce.' "

²⁹Zephaniah the priest, however, read the letter to Jeremiah the prophet. ³⁰Then the word of the LORD came to Jeremiah: ³¹"Send this message to all the exiles: 'This is what the LORD says about Shemaiah the Nehelamite: Because Shemaiah has prophesied to you, even though I did not send him, and has led you to believe a lie, ³²this is what the LORD says: I will surely punish Shemaiah the Nehelamite and his descendants. He will have no one left among this people, nor will he see the good things I will do for my people, declares the LORD, because he has preached rebellion against me.' "

ᵃ 14 Or will restore your fortunes

YOU WILL SEEK ME AND FIND ME
Mozarabic Sacramentary

VERSE: Jeremiah 29:11–12   **PASSAGE:** Jeremiah 29:10–14

For Hope

ord, when we think only of our own wants and desires, we are impatient to have them satisfied, yet in our hearts we know that such satisfaction will crumble to dust. Give us that spirit of hope which can enable us to want what you want, and to wait patiently on your time, in the knowledge that in you alone comes true and lasting pleasure.

For Love

O Lord, you have brought all your faithful people into a single, universal family, stretching across heaven and earth. Bind us together with a spiritual love which is stronger than any human love, that in serving one another we may neither count the cost nor seek reward, but think only of the common good.

For Peace

O God, through the death of your Son you reconciled us one to another, drawing us together in the bond of peace. In times of trouble and adversity, may your peace sustain us, calming our fretful and anxious hearts, and saving us from all hateful and violent activities.

For Purity

Make us, O Lord, flourish like pure, white lilies in the courts of your house, giving forth the sweet fragrance of your love to all who pass.

For Mercy

O God, in revealing to us the perfect spiritual beauty of your Son, you have shown the grotesque ugliness of our depravity, and so filled us with remorse. We beg you, Lord, to reach down to us in your mercy, re-creating us in the image of your Son, that we may be fit to live with him in your heavenly kingdom.

ADDITIONAL SCRIPTURE READING:
Isaiah 55:6–7; Amos 5:4–6; Luke 11:9–10

Go to page 892 for your next devotional reading.

Restoration of Israel

30 This is the word that came to Jeremiah from the LORD: 2"This is what the LORD, the God of Israel, says: 'Write in a book all the words I have spoken to you. 3The days are coming,' declares the LORD, 'when I will bring my people Israel and Judah back from captivity[a] and restore them to the land I gave their forefathers to possess,' says the LORD.'"

4These are the words the LORD spoke concerning Israel and Judah: 5"This is what the LORD says:

" 'Cries of fear are heard—
   terror, not peace.
6 Ask and see:
   Can a man bear children?
Then why do I see every strong man
   with his hands on his stomach like
      a woman in labor,
   every face turned deathly pale?
7 How awful that day will be!
   None will be like it.
It will be a time of trouble for Jacob,
   but he will be saved out of it.

8 " 'In that day,' declares the LORD
      Almighty,
   'I will break the yoke off their
      necks
and will tear off their bonds;
   no longer will foreigners enslave
      them.
9 Instead, they will serve the LORD
      their God
   and David their king,
   whom I will raise up for them.

10 " 'So do not fear, O Jacob my servant;
   do not be dismayed, O Israel,'
         declares the LORD.
'I will surely save you out of a distant
      place,
   your descendants from the land of
      their exile.
Jacob will again have peace and
      security,
   and no one will make him afraid.
11 I am with you and will save you,'
   declares the LORD.
'Though I completely destroy all the
      nations
   among which I scatter you,
   I will not completely destroy you.

I will discipline you but only with
      justice;
   I will not let you go entirely
      unpunished.'

12 "This is what the LORD says:

" 'Your wound is incurable,
   your injury beyond healing.
13 There is no one to plead your cause,
   no remedy for your sore,
   no healing for you.
14 All your allies have forgotten you;
   they care nothing for you.
I have struck you as an enemy would
   and punished you as would the
      cruel,
because your guilt is so great
   and your sins so many.
15 Why do you cry out over your
      wound,
   your pain that has no cure?
Because of your great guilt and many
      sins
   I have done these things to you.

16 " 'But all who devour you will be
      devoured;
   all your enemies will go into exile.
Those who plunder you will be
      plundered;
   all who make spoil of you I will
      despoil.
17 But I will restore you to health
   and heal your wounds,'
         declares the LORD,
'because you are called an outcast,
   Zion for whom no one cares.'

18 "This is what the LORD says:

" 'I will restore the fortunes of Jacob's
      tents
   and have compassion on his
      dwellings;
the city will be rebuilt on her ruins,
   and the palace will stand in its
      proper place.
19 From them will come songs of
      thanksgiving
   and the sound of rejoicing.
I will add to their numbers,
   and they will not be decreased;
I will bring them honor,
   and they will not be disdained.

---

a 3 Or will restore the fortunes of my people Israel and Judah

WEEKEND

A REST PREPARED FOR ME
John Wesley

VERSE: Psalm 62:1   **PASSAGE:** Psalm 62:1–2

ord, I believe a rest remains,
　　To all thy people known;
A rest where pure enjoyment reigns
　　And thou art loved alone,

A rest where all our soul's desire
　　Is fix'd on things above;
Where doubt and pain and fear expire,
　　Cast out by perfect love . . .

Come, O my Saviour, come away!
　　Into my soul descend!
No longer from thy creature stay,
　　My author and my end!

The bliss thou hast for me prepared,
　　No longer be delay'd;
Come, my exceeding great reward,
　　For whom I first was made.

Come, Father, Son, and Holy Ghost,
　　And seal me thine abode!
Let all I am in thee be lost:
　　Let all be lost in God!

ADDITIONAL SCRIPTURE READING:
Isaiah 43:1–3; Lamentations 3:22–23

Go to page 894 for your next devotional reading.

1700　　1900

²⁰ Their children will be as in days of
        old,
    and their community will be
        established before me;
    I will punish all who oppress them.
²¹ Their leader will be one of their own;
    their ruler will arise from among
        them.
  I will bring him near and he will
        come close to me,
    for who is he who will devote
        himself
    to be close to me?'
                          declares the LORD.
²² " 'So you will be my people,
    and I will be your God.' "

²³ See, the storm of the LORD
    will burst out in wrath,
  a driving wind swirling down
    on the heads of the wicked.
²⁴ The fierce anger of the LORD will not
        turn back
    until he fully accomplishes
    the purposes of his heart.
  In days to come
    you will understand this.

31 "At that time," declares the
    LORD, "I will be the God of all
the clans of Israel, and they will be my
people."
² This is what the LORD says:

  "The people who survive the sword
    will find favor in the desert;
    I will come to give rest to Israel."

³ The LORD appeared to us in the past,^a
saying:

  "I have loved you with an everlasting
        love;
    I have drawn you with loving-
        kindness.
⁴ I will build you up again
    and you will be rebuilt, O Virgin
        Israel.
  Again you will take up your
        tambourines
    and go out to dance with the joyful.
⁵ Again you will plant vineyards
    on the hills of Samaria;
  the farmers will plant them
    and enjoy their fruit.

⁶ There will be a day when watchmen
        cry out
    on the hills of Ephraim,
  'Come, let us go up to Zion,
    to the LORD our God.' "

⁷ This is what the LORD says:

  "Sing with joy for Jacob;
    shout for the foremost of the
        nations.
  Make your praises heard, and say,
    'O LORD, save your people,
    the remnant of Israel.'
⁸ See, I will bring them from the land
        of the north
    and gather them from the ends of
        the earth.
  Among them will be the blind and
        the lame,
    expectant mothers and women in
        labor;
    a great throng will return.
⁹ They will come with weeping;
    they will pray as I bring them back.
  I will lead them beside streams of
        water
    on a level path where they will not
        stumble,
  because I am Israel's father,
    and Ephraim is my firstborn son.

¹⁰ "Hear the word of the LORD,
        O nations;
    proclaim it in distant coastlands:
  'He who scattered Israel will gather
        them
    and will watch over his flock like a
        shepherd.'
¹¹ For the LORD will ransom Jacob
    and redeem them from the hand of
        those stronger than they.
¹² They will come and shout for joy on
        the heights of Zion;
    they will rejoice in the bounty of
        the LORD—
  the grain, the new wine and the oil,
    the young of the flocks and herds.
  They will be like a well-watered
        garden,
    and they will sorrow no more.
¹³ Then maidens will dance and be glad,
    young men and old as well.
  I will turn their mourning into
        gladness;

^a 3 Or LORD has appeared to us from afar

I will give them comfort and joy
    instead of sorrow.
¹⁴I will satisfy the priests with
        abundance,
    and my people will be filled with
        my bounty,"
                declares the LORD.

¹⁵This is what the LORD says:

"A voice is heard in Ramah,
    mourning and great weeping,
Rachel weeping for her children
    and refusing to be comforted,
    because her children are no more."

MONDAY

A PERSONAL PRAYER FOR LOVINGKINDNESS
John Baillie

VERSE: Jeremiah 31:3   **PASSAGE:** Jeremiah 31:3–4

 God, immortal, eternal, invisible, I remember with gladness and thanksgiving all that thou hast been to this world of men:

Companion of the brave:
Upholder of the loyal:
Light of the wanderer:
Joy of the pilgrim:
Guide of the pioneer:
Helper of laboring men:
Refuge of the broken-hearted:
Deliverer of the oppressed:
Succor of the tempted:
Strength of the victorious:
Ruler of rulers:
Friend of the poor:
Rescuer of the perishing:
Hope of the dying.

Give me faith now to believe that thou canst be all in all to me, according to my need, if only I renounce all proud self-dependence and put my trust in thee . . .

Show thy lovingkindness tonight, O Lord, to all who stand in need of thy help. Be with the weak to make them strong and with the strong to make them gentle. Cheer the lonely with thy company and the distracted with thy solitude. Prosper thy church in the fulfillment of her mighty task, and grant thy blessing to all who have toiled today in Christ's name. Amen.

ADDITIONAL SCRIPTURE READING:
Hosea 11:4; 1 Peter 1:3

Go to page 927 for your next devotional reading.

1900   Present

16This is what the LORD says:

"Restrain your voice from weeping
    and your eyes from tears,
for your work will be rewarded,"
                    declares the LORD.
"They will return from the land of
    the enemy.
17So there is hope for your future,"
                    declares the LORD.
"Your children will return to their
    own land.

18"I have surely heard Ephraim's
    moaning:
'You disciplined me like an unruly
    calf,
    and I have been disciplined.
Restore me, and I will return,
    because you are the LORD my God.
19After I strayed,
    I repented;
after I came to understand,
    I beat my breast.
I was ashamed and humiliated
    because I bore the disgrace of my
        youth.'
20Is not Ephraim my dear son,
    the child in whom I delight?
Though I often speak against him,
    I still remember him.
Therefore my heart yearns for him;
    I have great compassion for him,"
                    declares the LORD.

21"Set up road signs;
    put up guideposts.
Take note of the highway,
    the road that you take.
Return, O Virgin Israel,
    return to your towns.
22How long will you wander,
    O unfaithful daughter?
The LORD will create a new thing on
    earth—
    a woman will surround a man."

23This is what the LORD Almighty, the God of Israel, says: "When I bring them back from captivity,b the people in the land of Judah and in its towns will once again use these words: 'The LORD bless you, O righteous dwelling, O sacred mountain.' 24People will live together in Judah and all its towns—farmers and those who move about with their flocks. 25I will refresh the weary and satisfy the faint."

26At this I awoke and looked around. My sleep had been pleasant to me.

27"The days are coming," declares the LORD, "when I will plant the house of Israel and the house of Judah with the offspring of men and of animals. 28Just as I watched over them to uproot and tear down, and to overthrow, destroy and bring disaster, so I will watch over them to build and to plant," declares the LORD. 29"In those days people will no longer say,

'The fathers have eaten sour grapes,
    and the children's teeth are set on
        edge.'

30Instead, everyone will die for his own sin; whoever eats sour grapes—his own teeth will be set on edge.

31"The time is coming," declares the
        LORD,
    "when I will make a new
        covenant
with the house of Israel
    and with the house of Judah.
32It will not be like the covenant
    I made with their forefathers
when I took them by the hand
    to lead them out of Egypt,
because they broke my covenant,
    though I was a husband toc
    them,d "
                    declares the LORD.
33"This is the covenant I will make
    with the house of Israel
    after that time," declares the LORD.
"I will put my law in their minds
    and write it on their hearts.
I will be their God,
    and they will be my people.
34No longer will a man teach his
        neighbor,
    or a man his brother, saying, 'Know
        the LORD,'
because they will all know me,
    from the least of them to the
        greatest,"
                    declares the LORD.

"For I will forgive their wickedness
and will remember their sins no
more."

35This is what the LORD says,

he who appoints the sun
to shine by day,
who decrees the moon and stars
to shine by night,
who stirs up the sea
so that its waves roar—
the LORD Almighty is his name:
36"Only if these decrees vanish from
my sight,"
declares the LORD,
"will the descendants of Israel ever
cease
to be a nation before me."

37This is what the LORD says:

"Only if the heavens above can be
measured
and the foundations of the earth
below be searched out
will I reject all the descendants of
Israel
because of all they have done,"
declares the LORD.

38"The days are coming," declares the
LORD, "when this city will be rebuilt for
me from the Tower of Hananel to the
Corner Gate. 39The measuring line will
stretch from there straight to the hill of
Gareb and then turn to Goah. 40The
whole valley where dead bodies and
ashes are thrown, and all the terraces
out to the Kidron Valley on the east as
far as the corner of the Horse Gate, will
be holy to the LORD. The city will never
again be uprooted or demolished."

Jeremiah Buys a Field

32 This is the word that came to
Jeremiah from the LORD in
the tenth year of Zedekiah king of
Judah, which was the eighteenth year of
Nebuchadnezzar. 2The army of the king
of Babylon was then besieging Jerusalem, and Jeremiah the prophet was
confined in the courtyard of the guard in
the royal palace of Judah.

3Now Zedekiah king of Judah had

imprisoned him there, saying, "Why do
you prophesy as you do? You say, 'This is
what the LORD says: I am about to hand
this city over to the king of Babylon, and
he will capture it. 4Zedekiah king of
Judah will not escape out of the hands of
the Babylonians*a* but will certainly be
handed over to the king of Babylon, and
will speak with him face to face and see
him with his own eyes. 5He will take
Zedekiah to Babylon, where he will
remain until I deal with him, declares
the LORD. If you fight against the Babylonians, you will not succeed.' "

6Jeremiah said, "The word of the
LORD came to me: 7Hanamel son of
Shallum your uncle is going to come to
you and say, 'Buy my field at Anathoth,
because as nearest relative it is your
right and duty to buy it.'

8"Then, just as the LORD had said, my
cousin Hanamel came to me in the
courtyard of the guard and said, 'Buy my
field at Anathoth in the territory of Benjamin. Since it is your right to redeem it
and possess it, buy it for yourself.'

"I knew that this was the word of the
LORD; 9so I bought the field at Anathoth
from my cousin Hanamel and weighed
out for him seventeen shekels*b* of silver.
10I signed and sealed the deed, had it
witnessed, and weighed out the silver on
the scales. 11I took the deed of purchase—the sealed copy containing the
terms and conditions, as well as the
unsealed copy— 12and I gave this deed
to Baruch son of Neriah, the son of Mahseiah, in the presence of my cousin Hanamel and of the witnesses who had
signed the deed and of all the Jews sitting in the courtyard of the guard.

13"In their presence I gave Baruch
these instructions: 14'This is what the
LORD Almighty, the God of Israel, says:
Take these documents, both the sealed
and unsealed copies of the deed of purchase, and put them in a clay jar so they
will last a long time. 15For this is what
the LORD Almighty, the God of Israel,
says: Houses, fields and vineyards will
again be bought in this land.'

16"After I had given the deed of purchase to Baruch son of Neriah, I prayed
to the LORD:

a 4 Or *Chaldeans;* also in verses 5, 24, 25, 28, 29 and 43   *b 9* That is, about 7 ounces (about 200 grams)

17 "Ah, Sovereign LORD, you have made the heavens and the earth by your great power and outstretched arm. Nothing is too hard for you. 18 You show love to thousands but bring the punishment for the fathers' sins into the laps of their children after them. O great and powerful God, whose name is the LORD Almighty, 19 great are your purposes and mighty are your deeds. Your eyes are open to all the ways of men; you reward everyone according to his conduct and as his deeds deserve. 20 You performed miraculous signs and wonders in Egypt and have continued them to this day, both in Israel and among all mankind, and have gained the renown that is still yours. 21 You brought your people Israel out of Egypt with signs and wonders, by a mighty hand and an outstretched arm and with great terror. 22 You gave them this land you had sworn to give their forefathers, a land flowing with milk and honey. 23 They came in and took possession of it, but they did not obey you or follow your law; they did not do what you commanded them to do. So you brought all this disaster upon them.

24 "See how the siege ramps are built up to take the city. Because of the sword, famine and plague, the city will be handed over to the Babylonians who are attacking it. What you said has happened, as you now see. 25 And though the city will be handed over to the Babylonians, you, O Sovereign LORD, say to me, 'Buy the field with silver and have the transaction witnessed.' "

26 Then the word of the LORD came to Jeremiah: 27 "I am the LORD, the God of all mankind. Is anything too hard for me? 28 Therefore, this is what the LORD says: I am about to hand this city over to the Babylonians and to Nebuchadnezzar king of Babylon, who will capture it. 29 The Babylonians who are attacking this city will come in and set it on fire; they will burn it down, along with the houses where the people provoked me to anger by burning incense on the roofs to Baal and by pouring out drink offerings to other gods.

30 "The people of Israel and Judah have done nothing but evil in my sight from their youth; indeed, the people of Israel have done nothing but provoke me with what their hands have made, declares the LORD. 31 From the day it was built until now, this city has so aroused my anger and wrath that I must remove it from my sight. 32 The people of Israel and Judah have provoked me by all the evil they have done—they, their kings and officials, their priests and prophets, the men of Judah and the people of Jerusalem. 33 They turned their backs to me and not their faces; though I taught them again and again, they would not listen or respond to discipline. 34 They set up their abominable idols in the house that bears my Name and defiled it. 35 They built high places for Baal in the Valley of Ben Hinnom to sacrifice their sons and daughters[a] to Molech, though I never commanded, nor did it enter my mind, that they should do such a detestable thing and so make Judah sin.

36 "You are saying about this city, 'By the sword, famine and plague it will be handed over to the king of Babylon'; but this is what the LORD, the God of Israel, says: 37 I will surely gather them from all the lands where I banish them in my furious anger and great wrath; I will bring them back to this place and let them live in safety. 38 They will be my people, and I will be their God. 39 I will give them singleness of heart and action, so that they will always fear me for their own good and the good of their children after them. 40 I will make an everlasting covenant with them: I will never stop doing good to them, and I will inspire them to fear me, so that they will never turn away from me. 41 I will rejoice in doing them good and will assuredly plant them in this land with all my heart and soul.

42 "This is what the LORD says: As I have brought all this great calamity on this people, so I will give them all the prosperity I have promised them. 43 Once more fields will be bought in this land of which you say, 'It is a desolate waste, without men or animals, for

---

a 35 Or to make their sons and daughters pass through the fire

it has been handed over to the Babylonians.' **44**Fields will be bought for silver, and deeds will be signed, sealed and witnessed in the territory of Benjamin, in the villages around Jerusalem, in the towns of Judah and in the towns of the hill country, of the western foothills and of the Negev, because I will restore their fortunes,*a* declares the LORD."

Promise of Restoration

33 While Jeremiah was still confined in the courtyard of the guard, the word of the LORD came to him a second time: **2**"This is what the LORD says, he who made the earth, the LORD who formed it and established it— the LORD is his name: **3**'Call to me and I will answer you and tell you great and unsearchable things you do not know.' **4**For this is what the LORD, the God of Israel, says about the houses in this city and the royal palaces of Judah that have been torn down to be used against the siege ramps and the sword **5**in the fight with the Babylonians*b*: 'They will be filled with the dead bodies of the men I will slay in my anger and wrath. I will hide my face from this city because of all its wickedness.

6" 'Nevertheless, I will bring health and healing to it; I will heal my people and will let them enjoy abundant peace and security. **7**I will bring Judah and Israel back from captivity*c* and will rebuild them as they were before. **8**I will cleanse them from all the sin they have committed against me and will forgive all their sins of rebellion against me. **9**Then this city will bring me renown, joy, praise and honor before all nations on earth that hear of all the good things I do for it; and they will be in awe and will tremble at the abundant prosperity and peace I provide for it.'

10"This is what the LORD says: 'You say about this place, "It is a desolate waste, without men or animals." Yet in the towns of Judah and the streets of Jerusalem that are deserted, inhabited by neither men nor animals, there will be heard once more **11**the sounds of joy and gladness, the voices of bride and bridegroom, and the voices of those who

bring thank offerings to the house of the LORD, saying,

"Give thanks to the LORD Almighty,
 for the LORD is good;
 his love endures forever."

For I will restore the fortunes of the land as they were before,' says the LORD.

12"This is what the LORD Almighty says: 'In this place, desolate and without men or animals—in all its towns there will again be pastures for shepherds to rest their flocks. **13**In the towns of the hill country, of the western foothills and of the Negev, in the territory of Benjamin, in the villages around Jerusalem and in the towns of Judah, flocks will again pass under the hand of the one who counts them,' says the LORD.

14" 'The days are coming,' declares the LORD, 'when I will fulfill the gracious promise I made to the house of Israel and to the house of Judah.

15 " 'In those days and at that time
 I will make a righteous Branch
 sprout from David's line;
 he will do what is just and right in
 the land.
16In those days Judah will be saved
 and Jerusalem will live in safety.
 This is the name by which it*d* will be
 called:
 The LORD Our Righteousness.'

17For this is what the LORD says: 'David will never fail to have a man to sit on the throne of the house of Israel, **18**nor will the priests, who are Levites, ever fail to have a man to stand before me continually to offer burnt offerings, to burn grain offerings and to present sacrifices.' "

19The word of the LORD came to Jeremiah: **20**"This is what the LORD says: 'If you can break my covenant with the day and my covenant with the night, so that day and night no longer come at their appointed time, **21**then my covenant with David my servant—and my covenant with the Levites who are priests ministering before me—can be broken and David will no longer have a descendant to reign on his throne. **22**I

a 44 Or *will bring them back from captivity*   *b 5* Or *Chaldeans*   *c 7* Or *will restore the fortunes of Judah and Israel*   *d 16* Or *he* will make the descendants of David my servant and the Levites who minister before me as countless as the stars of the sky and as measureless as the sand on the seashore.' "

23 The word of the LORD came to Jeremiah: 24 "Have you not noticed that these people are saying, 'The LORD has rejected the two kingdoms*a* he chose'? So they despise my people and no longer regard them as a nation. 25 This is what the LORD says: 'If I have not established my covenant with day and night and the fixed laws of heaven and earth, 26 then I will reject the descendants of Jacob and David my servant and will not choose one of his sons to rule over the descendants of Abraham, Isaac and Jacob. For I will restore their fortunes*b* and have compassion on them.' "

Warning to Zedekiah

34 While Nebuchadnezzar king of Babylon and all his army and all the kingdoms and peoples in the empire he ruled were fighting against Jerusalem and all its surrounding towns, this word came to Jeremiah from the LORD: 2 "This is what the LORD, the God of Israel, says: Go to Zedekiah king of Judah and tell him, 'This is what the LORD says: I am about to hand this city over to the king of Babylon, and he will burn it down. 3 You will not escape from his grasp but will surely be captured and handed over to him. You will see the king of Babylon with your own eyes, and he will speak with you face to face. And you will go to Babylon.

4 " 'Yet hear the promise of the LORD, O Zedekiah king of Judah. This is what the LORD says concerning you: You will not die by the sword; 5 you will die peacefully. As people made a funeral fire in honor of your fathers, the former kings who preceded you, so they will make a fire in your honor and lament, "Alas, O master!" I myself make this promise, declares the LORD.' "

6 Then Jeremiah the prophet told all this to Zedekiah king of Judah, in Jerusalem, 7 while the army of the king of Babylon was fighting against Jerusalem and the other cities of Judah that were still holding out—Lachish and Azekah.

These were the only fortified cities left in Judah.

Freedom for Slaves

8 The word came to Jeremiah from the LORD after King Zedekiah had made a covenant with all the people in Jerusalem to proclaim freedom for the slaves. 9 Everyone was to free his Hebrew slaves, both male and female; no one was to hold a fellow Jew in bondage. 10 So all the officials and people who entered into this covenant agreed that they would free their male and female slaves and no longer hold them in bondage. They agreed, and set them free. 11 But afterward they changed their minds and took back the slaves they had freed and enslaved them again.

12 Then the word of the LORD came to Jeremiah: 13 "This is what the LORD, the God of Israel, says: I made a covenant with your forefathers when I brought them out of Egypt, out of the land of slavery. I said, 14 'Every seventh year each of you must free any fellow Hebrew who has sold himself to you. After he has served you six years, you must let him go free.'*c* Your fathers, however, did not listen to me or pay attention to me. 15 Recently you repented and did what is right in my sight: Each of you proclaimed freedom to his countrymen. You even made a covenant before me in the house that bears my Name. 16 But now you have turned around and profaned my name; each of you has taken back the male and female slaves you had set free to go where they wished. You have forced them to become your slaves again.

17 "Therefore, this is what the LORD says: You have not obeyed me; you have not proclaimed freedom for your fellow countrymen. So I now proclaim 'freedom' for you, declares the LORD—'freedom' to fall by the sword, plague and famine. I will make you abhorrent to all the kingdoms of the earth. 18 The men who have violated my covenant and have not fulfilled the terms of the covenant they made before me, I will treat like the calf they cut in two and then walked between its pieces. 19 The leaders of Judah and Jerusalem, the court officials, the priests and all the people of the

---

a 24 Or *families*   *b 26* Or *will bring them back from captivity*   *c 14* Deut. 15:12

land who walked between the pieces of the calf, 20I will hand over to their enemies who seek their lives. Their dead bodies will become food for the birds of the air and the beasts of the earth.

21"I will hand Zedekiah king of Judah and his officials over to their enemies who seek their lives, to the army of the king of Babylon, which has withdrawn from you. 22I am going to give the order, declares the LORD, and I will bring them back to this city. They will fight against it, take it and burn it down. And I will lay waste the towns of Judah so no one can live there."

The Recabites

35 This is the word that came to Jeremiah from the LORD during the reign of Jehoiakim son of Josiah king of Judah: 2"Go to the Recabite family and invite them to come to one of the side rooms of the house of the LORD and give them wine to drink."

3So I went to get Jaazaniah son of Jeremiah, the son of Habazziniah, and his brothers and all his sons—the whole family of the Recabites. 4I brought them into the house of the LORD, into the room of the sons of Hanan son of Igdaliah the man of God. It was next to the room of the officials, which was over that of Maaseiah son of Shallum the doorkeeper. 5Then I set bowls full of wine and some cups before the men of the Recabite family and said to them, "Drink some wine."

6But they replied, "We do not drink wine, because our forefather Jonadab son of Recab gave us this command: 'Neither you nor your descendants must ever drink wine. 7Also you must never build houses, sow seed or plant vineyards; you must never have any of these things, but must always live in tents. Then you will live a long time in the land where you are nomads.' 8We have obeyed everything our forefather Jonadab son of Recab commanded us. Neither we nor our wives nor our sons and daughters have ever drunk wine 9or built houses to live in or had vineyards, fields or crops. 10We have lived in tents and have fully obeyed everything our forefather Jonadab commanded us. 11But

when Nebuchadnezzar king of Babylon invaded this land, we said, 'Come, we must go to Jerusalem to escape the Babylonian*a* and Aramean armies.' So we have remained in Jerusalem."

12Then the word of the LORD came to Jeremiah, saying: 13"This is what the LORD Almighty, the God of Israel, says: Go and tell the men of Judah and the people of Jerusalem, 'Will you not learn a lesson and obey my words?' declares the LORD. 14'Jonadab son of Recab ordered his sons not to drink wine and this command has been kept. To this day they do not drink wine, because they obey their forefather's command. But I have spoken to you again and again, yet you have not obeyed me. 15Again and again I sent all my servants the prophets to you. They said, "Each of you must turn from your wicked ways and reform your actions; do not follow other gods to serve them. Then you will live in the land I have given to you and your fathers." But you have not paid attention or listened to me. 16The descendants of Jonadab son of Recab have carried out the command their forefather gave them, but these people have not obeyed me.'

17"Therefore, this is what the LORD God Almighty, the God of Israel, says: 'Listen! I am going to bring on Judah and on everyone living in Jerusalem every disaster I pronounced against them. I spoke to them, but they did not listen; I called to them, but they did not answer.' "

18Then Jeremiah said to the family of the Recabites, "This is what the LORD Almighty, the God of Israel, says: 'You have obeyed the command of your forefather Jonadab and have followed all his instructions and have done everything he ordered.' 19Therefore, this is what the LORD Almighty, the God of Israel, says: 'Jonadab son of Recab will never fail to have a man to serve me.' "

Jehoiakim Burns Jeremiah's Scroll

36 In the fourth year of Jehoiakim son of Josiah king of Judah, this word came to Jeremiah from the LORD: 2"Take a scroll and write on it all the words I have spoken to you concerning Israel, Judah and all the other nations from the time I began speaking to you in the reign of Josiah till now. 3Perhaps when the people of Judah hear about every disaster I plan to inflict on them, each of them will turn from his wicked way; then I will forgive their wickedness and their sin."

4So Jeremiah called Baruch son of Neriah, and while Jeremiah dictated all the words the LORD had spoken to him, Baruch wrote them on the scroll. 5Then Jeremiah told Baruch, "I am restricted; I cannot go to the LORD's temple. 6So you go to the house of the LORD on a day of fasting and read to the people from the scroll the words of the LORD that you wrote as I dictated. Read them to all the people of Judah who come in from their towns. 7Perhaps they will bring their petition before the LORD, and each will turn from his wicked ways, for the anger and wrath pronounced against this people by the LORD are great."

8Baruch son of Neriah did everything Jeremiah the prophet told him to do; at the LORD's temple he read the words of the LORD from the scroll. 9In the ninth month of the fifth year of Jehoiakim son of Josiah king of Judah, a time of fasting before the LORD was proclaimed for all the people in Jerusalem and those who had come from the towns of Judah. 10From the room of Gemariah son of Shaphan the secretary, which was in the upper courtyard at the entrance of the New Gate of the temple, Baruch read to all the people at the LORD's temple the words of Jeremiah from the scroll.

11When Micaiah son of Gemariah, the son of Shaphan, heard all the words of the LORD from the scroll, 12he went down to the secretary's room in the royal palace, where all the officials were sitting: Elishama the secretary, Delaiah son of Shemaiah, Elnathan son of Acbor, Gemariah son of Shaphan, Zedekiah son of Hananiah, and all the other officials. 13After Micaiah told them everything he had heard Baruch read to the people from the scroll, 14all the officials sent Jehudi son of Nethaniah, the son of Shelemiah, the son of Cushi, to say to Baruch, "Bring the scroll from which you have read to the people and come." So Baruch son of Neriah went to them with the scroll in his hand. 15They said to him, "Sit down, please, and read it to us."

So Baruch read it to them. 16When they heard all these words, they looked at each other in fear and said to Baruch, "We must report all these words to the king." 17Then they asked Baruch, "Tell us, how did you come to write all this? Did Jeremiah dictate it?"

18"Yes," Baruch replied, "he dictated all these words to me, and I wrote them in ink on the scroll."

19Then the officials said to Baruch, "You and Jeremiah, go and hide. Don't let anyone know where you are."

20After they put the scroll in the room of Elishama the secretary, they went to the king in the courtyard and reported everything to him. 21The king sent Jehudi to get the scroll, and Jehudi brought it from the room of Elishama the secretary and read it to the king and all the officials standing beside him. 22It was the ninth month and the king was sitting in the winter apartment, with a fire burning in the firepot in front of him. 23Whenever Jehudi had read three or four columns of the scroll, the king cut them off with a scribe's knife and threw them into the firepot, until the entire scroll was burned in the fire. 24The king and all his attendants who heard all these words showed no fear, nor did they tear their clothes. 25Even though Elnathan, Delaiah and Gemariah urged the king not to burn the scroll, he would not listen to them. 26Instead, the king commanded Jerahmeel, a son of the king, Seraiah son of Azriel and Shelemiah son of Abdeel to arrest Baruch the scribe and Jeremiah the prophet. But the LORD had hidden them.

27After the king burned the scroll containing the words that Baruch had written at Jeremiah's dictation, the word of the LORD came to Jeremiah: 28"Take another scroll and write on it all the words that were on the first scroll, which Jehoiakim king of Judah burned up. 29Also tell Jehoiakim king of Judah, 'This is what the LORD says: You burned that scroll and said, "Why did you write on it that the king of Babylon would certainly come and destroy this land and cut off both men and animals from it?" 30Therefore, this is what the LORD says about

Jehoiakim king of Judah: He will have no one to sit on the throne of David; his body will be thrown out and exposed to the heat by day and the frost by night. 31I will punish him and his children and his attendants for their wickedness; I will bring on them and those living in Jerusalem and the people of Judah every disaster I pronounced against them, because they have not listened.' "

32So Jeremiah took another scroll and gave it to the scribe Baruch son of Neriah, and as Jeremiah dictated, Baruch wrote on it all the words of the scroll that Jehoiakim king of Judah had burned in the fire. And many similar words were added to them.

Jeremiah in Prison

37 Zedekiah son of Josiah was made king of Judah by Nebuchadnezzar king of Babylon; he reigned in place of Jehoiachin*a* son of Jehoiakim. 2Neither he nor his attendants nor the people of the land paid any attention to the words the LORD had spoken through Jeremiah the prophet.

3King Zedekiah, however, sent Jehucal son of Shelemiah with the priest Zephaniah son of Maaseiah to Jeremiah the prophet with this message: "Please pray to the LORD our God for us."

4Now Jeremiah was free to come and go among the people, for he had not yet been put in prison. 5Pharaoh's army had marched out of Egypt, and when the Babylonians*b* who were besieging Jerusalem heard the report about them, they withdrew from Jerusalem.

6Then the word of the LORD came to Jeremiah the prophet: 7"This is what the LORD, the God of Israel, says: Tell the king of Judah, who sent you to inquire of me, 'Pharaoh's army, which has marched out to support you, will go back to its own land, to Egypt. 8Then the Babylonians will return and attack this city; they will capture it and burn it down.'

9"This is what the LORD says: Do not deceive yourselves, thinking, 'The Babylonians will surely leave us.' They will not! 10Even if you were to defeat the entire Babylonian*c* army that is attacking you and only wounded men were

left in their tents, they would come out and burn this city down."

11After the Babylonian army had withdrawn from Jerusalem because of Pharaoh's army, 12Jeremiah started to leave the city to go to the territory of Benjamin to get his share of the property among the people there. 13But when he reached the Benjamin Gate, the captain of the guard, whose name was Irijah son of Shelemiah, the son of Hananiah, arrested him and said, "You are deserting to the Babylonians!"

14"That's not true!" Jeremiah said. "I am not deserting to the Babylonians." But Irijah would not listen to him; instead, he arrested Jeremiah and brought him to the officials. 15They were angry with Jeremiah and had him beaten and imprisoned in the house of Jonathan the secretary, which they had made into a prison.

16Jeremiah was put into a vaulted cell in a dungeon, where he remained a long time. 17Then King Zedekiah sent for him and had him brought to the palace, where he asked him privately, "Is there any word from the LORD?"

"Yes," Jeremiah replied, "you will be handed over to the king of Babylon."

18Then Jeremiah said to King Zedekiah, "What crime have I committed against you or your officials or this people, that you have put me in prison? 19Where are your prophets who prophesied to you, 'The king of Babylon will not attack you or this land'? 20But now, my lord the king, please listen. Let me bring my petition before you: Do not send me back to the house of Jonathan the secretary, or I will die there."

21King Zedekiah then gave orders for Jeremiah to be placed in the courtyard of the guard and given bread from the street of the bakers each day until all the bread in the city was gone. So Jeremiah remained in the courtyard of the guard.

Jeremiah Thrown Into a Cistern

38 Shephatiah son of Mattan, Gedaliah son of Pashhur, Jehucal*d* son of Shelemiah, and Pashhur son of Malkijah heard what Jeremiah was telling all the people when he said,

---

a 1 Hebrew *Coniah*, a variant of *Jehoiachin*   *b 5* Or *Chaldeans*; also in verses 8, 9, 13 and 14
c 10 Or *Chaldean*; also in verse 11   *d 1* Hebrew *Jucal*, a variant of *Jehucal*

2"This is what the LORD says: 'Whoever stays in this city will die by the sword, famine or plague, but whoever goes over to the Babylonians[a] will live. He will escape with his life; he will live.' 3And this is what the LORD says: 'This city will certainly be handed over to the army of the king of Babylon, who will capture it.' "

4Then the officials said to the king, "This man should be put to death. He is discouraging the soldiers who are left in this city, as well as all the people, by the things he is saying to them. This man is not seeking the good of these people but their ruin."

5"He is in your hands," King Zedekiah answered. "The king can do nothing to oppose you."

6So they took Jeremiah and put him into the cistern of Malkijah, the king's son, which was in the courtyard of the guard. They lowered Jeremiah by ropes into the cistern; it had no water in it, only mud, and Jeremiah sank down into the mud.

7But Ebed-Melech, a Cushite,[b] an official[c] in the royal palace, heard that they had put Jeremiah into the cistern. While the king was sitting in the Benjamin Gate, 8Ebed-Melech went out of the palace and said to him, 9"My lord the king, these men have acted wickedly in all they have done to Jeremiah the prophet. They have thrown him into a cistern, where he will starve to death when there is no longer any bread in the city."

10Then the king commanded Ebed-Melech the Cushite, "Take thirty men from here with you and lift Jeremiah the prophet out of the cistern before he dies."

11So Ebed-Melech took the men with him and went to a room under the treasury in the palace. He took some old rags and worn-out clothes from there and let them down with ropes to Jeremiah in the cistern. 12Ebed-Melech the Cushite said to Jeremiah, "Put these old rags and worn-out clothes under your arms to pad the ropes." Jeremiah did so, 13and they pulled him up with the ropes and lifted him out of the cistern. And Jeremiah remained in the courtyard of the guard.

Zedekiah Questions Jeremiah Again

14Then King Zedekiah sent for Jeremiah the prophet and had him brought to the third entrance to the temple of the LORD. "I am going to ask you something," the king said to Jeremiah. "Do not hide anything from me."

15Jeremiah said to Zedekiah, "If I give you an answer, will you not kill me? Even if I did give you counsel, you would not listen to me."

16But King Zedekiah swore this oath secretly to Jeremiah: "As surely as the LORD lives, who has given us breath, I will neither kill you nor hand you over to those who are seeking your life."

17Then Jeremiah said to Zedekiah, "This is what the LORD God Almighty, the God of Israel, says: 'If you surrender to the officers of the king of Babylon, your life will be spared and this city will not be burned down; you and your family will live. 18But if you will not surrender to the officers of the king of Babylon, this city will be handed over to the Babylonians and they will burn it down; you yourself will not escape from their hands.' "

19King Zedekiah said to Jeremiah, "I am afraid of the Jews who have gone over to the Babylonians, for the Babylonians may hand me over to them and they will mistreat me."

20"They will not hand you over," Jeremiah replied. "Obey the LORD by doing what I tell you. Then it will go well with you, and your life will be spared. 21But if you refuse to surrender, this is what the LORD has revealed to me: 22All the women left in the palace of the king of Judah will be brought out to the officials of the king of Babylon. Those women will say to you:

" 'They misled you and overcame you—
    those trusted friends of yours.
Your feet are sunk in the mud;
    your friends have deserted you.'

23"All your wives and children will be brought out to the Babylonians. You yourself will not escape from their hands but will be captured by the king

---

[a] 2 Or *Chaldeans*; also in verses 18, 19 and 23   [b] 7 Probably from the upper Nile region   [c] 7 Or *a eunuch*

of Babylon; and this city will*a* be burned down."

24Then Zedekiah said to Jeremiah, "Do not let anyone know about this conversation, or you may die. 25If the officials hear that I talked with you, and they come to you and say, 'Tell us what you said to the king and what the king said to you; do not hide it from us or we will kill you,' 26then tell them, 'I was pleading with the king not to send me back to Jonathan's house to die there.' "

27All the officials did come to Jeremiah and question him, and he told them everything the king had ordered him to say. So they said no more to him, for no one had heard his conversation with the king.

28And Jeremiah remained in the courtyard of the guard until the day Jerusalem was captured.

The Fall of Jerusalem

39 This is how Jerusalem was taken: 1In the ninth year of Zedekiah king of Judah, in the tenth month, Nebuchadnezzar king of Babylon marched against Jerusalem with his whole army and laid siege to it. 2And on the ninth day of the fourth month of Zedekiah's eleventh year, the city wall was broken through. 3Then all the officials of the king of Babylon came and took seats in the Middle Gate: Nergal-Sharezer of Samgar, Nebo-Sarsekim*b* a chief officer, Nergal-Sharezer a high official and all the other officials of the king of Babylon. 4When Zedekiah king of Judah and all the soldiers saw them, they fled; they left the city at night by way of the king's garden, through the gate between the two walls, and headed toward the Arabah.*c*

5But the Babylonian*d* army pursued them and overtook Zedekiah in the plains of Jericho. They captured him and took him to Nebuchadnezzar king of Babylon at Riblah in the land of Hamath, where he pronounced sentence on him. 6There at Riblah the king of Babylon slaughtered the sons of Zedekiah before his eyes and also killed all the nobles of Judah. 7Then he put out Zedekiah's eyes

and bound him with bronze shackles to take him to Babylon.

8The Babylonians*e* set fire to the royal palace and the houses of the people and broke down the walls of Jerusalem. 9Nebuzaradan commander of the imperial guard carried into exile to Babylon the people who remained in the city, along with those who had gone over to him, and the rest of the people. 10But Nebuzaradan the commander of the guard left behind in the land of Judah some of the poor people, who owned nothing; and at that time he gave them vineyards and fields.

11Now Nebuchadnezzar king of Babylon had given these orders about Jeremiah through Nebuzaradan commander of the imperial guard: 12"Take him and look after him; don't harm him but do for him whatever he asks." 13So Nebuzaradan the commander of the guard, Nebushazban a chief officer, Nergal-Sharezer a high official and all the other officers of the king of Babylon 14sent and had Jeremiah taken out of the courtyard of the guard. They turned him over to Gedaliah son of Ahikam, the son of Shaphan, to take him back to his home. So he remained among his own people.

15While Jeremiah had been confined in the courtyard of the guard, the word of the LORD came to him: 16"Go and tell Ebed-Melech the Cushite, 'This is what the LORD Almighty, the God of Israel, says: I am about to fulfill my words against this city through disaster, not prosperity. At that time they will be fulfilled before your eyes. 17But I will rescue you on that day, declares the LORD; you will not be handed over to those you fear. 18I will save you; you will not fall by the sword but will escape with your life, because you trust in me, declares the LORD.' "

Jeremiah Freed

40 The word came to Jeremiah from the LORD after Nebuzaradan commander of the imperial guard had released him at Ramah. He had found Jeremiah bound in chains among all the captives from Jerusalem and Judah who were being carried into

---

a 23 Or *and you will cause this city to*   *b 3* Or *Nergal-Sharezer, Samgar-Nebo, Sarsekim*   *c 4* Or *the Jordan Valley*   *d 5* Or *Chaldean*   *e 8* Or *Chaldeans*

exile to Babylon. ²When the commander of the guard found Jeremiah, he said to him, "The LORD your God decreed this disaster for this place. ³And now the LORD has brought it about; he has done just as he said he would. All this happened because you people sinned against the LORD and did not obey him. ⁴But today I am freeing you from the chains on your wrists. Come with me to Babylon, if you like, and I will look after you; but if you do not want to, then don't come. Look, the whole country lies before you; go wherever you please." ⁵However, before Jeremiah turned to go,ᵃ Nebuzaradan added, "Go back to Gedaliah son of Ahikam, the son of Shaphan, whom the king of Babylon has appointed over the towns of Judah, and live with him among the people, or go anywhere else you please."

Then the commander gave him provisions and a present and let him go. ⁶So Jeremiah went to Gedaliah son of Ahikam at Mizpah and stayed with him among the people who were left behind in the land.

Gedaliah Assassinated

⁷When all the army officers and their men who were still in the open country heard that the king of Babylon had appointed Gedaliah son of Ahikam as governor over the land and had put him in charge of the men, women and children who were the poorest in the land and who had not been carried into exile to Babylon, ⁸they came to Gedaliah at Mizpah—Ishmael son of Nethaniah, Johanan and Jonathan the sons of Kareah, Seraiah son of Tanhumeth, the sons of Ephai the Netophathite, and Jaazaniahᵇ the son of the Maacathite, and their men. ⁹Gedaliah son of Ahikam, the son of Shaphan, took an oath to reassure them and their men. "Do not be afraid to serve the Babylonians,ᶜ" he said. "Settle down in the land and serve the king of Babylon, and it will go well with you. ¹⁰I myself will stay at Mizpah to represent you before the Babylonians who come to us, but you are to harvest the wine, summer fruit and oil, and put

them in your storage jars, and live in the towns you have taken over."

¹¹When all the Jews in Moab, Ammon, Edom and all the other countries heard that the king of Babylon had left a remnant in Judah and had appointed Gedaliah son of Ahikam, the son of Shaphan, as governor over them, ¹²they all came back to the land of Judah, to Gedaliah at Mizpah, from all the countries where they had been scattered. And they harvested an abundance of wine and summer fruit.

¹³Johanan son of Kareah and all the army officers still in the open country came to Gedaliah at Mizpah ¹⁴and said to him, "Don't you know that Baalis king of the Ammonites has sent Ishmael son of Nethaniah to take your life?" But Gedaliah son of Ahikam did not believe them.

¹⁵Then Johanan son of Kareah said privately to Gedaliah in Mizpah, "Let me go and kill Ishmael son of Nethaniah, and no one will know it. Why should he take your life and cause all the Jews who are gathered around you to be scattered and the remnant of Judah to perish?"

¹⁶But Gedaliah son of Ahikam said to Johanan son of Kareah, "Don't do such a thing! What you are saying about Ishmael is not true."

41 In the seventh month Ishmael son of Nethaniah, the son of Elishama, who was of royal blood and had been one of the king's officers, came with ten men to Gedaliah son of Ahikam at Mizpah. While they were eating together there, ²Ishmael son of Nethaniah and the ten men who were with him got up and struck down Gedaliah son of Ahikam, the son of Shaphan, with the sword, killing the one whom the king of Babylon had appointed as governor over the land. ³Ishmael also killed all the Jews who were with Gedaliah at Mizpah, as well as the Babylonianᵈ soldiers who were there.

⁴The day after Gedaliah's assassination, before anyone knew about it, ⁵eighty men who had shaved off their beards, torn their clothes and cut themselves came from Shechem, Shiloh and Samaria, bringing grain offerings and incense with them to the house of the

LORD. 6Ishmael son of Nethaniah went out from Mizpah to meet them, weeping as he went. When he met them, he said, "Come to Gedaliah son of Ahikam." 7When they went into the city, Ishmael son of Nethaniah and the men who were with him slaughtered them and threw them into a cistern. 8But ten of them said to Ishmael, "Don't kill us! We have wheat and barley, oil and honey, hidden in a field." So he let them alone and did not kill them with the others. 9Now the cistern where he threw all the bodies of the men he had killed along with Gedaliah was the one King Asa had made as part of his defense against Baasha king of Israel. Ishmael son of Nethaniah filled it with the dead.

10Ishmael made captives of all the rest of the people who were in Mizpah—the king's daughters along with all the others who were left there, over whom Nebuzaradan commander of the imperial guard had appointed Gedaliah son of Ahikam. Ishmael son of Nethaniah took them captive and set out to cross over to the Ammonites.

11When Johanan son of Kareah and all the army officers who were with him heard about all the crimes Ishmael son of Nethaniah had committed, 12they took all their men and went to fight Ishmael son of Nethaniah. They caught up with him near the great pool in Gibeon. 13When all the people Ishmael had with him saw Johanan son of Kareah and the army officers who were with him, they were glad. 14All the people Ishmael had taken captive at Mizpah turned and went over to Johanan son of Kareah. 15But Ishmael son of Nethaniah and eight of his men escaped from Johanan and fled to the Ammonites.

Flight to Egypt

16Then Johanan son of Kareah and all the army officers who were with him led away all the survivors from Mizpah whom he had recovered from Ishmael son of Nethaniah after he had assassinated Gedaliah son of Ahikam: the soldiers, women, children and court officials he had brought from Gibeon. 17And they went on, stopping at Geruth Kimham near Bethlehem on their way to Egypt 18to escape the Babylonians.*a* They were afraid of them because Ishmael son of Nethaniah had killed Gedaliah son of Ahikam, whom the king of Babylon had appointed as governor over the land.

42 Then all the army officers, including Johanan son of Kareah and Jezaniah*b* son of Hoshaiah, and all the people from the least to the greatest approached 2Jeremiah the prophet and said to him, "Please hear our petition and pray to the LORD your God for this entire remnant. For as you now see, though we were once many, now only a few are left. 3Pray that the LORD your God will tell us where we should go and what we should do."

4"I have heard you," replied Jeremiah the prophet. "I will certainly pray to the LORD your God as you have requested; I will tell you everything the LORD says and will keep nothing back from you."

5Then they said to Jeremiah, "May the LORD be a true and faithful witness against us if we do not act in accordance with everything the LORD your God sends you to tell us. 6Whether it is favorable or unfavorable, we will obey the LORD our God, to whom we are sending you, so that it will go well with us, for we will obey the LORD our God."

7Ten days later the word of the LORD came to Jeremiah. 8So he called together Johanan son of Kareah and all the army officers who were with him and all the people from the least to the greatest. 9He said to them, "This is what the LORD, the God of Israel, to whom you sent me to present your petition, says: 10'If you stay in this land, I will build you up and not tear you down; I will plant you and not uproot you, for I am grieved over the disaster I have inflicted on you. 11Do not be afraid of the king of Babylon, whom you now fear. Do not be afraid of him, declares the LORD, for I am with you and will save you and deliver you from his hands. 12I will show you compassion so that he will have compassion on you and restore you to your land.'

13"However, if you say, 'We will not stay in this land,' and so disobey the LORD your God, 14and if you say, 'No, we will go and live in Egypt, where we

---

a 18 Or *Chaldeans*   *b 1* Hebrew; Septuagint (see also 43:2) *Azariah*

will not see war or hear the trumpet or be hungry for bread,' [15]then hear the word of the LORD, O remnant of Judah. This is what the LORD Almighty, the God of Israel, says: 'If you are determined to go to Egypt and you do go to settle there, [16]then the sword you fear will overtake you there, and the famine you dread will follow you into Egypt, and there you will die. [17]Indeed, all who are determined to go to Egypt to settle there will die by the sword, famine and plague; not one of them will survive or escape the disaster I will bring on them.' [18]This is what the LORD Almighty, the God of Israel, says: 'As my anger and wrath have been poured out on those who lived in Jerusalem, so will my wrath be poured out on you when you go to Egypt. You will be an object of cursing and horror, of condemnation and reproach; you will never see this place again.'

[19]"O remnant of Judah, the LORD has told you, 'Do not go to Egypt.' Be sure of this: I warn you today [20]that you made a fatal mistake[a] when you sent me to the LORD your God and said, 'Pray to the LORD our God for us; tell us everything he says and we will do it.' [21]I have told you today, but you still have not obeyed the LORD your God in all he sent me to tell you. [22]So now, be sure of this: You will die by the sword, famine and plague in the place where you want to go to settle."

43 When Jeremiah finished telling the people all the words of the LORD their God—everything the LORD had sent him to tell them— [2]Azariah son of Hoshaiah and Johanan son of Kareah and all the arrogant men said to Jeremiah, "You are lying! The LORD our God has not sent you to say, 'You must not go to Egypt to settle there.' [3]But Baruch son of Neriah is inciting you against us to hand us over to the Babylonians,[b] so they may kill us or carry us into exile to Babylon."

[4]So Johanan son of Kareah and all the army officers and all the people disobeyed the LORD's command to stay in the land of Judah. [5]Instead, Johanan son of Kareah and all the army officers led away all the remnant of Judah who had come back to live in the land of Judah from all the nations where they had been scattered. [6]They also led away all the men, women and children and the king's daughters whom Nebuzaradan commander of the imperial guard had left with Gedaliah son of Ahikam, the son of Shaphan, and Jeremiah the prophet and Baruch son of Neriah. [7]So they entered Egypt in disobedience to the LORD and went as far as Tahpanhes.

[8]In Tahpanhes the word of the LORD came to Jeremiah: [9]"While the Jews are watching, take some large stones with you and bury them in clay in the brick pavement at the entrance to Pharaoh's palace in Tahpanhes. [10]Then say to them, 'This is what the LORD Almighty, the God of Israel, says: I will send for my servant Nebuchadnezzar king of Babylon, and I will set his throne over these stones I have buried here; he will spread his royal canopy above them. [11]He will come and attack Egypt, bringing death to those destined for death, captivity to those destined for captivity, and the sword to those destined for the sword. [12]He[c] will set fire to the temples of the gods of Egypt; he will burn their temples and take their gods captive. As a shepherd wraps his garment around him, so will he wrap Egypt around himself and depart from there unscathed. [13]There in the temple of the sun[d] in Egypt he will demolish the sacred pillars and will burn down the temples of the gods of Egypt.'"

Disaster Because of Idolatry

44 This word came to Jeremiah concerning all the Jews living in Lower Egypt—in Migdol, Tahpanhes and Memphis[e]—and in Upper Egypt[f]: [2]"This is what the LORD Almighty, the God of Israel, says: You saw the great disaster I brought on Jerusalem and on all the towns of Judah. Today they lie deserted and in ruins [3]because of the evil they have done. They provoked me to anger by burning incense and by worshiping other gods that neither they nor you nor your fathers ever knew. [4]Again and again I sent my servants the prophets, who said, 'Do not do this detestable

---

[a] 20 Or *you erred in your hearts*   [b] 3 Or *Chaldeans*   [c] 12 Or *I*   [d] 13 Or *in Heliopolis*
[e] 1 Hebrew *Noph*   [f] 1 Hebrew *in Pathros*

thing that I hate!' 5But they did not listen or pay attention; they did not turn from their wickedness or stop burning incense to other gods. 6Therefore, my fierce anger was poured out; it raged against the towns of Judah and the streets of Jerusalem and made them the desolate ruins they are today.

7"Now this is what the LORD God Almighty, the God of Israel, says: Why bring such great disaster on yourselves by cutting off from Judah the men and women, the children and infants, and so leave yourselves without a remnant? 8Why provoke me to anger with what your hands have made, burning incense to other gods in Egypt, where you have come to live? You will destroy yourselves and make yourselves an object of cursing and reproach among all the nations on earth. 9Have you forgotten the wickedness committed by your fathers and by the kings and queens of Judah and the wickedness committed by you and your wives in the land of Judah and the streets of Jerusalem? 10To this day they have not humbled themselves or shown reverence, nor have they followed my law and the decrees I set before you and your fathers.

11"Therefore, this is what the LORD Almighty, the God of Israel, says: I am determined to bring disaster on you and to destroy all Judah. 12I will take away the remnant of Judah who were determined to go to Egypt to settle there. They will all perish in Egypt; they will fall by the sword or die from famine. From the least to the greatest, they will die by sword or famine. They will become an object of cursing and horror, of condemnation and reproach. 13I will punish those who live in Egypt with the sword, famine and plague, as I punished Jerusalem. 14None of the remnant of Judah who have gone to live in Egypt will escape or survive to return to the land of Judah, to which they long to return and live; none will return except a few fugitives."

15Then all the men who knew that their wives were burning incense to other gods, along with all the women who were present—a large assembly—and all the people living in Lower and Upper Egypt,a said to Jeremiah, 16"We will not listen to the message you have spoken to us in the name of the LORD! 17We will certainly do everything we said we would: We will burn incense to the Queen of Heaven and will pour out drink offerings to her just as we and our fathers, our kings and our officials did in the towns of Judah and in the streets of Jerusalem. At that time we had plenty of food and were well off and suffered no harm. 18But ever since we stopped burning incense to the Queen of Heaven and pouring out drink offerings to her, we have had nothing and have been perishing by sword and famine."

19The women added, "When we burned incense to the Queen of Heaven and poured out drink offerings to her, did not our husbands know that we were making cakes like her image and pouring out drink offerings to her?"

20Then Jeremiah said to all the people, both men and women, who were answering him, 21"Did not the LORD remember and think about the incense burned in the towns of Judah and the streets of Jerusalem by you and your fathers, your kings and your officials and the people of the land? 22When the LORD could no longer endure your wicked actions and the detestable things you did, your land became an object of cursing and a desolate waste without inhabitants, as it is today. 23Because you have burned incense and have sinned against the LORD and have not obeyed him or followed his law or his decrees or his stipulations, this disaster has come upon you, as you now see."

24Then Jeremiah said to all the people, including the women, "Hear the word of the LORD, all you people of Judah in Egypt. 25This is what the LORD Almighty, the God of Israel, says: You and your wives have shown by your actions what you promised when you said, 'We will certainly carry out the vows we made to burn incense and pour out drink offerings to the Queen of Heaven.'

"Go ahead then, do what you promised! Keep your vows! 26But hear the word of the LORD, all Jews living in Egypt: 'I swear by my great name,' says the LORD, 'that no one from Judah living anywhere in Egypt will ever again invoke my name or swear, "As surely as the Sovereign LORD lives." ²⁷For I am watching over them for harm, not for good; the Jews in Egypt will perish by sword and famine until they are all destroyed. ²⁸Those who escape the sword and return to the land of Judah from Egypt will be very few. Then the whole remnant of Judah who came to live in Egypt will know whose word will stand—mine or theirs.

²⁹"'This will be the sign to you that I will punish you in this place,' declares the LORD, 'so that you will know that my threats of harm against you will surely stand.' ³⁰This is what the LORD says: 'I am going to hand Pharaoh Hophra king of Egypt over to his enemies who seek his life, just as I handed Zedekiah king of Judah over to Nebuchadnezzar king of Babylon, the enemy who was seeking his life.'"

A Message to Baruch

45 This is what Jeremiah the prophet told Baruch son of Neriah in the fourth year of Jehoiakim son of Josiah king of Judah, after Baruch had written on a scroll the words Jeremiah was then dictating: ²"This is what the LORD, the God of Israel, says to you, Baruch: ³You said, 'Woe to me! The LORD has added sorrow to my pain; I am worn out with groaning and find no rest.'"

⁴ₗThe LORD said,ⱼ "Say this to him: 'This is what the LORD says: I will overthrow what I have built and uproot what I have planted, throughout the land. ⁵Should you then seek great things for yourself? Seek them not. For I will bring disaster on all people, declares the LORD, but wherever you go I will let you escape with your life.'"

A Message About Egypt

46 This is the word of the LORD that came to Jeremiah the prophet concerning the nations:

²Concerning Egypt:

This is the message against the army of Pharaoh Neco king of Egypt, which was defeated at Carchemish on the

ᵃ 9 That is, the upper Nile region

Euphrates River by Nebuchadnezzar king of Babylon in the fourth year of Jehoiakim son of Josiah king of Judah:

³ "Prepare your shields, both large and small,
   and march out for battle!
⁴ Harness the horses,
   mount the steeds!
Take your positions
   with helmets on!
Polish your spears,
   put on your armor!
⁵ What do I see?
   They are terrified,
they are retreating,
   their warriors are defeated.
They flee in haste
   without looking back,
   and there is terror on every side,"
            declares the LORD.
⁶ "The swift cannot flee
   nor the strong escape.
In the north by the River Euphrates
   they stumble and fall.

⁷ "Who is this that rises like the Nile,
   like rivers of surging waters?
⁸ Egypt rises like the Nile,
   like rivers of surging waters.
She says, 'I will rise and cover the
      earth;
   I will destroy cities and their
      people.'
⁹ Charge, O horses!
   Drive furiously, O charioteers!
March on, O warriors—
   men of Cushᵃ and Put who carry
      shields,
   men of Lydia who draw the bow.
¹⁰ But that day belongs to the Lord, the
      LORD Almighty—
   a day of vengeance, for vengeance
      on his foes.
The sword will devour till it is
      satisfied,
   till it has quenched its thirst with
      blood.
For the Lord, the LORD Almighty,
   will offer sacrifice
in the land of the north by the
      River Euphrates.
¹¹ "Go up to Gilead and get balm,
   O Virgin Daughter of Egypt.
But you multiply remedies in vain;

there is no healing for you.
¹²The nations will hear of your shame;
    your cries will fill the earth.
One warrior will stumble over
    another;
    both will fall down together."

¹³This is the message the LORD spoke to Jeremiah the prophet about the coming of Nebuchadnezzar king of Babylon to attack Egypt:

¹⁴"Announce this in Egypt, and
    proclaim it in Migdol;
    proclaim it also in Memphis*ᵃ* and
    Tahpanhes:
'Take your positions and get ready,
    for the sword devours those around
    you.'
¹⁵Why will your warriors be laid low?
    They cannot stand, for the LORD
    will push them down.
¹⁶They will stumble repeatedly;
    they will fall over each other.
They will say, 'Get up, let us go back
    to our own people and our native
    lands,
    away from the sword of the
    oppressor.'
¹⁷There they will exclaim,
'Pharaoh king of Egypt is only a
    loud noise;
    he has missed his opportunity.'

¹⁸"As surely as I live," declares the
    King,
    whose name is the LORD Almighty,
"one will come who is like Tabor
    among the mountains,
    like Carmel by the sea.
¹⁹Pack your belongings for exile,
    you who live in Egypt,
for Memphis will be laid waste
    and lie in ruins without inhabitant.

²⁰"Egypt is a beautiful heifer,
    but a gadfly is coming
    against her from the north.
²¹The mercenaries in her ranks
    are like fattened calves.
They too will turn and flee together,
    they will not stand their ground,
for the day of disaster is coming upon
    them,
    the time for them to be punished.
²²Egypt will hiss like a fleeing serpent

as the enemy advances in force;
    they will come against her with axes,
    like men who cut down trees.
²³They will chop down her forest,"
                          declares the LORD,
"dense though it be.
They are more numerous than
    locusts,
    they cannot be counted.
²⁴The Daughter of Egypt will be put to
    shame,
    handed over to the people of the
    north."

²⁵The LORD Almighty, the God of Israel, says: "I am about to bring punishment on Amon god of Thebes,*ᵇ* on Pharaoh, on Egypt and her gods and her kings, and on those who rely on Pharaoh. ²⁶I will hand them over to those who seek their lives, to Nebuchadnezzar king of Babylon and his officers. Later, however, Egypt will be inhabited as in times past," declares the LORD.

²⁷"Do not fear, O Jacob my servant;
    do not be dismayed, O Israel.
I will surely save you out of a distant
    place,
    your descendants from the land of
    their exile.
Jacob will again have peace and
    security,
    and no one will make him afraid.
²⁸Do not fear, O Jacob my servant,
    for I am with you," declares the
    LORD.
"Though I completely destroy all the
    nations
    among which I scatter you,
    I will not completely destroy you.
I will discipline you but only with
    justice;
    I will not let you go entirely
    unpunished."

A Message About the Philistines

47 This is the word of the LORD that came to Jeremiah the prophet concerning the Philistines before Pharaoh attacked Gaza:

²This is what the LORD says:

"See how the waters are rising in the
    north;
    they will become an overflowing
        torrent.
They will overflow the land and
        everything in it,
    the towns and those who live in
        them.
The people will cry out;
    all who dwell in the land will wail
3 at the sound of the hoofs of galloping
        steeds,
    at the noise of enemy chariots
    and the rumble of their wheels.
Fathers will not turn to help their
        children;
    their hands will hang limp.
4 For the day has come
    to destroy all the Philistines
    and to cut off all survivors
    who could help Tyre and Sidon.
The LORD is about to destroy the
        Philistines,
    the remnant from the coasts of
        Caphtor.*a*
5 Gaza will shave her head in
        mourning;
    Ashkelon will be silenced.
O remnant on the plain,
    how long will you cut yourselves?

6 " 'Ah, sword of the LORD,' ⌐you cry,⌐
    'how long till you rest?
Return to your scabbard;
    cease and be still.'
7 But how can it rest
    when the LORD has commanded it,
    when he has ordered it
    to attack Ashkelon and the coast?"

A Message About Moab

48 Concerning Moab:

This is what the LORD Almighty, the
God of Israel, says:

"Woe to Nebo, for it will be ruined.
    Kiriathaim will be disgraced and
        captured;
    the stronghold*b* will be disgraced
        and shattered.
2 Moab will be praised no more;

in Heshbon*c* men will plot her
        downfall:
    'Come, let us put an end to that
        nation.'
You too, O Madmen,*d* will be
        silenced;
    the sword will pursue you.
3 Listen to the cries from Horonaim,
    cries of great havoc and
        destruction.
4 Moab will be broken;
    her little ones will cry out.*e*
5 They go up the way to Luhith,
    weeping bitterly as they go;
    on the road down to Horonaim
    anguished cries over the
        destruction are heard.
6 Flee! Run for your lives;
    become like a bush*f* in the desert.
7 Since you trust in your deeds and
        riches,
    you too will be taken captive,
    and Chemosh will go into exile,
    together with his priests and
        officials.
8 The destroyer will come against
        every town,
    and not a town will escape.
The valley will be ruined
    and the plateau destroyed,
    because the LORD has spoken.
9 Put salt on Moab,
    for she will be laid waste*g*;
    her towns will become desolate,
    with no one to live in them.

10 "A curse on him who is lax in doing
        the LORD's work!
    A curse on him who keeps his
        sword from bloodshed!

11 "Moab has been at rest from youth,
    like wine left on its dregs,
    not poured from one jar to another—
        she has not gone into exile.
So she tastes as she did,
    and her aroma is unchanged.
12 But days are coming,"
    declares the LORD,
"when I will send men who pour
        from jars,
    and they will pour her out;
    they will empty her jars
    and smash her jugs.

---

a 4 That is, Crete   *b 1* Or / *Misgab*   *c 2* The Hebrew for *Heshbon* sounds like the Hebrew for *plot*.
d 2 The name of the Moabite town Madmen sounds like the Hebrew for *be silenced*.   *e 4* Hebrew;
Septuagint / *proclaim it to Zoar*   *f 6* Or *like Aroer*   *g 9* Or *Give wings to Moab, / for she will fly
away*

13 Then Moab will be ashamed of
      Chemosh,
    as the house of Israel was ashamed
      when they trusted in Bethel.

14 "How can you say, 'We are warriors,
      men valiant in battle'?
15 Moab will be destroyed and her
      towns invaded;
    her finest young men will go down
      in the slaughter,"
    declares the King, whose name is
      the LORD Almighty.
16 "The fall of Moab is at hand;
      her calamity will come quickly.
17 Mourn for her, all who live around
      her,
    all who know her fame;
    say, 'How broken is the mighty
      scepter,
    how broken the glorious staff!'

18 "Come down from your glory
      and sit on the parched ground,
      O inhabitants of the Daughter of
        Dibon,
    for he who destroys Moab
      will come up against you
      and ruin your fortified cities.
19 Stand by the road and watch,
      you who live in Aroer.
    Ask the man fleeing and the woman
      escaping,
    ask them, 'What has happened?'
20 Moab is disgraced, for she is
      shattered.
    Wail and cry out!
    Announce by the Arnon
      that Moab is destroyed.
21 Judgment has come to the plateau—
      to Holon, Jahzah and Mephaath,
22   to Dibon, Nebo and Beth
        Diblathaim,
23   to Kiriathaim, Beth Gamul and
        Beth Meon,
24   to Kerioth and Bozrah—
    to all the towns of Moab, far and
      near.
25 Moab's horn*a* is cut off;
      her arm is broken,"
                  declares the LORD.

26 "Make her drunk,
      for she has defied the LORD.
    Let Moab wallow in her vomit;
      let her be an object of ridicule.

27 Was not Israel the object of your
      ridicule?
    Was she caught among thieves,
    that you shake your head in scorn
      whenever you speak of her?
28 Abandon your towns and dwell
      among the rocks,
      you who live in Moab.
    Be like a dove that makes its nest
      at the mouth of a cave.

29 "We have heard of Moab's pride—
      her overweening pride and conceit,
    her pride and arrogance
      and the haughtiness of her heart.
30 I know her insolence but it is futile,"
                  declares the LORD,
    "and her boasts accomplish
      nothing.
31 Therefore I wail over Moab,
      for all Moab I cry out,
    I moan for the men of Kir
      Hareseth.
32 I weep for you, as Jazer weeps,
      O vines of Sibmah.
    Your branches spread as far as the sea;
      they reached as far as the sea of
        Jazer.
    The destroyer has fallen
      on your ripened fruit and grapes.
33 Joy and gladness are gone
      from the orchards and fields of
        Moab.
    I have stopped the flow of wine from
      the presses;
      no one treads them with shouts of
        joy.
    Although there are shouts,
      they are not shouts of joy.

34 "The sound of their cry rises
      from Heshbon to Elealeh and Jahaz,
    from Zoar as far as Horonaim and
      Eglath Shelishiyah,
    for even the waters of Nimrim are
      dried up.
35 In Moab I will put an end
      to those who make offerings on the
        high places
      and burn incense to their gods,"
                  declares the LORD.
36 "So my heart laments for Moab like a
      flute;
    it laments like a flute for the men
      of Kir Hareseth.
    The wealth they acquired is gone.

---

a 25 Horn here symbolizes strength.

37 Every head is shaved
    and every beard cut off;
every hand is slashed
    and every waist is covered with
        sackcloth.
38 On all the roofs in Moab
    and in the public squares
there is nothing but mourning,
    for I have broken Moab
like a jar that no one wants,"
                    declares the LORD.
39 "How shattered she is! How they
        wail!
    How Moab turns her back in
        shame!
Moab has become an object of
        ridicule,
    an object of horror to all those
        around her."

40 This is what the LORD says:

"Look! An eagle is swooping down,
    spreading its wings over Moab.
41 Kerioth*a* will be captured
    and the strongholds taken.
In that day the hearts of Moab's
        warriors
    will be like the heart of a woman
        in labor.
42 Moab will be destroyed as a nation
    because she defied the LORD.
43 Terror and pit and snare await you,
    O people of Moab,"
                    declares the LORD.
44 "Whoever flees from the terror
    will fall into a pit,
whoever climbs out of the pit
    will be caught in a snare;
for I will bring upon Moab
    the year of her punishment,"
                    declares the LORD.

45 "In the shadow of Heshbon
    the fugitives stand helpless,
for a fire has gone out from Heshbon,
    a blaze from the midst of Sihon;
it burns the foreheads of Moab,
    the skulls of the noisy boasters.
46 Woe to you, O Moab!
    The people of Chemosh are
        destroyed;
your sons are taken into exile
    and your daughters into captivity.

47 "Yet I will restore the fortunes of
        Moab
    in days to come,"
                    declares the LORD.

Here ends the judgment on Moab.

A Message About Ammon

49 Concerning the Ammonites:

This is what the LORD says:

"Has Israel no sons?
    Has she no heirs?
Why then has Molech*b* taken
        possession of Gad?
    Why do his people live in its towns?
2 But the days are coming,"
    declares the LORD,
"when I will sound the battle cry
    against Rabbah of the Ammonites;
it will become a mound of ruins,
    and its surrounding villages will be
        set on fire.
Then Israel will drive out
    those who drove her out,"
                    says the LORD.
3 "Wail, O Heshbon, for Ai is destroyed!
    Cry out, O inhabitants of Rabbah!
Put on sackcloth and mourn;
    rush here and there inside the walls,
for Molech will go into exile,
    together with his priests and
        officials.
4 Why do you boast of your valleys,
    boast of your valleys so fruitful?
O unfaithful daughter,
    you trust in your riches and say,
    'Who will attack me?'
5 I will bring terror on you
    from all those around you,"
                    declares the Lord,
                    the LORD Almighty.
"Every one of you will be driven away,
    and no one will gather the fugitives.

6 "Yet afterward, I will restore the
        fortunes of the Ammonites,"
                    declares the LORD.

A Message About Edom

7 Concerning Edom:

This is what the LORD Almighty says:

"Is there no longer wisdom in Teman?

Has counsel perished from the
  prudent?
Has their wisdom decayed?
⁸Turn and flee, hide in deep caves,
  you who live in Dedan,
for I will bring disaster on Esau
  at the time I punish him.
⁹If grape pickers came to you,
  would they not leave a few grapes?
If thieves came during the night,
  would they not steal only as much
    as they wanted?
¹⁰But I will strip Esau bare;
  I will uncover his hiding places,
    so that he cannot conceal himself.
His children, relatives and neighbors
  will perish,
    and he will be no more.
¹¹Leave your orphans; I will protect
  their lives.
  Your widows too can trust in me."

¹²This is what the LORD says: "If those
who do not deserve to drink the cup
must drink it, why should you go
unpunished? You will not go unpunished, but must drink it. ¹³I swear by
myself," declares the LORD, "that Bozrah will become a ruin and an object of
horror, of reproach and of cursing; and
all its towns will be in ruins forever."

¹⁴I have heard a message from the LORD:
  An envoy was sent to the nations
    to say,
  "Assemble yourselves to attack it!
    Rise up for battle!"

¹⁵"Now I will make you small among
    the nations,
  despised among men.
¹⁶The terror you inspire
  and the pride of your heart have
    deceived you,
you who live in the clefts of the rocks,
  who occupy the heights of the hill.
Though you build your nest as high
    as the eagle's,
  from there I will bring you down,"
    declares the LORD.
¹⁷"Edom will become an object of
    horror;
  all who pass by will be appalled
    and will scoff
  because of all its wounds.

¹⁸As Sodom and Gomorrah were
    overthrown,
  along with their neighboring
    towns,"
        says the LORD,
  "so no one will live there;
    no man will dwell in it.

¹⁹"Like a lion coming up from Jordan's
    thickets
  to a rich pastureland,
I will chase Edom from its land in an
    instant.
  Who is the chosen one I will
    appoint for this?
Who is like me and who can
    challenge me?
  And what shepherd can stand
    against me?"
²⁰Therefore, hear what the LORD has
    planned against Edom,
  what he has purposed against those
    who live in Teman:
The young of the flock will be
    dragged away;
  he will completely destroy their
    pasture because of them.
²¹At the sound of their fall the earth
    will tremble;
  their cry will resound to the Red
    Sea.ᵃ
²²Look! An eagle will soar and swoop
    down,
  spreading its wings over Bozrah.
In that day the hearts of Edom's
    warriors
  will be like the heart of a woman
    in labor.

A Message About Damascus

²³Concerning Damascus:

"Hamath and Arpad are dismayed,
  for they have heard bad news.
They are disheartened,
  troubled likeᵇ the restless sea.
²⁴Damascus has become feeble,
  she has turned to flee
  and panic has gripped her;
anguish and pain have seized her,
  pain like that of a woman in labor.
²⁵Why has the city of renown not been
    abandoned,
  the town in which I delight?

_____
ᵃ 21 Hebrew *Yam Suph*; that is, Sea of Reeds   ᵇ 23 Hebrew *on* or *by*

26 Surely, her young men will fall in the
        streets;
    all her soldiers will be silenced in
        that day,"
            declares the LORD Almighty.
27 "I will set fire to the walls of
        Damascus;
    it will consume the fortresses of
        Ben-Hadad."

A Message About Kedar and Hazor

28 Concerning Kedar and the kingdoms of Hazor, which Nebuchadnezzar
king of Babylon attacked:

This is what the LORD says:

    "Arise, and attack Kedar
    and destroy the people of the East.
29 Their tents and their flocks will be
        taken;
    their shelters will be carried off
    with all their goods and camels.
    Men will shout to them,
    'Terror on every side!'

30 "Flee quickly away!
    Stay in deep caves, you who live in
        Hazor,"
            declares the LORD.
    "Nebuchadnezzar king of Babylon
        has plotted against you;
    he has devised a plan against you.

31 "Arise and attack a nation at ease,
    which lives in confidence,"
            declares the LORD,
    "a nation that has neither gates nor
        bars;
    its people live alone.
32 Their camels will become plunder,
    and their large herds will be booty.
    I will scatter to the winds those who
        are in distant places*a*
    and will bring disaster on them
        from every side,"
            declares the LORD.
33 "Hazor will become a haunt of
        jackals,
    a desolate place forever.
    No one will live there;
        no man will dwell in it."

A Message About Elam

34 This is the word of the LORD that
came to Jeremiah the prophet concerning

Elam, early in the reign of Zedekiah king
of Judah:

35 This is what the LORD Almighty
says:

    "See, I will break the bow of Elam,
    the mainstay of their might.
36 I will bring against Elam the four
        winds
    from the four quarters of the
        heavens;
    I will scatter them to the four winds,
    and there will not be a nation
    where Elam's exiles do not go.
37 I will shatter Elam before their foes,
    before those who seek their lives;
    I will bring disaster upon them,
        even my fierce anger,"
            declares the LORD.
    "I will pursue them with the sword
    until I have made an end of them.
38 I will set my throne in Elam
    and destroy her king and officials,"
            declares the LORD.

39 "Yet I will restore the fortunes of
        Elam
    in days to come,"
            declares the LORD.

A Message About Babylon

50 This is the word the LORD
spoke through Jeremiah the
prophet concerning Babylon and the
land of the Babylonians*b*:

2 "Announce and proclaim among the
        nations,
    lift up a banner and proclaim it;
    keep nothing back, but say,
    'Babylon will be captured;
    Bel will be put to shame,
    Marduk filled with terror.
    Her images will be put to shame
    and her idols filled with terror.'
3 A nation from the north will attack
        her
    and lay waste her land.
    No one will live in it;
    both men and animals will flee
        away.

4 "In those days, at that time,"
    declares the LORD,

a 32 Or *who clip the hair by their foreheads*   *b 1* Or *Chaldeans*; also in verses 8, 25, 35 and 45

"the people of Israel and the people of
   Judah together
will go in tears to seek the LORD
   their God.
5 They will ask the way to Zion
   and turn their faces toward it.
They will come and bind themselves
   to the LORD
in an everlasting covenant
   that will not be forgotten.

6 "My people have been lost sheep;
   their shepherds have led them
     astray
and caused them to roam on the
     mountains.
They wandered over mountain and
     hill
and forgot their own resting place.
7 Whoever found them devoured them;
   their enemies said, 'We are not
     guilty,
for they sinned against the LORD,
   their true pasture,
   the LORD, the hope of their fathers.'

8 "Flee out of Babylon;
   leave the land of the Babylonians,
and be like the goats that lead the
     flock.
9 For I will stir up and bring against
     Babylon
an alliance of great nations from
   the land of the north.
They will take up their positions
     against her,
and from the north she will be
     captured.
Their arrows will be like skilled
     warriors
who do not return empty-handed.
10 So Babylonia[a] will be plundered;
   all who plunder her will have their
     fill,"
                declares the LORD.

11 "Because you rejoice and are glad,
   you who pillage my inheritance,
because you frolic like a heifer
     threshing grain
and neigh like stallions,
12 your mother will be greatly ashamed;
   she who gave you birth will be
     disgraced.
She will be the least of the nations—
   a wilderness, a dry land, a desert.

13 Because of the LORD's anger she will
     not be inhabited
but will be completely desolate.
All who pass Babylon will be
     horrified and scoff
because of all her wounds.

14 "Take up your positions around
     Babylon,
all you who draw the bow.
Shoot at her! Spare no arrows,
   for she has sinned against the
     LORD.
15 Shout against her on every side!
   She surrenders, her towers fall,
   her walls are torn down.
Since this is the vengeance of the
     LORD,
take vengeance on her;
   do to her as she has done to others.
16 Cut off from Babylon the sower,
   and the reaper with his sickle at
     harvest.
Because of the sword of the oppressor
   let everyone return to his own
     people,
   let everyone flee to his own land.

17 "Israel is a scattered flock
   that lions have chased away.
The first to devour him
   was the king of Assyria;
the last to crush his bones
   was Nebuchadnezzar king of
     Babylon."

18 Therefore this is what the LORD
Almighty, the God of Israel, says:

"I will punish the king of Babylon
   and his land
as I punished the king of Assyria.
19 But I will bring Israel back to his own
     pasture
and he will graze on Carmel and
     Bashan;
his appetite will be satisfied
   on the hills of Ephraim and Gilead.
20 In those days, at that time,"
     declares the LORD,
"search will be made for Israel's guilt,
   but there will be none,
and for the sins of Judah,
   but none will be found,
for I will forgive the remnant I
     spare.

---

a 10 Or *Chaldea*

21 "Attack the land of Merathaim
     and those who live in Pekod.
   Pursue, kill and completely destroy[a]
     them,"
                          declares the LORD.
   "Do everything I have commanded
     you.
22 The noise of battle is in the land,
     the noise of great destruction!
23 How broken and shattered
     is the hammer of the whole earth!
   How desolate is Babylon
     among the nations!
24 I set a trap for you, O Babylon,
     and you were caught before you
       knew it;
   you were found and captured
     because you opposed the LORD.
25 The LORD has opened his arsenal
     and brought out the weapons of his
       wrath,
   for the Sovereign LORD Almighty has
       work to do
     in the land of the Babylonians.
26 Come against her from afar.
     Break open her granaries;
     pile her up like heaps of grain.
   Completely destroy her
     and leave her no remnant.
27 Kill all her young bulls;
     let them go down to the slaughter!
   Woe to them! For their day has come,
     the time for them to be punished.
28 Listen to the fugitives and refugees
     from Babylon
     declaring in Zion
   how the LORD our God has taken
       vengeance,
     vengeance for his temple.

29 "Summon archers against Babylon,
     all those who draw the bow.
   Encamp all around her;
     let no one escape.
   Repay her for her deeds;
     do to her as she has done.
   For she has defied the LORD,
     the Holy One of Israel.
30 Therefore, her young men will fall in
       the streets;
     all her soldiers will be silenced in
       that day,"
                          declares the LORD.
31 "See, I am against you, O arrogant
     one,"

declares the Lord, the LORD
     Almighty,
"for your day has come,
     the time for you to be punished.
32 The arrogant one will stumble and
     fall
     and no one will help her up;
   I will kindle a fire in her towns
     that will consume all who are
       around her."

33 This is what the LORD Almighty
says:

"The people of Israel are oppressed,
     and the people of Judah as well.
   All their captors hold them fast,
     refusing to let them go.
34 Yet their Redeemer is strong;
     the LORD Almighty is his name.
   He will vigorously defend their cause
     so that he may bring rest to their
       land,
     but unrest to those who live in
       Babylon.

35 "A sword against the Babylonians!"
     declares the LORD—
   "against those who live in Babylon
     and against her officials and wise
       men!
36 A sword against her false prophets!
     They will become fools.
   A sword against her warriors!
     They will be filled with terror.
37 A sword against her horses and
       chariots
     and all the foreigners in her ranks!
     They will become women.
   A sword against her treasures!
     They will be plundered.
38 A drought on[b] her waters!
     They will dry up.
   For it is a land of idols,
     idols that will go mad with terror.

39 "So desert creatures and hyenas will
       live there,
     and there the owl will dwell.
   It will never again be inhabited
     or lived in from generation to
       generation.
40 As God overthrew Sodom and
     Gomorrah

---

a 21 The Hebrew term refers to the irrevocable giving over of things or persons to the LORD, often by totally destroying them; also in verse 26.   b 38 Or A sword against

along with their neighboring
    towns,"
                declares the Lord,
"so no one will live there;
    no man will dwell in it.

41 "Look! An army is coming from the
    north;
    a great nation and many kings
    are being stirred up from the ends
        of the earth.
42 They are armed with bows and spears;
    they are cruel and without mercy.
They sound like the roaring sea
    as they ride on their horses;
they come like men in battle
    formation
    to attack you, O Daughter of
        Babylon.
43 The king of Babylon has heard
    reports about them,
    and his hands hang limp.
Anguish has gripped him,
    pain like that of a woman in labor.
44 Like a lion coming up from Jordan's
    thickets
    to a rich pastureland,
I will chase Babylon from its land in
    an instant.
Who is the chosen one I will
    appoint for this?
Who is like me and who can
    challenge me?
And what shepherd can stand
    against me?"
45 Therefore, hear what the Lord has
    planned against Babylon,
what he has purposed against the
    land of the Babylonians:
The young of the flock will be
    dragged away;
he will completely destroy their
    pasture because of them.
46 At the sound of Babylon's capture the
    earth will tremble;
    its cry will resound among the
        nations.

51

This is what the Lord says:

"See, I will stir up the spirit of a
    destroyer
against Babylon and the people of
    Leb Kamai.*a*

2 I will send foreigners to Babylon
    to winnow her and to devastate her
        land;
they will oppose her on every side
    in the day of her disaster.
3 Let not the archer string his bow,
    nor let him put on his armor.
Do not spare her young men;
    completely destroy*b* her army.
4 They will fall down slain in
    Babylon,*c*
    fatally wounded in her streets.
5 For Israel and Judah have not been
    forsaken
    by their God, the Lord Almighty,
though their land*d* is full of guilt
    before the Holy One of Israel.

6 "Flee from Babylon!
    Run for your lives!
    Do not be destroyed because of her
        sins.
It is time for the Lord's vengeance;
    he will pay her what she deserves.
7 Babylon was a gold cup in the Lord's
    hand;
    she made the whole earth drunk.
The nations drank her wine;
    therefore they have now gone mad.
8 Babylon will suddenly fall and be
    broken.
    Wail over her!
Get balm for her pain;
    perhaps she can be healed.

9 " 'We would have healed Babylon,
    but she cannot be healed;
let us leave her and each go to his
    own land,
    for her judgment reaches to the
        skies,
    it rises as high as the clouds.'

10 " 'The Lord has vindicated us;
    come, let us tell in Zion
    what the Lord our God has done.'

11 "Sharpen the arrows,
    take up the shields!
The Lord has stirred up the kings of
    the Medes,
    because his purpose is to destroy
        Babylon.
The Lord will take vengeance,
    vengeance for his temple.

---

a 1 Leb Kamai is a cryptogram for Chaldea, that is, Babylonia.   *b 3* The Hebrew term refers to the
irrevocable giving over of things or persons to the Lord, often by totally destroying them.   *c 4* Or
Chaldea   *d 5* Or / *and the land ,of the Babylonians⌉*

¹²Lift up a banner against the walls of
    Babylon!
  Reinforce the guard,
station the watchmen,
  prepare an ambush!
The LORD will carry out his purpose,
  his decree against the people of
    Babylon.
¹³You who live by many waters
  and are rich in treasures,
your end has come,
  the time for you to be cut off.
¹⁴The LORD Almighty has sworn by
    himself:
  I will surely fill you with men, as
    with a swarm of locusts,
  and they will shout in triumph
    over you.

¹⁵"He made the earth by his power;
  he founded the world by his
    wisdom
  and stretched out the heavens by
    his understanding.
¹⁶When he thunders, the waters in the
    heavens roar;
  he makes clouds rise from the ends
    of the earth.
He sends lightning with the rain
  and brings out the wind from his
    storehouses.

¹⁷"Every man is senseless and without
    knowledge;
  every goldsmith is shamed by his
    idols.
His images are a fraud;
  they have no breath in them.
¹⁸They are worthless, the objects of
    mockery;
  when their judgment comes, they
    will perish.
¹⁹He who is the Portion of Jacob is not
    like these,
  for he is the Maker of all things,
including the tribe of his
    inheritance—
  the LORD Almighty is his name.

²⁰"You are my war club,
  my weapon for battle—
with you I shatter nations,
  with you I destroy kingdoms,
²¹with you I shatter horse and rider,
  with you I shatter chariot and
    driver,

²²with you I shatter man and woman,
  with you I shatter old man and
    youth,
  with you I shatter young man and
    maiden,
²³with you I shatter shepherd and
    flock,
  with you I shatter farmer and oxen,
  with you I shatter governors and
    officials.

²⁴"Before your eyes I will repay Babylon and all who live in Babylonia[a] for all the wrong they have done in Zion," declares the LORD.

²⁵"I am against you, O destroying
    mountain,
  you who destroy the whole earth,"
                    declares the LORD.
"I will stretch out my hand against
    you,
  roll you off the cliffs,
  and make you a burned-out
    mountain.
²⁶No rock will be taken from you for a
    cornerstone,
  nor any stone for a foundation,
  for you will be desolate forever,"
                    declares the LORD.

²⁷"Lift up a banner in the land!
  Blow the trumpet among the
    nations!
Prepare the nations for battle against
    her;
  summon against her these
    kingdoms:
  Ararat, Minni and Ashkenaz.
Appoint a commander against her;
  send up horses like a swarm of
    locusts.
²⁸Prepare the nations for battle against
    her—
  the kings of the Medes,
their governors and all their officials,
  and all the countries they rule.
²⁹The land trembles and writhes,
  for the LORD's purposes against
    Babylon stand—
to lay waste the land of Babylon
  so that no one will live there.
³⁰Babylon's warriors have stopped
    fighting;
  they remain in their strongholds.

Their strength is exhausted;
　　they have become like women.
Her dwellings are set on fire;
　　the bars of her gates are broken.
31 One courier follows another
　　and messenger follows messenger
to announce to the king of Babylon
　　that his entire city is captured,
32 the river crossings seized,
　　the marshes set on fire,
　　and the soldiers terrified."

33 This is what the LORD Almighty, the
God of Israel, says:

"The Daughter of Babylon is like a
　　　threshing floor
　　at the time it is trampled;
　　the time to harvest her will soon
　　　come."

34 "Nebuchadnezzar king of Babylon
　　　has devoured us,
　　he has thrown us into confusion,
　　he has made us an empty jar.
Like a serpent he has swallowed us
　　and filled his stomach with our
　　　delicacies,
　　and then has spewed us out.
35 May the violence done to our flesh[a]
　　　be upon Babylon,"
　　say the inhabitants of Zion.
"May our blood be on those who live
　　　in Babylonia,"
　　says Jerusalem.

36 Therefore, this is what the LORD
says:

"See, I will defend your cause
　　and avenge you;
I will dry up her sea
　　and make her springs dry.
37 Babylon will be a heap of ruins,
　　a haunt of jackals,
an object of horror and scorn,
　　a place where no one lives.
38 Her people all roar like young lions,
　　they growl like lion cubs.
39 But while they are aroused,
　　I will set out a feast for them
　　and make them drunk,
so that they shout with laughter—
　　then sleep forever and not awake,"
　　　　　　　declares the LORD.

40 "I will bring them down
　　like lambs to the slaughter,
　　like rams and goats.
41 "How Sheshach[b] will be captured,
　　the boast of the whole earth seized!
What a horror Babylon will be
　　among the nations!
42 The sea will rise over Babylon;
　　its roaring waves will cover her.
43 Her towns will be desolate,
　　a dry and desert land,
a land where no one lives,
　　through which no man travels.
44 I will punish Bel in Babylon
　　and make him spew out what he
　　　has swallowed.
The nations will no longer stream to
　　　him.
　　And the wall of Babylon will fall.

45 "Come out of her, my people!
　　Run for your lives!
　　Run from the fierce anger of the
　　　LORD.
46 Do not lose heart or be afraid
　　when rumors are heard in the land;
one rumor comes this year, another
　　　the next,
　　rumors of violence in the land
　　and of ruler against ruler.
47 For the time will surely come
　　when I will punish the idols of
　　　Babylon;
her whole land will be disgraced
　　and her slain will all lie fallen
　　　within her.
48 Then heaven and earth and all that is
　　　in them
　　will shout for joy over Babylon,
for out of the north
　　destroyers will attack her,"
　　　　　　　　　　declares the LORD.
49 "Babylon must fall because of Israel's
　　　slain,
　　just as the slain in all the earth
　　have fallen because of Babylon.
50 You who have escaped the sword,
　　leave and do not linger!
Remember the LORD in a distant
　　　land,
　　and think on Jerusalem."

51 "We are disgraced,
　　for we have been insulted
　　and shame covers our faces,

---

[a] 35 Or done to us and to our children　　　[b] 41 Sheshach is a cryptogram for Babylon.

because foreigners have entered
  the holy places of the LORD's
  house."

⁵² "But days are coming," declares the
  LORD,
  "when I will punish her idols,
and throughout her land
  the wounded will groan.
⁵³ Even if Babylon reaches the sky
  and fortifies her lofty stronghold,
  I will send destroyers against her,"
                    declares the LORD.

⁵⁴ "The sound of a cry comes from
  Babylon,
  the sound of great destruction
  from the land of the Babylonians.ᵃ
⁵⁵ The LORD will destroy Babylon;
  he will silence her noisy din.
Waves ⌊of enemies⌋ will rage like
    great waters;
  the roar of their voices will resound.
⁵⁶ A destroyer will come against
  Babylon;
  her warriors will be captured,
  and their bows will be broken.
For the LORD is a God of retribution;
  he will repay in full.
⁵⁷ I will make her officials and wise
    men drunk,
  her governors, officers and warriors
    as well;
they will sleep forever and not
    awake,"
  declares the King, whose name is
    the LORD Almighty.

⁵⁸ This is what the LORD Almighty
says:

"Babylon's thick wall will be leveled
  and her high gates set on fire;
the peoples exhaust themselves for
    nothing,
  the nations' labor is only fuel for
    the flames."

⁵⁹ This is the message Jeremiah gave
to the staff officer Seraiah son of Neriah, the son of Mahseiah, when he went
to Babylon with Zedekiah king of Judah
in the fourth year of his reign. ⁶⁰ Jeremiah had written on a scroll about all
the disasters that would come upon

Babylon—all that had been recorded
concerning Babylon. ⁶¹ He said to Seraiah, "When you get to Babylon, see that
you read all these words aloud. ⁶² Then
say, 'O LORD, you have said you will
destroy this place, so that neither man
nor animal will live in it; it will be desolate forever.' ⁶³ When you finish reading this scroll, tie a stone to it and
throw it into the Euphrates. ⁶⁴ Then say,
'So will Babylon sink to rise no more
because of the disaster I will bring upon
her. And her people will fall.' "

The words of Jeremiah end here.

The Fall of Jerusalem

52 Zedekiah was twenty-one
years old when he became
king, and he reigned in Jerusalem
eleven years. His mother's name was
Hamutal daughter of Jeremiah; she was
from Libnah. ²He did evil in the eyes of
the LORD, just as Jehoiakim had done.
³It was because of the LORD's anger that
all this happened to Jerusalem and
Judah, and in the end he thrust them
from his presence.
  Now Zedekiah rebelled against the
king of Babylon.
  ⁴So in the ninth year of Zedekiah's
reign, on the tenth day of the tenth
month, Nebuchadnezzar king of Babylon marched against Jerusalem with
his whole army. They camped outside
the city and built siege works all around
it. ⁵The city was kept under siege until
the eleventh year of King Zedekiah.
  ⁶By the ninth day of the fourth month
the famine in the city had become so
severe that there was no food for the
people to eat. ⁷Then the city wall was
broken through, and the whole army
fled. They left the city at night through
the gate between the two walls near the
king's garden, though the Babyloniansᵇ
were surrounding the city. They fled
toward the Arabah,ᶜ ⁸but the Babylonianᵈ army pursued King Zedekiah and
overtook him in the plains of Jericho.
All his soldiers were separated from him
and scattered, ⁹and he was captured.
  He was taken to the king of Babylon
at Riblah in the land of Hamath, where
he pronounced sentence on him.

ᵃ 54 Or *Chaldeans*   ᵇ 7 Or *Chaldeans*; also in verse 17   ᶜ 7 Or *the Jordan Valley*   ᵈ 8 Or
Chaldean; also in verse 14

¹⁰There at Riblah the king of Babylon slaughtered the sons of Zedekiah before his eyes; he also killed all the officials of Judah. ¹¹Then he put out Zedekiah's eyes, bound him with bronze shackles and took him to Babylon, where he put him in prison till the day of his death.

¹²On the tenth day of the fifth month, in the nineteenth year of Nebuchadnezzar king of Babylon, Nebuzaradan commander of the imperial guard, who served the king of Babylon, came to Jerusalem. ¹³He set fire to the temple of the LORD, the royal palace and all the houses of Jerusalem. Every important building he burned down. ¹⁴The whole Babylonian army under the commander of the imperial guard broke down all the walls around Jerusalem. ¹⁵Nebuzaradan the commander of the guard carried into exile some of the poorest people and those who remained in the city, along with the rest of the craftsmen*a* and those who had gone over to the king of Babylon. ¹⁶But Nebuzaradan left behind the rest of the poorest people of the land to work the vineyards and fields.

¹⁷The Babylonians broke up the bronze pillars, the movable stands and the bronze Sea that were at the temple of the LORD and they carried all the bronze to Babylon. ¹⁸They also took away the pots, shovels, wick trimmers, sprinkling bowls, dishes and all the bronze articles used in the temple service. ¹⁹The commander of the imperial guard took away the basins, censers, sprinkling bowls, pots, lampstands, dishes and bowls used for drink offerings—all that were made of pure gold or silver.

²⁰The bronze from the two pillars, the Sea and the twelve bronze bulls under it, and the movable stands, which King Solomon had made for the temple of the LORD, was more than could be weighed. ²¹Each of the pillars was eighteen cubits high and twelve cubits in circumference*b*; each was four fingers thick, and hollow. ²²The bronze capital on top of the one pillar was five cubits*c* high and was decorated with a network and

pomegranates of bronze all around. The other pillar, with its pomegranates, was similar. ²³There were ninety-six pomegranates on the sides; the total number of pomegranates above the surrounding network was a hundred.

²⁴The commander of the guard took as prisoners Seraiah the chief priest, Zephaniah the priest next in rank and the three doorkeepers. ²⁵Of those still in the city, he took the officer in charge of the fighting men, and seven royal advisers. He also took the secretary who was chief officer in charge of conscripting the people of the land and sixty of his men who were found in the city. ²⁶Nebuzaradan the commander took them all and brought them to the king of Babylon at Riblah. ²⁷There at Riblah, in the land of Hamath, the king had them executed.

So Judah went into captivity, away from her land. ²⁸This is the number of the people Nebuchadnezzar carried into exile:

in the seventh year, 3,023 Jews;
²⁹in Nebuchadnezzar's eighteenth year,
832 people from Jerusalem;
³⁰in his twenty-third year,
745 Jews taken into exile by Nebuzaradan the commander of the imperial guard.
There were 4,600 people in all.

Jehoiachin Released

³¹In the thirty-seventh year of the exile of Jehoiachin king of Judah, in the year Evil-Merodach*d* became king of Babylon, he released Jehoiachin king of Judah and freed him from prison on the twenty-fifth day of the twelfth month. ³²He spoke kindly to him and gave him a seat of honor higher than those of the other kings who were with him in Babylon. ³³So Jehoiachin put aside his prison clothes and for the rest of his life ate regularly at the king's table. ³⁴Day by day the king of Babylon gave Jehoiachin a regular allowance as long as he lived, till the day of his death.

---

a 15 Or *populace*   *b 21* That is, about 27 feet (about 8.1 meters) high and 18 feet (about 5.4 meters) in circumference   *c 22* That is, about 7 1/2 feet (about 2.3 meters)   *d 31* Also called *Amel-Marduk*

LAMENTATIONS

AMENTATIONS IS THE ONLY OLD TESTA-
MENT BOOK THAT CONSISTS SOLELY OF
LAMENTS. ITS AUTHOR, TRADITIONALLY
THOUGHT TO BE JEREMIAH, "LAMENTS" THE
INTENSE SUFFERING OF GOD'S PEOPLE AND THE
UTTER DEVASTATION OF THE TEMPLE. KNOWING
THAT GOD IS MERCIFUL, HE APPEALS FOR MERCY
IN PRAYER. IN THE MIDDLE OF THE BOOK, JEREMI-
AH AFFIRMS GOD'S GOODNESS AND FAITHFUL-
NESS IN THE MIDST OF SUFFERING. HERE YOU
FIND A FAITH ROOTED IN GOD'S UNCHANGING
CHARACTER—A RINGING AFFIRMATION OF THE
GOD WHOSE "COMPASSIONS NEVER FAIL" (3:22).

1 *a* How deserted lies the city,
  once so full of people!
How like a widow is she,
  who once was great among the
    nations!
She who was queen among the
    provinces
  has now become a slave.

2 Bitterly she weeps at night,
  tears are upon her cheeks.
Among all her lovers
  there is none to comfort her.
All her friends have betrayed her;
  they have become her enemies.

3 After affliction and harsh labor,
  Judah has gone into exile.
She dwells among the nations;
  she finds no resting place.
All who pursue her have overtaken
    her
  in the midst of her distress.

4 The roads to Zion mourn,
  for no one comes to her appointed
    feasts.
All her gateways are desolate,
  her priests groan,
her maidens grieve,
  and she is in bitter anguish.

5 Her foes have become her masters;
  her enemies are at ease.
The LORD has brought her grief
  because of her many sins.
Her children have gone into exile,
  captive before the foe.

a This chapter is an acrostic poem, the verses of which begin with the successive letters of the Hebrew
alphabet.

⁶All the splendor has departed
  from the Daughter of Zion.
Her princes are like deer
  that find no pasture;
in weakness they have fled
  before the pursuer.

⁷In the days of her affliction and
    wandering
  Jerusalem remembers all the
    treasures
  that were hers in days of old.
When her people fell into enemy
    hands,
  there was no one to help her.
Her enemies looked at her
  and laughed at her destruction.

⁸Jerusalem has sinned greatly
  and so has become unclean.
All who honored her despise her,
  for they have seen her nakedness;
she herself groans
  and turns away.

⁹Her filthiness clung to her skirts;
  she did not consider her future.
Her fall was astounding;
  there was none to comfort her.
"Look, O LORD, on my affliction,
  for the enemy has triumphed."

¹⁰The enemy laid hands
  on all her treasures;
she saw pagan nations
  enter her sanctuary—
those you had forbidden
  to enter your assembly.

¹¹All her people groan
  as they search for bread;
they barter their treasures for food
  to keep themselves alive.
"Look, O LORD, and consider,
  for I am despised."

¹²"Is it nothing to you, all you who
    pass by?
  Look around and see.
Is any suffering like my suffering
  that was inflicted on me,
that the LORD brought on me
  in the day of his fierce anger?

¹³"From on high he sent fire,
  sent it down into my bones.
He spread a net for my feet
  and turned me back.

He made me desolate,
  faint all the day long.

¹⁴"My sins have been bound into a
    yokeᵃ;
  by his hands they were woven
    together.
They have come upon my neck
  and the Lord has sapped my
    strength.
He has handed me over
  to those I cannot withstand.

¹⁵"The Lord has rejected
  all the warriors in my midst;
he has summoned an army against me
  toᵇ crush my young men.
In his winepress the Lord has
    trampled
  the Virgin Daughter of Judah.

¹⁶"This is why I weep
  and my eyes overflow with tears.
No one is near to comfort me,
  no one to restore my spirit.
My children are destitute
  because the enemy has prevailed."

¹⁷Zion stretches out her hands,
  but there is no one to comfort her.
The LORD has decreed for Jacob
  that his neighbors become his foes;
Jerusalem has become
  an unclean thing among them.

¹⁸"The LORD is righteous,
  yet I rebelled against his command.
Listen, all you peoples;
  look upon my suffering.
My young men and maidens
  have gone into exile.

¹⁹"I called to my allies
  but they betrayed me.
My priests and my elders
  perished in the city
while they searched for food
  to keep themselves alive.

²⁰"See, O LORD, how distressed I am!
  I am in torment within,
and in my heart I am disturbed,
  for I have been most rebellious.
Outside, the sword bereaves;
  inside, there is only death.

²¹"People have heard my groaning,
  but there is no one to comfort me.

ᵃ 14 Most Hebrew manuscripts; Septuagint *He kept watch over my sins*   ᵇ 15 Or *has set a time for me
/ when he will*

All my enemies have heard of my
  distress;
  they rejoice at what you have done.
May you bring the day you have
  announced
  so they may become like me.
22 "Let all their wickedness come
  before you;
  deal with them
as you have dealt with me
  because of all my sins.
My groans are many
  and my heart is faint."

2 *a* How the Lord has covered the
  Daughter of Zion
with the cloud of his anger*b*!
He has hurled down the splendor of
  Israel
  from heaven to earth;
he has not remembered his footstool
  in the day of his anger.

2 Without pity the Lord has swallowed
  up
  all the dwellings of Jacob;
in his wrath he has torn down
  the strongholds of the Daughter of
  Judah.
He has brought her kingdom and its
  princes
  down to the ground in dishonor.

3 In fierce anger he has cut off
  every horn*c* of Israel.
He has withdrawn his right hand
  at the approach of the enemy.
He has burned in Jacob like a flaming
  fire
  that consumes everything around it.

4 Like an enemy he has strung his
  bow;
  his right hand is ready.
Like a foe he has slain
  all who were pleasing to the eye;
he has poured out his wrath like fire
  on the tent of the Daughter of Zion.

5 The Lord is like an enemy;
  he has swallowed up Israel.
He has swallowed up all her palaces
  and destroyed her strongholds.
He has multiplied mourning and
  lamentation

for the Daughter of Judah.

6 He has laid waste his dwelling like a
  garden;
  he has destroyed his place of
  meeting.
The LORD has made Zion forget
  her appointed feasts and her
  Sabbaths;
in his fierce anger he has spurned
  both king and priest.

7 The Lord has rejected his altar
  and abandoned his sanctuary.
He has handed over to the enemy
  the walls of her palaces;
they have raised a shout in the house
  of the LORD
  as on the day of an appointed feast.

8 The LORD determined to tear down
  the wall around the Daughter of
  Zion.
He stretched out a measuring line
  and did not withhold his hand
  from destroying.
He made ramparts and walls lament;
  together they wasted away.

9 Her gates have sunk into the ground;
  their bars he has broken and
  destroyed.
Her king and her princes are exiled
  among the nations,
  the law is no more,
and her prophets no longer find
  visions from the LORD.

10 The elders of the Daughter of Zion
  sit on the ground in silence;
they have sprinkled dust on their
  heads
  and put on sackcloth.
The young women of Jerusalem
  have bowed their heads to the
  ground.

11 My eyes fail from weeping,
  I am in torment within,
my heart is poured out on the ground
  because my people are destroyed,
because children and infants faint
  in the streets of the city.

12 They say to their mothers,
  "Where is bread and wine?"
as they faint like wounded men

---

a This chapter is an acrostic poem, the verses of which begin with the successive letters of the Hebrew
alphabet.   *b* 1 Or *How the Lord in his anger / has treated the Daughter of Zion with contempt*
c 3 Or / *all the strength*; or *every king*; *horn* here symbolizes strength.

in the streets of the city,
as their lives ebb away
in their mothers' arms.

¹³ What can I say for you?
With what can I compare you,
O Daughter of Jerusalem?
To what can I liken you,
that I may comfort you,
O Virgin Daughter of Zion?
Your wound is as deep as the sea.
Who can heal you?

¹⁴ The visions of your prophets
were false and worthless;
they did not expose your sin
to ward off your captivity.
The oracles they gave you
were false and misleading.

¹⁵ All who pass your way
clap their hands at you;
they scoff and shake their heads
at the Daughter of Jerusalem:
"Is this the city that was called
the perfection of beauty,
the joy of the whole earth?"

¹⁶ All your enemies open their mouths
wide against you;
they scoff and gnash their teeth
and say, "We have swallowed her
up.
This is the day we have waited for;
we have lived to see it."

¹⁷ The LORD has done what he planned;
he has fulfilled his word,
which he decreed long ago.
He has overthrown you without pity,
he has let the enemy gloat over
you,
he has exalted the horn^a of your
foes.

¹⁸ The hearts of the people
cry out to the Lord.
O wall of the Daughter of Zion,
let your tears flow like a river
day and night;
give yourself no relief,
your eyes no rest.

¹⁹ Arise, cry out in the night,
as the watches of the night begin;
pour out your heart like water
in the presence of the Lord.

Lift up your hands to him
for the lives of your children,
who faint from hunger
at the head of every street.

²⁰ "Look, O LORD, and consider:
Whom have you ever treated like
this?
Should women eat their offspring,
the children they have cared for?
Should priest and prophet be killed
in the sanctuary of the Lord?

²¹ "Young and old lie together
in the dust of the streets;
my young men and maidens
have fallen by the sword.
You have slain them in the day of
your anger;
you have slaughtered them
without pity.

²² "As you summon to a feast day,
so you summoned against me
terrors on every side.
In the day of the LORD's anger
no one escaped or survived;
those I cared for and reared,
my enemy has destroyed."

3^b I am the man who has seen
affliction
by the rod of his wrath.
² He has driven me away and made me
walk
in darkness rather than light;
³ indeed, he has turned his hand
against me
again and again, all day long.

⁴ He has made my skin and my flesh
grow old
and has broken my bones.
⁵ He has besieged me and surrounded
me
with bitterness and hardship.
⁶ He has made me dwell in darkness
like those long dead.

⁷ He has walled me in so I cannot
escape;
he has weighed me down with
chains.
⁸ Even when I call out or cry for help,
he shuts out my prayer.

---

^a 17 Horn here symbolizes strength.   ^b This chapter is an acrostic poem; the verses of each stanza begin with the successive letters of the Hebrew alphabet, and the verses within each stanza begin with the same letter.

9 He has barred my way with blocks of
    stone;
  he has made my paths crooked.

10 Like a bear lying in wait,
    like a lion in hiding,
11 he dragged me from the path and
    mangled me
  and left me without help.
12 He drew his bow

and made me the target for his
    arrows.

13 He pierced my heart
    with arrows from his quiver.
14 I became the laughingstock of all my
    people;
  they mock me in song all day long.
15 He has filled me with bitter herbs
    and sated me with gall.

TUESDAY

A TIME OF TEMPTATION
F. B. Meyer

VERSE: Lamentations 3:19   **PASSAGE:** Lamentations 3:19–26

ou will be tempted to the end of your life, and the nearer you live to Christ the more you will be tempted . . . The [one] who sees the heavenly vision is the [one] whom the devil will tempt to the uttermost. God will permit it because temptation does for us what the storms do for the oaks—it roots us—and what the fire does for the painting on porcelain—it makes us permanent. You never know that you have a grip on Christ, or that he has a grip on you so well as when the devil is using all his force to attract you from him; then you feel the pull of Christ's right hand.

As long as the soldier slinks outside the battle, he faces little danger, but let him plunge in and follow the captain and he will soon have the bullets flying about him. Some of us have had a good time because there was no use in the devil wasting powder and shot upon us; we haven't been doing him any harm. But once we begin to wake up and set to work for God, the devil will set a thousand evils to worrying us . . .

The nearer you get to Christ the more you will have to do with temptation. The closer you get into the heart of the fight the more the devil will torment you . . . But the virulence of the temptation means not that you are declining into sin, but that you are advancing in holiness; that the devil is afraid of you and hopes only to wound Christ by hurting you.

ADDITIONAL SCRIPTURE READING:
Psalm 119:105; Jeremiah 15:16; Matthew 4:1–4

Go to page 929 for your next devotional reading.

1700   1900

16 He has broken my teeth with gravel;
   he has trampled me in the dust.

AFFLICTION TEACHETH A WICKED PERSON SOME-
TIME TO PRAY: PROSPERITY NEVER. —Ben Johnson

---

17 I have been deprived of peace;
   I have forgotten what prosperity is.
18 So I say, "My splendor is gone
   and all that I had hoped from the
   LORD."

19 I remember my affliction and my
   wandering,
   the bitterness and the gall.
20 I well remember them,
   and my soul is downcast within me.
21 Yet this I call to mind
   and therefore I have hope:

22 Because of the LORD's great love we
   are not consumed,
   for his compassions never fail.
23 They are new every morning;
   great is your faithfulness.
24 I say to myself, "The LORD is my
   portion;
   therefore I will wait for him."

25 The LORD is good to those whose
   hope is in him,
   to the one who seeks him;
26 it is good to wait quietly
   for the salvation of the LORD.
27 It is good for a man to bear the yoke
   while he is young.

28 Let him sit alone in silence,
   for the LORD has laid it on him.
29 Let him bury his face in the dust—
   there may yet be hope.
30 Let him offer his cheek to one who
   would strike him,
   and let him be filled with disgrace.

31 For men are not cast off
   by the Lord forever.
32 Though he brings grief, he will show
   compassion,
   so great is his unfailing love.
33 For he does not willingly bring
   affliction
   or grief to the children of men.

34 To crush underfoot
   all prisoners in the land,
35 to deny a man his rights
   before the Most High,

36 to deprive a man of justice—
   would not the Lord see such things?

37 Who can speak and have it happen
   if the Lord has not decreed it?
38 Is it not from the mouth of the Most
   High
   that both calamities and good
   things come?
39 Why should any living man complain
   when punished for his sins?

40 Let us examine our ways and test
   them,
   and let us return to the LORD.
41 Let us lift up our hearts and our
   hands
   to God in heaven, and say:
42 "We have sinned and rebelled
   and you have not forgiven.

43 "You have covered yourself with
   anger and pursued us;
   you have slain without pity.
44 You have covered yourself with a
   cloud
   so that no prayer can get through.
45 You have made us scum and refuse
   among the nations.

46 "All our enemies have opened their
   mouths
   wide against us.
47 We have suffered terror and pitfalls,
   ruin and destruction."
48 Streams of tears flow from my eyes
   because my people are destroyed.

49 My eyes will flow unceasingly,
   without relief,
50 until the LORD looks down
   from heaven and sees.
51 What I see brings grief to my soul
   because of all the women of my
   city.

52 Those who were my enemies
   without cause
   hunted me like a bird.
53 They tried to end my life in a pit
   and threw stones at me;
54 the waters closed over my head,
   and I thought I was about to be cut
   off.

55 I called on your name, O LORD,
   from the depths of the pit.
56 You heard my plea: "Do not close
   your ears
   to my cry for relief."

57 You came near when I called you,
and you said, "Do not fear."

58 O Lord, you took up my case;
you redeemed my life.

59 You have seen, O LORD, the wrong
done to me.
Uphold my cause!

60 You have seen the depth of their
vengeance,
all their plots against me.

61 O LORD, you have heard their insults,
all their plots against me—

62 what my enemies whisper and mutter
against me all day long.

63 Look at them! Sitting or standing,
they mock me in their songs.

64 Pay them back what they deserve,
O LORD,
for what their hands have done.

65 Put a veil over their hearts,
and may your curse be on them!

66 Pursue them in anger and destroy
them
from under the heavens of the
LORD.

WEDNESDAY

THE HAND OF GOD ALSO WAITS
Frances Ridley Havergal

VERSE: Lamentations 3:24   **PASSAGE:** Lamentations 3:24–27

id you ever hear of anyone being much used for Christ who did not have some *special* waiting time, some complete *upset* of all his or her plans first; from St. Paul's being sent off into the desert of Arabia for three years, when he must have been boiling over with the glad tidings, down to the present day (see Galatians 1:17–18)?

You were looking forward to telling about trusting Jesus in Syria; now he says, "I want you to *show* what it is to trust me, without waiting for Syria."

My own case is far less severe, but the same in principle, that when I thought the door was flung open for me to go with a bound into literary work, it is opposed, and doctor steps in and says, simply, "Never! She must choose between writing and living; she can't do both" . . .

In 1869 [I] saw the evident wisdom of being kept waiting nine years in the shade. God's love being unchangeable, he is just as loving when we do not see or feel his love. Also his love and his sovereignty are co-equal and universal; so he withholds the enjoyment and conscious progress because he knows best what will really ripen and further his work in us.

ADDITIONAL SCRIPTURE READING:
1 Kings 17:3–6; Ezekiel 37:1; Acts 9:7–9

Go to page 947 for your next devotional reading.

1700   1900

4 [a] How the gold has lost its
luster,
the fine gold become dull!
The sacred gems are scattered
at the head of every street.

2 How the precious sons of Zion,
once worth their weight in gold,
are now considered as pots of clay,
the work of a potter's hands!

3 Even jackals offer their breasts
to nurse their young,
but my people have become heartless
like ostriches in the desert.

4 Because of thirst the infant's tongue
sticks to the roof of its mouth;
the children beg for bread,
but no one gives it to them.

5 Those who once ate delicacies
are destitute in the streets.
Those nurtured in purple
now lie on ash heaps.

6 The punishment of my people
is greater than that of Sodom,
which was overthrown in a moment
without a hand turned to help her.

7 Their princes were brighter than
snow
and whiter than milk,
their bodies more ruddy than rubies,
their appearance like sapphires. [b]

8 But now they are blacker than soot;
they are not recognized in the
streets.
Their skin has shriveled on their
bones;
it has become as dry as a stick.

9 Those killed by the sword are better
off
than those who die of famine;
racked with hunger, they waste
away
for lack of food from the field.

10 With their own hands compassionate
women
have cooked their own children,
who became their food
when my people were destroyed.

11 The LORD has given full vent to his
wrath;
he has poured out his fierce anger.
He kindled a fire in Zion
that consumed her foundations.

12 The kings of the earth did not
believe,
nor did any of the world's people,
that enemies and foes could enter
the gates of Jerusalem.

13 But it happened because of the sins of
her prophets
and the iniquities of her priests,
who shed within her
the blood of the righteous.

14 Now they grope through the streets
like men who are blind.
They are so defiled with blood
that no one dares to touch their
garments.

15 "Go away! You are unclean!" men
cry to them.
"Away! Away! Don't touch us!"
When they flee and wander about,
people among the nations say,
"They can stay here no longer."

16 The LORD himself has scattered
them;
he no longer watches over them.
The priests are shown no honor,
the elders no favor.

17 Moreover, our eyes failed,
looking in vain for help;
from our towers we watched
for a nation that could not save us.

18 Men stalked us at every step,
so we could not walk in our
streets.
Our end was near, our days were
numbered,
for our end had come.

19 Our pursuers were swifter
than eagles in the sky;
they chased us over the mountains
and lay in wait for us in the
desert.

20 The LORD's anointed, our very life
breath,
was caught in their traps.
We thought that under his shadow
we would live among the nations.

[a] This chapter is an acrostic poem, the verses of which begin with the successive letters of the Hebrew
alphabet.   [b] 7 Or *lapis lazuli*

²¹ Rejoice and be glad, O Daughter of
    Edom,
  you who live in the land of Uz.
But to you also the cup will be
    passed;
  you will be drunk and stripped
    naked.

²² O Daughter of Zion, your
    punishment will end;
  he will not prolong your exile.
But, O Daughter of Edom, he will
    punish your sin
  and expose your wickedness.

5 Remember, O LORD, what has
  happened to us;
  look, and see our disgrace.
² Our inheritance has been turned over
    to aliens,
  our homes to foreigners.
³ We have become orphans and
    fatherless,
  our mothers like widows.
⁴ We must buy the water we drink;
  our wood can be had only at a
    price.
⁵ Those who pursue us are at our
    heels;
  we are weary and find no rest.
⁶ We submitted to Egypt and Assyria
  to get enough bread.
⁷ Our fathers sinned and are no more,
  and we bear their punishment.
⁸ Slaves rule over us,
  and there is none to free us from
    their hands.

⁹ We get our bread at the risk of our
    lives
  because of the sword in the desert.
¹⁰ Our skin is hot as an oven,
  feverish from hunger.
¹¹ Women have been ravished in Zion,
  and virgins in the towns of Judah.
¹² Princes have been hung up by their
    hands;
  elders are shown no respect.
¹³ Young men toil at the millstones;
  boys stagger under loads of wood.
¹⁴ The elders are gone from the city
    gate;
  the young men have stopped their
    music.
¹⁵ Joy is gone from our hearts;
  our dancing has turned to
    mourning.
¹⁶ The crown has fallen from our head.
  Woe to us, for we have sinned!
¹⁷ Because of this our hearts are faint,
  because of these things our eyes
    grow dim
¹⁸ for Mount Zion, which lies desolate,
  with jackals prowling over it.

¹⁹ You, O LORD, reign forever;
  your throne endures from
    generation to generation.
²⁰ Why do you always forget us?
  Why do you forsake us so long?
²¹ Restore us to yourself, O LORD, that
    we may return;
  renew our days as of old
²² unless you have utterly rejected us
  and are angry with us beyond
    measure.

EZEKIEL

Z EKIEL WAS AMONG THE MORE THAN
3,000 JEWS EXILED TO BABYLON BY NEBU-
CHADNEZZAR IN 597 B.C., AND THERE
AMONG THE EXILES HE RECEIVED HIS CALL TO
BECOME A PROPHET. AS A PRIEST-PROPHET CALLED
TO MINISTER TO THE EXILES, HE USES WORDS,
VISIONS AND "MINI-DRAMAS" TO URGE THE PEOPLE
TO RENEW THEIR COMMITMENT TO GOD. NOWHERE
IN THE BIBLE IS GOD'S CONTROL OVER ALL CRE-
ATION EXPRESSED MORE CLEARLY THAN IN EZEKIEL.
WATCH FOR THE MESSAGE OF GOD'S MAJESTY AND
GLORY: ALL THIS WOULD HAPPEN SO THAT "THEY
WILL KNOW THAT I AM THE LORD" (6:10).

The Living Creatures and the Glory of the LORD

1 In the[a] thirtieth year, in the fourth month on the fifth day, while I was among the exiles by the Kebar River, the heavens were opened and I saw visions of God.

²On the fifth of the month—it was the fifth year of the exile of King Jehoiachin— ³the word of the LORD came to Ezekiel the priest, the son of Buzi,[b] by the Kebar River in the land of the Babylonians.[c] There the hand of the LORD was upon him.

⁴I looked, and I saw a windstorm coming out of the north—an immense cloud with flashing lightning and surrounded by brilliant light. The center of the fire looked like glowing metal, ⁵and in the fire was what looked like four living creatures. In appearance their form was that of a man, ⁶but each of them had four faces and four wings. ⁷Their legs were straight; their feet were like those of a calf and gleamed like burnished bronze. ⁸Under their wings on their four sides they had the hands of a man. All four of them had faces and wings, ⁹and their wings touched one another. Each one went straight ahead; they did not turn as they moved.

¹⁰Their faces looked like this: Each of the four had the face of a man, and on the right side each had the face of a lion, and on the left the face of an ox; each also had the face of an eagle. ¹¹Such were their faces. Their wings were

ᵃ 1 Or my ᵇ 3 Or Ezekiel son of Buzi the priest ᶜ 3 Or Chaldeans spread out upward; each had two wings, one touching the wing of another creature on either side, and two wings covering its body. 12Each one went straight ahead. Wherever the spirit would go, they would go, without turning as they went. 13The appearance of the living creatures was like burning coals of fire or like torches. Fire moved back and forth among the creatures; it was bright, and lightning flashed out of it. 14The creatures sped back and forth like flashes of lightning.

15As I looked at the living creatures, I saw a wheel on the ground beside each creature with its four faces. 16This was the appearance and structure of the wheels: They sparkled like chrysolite, and all four looked alike. Each appeared to be made like a wheel intersecting a wheel. 17As they moved, they would go in any one of the four directions the creatures faced; the wheels did not turn about*a* as the creatures went. 18Their rims were high and awesome, and all four rims were full of eyes all around.

19When the living creatures moved, the wheels beside them moved; and when the living creatures rose from the ground, the wheels also rose. 20Wherever the spirit would go, they would go, and the wheels would rise along with them, because the spirit of the living creatures was in the wheels. 21When the creatures moved, they also moved; when the creatures stood still, they also stood still; and when the creatures rose from the ground, the wheels rose along with them, because the spirit of the living creatures was in the wheels.

22Spread out above the heads of the living creatures was what looked like an expanse, sparkling like ice, and awesome. 23Under the expanse their wings were stretched out one toward the other, and each had two wings covering its body. 24When the creatures moved, I heard the sound of their wings, like the roar of rushing waters, like the voice of the Almighty,*b* like the tumult of an army. When they stood still, they lowered their wings.

25Then there came a voice from above the expanse over their heads as they stood with lowered wings. 26Above the expanse over their heads was what looked like a throne of sapphire,*c* and high above on the throne was a figure like that of a man. 27I saw that from what appeared to be his waist up he looked like glowing metal, as if full of fire, and that from there down he looked like fire; and brilliant light surrounded him. 28Like the appearance of a rainbow in the clouds on a rainy day, so was the radiance around him.

This was the appearance of the likeness of the glory of the LORD. When I saw it, I fell facedown, and I heard the voice of one speaking.

Ezekiel's Call

2 He said to me, "Son of man, stand up on your feet and I will speak to you." 2As he spoke, the Spirit came into me and raised me to my feet, and I heard him speaking to me.

3He said: "Son of man, I am sending you to the Israelites, to a rebellious nation that has rebelled against me; they and their fathers have been in revolt against me to this very day. 4The people to whom I am sending you are obstinate and stubborn. Say to them, 'This is what the Sovereign LORD says.' 5And whether they listen or fail to listen—for they are a rebellious house—they will know that a prophet has been among them. 6And you, son of man, do not be afraid of them or their words. Do not be afraid, though briers and thorns are all around you and you live among scorpions. Do not be afraid of what they say or terrified by them, though they are a rebellious house. 7You must speak my words to them, whether they listen or fail to listen, for they are rebellious. 8But you, son of man, listen to what I say to you. Do not rebel like that rebellious house; open your mouth and eat what I give you."

9Then I looked, and I saw a hand stretched out to me. In it was a scroll, 10which he unrolled before me. On both sides of it were written words of lament and mourning and woe.

3 And he said to me, "Son of man, eat what is before you, eat this scroll; then go and speak to the house of Israel." 2So I opened my mouth, and he gave me the scroll to eat.

---

a 17 Or *aside*   *b* 24 Hebrew *Shaddai*   *c* 26 Or *lapis lazuli*

³Then he said to me, "Son of man, eat this scroll I am giving you and fill your stomach with it." So I ate it, and it tasted as sweet as honey in my mouth.

⁴He then said to me: "Son of man, go now to the house of Israel and speak my words to them. ⁵You are not being sent to a people of obscure speech and difficult language, but to the house of Israel— ⁶not to many peoples of obscure speech and difficult language, whose words you cannot understand. Surely if I had sent you to them, they would have listened to you. ⁷But the house of Israel is not willing to listen to you because they are not willing to listen to me, for the whole house of Israel is hardened and obstinate. ⁸But I will make you as unyielding and hardened as they are. ⁹I will make your forehead like the hardest stone, harder than flint. Do not be afraid of them or terrified by them, though they are a rebellious house."

¹⁰And he said to me, "Son of man, listen carefully and take to heart all the words I speak to you. ¹¹Go now to your countrymen in exile and speak to them. Say to them, 'This is what the Sovereign LORD says,' whether they listen or fail to listen."

¹²Then the Spirit lifted me up, and I heard behind me a loud rumbling sound—May the glory of the LORD be praised in his dwelling place!— ¹³the sound of the wings of the living creatures brushing against each other and the sound of the wheels beside them, a loud rumbling sound. ¹⁴The Spirit then lifted me up and took me away, and I went in bitterness and in the anger of my spirit, with the strong hand of the LORD upon me. ¹⁵I came to the exiles who lived at Tel Abib near the Kebar River. And there, where they were living, I sat among them for seven days—overwhelmed.

Warning to Israel

¹⁶At the end of seven days the word of the LORD came to me: ¹⁷"Son of man, I have made you a watchman for the house of Israel; so hear the word I speak and give them warning from me. ¹⁸When I say to a wicked man, 'You will surely die,' and you do not warn him or speak out to dissuade him from his evil ways in order to save his life, that wicked man will die for*a* his sin, and I will hold you accountable for his blood. ¹⁹But if you do warn the wicked man and he does not turn from his wickedness or from his evil ways, he will die for his sin; but you will have saved yourself.

²⁰"Again, when a righteous man turns from his righteousness and does evil, and I put a stumbling block before him, he will die. Since you did not warn him, he will die for his sin. The righteous things he did will not be remembered, and I will hold you accountable for his blood. ²¹But if you do warn the righteous man not to sin and he does not sin, he will surely live because he took warning, and you will have saved yourself."

²²The hand of the LORD was upon me there, and he said to me, "Get up and go out to the plain, and there I will speak to you." ²³So I got up and went out to the plain. And the glory of the LORD was standing there, like the glory I had seen by the Kebar River, and I fell facedown. ²⁴Then the Spirit came into me and raised me to my feet. He spoke to me and said: "Go, shut yourself inside your house. ²⁵And you, son of man, they will tie with ropes; you will be bound so that you cannot go out among the people. ²⁶I will make your tongue stick to the roof of your mouth so that you will be silent and unable to rebuke them, though they are a rebellious house. ²⁷But when I speak to you, I will open your mouth and you shall say to them, 'This is what the Sovereign LORD says.' Whoever will listen let him listen, and whoever will refuse let him refuse; for they are a rebellious house.

Siege of Jerusalem Symbolized

4 "Now, son of man, take a clay tablet, put it in front of you and draw the city of Jerusalem on it. ²Then lay siege to it: Erect siege works against it, build a ramp up to it, set up camps against it and put battering rams around it. ³Then take an iron pan, place it as an iron wall between you and the city and turn your face toward it. It will be under siege, and you shall besiege it. This will be a sign to the house of Israel.

---

a 18 Or *in;* also in verses 19 and 20

4"Then lie on your left side and put the sin of the house of Israel upon yourself.*a* You are to bear their sin for the number of days you lie on your side. 5I have assigned you the same number of days as the years of their sin. So for 390 days you will bear the sin of the house of Israel.

6"After you have finished this, lie down again, this time on your right side, and bear the sin of the house of Judah. I have assigned you 40 days, a day for each year. 7Turn your face toward the siege of Jerusalem and with bared arm prophesy against her. 8I will tie you up with ropes so that you cannot turn from one side to the other until you have finished the days of your siege.

9"Take wheat and barley, beans and lentils, millet and spelt; put them in a storage jar and use them to make bread for yourself. You are to eat it during the 390 days you lie on your side. 10Weigh out twenty shekels*b* of food to eat each day and eat it at set times. 11Also measure out a sixth of a hin*c* of water and drink it at set times. 12Eat the food as you would a barley cake; bake it in the sight of the people, using human excrement for fuel." 13The LORD said, "In this way the people of Israel will eat defiled food among the nations where I will drive them."

14Then I said, "Not so, Sovereign LORD! I have never defiled myself. From my youth until now I have never eaten anything found dead or torn by wild animals. No unclean meat has ever entered my mouth."

15"Very well," he said, "I will let you bake your bread over cow manure instead of human excrement."

16He then said to me: "Son of man, I will cut off the supply of food in Jerusalem. The people will eat rationed food in anxiety and drink rationed water in despair, 17for food and water will be scarce. They will be appalled at the sight of each other and will waste away because of*d* their sin.

5 "Now, son of man, take a sharp sword and use it as a barber's razor to shave your head and your beard. Then take a set of scales and divide up

the hair. 2When the days of your siege come to an end, burn a third of the hair with fire inside the city. Take a third and strike it with the sword all around the city. And scatter a third to the wind. For I will pursue them with drawn sword. 3But take a few strands of hair and tuck them away in the folds of your garment. 4Again, take a few of these and throw them into the fire and burn them up. A fire will spread from there to the whole house of Israel.

5"This is what the Sovereign LORD says: This is Jerusalem, which I have set in the center of the nations, with countries all around her. 6Yet in her wickedness she has rebelled against my laws and decrees more than the nations and countries around her. She has rejected my laws and has not followed my decrees.

7"Therefore this is what the Sovereign LORD says: You have been more unruly than the nations around you and have not followed my decrees or kept my laws. You have not even*e* conformed to the standards of the nations around you.

8"Therefore this is what the Sovereign LORD says: I myself am against you, Jerusalem, and I will inflict punishment on you in the sight of the nations. 9Because of all your detestable idols, I will do to you what I have never done before and will never do again. 10Therefore in your midst fathers will eat their children, and children will eat their fathers. I will inflict punishment on you and will scatter all your survivors to the winds. 11Therefore as surely as I live, declares the Sovereign LORD, because you have defiled my sanctuary with all your vile images and detestable practices, I myself will withdraw my favor; I will not look on you with pity or spare you. 12A third of your people will die of the plague or perish by famine inside you; a third will fall by the sword outside your walls; and a third I will scatter to the winds and pursue with drawn sword.

13"Then my anger will cease and my wrath against them will subside, and I will be avenged. And when I have spent my wrath upon them, they will know that I the LORD have spoken in my zeal.

---

a 4 Or *your side*   *b 10* That is, about 8 ounces (about 0.2 kilogram)   *c 11* That is, about 2/3 quart (about 0.6 liter)   *d 17* Or *away in*   *e 7* Most Hebrew manuscripts; some Hebrew manuscripts and Syriac *You have*

14"I will make you a ruin and a reproach among the nations around you, in the sight of all who pass by. 15You will be a reproach and a taunt, a warning and an object of horror to the nations around you when I inflict punishment on you in anger and in wrath and with stinging rebuke. I the LORD have spoken. 16When I shoot at you with my deadly and destructive arrows of famine, I will shoot to destroy you. I will bring more and more famine upon you and cut off your supply of food. 17I will send famine and wild beasts against you, and they will leave you childless. Plague and bloodshed will sweep through you, and I will bring the sword against you. I the LORD have spoken."

A Prophecy Against the Mountains of Israel

6 The word of the LORD came to me: 2"Son of man, set your face against the mountains of Israel; prophesy against them 3and say: 'O mountains of Israel, hear the word of the Sovereign LORD. This is what the Sovereign LORD says to the mountains and hills, to the ravines and valleys: I am about to bring a sword against you, and I will destroy your high places. 4Your altars will be demolished and your incense altars will be smashed; and I will slay your people in front of your idols. 5I will lay the dead bodies of the Israelites in front of their idols, and I will scatter your bones around your altars. 6Wherever you live, the towns will be laid waste and the high places demolished, so that your altars will be laid waste and devastated, your idols smashed and ruined, your incense altars broken down, and what you have made wiped out. 7Your people will fall slain among you, and you will know that I am the LORD.

8" 'But I will spare some, for some of you will escape the sword when you are scattered among the lands and nations. 9Then in the nations where they have been carried captive, those who escape will remember me—how I have been grieved by their adulterous hearts, which have turned away from me, and by their eyes, which have lusted after

their idols. They will loathe themselves for the evil they have done and for all their detestable practices. 10And they will know that I am the LORD; I did not threaten in vain to bring this calamity on them.

11" 'This is what the Sovereign LORD says: Strike your hands together and stamp your feet and cry out "Alas!" because of all the wicked and detestable practices of the house of Israel, for they will fall by the sword, famine and plague. 12He that is far away will die of the plague, and he that is near will fall by the sword, and he that survives and is spared will die of famine. So will I spend my wrath upon them. 13And they will know that I am the LORD, when their people lie slain among their idols around their altars, on every high hill and on all the mountaintops, under every spreading tree and every leafy oak—places where they offered fragrant incense to all their idols. 14And I will stretch out my hand against them and make the land a desolate waste from the desert to Diblah*a*—wherever they live. Then they will know that I am the LORD.' "

The End Has Come

7 The word of the LORD came to me: 2"Son of man, this is what the Sovereign LORD says to the land of Israel: The end! The end has come upon the four corners of the land. 3The end is now upon you and I will unleash my anger against you. I will judge you according to your conduct and repay you for all your detestable practices. 4I will not look on you with pity or spare you; I will surely repay you for your conduct and the detestable practices among you. Then you will know that I am the LORD.

5"This is what the Sovereign LORD says: Disaster! An unheard-of*b* disaster is coming. 6The end has come! The end has come! It has roused itself against you. It has come! 7Doom has come upon you—you who dwell in the land. The time has come, the day is near; there is panic, not joy, upon the mountains. 8I am about to pour out my wrath on you and spend my anger against you; I will judge you according to your conduct and

---

a 14 Most Hebrew manuscripts; a few Hebrew manuscripts *Riblah*   *b 5* Most Hebrew manuscripts; some Hebrew manuscripts and Syriac *Disaster after*

repay you for all your detestable practices. ⁹I will not look on you with pity or spare you; I will repay you in accordance with your conduct and the detestable practices among you. Then you will know that it is I the LORD who strikes the blow.

¹⁰"The day is here! It has come! Doom has burst forth, the rod has budded, arrogance has blossomed! ¹¹Violence has grown intoᵃ a rod to punish wickedness; none of the people will be left, none of that crowd—no wealth, nothing of value. ¹²The time has come, the day has arrived. Let not the buyer rejoice nor the seller grieve, for wrath is upon the whole crowd. ¹³The seller will not recover the land he has sold as long as both of them live, for the vision concerning the whole crowd will not be reversed. Because of their sins, not one of them will preserve his life. ¹⁴Though they blow the trumpet and get everything ready, no one will go into battle, for my wrath is upon the whole crowd.

¹⁵"Outside is the sword, inside are plague and famine; those in the country will die by the sword, and those in the city will be devoured by famine and plague. ¹⁶All who survive and escape will be in the mountains, moaning like doves of the valleys, each because of his sins. ¹⁷Every hand will go limp, and every knee will become as weak as water. ¹⁸They will put on sackcloth and be clothed with terror. Their faces will be covered with shame and their heads will be shaved. ¹⁹They will throw their silver into the streets, and their gold will be an unclean thing. Their silver and gold will not be able to save them in the day of the LORD's wrath. They will not satisfy their hunger or fill their stomachs with it, for it has made them stumble into sin. ²⁰They were proud of their beautiful jewelry and used it to make their detestable idols and vile images. Therefore I will turn these into an unclean thing for them. ²¹I will hand it all over as plunder to foreigners and as loot to the wicked of the earth, and they will defile it. ²²I will turn my face away from them, and they will desecrate my treasured place; robbers will enter it and desecrate it.

²³"Prepare chains, because the land is full of bloodshed and the city is full of violence. ²⁴I will bring the most wicked of the nations to take possession of their houses; I will put an end to the pride of the mighty, and their sanctuaries will be desecrated. ²⁵When terror comes, they will seek peace, but there will be none. ²⁶Calamity upon calamity will come, and rumor upon rumor. They will try to get a vision from the prophet; the teaching of the law by the priest will be lost, as will the counsel of the elders. ²⁷The king will mourn, the prince will be clothed with despair, and the hands of the people of the land will tremble. I will deal with them according to their conduct, and by their own standards I will judge them. Then they will know that I am the LORD."

Idolatry in the Temple

8 In the sixth year, in the sixth month on the fifth day, while I was sitting in my house and the elders of Judah were sitting before me, the hand of the Sovereign LORD came upon me there. ²I looked, and I saw a figure like that of a man.ᵇ From what appeared to be his waist down he was like fire, and from there up his appearance was as bright as glowing metal. ³He stretched out what looked like a hand and took me by the hair of my head. The Spirit lifted me up between earth and heaven and in visions of God he took me to Jerusalem, to the entrance to the north gate of the inner court, where the idol that provokes to jealousy stood. ⁴And there before me was the glory of the God of Israel, as in the vision I had seen in the plain.

⁵Then he said to me, "Son of man, look toward the north." So I looked, and in the entrance north of the gate of the altar I saw this idol of jealousy.

⁶And he said to me, "Son of man, do you see what they are doing—the utterly detestable things the house of Israel is doing here, things that will drive me far from my sanctuary? But you will see things that are even more detestable."

⁷Then he brought me to the entrance to the court. I looked, and I saw a hole in the wall. ⁸He said to me, "Son of man,

---

ᵃ 11 Or *The violent one has become*   ᵇ 2 Or *saw a fiery figure* now dig into the wall." So I dug into the wall and saw a doorway there.

⁹And he said to me, "Go in and see the wicked and detestable things they are doing here." ¹⁰So I went in and looked, and I saw portrayed all over the walls all kinds of crawling things and detestable animals and all the idols of the house of Israel. ¹¹In front of them stood seventy elders of the house of Israel, and Jaazaniah son of Shaphan was standing among them. Each had a censer in his hand, and a fragrant cloud of incense was rising.

¹²He said to me, "Son of man, have you seen what the elders of the house of Israel are doing in the darkness, each at the shrine of his own idol? They say, 'The LORD does not see us; the LORD has forsaken the land.'" ¹³Again, he said, "You will see them doing things that are even more detestable."

¹⁴Then he brought me to the entrance to the north gate of the house of the LORD, and I saw women sitting there, mourning for Tammuz. ¹⁵He said to me, "Do you see this, son of man? You will see things that are even more detestable than this."

¹⁶He then brought me into the inner court of the house of the LORD, and there at the entrance to the temple, between the portico and the altar, were about twenty-five men. With their backs toward the temple of the LORD and their faces toward the east, they were bowing down to the sun in the east.

¹⁷He said to me, "Have you seen this, son of man? Is it a trivial matter for the house of Judah to do the detestable things they are doing here? Must they also fill the land with violence and continually provoke me to anger? Look at them putting the branch to their nose! ¹⁸Therefore I will deal with them in anger; I will not look on them with pity or spare them. Although they shout in my ears, I will not listen to them."

Idolaters Killed

9 Then I heard him call out in a loud voice, "Bring the guards of the city here, each with a weapon in his hand." ²And I saw six men coming from the direction of the upper gate, which

faces north, each with a deadly weapon in his hand. With them was a man clothed in linen who had a writing kit at his side. They came in and stood beside the bronze altar.

³Now the glory of the God of Israel went up from above the cherubim, where it had been, and moved to the threshold of the temple. Then the LORD called to the man clothed in linen who had the writing kit at his side ⁴and said to him, "Go throughout the city of Jerusalem and put a mark on the foreheads of those who grieve and lament over all the detestable things that are done in it."

⁵As I listened, he said to the others, "Follow him through the city and kill, without showing pity or compassion. ⁶Slaughter old men, young men and maidens, women and children, but do not touch anyone who has the mark. Begin at my sanctuary." So they began with the elders who were in front of the temple.

⁷Then he said to them, "Defile the temple and fill the courts with the slain. Go!" So they went out and began killing throughout the city. ⁸While they were killing and I was left alone, I fell facedown, crying out, "Ah, Sovereign LORD! Are you going to destroy the entire remnant of Israel in this outpouring of your wrath on Jerusalem?"

⁹He answered me, "The sin of the house of Israel and Judah is exceedingly great; the land is full of bloodshed and the city is full of injustice. They say, 'The LORD has forsaken the land; the LORD does not see.' ¹⁰So I will not look on them with pity or spare them, but I will bring down on their own heads what they have done."

¹¹Then the man in linen with the writing kit at his side brought back word, saying, "I have done as you commanded."

The Glory Departs From the Temple

10 I looked, and I saw the likeness of a throne of sapphire*a* above the expanse that was over the heads of the cherubim. ²The LORD said to the man clothed in linen, "Go in among the wheels beneath the cherubim. Fill your hands with burning coals

a 1 Or *lapis lazuli*

from among the cherubim and scatter them over the city." And as I watched, he went in.

³Now the cherubim were standing on the south side of the temple when the man went in, and a cloud filled the inner court. ⁴Then the glory of the LORD rose from above the cherubim and moved to the threshold of the temple. The cloud filled the temple, and the court was full of the radiance of the glory of the LORD. ⁵The sound of the wings of the cherubim could be heard as far away as the outer court, like the voice of God Almighty*a* when he speaks.

⁶When the LORD commanded the man in linen, "Take fire from among the wheels, from among the cherubim," the man went in and stood beside a wheel. ⁷Then one of the cherubim reached out his hand to the fire that was among them. He took up some of it and put it into the hands of the man in linen, who took it and went out. ⁸(Under the wings of the cherubim could be seen what looked like the hands of a man.)

⁹I looked, and I saw beside the cherubim four wheels, one beside each of the cherubim; the wheels sparkled like chrysolite. ¹⁰As for their appearance, the four of them looked alike; each was like a wheel intersecting a wheel. ¹¹As they moved, they would go in any one of the four directions the cherubim faced; the wheels did not turn about*b* as the cherubim went. The cherubim went in whatever direction the head faced, without turning as they went. ¹²Their entire bodies, including their backs, their hands and their wings, were completely full of eyes, as were their four wheels. ¹³I heard the wheels being called "the whirling wheels." ¹⁴Each of the cherubim had four faces: One face was that of a cherub, the second the face of a man, the third the face of a lion, and the fourth the face of an eagle.

¹⁵Then the cherubim rose upward. These were the living creatures I had seen by the Kebar River. ¹⁶When the cherubim moved, the wheels beside them moved; and when the cherubim spread their wings to rise from the ground, the wheels did not leave their side. ¹⁷When the cherubim stood still,

they also stood still; and when the cherubim rose, they rose with them, because the spirit of the living creatures was in them.

¹⁸Then the glory of the LORD departed from over the threshold of the temple and stopped above the cherubim. ¹⁹While I watched, the cherubim spread their wings and rose from the ground, and as they went, the wheels went with them. They stopped at the entrance to the east gate of the LORD's house, and the glory of the God of Israel was above them.

²⁰These were the living creatures I had seen beneath the God of Israel by the Kebar River, and I realized that they were cherubim. ²¹Each had four faces and four wings, and under their wings was what looked like the hands of a man. ²²Their faces had the same appearance as those I had seen by the Kebar River. Each one went straight ahead.

Judgment on Israel's Leaders

11 Then the Spirit lifted me up and brought me to the gate of the house of the LORD that faces east. There at the entrance to the gate were twenty-five men, and I saw among them Jaazaniah son of Azzur and Pelatiah son of Benaiah, leaders of the people. ²The LORD said to me, "Son of man, these are the men who are plotting evil and giving wicked advice in this city. ³They say, 'Will it not soon be time to build houses?*c* This city is a cooking pot, and we are the meat.' ⁴Therefore prophesy against them; prophesy, son of man."

⁵Then the Spirit of the LORD came upon me, and he told me to say: "This is what the LORD says: That is what you are saying, O house of Israel, but I know what is going through your mind. ⁶You have killed many people in this city and filled its streets with the dead.

⁷"Therefore this is what the Sovereign LORD says: The bodies you have thrown there are the meat and this city is the pot, but I will drive you out of it. ⁸You fear the sword, and the sword is what I will bring against you, declares the Sovereign LORD. ⁹I will drive you out of the city and hand you over to foreigners and inflict punishment on you. ¹⁰You will

---

a 5 Hebrew *El-Shaddai*   *b* 11 Or *aside*   *c* 3 Or *This is not the time to build houses.*

fall by the sword, and I will execute judgment on you at the borders of Israel. Then you will know that I am the LORD. ¹¹This city will not be a pot for you, nor will you be the meat in it; I will execute judgment on you at the borders of Israel. ¹²And you will know that I am the LORD, for you have not followed my decrees or kept my laws but have conformed to the standards of the nations around you."

¹³Now as I was prophesying, Pelatiah son of Benaiah died. Then I fell face-down and cried out in a loud voice, "Ah, Sovereign LORD! Will you completely destroy the remnant of Israel?"

¹⁴The word of the LORD came to me: ¹⁵"Son of man, your brothers—your brothers who are your blood relatives[a] and the whole house of Israel—are those of whom the people of Jerusalem have said, 'They are[b] far away from the LORD; this land was given to us as our possession.'

Promised Return of Israel

¹⁶"Therefore say: 'This is what the Sovereign LORD says: Although I sent them far away among the nations and scattered them among the countries, yet for a little while I have been a sanctuary for them in the countries where they have gone.'

¹⁷"Therefore say: 'This is what the Sovereign LORD says: I will gather you from the nations and bring you back from the countries where you have been scattered, and I will give you back the land of Israel again.'

¹⁸"They will return to it and remove all its vile images and detestable idols. ¹⁹I will give them an undivided heart and put a new spirit in them; I will remove from them their heart of stone and give them a heart of flesh. ²⁰Then they will follow my decrees and be careful to keep my laws. They will be my people, and I will be their God. ²¹But as for those whose hearts are devoted to their vile images and detestable idols, I will bring down on their own heads what they have done, declares the Sovereign LORD."

²²Then the cherubim, with the wheels

beside them, spread their wings, and the glory of the God of Israel was above them. ²³The glory of the LORD went up from within the city and stopped above the mountain east of it. ²⁴The Spirit lifted me up and brought me to the exiles in Babylonia[c] in the vision given by the Spirit of God.

Then the vision I had seen went up from me, ²⁵and I told the exiles everything the LORD had shown me.

The Exile Symbolized

12 The word of the LORD came to me: ²"Son of man, you are living among a rebellious people. They have eyes to see but do not see and ears to hear but do not hear, for they are a rebellious people.

NONE ARE SO DEAF AS THOSE WHO WILL NOT HEAR. —*Matthew Henry*

---

³"Therefore, son of man, pack your belongings for exile and in the daytime, as they watch, set out and go from where you are to another place. Perhaps they will understand, though they are a rebellious house. ⁴During the daytime, while they watch, bring out your belongings packed for exile. Then in the evening, while they are watching, go out like those who go into exile. ⁵While they watch, dig through the wall and take your belongings out through it. ⁶Put them on your shoulder as they are watching and carry them out at dusk. Cover your face so that you cannot see the land, for I have made you a sign to the house of Israel."

⁷So I did as I was commanded. During the day I brought out my things packed for exile. Then in the evening I dug through the wall with my hands. I took my belongings out at dusk, carrying them on my shoulders while they watched.

⁸In the morning the word of the LORD came to me: ⁹"Son of man, did not that rebellious house of Israel ask you, 'What are you doing?'

¹⁰"Say to them, 'This is what the

---

a 15 Or *are in exile with you* (see Septuagint and Syriac)   *b 15* Or *those to whom the people of Jerusalem have said, 'Stay*   *c 24* Or *Chaldea*

Sovereign LORD says: This oracle concerns the prince in Jerusalem and the whole house of Israel who are there.' 11Say to them, 'I am a sign to you.'

"As I have done, so it will be done to them. They will go into exile as captives.

12"The prince among them will put his things on his shoulder at dusk and leave, and a hole will be dug in the wall for him to go through. He will cover his face so that he cannot see the land. 13I will spread my net for him, and he will be caught in my snare; I will bring him to Babylonia, the land of the Chaldeans, but he will not see it, and there he will die. 14I will scatter to the winds all those around him—his staff and all his troops—and I will pursue them with drawn sword.

15"They will know that I am the LORD, when I disperse them among the nations and scatter them through the countries. 16But I will spare a few of them from the sword, famine and plague, so that in the nations where they go they may acknowledge all their detestable practices. Then they will know that I am the LORD."

17The word of the LORD came to me: 18"Son of man, tremble as you eat your food, and shudder in fear as you drink your water. 19Say to the people of the land: 'This is what the Sovereign LORD says about those living in Jerusalem and in the land of Israel: They will eat their food in anxiety and drink their water in despair, for their land will be stripped of everything in it because of the violence of all who live there. 20The inhabited towns will be laid waste and the land will be desolate. Then you will know that I am the LORD.' "

21The word of the LORD came to me: 22"Son of man, what is this proverb you have in the land of Israel: 'The days go by and every vision comes to nothing'? 23Say to them, 'This is what the Sovereign LORD says: I am going to put an end to this proverb, and they will no longer quote it in Israel.' Say to them, 'The days are near when every vision will be fulfilled. 24For there will be no more false visions or flattering divinations among the people of Israel. 25But I the LORD will speak what I will, and it shall

be fulfilled without delay. For in your days, you rebellious house, I will fulfill whatever I say, declares the Sovereign LORD.' "

26The word of the LORD came to me: 27"Son of man, the house of Israel is saying, 'The vision he sees is for many years from now, and he prophesies about the distant future.'

28"Therefore say to them, 'This is what the Sovereign LORD says: None of my words will be delayed any longer; whatever I say will be fulfilled, declares the Sovereign LORD.' "

False Prophets Condemned

13 The word of the LORD came to me: 2"Son of man, prophesy against the prophets of Israel who are now prophesying. Say to those who prophesy out of their own imagination: 'Hear the word of the LORD! 3This is what the Sovereign LORD says: Woe to the foolisha prophets who follow their own spirit and have seen nothing! 4Your prophets, O Israel, are like jackals among ruins. 5You have not gone up to the breaks in the wall to repair it for the house of Israel so that it will stand firm in the battle on the day of the LORD. 6Their visions are false and their divinations a lie. They say, "The LORD declares," when the LORD has not sent them; yet they expect their words to be fulfilled. 7Have you not seen false visions and uttered lying divinations when you say, "The LORD declares," though I have not spoken?

8" 'Therefore this is what the Sovereign LORD says: Because of your false words and lying visions, I am against you, declares the Sovereign LORD. 9My hand will be against the prophets who see false visions and utter lying divinations. They will not belong to the council of my people or be listed in the records of the house of Israel, nor will they enter the land of Israel. Then you will know that I am the Sovereign LORD.

10" 'Because they lead my people astray, saying, "Peace," when there is no peace, and because, when a flimsy wall is built, they cover it with whitewash, 11therefore tell those who cover it with whitewash that it is going to fall. Rain

a 3 Or wicked

will come in torrents, and I will send hailstones hurtling down, and violent winds will burst forth. [12]When the wall collapses, will people not ask you, "Where is the whitewash you covered it with?"

[13]" 'Therefore this is what the Sovereign LORD says: In my wrath I will unleash a violent wind, and in my anger hailstones and torrents of rain will fall with destructive fury. [14]I will tear down the wall you have covered with whitewash and will level it to the ground so that its foundation will be laid bare. When it[a] falls, you will be destroyed in it; and you will know that I am the LORD. [15]So I will spend my wrath against the wall and against those who covered it with whitewash. I will say to you, "The wall is gone and so are those who whitewashed it, [16]those prophets of Israel who prophesied to Jerusalem and saw visions of peace for her when there was no peace, declares the Sovereign LORD." '

[17]"Now, son of man, set your face against the daughters of your people who prophesy out of their own imagination. Prophesy against them [18]and say, 'This is what the Sovereign LORD says: Woe to the women who sew magic charms on all their wrists and make veils of various lengths for their heads in order to ensnare people. Will you ensnare the lives of my people but preserve your own? [19]You have profaned me among my people for a few handfuls of barley and scraps of bread. By lying to my people, who listen to lies, you have killed those who should not have died and have spared those who should not live.

[20]" 'Therefore this is what the Sovereign LORD says: I am against your magic charms with which you ensnare people like birds and I will tear them from your arms; I will set free the people that you ensnare like birds. [21]I will tear off your veils and save my people from your hands, and they will no longer fall prey to your power. Then you will know that I am the LORD. [22]Because you disheartened the righteous with your lies, when I had brought them no grief, and because you encouraged the wicked not to turn from their evil ways and so save their lives, [23]therefore you will no longer see false

visions or practice divination. I will save my people from your hands. And then you will know that I am the LORD.' "

Idolaters Condemned

14 Some of the elders of Israel came to me and sat down in front of me. [2]Then the word of the LORD came to me: [3]"Son of man, these men have set up idols in their hearts and put wicked stumbling blocks before their faces. Should I let them inquire of me at all? [4]Therefore speak to them and tell them, 'This is what the Sovereign LORD says: When any Israelite sets up idols in his heart and puts a wicked stumbling block before his face and then goes to a prophet, I the LORD will answer him myself in keeping with his great idolatry. [5]I will do this to recapture the hearts of the people of Israel, who have all deserted me for their idols.'

[6]"Therefore say to the house of Israel, 'This is what the Sovereign LORD says: Repent! Turn from your idols and renounce all your detestable practices!

[7]" 'When any Israelite or any alien living in Israel separates himself from me and sets up idols in his heart and puts a wicked stumbling block before his face and then goes to a prophet to inquire of me, I the LORD will answer him myself. [8]I will set my face against that man and make him an example and a byword. I will cut him off from my people. Then you will know that I am the LORD.

[9]" 'And if the prophet is enticed to utter a prophecy, I the LORD have enticed that prophet, and I will stretch out my hand against him and destroy him from among my people Israel. [10]They will bear their guilt—the prophet will be as guilty as the one who consults him. [11]Then the people of Israel will no longer stray from me, nor will they defile themselves anymore with all their sins. They will be my people, and I will be their God, declares the Sovereign LORD.' "

Judgment Inescapable

[12]The word of the LORD came to me: [13]"Son of man, if a country sins against me by being unfaithful and I stretch out my hand against it to cut off its food supply and send famine upon it and kill

---

[a] 14 Or *the city*

its men and their animals, **14**even if these three men—Noah, Daniel*a* and Job—were in it, they could save only themselves by their righteousness, declares the Sovereign LORD.

15"Or if I send wild beasts through that country and they leave it childless and it becomes desolate so that no one can pass through it because of the beasts, **16**as surely as I live, declares the Sovereign LORD, even if these three men were in it, they could not save their own sons or daughters. They alone would be saved, but the land would be desolate.

17"Or if I bring a sword against that country and say, 'Let the sword pass throughout the land,' and I kill its men and their animals, **18**as surely as I live, declares the Sovereign LORD, even if these three men were in it, they could not save their own sons or daughters. They alone would be saved.

19"Or if I send a plague into that land and pour out my wrath upon it through bloodshed, killing its men and their animals, **20**as surely as I live, declares the Sovereign LORD, even if Noah, Daniel and Job were in it, they could save neither son nor daughter. They would save only themselves by their righteousness.

21"For this is what the Sovereign LORD says: How much worse will it be when I send against Jerusalem my four dreadful judgments—sword and famine and wild beasts and plague—to kill its men and their animals! **22**Yet there will be some survivors—sons and daughters who will be brought out of it. They will come to you, and when you see their conduct and their actions, you will be consoled regarding the disaster I have brought upon Jerusalem—every disaster I have brought upon it. **23**You will be consoled when you see their conduct and their actions, for you will know that I have done nothing in it without cause, declares the Sovereign LORD."

Jerusalem, A Useless Vine

15 The word of the LORD came to me: **2**"Son of man, how is the wood of a vine better than that of a branch on any of the trees in the forest?

3Is wood ever taken from it to make anything useful? Do they make pegs from it to hang things on? **4**And after it is thrown on the fire as fuel and the fire burns both ends and chars the middle, is it then useful for anything? **5**If it was not useful for anything when it was whole, how much less can it be made into something useful when the fire has burned it and it is charred?

6"Therefore this is what the Sovereign LORD says: As I have given the wood of the vine among the trees of the forest as fuel for the fire, so will I treat the people living in Jerusalem. **7**I will set my face against them. Although they have come out of the fire, the fire will yet consume them. And when I set my face against them, you will know that I am the LORD. **8**I will make the land desolate because they have been unfaithful, declares the Sovereign LORD."

An Allegory of Unfaithful Jerusalem

16 The word of the LORD came to me: **2**"Son of man, confront Jerusalem with her detestable practices **3**and say, 'This is what the Sovereign LORD says to Jerusalem: Your ancestry and birth were in the land of the Canaanites; your father was an Amorite and your mother a Hittite. **4**On the day you were born your cord was not cut, nor were you washed with water to make you clean, nor were you rubbed with salt or wrapped in cloths. **5**No one looked on you with pity or had compassion enough to do any of these things for you. Rather, you were thrown out into the open field, for on the day you were born you were despised.

6" 'Then I passed by and saw you kicking about in your blood, and as you lay there in your blood I said to you, "Live!"*b* **7**I made you grow like a plant of the field. You grew up and developed and became the most beautiful of jewels.*c* Your breasts were formed and your hair grew, you who were naked and bare.

8" 'Later I passed by, and when I looked at you and saw that you were old enough for love, I spread the corner of my garment over you and covered your

---

a 14 Or *Daniel;* the Hebrew spelling may suggest a person other than the prophet Daniel; also in verse 20.
b 6 A few Hebrew manuscripts, Septuagint and Syriac; most Hebrew manuscripts *"Live!" And as you lay there in your blood I said to you, "Live!"*   *c 7* Or *became mature*

nakedness. I gave you my solemn oath and entered into a covenant with you, declares the Sovereign LORD, and you became mine.

⁹" 'I bathed*a* you with water and washed the blood from you and put ointments on you. ¹⁰I clothed you with an embroidered dress and put leather sandals on you. I dressed you in fine linen and covered you with costly garments. ¹¹I adorned you with jewelry: I put bracelets on your arms and a necklace around your neck, ¹²and I put a ring on your nose, earrings on your ears and a beautiful crown on your head. ¹³So you were adorned with gold and silver; your clothes were of fine linen and costly fabric and embroidered cloth. Your food was fine flour, honey and olive oil. You became very beautiful and rose to be a queen. ¹⁴And your fame spread among the nations on account of your beauty, because the splendor I had given you made your beauty perfect, declares the Sovereign LORD.

¹⁵" 'But you trusted in your beauty and used your fame to become a prostitute. You lavished your favors on anyone who passed by and your beauty became his.*b* ¹⁶You took some of your garments to make gaudy high places, where you carried on your prostitution. Such things should not happen, nor should they ever occur. ¹⁷You also took the fine jewelry I gave you, the jewelry made of my gold and silver, and you made for yourself male idols and engaged in prostitution with them. ¹⁸And you took your embroidered clothes to put on them, and you offered my oil and incense before them. ¹⁹Also the food I provided for you—the fine flour, olive oil and honey I gave you to eat—you offered as fragrant incense before them. That is what happened, declares the Sovereign LORD.

²⁰" 'And you took your sons and daughters whom you bore to me and sacrificed them as food to the idols. Was your prostitution not enough? ²¹You slaughtered my children and sacrificed them*c* to the idols. ²²In all your detestable practices and your prostitution you did not remember the days of your youth, when you were naked and bare, kicking about in your blood.

²³" 'Woe! Woe to you, declares the Sovereign LORD. In addition to all your other wickedness, ²⁴you built a mound for yourself and made a lofty shrine in every public square. ²⁵At the head of every street you built your lofty shrines and degraded your beauty, offering your body with increasing promiscuity to anyone who passed by. ²⁶You engaged in prostitution with the Egyptians, your lustful neighbors, and provoked me to anger with your increasing promiscuity. ²⁷So I stretched out my hand against you and reduced your territory; I gave you over to the greed of your enemies, the daughters of the Philistines, who were shocked by your lewd conduct. ²⁸You engaged in prostitution with the Assyrians too, because you were insatiable; and even after that, you still were not satisfied. ²⁹Then you increased your promiscuity to include Babylonia,*d* a land of merchants, but even with this you were not satisfied.

³⁰" 'How weak-willed you are, declares the Sovereign LORD, when you do all these things, acting like a brazen prostitute! ³¹When you built your mounds at the head of every street and made your lofty shrines in every public square, you were unlike a prostitute, because you scorned payment.

³²" 'You adulterous wife! You prefer strangers to your own husband! ³³Every prostitute receives a fee, but you give gifts to all your lovers, bribing them to come to you from everywhere for your illicit favors. ³⁴So in your prostitution you are the opposite of others; no one runs after you for your favors. You are the very opposite, for you give payment and none is given to you.

³⁵" 'Therefore, you prostitute, hear the word of the LORD! ³⁶This is what the Sovereign LORD says: Because you poured out your wealth*e* and exposed your nakedness in your promiscuity with your lovers, and because of all your detestable idols, and because you gave them your children's blood, ³⁷therefore I

---

a 9 Or *I had bathed*   *b* 15 Most Hebrew manuscripts; one Hebrew manuscript (see some Septuagint manuscripts) *by. Such a thing should not happen*   *c* 21 Or *and made them pass through the fire;*   *d* 29 Or *Chaldea*   *e* 36 Or *lust*

am going to gather all your lovers, with whom you found pleasure, those you loved as well as those you hated. I will gather them against you from all around and will strip you in front of them, and they will see all your nakedness. **38**I will sentence you to the punishment of women who commit adultery and who shed blood; I will bring upon you the blood vengeance of my wrath and jealous anger. **39**Then I will hand you over to your lovers, and they will tear down your mounds and destroy your lofty shrines. They will strip you of your clothes and take your fine jewelry and leave you naked and bare. **40**They will bring a mob against you, who will stone you and hack you to pieces with their swords. **41**They will burn down your houses and inflict punishment on you in the sight of many women. I will put a stop to your prostitution, and you will no longer pay your lovers. **42**Then my wrath against you will subside and my jealous anger will turn away from you; I will be calm and no longer angry.

43" 'Because you did not remember the days of your youth but enraged me with all these things, I will surely bring down on your head what you have done, declares the Sovereign LORD. Did you not add lewdness to all your other detestable practices?

44" 'Everyone who quotes proverbs will quote this proverb about you: "Like mother, like daughter." **45**You are a true daughter of your mother, who despised her husband and her children; and you are a true sister of your sisters, who despised their husbands and their children. Your mother was a Hittite and your father an Amorite. **46**Your older sister was Samaria, who lived to the north of you with her daughters; and your younger sister, who lived to the south of you with her daughters, was Sodom. **47**You not only walked in their ways and copied their detestable practices, but in all your ways you soon became more depraved than they. **48**As surely as I live, declares the Sovereign LORD, your sister Sodom and her daughters never did what you and your daughters have done.

49" 'Now this was the sin of your sister Sodom: She and her daughters were arrogant, overfed and unconcerned; they did not help the poor and needy. **50**They were haughty and did detestable things before me. Therefore I did away with them as you have seen. **51**Samaria did not commit half the sins you did. You have done more detestable things than they, and have made your sisters seem righteous by all these things you have done. **52**Bear your disgrace, for you have furnished some justification for your sisters. Because your sins were more vile than theirs, they appear more righteous than you. So then, be ashamed and bear your disgrace, for you have made your sisters appear righteous.

53" 'However, I will restore the fortunes of Sodom and her daughters and of Samaria and her daughters, and your fortunes along with them, **54**so that you may bear your disgrace and be ashamed of all you have done in giving them comfort. **55**And your sisters, Sodom with her daughters and Samaria with her daughters, will return to what they were before; and you and your daughters will return to what you were before. **56**You would not even mention your sister Sodom in the day of your pride, **57**before your wickedness was uncovered. Even so, you are now scorned by the daughters of Edom*a* and all her neighbors and the daughters of the Philistines—all those around you who despise you. **58**You will bear the consequences of your lewdness and your detestable practices, declares the LORD.

59" 'This is what the Sovereign LORD says: I will deal with you as you deserve, because you have despised my oath by breaking the covenant. **60**Yet I will remember the covenant I made with you in the days of your youth, and I will establish an everlasting covenant with you. **61**Then you will remember your ways and be ashamed when you receive your sisters, both those who are older than you and those who are younger. I will give them to you as daughters, but not on the basis of my covenant with you. **62**So I will establish my covenant with you, and you will know that I am the LORD. **63**Then, when I make atonement for you for all you have done, you will remember and be ashamed and

---

a 57 Many Hebrew manuscripts and Syriac; most Hebrew manuscripts, Septuagint and Vulgate *Aram*

never again open your mouth because of your humiliation, declares the Sovereign LORD.' "

Two Eagles and a Vine

17 The word of the LORD came to me: 2"Son of man, set forth an allegory and tell the house of Israel a parable. 3Say to them, 'This is what the Sovereign LORD says: A great eagle with powerful wings, long feathers and full plumage of varied colors came to Lebanon. Taking hold of the top of a cedar, 4he broke off its topmost shoot and carried it away to a land of merchants, where he planted it in a city of traders.

5" 'He took some of the seed of your land and put it in fertile soil. He planted it like a willow by abundant water, 6and it sprouted and became a low, spreading vine. Its branches turned toward him, but its roots remained under it. So it became a vine and produced branches and put out leafy boughs.

7" 'But there was another great eagle with powerful wings and full plumage. The vine now sent out its roots toward him from the plot where it was planted and stretched out its branches to him for water. 8It had been planted in good soil by abundant water so that it would produce branches, bear fruit and become a splendid vine.'

9"Say to them, 'This is what the Sovereign LORD says: Will it thrive? Will it not be uprooted and stripped of its fruit so that it withers? All its new growth will wither. It will not take a strong arm or many people to pull it up by the roots. 10Even if it is transplanted, will it thrive? Will it not wither completely when the east wind strikes it—wither away in the plot where it grew?' "

11Then the word of the LORD came to me: 12"Say to this rebellious house, 'Do you not know what these things mean?' Say to them: 'The king of Babylon went to Jerusalem and carried off her king and her nobles, bringing them back with him to Babylon. 13Then he took a member of the royal family and made a treaty with him, putting him under oath. He also carried away the leading men of the land, 14so that the kingdom would be brought low, unable to rise again, surviving only by keeping his treaty. 15But the king rebelled against him by sending his envoys to Egypt to get horses and a large army. Will he succeed? Will he who does such things escape? Will he break the treaty and yet escape?

16" 'As surely as I live, declares the Sovereign LORD, he shall die in Babylon, in the land of the king who put him on the throne, whose oath he despised and whose treaty he broke. 17Pharaoh with his mighty army and great horde will be of no help to him in war, when ramps are built and siege works erected to destroy many lives. 18He despised the oath by breaking the covenant. Because he had given his hand in pledge and yet did all these things, he shall not escape.

19" 'Therefore this is what the Sovereign LORD says: As surely as I live, I will bring down on his head my oath that he despised and my covenant that he broke. 20I will spread my net for him, and he will be caught in my snare. I will bring him to Babylon and execute judgment upon him there because he was unfaithful to me. 21All his fleeing troops will fall by the sword, and the survivors will be scattered to the winds. Then you will know that I the LORD have spoken.

22" 'This is what the Sovereign LORD says: I myself will take a shoot from the very top of a cedar and plant it; I will break off a tender sprig from its topmost shoots and plant it on a high and lofty mountain. 23On the mountain heights of Israel I will plant it; it will produce branches and bear fruit and become a splendid cedar. Birds of every kind will nest in it; they will find shelter in the shade of its branches. 24All the trees of the field will know that I the LORD bring down the tall tree and make the low tree grow tall. I dry up the green tree and make the dry tree flourish.

" 'I the LORD have spoken, and I will do it.' "

The Soul Who Sins Will Die

18 The word of the LORD came to me: 2"What do you people mean by quoting this proverb about the land of Israel:

" 'The fathers eat sour grapes,
    and the children's teeth are set on
        edge'?

³"As surely as I live, declares the Sovereign LORD, you will no longer quote this proverb in Israel. ⁴For every living soul belongs to me, the father as well as the son—both alike belong to me. The soul who sins is the one who will die.

⁵ "Suppose there is a righteous man
   who does what is just and right.
⁶ He does not eat at the mountain
      shrines
   or look to the idols of the house of
      Israel.
   He does not defile his neighbor's wife
   or lie with a woman during her
      period.
⁷ He does not oppress anyone,
   but returns what he took in pledge
      for a loan.
   He does not commit robbery
   but gives his food to the hungry
   and provides clothing for the
      naked.
⁸ He does not lend at usury
   or take excessive interest.ᵃ
   He withholds his hand from doing
      wrong
   and judges fairly between man and
      man.
⁹ He follows my decrees
   and faithfully keeps my laws.
   That man is righteous;
      he will surely live,
         declares the Sovereign LORD.

ᵃ 8 Or *take interest*; similarly in verses 13 and 17

THURSDAY

ALL SOULS ARE GOD'S
G. Campbell Morgan

VERSE: Ezekiel 18:4   **PASSAGE:** Ezekiel 18:3–9

very living soul belongs to me. The great truth revealed is that every individual has a relationship with God available, which is mightier than all the facts resulting from physical relationships. It may be true that in my physical being I have inherited tendencies to some forms of evil from my father; but in the fact of my essential relation to God there are forces available to me more and mightier than all these tendencies. Therefore if I die, it is not because of the sin of my father, but because I fail to avail myself of my resources in God; and if I live, it is because I have availed myself of these resources . . . The former [righteousness] results from right relationship with God, and the latter [evil] from failure to realize that relationship. All souls are his, and that means that every soul is made for first-hand personal dealing with him.

ADDITIONAL SCRIPTURE READING:
Numbers 16:22–33; Hebrews 12:9–10

Go to page 967 for your next devotional reading.

1900   Present

10"Suppose he has a violent son, who sheds blood or does any of these other things[a] 11(though the father has done none of them):

"He eats at the mountain shrines.
He defiles his neighbor's wife.
12 He oppresses the poor and needy.
He commits robbery.
He does not return what he took in
    pledge.
He looks to the idols.
He does detestable things.
13 He lends at usury and takes excessive
    interest.

Will such a man live? He will not! Because he has done all these detestable things, he will surely be put to death and his blood will be on his own head.

14"But suppose this son has a son who sees all the sins his father commits, and though he sees them, he does not do such things:

15 "He does not eat at the mountain
    shrines
    or look to the idols of the house of
    Israel.
He does not defile his neighbor's
    wife.
16 He does not oppress anyone
    or require a pledge for a loan.
He does not commit robbery
    but gives his food to the hungry
    and provides clothing for the
    naked.
17 He withholds his hand from sin[b]
    and takes no usury or excessive
    interest.
He keeps my laws and follows my
    decrees.

He will not die for his father's sin; he will surely live. 18But his father will die for his own sin, because he practiced extortion, robbed his brother and did what was wrong among his people.

19"Yet you ask, 'Why does the son not share the guilt of his father?' Since the son has done what is just and right and has been careful to keep all my decrees, he will surely live. 20The soul who sins is the one who will die. The son will not share the guilt of the father, nor will the father share the guilt of the son. The righteousness of the righteous man will be credited to him, and the wickedness of the wicked will be charged against him.

21"But if a wicked man turns away from all the sins he has committed and keeps all my decrees and does what is just and right, he will surely live; he will not die. 22None of the offenses he has committed will be remembered against him. Because of the righteous things he has done, he will live. 23Do I take any pleasure in the death of the wicked? declares the Sovereign LORD. Rather, am I not pleased when they turn from their ways and live?

24"But if a righteous man turns from his righteousness and commits sin and does the same detestable things the wicked man does, will he live? None of the righteous things he has done will be remembered. Because of the unfaithfulness he is guilty of and because of the sins he has committed, he will die.

25"Yet you say, 'The way of the Lord is not just.' Hear, O house of Israel: Is my way unjust? Is it not your ways that are unjust? 26If a righteous man turns from his righteousness and commits sin, he will die for it; because of the sin he has committed he will die. 27But if a wicked man turns away from the wickedness he has committed and does what is just and right, he will save his life. 28Because he considers all the offenses he has committed and turns away from them, he will surely live; he will not die. 29Yet the house of Israel says, 'The way of the Lord is not just.' Are my ways unjust, O house of Israel? Is it not your ways that are unjust?

30"Therefore, O house of Israel, I will judge you, each one according to his ways, declares the Sovereign LORD. Repent! Turn away from all your offenses; then sin will not be your downfall. 31Rid yourselves of all the offenses you have committed, and get a new heart and a new spirit. Why will you die, O house of Israel? 32For I take no pleasure in the death of anyone, declares the Sovereign LORD. Repent and live!

a 10 Or things to a brother   b 17 Septuagint (see also verse 8); Hebrew from the poor

A Lament for Israel's Princes

19 "Take up a lament concerning the princes of Israel ²and say:

" 'What a lioness was your mother
    among the lions!
She lay down among the young lions
    and reared her cubs.
³ She brought up one of her cubs,
    and he became a strong lion.
He learned to tear the prey
    and he devoured men.
⁴ The nations heard about him,
    and he was trapped in their pit.
They led him with hooks
    to the land of Egypt.

⁵ " 'When she saw her hope unfulfilled,
    her expectation gone,
she took another of her cubs
    and made him a strong lion.
⁶ He prowled among the lions,
    for he was now a strong lion.
He learned to tear the prey
    and he devoured men.
⁷ He broke down*ᵃ* their strongholds
    and devastated their towns.
The land and all who were in it
    were terrified by his roaring.
⁸ Then the nations came against him,
    those from regions round about.
They spread their net for him,
    and he was trapped in their pit.
⁹ With hooks they pulled him into a
    cage
    and brought him to the king of
    Babylon.
They put him in prison,
    so his roar was heard no longer
    on the mountains of Israel.

¹⁰ " 'Your mother was like a vine in
    your vineyard*ᵇ*
planted by the water;
it was fruitful and full of branches
    because of abundant water.
¹¹ Its branches were strong,
    fit for a ruler's scepter.
It towered high
    above the thick foliage,
conspicuous for its height
    and for its many branches.
¹² But it was uprooted in fury
    and thrown to the ground.

The east wind made it shrivel,
    it was stripped of its fruit;
its strong branches withered
    and fire consumed them.
¹³ Now it is planted in the desert,
    in a dry and thirsty land.
¹⁴ Fire spread from one of its main*ᶜ*
    branches
    and consumed its fruit.
No strong branch is left on it
    fit for a ruler's scepter.'

This is a lament and is to be used as a lament."

Rebellious Israel

20 In the seventh year, in the fifth month on the tenth day, some of the elders of Israel came to inquire of the LORD, and they sat down in front of me.

²Then the word of the LORD came to me: ³"Son of man, speak to the elders of Israel and say to them, 'This is what the Sovereign LORD says: Have you come to inquire of me? As surely as I live, I will not let you inquire of me, declares the Sovereign LORD.'

⁴"Will you judge them? Will you judge them, son of man? Then confront them with the detestable practices of their fathers ⁵and say to them: 'This is what the Sovereign LORD says: On the day I chose Israel, I swore with uplifted hand to the descendants of the house of Jacob and revealed myself to them in Egypt. With uplifted hand I said to them, "I am the LORD your God." ⁶On that day I swore to them that I would bring them out of Egypt into a land I had searched out for them, a land flowing with milk and honey, the most beautiful of all lands. ⁷And I said to them, "Each of you, get rid of the vile images you have set your eyes on, and do not defile yourselves with the idols of Egypt. I am the LORD your God."

⁸" 'But they rebelled against me and would not listen to me; they did not get rid of the vile images they had set their eyes on, nor did they forsake the idols of Egypt. So I said I would pour out my wrath on them and spend my anger against them in Egypt. ⁹But for the sake

---

ᵃ 7 Targum (see Septuagint); Hebrew *He knew*
manuscripts *your blood*   *ᶜ 14* Or *from under its*   *ᵇ 10* Two Hebrew manuscripts; most Hebrew

of my name I did what would keep it from being profaned in the eyes of the nations they lived among and in whose sight I had revealed myself to the Israelites by bringing them out of Egypt. 10Therefore I led them out of Egypt and brought them into the desert. 11I gave them my decrees and made known to them my laws, for the man who obeys them will live by them. 12Also I gave them my Sabbaths as a sign between us, so they would know that I the LORD made them holy.

13" 'Yet the people of Israel rebelled against me in the desert. They did not follow my decrees but rejected my laws—although the man who obeys them will live by them—and they utterly desecrated my Sabbaths. So I said I would pour out my wrath on them and destroy them in the desert. 14But for the sake of my name I did what would keep it from being profaned in the eyes of the nations in whose sight I had brought them out. 15Also with uplifted hand I swore to them in the desert that I would not bring them into the land I had given them—a land flowing with milk and honey, most beautiful of all lands— 16because they rejected my laws and did not follow my decrees and desecrated my Sabbaths. For their hearts were devoted to their idols. 17Yet I looked on them with pity and did not destroy them or put an end to them in the desert. 18I said to their children in the desert, "Do not follow the statutes of your fathers or keep their laws or defile yourselves with their idols. 19I am the LORD your God; follow my decrees and be careful to keep my laws. 20Keep my Sabbaths holy, that they may be a sign between us. Then you will know that I am the LORD your God."

21" 'But the children rebelled against me: They did not follow my decrees, they were not careful to keep my laws—although the man who obeys them will live by them—and they desecrated my Sabbaths. So I said I would pour out my wrath on them and spend my anger against them in the desert. 22But I withheld my hand, and for the sake of my name I did what would keep it from being profaned in the eyes of the nations in whose sight I had brought them out. 23Also with uplifted hand I swore to them in the desert that I would disperse them among the nations and scatter them through the countries, 24because they had not obeyed my laws but had rejected my decrees and desecrated my Sabbaths, and their eyes ˎlustedˌ after their fathers' idols. 25I also gave them over to statutes that were not good and laws they could not live by; 26I let them become defiled through their gifts—the sacrifice of every firstborn*a*—that I might fill them with horror so they would know that I am the LORD.'

27"Therefore, son of man, speak to the people of Israel and say to them, 'This is what the Sovereign LORD says: In this also your fathers blasphemed me by forsaking me: 28When I brought them into the land I had sworn to give them and they saw any high hill or any leafy tree, there they offered their sacrifices, made offerings that provoked me to anger, presented their fragrant incense and poured out their drink offerings. 29Then I said to them: What is this high place you go to?' " (It is called Bamah*b* to this day.)

Judgment and Restoration

30"Therefore say to the house of Israel: 'This is what the Sovereign LORD says: Will you defile yourselves the way your fathers did and lust after their vile images? 31When you offer your gifts—the sacrifice of your sons in*c* the fire—you continue to defile yourselves with all your idols to this day. Am I to let you inquire of me, O house of Israel? As surely as I live, declares the Sovereign LORD, I will not let you inquire of me.

32" 'You say, "We want to be like the nations, like the peoples of the world, who serve wood and stone." But what you have in mind will never happen. 33As surely as I live, declares the Sovereign LORD, I will rule over you with a mighty hand and an outstretched arm and with outpoured wrath. 34I will bring you from the nations and gather you from the countries where you have been scattered—with a mighty hand and an outstretched arm and with outpoured

---

a 26 Or —*making every firstborn pass through ˎthe fireˌ*   *b 29 Bamah* means *high place.*   *c 31* Or —*making your sons pass through*

wrath. ³⁵I will bring you into the desert of the nations and there, face to face, I will execute judgment upon you. ³⁶As I judged your fathers in the desert of the land of Egypt, so I will judge you, declares the Sovereign LORD. ³⁷I will take note of you as you pass under my rod, and I will bring you into the bond of the covenant. ³⁸I will purge you of those who revolt and rebel against me. Although I will bring them out of the land where they are living, yet they will not enter the land of Israel. Then you will know that I am the LORD.

³⁹" 'As for you, O house of Israel, this is what the Sovereign LORD says: Go and serve your idols, every one of you! But afterward you will surely listen to me and no longer profane my holy name with your gifts and idols. ⁴⁰For on my holy mountain, the high mountain of Israel, declares the Sovereign LORD, there in the land the entire house of Israel will serve me, and there I will accept them. There I will require your offerings and your choice gifts,ᵃ along with all your holy sacrifices. ⁴¹I will accept you as fragrant incense when I bring you out from the nations and gather you from the countries where you have been scattered, and I will show myself holy among you in the sight of the nations. ⁴²Then you will know that I am the LORD, when I bring you into the land of Israel, the land I had sworn with uplifted hand to give to your fathers. ⁴³There you will remember your conduct and all the actions by which you have defiled yourselves, and you will loathe yourselves for all the evil you have done. ⁴⁴You will know that I am the LORD, when I deal with you for my name's sake and not according to your evil ways and your corrupt practices, O house of Israel, declares the Sovereign LORD.' "

Prophecy Against the South

⁴⁵The word of the LORD came to me: ⁴⁶"Son of man, set your face toward the south; preach against the south and prophesy against the forest of the southland. ⁴⁷Say to the southern forest: 'Hear the word of the LORD. This is what the Sovereign LORD says: I am about to set fire to you, and it will consume all your trees, both green and dry. The blazing flame will not be quenched, and every face from south to north will be scorched by it. ⁴⁸Everyone will see that I the LORD have kindled it; it will not be quenched.' "

⁴⁹Then I said, "Ah, Sovereign LORD! They are saying of me, 'Isn't he just telling parables?' "

Babylon, God's Sword of Judgment

21 The word of the LORD came to me: ²"Son of man, set your face against Jerusalem and preach against the sanctuary. Prophesy against the land of Israel ³and say to her: 'This is what the LORD says: I am against you. I will draw my sword from its scabbard and cut off from you both the righteous and the wicked. ⁴Because I am going to cut off the righteous and the wicked, my sword will be unsheathed against everyone from south to north. ⁵Then all people will know that I the LORD have drawn my sword from its scabbard; it will not return again.'

⁶"Therefore groan, son of man! Groan before them with broken heart and bitter grief. ⁷And when they ask you, 'Why are you groaning?' you shall say, 'Because of the news that is coming. Every heart will melt and every hand go limp; every spirit will become faint and every knee become as weak as water.' It is coming! It will surely take place, declares the Sovereign LORD."

⁸The word of the LORD came to me: ⁹"Son of man, prophesy and say, 'This is what the Lord says:

" 'A sword, a sword,
    sharpened and polished—
¹⁰sharpened for the slaughter,
    polished to flash like lightning!

" 'Shall we rejoice in the scepter of my son ⌞Judah⌟? The sword despises every such stick.

¹¹" 'The sword is appointed to be polished,
    to be grasped with the hand;
it is sharpened and polished,
    made ready for the hand of the slayer.

ᵃ 40 Or and the gifts of your firstfruits

12 Cry out and wail, son of man,
   for it is against my people;
   it is against all the princes of Israel.
They are thrown to the sword
   along with my people.
Therefore beat your breast.

13 " 'Testing will surely come. And what if the scepter ⌞of Judah⌟, which the sword despises, does not continue? declares the Sovereign LORD.'

14 "So then, son of man, prophesy
   and strike your hands together.
Let the sword strike twice,
   even three times.
It is a sword for slaughter—
   a sword for great slaughter,
   closing in on them from every side.
15 So that hearts may melt
   and the fallen be many,
I have stationed the sword for
   slaughter*a*
   at all their gates.
Oh! It is made to flash like lightning,
   it is grasped for slaughter.
16 O sword, slash to the right,
   then to the left,
   wherever your blade is turned.
17 I too will strike my hands together,
   and my wrath will subside.
I the LORD have spoken."

18 The word of the LORD came to me: 19 "Son of man, mark out two roads for the sword of the king of Babylon to take, both starting from the same country. Make a signpost where the road branches off to the city. 20 Mark out one road for the sword to come against Rabbah of the Ammonites and another against Judah and fortified Jerusalem. 21 For the king of Babylon will stop at the fork in the road, at the junction of the two roads, to seek an omen: He will cast lots with arrows, he will consult his idols, he will examine the liver. 22 Into his right hand will come the lot for Jerusalem, where he is to set up battering rams, to give the command to slaughter, to sound the battle cry, to set battering rams against the gates, to build a ramp and to erect siege works. 23 It will seem like a false omen to those who have sworn allegiance to him, but he will remind them of their guilt and take them captive.

24 "Therefore this is what the Sovereign LORD says: 'Because you people have brought to mind your guilt by your open rebellion, revealing your sins in all that you do—because you have done this, you will be taken captive.

25 " 'O profane and wicked prince of Israel, whose day has come, whose time of punishment has reached its climax, 26 this is what the Sovereign LORD says: Take off the turban, remove the crown. It will not be as it was: The lowly will be exalted and the exalted will be brought low. 27 A ruin! A ruin! I will make it a ruin! It will not be restored until he comes to whom it rightfully belongs; to him I will give it.'

28 "And you, son of man, prophesy and say, 'This is what the Sovereign LORD says about the Ammonites and their insults:

" 'A sword, a sword,
   drawn for the slaughter,
polished to consume
   and to flash like lightning!
29 Despite false visions concerning you
   and lying divinations about you,
it will be laid on the necks
   of the wicked who are to be slain,
whose day has come,
   whose time of punishment has
      reached its climax.
30 Return the sword to its scabbard.
In the place where you were
      created,
in the land of your ancestry,
   I will judge you.
31 I will pour out my wrath upon you
   and breathe out my fiery anger
      against you;
I will hand you over to brutal men,
   men skilled in destruction.
32 You will be fuel for the fire,
   your blood will be shed in your
      land,
you will be remembered no more;
   for I the LORD have spoken.' "

Jerusalem's Sins

22 The word of the LORD came to me: 2 "Son of man, will you judge her? Will you judge this city of

---

a 15 Septuagint; the meaning of the Hebrew for this word is uncertain.

bloodshed? Then confront her with all her detestable practices ³and say: 'This is what the Sovereign LORD says: O city that brings on herself doom by shedding blood in her midst and defiles herself by making idols, ⁴you have become guilty because of the blood you have shed and have become defiled by the idols you have made. You have brought your days to a close, and the end of your years has come. Therefore I will make you an object of scorn to the nations and a laughingstock to all the countries. ⁵Those who are near and those who are far away will mock you, O infamous city, full of turmoil.

⁶" 'See how each of the princes of Israel who are in you uses his power to shed blood. ⁷In you they have treated father and mother with contempt; in you they have oppressed the alien and mistreated the fatherless and the widow. ⁸You have despised my holy things and desecrated my Sabbaths. ⁹In you are slanderous men bent on shedding blood; in you are those who eat at the mountain shrines and commit lewd acts. ¹⁰In you are those who dishonor their fathers' bed; in you are those who violate women during their period, when they are ceremonially unclean. ¹¹In you one man commits a detestable offense with his neighbor's wife, another shamefully defiles his daughter-in-law, and another violates his sister, his own father's daughter. ¹²In you men accept bribes to shed blood; you take usury and excessive interest*a* and make unjust gain from your neighbors by extortion. And you have forgotten me, declares the Sovereign LORD.

¹³" 'I will surely strike my hands together at the unjust gain you have made and at the blood you have shed in your midst. ¹⁴Will your courage endure or your hands be strong in the day I deal with you? I the LORD have spoken, and I will do it. ¹⁵I will disperse you among the nations and scatter you through the countries; and I will put an end to your uncleanness. ¹⁶When you have been defiled*b* in the eyes of the nations, you will know that I am the LORD.' "

¹⁷Then the word of the LORD came to me: ¹⁸"Son of man, the house of Israel has become dross to me; all of them are the copper, tin, iron and lead left inside a furnace. They are but the dross of silver. ¹⁹Therefore this is what the Sovereign LORD says: 'Because you have all become dross, I will gather you into Jerusalem. ²⁰As men gather silver, copper, iron, lead and tin into a furnace to melt it with a fiery blast, so will I gather you in my anger and my wrath and put you inside the city and melt you. ²¹I will gather you and I will blow on you with my fiery wrath, and you will be melted inside her. ²²As silver is melted in a furnace, so you will be melted inside her, and you will know that I the LORD have poured out my wrath upon you.' "

²³Again the word of the LORD came to me: ²⁴"Son of man, say to the land, 'You are a land that has had no rain or showers*c* in the day of wrath.' ²⁵There is a conspiracy of her princes*d* within her like a roaring lion tearing its prey; they devour people, take treasures and precious things and make many widows within her. ²⁶Her priests do violence to my law and profane my holy things; they do not distinguish between the holy and the common; they teach that there is no difference between the unclean and the clean; and they shut their eyes to the keeping of my Sabbaths, so that I am profaned among them. ²⁷Her officials within her are like wolves tearing their prey; they shed blood and kill people to make unjust gain. ²⁸Her prophets whitewash these deeds for them by false visions and lying divinations. They say, 'This is what the Sovereign LORD says'—when the LORD has not spoken. ²⁹The people of the land practice extortion and commit robbery; they oppress the poor and needy and mistreat the alien, denying them justice.

³⁰"I looked for a man among them who would build up the wall and stand before me in the gap on behalf of the land so I would not have to destroy it, but I found none. ³¹So I will pour out my wrath on them and consume them with my fiery anger, bringing down on their own heads all they have done, declares the Sovereign LORD."

---

a 12 Or *usury and interest*   *b* 16 Or *When I have allotted you your inheritance*   *c* 24 Septuagint; Hebrew *has not been cleansed or rained on*   *d* 25 Septuagint; Hebrew *prophets*

Two Adulterous Sisters

23 The word of the LORD came to me: ²"Son of man, there were two women, daughters of the same mother. ³They became prostitutes in Egypt, engaging in prostitution from their youth. In that land their breasts were fondled and their virgin bosoms caressed. ⁴The older was named Oholah, and her sister was Oholibah. They were mine and gave birth to sons and daughters. Oholah is Samaria, and Oholibah is Jerusalem.

⁵"Oholah engaged in prostitution while she was still mine; and she lusted after her lovers, the Assyrians—warriors ⁶clothed in blue, governors and commanders, all of them handsome young men, and mounted horsemen. ⁷She gave herself as a prostitute to all the elite of the Assyrians and defiled herself with all the idols of everyone she lusted after. ⁸She did not give up the prostitution she began in Egypt, when during her youth men slept with her, caressed her virgin bosom and poured out their lust upon her.

⁹"Therefore I handed her over to her lovers, the Assyrians, for whom she lusted. ¹⁰They stripped her naked, took away her sons and daughters and killed her with the sword. She became a byword among women, and punishment was inflicted on her.

¹¹"Her sister Oholibah saw this, yet in her lust and prostitution she was more depraved than her sister. ¹²She too lusted after the Assyrians—governors and commanders, warriors in full dress, mounted horsemen, all handsome young men. ¹³I saw that she too defiled herself; both of them went the same way.

¹⁴"But she carried her prostitution still further. She saw men portrayed on a wall, figures of Chaldeans[a] portrayed in red, ¹⁵with belts around their waists and flowing turbans on their heads; all of them looked like Babylonian chariot officers, natives of Chaldea.[b] ¹⁶As soon as she saw them, she lusted after them and sent messengers to them in Chaldea. ¹⁷Then the Babylonians came to her, to the bed of love, and in their lust they defiled her. After she had been defiled by them, she turned away from them in disgust. ¹⁸When she carried on her prostitution openly and exposed her nakedness, I turned away from her in disgust, just as I had turned away from her sister. ¹⁹Yet she became more and more promiscuous as she recalled the days of her youth, when she was a prostitute in Egypt. ²⁰There she lusted after her lovers, whose genitals were like those of donkeys and whose emission was like that of horses. ²¹So you longed for the lewdness of your youth, when in Egypt your bosom was caressed and your young breasts fondled.[c]

²²"Therefore, Oholibah, this is what the Sovereign LORD says: I will stir up your lovers against you, those you turned away from in disgust, and I will bring them against you from every side— ²³the Babylonians and all the Chaldeans, the men of Pekod and Shoa and Koa, and all the Assyrians with them, handsome young men, all of them governors and commanders, chariot officers and men of high rank, all mounted on horses. ²⁴They will come against you with weapons,[d] chariots and wagons and with a throng of people; they will take up positions against you on every side with large and small shields and with helmets. I will turn you over to them for punishment, and they will punish you according to their standards. ²⁵I will direct my jealous anger against you, and they will deal with you in fury. They will cut off your noses and your ears, and those of you who are left will fall by the sword. They will take away your sons and daughters, and those of you who are left will be consumed by fire. ²⁶They will also strip you of your clothes and take your fine jewelry. ²⁷So I will put a stop to the lewdness and prostitution you began in Egypt. You will not look on these things with longing or remember Egypt anymore.

²⁸"For this is what the Sovereign LORD says: I am about to hand you over to those you hate, to those you turned away from in disgust. ²⁹They will deal with you in hatred and take away everything you have worked for. They will leave you naked and bare, and the

---

shame of your prostitution will be exposed. Your lewdness and promiscuity ³⁰have brought this upon you, because you lusted after the nations and defiled yourself with their idols. ³¹You have gone the way of your sister; so I will put her cup into your hand.

³²"This is what the Sovereign LORD says:

"You will drink your sister's cup,
  a cup large and deep;
it will bring scorn and derision,
  for it holds so much.
³³You will be filled with drunkenness
    and sorrow,
  the cup of ruin and desolation,
  the cup of your sister Samaria.
³⁴You will drink it and drain it dry;
  you will dash it to pieces
  and tear your breasts.

I have spoken, declares the Sovereign LORD.

³⁵"Therefore this is what the Sovereign LORD says: Since you have forgotten me and thrust me behind your back, you must bear the consequences of your lewdness and prostitution."

³⁶The LORD said to me: "Son of man, will you judge Oholah and Oholibah? Then confront them with their detestable practices, ³⁷for they have committed adultery and blood is on their hands. They committed adultery with their idols; they even sacrificed their children, whom they bore to me,ᵃ as food for them. ³⁸They have also done this to me: At that same time they defiled my sanctuary and desecrated my Sabbaths. ³⁹On the very day they sacrificed their children to their idols, they entered my sanctuary and desecrated it. That is what they did in my house.

⁴⁰"They even sent messengers for men who came from far away, and when they arrived you bathed yourself for them, painted your eyes and put on your jewelry. ⁴¹You sat on an elegant couch, with a table spread before it on which you had placed the incense and oil that belonged to me.

⁴²"The noise of a carefree crowd was around her; Sabeansᵇ were brought from the desert along with men from the rabble, and they put bracelets on the arms of the woman and her sister and beautiful crowns on their heads. ⁴³Then I said about the one worn out by adultery, 'Now let them use her as a prostitute, for that is all she is.' ⁴⁴And they slept with her. As men sleep with a prostitute, so they slept with those lewd women, Oholah and Oholibah. ⁴⁵But righteous men will sentence them to the punishment of women who commit adultery and shed blood, because they are adulterous and blood is on their hands.

⁴⁶"This is what the Sovereign LORD says: Bring a mob against them and give them over to terror and plunder. ⁴⁷The mob will stone them and cut them down with their swords; they will kill their sons and daughters and burn down their houses.

⁴⁸"So I will put an end to lewdness in the land, that all women may take warning and not imitate you. ⁴⁹You will suffer the penalty for your lewdness and bear the consequences of your sins of idolatry. Then you will know that I am the Sovereign LORD."

The Cooking Pot

24 In the ninth year, in the tenth month on the tenth day, the word of the LORD came to me: ²"Son of man, record this date, this very date, because the king of Babylon has laid siege to Jerusalem this very day. ³Tell this rebellious house a parable and say to them: 'This is what the Sovereign LORD says:

" 'Put on the cooking pot; put it on
  and pour water into it.
⁴Put into it the pieces of meat,
  all the choice pieces—the leg and
    the shoulder.
Fill it with the best of these bones;
⁵ take the pick of the flock.
Pile wood beneath it for the bones;
  bring it to a boil
  and cook the bones in it.

⁶" 'For this is what the Sovereign LORD says:

" 'Woe to the city of bloodshed,

ᵃ 37 Or *even made the children they bore to me pass through the fire*   ᵇ 42 Or *drunkards*

to the pot now encrusted,
　whose deposit will not go away!
Empty it piece by piece
　without casting lots for them.

7 " 'For the blood she shed is in her
　　midst:
She poured it on the bare rock;
she did not pour it on the ground,
　where the dust would cover it.
8 To stir up wrath and take revenge
I put her blood on the bare rock,
　so that it would not be covered.

9 " 'Therefore this is what the Sovereign
LORD says:

" 'Woe to the city of bloodshed!
　I, too, will pile the wood high.
10 So heap on the wood
　and kindle the fire.
Cook the meat well,
　mixing in the spices;
　and let the bones be charred.
11 Then set the empty pot on the coals
　till it becomes hot and its copper
　　glows
so its impurities may be melted
　and its deposit burned away.
12 It has frustrated all efforts;
　its heavy deposit has not been
　　removed,
　not even by fire.

13 " 'Now your impurity is lewdness.
Because I tried to cleanse you but you
would not be cleansed from your impurity, you will not be clean again until
my wrath against you has subsided.

14 " 'I the LORD have spoken. The time
has come for me to act. I will not hold
back; I will not have pity, nor will I
relent. You will be judged according to
your conduct and your actions, declares
the Sovereign LORD.' "

Ezekiel's Wife Dies

15 The word of the LORD came to me:
16 "Son of man, with one blow I am about
to take away from you the delight of your
eyes. Yet do not lament or weep or shed
any tears. 17 Groan quietly; do not mourn
for the dead. Keep your turban fastened
and your sandals on your feet; do not

cover the lower part of your face or eat
the customary food ⌊of mourners⌋."

18 So I spoke to the people in the
morning, and in the evening my wife
died. The next morning I did as I had
been commanded.

19 Then the people asked me, "Won't
you tell us what these things have to do
with us?"

20 So I said to them, "The word of the
LORD came to me: 21 Say to the house of
Israel, 'This is what the Sovereign LORD
says: I am about to desecrate my sanctuary—the stronghold in which you take
pride, the delight of your eyes, the object
of your affection. The sons and daughters
you left behind will fall by the sword.
22 And you will do as I have done. You
will not cover the lower part of your face
or eat the customary food ⌊of mourners⌋.
23 You will keep your turbans on your
heads and your sandals on your feet. You
will not mourn or weep but will waste
away because of[a] your sins and groan
among yourselves. 24 Ezekiel will be a
sign to you; you will do just as he has
done. When this happens, you will know
that I am the Sovereign LORD.'

25 "And you, son of man, on the day I
take away their stronghold, their joy and
glory, the delight of their eyes, their
heart's desire, and their sons and daughters as well— 26 on that day a fugitive
will come to tell you the news. 27 At that
time your mouth will be opened; you
will speak with him and will no longer
be silent. So you will be a sign to them,
and they will know that I am the LORD."

A Prophecy Against Ammon

25 The word of the LORD came
to me: 2 "Son of man, set your
face against the Ammonites and prophesy against them. 3 Say to them, 'Hear the
word of the Sovereign LORD. This is
what the Sovereign LORD says: Because
you said "Aha!" over my sanctuary
when it was desecrated and over the
land of Israel when it was laid waste and
over the people of Judah when they
went into exile, 4 therefore I am going to
give you to the people of the East as a
possession. They will set up their camps
and pitch their tents among you; they
will eat your fruit and drink your milk.

a 23 Or away in

⁵I will turn Rabbah into a pasture for camels and Ammon into a resting place for sheep. Then you will know that I am the LORD. ⁶For this is what the Sovereign LORD says: Because you have clapped your hands and stamped your feet, rejoicing with all the malice of your heart against the land of Israel, ⁷therefore I will stretch out my hand against you and give you as plunder to the nations. I will cut you off from the nations and exterminate you from the countries. I will destroy you, and you will know that I am the LORD.' "

A Prophecy Against Moab

⁸"This is what the Sovereign LORD says: 'Because Moab and Seir said, "Look, the house of Judah has become like all the other nations," ⁹therefore I will expose the flank of Moab, beginning at its frontier towns—Beth Jeshimoth, Baal Meon and Kiriathaim—the glory of that land. ¹⁰I will give Moab along with the Ammonites to the people of the East as a possession, so that the Ammonites will not be remembered among the nations; ¹¹and I will inflict punishment on Moab. Then they will know that I am the LORD.' "

A Prophecy Against Edom

¹²"This is what the Sovereign LORD says: 'Because Edom took revenge on the house of Judah and became very guilty by doing so, ¹³therefore this is what the Sovereign LORD says: I will stretch out my hand against Edom and kill its men and their animals. I will lay it waste, and from Teman to Dedan they will fall by the sword. ¹⁴I will take vengeance on Edom by the hand of my people Israel, and they will deal with Edom in accordance with my anger and my wrath; they will know my vengeance, declares the Sovereign LORD.' "

A Prophecy Against Philistia

¹⁵"This is what the Sovereign LORD says: 'Because the Philistines acted in vengeance and took revenge with malice in their hearts, and with ancient hostility sought to destroy Judah, ¹⁶therefore this is what the Sovereign LORD says: I am about to stretch out my hand against the Philistines, and I will cut off the Kerethites and destroy those remaining along the coast. ¹⁷I will carry out great vengeance on them and punish them in my wrath. Then they will know that I am the LORD, when I take vengeance on them.' "

A Prophecy Against Tyre

26 In the eleventh year, on the first day of the month, the word of the LORD came to me: ²"Son of man, because Tyre has said of Jerusalem, 'Aha! The gate to the nations is broken, and its doors have swung open to me; now that she lies in ruins I will prosper,' ³therefore this is what the Sovereign LORD says: I am against you, O Tyre, and I will bring many nations against you, like the sea casting up its waves. ⁴They will destroy the walls of Tyre and pull down her towers; I will scrape away her rubble and make her a bare rock. ⁵Out in the sea she will become a place to spread fishnets, for I have spoken, declares the Sovereign LORD. She will become plunder for the nations, ⁶and her settlements on the mainland will be ravaged by the sword. Then they will know that I am the LORD.

⁷"For this is what the Sovereign LORD says: From the north I am going to bring against Tyre Nebuchadnezzar[a] king of Babylon, king of kings, with horses and chariots, with horsemen and a great army. ⁸He will ravage your settlements on the mainland with the sword; he will set up siege works against you, build a ramp up to your walls and raise his shields against you. ⁹He will direct the blows of his battering rams against your walls and demolish your towers with his weapons. ¹⁰His horses will be so many that they will cover you with dust. Your walls will tremble at the noise of the war horses, wagons and chariots when he enters your gates as men enter a city whose walls have been broken through. ¹¹The hoofs of his horses will trample all your streets; he will kill your people with the sword, and your strong pillars will fall to the ground. ¹²They will plunder your wealth

---

a 7 Hebrew *Nebuchadrezzar,* of which *Nebuchadnezzar* is a variant; here and often in Ezekiel and Jeremiah

and loot your merchandise; they will break down your walls and demolish your fine houses and throw your stones, timber and rubble into the sea. [13]I will put an end to your noisy songs, and the music of your harps will be heard no more. [14]I will make you a bare rock, and you will become a place to spread fishnets. You will never be rebuilt, for I the LORD have spoken, declares the Sovereign LORD.

[15]"This is what the Sovereign LORD says to Tyre: Will not the coastlands tremble at the sound of your fall, when the wounded groan and the slaughter takes place in you? [16]Then all the princes of the coast will step down from their thrones and lay aside their robes and take off their embroidered garments. Clothed with terror, they will sit on the ground, trembling every moment, appalled at you. [17]Then they will take up a lament concerning you and say to you:

" 'How you are destroyed, O city of
　　renown,
　peopled by men of the sea!
You were a power on the seas,
　you and your citizens;
you put your terror
　on all who lived there.
[18]Now the coastlands tremble
　on the day of your fall;
the islands in the sea
　are terrified at your collapse.'

[19]"This is what the Sovereign LORD says: When I make you a desolate city, like cities no longer inhabited, and when I bring the ocean depths over you and its vast waters cover you, [20]then I will bring you down with those who go down to the pit, to the people of long ago. I will make you dwell in the earth below, as in ancient ruins, with those who go down to the pit, and you will not return or take your place[a] in the land of the living. [21]I will bring you to a horrible end and you will be no more. You will be sought, but you will never again be found, declares the Sovereign LORD."

A Lament for Tyre

27 The word of the LORD came to me: [2]"Son of man, take up a lament concerning Tyre. [3]Say to Tyre, situated at the gateway to the sea, merchant of peoples on many coasts, 'This is what the Sovereign LORD says:

" 'You say, O Tyre,
　"I am perfect in beauty."
[4]Your domain was on the high seas;
　your builders brought your beauty
　　to perfection.
[5]They made all your timbers
　of pine trees from Senir[b];
they took a cedar from Lebanon
　to make a mast for you.
[6]Of oaks from Bashan
　they made your oars;
of cypress wood[c] from the coasts of
　　Cyprus[d]
　they made your deck, inlaid with
　　ivory.
[7]Fine embroidered linen from Egypt
　　was your sail
　and served as your banner;
your awnings were of blue and purple
　from the coasts of Elishah.
[8]Men of Sidon and Arvad were your
　　oarsmen;
　your skilled men, O Tyre, were
　　aboard as your seamen.
[9]Veteran craftsmen of Gebal[e] were on
　　board
　as shipwrights to caulk your
　　seams.
All the ships of the sea and their
　　sailors
　came alongside to trade for your
　　wares.
[10]" 'Men of Persia, Lydia and Put
　served as soldiers in your army.
They hung their shields and helmets
　　on your walls,
　bringing you splendor.
[11]Men of Arvad and Helech
　manned your walls on every side;
men of Gammad
　were in your towers.
They hung their shields around your
　　walls;
　they brought your beauty to
　　perfection.

---

[a] 20 Septuagint; Hebrew *return, and I will give glory*
Masoretic Text has a different division of the consonants.　　[b] 5 That is, Hermon　　[c] 6 Targum; the
[d] 6 Hebrew *Kittim*　　[e] 9 That is, Byblos

¹²" 'Tarshish did business with you because of your great wealth of goods; they exchanged silver, iron, tin and lead for your merchandise.

¹³" 'Greece, Tubal and Meshech traded with you; they exchanged slaves and articles of bronze for your wares.

¹⁴" 'Men of Beth Togarmah exchanged work horses, war horses and mules for your merchandise.

¹⁵" 'The men of Rhodes^a traded with you, and many coastlands were your customers; they paid you with ivory tusks and ebony.

¹⁶" 'Aram^b did business with you because of your many products; they exchanged turquoise, purple fabric, embroidered work, fine linen, coral and rubies for your merchandise.

¹⁷" 'Judah and Israel traded with you; they exchanged wheat from Minnith and confections,^c honey, oil and balm for your wares.

¹⁸" 'Damascus, because of your many products and great wealth of goods, did business with you in wine from Helbon and wool from Zahar.

¹⁹" 'Danites and Greeks from Uzal bought your merchandise; they exchanged wrought iron, cassia and calamus for your wares.

²⁰" 'Dedan traded in saddle blankets with you.

²¹" 'Arabia and all the princes of Kedar were your customers; they did business with you in lambs, rams and goats.

²²" 'The merchants of Sheba and Raamah traded with you; for your merchandise they exchanged the finest of all kinds of spices and precious stones, and gold.

²³" 'Haran, Canneh and Eden and merchants of Sheba, Asshur and Kilmad traded with you. ²⁴In your marketplace they traded with you beautiful garments, blue fabric, embroidered work and multicolored rugs with cords twisted and tightly knotted.

²⁵" 'The ships of Tarshish serve
    as carriers for your wares.
You are filled with heavy cargo
    in the heart of the sea.

²⁶Your oarsmen take you
    out to the high seas.
But the east wind will break you to
        pieces
    in the heart of the sea.
²⁷Your wealth, merchandise and wares,
    your mariners, seamen and
        shipwrights,
    your merchants and all your soldiers,
        and everyone else on board
will sink into the heart of the sea
    on the day of your shipwreck.
²⁸The shorelands will quake
    when your seamen cry out.
²⁹All who handle the oars
    will abandon their ships;
    the mariners and all the seamen
        will stand on the shore.
³⁰They will raise their voice
    and cry bitterly over you;
they will sprinkle dust on their heads
    and roll in ashes.
³¹They will shave their heads because
        of you
    and will put on sackcloth.
They will weep over you with
        anguish of soul
    and with bitter mourning.
³²As they wail and mourn over you,
    they will take up a lament
        concerning you:
"Who was ever silenced like Tyre,
    surrounded by the sea?"
³³When your merchandise went out on
        the seas,
    you satisfied many nations;
with your great wealth and your
        wares
    you enriched the kings of the
        earth.
³⁴Now you are shattered by the sea
    in the depths of the waters;
your wares and all your company
    have gone down with you.
³⁵All who live in the coastlands
    are appalled at you;
    their kings shudder with horror
        and their faces are distorted with
            fear.
³⁶The merchants among the nations
        hiss at you;
    you have come to a horrible end
        and will be no more.' "

---

^a 15 Septuagint; Hebrew *Dedan*   ^b 16 Most Hebrew manuscripts; some Hebrew manuscripts and Syriac *Edom*   ^c 17 The meaning of the Hebrew for this word is uncertain.

A Prophecy Against the King of Tyre

28 The word of the LORD came to me: 2"Son of man, say to the ruler of Tyre, 'This is what the Sovereign LORD says:

" 'In the pride of your heart
　　you say, "I am a god;
I sit on the throne of a god
　　in the heart of the seas."
But you are a man and not a god,
　　though you think you are as wise
　　　as a god.
3 Are you wiser than Daniel*a* ?
　　Is no secret hidden from you?
4 By your wisdom and understanding
　　you have gained wealth for yourself
and amassed gold and silver
　　in your treasuries.
5 By your great skill in trading
　　you have increased your wealth,
and because of your wealth
　　your heart has grown proud.

6 " 'Therefore this is what the Sovereign LORD says:

" 'Because you think you are wise,
　　as wise as a god,
7 I am going to bring foreigners against
　　you,
　　the most ruthless of nations;
they will draw their swords against
　　　your beauty and wisdom
　　and pierce your shining splendor.
8 They will bring you down to the pit,
　　and you will die a violent death
　　in the heart of the seas.
9 Will you then say, "I am a god,"
　　in the presence of those who kill
　　　you?
You will be but a man, not a god,
　　in the hands of those who slay you.
10 You will die the death of the
　　　uncircumcised
　　at the hands of foreigners.

I have spoken, declares the Sovereign LORD.' "

11 The word of the LORD came to me: 12"Son of man, take up a lament concerning the king of Tyre and say to him: 'This is what the Sovereign LORD says:

" 'You were the model of perfection,
　　full of wisdom and perfect in
　　　beauty.
13 You were in Eden,
　　the garden of God;
every precious stone adorned you:
　　ruby, topaz and emerald,
　　chrysolite, onyx and jasper,
　　sapphire,*b* turquoise and beryl.*c*
Your settings and mountings*d* were
　　　made of gold;
on the day you were created they
　　　were prepared.
14 You were anointed as a guardian
　　　cherub,
　　for so I ordained you.
You were on the holy mount of God;
　　you walked among the fiery stones.
15 You were blameless in your ways
　　from the day you were created
　　till wickedness was found in you.
16 Through your widespread trade
　　you were filled with violence,
　　and you sinned.
So I drove you in disgrace from the
　　　mount of God,
　　and I expelled you, O guardian
　　　cherub,
　　from among the fiery stones.
17 Your heart became proud
　　on account of your beauty,
and you corrupted your wisdom
　　because of your splendor.
So I threw you to the earth;
　　I made a spectacle of you before
　　　kings.
18 By your many sins and dishonest
　　　trade
　　you have desecrated your
　　　sanctuaries.
So I made a fire come out from you,
　　and it consumed you,
and I reduced you to ashes on the
　　　ground
　　in the sight of all who were
　　　watching.
19 All the nations who knew you
　　are appalled at you;
you have come to a horrible end
　　and will be no more.' "

---

a 3 Or *Danel*; the Hebrew spelling may suggest a person other than the prophet Daniel.　　*b 13* Or *lapis lazuli*　　*c 13* The precise identification of some of these precious stones is uncertain.　　*d 13* The meaning of the Hebrew for this phrase is uncertain.

A Prophecy Against Sidon

20The word of the LORD came to me: **21**"Son of man, set your face against Sidon; prophesy against her **22**and say: 'This is what the Sovereign LORD says:

" 'I am against you, O Sidon,
and I will gain glory within you.
They will know that I am the LORD,
when I inflict punishment on her
and show myself holy within her.
23I will send a plague upon her
and make blood flow in her streets.
The slain will fall within her,
with the sword against her on
every side.
Then they will know that I am the
LORD.

24" 'No longer will the people of Israel have malicious neighbors who are painful briers and sharp thorns. Then they will know that I am the Sovereign LORD.

25" 'This is what the Sovereign LORD says: When I gather the people of Israel from the nations where they have been scattered, I will show myself holy among them in the sight of the nations. Then they will live in their own land, which I gave to my servant Jacob. **26**They will live there in safety and will build houses and plant vineyards; they will live in safety when I inflict punishment on all their neighbors who maligned them. Then they will know that I am the LORD their God.' "

A Prophecy Against Egypt

29 In the tenth year, in the tenth month on the twelfth day, the word of the LORD came to me: **2**"Son of man, set your face against Pharaoh king of Egypt and prophesy against him and against all Egypt. **3**Speak to him and say: 'This is what the Sovereign LORD says:

" 'I am against you, Pharaoh king of
Egypt,
you great monster lying among
your streams.
You say, "The Nile is mine;
I made it for myself."
4But I will put hooks in your jaws
and make the fish of your streams
stick to your scales.
I will pull you out from among your
streams,
with all the fish sticking to your
scales.
5I will leave you in the desert,
you and all the fish of your
streams.
You will fall on the open field
and not be gathered or picked up.
I will give you as food
to the beasts of the earth and the
birds of the air.

6Then all who live in Egypt will know that I am the LORD.

" 'You have been a staff of reed for the house of Israel. **7**When they grasped you with their hands, you splintered and you tore open their shoulders; when they leaned on you, you broke and their backs were wrenched.*a*

8" 'Therefore this is what the Sovereign LORD says: I will bring a sword against you and kill your men and their animals. **9**Egypt will become a desolate wasteland. Then they will know that I am the LORD.

" 'Because you said, "The Nile is mine; I made it," **10**therefore I am against you and against your streams, and I will make the land of Egypt a ruin and a desolate waste from Migdol to Aswan, as far as the border of Cush.*b* **11**No foot of man or animal will pass through it; no one will live there for forty years. **12**I will make the land of Egypt desolate among devastated lands, and her cities will lie desolate forty years among ruined cities. And I will disperse the Egyptians among the nations and scatter them through the countries.

13" 'Yet this is what the Sovereign LORD says: At the end of forty years I will gather the Egyptians from the nations where they were scattered. **14**I will bring them back from captivity and return them to Upper Egypt,*c* the land of their ancestry. There they will be a lowly kingdom. **15**It will be the lowliest of kingdoms and will never again exalt itself above the other nations. I will make it so weak that it will never again rule over

a 7 Syriac (see also Septuagint and Vulgate); Hebrew *and you caused their backs to stand*   *b 10* That is, the upper Nile region   *c 14* Hebrew *to Pathros*

the nations. ¹⁶Egypt will no longer be a source of confidence for the people of Israel but will be a reminder of their sin in turning to her for help. Then they will know that I am the Sovereign Lord.' "

¹⁷In the twenty-seventh year, in the first month on the first day, the word of the Lord came to me: ¹⁸"Son of man, Nebuchadnezzar king of Babylon drove his army in a hard campaign against Tyre; every head was rubbed bare and every shoulder made raw. Yet he and his army got no reward from the campaign he led against Tyre. ¹⁹Therefore this is what the Sovereign Lord says: I am going to give Egypt to Nebuchadnezzar king of Babylon, and he will carry off its wealth. He will loot and plunder the land as pay for his army. ²⁰I have given him Egypt as a reward for his efforts because he and his army did it for me, declares the Sovereign Lord. ²¹"On that day I will make a horn*a* grow for the house of Israel, and I will open your mouth among them. Then they will know that I am the Lord."

A Lament for Egypt

30 The word of the Lord came to me: ²"Son of man, prophesy and say: 'This is what the Sovereign Lord says:

" 'Wail and say,
  "Alas for that day!"
³ For the day is near,
  the day of the Lord is near—
a day of clouds,
  a time of doom for the nations.
⁴ A sword will come against Egypt,
  and anguish will come upon Cush.*b*
When the slain fall in Egypt,
  her wealth will be carried away
  and her foundations torn down.

⁵Cush and Put, Lydia and all Arabia, Libya*c* and the people of the covenant land will fall by the sword along with Egypt.
⁶" 'This is what the Lord says:

" 'The allies of Egypt will fall
  and her proud strength will fail.

From Migdol to Aswan
  they will fall by the sword within her,
    declares the Sovereign Lord.
⁷ " 'They will be desolate
  among desolate lands,
and their cities will lie
  among ruined cities.
⁸ Then they will know that I am the Lord,
  when I set fire to Egypt
  and all her helpers are crushed.

⁹" 'On that day messengers will go out from me in ships to frighten Cush out of her complacency. Anguish will take hold of them on the day of Egypt's doom, for it is sure to come.

¹⁰" 'This is what the Sovereign Lord says:

" 'I will put an end to the hordes of Egypt
  by the hand of Nebuchadnezzar
    king of Babylon.
¹¹ He and his army—the most ruthless of nations—
  will be brought in to destroy the land.
They will draw their swords against Egypt
  and fill the land with the slain.
¹² I will dry up the streams of the Nile
  and sell the land to evil men;
by the hand of foreigners
  I will lay waste the land and
    everything in it.

I the Lord have spoken.

¹³" 'This is what the Sovereign Lord says:

" 'I will destroy the idols
  and put an end to the images in
    Memphis.*d*
No longer will there be a prince in Egypt,
  and I will spread fear throughout the land.
¹⁴ I will lay waste Upper Egypt,*e*
  set fire to Zoan
  and inflict punishment on Thebes.*f*

---

a 21 *Horn* here symbolizes strength.   *b* 4 That is, the upper Nile region; also in verses 5 and 9   *c* 5 Hebrew *Cub*   *d* 13 Hebrew *Noph;* also in verse 16   *e* 14 Hebrew *waste Pathros*   *f* 14 Hebrew *No;* also in verses 15 and 16

15 I will pour out my wrath on
   Pelusium,*a*
 the stronghold of Egypt,
 and cut off the hordes of Thebes.
16 I will set fire to Egypt;
   Pelusium will writhe in agony.
 Thebes will be taken by storm;
 Memphis will be in constant
   distress.
17 The young men of Heliopolis*b* and
   Bubastis*c*
 will fall by the sword,
 and the cities themselves will go
   into captivity.
18 Dark will be the day at Tahpanhes
 when I break the yoke of Egypt;
 there her proud strength will come
   to an end.
 She will be covered with clouds,
 and her villages will go into
   captivity.
19 So I will inflict punishment on Egypt,
 and they will know that I am the
   LORD.' "

20 In the eleventh year, in the first
month on the seventh day, the word of
the LORD came to me: 21 "Son of man, I
have broken the arm of Pharaoh king of
Egypt. It has not been bound up for healing or put in a splint so as to become
strong enough to hold a sword. 22 Therefore this is what the Sovereign LORD
says: I am against Pharaoh king of Egypt.
I will break both his arms, the good arm
as well as the broken one, and make the
sword fall from his hand. 23 I will disperse the Egyptians among the nations
and scatter them through the countries.
24 I will strengthen the arms of the king
of Babylon and put my sword in his
hand, but I will break the arms of Pharaoh, and he will groan before him like a
mortally wounded man. 25 I will
strengthen the arms of the king of Babylon, but the arms of Pharaoh will fall
limp. Then they will know that I am the
LORD, when I put my sword into the
hand of the king of Babylon and he bran-
dishes it against Egypt. 26 I will disperse
the Egyptians among the nations and
scatter them through the countries.
Then they will know that I am the
LORD."

A Cedar in Lebanon

31 In the eleventh year, in the
third month on the first day,
the word of the LORD came to me: 2 "Son
of man, say to Pharaoh king of Egypt and
to his hordes:

" 'Who can be compared with you in
   majesty?
3 Consider Assyria, once a cedar in
   Lebanon,
 with beautiful branches
   overshadowing the forest;
 it towered on high,
   its top above the thick foliage.
4 The waters nourished it,
   deep springs made it grow tall;
 their streams flowed
   all around its base
 and sent their channels
   to all the trees of the field.
5 So it towered higher
   than all the trees of the field;
 its boughs increased
   and its branches grew long,
 spreading because of abundant
   waters.
6 All the birds of the air
   nested in its boughs,
 all the beasts of the field
   gave birth under its branches;
 all the great nations
   lived in its shade.
7 It was majestic in beauty,
   with its spreading boughs,
 for its roots went down
   to abundant waters.
8 The cedars in the garden of God
   could not rival it,
 nor could the pine trees
   equal its boughs,
 nor could the plane trees
   compare with its branches—
 no tree in the garden of God
   could match its beauty.
9 I made it beautiful
   with abundant branches,
 the envy of all the trees of Eden
   in the garden of God.

10 " 'Therefore this is what the Sovereign LORD says: Because it towered on
high, lifting its top above the thick
foliage, and because it was proud of its
height, 11 I handed it over to the ruler of

---

a 15 Hebrew *Sin;* also in verse 16   *b* 17 Hebrew *Awen* (or *On*)   *c* 17 Hebrew *Pi Beseth*

the nations, for him to deal with according to its wickedness. I cast it aside, 12and the most ruthless of foreign nations cut it down and left it. Its boughs fell on the mountains and in all the valleys; its branches lay broken in all the ravines of the land. All the nations of the earth came out from under its shade and left it. 13All the birds of the air settled on the fallen tree, and all the beasts of the field were among its branches. 14Therefore no other trees by the waters are ever to tower proudly on high, lifting their tops above the thick foliage. No other trees so well-watered are ever to reach such a height; they are all destined for death, for the earth below, among mortal men, with those who go down to the pit.

15" 'This is what the Sovereign LORD says: On the day it was brought down to the grave*a* I covered the deep springs with mourning for it; I held back its streams, and its abundant waters were restrained. Because of it I clothed Lebanon with gloom, and all the trees of the field withered away. 16I made the nations tremble at the sound of its fall when I brought it down to the grave with those who go down to the pit. Then all the trees of Eden, the choicest and best of Lebanon, all the trees that were well-watered, were consoled in the earth below. 17Those who lived in its shade, its allies among the nations, had also gone down to the grave with it, joining those killed by the sword.

18" 'Which of the trees of Eden can be compared with you in splendor and majesty? Yet you, too, will be brought down with the trees of Eden to the earth below; you will lie among the uncircumcised, with those killed by the sword.

" 'This is Pharaoh and all his hordes, declares the Sovereign LORD.' "

A Lament for Pharaoh

32 In the twelfth year, in the twelfth month on the first day, the word of the LORD came to me: 2"Son of man, take up a lament concerning Pharaoh king of Egypt and say to him:

" 'You are like a lion among the nations;
you are like a monster in the seas
thrashing about in your streams,
	churning the water with your feet
	and muddying the streams.

3" 'This is what the Sovereign LORD says:

" 'With a great throng of people
	I will cast my net over you,
	and they will haul you up in my
		net.
4I will throw you on the land
	and hurl you on the open field.
I will let all the birds of the air settle
		on you
	and all the beasts of the earth gorge
		themselves on you.
5I will spread your flesh on the
		mountains
	and fill the valleys with your
		remains.
6I will drench the land with your
		flowing blood
	all the way to the mountains,
	and the ravines will be filled with
		your flesh.
7When I snuff you out, I will cover the
		heavens
	and darken their stars;
I will cover the sun with a cloud,
	and the moon will not give its light.
8All the shining lights in the heavens
	I will darken over you;
	I will bring darkness over your
		land,
		declares the Sovereign LORD.
9I will trouble the hearts of many
		peoples
	when I bring about your
		destruction among the
		nations,
	among*b* lands you have not known.
10I will cause many peoples to be
		appalled at you,
	and their kings will shudder with
		horror because of you
	when I brandish my sword before
		them.
On the day of your downfall
	each of them will tremble
	every moment for his life.

---

a 15 Hebrew *Sheol*; also in verses 16 and 17   *b* 9 Hebrew; Septuagint *bring you into captivity among the nations,* / *to*

11 " 'For this is what the Sovereign
LORD says:

" 'The sword of the king of Babylon
    will come against you.
12 I will cause your hordes to fall
    by the swords of mighty men—
    the most ruthless of all nations.
They will shatter the pride of Egypt,
    and all her hordes will be
        overthrown.
13 I will destroy all her cattle
    from beside abundant waters
no longer to be stirred by the foot of
        man
    or muddied by the hoofs of cattle.
14 Then I will let her waters settle
    and make her streams flow like oil,
        declares the Sovereign LORD.
15 When I make Egypt desolate
    and strip the land of everything in
        it,
    when I strike down all who live
        there,
    then they will know that I am the
        LORD.'

16 "This is the lament they will chant
for her. The daughters of the nations
will chant it; for Egypt and all her hordes
they will chant it, declares the Sovereign LORD."

17 In the twelfth year, on the fifteenth
day of the month, the word of the LORD
came to me: 18 "Son of man, wail for the
hordes of Egypt and consign to the earth
below both her and the daughters of
mighty nations, with those who go
down to the pit. 19 Say to them, 'Are you
more favored than others? Go down and
be laid among the uncircumcised.'
20 They will fall among those killed by
the sword. The sword is drawn; let her
be dragged off with all her hordes.
21 From within the grave*a* the mighty
leaders will say of Egypt and her allies,
'They have come down and they lie
with the uncircumcised, with those
killed by the sword.'
22 "Assyria is there with her whole
army; she is surrounded by the graves of
all her slain, all who have fallen by the
sword. 23 Their graves are in the depths
of the pit and her army lies around her

grave. All who had spread terror in the
land of the living are slain, fallen by the
sword.
24 "Elam is there, with all her hordes
around her grave. All of them are slain,
fallen by the sword. All who had spread
terror in the land of the living went
down uncircumcised to the earth below.
They bear their shame with those who
go down to the pit. 25 A bed is made for
her among the slain, with all her hordes
around her grave. All of them are uncircumcised, killed by the sword. Because
their terror had spread in the land of the
living, they bear their shame with those
who go down to the pit; they are laid
among the slain.
26 "Meshech and Tubal are there, with
all their hordes around their graves. All
of them are uncircumcised, killed by the
sword because they spread their terror in
the land of the living. 27 Do they not lie
with the other uncircumcised warriors
who have fallen, who went down to the
grave with their weapons of war, whose
swords were placed under their heads?
The punishment for their sins rested on
their bones, though the terror of these
warriors had stalked through the land of
the living.
28 "You too, O Pharaoh, will be broken
and will lie among the uncircumcised,
with those killed by the sword.
29 "Edom is there, her kings and all her
princes; despite their power, they are
laid with those killed by the sword.
They lie with the uncircumcised, with
those who go down to the pit.
30 "All the princes of the north and all
the Sidonians are there; they went down
with the slain in disgrace despite the terror caused by their power. They lie
uncircumcised with those killed by the
sword and bear their shame with those
who go down to the pit.
31 "Pharaoh—he and all his army—
will see them and he will be consoled
for all his hordes that were killed by the
sword, declares the Sovereign LORD.
32 Although I had him spread terror in
the land of the living, Pharaoh and all
his hordes will be laid among the uncircumcised, with those killed by the
sword, declares the Sovereign LORD."

a 21 Hebrew *Sheol*; also in verse 27

Ezekiel a Watchman

33 The word of the LORD came to me: 2"Son of man, speak to your countrymen and say to them: 'When I bring the sword against a land, and the people of the land choose one of their men and make him their watchman, 3and he sees the sword coming against the land and blows the trumpet to warn the people, 4then if anyone hears the trumpet but does not take warning and the sword comes and takes his life, his blood will be on his own head. 5Since he heard the sound of the trumpet but did not take warning, his blood will be on his own head. If he had taken warning, he would have saved himself. 6But if the watchman sees the sword coming and does not blow the trumpet to warn the people and the sword comes and takes the life of one of them, that man will be taken away because of his sin, but I will hold the watchman accountable for his blood.'

7"Son of man, I have made you a watchman for the house of Israel; so hear the word I speak and give them warning from me. 8When I say to the wicked, 'O wicked man, you will surely die,' and you do not speak out to dissuade him from his ways, that wicked man will die for*a* his sin, and I will hold you accountable for his blood. 9But if you do warn the wicked man to turn from his ways and he does not do so, he will die for his sin, but you will have saved yourself.

10"Son of man, say to the house of Israel, 'This is what you are saying: "Our offenses and sins weigh us down, and we are wasting away because of*b* them. How then can we live?" ' 11Say to them, 'As surely as I live, declares the Sovereign LORD, I take no pleasure in the death of the wicked, but rather that they turn from their ways and live. Turn! Turn from your evil ways! Why will you die, O house of Israel?'

12"Therefore, son of man, say to your countrymen, 'The righteousness of the righteous man will not save him when he disobeys, and the wickedness of the wicked man will not cause him to fall when he turns from it. The righteous man, if he sins, will not be allowed to live because of his former righteousness.'

13If I tell the righteous man that he will surely live, but then he trusts in his righteousness and does evil, none of the righteous things he has done will be remembered; he will die for the evil he has done. 14And if I say to the wicked man, 'You will surely die,' but he then turns away from his sin and does what is just and right— 15if he gives back what he took in pledge for a loan, returns what he has stolen, follows the decrees that give life, and does no evil, he will surely live; he will not die. 16None of the sins he has committed will be remembered against him. He has done what is just and right; he will surely live.

17"Yet your countrymen say, 'The way of the Lord is not just.' But it is their way that is not just. 18If a righteous man turns from his righteousness and does evil, he will die for it. 19And if a wicked man turns away from his wickedness and does what is just and right, he will live by doing so. 20Yet, O house of Israel, you say, 'The way of the Lord is not just.' But I will judge each of you according to his own ways."

Jerusalem's Fall Explained

21In the twelfth year of our exile, in the tenth month on the fifth day, a man who had escaped from Jerusalem came to me and said, "The city has fallen!" 22Now the evening before the man arrived, the hand of the LORD was upon me, and he opened my mouth before the man came to me in the morning. So my mouth was opened and I was no longer silent.

23Then the word of the LORD came to me: 24"Son of man, the people living in those ruins in the land of Israel are saying, 'Abraham was only one man, yet he possessed the land. But we are many; surely the land has been given to us as our possession.' 25Therefore say to them, 'This is what the Sovereign LORD says: Since you eat meat with the blood still in it and look to your idols and shed blood, should you then possess the land? 26You rely on your sword, you do detestable things, and each of you defiles his neighbor's wife. Should you then possess the land?'

27"Say this to them: 'This is what the Sovereign LORD says: As surely as I live,

---

a 8 Or *in;* also in verse 9   *b* 10 Or *away in*

THE WATCHMAN OF THE SOCIETY OF FRIENDS
John Woolman

VERSE: Ezekiel 33:6   **PASSAGE:** Ezekiel 33:1–12

 bout the twenty-third year of my age, I had many fresh and heavenly openings, in respect to the care and providence of the Almighty over his creatures in general, and over man as the most noble amongst those which are visible. And being clearly convinced in my judgment, that to place my whole trust in God was best for me, I felt renewed engagements, that in all things I might act on an inward principle of virtue, and pursue worldly business no farther, than as truth opened my way therein.

About the time called *Christmas*, I observed many people from the country, and dwellers in town, who, resorting to public houses, spent their time in drinking and vain sports, tending to corrupt one another; on which account I was much troubled. At one house, in particular, there was much disorder; and I believed it was a duty incumbent on me to go and speak to the master of that house. I considered I was young, and that several elderly friends in town had opportunity to see these things; but though I would gladly have been excused, yet I could not feel my mind clear.

The exercise was heavy; and as I was reading what the Almighty said to *Ezekiel*, respecting his duty as a watchman, the matter was set home more clearly; and then, with prayers and tears, I besought the Lord for his assistance, who, in loving-kindness, gave me a resigned heart. Then, at a suitable opportunity, I went to the public house, and, seeing the man amongst much company, I went to him, and told him, I wanted to speak with him; so we went aside, and there, in the fear of the Almighty, I expressed to him what rested on my mind; which he took kindly, and afterward showed more regard to me than before. In a few years afterwards he died, middle-aged; and I often thought that, had I neglected my duty in that case, it would have given me great trouble; and I was humbly thankful to my gracious Father, who had supported me herein.

ADDITIONAL SCRIPTURE READING:
Nehemiah 7:3; Isaiah 62:6

Go to page 977 for your next devotional reading.

1700   1900

those who are left in the ruins will fall by the sword, those out in the country I will give to the wild animals to be devoured, and those in strongholds and caves will die of a plague. ²⁸I will make the land a desolate waste, and her proud strength will come to an end, and the mountains of Israel will become desolate so that no one will cross them. ²⁹Then they will know that I am the LORD, when I have made the land a desolate waste because of all the detestable things they have done.'

³⁰"As for you, son of man, your countrymen are talking together about you by the walls and at the doors of the houses, saying to each other, 'Come and hear the message that has come from the LORD.' ³¹My people come to you, as they usually do, and sit before you to listen to your words, but they do not put them into practice. With their mouths they express devotion, but their hearts are greedy for unjust gain. ³²Indeed, to them you are nothing more than one who sings love songs with a beautiful voice and plays an instrument well, for they hear your words but do not put them into practice.

³³"When all this comes true—and it surely will—then they will know that a prophet has been among them."

Shepherds and Sheep

34 The word of the LORD came to me: ²"Son of man, prophesy against the shepherds of Israel; prophesy and say to them: 'This is what the Sovereign LORD says: Woe to the shepherds of Israel who only take care of themselves! Should not shepherds take care of the flock? ³You eat the curds, clothe yourselves with the wool and slaughter the choice animals, but you do not take care of the flock. ⁴You have not strengthened the weak or healed the sick or bound up the injured. You have not brought back the strays or searched for the lost. You have ruled them harshly and brutally. ⁵So they were scattered because there was no shepherd, and when they were scattered they became food for all the wild animals. ⁶My sheep wandered over all the mountains and on every high hill. They were scattered over the whole earth, and no one searched or looked for them.

⁷"'Therefore, you shepherds, hear the word of the LORD: ⁸As surely as I live, declares the Sovereign LORD, because my flock lacks a shepherd and so has been plundered and has become food for all the wild animals, and because my shepherds did not search for my flock but cared for themselves rather than for my flock, ⁹therefore, O shepherds, hear the word of the LORD: ¹⁰This is what the Sovereign LORD says: I am against the shepherds and will hold them accountable for my flock. I will remove them from tending the flock so that the shepherds can no longer feed themselves. I will rescue my flock from their mouths, and it will no longer be food for them.

¹¹"'For this is what the Sovereign LORD says: I myself will search for my sheep and look after them. ¹²As a shepherd looks after his scattered flock when he is with them, so will I look after my sheep. I will rescue them from all the places where they were scattered on a day of clouds and darkness. ¹³I will bring them out from the nations and gather them from the countries, and I will bring them into their own land. I will pasture them on the mountains of Israel, in the ravines and in all the settlements in the land. ¹⁴I will tend them in a good pasture, and the mountain heights of Israel will be their grazing land. There they will lie down in good grazing land, and there they will feed in a rich pasture on the mountains of Israel. ¹⁵I myself will tend my sheep and have them lie down, declares the Sovereign LORD. ¹⁶I will search for the lost and bring back the strays. I will bind up the injured and strengthen the weak, but the sleek and the strong I will destroy. I will shepherd the flock with justice.

¹⁷"'As for you, my flock, this is what the Sovereign LORD says: I will judge between one sheep and another, and between rams and goats. ¹⁸Is it not enough for you to feed on the good pasture? Must you also trample the rest of your pasture with your feet? Is it not enough for you to drink clear water? Must you also muddy the rest with your feet? ¹⁹Must my flock feed on what you

have trampled and drink what you have muddied with your feet?

20" 'Therefore this is what the Sovereign LORD says to them: See, I myself will judge between the fat sheep and the lean sheep. 21Because you shove with flank and shoulder, butting all the weak sheep with your horns until you have driven them away, 22I will save my flock, and they will no longer be plundered. I will judge between one sheep and another. 23I will place over them one shepherd, my servant David, and he will tend them; he will tend them and be their shepherd. 24I the LORD will be their God, and my servant David will be prince among them. I the LORD have spoken.

25" 'I will make a covenant of peace with them and rid the land of wild beasts so that they may live in the desert and sleep in the forests in safety. 26I will bless them and the places surrounding my hill.*a* I will send down showers in season; there will be showers of blessing. 27The trees of the field will yield their fruit and the ground will yield its crops; the people will be secure in their land. They will know that I am the LORD, when I break the bars of their yoke and rescue them from the hands of those who enslaved them. 28They will no longer be plundered by the nations, nor will wild animals devour them. They will live in safety, and no one will make them afraid. 29I will provide for them a land renowned for its crops, and they will no longer be victims of famine in the land or bear the scorn of the nations. 30Then they will know that I, the LORD their God, am with them and that they, the house of Israel, are my people, declares the Sovereign LORD. 31You my sheep, the sheep of my pasture, are people, and I am your God, declares the Sovereign LORD.' "

A Prophecy Against Edom

35 The word of the LORD came to me: 2"Son of man, set your face against Mount Seir; prophesy against it 3and say: 'This is what the Sovereign LORD says: I am against you, Mount Seir, and I will stretch out my hand against you and make you a desolate waste. 4I will turn your towns into

ruins and you will be desolate. Then you will know that I am the LORD.

5" 'Because you harbored an ancient hostility and delivered the Israelites over to the sword at the time of their calamity, the time their punishment reached its climax, 6therefore as surely as I live, declares the Sovereign LORD, I will give you over to bloodshed and it will pursue you. Since you did not hate bloodshed, bloodshed will pursue you. 7I will make Mount Seir a desolate waste and cut off from it all who come and go. 8I will fill your mountains with the slain; those killed by the sword will fall on your hills and in your valleys and in all your ravines. 9I will make you desolate forever; your towns will not be inhabited. Then you will know that I am the LORD.

10" 'Because you have said, "These two nations and countries will be ours and we will take possession of them," even though I the LORD was there, 11therefore as surely as I live, declares the Sovereign LORD, I will treat you in accordance with the anger and jealousy you showed in your hatred of them and I will make myself known among them when I judge you. 12Then you will know that I the LORD have heard all the contemptible things you have said against the mountains of Israel. You said, "They have been laid waste and have been given over to us to devour." 13You boasted against me and spoke against me without restraint, and I heard it. 14This is what the Sovereign LORD says: While the whole earth rejoices, I will make you desolate. 15Because you rejoiced when the inheritance of the house of Israel became desolate, that is how I will treat you. You will be desolate, O Mount Seir, you and all of Edom. Then they will know that I am the LORD.' "

A Prophecy to the Mountains of Israel

36 "Son of man, prophesy to the mountains of Israel and say, 'O mountains of Israel, hear the word of the LORD. 2This is what the Sovereign LORD says: The enemy said of you, "Aha! The ancient heights have become our possession." ' 3Therefore prophesy and say, 'This is what the Sovereign

---

a 26 Or *I will make them and the places surrounding my hill a blessing*

LORD says: Because they ravaged and hounded you from every side so that you became the possession of the rest of the nations and the object of people's malicious talk and slander, 4therefore, O mountains of Israel, hear the word of the Sovereign LORD: This is what the Sovereign LORD says to the mountains and hills, to the ravines and valleys, to the desolate ruins and the deserted towns that have been plundered and ridiculed by the rest of the nations around you— 5this is what the Sovereign LORD says: In my burning zeal I have spoken against the rest of the nations, and against all Edom, for with glee and with malice in their hearts they made my land their own possession so that they might plunder its pastureland.' 6Therefore prophesy concerning the land of Israel and say to the mountains and hills, to the ravines and valleys: 'This is what the Sovereign LORD says: I speak in my jealous wrath because you have suffered the scorn of the nations. 7Therefore this is what the Sovereign LORD says: I swear with uplifted hand that the nations around you will also suffer scorn.

8" 'But you, O mountains of Israel, will produce branches and fruit for my people Israel, for they will soon come home. 9I am concerned for you and will look on you with favor; you will be plowed and sown, 10and I will multiply the number of people upon you, even the whole house of Israel. The towns will be inhabited and the ruins rebuilt. 11I will increase the number of men and animals upon you, and they will be fruitful and become numerous. I will settle people on you as in the past and will make you prosper more than before. Then you will know that I am the LORD. 12I will cause people, my people Israel, to walk upon you. They will possess you, and you will be their inheritance; you will never again deprive them of their children.

13" 'This is what the Sovereign LORD says: Because people say to you, "You devour men and deprive your nation of its children," 14therefore you will no longer devour men or make your nation childless, declares the Sovereign LORD. 15No longer will I make you hear the taunts of the nations, and no longer will you suffer the scorn of the peoples or cause your nation to fall, declares the Sovereign LORD.' "

16Again the word of the LORD came to me: 17"Son of man, when the people of Israel were living in their own land, they defiled it by their conduct and their actions. Their conduct was like a woman's monthly uncleanness in my sight. 18So I poured out my wrath on them because they had shed blood in the land and because they had defiled it with their idols. 19I dispersed them among the nations, and they were scattered through the countries; I judged them according to their conduct and their actions. 20And wherever they went among the nations they profaned my holy name, for it was said of them, 'These are the LORD's people, and yet they had to leave his land.' 21I had concern for my holy name, which the house of Israel profaned among the nations where they had gone.

22"Therefore say to the house of Israel, 'This is what the Sovereign LORD says: It is not for your sake, O house of Israel, that I am going to do these things, but for the sake of my holy name, which you have profaned among the nations where you have gone. 23I will show the holiness of my great name, which has been profaned among the nations, the name you have profaned among them. Then the nations will know that I am the LORD, declares the Sovereign LORD, when I show myself holy through you before their eyes.

24" 'For I will take you out of the nations; I will gather you from all the countries and bring you back into your own land. 25I will sprinkle clean water on you, and you will be clean; I will cleanse you from all your impurities and from all your idols. 26I will give you a new heart and put a new spirit in you; I will remove from you your heart of stone and give you a heart of flesh. 27And I will put my Spirit in you and move you to follow my decrees and be careful to keep my laws. 28You will live in the land I gave your forefathers; you will be my people, and I will be your God. 29I will save you from all your uncleanness. I will call for the grain and make it plentiful and will not bring famine upon you. ³⁰I will increase the fruit of the trees and the crops of the field, so that you will no longer suffer disgrace among the nations because of famine. ³¹Then you will remember your evil ways and wicked deeds, and you will loathe yourselves for your sins and detestable practices. ³²I want you to know that I am not doing this for your sake, declares the Sovereign LORD. Be ashamed and disgraced for your conduct, O house of Israel!

³³ 'This is what the Sovereign LORD says: On the day I cleanse you from all your sins, I will resettle your towns, and the ruins will be rebuilt. ³⁴The desolate land will be cultivated instead of lying desolate in the sight of all who pass through it. ³⁵They will say, "This land that was laid waste has become like the garden of Eden; the cities that were lying in ruins, desolate and destroyed, are now fortified and inhabited." ³⁶Then the nations around you that remain will know that I the LORD have rebuilt what was destroyed and have replanted what was desolate. I the LORD have spoken, and I will do it.'

³⁷"This is what the Sovereign LORD says: Once again I will yield to the plea of the house of Israel and do this for them: I will make their people as numerous as sheep, ³⁸as numerous as the flocks for offerings at Jerusalem during her appointed feasts. So will the ruined cities be filled with flocks of people. Then they will know that I am the LORD."

The Valley of Dry Bones

37 The hand of the LORD was upon me, and he brought me out by the Spirit of the LORD and set me in the middle of a valley; it was full of bones. ²He led me back and forth among them, and I saw a great many bones on the floor of the valley, bones that were very dry. ³He asked me, "Son of man, can these bones live?"

I said, "O Sovereign LORD, you alone know."

⁴Then he said to me, "Prophesy to these bones and say to them, 'Dry bones, hear the word of the LORD! ⁵This is what the Sovereign LORD says to these bones: I will make breath^a enter you, and you will come to life. ⁶I will attach tendons to you and make flesh come upon you and cover you with skin; I will put breath in you, and you will come to life. Then you will know that I am the LORD.' "

⁷So I prophesied as I was commanded. And as I was prophesying, there was a noise, a rattling sound, and the bones came together, bone to bone. ⁸I looked, and tendons and flesh appeared on them and skin covered them, but there was no breath in them.

⁹Then he said to me, "Prophesy to the breath; prophesy, son of man, and say to it, 'This is what the Sovereign LORD says: Come from the four winds, O breath, and breathe into these slain, that they may live.' " ¹⁰So I prophesied as he commanded me, and breath entered them; they came to life and stood up on their feet—a vast army.

¹¹Then he said to me: "Son of man, these bones are the whole house of Israel. They say, 'Our bones are dried up and our hope is gone; we are cut off.' ¹²Therefore prophesy and say to them: 'This is what the Sovereign LORD says: O my people, I am going to open your graves and bring you up from them; I will bring you back to the land of Israel. ¹³Then you, my people, will know that I am the LORD, when I open your graves and bring you up from them. ¹⁴I will put my Spirit in you and you will live, and I will settle you in your own land. Then you will know that I the LORD have spoken, and I have done it, declares the LORD.' "

One Nation Under One King

¹⁵The word of the LORD came to me: ¹⁶"Son of man, take a stick of wood and write on it, 'Belonging to Judah and the Israelites associated with him.' Then take another stick of wood, and write on it, 'Ephraim's stick, belonging to Joseph and all the house of Israel associated with him.' ¹⁷Join them together into one stick so that they will become one in your hand.

¹⁸"When your countrymen ask you, 'Won't you tell us what you mean by this?' ¹⁹say to them, 'This is what the Sovereign LORD says: I am going to take

---

^a 5 The Hebrew for this word can also mean *wind* or *spirit* (see verses 6–14).

the stick of Joseph—which is in Ephraim's hand—and of the Israelite tribes associated with him, and join it to Judah's stick, making them a single stick of wood, and they will become one in my hand.' ²⁰Hold before their eyes the sticks you have written on ²¹and say to them, 'This is what the Sovereign LORD says: I will take the Israelites out of the nations where they have gone. I will gather them from all around and bring them back into their own land. ²²I will make them one nation in the land, on the mountains of Israel. There will be one king over all of them and they will never again be two nations or be divided into two kingdoms. ²³They will no longer defile themselves with their idols and vile images or with any of their offenses, for I will save them from all their sinful backsliding,ᵃ and I will cleanse them. They will be my people, and I will be their God.

²⁴" 'My servant David will be king over them, and they will all have one shepherd. They will follow my laws and be careful to keep my decrees. ²⁵They will live in the land I gave to my servant Jacob, the land where your fathers lived. They and their children and their children's children will live there forever, and David my servant will be their prince forever. ²⁶I will make a covenant of peace with them; it will be an everlasting covenant. I will establish them and increase their numbers, and I will put my sanctuary among them forever. ²⁷My dwelling place will be with them; I will be their God, and they will be my people. ²⁸Then the nations will know that I the LORD make Israel holy, when my sanctuary is among them forever.' "

A Prophecy Against Gog

38 The word of the LORD came to me: ²"Son of man, set your face against Gog, of the land of Magog, the chief prince ofᵇ Meshech and Tubal; prophesy against him ³and say: 'This is what the Sovereign LORD says: I am against you, O Gog, chief prince ofᶜ Meshech and Tubal. ⁴I will turn you around, put hooks in your jaws and

bring you out with your whole army—your horses, your horsemen fully armed, and a great horde with large and small shields, all of them brandishing their swords. ⁵Persia, Cushᵈ and Put will be with them, all with shields and helmets, ⁶also Gomer with all its troops, and Beth Togarmah from the far north with all its troops—the many nations with you.

⁷" 'Get ready; be prepared, you and all the hordes gathered about you, and take command of them. ⁸After many days you will be called to arms. In future years you will invade a land that has recovered from war, whose people were gathered from many nations to the mountains of Israel, which had long been desolate. They had been brought out from the nations, and now all of them live in safety. ⁹You and all your troops and the many nations with you will go up, advancing like a storm; you will be like a cloud covering the land.

¹⁰" 'This is what the Sovereign LORD says: On that day thoughts will come into your mind and you will devise an evil scheme. ¹¹You will say, "I will invade a land of unwalled villages; I will attack a peaceful and unsuspecting people—all of them living without walls and without gates and bars. ¹²I will plunder and loot and turn my hand against the resettled ruins and the people gathered from the nations, rich in livestock and goods, living at the center of the land." ¹³Sheba and Dedan and the merchants of Tarshish and all her villagesᵉ will say to you, "Have you come to plunder? Have you gathered your hordes to loot, to carry off silver and gold, to take away livestock and goods and to seize much plunder?" '

¹⁴"Therefore, son of man, prophesy and say to Gog: 'This is what the Sovereign LORD says: In that day, when my people Israel are living in safety, will you not take notice of it? ¹⁵You will come from your place in the far north, you and many nations with you, all of them riding on horses, a great horde, a mighty army. ¹⁶You will advance against my people Israel like a cloud that covers the land. In days to come,

---

ᵃ 23 Many Hebrew manuscripts (see also Septuagint); most Hebrew manuscripts *all their dwelling places where they sinned*   ᵇ 2 Or *the prince of Rosh,*   ᶜ 3 Or *Gog, prince of Rosh,*   ᵈ 5 That is, the upper Nile region   ᵉ 13 Or *her strong lions*

O Gog, I will bring you against my land, so that the nations may know me when I show myself holy through you before their eyes.

17" 'This is what the Sovereign LORD says: Are you not the one I spoke of in former days by my servants the prophets of Israel? At that time they prophesied for years that I would bring you against them. 18This is what will happen in that day: When Gog attacks the land of Israel, my hot anger will be aroused, declares the Sovereign LORD. 19In my zeal and fiery wrath I declare that at that time there shall be a great earthquake in the land of Israel. 20The fish of the sea, the birds of the air, the beasts of the field, every creature that moves along the ground, and all the people on the face of the earth will tremble at my presence. The mountains will be overturned, the cliffs will crumble and every wall will fall to the ground. 21I will summon a sword against Gog on all my mountains, declares the Sovereign LORD. Every man's sword will be against his brother. 22I will execute judgment upon him with plague and bloodshed; I will pour down torrents of rain, hailstones and burning sulfur on him and on his troops and on the many nations with him. 23And so I will show my greatness and my holiness, and I will make myself known in the sight of many nations. Then they will know that I am the LORD.'

39 "Son of man, prophesy against Gog and say: 'This is what the Sovereign LORD says: I am against you, O Gog, chief prince of[a] Meshech and Tubal. 2I will turn you around and drag you along. I will bring you from the far north and send you against the mountains of Israel. 3Then I will strike your bow from your left hand and make your arrows drop from your right hand. 4On the mountains of Israel you will fall, you and all your troops and the nations with you. I will give you as food to all kinds of carrion birds and to the wild animals. 5You will fall in the open field, for I have spoken, declares the Sovereign LORD. 6I will send fire on Magog and on those who live in safety

in the coastlands, and they will know that I am the LORD.

7" 'I will make known my holy name among my people Israel. I will no longer let my holy name be profaned, and the nations will know that I the LORD am the Holy One in Israel. 8It is coming! It will surely take place, declares the Sovereign LORD. This is the day I have spoken of.

9" 'Then those who live in the towns of Israel will go out and use the weapons for fuel and burn them up—the small and large shields, the bows and arrows, the war clubs and the spears. For seven years they will use them for fuel. 10They will not need to gather wood from the fields or cut it from the forests, because they will use the weapons for fuel. And they will plunder those who plundered them and loot those who looted them, declares the Sovereign LORD.

11" 'On that day I will give Gog a burial place in Israel, in the valley of those who travel east toward[b] the Sea.[c] It will block the way of travelers, because Gog and all his hordes will be buried there. So it will be called the Valley of Hamon Gog.[d]

12" 'For seven months the house of Israel will be burying them in order to cleanse the land. 13All the people of the land will bury them, and the day I am glorified will be a memorable day for them, declares the Sovereign LORD.

14" 'Men will be regularly employed to cleanse the land. Some will go throughout the land and, in addition to them, others will bury those that remain on the ground. At the end of the seven months they will begin their search. 15As they go through the land and one of them sees a human bone, he will set up a marker beside it until the gravediggers have buried it in the Valley of Hamon Gog. 16(Also a town called Hamonah[e] will be there.) And so they will cleanse the land.'

17"Son of man, this is what the Sovereign LORD says: Call out to every kind of bird and all the wild animals: 'Assemble and come together from all around to the sacrifice I am preparing for you, the great sacrifice on the mountains of Israel. There you will eat flesh and drink blood. 18You will eat the flesh of mighty

---

a 1 Or Gog, prince of Rosh,   b 11 Or of   c 11 That is, the Dead Sea   d 11 Hamon Gog means hordes of Gog.   e 16 Hamonah means horde.

men and drink the blood of the princes of the earth as if they were rams and lambs, goats and bulls—all of them fattened animals from Bashan. ¹⁹At the sacrifice I am preparing for you, you will eat fat till you are glutted and drink blood till you are drunk. ²⁰At my table you will eat your fill of horses and riders, mighty men and soldiers of every kind,' declares the Sovereign LORD.

²¹"I will display my glory among the nations, and all the nations will see the punishment I inflict and the hand I lay upon them. ²²From that day forward the house of Israel will know that I am the LORD their God. ²³And the nations will know that the people of Israel went into exile for their sin, because they were unfaithful to me. So I hid my face from them and handed them over to their enemies, and they all fell by the sword. ²⁴I dealt with them according to their uncleanness and their offenses, and I hid my face from them.

²⁵"Therefore this is what the Sovereign LORD says: I will now bring Jacob back from captivity*a* and will have compassion on all the people of Israel, and I will be zealous for my holy name. ²⁶They will forget their shame and all the unfaithfulness they showed toward me when they lived in safety in their land with no one to make them afraid.

FOR JUST AS BY THE COURTESY OF GOD HE FORGETTETH OUR SIN AFTER THE TIME THAT WE OURSELVES REPENT, SO WILLETH HE THAT WE FORGET OUR SIN IN REGARD TO OUR STUPID DEPRESSION AND OUR DOUBTFUL FEARS.

—*Julian of Norwich*

---

²⁷When I have brought them back from the nations and have gathered them from the countries of their enemies, I will show myself holy through them in the sight of many nations. ²⁸Then they will know that I am the LORD their God, for though I sent them into exile among the nations, I will gather them to their own land, not leaving any behind. ²⁹I

will no longer hide my face from them, for I will pour out my Spirit on the house of Israel, declares the Sovereign LORD."

The New Temple Area

40 In the twenty-fifth year of our exile, at the beginning of the year, on the tenth of the month, in the fourteenth year after the fall of the city— on that very day the hand of the LORD was upon me and he took me there. ²In visions of God he took me to the land of Israel and set me on a very high mountain, on whose south side were some buildings that looked like a city. ³He took me there, and I saw a man whose appearance was like bronze; he was standing in the gateway with a linen cord and a measuring rod in his hand. ⁴The man said to me, "Son of man, look with your eyes and hear with your ears and pay attention to everything I am going to show you, for that is why you have been brought here. Tell the house of Israel everything you see."

The East Gate to the Outer Court

⁵I saw a wall completely surrounding the temple area. The length of the measuring rod in the man's hand was six long cubits, each of which was a cubit*b* and a handbreadth.*c* He measured the wall; it was one measuring rod thick and one rod high.

⁶Then he went to the gate facing east. He climbed its steps and measured the threshold of the gate; it was one rod deep.*d* ⁷The alcoves for the guards were one rod long and one rod wide, and the projecting walls between the alcoves were five cubits thick. And the threshold of the gate next to the portico facing the temple was one rod deep.

⁸Then he measured the portico of the gateway; ⁹it*e* was eight cubits deep and its jambs were two cubits thick. The portico of the gateway faced the temple.

¹⁰Inside the east gate were three alcoves on each side; the three had the same measurements; and the faces of the projecting walls on each side had the

---

a 25 Or *now restore the fortunes of Jacob*   *b* 5 The common cubit was about 1 1/2 feet (about 0.5 meter).   *c* 5 That is, about 3 inches (about 8 centimeters)   *d* 6 Septuagint; Hebrew *deep, the first threshold, one rod deep*   *e* 8,9 Many Hebrew manuscripts, Septuagint, Vulgate and Syriac; most Hebrew manuscripts *gateway facing the temple; it was one rod deep.* ⁹*Then he measured the portico of the gateway; it*

same measurements. ¹¹Then he measured the width of the entrance to the gateway; it was ten cubits and its length was thirteen cubits. ¹²In front of each alcove was a wall one cubit high, and the alcoves were six cubits square. ¹³Then he measured the gateway from the top of the rear wall of one alcove to the top of the opposite one; the distance was twenty-five cubits from one parapet opening to the opposite one. ¹⁴He measured along the faces of the projecting walls all around the inside of the gateway—sixty cubits. The measurement was up to the portico*ᵃ* facing the courtyard.*ᵇ* ¹⁵The distance from the entrance of the gateway to the far end of its portico was fifty cubits. ¹⁶The alcoves and the projecting walls inside the gateway were surmounted by narrow parapet openings all around, as was the portico; the openings all around faced inward. The faces of the projecting walls were decorated with palm trees.

The Outer Court

¹⁷Then he brought me into the outer court. There I saw some rooms and a pavement that had been constructed all around the court; there were thirty rooms along the pavement. ¹⁸It abutted the sides of the gateways and was as wide as they were long; this was the lower pavement. ¹⁹Then he measured the distance from the inside of the lower gateway to the outside of the inner court; it was a hundred cubits on the east side as well as on the north.

The North Gate

²⁰Then he measured the length and width of the gate facing north, leading into the outer court. ²¹Its alcoves—three on each side—its projecting walls and its portico had the same measurements as those of the first gateway. It was fifty cubits long and twenty-five cubits wide. ²²Its openings, its portico and its palm tree decorations had the same measurements as those of the gate facing east. Seven steps led up to it, with its portico opposite them. ²³There was a gate to the inner court facing the north gate, just as there was on the east. He measured from one gate to the opposite one; it was a hundred cubits.

The South Gate

²⁴Then he led me to the south side and I saw a gate facing south. He measured its jambs and its portico, and they had the same measurements as the others. ²⁵The gateway and its portico had narrow openings all around, like the openings of the others. It was fifty cubits long and twenty-five cubits wide. ²⁶Seven steps led up to it, with its portico opposite them; it had palm tree decorations on the faces of the projecting walls on each side. ²⁷The inner court also had a gate facing south, and he measured from this gate to the outer gate on the south side; it was a hundred cubits.

Gates to the Inner Court

²⁸Then he brought me into the inner court through the south gate, and he measured the south gate; it had the same measurements as the others. ²⁹Its alcoves, its projecting walls and its portico had the same measurements as the others. The gateway and its portico had openings all around. It was fifty cubits long and twenty-five cubits wide. ³⁰(The porticoes of the gateways around the inner court were twenty-five cubits wide and five cubits deep.) ³¹Its portico faced the outer court; palm trees decorated its jambs, and eight steps led up to it.

³²Then he brought me to the inner court on the east side, and he measured the gateway; it had the same measurements as the others. ³³Its alcoves, its projecting walls and its portico had the same measurements as the others. The gateway and its portico had openings all around. It was fifty cubits long and twenty-five cubits wide. ³⁴Its portico faced the outer court; palm trees decorated the jambs on either side, and eight steps led up to it.

³⁵Then he brought me to the north gate and measured it. It had the same measurements as the others, ³⁶as did its alcoves, its projecting walls and its portico, and it had openings all around. It was fifty cubits long and twenty-five cubits wide. ³⁷Its portico*ᶜ* faced the

---

a 14 Septuagint; Hebrew *projecting wall*   *b 14* The meaning of the Hebrew for this verse is uncertain.
c 37 Septuagint (see also verses 31 and 34); Hebrew *jambs*

outer court; palm trees decorated the
jambs on either side, and eight steps led
up to it.

The Rooms for Preparing Sacrifices

38A room with a doorway was by the
portico in each of the inner gateways,
where the burnt offerings were washed.
39In the portico of the gateway were two
tables on each side, on which the burnt
offerings, sin offerings and guilt offerings
were slaughtered. **40**By the outside wall
of the portico of the gateway, near the
steps at the entrance to the north gateway were two tables, and on the other
side of the steps were two tables. **41**So
there were four tables on one side of the
gateway and four on the other—eight
tables in all—on which the sacrifices
were slaughtered. **42**There were also four
tables of dressed stone for the burnt
offerings, each a cubit and a half long, a
cubit and a half wide and a cubit high.
On them were placed the utensils for
slaughtering the burnt offerings and the
other sacrifices. **43**And double-pronged
hooks, each a handbreadth long, were
attached to the wall all around. The
tables were for the flesh of the offerings.

Rooms for the Priests

44Outside the inner gate, within the
inner court, were two rooms, one*a* at the
side of the north gate and facing south,
and another at the side of the south*b*
gate and facing north. **45**He said to me,
"The room facing south is for the priests
who have charge of the temple, **46**and
the room facing north is for the priests
who have charge of the altar. These are
the sons of Zadok, who are the only
Levites who may draw near to the LORD
to minister before him."

47Then he measured the court: It was
square—a hundred cubits long and a
hundred cubits wide. And the altar was
in front of the temple.

The Temple

48He brought me to the portico of the
temple and measured the jambs of the
portico; they were five cubits wide on

either side. The width of the entrance
was fourteen cubits and its projecting
walls were*c* three cubits wide on either
side. **49**The portico was twenty cubits
wide, and twelve*d* cubits from front to
back. It was reached by a flight of stairs,*e*
and there were pillars on each side of the
jambs.

41 Then the man brought me to
the outer sanctuary and measured the jambs; the width of the jambs
was six cubits*f* on each side.*g* **2**The
entrance was ten cubits wide, and the
projecting walls on each side of it were
five cubits wide. He also measured the
outer sanctuary; it was forty cubits long
and twenty cubits wide.

3Then he went into the inner sanctuary and measured the jambs of the
entrance; each was two cubits wide. The
entrance was six cubits wide, and the
projecting walls on each side of it were
seven cubits wide. **4**And he measured
the length of the inner sanctuary; it was
twenty cubits, and its width was twenty
cubits across the end of the outer sanctuary. He said to me, "This is the Most
Holy Place."

5Then he measured the wall of the
temple; it was six cubits thick, and each
side room around the temple was four
cubits wide. **6**The side rooms were on
three levels, one above another, thirty
on each level. There were ledges all
around the wall of the temple to serve as
supports for the side rooms, so that the
supports were not inserted into the wall
of the temple. **7**The side rooms all
around the temple were wider at each
successive level. The structure surrounding the temple was built in
ascending stages, so that the rooms
widened as one went upward. A stairway went up from the lowest floor to
the top floor through the middle floor.

8I saw that the temple had a raised base
all around it, forming the foundation of
the side rooms. It was the length of the
rod, six long cubits. **9**The outer wall of
the side rooms was five cubits thick. The
open area between the side rooms of the
temple **10**and the ⌐priests'⌐ rooms was
twenty cubits wide all around the

WEEKEND

THE SOWER
William Cowper

VERSE: Matthew 13:3   **PASSAGE:** Matthew 13:1–9

e sons of earth prepare the plough,
    Break up your fallow ground!
The sower is gone forth to sow,
    And scatter blessings round.

The seed that finds a stony soil,
    Shoots forth a hasty blade;
But ill repays the sower's toil,
    Soon withered, scorched, and dead.

The thorny ground is sure to balk
    All hopes of harvest there;
We find a tall and sickly stalk,
    But not the fruitful ear.

The beaten path and highway side
    Receive the trust in vain;
The watchful birds the spoil divide,
    And pick up all the grain.

But where the Lord of grace and power
    Has blessed the happy field;
How plenteous is the golden store
    The deep-wrought furrows yield!

Father of mercies we have need
    Of thy preparing grace;
Let the same hand that gives the seed,
    Provide a fruitful place.

ADDITIONAL SCRIPTURE READING:
Matthew 13:18–23; Mark 4:1–12; Luke 8:5–8

Go to page 989 for your next devotional reading.

1700   1900

temple. **11**There were entrances to the side rooms from the open area, one on the north and another on the south; and the base adjoining the open area was five cubits wide all around.

12The building facing the temple courtyard on the west side was seventy cubits wide. The wall of the building was five cubits thick all around, and its length was ninety cubits.

13Then he measured the temple; it was a hundred cubits long, and the temple courtyard and the building with its walls were also a hundred cubits long. **14**The width of the temple courtyard on the east, including the front of the temple, was a hundred cubits.

15Then he measured the length of the building facing the courtyard at the rear of the temple, including its galleries on each side; it was a hundred cubits.

The outer sanctuary, the inner sanctuary and the portico facing the court, **16**as well as the thresholds and the narrow windows and galleries around the three of them—everything beyond and including the threshold was covered with wood. The floor, the wall up to the windows, and the windows were covered. **17**In the space above the outside of the entrance to the inner sanctuary and on the walls at regular intervals all around the inner and outer sanctuary **18**were carved cherubim and palm trees. Palm trees alternated with cherubim. Each cherub had two faces: **19**the face of a man toward the palm tree on one side and the face of a lion toward the palm tree on the other. They were carved all around the whole temple. **20**From the floor to the area above the entrance, cherubim and palm trees were carved on the wall of the outer sanctuary.

21The outer sanctuary had a rectangular doorframe, and the one at the front of the Most Holy Place was similar. **22**There was a wooden altar three cubits high and two cubits square*a*; its corners, its base*b* and its sides were of wood. The man said to me, "This is the table that is before the LORD." **23**Both the outer sanctuary and the Most Holy Place had double doors. **24**Each door had two leaves—

two hinged leaves for each door. **25**And on the doors of the outer sanctuary were carved cherubim and palm trees like those carved on the walls, and there was a wooden overhang on the front of the portico. **26**On the sidewalls of the portico were narrow windows with palm trees carved on each side. The side rooms of the temple also had overhangs.

Rooms for the Priests

42 Then the man led me northward into the outer court and brought me to the rooms opposite the temple courtyard and opposite the outer wall on the north side. **2**The building whose door faced north was a hundred cubits*c* long and fifty cubits wide. **3**Both in the section twenty cubits from the inner court and in the section opposite the pavement of the outer court, gallery faced gallery at the three levels. **4**In front of the rooms was an inner passageway ten cubits wide and a hundred cubits*d* long. Their doors were on the north. **5**Now the upper rooms were narrower, for the galleries took more space from them than from the rooms on the lower and middle floors of the building. **6**The rooms on the third floor had no pillars, as the courts had; so they were smaller in floor space than those on the lower and middle floors. **7**There was an outer wall parallel to the rooms and the outer court; it extended in front of the rooms for fifty cubits. **8**While the row of rooms on the side next to the outer court was fifty cubits long, the row on the side nearest the sanctuary was a hundred cubits long. **9**The lower rooms had an entrance on the east side as one enters them from the outer court.

10On the south side*e* along the length of the wall of the outer court, adjoining the temple courtyard and opposite the outer wall, were rooms **11**with a passageway in front of them. These were like the rooms on the north; they had the same length and width, with similar exits and dimensions. Similar to the doorways on the north **12**were the doorways of the rooms on the south. There was a doorway at the beginning of the

---

a 22 Septuagint; Hebrew *long*　　*b* 22 Septuagint; Hebrew *length*　　*c* 2 The common cubit was about 1 1/2 feet (about 0.5 meter).　　*d* 4 Septuagint and Syriac; Hebrew *and one cubit*　　*e* 10 Septuagint; Hebrew *Eastward*

passageway that was parallel to the corresponding wall extending eastward, by which one enters the rooms.

13 Then he said to me, "The north and south rooms facing the temple courtyard are the priests' rooms, where the priests who approach the LORD will eat the most holy offerings. There they will put the most holy offerings—the grain offerings, the sin offerings and the guilt offerings—for the place is holy. 14 Once the priests enter the holy precincts, they are not to go into the outer court until they leave behind the garments in which they minister, for these are holy. They are to put on other clothes before they go near the places that are for the people."

15 When he had finished measuring what was inside the temple area, he led me out by the east gate and measured the area all around: 16 He measured the east side with the measuring rod; it was five hundred cubits.[a] 17 He measured the north side; it was five hundred cubits[b] by the measuring rod. 18 He measured the south side; it was five hundred cubits by the measuring rod. 19 Then he turned to the west side and measured; it was five hundred cubits by the measuring rod. 20 So he measured the area on all four sides. It had a wall around it, five hundred cubits long and five hundred cubits wide, to separate the holy from the common.

The Glory Returns to the Temple

43 Then the man brought me to the gate facing east, 2 and I saw the glory of the God of Israel coming from the east. His voice was like the roar of rushing waters, and the land was radiant with his glory. 3 The vision I saw was like the vision I had seen when he[c] came to destroy the city and like the visions I had seen by the Kebar River, and I fell facedown. 4 The glory of the LORD entered the temple through the gate facing east. 5 Then the Spirit lifted me up and brought me into the inner court, and the glory of the LORD filled the temple.

6 While the man was standing beside me, I heard someone speaking to me from inside the temple. 7 He said: "Son of man, this is the place of my throne and the place for the soles of my feet. This is where I will live among the Israelites forever. The house of Israel will never again defile my holy name—neither they nor their kings—by their prostitution[d] and the lifeless idols[e] of their kings at their high places. 8 When they placed their threshold next to my threshold and their doorposts beside my doorposts, with only a wall between me and them, they defiled my holy name by their detestable practices. So I destroyed them in my anger. 9 Now let them put away from me their prostitution and the lifeless idols of their kings, and I will live among them forever.

10 "Son of man, describe the temple to the people of Israel, that they may be ashamed of their sins. Let them consider the plan, 11 and if they are ashamed of all they have done, make known to them the design of the temple—its arrangement, its exits and entrances—its whole design and all its regulations[f] and laws. Write these down before them so that they may be faithful to its design and follow all its regulations.

12 "This is the law of the temple: All the surrounding area on top of the mountain will be most holy. Such is the law of the temple.

The Altar

13 "These are the measurements of the altar in long cubits, that cubit being a cubit[g] and a handbreadth[h]: Its gutter is a cubit deep and a cubit wide, with a rim of one span[i] around the edge. And this is the height of the altar: 14 From the gutter on the ground up to the lower ledge it is two cubits high and a cubit wide, and from the smaller ledge up to the larger ledge it is four cubits high and a cubit wide. 15 The altar hearth is four cubits high, and four horns project upward from the hearth. 16 The altar hearth is square, twelve cubits long and twelve

a 16 See Septuagint of verse 17; Hebrew *rods;* also in verses 18 and 19.   *b 17* Septuagint; Hebrew *rods*
c 3 Some Hebrew manuscripts and Vulgate; most Hebrew manuscripts *I*   *d 7* Or *their spiritual*
adultery; also in verse 9   *e 7* Or *the corpses;* also in verse 9   *f 11* Some Hebrew manuscripts and
Septuagint; most Hebrew manuscripts *regulations and its whole design*   *g 13* The common cubit was
about 1 1/2 feet (about 0.5 meter).   *h 13* That is, about 3 inches (about 8 centimeters)   *i 13* That is,
about 9 inches (about 22 centimeters)

cubits wide. 17The upper ledge also is square, fourteen cubits long and fourteen cubits wide, with a rim of half a cubit and a gutter of a cubit all around. The steps of the altar face east."

18Then he said to me, "Son of man, this is what the Sovereign Lord says: These will be the regulations for sacrificing burnt offerings and sprinkling blood upon the altar when it is built: 19You are to give a young bull as a sin offering to the priests, who are Levites, of the family of Zadok, who come near to minister before me, declares the Sovereign Lord. 20You are to take some of its blood and put it on the four horns of the altar and on the four corners of the upper ledge and all around the rim, and so purify the altar and make atonement for it. 21You are to take the bull for the sin offering and burn it in the designated part of the temple area outside the sanctuary.

22"On the second day you are to offer a male goat without defect for a sin offering, and the altar is to be purified as it was purified with the bull. 23When you have finished purifying it, you are to offer a young bull and a ram from the flock, both without defect. 24You are to offer them before the Lord, and the priests are to sprinkle salt on them and sacrifice them as a burnt offering to the Lord.

25"For seven days you are to provide a male goat daily for a sin offering; you are also to provide a young bull and a ram from the flock, both without defect. 26For seven days they are to make atonement for the altar and cleanse it; thus they will dedicate it. 27At the end of these days, from the eighth day on, the priests are to present your burnt offerings and fellowship offeringsᵃ on the altar. Then I will accept you, declares the Sovereign Lord."

The Prince, the Levites, the Priests

44 Then the man brought me back to the outer gate of the sanctuary, the one facing east, and it was shut. 2The Lord said to me, "This gate is to remain shut. It must not be opened; no one may enter through it. It is to remain shut because the Lord, the God of Israel, has entered through it. 3The prince himself is the only one who may

sit inside the gateway to eat in the presence of the Lord. He is to enter by way of the portico of the gateway and go out the same way."

4Then the man brought me by way of the north gate to the front of the temple. I looked and saw the glory of the Lord filling the temple of the Lord, and I fell facedown.

5The Lord said to me, "Son of man, look carefully, listen closely and give attention to everything I tell you concerning all the regulations regarding the temple of the Lord. Give attention to the entrance of the temple and all the exits of the sanctuary. 6Say to the rebellious house of Israel, 'This is what the Sovereign Lord says: Enough of your detestable practices, O house of Israel! 7In addition to all your other detestable practices, you brought foreigners uncircumcised in heart and flesh into my sanctuary, desecrating my temple while you offered me food, fat and blood, and you broke my covenant. 8Instead of carrying out your duty in regard to my holy things, you put others in charge of my sanctuary. 9This is what the Sovereign Lord says: No foreigner uncircumcised in heart and flesh is to enter my sanctuary, not even the foreigners who live among the Israelites.

10" 'The Levites who went far from me when Israel went astray and who wandered from me after their idols must bear the consequences of their sin. 11They may serve in my sanctuary, having charge of the gates of the temple and serving in it; they may slaughter the burnt offerings and sacrifices for the people and stand before the people and serve them. 12But because they served them in the presence of their idols and made the house of Israel fall into sin, therefore I have sworn with uplifted hand that they must bear the consequences of their sin, declares the Sovereign Lord. 13They are not to come near to serve me as priests or come near any of my holy things or my most holy offerings; they must bear the shame of their detestable practices. 14Yet I will put them in charge of the duties of the temple and all the work that is to be done in it.

ᵃ 27 Traditionally *peace offerings*

15" 'But the priests, who are Levites and descendants of Zadok and who faithfully carried out the duties of my sanctuary when the Israelites went astray from me, are to come near to minister before me; they are to stand before me to offer sacrifices of fat and blood, declares the Sovereign LORD. 16They alone are to enter my sanctuary; they alone are to come near my table to minister before me and perform my service.

17" 'When they enter the gates of the inner court, they are to wear linen clothes; they must not wear any woolen garment while ministering at the gates of the inner court or inside the temple. 18They are to wear linen turbans on their heads and linen undergarments around their waists. They must not wear anything that makes them perspire. 19When they go out into the outer court where the people are, they are to take off the clothes they have been ministering in and are to leave them in the sacred rooms, and put on other clothes, so that they do not consecrate the people by means of their garments.

20" 'They must not shave their heads or let their hair grow long, but they are to keep the hair of their heads trimmed. 21No priest is to drink wine when he enters the inner court. 22They must not marry widows or divorced women; they may marry only virgins of Israelite descent or widows of priests. 23They are to teach my people the difference between the holy and the common and show them how to distinguish between the unclean and the clean.

24" 'In any dispute, the priests are to serve as judges and decide it according to my ordinances. They are to keep my laws and my decrees for all my appointed feasts, and they are to keep my Sabbaths holy.

25" 'A priest must not defile himself by going near a dead person; however, if the dead person was his father or mother, son or daughter, brother or unmarried sister, then he may defile himself. 26After he is cleansed, he must wait seven days. 27On the day he goes into the inner court of the sanctuary to minister

in the sanctuary, he is to offer a sin offering for himself, declares the Sovereign LORD.

28" 'I am to be the only inheritance the priests have. You are to give them no possession in Israel; I will be their possession. 29They will eat the grain offerings, the sin offerings and the guilt offerings; and everything in Israel devoted[a] to the LORD will belong to them. 30The best of all the firstfruits and of all your special gifts will belong to the priests. You are to give them the first portion of your ground meal so that a blessing may rest on your household. 31The priests must not eat anything, bird or animal, found dead or torn by wild animals.

Division of the Land

45 " 'When you allot the land as an inheritance, you are to present to the LORD a portion of the land as a sacred district, 25,000 cubits long and 20,000[b] cubits wide; the entire area will be holy. 2Of this, a section 500 cubits square is to be for the sanctuary, with 50 cubits around it for open land. 3In the sacred district, measure off a section 25,000 cubits[c] long and 10,000 cubits[d] wide. In it will be the sanctuary, the Most Holy Place. 4It will be the sacred portion of the land for the priests, who minister in the sanctuary and who draw near to minister before the LORD. It will be a place for their houses as well as a holy place for the sanctuary. 5An area 25,000 cubits long and 10,000 cubits wide will belong to the Levites, who serve in the temple, as their possession for towns to live in.[e]

6" 'You are to give the city as its property an area 5,000 cubits wide and 25,000 cubits long, adjoining the sacred portion; it will belong to the whole house of Israel.

7" 'The prince will have the land bordering each side of the area formed by the sacred district and the property of the city. It will extend westward from the west side and eastward from the east side, running lengthwise from the western to the eastern border parallel to one

---

a 29 The Hebrew term refers to the irrevocable giving over of things or persons to the LORD.
b 1 Septuagint (see also verses 3 and 5 and 48:9); Hebrew *10,000*   *c 3* That is, about 7 miles (about 12 kilometers)   *d 3* That is, about 3 miles (about 5 kilometers)   *e 5* Septuagint; Hebrew *temple; they will have as their possession 20 rooms*

of the tribal portions. ⁸This land will be his possession in Israel. And my princes will no longer oppress my people but will allow the house of Israel to possess the land according to their tribes.

⁹" 'This is what the Sovereign LORD says: You have gone far enough, O princes of Israel! Give up your violence and oppression and do what is just and right. Stop dispossessing my people, declares the Sovereign LORD. ¹⁰You are to use accurate scales, an accurate ephah*ᵃ* and an accurate bath.*ᵇ* ¹¹The ephah and the bath are to be the same size, the bath containing a tenth of a homer*ᶜ* and the ephah a tenth of a homer; the homer is to be the standard measure for both. ¹²The shekel*ᵈ* is to consist of twenty gerahs. Twenty shekels plus twenty-five shekels plus fifteen shekels equal one mina.*ᵉ*

Offerings and Holy Days

¹³" 'This is the special gift you are to offer: a sixth of an ephah from each homer of wheat and a sixth of an ephah from each homer of barley. ¹⁴The prescribed portion of oil, measured by the bath, is a tenth of a bath from each cor (which consists of ten baths or one homer, for ten baths are equivalent to a homer). ¹⁵Also one sheep is to be taken from every flock of two hundred from the well-watered pastures of Israel. These will be used for the grain offerings, burnt offerings and fellowship offerings*ᶠ* to make atonement for the people, declares the Sovereign LORD. ¹⁶All the people of the land will participate in this special gift for the use of the prince in Israel. ¹⁷It will be the duty of the prince to provide the burnt offerings, grain offerings and drink offerings at the festivals, the New Moons and the Sabbaths—at all the appointed feasts of the house of Israel. He will provide the sin offerings, grain offerings, burnt offerings and fellowship offerings to make atonement for the house of Israel.

¹⁸" 'This is what the Sovereign LORD says: In the first month on the first day you are to take a young bull without defect and purify the sanctuary. ¹⁹The priest is to take some of the blood of the sin offering and put it on the doorposts of the temple, on the four corners of the upper ledge of the altar and on the gateposts of the inner court. ²⁰You are to do the same on the seventh day of the month for anyone who sins unintentionally or through ignorance; so you are to make atonement for the temple.

²¹" 'In the first month on the fourteenth day you are to observe the Passover, a feast lasting seven days, during which you shall eat bread made without yeast. ²²On that day the prince is to provide a bull as a sin offering for himself and for all the people of the land. ²³Every day during the seven days of the Feast he is to provide seven bulls and seven rams without defect as a burnt offering to the LORD, and a male goat for a sin offering. ²⁴He is to provide as a grain offering an ephah for each bull and an ephah for each ram, along with a hin*ᵍ* of oil for each ephah.

²⁵" 'During the seven days of the Feast, which begins in the seventh month on the fifteenth day, he is to make the same provision for sin offerings, burnt offerings, grain offerings and oil.

46 " 'This is what the Sovereign LORD says: The gate of the inner court facing east is to be shut on the six working days, but on the Sabbath day and on the day of the New Moon it is to be opened. ²The prince is to enter from the outside through the portico of the gateway and stand by the gatepost. The priests are to sacrifice his burnt offering and his fellowship offerings.*ʰ* He is to worship at the threshold of the gateway and then go out, but the gate will not be shut until evening. ³On the Sabbaths and New Moons the people of the land are to worship in the presence of the LORD at the entrance to that gateway. ⁴The burnt offering the prince brings to the LORD on the Sabbath day is to be six male lambs and a ram, all without defect. ⁵The grain offering given with the ram is to be an ephah,*ⁱ* and the grain offering with the lambs is to be as

---

ᵃ 10 An ephah was a dry measure.   *ᵇ 10* A bath was a liquid measure.   *ᶜ 11* A homer was a dry measure.   *ᵈ 12* A shekel weighed about 2/5 ounce (about 11.5 grams).   *ᵉ 12* That is, 60 shekels; the common mina was 50 shekels.   *ᶠ 15* Traditionally *peace offerings;* also in verse 17   *ᵍ 24* That is, probably about 4 quarts (about 4 liters)   *ʰ 2* Traditionally *peace offerings;* also in verse 12   *ⁱ 5* That is, probably about 3/5 bushel (about 22 liters)

much as he pleases, along with a hin*a* of oil for each ephah. 6On the day of the New Moon he is to offer a young bull, six lambs and a ram, all without defect. 7He is to provide as a grain offering one ephah with the bull, one ephah with the ram, and with the lambs as much as he wants to give, along with a hin of oil with each ephah. 8When the prince enters, he is to go in through the portico of the gateway, and he is to come out the same way.

9" 'When the people of the land come before the LORD at the appointed feasts, whoever enters by the north gate to worship is to go out the south gate; and whoever enters by the south gate is to go out the north gate. No one is to return through the gate by which he entered, but each is to go out the opposite gate. 10The prince is to be among them, going in when they go in and going out when they go out.

11" 'At the festivals and the appointed feasts, the grain offering is to be an ephah with a bull, an ephah with a ram, and with the lambs as much as one pleases, along with a hin of oil for each ephah. 12When the prince provides a freewill offering to the LORD—whether a burnt offering or fellowship offerings—the gate facing east is to be opened for him. He shall offer his burnt offering or his fellowship offerings as he does on the Sabbath day. Then he shall go out, and after he has gone out, the gate will be shut.

13" 'Every day you are to provide a year-old lamb without defect for a burnt offering to the LORD; morning by morning you shall provide it. 14You are also to provide with it morning by morning a grain offering, consisting of a sixth of an ephah with a third of a hin of oil to moisten the flour. The presenting of this grain offering to the LORD is a lasting ordinance. 15So the lamb and the grain offering and the oil shall be provided morning by morning for a regular burnt offering.

16" 'This is what the Sovereign LORD says: If the prince makes a gift from his inheritance to one of his sons, it will also belong to his descendants; it is to be their property by inheritance. 17If, however, he makes a gift from his inheritance to one

of his servants, the servant may keep it until the year of freedom; then it will revert to the prince. His inheritance belongs to his sons only; it is theirs. 18The prince must not take any of the inheritance of the people, driving them off their property. He is to give his sons their inheritance out of his own property, so that none of my people will be separated from his property.' "

19Then the man brought me through the entrance at the side of the gate to the sacred rooms facing north, which belonged to the priests, and showed me a place at the western end. 20He said to me, "This is the place where the priests will cook the guilt offering and the sin offering and bake the grain offering, to avoid bringing them into the outer court and consecrating the people."

21He then brought me to the outer court and led me around to its four corners, and I saw in each corner another court. 22In the four corners of the outer court were enclosed*b* courts, forty cubits long and thirty cubits wide; each of the courts in the four corners was the same size. 23Around the inside of each of the four courts was a ledge of stone, with places for fire built all around under the ledge. 24He said to me, "These are the kitchens where those who minister at the temple will cook the sacrifices of the people."

The River From the Temple

47 The man brought me back to the entrance of the temple, and I saw water coming out from under the threshold of the temple toward the east (for the temple faced east). The water was coming down from under the south side of the temple, south of the altar. 2He then brought me out through the north gate and led me around the outside to the outer gate facing east, and the water was flowing from the south side.

3As the man went eastward with a measuring line in his hand, he measured off a thousand cubits*c* and then led me through water that was ankle-deep. 4He measured off another thousand cubits and led me through water that was knee-deep. He measured off another

---

a 5 That is, probably about 4 quarts (about 4 liters) uncertain.   *c 3* That is, about 1,500 feet (about 450 meters)   *b 22* The meaning of the Hebrew for this word is

thousand and led me through water that was up to the waist. ⁵He measured off another thousand, but now it was a river that I could not cross, because the water had risen and was deep enough to swim in—a river that no one could cross. ⁶He asked me, "Son of man, do you see this?"

Then he led me back to the bank of the river. ⁷When I arrived there, I saw a great number of trees on each side of the river. ⁸He said to me, "This water flows toward the eastern region and goes down into the Arabah,ᵃ where it enters the Sea.ᵇ When it empties into the Sea,ᵇ the water there becomes fresh. ⁹Swarms of living creatures will live wherever the river flows. There will be large numbers of fish, because this water flows there and makes the salt water fresh; so where the river flows everything will live. ¹⁰Fishermen will stand along the shore; from En Gedi to En Eglaim there will be places for spreading nets. The fish will be of many kinds—like the fish of the Great Sea.ᶜ ¹¹But the swamps and marshes will not become fresh; they will be left for salt. ¹²Fruit trees of all kinds will grow on both banks of the river. Their leaves will not wither, nor will their fruit fail. Every month they will bear, because the water from the sanctuary flows to them. Their fruit will serve for food and their leaves for healing."

The Boundaries of the Land

¹³This is what the Sovereign LORD says: "These are the boundaries by which you are to divide the land for an inheritance among the twelve tribes of Israel, with two portions for Joseph. ¹⁴You are to divide it equally among them. Because I swore with uplifted hand to give it to your forefathers, this land will become your inheritance.

¹⁵"This is to be the boundary of the land:

"On the north side it will run from the Great Sea by the Hethlon road past Leboᵈ Hamath to Zedad, ¹⁶Berothahᵉ and Sibraim (which lies on the border between Damascus and Hamath), as far as Hazer Hatticon, which is on the border of Hauran. ¹⁷The boundary will extend from the sea to Hazar Enan,ᶠ along the northern border of Damascus, with the border of Hamath to the north. This will be the north boundary.

¹⁸"On the east side the boundary will run between Hauran and Damascus, along the Jordan between Gilead and the land of Israel, to the eastern sea and as far as Tamar.ᵍ This will be the east boundary.

¹⁹"On the south side it will run from Tamar as far as the waters of Meribah Kadesh, then along the Wadi ᵢof Egyptᵢ to the Great Sea. This will be the south boundary.

²⁰"On the west side, the Great Sea will be the boundary to a point opposite Leboʰ Hamath. This will be the west boundary.

²¹"You are to distribute this land among yourselves according to the tribes of Israel. ²²You are to allot it as an inheritance for yourselves and for the aliens who have settled among you and who have children. You are to consider them as native-born Israelites; along with you they are to be allotted an inheritance among the tribes of Israel. ²³In whatever tribe the alien settles, there you are to give him his inheritance," declares the Sovereign LORD.

The Division of the Land

48 "These are the tribes, listed by name: At the northern frontier, Dan will have one portion; it will follow the Hethlon road to Leboⁱ Hamath; Hazar Enan and the northern border of Damascus next to Hamath will be part of its border from the east side to the west side.

²"Asher will have one portion; it will border the territory of Dan from east to west.

³"Naphtali will have one portion; it

ᵃ 8 Or *the Jordan Valley*   ᵇ 8 That is, the Dead Sea   ᶜ 10 That is, the Mediterranean; also in verses 15, 19 and 20   ᵈ 15 Or *past the entrance to*   ᵉ 15,16 See Septuagint and Ezekiel 48:1; Hebrew *road to go into Zedad,* ¹⁶*Hamath, Berothah*   ᶠ 17 Hebrew *Enon,* a variant of *Enan*   ᵍ 18 Septuagint and Syriac; Hebrew *Israel. You will measure to the eastern sea*   ʰ 20 Or *opposite the entrance to*   ⁱ 1 Or *to the entrance to*

will border the territory of Asher from east to west.

4 "Manasseh will have one portion; it will border the territory of Naphtali from east to west.

5 "Ephraim will have one portion; it will border the territory of Manasseh from east to west.

6 "Reuben will have one portion; it will border the territory of Ephraim from east to west.

7 "Judah will have one portion; it will border the territory of Reuben from east to west.

8 "Bordering the territory of Judah from east to west will be the portion you are to present as a special gift. It will be 25,000 cubits^a wide, and its length from east to west will equal one of the tribal portions; the sanctuary will be in the center of it.

9 "The special portion you are to offer to the LORD will be 25,000 cubits long and 10,000 cubits^b wide. 10 This will be the sacred portion for the priests. It will be 25,000 cubits long on the north side, 10,000 cubits wide on the west side, 10,000 cubits wide on the east side and 25,000 cubits long on the south side. In the center of it will be the sanctuary of the LORD. 11 This will be for the consecrated priests, the Zadokites, who were faithful in serving me and did not go astray as the Levites did when the Israelites went astray. 12 It will be a special gift to them from the sacred portion of the land, a most holy portion, bordering the territory of the Levites.

13 "Alongside the territory of the priests, the Levites will have an allotment 25,000 cubits long and 10,000 cubits wide. Its total length will be 25,000 cubits and its width 10,000 cubits. 14 They must not sell or exchange any of it. This is the best of the land and must not pass into other hands, because it is holy to the LORD.

15 "The remaining area, 5,000 cubits wide and 25,000 cubits long, will be for the common use of the city, for houses and for pastureland. The city will be in the center of it 16 and will have these measurements: the north side 4,500 cubits, the south side 4,500 cubits, the east side 4,500 cubits, and the west side 4,500 cubits. 17 The pastureland for the city will be 250 cubits on the north, 250 cubits on the south, 250 cubits on the east, and 250 cubits on the west. 18 What remains of the area, bordering on the sacred portion and running the length of it, will be 10,000 cubits on the east side and 10,000 cubits on the west side. Its produce will supply food for the workers of the city. 19 The workers from the city who farm it will come from all the tribes of Israel. 20 The entire portion will be a square, 25,000 cubits on each side. As a special gift you will set aside the sacred portion, along with the property of the city.

21 "What remains on both sides of the area formed by the sacred portion and the city property will belong to the prince. It will extend eastward from the 25,000 cubits of the sacred portion to the eastern border, and westward from the 25,000 cubits to the western border. Both these areas running the length of the tribal portions will belong to the prince, and the sacred portion with the temple sanctuary will be in the center of them. 22 So the property of the Levites and the property of the city will lie in the center of the area that belongs to the prince. The area belonging to the prince will lie between the border of Judah and the border of Benjamin.

23 "As for the rest of the tribes: Benjamin will have one portion; it will extend from the east side to the west side.

24 "Simeon will have one portion; it will border the territory of Benjamin from east to west.

25 "Issachar will have one portion; it will border the territory of Simeon from east to west.

26 "Zebulun will have one portion; it will border the territory of Issachar from east to west.

27 "Gad will have one portion; it will border the territory of Zebulun from east to west.

28 "The southern boundary of Gad will run south from Tamar to the waters of Meribah Kadesh, then along the Wadi ⸤of Egypt⸥ to the Great Sea.^{c}

^{a} 8 That is, about 7 miles (about 12 kilometers) ^{b} 9 That is, about 3 miles (about 5 kilometers)
^{c} 28 That is, the Mediterranean

²⁹"This is the land you are to allot as an inheritance to the tribes of Israel, and these will be their portions," declares the Sovereign LORD.

The Gates of the City

³⁰"These will be the exits of the city: Beginning on the north side, which is 4,500 cubits long, ³¹the gates of the city will be named after the tribes of Israel. The three gates on the north side will be the gate of Reuben, the gate of Judah and the gate of Levi.

³²"On the east side, which is 4,500 cubits long, will be three gates: the gate of Joseph, the gate of Benjamin and the gate of Dan.

³³"On the south side, which measures 4,500 cubits, will be three gates: the gate of Simeon, the gate of Issachar and the gate of Zebulun.

³⁴"On the west side, which is 4,500 cubits long, will be three gates: the gate of Gad, the gate of Asher and the gate of Naphtali.

³⁵"The distance all around will be 18,000 cubits.

"And the name of the city from that time on will be:

THE LORD IS THERE."

DANIEL

ANIEL RECORDS EVENTS THAT TOOK
PLACE DURING ISRAEL'S CAPTIVITY
AND ENCOURAGES THE PEOPLE TO
TRUST IN THE GOD WHO CONTROLS ALL OF
HISTORY. DANIEL'S VISIONS ALWAYS SHOW
GOD AS TRIUMPHANT. AS YOU READ THIS
BOOK BE ENCOURAGED THAT GOD STILL
SHOWS HIS FAITHFULNESS AND HIS PROTEC-
TION TODAY, AS HE KEEPS HIS PROMISE
NEVER TO DESERT YOU. HE GIVES YOU THE
STRENGTH TO STAND FIRM IN HIM AS YOU
SERVE AND OBEY HIM DAY BY DAY.

Daniel's Training in Babylon

1 In the third year of the reign of Jehoiakim king of Judah, Nebuchadnezzar king of Babylon came to Jerusalem and besieged it. ²And the Lord delivered Jehoiakim king of Judah into his hand, along with some of the articles from the temple of God. These he carried off to the temple of his god in Babylonia*a* and put in the treasure house of his god.

³Then the king ordered Ashpenaz, chief of his court officials, to bring in some of the Israelites from the royal family and the nobility— ⁴young men without any physical defect, handsome, showing aptitude for every kind of learning, well informed, quick to understand, and qualified to serve in the king's palace. He was to teach them the language and literature of the Babylonians.*b* ⁵The king assigned them a daily amount of food and wine from the king's table. They were to be trained for three years, and after that they were to enter the king's service.

⁶Among these were some from Judah: Daniel, Hananiah, Mishael and Azariah. ⁷The chief official gave them new names: to Daniel, the name Belteshazzar; to Hananiah, Shadrach; to Mishael, Meshach; and to Azariah, Abednego.

⁸But Daniel resolved not to defile himself with the royal food and wine, and he asked the chief official for permission not to defile himself this way. ⁹Now God had caused the official to show favor and sympathy to Daniel, ¹⁰but the official

a 2 Hebrew Shinar   b 4 Or Chaldeans

told Daniel, "I am afraid of my lord the king, who has assigned your[a] food and drink. Why should he see you looking worse than the other young men your age? The king would then have my head because of you."

[11]Daniel then said to the guard whom the chief official had appointed over Daniel, Hananiah, Mishael and Azariah, [12]"Please test your servants for ten days: Give us nothing but vegetables to eat and water to drink. [13]Then compare our appearance with that of the young men who eat the royal food, and treat your servants in accordance with what you see." [14]So he agreed to this and tested them for ten days.

[15]At the end of the ten days they looked healthier and better nourished than any of the young men who ate the royal food. [16]So the guard took away their choice food and the wine they were to drink and gave them vegetables instead.

[17]To these four young men God gave knowledge and understanding of all kinds of literature and learning. And Daniel could understand visions and dreams of all kinds.

[18]At the end of the time set by the king to bring them in, the chief official presented them to Nebuchadnezzar. [19]The king talked with them, and he found none equal to Daniel, Hananiah, Mishael and Azariah; so they entered the king's service. [20]In every matter of wisdom and understanding about which the king questioned them, he found them ten times better than all the magicians and enchanters in his whole kingdom.

[21]And Daniel remained there until the first year of King Cyrus.

Nebuchadnezzar's Dream

2 In the second year of his reign, Nebuchadnezzar had dreams; his mind was troubled and he could not sleep. [2]So the king summoned the magicians, enchanters, sorcerers and astrologers[b] to tell him what he had dreamed. When they came in and stood before the king, [3]he said to them, "I have had a dream that troubles me and I want to know what it means.[c] "

[4]Then the astrologers answered the king in Aramaic,[d] "O king, live forever! Tell your servants the dream, and we will interpret it."

[5]The king replied to the astrologers, "This is what I have firmly decided: If you do not tell me what my dream was and interpret it, I will have you cut into pieces and your houses turned into piles of rubble. [6]But if you tell me the dream and explain it, you will receive from me gifts and rewards and great honor. So tell me the dream and interpret it for me."

[7]Once more they replied, "Let the king tell his servants the dream, and we will interpret it."

[8]Then the king answered, "I am certain that you are trying to gain time, because you realize that this is what I have firmly decided: [9]If you do not tell me the dream, there is just one penalty for you. You have conspired to tell me misleading and wicked things, hoping the situation will change. So then, tell me the dream, and I will know that you can interpret it for me."

[10]The astrologers answered the king, "There is not a man on earth who can do what the king asks! No king, however great and mighty, has ever asked such a thing of any magician or enchanter or astrologer. [11]What the king asks is too difficult. No one can reveal it to the king except the gods, and they do not live among men."

[12]This made the king so angry and furious that he ordered the execution of all the wise men of Babylon. [13]So the decree was issued to put the wise men to death, and men were sent to look for Daniel and his friends to put them to death.

[14]When Arioch, the commander of the king's guard, had gone out to put to death the wise men of Babylon, Daniel spoke to him with wisdom and tact. [15]He asked the king's officer, "Why did the king issue such a harsh decree?" Arioch then explained the matter to Daniel. [16]At this, Daniel went in to the king and asked for time, so that he might interpret the dream for him.

[17]Then Daniel returned to his house and explained the matter to his friends Hananiah, Mishael and Azariah. [18]He urged them to plead for mercy from the

---

a 10 The Hebrew for *your* and *you* in this verse is plural.   *b 2* Or *Chaldeans;* also in verses 4, 5 and 10
c 3 Or *was*   *d 4* The text from here through chapter 7 is in Aramaic.

God of heaven concerning this mystery, so that he and his friends might not be executed with the rest of the wise men of Babylon. ¹⁹During the night the mystery was revealed to Daniel in a vision. Then Daniel praised the God of heaven ²⁰and said:

"Praise be to the name of God for
　　ever and ever;
　　wisdom and power are his.

²¹He changes times and seasons;
　　he sets up kings and deposes them.
He gives wisdom to the wise
　　and knowledge to the discerning.
²²He reveals deep and hidden things;
　　he knows what lies in darkness,
　　and light dwells with him.
²³I thank and praise you, O God of my
　　fathers:
　　You have given me wisdom and
　　power,

MONDAY

THE HEARER AND ANSWERER OF PRAYER
Dwight L. Moody

VERSE: Daniel 2:22　　　　　　　　　　**PASSAGE:** Daniel 2:1–23

ne of [God's] greatest and most wonderful characteristics [is that] he is the hearer and answerer of prayer. As an instance of this, see Daniel 2:18, where there is a prayer that God would reveal to his servants, not only the interpretation of a dream, but even the dream itself. "Is there anything too hard for the LORD?" (Genesis 18:14). No. In the very next verse we have the answer right back, as it were, by telegraph from heaven: "During the night the mystery was revealed to Daniel in a vision."

The Scripture is full of such answers; every page of it encourages prayer. God will have us pray, and he will answer prayer. Surely we have all found that out in our experience; if not, it is our own fault. "Surely the arm of the LORD is not too short to save, nor his ear too dull to hear" (Isaiah 59:1). It is our own prayers that are shortened and that are weak and faithless. Oh, let us "ask in faith, nothing wavering!" (James 1:6, KJV). Some people are like the disciples in Jerusalem praying for the release of Peter; their prayers were answered, and Peter stood at the door, but they could not believe it; they said it must be his spirit (see Acts 12:5–14). Oh, let us take God at his word! He says, "While they are still speaking I will hear" (Isaiah 65:24). Is not that encouraging? He delights to hear our prayers; he will not weary with our often coming.

ADDITIONAL SCRIPTURE READING:
Daniel 4:9; Amos 3:7; 1 Corinthians 2:9–10

Go to page 996 for your next devotional reading.

1900　　Present

you have made known to me what
        we asked of you,
you have made known to us the
        dream of the king."

Daniel Interprets the Dream

24 Then Daniel went to Arioch, whom
the king had appointed to execute the
wise men of Babylon, and said to him,
"Do not execute the wise men of Babylon. Take me to the king, and I will
interpret his dream for him."
25 Arioch took Daniel to the king at
once and said, "I have found a man
among the exiles from Judah who can
tell the king what his dream means."
26 The king asked Daniel (also called
Belteshazzar), "Are you able to tell me
what I saw in my dream and interpret it?"
27 Daniel replied, "No wise man,
enchanter, magician or diviner can
explain to the king the mystery he has
asked about, 28 but there is a God in
heaven who reveals mysteries. He has
shown King Nebuchadnezzar what will
happen in days to come. Your dream and
the visions that passed through your
mind as you lay on your bed are these:
29 "As you were lying there, O king,
your mind turned to things to come, and
the revealer of mysteries showed you
what is going to happen. 30 As for me,
this mystery has been revealed to me,
not because I have greater wisdom than
other living men, but so that you,
O king, may know the interpretation
and that you may understand what went
through your mind.
31 "You looked, O king, and there
before you stood a large statue—an enormous, dazzling statue, awesome in
appearance. 32 The head of the statue
was made of pure gold, its chest and
arms of silver, its belly and thighs of
bronze, 33 its legs of iron, its feet partly of
iron and partly of baked clay. 34 While
you were watching, a rock was cut out,
but not by human hands. It struck the
statue on its feet of iron and clay and
smashed them. 35 Then the iron, the
clay, the bronze, the silver and the gold
were broken to pieces at the same time
and became like chaff on a threshing
floor in the summer. The wind swept
them away without leaving a trace. But

the rock that struck the statue became a
huge mountain and filled the whole
earth.
36 "This was the dream, and now we
will interpret it to the king. 37 You,
O king, are the king of kings. The God of
heaven has given you dominion and
power and might and glory; 38 in your
hands he has placed mankind and the
beasts of the field and the birds of the
air. Wherever they live, he has made you
ruler over them all. You are that head of
gold.
39 "After you, another kingdom will
rise, inferior to yours. Next, a third kingdom, one of bronze, will rule over the
whole earth. 40 Finally, there will be a
fourth kingdom, strong as iron—for iron
breaks and smashes everything—and as
iron breaks things to pieces, so it will
crush and break all the others. 41 Just as
you saw that the feet and toes were partly of baked clay and partly of iron, so
this will be a divided kingdom; yet it
will have some of the strength of iron in
it, even as you saw iron mixed with clay.
42 As the toes were partly iron and partly
clay, so this kingdom will be partly
strong and partly brittle. 43 And just as
you saw the iron mixed with baked clay,
so the people will be a mixture and will
not remain united, any more than iron
mixes with clay.
44 "In the time of those kings, the God
of heaven will set up a kingdom that
will never be destroyed, nor will it be
left to another people. It will crush all
those kingdoms and bring them to an
end, but it will itself endure forever.
45 This is the meaning of the vision of
the rock cut out of a mountain, but not
by human hands—a rock that broke the
iron, the bronze, the clay, the silver and
the gold to pieces.
"The great God has shown the king
what will take place in the future. The
dream is true and the interpretation is
trustworthy."
46 Then King Nebuchadnezzar fell
prostrate before Daniel and paid him
honor and ordered that an offering and
incense be presented to him. 47 The king
said to Daniel, "Surely your God is the
God of gods and the Lord of kings and a
revealer of mysteries, for you were able
to reveal this mystery."

⁴⁸Then the king placed Daniel in a high position and lavished many gifts on him. He made him ruler over the entire province of Babylon and placed him in charge of all its wise men. ⁴⁹Moreover, at Daniel's request the king appointed Shadrach, Meshach and Abednego administrators over the province of Babylon, while Daniel himself remained at the royal court.

The Image of Gold and the Fiery Furnace

3 King Nebuchadnezzar made an image of gold, ninety feet high and nine feet^a wide, and set it up on the plain of Dura in the province of Babylon. ²He then summoned the satraps, prefects, governors, advisers, treasurers, judges, magistrates and all the other provincial officials to come to the dedication of the image he had set up. ³So the satraps, prefects, governors, advisers, treasurers, judges, magistrates and all the other provincial officials assembled for the dedication of the image that King Nebuchadnezzar had set up, and they stood before it.

⁴Then the herald loudly proclaimed, "This is what you are commanded to do, O peoples, nations and men of every language: ⁵As soon as you hear the sound of the horn, flute, zither, lyre, harp, pipes and all kinds of music, you must fall down and worship the image of gold that King Nebuchadnezzar has set up. ⁶Whoever does not fall down and worship will immediately be thrown into a blazing furnace."

⁷Therefore, as soon as they heard the sound of the horn, flute, zither, lyre, harp and all kinds of music, all the peoples, nations and men of every language fell down and worshiped the image of gold that King Nebuchadnezzar had set up.

⁸At this time some astrologers^b came forward and denounced the Jews. ⁹They said to King Nebuchadnezzar, "O king, live forever! ¹⁰You have issued a decree, O king, that everyone who hears the sound of the horn, flute, zither, lyre, harp, pipes and all kinds of music must fall down and worship the image of gold,

¹¹and that whoever does not fall down and worship will be thrown into a blazing furnace. ¹²But there are some Jews whom you have set over the affairs of the province of Babylon—Shadrach, Meshach and Abednego—who pay no attention to you, O king. They neither serve your gods nor worship the image of gold you have set up."

¹³Furious with rage, Nebuchadnezzar summoned Shadrach, Meshach and Abednego. So these men were brought before the king, ¹⁴and Nebuchadnezzar said to them, "Is it true, Shadrach, Meshach and Abednego, that you do not serve my gods or worship the image of gold I have set up? ¹⁵Now when you hear the sound of the horn, flute, zither, lyre, harp, pipes and all kinds of music, if you are ready to fall down and worship the image I made, very good. But if you do not worship it, you will be thrown immediately into a blazing furnace. Then what god will be able to rescue you from my hand?"

¹⁶Shadrach, Meshach and Abednego replied to the king, "O Nebuchadnezzar, we do not need to defend ourselves before you in this matter. ¹⁷If we are thrown into the blazing furnace, the God we serve is able to save us from it, and he will rescue us from your hand, O king. ¹⁸But even if he does not, we want you to know, O king, that we will not serve your gods or worship the image of gold you have set up."

¹⁹Then Nebuchadnezzar was furious with Shadrach, Meshach and Abednego, and his attitude toward them changed. He ordered the furnace heated seven times hotter than usual ²⁰and commanded some of the strongest soldiers in his army to tie up Shadrach, Meshach and Abednego and throw them into the blazing furnace. ²¹So these men, wearing their robes, trousers, turbans and other clothes, were bound and thrown into the blazing furnace. ²²The king's command was so urgent and the furnace so hot that the flames of the fire killed the soldiers who took up Shadrach, Meshach and Abednego, ²³and these three men, firmly tied, fell into the blazing furnace.

^a 1 Aramaic *sixty cubits high and six cubits wide* (about 27 meters high and 2.7 meters wide)   ^b 8 Or *Chaldeans*

²⁴Then King Nebuchadnezzar leaped to his feet in amazement and asked his advisers, "Weren't there three men that we tied up and threw into the fire?"

They replied, "Certainly, O king."

²⁵He said, "Look! I see four men walking around in the fire, unbound and unharmed, and the fourth looks like a son of the gods."

AS SURE AS EVER GOD PUTS HIS CHILDREN IN THE FURNACE, HE WILL BE IN THE FURNACE WITH THEM.   —*C. H. Spurgeon*

---

²⁶Nebuchadnezzar then approached the opening of the blazing furnace and shouted, "Shadrach, Meshach and Abednego, servants of the Most High God, come out! Come here!"

So Shadrach, Meshach and Abednego came out of the fire, ²⁷and the satraps, prefects, governors and royal advisers crowded around them. They saw that the fire had not harmed their bodies, nor was a hair of their heads singed; their robes were not scorched, and there was no smell of fire on them.

²⁸Then Nebuchadnezzar said, "Praise be to the God of Shadrach, Meshach and Abednego, who has sent his angel and rescued his servants! They trusted in him and defied the king's command and were willing to give up their lives rather than serve or worship any god except their own God. ²⁹Therefore I decree that the people of any nation or language who say anything against the God of Shadrach, Meshach and Abednego be cut into pieces and their houses be turned into piles of rubble, for no other god can save in this way."

³⁰Then the king promoted Shadrach, Meshach and Abednego in the province of Babylon.

Nebuchadnezzar's Dream of a Tree

4 King Nebuchadnezzar,

To the peoples, nations and men of every language, who live in all the world:

May you prosper greatly!

²It is my pleasure to tell you about the miraculous signs and wonders that the Most High God has performed for me.

³How great are his signs,
  how mighty his wonders!
His kingdom is an eternal
    kingdom;
  his dominion endures from
    generation to generation.

⁴I, Nebuchadnezzar, was at home in my palace, contented and prosperous. ⁵I had a dream that made me afraid. As I was lying in my bed, the images and visions that passed through my mind terrified me. ⁶So I commanded that all the wise men of Babylon be brought before me to interpret the dream for me. ⁷When the magicians, enchanters, astrologers[a] and diviners came, I told them the dream, but they could not interpret it for me. ⁸Finally, Daniel came into my presence and I told him the dream. (He is called Belteshazzar, after the name of my god, and the spirit of the holy gods is in him.)

⁹I said, "Belteshazzar, chief of the magicians, I know that the spirit of the holy gods is in you, and no mystery is too difficult for you. Here is my dream; interpret it for me. ¹⁰These are the visions I saw while lying in my bed: I looked, and there before me stood a tree in the middle of the land. Its height was enormous. ¹¹The tree grew large and strong and its top touched the sky; it was visible to the ends of the earth. ¹²Its leaves were beautiful, its fruit abundant, and on it was food for all. Under it the beasts of the field found shelter, and the birds of the air lived in its branches; from it every creature was fed.

¹³"In the visions I saw while lying in my bed, I looked, and there before me was a messenger,[b] a holy one, coming down from heaven. ¹⁴He called in a loud voice: 'Cut down the tree and trim off its branches; strip off its leaves and

---

a 7 Or *Chaldeans*   *b* 13 Or *watchman*; also in verses 17 and 23

scatter its fruit. Let the animals flee from under it and the birds from its branches. 15But let the stump and its roots, bound with iron and bronze, remain in the ground, in the grass of the field.

" 'Let him be drenched with the dew of heaven, and let him live with the animals among the plants of the earth. 16Let his mind be changed from that of a man and let him be given the mind of an animal, till seven times*a* pass by for him.

17" 'The decision is announced by messengers, the holy ones declare the verdict, so that the living may know that the Most High is sovereign over the kingdoms of men and gives them to anyone he wishes and sets over them the lowliest of men.'

18"This is the dream that I, King Nebuchadnezzar, had. Now, Belteshazzar, tell me what it means, for none of the wise men in my kingdom can interpret it for me. But you can, because the spirit of the holy gods is in you."

Daniel Interprets the Dream

19Then Daniel (also called Belteshazzar) was greatly perplexed for a time, and his thoughts terrified him. So the king said, "Belteshazzar, do not let the dream or its meaning alarm you."

Belteshazzar answered, "My lord, if only the dream applied to your enemies and its meaning to your adversaries! 20The tree you saw, which grew large and strong, with its top touching the sky, visible to the whole earth, 21with beautiful leaves and abundant fruit, providing food for all, giving shelter to the beasts of the field, and having nesting places in its branches for the birds of the air— 22you, O king, are that tree! You have become great and strong; your greatness has grown until it reaches the sky, and your dominion extends to distant parts of the earth.

23"You, O king, saw a messenger, a holy one, coming down from

heaven and saying, 'Cut down the tree and destroy it, but leave the stump, bound with iron and bronze, in the grass of the field, while its roots remain in the ground. Let him be drenched with the dew of heaven; let him live like the wild animals, until seven times pass by for him.'

24"This is the interpretation, O king, and this is the decree the Most High has issued against my lord the king: 25You will be driven away from people and will live with the wild animals; you will eat grass like cattle and be drenched with the dew of heaven. Seven times will pass by for you until you acknowledge that the Most High is sovereign over the kingdoms of men and gives them to anyone he wishes. 26The command to leave the stump of the tree with its roots means that your kingdom will be restored to you when you acknowledge that Heaven rules. 27Therefore, O king, be pleased to accept my advice: Renounce your sins by doing what is right, and your wickedness by being kind to the oppressed. It may be that then your prosperity will continue."

The Dream Is Fulfilled

28All this happened to King Nebuchadnezzar. 29Twelve months later, as the king was walking on the roof of the royal palace of Babylon, 30he said, "Is not this the great Babylon I have built as the royal residence, by my mighty power and for the glory of my majesty?"

31The words were still on his lips when a voice came from heaven, "This is what is decreed for you, King Nebuchadnezzar: Your royal authority has been taken from you. 32You will be driven away from people and will live with the wild animals; you will eat grass like cattle. Seven times will pass by for you until you acknowledge that the Most High is sovereign over the kingdoms of men and gives them to anyone he wishes."

a 16 Or *years;* also in verses 23, 25 and 32

33Immediately what had been said about Nebuchadnezzar was fulfilled. He was driven away from people and ate grass like cattle. His body was drenched with the dew of heaven until his hair grew like the feathers of an eagle and his nails like the claws of a bird.

34At the end of that time, I, Nebuchadnezzar, raised my eyes toward heaven, and my sanity was restored. Then I praised the Most High; I honored and glorified him who lives forever.

His dominion is an eternal dominion;
  his kingdom endures from
      generation to generation.
35All the peoples of the earth
    are regarded as nothing.
He does as he pleases
  with the powers of heaven
  and the peoples of the earth.
No one can hold back his hand
  or say to him: "What have you
      done?"

36At the same time that my sanity was restored, my honor and splendor were returned to me for the glory of my kingdom. My advisers and nobles sought me out, and I was restored to my throne and became even greater than before. 37Now I, Nebuchadnezzar, praise and exalt and glorify the King of heaven, because everything he does is right and all his ways are just. And those who walk in pride he is able to humble.

The Writing on the Wall

5 King Belshazzar gave a great banquet for a thousand of his nobles and drank wine with them. 2While Belshazzar was drinking his wine, he gave orders to bring in the gold and silver goblets that Nebuchadnezzar his father*a* had taken from the temple in Jerusalem, so that the king and his nobles, his wives and his concubines might drink from them. 3So they brought in the gold goblets that had been taken from the temple of God in

Jerusalem, and the king and his nobles, his wives and his concubines drank from them. 4As they drank the wine, they praised the gods of gold and silver, of bronze, iron, wood and stone.

5Suddenly the fingers of a human hand appeared and wrote on the plaster of the wall, near the lampstand in the royal palace. The king watched the hand as it wrote. 6His face turned pale and he was so frightened that his knees knocked together and his legs gave way.

7The king called out for the enchanters, astrologers*b* and diviners to be brought and said to these wise men of Babylon, "Whoever reads this writing and tells me what it means will be clothed in purple and have a gold chain placed around his neck, and he will be made the third highest ruler in the kingdom."

8Then all the king's wise men came in, but they could not read the writing or tell the king what it meant. 9So King Belshazzar became even more terrified and his face grew more pale. His nobles were baffled.

10The queen,*c* hearing the voices of the king and his nobles, came into the banquet hall. "O king, live forever!" she said. "Don't be alarmed! Don't look so pale! 11There is a man in your kingdom who has the spirit of the holy gods in him. In the time of your father he was found to have insight and intelligence and wisdom like that of the gods. King Nebuchadnezzar your father—your father the king, I say—appointed him chief of the magicians, enchanters, astrologers and diviners. 12This man Daniel, whom the king called Belteshazzar, was found to have a keen mind and knowledge and understanding, and also the ability to interpret dreams, explain riddles and solve difficult problems. Call for Daniel, and he will tell you what the writing means."

13So Daniel was brought before the king, and the king said to him, "Are you Daniel, one of the exiles my father the king brought from Judah? 14I have heard that the spirit of the gods is in you and that you have insight, intelligence and outstanding wisdom. 15The wise men

---

a 2 Or *ancestor;* or *predecessor;* also in verses 11, 13 and 18   *b* 7 Or *Chaldeans;* also in verse 11
c 10 Or *queen mother*

and enchanters were brought before me to read this writing and tell me what it means, but they could not explain it. 16Now I have heard that you are able to give interpretations and to solve difficult problems. If you can read this writing and tell me what it means, you will be clothed in purple and have a gold chain placed around your neck, and you will be made the third highest ruler in the kingdom."

17Then Daniel answered the king, "You may keep your gifts for yourself and give your rewards to someone else. Nevertheless, I will read the writing for the king and tell him what it means.

18"O king, the Most High God gave your father Nebuchadnezzar sovereignty and greatness and glory and splendor. 19Because of the high position he gave him, all the peoples and nations and men of every language dreaded and feared him. Those the king wanted to put to death, he put to death; those he wanted to spare, he spared; those he wanted to promote, he promoted; and those he wanted to humble, he humbled. 20But when his heart became arrogant and hardened with pride, he was deposed from his royal throne and stripped of his glory. 21He was driven away from people and given the mind of an animal; he lived with the wild donkeys and ate grass like cattle; and his body was drenched with the dew of heaven, until he acknowledged that the Most High God is sovereign over the kingdoms of men and sets over them anyone he wishes.

22"But you his son,a O Belshazzar, have not humbled yourself, though you knew all this. 23Instead, you have set yourself up against the Lord of heaven. You had the goblets from his temple brought to you, and you and your nobles, your wives and your concubines drank wine from them. You praised the gods of silver and gold, of bronze, iron, wood and stone, which cannot see or hear or understand. But you did not honor the God who holds in his hand your life and all your ways. 24Therefore he sent the hand that wrote the inscription.

25"This is the inscription that was written:

MENE, MENE, TEKEL, PARSINb

26"This is what these words mean:

Menec: God has numbered the days of your reign and brought it to an end.
27 Tekeld: You have been weighed on the scales and found wanting.
28 Perese: Your kingdom is divided and given to the Medes and Persians."

29Then at Belshazzar's command, Daniel was clothed in purple, a gold chain was placed around his neck, and he was proclaimed the third highest ruler in the kingdom.

30That very night Belshazzar, king of the Babylonians,f was slain, 31and Darius the Mede took over the kingdom, at the age of sixty-two.

Daniel in the Den of Lions

6 It pleased Darius to appoint 120 satraps to rule throughout the kingdom, 2with three administrators over them, one of whom was Daniel. The satraps were made accountable to them so that the king might not suffer loss. 3Now Daniel so distinguished himself among the administrators and the satraps by his exceptional qualities that the king planned to set him over the whole kingdom. 4At this, the administrators and the satraps tried to find grounds for charges against Daniel in his conduct of government affairs, but they were unable to do so. They could find no corruption in him, because he was trustworthy and neither corrupt nor negligent. 5Finally these men said, "We will never find any basis for charges against this man Daniel unless it has something to do with the law of his God."

6So the administrators and the satraps went as a group to the king and said: "O King Darius, live forever! 7The royal administrators, prefects, satraps, advisers and governors have all agreed that the king should issue an edict and

a 22 Or descendant; or successor   b 25 Aramaic UPARSIN (that is, AND PARSIN)   c 26 Mene can mean numbered or mina (a unit of money).   d 27 Tekel can mean weighed or shekel.   e 28 Peres (the singular of Parsin) can mean divided or Persia or a half mina or a half shekel.   f 30 Or Chaldeans

enforce the decree that anyone who prays to any god or man during the next thirty days, except to you, O king, shall be thrown into the lions' den. ⁸Now, O king, issue the decree and put it in writing so that it cannot be altered—in accordance with the laws of the Medes and Persians, which cannot be repealed." ⁹So King Darius put the decree in writing.

¹⁰Now when Daniel learned that the decree had been published, he went home to his upstairs room where the windows opened toward Jerusalem. Three times a day he got down on his knees and prayed, giving thanks to his God, just as he had done before. ¹¹Then these men went as a group and found Daniel praying and asking God for help. ¹²So they went to the king and spoke to him about his royal decree: "Did you not publish a decree that during the next

---

TUESDAY

ARE YOU FIT FOR HEAVEN?
J. C. Ryle

VERSE: Daniel 5:23   **PASSAGE:** Daniel 5:18–31

elshazzar had Daniel the prophet hard by his door— Ananias and Sapphira joined the church in the days when the apostles were working miracles—Judas Iscariot was a chosen companion of our Lord Jesus Christ himself (see also Matthew 26:14; Acts 5:1–10). But they all sinned with a high hand against light and knowledge; and they were all suddenly destroyed without remedy. They had no time or space for repentance. As they lived, so they died: as they were, they hurried away to meet God. They went with all their sins upon them, unpardoned, unrenewed, and utterly unfit for heaven . . .

Oh, that you would be wise! Oh, that you would consider your latter end! . . . There is a love in God towards sinners which is unspeakable and unsearchable—but it is for those who "hear Christ's voice and follow him." Seek to have an interest in that love. Break off every known sin; come out boldly from the world; cry mightily to God in prayer; cast yourself wholly and unreservedly on the Lord Jesus for time and eternity; lay aside every weight. Cling to nothing, however dear, which interferes with your soul's salvation; give up everything, however precious, which comes between you and heaven. This old shipwrecked world is fast sinking beneath your feet: the one thing needful is to have a place in the lifeboat and get safe to shore.

ADDITIONAL SCRIPTURE READING:
Psalm 18:23; Daniel 2:47; Hebrews 12:1

Go to page 1001 for your next devotional reading.

1900   Present

thirty days anyone who prays to any god or man except to you, O king, would be thrown into the lions' den?"

The king answered, "The decree stands—in accordance with the laws of the Medes and Persians, which cannot be repealed."

¹³Then they said to the king, "Daniel, who is one of the exiles from Judah, pays no attention to you, O king, or to the decree you put in writing. He still prays three times a day." ¹⁴When the king heard this, he was greatly distressed; he was determined to rescue Daniel and made every effort until sundown to save him.

¹⁵Then the men went as a group to the king and said to him, "Remember, O king, that according to the law of the Medes and Persians no decree or edict that the king issues can be changed."

¹⁶So the king gave the order, and they brought Daniel and threw him into the lions' den. The king said to Daniel, "May your God, whom you serve continually, rescue you!"

¹⁷A stone was brought and placed over the mouth of the den, and the king sealed it with his own signet ring and with the rings of his nobles, so that Daniel's situation might not be changed. ¹⁸Then the king returned to his palace and spent the night without eating and without any entertainment being brought to him. And he could not sleep.

¹⁹At the first light of dawn, the king got up and hurried to the lions' den. ²⁰When he came near the den, he called to Daniel in an anguished voice, "Daniel, servant of the living God, has your God, whom you serve continually, been able to rescue you from the lions?"

²¹Daniel answered, "O king, live forever! ²²My God sent his angel, and he shut the mouths of the lions. They have not hurt me, because I was found innocent in his sight. Nor have I ever done any wrong before you, O king."

²³The king was overjoyed and gave orders to lift Daniel out of the den. And when Daniel was lifted from the den, no wound was found on him, because he had trusted in his God.

²⁴At the king's command, the men who had falsely accused Daniel were brought in and thrown into the lions' den, along with their wives and children. And before they reached the floor of the den, the lions overpowered them and crushed all their bones.

²⁵Then King Darius wrote to all the peoples, nations and men of every language throughout the land:

"May you prosper greatly!

²⁶"I issue a decree that in every part of my kingdom people must fear and reverence the God of Daniel.

"For he is the living God
   and he endures forever;
his kingdom will not be destroyed,
   his dominion will never end.
²⁷He rescues and he saves;
   he performs signs and wonders
   in the heavens and on the earth.
He has rescued Daniel
   from the power of the lions."

²⁸So Daniel prospered during the reign of Darius and the reign of Cyrus*a* the Persian.

Daniel's Dream of Four Beasts

7 In the first year of Belshazzar king of Babylon, Daniel had a dream, and visions passed through his mind as he was lying on his bed. He wrote down the substance of his dream.

²Daniel said: "In my vision at night I looked, and there before me were the four winds of heaven churning up the great sea. ³Four great beasts, each different from the others, came up out of the sea.

⁴"The first was like a lion, and it had the wings of an eagle. I watched until its wings were torn off and it was lifted from the ground so that it stood on two feet like a man, and the heart of a man was given to it.

⁵"And there before me was a second beast, which looked like a bear. It was raised up on one of its sides, and it had three ribs in its mouth between its teeth. It was told, 'Get up and eat your fill of flesh!'

⁶"After that, I looked, and there before me was another beast, one that looked like a leopard. And on its back it had

---

a 28 Or *Darius, that is, the reign of Cyrus*

four wings like those of a bird. This beast had four heads, and it was given authority to rule.

7"After that, in my vision at night I looked, and there before me was a fourth beast—terrifying and frightening and very powerful. It had large iron teeth; it crushed and devoured its victims and trampled underfoot whatever was left. It was different from all the former beasts, and it had ten horns.

8"While I was thinking about the horns, there before me was another horn, a little one, which came up among them; and three of the first horns were uprooted before it. This horn had eyes like the eyes of a man and a mouth that spoke boastfully.

9"As I looked,

"thrones were set in place,
    and the Ancient of Days took his
        seat.
His clothing was as white as snow;
    the hair of his head was white like
        wool.
His throne was flaming with fire,
    and its wheels were all ablaze.
10 A river of fire was flowing,
    coming out from before him.
Thousands upon thousands attended
        him;
    ten thousand times ten thousand
        stood before him.
The court was seated,
    and the books were opened.

11"Then I continued to watch because of the boastful words the horn was speaking. I kept looking until the beast was slain and its body destroyed and thrown into the blazing fire. 12(The other beasts had been stripped of their authority, but were allowed to live for a period of time.)

13"In my vision at night I looked, and there before me was one like a son of man, coming with the clouds of heaven. He approached the Ancient of Days and was led into his presence. 14He was given authority, glory and sovereign power; all peoples, nations and men of every language worshiped him. His dominion is an everlasting dominion that will not pass away, and his kingdom is one that will never be destroyed.

The Interpretation of the Dream

15"I, Daniel, was troubled in spirit, and the visions that passed through my mind disturbed me. 16I approached one of those standing there and asked him the true meaning of all this.

"So he told me and gave me the interpretation of these things: 17'The four great beasts are four kingdoms that will rise from the earth. 18But the saints of the Most High will receive the kingdom and will possess it forever—yes, for ever and ever.'

19"Then I wanted to know the true meaning of the fourth beast, which was different from all the others and most terrifying, with its iron teeth and bronze claws—the beast that crushed and devoured its victims and trampled underfoot whatever was left. 20I also wanted to know about the ten horns on its head and about the other horn that came up, before which three of them fell—the horn that looked more imposing than the others and that had eyes and a mouth that spoke boastfully. 21As I watched, this horn was waging war against the saints and defeating them, 22until the Ancient of Days came and pronounced judgment in favor of the saints of the Most High, and the time came when they possessed the kingdom.

23"He gave me this explanation: 'The fourth beast is a fourth kingdom that will appear on earth. It will be different from all the other kingdoms and will devour the whole earth, trampling it down and crushing it. 24The ten horns are ten kings who will come from this kingdom. After them another king will arise, different from the earlier ones; he will subdue three kings. 25He will speak against the Most High and oppress his saints and try to change the set times and the laws. The saints will be handed over to him for a time, times and half a time.a

26" 'But the court will sit, and his power will be taken away and completely destroyed forever. 27Then the sovereignty, power and greatness of the kingdoms under the whole heaven will be handed over to the saints, the people of

---

a 25 Or for a year, two years and half a year

the Most High. His kingdom will be an everlasting kingdom, and all rulers will worship and obey him.'

28"This is the end of the matter. I, Daniel, was deeply troubled by my thoughts, and my face turned pale, but I kept the matter to myself."

Daniel's Vision of a Ram and a Goat

8 In the third year of King Belshazzar's reign, I, Daniel, had a vision, after the one that had already appeared to me. 2In my vision I saw myself in the citadel of Susa in the province of Elam; in the vision I was beside the Ulai Canal. 3I looked up, and there before me was a ram with two horns, standing beside the canal, and the horns were long. One of the horns was longer than the other but grew up later. 4I watched the ram as he charged toward the west and the north and the south. No animal could stand against him, and none could rescue from his power. He did as he pleased and became great.

5As I was thinking about this, suddenly a goat with a prominent horn between his eyes came from the west, crossing the whole earth without touching the ground. 6He came toward the two-horned ram I had seen standing beside the canal and charged at him in great rage. 7I saw him attack the ram furiously, striking the ram and shattering his two horns. The ram was powerless to stand against him; the goat knocked him to the ground and trampled on him, and none could rescue the ram from his power. 8The goat became very great, but at the height of his power his large horn was broken off, and in its place four prominent horns grew up toward the four winds of heaven.

9Out of one of them came another horn, which started small but grew in power to the south and to the east and toward the Beautiful Land. 10It grew until it reached the host of the heavens, and it threw some of the starry host down to the earth and trampled on them. 11It set itself up to be as great as the Prince of the host; it took away the daily sacrifice from him, and the place of his sanctuary was brought low. 12Because of

rebellion, the host ᴸof the saintsᴶᵃ and the daily sacrifice were given over to it. It prospered in everything it did, and truth was thrown to the ground.

13Then I heard a holy one speaking, and another holy one said to him, "How long will it take for the vision to be fulfilled—the vision concerning the daily sacrifice, the rebellion that causes desolation, and the surrender of the sanctuary and of the host that will be trampled underfoot?"

14He said to me, "It will take 2,300 evenings and mornings; then the sanctuary will be reconsecrated."

The Interpretation of the Vision

15While I, Daniel, was watching the vision and trying to understand it, there before me stood one who looked like a man. 16And I heard a man's voice from the Ulai calling, "Gabriel, tell this man the meaning of the vision."

17As he came near the place where I was standing, I was terrified and fell prostrate. "Son of man," he said to me, "understand that the vision concerns the time of the end."

18While he was speaking to me, I was in a deep sleep, with my face to the ground. Then he touched me and raised me to my feet.

19He said: "I am going to tell you what will happen later in the time of wrath, because the vision concerns the appointed time of the end.ᵇ 20The two-horned ram that you saw represents the kings of Media and Persia. 21The shaggy goat is the king of Greece, and the large horn between his eyes is the first king. 22The four horns that replaced the one that was broken off represent four kingdoms that will emerge from his nation but will not have the same power.

23"In the latter part of their reign, when rebels have become completely wicked, a stern-faced king, a master of intrigue, will arise. 24He will become very strong, but not by his own power. He will cause astounding devastation and will succeed in whatever he does. He will destroy the mighty men and the holy people. 25He will cause deceit to prosper, and he will consider himself superior. When they feel secure, he will

ᵃ 12 Or rebellion, the armies   ᵇ 19 Or because the end will be at the appointed time destroy many and take his stand against the Prince of princes. Yet he will be destroyed, but not by human power.

26"The vision of the evenings and mornings that has been given you is true, but seal up the vision, for it concerns the distant future."

27I, Daniel, was exhausted and lay ill for several days. Then I got up and went about the king's business. I was appalled by the vision; it was beyond understanding.

Daniel's Prayer

9 In the first year of Darius son of Xerxes[a] (a Mede by descent), who was made ruler over the Babylonian[b] kingdom— 2in the first year of his reign, I, Daniel, understood from the Scriptures, according to the word of the LORD given to Jeremiah the prophet, that the desolation of Jerusalem would last seventy years. 3So I turned to the Lord God and pleaded with him in prayer and petition, in fasting, and in sackcloth and ashes.

YOU ART COMING TO A KING,

LARGE PETITIONS WITH YOU BRING

FOR HIS GRACE AND POWER ARE SUCH

NONE CAN EVER ASK TOO MUCH.   —John Newton

4I prayed to the LORD my God and confessed:

"O Lord, the great and awesome God, who keeps his covenant of love with all who love him and obey his commands, 5we have sinned and done wrong. We have been wicked and have rebelled; we have turned away from your commands and laws. 6We have not listened to your servants the prophets, who spoke in your name to our kings, our princes and our fathers, and to all the people of the land.

7"Lord, you are righteous, but this day we are covered with shame— the men of Judah and people of Jerusalem and all Israel, both near and far, in all the countries where you have scattered us because of our unfaithfulness to you. 8O LORD, we and our kings, our princes and our fathers are covered with shame because we have sinned against you. 9The Lord our God is merciful and forgiving, even though we have rebelled against him; 10we have not obeyed the LORD our God or kept the laws he gave us through his servants the prophets. 11All Israel has transgressed your law and turned away, refusing to obey you.

"Therefore the curses and sworn judgments written in the Law of Moses, the servant of God, have been poured out on us, because we have sinned against you. 12You have fulfilled the words spoken against us and against our rulers by bringing upon us great disaster. Under the whole heaven nothing has ever been done like what has been done to Jerusalem. 13Just as it is written in the Law of Moses, all this disaster has come upon us, yet we have not sought the favor of the LORD our God by turning from our sins and giving attention to your truth. 14The LORD did not hesitate to bring the disaster upon us, for the LORD our God is righteous in everything he does; yet we have not obeyed him.

15"Now, O Lord our God, who brought your people out of Egypt with a mighty hand and who made for yourself a name that endures to this day, we have sinned, we have done wrong. 16O Lord, in keeping with all your righteous acts, turn away your anger and your wrath from Jerusalem, your city, your holy hill. Our sins and the iniquities of our fathers have made Jerusalem and your people an object of scorn to all those around us.

17"Now, our God, hear the prayers and petitions of your servant. For your sake, O Lord, look with favor on your desolate sanctuary. 18Give ear, O God, and hear; open your eyes and see the desolation of the city that bears your Name. We do not make requests of you because we are righteous, but because of your great

---

a 1 Hebrew *Ahasuerus*   *b* 1 Or *Chaldean*

mercy. ¹⁹O Lord, listen! O Lord, forgive! O Lord, hear and act! For your sake, O my God, do not delay, because your city and your people bear your Name."

The Seventy "Sevens"

²⁰While I was speaking and praying, confessing my sin and the sin of my people Israel and making my request to the LORD my God for his holy hill— ²¹while I was still in prayer, Gabriel, the man I had seen in the earlier vision, came to me in swift flight about the time of the evening sacrifice. ²²He instructed me and said to me, "Daniel, I have now come to give you insight and understanding. ²³As soon as you began to pray, an answer was given, which I have come to tell you, for you are highly esteemed. Therefore, consider the message and understand the vision:

²⁴"Seventy 'sevens'ᵃ are decreed for your people and your holy city to finishᵇ transgression, to put an end to sin, to atone for wickedness, to bring in everlasting righteousness, to seal up vision and prophecy and to anoint the most holy.ᶜ

²⁵"Know and understand this: From the issuing of the decreeᵈ to restore and rebuild Jerusalem until the Anointed

---

ᵃ 24 Or 'weeks'; also in verses 25 and 26   ᵇ 24 Or restrain   ᶜ 24 Or Most Holy Place; or most holy One   ᵈ 25 Or word

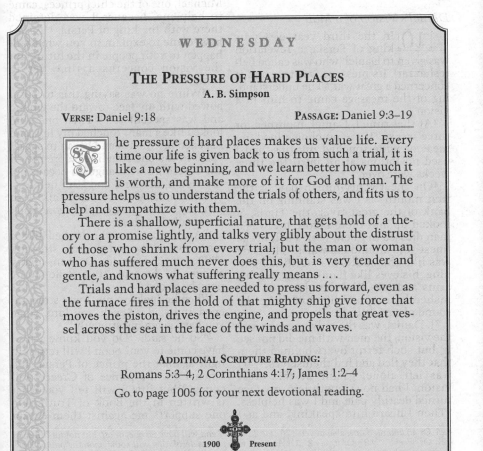

WEDNESDAY

THE PRESSURE OF HARD PLACES
A. B. Simpson

VERSE: Daniel 9:18   **PASSAGE:** Daniel 9:3–19

The pressure of hard places makes us value life. Every time our life is given back to us from such a trial, it is like a new beginning, and we learn better how much it is worth, and make more of it for God and man. The pressure helps us to understand the trials of others, and fits us to help and sympathize with them.

There is a shallow, superficial nature, that gets hold of a theory or a promise lightly, and talks very glibly about the distrust of those who shrink from every trial; but the man or woman who has suffered much never does this, but is very tender and gentle, and knows what suffering really means . . .

Trials and hard places are needed to press us forward, even as the furnace fires in the hold of that mighty ship give force that moves the piston, drives the engine, and propels that great vessel across the sea in the face of the winds and waves.

ADDITIONAL SCRIPTURE READING:
Romans 5:3–4; 2 Corinthians 4:17; James 1:2–4

Go to page 1005 for your next devotional reading.

1900   Present

One,*a* the ruler, comes, there will be seven 'sevens,' and sixty-two 'sevens.' It will be rebuilt with streets and a trench, but in times of trouble. 26After the sixty-two 'sevens,' the Anointed One will be cut off and will have nothing.*b* The people of the ruler who will come will destroy the city and the sanctuary. The end will come like a flood: War will continue until the end, and desolations have been decreed. 27He will confirm a covenant with many for one 'seven.'*c* In the middle of the 'seven'*c* he will put an end to sacrifice and offering. And on a wing ᴸof the templeᴶ he will set up an abomination that causes desolation, until the end that is decreed is poured out on him.*d* "*e*

Daniel's Vision of a Man

10 In the third year of Cyrus king of Persia, a revelation was given to Daniel (who was called Belteshazzar). Its message was true and it concerned a great war.*f* The understanding of the message came to him in a vision.

2At that time I, Daniel, mourned for three weeks. 3I ate no choice food; no meat or wine touched my lips; and I used no lotions at all until the three weeks were over.

4On the twenty-fourth day of the first month, as I was standing on the bank of the great river, the Tigris, 5I looked up and there before me was a man dressed in linen, with a belt of the finest gold around his waist. 6His body was like chrysolite, his face like lightning, his eyes like flaming torches, his arms and legs like the gleam of burnished bronze, and his voice like the sound of a multitude.

7I, Daniel, was the only one who saw the vision; the men with me did not see it, but such terror overwhelmed them that they fled and hid themselves. 8So I was left alone, gazing at this great vision; I had no strength left, my face turned deathly pale and I was helpless. 9Then I heard him speaking, and as I listened to him, I fell into a deep sleep, my face to the ground.

10A hand touched me and set me trembling on my hands and knees. 11He said, "Daniel, you who are highly esteemed, consider carefully the words I am about to speak to you, and stand up, for I have now been sent to you." And when he said this to me, I stood up trembling.

12Then he continued, "Do not be afraid, Daniel. Since the first day that you set your mind to gain understanding and to humble yourself before your God, your words were heard, and I have come in response to them. 13But the prince of the Persian kingdom resisted me twenty-one days. Then Michael, one of the chief princes, came to help me, because I was detained there with the king of Persia. 14Now I have come to explain to you what will happen to your people in the future, for the vision concerns a time yet to come."

15While he was saying this to me, I bowed with my face toward the ground and was speechless. 16Then one who looked like a man*g* touched my lips, and I opened my mouth and began to speak. I said to the one standing before me, "I am overcome with anguish because of the vision, my lord, and I am helpless. 17How can I, your servant, talk with you, my lord? My strength is gone and I can hardly breathe."

18Again the one who looked like a man touched me and gave me strength. 19"Do not be afraid, O man highly esteemed," he said. "Peace! Be strong now; be strong."

When he spoke to me, I was strengthened and said, "Speak, my lord, since you have given me strength."

20So he said, "Do you know why I have come to you? Soon I will return to fight against the prince of Persia, and when I go, the prince of Greece will come; 21but first I will tell you what is written in the Book of Truth. (No one supports me against them except

---

a 25 Or *an anointed one*; also in verse 26   *b* 26 Or *off and will have no one*; or *off, but not for himself*   *c* 27 Or 'week'   *d* 27 Or *it*   *e* 27 Or *And one who causes desolation will come upon the pinnacle of the abominable ᴸtempleᴶ, until the end that is decreed is poured out on the desolated ᴸcityᴶ*   *f* 1 Or *true and burdensome*   *g* 16 Most manuscripts of the Masoretic Text; one manuscript of the Masoretic Text, Dead Sea Scrolls and Septuagint *Then something that looked like a man's hand*

11 Michael, your prince. ¹And in the first year of Darius the Mede, I took my stand to support and protect him.)

The Kings of the South and the North

²"Now then, I tell you the truth: Three more kings will appear in Persia, and then a fourth, who will be far richer than all the others. When he has gained power by his wealth, he will stir up everyone against the kingdom of Greece. ³Then a mighty king will appear, who will rule with great power and do as he pleases. ⁴After he has appeared, his empire will be broken up and parceled out toward the four winds of heaven. It will not go to his descendants, nor will it have the power he exercised, because his empire will be uprooted and given to others.

⁵"The king of the South will become strong, but one of his commanders will become even stronger than he and will rule his own kingdom with great power. ⁶After some years, they will become allies. The daughter of the king of the South will go to the king of the North to make an alliance, but she will not retain her power, and he and his power[a] will not last. In those days she will be handed over, together with her royal escort and her father[b] and the one who supported her.

⁷"One from her family line will arise to take her place. He will attack the forces of the king of the North and enter his fortress; he will fight against them and be victorious. ⁸He will also seize their gods, their metal images and their valuable articles of silver and gold and carry them off to Egypt. For some years he will leave the king of the North alone. ⁹Then the king of the North will invade the realm of the king of the South but will retreat to his own country. ¹⁰His sons will prepare for war and assemble a great army, which will sweep on like an irresistible flood and carry the battle as far as his fortress.

¹¹"Then the king of the South will march out in a rage and fight against the king of the North, who will raise a large army, but it will be defeated. ¹²When the army is carried off, the king of the South will be filled with pride and will slaughter many thousands, yet he will not remain triumphant. ¹³For the king of the North will muster another army, larger than the first; and after several years, he will advance with a huge army fully equipped.

¹⁴"In those times many will rise against the king of the South. The violent men among your own people will rebel in fulfillment of the vision, but without success. ¹⁵Then the king of the North will come and build up siege ramps and will capture a fortified city. The forces of the South will be powerless to resist; even their best troops will not have the strength to stand. ¹⁶The invader will do as he pleases; no one will be able to stand against him. He will establish himself in the Beautiful Land and will have the power to destroy it. ¹⁷He will determine to come with the might of his entire kingdom and will make an alliance with the king of the South. And he will give him a daughter in marriage in order to overthrow the kingdom, but his plans[c] will not succeed or help him. ¹⁸Then he will turn his attention to the coastlands and will take many of them, but a commander will put an end to his insolence and will turn his insolence back upon him. ¹⁹After this, he will turn back toward the fortresses of his own country but will stumble and fall, to be seen no more.

²⁰"His successor will send out a tax collector to maintain the royal splendor. In a few years, however, he will be destroyed, yet not in anger or in battle.

²¹"He will be succeeded by a contemptible person who has not been given the honor of royalty. He will invade the kingdom when its people feel secure, and he will seize it through intrigue. ²²Then an overwhelming army will be swept away before him; both it and a prince of the covenant will be destroyed. ²³After coming to an agreement with him, he will act deceitfully, and with only a few people he will rise to power. ²⁴When the richest provinces feel secure, he will invade them and will achieve what neither his fathers nor his forefathers did. He will

distribute plunder, loot and wealth among his followers. He will plot the overthrow of fortresses—but only for a time. [25]"With a large army he will stir up his strength and courage against the king of the South. The king of the South will wage war with a large and very powerful army, but he will not be able to stand because of the plots devised against him. [26]Those who eat from the king's provisions will try to destroy him; his army will be swept away, and many will fall in battle. [27]The two kings, with their hearts bent on evil, will sit at the same table and lie to each other, but to no avail, because an end will still come at the appointed time. [28]The king of the North will return to his own country with great wealth, but his heart will be set against the holy covenant. He will take action against it and then return to his own country.

[29]"At the appointed time he will invade the South again, but this time the outcome will be different from what it was before. [30]Ships of the western coastlands[a] will oppose him, and he will lose heart. Then he will turn back and vent his fury against the holy covenant. He will return and show favor to those who forsake the holy covenant.

[31]"His armed forces will rise up to desecrate the temple fortress and will abolish the daily sacrifice. Then they will set up the abomination that causes desolation. [32]With flattery he will corrupt those who have violated the covenant, but the people who know their God will firmly resist him.

[33]"Those who are wise will instruct many, though for a time they will fall by the sword or be burned or captured or plundered. [34]When they fall, they will receive a little help, and many who are not sincere will join them. [35]Some of the wise will stumble, so that they may be refined, purified and made spotless until the time of the end, for it will still come at the appointed time.

The King Who Exalts Himself

[36]"The king will do as he pleases. He will exalt and magnify himself above every god and will say unheard-of things against the God of gods. He will be successful until the time of wrath is completed, for what has been determined must take place. [37]He will show no regard for the gods of his fathers or for the one desired by women, nor will he regard any god, but will exalt himself above them all. [38]Instead of them, he will honor a god of fortresses; a god unknown to his fathers he will honor with gold and silver, with precious stones and costly gifts. [39]He will attack the mightiest fortresses with the help of a foreign god and will greatly honor those who acknowledge him. He will make them rulers over many people and will distribute the land at a price.[b]

[40]"At the time of the end the king of the South will engage him in battle, and the king of the North will storm out against him with chariots and cavalry and a great fleet of ships. He will invade many countries and sweep through them like a flood. [41]He will also invade the Beautiful Land. Many countries will fall, but Edom, Moab and the leaders of Ammon will be delivered from his hand. [42]He will extend his power over many countries; Egypt will not escape. [43]He will gain control of the treasures of gold and silver and all the riches of Egypt, with the Libyans and Nubians in submission. [44]But reports from the east and the north will alarm him, and he will set out in a great rage to destroy and annihilate many. [45]He will pitch his royal tents between the seas at[c] the beautiful holy mountain. Yet he will come to his end, and no one will help him.

The End Times

12 "At that time Michael, the great prince who protects your people, will arise. There will be a time of distress such as has not happened from the beginning of nations until then. But at that time your people—everyone whose name is found written in the book—will be delivered. [2]Multitudes who sleep in the dust of the earth will awake: some to everlasting life, others to shame and everlasting contempt. [3]Those who are wise[d] will

---

[a] 30 Hebrew of Kittim   [b] 39 Or land for a reward wisdom   [c] 45 Or the sea and   [d] 3 Or who impart

shine like the brightness of the heavens, and those who lead many to righteousness, like the stars for ever and ever. [4]But you, Daniel, close up and seal the words of the scroll until the time of the end. Many will go here and there to increase knowledge."

[5]Then I, Daniel, looked, and there before me stood two others, one on this bank of the river and one on the opposite bank. [6]One of them said to the man clothed in linen, who was above the waters of the river, "How long will it be before these astonishing things are fulfilled?"

[7]The man clothed in linen, who was above the waters of the river, lifted his right hand and his left hand toward heaven, and I heard him swear by him who lives forever, saying, "It will be for a time, times and half a time.[a] When the power of the holy people has been finally broken, all these things will be completed."

[8]I heard, but I did not understand. So I

[a] 7 Or *a year, two years and half a year*

THURSDAY

BLESSED IS THE ONE WHO WAITS
Charles H. Spurgeon

VERSE: Daniel 12:6   PASSAGE: Daniel 12:1–13

It may seem an easy thing to *wait*, but it is one of the postures which a Christian soldier does not learn without years of teaching. Marching and quick-marching are much easier to God's warriors than standing still. There are hours of perplexity when the most willing spirit, anxiously desirous to serve the Lord, knows not what part to take. Then what shall it do? Vex itself by despair? Fly back in cowardice, turn to the right hand in fear, or rush forward in presumption? No, only simply wait.

Wait in prayer, however. Call on God, and spread the case before him; tell him your difficulty and plead his promise of aid. In dilemmas between one duty and another, it is sweet to be humble as a child and *wait with simplicity of soul* on the Lord. It is sure to be well with us when we feel and know our own folly, and are heartily willing to be guided by the will of God.

But *wait in faith*. Express your unstaggering confidence in him, for unfaithful, untrusting waiting is but an insult to the Lord. Believe that if he keeps you tarrying even till midnight, yet he will come at the right time; the vision will come and will not tarry.

ADDITIONAL SCRIPTURE READING:
Psalms 27:14; 37:34; 1 Corinthians 1:7

Go to page 1010 for your next devotional reading.

1700   1900

asked, "My lord, what will the outcome of all this be?"

⁹He replied, "Go your way, Daniel, because the words are closed up and sealed until the time of the end. ¹⁰Many will be purified, made spotless and refined, but the wicked will continue to be wicked. None of the wicked will understand, but those who are wise will understand.

¹¹"From the time that the daily sacrifice is abolished and the abomination that causes desolation is set up, there will be 1,290 days. ¹²Blessed is the one who waits for and reaches the end of the 1,335 days.

¹³"As for you, go your way till the end. You will rest, and then at the end of the days you will rise to receive your allotted inheritance."

HOSEA

 HE BOOK IS NAMED AFTER THE
PROPHET WHOSE MESSAGE IT PRE-
SERVES. HOSEA PROPHESIED JUST
BEFORE THE NORTHERN KINGDOM OF ISRAEL
WAS CONQUERED BY THE ASSYRIANS. THE
STORY OF HOSEA'S FAMILY LIFE ILLUSTRATES
ANOTHER LOVE STORY—THAT GOD LOVES US,
EVEN WHEN OUR SINS HAVE BROKEN HIS
HEART. LOOK BEYOND HOSEA'S SUFFERING TO
SEE A STARTLING EXAMPLE OF LOVE THAT WILL
NOT QUIT. TAKE COURAGE IN KNOWING THAT
GOD'S LOVE AND HEALING ARE AVAILABLE TO
YOU TODAY.

1 The word of the LORD that came to Hosea son of Beeri during the reigns of Uzziah, Jotham, Ahaz and Hezekiah, kings of Judah, and during the reign of Jeroboam son of Jehoash[a] king of Israel:

Hosea's Wife and Children

2When the LORD began to speak through Hosea, the LORD said to him, "Go, take to yourself an adulterous wife and children of unfaithfulness, because the land is guilty of the vilest adultery in departing from the LORD." 3So he married Gomer daughter of Diblaim, and she conceived and bore him a son.

4Then the LORD said to Hosea, "Call him Jezreel, because I will soon punish the house of Jehu for the massacre at Jezreel, and I will put an end to the kingdom of Israel. 5In that day I will break Israel's bow in the Valley of Jezreel."

6Gomer conceived again and gave birth to a daughter. Then the LORD said to Hosea, "Call her Lo-Ruhamah,[b] for I will no longer show love to the house of Israel, that I should at all forgive them. 7Yet I will show love to the house of Judah; and I will save them—not by bow, sword or battle, or by horses and horsemen, but by the LORD their God."

8After she had weaned Lo-Ruhamah, Gomer had another son. 9Then the LORD said, "Call him Lo-Ammi,[c] for you are not my people, and I am not your God. 10"Yet the Israelites will be like the sand on the seashore, which cannot be measured or counted. In the place where it was said to them, 'You are not my people,' they will be called 'sons of the living God.' [11] The people of Judah and the people of Israel will be reunited, and they will appoint one leader and will come up out of the land, for great will be the day of Jezreel.

2 "Say of your brothers, 'My people,' and of your sisters, 'My loved one.'

Israel Punished and Restored

2 "Rebuke your mother, rebuke her,
 for she is not my wife,
 and I am not her husband.
Let her remove the adulterous look
 from her face
 and the unfaithfulness from
  between her breasts.
[3] Otherwise I will strip her naked
 and make her as bare as on the day
  she was born;
I will make her like a desert,
 turn her into a parched land,
 and slay her with thirst.
[4] I will not show my love to her
 children,
 because they are the children of
  adultery.
[5] Their mother has been unfaithful
 and has conceived them in
  disgrace.
She said, 'I will go after my lovers,
 who give me my food and my
  water,
 my wool and my linen, my oil and
  my drink.'
[6] Therefore I will block her path with
 thornbushes;
 I will wall her in so that she cannot
  find her way.
[7] She will chase after her lovers but
 not catch them;
 she will look for them but not find
  them.
Then she will say,
 'I will go back to my husband as at
  first,
 for then I was better off than now.'
[8] She has not acknowledged that I was
 the one
 who gave her the grain, the new
  wine and oil,

who lavished on her the silver and
 gold—
 which they used for Baal.
[9] "Therefore I will take away my grain
 when it ripens,
 and my new wine when it is ready.
I will take back my wool and my
 linen,
 intended to cover her nakedness.
[10] So now I will expose her lewdness
 before the eyes of her lovers;
 no one will take her out of my
  hands.
[11] I will stop all her celebrations:
 her yearly festivals, her New
  Moons,
 her Sabbath days—all her
  appointed feasts.
[12] I will ruin her vines and her fig trees,
 which she said were her pay from
  her lovers;
I will make them a thicket,
 and wild animals will devour
  them.
[13] I will punish her for the days
 she burned incense to the Baals;
she decked herself with rings and
 jewelry,
 and went after her lovers,
 but me she forgot,"
      declares the LORD.

[14] "Therefore I am now going to allure
 her;
 I will lead her into the desert
 and speak tenderly to her.
[15] There I will give her back her
 vineyards,
 and will make the Valley of Achor[a]
  a door of hope.
There she will sing[b] as in the days of
 her youth,
 as in the day she came up out of
  Egypt.

[16] "In that day," declares the LORD,
 "you will call me 'my husband';
 you will no longer call me 'my
  master.[c] '
[17] I will remove the names of the Baals
 from her lips;
 no longer will their names be
  invoked.
[18] In that day I will make a covenant for
 them

---

[a] 15 Achor means trouble. [b] 15 Or respond [c] 16 Hebrew baal

with the beasts of the field and the
    birds of the air
  and the creatures that move along
    the ground.
Bow and sword and battle
  I will abolish from the land,
    so that all may lie down in safety.
¹⁹ I will betroth you to me forever;
  I will betroth you in*a* righteousness
    and justice,
  in*b* love and compassion.
²⁰ I will betroth you in faithfulness,
  and you will acknowledge the
    LORD.

²¹ "In that day I will respond,"
    declares the LORD—
  "I will respond to the skies,
    and they will respond to the earth;
²² and the earth will respond to the
    grain,
  the new wine and oil,
    and they will respond to Jezreel.*c*
²³ I will plant her for myself in the land;
  I will show my love to the one I
    called 'Not my loved one.'*d*
I will say to those called 'Not my
    people,'*e* 'You are my people';
  and they will say, 'You are my
    God.' "

Hosea's Reconciliation With His Wife

3 The LORD said to me, "Go, show
your love to your wife again,
though she is loved by another and is an
adulteress. Love her as the LORD loves the
Israelites, though they turn to other gods
and love the sacred raisin cakes."

²So I bought her for fifteen shekels*f* of
silver and about a homer and a lethek*g*
of barley. ³Then I told her, "You are to
live with*h* me many days; you must not
be a prostitute or be intimate with any
man, and I will live with*h* you."

⁴For the Israelites will live many days
without king or prince, without sacrifice
or sacred stones, without ephod or idol.
⁵Afterward the Israelites will return and
seek the LORD their God and David their
king. They will come trembling to the
LORD and to his blessings in the last days.

The Charge Against Israel

4 Hear the word of the LORD, you
  Israelites,
  because the LORD has a charge to
    bring
  against you who live in the land:
"There is no faithfulness, no love,
  no acknowledgment of God in the
    land.
² There is only cursing,*i* lying and
    murder,
  stealing and adultery;
they break all bounds,
  and bloodshed follows bloodshed.
³ Because of this the land mourns,*j*
  and all who live in it waste away;
the beasts of the field and the birds of
    the air
  and the fish of the sea are dying.

⁴ "But let no man bring a charge,
  let no man accuse another,
for your people are like those
  who bring charges against a priest.
⁵ You stumble day and night,
  and the prophets stumble with
    you.
So I will destroy your mother—
⁶   my people are destroyed from lack
    of knowledge.

"Because you have rejected
    knowledge,
  I also reject you as my priests;
because you have ignored the law of
    your God,
  I also will ignore your children.
⁷ The more the priests increased,
  the more they sinned against me;
  they exchanged*k* their*l* Glory for
    something disgraceful.
⁸ They feed on the sins of my people
  and relish their wickedness.
⁹ And it will be: Like people, like
    priests.
  I will punish both of them for their
    ways
  and repay them for their deeds.

¹⁰ "They will eat but not have enough;
  they will engage in prostitution
    but not increase,
because they have deserted the LORD

---

a 19 Or *with*; also in verse 20   *b* 19 Or *with*   *c* 22 *Jezreel* means *God plants.*   *d* 23 Hebrew *Lo-
Ruhamah*   *e* 23 Hebrew *Lo-Ammi*   *f* 2 That is, about 6 ounces (about 170 grams)   *g* 2 That is,
probably about 10 bushels (about 330 liters)   *h* 3 Or *wait for*   *i* 2 That is, to pronounce a curse upon
j 3 Or *dries up*   *k* 7 Syriac and an ancient Hebrew scribal tradition; Masoretic Text *I will exchange*
l 7 Masoretic Text; an ancient Hebrew scribal tradition *my*

to give themselves ¹¹to
      prostitution,
to old wine and new,
      which take away the
            understanding ¹²of my people.
They consult a wooden idol
      and are answered by a stick of
            wood.
A spirit of prostitution leads them
      astray;
      they are unfaithful to their God.
¹³They sacrifice on the mountaintops
      and burn offerings on the hills,
under oak, poplar and terebinth,
      where the shade is pleasant.

Therefore your daughters turn to
      prostitution
      and your daughters-in-law to
            adultery.

¹⁴"I will not punish your daughters
      when they turn to prostitution,
nor your daughters-in-law
      when they commit adultery,
because the men themselves consort
      with harlots
and sacrifice with shrine
      prostitutes—
a people without understanding
      will come to ruin!

FRIDAY

SENSITIVE SENSES
F. B. Meyer

VERSE: Hosea 4:6   **PASSAGE:** Hosea 4:4–9

Most of us never use our spiritual sense. God has given us a nose to smell with, eyes to see with, hands to feel with, a tongue to taste with. We are made in three parts—body, soul, and spirit. The soul has senses equivalent to those of the body, and the spirit behind that has a third set of senses that an unregenerate man has not commenced to use. But if you are a spiritual man you will use these spiritual senses to discriminate the thoughts as they come to your heart. "By reason of use" you will have your senses exercised to discern both good and evil . . .

If you live in the midst of bad people, bad books, and bad things, you lose your power of detecting bad thoughts when they come teeming about you like microbes. But if every day you spend an hour on God's mountains or upon the broad sea of the Bible, and get some of God's accurate senses into you, you will be able to detect things which are wrong that other people, even Christians, pass without seeing as wrong.

ADDITIONAL SCRIPTURE READING:
Psalm 119:105; Hebrews 4:12

Go to page 1013 for your next devotional reading.

1700   1900

15 "Though you commit adultery,
    O Israel,
  let not Judah become guilty.

  "Do not go to Gilgal;
    do not go up to Beth Aven.*a*
    And do not swear, 'As surely as the
    LORD lives!'
16 The Israelites are stubborn,
    like a stubborn heifer.
  How then can the LORD pasture them
    like lambs in a meadow?
17 Ephraim is joined to idols;
    leave him alone!
18 Even when their drinks are gone,
    they continue their prostitution;
    their rulers dearly love shameful
      ways.
19 A whirlwind will sweep them away,
    and their sacrifices will bring them
      shame.

Judgment Against Israel

5 "Hear this, you priests!
  Pay attention, you Israelites!
  Listen, O royal house!
    This judgment is against you:
  You have been a snare at Mizpah,
    a net spread out on Tabor.
2 The rebels are deep in slaughter.
    I will discipline all of them.
3 I know all about Ephraim;
    Israel is not hidden from me.
  Ephraim, you have now turned to
    prostitution;
    Israel is corrupt.

4 "Their deeds do not permit them
    to return to their God.
  A spirit of prostitution is in their
    heart;
    they do not acknowledge the LORD.
5 Israel's arrogance testifies against
    them;
    the Israelites, even Ephraim,
      stumble in their sin;
    Judah also stumbles with them.
6 When they go with their flocks and
    herds
    to seek the LORD,
  they will not find him;
    he has withdrawn himself from
      them.
7 They are unfaithful to the LORD;

they give birth to illegitimate
    children.
  Now their New Moon festivals
    will devour them and their fields.

8 "Sound the trumpet in Gibeah,
    the horn in Ramah.
  Raise the battle cry in Beth Aven*a*;
    lead on, O Benjamin.
9 Ephraim will be laid waste
    on the day of reckoning.
  Among the tribes of Israel
    I proclaim what is certain.
10 Judah's leaders are like those
    who move boundary stones.
  I will pour out my wrath on them
    like a flood of water.
11 Ephraim is oppressed,
    trampled in judgment,
    intent on pursuing idols.*b*
12 I am like a moth to Ephraim,
    like rot to the people of Judah.

13 "When Ephraim saw his sickness,
    and Judah his sores,
  then Ephraim turned to Assyria,
    and sent to the great king for help.
  But he is not able to cure you,
    not able to heal your sores.
14 For I will be like a lion to Ephraim,
    like a great lion to Judah.
  I will tear them to pieces and go
      away;
    I will carry them off, with no one
      to rescue them.
15 Then I will go back to my place
    until they admit their guilt.
  And they will seek my face;
    in their misery they will earnestly
      seek me."

Israel Unrepentant

6 "Come, let us return to the
  LORD.
  He has torn us to pieces
    but he will heal us;
  he has injured us
    but he will bind up our wounds.
2 After two days he will revive us;
    on the third day he will restore us,
    that we may live in his presence.
3 Let us acknowledge the LORD;
    let us press on to acknowledge him.
  As surely as the sun rises,
    he will appear;

---

a 15,8 Beth Aven means *house of wickedness* (a name for Bethel, which means *house of God*).
b 11 The meaning of the Hebrew for this word is uncertain.

he will come to us like the winter
    rains,
  like the spring rains that water the
    earth."

⁴ "What can I do with you, Ephraim?
  What can I do with you, Judah?
  Your love is like the morning mist,
  like the early dew that disappears.
⁵ Therefore I cut you in pieces with my
    prophets,
  I killed you with the words of my
    mouth;
  my judgments flashed like
    lightning upon you.
⁶ For I desire mercy, not sacrifice,
  and acknowledgment of God rather
    than burnt offerings.
⁷ Like Adam,ᵃ they have broken the
    covenant—
  they were unfaithful to me there.
⁸ Gilead is a city of wicked men,
  stained with footprints of blood.
⁹ As marauders lie in ambush for a
    man,
  so do bands of priests;
  they murder on the road to Shechem,
  committing shameful crimes.
¹⁰ I have seen a horrible thing
  in the house of Israel.
  There Ephraim is given to
    prostitution
  and Israel is defiled.

¹¹ "Also for you, Judah,
  a harvest is appointed.

"Whenever I would restore the
    fortunes of my people,
7 ¹ whenever I would heal Israel,
  the sins of Ephraim are exposed
  and the crimes of Samaria revealed.
They practice deceit,
  thieves break into houses,
  bandits rob in the streets;
² but they do not realize
  that I remember all their evil deeds.
Their sins engulf them;
  they are always before me.

³ "They delight the king with their
    wickedness,
  the princes with their lies.
⁴ They are all adulterers,
  burning like an oven
  whose fire the baker need not stir

from the kneading of the dough till
  it rises.
⁵ On the day of the festival of our king
  the princes become inflamed with
    wine,
  and he joins hands with the
    mockers.
⁶ Their hearts are like an oven;
  they approach him with intrigue.
Their passion smolders all night;
  in the morning it blazes like a
    flaming fire.
⁷ All of them are hot as an oven;
  they devour their rulers.
All their kings fall,
  and none of them calls on me.

⁸ "Ephraim mixes with the nations;
  Ephraim is a flat cake not turned
    over.
⁹ Foreigners sap his strength,
  but he does not realize it.
His hair is sprinkled with gray,
  but he does not notice.
¹⁰ Israel's arrogance testifies against him,
  but despite all this
he does not return to the Lᴏʀᴅ his
    God
  or search for him.

¹¹ "Ephraim is like a dove,
  easily deceived and senseless—
now calling to Egypt,
  now turning to Assyria.
¹² When they go, I will throw my net
    over them;
  I will pull them down like birds of
    the air.
When I hear them flocking together,
  I will catch them.
¹³ Woe to them,
  because they have strayed from me!
Destruction to them,
  because they have rebelled against
    me!
I long to redeem them
  but they speak lies against me.
¹⁴ They do not cry out to me from their
    hearts
  but wail upon their beds.
They gather togetherᵇ for grain and
    new wine
  but turn away from me.
¹⁵ I trained them and strengthened them,
  but they plot evil against me.

ᵃ 7 Or *As at Adam*; or *Like men*   ᵇ 14 Most Hebrew manuscripts; some Hebrew manuscripts and
Septuagint *They slash themselves*

WEEKEND

DEWDROP CHRISTIANITY
Horatius Bonar

VERSE: Hosea 6:4   **PASSAGE:** Hosea 6:1–6

There is some danger of falling into a soft Christianity, under the plea of a lofty and ethereal theology. Christianity was born for endurance; it is not an exotic, but a hardy plant, braced by the keen wind; not languid, nor childish, nor cowardly. It walks with strong step and erect frame; it is kindly, but firm; it is gentle, but honest; it is calm, but not facile; decided, but not churlish. It does not fear to speak the stern word of condemnation against error, nor to raise its voice against surrounding evils, knowing that it is not of this world. It does not shrink from giving honest reproof, lest it come under the charge of displaying an unchristian spirit . . . The religion of both Old and New Testament is marked by fervent outspoken testimonies against evil. To speak smooth things in such a case may be sentimentalism, but it is not Christianity. It is a betrayal of the cause of truth and righteousness.

If anyone should be frank, manly, honest, cheerful (I do not say blunt or rude, for a Christian must be courteous and polite), it is he who has tasted that the Lord is gracious.

ADDITIONAL SCRIPTURE READING:
Hosea 13:3; Luke 8:13–15

Go to page 1017 for your next devotional reading.

1700   1900

16 They do not turn to the Most High;
　　they are like a faulty bow.
　Their leaders will fall by the sword
　　because of their insolent words.
　For this they will be ridiculed
　　in the land of Egypt.

Israel to Reap the Whirlwind

8 "Put the trumpet to your lips!
　An eagle is over the house of
　　the LORD
because the people have broken my
　　covenant
　and rebelled against my law.
2 Israel cries out to me,
　　'O our God, we acknowledge you!'
3 But Israel has rejected what is good;
　　an enemy will pursue him.
4 They set up kings without my
　　consent;
　they choose princes without my
　　approval.
　With their silver and gold
　　they make idols for themselves
　　to their own destruction.
5 Throw out your calf-idol, O Samaria!
　　My anger burns against them.
　How long will they be incapable of
　　purity?
6　They are from Israel!
　This calf—a craftsman has made it;
　　it is not God.
　It will be broken in pieces,
　　that calf of Samaria.

7 "They sow the wind
　　and reap the whirlwind.
　The stalk has no head;
　　it will produce no flour.
　Were it to yield grain,
　　foreigners would swallow it up.
8 Israel is swallowed up;
　　now she is among the nations
　　like a worthless thing.
9 For they have gone up to Assyria
　　like a wild donkey wandering alone.
　Ephraim has sold herself to lovers.
10 Although they have sold themselves
　　among the nations,
　I will now gather them together.
　They will begin to waste away
　　under the oppression of the mighty
　　king.

11 "Though Ephraim built many altars
　　for sin offerings,

these have become altars for
　　sinning.
12 I wrote for them the many things of
　　my law,
　but they regarded them as
　　something alien.
13 They offer sacrifices given to me
　　and they eat the meat,
　but the LORD is not pleased with
　　them.
　Now he will remember their
　　wickedness
　and punish their sins:
　　They will return to Egypt.
14 Israel has forgotten his Maker
　　and built palaces;
　Judah has fortified many towns.
　But I will send fire upon their cities
　　that will consume their fortresses."

Punishment for Israel

9 Do not rejoice, O Israel;
　do not be jubilant like the
　　other nations.
For you have been unfaithful to your
　　God;
　you love the wages of a prostitute
　　at every threshing floor.
2 Threshing floors and winepresses
　　will not feed the people;
　the new wine will fail them.
3 They will not remain in the LORD's
　　land;
　Ephraim will return to Egypt
　and eat unclean[a] food in Assyria.
4 They will not pour out wine offerings
　　to the LORD,
　nor will their sacrifices please him.
　Such sacrifices will be to them like
　　the bread of mourners;
　all who eat them will be unclean.
　This food will be for themselves;
　　it will not come into the temple of
　　the LORD.

5 What will you do on the day of your
　　appointed feasts,
　on the festival days of the LORD?
6 Even if they escape from destruction,
　　Egypt will gather them,
　and Memphis will bury them.
　Their treasures of silver will be taken
　　over by briers,
　and thorns will overrun their tents.
7 The days of punishment are coming,

---

a 3 That is, ceremonially unclean

the days of reckoning are at hand.
Let Israel know this.
Because your sins are so many
and your hostility so great,
the prophet is considered a fool,
the inspired man a maniac.
⁸ The prophet, along with my God,
is the watchman over Ephraim,*ᵃ*
yet snares await him on all his paths,
and hostility in the house of his
God.
⁹ They have sunk deep into corruption,
as in the days of Gibeah.
God will remember their wickedness
and punish them for their sins.

¹⁰ "When I found Israel,
it was like finding grapes in the
desert;
when I saw your fathers,
it was like seeing the early fruit on
the fig tree.
But when they came to Baal Peor,
they consecrated themselves to
that shameful idol
and became as vile as the thing
they loved.
¹¹ Ephraim's glory will fly away like a
bird—
no birth, no pregnancy, no
conception.
¹² Even if they rear children,
I will bereave them of every one.
Woe to them
when I turn away from them!
¹³ I have seen Ephraim, like Tyre,
planted in a pleasant place.
But Ephraim will bring out
their children to the slayer."

¹⁴ Give them, O LORD—
what will you give them?
Give them wombs that miscarry
and breasts that are dry.

¹⁵ "Because of all their wickedness in
Gilgal,
I hated them there.
Because of their sinful deeds,
I will drive them out of my house.
I will no longer love them;
all their leaders are rebellious.
¹⁶ Ephraim is blighted,
their root is withered,
they yield no fruit.

Even if they bear children,
I will slay their cherished
offspring."

¹⁷ My God will reject them
because they have not obeyed him;
they will be wanderers among the
nations.

10 Israel was a spreading vine;
he brought forth fruit for
himself.
As his fruit increased,
he built more altars;
as his land prospered,
he adorned his sacred stones.
² Their heart is deceitful,
and now they must bear their guilt.
The LORD will demolish their altars
and destroy their sacred stones.

³ Then they will say, "We have no king
because we did not revere the LORD.
But even if we had a king,
what could he do for us?"
⁴ They make many promises,
take false oaths
and make agreements;
therefore lawsuits spring up
like poisonous weeds in a plowed
field.
⁵ The people who live in Samaria fear
for the calf-idol of Beth Aven.*ᵇ*
Its people will mourn over it,
and so will its idolatrous priests,
those who had rejoiced over its
splendor,
because it is taken from them into
exile.
⁶ It will be carried to Assyria
as tribute for the great king.
Ephraim will be disgraced;
Israel will be ashamed of its
wooden idols.*ᶜ*
⁷ Samaria and its king will float away
like a twig on the surface of the
waters.
⁸ The high places of wickedness*ᵈ* will
be destroyed—
it is the sin of Israel.
Thorns and thistles will grow up
and cover their altars.
Then they will say to the mountains,
"Cover us!"
and to the hills, "Fall on us!"

ᵃ 8 Or *The prophet is the watchman over Ephraim, / the people of my God*   *ᵇ 5 Beth Aven* means
house of wickedness (a name for Bethel, which means *house of God*).   *ᶜ 6* Or *its counsel*
ᵈ 8 Hebrew *aven,* a reference to Beth Aven (a derogatory name for Bethel)

9 "Since the days of Gibeah, you have
      sinned, O Israel,
   and there you have remained.ᵃ
Did not war overtake
   the evildoers in Gibeah?
10 When I please, I will punish them;
   nations will be gathered against
      them
   to put them in bonds for their
      double sin.
11 Ephraim is a trained heifer
      that loves to thresh;
   so I will put a yoke
      on her fair neck.
   I will drive Ephraim,
      Judah must plow,
   and Jacob must break up the
      ground.
12 Sow for yourselves righteousness,
   reap the fruit of unfailing love,
   and break up your unplowed ground;
   for it is time to seek the LORD,
   until he comes
   and showers righteousness on you.
13 But you have planted wickedness,
   you have reaped evil,
   you have eaten the fruit of
      deception.
   Because you have depended on your
      own strength
   and on your many warriors,
14 the roar of battle will rise against
      your people,
   so that all your fortresses will be
      devastated—
   as Shalman devastated Beth Arbel on
      the day of battle,
   when mothers were dashed to the
      ground with their children.
15 Thus will it happen to you, O Bethel,
   because your wickedness is great.
   When that day dawns,
      the king of Israel will be
         completely destroyed.

God's Love for Israel

11 "When Israel was a child, I
      loved him,
   and out of Egypt I called my son.
2 But the more Iᵇ called Israel,
   the further they went from me.ᶜ
   They sacrificed to the Baals
   and they burned incense to images.
3 It was I who taught Ephraim to walk,

taking them by the arms;
but they did not realize
   it was I who healed them.
4 I led them with cords of human
      kindness,
   with ties of love;
I lifted the yoke from their neck
   and bent down to feed them.

5 "Will they not return to Egypt
   and will not Assyria rule over them
   because they refuse to repent?
6 Swords will flash in their cities,
   will destroy the bars of their gates
   and put an end to their plans.
7 My people are determined to turn
      from me.
   Even if they call to the Most High,
   he will by no means exalt them.

8 "How can I give you up, Ephraim?
   How can I hand you over, Israel?
   How can I treat you like Admah?
   How can I make you like Zeboiim?
   My heart is changed within me;
   all my compassion is aroused.
9 I will not carry out my fierce anger,
   nor will I turn and devastate
      Ephraim.
   For I am God, and not man—
   the Holy One among you.
   I will not come in wrath.ᵈ
10 They will follow the LORD;
   he will roar like a lion.
   When he roars,
   his children will come trembling
      from the west.
11 They will come trembling
   like birds from Egypt,
   like doves from Assyria.
   I will settle them in their homes,"
declares the LORD.

Israel's Sin

12 Ephraim has surrounded me with
      lies,
   the house of Israel with deceit.
   And Judah is unruly against God,
   even against the faithful Holy One.

12 ¹Ephraim feeds on the wind;
   he pursues the east wind all
      day
   and multiplies lies and violence.
   He makes a treaty with Assyria
   and sends olive oil to Egypt.

ᵃ 9 Or there a stand was taken   ᵇ 2 Some Septuagint manuscripts; Hebrew they   ᶜ 2 Septuagint;
Hebrew them   ᵈ 9 Or come against any city

2 The LORD has a charge to bring
   against Judah;
   he will punish Jacob[a] according to
      his ways
   and repay him according to his
      deeds.
3 In the womb he grasped his brother's
      heel;
   as a man he struggled with God.
4 He struggled with the angel and
      overcame him;
   he wept and begged for his favor.
   He found him at Bethel
   and talked with him there—

5 the LORD God Almighty,
   the LORD is his name of renown!
6 But you must return to your God;
   maintain love and justice,
   and wait for your God always.

7 The merchant uses dishonest scales;
   he loves to defraud.
8 Ephraim boasts,
   "I am very rich; I have become
      wealthy.
   With all my wealth they will not find
      in me
   any iniquity or sin."

---

a 2 *Jacob* means *he grasps the heel* (figuratively, *he deceives*).

MONDAY

THE DEPTHS OF HUMAN NATURE
Francis Schaeffer

VERSE: Hosea 12:8   **PASSAGE:** Hosea 11:12—12:8

he more the Holy Spirit puts his finger on my life and goes down deep into my life, the more I understand that there are deep wells to my nature. Modern psychology has dealt with these under the terms unconscious and subconscious, and though the philosophy behind modern psychology is often fundamentally wrong, surely it is right in pointing out that we are more than merely that which is on the surface. We are like the iceberg: one-tenth above and nine-tenths below. It is a very, very simple thing to fool ourselves, and that is why we must question this word "known." If I say I can have freedom from all "known" sin, surely I must acknowledge the meaningfulness of the question: *What do I know?* Until I can describe what I know, I cannot go on meaningfully to ask whether I can have freedom from "known" sin. As the Holy Spirit has wrestled with me down through the years, more and more I am aware of the depths of my own nature, and the depths of the results of that awful fall in the Garden of Eden. Man is separated from him.

ADDITIONAL SCRIPTURE READING:
Deuteronomy 8:17–18; Luke 16:15; Romans 8:26–27

Go to page 1019 for your next devotional reading.

1900   Present

9 "I am the LORD your God,
⌞who brought you⌟ out of*a* Egypt;
I will make you live in tents again,
as in the days of your appointed
feasts.
10 I spoke to the prophets,
gave them many visions
and told parables through them."

11 Is Gilead wicked?
Its people are worthless!
Do they sacrifice bulls in Gilgal?
Their altars will be like piles of
stones
on a plowed field.
12 Jacob fled to the country of Aram*b*;
Israel served to get a wife,
and to pay for her he tended sheep.
13 The LORD used a prophet to bring
Israel up from Egypt,
by a prophet he cared for him.
14 But Ephraim has bitterly provoked
him to anger;
his Lord will leave upon him the
guilt of his bloodshed
and will repay him for his
contempt.

The LORD's Anger Against Israel

13 When Ephraim spoke, men
trembled;
he was exalted in Israel.
But he became guilty of Baal
worship and died.
2 Now they sin more and more;
they make idols for themselves
from their silver,
cleverly fashioned images,
all of them the work of craftsmen.
It is said of these people,
"They offer human sacrifice
and kiss*c* the calf-idols."
3 Therefore they will be like the
morning mist,
like the early dew that disappears,
like chaff swirling from a threshing
floor,
like smoke escaping through a
window.

4 "But I am the LORD your God,
⌞who brought you⌟ out of*a* Egypt.
You shall acknowledge no God but
me,
no Savior except me.

5 I cared for you in the desert,
in the land of burning heat.
6 When I fed them, they were satisfied;
when they were satisfied, they
became proud;
then they forgot me.
7 So I will come upon them like a lion,
like a leopard I will lurk by the
path.
8 Like a bear robbed of her cubs,
I will attack them and rip them
open.
Like a lion I will devour them;
a wild animal will tear them apart.

9 "You are destroyed, O Israel,
because you are against me, against
your helper.
10 Where is your king, that he may save
you?
Where are your rulers in all your
towns,
of whom you said,
'Give me a king and princes'?
11 So in my anger I gave you a king,
and in my wrath I took him away.
12 The guilt of Ephraim is stored up,
his sins are kept on record.
13 Pains as of a woman in childbirth
come to him,
but he is a child without wisdom;
when the time arrives,
he does not come to the opening of
the womb.

14 "I will ransom them from the power
of the grave*d*;
I will redeem them from death.
Where, O death, are your plagues?
Where, O grave,*d* is your
destruction?

"I will have no compassion,
15 even though he thrives among his
brothers.
An east wind from the LORD will
come,
blowing in from the desert;
his spring will fail
and his well dry up.
His storehouse will be plundered
of all its treasures.
16 The people of Samaria must bear
their guilt,
because they have rebelled against
their God.

---

a 9,4 Or *God / ever since you were in*
b 12 That is, Northwest Mesopotamia   *c* 2 Or "Men who
sacrifice / kiss   *d* 14 Hebrew *Sheol*

They will fall by the sword;
   their little ones will be dashed to
      the ground,
   their pregnant women ripped open."

Repentance to Bring Blessing

 14 Return, O Israel, to the Lord
      your God.
   Your sins have been your downfall!
² Take words with you
   and return to the Lord.

Say to him:
   "Forgive all our sins
and receive us graciously,
   that we may offer the fruit of our
      lips.*ᵃ*
³ Assyria cannot save us;
   we will not mount war-horses.
We will never again say 'Our gods'
   to what our own hands have made,
for in you the fatherless find
   compassion."

ᵃ 2 Or offer our lips as sacrifices of bulls

TUESDAY

GOD LOVES THE BACKSLIDER
Dwight L. Moody

VERSE: Hosea 14:4   **PASSAGE:** Hosea 14

backslider came into the inquiry room night before last, and I was trying to tell him God loved him. He would hardly believe me. He thought because he had not kept up his love and faithfulness to God, and to his own vows, that God had stopped loving him.

Now, it says in John 13:1 (KJV), "He loved them unto the end," that is, his love was unchangeable. You may have forgotten him and betrayed him and denied him, but nevertheless, he loves you; he loves the backslider. There is not a man here who has wandered from God and betrayed him but what the Lord Jesus loves him and wants him to come back.

Now, in Hosea 14:4, God says that he will heal every backslider. "I will . . . love them freely." So the Lord tells the backsliders, "If you will only come back to me, I will forgive you." It was thus with Peter who denied his Lord. The Savior forgave him and sent him to preach his glorious gospel on the day of Pentecost when 3,000 were won to Christ under one sermon of a backslider (see John 18:25–27; 21:15–19; Acts 2:14–39).

Don't let a backslider go out of this hall this evening with such hard talk about the Lord. No backslider can say God has left him. He may think so, but it is one of the devil's lies. The Lord has never left a man yet.

ADDITIONAL SCRIPTURE READING:
Isaiah 57:18; Jeremiah 3:22; 17:14

Go to page 1024 for your next devotional reading.

1900   Present

4 "I will heal their waywardness
   and love them freely,
     for my anger has turned away from
      them.
5 I will be like the dew to Israel;
   he will blossom like a lily.
  Like a cedar of Lebanon
   he will send down his roots;
6   his young shoots will grow.
  His splendor will be like an olive
     tree,
   his fragrance like a cedar of
     Lebanon.
7 Men will dwell again in his shade.
  He will flourish like the grain.
  He will blossom like a vine,

and his fame will be like the wine
   from Lebanon.
8 O Ephraim, what more have I*a* to do
   with idols?
  I will answer him and care for
    him.
  I am like a green pine tree;
   your fruitfulness comes from me."

9 Who is wise? He will realize these
   things.
  Who is discerning? He will
   understand them.
The ways of the LORD are right;
  the righteous walk in them,
  but the rebellious stumble in
   them.

---

a 8 Or *What more has Ephraim*

JOEL

THE PROPHET JOEL URGED THE PEOPLE OF JUDAH TO TURN AGAIN TO GOD AND WARNED THEM THAT JUDGMENT WAS AT HAND. HE DESCRIBED THIS JUDGMENT AS "THE GREAT AND DREADFUL DAY OF THE LORD" (2:31). HE WARNED THAT THE DAY OF PUNISHMENT WOULD COME NOT ONLY ON OTHER NATIONS, BUT ON UNFAITHFUL ISRAEL AS WELL, AND HE CALLED UPON EVERYONE TO REPENT. AS YOU READ THE BOOK OF JOEL, YOU WILL SEE GOD'S INTENSE DESIRE FOR INTIMACY WITH ALL OF HIS PEOPLE.

1

The word of the LORD that came to Joel son of Pethuel.

An Invasion of Locusts

² Hear this, you elders;
  listen, all who live in the land.
Has anything like this ever happened
      in your days
  or in the days of your forefathers?
³ Tell it to your children,
    and let your children tell it to their
      children,
  and their children to the next
      generation.
⁴ What the locust swarm has left
    the great locusts have eaten;
  what the great locusts have left
    the young locusts have eaten;

what the young locusts have left
    other locusts*a* have eaten.

⁵ Wake up, you drunkards, and weep!
    Wail, all you drinkers of wine;
  wail because of the new wine,
    for it has been snatched from your
      lips.
⁶ A nation has invaded my land,
    powerful and without number;
  it has the teeth of a lion,
    the fangs of a lioness.
⁷ It has laid waste my vines
    and ruined my fig trees.
  It has stripped off their bark
    and thrown it away,
    leaving their branches white.
⁸ Mourn like a virgin*b* in sackcloth

---

a 4 The precise meaning of the four Hebrew words used here for locusts is uncertain.   *b 8* Or *young woman*

grieving for the husband*a* of her
  youth.
⁹ Grain offerings and drink offerings
  are cut off from the house of the
  LORD.
The priests are in mourning,
  those who minister before the
  LORD.
¹⁰ The fields are ruined,
  the ground is dried up*b*;
the grain is destroyed,
  the new wine is dried up,
  the oil fails.
¹¹ Despair, you farmers,
  wail, you vine growers;
grieve for the wheat and the barley,
  because the harvest of the field is
  destroyed.
¹² The vine is dried up
  and the fig tree is withered;
the pomegranate, the palm and the
  apple tree—
  all the trees of the field—are dried
  up.
Surely the joy of mankind
  is withered away.

A Call to Repentance

¹³ Put on sackcloth, O priests, and
  mourn;
  wail, you who minister before the
  altar.
Come, spend the night in sackcloth,
  you who minister before my God;
for the grain offerings and drink
  offerings
  are withheld from the house of
  your God.
¹⁴ Declare a holy fast;
  call a sacred assembly.
Summon the elders
  and all who live in the land
to the house of the LORD your God,
  and cry out to the LORD.

¹⁵ Alas for that day!
  For the day of the LORD is near;
  it will come like destruction from
  the Almighty.*c*

¹⁶ Has not the food been cut off
  before our very eyes—
joy and gladness
  from the house of our God?
¹⁷ The seeds are shriveled

beneath the clods.*d*
The storehouses are in ruins,
  the granaries have been broken
  down,
  for the grain has dried up.
¹⁸ How the cattle moan!
The herds mill about
  because they have no pasture;
  even the flocks of sheep are
  suffering.

¹⁹ To you, O LORD, I call,
  for fire has devoured the open
  pastures
  and flames have burned up all the
  trees of the field.
²⁰ Even the wild animals pant for you;
  the streams of water have dried up
  and fire has devoured the open
  pastures.

An Army of Locusts

2 Blow the trumpet in Zion;
  sound the alarm on my holy
  hill.
Let all who live in the land tremble,
  for the day of the LORD is coming.
It is close at hand—
²   a day of darkness and gloom,
  a day of clouds and blackness.
Like dawn spreading across the
  mountains
  a large and mighty army comes,
such as never was of old
  nor ever will be in ages to come.

³ Before them fire devours,
  behind them a flame blazes.
Before them the land is like the
  garden of Eden,
  behind them, a desert waste—
  nothing escapes them.
⁴ They have the appearance of horses;
  they gallop along like cavalry.
⁵ With a noise like that of chariots
  they leap over the mountaintops,
like a crackling fire consuming
  stubble,
  like a mighty army drawn up for
  battle.

⁶ At the sight of them, nations are in
  anguish;
  every face turns pale.
⁷ They charge like warriors;
  they scale walls like soldiers.

---

a 8 Or *betrothed*   *b 10* Or *ground mourns*   *c 15* Hebrew *Shaddai*   *d 17* The meaning of the
Hebrew for this word is uncertain.

They all march in line,
 not swerving from their course.
⁸ They do not jostle each other;
 each marches straight ahead.
They plunge through defenses
 without breaking ranks.
⁹ They rush upon the city;
 they run along the wall.
They climb into the houses;
 like thieves they enter through the
 windows.

¹⁰ Before them the earth shakes,
 the sky trembles,
the sun and moon are darkened,
 and the stars no longer shine.
¹¹ The LORD thunders
 at the head of his army;
his forces are beyond number,
 and mighty are those who obey his
 command.
The day of the LORD is great;
 it is dreadful.
Who can endure it?

Rend Your Heart

¹² "Even now," declares the LORD,
 "return to me with all your heart,
 with fasting and weeping and
 mourning."

¹³ Rend your heart
 and not your garments.
Return to the LORD your God,
 for he is gracious and
 compassionate,
slow to anger and abounding in love,
 and he relents from sending
 calamity.
¹⁴ Who knows? He may turn and have
 pity
 and leave behind a blessing—
grain offerings and drink offerings
 for the LORD your God.

¹⁵ Blow the trumpet in Zion,
 declare a holy fast,
 call a sacred assembly.
¹⁶ Gather the people,
 consecrate the assembly;
bring together the elders,
 gather the children,
 those nursing at the breast.
Let the bridegroom leave his room
 and the bride her chamber.

¹⁷ Let the priests, who minister before
 the LORD,
 weep between the temple porch
 and the altar.
Let them say, "Spare your people,
 O LORD.
Do not make your inheritance an
 object of scorn,
 a byword among the nations.
Why should they say among the
 peoples,
 'Where is their God?' "

The LORD's Answer

¹⁸ Then the LORD will be jealous for his
 land
 and take pity on his people.

¹⁹ The LORD will reply[a] to them:

"I am sending you grain, new wine
 and oil,
 enough to satisfy you fully;
never again will I make you
 an object of scorn to the nations.

²⁰ "I will drive the northern army far
 from you,
 pushing it into a parched and
 barren land,
with its front columns going into the
 eastern sea[b]
 and those in the rear into the
 western sea.[c]
And its stench will go up;
 its smell will rise."

Surely he has done great things.[d]
²¹   Be not afraid, O land;
 be glad and rejoice.
Surely the LORD has done great
 things.
²²   Be not afraid, O wild animals,
 for the open pastures are becoming
 green.
The trees are bearing their fruit;
 the fig tree and the vine yield their
 riches.
²³ Be glad, O people of Zion,
 rejoice in the LORD your God,
for he has given you
 the autumn rains in
 righteousness.[e]
He sends you abundant showers,

---

a 18,19 Or LORD was jealous . . . / and took pity . . . / ¹⁹The LORD replied   b 20 That is, the Dead Sea
c 20 That is, the Mediterranean   d 20 Or rise. / Surely it has done great things."   e 23 Or / the
teacher for righteousness:

both autumn and spring rains, as
    before.
24 The threshing floors will be filled
    with grain;
the vats will overflow with new
    wine and oil.

25 "I will repay you for the years the
    locusts have eaten—
the great locust and the young
    locust,
the other locusts and the locust
    swarm[a]—
my great army that I sent among you.
26 You will have plenty to eat, until you
    are full,
and you will praise the name of the
    LORD your God,
who has worked wonders for you;
never again will my people be
    shamed.

[a] 25 The precise meaning of the four Hebrew words used here for locusts is uncertain.

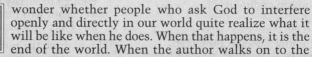

WHEN THE AUTHOR WALKS ON THE STAGE
C. S. Lewis

VERSE: Joel 2:11   PASSAGE: Joel 2:1–11

I wonder whether people who ask God to interfere openly and directly in our world quite realize what it will be like when he does. When that happens, it is the end of the world. When the author walks on to the stage the play is over. God is going to invade, all right: but what is the good of saying you are on his side then, when you see the whole natural universe melting away like a dream and something else—something it never entered your head to conceive—comes crashing in; something so beautiful to some of us and so terrible to others that none of us will have any choice left? For this time it will be God without disguise; something so overwhelming that it will strike either irresistible love or irresistible horror into every creature. It will be too late then to choose your side. There is no use saying you choose to lie down when it has become impossible to stand up. That will not be the time for choosing: it will be the time when we discover which side we really have chosen, whether we realized it before or not. Now, today, this moment, is our chance to choose the right side. God is holding back to give us that chance. It will not last for ever. We must take it or leave it.

ADDITIONAL SCRIPTURE READING:
Isaiah 49:8; 2 Corinthians 6:2; Hebrews 4:7

Go to page 1032 for your next devotional reading.

1900   Present

27 Then you will know that I am in
    Israel,
    that I am the LORD your God,
    and that there is no other;
    never again will my people be
    shamed.

The Day of the LORD

28 "And afterward,
    I will pour out my Spirit on all
    people.
    Your sons and daughters will
    prophesy,
    your old men will dream dreams,
    your young men will see visions.
29 Even on my servants, both men and
    women,
    I will pour out my Spirit in those
    days.
30 I will show wonders in the heavens
    and on the earth,
    blood and fire and billows of smoke.
31 The sun will be turned to darkness
    and the moon to blood
    before the coming of the great and
    dreadful day of the LORD.
32 And everyone who calls
    on the name of the LORD will be
    saved;
    for on Mount Zion and in Jerusalem
    there will be deliverance,
    as the LORD has said,
    among the survivors
    whom the LORD calls.

The Nations Judged

3 "In those days and at that time,
    when I restore the fortunes of
    Judah and Jerusalem,
2 I will gather all nations
    and bring them down to the Valley
    of Jehoshaphat.ᵃ
    There I will enter into judgment
    against them
    concerning my inheritance, my
    people Israel,
    for they scattered my people among
    the nations
    and divided up my land.
3 They cast lots for my people
    and traded boys for prostitutes;
    they sold girls for wine
    that they might drink.

4 "Now what have you against me,

O Tyre and Sidon and all you regions of
Philistia? Are you repaying me for something I have done? If you are paying me
back, I will swiftly and speedily return
on your own heads what you have done.
5 For you took my silver and my gold and
carried off my finest treasures to your
temples. 6 You sold the people of Judah
and Jerusalem to the Greeks, that you
might send them far from their homeland.

7 "See, I am going to rouse them out of
the places to which you sold them, and I
will return on your own heads what you
have done. 8 I will sell your sons and
daughters to the people of Judah, and
they will sell them to the Sabeans, a
nation far away." The LORD has spoken.

9 Proclaim this among the nations:
    Prepare for war!
    Rouse the warriors!
    Let all the fighting men draw near
    and attack.
10 Beat your plowshares into swords
    and your pruning hooks into spears.
    Let the weakling say,
    "I am strong!"
11 Come quickly, all you nations from
    every side,
    and assemble there.

    Bring down your warriors, O LORD!

12 "Let the nations be roused;
    let them advance into the Valley of
    Jehoshaphat,
    for there I will sit
    to judge all the nations on every
    side.
13 Swing the sickle,
    for the harvest is ripe.
    Come, trample the grapes,
    for the winepress is full
    and the vats overflow—
    so great is their wickedness!"

14 Multitudes, multitudes
    in the valley of decision!
    For the day of the LORD is near
    in the valley of decision.
15 The sun and moon will be darkened,
    and the stars no longer shine.
16 The LORD will roar from Zion
    and thunder from Jerusalem;
    the earth and the sky will tremble.

ᵃ 2 *Jehoshaphat* means *the LORD judges*; also in verse 12.

But the LORD will be a refuge for his
people,
　a stronghold for the people of
　　Israel.

Blessings for God's People

17 "Then you will know that I, the
　　LORD your God,
　dwell in Zion, my holy hill.
Jerusalem will be holy;
　never again will foreigners invade
　　her.

18 "In that day the mountains will drip
　　new wine,
　and the hills will flow with milk;
　all the ravines of Judah will run
　　with water.

A fountain will flow out of the
　　LORD's house
　and will water the valley of
　　acacias. a
19 But Egypt will be desolate,
　Edom a desert waste,
because of violence done to the
　　people of Judah,
　in whose land they shed innocent
　　blood.
20 Judah will be inhabited forever
　and Jerusalem through all
　　generations.
21 Their bloodguilt, which I have not
　　pardoned,
　I will pardon."

The LORD dwells in Zion!

---

a 18 Or *Valley of Shittim*

AMOS

MOS, A SHEPHERD FROM THE SMALL
TOWN OF TEKOA; WAS SENT TO
ANNOUNCE GOD'S JUDGMENT ON
THE NORTHERN KINGDOM OF ISRAEL. WITH
STRONG POETIC IMAGERY, AMOS SPEAKS PAS-
SIONATELY ABOUT GOD'S CONCERN FOR THE
POOR AND URGES A RETURN TO RIGHTEOUS-
NESS AND JUSTICE. AS YOU READ THIS BOOK,
LOOK FOR GOD'S PERSPECTIVE ON ISSUES
OF SOCIAL JUSTICE, AND BE PREPARED TO
RESPOND WITH A HEART OF COMPASSION.

1 The words of Amos, one of the
shepherds of Tekoa—what he
saw concerning Israel two years before
the earthquake, when Uzziah was king
of Judah and Jeroboam son of Jehoash*a*
was king of Israel.
²He said:

"The LORD roars from Zion
and thunders from Jerusalem;
the pastures of the shepherds dry up,*b*
and the top of Carmel withers."

Judgment on Israel's Neighbors

³This is what the LORD says:

"For three sins of Damascus,
even for four, I will not turn back
⌊my wrath⌋.
Because she threshed Gilead
with sledges having iron teeth,
⁴I will send fire upon the house of
Hazael
that will consume the fortresses of
Ben-Hadad.
⁵I will break down the gate of
Damascus;
I will destroy the king who is in*c*
the Valley of Aven*d*
and the one who holds the scepter in
Beth Eden.
The people of Aram will go into
exile to Kir,"
says the LORD.

6This is what the LORD says:

"For three sins of Gaza,
　even for four, I will not turn back
　⌐my wrath⌐.
Because she took captive whole
　communities
and sold them to Edom,
7I will send fire upon the walls of
　Gaza
that will consume her fortresses.
8I will destroy the king*a* of Ashdod
and the one who holds the scepter
　in Ashkelon.
I will turn my hand against Ekron,
　till the last of the Philistines is
　dead,"
　　　　　says the Sovereign LORD.

9This is what the LORD says:

"For three sins of Tyre,
　even for four, I will not turn back
　⌐my wrath⌐.
Because she sold whole communities
　of captives to Edom,
disregarding a treaty of
　brotherhood,
10I will send fire upon the walls of Tyre
that will consume her fortresses."

11This is what the LORD says:

"For three sins of Edom,
　even for four, I will not turn back
　⌐my wrath⌐.
Because he pursued his brother with
　a sword,
stifling all compassion,*b*
because his anger raged continually
and his fury flamed unchecked,
12I will send fire upon Teman
that will consume the fortresses of
　Bozrah."

13This is what the LORD says:

"For three sins of Ammon,
　even for four, I will not turn back
　⌐my wrath⌐.
Because he ripped open the pregnant
　women of Gilead
in order to extend his borders,
14I will set fire to the walls of Rabbah

that will consume her fortresses
amid war cries on the day of battle,
　amid violent winds on a stormy
　day.
15Her king*c* will go into exile,
　he and his officials together,"
　　　　　says the LORD.

2 This is what the LORD says:

"For three sins of Moab,
　even for four, I will not turn back
　⌐my wrath⌐.
Because he burned, as if to lime,
　the bones of Edom's king,
2I will send fire upon Moab
　that will consume the fortresses of
　Kerioth.*d*
Moab will go down in great tumult
　amid war cries and the blast of the
　trumpet.
3I will destroy her ruler
　and kill all her officials with him,"
　　　　　says the LORD.

4This is what the LORD says:

"For three sins of Judah,
　even for four, I will not turn back
　⌐my wrath⌐.
Because they have rejected the law of
　the LORD
and have not kept his decrees,
because they have been led astray by
　false gods,*e*
　the gods*f* their ancestors followed,
5I will send fire upon Judah
　that will consume the fortresses of
　Jerusalem."

Judgment on Israel

6This is what the LORD says:

"For three sins of Israel,
　even for four, I will not turn back
　⌐my wrath⌐.
They sell the righteous for silver,
　and the needy for a pair of sandals.
7They trample on the heads of the
　poor
as upon the dust of the ground
and deny justice to the oppressed.
Father and son use the same girl
and so profane my holy name.

---

a 8 Or *inhabitants*　　*b* 11 Or *sword / and destroyed his allies*　　*c* 15 Or / *Molech*; Hebrew *malcam*
d 2 Or *of her cities*　　*e* 4 Or *by lies*　　*f* 4 Or *lies*

8 They lie down beside every altar
  on garments taken in pledge.
In the house of their god
  they drink wine taken as fines.

9 "I destroyed the Amorite before
      them,
  though he was tall as the cedars
  and strong as the oaks.
I destroyed his fruit above
  and his roots below.

10 "I brought you up out of Egypt,
  and I led you forty years in the
      desert
  to give you the land of the
      Amorites.

11 I also raised up prophets from among
      your sons
  and Nazirites from among your
      young men.
Is this not true, people of Israel?"
                    declares the LORD.

12 "But you made the Nazirites drink
      wine
  and commanded the prophets not
      to prophesy.

13 "Now then, I will crush you
  as a cart crushes when loaded with
      grain.

14 The swift will not escape,
  the strong will not muster their
      strength,
  and the warrior will not save his
      life.

15 The archer will not stand his ground,
  the fleet-footed soldier will not get
      away,
  and the horseman will not save his
      life.

16 Even the bravest warriors
  will flee naked on that day,"
                    declares the LORD.

Witnesses Summoned Against Israel

3 Hear this word the LORD has
spoken against you, O people of
Israel—against the whole family I
brought up out of Egypt:

2 "You only have I chosen
  of all the families of the earth;
  therefore I will punish you
  for all your sins."

3 Do two walk together
  unless they have agreed to do so?

4 Does a lion roar in the thicket
  when he has no prey?
Does he growl in his den
  when he has caught nothing?

5 Does a bird fall into a trap on the
      ground
  where no snare has been set?
Does a trap spring up from the earth
  when there is nothing to catch?

6 When a trumpet sounds in a city,
  do not the people tremble?
When disaster comes to a city,
  has not the LORD caused it?

7 Surely the Sovereign LORD does
      nothing
  without revealing his plan
  to his servants the prophets.

8 The lion has roared—
  who will not fear?
The Sovereign LORD has spoken—
  who can but prophesy?

9 Proclaim to the fortresses of Ashdod
  and to the fortresses of Egypt:
"Assemble yourselves on the
      mountains of Samaria;
  see the great unrest within her
  and the oppression among her
      people."

10 "They do not know how to do right,"
      declares the LORD,
  "who hoard plunder and loot in
      their fortresses."

11 Therefore this is what the Sovereign
LORD says:

"An enemy will overrun the land;
  he will pull down your strongholds
  and plunder your fortresses."

12 This is what the LORD says:

"As a shepherd saves from the lion's
      mouth
  only two leg bones or a piece of an
      ear,
so will the Israelites be saved,
those who sit in Samaria
  on the edge of their beds
  and in Damascus on their
      couches.ª"

ª 12 The meaning of the Hebrew for this line is uncertain.

13 "Hear this and testify against the house of Jacob," declares the Lord, the LORD God Almighty.

14 "On the day I punish Israel for her sins,
 I will destroy the altars of Bethel;
the horns of the altar will be cut off
 and fall to the ground.
15 I will tear down the winter house
 along with the summer house;
the houses adorned with ivory will
 be destroyed
and the mansions will be
 demolished,"
                    declares the LORD.

Israel Has Not Returned to God

4 Hear this word, you cows of Bashan on Mount Samaria,
you women who oppress the poor
 and crush the needy
and say to your husbands, "Bring
 us some drinks!"
2 The Sovereign LORD has sworn by his
 holiness:
 "The time will surely come
when you will be taken away with
 hooks,
 the last of you with fishhooks.
3 You will each go straight out
 through breaks in the wall,
and you will be cast out toward
 Harmon,a "
                    declares the LORD.
4 "Go to Bethel and sin;
 go to Gilgal and sin yet more.
Bring your sacrifices every morning,
 your tithes every three years.b
5 Burn leavened bread as a thank
 offering
and brag about your freewill
 offerings—
boast about them, you Israelites,
 for this is what you love to do,"
                    declares the Sovereign LORD.

6 "I gave you empty stomachsc in
 every city
and lack of bread in every town,
 yet you have not returned to me,"
                    declares the LORD.

7 "I also withheld rain from you
 when the harvest was still three
 months away.
I sent rain on one town,
 but withheld it from another.
One field had rain;
 another had none and dried up.
8 People staggered from town to town
 for water
but did not get enough to drink,
 yet you have not returned to me,"
                    declares the LORD.

9 "Many times I struck your gardens
 and vineyards,
I struck them with blight and
 mildew.
Locusts devoured your fig and olive
 trees,
 yet you have not returned to me,"
                    declares the LORD.

10 "I sent plagues among you
 as I did to Egypt.
I killed your young men with the
 sword,
along with your captured horses.
I filled your nostrils with the stench
 of your camps,
 yet you have not returned to me,"
                    declares the LORD.

11 "I overthrew some of you
 as Id overthrew Sodom and
 Gomorrah.
You were like a burning stick
 snatched from the fire,
 yet you have not returned to me,"
                    declares the LORD.

12 "Therefore this is what I will do to
 you, Israel,
and because I will do this to you,
 prepare to meet your God,
 O Israel."

13 He who forms the mountains,
 creates the wind,
 and reveals his thoughts to man,
he who turns dawn to darkness,
 and treads the high places of the
 earth—
 the LORD God Almighty is his
 name.

---

a 3 Masoretic Text; with a different word division of the Hebrew (see Septuagint) out, O mountain of oppression   b 4 Or tithes on the third day   c 6 Hebrew you cleanness of teeth   d 11 Hebrew God

A Lament and Call to Repentance

5 Hear this word, O house of Israel, this lament I take up concerning you:

2 "Fallen is Virgin Israel,
    never to rise again,
deserted in her own land,
    with no one to lift her up."

3 This is what the Sovereign Lord says:

"The city that marches out a
        thousand strong for Israel
will have only a hundred left;
the town that marches out a hundred
        strong
will have only ten left."

4 This is what the Lord says to the house of Israel:

"Seek me and live;
5   do not seek Bethel,
do not go to Gilgal,
    do not journey to Beersheba.
For Gilgal will surely go into exile,
    and Bethel will be reduced to
        nothing.ᵃ"
6 Seek the Lord and live,
    or he will sweep through the house
        of Joseph like a fire;
it will devour,
    and Bethel will have no one to
        quench it.

7 You who turn justice into bitterness
    and cast righteousness to the
        ground
8 (he who made the Pleiades and
        Orion,
    who turns blackness into dawn
    and darkens day into night,
who calls for the waters of the sea
    and pours them out over the face of
        the land—
    the Lord is his name—
9 he flashes destruction on the
        stronghold
    and brings the fortified city to
        ruin),
10 you hate the one who reproves in
        court
    and despise him who tells the
        truth.

11 You trample on the poor
    and force him to give you grain.
Therefore, though you have built
        stone mansions,
    you will not live in them;
though you have planted lush
        vineyards,
    you will not drink their wine.
12 For I know how many are your
        offenses
    and how great your sins.

You oppress the righteous and take
        bribes
    and you deprive the poor of justice
        in the courts.
13 Therefore the prudent man keeps
        quiet in such times,
    for the times are evil.

14 Seek good, not evil,
    that you may live.
Then the Lord God Almighty will be
        with you,
    just as you say he is.
15 Hate evil, love good;
    maintain justice in the courts.
Perhaps the Lord God Almighty will
        have mercy
    on the remnant of Joseph.

16 Therefore this is what the Lord, the
Lord God Almighty, says:

"There will be wailing in all the
        streets
    and cries of anguish in every public
        square.
The farmers will be summoned to
        weep
    and the mourners to wail.
17 There will be wailing in all the
        vineyards,
    for I will pass through your midst,"
                        says the Lord.

The Day of the Lord

18 Woe to you who long
    for the day of the Lord!
Why do you long for the day of the
        Lord?
    That day will be darkness, not light.
19 It will be as though a man fled from a
        lion
    only to meet a bear,
as though he entered his house

ᵃ 5 Or grief; or wickedness; Hebrew aven, a reference to Beth Aven (a derogatory name for Bethel)

HE WHO TURNS BLACKNESS INTO DAWN
Martin Luther King, Jr.

VERSE: Amos 5:8   **PASSAGE:** Amos 5:4–17

idnight is a confusing hour when it is difficult to be faithful. The most inspiring word that the church may speak is that no midnight long remains. The weary traveler by midnight who asks for bread is really seeking the dawn. Our eternal message of hope is that dawn will come. Our slave foreparents realized this. They were never unmindful of the fact of midnight, for always there was the rawhide whip of the overseer and the auction block where families were torn asunder to remind them of its reality. When they thought of the agonizing darkness of midnight, they sang:

> Oh, nobody knows de trouble I've seen,
>   Glory hallelujah!
> Sometimes I'm up, sometimes I'm down,
>   Oh, yes, Lord,
> Sometimes I'm almost to de groun',
>   Oh, yes, Lord,
> Oh, nobody knows de trouble I've seen,
>   Glory hallelujah!

Encompassed by a staggering midnight but believing that morning would come, they sang:

> I'm so glad trouble don't last alway.
> O my Lord, O my Lord, what shall I do?

Their positive belief in the dawn was the growing edge of hope that kept the slaves faithful amid the most barren and tragic circumstances.

Faith in the dawn arises from the faith that God is good and just. When one believes this, he knows that the contradictions of life are neither final nor ultimate. He can walk through the dark night and the radiant conviction that all things work together for good for those that love God. Even the most starless midnight may herald the dawn of some great fulfillment.

ADDITIONAL SCRIPTURE READING:
Psalms 30:5; 126:5–6; Amos 4:13

Go to page 1035 for your next devotional reading.

1900   Present

and rested his hand on the wall
  only to have a snake bite him.
20 Will not the day of the LORD be
    darkness, not light—
  pitch-dark, without a ray of
    brightness?

21 "I hate, I despise your religious feasts;
  I cannot stand your assemblies.
22 Even though you bring me burnt
      offerings and grain offerings,
  I will not accept them.
  Though you bring choice fellowship
      offerings,[a]
  I will have no regard for them.
23 Away with the noise of your songs!
  I will not listen to the music of
    your harps.
24 But let justice roll on like a river,
  righteousness like a never-failing
    stream!

WE WILL NOT BE SATISFIED UNTIL JUSTICE ROLLS
DOWN LIKE WATERS, AND RIGHTEOUSNESS LIKE A
MIGHTY STREAM.   —*Martin Luther King, Jr.*

---

25 "Did you bring me sacrifices and
      offerings
  forty years in the desert, O house
    of Israel?
26 You have lifted up the shrine of your
      king,
  the pedestal of your idols,
  the star of your god[b]—
  which you made for yourselves.
27 Therefore I will send you into exile
    beyond Damascus,"
  says the LORD, whose name is God
    Almighty.

Woe to the Complacent

6 Woe to you who are
    complacent in Zion,
  and to you who feel secure on
    Mount Samaria,
  you notable men of the foremost
    nation,
  to whom the people of Israel come!
2 Go to Calneh and look at it;
  go from there to great Hamath,
  and then go down to Gath in
    Philistia.

Are they better off than your two
    kingdoms?
  Is their land larger than yours?
3 You put off the evil day
  and bring near a reign of terror.
4 You lie on beds inlaid with ivory
  and lounge on your couches.
  You dine on choice lambs
    and fattened calves.
5 You strum away on your harps like
      David
  and improvise on musical
    instruments.
6 You drink wine by the bowlful
  and use the finest lotions,
  but you do not grieve over the ruin
    of Joseph.
7 Therefore you will be among the first
    to go into exile;
  your feasting and lounging will
    end.

The LORD Abhors the Pride of Israel

8 The Sovereign LORD has sworn by
himself—the LORD God Almighty
declares:

  "I abhor the pride of Jacob
    and detest his fortresses;
  I will deliver up the city
    and everything in it."

9 If ten men are left in one house, they
too will die. 10 And if a relative who is to
burn the bodies comes to carry them out
of the house and asks anyone still hiding
there, "Is anyone with you?" and he says,
"No," then he will say, "Hush! We must
not mention the name of the LORD."

11 For the LORD has given the
      command,
  and he will smash the great house
    into pieces
  and the small house into bits.

12 Do horses run on the rocky crags?
  Does one plow there with oxen?
  But you have turned justice into
    poison
  and the fruit of righteousness into
    bitterness—
13 you who rejoice in the conquest of Lo
    Debar[c]

---

a 22 Traditionally *peace offerings*   *b 26* Or *lifted up Sakkuth your king / and Kaiwan your idols, / your star-gods;* Septuagint *lifted up the shrine of Molech / and the star of your god Rephan, / their idols*
c 13 Lo Debar *means* nothing.

and say, "Did we not take Karnaim^a by our own strength?"

¹⁴For the LORD God Almighty declares,
"I will stir up a nation against you,
  O house of Israel,
that will oppress you all the way
  from Lebo^b Hamath to the valley
  of the Arabah."

Locusts, Fire and a Plumb Line

7 This is what the Sovereign LORD showed me: He was preparing swarms of locusts after the king's share had been harvested and just as the second crop was coming up. ²When they had stripped the land clean, I cried out, "Sovereign LORD, forgive! How can Jacob survive? He is so small!"

³So the LORD relented.

"This will not happen," the LORD said.

⁴This is what the Sovereign LORD showed me: The Sovereign LORD was calling for judgment by fire; it dried up the great deep and devoured the land. ⁵Then I cried out, "Sovereign LORD, I beg you, stop! How can Jacob survive? He is so small!"

⁶So the LORD relented.

"This will not happen either," the Sovereign LORD said.

⁷This is what he showed me: The Lord was standing by a wall that had been built true to plumb, with a plumb line in his hand. ⁸And the LORD asked me, "What do you see, Amos?"

"A plumb line," I replied.

Then the Lord said, "Look, I am setting a plumb line among my people Israel; I will spare them no longer.

⁹"The high places of Isaac will be
  destroyed
and the sanctuaries of Israel will be
  ruined;
with my sword I will rise against
  the house of Jeroboam."

Amos and Amaziah

¹⁰Then Amaziah the priest of Bethel sent a message to Jeroboam king of Israel: "Amos is raising a conspiracy against you in the very heart of Israel. The land cannot bear all his words. ¹¹For this is what Amos is saying:

" 'Jeroboam will die by the sword,
  and Israel will surely go into exile,
  away from their native land.' "

¹²Then Amaziah said to Amos, "Get out, you seer! Go back to the land of Judah. Earn your bread there and do your prophesying there. ¹³Don't prophesy anymore at Bethel, because this is the king's sanctuary and the temple of the kingdom."

¹⁴Amos answered Amaziah, "I was neither a prophet nor a prophet's son, but I was a shepherd, and I also took care of sycamore-fig trees. ¹⁵But the LORD took me from tending the flock and said to me, 'Go, prophesy to my people Israel.' ¹⁶Now then, hear the word of the LORD. You say,

" 'Do not prophesy against Israel,
  and stop preaching against the
    house of Isaac.'

¹⁷"Therefore this is what the LORD says:

" 'Your wife will become a prostitute
    in the city,
  and your sons and daughters will
    fall by the sword.
Your land will be measured and
    divided up,
  and you yourself will die in a
    pagan^c country.
And Israel will certainly go into
    exile,
  away from their native land.' "

A Basket of Ripe Fruit

8 This is what the Sovereign LORD showed me: a basket of ripe fruit. ²"What do you see, Amos?" he asked.

"A basket of ripe fruit," I answered.

Then the LORD said to me, "The time is ripe for my people Israel; I will spare them no longer.

³"In that day," declares the Sovereign LORD, "the songs in the temple will turn

^a 13 *Karnaim* means *horns; horn* here symbolizes strength.   ^b 14 Or *from the entrance to*
^c 17 Hebrew *an unclean*

to wailing.*a* Many, many bodies—flung everywhere! Silence!"

4 Hear this, you who trample the needy
    and do away with the poor of the
    land,

5 saying,

"When will the New Moon be over
    that we may sell grain,
and the Sabbath be ended
    that we may market wheat?"—

a 3 Or "the temple singers will wail

FRIDAY

THE ENDS ARE SWALLOWED IN THE MEANS
Martin Luther King, Jr.

VERSE: Amos 8:4   **PASSAGE:** Amos 8:4–7

nly an irrelevant religion fails to be concerned about man's economic well-being. Religion at its best realizes that the soul is crushed as long as the body is tortured with hunger pangs and harrowed with the need for shelter. Jesus realized that we need food, clothing, shelter, and economic security. He said in clear and concise terms: "Your Father knows what you need" (Matthew 6:8). But Jesus knew that man was more than a dog to be satisfied by a few economic bones. He realized that the internal of a man's life is as significant as the external. So he added, "Seek first his kingdom and his righteousness, and all these things will be given to you as well" (v. 33). The tragedy of the rich man was that he sought the means first, and in the process the ends were swallowed in the means.

The richer this man became materially the poorer he became intellectually and spiritually. He may have been married, but he probably could not love his wife. It is possible that he gave her countless material gifts, but he could not give her that which she needed most, love and affection. He may have had children, but he probably did not appreciate them. He may have had the great books of the ages shelved neatly in his library, but he never read them. He may have had access to great music, but he did not listen. His eyes did not behold the majestic splendor of the skies. His ears were not attuned to the melodious sweetness of heavenly music. His mind was closed to the insights of poets, prophets, and philosophers. His title was justly merited—"You fool!"

ADDITIONAL SCRIPTURE READING:
Matthew 6:28–34; Luke 12:27–31

Go to page 1037 for your next devotional reading.

1900   Present

skimping the measure,
  boosting the price
  and cheating with dishonest scales,
6 buying the poor with silver
  and the needy for a pair of sandals,
  selling even the sweepings with
    the wheat.

7 The Lord has sworn by the Pride of
Jacob: "I will never forget anything they
have done.

8 "Will not the land tremble for this,
  and all who live in it mourn?
The whole land will rise like the
    Nile;
  it will be stirred up and then sink
  like the river of Egypt.

9 "In that day," declares the Sovereign
Lord,

"I will make the sun go down at
    noon
  and darken the earth in broad
    daylight.
10 I will turn your religious feasts into
    mourning
  and all your singing into weeping.
I will make all of you wear sackcloth
  and shave your heads.
I will make that time like mourning
    for an only son
  and the end of it like a bitter day.

11 "The days are coming," declares the
    Sovereign Lord,
  "when I will send a famine
    through the land—
not a famine of food or a thirst for
    water,
  but a famine of hearing the words
  of the Lord.
12 Men will stagger from sea to sea
  and wander from north to east,
searching for the word of the Lord,
  but they will not find it.

13 "In that day

"the lovely young women and strong
    young men
  will faint because of thirst.
14 They who swear by the shame^a of
    Samaria,

or say, 'As surely as your god lives,
    O Dan,'
or, 'As surely as the god^b of
    Beersheba lives'—
they will fall,
  never to rise again."

Israel to Be Destroyed

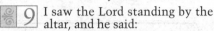 **9** I saw the Lord standing by the
altar, and he said:

"Strike the tops of the pillars
  so that the thresholds shake.
Bring them down on the heads of all
    the people;
  those who are left I will kill with
  the sword.
Not one will get away,
  none will escape.
2 Though they dig down to the depths
    of the grave,^c
  from there my hand will take
    them.
Though they climb up to the
    heavens,
  from there I will bring them down.
3 Though they hide themselves on the
    top of Carmel,
  there I will hunt them down and
  seize them.
Though they hide from me at the
    bottom of the sea,
  there I will command the serpent
  to bite them.
4 Though they are driven into exile by
    their enemies,
  there I will command the sword to
  slay them.
I will fix my eyes upon them
  for evil and not for good."

5 The Lord, the Lord Almighty,
  he who touches the earth and it
    melts,
  and all who live in it mourn—
the whole land rises like the Nile,
  then sinks like the river of Egypt—
6 he who builds his lofty palace^d in the
    heavens
  and sets its foundation^e on the
    earth,
who calls for the waters of the sea
  and pours them out over the face of
    the land—
  the Lord is his name.

---

^a 14 Or *by Ashima;* or *by the idol*   ^b 14 Or *power*   ^c 2 Hebrew *to Sheol*   ^d 6 The meaning of the
Hebrew for this phrase is uncertain.   ^e 6 The meaning of the Hebrew for this word is uncertain.

WEEKEND

WE GIVE THEE THANKS, O LORD
Horatius Bonar

VERSE: Matthew 26:26   **PASSAGE:** Matthew 26:26–30

or the bread and for the wine,
For the pledge that seals him mine,
For the words of love divine,
We give thee thanks, O Lord.

Only bread and only wine,
Yet to faith, the solemn sign
Of the heav'nly and divine!
We give thee thanks, O Lord.

For the words that turn our eye
To the cross of Calvary,
Bidding us in faith draw nigh,
We give thee thanks, O Lord . . .

For thy words in Spirit shown,
For thy will to us made known.
"Do ye this until I come,"
We give thee thanks, O Lord.

Till he come we take the bread,
Type of him on whom we feed,
Him who liveth and was dead!
We give thee thanks, O Lord.

Till he come we take the cup;
As we at his table sup,
Eye and heart are lifted up!
We give thee thanks, O Lord.

For that coming, here foreshown,
For that day to man unknown,
For the glory and the throne,
We give thee thanks, O Lord.

ADDITIONAL SCRIPTURE READING:
John 6:33–35; 1 Corinthians 11:26–29

Go to page 1040 for your next devotional reading.

1700   1900

7 "Are not you Israelites
   the same to me as the Cushites[a] ?"
      declares the LORD.
"Did I not bring Israel up from Egypt,
   the Philistines from Caphtor[b]
   and the Arameans from Kir?

8 "Surely the eyes of the Sovereign
      LORD
   are on the sinful kingdom.
I will destroy it
   from the face of the earth—
yet I will not totally destroy
   the house of Jacob,"
      declares the LORD.
9 "For I will give the command,
   and I will shake the house of Israel
      among all the nations
   as grain is shaken in a sieve,
      and not a pebble will reach the
         ground.
10 All the sinners among my people
   will die by the sword,
all those who say,
   'Disaster will not overtake or meet
      us.'

Israel's Restoration

11 "In that day I will restore
   David's fallen tent.
I will repair its broken places,
restore its ruins,
   and build it as it used to be,
12 so that they may possess the
      remnant of Edom
   and all the nations that bear my
      name,[c]"
         declares the LORD,
         who will do these things.

13 "The days are coming," declares the
LORD,

"when the reaper will be overtaken
      by the plowman
   and the planter by the one treading
      grapes.
New wine will drip from the
      mountains
   and flow from all the hills.
14 I will bring back my exiled[d] people
      Israel;
   they will rebuild the ruined cities
      and live in them.
They will plant vineyards and drink
      their wine;
   they will make gardens and eat
      their fruit.
15 I will plant Israel in their own land,
   never again to be uprooted
from the land I have given them,"
      says the LORD your God.

---

[a] 7 That is, people from the upper Nile region   [b] 7 That is, Crete   [c] 12 Hebrew; Septuagint *so that the remnant of men / and all the nations that bear my name may seek ⌐the Lord⌐*   [d] 14 Or *will restore the fortunes of my*

OBADIAH

O BADIAH'S PROPHECY CENTERS AROUND AN ANCIENT FEUD BETWEEN EDOM AND ISRAEL. AS DESCENDANTS OF ESAU, THE EDOMITES HELD A GRUDGE AGAINST ISRAEL BECAUSE JACOB HAD CHEATED THEIR ANCESTOR OUT OF HIS BIRTHRIGHT. OBADIAH PROPHESIES JUDGMENT AGAINST EDOM, REMINDING THE PEOPLE OF EDOM THAT GOD IS IN CONTROL OF THE WORLD. EDOM HERSELF WILL BE DESTROYED, BUT MOUNT ZION AND ISRAEL WILL BE DELIVERED, AND GOD'S KINGDOM WILL TRIUMPH.

---

¹The vision of Obadiah.

This is what the Sovereign Lord says about Edom—

We have heard a message from the
  Lord:
  An envoy was sent to the nations
    to say,
"Rise, and let us go against her for
    battle"—

² "See, I will make you small among
    the nations;
  you will be utterly despised.
³ The pride of your heart has deceived
    you,
  you who live in the clefts of the
    rocks*a*

and make your home on the
    heights,
  you who say to yourself,
  'Who can bring me down to the
    ground?'

⁴ Though you soar like the eagle
  and make your nest among the
    stars,
  from there I will bring you down,"
            declares the Lord.
⁵ "If thieves came to you,
  if robbers in the night—
  Oh, what a disaster awaits you—

---

a 3 Or *of Sela*

would they not steal only as much
as they wanted?
If grape pickers came to you,
would they not leave a few grapes?
6 But how Esau will be ransacked,
his hidden treasures pillaged!
7 All your allies will force you to the
border;
your friends will deceive and
overpower you;
those who eat your bread will set a
trap for you,*a*
but you will not detect it.

8 "In that day," declares the LORD,
"will I not destroy the wise men of
Edom,
men of understanding in the
mountains of Esau?

9 Your warriors, O Teman, will be
terrified,
and everyone in Esau's mountains
will be cut down in the slaughter.
10 Because of the violence against your
brother Jacob,
you will be covered with shame;
you will be destroyed forever.
11 On the day you stood aloof
while strangers carried off his
wealth
and foreigners entered his gates
and cast lots for Jerusalem,
you were like one of them.
12 You should not look down on your
brother
in the day of his misfortune,
nor rejoice over the people of Judah

a 7 The meaning of the Hebrew for this clause is uncertain.

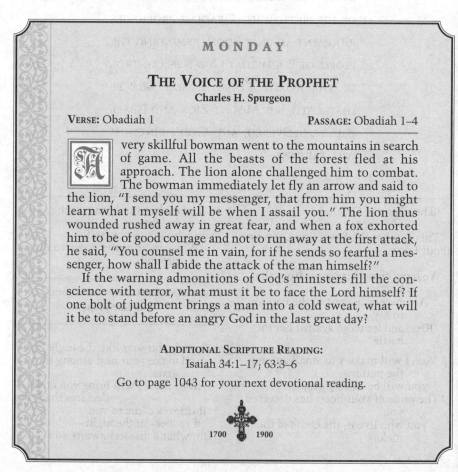

MONDAY

THE VOICE OF THE PROPHET
Charles H. Spurgeon

VERSE: Obadiah 1   **PASSAGE:** Obadiah 1–4

A very skillful bowman went to the mountains in search
of game. All the beasts of the forest fled at his
approach. The lion alone challenged him to combat.
The bowman immediately let fly an arrow and said to
the lion, "I send you my messenger, that from him you might
learn what I myself will be when I assail you." The lion thus
wounded rushed away in great fear, and when a fox exhorted
him to be of good courage and not to run away at the first attack,
he said, "You counsel me in vain, for if he sends so fearful a messenger, how shall I abide the attack of the man himself?"

If the warning admonitions of God's ministers fill the conscience with terror, what must it be to face the Lord himself? If
one bolt of judgment brings a man into a cold sweat, what will
it be to stand before an angry God in the last great day?

ADDITIONAL SCRIPTURE READING:
Isaiah 34:1–17; 63:3–6

Go to page 1043 for your next devotional reading.

1700   1900

in the day of their destruction,
nor boast so much
in the day of their trouble.
13 You should not march through the
gates of my people
in the day of their disaster,
nor look down on them in their
calamity
in the day of their disaster,
nor seize their wealth
in the day of their disaster.
14 You should not wait at the crossroads
to cut down their fugitives,
nor hand over their survivors
in the day of their trouble.

15 "The day of the LORD is near
for all nations.
As you have done, it will be done to
you;
your deeds will return upon your
own head.
16 Just as you drank on my holy hill,
so all the nations will drink
continually;
they will drink and drink
and be as if they had never been.
17 But on Mount Zion will be
deliverance;
it will be holy,
and the house of Jacob

will possess its inheritance.
18 The house of Jacob will be a fire
and the house of Joseph a flame;
the house of Esau will be stubble,
and they will set it on fire and
consume it.
There will be no survivors
from the house of Esau."
The LORD has spoken.

19 People from the Negev will occupy
the mountains of Esau,
and people from the foothills will
possess
the land of the Philistines.
They will occupy the fields of
Ephraim and Samaria,
and Benjamin will possess Gilead.
20 This company of Israelite exiles who
are in Canaan
will possess ⌊the land⌋ as far as
Zarephath;
the exiles from Jerusalem who are in
Sepharad
will possess the towns of the
Negev.
21 Deliverers will go up on[a] Mount
Zion
to govern the mountains of Esau.
And the kingdom will be the
LORD's.

---

a 21 Or from

JONAH

HEN GOD SENT HIM TO WARN THE PEOPLE OF NINEVEH TO REPENT, JONAH RAN IN THE OPPO-SITE DIRECTION. BUT GOD USED A RELUC-TANT PROPHET AS A VEHICLE OF HIS GRACE. AS YOU READ THIS BOOK, NOTE GOD'S GREAT COMPASSION FOR ALL PEOPLE AND HIS DESIRE FOR SINCERE REPENTANCE REGARD-LESS OF WHAT SOMEONE HAS DONE. AND THANK HIM FOR REACHING OUT TO YOU IN LOVE AND CALLING YOU TO TELL OTHERS ABOUT HIS GRACE FOR THEM.

Jonah Flees From the LORD

1 The word of the LORD came to Jonah son of Amittai: 2"Go to the great city of Nineveh and preach against it, because its wickedness has come up before me."

3But Jonah ran away from the LORD and headed for Tarshish. He went down to Joppa, where he found a ship bound for that port. After paying the fare, he went aboard and sailed for Tarshish to flee from the LORD.

4Then the LORD sent a great wind on the sea, and such a violent storm arose that the ship threatened to break up. 5All the sailors were afraid and each cried out to his own god. And they threw the cargo into the sea to lighten the ship.

But Jonah had gone below deck, where he lay down and fell into a deep sleep. 6The captain went to him and said, "How can you sleep? Get up and call on your god! Maybe he will take notice of us, and we will not perish."

7Then the sailors said to each other, "Come, let us cast lots to find out who is responsible for this calamity." They cast lots and the lot fell on Jonah.

8So they asked him, "Tell us, who is responsible for making all this trouble for us? What do you do? Where do you come from? What is your country? From what people are you?"

9He answered, "I am a Hebrew and I worship the LORD, the God of heaven, who made the sea and the land."

10This terrified them and they asked, "What have you done?" (They knew he was running away from the LORD, because he had already told them so.)

¹¹The sea was getting rougher and rougher. So they asked him, "What should we do to you to make the sea calm down for us?"

¹²"Pick me up and throw me into the sea," he replied, "and it will become calm. I know that it is my fault that this great storm has come upon you."

¹³Instead, the men did their best to row back to land. But they could not, for the sea grew even wilder than before. ¹⁴Then they cried to the LORD, "O LORD,

TUESDAY

KEPT SECURE IN OUR STRUGGLES
Julian of Norwich

VERSE: Jonah 1:3   **PASSAGE:** Jonah 1:1–3

n this life there is within us who are to be saved a surprising mixture of good and bad. We have our risen Lord; we have the wretchedness and mischief done by Adam's fall and death. Kept secure by Christ we are assured, by his touch of grace, of salvation; broken by Adam's fall, and in many ways by our own sins and sorrows, we are so darkened and blinded that we can hardly find any comfort. But in our heart we abide in God, and confidently trust to his mercy and grace—and this is his working in us. And of his goodness he opens the eye of our understanding so that we can see; sometimes it is less, sometimes more, according to our God-given ability to receive it. Now we are uplifted by the one; now we are allowed to fall into the other. And this fluctuating is so baffling that we are hard put to know where we stand, whether we are thinking of ourselves or of our fellow believers. It certainly is a marvelous mix up! But the one thing that matters is that we always say "Yes" to God whenever we experience him, and really do will to be with him, with all our heart and soul and strength. It is then that we hate and despise our evil inclinations, and all else that might make us sin, physically or spiritually. Yet, when this sweetness vanishes, we fall back into our blind state, and so into all sorts of distress and trouble. At such a time this is our strength—we know by faith that, through the virtue of Christ our guardian, we never really accept this situation; but, protesting against it, we hang on and pray through all this trouble and grief, until such time as once again God will reveal himself to us.

ADDITIONAL SCRIPTURE READING:
Genesis 3:8–9; Psalm 139:7–12

Go to page 1045 for your next devotional reading.

500   1500

please do not let us die for taking this man's life. Do not hold us accountable for killing an innocent man, for you, O LORD, have done as you pleased." ¹⁵Then they took Jonah and threw him overboard, and the raging sea grew calm. ¹⁶At this the men greatly feared the LORD, and they offered a sacrifice to the LORD and made vows to him.

¹⁷But the LORD provided a great fish to swallow Jonah, and Jonah was inside the fish three days and three nights.

Jonah's Prayer

2 From inside the fish Jonah prayed to the LORD his God. ²He said:

"In my distress I called to the LORD,
    and he answered me.
From the depths of the grave[a] I called
        for help,
    and you listened to my cry.
³ You hurled me into the deep,
        into the very heart of the seas,
        and the currents swirled about me;
    all your waves and breakers
        swept over me.
⁴ I said, 'I have been banished
        from your sight;
    yet I will look again
        toward your holy temple.'
⁵ The engulfing waters threatened me,[b]
        the deep surrounded me;
    seaweed was wrapped around my
        head.
⁶ To the roots of the mountains I sank
        down;
    the earth beneath barred me in
        forever.
But you brought my life up from the
        pit,
    O LORD my God.

⁷ "When my life was ebbing away,
    I remembered you, LORD,
and my prayer rose to you,
    to your holy temple.

⁸ "Those who cling to worthless idols
    forfeit the grace that could be
        theirs.
⁹ But I, with a song of thanksgiving,
    will sacrifice to you.
What I have vowed I will make good.
    Salvation comes from the LORD."

¹⁰And the LORD commanded the fish, and it vomited Jonah onto dry land.

Jonah Goes to Nineveh

3 Then the word of the LORD came to Jonah a second time: ²"Go to the great city of Nineveh and proclaim to it the message I give you."

³Jonah obeyed the word of the LORD and went to Nineveh. Now Nineveh was a very important city—a visit required three days. ⁴On the first day, Jonah started into the city. He proclaimed: "Forty more days and Nineveh will be overturned." ⁵The Ninevites believed God. They declared a fast, and all of them, from the greatest to the least, put on sackcloth.

⁶When the news reached the king of Nineveh, he rose from his throne, took off his royal robes, covered himself with sackcloth and sat down in the dust. ⁷Then he issued a proclamation in Nineveh:

"By the decree of the king and his nobles:

Do not let any man or beast, herd or flock, taste anything; do not let them eat or drink. ⁸But let man and beast be covered with sackcloth. Let everyone call urgently on God. Let them give up their evil ways and their violence. ⁹Who knows? God may yet relent and with compassion turn from his fierce anger so that we will not perish."

¹⁰When God saw what they did and how they turned from their evil ways, he had compassion and did not bring upon them the destruction he had threatened.

MAN MAY DISMISS COMPASSION FROM HIS HEART,
BUT GOD WILL NEVER.   —*William Cowper*

Jonah's Anger at the LORD's Compassion

4 But Jonah was greatly displeased and became angry. ²He prayed to the LORD, "O LORD, is this not what I said when I was still at home? That is why I was so quick to flee to Tar-

---

a 2 Hebrew *Sheol*   *b 5* Or *waters were at my throat*

shish. I knew that you are a gracious and compassionate God, slow to anger and abounding in love, a God who relents from sending calamity. ³Now, O LORD, take away my life, for it is better for me to die than to live."

⁴But the LORD replied, "Have you any right to be angry?"

⁵Jonah went out and sat down at a place east of the city. There he made himself a shelter, sat in its shade and waited to see what would happen to the city. ⁶Then the LORD God provided a vine and made it grow up over Jonah to give shade for his head to ease his discomfort, and Jonah was very happy about the vine. ⁷But at dawn the next day God provided a worm, which

---

ALWAYS PRAY
Sojourner Truth

VERSE: Jonah 2:7   **PASSAGE:** Jonah 2:1–9

sabella avers that, in her darkest hours, she had no fear of any worse hell than the one she then carried in her bosom; though it had ever been pictured to her in its deepest colors, and threatened her as a reward for all her misdemeanors. Her vileness and God's holiness and all pervading presence, which filled immensity, and threatened her with instant annihilation, composed the burden of her vision of terror. Her faith in prayer is equal to her faith in the love of Jesus. Her language is, "Let others say what they will of the efficacy of prayer, *I* believe in it, and *I* shall pray. Thank God! Yes, *I shall always pray*," she exclaims, putting her hands together with the greatest enthusiasm.

For some time subsequent to the happy change we have spoken of, Isabella's prayers partook largely of their former character; and while, in deep affliction, she labored for the recovery of her son, she prayed with constancy and fervor; and the following may be taken as a specimen:—"Oh, God, you know how much I am distressed, for I have told you again and again. Now, God, help me get my son. If you were in trouble, as I am, and I could help you, as you can me, think I wouldn't do it? Yes, God, you *know* I would do it. Oh, God, you know I have no money, but you can make the people do for me, and you must make the people do for me. I will never give you peace till you do, God. Oh, God, make the people hear me—don't let them turn me off, without hearing and helping me."

ADDITIONAL SCRIPTURE READING:
2 Chronicles 20:27; Psalm 18:6; Luke 18:1–8

Go to page 1053 for your next devotional reading.

1700   1900

chewed the vine so that it withered. ⁸When the sun rose, God provided a scorching east wind, and the sun blazed on Jonah's head so that he grew faint. He wanted to die, and said, "It would be better for me to die than to live."

⁹But God said to Jonah, "Do you have a right to be angry about the vine?"

"I do," he said. "I am angry enough to die."

¹⁰But the LORD said, "You have been concerned about this vine, though you did not tend it or make it grow. It sprang up overnight and died overnight. ¹¹But Nineveh has more than a hundred and twenty thousand people who cannot tell their right hand from their left, and many cattle as well. Should I not be concerned about that great city?"

MICAH

T HE PROPHET MICAH WROTE TO THE
PEOPLE OF JUDAH TO WARN THEM
THAT GOD'S JUDGMENT WAS NEAR
BECAUSE THEY HAD REJECTED GOD AND HIS
LAW. HIS MESSAGE ALTERNATED BETWEEN
ORACLES OF DOOM AND ORACLES OF HOPE,
STRESSING THAT GOD HATES IDOLATRY,
INJUSTICE, REBELLION AND EMPTY RITUALISM,
BUT HE DELIGHTS IN FORGIVING THOSE WHO
RETURN TO HIM. AS YOU READ THIS BOOK,
TAKE COMFORT THAT GOD OFFERS HOPE FOR
THOSE WHO REMAIN FAITHFUL TO HIM.

1 The word of the LORD that
came to Micah of Moresheth
during the reigns of Jotham, Ahaz and
Hezekiah, kings of Judah—the vision he
saw concerning Samaria and Jerusalem.

2 Hear, O peoples, all of you,
    listen, O earth and all who are in
    it,
  that the Sovereign LORD may witness
    against you,
    the Lord from his holy temple.

Judgment Against Samaria and Jerusalem

3 Look! The LORD is coming from his
    dwelling place;
  he comes down and treads the high
    places of the earth.
4 The mountains melt beneath him

and the valleys split apart,
  like wax before the fire,
    like water rushing down a slope.
5 All this is because of Jacob's
    transgression,
  because of the sins of the house of
    Israel.
  What is Jacob's transgression?
    Is it not Samaria?
  What is Judah's high place?
    Is it not Jerusalem?

6 "Therefore I will make Samaria a
    heap of rubble,
  a place for planting vineyards.
  I will pour her stones into the valley
    and lay bare her foundations.
7 All her idols will be broken to pieces;
  all her temple gifts will be burned
    with fire;
  I will destroy all her images.

Since she gathered her gifts from the
wages of prostitutes,
as the wages of prostitutes they
will again be used."

Weeping and Mourning

8 Because of this I will weep and wail;
I will go about barefoot and naked.
I will howl like a jackal
and moan like an owl.
9 For her wound is incurable;
it has come to Judah.
It*a* has reached the very gate of my
people,
even to Jerusalem itself.
10 Tell it not in Gath*b*;
weep not at all.*c*
In Beth Ophrah*d*
roll in the dust.
11 Pass on in nakedness and shame,
you who live in Shaphir.*e*
Those who live in Zaanan*f*
will not come out.
Beth Ezel is in mourning;
its protection is taken from you.
12 Those who live in Maroth*g* writhe in
pain,
waiting for relief,
because disaster has come from the
LORD,
even to the gate of Jerusalem.
13 You who live in Lachish,*h*
harness the team to the chariot.
You were the beginning of sin
to the Daughter of Zion,
for the transgressions of Israel
were found in you.
14 Therefore you will give parting gifts
to Moresheth Gath.
The town of Aczib*i* will prove
deceptive
to the kings of Israel.
15 I will bring a conqueror against you
who live in Mareshah.*j*
He who is the glory of Israel
will come to Adullam.
16 Shave your heads in mourning
for the children in whom you
delight;
make yourselves as bald as the
vulture,
for they will go from you into exile.

Man's Plans and God's

2 Woe to those who plan iniquity,
to those who plot evil on their
beds!
At morning's light they carry it out
because it is in their power to do it.
2 They covet fields and seize them,
and houses, and take them.
They defraud a man of his home,
a fellowman of his inheritance.

3 Therefore, the LORD says:

"I am planning disaster against this
people,
from which you cannot save
yourselves.
You will no longer walk proudly,
for it will be a time of calamity.
4 In that day men will ridicule you;
they will taunt you with this
mournful song:
'We are utterly ruined;
my people's possession is divided
up.
He takes it from me!
He assigns our fields to traitors.' "

5 Therefore you will have no one in the
assembly of the LORD
to divide the land by lot.

False Prophets

6 "Do not prophesy," their prophets
say.
"Do not prophesy about these
things;
disgrace will not overtake us."
7 Should it be said, O house of Jacob:
"Is the Spirit of the LORD angry?
Does he do such things?"

"Do not my words do good
to him whose ways are upright?
8 Lately my people have risen up
like an enemy.
You strip off the rich robe
from those who pass by without a
care,
like men returning from battle.
9 You drive the women of my people
from their pleasant homes.

---

a 9 Or *He*   *b 10 Gath* sounds like the Hebrew for *tell.*   *c 10* Hebrew; Septuagint may suggest *not in
Acco.* The Hebrew for *in Acco* sounds like the Hebrew for *weep.*   *d 10 Beth Ophrah* means *house of
dust.*   *e 11 Shaphir* means *pleasant.*   *f 11 Zaanan* sounds like the Hebrew for *come out.*
g 12 Maroth sounds like the Hebrew for *bitter.*   *h 13 Lachish* sounds like the Hebrew for *team.*
i 14 Aczib means *deception.*   *j 15 Mareshah* sounds like the Hebrew for *conqueror.*

You take away my blessing
  from their children forever.
10 Get up, go away!
  For this is not your resting place,
because it is defiled,
  it is ruined, beyond all remedy.
11 If a liar and deceiver comes and says,
  'I will prophesy for you plenty of
    wine and beer,'
  he would be just the prophet for
    this people!

Deliverance Promised

12 "I will surely gather all of you,
  O Jacob;
  I will surely bring together the
    remnant of Israel.
I will bring them together like sheep
    in a pen,
  like a flock in its pasture;
  the place will throng with people.
13 One who breaks open the way will go
    up before them;
  they will break through the gate
    and go out.
Their king will pass through before
    them,
  the LORD at their head."

Leaders and Prophets Rebuked

3 Then I said,

"Listen, you leaders of Jacob,
  you rulers of the house of Israel.
Should you not know justice,
2   you who hate good and love evil;
who tear the skin from my people
  and the flesh from their bones;
3 who eat my people's flesh,
  strip off their skin
  and break their bones in pieces;
who chop them up like meat for the
    pan,
  like flesh for the pot?"

4 Then they will cry out to the LORD,
  but he will not answer them.
At that time he will hide his face
    from them
  because of the evil they have done.

5 This is what the LORD says:

"As for the prophets
  who lead my people astray,
if one feeds them,
  they proclaim 'peace';

if he does not,
  they prepare to wage war against
    him.
6 Therefore night will come over you,
  without visions,
  and darkness, without divination.
The sun will set for the prophets,
  and the day will go dark for them.
7 The seers will be ashamed
  and the diviners disgraced.
They will all cover their faces
  because there is no answer from
    God."

8 But as for me, I am filled with power,
  with the Spirit of the LORD,
  and with justice and might,
to declare to Jacob his transgression,
  to Israel his sin.
9 Hear this, you leaders of the house of
    Jacob,
  you rulers of the house of Israel,
who despise justice
  and distort all that is right;
10 who build Zion with bloodshed,
  and Jerusalem with wickedness.
11 Her leaders judge for a bribe,
  her priests teach for a price,
  and her prophets tell fortunes for
    money.
Yet they lean upon the LORD and say,
  "Is not the LORD among us?
  No disaster will come upon us."
12 Therefore because of you,
  Zion will be plowed like a field,
Jerusalem will become a heap of
    rubble,
  the temple hill a mound overgrown
    with thickets.

The Mountain of the LORD

4 In the last days

the mountain of the LORD's temple
    will be established
  as chief among the mountains;
it will be raised above the hills,
  and peoples will stream to it.

2 Many nations will come and say,

"Come, let us go up to the mountain
    of the LORD,
  to the house of the God of Jacob.
He will teach us his ways,
  so that we may walk in his paths."
The law will go out from Zion,

the word of the LORD from
  Jerusalem.
³ He will judge between many peoples
  and will settle disputes for strong
    nations far and wide.
They will beat their swords into
  plowshares
  and their spears into pruning
    hooks.
Nation will not take up sword
  against nation,
  nor will they train for war
    anymore.
⁴ Every man will sit under his own
  vine
  and under his own fig tree,
and no one will make them afraid,
  for the LORD Almighty has spoken.
⁵ All the nations may walk
  in the name of their gods;
we will walk in the name of the LORD
  our God for ever and ever.

The LORD's Plan

⁶ "In that day," declares the LORD,

"I will gather the lame;
  I will assemble the exiles
  and those I have brought to grief.
⁷ I will make the lame a remnant,
  those driven away a strong nation.
The LORD will rule over them in
    Mount Zion
  from that day and forever.
⁸ As for you, O watchtower of the flock,
  O stronghold*ᵃ* of the Daughter of
    Zion,
the former dominion will be restored
  to you;
  kingship will come to the
    Daughter of Jerusalem."

⁹ Why do you now cry aloud—
  have you no king?
Has your counselor perished,
  that pain seizes you like that of a
    woman in labor?
¹⁰ Writhe in agony, O Daughter of Zion,
  like a woman in labor,
for now you must leave the city
  to camp in the open field.
You will go to Babylon;
  there you will be rescued.
There the LORD will redeem you
  out of the hand of your enemies.

¹¹ But now many nations
  are gathered against you.
They say, "Let her be defiled,
  let our eyes gloat over Zion!"
¹² But they do not know
  the thoughts of the LORD;
they do not understand his plan,
  he who gathers them like sheaves
    to the threshing floor.
¹³ "Rise and thresh, O Daughter of Zion,
  for I will give you horns of iron;
I will give you hoofs of bronze
  and you will break to pieces many
    nations."

You will devote their ill-gotten gains
  to the LORD,
  their wealth to the Lord of all the
    earth.

A Promised Ruler From Bethlehem

5 Marshal your troops, O city of
  troops,*ᵇ*
for a siege is laid against us.
They will strike Israel's ruler
  on the cheek with a rod.

² "But you, Bethlehem Ephrathah,
  though you are small among the
    clans*ᶜ* of Judah,
out of you will come for me
  one who will be ruler over Israel,
whose origins*ᵈ* are from of old,
  from ancient times.*ᵉ* "

³ Therefore Israel will be abandoned
  until the time when she who is in
    labor gives birth
and the rest of his brothers return
  to join the Israelites.

⁴ He will stand and shepherd his flock
  in the strength of the LORD,
  in the majesty of the name of the
    LORD his God.
And they will live securely, for then
  his greatness
  will reach to the ends of the earth.
⁵   And he will be their peace.

Deliverance and Destruction

When the Assyrian invades our land
  and marches through our fortresses,
we will raise against him seven
  shepherds,
  even eight leaders of men.

ᵃ 8 Or *hill*   *ᵇ* 1 Or *Strengthen your walls, O walled city*   *ᶜ* 2 Or *rulers*   *ᵈ* 2 Hebrew *goings out*
ᵉ 2 Or *from days of eternity*

6 They will rule*a* the land of Assyria
    with the sword,
  the land of Nimrod with drawn
    sword.*b*
He will deliver us from the Assyrian
  when he invades our land
  and marches into our borders.

7 The remnant of Jacob will be
  in the midst of many peoples
like dew from the LORD,
  like showers on the grass,
which do not wait for man
  or linger for mankind.

8 The remnant of Jacob will be among
    the nations,
  in the midst of many peoples,
like a lion among the beasts of the
    forest,
  like a young lion among flocks of
    sheep,
which mauls and mangles as it goes,
  and no one can rescue.

9 Your hand will be lifted up in
    triumph over your enemies,
  and all your foes will be destroyed.

10 "In that day," declares the LORD,

"I will destroy your horses from
    among you
  and demolish your chariots.
11 I will destroy the cities of your land
  and tear down all your strongholds.
12 I will destroy your witchcraft
  and you will no longer cast spells.
13 I will destroy your carved images
  and your sacred stones from among
    you;
you will no longer bow down
  to the work of your hands.
14 I will uproot from among you your
    Asherah poles*c*
  and demolish your cities.
15 I will take vengeance in anger and
    wrath
  upon the nations that have not
    obeyed me."

The LORD's Case Against Israel

6 Listen to what the LORD says:

"Stand up, plead your case before the
  mountains;

let the hills hear what you have to
  say.
2 Hear, O mountains, the LORD's
    accusation;
  listen, you everlasting foundations
    of the earth.
For the LORD has a case against his
    people;
  he is lodging a charge against Israel.

3 "My people, what have I done to
    you?
  How have I burdened you? Answer
    me.
4 I brought you up out of Egypt
  and redeemed you from the land of
    slavery.
I sent Moses to lead you,
  also Aaron and Miriam.
5 My people, remember
  what Balak king of Moab
    counseled
and what Balaam son of Beor
  answered.
Remember ˻your journey˼ from
    Shittim to Gilgal,
  that you may know the righteous
    acts of the LORD."

6 With what shall I come before the
    LORD
  and bow down before the exalted
    God?
Shall I come before him with burnt
    offerings,
  with calves a year old?
7 Will the LORD be pleased with
    thousands of rams,
  with ten thousand rivers of oil?
Shall I offer my firstborn for my
    transgression,
  the fruit of my body for the sin of
    my soul?
8 He has showed you, O man, what is
    good.
  And what does the LORD require of
    you?
To act justly and to love mercy
  and to walk humbly with your
    God.

Israel's Guilt and Punishment

9 Listen! The LORD is calling to the
    city—
  and to fear your name is wisdom—

---

a 6 Or *crush*   *b 6* Or *Nimrod in its gates*   *c 14* That is, symbols of the goddess Asherah

"Heed the rod and the One who
    appointed it.*a*
10 Am I still to forget, O wicked house,
    your ill-gotten treasures
and the short ephah,*b* which is
    accursed?
11 Shall I acquit a man with dishonest
    scales,
    with a bag of false weights?
12 Her rich men are violent;
    her people are liars
and their tongues speak deceitfully.
13 Therefore, I have begun to destroy
    you,
    to ruin you because of your sins.
14 You will eat but not be satisfied;
    your stomach will still be empty.*c*
You will store up but save nothing,
    because what you save I will give
    to the sword.
15 You will plant but not harvest;
    you will press olives but not use
    the oil on yourselves,
    you will crush grapes but not drink
    the wine.
16 You have observed the statutes of
    Omri
and all the practices of Ahab's
    house,
and you have followed their
    traditions.
Therefore I will give you over to ruin
and your people to derision;
    you will bear the scorn of the
    nations.*d* "

Israel's Misery

7 What misery is mine!
    I am like one who gathers
    summer fruit
    at the gleaning of the vineyard;
there is no cluster of grapes to eat,
    none of the early figs that I crave.
2 The godly have been swept from the
    land;
    not one upright man remains.
All men lie in wait to shed blood;
    each hunts his brother with a net.
3 Both hands are skilled in doing evil;
    the ruler demands gifts,
    the judge accepts bribes,
    the powerful dictate what they
    desire—

    they all conspire together.
4 The best of them is like a brier,
    the most upright worse than a
    thorn hedge.
The day of your watchmen has come,
    the day God visits you.
Now is the time of their confusion.
5 Do not trust a neighbor;
    put no confidence in a friend.
Even with her who lies in your
    embrace
    be careful of your words.
6 For a son dishonors his father,
    a daughter rises up against her
    mother,
    a daughter-in-law against her
    mother-in-law—
a man's enemies are the members
    of his own household.

7 But as for me, I watch in hope for the
    Lord,
I wait for God my Savior;
    my God will hear me.

Israel Will Rise

8 Do not gloat over me, my enemy!
    Though I have fallen, I will rise.
Though I sit in darkness,
    the Lord will be my light.
9 Because I have sinned against him,
    I will bear the Lord's wrath,
until he pleads my case
    and establishes my right.
He will bring me out into the light;
    I will see his righteousness.

MOST HIGH, GLORIOUS GOD, ENLIGHTEN THE
DARKNESS OF MY HEART AND GIVE ME, LORD, A
CORRECT FAITH, A CERTAIN HOPE, A PERFECT
CHARITY, SENSE AND KNOWLEDGE, SO THAT I MAY
CARRY OUT YOUR HOLY AND TRUE COMMAND.

    —Francis of Assisi

---

10 Then my enemy will see it
    and will be covered with shame,
she who said to me,
    "Where is the Lord your God?"
My eyes will see her downfall;
    even now she will be trampled
    underfoot
    like mire in the streets.

a 9 The meaning of the Hebrew for this line is uncertain.   *b 10* An ephah was a dry measure.
c 14 The meaning of the Hebrew for this word is uncertain.   *d 16* Septuagint; Hebrew *scorn due my*
people

11 The day for building your walls will
        come,
    the day for extending your
        boundaries.
12 In that day people will come to you
    from Assyria and the cities of Egypt,

even from Egypt to the Euphrates
    and from sea to sea
    and from mountain to mountain.
13 The earth will become desolate
    because of its inhabitants,
    as the result of their deeds.

THURSDAY

LOOK TO THE LORD
Mrs. Charles E. Cowman

VERSE: Micah 7:7   PASSAGE: Micah 7:1–7

everal years ago while visiting certain of the Northern European countries, it was necessary for me to cross the North Sea in a large ocean liner. During the first days of the voyage we sped along over calm seas, but suddenly we were overtaken by a frightening tempest. The waves were like great mountains, and we were lifted to their heights. The great ship rocked and rolled, creaked and groaned. The faces of the passengers were blanched white with fear. Even the little ones clung to their mothers, sensing the nearness of danger—the very air was surcharged by an ominous foreboding of impending destruction. When it seemed that surely the ship had endured to the very limit, a man appeared on the scene. There was no trace of anxiety or concern on his face. His presence radiated calmness, rest and peace. With a voice full of gentleness he assured us, "all's well," and our fears disappeared.

Who was that man? The captain. He had taken that vessel through many a long voyage, plowed rough seas, met terrible storms, and had always arrived safely into port . . .

What have we to fear? . . . Is not our Captain on board? . . . With Christ in the vessel we smile at the storm.

Yes, one whose faith is continually stimulated by *the upward look* gives no ground to the attempted encroachment of despair. No matter how great the trouble or how dark the outlook, a quick lifting of the heart to God in a moment of real actual faith in him will completely alter any situation and turn the darkness of midnight into glorious sunrise.

ADDITIONAL SCRIPTURE READING:
Psalms 31:5; 37:5; Isaiah 65:24

Go to page 1056 for your next devotional reading.

1900   Present

Prayer and Praise

14 Shepherd your people with your staff,
   the flock of your inheritance,
which lives by itself in a forest,
   in fertile pasturelands.*a*
Let them feed in Bashan and Gilead
   as in days long ago.

15 "As in the days when you came out
      of Egypt,
   I will show them my wonders."

16 Nations will see and be ashamed,
   deprived of all their power.
They will lay their hands on their
      mouths
   and their ears will become deaf.
17 They will lick dust like a snake,
   like creatures that crawl on the
      ground.
They will come trembling out of
   their dens;
they will turn in fear to the LORD
      our God
   and will be afraid of you.
18 Who is a God like you,
   who pardons sin and forgives the
      transgression
of the remnant of his inheritance?
You do not stay angry forever
   but delight to show mercy.
19 You will again have compassion on
   us;
you will tread our sins underfoot
   and hurl all our iniquities into the
      depths of the sea.
20 You will be true to Jacob,
   and show mercy to Abraham,
as you pledged on oath to our fathers
   in days long ago.

---

a 14 Or *in the middle of Carmel*

NAHUM

AHUM (MEANING "COMFORT")
PROPHESIES AGAINST THE CRUEL
NATION OF ASSYRIA. HE REMINDS
THE PEOPLE OF JUDAH THAT GOD IS IN CON-
TROL OF HISTORY AND WILL NOT ALLOW EVIL
TO PREVAIL FOREVER. NAHUM PROPHESIED
THAT NINEVEH WOULD FALL, WHICH DID
HAPPEN IN 612 B.C. KINGDOMS BUILT ON
WICKEDNESS AND TYRANNY MUST EVENTU-
ALLY FALL, AS ASSYRIA DID. AS YOU READ
THIS BOOK, TAKE COMFORT THAT GOD IS
THE LORD OF HISTORY AND HE WILL HAVE
HIS WAY.

1 An oracle concerning Nineveh. The book of the vision of Nahum the Elkoshite.

The LORD's Anger Against Nineveh

2 The LORD is a jealous and avenging
  God;
    the LORD takes vengeance and is
    filled with wrath.
  The LORD takes vengeance on his
    foes
    and maintains his wrath against
    his enemies.
3 The LORD is slow to anger and great
    in power;
    the LORD will not leave the guilty
    unpunished.
  His way is in the whirlwind and the
    storm,
    and clouds are the dust of his feet.
4 He rebukes the sea and dries it up;
    he makes all the rivers run dry.
  Bashan and Carmel wither
    and the blossoms of Lebanon fade.
5 The mountains quake before him
    and the hills melt away.
  The earth trembles at his presence,
    the world and all who live in it.
6 Who can withstand his indignation?
    Who can endure his fierce anger?
  His wrath is poured out like fire;
    the rocks are shattered before
    him.

7 The LORD is good,
    a refuge in times of trouble.
  He cares for those who trust in him,
8   but with an overwhelming flood
  he will make an end of ˻Nineveh˼;
    he will pursue his foes into
    darkness.

TRUST IN THE GOODNESS OF GOD
François Fénelon

VERSE: Nahum 1:7   **PASSAGE:** Nahum 1:2–8

he best and highest use of your mind is to learn to distrust yourself, to renounce your own will, to submit to the will of God, and to become as a little child. It is not of doing difficult things that I speak, but of performing the most common actions with your heart fixed on God, and as one who is accomplishing the end of his being. You will act as others do, except that you will never sin . . . You will be moderate at table, moderate in speaking, moderate in expense, moderate in judging, moderate in your diversions; sober even in your wisdom and foresight. It is this universal sobriety in the use of the best things that is taught us by the true love of God. We are neither austere, nor fretful, nor scrupulous, but have within ourselves a principle of love that enlarges the heart and sheds a gentle influence upon everything; that, without constraint or effort, inspires a delicate apprehension lest we should displease God; and that arrests us if we are tempted to do wrong.

In this state we suffer, as other people do, from fatigue, embarrassments, misfortunes, bodily infirmities, trials from ourselves and trials from others, temptations, disgusts, and sometimes discouragements. But though our crosses are the same with those of the rest of the world, our motives for supporting them are very different. We have learned from Jesus Christ how to endure. This can purify, this can detach us from self and renew the spirit of our minds. We see God in everything, but we have the clearest vision of him in suffering and in our humiliations . . .

Put your trust not in your resolutions or your own strength, but in the goodness of God, who has loved you when you thought not of him, and before you could love him.

ADDITIONAL SCRIPTURE READING:
2 Chronicles 32:8–11; Jeremiah 17:7–8

Go to page 1058 for your next devotional reading.

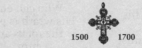

1500   1700

⁹ Whatever they plot against the LORD
    heᵃ will bring to an end;
    trouble will not come a second
      time.
¹⁰ They will be entangled among thorns
    and drunk from their wine;
    they will be consumed like dry
      stubble.ᵇ
¹¹ From you, ⌞O Nineveh,⌟ has one
    come forth
    who plots evil against the LORD
    and counsels wickedness.

¹² This is what the LORD says:

"Although they have allies and are
    numerous,
    they will be cut off and pass away.
Although I have afflicted you,
    ⌞O Judah,⌟
    I will afflict you no more.
¹³ Now I will break their yoke from
    your neck
    and tear your shackles away."

¹⁴ The LORD has given a command
    concerning you, ⌞Nineveh⌟:
    "You will have no descendants to
      bear your name.
I will destroy the carved images and
    cast idols
    that are in the temple of your gods.
I will prepare your grave,
    for you are vile."

¹⁵ Look, there on the mountains,
    the feet of one who brings good
      news,
    who proclaims peace!
Celebrate your festivals, O Judah,
    and fulfill your vows.
No more will the wicked invade you;
    they will be completely destroyed.

Nineveh to Fall

2 An attacker advances against
    you, ⌞Nineveh⌟.
    Guard the fortress,
    watch the road,
    brace yourselves,
    marshal all your strength!

² The LORD will restore the splendor of
    Jacob
    like the splendor of Israel,

though destroyers have laid them
    waste
    and have ruined their vines.

³ The shields of his soldiers are red;
    the warriors are clad in scarlet.
The metal on the chariots flashes
    on the day they are made ready;
    the spears of pine are brandished.ᶜ
⁴ The chariots storm through the
    streets,
    rushing back and forth through the
      squares.
They look like flaming torches;
    they dart about like lightning.

⁵ He summons his picked troops,
    yet they stumble on their way.
They dash to the city wall;
    the protective shield is put in
      place.
⁶ The river gates are thrown open
    and the palace collapses.
⁷ It is decreedᵈ that ⌞the city⌟
    be exiled and carried away.
Its slave girls moan like doves
    and beat upon their breasts.
⁸ Nineveh is like a pool,
    and its water is draining away.
"Stop! Stop!" they cry,
    but no one turns back.
⁹ Plunder the silver!
    Plunder the gold!
The supply is endless,
    the wealth from all its treasures!
¹⁰ She is pillaged, plundered, stripped!
    Hearts melt, knees give way,
    bodies tremble, every face grows
      pale.

¹¹ Where now is the lions' den,
    the place where they fed their
      young,
    where the lion and lioness went,
    and the cubs, with nothing to fear?
¹² The lion killed enough for his cubs
    and strangled the prey for his mate,
filling his lairs with the kill
    and his dens with the prey.

¹³ "I am against you,"
    declares the LORD Almighty.
"I will burn up your chariots in
    smoke,

ᵃ 9 Or *What do you foes plot against the LORD? / He*
uncertain.   ᶜ 3 Hebrew; Septuagint and Syriac / *the horsemen rush to and fro*   ᵈ 7 The meaning of
the Hebrew for this word is uncertain.   ᵇ 10 The meaning of the Hebrew for this verse is

WEEKEND

BEAUTIFUL FEET
Frances Ridley Havergal

VERSE: Nahum 1:15   **PASSAGE:** Nahum 1:14–15

ur Lord has many uses for what is kept for himself. How beautiful are the feet of them that bring glad tidings of good things! That is the best use of all, and I expect the angels think those feet beautiful, even if they are cased in muddy boots or galoshes . . .

If we want to have these beautiful feet, we must have the tidings ready which they are to bear. Let us ask him to keep our hearts so freshly full of his good news of salvation that our mouths may speak out of their abundance. If the clouds be full of rain, they empty themselves upon the earth. May we be so filled with the Spirit that we may have much to pour out for others.

Besides the privilege of carrying water from the wells of salvation, there are plenty of cups of cold water to be carried in all directions; not to the poor only—ministries of love are often as much needed by a rich friend. But the feet must be kept for these; they will be too tired for them if they are tired out for self-pleasing. In such services we are treading in the blessed steps of Christ, who went about doing good.

ADDITIONAL SCRIPTURE READING:
Isaiah 52:7; Romans 10:15

Go to page 1062 for your next devotional reading.

1700   1900

and the sword will devour your
   young lions.
I will leave you no prey on the earth.
The voices of your messengers
   will no longer be heard."

Woe to Nineveh

3 Woe to the city of blood,
      full of lies,
   full of plunder,
      never without victims!
2 The crack of whips,
      the clatter of wheels,
   galloping horses
      and jolting chariots!
3 Charging cavalry,
      flashing swords
      and glittering spears!
   Many casualties,
      piles of dead,
   bodies without number,
      people stumbling over the corpses—
4 all because of the wanton lust of a
      harlot,
      alluring, the mistress of sorceries,
   who enslaved nations by her
      prostitution
      and peoples by her witchcraft.

5 "I am against you," declares the
      LORD Almighty.
   "I will lift your skirts over your
      face.
   I will show the nations your
      nakedness
      and the kingdoms your shame.
6 I will pelt you with filth,
      I will treat you with contempt
      and make you a spectacle.

IF WE HAVE NOT QUIET IN OUR MINDS, OUTWARD
COMFORT WILL DO NO MORE FOR US THAN A
GOLDEN SLIPPER ON A GOUTY FOOT.

—John Bunyan

---

7 All who see you will flee from you
      and say,
   'Nineveh is in ruins—who will
      mourn for her?'
   Where can I find anyone to comfort
      you?"

8 Are you better than Thebes,[a]
   situated on the Nile,

with water around her?
The river was her defense,
   the waters her wall.
9 Cush[b] and Egypt were her boundless
      strength;
   Put and Libya were among her
      allies.
10 Yet she was taken captive
      and went into exile.
   Her infants were dashed to pieces
      at the head of every street.
   Lots were cast for her nobles,
      and all her great men were put in
      chains.
11 You too will become drunk;
      you will go into hiding
      and seek refuge from the enemy.

12 All your fortresses are like fig trees
      with their first ripe fruit;
   when they are shaken,
      the figs fall into the mouth of the
      eater.
13 Look at your troops—
      they are all women!
   The gates of your land
      are wide open to your enemies;
      fire has consumed their bars.

14 Draw water for the siege,
      strengthen your defenses!
   Work the clay,
      tread the mortar,
      repair the brickwork!
15 There the fire will devour you;
      the sword will cut you down
      and, like grasshoppers, consume
      you.
   Multiply like grasshoppers,
      multiply like locusts!
16 You have increased the number of
      your merchants
      till they are more than the stars of
      the sky,
   but like locusts they strip the land
      and then fly away.
17 Your guards are like locusts,
      your officials like swarms of locusts
   that settle in the walls on a cold
      day—
   but when the sun appears they fly
      away,
      and no one knows where.

18 O king of Assyria, your shepherds[c]
      slumber;
   your nobles lie down to rest.

---

a 8 Hebrew *No Amon*   *b 9* That is, the upper Nile region   *c 18* Or *rulers*

Your people are scattered on the
    mountains
    with no one to gather them.
19 Nothing can heal your wound;
    your injury is fatal.

Everyone who hears the news about
    you
    claps his hands at your fall,
for who has not felt
    your endless cruelty?

HABAKKUK

ABAKKUK PRAYED AND PROPHESIED
IN TIMES OF CRISIS. THE INTERNA-
TIONAL SCENE WAS SHOCKED BY
EVENTS OF FAR-REACHING IMPORT. INTER-
NALLY THE PEOPLE OF GOD WERE CAUGHT
UP IN A CRISIS OF RELIGIOUS AND MORAL
BEWILDERMENT. IT WAS INTO THAT TROU-
BLED SCENE THAT HABAKKUK STEPPED WITH
HIS EXPRESSIONS OF CONFUSION AND COM-
PLAINT. AS YOU READ THIS BOOK, NOTICE
GOD'S UNEXPECTED ANSWER AND THE HOPE
HABAKKUK FINALLY DISCOVERED.

1

The oracle that Habakkuk the prophet received.

Habakkuk's Complaint

2 How long, O LORD, must I call for
    help,
  but you do not listen?
  Or cry out to you, "Violence!"
  but you do not save?
3 Why do you make me look at
    injustice?
  Why do you tolerate wrong?
  Destruction and violence are before
    me;
  there is strife, and conflict abounds.
4 Therefore the law is paralyzed,
  and justice never prevails.
  The wicked hem in the righteous,
  so that justice is perverted.

The LORD's Answer

5 "Look at the nations and watch—
  and be utterly amazed.
  For I am going to do something in
    your days
  that you would not believe,
  even if you were told.
6 I am raising up the Babylonians,[a]
  that ruthless and impetuous
    people,
  who sweep across the whole earth
  to seize dwelling places not their
    own.
7 They are a feared and dreaded people;
  they are a law to themselves
  and promote their own honor.
8 Their horses are swifter than leopards,
  fiercer than wolves at dusk.

a 6 Or *Chaldeans*

Their cavalry gallops headlong;
 their horsemen come from afar.
They fly like a vulture swooping to
 devour;
9 they all come bent on violence.

Their hordes[a] advance like a desert
 wind
 and gather prisoners like sand.
10 They deride kings
 and scoff at rulers.

[a] 9 The meaning of the Hebrew for this word is uncertain.

MONDAY

Ivan Has No God. He Has an Idea.
Fyodor Dostoyevsky

Verse: Habakkuk 1:11   **Passage:** Habakkuk 1:5–11

ou see, I never had any of these doubts before, but it was all hidden away in me. It was perhaps just because I did not understand these ideas surging up in me that I used to drink and fight and rage. It was to stifle them in myself, to still them, to smother them. There is an idea in Ivan; he is not Rakitin. But Ivan is a sphinx and is silent; he is always silent. It's God that's worrying me. That's the only thing that's worrying me. What if he doesn't exist? What if Rakitin's right—that it's an idea made up by men? Then, if he doesn't exist, man is the chief of the earth, of the universe. Magnificent! Only how is he going to be good without God? That's the question. I always come back to that. For whom is man going to love then? To whom will he be thankful? To whom will he sing the hymn? Rakitin laughs, Rakitin says that one can love humanity without God. Well, only a sniveling idiot can maintain that. I can't understand it. Life's easy for Rakitin—"You'd better think about the extension of civic rights," he says, "or even of keeping down the price of meat. You will show your love for humanity more simply and directly by that than by philosophy." I answered him, "Well, but you without a God, are more likely to raise the price of meat if it suits you and make a ruble on every kopeck." He lost his temper. But after all, what is goodness? Answer me that, Alexey. Goodness is one thing with me and another with a Chinaman, so it's a relative thing. Or isn't it? Is it not relative? A treacherous question! You won't laugh if I tell you it's kept me awake two nights. I only wonder now how people can live and think nothing about it. Vanity! Ivan has no God. He has an idea.

Additional Scripture Reading:
Daniel 5:4; Lamentations 5:19; Hebrews 1:10–12

Go to page 1065 for your next devotional reading.

1700   1900

They laugh at all fortified cities;
   they build earthen ramps and
     capture them.
11 Then they sweep past like the wind
   and go on—
   guilty men, whose own strength is
     their god."

Habakkuk's Second Complaint

12 O LORD, are you not from
   everlasting?
   My God, my Holy One, we will
     not die.
O LORD, you have appointed them to
   execute judgment;
   O Rock, you have ordained them
     to punish.
13 Your eyes are too pure to look on
   evil;
   you cannot tolerate wrong.
Why then do you tolerate the
   treacherous?
   Why are you silent while the
     wicked
   swallow up those more righteous
     than themselves?
14 You have made men like fish in the
   sea,
   like sea creatures that have no ruler.
15 The wicked foe pulls all of them up
   with hooks,
   he catches them in his net,
he gathers them up in his dragnet;
   and so he rejoices and is glad.
16 Therefore he sacrifices to his net
   and burns incense to his dragnet,
for by his net he lives in luxury
   and enjoys the choicest food.
17 Is he to keep on emptying his net,
   destroying nations without mercy?

2 I will stand at my watch
   and station myself on the
     ramparts;
I will look to see what he will say to
   me,
   and what answer I am to give to
     this complaint.[a]

The LORD's Answer

2 Then the LORD replied:

"Write down the revelation
   and make it plain on tablets
   so that a herald[b] may run with it.

3 For the revelation awaits an
   appointed time;
   it speaks of the end
   and will not prove false.
Though it linger, wait for it;
   it[c] will certainly come and will not
     delay.

4 "See, he is puffed up;
   his desires are not upright—
   but the righteous will live by his
     faith[d]—
5 indeed, wine betrays him;
   he is arrogant and never at rest.
Because he is as greedy as the grave[e]
   and like death is never satisfied,
he gathers to himself all the nations
   and takes captive all the peoples.

6 "Will not all of them taunt him with
ridicule and scorn, saying,

   " 'Woe to him who piles up stolen
     goods
   and makes himself wealthy by
     extortion!
   How long must this go on?'
7 Will not your debtors[f] suddenly
   arise?
   Will they not wake up and make
     you tremble?
   Then you will become their victim.
8 Because you have plundered many
   nations,
   the peoples who are left will
     plunder you.
For you have shed man's blood;
   you have destroyed lands and cities
     and everyone in them.

9 "Woe to him who builds his realm by
     unjust gain
   to set his nest on high,
   to escape the clutches of ruin!
10 You have plotted the ruin of many
   peoples,
   shaming your own house and
     forfeiting your life.
11 The stones of the wall will cry out,
   and the beams of the woodwork
     will echo it.

12 "Woe to him who builds a city with
     bloodshed
   and establishes a town by crime!

---

a 1 Or and what to answer when I am rebuked
linger, wait for him; / he   *d 4 Or faithfulness*   *b 2 Or so that whoever reads it*   *c 3 Or Though he*
e 5 Hebrew Sheol   *f 7 Or creditors*

¹³ Has not the LORD Almighty
determined
that the people's labor is only fuel
for the fire,
that the nations exhaust
themselves for nothing?
¹⁴ For the earth will be filled with the
knowledge of the glory of the
LORD,
as the waters cover the sea.

¹⁵ "Woe to him who gives drink to his
neighbors,
pouring it from the wineskin till
they are drunk,
so that he can gaze on their naked
bodies.
¹⁶ You will be filled with shame instead
of glory.
Now it is your turn! Drink and be
exposed*a* !
The cup from the LORD's right hand
is coming around to you,
and disgrace will cover your glory.
¹⁷ The violence you have done to
Lebanon will overwhelm you,
and your destruction of animals
will terrify you.
For you have shed man's blood;
you have destroyed lands and cities
and everyone in them.

¹⁸ "Of what value is an idol, since a
man has carved it?
Or an image that teaches lies?
For he who makes it trusts in his
own creation;
he makes idols that cannot speak.
¹⁹ Woe to him who says to wood,
'Come to life!'
Or to lifeless stone, 'Wake up!'
Can it give guidance?
It is covered with gold and silver;
there is no breath in it.
²⁰ But the LORD is in his holy temple;
let all the earth be silent before
him."

Habakkuk's Prayer

3 A prayer of Habakkuk the
prophet. On *shigionoth*.*b*

² LORD, I have heard of your fame;

I stand in awe of your deeds,
O LORD.
Renew them in our day,
in our time make them known;
in wrath remember mercy.

³ God came from Teman,
the Holy One from Mount Paran.
*Selah*c
His glory covered the heavens
and his praise filled the earth.
⁴ His splendor was like the sunrise;
rays flashed from his hand,
where his power was hidden.
⁵ Plague went before him;
pestilence followed his steps.
⁶ He stood, and shook the earth;
he looked, and made the nations
tremble.
The ancient mountains crumbled
and the age-old hills collapsed.
His ways are eternal.
⁷ I saw the tents of Cushan in distress,
the dwellings of Midian in anguish.

⁸ Were you angry with the rivers,
O LORD?
Was your wrath against the
streams?
Did you rage against the sea
when you rode with your horses
and your victorious chariots?
⁹ You uncovered your bow,
you called for many arrows.   *Selah*
You split the earth with rivers;
¹⁰   the mountains saw you and
writhed.
Torrents of water swept by;
the deep roared
and lifted its waves on high.

¹¹ Sun and moon stood still in the
heavens
at the glint of your flying arrows,
at the lightning of your flashing
spear.
¹² In wrath you strode through the
earth
and in anger you threshed the
nations.
¹³ You came out to deliver your people,
to save your anointed one.
You crushed the leader of the land of
wickedness,

---

a 16 Masoretic Text; Dead Sea Scrolls, Aquila, Vulgate and Syriac (see also Septuagint) *and stagger*
b 1 Probably a literary or musical term   *c 3* A word of uncertain meaning; possibly a musical term;
also in verses 9 and 13

THE ARRIVAL AT THE HIGH PLACES
Hannah Hurnard

VERSE: Habakkuk 3:19   PASSAGE: Habakkuk 3:18–19

hen he had finished, Much-Afraid lifted her face toward the high places which were quite invisible and spoke quietly through the mist. "My Lord, behold me—here I am, in the place thou didst send me to—doing the thing thou didst tell me to do for 'where you die I will die, and there I will be buried. May the LORD deal with me, be it ever so severely, if anything but death separates you and me' " (Ruth 1:17).

Still there was silence, a silence as of the grave, for indeed she was in the grave of her own hopes and still without the promised hinds' feet, still outside the high places with even the promise to be laid down on the altar. This was the place to which the long, heartbreaking journey had led her. Yet just once more before she laid it down on the altar, Much-Afraid repeated the glorious promise which had been the cause of her starting for the high places. "The Sovereign LORD is my strength; he makes my feet like the feet of a deer, he enables me to go on the heights" (Habakkuk 3:19).

The priest put forth a hand of steel, right into her heart. There was a sound of rending and tearing, and the human love, with all its myriad rootlets and fibers, came forth. He held it for a moment and then said, "Yes, it was ripe for removal, the time had come. There is not a rootlet torn or missing."

When he had said this he cast it down on the altar and spread his hands above it. There came a flash of fire which seemed to rend the altar; after that, nothing but ashes remained, either of the love itself, which had been so deeply planted in her heart, or of the suffering and sorrow which had been her companions on that long, strange journey. A sense of utter, overwhelming rest and peace engulfed Much-Afraid. At last, the offering had been made and there was nothing left to be done. When the priest had unbound her she leaned forward over the ashes on the altar and said with complete thanksgiving, "It is finished."

Then, utterly exhausted, she fell asleep.

ADDITIONAL SCRIPTURE READING:
Deuteronomy 32:13; Isaiah 58:14; 2 Corinthians 12:9–10

Go to page 1069 for your next devotional reading.

1900   Present

you stripped him from head to
foot. *Selah*
14 With his own spear you pierced his
head
when his warriors stormed out to
scatter us,
gloating as though about to devour
the wretched who were in hiding.
15 You trampled the sea with your
horses,
churning the great waters.

16 I heard and my heart pounded,
my lips quivered at the sound;
decay crept into my bones,
and my legs trembled.
Yet I will wait patiently for the day of
calamity

to come on the nation invading us.
17 Though the fig tree does not bud
and there are no grapes on the
vines,
though the olive crop fails
and the fields produce no food,
though there are no sheep in the pen
and no cattle in the stalls,
18 yet I will rejoice in the LORD,
I will be joyful in God my Savior.

19 The Sovereign LORD is my strength;
he makes my feet like the feet of a
deer,
he enables me to go on the heights.

For the director of music. On my
stringed instruments.

ZEPHANIAH

EPHANIAH WROTE TO THE PEOPLE OF JUDAH, WARNING THEM OF JUDGMENT AND A TERRIBLE "DAY OF THE LORD" THAT WAS TO COME—A DAY WHEN GOD WOULD SEVERELY PUNISH THE NATIONS. AS YOU READ THIS BOOK, LOOK FOR THE NOTE OF HOPE THAT GOD'S JUDGMENT WOULD PAVE THE WAY FOR A NEW SOCIETY IN WHICH JUSTICE WOULD PREVAIL AND ALL PEOPLE WOULD WORSHIP THE LORD.

1 The word of the LORD that came to Zephaniah son of Cushi, the son of Gedaliah, the son of Amariah, the son of Hezekiah, during the reign of Josiah son of Amon king of Judah:

Warning of Coming Destruction

2 "I will sweep away everything
 from the face of the earth,"
  declares the LORD.
3 "I will sweep away both men and
  animals;
 I will sweep away the birds of the
  air
 and the fish of the sea.
 The wicked will have only heaps of
  rubble[a]

when I cut off man from the face of
  the earth,"
  declares the LORD.

Against Judah

4 "I will stretch out my hand against
  Judah
 and against all who live in
  Jerusalem.
 I will cut off from this place every
  remnant of Baal,
 the names of the pagan and the
  idolatrous priests—
5 those who bow down on the roofs
 to worship the starry host,
 those who bow down and swear by
  the LORD
 and who also swear by Molech,[b]

---

a 3 The meaning of the Hebrew for this line is uncertain.   b 5 Hebrew *Malcam*, that is, Milcom

6 those who turn back from following
the LORD
and neither seek the LORD nor
inquire of him.
7 Be silent before the Sovereign LORD,
for the day of the LORD is near.
The LORD has prepared a sacrifice;
he has consecrated those he has
invited.
8 On the day of the LORD's sacrifice
I will punish the princes
and the king's sons
and all those clad
in foreign clothes.
9 On that day I will punish
all who avoid stepping on the
threshold,[a]
who fill the temple of their gods
with violence and deceit.

10 "On that day," declares the LORD,
"a cry will go up from the Fish
Gate,
wailing from the New Quarter,
and a loud crash from the hills.
11 Wail, you who live in the market
district[b];
all your merchants will be wiped
out,
all who trade with[c] silver will be
ruined.
12 At that time I will search Jerusalem
with lamps
and punish those who are
complacent,
who are like wine left on its dregs,
who think, 'The LORD will do
nothing,
either good or bad.'
13 Their wealth will be plundered,
their houses demolished.
They will build houses
but not live in them;
they will plant vineyards
but not drink the wine.

The Great Day of the LORD

14 "The great day of the LORD is near—
near and coming quickly.
Listen! The cry on the day of the
LORD will be bitter,
the shouting of the warrior there.
15 That day will be a day of wrath,
a day of distress and anguish,
a day of trouble and ruin,

a day of darkness and gloom,
a day of clouds and blackness,
16 a day of trumpet and battle cry
against the fortified cities
and against the corner towers.
17 I will bring distress on the people
and they will walk like blind men,
because they have sinned against
the LORD.
Their blood will be poured out like
dust
and their entrails like filth.
18 Neither their silver nor their gold
will be able to save them
on the day of the LORD's wrath.
In the fire of his jealousy
the whole world will be consumed,
for he will make a sudden end
of all who live in the earth."

2 Gather together, gather
together,
O shameful nation,
2 before the appointed time arrives
and that day sweeps on like chaff,
before the fierce anger of the LORD
comes upon you,
before the day of the LORD's wrath
comes upon you.
3 Seek the LORD, all you humble of the
land,
you who do what he commands.
Seek righteousness, seek humility;
perhaps you will be sheltered
on the day of the LORD's anger.

Against Philistia

4 Gaza will be abandoned
and Ashkelon left in ruins.
At midday Ashdod will be emptied
and Ekron uprooted.
5 Woe to you who live by the sea,
O Kerethite people;
the word of the LORD is against you,
O Canaan, land of the Philistines.
"I will destroy you,
and none will be left."
6 The land by the sea, where the
Kerethites[d] dwell,
will be a place for shepherds and
sheep pens.
7 It will belong to the remnant of the
house of Judah;
there they will find pasture.

---

[a] 9 See 1 Samuel 5:5.　　[b] 11 Or the Mortar　　[c] 11 Or in　　[d] 6 The meaning of the Hebrew for this
word is uncertain.

THE MOMENT OF MEANING
T. S. Eliot

VERSE: Zephaniah 1:14   **PASSAGE:** Zephaniah 1:14—2:3

hen came, at a predetermined moment, a moment in
      time and of time,
A moment not out of time, but in time, in what we call
      history: transecting, bisecting the world of time,
      a moment in time but not like a moment of time,
A moment in time but time was made through that
      moment; for without the meaning there is no
      time, and that moment of time gave the
      meaning.
Then it seemed as if men must proceed from light to light,
      in the light of the Word,
Through the passion and sacrifice saved in spite of their
      negative being:
Bestial as ever before, carnal, self-seeking as always before,
      selfish and purblind as ever before,
Yet always struggling, always reaffirming, always resuming
      their march on the way that was lit by the light;
Often halting, loitering, straying, delaying, returning, yet
      following no other way.
But it seems that something has happened that has never
      happened before: though we know not just
      when, or why, or where.
Men have left God not for other gods, they say, but for no
      god; and this has never happened before
That men both deny gods and worship gods, professing first
      reason,
And then money, and power, and what they call life, or race,
      or dialectic.
The church disowned, the tower overthrown, the bells
      upturned, what have we to do
But stand with empty hands and palms turned upwards
In an age which advances progressively backwards?

ADDITIONAL SCRIPTURE READING:
Jeremiah 30:7; Zephaniah 1:7; Acts 2:20–21

Go to page 1073 for your next devotional reading.

1900   Present

In the evening they will lie down
   in the houses of Ashkelon.
The LORD their God will care for
   them;
   he will restore their fortunes.*a*

Against Moab and Ammon

8 "I have heard the insults of Moab
   and the taunts of the Ammonites,
who insulted my people
   and made threats against their
      land.
9 Therefore, as surely as I live,"
   declares the LORD Almighty, the
      God of Israel,
"surely Moab will become like
      Sodom,
   the Ammonites like Gomorrah—
a place of weeds and salt pits,
   a wasteland forever.
The remnant of my people will
      plunder them;
   the survivors of my nation will
      inherit their land."

10 This is what they will get in return
   for their pride,
   for insulting and mocking the
      people of the LORD Almighty.
11 The LORD will be awesome to them
   when he destroys all the gods of
      the land.
The nations on every shore will
      worship him,
   every one in its own land.

Against Cush

12 "You too, O Cushites,*b*
   will be slain by my sword."

Against Assyria

13 He will stretch out his hand against
      the north
   and destroy Assyria,
leaving Nineveh utterly desolate
   and dry as the desert.
14 Flocks and herds will lie down there,
   creatures of every kind.
The desert owl and the screech owl
   will roost on her columns.
Their calls will echo through the
      windows,
   rubble will be in the doorways,
   the beams of cedar will be exposed.

15 This is the carefree city
   that lived in safety.
She said to herself,
   "I am, and there is none besides
      me."
What a ruin she has become,
   a lair for wild beasts!
All who pass by her scoff
   and shake their fists.

The Future of Jerusalem

3 Woe to the city of oppressors,
   rebellious and defiled!
2 She obeys no one,
   she accepts no correction.
She does not trust in the LORD,
   she does not draw near to her God.
3 Her officials are roaring lions,
   her rulers are evening wolves,
who leave nothing for the
      morning.
4 Her prophets are arrogant;
   they are treacherous men.
Her priests profane the sanctuary
   and do violence to the law.
5 The LORD within her is righteous;
   he does no wrong.
Morning by morning he dispenses his
      justice,
   and every new day he does not fail,
   yet the unrighteous know no
      shame.

6 "I have cut off nations;
   their strongholds are demolished.
I have left their streets deserted,
   with no one passing through.
Their cities are destroyed;
   no one will be left—no one at all.
7 I said to the city,
   'Surely you will fear me
   and accept correction!'
Then her dwelling would not be cut
      off,
   nor all my punishments come
      upon her.
But they were still eager
   to act corruptly in all they did.
8 Therefore wait for me," declares the
      LORD,
   "for the day I will stand up to
      testify.*c*
I have decided to assemble the
      nations,
   to gather the kingdoms

---

a 7 Or *will bring back their captives*   *b 12* That is, people from the upper Nile region
c 8 Septuagint and Syriac; Hebrew *will rise up to plunder*

and to pour out my wrath on them—
    all my fierce anger.
The whole world will be consumed
    by the fire of my jealous anger.

9 "Then will I purify the lips of the
    peoples,
    that all of them may call on the
        name of the LORD
and serve him shoulder to
    shoulder.
10 From beyond the rivers of Cush*a*
    my worshipers, my scattered
      people,
    will bring me offerings.
11 On that day you will not be put to
    shame
    for all the wrongs you have done to
      me,
because I will remove from this city
    those who rejoice in their pride.
Never again will you be haughty
    on my holy hill.
12 But I will leave within you
    the meek and humble,
    who trust in the name of the LORD.
13 The remnant of Israel will do no
    wrong;
    they will speak no lies,
    nor will deceit be found in their
      mouths.
They will eat and lie down
    and no one will make them afraid."

14 Sing, O Daughter of Zion;
    shout aloud, O Israel!
Be glad and rejoice with all your heart,
    O Daughter of Jerusalem!

15 The LORD has taken away your
    punishment,
    he has turned back your enemy.
The LORD, the King of Israel, is with
    you;
    never again will you fear any harm.
16 On that day they will say to
    Jerusalem,
"Do not fear, O Zion;
    do not let your hands hang limp.
17 The LORD your God is with you,
    he is mighty to save.
He will take great delight in you,
    he will quiet you with his love,
    he will rejoice over you with
      singing."

18 "The sorrows for the appointed feasts
    I will remove from you;
    they are a burden and a reproach to
      you.*b*
19 At that time I will deal
    with all who oppressed you;
I will rescue the lame
    and gather those who have been
      scattered.
I will give them praise and honor
    in every land where they were put
      to shame.
20 At that time I will gather you;
    at that time I will bring you home.
I will give you honor and praise
    among all the peoples of the earth
when I restore your fortunes*c*
    before your very eyes,"
                  says the LORD.

---

a 10 That is, the upper Nile region   *b 18* Or "I will gather you who mourn for the appointed feasts; /
your reproach is a burden to you   *c 20* Or I bring back your captives

HAGGAI

 AGGAI WAS A PROPHET WHO, ALONG
WITH ZECHARIAH, ENCOURAGED THE
RETURNED EXILES TO REBUILD THE TEM-
PLE. THE MESSAGES OF HAGGAI WERE GIVEN DUR-
ING A FOUR-MONTH PERIOD IN 520 B.C. HAGGAI
CLEARLY SHOWS THE CONSEQUENCES OF DISOBE-
DIENCE AND THE BLESSINGS OF OBEDIENCE, AS HE
TELLS THE PEOPLE THAT THEY HAVE DEPRIVED
THEMSELVES OF GOD'S BLESSINGS BY FORSAKING
THE TEMPLE BUILDING PROJECT. WHEN THE PEO-
PLE GIVE PRIORITY TO GOD AND HIS HOUSE, THEY
ARE BLESSED. OBEDIENCE BRINGS THE ENCOUR-
AGEMENT AND STRENGTH OF GOD'S SPIRIT.

A Call to Build the House of the LORD

1 In the second year of King Darius, on the first day of the sixth month, the word of the LORD came through the prophet Haggai to Zerubbabel son of Shealtiel, governor of Judah, and to Joshua[a] son of Jehozadak, the high priest:

²This is what the LORD Almighty says: "These people say, 'The time has not yet come for the LORD's house to be built.' "

³Then the word of the LORD came through the prophet Haggai: ⁴"Is it a time for you yourselves to be living in your paneled houses, while this house remains a ruin?"

⁵Now this is what the LORD Almighty says: "Give careful thought to your ways. ⁶You have planted much, but have harvested little. You eat, but never have enough. You drink, but never have your fill. You put on clothes, but are not warm. You earn wages, only to put them in a purse with holes in it."

⁷This is what the LORD Almighty says: "Give careful thought to your ways. ⁸Go up into the mountains and bring down timber and build the house, so that I may take pleasure in it and be honored," says the LORD. ⁹"You expected much, but see, it turned out to be little. What you brought home, I blew away. Why?" declares the LORD Almighty. "Because of my house, which remains a ruin, while each of you is busy with his own house. ¹⁰Therefore,

because of you the heavens have withheld their dew and the earth its crops. ¹¹I called for a drought on the fields and the mountains, on the grain, the new wine, the oil and whatever the ground produces, on men and cattle, and on the labor of your hands."

¹²Then Zerubbabel son of Shealtiel, Joshua son of Jehozadak, the high priest,

THURSDAY

THE SHAKING OF THE THINGS THAT ARE MADE
Hannah Whitall Smith

VERSE: Haggai 2:6–7   **PASSAGE:** Haggai 2:6–9, 21–22

he "foundation of God standeth sure" (2 Timothy 2:19, KJV), and it is the only foundation that does. Therefore, we need to be "shaken" from off every other foundation in order that we may be forced to rest on the foundation of God alone. And this explains the necessity for those "shakings" through which so many Christians seem called to pass. The Lord sees that they are building their spiritual houses on flimsy foundations, which will not be able to withstand the "vehement beating" of the storms of life; and not in anger but in tenderest love, he shakes our earth and our heaven until all that "can be shaken" is removed, and only those "things which cannot be shaken" are left behind.

The apostle tells us that the things that are shaken are the "things that are made" (Hebrews 12:27, KJV); that is, the things that are manufactured by our own efforts, feelings that we get up, doctrines that we elaborate, good works that we perform. It is not that these things are bad things in themselves. It is only when the soul begins to rest on them instead of upon the Lord that he is compelled to "shake" us from off them. And this shaking applies, we are told, "not to the earth only, but also to heaven." This means, I am sure, that it is possible to have "things that are made" even in religious matters.

How much of the so-called religiousness of many Christians consists of these "things that are made," I cannot say; but I sometimes think the great overturnings and tossings in matters of faith, which so distress Christians in these times, may be only the necessary shaking of the "things that are made," in order that only that which "cannot be shaken" may remain.

ADDITIONAL SCRIPTURE READING:
Psalm 125:1; Hebrews 12:27–28

Go to page 1076 for your next devotional reading.

1700   1900

and the whole remnant of the people obeyed the voice of the LORD their God and the message of the prophet Haggai, because the LORD their God had sent him. And the people feared the LORD.

13Then Haggai, the LORD's messenger, gave this message of the LORD to the people: "I am with you," declares the LORD. 14So the LORD stirred up the spirit of Zerubbabel son of Shealtiel, governor of Judah, and the spirit of Joshua son of Jehozadak, the high priest, and the spirit of the whole remnant of the people. They came and began to work on the house of the LORD Almighty, their God, 15on the twenty-fourth day of the sixth month in the second year of King Darius.

The Promised Glory of the New House

2 On the twenty-first day of the seventh month, the word of the LORD came through the prophet Haggai: 2"Speak to Zerubbabel son of Shealtiel, governor of Judah, to Joshua son of Jehozadak, the high priest, and to the remnant of the people. Ask them, 3'Who of you is left who saw this house in its former glory? How does it look to you now? Does it not seem to you like nothing? 4But now be strong, O Zerubbabel,' declares the LORD. 'Be strong, O Joshua son of Jehozadak, the high priest. Be strong, all you people of the land,' declares the LORD, 'and work. For I am with you,' declares the LORD Almighty. 5'This is what I covenanted with you when you came out of Egypt. And my Spirit remains among you. Do not fear.'

6"This is what the LORD Almighty says: 'In a little while I will once more shake the heavens and the earth, the sea and the dry land. 7I will shake all nations, and the desired of all nations will come, and I will fill this house with glory,' says the LORD Almighty. 8'The silver is mine and the gold is mine,' declares the LORD Almighty. 9'The glory of this present house will be greater than the glory of the former house,' says the LORD Almighty. 'And in this place I will grant peace,' declares the LORD Almighty."

Blessings for a Defiled People

10On the twenty-fourth day of the ninth month, in the second year of Darius, the word of the LORD came to the prophet Haggai: 11"This is what the LORD Almighty says: 'Ask the priests what the law says: 12If a person carries consecrated meat in the fold of his garment, and that fold touches some bread or stew, some wine, oil or other food, does it become consecrated?' "

The priests answered, "No."

13Then Haggai said, "If a person defiled by contact with a dead body touches one of these things, does it become defiled?"

"Yes," the priests replied, "it becomes defiled."

14Then Haggai said, " 'So it is with this people and this nation in my sight,' declares the LORD. 'Whatever they do and whatever they offer there is defiled.

15" 'Now give careful thought to this from this day on*a*—consider how things were before one stone was laid on another in the LORD's temple. 16When anyone came to a heap of twenty measures, there were only ten. When anyone went to a wine vat to draw fifty measures, there were only twenty. 17I struck all the work of your hands with blight, mildew and hail, yet you did not turn to me,' declares the LORD. 18'From this day on, from this twenty-fourth day of the ninth month, give careful thought to the day when the foundation of the LORD's temple was laid. Give careful thought: 19Is there yet any seed left in the barn? Until now, the vine and the fig tree, the pomegranate and the olive tree have not borne fruit.

" 'From this day on I will bless you.' "

Zerubbabel the LORD's Signet Ring

20The word of the LORD came to Haggai a second time on the twenty-fourth day of the month: 21"Tell Zerubbabel governor of Judah that I will shake the heavens and the earth. 22I will overturn royal thrones and shatter the power of the foreign kingdoms. I will overthrow chariots and their drivers; horses and their riders will fall, each by the sword of his brother. 23" 'On that day,' declares the LORD Almighty, 'I will take you, my servant Zerubbabel son of Shealtiel,' declares the LORD, 'and I will make you like my signet ring, for I have chosen you,' declares the LORD Almighty."

a 15 Or *to the days past*

ZECHARIAH

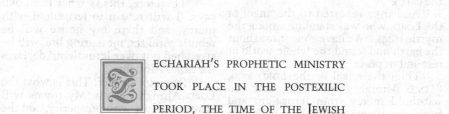

ECHARIAH'S PROPHETIC MINISTRY TOOK PLACE IN THE POSTEXILIC PERIOD, THE TIME OF THE JEWISH RESTORATION FROM BABYLONIAN CAPTIVITY. HIS PROPHECIES BEGAN TWO MONTHS AFTER HAGGAI'S FIRST MESSAGE. TO A PEOPLE DISCOURAGED ABOUT THEIR TASK OF REBUILDING THE TEMPLE, ZECHARIAH SPOKE WORDS OF ENCOURAGEMENT AND MOTIVATION. LOOK FOR THE MANY PREDICTIONS CONCERNING THE COMING MESSIAH, AS ZECHARIAH GAVE HIS PEOPLE A VISION OF GOD'S PURPOSES BEYOND THE RESTORED TEMPLE.

A Call to Return to the LORD

1 In the eighth month of the second year of Darius, the word of the LORD came to the prophet Zechariah son of Berekiah, the son of Iddo:

2"The LORD was very angry with your forefathers. 3Therefore tell the people: This is what the LORD Almighty says: 'Return to me,' declares the LORD Almighty, 'and I will return to you,' says the LORD Almighty. 4Do not be like your forefathers, to whom the earlier prophets proclaimed: This is what the LORD Almighty says: 'Turn from your evil ways and your evil practices.' But they would not listen or pay attention to me, declares the LORD. 5Where are your forefathers now? And the prophets, do they live forever? 6But did not my words and my decrees, which I commanded my servants the prophets, overtake your forefathers?

"Then they repented and said, 'The LORD Almighty has done to us what our ways and practices deserve, just as he determined to do.' "

The Man Among the Myrtle Trees

7On the twenty-fourth day of the eleventh month, the month of Shebat, in the second year of Darius, the word of the LORD came to the prophet Zechariah son of Berekiah, the son of Iddo.

8During the night I had a vision—and there before me was a man riding a red horse! He was standing among the myrtle trees in a ravine. Behind him were red, brown and white horses.

9I asked, "What are these, my lord?"

The angel who was talking with me

answered, "I will show you what they are."

¹⁰Then the man standing among the myrtle trees explained, "They are the ones the LORD has sent to go throughout the earth."

¹¹And they reported to the angel of the LORD, who was standing among the myrtle trees, "We have gone throughout the earth and found the whole world at rest and in peace."

¹²Then the angel of the LORD said, "LORD Almighty, how long will you withhold mercy from Jerusalem and from the towns of Judah, which you have been angry with these seventy years?" ¹³So the LORD spoke kind and comforting words to the angel who talked with me.

¹⁴Then the angel who was speaking to me said, "Proclaim this word: This is what the LORD Almighty says: 'I am very jealous for Jerusalem and Zion, ¹⁵but I am very angry with the nations that feel secure. I was only a little angry, but they added to the calamity.'

¹⁶"Therefore, this is what the LORD says: 'I will return to Jerusalem with mercy, and there my house will be rebuilt. And the measuring line will be stretched out over Jerusalem,' declares the LORD Almighty.

¹⁷"Proclaim further: This is what the LORD Almighty says: 'My towns will again overflow with prosperity, and the LORD will again comfort Zion and choose Jerusalem.'"

Four Horns and Four Craftsmen

¹⁸Then I looked up—and there before me were four horns! ¹⁹I asked the angel

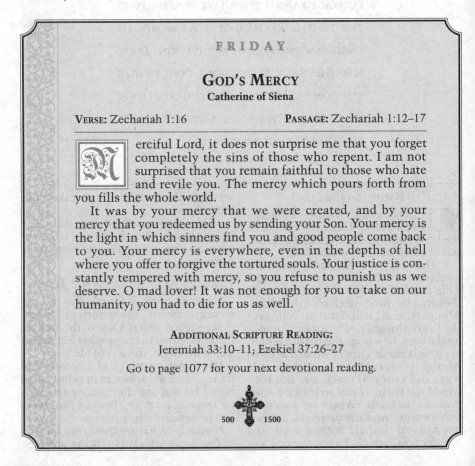

FRIDAY

GOD'S MERCY
Catherine of Siena

VERSE: Zechariah 1:16   **PASSAGE:** Zechariah 1:12–17

Merciful Lord, it does not surprise me that you forget completely the sins of those who repent. I am not surprised that you remain faithful to those who hate and revile you. The mercy which pours forth from you fills the whole world.

It was by your mercy that we were created, and by your mercy that you redeemed us by sending your Son. Your mercy is the light in which sinners find you and good people come back to you. Your mercy is everywhere, even in the depths of hell where you offer to forgive the tortured souls. Your justice is constantly tempered with mercy, so you refuse to punish us as we deserve. O mad lover! It was not enough for you to take on our humanity; you had to die for us as well.

ADDITIONAL SCRIPTURE READING:
Jeremiah 33:10–11; Ezekiel 37:26–27

Go to page 1077 for your next devotional reading.

500   1500

WEEKEND

HIS SAVIOR'S WORDS, GOING TO THE CROSS
Robert Herrick

VERSE: Luke 23:27   **PASSAGE:** Luke 23:26–31

ave, have ye no regard, all ye
Who pass this way, to pity me,
Who am a man of misery!

A man both bruised, and broke, and one
Who suffers not here for mine own,
But for my friends' transgression!

Ah! Zion's Daughters, do not fear
The cross, the cords, the nails, the spear,
The myrrh, the gall, the vinegar:

For Christ, your loving Savior, hath
Drunk up the wine of God's fierce wrath;
Only, there's left a little froth,

Less for to taste, than for to show,
What bitter cups had been your due,
Had he not drank them up for you.

ADDITIONAL SCRIPTURE READING:
Matthew 27:33–37; Mark 15:22–26

Go to page 1079 for your next devotional reading.

1500   1700

who was speaking to me, "What are these?"

He answered me, "These are the horns that scattered Judah, Israel and Jerusalem."

²⁰Then the LORD showed me four craftsmen. ²¹I asked, "What are these coming to do?"

He answered, "These are the horns that scattered Judah so that no one could raise his head, but the craftsmen have come to terrify them and throw down these horns of the nations who lifted up their horns against the land of Judah to scatter its people."

A Man With a Measuring Line

2 Then I looked up—and there before me was a man with a measuring line in his hand! ²I asked, "Where are you going?"

He answered me, "To measure Jerusalem, to find out how wide and how long it is."

³Then the angel who was speaking to me left, and another angel came to meet him ⁴and said to him: "Run, tell that young man, 'Jerusalem will be a city without walls because of the great number of men and livestock in it. ⁵And I myself will be a wall of fire around it,' declares the LORD, 'and I will be its glory within.'

⁶"Come! Come! Flee from the land of the north," declares the LORD, "for I have scattered you to the four winds of heaven," declares the LORD.

⁷"Come, O Zion! Escape, you who live in the Daughter of Babylon!" ⁸For this is what the LORD Almighty says: "After he has honored me and has sent me against the nations that have plundered you—for whoever touches you touches the apple of his eye— ⁹I will surely raise my hand against them so that their slaves will plunder them.ᵃ Then you will know that the LORD Almighty has sent me.

¹⁰"Shout and be glad, O Daughter of Zion. For I am coming, and I will live among you," declares the LORD. ¹¹"Many nations will be joined with the LORD in that day and will become my people. I will live among you and you

will know that the LORD Almighty has sent me to you. ¹²The LORD will inherit Judah as his portion in the holy land and will again choose Jerusalem. ¹³Be still before the LORD, all mankind, because he has roused himself from his holy dwelling."

Clean Garments for the High Priest

3 Then he showed me Joshuaᵇ the high priest standing before the angel of the LORD, and Satanᶜ standing at his right side to accuse him. ²The LORD said to Satan, "The LORD rebuke you, Satan! The LORD, who has chosen Jerusalem, rebuke you! Is not this man a burning stick snatched from the fire?"

³Now Joshua was dressed in filthy clothes as he stood before the angel. ⁴The angel said to those who were standing before him, "Take off his filthy clothes."

Then he said to Joshua, "See, I have taken away your sin, and I will put rich garments on you."

⁵Then I said, "Put a clean turban on his head." So they put a clean turban on his head and clothed him, while the angel of the LORD stood by.

⁶The angel of the LORD gave this charge to Joshua: ⁷"This is what the LORD Almighty says: 'If you will walk in my ways and keep my requirements, then you will govern my house and have charge of my courts, and I will give you a place among these standing here.

⁸" 'Listen, O high priest Joshua and your associates seated before you, who are men symbolic of things to come: I am going to bring my servant, the Branch. ⁹See, the stone I have set in front of Joshua! There are seven eyesᵈ on that one stone, and I will engrave an inscription on it,' says the LORD Almighty, 'and I will remove the sin of this land in a single day.

¹⁰" 'In that day each of you will invite his neighbor to sit under his vine and fig tree,' declares the LORD Almighty."

ᵃ 8,9 Or says after . . . eye: ⁹"I . . . plunder them."   ᵇ 1 A variant of Jeshua; here and elsewhere in Zechariah   ᶜ 1 Satan means accuser.   ᵈ 9 Or facets

CHRISTIAN'S BURDEN IS LOOSED
John Bunyan

VERSE: Zechariah 3:4   **PASSAGE:** Zechariah 3:3–5

 ow I saw in my dream, that the highway up which Christian was to go was fenced on either side with a wall; and that wall was called "Salvation" (Isaiah 26:1). Up this way, therefore, did burdened Christian run; but not without great difficulty, because of the load on his back.

He ran thus till he came at a place somewhat ascending; and upon that place stood a cross, and a little below, in the bottom, a sepulcher. So I saw in my dream, that just as Christian came up with the cross, his burden loosed from off his shoulders, and fell from off his back, and began to tumble; and so continued to do till it came to the mouth of the sepulcher, where it fell in, and I saw it no more.

Then was Christian glad and lightsome, and said, with a merry heart,

He hath given me rest by his sorrow,
And life by his death . . .

Now, as he stood looking and weeping, behold three shining ones came to him, and saluted him with, "Peace be to thee!" so the first said to him, "Your sins are forgiven" (Mark 2:5); the second stripped him of his rags, and clothed him with change of raiment (Zechariah 3:4); the third also set a mark in his forehead, and gave him a roll with a seal upon it (Ephesians 1:13), which he bade him look on as he ran, and that he should give it in the Celestial Gate: so they went their way. Then Christian gave three leaps for joy, and went on singing:

Thus far did I come laden with my sin,
Nor could aught ease the grief that I was in,
Till I came hither. What a place is this!
Must here be the beginning of my bliss!
Must here the burden fall from off my back!
Must here the strings that bound it to me crack!
Blest cross! blest sepulcher! blest rather be
The man that there was put to shame for me!

ADDITIONAL SCRIPTURE READING:
Psalm 32:1–2; Matthew 11:30

Go to page 1084 for your next devotional reading.

1500   1700

The Gold Lampstand and the Two Olive Trees

4 Then the angel who talked with me returned and wakened me, as a man is wakened from his sleep. ²He asked me, "What do you see?"

I answered, "I see a solid gold lampstand with a bowl at the top and seven lights on it, with seven channels to the lights. ³Also there are two olive trees by it, one on the right of the bowl and the other on its left."

⁴I asked the angel who talked with me, "What are these, my lord?"

⁵He answered, "Do you not know what these are?"

"No, my lord," I replied.

⁶So he said to me, "This is the word of the LORD to Zerubbabel: 'Not by might nor by power, but by my Spirit,' says the LORD Almighty.

⁷"What*ᵃ* are you, O mighty mountain? Before Zerubbabel you will become level ground. Then he will bring out the capstone to shouts of 'God bless it! God bless it!' "

⁸Then the word of the LORD came to me: ⁹"The hands of Zerubbabel have laid the foundation of this temple; his hands will also complete it. Then you will know that the LORD Almighty has sent me to you.

¹⁰"Who despises the day of small things? Men will rejoice when they see the plumb line in the hand of Zerubbabel.

"(These seven are the eyes of the LORD, which range throughout the earth.)"

¹¹Then I asked the angel, "What are these two olive trees on the right and the left of the lampstand?"

¹²Again I asked him, "What are these two olive branches beside the two gold pipes that pour out golden oil?"

¹³He replied, "Do you not know what these are?"

"No, my lord," I said.

¹⁴So he said, "These are the two who are anointed toᵇ serve the Lord of all the earth."

The Flying Scroll

5 I looked again—and there before me was a flying scroll! ²He asked me, "What do you see?"

I answered, "I see a flying scroll, thirty feet long and fifteen feet wide.ᶜ"

³And he said to me, "This is the curse that is going out over the whole land; for according to what it says on one side, every thief will be banished, and according to what it says on the other, everyone who swears falsely will be banished. ⁴The LORD Almighty declares, 'I will send it out, and it will enter the house of the thief and the house of him who swears falsely by my name. It will remain in his house and destroy it, both its timbers and its stones.' "

The Woman in a Basket

⁵Then the angel who was speaking to me came forward and said to me, "Look up and see what this is that is appearing."

⁶I asked, "What is it?"

He replied, "It is a measuring basket.ᵈ" And he added, "This is the iniquityᵉ of the people throughout the land."

⁷Then the cover of lead was raised, and there in the basket sat a woman! ⁸He said, "This is wickedness," and he pushed her back into the basket and pushed the lead cover down over its mouth.

⁹Then I looked up—and there before me were two women, with the wind in their wings! They had wings like those of a stork, and they lifted up the basket between heaven and earth.

¹⁰"Where are they taking the basket?" I asked the angel who was speaking to me.

¹¹He replied, "To the country of Babyloniaᶠ to build a house for it. When it is ready, the basket will be set there in its place."

Four Chariots

6 I looked up again—and there before me were four chariots coming out from between two mountains—mountains of bronze! ²The first chariot had red horses, the second black, ³the third white, and the fourth

---

ᵃ 7 Or *Who*　　ᵇ 14 Or *two who bring oil and*　　ᶜ 2 Hebrew *twenty cubits long and ten cubits wide* (about 9 meters long and 4.5 meters wide)　　ᵈ 6 Hebrew *an ephah*; also in verses 7–11　　ᵉ 6 Or *appearance*　　ᶠ 11 Hebrew *Shinar*

dappled—all of them powerful. **4**I asked the angel who was speaking to me, "What are these, my lord?"

5The angel answered me, "These are the four spirits*a* of heaven, going out from standing in the presence of the Lord of the whole world. **6**The one with the black horses is going toward the north country, the one with the white horses toward the west,*b* and the one with the dappled horses toward the south."

7When the powerful horses went out, they were straining to go throughout the earth. And he said, "Go throughout the earth!" So they went throughout the earth.

8Then he called to me, "Look, those going toward the north country have given my Spirit*c* rest in the land of the north."

A Crown for Joshua

9The word of the LORD came to me: **10**"Take ₁silver and gold₁ from the exiles Heldai, Tobijah and Jedaiah, who have arrived from Babylon. Go the same day to the house of Josiah son of Zephaniah. **11**Take the silver and gold and make a crown, and set it on the head of the high priest, Joshua son of Jehozadak. **12**Tell him this is what the LORD Almighty says: 'Here is the man whose name is the Branch, and he will branch out from his place and build the temple of the LORD. **13**It is he who will build the temple of the LORD, and he will be clothed with majesty and will sit and rule on his throne. And he will be a priest on his throne. And there will be harmony between the two.' **14**The crown will be given to Heldai,*d* Tobijah, Jedaiah and Hen*e* son of Zephaniah as a memorial in the temple of the LORD. **15**Those who are far away will come and help to build the temple of the LORD, and you will know that the LORD Almighty has sent me to you. This will happen if you diligently obey the LORD your God."

Justice and Mercy, Not Fasting

7 In the fourth year of King Darius, the word of the LORD came to Zechariah on the fourth day of the

ninth month, the month of Kislev. **2**The people of Bethel had sent Sharezer and Regem-Melech, together with their men, to entreat the LORD **3**by asking the priests of the house of the LORD Almighty and the prophets, "Should I mourn and fast in the fifth month, as I have done for so many years?"

4Then the word of the LORD Almighty came to me: **5**"Ask all the people of the land and the priests, 'When you fasted and mourned in the fifth and seventh months for the past seventy years, was it really for me that you fasted? **6**And when you were eating and drinking, were you not just feasting for yourselves? **7**Are these not the words the LORD proclaimed through the earlier prophets when Jerusalem and its surrounding towns were at rest and prosperous, and the Negev and the western foothills were settled?' "

COMPASSION MEANS JUSTICE.

—Meister Eckhart

8And the word of the LORD came again to Zechariah: **9**"This is what the LORD Almighty says: 'Administer true justice; show mercy and compassion to one another. **10**Do not oppress the widow or the fatherless, the alien or the poor. In your hearts do not think evil of each other.'

11"But they refused to pay attention; stubbornly they turned their backs and stopped up their ears. **12**They made their hearts as hard as flint and would not listen to the law or to the words that the LORD Almighty had sent by his Spirit through the earlier prophets. So the LORD Almighty was very angry.

13" 'When I called, they did not listen; so when they called, I would not listen,' says the LORD Almighty. **14**'I scattered them with a whirlwind among all the nations, where they were strangers. The land was left so desolate behind them that no one could come or go. This is how they made the pleasant land desolate.' "

---

a 5 Or *winds*   *b 6* Or *horses after them*   *c 8* Or *spirit*   *d 14* Syriac; Hebrew *Helem*   *e 14* Or *and the gracious one, the*

The LORD Promises to Bless Jerusalem

8 Again the word of the LORD Almighty came to me. ²This is what the LORD Almighty says: "I am very jealous for Zion; I am burning with jealousy for her."

³This is what the LORD says: "I will return to Zion and dwell in Jerusalem. Then Jerusalem will be called the City of Truth, and the mountain of the LORD Almighty will be called the Holy Mountain."

⁴This is what the LORD Almighty says: "Once again men and women of ripe old age will sit in the streets of Jerusalem, each with cane in hand because of his age. ⁵The city streets will be filled with boys and girls playing there."

⁶This is what the LORD Almighty says: "It may seem marvelous to the remnant of this people at that time, but will it seem marvelous to me?" declares the LORD Almighty.

⁷This is what the LORD Almighty says: "I will save my people from the countries of the east and the west. ⁸I will bring them back to live in Jerusalem; they will be my people, and I will be faithful and righteous to them as their God."

⁹This is what the LORD Almighty says: "You who now hear these words spoken by the prophets who were there when the foundation was laid for the house of the LORD Almighty, let your hands be strong so that the temple may be built. ¹⁰Before that time there were no wages for man or beast. No one could go about his business safely because of his enemy, for I had turned every man against his neighbor. ¹¹But now I will not deal with the remnant of this people as I did in the past," declares the LORD Almighty.

¹²"The seed will grow well, the vine will yield its fruit, the ground will produce its crops, and the heavens will drop their dew. I will give all these things as an inheritance to the remnant of this people. ¹³As you have been an object of cursing among the nations, O Judah and Israel, so will I save you, and you will be a blessing. Do not be afraid, but let your hands be strong."

¹⁴This is what the LORD Almighty says: "Just as I had determined to bring disaster upon you and showed no pity when your fathers angered me," says the LORD Almighty, ¹⁵"so now I have determined to do good again to Jerusalem and Judah. Do not be afraid. ¹⁶These are the things you are to do: Speak the truth to each other, and render true and sound judgment in your courts; ¹⁷do not plot evil against your neighbor, and do not love to swear falsely. I hate all this," declares the LORD.

¹⁸Again the word of the LORD Almighty came to me. ¹⁹This is what the LORD Almighty says: "The fasts of the fourth, fifth, seventh and tenth months will become joyful and glad occasions and happy festivals for Judah. Therefore love truth and peace."

²⁰This is what the LORD Almighty says: "Many peoples and the inhabitants of many cities will yet come, ²¹and the inhabitants of one city will go to another and say, 'Let us go at once to entreat the LORD and seek the LORD Almighty. I myself am going.' ²²And many peoples and powerful nations will come to Jerusalem to seek the LORD Almighty and to entreat him."

²³This is what the LORD Almighty says: "In those days ten men from all languages and nations will take firm hold of one Jew by the hem of his robe and say, 'Let us go with you, because we have heard that God is with you.' "

Judgment on Israel's Enemies
An Oracle

9 The word of the LORD is
   against the land of Hadrach
and will rest upon Damascus—
   for the eyes of men and all the tribes
     of Israel
are on the LORD—ᵃ
² and upon Hamath too, which borders
     on it,
   and upon Tyre and Sidon, though
     they are very skillful.
³ Tyre has built herself a stronghold;
   she has heaped up silver like dust,
   and gold like the dirt of the streets.
⁴ But the Lord will take away her
     possessions

ᵃ 1 Or Damascus. / For the eye of the LORD is on all mankind, / as well as on the tribes of Israel,

and destroy her power on the sea,
and she will be consumed by fire.
5 Ashkelon will see it and fear;
Gaza will writhe in agony,
and Ekron too, for her hope will
wither.
Gaza will lose her king
and Ashkelon will be deserted.
6 Foreigners will occupy Ashdod,
and I will cut off the pride of the
Philistines.
7 I will take the blood from their
mouths,
the forbidden food from between
their teeth.
Those who are left will belong to our
God
and become leaders in Judah,
and Ekron will be like the Jebusites.
8 But I will defend my house
against marauding forces.
Never again will an oppressor
overrun my people,
for now I am keeping watch.

The Coming of Zion's King

9 Rejoice greatly, O Daughter of Zion!
Shout, Daughter of Jerusalem!
See, your king*a* comes to you,
righteous and having salvation,
gentle and riding on a donkey,
on a colt, the foal of a donkey.
10 I will take away the chariots from
Ephraim
and the war-horses from Jerusalem,
and the battle bow will be broken.
He will proclaim peace to the
nations.
His rule will extend from sea to sea
and from the River*b* to the ends of
the earth.*c*
11 As for you, because of the blood of
my covenant with you,
I will free your prisoners from the
waterless pit.
12 Return to your fortress, O prisoners
of hope;
even now I announce that I will
restore twice as much to you.
13 I will bend Judah as I bend my bow
and fill it with Ephraim.
I will rouse your sons, O Zion,
against your sons, O Greece,
and make you like a warrior's
sword.

The LORD Will Appear

14 Then the LORD will appear over
them;
his arrow will flash like lightning.
The Sovereign LORD will sound the
trumpet;
he will march in the storms of the
south,
15   and the LORD Almighty will shield
them.
They will destroy
and overcome with slingstones.
They will drink and roar as with
wine;
they will be full like a bowl
used for sprinkling*d* the corners of
the altar.
16 The LORD their God will save them
on that day
as the flock of his people.
They will sparkle in his land
like jewels in a crown.
17 How attractive and beautiful they
will be!
Grain will make the young men
thrive,
and new wine the young women.

The LORD Will Care for Judah

10 Ask the LORD for rain in the
springtime;
it is the LORD who makes the
storm clouds.
He gives showers of rain to men,
and plants of the field to everyone.
2 The idols speak deceit,
diviners see visions that lie;
they tell dreams that are false,
they give comfort in vain.
Therefore the people wander like
sheep
oppressed for lack of a shepherd.

3 "My anger burns against the
shepherds,
and I will punish the leaders;
for the LORD Almighty will care
for his flock, the house of Judah,
and make them like a proud horse
in battle.
4 From Judah will come the
cornerstone,
from him the tent peg,
from him the battle bow,
from him every ruler.

---

a 9 Or *King*   *b 10* That is, the Euphrates   *c 10* Or *the end of the land*   *d 15* Or *bowl, / like*

5 Together they*a* will be like mighty
    men
    trampling the muddy streets in
        battle.
Because the LORD is with them,
    they will fight and overthrow the
        horsemen.
6 "I will strengthen the house of Judah
    and save the house of Joseph.
I will restore them
    because I have compassion on
        them.

a 4,5 Or ruler, all of them together. / 5They

They will be as though
    I had not rejected them,
for I am the LORD their God
    and I will answer them.
7 The Ephraimites will become like
    mighty men,
    and their hearts will be glad as
        with wine.
Their children will see it and be
    joyful;
    their hearts will rejoice in the LORD.
8 I will signal for them
    and gather them in.

TUESDAY

PRECIOUS JEWELS
William O. Cushing

VERSE: Zechariah 9:16   **PASSAGE:** Zechariah 9:15–17

hen he cometh, when he cometh
To make up his jewels,
All his jewels, precious jewels,
His loved and his own.

He will gather, he will gather
The gems for his kingdom,
All the pure ones, all the bright ones,
His loved and his own.

Little children, little children
Who love their Redeemer
Are the jewels, precious jewels,
His loved and his own.

Like the stars of the morning,
His bright crown adorning,
They shall shine in their beauty—
Bright gems for his crown.

ADDITIONAL SCRIPTURE READING:
Isaiah 25:6–8; 62:3; Haggai 2:23

Go to page 1086 for your next devotional reading.

1700   1900

Surely I will redeem them;
  they will be as numerous as before.
9 Though I scatter them among the
      peoples,
  yet in distant lands they will
      remember me.
They and their children will survive,
  and they will return.
10 I will bring them back from Egypt
  and gather them from Assyria.
I will bring them to Gilead and
      Lebanon,
  and there will not be room enough
      for them.
11 They will pass through the sea of
      trouble;
  the surging sea will be subdued
  and all the depths of the Nile will
      dry up.
Assyria's pride will be brought down
  and Egypt's scepter will pass away.
12 I will strengthen them in the LORD
  and in his name they will walk,"
                  declares the LORD.

11 Open your doors, O Lebanon,
      so that fire may devour your
    cedars!
2 Wail, O pine tree, for the cedar has
      fallen;
  the stately trees are ruined!
Wail, oaks of Bashan;
  the dense forest has been cut down!
3 Listen to the wail of the shepherds;
  their rich pastures are destroyed!
Listen to the roar of the lions;
  the lush thicket of the Jordan is
      ruined!

Two Shepherds

4 This is what the LORD my God says:
"Pasture the flock marked for slaughter.
5 Their buyers slaughter them and go
unpunished. Those who sell them say,
'Praise the LORD, I am rich!' Their own
shepherds do not spare them. 6 For I will
no longer have pity on the people of the
land," declares the LORD. "I will hand
everyone over to his neighbor and his
king. They will oppress the land, and I
will not rescue them from their hands."

7 So I pastured the flock marked for
slaughter, particularly the oppressed of
the flock. Then I took two staffs and
called one Favor and the other Union,
and I pastured the flock. 8 In one month I
got rid of the three shepherds.

The flock detested me, and I grew
weary of them 9 and said, "I will not be
your shepherd. Let the dying die, and
the perishing perish. Let those who are
left eat one another's flesh."

10 Then I took my staff called Favor
and broke it, revoking the covenant I
had made with all the nations. 11 It was
revoked on that day, and so the afflicted
of the flock who were watching me
knew it was the word of the LORD.

12 I told them, "If you think it best,
give me my pay; but if not, keep it." So
they paid me thirty pieces of silver.

13 And the LORD said to me, "Throw it
to the potter"—the handsome price at
which they priced me! So I took the thirty pieces of silver and threw them into
the house of the LORD to the potter.
14 Then I broke my second staff called
Union, breaking the brotherhood between Judah and Israel.

15 Then the LORD said to me, "Take
again the equipment of a foolish shepherd. 16 For I am going to raise up a shepherd over the land who will not care for
the lost, or seek the young, or heal the
injured, or feed the healthy, but will eat
the meat of the choice sheep, tearing off
their hoofs.

17 "Woe to the worthless shepherd,
      who deserts the flock!
May the sword strike his arm and his
      right eye!
May his arm be completely
      withered,
  his right eye totally blinded!"

Jerusalem's Enemies to Be Destroyed

An Oracle

12 This is the word of the LORD
      concerning Israel. The LORD,
who stretches out the heavens, who lays
the foundation of the earth, and who
forms the spirit of man within him,
declares: 2 "I am going to make Jerusalem a cup that sends all the surrounding peoples reeling. Judah will be
besieged as well as Jerusalem. 3 On that
day, when all the nations of the earth are
gathered against her, I will make Jerusalem an immovable rock for all the
nations. All who try to move it will
injure themselves. 4 On that day I will
strike every horse with panic and its

rider with madness," declares the LORD. "I will keep a watchful eye over the house of Judah, but I will blind all the horses of the nations. ⁵Then the leaders of Judah will say in their hearts, 'The people of Jerusalem are strong, because the LORD Almighty is their God.'

⁶"On that day I will make the leaders of Judah like a firepot in a woodpile, like a flaming torch among sheaves. They will consume right and left all the surrounding peoples, but Jerusalem will remain intact in her place.

⁷"The LORD will save the dwellings of Judah first, so that the honor of the house of David and of Jerusalem's inhabitants may not be greater than that of Judah.

⁸On that day the LORD will shield those who live in Jerusalem, so that the feeblest among them will be like David, and the house of David will be like God, like the Angel of the LORD going before them. ⁹On that day I will set out to destroy all the nations that attack Jerusalem.

Mourning for the One They Pierced

¹⁰"And I will pour out on the house of David and the inhabitants of Jerusalem a spirit*a* of grace and supplication. They will look on*b* me, the one they have pierced, and they will mourn for him as one mourns for an only child, and grieve bitterly for him as one grieves for a firstborn son. ¹¹On that day the weeping in

a 10 Or *the Spirit*   *b 10* Or *to*

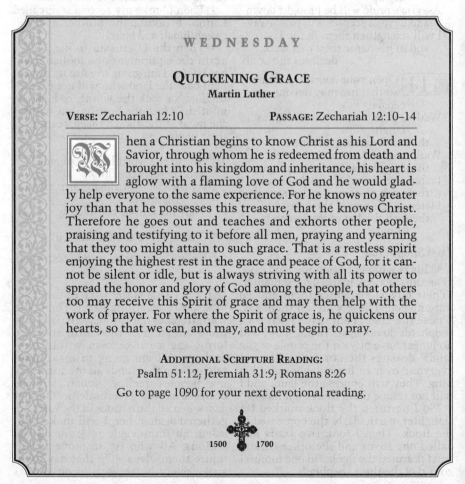

WEDNESDAY

QUICKENING GRACE
Martin Luther

VERSE: Zechariah 12:10   **PASSAGE:** Zechariah 12:10–14

When a Christian begins to know Christ as his Lord and Savior, through whom he is redeemed from death and brought into his kingdom and inheritance, his heart is aglow with a flaming love of God and he would gladly help everyone to the same experience. For he knows no greater joy than that he possesses this treasure, that he knows Christ. Therefore he goes out and teaches and exhorts other people, praising and testifying to it before all men, praying and yearning that they too might attain to such grace. That is a restless spirit enjoying the highest rest in the grace and peace of God, for it cannot be silent or idle, but is always striving with all its power to spread the honor and glory of God among the people, that others too may receive this Spirit of grace and may then help with the work of prayer. For where the Spirit of grace is, he quickens our hearts, so that we can, and may, and must begin to pray.

ADDITIONAL SCRIPTURE READING:
Psalm 51:12; Jeremiah 31:9; Romans 8:26

Go to page 1090 for your next devotional reading.

1500   1700

Jerusalem will be great, like the weeping of Hadad Rimmon in the plain of Megiddo. 12 The land will mourn, each clan by itself, with their wives by themselves: the clan of the house of David and their wives, the clan of the house of Nathan and their wives, 13 the clan of the house of Levi and their wives, the clan of Shimei and their wives, 14 and all the rest of the clans and their wives.

Cleansing From Sin

13 "On that day a fountain will be opened to the house of David and the inhabitants of Jerusalem, to cleanse them from sin and impurity.

2 "On that day, I will banish the names of the idols from the land, and they will be remembered no more," declares the LORD Almighty. "I will remove both the prophets and the spirit of impurity from the land. 3 And if anyone still prophesies, his father and mother, to whom he was born, will say to him, 'You must die, because you have told lies in the LORD's name.' When he prophesies, his own parents will stab him.

4 "On that day every prophet will be ashamed of his prophetic vision. He will not put on a prophet's garment of hair in order to deceive. 5 He will say, 'I am not a prophet. I am a farmer; the land has been my livelihood since my youth.*a* ' 6 If someone asks him, 'What are these wounds on your body*b* ?' he will answer, 'The wounds I was given at the house of my friends.'

The Shepherd Struck, the Sheep Scattered

7 "Awake, O sword, against my shepherd,
   against the man who is close to me!"
   declares the LORD Almighty.
"Strike the shepherd,
   and the sheep will be scattered,
   and I will turn my hand against the little ones.
8 In the whole land," declares the LORD,
   "two-thirds will be struck down and perish;
   yet one-third will be left in it.

9 This third I will bring into the fire;
   I will refine them like silver
   and test them like gold.
They will call on my name
   and I will answer them;
I will say, 'They are my people,'
   and they will say, 'The LORD is our God.' "

The LORD Comes and Reigns

14 A day of the LORD is coming when your plunder will be divided among you.

2 I will gather all the nations to Jerusalem to fight against it; the city will be captured, the houses ransacked, and the women raped. Half of the city will go into exile, but the rest of the people will not be taken from the city. 3 Then the LORD will go out and fight against those nations, as he fights in the day of battle. 4 On that day his feet will stand on the Mount of Olives, east of Jerusalem, and the Mount of Olives will be split in two from east to west, forming a great valley, with half of the mountain moving north and half moving south. 5 You will flee by my mountain valley, for it will extend to Azel. You will flee as you fled from the earthquake*c* in the days of Uzziah king of Judah. Then the LORD my God will come, and all the holy ones with him.

6 On that day there will be no light, no cold or frost. 7 It will be a unique day, without daytime or nighttime—a day known to the LORD. When evening comes, there will be light.

8 On that day living water will flow out from Jerusalem, half to the eastern sea*d* and half to the western sea,*e* in summer and in winter. 9 The LORD will be king over the whole earth. On that day there will be one LORD, and his name the only name.

10 The whole land, from Geba to Rimmon, south of Jerusalem, will become like the Arabah. But Jerusalem will be raised up and remain in its place, from the Benjamin Gate to the site of the First Gate, to the Corner Gate, and from the Tower of Hananel to the royal winepresses. 11 It will be inhabited; never

---

a 5 Or *farmer; a man sold me in my youth*   *b* 6 Or *wounds between your hands*   *c* 5 Or *5My mountain valley will be blocked and will extend to Azel. It will be blocked as it was blocked because of the earthquake*   *d* 8 That is, the Dead Sea   *e* 8 That is, the Mediterranean

again will it be destroyed. Jerusalem will be secure.

12This is the plague with which the LORD will strike all the nations that fought against Jerusalem: Their flesh will rot while they are still standing on their feet, their eyes will rot in their sockets, and their tongues will rot in their mouths. 13On that day men will be stricken by the LORD with great panic. Each man will seize the hand of another, and they will attack each other. 14Judah too will fight at Jerusalem. The wealth of all the surrounding nations will be collected—great quantities of gold and silver and clothing. 15A similar plague will strike the horses and mules, the camels and donkeys, and all the animals in those camps.

16Then the survivors from all the nations that have attacked Jerusalem will go up year after year to worship the King, the LORD Almighty, and to celebrate the Feast of Tabernacles. 17If any of the peoples of the earth do not go up to Jerusalem to worship the King, the LORD Almighty, they will have no rain. 18If the Egyptian people do not go up and take part, they will have no rain. The LORD*a* will bring on them the plague he inflicts on the nations that do not go up to celebrate the Feast of Tabernacles. 19This will be the punishment of Egypt and the punishment of all the nations that do not go up to celebrate the Feast of Tabernacles.

20On that day HOLY TO THE LORD will be inscribed on the bells of the horses, and the cooking pots in the LORD's house will be like the sacred bowls in front of the altar. 21Every pot in Jerusalem and Judah will be holy to the LORD Almighty, and all who come to sacrifice will take some of the pots and cook in them. And on that day there will no longer be a Canaanite*b* in the house of the LORD Almighty.

MALACHI

HE TEMPLE HAD BEEN REBUILT, BUT TIMES OF PROSPERITY HAD NOT COME. THE PEOPLE WERE SUFFERING DROUGHT AND FAMINE, AND THEY RESPONDED WITH INDIFFERENCE AND SPIRITUAL LETHARGY. THEY HAD FORGOTTEN GOD AND TREATED HIM WITH DISHONOR. AGAINST SUCH A BACKGROUND MALACHI, MEANING "MY MESSENGER," WAS WRITTEN. WHILE MALACHI'S MESSAGE IS FILLED WITH INDICTMENTS AND WARNINGS, BE ALERT TO GOD'S PASSIONATE LOVE FOR HIS PEOPLE AND HIS DESIRE THAT WE RETURN THAT LOVE WITH OUR OWN WHOLEHEARTED LOVE AND OBEDIENCE.

1 An oracle: The word of the LORD to Israel through Malachi.*a*

Jacob Loved, Esau Hated

2"I have loved you," says the LORD.

"But you ask, 'How have you loved us?'

"Was not Esau Jacob's brother?" the LORD says. "Yet I have loved Jacob, 3but Esau I have hated, and I have turned his mountains into a wasteland and left his inheritance to the desert jackals."

4Edom may say, "Though we have been crushed, we will rebuild the ruins."

But this is what the LORD Almighty says: "They may build, but I will demolish. They will be called the Wicked Land, a people always under the wrath of the LORD. 5You will see it with your own eyes and say, 'Great is the LORD—even beyond the borders of Israel!'

Blemished Sacrifices

6"A son honors his father, and a servant his master. If I am a father, where is the honor due me? If I am a master, where is the respect due me?" says the LORD Almighty. "It is you, O priests, who show contempt for my name.

"But you ask, 'How have we shown contempt for your name?'

7"You place defiled food on my altar.

"But you ask, 'How have we defiled you?'

"By saying that the LORD's table is contemptible. 8When you bring blind animals for sacrifice, is that not wrong? When you sacrifice crippled or diseased animals, is that not wrong? Try offering them to your governor! Would he be pleased with you? Would he accept you?" says the LORD Almighty.

9"Now implore God to be gracious to us. With such offerings from your hands, will he accept you?"—says the LORD Almighty.

10"Oh, that one of you would shut the temple doors, so that you would not light useless fires on my altar! I am not pleased with you," says the LORD Almighty, "and I will accept no offering from your hands. 11My name will be great among the nations, from the rising to the setting of the sun. In every place incense and pure offerings will be brought to my name, because my name will be great among the nations," says the LORD Almighty.

12"But you profane it by saying of the Lord's table, 'It is defiled,' and of its food, 'It is contemptible.' 13And you say, 'What a burden!' and you sniff at it contemptuously," says the LORD Almighty.

"When you bring injured, crippled or diseased animals and offer them as sacrifices, should I accept them from your hands?" says the LORD. 14"Cursed is the cheat who has an acceptable male in his

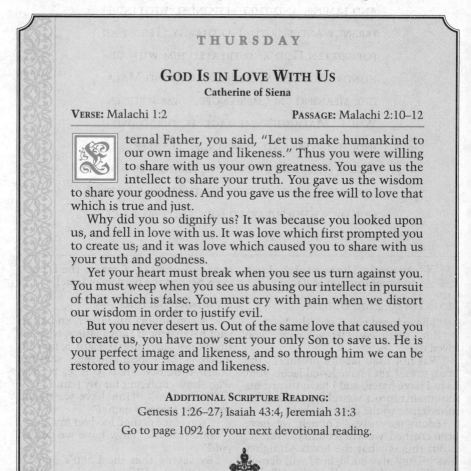

THURSDAY

GOD IS IN LOVE WITH US
Catherine of Siena

VERSE: Malachi 1:2   **PASSAGE:** Malachi 2:10–12

ternal Father, you said, "Let us make humankind to our own image and likeness." Thus you were willing to share with us your own greatness. You gave us the intellect to share your truth. You gave us the wisdom to share your goodness. And you gave us the free will to love that which is true and just.

Why did you so dignify us? It was because you looked upon us, and fell in love with us. It was love which first prompted you to create us; and it was love which caused you to share with us your truth and goodness.

Yet your heart must break when you see us turn against you. You must weep when you see us abusing our intellect in pursuit of that which is false. You must cry with pain when we distort our wisdom in order to justify evil.

But you never desert us. Out of the same love that caused you to create us, you have now sent your only Son to save us. He is your perfect image and likeness, and so through him we can be restored to your image and likeness.

ADDITIONAL SCRIPTURE READING:
Genesis 1:26–27; Isaiah 43:4; Jeremiah 31:3

Go to page 1092 for your next devotional reading.

500   1500

flock and vows to give it, but then sacrifices a blemished animal to the Lord. For I am a great king," says the LORD Almighty, "and my name is to be feared among the nations.

Admonition for the Priests

2 "And now this admonition is for you, O priests. ²If you do not listen, and if you do not set your heart to honor my name," says the LORD Almighty, "I will send a curse upon you, and I will curse your blessings. Yes, I have already cursed them, because you have not set your heart to honor me.

³"Because of you I will rebuke[a] your descendants[b]; I will spread on your faces the offal from your festival sacrifices, and you will be carried off with it. ⁴And you will know that I have sent you this admonition so that my covenant with Levi may continue," says the LORD Almighty. ⁵"My covenant was with him, a covenant of life and peace, and I gave them to him; this called for reverence and he revered me and stood in awe of my name. ⁶True instruction was in his mouth and nothing false was found on his lips. He walked with me in peace and uprightness, and turned many from sin.

⁷"For the lips of a priest ought to preserve knowledge, and from his mouth men should seek instruction—because he is the messenger of the LORD Almighty. ⁸But you have turned from the way and by your teaching have caused many to stumble; you have violated the covenant with Levi," says the LORD Almighty. ⁹"So I have caused you to be despised and humiliated before all the people, because you have not followed my ways but have shown partiality in matters of the law."

Judah Unfaithful

¹⁰Have we not all one Father[c]? Did not one God create us? Why do we profane the covenant of our fathers by breaking faith with one another?

¹¹Judah has broken faith. A detestable thing has been committed in Israel and in Jerusalem: Judah has desecrated the sanctuary the LORD loves, by marrying the daughter of a foreign god. ¹²As for the man who does this, whoever he may be, may the LORD cut him off from the tents of Jacob[d]—even though he brings offerings to the LORD Almighty.

¹³Another thing you do: You flood the LORD's altar with tears. You weep and wail because he no longer pays attention to your offerings or accepts them with pleasure from your hands. ¹⁴You ask, "Why?" It is because the LORD is acting as the witness between you and the wife of your youth, because you have broken faith with her, though she is your partner, the wife of your marriage covenant.

¹⁵Has not ⌊the LORD⌋ made them one? In flesh and spirit they are his. And why one? Because he was seeking godly offspring.[e] So guard yourself in your spirit, and do not break faith with the wife of your youth.

THE FORM OF MARRIAGE LIES IN AN INSEPARABLE UNION OF MINDS BY WHICH EITHER IS UNALTERABLY PLIGHTED TO SERVE THE OTHER LOYALLY.

—*Thomas Aquinas*

---

¹⁶"I hate divorce," says the LORD God of Israel, "and I hate a man's covering himself[f] with violence as well as with his garment," says the LORD Almighty.

So guard yourself in your spirit, and do not break faith.

The Day of Judgment

¹⁷You have wearied the LORD with your words.

"How have we wearied him?" you ask.

By saying, "All who do evil are good in the eyes of the LORD, and he is pleased with them" or "Where is the God of justice?"

3 "See, I will send my messenger, who will prepare the way before me. Then suddenly the Lord you are seeking will come to his temple; the messenger of the covenant, whom you desire, will come," says the LORD Almighty.

---

a 3 Or *cut off* (see Septuagint)   *b 3* Or *will blight your grain*   *c 10* Or *father*   *d 12* Or *¹²May the LORD cut off from the tents of Jacob anyone who gives testimony in behalf of the man who does this*   *e 15* Or *¹⁵But the one ⌊who is our father⌋ did not do this, not as long as life remained in him. And what was he seeking? An offspring from God*   *f 16* Or *his wife*

²But who can endure the day of his coming? Who can stand when he appears? For he will be like a refiner's fire or a launderer's soap. ³He will sit as a refiner and purifier of silver; he will purify the Levites and refine them like gold and silver. Then the LORD will have men who will bring offerings in righteousness, ⁴and the offerings of Judah and Jerusalem will be acceptable to the LORD, as in days gone by, as in former years.

⁵"So I will come near to you for judgment. I will be quick to testify against sorcerers, adulterers and perjurers, against those who defraud laborers of their wages, who oppress the widows and the fatherless, and deprive aliens of justice, but do not fear me," says the LORD Almighty.

FRIDAY

GOD THE REMEDY
Henry Ward Beecher

VERSE: Malachi 4:2   PASSAGE: Malachi 4:1–3

od is himself a vast medicine. God's soul and nature are the blood of the universe. Ask the physician what it is that he trusts to throw out deadly influences from the human system. If there are diseased organs, what cures them? Do you think pills do the work? They do but little except to say to the lazy organ, "Wake up and go to work, and throw out the enemy that is preying upon you." What is medicine? It is merely a coaxer. Its business is to say to the part affected, "Lazy dog! Wake up and get well."

If a man gets well, he cures himself—often, thanks to the doctor; more often, thanks to the nurse; always, thanks to nature. That does the work, if it is done at all. What is the stream that carries reparation to the wasted parts, that carries stimulation to the dormant parts, that carries nutrition to the exhausted parts? What is it that fights? It is the blood.

And throughout the vast heaven, throughout time and the universe, the blood of the world comes from the heart of God. The mercies of the loving God throb everywhere—above and below, within and without, endless in circuits, vast in distribution, infinitely potential. It is the heart of God that carries restoration, inspiration, aspiration, and final victory. And as long as God lives, and is what he is "the Father of mercies, and the God of all comfort" (see 2 Corinthians 1:3)—this world will not go to rack and ruin.

ADDITIONAL SCRIPTURE READING:
Psalm 103:1–3; Isaiah 53:5; Hosea 6:1–3

Go to page 1098 for your next devotional reading.

1700   1900

Robbing God

6"I the LORD do not change. So you, O descendants of Jacob, are not destroyed. **7**Ever since the time of your forefathers you have turned away from my decrees and have not kept them. Return to me, and I will return to you," says the LORD Almighty.

"But you ask, 'How are we to return?'

8"Will a man rob God? Yet you rob me.

"But you ask, 'How do we rob you?'

"In tithes and offerings. **9**You are under a curse—the whole nation of you—because you are robbing me. **10**Bring the whole tithe into the storehouse, that there may be food in my house. Test me in this," says the LORD Almighty, "and see if I will not throw open the floodgates of heaven and pour out so much blessing that you will not have room enough for it. **11**I will prevent pests from devouring your crops, and the vines in your fields will not cast their fruit," says the LORD Almighty. **12**"Then all the nations will call you blessed, for yours will be a delightful land," says the LORD Almighty.

13"You have said harsh things against me," says the LORD.

"Yet you ask, 'What have we said against you?'

14"You have said, 'It is futile to serve God. What did we gain by carrying out his requirements and going about like mourners before the LORD Almighty? **15**But now we call the arrogant blessed. Certainly the evildoers prosper, and even those who challenge God escape.' "

16Then those who feared the LORD talked with each other, and the LORD listened and heard. A scroll of remembrance was written in his presence concerning those who feared the LORD and honored his name.

17"They will be mine," says the LORD Almighty, "in the day when I make up my treasured possession.*a* I will spare them, just as in compassion a man spares his son who serves him. **18**And you will again see the distinction between the righteous and the wicked, between those who serve God and those who do not.

The Day of the LORD

4 "Surely the day is coming; it will burn like a furnace. All the arrogant and every evildoer will be stubble, and that day that is coming will set them on fire," says the LORD Almighty. "Not a root or a branch will be left to them. **2**But for you who revere my name, the sun of righteousness will rise with healing in its wings. And you will go out and leap like calves released from the stall. **3**Then you will trample down the wicked; they will be ashes under the soles of your feet on the day when I do these things," says the LORD Almighty.

4"Remember the law of my servant Moses, the decrees and laws I gave him at Horeb for all Israel.

5"See, I will send you the prophet Elijah before that great and dreadful day of the LORD comes. **6**He will turn the hearts of the fathers to their children, and the hearts of the children to their fathers; or else I will come and strike the land with a curse."

---

a 17 Or *Almighty, "my treasured possession, in the day when I act*

NEW
TESTAMENT

MATTHEW

 ATTHEW WRITES THIS GOSPEL TO REVEAL JESUS AS THE PROMISED MESSIAH AND KING. HE ALSO TELLS US MUCH ABOUT THE LIFE AND MINISTRY OF JESUS, ESPECIALLY HOW HE FULFILLS THE PROMISES OF THE OLD TESTAMENT, AND ABOUT HOW HIS FOLLOWERS SHOULD CONDUCT THEIR LIVES AS CITIZENS OF GOD'S KINGDOM. MATTHEW BEGINS HIS GOSPEL WITH THE BIRTH OF JESUS, WHO IS CALLED "IMMANUEL" (1:23), OR "GOD WITH US," AND CLOSES HIS STORY WITH JESUS' REASSURING PROMISE, "I AM WITH YOU ALWAYS" (28:20).

The Genealogy of Jesus

1 A record of the genealogy of Jesus Christ the son of David, the son of Abraham:

2 Abraham was the father of Isaac,
Isaac the father of Jacob,
Jacob the father of Judah and his brothers,
3 Judah the father of Perez and Zerah, whose mother was Tamar,
Perez the father of Hezron,
Hezron the father of Ram,
4 Ram the father of Amminadab,
Amminadab the father of Nahshon,
Nahshon the father of Salmon,
5 Salmon the father of Boaz, whose mother was Rahab,
Boaz the father of Obed, whose mother was Ruth,
Obed the father of Jesse,
6 and Jesse the father of King David.

David was the father of Solomon, whose mother had been Uriah's wife,
7 Solomon the father of Rehoboam,
Rehoboam the father of Abijah,
Abijah the father of Asa,
8 Asa the father of Jehoshaphat,
Jehoshaphat the father of Jehoram,
Jehoram the father of Uzziah,
9 Uzziah the father of Jotham,
Jotham the father of Ahaz,
Ahaz the father of Hezekiah,
10 Hezekiah the father of Manasseh,
Manasseh the father of Amon,
Amon the father of Josiah,

WEEKEND

THE SONG OF THE VIRGIN MARY
Miles Coverdale

VERSE: Luke 1:46   **PASSAGE:** Luke 1:46–55

y soul doth magnify the Lord,
My spirit rejoiceth greatly
In God my Savior and his word;
For he hath seen the low degree
Of me his handmaiden truly.
Behold now, after this day,
All generations shall speak of me,
And call me blessed alway.

For he that is only of might
Hath done great things for me;
And holy is his name by right:
As for his endless mercy,
It endureth perpetually,
In every generation,
On them that fear him unfeignedly
Without dissimulation.

He showeth strength with his great arm,
Declaring himself to be of power;
He scattereth the proud to their own harm,
Even with the wicked behavior
Of their own hearts every hour
He putteth down the mighty
From their high seat and great honor,
Exalting them of low degree.

The hungry filleth he with good,
And letteth the rich go empty,
Where his own people want no food:
He thinketh upon his mercy,
And helpeth his servant truly,
Even Israel, as he promised
Unto our fathers perpetually,
Abraham and to his seed.

ADDITIONAL SCRIPTURE READING:
Exodus 15:21; 1 Samuel 2:1

Go to page 1100 for your next devotional reading.

1500   1700

11 and Josiah the father of Jeconiah[a] and his brothers at the time of the exile to Babylon.

12 After the exile to Babylon:
Jeconiah was the father of Shealtiel,
Shealtiel the father of Zerubbabel,
13 Zerubbabel the father of Abiud,
Abiud the father of Eliakim,
Eliakim the father of Azor,
14 Azor the father of Zadok,
Zadok the father of Akim,
Akim the father of Eliud,
15 Eliud the father of Eleazar,
Eleazar the father of Matthan,
Matthan the father of Jacob,
16 and Jacob the father of Joseph, the husband of Mary, of whom was born Jesus, who is called Christ.

17 Thus there were fourteen generations in all from Abraham to David, fourteen from David to the exile to Babylon, and fourteen from the exile to the Christ.[b]

The Birth of Jesus Christ

18 This is how the birth of Jesus Christ came about: His mother Mary was pledged to be married to Joseph, but before they came together, she was found to be with child through the Holy Spirit. 19 Because Joseph her husband was a righteous man and did not want to expose her to public disgrace, he had in mind to divorce her quietly.

20 But after he had considered this, an angel of the Lord appeared to him in a dream and said, "Joseph son of David, do not be afraid to take Mary home as your wife, because what is conceived in her is from the Holy Spirit. 21 She will give birth to a son, and you are to give him the name Jesus,[c] because he will save his people from their sins."

22 All this took place to fulfill what the Lord had said through the prophet: 23 "The virgin will be with child and will give birth to a son, and they will call him Immanuel"[d]—which means, "God with us."

24 When Joseph woke up, he did what the angel of the Lord had commanded him and took Mary home as his wife. 25 But he had no union with her until she gave birth to a son. And he gave him the name Jesus.

The Visit of the Magi

2 After Jesus was born in Bethlehem in Judea, during the time of King Herod, Magi[e] from the east came to Jerusalem 2 and asked, "Where is the one who has been born king of the Jews? We saw his star in the east[f] and have come to worship him."

3 When King Herod heard this he was disturbed, and all Jerusalem with him. 4 When he had called together all the people's chief priests and teachers of the law, he asked them where the Christ[g] was to be born. 5 "In Bethlehem in Judea," they replied, "for this is what the prophet has written:

6 " 'But you, Bethlehem, in the land of Judah,
    are by no means least among the rulers of Judah;
for out of you will come a ruler
    who will be the shepherd of my people Israel.'[h]"

7 Then Herod called the Magi secretly and found out from them the exact time the star had appeared. 8 He sent them to Bethlehem and said, "Go and make a careful search for the child. As soon as you find him, report to me, so that I too may go and worship him."

9 After they had heard the king, they went on their way, and the star they had seen in the east[i] went ahead of them until it stopped over the place where the child was. 10 When they saw the star, they were overjoyed. 11 On coming to the house, they saw the child with his mother Mary, and they bowed down and worshiped him. Then they opened their treasures and presented him with gifts of gold and of incense and of myrrh. 12 And having been warned in a dream not to go back to Herod, they returned to their country by another route.

The Escape to Egypt

13When they had gone, an angel of the Lord appeared to Joseph in a dream. "Get up," he said, "take the child and his mother and escape to Egypt. Stay there until I tell you, for Herod is going to search for the child to kill him."

14So he got up, took the child and his mother during the night and left for Egypt, **15**where he stayed until the death of Herod. And so was fulfilled what the Lord had said through the prophet: "Out of Egypt I called my son."[a]

16When Herod realized that he had

a 15 Hosea 11:1

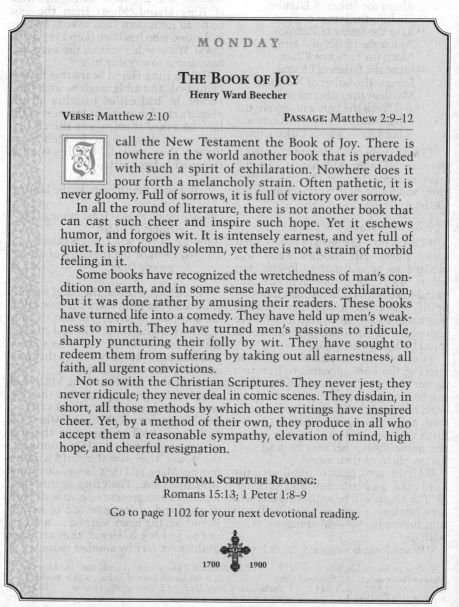

MONDAY

THE BOOK OF JOY
Henry Ward Beecher

VERSE: Matthew 2:10 **PASSAGE:** Matthew 2:9–12

I call the New Testament the Book of Joy. There is nowhere in the world another book that is pervaded with such a spirit of exhilaration. Nowhere does it pour forth a melancholy strain. Often pathetic, it is never gloomy. Full of sorrows, it is full of victory over sorrow.

In all the round of literature, there is not another book that can cast such cheer and inspire such hope. Yet it eschews humor, and forgoes wit. It is intensely earnest, and yet full of quiet. It is profoundly solemn, yet there is not a strain of morbid feeling in it.

Some books have recognized the wretchedness of man's condition on earth, and in some sense have produced exhilaration; but it was done rather by amusing their readers. These books have turned life into a comedy. They have held up men's weakness to mirth. They have turned men's passions to ridicule, sharply puncturing their folly by wit. They have sought to redeem them from suffering by taking out all earnestness, all faith, all urgent convictions.

Not so with the Christian Scriptures. They never jest; they never ridicule; they never deal in comic scenes. They disdain, in short, all those methods by which other writings have inspired cheer. Yet, by a method of their own, they produce in all who accept them a reasonable sympathy, elevation of mind, high hope, and cheerful resignation.

ADDITIONAL SCRIPTURE READING:
Romans 15:13; 1 Peter 1:8–9

Go to page 1102 for your next devotional reading.

1700 1900

been outwitted by the Magi, he was furious, and he gave orders to kill all the boys in Bethlehem and its vicinity who were two years old and under, in accordance with the time he had learned from the Magi. 17Then what was said through the prophet Jeremiah was fulfilled:

18 "A voice is heard in Ramah,
   weeping and great mourning,
   Rachel weeping for her children
   and refusing to be comforted,
   because they are no more."a

The Return to Nazareth

19After Herod died, an angel of the Lord appeared in a dream to Joseph in Egypt 20and said, "Get up, take the child and his mother and go to the land of Israel, for those who were trying to take the child's life are dead."

21So he got up, took the child and his mother and went to the land of Israel. 22But when he heard that Archelaus was reigning in Judea in place of his father Herod, he was afraid to go there. Having been warned in a dream, he withdrew to the district of Galilee, 23and he went and lived in a town called Nazareth. So was fulfilled what was said through the prophets: "He will be called a Nazarene."

John the Baptist Prepares the Way

3 In those days John the Baptist came, preaching in the Desert of Judea 2and saying, "Repent, for the kingdom of heaven is near." 3This is he who was spoken of through the prophet Isaiah:

   "A voice of one calling in the desert,
   'Prepare the way for the Lord,
      make straight paths for him.' "b

4John's clothes were made of camel's hair, and he had a leather belt around his waist. His food was locusts and wild honey. 5People went out to him from Jerusalem and all Judea and the whole region of the Jordan. 6Confessing their sins, they were baptized by him in the Jordan River.

7But when he saw many of the Pharisees and Sadducees coming to where he was baptizing, he said to them: "You brood of vipers! Who warned you to flee from the coming wrath? 8Produce fruit in keeping with repentance. 9And do not think you can say to yourselves, 'We have Abraham as our father.' I tell you that out of these stones God can raise up children for Abraham. 10The ax is already at the root of the trees, and every tree that does not produce good fruit will be cut down and thrown into the fire.

11"I baptize you withc water for repentance. But after me will come one who is more powerful than I, whose sandals I am not fit to carry. He will baptize you with the Holy Spirit and with fire. 12His winnowing fork is in his hand, and he will clear his threshing floor, gathering his wheat into the barn and burning up the chaff with unquenchable fire."

The Baptism of Jesus

13Then Jesus came from Galilee to the Jordan to be baptized by John. 14But John tried to deter him, saying, "I need to be baptized by you, and do you come to me?"

15Jesus replied, "Let it be so now; it is proper for us to do this to fulfill all righteousness." Then John consented.

16As soon as Jesus was baptized, he went up out of the water. At that moment heaven was opened, and he saw the Spirit of God descending like a dove and lighting on him. 17And a voice from heaven said, "This is my Son, whom I love; with him I am well pleased."

The Temptation of Jesus

4 Then Jesus was led by the Spirit into the desert to be tempted by the devil. 2After fasting forty days and forty nights, he was hungry. 3The tempter came to him and said, "If you are the Son of God, tell these stones to become bread."

4Jesus answered, "It is written: 'Man does not live on bread alone, but on every word that comes from the mouth of God.'d"

5Then the devil took him to the holy city and had him stand on the highest point of the temple. 6"If you are the Son of God," he said, "throw yourself down. For it is written:

a 18 Jer. 31:15   b 3 Isaiah 40:3   c 11 Or in   d 4 Deut. 8:3

" 'He will command his angels
    concerning you,
and they will lift you up in their
    hands,
so that you will not strike your foot
    against a stone.'ᵃ"

⁷Jesus answered him, "It is also written: 'Do not put the Lord your God to
the test.'ᵇ "

⁸Again, the devil took him to a very
high mountain and showed him all the
kingdoms of the world and their splendor. ⁹"All this I will give you," he said,
"if you will bow down and worship me."
¹⁰Jesus said to him, "Away from me,
Satan! For it is written: 'Worship the
Lord your God, and serve him only.'ᶜ "
¹¹Then the devil left him, and angels
came and attended him.

ᵃ 6 Psalm 91:11,12   ᵇ 7 Deut. 6:16   ᶜ 10 Deut. 6:13

TUESDAY

THE SON OF GOD IS GOD AND MAN
From Athanasian Creed

VERSE: Matthew 3:17   **PASSAGE:** Matthew 3:13–17

he Father is made of none, neither created nor begotten.
The Son is of the Father alone, not made, nor created,
but begotten.
    The Holy Ghost is of the Father and of the Son, neither
made, nor created nor begotten, but proceeding.
    So there is one Father, not three Fathers; one Son, not three
Sons; one Holy Ghost, not three Holy Ghosts.
    And in this Trinity none is afore, or after other; none is
greater, or less than another; but the whole three persons are co-
eternal together and co-equal . . .
    He therefore that will be saved must thus think of the Trinity.
    Furthermore, it is necessary to everlasting salvation that he
also believe rightly the incarnation of our Lord Jesus Christ. For
the right faith is, that we believe and confess, that our Lord Jesus
Christ, the Son of God, is God and Man;
    God, of the substance of the Father, begotten before the
worlds; and Man, of the substance of his mother, born in the
world; perfect God and perfect Man, of a reasonable soul and
human flesh subsisting; equal to the Father, as touching his
Godhead; and inferior to the Father, as touching his Manhood.
Who although he be God and Man, yet he is not two, but one
Christ . . .

ADDITIONAL SCRIPTURE READING:
Psalm 2:2–12; 1 John 5:20

Go to page 1104 for your next devotional reading.

100   500

Jesus Begins to Preach

12When Jesus heard that John had been put in prison, he returned to Galilee. 13Leaving Nazareth, he went and

---

THE ANGELS ARE THE DISPENSERS AND ADMINIS-
TRATORS OF THE DIVINE BENEFICENCE TOWARD
US; THEY REGARD OUR SAFETY, UNDERTAKE OUR
DEFENSE, DIRECT OUR WAYS, AND EXERCISE A
CONSTANT SOLICITUDE THAT NO EVIL BEFALL US.

—John Calvin

---

lived in Capernaum, which was by the lake in the area of Zebulun and Naphtali— 14to fulfill what was said through the prophet Isaiah:

15 "Land of Zebulun and land of
      Naphtali,
   the way to the sea, along the
      Jordan,
   Galilee of the Gentiles—
16 the people living in darkness
      have seen a great light;
   on those living in the land of the
      shadow of death
   a light has dawned." a

17From that time on Jesus began to preach, "Repent, for the kingdom of heaven is near."

The Calling of the First Disciples

18As Jesus was walking beside the Sea of Galilee, he saw two brothers, Simon called Peter and his brother Andrew. They were casting a net into the lake, for they were fishermen. 19"Come, follow me," Jesus said, "and I will make you fishers of men." 20At once they left their nets and followed him.

21Going on from there, he saw two other brothers, James son of Zebedee and his brother John. They were in a boat with their father Zebedee, preparing their nets. Jesus called them, 22and immediately they left the boat and their father and followed him.

Jesus Heals the Sick

23Jesus went throughout Galilee, teaching in their synagogues, preaching the good news of the kingdom, and healing every disease and sickness among the people. 24News about him spread all over Syria, and people brought to him all who were ill with various diseases, those suffering severe pain, the demon-possessed, those having seizures, and the paralyzed, and he healed them. 25Large crowds from Galilee, the Decapolis, b Jerusalem, Judea and the region across the Jordan followed him.

The Beatitudes

5 Now when he saw the crowds, he went up on a mountainside and sat down. His disciples came to him, 2and he began to teach them, saying:

3 "Blessed are the poor in spirit,
      for theirs is the kingdom of
      heaven.

THE MAN WHO IS POOR IN SPIRIT IS THE MAN
WHO HAS REALIZED THAT THINGS MEAN NOTH-
ING, AND THAT GOD MEANS EVERYTHING.

—William Barclay

---

4 Blessed are those who mourn,
      for they will be comforted.
5 Blessed are the meek,
      for they will inherit the earth.
6 Blessed are those who hunger and
         thirst for righteousness,
      for they will be filled.
7 Blessed are the merciful,
      for they will be shown mercy.
8 Blessed are the pure in heart,
      for they will see God.
9 Blessed are the peacemakers,
      for they will be called sons of
         God.
10 Blessed are those who are persecuted
         because of righteousness,
      for theirs is the kingdom of
         heaven.

11"Blessed are you when people insult you, persecute you and falsely say all kinds of evil against you because of me. 12Rejoice and be glad, because great is your reward in heaven, for in the same way they persecuted the prophets who were before you.

---

a 16 Isaiah 9:1,2   b 25 That is, the Ten Cities

Salt and Light

13"You are the salt of the earth. But if the salt loses its saltiness, how can it be made salty again? It is no longer good for anything, except to be thrown out and trampled by men.

14"You are the light of the world. A city on a hill cannot be hidden. 15Neither

---

WEDNESDAY

THE PROPERTY OF LIGHT
Dietrich Bonhoeffer

VERSE: Matthew 5:14   **PASSAGE:** Matthew 5:14–16

The call of Jesus makes the disciple community not only the salt but also the light of the world: their activity is visible, as well as imperceptible. "You *are* the light." Once again it is not: "You are to be the light," they are already the light because Christ has called them, they are a light which is seen of men, they cannot be otherwise, and if they were it would be a sign that they had not been called. How impossible, how utterly absurd it would be for the disciples—*these* disciples, such men as these!—to try and *become* the light of the world! No, they are already the light, and the call has made them so. Nor does Jesus say: "You *have* the light." The light is not an instrument which has been put into their hands, such as their preaching. It is the disciples themselves. The same Jesus who, speaking of himself, said, "I am the light," says to his followers: "You are the light in your whole existence, provided you remain faithful to your calling (see also John 8:12). And since you are that light, you can no longer remain hidden, even if you want to." It is the property of light to shine. A city set on a hill cannot be hid; it can be seen for miles away, whether it is a fortified burgh, a stronghold or a tottering ruin. This city set on the hill (the Israelite would instinctively think of "Jerusalem on high") is the disciple community. But this is not to say that the disciples have now to make their first decision. The only necessary decision has already been taken. Now they must be what they really are—otherwise they are not followers of Jesus. The followers are a visible community; their discipleship visible in action which lifts them out of the world—otherwise it would not be discipleship.

ADDITIONAL SCRIPTURE READING:
Luke 8:16; John 8:12

Go to page 1110 for your next devotional reading.

1900   Present

do people light a lamp and put it under a bowl. Instead they put it on its stand, and it gives light to everyone in the house. 16In the same way, let your light shine before men, that they may see your good deeds and praise your Father in heaven.

The Fulfillment of the Law

17"Do not think that I have come to abolish the Law or the Prophets; I have not come to abolish them but to fulfill them. 18I tell you the truth, until heaven and earth disappear, not the smallest letter, not the least stroke of a pen, will by any means disappear from the Law until everything is accomplished. 19Anyone who breaks one of the least of these commandments and teaches others to do the same will be called least in the kingdom of heaven, but whoever practices and teaches these commands will be called great in the kingdom of heaven. 20For I tell you that unless your righteousness surpasses that of the Pharisees and the teachers of the law, you will certainly not enter the kingdom of heaven.

Murder

21"You have heard that it was said to the people long ago, 'Do not murder,a and anyone who murders will be subject to judgment.' 22But I tell you that anyone who is angry with his brotherb will be subject to judgment. Again, anyone who says to his brother, 'Raca,c ' is answerable to the Sanhedrin. But anyone who says, 'You fool!' will be in danger of the fire of hell.

23"Therefore, if you are offering your gift at the altar and there remember that your brother has something against you, 24leave your gift there in front of the altar. First go and be reconciled to your brother; then come and offer your gift.

25"Settle matters quickly with your adversary who is taking you to court. Do it while you are still with him on the way, or he may hand you over to the judge, and the judge may hand you over to the officer, and you may be thrown into prison. 26I tell you the truth, you will not get out until you have paid the last penny.d

Adultery

27"You have heard that it was said, 'Do not commit adultery.'e 28But I tell you that anyone who looks at a woman lustfully has already committed adultery with her in his heart. 29If your right eye causes you to sin, gouge it out and throw it away. It is better for you to lose one part of your body than for your whole body to be thrown into hell. 30And if your right hand causes you to sin, cut it off and throw it away. It is better for you to lose one part of your body than for your whole body to go into hell.

Divorce

31"It has been said, 'Anyone who divorces his wife must give her a certificate of divorce.'f 32But I tell you that anyone who divorces his wife, except for marital unfaithfulness, causes her to become an adulteress, and anyone who marries the divorced woman commits adultery.

Oaths

33"Again, you have heard that it was said to the people long ago, 'Do not break your oath, but keep the oaths you have made to the Lord.' 34But I tell you, Do not swear at all: either by heaven, for it is God's throne; 35or by the earth, for it is his footstool; or by Jerusalem, for it is the city of the Great King. 36And do not swear by your head, for you cannot make even one hair white or black. 37Simply let your 'Yes' be 'Yes,' and your 'No,' 'No'; anything beyond this comes from the evil one.

An Eye for an Eye

38"You have heard that it was said, 'Eye for eye, and tooth for tooth.'g 39But I tell you, Do not resist an evil person. If someone strikes you on the right cheek, turn to him the other also. 40And if someone wants to sue you and take your tunic, let him have your cloak as well. 41If someone forces you to go one mile, go with him two miles. 42Give to the one who asks you, and do not turn away from the one who wants to borrow from you.

---

a 21 Exodus 20:13   b 22 Some manuscripts brother without cause   c 22 An Aramaic term of contempt   d 26 Greek kodrantes   e 27 Exodus 20:14   f 31 Deut. 24:1   g 38 Exodus 21:24; Lev. 24:20; Deut. 19:21

Love for Enemies

43"You have heard that it was said, 'Love your neighbor[a] and hate your enemy.' 44But I tell you: Love your enemies[b] and pray for those who persecute you, 45that you may be sons of your Father in heaven. He causes his sun to rise on the evil and the good, and sends rain on the righteous and the unrighteous. 46If you love those who love you, what reward will you get? Are not even the tax collectors doing that? 47And if you greet only your brothers, what are you doing more than others? Do not even pagans do that? 48Be perfect, therefore, as your heavenly Father is perfect.

Giving to the Needy

6 "Be careful not to do your 'acts of righteousness' before men, to be seen by them. If you do, you will have no reward from your Father in heaven.

2"So when you give to the needy, do not announce it with trumpets, as the hypocrites do in the synagogues and on the streets, to be honored by men. I tell you the truth, they have received their reward in full. 3But when you give to the needy, do not let your left hand know what your right hand is doing, 4so that your giving may be in secret. Then your Father, who sees what is done in secret, will reward you.

Prayer

5"And when you pray, do not be like the hypocrites, for they love to pray standing in the synagogues and on the street corners to be seen by men. I tell you the truth, they have received their reward in full. 6But when you pray, go into your room, close the door and pray to your Father, who is unseen. Then your Father, who sees what is done in

THE FEWER WORDS, THE BETTER PRAYER.

—Martin Luther

secret, will reward you. 7And when you pray, do not keep on babbling like pagans, for they think they will be heard because of their many words. 8Do not be like them, for your Father knows what you need before you ask him.

9"This, then, is how you should pray:

" 'Our Father in heaven,
    hallowed be your name,
10your kingdom come,
    your will be done
        on earth as it is in heaven.
11Give us today our daily bread.
12Forgive us our debts,
        as we also have forgiven our
            debtors.
13And lead us not into temptation,
        but deliver us from the evil one.[c] '

14For if you forgive men when they sin against you, your heavenly Father will also forgive you. 15But if you do not forgive men their sins, your Father will not forgive your sins.

Fasting

16"When you fast, do not look somber as the hypocrites do, for they disfigure their faces to show men they are fasting. I tell you the truth, they have received their reward in full. 17But when you fast, put oil on your head and wash your face, 18so that it will not be obvious to men that you are fasting, but only to your Father, who is unseen; and your Father, who sees what is done in secret, will reward you.

Treasures in Heaven

19"Do not store up for yourselves treasures on earth, where moth and rust destroy, and where thieves break in and steal. 20But store up for yourselves treasures in heaven, where moth and rust do not destroy, and where thieves do not break in and steal. 21For where your treasure is, there your heart will be also.

22"The eye is the lamp of the body. If your eyes are good, your whole body will be full of light. 23But if your eyes are bad, your whole body will be full of darkness. If then the light within you is darkness, how great is that darkness!

24"No one can serve two masters. Either he will hate the one and love the

---

a 43 Lev. 19:18   b 44 Some late manuscripts enemies, bless those who curse you, do good to those who hate you   c 13 Or from evil; some late manuscripts one, / for yours is the kingdom and the power and the glory forever. Amen.

other, or he will be devoted to the one and despise the other. You cannot serve both God and Money.

Do Not Worry

25 "Therefore I tell you, do not worry about your life, what you will eat or drink; or about your body, what you will wear. Is not life more important than food, and the body more important than clothes? 26 Look at the birds of the air; they do not sow or reap or store away in barns, and yet your heavenly Father feeds them. Are you not much more valuable than they? 27 Who of you by worrying can add a single hour to his life[a]?

28 "And why do you worry about clothes? See how the lilies of the field grow. They do not labor or spin. 29 Yet I tell you that not even Solomon in all his splendor was dressed like one of these. 30 If that is how God clothes the grass of the field, which is here today and tomorrow is thrown into the fire, will he not much more clothe you, O you of little faith? 31 So do not worry, saying, 'What shall we eat?' or 'What shall we drink?' or 'What shall we wear?' 32 For the pagans run after all these things, and your heavenly Father knows that you need them. 33 But seek first his kingdom and his righteousness, and all these things will be

---

ANXIETY DOES NOT EMPTY TOMORROW OF ITS SORROWS BUT ONLY EMPTIES TODAY OF ITS STRENGTH.   —C. H. Spurgeon

---

given to you as well. 34 Therefore do not worry about tomorrow, for tomorrow will worry about itself. Each day has enough trouble of its own.

Judging Others

7 "Do not judge, or you too will be judged. 2 For in the same way you judge others, you will be judged, and with the measure you use, it will be measured to you.

3 "Why do you look at the speck of sawdust in your brother's eye and pay no attention to the plank in your own eye? 4 How can you say to your brother, 'Let me take the speck out of your eye,'

when all the time there is a plank in your own eye? 5 You hypocrite, first take the plank out of your own eye, and then you will see clearly to remove the speck from your brother's eye.

6 "Do not give dogs what is sacred; do not throw your pearls to pigs. If you do, they may trample them under their feet, and then turn and tear you to pieces.

Ask, Seek, Knock

7 "Ask and it will be given to you; seek and you will find; knock and the door will be opened to you. 8 For everyone who asks receives; he who seeks finds; and to him who knocks, the door will be opened.

9 "Which of you, if his son asks for bread, will give him a stone? 10 Or if he asks for a fish, will give him a snake? 11 If you, then, though you are evil, know how to give good gifts to your children, how much more will your Father in heaven give good gifts to those who ask him! 12 So in everything, do to others what you would have them do to you, for this sums up the Law and the Prophets.

The Narrow and Wide Gates

13 "Enter through the narrow gate. For wide is the gate and broad is the road that leads to destruction, and many enter through it. 14 But small is the gate and narrow the road that leads to life, and only a few find it.

A Tree and Its Fruit

15 "Watch out for false prophets. They come to you in sheep's clothing, but inwardly they are ferocious wolves. 16 By their fruit you will recognize them. Do people pick grapes from thornbushes, or figs from thistles? 17 Likewise every good tree bears good fruit, but a bad tree bears bad fruit. 18 A good tree cannot bear bad fruit, and a bad tree cannot bear good fruit. 19 Every tree that does not bear good fruit is cut down and thrown into the fire. 20 Thus, by their fruit you will recognize them.

21 "Not everyone who says to me, 'Lord, Lord,' will enter the kingdom of heaven, but only he who does the will of my Father who is in heaven. 22 Many will say to me on that day, 'Lord, Lord,

---

a 27 Or single cubit to his height

did we not prophesy in your name, and in your name drive out demons and perform many miracles?' ²³Then I will tell them plainly, 'I never knew you. Away from me, you evildoers!'

The Wise and Foolish Builders

²⁴"Therefore everyone who hears these words of mine and puts them into practice is like a wise man who built his house on the rock. ²⁵The rain came down, the streams rose, and the winds blew and beat against that house; yet it did not fall, because it had its foundation on the rock. ²⁶But everyone who hears these words of mine and does not put them into practice is like a foolish man who built his house on sand. ²⁷The rain came down, the streams rose, and the winds blew and beat against that house, and it fell with a great crash."

²⁸When Jesus had finished saying these things, the crowds were amazed at his teaching, ²⁹because he taught as one who had authority, and not as their teachers of the law.

The Man With Leprosy

8 When he came down from the mountainside, large crowds followed him. ²A man with leprosy*a* came and knelt before him and said, "Lord, if you are willing, you can make me clean."

³Jesus reached out his hand and touched the man. "I am willing," he said. "Be clean!" Immediately he was cured*b* of his leprosy. ⁴Then Jesus said to him, "See that you don't tell anyone. But go, show yourself to the priest and offer the gift Moses commanded, as a testimony to them."

The Faith of the Centurion

⁵When Jesus had entered Capernaum, a centurion came to him, asking for help. ⁶"Lord," he said, "my servant lies at home paralyzed and in terrible suffering."

⁷Jesus said to him, "I will go and heal him."

⁸The centurion replied, "Lord, I do not deserve to have you come under my roof. But just say the word, and my servant will be healed. ⁹For I myself am a man under authority, with soldiers under me. I tell this one, 'Go,' and he goes; and that one, 'Come,' and he comes. I say to my servant, 'Do this,' and he does it."

¹⁰When Jesus heard this, he was astonished and said to those following him, "I tell you the truth, I have not found anyone in Israel with such great faith. ¹¹I say to you that many will come from the east and the west, and will take their places at the feast with Abraham, Isaac and Jacob in the kingdom of heaven. ¹²But the subjects of the kingdom will be thrown outside, into the darkness, where there will be weeping and gnashing of teeth."

¹³Then Jesus said to the centurion, "Go! It will be done just as you believed it would." And his servant was healed at that very hour.

Jesus Heals Many

¹⁴When Jesus came into Peter's house, he saw Peter's mother-in-law lying in bed with a fever. ¹⁵He touched her hand and the fever left her, and she got up and began to wait on him.

¹⁶When evening came, many who were demon-possessed were brought to him, and he drove out the spirits with a word and healed all the sick. ¹⁷This was to fulfill what was spoken through the prophet Isaiah:

"He took up our infirmities
and carried our diseases."*c*

The Cost of Following Jesus

¹⁸When Jesus saw the crowd around him, he gave orders to cross to the other side of the lake. ¹⁹Then a teacher of the law came to him and said, "Teacher, I will follow you wherever you go."

²⁰Jesus replied, "Foxes have holes and birds of the air have nests, but the Son of Man has no place to lay his head."

²¹Another disciple said to him, "Lord, first let me go and bury my father."

²²But Jesus told him, "Follow me, and let the dead bury their own dead."

---

a 2 The Greek word was used for various diseases affecting the skin—not necessarily leprosy.
b 3 Greek *made clean*   *c 17* Isaiah 53:4

Jesus Calms the Storm

23Then he got into the boat and his disciples followed him. 24Without warning, a furious storm came up on the lake, so that the waves swept over the boat. But Jesus was sleeping. 25The disciples went and woke him, saying, "Lord, save us! We're going to drown!"

26He replied, "You of little faith, why are you so afraid?" Then he got up and rebuked the winds and the waves, and it was completely calm.

27The men were amazed and asked, "What kind of man is this? Even the winds and the waves obey him!"

The Healing of Two Demon-possessed Men

28When he arrived at the other side in the region of the Gadarenes,*a* two demon-possessed men coming from the tombs met him. They were so violent that no one could pass that way. 29"What do you want with us, Son of God?" they shouted. "Have you come here to torture us before the appointed time?"

30Some distance from them a large herd of pigs was feeding. 31The demons begged Jesus, "If you drive us out, send us into the herd of pigs."

32He said to them, "Go!" So they came out and went into the pigs, and the whole herd rushed down the steep bank into the lake and died in the water. 33Those tending the pigs ran off, went into the town and reported all this, including what had happened to the demon-possessed men. 34Then the whole town went out to meet Jesus. And when they saw him, they pleaded with him to leave their region.

Jesus Heals a Paralytic

9 Jesus stepped into a boat, crossed over and came to his own town. 2Some men brought to him a paralytic, lying on a mat. When Jesus saw their faith, he said to the paralytic, "Take heart, son; your sins are forgiven."

3At this, some of the teachers of the law said to themselves, "This fellow is blaspheming!"

4Knowing their thoughts, Jesus said, "Why do you entertain evil thoughts in your hearts? 5Which is easier: to say, 'Your sins are forgiven,' or to say, 'Get up and walk'? 6But so that you may know that the Son of Man has authority on earth to forgive sins. . . ." Then he said to the paralytic, "Get up, take your mat and go home." 7And the man got up and went home. 8When the crowd saw this, they were filled with awe; and they praised God, who had given such authority to men.

The Calling of Matthew

9As Jesus went on from there, he saw a man named Matthew sitting at the tax collector's booth. "Follow me," he told him, and Matthew got up and followed him.

10While Jesus was having dinner at Matthew's house, many tax collectors and "sinners" came and ate with him and his disciples. 11When the Pharisees saw this, they asked his disciples, "Why does your teacher eat with tax collectors and 'sinners'?"

12On hearing this, Jesus said, "It is not the healthy who need a doctor, but the sick. 13But go and learn what this means: 'I desire mercy, not sacrifice.'*b* For I have not come to call the righteous, but sinners."

Jesus Questioned About Fasting

14Then John's disciples came and asked him, "How is it that we and the Pharisees fast, but your disciples do not fast?"

15Jesus answered, "How can the guests of the bridegroom mourn while he is with them? The time will come when the bridegroom will be taken from them; then they will fast.

16"No one sews a patch of unshrunk cloth on an old garment, for the patch will pull away from the garment, making the tear worse. 17Neither do men pour new wine into old wineskins. If they do, the skins will burst, the wine will run out and the wineskins will be ruined. No, they pour new wine into new wineskins, and both are preserved."

A Dead Girl and a Sick Woman

18While he was saying this, a ruler came and knelt before him and said, "My daughter has just died. But come

---

a 28 Some manuscripts *Gergesenes;* others *Gerasenes*   *b 13* Hosea 6:6

A TRUE RELATION WITH CHRIST
Dietrich Bonhoeffer

VERSE: Matthew 9:9   **PASSAGE:** Matthew 9:9–13

hen we are called to follow Christ, we are summoned to an exclusive attachment to his person. The grace of his call bursts all the bonds of legalism. It is a gracious call, a gracious commandment. It transcends the difference between the law and the gospel. Christ calls, the disciple follows; that is grace and commandment in one. "I will walk about in freedom, for I have sought out your precepts" (Psalm 119:45).

Discipleship means adherence to Christ, and, because Christ is the object of that adherence, it must take the form of discipleship. An abstract Christology, a doctrinal system, a general religious knowledge on the subject of grace or on the forgiveness of sins, render discipleship superfluous, and in fact they positively exclude any idea of discipleship whatever, and are essentially inimical to the whole conception of following Christ. With an abstract idea it is possible to enter into a relation of formal knowledge, to become enthusiastic about it, and perhaps even to put it into practice; but it can never be followed in personal obedience. Christianity without the living Christ is inevitably Christianity without discipleship, and Christianity without discipleship is always Christianity without Christ. It remains an abstract idea, a myth which has a place for the Fatherhood of God, but omits Christ as the living Son. And a Christianity of that kind is nothing more or less than the end of discipleship. In such a religion there is trust in God, but no following of Christ. Because the Son of God became man, because he is the mediator, for that reason alone the only true relation we can have with him is to follow him. Discipleship is bound to Christ as the mediator, and where it is properly understood, it necessarily implies faith in the Son of God as the mediator. Only the mediator, the God-man, can call men to follow him.

ADDITIONAL SCRIPTURE READING:
Luke 5:27–28; John 13:34–35

Go to page 1114 for your next devotional reading.

1900   Present

and put your hand on her, and she will live." ¹⁹Jesus got up and went with him, and so did his disciples.

²⁰Just then a woman who had been subject to bleeding for twelve years came up behind him and touched the edge of his cloak. ²¹She said to herself, "If I only touch his cloak, I will be healed." ²²Jesus turned and saw her. "Take heart, daughter," he said, "your faith has healed you." And the woman was healed from that moment.

²³When Jesus entered the ruler's house and saw the flute players and the noisy crowd, ²⁴he said, "Go away. The girl is not dead but asleep." But they laughed at him. ²⁵After the crowd had been put outside, he went in and took the girl by the hand, and she got up. ²⁶News of this spread through all that region.

Jesus Heals the Blind and Mute

²⁷As Jesus went on from there, two blind men followed him, calling out, "Have mercy on us, Son of David!"

²⁸When he had gone indoors, the blind men came to him, and he asked them, "Do you believe that I am able to do this?"

"Yes, Lord," they replied.

²⁹Then he touched their eyes and said, "According to your faith will it be done to you"; ³⁰and their sight was restored. Jesus warned them sternly, "See that no one knows about this." ³¹But they went out and spread the news about him all over that region.

³²While they were going out, a man who was demon-possessed and could not talk was brought to Jesus. ³³And when the demon was driven out, the man who had been mute spoke. The crowd was amazed and said, "Nothing like this has ever been seen in Israel."

³⁴But the Pharisees said, "It is by the prince of demons that he drives out demons."

The Workers Are Few

³⁵Jesus went through all the towns and villages, teaching in their synagogues, preaching the good news of the kingdom and healing every disease and sickness. ³⁶When he saw the crowds, he had compassion on them, because they were harassed and helpless, like sheep without a shepherd. ³⁷Then he said to his disciples, "The harvest is plentiful but the workers are few. ³⁸Ask the Lord of the harvest, therefore, to send out workers into his harvest field."

Jesus Sends Out the Twelve

10 He called his twelve disciples to him and gave them authority to drive out evil[a] spirits and to heal every disease and sickness.

²These are the names of the twelve apostles: first, Simon (who is called Peter) and his brother Andrew; James son of Zebedee, and his brother John; ³Philip and Bartholomew; Thomas and Matthew the tax collector; James son of Alphaeus, and Thaddaeus; ⁴Simon the Zealot and Judas Iscariot, who betrayed him.

⁵These twelve Jesus sent out with the following instructions: "Do not go among the Gentiles or enter any town of the Samaritans. ⁶Go rather to the lost sheep of Israel. ⁷As you go, preach this message: 'The kingdom of heaven is near.' ⁸Heal the sick, raise the dead, cleanse those who have leprosy,[b] drive out demons. Freely you have received, freely give. ⁹Do not take along any gold or silver or copper in your belts; ¹⁰take no bag for the journey, or extra tunic, or sandals or a staff; for the worker is worth his keep.

¹¹"Whatever town or village you enter, search for some worthy person there and stay at his house until you leave. ¹²As you enter the home, give it your greeting. ¹³If the home is deserving, let your peace rest on it; if it is not, let your peace return to you. ¹⁴If anyone will not welcome you or listen to your words, shake the dust off your feet when you leave that home or town. ¹⁵I tell you the truth, it will be more bearable for Sodom and Gomorrah on the day of judgment than for that town. ¹⁶I am sending you out like sheep among wolves. Therefore be as shrewd as snakes and as innocent as doves.

¹⁷"Be on your guard against men; they will hand you over to the local councils and flog you in their synagogues. ¹⁸On

my account you will be brought before governors and kings as witnesses to them and to the Gentiles. ¹⁹But when they arrest you, do not worry about what to say or how to say it. At that time you will be given what to say, ²⁰for it will not be you speaking, but the Spirit of your Father speaking through you.

²¹"Brother will betray brother to death, and a father his child; children will rebel against their parents and have them put to death. ²²All men will hate you because of me, but he who stands firm to the end will be saved. ²³When you are persecuted in one place, flee to another. I tell you the truth, you will not finish going through the cities of Israel before the Son of Man comes.

²⁴"A student is not above his teacher, nor a servant above his master. ²⁵It is enough for the student to be like his teacher, and the servant like his master. If the head of the house has been called Beelzebub,^a how much more the members of his household!

²⁶"So do not be afraid of them. There is nothing concealed that will not be disclosed, or hidden that will not be made known. ²⁷What I tell you in the dark, speak in the daylight; what is whispered in your ear, proclaim from the roofs. ²⁸Do not be afraid of those who kill the body but cannot kill the soul. Rather, be afraid of the One who can destroy both soul and body in hell. ²⁹Are not two sparrows sold for a penny^b? Yet not one of them will fall to the ground apart from the will of your Father. ³⁰And even the very hairs of your head are all numbered. ³¹So don't be afraid; you are worth more than many sparrows.

³²"Whoever acknowledges me before men, I will also acknowledge him before my Father in heaven. ³³But whoever disowns me before men, I will disown him before my Father in heaven.

³⁴"Do not suppose that I have come to bring peace to the earth. I did not come to bring peace, but a sword. ³⁵For I have come to turn

" 'a man against his father,
   a daughter against her mother,

a daughter-in-law against her
   mother-in-law—
³⁶   a man's enemies will be the
   members of his own
   household.'^c

³⁷"Anyone who loves his father or mother more than me is not worthy of me; anyone who loves his son or daughter more than me is not worthy of me; ³⁸and anyone who does not take his cross and follow me is not worthy of me. ³⁹Whoever finds his life will lose it, and whoever loses his life for my sake will find it.

⁴⁰"He who receives you receives me, and he who receives me receives the one who sent me. ⁴¹Anyone who receives a prophet because he is a prophet will receive a prophet's reward, and anyone who receives a righteous man because he is a righteous man will receive a righteous man's reward. ⁴²And if anyone gives even a cup of cold water to one of these little ones because he is my disciple, I tell you the truth, he will certainly not lose his reward."

Jesus and John the Baptist

11 After Jesus had finished instructing his twelve disciples, he went on from there to teach and preach in the towns of Galilee.^d

²When John heard in prison what Christ was doing, he sent his disciples ³to ask him, "Are you the one who was to come, or should we expect someone else?"

⁴Jesus replied, "Go back and report to John what you hear and see: ⁵The blind receive sight, the lame walk, those who have leprosy^e are cured, the deaf hear, the dead are raised, and the good news is preached to the poor. ⁶Blessed is the man who does not fall away on account of me."

⁷As John's disciples were leaving, Jesus began to speak to the crowd about John: "What did you go out into the desert to see? A reed swayed by the wind? ⁸If not, what did you go out to see? A man dressed in fine clothes? No, those who wear fine clothes are in kings' palaces. ⁹Then what did you go

---

^a 25 Greek *Beezeboul* or *Beelzeboul*   ^b 29 Greek *an assarion*   ^c 36 Micah 7:6   ^d 1 Greek *in their towns*   ^e 5 The Greek word was used for various diseases affecting the skin—not necessarily leprosy.

out to see? A prophet? Yes, I tell you, and more than a prophet. [10]This is the one about whom it is written:

" 'I will send my messenger ahead of
    you,
who will prepare your way before
    you.'[a]

[11]I tell you the truth: Among those born of women there has not risen anyone greater than John the Baptist; yet he who is least in the kingdom of heaven is greater than he. [12]From the days of John the Baptist until now, the kingdom of heaven has been forcefully advancing, and forceful men lay hold of it. [13]For all the Prophets and the Law prophesied until John. [14]And if you are willing to accept it, he is the Elijah who was to come. [15]He who has ears, let him hear.

[16]"To what can I compare this generation? They are like children sitting in the marketplaces and calling out to others:

[17]" 'We played the flute for you,
    and you did not dance;
we sang a dirge,
    and you did not mourn.'

[18]For John came neither eating nor drinking, and they say, 'He has a demon.' [19]The Son of Man came eating and drinking, and they say, 'Here is a glutton and a drunkard, a friend of tax collectors and "sinners." ' But wisdom is proved right by her actions."

Woe on Unrepentant Cities

[20]Then Jesus began to denounce the cities in which most of his miracles had been performed, because they did not repent. [21]"Woe to you, Korazin! Woe to you, Bethsaida! If the miracles that were performed in you had been performed in Tyre and Sidon, they would have repented long ago in sackcloth and ashes. [22]But I tell you, it will be more bearable for Tyre and Sidon on the day of judgment than for you. [23]And you, Capernaum, will you be lifted up to the skies? No, you will go down to the depths.[b] If the miracles that were performed in you had been performed in Sodom, it would have remained to this day. [24]But I tell you

that it will be more bearable for Sodom on the day of judgment than for you."

Rest for the Weary

[25]At that time Jesus said, "I praise you, Father, Lord of heaven and earth, because you have hidden these things from the wise and learned, and revealed them to little children. [26]Yes, Father, for this was your good pleasure.

[27]"All things have been committed to me by my Father. No one knows the Son except the Father, and no one knows the Father except the Son and those to whom the Son chooses to reveal him.

[28]"Come to me, all you who are weary and burdened, and I will give you rest. [29]Take my yoke upon you and learn from me, for I am gentle and humble in

---

I HAVE READ IN PLATO AND CICERO SAYINGS THAT ARE VERY WISE AND VERY BEAUTIFUL; BUT I NEVER READ IN EITHER OF THEM: "COME UNTO ME ALL YE THAT LABOR AND ARE HEAVY LADEN."

—*Augustine*

---

heart, and you will find rest for your souls. [30]For my yoke is easy and my burden is light."

Lord of the Sabbath

12 At that time Jesus went through the grainfields on the Sabbath. His disciples were hungry and began to pick some heads of grain and eat them. [2]When the Pharisees saw this, they said to him, "Look! Your disciples are doing what is unlawful on the Sabbath."

[3]He answered, "Haven't you read what David did when he and his companions were hungry? [4]He entered the house of God, and he and his companions ate the consecrated bread—which was not lawful for them to do, but only for the priests. [5]Or haven't you read in the Law that on the Sabbath the priests in the temple desecrate the day and yet are innocent? [6]I tell you that one[c] greater than the temple is here. [7]If you had known what these words mean, 'I desire mercy, not sacrifice,'[d] you would

not have condemned the innocent. **8**For the Son of Man is Lord of the Sabbath."

9Going on from that place, he went into their synagogue, **10**and a man with a shriveled hand was there. Looking for a reason to accuse Jesus, they asked him, "Is it lawful to heal on the Sabbath?"

11He said to them, "If any of you has a sheep and it falls into a pit on the Sabbath, will you not take hold of it and lift

---

FRIDAY

SELF-CONSCIOUSNESS VS. CHRIST-CONSCIOUSNESS
Oswald Chambers

VERSE: Matthew 11:28   **PASSAGE:** Matthew 11:25–30

henever anything begins to disintegrate your life with Jesus Christ, turn to him at once, asking him to re-establish your rest. Never allow anything to remain in your life that is causing the unrest. Think of every detail of your life that is causing the disintegration as something to fight against, not as something you should allow to remain. Ask the Lord to put awareness of himself in you, and your self-awareness will disappear. Then he will be your all in all. Beware of allowing your self-awareness to continue, because slowly but surely it will awaken self-pity, and self-pity is satanic . . . Ask the Lord to give you Christ-awareness, and he will steady you until your completeness in him is absolute.

A complete life is the life of a child. When I am fully conscious of my awareness of Christ, there is something wrong. It is the sick person who really knows what health is. A child of God is not aware of the will of God because he *is* the will of God. When we have deviated even slightly from the will of God, we begin to ask, "Lord, what is your will?" A child of God never prays to be made aware of the fact that God answers prayer, because he is so restfully certain that God always answers prayer.

If we try to overcome self-awareness through any of our own commonsense methods, we will only serve to strengthen our self-awareness tremendously. Jesus says, "Come to me . . . and I will give you rest," that is, Christ-awareness will take the place of self-awareness. Wherever Jesus comes he establishes rest— the rest of the completion of activity in our lives that is never aware of itself.

ADDITIONAL SCRIPTURE READING:
Psalm 116:7–9; John 14:27

Go to page 1119 for your next devotional reading.

1900   Present

it out? [12]How much more valuable is a man than a sheep! Therefore it is lawful to do good on the Sabbath."

[13]Then he said to the man, "Stretch out your hand." So he stretched it out and it was completely restored, just as sound as the other. [14]But the Pharisees went out and plotted how they might kill Jesus.

God's Chosen Servant

[15]Aware of this, Jesus withdrew from that place. Many followed him, and he healed all their sick, [16]warning them not to tell who he was. [17]This was to fulfill what was spoken through the prophet Isaiah:

[18] "Here is my servant whom I have
　　chosen,
　　the one I love, in whom I delight;
　I will put my Spirit on him,
　　and he will proclaim justice to the
　　nations.
[19] He will not quarrel or cry out;
　　no one will hear his voice in the
　　streets.
[20] A bruised reed he will not break,
　　and a smoldering wick he will not
　　snuff out,
　till he leads justice to victory.
[21]　In his name the nations will put
　　their hope." [a]

Jesus and Beelzebub

[22]Then they brought him a demon-possessed man who was blind and mute, and Jesus healed him, so that he could both talk and see. [23]All the people were astonished and said, "Could this be the Son of David?"

[24]But when the Pharisees heard this, they said, "It is only by Beelzebub,[b] the prince of demons, that this fellow drives out demons."

[25]Jesus knew their thoughts and said to them, "Every kingdom divided against itself will be ruined, and every city or household divided against itself will not stand. [26]If Satan drives out Satan, he is divided against himself. How then can his kingdom stand? [27]And if I drive out demons by Beelzebub, by whom do your people drive them out? So then, they will be your judges. [28]But if I drive out demons by the Spirit of God, then the kingdom of God has come upon you.

[29] "Or again, how can anyone enter a strong man's house and carry off his possessions unless he first ties up the strong man? Then he can rob his house.

[30] "He who is not with me is against me, and he who does not gather with me scatters. [31]And so I tell you, every sin and blasphemy will be forgiven men, but the blasphemy against the Spirit will not be forgiven. [32]Anyone who speaks a word against the Son of Man will be forgiven, but anyone who speaks against the Holy Spirit will not be forgiven, either in this age or in the age to come.

[33] "Make a tree good and its fruit will be good, or make a tree bad and its fruit will be bad, for a tree is recognized by its fruit. [34]You brood of vipers, how can you who are evil say anything good? For out of the overflow of the heart the mouth speaks. [35]The good man brings good things out of the good stored up in him, and the evil man brings evil things out of the evil stored up in him. [36]But I tell you that men will have to give account on the day of judgment for every careless word they have spoken. [37]For by your words you will be acquitted, and by your words you will be condemned."

The Sign of Jonah

[38]Then some of the Pharisees and teachers of the law said to him, "Teacher, we want to see a miraculous sign from you."

[39]He answered, "A wicked and adulterous generation asks for a miraculous sign! But none will be given it except the sign of the prophet Jonah. [40]For as Jonah was three days and three nights in the belly of a huge fish, so the Son of Man will be three days and three nights in the heart of the earth. [41]The men of Nineveh will stand up at the judgment with this generation and condemn it; for they repented at the preaching of Jonah, and now one[c] greater than Jonah is here. [42]The Queen of the South will rise at the judgment with this generation and condemn it; for she came from the ends of the earth to listen to Solomon's wisdom,

---

[a] 21 Isaiah 42:1–4　　[b] 24 Greek Beezeboul or Beelzeboul; also in verse 27　　[c] 41 Or something; also in verse 42

and now one greater than Solomon is here.

⁴³"When an evil*ᵃ* spirit comes out of a man, it goes through arid places seeking rest and does not find it. ⁴⁴Then it says, 'I will return to the house I left.' When it arrives, it finds the house unoccupied, swept clean and put in order. ⁴⁵Then it goes and takes with it seven other spirits more wicked than itself, and they go in and live there. And the final condition of that man is worse than the first. That is how it will be with this wicked generation."

Jesus' Mother and Brothers

⁴⁶While Jesus was still talking to the crowd, his mother and brothers stood outside, wanting to speak to him. ⁴⁷Someone told him, "Your mother and brothers are standing outside, wanting to speak to you."*ᵇ*

⁴⁸He replied to him, "Who is my mother, and who are my brothers?" ⁴⁹Pointing to his disciples, he said, "Here are my mother and my brothers. ⁵⁰For whoever does the will of my Father in heaven is my brother and sister and mother."

The Parable of the Sower

13 That same day Jesus went out of the house and sat by the lake. ²Such large crowds gathered around him that he got into a boat and sat in it, while all the people stood on the shore. ³Then he told them many things in parables, saying: "A farmer went out to sow his seed. ⁴As he was scattering the seed, some fell along the path, and the birds came and ate it up. ⁵Some fell on rocky places, where it did not have much soil. It sprang up quickly, because the soil was shallow. ⁶But when the sun came up, the plants were scorched, and they withered because they had no root. ⁷Other seed fell among thorns, which grew up and choked the plants. ⁸Still other seed fell on good soil, where it produced a crop—a hundred, sixty or thirty times what was sown. ⁹He who has ears, let him hear."

¹⁰The disciples came to him and asked, "Why do you speak to the people in parables?"

¹¹He replied, "The knowledge of the secrets of the kingdom of heaven has been given to you, but not to them. ¹²Whoever has will be given more, and he will have an abundance. Whoever does not have, even what he has will be taken from him. ¹³This is why I speak to them in parables:

"Though seeing, they do not see;
    though hearing, they do not hear or
        understand.

¹⁴In them is fulfilled the prophecy of Isaiah:

" 'You will be ever hearing but never
        understanding;
    you will be ever seeing but never
        perceiving.
¹⁵ For this people's heart has become
        calloused;
    they hardly hear with their ears,
    and they have closed their eyes.
Otherwise they might see with their
        eyes,
    hear with their ears,
    understand with their hearts
and turn, and I would heal them.'*ᶜ*

¹⁶But blessed are your eyes because they see, and your ears because they hear. ¹⁷For I tell you the truth, many prophets and righteous men longed to see what you see but did not see it, and to hear what you hear but did not hear it.

¹⁸"Listen then to what the parable of the sower means: ¹⁹When anyone hears the message about the kingdom and does not understand it, the evil one comes and snatches away what was sown in his heart. This is the seed sown along the path. ²⁰The one who received the seed that fell on rocky places is the man who hears the word and at once receives it with joy. ²¹But since he has no root, he lasts only a short time. When trouble or persecution comes because of the word, he quickly falls away. ²²The one who received the seed that fell among the thorns is the man who hears the word, but the worries of this life and the deceitfulness of wealth choke it, making it unfruitful. ²³But the one who received the seed that fell on good soil is

---

ᵃ 43 Greek *unclean*   *ᵇ 47* Some manuscripts do not have verse 47.   *ᶜ 15* Isaiah 6:9,10

the man who hears the word and understands it. He produces a crop, yielding a hundred, sixty or thirty times what was sown."

The Parable of the Weeds

24Jesus told them another parable: "The kingdom of heaven is like a man who sowed good seed in his field. 25But while everyone was sleeping, his enemy came and sowed weeds among the wheat, and went away. 26When the wheat sprouted and formed heads, then the weeds also appeared.

27"The owner's servants came to him and said, 'Sir, didn't you sow good seed in your field? Where then did the weeds come from?'

28" 'An enemy did this,' he replied.

"The servants asked him, 'Do you want us to go and pull them up?'

29" 'No,' he answered, 'because while you are pulling the weeds, you may root up the wheat with them. 30Let both grow together until the harvest. At that time I will tell the harvesters: First collect the weeds and tie them in bundles to be burned; then gather the wheat and bring it into my barn.' "

The Parables of the Mustard Seed and the Yeast

31He told them another parable: "The kingdom of heaven is like a mustard seed, which a man took and planted in his field. 32Though it is the smallest of all your seeds, yet when it grows, it is the largest of garden plants and becomes a tree, so that the birds of the air come and perch in its branches."

33He told them still another parable: "The kingdom of heaven is like yeast that a woman took and mixed into a large amount[a] of flour until it worked all through the dough."

34Jesus spoke all these things to the crowd in parables; he did not say anything to them without using a parable. 35So was fulfilled what was spoken through the prophet:

"I will open my mouth in parables,
    I will utter things hidden since the
    creation of the world."[b]

The Parable of the Weeds Explained

36Then he left the crowd and went into the house. His disciples came to him and said, "Explain to us the parable of the weeds in the field."

37He answered, "The one who sowed the good seed is the Son of Man. 38The field is the world, and the good seed stands for the sons of the kingdom. The weeds are the sons of the evil one, 39and the enemy who sows them is the devil. The harvest is the end of the age, and the harvesters are angels.

40"As the weeds are pulled up and burned in the fire, so it will be at the end of the age. 41The Son of Man will send out his angels, and they will weed out of his kingdom everything that causes sin and all who do evil. 42They will throw them into the fiery furnace, where there will be weeping and gnashing of teeth. 43Then the righteous will shine like the sun in the kingdom of their Father. He who has ears, let him hear.

The Parables of the Hidden Treasure and the Pearl

44"The kingdom of heaven is like treasure hidden in a field. When a man found it, he hid it again, and then in his joy went and sold all he had and bought that field.

COSTLY GRACE IS THE TREASURE HIDDEN IN THE FIELD; FOR THE SAKE OF IT A MAN WILL GLADLY GO AND SELL ALL THAT HE HAS. IT IS COSTLY BECAUSE IT COSTS A MAN HIS LIFE, AND IT IS GRACE BECAUSE IT GIVES A MAN THE ONLY TRUE LIFE.   —Dietrich Bonhoeffer

---

45"Again, the kingdom of heaven is like a merchant looking for fine pearls. 46When he found one of great value, he went away and sold everything he had and bought it.

The Parable of the Net

47"Once again, the kingdom of heaven is like a net that was let down into the lake and caught all kinds of fish. 48When it was full, the fishermen pulled it up on the shore. Then they sat

---

a 33 Greek three satas (probably about 1/2 bushel or 22 liters)   b 35 Psalm 78:2

down and collected the good fish in baskets, but threw the bad away. ⁴⁹This is how it will be at the end of the age. The angels will come and separate the wicked from the righteous ⁵⁰and throw them into the fiery furnace, where there will be weeping and gnashing of teeth.

⁵¹"Have you understood all these things?" Jesus asked.

"Yes," they replied.

⁵²He said to them, "Therefore every teacher of the law who has been instructed about the kingdom of heaven is like the owner of a house who brings out of his storeroom new treasures as well as old."

A Prophet Without Honor

⁵³When Jesus had finished these parables, he moved on from there. ⁵⁴Coming to his hometown, he began teaching the people in their synagogue, and they were amazed. "Where did this man get this wisdom and these miraculous powers?" they asked. ⁵⁵"Isn't this the carpenter's son? Isn't his mother's name Mary, and aren't his brothers James, Joseph, Simon and Judas? ⁵⁶Aren't all his sisters with us? Where then did this man get all these things?" ⁵⁷And they took offense at him.

But Jesus said to them, "Only in his hometown and in his own house is a prophet without honor."

⁵⁸And he did not do many miracles there because of their lack of faith.

John the Baptist Beheaded

14 At that time Herod the tetrarch heard the reports about Jesus, ²and he said to his attendants, "This is John the Baptist; he has risen from the dead! That is why miraculous powers are at work in him."

³Now Herod had arrested John and bound him and put him in prison because of Herodias, his brother Philip's wife, ⁴for John had been saying to him: "It is not lawful for you to have her." ⁵Herod wanted to kill John, but he was afraid of the people, because they considered him a prophet.

⁶On Herod's birthday the daughter of Herodias danced for them and pleased Herod so much ⁷that he promised with an oath to give her whatever she asked.

⁸Prompted by her mother, she said, "Give me here on a platter the head of John the Baptist." ⁹The king was distressed, but because of his oaths and his dinner guests, he ordered that her request be granted ¹⁰and had John beheaded in the prison. ¹¹His head was brought in on a platter and given to the girl, who carried it to her mother. ¹²John's disciples came and took his body and buried it. Then they went and told Jesus.

Jesus Feeds the Five Thousand

¹³When Jesus heard what had happened, he withdrew by boat privately to a solitary place. Hearing of this, the crowds followed him on foot from the towns. ¹⁴When Jesus landed and saw a large crowd, he had compassion on them and healed their sick.

¹⁵As evening approached, the disciples came to him and said, "This is a remote place, and it's already getting late. Send the crowds away, so they can go to the villages and buy themselves some food."

¹⁶Jesus replied, "They do not need to go away. You give them something to eat."

¹⁷"We have here only five loaves of bread and two fish," they answered.

¹⁸"Bring them here to me," he said. ¹⁹And he directed the people to sit down on the grass. Taking the five loaves and the two fish and looking up to heaven, he gave thanks and broke the loaves. Then he gave them to the disciples, and the disciples gave them to the people. ²⁰They all ate and were satisfied, and the disciples picked up twelve basketfuls of broken pieces that were left over. ²¹The number of those who ate was about five thousand men, besides women and children.

Jesus Walks on the Water

²²Immediately Jesus made the disciples get into the boat and go on ahead of him to the other side, while he dismissed the crowd. ²³After he had dismissed them, he went up on a mountainside by himself to pray. When evening came, he was there alone, ²⁴but the boat was already a considerable distance[a] from land, buffeted by the waves because the wind was against it.

a 24 Greek *many stadia*

WEEKEND

A SONG FOR SIMEON
T. S. Eliot

VERSE: Luke 2:25   **PASSAGE:** Luke 2:25–34

ord, the Roman hyacinths are blooming in
      bowls and
The winter sun creeps by the snow hills;
The stubborn season has made stand.
My life is light, waiting for the death wind,
Like a feather on the back of my hand.
Dust in sunlight and memory in corners
Wait for the wind that chills towards the dead land . . .

Before the time of cords and scourges and lamentation
Grant us thy peace.
Before the stations of the mountain of desolation,
Before the certain hour of maternal sorrow,
Now at this birth season of decease,
Let the infant, the still unspeaking and unspoken
        Word,
Grant Israel's consolation
To one who has eighty years and no tomorrow . . .

I am tired with my own life and the lives of those
        after me,
I am dying in my own death and the deaths of those
        after me.
Let thy servant depart,
Having seen thy salvation.

ADDITIONAL SCRIPTURE READING:
Isaiah 44:23; 52:9

Go to page 1123 for your next devotional reading.

1900   Present

25During the fourth watch of the night Jesus went out to them, walking on the lake. 26When the disciples saw him walking on the lake, they were terrified. "It's a ghost," they said, and cried out in fear.

27But Jesus immediately said to them: "Take courage! It is I. Don't be afraid."

28"Lord, if it's you," Peter replied, "tell me to come to you on the water."

29"Come," he said.

Then Peter got down out of the boat, walked on the water and came toward Jesus. 30But when he saw the wind, he was afraid and, beginning to sink, cried out, "Lord, save me!"

31Immediately Jesus reached out his hand and caught him. "You of little faith," he said, "why did you doubt?"

32And when they climbed into the boat, the wind died down. 33Then those who were in the boat worshiped him, saying, "Truly you are the Son of God."

34When they had crossed over, they landed at Gennesaret. 35And when the men of that place recognized Jesus, they sent word to all the surrounding country. People brought all their sick to him 36and begged him to let the sick just touch the edge of his cloak, and all who touched him were healed.

Clean and Unclean

15 Then some Pharisees and teachers of the law came to Jesus from Jerusalem and asked, 2"Why do your disciples break the tradition of the elders? They don't wash their hands before they eat!"

3Jesus replied, "And why do you break the command of God for the sake of your tradition? 4For God said, 'Honor your father and mother'*a* and 'Anyone who curses his father or mother must be put to death.'*b* 5But you say that if a man says to his father or mother, 'Whatever help you might otherwise have received from me is a gift devoted to God,' 6he is not to 'honor his father*c*' with it. Thus you nullify the word of God for the sake of your tradition. 7You hypocrites! Isaiah was right when he prophesied about you:

8" 'These people honor me with their lips,
   but their hearts are far from me.
9They worship me in vain;
   their teachings are but rules taught
      by men.'*d*"

10Jesus called the crowd to him and said, "Listen and understand. 11What goes into a man's mouth does not make him 'unclean,' but what comes out of his mouth, that is what makes him 'unclean.' "

12Then the disciples came to him and asked, "Do you know that the Pharisees were offended when they heard this?"

13He replied, "Every plant that my heavenly Father has not planted will be pulled up by the roots. 14Leave them; they are blind guides.*e* If a blind man leads a blind man, both will fall into a pit."

15Peter said, "Explain the parable to us."

16"Are you still so dull?" Jesus asked them. 17"Don't you see that whatever enters the mouth goes into the stomach and then out of the body? 18But the things that come out of the mouth come from the heart, and these make a man 'unclean.' 19For out of the heart come evil thoughts, murder, adultery, sexual immorality, theft, false testimony, slander. 20These are what make a man 'unclean'; but eating with unwashed hands does not make him 'unclean.' "

The Faith of the Canaanite Woman

21Leaving that place, Jesus withdrew to the region of Tyre and Sidon. 22A Canaanite woman from that vicinity came to him, crying out, "Lord, Son of David, have mercy on me! My daughter is suffering terribly from demon-possession."

23Jesus did not answer a word. So his disciples came to him and urged him, "Send her away, for she keeps crying out after us."

24He answered, "I was sent only to the lost sheep of Israel."

25The woman came and knelt before him. "Lord, help me!" she said.

26He replied, "It is not right to take the children's bread and toss it to their dogs."

---

a 4 Exodus 20:12; Deut. 5:16   *b 4* Exodus 21:17; Lev. 20:9   *c 6* Some manuscripts *father or his mother*   *d 9* Isaiah 29:13   *e 14* Some manuscripts *guides of the blind*

27"Yes, Lord," she said, "but even the dogs eat the crumbs that fall from their masters' table."

28Then Jesus answered, "Woman, you have great faith! Your request is granted." And her daughter was healed from that very hour.

Jesus Feeds the Four Thousand

29Jesus left there and went along the Sea of Galilee. Then he went up on a mountainside and sat down. 30Great crowds came to him, bringing the lame, the blind, the crippled, the mute and many others, and laid them at his feet; and he healed them. 31The people were amazed when they saw the mute speaking, the crippled made well, the lame walking and the blind seeing. And they praised the God of Israel.

32Jesus called his disciples to him and said, "I have compassion for these people; they have already been with me three days and have nothing to eat. I do not want to send them away hungry, or they may collapse on the way."

33His disciples answered, "Where could we get enough bread in this remote place to feed such a crowd?"

34"How many loaves do you have?" Jesus asked.

"Seven," they replied, "and a few small fish."

35He told the crowd to sit down on the ground. 36Then he took the seven loaves and the fish, and when he had given thanks, he broke them and gave them to the disciples, and they in turn to the people. 37They all ate and were satisfied. Afterward the disciples picked up seven basketfuls of broken pieces that were left over. 38The number of those who ate was four thousand, besides women and children. 39After Jesus had sent the crowd away, he got into the boat and went to the vicinity of Magadan.

The Demand for a Sign

16 The Pharisees and Sadducees came to Jesus and tested him by asking him to show them a sign from heaven.

2He replied,a "When evening comes, you say, 'It will be fair weather, for the sky is red,' 3and in the morning, 'Today it will be stormy, for the sky is red and overcast.' You know how to interpret the appearance of the sky, but you cannot interpret the signs of the times. 4A wicked and adulterous generation looks for a miraculous sign, but none will be given it except the sign of Jonah." Jesus then left them and went away.

The Yeast of the Pharisees and Sadducees

5When they went across the lake, the disciples forgot to take bread. 6"Be careful," Jesus said to them. "Be on your guard against the yeast of the Pharisees and Sadducees."

7They discussed this among themselves and said, "It is because we didn't bring any bread."

8Aware of their discussion, Jesus asked, "You of little faith, why are you talking among yourselves about having no bread? 9Do you still not understand? Don't you remember the five loaves for the five thousand, and how many basketfuls you gathered? 10Or the seven loaves for the four thousand, and how many basketfuls you gathered? 11How is it you don't understand that I was not talking to you about bread? But be on your guard against the yeast of the Pharisees and Sadducees." 12Then they understood that he was not telling them to guard against the yeast used in bread, but against the teaching of the Pharisees and Sadducees.

Peter's Confession of Christ

13When Jesus came to the region of Caesarea Philippi, he asked his disciples, "Who do people say the Son of Man is?"

14They replied, "Some say John the Baptist; others say Elijah; and still others, Jeremiah or one of the prophets."

15"But what about you?" he asked. "Who do you say I am?"

16Simon Peter answered, "You are the Christ,b the Son of the living God."

17Jesus replied, "Blessed are you, Simon son of Jonah, for this was not revealed to you by man, but by my Father in heaven. 18And I tell you that you are Peter,c and on this rock I will

---

a 2 Some early manuscripts do not have the rest of verse 2 and all of verse 3.   b 16 Or Messiah; also in verse 20   c 18 Peter means rock.

build my church, and the gates of Hades[a] will not overcome it.[b] 19I will give you the keys of the kingdom of heaven; whatever you bind on earth will be[c] bound in heaven, and whatever you loose on earth will be[c] loosed in heaven." 20Then he warned his disciples not to tell anyone that he was the Christ.

Jesus Predicts His Death

21From that time on Jesus began to explain to his disciples that he must go to Jerusalem and suffer many things at the hands of the elders, chief priests and teachers of the law, and that he must be killed and on the third day be raised to life.

22Peter took him aside and began to rebuke him. "Never, Lord!" he said. "This shall never happen to you!"

23Jesus turned and said to Peter, "Get behind me, Satan! You are a stumbling block to me; you do not have in mind the things of God, but the things of men."

24Then Jesus said to his disciples, "If anyone would come after me, he must deny himself and take up his cross and follow me. 25For whoever wants to save his life[d] will lose it, but whoever loses his life for me will find it. 26What good will it be for a man if he gains the whole world, yet forfeits his soul? Or what can a man give in exchange for his soul? 27For the Son of Man is going to come in his Father's glory with his angels, and then he will reward each person according to what he has done. 28I tell you the truth, some who are standing here will not taste death before they see the Son of Man coming in his kingdom."

The Transfiguration

17 After six days Jesus took with him Peter, James and John the brother of James, and led them up a high mountain by themselves. 2There he was transfigured before them. His face shone like the sun, and his clothes became as white as the light. 3Just then there appeared before them Moses and Elijah, talking with Jesus.

4Peter said to Jesus, "Lord, it is good for us to be here. If you wish, I will put up three shelters—one for you, one for Moses and one for Elijah."

5While he was still speaking, a bright cloud enveloped them, and a voice from the cloud said, "This is my Son, whom I love; with him I am well pleased. Listen to him!"

6When the disciples heard this, they fell facedown to the ground, terrified. 7But Jesus came and touched them. "Get up," he said. "Don't be afraid." 8When they looked up, they saw no one except Jesus.

9As they were coming down the mountain, Jesus instructed them, "Don't tell anyone what you have seen, until the Son of Man has been raised from the dead."

10The disciples asked him, "Why then do the teachers of the law say that Elijah must come first?"

11Jesus replied, "To be sure, Elijah comes and will restore all things. 12But I tell you, Elijah has already come, and they did not recognize him, but have done to him everything they wished. In the same way the Son of Man is going to suffer at their hands." 13Then the disciples understood that he was talking to them about John the Baptist.

The Healing of a Boy With a Demon

14When they came to the crowd, a man approached Jesus and knelt before him. 15"Lord, have mercy on my son," he said. "He has seizures and is suffering greatly. He often falls into the fire or into the water. 16I brought him to your disciples, but they could not heal him."

17"O unbelieving and perverse generation," Jesus replied, "how long shall I stay with you? How long shall I put up with you? Bring the boy here to me." 18Jesus rebuked the demon, and it came out of the boy, and he was healed from that moment.

19Then the disciples came to Jesus in private and asked, "Why couldn't we drive it out?"

20He replied, "Because you have so little faith. I tell you the truth, if you have faith as small as a mustard seed, you can say to this mountain, 'Move from here

EXPERIENCING THE LORD
A. B. Simpson

VERSE: Matthew 17:8   **PASSAGE:** Matthew 17:1–8

nce it was the blessing, now it is the Lord;
Once it was the feeling, now it is his word;
Once his gift I wanted, now, the Giver own;
Once I sought for healing, now himself alone.

Once 'twas painful trying, now 'tis perfect trust;
Once a half salvation, now the uttermost;
Once 'twas ceaseless holding, now he holds me fast;
Once 'twas constant drifting, now my anchor's cast.

Once 'twas busy planning, now 'tis trustful prayer;
Once 'twas anxious caring, now he has the care;
Once 'twas what I wanted, now what Jesus says;
Once 'twas constant asking, now 'tis ceaseless praise.

Once I hoped in Jesus, now I know he's mine;
Once my lamps were dying, now they brightly shine;
Once for death I waited, now his coming hail;
And my hopes are anchored safe within the veil.

All in all forever,
Only Christ I'll sing;
Ev'rything is in Christ,
And Christ is ev'rything.

ADDITIONAL SCRIPTURE READING:
Philippians 3:7–11; 1 Peter 5:7

Go to page 1127 for your next devotional reading.

1900   Present

to there' and it will move. Nothing will be impossible for you.*a*"

22When they came together in Galilee, he said to them, "The Son of Man is going to be betrayed into the hands of men. 23They will kill him, and on the third day he will be raised to life." And the disciples were filled with grief.

The Temple Tax

24After Jesus and his disciples arrived in Capernaum, the collectors of the two-drachma tax came to Peter and asked, "Doesn't your teacher pay the temple tax*b*?"

25"Yes, he does," he replied.

When Peter came into the house, Jesus was the first to speak. "What do you think, Simon?" he asked. "From whom do the kings of the earth collect duty and taxes—from their own sons or from others?"

26"From others," Peter answered.

"Then the sons are exempt," Jesus said to him. 27"But so that we may not offend them, go to the lake and throw out your line. Take the first fish you catch; open its mouth and you will find a four-drachma coin. Take it and give it to them for my tax and yours."

The Greatest in the Kingdom of Heaven

18 At that time the disciples came to Jesus and asked, "Who is the greatest in the kingdom of heaven?"

2He called a little child and had him stand among them. 3And he said: "I tell you the truth, unless you change and become like little children, you will never enter the kingdom of heaven. 4Therefore, whoever humbles himself like this child is the greatest in the kingdom of heaven.

5"And whoever welcomes a little child like this in my name welcomes me. 6But if anyone causes one of these little ones who believe in me to sin, it would be better for him to have a large millstone hung around his neck and to be drowned in the depths of the sea.

7"Woe to the world because of the things that cause people to sin! Such things must come, but woe to the man through whom they come! 8If your hand or your foot causes you to sin, cut it off and throw it away. It is better for you to enter life maimed or crippled than to have two hands or two feet and be thrown into eternal fire. 9And if your eye causes you to sin, gouge it out and throw it away. It is better for you to enter life with one eye than to have two eyes and be thrown into the fire of hell.

The Parable of the Lost Sheep

10"See that you do not look down on one of these little ones. For I tell you that their angels in heaven always see the face of my Father in heaven.*c*

12"What do you think? If a man owns a hundred sheep, and one of them wanders away, will he not leave the ninety-nine on the hills and go to look for the one that wandered off? 13And if he finds it, I tell you the truth, he is happier about that one sheep than about the ninety-nine that did not wander off. 14In the same way your Father in heaven is not willing that any of these little ones should be lost.

A Brother Who Sins Against You

15"If your brother sins against you,*d* go and show him his fault, just between the two of you. If he listens to you, you have won your brother over. 16But if he will not listen, take one or two others along, so that 'every matter may be established by the testimony of two or three witnesses.'*e* 17If he refuses to listen to them, tell it to the church; and if he refuses to listen even to the church, treat him as you would a pagan or a tax collector.

18"I tell you the truth, whatever you bind on earth will be*f* bound in heaven, and whatever you loose on earth will be*f* loosed in heaven.

19"Again, I tell you that if two of you on earth agree about anything you ask for, it will be done for you by my Father in heaven. 20For where two or three come together in my name, there am I with them."

a 20 Some manuscripts *you.* *21But this kind does not go out except by prayer and fasting.*   *b* 24 Greek *the two drachmas*   *c* 10 Some manuscripts *heaven.* *11The Son of Man came to save what was lost.*   *d* 15 Some manuscripts do not have *against you.*   *e* 16 Deut. 19:15   *f* 18 Or *have been*

The Parable of the Unmerciful Servant

21Then Peter came to Jesus and asked, "Lord, how many times shall I forgive my brother when he sins against me? Up to seven times?"

22Jesus answered, "I tell you, not seven times, but seventy-seven times.*a*

23"Therefore, the kingdom of heaven is like a king who wanted to settle accounts with his servants. 24As he began the settlement, a man who owed him ten thousand talents*b* was brought to him. 25Since he was not able to pay, the master ordered that he and his wife and his children and all that he had be sold to repay the debt.

26"The servant fell on his knees before him. 'Be patient with me,' he begged, 'and I will pay back everything.' 27The servant's master took pity on him, canceled the debt and let him go.

28"But when that servant went out, he found one of his fellow servants who owed him a hundred denarii.*c* He grabbed him and began to choke him. 'Pay back what you owe me!' he demanded.

29"His fellow servant fell on his knees and begged him, 'Be patient with me, and I will pay you back.'

30"But he refused. Instead, he went off and had the man thrown into prison until he could pay the debt. 31When the other servants saw what had happened, they were greatly distressed and went and told their master everything that had happened.

32"Then the master called the servant in. 'You wicked servant,' he said, 'I canceled all that debt of yours because you begged me to. 33Shouldn't you have had mercy on your fellow servant just as I had on you?' 34In anger his master turned him over to the jailers to be tortured, until he should pay back all he owed.

35"This is how my heavenly Father will treat each of you unless you forgive your brother from your heart."

Divorce

19 When Jesus had finished saying these things, he left Galilee and went into the region of Judea to the other side of the Jordan. 2Large crowds followed him, and he healed them there.

3Some Pharisees came to him to test him. They asked, "Is it lawful for a man to divorce his wife for any and every reason?"

4"Haven't you read," he replied, "that at the beginning the Creator 'made them male and female,'*d* 5and said, 'For this reason a man will leave his father and mother and be united to his wife, and the two will become one flesh'*e*? 6So they are no longer two, but one. Therefore what God has joined together, let man not separate."

7"Why then," they asked, "did Moses command that a man give his wife a certificate of divorce and send her away?"

8Jesus replied, "Moses permitted you to divorce your wives because your hearts were hard. But it was not this way from the beginning. 9I tell you that anyone who divorces his wife, except for marital unfaithfulness, and marries another woman commits adultery."

10The disciples said to him, "If this is the situation between a husband and wife, it is better not to marry."

11Jesus replied, "Not everyone can accept this word, but only those to whom it has been given. 12For some are eunuchs because they were born that way; others were made that way by men; and others have renounced marriage*f* because of the kingdom of heaven. The one who can accept this should accept it."

The Little Children and Jesus

13Then little children were brought to Jesus for him to place his hands on them and pray for them. But the disciples rebuked those who brought them.

14Jesus said, "Let the little children come to me, and do not hinder them, for the kingdom of heaven belongs to such as these." 15When he had placed his hands on them, he went on from there.

The Rich Young Man

16Now a man came up to Jesus and asked, "Teacher, what good thing must I do to get eternal life?"

17"Why do you ask me about what is

a 22 Or *seventy times seven*   *b 24* That is, millions of dollars   *c 28* That is, a few dollars
d 4 Gen. 1:27   *e 5* Gen. 2:24   *f 12* Or *have made themselves eunuchs*

good?" Jesus replied. "There is only One who is good. If you want to enter life, obey the commandments."

18"Which ones?" the man inquired.

Jesus replied, " 'Do not murder, do not commit adultery, do not steal, do not give false testimony, 19honor your father and mother,'ᵃ and 'love your neighbor as yourself.'ᵇ "

20"All these I have kept," the young man said. "What do I still lack?"

21Jesus answered, "If you want to be perfect, go, sell your possessions and give to the poor, and you will have treasure in heaven. Then come, follow me."

22When the young man heard this, he went away sad, because he had great wealth.

23Then Jesus said to his disciples, "I tell you the truth, it is hard for a rich man to enter the kingdom of heaven. 24Again I tell you, it is easier for a camel to go through the eye of a needle than for a rich man to enter the kingdom of God."

25When the disciples heard this, they were greatly astonished and asked, "Who then can be saved?"

26Jesus looked at them and said, "With man this is impossible, but with God all things are possible."

27Peter answered him, "We have left everything to follow you! What then will there be for us?"

28Jesus said to them, "I tell you the truth, at the renewal of all things, when the Son of Man sits on his glorious throne, you who have followed me will also sit on twelve thrones, judging the twelve tribes of Israel. 29And everyone who has left houses or brothers or sisters or father or motherᶜ or children or fields for my sake will receive a hundred times as much and will inherit eternal life. 30But many who are first will be last, and many who are last will be first.

The Parable of the Workers in the Vineyard

20 "For the kingdom of heaven is like a landowner who went out early in the morning to hire men to work in his vineyard. 2He agreed to pay them a denarius for the day and sent them into his vineyard.

3"About the third hour he went out and saw others standing in the market-place doing nothing. 4He told them, 'You also go and work in my vineyard, and I will pay you whatever is right.' 5So they went.

"He went out again about the sixth hour and the ninth hour and did the same thing. 6About the eleventh hour he went out and found still others standing around. He asked them, 'Why have you been standing here all day long doing nothing?'

7" 'Because no one has hired us,' they answered.

"He said to them, 'You also go and work in my vineyard.'

8"When evening came, the owner of the vineyard said to his foreman, 'Call the workers and pay them their wages, beginning with the last ones hired and going on to the first.'

9"The workers who were hired about the eleventh hour came and each received a denarius. 10So when those came who were hired first, they expected to receive more. But each one of them also received a denarius. 11When they received it, they began to grumble against the landowner. 12'These men who were hired last worked only one hour,' they said, 'and you have made them equal to us who have borne the burden of the work and the heat of the day.'

13"But he answered one of them, 'Friend, I am not being unfair to you. Didn't you agree to work for a denarius? 14Take your pay and go. I want to give the man who was hired last the same as I gave you. 15Don't I have the right to do

---

ᵃ 19 Exodus 20:12–16; Deut. 5:16–20   ᵇ 19 Lev. 19:18   ᶜ 29 Some manuscripts *mother or wife*

what I want with my own money? Or are you envious because I am generous?'

¹⁶"So the last will be first, and the first will be last."

Jesus Again Predicts His Death

¹⁷Now as Jesus was going up to Jerusalem, he took the twelve disciples aside and said to them, ¹⁸"We are going up to Jerusalem, and the Son of Man will be betrayed to the chief priests and the teachers of the law. They will condemn him to death ¹⁹and will turn him over to the Gentiles to be mocked and flogged and crucified. On the third day he will be raised to life!"

A Mother's Request

²⁰Then the mother of Zebedee's sons came to Jesus with her sons and, kneeling down, asked a favor of him.

²¹"What is it you want?" he asked.

She said, "Grant that one of these two sons of mine may sit at your right and the other at your left in your kingdom."

²²"You don't know what you are

TUESDAY

THOU SHALT NOT COVET
Richard Pynson

VERSE: Matthew 19:21–22   **PASSAGE:** Matthew 19:16–24

he riches and wealth of this world are like the minstrel's horse. Once upon a time there came a proud thief into a stable and found a minstrel's horse standing next to his own. And since the minstrel's horse was the finer of the two, he took it and rode away on it, leaving his own feeble horse in the stable. The minstrel, who happened to see all this, ran by way of a short cut and met the thief as he was crossing a river. The minstrel cried, "Let us kneel!" The horse, who knew his master's voice well, kneeled down in the river, as he was accustomed to do when playing with his master. Then the minstrel said, "Arise!" and immediately the horse stood up, as he had been taught, and threw the proud thief into the water and ran again to his master.

This minstrel is the world, which plays with the folk of this world as does a minstrel or a juggler or a gambler. His horse is this world's wealth, which often, upon hearing the voice of its master, the world, plays "let us kneel" and brings people low and into great poverty and forsakes them in their greatest need and follows after the play of this world and not after the will of the covetous that would possess it. But often, those who toil most to be rich become the poorest.

ADDITIONAL SCRIPTURE READING:
Matthew 6:24; 1 Timothy 6:10

Go to page 1129 for your next devotional reading.

1500   1700

asking," Jesus said to them. "Can you drink the cup I am going to drink?"

"We can," they answered.

²³Jesus said to them, "You will indeed drink from my cup, but to sit at my right or left is not for me to grant. These places belong to those for whom they have been prepared by my Father."

²⁴When the ten heard about this, they were indignant with the two brothers. ²⁵Jesus called them together and said, "You know that the rulers of the Gentiles lord it over them, and their high officials exercise authority over them. ²⁶Not so with you. Instead, whoever wants to become great among you must be your servant, ²⁷and whoever wants to be first must be your slave— ²⁸just as the Son of Man did not come to be served, but to serve, and to give his life as a ransom for many."

Two Blind Men Receive Sight

²⁹As Jesus and his disciples were leaving Jericho, a large crowd followed him. ³⁰Two blind men were sitting by the roadside, and when they heard that Jesus was going by, they shouted, "Lord, Son of David, have mercy on us!"

³¹The crowd rebuked them and told them to be quiet, but they shouted all the louder, "Lord, Son of David, have mercy on us!"

³²Jesus stopped and called them. "What do you want me to do for you?" he asked.

³³"Lord," they answered, "we want our sight."

³⁴Jesus had compassion on them and touched their eyes. Immediately they received their sight and followed him.

The Triumphal Entry

21 As they approached Jerusalem and came to Bethphage on the Mount of Olives, Jesus sent two disciples, ²saying to them, "Go to the village ahead of you, and at once you will find a donkey tied there, with her colt by her. Untie them and bring them to me. ³If anyone says anything to you, tell him that the Lord needs them, and he will send them right away."

⁴This took place to fulfill what was spoken through the prophet:

⁵ "Say to the Daughter of Zion,
    'See, your king comes to you,
gentle and riding on a donkey,
    on a colt, the foal of a donkey.' " ᵃ

⁶The disciples went and did as Jesus had instructed them. ⁷They brought the donkey and the colt, placed their cloaks on them, and Jesus sat on them. ⁸A very large crowd spread their cloaks on the road, while others cut branches from the trees and spread them on the road. ⁹The crowds that went ahead of him and those that followed shouted,

"Hosanna[b] to the Son of David!"

"Blessed is he who comes in the
    name of the Lord!"[c]

"Hosanna[b] in the highest!"

¹⁰When Jesus entered Jerusalem, the whole city was stirred and asked, "Who is this?"

¹¹The crowds answered, "This is Jesus, the prophet from Nazareth in Galilee."

Jesus at the Temple

¹²Jesus entered the temple area and drove out all who were buying and selling there. He overturned the tables of the money changers and the benches of those selling doves. ¹³"It is written," he said to them, " 'My house will be called a house of prayer,'[d] but you are making it a 'den of robbers.'[e] "

¹⁴The blind and the lame came to him at the temple, and he healed them. ¹⁵But when the chief priests and the teachers of the law saw the wonderful things he did and the children shouting in the temple area, "Hosanna to the Son of David," they were indignant.

¹⁶"Do you hear what these children are saying?" they asked him.

"Yes," replied Jesus, "have you never read,

" 'From the lips of children and
    infants
    you have ordained praise'[f] ?"

ᵃ 5 Zech. 9:9   ᵇ 9 A Hebrew expression meaning "Save!" which became an exclamation of praise; also in verse 15   ᶜ 9 Psalm 118:26   ᵈ 13 Isaiah 56:7   ᵉ 13 Jer. 7:11   ᶠ 16 Psalm 8:2

THE HOUSE OF PRAYER
William Cowper

VERSE: Matthew 21:13   **PASSAGE:** Matthew 21:12–17

Thy mansion is the Christian's heart,
O Lord, thy dwelling-place secure!
Bid the unruly throng depart,
And leave the consecrated door.

Devoted as it is to thee,
A thievish swarm frequents the place;
They steal away my joys from me,
And rob my Savior of his praise.

There too a sharp designing trade
Sin, Satan, and the world maintain;
Nor cease to press me, and persuade,
To part with ease and purchase pain.

I know them, and I hate their din,
Am weary of the bustling crowd;
But while their voice is heard within,
I cannot serve thee as I would.

Oh! for the joy thy presence gives,
What peace shall reign when thou art here!
Thy presence makes this den of thieves,
A calm delightful house of prayer.

And if thou make thy temple shine,
Yet, self-abased, will I adore;
The gold and silver are not mine,
I give thee what was thine before.

ADDITIONAL SCRIPTURE READING:
Psalm 93:5; Isaiah 56:7

Go to page 1135 for your next devotional reading.

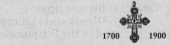

1700   1900

¹⁷And he left them and went out of the city to Bethany, where he spent the night.

The Fig Tree Withers

¹⁸Early in the morning, as he was on his way back to the city, he was hungry. ¹⁹Seeing a fig tree by the road, he went up to it but found nothing on it except leaves. Then he said to it, "May you never bear fruit again!" Immediately the tree withered.

²⁰When the disciples saw this, they were amazed. "How did the fig tree wither so quickly?" they asked.

²¹Jesus replied, "I tell you the truth, if you have faith and do not doubt, not only can you do what was done to the fig tree, but also you can say to this mountain, 'Go, throw yourself into the sea,' and it will be done. ²²If you believe, you will receive whatever you ask for in prayer."

The Authority of Jesus Questioned

²³Jesus entered the temple courts, and, while he was teaching, the chief priests and the elders of the people came to him. "By what authority are you doing these things?" they asked. "And who gave you this authority?"

²⁴Jesus replied, "I will also ask you one question. If you answer me, I will tell you by what authority I am doing these things. ²⁵John's baptism—where did it come from? Was it from heaven, or from men?"

They discussed it among themselves and said, "If we say, 'From heaven,' he will ask, 'Then why didn't you believe him?' ²⁶But if we say, 'From men'—we are afraid of the people, for they all hold that John was a prophet."

²⁷So they answered Jesus, "We don't know."

Then he said, "Neither will I tell you by what authority I am doing these things.

The Parable of the Two Sons

²⁸"What do you think? There was a man who had two sons. He went to the first and said, 'Son, go and work today in the vineyard.'

²⁹" 'I will not,' he answered, but later he changed his mind and went.

³⁰"Then the father went to the other son and said the same thing. He answered, 'I will, sir,' but he did not go.

³¹"Which of the two did what his father wanted?"

"The first," they answered.

Jesus said to them, "I tell you the truth, the tax collectors and the prostitutes are entering the kingdom of God ahead of you. ³²For John came to you to show you the way of righteousness, and you did not believe him, but the tax collectors and the prostitutes did. And even after you saw this, you did not repent and believe him.

The Parable of the Tenants

³³"Listen to another parable: There was a landowner who planted a vineyard. He put a wall around it, dug a winepress in it and built a watchtower. Then he rented the vineyard to some farmers and went away on a journey. ³⁴When the harvest time approached, he sent his servants to the tenants to collect his fruit.

³⁵"The tenants seized his servants; they beat one, killed another, and stoned a third. ³⁶Then he sent other servants to them, more than the first time, and the tenants treated them the same way. ³⁷Last of all, he sent his son to them. 'They will respect my son,' he said.

³⁸"But when the tenants saw the son, they said to each other, 'This is the heir. Come, let's kill him and take his inheritance.' ³⁹So they took him and threw him out of the vineyard and killed him.

⁴⁰"Therefore, when the owner of the vineyard comes, what will he do to those tenants?"

⁴¹"He will bring those wretches to a wretched end," they replied, "and he will rent the vineyard to other tenants, who will give him his share of the crop at harvest time."

⁴²Jesus said to them, "Have you never read in the Scriptures:

" 'The stone the builders rejected
   has become the capstone*ᵃ*;
the Lord has done this,
   and it is marvelous in our eyes'*ᵇ*?

⁴³"Therefore I tell you that the kingdom of God will be taken away from

---

ᵃ 42 Or *cornerstone*   *ᵇ 42* Psalm 118:22,23

you and given to a people who will produce its fruit. 44He who falls on this stone will be broken to pieces, but he on whom it falls will be crushed."*a*

45When the chief priests and the Pharisees heard Jesus' parables, they knew he was talking about them. 46They looked for a way to arrest him, but they were afraid of the crowd because the people held that he was a prophet.

The Parable of the Wedding Banquet

22 Jesus spoke to them again in parables, saying: 2"The kingdom of heaven is like a king who prepared a wedding banquet for his son. 3He sent his servants to those who had been invited to the banquet to tell them to come, but they refused to come.

4"Then he sent some more servants and said, 'Tell those who have been invited that I have prepared my dinner: My oxen and fattened cattle have been butchered, and everything is ready. Come to the wedding banquet.'

5"But they paid no attention and went off—one to his field, another to his business. 6The rest seized his servants, mistreated them and killed them. 7The king was enraged. He sent his army and destroyed those murderers and burned their city.

8"Then he said to his servants, 'The wedding banquet is ready, but those I invited did not deserve to come. 9Go to the street corners and invite to the banquet anyone you find.' 10So the servants went out into the streets and gathered all the people they could find, both good and bad, and the wedding hall was filled with guests.

11"But when the king came in to see the guests, he noticed a man there who was not wearing wedding clothes. 12'Friend,' he asked, 'how did you get in here without wedding clothes?' The man was speechless.

13"Then the king told the attendants, 'Tie him hand and foot, and throw him outside, into the darkness, where there will be weeping and gnashing of teeth.'

14"For many are invited, but few are chosen."

Paying Taxes to Caesar

15Then the Pharisees went out and laid plans to trap him in his words. 16They sent their disciples to him along with the Herodians. "Teacher," they said, "we know you are a man of integrity and that you teach the way of God in accordance with the truth. You aren't swayed by men, because you pay no attention to who they are. 17Tell us then, what is your opinion? Is it right to pay taxes to Caesar or not?"

18But Jesus, knowing their evil intent, said, "You hypocrites, why are you trying to trap me? 19Show me the coin used for paying the tax." They brought him a denarius, 20and he asked them, "Whose portrait is this? And whose inscription?"

21"Caesar's," they replied.

Then he said to them, "Give to Caesar what is Caesar's, and to God what is God's."

22When they heard this, they were amazed. So they left him and went away.

Marriage at the Resurrection

23That same day the Sadducees, who say there is no resurrection, came to him with a question. 24"Teacher," they said, "Moses told us that if a man dies without having children, his brother must marry the widow and have children for him. 25Now there were seven brothers among us. The first one married and died, and since he had no children, he left his wife to his brother. 26The same thing happened to the second and third brother, right on down to the seventh. 27Finally, the woman died. 28Now then, at the resurrection, whose wife will she be of the seven, since all of them were married to her?"

29Jesus replied, "You are in error because you do not know the Scriptures or the power of God. 30At the resurrection people will neither marry nor be given in marriage; they will be like the angels in heaven. 31But about the resurrection of the dead—have you not read what God said to you, 32'I am the God of Abraham, the God of Isaac, and the God of Jacob'*b*? He is not the God of the dead but of the living."

a 44 Some manuscripts do not have verse 44.   *b 32* Exodus 3:6

33When the crowds heard this, they were astonished at his teaching.

The Greatest Commandment

34Hearing that Jesus had silenced the Sadducees, the Pharisees got together. 35One of them, an expert in the law, tested him with this question: 36"Teacher, which is the greatest commandment in the Law?"

37Jesus replied: " 'Love the Lord your God with all your heart and with all your soul and with all your mind.'a 38This is the first and greatest commandment. 39And the second is like it: 'Love your neighbor as yourself.'b 40All the Law and the Prophets hang on these two commandments."

Whose Son Is the Christ?

41While the Pharisees were gathered together, Jesus asked them, 42"What do you think about the Christc? Whose son is he?"

"The son of David," they replied.

43He said to them, "How is it then that David, speaking by the Spirit, calls him 'Lord'? For he says,

44 " 'The Lord said to my Lord:
     "Sit at my right hand
     until I put your enemies
         under your feet." 'd

45If then David calls him 'Lord,' how can he be his son?" 46No one could say a word in reply, and from that day on no one dared to ask him any more questions.

Seven Woes

23 Then Jesus said to the crowds and to his disciples: 2"The teachers of the law and the Pharisees sit in Moses' seat. 3So you must obey them and do everything they tell you. But do not do what they do, for they do not practice what they preach. 4They tie up heavy loads and put them on men's shoulders, but they themselves are not willing to lift a finger to move them.

5"Everything they do is done for men to see: They make their phylacteriese wide and the tassels on their garments long; 6they love the place of honor at banquets and the most important seats in the synagogues; 7they love to be greeted in the marketplaces and to have men call them 'Rabbi.'

8"But you are not to be called 'Rabbi,' for you have only one Master and you are all brothers. 9And do not call anyone on earth 'father,' for you have one Father, and he is in heaven. 10Nor are you to be called 'teacher,' for you have one Teacher, the Christ.c 11The greatest among you will be your servant. 12For whoever exalts himself will be humbled, and whoever humbles himself will be exalted.

13"Woe to you, teachers of the law and Pharisees, you hypocrites! You shut the kingdom of heaven in men's faces. You yourselves do not enter, nor will you let those enter who are trying to.f

15"Woe to you, teachers of the law and Pharisees, you hypocrites! You travel over land and sea to win a single convert, and when he becomes one, you make him twice as much a son of hell as you are.

16"Woe to you, blind guides! You say, 'If anyone swears by the temple, it means nothing; but if anyone swears by the gold of the temple, he is bound by his oath.' 17You blind fools! Which is greater: the gold, or the temple that makes the gold sacred? 18You also say, 'If anyone swears by the altar, it means nothing; but if anyone swears by the gift on it, he is bound by his oath.' 19You blind men! Which is greater: the gift, or the altar that makes the gift sacred? 20Therefore, he who swears by the altar swears by it and by everything on it. 21And he who swears by the temple swears by it and by the one who dwells in it. 22And he who swears by heaven swears by God's throne and by the one who sits on it.

23"Woe to you, teachers of the law and Pharisees, you hypocrites! You give a tenth of your spices—mint, dill and cummin. But you have neglected the more important matters of the law—justice, mercy and faithfulness. You should have practiced the latter, with-

---

a 37 Deut. 6:5   b 39 Lev. 19:18   c 42,10 Or Messiah   d 44 Psalm 110:1   e 5 That is, boxes containing Scripture verses, worn on forehead and arm   f 13 Some manuscripts to. 14Woe to you, teachers of the law and Pharisees, you hypocrites! You devour widows' houses and for a show make lengthy prayers. Therefore you will be punished more severely.

out neglecting the former. 24You blind guides! You strain out a gnat but swallow a camel.

25"Woe to you, teachers of the law and Pharisees, you hypocrites! You clean the outside of the cup and dish, but inside they are full of greed and self-indulgence. 26Blind Pharisee! First clean the inside of the cup and dish, and then the outside also will be clean.

27"Woe to you, teachers of the law and Pharisees, you hypocrites! You are like whitewashed tombs, which look beautiful on the outside but on the inside are full of dead men's bones and everything unclean. 28In the same way, on the outside you appear to people as righteous but on the inside you are full of hypocrisy and wickedness.

29"Woe to you, teachers of the law and Pharisees, you hypocrites! You build tombs for the prophets and decorate the graves of the righteous. 30And you say, 'If we had lived in the days of our forefathers, we would not have taken part with them in shedding the blood of the prophets.' 31So you testify against yourselves that you are the descendants of those who murdered the prophets. 32Fill up, then, the measure of the sin of your forefathers!

33"You snakes! You brood of vipers! How will you escape being condemned to hell? 34Therefore I am sending you prophets and wise men and teachers. Some of them you will kill and crucify; others you will flog in your synagogues and pursue from town to town. 35And so upon you will come all the righteous blood that has been shed on earth, from the blood of righteous Abel to the blood of Zechariah son of Berekiah, whom you murdered between the temple and the altar. 36I tell you the truth, all this will come upon this generation.

37"O Jerusalem, Jerusalem, you who kill the prophets and stone those sent to you, how often I have longed to gather your children together, as a hen gathers her chicks under her wings, but you were not willing. 38Look, your house is left to you desolate. 39For I tell you, you will not see me again until you say, 'Blessed is he who comes in the name of the Lord.'ᵃ "

Signs of the End of the Age

24 Jesus left the temple and was walking away when his disciples came up to him to call his attention to its buildings. 2"Do you see all these things?" he asked. "I tell you the truth, not one stone here will be left on another; every one will be thrown down."

3As Jesus was sitting on the Mount of Olives, the disciples came to him privately. "Tell us," they said, "when will this happen, and what will be the sign of your coming and of the end of the age?"

4Jesus answered: "Watch out that no one deceives you. 5For many will come in my name, claiming, 'I am the Christ,ᵇ' and will deceive many. 6You will hear of wars and rumors of wars, but see to it that you are not alarmed. Such things must happen, but the end is still to come. 7Nation will rise against nation, and kingdom against kingdom. There will be famines and earthquakes in various places. 8All these are the beginning of birth pains.

9"Then you will be handed over to be persecuted and put to death, and you will be hated by all nations because of me. 10At that time many will turn away from the faith and will betray and hate each other, 11and many false prophets will appear and deceive many people. 12Because of the increase of wickedness, the love of most will grow cold, 13but he who stands firm to the end will be saved. 14And this gospel of the kingdom will be preached in the whole world as a testimony to all nations, and then the end will come.

15"So when you see standing in the holy place 'the abomination that causes desolation,'ᶜ spoken of through the prophet Daniel—let the reader understand— 16then let those who are in Judea flee to the mountains. 17Let no one on the roof of his house go down to take anything out of the house. 18Let no one in the field go back to get his cloak. 19How dreadful it will be in those days for pregnant women and nursing mothers! 20Pray that your flight will not take place in winter or on the Sabbath. 21For then there will be great distress, unequaled from the beginning of the world until now—and never to be equaled again. 22If

---

ᵃ 39 Psalm 118:26   ᵇ 5 Or *Messiah*; also in verse 23   ᶜ 15 Daniel 9:27; 11:31; 12:11

those days had not been cut short, no one would survive, but for the sake of the elect those days will be shortened. 23At that time if anyone says to you, 'Look, here is the Christ!' or, 'There he is!' do not believe it. 24For false Christs and false prophets will appear and perform great signs and miracles to deceive even the elect—if that were possible. 25See, I have told you ahead of time.

26"So if anyone tells you, 'There he is, out in the desert,' do not go out; or, 'Here he is, in the inner rooms,' do not believe it. 27For as lightning that comes from the east is visible even in the west, so will be the coming of the Son of Man. 28Wherever there is a carcass, there the vultures will gather.

29"Immediately after the distress of those days

" 'the sun will be darkened,
    and the moon will not give its
        light;
the stars will fall from the sky,
    and the heavenly bodies will be
        shaken.'a

30"At that time the sign of the Son of Man will appear in the sky, and all the nations of the earth will mourn. They will see the Son of Man coming on the clouds of the sky, with power and great glory. 31And he will send his angels with a loud trumpet call, and they will gather his elect from the four winds, from one end of the heavens to the other.

32"Now learn this lesson from the fig tree: As soon as its twigs get tender and its leaves come out, you know that summer is near. 33Even so, when you see all these things, you know that itb is near, right at the door. 34I tell you the truth, this generationc will certainly not pass away until all these things have happened. 35Heaven and earth will pass away, but my words will never pass away.

The Day and Hour Unknown

36"No one knows about that day or hour, not even the angels in heaven, nor the Son,d but only the Father. 37As it was in the days of Noah, so it will be at the coming of the Son of Man. 38For in the days before the flood, people were eating and drinking, marrying and giving in marriage, up to the day Noah entered the ark; 39and they knew nothing about what would happen until the flood came and took them all away. That is how it will be at the coming of the Son of Man. 40Two men will be in the field; one will be taken and the other left. 41Two women will be grinding with a hand mill; one will be taken and the other left.

42"Therefore keep watch, because you do not know on what day your Lord will come. 43But understand this: If the owner of the house had known at what time of night the thief was coming, he would have kept watch and would not have let his house be broken into. 44So you also must be ready, because the Son of Man will come at an hour when you do not expect him.

45"Who then is the faithful and wise servant, whom the master has put in charge of the servants in his household to give them their food at the proper time? 46It will be good for that servant whose master finds him doing so when he returns. 47I tell you the truth, he will put him in charge of all his possessions. 48But suppose that servant is wicked and says to himself, 'My master is staying away a long time,' 49and he then begins to beat his fellow servants and to eat and drink with drunkards. 50The master of that servant will come on a day when he does not expect him and at an hour he is not aware of. 51He will cut him to pieces and assign him a place with the hypocrites, where there will be weeping and gnashing of teeth.

The Parable of the Ten Virgins

25 "At that time the kingdom of heaven will be like ten virgins who took their lamps and went out to meet the bridegroom. 2Five of them were foolish and five were wise. 3The foolish ones took their lamps but did not take any oil with them. 4The wise, however, took oil in jars along with their lamps. 5The bridegroom was a long time in coming, and they all became drowsy and fell asleep.

a 29 Isaiah 13:10; 34:4   b 33 Or he   c 34 Or race   d 36 Some manuscripts do not have nor the Son.

6"At midnight the cry rang out: 'Here's the bridegroom! Come out to meet him!'

7"Then all the virgins woke up and trimmed their lamps. 8The foolish ones said to the wise, 'Give us some of your oil; our lamps are going out.'

9" 'No,' they replied, 'there may not be enough for both us and you. Instead, go to those who sell oil and buy some for yourselves.'

10"But while they were on their way to buy the oil, the bridegroom arrived. The virgins who were ready went in with him to the wedding banquet. And the door was shut.

11"Later the others also came. 'Sir! Sir!' they said. 'Open the door for us!'

12"But he replied, 'I tell you the truth, I don't know you.'

13"Therefore keep watch, because you do not know the day or the hour.

The Parable of the Talents

14"Again, it will be like a man going on a journey, who called his servants and entrusted his property to them. 15To one he gave five talents[a] of money, to another two talents, and to another one talent, each according to his ability. Then he went on his journey. 16The man who had received the five talents went at once and put his money to work and gained five more. 17So also, the one with the two talents gained two more. 18But the man who had received the one

a 15 A talent was worth more than a thousand dollars.

THURSDAY

A SONNET

John Milton

VERSE: Matthew 25:10   **PASSAGE:** Matthew 25:1–30

ady that in the prime of earliest youth,
　　Wisely hast shunned the broad way and the green,
　　And with those few art eminently seen
　　That labor up the hill of heavenly truth,
The better part with Mary and with Ruth
　　Chosen thou hast; and they that overween,
　　And at thy growing virtues fret their spleen,
　　No anger find in thee, but pity and ruth.
Thy care is fixed and zealously attends
　　To fill thy odorous lamp with deeds of light,
　　And hope that reaps not shame. Therefore be sure
Thou, when the bridegroom with his feastful friends
　　Passes to bliss at the mid-hour of night,
　　Hast gained thy entrance, virgin wise and pure.

ADDITIONAL SCRIPTURE READING:
Psalm 18:28; 1 Timothy 4:12

Go to page 1137 for your next devotional reading.

1500   1700

talent went off, dug a hole in the ground and hid his master's money.

19 "After a long time the master of those servants returned and settled accounts with them. 20 The man who had received the five talents brought the other five. 'Master,' he said, 'you entrusted me with five talents. See, I have gained five more.'

21 "His master replied, 'Well done, good and faithful servant! You have been faithful with a few things; I will put you in charge of many things. Come and share your master's happiness!'

22 "The man with the two talents also came. 'Master,' he said, 'you entrusted me with two talents; see, I have gained two more.'

23 "His master replied, 'Well done, good and faithful servant! You have been faithful with a few things; I will put you in charge of many things. Come and share your master's happiness!'

24 "Then the man who had received the one talent came. 'Master,' he said, 'I knew that you are a hard man, harvesting where you have not sown and gathering where you have not scattered seed. 25 So I was afraid and went out and hid your talent in the ground. See, here is what belongs to you.'

26 "His master replied, 'You wicked, lazy servant! So you knew that I harvest where I have not sown and gather where I have not scattered seed? 27 Well then, you should have put my money on deposit with the bankers, so that when I returned I would have received it back with interest.

28 "'Take the talent from him and give it to the one who has the ten talents. 29 For everyone who has will be given more, and he will have an abundance. Whoever does not have, even what he has will be taken from him. 30 And throw that worthless servant outside, into the darkness, where there will be weeping and gnashing of teeth.'

The Sheep and the Goats

31 "When the Son of Man comes in his glory, and all the angels with him, he will sit on his throne in heavenly glory. 32 All the nations will be gathered before him, and he will separate the people one from another as a shepherd separates the sheep from the goats. 33 He will put the sheep on his right and the goats on his left.

34 "Then the King will say to those on his right, 'Come, you who are blessed by my Father; take your inheritance, the kingdom prepared for you since the creation of the world. 35 For I was hungry and you gave me something to eat, I was thirsty and you gave me something to drink, I was a stranger and you invited me in, 36 I needed clothes and you clothed me, I was sick and you looked after me, I was in prison and you came to visit me.'

37 "Then the righteous will answer him, 'Lord, when did we see you hungry and feed you, or thirsty and give you something to drink? 38 When did we see you a stranger and invite you in, or needing clothes and clothe you? 39 When did we see you sick or in prison and go to visit you?'

40 "The King will reply, 'I tell you the truth, whatever you did for one of the least of these brothers of mine, you did for me.'

41 "Then he will say to those on his left, 'Depart from me, you who are cursed, into the eternal fire prepared for the devil and his angels. 42 For I was hungry and you gave me nothing to eat, I was thirsty and you gave me nothing to drink, 43 I was a stranger and you did not invite me in, I needed clothes and you did not clothe me, I was sick and in prison and you did not look after me.'

44 "They also will answer, 'Lord, when did we see you hungry or thirsty or a stranger or needing clothes or sick or in prison, and did not help you?'

45 "He will reply, 'I tell you the truth, whatever you did not do for one of the least of these, you did not do for me.'

46 "Then they will go away to eternal punishment, but the righteous to eternal life."

The Plot Against Jesus

26 When Jesus had finished saying all these things, he said to his disciples, 2 "As you know, the Passover is two days away—and the Son of Man will be handed over to be crucified."

3 Then the chief priests and the elders of the people assembled in the palace of

"WHATEVER YOU DID NOT DO"
William Temple

VERSE: Matthew 25:44–45 **PASSAGE:** Matthew 25:31–46

---

t is Christ who pines when the poor are hungry; it is Christ who is repulsed when strangers are not welcome; it is Christ who suffers when rags fail to keep out the cold; it is Christ who is in anguish in the long-drawn illness; it is Christ who waits behind the prison doors. You come upon one of those who have been broken by the tempests of life, and if you look with eyes of Christian faith and love, he will lift a brow "luminous and imperial from the rags," and you will know that you are standing before the King of kings, Lord of lords.

Christ brought to the world a new conception of royalty. He rules by love and not by force. That, as he expressly said, is the difference between his kingdom and the kingdoms of this world. His most regal act was the supreme self-sacrifice whereby he would draw all men to himself and make them willingly obedient to him forever (see John 12:32). In full harmony with this, he never speaks of himself as King except on one occasion only, . . . when, in the parable of the sheep and the goats, he identifies himself with the failures of the world and the outcasts of society. "Then the King will say to those on his right . . . I was hungry and you gave me something to eat, I was thirsty and you gave me something to drink, I was a stranger and you invited me in, I needed clothes and you clothed me, I was sick and you looked after me, I was in prison and you came to visit me" (Matthew 25:34–36).

Civilization, as we know it, produces much human refuse. Slum dwellings, long hours of work, underpayment, child labor, lack of education, prostitution—all these evils are responsible for stunting and warping the development of souls. Things are improving, we hope. But unless we are exerting all the strength that Christ gives us in ending these bad conditions, then the responsibility for wasted lives lies at our door, and from the streets of cities or the lanes of countrysides the cry goes up through the lips of their Savior and our Judge: "Whatever you did not do for one of the least of these, you did not do for me."

ADDITIONAL SCRIPTURE READING:
Luke 10:25–37; Hebrews 13:1–3

Go to page 1140 for your next devotional reading.

1900 Present

the high priest, whose name was Caia-phas, [4]and they plotted to arrest Jesus in some sly way and kill him. [5]"But not during the Feast," they said, "or there may be a riot among the people."

Jesus Anointed at Bethany

[6]While Jesus was in Bethany in the home of a man known as Simon the Leper, [7]a woman came to him with an alabaster jar of very expensive perfume, which she poured on his head as he was reclining at the table.

[8]When the disciples saw this, they were indignant. "Why this waste?" they asked. [9]"This perfume could have been sold at a high price and the money given to the poor."

[10]Aware of this, Jesus said to them, "Why are you bothering this woman? She has done a beautiful thing to me. [11]The poor you will always have with you, but you will not always have me. [12]When she poured this perfume on my body, she did it to prepare me for burial. [13]I tell you the truth, wherever this gospel is preached throughout the world, what she has done will also be told, in memory of her."

Judas Agrees to Betray Jesus

[14]Then one of the Twelve—the one called Judas Iscariot—went to the chief priests [15]and asked, "What are you will-ing to give me if I hand him over to you?" So they counted out for him thirty silver coins. [16]From then on Judas watched for an opportunity to hand him over.

The Lord's Supper

[17]On the first day of the Feast of Unleavened Bread, the disciples came to Jesus and asked, "Where do you want us to make preparations for you to eat the Passover?"

[18]He replied, "Go into the city to a certain man and tell him, 'The Teacher says: My appointed time is near. I am going to celebrate the Passover with my disciples at your house.' " [19]So the disci-ples did as Jesus had directed them and prepared the Passover.

[20]When evening came, Jesus was reclining at the table with the Twelve. [21]And while they were eating, he said, "I tell you the truth, one of you will betray me."

[22]They were very sad and began to say to him one after the other, "Surely not I, Lord?"

[23]Jesus replied, "The one who has dipped his hand into the bowl with me will betray me. [24]The Son of Man will go just as it is written about him. But woe to that man who betrays the Son of Man! It would be better for him if he had not been born."

[25]Then Judas, the one who would betray him, said, "Surely not I, Rabbi?" Jesus answered, "Yes, it is you."[a]

[26]While they were eating, Jesus took bread, gave thanks and broke it, and gave it to his disciples, saying, "Take and eat; this is my body."

[27]Then he took the cup, gave thanks and offered it to them, saying, "Drink from it, all of you. [28]This is my blood of the[b] covenant, which is poured out for many for the forgiveness of sins. [29]I tell you, I will not drink of this fruit of the vine from now on until that day when I drink it anew with you in my Father's kingdom."

[30]When they had sung a hymn, they went out to the Mount of Olives.

Jesus Predicts Peter's Denial

[31]Then Jesus told them, "This very night you will all fall away on account of me, for it is written:

" 'I will strike the shepherd,
    and the sheep of the flock will be
        scattered.'[c]

[32]But after I have risen, I will go ahead of you into Galilee."

[33]Peter replied, "Even if all fall away on account of you, I never will."

[34]"I tell you the truth," Jesus answered, "this very night, before the rooster crows, you will disown me three times."

[35]But Peter declared, "Even if I have to die with you, I will never disown you." And all the other disciples said the same.

Gethsemane

[36]Then Jesus went with his disciples to a place called Gethsemane, and he said to

---

[a] 25 Or "You yourself have said it"   [b] 28 Some manuscripts the new   [c] 31 Zech. 13:7

them, "Sit here while I go over there and pray." 37He took Peter and the two sons of Zebedee along with him, and he began to be sorrowful and troubled. 38Then he said to them, "My soul is overwhelmed with sorrow to the point of death. Stay here and keep watch with me."

39Going a little farther, he fell with his face to the ground and prayed, "My Father, if it is possible, may this cup be taken from me. Yet not as I will, but as you will."

SPREAD OUT YOUR PETITION BEFORE GOD, AND THEN SAY, "THY WILL, NOT MINE, BE DONE." THE SWEETEST LESSON I HAVE LEARNED IN GOD'S SCHOOL IS TO LET THE LORD CHOOSE FOR ME.

—*Dwight L. Moody*

40Then he returned to his disciples and found them sleeping. "Could you men not keep watch with me for one hour?" he asked Peter. 41"Watch and pray so that you will not fall into temptation. The spirit is willing, but the body is weak."

42He went away a second time and prayed, "My Father, if it is not possible for this cup to be taken away unless I drink it, may your will be done."

43When he came back, he again found them sleeping, because their eyes were heavy. 44So he left them and went away once more and prayed the third time, saying the same thing.

45Then he returned to the disciples and said to them, "Are you still sleeping and resting? Look, the hour is near, and the Son of Man is betrayed into the hands of sinners. 46Rise, let us go! Here comes my betrayer!"

Jesus Arrested

47While he was still speaking, Judas, one of the Twelve, arrived. With him was a large crowd armed with swords and clubs, sent from the chief priests and the elders of the people. 48Now the betrayer had arranged a signal with them: "The one I kiss is the man; arrest him." 49Going at once to Jesus, Judas said, "Greetings, Rabbi!" and kissed him.

50Jesus replied, "Friend, do what you came for."*a*

Then the men stepped forward, seized Jesus and arrested him. 51With that, one of Jesus' companions reached for his sword, drew it out and struck the servant of the high priest, cutting off his ear.

52"Put your sword back in its place," Jesus said to him, "for all who draw the sword will die by the sword. 53Do you think I cannot call on my Father, and he will at once put at my disposal more than twelve legions of angels? 54But how then would the Scriptures be fulfilled that say it must happen in this way?"

55At that time Jesus said to the crowd, "Am I leading a rebellion, that you have come out with swords and clubs to capture me? Every day I sat in the temple courts teaching, and you did not arrest me. 56But this has all taken place that the writings of the prophets might be fulfilled." Then all the disciples deserted him and fled.

Before the Sanhedrin

57Those who had arrested Jesus took him to Caiaphas, the high priest, where the teachers of the law and the elders had assembled. 58But Peter followed him at a distance, right up to the courtyard of the high priest. He entered and sat down with the guards to see the outcome.

59The chief priests and the whole Sanhedrin were looking for false evidence against Jesus so that they could put him to death. 60But they did not find any, though many false witnesses came forward.

Finally two came forward 61and declared, "This fellow said, 'I am able to destroy the temple of God and rebuild it in three days.' "

WHENEVER ANYTHING DISAGREEABLE OR DISPLEASING HAPPENS TO YOU, REMEMBER CHRIST CRUCIFIED AND BE SILENT.   —*John of the Cross*

62Then the high priest stood up and said to Jesus, "Are you not going to answer? What is this testimony that these men are bringing against you?" 63But Jesus remained silent.

---

a 50 Or *"Friend, why have you come?"*

To His Savior, a Child;
a Present, by a Child
Robert Herrick

Verse: Luke 2:27   **Passage:** Luke 2:25–32

Go pretty child, and bear this flower
Unto thy little Savior;
And tell him, by that bud now blown,
He is the Rose of Sharon known:
When thou hast said so, stick it there
Upon his bib, or stomacher:
And tell him, (for good handsell too)
That thou hast brought a whistle new,
Made of a clean strait oaten reed,
To charm his cries, (at time of need:)
Tell him, for coral, thou hast none;
But if thou hadst, he should have one;
But poor thou art, and known to be
Even as moneyless, as he.
Lastly, if thou canst win a kiss
From those mellifluous lips of his;
Then never take a second on,
To spoil the first impression.

Additional Scripture Reading:
Acts 2:36; Hebrews 1:8

Go to page 1143 for your next devotional reading.

1500   1700

The high priest said to him, "I charge you under oath by the living God: Tell us if you are the Christ,[a] the Son of God."

64"Yes, it is as you say," Jesus replied. "But I say to all of you: In the future you will see the Son of Man sitting at the right hand of the Mighty One and coming on the clouds of heaven."

65Then the high priest tore his clothes and said, "He has spoken blasphemy! Why do we need any more witnesses? Look, now you have heard the blasphemy. 66What do you think?"

"He is worthy of death," they answered.

67Then they spit in his face and struck him with their fists. Others slapped him 68and said, "Prophesy to us, Christ. Who hit you?"

Peter Disowns Jesus

69Now Peter was sitting out in the courtyard, and a servant girl came to him. "You also were with Jesus of Galilee," she said.

70But he denied it before them all. "I don't know what you're talking about," he said.

71Then he went out to the gateway, where another girl saw him and said to the people there, "This fellow was with Jesus of Nazareth."

72He denied it again, with an oath: "I don't know the man!"

73After a little while, those standing there went up to Peter and said, "Surely you are one of them, for your accent gives you away."

74Then he began to call down curses on himself and he swore to them, "I don't know the man!"

Immediately a rooster crowed. 75Then Peter remembered the word Jesus had spoken: "Before the rooster crows, you will disown me three times." And he went outside and wept bitterly.

Judas Hangs Himself

27 Early in the morning, all the chief priests and the elders of the people came to the decision to put Jesus to death. 2They bound him, led him away and handed him over to Pilate, the governor.

3When Judas, who had betrayed him, saw that Jesus was condemned, he was seized with remorse and returned the thirty silver coins to the chief priests and the elders. 4"I have sinned," he said, "for I have betrayed innocent blood."

"What is that to us?" they replied. "That's your responsibility."

5So Judas threw the money into the temple and left. Then he went away and hanged himself.

6The chief priests picked up the coins and said, "It is against the law to put this into the treasury, since it is blood money." 7So they decided to use the money to buy the potter's field as a burial place for foreigners. 8That is why it has been called the Field of Blood to this day. 9Then what was spoken by Jeremiah the prophet was fulfilled: "They took the thirty silver coins, the price set on him by the people of Israel, 10and they used them to buy the potter's field, as the Lord commanded me."[b]

Jesus Before Pilate

11Meanwhile Jesus stood before the governor, and the governor asked him, "Are you the king of the Jews?"

"Yes, it is as you say," Jesus replied.

12When he was accused by the chief priests and the elders, he gave no answer. 13Then Pilate asked him, "Don't you hear the testimony they are bringing against you?" 14But Jesus made no reply, not even to a single charge—to the great amazement of the governor.

15Now it was the governor's custom at the Feast to release a prisoner chosen by the crowd. 16At that time they had a notorious prisoner, called Barabbas. 17So when the crowd had gathered, Pilate asked them, "Which one do you want me to release to you: Barabbas, or Jesus who is called Christ?" 18For he knew it was out of envy that they had handed Jesus over to him.

19While Pilate was sitting on the judge's seat, his wife sent him this message: "Don't have anything to do with that innocent man, for I have suffered a great deal today in a dream because of him."

20But the chief priests and the elders persuaded the crowd to ask for Barabbas and to have Jesus executed.

a 63 Or Messiah; also in verse 68   b 10 See Zech. 11:12,13; Jer. 19:1–13; 32:6–9.

21"Which of the two do you want me to release to you?" asked the governor.

"Barabbas," they answered.

22"What shall I do, then, with Jesus who is called Christ?" Pilate asked.

They all answered, "Crucify him!"

23"Why? What crime has he committed?" asked Pilate.

But they shouted all the louder, "Crucify him!"

24When Pilate saw that he was getting nowhere, but that instead an uproar was starting, he took water and washed his hands in front of the crowd. "I am innocent of this man's blood," he said. "It is your responsibility!"

25All the people answered, "Let his blood be on us and on our children!"

26Then he released Barabbas to them. But he had Jesus flogged, and handed him over to be crucified.

The Soldiers Mock Jesus

27Then the governor's soldiers took Jesus into the Praetorium and gathered the whole company of soldiers around him. 28They stripped him and put a scarlet robe on him, 29and then twisted together a crown of thorns and set it on his head. They put a staff in his right hand and knelt in front of him and mocked him. "Hail, king of the Jews!" they said. 30They spit on him, and took the staff and struck him on the head again and again. 31After they had mocked him, they took off the robe and put his own clothes on him. Then they led him away to crucify him.

The Crucifixion

32As they were going out, they met a man from Cyrene, named Simon, and they forced him to carry the cross. 33They came to a place called Golgotha (which means The Place of the Skull). 34There they offered Jesus wine to drink, mixed with gall; but after tasting it, he refused to drink it. 35When they had crucified him, they divided up his clothes by casting lots.*a* 36And sitting down, they kept watch over him there. 37Above his head they placed the written charge against him: THIS IS JESUS, THE KING OF THE

JEWS. 38Two robbers were crucified with him, one on his right and one on his left. 39Those who passed by hurled insults at him, shaking their heads 40and saying, "You who are going to destroy the temple and build it in three days, save yourself! Come down from the cross, if you are the Son of God!"

41In the same way the chief priests, the teachers of the law and the elders mocked him. 42"He saved others," they said, "but he can't save himself! He's the King of Israel! Let him come down now from the cross, and we will believe in him. 43He trusts in God. Let God rescue him now if he wants him, for he said, 'I am the Son of God.' " 44In the same way the robbers who were crucified with him also heaped insults on him.

The Death of Jesus

45From the sixth hour until the ninth hour darkness came over all the land. 46About the ninth hour Jesus cried out in a loud voice, "Eloi, Eloi,*b* lama sabachthani?"—which means, "My God, my God, why have you forsaken me?"*c*

47When some of those standing there heard this, they said, "He's calling Elijah."

48Immediately one of them ran and got a sponge. He filled it with wine vinegar, put it on a stick, and offered it to Jesus to drink. 49The rest said, "Now leave him alone. Let's see if Elijah comes to save him."

50And when Jesus had cried out again in a loud voice, he gave up his spirit.

51At that moment the curtain of the temple was torn in two from top to bottom. The earth shook and the rocks split. 52The tombs broke open and the bodies of many holy people who had died were raised to life. 53They came out of the tombs, and after Jesus' resurrection they went into the holy city and appeared to many people.

54When the centurion and those with him who were guarding Jesus saw the earthquake and all that had happened, they were terrified, and exclaimed, "Surely he was the Son*d* of God!"

---

a 35 A few late manuscripts *lots that the word spoken by the prophet might be fulfilled: "They divided my garments among themselves and cast lots for my clothing"* (Psalm 22:18)   *b 46* Some manuscripts *Eli, Eli*   *c 46* Psalm 22:1   *d 54* Or *a son*

55Many women were there, watching from a distance. They had followed Jesus from Galilee to care for his needs. 56Among them were Mary Magdalene, Mary the mother of James and Joses, and the mother of Zebedee's sons.

The Burial of Jesus

57As evening approached, there came a rich man from Arimathea, named Joseph, who had himself become a disciple of Jesus. 58Going to Pilate, he asked for Jesus' body, and Pilate ordered that it be given to him. 59Joseph took the body, wrapped it in a clean linen cloth, 60and placed it in his own new tomb that he had cut out of the rock. He rolled a big stone in front of the entrance to the tomb and went away. 61Mary Magdalene and the other Mary were sitting there opposite the tomb.

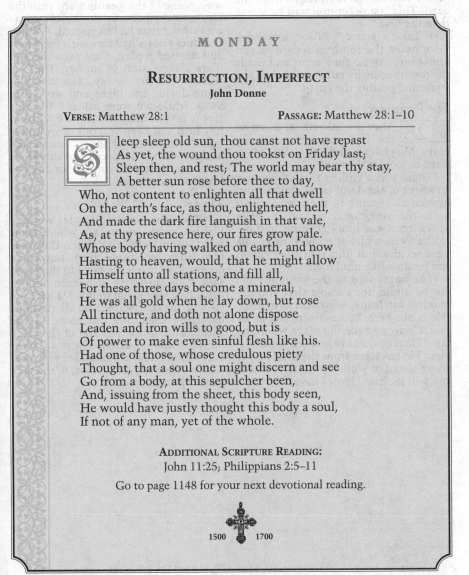

MONDAY

RESURRECTION, IMPERFECT
John Donne

VERSE: Matthew 28:1   **PASSAGE:** Matthew 28:1–10

leep sleep old sun, thou canst not have repast
As yet, the wound thou tookst on Friday last;
Sleep then, and rest; The world may bear thy stay,
A better sun rose before thee to day,
Who, not content to enlighten all that dwell
On the earth's face, as thou, enlightened hell,
And made the dark fire languish in that vale,
As, at thy presence here, our fires grow pale.
Whose body having walked on earth, and now
Hasting to heaven, would, that he might allow
Himself unto all stations, and fill all,
For these three days become a mineral;
He was all gold when he lay down, but rose
All tincture, and doth not alone dispose
Leaden and iron wills to good, but is
Of power to make even sinful flesh like his.
Had one of those, whose credulous piety
Thought, that a soul one might discern and see
Go from a body, at this sepulcher been,
And, issuing from the sheet, this body seen,
He would have justly thought this body a soul,
If not of any man, yet of the whole.

ADDITIONAL SCRIPTURE READING:
John 11:25; Philippians 2:5–11

Go to page 1148 for your next devotional reading.

1500   1700

The Guard at the Tomb

⁶²The next day, the one after Preparation Day, the chief priests and the Pharisees went to Pilate. ⁶³"Sir," they said, "we remember that while he was still alive that deceiver said, 'After three days I will rise again.' ⁶⁴So give the order for the tomb to be made secure until the third day. Otherwise, his disciples may come and steal the body and tell the people that he has been raised from the dead. This last deception will be worse than the first."

⁶⁵"Take a guard," Pilate answered. "Go, make the tomb as secure as you know how." ⁶⁶So they went and made the tomb secure by putting a seal on the stone and posting the guard.

The Resurrection

28 After the Sabbath, at dawn on the first day of the week, Mary Magdalene and the other Mary went to look at the tomb.

²There was a violent earthquake, for an angel of the Lord came down from heaven and, going to the tomb, rolled back the stone and sat on it. ³His appearance was like lightning, and his clothes were white as snow. ⁴The guards were so afraid of him that they shook and became like dead men.

⁵The angel said to the women, "Do not be afraid, for I know that you are looking for Jesus, who was crucified. ⁶He is not here; he has risen, just as he said. Come and see the place where he lay. ⁷Then go quickly and tell his disciples: 'He has risen from the dead and is going ahead of you into Galilee. There you will see him.' Now I have told you."

⁸So the women hurried away from the tomb, afraid yet filled with joy, and ran to tell his disciples. ⁹Suddenly Jesus met them. "Greetings," he said. They came to him, clasped his feet and worshiped him. ¹⁰Then Jesus said to them, "Do not be afraid. Go and tell my brothers to go to Galilee; there they will see me."

The Guards' Report

¹¹While the women were on their way, some of the guards went into the city and reported to the chief priests everything that had happened. ¹²When the chief priests had met with the elders and devised a plan, they gave the soldiers a large sum of money, ¹³telling them, "You are to say, 'His disciples came during the night and stole him away while we were asleep.' ¹⁴If this report gets to the governor, we will satisfy him and keep you out of trouble." ¹⁵So the soldiers took the money and did as they were instructed. And this story has been widely circulated among the Jews to this very day.

The Great Commission

¹⁶Then the eleven disciples went to Galilee, to the mountain where Jesus had told them to go. ¹⁷When they saw him, they worshiped him; but some doubted. ¹⁸Then Jesus came to them and said, "All authority in heaven and on earth has been given to me. ¹⁹Therefore go and make disciples of all nations, baptizing them in*ᵃ* the name of the Father and of the Son and of the Holy Spirit, ²⁰and teaching them to obey everything I have commanded you. And surely I am with you always, to the very end of the age."

ᵃ 19 Or *into;* see Acts 8:16; 19:5; Romans 6:3; 1 Cor. 1:13; 10:2 and Gal. 3:27.

MARK

THE GOSPEL OF MARK TAKES A FAST-PACED
APPROACH TO INTRODUCING JESUS CHRIST,
THE SON OF GOD. MARK SHOWS JESUS
MOVING QUICKLY FROM TEACHING HIS DISCIPLES TO
HEALING SICK PEOPLE TO CONFRONTING RELIGIOUS
LEADERS ON HIS WAY TO DEATH ON THE CROSS.
NOTE MARK'S SENSITIVE PORTRAYAL OF THE COM-
PASSIONATE SUFFERING SERVANT, JESUS, FULL OF LIFE
AND EMOTION AND PURPOSE, AND OUR CALL TO BE
DISCIPLES OF JESUS. KEEP IN MIND THE LOVE JESUS
SHOWED HIS DISCIPLES AND ASK YOURSELF, "IF JESUS
WAS WILLING TO SUFFER FOR ME, WHAT AM I WILLING
TO DO AS HIS DISCIPLE?"

John the Baptist Prepares the Way

1 The beginning of the gospel
about Jesus Christ, the Son of
God.*a*

²It is written in Isaiah the prophet:

"I will send my messenger ahead of
you,
who will prepare your way"*b*—
³ "a voice of one calling in the desert,
'Prepare the way for the Lord,
make straight paths for him.' "*c*

⁴And so John came, baptizing in the
desert region and preaching a baptism of
repentance for the forgiveness of sins.
⁵The whole Judean countryside and all

the people of Jerusalem went out to him.
Confessing their sins, they were baptized
by him in the Jordan River. ⁶John wore
clothing made of camel's hair, with a
leather belt around his waist, and he ate
locusts and wild honey. ⁷And this was his
message: "After me will come one more
powerful than I, the thongs of whose sandals I am not worthy to stoop down and
untie. ⁸I baptize you with*d* water, but he
will baptize you with the Holy Spirit."

The Baptism and Temptation
of Jesus

⁹At that time Jesus came from Nazareth in Galilee and was baptized by John
in the Jordan. ¹⁰As Jesus was coming up
out of the water, he saw heaven being
torn open and the Spirit descending on

---

a 1 Some manuscripts do not have *the Son of God.*   *b 2* Mal. 3:1   *c 3* Isaiah 40:3   *d 8* Or *in*

him like a dove. ¹¹And a voice came from heaven: "You are my Son, whom I love; with you I am well pleased."

¹²At once the Spirit sent him out into the desert, ¹³and he was in the desert forty days, being tempted by Satan. He was with the wild animals, and angels attended him.

The Calling of the First Disciples

¹⁴After John was put in prison, Jesus went into Galilee, proclaiming the good news of God. ¹⁵"The time has come," he said. "The kingdom of God is near. Repent and believe the good news!"

¹⁶As Jesus walked beside the Sea of Galilee, he saw Simon and his brother Andrew casting a net into the lake, for they were fishermen. ¹⁷"Come, follow me," Jesus said, "and I will make you fishers of men." ¹⁸At once they left their nets and followed him.

ONE DAY THERE CAME ALONG THAT SILENT
    SHORE,
WHILE I MY NET WAS CASTING IN THE SEA,
A MAN WHO SPOKE AS NEVER MAN BEFORE,
I FOLLOWED HIM; NEW LIFE BEGAN IN ME.
MINE WAS THE BOAT, BUT HIS THE VOICE,
    AND HIS THE CALL, YET MINE THE CHOICE.

        —*George MacDonald*

---

¹⁹When he had gone a little farther, he saw James son of Zebedee and his brother John in a boat, preparing their nets. ²⁰Without delay he called them, and they left their father Zebedee in the boat with the hired men and followed him.

Jesus Drives Out an Evil Spirit

²¹They went to Capernaum, and when the Sabbath came, Jesus went into the synagogue and began to teach. ²²The people were amazed at his teaching, because he taught them as one who had authority, not as the teachers of the law. ²³Just then a man in their synagogue who was possessed by an evil[a] spirit cried out, ²⁴"What do you want with us, Jesus of Nazareth? Have you come to destroy us? I know who you are—the Holy One of God!"

²⁵"Be quiet!" said Jesus sternly. "Come out of him!" ²⁶The evil spirit shook the man violently and came out of him with a shriek.

²⁷The people were all so amazed that they asked each other, "What is this? A new teaching—and with authority! He even gives orders to evil spirits and they obey him." ²⁸News about him spread quickly over the whole region of Galilee.

Jesus Heals Many

²⁹As soon as they left the synagogue, they went with James and John to the home of Simon and Andrew. ³⁰Simon's mother-in-law was in bed with a fever, and they told Jesus about her. ³¹So he went to her, took her hand and helped her up. The fever left her and she began to wait on them.

³²That evening after sunset the people brought to Jesus all the sick and demon-possessed. ³³The whole town gathered at the door, ³⁴and Jesus healed many who had various diseases. He also drove out many demons, but he would not let the demons speak because they knew who he was.

Jesus Prays in a Solitary Place

³⁵Very early in the morning, while it was still dark, Jesus got up, left the house and went off to a solitary place, where he prayed. ³⁶Simon and his companions went to look for him, ³⁷and when they found him, they exclaimed: "Everyone is looking for you!"

³⁸Jesus replied, "Let us go somewhere else—to the nearby villages—so I can preach there also. That is why I have come." ³⁹So he traveled throughout Galilee, preaching in their synagogues and driving out demons.

A Man With Leprosy

⁴⁰A man with leprosy[b] came to him and begged him on his knees, "If you are willing, you can make me clean."

⁴¹Filled with compassion, Jesus reached out his hand and touched the man. "I am willing," he said. "Be clean!"

---

a 23 Greek *unclean;* also in verses 26 and 27 affecting the skin—not necessarily leprosy.   *b 40* The Greek word was used for various diseases

⁴²Immediately the leprosy left him and he was cured.

⁴³Jesus sent him away at once with a strong warning: ⁴⁴"See that you don't tell this to anyone. But go, show yourself to the priest and offer the sacrifices that Moses commanded for your cleansing, as a testimony to them." ⁴⁵Instead he went out and began to talk freely, spreading the news. As a result, Jesus could no longer enter a town openly but stayed outside in lonely places. Yet the people still came to him from everywhere.

Jesus Heals a Paralytic

2 A few days later, when Jesus again entered Capernaum, the people heard that he had come home. ²So many gathered that there was no room left, not even outside the door, and he preached the word to them. ³Some men came, bringing to him a paralytic, carried by four of them. ⁴Since they could not get him to Jesus because of the crowd, they made an opening in the roof above Jesus and, after digging through it, lowered the mat the paralyzed man was lying on. ⁵When Jesus saw their faith, he said to the paralytic, "Son, your sins are forgiven."

⁶Now some teachers of the law were sitting there, thinking to themselves, ⁷"Why does this fellow talk like that? He's blaspheming! Who can forgive sins but God alone?"

⁸Immediately Jesus knew in his spirit that this was what they were thinking in their hearts, and he said to them, "Why are you thinking these things? ⁹Which is easier: to say to the paralytic, 'Your sins are forgiven,' or to say, 'Get up, take your mat and walk'? ¹⁰But that you may know that the Son of Man has authority on earth to forgive sins . . . ." He said to the paralytic, ¹¹"I tell you, get up, take your mat and go home." ¹²He got up, took his mat and walked out in full view of them all. This amazed everyone and they praised God, saying, "We have never seen anything like this!"

The Calling of Levi

¹³Once again Jesus went out beside the lake. A large crowd came to him, and he began to teach them. ¹⁴As he walked along, he saw Levi son of Alphaeus sitting at the tax collector's booth. "Follow me," Jesus told him, and Levi got up and followed him.

¹⁵While Jesus was having dinner at Levi's house, many tax collectors and "sinners" were eating with him and his disciples, for there were many who followed him. ¹⁶When the teachers of the law who were Pharisees saw him eating with the "sinners" and tax collectors, they asked his disciples: "Why does he eat with tax collectors and 'sinners'?"

¹⁷On hearing this, Jesus said to them, "It is not the healthy who need a doctor, but the sick. I have not come to call the righteous, but sinners."

Jesus Questioned About Fasting

¹⁸Now John's disciples and the Pharisees were fasting. Some people came and asked Jesus, "How is it that John's disciples and the disciples of the Pharisees are fasting, but yours are not?"

¹⁹Jesus answered, "How can the guests of the bridegroom fast while he is with them? They cannot, so long as they have him with them. ²⁰But the time will come when the bridegroom will be taken from them, and on that day they will fast.

²¹"No one sews a patch of unshrunk cloth on an old garment. If he does, the new piece will pull away from the old, making the tear worse. ²²And no one pours new wine into old wineskins. If he does, the wine will burst the skins, and both the wine and the wineskins will be ruined. No, he pours new wine into new wineskins."

Lord of the Sabbath

²³One Sabbath Jesus was going through the grainfields, and as his disciples walked along, they began to pick some heads of grain. ²⁴The Pharisees said to him, "Look, why are they doing what is unlawful on the Sabbath?"

²⁵He answered, "Have you never read what David did when he and his companions were hungry and in need? ²⁶In the days of Abiathar the high priest, he entered the house of God and ate the consecrated bread, which is lawful only for priests to eat. And he also gave some to his companions."

²⁷Then he said to them, "The Sabbath

was made for man, not man for the Sabbath. ²⁸So the Son of Man is Lord even of the Sabbath."

3 Another time he went into the synagogue, and a man with a shriveled hand was there. ²Some of them were looking for a reason to accuse Jesus, so they watched him closely to see if he would heal him on the Sabbath. ³Jesus said to the man with the shriveled hand, "Stand up in front of everyone."

⁴Then Jesus asked them, "Which is lawful on the Sabbath: to do good or to do evil, to save life or to kill?" But they remained silent.

⁵He looked around at them in anger and, deeply distressed at their stubborn hearts, said to the man, "Stretch out your hand." He stretched it out, and his hand was completely restored. ⁶Then the Pharisees went out and began to plot with the Herodians how they might kill Jesus.

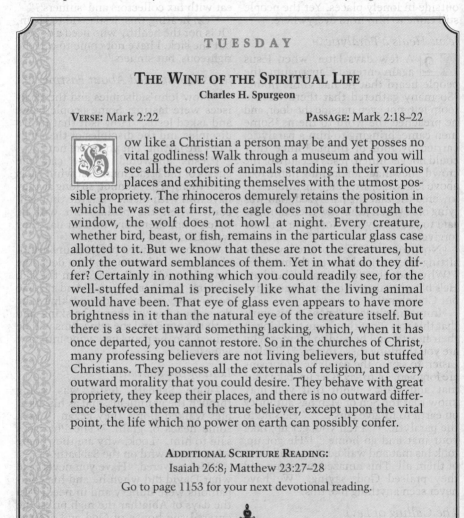

TUESDAY

THE WINE OF THE SPIRITUAL LIFE
Charles H. Spurgeon

VERSE: Mark 2:22   **PASSAGE:** Mark 2:18–22

How like a Christian a person may be and yet posses no vital godliness! Walk through a museum and you will see all the orders of animals standing in their various places and exhibiting themselves with the utmost possible propriety. The rhinoceros demurely retains the position in which he was set at first, the eagle does not soar through the window, the wolf does not howl at night. Every creature, whether bird, beast, or fish, remains in the particular glass case allotted to it. But we know that these are not the creatures, but only the outward semblances of them. Yet in what do they differ? Certainly in nothing which you could readily see, for the well-stuffed animal is precisely like what the living animal would have been. That eye of glass even appears to have more brightness in it than the natural eye of the creature itself. But there is a secret inward something lacking, which, when it has once departed, you cannot restore. So in the churches of Christ, many professing believers are not living believers, but stuffed Christians. They possess all the externals of religion, and every outward morality that you could desire. They behave with great propriety, they keep their places, and there is no outward difference between them and the true believer, except upon the vital point, the life which no power on earth can possibly confer.

ADDITIONAL SCRIPTURE READING:
Isaiah 26:8; Matthew 23:27–28

Go to page 1153 for your next devotional reading.

1700   1900

Crowds Follow Jesus

[7]Jesus withdrew with his disciples to the lake, and a large crowd from Galilee followed. [8]When they heard all he was doing, many people came to him from Judea, Jerusalem, Idumea, and the regions across the Jordan and around Tyre and Sidon. [9]Because of the crowd he told his disciples to have a small boat ready for him, to keep the people from crowding him. [10]For he had healed many, so that those with diseases were pushing forward to touch him. [11]Whenever the evil[a] spirits saw him, they fell down before him and cried out, "You are the Son of God." [12]But he gave them strict orders not to tell who he was.

The Appointing of the Twelve Apostles

[13]Jesus went up on a mountainside and called to him those he wanted, and they came to him. [14]He appointed twelve—designating them apostles[b]—that they might be with him and that he might send them out to preach [15]and to have authority to drive out demons. [16]These are the twelve he appointed: Simon (to whom he gave the name Peter); [17]James son of Zebedee and his brother John (to them he gave the name Boanerges, which means Sons of Thunder); [18]Andrew, Philip, Bartholomew, Matthew, Thomas, James son of Alphaeus, Thaddaeus, Simon the Zealot [19]and Judas Iscariot, who betrayed him.

Jesus and Beelzebub

[20]Then Jesus entered a house, and again a crowd gathered, so that he and his disciples were not even able to eat. [21]When his family heard about this, they went to take charge of him, for they said, "He is out of his mind."

[22]And the teachers of the law who came down from Jerusalem said, "He is possessed by Beelzebub[c]! By the prince of demons he is driving out demons."

[23]So Jesus called them and spoke to them in parables: "How can Satan drive out Satan? [24]If a kingdom is divided against itself, that kingdom cannot stand. [25]If a house is divided against itself, that house cannot stand. [26]And if Satan opposes himself and is divided, he cannot stand; his end has come. [27]In fact, no one can enter a strong man's house and carry off his possessions unless he first ties up the strong man. Then he can rob his house. [28]I tell you the truth, all the sins and blasphemies of men will be forgiven them. [29]But whoever blasphemes against the Holy Spirit will never be forgiven; he is guilty of an eternal sin."

[30]He said this because they were saying, "He has an evil spirit."

Jesus' Mother and Brothers

[31]Then Jesus' mother and brothers arrived. Standing outside, they sent someone in to call him. [32]A crowd was sitting around him, and they told him, "Your mother and brothers are outside looking for you."

[33]"Who are my mother and my brothers?" he asked.

[34]Then he looked at those seated in a circle around him and said, "Here are my mother and my brothers! [35]Whoever does God's will is my brother and sister and mother."

The Parable of the Sower

4 Again Jesus began to teach by the lake. The crowd that gathered around him was so large that he got into a boat and sat in it out on the lake, while all the people were along the shore at the water's edge. [2]He taught them many things by parables, and in his teaching said: [3]"Listen! A farmer went out to sow his seed. [4]As he was scattering the seed, some fell along the path, and the birds came and ate it up. [5]Some fell on rocky places, where it did not have much soil. It sprang up quickly, because the soil was shallow. [6]But when the sun came up, the plants were scorched, and they withered because they had no root. [7]Other seed fell among thorns, which grew up and choked the plants, so that they did not bear grain. [8]Still other seed fell on good soil. It came up, grew and produced a crop, multiplying thirty, sixty, or even a hundred times."

---

[a] 11 Greek unclean; also in verse 30   [b] 14 Some manuscripts do not have designating them apostles.
[c] 22 Greek Beezeboul or Beelzeboul

[9]Then Jesus said, "He who has ears to hear, let him hear."

[10]When he was alone, the Twelve and the others around him asked him about the parables. [11]He told them, "The secret of the kingdom of God has been given to you. But to those on the outside everything is said in parables [12]so that,

" 'they may be ever seeing but never
     perceiving,
and ever hearing but never
     understanding;
otherwise they might turn and be
     forgiven!'[a] "

[13]Then Jesus said to them, "Don't you understand this parable? How then will you understand any parable? [14]The farmer sows the word. [15]Some people are like seed along the path, where the word is sown. As soon as they hear it, Satan comes and takes away the word that was sown in them. [16]Others, like seed sown on rocky places, hear the word and at once receive it with joy. [17]But since they have no root, they last only a short time. When trouble or persecution comes because of the word, they quickly fall away. [18]Still others, like seed sown among thorns, hear the word; [19]but the worries of this life, the deceitfulness of wealth and the desires for other things come in and choke the word, making it unfruitful. [20]Others, like seed sown on good soil, hear the word, accept it, and produce a crop—thirty, sixty or even a hundred times what was sown."

A Lamp on a Stand

[21]He said to them, "Do you bring in a lamp to put it under a bowl or a bed? Instead, don't you put it on its stand? [22]For whatever is hidden is meant to be disclosed, and whatever is concealed is meant to be brought out into the open. [23]If anyone has ears to hear, let him hear."

[24]"Consider carefully what you hear," he continued. "With the measure you use, it will be measured to you—and even more. [25]Whoever has will be given more; whoever does not have, even what he has will be taken from him."

The Parable of the Growing Seed

[26]He also said, "This is what the kingdom of God is like. A man scatters seed on the ground. [27]Night and day, whether he sleeps or gets up, the seed sprouts and grows, though he does not know how. [28]All by itself the soil produces grain—first the stalk, then the head, then the full kernel in the head. [29]As soon as the grain is ripe, he puts the sickle to it, because the harvest has come."

The Parable of the Mustard Seed

[30]Again he said, "What shall we say the kingdom of God is like, or what parable shall we use to describe it? [31]It is like a mustard seed, which is the smallest seed you plant in the ground. [32]Yet when planted, it grows and becomes the largest of all garden plants, with such big branches that the birds of the air can perch in its shade."

[33]With many similar parables Jesus spoke the word to them, as much as they could understand. [34]He did not say anything to them without using a parable. But when he was alone with his own disciples, he explained everything.

HOW OFTEN WE LOOK UPON GOD AS OUR LAST AND FEEBLEST RESOURCE! WE GO TO HIM BECAUSE WE HAVE NOWHERE ELSE TO GO. AND THEN WE LEARN THAT THE STORMS OF LIFE HAVE DRIVEN US, NOT UPON THE ROCKS, BUT INTO THE DESIRED HAVEN.   —*George MacDonald*

Jesus Calms the Storm

[35]That day when evening came, he said to his disciples, "Let us go over to the other side." [36]Leaving the crowd behind, they took him along, just as he was, in the boat. There were also other boats with him. [37]A furious squall came up, and the waves broke over the boat, so that it was nearly swamped. [38]Jesus was in the stern, sleeping on a cushion. The disciples woke him and said to him, "Teacher, don't you care if we drown?"

[39]He got up, rebuked the wind and said to the waves, "Quiet! Be still!" Then the wind died down and it was completely calm.

[a] *12* Isaiah 6:9,10

[40] He said to his disciples, "Why are you so afraid? Do you still have no faith?"

[41] They were terrified and asked each other, "Who is this? Even the wind and the waves obey him!"

The Healing of a Demon-possessed Man

5 They went across the lake to the region of the Gerasenes.[a] [2] When Jesus got out of the boat, a man with an evil[b] spirit came from the tombs to meet him. [3] This man lived in the tombs, and no one could bind him any more, not even with a chain. [4] For he had often been chained hand and foot, but he tore the chains apart and broke the irons on his feet. No one was strong enough to subdue him. [5] Night and day among the tombs and in the hills he would cry out and cut himself with stones.

[6] When he saw Jesus from a distance, he ran and fell on his knees in front of him. [7] He shouted at the top of his voice, "What do you want with me, Jesus, Son of the Most High God? Swear to God that you won't torture me!" [8] For Jesus had said to him, "Come out of this man, you evil spirit!"

[9] Then Jesus asked him, "What is your name?"

"My name is Legion," he replied, "for we are many." [10] And he begged Jesus again and again not to send them out of the area.

[11] A large herd of pigs was feeding on the nearby hillside. [12] The demons begged Jesus, "Send us among the pigs; allow us to go into them." [13] He gave them permission, and the evil spirits came out and went into the pigs. The herd, about two thousand in number, rushed down the steep bank into the lake and were drowned.

[14] Those tending the pigs ran off and reported this in the town and countryside, and the people went out to see what had happened. [15] When they came to Jesus, they saw the man who had been possessed by the legion of demons, sitting there, dressed and in his right mind; and they were afraid. [16] Those who had seen it told the people what had happened to the demon-possessed man—and told about the pigs as well. [17] Then the people began to plead with Jesus to leave their region.

[18] As Jesus was getting into the boat, the man who had been demon-possessed begged to go with him. [19] Jesus did not let him, but said, "Go home to your family and tell them how much the Lord has done for you, and how he has had mercy on you." [20] So the man went away and began to tell in the Decapolis[c] how much Jesus had done for him. And all the people were amazed.

A Dead Girl and a Sick Woman

[21] When Jesus had again crossed over by boat to the other side of the lake, a large crowd gathered around him while he was by the lake. [22] Then one of the synagogue rulers, named Jairus, came there. Seeing Jesus, he fell at his feet [23] and pleaded earnestly with him, "My little daughter is dying. Please come and put your hands on her so that she will be healed and live." [24] So Jesus went with him.

A large crowd followed and pressed around him. [25] And a woman was there who had been subject to bleeding for twelve years. [26] She had suffered a great deal under the care of many doctors and had spent all she had, yet instead of getting better she grew worse. [27] When she heard about Jesus, she came up behind him in the crowd and touched his cloak, [28] because she thought, "If I just touch his clothes, I will be healed." [29] Immediately her bleeding stopped and she felt in her body that she was freed from her suffering.

[30] At once Jesus realized that power had gone out from him. He turned around in the crowd and asked, "Who touched my clothes?"

[31] "You see the people crowding against you," his disciples answered, "and yet you can ask, 'Who touched me?'"

[32] But Jesus kept looking around to see who had done it. [33] Then the woman, knowing what had happened to her, came and fell at his feet and, trembling with fear, told him the whole truth. [34] He said to her, "Daughter, your faith

a 1 Some manuscripts *Gadarenes*; other manuscripts *Gergesenes*   *b 2* Greek *unclean*; also in verses 8 and 13   *c 20* That is, the Ten Cities

has healed you. Go in peace and be freed from your suffering."

35While Jesus was still speaking, some men came from the house of Jairus, the synagogue ruler. "Your daughter is dead," they said. "Why bother the teacher any more?"

36Ignoring what they said, Jesus told the synagogue ruler, "Don't be afraid; just believe."

37He did not let anyone follow him except Peter, James and John the brother of James. 38When they came to the home of the synagogue ruler, Jesus saw a commotion, with people crying and wailing loudly. 39He went in and said to them, "Why all this commotion and wailing? The child is not dead but asleep." 40But they laughed at him.

After he put them all out, he took the child's father and mother and the disciples who were with him, and went in where the child was. 41He took her by the hand and said to her, *"Talitha koum!"* (which means, "Little girl, I say to you, get up!"). 42Immediately the girl stood up and walked around (she was twelve years old). At this they were completely astonished. 43He gave strict orders not to let anyone know about this, and told them to give her something to eat.

A Prophet Without Honor

6 Jesus left there and went to his hometown, accompanied by his disciples. 2When the Sabbath came, he began to teach in the synagogue, and many who heard him were amazed.

"Where did this man get these things?" they asked. "What's this wisdom that has been given him, that he even does miracles! 3Isn't this the carpenter? Isn't this Mary's son and the brother of James, Joseph,*a* Judas and Simon? Aren't his sisters here with us?" And they took offense at him.

4Jesus said to them, "Only in his hometown, among his relatives and in his own house is a prophet without honor." 5He could not do any miracles there, except lay his hands on a few sick people and heal them. 6And he was amazed at their lack of faith.

Jesus Sends Out the Twelve

Then Jesus went around teaching from village to village. 7Calling the Twelve to him, he sent them out two by two and gave them authority over evil*b* spirits.

8These were his instructions: "Take nothing for the journey except a staff— no bread, no bag, no money in your belts. 9Wear sandals but not an extra tunic. 10Whenever you enter a house, stay there until you leave that town. 11And if any place will not welcome you or listen to you, shake the dust off your feet when you leave, as a testimony against them."

12They went out and preached that people should repent. 13They drove out many demons and anointed many sick people with oil and healed them.

John the Baptist Beheaded

14King Herod heard about this, for Jesus' name had become well known. Some were saying,*c* "John the Baptist has been raised from the dead, and that is why miraculous powers are at work in him."

15Others said, "He is Elijah."

And still others claimed, "He is a prophet, like one of the prophets of long ago."

16But when Herod heard this, he said, "John, the man I beheaded, has been raised from the dead!"

17For Herod himself had given orders to have John arrested, and he had him bound and put in prison. He did this because of Herodias, his brother Philip's wife, whom he had married. 18For John had been saying to Herod, "It is not lawful for you to have your brother's wife." 19So Herodias nursed a grudge against John and wanted to kill him. But she was not able to, 20because Herod feared John and protected him, knowing him to be a righteous and holy man. When Herod heard John, he was greatly puzzled*d*; yet he liked to listen to him.

21Finally the opportune time came. On his birthday Herod gave a banquet for his high officials and military commanders and the leading men of Galilee.

---

a 3 Greek *Joses,* a variant of *Joseph*   *b 7* Greek *unclean*   *c 14* Some early manuscripts *He was saying*
d 20 Some early manuscripts *he did many things*

22When the daughter of Herodias came in and danced, she pleased Herod and his dinner guests.

The king said to the girl, "Ask me for anything you want, and I'll give it to you." 23And he promised her with an oath, "Whatever you ask I will give you, up to half my kingdom."

24She went out and said to her mother, "What shall I ask for?"

"The head of John the Baptist," she answered.

25At once the girl hurried in to the king with the request: "I want you to give me right now the head of John the Baptist on a platter."

WEDNESDAY

THE REPENTANCE OF THOMAS MORE
Thomas More

VERSE: Mark 6:12   **PASSAGE:** Mark 6:7–12

ood and gracious Lord, as you give me grace to acknowledge my sins, so give me grace in both word and heart to repent them and utterly forsake them. And forgive me those sins which my pride blinds me from discerning.

Glorious God, give me your grace to turn my back on the things of this world, and to fix my heart solely on you.

Give me your grace to amend my life, so that I can approach death without resentment, knowing that in you it is the gateway to eternal riches.

Glorious God, take from me all sinful fear, all sinful sorrow and self-pity, all sinful hope and all sinful desire. Instead give me such fear, such sorrow, such pity, such hope and such desire as may be profitable for my soul.

Good Lord, give me this grace, in all my fear and agony, to find strength in that great fear and agony which you, sweet Savior, had on the Mount of Olives before your bitter passion.

Almighty God, take from me all desire for worldly praise, and all emotions of anger and revenge. Give me a humble, lowly, quiet, peaceable, patient, generous, kind, tender and compassionate mind.

Grant me, good Lord, a full faith, a firm hope and a fervent love, that I may desire only that which gives you pleasure and conforms to your will.

And, above all, look upon me with your love and your favor.

ADDITIONAL SCRIPTURE READING:
Jeremiah 15:19; John 14:1–4

Go to page 1159 for your next devotional reading.

1500   1700

26The king was greatly distressed, but because of his oaths and his dinner guests, he did not want to refuse her. **27**So he immediately sent an executioner with orders to bring John's head. The man went, beheaded John in the prison, **28**and brought back his head on a platter. He presented it to the girl, and she gave it to her mother. **29**On hearing of this, John's disciples came and took his body and laid it in a tomb.

Jesus Feeds the Five Thousand

30The apostles gathered around Jesus and reported to him all they had done and taught. **31**Then, because so many people were coming and going that they did not even have a chance to eat, he said to them, "Come with me by yourselves to a quiet place and get some rest."

32So they went away by themselves in a boat to a solitary place. **33**But many who saw them leaving recognized them and ran on foot from all the towns and got there ahead of them. **34**When Jesus landed and saw a large crowd, he had compassion on them, because they were like sheep without a shepherd. So he began teaching them many things.

35By this time it was late in the day, so his disciples came to him. "This is a remote place," they said, "and it's already very late. **36**Send the people away so they can go to the surrounding countryside and villages and buy themselves something to eat."

37But he answered, "You give them something to eat."

They said to him, "That would take eight months of a man's wages*a*! Are we to go and spend that much on bread and give it to them to eat?"

38"How many loaves do you have?" he asked. "Go and see."

When they found out, they said, "Five—and two fish."

39Then Jesus directed them to have all the people sit down in groups on the green grass. **40**So they sat down in groups of hundreds and fifties. **41**Taking the five loaves and the two fish and looking up to heaven, he gave thanks and broke the loaves. Then he gave them to his disciples to set before the people. He also divided the two fish among them all. **42**They all ate and were satisfied, **43**and the disciples picked up twelve basketfuls of broken pieces of bread and fish. **44**The number of the men who had eaten was five thousand.

Jesus Walks on the Water

45Immediately Jesus made his disciples get into the boat and go on ahead of him to Bethsaida, while he dismissed the crowd. **46**After leaving them, he went up on a mountainside to pray.

47When evening came, the boat was in the middle of the lake, and he was alone on land. **48**He saw the disciples straining at the oars, because the wind was against them. About the fourth watch of the night he went out to them, walking on the lake. He was about to pass by them, **49**but when they saw him walking on the lake, they thought he was a ghost. They cried out, **50**because they all saw him and were terrified.

Immediately he spoke to them and said, "Take courage! It is I. Don't be afraid." **51**Then he climbed into the boat with them, and the wind died down. They were completely amazed, **52**for they had not understood about the loaves; their hearts were hardened.

53When they had crossed over, they landed at Gennesaret and anchored there. **54**As soon as they got out of the boat, people recognized Jesus. **55**They ran throughout that whole region and carried the sick on mats to wherever they heard he was. **56**And wherever he went—into villages, towns or countryside—they placed the sick in the marketplaces. They begged him to let them touch even the edge of his cloak, and all who touched him were healed.

Clean and Unclean

7 The Pharisees and some of the teachers of the law who had come from Jerusalem gathered around Jesus and **2**saw some of his disciples eating food with hands that were "unclean," that is, unwashed. **3**(The Pharisees and all the Jews do not eat unless they give their hands a ceremonial washing, holding to the tradition of the elders. **4**When they come from the marketplace they do not eat unless they

---

a 37 Greek *take two hundred denarii*

wash. And they observe many other traditions, such as the washing of cups, pitchers and kettles.*ᵃ)*

⁵So the Pharisees and teachers of the law asked Jesus, "Why don't your disciples live according to the tradition of the elders instead of eating their food with 'unclean' hands?"

⁶He replied, "Isaiah was right when he prophesied about you hypocrites; as it is written:

" 'These people honor me with their
     lips,
   but their hearts are far from me.
⁷They worship me in vain;
     their teachings are but rules taught
       by men.'ᵇ

⁸You have let go of the commands of God and are holding on to the traditions of men."

⁹And he said to them: "You have a fine way of setting aside the commands of God in order to observeᶜ your own traditions! ¹⁰For Moses said, 'Honor your father and your mother,'ᵈ and, 'Anyone who curses his father or mother must be put to death.'ᵉ ¹¹But you say that if a man says to his father or mother: 'Whatever help you might otherwise have received from me is Corban' (that is, a gift devoted to God), ¹²then you no longer let him do anything for his father or mother. ¹³Thus you nullify the word of God by your tradition that you have handed down. And you do many things like that."

¹⁴Again Jesus called the crowd to him and said, "Listen to me, everyone, and understand this. ¹⁵Nothing outside a man can make him 'unclean' by going into him. Rather, it is what comes out of a man that makes him 'unclean.'ᶠ "

¹⁷After he had left the crowd and entered the house, his disciples asked him about this parable. ¹⁸"Are you so dull?" he asked. "Don't you see that nothing that enters a man from the outside can make him 'unclean'? ¹⁹For it doesn't go into his heart but into his stomach, and then out of his body." (In

saying this, Jesus declared all foods "clean.")

²⁰He went on: "What comes out of a man is what makes him 'unclean.' ²¹For from within, out of men's hearts, come evil thoughts, sexual immorality, theft, murder, adultery, ²²greed, malice, deceit, lewdness, envy, slander, arrogance and folly. ²³All these evils come from inside and make a man 'unclean.' "

The Faith of a Syrophoenician Woman

²⁴Jesus left that place and went to the vicinity of Tyre.ᵍ He entered a house and did not want anyone to know it; yet he could not keep his presence secret. ²⁵In fact, as soon as she heard about him, a woman whose little daughter was possessed by an evilʰ spirit came and fell at his feet. ²⁶The woman was a Greek, born in Syrian Phoenicia. She begged Jesus to drive the demon out of her daughter.

²⁷"First let the children eat all they want," he told her, "for it is not right to take the children's bread and toss it to their dogs."

²⁸"Yes, Lord," she replied, "but even the dogs under the table eat the children's crumbs."

²⁹Then he told her, "For such a reply, you may go; the demon has left your daughter."

³⁰She went home and found her child lying on the bed, and the demon gone.

The Healing of a Deaf and Mute Man

³¹Then Jesus left the vicinity of Tyre and went through Sidon, down to the Sea of Galilee and into the region of the Decapolis.ⁱ ³²There some people brought to him a man who was deaf and could hardly talk, and they begged him to place his hand on the man.

³³After he took him aside, away from the crowd, Jesus put his fingers into the man's ears. Then he spit and touched the man's tongue. ³⁴He looked up to heaven and with a deep sigh said to him, *"Ephphatha!"* (which means, "Be

ᵃ 4 Some early manuscripts *pitchers, kettles and dining couches*   ᵇ 6,7 Isaiah 29:13   ᶜ 9 Some manuscripts *set up*   ᵈ 10 Exodus 20:12; Deut. 5:16   ᵉ 10 Exodus 21:17; Lev. 20:9   ᶠ 15 Some early manuscripts *'unclean.' ¹⁶If anyone has ears to hear, let him hear.*   ᵍ 24 Many early manuscripts *Tyre and Sidon*   ʰ 25 Greek *unclean*   ⁱ 31 That is, the Ten Cities

opened!"). 35At this, the man's ears were opened, his tongue was loosened and he began to speak plainly.

36Jesus commanded them not to tell anyone. But the more he did so, the more they kept talking about it. 37People were overwhelmed with amazement. "He has done everything well," they said. "He even makes the deaf hear and the mute speak."

Jesus Feeds the Four Thousand

8 During those days another large crowd gathered. Since they had nothing to eat, Jesus called his disciples to him and said, 2"I have compassion for these people; they have already been with me three days and have nothing to eat. 3If I send them home hungry, they will collapse on the way, because some of them have come a long distance."

4His disciples answered, "But where in this remote place can anyone get enough bread to feed them?"

5"How many loaves do you have?" Jesus asked.

"Seven," they replied.

6He told the crowd to sit down on the ground. When he had taken the seven loaves and given thanks, he broke them and gave them to his disciples to set before the people, and they did so. 7They had a few small fish as well; he gave thanks for them also and told the disciples to distribute them. 8The people ate and were satisfied. Afterward the disciples picked up seven basketfuls of broken pieces that were left over. 9About four thousand men were present. And having sent them away, 10he got into the boat with his disciples and went to the region of Dalmanutha.

11The Pharisees came and began to question Jesus. To test him, they asked him for a sign from heaven. 12He sighed deeply and said, "Why does this generation ask for a miraculous sign? I tell you the truth, no sign will be given to it." 13Then he left them, got back into the boat and crossed to the other side.

The Yeast of the Pharisees and Herod

14The disciples had forgotten to bring bread, except for one loaf they had with them in the boat. 15"Be careful," Jesus warned them. "Watch out for the yeast of the Pharisees and that of Herod."

16They discussed this with one another and said, "It is because we have no bread."

17Aware of their discussion, Jesus asked them: "Why are you talking about having no bread? Do you still not see or understand? Are your hearts hardened? 18Do you have eyes but fail to see, and ears but fail to hear? And don't you remember? 19When I broke the five loaves for the five thousand, how many basketfuls of pieces did you pick up?"

"Twelve," they replied.

20"And when I broke the seven loaves for the four thousand, how many basketfuls of pieces did you pick up?"

They answered, "Seven."

21He said to them, "Do you still not understand?"

The Healing of a Blind Man at Bethsaida

22They came to Bethsaida, and some people brought a blind man and begged Jesus to touch him. 23He took the blind man by the hand and led him outside the village. When he had spit on the man's eyes and put his hands on him, Jesus asked, "Do you see anything?"

24He looked up and said, "I see people; they look like trees walking around."

25Once more Jesus put his hands on the man's eyes. Then his eyes were opened, his sight was restored, and he saw everything clearly. 26Jesus sent him home, saying, "Don't go into the village.*a*"

Peter's Confession of Christ

27Jesus and his disciples went on to the villages around Caesarea Philippi. On the way he asked them, "Who do people say I am?"

28They replied, "Some say John the Baptist; others say Elijah; and still others, one of the prophets."

29"But what about you?" he asked. "Who do you say I am?"

Peter answered, "You are the Christ.*b*"

30Jesus warned them not to tell anyone about him.

---

a 26 Some manuscripts *Don't go and tell anyone in the village*   *b* 29 Or *Messiah*. "The Christ" (Greek) and "the Messiah" (Hebrew) both mean "the Anointed One."

Jesus Predicts His Death

31He then began to teach them that the Son of Man must suffer many things and be rejected by the elders, chief priests and teachers of the law, and that he must be killed and after three days rise again. **32**He spoke plainly about this, and Peter took him aside and began to rebuke him.

33But when Jesus turned and looked at his disciples, he rebuked Peter. "Get behind me, Satan!" he said. "You do not have in mind the things of God, but the things of men."

34Then he called the crowd to him along with his disciples and said: "If anyone would come after me, he must deny himself and take up his cross and follow me. **35**For whoever wants to save his life*a* will lose it, but whoever loses his life for me and for the gospel will save it. **36**What good is it for a man to gain the whole world, yet forfeit his soul? **37**Or what can a man give in

---

THE CHRISTIAN HAS GREATLY THE ADVANTAGE OF THE UNBELIEVER, HAVING EVERYTHING TO GAIN AND NOTHING TO LOSE.   —*Lord Byron*

---

exchange for his soul? **38**If anyone is ashamed of me and my words in this adulterous and sinful generation, the Son of Man will be ashamed of him when he comes in his Father's glory with the holy angels."

9 And he said to them, "I tell you the truth, some who are standing here will not taste death before they see the kingdom of God come with power."

The Transfiguration

2After six days Jesus took Peter, James and John with him and led them up a high mountain, where they were all alone. There he was transfigured before them. **3**His clothes became dazzling white, whiter than anyone in the world could bleach them. **4**And there appeared before them Elijah and Moses, who were talking with Jesus.

5Peter said to Jesus, "Rabbi, it is good for us to be here. Let us put up three shelters—one for you, one for Moses and one for Elijah." **6**(He did not know what to say, they were so frightened.)

7Then a cloud appeared and enveloped them, and a voice came from the cloud: "This is my Son, whom I love. Listen to him!"

8Suddenly, when they looked around, they no longer saw anyone with them except Jesus.

9As they were coming down the mountain, Jesus gave them orders not to tell anyone what they had seen until the Son of Man had risen from the dead. **10**They kept the matter to themselves, discussing what "rising from the dead" meant.

11And they asked him, "Why do the teachers of the law say that Elijah must come first?"

12Jesus replied, "To be sure, Elijah does come first, and restores all things. Why then is it written that the Son of Man must suffer much and be rejected? **13**But I tell you, Elijah has come, and they have done to him everything they wished, just as it is written about him."

The Healing of a Boy With an Evil Spirit

14When they came to the other disciples, they saw a large crowd around them and the teachers of the law arguing with them. **15**As soon as all the people saw Jesus, they were overwhelmed with wonder and ran to greet him.

16"What are you arguing with them about?" he asked.

17A man in the crowd answered, "Teacher, I brought you my son, who is possessed by a spirit that has robbed him of speech. **18**Whenever it seizes him, it throws him to the ground. He foams at the mouth, gnashes his teeth and becomes rigid. I asked your disciples to drive out the spirit, but they could not."

19"O unbelieving generation," Jesus replied, "how long shall I stay with you? How long shall I put up with you? Bring the boy to me."

20So they brought him. When the spirit saw Jesus, it immediately threw the boy into a convulsion. He fell to the

---

a 35 The Greek word means either *life* or *soul;* also in verse 36.

ground and rolled around, foaming at the mouth.

²¹Jesus asked the boy's father, "How long has he been like this?"

"From childhood," he answered. ²²"It has often thrown him into fire or water to kill him. But if you can do anything, take pity on us and help us."

²³" 'If you can'?" said Jesus. "Everything is possible for him who believes."

²⁴Immediately the boy's father exclaimed, "I do believe; help me overcome my unbelief!"

²⁵When Jesus saw that a crowd was running to the scene, he rebuked the evil*a* spirit. "You deaf and mute spirit," he said, "I command you, come out of him and never enter him again."

²⁶The spirit shrieked, convulsed him violently and came out. The boy looked so much like a corpse that many said, "He's dead." ²⁷But Jesus took him by the hand and lifted him to his feet, and he stood up.

²⁸After Jesus had gone indoors, his disciples asked him privately, "Why couldn't we drive it out?"

²⁹He replied, "This kind can come out only by prayer.*b*"

³⁰They left that place and passed through Galilee. Jesus did not want anyone to know where they were, ³¹because he was teaching his disciples. He said to them, "The Son of Man is going to be betrayed into the hands of men. They will kill him, and after three days he will rise." ³²But they did not understand what he meant and were afraid to ask him about it.

Who Is the Greatest?

³³They came to Capernaum. When he was in the house, he asked them, "What were you arguing about on the road?" ³⁴But they kept quiet because on the way they had argued about who was the greatest.

³⁵Sitting down, Jesus called the Twelve and said, "If anyone wants to be first, he must be the very last, and the servant of all."

³⁶He took a little child and had him stand among them. Taking him in his arms, he said to them, ³⁷"Whoever welcomes one of these little children in my name welcomes me; and whoever welcomes me does not welcome me but the one who sent me."

Whoever Is Not Against Us Is for Us

³⁸"Teacher," said John, "we saw a man driving out demons in your name and we told him to stop, because he was not one of us."

³⁹"Do not stop him," Jesus said. "No one who does a miracle in my name can in the next moment say anything bad about me, ⁴⁰for whoever is not against us is for us. ⁴¹I tell you the truth, anyone who gives you a cup of water in my name because you belong to Christ will certainly not lose his reward.

Causing to Sin

⁴²"And if anyone causes one of these little ones who believe in me to sin, it would be better for him to be thrown into the sea with a large millstone tied around his neck. ⁴³If your hand causes you to sin, cut it off. It is better for you to enter life maimed than with two hands to go into hell, where the fire never goes out.*c* ⁴⁵And if your foot causes you to sin, cut it off. It is better for you to enter life crippled than to have two feet and be thrown into hell.*d* ⁴⁷And if your eye causes you to sin, pluck it out. It is better for you to enter the kingdom of God with one eye than to have two eyes and be thrown into hell, ⁴⁸where

" 'their worm does not die,
  and the fire is not quenched.'*e*

⁴⁹Everyone will be salted with fire.

⁵⁰"Salt is good, but if it loses its saltiness, how can you make it salty again? Have salt in yourselves, and be at peace with each other."

Divorce

10 Jesus then left that place and went into the region of Judea and across the Jordan. Again crowds of

---

a 25 Greek *unclean*   *b 29* Some manuscripts *prayer and fasting*   *c 43* Some manuscripts *out,* *⁴⁴where / " 'their worm does not die, / and the fire is not quenched.'*   *d 45* Some manuscripts *hell, ⁴⁶where / " 'their worm does not die, / and the fire is not quenched.'*   *e 48* Isaiah 66:24

people came to him, and as was his custom, he taught them.

²Some Pharisees came and tested him by asking, "Is it lawful for a man to divorce his wife?"

³"What did Moses command you?" he replied.

⁴They said, "Moses permitted a man to write a certificate of divorce and send her away."

⁵"It was because your hearts were hard that Moses wrote you this law," Jesus replied. ⁶"But at the beginning of creation God 'made them male and female.'ᵃ ⁷'For this reason a man will leave his father and mother and be united to his wife,ᵇ

ᵃ 6 Gen. 1:27   ᵇ 7 Some early manuscripts do not have *and be united to his wife.*

THURSDAY

MAKE US LIKE CHILDREN AGAIN
Peter Marshall

VERSE: Mark 9:37   **PASSAGE:** Mark 9:35–37

orgive us, Lord, that as we grow to maturity, our faith is blighted with doubts, withered with worry, tainted with sophistication. We pray that thou wilt make us like children again in faith—not childish, but childlike in the simplicity of a faith that is willing to trust thee even though we cannot see what tomorrow will bring.

We ask thee to give to each of us that childlike faith, that simplicity of mind which is willing to lay aside all egotism and conceit, which recognizes vanity for what it is—an empty show, which knows that we are incapable of thinking the thoughts of God, which is willing to be humble again.

Then may we feel once more as do our children who whisper their love to thee, who trace with chubby little fingers the pictures of Jesus in a picture book—those pictures that portray thee, Lord Jesus, with a hurt lamb in thy arms or a child on thy knee. Help us, even now, to feel again like that, that we may be as loving, as trusting, as innocent, as grateful, as affectionate.

And as we are willing to kneel again as children, then shall we discover for ourselves the glory thou hast revealed, and find the wonder of it gripping our hearts and preparing them for thy peace. So shall we, along with our children, enter into the kingdom of God, and know it, and feel it, and rejoice in it. In thy name, who didst dare to come to earth as a little child, we pray. Amen.

ADDITIONAL SCRIPTURE READING:
Matthew 18:3; 1 John 3:1

Go to page 1164 for your next devotional reading.

1900   Present

[8]and the two will become one flesh.'[a] So they are no longer two, but one. [9]Therefore what God has joined together, let man not separate."

[10]When they were in the house again, the disciples asked Jesus about this. [11]He answered, "Anyone who divorces his wife and marries another woman commits adultery against her. [12]And if she divorces her husband and marries another man, she commits adultery."

The Little Children and Jesus

[13]People were bringing little children to Jesus to have him touch them, but the disciples rebuked them. [14]When Jesus saw this, he was indignant. He said to them, "Let the little children come to me, and do not hinder them, for the kingdom of God belongs to such as these. [15]I tell you the truth, anyone who will not receive the kingdom of God like a little child will never enter it." [16]And he took the children in his arms, put his hands on them and blessed them.

The Rich Young Man

[17]As Jesus started on his way, a man ran up to him and fell on his knees before him. "Good teacher," he asked, "what must I do to inherit eternal life?"

[18]"Why do you call me good?" Jesus answered. "No one is good—except God alone. [19]You know the commandments: 'Do not murder, do not commit adultery, do not steal, do not give false testimony, do not defraud, honor your father and mother.'[b]"

[20]"Teacher," he declared, "all these I have kept since I was a boy."

[21]Jesus looked at him and loved him. "One thing you lack," he said. "Go, sell everything you have and give to the poor, and you will have treasure in heaven. Then come, follow me."

[22]At this the man's face fell. He went away sad, because he had great wealth.

[23]Jesus looked around and said to his disciples, "How hard it is for the rich to enter the kingdom of God!"

[24]The disciples were amazed at his words. But Jesus said again, "Children, how hard it is[c] to enter the kingdom of God! [25]It is easier for a camel to go

through the eye of a needle than for a rich man to enter the kingdom of God."

[26]The disciples were even more amazed, and said to each other, "Who then can be saved?"

[27]Jesus looked at them and said, "With man this is impossible, but not with God; all things are possible with God."

[28]Peter said to him, "We have left everything to follow you!"

[29]"I tell you the truth," Jesus replied, "no one who has left home or brothers or sisters or mother or father or children or fields for me and the gospel [30]will fail to receive a hundred times as much in this present age (homes, brothers, sisters, mothers, children and fields—and with them, persecutions) and in the age to come, eternal life. [31]But many who are first will be last, and the last first."

Jesus Again Predicts His Death

[32]They were on their way up to Jerusalem, with Jesus leading the way, and the disciples were astonished, while those who followed were afraid. Again he took the Twelve aside and told them what was going to happen to him. [33]"We are going up to Jerusalem," he said, "and the Son of Man will be betrayed to the chief priests and teachers of the law. They will condemn him to death and will hand him over to the Gentiles, [34]who will mock him and spit on him, flog him and kill him. Three days later he will rise."

The Request of James and John

[35]Then James and John, the sons of Zebedee, came to him. "Teacher," they said, "we want you to do for us whatever we ask."

[36]"What do you want me to do for you?" he asked.

[37]They replied, "Let one of us sit at your right and the other at your left in your glory."

[38]"You don't know what you are asking," Jesus said. "Can you drink the cup I drink or be baptized with the baptism I am baptized with?"

[39]"We can," they answered.

Jesus said to them, "You will drink the cup I drink and be baptized with the

---

[a] 8 Gen. 2:24   [b] 19 Exodus 20:12–16; Deut. 5:16–20   [c] 24 Some manuscripts is for those who trust in riches

baptism I am baptized with, **40**but to sit at my right or left is not for me to grant. These places belong to those for whom they have been prepared."

41When the ten heard about this, they became indignant with James and John. **42**Jesus called them together and said, "You know that those who are regarded as rulers of the Gentiles lord it over them, and their high officials exercise authority over them. **43**Not so with you. Instead, whoever wants to become great among you must be your servant, **44**and whoever wants to be first must be slave of all. **45**For even the Son of Man did not come to be served, but to serve, and to give his life as a ransom for many."

Blind Bartimaeus Receives His Sight

46Then they came to Jericho. As Jesus and his disciples, together with a large crowd, were leaving the city, a blind man, Bartimaeus (that is, the Son of Timaeus), was sitting by the roadside begging. **47**When he heard that it was Jesus of Nazareth, he began to shout, "Jesus, Son of David, have mercy on me!"

48Many rebuked him and told him to be quiet, but he shouted all the more, "Son of David, have mercy on me!"

49Jesus stopped and said, "Call him."

So they called to the blind man, "Cheer up! On your feet! He's calling you." **50**Throwing his cloak aside, he jumped to his feet and came to Jesus.

51"What do you want me to do for you?" Jesus asked him.

The blind man said, "Rabbi, I want to see."

52"Go," said Jesus, "your faith has healed you." Immediately he received his sight and followed Jesus along the road.

The Triumphal Entry

11 As they approached Jerusalem and came to Bethphage and Bethany at the Mount of Olives, Jesus sent two of his disciples, **2**saying to them, "Go to the village ahead of you, and just as you enter it, you will find a colt tied there, which no one has ever ridden. Untie it and bring it here. **3**If

anyone asks you, 'Why are you doing this?' tell him, 'The Lord needs it and will send it back here shortly.' "

4They went and found a colt outside in the street, tied at a doorway. As they untied it, **5**some people standing there asked, "What are you doing, untying that colt?" **6**They answered as Jesus had told them to, and the people let them go. **7**When they brought the colt to Jesus and threw their cloaks over it, he sat on it. **8**Many people spread their cloaks on the road, while others spread branches they had cut in the fields. **9**Those who went ahead and those who followed shouted,

"Hosanna!*a*"

"Blessed is he who comes in the name of the Lord!"*b*

10"Blessed is the coming kingdom of our father David!"

"Hosanna in the highest!"

11Jesus entered Jerusalem and went to the temple. He looked around at everything, but since it was already late, he went out to Bethany with the Twelve.

Jesus Clears the Temple

12The next day as they were leaving Bethany, Jesus was hungry. **13**Seeing in the distance a fig tree in leaf, he went to find out if it had any fruit. When he reached it, he found nothing but leaves, because it was not the season for figs. **14**Then he said to the tree, "May no one ever eat fruit from you again." And his disciples heard him say it.

15On reaching Jerusalem, Jesus entered the temple area and began driving out those who were buying and selling there. He overturned the tables of the money changers and the benches of those selling doves, **16**and would not allow anyone to carry merchandise through the temple courts. **17**And as he taught them, he said, "Is it not written:

" 'My house will be called a house of prayer for all nations'*c*?

But you have made it 'a den of robbers.'*d*"

---

a 9 A Hebrew expression meaning "Save!" which became an exclamation of praise; also in verse 10
b 9 Psalm 118:25,26 *c 17* Isaiah 56:7 *d 17* Jer. 7:11

18The chief priests and the teachers of the law heard this and began looking for a way to kill him, for they feared him, because the whole crowd was amazed at his teaching.

19When evening came, they*a* went out of the city.

The Withered Fig Tree

20In the morning, as they went along, they saw the fig tree withered from the roots. 21Peter remembered and said to Jesus, "Rabbi, look! The fig tree you cursed has withered!"

22"Have*b* faith in God," Jesus answered. 23"I tell you the truth, if anyone says to this mountain, 'Go, throw yourself into the sea,' and does not doubt in his heart but believes that what he says will happen, it will be done for him. 24Therefore I tell you, whatever you ask for in prayer, believe that you have received it, and it will be yours. 25And when you stand praying, if you hold anything against anyone, forgive him, so that your Father in heaven may forgive you your sins.*c* "

I FIRMLY BELIEVE A GREAT MANY PRAYERS ARE NOT ANSWERED BECAUSE WE ARE NOT WILLING TO FORGIVE SOMEONE.   —*Dwight L. Moody*

The Authority of Jesus Questioned

27They arrived again in Jerusalem, and while Jesus was walking in the temple courts, the chief priests, the teachers of the law and the elders came to him. 28"By what authority are you doing these things?" they asked. "And who gave you authority to do this?"

29Jesus replied, "I will ask you one question. Answer me, and I will tell you by what authority I am doing these things. 30John's baptism—was it from heaven, or from men? Tell me!"

31They discussed it among themselves and said, "If we say, 'From heaven,' he will ask, 'Then why didn't you believe him?' 32But if we say, 'From men' . . . ." (They feared the people, for everyone held that John really was a prophet.)

33So they answered Jesus, "We don't know."

Jesus said, "Neither will I tell you by what authority I am doing these things."

The Parable of the Tenants

12 He then began to speak to them in parables: "A man planted a vineyard. He put a wall around it, dug a pit for the winepress and built a watchtower. Then he rented the vineyard to some farmers and went away on a journey. 2At harvest time he sent a servant to the tenants to collect from them some of the fruit of the vineyard. 3But they seized him, beat him and sent him away empty-handed. 4Then he sent another servant to them; they struck this man on the head and treated him shamefully. 5He sent still another, and that one they killed. He sent many others; some of them they beat, others they killed.

6"He had one left to send, a son, whom he loved. He sent him last of all, saying, 'They will respect my son.'

7"But the tenants said to one another, 'This is the heir. Come, let's kill him, and the inheritance will be ours.' 8So they took him and killed him, and threw him out of the vineyard.

9"What then will the owner of the vineyard do? He will come and kill those tenants and give the vineyard to others. 10Haven't you read this scripture:

" 'The stone the builders rejected
    has become the capstone*d*;
11the Lord has done this,
    and it is marvelous in our eyes'*e*?"

12Then they looked for a way to arrest him because they knew he had spoken the parable against them. But they were afraid of the crowd; so they left him and went away.

Paying Taxes to Caesar

13Later they sent some of the Pharisees and Herodians to Jesus to catch him in his words. 14They came to him and said, "Teacher, we know you are a man of integrity. You aren't swayed by men, because you pay no attention to

---

a 19 Some early manuscripts *he*   *b 22* Some early manuscripts *If you have*   *c 25* Some manuscripts *sins. 26But if you do not forgive, neither will your Father who is in heaven forgive your sins.*   *d 10* Or *cornerstone*   *e 11* Psalm 118:22,23

who they are; but you teach the way of God in accordance with the truth. Is it right to pay taxes to Caesar or not? ¹⁵Should we pay or shouldn't we?"

But Jesus knew their hypocrisy. "Why are you trying to trap me?" he asked. "Bring me a denarius and let me look at it." ¹⁶They brought the coin, and he asked them, "Whose portrait is this? And whose inscription?"

"Caesar's," they replied.

¹⁷Then Jesus said to them, "Give to Caesar what is Caesar's and to God what is God's."

And they were amazed at him.

Marriage at the Resurrection

¹⁸Then the Sadducees, who say there is no resurrection, came to him with a question. ¹⁹"Teacher," they said, "Moses wrote for us that if a man's brother dies and leaves a wife but no children, the man must marry the widow and have children for his brother. ²⁰Now there were seven brothers. The first one married and died without leaving any children. ²¹The second one married the widow, but he also died, leaving no child. It was the same with the third. ²²In fact, none of the seven left any children. Last of all, the woman died too. ²³At the resurrection*a* whose wife will she be, since the seven were married to her?"

²⁴Jesus replied, "Are you not in error because you do not know the Scriptures or the power of God? ²⁵When the dead rise, they will neither marry nor be given in marriage; they will be like the angels in heaven. ²⁶Now about the dead rising—have you not read in the book of Moses, in the account of the bush, how God said to him, 'I am the God of Abraham, the God of Isaac, and the God of Jacob'*b*? ²⁷He is not the God of the dead, but of the living. You are badly mistaken!"

The Greatest Commandment

²⁸One of the teachers of the law came and heard them debating. Noticing that Jesus had given them a good answer, he asked him, "Of all the commandments, which is the most important?"

²⁹"The most important one," answered Jesus, "is this: 'Hear, O Israel, the Lord our God, the Lord is one.*c* ³⁰Love the Lord your God with all your heart and with all your soul and with all your mind and with all your strength.'*d* ³¹The second is this: 'Love your neighbor as yourself.'*e* There is no commandment greater than these."

³²"Well said, teacher," the man replied. "You are right in saying that God is one and there is no other but him. ³³To love him with all your heart, with all your understanding and with all your strength, and to love your neighbor as yourself is more important than all burnt offerings and sacrifices."

³⁴When Jesus saw that he had answered wisely, he said to him, "You are not far from the kingdom of God." And from then on no one dared ask him any more questions.

Whose Son Is the Christ?

³⁵While Jesus was teaching in the temple courts, he asked, "How is it that the teachers of the law say that the Christ*f* is the son of David? ³⁶David himself, speaking by the Holy Spirit, declared:

" 'The Lord said to my Lord:
"Sit at my right hand
until I put your enemies
under your feet." '*g*

³⁷David himself calls him 'Lord.' How then can he be his son?"

The large crowd listened to him with delight.

³⁸As he taught, Jesus said, "Watch out for the teachers of the law. They like to walk around in flowing robes and be greeted in the marketplaces, ³⁹and have the most important seats in the synagogues and the places of honor at banquets. ⁴⁰They devour widows' houses and for a show make lengthy prayers. Such men will be punished most severely."

The Widow's Offering

⁴¹Jesus sat down opposite the place where the offerings were put and watched the crowd putting their money into the temple treasury. Many rich people threw in large amounts. ⁴²But a poor

widow came and put in two very small copper coins,*a* worth only a fraction of a penny.*b*

43Calling his disciples to him, Jesus said, "I tell you the truth, this poor widow has put more into the treasury than all the others. **44**They all gave out of their wealth; but she, out of her poverty, put in everything—all she had to live on."

Signs of the End of the Age

13 As he was leaving the temple, one of his disciples said to him, "Look, Teacher! What massive stones! What magnificent buildings!"

a 42 Greek *two lepta*   *b 42* Greek *kodrantes*

FRIDAY

THE LAW OF LOVE IS GOOD AND SWEET
Bernard of Clairvaux

VERSE: Mark 12:30   **PASSAGE:** Mark 12:28–31

he law of love is good and sweet. It is not only borne lightly and easily, but it also makes bearable the laws which make men into slaves and hirelings. It does not destroy them; it fulfills them. As the Lord says, "I have not come to take away the law but to fulfill it" (Matthew 5:17). It tempers the slave's law and makes the hireling's law orderly. It lightens both. For there will never be any love without fear but chaste love. There will never be love without greed unless it is kept within bounds. Therefore love fulfills the slave's law when it overflows in devotion. It fulfills the hireling's law when it sets limits to greed.

Devotion mixed with fear does not remove the fear but purifies it. Punishment is lifted, for while law was servitude it could not function without it. Fear remains forever, but a pure and filial fear. For we read that "perfect love casts out fear" (1 John 4:18). This is to be understood to refer to the punishment which is never absent from servile fear, as I have said—by that mode of speaking by which the cause is often given for the effect.

Greed is brought to order when love overshadows it and evils are condemned and what is better is preferred to what is merely good, and the good is desired only for the sake of what is better. When by the grace of God this is fully achieved, the body is loved, and all the goods of the body for the sake of the soul, and the goods of the soul for the sake of God, and God for his own sake.

ADDITIONAL SCRIPTURE READING:
Matthew 5:17; 1 John 4:18

Go to page 1166 for your next devotional reading.

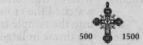

500   1500

2"Do you see all these great buildings?" replied Jesus. "Not one stone here will be left on another; every one will be thrown down."

3As Jesus was sitting on the Mount of Olives opposite the temple, Peter, James, John and Andrew asked him privately, 4"Tell us, when will these things happen? And what will be the sign that they are all about to be fulfilled?"

5Jesus said to them: "Watch out that no one deceives you. 6Many will come in my name, claiming, 'I am he,' and will deceive many. 7When you hear of wars and rumors of wars, do not be alarmed. Such things must happen, but the end is still to come. 8Nation will rise against nation, and kingdom against kingdom. There will be earthquakes in various places, and famines. These are the beginning of birth pains.

9"You must be on your guard. You will be handed over to the local councils and flogged in the synagogues. On account of me you will stand before governors and kings as witnesses to them. 10And the gospel must first be preached to all nations. 11Whenever you are arrested and brought to trial, do not worry beforehand about what to say. Just say whatever is given you at the time, for it is not you speaking, but the Holy Spirit.

12"Brother will betray brother to death, and a father his child. Children will rebel against their parents and have them put to death. 13All men will hate you because of me, but he who stands firm to the end will be saved.

14"When you see 'the abomination that causes desolation'a standing where itb does not belong—let the reader understand—then let those who are in Judea flee to the mountains. 15Let no one on the roof of his house go down or enter the house to take anything out. 16Let no one in the field go back to get his cloak. 17How dreadful it will be in those days for pregnant women and nursing mothers! 18Pray that this will not take place in winter, 19because those will be days of distress unequaled from the beginning, when God created the world, until now—and never to be equaled again. 20If the Lord had not cut

short those days, no one would survive. But for the sake of the elect, whom he has chosen, he has shortened them. 21At that time if anyone says to you, 'Look, here is the Christc!' or, 'Look, there he is!' do not believe it. 22For false Christs and false prophets will appear and perform signs and miracles to deceive the elect—if that were possible. 23So be on your guard; I have told you everything ahead of time.

24"But in those days, following that distress,

" 'the sun will be darkened,
    and the moon will not give its
      light;
25the stars will fall from the sky,
    and the heavenly bodies will be
      shaken.'d

26"At that time men will see the Son of Man coming in clouds with great power and glory. 27And he will send his angels and gather his elect from the four winds, from the ends of the earth to the ends of the heavens.

28"Now learn this lesson from the fig tree: As soon as its twigs get tender and its leaves come out, you know that summer is near. 29Even so, when you see these things happening, you know that it is near, right at the door. 30I tell you the truth, this generatione will certainly not pass away until all these things have happened. 31Heaven and earth will pass away, but my words will never pass away.

The Day and Hour Unknown

32"No one knows about that day or hour, not even the angels in heaven, nor the Son, but only the Father. 33Be on guard! Be alertf! You do not know when that time will come. 34It's like a man going away: He leaves his house and puts his servants in charge, each with his assigned task, and tells the one at the door to keep watch.

35"Therefore keep watch because you do not know when the owner of the house will come back—whether in the evening, or at midnight, or when the rooster crows, or at dawn. 36If he comes

a 14 Daniel 9:27; 11:31; 12:11   b 14 Or he; also in verse 29   c 21 Or Messiah   d 25 Isaiah 13:10;
34:4   e 30 Or race   f 33 Some manuscripts alert and pray

WEEKEND

A HYMN ON THE NATIVITY OF MY SAVIOR
Ben Jonson

VERSE: Luke 2:7   **PASSAGE:** Luke 2:1–7

 sing the birth, was born tonight,
The author both of life, and light;
   The angels so did sound it,
And like the ravished shepherds said,
Who saw the light, and were afraid,
   Yet searched, and true they found it.

The Son of God, th' Eternal King,
That did us all salvation bring,
   And freed the soul from danger;
He whom the whole world could not take,
The Word, which heaven, and earth did make,
   Was now laid in a manger.

The Father's wisdom willed it so,
The Son's obedience knew no No,
   Both wills were in one stature,
And as that wisdom had decreed,
The Word was now made flesh indeed,
   And took on him our nature.

What comfort by him do we win?
Who made himself the prince of sin,
   To make us heirs of glory?
To see this babe, all innocence;
A martyr born in our defense;
   Can man forget this story?

ADDITIONAL SCRIPTURE READING:
Isaiah 7:14; Galatians 4:4

Go to page 1168 for your next devotional reading.

1500   1700

suddenly, do not let him find you sleeping. 37What I say to you, I say to everyone: 'Watch!' "

Jesus Anointed at Bethany

14 Now the Passover and the Feast of Unleavened Bread were only two days away, and the chief priests and the teachers of the law were looking for some sly way to arrest Jesus and kill him. 2"But not during the Feast," they said, "or the people may riot."

3While he was in Bethany, reclining at the table in the home of a man known as Simon the Leper, a woman came with an alabaster jar of very expensive perfume, made of pure nard. She broke the jar and poured the perfume on his head.

4Some of those present were saying indignantly to one another, "Why this waste of perfume? 5It could have been sold for more than a year's wages*a* and the money given to the poor." And they rebuked her harshly.

6"Leave her alone," said Jesus. "Why are you bothering her? She has done a beautiful thing to me. 7The poor you will always have with you, and you can help them any time you want. But you will not always have me. 8She did what she could. She poured perfume on my body beforehand to prepare for my burial. 9I tell you the truth, wherever the gospel is preached throughout the world, what she has done will also be told, in memory of her."

10Then Judas Iscariot, one of the Twelve, went to the chief priests to betray Jesus to them. 11They were delighted to hear this and promised to give him money. So he watched for an opportunity to hand him over.

The Lord's Supper

12On the first day of the Feast of Unleavened Bread, when it was customary to sacrifice the Passover lamb, Jesus' disciples asked him, "Where do you want us to go and make preparations for you to eat the Passover?"

13So he sent two of his disciples, telling them, "Go into the city, and a man carrying a jar of water will meet you. Follow him. 14Say to the owner of the house he enters, 'The Teacher asks: Where is my guest room, where I may eat the Passover with my disciples?' 15He will show you a large upper room, furnished and ready. Make preparations for us there."

16The disciples left, went into the city and found things just as Jesus had told them. So they prepared the Passover.

17When evening came, Jesus arrived with the Twelve. 18While they were reclining at the table eating, he said, "I tell you the truth, one of you will betray me—one who is eating with me."

19They were saddened, and one by one they said to him, "Surely not I?"

20"It is one of the Twelve," he replied, "one who dips bread into the bowl with me. 21The Son of Man will go just as it is written about him. But woe to that man who betrays the Son of Man! It would be better for him if he had not been born."

22While they were eating, Jesus took bread, gave thanks and broke it, and gave it to his disciples, saying, "Take it; this is my body."

BREAKING ONE BREAD, WHICH IS THE MEDICINE OF IMMORTALITY, THE ANTIDOTE AGAINST DEATH WHICH GIVES ETERNAL LIFE IN JESUS CHRIST.   —*Irenaeus of Lyons*

23Then he took the cup, gave thanks and offered it to them, and they all drank from it.

24"This is my blood of the*b* covenant, which is poured out for many," he said to them. 25"I tell you the truth, I will not drink again of the fruit of the vine until that day when I drink it anew in the kingdom of God."

26When they had sung a hymn, they went out to the Mount of Olives.

Jesus Predicts Peter's Denial

27"You will all fall away," Jesus told them, "for it is written:

" 'I will strike the shepherd,
    and the sheep will be scattered.'*c*

28But after I have risen, I will go ahead of you into Galilee."

---

a 5 Greek *than three hundred denarii*   *b 24* Some manuscripts *the new*   *c 27* Zech. 13:7

²⁹Peter declared, "Even if all fall away, I will not."

³⁰"I tell you the truth," Jesus answered, "today—yes, tonight—before the rooster crows twice[a] you yourself will disown me three times."

³¹But Peter insisted emphatically, "Even if I have to die with you, I will never disown you." And all the others said the same.

Gethsemane

³²They went to a place called Geth-semane, and Jesus said to his disciples, "Sit here while I pray." ³³He took Peter, James and John along with him, and he began to be deeply distressed and troubled. ³⁴"My soul is overwhelmed with sorrow to the point of death," he said to them. "Stay here and keep watch."

³⁵Going a little farther, he fell to the ground and prayed that if possible the hour might pass from him. ³⁶"Abba,[b] Father," he said, "everything is possible for you. Take this cup from me. Yet not what I will, but what you will."

a 30 Some early manuscripts do not have *twice.*   *b 36* Aramaic for *Father*

MONDAY

HUMBLY I ADORE THEE, VERITY UNSEEN
Thomas Aquinas

VERSE: Mark 14:22   **PASSAGE:** Mark 14:22–26

umbly I adore thee, verity unseen,
who thy glory hidest 'neath these shadows mean;
lo, to thee surrendered, my whole heart is bowed,
tranced as it beholds thee, shrined within the cloud.

Taste and touch and vision to discern thee fail;
faith, that comes by hearing, pierces through the veil.
I believe whate'er the Son of God hath told;
what the truth hath spoken, that for truth I hold.

O memorial wondrous of the Lord's own death;
living bread that givest all thy creatures breath,
grant my spirit ever by the life may live,
to my taste thy sweetness never failing give.

Jesus, whom now hidden, I by faith behold,
what my soul doth long for, that thy word foretold:
face to face thy splendor, I at last shall see,
in the glorious vision, blessed Lord, of thee.

ADDITIONAL SCRIPTURE READING:
John 6:48–51; 1 Corinthians 11:23–28

Go to page 1171 for your next devotional reading.

500   1500

37Then he returned to his disciples and found them sleeping. "Simon," he said to Peter, "are you asleep? Could you not keep watch for one hour? 38Watch and pray so that you will not fall into temptation. The spirit is willing, but the body is weak."

39Once more he went away and prayed the same thing. 40When he came back, he again found them sleeping, because their eyes were heavy. They did not know what to say to him.

41Returning the third time, he said to them, "Are you still sleeping and resting? Enough! The hour has come. Look, the Son of Man is betrayed into the hands of sinners. 42Rise! Let us go! Here comes my betrayer!"

Jesus Arrested

43Just as he was speaking, Judas, one of the Twelve, appeared. With him was a crowd armed with swords and clubs, sent from the chief priests, the teachers of the law, and the elders.

44Now the betrayer had arranged a signal with them: "The one I kiss is the man; arrest him and lead him away under guard." 45Going at once to Jesus, Judas said, "Rabbi!" and kissed him. 46The men seized Jesus and arrested him. 47Then one of those standing near drew his sword and struck the servant of the high priest, cutting off his ear.

48"Am I leading a rebellion," said Jesus, "that you have come out with swords and clubs to capture me? 49Every day I was with you, teaching in the temple courts, and you did not arrest me. But the Scriptures must be fulfilled." 50Then everyone deserted him and fled.

51A young man, wearing nothing but a linen garment, was following Jesus. When they seized him, 52he fled naked, leaving his garment behind.

Before the Sanhedrin

53They took Jesus to the high priest, and all the chief priests, elders and teachers of the law came together. 54Peter followed him at a distance, right into the courtyard of the high priest. There he sat with the guards and warmed himself at the fire.

55The chief priests and the whole Sanhedrin were looking for evidence against Jesus so that they could put him to death, but they did not find any. 56Many testified falsely against him, but their statements did not agree.

57Then some stood up and gave this false testimony against him: 58"We heard him say, 'I will destroy this man-made temple and in three days will build another, not made by man.' " 59Yet even then their testimony did not agree.

60Then the high priest stood up before them and asked Jesus, "Are you not going to answer? What is this testimony that these men are bringing against you?" 61But Jesus remained silent and gave no answer.

Again the high priest asked him, "Are you the Christ,a the Son of the Blessed One?"

62"I am," said Jesus. "And you will see the Son of Man sitting at the right hand of the Mighty One and coming on the clouds of heaven."

63The high priest tore his clothes. "Why do we need any more witnesses?" he asked. 64"You have heard the blasphemy. What do you think?"

They all condemned him as worthy of death. 65Then some began to spit at him; they blindfolded him, struck him with their fists, and said, "Prophesy!" And the guards took him and beat him.

Peter Disowns Jesus

66While Peter was below in the courtyard, one of the servant girls of the high priest came by. 67When she saw Peter warming himself, she looked closely at him.

"You also were with that Nazarene, Jesus," she said.

68But he denied it. "I don't know or understand what you're talking about," he said, and went out into the entryway.b

69When the servant girl saw him there, she said again to those standing around, "This fellow is one of them." 70Again he denied it.

After a little while, those standing near said to Peter, "Surely you are one of them, for you are a Galilean."

71He began to call down curses on himself, and he swore to them, "I don't know this man you're talking about."

a 61 Or Messiah   b 68 Some early manuscripts entryway and the rooster crowed

[72]Immediately the rooster crowed the second time.[a] Then Peter remembered the word Jesus had spoken to him: "Before the rooster crows twice[b] you will disown me three times." And he broke down and wept.

Jesus Before Pilate

15 Very early in the morning, the chief priests, with the elders, the teachers of the law and the whole Sanhedrin, reached a decision. They bound Jesus, led him away and handed him over to Pilate.

[2]"Are you the king of the Jews?" asked Pilate.

"Yes, it is as you say," Jesus replied.

[3]The chief priests accused him of many things. [4]So again Pilate asked him, "Aren't you going to answer? See how many things they are accusing you of."

[5]But Jesus still made no reply, and Pilate was amazed.

[6]Now it was the custom at the Feast to release a prisoner whom the people requested. [7]A man called Barabbas was in prison with the insurrectionists who had committed murder in the uprising. [8]The crowd came up and asked Pilate to do for them what he usually did.

[9]"Do you want me to release to you the king of the Jews?" asked Pilate, [10]knowing it was out of envy that the chief priests had handed Jesus over to him. [11]But the chief priests stirred up the crowd to have Pilate release Barabbas instead.

[12]"What shall I do, then, with the one you call the king of the Jews?" Pilate asked them.

[13]"Crucify him!" they shouted.

[14]"Why? What crime has he committed?" asked Pilate.

But they shouted all the louder, "Crucify him!"

[15]Wanting to satisfy the crowd, Pilate released Barabbas to them. He had Jesus flogged, and handed him over to be crucified.

The Soldiers Mock Jesus

[16]The soldiers led Jesus away into the palace (that is, the Praetorium) and called together the whole company of soldiers. [17]They put a purple robe on him, then twisted together a crown of thorns and set it on him. [18]And they began to call out to him, "Hail, king of the Jews!" [19]Again and again they struck him on the head with a staff and spit on him. Falling on their knees, they paid homage to him. [20]And when they had mocked him, they took off the purple robe and put his own clothes on him. Then they led him out to crucify him.

The Crucifixion

[21]A certain man from Cyrene, Simon, the father of Alexander and Rufus, was passing by on his way in from the country, and they forced him to carry the cross. [22]They brought Jesus to the place called Golgotha (which means The Place of the Skull). [23]Then they offered him wine mixed with myrrh, but he did not take it. [24]And they crucified him. Dividing up his clothes, they cast lots to see what each would get.

[25]It was the third hour when they crucified him. [26]The written notice of the charge against him read: THE KING OF THE JEWS. [27]They crucified two robbers with him, one on his right and one on his left.[c] [29]Those who passed by hurled insults at him, shaking their heads and saying, "So! You who are going to destroy the temple and build it in three days, [30]come down from the cross and save yourself!"

[31]In the same way the chief priests and the teachers of the law mocked him among themselves. "He saved others," they said, "but he can't save himself! [32]Let this Christ,[d] this King of Israel, come down now from the cross, that we may see and believe." Those crucified with him also heaped insults on him.

The Death of Jesus

[33]At the sixth hour darkness came over the whole land until the ninth hour. [34]And at the ninth hour Jesus cried out in a loud voice, "*Eloi, Eloi, lama sabachthani?*"—which means,

---

[a] 72 Some early manuscripts do not have *the second time.*   [b] 72 Some early manuscripts do not have *twice.*   [c] 27 Some manuscripts *left,* [28]*and the scripture was fulfilled which says, "He was counted with the lawless ones"* (Isaiah 53:12)   [d] 32 Or *Messiah*

GOOD FRIDAY, 1613. RIDING WESTWARD
John Donne

VERSE: Mark 15:37   **PASSAGE:** Mark 15:33–41

ence is't, that I am carried towards the West
This day, when my soul's form bends towards the East.
There I should see a sun, by rising, set,
And by that setting endless day beget:
But that Christ on this cross did rise and fall,
Sin had eternally benighted all.
Yet dare I almost be glad I do not see
That spectacle, of too much weight for me.
Who sees God's face, that is self life, must die;
What a death were it then to see God die?
It made his own lieutenant nature, shrink;
It made his footstool crack, and the sun wink.
Could I behold those hands which span the poles,
And tune all spheres at once, pierced with those holes?
Could I behold that endless height which is
Zenith to us, and our Antipodes,
Humbled below us? Or that blood which is
The seat of all our souls, if not of his,
Make dirt of dust, or that flesh which was worn
By God, for his apparel, ragged and torn?
If on these things I durst not look, durst I
Upon his miserable mother cast mine eye,
Who was God's partner here, and furnished thus
Half of that sacrifice which ransomed us?
Though these things, as I ride, be from mine eye,
They are present yet unto my memory,
For that looks towards them; and thou lookst towards me,
O Savior, as thou hangst upon the tree.
I turn my back to thee but to receive
Corrections, till thy mercies bid thee leave.
O think me worth thine anger; punish me;
Burn off my rusts, and my deformity,
Restore thine Image so much, by thy grace
That thou mayst know me, and I'll turn my face.

ADDITIONAL SCRIPTURE READING:
Exodus 40:21; Hebrews 4:14–16

Go to page 1176 for your next devotional reading.

1500   1700

"My God, my God, why have you forsaken me?"[a]

35When some of those standing near heard this, they said, "Listen, he's calling Elijah."

36One man ran, filled a sponge with wine vinegar, put it on a stick, and offered it to Jesus to drink. "Now leave him alone. Let's see if Elijah comes to take him down," he said.

37With a loud cry, Jesus breathed his last.

38The curtain of the temple was torn in two from top to bottom. 39And when the centurion, who stood there in front of Jesus, heard his cry and[b] saw how he died, he said, "Surely this man was the Son[c] of God!"

40Some women were watching from a distance. Among them were Mary Magdalene, Mary the mother of James the younger and of Joses, and Salome. 41In Galilee these women had followed him and cared for his needs. Many other women who had come up with him to Jerusalem were also there.

The Burial of Jesus

42It was Preparation Day (that is, the day before the Sabbath). So as evening approached, 43Joseph of Arimathea, a prominent member of the Council, who was himself waiting for the kingdom of God, went boldly to Pilate and asked for Jesus' body. 44Pilate was surprised to hear that he was already dead. Summoning the centurion, he asked him if Jesus had already died. 45When he learned from the centurion that it was so, he gave the body to Joseph. 46So Joseph bought some linen cloth, took down the body, wrapped it in the linen, and placed it in a tomb cut out of rock. Then he rolled a stone against the entrance of the tomb. 47Mary Magdalene and Mary the mother of Joses saw where he was laid.

The Resurrection

16 When the Sabbath was over, Mary Magdalene, Mary the mother of James, and Salome bought spices so that they might go to anoint Jesus' body. 2Very early on the first day of the week, just after sunrise, they were on their way to the tomb 3and they asked each other, "Who will roll the stone away from the entrance of the tomb?"

4But when they looked up, they saw that the stone, which was very large, had been rolled away. 5As they entered the tomb, they saw a young man dressed in a white robe sitting on the right side, and they were alarmed.

6"Don't be alarmed," he said. "You are looking for Jesus the Nazarene, who was crucified. He has risen! He is not here. See the place where they laid him. 7But go, tell his disciples and Peter, 'He is going ahead of you into Galilee. There you will see him, just as he told you.' "

8Trembling and bewildered, the women went out and fled from the tomb. They said nothing to anyone, because they were afraid.

[The earliest manuscripts and some other ancient witnesses do not have Mark 16:9–20.]

9When Jesus rose early on the first day of the week, he appeared first to Mary Magdalene, out of whom he had driven seven demons. 10She went and told those who had been with him and who were mourning and weeping. 11When they heard that Jesus was alive and that she had seen him, they did not believe it.

12Afterward Jesus appeared in a different form to two of them while they were walking in the country. 13These returned and reported it to the rest; but they did not believe them either.

14Later Jesus appeared to the Eleven as they were eating; he rebuked them for their lack of faith and their stubborn refusal to believe those who had seen him after he had risen.

15He said to them, "Go into all the world and preach the good news to all creation. 16Whoever believes and is baptized will be saved, but whoever does not believe will be condemned. 17And these signs will accompany those who believe: In my name they

---

a 34 Psalm 22:1   b 39 Some manuscripts do not have *heard his cry and*   c 39 Or *a son*

will drive out demons; they will speak in new tongues; **18**they will pick up snakes with their hands; and when they drink deadly poison, it will not hurt them at all; they will place their hands on sick people, and they will get well."

19After the Lord Jesus had spoken to them, he was taken up into heaven and he sat at the right hand of God. **20**Then the disciples went out and preached everywhere, and the Lord worked with them and confirmed his word by the signs that accompanied it.

LUKE

L UKE WRITES HIS GOSPEL TO SHARE THE GOOD NEWS OF SALVATION—A MESSAGE INTENDED FOR EVERYONE. A PHYSICIAN BY PROFESSION, LUKE DISPLAYS GOOD "BEDSIDE MAN-NERS" BY SHOWING COMPASSION FOR PEOPLE CON-SIDERED OUTCASTS, INCLUDING TAX COLLECTORS, WOMEN, CHILDREN AND THE POOR. NOT ONLY DOES LUKE SHOW GREAT REGARD FOR PEOPLE, BUT HE ALSO SHOWS A DEEP CONCERN FOR PRAYER, DISCIPLE-SHIP, JOY AND THE MINISTRY OF THE SPIRIT. AS YOU READ LUKE'S ACCOUNT OF THE LIFE OF JESUS, MAY YOU BE LIKE HIM WHO WAS "FULL OF JOY THROUGH THE HOLY SPIRIT" (10:21).

Introduction

1 Many have undertaken to draw up an account of the things that have been fulfilled*a* among us, ²just as they were handed down to us by those who from the first were eyewitnesses and servants of the word. ³Therefore, since I myself have carefully investigated every-thing from the beginning, it seemed good also to me to write an orderly account for you, most excellent Theophilus, ⁴so that you may know the certainty of the things you have been taught.

The Birth of John the Baptist Foretold

⁵In the time of Herod king of Judea there was a priest named Zechariah, who belonged to the priestly division of Abi-jah; his wife Elizabeth was also a descen-dant of Aaron. ⁶Both of them were upright in the sight of God, observing all the Lord's commandments and regula-tions blamelessly. ⁷But they had no chil-dren, because Elizabeth was barren; and they were both well along in years.

⁸Once when Zechariah's division was on duty and he was serving as priest before God, ⁹he was chosen by lot, according to the custom of the priest-hood, to go into the temple of the Lord and burn incense. ¹⁰And when the time for the burning of incense came, all the assembled worshipers were praying out-side.

¹¹Then an angel of the Lord appeared to him, standing at the right side of the

a 1 Or *been surely believed*

altar of incense. 12When Zechariah saw him, he was startled and was gripped with fear. 13But the angel said to him: "Do not be afraid, Zechariah; your prayer has been heard. Your wife Elizabeth will bear you a son, and you are to give him the name John. 14He will be a joy and delight to you, and many will rejoice because of his birth, 15for he will be great in the sight of the Lord. He is never to take wine or other fermented drink, and he will be filled with the Holy Spirit even from birth.*a* 16Many of the people of Israel will he bring back to the Lord their God. 17And he will go on before the Lord, in the spirit and power of Elijah, to turn the hearts of the fathers to their children and the disobedient to the wisdom of the righteous—to make ready a people prepared for the Lord."

18Zechariah asked the angel, "How can I be sure of this? I am an old man and my wife is well along in years."

19The angel answered, "I am Gabriel. I stand in the presence of God, and I have been sent to speak to you and to tell you this good news. 20And now you will be silent and not able to speak until the day this happens, because you did not believe my words, which will come true at their proper time."

21Meanwhile, the people were waiting for Zechariah and wondering why he stayed so long in the temple. 22When he came out, he could not speak to them. They realized he had seen a vision in the temple, for he kept making signs to them but remained unable to speak.

23When his time of service was completed, he returned home. 24After this his wife Elizabeth became pregnant and for five months remained in seclusion. 25"The Lord has done this for me," she said. "In these days he has shown his favor and taken away my disgrace among the people."

The Birth of Jesus Foretold

26In the sixth month, God sent the angel Gabriel to Nazareth, a town in Galilee, 27to a virgin pledged to be married to a man named Joseph, a descendant of David. The virgin's name was Mary. 28The angel went to her and said,

"Greetings, you who are highly favored! The Lord is with you."

29Mary was greatly troubled at his words and wondered what kind of greeting this might be. 30But the angel said to her, "Do not be afraid, Mary, you have found favor with God. 31You will be with child and give birth to a son, and you are to give him the name Jesus. 32He will be great and will be called the Son of the Most High. The Lord God will give him the throne of his father David, 33and he will reign over the house of Jacob forever; his kingdom will never end."

34"How will this be," Mary asked the angel, "since I am a virgin?"

35The angel answered, "The Holy Spirit will come upon you, and the power of the Most High will overshadow you. So the holy one to be born will be called*b* the Son of God. 36Even Elizabeth your relative is going to have a child in her old age, and she who was said to be barren is in her sixth month. 37For nothing is impossible with God."

38"I am the Lord's servant," Mary answered. "May it be to me as you have said." Then the angel left her.

Mary Visits Elizabeth

39At that time Mary got ready and hurried to a town in the hill country of Judea, 40where she entered Zechariah's home and greeted Elizabeth. 41When Elizabeth heard Mary's greeting, the baby leaped in her womb, and Elizabeth was filled with the Holy Spirit. 42In a loud voice she exclaimed: "Blessed are you among women, and blessed is the child you will bear! 43But why am I so favored, that the mother of my Lord should come to me? 44As soon as the sound of your greeting reached my ears, the baby in my womb leaped for joy. 45Blessed is she who has believed that what the Lord has said to her will be accomplished!"

Mary's Song

46And Mary said:

"My soul glorifies the Lord
47   and my spirit rejoices in God my
         Savior,
48for he has been mindful
         of the humble state of his servant.

---

a 15 Or from his mother's womb   b 35 Or So the child to be born will be called holy.

From now on all generations will call
me blessed,
⁴⁹ for the Mighty One has done great
things for me—
holy is his name.
⁵⁰ His mercy extends to those who fear
him,
from generation to generation.
⁵¹ He has performed mighty deeds with
his arm;
he has scattered those who are
proud in their inmost
thoughts.
⁵² He has brought down rulers from
their thrones
but has lifted up the humble.

⁵³ He has filled the hungry with good
things
but has sent the rich away empty.
⁵⁴ He has helped his servant Israel,
remembering to be merciful
⁵⁵ to Abraham and his descendants
forever,
even as he said to our fathers."

⁵⁶ Mary stayed with Elizabeth for about
three months and then returned home.

The Birth of John the Baptist

⁵⁷ When it was time for Elizabeth to
have her baby, she gave birth to a son.
⁵⁸ Her neighbors and relatives heard that

WEDNESDAY

A GOD-MAN BORN OF A VIRGIN WOMAN
Anselm of Canterbury

VERSE: Luke 1:26–27   **PASSAGE:** Luke 1:26–38

xercise your pictorial art, then, not on an empty fiction, but upon a solid truth, and say that it is extremely fitting that, as the sin of man and the cause of our
condemnation took their origin from a woman, so the
cure for sin and the cause of our salvation must be born of a
woman. And so that women may not despair of attaining to the
lot of the blessed, because such great evil has issued from a
woman, it was fitting that such a great good should issue from a
woman, to revitalize their hope. Add this to your painting: If it
was a virgin who was the cause of all evil to the human race, it is
far more fitting that it be a virgin who will be the cause of all
good. Depict this also: If the woman whom God made from a
man without a woman was made from a virgin, it is also
extremely fitting that the man who will originate from a woman
without a man be born of a virgin. But for the present let these
examples suffice of the pictures that can be depicted on the fact
that the God-man must be born of a virgin woman.

ADDITIONAL SCRIPTURE READING:
Genesis 3:11–13; Luke 1:46–55

Go to page 1185 for your next devotional reading.

500   1500

the Lord had shown her great mercy, and they shared her joy.

59On the eighth day they came to circumcise the child, and they were going to name him after his father Zechariah, 60but his mother spoke up and said, "No! He is to be called John."

61They said to her, "There is no one among your relatives who has that name."

62Then they made signs to his father, to find out what he would like to name the child. 63He asked for a writing tablet, and to everyone's astonishment he wrote, "His name is John." 64Immediately his mouth was opened and his tongue was loosed, and he began to speak, praising God. 65The neighbors were all filled with awe, and throughout the hill country of Judea people were talking about all these things. 66Everyone who heard this wondered about it, asking, "What then is this child going to be?" For the Lord's hand was with him.

Zechariah's Song

67His father Zechariah was filled with the Holy Spirit and prophesied:

68 "Praise be to the Lord, the God of
    Israel,
  because he has come and has
    redeemed his people.
69 He has raised up a horn*a* of salvation
    for us
  in the house of his servant David
70 (as he said through his holy prophets
    of long ago),
71 salvation from our enemies
  and from the hand of all who hate
    us—
72 to show mercy to our fathers
  and to remember his holy
    covenant,
73   the oath he swore to our father
    Abraham:
74 to rescue us from the hand of our
    enemies,
  and to enable us to serve him
    without fear
75   in holiness and righteousness
    before him all our days.

76 And you, my child, will be called a
    prophet of the Most High;
  for you will go on before the Lord
    to prepare the way for him,
77 to give his people the knowledge of
    salvation
  through the forgiveness of their
    sins,
78 because of the tender mercy of our
    God,
  by which the rising sun will come
    to us from heaven
79 to shine on those living in darkness
  and in the shadow of death,
  to guide our feet into the path of
    peace."

80 And the child grew and became strong in spirit; and he lived in the desert until he appeared publicly to Israel.

The Birth of Jesus

2 In those days Caesar Augustus issued a decree that a census should be taken of the entire Roman world. 2(This was the first census that took place while Quirinius was governor of Syria.) 3And everyone went to his own town to register.

4So Joseph also went up from the town of Nazareth in Galilee to Judea, to Bethlehem the town of David, because he belonged to the house and line of David. 5He went there to register with Mary, who was pledged to be married to him and was expecting a child. 6While they were there, the time came for the baby to be born, 7and she gave birth to her firstborn, a son. She wrapped him in cloths and placed him in a manger, because there was no room for them in the inn.

The Shepherds and the Angels

8And there were shepherds living out in the fields nearby, keeping watch over their flocks at night. 9An angel of the Lord appeared to them, and the glory of the Lord shone around them, and they were terrified. 10But the angel said to them, "Do not be afraid. I bring you good news of great joy that will be for all the people. 11Today in the town of David a Savior has been born to you; he is Christ*b* the Lord. 12This will be a sign

---

a 69 Horn here symbolizes strength.   *b 11* Or *Messiah.* "The Christ" (Greek) and "the Messiah" (Hebrew) both mean "the Anointed One"; also in verse 26.

to you: You will find a baby wrapped in cloths and lying in a manger."

¹³Suddenly a great company of the heavenly host appeared with the angel, praising God and saying,

¹⁴"Glory to God in the highest,
  and on earth peace to men on
    whom his favor rests."

¹⁵When the angels had left them and gone into heaven, the shepherds said to one another, "Let's go to Bethlehem and see this thing that has happened, which the Lord has told us about."

¹⁶So they hurried off and found Mary and Joseph, and the baby, who was lying in the manger. ¹⁷When they had seen him, they spread the word concerning what had been told them about this child, ¹⁸and all who heard it were amazed at what the shepherds said to them. ¹⁹But Mary treasured up all these things and pondered them in her heart. ²⁰The shepherds returned, glorifying and praising God for all the things they had heard and seen, which were just as they had been told.

Jesus Presented in the Temple

²¹On the eighth day, when it was time to circumcise him, he was named Jesus, the name the angel had given him before he had been conceived.

²²When the time of their purification according to the Law of Moses had been completed, Joseph and Mary took him to Jerusalem to present him to the Lord ²³(as it is written in the Law of the Lord, "Every firstborn male is to be consecrated to the Lord"[a]), ²⁴and to offer a sacrifice in keeping with what is said in the Law of the Lord: "a pair of doves or two young pigeons."[b]

²⁵Now there was a man in Jerusalem called Simeon, who was righteous and devout. He was waiting for the consolation of Israel, and the Holy Spirit was upon him. ²⁶It had been revealed to him by the Holy Spirit that he would not die before he had seen the Lord's Christ. ²⁷Moved by the Spirit, he went into the temple courts. When the parents brought in the child Jesus to do for him

what the custom of the Law required, ²⁸Simeon took him in his arms and praised God, saying:

²⁹"Sovereign Lord, as you have
      promised,
    you now dismiss[c] your servant in
      peace.
³⁰For my eyes have seen your salvation,
³¹ which you have prepared in the
      sight of all people,
³²a light for revelation to the Gentiles
    and for glory to your people Israel."

³³The child's father and mother marveled at what was said about him. ³⁴Then Simeon blessed them and said to Mary, his mother: "This child is destined to cause the falling and rising of many in Israel, and to be a sign that will be spoken against, ³⁵so that the thoughts of many hearts will be revealed. And a sword will pierce your own soul too."

³⁶There was also a prophetess, Anna, the daughter of Phanuel, of the tribe of Asher. She was very old; she had lived with her husband seven years after her marriage, ³⁷and then was a widow until she was eighty-four.[d] She never left the temple but worshiped night and day, fasting and praying. ³⁸Coming up to them at that very moment, she gave thanks to God and spoke about the child to all who were looking forward to the redemption of Jerusalem.

³⁹When Joseph and Mary had done everything required by the Law of the Lord, they returned to Galilee to their own town of Nazareth. ⁴⁰And the child grew and became strong; he was filled with wisdom, and the grace of God was upon him.

The Boy Jesus at the Temple

⁴¹Every year his parents went to Jerusalem for the Feast of the Passover. ⁴²When he was twelve years old, they went up to the Feast, according to the custom. ⁴³After the Feast was over, while his parents were returning home, the boy Jesus stayed behind in Jerusalem, but they were unaware of it. ⁴⁴Thinking he was in their company, they traveled on for a day. Then they

---

^a 23 Exodus 13:2,12   ^b 24 Lev. 12:8   ^c 29 Or promised, / now dismiss   ^d 37 Or widow for eighty-four years

began looking for him among their relatives and friends. 45When they did not find him, they went back to Jerusalem to look for him. 46After three days they found him in the temple courts, sitting among the teachers, listening to them and asking them questions. 47Everyone who heard him was amazed at his understanding and his answers. 48When his parents saw him, they were astonished. His mother said to him, "Son, why have you treated us like this? Your father and I have been anxiously searching for you."

49"Why were you searching for me?" he asked. "Didn't you know I had to be in my Father's house?" 50But they did not understand what he was saying to them.

51Then he went down to Nazareth with them and was obedient to them. But his mother treasured all these things in her heart. 52And Jesus grew in wisdom and stature, and in favor with God and men.

John the Baptist Prepares the Way

3 In the fifteenth year of the reign of Tiberius Caesar—when Pontius Pilate was governor of Judea, Herod tetrarch of Galilee, his brother Philip tetrarch of Iturea and Traconitis, and Lysanias tetrarch of Abilene— 2during the high priesthood of Annas and Caiaphas, the word of God came to John son of Zechariah in the desert. 3He went into all the country around the Jordan, preaching a baptism of repentance for the forgiveness of sins. 4As is written in the book of the words of Isaiah the prophet:

"A voice of one calling in the desert,
    'Prepare the way for the Lord,
      make straight paths for him.
5 Every valley shall be filled in,
      every mountain and hill made low.
    The crooked roads shall become
        straight,
      the rough ways smooth.
6 And all mankind will see God's
        salvation.' "a

7John said to the crowds coming out to be baptized by him, "You brood of vipers! Who warned you to flee from the coming wrath? 8Produce fruit in keeping with repentance. And do not begin to say to yourselves, 'We have Abraham as our father.' For I tell you that out of these stones God can raise up children for Abraham. 9The ax is already at the root of the trees, and every tree that does not produce good fruit will be cut down and thrown into the fire."

10"What should we do then?" the crowd asked.

11John answered, "The man with two tunics should share with him who has none, and the one who has food should do the same."

12Tax collectors also came to be baptized. "Teacher," they asked, "what should we do?"

13"Don't collect any more than you are required to," he told them.

14Then some soldiers asked him, "And what should we do?"

He replied, "Don't extort money and don't accuse people falsely—be content with your pay."

15The people were waiting expectantly and were all wondering in their hearts if John might possibly be the Christ.b 16John answered them all, "I baptize you withc water. But one more powerful than I will come, the thongs of whose sandals I am not worthy to untie. He will baptize you with the Holy Spirit and with fire. 17His winnowing fork is in his hand to clear his threshing floor and to gather the wheat into his barn, but he will burn up the chaff with unquenchable fire." 18And with many other words John exhorted the people and preached the good news to them.

19But when John rebuked Herod the tetrarch because of Herodias, his brother's wife, and all the other evil things he had done, 20Herod added this to them all: He locked John up in prison.

The Baptism and Genealogy of Jesus

21When all the people were being baptized, Jesus was baptized too. And as he was praying, heaven was opened 22and the Holy Spirit descended on him in bodily form like a dove. And a voice came from heaven: "You are my Son, whom I love; with you I am well pleased."

23Now Jesus himself was about thirty years old when he began his ministry.

a 6 Isaiah 40:3-5   b 15 Or Messiah   c 16 Or in

He was the son, so it was thought, of Joseph,

the son of Heli, **24**the son of Matthat,
the son of Levi, the son of Melki,
the son of Jannai, the son of Joseph,
25 the son of Mattathias, the son of Amos,
the son of Nahum, the son of Esli,
the son of Naggai, **26**the son of Maath,
the son of Mattathias, the son of Semein,
the son of Josech, the son of Joda,
27 the son of Joanan, the son of Rhesa,
the son of Zerubbabel, the son of Shealtiel,
the son of Neri, **28**the son of Melki,
the son of Addi, the son of Cosam,
the son of Elmadam, the son of Er,
29 the son of Joshua, the son of Eliezer,
the son of Jorim, the son of Matthat,
the son of Levi, **30**the son of Simeon,
the son of Judah, the son of Joseph,
the son of Jonam, the son of Eliakim,
31 the son of Melea, the son of Menna,
the son of Mattatha, the son of Nathan,
the son of David, **32**the son of Jesse,
the son of Obed, the son of Boaz,
the son of Salmon,*a* the son of Nahshon,
33 the son of Amminadab, the son of Ram,*b*
the son of Hezron, the son of Perez,
the son of Judah, **34**the son of Jacob,
the son of Isaac, the son of Abraham,
the son of Terah, the son of Nahor,
35 the son of Serug, the son of Reu,
the son of Peleg, the son of Eber,
the son of Shelah, **36**the son of Cainan,
the son of Arphaxad, the son of Shem,
the son of Noah, the son of Lamech,
37 the son of Methuselah, the son of Enoch,
the son of Jared, the son of Mahalalel,
the son of Kenan, **38**the son of Enosh,
the son of Seth, the son of Adam,
the son of God.

The Temptation of Jesus

4 Jesus, full of the Holy Spirit, returned from the Jordan and was led by the Spirit in the desert, **2**where for forty days he was tempted by the devil. He ate nothing during those days, and at the end of them he was hungry.

3The devil said to him, "If you are the Son of God, tell this stone to become bread."

4Jesus answered, "It is written: 'Man does not live on bread alone.'*c* "

5The devil led him up to a high place and showed him in an instant all the kingdoms of the world. **6**And he said to him, "I will give you all their authority and splendor, for it has been given to me, and I can give it to anyone I want to. **7**So if you worship me, it will all be yours."

8Jesus answered, "It is written: 'Worship the Lord your God and serve him only.'*d* "

9The devil led him to Jerusalem and had him stand on the highest point of the temple. "If you are the Son of God," he said, "throw yourself down from here. **10**For it is written:

" 'He will command his angels
    concerning you
  to guard you carefully;
11 they will lift you up in their hands,
  so that you will not strike your
    foot against a stone.'*e* "

12Jesus answered, "It says: 'Do not put the Lord your God to the test.'*f* "

13When the devil had finished all this tempting, he left him until an opportune time.

Jesus Rejected at Nazareth

14Jesus returned to Galilee in the power of the Spirit, and news about him spread through the whole countryside. **15**He taught in their synagogues, and everyone praised him.

16He went to Nazareth, where he had been brought up, and on the Sabbath day he went into the synagogue, as was his custom. And he stood up to read. **17**The scroll of the prophet Isaiah was handed

---

a 32 Some early manuscripts *Sala*   *b 33* Some manuscripts *Amminadab, the son of Admin, the son of Arni;* other manuscripts vary widely.   *c 4* Deut. 8:3   *d 8* Deut. 6:13   *e 11* Psalm 91:11,12
f 12 Deut. 6:16

to him. Unrolling it, he found the place where it is written:

18 "The Spirit of the Lord is on me,
   because he has anointed me
   to preach good news to the poor.
He has sent me to proclaim freedom
   for the prisoners
   and recovery of sight for the blind,
   to release the oppressed,
19   to proclaim the year of the Lord's
   favor."[a]

20Then he rolled up the scroll, gave it back to the attendant and sat down. The eyes of everyone in the synagogue were fastened on him, 21and he began by saying to them, "Today this scripture is fulfilled in your hearing."

22All spoke well of him and were amazed at the gracious words that came from his lips. "Isn't this Joseph's son?" they asked.

23Jesus said to them, "Surely you will quote this proverb to me: 'Physician, heal yourself! Do here in your hometown what we have heard that you did in Capernaum.' "

24"I tell you the truth," he continued, "no prophet is accepted in his hometown. 25I assure you that there were many widows in Israel in Elijah's time, when the sky was shut for three and a half years and there was a severe famine throughout the land. 26Yet Elijah was not sent to any of them, but to a widow in Zarephath in the region of Sidon. 27And there were many in Israel with leprosy[b] in the time of Elisha the prophet, yet not one of them was cleansed— only Naaman the Syrian."

28All the people in the synagogue were furious when they heard this. 29They got up, drove him out of the town, and took him to the brow of the hill on which the town was built, in order to throw him down the cliff. 30But he walked right through the crowd and went on his way.

Jesus Drives Out an Evil Spirit

31Then he went down to Capernaum, a town in Galilee, and on the Sabbath began to teach the people. 32They were amazed at his teaching, because his message had authority.

33In the synagogue there was a man possessed by a demon, an evil[c] spirit. He cried out at the top of his voice, 34"Ha! What do you want with us, Jesus of Nazareth? Have you come to destroy us? I know who you are—the Holy One of God!"

35"Be quiet!" Jesus said sternly. "Come out of him!" Then the demon threw the man down before them all and came out without injuring him.

36All the people were amazed and said to each other, "What is this teaching? With authority and power he gives orders to evil spirits and they come out!" 37And the news about him spread throughout the surrounding area.

Jesus Heals Many

38Jesus left the synagogue and went to the home of Simon. Now Simon's mother-in-law was suffering from a high fever, and they asked Jesus to help her. 39So he bent over her and rebuked the fever, and it left her. She got up at once and began to wait on them.

40When the sun was setting, the people brought to Jesus all who had various kinds of sickness, and laying his hands on each one, he healed them. 41Moreover, demons came out of many people, shouting, "You are the Son of God!" But he rebuked them and would not allow them to speak, because they knew he was the Christ.[d]

42At daybreak Jesus went out to a solitary place. The people were looking for him and when they came to where he was, they tried to keep him from leaving them. 43But he said, "I must preach the good news of the kingdom of God to the other towns also, because that is why I was sent." 44And he kept on preaching in the synagogues of Judea.[e]

The Calling of the First Disciples

5 One day as Jesus was standing by the Lake of Gennesaret,[f] with the people crowding around him and listening to the word of God, 2he

---

[a] 19 Isaiah 61:1,2   [b] 27 The Greek word was used for various diseases affecting the skin—not necessarily leprosy.   [c] 33 Greek unclean; also in verse 36   [d] 41 Or Messiah   [e] 44 Or the land of the Jews; some manuscripts Galilee   [f] 1 That is, Sea of Galilee

saw at the water's edge two boats, left there by the fishermen, who were washing their nets. ³He got into one of the boats, the one belonging to Simon, and asked him to put out a little from shore. Then he sat down and taught the people from the boat.

⁴When he had finished speaking, he said to Simon, "Put out into deep water, and let down*a* the nets for a catch."

⁵Simon answered, "Master, we've worked hard all night and haven't caught anything. But because you say so, I will let down the nets."

⁶When they had done so, they caught such a large number of fish that their nets began to break. ⁷So they signaled their partners in the other boat to come and help them, and they came and filled both boats so full that they began to sink.

⁸When Simon Peter saw this, he fell at Jesus' knees and said, "Go away from me, Lord; I am a sinful man!" ⁹For he and all his companions were astonished at the catch of fish they had taken, ¹⁰and so were James and John, the sons of Zebedee, Simon's partners.

Then Jesus said to Simon, "Don't be afraid; from now on you will catch men." ¹¹So they pulled their boats up on shore, left everything and followed him.

The Man With Leprosy

¹²While Jesus was in one of the towns, a man came along who was covered with leprosy.*b* When he saw Jesus, he fell with his face to the ground and begged him, "Lord, if you are willing, you can make me clean."

¹³Jesus reached out his hand and touched the man. "I am willing," he said. "Be clean!" And immediately the leprosy left him.

¹⁴Then Jesus ordered him, "Don't tell anyone, but go, show yourself to the priest and offer the sacrifices that Moses commanded for your cleansing, as a testimony to them."

¹⁵Yet the news about him spread all the more, so that crowds of people came to hear him and to be healed of their sicknesses. ¹⁶But Jesus often withdrew to lonely places and prayed.

Jesus Heals a Paralytic

¹⁷One day as he was teaching, Pharisees and teachers of the law, who had come from every village of Galilee and from Judea and Jerusalem, were sitting there. And the power of the Lord was present for him to heal the sick. ¹⁸Some men came carrying a paralytic on a mat and tried to take him into the house to lay him before Jesus. ¹⁹When they could not find a way to do this because of the crowd, they went up on the roof and lowered him on his mat through the tiles into the middle of the crowd, right in front of Jesus.

²⁰When Jesus saw their faith, he said, "Friend, your sins are forgiven."

²¹The Pharisees and the teachers of the law began thinking to themselves, "Who is this fellow who speaks blasphemy? Who can forgive sins but God alone?"

²²Jesus knew what they were thinking and asked, "Why are you thinking these things in your hearts? ²³Which is easier: to say, 'Your sins are forgiven,' or to say, 'Get up and walk'? ²⁴But that you may know that the Son of Man has authority on earth to forgive sins. . . ." He said to the paralyzed man, "I tell you, get up, take your mat and go home." ²⁵Immediately he stood up in front of them, took what he had been lying on and went home praising God. ²⁶Everyone was amazed and gave praise to God. They were filled with awe and said, "We have seen remarkable things today."

The Calling of Levi

²⁷After this, Jesus went out and saw a tax collector by the name of Levi sitting at his tax booth. "Follow me," Jesus said to him, ²⁸and Levi got up, left everything and followed him.

²⁹Then Levi held a great banquet for Jesus at his house, and a large crowd of tax collectors and others were eating with them. ³⁰But the Pharisees and the teachers of the law who belonged to their sect complained to his disciples, "Why do you eat and drink with tax collectors and 'sinners'?"

³¹Jesus answered them, "It is not the healthy who need a doctor, but the sick.

---

a 4 The Greek verb is plural.   *b 12* The Greek word was used for various diseases affecting the skin—not necessarily leprosy.

32I have not come to call the righteous, but sinners to repentance."

Jesus Questioned About Fasting

33They said to him, "John's disciples often fast and pray, and so do the disciples of the Pharisees, but yours go on eating and drinking."

34Jesus answered, "Can you make the guests of the bridegroom fast while he is with them? 35But the time will come when the bridegroom will be taken from them; in those days they will fast."

36He told them this parable: "No one tears a patch from a new garment and sews it on an old one. If he does, he will have torn the new garment, and the patch from the new will not match the old. 37And no one pours new wine into old wineskins. If he does, the new wine will burst the skins, the wine will run out and the wineskins will be ruined. 38No, new wine must be poured into new wineskins. 39And no one after drinking old wine wants the new, for he says, 'The old is better.' "

Lord of the Sabbath

6 One Sabbath Jesus was going through the grainfields, and his disciples began to pick some heads of grain, rub them in their hands and eat the kernels. 2Some of the Pharisees asked, "Why are you doing what is unlawful on the Sabbath?"

3Jesus answered them, "Have you never read what David did when he and his companions were hungry? 4He entered the house of God, and taking the consecrated bread, he ate what is lawful only for priests to eat. And he also gave some to his companions." 5Then Jesus said to them, "The Son of Man is Lord of the Sabbath."

6On another Sabbath he went into the synagogue and was teaching, and a man was there whose right hand was shriveled. 7The Pharisees and the teachers of the law were looking for a reason to accuse Jesus, so they watched him closely to see if he would heal on the Sabbath. 8But Jesus knew what they were thinking and said to the man with the shriveled hand, "Get up and stand in

front of everyone." So he got up and stood there.

9Then Jesus said to them, "I ask you, which is lawful on the Sabbath: to do good or to do evil, to save life or to destroy it?"

10He looked around at them all, and then said to the man, "Stretch out your hand." He did so, and his hand was completely restored. 11But they were furious and began to discuss with one another what they might do to Jesus.

The Twelve Apostles

12One of those days Jesus went out to a mountainside to pray, and spent the night praying to God. 13When morning came, he called his disciples to him and chose twelve of them, whom he also designated apostles: 14Simon (whom he named Peter), his brother Andrew, James, John, Philip, Bartholomew, 15Matthew, Thomas, James son of Alphaeus, Simon who was called the Zealot, 16Judas son of James, and Judas Iscariot, who became a traitor.

Blessings and Woes

17He went down with them and stood on a level place. A large crowd of his disciples was there and a great number of people from all over Judea, from Jerusalem, and from the coast of Tyre and Sidon, 18who had come to hear him and to be healed of their diseases. Those troubled by evil*a* spirits were cured, 19and the people all tried to touch him, because power was coming from him and healing them all.

20Looking at his disciples, he said:

"Blessed are you who are poor,
    for yours is the kingdom of God.
21Blessed are you who hunger now,
    for you will be satisfied.
Blessed are you who weep now,
    for you will laugh.
22Blessed are you when men hate you,
    when they exclude you and insult
        you
    and reject your name as evil,
        because of the Son of Man.

23"Rejoice in that day and leap for joy, because great is your reward in heaven.

For that is how their fathers treated the prophets.

24 "But woe to you who are rich,
for you have already received your comfort.
25 Woe to you who are well fed now,
for you will go hungry.
Woe to you who laugh now,
for you will mourn and weep.
26 Woe to you when all men speak well of you,
for that is how their fathers treated the false prophets.

Love for Enemies

27 "But I tell you who hear me: Love your enemies, do good to those who hate you, 28 bless those who curse you, pray for those who mistreat you. 29 If someone strikes you on one cheek, turn to him the other also. If someone takes your cloak, do not stop him from taking your tunic. 30 Give to everyone who asks you, and if anyone takes what belongs to you, do not demand it back. 31 Do to others as you would have them do to you.

32 "If you love those who love you, what credit is that to you? Even 'sinners' love those who love them. 33 And if you do good to those who are good to you, what credit is that to you? Even 'sinners' do that. 34 And if you lend to those from whom you expect repayment, what credit is that to you? Even 'sinners' lend to 'sinners,' expecting to be repaid in full. 35 But love your enemies, do good to them, and lend to them without expecting to get anything back. Then your reward will be great, and you will be sons of the Most High, because he is kind to the ungrateful and wicked. 36 Be merciful, just as your Father is merciful.

Judging Others

37 "Do not judge, and you will not be judged. Do not condemn, and you will not be condemned. Forgive, and you will be forgiven. 38 Give, and it will be given to you. A good measure, pressed down, shaken together and running over, will be poured into your lap. For with the measure you use, it will be measured to you."

39 He also told them this parable: "Can a blind man lead a blind man? Will they not both fall into a pit? 40 A student is not above his teacher, but everyone who is fully trained will be like his teacher.

41 "Why do you look at the speck of sawdust in your brother's eye and pay no attention to the plank in your own eye? 42 How can you say to your brother, 'Brother, let me take the speck out of your eye,' when you yourself fail to see the plank in your own eye? You hypocrite, first take the plank out of your eye, and then you will see clearly to remove the speck from your brother's eye.

A Tree and Its Fruit

43 "No good tree bears bad fruit, nor does a bad tree bear good fruit. 44 Each tree is recognized by its own fruit. People do not pick figs from thornbushes, or grapes from briers. 45 The good man brings good things out of the good stored up in his heart, and the evil man brings evil things out of the evil stored up in his heart. For out of the overflow of his heart his mouth speaks.

The Wise and Foolish Builders

46 "Why do you call me, 'Lord, Lord,' and do not do what I say? 47 I will show you what he is like who comes to me and hears my words and puts them into practice. 48 He is like a man building a house, who dug down deep and laid the foundation on rock. When a flood came, the torrent struck that house but could not shake it, because it was well built. 49 But the one who hears my words and does not put them into practice is like a man who built a house on the ground without a foundation. The moment the torrent struck that house, it collapsed and its destruction was complete."

The Faith of the Centurion

7 When Jesus had finished saying all this in the hearing of the people, he entered Capernaum. 2 There a centurion's servant, whom his master valued highly, was sick and about to die. 3 The centurion heard of Jesus and sent

some elders of the Jews to him, asking him to come and heal his servant. 4When they came to Jesus, they pleaded earnestly with him, "This man deserves to have you do this, 5because he loves our nation and has built our synagogue." 6So Jesus went with them.

He was not far from the house when the centurion sent friends to say to him: "Lord, don't trouble yourself, for I do not deserve to have you come under my roof. 7That is why I did not even consider myself worthy to come to you. But say the word, and my servant will be healed. 8For I myself am a man under authority, with soldiers under me. I tell this one, 'Go,' and he goes; and that one, 'Come,' and he comes. I say to my servant, 'Do this,' and he does it."

9When Jesus heard this, he was

THURSDAY

PRAYER OF A PEACEMAKER
Martin Luther King, Jr.

VERSE: Luke 6:31   **PASSAGE:** Luke 6:27–36

God, our Heavenly Father, we thank thee for this golden privilege to worship thee, the only true God of the universe. We come to thee today, grateful that thou hast kept us through the long night of the past and ushered us into the challenge of the present and the bright hope of the future. We are mindful, O God, that man cannot save himself, for man is not the measure of things and humanity is not God. Bound by our chains of sins and finiteness, we know we need a Savior. We thank thee, O God, for the spiritual nature of man. We are in nature but we live above nature. Help us never to let anybody or any condition pull us so low as to cause us to hate. Give us strength to love our enemies and to do good to those who despitefully use us and persecute us. We thank thee for thy church, founded upon thy Word, that challenges us to do more than sing and pray, but go out and work as though the very answer to our prayers depended on us and not upon thee. Then, finally, help us to realize that man was created to shine like stars and live on through all eternity. Keep us, we pray, in perfect peace, help us to walk together, pray together, sing together, and live together until that day when all God's children, Black, White, Red, and Yellow will rejoice in one common band of humanity in the kingdom of our Lord and of our God, we pray. Amen.

ADDITIONAL SCRIPTURE READING:
Matthew 5:9; Titus 3:1–2

Go to page 1187 for your next devotional reading.

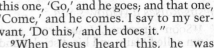

1900   Present

amazed at him, and turning to the crowd following him, he said, "I tell you, I have not found such great faith even in Israel." 10Then the men who had been sent returned to the house and found the servant well.

Jesus Raises a Widow's Son

11Soon afterward, Jesus went to a town called Nain, and his disciples and a large crowd went along with him. 12As he approached the town gate, a dead person was being carried out—the only son of his mother, and she was a widow. And a large crowd from the town was with her. 13When the Lord saw her, his heart went out to her and he said, "Don't cry."

14Then he went up and touched the coffin, and those carrying it stood still. He said, "Young man, I say to you, get up!" 15The dead man sat up and began to talk, and Jesus gave him back to his mother.

16They were all filled with awe and praised God. "A great prophet has appeared among us," they said. "God has come to help his people." 17This news about Jesus spread throughout Judea[a] and the surrounding country.

Jesus and John the Baptist

18John's disciples told him about all these things. Calling two of them, 19he sent them to the Lord to ask, "Are you the one who was to come, or should we expect someone else?"

20When the men came to Jesus, they said, "John the Baptist sent us to you to ask, 'Are you the one who was to come, or should we expect someone else?'"

21At that very time Jesus cured many who had diseases, sicknesses and evil spirits, and gave sight to many who were blind. 22So he replied to the messengers, "Go back and report to John what you have seen and heard: The blind receive sight, the lame walk, those who have leprosy[b] are cured, the deaf hear, the dead are raised, and the good news is preached to the poor. 23Blessed is the man who does not fall away on account of me."

24After John's messengers left, Jesus began to speak to the crowd about John: "What did you go out into the desert to see? A reed swayed by the wind? 25If not, what did you go out to see? A man dressed in fine clothes? No, those who wear expensive clothes and indulge in luxury are in palaces. 26But what did you go out to see? A prophet? Yes, I tell you, and more than a prophet. 27This is the one about whom it is written:

" 'I will send my messenger ahead of
    you,
  who will prepare your way before
    you.'[c]

28I tell you, among those born of women there is no one greater than John; yet the one who is least in the kingdom of God is greater than he."

29(All the people, even the tax collectors, when they heard Jesus' words, acknowledged that God's way was right, because they had been baptized by John. 30But the Pharisees and experts in the law rejected God's purpose for themselves, because they had not been baptized by John.)

31"To what, then, can I compare the people of this generation? What are they like? 32They are like children sitting in the marketplace and calling out to each other:

" 'We played the flute for you,
  and you did not dance;
we sang a dirge,
  and you did not cry.'

33For John the Baptist came neither eating bread nor drinking wine, and you say, 'He has a demon.' 34The Son of Man came eating and drinking, and you say, 'Here is a glutton and a drunkard, a friend of tax collectors and "sinners." ' 35But wisdom is proved right by all her children."

Jesus Anointed by a Sinful Woman

36Now one of the Pharisees invited Jesus to have dinner with him, so he went to the Pharisee's house and reclined at the table. 37When a woman who had lived a sinful life in that town

a 17 Or the land of the Jews   b 22 The Greek word was used for various diseases affecting the skin—not necessarily leprosy.   c 27 Mal. 3:1

TEMPERANCE: ONE OF THE "CARDINAL VIRTUES"
C. S. Lewis

VERSE: Luke 7:34   **PASSAGE:** Luke 7:31–35

emperance is, unfortunately, one of those words that has changed its meaning. It now usually means teetotalism. But in the days when the second cardinal virtue was christened "temperance," it meant nothing of the sort. Temperance referred not specially to drink, but to all pleasures; and it meant not abstaining, but going the right length and no further. It is a mistake to think that Christians ought all to be teetotallers; Mohammedanism, not Christianity, is the teetotal religion. Of course it may be the duty of a particular Christian or of any Christian, at a particular time, to abstain from strong drink, either because he is the sort of man who cannot drink at all without drinking too much, or because he wants to give the money to the poor, or because he is with people who are inclined to drunkenness and must not encourage them by drinking himself. But the whole point is that he is abstaining, for a good reason, from something which he does not condemn and which he likes to see other people enjoying. One of the marks of a certain type of bad man is that he cannot give up a thing himself without wanting every one else to give it up. That is not the Christian way. An individual Christian may see fit to give up all sorts of things for special reasons—marriage, or meat, or beer, or the cinema; but the moment he starts saying the things are bad in themselves, or looking down his nose at other people who do use them, he has taken the wrong turning.

One great piece of mischief has been done by the modern restriction of the word temperance to the question of drink. It helps people to forget that you can be just as intemperate about lots of other things. A man who makes his golf or his motorbicycle the center of his life, or a woman who devotes all her thoughts to clothes or bridge or her dog, is being just as "intemperate" as someone who gets drunk every evening. Of course, it does not show on the outside so easily: bridge-mania or golfmania do not make you fall down in the middle of the road. But God is not deceived by externals.

ADDITIONAL SCRIPTURE READING:
Proverbs 25:28; Titus 3:3–5

Go to page 1191 for your next devotional reading.

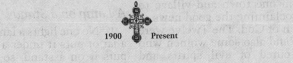

1900   Present

learned that Jesus was eating at the Pharisee's house, she brought an alabaster jar of perfume, ³⁸and as she stood behind him at his feet weeping, she began to wet his feet with her tears. Then she wiped them with her hair, kissed them and poured perfume on them.

³⁹When the Pharisee who had invited him saw this, he said to himself, "If this man were a prophet, he would know who is touching him and what kind of woman she is—that she is a sinner."

⁴⁰Jesus answered him, "Simon, I have something to tell you."

"Tell me, teacher," he said.

⁴¹"Two men owed money to a certain moneylender. One owed him five hundred denarii,ᵃ and the other fifty. ⁴²Neither of them had the money to pay him back, so he canceled the debts of both. Now which of them will love him more?"

⁴³Simon replied, "I suppose the one who had the bigger debt canceled."

"You have judged correctly," Jesus said.

⁴⁴Then he turned toward the woman and said to Simon, "Do you see this woman? I came into your house. You did not give me any water for my feet, but she wet my feet with her tears and wiped them with her hair. ⁴⁵You did not give me a kiss, but this woman, from the time I entered, has not stopped kissing my feet. ⁴⁶You did not put oil on my head, but she has poured perfume on my feet. ⁴⁷Therefore, I tell you, her many sins have been forgiven—for she loved much. But he who has been forgiven little loves little."

⁴⁸Then Jesus said to her, "Your sins are forgiven."

⁴⁹The other guests began to say among themselves, "Who is this who even forgives sins?"

⁵⁰Jesus said to the woman, "Your faith has saved you; go in peace."

The Parable of the Sower

8 After this, Jesus traveled about from one town and village to another, proclaiming the good news of the kingdom of God. The Twelve were with him, ²and also some women who had been cured of evil spirits and diseases: Mary (called Magdalene) from whom seven demons had come out; ³Joanna the wife of Cuza, the manager of Herod's household; Susanna; and many others. These women were helping to support them out of their own means.

⁴While a large crowd was gathering and people were coming to Jesus from town after town, he told this parable: ⁵"A farmer went out to sow his seed. As he was scattering the seed, some fell along the path; it was trampled on, and the birds of the air ate it up. ⁶Some fell on rock, and when it came up, the plants withered because they had no moisture. ⁷Other seed fell among thorns, which grew up with it and choked the plants. ⁸Still other seed fell on good soil. It came up and yielded a crop, a hundred times more than was sown."

When he said this, he called out, "He who has ears to hear, let him hear."

⁹His disciples asked him what this parable meant. ¹⁰He said, "The knowledge of the secrets of the kingdom of God has been given to you, but to others I speak in parables, so that,

" 'though seeing, they may not see;
though hearing, they may not understand.'ᵇ

¹¹"This is the meaning of the parable: The seed is the word of God. ¹²Those along the path are the ones who hear, and then the devil comes and takes away the word from their hearts, so that they may not believe and be saved. ¹³Those on the rock are the ones who receive the word with joy when they hear it, but they have no root. They believe for a while, but in the time of testing they fall away. ¹⁴The seed that fell among thorns stands for those who hear, but as they go on their way they are choked by life's worries, riches and pleasures, and they do not mature. ¹⁵But the seed on good soil stands for those with a noble and good heart, who hear the word, retain it, and by persevering produce a crop.

A Lamp on a Stand

¹⁶"No one lights a lamp and hides it in a jar or puts it under a bed. Instead, he puts it on a stand, so that those who

ᵃ 41 A denarius was a coin worth about a day's wages.   ᵇ 10 Isaiah 6:9

come in can see the light. 17For there is nothing hidden that will not be disclosed, and nothing concealed that will not be known or brought out into the open. 18Therefore consider carefully how you listen. Whoever has will be given more; whoever does not have, even what he thinks he has will be taken from him."

I HAVE NOW DISPOSED OF ALL MY PROPERTY TO MY FAMILY. THERE IS ONE THING MORE I WISH I COULD GIVE THEM AND THAT IS THE CHRISTIAN RELIGION. IF THEY HAD THAT, AND I HAD NOT GIVEN THEM ONE SHILLING, THEY WOULD HAVE BEEN RICH; AND IF THEY HAD NOT THAT, AND I HAD GIVEN THEM ALL THE WORLD, THEY WOULD BE POOR.   —*Patrick Henry*

Jesus' Mother and Brothers

19Now Jesus' mother and brothers came to see him, but they were not able to get near him because of the crowd. 20Someone told him, "Your mother and brothers are standing outside, wanting to see you."

21He replied, "My mother and brothers are those who hear God's word and put it into practice."

Jesus Calms the Storm

22One day Jesus said to his disciples, "Let's go over to the other side of the lake." So they got into a boat and set out. 23As they sailed, he fell asleep. A squall came down on the lake, so that the boat was being swamped, and they were in great danger.

24The disciples went and woke him, saying, "Master, Master, we're going to drown!"

He got up and rebuked the wind and the raging waters; the storm subsided, and all was calm. 25"Where is your faith?" he asked his disciples.

In fear and amazement they asked one another, "Who is this? He commands even the winds and the water, and they obey him."

The Healing of a Demon-possessed Man

26They sailed to the region of the Gerasenes,*a* which is across the lake from Galilee. 27When Jesus stepped ashore, he was met by a demon-possessed man from the town. For a long time this man had not worn clothes or lived in a house, but had lived in the tombs. 28When he saw Jesus, he cried out and fell at his feet, shouting at the top of his voice, "What do you want with me, Jesus, Son of the Most High God? I beg you, don't torture me!" 29For Jesus had commanded the evil*b* spirit to come out of the man. Many times it had seized him, and though he was chained hand and foot and kept under guard, he had broken his chains and had been driven by the demon into solitary places.

30Jesus asked him, "What is your name?"

"Legion," he replied, because many demons had gone into him. 31And they begged him repeatedly not to order them to go into the Abyss.

32A large herd of pigs was feeding there on the hillside. The demons begged Jesus to let them go into them, and he gave them permission. 33When the demons came out of the man, they went into the pigs, and the herd rushed down the steep bank into the lake and was drowned.

34When those tending the pigs saw what had happened, they ran off and reported this in the town and countryside, 35and the people went out to see what had happened. When they came to Jesus, they found the man from whom the demons had gone out, sitting at Jesus' feet, dressed and in his right mind; and they were afraid. 36Those who had seen it told the people how the demon-possessed man had been cured. 37Then all the people of the region of the Gerasenes asked Jesus to leave them, because they were overcome with fear. So he got into the boat and left.

38The man from whom the demons had gone out begged to go with him, but Jesus sent him away, saying, 39"Return home and tell how much God has done for you." So the man went away and told all over town how much Jesus had done for him.

---

a 26 Some manuscripts *Gadarenes;* other manuscripts *Gergesenes;* also in verse 37   *b 29* Greek *unclean*

A Dead Girl and a Sick Woman

40Now when Jesus returned, a crowd welcomed him, for they were all expecting him. **41**Then a man named Jairus, a ruler of the synagogue, came and fell at Jesus' feet, pleading with him to come to his house **42**because his only daughter, a girl of about twelve, was dying.

As Jesus was on his way, the crowds almost crushed him. **43**And a woman was there who had been subject to bleeding for twelve years,*a* but no one could heal her. **44**She came up behind him and touched the edge of his cloak, and immediately her bleeding stopped.

45"Who touched me?" Jesus asked.

When they all denied it, Peter said, "Master, the people are crowding and pressing against you."

46But Jesus said, "Someone touched me; I know that power has gone out from me."

47Then the woman, seeing that she could not go unnoticed, came trembling and fell at his feet. In the presence of all the people, she told why she had touched him and how she had been instantly healed. **48**Then he said to her, "Daughter, your faith has healed you. Go in peace."

49While Jesus was still speaking, someone came from the house of Jairus, the synagogue ruler. "Your daughter is dead," he said. "Don't bother the teacher any more."

50Hearing this, Jesus said to Jairus, "Don't be afraid; just believe, and she will be healed."

51When he arrived at the house of Jairus, he did not let anyone go in with him except Peter, John and James, and the child's father and mother. **52**Meanwhile, all the people were wailing and mourning for her. "Stop wailing," Jesus said. "She is not dead but asleep."

53They laughed at him, knowing that she was dead. **54**But he took her by the hand and said, "My child, get up!" **55**Her spirit returned, and at once she stood up. Then Jesus told them to give her something to eat. **56**Her parents were astonished, but he ordered them not to tell anyone what had happened.

Jesus Sends Out the Twelve

9 When Jesus had called the Twelve together, he gave them power and authority to drive out all demons and to cure diseases, **2**and he sent them out to preach the kingdom of God and to heal the sick. **3**He told them: "Take nothing for the journey—no staff, no bag, no bread, no money, no extra tunic. **4**Whatever house you enter, stay there until you leave that town. **5**If people do not welcome you, shake the dust off your feet when you leave their town, as a testimony against them." **6**So they set out and went from village to village, preaching the gospel and healing people everywhere.

7Now Herod the tetrarch heard about all that was going on. And he was perplexed, because some were saying that John had been raised from the dead, **8**others that Elijah had appeared, and still others that one of the prophets of long ago had come back to life. **9**But Herod said, "I beheaded John. Who, then, is this I hear such things about?" And he tried to see him.

Jesus Feeds the Five Thousand

10When the apostles returned, they reported to Jesus what they had done. Then he took them with him and they withdrew by themselves to a town called Bethsaida, **11**but the crowds learned about it and followed him. He welcomed them and spoke to them about the kingdom of God, and healed those who needed healing.

12Late in the afternoon the Twelve came to him and said, "Send the crowd away so they can go to the surrounding villages and countryside and find food and lodging, because we are in a remote place here."

13He replied, "You give them something to eat."

They answered, "We have only five loaves of bread and two fish—unless we go and buy food for all this crowd." **14**(About five thousand men were there.)

But he said to his disciples, "Have them sit down in groups of about fifty each." **15**The disciples did so, and everybody sat down. **16**Taking the five loaves

a 43 Many manuscripts *years, and she had spent all she had on doctors*

WEEKEND

GODHEAD HERE IN HIDING
Thomas Aquinas

VERSE: Luke 23:42   **PASSAGE:** Luke 23:39–43

odhead here in hiding, whom I do adore
Masked by these bare shadows, shape and
   nothing more,
   See, Lord, at thy service low lies here a heart
Lost, all lost in wonder at the God thou art.

Seeing, touching, tasting are in thee deceived;
How says trusty hearing? that shall be believed;
What God's Son has told me, take for true I do;
Truth himself speaks truly or there's nothing true.

On the cross thy godhead made no sign to men;
Here thy very manhood steals from human ken:
Both are my confession, both are my belief,
And I pray the prayer of the dying thief.

I am not like Thomas, wounds I cannot see,
But can plainly call thee God and Lord as he:
This faith each day deeper be my holding of,
Daily make me harder hope and dearer love.

O thou our reminder of Christ crucified,
Living Bread the life of us for whom he died,
Lend this life to me then: feed and feast my mind,
There be thou the sweetness man was meant to find . . .

Jesu, whom I look at shrouded here below,
I beseech thee send me what I thirst for so,
Some day to gaze on thee face to face in light,
And be blest for ever with thy glory's light.

ADDITIONAL SCRIPTURE READING:
John 3:16; 20:24–29

Go to page 1195 for your next devotional reading.

500   1500

and the two fish and looking up to heaven, he gave thanks and broke them. Then he gave them to the disciples to set before the people. ¹⁷They all ate and were satisfied, and the disciples picked up twelve basketfuls of broken pieces that were left over.

Peter's Confession of Christ

¹⁸Once when Jesus was praying in private and his disciples were with him, he asked them, "Who do the crowds say I am?"

¹⁹They replied, "Some say John the Baptist; others say Elijah; and still others, that one of the prophets of long ago has come back to life."

²⁰"But what about you?" he asked. "Who do you say I am?"

Peter answered, "The Christ*a* of God."

²¹Jesus strictly warned them not to tell this to anyone. ²²And he said, "The Son of Man must suffer many things and be rejected by the elders, chief priests and teachers of the law, and he must be killed and on the third day be raised to life."

²³Then he said to them all: "If anyone would come after me, he must deny himself and take up his cross daily and follow me. ²⁴For whoever wants to save his life will lose it, but whoever loses his life for me will save it. ²⁵What good is it for a man to gain the whole world, and yet lose or forfeit his very self? ²⁶If anyone is ashamed of me and my words, the Son of Man will be ashamed of him when he comes in his glory and in the glory of the Father and of the holy angels. ²⁷I tell you the truth, some who are standing here will not taste death before they see the kingdom of God."

The Transfiguration

²⁸About eight days after Jesus said this, he took Peter, John and James with him and went up onto a mountain to pray. ²⁹As he was praying, the appearance of his face changed, and his clothes became as bright as a flash of lightning. ³⁰Two men, Moses and Elijah, ³¹appeared in glorious splendor, talking with Jesus. They spoke about his departure, which he was about to bring to fulfillment at Jerusalem. ³²Peter and his companions were very

sleepy, but when they became fully awake, they saw his glory and the two men standing with him. ³³As the men were leaving Jesus, Peter said to him, "Master, it is good for us to be here. Let us put up three shelters—one for you, one for Moses and one for Elijah." (He did not know what he was saying.)

³⁴While he was speaking, a cloud appeared and enveloped them, and they were afraid as they entered the cloud. ³⁵A voice came from the cloud, saying, "This is my Son, whom I have chosen; listen to him." ³⁶When the voice had spoken, they found that Jesus was alone. The disciples kept this to themselves, and told no one at that time what they had seen.

The Healing of a Boy With an Evil Spirit

³⁷The next day, when they came down from the mountain, a large crowd met him. ³⁸A man in the crowd called out, "Teacher, I beg you to look at my son, for he is my only child. ³⁹A spirit seizes him and he suddenly screams; it throws him into convulsions so that he foams at the mouth. It scarcely ever leaves him and is destroying him. ⁴⁰I begged your disciples to drive it out, but they could not."

⁴¹"O unbelieving and perverse generation," Jesus replied, "how long shall I stay with you and put up with you? Bring your son here."

⁴²Even while the boy was coming, the demon threw him to the ground in a convulsion. But Jesus rebuked the evil*b* spirit, healed the boy and gave him back to his father. ⁴³And they were all amazed at the greatness of God.

While everyone was marveling at all that Jesus did, he said to his disciples, ⁴⁴"Listen carefully to what I am about to tell you: The Son of Man is going to be betrayed into the hands of men." ⁴⁵But they did not understand what this meant. It was hidden from them, so that they did not grasp it, and they were afraid to ask him about it.

Who Will Be the Greatest?

⁴⁶An argument started among the disciples as to which of them would be the greatest. ⁴⁷Jesus, knowing their thoughts,

a 20 Or *Messiah*   *b 42* Greek *unclean*

took a little child and had him stand beside him. 48Then he said to them, "Whoever welcomes this little child in my name welcomes me; and whoever welcomes me welcomes the one who sent me. For he who is least among you all—he is the greatest."

49"Master," said John, "we saw a man driving out demons in your name and we tried to stop him, because he is not one of us."

50"Do not stop him," Jesus said, "for whoever is not against you is for you."

Samaritan Opposition

51As the time approached for him to be taken up to heaven, Jesus resolutely set out for Jerusalem. 52And he sent messengers on ahead, who went into a Samaritan village to get things ready for him; 53but the people there did not welcome him, because he was heading for Jerusalem. 54When the disciples James and John saw this, they asked, "Lord, do you want us to call fire down from heaven to destroy them*a*?" 55But Jesus turned and rebuked them, 56and*b* they went to another village.

The Cost of Following Jesus

57As they were walking along the road, a man said to him, "I will follow you wherever you go."

58Jesus replied, "Foxes have holes and birds of the air have nests, but the Son of Man has no place to lay his head."

59He said to another man, "Follow me."

But the man replied, "Lord, first let me go and bury my father."

60Jesus said to him, "Let the dead bury their own dead, but you go and proclaim the kingdom of God."

TO HOLD ON TO THE PLOUGH WHILE WIPING OUR TEARS—THIS IS CHRISTIANITY.   —*Watchman Nee*

61Still another said, "I will follow you, Lord; but first let me go back and say good-by to my family."

62Jesus replied, "No one who puts his hand to the plow and looks back is fit for service in the kingdom of God."

Jesus Sends Out the Seventy-two

10 After this the Lord appointed seventy-two*c* others and sent them two by two ahead of him to every town and place where he was about to go. 2He told them, "The harvest is plentiful, but the workers are few. Ask the Lord of the harvest, therefore, to send out workers into his harvest field. 3Go! I am sending you out like lambs among wolves. 4Do not take a purse or bag or sandals; and do not greet anyone on the road.

5"When you enter a house, first say, 'Peace to this house.' 6If a man of peace is there, your peace will rest on him; if not, it will return to you. 7Stay in that house, eating and drinking whatever they give you, for the worker deserves his wages. Do not move around from house to house.

8"When you enter a town and are welcomed, eat what is set before you. 9Heal the sick who are there and tell them, 'The kingdom of God is near you.' 10But when you enter a town and are not welcomed, go into its streets and say, 11'Even the dust of your town that sticks to our feet we wipe off against you. Yet be sure of this: The kingdom of God is near.' 12I tell you, it will be more bearable on that day for Sodom than for that town.

13"Woe to you, Korazin! Woe to you, Bethsaida! For if the miracles that were performed in you had been performed in Tyre and Sidon, they would have repented long ago, sitting in sackcloth and ashes. 14But it will be more bearable for Tyre and Sidon at the judgment than for you. 15And you, Capernaum, will you be lifted up to the skies? No, you will go down to the depths.*d*

16"He who listens to you listens to me; he who rejects you rejects me; but he who rejects me rejects him who sent me."

17The seventy-two returned with joy and said, "Lord, even the demons submit to us in your name."

18He replied, "I saw Satan fall like lightning from heaven. 19I have given

a 54 Some manuscripts *them, even as Elijah did*   *b 55,56* Some manuscripts *them. And he said, "You do not know what kind of spirit you are of, for the Son of Man did not come to destroy men's lives, but to save them." 56And*   *c 1* Some manuscripts *seventy; also in verse 17*   *d 15* Greek *Hades*

you authority to trample on snakes and scorpions and to overcome all the power of the enemy; nothing will harm you. ²⁰However, do not rejoice that the spirits submit to you, but rejoice that your names are written in heaven."

²¹At that time Jesus, full of joy through the Holy Spirit, said, "I praise you, Father, Lord of heaven and earth, because you have hidden these things from the wise and learned, and revealed them to little children. Yes, Father, for this was your good pleasure.

²²"All things have been committed to me by my Father. No one knows who the Son is except the Father, and no one knows who the Father is except the Son and those to whom the Son chooses to reveal him."

²³Then he turned to his disciples and said privately, "Blessed are the eyes that see what you see. ²⁴For I tell you that many prophets and kings wanted to see what you see but did not see it, and to hear what you hear but did not hear it."

The Parable of the Good Samaritan

²⁵On one occasion an expert in the law stood up to test Jesus. "Teacher," he asked, "what must I do to inherit eternal life?"

²⁶"What is written in the Law?" he replied. "How do you read it?"

²⁷He answered: " 'Love the Lord your God with all your heart and with all your soul and with all your strength and with all your mind'ᵃ; and, 'Love your neighbor as yourself.'ᵇ"

²⁸"You have answered correctly," Jesus replied. "Do this and you will live."

²⁹But he wanted to justify himself, so he asked Jesus, "And who is my neighbor?"

³⁰In reply Jesus said: "A man was going down from Jerusalem to Jericho, when he fell into the hands of robbers. They stripped him of his clothes, beat him and went away, leaving him half dead. ³¹A priest happened to be going down the same road, and when he saw the man, he passed by on the other side. ³²So too, a Levite, when he came to the

place and saw him, passed by on the other side. ³³But a Samaritan, as he traveled, came where the man was; and when he saw him, he took pity on him. ³⁴He went to him and bandaged his wounds, pouring on oil and wine. Then he put the man on his own donkey, took him to an inn and took care of him. ³⁵The next day he took out two silver coinsᶜ and gave them to the innkeeper. 'Look after him,' he said, 'and when I return, I will reimburse you for any extra expense you may have.'

³⁶"Which of these three do you think was a neighbor to the man who fell into the hands of robbers?"

³⁷The expert in the law replied, "The one who had mercy on him."

Jesus told him, "Go and do likewise."

At the Home of Martha and Mary

³⁸As Jesus and his disciples were on their way, he came to a village where a woman named Martha opened her home to him. ³⁹She had a sister called Mary, who sat at the Lord's feet listening to what he said. ⁴⁰But Martha was distracted by all the preparations that had to be made. She came to him and asked, "Lord, don't you care that my sister has left me to do the work by myself? Tell her to help me!"

⁴¹"Martha, Martha," the Lord answered, "you are worried and upset about many things, ⁴²but only one thing is needed.ᵈ Mary has chosen what is better, and it will not be taken away from her."

Jesus' Teaching on Prayer

11 One day Jesus was praying in a certain place. When he finished, one of his disciples said to him, "Lord, teach us to pray, just as John taught his disciples."

²He said to them, "When you pray, say:

" 'Father,ᵉ
hallowed be your name,
    your kingdom come.ᶠ
³Give us each day our daily bread.
⁴Forgive us our sins,

ᵃ 27 Deut. 6:5   ᵇ 27 Lev. 19:18   ᶜ 35 Greek two denarii   ᵈ 42 Some manuscripts but few things are needed—or only one   ᵉ 2 Some manuscripts Our Father in heaven   ᶠ 2 Some manuscripts come. May your will be done on earth as it is in heaven.

WHO IS A LOVABLE NEIGHBOR?
Thomas Merton

VERSE: Luke 10:29   **PASSAGE:** Luke 10:25–37

 onsider the question that was asked: "Who is my neighbor?" This was, in fact, the second question which a lawyer asked of Christ. His first, intended as a temptation or an embarrassment, was, "How shall I obtain eternal life?" This is an important question, and so important that nobody can be without the answer to it. And note that he asks this question of him of whom we read: "This is eternal life: that they may know you, the only true God, and Jesus Christ whom you have sent" (John 17:3). Since the answer to the most important of questions is accessible to everyone, the lawyer should have known it. And he did know it. He had no need to ask it at all. The Lord made this clear, for he said: "What is the first commandment?" When the lawyer replied, saying that the first commandment was the love of God and of our neighbor, then Christ told him to keep that commandment and he would have eternal life. In this way it became clear that the question was not necessary. But in order to prove that he had a real problem, the lawyer asked again: "Who is my neighbor?"

We can perhaps assume that he meant by this he had no problem about loving God, since "God is good," but that he was perplexed about loving his neighbor, since some men are better than others and all are imperfect. This being the case, in order to protect himself against loving an unworthy object and thus wasting his love, he wanted to know where to draw the line. Who is the neighbor to be loved, who is the alien not to be loved? The question is a matter of classification. Therefore it is a matter of judgment also, for to classify is to judge. How then does one classify people, and judge them accurately as worthy of love, or of hatred, or of indifference? This is a pretty question. But to the Lord it was a question that had no meaning, for he said, "Do not judge, or you too will be judged" (Matthew 7:1). Do not classify, and do not be classified.

ADDITIONAL SCRIPTURE READING:
Matthew 7:1; Mark 12:30–31

Go to page 1197 for your next devotional reading.

1900   Present

for we also forgive everyone who sins against us.ᵃ

And lead us not into temptation.ᵇʹ "

⁵Then he said to them, "Suppose one of you has a friend, and he goes to him at midnight and says, 'Friend, lend me three loaves of bread, ⁶because a friend of mine on a journey has come to me, and I have nothing to set before him.'

⁷"Then the one inside answers, 'Don't bother me. The door is already locked, and my children are with me in bed. I can't get up and give you anything.' ⁸I tell you, though he will not get up and give him the bread because he is his friend, yet because of the man's boldnessᶜ he will get up and give him as much as he needs.

⁹"So I say to you: Ask and it will be given to you; seek and you will find; knock and the door will be opened to you. ¹⁰For everyone who asks receives; he who seeks finds; and to him who knocks, the door will be opened.

¹¹"Which of you fathers, if your son asks forᵈ a fish, will give him a snake instead? ¹²Or if he asks for an egg, will give him a scorpion? ¹³If you then, though you are evil, know how to give good gifts to your children, how much more will your Father in heaven give the Holy Spirit to those who ask him!"

THAT GIFT OF HIS, FROM GOD DESCENDED:

AH FRIEND, WHAT GIFT OF MAN'S DOES NOT?

—*Robert Browning*

Jesus and Beelzebub

¹⁴Jesus was driving out a demon that was mute. When the demon left, the man who had been mute spoke, and the crowd was amazed. ¹⁵But some of them said, "By Beelzebub,ᵉ the prince of demons, he is driving out demons." ¹⁶Others tested him by asking for a sign from heaven.

¹⁷Jesus knew their thoughts and said to them: "Any kingdom divided against itself will be ruined, and a house divided against itself will fall. ¹⁸If Satan is divided against himself, how can his kingdom stand? I say this because you claim that I drive out demons by Beelzebub. ¹⁹Now if I drive out demons by Beelzebub, by whom do your followers drive them out? So then, they will be your judges. ²⁰But if I drive out demons by the finger of God, then the kingdom of God has come to you.

²¹"When a strong man, fully armed, guards his own house, his possessions are safe. ²²But when someone stronger attacks and overpowers him, he takes away the armor in which the man trusted and divides up the spoils.

²³"He who is not with me is against me, and he who does not gather with me, scatters.

²⁴"When an evilᶠ spirit comes out of a man, it goes through arid places seeking rest and does not find it. Then it says, 'I will return to the house I left.' ²⁵When it arrives, it finds the house swept clean and put in order. ²⁶Then it goes and takes seven other spirits more wicked than itself, and they go in and live there. And the final condition of that man is worse than the first."

²⁷As Jesus was saying these things, a woman in the crowd called out, "Blessed is the mother who gave you birth and nursed you."

²⁸He replied, "Blessed rather are those who hear the word of God and obey it."

The Sign of Jonah

²⁹As the crowds increased, Jesus said, "This is a wicked generation. It asks for a miraculous sign, but none will be given it except the sign of Jonah. ³⁰For as Jonah was a sign to the Ninevites, so also will the Son of Man be to this generation. ³¹The Queen of the South will rise at the judgment with the men of this generation and condemn them; for she came from the ends of the earth to listen to Solomon's wisdom, and now oneᵍ greater than Solomon is here. ³²The men of Nineveh will stand up at the judgment with this generation and condemn it; for they repented at the

---

ᵃ *4* Greek *everyone who is indebted to us*   ᵇ *4* Some manuscripts *temptation but deliver us from the evil one*   ᶜ *8* Or *persistence*   ᵈ *11* Some manuscripts *for bread, will give him a stone; or if he asks for*   ᵉ *15* Greek *Beezeboul* or *Beelzeboul;* also in verses 18 and 19   ᶠ *24* Greek *unclean*   ᵍ *31* Or *something;* also in verse 32

preaching of Jonah, and now one greater than Jonah is here.

The Lamp of the Body

33 "No one lights a lamp and puts it in a place where it will be hidden, or under a bowl. Instead he puts it on its stand, so that those who come in may see the light. 34 Your eye is the lamp of your body. When your eyes are good, your whole body also is full of light. But when they are bad, your body also is full of darkness. 35 See to it, then, that the light within you is not darkness.

36 Therefore, if your whole body is full of light, and no part of it dark, it will be completely lighted, as when the light of a lamp shines on you."

Six Woes

37 When Jesus had finished speaking, a Pharisee invited him to eat with him; so he went in and reclined at the table. 38 But the Pharisee, noticing that Jesus did not first wash before the meal, was surprised. 39 Then the Lord said to him, "Now then, you Pharisees clean the outside of the cup and dish, but inside you are full

---

TUESDAY

EMPTINESS BEFORE FULLNESS
A. W. Tozer

VERSE: Luke 11:13   **PASSAGE:** Luke 11:11–13

efore there can be fullness there must be emptiness. Before God can fill us with himself we must first be emptied of ourselves. It is this emptying that brings the painful disappointment and despair of self of which so many persons have complained just prior to their new and radiant experience.

There must come a total of self-devaluation, a death to all things without us and within us, or there can never be real filling with the Holy Spirit . . .

While I shy away from "how to" formulas in spiritual things, I believe the answer to the question "How can I be filled?" may be answered in four words, all of them active verbs. They are these: (1) *surrender* (Romans 12:1–2), (2) *ask* (Luke 11:13), (3) *obey* (Acts 5:32), (4) believe (Galatians 3:2) . . .

Complete and ungrudging obedience to the will of God is absolutely indispensable to the reception of the Spirit's anointing. As we wait before God we should reverently search the Scriptures and listen for the voice of gentle stillness to learn what our heavenly Father expects of us. Then, trusting in his enabling, we should obey to the best of our ability and understanding.

ADDITIONAL SCRIPTURE READING:
Ezekiel 36:26–27; John 7:37–39; Ephesians 5:18

1900   Present

of greed and wickedness. **40**You foolish people! Did not the one who made the outside make the inside also? **41**But give what is inside ⌞the dish⌟*a* to the poor, and everything will be clean for you.

42"Woe to you Pharisees, because you give God a tenth of your mint, rue and all other kinds of garden herbs, but you neglect justice and the love of God. You should have practiced the latter without leaving the former undone.

43"Woe to you Pharisees, because you love the most important seats in the synagogues and greetings in the marketplaces.

44"Woe to you, because you are like unmarked graves, which men walk over without knowing it."

45One of the experts in the law answered him, "Teacher, when you say these things, you insult us also."

46Jesus replied, "And you experts in the law, woe to you, because you load people down with burdens they can hardly carry, and you yourselves will not lift one finger to help them.

47"Woe to you, because you build tombs for the prophets, and it was your forefathers who killed them. **48**So you testify that you approve of what your forefathers did; they killed the prophets, and you build their tombs. **49**Because of this, God in his wisdom said, 'I will send them prophets and apostles, some of whom they will kill and others they will persecute.' **50**Therefore this generation will be held responsible for the blood of all the prophets that has been shed since the beginning of the world, **51**from the blood of Abel to the blood of Zechariah, who was killed between the altar and the sanctuary. Yes, I tell you, this generation will be held responsible for it all.

52"Woe to you experts in the law, because you have taken away the key to knowledge. You yourselves have not entered, and you have hindered those who were entering."

53When Jesus left there, the Pharisees and the teachers of the law began to oppose him fiercely and to besiege him with questions, **54**waiting to catch him in something he might say.

Warnings and Encouragements

12 Meanwhile, when a crowd of many thousands had gathered, so that they were trampling on one another, Jesus began to speak first to his disciples, saying: "Be on your guard against the yeast of the Pharisees, which is hypocrisy. **2**There is nothing concealed that will not be disclosed, or hidden that will not be made known. **3**What you have said in the dark will be heard in the daylight, and what you have whispered in the ear in the inner rooms will be proclaimed from the roofs.

4"I tell you, my friends, do not be afraid of those who kill the body and after that can do no more. **5**But I will show you whom you should fear: Fear him who, after the killing of the body, has power to throw you into hell. Yes, I tell you, fear him. **6**Are not five sparrows sold for two pennies*b*? Yet not one of them is forgotten by God. **7**Indeed, the very hairs of your head are all numbered. Don't be afraid; you are worth more than many sparrows.

8"I tell you, whoever acknowledges me before men, the Son of Man will also acknowledge him before the angels of God. **9**But he who disowns me before men will be disowned before the angels of God. **10**And everyone who speaks a word against the Son of Man will be forgiven, but anyone who blasphemes against the Holy Spirit will not be forgiven.

11"When you are brought before synagogues, rulers and authorities, do not worry about how you will defend yourselves or what you will say, **12**for the Holy Spirit will teach you at that time what you should say."

The Parable of the Rich Fool

13Someone in the crowd said to him, "Teacher, tell my brother to divide the inheritance with me."

14Jesus replied, "Man, who appointed me a judge or an arbiter between you?" **15**Then he said to them, "Watch out! Be on your guard against all kinds of greed; a man's life does not consist in the abundance of his possessions."

---

a 41 Or *what you have*   *b* 6 Greek *two assaria*

16And he told them this parable: "The ground of a certain rich man produced a good crop. 17He thought to himself, 'What shall I do? I have no place to store my crops.'

18"Then he said, 'This is what I'll do. I will tear down my barns and build bigger ones, and there I will store all my grain and my goods. 19And I'll say to myself, "You have plenty of good things laid up for many years. Take life easy; eat, drink and be merry." '

20"But God said to him, 'You fool! This very night your life will be demanded from you. Then who will get what you have prepared for yourself?'

21"This is how it will be with anyone who stores up things for himself but is not rich toward God."

Do Not Worry

22Then Jesus said to his disciples: "Therefore I tell you, do not worry about your life, what you will eat; or about your body, what you will wear. 23Life is more than food, and the body more than clothes. 24Consider the ravens: They do not sow or reap, they have no storeroom or barn; yet God feeds them. And how much more valuable you are than birds! 25Who of you by worrying can add a single hour to his life[a]? 26Since you cannot do this very little thing, why do you worry about the rest?

ANXIETY IS NOT ONLY A PAIN WHICH WE MUST ASK GOD TO ASSUAGE BUT ALSO A WEAKNESS WE MUST ASK HIM TO PARDON—FOR HE'S TOLD US TO TAKE NO CARE FOR THE MORROW. —C. S. Lewis

---

27"Consider how the lilies grow. They do not labor or spin. Yet I tell you, not even Solomon in all his splendor was dressed like one of these. 28If that is how God clothes the grass of the field, which is here today, and tomorrow is thrown into the fire, how much more will he clothe you, O you of little faith! 29And do not set your heart on what you will eat or drink; do not worry about it. 30For the pagan world runs after all such things, and your Father knows that you

need them. 31But seek his kingdom, and these things will be given to you as well.

32"Do not be afraid, little flock, for your Father has been pleased to give you the kingdom. 33Sell your possessions and give to the poor. Provide purses for yourselves that will not wear out, a treasure in heaven that will not be exhausted, where no thief comes near and no moth destroys. 34For where your treasure is, there your heart will be also.

Watchfulness

35"Be dressed ready for service and keep your lamps burning, 36like men waiting for their master to return from a wedding banquet, so that when he comes and knocks they can immediately open the door for him. 37It will be good for those servants whose master finds them watching when he comes. I tell you the truth, he will dress himself to serve, will have them recline at the table and will come and wait on them. 38It will be good for those servants whose master finds them ready, even if he comes in the second or third watch of the night. 39But understand this: If the owner of the house had known at what hour the thief was coming, he would not have let his house be broken into. 40You also must be ready, because the Son of Man will come at an hour when you do not expect him."

41Peter asked, "Lord, are you telling this parable to us, or to everyone?"

42The Lord answered, "Who then is the faithful and wise manager, whom the master puts in charge of his servants to give them their food allowance at the proper time? 43It will be good for that servant whom the master finds doing so when he returns. 44I tell you the truth, he will put him in charge of all his possessions. 45But suppose the servant says to himself, 'My master is taking a long time in coming,' and he then begins to beat the menservants and maidservants and to eat and drink and get drunk. 46The master of that servant will come on a day when he does not expect him and at an hour he is not aware of. He will cut him to pieces and assign him a place with the unbelievers.

47"That servant who knows his master's will and does not get ready or does

a 25 Or single cubit to his height

not do what his master wants will be beaten with many blows. **48**But the one who does not know and does things deserving punishment will be beaten with few blows. From everyone who has been given much, much will be demanded; and from the one who has been entrusted with much, much more will be asked.

Not Peace but Division

49"I have come to bring fire on the earth, and how I wish it were already kindled! **50**But I have a baptism to undergo, and how distressed I am until it is completed! **51**Do you think I came to bring peace on earth? No, I tell you, but division. **52**From now on there will be five in one family divided against each other, three against two and two against three. **53**They will be divided, father against son and son against father, mother against daughter and daughter against mother, mother-in-law against daughter-in-law and daughter-in-law against mother-in-law."

Interpreting the Times

54He said to the crowd: "When you see a cloud rising in the west, immediately you say, 'It's going to rain,' and it does. **55**And when the south wind blows, you say, 'It's going to be hot,' and it is. **56**Hypocrites! You know how to interpret the appearance of the earth and the sky. How is it that you don't know how to interpret this present time?

57"Why don't you judge for yourselves what is right? **58**As you are going with your adversary to the magistrate, try hard to be reconciled to him on the way, or he may drag you off to the judge, and the judge turn you over to the officer, and the officer throw you into prison. **59**I tell you, you will not get out until you have paid the last penny.*a*"

Repent or Perish

13 Now there were some present at that time who told Jesus about the Galileans whose blood Pilate had mixed with their sacrifices. **2**Jesus answered, "Do you think that these Galileans were worse sinners than all the other Galileans because

they suffered this way? **3**I tell you, no! But unless you repent, you too will all perish. **4**Or those eighteen who died when the tower in Siloam fell on them—do you think they were more guilty than all the others living in Jerusalem? **5**I tell you, no! But unless you repent, you too will all perish."

6Then he told this parable: "A man had a fig tree, planted in his vineyard, and he went to look for fruit on it, but did not find any. **7**So he said to the man who took care of the vineyard, 'For three years now I've been coming to look for fruit on this fig tree and haven't found any. Cut it down! Why should it use up the soil?'

8"'Sir,' the man replied, 'leave it alone for one more year, and I'll dig around it and fertilize it. **9**If it bears fruit next year, fine! If not, then cut it down.'"

A Crippled Woman Healed on the Sabbath

10On a Sabbath Jesus was teaching in one of the synagogues, **11**and a woman was there who had been crippled by a spirit for eighteen years. She was bent over and could not straighten up at all. **12**When Jesus saw her, he called her forward and said to her, "Woman, you are set free from your infirmity." **13**Then he put his hands on her, and immediately she straightened up and praised God.

14Indignant because Jesus had healed on the Sabbath, the synagogue ruler said to the people, "There are six days for work. So come and be healed on those days, not on the Sabbath."

15The Lord answered him, "You hypocrites! Doesn't each of you on the Sabbath untie his ox or donkey from the stall and lead it out to give it water? **16**Then should not this woman, a daughter of Abraham, whom Satan has kept bound for eighteen long years, be set free on the Sabbath day from what bound her?"

17When he said this, all his opponents were humiliated, but the people were delighted with all the wonderful things he was doing.

a 59 Greek *lepton*

The Parables of the Mustard Seed and the Yeast

18Then Jesus asked, "What is the kingdom of God like? What shall I compare it to? **19**It is like a mustard seed, which a man took and planted in his garden. It grew and became a tree, and the birds of the air perched in its branches."

20Again he asked, "What shall I compare the kingdom of God to? **21**It is like yeast that a woman took and mixed into a large amount*a* of flour until it worked all through the dough."

The Narrow Door

22Then Jesus went through the towns and villages, teaching as he made his way to Jerusalem. **23**Someone asked him, "Lord, are only a few people going to be saved?"

He said to them, **24**"Make every effort to enter through the narrow door, because many, I tell you, will try to enter and will not be able to. **25**Once the owner of the house gets up and closes the door, you will stand outside knocking and pleading, 'Sir, open the door for us.'

"But he will answer, 'I don't know you or where you come from.'

26"Then you will say, 'We ate and drank with you, and you taught in our streets.'

27"But he will reply, 'I don't know you or where you come from. Away from me, all you evildoers!'

28"There will be weeping there, and gnashing of teeth, when you see Abraham, Isaac and Jacob and all the prophets in the kingdom of God, but you yourselves thrown out. **29**People will come from east and west and north and south, and will take their places at the feast in the kingdom of God. **30**Indeed there are those who are last who will be first, and first who will be last."

Jesus' Sorrow for Jerusalem

31At that time some Pharisees came to Jesus and said to him, "Leave this place and go somewhere else. Herod wants to kill you."

32He replied, "Go tell that fox, 'I will drive out demons and heal people today and tomorrow, and on the third day I will reach my goal.' **33**In any case, I must keep going today and tomorrow and the next day—for surely no prophet can die outside Jerusalem!

34"O Jerusalem, Jerusalem, you who kill the prophets and stone those sent to you, how often I have longed to gather your children together, as a hen gathers her chicks under her wings, but you were not willing! **35**Look, your house is left to you desolate. I tell you, you will not see me again until you say, 'Blessed is he who comes in the name of the Lord.'*b*"

Jesus at a Pharisee's House

14 One Sabbath, when Jesus went to eat in the house of a prominent Pharisee, he was being carefully watched. **2**There in front of him was a man suffering from dropsy. **3**Jesus asked the Pharisees and experts in the law, "Is it lawful to heal on the Sabbath or not?" **4**But they remained silent. So taking hold of the man, he healed him and sent him away.

5Then he asked them, "If one of you has a son*c* or an ox that falls into a well on the Sabbath day, will you not immediately pull him out?" **6**And they had nothing to say.

7When he noticed how the guests picked the places of honor at the table, he told them this parable: **8**"When someone invites you to a wedding feast, do not take the place of honor, for a person more distinguished than you may have been invited. **9**If so, the host who invited both of you will come and say to you, 'Give this man your seat.' Then, humiliated, you will have to take the least important place. **10**But when you are invited, take the lowest place, so that when your host comes, he will say to you, 'Friend, move up to a better place.' Then you will be honored in the presence of all your fellow guests. **11**For everyone who exalts himself will be humbled, and he who humbles himself will be exalted."

12Then Jesus said to his host, "When you give a luncheon or dinner, do not invite your friends, your brothers or relatives, or your rich neighbors; if you do, they may invite you back and so you will be repaid. **13**But when you give a

---

a 21 Greek *three satas* (probably about 1/2 bushel or 22 liters)   *b 35* Psalm 118:26   *c 5* Some manuscripts *donkey*

banquet, invite the poor, the crippled, the lame, the blind, **14**and you will be blessed. Although they cannot repay you, you will be repaid at the resurrection of the righteous."

The Parable of the Great Banquet

15When one of those at the table with him heard this, he said to Jesus, "Blessed is the man who will eat at the feast in the kingdom of God."

16Jesus replied: "A certain man was preparing a great banquet and invited many guests. **17**At the time of the banquet he sent his servant to tell those who had been invited, 'Come, for everything is now ready.'

18"But they all alike began to make excuses. The first said, 'I have just bought a field, and I must go and see it. Please excuse me.'

19"Another said, 'I have just bought five yoke of oxen, and I'm on my way to try them out. Please excuse me.'

20"Still another said, 'I just got married, so I can't come.'

21"The servant came back and reported this to his master. Then the owner of the house became angry and ordered his servant, 'Go out quickly into the streets and alleys of the town and bring in the poor, the crippled, the blind and the lame.'

22" 'Sir,' the servant said, 'what you ordered has been done, but there is still room.'

23"Then the master told his servant, 'Go out to the roads and country lanes and make them come in, so that my house will be full. **24**I tell you, not one of those men who were invited will get a taste of my banquet.' "

I DO NOT PRAY FOR A LIGHTER LOAD, BUT FOR A STRONGER BACK.   —*Phillips Brooks*

The Cost of Being a Disciple

25Large crowds were traveling with Jesus, and turning to them he said: **26**"If anyone comes to me and does not hate his father and mother, his wife and children, his brothers and sisters—yes, even his own life—he cannot be my disciple.

27And anyone who does not carry his cross and follow me cannot be my disciple.

28"Suppose one of you wants to build a tower. Will he not first sit down and estimate the cost to see if he has enough money to complete it? **29**For if he lays the foundation and is not able to finish it, everyone who sees it will ridicule him, **30**saying, 'This fellow began to build and was not able to finish.'

31"Or suppose a king is about to go to war against another king. Will he not first sit down and consider whether he is able with ten thousand men to oppose the one coming against him with twenty thousand? **32**If he is not able, he will send a delegation while the other is still a long way off and will ask for terms of peace. **33**In the same way, any of you who does not give up everything he has cannot be my disciple.

34"Salt is good, but if it loses its saltiness, how can it be made salty again? **35**It is fit neither for the soil nor for the manure pile; it is thrown out.

"He who has ears to hear, let him hear."

The Parable of the Lost Sheep

15 Now the tax collectors and "sinners" were all gathering around to hear him. **2**But the Pharisees and the teachers of the law muttered, "This man welcomes sinners and eats with them."

3Then Jesus told them this parable: **4**"Suppose one of you has a hundred sheep and loses one of them. Does he not leave the ninety-nine in the open country and go after the lost sheep until he finds it? **5**And when he finds it, he joyfully puts it on his shoulders **6**and goes home. Then he calls his friends and neighbors together and says, 'Rejoice with me; I have found my lost sheep.' **7**I tell you that in the same way there will be more rejoicing in heaven over one sinner who repents than over ninety-nine righteous persons who do not need to repent.

The Parable of the Lost Coin

8"Or suppose a woman has ten silver coins*a* and loses one. Does she not light

---

a 8 Greek *ten drachmas,* each worth about a day's wages

a lamp, sweep the house and search carefully until she finds it? ⁹And when she finds it, she calls her friends and neighbors together and says, 'Rejoice with me; I have found my lost coin.' ¹⁰In the same way, I tell you, there is rejoicing in the presence of the angels of God over one sinner who repents.''

The Parable of the Lost Son

¹¹Jesus continued: "There was a man who had two sons. ¹²The younger one said to his father, 'Father, give me my share of the estate.' So he divided his property between them.

¹³"Not long after that, the younger son got together all he had, set off for a distant country and there squandered his wealth in wild living. ¹⁴After he had spent everything, there was a severe famine in that whole country, and he began to be in need. ¹⁵So he went and hired himself out to a citizen of that country, who sent him to his fields to feed pigs. ¹⁶He longed to fill his stomach with the pods that the pigs were eating, but no one gave him anything.

¹⁷"When he came to his senses, he said, 'How many of my father's hired men have food to spare, and here I am starving to death! ¹⁸I will set out and go back to my father and say to him: Father, I have sinned against heaven and against you. ¹⁹I am no longer worthy to be called your son; make me like one of your hired men.' ²⁰So he got up and went to his father.

"But while he was still a long way off, his father saw him and was filled with compassion for him; he ran to his son, threw his arms around him and kissed him.

²¹"The son said to him, 'Father, I have sinned against heaven and against you. I am no longer worthy to be called your son.ᵃ'

²²"But the father said to his servants, 'Quick! Bring the best robe and put it on him. Put a ring on his finger and sandals on his feet. ²³Bring the fattened calf and kill it. Let's have a feast and celebrate. ²⁴For this son of mine was dead and is alive again; he was lost and is found.' So they began to celebrate.

²⁵"Meanwhile, the older son was in the field. When he came near the house, he heard music and dancing. ²⁶So he called one of the servants and asked him what was going on. ²⁷'Your brother has come,' he replied, 'and your father has killed the fattened calf because he has him back safe and sound.'

²⁸"The older brother became angry and refused to go in. So his father went out and pleaded with him. ²⁹But he answered his father, 'Look! All these years I've been slaving for you and never disobeyed your orders. Yet you never gave me even a young goat so I could celebrate with my friends. ³⁰But when this son of yours who has squandered your property with prostitutes comes home, you kill the fattened calf for him!'

³¹" 'My son,' the father said, 'you are always with me, and everything I have is yours. ³²But we had to celebrate and be glad, because this brother of yours was dead and is alive again; he was lost and is found.' "

The Parable of the Shrewd Manager

16 Jesus told his disciples: "There was a rich man whose manager was accused of wasting his possessions. ²So he called him in and asked him, 'What is this I hear about you? Give an account of your management, because you cannot be manager any longer.'

³"The manager said to himself, 'What shall I do now? My master is taking away my job. I'm not strong enough to dig, and I'm ashamed to beg— ⁴I know what I'll do so that, when I lose my job here, people will welcome me into their houses.'

⁵"So he called in each one of his master's debtors. He asked the first, 'How much do you owe my master?'

⁶" 'Eight hundred gallonsᵇ of olive oil,' he replied.

"The manager told him, 'Take your bill, sit down quickly, and make it four hundred.'

⁷"Then he asked the second, 'And how much do you owe?'

" 'A thousand bushelsᶜ of wheat,' he replied.

ᵃ 21 Some early manuscripts son. Make me like one of your hired men.   ᵇ 6 Greek one hundred batous (probably about 3 kiloliters)   ᶜ 7 Greek one hundred korous (probably about 35 kiloliters)

"He told him, 'Take your bill and make it eight hundred.'

8 "The master commended the dishonest manager because he had acted shrewdly. For the people of this world are more shrewd in dealing with their own kind than are the people of the light. 9 I tell you, use worldly wealth to gain friends for yourselves, so that when it is gone, you will be welcomed into eternal dwellings.

10 "Whoever can be trusted with very little can also be trusted with much, and whoever is dishonest with very little will also be dishonest with much. 11 So if you have not been trustworthy in handling worldly wealth, who will trust you with true riches? 12 And if you have not been trustworthy with someone else's property, who will give you property of your own?

13 "No servant can serve two masters. Either he will hate the one and love the other, or he will be devoted to the one and despise the other. You cannot serve both God and Money."

14 The Pharisees, who loved money, heard all this and were sneering at Jesus. 15 He said to them, "You are the ones who justify yourselves in the eyes of men, but God knows your hearts. What is highly valued among men is detestable in God's sight.

Additional Teachings

16 "The Law and the Prophets were proclaimed until John. Since that time, the good news of the kingdom of God is being preached, and everyone is forcing his way into it. 17 It is easier for heaven and earth to disappear than for the least stroke of a pen to drop out of the Law.

18 "Anyone who divorces his wife and marries another woman commits adultery, and the man who marries a divorced woman commits adultery.

The Rich Man and Lazarus

19 "There was a rich man who was dressed in purple and fine linen and lived in luxury every day. 20 At his gate was laid a beggar named Lazarus, covered with sores 21 and longing to eat what fell from the rich man's table. Even the dogs came and licked his sores.

22 "The time came when the beggar died and the angels carried him to Abraham's side. The rich man also died and was buried. 23 In hell,a where he was in torment, he looked up and saw Abraham far away, with Lazarus by his side. 24 So he called to him, 'Father Abraham, have pity on me and send Lazarus to dip the tip of his finger in water and cool my tongue, because I am in agony in this fire.'

25 "But Abraham replied, 'Son, remember that in your lifetime you received your good things, while Lazarus received bad things, but now he is comforted here and you are in agony. 26 And besides all this, between us and you a great chasm has been fixed, so that those who want to go from here to you cannot, nor can anyone cross over from there to us.'

27 "He answered, 'Then I beg you, father, send Lazarus to my father's house, 28 for I have five brothers. Let him warn them, so that they will not also come to this place of torment.'

29 "Abraham replied, 'They have Moses and the Prophets; let them listen to them.'

30 " 'No, father Abraham,' he said, 'but if someone from the dead goes to them, they will repent.'

31 "He said to him, 'If they do not listen to Moses and the Prophets, they will not be convinced even if someone rises from the dead.' "

Sin, Faith, Duty

17 Jesus said to his disciples: "Things that cause people to sin are bound to come, but woe to that person through whom they come. 2 It would be better for him to be thrown into the sea with a millstone tied around his neck than for him to cause one of these little ones to sin. 3 So watch yourselves.

"If your brother sins, rebuke him, and if he repents, forgive him. 4 If he sins against you seven times in a day, and seven times comes back to you and says, 'I repent,' forgive him."

5 The apostles said to the Lord, "Increase our faith!"

6 He replied, "If you have faith as small as a mustard seed, you can say to

a 23 Greek Hades

this mulberry tree, 'Be uprooted and planted in the sea,' and it will obey you.

7"Suppose one of you had a servant plowing or looking after the sheep. Would he say to the servant when he comes in from the field, 'Come along now and sit down to eat'? 8Would he not rather say, 'Prepare my supper, get yourself ready and wait on me while I eat and drink; after that you may eat and drink'? 9Would he thank the servant because he did what he was told to do? 10So you also, when you have done everything you were told to do, should say, 'We are unworthy servants; we have only done our duty.' "

Ten Healed of Leprosy

11Now on his way to Jerusalem, Jesus traveled along the border between Samaria and Galilee. 12As he was going into a village, ten men who had leprosy^a met him. They stood at a distance 13and called out in a loud voice, "Jesus, Master, have pity on us!"

14When he saw them, he said, "Go, show yourselves to the priests." And as they went, they were cleansed.

15One of them, when he saw he was healed, came back, praising God in a loud voice. 16He threw himself at Jesus' feet and thanked him—and he was a Samaritan.

17Jesus asked, "Were not all ten cleansed? Where are the other nine? 18Was no one found to return and give praise to God except this foreigner?" 19Then he said to him, "Rise and go; your faith has made you well."

The Coming of the Kingdom of God

20Once, having been asked by the Pharisees when the kingdom of God would come, Jesus replied, "The kingdom of God does not come with your careful observation, 21nor will people say, 'Here it is,' or 'There it is,' because the kingdom of God is within^b you."

22Then he said to his disciples, "The time is coming when you will long to see one of the days of the Son of Man, but you will not see it. 23Men will tell you, 'There he is!' or 'Here he is!' Do not

go running off after them. 24For the Son of Man in his day^c will be like the lightning, which flashes and lights up the sky from one end to the other. 25But first he must suffer many things and be rejected by this generation.

26"Just as it was in the days of Noah, so also will it be in the days of the Son of Man. 27People were eating, drinking, marrying and being given in marriage up to the day Noah entered the ark. Then the flood came and destroyed them all.

28"It was the same in the days of Lot. People were eating and drinking, buying and selling, planting and building. 29But the day Lot left Sodom, fire and sulfur rained down from heaven and destroyed them all.

30"It will be just like this on the day the Son of Man is revealed. 31On that day no one who is on the roof of his house, with his goods inside, should go down to get them. Likewise, no one in the field should go back for anything. 32Remember Lot's wife! 33Whoever tries to keep his life will lose it, and whoever loses his life will preserve it. 34I tell you, on that night two people will be in one bed; one will be taken and the other left. 35Two women will be grinding grain together; one will be taken and the other left.^d

37"Where, Lord?" they asked.

He replied, "Where there is a dead body, there the vultures will gather."

The Parable of the Persistent Widow

18 Then Jesus told his disciples a parable to show them that they should always pray and not give up.

WE OUGHT NOT TO TOLERATE FOR A MINUTE THE GHASTLY AND GRIEVOUS THOUGHT THAT GOD WILL NOT ANSWER PRAYER. HISTORY, AS MANIFESTED IN CHRIST JESUS, DEMANDS IT.

—*C. H. Spurgeon*

2He said: "In a certain town there was a judge who neither feared God nor cared about men. 3And there was a widow in that town who kept coming to him with the plea, 'Grant me justice against my adversary.'

---

^a 12 The Greek word was used for various diseases affecting the skin—not necessarily leprosy.
^b 21 Or *among*   ^c 24 Some manuscripts do not have *in his day.*   ^d 35 Some manuscripts *left.* 36*Two men will be in the field; one will be taken and the other left.*

[4]"For some time he refused. But finally he said to himself, 'Even though I don't fear God or care about men, [5]yet because this widow keeps bothering me, I will see that she gets justice, so that she won't eventually wear me out with her coming!' "

[6]And the Lord said, "Listen to what the unjust judge says. [7]And will not God bring about justice for his chosen ones, who cry out to him day and night? Will he keep putting them off? [8]I tell you, he will see that they get justice, and quickly. However, when the Son of Man comes, will he find faith on the earth?"

The Parable of the Pharisee and the Tax Collector

[9]To some who were confident of their own righteousness and looked down on everybody else, Jesus told this parable: [10]"Two men went up to the temple to pray, one a Pharisee and the other a tax collector. [11]The Pharisee stood up and prayed about[a] himself: 'God, I thank you that I am not like other men—robbers, evildoers, adulterers—or even like this tax collector. [12]I fast twice a week and give a tenth of all I get.'

IF YOUR PRAYER IS SELFISH, THE ANSWER WILL BE SOMETHING THAT WILL REBUKE YOUR SELFISHNESS. YOU MAY NOT RECOGNIZE IT AS HAVING COME AT ALL, BUT IT IS SURE TO BE THERE.

—*William Temple*

---

[13]"But the tax collector stood at a distance. He would not even look up to heaven, but beat his breast and said, 'God, have mercy on me, a sinner.'

[14]"I tell you that this man, rather than the other, went home justified before God. For everyone who exalts himself will be humbled, and he who humbles himself will be exalted."

The Little Children and Jesus

[15]People were also bringing babies to Jesus to have him touch them. When the disciples saw this, they rebuked them. [16]But Jesus called the children to him and said, "Let the little children come to me, and do not hinder them, for the kingdom of God belongs to such as these. [17]I tell you the truth, anyone who will not receive the kingdom of God like a little child will never enter it."

The Rich Ruler

[18]A certain ruler asked him, "Good teacher, what must I do to inherit eternal life?"

[19]"Why do you call me good?" Jesus answered. "No one is good—except God alone. [20]You know the commandments: 'Do not commit adultery, do not murder, do not steal, do not give false testimony, honor your father and mother.'[b]"

[21]"All these I have kept since I was a boy," he said.

[22]When Jesus heard this, he said to him, "You still lack one thing. Sell everything you have and give to the poor, and you will have treasure in heaven. Then come, follow me."

[23]When he heard this, he became very sad, because he was a man of great wealth. [24]Jesus looked at him and said, "How hard it is for the rich to enter the kingdom of God! [25]Indeed, it is easier for a camel to go through the eye of a needle than for a rich man to enter the kingdom of God."

[26]Those who heard this asked, "Who then can be saved?"

[27]Jesus replied, "What is impossible with men is possible with God."

[28]Peter said to him, "We have left all we had to follow you!"

[29]"I tell you the truth," Jesus said to them, "no one who has left home or wife or brothers or parents or children for the sake of the kingdom of God [30]will fail to receive many times as much in this age and, in the age to come, eternal life."

Jesus Again Predicts His Death

[31]Jesus took the Twelve aside and told them, "We are going up to Jerusalem, and everything that is written by the prophets about the Son of Man will be fulfilled. [32]He will be handed over to the Gentiles. They will mock him, insult him, spit on him, flog him and kill him. [33]On the third day he will rise again."

[34]The disciples did not understand

---

[a] 11 Or *to*   [b] 20 Exodus 20:12–16; Deut. 5:16–20

any of this. Its meaning was hidden from them, and they did not know what he was talking about.

A Blind Beggar Receives His Sight

35 As Jesus approached Jericho, a blind man was sitting by the roadside begging.

36 When he heard the crowd going by, he asked what was happening. 37 They told him, "Jesus of Nazareth is passing by."

38 He called out, "Jesus, Son of David, have mercy on me!"

39 Those who led the way rebuked him and told him to be quiet, but he shouted

---

WEDNESDAY

LUTHER ON PRAYER
Martin Luther

VERSE: Luke 18:1   **PASSAGE:** Luke 18:1–14

pright Christians pray without ceasing; though they pray not always with their mouths, yet their hearts pray continually, sleeping and waking; for the sigh of a true Christian is a prayer. As the Psalm saith: "Because of the deep sighing of the poor, I will rise up, saith the Lord," etc. (see Psalm 12:5, KJV). In like manner a true Christian always carries the cross, though he feel it not always.

The Lord's Prayer binds the people together, and knits them one to another, so that one prays for another and together one with another; and it is so strong and powerful that it even drives away the fear of death.

Prayer preserves the church, and hitherto has done the best for the church; therefore we must continually pray. Hence Christ says: "Ask, and ye shall have; seek, and ye shall find; knock, and it shall be opened unto you" (see Luke 11:9, KJV).

First, when we are in trouble, he will have us to pray; for God often, as it were, hides himself, and will not hear; yea, will not suffer himself to be found. Then we must seek him; that is, we must continue in prayer. When we seek him, he often locks himself up, as it were, in a private chamber; if we intend to come in unto him, then we must knock, and when we have knocked once or twice, then he begins a little to hear. At last, when we make much knocking, then he opens, and says: What will ye have? Lord, say we, we would have this or that; then, says he, Take it unto you. In such sort must we persist in praying, and waken God up.

ADDITIONAL SCRIPTURE READING:
Matthew 7:7–11; 1 Thessalonians 5:16–18

Go to page 1215 for your next devotional reading.

1500   1700

all the more, "Son of David, have mercy on me!"

⁴⁰Jesus stopped and ordered the man to be brought to him. When he came near, Jesus asked him, ⁴¹"What do you want me to do for you?"

"Lord, I want to see," he replied.

⁴²Jesus said to him, "Receive your sight; your faith has healed you." ⁴³Immediately he received his sight and followed Jesus, praising God. When all the people saw it, they also praised God.

Zacchaeus the Tax Collector

19 Jesus entered Jericho and was passing through. ²A man was there by the name of Zacchaeus; he was a chief tax collector and was wealthy. ³He wanted to see who Jesus was, but being a short man he could not, because of the crowd. ⁴So he ran ahead and climbed a sycamore-fig tree to see him, since Jesus was coming that way.

⁵When Jesus reached the spot, he looked up and said to him, "Zacchaeus, come down immediately. I must stay at your house today." ⁶So he came down at once and welcomed him gladly.

⁷All the people saw this and began to mutter, "He has gone to be the guest of a 'sinner.' "

⁸But Zacchaeus stood up and said to the Lord, "Look, Lord! Here and now I give half of my possessions to the poor, and if I have cheated anybody out of anything, I will pay back four times the amount."

⁹Jesus said to him, "Today salvation has come to this house, because this man, too, is a son of Abraham. ¹⁰For the Son of Man came to seek and to save what was lost."

The Parable of the Ten Minas

¹¹While they were listening to this, he went on to tell them a parable, because he was near Jerusalem and the people thought that the kingdom of God was going to appear at once. ¹²He said: "A man of noble birth went to a distant country to have himself appointed king and then to return. ¹³So he called ten of his servants and gave them ten minas.ᵃ 'Put this money to work,' he said, 'until I come back.'

¹⁴"But his subjects hated him and sent a delegation after him to say, 'We don't want this man to be our king.'

¹⁵"He was made king, however, and returned home. Then he sent for the servants to whom he had given the money, in order to find out what they had gained with it.

¹⁶"The first one came and said, 'Sir, your mina has earned ten more.'

¹⁷" 'Well done, my good servant!' his master replied. 'Because you have been trustworthy in a very small matter, take charge of ten cities.'

¹⁸"The second came and said, 'Sir, your mina has earned five more.'

¹⁹"His master answered, 'You take charge of five cities.'

²⁰"Then another servant came and said, 'Sir, here is your mina; I have kept it laid away in a piece of cloth. ²¹I was afraid of you, because you are a hard man. You take out what you did not put in and reap what you did not sow.'

²²"His master replied, 'I will judge you by your own words, you wicked servant! You knew, did you, that I am a hard man, taking out what I did not put in, and reaping what I did not sow? ²³Why then didn't you put my money on deposit, so that when I came back, I could have collected it with interest?'

²⁴"Then he said to those standing by, 'Take his mina away from him and give it to the one who has ten minas.'

²⁵" 'Sir,' they said, 'he already has ten!'

²⁶"He replied, 'I tell you that to everyone who has, more will be given, but as for the one who has nothing, even what he has will be taken away. ²⁷But those enemies of mine who did not want me to be king over them—bring them here and kill them in front of me.' "

The Triumphal Entry

²⁸After Jesus had said this, he went on ahead, going up to Jerusalem. ²⁹As he approached Bethphage and Bethany at the hill called the Mount of Olives, he sent two of his disciples, saying to them, ³⁰"Go to the village ahead of you, and as you enter it, you will find a colt tied there, which no one has ever ridden. Untie it and bring it here. ³¹If anyone

---

ᵃ 13 A mina was about three months' wages.

asks you, 'Why are you untying it?' tell him, 'The Lord needs it.' "

³²Those who were sent ahead went and found it just as he had told them. ³³As they were untying the colt, its owners asked them, "Why are you untying the colt?"

³⁴They replied, "The Lord needs it."

³⁵They brought it to Jesus, threw their cloaks on the colt and put Jesus on it. ³⁶As he went along, people spread their cloaks on the road.

³⁷When he came near the place where the road goes down the Mount of Olives, the whole crowd of disciples began joyfully to praise God in loud voices for all the miracles they had seen:

³⁸"Blessed is the king who comes in the name of the Lord!"ᵃ

"Peace in heaven and glory in the highest!"

³⁹Some of the Pharisees in the crowd said to Jesus, "Teacher, rebuke your disciples!"

⁴⁰"I tell you," he replied, "if they keep quiet, the stones will cry out."

⁴¹As he approached Jerusalem and saw the city, he wept over it ⁴²and said, "If you, even you, had only known on this day what would bring you peace—but now it is hidden from your eyes. ⁴³The days will come upon you when your enemies will build an embankment against you and encircle you and hem you in on every side. ⁴⁴They will dash you to the ground, you and the children within your walls. They will not leave one stone on another, because you did not recognize the time of God's coming to you."

Jesus at the Temple

⁴⁵Then he entered the temple area and began driving out those who were selling. ⁴⁶"It is written," he said to them, " 'My house will be a house of prayer'ᵇ; but you have made it 'a den of robbers.'ᶜ "

⁴⁷Every day he was teaching at the temple. But the chief priests, the teachers of the law and the leaders among the people were trying to kill him. ⁴⁸Yet they could not find any way to do it, because all the people hung on his words.

The Authority of Jesus Questioned

20 One day as he was teaching the people in the temple courts and preaching the gospel, the chief priests and the teachers of the law, together with the elders, came up to him. ²"Tell us by what authority you are doing these things," they said. "Who gave you this authority?"

³He replied, "I will also ask you a question. Tell me, ⁴John's baptism—was it from heaven, or from men?"

⁵They discussed it among themselves and said, "If we say, 'From heaven,' he will ask, 'Why didn't you believe him?' ⁶But if we say, 'From men,' all the people will stone us, because they are persuaded that John was a prophet."

⁷So they answered, "We don't know where it was from."

⁸Jesus said, "Neither will I tell you by what authority I am doing these things."

The Parable of the Tenants

⁹He went on to tell the people this parable: "A man planted a vineyard, rented it to some farmers and went away for a long time. ¹⁰At harvest time he sent a servant to the tenants so they would give him some of the fruit of the vineyard. But the tenants beat him and sent him away empty-handed. ¹¹He sent another servant, but that one also they beat and treated shamefully and sent away empty-handed. ¹²He sent still a third, and they wounded him and threw him out.

¹³"Then the owner of the vineyard said, 'What shall I do? I will send my son, whom I love; perhaps they will respect him.'

¹⁴"But when the tenants saw him, they talked the matter over. 'This is the heir,' they said. 'Let's kill him, and the inheritance will be ours.' ¹⁵So they threw him out of the vineyard and killed him.

"What then will the owner of the vineyard do to them? ¹⁶He will come and kill those tenants and give the vineyard to others."

When the people heard this, they said, "May this never be!"

ᵃ 38 Psalm 118:26   ᵇ 46 Isaiah 56:7   ᶜ 46 Jer. 7:11

17Jesus looked directly at them and asked, "Then what is the meaning of that which is written:

" 'The stone the builders rejected
    has become the capstone*a'b*?

18Everyone who falls on that stone will be broken to pieces, but he on whom it falls will be crushed."

19The teachers of the law and the chief priests looked for a way to arrest him immediately, because they knew he had spoken this parable against them. But they were afraid of the people.

Paying Taxes to Caesar

20Keeping a close watch on him, they sent spies, who pretended to be honest. They hoped to catch Jesus in something he said so that they might hand him over to the power and authority of the governor. **21**So the spies questioned him: "Teacher, we know that you speak and teach what is right, and that you do not show partiality but teach the way of God in accordance with the truth. **22**Is it right for us to pay taxes to Caesar or not?"

23He saw through their duplicity and said to them, **24**"Show me a denarius. Whose portrait and inscription are on it?"

25"Caesar's," they replied.

He said to them, "Then give to Caesar what is Caesar's, and to God what is God's."

26They were unable to trap him in what he had said there in public. And astonished by his answer, they became silent.

The Resurrection and Marriage

27Some of the Sadducees, who say there is no resurrection, came to Jesus with a question. **28**"Teacher," they said, "Moses wrote for us that if a man's brother dies and leaves a wife but no children, the man must marry the widow and have children for his brother. **29**Now there were seven brothers. The first one married a woman and died childless. **30**The second **31**and then the third married her, and in the same way the seven died, leaving no children. **32**Finally, the woman died too. **33**Now

then, at the resurrection whose wife will she be, since the seven were married to her?"

34Jesus replied, "The people of this age marry and are given in marriage. **35**But those who are considered worthy of taking part in that age and in the resurrection from the dead will neither marry nor be given in marriage, **36**and they can no longer die; for they are like the angels. They are God's children, since they are children of the resurrection. **37**But in the account of the bush, even Moses showed that the dead rise, for he calls the Lord 'the God of Abraham, and the God of Isaac, and the God of Jacob.'*c* **38**He is not the God of the dead, but of the living, for to him all are alive."

39Some of the teachers of the law responded, "Well said, teacher!" **40**And no one dared to ask him any more questions.

Whose Son Is the Christ?

41Then Jesus said to them, "How is it that they say the Christ*d* is the Son of David? **42**David himself declares in the Book of Psalms:

" 'The Lord said to my Lord:
    "Sit at my right hand
43until I make your enemies
    a footstool for your feet." '*e*

44David calls him 'Lord.' How then can he be his son?"

45While all the people were listening, Jesus said to his disciples, **46**"Beware of the teachers of the law. They like to walk around in flowing robes and love to be greeted in the marketplaces and have the most important seats in the synagogues and the places of honor at banquets. **47**They devour widows' houses and for a show make lengthy prayers. Such men will be punished most severely."

The Widow's Offering

21 As he looked up, Jesus saw the rich putting their gifts into the temple treasury. **2**He also saw a poor widow put in two very small copper coins.*f* **3**"I tell you the truth," he

---

a 17 Or *cornerstone*   *b 17* Psalm 118:22   *c 37* Exodus 3:6   *d 41* Or *Messiah*   *e 43* Psalm 110:1
f 2 Greek *two lepta*

said, "this poor widow has put in more than all the others. 4All these people gave their gifts out of their wealth; but she out of her poverty put in all she had to live on."

Signs of the End of the Age

5Some of his disciples were remarking about how the temple was adorned with beautiful stones and with gifts dedicated to God. But Jesus said, 6"As for what you see here, the time will come when not one stone will be left on another; every one of them will be thrown down."

7"Teacher," they asked, "when will these things happen? And what will be the sign that they are about to take place?"

8He replied: "Watch out that you are not deceived. For many will come in my name, claiming, 'I am he,' and, 'The time is near.' Do not follow them. 9When you hear of wars and revolutions, do not be frightened. These things must happen first, but the end will not come right away."

10Then he said to them: "Nation will rise against nation, and kingdom against kingdom. 11There will be great earthquakes, famines and pestilences in various places, and fearful events and great signs from heaven.

12"But before all this, they will lay hands on you and persecute you. They will deliver you to synagogues and prisons, and you will be brought before kings and governors, and all on account of my name. 13This will result in your being witnesses to them. 14But make up your mind not to worry beforehand how you will defend yourselves. 15For I will give you words and wisdom that none of your adversaries will be able to resist or contradict. 16You will be betrayed even by parents, brothers, relatives and friends, and they will put some of you to death. 17All men will hate you because of me. 18But not a hair of your head will perish. 19By standing firm you will gain life.

20"When you see Jerusalem being surrounded by armies, you will know that its desolation is near. 21Then let those who are in Judea flee to the mountains, let those in the city get out, and let those in the country not enter the city. 22For this is the time of punishment in fulfillment of all that has been written. 23How dreadful it will be in those days for pregnant women and nursing mothers! There will be great distress in the land and wrath against this people. 24They will fall by the sword and will be taken as prisoners to all the nations. Jerusalem will be trampled on by the Gentiles until the times of the Gentiles are fulfilled.

25"There will be signs in the sun, moon and stars. On the earth, nations will be in anguish and perplexity at the roaring and tossing of the sea. 26Men will faint from terror, apprehensive of what is coming on the world, for the heavenly bodies will be shaken. 27At that time they will see the Son of Man coming in a cloud with power and great glory. 28When these things begin to take place, stand up and lift up your heads, because your redemption is drawing near."

29He told them this parable: "Look at the fig tree and all the trees. 30When they sprout leaves, you can see for yourselves and know that summer is near. 31Even so, when you see these things happening, you know that the kingdom of God is near.

32"I tell you the truth, this generation*a* will certainly not pass away until all these things have happened. 33Heaven and earth will pass away, but my words will never pass away.

34"Be careful, or your hearts will be weighed down with dissipation, drunkenness and the anxieties of life, and that day will close on you unexpectedly like a trap. 35For it will come upon all those who live on the face of the whole earth. 36Be always on the watch, and pray that you may be able to escape all that is about to happen, and that you may be able to stand before the Son of Man."

37Each day Jesus was teaching at the temple, and each evening he went out to spend the night on the hill called the Mount of Olives, 38and all the people came early in the morning to hear him at the temple.

Judas Agrees to Betray Jesus

22 Now the Feast of Unleavened Bread, called the Passover, was approaching, 2and the chief priests

a 32 Or *race*

and the teachers of the law were looking for some way to get rid of Jesus, for they were afraid of the people. ³Then Satan entered Judas, called Iscariot, one of the Twelve. ⁴And Judas went to the chief priests and the officers of the temple guard and discussed with them how he might betray Jesus. ⁵They were delighted and agreed to give him money. ⁶He consented, and watched for an opportunity to hand Jesus over to them when no crowd was present.

The Last Supper

⁷Then came the day of Unleavened Bread on which the Passover lamb had to be sacrificed. ⁸Jesus sent Peter and John, saying, "Go and make preparations for us to eat the Passover."

⁹"Where do you want us to prepare for it?" they asked.

¹⁰He replied, "As you enter the city, a man carrying a jar of water will meet you. Follow him to the house that he enters, ¹¹and say to the owner of the house, 'The Teacher asks: Where is the guest room, where I may eat the Passover with my disciples?' ¹²He will show you a large upper room, all furnished. Make preparations there."

¹³They left and found things just as Jesus had told them. So they prepared the Passover.

¹⁴When the hour came, Jesus and his apostles reclined at the table. ¹⁵And he said to them, "I have eagerly desired to eat this Passover with you before I suffer. ¹⁶For I tell you, I will not eat it again until it finds fulfillment in the kingdom of God."

¹⁷After taking the cup, he gave thanks and said, "Take this and divide it among you. ¹⁸For I tell you I will not drink again of the fruit of the vine until the kingdom of God comes."

¹⁹And he took bread, gave thanks and broke it, and gave it to them, saying, "This is my body given for you; do this in remembrance of me."

²⁰In the same way, after the supper he took the cup, saying, "This cup is the new covenant in my blood, which is poured out for you. ²¹But the hand of him who is going to betray me is with mine on the table. ²²The Son of Man will go as it has been decreed, but woe to that man who betrays him." ²³They began to question among themselves which of them it might be who would do this.

²⁴Also a dispute arose among them as to which of them was considered to be greatest. ²⁵Jesus said to them, "The kings of the Gentiles lord it over them; and those who exercise authority over them call themselves Benefactors. ²⁶But you are not to be like that. Instead, the greatest among you should be like the youngest, and the one who rules like the one who serves. ²⁷For who is greater, the one who is at the table or the one who serves? Is it not the one who is at the table? But I am among you as one who serves. ²⁸You are those who have stood by me in my trials. ²⁹And I confer on you a kingdom, just as my Father conferred one on me, ³⁰so that you may eat and drink at my table in my kingdom and sit on thrones, judging the twelve tribes of Israel.

³¹"Simon, Simon, Satan has asked to sift you*ᵃ* as wheat. ³²But I have prayed for you, Simon, that your faith may not fail. And when you have turned back, strengthen your brothers."

³³But he replied, "Lord, I am ready to go with you to prison and to death."

³⁴Jesus answered, "I tell you, Peter, before the rooster crows today, you will deny three times that you know me."

³⁵Then Jesus asked them, "When I sent you without purse, bag or sandals, did you lack anything?"

"Nothing," they answered.

³⁶He said to them, "But now if you have a purse, take it, and also a bag; and if you don't have a sword, sell your cloak and buy one. ³⁷It is written: 'And he was numbered with the transgressors'*ᵇ*; and I tell you that this must be fulfilled in me. Yes, what is written about me is reaching its fulfillment."

³⁸The disciples said, "See, Lord, here are two swords."

"That is enough," he replied.

Jesus Prays on the Mount of Olives

³⁹Jesus went out as usual to the Mount of Olives, and his disciples followed him. ⁴⁰On reaching the place, he said to them, "Pray that you will not fall

---

ᵃ 31 The Greek is plural.   *ᵇ 37* Isaiah 53:12

into temptation." ⁴¹He withdrew about a stone's throw beyond them, knelt down and prayed, ⁴²"Father, if you are willing, take this cup from me; yet not my will, but yours be done." ⁴³An angel from heaven appeared to him and strengthened him. ⁴⁴And being in anguish, he prayed more earnestly, and his sweat was like drops of blood falling to the ground.ᵃ

⁴⁵When he rose from prayer and went back to the disciples, he found them asleep, exhausted from sorrow. ⁴⁶"Why are you sleeping?" he asked them. "Get up and pray so that you will not fall into temptation."

Jesus Arrested

⁴⁷While he was still speaking a crowd came up, and the man who was called Judas, one of the Twelve, was leading them. He approached Jesus to kiss him, ⁴⁸but Jesus asked him, "Judas, are you betraying the Son of Man with a kiss?"

⁴⁹When Jesus' followers saw what was going to happen, they said, "Lord, should we strike with our swords?" ⁵⁰And one of them struck the servant of the high priest, cutting off his right ear.

⁵¹But Jesus answered, "No more of this!" And he touched the man's ear and healed him.

⁵²Then Jesus said to the chief priests, the officers of the temple guard, and the elders, who had come for him, "Am I leading a rebellion, that you have come with swords and clubs? ⁵³Every day I was with you in the temple courts, and you did not lay a hand on me. But this is your hour—when darkness reigns."

Peter Disowns Jesus

⁵⁴Then seizing him, they led him away and took him into the house of the high priest. Peter followed at a distance. ⁵⁵But when they had kindled a fire in the middle of the courtyard and had sat down together, Peter sat down with them. ⁵⁶A servant girl saw him seated there in the firelight. She looked closely at him and said, "This man was with him."

⁵⁷But he denied it. "Woman, I don't know him," he said.

⁵⁸A little later someone else saw him and said, "You also are one of them."

"Man, I am not!" Peter replied.

⁵⁹About an hour later another asserted, "Certainly this fellow was with him, for he is a Galilean."

⁶⁰Peter replied, "Man, I don't know what you're talking about!" Just as he was speaking, the rooster crowed. ⁶¹The Lord turned and looked straight at Peter. Then Peter remembered the word the Lord had spoken to him: "Before the rooster crows today, you will disown me three times." ⁶²And he went outside and wept bitterly.

The Guards Mock Jesus

⁶³The men who were guarding Jesus began mocking and beating him. ⁶⁴They blindfolded him and demanded, "Prophesy! Who hit you?" ⁶⁵And they said many other insulting things to him.

Jesus Before Pilate and Herod

⁶⁶At daybreak the council of the elders of the people, both the chief priests and teachers of the law, met together, and Jesus was led before them. ⁶⁷"If you are the Christ,ᵇ" they said, "tell us."

Jesus answered, "If I tell you, you will not believe me, ⁶⁸and if I asked you, you would not answer. ⁶⁹But from now on, the Son of Man will be seated at the right hand of the mighty God."

⁷⁰They all asked, "Are you then the Son of God?"

He replied, "You are right in saying I am."

⁷¹Then they said, "Why do we need any more testimony? We have heard it from his own lips."

23 Then the whole assembly rose and led him off to Pilate. ²And they began to accuse him, saying, "We have found this man subverting our nation. He opposes payment of taxes to Caesar and claims to be Christ,ᶜ a king."

³So Pilate asked Jesus, "Are you the king of the Jews?"

"Yes, it is as you say," Jesus replied.

⁴Then Pilate announced to the chief

ᵃ 44 Some early manuscripts do not have verses 43 and 44. in verses 35 and 39   ᵇ 67 Or *Messiah*   ᶜ 2 Or *Messiah*; also

priests and the crowd, "I find no basis for a charge against this man."

⁵But they insisted, "He stirs up the people all over Judea*a* by his teaching. He started in Galilee and has come all the way here."

⁶On hearing this, Pilate asked if the man was a Galilean. ⁷When he learned that Jesus was under Herod's jurisdiction, he sent him to Herod, who was also in Jerusalem at that time.

⁸When Herod saw Jesus, he was greatly pleased, because for a long time he had been wanting to see him. From what he had heard about him, he hoped to see him perform some miracle. ⁹He plied him with many questions, but Jesus gave him no answer. ¹⁰The chief priests and the teachers of the law were standing there, vehemently accusing him. ¹¹Then Herod and his soldiers ridiculed and mocked him. Dressing him in an elegant robe, they sent him back to Pilate. ¹²That day Herod and Pilate became friends—before this they had been enemies.

¹³Pilate called together the chief priests, the rulers and the people, ¹⁴and said to them, "You brought me this man as one who was inciting the people to rebellion. I have examined him in your presence and have found no basis for your charges against him. ¹⁵Neither has Herod, for he sent him back to us; as you can see, he has done nothing to deserve death. ¹⁶Therefore, I will punish him and then release him.*b*"

¹⁸With one voice they cried out, "Away with this man! Release Barabbas to us!" ¹⁹(Barabbas had been thrown into prison for an insurrection in the city, and for murder.)

²⁰Wanting to release Jesus, Pilate appealed to them again. ²¹But they kept shouting, "Crucify him! Crucify him!"

²²For the third time he spoke to them: "Why? What crime has this man committed? I have found in him no grounds for the death penalty. Therefore I will have him punished and then release him."

²³But with loud shouts they insistently demanded that he be crucified, and their shouts prevailed. ²⁴So Pilate decided to grant their demand. ²⁵He released the man who had been thrown into prison for insurrection and murder, the one they asked for, and surrendered Jesus to their will.

The Crucifixion

²⁶As they led him away, they seized Simon from Cyrene, who was on his way in from the country, and put the cross on him and made him carry it behind Jesus. ²⁷A large number of people followed him, including women who mourned and wailed for him. ²⁸Jesus turned and said to them, "Daughters of Jerusalem, do not weep for me; weep for yourselves and for your children. ²⁹For the time will come when you will say, 'Blessed are the barren women, the wombs that never bore and the breasts that never nursed!' ³⁰Then

" 'they will say to the mountains,
    "Fall on us!"
and to the hills, "Cover us!" '*c*

³¹For if men do these things when the tree is green, what will happen when it is dry?"

³²Two other men, both criminals, were also led out with him to be executed. ³³When they came to the place called the Skull, there they crucified him, along with the criminals—one on his right, the other on his left. ³⁴Jesus said, "Father, forgive them, for they do not know what they are doing."*d* And they divided up his clothes by casting lots.

³⁵The people stood watching, and the rulers even sneered at him. They said, "He saved others; let him save himself if he is the Christ of God, the Chosen One."

³⁶The soldiers also came up and mocked him. They offered him wine vinegar ³⁷and said, "If you are the king of the Jews, save yourself."

³⁸There was a written notice above him, which read: THIS IS THE KING OF THE JEWS.

³⁹One of the criminals who hung there hurled insults at him: "Aren't you the Christ? Save yourself and us!"

⁴⁰But the other criminal rebuked him. "Don't you fear God," he said, "since

GOOD AND EVIL CHANGED PLACES
Leo Tolstoy

VERSE: Luke 23:43   PASSAGE: Luke 23:39–43

 ive years ago I came to believe in Christ's teaching, and my life suddenly changed; I ceased to desire what I had previously desired, and began to desire what I formerly did not want. What had previously seemed to me good seemed evil, and what had seemed evil seemed good. It happened to me as it happens to a man who goes out on some business and on the way suddenly decides that the business is unnecessary and returns home. All that was on his right is now on his left, and all that was on his left is now on his right; his former wish to get as far as possible from home has changed into a wish to be as near as possible to it. The direction of my life and my desires became different, and good and evil changed places . . .

I, like that thief on the cross, have believed Christ's teaching and been saved. And this is no far-fetched comparison, but the closest expression of the condition of spiritual despair and horror at the problem of life and death in which I lived formerly, and of the condition of peace and happiness in which I am now. I, like the thief, knew that I was unhappy and suffering . . . I, like the thief to the cross, was nailed by some force to that life of suffering and evil. And as, after the meaningless sufferings and evils of life, the thief awaited the terrible darkness of death, so did I await the same thing.

In all this I was exactly like the thief, but the difference was that the thief was already dying, while I was still living. The thief might believe that his salvation lay there beyond the grave, but I could not be satisfied with that, because besides a life beyond the grave life still awaited me here. But I did not understand that life. It seemed to me terrible. And suddenly I heard the words of Christ and understood them, and life and death ceased to seem to me evil, and instead of despair I experienced happiness and the joy of life undisturbed by death.

ADDITIONAL SCRIPTURE READING:
Psalm 56:13; 1 Peter 1:8–9

Go to page 1217 for your next devotional reading.

1700   1900

you are under the same sentence? **41**We are punished justly, for we are getting what our deeds deserve. But this man has done nothing wrong."

42Then he said, "Jesus, remember me when you come into your kingdom.*a*"

43Jesus answered him, "I tell you the truth, today you will be with me in paradise."

Jesus' Death

44It was now about the sixth hour, and darkness came over the whole land until the ninth hour, **45**for the sun stopped shining. And the curtain of the temple was torn in two. **46**Jesus called out with a loud voice, "Father, into your hands I commit my spirit." When he had said this, he breathed his last.

47The centurion, seeing what had happened, praised God and said, "Surely this was a righteous man." **48**When all the people who had gathered to witness this sight saw what took place, they beat their breasts and went away. **49**But all those who knew him, including the women who had followed him from Galilee, stood at a distance, watching these things.

Jesus' Burial

50Now there was a man named Joseph, a member of the Council, a good and upright man, **51**who had not consented to their decision and action. He came from the Judean town of Arimathea and he was waiting for the kingdom of God. **52**Going to Pilate, he asked for Jesus' body. **53**Then he took it down, wrapped it in linen cloth and placed it in a tomb cut in the rock, one in which no one had yet been laid. **54**It was Preparation Day, and the Sabbath was about to begin.

55The women who had come with Jesus from Galilee followed Joseph and saw the tomb and how his body was laid in it. **56**Then they went home and prepared spices and perfumes. But they rested on the Sabbath in obedience to the commandment.

The Resurrection

24 On the first day of the week, very early in the morning, the women took the spices they had prepared and went to the tomb. **2**They found the stone rolled away from the tomb, **3**but when they entered, they did not find the body of the Lord Jesus. **4**While they were wondering about this, suddenly two men in clothes that gleamed like lightning stood beside them. **5**In their fright the women bowed down with their faces to the ground, but the men said to them, "Why do you look for the living among the dead? **6**He is not here; he has risen! Remember how he told you, while he was still with you in Galilee: **7**'The Son of Man must be delivered into the hands of sinful men, be crucified and on the third day be raised again.' " **8**Then they remembered his words.

TOMB, THOU SHALT NOT HOLD HIM LONGER;
DEATH IS STRONG, BUT LIFE IS STRONGER;
STRONGER THAN THE DARK, THE LIGHT;
STRONGER THAN THE WRONG, THE RIGHT;
FAITH AND HOPE TRIUMPHANT SAY
CHRIST WILL RISE ON EASTER DAY.
—*Phillips Brooks*

9When they came back from the tomb, they told all these things to the Eleven and to all the others. **10**It was Mary Magdalene, Joanna, Mary the mother of James, and the others with them who told this to the apostles. **11**But they did not believe the women, because their words seemed to them like nonsense. **12**Peter, however, got up and ran to the tomb. Bending over, he saw the strips of linen lying by themselves, and he went away, wondering to himself what had happened.

On the Road to Emmaus

13Now that same day two of them were going to a village called Emmaus, about seven miles*b* from Jerusalem. **14**They were talking with each other about everything that had happened. **15**As they talked and discussed these things with each other, Jesus himself came up and walked along with them; **16**but they were kept from recognizing him. **17**He asked them, "What are you discussing together as you walk along?"

---

a 42 Some manuscripts *come with your kingly power*   *b 13* Greek *sixty stadia* (about 11 kilometers)

WALKING WITH JESUS
Jacob Boehme

VERSE: Luke 24:15   **PASSAGE:** Luke 24:13–16

At Noon

God, the source of eternal light, you provide temporal light for the earth, ruling over the sun and the
moon that all creatures may live and thrive. The
warmth and brightness of the sun makes the flowers
bloom and the crops grow. And the gentle beams of the moon
and stars remind us that your Word is alive and active even
when we can see only dimly. Guide me to find my rightful
place in your creation, that in some small way I may add to
the beauty of your handiwork. And may your eternal light
shine in the darkest corners of my soul, that all shadow of sin
may be expelled.

At Evening

I thank you, O God, for your care and protection this day, keeping me from physical harm and spiritual corruption. I now place
the work of the day into your hands, trusting that you will
redeem my errors and turn my achievements to your glory. And
I now ask you to work within me, trusting that you will use the
hours of rest to create in me a new heart and new soul. Let my
mind, which through the day has been directed to my work,
through the evening be wholly directed at you.

At Bedtime

As I take off my dusty, dirty clothes, let me also be stripped of
the sins I have committed this day. I confess, dear Lord, that in
so many ways my thoughts and actions have been impure. Now
I come before you, naked in body and bare in soul, to be washed
clean. Let me rest tonight in your arms, and so may the dreams
that pass through my mind be holy. And let me awake tomorrow, strong and eager to serve you.

ADDITIONAL SCRIPTURE READING:
Psalms 15:1–3; 43:3

Go to page 1220 for your next devotional reading.

1500   1700

They stood still, their faces downcast. ¹⁸One of them, named Cleopas, asked him, "Are you only a visitor to Jerusalem and do not know the things that have happened there in these days?"

¹⁹"What things?" he asked.

"About Jesus of Nazareth," they replied. "He was a prophet, powerful in word and deed before God and all the people. ²⁰The chief priests and our rulers handed him over to be sentenced to death, and they crucified him; ²¹but we had hoped that he was the one who was going to redeem Israel. And what is more, it is the third day since all this took place. ²²In addition, some of our women amazed us. They went to the tomb early this morning ²³but didn't find his body. They came and told us that they had seen a vision of angels, who said he was alive. ²⁴Then some of our companions went to the tomb and found it just as the women had said, but him they did not see."

²⁵He said to them, "How foolish you are, and how slow of heart to believe all that the prophets have spoken! ²⁶Did not the Christ*a* have to suffer these things and then enter his glory?" ²⁷And beginning with Moses and all the Prophets, he explained to them what was said in all the Scriptures concerning himself.

²⁸As they approached the village to which they were going, Jesus acted as if he were going farther. ²⁹But they urged him strongly, "Stay with us, for it is nearly evening; the day is almost over." So he went in to stay with them.

³⁰When he was at the table with them, he took bread, gave thanks, broke it and began to give it to them. ³¹Then their eyes were opened and they recognized him, and he disappeared from their sight. ³²They asked each other, "Were not our hearts burning within us while he talked with us on the road and opened the Scriptures to us?"

³³They got up and returned at once to Jerusalem. There they found the Eleven and those with them, assembled together ³⁴and saying, "It is true! The Lord has risen and has appeared to Simon." ³⁵Then the two told what had happened on the way, and how Jesus was recognized by them when he broke the bread.

Jesus Appears to the Disciples

³⁶While they were still talking about this, Jesus himself stood among them and said to them, "Peace be with you."

³⁷They were startled and frightened, thinking they saw a ghost. ³⁸He said to them, "Why are you troubled, and why do doubts rise in your minds? ³⁹Look at my hands and my feet. It is I myself! Touch me and see; a ghost does not have flesh and bones, as you see I have."

⁴⁰When he had said this, he showed them his hands and feet. ⁴¹And while they still did not believe it because of joy and amazement, he asked them, "Do you have anything here to eat?" ⁴²They gave him a piece of broiled fish, ⁴³and he took it and ate it in their presence.

⁴⁴He said to them, "This is what I told you while I was still with you: Everything must be fulfilled that is written about me in the Law of Moses, the Prophets and the Psalms."

⁴⁵Then he opened their minds so they could understand the Scriptures. ⁴⁶He told them, "This is what is written: The Christ will suffer and rise from the dead on the third day, ⁴⁷and repentance and forgiveness of sins will be preached in his name to all nations, beginning at Jerusalem. ⁴⁸You are witnesses of these things. ⁴⁹I am going to send you what my Father has promised; but stay in the city until you have been clothed with power from on high."

IN THE OLD TESTAMENT THE NEW LIES HIDDEN, IN THE NEW TESTAMENT THE OLD IS LAID OPEN.

—*Augustine*

The Ascension

⁵⁰When he had led them out to the vicinity of Bethany, he lifted up his hands and blessed them. ⁵¹While he was blessing them, he left them and was taken up into heaven. ⁵²Then they worshiped him and returned to Jerusalem with great joy. ⁵³And they stayed continually at the temple, praising God.

a 26 Or *Messiah*; also in verse 46

JOHN

HY DID GOD'S SON COME TO
EARTH? JOHN'S GOSPEL HAS THE
ANSWER. "FOR GOD SO LOVED THE
WORLD THAT HE GAVE HIS ONE AND ONLY
SON, THAT WHOEVER BELIEVES IN HIM SHALL
NOT PERISH BUT HAVE ETERNAL LIFE" (3:16).
JOHN'S WRITINGS ARE DESIGNED TO CON-
VINCE PEOPLE TO BELIEVE IN JESUS AS GOD IN
HUMAN FORM AND TO "HAVE LIFE" AS A
RESULT (20:31). REFLECT ON THE ONE WHO
ONCE LIVED AMONG PEOPLE LIKE US, AND
RENEW YOUR TRUST THAT HE WILL GIVE YOU
LIFE TO THE FULL.

The Word Became Flesh

1 In the beginning was the Word, and the Word was with God, and the Word was God. ²He was with God in the beginning.

³Through him all things were made; without him nothing was made that has been made. ⁴In him was life, and that life was the light of men. ⁵The light shines in the darkness, but the darkness has not understood*a* it.

⁶There came a man who was sent from God; his name was John. ⁷He came as a witness to testify concerning that light, so that through him all men might believe. ⁸He himself was not the light; he came only as a witness to the light.

⁹The true light that gives light to every man was coming into the world.*b*

¹⁰He was in the world, and though the world was made through him, the world did not recognize him. ¹¹He came to that which was his own, but his own did not receive him. ¹²Yet to all who received him, to those who believed in his name, he gave the right to become children of God— ¹³children born not of natural descent,*c* nor of human decision or a husband's will, but born of God.

¹⁴The Word became flesh and made his dwelling among us. We have seen his glory, the glory of the One and Only,*d* who came from the Father, full of grace and truth.

¹⁵John testifies concerning him. He

---

a 5 Or *darkness, and the darkness has not overcome every man who comes into the world*   *b 9* Or *This was the true light that gives light to*   *c 13* Greek *of bloods*   *d 14* Or *the Only Begotten*

WEEKEND

THE WORD OF GOD IS GOD IN ACTION
F. F. Bruce

VERSE: John 1:1   **PASSAGE:** John 1:1–2

---

 n the beginning," . . . when the universe was brought into existence, the divine Word by which it was brought into existence was already there. And the language which follows shows that our Evangelist has no mere literary personification in mind. The personal status which he ascribes to the Word is a matter of real existence; the relation which the Word bears to God is a personal relation: "the Word was with God."

This statement has profound theological implications . . . The Word of God is distinguished from God himself, and yet exists in a close personal relation with him; moreover, the Word shares the very nature of God, for "the Word was *God*."

The structure of the third clause in verse 1 . . . demands the translation "the Word was God." Since *logos* [Word] has the article preceding it, it is marked out as the subject . . . Had *theos* [God] as well as *logos* been preceded by the article the meaning would have been that the Word was completely identical with God, which is impossible if the Word was also "with God." What is meant is that the Word shared the nature and being of God, or (to use a piece of modern jargon) was an extension of the personality of God . . .

So, when heaven and earth were created, there was the Word of God, already existing in the closest association with God and partaking of the essence of God. No matter how far back we may try to push our imagination, we can never reach a point at which we could say of the Divine Word, as Arius did, "There was once when he was not."

ADDITIONAL SCRIPTURE READING:
Isaiah 55:11; Revelation 1:8

Go to page 1224 for your next devotional reading.

1900   Present

cries out, saying, "This was he of whom I said, 'He who comes after me has surpassed me because he was before me.' " [16]From the fullness of his grace we have all received one blessing after another. [17]For the law was given through Moses; grace and truth came through Jesus Christ. [18]No one has ever seen God, but God the One and Only,[a,b] who is at the Father's side, has made him known.

DEITY INDWELLING MEN! THAT, I SAY IS CHRISTIANITY!   —A. W. Tozer

---

John the Baptist Denies Being the Christ

[19]Now this was John's testimony when the Jews of Jerusalem sent priests and Levites to ask him who he was. [20]He did not fail to confess, but confessed freely, "I am not the Christ.[c] "

[21]They asked him, "Then who are you? Are you Elijah?"

He said, "I am not."

"Are you the Prophet?"

He answered, "No."

[22]Finally they said, "Who are you? Give us an answer to take back to those who sent us. What do you say about yourself?"

[23]John replied in the words of Isaiah the prophet, "I am the voice of one calling in the desert, 'Make straight the way for the Lord.' "[d]

[24]Now some Pharisees who had been sent [25]questioned him, "Why then do you baptize if you are not the Christ, nor Elijah, nor the Prophet?"

[26]"I baptize with[e] water," John replied, "but among you stands one you do not know. [27]He is the one who comes after me, the thongs of whose sandals I am not worthy to untie."

[28]This all happened at Bethany on the other side of the Jordan, where John was baptizing.

Jesus the Lamb of God

[29]The next day John saw Jesus coming toward him and said, "Look, the Lamb of God, who takes away the sin of the world! [30]This is the one I meant when I said, 'A man who comes after me has surpassed me because he was before me.' [31]I myself did not know him, but the reason I came baptizing with water was that he might be revealed to Israel."

[32]Then John gave this testimony: "I saw the Spirit come down from heaven as a dove and remain on him. [33]I would not have known him, except that the one who sent me to baptize with water told me, 'The man on whom you see the Spirit come down and remain is he who will baptize with the Holy Spirit.' [34]I have seen and I testify that this is the Son of God."

Jesus' First Disciples

[35]The next day John was there again with two of his disciples. [36]When he saw Jesus passing by, he said, "Look, the Lamb of God!"

[37]When the two disciples heard him say this, they followed Jesus. [38]Turning around, Jesus saw them following and asked, "What do you want?"

They said, "Rabbi" (which means Teacher), "where are you staying?"

[39]"Come," he replied, "and you will see."

So they went and saw where he was staying, and spent that day with him. It was about the tenth hour.

[40]Andrew, Simon Peter's brother, was one of the two who heard what John had said and who had followed Jesus. [41]The first thing Andrew did was to find his brother Simon and tell him, "We have found the Messiah" (that is, the Christ). [42]And he brought him to Jesus.

Jesus looked at him and said, "You are Simon son of John. You will be called Cephas" (which, when translated, is Peter[f]).

Jesus Calls Philip and Nathanael

[43]The next day Jesus decided to leave for Galilee. Finding Philip, he said to him, "Follow me."

[44]Philip, like Andrew and Peter, was from the town of Bethsaida. [45]Philip

---

[a] 18 Or the Only Begotten   [b] 18 Some manuscripts but the only (or only begotten) Son   [c] 20 Or Messiah. "The Christ" (Greek) and "the Messiah" (Hebrew) both mean "the Anointed One"; also in verse 25.   [d] 23 Isaiah 40:3   [e] 26 Or in; also in verses 31 and 33   [f] 42 Both Cephas (Aramaic) and Peter (Greek) mean rock.

found Nathanael and told him, "We have found the one Moses wrote about in the Law, and about whom the prophets also wrote—Jesus of Nazareth, the son of Joseph."

46"Nazareth! Can anything good come from there?" Nathanael asked.

"Come and see," said Philip.

47When Jesus saw Nathanael approaching, he said of him, "Here is a true Israelite, in whom there is nothing false."

48"How do you know me?" Nathanael asked.

Jesus answered, "I saw you while you were still under the fig tree before Philip called you."

49Then Nathanael declared, "Rabbi, you are the Son of God; you are the King of Israel."

50Jesus said, "You believe*a* because I told you I saw you under the fig tree. You shall see greater things than that." 51He then added, "I tell you*b* the truth, you*b* shall see heaven open, and the angels of God ascending and descending on the Son of Man."

Jesus Changes Water to Wine

2 On the third day a wedding took place at Cana in Galilee. Jesus' mother was there, 2and Jesus and his disciples had also been invited to the wedding. 3When the wine was gone, Jesus' mother said to him, "They have no more wine."

4"Dear woman, why do you involve me?" Jesus replied. "My time has not yet come."

5His mother said to the servants, "Do whatever he tells you."

6Nearby stood six stone water jars, the kind used by the Jews for ceremonial washing, each holding from twenty to thirty gallons.*c*

7Jesus said to the servants, "Fill the jars with water"; so they filled them to the brim.

8Then he told them, "Now draw some out and take it to the master of the banquet."

They did so, 9and the master of the banquet tasted the water that had been turned into wine. He did not realize where it had come from, though the ser-

vants who had drawn the water knew. Then he called the bridegroom aside 10and said, "Everyone brings out the choice wine first and then the cheaper wine after the guests have had too much to drink; but you have saved the best till now."

11This, the first of his miraculous signs, Jesus performed at Cana in Galilee. He thus revealed his glory, and his disciples put their faith in him.

Jesus Clears the Temple

12After this he went down to Capernaum with his mother and brothers and his disciples. There they stayed for a few days.

13When it was almost time for the Jewish Passover, Jesus went up to Jerusalem. 14In the temple courts he found men selling cattle, sheep and doves, and others sitting at tables exchanging money. 15So he made a whip out of cords, and drove all from the temple area, both sheep and cattle; he scattered the coins of the money changers and overturned their tables. 16To those who sold doves he said, "Get these out of here! How dare you turn my Father's house into a market!"

17His disciples remembered that it is written: "Zeal for your house will consume me."*d*

18Then the Jews demanded of him, "What miraculous sign can you show us to prove your authority to do all this?"

19Jesus answered them, "Destroy this temple, and I will raise it again in three days."

20The Jews replied, "It has taken forty-six years to build this temple, and you are going to raise it in three days?" 21But the temple he had spoken of was his body. 22After he was raised from the dead, his disciples recalled what he had said. Then they believed the Scripture and the words that Jesus had spoken.

23Now while he was in Jerusalem at the Passover Feast, many people saw the miraculous signs he was doing and believed in his name.*e* 24But Jesus would not entrust himself to them, for he knew all men. 25He did not need man's testimony about man, for he knew what was in a man.

---

a 50 Or *Do you believe . . . ?*   *b* 51 The Greek is plural.   *c* 6 Greek *two to three metretes* (probably about 75 to 115 liters)   *d* 17 Psalm 69:9   *e* 23 Or *and believed in him*

Jesus Teaches Nicodemus

3 Now there was a man of the Pharisees named Nicodemus, a member of the Jewish ruling council. ²He came to Jesus at night and said, "Rabbi, we know you are a teacher who has come from God. For no one could perform the miraculous signs you are doing if God were not with him."

³In reply Jesus declared, "I tell you the truth, no one can see the kingdom of God unless he is born again.*ᵃ*"

⁴"How can a man be born when he is old?" Nicodemus asked. "Surely he cannot enter a second time into his mother's womb to be born!"

⁵Jesus answered, "I tell you the truth, no one can enter the kingdom of God unless he is born of water and the Spirit. ⁶Flesh gives birth to flesh, but the Spirit*ᵇ* gives birth to spirit. ⁷You should not be surprised at my saying, 'You*ᶜ* must be born again.' ⁸The wind blows wherever it pleases. You hear its sound, but you cannot tell where it comes from or where it is going. So it is with everyone born of the Spirit."

THE EGG'S NO CHICK BY FALLING FROM THE
HEN,

NOR MAN A CHRISTIAN TILL HE'S BORN AGAIN.

—*John Bunyan*

---

⁹"How can this be?" Nicodemus asked.

¹⁰"You are Israel's teacher," said Jesus, "and do you not understand these things? ¹¹I tell you the truth, we speak of what we know, and we testify to what we have seen, but still you people do not accept our testimony. ¹²I have spoken to you of earthly things and you do not believe; how then will you believe if I speak of heavenly things? ¹³No one has ever gone into heaven except the one who came from heaven—the Son of Man.*ᵈ* ¹⁴Just as Moses lifted up the snake in the desert, so the Son of Man must be lifted up, ¹⁵that everyone who believes in him may have eternal life.*ᵉ*

¹⁶"For God so loved the world that he gave his one and only Son,*ᶠ* that whoever believes in him shall not perish but have eternal life. ¹⁷For God did not send his Son into the world to condemn the world, but to save the world through him. ¹⁸Whoever believes in him is not condemned, but whoever does not believe stands condemned already because he has not believed in the name of God's one and only Son.*ᵍ* ¹⁹This is the verdict: Light has come into the world, but men loved darkness instead of light because their deeds were evil. ²⁰Everyone who does evil hates the light, and will not come into the light for fear that his deeds will be exposed. ²¹But whoever lives by the truth comes into the light, so that it may be seen plainly that what he has done has been done through God."*ʰ*

John the Baptist's Testimony About Jesus

²²After this, Jesus and his disciples went out into the Judean countryside, where he spent some time with them, and baptized. ²³Now John also was baptizing at Aenon near Salim, because there was plenty of water, and people were constantly coming to be baptized. ²⁴(This was before John was put in prison.) ²⁵An argument developed between some of John's disciples and a certain Jew*ⁱ* over the matter of ceremonial washing. ²⁶They came to John and said to him, "Rabbi, that man who was with you on the other side of the Jordan—the one you testified about—well, he is baptizing, and everyone is going to him."

²⁷To this John replied, "A man can receive only what is given him from heaven. ²⁸You yourselves can testify that I said, 'I am not the Christ*ʲ* but am sent ahead of him.' ²⁹The bride belongs to the bridegroom. The friend who attends the bridegroom waits and listens for him, and is full of joy when he hears the bridegroom's voice. That joy is mine, and it is now complete. ³⁰He must become greater; I must become less.

³¹"The one who comes from above is above all; the one who is from the earth

---

ᵃ 3 Or *born from above;* also in verse 7   *ᵇ 6* Or *but spirit*   *ᶜ 7* The Greek is plural.   *ᵈ 13* Some manuscripts *Man, who is in heaven*   *ᵉ 15* Or *believes may have eternal life in him*   *ᶠ 16* Or *his only begotten Son*   *ᵍ 18* Or *God's only begotten Son*   *ʰ 21* Some interpreters end the quotation after verse 15.   *ⁱ 25* Some manuscripts *and certain Jews*   *ʲ 28* Or *Messiah*

belongs to the earth, and speaks as one from the earth. The one who comes from heaven is above all. ³²He testifies to what he has seen and heard, but no one accepts his testimony. ³³The man who has accepted it has certified that

MONDAY

A WAY OF LIFE
Sir William Osler

VERSE: John 3:5   **PASSAGE:** John 3:1–7

 o you remember that most touching of all incidents in Christ's ministry, when the anxious ruler Nicodemus came by night, worried lest the things that pertained to his everlasting peace were not a part of his busy and successful life? Christ's message to him is his message to the world—never more needed than at present: "You must be born of the Spirit." You wish to be with the leaders . . . know the great souls that make up the moral radium of the world. You must be born of their spirit, initiated into their fraternity, whether of the spiritually minded followers of the Nazarene or of that larger company, elect from every nation, seen by St. John.

Begin the day with Christ and [the Lord's] prayer—you need no other. Creedless, with it you have religion; creed-stuffed, it will leaven any theological dough in which you stick. As the soul is dyed by the thoughts, let no day pass without contact with the best literature of the world. Learn to know your Bible, though not perhaps as your fathers did. In forming character and in shaping conduct, its touch has still its ancient power. Of the kindred of Ram and sons of Elihu, you should know its beauties and its strength. Fifteen or twenty minutes day by day will give you fellowship with the great minds of the race, and little by little as the years pass you extend your friendship with the immortal dead. They will give you faith in your own day. Listen while they speak to you of the fathers . . . Mankind, it has been said, is always advancing, man is always the same. The love, hope, fear, and faith that make humanity, and the elemental passions of the human heart, remain unchanged, and the secret of inspiration in any literature is the capacity to touch the cord that vibrates in a sympathy that knows no time nor place . . .

ADDITIONAL SCRIPTURE READING:
2 Timothy 3:16; James 1:22–25

Go to page 1226 for your next devotional reading.

1900   Present

God is truthful. **34**For the one whom God has sent speaks the words of God, for God*a* gives the Spirit without limit. **35**The Father loves the Son and has placed everything in his hands. **36**Whoever believes in the Son has eternal life, but whoever rejects the Son will not see life, for God's wrath remains on him."*b*

Jesus Talks With a Samaritan Woman

4 The Pharisees heard that Jesus was gaining and baptizing more disciples than John, **2**although in fact it was not Jesus who baptized, but his disciples. **3**When the Lord learned of this, he left Judea and went back once more to Galilee.

4Now he had to go through Samaria. **5**So he came to a town in Samaria called Sychar, near the plot of ground Jacob had given to his son Joseph. **6**Jacob's well was there, and Jesus, tired as he was from the journey, sat down by the well. It was about the sixth hour.

7When a Samaritan woman came to draw water, Jesus said to her, "Will you give me a drink?" **8**(His disciples had gone into the town to buy food.)

9The Samaritan woman said to him, "You are a Jew and I am a Samaritan woman. How can you ask me for a drink?" (For Jews do not associate with Samaritans.*c*)

10Jesus answered her, "If you knew the gift of God and who it is that asks you for a drink, you would have asked him and he would have given you living water."

11"Sir," the woman said, "you have nothing to draw with and the well is deep. Where can you get this living water? **12**Are you greater than our father Jacob, who gave us the well and drank from it himself, as did also his sons and his flocks and herds?"

13Jesus answered, "Everyone who drinks this water will be thirsty again, **14**but whoever drinks the water I give him will never thirst. Indeed, the water I give him will become in him a spring of water welling up to eternal life."

15The woman said to him, "Sir, give me this water so that I won't get thirsty

and have to keep coming here to draw water."

16He told her, "Go, call your husband and come back."

17"I have no husband," she replied.

Jesus said to her, "You are right when you say you have no husband. **18**The fact is, you have had five husbands, and the man you now have is not your husband. What you have just said is quite true."

19"Sir," the woman said, "I can see that you are a prophet. **20**Our fathers worshiped on this mountain, but you Jews claim that the place where we must worship is in Jerusalem."

21Jesus declared, "Believe me, woman, a time is coming when you will worship the Father neither on this mountain nor in Jerusalem. **22**You Samaritans worship what you do not know; we worship what we do know, for salvation is from the Jews. **23**Yet a time is coming and has now come when the true worshipers will worship the Father in spirit and truth, for they are the kind of worshipers the Father seeks. **24**God is spirit, and his worshipers must worship in spirit and in truth."

25The woman said, "I know that Messiah" (called Christ) "is coming. When he comes, he will explain everything to us."

26Then Jesus declared, "I who speak to you am he."

The Disciples Rejoin Jesus

27Just then his disciples returned and were surprised to find him talking with a woman. But no one asked, "What do you want?" or "Why are you talking with her?"

28Then, leaving her water jar, the woman went back to the town and said to the people, **29**"Come, see a man who told me everything I ever did. Could this be the Christ*d*?" **30**They came out of the town and made their way toward him.

31Meanwhile his disciples urged him, "Rabbi, eat something."

32But he said to them, "I have food to eat that you know nothing about."

33Then his disciples said to each other, "Could someone have brought him food?"

---

a 34 Greek *he*   *b 36* Some interpreters end the quotation after verse 30.   *c 9* Or *do not use dishes Samaritans have used*   *d 29* Or *Messiah*

THE ESSENCE OF TRUE WORSHIP
F. F. Bruce

VERSE: John 4:24   **PASSAGE:** John 4:21–24

he answer [about worship] that the Samaritan woman received was quite different from anything that she could have expected. The time when there was any point in the argument about the claims of Gerizim versus those of Zion had come to an end. A new order was now being introduced which rendered such questions out-of-date and meaningless. The important question is not *where* people worship God but *how* they worship him . . .

The prophets had spoken of a coming day when not one central sanctuary alone, but the whole earth, would be the habitation of the name and glory of God (see Isaiah 6:3; Habakkuk 2:14). While the manifest consummation of this hope, associated as it is with the universal knowledge of God, lies in the future even from our perspective, yet to faith the conditions of that coming age are present already . . . Spiritual worship, genuine worship, cannot be tied to set places and seasons. And such worship is seen to be the more appropriate when we consider the nature of the God to whom it is offered.

"God is spirit": it is not merely that he is *a* spirit among other spirits; rather, God himself is pure spirit, and the worship in which he takes delight is accordingly spiritual worship—the sacrifice of a humble, contrite, grateful and adoring spirit. This affirmation of our Lord's was not entirely new; it but crowns the witness of psalmists and prophets in earlier ages, who saw that material things could at best be the vehicle of true worship but could never belong to its essence. Sincere heart-devotion, whenever and wherever found, is indispensable if men and woman would present to God worship which he can accept.

ADDITIONAL SCRIPTURE READING:
Psalm 86:9; Romans 12:1

Go to page 1234 for your next devotional reading.

1900   Present

³⁴"My food," said Jesus, "is to do the will of him who sent me and to finish his work. ³⁵Do you not say, 'Four months more and then the harvest'? I tell you, open your eyes and look at the fields! They are ripe for harvest. ³⁶Even now the reaper draws his wages, even now he harvests the crop for eternal life, so that the sower and the reaper may be glad together. ³⁷Thus the saying 'One sows and another reaps' is true. ³⁸I sent you to reap what you have not worked for. Others have done the hard work, and you have reaped the benefits of their labor."

Many Samaritans Believe

³⁹Many of the Samaritans from that town believed in him because of the woman's testimony, "He told me everything I ever did." ⁴⁰So when the Samaritans came to him, they urged him to stay with them, and he stayed two days. ⁴¹And because of his words many more became believers.

⁴²They said to the woman, "We no longer believe just because of what you said; now we have heard for ourselves, and we know that this man really is the Savior of the world."

Jesus Heals the Official's Son

⁴³After the two days he left for Galilee. ⁴⁴(Now Jesus himself had pointed out that a prophet has no honor in his own country.) ⁴⁵When he arrived in Galilee, the Galileans welcomed him. They had seen all that he had done in Jerusalem at the Passover Feast, for they also had been there.

⁴⁶Once more he visited Cana in Galilee, where he had turned the water into wine. And there was a certain royal official whose son lay sick at Capernaum. ⁴⁷When this man heard that Jesus had arrived in Galilee from Judea, he went to him and begged him to come and heal his son, who was close to death.

⁴⁸"Unless you people see miraculous signs and wonders," Jesus told him, "you will never believe."

⁴⁹The royal official said, "Sir, come down before my child dies."

⁵⁰Jesus replied, "You may go. Your son will live."

The man took Jesus at his word and departed. ⁵¹While he was still on the way, his servants met him with the news that his boy was living. ⁵²When he inquired as to the time when his son got better, they said to him, "The fever left him yesterday at the seventh hour."

⁵³Then the father realized that this was the exact time at which Jesus had said to him, "Your son will live." So he and all his household believed.

⁵⁴This was the second miraculous sign that Jesus performed, having come from Judea to Galilee.

The Healing at the Pool

5 Some time later, Jesus went up to Jerusalem for a feast of the Jews. ²Now there is in Jerusalem near the Sheep Gate a pool, which in Aramaic is called Bethesda^a^ and which is surrounded by five covered colonnades. ³Here a great number of disabled people used to lie—the blind, the lame, the paralyzed.^b^ ⁵One who was there had been an invalid for thirty-eight years. ⁶When Jesus saw him lying there and learned that he had been in this condition for a long time, he asked him, "Do you want to get well?"

⁷"Sir," the invalid replied, "I have no one to help me into the pool when the water is stirred. While I am trying to get in, someone else goes down ahead of me."

⁸Then Jesus said to him, "Get up! Pick up your mat and walk." ⁹At once the man was cured; he picked up his mat and walked.

The day on which this took place was a Sabbath, ¹⁰and so the Jews said to the man who had been healed, "It is the Sabbath; the law forbids you to carry your mat."

¹¹But he replied, "The man who made me well said to me, 'Pick up your mat and walk.' "

¹²So they asked him, "Who is this fellow who told you to pick it up and walk?"

---

^a^ 2 Some manuscripts *Bethzatha*; other manuscripts *Bethsaida*   ^b^ 3 Some less important manuscripts *paralyzed—and they waited for the moving of the waters.* ⁴*From time to time an angel of the Lord would come down and stir up the waters. The first one into the pool after each such disturbance would be cured of whatever disease he had.*

[13]The man who was healed had no idea who it was, for Jesus had slipped away into the crowd that was there.

[14]Later Jesus found him at the temple and said to him, "See, you are well again. Stop sinning or something worse may happen to you." [15]The man went away and told the Jews that it was Jesus who had made him well.

Life Through the Son

[16]So, because Jesus was doing these things on the Sabbath, the Jews persecuted him. [17]Jesus said to them, "My Father is always at his work to this very day, and I, too, am working." [18]For this reason the Jews tried all the harder to kill him; not only was he breaking the Sabbath, but he was even calling God his own Father, making himself equal with God.

[19]Jesus gave them this answer: "I tell you the truth, the Son can do nothing by himself; he can do only what he sees his Father doing, because whatever the Father does the Son also does. [20]For the Father loves the Son and shows him all he does. Yes, to your amazement he will show him even greater things than these. [21]For just as the Father raises the dead and gives them life, even so the Son gives life to whom he is pleased to give it. [22]Moreover, the Father judges no one, but has entrusted all judgment to the Son, [23]that all may honor the Son just as they honor the Father. He who does not honor the Son does not honor the Father, who sent him.

[24]"I tell you the truth, whoever hears my word and believes him who sent me has eternal life and will not be condemned; he has crossed over from death to life. [25]I tell you the truth, a time is coming and has now come when the dead will hear the voice of the Son of God and those who hear will live. [26]For as the Father has life in himself, so he has granted the Son to have life in himself. [27]And he has given him authority to judge because he is the Son of Man.

[28]"Do not be amazed at this, for a time is coming when all who are in their graves will hear his voice [29]and come out—those who have done good will rise to live, and those who have done evil will rise to be condemned. [30]By myself I can do nothing; I judge only as I hear, and my judgment is just, for I seek not to please myself but him who sent me.

Testimonies About Jesus

[31]"If I testify about myself, my testimony is not valid. [32]There is another who testifies in my favor, and I know that his testimony about me is valid.

[33]"You have sent to John and he has testified to the truth. [34]Not that I accept human testimony; but I mention it that you may be saved. [35]John was a lamp that burned and gave light, and you chose for a time to enjoy his light.

[36]"I have testimony weightier than that of John. For the very work that the Father has given me to finish, and which I am doing, testifies that the Father has sent me. [37]And the Father who sent me has himself testified concerning me. You have never heard his voice nor seen his form, [38]nor does his word dwell in you, for you do not believe the one he sent. [39]You diligently study[a] the Scriptures because you think that by them you possess eternal life. These are the Scriptures that testify about me, [40]yet you refuse to come to me to have life.

[41]"I do not accept praise from men, [42]but I know you. I know that you do not have the love of God in your hearts. [43]I have come in my Father's name, and you do not accept me; but if someone else comes in his own name, you will accept him. [44]How can you believe if you accept praise from one another, yet make no effort to obtain the praise that comes from the only God[b]?

[45]"But do not think I will accuse you before the Father. Your accuser is Moses, on whom your hopes are set. [46]If you believed Moses, you would believe me, for he wrote about me. [47]But since you do not believe what he wrote, how are you going to believe what I say?"

Jesus Feeds the Five Thousand

6 Some time after this, Jesus crossed to the far shore of the Sea of Galilee (that is, the Sea of Tiberias), [2]and a great crowd of people followed him because they saw the miraculous signs he had performed on the sick. [3]Then Jesus went up on a mountainside

---

[a] 39 Or Study diligently (the imperative)   [b] 44 Some early manuscripts the Only One

and sat down with his disciples. 4The Jewish Passover Feast was near.

5When Jesus looked up and saw a great crowd coming toward him, he said to Philip, "Where shall we buy bread for these people to eat?" 6He asked this only to test him, for he already had in mind what he was going to do.

7Philip answered him, "Eight months' wages[a] would not buy enough bread for each one to have a bite!"

8Another of his disciples, Andrew, Simon Peter's brother, spoke up, 9"Here is a boy with five small barley loaves and two small fish, but how far will they go among so many?"

10Jesus said, "Have the people sit down." There was plenty of grass in that place, and the men sat down, about five thousand of them. 11Jesus then took the loaves, gave thanks, and distributed to those who were seated as much as they wanted. He did the same with the fish.

12When they had all had enough to eat, he said to his disciples, "Gather the pieces that are left over. Let nothing be wasted." 13So they gathered them and filled twelve baskets with the pieces of the five barley loaves left over by those who had eaten.

14After the people saw the miraculous sign that Jesus did, they began to say, "Surely this is the Prophet who is to come into the world." 15Jesus, knowing that they intended to come and make him king by force, withdrew again to a mountain by himself.

Jesus Walks on the Water

16When evening came, his disciples went down to the lake, 17where they got into a boat and set off across the lake for Capernaum. By now it was dark, and Jesus had not yet joined them. 18A strong wind was blowing and the waters grew rough. 19When they had rowed three or three and a half miles,[b] they saw Jesus approaching the boat, walking on the water; and they were terrified. 20But he said to them, "It is I; don't be afraid." 21Then they were willing to take him into the boat, and immediately the boat reached the shore where they were heading.

22The next day the crowd that had stayed on the opposite shore of the lake realized that only one boat had been there, and that Jesus had not entered it with his disciples, but that they had gone away alone. 23Then some boats from Tiberias landed near the place where the people had eaten the bread after the Lord had given thanks. 24Once the crowd realized that neither Jesus nor his disciples were there, they got into the boats and went to Capernaum in search of Jesus.

Jesus the Bread of Life

25When they found him on the other side of the lake, they asked him, "Rabbi, when did you get here?"

26Jesus answered, "I tell you the truth, you are looking for me, not because you saw miraculous signs but because you ate the loaves and had your fill. 27Do not work for food that spoils, but for food that endures to eternal life, which the Son of Man will give you. On him God the Father has placed his seal of approval."

28Then they asked him, "What must we do to do the works God requires?"

29Jesus answered, "The work of God is this: to believe in the one he has sent."

30So they asked him, "What miraculous sign then will you give that we may see it and believe you? What will you do? 31Our forefathers ate the manna in the desert; as it is written: 'He gave them bread from heaven to eat.'[c] "

MY SPIRIT HAS BECOME DRY BECAUSE IT FORGETS TO FEED ON YOU.   —*John of the Cross*

32Jesus said to them, "I tell you the truth, it is not Moses who has given you the bread from heaven, but it is my Father who gives you the true bread from heaven. 33For the bread of God is he who comes down from heaven and gives life to the world."

34"Sir," they said, "from now on give us this bread."

35Then Jesus declared, "I am the bread of life. He who comes to me will never

---

a 7 Greek *two hundred denarii*   *b 19* Greek *rowed twenty-five or thirty stadia* (about 5 or 6 kilometers)   *c 31* Exodus 16:4; Neh. 9:15; Psalm 78:24,25

go hungry, and he who believes in me will never be thirsty. 36But as I told you, you have seen me and still you do not believe. 37All that the Father gives me will come to me, and whoever comes to me I will never drive away. 38For I have come down from heaven not to do my will but to do the will of him who sent me. 39And this is the will of him who sent me, that I shall lose none of all that he has given me, but raise them up at the last day. 40For my Father's will is that everyone who looks to the Son and believes in him shall have eternal life, and I will raise him up at the last day."

41At this the Jews began to grumble about him because he said, "I am the bread that came down from heaven." 42They said, "Is this not Jesus, the son of Joseph, whose father and mother we know? How can he now say, 'I came down from heaven'?"

43"Stop grumbling among yourselves," Jesus answered. 44"No one can come to me unless the Father who sent me draws him, and I will raise him up at the last day. 45It is written in the Prophets: 'They will all be taught by God.'a Everyone who listens to the Father and learns from him comes to me. 46No one has seen the Father except the one who is from God; only he has seen the Father. 47I tell you the truth, he who believes has everlasting life. 48I am the bread of life. 49Your forefathers ate the manna in the desert, yet they died. 50But here is the bread that comes down from heaven, which a man may eat and not die. 51I am the living bread that came down from heaven. If anyone eats of this bread, he will live forever. This bread is my flesh, which I will give for the life of the world."

52Then the Jews began to argue sharply among themselves, "How can this man give us his flesh to eat?"

53Jesus said to them, "I tell you the truth, unless you eat the flesh of the Son of Man and drink his blood, you have no life in you. 54Whoever eats my flesh and drinks my blood has eternal life, and I will raise him up at the last day. 55For my flesh is real food and my blood is real drink. 56Whoever eats my flesh and drinks my blood remains in me, and I in him. 57Just as the living Father sent me

and I live because of the Father, so the one who feeds on me will live because of me. 58This is the bread that came down from heaven. Your forefathers ate manna and died, but he who feeds on this bread will live forever." 59He said this while teaching in the synagogue in Capernaum.

Many Disciples Desert Jesus

60On hearing it, many of his disciples said, "This is a hard teaching. Who can accept it?"

61Aware that his disciples were grumbling about this, Jesus said to them, "Does this offend you? 62What if you see the Son of Man ascend to where he was before! 63The Spirit gives life; the flesh counts for nothing. The words I have spoken to you are spiritb and they are life. 64Yet there are some of you who do not believe." For Jesus had known from the beginning which of them did not believe and who would betray him. 65He went on to say, "This is why I told you that no one can come to me unless the Father has enabled him."

66From this time many of his disciples turned back and no longer followed him.

67"You do not want to leave too, do you?" Jesus asked the Twelve.

68Simon Peter answered him, "Lord, to whom shall we go? You have the words of eternal life. 69We believe and know that you are the Holy One of God."

70Then Jesus replied, "Have I not chosen you, the Twelve? Yet one of you is a devil!" 71(He meant Judas, the son of Simon Iscariot, who, though one of the Twelve, was later to betray him.)

Jesus Goes to the Feast of Tabernacles

7 After this, Jesus went around in Galilee, purposely staying away from Judea because the Jews there were waiting to take his life. 2But when the Jewish Feast of Tabernacles was near, 3Jesus' brothers said to him, "You ought to leave here and go to Judea, so that your disciples may see the miracles you do. 4No one who wants to become a public figure acts in secret. Since you are doing these things, show yourself to the world." 5For even his own brothers did not believe in him.

a 45 Isaiah 54:13   b 63 Or Spirit

⁶Therefore Jesus told them, "The right time for me has not yet come; for you any time is right. ⁷The world cannot hate you, but it hates me because I testify that what it does is evil. ⁸You go to the Feast. I am not yet*a* going up to this Feast, because for me the right time has not yet come." ⁹Having said this, he stayed in Galilee.

¹⁰However, after his brothers had left for the Feast, he went also, not publicly, but in secret. ¹¹Now at the Feast the Jews were watching for him and asking, "Where is that man?"

¹²Among the crowds there was widespread whispering about him. Some said, "He is a good man."

Others replied, "No, he deceives the people." ¹³But no one would say anything publicly about him for fear of the Jews.

Jesus Teaches at the Feast

¹⁴Not until halfway through the Feast did Jesus go up to the temple courts and begin to teach. ¹⁵The Jews were amazed and asked, "How did this man get such learning without having studied?"

¹⁶Jesus answered, "My teaching is not my own. It comes from him who sent me. ¹⁷If anyone chooses to do God's will, he will find out whether my teaching comes from God or whether I speak on my own. ¹⁸He who speaks on his own does so to gain honor for himself, but he who works for the honor of the one who sent him is a man of truth; there is nothing false about him. ¹⁹Has not Moses given you the law? Yet not one of you keeps the law. Why are you trying to kill me?"

²⁰"You are demon-possessed," the crowd answered. "Who is trying to kill you?"

²¹Jesus said to them, "I did one miracle, and you are all astonished. ²²Yet, because Moses gave you circumcision (though actually it did not come from Moses, but from the patriarchs), you circumcise a child on the Sabbath. ²³Now if a child can be circumcised on the Sabbath so that the law of Moses may not be broken, why are you angry with me for healing the whole man on the Sabbath? ²⁴Stop judging by mere appearances, and make a right judgment."

Is Jesus the Christ?

²⁵At that point some of the people of Jerusalem began to ask, "Isn't this the man they are trying to kill? ²⁶Here he is, speaking publicly, and they are not saying a word to him. Have the authorities really concluded that he is the Christ*b*? ²⁷But we know where this man is from; when the Christ comes, no one will know where he is from."

²⁸Then Jesus, still teaching in the temple courts, cried out, "Yes, you know me, and you know where I am from. I am not here on my own, but he who sent me is true. You do not know him, ²⁹but I know him because I am from him and he sent me."

³⁰At this they tried to seize him, but no one laid a hand on him, because his time had not yet come. ³¹Still, many in the crowd put their faith in him. They said, "When the Christ comes, will he do more miraculous signs than this man?"

³²The Pharisees heard the crowd whispering such things about him. Then the chief priests and the Pharisees sent temple guards to arrest him.

³³Jesus said, "I am with you for only a short time, and then I go to the one who sent me. ³⁴You will look for me, but you will not find me; and where I am, you cannot come."

³⁵The Jews said to one another, "Where does this man intend to go that we cannot find him? Will he go where our people live scattered among the Greeks, and teach the Greeks? ³⁶What did he mean when he said, 'You will look for me, but you will not find me,' and 'Where I am, you cannot come'?"

³⁷On the last and greatest day of the Feast, Jesus stood and said in a loud voice, "If anyone is thirsty, let him come to me and drink. ³⁸Whoever believes in me, as*c* the Scripture has said, streams of living water will flow from within him." ³⁹By this he meant the Spirit, whom those who believed in him were later to receive. Up to that time the Spirit had not been given, since Jesus had not yet been glorified.

a 8 Some early manuscripts do not have *yet*.   *b* 26 Or *Messiah*; also in verses 27, 31, 41 and 42
c 37,38 Or / *If anyone is thirsty, let him come to me. / And let him drink, ³⁸who believes in me. / As*

40On hearing his words, some of the people said, "Surely this man is the Prophet."

41Others said, "He is the Christ."

Still others asked, "How can the Christ come from Galilee? **42**Does not the Scripture say that the Christ will come from David's family*a* and from Bethlehem, the town where David lived?" **43**Thus the people were divided because of Jesus. **44**Some wanted to seize him, but no one laid a hand on him.

Unbelief of the Jewish Leaders

45Finally the temple guards went back to the chief priests and Pharisees, who asked them, "Why didn't you bring him in?"

46"No one ever spoke the way this man does," the guards declared.

47"You mean he has deceived you also?" the Pharisees retorted. **48**"Has any of the rulers or of the Pharisees believed in him? **49**No! But this mob that knows nothing of the law—there is a curse on them."

50Nicodemus, who had gone to Jesus earlier and who was one of their own number, asked, **51**"Does our law condemn anyone without first hearing him to find out what he is doing?"

52They replied, "Are you from Galilee, too? Look into it, and you will find that a prophet*b* does not come out of Galilee."

[The earliest manuscripts and many other ancient witnesses do not have John 7:53–8:11.]

53Then each went to his own home.

8 But Jesus went to the Mount of Olives. **2**At dawn he appeared again in the temple courts, where all the people gathered around him, and he sat down to teach them. **3**The teachers of the law and the Pharisees brought in a woman caught in adultery. They made her stand before the group **4**and said to Jesus, "Teacher, this woman was caught in the act of adultery. **5**In the Law Moses commanded us to stone such women. Now what do you say?" **6**They were using this question as a trap, in order to have a basis for accusing him.

But Jesus bent down and started to write on the ground with his finger. **7**When they kept on questioning him, he straightened up and said to them, "If any one of you is without sin, let him be the first to throw a stone at her." **8**Again he stooped down and wrote on the ground.

9At this, those who heard began to go away one at a time, the older ones first, until only Jesus was left, with the woman still standing there. **10**Jesus straightened up and asked her, "Woman, where are they? Has no one condemned you?"

11"No one, sir," she said.

"Then neither do I condemn you," Jesus declared. "Go now and leave your life of sin."

The Validity of Jesus' Testimony

12When Jesus spoke again to the people, he said, "I am the light of the world. Whoever follows me will never walk in darkness, but will have the light of life."

13The Pharisees challenged him, "Here you are, appearing as your own witness; your testimony is not valid."

14Jesus answered, "Even if I testify on my own behalf, my testimony is valid, for I know where I came from and where I am going. But you have no idea where I come from or where I am going. **15**You judge by human standards; I pass judgment on no one. **16**But if I do judge, my decisions are right, because I am not alone. I stand with the Father, who sent me. **17**In your own Law it is written that the testimony of two men is valid. **18**I am one who testifies for myself; my other witness is the Father, who sent me."

19Then they asked him, "Where is your father?"

"You do not know me or my Father," Jesus replied. "If you knew me, you would know my Father also." **20**He spoke these words while teaching in the temple area near the place where the offerings were put. Yet no one seized him, because his time had not yet come.

21Once more Jesus said to them, "I am going away, and you will look for me,

---

a 42 Greek *seed*   *b 52* Two early manuscripts *the Prophet* and you will die in your sin. Where I go, you cannot come."

²²This made the Jews ask, "Will he kill himself? Is that why he says, 'Where I go, you cannot come'?"

²³But he continued, "You are from below; I am from above. You are of this world; I am not of this world. ²⁴I told you that you would die in your sins; if you do not believe that I am ˻the one I claim to be˼,ᵃ you will indeed die in your sins."

²⁵"Who are you?" they asked.

"Just what I have been claiming all along," Jesus replied. ²⁶"I have much to say in judgment of you. But he who sent me is reliable, and what I have heard from him I tell the world."

²⁷They did not understand that he was telling them about his Father. ²⁸So Jesus said, "When you have lifted up the Son of Man, then you will know that I am ˻the one I claim to be˼ and that I do nothing on my own but speak just what the Father has taught me. ²⁹The one who sent me is with me; he has not left me alone, for I always do what pleases him." ³⁰Even as he spoke, many put their faith in him.

The Children of Abraham

³¹To the Jews who had believed him, Jesus said, "If you hold to my teaching, you are really my disciples. ³²Then you will know the truth, and the truth will set you free."

³³They answered him, "We are Abraham's descendantsᵇ and have never been slaves of anyone. How can you say that we shall be set free?"

³⁴Jesus replied, "I tell you the truth, everyone who sins is a slave to sin. ³⁵Now a slave has no permanent place in the family, but a son belongs to it forever. ³⁶So if the Son sets you free, you will be free indeed. ³⁷I know you are Abraham's descendants. Yet you are ready to kill me, because you have no room for my word. ³⁸I am telling you what I have seen in the Father's presence, and you do what you have heard from your father.ᶜ"

³⁹"Abraham is our father," they answered.

"If you were Abraham's children," said Jesus, "then you wouldᵈ do the things Abraham did. ⁴⁰As it is, you are determined to kill me, a man who has told you the truth that I heard from God. Abraham did not do such things. ⁴¹You are doing the things your own father does."

"We are not illegitimate children," they protested. "The only Father we have is God himself."

The Children of the Devil

⁴²Jesus said to them, "If God were your Father, you would love me, for I came from God and now am here. I have not come on my own; but he sent me. ⁴³Why is my language not clear to you? Because you are unable to hear what I say. ⁴⁴You belong to your father, the devil, and you want to carry out your father's desire. He was a murderer from the beginning, not holding to the truth, for there is no truth in him. When he lies, he speaks his native language, for he is a liar and the father of lies. ⁴⁵Yet because I tell the truth, you do not believe me! ⁴⁶Can any of you prove me guilty of sin? If I am telling the truth, why don't you believe me? ⁴⁷He who belongs to God hears what God says. The reason you do not hear is that you do not belong to God."

The Claims of Jesus About Himself

⁴⁸The Jews answered him, "Aren't we right in saying that you are a Samaritan and demon-possessed?"

⁴⁹"I am not possessed by a demon," said Jesus, "but I honor my Father and you dishonor me. ⁵⁰I am not seeking glory for myself; but there is one who seeks it, and he is the judge. ⁵¹I tell you the truth, if anyone keeps my word, he will never see death."

⁵²At this the Jews exclaimed, "Now we know that you are demon-possessed! Abraham died and so did the prophets, yet you say that if anyone keeps your word, he will never taste death. ⁵³Are you greater than our father Abraham? He died, and so did the prophets. Who do you think you are?"

ᵃ 24 Or I am he; also in verse 28   ᵇ 33 Greek seed; also in verse 37   ᶜ 38 Or presence. Therefore do what you have heard from the Father.   ᵈ 39 Some early manuscripts "If you are Abraham's children," said Jesus, "then

⁵⁴Jesus replied, "If I glorify myself, my glory means nothing. My Father, whom you claim as your God, is the one who glorifies me. ⁵⁵Though you do not know him, I know him. If I said I did not, I would be a liar like you, but I do know him and keep his word. ⁵⁶Your father Abraham rejoiced at the thought of seeing my day; he saw it and was glad."

⁵⁷"You are not yet fifty years old," the

WEDNESDAY

THE WHOLESOME PRECEPT OF OUR LORD
Cyprian

VERSE: John 8:31   **PASSAGE:** John 8:31–41

t is the wholesome precept of our Lord and Master: "He that endureth," saith he, "unto the end the same shall be saved" (see Matthew 10:22); and again, "If ye continue," saith he, "in my word ye shall be truly my disciples; and ye shall know the truth, and the truth shall make you free." We must endure and persevere, beloved brethren, in order that, being admitted to the hope of truth and liberty, we may attain to the truth and liberty itself; for that very fact that we are Christians is the substance of faith and hope. But that hope and faith may attain to their result, there is need of patience. For we are not following after present glory, but future, according to what Paul the apostle also warns us, and says, "We are saved by hope; but hope that is seen is not hope: for what a man seeth, why doth he hope for? But if we hope for that which we see not, then do we by patience wait for it" (see Romans 8:24). Therefore, waiting and patience are needful, that we may fulfill that which we have begun to be, and may receive that which we believe and hope for, according to God's own showing . . . [Paul] admonishes that no man should impatiently faint in his labor, that none should be either called off or overcome by temptations and desist in the midst of the praise and in the way of glory; and the things that are past perish, while those which have begun cease to be perfect; as it is written, "The righteousness of the righteous shall not deliver him in whatever day he shall transgress" (see Ezekiel 33:12); and again, "Hold that which thou hast, that another take not thy crown" (see Revelation 3:11). Which word exhorts us to persevere with patience and courage, so that he who strives towards the crown with the praise now near at hand, may be crowned by the continuance of patience.

ADDITIONAL SCRIPTURE READING:
2 Chronicles 20:17; 2 Thessalonians 2:15

Go to page 1238 for your next devotional reading.

100   500

Jews said to him, "and you have seen Abraham!"

⁵⁸"I tell you the truth," Jesus answered, "before Abraham was born, I am!" ⁵⁹At this, they picked up stones to stone him, but Jesus hid himself, slipping away from the temple grounds.

Jesus Heals a Man Born Blind

9 As he went along, he saw a man blind from birth. ²His disciples asked him, "Rabbi, who sinned, this man or his parents, that he was born blind?"

³"Neither this man nor his parents sinned," said Jesus, "but this happened so that the work of God might be displayed in his life. ⁴As long as it is day, we must do the work of him who sent me. Night is coming, when no one can work. ⁵While I am in the world, I am the light of the world."

⁶Having said this, he spit on the ground, made some mud with the saliva, and put it on the man's eyes. ⁷"Go," he told him, "wash in the Pool of Siloam" (this word means Sent). So the man went and washed, and came home seeing.

⁸His neighbors and those who had formerly seen him begging asked, "Isn't this the same man who used to sit and beg?" ⁹Some claimed that he was.

Others said, "No, he only looks like him."

But he himself insisted, "I am the man."

¹⁰"How then were your eyes opened?" they demanded.

¹¹He replied, "The man they call Jesus made some mud and put it on my eyes. He told me to go to Siloam and wash. So I went and washed, and then I could see."

¹²"Where is this man?" they asked him.

"I don't know," he said.

The Pharisees Investigate the Healing

¹³They brought to the Pharisees the man who had been blind. ¹⁴Now the day on which Jesus had made the mud and opened the man's eyes was a Sabbath. ¹⁵Therefore the Pharisees also asked him how he had received his sight. "He put mud on my eyes," the man replied, "and I washed, and now I see."

¹⁶Some of the Pharisees said, "This man is not from God, for he does not keep the Sabbath."

But others asked, "How can a sinner do such miraculous signs?" So they were divided.

¹⁷Finally they turned again to the blind man, "What have you to say about him? It was your eyes he opened."

The man replied, "He is a prophet."

¹⁸The Jews still did not believe that he had been blind and had received his sight until they sent for the man's parents. ¹⁹"Is this your son?" they asked. "Is this the one you say was born blind? How is it that now he can see?"

²⁰"We know he is our son," the parents answered, "and we know he was born blind. ²¹But how he can see now, or who opened his eyes, we don't know. Ask him. He is of age; he will speak for himself." ²²His parents said this because they were afraid of the Jews, for already the Jews had decided that anyone who acknowledged that Jesus was the Christ*a* would be put out of the synagogue. ²³That was why his parents said, "He is of age; ask him."

²⁴A second time they summoned the man who had been blind. "Give glory to God,*b*" they said. "We know this man is a sinner."

²⁵He replied, "Whether he is a sinner or not, I don't know. One thing I do know. I was blind but now I see!"

²⁶Then they asked him, "What did he do to you? How did he open your eyes?"

²⁷He answered, "I have told you already and you did not listen. Why do you want to hear it again? Do you want to become his disciples, too?"

²⁸Then they hurled insults at him and said, "You are this fellow's disciple! We are disciples of Moses! ²⁹We know that God spoke to Moses, but as for this fellow, we don't even know where he comes from."

³⁰The man answered, "Now that is remarkable! You don't know where he comes from, yet he opened my eyes. ³¹We know that God does not listen to sinners. He listens to the godly man who does his will. ³²Nobody has ever heard of opening the eyes of a man born

---

a 22 Or *Messiah*   *b* 24 A solemn charge to tell the truth (see Joshua 7:19)

blind. [33]If this man were not from God, he could do nothing."

[34]To this they replied, "You were steeped in sin at birth; how dare you lecture us!" And they threw him out.

Spiritual Blindness

[35]Jesus heard that they had thrown him out, and when he found him, he said, "Do you believe in the Son of Man?"

[36]"Who is he, sir?" the man asked. "Tell me so that I may believe in him."

[37]Jesus said, "You have now seen him; in fact, he is the one speaking with you."

[38]Then the man said, "Lord, I believe," and he worshiped him.

[39]Jesus said, "For judgment I have come into this world, so that the blind will see and those who see will become blind."

[40]Some Pharisees who were with him heard him say this and asked, "What? Are we blind too?"

[41]Jesus said, "If you were blind, you would not be guilty of sin; but now that you claim you can see, your guilt remains.

The Shepherd and His Flock

10 "I tell you the truth, the man who does not enter the sheep pen by the gate, but climbs in by some other way, is a thief and a robber. [2]The man who enters by the gate is the shepherd of his sheep. [3]The watchman opens the gate for him, and the sheep listen to his voice. He calls his own sheep by name and leads them out. [4]When he has brought out all his own, he goes on ahead of them, and his sheep follow him because they know his voice. [5]But they will never follow a stranger; in fact, they will run away from him because they do not recognize a stranger's voice." [6]Jesus used this figure of speech, but they did not understand what he was telling them.

[7]Therefore Jesus said again, "I tell you the truth, I am the gate for the sheep. [8]All who ever came before me were thieves and robbers, but the sheep did not listen to them. [9]I am the gate; whoever enters through me will be saved.[a]

He will come in and go out, and find pasture. [10]The thief comes only to steal and kill and destroy; I have come that they may have life, and have it to the full.

[11]"I am the good shepherd. The good shepherd lays down his life for the sheep. [12]The hired hand is not the shepherd who owns the sheep. So when he sees the wolf coming, he abandons the sheep and runs away. Then the wolf attacks the flock and scatters it. [13]The man runs away because he is a hired hand and cares nothing for the sheep.

[14]"I am the good shepherd; I know my sheep and my sheep know me— [15]just as the Father knows me and I know the Father—and I lay down my life for the sheep. [16]I have other sheep that are not of this sheep pen. I must bring them also. They too will listen to my voice, and there shall be one flock and one shepherd. [17]The reason my Father loves me is that I lay down my life—only to take it up again. [18]No one takes it from me, but I lay it down of my own accord. I have authority to lay it down and authority to take it up again. This command I received from my Father."

[19]At these words the Jews were again divided. [20]Many of them said, "He is demon-possessed and raving mad. Why listen to him?"

[21]But others said, "These are not the sayings of a man possessed by a demon. Can a demon open the eyes of the blind?"

The Unbelief of the Jews

[22]Then came the Feast of Dedication[b] at Jerusalem. It was winter, [23]and Jesus was in the temple area walking in Solomon's Colonnade. [24]The Jews gathered around him, saying, "How long will you keep us in suspense? If you are the Christ,[c] tell us plainly."

[25]Jesus answered, "I did tell you, but you do not believe. The miracles I do in my Father's name speak for me, [26]but you do not believe because you are not my sheep. [27]My sheep listen to my voice; I know them, and they follow me. [28]I give them eternal life, and they shall never perish; no one can snatch them out of my hand. [29]My Father, who has given them to me, is greater than all[d]; no

---

[a] 9 Or kept safe   [b] 22 That is, Hanukkah   [c] 24 Or Messiah   [d] 29 Many early manuscripts What my Father has given me is greater than all

one can snatch them out of my Father's hand. ³⁰I and the Father are one."

³¹Again the Jews picked up stones to stone him, ³²but Jesus said to them, "I have shown you many great miracles from the Father. For which of these do you stone me?"

³³"We are not stoning you for any of these," replied the Jews, "but for blasphemy, because you, a mere man, claim to be God."

³⁴Jesus answered them, "Is it not written in your Law, 'I have said you are gods'ᵃ? ³⁵If he called them 'gods,' to whom the word of God came—and the Scripture cannot be broken— ³⁶what about the one whom the Father set apart as his very own and sent into the world? Why then do you accuse me of blasphemy because I said, 'I am God's Son'? ³⁷Do not believe me unless I do what my Father does. ³⁸But if I do it, even though you do not believe me, believe the miracles, that you may know and understand that the Father is in me, and I in the Father." ³⁹Again they tried to seize him, but he escaped their grasp.

⁴⁰Then Jesus went back across the Jordan to the place where John had been baptizing in the early days. Here he stayed ⁴¹and many people came to him. They said, "Though John never performed a miraculous sign, all that John said about this man was true." ⁴²And in that place many believed in Jesus.

The Death of Lazarus

11 Now a man named Lazarus was sick. He was from Bethany, the village of Mary and her sister Martha. ²This Mary, whose brother Lazarus now lay sick, was the same one who poured perfume on the Lord and wiped his feet with her hair. ³So the sisters sent word to Jesus, "Lord, the one you love is sick."

⁴When he heard this, Jesus said, "This sickness will not end in death. No, it is for God's glory so that God's Son may be glorified through it." ⁵Jesus loved Martha and her sister and Lazarus. ⁶Yet when he heard that Lazarus was sick, he stayed where he was two more days.

⁷Then he said to his disciples, "Let us go back to Judea."

⁸"But Rabbi," they said, "a short while ago the Jews tried to stone you, and yet you are going back there?"

⁹Jesus answered, "Are there not twelve hours of daylight? A man who walks by day will not stumble, for he sees by this world's light. ¹⁰It is when he walks by night that he stumbles, for he has no light."

¹¹After he had said this, he went on to tell them, "Our friend Lazarus has fallen asleep; but I am going there to wake him up."

¹²His disciples replied, "Lord, if he sleeps, he will get better." ¹³Jesus had been speaking of his death, but his disciples thought he meant natural sleep.

¹⁴So then he told them plainly, "Lazarus is dead, ¹⁵and for your sake I am glad I was not there, so that you may believe. But let us go to him."

¹⁶Then Thomas (called Didymus) said to the rest of the disciples, "Let us also go, that we may die with him."

Jesus Comforts the Sisters

¹⁷On his arrival, Jesus found that Lazarus had already been in the tomb for four days. ¹⁸Bethany was less than two milesᵇ from Jerusalem, ¹⁹and many Jews had come to Martha and Mary to comfort them in the loss of their brother. ²⁰When Martha heard that Jesus was coming, she went out to meet him, but Mary stayed at home.

²¹"Lord," Martha said to Jesus, "if you had been here, my brother would not have died. ²²But I know that even now God will give you whatever you ask."

²³Jesus said to her, "Your brother will rise again."

²⁴Martha answered, "I know he will rise again in the resurrection at the last day."

²⁵Jesus said to her, "I am the resurrection and the life. He who believes in me will live, even though he dies; ²⁶and whoever lives and believes in me will never die. Do you believe this?"

²⁷"Yes, Lord," she told him, "I believe that you are the Christ,ᶜ the Son of God, who was to come into the world."

²⁸And after she had said this, she went back and called her sister Mary aside. "The Teacher is here," she said, "and is

---

ᵃ 34 Psalm 82:6   ᵇ 18 Greek *fifteen stadia* (about 3 kilometers)   ᶜ 27 Or *Messiah* asking for you." 29When Mary heard this, she got up quickly and went to him. 30Now Jesus had not yet entered the village, but was still at the place where Martha had met him. 31When the Jews who had been with Mary in the house, comforting her, noticed how quickly she got up and went out, they followed her, supposing she was going to the tomb to mourn there.

32When Mary reached the place where Jesus was and saw him, she fell at his

---

THURSDAY

THE MELDING OF MARTHA AND MARY
Evelyn Underhill

VERSE: John 11:20   **PASSAGE:** John 11:17–31

St. Theresa said that to give our Lord a perfect service, Martha and Mary must combine. The modern tendency is to turn from the attitude and the work of Mary; and even call it—as I have heard it called by busy social Christians—a form of spiritual selfishness. Thousands of devoted men and women today believe that the really good part is to keep busy, and give themselves no time to take what is offered to those who abide quietly with Christ; because there seem such a lot of urgent jobs for Martha to do. The result of this can only be a maiming of their human nature, exhaustion, loss of depth and of vision; and it is seen in the vagueness and ineffectuality of a great deal of the work that is done for God. It means a total surrender to the busy click-click of the life of succession; nowhere, in the end, more deadly than in the religious sphere. I insist on this because I feel, more and more, the danger in which we stand of developing a lopsided Christianity; so concentrated on service, and on this-world obligations, as to forget the needs of constant willed and quiet contact with that other world, wherefrom the sanctions of service and the power in which to do it proceed. We mostly spend those lives conjugating three verbs: to Want, to Have, and to Do. Craving, clutching, and fussing, on the material, political, social, emotional, intellectual—even on the religious—plane, we are kept in perpetual unrest: forgetting that none of these verbs has ultimate significance, except so far as they are transcended by and included in, the fundamental verb, to Be: and that Being, not wanting, having, and doing, is the essence of a spiritual life.

ADDITIONAL SCRIPTURE READING:
Luke 10:38–42; John 15:4

Go to page 1240 for your next devotional reading.

1900   Present

feet and said, "Lord, if you had been here, my brother would not have died."

33When Jesus saw her weeping, and the Jews who had come along with her also weeping, he was deeply moved in spirit and troubled. 34"Where have you laid him?" he asked.

"Come and see, Lord," they replied.

35Jesus wept.

36Then the Jews said, "See how he loved him!"

37But some of them said, "Could not he who opened the eyes of the blind man have kept this man from dying?"

Jesus Raises Lazarus From the Dead

38Jesus, once more deeply moved, came to the tomb. It was a cave with a stone laid across the entrance. 39"Take away the stone," he said.

"But, Lord," said Martha, the sister of the dead man, "by this time there is a bad odor, for he has been there four days."

40Then Jesus said, "Did I not tell you that if you believed, you would see the glory of God?"

41So they took away the stone. Then Jesus looked up and said, "Father, I thank you that you have heard me. 42I knew that you always hear me, but I said this for the benefit of the people standing here, that they may believe that you sent me."

43When he had said this, Jesus called in a loud voice, "Lazarus, come out!" 44The dead man came out, his hands and feet wrapped with strips of linen, and a cloth around his face.

Jesus said to them, "Take off the grave clothes and let him go."

WHAT IS SO INTRICATE, SO ENTANGLING AS
DEATH? WHOEVER GOT OUT OF A WINDING
SHEET?   —John Donne

The Plot to Kill Jesus

45Therefore many of the Jews who had come to visit Mary, and had seen what Jesus did, put their faith in him. 46But some of them went to the Pharisees and told them what Jesus had done. 47Then the chief priests and the Pharisees called a meeting of the Sanhedrin.

"What are we accomplishing?" they asked. "Here is this man performing many miraculous signs. 48If we let him go on like this, everyone will believe in him, and then the Romans will come and take away both our place*a* and our nation."

49Then one of them, named Caiaphas, who was high priest that year, spoke up, "You know nothing at all! 50You do not realize that it is better for you that one man die for the people than that the whole nation perish."

51He did not say this on his own, but as high priest that year he prophesied that Jesus would die for the Jewish nation, 52and not only for that nation but also for the scattered children of God, to bring them together and make them one. 53So from that day on they plotted to take his life.

54Therefore Jesus no longer moved about publicly among the Jews. Instead he withdrew to a region near the desert, to a village called Ephraim, where he stayed with his disciples.

55When it was almost time for the Jewish Passover, many went up from the country to Jerusalem for their ceremonial cleansing before the Passover. 56They kept looking for Jesus, and as they stood in the temple area they asked one another, "What do you think? Isn't he coming to the Feast at all?" 57But the chief priests and Pharisees had given orders that if anyone found out where Jesus was, he should report it so that they might arrest him.

Jesus Anointed at Bethany

12 Six days before the Passover, Jesus arrived at Bethany, where Lazarus lived, whom Jesus had raised from the dead. 2Here a dinner was given in Jesus' honor. Martha served, while Lazarus was among those reclining at the table with him. 3Then Mary took about a pint*b* of pure nard, an expensive perfume; she poured it on Jesus' feet and wiped his feet with her hair. And the house was filled with the fragrance of the perfume.

---

a 48 Or temple   *b* 3 Greek a litra (probably about 0.5 liter)

⁴But one of his disciples, Judas Iscariot, who was later to betray him, objected, ⁵"Why wasn't this perfume sold and the money given to the poor? It was worth a year's wages.ᵃ" ⁶He did not say this because he cared about the poor but

ᵃ 5 Greek *three hundred denarii*

THE FRAGRANCE OF GOD
Watchman Nee

VERSE: John 12:3   **PASSAGE:** John 12:1–8

here must be something—a willingness to yield, a breaking and a pouring out of everything to him—which gives release to that fragrance of Christ and produces in other lives an awareness of need, drawing them out and on to know the Lord. This is what I feel to be the heart of everything. The gospel has as its one object the producing in us sinners of a condition that will satisfy the heart of our God. In order that he may have that, we come to him with all we have, all we are—yes, even the most cherished things in our spiritual experience—and we make known to him: "Lord, I am willing to let go all of this for you: not just for your work, not for your children, not for anything else at all, but altogether and only for yourself!"

Oh, to be wasted! It is a blessed thing to be wasted for the Lord. So many who have been prominent in the Christian world know nothing of this. Many of us have been used to the full—have been used, I would say, too much—but we do not know what it means to be "wasted on God." We like to be always "on the go": the Lord would sometimes prefer to have us in prison. We think in terms of apostolic journeys: God dares to put his greatest ambassadors in chains.

"But thanks be to God, who always leads us in triumphal procession in Christ and through us spreads everywhere the fragrance of the knowledge of him" (2 Corinthians 2:14).

"And the house was filled with the fragrance of the perfume" (John 12:3).

The Lord grant us grace that we may learn how to please him. When, like Paul, we make this our supreme aim (2 Corinthians 5:9), the gospel will have achieved its end.

ADDITIONAL SCRIPTURE READING:
Philippians 2:14–18; Hebrews 13:15

Go to page 1242 for your next devotional reading.

1900   Present

because he was a thief; as keeper of the money bag, he used to help himself to what was put into it.

7 "Leave her alone," Jesus replied. "⌐It was intended⌐ that she should save this perfume for the day of my burial. 8 You will always have the poor among you, but you will not always have me."

9 Meanwhile a large crowd of Jews found out that Jesus was there and came, not only because of him but also to see Lazarus, whom he had raised from the dead. 10 So the chief priests made plans to kill Lazarus as well, 11 for on account of him many of the Jews were going over to Jesus and putting their faith in him.

The Triumphal Entry

12 The next day the great crowd that had come for the Feast heard that Jesus was on his way to Jerusalem. 13 They took palm branches and went out to meet him, shouting,

"Hosanna!ª"

"Blessed is he who comes in the
    name of the Lord!"ᵇ

"Blessed is the King of Israel!"

14 Jesus found a young donkey and sat upon it, as it is written,

15 "Do not be afraid, O Daughter of
    Zion;
see, your king is coming,
    seated on a donkey's colt."ᶜ

16 At first his disciples did not understand all this. Only after Jesus was glorified did they realize that these things had been written about him and that they had done these things to him.

17 Now the crowd that was with him when he called Lazarus from the tomb and raised him from the dead continued to spread the word. 18 Many people, because they had heard that he had given this miraculous sign, went out to meet him. 19 So the Pharisees said to one another, "See, this is getting us nowhere. Look how the whole world has gone after him!"

Jesus Predicts His Death

20 Now there were some Greeks among those who went up to worship at the Feast. 21 They came to Philip, who was from Bethsaida in Galilee, with a request. "Sir," they said, "we would like to see Jesus." 22 Philip went to tell Andrew; Andrew and Philip in turn told Jesus.

23 Jesus replied, "The hour has come for the Son of Man to be glorified. 24 I tell you the truth, unless a kernel of wheat falls to the ground and dies, it remains only a single seed. But if it dies, it produces many seeds. 25 The man who loves his life will lose it, while the man who hates his life in this world will keep it for eternal life. 26 Whoever serves me must follow me; and where I am, my servant also will be. My Father will honor the one who serves me.

27 "Now my heart is troubled, and what shall I say? 'Father, save me from this hour'? No, it was for this very reason I came to this hour. 28 Father, glorify your name!"

Then a voice came from heaven, "I have glorified it, and will glorify it again." 29 The crowd that was there and heard it said it had thundered; others said an angel had spoken to him.

30 Jesus said, "This voice was for your benefit, not mine. 31 Now is the time for judgment on this world; now the prince of this world will be driven out. 32 But I, when I am lifted up from the earth, will draw all men to myself." 33 He said this to show the kind of death he was going to die.

34 The crowd spoke up, "We have heard from the Law that the Christᵈ will remain forever, so how can you say, 'The Son of Man must be lifted up'? Who is this 'Son of Man'?"

35 Then Jesus told them, "You are going to have the light just a little while longer. Walk while you have the light, before darkness overtakes you. The man who walks in the dark does not know where he is going. 36 Put your trust in the light while you have it, so that you may become sons of light." When he had finished speaking, Jesus left and hid himself from them.

ª 13 A Hebrew expression meaning "Save!" which became an exclamation of praise   ᵇ 13 Psalm 118:25, 26   ᶜ 15 Zech. 9:9   ᵈ 34 Or *Messiah*

WEEKEND

THE DONKEY
G. K. Chesterton

VERSE: John 12:14   **PASSAGE:** John 12:12–16

hen fishes flew and forests walked
    And figs grew upon thorn,
Some moment when the moon was blood,
    Then surely I was born;

With monstrous head and sickening cry
    And ears like errant wings,
The devil's walking parody
    On all four-footed things.

The tattered outlaw of the earth,
    Of ancient crooked will;
Starve, scourge, deride me: I am dumb,
    I keep my secret still.

Fools! For I also had my hour;
    One far fierce hour and sweet:
There was a shout about my ears,
    And palms before my feet!

ADDITIONAL SCRIPTURE READING:
Zechariah 9:9; Matthew 21:5–6

Go to page 1245 for your next devotional reading.

1900   Present

The Jews Continue in Their Unbelief

37Even after Jesus had done all these miraculous signs in their presence, they still would not believe in him. **38**This was to fulfill the word of Isaiah the prophet:

"Lord, who has believed our message
    and to whom has the arm of the
    Lord been revealed?"*a*

39For this reason they could not believe, because, as Isaiah says elsewhere:

40"He has blinded their eyes
    and deadened their hearts,
  so they can neither see with their
        eyes,
    nor understand with their hearts,
    nor turn—and I would heal
        them."*b*

41Isaiah said this because he saw Jesus' glory and spoke about him.

42Yet at the same time many even among the leaders believed in him. But because of the Pharisees they would not confess their faith for fear they would be put out of the synagogue; **43**for they loved praise from men more than praise from God.

44Then Jesus cried out, "When a man believes in me, he does not believe in me only, but in the one who sent me. **45**When he looks at me, he sees the one who sent me. **46**I have come into the world as a light, so that no one who believes in me should stay in darkness.

47"As for the person who hears my words but does not keep them, I do not judge him. For I did not come to judge the world, but to save it. **48**There is a judge for the one who rejects me and does not accept my words; that very word which I spoke will condemn him at the last day. **49**For I did not speak of my own accord, but the Father who sent me commanded me what to say and how to say it. **50**I know that his command leads to eternal life. So whatever I say is just what the Father has told me to say."

Jesus Washes His Disciples' Feet

13 It was just before the Passover Feast. Jesus knew that the time had come for him to leave this world and go to the Father. Having loved his own who were in the world, he now showed them the full extent of his love.*c*

2The evening meal was being served, and the devil had already prompted Judas Iscariot, son of Simon, to betray Jesus. **3**Jesus knew that the Father had put all things under his power, and that he had come from God and was returning to God; **4**so he got up from the meal, took off his outer clothing, and wrapped a towel around his waist. **5**After that, he poured water into a basin and began to wash his disciples' feet, drying them with the towel that was wrapped around him.

6He came to Simon Peter, who said to him, "Lord, are you going to wash my feet?"

7Jesus replied, "You do not realize now what I am doing, but later you will understand."

8"No," said Peter, "you shall never wash my feet."

Jesus answered, "Unless I wash you, you have no part with me."

9"Then, Lord," Simon Peter replied, "not just my feet but my hands and my head as well!"

10Jesus answered, "A person who has had a bath needs only to wash his feet; his whole body is clean. And you are clean, though not every one of you." **11**For he knew who was going to betray him, and that was why he said not every one was clean.

12When he had finished washing their feet, he put on his clothes and returned to his place. "Do you understand what I have done for you?" he asked them. **13**"You call me 'Teacher' and 'Lord,' and rightly so, for that is what I am. **14**Now that I, your Lord and Teacher, have washed your feet, you also should wash one another's feet. **15**I have set you an example that you should do as I have done for you. **16**I tell you the truth, no servant is greater than his master, nor is a messenger greater than the one who sent him. **17**Now that you know these things, you will be blessed if you do them.

a 38 Isaiah 53:1   *b 40* Isaiah 6:10   *c 1* Or *he loved them to the last*

Jesus Predicts His Betrayal

18"I am not referring to all of you; I know those I have chosen. But this is to fulfill the scripture: 'He who shares my bread has lifted up his heel against me.'ᵃ

19"I am telling you now before it happens, so that when it does happen you will believe that I am He. 20I tell you the truth, whoever accepts anyone I send accepts me; and whoever accepts me accepts the one who sent me."

21After he had said this, Jesus was troubled in spirit and testified, "I tell you the truth, one of you is going to betray me."

22His disciples stared at one another, at a loss to know which of them he meant. 23One of them, the disciple whom Jesus loved, was reclining next to him. 24Simon Peter motioned to this disciple and said, "Ask him which one he means."

25Leaning back against Jesus, he asked him, "Lord, who is it?"

26Jesus answered, "It is the one to whom I will give this piece of bread when I have dipped it in the dish." Then, dipping the piece of bread, he gave it to Judas Iscariot, son of Simon. 27As soon as Judas took the bread, Satan entered into him.

"What you are about to do, do quickly," Jesus told him, 28but no one at the meal understood why Jesus said this to him. 29Since Judas had charge of the money, some thought Jesus was telling him to buy what was needed for the Feast, or to give something to the poor. 30As soon as Judas had taken the bread, he went out. And it was night.

Jesus Predicts Peter's Denial

31When he was gone, Jesus said, "Now is the Son of Man glorified and God is glorified in him. 32If God is glorified in him,ᵇ God will glorify the Son in himself, and will glorify him at once. 33"My children, I will be with you only a little longer. You will look for me, and just as I told the Jews, so I tell you now: Where I am going, you cannot come.

34"A new command I give you: Love one another. As I have loved you, so you must love one another. 35By this all men will know that you are my disciples, if you love one another."

36Simon Peter asked him, "Lord, where are you going?"

Jesus replied, "Where I am going, you cannot follow now, but you will follow later."

37Peter asked, "Lord, why can't I follow you now? I will lay down my life for you."

38Then Jesus answered, "Will you really lay down your life for me? I tell you the truth, before the rooster crows, you will disown me three times!

Jesus Comforts His Disciples

14 "Do not let your hearts be troubled. Trust in Godᶜ; trust also in me. 2In my Father's house are many rooms; if it were not so, I would have told you. I am going there to prepare a place for you. 3And if I go and prepare a place for you, I will come back and take you to be with me that you also may be where I am. 4You know the way to the place where I am going."

Jesus the Way to the Father

5Thomas said to him, "Lord, we don't know where you are going, so how can we know the way?"

6Jesus answered, "I am the way and the truth and the life. No one comes to the Father except through me. 7If you really knew me, you would knowᵈ my Father as well. From now on, you do know him and have seen him."

8Philip said, "Lord, show us the Father and that will be enough for us."

9Jesus answered: "Don't you know me, Philip, even after I have been among you such a long time? Anyone who has seen me has seen the Father. How can you say, 'Show us the Father'? 10Don't you believe that I am in the Father, and that the Father is in me? The words I say to you are not just my own. Rather, it is the Father, living in me, who is doing his work. 11Believe me when I say that I am in the Father and the Father is in me; or at least believe on the evidence of the miracles themselves. 12I tell you the truth, anyone who has faith in me will do what I have been doing. He will do

---

ᵃ 18 Psalm 41:9   ᵇ 32 Many early manuscripts do not have *If God is glorified in him.*   ᶜ 1 Or *You trust in God*   ᵈ 7 Some early manuscripts *If you really have known me, you will know*

THE INCARNATE TRUTH AND LIFE
F. F. Bruce

VERSE: John 14:6   **PASSAGE:** John 14:5–14

 homas's bewildered question, like many questions in the Fourth Gospel, provides Jesus with the opportunity of expanding and elucidating what he has just said. Jesus is going to the Father, and his disciples are to follow him; for them he is himself the way to the Father. He is, in fact, the only way by which men and women may come to the Father; there is no other way. If this seems offensively exclusive, let it be borne in mind that the one who makes this claim is the incarnate Word, the revealer of the Father. If God has no avenue of communication with mankind apart from his Word (incarnate or otherwise), mankind has no avenue of approach to God apart from that same Word, who became flesh and dwelt among us in order to supply such an avenue of approach. Jesus' claim, understood in the light of the prologue to the Gospel, is inclusive, not exclusive. All truth is God's truth, as all life is God's life; but God's truth and God's life are incarnate in Jesus.

It has been suggested that, in the Semitic language which Jesus spoke, the nouns "truth" and "life" were governed by "the way," as though he said, "I am the way of truth and life"—"I am the true and living way." This is no doubt an attractive suggestion . . . but that is not how [John] understood the words. For him the three nouns are co-ordinate, and are best understood by us as they were by him: "I am the way and the truth and the life." Jesus is not only the way to God; he is the truth of God—how could he be otherwise, since he is the embodiment of God's self-revelation?—and he is the life of God, "the true God and eternal life" (1 John 5:20), manifested on earth to give his flesh "for the life of the world" (John 6:51) . . .

To come to God by this way is to know him. The disciples have already begun to know the Father because they have come to know the Son; in fact (although they do not realize it yet) in the Son they have seen the Father.

ADDITIONAL SCRIPTURE READING:
John 10:9; Hebrews 10:19–22

Go to page 1247 for your next devotional reading.

1900   Present

even greater things than these, because I am going to the Father. [13]And I will do whatever you ask in my name, so that the Son may bring glory to the Father. [14]You may ask me for anything in my name, and I will do it.

Jesus Promises the Holy Spirit

[15]"If you love me, you will obey what I command. [16]And I will ask the Father, and he will give you another Counselor to be with you forever— [17]the Spirit of truth. The world cannot accept him, because it neither sees him nor knows him. But you know him, for he lives with you and will be[a] in you. [18]I will not leave you as orphans; I will come to you. [19]Before long, the world will not see me anymore, but you will see me. Because I live, you also will live. [20]On that day you will realize that I am in my Father, and you are in me, and I am in you. [21]Whoever has my commands and obeys them, he is the one who loves me. He who loves me will be loved by my Father, and I too will love him and show myself to him."

[22]Then Judas (not Judas Iscariot) said, "But, Lord, why do you intend to show yourself to us and not to the world?"

[23]Jesus replied, "If anyone loves me, he will obey my teaching. My Father will love him, and we will come to him and make our home with him. [24]He who does not love me will not obey my teaching. These words you hear are not my own; they belong to the Father who sent me.

[25]"All this I have spoken while still with you. [26]But the Counselor, the Holy Spirit, whom the Father will send in my name, will teach you all things and will remind you of everything I have said to you. [27]Peace I leave with you; my peace I give you. I do not give to you as the world gives. Do not let your hearts be troubled and do not be afraid.

[28]"You heard me say, 'I am going away and I am coming back to you.' If you loved me, you would be glad that I am going to the Father, for the Father is greater than I. [29]I have told you now before it happens, so that when it does happen you will believe. [30]I will not speak with you much longer, for the prince of this world is coming. He has no

hold on me, [31]but the world must learn that I love the Father and that I do exactly what my Father has commanded me.

"Come now; let us leave.

The Vine and the Branches

15 "I am the true vine, and my Father is the gardener. [2]He cuts off every branch in me that bears no fruit, while every branch that does bear fruit he prunes[b] so that it will be even more fruitful. [3]You are already clean because of the word I have spoken to you. [4]Remain in me, and I will remain in you. No branch can bear fruit by itself; it must remain in the vine. Neither can you bear fruit unless you remain in me.

[5]"I am the vine; you are the branches. If a man remains in me and I in him, he will bear much fruit; apart from me you can do nothing. [6]If anyone does not remain in me, he is like a branch that is thrown away and withers; such branches are picked up, thrown into the fire and burned. [7]If you remain in me and my words remain in you, ask whatever you wish, and it will be given you. [8]This is to my Father's glory, that you bear much fruit, showing yourselves to be my disciples.

[9]"As the Father has loved me, so have I loved you. Now remain in my love. [10]If you obey my commands, you will remain in my love, just as I have obeyed my Father's commands and remain in his love. [11]I have told you this so that my joy may be in you and that your joy may be complete. [12]My command is this: Love each other as I have loved you. [13]Greater love has no one than this, that he lay down his life for his friends. [14]You are my friends if you do what I command. [15]I no longer call you servants, because a servant does not know his master's business. Instead, I have called you friends, for everything that I learned from my Father I have made known to you. [16]You did not choose me, but I chose you and appointed you to go and bear fruit—fruit that will last. Then the Father will give you whatever you ask in my name. [17]This is my command: Love each other.

---

[a] 17 Some early manuscripts *and is*   [b] 2 The Greek for *prunes* also means *cleans.*

The World Hates the Disciples

18"If the world hates you, keep in mind that it hated me first. 19If you belonged to the world, it would love you as its own. As it is, you do not belong to the world, but I have chosen you out of the world. That is why the world hates you. 20Remember the words I spoke to you: 'No servant is greater than his master.'*a* If they persecuted me, they will persecute you also. If they obeyed my teaching, they will obey yours also. 21They will treat you this way because of my name, for they do not know the One who sent me. 22If I had not come and spoken to them, they would not be guilty of sin. Now, however, they have no excuse for their sin. 23He who hates me hates my Father as well. 24If I had not done among them what no one else did, they would not be guilty of sin. But now they have seen these miracles, and yet they have hated both me and my

a 20 John 13:16

TUESDAY

WITHOUT ME YOU CAN DO NOTHING
Andrew Murray

VERSE: John 15:5   **PASSAGE:** John 15:1–8

ithout the vine the branch can do nothing. To the vine it owes its right of place in the vineyard, its life and its fruitfulness. And so the Lord says, "Apart from me you can do nothing." The believer can each day be pleasing to God only in that which he does through the power of Christ dwelling in him. The daily inflowing of the life-sap of the Holy Spirit is his only power to bring forth fruit. He lives fully in him and is for each moment dependent on him alone.

Without the branch the vine can also do nothing. A vine without branches can bear no fruit. No less indispensable than the vine to the branch is the branch to the vine. Such is the wonderful condescension of the grace of Jesus that, just as his people are dependent on him, he has made himself dependent on them. Without his disciples he cannot dispense his blessing to the world . . . This is the high honor to which he has called his redeemed ones, that as indispensable as he is to them in heaven, that *from* him their fruit may be found, so indispensable also are they to him on earth, that *through* them his fruit may be found. Believers, meditate on this until your soul bows to worship in presence of the mystery of the perfect union between Christ and the believer.

ADDITIONAL SCRIPTURE READING:
Psalm 1:1–3; Colossians 3:3

Go to page 1250 for your next devotional reading.

1900   Present

Father. 25But this is to fulfill what is written in their Law: 'They hated me without reason.'*a*

26"When the Counselor comes, whom I will send to you from the Father, the Spirit of truth who goes out from the Father, he will testify about me. 27And you also must testify, for you have been with me from the beginning.

16 "All this I have told you so that you will not go astray. 2They will put you out of the synagogue; in fact, a time is coming when anyone who kills you will think he is offering a service to God. 3They will do such things because they have not known the Father or me. 4I have told you this, so that when the time comes you will remember that I warned you. I did not tell you this at first because I was with you.

The Work of the Holy Spirit

5"Now I am going to him who sent me, yet none of you asks me, 'Where are you going?' 6Because I have said these things, you are filled with grief. 7But I tell you the truth: It is for your good that I am going away. Unless I go away, the Counselor will not come to you; but if I go, I will send him to you. 8When he comes, he will convict the world of guilt*b* in regard to sin and righteousness and judgment: 9in regard to sin, because men do not believe in me; 10in regard to righteousness, because I am going to the Father, where you can see me no longer; 11and in regard to judgment, because the prince of this world now stands condemned.

12"I have much more to say to you, more than you can now bear. 13But

---

COME, HOLY GHOST, FOR MOVED BY THEE
THE PROPHET WROTE AND SPOKE;
UNLOCK THE TRUTH, THYSELF THE KEY,
UNSEAL THE SACRED BOOK.

—*John Calvin*

---

when he, the Spirit of truth, comes, he will guide you into all truth. He will not speak on his own; he will speak only what he hears, and he will tell you what

is yet to come. 14He will bring glory to me by taking from what is mine and making it known to you. 15All that belongs to the Father is mine. That is why I said the Spirit will take from what is mine and make it known to you.

16"In a little while you will see me no more, and then after a little while you will see me."

The Disciples' Grief Will Turn to Joy

17Some of his disciples said to one another, "What does he mean by saying, 'In a little while you will see me no more, and then after a little while you will see me,' and 'Because I am going to the Father'?" 18They kept asking, "What does he mean by 'a little while'? We don't understand what he is saying."

19Jesus saw that they wanted to ask him about this, so he said to them, "Are you asking one another what I meant when I said, 'In a little while you will see me no more, and then after a little while you will see me'? 20I tell you the truth, you will weep and mourn while the world rejoices. You will grieve, but your grief will turn to joy. 21A woman giving birth to a child has pain because her time has come; but when her baby is born she forgets the anguish because of her joy that a child is born into the world. 22So with you: Now is your time of grief, but I will see you again and you will rejoice, and no one will take away your joy. 23In that day you will no longer ask me anything. I tell you the truth, my Father will give you whatever you ask in my name. 24Until now you have not asked for anything in my name. Ask and you will receive, and your joy will be complete.

25"Though I have been speaking figuratively, a time is coming when I will no longer use this kind of language but will tell you plainly about my Father. 26In that day you will ask in my name. I am not saying that I will ask the Father on your behalf. 27No, the Father himself loves you because you have loved me and have believed that I came from God. 28I came from the Father and entered the world; now I am leaving the world and going back to the Father."

29Then Jesus' disciples said, "Now you are speaking clearly and without figures

---

a 25 Psalms 35:19; 69:4   *b 8* Or *will expose the guilt of the world* of speech. 30Now we can see that you know all things and that you do not even need to have anyone ask you questions. This makes us believe that you came from God."

31"You believe at last!"*a* Jesus answered. 32"But a time is coming, and has come, when you will be scattered, each to his own home. You will leave me all alone. Yet I am not alone, for my Father is with me.

33"I have told you these things, so that in me you may have peace. In this world you will have trouble. But take heart! I have overcome the world."

Jesus Prays for Himself

17 After Jesus said this, he looked toward heaven and prayed:

"Father, the time has come. Glorify your Son, that your Son may glorify you. 2For you granted him authority over all people that he might give eternal life to all those you have given him. 3Now this is eternal life: that they may know you, the only true God, and Jesus Christ, whom you have sent. 4I have brought you glory on earth by completing the work you gave me to do. 5And now, Father, glorify me in your presence with the glory I had with you before the world began.

Jesus Prays for His Disciples

6"I have revealed you*b* to those whom you gave me out of the world. They were yours; you gave them to me and they have obeyed your word. 7Now they know that everything you have given me comes from you. 8For I gave them the words you gave me and they accepted them. They knew with certainty that I came from you, and they believed that you sent me. 9I pray for them. I am not praying for the world, but for those you have given me, for they are yours. 10All I have is yours, and all you have is mine. And glory has come to me through them. 11I will remain in the world no longer, but they are still in the world, and I am coming to you. Holy Father, protect them by the power of your name—the name you gave me—so that they may be one as we are one. 12While I was with them, I protected them and kept them safe by that name you gave me. None has been lost except the one doomed to destruction so that Scripture would be fulfilled.

13"I am coming to you now, but I say these things while I am still in the world, so that they may have the full measure of my joy within them. 14I have given them your word and the world has hated them, for they are not of the world any more than I am of the world. 15My prayer is not that you take them out of the world but that you protect them from the evil one. 16They are not of the world, even as I am not of it. 17Sanctify*c* them by the truth; your word is truth. 18As you sent me into the world, I have sent them into the world. 19For them I sanctify myself, that they too may be truly sanctified.

Jesus Prays for All Believers

20"My prayer is not for them alone. I pray also for those who will believe in me through their message, 21that all of them may be one, Father, just as you are in me and I am in you. May they also be in us so that the world may believe that you have sent me. 22I have given them the glory that you gave me, that they may be one as we are one: 23I in them and you in me. May they be brought to complete unity to let the world know that you sent me and have loved them even as you have loved me.

24"Father, I want those you have given me to be with me where I am, and to see my glory, the glory you have given me because you loved me before the creation of the world.

25"Righteous Father, though the world does not know you, I know

---

a 31 Or *"Do you now believe?"*   *b 6* Greek *your name;* also in verse 26   *c 17* Greek *hagiazo (set apart for sacred use* or *make holy);* also in verse 19

you, and they know that you have sent me. ²⁶I have made you known to them, and will continue to make you known in order that the love you have for me may be in them and that I myself may be in them."

WEDNESDAY

A SPLENDOR OF HOPE
George MacDonald

VERSE: John 17:24   **PASSAGE:** John 17:20–26

 et us note . . . that the dwelling of Jesus in us is the power of the Spirit of God upon us; for "the Lord is the Spirit," and "this comes from the Lord, who is the Spirit" (2 Corinthians 3:18). When we think Christ, Christ comes; when we receive his image into our spiritual mirror, he enters with it.

When our hearts turn to him, that is opening the door to him, that is holding up our mirror to him; then he comes in, not by our thought only, not in our idea only, but he comes himself, and of his own will. Thus the Lord, the Spirit, becomes the soul of our souls, becomes spiritually what he always was creatively; and as our spirit informs, gives shape to our bodies, in like manner his soul informs, gives shape to our souls.

In this there is nothing unnatural, nothing at conflict with our being. It is but that the deeper soul that willed and wills our souls, rises up, the infinite Life, into the self we call *I* and *me*, makes the *I* and *me* more and more his, and himself more and more ours; until at length the glory of our existence flashes upon us, we face full to the sun that enlightens what it sent forth, and know ourselves alive with an infinite life, even the life of the Father. Then indeed we *are*; then indeed we have life; the life of Jesus has, through light, become life in us; the glory of God in the face of Jesus, mirrored in our hearts, has made us alive; we are one with God for ever and ever.

What less than such a splendor of hope would be worthy the revelation of Jesus? Filled with the soul of their Father, men shall inherit the glory of their Father; filled with themselves, they cast him out, and rot. No other saving can save them. They must receive the Son and through the Son the Father.

ADDITIONAL SCRIPTURE READING:
Colossians 2:13; Revelation 3:20

Go to page 1254 for your next devotional reading.

1700   1900

Jesus Arrested

18 When he had finished praying, Jesus left with his disciples and crossed the Kidron Valley. On the other side there was an olive grove, and he and his disciples went into it.

2Now Judas, who betrayed him, knew the place, because Jesus had often met there with his disciples. 3So Judas came to the grove, guiding a detachment of soldiers and some officials from the chief priests and Pharisees. They were carrying torches, lanterns and weapons.

4Jesus, knowing all that was going to happen to him, went out and asked them, "Who is it you want?"

5"Jesus of Nazareth," they replied.

"I am he," Jesus said. (And Judas the traitor was standing there with them.) 6When Jesus said, "I am he," they drew back and fell to the ground.

7Again he asked them, "Who is it you want?"

And they said, "Jesus of Nazareth."

8"I told you that I am he," Jesus answered. "If you are looking for me, then let these men go." 9This happened so that the words he had spoken would be fulfilled: "I have not lost one of those you gave me."*a*

10Then Simon Peter, who had a sword, drew it and struck the high priest's servant, cutting off his right ear. (The servant's name was Malchus.)

11Jesus commanded Peter, "Put your sword away! Shall I not drink the cup the Father has given me?"

Jesus Taken to Annas

12Then the detachment of soldiers with its commander and the Jewish officials arrested Jesus. They bound him 13and brought him first to Annas, who was the father-in-law of Caiaphas, the high priest that year. 14Caiaphas was the one who had advised the Jews that it would be good if one man died for the people.

Peter's First Denial

15Simon Peter and another disciple were following Jesus. Because this disciple was known to the high priest, he went with Jesus into the high priest's courtyard, 16but Peter had to wait outside at the door. The other disciple, who was known to the high priest, came back, spoke to the girl on duty there and brought Peter in.

17"You are not one of his disciples, are you?" the girl at the door asked Peter.

He replied, "I am not."

18It was cold, and the servants and officials stood around a fire they had made to keep warm. Peter also was standing with them, warming himself.

The High Priest Questions Jesus

19Meanwhile, the high priest questioned Jesus about his disciples and his teaching.

20"I have spoken openly to the world," Jesus replied. "I always taught in synagogues or at the temple, where all the Jews come together. I said nothing in secret. 21Why question me? Ask those who heard me. Surely they know what I said."

22When Jesus said this, one of the officials nearby struck him in the face. "Is this the way you answer the high priest?" he demanded.

23"If I said something wrong," Jesus replied, "testify as to what is wrong. But if I spoke the truth, why did you strike me?" 24Then Annas sent him, still bound, to Caiaphas the high priest.*b*

Peter's Second and Third Denials

25As Simon Peter stood warming himself, he was asked, "You are not one of his disciples, are you?"

He denied it, saying, "I am not."

26One of the high priest's servants, a relative of the man whose ear Peter had cut off, challenged him, "Didn't I see you with him in the olive grove?" 27Again Peter denied it, and at that moment a rooster began to crow.

Jesus Before Pilate

28Then the Jews led Jesus from Caiaphas to the palace of the Roman governor. By now it was early morning, and to avoid ceremonial uncleanness the Jews did not enter the palace; they wanted to be able to eat the Passover. 29So Pilate came out to them and asked, "What

a 9 John 6:39　　*b 24* Or *(Now Annas had sent him, still bound, to Caiaphas the high priest.)*

charges are you bringing against this man?"

³⁰"If he were not a criminal," they replied, "we would not have handed him over to you."

³¹Pilate said, "Take him yourselves and judge him by your own law."

"But we have no right to execute anyone," the Jews objected. ³²This happened so that the words Jesus had spoken indicating the kind of death he was going to die would be fulfilled.

³³Pilate then went back inside the palace, summoned Jesus and asked him, "Are you the king of the Jews?"

³⁴"Is that your own idea," Jesus asked, "or did others talk to you about me?"

³⁵"Am I a Jew?" Pilate replied. "It was your people and your chief priests who handed you over to me. What is it you have done?"

³⁶Jesus said, "My kingdom is not of this world. If it were, my servants would fight to prevent my arrest by the Jews. But now my kingdom is from another place."

³⁷"You are a king, then!" said Pilate.

Jesus answered, "You are right in saying I am a king. In fact, for this reason I was born, and for this I came into the world, to testify to the truth. Everyone on the side of truth listens to me."

³⁸"What is truth?" Pilate asked. With this he went out again to the Jews and said, "I find no basis for a charge against him. ³⁹But it is your custom for me to release to you one prisoner at the time of the Passover. Do you want me to release 'the king of the Jews'?"

⁴⁰They shouted back, "No, not him! Give us Barabbas!" Now Barabbas had taken part in a rebellion.

Jesus Sentenced to be Crucified

19 Then Pilate took Jesus and had him flogged. ²The soldiers twisted together a crown of thorns and put it on his head. They clothed him in a purple robe ³and went up to him again and again, saying, "Hail, king of the Jews!" And they struck him in the face.

⁴Once more Pilate came out and said to the Jews, "Look, I am bringing him out to you to let you know that I find no basis for a charge against him." ⁵When Jesus came out wearing the crown of thorns and the purple robe, Pilate said to them, "Here is the man!"

⁶As soon as the chief priests and their officials saw him, they shouted, "Crucify! Crucify!"

But Pilate answered, "You take him and crucify him. As for me, I find no basis for a charge against him."

⁷The Jews insisted, "We have a law, and according to that law he must die, because he claimed to be the Son of God."

⁸When Pilate heard this, he was even more afraid, ⁹and he went back inside the palace. "Where do you come from?" he asked Jesus, but Jesus gave him no answer. ¹⁰"Do you refuse to speak to me?" Pilate said. "Don't you realize I have power either to free you or to crucify you?"

¹¹Jesus answered, "You would have no power over me if it were not given to you from above. Therefore the one who handed me over to you is guilty of a greater sin."

¹²From then on, Pilate tried to set Jesus free, but the Jews kept shouting, "If you let this man go, you are no friend of Caesar. Anyone who claims to be a king opposes Caesar."

¹³When Pilate heard this, he brought Jesus out and sat down on the judge's seat at a place known as the Stone Pavement (which in Aramaic is Gabbatha). ¹⁴It was the day of Preparation of Passover Week, about the sixth hour.

"Here is your king," Pilate said to the Jews.

¹⁵But they shouted, "Take him away! Take him away! Crucify him!"

"Shall I crucify your king?" Pilate asked.

"We have no king but Caesar," the chief priests answered.

¹⁶Finally Pilate handed him over to them to be crucified.

The Crucifixion

So the soldiers took charge of Jesus. ¹⁷Carrying his own cross, he went out to the place of the Skull (which in Aramaic is called Golgotha). ¹⁸Here they crucified him, and with him two others—one on each side and Jesus in the middle.

¹⁹Pilate had a notice prepared and fastened to the cross. It read: JESUS OF

NAZARETH, THE KING OF THE JEWS. 20Many of the Jews read this sign, for the place where Jesus was crucified was near the city, and the sign was written in Aramaic, Latin and Greek. 21The chief priests of the Jews protested to Pilate, "Do not write 'The King of the Jews,' but that this man claimed to be king of the Jews."

WHERE LIFE WAS SLAIN AND TRUTH WAS

SLANDERED

ON THAT ONE HOLIER HILL THAN ROME.

—G. K. Chesterton

22Pilate answered, "What I have written, I have written."

23When the soldiers crucified Jesus, they took his clothes, dividing them into four shares, one for each of them, with the undergarment remaining. This garment was seamless, woven in one piece from top to bottom.

24"Let's not tear it," they said to one another. "Let's decide by lot who will get it."

This happened that the scripture might be fulfilled which said,

"They divided my garments among
them
and cast lots for my clothing."a

So this is what the soldiers did.

25Near the cross of Jesus stood his mother, his mother's sister, Mary the wife of Clopas, and Mary Magdalene. 26When Jesus saw his mother there, and the disciple whom he loved standing nearby, he said to his mother, "Dear woman, here is your son," 27and to the disciple, "Here is your mother." From that time on, this disciple took her into his home.

The Death of Jesus

28Later, knowing that all was now completed, and so that the Scripture would be fulfilled, Jesus said, "I am thirsty." 29A jar of wine vinegar was there, so they soaked a sponge in it, put the sponge on a stalk of the hyssop plant, and lifted it to Jesus' lips. 30When he had received the drink, Jesus said, "It is finished." With that, he bowed his head and gave up his spirit.

31Now it was the day of Preparation, and the next day was to be a special Sabbath. Because the Jews did not want the bodies left on the crosses during the Sabbath, they asked Pilate to have the legs broken and the bodies taken down. 32The soldiers therefore came and broke the legs of the first man who had been crucified with Jesus, and then those of the other. 33But when they came to Jesus and found that he was already dead, they did not break his legs. 34Instead, one of the soldiers pierced Jesus' side with a spear, bringing a sudden flow of blood and water. 35The man who saw it has given testimony, and his testimony is true. He knows that he tells the truth, and he testifies so that you also may believe. 36These things happened so that the scripture would be fulfilled: "Not one of his bones will be broken,"b 37and, as another scripture says, "They will look on the one they have pierced."c

NO PAIN, NO PALM; NO THORNS, NO THRONE; NO

GALL, NO GLORY; NO CROSS, NO CROWN.

—William Penn

The Burial of Jesus

38Later, Joseph of Arimathea asked Pilate for the body of Jesus. Now Joseph was a disciple of Jesus, but secretly because he feared the Jews. With Pilate's permission, he came and took the body away. 39He was accompanied by Nicodemus, the man who earlier had visited Jesus at night. Nicodemus brought a mixture of myrrh and aloes, about seventy-five pounds.d 40Taking Jesus' body, the two of them wrapped it, with the spices, in strips of linen. This was in accordance with Jewish burial customs. 41At the place where Jesus was crucified, there was a garden, and in the garden a new tomb, in which no one had ever been laid. 42Because it was the Jewish day of Preparation and since the tomb was nearby, they laid Jesus there.

a 24 Psalm 22:18   b 36 Exodus 12:46; Num. 9:12; Psalm 34:20   c 37 Zech. 12:10   d 39 Greek a hundred litrai (about 34 kilograms)

PRAYERS ON THE DEATH OF CHRIST
Bonaventura

VERSE: John 19:30   **PASSAGE:** John 19:28–42

Gethsemane

ord Jesus, you have shaped our faith, by making us believe you shared our mortal nature. In Gethsemane real drops of sweat fell from your body.

Lord Jesus, you have given us hope, because you endured all the spiritual and physical hardships which mortal nature can suffer. In Gethsemane your soul was in torment, and your heart shook at the prospect of the physical pain to come.

You showed all the natural weaknesses of the flesh, that we might know that you have truly borne our sorrows.

Trial

Sweet Jesus, what soul can be so hardened as not to cry out at your plight?

Sweet Jesus, what heart can be so hardened as not to groan with compassion for you?

Sweet Jesus, my ears can hardly bear to hear those horrible shouts:

"Away with him. Away with him. Crucify him."

Crucifixion

O Lord, holy Father, show us what kind of man it is who is hanging for our sakes on the cross, whose suffering causes the rocks themselves to crack and crumble with compassion, whose death brings the dead back to life.

Let my heart crack and crumble at the sight of him. Let my soul break apart with compassion for his suffering. Let it be shattered with grief at my sins for which he dies. And finally let it be softened with devoted love for him.

Burial

O my God, Jesus, I am in every way unworthy of you. Yet, like Joseph of Arimathea, I want to offer a space for you. He offered his own tomb; I offer my heart.

Enter the darkness of my heart, as your body entered the darkness of Joseph's tomb. And make me worthy to receive you, driving out all sin that I may be filled with your spiritual light.

ADDITIONAL SCRIPTURE READING:
Psalm 22; 1 Peter 2:21–24

Go to page 1256 for your next devotional reading.

The Empty Tomb

20 Early on the first day of the week, while it was still dark, Mary Magdalene went to the tomb and saw that the stone had been removed from the entrance. ²So she came running to Simon Peter and the other disciple, the one Jesus loved, and said, "They have taken the Lord out of the tomb, and we don't know where they have put him!"

³So Peter and the other disciple started for the tomb. ⁴Both were running, but the other disciple outran Peter and reached the tomb first. ⁵He bent over and looked in at the strips of linen lying there but did not go in. ⁶Then Simon Peter, who was behind him, arrived and went into the tomb. He saw the strips of linen lying there, ⁷as well as the burial cloth that had been around Jesus' head. The cloth was folded up by itself, separate from the linen. ⁸Finally the other disciple, who had reached the tomb first, also went inside. He saw and believed. ⁹(They still did not understand from Scripture that Jesus had to rise from the dead.)

Jesus Appears to Mary Magdalene

¹⁰Then the disciples went back to their homes, ¹¹but Mary stood outside the tomb crying. As she wept, she bent over to look into the tomb ¹²and saw two angels in white, seated where Jesus' body had been, one at the head and the other at the foot.

¹³They asked her, "Woman, why are you crying?"

"They have taken my Lord away," she said, "and I don't know where they have put him." ¹⁴At this, she turned around and saw Jesus standing there, but she did not realize that it was Jesus.

¹⁵"Woman," he said, "why are you crying? Who is it you are looking for?"

Thinking he was the gardener, she said, "Sir, if you have carried him away, tell me where you have put him, and I will get him."

¹⁶Jesus said to her, "Mary."

She turned toward him and cried out in Aramaic, "Rabboni!" (which means Teacher).

¹⁷Jesus said, "Do not hold on to me, for I have not yet returned to the Father. Go instead to my brothers and tell them, 'I am returning to my Father and your Father, to my God and your God.' "

¹⁸Mary Magdalene went to the disciples with the news: "I have seen the Lord!" And she told them that he had said these things to her.

Jesus Appears to His Disciples

¹⁹On the evening of that first day of the week, when the disciples were together, with the doors locked for fear of the Jews, Jesus came and stood among them and said, "Peace be with you!" ²⁰After he said this, he showed them his hands and side. The disciples were overjoyed when they saw the Lord.

²¹Again Jesus said, "Peace be with you! As the Father has sent me, I am sending you." ²²And with that he breathed on them and said, "Receive the Holy Spirit. ²³If you forgive anyone his sins, they are forgiven; if you do not forgive them, they are not forgiven."

Jesus Appears to Thomas

²⁴Now Thomas (called Didymus), one of the Twelve, was not with the disciples when Jesus came. ²⁵So the other disciples told him, "We have seen the Lord!"

But he said to them, "Unless I see the nail marks in his hands and put my finger where the nails were, and put my hand into his side, I will not believe it."

²⁶A week later his disciples were in the house again, and Thomas was with them. Though the doors were locked, Jesus came and stood among them and said, "Peace be with you!" ²⁷Then he said to Thomas, "Put your finger here; see my hands. Reach out your hand and put it into my side. Stop doubting and believe."

²⁸Thomas said to him, "My Lord and my God!"

CHRISTIANITY, IF FALSE, IS OF NO IMPORTANCE, AND, IF TRUE, OF INFINITE IMPORTANCE. THE ONE THING IT CANNOT BE IS MODERATELY IMPORTANT.
                                    —C. S. Lewis

---

²⁹Then Jesus told him, "Because you have seen me, you have believed; blessed are those who have not seen and yet have believed."

³⁰Jesus did many other miraculous signs in the presence of his disciples,

THE HOLINESS OF HOME
Gregory of Nyssa

VERSE: John 20:29   **PASSAGE:** John 20:24–29

e confessed that the Christ who was manifested is very God, as much before as after our sojourn at Jerusalem; our faith in him was not increased afterwards any more than it was diminished. Before we saw Bethlehem we knew his being made man by means of the Virgin; before we saw his grave we believed in his resurrection from the dead; apart from seeing the Mount of Olives, we confessed that his ascension into heaven was real. We derived only thus much of profit from our traveling thither, namely that we came to know by being able to compare them, that our own places are far holier than those abroad. Wherefore, O ye who fear the Lord, praise him in the places where ye now are. Change of place does not effect any drawing nearer unto God, but wherever thou mayest be, God will come to thee, if the chambers of thy soul be found of such a sort that he can dwell in thee and walk in thee. But if thou keepest thine inner man full of wicked thoughts, even if thou wast on Golgotha, even if thou wast on the Mount of Olives, even if thou stoodest on the memorial-rock of the resurrection, thou wilt be as far away from receiving Christ into thyself, as one who has not even begun to confess him . . . Inasmuch as the gift and the distribution of the Holy Spirit had not yet passed upon the apostles, our Lord commanded them to remain in the same place, until they should have been endued with power from on high (see Acts 1:4). Now, if that which happened at the beginning, when the Holy Spirit was dispensing each of his gifts under the appearance of a flame, continued until now, it would be right for all to remain in that place where that dispensing took place; but if the Spirit "bloweth" where he "listeth," those, too, who have become believers here are made partakers of that gift; and that according to the proportion of their faith, not in consequence of their pilgrimage to Jerusalem.

ADDITIONAL SCRIPTURE READING:
1 Chronicles 17:4–6; Revelation 21:1–3

Go to page 1258 for your next devotional reading.

100   500

which are not recorded in this book. 31But these are written that you may*a* believe that Jesus is the Christ, the Son of God, and that by believing you may have life in his name.

Jesus and the Miraculous Catch of Fish

21 Afterward Jesus appeared again to his disciples, by the Sea of Tiberias.*b* It happened this way: 2Simon Peter, Thomas (called Didymus), Nathanael from Cana in Galilee, the sons of Zebedee, and two other disciples were together. 3"I'm going out to fish," Simon Peter told them, and they said, "We'll go with you." So they went out and got into the boat, but that night they caught nothing.

4Early in the morning, Jesus stood on the shore, but the disciples did not realize that it was Jesus.

5He called out to them, "Friends, haven't you any fish?"

"No," they answered.

6He said, "Throw your net on the right side of the boat and you will find some." When they did, they were unable to haul the net in because of the large number of fish.

7Then the disciple whom Jesus loved said to Peter, "It is the Lord!" As soon as Simon Peter heard him say, "It is the Lord," he wrapped his outer garment around him (for he had taken it off) and jumped into the water. 8The other disciples followed in the boat, towing the net full of fish, for they were not far from shore, about a hundred yards.*c* 9When they landed, they saw a fire of burning coals there with fish on it, and some bread.

10Jesus said to them, "Bring some of the fish you have just caught."

11Simon Peter climbed aboard and dragged the net ashore. It was full of large fish, 153, but even with so many the net was not torn. 12Jesus said to them, "Come and have breakfast." None of the disciples dared ask him, "Who are you?" They knew it was the Lord. 13Jesus came, took the bread and gave it to them, and did the same with the fish. 14This was now the third time Jesus appeared to his disciples after he was raised from the dead.

Jesus Reinstates Peter

15When they had finished eating, Jesus said to Simon Peter, "Simon son of John, do you truly love me more than these?"

"Yes, Lord," he said, "you know that I love you."

Jesus said, "Feed my lambs."

16Again Jesus said, "Simon son of John, do you truly love me?"

He answered, "Yes, Lord, you know that I love you."

Jesus said, "Take care of my sheep."

17The third time he said to him, "Simon son of John, do you love me?"

Peter was hurt because Jesus asked him the third time, "Do you love me?" He said, "Lord, you know all things; you know that I love you."

Jesus said, "Feed my sheep. 18I tell you the truth, when you were younger you dressed yourself and went where you wanted; but when you are old you will stretch out your hands, and someone else will dress you and lead you where you do not want to go." 19Jesus said this to indicate the kind of death by which Peter would glorify God. Then he said to him, "Follow me!"

20Peter turned and saw that the disciple whom Jesus loved was following them. (This was the one who had leaned back against Jesus at the supper and had said, "Lord, who is going to betray you?") 21When Peter saw him, he asked, "Lord, what about him?"

22Jesus answered, "If I want him to remain alive until I return, what is that to you? You must follow me." 23Because of this, the rumor spread among the brothers that this disciple would not die. But Jesus did not say that he would not die; he only said, "If I want him to remain alive until I return, what is that to you?"

24This is the disciple who testifies to these things and who wrote them down. We know that his testimony is true.

25Jesus did many other things as well. If every one of them were written down, I suppose that even the whole world would not have room for the books that would be written.

---

a 31 Some manuscripts *may continue to cubits* (about 90 meters)   *b 1* That is, Sea of Galilee   *c 8* Greek *about two hundred*

WEEKEND

An Hymne of Heavenly Love
Edmund Spenser

Verse: John 21:15   **Passage:** John 21:15–17

im first to love great right and reason is,
Who first to us our life and being gave,
And after, when we fared had amiss,
Us wretches from the second death did save;
And last the food of life, which now we have,
Even he himself, in his dear sacrament,
To feed our hungry souls, unto us lent.

Then next, to love our brethren that were made
Of that self mould, and that self Maker's hand,
That we, and to the same again shall fade,
Where they shall have like heritage of land,
However here on higher steps we stand;
Which also were with self-same price redeemed
That we, however of us light esteemed.

And were they not, yet since that loving Lord
Commanded us to love them for his sake,
Even for his sake, and for his sacred word,
Which in his last bequest he to us spake,
We should them love, and with their needs partake;
Knowing that whatso'er to them we give,
We give to him by whom we all do live.

Such mercy he by his most holy rede
Unto us taught, and to approve it true,
Ensampled it by his most righteous deed,
Showing us mercy (miserable crew!)
That we the like should to the wretches show,
And love our brethren; thereby to approve
How much himself that loved us we love.

Additional Scripture Reading:
Ephesians 3:14–19; 1 John 4:19–21

Go to page 1263 for your next devotional reading.

1500   1700

ACTS

IKE A SEQUEL TO A MOVIE, ACTS
PICKS UP THE ACTION BEGUN IN
LUKE'S GOSPEL. SOME REFER TO
THE BOOK OF ACTS AS "THE ACTS OF THE
HOLY SPIRIT," BECAUSE IT FOCUSES ON THE
COMING OF THE SPIRIT ON GOD'S PEOPLE,
THE CHURCH, IN A NEW AND POWERFUL
WAY. IN THIS BOOK LUKE RECORDS CHRIS-
TIANITY'S AMAZING GROWTH, SHOWING
HOW REVIVAL COMES NOT BY HUMAN EFFORT
BUT BY THE POWER OF THE HOLY SPIRIT. THE
SPIRIT SO ACTIVE IN ACTS IS THE SAME SPIR-
IT AT WORK IN YOUR LIFE TODAY.

Jesus Taken Up Into Heaven

1 In my former book, Theophilus,
I wrote about all that Jesus began
to do and to teach ²until the day he was
taken up to heaven, after giving instructions through the Holy Spirit to the apostles he had chosen. ³After his suffering,
he showed himself to these men and gave
many convincing proofs that he was
alive. He appeared to them over a period
of forty days and spoke about the kingdom of God. ⁴On one occasion, while he
was eating with them, he gave them this
command: "Do not leave Jerusalem, but
wait for the gift my Father promised,
which you have heard me speak about.
⁵For John baptized with*ᵃ* water, but in a

few days you will be baptized with the
Holy Spirit."

⁶So when they met together, they
asked him, "Lord, are you at this time
going to restore the kingdom to Israel?"

⁷He said to them: "It is not for you to
know the times or dates the Father has
set by his own authority. ⁸But you will
receive power when the Holy Spirit
comes on you; and you will be my witnesses in Jerusalem, and in all Judea and
Samaria, and to the ends of the earth."

⁹After he said this, he was taken up
before their very eyes, and a cloud hid
him from their sight.

¹⁰They were looking intently up into
the sky as he was going, when suddenly
two men dressed in white stood beside
them. ¹¹"Men of Galilee," they said,

ᵃ 5 Or in

"why do you stand here looking into the sky? This same Jesus, who has been taken from you into heaven, will come back in the same way you have seen him go into heaven."

Matthias Chosen to Replace Judas

12Then they returned to Jerusalem from the hill called the Mount of Olives, a Sabbath day's walk*a* from the city. 13When they arrived, they went upstairs to the room where they were staying. Those present were Peter, John, James and Andrew; Philip and Thomas, Bartholomew and Matthew; James son of Alphaeus and Simon the Zealot, and Judas son of James. 14They all joined together constantly in prayer, along with the women and Mary the mother of Jesus, and with his brothers.

15In those days Peter stood up among the believers*b* (a group numbering about a hundred and twenty) 16and said, "Brothers, the Scripture had to be fulfilled which the Holy Spirit spoke long ago through the mouth of David concerning Judas, who served as guide for those who arrested Jesus— 17he was one of our number and shared in this ministry."

18(With the reward he got for his wickedness, Judas bought a field; there he fell headlong, his body burst open and all his intestines spilled out. 19Everyone in Jerusalem heard about this, so they called that field in their language Akeldama, that is, Field of Blood.)

20"For," said Peter, "it is written in the book of Psalms,

" 'May his place be deserted;
    let there be no one to dwell in it,'*c*

and,

" 'May another take his place of
    leadership.'*d*

21Therefore it is necessary to choose one of the men who have been with us the whole time the Lord Jesus went in and out among us, 22beginning from John's baptism to the time when Jesus was taken up from us. For one of these must become a witness with us of his resurrection."

23So they proposed two men: Joseph called Barsabbas (also known as Justus) and Matthias. 24Then they prayed, "Lord, you know everyone's heart. Show us which of these two you have chosen 25to take over this apostolic ministry, which Judas left to go where he belongs." 26Then they cast lots, and the lot fell to Matthias; so he was added to the eleven apostles.

The Holy Spirit Comes at Pentecost

2 When the day of Pentecost came, they were all together in one place. 2Suddenly a sound like the blowing of a violent wind came from heaven and filled the whole house where they were sitting. 3They saw what seemed to be tongues of fire that separated and came to rest on each of them. 4All of them were filled with the Holy Spirit and began to speak in other tongues*e* as the Spirit enabled them.

5Now there were staying in Jerusalem God-fearing Jews from every nation under heaven. 6When they heard this sound, a crowd came together in bewilderment, because each one heard them speaking in his own language. 7Utterly amazed, they asked: "Are not all these men who are speaking Galileans? 8Then how is it that each of us hears them in his own native language? 9Parthians, Medes and Elamites; residents of Mesopotamia, Judea and Cappadocia, Pontus and Asia, 10Phrygia and Pamphylia, Egypt and the parts of Libya near Cyrene; visitors from Rome 11(both Jews and converts to Judaism); Cretans and Arabs—we hear them declaring the wonders of God in our own tongues!" 12Amazed and perplexed, they asked one another, "What does this mean?"

13Some, however, made fun of them and said, "They have had too much wine.*f* "

---

a 12 That is, about 3/4 mile (about 1,100 meters)   *b 15* Greek *brothers*   *c 20* Psalm 69:25
d 20 Psalm 109:8   *e 4* Or *languages;* also in verse 11   *f 13* Or *sweet wine*

Peter Addresses the Crowd

14Then Peter stood up with the Eleven, raised his voice and addressed the crowd: "Fellow Jews and all of you who live in Jerusalem, let me explain this to you; listen carefully to what I say. **15**These men are not drunk, as you suppose. It's only nine in the morning! **16**No, this is what was spoken by the prophet Joel:

17 " 'In the last days, God says,
  I will pour out my Spirit on all
    people.
  Your sons and daughters will
    prophesy,
  your young men will see visions,
  your old men will dream dreams.
18Even on my servants, both men and
    women,
  I will pour out my Spirit in those
    days,
  and they will prophesy.
19I will show wonders in the heaven
    above
  and signs on the earth below,
  blood and fire and billows of
    smoke.
20The sun will be turned to darkness
  and the moon to blood
  before the coming of the great and
    glorious day of the Lord.
21And everyone who calls
  on the name of the Lord will be
    saved.'[a]

22"Men of Israel, listen to this: Jesus of Nazareth was a man accredited by God to you by miracles, wonders and signs, which God did among you through him, as you yourselves know. **23**This man was handed over to you by God's set purpose and foreknowledge; and you, with the help of wicked men,[b] put him to death by nailing him to the cross. **24**But God raised him from the dead, freeing him from the agony of death, because it was impossible for death to keep its hold on him. **25**David said about him:

" 'I saw the Lord always before me.
  Because he is at my right hand,

I will not be shaken.
26Therefore my heart is glad and my
    tongue rejoices;
  my body also will live in hope,
27because you will not abandon me to
    the grave,
  nor will you let your Holy One see
    decay.
28You have made known to me the
    paths of life;
  you will fill me with joy in your
    presence.'[c]

29"Brothers, I can tell you confidently that the patriarch David died and was buried, and his tomb is here to this day. **30**But he was a prophet and knew that God had promised him on oath that he would place one of his descendants on his throne. **31**Seeing what was ahead, he spoke of the resurrection of the Christ,[d] that he was not abandoned to the grave, nor did his body see decay. **32**God has raised this Jesus to life, and we are all witnesses of the fact. **33**Exalted to the right hand of God, he has received from the Father the promised Holy Spirit and has poured out what you now see and hear. **34**For David did not ascend to heaven, and yet he said,

" 'The Lord said to my Lord:
  "Sit at my right hand
35until I make your enemies
  a footstool for your feet." '[e]

36"Therefore let all Israel be assured of this: God has made this Jesus, whom you crucified, both Lord and Christ."

37When the people heard this, they were cut to the heart and said to Peter and the other apostles, "Brothers, what shall we do?"

38Peter replied, "Repent and be baptized, every one of you, in the name of Jesus Christ for the forgiveness of your sins. And you will receive the gift of the Holy Spirit. **39**The promise is for you and your children and for all who are far off— for all whom the Lord our God will call."

40With many other words he warned them; and he pleaded with them, "Save yourselves from this corrupt generation."

21 Joel 2:28–32   b 23 Or *of those not having the law* (that is, Gentiles)   c 28 Psalm 16:8–11
d 31 Or *Messiah.* "The Christ" (Greek) and "the Messiah" (Hebrew) both mean "the Anointed One"; also in verse 36.   e 35 Psalm 110:1

⁴¹Those who accepted his message were baptized, and about three thousand were added to their number that day.

The Fellowship of the Believers

⁴²They devoted themselves to the apostles' teaching and to the fellowship, to the breaking of bread and to prayer. ⁴³Everyone was filled with awe, and many wonders and miraculous signs were done by the apostles. ⁴⁴All the believers were together and had everything in common. ⁴⁵Selling their possessions and goods, they gave to anyone as he had need. ⁴⁶Every day they continued to meet together in the temple courts. They broke bread in their homes and ate together with glad and sincere hearts, ⁴⁷praising God and enjoying the favor of all the people. And the Lord added to their number daily those who were being saved.

THERE IS NO LIFE THAT IS NOT IN COMMUNITY. AND NO COMMUNITY NOT LIVED IN PRAISE OF GOD.   —*T. S. Eliot*

Peter Heals the Crippled Beggar

3 One day Peter and John were going up to the temple at the time of prayer—at three in the afternoon. ²Now a man crippled from birth was being carried to the temple gate called Beautiful, where he was put every day to beg from those going into the temple courts. ³When he saw Peter and John about to enter, he asked them for money. ⁴Peter looked straight at him, as did John. Then Peter said, "Look at us!" ⁵So the man gave them his attention, expecting to get something from them.

⁶Then Peter said, "Silver or gold I do not have, but what I have I give you. In the name of Jesus Christ of Nazareth, walk." ⁷Taking him by the right hand, he helped him up, and instantly the man's feet and ankles became strong. ⁸He jumped to his feet and began to walk. Then he went with them into the temple courts, walking and jumping, and praising God. ⁹When all the people saw him walking and praising God,

¹⁰they recognized him as the same man who used to sit begging at the temple gate called Beautiful, and they were filled with wonder and amazement at what had happened to him.

Peter Speaks to the Onlookers

¹¹While the beggar held on to Peter and John, all the people were astonished and came running to them in the place called Solomon's Colonnade. ¹²When Peter saw this, he said to them: "Men of Israel, why does this surprise you? Why do you stare at us as if by our own power or godliness we had made this man walk? ¹³The God of Abraham, Isaac and Jacob, the God of our fathers, has glorified his servant Jesus. You handed him over to be killed, and you disowned him before Pilate, though he had decided to let him go. ¹⁴You disowned the Holy and Righteous One and asked that a murderer be released to you. ¹⁵You killed the author of life, but God raised him from the dead. We are witnesses of this. ¹⁶By faith in the name of Jesus, this man whom you see and know was made strong. It is Jesus' name and the faith that comes through him that has given this complete healing to him, as you can all see.

¹⁷"Now, brothers, I know that you acted in ignorance, as did your leaders. ¹⁸But this is how God fulfilled what he had foretold through all the prophets, saying that his Christ*ᵃ* would suffer. ¹⁹Repent, then, and turn to God, so that your sins may be wiped out, that times of refreshing may come from the Lord, ²⁰and that he may send the Christ, who has been appointed for you—even Jesus. ²¹He must remain in heaven until the time comes for God to restore everything, as he promised long ago through his holy prophets. ²²For Moses said, 'The Lord your God will raise up for you a prophet like me from among your own people; you must listen to everything he tells you. ²³Anyone who does not listen to him will be completely cut off from among his people.'*ᵇ*

²⁴"Indeed, all the prophets from Samuel on, as many as have spoken, have foretold these days. ²⁵And you are heirs of the prophets and of the covenant God

---

ᵃ 18 Or *Messiah;* also in verse 20   *ᵇ 23* Deut. 18:15,18,19

DEVOTED TO THE BREAKING OF BREAD
The Didache

VERSE: Acts 2:42   **PASSAGE:** Acts 2:42–47

 ow about the Eucharist: This is how to give thanks: First in connection with the cup: "We thank you, our Father, for the holy vine of David, your child, which you have revealed through Jesus, your child. To you be glory forever."

Then in connection with the piece [broken off the loaf]: "We thank you, our Father, for the life and knowledge which you have revealed through Jesus, your child. To you be glory forever. As this piece [of bread] was scattered over the hills and then was brought together and made one, so let your church be brought together from the ends of the earth into your kingdom. For yours is the glory and the power through Jesus Christ forever."

You must not let anyone eat or drink of your Eucharist except those baptized in the Lord's name. For in reference to this the Lord said, "Do not give what is sacred to dogs" (see Matthew 7:6).

After you have finished your meal, say grace in this way: "We thank you, holy Father, for your sacred name which you have lodged in our hearts, and for the knowledge and faith and immortality which you have revealed through Jesus, your child. To you be glory forever. Almighty Master, you have created everything for the sake of your name, and have given men food and drink to enjoy that they may thank you. But to us you have given spiritual food and drink and eternal life through Jesus, your child. Above all, we thank you that you are mighty. To you be glory forever.

"Remember, Lord, your church, to save it from all evil and to make it perfect by your love. Make it holy, and gather it together from the four winds into your kingdom which you have made ready for it. For yours is the power and the glory forever.

"Let grace come and let this world pass away.

"Hosanna to the God of David!

"If anyone is holy, let him come. If not, let him repent.

"Our Lord, come!

"Amen."

ADDITIONAL SCRIPTURE READING:
Matthew 26:26–29; 1 Corinthians 11:17–34

Go to page 1265 for your next devotional reading.

made with your fathers. He said to Abraham, 'Through your offspring all peoples on earth will be blessed.'*a* 26When God raised up his servant, he sent him first to you to bless you by turning each of you from your wicked ways."

Peter and John Before the Sanhedrin

4 The priests and the captain of the temple guard and the Sadducees came up to Peter and John while they were speaking to the people. 2They were greatly disturbed because the apostles were teaching the people and proclaiming in Jesus the resurrection of the dead. 3They seized Peter and John, and because it was evening, they put them in jail until the next day. 4But many who heard the message believed, and the number of men grew to about five thousand.

5The next day the rulers, elders and teachers of the law met in Jerusalem. 6Annas the high priest was there, and so were Caiaphas, John, Alexander and the other men of the high priest's family. 7They had Peter and John brought before them and began to question them: "By what power or what name did you do this?"

8Then Peter, filled with the Holy Spirit, said to them: "Rulers and elders of the people! 9If we are being called to account today for an act of kindness shown to a cripple and are asked how he was healed, 10then know this, you and all the people of Israel: It is by the name of Jesus Christ of Nazareth, whom you crucified but whom God raised from the dead, that this man stands before you healed. 11He is

" 'the stone you builders rejected,
   which has become the capstone.'*b*'*c*

12Salvation is found in no one else, for there is no other name under heaven given to men by which we must be saved."

13When they saw the courage of Peter and John and realized that they were unschooled, ordinary men, they were astonished and they took note that these men had been with Jesus. 14But

since they could see the man who had been healed standing there with them, there was nothing they could say. 15So they ordered them to withdraw from the Sanhedrin and then conferred together. 16"What are we going to do with these men?" they asked. "Everybody living in Jerusalem knows they have done an outstanding miracle, and we cannot deny it. 17But to stop this thing from spreading any further among the people, we must warn these men to speak no longer to anyone in this name."

18Then they called them in again and commanded them not to speak or teach at all in the name of Jesus. 19But Peter and John replied, "Judge for yourselves whether it is right in God's sight to obey you rather than God. 20For we cannot help speaking about what we have seen and heard."

21After further threats they let them go. They could not decide how to punish them, because all the people were praising God for what had happened. 22For the man who was miraculously healed was over forty years old.

The Believers' Prayer

23On their release, Peter and John went back to their own people and reported all that the chief priests and elders had said to them. 24When they heard this, they raised their voices together in prayer to God. "Sovereign Lord," they said, "you made the heaven and the earth and the sea, and everything in them. 25You spoke by the Holy Spirit through the mouth of your servant, our father David:

" 'Why do the nations rage
   and the peoples plot in vain?
26The kings of the earth take their
      stand
   and the rulers gather together
against the Lord
   and against his Anointed One.'*d*'*e*

27Indeed Herod and Pontius Pilate met together with the Gentiles and the people*f* of Israel in this city to conspire against your holy servant Jesus, whom

---

a 25 Gen. 22:18; 26:4   *b 11* Or *cornerstone*   *c 11* Psalm 118:22   *d 26* That is, Christ or Messiah
e 26 Psalm 2:1,2   *f 27* The Greek is plural.

you anointed. ²⁸They did what your power and will had decided beforehand should happen. ²⁹Now, Lord, consider their threats and enable your servants to speak your word with great boldness. ³⁰Stretch out your hand to heal and

---

TUESDAY

ARRESTED IN THE STEEPLEHOUSE
George Fox

VERSE: Acts: 4:3   PASSAGE: Acts 4:1–4

ow while I was at Mansfield-Woodhouse, I was moved to go to the steeplehouse there on a First-day, out of the meeting in Mansfield, and when the priest had done I declared the truth to the priest and people. But the people fell upon me with their fists, books, and without compassion or mercy beat me down in the steeplehouse and almost smothered me in it, being under them . . . Then they punched and thrust and struck me up and down and they set me in the stocks and brought a whip to whip me, but did not. And as I sat in the stocks they threw stones at me, and my head, arms, breast, shoulders, back, and sides were so bruised that I was mazed and dazzled with the blows . . .

After some time they had me before the magistrate, at a knight's house and examined me, where were many great persons, and I reasoned with them of the things of God and his teachings, and Christ's, and how that God that made the world did not well in temples made with hands (see Acts 17:24); and of divers things of the truth I spake to them, and they, seeing how evilly I had been used, set me at liberty. The rude people were ready to fall upon me with staves but the constable kept them off. And when they had set me at liberty, they threatened me with pistols, if ever I came again they would kill me and shoot me; and they would carry their pistols to the steeplehouse . . . I was scarce able to go or well to stand, by reason of ill-usage. Yet with much ado I got about a mile from the town, and as I was passing along the fields friends met me. I was so bruised that I could not turn in my bed, and bruised inwardly at my heart, but after a while the power of the Lord went through me and healed me, that I was well, glory be to the Lord forever.

ADDITIONAL SCRIPTURE READING:
2 Corinthians 6:4–10; 2 Timothy 3:12–14

Go to page 1271 for your next devotional reading.

1500   1700

perform miraculous signs and wonders through the name of your holy servant Jesus."

31After they prayed, the place where they were meeting was shaken. And they were all filled with the Holy Spirit and spoke the word of God boldly.

The Believers Share Their Possessions

32All the believers were one in heart and mind. No one claimed that any of his possessions was his own, but they shared everything they had. 33With great power the apostles continued to testify to the resurrection of the Lord Jesus, and much grace was upon them all. 34There were no needy persons among them. For from time to time those who owned lands or houses sold them, brought the money from the sales 35and put it at the apostles' feet, and it was distributed to anyone as he had need.

36Joseph, a Levite from Cyprus, whom the apostles called Barnabas (which means Son of Encouragement), 37sold a field he owned and brought the money and put it at the apostles' feet.

Ananias and Sapphira

5 Now a man named Ananias, together with his wife Sapphira, also sold a piece of property. 2With his wife's full knowledge he kept back part of the money for himself, but brought the rest and put it at the apostles' feet.

3Then Peter said, "Ananias, how is it that Satan has so filled your heart that you have lied to the Holy Spirit and have kept for yourself some of the money you received for the land? 4Didn't it belong to you before it was sold? And after it was sold, wasn't the money at your disposal? What made you think of doing such a thing? You have not lied to men but to God."

5When Ananias heard this, he fell down and died. And great fear seized all who heard what had happened. 6Then the young men came forward, wrapped up his body, and carried him out and buried him.

7About three hours later his wife came in, not knowing what had happened.

8Peter asked her, "Tell me, is this the price you and Ananias got for the land?"

"Yes," she said, "that is the price."

9Peter said to her, "How could you agree to test the Spirit of the Lord? Look! The feet of the men who buried your husband are at the door, and they will carry you out also."

10At that moment she fell down at his feet and died. Then the young men came in and, finding her dead, carried her out and buried her beside her husband. 11Great fear seized the whole church and all who heard about these events.

The Apostles Heal Many

12The apostles performed many miraculous signs and wonders among the people. And all the believers used to meet together in Solomon's Colonnade. 13No one else dared join them, even though they were highly regarded by the people. 14Nevertheless, more and more men and women believed in the Lord and were added to their number. 15As a result, people brought the sick into the streets and laid them on beds and mats so that at least Peter's shadow might fall on some of them as he passed by. 16Crowds gathered also from the towns around Jerusalem, bringing their sick and those tormented by evil*a* spirits, and all of them were healed.

The Apostles Persecuted

17Then the high priest and all his associates, who were members of the party of the Sadducees, were filled with jealousy. 18They arrested the apostles and put them in the public jail. 19But during the night an angel of the Lord opened the doors of the jail and brought them out. 20"Go, stand in the temple courts," he said, "and tell the people the full message of this new life."

21At daybreak they entered the temple courts, as they had been told, and began to teach the people.

When the high priest and his associates arrived, they called together the Sanhedrin—the full assembly of the elders of Israel—and sent to the jail for the apostles. 22But on arriving at the jail, the officers did not find them there. So they went back and reported, 23"We

a 16 Greek unclean

found the jail securely locked, with the guards standing at the doors; but when we opened them, we found no one inside." ²⁴On hearing this report, the captain of the temple guard and the chief priests were puzzled, wondering what would come of this.

²⁵Then someone came and said, "Look! The men you put in jail are standing in the temple courts teaching the people." ²⁶At that, the captain went with his officers and brought the apostles. They did not use force, because they feared that the people would stone them.

²⁷Having brought the apostles, they made them appear before the Sanhedrin to be questioned by the high priest. ²⁸"We gave you strict orders not to teach in this name," he said. "Yet you have filled Jerusalem with your teaching and are determined to make us guilty of this man's blood."

²⁹Peter and the other apostles replied: "We must obey God rather than men! ³⁰The God of our fathers raised Jesus from the dead—whom you had killed by hanging him on a tree. ³¹God exalted him to his own right hand as Prince and Savior that he might give repentance and forgiveness of sins to Israel. ³²We are witnesses of these things, and so is the Holy Spirit, whom God has given to those who obey him."

³³When they heard this, they were furious and wanted to put them to death. ³⁴But a Pharisee named Gamaliel, a teacher of the law, who was honored by all the people, stood up in the Sanhedrin and ordered that the men be put outside for a little while. ³⁵Then he addressed them: "Men of Israel, consider carefully what you intend to do to these men. ³⁶Some time ago Theudas appeared, claiming to be somebody, and about four hundred men rallied to him. He was killed, all his followers were dispersed, and it all came to nothing. ³⁷After him, Judas the Galilean appeared in the days of the census and led a band of people in revolt. He too was killed, and all his followers were scattered. ³⁸Therefore, in the present case I advise you: Leave these men alone! Let them go! For if their purpose or activity is of

human origin, it will fail. ³⁹But if it is from God, you will not be able to stop these men; you will only find yourselves fighting against God."

⁴⁰His speech persuaded them. They called the apostles in and had them flogged. Then they ordered them not to speak in the name of Jesus, and let them go.

⁴¹The apostles left the Sanhedrin, rejoicing because they had been counted worthy of suffering disgrace for the Name. ⁴²Day after day, in the temple courts and from house to house, they never stopped teaching and proclaiming the good news that Jesus is the Christ.ᵃ

The Choosing of the Seven

6 In those days when the number of disciples was increasing, the Grecian Jews among them complained against the Hebraic Jews because their widows were being overlooked in the daily distribution of food. ²So the Twelve gathered all the disciples together and said, "It would not be right for us to neglect the ministry of the word of God in order to wait on tables. ³Brothers, choose seven men from among you who are known to be full of the Spirit and wisdom. We will turn this responsibility over to them ⁴and will give our attention to prayer and the ministry of the word."

⁵This proposal pleased the whole group. They chose Stephen, a man full of faith and of the Holy Spirit; also Philip, Procorus, Nicanor, Timon, Parmenas, and Nicolas from Antioch, a convert to Judaism. ⁶They presented these men to the apostles, who prayed and laid their hands on them.

⁷So the word of God spread. The number of disciples in Jerusalem increased rapidly, and a large number of priests became obedient to the faith.

Stephen Seized

⁸Now Stephen, a man full of God's grace and power, did great wonders and miraculous signs among the people. ⁹Opposition arose, however, from members of the Synagogue of the Freedmen (as it was called)—Jews of Cyrene and Alexandria as well as the provinces of Cilicia and Asia. These men began to

ᵃ 42 Or *Messiah*

argue with Stephen, ¹⁰but they could not stand up against his wisdom or the Spirit by whom he spoke.

¹¹Then they secretly persuaded some men to say, "We have heard Stephen speak words of blasphemy against Moses and against God."

¹²So they stirred up the people and the elders and the teachers of the law. They seized Stephen and brought him before the Sanhedrin. ¹³They produced false witnesses, who testified, "This fellow never stops speaking against this holy place and against the law. ¹⁴For we have heard him say that this Jesus of Nazareth will destroy this place and change the customs Moses handed down to us."

¹⁵All who were sitting in the Sanhedrin looked intently at Stephen, and they saw that his face was like the face of an angel.

Stephen's Speech to the Sanhedrin

7 Then the high priest asked him, "Are these charges true?"

²To this he replied: "Brothers and fathers, listen to me! The God of glory appeared to our father Abraham while he was still in Mesopotamia, before he lived in Haran. ³'Leave your country and your people,' God said, 'and go to the land I will show you.'ᵃ

⁴"So he left the land of the Chaldeans and settled in Haran. After the death of his father, God sent him to this land where you are now living. ⁵He gave him no inheritance here, not even a foot of ground. But God promised him that he and his descendants after him would possess the land, even though at that time Abraham had no child. ⁶God spoke to him in this way: 'Your descendants will be strangers in a country not their own, and they will be enslaved and mistreated four hundred years. ⁷But I will punish the nation they serve as slaves,' God said, 'and afterward they will come out of that country and worship me in this place.'ᵇ ⁸Then he gave Abraham the covenant of circumcision. And Abraham became the father of Isaac and circumcised him eight days after his birth. Later Isaac became the father of Jacob, and Jacob became the father of the twelve patriarchs.

⁹"Because the patriarchs were jealous of Joseph, they sold him as a slave into Egypt. But God was with him ¹⁰and rescued him from all his troubles. He gave Joseph wisdom and enabled him to gain the goodwill of Pharaoh king of Egypt; so he made him ruler over Egypt and all his palace.

¹¹"Then a famine struck all Egypt and Canaan, bringing great suffering, and our fathers could not find food. ¹²When Jacob heard that there was grain in Egypt, he sent our fathers on their first visit. ¹³On their second visit, Joseph told his brothers who he was, and Pharaoh learned about Joseph's family. ¹⁴After this, Joseph sent for his father Jacob and his whole family, seventy-five in all. ¹⁵Then Jacob went down to Egypt, where he and our fathers died. ¹⁶Their bodies were brought back to Shechem and placed in the tomb that Abraham had bought from the sons of Hamor at Shechem for a certain sum of money.

¹⁷"As the time drew near for God to fulfill his promise to Abraham, the number of our people in Egypt greatly increased. ¹⁸Then another king, who knew nothing about Joseph, became ruler of Egypt. ¹⁹He dealt treacherously with our people and oppressed our forefathers by forcing them to throw out their newborn babies so that they would die.

²⁰"At that time Moses was born, and he was no ordinary child.ᶜ For three months he was cared for in his father's house. ²¹When he was placed outside, Pharaoh's daughter took him and brought him up as her own son. ²²Moses was educated in all the wisdom of the Egyptians and was powerful in speech and action.

²³"When Moses was forty years old, he decided to visit his fellow Israelites. ²⁴He saw one of them being mistreated by an Egyptian, so he went to his defense and avenged him by killing the Egyptian. ²⁵Moses thought that his own people would realize that God was using him to rescue them, but they did not. ²⁶The next day Moses came upon two Israelites who were fighting. He tried to reconcile them by saying, 'Men, you are

---

ᵃ 3 Gen. 12:1   ᵇ 7 Gen. 15:13,14   ᶜ 20 Or *was fair in the sight of God*

brothers; why do you want to hurt each other?'

27"But the man who was mistreating the other pushed Moses aside and said, 'Who made you ruler and judge over us? 28Do you want to kill me as you killed the Egyptian yesterday?'a 29When Moses heard this, he fled to Midian, where he settled as a foreigner and had two sons.

30"After forty years had passed, an angel appeared to Moses in the flames of a burning bush in the desert near Mount Sinai. 31When he saw this, he was amazed at the sight. As he went over to look more closely, he heard the Lord's voice: 32'I am the God of your fathers, the God of Abraham, Isaac and Jacob.'b Moses trembled with fear and did not dare to look.

33"Then the Lord said to him, 'Take off your sandals; the place where you are standing is holy ground. 34I have indeed seen the oppression of my people in Egypt. I have heard their groaning and have come down to set them free. Now come, I will send you back to Egypt.'c

35"This is the same Moses whom they had rejected with the words, 'Who made you ruler and judge?' He was sent to be their ruler and deliverer by God himself, through the angel who appeared to him in the bush. 36He led them out of Egypt and did wonders and miraculous signs in Egypt, at the Red Sead and for forty years in the desert.

37"This is that Moses who told the Israelites, 'God will send you a prophet like me from your own people.'e 38He was in the assembly in the desert, with the angel who spoke to him on Mount Sinai, and with our fathers; and he received living words to pass on to us.

39"But our fathers refused to obey him. Instead, they rejected him and in their hearts turned back to Egypt. 40They told Aaron, 'Make us gods who will go before us. As for this fellow Moses who led us out of Egypt—we don't know what has happened to him!'f 41That was the time they made an idol in the form of a calf. They brought sacrifices to it and held a celebration in honor of what their hands had made.

42But God turned away and gave them over to the worship of the heavenly bodies. This agrees with what is written in the book of the prophets:

" 'Did you bring me sacrifices and
    offerings
    forty years in the desert, O house
        of Israel?
43 You have lifted up the shrine of
    Molech
    and the star of your god Rephan,
    the idols you made to worship.
Therefore I will send you into exile'g
    beyond Babylon.

44"Our forefathers had the tabernacle of the Testimony with them in the desert. It had been made as God directed Moses, according to the pattern he had seen. 45Having received the tabernacle, our fathers under Joshua brought it with them when they took the land from the nations God drove out before them. It remained in the land until the time of David, 46who enjoyed God's favor and asked that he might provide a dwelling place for the God of Jacob.h 47But it was Solomon who built the house for him.

48"However, the Most High does not live in houses made by men. As the prophet says:

49 " 'Heaven is my throne,
    and the earth is my footstool.
What kind of house will you build for
    me?
                    says the Lord.
Or where will my resting place be?
50 Has not my hand made all these
        things?'i

51"You stiff-necked people, with uncircumcised hearts and ears! You are just like your fathers: You always resist the Holy Spirit! 52Was there ever a prophet your fathers did not persecute? They even killed those who predicted the coming of the Righteous One. And now you have betrayed and murdered him— 53you who have received the law that was put into effect through angels but have not obeyed it."

a 28 Exodus 2:14   b 32 Exodus 3:6   c 34 Exodus 3:5,7,8,10   d 36 That is, Sea of Reeds
e 37 Deut. 18:15   f 40 Exodus 32:1   g 43 Amos 5:25–27   h 46 Some early manuscripts the house
of Jacob   i 50 Isaiah 66:1,2

The Stoning of Stephen

54When they heard this, they were furious and gnashed their teeth at him. 55But Stephen, full of the Holy Spirit, looked up to heaven and saw the glory of God, and Jesus standing at the right hand of God. 56"Look," he said, "I see heaven open and the Son of Man standing at the right hand of God."

57At this they covered their ears and, yelling at the top of their voices, they all rushed at him, 58dragged him out of the city and began to stone him. Meanwhile, the witnesses laid their clothes at the feet of a young man named Saul.

59While they were stoning him, Stephen prayed, "Lord Jesus, receive my spirit." 60Then he fell on his knees and cried out, "Lord, do not hold this sin against them." When he had said this, he fell asleep.

8 And Saul was there, giving approval to his death.

The Church Persecuted and Scattered

On that day a great persecution broke out against the church at Jerusalem, and all except the apostles were scattered throughout Judea and Samaria. 2Godly men buried Stephen and mourned deeply for him. 3But Saul began to destroy the church. Going from house to house, he dragged off men and women and put them in prison.

Philip in Samaria

4Those who had been scattered preached the word wherever they went. 5Philip went down to a city in Samaria and proclaimed the Christ*a* there. 6When the crowds heard Philip and saw the miraculous signs he did, they all paid close attention to what he said. 7With shrieks, evil*b* spirits came out of many, and many paralytics and cripples were healed. 8So there was great joy in that city.

Simon the Sorcerer

9Now for some time a man named Simon had practiced sorcery in the city and amazed all the people of Samaria.

He boasted that he was someone great, 10and all the people, both high and low, gave him their attention and exclaimed, "This man is the divine power known as the Great Power." 11They followed him because he had amazed them for a long time with his magic. 12But when they believed Philip as he preached the good news of the kingdom of God and the name of Jesus Christ, they were baptized, both men and women. 13Simon himself believed and was baptized. And he followed Philip everywhere, astonished by the great signs and miracles he saw.

HOW SWEET THE NAME OF JESUS SOUNDS
IN A BELIEVER'S EAR!
IT SOOTHES HIS SORROWS, HEALS HIS WOUNDS,
AND DRIVES AWAY HIS FEAR!
—*John Newton*

14When the apostles in Jerusalem heard that Samaria had accepted the word of God, they sent Peter and John to them. 15When they arrived, they prayed for them that they might receive the Holy Spirit, 16because the Holy Spirit had not yet come upon any of them; they had simply been baptized into*c* the name of the Lord Jesus. 17Then Peter and John placed their hands on them, and they received the Holy Spirit.

18When Simon saw that the Spirit was given at the laying on of the apostles' hands, he offered them money 19and said, "Give me also this ability so that everyone on whom I lay my hands may receive the Holy Spirit."

20Peter answered: "May your money perish with you, because you thought you could buy the gift of God with money! 21You have no part or share in this ministry, because your heart is not right before God. 22Repent of this wickedness and pray to the Lord. Perhaps he will forgive you for having such a thought in your heart. 23For I see that you are full of bitterness and captive to sin."

24Then Simon answered, "Pray to the

a 5 Or *Messiah*   *b* 7 Greek *unclean*   *c* 16 Or *in*

Lord for me so that nothing you have said may happen to me."

25When they had testified and proclaimed the word of the Lord, Peter and John returned to Jerusalem, preaching the gospel in many Samaritan villages.

Philip and the Ethiopian

26Now an angel of the Lord said to Philip, "Go south to the road—the desert road—that goes down from Jerusalem to Gaza." 27So he started out, and on his way he met an Ethiopian*a* eunuch, an important official in charge of all the treasury of Candace, queen of the Ethiopians. This man had gone to Jerusalem to worship, 28and on his way home was sitting in his chariot reading

a 27 That is, from the upper Nile region

WEDNESDAY

A MARTYR'S PRAYER
Polycarp of Smyrna

VERSE: Acts 7:60   PASSAGE: Acts 7:54—8:1

At the Stake

ord God Almighty, we have come to know you through that dear child of yours, Jesus Christ, and he has led us to you. I bless you because you have thought me worthy of this day and hour, worthy to be numbered among the martyrs and then to drink out of the cup that Jesus has drunk from; so with him you have counted me worthy to rise and live for ever.

May I be admitted to your presence today, a satisfactory and welcome sacrifice. You have made my life a preparation for this. You showed me that this was my destiny, and now, true to your word, you have brought it about. For this and all your blessings I praise you and give you glory.

As the Flames Rose

Lord Jesus Christ, receive my soul.
　　Blessings to you, Lord Jesus Christ, that you have thought me
　　　fit to share this fate with you, sinner that I am.
　　Lord, Lord, Lord, come to my help; I turn to you for refuge.

ADDITIONAL SCRIPTURE READING:
Romans 14:8; Philippians 1:21

Go to page 1275 for your next devotional reading.

100 　 500

the book of Isaiah the prophet. 29The Spirit told Philip, "Go to that chariot and stay near it."

30Then Philip ran up to the chariot and heard the man reading Isaiah the prophet. "Do you understand what you are reading?" Philip asked.

31"How can I," he said, "unless someone explains it to me?" So he invited Philip to come up and sit with him.

32The eunuch was reading this passage of Scripture:

"He was led like a sheep to the
    slaughter,
  and as a lamb before the shearer is
    silent,
  so he did not open his mouth.
33In his humiliation he was deprived of
    justice.
  Who can speak of his
    descendants?
  For his life was taken from the
    earth."a

34The eunuch asked Philip, "Tell me, please, who is the prophet talking about, himself or someone else?" 35Then Philip began with that very passage of Scripture and told him the good news about Jesus.

36As they traveled along the road, they came to some water and the eunuch said, "Look, here is water. Why shouldn't I be baptized?"b 38And he gave orders to stop the chariot. Then both Philip and the eunuch went down into the water and Philip baptized him. 39When they came up out of the water, the Spirit of the Lord suddenly took Philip away, and the eunuch did not see him again, but went on his way rejoicing. 40Philip, however, appeared at Azotus and traveled about, preaching the gospel in all the towns until he reached Caesarea.

Saul's Conversion

9 Meanwhile, Saul was still breathing out murderous threats against the Lord's disciples. He went to the high priest 2and asked him for letters to the synagogues in Damascus, so that if he found any there who belonged to the

Way, whether men or women, he might take them as prisoners to Jerusalem. 3As he neared Damascus on his journey, suddenly a light from heaven flashed around him. 4He fell to the ground and heard a voice say to him, "Saul, Saul, why do you persecute me?"

5"Who are you, Lord?" Saul asked.

"I am Jesus, whom you are persecuting," he replied. 6"Now get up and go into the city, and you will be told what you must do."

7The men traveling with Saul stood there speechless; they heard the sound but did not see anyone. 8Saul got up from the ground, but when he opened his eyes he could see nothing. So they led him by the hand into Damascus. 9For three days he was blind, and did not eat or drink anything.

10In Damascus there was a disciple named Ananias. The Lord called to him in a vision, "Ananias!"

"Yes, Lord," he answered.

11The Lord told him, "Go to the house of Judas on Straight Street and ask for a man from Tarsus named Saul, for he is praying. 12In a vision he has seen a man named Ananias come and place his hands on him to restore his sight."

13"Lord," Ananias answered, "I have heard many reports about this man and all the harm he has done to your saints in Jerusalem. 14And he has come here with authority from the chief priests to arrest all who call on your name."

15But the Lord said to Ananias, "Go! This man is my chosen instrument to carry my name before the Gentiles and their kings and before the people of Israel. 16I will show him how much he must suffer for my name."

17Then Ananias went to the house and entered it. Placing his hands on Saul, he said, "Brother Saul, the Lord—Jesus, who appeared to you on the road as you were coming here—has sent me so that you may see again and be filled with the Holy Spirit." 18Immediately, something like scales fell from Saul's eyes, and he could see again. He got up and was baptized, 19and after taking some food, he regained his strength.

a 33 Isaiah 53:7,8   b 36 Some late manuscripts baptized?" 37Philip said, "If you believe with all your heart, you may." The eunuch answered, "I believe that Jesus Christ is the Son of God."

Saul in Damascus and Jerusalem

Saul spent several days with the disciples in Damascus. [20] At once he began to preach in the synagogues that Jesus is the Son of God. [21] All those who heard him were astonished and asked, "Isn't he the man who raised havoc in Jerusalem among those who call on this name? And hasn't he come here to take them as prisoners to the chief priests?" [22] Yet Saul grew more and more powerful and baffled the Jews living in Damascus by proving that Jesus is the Christ.[a]

[23] After many days had gone by, the Jews conspired to kill him, [24] but Saul learned of their plan. Day and night they kept close watch on the city gates in order to kill him. [25] But his followers took him by night and lowered him in a basket through an opening in the wall.

[26] When he came to Jerusalem, he tried to join the disciples, but they were all afraid of him, not believing that he really was a disciple. [27] But Barnabas took him and brought him to the apostles. He told them how Saul on his journey had seen the Lord and that the Lord had spoken to him, and how in Damascus he had preached fearlessly in the name of Jesus. [28] So Saul stayed with them and moved about freely in Jerusalem, speaking boldly in the name of the Lord. [29] He talked and debated with the Grecian Jews, but they tried to kill him. [30] When the brothers learned of this, they took him down to Caesarea and sent him off to Tarsus.

[31] Then the church throughout Judea, Galilee and Samaria enjoyed a time of peace. It was strengthened; and encouraged by the Holy Spirit, it grew in numbers, living in the fear of the Lord.

Aeneas and Dorcas

[32] As Peter traveled about the country, he went to visit the saints in Lydda. [33] There he found a man named Aeneas, a paralytic who had been bedridden for eight years. [34] "Aeneas," Peter said to him, "Jesus Christ heals you. Get up and take care of your mat." Immediately Aeneas got up. [35] All those who lived in Lydda and Sharon saw him and turned to the Lord.

[36] In Joppa there was a disciple named Tabitha (which, when translated, is Dorcas[b]), who was always doing good and helping the poor. [37] About that time she became sick and died, and her body was washed and placed in an upstairs room. [38] Lydda was near Joppa; so when the disciples heard that Peter was in Lydda, they sent two men to him and urged him, "Please come at once!"

[39] Peter went with them, and when he arrived he was taken upstairs to the room. All the widows stood around him, crying and showing him the robes and other clothing that Dorcas had made while she was still with them.

[40] Peter sent them all out of the room; then he got down on his knees and prayed. Turning toward the dead woman, he said, "Tabitha, get up." She opened her eyes, and seeing Peter she sat up. [41] He took her by the hand and helped her to her feet. Then he called the believers and the widows and presented her to them alive. [42] This became known all over Joppa, and many people believed in the Lord. [43] Peter stayed in Joppa for some time with a tanner named Simon.

Cornelius Calls for Peter

10 At Caesarea there was a man named Cornelius, a centurion in what was known as the Italian Regiment. [2] He and all his family were devout and God-fearing; he gave generously to those in need and prayed to God regularly. [3] One day at about three in the afternoon he had a vision. He distinctly saw an angel of God, who came to him and said, "Cornelius!"

[4] Cornelius stared at him in fear. "What is it, Lord?" he asked.

The angel answered, "Your prayers and gifts to the poor have come up as a memorial offering before God. [5] Now send men to Joppa to bring back a man named Simon who is called Peter. [6] He is staying with Simon the tanner, whose house is by the sea."

[7] When the angel who spoke to him had gone, Cornelius called two of his servants and a devout soldier who was one of his attendants. [8] He told them everything that had happened and sent them to Joppa.

a 22 Or *Messiah*   *b 36* Both *Tabitha* (Aramaic) and *Dorcas* (Greek) mean *gazelle.*

Peter's Vision

9About noon the following day as they were on their journey and approaching the city, Peter went up on the roof to pray. 10He became hungry and wanted something to eat, and while the meal was being prepared, he fell into a trance. 11He saw heaven opened and something like a large sheet being let down to earth by its four corners. 12It contained all kinds of four-footed animals, as well as reptiles of the earth and birds of the air. 13Then a voice told him, "Get up, Peter. Kill and eat."

14"Surely not, Lord!" Peter replied. "I have never eaten anything impure or unclean."

15The voice spoke to him a second time, "Do not call anything impure that God has made clean."

16This happened three times, and immediately the sheet was taken back to heaven.

17While Peter was wondering about the meaning of the vision, the men sent by Cornelius found out where Simon's house was and stopped at the gate. 18They called out, asking if Simon who was known as Peter was staying there.

19While Peter was still thinking about the vision, the Spirit said to him, "Simon, three*a* men are looking for you. 20So get up and go downstairs. Do not hesitate to go with them, for I have sent them."

21Peter went down and said to the men, "I'm the one you're looking for. Why have you come?"

22The men replied, "We have come from Cornelius the centurion. He is a righteous and God-fearing man, who is respected by all the Jewish people. A holy angel told him to have you come to his house so that he could hear what you have to say." 23Then Peter invited the men into the house to be his guests.

Peter at Cornelius' House

The next day Peter started out with them, and some of the brothers from Joppa went along. 24The following day he arrived in Caesarea. Cornelius was expecting them and had called together his relatives and close friends. 25As Peter entered the house, Cornelius met him and fell at his feet in reverence. 26But Peter made him get up. "Stand up," he said, "I am only a man myself."

27Talking with him, Peter went inside and found a large gathering of people. 28He said to them: "You are well aware that it is against our law for a Jew to associate with a Gentile or visit him. But God has shown me that I should not call any man impure or unclean. 29So when I was sent for, I came without raising any objection. May I ask why you sent for me?"

30Cornelius answered: "Four days ago I was in my house praying at this hour, at three in the afternoon. Suddenly a man in shining clothes stood before me 31and said, 'Cornelius, God has heard your prayer and remembered your gifts to the poor. 32Send to Joppa for Simon who is called Peter. He is a guest in the home of Simon the tanner, who lives by the sea.' 33So I sent for you immediately, and it was good of you to come. Now we are all here in the presence of God to listen to everything the Lord has commanded you to tell us."

34Then Peter began to speak: "I now realize how true it is that God does not show favoritism 35but accepts men from every nation who fear him and do what is right. 36You know the message God sent to the people of Israel, telling the good news of peace through Jesus Christ, who is Lord of all. 37You know what has happened throughout Judea, beginning in Galilee after the baptism that John preached— 38how God anointed Jesus of Nazareth with the Holy Spirit and power, and how he went around doing good and healing all who were under the power of the devil, because God was with him.

39"We are witnesses of everything he did in the country of the Jews and in Jerusalem. They killed him by hanging him on a tree, 40but God raised him from the dead on the third day and caused him to be seen. 41He was not seen by all the people, but by witnesses whom God had already chosen—by us who ate and drank with him after he rose from the dead. 42He commanded us to preach to the people and to testify

---

a 19 One early manuscript *two;* other manuscripts do not have the number.

AT THE CENTER
Thomas R. Kelly

VERSE: Acts 10:34   **PASSAGE:** Acts 10:24–35

n the Fellowship, cultural and educational and national and racial differences are leveled. Unlettered men are at ease with the truly humble scholar . . . , and the scholar listens with joy and openness to the precious experiences of God's dealing with the workingman. We find men with chilly theologies but with glowing hearts. We overleap the boundaries of church membership and find Lutherans and Roman Catholics, Jews and Christians, within the Fellowship. We reread the poets and the saints, and the Fellowship is enlarged. With urgent hunger we read the Scriptures, with no thought of pious exercise, but in order to find more friends for the soul. We brush past our historical learning in the Scriptures, to seize upon those writers who lived in the Center, in the Life and in the Power. Particularly does devotional literature become illuminated, for *The Imitation of Christ*, and Augustine's *Confessions*, and Brother Lawrence's *Practice of the Presence of God* speak the language of the souls who live at the Center. Time telescopes and vanishes, centuries and creeds are overleaped. The incident of death puts no boundaries to the Blessed Community, wherein men and women live and love and work and pray in that Life and Power which gave forth the Scriptures. And we wonder and grieve at the overwhelmingly heady preoccupation of religious people with problems, problems, unless they have first come into the Fellowship of the Light.

The final grounds of holy Fellowship are in God. Lives immersed and drowned in God are drowned in love, and know one another in him, and know one another in love. God is the medium, the matrix, the focus, the solvent. As Meister Eckhart suggests, he who is wholly surrounded by God, enveloped by God, clothed with God, glowing in selfless love toward him—such a man no one can touch except he touch God also.

ADDITIONAL SCRIPTURE READING:
John 3:16; Colossians 3:12–15

Go to page 1280 for your next devotional reading.

1900   Present

that he is the one whom God appointed as judge of the living and the dead. [43]All the prophets testify about him that everyone who believes in him receives forgiveness of sins through his name."

[44]While Peter was still speaking these words, the Holy Spirit came on all who heard the message. [45]The circumcised believers who had come with Peter were astonished that the gift of the Holy Spirit had been poured out even on the Gentiles. [46]For they heard them speaking in tongues[a] and praising God.

Then Peter said, [47]"Can anyone keep these people from being baptized with water? They have received the Holy Spirit just as we have." [48]So he ordered that they be baptized in the name of Jesus Christ. Then they asked Peter to stay with them for a few days.

Peter Explains His Actions

11 The apostles and the brothers throughout Judea heard that the Gentiles also had received the word of God. [2]So when Peter went up to Jerusalem, the circumcised believers criticized him [3]and said, "You went into the house of uncircumcised men and ate with them."

[4]Peter began and explained everything to them precisely as it had happened: [5]"I was in the city of Joppa praying, and in a trance I saw a vision. I saw something like a large sheet being let down from heaven by its four corners, and it came down to where I was. [6]I looked into it and saw four-footed animals of the earth, wild beasts, reptiles, and birds of the air. [7]Then I heard a voice telling me, 'Get up, Peter. Kill and eat.'

[8]"I replied, 'Surely not, Lord! Nothing impure or unclean has ever entered my mouth.'

[9]"The voice spoke from heaven a second time, 'Do not call anything impure that God has made clean.' [10]This happened three times, and then it was all pulled up to heaven again.

[11]"Right then three men who had been sent to me from Caesarea stopped at the house where I was staying. [12]The Spirit told me to have no hesitation about going with them. These six brothers also went with me, and we entered

the man's house. [13]He told us how he had seen an angel appear in his house and say, 'Send to Joppa for Simon who is called Peter. [14]He will bring you a message through which you and all your household will be saved.'

[15]"As I began to speak, the Holy Spirit came on them as he had come on us at the beginning. [16]Then I remembered what the Lord had said: 'John baptized with[b] water, but you will be baptized with the Holy Spirit.' [17]So if God gave them the same gift as he gave us, who believed in the Lord Jesus Christ, who was I to think that I could oppose God?"

[18]When they heard this, they had no further objections and praised God, saying, "So then, God has granted even the Gentiles repentance unto life."

The Church in Antioch

[19]Now those who had been scattered by the persecution in connection with Stephen traveled as far as Phoenicia, Cyprus and Antioch, telling the message only to Jews. [20]Some of them, however, men from Cyprus and Cyrene, went to Antioch and began to speak to Greeks also, telling them the good news about the Lord Jesus. [21]The Lord's hand was with them, and a great number of people believed and turned to the Lord.

[22]News of this reached the ears of the church at Jerusalem, and they sent Barnabas to Antioch. [23]When he arrived and saw the evidence of the grace of God, he was glad and encouraged them all to remain true to the Lord with all their hearts. [24]He was a good man, full of the Holy Spirit and faith, and a great number of people were brought to the Lord.

[25]Then Barnabas went to Tarsus to look for Saul, [26]and when he found him, he brought him to Antioch. So for a whole year Barnabas and Saul met with the church and taught great numbers of people. The disciples were called Christians first at Antioch.

[27]During this time some prophets came down from Jerusalem to Antioch. [28]One of them, named Agabus, stood up and through the Spirit predicted that a severe famine would spread over the entire Roman world. (This happened during the reign of Claudius.) [29]The

disciples, each according to his ability, decided to provide help for the brothers living in Judea. 30This they did, sending their gift to the elders by Barnabas and Saul.

Peter's Miraculous Escape From Prison

12 It was about this time that King Herod arrested some who belonged to the church, intending to persecute them. 2He had James, the brother of John, put to death with the sword. 3When he saw that this pleased the Jews, he proceeded to seize Peter also. This happened during the Feast of Unleavened Bread. 4After arresting him, he put him in prison, handing him over to be guarded by four squads of four soldiers each. Herod intended to bring him out for public trial after the Passover.

5So Peter was kept in prison, but the church was earnestly praying to God for him.

6The night before Herod was to bring him to trial, Peter was sleeping between two soldiers, bound with two chains, and sentries stood guard at the entrance. 7Suddenly an angel of the Lord appeared and a light shone in the cell. He struck Peter on the side and woke him up. "Quick, get up!" he said, and the chains fell off Peter's wrists.

8Then the angel said to him, "Put on your clothes and sandals." And Peter did so. "Wrap your cloak around you and follow me," the angel told him. 9Peter followed him out of the prison, but he had no idea that what the angel was doing was really happening; he thought he was seeing a vision. 10They passed the first and second guards and came to the iron gate leading to the city. It opened for them by itself, and they went through it. When they had walked the length of one street, suddenly the angel left him.

11Then Peter came to himself and said, "Now I know without a doubt that the Lord sent his angel and rescued me from Herod's clutches and from everything the Jewish people were anticipating."

12When this had dawned on him, he went to the house of Mary the mother of John, also called Mark, where many people had gathered and were praying.

13Peter knocked at the outer entrance, and a servant girl named Rhoda came to answer the door. 14When she recognized Peter's voice, she was so overjoyed she ran back without opening it and exclaimed, "Peter is at the door!"

15"You're out of your mind," they told her. When she kept insisting that it was so, they said, "It must be his angel."

16But Peter kept on knocking, and when they opened the door and saw him, they were astonished. 17Peter motioned with his hand for them to be quiet and described how the Lord had brought him out of prison. "Tell James and the brothers about this," he said, and then he left for another place.

18In the morning, there was no small commotion among the soldiers as to what had become of Peter. 19After Herod had a thorough search made for him and did not find him, he cross-examined the guards and ordered that they be executed.

Herod's Death

Then Herod went from Judea to Caesarea and stayed there a while. 20He had been quarreling with the people of Tyre and Sidon; they now joined together and sought an audience with him. Having secured the support of Blastus, a trusted personal servant of the king, they asked for peace, because they depended on the king's country for their food supply.

21On the appointed day Herod, wearing his royal robes, sat on his throne and delivered a public address to the people. 22They shouted, "This is the voice of a god, not of a man." 23Immediately, because Herod did not give praise to God, an angel of the Lord struck him down, and he was eaten by worms and died.

24But the word of God continued to increase and spread.

25When Barnabas and Saul had finished their mission, they returned from*a* Jerusalem, taking with them John, also called Mark.

Barnabas and Saul Sent Off

13 In the church at Antioch there were prophets and teachers: Barnabas, Simeon called Niger, Lucius of Cyrene, Manaen (who had been brought up with Herod the

a 25 Some manuscripts *to*

tetrarch) and Saul. ²While they were worshiping the Lord and fasting, the Holy Spirit said, "Set apart for me Barnabas and Saul for the work to which I have called them." ³So after they had fasted and prayed, they placed their hands on them and sent them off.

On Cyprus

⁴The two of them, sent on their way by the Holy Spirit, went down to Seleucia and sailed from there to Cyprus. ⁵When they arrived at Salamis, they proclaimed the word of God in the Jewish synagogues. John was with them as their helper.

⁶They traveled through the whole island until they came to Paphos. There they met a Jewish sorcerer and false prophet named Bar-Jesus, ⁷who was an attendant of the proconsul, Sergius Paulus. The proconsul, an intelligent man, sent for Barnabas and Saul because he wanted to hear the word of God. ⁸But Elymas the sorcerer (for that is what his name means) opposed them and tried to turn the proconsul from the faith. ⁹Then Saul, who was also called Paul, filled with the Holy Spirit, looked straight at Elymas and said, ¹⁰"You are a child of the devil and an enemy of everything that is right! You are full of all kinds of deceit and trickery. Will you never stop perverting the right ways of the Lord? ¹¹Now the hand of the Lord is against you. You are going to be blind, and for a time you will be unable to see the light of the sun."

Immediately mist and darkness came over him, and he groped about, seeking someone to lead him by the hand. ¹²When the proconsul saw what had happened, he believed, for he was amazed at the teaching about the Lord.

In Pisidian Antioch

¹³From Paphos, Paul and his companions sailed to Perga in Pamphylia, where John left them to return to Jerusalem. ¹⁴From Perga they went on to Pisidian Antioch. On the Sabbath they entered the synagogue and sat down. ¹⁵After the reading from the Law and the Prophets, the synagogue rulers sent word to them, saying, "Brothers, if you have a message of encouragement for the people, please speak."

¹⁶Standing up, Paul motioned with his hand and said: "Men of Israel and you Gentiles who worship God, listen to me! ¹⁷The God of the people of Israel chose our fathers; he made the people prosper during their stay in Egypt, with mighty power he led them out of that country, ¹⁸he endured their conduct*a* for about forty years in the desert, ¹⁹he overthrew seven nations in Canaan and gave their land to his people as their inheritance. ²⁰All this took about 450 years.

"After this, God gave them judges until the time of Samuel the prophet. ²¹Then the people asked for a king, and he gave them Saul son of Kish, of the tribe of Benjamin, who ruled forty years. ²²After removing Saul, he made David their king. He testified concerning him: 'I have found David son of Jesse a man after my own heart; he will do everything I want him to do.'

²³"From this man's descendants God has brought to Israel the Savior Jesus, as he promised. ²⁴Before the coming of Jesus, John preached repentance and baptism to all the people of Israel. ²⁵As John was completing his work, he said: 'Who do you think I am? I am not that one. No, but he is coming after me, whose sandals I am not worthy to untie.'

²⁶"Brothers, children of Abraham, and you God-fearing Gentiles, it is to us that this message of salvation has been sent. ²⁷The people of Jerusalem and their rulers did not recognize Jesus, yet in condemning him they fulfilled the words of the prophets that are read every Sabbath. ²⁸Though they found no proper ground for a death sentence, they asked Pilate to have him executed. ²⁹When they had carried out all that was written about him, they took him down from the tree and laid him in a tomb. ³⁰But God raised him from the dead, ³¹and for many days he was seen by those who had traveled with him from Galilee to Jerusalem. They are now his witnesses to our people.

³²"We tell you the good news: What God promised our fathers ³³he has fulfilled for us, their children, by raising up

a 18 Some manuscripts *and cared for them*

Jesus. As it is written in the second Psalm:

" 'You are my Son;
today I have become your Father.'$^{a'b}$

34The fact that God raised him from the dead, never to decay, is stated in these words:

" 'I will give you the holy and sure
blessings promised to David.'^{c}

35So it is stated elsewhere:

" 'You will not let your Holy One see
decay.'^{d}

36"For when David had served God's purpose in his own generation, he fell asleep; he was buried with his fathers and his body decayed; 37But the one whom God raised from the dead did not see decay.

38"Therefore, my brothers, I want you to know that through Jesus the forgiveness of sins is proclaimed to you. 39Through him everyone who believes is justified from everything you could not be justified from by the law of Moses. 40Take care that what the prophets have said does not happen to you:

41" 'Look, you scoffers,
wonder and perish,
for I am going to do something in
your days
that you would never believe,
even if someone told you.'^{e}"

42As Paul and Barnabas were leaving the synagogue, the people invited them to speak further about these things on the next Sabbath. 43When the congregation was dismissed, many of the Jews and devout converts to Judaism followed Paul and Barnabas, who talked with them and urged them to continue in the grace of God.

44On the next Sabbath almost the whole city gathered to hear the word of the Lord. 45When the Jews saw the crowds, they were filled with jealousy

and talked abusively against what Paul was saying.

46Then Paul and Barnabas answered them boldly: "We had to speak the word of God to you first. Since you reject it and do not consider yourselves worthy of eternal life, we now turn to the Gentiles. 47For this is what the Lord has commanded us:

" 'I have made you^f a light for the
Gentiles,
that you^f may bring salvation to
the ends of the earth.'^{g}"

48When the Gentiles heard this, they were glad and honored the word of the Lord; and all who were appointed for eternal life believed.

49The word of the Lord spread through the whole region. 50But the Jews incited the God-fearing women of high standing and the leading men of the city. They stirred up persecution against Paul and Barnabas, and expelled them from their region. 51So they shook the dust from their feet in protest against them and went to Iconium. 52And the disciples were filled with joy and with the Holy Spirit.

In Iconium

14 At Iconium Paul and Barnabas went as usual into the Jewish synagogue. There they spoke so effectively that a great number of Jews and Gentiles believed. 2But the Jews who refused to believe stirred up the Gentiles and poisoned their minds against the brothers. 3So Paul and Barnabas spent considerable time there, speaking boldly for the Lord, who confirmed the message of his grace by enabling them to do miraculous signs and wonders. 4The people of the city were divided; some sided with the Jews, others with the apostles. 5There was a plot afoot among the Gentiles and Jews, together with their leaders, to mistreat them and stone them. 6But they found out about it and fled to the Lycaonian cities of Lystra and Derbe and to the surrounding country, 7where they continued to preach the good news.

FAITH AND ELECTION
John Calvin

VERSE: Acts 13:48   **PASSAGE:** Acts13:46–52

t is objected by some, that God will be inconsistent with himself, if he invites all men universally to come to him, and receives only a few elect, . . . that by external preaching all are called to repentance and faith, and yet that the spirit of repentance and faith is not given to all . . . What they assume, I deny as being false in two respects. For he who threatens drought to one city while it rains upon another, and who denounces to another place a famine of doctrine, lays himself under no positive obligation to call all men alike. And he who, forbidding Paul to preach the word in Asia, and suffering him not to go into Bithynia, calls him into Macedonia, demonstrates his right to distribute this treasure to whom he pleases (see Acts 16:7–9). In Isaiah, he still more fully declares his destination of the promises of salvation exclusively for the elect (see Isaiah 26:19); for of them only, and not indiscriminately of all mankind, he declares that they shall be his disciples. Whence it appears, that when the doctrine of salvation is offered to all for their effectual benefit, it is a corrupt prostitution of that which is declared to be reserved particularly for the children of the church . . . Let this suffice, that though the voice of the gospel addresses all men generally, yet the gift of faith is bestowed on few . . . It is no new thing for the seed to fall among thorns or in stony places; not only because most men are evidently in actual rebellion against God, but because they are not all endued with eyes and ears. Where, then, will be the consistency of God's calling to himself such as he knows will never come? . . . Faith, indeed, is properly connected with election, provided it occupies the second place. This order is clearly expressed in these words of Christ: "This is the Father's will, that of all which he hath given me, I should lose nothing . . . And this is the will of him that sent me, that every one which believeth on the son, may have everlasting life" (John 6:39–40, KJV).

ADDITIONAL SCRIPTURE READING:
Isaiah 42:1, 6–7; 2 Thessalonians 2:13–15

Go to page 1284 for your next devotional reading.

1500   1700

In Lystra and Derbe

8In Lystra there sat a man crippled in his feet, who was lame from birth and had never walked. 9He listened to Paul as he was speaking. Paul looked directly at him, saw that he had faith to be healed 10and called out, "Stand up on your feet!" At that, the man jumped up and began to walk.

11When the crowd saw what Paul had done, they shouted in the Lycaonian language, "The gods have come down to us in human form!" 12Barnabas they called Zeus, and Paul they called Hermes because he was the chief speaker. 13The priest of Zeus, whose temple was just outside the city, brought bulls and wreaths to the city gates because he and the crowd wanted to offer sacrifices to them.

14But when the apostles Barnabas and Paul heard of this, they tore their clothes and rushed out into the crowd, shouting: 15"Men, why are you doing this? We too are only men, human like you. We are bringing you good news, telling you to turn from these worthless things to the living God, who made heaven and earth and sea and everything in them. 16In the past, he let all nations go their own way. 17Yet he has not left himself without testimony: He has shown kindness by giving you rain from heaven and crops in their seasons; he provides you with plenty of food and fills your hearts with joy." 18Even with these words, they had difficulty keeping the crowd from sacrificing to them.

19Then some Jews came from Antioch and Iconium and won the crowd over. They stoned Paul and dragged him outside the city, thinking he was dead. 20But after the disciples had gathered around him, he got up and went back into the city. The next day he and Barnabas left for Derbe.

The Return to Antioch in Syria

21They preached the good news in that city and won a large number of disciples. Then they returned to Lystra, Iconium and Antioch, 22strengthening the disciples and encouraging them to remain true to the faith. "We must go through many hardships to enter the kingdom of God," they said. 23Paul and Barnabas appointed elders*a* for them in each church and, with prayer and fasting, committed them to the Lord, in whom they had put their trust. 24After going through Pisidia, they came into Pamphylia, 25and when they had preached the word in Perga, they went down to Attalia.

26From Attalia they sailed back to Antioch, where they had been committed to the grace of God for the work they had now completed. 27On arriving there, they gathered the church together and reported all that God had done through them and how he had opened the door of faith to the Gentiles. 28And they stayed there a long time with the disciples.

The Council at Jerusalem

15 Some men came down from Judea to Antioch and were teaching the brothers: "Unless you are circumcised, according to the custom taught by Moses, you cannot be saved." 2This brought Paul and Barnabas into sharp dispute and debate with them. So Paul and Barnabas were appointed, along with some other believers, to go up to Jerusalem to see the apostles and elders about this question. 3The church sent them on their way, and as they traveled through Phoenicia and Samaria, they told how the Gentiles had been converted. This news made all the brothers very glad. 4When they came to Jerusalem, they were welcomed by the church and the apostles and elders, to whom they reported everything God had done through them.

5Then some of the believers who belonged to the party of the Pharisees stood up and said, "The Gentiles must be circumcised and required to obey the law of Moses."

6The apostles and elders met to consider this question. 7After much discussion, Peter got up and addressed them: "Brothers, you know that some time ago God made a choice among you that the Gentiles might hear from my lips the message of the gospel and believe. 8God, who knows the heart, showed that he accepted them by giving the Holy Spirit

a 23 Or Barnabas ordained elders; or Barnabas had elders elected to them, just as he did to us. [9]He made no distinction between us and them, for he purified their hearts by faith. [10]Now then, why do you try to test God by putting on the necks of the disciples a yoke that neither we nor our fathers have been able to bear? [11]No! We believe it is through the grace of our Lord Jesus that we are saved, just as they are."

[12]The whole assembly became silent as they listened to Barnabas and Paul telling about the miraculous signs and wonders God had done among the Gentiles through them. [13]When they finished, James spoke up: "Brothers, listen to me. [14]Simon[a] has described to us how God at first showed his concern by taking from the Gentiles a people for himself. [15]The words of the prophets are in agreement with this, as it is written:

[16]" 'After this I will return
    and rebuild David's fallen tent.
Its ruins I will rebuild,
    and I will restore it,
[17]that the remnant of men may seek
      the Lord,
    and all the Gentiles who bear my
      name,
says the Lord, who does these things'[b]
[18]   that have been known for ages.[c]

[19]"It is my judgment, therefore, that we should not make it difficult for the Gentiles who are turning to God. [20]Instead we should write to them, telling them to abstain from food polluted by idols, from sexual immorality, from the meat of strangled animals and from blood. [21]For Moses has been preached in every city from the earliest times and is read in the synagogues on every Sabbath."

The Council's Letter to Gentile Believers

[22]Then the apostles and elders, with the whole church, decided to choose some of their own men and send them to Antioch with Paul and Barnabas. They chose Judas (called Barsabbas) and Silas, two men who were leaders among the brothers. [23]With them they sent the following letter:

The apostles and elders, your brothers,

To the Gentile believers in Antioch, Syria and Cilicia:

Greetings.

[24]We have heard that some went out from us without our authorization and disturbed you, troubling your minds by what they said. [25]So we all agreed to choose some men and send them to you with our dear friends Barnabas and Paul— [26]men who have risked their lives for the name of our Lord Jesus Christ. [27]Therefore we are sending Judas and Silas to confirm by word of mouth what we are writing. [28]It seemed good to the Holy Spirit and to us not to burden you with anything beyond the following requirements: [29]You are to abstain from food sacrificed to idols, from blood, from the meat of strangled animals and from sexual immorality. You will do well to avoid these things.

Farewell.

[30]The men were sent off and went down to Antioch, where they gathered the church together and delivered the letter. [31]The people read it and were glad for its encouraging message. [32]Judas and Silas, who themselves were prophets, said much to encourage and strengthen the brothers. [33]After spending some time there, they were sent off by the brothers with the blessing of peace to return to those who had sent them.[d] [35]But Paul and Barnabas remained in Antioch, where they and many others taught and preached the word of the Lord.

Disagreement Between Paul and Barnabas

[36]Some time later Paul said to Barnabas, "Let us go back and visit the brothers in all the towns where we preached

---

[a] 14 Greek Simeon, a variant of Simon; that is, Peter things'— / [18]known to the Lord for ages is his work to remain there

[b] 17 Amos 9:11,12   [c] 17,18 Some manuscripts [d] 33 Some manuscripts them, [34]but Silas decided

the word of the Lord and see how they are doing." 37Barnabas wanted to take John, also called Mark, with them, 38but Paul did not think it wise to take him, because he had deserted them in Pamphylia and had not continued with them in the work. 39They had such a sharp disagreement that they parted company. Barnabas took Mark and sailed for Cyprus, 40but Paul chose Silas and left, commended by the brothers to the grace of the Lord. 41He went through Syria and Cilicia, strengthening the churches.

Timothy Joins Paul and Silas

16 He came to Derbe and then to Lystra, where a disciple named Timothy lived, whose mother was a Jewess and a believer, but whose father was a Greek. 2The brothers at Lystra and Iconium spoke well of him. 3Paul wanted to take him along on the journey, so he circumcised him because of the Jews who lived in that area, for they all knew that his father was a Greek. 4As they traveled from town to town, they delivered the decisions reached by the apostles and elders in Jerusalem for the people to obey. 5So the churches were strengthened in the faith and grew daily in numbers.

Paul's Vision of the Man of Macedonia

6Paul and his companions traveled throughout the region of Phrygia and Galatia, having been kept by the Holy Spirit from preaching the word in the province of Asia. 7When they came to the border of Mysia, they tried to enter Bithynia, but the Spirit of Jesus would not allow them to. 8So they passed by Mysia and went down to Troas. 9During the night Paul had a vision of a man of Macedonia standing and begging him, "Come over to Macedonia and help us." 10After Paul had seen the vision, we got ready at once to leave for Macedonia, concluding that God had called us to preach the gospel to them.

Lydia's Conversion in Philippi

11From Troas we put out to sea and sailed straight for Samothrace, and the next day on to Neapolis. 12From there we traveled to Philippi, a Roman colony and the leading city of that district of Macedonia. And we stayed there several days. 13On the Sabbath we went outside the city gate to the river, where we expected to find a place of prayer. We sat down and began to speak to the women who had gathered there. 14One of those listening was a woman named Lydia, a dealer in purple cloth from the city of Thyatira, who was a worshiper of God. The Lord opened her heart to respond to Paul's message. 15When she and the members of her household were baptized, she invited us to her home. "If you consider me a believer in the Lord," she said, "come and stay at my house." And she persuaded us.

Paul and Silas in Prison

16Once when we were going to the place of prayer, we were met by a slave girl who had a spirit by which she predicted the future. She earned a great deal of money for her owners by fortune-telling. 17This girl followed Paul and the rest of us, shouting, "These men are servants of the Most High God, who are telling you the way to be saved." 18She kept this up for many days. Finally Paul became so troubled that he turned around and said to the spirit, "In the name of Jesus Christ I command you to come out of her!" At that moment the spirit left her.

19When the owners of the slave girl realized that their hope of making money was gone, they seized Paul and Silas and dragged them into the marketplace to face the authorities. 20They brought them before the magistrates and said, "These men are Jews, and are throwing our city into an uproar 21by advocating customs unlawful for us Romans to accept or practice."

22The crowd joined in the attack against Paul and Silas, and the magistrates ordered them to be stripped and beaten. 23After they had been severely flogged, they were thrown into prison, and the jailer was commanded to guard them carefully. 24Upon receiving such orders, he put them in the inner cell and fastened their feet in the stocks.

25About midnight Paul and Silas were praying and singing hymns to God, and the other prisoners were listening to

EVENING ON CALAIS BEACH
William Wordsworth

VERSE: John 20:13–14   **PASSAGE:** John 20

I t is a beauteous evening, calm and free,
    The holy time is quiet as a Nun
    Breathless with adoration; the broad sun
Is sinking down in its tranquility;
The gentleness of heaven broods o'er the sea:
    Listen! the mighty Being is awake,
    And doth with his eternal motion make
A sound like thunder—everlastingly.
Dear child! dear girl! that walkest with me here,
    If thou appear untouched by solemn thought,
    Thy nature is not therefore less divine:
Thou liest in Abraham's bosom all the year;
    And worship'st at the Temple's inner shrine,
    God being with thee when we know it not.

ADDITIONAL SCRIPTURE READING:
Matthew 27:55–56; Luke 8:1–3

Go to page 1287 for your next devotional reading.

1700   1900

them. 26Suddenly there was such a violent earthquake that the foundations of the prison were shaken. At once all the prison doors flew open, and everybody's chains came loose. 27The jailer woke up, and when he saw the prison doors open, he drew his sword and was about to kill himself because he thought the prisoners had escaped. 28But Paul shouted, "Don't harm yourself! We are all here!"

29The jailer called for lights, rushed in and fell trembling before Paul and Silas. 30He then brought them out and asked, "Sirs, what must I do to be saved?"

31They replied, "Believe in the Lord Jesus, and you will be saved—you and your household." 32Then they spoke the word of the Lord to him and to all the others in his house. 33At that hour of the night the jailer took them and washed their wounds; then immediately he and all his family were baptized. 34The jailer brought them into his house and set a meal before them; he was filled with joy because he had come to believe in God—he and his whole family.

35When it was daylight, the magistrates sent their officers to the jailer with the order: "Release those men." 36The jailer told Paul, "The magistrates have ordered that you and Silas be released. Now you can leave. Go in peace."

37But Paul said to the officers: "They beat us publicly without a trial, even though we are Roman citizens, and threw us into prison. And now do they want to get rid of us quietly? No! Let them come themselves and escort us out."

38The officers reported this to the magistrates, and when they heard that Paul and Silas were Roman citizens, they were alarmed. 39They came to appease them and escorted them from the prison, requesting them to leave the city. 40After Paul and Silas came out of the prison, they went to Lydia's house, where they met with the brothers and encouraged them. Then they left.

In Thessalonica

17 When they had passed through Amphipolis and Apollonia, they came to Thessalonica, where there was a Jewish synagogue.

2As his custom was, Paul went into the synagogue, and on three Sabbath days he reasoned with them from the Scriptures, 3explaining and proving that the Christ[a] had to suffer and rise from the dead. "This Jesus I am proclaiming to you is the Christ,[a'] he said. 4Some of the Jews were persuaded and joined Paul and Silas, as did a large number of God-fearing Greeks and not a few prominent women.

5But the Jews were jealous; so they rounded up some bad characters from the marketplace, formed a mob and started a riot in the city. They rushed to Jason's house in search of Paul and Silas in order to bring them out to the crowd.[b] 6But when they did not find them, they dragged Jason and some other brothers before the city officials, shouting: "These men who have caused trouble all over the world have now come here, 7and Jason has welcomed them into his house. They are all defying Caesar's decrees, saying that there is another king, one called Jesus." 8When they heard this, the crowd and the city officials were thrown into turmoil. 9Then they made Jason and the others post bond and let them go.

In Berea

10As soon as it was night, the brothers sent Paul and Silas away to Berea. On arriving there, they went to the Jewish synagogue. 11Now the Bereans were of more noble character than the Thessalonians, for they received the message with great eagerness and examined the Scriptures every day to see if what Paul said was true. 12Many of the Jews believed, as did also a number of prominent Greek women and many Greek men.

13When the Jews in Thessalonica learned that Paul was preaching the word of God at Berea, they went there too, agitating the crowds and stirring them up. 14The brothers immediately sent Paul to the coast, but Silas and Timothy stayed at Berea. 15The men who escorted Paul brought him to Athens and then left with instructions for Silas and Timothy to join him as soon as possible.

a 3 Or *Messiah*   *b 5* Or *the assembly of the people*

In Athens

16While Paul was waiting for them in Athens, he was greatly distressed to see that the city was full of idols. 17So he reasoned in the synagogue with the Jews and the God-fearing Greeks, as well as in the marketplace day by day with those who happened to be there. 18A group of Epicurean and Stoic philosophers began to dispute with him. Some of them asked, "What is this babbler trying to say?" Others remarked, "He seems to be advocating foreign gods." They said this because Paul was preaching the good news about Jesus and the resurrection. 19Then they took him and brought him to a meeting of the Areopagus, where they said to him, "May we know what this new teaching is that you are presenting? 20You are bringing some strange ideas to our ears, and we want to know what they mean." 21(All the Athenians and the foreigners who lived there spent their time doing nothing but talking about and listening to the latest ideas.)

22Paul then stood up in the meeting of the Areopagus and said: "Men of Athens! I see that in every way you are very religious. 23For as I walked around and looked carefully at your objects of worship, I even found an altar with this inscription: TO AN UNKNOWN GOD. Now what you worship as something unknown I am going to proclaim to you.

24"The God who made the world and everything in it is the Lord of heaven and earth and does not live in temples built by hands. 25And he is not served by human hands, as if he needed anything, because he himself gives all men life and breath and everything else. 26From one man he made every nation of men, that they should inhabit the whole earth; and he determined the times set for them and the exact places where they should live. 27God did this so that men would seek him and perhaps reach out for him and find him, though he is not far from each one of us. 28'For in him we live and move and have our being.' As some of your own poets have said, 'We are his offspring.'

29"Therefore since we are God's offspring, we should not think that the divine being is like gold or silver or stone—an image made by man's design and skill. 30In the past God overlooked such ignorance, but now he commands all people everywhere to repent. 31For he has set a day when he will judge the world with justice by the man he has appointed. He has given proof of this to all men by raising him from the dead."

GOD, OF YOUR GOODNESS, GIVE ME YOURSELF FOR YOU ARE SUFFICIENT FOR ME. I CANNOT PROPERLY ASK ANYTHING LESS, TO BE WORTHY OF YOU. IF I WERE TO ASK LESS, I SHOULD ALWAYS BE IN WANT. IN YOU ALONE DO I HAVE ALL.

—Julian of Norwich

32When they heard about the resurrection of the dead, some of them sneered, but others said, "We want to hear you again on this subject." 33At that, Paul left the Council. 34A few men became followers of Paul and believed. Among them was Dionysius, a member of the Areopagus, also a woman named Damaris, and a number of others.

In Corinth

18 After this, Paul left Athens and went to Corinth. 2There he met a Jew named Aquila, a native of Pontus, who had recently come from Italy with his wife Priscilla, because Claudius had ordered all the Jews to leave Rome. Paul went to see them, 3and because he was a tentmaker as they were, he stayed and worked with them. 4Every Sabbath he reasoned in the synagogue, trying to persuade Jews and Greeks.

5When Silas and Timothy came from Macedonia, Paul devoted himself exclusively to preaching, testifying to the Jews that Jesus was the Christ.[a] 6But when the Jews opposed Paul and became abusive, he shook out his clothes in protest and said to them, "Your blood be on your own heads! I am clear of my responsibility. From now on I will go to the Gentiles."

7Then Paul left the synagogue and went next door to the house of Titius Justus, a worshiper of God. 8Crispus, the

a 5 Or Messiah; also in verse 28

WHY CHRISTIANS LOSE REALITY
Francis Schaeffer

VERSE: Acts 17:29   **PASSAGE:** Acts 17:22–31

 ur generation is overwhelmingly naturalistic. There is an almost complete commitment to the concept of the uniformity of natural causes in a closed system. This is its distinguishing mark. If we are not careful, even though we say we are Biblical Christians and supernaturalists, nevertheless the naturalism of our generation tends to come in upon us. It may infiltrate our thinking without our recognizing its coming, like a fog creeping in through a window opened only half an inch. As soon as this happens, Christians begin to lose the reality of their Christian lives . . . All too often the reality is lost because the "ceiling" is down too close upon our heads. It is too low. And the "ceiling" which closes us in is the naturalistic type of thinking.

Now the Christian's spirituality . . . does not stand alone. It is related to the unity of the Bible's view of the universe. This means that we must understand—intellectually, with the windows open—that the universe is not what our generation says it is, seeing only the naturalistic universe . . . For example, we have said that we are to love God enough to say, "Thank you" even for the difficult things. We must immediately understand, as we say this, that this has no meaning whatsoever unless we live in a personal universe in which there is a personal God who objectively exists . . .

We have also considered Christ's redemptive death, which has no meaning whatsoever outside the relationship of a supernatural world. The only reason the words "redemptive death" have any meaning is that there is a personal God who exists and, more than that, has a character. He is not morally neutral. When man sins against that character, which is the law of the universe, he is guilty, and God will judge that man on the basis of true moral guilt. In such a setting, the words "the redemptive death of Christ" have meaning, otherwise they cannot.

ADDITIONAL SCRIPTURE READING:
2 Kings 6:15–23; Titus 2:11–14

Go to page 1291 for your next devotional reading.

1900   Present

synagogue ruler, and his entire household believed in the Lord; and many of the Corinthians who heard him believed and were baptized.

⁹One night the Lord spoke to Paul in a vision: "Do not be afraid; keep on speaking, do not be silent. ¹⁰For I am with you, and no one is going to attack and harm you, because I have many people in this city." ¹¹So Paul stayed for a year and a half, teaching them the word of God.

¹²While Gallio was proconsul of Achaia, the Jews made a united attack on Paul and brought him into court. ¹³"This man," they charged, "is persuading the people to worship God in ways contrary to the law."

¹⁴Just as Paul was about to speak, Gallio said to the Jews, "If you Jews were making a complaint about some misdemeanor or serious crime, it would be reasonable for me to listen to you. ¹⁵But since it involves questions about words and names and your own law—settle the matter yourselves. I will not be a judge of such things." ¹⁶So he had them ejected from the court. ¹⁷Then they all turned on Sosthenes the synagogue ruler and beat him in front of the court. But Gallio showed no concern whatever.

Priscilla, Aquila and Apollos

¹⁸Paul stayed on in Corinth for some time. Then he left the brothers and sailed for Syria, accompanied by Priscilla and Aquila. Before he sailed, he had his hair cut off at Cenchrea because of a vow he had taken. ¹⁹They arrived at Ephesus, where Paul left Priscilla and Aquila. He himself went into the synagogue and reasoned with the Jews. ²⁰When they asked him to spend more time with them, he declined. ²¹But as he left, he promised, "I will come back if it is God's will." Then he set sail from Ephesus. ²²When he landed at Caesarea, he went up and greeted the church and then went down to Antioch.

²³After spending some time in Antioch, Paul set out from there and traveled from place to place throughout the region of Galatia and Phrygia, strengthening all the disciples.

²⁴Meanwhile a Jew named Apollos, a native of Alexandria, came to Ephesus.

He was a learned man, with a thorough knowledge of the Scriptures. ²⁵He had been instructed in the way of the Lord, and he spoke with great fervor*a* and taught about Jesus accurately, though he knew only the baptism of John. ²⁶He began to speak boldly in the synagogue. When Priscilla and Aquila heard him, they invited him to their home and explained to him the way of God more adequately.

²⁷When Apollos wanted to go to Achaia, the brothers encouraged him and wrote to the disciples there to welcome him. On arriving, he was a great help to those who by grace had believed. ²⁸For he vigorously refuted the Jews in public debate, proving from the Scriptures that Jesus was the Christ.

Paul in Ephesus

19 While Apollos was at Corinth, Paul took the road through the interior and arrived at Ephesus. There he found some disciples ²and asked them, "Did you receive the Holy Spirit when*b* you believed?"

They answered, "No, we have not even heard that there is a Holy Spirit."

³So Paul asked, "Then what baptism did you receive?"

"John's baptism," they replied.

⁴Paul said, "John's baptism was a baptism of repentance. He told the people to believe in the one coming after him, that is, in Jesus." ⁵On hearing this, they were baptized into*c* the name of the Lord Jesus. ⁶When Paul placed his hands on them, the Holy Spirit came on them, and they spoke in tongues*d* and prophesied. ⁷There were about twelve men in all.

⁸Paul entered the synagogue and spoke boldly there for three months, arguing persuasively about the kingdom of God. ⁹But some of them became obstinate; they refused to believe and publicly maligned the Way. So Paul left them. He took the disciples with him and had discussions daily in the lecture hall of Tyrannus. ¹⁰This went on for two years, so that all the Jews and Greeks who lived in the province of Asia heard the word of the Lord.

¹¹God did extraordinary miracles

a 25 Or *with fervor in the Spirit*   *b 2* Or *after*   *c 5* Or *in*   *d 6* Or *other languages* through Paul, [12]so that even handkerchiefs and aprons that had touched him were taken to the sick, and their illnesses were cured and the evil spirits left them.

[13]Some Jews who went around driving out evil spirits tried to invoke the name of the Lord Jesus over those who were demon-possessed. They would say, "In the name of Jesus, whom Paul preaches, I command you to come out." [14]Seven sons of Sceva, a Jewish chief priest, were doing this. [15]One day the evil spirit answered them, "Jesus I know, and I know about Paul, but who are you?" [16]Then the man who had the evil spirit jumped on them and overpowered them all. He gave them such a beating that they ran out of the house naked and bleeding.

[17]When this became known to the Jews and Greeks living in Ephesus, they were all seized with fear, and the name of the Lord Jesus was held in high honor. [18]Many of those who believed now came and openly confessed their evil deeds. [19]A number who had practiced sorcery brought their scrolls together and burned them publicly. When they calculated the value of the scrolls, the total came to fifty thousand drachmas.[a] [20]In this way the word of the Lord spread widely and grew in power.

[21]After all this had happened, Paul decided to go to Jerusalem, passing through Macedonia and Achaia. "After I have been there," he said, "I must visit Rome also." [22]He sent two of his helpers, Timothy and Erastus, to Macedonia, while he stayed in the province of Asia a little longer.

The Riot in Ephesus

[23]About that time there arose a great disturbance about the Way. [24]A silversmith named Demetrius, who made silver shrines of Artemis, brought in no little business for the craftsmen. [25]He called them together, along with the workmen in related trades, and said: "Men, you know we receive a good income from this business. [26]And you see and hear how this fellow Paul has convinced and led astray large numbers of people here in Ephesus and in practically the whole province of Asia. He

says that man-made gods are no gods at all. [27]There is danger not only that our trade will lose its good name, but also that the temple of the great goddess Artemis will be discredited, and the goddess herself, who is worshiped throughout the province of Asia and the world, will be robbed of her divine majesty."

[28]When they heard this, they were furious and began shouting: "Great is Artemis of the Ephesians!" [29]Soon the whole city was in an uproar. The people seized Gaius and Aristarchus, Paul's traveling companions from Macedonia, and rushed as one man into the theater. [30]Paul wanted to appear before the crowd, but the disciples would not let him. [31]Even some of the officials of the province, friends of Paul, sent him a message begging him not to venture into the theater.

[32]The assembly was in confusion: Some were shouting one thing, some another. Most of the people did not even know why they were there. [33]The Jews pushed Alexander to the front, and some of the crowd shouted instructions to him. He motioned for silence in order to make a defense before the people. [34]But when they realized he was a Jew, they all shouted in unison for about two hours: "Great is Artemis of the Ephesians!"

[35]The city clerk quieted the crowd and said: "Men of Ephesus, doesn't all the world know that the city of Ephesus is the guardian of the temple of the great Artemis and of her image, which fell from heaven? [36]Therefore, since these facts are undeniable, you ought to be quiet and not do anything rash. [37]You have brought these men here, though they have neither robbed temples nor blasphemed our goddess. [38]If, then, Demetrius and his fellow craftsmen have a grievance against anybody, the courts are open and there are proconsuls. They can press charges. [39]If there is anything further you want to bring up, it must be settled in a legal assembly. [40]As it is, we are in danger of being charged with rioting because of today's events. In that case we would not be able to account for this commotion, since there is no reason for it." [41]After he had said this, he dismissed the assembly.

[a] 19 A drachma was a silver coin worth about a day's wages.

Through Macedonia and Greece

20 When the uproar had ended, Paul sent for the disciples and, after encouraging them, said goodby and set out for Macedonia. ²He traveled through that area, speaking many words of encouragement to the people, and finally arrived in Greece, ³where he stayed three months. Because the Jews made a plot against him just as he was about to sail for Syria, he decided to go back through Macedonia. ⁴He was accompanied by Sopater son of Pyrrhus from Berea, Aristarchus and Secundus from Thessalonica, Gaius from Derbe, Timothy also, and Tychicus and Trophimus from the province of Asia. ⁵These men went on ahead and waited for us at Troas. ⁶But we sailed from Philippi after the Feast of Unleavened Bread, and five days later joined the others at Troas, where we stayed seven days.

Eutychus Raised From the Dead at Troas

⁷On the first day of the week we came together to break bread. Paul spoke to the people and, because he intended to leave the next day, kept on talking until midnight. ⁸There were many lamps in the upstairs room where we were meeting. ⁹Seated in a window was a young man named Eutychus, who was sinking into a deep sleep as Paul talked on and on. When he was sound asleep, he fell to the ground from the third story and was picked up dead. ¹⁰Paul went down, threw himself on the young man and put his arms around him. "Don't be alarmed," he said. "He's alive!" ¹¹Then he went upstairs again and broke bread and ate. After talking until daylight, he left. ¹²The people took the young man home alive and were greatly comforted.

Paul's Farewell to the Ephesian Elders

¹³We went on ahead to the ship and sailed for Assos, where we were going to take Paul aboard. He had made this arrangement because he was going there on foot. ¹⁴When he met us at Assos, we took him aboard and went on to Mitylene. ¹⁵The next day we set sail from there

and arrived off Kios. The day after that we crossed over to Samos, and on the following day arrived at Miletus. ¹⁶Paul had decided to sail past Ephesus to avoid spending time in the province of Asia, for he was in a hurry to reach Jerusalem, if possible, by the day of Pentecost.

¹⁷From Miletus, Paul sent to Ephesus for the elders of the church. ¹⁸When they arrived, he said to them: "You know how I lived the whole time I was with you, from the first day I came into the province of Asia. ¹⁹I served the Lord with great humility and with tears, although I was severely tested by the plots of the Jews. ²⁰You know that I have not hesitated to preach anything that would be helpful to you but have taught you publicly and from house to house. ²¹I have declared to both Jews and Greeks that they must turn to God in repentance and have faith in our Lord Jesus.

²²"And now, compelled by the Spirit, I am going to Jerusalem, not knowing what will happen to me there. ²³I only know that in every city the Holy Spirit warns me that prison and hardships are facing me. ²⁴However, I consider my life worth nothing to me, if only I may finish the race and complete the task the Lord Jesus has given me—the task of testifying to the gospel of God's grace.

²⁵"Now I know that none of you among whom I have gone about preaching the kingdom will ever see me again. ²⁶Therefore, I declare to you today that I am innocent of the blood of all men. ²⁷For I have not hesitated to proclaim to you the whole will of God. ²⁸Keep watch over yourselves and all the flock of which the Holy Spirit has made you overseers.ᵃ Be shepherds of the church of God,ᵇ which he bought with his own blood. ²⁹I know that after I leave, savage wolves will come in among you and will not spare the flock. ³⁰Even from your own number men will arise and distort the truth in order to draw away disciples after them. ³¹So be on your guard! Remember that for three years I never stopped warning each of you night and day with tears.

³²"Now I commit you to God and to the word of his grace, which can build you up and give you an inheritance

---

ᵃ 28 Traditionally *bishops*   ᵇ 28 Many manuscripts *of the Lord* among all those who are sanctified. [33]I have not coveted anyone's silver or gold or clothing. [34]You yourselves know that these hands of mine have supplied my own needs and the needs of my companions. [35]In everything I did, I showed you that by this kind of hard work we must help the weak, remembering the words

TUESDAY

SATURATED WITH THE SPIRIT
Hilary of Poitiers

VERSE: Acts 20:24   **PASSAGE:** Acts 20:17–24

Hoisting My Sails

he chief service I owe you, O God, is that every thought and word of mine should speak of you. The power of speech which you have bestowed on me can give me no greater pleasure than to serve you by preaching your gospel.

But in saying this, I am merely expressing what I want to do. If I am actually to use this gift, I must ask you for your help—ask you to fill the sails I have hoisted for you with the wind of your Holy Spirit, inspiring my mind and my voice. I know that I am often heavy with stupor, so that I am too lazy to speak of you. And I do not spend sufficient time studying your Scriptures, to ensure that my words conform to your Word. Give me the energy and the courage to share the spirit of the apostles, that like them I may truly be an ambassador of your grace.

Saturated in His Love

Although I am dust and ashes, Lord, I am tied to you by bonds of love. Therefore I feel I can speak freely to you. Before I came to know you, I was nothing. I did not know the meaning of life, and I had no understanding of myself. I have no doubt that you had a purpose in causing me to be born; yet you had no need of me, and on my own I was of no use to you.

But then you decided that I should hear the words of your Son, Jesus Christ. And that as I heard his words, you enabled his love to penetrate my heart. Now I am completely saturated in his love and faith, and there is no remedy. Now, Lord, I cannot change my attitude to my faith; I can only die for it.

ADDITIONAL SCRIPTURE READING:
Psalm 139; Philippians 1:21–26

Go to page 1295 for your next devotional reading.

100   500

the Lord Jesus himself said: 'It is more blessed to give than to receive.' "

36When he had said this, he knelt down with all of them and prayed. 37They all wept as they embraced him and kissed him. 38What grieved them most was his statement that they would never see his face again. Then they accompanied him to the ship.

On to Jerusalem

21 After we had torn ourselves away from them, we put out to sea and sailed straight to Cos. The next day we went to Rhodes and from there to Patara. 2We found a ship crossing over to Phoenicia, went on board and set sail. 3After sighting Cyprus and passing to the south of it, we sailed on to Syria. We landed at Tyre, where our ship was to unload its cargo. 4Finding the disciples there, we stayed with them seven days. Through the Spirit they urged Paul not to go on to Jerusalem. 5But when our time was up, we left and continued on our way. All the disciples and their wives and children accompanied us out of the city, and there on the beach we knelt to pray. 6After saying good-by to each other, we went aboard the ship, and they returned home.

7We continued our voyage from Tyre and landed at Ptolemais, where we greeted the brothers and stayed with them for a day. 8Leaving the next day, we reached Caesarea and stayed at the house of Philip the evangelist, one of the Seven. 9He had four unmarried daughters who prophesied.

10After we had been there a number of days, a prophet named Agabus came down from Judea. 11Coming over to us, he took Paul's belt, tied his own hands and feet with it and said, "The Holy Spirit says, 'In this way the Jews of Jerusalem will bind the owner of this belt and will hand him over to the Gentiles.' "

12When we heard this, we and the people there pleaded with Paul not to go up to Jerusalem. 13Then Paul answered, "Why are you weeping and breaking my heart? I am ready not only to be bound, but also to die in Jerusalem for the name of the Lord Jesus." 14When he would not be dissuaded, we gave up and said, "The Lord's will be done."

15After this, we got ready and went up to Jerusalem. 16Some of the disciples from Caesarea accompanied us and brought us to the home of Mnason, where we were to stay. He was a man from Cyprus and one of the early disciples.

Paul's Arrival at Jerusalem

17When we arrived at Jerusalem, the brothers received us warmly. 18The next day Paul and the rest of us went to see James, and all the elders were present. 19Paul greeted them and reported in detail what God had done among the Gentiles through his ministry.

20When they heard this, they praised God. Then they said to Paul: "You see, brother, how many thousands of Jews have believed, and all of them are zealous for the law. 21They have been informed that you teach all the Jews who live among the Gentiles to turn away from Moses, telling them not to circumcise their children or live according to our customs. 22What shall we do? They will certainly hear that you have come, 23so do what we tell you. There are four men with us who have made a vow. 24Take these men, join in their purification rites and pay their expenses, so that they can have their heads shaved. Then everybody will know there is no truth in these reports about you, but that you yourself are living in obedience to the law. 25As for the Gentile believers, we have written to them our decision that they should abstain from food sacrificed to idols, from blood, from the meat of strangled animals and from sexual immorality."

26The next day Paul took the men and purified himself along with them. Then he went to the temple to give notice of the date when the days of purification would end and the offering would be made for each of them.

Paul Arrested

27When the seven days were nearly over, some Jews from the province of Asia saw Paul at the temple. They stirred up the whole crowd and seized him, 28shouting, "Men of Israel, help us! This is the man who teaches all men everywhere against our people and our law and this place. And besides, he has brought Greeks into the temple area and defiled this holy place." 29(They had previously seen Trophimus the Ephesian in the city with Paul and assumed that Paul had brought him into the temple area.)

30The whole city was aroused, and the people came running from all directions. Seizing Paul, they dragged him from the temple, and immediately the gates were shut. 31While they were trying to kill him, news reached the commander of the Roman troops that the whole city of Jerusalem was in an uproar. 32He at once took some officers and soldiers and ran down to the crowd. When the rioters saw the commander and his soldiers, they stopped beating Paul.

33The commander came up and arrested him and ordered him to be bound with two chains. Then he asked who he was and what he had done. 34Some in the crowd shouted one thing and some another, and since the commander could not get at the truth because of the uproar, he ordered that Paul be taken into the barracks. 35When Paul reached the steps, the violence of the mob was so great he had to be carried by the soldiers. 36The crowd that followed kept shouting, "Away with him!"

Paul Speaks to the Crowd

37As the soldiers were about to take Paul into the barracks, he asked the commander, "May I say something to you?"

"Do you speak Greek?" he replied. 38"Aren't you the Egyptian who started a revolt and led four thousand terrorists out into the desert some time ago?"

39Paul answered, "I am a Jew, from Tarsus in Cilicia, a citizen of no ordinary city. Please let me speak to the people."

40Having received the commander's permission, Paul stood on the steps and motioned to the crowd. When they were all silent, he said to them in Aramaic[a]:

22 1"Brothers and fathers, listen now to my defense."

2When they heard him speak to them in Aramaic, they became very quiet.

Then Paul said: 3"I am a Jew, born in Tarsus of Cilicia, but brought up in this city. Under Gamaliel I was thoroughly trained in the law of our fathers and was just as zealous for God as any of you are today. 4I persecuted the followers of this Way to their death, arresting both men and women and throwing them into prison, 5as also the high priest and all the Council can testify. I even obtained letters from them to their brothers in Damascus, and went there to bring these people as prisoners to Jerusalem to be punished.

6"About noon as I came near Damascus, suddenly a bright light from heaven flashed around me. 7I fell to the ground and heard a voice say to me, 'Saul! Saul! Why do you persecute me?'

8"'Who are you, Lord?' I asked.

"'I am Jesus of Nazareth, whom you are persecuting,' he replied. 9My companions saw the light, but they did not understand the voice of him who was speaking to me.

10"'What shall I do, Lord?' I asked.

"'Get up,' the Lord said, 'and go into Damascus. There you will be told all that you have been assigned to do.' 11My companions led me by the hand into Damascus, because the brilliance of the light had blinded me.

12"A man named Ananias came to see me. He was a devout observer of the law and highly respected by all the Jews living there. 13He stood beside me and said, 'Brother Saul, receive your sight!' And at that very moment I was able to see him.

14"Then he said: 'The God of our fathers has chosen you to know his will and to see the Righteous One and to hear words from his mouth. 15You will be his witness to all men of what you have seen and heard. 16And now what are you waiting for? Get up, be baptized and wash your sins away, calling on his name.'

17"When I returned to Jerusalem and was praying at the temple, I fell into a trance 18and saw the Lord speaking. 'Quick!' he said to me. 'Leave Jerusalem immediately, because they will not accept your testimony about me.'

19"'Lord,' I replied, 'these men know that I went from one synagogue to another to imprison and beat those who believe in you. 20And when the blood of your martyr[b] Stephen was shed, I stood there giving my approval and guarding

---

a 40 Or possibly Hebrew; also in 22:2   b 20 Or witness

the clothes of those who were killing him.'

21"Then the Lord said to me, 'Go; I will send you far away to the Gentiles.' "

Paul the Roman Citizen

22The crowd listened to Paul until he said this. Then they raised their voices and shouted, "Rid the earth of him! He's not fit to live!"

23As they were shouting and throwing off their cloaks and flinging dust into the air, 24the commander ordered Paul to be taken into the barracks. He directed that he be flogged and questioned in order to find out why the people were shouting at him like this. 25As they stretched him out to flog him, Paul said to the centurion standing there, "Is it legal for you to flog a Roman citizen who hasn't even been found guilty?"

26When the centurion heard this, he went to the commander and reported it. "What are you going to do?" he asked. "This man is a Roman citizen."

27The commander went to Paul and asked, "Tell me, are you a Roman citizen?"

"Yes, I am," he answered.

28Then the commander said, "I had to pay a big price for my citizenship."

"But I was born a citizen," Paul replied.

29Those who were about to question him withdrew immediately. The commander himself was alarmed when he realized that he had put Paul, a Roman citizen, in chains.

Before the Sanhedrin

30The next day, since the commander wanted to find out exactly why Paul was being accused by the Jews, he released him and ordered the chief priests and all the Sanhedrin to assemble. Then he brought Paul and had him stand before them.

23 Paul looked straight at the Sanhedrin and said, "My brothers, I have fulfilled my duty to God in all good conscience to this day." 2At this the high priest Ananias ordered those standing near Paul to strike him on the mouth. 3Then Paul said to him, "God will strike you, you whitewashed

wall! You sit there to judge me according to the law, yet you yourself violate the law by commanding that I be struck!"

4Those who were standing near Paul said, "You dare to insult God's high priest?"

5Paul replied, "Brothers, I did not realize that he was the high priest; for it is written: 'Do not speak evil about the ruler of your people.'*a* "

6Then Paul, knowing that some of them were Sadducees and the others Pharisees, called out in the Sanhedrin, "My brothers, I am a Pharisee, the son of a Pharisee. I stand on trial because of my hope in the resurrection of the dead." 7When he said this, a dispute broke out between the Pharisees and the Sadducees, and the assembly was divided. 8(The Sadducees say that there is no resurrection, and that there are neither angels nor spirits, but the Pharisees acknowledge them all.)

9There was a great uproar, and some of the teachers of the law who were Pharisees stood up and argued vigorously. "We find nothing wrong with this man," they said. "What if a spirit or an angel has spoken to him?" 10The dispute became so violent that the commander was afraid Paul would be torn to pieces by them. He ordered the troops to go down and take him away from them by force and bring him into the barracks.

11The following night the Lord stood near Paul and said, "Take courage! As you have testified about me in Jerusalem, so you must also testify in Rome."

The Plot to Kill Paul

12The next morning the Jews formed a conspiracy and bound themselves with an oath not to eat or drink until they had killed Paul. 13More than forty men were involved in this plot. 14They went to the chief priests and elders and said, "We have taken a solemn oath not to eat anything until we have killed Paul. 15Now then, you and the Sanhedrin petition the commander to bring him before you on the pretext of wanting more accurate information about his case. We are ready to kill him before he gets here."

a 5 Exodus 22:28

16But when the son of Paul's sister heard of this plot, he went into the barracks and told Paul.

17Then Paul called one of the centurions and said, "Take this young man to the commander; he has something to tell him." 18So he took him to the commander.

THE HOPE OF THE RESURRECTION
Reinhold Niebuhr

VERSE: Acts 23:6   **PASSAGE:** Acts 23:6–8

he idea of the resurrection of the body is a Biblical symbol in which modern minds take the greatest offense and which has long since been displaced in most modern versions of the Christian faith by the idea of the immortality of the soul. The latter idea is regarded as a more plausible expression of the hope of everlasting life. It is true of course that the idea of the resurrection transcends the limits of the conceivable; but it is not always appreciated that this is equally true of the idea of an immortal soul. The fact is that the unity of historical existence, despite its involvement in and transcendence over nature, makes it no more possible to conceive transcendent spirit, completely freed of the conditions of nature, than to conceive the conditions of nature transmuted into an eternal consummation. Either idea, as every other idea, which points to the consummation beyond history, is beyond logical conception. The hope of the resurrection nevertheless embodies the very genius of the Christian idea of the historical. On the one hand it implies that eternity will fulfill and not annul the richness and variety which the temporal process has elaborated. On the other it implies that the condition of finiteness and freedom, which lies at the basis of historical existence, is a problem for which there is no solution by any human power. Only God can save this problem. From the human perspective it can only be solved by faith. All structures of meaning and realms of coherence, which human reason constructs, face the chasm of meaninglessness when men discover that the tangents of meaning transcend the limits of existence. Only faith has an answer for this problem. The Christian answer is faith in the God who is revealed in Christ and from whose love neither life nor death can separate us.

ADDITIONAL SCRIPTURE READING:
1 Corinthians 15:12–14; Philippians 3:8–11

Go to page 1301 for your next devotional reading.

1900   Present

The centurion said, "Paul, the prisoner, sent for me and asked me to bring this young man to you because he has something to tell you."

¹⁹The commander took the young man by the hand, drew him aside and asked, "What is it you want to tell me?"

²⁰He said: "The Jews have agreed to ask you to bring Paul before the Sanhedrin tomorrow on the pretext of wanting more accurate information about him. ²¹Don't give in to them, because more than forty of them are waiting in ambush for him. They have taken an oath not to eat or drink until they have killed him. They are ready now, waiting for your consent to their request."

²²The commander dismissed the young man and cautioned him, "Don't tell anyone that you have reported this to me."

Paul Transferred to Caesarea

²³Then he called two of his centurions and ordered them, "Get ready a detachment of two hundred soldiers, seventy horsemen and two hundred spearmen*a* to go to Caesarea at nine tonight. ²⁴Provide mounts for Paul so that he may be taken safely to Governor Felix."

²⁵He wrote a letter as follows:

²⁶Claudius Lysias,

To His Excellency, Governor Felix:

Greetings.

²⁷This man was seized by the Jews and they were about to kill him, but I came with my troops and rescued him, for I had learned that he is a Roman citizen. ²⁸I wanted to know why they were accusing him, so I brought him to their Sanhedrin. ²⁹I found that the accusation had to do with questions about their law, but there was no charge against him that deserved death or imprisonment. ³⁰When I was informed of a plot to be carried out against the man, I sent him to you at once. I also ordered his accusers to present to you their case against him.

³¹So the soldiers, carrying out their orders, took Paul with them during the night and brought him as far as Antipatris. ³²The next day they let the cavalry go on with him, while they returned to the barracks. ³³When the cavalry arrived in Caesarea, they delivered the letter to the governor and handed Paul over to him. ³⁴The governor read the letter and asked what province he was from. Learning that he was from Cilicia, ³⁵he said, "I will hear your case when your accusers get here." Then he ordered that Paul be kept under guard in Herod's palace.

The Trial Before Felix

24 Five days later the high priest Ananias went down to Caesarea with some of the elders and a lawyer named Tertullus, and they brought their charges against Paul before the governor. ²When Paul was called in, Tertullus presented his case before Felix: "We have enjoyed a long period of peace under you, and your foresight has brought about reforms in this nation. ³Everywhere and in every way, most excellent Felix, we acknowledge this with profound gratitude. ⁴But in order not to weary you further, I would request that you be kind enough to hear us briefly.

⁵"We have found this man to be a troublemaker, stirring up riots among the Jews all over the world. He is a ringleader of the Nazarene sect ⁶and even tried to desecrate the temple; so we seized him. ⁸By*b* examining him yourself you will be able to learn the truth about all these charges we are bringing against him."

⁹The Jews joined in the accusation, asserting that these things were true.

¹⁰When the governor motioned for him to speak, Paul replied: "I know that for a number of years you have been a judge over this nation; so I gladly make my defense. ¹¹You can easily verify that no more than twelve days ago I went up to Jerusalem to worship. ¹²My accusers did not find me arguing with anyone at the temple, or stirring up a crowd in the synagogues or anywhere else in the city.

---

a 23 The meaning of the Greek for this word is uncertain.   *b* 6–8 Some manuscripts *him and wanted to judge him according to our law.* ⁷*But the commander, Lysias, came and with the use of much force snatched him from our hands* ⁸*and ordered his accusers to come before you. By*

¹³And they cannot prove to you the charges they are now making against me. ¹⁴However, I admit that I worship the God of our fathers as a follower of the Way, which they call a sect. I believe everything that agrees with the Law and that is written in the Prophets, ¹⁵and I have the same hope in God as these men, that there will be a resurrection of both the righteous and the wicked. ¹⁶So I strive always to keep my conscience clear before God and man.

AND I WILL PLACE WITHIN THEM AS A GUIDE
MY UMPIRE CONSCIENCE, WHOM IF THEY WILL
    HEAR,
LIGHT AFTER LIGHT WELL US'D THEY SHALL
    ATTAIN,
AND TO THE END PERSISTING, SAFE ARRIVE.

—*John Milton*

---

¹⁷"After an absence of several years, I came to Jerusalem to bring my people gifts for the poor and to present offerings. ¹⁸I was ceremonially clean when they found me in the temple courts doing this. There was no crowd with me, nor was I involved in any disturbance. ¹⁹But there are some Jews from the province of Asia, who ought to be here before you and bring charges if they have anything against me. ²⁰Or these who are here should state what crime they found in me when I stood before the Sanhedrin— ²¹unless it was this one thing I shouted as I stood in their presence: 'It is concerning the resurrection of the dead that I am on trial before you today.'"

²²Then Felix, who was well acquainted with the Way, adjourned the proceedings. "When Lysias the commander comes," he said, "I will decide your case." ²³He ordered the centurion to keep Paul under guard but to give him some freedom and permit his friends to take care of his needs.

²⁴Several days later Felix came with his wife Drusilla, who was a Jewess. He sent for Paul and listened to him as he spoke about faith in Christ Jesus. ²⁵As Paul discoursed on righteousness, self-control and the judgment to come, Felix was afraid and said, "That's enough for

now! You may leave. When I find it convenient, I will send for you." ²⁶At the same time he was hoping that Paul would offer him a bribe, so he sent for him frequently and talked with him.

²⁷When two years had passed, Felix was succeeded by Porcius Festus, but because Felix wanted to grant a favor to the Jews, he left Paul in prison.

The Trial Before Festus

25 Three days after arriving in the province, Festus went up from Caesarea to Jerusalem, ²where the chief priests and Jewish leaders appeared before him and presented the charges against Paul. ³They urgently requested Festus, as a favor to them, to have Paul transferred to Jerusalem, for they were preparing an ambush to kill him along the way. ⁴Festus answered, "Paul is being held at Caesarea, and I myself am going there soon. ⁵Let some of your leaders come with me and press charges against the man there, if he has done anything wrong."

⁶After spending eight or ten days with them, he went down to Caesarea, and the next day he convened the court and ordered that Paul be brought before him. ⁷When Paul appeared, the Jews who had come down from Jerusalem stood around him, bringing many serious charges against him, which they could not prove.

⁸Then Paul made his defense: "I have done nothing wrong against the law of the Jews or against the temple or against Caesar."

⁹Festus, wishing to do the Jews a favor, said to Paul, "Are you willing to go up to Jerusalem and stand trial before me there on these charges?"

¹⁰Paul answered: "I am now standing before Caesar's court, where I ought to be tried. I have not done any wrong to the Jews, as you yourself know very well. ¹¹If, however, I am guilty of doing anything deserving death, I do not refuse to die. But if the charges brought against me by these Jews are not true, no one has the right to hand me over to them. I appeal to Caesar!"

¹²After Festus had conferred with his council, he declared: "You have appealed to Caesar. To Caesar you will go!"

Festus Consults King Agrippa

13A few days later King Agrippa and Bernice arrived at Caesarea to pay their respects to Festus. 14Since they were spending many days there, Festus discussed Paul's case with the king. He said: "There is a man here whom Felix left as a prisoner. 15When I went to Jerusalem, the chief priests and elders of the Jews brought charges against him and asked that he be condemned.

16"I told them that it is not the Roman custom to hand over any man before he has faced his accusers and has had an opportunity to defend himself against their charges. 17When they came here with me, I did not delay the case, but convened the court the next day and ordered the man to be brought in. 18When his accusers got up to speak, they did not charge him with any of the crimes I had expected. 19Instead, they had some points of dispute with him about their own religion and about a dead man named Jesus who Paul claimed was alive. 20I was at a loss how to investigate such matters; so I asked if he would be willing to go to Jerusalem and stand trial there on these charges. 21When Paul made his appeal to be held over for the Emperor's decision, I ordered him held until I could send him to Caesar."

22Then Agrippa said to Festus, "I would like to hear this man myself."

He replied, "Tomorrow you will hear him."

Paul Before Agrippa

23The next day Agrippa and Bernice came with great pomp and entered the audience room with the high ranking officers and the leading men of the city. At the command of Festus, Paul was brought in. 24Festus said: "King Agrippa, and all who are present with us, you see this man! The whole Jewish community has petitioned me about him in Jerusalem and here in Caesarea, shouting that he ought not to live any longer. 25I found he had done nothing deserving of death, but because he made his appeal to the Emperor I decided to send him to Rome. 26But I have nothing definite to write to His Majesty about him. Therefore I have brought him before all of you,

and especially before you, King Agrippa, so that as a result of this investigation I may have something to write. 27For I think it is unreasonable to send on a prisoner without specifying the charges against him."

26 Then Agrippa said to Paul, "You have permission to speak for yourself."

So Paul motioned with his hand and began his defense: 2"King Agrippa, I consider myself fortunate to stand before you today as I make my defense against all the accusations of the Jews, 3and especially so because you are well acquainted with all the Jewish customs and controversies. Therefore, I beg you to listen to me patiently.

4"The Jews all know the way I have lived ever since I was a child, from the beginning of my life in my own country, and also in Jerusalem. 5They have known me for a long time and can testify, if they are willing, that according to the strictest sect of our religion, I lived as a Pharisee. 6And now it is because of my hope in what God has promised our fathers that I am on trial today. 7This is the promise our twelve tribes are hoping to see fulfilled as they earnestly serve God day and night. O king, it is because of this hope that the Jews are accusing me. 8Why should any of you consider it incredible that God raises the dead?

9"I too was convinced that I ought to do all that was possible to oppose the name of Jesus of Nazareth. 10And that is just what I did in Jerusalem. On the authority of the chief priests I put many of the saints in prison, and when they were put to death, I cast my vote against them. 11Many a time I went from one synagogue to another to have them punished, and I tried to force them to blaspheme. In my obsession against them, I even went to foreign cities to persecute them.

12"On one of these journeys I was going to Damascus with the authority and commission of the chief priests. 13About noon, O king, as I was on the road, I saw a light from heaven, brighter than the sun, blazing around me and my companions. 14We all fell to the ground, and I heard a voice saying to me in Aramaic,[a] 'Saul, Saul, why do you persecute me? It is hard for you to kick against the goads.'

15 "Then I asked, 'Who are you, Lord?'

" 'I am Jesus, whom you are persecuting,' the Lord replied. 16 'Now get up and stand on your feet. I have appeared to you to appoint you as a servant and as a witness of what you have seen of me and what I will show you. 17 I will rescue you from your own people and from the Gentiles. I am sending you to them 18 to open their eyes and turn them from darkness to light, and from the power of Satan to God, so that they may receive forgiveness of sins and a place among those who are sanctified by faith in me.'

19 "So then, King Agrippa, I was not disobedient to the vision from heaven. 20 First to those in Damascus, then to those in Jerusalem and in all Judea, and to the Gentiles also, I preached that they should repent and turn to God and prove their repentance by their deeds. 21 That is why the Jews seized me in the temple courts and tried to kill me. 22 But I have had God's help to this very day, and so I stand here and testify to small and great alike. I am saying nothing beyond what the prophets and Moses said would happen— 23 that the Christ[b] would suffer and, as the first to rise from the dead, would proclaim light to his own people and to the Gentiles."

24 At this point Festus interrupted Paul's defense. "You are out of your mind, Paul!" he shouted. "Your great learning is driving you insane."

25 "I am not insane, most excellent Festus," Paul replied. "What I am saying is true and reasonable. 26 The king is familiar with these things, and I can speak freely to him. I am convinced that none of this has escaped his notice, because it was not done in a corner. 27 King Agrippa, do you believe the prophets? I know you do."

28 Then Agrippa said to Paul, "Do you think that in such a short time you can persuade me to be a Christian?"

29 Paul replied, "Short time or long—I pray God that not only you but all who are listening to me today may become what I am, except for these chains."

30 The king rose, and with him the governor and Bernice and those sitting with them. 31 They left the room, and while talking with one another, they said, "This man is not doing anything that deserves death or imprisonment."

THERE ARE TWO KINDS OF PEOPLE IN THIS WORLD, THE CONSCIOUS DOGMATISTS AND THE UNCONSCIOUS DOGMATISTS. I HAVE ALWAYS FOUND MYSELF THAT THE UNCONSCIOUS DOGMATISTS WERE BY FAR THE MOST DOGMATIC.

—G. K. Chesterton

---

32 Agrippa said to Festus, "This man could have been set free if he had not appealed to Caesar."

Paul Sails for Rome

27 When it was decided that we would sail for Italy, Paul and some other prisoners were handed over to a centurion named Julius, who belonged to the Imperial Regiment. 2 We boarded a ship from Adramyttium about to sail for ports along the coast of the province of Asia, and we put out to sea. Aristarchus, a Macedonian from Thessalonica, was with us.

3 The next day we landed at Sidon; and Julius, in kindness to Paul, allowed him to go to his friends so they might provide for his needs. 4 From there we put out to sea again and passed to the lee of Cyprus because the winds were against us. 5 When we had sailed across the open sea off the coast of Cilicia and Pamphylia, we landed at Myra in Lycia. 6 There the centurion found an Alexandrian ship sailing for Italy and put us on board. 7 We made slow headway for many days and had difficulty arriving off Cnidus. When the wind did not allow us to hold our course, we sailed to the lee of Crete, opposite Salmone. 8 We moved along the coast with difficulty and came to a place called Fair Havens, near the town of Lasea.

9 Much time had been lost, and sailing had already become dangerous because by now it was after the Fast.[c] So Paul warned them, 10 "Men, I can see that our voyage is going to be disastrous and bring great loss to ship and cargo, and to

---

[a] 14 Or Hebrew   [b] 23 Or Messiah   [c] 9 That is, the Day of Atonement (Yom Kippur)

our own lives also." ¹¹But the centurion, instead of listening to what Paul said, followed the advice of the pilot and of the owner of the ship. ¹²Since the harbor was unsuitable to winter in, the majority decided that we should sail on, hoping to reach Phoenix and winter there. This was a harbor in Crete, facing both southwest and northwest.

The Storm

¹³When a gentle south wind began to blow, they thought they had obtained what they wanted; so they weighed anchor and sailed along the shore of Crete. ¹⁴Before very long, a wind of hurricane force, called the "northeaster," swept down from the island. ¹⁵The ship was caught by the storm and could not head into the wind; so we gave way to it and were driven along. ¹⁶As we passed to the lee of a small island called Cauda, we were hardly able to make the lifeboat secure. ¹⁷When the men had hoisted it aboard, they passed ropes under the ship itself to hold it together. Fearing that they would run aground on the sandbars of Syrtis, they lowered the sea anchor and let the ship be driven along. ¹⁸We took such a violent battering from the storm that the next day they began to throw the cargo overboard. ¹⁹On the third day, they threw the ship's tackle overboard with their own hands. ²⁰When neither sun nor stars appeared for many days and the storm continued raging, we finally gave up all hope of being saved.

²¹After the men had gone a long time without food, Paul stood up before them and said: "Men, you should have taken my advice not to sail from Crete; then you would have spared yourselves this damage and loss. ²²But now I urge you to keep up your courage, because not one of you will be lost; only the ship will be destroyed. ²³Last night an angel of the God whose I am and whom I serve stood beside me ²⁴and said, 'Do not be afraid, Paul. You must stand trial before Caesar; and God has graciously given you the lives of all who sail with you.' ²⁵So keep up your courage, men, for I have faith in God that it will happen just as

he told me. ²⁶Nevertheless, we must run aground on some island."

The Shipwreck

²⁷On the fourteenth night we were still being driven across the Adriatic[a] Sea, when about midnight the sailors sensed they were approaching land. ²⁸They took soundings and found that the water was a hundred and twenty feet[b] deep. A short time later they took soundings again and found it was ninety feet[c] deep. ²⁹Fearing that we would be dashed against the rocks, they dropped four anchors from the stern and prayed for daylight. ³⁰In an attempt to escape from the ship, the sailors let the lifeboat down into the sea, pretending they were going to lower some anchors from the bow. ³¹Then Paul said to the centurion and the soldiers, "Unless these men stay with the ship, you cannot be saved." ³²So the soldiers cut the ropes that held the lifeboat and let it fall away.

³³Just before dawn Paul urged them all to eat. "For the last fourteen days," he said, "you have been in constant suspense and have gone without food—you haven't eaten anything. ³⁴Now I urge you to take some food. You need it to survive. Not one of you will lose a single hair from his head." ³⁵After he said this, he took some bread and gave thanks to God in front of them all. Then he broke it and began to eat. ³⁶They were all encouraged and ate some food themselves. ³⁷Altogether there were 276 of us on board. ³⁸When they had eaten as much as they wanted, they lightened the ship by throwing the grain into the sea.

³⁹When daylight came, they did not recognize the land, but they saw a bay with a sandy beach, where they decided to run the ship aground if they could. ⁴⁰Cutting loose the anchors, they left them in the sea and at the same time untied the ropes that held the rudders. Then they hoisted the foresail to the wind and made for the beach. ⁴¹But the ship struck a sandbar and ran aground. The bow stuck fast and would not

---

a 27 In ancient times the name referred to an area extending well south of Italy.   *b 28* Greek *twenty orguias* (about 37 meters)   *c 28* Greek *fifteen orguias* (about 27 meters)

THE MINISTER IN HIS STUDY
W. W. Staley

VERSE: Acts 27:23–24   **PASSAGE:** Acts 27:1–42

 mighty host surrounds me in my library. Peter, James, and John did not see as much nor hear as much as the minister in his library. Jesus is here too, in the Bible and by the Spirit. There are more people in my library than in my church. They speak to me; they kindle the fires of my imagination; they quicken my faith, humble my pride, rebuke my wrong-doing and wrong-thinking, warn me against sin, and point my soul to the living Christ. I find tombs with angels, deserts with fountains, gardens with Saviors, prisons with praises, and crosses with crowns. Above the roar of the tempest, the flap of the split sails, the creak of the breaking timbers, and the cry of endangered men, I hear Jesus say, "Quiet! Be still" (Mark 4:39). I hear Nebuchadnezzar say, "Look! I see four men walking around in the fire, unbound and unharmed, and the fourth looks like a son of the gods" (Daniel 3:25). I hear Paul, in the midst of darkness and the raging sea, say, "Last night an angel of the God whose I am and who I serve stood beside me and said, 'Do not be afraid'" (Acts 27:23–24). The past is a mighty host, their thought, faith, love, and lives still speaking to our own.

The library is a transfiguration scene, crowning lofty summits, silently and sweetly speaking to the minister so as to inspire him with renewed strength and satisfaction that arms him for the good fight of faith. Beyond this teeming past are the living millions moving to and fro, loving and hating, helping and hindering, neglecting age, crushing childhood, desecrating the Sabbath, greedily preying upon their fellows, preparing for war, and killing the flower of age . . . The minister should seek to interpret the present age in the light of the Gospel and past civilizations. From his study as a tower, he should get his vision of mankind and God, and then go forth to preach salvation to a sinning world. His sermon should be a message from God, supported by His word, fired by His Spirit, and delivered in the spirit of love.

ADDITIONAL SCRIPTURE READING:
Matthew 28:19; Ephesians 4:11–16

Go to page 1306 for your next devotional reading.

1900   Present

move, and the stern was broken to pieces by the pounding of the surf.

⁴²The soldiers planned to kill the prisoners to prevent any of them from swimming away and escaping. ⁴³But the centurion wanted to spare Paul's life and kept them from carrying out their plan. He ordered those who could swim to jump overboard first and get to land. ⁴⁴The rest were to get there on planks or on pieces of the ship. In this way everyone reached land in safety.

Ashore on Malta

28 Once safely on shore, we found out that the island was called Malta. ²The islanders showed us unusual kindness. They built a fire and welcomed us all because it was raining and cold. ³Paul gathered a pile of brushwood and, as he put it on the fire, a viper, driven out by the heat, fastened itself on his hand. ⁴When the islanders saw the snake hanging from his hand, they said to each other, "This man must be a murderer; for though he escaped from the sea, Justice has not allowed him to live." ⁵But Paul shook the snake off into the fire and suffered no ill effects. ⁶The people expected him to swell up or suddenly fall dead, but after waiting a long time and seeing nothing unusual happen to him, they changed their minds and said he was a god.

⁷There was an estate nearby that belonged to Publius, the chief official of the island. He welcomed us to his home and for three days entertained us hospitably. ⁸His father was sick in bed, suffering from fever and dysentery. Paul went in to see him and, after prayer, placed his hands on him and healed him. ⁹When this had happened, the rest of the sick on the island came and were cured. ¹⁰They honored us in many ways and when we were ready to sail, they furnished us with the supplies we needed.

Arrival at Rome

¹¹After three months we put out to sea in a ship that had wintered in the island. It was an Alexandrian ship with the figurehead of the twin gods Castor and Pollux. ¹²We put in at Syracuse and stayed there three days. ¹³From there we set sail and arrived at Rhegium. The next day the south wind came up, and on the following day we reached Puteoli. ¹⁴There we found some brothers who invited us to spend a week with them. And so we came to Rome. ¹⁵The brothers there had heard that we were coming, and they traveled as far as the Forum of Appius and the Three Taverns to meet us. At the sight of these men Paul thanked God and was encouraged. ¹⁶When we got to Rome, Paul was allowed to live by himself, with a soldier to guard him.

Paul Preaches at Rome Under Guard

¹⁷Three days later he called together the leaders of the Jews. When they had assembled, Paul said to them: "My brothers, although I have done nothing against our people or against the customs of our ancestors, I was arrested in Jerusalem and handed over to the Romans. ¹⁸They examined me and wanted to release me, because I was not guilty of any crime deserving death. ¹⁹But when the Jews objected, I was compelled to appeal to Caesar—not that I had any charge to bring against my own people. ²⁰For this reason I have asked to see you and talk with you. It is because of the hope of Israel that I am bound with this chain." ²¹They replied, "We have not received any letters from Judea concerning you, and none of the brothers who have come from there has reported or said anything bad about you. ²²But we want to hear what your views are, for we know that people everywhere are talking against this sect."

²³They arranged to meet Paul on a certain day, and came in even larger numbers to the place where he was staying. From morning till evening he explained and declared to them the kingdom of God and tried to convince them about Jesus from the Law of Moses and from the Prophets. ²⁴Some were convinced by what he said, but others would not believe. ²⁵They disagreed among themselves and began to leave after Paul had made this final statement: "The Holy Spirit spoke the truth to your forefathers when he said through Isaiah the prophet:

26 " 'Go to this people and say,
    "You will be ever hearing but never
        understanding;
    you will be ever seeing but never
        perceiving."
27 For this people's heart has become
        calloused;
    they hardly hear with their ears,
    and they have closed their eyes.
    Otherwise they might see with their
        eyes,
    hear with their ears,

understand with their hearts
    and turn, and I would heal them.'*a*

28 "Therefore I want you to know that
God's salvation has been sent to the
Gentiles, and they will listen!"*b*
30 For two whole years Paul stayed
there in his own rented house and welcomed all who came to see him. 31 Boldly and without hindrance he preached
the kingdom of God and taught about
the Lord Jesus Christ.

---

a 27 Isaiah 6:9,10   *b* 28 Some manuscripts *listen!"* 29*After he said this, the Jews left, arguing
vigorously among themselves.*

ROMANS

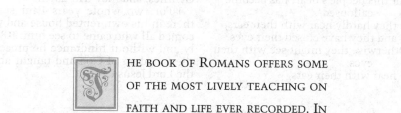

HE BOOK OF ROMANS OFFERS SOME
OF THE MOST LIVELY TEACHING ON
FAITH AND LIFE EVER RECORDED. IN
THIS LETTER PAUL TELLS OF GOD'S WONDER-
FUL PLAN FOR REDEEMING HIS PEOPLE AND
SETTING THEM FREE FOR SERVICE THROUGH
THE POWER OF HIS SPIRIT. AS YOU READ
ABOUT THE RICHES OF GOD'S GRACE, BE COM-
FORTED THAT NOTHING "WILL BE ABLE TO
SEPARATE US FROM THE LOVE OF GOD THAT
IS IN CHRIST JESUS OUR LORD" (8:39). THEN
RESPOND TO HIS LOVE WITH A TRANSFORMED
LIFE OF SERVICE.

---

1 Paul, a servant of Christ Jesus, called to be an apostle and set apart for the gospel of God— ²the gospel he promised beforehand through his prophets in the Holy Scriptures ³regarding his Son, who as to his human nature was a descendant of David, ⁴and who through the Spirit*ᵃ* of holiness was declared with power to be the Son of God*ᵇ* by his resurrection from the dead: Jesus Christ our Lord. ⁵Through him and for his name's sake, we received grace and apostleship to call people from among all the Gentiles to the obedience that comes from faith. ⁶And you also are among those who are called to belong to Jesus Christ.

⁷To all in Rome who are loved by God and called to be saints:

Grace and peace to you from God our Father and from the Lord Jesus Christ.

Paul's Longing to Visit Rome

⁸First, I thank my God through Jesus Christ for all of you, because your faith is being reported all over the world. ⁹God, whom I serve with my whole heart in preaching the gospel of his Son, is my witness how constantly I remember you ¹⁰in my prayers at all times; and I pray that now at last by God's will the way may be opened for me to come to you.

¹¹I long to see you so that I may impart to you some spiritual gift to make you strong— ¹²that is, that you

---

ᵃ 4 Or *who as to his spirit*   *ᵇ 4* Or *was appointed to be the Son of God with power*

and I may be mutually encouraged by each other's faith. [13]I do not want you to be unaware, brothers, that I planned many times to come to you (but have been prevented from doing so until now) in order that I might have a harvest among you, just as I have had among the other Gentiles.

[14]I am obligated both to Greeks and non-Greeks, both to the wise and the foolish. [15]That is why I am so eager to preach the gospel also to you who are at Rome.

[16]I am not ashamed of the gospel, because it is the power of God for the salvation of everyone who believes: first for the Jew, then for the Gentile. [17]For in the gospel a righteousness from God is revealed, a righteousness that is by faith from first to last,[a] just as it is written: "The righteous will live by faith."[b]

God's Wrath Against Mankind

[18]The wrath of God is being revealed from heaven against all the godlessness and wickedness of men who suppress the truth by their wickedness, [19]since what may be known about God is plain to them, because God has made it plain to them. [20]For since the creation of the world God's invisible qualities—his eternal power and divine nature—have been clearly seen, being understood from what has been made, so that men are without excuse.

REALLY, A YOUNG ATHEIST CANNOT GUARD HIS FAITH TOO CAREFULLY.   —C. S. Lewis

[21]For although they knew God, they neither glorified him as God nor gave thanks to him, but their thinking became futile and their foolish hearts were darkened. [22]Although they claimed to be wise, they became fools [23]and exchanged the glory of the immortal God for images made to look like mortal man and birds and animals and reptiles.

[24]Therefore God gave them over in the sinful desires of their hearts to sexual impurity for the degrading of their bodies with one another. [25]They exchanged the truth of God for a lie, and worshiped and served created things rather than the Creator—who is forever praised. Amen.

[26]Because of this, God gave them over to shameful lusts. Even their women exchanged natural relations for unnatural ones. [27]In the same way the men also abandoned natural relations with women and were inflamed with lust for one another. Men committed indecent acts with other men, and received in themselves the due penalty for their perversion.

[28]Furthermore, since they did not think it worthwhile to retain the knowledge of God, he gave them over to a depraved mind, to do what ought not to be done. [29]They have become filled with every kind of wickedness, evil, greed and depravity. They are full of envy, murder, strife, deceit and malice. They are gossips, [30]slanderers, God-haters, insolent, arrogant and boastful; they invent ways of doing evil; they disobey their parents; [31]they are senseless, faithless, heartless, ruthless. [32]Although they know God's righteous decree that those who do such things deserve death, they not only continue to do these very things but also approve of those who practice them.

God's Righteous Judgment

2 You, therefore, have no excuse, you who pass judgment on someone else, for at whatever point you judge the other, you are condemning yourself, because you who pass judgment do the same things. [2]Now we know that God's judgment against those who do such things is based on truth. [3]So when you, a mere man, pass judgment on them and yet do the same things, do you think you will escape God's judgment? [4]Or do you show contempt for the riches of his kindness, tolerance and patience, not realizing that God's kindness leads you toward repentance?

[5]But because of your stubbornness and your unrepentant heart, you are storing up wrath against yourself for the day of God's wrath, when his righteous judgment will be revealed. [6]God "will give to each person according to what he has done."[c] [7]To those who by persistence in doing good seek glory, honor

THE IMPEACHMENT OF ST. PAUL

C. S. Lewis

VERSE: Romans 1:1–2   **PASSAGE:** Romans 1:1–7

 most astonishing misconception has long dominated the modern mind on the subject of St. Paul. It is to this effect: that Jesus preached a kindly and simple religion (found in the gospels) and that St. Paul afterwards corrupted it into a cruel and complicated religion (found in the epistles). This is really quite untenable. All the most terrifying texts came from the mouth of our Lord: all the texts on which we can base such warrant as we have for hoping that all men will be saved come from St. Paul . . . There is no real evidence for a pre-Pauline doctrine different from St. Paul's. The epistles are, for the most part, the earliest Christian documents we possess. The gospels come later. They are not "the gospel," the statement of the Christian belief. They were written for those who had already been converted, who had already accepted "the gospel." They leave out many of the "complications" (that is, the theology) because they are intended for readers who have already been instructed in it. In that sense the epistles are more primitive and more central than the gospels—though not, of course, than the great events which the gospels recount . . . In the earlier history of every rebellion there is a stage at which you do not yet attack the King in person. You say: "The King is all right. It is his ministers who are wrong. They misrepresent him and corrupt all his plans—which, I'm sure, are good plans if only the ministers would let them take effect." And the first victory consists in beheading a few ministers: only at a later stage do you go on and behead the King himself. In the same way, the nineteenth-century attack on St. Paul was really only a stage in the revolt against Christ . . . It was unfortunate that [the attack] could not impress anyone who had really read the gospels and the epistles with attention: but apparently few people had, and so the first victory was won. St. Paul was impeached and banished and the world went on to the next step—the attack on the King himself.

ADDITIONAL SCRIPTURE READING:
Psalm 14:1–5; Acts 9:1–19

Go to page 1308 for your next devotional reading.

1900   Present

and immortality, he will give eternal life. [8]But for those who are self-seeking and who reject the truth and follow evil, there will be wrath and anger. [9]There will be trouble and distress for every human being who does evil: first for the Jew, then for the Gentile; [10]but glory, honor and peace for everyone who does good: first for the Jew, then for the Gentile. [11]For God does not show favoritism.

[12]All who sin apart from the law will also perish apart from the law, and all who sin under the law will be judged by the law. [13]For it is not those who hear the law who are righteous in God's sight, but it is those who obey the law who will be declared righteous. [14](Indeed, when Gentiles, who do not have the law, do by nature things required by the law, they are a law for themselves, even though they do not have the law, [15]since they show that the requirements of the law are written on their hearts, their consciences also bearing witness, and their thoughts now accusing, now even defending them.) [16]This will take place on the day when God will judge men's secrets through Jesus Christ, as my gospel declares.

The Jews and the Law

[17]Now you, if you call yourself a Jew; if you rely on the law and brag about your relationship to God; [18]if you know his will and approve of what is superior because you are instructed by the law; [19]if you are convinced that you are a guide for the blind, a light for those who are in the dark, [20]an instructor of the foolish, a teacher of infants, because you have in the law the embodiment of knowledge and truth— [21]you, then, who teach others, do you not teach yourself? You who preach against stealing, do you steal? [22]You who say that people should not commit adultery, do you commit adultery? You who abhor idols, do you rob temples? [23]You who brag about the law, do you dishonor God by breaking the law? [24]As it is written: "God's name is blasphemed among the Gentiles because of you."[a]

[25]Circumcision has value if you observe the law, but if you break the law, you have become as though you had not been circumcised. [26]If those who are not circumcised keep the law's requirements, will they not be regarded as though they were circumcised? [27]The one who is not circumcised physically and yet obeys the law will condemn you who, even though you have the[b] written code and circumcision, are a lawbreaker.

[28]A man is not a Jew if he is only one outwardly, nor is circumcision merely outward and physical. [29]No, a man is a Jew if he is one inwardly; and circumcision is circumcision of the heart, by the Spirit, not by the written code. Such a man's praise is not from men, but from God.

God's Faithfulness

3 What advantage, then, is there in being a Jew, or what value is there in circumcision? [2]Much in every way! First of all, they have been entrusted with the very words of God.

[3]What if some did not have faith? Will their lack of faith nullify God's faithfulness? [4]Not at all! Let God be true, and every man a liar. As it is written:

"So that you may be proved right
when you speak
and prevail when you judge."[c]

[5]But if our unrighteousness brings out God's righteousness more clearly, what shall we say? That God is unjust in bringing his wrath on us? (I am using a human argument.) [6]Certainly not! If that were so, how could God judge the world? [7]Someone might argue, "If my falsehood enhances God's truthfulness and so increases his glory, why am I still condemned as a sinner?" [8]Why not say—as we are being slanderously reported as saying and as some claim that we say—"Let us do evil that good may result"? Their condemnation is deserved.

No One Is Righteous

[9]What shall we conclude then? Are we any better[d]? Not at all! We have already made the charge that Jews and Gentiles alike are all under sin. [10]As it is written:

---

[a] 24 Isaiah 52:5; Ezek. 36:22   [b] 27 Or who, by means of a   [c] 4 Psalm 51:4   [d] 9 Or worse

St. Paul

Thomas Merton

hen I was Saul, and sat among the cloaks,
My eyes were stones, I saw no sight of heaven
Open to take the spirit of the twisting Stephen.
When I was Saul, and sat among the rocks,
I locked my eyes, and made my brain my tomb,
Sealed with what boulders rolled across my reason!

When I was Saul and walked upon the blazing desert
My road was quiet as a trap.
I feared what word would split high noon with light
And lock my life, and try to drive me mad:
And thus I saw the Voice that struck me dead.

Tie up my breath, and wind me in white sheets of
           anguish,
And lay me in my three days' sepulchre
Until I find my Easter in a vision.

Oh Christ! Give back my life, go, cross Damascus,
Find out my Ananias in that other room:
Command him, as you do, in this my dream;
He knows my locks, and owns my ransom,
Waits for Your word to take his keys and come.

Additional Scripture Reading:
Acts 7:54—8:1; Philippians 1:21–24

Go to page 1310 for your next devotional reading.

1900   Present

"There is no one righteous, not even
  one;
11   there is no one who understands,
     no one who seeks God.
12 All have turned away,
     they have together become
       worthless;
   there is no one who does good,
     not even one."*a*
13 "Their throats are open graves;
     their tongues practice deceit."*b*
   "The poison of vipers is on their
     lips."*c*
14   "Their mouths are full of cursing
       and bitterness."*d*
15 "Their feet are swift to shed blood;
16   ruin and misery mark their ways,
17 and the way of peace they do not
       know."*e*
18   "There is no fear of God before
       their eyes."*f*

19Now we know that whatever the
law says, it says to those who are under
the law, so that every mouth may be
silenced and the whole world held
accountable to God. 20Therefore no one
will be declared righteous in his sight by
observing the law; rather, through the
law we become conscious of sin.

Righteousness Through Faith

21But now a righteousness from God,
apart from law, has been made known,
to which the Law and the Prophets testify. 22This righteousness from God
comes through faith in Jesus Christ to
all who believe. There is no difference,
23for all have sinned and fall short of the
glory of God, 24and are justified freely by
his grace through the redemption that
came by Christ Jesus. 25God presented
him as a sacrifice of atonement,*g*
through faith in his blood. He did this to
demonstrate his justice, because in his
forbearance he had left the sins committed beforehand unpunished— 26he did it
to demonstrate his justice at the present
time, so as to be just and the one who
justifies those who have faith in Jesus.
27Where, then, is boasting? It is
excluded. On what principle? On that of
observing the law? No, but on that of

faith. 28For we maintain that a man is
justified by faith apart from observing
the law. 29Is God the God of Jews only?
Is he not the God of Gentiles too? Yes, of
Gentiles too, 30since there is only one
God, who will justify the circumcised
by faith and the uncircumcised through
that same faith. 31Do we, then, nullify
the law by this faith? Not at all! Rather,
we uphold the law.

Abraham Justified by Faith

4 What then shall we say that
Abraham, our forefather, discovered in this matter? 2If, in fact, Abraham was justified by works, he had
something to boast about—but not
before God. 3What does the Scripture
say? "Abraham believed God, and it was
credited to him as righteousness."*h*
4Now when a man works, his wages
are not credited to him as a gift, but as
an obligation. 5However, to the man
who does not work but trusts God who
justifies the wicked, his faith is credited
as righteousness. 6David says the same
thing when he speaks of the blessedness
of the man to whom God credits righteousness apart from works:

7 "Blessed are they
     whose transgressions are forgiven,
     whose sins are covered.
8 Blessed is the man
     whose sin the Lord will never
       count against him."*i*

9Is this blessedness only for the circumcised, or also for the uncircumcised? We have been saying that Abraham's faith was credited to him as
righteousness. 10Under what circumstances was it credited? Was it after he
was circumcised, or before? It was not
after, but before! 11And he received the
sign of circumcision, a seal of the righteousness that he had by faith while he
was still uncircumcised. So then, he is
the father of all who believe but have
not been circumcised, in order that righteousness might be credited to them.
12And he is also the father of the circumcised who not only are circumcised

---

a 12 Psalms 14:1–3; 53:1–3; Eccles. 7:20   *b 13* Psalm 5:9   *c 13* Psalm 140:3   *d 14* Psalm 10:7
e 17 Isaiah 59:7,8   *f 18* Psalm 36:1   *g 25* Or *as the one who would turn aside his wrath, taking away*
sin   *h 3* Gen. 15:6; also in verse 22   *i 8* Psalm 32:1,2

but who also walk in the footsteps of the faith that our father Abraham had before he was circumcised.

¹³It was not through law that Abraham and his offspring received the promise that he would be heir of the world, but through the righteousness that comes by faith. ¹⁴For if those who live by law are

---

GOD'S JUSTICE AND HUMAN SIGNIFICANCE
Francis Schaeffer

VERSE: Romans 3:26   **PASSAGE:** Romans 3:21–26

f there is true moral guilt in the presence of a personal God (rather than a metaphysical intrinsic situation of what is and always has been), then perhaps there will be a solution from God's side. And God says to man that there is a solution. That solution rests upon God saying that he is holy and he is love, and in his love he has loved the world, and he sent his son. Now in history, there on Calvary's cross, in space and time, Jesus died. And we should never speak of Jesus' death without linking it to his person. This is the eternal Second Person of the Trinity. When he died, with the division that man has caused by his revolt now carried up into the Trinity itself, there in expiation, in propitiation and substitution, the true moral guilt is met by the *infinite* value of Jesus' death. Thus Jesus says: "It is finished" (John 19:30).

Romans 3:26 is a verse that we tend to pass by too quickly in the midst of the structure of the first three chapters of Romans. These chapters tell us first why man is lost, and then the solution in the propitiatory death of Jesus Christ. At this point Paul can say: "that he himself might be just and *yet* (the force of the Greek construction) the justifier of him who has faith in Jesus." On the one hand, because of the infinite value of Christ's holy death, God does not have to surrender his absolute holy character; and on the other, he does not have to violate man's significance in order for him to be able to pardon guilt and restore man's broken relationship to himself. This is the very opposite of the denial of antithesis and significance in modern man's leap into the dark, which says that somehow we must believe, without reason, that God is love. A moral absolute remains, and yet there is a solution to man's dilemma.

ADDITIONAL SCRIPTURE READING:
Matthew 27:50–54; 1 John 4:8–10

Go to page 1313 for your next devotional reading.

1900   Present

heirs, faith has no value and the promise is worthless, 15because law brings wrath. And where there is no law there is no transgression.

16Therefore, the promise comes by faith, so that it may be by grace and may be guaranteed to all Abraham's offspring—not only to those who are of the law but also to those who are of the faith of Abraham. He is the father of us all. 17As it is written: "I have made you a father of many nations."a He is our father in the sight of God, in whom he believed—the God who gives life to the dead and calls things that are not as though they were.

18Against all hope, Abraham in hope believed and so became the father of many nations, just as it had been said to him, "So shall your offspring be."b 19Without weakening in his faith, he faced the fact that his body was as good as dead—since he was about a hundred years old—and that Sarah's womb was also dead. 20Yet he did not waver through unbelief regarding the promise of God, but was strengthened in his faith and gave glory to God, 21being fully persuaded that God had power to do what he had promised. 22This is why "it was credited to him as righteousness." 23The words "it was credited to him" were written not for him alone, 24but also for us, to whom God will credit righteousness—for us who believe in him who raised Jesus our Lord from the dead. 25He was delivered over to death for our sins and was raised to life for our justification.

Peace and Joy

5 Therefore, since we have been justified through faith, wec have peace with God through our Lord Jesus Christ, 2through whom we have gained access by faith into this grace in which we now stand. And wec rejoice in the hope of the glory of God. 3Not only so, but wec also rejoice in our sufferings, because we know that suffering produces perseverance; 4perseverance, character; and character, hope. 5And hope does not disappoint us, because God has poured out his love into our hearts by the Holy Spirit, whom he has given us.

6You see, at just the right time, when we were still powerless, Christ died for the ungodly. 7Very rarely will anyone die for a righteous man, though for a good man someone might possibly dare to die. 8But God demonstrates his own love for us in this: While we were still sinners, Christ died for us.

WE ARE ALWAYS IN THE FORGE, OR ON THE ANVIL; BY TRIALS GOD IS SHAPING US FOR HIGHER THINGS.   —Henry Ward Beecher

9Since we have now been justified by his blood, how much more shall we be saved from God's wrath through him! 10For if, when we were God's enemies, we were reconciled to him through the death of his Son, how much more, having been reconciled, shall we be saved through his life! 11Not only is this so, but we also rejoice in God through our Lord Jesus Christ, through whom we have now received reconciliation.

Death Through Adam, Life Through Christ

12Therefore, just as sin entered the world through one man, and death through sin, and in this way death came to all men, because all sinned— 13for before the law was given, sin was in the world. But sin is not taken into account when there is no law. 14Nevertheless, death reigned from the time of Adam to the time of Moses, even over those who did not sin by breaking a command, as did Adam, who was a pattern of the one to come.

15But the gift is not like the trespass. For if the many died by the trespass of the one man, how much more did God's grace and the gift that came by the grace of the one man, Jesus Christ, overflow to the many! 16Again, the gift of God is not like the result of the one man's sin: The judgment followed one sin and brought condemnation, but the gift followed many trespasses and brought justification. 17For if, by the trespass of the one man, death reigned through that one man, how much more will those who receive God's abundant provision

a 17 Gen. 17:5   b 18 Gen. 15:5   c 1,2,3 Or let us

of grace and of the gift of righteousness reign in life through the one man, Jesus Christ.

[18]Consequently, just as the result of one trespass was condemnation for all men, so also the result of one act of righteousness was justification that brings life for all men. [19]For just as through the disobedience of the one man the many were made sinners, so also through the obedience of the one man the many will be made righteous.

[20]The law was added so that the trespass might increase. But where sin increased, grace increased all the more, [21]so that, just as sin reigned in death, so also grace might reign through righteousness to bring eternal life through Jesus Christ our Lord.

Dead to Sin, Alive in Christ

6 What shall we say, then? Shall we go on sinning so that grace may increase? [2]By no means! We died to sin; how can we live in it any longer? [3]Or don't you know that all of us who were baptized into Christ Jesus were baptized into his death? [4]We were therefore buried with him through baptism into death in order that, just as Christ was raised from the dead through the glory of the Father, we too may live a new life.

[5]If we have been united with him like this in his death, we will certainly also be united with him in his resurrection. [6]For we know that our old self was crucified with him so that the body of sin might be done away with,[a] that we should no longer be slaves to sin— [7]because anyone who has died has been freed from sin.

[8]Now if we died with Christ, we believe that we will also live with him. [9]For we know that since Christ was raised from the dead, he cannot die again; death no longer has mastery over him. [10]The death he died, he died to sin once for all; but the life he lives, he lives to God.

[11]In the same way, count yourselves dead to sin but alive to God in Christ Jesus. [12]Therefore do not let sin reign in your mortal body so that you obey its evil desires. [13]Do not offer the parts of your body to sin, as instruments of wickedness, but rather offer yourselves to God, as those who have been brought from death to life; and offer the parts of your body to him as instruments of righteousness. [14]For sin shall not be your master, because you are not under law, but under grace.

Slaves to Righteousness

[15]What then? Shall we sin because we are not under law but under grace? By no means! [16]Don't you know that when you offer yourselves to someone to obey him as slaves, you are slaves to the one whom you obey—whether you are slaves to sin, which leads to death, or to obedience, which leads to righteousness? [17]But thanks be to God that,

---

WHAT CAN I GIVE HIM,
   POOR AS I AM?
IF I WERE A SHEPHERD,
   I WOULD BRING A LAMB;
IF I WERE A WISE MAN,
   I WOULD DO MY PART;
YET WHAT I CAN I GIVE HIM—
   GIVE MY HEART.   —*Christina Georgina Rossetti*

---

though you used to be slaves to sin, you wholeheartedly obeyed the form of teaching to which you were entrusted. [18]You have been set free from sin and have become slaves to righteousness.

[19]I put this in human terms because you are weak in your natural selves. Just as you used to offer the parts of your body in slavery to impurity and to ever-increasing wickedness, so now offer them in slavery to righteousness leading to holiness. [20]When you were slaves to sin, you were free from the control of righteousness. [21]What benefit did you reap at that time from the things you are now ashamed of? Those things result in death! [22]But now that you have been set free from sin and have become slaves to God, the benefit you reap leads to holiness, and the result is eternal life. [23]For the wages of sin is death, but the gift of God is eternal life in[b] Christ Jesus our Lord.

---

a 6 Or *be rendered powerless*   *b 23* Or *through*

TUESDAY

A CIVIL WAR WITHIN THE SELF
E. Stanley Jones

VERSE: Romans 7:19   **PASSAGE:** Romans 7:7–25

nto the conscious mind is introduced by conversion a new sense of conscious cleanness, a new loyalty, a new love. This introduction is so real, so satisfying, so conduct-determining, that the converted think the battle is over, that life is now to be one glad song of victory. Those honeymoon days come to an end, usually within a year. The subconscious urges, which have been laying low, apparently stunned into insensibility by the introduction of this new and different and authoritative life in the conscious mind, now begin to reassert themselves. Tempers, moods, fears, resentments, which we thought were gone forever, now lift their heads from the storm cellars of the subconscious, and the struggle between the conscious and the subconscious ensues. Paul calls it the war between "spirit" and "flesh" . . .

Many take it for granted that this stalemate is the best that the Christian faith offers. So they settle down to the state of being canceled out by this inevitable conflict. The seventh chapter of Romans is their escape and their excuse—Paul had this conflict, why shouldn't we? If the seventh of Romans were the only gospel Paul had to preach we would never have heard of him again. But the seventh of Romans is pre-Christian and sub-Christian—a man under the law fighting with sin in the subconscious with no resources of Christ at his disposal. It depicts the whole world experience without Christ. Does the Christian faith provide a way out of this dilemma? It can only if it provides for the conversion of the subconscious, and it does provide for just that. The area of the work of the Holy Spirit is largely, if not entirely, in the subconscious. He who made the subconscious has made plans for its redemption, its conversion, its sanctification. What kind of Creator would he have been if he had created the subconscious and then had not provided for its redemption in case evil should invade it?

ADDITIONAL SCRIPTURE READING:
Galatians 5:13–18; James 1:13–15

Go to page 1315 for your next devotional reading.

1900   Present

An Illustration From Marriage

7 Do you not know, brothers—for I am speaking to men who know the law—that the law has authority over a man only as long as he lives? ²For example, by law a married woman is bound to her husband as long as he is alive, but if her husband dies, she is released from the law of marriage. ³So then, if she marries another man while her husband is still alive, she is called an adulteress. But if her husband dies, she is released from that law and is not an adulteress, even though she marries another man.

⁴So, my brothers, you also died to the law through the body of Christ, that you might belong to another, to him who was raised from the dead, in order that we might bear fruit to God. ⁵For when we were controlled by the sinful nature,ᵃ the sinful passions aroused by the law were at work in our bodies, so that we bore fruit for death. ⁶But now, by dying to what once bound us, we have been released from the law so that we serve in the new way of the Spirit, and not in the old way of the written code.

Struggling With Sin

⁷What shall we say, then? Is the law sin? Certainly not! Indeed I would not have known what sin was except through the law. For I would not have known what coveting really was if the law had not said, "Do not covet."ᵇ ⁸But sin, seizing the opportunity afforded by the commandment, produced in me every kind of covetous desire. For apart from law, sin is dead. ⁹Once I was alive apart from law; but when the commandment came, sin sprang to life and I died. ¹⁰I found that the very commandment that was intended to bring life actually brought death. ¹¹For sin, seizing the opportunity afforded by the commandment, deceived me, and through the commandment put me to death. ¹²So then, the law is holy, and the commandment is holy, righteous and good.

¹³Did that which is good, then, become death to me? By no means! But in order that sin might be recognized as sin, it produced death in me through what was good, so that through the commandment sin might become utterly sinful.

¹⁴We know that the law is spiritual; but I am unspiritual, sold as a slave to sin. ¹⁵I do not understand what I do. For what I want to do I do not do, but what I hate I do. ¹⁶And if I do what I do not want to do, I agree that the law is good. ¹⁷As it is, it is no longer I myself who do it, but it is sin living in me. ¹⁸I know that nothing good lives in me, that is, in my sinful nature.ᶜ For I have the desire to do what is good, but I cannot carry it out. ¹⁹For what I do is not the good I want to do; no, the evil I do not want to do—this I keep on doing. ²⁰Now if I do what I do not want to do, it is no longer I who do it, but it is sin living in me that does it.

²¹So I find this law at work: When I want to do good, evil is right there with me. ²²For in my inner being I delight in God's law; ²³but I see another law at work in the members of my body, waging war against the law of my mind and making me a prisoner of the law of sin at work within my members. ²⁴What a wretched man I am! Who will rescue me from this body of death? ²⁵Thanks be to God—through Jesus Christ our Lord!

So then, I myself in my mind am a slave to God's law, but in the sinful nature a slave to the law of sin.

Life Through the Spirit

8 Therefore, there is now no condemnation for those who are in Christ Jesus,ᵈ ²because through Christ Jesus the law of the Spirit of life set me free from the law of sin and death. ³For what the law was powerless to do in that it was weakened by the sinful nature,ᵉ God did by sending his own Son in the likeness of sinful man to be a sin offering.ᶠ And so he condemned sin in sinful man,ᵍ ⁴in order that the righteous requirements of the law might be fully met in us, who do not live according to the sinful nature but according to the Spirit.

⁵Those who live according to the sinful nature have their minds set on what

---

ᵃ 5 Or *the flesh;* also in verse 25   ᵇ 7 Exodus 20:17; Deut. 5:21   ᶜ 18 Or *my flesh*   ᵈ 1 Some later manuscripts *Jesus, who do not live according to the sinful nature but according to the Spirit,*   ᵉ 3 Or *the flesh;* also in verses 4, 5, 8, 9, 12 and 13   ᶠ 3 Or *man, for sin*   ᵍ 3 Or *in the flesh*

that nature desires; but those who live in accordance with the Spirit have their minds set on what the Spirit desires. [6]The mind of sinful man[a] is death, but the mind controlled by the Spirit is life and peace; [7]the sinful mind[b] is hostile to God. It does not submit to God's law, nor can it do so. [8]Those controlled by the sinful nature cannot please God.

[9]You, however, are controlled not by

[a] 6 Or *mind set on the flesh*   [b] 7 Or *the mind set on the flesh*

WEDNESDAY

FROM ASLEEP IN JESUS
Abraham Kuyper

VERSE: Romans 8:29   **PASSAGE:** Romans 8:28–34

o one on earth has ever fathomed his own being. Until we die we remain to ourselves the *deepest* mystery.

But this then is the glory that awaits us after dying— that the veil will be taken away from our face, and as in a clear mirror God will show us our own being (see 1 Corinthians 13:12).

Then only. Not before.

And herein is grace. If here on earth we were ever to have a sight of our own being as we actually are, we would be terrified at ourselves. Even as the loving wife, hastening to the hospital to see her husband who had been wounded on the field of battle— when she saw his misshapen, bandaged face, involuntarily recoiled; so would our soul shrink back from ourselves if we were to see in clearness our own being soiled by sin and enwound by grace.

And therefore Jesus tarries. And he will only let you see yourself when the latest trace of sin is gone and the last bandage has been removed and you can see yourself as a model of Christ's redeeming love, altogether sound and altogether healed.

Then the mystery of your person falls away from before you.

And God who *alone* knows your being, because he himself has foreordained and created you and has kept you and has restored you, will then discover you to yourself, reveal your own being to you and in your own being, *for God's sake*, make you rich.

ADDITIONAL SCRIPTURE READING:
Galatians 4:1–6; Ephesians 2:1–10

Go to page 1319 for your next devotional reading.

1900   Present

the sinful nature but by the Spirit, if the Spirit of God lives in you. And if anyone does not have the Spirit of Christ, he does not belong to Christ. ¹⁰But if Christ is in you, your body is dead because of sin, yet your spirit is alive because of righteousness. ¹¹And if the Spirit of him who raised Jesus from the dead is living in you, he who raised Christ from the dead will also give life to your mortal bodies through his Spirit, who lives in you.

¹²Therefore, brothers, we have an obligation—but it is not to the sinful nature, to live according to it. ¹³For if you live according to the sinful nature, you will die; but if by the Spirit you put to death the misdeeds of the body, you will live, ¹⁴because those who are led by the Spirit of God are sons of God. ¹⁵For you did not receive a spirit that makes you a slave again to fear, but you received the Spirit of sonship.ᵃ And by him we cry, "Abba,ᵇ Father." ¹⁶The Spirit himself testifies with our spirit that we are God's children. ¹⁷Now if we are children, then we are heirs—heirs of God and co-heirs with Christ, if indeed we share in his sufferings in order that we may also share in his glory.

Future Glory

¹⁸I consider that our present sufferings are not worth comparing with the glory that will be revealed in us. ¹⁹The creation waits in eager expectation for the sons of God to be revealed. ²⁰For the creation was subjected to frustration, not by its own choice, but by the will of the one who subjected it, in hope ²¹thatᶜ the creation itself will be liberated from its bondage to decay and brought into the glorious freedom of the children of God.

²²We know that the whole creation has been groaning as in the pains of childbirth right up to the present time. ²³Not only so, but we ourselves, who have the firstfruits of the Spirit, groan inwardly as we wait eagerly for our adoption as sons, the redemption of our bodies. ²⁴For in this hope we were saved. But hope that is seen is no hope at all. Who hopes for what he already has?

²⁵But if we hope for what we do not yet have, we wait for it patiently.

²⁶In the same way, the Spirit helps us in our weakness. We do not know what we ought to pray for, but the Spirit himself intercedes for us with groans that words cannot express. ²⁷And he who searches our hearts knows the mind of the Spirit, because the Spirit intercedes for the saints in accordance with God's will.

More Than Conquerors

²⁸And we know that in all things God works for the good of those who love him,ᵈ whoᵉ have been called according to his purpose. ²⁹For those God foreknew he also predestined to be conformed to the likeness of his Son, that he might be the firstborn among many brothers. ³⁰And those he predestined, he also called; those he called, he also justified; those he justified, he also glorified.

³¹What, then, shall we say in response to this? If God is for us, who can be against us? ³²He who did not spare his own Son, but gave him up for us all—how will he not also, along with him, graciously give us all things? ³³Who will bring any charge against those whom God has chosen? It is God who justifies. ³⁴Who is he that condemns? Christ Jesus, who died—more than that, who was raised to life—is at the right hand of God and is also interceding for us. ³⁵Who shall separate us from the love of Christ? Shall trouble or hardship or persecution or famine or nakedness or danger or sword? ³⁶As it is written:

"For your sake we face death all day
        long;
    we are considered as sheep to be
        slaughtered."ᶠ

³⁷No, in all these things we are more than conquerors through him who loved us. ³⁸For I am convinced that neither death nor life, neither angels nor demons,ᵍ neither the present nor the future, nor any powers, ³⁹neither height nor depth, nor anything else in

---

ᵃ 15 Or adoption   ᵇ 15 Aramaic for Father   ᶜ 20,21 Or subjected it in hope. ²¹For   ᵈ 28 Some manuscripts And we know that all things work together for good to those who love God   ᵉ 28 Or works together with those who love him to bring about what is good—with those who
ᶠ 36 Psalm 44:22   ᵍ 38 Or nor heavenly rulers

all creation, will be able to separate us from the love of God that is in Christ Jesus our Lord.

God's Sovereign Choice

9 I speak the truth in Christ—I am not lying, my conscience confirms it in the Holy Spirit— ²I have great sorrow and unceasing anguish in my heart. ³For I could wish that I myself were cursed and cut off from Christ for the sake of my brothers, those of my own race, ⁴the people of Israel. Theirs is the adoption as sons; theirs the divine glory, the covenants, the receiving of the law, the temple worship and the promises. ⁵Theirs are the patriarchs, and from them is traced the human ancestry of Christ, who is God over all, forever praised!ᵃ Amen.

⁶It is not as though God's word had failed. For not all who are descended from Israel are Israel. ⁷Nor because they are his descendants are they all Abraham's children. On the contrary, "It is through Isaac that your offspring will be reckoned."ᵇ ⁸In other words, it is not the natural children who are God's children, but it is the children of the promise who are regarded as Abraham's offspring. ⁹For this was how the promise was stated: "At the appointed time I will return, and Sarah will have a son."ᶜ

¹⁰Not only that, but Rebekah's children had one and the same father, our father Isaac. ¹¹Yet, before the twins were born or had done anything good or bad—in order that God's purpose in election might stand: ¹²not by works but by him who calls—she was told, "The older will serve the younger."ᵈ ¹³Just as it is written: "Jacob I loved, but Esau I hated."ᵉ

¹⁴What then shall we say? Is God unjust? Not at all! ¹⁵For he says to Moses,

"I will have mercy on whom I have
    mercy,
and I will have compassion on
    whom I have compassion."ᶠ

¹⁶It does not, therefore, depend on man's desire or effort, but on God's mercy. ¹⁷For the Scripture says to Pharaoh: "I raised you up for this very purpose, that I might display my power in you and that my name might be proclaimed in all the earth."ᵍ ¹⁸Therefore God has mercy on whom he wants to have mercy, and he hardens whom he wants to harden.

¹⁹One of you will say to me: "Then why does God still blame us? For who resists his will?" ²⁰But who are you, O man, to talk back to God? "Shall what is formed say to him who formed it, 'Why did you make me like this?' "ʰ ²¹Does not the potter have the right to make out of the same lump of clay some pottery for noble purposes and some for common use?

²²What if God, choosing to show his wrath and make his power known, bore with great patience the objects of his wrath—prepared for destruction? ²³What if he did this to make the riches of his glory known to the objects of his mercy, whom he prepared in advance for glory— ²⁴even us, whom he also called, not only from the Jews but also from the Gentiles? ²⁵As he says in Hosea:

"I will call them 'my people' who are
    not my people;
and I will call her 'my loved one'
    who is not my loved one,"ⁱ

²⁶and,

"It will happen that in the very place
    where it was said to them,
    'You are not my people,'
they will be called 'sons of the living
    God.' "ʲ

²⁷Isaiah cries out concerning Israel:

"Though the number of the Israelites
    be like the sand by the sea,
only the remnant will be saved.
²⁸For the Lord will carry out
    his sentence on earth with speed
    and finality."ᵏ

²⁹It is just as Isaiah said previously:

"Unless the Lord Almighty

ᵃ 5 Or Christ, who is over all. God be forever praised! Or Christ. God who is over all be forever praised!   ᵇ 7 Gen. 21:12   ᶜ 9 Gen. 18:10,14   ᵈ 12 Gen. 25:23   ᵉ 13 Mal. 1:2,3   ᶠ 15 Exodus 33:19
ᵍ 17 Exodus 9:16   ʰ 20 Isaiah 29:16; 45:9   ⁱ 25 Hosea 2:23   ʲ 26 Hosea 1:10   ᵏ 28 Isaiah 10:22,23

had left us descendants,
  we would have become like Sodom,
  we would have been like
    Gomorrah."*a*

Israel's Unbelief

30What then shall we say? That the
Gentiles, who did not pursue righteousness, have obtained it, a righteousness
that is by faith; 31but Israel, who pursued a law of righteousness, has not
attained it. 32Why not? Because they
pursued it not by faith but as if it were
by works. They stumbled over the
"stumbling stone." 33As it is written:

  "See, I lay in Zion a stone that causes
    men to stumble
  and a rock that makes them fall,
  and the one who trusts in him will
    never be put to shame."*b*

10 Brothers, my heart's desire
  and prayer to God for the Israelites is that they may be saved. 2For I
can testify about them that they are
zealous for God, but their zeal is not
based on knowledge. 3Since they did not
know the righteousness that comes
from God and sought to establish their
own, they did not submit to God's righteousness. 4Christ is the end of the law
so that there may be righteousness for
everyone who believes.

5Moses describes in this way the righteousness that is by the law: "The man
who does these things will live by
them."*c* 6But the righteousness that is
by faith says: "Do not say in your heart,
'Who will ascend into heaven?'*d*" (that
is, to bring Christ down) 7"or 'Who will
descend into the deep?'*e*" (that is, to
bring Christ up from the dead). 8But
what does it say? "The word is near you;
it is in your mouth and in your heart,"*f*
that is, the word of faith we are proclaiming: 9That if you confess with your
mouth, "Jesus is Lord," and believe in
your heart that God raised him from the
dead, you will be saved. 10For it is with
your heart that you believe and are justified, and it is with your mouth that you
confess and are saved. 11As the Scripture

says, "Anyone who trusts in him will
never be put to shame."*g* 12For there is
no difference between Jew and Gentile—the same Lord is Lord of all and
richly blesses all who call on him, 13for,
"Everyone who calls on the name of the
Lord will be saved."*h*

14How, then, can they call on the one
they have not believed in? And how can
they believe in the one of whom they
have not heard? And how can they hear
without someone preaching to them?
15And how can they preach unless they
are sent? As it is written, "How beautiful are the feet of those who bring good
news!"*i*

16But not all the Israelites accepted
the good news. For Isaiah says, "Lord,
who has believed our message?"*j* 17Con-
sequently, faith comes from hearing the
message, and the message is heard
through the word of Christ. 18But I ask:
Did they not hear? Of course they did:

  "Their voice has gone out into all the
    earth,
    their words to the ends of the
      world."*k*

19Again I ask: Did Israel not understand?
First, Moses says,

  "I will make you envious by those
    who are not a nation;
  I will make you angry by a nation
    that has no understanding."*l*

20And Isaiah boldly says,

  "I was found by those who did not
    seek me;
  I revealed myself to those who did
    not ask for me."*m*

21But concerning Israel he says,

  "All day long I have held out my
    hands
  to a disobedient and obstinate
    people."*n*

a 29 Isaiah 1:9   *b* 33 Isaiah 8:14; 28:16   *c* 5 Lev. 18:5   *d* 6 Deut. 30:12   *e* 7 Deut. 30:13
f 8 Deut. 30:14   *g* 11 Isaiah 28:16   *h* 13 Joel 2:32   *i* 15 Isaiah 52:7   *j* 16 Isaiah 53:1
k 18 Psalm 19:4   *l* 19 Deut. 32:21   *m* 20 Isaiah 65:1   *n* 21 Isaiah 65:2

The Remnant of Israel

11 I ask then: Did God reject his people? By no means! I am an Israelite myself, a descendant of Abraham, from the tribe of Benjamin. ²God did not reject his people, whom he foreknew. Don't you know what the Scripture says in the passage about Elijah—how he appealed to God against Israel: ³"Lord, they have killed your prophets and torn down your altars; I am the only one left, and they are trying to kill me"*a*? ⁴And what was God's answer to him? "I have reserved for myself seven thousand who have not bowed the knee to Baal."*b* ⁵So too, at the present time there is a remnant chosen by grace. ⁶And if by grace, then it is no longer by

a 3 1 Kings 19:10,14   *b 4* 1 Kings 19:18

YOU HAVE BEEN SAVED
Karl Barth

VERSE: Romans 10:9   **PASSAGE:** Romans 10:9–13

ou probably all know the legend of the rider who crossed the frozen Lake of Constance by night without knowing it. When he reached the opposite shore and was told whence he came, he broke down, horrified. This is the human situation when the sky opens and the earth is bright, when we may hear: *By grace you have been saved!* In such a moment we are like that terrified rider. When we hear this word we involuntarily look back, do we not, asking ourselves: Where have I been? Over an abyss, in mortal danger! What did I do? The most foolish thing I ever attempted! What happened? I was doomed and miraculously escaped and now I am safe! You ask: "Do we really live in such danger?" Yes, we live on the brink of death. But we have been saved. Look at our Savior and at our Salvation! Look at Jesus Christ on the cross, accused, sentenced, and punished instead of us! Do you know for whose sake he is hanging there? For *our* sake—because of *our* sin—sharing *our* captivity—burdened with *our* suffering! He nails *our* life to the cross. This is how God had to deal with *us*. From this darkness he has saved *us*. He who is not shattered after hearing this news may not yet have grasped the word of God: *By grace you have been saved.*

ADDITIONAL SCRIPTURE READING:
Psalm 23; Ephesians 2:8–9

Go to page 1321 for your next devotional reading.

1900   Present

works; if it were, grace would no longer be grace.*a*

⁷What then? What Israel sought so earnestly it did not obtain, but the elect did. The others were hardened, ⁸as it is written:

> "God gave them a spirit of stupor,
>   eyes so that they could not see
>   and ears so that they could not hear,
> to this very day."*b*

⁹And David says:

> "May their table become a snare and
>   a trap,
>   a stumbling block and a retribution
>   for them.
> ¹⁰May their eyes be darkened so they
>   cannot see,
>   and their backs be bent forever."*c*

Ingrafted Branches

¹¹Again I ask: Did they stumble so as to fall beyond recovery? Not at all! Rather, because of their transgression, salvation has come to the Gentiles to make Israel envious. ¹²But if their transgression means riches for the world, and their loss means riches for the Gentiles, how much greater riches will their fullness bring!

¹³I am talking to you Gentiles. Inasmuch as I am the apostle to the Gentiles, I make much of my ministry ¹⁴in the hope that I may somehow arouse my own people to envy and save some of them. ¹⁵For if their rejection is the reconciliation of the world, what will their acceptance be but life from the dead? ¹⁶If the part of the dough offered as firstfruits is holy, then the whole batch is holy; if the root is holy, so are the branches.

¹⁷If some of the branches have been broken off, and you, though a wild olive shoot, have been grafted in among the others and now share in the nourishing sap from the olive root, ¹⁸do not boast over those branches. If you do, consider this: You do not support the root, but the root supports you. ¹⁹You will say then, "Branches were broken off so that I could be grafted in." ²⁰Granted. But

they were broken off because of unbelief, and you stand by faith. Do not be arrogant, but be afraid. ²¹For if God did not spare the natural branches, he will not spare you either.

²²Consider therefore the kindness and sternness of God: sternness to those who fell, but kindness to you, provided that you continue in his kindness. Otherwise, you also will be cut off. ²³And if they do not persist in unbelief, they will be grafted in, for God is able to graft them in again. ²⁴After all, if you were cut out of an olive tree that is wild by nature, and contrary to nature were grafted into a cultivated olive tree, how much more readily will these, the natural branches, be grafted into their own olive tree!

All Israel Will Be Saved

²⁵I do not want you to be ignorant of this mystery, brothers, so that you may not be conceited: Israel has experienced a hardening in part until the full number of the Gentiles has come in. ²⁶And so all Israel will be saved, as it is written:

> "The deliverer will come from Zion;
>   he will turn godlessness away from
>   Jacob.
> ²⁷And this is*d* my covenant with them
>   when I take away their sins."*e*

²⁸As far as the gospel is concerned, they are enemies on your account; but as far as election is concerned, they are loved on account of the patriarchs, ²⁹for God's gifts and his call are irrevocable. ³⁰Just as you who were at one time disobedient to God have now received mercy as a result of their disobedience, ³¹so they too have now become disobedient in order that they too may now*f* receive mercy as a result of God's mercy to you. ³²For God has bound all men over to disobedience so that he may have mercy on them all.

Doxology

³³Oh, the depth of the riches of the
    wisdom and*g* knowledge of
    God!
  How unsearchable his judgments,

---

a 6 Some manuscripts *by grace. But if by works, then it is no longer grace; if it were, work would no longer be work.*   *b 8* Deut. 29:4; Isaiah 29:10   *c 10* Psalm 69:22,23   *d 27* Or *will be*   *e 27* Isaiah 59:20,21; 27:9; Jer. 31:33,34   *f 31* Some manuscripts do not have *now.*   *g 33* Or *riches and the wisdom and the*

and his paths beyond tracing out!   Or who has been his counselor?"*a*
34 "Who has known the mind of the   35 "Who has ever given to God,
    Lord?   that God should repay him?"*b*

a 34 Isaiah 40:13   *b 35* Job 41:11

FRIDAY

FROM PAUL'S LETTER TO AMERICAN CHRISTIANS
Martin Luther King, Jr.

VERSE: Romans 12:2   PASSAGE: Romans 12:1–2

find it necessary to remind you of the responsibility laid upon you to represent the ethical principles of Christianity amid a time that popularly disregards them. That was a task laid on me. I understand that there are many Christians in America who give their ultimate allegiance to man-made systems and customs. They are afraid to be different. Their great concern is to be accepted socially. They live by some such principle as this: "Everybody is doing it, so it must be all right." For so many of you morality merely reflects group consensus. In your modern sociological lingo, the mores are accepted as the right ways. You have unconsciously come to believe that what is right is determined by Gallup polls.

American Christians, I must say to you what I wrote to the Roman Christians years ago: "Do not conform any longer to the pattern of this world, but be transformed by the renewing of your mind" (Romans 12:2). You have a duel citizenry. You live both in time and eternity. Your highest loyalty is to God, and not to the mores or the folkways, the state or the nation, or any man-made institution. If any earthly institution or custom conflicts with God's will, it is your Christian duty to oppose it. You must never allow the transitory, evanescent demands of man-made institutions to take precedence over the eternal demands of the Almighty God. In a time when men are surrendering the high values of the faith you must cling to them, and despite the pressure of an alien generation preserve them for children yet unborn. You must be willing to challenge unjust mores, to champion unpopular causes, and to buck the status quo. You are called to be the salt of the earth. You are to be the light of the world. You are to be that vitally active leaven in the lump of the nation.

ADDITIONAL SCRIPTURE READING:
Matthew 5:11–16; Ephesians 4:21–24

Go to page 1323 for your next devotional reading.

1900   Present

36 For from him and through him and to him are all things.
To him be the glory forever! Amen.

Living Sacrifices

12 Therefore, I urge you, brothers, in view of God's mercy, to offer your bodies as living sacrifices, holy and pleasing to God—this is your spiritual[a] act of worship. 2 Do not conform any longer to the pattern of this world, but be transformed by the renewing of your mind. Then you will be able to test and approve what God's will is—his good, pleasing and perfect will.

3 For by the grace given me I say to every one of you: Do not think of yourself more highly than you ought, but rather think of yourself with sober judgment, in accordance with the measure of faith God has given you. 4 Just as each of us has one body with many members, and these members do not all have the same function, 5 so in Christ we who are many form one body, and each member belongs to all the others. 6 We have different gifts, according to the grace given us. If a man's gift is prophesying, let him use it in proportion to his[b] faith. 7 If it is serving, let him serve; if it is teaching, let him teach; 8 if it is encouraging, let him encourage; if it is contributing to the needs of others, let him give generously; if it is leadership, let him govern diligently; if it is showing mercy, let him do it cheerfully.

IT IS VERY EASY TO OVERESTIMATE THE IMPORTANCE OF OUR OWN ACHIEVEMENTS IN COMPARISON WITH WHAT WE OWE OTHERS.

—Dietrich Bonhoeffer

Love

9 Love must be sincere. Hate what is evil; cling to what is good. 10 Be devoted to one another in brotherly love. Honor one another above yourselves. 11 Never be lacking in zeal, but keep your spiritual fervor, serving the Lord. 12 Be joyful in hope, patient in affliction, faithful in prayer. 13 Share with God's people who are in need. Practice hospitality.

14 Bless those who persecute you; bless and do not curse. 15 Rejoice with those who rejoice; mourn with those who mourn. 16 Live in harmony with one another. Do not be proud, but be willing to associate with people of low position.[c] Do not be conceited.

17 Do not repay anyone evil for evil. Be careful to do what is right in the eyes of everybody. 18 If it is possible, as far as it depends on you, live at peace with everyone. 19 Do not take revenge, my friends, but leave room for God's wrath, for it is written: "It is mine to avenge; I will repay,"[d] says the Lord. 20 On the contrary:

"If your enemy is hungry, feed him;
   if he is thirsty, give him something
     to drink.
In doing this, you will heap burning
   coals on his head."[e]

21 Do not be overcome by evil, but overcome evil with good.

Submission to the Authorities

13 Everyone must submit himself to the governing authorities, for there is no authority except that which God has established. The authorities that exist have been established by God. 2 Consequently, he who rebels against the authority is rebelling against what God has instituted, and those who do so will bring judgment on themselves. 3 For rulers hold no terror for those who do right, but for those who do wrong. Do you want to be free from fear of the one in authority? Then do what is right and he will commend you. 4 For he is God's servant to do you good. But if you do wrong, be afraid, for he does not bear the sword for nothing. He is God's servant, an agent of wrath to bring punishment on the wrongdoer. 5 Therefore, it is necessary to submit to the authorities, not only because of possible punishment but also because of conscience.

6 This is also why you pay taxes, for the authorities are God's servants, who give their full time to governing. 7 Give everyone what you owe him: If you owe taxes, pay taxes; if revenue, then rev-

---

a 1 Or *reasonable*   b 6 Or *in agreement with the*   c 16 Or *willing to do menial work*
d 19 Deut. 32:35   e 20 Prov. 25:21,22

WEEKEND

THE SOUND OF THE BELL
John Donne

VERSE: Acts 17:26   **PASSAGE:** Acts 17:24–28

ow, this Bell tolling softly for another, saies to me, Thou must die.

Perchance hee for whom this *Bell* tolls, may bee so ill, as that he knowes not it *tolls* for him; And perchance I may thinke my selfe so much better than I am, as that they who are about mee, and see my state, may have caused it to toll for mee, and I know not that . . . As therefore the *Bell* that rings to a *Sermon*, calls not upon the *Preacher* onely, but upon the *Congregation* to come; so this *Bell* calls us all: but how much more *mee*, who am brought so neere the *doore* by this *sicknesse* . . . No man is an *Iland*, intire of it selfe; every man is a peece of the *Continent*, a part of the *maine*; if a *Clod* bee washed away by the *Sea*, *Europe* is the lesse, as well as if a *Promontorie* were, as well as if a *Mannor* of thy *friends*, or of *thine owne* were; Any Mans *deathe* diminishes *me*, because I am involved in *Mankinde*; And therefore never send to know for whom the *bell* tolls; It tolls for *thee*.

ADDITIONAL SCRIPTURE READING:
Psalm 13:1–6; Revelation 21:1–4

Go to page 1325 for your next devotional reading.

1500   1700

enue; if respect, then respect; if honor, then honor.

Love, for the Day Is Near

[8]Let no debt remain outstanding, except the continuing debt to love one another, for he who loves his fellowman has fulfilled the law. [9]The commandments, "Do not commit adultery," "Do not murder," "Do not steal," "Do not covet,"[a] and whatever other commandment there may be, are summed up in this one rule: "Love your neighbor as yourself."[b] [10]Love does no harm to its neighbor. Therefore love is the fulfillment of the law.

IF THERE IS NO ELEMENT OF ASCETICISM IN OUR LIVES, IF WE GIVE FREE REIN TO THE DESIRES OF THE FLESH . . . WE SHALL FIND IT HARD TO TRAIN FOR THE SERVICE OF CHRIST. —*Dietrich Bonhoeffer*

[11]And do this, understanding the present time. The hour has come for you to wake up from your slumber, because our salvation is nearer now than when we first believed. [12]The night is nearly over; the day is almost here. So let us put aside the deeds of darkness and put on the armor of light. [13]Let us behave decently, as in the daytime, not in orgies and drunkenness, not in sexual immorality and debauchery, not in dissension and jealousy. [14]Rather, clothe yourselves with the Lord Jesus Christ, and do not think about how to gratify the desires of the sinful nature.[c]

The Weak and the Strong

14 Accept him whose faith is weak, without passing judgment on disputable matters. [2]One man's faith allows him to eat everything, but another man, whose faith is weak, eats only vegetables. [3]The man who eats everything must not look down on him who does not, and the man who does not eat everything must not condemn the man who does, for God has accepted him. [4]Who are you to judge someone else's servant? To his own master he stands or falls. And he

will stand, for the Lord is able to make him stand.

[5]One man considers one day more sacred than another; another man considers every day alike. Each one should be fully convinced in his own mind. [6]He who regards one day as special, does so to the Lord. He who eats meat, eats to the Lord, for he gives thanks to God; and he who abstains, does so to the Lord and gives thanks to God. [7]For none of us lives to himself alone and none of us dies to himself alone. [8]If we live, we live to the Lord; and if we die, we die to the Lord. So, whether we live or die, we belong to the Lord.

[9]For this very reason, Christ died and returned to life so that he might be the Lord of both the dead and the living. [10]You, then, why do you judge your brother? Or why do you look down on your brother? For we will all stand before God's judgment seat. [11]It is written:

" 'As surely as I live,' says the Lord,
'every knee will bow before me;
　every tongue will confess to
　　God.' "[d]

[12]So then, each of us will give an account of himself to God.

AT THE DAY OF JUDGMENT WE SHALL NOT BE ASKED WHAT WE HAVE READ BUT WHAT WE HAVE DONE. —*Thomas à Kempis*

[13]Therefore let us stop passing judgment on one another. Instead, make up your mind not to put any stumbling block or obstacle in your brother's way. [14]As one who is in the Lord Jesus, I am fully convinced that no food[e] is unclean in itself. But if anyone regards something as unclean, then for him it is unclean. [15]If your brother is distressed because of what you eat, you are no longer acting in love. Do not by your eating destroy your brother for whom Christ died. [16]Do not allow what you consider good to be spoken of as evil. [17]For the kingdom of God is not a matter of eating and drinking, but of righ-

---

[a] 9 Exodus 20:13–15,17; Deut. 5:17–19,21　　[b] 9 Lev. 19:18　　[c] 14 Or *the flesh*　　[d] 11 Isaiah 45:23
[e] 14 Or *that nothing*

teousness, peace and joy in the Holy Spirit, [18]because anyone who serves Christ in this way is pleasing to God and approved by men.

[19]Let us therefore make every effort to do what leads to peace and to mutual edification. [20]Do not destroy the work of God for the sake of food. All food is clean, but it is wrong for a man to eat anything that causes someone else to

MONDAY

SCREWTAPE'S STRATEGY
C. S. Lewis

VERSE: Romans 13:8   **PASSAGE:** Romans 13:8–10

[Satan writes to one of his minions:]

y Dear Wormwood,

. . . The "Historical Jesus," however dangerous he may seem to be to us at some particular point, is always to be encouraged. About the general connection between Christianity and politics, our position is more delicate. Certainly we do not want men to allow their Christianity to flow over into their political life, for the establishment of anything like a really just society would be a major disaster. On the other hand we do want, and want very much, to make men treat Christianity as a means; preferably, of course, as a means to their own advancement, but, failing that, as a means to anything—even to social justice. The thing to do is to get a man at first to value social justice as a thing which the Enemy [God] demands, and then work him on to the stage at which he values Christianity because it may produce social justice. For the Enemy will not be used as a convenience. Men or nations who think they can revive the faith in order to make a good society might just as well think they can use the stairs of heaven as a short cut to the nearest chemist's shop. Fortunately it is quite easy to coax humans round this little corner. Only today I have found a passage in a Christian writer where he recommends his own version of Christianity on the ground that "only such a faith can outlast the death of old cultures and the birth of new civilizations." You see the little rift? "Believe this, not because it is true, but for some other reason." That's the game,

Your affectionate uncle
Screwtape

ADDITIONAL SCRIPTURE READING:
Galatians 6:7–8; Hebrews 10:22–24

Go to page 1327 for your next devotional reading.

1900   Present

stumble. 21It is better not to eat meat or drink wine or to do anything else that will cause your brother to fall.

22So whatever you believe about these things keep between yourself and God. Blessed is the man who does not condemn himself by what he approves. 23But the man who has doubts is condemned if he eats, because his eating is not from faith; and everything that does not come from faith is sin.

15 We who are strong ought to bear with the failings of the weak and not to please ourselves. 2Each of us should please his neighbor for his good, to build him up. 3For even Christ did not please himself but, as it is written: "The insults of those who insult you have fallen on me."[a] 4For everything that was written in the past was written to teach us, so that through endurance and the encouragement of the Scriptures we might have hope.

5May the God who gives endurance and encouragement give you a spirit of unity among yourselves as you follow Christ Jesus, 6so that with one heart and mouth you may glorify the God and Father of our Lord Jesus Christ.

7Accept one another, then, just as Christ accepted you, in order to bring praise to God. 8For I tell you that Christ has become a servant of the Jews[b] on behalf of God's truth, to confirm the promises made to the patriarchs 9so that the Gentiles may glorify God for his mercy, as it is written:

"Therefore I will praise you among
    the Gentiles;
I will sing hymns to your name."[c]

10Again, it says,

"Rejoice, O Gentiles, with his
    people."[d]

11And again,

"Praise the Lord, all you Gentiles,
    and sing praises to him, all you
    peoples."[e]

12And again, Isaiah says,

"The Root of Jesse will spring up,
    one who will arise to rule over the
    nations;
the Gentiles will hope in him."[f]

13May the God of hope fill you with all joy and peace as you trust in him, so that you may overflow with hope by the power of the Holy Spirit.

Paul the Minister to the Gentiles

14I myself am convinced, my brothers, that you yourselves are full of goodness, complete in knowledge and competent to instruct one another. 15I have written you quite boldly on some points, as if to remind you of them again, because of the grace God gave me 16to be a minister of Christ Jesus to the Gentiles with the priestly duty of proclaiming the gospel of God, so that the Gentiles might become an offering acceptable to God, sanctified by the Holy Spirit.

17Therefore I glory in Christ Jesus in my service to God. 18I will not venture to speak of anything except what Christ has accomplished through me in leading the Gentiles to obey God by what I have said and done— 19by the power of signs and miracles, through the power of the Spirit. So from Jerusalem all the way around to Illyricum, I have fully proclaimed the gospel of Christ. 20It has always been my ambition to preach the gospel where Christ was not known, so that I would not be building on someone else's foundation. 21Rather, as it is written:

"Those who were not told about him
    will see,
and those who have not heard will
    understand."[g]

22This is why I have often been hindered from coming to you.

Paul's Plan to Visit Rome

23But now that there is no more place for me to work in these regions, and since I have been longing for many years to see you, 24I plan to do so when I go to Spain. I hope to visit you while passing through and to have you assist me on

a 3 Psalm 69:9   b 8 Greek circumcision   c 9 2 Samuel 22:50; Psalm 18:49   d 10 Deut. 32:43
e 11 Psalm 117:1   f 12 Isaiah 11:10   g 21 Isaiah 52:15

THE WIDENING CIRCLE OF RIPPLES
IN THE POOL OF HISTORY
Karl Barth

VERSE: Romans 15:20   **PASSAGE:** Romans 15:17–21

e all know the curiosity that comes over us when from a window we see the people in the street suddenly stop and look up—shade their eyes with their hands and look straight up into the sky toward something which is hidden from us by the roof. Our curiosity is superfluous, for what they see is doubtless an airplane. But as to the sudden stopping, looking up, and tense attention characteristic of the people of the Bible, our wonder will not be so lightly dismissed. To me personally it came first with Paul: this man evidently sees and hears something which is above everything, which is absolutely beyond the range of my observation and the measure of my thought. Let me place myself as I will to this coming something that in enigmatical words he insists he sees and hears, I am still taken by the fact that he, Paul, or whoever it was who wrote the epistle to the Ephesians, for example, is eye and ear in a state which expressions such as inspiration, alarm, or stirring or overwhelming emotion, do not satisfactorily describe. I seem to see within so transparent a piece of literature a personality who is actually thrown out of his course by seeing and hearing what I for my part do not see and hear—who is, so to speak, captured, in order to be dragged as a prisoner from land to land for strange, intense, uncertain, and yet mysteriously well-planned service.

And if ever I come to fear lest mine is a case of self-hallucination, one glance at the secular events of those times, one glance at the widening circle of ripples in the pool of history, tells me of a certainty that a stone of unusual weight must have been dropped into deep water somewhere—tells me that, among all the hundreds of peripatetic preachers and miracle-workers from the Near East who in that day must have gone along the same Appian Way into imperial Rome, it was this one Paul, seeing and hearing what he did, who was the cause, if not of all, yet of the most important developments in that city's future.

ADDITIONAL SCRIPTURE READING:
Galatians 1:13–17; Ephesians 3:7–10

Go to page 1328 for your next devotional reading.

1900   Present

my journey there, after I have enjoyed your company for a while. 25Now, however, I am on my way to Jerusalem in the service of the saints there. 26For Macedonia and Achaia were pleased to make a contribution for the poor among the saints in Jerusalem. 27They were pleased to do it, and indeed they owe it to them. For if the Gentiles have shared in the Jews' spiritual blessings, they owe it to the Jews to share with them their material blessings. 28So after I have completed this task and have made sure that they have received this fruit, I will go to Spain and visit you on the way. 29I know that when I come to you, I will come in the full measure of the blessing of Christ.

30I urge you, brothers, by our Lord Jesus Christ and by the love of the Spirit, to join me in my struggle by praying to God for me. 31Pray that I may be rescued from the unbelievers in Judea and that my service in Jerusalem may be acceptable to the saints there, 32so that by God's will I may come to you with joy and together with you be refreshed. 33The God of peace be with you all. Amen.

WEDNESDAY

CHRIST, OUR DELIVERER
Hippolytus

VERSE: Romans 16:20   **PASSAGE:** Romans 16:20, 25–27

 e give you thanks, O God, through your dear child, Jesus Christ, who in these last days you sent to save us and instruct us. He is your word, inseparable from you; you made all things through him, and you were well pleased with him.

You sent him from heaven to a virgin's womb. He lay in that womb and took flesh, and you were presented with a son, born of the Holy Spirit and of a virgin. He did what you wanted him to do. When he suffered, he stretched out his hands to free those who believed in you from suffering. When he died he destroyed death, breaking the chains of the devil which held us and crushing hell beneath his feet. When he rose again he gave light to the righteous, revealing his new covenant with mankind.

Thus, calling to mind his death and resurrection, we offer you bread and wine, thanking you for enabling us to stand before you and serve you. We ask you to send down your Holy Spirit on the offering which we make to you, uniting all who receive Holy Communion in the bond of your truth.

ADDITIONAL SCRIPTURE READING:
Luke 22:14–20; John 1:1–3,14

Go to page 1332 for your next devotional reading.

100   500

Personal Greetings

16 I commend to you our sister Phoebe, a servant[a] of the church in Cenchrea. [2]I ask you to receive her in the Lord in a way worthy of the saints and to give her any help she may need from you, for she has been a great help to many people, including me.

[3]Greet Priscilla[b] and Aquila, my fellow workers in Christ Jesus. [4]They risked their lives for me. Not only I but all the churches of the Gentiles are grateful to them.

[5]Greet also the church that meets at their house.

Greet my dear friend Epenetus, who was the first convert to Christ in the province of Asia.

[6]Greet Mary, who worked very hard for you.

[7]Greet Andronicus and Junias, my relatives who have been in prison with me. They are outstanding among the apostles, and they were in Christ before I was.

[8]Greet Ampliatus, whom I love in the Lord.

[9]Greet Urbanus, our fellow worker in Christ, and my dear friend Stachys.

[10]Greet Apelles, tested and approved in Christ.

Greet those who belong to the household of Aristobulus.

[11]Greet Herodion, my relative.

Greet those in the household of Narcissus who are in the Lord.

[12]Greet Tryphena and Tryphosa, those women who work hard in the Lord.

Greet my dear friend Persis, another woman who has worked very hard in the Lord.

[13]Greet Rufus, chosen in the Lord, and his mother, who has been a mother to me, too.

[14]Greet Asyncritus, Phlegon, Hermes, Patrobas, Hermas and the brothers with them.

[15]Greet Philologus, Julia, Nereus and his sister, and Olympas and all the saints with them.

[16]Greet one another with a holy kiss.

All the churches of Christ send greetings.

[17]I urge you, brothers, to watch out for those who cause divisions and put obstacles in your way that are contrary to the teaching you have learned. Keep away from them. [18]For such people are not serving our Lord Christ, but their own appetites. By smooth talk and flattery they deceive the minds of naive people. [19]Everyone has heard about your obedience, so I am full of joy over you; but I want you to be wise about what is good, and innocent about what is evil.

[20]The God of peace will soon crush Satan under your feet.

The grace of our Lord Jesus be with you.

[21]Timothy, my fellow worker, sends his greetings to you, as do Lucius, Jason and Sosipater, my relatives.

[22]I, Tertius, who wrote down this letter, greet you in the Lord.

[23]Gaius, whose hospitality I and the whole church here enjoy, sends you his greetings.

Erastus, who is the city's director of public works, and our brother Quartus send you their greetings.[c]

[25]Now to him who is able to establish you by my gospel and the proclamation of Jesus Christ, according to the revelation of the mystery hidden for long ages past, [26]but now revealed and made known through the prophetic writings by the command of the eternal God, so that all nations might believe and obey him— [27]to the only wise God be glory forever through Jesus Christ! Amen.

---

a 1 Or *deaconess*   *b 3* Greek *Prisca,* a variant of *Priscilla*   *c 23* Some manuscripts *their greetings.*
24May the grace of our Lord Jesus Christ be with all of you. Amen.

1 CORINTHIANS

AUL WROTE TO THE CHURCH HE'D STARTED IN CORINTH (ACTS 18:1–17), A CHURCH NOW STRUGGLING TO LIVE IN OBEDIENCE. IN A LETTER MARKED BY LOVING CONCERN AND A TRUE PASTOR'S HEART, PAUL ADDRESSES PROBLEMS IN CHRISTIAN CONDUCT AND CHARACTER. LOOK FOR PRACTICAL INFORMATION RELEVANT TO CHRISTIAN LIVING AND RELATIONSHIPS, AS WELL AS UPLIFTING WORDS ABOUT LOVE (CHAPTER 13) AND THE RESURRECTION (CHAPTER 15).

1 Paul, called to be an apostle of Christ Jesus by the will of God, and our brother Sosthenes,

2To the church of God in Corinth, to those sanctified in Christ Jesus and called to be holy, together with all those everywhere who call on the name of our Lord Jesus Christ—their Lord and ours:

3Grace and peace to you from God our Father and the Lord Jesus Christ.

Thanksgiving

4I always thank God for you because of his grace given you in Christ Jesus. 5For in him you have been enriched in every way—in all your speaking and in all your knowledge— 6because our testimony about Christ was confirmed in you. 7Therefore you do not lack any spiritual gift as you eagerly wait for our Lord Jesus Christ to be revealed. 8He will keep you strong to the end, so that you will be blameless on the day of our Lord Jesus Christ. 9God, who has called you into fellowship with his Son Jesus Christ our Lord, is faithful.

Divisions in the Church

10I appeal to you, brothers, in the name of our Lord Jesus Christ, that all of you agree with one another so that there may be no divisions among you and that you may be perfectly united in mind and thought. 11My brothers, some from Chloe's household have informed me that there are quarrels among you. 12What I mean is this: One of you says, "I follow Paul"; another, "I follow Apollos";

another, "I follow Cephas[a]"; still another, "I follow Christ."

[13]Is Christ divided? Was Paul crucified for you? Were you baptized into[b] the name of Paul? [14]I am thankful that I did not baptize any of you except Crispus and Gaius, [15]so no one can say that you were baptized into my name. [16](Yes, I also baptized the household of Stephanas; beyond that, I don't remember if I baptized anyone else.) [17]For Christ did not send me to baptize, but to preach the gospel—not with words of human wisdom, lest the cross of Christ be emptied of its power.

Christ the Wisdom and Power of God

[18]For the message of the cross is foolishness to those who are perishing, but to us who are being saved it is the power of God. [19]For it is written:

"I will destroy the wisdom of the
    wise;
  the intelligence of the intelligent I
    will frustrate."[c]

[20]Where is the wise man? Where is the scholar? Where is the philosopher of this age? Has not God made foolish the wisdom of the world? [21]For since in the wisdom of God the world through its wisdom did not know him, God was pleased through the foolishness of what was preached to save those who believe. [22]Jews demand miraculous signs and Greeks look for wisdom, [23]but we preach Christ crucified: a stumbling block to Jews and foolishness to Gentiles, [24]but to those whom God has called, both Jews and Greeks, Christ the power of God and the wisdom of God. [25]For the foolishness

---

---

of God is wiser than man's wisdom, and the weakness of God is stronger than man's strength.

[26]Brothers, think of what you were when you were called. Not many of you were wise by human standards; not many were influential; not many were of noble birth. [27]But God chose the foolish things of the world to shame the wise; God chose the weak things of the world to shame the strong. [28]He chose the lowly things of this world and the despised things—and the things that are not—to nullify the things that are, [29]so that no one may boast before him. [30]It is because of him that you are in Christ Jesus, who has become for us wisdom from God—that is, our righteousness, holiness and redemption. [31]Therefore, as it is written: "Let him who boasts boast in the Lord."[d]

2 When I came to you, brothers, I did not come with eloquence or superior wisdom as I proclaimed to you the testimony about God.[e] [2]For I resolved to know nothing while I was with you except Jesus Christ and him crucified. [3]I came to you in weakness and fear, and with much trembling. [4]My message and my preaching were not with wise and persuasive words, but with a demonstration of the Spirit's power, [5]so that your faith might not rest on men's wisdom, but on God's power.

Wisdom From the Spirit

[6]We do, however, speak a message of wisdom among the mature, but not the wisdom of this age or of the rulers of this age, who are coming to nothing. [7]No, we speak of God's secret wisdom, a wisdom that has been hidden and that God destined for our glory before time began. [8]None of the rulers of this age understood it, for if they had, they would not have crucified the Lord of glory. [9]However, as it is written:

"No eye has seen,
  no ear has heard,
no mind has conceived
  what God has prepared for those
    who love him"[f]—

[10]but God has revealed it to us by his Spirit.

The Spirit searches all things, even the

---

a 12 That is, Peter   b 13 Or in; also in verse 15   c 19 Isaiah 29:14   d 31 Jer. 9:24   e 1 Some
manuscripts as I proclaimed to you God's mystery   f 9 Isaiah 64:4

deep things of God. **11**For who among men knows the thoughts of a man except the man's spirit within him? In the same way no one knows the thoughts of God except the Spirit of God. **12**We have not received the spirit of the world but the Spirit who is from God, that we may understand what God has freely given us.

THURSDAY

CHRIST IS OUR WISDOM
George Whitefield

VERSE: 1 Corinthians 1:30   **PASSAGE:** 1 Corinthians 1:26–31

herein does true wisdom consist? Were I to ask some of you, perhaps you would say, in indulging the lust of the flesh, and saying to your souls, eat, drink, and be merry: but this is only the wisdom of brutes; they have as good a gust and relish for sensual pleasures, as the greatest epicure on earth. Others would tell me, true wisdom consisted in adding house to house, and field to field, and calling lands after their own names: but this cannot be true wisdom; for riches often take to themselves wings, and fly away, like an eagle towards heaven . . .

But perhaps you despise riches and pleasure, and therefore place wisdom in the knowledge of books: but . . . learned men are not always wise; nay, our common learning, so much cried up, makes men only so many accomplished fools; to keep you therefore no longer in suspense, and withal to humble you, I will send you to a heathen to school, to learn what true wisdom is: "Know thyself," was a saying of one of the wise men of Greece; this is certainly true wisdom, and this is that wisdom spoken of in the text, and which Jesus Christ is made to all elect sinners—they are made to know themselves, so as not to think more highly of themselves than they ought to think. Before, they were darkness; now, they are light in the Lord; and in that light they see their own darkness; they now bewail themselves as fallen creatures by nature, dead in trespasses and sins, sons and heirs of hell, and children of wrath; they now see that all their righteousnesses are but as filthy rags; that there is no health in their souls; that they are poor and miserable, blind and naked; and that there is no name given under heaven, whereby they can be saved, but that of Jesus Christ . . . thus Christ is made to them wisdom.

ADDITIONAL SCRIPTURE READING:
Proverbs 1:7–9; Ecclesiastes 12:13

Go to page 1334 for your next devotional reading.

1700   1900

13This is what we speak, not in words taught us by human wisdom but in words taught by the Spirit, expressing spiritual truths in spiritual words.ᵃ 14The man without the Spirit does not accept the things that come from the Spirit of God, for they are foolishness to him, and he cannot understand them, because they are spiritually discerned. 15The spiritual man makes judgments about all things, but he himself is not subject to any man's judgment:

16 "For who has known the mind of the
   Lord
   that he may instruct him?"ᵇ

But we have the mind of Christ.

On Divisions in the Church

3 Brothers, I could not address you as spiritual but as worldly—mere infants in Christ. 2I gave you milk, not solid food, for you were not yet ready for it. Indeed, you are still not ready. 3You are still worldly. For since there is jealousy and quarreling among you, are you not worldly? Are you not acting like mere men? 4For when one says, "I follow Paul," and another, "I follow Apollos," are you not mere men?

5What, after all, is Apollos? And what is Paul? Only servants, through whom you came to believe—as the Lord has assigned to each his task. 6I planted the seed, Apollos watered it, but God made it grow. 7So neither he who plants nor he who waters is anything, but only God, who makes things grow. 8The man who plants and the man who waters have one purpose, and each will be rewarded according to his own labor. 9For we are God's fellow workers; you are God's field, God's building.

10By the grace God has given me, I laid a foundation as an expert builder, and someone else is building on it. But each one should be careful how he builds. 11For no one can lay any foundation other than the one already laid, which is Jesus Christ. 12If any man builds on this foundation using gold, silver, costly stones, wood, hay or straw, 13his work will be shown for what it is, because the Day will bring it to light. It will be revealed with fire, and the fire will test the quality of each man's work. 14If what he has built survives, he will receive his reward. 15If it is burned up, he will suffer loss; he himself will be saved, but only as one escaping through the flames.

> NO MATTER WHAT A MAN DOES, NO MATTER HOW SUCCESSFUL HE SEEMS TO BE IN ANY FIELD, IF THE HOLY SPIRIT IS NOT THE CHIEF ENERGIZER OF HIS ACTIVITY, IT WILL ALL FALL APART WHEN HE DIES.
>
> —A. W. Tozer

16Don't you know that you yourselves are God's temple and that God's Spirit lives in you? 17If anyone destroys God's temple, God will destroy him; for God's temple is sacred, and you are that temple.

18Do not deceive yourselves. If any one of you thinks he is wise by the standards of this age, he should become a "fool" so that he may become wise. 19For the wisdom of this world is foolishness in God's sight. As it is written: "He catches the wise in their craftiness"ᶜ; 20and again, "The Lord knows that the thoughts of the wise are futile."ᵈ 21So then, no more boasting about men! All things are yours, 22whether Paul or Apollos or Cephasᵉ or the world or life or death or the present or the future—all are yours, 23and you are of Christ, and Christ is of God.

Apostles of Christ

4 So then, men ought to regard us as servants of Christ and as those entrusted with the secret things of God. 2Now it is required that those who have been given a trust must prove faithful. 3I care very little if I am judged by you or by any human court; indeed, I do not even judge myself. 4My conscience is clear, but that does not make me innocent. It is the Lord who judges me. 5Therefore judge nothing before the appointed time; wait till the Lord comes. He will bring to light what is hidden in darkness and will expose the motives of men's hearts. At that time each will receive his praise from God.

ᵃ 13 Or Spirit, interpreting spiritual truths to spiritual men   ᵇ 16 Isaiah 40:13   ᶜ 19 Job 5:13
ᵈ 20 Psalm 94:11   ᵉ 22 That is, Peter

⁶Now, brothers, I have applied these things to myself and Apollos for your benefit, so that you may learn from us the meaning of the saying, "Do not go beyond what is written." Then you will not take pride in one man over against

---

FROM APOLOGY FOR MY FLIGHT
Athanasius

VERSE: 1 Corinthians 4:9　　　　　　　**PASSAGE:** 1 Corinthians 4:9–13

he flight of the saints was neither blamable nor unprofitable. If they had not avoided their persecutors, who would have preached the glad tiding of the Word of Truth? It was for this that the persecutors sought after the saints—that there might be no one to teach [the Word]. For this cause the saints endured all things, that the Gospel might be preached. Behold, while they were thus engaged in conflict with their enemies, they passed not the time of their flight unprofitably; nor while they were persecuted, did they forget the welfare of others. But as ministers of the Good Word, they grudged not to communicate it to all men; so that even while they fled, they preached the Gospel and gave warning of the wickedness of those who conspired against them and confirmed the faithful by their exhortations. Thus, the blessed Paul, having found it so by experience, declared, "All that will live godly in Christ shall suffer persecution" (2 Timothy 3:12, KJV). And straightway he prepared those who fled for the trial, saying, "Let us run with patience the race that is set before us" (Hebrews 12:1, KJV); for although there be continual tribulations, yet "tribulation worketh patience, and patience experience, and experience hope, and hope maketh not ashamed" (Romans 5:3–5, KJV) . . .

Thus the saints were abundantly preserved in their flight by the providence of God, as physicians for the sake of them that had need . . . This rule the blessed martyrs observed in their persecutions: When persecuted they fled; while concealing themselves they showed fortitude; and when discovered they submitted to martyrdom.

ADDITIONAL SCRIPTURE READING:
1 Peter 4:12–19; James 1:12

Go to page 1336 for your next devotional reading.

100　　500

another. 7For who makes you different from anyone else? What do you have that you did not receive? And if you did receive it, why do you boast as though you did not?

8Already you have all you want! Already you have become rich! You have become kings—and that without us! How I wish that you really had become kings so that we might be kings with you! 9For it seems to me that God has put us apostles on display at the end of the procession, like men condemned to die in the arena. We have been made a spectacle to the whole universe, to angels as well as to men. 10We are fools for Christ, but you are so wise in Christ! We are weak, but you are strong! You are honored, we are dishonored! 11To this very hour we go hungry and thirsty, we are in rags, we are brutally treated, we are homeless. 12We work hard with our own hands. When we are cursed, we bless; when we are persecuted, we endure it; 13when we are slandered, we answer kindly. Up to this moment we have become the scum of the earth, the refuse of the world.

14I am not writing this to shame you, but to warn you, as my dear children. 15Even though you have ten thousand guardians in Christ, you do not have many fathers, for in Christ Jesus I became your father through the gospel. 16Therefore I urge you to imitate me. 17For this reason I am sending to you Timothy, my son whom I love, who is faithful in the Lord. He will remind you of my way of life in Christ Jesus, which agrees with what I teach everywhere in every church.

18Some of you have become arrogant, as if I were not coming to you. 19But I will come to you very soon, if the Lord is willing, and then I will find out not only how these arrogant people are talking, but what power they have. 20For the kingdom of God is not a matter of talk but of power. 21What do you prefer? Shall I come to you with a whip, or in love and with a gentle spirit?

Expel the Immoral Brother!

5 It is actually reported that there is sexual immorality among you, and of a kind that does not occur even among pagans: A man has his father's wife. 2And you are proud! Shouldn't you rather have been filled with grief and have put out of your fellowship the man who did this? 3Even though I am not physically present, I am with you in spirit. And I have already passed judgment on the one who did this, just as if I were present. 4When you are assembled in the name of our Lord Jesus and I am with you in spirit, and the power of our Lord Jesus is present, 5hand this man over to Satan, so that the sinful nature*a* may be destroyed and his spirit saved on the day of the Lord.

6Your boasting is not good. Don't you know that a little yeast works through the whole batch of dough? 7Get rid of the old yeast that you may be a new batch without yeast—as you really are. For Christ, our Passover lamb, has been sacrificed. 8Therefore let us keep the Festival, not with the old yeast, the yeast of malice and wickedness, but with bread without yeast, the bread of sincerity and truth.

9I have written you in my letter not to associate with sexually immoral people— 10not at all meaning the people of this world who are immoral, or the greedy and swindlers, or idolaters. In that case you would have to leave this world. 11But now I am writing you that you must not associate with anyone who calls himself a brother but is sexually immoral or greedy, an idolater or a slanderer, a drunkard or a swindler. With such a man do not even eat.

12What business is it of mine to judge those outside the church? Are you not to judge those inside? 13God will judge those outside. "Expel the wicked man from among you."*b*

Lawsuits Among Believers

6 If any of you has a dispute with another, dare he take it before the ungodly for judgment instead of before the saints? 2Do you not know that the saints will judge the world? And if you are to judge the world, are you not competent to judge trivial cases? 3Do you not know that we will judge angels? How much more the things of this life! 4Therefore, if you have disputes about

---

a 5 Or *that his body;* or *that the flesh*   *b 13* Deut. 17:7; 19:19; 21:21; 22:21,24; 24:7

WEEKEND

THE WONDROUS CROSS
Isaac Watts

VERSE: 1 Corinthians 1:18   **PASSAGE:** 1 Corinthians 1:18–25

hen I survey the wondrous cross
On which the Prince of glory died,
My richest gain I count but loss,
And pour contempt on all my pride.

Forbid it, Lord, that I should boast,
Save in the cross of Christ my God;
All the vain things that charm me most,
I sacrifice them to his blood.

See from his head, his hands, his feet,
Sorrow and love flow mingled down;
Did e'er such love and sorrow meet,
Or thorns compose so rich a crown?

His dying crimson like a robe,
Spreads o'er his body on the tree;
Then am I dead to all the globe,
And all the globe is dead to me.

Were the whole realm of nature mine,
That were an offering far too small;
Love so amazing, so divine,
Demands my heart, my life, my all!

ADDITIONAL SCRIPTURE READING:
Isaiah 29:14; Mark 15:37–39

Go to page 1338 for your next devotional reading.

1700   1900

such matters, appoint as judges even men of little account in the church![a] [5]I say this to shame you. Is it possible that there is nobody among you wise enough to judge a dispute between believers? [6]But instead, one brother goes to law against another—and this in front of unbelievers!

[7]The very fact that you have lawsuits among you means you have been completely defeated already. Why not rather be wronged? Why not rather be cheated? [8]Instead, you yourselves cheat and do wrong, and you do this to your brothers.

[9]Do you not know that the wicked will not inherit the kingdom of God? Do not be deceived: Neither the sexually immoral nor idolaters nor adulterers nor male prostitutes nor homosexual offenders [10]nor thieves nor the greedy nor drunkards nor slanderers nor swindlers will inherit the kingdom of God. [11]And that is what some of you were. But you were washed, you were sanctified, you were justified in the name of the Lord Jesus Christ and by the Spirit of our God.

Sexual Immorality

[12]"Everything is permissible for me"—but not everything is beneficial. "Everything is permissible for me"—but I will not be mastered by anything. [13]"Food for the stomach and the stomach for food"—but God will destroy them both. The body is not meant for sexual immorality, but for the Lord, and the Lord for the body. [14]By his power God raised the Lord from the dead, and he will raise us also. [15]Do you not know that your bodies are members of Christ himself? Shall I then take the members of Christ and unite them with a prostitute? Never! [16]Do you not know that he who unites himself with a prostitute is one with her in body? For it is said, "The two will become one flesh."[b] [17]But he who unites himself with the Lord is one with him in spirit.

[18]Flee from sexual immorality. All other sins a man commits are outside his body, but he who sins sexually sins against his own body. [19]Do you not know that your body is a temple of the Holy Spirit, who is in you, whom you have received from God? You are not your own; [20]you were bought at a price. Therefore honor God with your body.

Marriage

7 Now for the matters you wrote about: It is good for a man not to marry.[c] [2]But since there is so much immorality, each man should have his own wife, and each woman her own husband. [3]The husband should fulfill his marital duty to his wife, and likewise the wife to her husband. [4]The wife's body does not belong to her alone but also to her husband. In the same way, the husband's body does not belong to him alone but also to his wife. [5]Do not deprive each other except by mutual consent and for a time, so that you may devote yourselves to prayer. Then come together again so that Satan will not tempt you because of your lack of self-control. [6]I say this as a concession, not as a command. [7]I wish that all men were as I am. But each man has his own gift from God; one has this gift, another has that.

[8]Now to the unmarried and the widows I say: It is good for them to stay unmarried, as I am. [9]But if they cannot control themselves, they should marry, for it is better to marry than to burn with passion.

[10]To the married I give this command (not I, but the Lord): A wife must not separate from her husband. [11]But if she does, she must remain unmarried or else be reconciled to her husband. And a husband must not divorce his wife.

[12]To the rest I say this (I, not the Lord): If any brother has a wife who is not a believer and she is willing to live with him, he must not divorce her. [13]And if a woman has a husband who is not a believer and he is willing to live with her, she must not divorce him. [14]For the unbelieving husband has been sanctified through his wife, and the unbelieving wife has been sanctified through her believing husband. Otherwise your children would be unclean, but as it is, they are holy.

[15]But if the unbeliever leaves, let him do so. A believing man or woman is not

---

[a] 4 Or *matters, do you appoint as judges men of little account in the church?*   [b] 16 Gen. 2:24
[c] 1 Or *"It is good for a man not to have sexual relations with a woman."*

bound in such circumstances; God has called us to live in peace. ¹⁶How do you know, wife, whether you will save your husband? Or, how do you know, husband, whether you will save your wife?

¹⁷Nevertheless, each one should

MONDAY

THE EXHORTATION OF A FATHER TO HIS CHILDREN
Robert Smith

VERSE: 1 Corinthians 6:19   **PASSAGE:** 1 Corinthians 6:19–20

Ye are the temples of the Lord,
      For ye are dearly bought;
And they that do defile the same
      Shall surely come to naught.

Possess not pride in any wise,
      Build not your house too high;
But have always before your eyes
      That ye be born to die.

Defraud not him that hired is,
      Your labor to sustain
But give him always out of hand,
      His penny for his pain.

And as you would that other men
      Against you should proceed,
Do you the same to them again
      When they do stand in need.

And part your portion with the poor
      In money and in meat;
And feed the fainted feeble soul
      With that which ye should eat.

Ask counsel always of the wise,
      Give ear unto the end;
Refuse not you the sweet rebuke
      of him that is your friend.

Be thankful always to the Lord,
      With prayer and with praise,
Desiring him in all your works
      For to direct your ways.

ADDITIONAL SCRIPTURE READING:
2 Corinthians 6:16–18; Romans 15:5–6

Go to page 1340 for your next devotional reading.

1500   1700

retain the place in life that the Lord assigned to him and to which God has called him. This is the rule I lay down in all the churches. ¹⁸Was a man already circumcised when he was called? He should not become uncircumcised. Was a man uncircumcised when he was called? He should not be circumcised. ¹⁹Circumcision is nothing and uncircumcision is nothing. Keeping God's commands is what counts. ²⁰Each one should remain in the situation which he was in when God called him. ²¹Were you a slave when you were called? Don't let it trouble you—although if you can gain your freedom, do so. ²²For he who was a slave when he was called by the Lord is the Lord's freedman; similarly, he who was a free man when he was called is Christ's slave. ²³You were bought at a price; do not become slaves of men. ²⁴Brothers, each man, as responsible to God, should remain in the situation God called him to.

²⁵Now about virgins: I have no command from the Lord, but I give a judgment as one who by the Lord's mercy is trustworthy. ²⁶Because of the present crisis, I think that it is good for you to remain as you are. ²⁷Are you married? Do not seek a divorce. Are you unmarried? Do not look for a wife. ²⁸But if you do marry, you have not sinned; and if a virgin marries, she has not sinned. But those who marry will face many troubles in this life, and I want to spare you this.

²⁹What I mean, brothers, is that the time is short. From now on those who have wives should live as if they had none; ³⁰those who mourn, as if they did not; those who are happy, as if they were not; those who buy something, as if it were not theirs to keep; ³¹those who use the things of the world, as if not engrossed in them. For this world in its present form is passing away.

³²I would like you to be free from concern. An unmarried man is concerned about the Lord's affairs—how he can please the Lord. ³³But a married man is concerned about the affairs of this world—how he can please his wife—³⁴and his interests are divided. An unmarried woman or virgin is concerned about the Lord's affairs: Her aim is to be devoted to the Lord in both body and spirit. But a married woman is concerned about the affairs of this world—how she can please her husband. ³⁵I am saying this for your own good, not to restrict you, but that you may live in a right way in undivided devotion to the Lord.

³⁶If anyone thinks he is acting improperly toward the virgin he is engaged to, and if she is getting along in years and he feels he ought to marry, he should do as he wants. He is not sinning. They should get married. ³⁷But the man who has settled the matter in his own mind, who is under no compulsion but has control over his own will, and who has made up his mind not to marry the virgin—this man also does the right thing. ³⁸So then, he who marries the virgin does right, but he who does not marry her does even better.ᵃ

³⁹A woman is bound to her husband as long as he lives. But if her husband dies, she is free to marry anyone she wishes, but he must belong to the Lord. ⁴⁰In my judgment, she is happier if she stays as she is—and I think that I too have the Spirit of God.

Food Sacrificed to Idols

8 Now about food sacrificed to idols: We know that we all possess knowledge.ᵇ Knowledge puffs up, but love builds up. ²The man who thinks he knows something does not yet know as he ought to know. ³But the man who loves God is known by God.

⁴So then, about eating food sacrificed to idols: We know that an idol is nothing at all in the world and that there is no God but one. ⁵For even if there are so-called gods, whether in heaven or on earth (as indeed there are many "gods" and many "lords"), ⁶yet for us there is but one God, the Father, from whom all

---

ᵃ 36–38 Or ³⁶If anyone thinks he is not treating his daughter properly, and if she is getting along in years, and he feels she ought to marry, he should do as he wants. He is not sinning. He should let her get married. ³⁷But the man who has settled the matter in his own mind, who is under no compulsion but has control over his own will, and who has made up his mind to keep the virgin unmarried—this man also does the right thing. ³⁸So then, he who gives his virgin in marriage does right, but he who does not give her in marriage does even better.   ᵇ 1 Or "We all possess knowledge," as you say

things came and for whom we live; and there is but one Lord, Jesus Christ, through whom all things came and through whom we live.

⁷But not everyone knows this. Some people are still so accustomed to idols that when they eat such food they think of it as having been sacrificed to an idol, and since their conscience is weak, it is defiled. ⁸But food does not bring us near to God; we are no worse if we do not eat, and no better if we do.

⁹Be careful, however, that the exercise of your freedom does not become a stumbling block to the weak. ¹⁰For if anyone with a weak conscience sees you

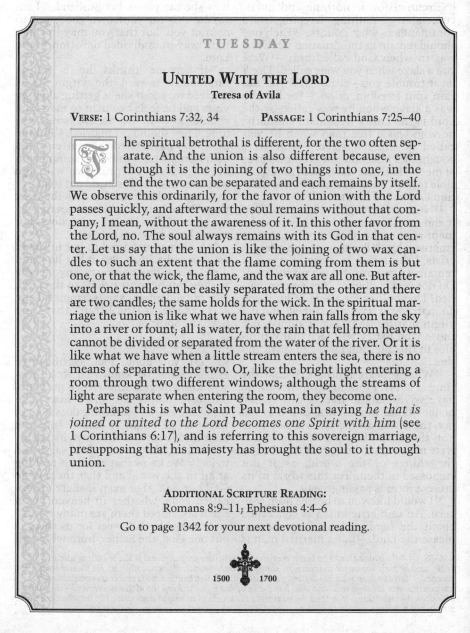

TUESDAY

UNITED WITH THE LORD
Teresa of Avila

VERSE: 1 Corinthians 7:32, 34   PASSAGE: 1 Corinthians 7:25–40

he spiritual betrothal is different, for the two often separate. And the union is also different because, even though it is the joining of two things into one, in the end the two can be separated and each remains by itself. We observe this ordinarily, for the favor of union with the Lord passes quickly, and afterward the soul remains without that company; I mean, without the awareness of it. In this other favor from the Lord, no. The soul always remains with its God in that center. Let us say that the union is like the joining of two wax candles to such an extent that the flame coming from them is but one, or that the wick, the flame, and the wax are all one. But afterward one candle can be easily separated from the other and there are two candles; the same holds for the wick. In the spiritual marriage the union is like what we have when rain falls from the sky into a river or fount; all is water, for the rain that fell from heaven cannot be divided or separated from the water of the river. Or it is like what we have when a little stream enters the sea, there is no means of separating the two. Or, like the bright light entering a room through two different windows; although the streams of light are separate when entering the room, they become one.

Perhaps this is what Saint Paul means in saying *he that is joined or united to the Lord becomes one Spirit with him* (see 1 Corinthians 6:17), and is referring to this sovereign marriage, presupposing that his majesty has brought the soul to it through union.

ADDITIONAL SCRIPTURE READING:
Romans 8:9–11; Ephesians 4:4–6

Go to page 1342 for your next devotional reading.

1500   1700

who have this knowledge eating in an idol's temple, won't he be emboldened to eat what has been sacrificed to idols? [11]So this weak brother, for whom Christ died, is destroyed by your knowledge. [12]When you sin against your brothers in this way and wound their weak conscience, you sin against Christ. [13]Therefore, if what I eat causes my brother to fall into sin, I will never eat meat again, so that I will not cause him to fall.

The Rights of an Apostle

9 Am I not free? Am I not an apostle? Have I not seen Jesus our Lord? Are you not the result of my work in the Lord? [2]Even though I may not be an apostle to others, surely I am to you! For you are the seal of my apostleship in the Lord.

[3]This is my defense to those who sit in judgment on me. [4]Don't we have the right to food and drink? [5]Don't we have the right to take a believing wife along with us, as do the other apostles and the Lord's brothers and Cephas[a]? [6]Or is it only I and Barnabas who must work for a living?

[7]Who serves as a soldier at his own expense? Who plants a vineyard and does not eat of its grapes? Who tends a flock and does not drink of the milk? [8]Do I say this merely from a human point of view? Doesn't the Law say the same thing? [9]For it is written in the Law of Moses: "Do not muzzle an ox while it is treading out the grain."[b] Is it about oxen that God is concerned? [10]Surely he says this for us, doesn't he? Yes, this was written for us, because when the plowman plows and the thresher threshes, they ought to do so in the hope of sharing in the harvest. [11]If we have sown spiritual seed among you, is it too much if we reap a material harvest from you? [12]If others have this right of support from you, shouldn't we have it all the more?

But we did not use this right. On the contrary, we put up with anything rather than hinder the gospel of Christ. [13]Don't you know that those who work in the temple get their food from the temple, and those who serve at the altar share in what is offered on the altar? [14]In the same way, the Lord has commanded that those who preach the gospel should receive their living from the gospel.

[15]But I have not used any of these rights. And I am not writing this in the hope that you will do such things for me. I would rather die than have anyone deprive me of this boast. [16]Yet when I preach the gospel, I cannot boast, for I am compelled to preach. Woe to me if I do not preach the gospel! [17]If I preach voluntarily, I have a reward; if not voluntarily, I am simply discharging the trust committed to me. [18]What then is my reward? Just this: that in preaching the gospel I may offer it free of charge, and so not make use of my rights in preaching it.

[19]Though I am free and belong to no man, I make myself a slave to everyone, to win as many as possible. [20]To the Jews I became like a Jew, to win the Jews. To those under the law I became like one under the law (though I myself am not under the law), so as to win those under the law. [21]To those not having the law I became like one not having the law (though I am not free from God's law but am under Christ's law), so as to win those not having the law. [22]To the weak I became weak, to win the weak. I have become all things to all men so that by all possible means I might save some. [23]I do all this for the sake of the gospel, that I may share in its blessings.

[24]Do you not know that in a race all the runners run, but only one gets the prize? Run in such a way as to get the prize. [25]Everyone who competes in the games goes into strict training. They do it to get a crown that will not last; but we do it to get a crown that will last forever. [26]Therefore I do not run like a man running aimlessly; I do not fight like a

---

WHEN THE FIGHT BEGINS WITHIN HIMSELF, A MAN'S WORTH SOMETHING.   —*Robert Browning*

---

man beating the air. [27]No, I beat my body and make it my slave so that after I have preached to others, I myself will not be disqualified for the prize.

---

[a] 5 That is, Peter   [b] 9 Deut. 25:4

Warnings From Israel's History

10 For I do not want you to be ignorant of the fact, brothers, that our forefathers were all under the cloud and that they all passed through the sea. [2]They were all baptized into Moses in the cloud and in the sea. [3]They all ate the same spiritual food [4]and drank the same spiritual drink; for they drank from the spiritual rock that accompanied them, and that rock was Christ. [5]Nevertheless, God was not pleased with most of them; their bodies were scattered over the desert.

[6]Now these things occurred as examples[a] to keep us from setting our hearts

[a] 6 Or *types*; also in verse 11

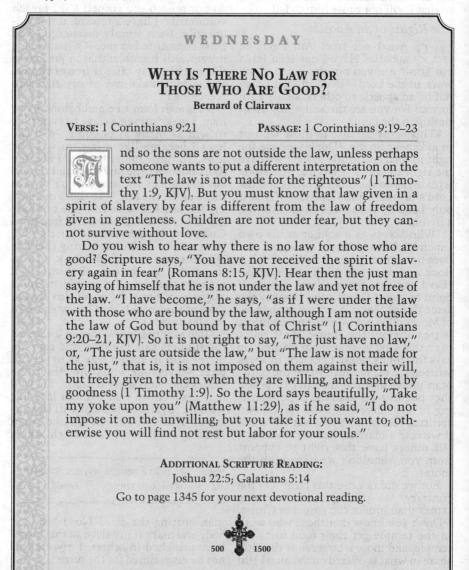

WEDNESDAY

WHY IS THERE NO LAW FOR THOSE WHO ARE GOOD?
Bernard of Clairvaux

VERSE: 1 Corinthians 9:21   **PASSAGE:** 1 Corinthians 9:19–23

And so the sons are not outside the law, unless perhaps someone wants to put a different interpretation on the text "The law is not made for the righteous" (1 Timothy 1:9, KJV). But you must know that law given in a spirit of slavery by fear is different from the law of freedom given in gentleness. Children are not under fear, but they cannot survive without love.

Do you wish to hear why there is no law for those who are good? Scripture says, "You have not received the spirit of slavery again in fear" (Romans 8:15, KJV). Hear then the just man saying of himself that he is not under the law and yet not free of the law. "I have become," he says, "as if I were under the law with those who are bound by the law, although I am not outside the law of God but bound by that of Christ" (1 Corinthians 9:20–21, KJV). So it is not right to say, "The just have no law," or, "The just are outside the law," but "The law is not made for the just," that is, it is not imposed on them against their will, but freely given to them when they are willing, and inspired by goodness (1 Timothy 1:9). So the Lord says beautifully, "Take my yoke upon you" (Matthew 11:29), as if he said, "I do not impose it on the unwilling; but you take it if you want to; otherwise you will find not rest but labor for your souls."

ADDITIONAL SCRIPTURE READING:
Joshua 22:5; Galatians 5:14

Go to page 1345 for your next devotional reading.

500 ✦ 1500

on evil things as they did. 7Do not be idolaters, as some of them were; as it is written: "The people sat down to eat and drink and got up to indulge in pagan revelry."*a* 8We should not commit sexual immorality, as some of them did—and in one day twenty-three thousand of them died. 9We should not test the Lord, as some of them did—and were killed by snakes. 10And do not grumble, as some of them did—and were killed by the destroying angel.

11These things happened to them as examples and were written down as warnings for us, on whom the fulfillment of the ages has come. 12So, if you think you are standing firm, be careful that you don't fall! 13No temptation has seized you except what is common to man. And God is faithful; he will not let you be tempted beyond what you can bear. But when you are tempted, he will also provide a way out so that you can stand up under it.

HE SAID NOT, THOU SHALL NOT BE TEMPESTED,

THOU SHALL NOT BE TRAVAILED,

THOU SHALL NOT BE AFFLICTED,

BUT HE SAID, THOU SHALL NOT BE OVERCOME.

—*Julian of Norwich*

Idol Feasts and the Lord's Supper

14Therefore, my dear friends, flee from idolatry. 15I speak to sensible people; judge for yourselves what I say. 16Is not the cup of thanksgiving for which we give thanks a participation in the blood of Christ? And is not the bread that we break a participation in the body of Christ? 17Because there is one loaf, we, who are many, are one body, for we all partake of the one loaf.

18Consider the people of Israel: Do not those who eat the sacrifices participate in the altar? 19Do I mean then that a sacrifice offered to an idol is anything, or that an idol is anything? 20No, but the sacrifices of pagans are offered to demons, not to God, and I do not want you to be participants with demons. 21You cannot drink the cup of the Lord and the cup of demons too; you cannot

have a part in both the Lord's table and the table of demons. 22Are we trying to arouse the Lord's jealousy? Are we stronger than he?

The Believer's Freedom

23"Everything is permissible"—but not everything is beneficial. "Everything is permissible"—but not everything is constructive. 24Nobody should seek his own good, but the good of others.

25Eat anything sold in the meat market without raising questions of conscience, 26for, "The earth is the Lord's, and everything in it."*b* 27If some unbeliever invites you to a meal and you want to go, eat whatever is put before you without raising questions of conscience. 28But if anyone says to you, "This has been offered in sacrifice," then do not eat it, both for the sake of the man who told you and for conscience' sake*c*— 29the other man's conscience, I mean, not yours. For why should my freedom be judged by another's conscience? 30If I take part in the meal with thankfulness, why am I denounced because of something I thank God for?

31So whether you eat or drink or whatever you do, do it all for the glory of God. 32Do not cause anyone to stumble, whether Jews, Greeks or the church of God— 33even as I try to please everybody in every way. For I am not seeking my own good but the good of many, so that they may be saved. 1Follow my example, as I follow the example of Christ.

Propriety in Worship

2I praise you for remembering me in everything and for holding to the teachings,*d* just as I passed them on to you. 3Now I want you to realize that the head of every man is Christ, and the head of the woman is man, and the head of Christ is God. 4Every man who prays or prophesies with his head covered dishonors his head. 5And every woman who prays or prophesies with her head uncovered dishonors her head—it is just as though her head were shaved. 6If a woman does not cover her head, she

---

a 7 Exodus 32:6   *b* 26 Psalm 24:1   *c* 28 Some manuscripts *conscience' sake, for "the earth is the Lord's and everything in it"*   *d* 2 Or *traditions*

should have her hair cut off; and if it is a disgrace for a woman to have her hair cut or shaved off, she should cover her head. 7A man ought not to cover his head,[a] since he is the image and glory of God; but the woman is the glory of man. 8For man did not come from woman, but woman from man; 9neither was man created for woman, but woman for man. 10For this reason, and because of the angels, the woman ought to have a sign of authority on her head.

11In the Lord, however, woman is not independent of man, nor is man independent of woman. 12For as woman came from man, so also man is born of woman. But everything comes from God. 13Judge for yourselves: Is it proper for a woman to pray to God with her head uncovered? 14Does not the very nature of things teach you that if a man has long hair, it is a disgrace to him, 15but that if a woman has long hair, it is her glory? For long hair is given to her as a covering. 16If anyone wants to be contentious about this, we have no other practice—nor do the churches of God.

The Lord's Supper

17In the following directives I have no praise for you, for your meetings do more harm than good. 18In the first place, I hear that when you come together as a church, there are divisions among you, and to some extent I believe it. 19No doubt there have to be differences among you to show which of you have God's approval. 20When you come together, it is not the Lord's Supper you eat, 21for as you eat, each of you goes ahead without waiting for anybody else. One remains hungry, another gets drunk. 22Don't you have homes to eat and drink in? Or do you despise the church of God and humiliate those who have nothing? What shall I say to you? Shall I praise you for this? Certainly not!

23For I received from the Lord what I also passed on to you: The Lord Jesus, on the night he was betrayed, took bread, 24and when he had given thanks, he broke it and said, "This is my body,

which is for you; do this in remembrance of me." 25In the same way, after supper he took the cup, saying, "This cup is the new covenant in my blood; do this, whenever you drink it, in remembrance of me." 26For whenever you eat this bread and drink this cup, you proclaim the Lord's death until he comes.

27Therefore, whoever eats the bread or drinks the cup of the Lord in an unworthy manner will be guilty of sinning against the body and blood of the Lord. 28A man ought to examine himself before he eats of the bread and drinks of the cup. 29For anyone who eats and drinks without recognizing the body of the Lord eats and drinks judgment on himself. 30That is why many among you are weak and sick, and a number of you have fallen asleep. 31But if we judged ourselves, we would not come under judgment. 32When we are judged by the Lord, we are being disciplined so that we will not be condemned with the world.

33So then, my brothers, when you come together to eat, wait for each other. 34If anyone is hungry, he should eat at home, so that when you meet together it may not result in judgment.

And when I come I will give further directions.

Spiritual Gifts

12 Now about spiritual gifts, brothers, I do not want you to be ignorant. 2You know that when you were pagans, somehow or other you were influenced and led astray to mute idols. 3Therefore I tell you that no one who is speaking by the Spirit of God says, "Jesus be cursed," and no one can say, "Jesus is Lord," except by the Holy Spirit.

4There are different kinds of gifts, but the same Spirit. 5There are different kinds of service, but the same Lord. 6There are different kinds of working, but the same God works all of them in all men.

7Now to each one the manifestation of the Spirit is given for the common good. 8To one there is given through the

---

a 4–7 Or 4Every man who prays or prophesies with long hair dishonors his head. 5And every woman who prays or prophesies with no covering ⌐of hair⌐ on her head dishonors her head—she is just like one of the "shorn women." 6If a woman has no covering, let her be for now with short hair, but since it is a disgrace for a woman to have her hair shorn or shaved, she should grow it again. 7A man ought not to have long hair

Spirit the message of wisdom, to another the message of knowledge by means of the same Spirit, [9]to another faith by the same Spirit, to another gifts of healing by that one Spirit, [10]to another miraculous powers, to another prophe-

---

ou think the Bible hasn't much to say about health, fortune, vigor, etc . . . It's certainly not true of the Old Testament. The intermediate theological category between God and human fortune is, as far as I can see, that of blessing. In the Old Testament—for example among the patriarchs—there's a concern not for fortune, but for God's blessing, which includes in itself all earthly good. In that blessing the whole of the earthly life is claimed for God, and it includes all his promises. It would be natural to suppose that, as usual, the New Testament spiritualizes the teaching of the Old Testament here, and therefore to regard the Old Testament blessing as superseded in the New. But is it an accident that sickness and death are mentioned in connection with the misuse of the Lord's Supper ("the cup of *blessing*," 1 Corinthians 10:16, KJV; 11:30, emphasis added), that Jesus restored people's health, and that while his disciples were with him they "lacked nothing"? Now, is it right to set the Old Testament blessing against the cross? That is what Kierkegaard did. That makes the cross, or at least suffering, an abstract principle; and that is just what gives rise to an unhealthy methodism, which deprives suffering of its element of contingency as a divine ordinance. It is true that in the Old Testament the person who receives the blessing has to endure a great deal of suffering (e.g. Abraham, Isaac, Jacob, and Joseph), but this never leads to the idea that fortune and suffering, blessing and cross are mutually exclusive and contradictory—nor does it in the New Testament. Indeed, the only difference between the Old and New Testaments in this respect is that in the Old blessing includes the cross, and in the New the cross includes the blessing . . .

Go to page 1347 for your next devotional reading.

1900   Present

cy, to another distinguishing between spirits, to another speaking in different kinds of tongues,[a] and to still another the interpretation of tongues.[a] 11All these are the work of one and the same Spirit, and he gives them to each one, just as he determines.

One Body, Many Parts

12The body is a unit, though it is made up of many parts; and though all its parts are many, they form one body. So it is with Christ. 13For we were all baptized by[b] one Spirit into one body—whether Jews or Greeks, slave or free—and we were all given the one Spirit to drink.

14Now the body is not made up of one part but of many. 15If the foot should say, "Because I am not a hand, I do not belong to the body," it would not for that reason cease to be part of the body. 16And if the ear should say, "Because I am not an eye, I do not belong to the body," it would not for that reason cease to be part of the body. 17If the whole body were an eye, where would the sense of hearing be? If the whole body were an ear, where would the sense of smell be? 18But in fact God has arranged the parts in the body, every one of them, just as he wanted them to be. 19If they were all one part, where would the body be? 20As it is, there are many parts, but one body.

21The eye cannot say to the hand, "I don't need you!" And the head cannot say to the feet, "I don't need you!" 22On the contrary, those parts of the body that seem to be weaker are indispensable, 23and the parts that we think are less honorable we treat with special honor. And the parts that are unpresentable are treated with special modesty, 24while our presentable parts need no special treatment. But God has combined the members of the body and has given greater honor to the parts that lacked it, 25so that there should be no division in the body, but that its parts should have equal concern for each other. 26If one part suffers, every part suffers with it; if one part is honored, every part rejoices with it.

27Now you are the body of Christ, and each one of you is a part of it. 28And in the church God has appointed first of all apostles, second prophets, third teachers, then workers of miracles, also those having gifts of healing, those able to help others, those with gifts of administration, and those speaking in different kinds of tongues. 29Are all apostles? Are all prophets? Are all teachers? Do all work miracles? 30Do all have gifts of healing? Do all speak in tongues[c]? Do all interpret? 31But eagerly desire[d] the greater gifts.

Love

And now I will show you the most excellent way.

13 If I speak in the tongues[e] of men and of angels, but have not love, I am only a resounding gong or a clanging cymbal. 2If I have the gift of prophecy and can fathom all mysteries and all knowledge, and if I have a faith that can move mountains, but have not love, I am nothing. 3If I give all I possess to the poor and surrender my body to the flames,[f] but have not love, I gain nothing.

4Love is patient, love is kind. It does not envy, it does not boast, it is not proud. 5It is not rude, it is not self-seeking, it is not easily angered, it keeps no record of wrongs. 6Love does not delight in evil but rejoices with the truth. 7It always protects, always trusts, always hopes, always perseveres.

CHARITY IS THE SCOPE OF ALL GOD'S COMMANDS.

—*John Chrysostom*

8Love never fails. But where there are prophecies, they will cease; where there are tongues, they will be stilled; where there is knowledge, it will pass away. 9For we know in part and we prophesy in part, 10but when perfection comes, the imperfect disappears. 11When I was a child, I talked like a child, I thought like a child, I reasoned like a child. When I became a man, I put childish ways behind me. 12Now we see but a poor reflection as in a mirror; then we

---

a 10 Or *languages*; also in verse 28   b 13 Or *with*; or *in*   c 30 Or *other languages*   d 31 Or *But you are eagerly desiring*   e 1 Or *languages*   f 3 Some early manuscripts *body that I may boast*

shall see face to face. Now I know in part; then I shall know fully, even as I am fully known.

13 And now these three remain: faith, hope and love. But the greatest of these is love.

FROM THE SAINTS' EVERLASTING REST
Richard Baxter

VERSE: 1 Corinthians 13:8   **PASSAGE:** 1 Corinthians 13:8–10

It is a question with some whether or not we shall know each other in heaven. Surely, no knowledge shall cease that we now have, but only that which implies our imperfection; and what imperfection can this imply? Nay, our present knowledge shall be increased beyond belief. It shall indeed be done away, but only as the light of candles and stars is done away by the rising of the sun; which is more properly a doing away of our ignorance than of our knowledge.

Indeed, we shall not know each other after the flesh, not by stature, voice, color, complexion, visage, or outward shape. If we had so known Christ, we should know him no more; not by parts and gifts of learning, nor titles of honor or worldly dignity; nor by terms of affinity and consanguinity, nor benefits, nor such relations; nor by youth or age; nor, I think, by sex; but by the image of Christ and spiritual relation and former faithfulness in improving our talents, beyond doubt, we shall know and be known.

Nor is it only our old acquaintance, but all the saints of all the ages, whose faces in the flesh we never saw, whom we shall there both know and comfortably enjoy . . . Those who now are willingly ministering spirits for our good will willingly then be our companions in joy for the perfecting of our good; and they who had such joy in heaven for our conversion will gladly rejoice with us in our glorification. I think, Christian, this will be a more honorable assembly than ever you beheld and a more happy society than you were ever in before . . .

What a day will it be when we shall join with them in praises to our Lord in and for that kingdom! So then I conclude, this is one singular excellency of the Rest of heaven, that we are "fellow citizens with the saints, and of the household of God" (Ephesians 2:19, KJV).

ADDITIONAL SCRIPTURE READING:
Isaiah 29:13–14; 1 Corinthians 13:2

Go to page 1349 for your next devotional reading.

1500   1700

Gifts of Prophecy and Tongues

14 Follow the way of love and eagerly desire spiritual gifts, especially the gift of prophecy. 2For anyone who speaks in a tongue*a* does not speak to men but to God. Indeed, no one understands him; he utters mysteries with his spirit.*b* 3But everyone who prophesies speaks to men for their strengthening, encouragement and comfort. 4He who speaks in a tongue edifies himself, but he who prophesies edifies the church. 5I would like every one of you to speak in tongues,*c* but I would rather have you prophesy. He who prophesies is greater than one who speaks in tongues,*c* unless he interprets, so that the church may be edified.

6Now, brothers, if I come to you and speak in tongues, what good will I be to you, unless I bring you some revelation or knowledge or prophecy or word of instruction? 7Even in the case of lifeless things that make sounds, such as the flute or harp, how will anyone know what tune is being played unless there is a distinction in the notes? 8Again, if the trumpet does not sound a clear call, who will get ready for battle? 9So it is with you. Unless you speak intelligible words with your tongue, how will anyone know what you are saying? You will just be speaking into the air. 10Undoubtedly there are all sorts of languages in the world, yet none of them is without meaning. 11If then I do not grasp the meaning of what someone is saying, I am a foreigner to the speaker, and he is a foreigner to me. 12So it is with you. Since you are eager to have spiritual gifts, try to excel in gifts that build up the church.

13For this reason anyone who speaks in a tongue should pray that he may interpret what he says. 14For if I pray in a tongue, my spirit prays, but my mind is unfruitful. 15So what shall I do? I will pray with my spirit, but I will also pray with my mind; I will sing with my spirit, but I will also sing with my mind. 16If you are praising God with your spirit, how can one who finds himself among those who do not understand*d* say "Amen" to your thanksgiving, since he

does not know what you are saying? 17You may be giving thanks well enough, but the other man is not edified. 18I thank God that I speak in tongues more than all of you. 19But in the church I would rather speak five intelligible words to instruct others than ten thousand words in a tongue.

20Brothers, stop thinking like children. In regard to evil be infants, but in your thinking be adults. 21In the Law it is written:

"Through men of strange tongues
    and through the lips of foreigners
I will speak to this people,
    but even then they will not listen
        to me,"*e*

says the Lord.

22Tongues, then, are a sign, not for believers but for unbelievers; prophecy, however, is for believers, not for unbelievers. 23So if the whole church comes together and everyone speaks in tongues, and some who do not understand*f* or some unbelievers come in, will they not say that you are out of your mind? 24But if an unbeliever or someone who does not understand*g* comes in while everybody is prophesying, he will be convinced by all that he is a sinner and will be judged by all, 25and the secrets of his heart will be laid bare. So he will fall down and worship God, exclaiming, "God is really among you!"

Orderly Worship

26What then shall we say, brothers? When you come together, everyone has a hymn, or a word of instruction, a revelation, a tongue or an interpretation. All of these must be done for the strengthening of the church. 27If anyone speaks in a tongue, two—or at the most three—should speak, one at a time, and someone must interpret. 28If there is no interpreter, the speaker should keep quiet in the church and speak to himself and God. 29Two or three prophets should speak, and the others should weigh carefully what is said. 30And if a revelation comes to someone who is sitting down, the

---

a 2 Or *another language;* also in verses 4, 13, 14, 19, 26 and 27   *b* 2 Or *by the Spirit*   *c* 5 Or *other languages;* also in verses 6, 18, 22, 23 and 39   *d* 16 Or *among the inquirers*   *e* 21 Isaiah 28:11,12
f 23 Or *some inquirers*   *g* 24 Or *or some inquirer*

WEEKEND

THE HABIT OF PERFECTION
Gerard Manley Hopkins

VERSE: 1 Corinthians 13:10   **PASSAGE:** 1 Corinthians 13:1–10

lected Silence, sing to me
And beat upon my whorlèd ear,
Pipe me to measures still and be
The music that I care to hear.

Shape nothing, lips; be lovely-dumb:
It is the shut, the curfew sent
From there where all surrenders come
Which only makes you eloquent.

Be shellèd, eyes, with double dark
And find the uncreated light:
This ruck and reel which you remark
Coils, keeps, and teases simple sight.

Palate, the hutch of tasty lust,
Desire not to be rinsed with wine:
The can must be so sweet, the crust
So fresh that come in fasts divine!

Nostrils, your careless breath that spend
Upon the stir and keep of pride,
What relish shall the censers send
Along the sanctuary side!

O feel-of-primrose hands, O feet
That want the yield of plushy sward,
But you shall walk the golden street
And you unhouse and house the Lord.

And, Poverty, be thou the bride
And now the marriage feast begun,
And lily-colored clothes provide
Your spouse not labored-at nor spun.

ADDITIONAL SCRIPTURE READING:
Colossians 1:28; Hebrews 12:22–23

Go to page 1552 for your next devotional reading.

1700   1900

first speaker should stop. 31For you can all prophesy in turn so that everyone may be instructed and encouraged. 32The spirits of prophets are subject to the control of prophets. 33For God is not a God of disorder but of peace.

As in all the congregations of the saints, 34women should remain silent in the churches. They are not allowed to speak, but must be in submission, as the Law says. 35If they want to inquire about something, they should ask their own husbands at home; for it is disgraceful for a woman to speak in the church.

36Did the word of God originate with you? Or are you the only people it has reached? 37If anybody thinks he is a prophet or spiritually gifted, let him acknowledge that what I am writing to you is the Lord's command. 38If he ignores this, he himself will be ignored.*a*

39Therefore, my brothers, be eager to prophesy, and do not forbid speaking in tongues. 40But everything should be done in a fitting and orderly way.

The Resurrection of Christ

15 Now, brothers, I want to remind you of the gospel I preached to you, which you received and on which you have taken your stand. 2By this gospel you are saved, if you hold firmly to the word I preached to you. Otherwise, you have believed in vain.

3For what I received I passed on to you as of first importance*b*: that Christ died for our sins according to the Scriptures, 4that he was buried, that he was raised on the third day according to the Scriptures, 5and that he appeared to Peter,*c* and then to the Twelve. 6After that, he appeared to more than five hundred of the brothers at the same time, most of whom are still living, though some have fallen asleep. 7Then he appeared to James, then to all the apostles, 8and last of all he appeared to me also, as to one abnormally born.

9For I am the least of the apostles and do not even deserve to be called an apostle, because I persecuted the church of God. 10But by the grace of God I am what I am, and his grace to me was not without effect. No, I worked harder than

all of them—yet not I, but the grace of God that was with me. 11Whether, then, it was I or they, this is what we preach, and this is what you believed.

THE PRIMARY DECLARATION OF CHRISTIANITY IS NOT "THIS DO!" BUT "THIS HAPPENED!"

—*Evelyn Underhill*

The Resurrection of the Dead

12But if it is preached that Christ has been raised from the dead, how can some of you say that there is no resurrection of the dead? 13If there is no resurrection of the dead, then not even Christ has been raised. 14And if Christ has not been raised, our preaching is useless and so is your faith. 15More than that, we are then found to be false witnesses about God, for we have testified about God that he raised Christ from the dead. But he did not raise him if in fact the dead are not raised. 16For if the dead are not raised, then Christ has not been raised either. 17And if Christ has not been raised, your faith is futile; you are still in your sins. 18Then those also who have fallen asleep in Christ are lost. 19If only for this life we have hope in Christ, we are to be pitied more than all men.

20But Christ has indeed been raised from the dead, the firstfruits of those

---

WHAT REASON HAVE ATHEISTS FOR SAYING THAT WE CANNOT RISE AGAIN? WHICH IS THE MORE DIFFICULT, TO BE BORN, OR TO RISE AGAIN? THAT WHAT HAS NEVER BEEN, SHOULD BE, OR THAT WHAT HAS BEEN SHOULD BE AGAIN? IS IT MORE DIFFICULT TO COME INTO BEING THAN TO RETURN TO IT?　　　　—*Blaise Pascal*

---

who have fallen asleep. 21For since death came through a man, the resurrection of the dead comes also through a man. 22For as in Adam all die, so in Christ all will be made alive. 23But each in his own turn: Christ, the firstfruits; then, when he comes, those who belong to him. 24Then the end will come, when he

---

a 38 Some manuscripts *If he is ignorant of this, let him be ignorant*　　*b 3* Or *you at the first*
c 5 Greek *Cephas*

hands over the kingdom to God the Father after he has destroyed all dominion, authority and power. 25For he must reign until he has put all his enemies under his feet. 26The last enemy to be destroyed is death. 27For he "has put everything under his feet."ᵃ Now when it says that "everything" has been put under him, it is clear that this does not include God himself, who put everything under Christ. 28When he has done this, then the Son himself will be made subject to him who put everything under him, so that God may be all in all.

29Now if there is no resurrection, what will those do who are baptized for the dead? If the dead are not raised at all, why are people baptized for them? 30And as for us, why do we endanger ourselves every hour? 31I die every day— I mean that, brothers—just as surely as I glory over you in Christ Jesus our Lord. 32If I fought wild beasts in Ephesus for merely human reasons, what have I gained? If the dead are not raised,

"Let us eat and drink,
    for tomorrow we die."ᵇ

33Do not be misled: "Bad company corrupts good character." 34Come back to your senses as you ought, and stop sinning; for there are some who are ignorant of God—I say this to your shame.

The Resurrection Body

35But someone may ask, "How are the dead raised? With what kind of body will they come?" 36How foolish! What you sow does not come to life unless it dies. 37When you sow, you do not plant the body that will be, but just a seed, perhaps of wheat or of something else. 38But God gives it a body as he has determined, and to each kind of seed he gives its own body. 39All flesh is not the same: Men have one kind of flesh, animals have another, birds another and fish another. 40There are also heavenly bodies and there are earthly bodies; but the splendor of the heavenly bodies is one kind, and the splendor of the earthly bodies is another. 41The sun has one kind of splendor, the moon another and the stars another; and star differs from star in splendor.

42So will it be with the resurrection of the dead. The body that is sown is perishable, it is raised imperishable; 43it is sown in dishonor, it is raised in glory; it is sown in weakness, it is raised in power; 44it is sown a natural body, it is raised a spiritual body.

If there is a natural body, there is also a spiritual body. 45So it is written: "The first man Adam became a living being"ᶜ; the last Adam, a life-giving spirit. 46The spiritual did not come first, but the natural, and after that the spiritual. 47The first man was of the dust of the earth, the second man from heaven. 48As was the earthly man, so are those who are of the earth; and as is the man from heaven, so also are those who are of heaven. 49And just as we have borne the likeness of the earthly man, so shall weᵈ bear the likeness of the man from heaven.

50I declare to you, brothers, that flesh and blood cannot inherit the kingdom of God, nor does the perishable inherit the imperishable. 51Listen, I tell you a mystery: We will not all sleep, but we will all be changed— 52in a flash, in the twinkling of an eye, at the last trumpet. For the trumpet will sound, the dead will be raised imperishable, and we will be changed. 53For the perishable must clothe itself with the imperishable, and the mortal with immortality. 54When the perishable has been clothed with the

---

ONE SHORT SLEEP PAST, WE WAKE ETERNALLY, AND DEATH SHALL BE NO MORE: DEATH, THOU SHALT DIE!

—*John Donne*

---

imperishable, and the mortal with immortality, then the saying that is written will come true: "Death has been swallowed up in victory."ᵉ

55 "Where, O death, is your victory?
    Where, O death, is your sting?"ᶠ

56The sting of death is sin, and the power of sin is the law. 57But thanks be

---

ᵃ 27 Psalm 8:6   ᵇ 32 Isaiah 22:13   ᶜ 45 Gen. 2:7   ᵈ 49 Some early manuscripts *so let us*
ᵉ 54 Isaiah 25:8   ᶠ 55 Hosea 13:14

to God! He gives us the victory through our Lord Jesus Christ.

⁵⁸Therefore, my dear brothers, stand firm. Let nothing move you. Always give yourselves fully to the work of the Lord, because you know that your labor in the Lord is not in vain.

The Collection for God's People

 16 Now about the collection for God's people: Do what I told the Galatian churches to do. ²On the first day of every week, each one of you should set aside a sum of money in keeping with his income, saving it up, so that when I come no collections will have to be made. ³Then, when I arrive, I will give letters of introduction to the men you approve and send them with your gift to Jerusalem. ⁴If it seems advisable for me to go also, they will accompany me.

Personal Requests

⁵After I go through Macedonia, I will come to you—for I will be going

---

MONDAY

THE REALITY OF CHRIST
Ignatius of Antioch

VERSE: 1 Corinthians 15:32   **PASSAGE:** 1 Corinthians 15:29–34

e deaf, therefore, whenever anyone speaks to you apart from Jesus Christ, who was of the family of David, who was the son of Mary; who really was born, who both ate and drank; who really was persecuted under Pontius Pilate, who really was crucified and died while those in heaven and on earth looked on; who, moreover, really was raised from the dead when his Father raised him up, who—his Father, that is—in the same way will likewise also raise us up in Christ Jesus who believe in him, apart from whom we have no true life.

But if, as some atheists (that is, unbelievers) say, he suffered in appearance only (while they exist in appearance only!), why am I in chains? And why do I want to fight with wild beasts? If that is the case, I die for no reason; what is more, I am telling lies about the Lord.

Flee, therefore, from these wicked offshoots that bear deadly fruit; if anyone even tastes it, he dies on the spot. These people are not the Father's planting. For if they were, they would appear as branches of the cross, and their fruit would be imperishable— the same cross by which he, through his suffering, calls you who are his members. The head, therefore, cannot be born without members, since God promises unity, which he himself is.

ADDITIONAL SCRIPTURE READING:
2 Corinthians 4:14; Colossians 1:21–22

Go to page 1356 for your next devotional reading.

100   500

through Macedonia. [6]Perhaps I will stay with you awhile, or even spend the winter, so that you can help me on my journey, wherever I go. [7]I do not want to see you now and make only a passing visit; I hope to spend some time with you, if the Lord permits. [8]But I will stay on at Ephesus until Pentecost, [9]because a great door for effective work has opened to me, and there are many who oppose me.

[10]If Timothy comes, see to it that he has nothing to fear while he is with you, for he is carrying on the work of the Lord, just as I am. [11]No one, then, should refuse to accept him. Send him on his way in peace so that he may return to me. I am expecting him along with the brothers.

[12]Now about our brother Apollos: I strongly urged him to go to you with the brothers. He was quite unwilling to go now, but he will go when he has the opportunity.

[13]Be on your guard; stand firm in the faith; be men of courage; be strong. [14]Do everything in love.

[15]You know that the household of Stephanas were the first converts in Achaia, and they have devoted themselves to the service of the saints. I urge you, brothers, [16]to submit to such as these and to everyone who joins in the work, and labors at it. [17]I was glad when Stephanas, Fortunatus and Achaicus arrived, because they have supplied what was lacking from you. [18]For they refreshed my spirit and yours also. Such men deserve recognition.

Final Greetings

[19]The churches in the province of Asia send you greetings. Aquila and Priscilla[a] greet you warmly in the Lord, and so does the church that meets at their house. [20]All the brothers here send you greetings. Greet one another with a holy kiss.

[21]I, Paul, write this greeting in my own hand.

[22]If anyone does not love the Lord—a curse be on him. Come, O Lord[b]!

[23]The grace of the Lord Jesus be with you.

[24]My love to all of you in Christ Jesus. Amen.[c]

---

[a] 19 Greek *Prisca*, a variant of *Priscilla*   [b] 22 In Aramaic the expression *Come, O Lord* is *Marana tha.*
[c] 24 Some manuscripts do not have *Amen.*

2 CORINTHIANS

 AUL WROTE THIS SECOND LETTER TO THE CORINTHIANS A FEW MONTHS AFTER THE FIRST LETTER. THE DIVISIONS AND PROBLEMS ADDRESSED IN 1 CORINTHIANS WERE STILL PRESENT IN THE CHURCH AND FALSE TEACHERS WERE CHALLENGING PAUL'S INTEGRITY AND HIS AUTHORITY AS AN APOSTLE. WITH PASSIONATE EMOTION, PAUL MOVES BACK AND FORTH BETWEEN DESPAIR AND ECSTATIC JOY. WATCH FOR PRACTICAL ADVICE ON RESOLVING CONFLICT WITHIN THE CHURCH AND PROVIDING FINANCIAL SUPPORT FOR THE CHURCH AND FOR THE POOR.

1 Paul, an apostle of Christ Jesus by the will of God, and Timothy our brother,

To the church of God in Corinth, together with all the saints throughout Achaia:

²Grace and peace to you from God our Father and the Lord Jesus Christ.

The God of All Comfort

³Praise be to the God and Father of our Lord Jesus Christ, the Father of compassion and the God of all comfort, ⁴who comforts us in all our troubles, so that we can comfort those in any trouble with the comfort we ourselves have received from God. ⁵For just as the sufferings of Christ flow over into our lives, so also through Christ our comfort overflows. ⁶If we are distressed, it is for your comfort and salvation; if we are comforted, it is for your comfort, which produces in you patient endurance of the same sufferings we suffer. ⁷And our hope for you is firm, because we know that just as you share in our sufferings, so also you share in our comfort.

⁸We do not want you to be uninformed, brothers, about the hardships we suffered in the province of Asia. We were under great pressure, far beyond our ability to endure, so that we despaired even of life. ⁹Indeed, in our hearts we felt the sentence of death. But this happened that we might not rely on ourselves but on God, who raises the dead. ¹⁰He has delivered us from such a deadly peril, and he will deliver us. On him we have set our hope that he will continue to

deliver us, [11]as you help us by your prayers. Then many will give thanks on our[a] behalf for the gracious favor granted us in answer to the prayers of many.

Paul's Change of Plans

[12]Now this is our boast: Our conscience testifies that we have conducted ourselves in the world, and especially in our relations with you, in the holiness and sincerity that are from God. We have done so not according to worldly wisdom but according to God's grace. [13]For we do not write you anything you cannot read or understand. And I hope that, [14]as you have understood us in part, you will come to understand fully that you can boast of us just as we will boast of you in the day of the Lord Jesus.

[15]Because I was confident of this, I planned to visit you first so that you might benefit twice. [16]I planned to visit you on my way to Macedonia and to come back to you from Macedonia, and then to have you send me on my way to Judea. [17]When I planned this, did I do it lightly? Or do I make my plans in a worldly manner so that in the same breath I say, "Yes, yes" and "No, no"?

[18]But as surely as God is faithful, our message to you is not "Yes" and "No." [19]For the Son of God, Jesus Christ, who was preached among you by me and Silas[b] and Timothy, was not "Yes" and "No," but in him it has always been "Yes." [20]For no matter how many promises God has made, they are "Yes" in Christ. And so through him the "Amen" is spoken by us to the glory of God. [21]Now it is God who makes both us and you stand firm in Christ. He anointed us, [22]set his seal of ownership on us, and put his Spirit in our hearts as a deposit, guaranteeing what is to come.

[23]I call God as my witness that it was in order to spare you that I did not return to Corinth. [24]Not that we lord it over your faith, but we work with you for your joy, because it is by faith you **2** stand firm. [1]So I made up my mind that I would not make another painful visit to you. [2]For if I grieve you, who is left to make me glad but you whom I have grieved? [3]I wrote as I did so that when I came I should not

be distressed by those who ought to make me rejoice. I had confidence in all of you, that you would all share my joy. [4]For I wrote you out of great distress and anguish of heart and with many tears, not to grieve you but to let you know the depth of my love for you.

Forgiveness for the Sinner

[5]If anyone has caused grief, he has not so much grieved me as he has grieved all of you, to some extent—not to put it too severely. [6]The punishment inflicted on him by the majority is sufficient for him. [7]Now instead, you ought to forgive and comfort him, so that he will not be overwhelmed by excessive sorrow. [8]I urge you, therefore, to reaffirm your love for him. [9]The reason I wrote you was to see if you would stand the test and be obedient in everything. [10]If you forgive anyone, I also forgive him. And what I have forgiven—if there was anything to forgive—I have forgiven in the sight of Christ for your sake, [11]in order that Satan might not outwit us. For we are not unaware of his schemes.

Ministers of the New Covenant

[12]Now when I went to Troas to preach the gospel of Christ and found that the Lord had opened a door for me, [13]I still had no peace of mind, because I did not find my brother Titus there. So I said good-by to them and went on to Macedonia.

[14]But thanks be to God, who always leads us in triumphal procession in Christ and through us spreads everywhere the fragrance of the knowledge of him. [15]For we are to God the aroma of Christ among those who are being saved and those who are perishing. [16]To the one we are the smell of death; to the other, the fragrance of life. And who is equal to such a task? [17]Unlike so many, we do not peddle the word of God for profit. On the contrary, in Christ we speak before God with sincerity, like men sent from God.

3 Are we beginning to commend ourselves again? Or do we need, like some people, letters of recommendation to you or from you? [2]You yourselves are our letter, written on our

THE DIVINE *YES* HAS SOUNDED
E. Stanley Jones

VERSE: 2 Corinthians 1:20   **PASSAGE:** 2 Corinthians 1:18–22

 all the roll of the ancient philosophies—and the modern—and they nearly all come out to a *No*. The note of pessimism about life sounds in them all. Take Buddhism: Buddha, in his meditation under the Bo tree at Gaya, India, came to the startling conclusion: "Existence and suffering are one," inextricably bound up together. The only way to get out of suffering is to get out of life. So cut the root of desire and become desireless, even for life, and then you go out into that state, literally, "of the snuffed-out candle"—Nirvana. This is the most decisive No ever uttered about life. And yet hundreds of millions cling to this vast No as emancipation, for they feel life is saying the same, life is a No. Take the Vedanta philosophy, the outstanding philosophy of India. It says that you are to lose your separate individual personality and be absorbed into the impersonal essence, called Brahma. So you as a person are wiped out—like a raindrop you are lost in the ocean of the impersonal. It, too, is a vast No. Take Islam: Fundamentally Islam means submission—submission to the sovereign will of God. Your will is gone; his will is the all. For all intents and purposes the individual is swamped in the divine. This, too, is a vast No. Take Stoicism: To shut out sorrow and suffering, the Stoic had to shut out love and pity too, for if love and pity came in, then sorrow and suffering would come trooping in behind. This, too, is a No to the "greatest thing in the world"—love. Schopenhauer, the apostle of pessimism, seated on a park bench was asked by a policeman who thought him a tramp: "Who are you, and what are you here for?" Schopenhauer replied sadly, "I wish I knew." His was a No—a sad question mark. The loudest and saddest No that has been sounded on our planet is the latest: "God is dead." It is not only a No to life, but to God, the author of life; both God and life are dead. This is the nadir of the No.

Now in the midst of this world chorus of No, at last—at long last—"the divine 'yes' has sounded." And Jesus is that Yes.

ADDITIONAL SCRIPTURE READING:
John 14:6; 1 Timothy 4:9–10

Go to page 1358 for your next devotional reading.

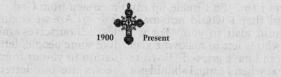

1900   Present

hearts, known and read by everybody. ³You show that you are a letter from Christ, the result of our ministry, written not with ink but with the Spirit of the living God, not on tablets of stone but on tablets of human hearts.

⁴Such confidence as this is ours through Christ before God. ⁵Not that we are competent in ourselves to claim anything for ourselves, but our competence comes from God. ⁶He has made us competent as ministers of a new covenant— not of the letter but of the Spirit; for the letter kills, but the Spirit gives life.

The Glory of the New Covenant

⁷Now if the ministry that brought death, which was engraved in letters on stone, came with glory, so that the Israelites could not look steadily at the face of Moses because of its glory, fading though it was, ⁸will not the ministry of the Spirit be even more glorious? ⁹If the ministry that condemns men is glorious, how much more glorious is the ministry that brings righteousness! ¹⁰For what was glorious has no glory now in comparison with the surpassing glory. ¹¹And if what was fading away came with glory, how much greater is the glory of that which lasts!

¹²Therefore, since we have such a hope, we are very bold. ¹³We are not like Moses, who would put a veil over his face to keep the Israelites from gazing at it while the radiance was fading away. ¹⁴But their minds were made dull, for to this day the same veil remains when the old covenant is read. It has not been removed, because only in Christ is it taken away. ¹⁵Even to this day when Moses is read, a veil covers their hearts. ¹⁶But whenever anyone turns to the Lord, the veil is taken away. ¹⁷Now the Lord is the Spirit, and where the Spirit of the Lord is, there is freedom. ¹⁸And we, who with unveiled faces all reflect*ᵃ* the Lord's glory, are being transformed into his likeness with ever-increasing glory, which comes from the Lord, who is the Spirit.

Treasures in Jars of Clay

4 Therefore, since through God's mercy we have this ministry, we do not lose heart. ²Rather, we have renounced secret and shameful ways; we do not use deception, nor do we distort the word of God. On the contrary, by setting forth the truth plainly we

---

A DOG BARKS WHEN HIS MASTER IS ATTACKED. I WOULD BE A COWARD IF I SAW THAT GOD'S TRUTH IS ATTACKED AND YET WOULD REMAIN SILENT.   —John Calvin

---

commend ourselves to every man's conscience in the sight of God. ³And even if our gospel is veiled, it is veiled to those who are perishing. ⁴The god of this age has blinded the minds of unbelievers, so that they cannot see the light of the gospel of the glory of Christ, who is the image of God. ⁵For we do not preach ourselves, but Jesus Christ as Lord, and ourselves as your servants for Jesus' sake. ⁶For God, who said, "Let light shine out of darkness,"*ᵇ* made his light shine in our hearts to give us the light of the knowledge of the glory of God in the face of Christ.

⁷But we have this treasure in jars of clay to show that this all-surpassing power is from God and not from us. ⁸We are hard pressed on every side, but not crushed; perplexed, but not in despair; ⁹persecuted, but not abandoned; struck down, but not destroyed. ¹⁰We always carry around in our body the death of Jesus, so that the life of Jesus may also be revealed in our body. ¹¹For we who are alive are always being given over to death for Jesus' sake, so that his life may be revealed in our mortal body. ¹²So then, death is at work in us, but life is at work in you.

ALMIGHTY GOD, BESTOW UPON US THE MEANING OF WORDS, THE LIGHT OF UNDERSTANDING, THE NOBILITY OF DICTION AND THE FAITH OF THE TRUE NATURE. AND GRANT THAT WHAT WE BELIEVE WE MAY ALSO SPEAK.

—Hilary of Poitiers

---

¹³It is written: "I believed; therefore I have spoken."*ᶜ* With that same spirit of faith we also believe and therefore

---

ᵃ 18 Or contemplate   ᵇ 6 Gen. 1:3   ᶜ 13 Psalm 116:10

speak, [14]because we know that the one who raised the Lord Jesus from the dead will also raise us with Jesus and present us with you in his presence. [15]All this is for your benefit, so that the grace that is reaching more and more people may cause thanksgiving to overflow to the glory of God.

[16]Therefore we do not lose heart. Though outwardly we are wasting away, yet inwardly we are being renewed day by day. [17]For our light and momentary troubles are achieving for us an eternal glory that far outweighs them all. [18]So we fix our eyes not on what is seen, but on what is unseen. For what is seen is temporary, but what is unseen is eternal.

Our Heavenly Dwelling

5 Now we know that if the earthly tent we live in is destroyed, we have a building from God, an eternal house in heaven, not built by human hands. [2]Meanwhile we groan, longing to

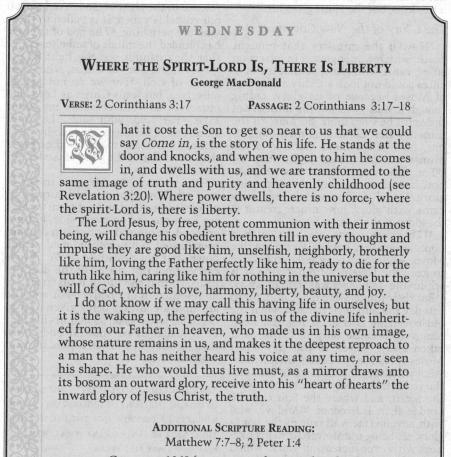

WEDNESDAY

WHERE THE SPIRIT-LORD IS, THERE IS LIBERTY
George MacDonald

VERSE: 2 Corinthians 3:17   **PASSAGE:** 2 Corinthians 3:17–18

hat it cost the Son to get so near to us that we could say *Come in*, is the story of his life. He stands at the door and knocks, and when we open to him he comes in, and dwells with us, and we are transformed to the same image of truth and purity and heavenly childhood (see Revelation 3:20). Where power dwells, there is no force; where the spirit-Lord is, there is liberty.

The Lord Jesus, by free, potent communion with their inmost being, will change his obedient brethren till in every thought and impulse they are good like him, unselfish, neighborly, brotherly like him, loving the Father perfectly like him, ready to die for the truth like him, caring like him for nothing in the universe but the will of God, which is love, harmony, liberty, beauty, and joy.

I do not know if we may call this having life in ourselves; but it is the waking up, the perfecting in us of the divine life inherited from our Father in heaven, who made us in his own image, whose nature remains in us, and makes it the deepest reproach to a man that he has neither heard his voice at any time, nor seen his shape. He who would thus live must, as a mirror draws into its bosom an outward glory, receive into his "heart of hearts" the inward glory of Jesus Christ, the truth.

ADDITIONAL SCRIPTURE READING:
Matthew 7:7–8; 2 Peter 1:4

Go to page 1360 for your next devotional reading.

1700   1900

be clothed with our heavenly dwelling, ³because when we are clothed, we will not be found naked. ⁴For while we are in this tent, we groan and are burdened, because we do not wish to be unclothed but to be clothed with our heavenly dwelling, so that what is mortal may be swallowed up by life. ⁵Now it is God who has made us for this very purpose and has given us the Spirit as a deposit, guaranteeing what is to come.

⁶Therefore we are always confident and know that as long as we are at home in the body we are away from the Lord. ⁷We live by faith, not by sight. ⁸We are confident, I say, and would prefer to be away from the body and at home with the Lord. ⁹So we make it our goal to please him, whether we are at home in the body or away from it. ¹⁰For we must all appear before the judgment seat of Christ, that each one may receive what is due him for the things done while in the body, whether good or bad.

The Ministry of Reconciliation

¹¹Since, then, we know what it is to fear the Lord, we try to persuade men. What we are is plain to God, and I hope it is also plain to your conscience. ¹²We are not trying to commend ourselves to you again, but are giving you an opportunity to take pride in us, so that you can answer those who take pride in what is seen rather than in what is in the heart. ¹³If we are out of our mind, it is for the sake of God; if we are in our right mind, it is for you. ¹⁴For Christ's love compels us, because we are convinced that one died for all, and therefore all died. ¹⁵And he died for all, that those who live should no longer live for themselves but for him who died for them and was raised again.

¹⁶So from now on we regard no one from a worldly point of view. Though we once regarded Christ in this way, we do so no longer. ¹⁷Therefore, if anyone is in Christ, he is a new creation; the old has gone, the new has come! ¹⁸All this is from God, who reconciled us to himself through Christ and gave us the ministry of reconciliation: ¹⁹that God was reconciling the world to himself in Christ, not counting men's sins against them. And

he has committed to us the message of reconciliation. ²⁰We are therefore Christ's ambassadors, as though God were making his appeal through us. We implore you on Christ's behalf: Be reconciled to God. ²¹God made him who had no sin to be sin[a] for us, so that in him we might become the righteousness of God.

6 As God's fellow workers we urge you not to receive God's grace in vain. ²For he says,

"In the time of my favor I heard you,
  and in the day of salvation I helped
  you."[b]

I tell you, now is the time of God's favor, now is the day of salvation.

Paul's Hardships

³We put no stumbling block in anyone's path, so that our ministry will not be discredited. ⁴Rather, as servants of God we commend ourselves in every way: in great endurance; in troubles, hardships and distresses; ⁵in beatings, imprisonments and riots; in hard work, sleepless nights and hunger; ⁶in purity, understanding, patience and kindness; in the Holy Spirit and in sincere love; ⁷in truthful speech and in the power of God; with weapons of righteousness in the right hand and in the left; ⁸through glory and dishonor, bad report and good report; genuine, yet regarded as impostors; ⁹known, yet regarded as unknown; dying, and yet we live on; beaten, and yet not killed; ¹⁰sorrowful, yet always rejoicing; poor, yet making many rich; having nothing, and yet possessing everything.

¹¹We have spoken freely to you, Corinthians, and opened wide our hearts to you. ¹²We are not withholding our affection from you, but you are withholding yours from us. ¹³As a fair exchange—I speak as to my children—open wide your hearts also.

Do Not Be Yoked With Unbelievers

¹⁴Do not be yoked together with unbelievers. For what do righteousness and wickedness have in common? Or what fellowship can light have with darkness? ¹⁵What harmony is there

---

a 21 Or *be a sin offering*   *b 2* Isaiah 49:8

between Christ and Belial[a]? What does a believer have in common with an unbeliever? [16]What agreement is there between the temple of God and idols? For we are the temple of the living God. As God has said: "I will live with them and walk among them, and I will be their God, and they will be my people."[b]

[17] "Therefore come out from them
    and be separate,
             says the Lord.
Touch no unclean thing,
    and I will receive you."[c]
[18] "I will be a Father to you,
    and you will be my sons and
      daughters,
          says the Lord Almighty."[d]

[a] 15 Greek Beliar, a variant of Belial   [b] 16 Lev. 26:12; Jer. 32:38; Ezek. 37:27   [c] 17 Isaiah 52:11; Ezek. 20:34,41   [d] 18 2 Samuel 7:14; 7:8

THURSDAY

THE CONSOLATIONS WHICH THE WORLD KNOWS NOT
Anne Bradstreet

VERSE: 2 Corinthians 6:18   **PASSAGE:** 2 Corinthians 6:14–18

ord, why should I doubt any more when thou hast given me such assured pledges of thy love? First, thou art my Creator, I thy creature, thou my master, I thy servant. But hence arises not my comfort, thou art my Father, I thy child; "Ye shall be my sons and daughters" (Romans 9:26, KJV) saith the Lord Almighty. Christ is my brother, I ascend unto my Father, and your Father, unto my God and your God; but lest this should not be enough, thy maker is thy husband. Nay more, I am a member of his body, he my head. Such privileges had not the Word of truth made them known, who or where is the man that durst in his heart have presumed to have thought it? So wonderful are these thoughts that my spirit fails in me at the consideration thereof, and I am confounded to think that God, who hath done so much for me, should have so little from me. But this is my comfort, when I come to heaven, I shall understand perfectly what he hath done for me, and then shall I be able to praise him as I ought. Lord, having this hope, let me purify myself as thou art pure, and let me be no more afraid of death, but even desire to be dissolved and be with thee, which is best of all.

ADDITIONAL SCRIPTURE READING:
Psalm 51:10; Romans 9:26

Go to page 1362 for your next devotional reading.

1500   1700

7 Since we have these promises, dear friends, let us purify ourselves from everything that contaminates body and spirit, perfecting holiness out of reverence for God.

Paul's Joy

2Make room for us in your hearts. We have wronged no one, we have corrupted no one, we have exploited no one. 3I do not say this to condemn you; I have said before that you have such a place in our hearts that we would live or die with you. 4I have great confidence in you; I take great pride in you. I am greatly encouraged; in all our troubles my joy knows no bounds.

5For when we came into Macedonia, this body of ours had no rest, but we were harassed at every turn—conflicts on the outside, fears within. 6But God, who comforts the downcast, comforted us by the coming of Titus, 7and not only by his coming but also by the comfort you had given him. He told us about your longing for me, your deep sorrow, your ardent concern for me, so that my joy was greater than ever.

8Even if I caused you sorrow by my letter, I do not regret it. Though I did regret it—I see that my letter hurt you, but only for a little while— 9yet now I am happy, not because you were made sorry, but because your sorrow led you to repentance. For you became sorrowful as God intended and so were not harmed in any way by us. 10Godly sorrow brings repentance that leads to salvation and leaves no regret, but worldly sorrow brings death. 11See what this godly sorrow has produced in you: what earnestness, what eagerness to clear yourselves, what indignation, what alarm, what longing, what concern, what readiness to see justice done. At every point you have proved yourselves to be innocent in this matter. 12So even though I wrote to you, it was not on account of the one who did the wrong or of the injured party, but rather that before God you could see for yourselves how devoted to us you are. 13By all this we are encouraged.

In addition to our own encouragement, we were especially delighted to see how happy Titus was, because his spirit has been refreshed by all of you. 14I had boasted to him about you, and you have not embarrassed me. But just as everything we said to you was true, so our boasting about you to Titus has proved to be true as well. 15And his affection for you is all the greater when he remembers that you were all obedient, receiving him with fear and trembling. 16I am glad I can have complete confidence in you.

Generosity Encouraged

8 And now, brothers, we want you to know about the grace that God has given the Macedonian churches. 2Out of the most severe trial, their overflowing joy and their extreme poverty welled up in rich generosity. 3For I testify that they gave as much as they were able, and even beyond their ability. Entirely on their own, 4they urgently pleaded with us for the privilege of sharing in this service to the saints. 5And they did not do as we expected, but they gave themselves first to the Lord and then to us in keeping with God's will. 6So we urged Titus, since he had earlier made a beginning, to bring also to completion this act of grace on your part. 7But just as you excel in everything—in faith, in speech, in knowledge, in complete earnestness and in your love for us*a*—see that you also excel in this grace of giving.

8I am not commanding you, but I want to test the sincerity of your love by comparing it with the earnestness of others. 9For you know the grace of our Lord Jesus Christ, that though he was rich, yet for your sakes he became poor, so that you through his poverty might become rich.

10And here is my advice about what is best for you in this matter: Last year you were the first not only to give but also to have the desire to do so. 11Now finish the work, so that your eager willingness to do it may be matched by your completion of it, according to your means. 12For if the willingness is there, the gift is acceptable according to what one has, not according to what he does not have. 13Our desire is not that others might

---

a 7 Some manuscripts *in our love for you*

THE MEMORIAL TO THE MACEDONIANS' LIBERALITY
W. J. Conybeare and J. S. Howson

VERSE: 2 Corinthians 8:1   **PASSAGE:** 2 Corinthians 8:1–5

n writing to the Corinthians, [Paul] delicately contrasts their wealth with the poverty of the Macedonians. In speaking to the Macedonians themselves, such a mode of appeal was less natural, for they were poorer and more generous. Yet them also he endeavored to rouse to a generous rivalry, by telling them of the zeal of Achaia (2 Corinthians 8:24, 9:2) . . . Nor ought we, when speaking of the instruction to be gathered from this charitable undertaking, to leave unnoticed the calmness and deliberation of the method which he recommends of laying aside, week by week, what is devoted to God (1 Corinthians 16:2),—a practice equally remote from the excitement of popular appeals, and the mere impulse of instinctive benevolence.

The Macedonian Christians responded nobly to the appeal which was made to them by St. Paul. The zeal of their brethren in Achaia "stirred most of them to action" (2 Corinthians 9:2). God's grace was abundantly "manifested in the churches" on the north of the Aegean (2 Corinthians 8:1). Their conduct in this matter, as described to us by the apostle's pen, rises to the point of the highest praise. It was a time, not of prosperity, but of great affliction, to the Macedonian churches; nor were they wealthy communities like the church of Corinth; yet, "out of the most severe trial, their overflowing joy and their extreme poverty welled up in rich generosity" (v. 2). Their contribution was no niggardly gift, wrung from their covetousness (v. 5); but they gave honestly "as much as they were able" (v. 3), and not only so, but even "beyond their ability" (v. 3); nor did they give grudgingly, under the pressure of the apostle's urgency, but "entirely on their own, they urgently pleaded with us for the privilege of sharing in this service to the saints" (8:3–4). And this liberality arose from that which is the basis of all true Christian charity. "They gave themselves first to the Lord Jesus Christ, by the will of God" (see v. 5).

ADDITIONAL SCRIPTURE READING:
Luke 21:1–4; 1 Corinthians 16:2

Go to page 1365 for your next devotional reading.

1700   1900

be relieved while you are hard pressed, but that there might be equality. [14]At the present time your plenty will supply what they need, so that in turn their plenty will supply what you need. Then there will be equality, [15]as it is written: "He who gathered much did not have too much, and he who gathered little did not have too little."[a]

Titus Sent to Corinth

[16]I thank God, who put into the heart of Titus the same concern I have for you. [17]For Titus not only welcomed our appeal, but he is coming to you with much enthusiasm and on his own initiative. [18]And we are sending along with him the brother who is praised by all the churches for his service to the gospel. [19]What is more, he was chosen by the churches to accompany us as we carry the offering, which we administer in order to honor the Lord himself and to show our eagerness to help. [20]We want to avoid any criticism of the way we administer this liberal gift. [21]For we are taking pains to do what is right, not only in the eyes of the Lord but also in the eyes of men.

[22]In addition, we are sending with them our brother who has often proved to us in many ways that he is zealous, and now even more so because of his great confidence in you. [23]As for Titus, he is my partner and fellow worker among you; as for our brothers, they are representatives of the churches and an honor to Christ. [24]Therefore show these men the proof of your love and the reason for our pride in you, so that the churches can see it.

9 There is no need for me to write to you about this service to the saints. [2]For I know your eagerness to help, and I have been boasting about it to the Macedonians, telling them that since last year you in Achaia were ready to give; and your enthusiasm has stirred most of them to action. [3]But I am sending the brothers in order that our boasting about you in this matter should not prove hollow, but that you may be ready, as I said you would be. [4]For if any Macedonians come with me and find you unprepared, we—not to say anything

about you—would be ashamed of having been so confident. [5]So I thought it necessary to urge the brothers to visit you in advance and finish the arrangements for the generous gift you had promised. Then it will be ready as a generous gift, not as one grudgingly given.

Sowing Generously

[6]Remember this: Whoever sows sparingly will also reap sparingly, and whoever sows generously will also reap generously. [7]Each man should give what he has decided in his heart to give, not reluctantly or under compulsion, for

---

IT IS NOT MY ABILITY, BUT MY RESPONSE TO GOD'S ABILITY, THAT COUNTS. —*Corrie ten Boom*

God loves a cheerful giver. [8]And God is able to make all grace abound to you, so that in all things at all times, having all that you need, you will abound in every good work. [9]As it is written:

"He has scattered abroad his gifts to
　　the poor;
　his righteousness endures
　　forever."[b]

[10]Now he who supplies seed to the sower and bread for food will also supply and increase your store of seed and will enlarge the harvest of your righteousness. [11]You will be made rich in every way so that you can be generous on every occasion, and through us your generosity will result in thanksgiving to God.

[12]This service that you perform is not only supplying the needs of God's people but is also overflowing in many expressions of thanks to God. [13]Because of the service by which you have proved yourselves, men will praise God for the obedience that accompanies your confession of the gospel of Christ, and for your generosity in sharing with them and with everyone else. [14]And in their prayers for you their hearts will go out to you, because of the surpassing grace God has given you. [15]Thanks be to God for his indescribable gift!

---

a 15 Exodus 16:18　　*b 9* Psalm 112:9

Paul's Defense of His Ministry

10 By the meekness and gentleness of Christ, I appeal to you—I, Paul, who am "timid" when face to face with you, but "bold" when away! ²I beg you that when I come I may not have to be as bold as I expect to be toward some people who think that we live by the standards of this world. ³For though we live in the world, we do not wage war as the world does. ⁴The weapons we fight with are not the weapons of the world. On the contrary, they have divine power to demolish strongholds. ⁵We demolish arguments and every pretension that sets itself up against the knowledge of God, and we take captive every thought to make it obedient to Christ. ⁶And we will be ready to punish every act of disobedience, once your obedience is complete.

WE ARE CALLED TO BE GOD'S TRANSMITTERS, TO BE COMPLETELY SEPARATED FROM ALL THOUGHTS WHICH ARE CONTRARY TO HIS THINKING, SO THAT WE MAY TRANSMIT HIS THOUGHTS TO OTHERS.   —*Hannah Hurnard*

---

⁷You are looking only on the surface of things.ᵃ If anyone is confident that he belongs to Christ, he should consider again that we belong to Christ just as much as he. ⁸For even if I boast somewhat freely about the authority the Lord gave us for building you up rather than pulling you down, I will not be ashamed of it. ⁹I do not want to seem to be trying to frighten you with my letters. ¹⁰For some say, "His letters are weighty and forceful, but in person he is unimpressive and his speaking amounts to nothing." ¹¹Such people should realize that what we are in our letters when we are absent, we will be in our actions when we are present.

¹²We do not dare to classify or compare ourselves with some who commend themselves. When they measure themselves by themselves and compare themselves with themselves, they are not wise. ¹³We, however, will not boast beyond proper limits, but will confine our boasting to the field God has assigned to us, a field that reaches even to you. ¹⁴We are not going too far in our boasting, as would be the case if we had not come to you, for we did get as far as you with the gospel of Christ. ¹⁵Neither do we go beyond our limits by boasting of work done by others.ᵇ Our hope is that, as your faith continues to grow, our area of activity among you will greatly expand, ¹⁶so that we can preach the gospel in the regions beyond you. For we do not want to boast about work already done in another man's territory. ¹⁷But, "Let him who boasts boast in the Lord."ᶜ ¹⁸For it is not the one who commends himself who is approved, but the one whom the Lord commends.

Paul and the False Apostles

11 I hope you will put up with a little of my foolishness; but you are already doing that. ²I am jealous for you with a godly jealousy. I promised you to one husband, to Christ, so that I might present you as a pure virgin to him. ³But I am afraid that just as Eve was deceived by the serpent's cunning, your minds may somehow be led astray from your sincere and pure devotion to Christ. ⁴For if someone comes to you and preaches a Jesus other than the Jesus we preached, or if you receive a different spirit from the one you received, or a different gospel from the one you accepted, you put up with it easily enough. ⁵But I do not think I am in the least inferior to those "super-apostles." ⁶I may not be a trained speaker, but I do have knowledge. We have made this perfectly clear to you in every way.

⁷Was it a sin for me to lower myself in order to elevate you by preaching the gospel of God to you free of charge? ⁸I robbed other churches by receiving support from them so as to serve you. ⁹And when I was with you and needed something, I was not a burden to anyone, for the brothers who came from Macedonia supplied what I needed. I have kept

---

ᵃ 7 Or *Look at the obvious facts*   ᵇ 13–15 Or ¹³*We, however, will not boast about things that cannot be measured, but we will boast according to the standard of measurement that the God of measure has assigned us—a measurement that relates even to you.* ¹⁴ . . . . ¹⁵*Neither do we boast about things that cannot be measured in regard to the work done by others.*   ᶜ 17 Jer. 9:24

WEEKEND

AT THE LORD'S TABLE
Horatius Bonar

VERSE: 1 Corinthians 11:26 **PASSAGE:** 1 Corinthians 11:23–26

ere, O my Lord, I see thee face to face;
 Here would I touch and handle things
  unseen,
  Here grasp with firmer hand the eternal grace,
And all my weariness upon thee lean.

Here would I feed upon the bread of God,
 Here drink with thee the royal wine of heaven;
Here would I lay aside each earthly load,
 Here taste afresh the calm of sin forgiven.

This is the hour of banquet and of song;
 This is the heavenly table spread for me;
Here let me feast, and feasting, still prolong
 The brief bright hour of fellowship with thee.

Too soon we rise; the symbols disappear;
 The feast, though not the love, is past and gone;
The bread and wine remove, but thou are here,
 Nearer than ever; still my Shield and Sun.

I have no help but thine; nor do I need
 Another arm save thine to lean upon;
It is enough, my Lord, enough indeed;
 My strength is in thy might, thy might alone.

Mine is the sin, but thine the righteousness;
 Mine is the guilt, but thine the cleansing blood;
Here is my robe, my refuge, and my peace,—
 Thy blood, thy righteousness, O Lord my God.

Feast after feast thus comes and passes by,
 Yet, passing, points to the glad feast above,
Giving sweet foretaste of the festal joy,
 The Lamb's great bridal feast of bliss and love.

ADDITIONAL SCRIPTURE READING:
John 6:35; Ephesians 1:7–8

Go to page 1367 for your next devotional reading.

1700   1900

myself from being a burden to you in any way, and will continue to do so. 10As surely as the truth of Christ is in me, nobody in the regions of Achaia will stop this boasting of mine. 11Why? Because I do not love you? God knows I do! 12And I will keep on doing what I am doing in order to cut the ground from under those who want an opportunity to be considered equal with us in the things they boast about.

13For such men are false apostles, deceitful workmen, masquerading as apostles of Christ. 14And no wonder, for Satan himself masquerades as an angel of light. 15It is not surprising, then, if his servants masquerade as servants of righteousness. Their end will be what their actions deserve.

Paul Boasts About His Sufferings

16I repeat: Let no one take me for a fool. But if you do, then receive me just as you would a fool, so that I may do a little boasting. 17In this self-confident boasting I am not talking as the Lord would, but as a fool. 18Since many are boasting in the way the world does, I too will boast. 19You gladly put up with fools since you are so wise! 20In fact, you even put up with anyone who enslaves you or exploits you or takes advantage of you or pushes himself forward or slaps you in the face. 21To my shame I admit that we were too weak for that!

What anyone else dares to boast about—I am speaking as a fool—I also dare to boast about. 22Are they Hebrews? So am I. Are they Israelites? So am I. Are they Abraham's descendants? So am I. 23Are they servants of Christ? (I am out of my mind to talk like this.) I am more. I have worked much harder, been in prison more frequently, been flogged more severely, and been exposed to death again and again. 24Five times I received from the Jews the forty lashes minus one. 25Three times I was beaten with rods, once I was stoned, three times I was shipwrecked, I spent a night and a day in the open sea, 26I have been constantly on the move. I have been in danger from rivers, in danger from bandits, in danger from my own countrymen, in danger from Gentiles; in danger in the city, in danger in the country, in danger

at sea; and in danger from false brothers. 27I have labored and toiled and have often gone without sleep; I have known hunger and thirst and have often gone without food; I have been cold and naked. 28Besides everything else, I face daily the pressure of my concern for all the churches. 29Who is weak, and I do not feel weak? Who is led into sin, and I do not inwardly burn?

30If I must boast, I will boast of the things that show my weakness. 31The God and Father of the Lord Jesus, who is to be praised forever, knows that I am not lying. 32In Damascus the governor under King Aretas had the city of the Damascenes guarded in order to arrest me. 33But I was lowered in a basket from a window in the wall and slipped through his hands.

Paul's Vision and His Thorn

12 I must go on boasting. Although there is nothing to be gained, I will go on to visions and revelations from the Lord. 2I know a man in Christ who fourteen years ago was caught up to the third heaven. Whether it was in the body or out of the body I do not know—God knows. 3And I know that this man—whether in the body or apart from the body I do not know, but God knows— 4was caught up to paradise. He heard inexpressible things, things that man is not permitted to tell. 5I will boast about a man like that, but I will not boast about myself, except about my weaknesses. 6Even if I should choose to boast, I would not be a fool, because I would be speaking the truth. But I refrain, so no one will think more of me than is warranted by what I do or say.

7To keep me from becoming conceited because of these surpassingly great revelations, there was given me a thorn in my flesh, a messenger of Satan, to torment me. 8Three times I pleaded with the Lord to take it away from me. 9But he said to me, "My grace is sufficient for you, for my power is made perfect in weakness." Therefore I will boast all the more gladly about my weaknesses, so that Christ's power may rest on me. 10That is why, for Christ's sake, I delight in weaknesses, in insults, in hardships, in persecutions, in difficulties. For when I am weak, then I am strong.

GOD IS SUFFICIENT FOR ALL OUR NEEDS, FOR EVERY PROBLEM, AND FOR EVERY DIFFICULTY, FOR EVERY BROKEN HEART, AND FOR EVERY HUMAN SORROW.   —*Peter Marshall*

Paul's Concern for the Corinthians

¹¹I have made a fool of myself, but you drove me to it. I ought to have been commended by you, for I am not in the least inferior to the "super-apostles," even though I am nothing. ¹²The things that mark an apostle—signs, wonders and miracles—were done among you with great perseverance. ¹³How were you inferior to the other churches, except that I was never a burden to you? Forgive me this wrong!

¹⁴Now I am ready to visit you for the third time, and I will not be a burden to you, because what I want is not your possessions but you. After all, children should not have to save up for their parents, but parents for their children. ¹⁵So I will very gladly spend for you everything I have and expend myself as well.

MONDAY

SIX WORDS ARE ENOUGH
Karl Barth

VERSE: 2 Corinthians 12:9   **PASSAGE:** 2 Corinthians 12:7–10

"My grace is sufficient for you" (2 Corinthians 12:9). This is a very short text—a mere six words—the shortest I have ever preached on. The brevity is an advantage for you; you can retain it better. I might say in passing that every time I come here I am very concerned that not so much my sermon but the text that it follows may really sink in and go with you. This time then: "My grace is sufficient for you." The wonderful spice of this saying lies in its brevity. The six words are enough. Some of you may have heard that in the last forty years I have written many books, some large. I will freely and frankly and gladly admit that these six words say much more and much better things than all the heaps of paper with which I have surrounded myself. They are enough—which cannot be said even remotely of my books. What may be good in my books can be at most that from afar they point to what these six words say. And when my books are long since outdated and forgotten, and every book in the world with them, these words will still shine with everlasting fullness: "My grace is sufficient for you."

ADDITIONAL SCRIPTURE READING:
Romans 5:20–21; Hebrews 4:16

Go to page 1370 for your next devotional reading.

1900   Present

If I love you more, will you love me less? [16]Be that as it may, I have not been a burden to you. Yet, crafty fellow that I am, I caught you by trickery! [17]Did I exploit you through any of the men I sent you? [18]I urged Titus to go to you and I sent our brother with him. Titus did not exploit you, did he? Did we not act in the same spirit and follow the same course?

[19]Have you been thinking all along that we have been defending ourselves to you? We have been speaking in the sight of God as those in Christ; and everything we do, dear friends, is for your strengthening. [20]For I am afraid that when I come I may not find you as I want you to be, and you may not find me as you want me to be. I fear that there may be quarreling, jealousy, outbursts of anger, factions, slander, gossip, arrogance and disorder. [21]I am afraid that when I come again my God will humble me before you, and I will be grieved over many who have sinned earlier and have not repented of the impurity, sexual sin and debauchery in which they have indulged.

Final Warnings

13 This will be my third visit to you. "Every matter must be established by the testimony of two or three witnesses."[a] [2]I already gave you a warning when I was with you the second time. I now repeat it while absent: On my return I will not spare those who sinned earlier or any of the others, [3]since you are demanding proof that Christ is speaking through me. He is not weak in dealing with you, but is powerful among you. [4]For to be sure, he was crucified in weakness, yet he lives by God's power. Likewise, we are weak in him, yet by God's power we will live with him to serve you.

[5]Examine yourselves to see whether you are in the faith; test yourselves. Do you not realize that Christ Jesus is in you—unless, of course, you fail the test? [6]And I trust that you will discover that we have not failed the test. [7]Now we pray to God that you will not do anything wrong. Not that people will see that we have stood the test but that you will do what is right even though we may seem to have failed. [8]For we cannot do anything against the truth, but only for the truth. [9]We are glad whenever we are weak but you are strong; and our prayer is for your perfection. [10]This is why I write these things when I am absent, that when I come I may not have to be harsh in my use of authority—the authority the Lord gave me for building you up, not for tearing you down.

Final Greetings

[11]Finally, brothers, good-by. Aim for perfection, listen to my appeal, be of one mind, live in peace. And the God of love and peace will be with you.

[12]Greet one another with a holy kiss. [13]All the saints send their greetings.

[14]May the grace of the Lord Jesus Christ, and the love of God, and the fellowship of the Holy Spirit be with you all.

_a 1_ Deut. 19:15

GALATIANS

AUL'S LETTER TO THE CHURCHES HE ESTABLISHED IN GALATIA (ACTS 13:13—14:28) CONTAINS HIS CLASSIC STATEMENT OF THE FOUNDATIONAL BIBLICAL TRUTH THAT A PERSON IS JUSTIFIED BY FAITH IN CHRIST. AFTER WARNING THE GALATIANS NOT TO DESERT THE GOSPEL, PAUL ENCOURAGES THEM TO LIVE OUT THE FREEDOM THEY HAVE IN CHRIST. AS YOU READ THIS LETTER, ASK GOD TO HELP YOU ENJOY THE FREEDOM YOU HAVE IN CHRIST AS YOU LIVE A SPIRIT-FILLED LIFE (5:22–23).

1 Paul, an apostle—sent not from men nor by man, but by Jesus Christ and God the Father, who raised him from the dead— 2and all the brothers with me,

To the churches in Galatia:

3Grace and peace to you from God our Father and the Lord Jesus Christ, 4who gave himself for our sins to rescue us from the present evil age, according to the will of our God and Father, 5to whom be glory for ever and ever. Amen.

No Other Gospel

6I am astonished that you are so quickly deserting the one who called you by the grace of Christ and are turning to a different gospel— 7which is really no gospel at all. Evidently some people are throwing you into confusion and are trying to pervert the gospel of Christ. 8But even if we or an angel from heaven should preach a gospel other than the one we preached to you, let him be eternally condemned! 9As we have already said, so now I say again: If anybody is preaching to you a gospel other than what you accepted, let him be eternally condemned!

YOU CANNOT HAVE CHRISTIAN PRINCIPLES WITHOUT CHRIST.   —*Dorothy L. Sayers*

10Am I now trying to win the approval of men, or of God? Or am I trying to please men? If I were still trying to please men, I would not be a servant of Christ.

Paul Called by God

¹¹I want you to know, brothers, that the gospel I preached is not something that man made up. ¹²I did not receive it from any man, nor was I taught it; rather, I received it by revelation from Jesus Christ.

¹³For you have heard of my previous way of life in Judaism, how intensely I persecuted the church of God and tried to destroy it. ¹⁴I was advancing in Judaism beyond many Jews of my own age and was extremely zealous for the traditions of my fathers. ¹⁵But when God,

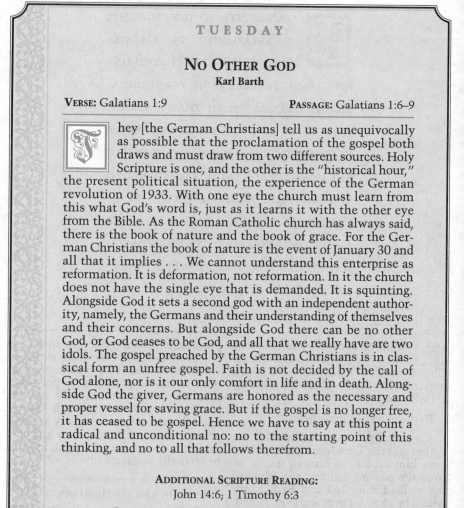

TUESDAY

NO OTHER GOD
Karl Barth

VERSE: Galatians 1:9   **PASSAGE:** Galatians 1:6–9

hey [the German Christians] tell us as unequivocally as possible that the proclamation of the gospel both draws and must draw from two different sources. Holy Scripture is one, and the other is the "historical hour," the present political situation, the experience of the German revolution of 1933. With one eye the church must learn from this what God's word is, just as it learns it with the other eye from the Bible. As the Roman Catholic church has always said, there is the book of nature and the book of grace. For the German Christians the book of nature is the event of January 30 and all that it implies . . . We cannot understand this enterprise as reformation. It is deformation, not reformation. In it the church does not have the single eye that is demanded. It is squinting. Alongside God it sets a second god with an independent authority, namely, the Germans and their understanding of themselves and their concerns. But alongside God there can be no other God, or God ceases to be God, and all that we really have are two idols. The gospel preached by the German Christians is in classical form an unfree gospel. Faith is not decided by the call of God alone, nor is it our only comfort in life and in death. Alongside God the giver, Germans are honored as the necessary and proper vessel for saving grace. But if the gospel is no longer free, it has ceased to be gospel. Hence we have to say at this point a radical and unconditional no: no to the starting point of this thinking, and no to all that follows therefrom.

ADDITIONAL SCRIPTURE READING:
John 14:6; 1 Timothy 6:3

Go to page 1374 for your next devotional reading.

1900   Present

who set me apart from birth*a* and called me by his grace, was pleased 16to reveal his Son in me so that I might preach him among the Gentiles, I did not consult any man, 17nor did I go up to Jerusalem to see those who were apostles before I was, but I went immediately into Arabia and later returned to Damascus.

18Then after three years, I went up to Jerusalem to get acquainted with Peter*b* and stayed with him fifteen days. 19I saw none of the other apostles—only James, the Lord's brother. 20I assure you before God that what I am writing you is no lie. 21Later I went to Syria and Cilicia. 22I was personally unknown to the churches of Judea that are in Christ. 23They only heard the report: "The man who formerly persecuted us is now preaching the faith he once tried to destroy." 24And they praised God because of me.

Paul Accepted by the Apostles

2 Fourteen years later I went up again to Jerusalem, this time with Barnabas. I took Titus along also. 2I went in response to a revelation and set before them the gospel that I preach among the Gentiles. But I did this privately to those who seemed to be leaders, for fear that I was running or had run my race in vain. 3Yet not even Titus, who was with me, was compelled to be circumcised, even though he was a Greek. 4This matter arose because some false brothers had infiltrated our ranks to spy on the freedom we have in Christ Jesus and to make us slaves. 5We did not give in to them for a moment, so that the truth of the gospel might remain with you.

6As for those who seemed to be important—whatever they were makes no difference to me; God does not judge by external appearance—those men added nothing to my message. 7On the contrary, they saw that I had been entrusted with the task of preaching the gospel to the Gentiles,*c* just as Peter had been to the Jews.*d* 8For God, who was at work in the ministry of Peter as an apostle to the Jews, was also at work in my ministry as an apostle to the Gentiles. 9James, Peter*e* and John, those reputed to be pillars,

gave me and Barnabas the right hand of fellowship when they recognized the grace given to me. They agreed that we should go to the Gentiles, and they to the Jews. 10All they asked was that we should continue to remember the poor, the very thing I was eager to do.

Paul Opposes Peter

11When Peter came to Antioch, I opposed him to his face, because he was clearly in the wrong. 12Before certain men came from James, he used to eat with the Gentiles. But when they arrived, he began to draw back and separate himself from the Gentiles because he was afraid of those who belonged to the circumcision group. 13The other Jews joined him in his hypocrisy, so that by their hypocrisy even Barnabas was led astray.

14When I saw that they were not acting in line with the truth of the gospel, I said to Peter in front of them all, "You are a Jew, yet you live like a Gentile and not like a Jew. How is it, then, that you force Gentiles to follow Jewish customs?

15"We who are Jews by birth and not 'Gentile sinners' 16know that a man is not justified by observing the law, but by faith in Jesus Christ. So we, too, have put our faith in Christ Jesus that we may be justified by faith in Christ and not by observing the law, because by observing the law no one will be justified.

IT IS THROUGH ACCEPTING THE CIRCUMSTANCES THAT COME TO US IN LIFE THAT SELF IS CRUCIFIED.   —*Hannah Hurnard*

17"If, while we seek to be justified in Christ, it becomes evident that we ourselves are sinners, does that mean that Christ promotes sin? Absolutely not! 18If I rebuild what I destroyed, I prove that I am a lawbreaker. 19For through the law I died to the law so that I might live for God. 20I have been crucified with Christ and I no longer live, but Christ lives in me. The life I live in the body, I live by faith in the Son of God, who loved me and gave himself for me. 21I do not set aside the grace of God, for

---

a 15 Or *from my mother's womb*   *b* 18 Greek *Cephas*   *c* 7 Greek *uncircumcised*   *d* 7 Greek *circumcised*; also in verses 8 and 9   *e* 9 Greek *Cephas*; also in verses 11 and 14

if righteousness could be gained through the law, Christ died for nothing!"[a]

Faith or Observance of the Law

3 You foolish Galatians! Who has bewitched you? Before your very eyes Jesus Christ was clearly portrayed as crucified. [2]I would like to learn just one thing from you: Did you receive the Spirit by observing the law, or by believing what you heard? [3]Are you so foolish? After beginning with the Spirit, are you now trying to attain your goal by human effort? [4]Have you suffered so much for nothing—if it really was for nothing? [5]Does God give you his Spirit and work miracles among you because you observe the law, or because you believe what you heard?

[6]Consider Abraham: "He believed God, and it was credited to him as righteousness."[b] [7]Understand, then, that those who believe are children of Abraham. [8]The Scripture foresaw that God would justify the Gentiles by faith, and announced the gospel in advance to Abraham: "All nations will be blessed through you."[c] [9]So those who have faith are blessed along with Abraham, the man of faith.

[10]All who rely on observing the law are under a curse, for it is written: "Cursed is everyone who does not continue to do everything written in the Book of the Law."[d] [11]Clearly no one is justified before God by the law, because, "The righteous will live by faith."[e] [12]The law is not based on faith; on the contrary, "The man who does these things will live by them."[f] [13]Christ redeemed us from the curse of the law by becoming a curse for us, for it is written: "Cursed is everyone who is hung on a tree."[g] [14]He redeemed us in order that the blessing given to Abraham might come to the Gentiles through Christ Jesus, so that by faith we might receive the promise of the Spirit.

The Law and the Promise

[15]Brothers, let me take an example from everyday life. Just as no one can set aside or add to a human covenant that has been duly established, so it is in this case. [16]The promises were spoken to Abraham and to his seed. The Scripture does not say "and to seeds," meaning many people, but "and to your seed,"[h] meaning one person, who is Christ. [17]What I mean is this: The law, introduced 430 years later, does not set aside the covenant previously established by God and thus do away with the promise. [18]For if the inheritance depends on the law, then it no longer depends on a promise; but God in his grace gave it to Abraham through a promise.

[19]What, then, was the purpose of the law? It was added because of transgressions until the Seed to whom the promise referred had come. The law was put into effect through angels by a mediator. [20]A mediator, however, does not represent just one party; but God is one.

[21]Is the law, therefore, opposed to the promises of God? Absolutely not! For if a law had been given that could impart life, then righteousness would certainly have come by the law. [22]But the Scripture declares that the whole world is a prisoner of sin, so that what was promised, being given through faith in Jesus Christ, might be given to those who believe.

[23]Before this faith came, we were held prisoners by the law, locked up until faith should be revealed. [24]So the law was put in charge to lead us to Christ[i] that we might be justified by faith. [25]Now that faith has come, we are no longer under the supervision of the law.

Sons of God

[26]You are all sons of God through faith in Christ Jesus, [27]for all of you who were baptized into Christ have clothed yourselves with Christ. [28]There is neither Jew nor Greek, slave nor free, male nor female, for you are all one in Christ Jesus. [29]If you belong to Christ, then you are Abraham's seed, and heirs according to the promise.

4 What I am saying is that as long as the heir is a child, he is no different from a slave, although he owns the whole estate. [2]He is subject to

a 21 Some interpreters end the quotation after verse 14.   b 6 Gen. 15:6   c 8 Gen. 12:3; 18:18; 22:18
d 10 Deut. 27:26   e 11 Hab. 2:4   f 12 Lev. 18:5   g 13 Deut. 21:23   h 16 Gen. 12:7; 13:15; 24:7
i 24 Or charge until Christ came

guardians and trustees until the time set by his father. ³So also, when we were children, we were in slavery under the basic principles of the world. ⁴But when the time had fully come, God sent his Son, born of a woman, born under law, ⁵to redeem those under law, that we might receive the full rights of sons. ⁶Because you are sons, God sent the Spirit of his Son into our hearts, the Spirit who calls out, "Abba,ᵃ Father." ⁷So you are no longer a slave, but a son; and since you are a son, God has made you also an heir.

Paul's Concern for the Galatians

⁸Formerly, when you did not know God, you were slaves to those who by nature are not gods. ⁹But now that you know God—or rather are known by God—how is it that you are turning back to those weak and miserable principles? Do you wish to be enslaved by them all over again? ¹⁰You are observing special days and months and seasons and years! ¹¹I fear for you, that somehow I have wasted my efforts on you.

¹²I plead with you, brothers, become like me, for I became like you. You have done me no wrong. ¹³As you know, it was because of an illness that I first preached the gospel to you. ¹⁴Even though my illness was a trial to you, you did not treat me with contempt or scorn. Instead, you welcomed me as if I were an angel of God, as if I were Christ Jesus himself. ¹⁵What has happened to all your joy? I can testify that, if you could have done so, you would have torn out your eyes and given them to me. ¹⁶Have I now become your enemy by telling you the truth?

¹⁷Those people are zealous to win you over, but for no good. What they want is to alienate you ⌊from us⌋, so that you may be zealous for them. ¹⁸It is fine to be zealous, provided the purpose is good, and to be so always and not just when I am with you. ¹⁹My dear children, for whom I am again in the pains of childbirth until Christ is formed in you, ²⁰how I wish I could be with you now and change my tone, because I am perplexed about you!

Hagar and Sarah

²¹Tell me, you who want to be under the law, are you not aware of what the law says? ²²For it is written that Abraham had two sons, one by the slave woman and the other by the free woman. ²³His son by the slave woman was born in the ordinary way; but his son by the free woman was born as the result of a promise.

²⁴These things may be taken figuratively, for the women represent two covenants. One covenant is from Mount Sinai and bears children who are to be slaves: This is Hagar. ²⁵Now Hagar stands for Mount Sinai in Arabia and corresponds to the present city of Jerusalem, because she is in slavery with her children. ²⁶But the Jerusalem that is above is free, and she is our mother. ²⁷For it is written:

"Be glad, O barren woman,
    who bears no children;
break forth and cry aloud,
    you who have no labor pains;
because more are the children of the
        desolate woman
    than of her who has a husband."ᵇ

²⁸Now you, brothers, like Isaac, are children of promise. ²⁹At that time the son born in the ordinary way persecuted the son born by the power of the Spirit. It is the same now. ³⁰But what does the Scripture say? "Get rid of the slave woman and her son, for the slave woman's son will never share in the inheritance with the free woman's son."ᶜ ³¹Therefore, brothers, we are not children of the slave woman, but of the free woman.

WHAT HAVE WE, SONS OF GOD, TO DO WITH LAW?
—John Milton

Freedom in Christ

5 It is for freedom that Christ has set us free. Stand firm, then, and do not let yourselves be burdened again by a yoke of slavery.

²Mark my words! I, Paul, tell you that

ᵃ 6 Aramaic for *Father*   ᵇ 27 Isaiah 54:1   ᶜ 30 Gen. 21:10

if you let yourselves be circumcised, Christ will be of no value to you at all. ³Again I declare to every man who lets himself be circumcised that he is obligated to obey the whole law. ⁴You who are trying to be justified by law have been alienated from Christ; you have fallen away from grace. ⁵But by faith we eagerly await through the Spirit the righteousness for which we hope. ⁶For in Christ Jesus neither circumcision nor uncircumcision has any value. The only thing that counts is faith expressing itself through love.

⁷You were running a good race. Who cut in on you and kept you from obeying the truth? ⁸That kind of persuasion does not come from the one who calls you. ⁹"A little yeast works through the whole batch of dough." ¹⁰I am confident

WEDNESDAY

CHARACTERISTICS OF THE CHRISTIAN COMMUNITY
Epistle to Diognetus

VERSE: Galatians 5:16   **PASSAGE:** Galatians 5:16–26

 he relation of Christians to the world is that of a soul to the body. As the soul is diffused through every part of the body, so are Christians through all the cities of the world. The soul, too, inhabits the body, while at the same time forming no part of it; and Christians inhabit the world, but they are not part of the world. The soul, invisible herself, is immured within a visible body; so Christians can be recognized in the world, but their Christianity itself remains hidden from the eye. The flesh hates the soul, and wars against her without any provocation, because she is an obstacle to its own self-indulgence; and the world similarly hates the Christians without provocation, because they are opposed to its pleasures. All the same, the soul loves the flesh and all its members, despite their hatred for her; and Christians, too, love those who hate them. The soul, shut up inside the body, nevertheless holds the body together; and though they are confined within the world as in a dungeon, it is Christians who hold the world together. The soul, which is immortal, must dwell in a mortal tabernacle; and Christians, as they sojourn for a while in the midst of corruptibility here, look for incorruptibility in the heavens. Finally, just as to be stinted of food and drink makes for the soul's improvement, so when Christians are every day subjected to ill-treatment, they increase the more in numbers. Such is the high post of duty in which God has placed them, and it is their moral duty not to shrink from it.

ADDITIONAL SCRIPTURE READING:
John 18:36; 1 John 2:15–17

Go to page 1377 for your next devotional reading.

100   500

in the Lord that you will take no other view. The one who is throwing you into confusion will pay the penalty, whoever he may be. [11]Brothers, if I am still preaching circumcision, why am I still being persecuted? In that case the offense of the cross has been abolished. [12]As for those agitators, I wish they would go the whole way and emasculate themselves!

[13]You, my brothers, were called to be free. But do not use your freedom to indulge the sinful nature[a]; rather, serve one another in love. [14]The entire law is summed up in a single command: "Love your neighbor as yourself."[b] [15]If you keep on biting and devouring each other, watch out or you will be destroyed by each other.

Life by the Spirit

[16]So I say, live by the Spirit, and you will not gratify the desires of the sinful nature. [17]For the sinful nature desires what is contrary to the Spirit, and the Spirit what is contrary to the sinful nature. They are in conflict with each other, so that you do not do what you want. [18]But if you are led by the Spirit, you are not under law.

[19]The acts of the sinful nature are obvious: sexual immorality, impurity and debauchery; [20]idolatry and witchcraft; hatred, discord, jealousy, fits of rage, selfish ambition, dissensions, factions [21]and envy; drunkenness, orgies, and the like. I warn you, as I did before, that those who live like this will not inherit the kingdom of God.

[22]But the fruit of the Spirit is love, joy, peace, patience, kindness, goodness, faithfulness, [23]gentleness and self-control. Against such things there is no law. [24]Those who belong to Christ Jesus have crucified the sinful nature with its passions and desires. [25]Since we live by the Spirit, let us keep in step with the Spirit. [26]Let us not become conceited, provoking and envying each other.

Doing Good to All

6 Brothers, if someone is caught in a sin, you who are spiritual should restore him gently. But watch yourself, or you also may be tempted. [2]Carry each other's burdens, and in this way you will fulfill the law of Christ. [3]If anyone thinks he is something when he is nothing, he deceives himself. [4]Each one should test his own actions. Then he can take pride in himself, without comparing himself to somebody else, [5]for each one should carry his own load.

[6]Anyone who receives instruction in the word must share all good things with his instructor.

[7]Do not be deceived: God cannot be mocked. A man reaps what he sows. [8]The one who sows to please his sinful nature, from that nature[c] will reap destruction; the one who sows to please the Spirit, from the Spirit will reap eternal life. [9]Let us not become weary in doing good, for at the proper time we will reap a harvest if we do not give up. [10]Therefore, as we have opportunity, let us do good to all people, especially to those who belong to the family of believers.

Not Circumcision but a New Creation

[11]See what large letters I use as I write to you with my own hand!

[12]Those who want to make a good impression outwardly are trying to compel you to be circumcised. The only reason they do this is to avoid being persecuted for the cross of Christ. [13]Not even those who are circumcised obey the law, yet they want you to be circumcised that they may boast about your flesh. [14]May I never boast except in the cross of our Lord Jesus Christ, through which[d] the world has been crucified to me, and I to the world. [15]Neither circumcision nor uncircumcision means anything; what counts is a new creation. [16]Peace and mercy to all who follow this rule, even to the Israel of God.

[17]Finally, let no one cause me trouble, for I bear on my body the marks of Jesus.

[18]The grace of our Lord Jesus Christ be with your spirit, brothers. Amen.

---

a 13 Or *the flesh;* also in verses 16, 17, 19 and 24   *b 14* Lev. 19:18   *c 8* Or *his flesh, from the flesh*
d 14 Or *whom*

EPHESIANS

AUL WRITES THIS LETTER SO THAT HIS READERS MIGHT BETTER UNDERSTAND GOD'S ETERNAL PURPOSES FOR THE CHURCH. ONE OF THOSE PURPOSES IS TO RECONCILE PEOPLE TO GOD AND TO EACH OTHER THROUGH THE WORK OF JESUS ON THE CROSS. THINK ABOUT YOUR OWN RELATIONSHIP TO GOD AND OTHERS AND YOUR OWN NEED FOR RECONCILIATION. LOOK FOR PAUL'S PRACTICAL ADVICE ON HOW TO LIVE IN UNITY WITH GOD AND ONE ANOTHER.

1 Paul, an apostle of Christ Jesus by the will of God,

To the saints in Ephesus,*a* the faithful*b* in Christ Jesus:

²Grace and peace to you from God our Father and the Lord Jesus Christ.

Spiritual Blessings in Christ

³Praise be to the God and Father of our Lord Jesus Christ, who has blessed us in the heavenly realms with every spiritual blessing in Christ. ⁴For he chose us in him before the creation of the world to be holy and blameless in his sight. In love ⁵he*c* predestined us to be adopted as his sons through Jesus Christ, in accordance with his pleasure and will— ⁶to the praise of his glorious grace, which he has freely given us in the One he loves. ⁷In him we have redemption through his blood, the forgiveness of sins, in accordance with the riches of God's grace ⁸that he lavished on us with all wisdom and understanding. ⁹And he*d* made known to us the mystery of his will according to his good pleasure, which he purposed in Christ, ¹⁰to be put into effect when the times will have reached their fulfillment—to bring all things in heaven and on earth together under one head, even Christ.

¹¹In him we were also chosen,*e* having been predestined according to the plan of him who works out everything in conformity with the purpose of his will,

---

a 1 Some early manuscripts do not have *in Ephesus.*   *b* 1 Or *believers who are*   *c* 4,5 Or *sight in love.* ⁵*He*   *d* 8,9 Or *us. With all wisdom and understanding,* ⁹*he*   *e* 11 Or *were made heirs*

HYMN TO CHRIST
Clement of Alexandria

VERSE: Ephesians 1:17   **PASSAGE:** Ephesians 1:15–23

ou who bridles untamed colts,
Who gives flight to birds,
Who steers ships along their course,
Tame our wild hearts,
Lift our souls to you,
Steer us towards the safe harbor of your love.

King of the saints,
Invincible Lord of the Father,
Prince of wisdom,
Source of joy,
Savior of our race,
Cultivator of all life,
Guardian of our desires.
Whose sure hand guides us to heaven.

Fisher of men,
You cast out the sweet bait of your gospel,
You draw us out of the waters of sin,
Shepherd of men,
You call us with your sweet, gentle voice,
You invite us into your eternal sheepfold.

Fountain of mercy,
Light of truth,
Faith without limits,
Love without end,
Exemplar of virtue,
Proclaimer of justice,
Leader of men,
Your footprints show the way to heaven.

Mother of your people,
Your celestial breasts give pure spiritual milk.
You slake the thirst of all who have faith.
Bridegroom of your people,
Your celestial beauty inspires us to sing your praises,
You lift our voices with hymns of everlasting praise.

ADDITIONAL SCRIPTURE READING:
Psalms 19:14; 23:3

Go to page 1379 for your next devotional reading.

[12]in order that we, who were the first to hope in Christ, might be for the praise of his glory. [13]And you also were included in Christ when you heard the word of truth, the gospel of your salvation. Having believed, you were marked in him with a seal, the promised Holy Spirit, [14]who is a deposit guaranteeing our inheritance until the redemption of those who are God's possession—to the praise of his glory.

Thanksgiving and Prayer

[15]For this reason, ever since I heard about your faith in the Lord Jesus and your love for all the saints, [16]I have not stopped giving thanks for you, remembering you in my prayers. [17]I keep asking that the God of our Lord Jesus Christ, the glorious Father, may give you the Spirit[a] of wisdom and revelation, so that you may know him better. [18]I pray also that the eyes of your heart may be enlightened in order that you may know the hope to which he has called you, the riches of his glorious inheritance in the saints, [19]and his incomparably great power for us who believe. That power is like the working of his mighty strength, [20]which he exerted in Christ when he raised him from the dead and seated him at his right hand in the heavenly realms, [21]far above all rule and authority, power and dominion, and every title that can be given, not only in the present age but also in the one to come. [22]And God placed all things under his feet and appointed him to be head over everything for the church, [23]which is his body, the fullness of him who fills everything in every way.

Made Alive in Christ

2 As for you, you were dead in your transgressions and sins, [2]in which you used to live when you followed the ways of this world and of the ruler of the kingdom of the air, the spirit who is now at work in those who are disobedient. [3]All of us also lived among them at one time, gratifying the cravings of our sinful nature[b] and following its desires and thoughts. Like the rest, we were by nature objects of wrath. [4]But because of his great love for us, God, who is rich in mercy, [5]made us alive with Christ even when we were dead in transgressions—it is by grace you have been saved. [6]And God raised us up with Christ and seated us with him in the heavenly realms in Christ Jesus, [7]in order that in the coming ages he might show the incomparable riches of his grace, expressed in his kindness to us in Christ Jesus. [8]For it is by grace you have been saved, through faith—and this not from yourselves, it is the gift of God— [9]not by works, so that no one can boast. [10]For we are God's workmanship, created in Christ Jesus to do good works, which God prepared in advance for us to do.

NO MAN EVER BELIEVES WITH A TRUE AND SAVING FAITH UNLESS GOD INCLINES HIS HEART; AND NO MAN WHEN GOD DOES INCLINE HIS HEART CAN REFRAIN FROM BELIEVING.   —*Blaise Pascal*

One in Christ

[11]Therefore, remember that formerly you who are Gentiles by birth and called "uncircumcised" by those who call themselves "the circumcision" (that done in the body by the hands of men)— [12]remember that at that time you were separate from Christ, excluded from citizenship in Israel and foreigners to the covenants of the promise, without hope and without God in the world. [13]But now in Christ Jesus you who once were far away have been brought near through the blood of Christ.

[14]For he himself is our peace, who has made the two one and has destroyed the barrier, the dividing wall of hostility, [15]by abolishing in his flesh the law with its commandments and regulations. His purpose was to create in himself one new man out of the two, thus making peace, [16]and in this one body to reconcile both of them to God through the cross, by which he put to death their hostility. [17]He came and preached peace to you who were far away and peace to those who were near. [18]For through him we both have access to the Father by one Spirit.

_a 17_ Or _a spirit_   _b 3_ Or _our flesh_

THE UNSEARCHABLE RICHES OF CHRIST
James Hudson Taylor

VERSE: Ephesians 3:8   **PASSAGE:** Ephesians 3:7–13

 t is a wonderful thing to be really one with a risen and exalted Savior, to be a member of Christ! Think what it involves. Can Christ be rich and I poor? Can your right hand be rich and the left poor? or your head be well fed while your body starves? Again, think of its bearing on prayer. Could a bank clerk say to a customer, "It was only your hand, not you that wrote that check"; or "I cannot pay this sum to your hand, but only to yourself"? No more can your prayers or mine be discredited if offered in the name of Jesus (i.e., not for the sake of Jesus merely, but on the ground that we are his, his members) so long as we keep within the limits of Christ's credit—a tolerably wide limit! If we ask for anything unscriptural, or not in accordance with the will of God, Christ himself could not do that. But "if we ask anything according to his will . . . we know that we have the petitions that we desired of him" (1 John 5:14–15, KJV).

The sweetest part, if one may speak of one part being sweeter than another, is the rest which full identification with Christ brings. I am no longer anxious about anything, as I realize this; for he, I know, is able to carry out his will, and his will is mine. It makes no matter where he places me, or how. That is rather for him to consider than for me; for in the easiest position he must give me his grace, and in the most difficult his grace is sufficient . . . If God should place me in serious perplexity, must he not give me much guidance; in positions of great difficulty, much grace; in circumstances of great pressure and trial, much strength? No fear that his resources will prove unequal to the emergency! And his resources are mine, for he is mine, and is with me and dwells in me.

ADDITIONAL SCRIPTURE READING:
2 Corinthians 9:1; Philippians 4:6

Go to page 1381 for your next devotional reading.

1700   1900

[19]Consequently, you are no longer foreigners and aliens, but fellow citizens with God's people and members of God's household, [20]built on the foundation of the apostles and prophets, with Christ Jesus himself as the chief cornerstone. [21]In him the whole building is joined together and rises to become a holy temple in the Lord. [22]And in him you too are being built together to become a dwelling in which God lives by his Spirit.

Paul the Preacher to the Gentiles

3 For this reason I, Paul, the prisoner of Christ Jesus for the sake of you Gentiles—

[2]Surely you have heard about the administration of God's grace that was given to me for you, [3]that is, the mystery made known to me by revelation, as I have already written briefly. [4]In reading this, then, you will be able to understand my insight into the mystery of Christ, [5]which was not made known to men in other generations as it has now been revealed by the Spirit to God's holy apostles and prophets. [6]This mystery is that through the gospel the Gentiles are heirs together with Israel, members together of one body, and sharers together in the promise in Christ Jesus.

[7]I became a servant of this gospel by the gift of God's grace given me through the working of his power. [8]Although I am less than the least of all God's people, this grace was given me: to preach to the Gentiles the unsearchable riches of Christ, [9]and to make plain to everyone the administration of this mystery, which for ages past was kept hidden in God, who created all things. [10]His intent was that now, through the church, the manifold wisdom of God should be made known to the rulers and authorities in the heavenly realms, [11]according to his eternal purpose which he accomplished in Christ Jesus our Lord. [12]In him and through faith in him we may approach God with freedom and confidence. [13]I ask you, therefore, not to be discouraged because of my sufferings for you, which are your glory.

A Prayer for the Ephesians

[14]For this reason I kneel before the Father, [15]from whom his whole family[a] in heaven and on earth derives its name. [16]I pray that out of his glorious riches he may strengthen you with power through his Spirit in your inner being, [17]so that Christ may dwell in your hearts through faith. And I pray that you, being rooted and established in love, [18]may have power, together with all the saints, to grasp how wide and long and high and deep is the love of Christ, [19]and to know this love that surpasses knowledge—that you may be filled to the measure of all the fullness of God.

AH! DEAREST JESUS, HOLY CHILD,

MAKE THEE A BED, SOFT, UNDEFILED,

WITHIN MY HEART, THAT IT MAY BE

A QUIET CHAMBER KEPT FOR THEE.

—*Martin Luther*

---

[20]Now to him who is able to do immeasurably more than all we ask or imagine, according to his power that is at work within us, [21]to him be glory in the church and in Christ Jesus throughout all generations, for ever and ever! Amen.

Unity in the Body of Christ

4 As a prisoner for the Lord, then, I urge you to live a life worthy of the calling you have received. [2]Be completely humble and gentle; be patient, bearing with one another in love. [3]Make every effort to keep the unity of the Spirit through the bond of peace. [4]There is one body and one Spirit— just as you were called to one hope when you were called— [5]one Lord, one faith, one baptism; [6]one God and Father of all, who is over all and through all and in all.

[7]But to each one of us grace has been given as Christ apportioned it. [8]This is why it[b] says:

"When he ascended on high,
he led captives in his train
and gave gifts to men."[c]

---

a 15 Or *whom all fatherhood*   *b* 8 Or *God*   *c* 8 Psalm 68:18

WEEKEND

THE NICENE CREED

VERSE: Galatians 4:4   **PASSAGE:** Galatians 4:4–6

e believe in one God,
  the Father, the Almighty,
  maker of heaven and earth,
  of all that is, seen and unseen.

We believe in one Lord, Jesus Christ,
  the only Son of God,
  eternally begotten of the Father,
  God from God, light from light,
  true God from true God,
  begotten, not made,
  of one being with the Father.
  Through him all things were made.
  For us and for our salvation
    he came down from heaven:
  by the power of the Holy Spirit
    he became incarnate from the Virgin Mary,
    and was made man.
  For our sake he was crucified under Pontius Pilate;
    he suffered death and was buried.
    On the third day he rose again
      in accordance with the Scriptures;
    he ascended into heaven
      and is seated at the right hand of the Father.
  He will come again in glory to judge the living and
      the dead,
    and his kingdom will have no end.

We believe in the Holy Spirit, the Lord, the giver of life,
  who proceeds from the Father and the Son
  With the Father and the Son he is worshiped and
      glorified.
  He has spoken through the Prophets.
  We believe in one holy catholic and apostolic church.
  We acknowledge one baptism for the forgiveness
      of sins,
  We look for the resurrection of the dead,
    and the life of the world to come. Amen.

ADDITIONAL SCRIPTURE READING:
Ephesians 4:3–6; Philippians 2:5–11

Go to page 1384 for your next devotional reading.

100   500

⁹(What does "he ascended" mean except that he also descended to the lower, earthly regions*a*? ¹⁰He who descended is the very one who ascended higher than all the heavens, in order to fill the whole universe.) ¹¹It was he who gave some to be apostles, some to be prophets, some to be evangelists, and some to be pastors and teachers, ¹²to prepare God's people for works of service, so that the body of Christ may be built up ¹³until we all reach unity in the faith and in the knowledge of the Son of God and become mature, attaining to the whole measure of the fullness of Christ.

¹⁴Then we will no longer be infants, tossed back and forth by the waves, and blown here and there by every wind of teaching and by the cunning and craftiness of men in their deceitful scheming. ¹⁵Instead, speaking the truth in love, we will in all things grow up into him who is the Head, that is, Christ. ¹⁶From him the whole body, joined and held together by every supporting ligament, grows and builds itself up in love, as each part does its work.

Living as Children of Light

¹⁷So I tell you this, and insist on it in the Lord, that you must no longer live as the Gentiles do, in the futility of their thinking. ¹⁸They are darkened in their understanding and separated from the life of God because of the ignorance that is in them due to the hardening of their hearts. ¹⁹Having lost all sensitivity, they have given themselves over to sensuality so as to indulge in every kind of impurity, with a continual lust for more.

²⁰You, however, did not come to know Christ that way. ²¹Surely you heard of him and were taught in him in accordance with the truth that is in Jesus. ²²You were taught, with regard to your former way of life, to put off your old self, which is being corrupted by its deceitful desires; ²³to be made new in the attitude of your minds; ²⁴and to put on the new self, created to be like God in true righteousness and holiness.

²⁵Therefore each of you must put off falsehood and speak truthfully to his neighbor, for we are all members of one body. ²⁶"In your anger do not sin"*b*: Do not let the sun go down while you are still angry, ²⁷and do not give the devil a foothold. ²⁸He who has been stealing must steal no longer, but must work, doing something useful with his own hands, that he may have something to share with those in need.

²⁹Do not let any unwholesome talk come out of your mouths, but only what is helpful for building others up according to their needs, that it may benefit those who listen. ³⁰And do not grieve the Holy Spirit of God, with whom you were sealed for the day of redemption. ³¹Get rid of all bitterness, rage and anger, brawling and slander, along with every form of malice. ³²Be kind and compassionate to one another, forgiving each other, just as in Christ God forgave you.

WHEN ANGER ENTERS THE MIND, WISDOM DEPARTS.   —*Thomas à Kempis*

---

5 Be imitators of God, therefore, as dearly loved children ²and live a life of love, just as Christ loved us and gave himself up for us as a fragrant offering and sacrifice to God.

³But among you there must not be even a hint of sexual immorality, or of any kind of impurity, or of greed, because these are improper for God's holy people. ⁴Nor should there be obscenity, foolish talk or coarse joking, which are out of place, but rather thanksgiving. ⁵For of this you can be sure: No immoral, impure or greedy person—such a man is an idolater—has any inheritance in the kingdom of Christ and of God.*c* ⁶Let no one deceive you with empty words, for because of such things God's wrath comes on those who are disobedient. ⁷Therefore do not be partners with them.

⁸For you were once darkness, but now you are light in the Lord. Live as children of light ⁹(for the fruit of the light consists in all goodness, righteousness and truth) ¹⁰and find out what pleases the Lord. ¹¹Have nothing to do with the fruitless deeds of darkness, but rather expose them. ¹²For it is shameful even to mention what the disobedient do in

---

a 9 Or *the depths of the earth*   *b* 26 Psalm 4:4   *c* 5 Or *kingdom of the Christ and God*

secret. 13But everything exposed by the light becomes visible, 14for it is light that makes everything visible. This is why it is said:

"Wake up, O sleeper,
 rise from the dead,
 and Christ will shine on you."

15Be very careful, then, how you live—not as unwise but as wise, 16making the most of every opportunity, because the days are evil. 17Therefore do not be foolish, but understand what the Lord's will is. 18Do not get drunk on wine, which leads to debauchery. Instead, be filled with the Spirit. 19Speak to one another with psalms, hymns and spiritual songs. Sing and make music in your heart to the Lord, 20always giving thanks to God the Father for everything, in the name of our Lord Jesus Christ.

21Submit to one another out of reverence for Christ.

Wives and Husbands

22Wives, submit to your husbands as to the Lord. 23For the husband is the head of the wife as Christ is the head of the church, his body, of which he is the Savior. 24Now as the church submits to Christ, so also wives should submit to their husbands in everything.

25Husbands, love your wives, just as Christ loved the church and gave himself up for her 26to make her holy, cleansing*a* her by the washing with water through the word, 27and to present her to himself as a radiant church, without stain or wrinkle or any other blemish, but holy and blameless. 28In this same way, husbands ought to love their wives as their own bodies. He who loves his wife loves himself. 29After all, no one ever hated his own body, but he feeds and cares for it, just as Christ does the church— 30for we are members of his body. 31"For this reason a man will leave his father and mother and be united to his wife, and the two will become one flesh."*b* 32This is a profound mystery— but I am talking about Christ and the church. 33However, each one of you also must love his wife as he loves himself, and the wife must respect her husband.

Children and Parents

6 Children, obey your parents in the Lord, for this is right. 2"Honor your father and mother"— which is the first commandment with a promise— 3"that it may go well with you and that you may enjoy long life on the earth."*c*

4Fathers, do not exasperate your children; instead, bring them up in the training and instruction of the Lord.

Slaves and Masters

5Slaves, obey your earthly masters with respect and fear, and with sincerity of heart, just as you would obey Christ. 6Obey them not only to win their favor when their eye is on you, but like slaves of Christ, doing the will of God from your heart. 7Serve wholeheartedly, as if you were serving the Lord, not men, 8because you know that the Lord will reward everyone for whatever good he does, whether he is slave or free.

9And masters, treat your slaves in the same way. Do not threaten them, since you know that he who is both their Master and yours is in heaven, and there is no favoritism with him.

The Armor of God

10Finally, be strong in the Lord and in his mighty power. 11Put on the full armor of God so that you can take your stand against the devil's schemes. 12For our struggle is not against flesh and blood, but against the rulers, against the authorities, against the powers of this dark world and against the spiritual forces of evil in the heavenly realms. 13Therefore put on the full armor of God, so that when the day of evil comes, you may be able to stand your ground, and after you have done everything, to stand. 14Stand firm then, with the belt of truth buckled around your waist, with the breastplate of righteousness in place, 15and with your feet fitted with the readiness that comes from the gospel of peace. 16In addition to all this, take up the shield of faith, with which you can extinguish all the flaming arrows of the evil one. 17Take the helmet of salvation and the sword of the

---

a 26 Or *having cleansed*   *b 31* Gen. 2:24   *c 3* Deut. 5:16

THE LORD'S INVITATION
Benedict of Nursia

VERSE: Ephesians 5:14   **PASSAGE:** Ephesians 5:8–14

et us then rise at length, since the Scripture arouseth us, saying: "It is now the hour for us to rise from sleep;" and having opened our eyes to the deifying light, let us hear with awestruck ears what the divine voice, crying our daily, doth admonish us, saying: "Today, if you shall hear his voice, harden not your hearts" (Hebrews 3:15, KJV). And again: "He that hath ears to hear let him hear what the Spirit saith to the churches" (see Revelation 2:7). And what doth he say?—"Come, children, hearken unto me, I will teach you the fear of the Lord" (Psalm 34:11). "Run whilst you have the light of life, that the darkness of death overtake you not."

And the Lord seeking his workman in the multitude of the people, to whom he proclaimeth these words, saith again: "Who is the man that desireth life and loveth to see good days?" (see 1 Peter 3:10). If hearing this thou answerest, "I am he," God saith to thee: "If thou wilt have true and everlasting life, keep thy tongue from evil, and thy lips from speaking guile; turn away from evil and do good; seek after peace and pursue it" (see Psalm 34:12–14). And when you shall have done these things, my eyes shall be upon you, and my ears unto your prayers. And before you shall call upon me I will say: "Behold, I am here."

What, dearest brethren, can be sweeter to us than this voice of the Lord inviting us? See, in his loving kindness, the Lord showeth us the way to life. Therefore, having our loins girt with faith and the performance of good works, let us walk his ways under the guidance of the gospel, that we may be found worthy of seeing him who hath called us to his kingdom. If we desire to dwell in the tabernacle of his kingdom, we cannot reach it in any way, unless we run thither by good works. But let us ask the Lord with the prophet, saying to him: "Lord, who shall dwell in thy tabernacle, or who shall rest in thy holy hill?" (Psalm 15:1).

ADDITIONAL SCRIPTURE READING:
Psalm 23:6; 1 Peter 3:11

Go to page 1387 for your next devotional reading.

Spirit, which is the word of God. [18]And pray in the Spirit on all occasions with all kinds of prayers and requests. With this in mind, be alert and always keep on praying for all the saints.

THE CHRISTIAN PRAYS IN EVERY SITUATION, IN HIS WALKS FOR RECREATION, IN HIS DEALINGS WITH OTHERS, IN SILENCE, IN READING, IN ALL RATIONAL PURSUITS.   —Clement of Alexandria

---

[19]Pray also for me, that whenever I open my mouth, words may be given me so that I will fearlessly make known the mystery of the gospel, [20]for which I am an ambassador in chains. Pray that I may declare it fearlessly, as I should.

Final Greetings

[21]Tychicus, the dear brother and faithful servant in the Lord, will tell you everything, so that you also may know how I am and what I am doing. [22]I am sending him to you for this very purpose, that you may know how we are, and that he may encourage you.

[23]Peace to the brothers, and love with faith from God the Father and the Lord Jesus Christ. [24]Grace to all who love our Lord Jesus Christ with an undying love.

PHILIPPIANS

AUL WROTE TO THE PHILIPPIANS DURING HIS FIRST ROMAN IM-PRISONMENT TO THANK THEM FOR THEIR LOVE AND HELP AND TO WARN THEM AGAINST FALSE TEACHERS. THE THEME OF THE BOOK IS "JOY" (THE WORD "JOY" IN ITS VARIOUS FORMS OCCURS 16 TIMES). BE ALERT TO PAUL'S WARNINGS AGAINST PRIDE AND A SELF-SEEKING ATTITUDE THAT CAN LEAD TO HARMFUL DIVISIONS. HOLD ON TO THE PRACTICAL TOOLS PAUL PROVIDES TO HELP YOU RESHAPE YOUR THINKING ACCORD-ING TO GOD'S WAYS.

1

Paul and Timothy, servants of Christ Jesus,

To all the saints in Christ Jesus at Philippi, together with the overseers*a* and deacons:

²Grace and peace to you from God our Father and the Lord Jesus Christ.

Thanksgiving and Prayer

³I thank my God every time I remember you. ⁴In all my prayers for all of you, I always pray with joy ⁵because of your partnership in the gospel from the first day until now, ⁶being confident of this, that he who began a good work in you will carry it on to completion until the day of Christ Jesus.

⁷It is right for me to feel this way about all of you, since I have you in my heart; for whether I am in chains or defending and confirming the gospel, all of you share in God's grace with me.

> A CHRISTIAN IS NEVER IN A STATE OF COMPLE-TION BUT ALWAYS IN THE PROCESS OF BECOMING.
> —*Martin Luther*

⁸God can testify how I long for all of you with the affection of Christ Jesus.

⁹And this is my prayer: that your love may abound more and more in knowledge and depth of insight, ¹⁰so that you may be able to discern what is best and may be pure and blameless until the day

---

a 1 Traditionally *bishops*

of Christ, [11]filled with the fruit of righteousness that comes through Jesus Christ—to the glory and praise of God.

Paul's Chains Advance the Gospel

[12]Now I want you to know, brothers, that what has happened to me has really served to advance the gospel. [13]As a result, it has become clear throughout the whole palace guard[a] and to everyone else that I am in chains for Christ. [14]Because of my chains, most of the brothers in the Lord have been encouraged to speak the word of God more courageously and fearlessly.

[15]It is true that some preach Christ out of envy and rivalry, but others out of goodwill. [16]The latter do so in love, knowing that I am put here for the defense of the gospel. [17]The former

a 13 Or *whole palace*

TUESDAY

THE WONDERFUL, UNSPEAKABLE MYSTERY
Martin Luther

VERSE: Philippians 2:8 **PASSAGE:** Philippians 2:6–10

All the wisdom of the world is childish foolishness in comparison with the acknowledgment of Christ. For what is more wonderful than the unspeakable mystery, that the Son of God, the image of the eternal Father, took upon him the nature of man. Doubtless, he helped his supposed father, Joseph, to build houses; for Joseph was a carpenter. What will they of Nazareth think at the day of judgment, when they shall see Christ sitting in his divine majesty; surely they will be astonished, and say: Lord, thou helpest build my house, how comest thou now to this high honor?

When Jesus was born, doubtless, he cried and wept like other children, and his mother tended him as other mothers tend their children. As he grew up, he was submissive to his parents, and waited on them, and carried his supposed father's dinner to him, and when he came back, Mary, no doubt, often said: "My dear little Jesus, where hast thou been?" (see Luke 2:48). He that takes not offense at the simple, lowly, and mean course of the life of Christ, is endued with high divine art and wisdom; yea, has a special gift of God in the Holy Ghost. Let us ever bear in mind, that our blessed Savior thus humbled and abased himself, yielding even to the contumelious death of the cross, for the comfort of us poor, miserable, and damned creatures.

ADDITIONAL SCRIPTURE READING:
John 10:9–10; 1 Corinthians 2:1–10

Go to page 1389 for your next devotional reading.

1500   1700

preach Christ out of selfish ambition, not sincerely, supposing that they can stir up trouble for me while I am in chains.[a] [18]But what does it matter? The important thing is that in every way, whether from false motives or true, Christ is preached. And because of this I rejoice.

WHEREVER THE WORD OF GOD IS PREACHED AND HEARD, THERE A CHURCH OF GOD EXISTS, EVEN IF IT SWARMS WITH MANY FAULTS.   —*John Calvin*

Yes, and I will continue to rejoice, [19]for I know that through your prayers and the help given by the Spirit of Jesus Christ, what has happened to me will turn out for my deliverance.[b] [20]I eagerly expect and hope that I will in no way be ashamed, but will have sufficient courage so that now as always Christ will be exalted in my body, whether by life or by death. [21]For to me, to live is Christ and to die is gain. [22]If I am to go on living in the body, this will mean fruitful labor for me. Yet what shall I choose? I do not know! [23]I am torn between the two: I desire to depart and be with Christ, which is better by far; [24]but it is more necessary for you that I remain in the body. [25]Convinced of this, I know that I will remain, and I will continue with all of you for your progress and joy in the faith, [26]so that through my being with you again your joy in Christ Jesus will overflow on account of me.

[27]Whatever happens, conduct yourselves in a manner worthy of the gospel of Christ. Then, whether I come and see you or only hear about you in my absence, I will know that you stand firm in one spirit, contending as one man for the faith of the gospel [28]without being frightened in any way by those who oppose you. This is a sign to them that they will be destroyed, but that you will be saved—and that by God. [29]For it has been granted to you on behalf of Christ not only to believe on him, but also to suffer for him, [30]since you are going through the same struggle you saw I had, and now hear that I still have.

Imitating Christ's Humility

2 If you have any encouragement from being united with Christ, if any comfort from his love, if any fellowship with the Spirit, if any tenderness and compassion, [2]then make my joy complete by being like-minded, having the same love, being one in spirit and purpose. [3]Do nothing out of selfish ambition or vain conceit, but in humility consider others better than yourselves. [4]Each of you should look not only to your own interests, but also to the interests of others.

[5]Your attitude should be the same as that of Christ Jesus:

[6]Who, being in very nature[c] God,
did not consider equality with God
something to be grasped,
[7]but made himself nothing,
taking the very nature[d] of a
servant,
being made in human likeness.
[8]And being found in appearance as a
man,
he humbled himself
and became obedient to death—
even death on a cross!
[9]Therefore God exalted him to the
highest place
and gave him the name that is
above every name,

HE LEFT HIS FATHER'S THRONE ABOVE,
SO FREE, SO INFINITE HIS GRACE!
EMPTIED HIMSELF OF ALL BUT LOVE,
AND BLED FOR ADAM'S HELPLESS RACE.
—*Charles Wesley*

---

[10]that at the name of Jesus every knee
should bow,
in heaven and on earth and under
the earth,
[11]and every tongue confess that Jesus
Christ is Lord,
to the glory of God the Father.

Shining as Stars

[12]Therefore, my dear friends, as you have always obeyed—not only in my

---

[a] *16,17* Some late manuscripts have verses 16 and 17 in reverse order.   [b] *19* Or *salvation*   [c] *6* Or *in the form of*   [d] *7* Or *the form*

presence, but now much more in my absence—continue to work out your salvation with fear and trembling, 13for it is God who works in you to will and to act according to his good purpose.

14Do everything without complaining or arguing, 15so that you may become blameless and pure, children of God without fault in a crooked and depraved generation, in which you shine like stars in the universe 16as you hold out*a* the word of life—in order that I may boast

a 16 Or *hold on to*

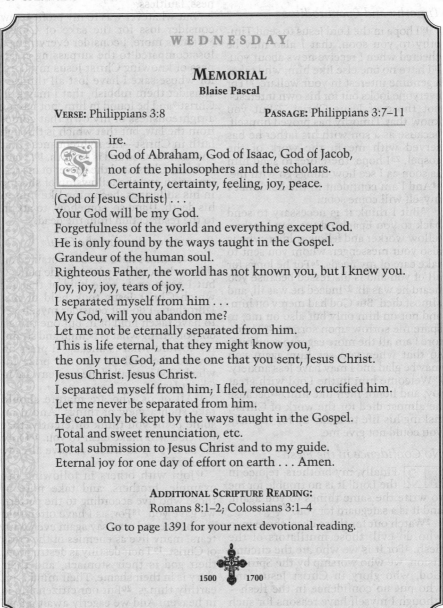

WEDNESDAY

MEMORIAL
Blaise Pascal

VERSE: Philippians 3:8   **PASSAGE:** Philippians 3:7–11

ire.
God of Abraham, God of Isaac, God of Jacob,
not of the philosophers and the scholars.
Certainty, certainty, feeling, joy, peace.
(God of Jesus Christ) . . .
Your God will be my God.
Forgetfulness of the world and everything except God.
He is only found by the ways taught in the Gospel.
Grandeur of the human soul.
Righteous Father, the world has not known you, but I knew you.
Joy, joy, joy, tears of joy.
I separated myself from him . . .
My God, will you abandon me?
Let me not be eternally separated from him.
This is life eternal, that they might know you,
the only true God, and the one that you sent, Jesus Christ.
Jesus Christ. Jesus Christ.
I separated myself from him; I fled, renounced, crucified him.
Let me never be separated from him.
He can only be kept by the ways taught in the Gospel.
Total and sweet renunciation, etc.
Total submission to Jesus Christ and to my guide.
Eternal joy for one day of effort on earth . . . Amen.

ADDITIONAL SCRIPTURE READING:
Romans 8:1–2; Colossians 3:1–4

Go to page 1391 for your next devotional reading.

1500   1700

on the day of Christ that I did not run or labor for nothing. [17]But even if I am being poured out like a drink offering on the sacrifice and service coming from your faith, I am glad and rejoice with all of you. [18]So you too should be glad and rejoice with me.

Timothy and Epaphroditus

[19]I hope in the Lord Jesus to send Timothy to you soon, that I also may be cheered when I receive news about you. [20]I have no one else like him, who takes a genuine interest in your welfare. [21]For everyone looks out for his own interests, not those of Jesus Christ. [22]But you know that Timothy has proved himself, because as a son with his father he has served with me in the work of the gospel. [23]I hope, therefore, to send him as soon as I see how things go with me. [24]And I am confident in the Lord that I myself will come soon.

[25]But I think it is necessary to send back to you Epaphroditus, my brother, fellow worker and fellow soldier, who is also your messenger, whom you sent to take care of my needs. [26]For he longs for all of you and is distressed because you heard he was ill. [27]Indeed he was ill, and almost died. But God had mercy on him, and not on him only but also on me, to spare me sorrow upon sorrow. [28]Therefore I am all the more eager to send him, so that when you see him again you may be glad and I may have less anxiety. [29]Welcome him in the Lord with great joy, and honor men like him, [30]because he almost died for the work of Christ, risking his life to make up for the help you could not give me.

No Confidence in the Flesh

3 Finally, my brothers, rejoice in the Lord! It is no trouble for me to write the same things to you again, and it is a safeguard for you.

[2]Watch out for those dogs, those men who do evil, those mutilators of the flesh. [3]For it is we who are the circumcision, we who worship by the Spirit of God, who glory in Christ Jesus, and who put no confidence in the flesh— [4]though I myself have reasons for such confidence.

If anyone else thinks he has reasons to put confidence in the flesh, I have more: [5]circumcised on the eighth day, of the people of Israel, of the tribe of Benjamin, a Hebrew of Hebrews; in regard to the law, a Pharisee; [6]as for zeal, persecuting the church; as for legalistic righteousness, faultless.

[7]But whatever was to my profit I now consider loss for the sake of Christ. [8]What is more, I consider everything a loss compared to the surpassing greatness of knowing Christ Jesus my Lord, for whose sake I have lost all things. I consider them rubbish, that I may gain Christ [9]and be found in him, not having a righteousness of my own that comes from the law, but that which is through faith in Christ—the righteousness that comes from God and is by faith. [10]I want to know Christ and the power of his resurrection and the fellowship of sharing in his sufferings, becoming like him in his death, [11]and so, somehow, to attain to the resurrection from the dead.

Pressing on Toward the Goal

[12]Not that I have already obtained all this, or have already been made perfect, but I press on to take hold of that for which Christ Jesus took hold of me. [13]Brothers, I do not consider myself yet to have taken hold of it. But one thing I do: Forgetting what is behind and straining toward what is ahead, [14]I press on toward the goal to win the prize for which God has called me heavenward in Christ Jesus.

[15]All of us who are mature should take such a view of things. And if on some point you think differently, that too God will make clear to you. [16]Only let us live up to what we have already attained.

[17]Join with others in following my example, brothers, and take note of those who live according to the pattern we gave you. [18]For, as I have often told you before and now say again even with tears, many live as enemies of the cross of Christ. [19]Their destiny is destruction, their god is their stomach, and their glory is in their shame. Their mind is on earthly things. [20]But our citizenship is in heaven. And we eagerly await a Savior from there, the Lord Jesus Christ,

21who, by the power that enables him to bring everything under his control, will transform our lowly bodies so that they will be like his glorious body.

4 Therefore, my brothers, you whom I love and long for, my joy and crown, that is how you should stand firm in the Lord, dear friends!

THE ESSENCE OF THE GOSPEL
Dietrich Bonhoeffer

VERSE: Philippians 4:6   **PASSAGE:** Philippians 4:4–7

Anxiety is characteristic of the Gentiles, for they rely on their own strength and work instead of relying on God. They do not know that the Father knows that we have need of all these things, and so they try to do for themselves what they do not expect from God. But the disciples know that the rule is "Seek first his kingdom and his righteousness, and all these things will be given to you as well" (Matthew 6:33). Anxiety for food and clothing is clearly not the same thing as anxiety for the kingdom of God, however much we should like to persuade ourselves that when we are working for our families and concerning ourselves with bread and houses we are thereby building the kingdom, as though the kingdom could be realized only through our worldly cares. The kingdom of God and his righteousness are sharply distinguished from the gifts of the world which come our way. That kingdom is none other than the righteousness of Matthew 5 and 6, the righteousness of the cross and of following Christ beneath that cross. Fellowship with Jesus and obedience to his commandment come first, and all else follows. Worldly cares are not a part of our discipleship, but distinct and subordinate concerns. Before we start taking thought for our life, our food and clothing, our work and families, we must seek the righteousness of Christ . . . If we follow Jesus and look only to his righteousness, we are in his hands and under the protection of him and his Father. And if we are in communion with the Father, nought can harm us. We shall always be assured that he can feed his children and will not suffer them to hunger. God will help us in the hour of need, and he knows our needs.

ADDITIONAL SCRIPTURE READING:
Psalm 111:5; 1 Peter 5:7

Go to page 1395 for your next devotional reading.

1900   Present

Exhortations

2I plead with Euodia and I plead with Syntyche to agree with each other in the Lord. **3**Yes, and I ask you, loyal yokefellow,*a* help these women who have contended at my side in the cause of the gospel, along with Clement and the rest of my fellow workers, whose names are in the book of life.

4Rejoice in the Lord always. I will say it again: Rejoice! **5**Let your gentleness be evident to all. The Lord is near. **6**Do not be anxious about anything, but in everything, by prayer and petition, with thanksgiving, present your requests to God. **7**And the peace of God, which transcends all understanding, will guard your hearts and your minds in Christ Jesus.

THE BEGINNING OF ANXIETY IS THE END OF FAITH; AND THE BEGINNING OF TRUE FAITH IS THE END OF ANXIETY. —*George Muller*

8Finally, brothers, whatever is true, whatever is noble, whatever is right, whatever is pure, whatever is lovely, whatever is admirable—if anything is excellent or praiseworthy—think about such things. **9**Whatever you have learned or received or heard from me, or seen in me—put it into practice. And the God of peace will be with you.

Thanks for Their Gifts

10I rejoice greatly in the Lord that at last you have renewed your concern for me. Indeed, you have been concerned, but you had no opportunity to show it. **11**I am not saying this because I am in need, for I have learned to be content whatever the circumstances. **12**I know what it is to be in need, and I know what it is to have plenty. I have learned the secret of being content in any and every situation, whether well fed or hungry, whether living in plenty or in want. **13**I can do everything through him who gives me strength.

IF WE HAD NOT WINTER, THE SPRING WOULD NOT BE SO PLEASANT; IF WE DID NOT SOMETIMES TASTE OF ADVERSITY, PROSPERITY WOULD NOT BE SO WELCOME. —*Anne Bradstreet*

14Yet it was good of you to share in my troubles. **15**Moreover, as you Philippians know, in the early days of your acquaintance with the gospel, when I set out from Macedonia, not one church shared with me in the matter of giving and receiving, except you only; **16**for even when I was in Thessalonica, you sent me aid again and again when I was in need. **17**Not that I am looking for a gift, but I am looking for what may be credited to your account. **18**I have received full payment and even more; I am amply supplied, now that I have received from Epaphroditus the gifts you sent. They are a fragrant offering, an acceptable sacrifice, pleasing to God. **19**And my God will meet all your needs according to his glorious riches in Christ Jesus.

20To our God and Father be glory for ever and ever. Amen.

Final Greetings

21Greet all the saints in Christ Jesus. The brothers who are with me send greetings. **22**All the saints send you greetings, especially those who belong to Caesar's household.

23The grace of the Lord Jesus Christ be with your spirit. Amen.*b*

COLOSSIANS

URING PAUL'S THREE-YEAR MINISTRY IN EPHESUS, EPAPHRAS HAD BEEN CONVERTED AND HAD CARRIED THE GOSPEL TO COLOSSE. THE YOUNG CHURCH THAT RESULTED THEN BECAME THE TARGET OF HERETICAL ATTACK, WHICH LED TO THE PENNING OF THIS LETTER. PAUL'S PURPOSE IS TO REFUTE THE FALSE TEACHERS, WHICH HE DOES BY ASSERTING THE SUPREMACY OF CHRIST AND EXAMINING WHAT THAT MEANS FOR EVERYDAY LIVING. AS YOU READ THIS LETTER, LOOK FOR INSIGHTS ON WAYS TO FORM ATTITUDES AND CARRY OUT ACTIONS THAT HONOR THE LORD.

1 Paul, an apostle of Christ Jesus by the will of God, and Timothy our brother,

2To the holy and faithful*a* brothers in Christ at Colosse:

Grace and peace to you from God our Father.*b*

Thanksgiving and Prayer

3We always thank God, the Father of our Lord Jesus Christ, when we pray for you, 4because we have heard of your faith in Christ Jesus and of the love you have for all the saints— 5the faith and love that spring from the hope that is stored up for you in heaven and that you have already heard about in the word of truth, the gospel 6that has come to you. All over the world this gospel is bearing fruit and growing, just as it has been doing among you since the day you heard it and understood God's grace in all its truth. 7You learned it from Epaphras, our dear fellow servant, who is a faithful minister of Christ on our*c* behalf, 8and who also told us of your love in the Spirit.

9For this reason, since the day we heard about you, we have not stopped praying for you and asking God to fill you with the knowledge of his will through all spiritual wisdom and understanding. 10And we pray this in order that you may live a life worthy of the Lord and may please him in every way:

---

a 2 Or *believing*   *b 2* Some manuscripts *Father and the Lord Jesus Christ*   *c 7* Some manuscripts *your* bearing fruit in every good work, growing in the knowledge of God, [11]being strengthened with all power according to his glorious might so that you may have great endurance and patience, and joyfully [12]giving thanks to the Father, who has qualified you[a] to share in the inheritance of the saints in the kingdom of light. [13]For he has rescued us from the dominion of darkness and brought us into the kingdom of the Son he loves, [14]in whom we have redemption,[b] the forgiveness of sins.

> I BELIEVE IN THE FORGIVENESS OF SINS.
> —*The Apostles' Creed*

The Supremacy of Christ

[15]He is the image of the invisible God, the firstborn over all creation. [16]For by him all things were created: things in heaven and on earth, visible and invisible, whether thrones or powers or rulers or authorities; all things were created by him and for him. [17]He is before all things, and in him all things hold together. [18]And he is the head of the body, the church; he is the beginning and the firstborn from among the dead, so that in everything he might have the supremacy. [19]For God was pleased to have all his fullness dwell in him, [20]and through him to reconcile to himself all things, whether things on earth or things in heaven, by making peace through his blood, shed on the cross. [21]Once you were alienated from God and were enemies in your minds because of[c] your evil behavior. [22]But now he has reconciled you by Christ's physical body through death to present you holy in his sight, without blemish and free from accusation— [23]if you continue in your faith, established and firm, not moved from the hope held out in the gospel. This is the gospel that you heard and that has been proclaimed to every creature under heaven, and of which I, Paul, have become a servant.

Paul's Labor for the Church

[24]Now I rejoice in what was suffered for you, and I fill up in my flesh what is still lacking in regard to Christ's afflictions, for the sake of his body, which is the church. [25]I have become its servant by the commission God gave me to present to you the word of God in its fullness— [26]the mystery that has been kept hidden for ages and generations, but is now disclosed to the saints. [27]To them God has chosen to make known among the Gentiles the glorious riches of this mystery, which is Christ in you, the hope of glory.

[28]We proclaim him, admonishing and teaching everyone with all wisdom, so that we may present everyone perfect in Christ. [29]To this end I labor, struggling with all his energy, which so powerfully works in me.

2 I want you to know how much I am struggling for you and for those at Laodicea, and for all who have not met me personally. [2]My purpose is that they may be encouraged in heart and united in love, so that they may have the full riches of complete understanding, in order that they may know the mystery of God, namely, Christ, [3]in whom are hidden all the treasures of wisdom and knowledge. [4]I tell you this so that no one may deceive you by fine-sounding arguments. [5]For though I am absent from you in body, I am present with you in spirit and delight to see how orderly you are and how firm your faith in Christ is.

Freedom From Human Regulations Through Life With Christ

[6]So then, just as you received Christ Jesus as Lord, continue to live in him, [7]rooted and built up in him, strengthened in the faith as you were taught, and overflowing with thankfulness.

[8]See to it that no one takes you captive through hollow and deceptive philosophy, which depends on human tradition and the basic principles of this world rather than on Christ.

[9]For in Christ all the fullness of the Deity lives in bodily form, [10]and you have been given fullness in Christ, who is the head over every power and authority. [11]In him you were also circumcised,

---

[a] 12 Some manuscripts *us*   [b] 14 A few late manuscripts *redemption through his blood*   [c] 21 Or *minds, as shown by*

in the putting off of the sinful nature,[a] not with a circumcision done by the hands of men but with the circumcision done by Christ, [12]having been buried with him in baptism and raised with him through your faith in the power of God, who raised him from the dead.

[13]When you were dead in your sins and in the uncircumcision of your sinful nature,[b] God made you[c] alive with Christ. He forgave us all our sins, [14]having canceled the written code, with its regulations, that was against us and that stood opposed to us; he took it away, nailing it to the cross. [15]And having disarmed the powers and authorities, he made a public spectacle of them, triumphing over them by the cross.[d]

[16]Therefore do not let anyone judge you by what you eat or drink, or with regard to a religious festival, a New Moon celebration or a Sabbath day. [17]These are a shadow of the things that were to come; the reality, however, is found in Christ. [18]Do not let anyone who delights in false humility and the worship of angels disqualify you for the prize. Such a person goes into great detail about what he has seen, and his unspiritual mind puffs him up with idle notions. [19]He has lost connection with the Head, from whom the whole body, supported and held together by its ligaments and sinews, grows as God causes it to grow.

[20]Since you died with Christ to the basic principles of this world, why, as though you still belonged to it, do you submit to its rules: [21]"Do not handle! Do not taste! Do not touch!"? [22]These are all destined to perish with use,

a 11 Or *the flesh*   *b* 13 Or *your flesh*   *c* 13 Some manuscripts *us*   *d* 15 Or *them in him*

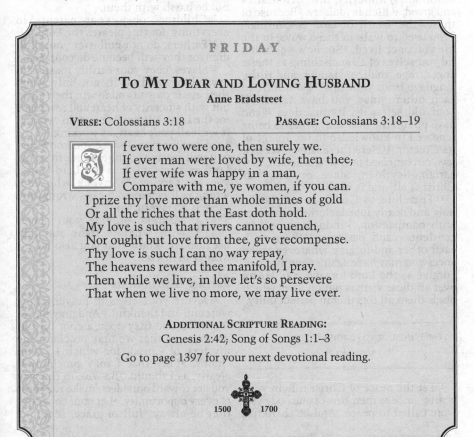

FRIDAY

TO MY DEAR AND LOVING HUSBAND
Anne Bradstreet

VERSE: Colossians 3:18   **PASSAGE:** Colossians 3:18–19

If ever two were one, then surely we.
If ever man were loved by wife, then thee;
If ever wife was happy in a man,
Compare with me, ye women, if you can.
I prize thy love more than whole mines of gold
Or all the riches that the East doth hold.
My love is such that rivers cannot quench,
Nor ought but love from thee, give recompense.
Thy love is such I can no way repay,
The heavens reward thee manifold, I pray.
Then while we live, in love let's so persevere
That when we live no more, we may live ever.

ADDITIONAL SCRIPTURE READING:
Genesis 2:42; Song of Songs 1:1–3

Go to page 1397 for your next devotional reading.

1500   1700

because they are based on human commands and teachings. 23Such regulations indeed have an appearance of wisdom, with their self-imposed worship, their false humility and their harsh treatment of the body, but they lack any value in restraining sensual indulgence.

Rules for Holy Living

3 Since, then, you have been raised with Christ, set your hearts on things above, where Christ is seated at the right hand of God. 2Set your minds on things above, not on earthly things. 3For you died, and your life is now hidden with Christ in God. 4When Christ, who is your*a* life, appears, then you also will appear with him in glory.

5Put to death, therefore, whatever belongs to your earthly nature: sexual immorality, impurity, lust, evil desires and greed, which is idolatry. 6Because of these, the wrath of God is coming.*b* 7You used to walk in these ways, in the life you once lived. 8But now you must rid yourselves of all such things as these: anger, rage, malice, slander, and filthy language from your lips. 9Do not lie to each other, since you have taken off your old self with its practices 10and have put on the new self, which is being renewed in knowledge in the image of its Creator. 11Here there is no Greek or Jew, circumcised or uncircumcised, barbarian, Scythian, slave or free, but Christ is all, and is in all.

12Therefore, as God's chosen people, holy and dearly loved, clothe yourselves with compassion, kindness, humility, gentleness and patience. 13Bear with each other and forgive whatever grievances you may have against one another. Forgive as the Lord forgave you. 14And over all these virtues put on love, which binds them all together in perfect unity.

TO ERR IS HUMAN, TO FORGIVE DIVINE.

—*Alexander Pope*

15Let the peace of Christ rule in your hearts, since as members of one body you were called to peace. And be thankful.

16Let the word of Christ dwell in you richly as you teach and admonish one another with all wisdom, and as you sing psalms, hymns and spiritual songs with gratitude in your hearts to God. 17And whatever you do, whether in word or deed, do it all in the name of the Lord Jesus, giving thanks to God the Father through him.

A CHILD OF GOD SHOULD BE A VISIBLE BEATITUDE FOR JOY AND HAPPINESS, AND A LIVING DOXOLOGY FOR GRATITUDE AND ADORATION.

—*C. H. Spurgeon*

Rules for Christian Households

18Wives, submit to your husbands, as is fitting in the Lord.

19Husbands, love your wives and do not be harsh with them.

20Children, obey your parents in everything, for this pleases the Lord.

21Fathers, do not embitter your children, or they will become discouraged.

22Slaves, obey your earthly masters in everything; and do it, not only when their eye is on you and to win their favor, but with sincerity of heart and reverence for the Lord. 23Whatever you do, work at it with all your heart, as working for the Lord, not for men, 24since you know that you will receive an inheritance from the Lord as a reward. It is the Lord Christ you are serving. 25Anyone who does wrong will be repaid for his wrong, and there is no favoritism.

4 Masters, provide your slaves with what is right and fair, because you know that you also have a Master in heaven.

Further Instructions

2Devote yourselves to prayer, being watchful and thankful. 3And pray for us, too, that God may open a door for our message, so that we may proclaim the mystery of Christ, for which I am in chains. 4Pray that I may proclaim it clearly, as I should. 5Be wise in the way you act toward outsiders; make the most of every opportunity. 6Let your conversation be always full of grace, seasoned

---

a 4 Some manuscripts *our*   *b* 6 Some early manuscripts *coming on those who are disobedient*

WEEKEND

SAVED BY GRACE
Fanny Crosby

VERSE: Ephesians 2:8   **PASSAGE:** Ephesians 2:4–10

omeday the silver cord will break,
And I no more as now shall sing.
But, oh, the joy when I shall wake
Within the palace of the King!

Someday my earthly house will fall;
I cannot tell how soon 'twill be,
But this I know—my All in All
Has now a place in heav'n for me.

Someday, when fades the golden sun
Beneath the rosy-tinted west,
My blessed Lord will say, "Well done!"
And I shall enter into rest.

Someday, till then I'll watch and wait,
My lamp all trimmed and burning bright,
That when my Savior opes the gate,
My soul to him may take its flight.

And I shall see him face to face,
And tell the story—saved by grace:
And I shall see him face to face,
And tell the story—saved by grace.

ADDITIONAL SCRIPTURE READING:
John 14:23; 1 Corinthians 13:12

Go to page 1400 for your next devotional reading.

1700   1900

with salt, so that you may know how to answer everyone.

Final Greetings

7Tychicus will tell you all the news about me. He is a dear brother, a faithful minister and fellow servant in the Lord. 8I am sending him to you for the express purpose that you may know about our*a* circumstances and that he may encourage your hearts. 9He is coming with Onesimus, our faithful and dear brother, who is one of you. They will tell you everything that is happening here.

10My fellow prisoner Aristarchus sends you his greetings, as does Mark, the cousin of Barnabas. (You have received instructions about him; if he comes to you, welcome him.) 11Jesus, who is called Justus, also sends greetings. These are the only Jews among my fellow workers for the kingdom of God, and they have proved a comfort to me.

12Epaphras, who is one of you and a servant of Christ Jesus, sends greetings. He is always wrestling in prayer for you, that you may stand firm in all the will of God, mature and fully assured. 13I vouch for him that he is working hard for you and for those at Laodicea and Hierapolis. 14Our dear friend Luke, the doctor, and Demas send greetings. 15Give my greetings to the brothers at Laodicea, and to Nympha and the church in her house.

16After this letter has been read to you, see that it is also read in the church of the Laodiceans and that you in turn read the letter from Laodicea.

17Tell Archippus: "See to it that you complete the work you have received in the Lord."

18I, Paul, write this greeting in my own hand. Remember my chains. Grace be with you.

---

a 8 Some manuscripts *that he may know about your*

1 THESSALONIANS

PAUL FOUNDED THE CHURCH AT THESSALONICA DURING HIS SECOND MISSIONARY JOURNEY. HE WRITES THIS LETTER TO COMMEND THE BELIEVERS THERE FOR GROWING IN THE LORD AND ALSO TO CORRECT SOME MISUNDERSTANDINGS. THE SUBJECT OF CHRIST'S SECOND COMING PERMEATES THE LETTER, WITH EVERY CHAPTER REFERRING TO IT. LOOK FOR GUIDELINES ON CHRISTIAN RELATIONSHIPS AND FOR A PERSPECTIVE ON LIFE THAT IS SHAPED BY PAUL'S EMPHASIS ON ETERNITY.

1

Paul, Silas*a* and Timothy,

To the church of the Thessalonians in God the Father and the Lord Jesus Christ:

Grace and peace to you.*b*

Thanksgiving for the Thessalonians' Faith

2We always thank God for all of you, mentioning you in our prayers. 3We continually remember before our God and Father your work produced by faith, your labor prompted by love, and your endurance inspired by hope in our Lord Jesus Christ.

4For we know, brothers loved by God, that he has chosen you, 5because our gospel came to you not simply with words, but also with power, with the Holy Spirit and with deep conviction. You know how we lived among you for your sake. 6You became imitators of us and of the Lord; in spite of severe suffering, you welcomed the message with the joy given by the Holy Spirit. 7And so you became a model to all the believers in Macedonia and Achaia. 8The Lord's message rang out from you not only in Macedonia and Achaia—your faith in God has become known everywhere. Therefore we do not need to say anything about it, 9for they themselves report what kind of reception you gave us. They tell how you turned to God from idols to serve the living and true God, 10and to wait for his

---

a 1 Greek *Silvanus*, a variant of *Silas*   *b* 1 Some early manuscripts *you from God our Father and the Lord Jesus Christ*

Son from heaven, whom he raised from the dead—Jesus, who rescues us from the coming wrath.

Paul's Ministry in Thessalonica

2 You know, brothers, that our visit to you was not a failure. ²We had previously suffered and been insulted in Philippi, as you know, but with the help of our God we dared to tell you his gospel in spite of strong opposition. ³For the appeal we make does not spring from error or impure motives, nor are we trying to trick you. ⁴On the contrary, we speak as men approved by God to be entrusted with the gospel. We are

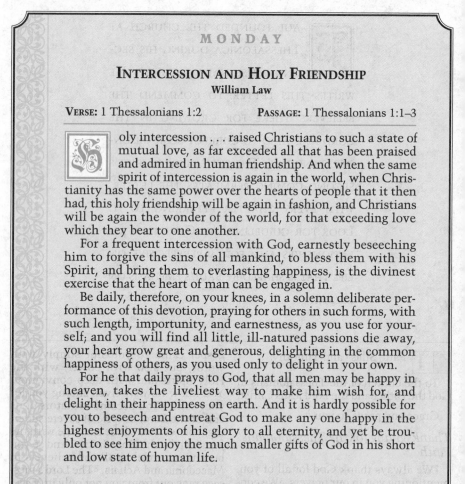

MONDAY

INTERCESSION AND HOLY FRIENDSHIP
William Law

VERSE: 1 Thessalonians 1:2   **PASSAGE:** 1 Thessalonians 1:1–3

oly intercession . . . raised Christians to such a state of mutual love, as far exceeded all that has been praised and admired in human friendship. And when the same spirit of intercession is again in the world, when Christianity has the same power over the hearts of people that it then had, this holy friendship will be again in fashion, and Christians will be again the wonder of the world, for that exceeding love which they bear to one another.

For a frequent intercession with God, earnestly beseeching him to forgive the sins of all mankind, to bless them with his Spirit, and bring them to everlasting happiness, is the divinest exercise that the heart of man can be engaged in.

Be daily, therefore, on your knees, in a solemn deliberate performance of this devotion, praying for others in such forms, with such length, importunity, and earnestness, as you use for yourself; and you will find all little, ill-natured passions die away, your heart grow great and generous, delighting in the common happiness of others, as you used only to delight in your own.

For he that daily prays to God, that all men may be happy in heaven, takes the liveliest way to make him wish for, and delight in their happiness on earth. And it is hardly possible for you to beseech and entreat God to make any one happy in the highest enjoyments of his glory to all eternity, and yet be troubled to see him enjoy the much smaller gifts of God in his short and low state of human life.

ADDITIONAL SCRIPTURE READING:
Romans 8:26–27; Hebrews 7:24–25

Go to page 1402 for your next devotional reading.

1700   1900

not trying to please men but God, who tests our hearts. ⁵You know we never used flattery, nor did we put on a mask to cover up greed—God is our witness.

WHAT MEN CALL FAME IS, AFTER ALL, BUT A VERY WINDY THING. A MAN THINKS THAT MANY ARE PRAISING HIM, AND TALKING OF HIM ALONE, AND YET THEY SPEND BUT A VERY SMALL PART OF THE DAY THINKING OF HIM, BEING OCCUPIED WITH THINGS OF THEIR OWN.   —*Thomas More*

---

⁶We were not looking for praise from men, not from you or anyone else.

As apostles of Christ we could have been a burden to you, ⁷but we were gentle among you, like a mother caring for her little children. ⁸We loved you so much that we were delighted to share with you not only the gospel of God but our lives as well, because you had become so dear to us. ⁹Surely you remember, brothers, our toil and hardship; we worked night and day in order not to be a burden to anyone while we preached the gospel of God to you.

¹⁰You are witnesses, and so is God, of how holy, righteous and blameless we were among you who believed. ¹¹For you know that we dealt with each of you as a father deals with his own children, ¹²encouraging, comforting and urging you to live lives worthy of God, who calls you into his kingdom and glory.

¹³And we also thank God continually because, when you received the word of God, which you heard from us, you accepted it not as the word of men, but as it actually is, the word of God, which is at work in you who believe. ¹⁴For you, brothers, became imitators of God's churches in Judea, which are in Christ Jesus: You suffered from your own countrymen the same things those churches suffered from the Jews, ¹⁵who killed the Lord Jesus and the prophets and also drove us out. They displease God and are hostile to all men ¹⁶in their effort to keep us from speaking to the Gentiles so that they may be saved. In this way they always heap up their sins to the limit.

The wrath of God has come upon them at last.*a*

Paul's Longing to See the Thessalonians

¹⁷But, brothers, when we were torn away from you for a short time (in person, not in thought), out of our intense longing we made every effort to see you. ¹⁸For we wanted to come to you—certainly I, Paul, did, again and again—but Satan stopped us. ¹⁹For what is our hope, our joy, or the crown in which we will glory in the presence of our Lord Jesus when he comes? Is it not you? ²⁰Indeed, you are our glory and joy.

3 So when we could stand it no longer, we thought it best to be left by ourselves in Athens. ²We sent Timothy, who is our brother and God's fellow worker*b* in spreading the gospel of Christ, to strengthen and encourage you in your faith, ³so that no one would be unsettled by these trials. You know quite well that we were destined for them. ⁴In fact, when we were with you, we kept telling you that we would be persecuted. And it turned out that way, as you well know. ⁵For this reason, when I could stand it no longer, I sent to find out about your faith. I was afraid that in some way the tempter might have tempted you and our efforts might have been useless.

Timothy's Encouraging Report

⁶But Timothy has just now come to us from you and has brought good news about your faith and love. He has told us that you always have pleasant memories of us and that you long to see us, just as we also long to see you. ⁷Therefore, brothers, in all our distress and persecution we were encouraged about you because of your faith. ⁸For now we really live, since you are standing firm in the Lord. ⁹How can we thank God enough for you in return for all the joy we have in the presence of our God because of you? ¹⁰Night and day we pray most earnestly that we may see you again and supply what is lacking in your faith.

---

a 16 Or *them fully*   *b* 2 Some manuscripts *brother and fellow worker;* other manuscripts *brother and God's servant*

THE NEEDLE TOUCHED WITH THE LODESTONE
John Owen

VERSE: 1 Thessalonians 4:17 **PASSAGE:** 1 Thessalonians 4:13–18

las! we cannot here think of Christ but we are quickly ashamed of and troubled at our own thoughts: so confused are they, so unsteady, so imperfect. Commonly they issue in a groan or a sigh: "Oh when shall we come unto him? When shall we be ever with him? When shall we see him as he is?" And if at any time he begins to give more than ordinary evidences and intimations of his glory and love unto our souls, we are not able to bear them, so as to give them any abiding residence in our minds. But ordinarily this trouble and groaning is amongst our best attainments in this world, a trouble which, I pray God, I may never be delivered from until deliverance does come at once from this state of mortality. Yea, the good Lord increases this trouble more and more in all that believe.

The heart of a believer affected with the glory of Christ is like the needle touched with the lodestone. It can no longer be quiet, no longer be satisfied in a distance from him. It is put into a continual motion towards him. The motion indeed is weak and tremulous. Pantings, breathings, sighings, groanings, in prayer, in meditations, in the secret recesses of our minds, are the life of it. However, it is continually pressing towards him. But it obtains not its point, it comes not to its center and rest in this world.

But now above, all things are clear and serene, all plain and evident in our beholding the glory of Christ; we shall be ever with him, and see him as he is. This is heaven, this is blessedness, this is eternal rest . . .

But alas! here at present our minds recoil, our meditations fail, our hearts are overcome, our thoughts confused, and our eyes turn aside from the luster of this glory. But there, an immediate, constant view of it will bring in everlasting refreshment and joy unto our whole souls.

ADDITIONAL SCRIPTURE READING:
Job 19:25–27; Philippians 3:12–14

Go to page 1404 for your next devotional reading.

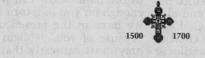

[11] Now may our God and Father himself and our Lord Jesus clear the way for us to come to you. [12] May the Lord make your love increase and overflow for each other and for everyone else, just as ours does for you. [13] May he strengthen your hearts so that you will be blameless and holy in the presence of our God and Father when our Lord Jesus comes with all his holy ones.

Living to Please God

4 Finally, brothers, we instructed you how to live in order to please God, as in fact you are living. Now we ask you and urge you in the Lord Jesus to do this more and more. [2] For you know what instructions we gave you by the authority of the Lord Jesus.

IF YOU BELIEVE WHAT YOU LIKE IN THE GOSPEL, AND REJECT WHAT YOU DON'T LIKE, IT IS NOT THE GOSPEL YOU BELIEVE, BUT YOURSELF.

—*Augustine*

---

[3] It is God's will that you should be sanctified: that you should avoid sexual immorality; [4] that each of you should learn to control his own body[a] in a way that is holy and honorable, [5] not in passionate lust like the heathen, who do not know God; [6] and that in this matter no one should wrong his brother or take advantage of him. The Lord will punish men for all such sins, as we have already told you and warned you. [7] For God did not call us to be impure, but to live a holy life. [8] Therefore, he who rejects this instruction does not reject man but God, who gives you his Holy Spirit.

[9] Now about brotherly love we do not need to write to you, for you yourselves have been taught by God to love each other. [10] And in fact, you do love all the brothers throughout Macedonia. Yet we urge you, brothers, to do so more and more. [11] Make it your ambition to lead a quiet life, to mind your own business and to work with your hands, just as we told you, [12] so that your daily life may win the respect of outsiders and so that you will not be dependent on anybody.

The Coming of the Lord

[13] Brothers, we do not want you to be ignorant about those who fall asleep, or to grieve like the rest of men, who have no hope. [14] We believe that Jesus died and rose again and so we believe that God will bring with Jesus those who have fallen asleep in him. [15] According to the Lord's own word, we tell you that we who are still alive, who are left till the coming of the Lord, will certainly not precede those who have fallen asleep. [16] For the Lord himself will come down from heaven, with a loud command, with the voice of the archangel and with the trumpet call of God, and the dead in Christ will rise first. [17] After that, we who are still alive and are left will be caught up together with them in the clouds to meet the Lord in the air. And so we will be with the Lord forever. [18] Therefore encourage each other with these words.

5 Now, brothers, about times and dates we do not need to write to you, [2] for you know very well that the day of the Lord will come like a thief in the night. [3] While people are saying, "Peace and safety," destruction will come on them suddenly, as labor pains on a pregnant woman, and they will not escape.

[4] But you, brothers, are not in darkness so that this day should surprise you like a thief. [5] You are all sons of the light and sons of the day. We do not belong to the night or to the darkness. [6] So then, let us not be like others, who are asleep, but let us be alert and self-controlled. [7] For those who sleep, sleep at night, and those who get drunk, get drunk at night.

IT IS STILL ONE OF THE TRAGEDIES OF HUMAN HISTORY THAT THE "CHILDREN OF DARKNESS" ARE FREQUENTLY MORE DETERMINED AND ZEALOUS THAN THE "CHILDREN OF LIGHT."

—*Martin Luther King, Jr.*

---

[8] But since we belong to the day, let us be self-controlled, putting on faith and love

---

a 4 Or *learn to live with his own wife;* or *learn to acquire a wife*

CHRIST IS OUR SANCTIFICATION
George Whitefield

VERSE: 1 Thessalonians 5:23   PASSAGE: 1 Thessalonians 5:23–24

 y sanctification I mean a total renovation of the whole man: by the righteousness of Christ, believers come legally, by sanctification they are made spiritually, alive; by the one they are entitled to, by the other they are made meet for, glory. They are sanctified, therefore, throughout, in spirit, soul, and body.

Their understandings, which were dark before, now become light in the Lord; and their wills, before contrary to, now become one with the will of God; their affections are now set on things above; their memory is now filled with divine things; their natural consciences are now enlightened; their members, which were before instruments of uncleanness, and of iniquity into iniquity, are now new creatures; "old things are passed away; all things are become new" (2 Corinthians 5:17, KJV) in their hearts: sin has now no longer dominion over them; they are freed from the power, though not the indwelling and being, of it; they are holy both in heart and life, in all manner of conversation; they are made partakers of a divine nature, and from Jesus Christ, they receive grace; and every grace that is in Christ, is copied and transcribed into their souls; they are transformed into his likeness; he is formed within them; they dwell in him, and he in them; they are led by the Spirit, and bring forth the fruits thereof; they know that Christ is their Emmanuel, God with and in them; they are living temples of the Holy Ghost. And therefore, being a holy habitation unto the Lord, the whole Trinity dwells and walks in them; even here, they sit together with Christ in heavenly places, and are vitally united to him, their head, by a living faith; their Redeemer, their Maker, is their husband; they are flesh of his flesh, bone of his bone; they talk, they walk with him, as a man talketh and walketh with his friend; in short, they are one with Christ, even as Jesus Christ and the Father are one.

ADDITIONAL SCRIPTURE READING:
1 Corinthians 6:11; 1 Thessalonians 5:23

Go to page 1407 for your next devotional reading.

1700   1900

as a breastplate, and the hope of salvation as a helmet. ⁹For God did not appoint us to suffer wrath but to receive salvation through our Lord Jesus Christ. ¹⁰He died for us so that, whether we are awake or asleep, we may live together with him. ¹¹Therefore encourage one another and build each other up, just as in fact you are doing.

Final Instructions

¹²Now we ask you, brothers, to respect those who work hard among you, who are over you in the Lord and who admonish you. ¹³Hold them in the highest regard in love because of their work. Live in peace with each other. ¹⁴And we urge you, brothers, warn those who are idle, encourage the timid, help the weak, be patient with everyone. ¹⁵Make sure that nobody pays back wrong for wrong, but always try to be kind to each other and to everyone else.

¹⁶Be joyful always; ¹⁷pray continually; ¹⁸give thanks in all circumstances, for this is God's will for you in Christ Jesus.

BE CAREFUL FOR NOTHING, PRAYERFUL FOR EVERYTHING, THANKFUL FOR ANYTHING.
—*Dwight L. Moody*

---

¹⁹Do not put out the Spirit's fire; ²⁰do not treat prophecies with contempt. ²¹Test everything. Hold on to the good. ²²Avoid every kind of evil.

²³May God himself, the God of peace, sanctify you through and through. May your whole spirit, soul and body be kept blameless at the coming of our Lord Jesus Christ. ²⁴The one who calls you is faithful and he will do it.

²⁵Brothers, pray for us. ²⁶Greet all the brothers with a holy kiss. ²⁷I charge you before the Lord to have this letter read to all the brothers.

²⁸The grace of our Lord Jesus Christ be with you.

2 THESSALONIANS

AUL WRITES THIS SECOND LETTER TO THOSE BELIEVERS AT THESSALONICA WHO NEED CLARIFICATION ON THE ADVICE GIVEN IN HIS FIRST LETTER. SOME PEOPLE MISUNDERSTOOD PAUL AND WERE SO SURE JESUS WAS COMING SOON THAT THEY STOPPED WORKING. WHILE ASSURING THE THESSALONIANS THAT JESUS IS IN FACT COMING AGAIN, PAUL URGES HIS READERS TO TAKE RESPONSIBILITY FOR WHAT THEY NEED TO DO TODAY.

1 Paul, Silas*a* and Timothy,

To the church of the Thessalonians in God our Father and the Lord Jesus Christ:

²Grace and peace to you from God the Father and the Lord Jesus Christ.

Thanksgiving and Prayer

³We ought always to thank God for you, brothers, and rightly so, because your faith is growing more and more, and the love every one of you has for each other is increasing. ⁴Therefore, among God's churches we boast about your perseverance and faith in all the persecutions and trials you are enduring.

⁵All this is evidence that God's judgment is right, and as a result you will be counted worthy of the kingdom of God, for which you are suffering. ⁶God is just: He will pay back trouble to those who trouble you ⁷and give relief to you who are troubled, and to us as well. This will happen when the Lord Jesus is revealed from heaven in blazing fire with his powerful angels. ⁸He will punish those who do not know God and do not obey the gospel of our Lord Jesus. ⁹They will be punished with everlasting destruction and shut out from the presence of the Lord and from the majesty of his power ¹⁰on the day he comes to be glorified in his holy people and to be marveled at among all those who have believed. This includes you, because you believed our testimony to you.

¹¹With this in mind, we constantly

pray for you, that our God may count you worthy of his calling, and that by his power he may fulfill every good purpose of yours and every act prompted by your faith. [12]We pray this so that the name of our Lord Jesus may be glorified in you, and you in him, according to the grace of our God and the Lord Jesus Christ.[a]

The Man of Lawlessness

2 Concerning the coming of our Lord Jesus Christ and our being gathered to him, we ask you, brothers, [2]not to become easily unsettled or alarmed by some prophecy, report or letter supposed to have come from us, saying that the day of the Lord has already come. [3]Don't let anyone deceive you in any way, for ιthat day will not comeι until the rebellion occurs and the man of lawlessness[b] is revealed, the man doomed to destruction. [4]He will oppose and will exalt himself over everything that is called God or is worshiped, so that he sets himself up in God's temple, proclaiming himself to be God.

[5]Don't you remember that when I was with you I used to tell you these things? [6]And now you know what is holding him back, so that he may be revealed at the proper time. [7]For the secret power of

[a] 12 Or God and Lord, Jesus Christ   [b] 3 Some manuscripts sin

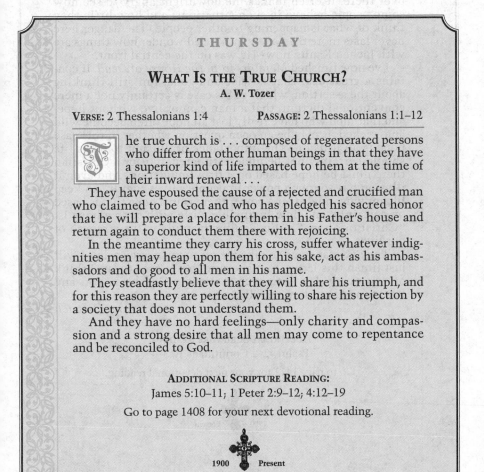

THURSDAY

WHAT IS THE TRUE CHURCH?
A. W. Tozer

VERSE: 2 Thessalonians 1:4   **PASSAGE:** 2 Thessalonians 1:1–12

he true church is . . . composed of regenerated persons who differ from other human beings in that they have a superior kind of life imparted to them at the time of their inward renewal . . .

They have espoused the cause of a rejected and crucified man who claimed to be God and who has pledged his sacred honor that he will prepare a place for them in his Father's house and return again to conduct them there with rejoicing.

In the meantime they carry his cross, suffer whatever indignities men may heap upon them for his sake, act as his ambassadors and do good to all men in his name.

They steadfastly believe that they will share his triumph, and for this reason they are perfectly willing to share his rejection by a society that does not understand them.

And they have no hard feelings—only charity and compassion and a strong desire that all men may come to repentance and be reconciled to God.

ADDITIONAL SCRIPTURE READING:
James 5:10–11; 1 Peter 2:9–12; 4:12–19

Go to page 1408 for your next devotional reading.

1900   Present

CHRIST OUR HOPE
Dietrich Bonhoeffer

VERSE: 2 Thessalonians 2:16   **PASSAGE:** 2 Thessalonians 2:16–17

ear Eberhard,
    I like to write to you as often as I can now, because I think you're always glad to hear from me. There's nothing special to report about myself nor about the family, as far as I know . . . I expect that Aunt Elisabeth will soon be visiting my parents.

During the last few nights it's been our turn again round here. When the bombs come shrieking down, I always think how trivial it all is compared with what you're going through over there. It often makes me downright angry to see how some people behave in such situations, and how little they think of what is happening to other people. The danger here never lasts more than a few minutes. I wonder how things are with Jochen Kanitz now? He was on the central front.

I've now finished *Memoirs from the House of Dead*. It contains a great deal that is wise and good. I'm still thinking about the assertion, which in his case is certainly not a mere conventional dictum, that a man cannot live without hope, and that men who have really lost all hope often become wild and wicked. It may be an open question whether in this case hope is an illusion. The importance of illusion to one's life should certainly not be underestimated; but for a Christian there must be hope based on a firm foundation. And even if illusion has so much power in people's lives that it can keep life moving, how great a power there is in a hope that is based on certainty, and how invincible a life with such a hope is. "Christ our hope"—this Pauline formula is the strength of our lives.

They've just come to take me off to my exercise, but I will just finish this letter, to make sure that it goes today. I think of you every day with true gratitude. God bless you and Renate and your boy and all of us.

Your Dietrich

ADDITIONAL SCRIPTURE READING:
Psalm 42; 2 Corinthians 10:3–4

Go to page 1411 for your next devotional reading.

1900   Present

lawlessness is already at work; but the one who now holds it back will continue to do so till he is taken out of the way. [8]And then the lawless one will be revealed, whom the Lord Jesus will overthrow with the breath of his mouth and destroy by the splendor of his coming. [9]The coming of the lawless one will be in accordance with the work of Satan displayed in all kinds of counterfeit miracles, signs and wonders, [10]and in every sort of evil that deceives those who are perishing. They perish because they refused to love the truth and so be saved. [11]For this reason God sends them a powerful delusion so that they will believe the lie [12]and so that all will be condemned who have not believed the truth but have delighted in wickedness.

Stand Firm

[13]But we ought always to thank God for you, brothers loved by the Lord, because from the beginning God chose you[a] to be saved through the sanctifying work of the Spirit and through belief in the truth. [14]He called you to this through our gospel, that you might share in the glory of our Lord Jesus Christ. [15]So then, brothers, stand firm and hold to the teachings[b] we passed on to you, whether by word of mouth or by letter.

IF A MAN CANNOT BE A CHRISTIAN IN THE PLACE WHERE HE IS, HE CANNOT BE A CHRISTIAN ANYWHERE.   —*Henry Ward Beecher*

---

[16]May our Lord Jesus Christ himself and God our Father, who loved us and by his grace gave us eternal encouragement and good hope, [17]encourage your hearts and strengthen you in every good deed and word.

Request for Prayer

3 Finally, brothers, pray for us that the message of the Lord may spread rapidly and be honored, just as it was with you. [2]And pray that we may be delivered from wicked and evil

men, for not everyone has faith. [3]But the Lord is faithful, and he will strengthen and protect you from the evil one. [4]We have confidence in the Lord that you are doing and will continue to do the things we command. [5]May the Lord direct your hearts into God's love and Christ's perseverance.

Warning Against Idleness

[6]In the name of the Lord Jesus Christ, we command you, brothers, to keep away from every brother who is idle and does not live according to the teaching[c] you received from us. [7]For you yourselves know how you ought to follow our example. We were not idle when we were with you, [8]nor did we eat anyone's food without paying for it. On the contrary, we worked night and day, laboring and toiling so that we would not be a burden to any of you. [9]We did this, not because we do not have the right to such help, but in order to make ourselves a model for you to follow. [10]For even when we were with you, we gave you this rule: "If a man will not work, he shall not eat."

[11]We hear that some among you are idle. They are not busy; they are busybodies. [12]Such people we command and urge in the Lord Jesus Christ to settle down and earn the bread they eat. [13]And as for you, brothers, never tire of doing what is right.

[14]If anyone does not obey our instruction in this letter, take special note of him. Do not associate with him, in order that he may feel ashamed. [15]Yet do not regard him as an enemy, but warn him as a brother.

Final Greetings

[16]Now may the Lord of peace himself give you peace at all times and in every way. The Lord be with all of you.

[17]I, Paul, write this greeting in my own hand, which is the distinguishing mark in all my letters. This is how I write.

[18]The grace of our Lord Jesus Christ be with you all.

---

[a] 13 Some manuscripts *because God chose you as his firstfruits*   [b] 15 Or *traditions*   [c] 6 Or *tradition*

1 TIMOTHY

AUL WROTE TO TIMOTHY WITH AFFIRMATION AND ADVICE ON HOW TO LEAD THE CHURCH AT EPHESUS. HERE YOU WILL FIND GUIDELINES FOR RUNNING A CHURCH, PRACTICAL HELP FOR BELIEVERS IN THEIR RELATIONSHIPS WITH OTHERS AND ADVICE ON DEALING WITH FALSE TEACHERS. LOOK FOR THE UNDERLYING PRINCIPLES THAT YOU CAN APPLY IN YOUR EVERYDAY LIFE AS YOU SEEK TO BE TRUE TO THE FAITH.

1 Paul, an apostle of Christ Jesus by the command of God our Savior and of Christ Jesus our hope,

²To Timothy my true son in the faith:

Grace, mercy and peace from God the Father and Christ Jesus our Lord.

Warning Against False Teachers of the Law

³As I urged you when I went into Macedonia, stay there in Ephesus so that you may command certain men not to teach false doctrines any longer ⁴nor to devote themselves to myths and endless genealogies. These promote controversies rather than God's work—which is by faith. ⁵The goal of this command is love, which comes from a pure heart and a good conscience and a sincere faith. ⁶Some have wandered away from these and turned to meaningless talk. ⁷They want to be teachers of the law, but they do not know what they are talking about or what they so confidently affirm.

⁸We know that the law is good if one uses it properly. ⁹We also know that law*a* is made not for the righteous but for lawbreakers and rebels, the ungodly and sinful, the unholy and irreligious; for those who kill their fathers or mothers, for murderers, ¹⁰for adulterers and perverts, for slave traders and liars and perjurers—and for whatever else is contrary to the sound doctrine ¹¹that conforms to the glorious gospel of the blessed God, which he entrusted to me.

a 9 Or that the law

WEEKEND

TO HEAVEN
Ben Jonson

VERSE: Philippians 1:23   **PASSAGE:** Philippians 1:20–26

ood and great God, can I not think of thee
    But it must, straight, my melancholy be?
Is it interpreted in my disease
    That, laden with my sins, I seek for ease?
O be thou witness, that the reins dost know
    And hearts of all, if I be sad for show,
And judge me after, if I dare pretend
    To aught but grace, or aim at other end.
As thou art all, so be thou all to me,
    First, midst, and last, converted, one and three;
My faith, my hope, my love; and in this state
    My judge, my witness, and my advocate.
Where have I been this while exil'd from thee,
    And whither rap'd, now thou but stoop'st to
      me?
Dwell, dwell here still, O being everywhere,
    How can I doubt to find thee ever, here?
I know my state, both full of shame and scorn
    Conceiv'd in sin, and unto labor born,
Standing with fear, and must with horror fall,
    And destin'd unto judgment, after all.
I feel my griefs too, and there scarce is ground
    Upon my flesh t'inflict another wound.
Yet dare I not complain, or wish for death
    With holy Paul, lest it be thought the breath
Of discontent; or that these prayers be
    For weariness of life, not love of thee.

ADDITIONAL SCRIPTURE READING:
Matthew 11:28; Galatians 6:9

Go to page 1413 for your next devotional reading.

1500   1700

The Lord's Grace to Paul

¹²I thank Christ Jesus our Lord, who has given me strength, that he considered me faithful, appointing me to his service. ¹³Even though I was once a blasphemer and a persecutor and a violent man, I was shown mercy because I acted in ignorance and unbelief. ¹⁴The grace of our Lord was poured out on me abundantly, along with the faith and love that are in Christ Jesus.

¹⁵Here is a trustworthy saying that deserves full acceptance: Christ Jesus came into the world to save sinners—of whom I am the worst. ¹⁶But for that very reason I was shown mercy so that in me, the worst of sinners, Christ Jesus might display his unlimited patience as an example for those who would believe on him and receive eternal life. ¹⁷Now to the King eternal, immortal, invisible, the only God, be honor and glory for ever and ever. Amen.

¹⁸Timothy, my son, I give you this instruction in keeping with the prophecies once made about you, so that by following them you may fight the good fight, ¹⁹holding on to faith and a good conscience. Some have rejected these and so have shipwrecked their faith. ²⁰Among them are Hymenaeus and Alexander, whom I have handed over to Satan to be taught not to blaspheme.

Instructions on Worship

2 I urge, then, first of all, that requests, prayers, intercession and thanksgiving be made for everyone— ²for kings and all those in authority, that we may live peaceful and quiet lives in all godliness and holiness. ³This is good, and pleases God our Savior, ⁴who wants all men to be saved and to come to a knowledge of the truth. ⁵For there is one God and one mediator between God and men, the man Christ Jesus, ⁶who gave himself as a ransom for all men—the testimony given in its proper time. ⁷And for this purpose I was appointed a herald and an apostle—I am telling the truth, I am not lying—and a teacher of the true faith to the Gentiles.

⁸I want men everywhere to lift up holy hands in prayer, without anger or disputing.

⁹I also want women to dress modestly, with decency and propriety, not with braided hair or gold or pearls or expensive clothes, ¹⁰but with good deeds, appropriate for women who profess to worship God.

TO LIFT UP THE HANDS IN PRAYER GIVES GOD GLORY, BUT A MAN WITH A DUNGFORK IN HIS HAND, A WOMAN WITH A SLOP PAIL, GIVES HIM GLORY TOO. HE IS SO GREAT THAT ALL THINGS GIVE HIM GLORY IF YOU MEAN THEY SHOULD.

—*Gerard Manley Hopkins*

---

¹¹A woman should learn in quietness and full submission. ¹²I do not permit a woman to teach or to have authority over a man; she must be silent. ¹³For Adam was formed first, then Eve. ¹⁴And Adam was not the one deceived; it was the woman who was deceived and became a sinner. ¹⁵But women*ᵃ* will be saved*ᵇ* through childbearing—if they continue in faith, love and holiness with propriety.

Overseers and Deacons

3 Here is a trustworthy saying: If anyone sets his heart on being an overseer,*ᶜ* he desires a noble task. ²Now the overseer must be above reproach, the husband of but one wife, temperate, self-controlled, respectable, hospitable, able to teach, ³not given to drunkenness, not violent but gentle, not quarrelsome, not a lover of money. ⁴He must manage his own family well and see that his children obey him with proper respect. ⁵(If anyone does not know how to manage his own family, how can he take care of God's church?) ⁶He must not be a recent convert, or he may become conceited and fall under the same judgment as the devil. ⁷He must also have a good reputation with outsiders, so that he will not fall into disgrace and into the devil's trap.

⁸Deacons, likewise, are to be men worthy of respect, sincere, not indulging in much wine, and not pursuing dishonest gain. ⁹They must keep hold of the deep truths of the faith with a clear

---

ᵃ 15 Greek *she*   *ᵇ* 15 Or *restored*   *ᶜ* 1 Traditionally *bishop*; also in verse 2

THE MAN-GOD
Anselm of Canterbury

VERSE: 1 Timothy 2:5   **PASSAGE:** 1 Timothy 2:5–6

 e must inquire now, how there can be a God-man. For divine nature and human nature cannot be changed into each other, so that the divine nature would become human or the human divine. Neither can they be so mingled that the two would constitute some third sort of nature which is neither entirely divine nor entirely human. In brief, if it were possible that one were changed into the other, it would be only God and not man, or only man and not God . . . The man-God we are looking for cannot arise out of divine and human nature either by change of one into the other, or by a corruptive mingling of both into a third, because these things are impossible; or if they are possible, they are totally unable to explain our problem.

Now, if we say these two complete natures are joined in some way or other, yet in such a way that the human nature is one being and the divine nature is another, and it is not the same person who is both God and man, it is impossible for the two natures to accomplish what must be accomplished. God, surely, will not accomplish it because it is not his obligation; and man will not accomplish it because he has not the ability. In order that a God-man accomplish it, therefore, it is necessary that one and the same person be perfect God and perfect man to make this satisfaction. For no one can make the satisfaction unless he is truly God, and no one has the obligation unless he is truly man. While therefore, it is necessary to find a God-man, with the integrity of both natures preserved, it is no less necessary that these two complete natures be united in one person—just as the body and rational soul are united in one man—because otherwise it is impossible for the same person to be perfect God and perfect man.

ADDITIONAL SCRIPTURE READING:
John 1:1; Hebrews 4:15

Go to page 1418 for your next devotional reading.

500   1500

conscience. ¹⁰They must first be tested; and then if there is nothing against them, let them serve as deacons.

---

¹¹In the same way, their wives*a* are to be women worthy of respect, not malicious talkers but temperate and trustworthy in everything.

¹²A deacon must be the husband of but one wife and must manage his children and his household well. ¹³Those who have served well gain an excellent standing and great assurance in their faith in Christ Jesus.

¹⁴Although I hope to come to you soon, I am writing you these instructions so that, ¹⁵if I am delayed, you will know how people ought to conduct themselves in God's household, which is the church of the living God, the pillar and foundation of the truth. ¹⁶Beyond all question, the mystery of godliness is great:

He*b* appeared in a body,*c*
    was vindicated by the Spirit,
was seen by angels,
    was preached among the nations,
was believed on in the world,
    was taken up in glory.

Instructions to Timothy

4 The Spirit clearly says that in later times some will abandon the faith and follow deceiving spirits and things taught by demons. ²Such teachings come through hypocritical liars, whose consciences have been seared as with a hot iron. ³They forbid people to marry and order them to abstain from certain foods, which God created to be received with thanksgiving by those who believe and who know the truth. ⁴For everything God created is good, and nothing is to be rejected if it is received with thanksgiving, ⁵because it is consecrated by the word of God and prayer.

⁶If you point these things out to the brothers, you will be a good minister of Christ Jesus, brought up in the truths of the faith and of the good teaching that you have followed. ⁷Have nothing to do with godless myths and old wives' tales; rather, train yourself to be godly. ⁸For physical training is of some value, but godliness has value for all things, holding promise for both the present life and the life to come.

⁹This is a trustworthy saying that deserves full acceptance ¹⁰(and for this we labor and strive), that we have put our hope in the living God, who is the Savior of all men, and especially of those who believe.

¹¹Command and teach these things. ¹²Don't let anyone look down on you because you are young, but set an example for the believers in speech, in life, in love, in faith and in purity. ¹³Until I come, devote yourself to the public reading of Scripture, to preaching and to teaching. ¹⁴Do not neglect your gift, which was given you through a prophetic message when the body of elders laid their hands on you.

¹⁵Be diligent in these matters; give yourself wholly to them, so that everyone may see your progress. ¹⁶Watch your life and doctrine closely. Persevere in them, because if you do, you will save both yourself and your hearers.

Advice About Widows, Elders and Slaves

5 Do not rebuke an older man harshly, but exhort him as if he were your father. Treat younger men as brothers, ²older women as mothers, and younger women as sisters, with absolute purity.

³Give proper recognition to those widows who are really in need. ⁴But if a widow has children or grandchildren, these should learn first of all to put their religion into practice by caring for their own family and so repaying their parents and grandparents, for this is pleasing to God. ⁵The widow who is really in need and left all alone puts her hope in God and continues night and day to pray and to ask God for help. ⁶But the widow who lives for pleasure is dead even while she lives. ⁷Give the people these

instructions, too, so that no one may be open to blame. [8]If anyone does not provide for his relatives, and especially for his immediate family, he has denied the faith and is worse than an unbeliever.

[9]No widow may be put on the list of widows unless she is over sixty, has been faithful to her husband,[a] [10]and is well known for her good deeds, such as bringing up children, showing hospitality, washing the feet of the saints, helping those in trouble and devoting herself to all kinds of good deeds.

[11]As for younger widows, do not put them on such a list. For when their sensual desires overcome their dedication to Christ, they want to marry. [12]Thus they bring judgment on themselves, because they have broken their first pledge. [13]Besides, they get into the habit of being idle and going about from house to house. And not only do they become idlers, but also gossips and busybodies, saying things they ought not to. [14]So I counsel younger widows to marry, to have children, to manage their homes and to give the enemy no opportunity for slander. [15]Some have in fact already turned away to follow Satan.

BE NOT CURIOUS ABOUT MATTERS THAT DO NOT CONCERN THEE; NEVER SPEAK OF THEM, AND DO NOT ASK ABOUT THEM.   —*Teresa of Avila*

---

[16]If any woman who is a believer has widows in her family, she should help them and not let the church be burdened with them, so that the church can help those widows who are really in need.

[17]The elders who direct the affairs of the church well are worthy of double honor, especially those whose work is preaching and teaching. [18]For the Scripture says, "Do not muzzle the ox while it is treading out the grain,"[b] and "The worker deserves his wages."[c] [19]Do not entertain an accusation against an elder unless it is brought by two or three witnesses. [20]Those who sin are to be rebuked publicly, so that the others may take warning.

[21]I charge you, in the sight of God and Christ Jesus and the elect angels, to keep these instructions without partiality, and to do nothing out of favoritism.

[22]Do not be hasty in the laying on of hands, and do not share in the sins of others. Keep yourself pure.

[23]Stop drinking only water, and use a little wine because of your stomach and your frequent illnesses.

[24]The sins of some men are obvious, reaching the place of judgment ahead of them; the sins of others trail behind them. [25]In the same way, good deeds are obvious, and even those that are not cannot be hidden.

6 All who are under the yoke of slavery should consider their masters worthy of full respect, so that God's name and our teaching may not be slandered. [2]Those who have believing masters are not to show less respect for them because they are brothers. Instead, they are to serve them even better, because those who benefit from their service are believers, and dear to them. These are the things you are to teach and urge on them.

Love of Money

[3]If anyone teaches false doctrines and does not agree to the sound instruction of our Lord Jesus Christ and to godly teaching, [4]he is conceited and understands nothing. He has an unhealthy interest in controversies and quarrels about words that result in envy, strife, malicious talk, evil suspicions [5]and constant friction between men of corrupt mind, who have been robbed of the truth and who think that godliness is a means to financial gain.

[6]But godliness with contentment is great gain. [7]For we brought nothing into the world, and we can take nothing out of it. [8]But if we have food and clothing, we will be content with that. [9]People who want to get rich fall into temptation and a trap and into many foolish and harmful desires that plunge men into ruin and destruction. [10]For the love of money is a root of all kinds of evil. Some people, eager for money, have wandered from the faith and pierced themselves with many griefs.

---

[a] 9 Or *has had but one husband*   [b] 18 Deut. 25:4   [c] 18 Luke 10:7

Paul's Charge to Timothy

11But you, man of God, flee from all this, and pursue righteousness, godliness, faith, love, endurance and gentleness. 12Fight the good fight of the faith. Take hold of the eternal life to which you were called when you made your good confession in the presence of many witnesses. 13In the sight of God, who gives life to everything, and of Christ Jesus, who while testifying before Pontius Pilate made the good confession, I charge you 14to keep this command without spot or blame until the appearing of our Lord Jesus Christ, 15which God will bring about in his own time— God, the blessed and only Ruler, the King of kings and Lord of lords, 16who alone is immortal and who lives in unapproachable light, whom no one has seen or can see. To him be honor and might forever. Amen.

17Command those who are rich in this present world not to be arrogant nor to put their hope in wealth, which is so uncertain, but to put their hope in God, who richly provides us with everything for our enjoyment. 18Command them to do good, to be rich in good deeds, and to be generous and willing to share. 19In this way they will lay up treasure for themselves as a firm foundation for the coming age, so that they may take hold of the life that is truly life.

20Timothy, guard what has been entrusted to your care. Turn away from godless chatter and the opposing ideas of what is falsely called knowledge, 21which some have professed and in so doing have wandered from the faith.

Grace be with you.

2 TIMOTHY

AUL'S SECOND LETTER TO TIMO-
THY, WRITTEN SHORTLY BEFORE
PAUL'S DEATH, REPRESENTS THE
ADVICE OF SOMEONE WHO KNOWS HE'S AT
THE END OF HIS LIFE. LANGUISHING IN A
COLD DUNGEON, CHAINED LIKE A COMMON
CRIMINAL, PAUL KNOWS THAT HIS WORK IS
DONE. HE CHALLENGES TIMOTHY TO A MORE
EFFECTIVE MINISTRY AND ENCOURAGES HIM
TO PERSEVERE IN HIS WALK WITH GOD. ASK
GOD TO GIVE YOU DAILY STRENGTH TO KEEP
WALKING WITH HIM, SECURE IN THE HOPE
THAT IS YOURS IN CHRIST.

---

1 Paul, an apostle of Christ Jesus by the will of God, according to the promise of life that is in Christ Jesus,

²To Timothy, my dear son:

Grace, mercy and peace from God the Father and Christ Jesus our Lord.

Encouragement to Be Faithful

³I thank God, whom I serve, as my forefathers did, with a clear conscience, as night and day I constantly remember you in my prayers. ⁴Recalling your tears, I long to see you, so that I may be filled with joy. ⁵I have been reminded of your sincere faith, which first lived in your grandmother Lois and in your mother Eunice and, I am persuaded, now lives in you also. ⁶For this reason I remind you to fan into flame the gift of God, which is in you through the laying on of my hands. ⁷For God did not give us a spirit of timidity, but a spirit of power, of love and of self-discipline.

⁸So do not be ashamed to testify about our Lord, or ashamed of me his prisoner. But join with me in suffering for the gospel, by the power of God, ⁹who has saved us and called us to a holy life—not because of anything we have done but because of his own purpose and grace. This grace was given us in Christ Jesus before the beginning of time, ¹⁰but it has now been revealed through the appearing of our Savior, Christ Jesus, who has destroyed death and has brought life and immortality to light through the gospel. ¹¹And of this gospel I was appointed a herald and an apostle and a teacher. ¹²That is why I am suffering as I am. Yet

As I Read, I Saw It All!
James Hudson Taylor

VERSE: 2 Timothy 2:13   **PASSAGE:** 2 Timothy 2:11–13

 ctober 17th, 1869: . . . My mind has been greatly exercised for six or eight months past, feeling the need personally, and for our mission, of more holiness, life, power in our souls. But personal need stood first and was the greatest. I felt the ingratitude, the danger, the sin of not living nearer to God. I prayed, agonized, fasted, strove, made resolutions, read the Word more diligently, sought more time for retirement and meditation—but all was without effect. Every day, almost every hour, the consciousness of sin oppressed me. I knew that if I could only abide in Christ all would be well, but I *could not* . . . Each day brought its register of sin and failure, of lack of power. To will was indeed present with me, but how to perform I found not.

Then came the question, "Is there *no* rescue? Must it be thus to the end—constant conflict and, instead of victory, too often defeat?" How, too, could I preach with sincerity that to those who receive Jesus, "to them gave he power to become the sons of God" (*i.e.*, God-like) (John 1:12, KJV) when it was not so in my own experience? . . .

When my agony of soul was at its height, a sentence in a letter from dear McCarthy was used to remove the scales from my eyes, and the Spirit of God revealed the truth of *our oneness* with *Jesus* as I had never known it before. McCarthy, who had been much exercised by the same sense of failure, but saw the light before I did, wrote (I quote from memory):

> But how to get faith strengthened? Not by striving after faith, but by resting on the Faithful One.

As I read I saw it all! "If we believe not, *yet* he abideth" (2 Timothy 2:13, KJV). I looked to Jesus and saw (and when I saw, oh, how the joy flowed!) that he had said, "*I* will never leave *you*" (Hebrews 13:5). "Ah, *there* is rest!" I thought. "I have striven in vain to rest in him. I'll strive no more. For has *he* not promised to abide with me—never to leave me, never to fail me?" And, dearie, *he never will!*

ADDITIONAL SCRIPTURE READING:
Isaiah 40:29–31; Ephesians 6:10–11

Go to page 1420 for your next devotional reading.

1700   1900

I am not ashamed, because I know whom I have believed, and am convinced that he is able to guard what I have entrusted to him for that day.

¹³What you heard from me, keep as the pattern of sound teaching, with faith and love in Christ Jesus. ¹⁴Guard the good deposit that was entrusted to you—guard it with the help of the Holy Spirit who lives in us.

¹⁵You know that everyone in the province of Asia has deserted me, including Phygelus and Hermogenes.

¹⁶May the Lord show mercy to the household of Onesiphorus, because he often refreshed me and was not ashamed of my chains. ¹⁷On the contrary, when he was in Rome, he searched hard for me until he found me. ¹⁸May the Lord grant that he will find mercy from the Lord on that day! You know very well in how many ways he helped me in Ephesus.

2 You then, my son, be strong in the grace that is in Christ Jesus. ²And the things you have heard me say in the presence of many witnesses entrust to reliable men who will also be qualified to teach others. ³Endure hardship with us like a good soldier of Christ Jesus. ⁴No one serving as a soldier gets involved in civilian affairs—he wants to please his commanding officer. ⁵Similarly, if anyone competes as an athlete, he does not receive the victor's crown unless he competes according to the rules. ⁶The hardworking farmer should be the first to receive a share of the crops. ⁷Reflect on what I am saying, for the Lord will give you insight into all this.

⁸Remember Jesus Christ, raised from the dead, descended from David. This is my gospel, ⁹for which I am suffering even to the point of being chained like a criminal. But God's word is not chained. ¹⁰Therefore I endure everything for the sake of the elect, that they too may obtain the salvation that is in Christ Jesus, with eternal glory.

¹¹Here is a trustworthy saying:

If we died with him,
    we will also live with him;
¹²if we endure,
    we will also reign with him.

If we disown him,
    he will also disown us;
¹³if we are faithless,
    he will remain faithful,
    for he cannot disown himself.

IT IS OUR BEST WORK THAT GOD WANTS, NOT THE DREGS OF OUR EXHAUSTION. I THINK HE MUST PREFER QUALITY TO QUANTITY.
                                —*George MacDonald*

A Workman Approved by God

¹⁴Keep reminding them of these things. Warn them before God against quarreling about words; it is of no value, and only ruins those who listen. ¹⁵Do your best to present yourself to God as one approved, a workman who does not need to be ashamed and who correctly handles the word of truth. ¹⁶Avoid godless chatter, because those who indulge in it will become more and more ungodly. ¹⁷Their teaching will spread like gangrene. Among them are Hymenaeus and Philetus, ¹⁸who have wandered away from the truth. They say that the resurrection has already taken place, and they destroy the faith of some. ¹⁹Nevertheless, God's solid foundation stands firm, sealed with this inscription: "The Lord knows those who are his,"ᵃ and, "Everyone who confesses the name of the Lord must turn away from wickedness."

²⁰In a large house there are articles not only of gold and silver, but also of wood and clay; some are for noble purposes and some for ignoble. ²¹If a man cleanses himself from the latter, he will be an instrument for noble purposes, made holy, useful to the Master and prepared to do any good work.

²²Flee the evil desires of youth, and pursue righteousness, faith, love and peace, along with those who call on the Lord out of a pure heart. ²³Don't have anything to do with foolish and stupid arguments, because you know they produce quarrels. ²⁴And the Lord's servant must not quarrel; instead, he must be kind to everyone, able to teach, not resentful. ²⁵Those who oppose him he must gently instruct, in the hope that

ᵃ *19* Num. 16:5 (see Septuagint)

INVOLVED WITH INSPIRATION

F. F. Bruce

VERSE: 2 Timothy 3:16   **PASSAGE:** 2 Timothy 3:14–17

 or many years now the greater part of my time has been devoted to the study and interpretation of the Bible, in academic and non-academic settings alike. I regard this as a most worthwhile and rewarding occupation. There is only one form of ministry which I should rate more highly; that is the work of an evangelist, to which I have not been called. (About a hundred years ago, J. N. Darby remarked, in the course of a Bible reading in Edinburgh, that he considered the gift of an evangelist to be the highest gift in the church today. He was heard with keen delight by W. T. P. Wolston, who thought that some of his brethren should take this to heart and accordingly interposed: "Would you please say that again, Mr. Darby?" "No, my dear young brother," said the great man; "I won't flatter your vanity.")

I should not find the career of a Bible teacher so satisfying as I do if I were not persuaded that the Bible is God's word written. The fact that I am so persuaded means that I must not come to the Bible with my own preconceptions of what the Bible, as God's word written, can or cannot say. It is important to determine, by the canons of grammatical, textual, historical and literary study, what it actually does say. Occasionally, when I have expounded the meaning of some Biblical passage in a particular way, I have been asked, "But how does that square with inspiration?" But inspiration is not a concept of which I have a clear understanding before I come to the study of the text, so that I know in advance what limits are placed on the meaning of the text by the requirements of inspiration. On the contrary, it is by the patient study of the text that I come to understand better not only what the text itself means but also what is involved in biblical inspiration. My doctrine of Scripture is based on my study of Scripture, not *vice versa*.

ADDITIONAL SCRIPTURE READING:
Psalm 119:105; 2 Peter 1:21

Go to page 1422 for your next devotional reading.

1900   Present

God will grant them repentance leading them to a knowledge of the truth, 26and that they will come to their senses and escape from the trap of the devil, who has taken them captive to do his will.

Godlessness in the Last Days

3 But mark this: There will be terrible times in the last days. 2People will be lovers of themselves, lovers of money, boastful, proud, abusive, disobedient to their parents, ungrateful, unholy, 3without love, unforgiving, slanderous, without self-control, brutal, not lovers of the good, 4treacherous, rash, conceited, lovers of pleasure rather than lovers of God— 5having a form of godliness but denying its power. Have nothing to do with them.

6They are the kind who worm their way into homes and gain control over weak-willed women, who are loaded down with sins and are swayed by all kinds of evil desires, 7always learning but never able to acknowledge the truth. 8Just as Jannes and Jambres opposed Moses, so also these men oppose the truth—men of depraved minds, who, as far as the faith is concerned, are rejected. 9But they will not get very far because, as in the case of those men, their folly will be clear to everyone.

Paul's Charge to Timothy

10You, however, know all about my teaching, my way of life, my purpose, faith, patience, love, endurance, 11persecutions, sufferings—what kinds of things happened to me in Antioch, Iconium and Lystra, the persecutions I endured. Yet the Lord rescued me from all of them. 12In fact, everyone who wants to live a godly life in Christ Jesus will be persecuted, 13while evil men and impostors will go from bad to worse, deceiving and being deceived. 14But as for you, continue in what you have learned and have become convinced of, because you know those from whom you learned it, 15and how from infancy you have known the holy Scriptures, which are able to make you wise for salvation through faith in Christ Jesus. 16All Scripture is God-breathed and is useful for teaching, rebuking, correcting and training in righteousness, 17so that

the man of God may be thoroughly equipped for every good work.

4 In the presence of God and of Christ Jesus, who will judge the living and the dead, and in view of his appearing and his kingdom, I give you this charge: 2Preach the Word; be prepared in season and out of season; correct, rebuke and encourage—with great patience and careful instruction. 3For the time will come when men will not put up with sound doctrine. Instead, to suit their own desires, they will gather around them a great number of teachers to say what their itching ears want to hear. 4They will turn their ears away from the truth and turn aside to myths. 5But you, keep your head in all situations, endure hardship, do the work of an evangelist, discharge all the duties of your ministry.

6For I am already being poured out like a drink offering, and the time has come for my departure. 7I have fought the good fight, I have finished the race, I have kept the faith. 8Now there is in store for me the crown of righteousness,

> YOU ARE BUT A POOR SOLDIER OF CHRIST IF YOU THINK YOU CAN OVERCOME WITHOUT FIGHTING, AND SUPPOSE YOU CAN HAVE THE CROWN WITHOUT THE CONFLICT.   —John Chrysostom

which the Lord, the righteous Judge, will award to me on that day—and not only to me, but also to all who have longed for his appearing.

Personal Remarks

9Do your best to come to me quickly, 10for Demas, because he loved this world, has deserted me and has gone to Thessalonica. Crescens has gone to Galatia, and Titus to Dalmatia. 11Only Luke is with me. Get Mark and bring him with you, because he is helpful to me in my ministry. 12I sent Tychicus to Ephesus. 13When you come, bring the cloak that I left with Carpus at Troas, and my scrolls, especially the parchments.

14Alexander the metalworker did me a great deal of harm. The Lord will repay him for what he has done. 15You too should be on your guard against him, because he strongly opposed our message.

¹⁶At my first defense, no one came to my support, but everyone deserted me. May it not be held against them. ¹⁷But the Lord stood at my side and gave me strength, so that through me the message might be fully proclaimed and all the Gentiles might hear it. And I was delivered from the lion's mouth. ¹⁸The Lord will rescue me from every evil attack and will bring me safely to his heavenly kingdom. To him be glory for ever and ever. Amen.

THURSDAY

FROM REVELATIONS OF DIVINE LOVE
Julian of Norwich

VERSE: 2 Timothy 4:18   **PASSAGE:** 2 Timothy 4:17–18

One time our Lord said to me, "All things shall be well." And another time he said, "You yourself shall see that all manner of things shall be well," and my soul understood these two sayings to mean several different things.

One meaning was that his will is for us to know that he takes notice not only of great and noble things, but of little and small things as well, low and simple things, one and the other. And so this is what he meant by saying, "All manner of things shall be well." For it is his will that we know even the smallest of things will not be forgotten.

Another meaning was this: We see many evil deeds done all around us, deeds that cause great harm, and sometimes it seems impossible that they should ever result in anything good. Sometimes when we see these evils, sorrowing and mourning because of them, we find it difficult to concentrate on beholding God blissfully, which is something we should do. And the cause of this is that our reasoning capacity is now so blind, low, and simple that we cannot know his high and marvelous wisdom, the power and the goodness of the blissful Trinity. And this is what he meant when he said, "You yourself shall see that all manner of things shall be well." It was as if he had said, "Take heed faithfully and trustingly now, and at the end of all things, you will truly see them in the fullness of joy."

ADDITIONAL SCRIPTURE READING:
Psalm 121; Romans 8:28, 37–39

Go to page 1425 for your next devotional reading.

500   1500

Final Greetings

[19]Greet Priscilla[a] and Aquila and the household of Onesiphorus. [20]Erastus stayed in Corinth, and I left Trophimus sick in Miletus. [21]Do your best to get here before winter. Eubulus greets you, and so do Pudens, Linus, Claudia and all the brothers.

[22]The Lord be with your spirit. Grace be with you.

TITUS

ITUS, A CLOSE FRIEND OF PAUL, HELPED PAUL ORGANIZE AND LEAD CHURCHES IN THE EASTERN HALF OF THE ROMAN EMPIRE. PAUL WROTE THIS LETTER TO TITUS TO HELP HIM LEAD THE TROUBLED CHURCH ON THE ISLAND OF CRETE. PAUL COVERS SUCH MATTERS AS QUALIFICATIONS OF CHURCH LEADERS, GUIDELINES FOR A GODLY LIFE AND AN EMPHASIS ON FAITH THAT OVERCOMES DIVISION AMONG BELIEVERS.

1 Paul, a servant of God and an apostle of Jesus Christ for the faith of God's elect and the knowledge of the truth that leads to godliness— ²a faith and knowledge resting on the hope of eternal life, which God, who does not lie, promised before the beginning of time, ³and at his appointed season he brought his word to light through the preaching entrusted to me by the command of God our Savior,

⁴To Titus, my true son in our common faith:

Grace and peace from God the Father and Christ Jesus our Savior.

Titus' Task on Crete

⁵The reason I left you in Crete was that you might straighten out what was left unfinished and appoint*a* elders in every town, as I directed you. ⁶An elder

---

THE SERVANT OF GOD HAS A GOOD MASTER.
—*Blaise Pascal*

---

must be blameless, the husband of but one wife, a man whose children believe and are not open to the charge of being wild and disobedient. ⁷Since an overseer*b* is entrusted with God's work, he must be blameless—not overbearing, not quick-tempered, not given to drunkenness, not violent, not pursuing dishonest gain. ⁸Rather he must be hospitable, one who loves what is good,

---

a 5 Or *ordain*   *b* 7 Traditionally *bishop*

who is self-controlled, upright, holy and disciplined. ⁹He must hold firmly to the trustworthy message as it has been taught, so that he can encourage others by sound doctrine and refute those who oppose it.

¹⁰For there are many rebellious people, mere talkers and deceivers, especially those of the circumcision group. ¹¹They must be silenced, because they are ruining whole households by teaching things they ought not to teach—and that for the sake of dishonest gain. ¹²Even one of their own prophets has said, "Cretans are always liars, evil brutes, lazy gluttons." ¹³This testimony is true. Therefore, rebuke them sharply, so that they will be sound in the faith ¹⁴and will pay no attention to Jewish myths or to the commands of those who reject the truth. ¹⁵To the pure, all things are pure, but to those who are corrupted and do not believe, nothing is pure. In fact, both their minds and consciences are corrupted. ¹⁶They claim to know God, but by their actions they deny him. They are detestable, disobedient and unfit for doing anything good.

What Must Be Taught to Various Groups

2 You must teach what is in accord with sound doctrine. ²Teach the older men to be temperate, worthy of respect, self-controlled, and sound in faith, in love and in endurance.

³Likewise, teach the older women to be reverent in the way they live, not to

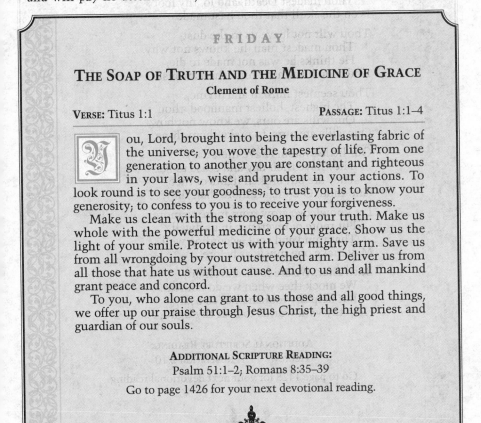

FRIDAY

THE SOAP OF TRUTH AND THE MEDICINE OF GRACE
Clement of Rome

VERSE: Titus 1:1   **PASSAGE:** Titus 1:1–4

You, Lord, brought into being the everlasting fabric of the universe; you wove the tapestry of life. From one generation to another you are constant and righteous in your laws, wise and prudent in your actions. To look round is to see your goodness; to trust you is to know your generosity; to confess to you is to receive your forgiveness.

Make us clean with the strong soap of your truth. Make us whole with the powerful medicine of your grace. Show us the light of your smile. Protect us with your mighty arm. Save us from all wrongdoing by your outstretched arm. Deliver us from all those that hate us without cause. And to us and all mankind grant peace and concord.

To you, who alone can grant to us those and all good things, we offer up our praise through Jesus Christ, the high priest and guardian of our souls.

ADDITIONAL SCRIPTURE READING:
Psalm 51:1–2; Romans 8:35–39

Go to page 1426 for your next devotional reading.

100   500

WEEKEND

STRONG SON OF GOD
Alfred, Lord Tennyson

VERSE: Colossians 1:16   PASSAGE: Colossians 1:15–20

trong Son of God, immortal Love,
    Whom we, that have not seen thy face,
    By faith, and faith alone, embrace,
Believing where we cannot prove;

Thine are these orbs of light and shade;
    Thou madest Life in man and brute;
    Thou madest Death; and lo, thy foot
Is on the skull that thou hast made.

Thou wilt not leave us in the dust;
    Thou madest man, he knows not why,
    He thinks he was not made to die;
And thou hast made him: thou art just.

Thou seemest human and divine,
    The highest, holiest manhood, thou.
    Our wills are ours, we know not how,
Our wills are ours, to make them thine.

Our little systems have their day;
    They have their day and cease to be:
    They are but broken lights of thee,
And thou, O Lord, art more than they. . .

Let knowledge grow from more to more,
    But more of reverence in us dwell;
    That mind and soul, according well,
May make one music as before,

But vaster. We are fools and slight;
    We mock thee when we do not fear:
    But help thy foolish ones to bear;
Help thy vain worlds to bear thy light . . .

ADDITIONAL SCRIPTURE READING:
Hebrews 11:1; Revelation 2:10

Go to page 1428 for your next devotional reading.

1700   1900

be slanderers or addicted to much wine, but to teach what is good. [4]Then they can train the younger women to love their husbands and children, [5]to be self-controlled and pure, to be busy at home, to be kind, and to be subject to their husbands, so that no one will malign the word of God.

[6]Similarly, encourage the young men to be self-controlled. [7]In everything set them an example by doing what is good. In your teaching show integrity, seriousness [8]and soundness of speech that cannot be condemned, so that those who oppose you may be ashamed because they have nothing bad to say about us.

[9]Teach slaves to be subject to their masters in everything, to try to please them, not to talk back to them, [10]and not to steal from them, but to show that they can be fully trusted, so that in every way they will make the teaching about God our Savior attractive.

[11]For the grace of God that brings salvation has appeared to all men. [12]It teaches us to say "No" to ungodliness and worldly passions, and to live self-controlled, upright and godly lives in this present age, [13]while we wait for the blessed hope—the glorious appearing of our great God and Savior, Jesus Christ, [14]who gave himself for us to redeem us from all wickedness and to purify for himself a people that are his very own, eager to do what is good.

THE CHURCH IS NOT A GALLERY FOR THE EXHIBITION OF EMINENT CHRISTIANS, BUT A SCHOOL FOR THE EDUCATION OF IMPERFECT ONES.

—*Henry Ward Beecher*

---

[15]These, then, are the things you should teach. Encourage and rebuke with all authority. Do not let anyone despise you.

Doing What Is Good

3 Remind the people to be subject to rulers and authorities, to be obedient, to be ready to do whatever is good, [2]to slander no one, to be peaceable and considerate, and to show true humility toward all men.

[3]At one time we too were foolish, disobedient, deceived and enslaved by all kinds of passions and pleasures. We lived in malice and envy, being hated and hating one another. [4]But when the kindness and love of God our Savior appeared, [5]he saved us, not because of righteous things we had done, but because of his mercy. He saved us through the washing of rebirth and renewal by the Holy Spirit, [6]whom he poured out on us generously through Jesus Christ our Savior, [7]so that, having been justified by his grace, we might become heirs having the hope of eternal life. [8]This is a trustworthy saying. And I want you to stress these things, so that those who have trusted in God may be careful to devote themselves to doing what is good. These things are excellent and profitable for everyone.

[9]But avoid foolish controversies and genealogies and arguments and quarrels about the law, because these are unprofitable and useless. [10]Warn a divisive person once, and then warn him a second time. After that, have nothing to do with him. [11]You may be sure that such a man is warped and sinful; he is self-condemned.

Final Remarks

[12]As soon as I send Artemas or Tychicus to you, do your best to come to me at Nicopolis, because I have decided to winter there. [13]Do everything you can to help Zenas the lawyer and Apollos on their way and see that they have everything they need. [14]Our people must learn to devote themselves to doing what is good, in order that they may provide for daily necessities and not live unproductive lives.

[15]Everyone with me sends you greetings. Greet those who love us in the faith.

Grace be with you all.

THE EXAMPLE OF GOD'S ADORNMENT
Clement of Rome

VERSE: Titus 3:14   **PASSAGE:** Titus 3:12–15

hat must we do, then, my brothers? Should we relax our efforts at well-doing, and cease to exercise Christian love? God forbid that we, at least, should ever come to such a pass. On the contrary, let us be earnestly, even passionately, eager to set about any kind of activity that is good. Even the Architect and Lord of the universe himself takes a delight in working. In his supreme power he has established the heavens, and in his unsearchable wisdom set them in order. He divided the earth from the waters around it, and settled it securely on the firm foundation of his will, and at his word he called to life the beasts of the field that roam its surface. He formed the sea and its creatures, and confined them by his power. Above all, with his own sacred and immaculate hands he fashioned man, who in virtue of his intelligence is the chiefest and greatest of all his works and the very likeness of his own image; for God said, *Let us make man in our image and likeness; and God created man, male and female he created them* (Genesis 1:26–27, KJV). And when he had made an end of all his works, he gave them his approval and his blessing, saying, *Increase and multiply* (Genesis 1:28). We see, then, that good works have not only embellished the lives of all just men, but are an adornment with which even the Lord has delighted to deck himself; and therefore, with such an example before us, let us spare no effort to obey his will, but put all our energies into the work of righteousness.

ADDITIONAL SCRIPTURE READING:
Matthew 5:6; 2 Timothy 2:22

Go to page 1430 for your next devotional reading.

100 500

PHILEMON

PHILEMON, A BELIEVER IN COLOSSE, OWNED A SLAVE NAMED ONESIMUS WHO HAD APPARENTLY STOLEN FROM HIM AND THEN RUN AWAY. BUT ONESIMUS MET PAUL AND THROUGH HIS MINISTRY BECAME A CHRISTIAN. NOW HE WAS WILLING TO RETURN TO HIS MASTER. PAUL WRITES THIS PERSONAL APPEAL TO ASK PHILEMON TO ACCEPT ONESIMUS AS A CHRISTIAN BROTHER, NOT AS A SLAVE. READ THIS LETTER AS A CASE STUDY IN THE COST OF ASKING FOR FORGIVENESS AND OF GRANTING IT.

---

¹Paul, a prisoner of Christ Jesus, and Timothy our brother,

To Philemon our dear friend and fellow worker, ²to Apphia our sister, to Archippus our fellow soldier and to the church that meets in your home:

³Grace to you and peace from God our Father and the Lord Jesus Christ.

Thanksgiving and Prayer

⁴I always thank my God as I remember you in my prayers, ⁵because I hear about your faith in the Lord Jesus and your love for all the saints. ⁶I pray that you may be active in sharing your faith, so that you will have a full understanding of every good thing we have in Christ. ⁷Your love has given me great joy and encouragement, because you, brother, have refreshed the hearts of the saints.

Paul's Plea for Onesimus

⁸Therefore, although in Christ I could be bold and order you to do what you ought to do, ⁹yet I appeal to you on the basis of love. I then, as Paul—an old man and now also a prisoner of Christ Jesus— ¹⁰I appeal to you for my son Onesimus,ᵃ who became my son while I was in chains. ¹¹Formerly he was useless to you, but now he has become useful both to you and to me.

¹²I am sending him—who is my very heart—back to you. ¹³I would have liked to keep him with me so that he could take your place in helping me

ᵃ 10 *Onesimus* means *useful.*

PRAYER OF A SLAVE
Frederick Douglass

VERSE: Philemon 17 **PASSAGE:** Philemon 8–21

ur house stood within a few rods of the Chesapeake Bay, whose broad bosom was ever white with sails from every quarter of the habitable globe. Those beautiful vessels, robed in white, and so delightful to the eyes of freemen, were to me so many shrouded ghosts, to terrify and torment me with thoughts of my wretched condition. I have often, in the deep stillness of a summer's Sabbath, stood all alone upon the banks of that noble bay, and traced, with saddened heart and tearful eye, the countless number of sails moving off to the mighty ocean. The sight of these always affected me powerfully. My thoughts would compel utterance; and there, with no audience but the Almighty, I would pour out my soul's complaint in my rude way with an apostrophe to the multitude of ships.

"You are loosed from your moorings, and free. I am fast in my chains, and am a slave! You move merrily before the gentle gale, and I sadly before the bloody whip. You are freedom's swift-winged angels, that fly around the world; I am confined in bonds of iron. O, that I were free! O, that I were one of your gallant decks, and under your protecting wing. Alas! betwixt me and you the turbid waters roll. Go on, go on; O, that I could also go! Could I but swim! If I could fly! O, why was I born a man, of whom to make a brute! The glad ship is gone: she hides in the dim distance. I am left in the hell of unending slavery. O, God, save me! God, deliver me! Let me be free!—Is there any God? Why am I a slave? I will run away. I will not stand it. Get caught or get clear, I'll try it. I had as well die with ague as with fever. I have only one life to lose. I had as well be killed running as die standing. Only think of it: one hundred miles north, and I am free! Try it? Yes! God helping me, I will. It cannot be that I shall live and die a slave. I will take to the water. This very bay shall yet bear me into freedom.

ADDITIONAL SCRIPTURE READING:
Romans 7:24–25; 1 Corinthians 7:21–23

Go to page 1435 for your next devotional reading.

1700   1900

while I am in chains for the gospel.
¹⁴But I did not want to do anything
without your consent, so that any favor
you do will be spontaneous and not
forced. ¹⁵Perhaps the reason he was separated from you for a little while was
that you might have him back for
good— ¹⁶no longer as a slave, but better
than a slave, as a dear brother. He is
very dear to me but even dearer to you,
both as a man and as a brother in the
Lord.

¹⁷So if you consider me a partner, wel-
come him as you would welcome me.
¹⁸If he has done you any wrong or owes
you anything, charge it to me. ¹⁹I, Paul,
am writing this with my own hand. I
will pay it back—not to mention that
you owe me your very self. ²⁰I do wish,
brother, that I may have some benefit
from you in the Lord; refresh my heart
in Christ. ²¹Confident of your obedience, I write to you, knowing that you
will do even more than I ask.

²²And one thing more: Prepare a guest
room for me, because I hope to be restored to you in answer to your prayers.

²³Epaphras, my fellow prisoner in
Christ Jesus, sends you greetings. ²⁴And
so do Mark, Aristarchus, Demas and
Luke, my fellow workers.

²⁵The grace of the Lord Jesus Christ be
with your spirit.

HEBREWS

THE FIRST-CENTURY CHURCH SUFFERED SEVERE PERSECUTION, AND THIS LETTER WAS WRITTEN IN THAT SETTING. THE INTENDED READERS SEEM TO HAVE BEEN JEWISH CHRISTIANS WHO WERE THINKING OF ABANDONING THEIR FAITH AND LAPSING BACK INTO JUDAISM. SO THE AUTHOR EXHORTS THEM TO HOLD FAST TO THEIR CONFESSION OF CHRIST AS SAVIOR AND LORD. THE THEME OF HEBREWS IS THE ABSOLUTE SUPREMACY AND SUFFICIENCY OF JESUS CHRIST AS REVEALER AND AS MEDIATOR OF GOD'S GRACE. AS YOU READ THIS BOOK, LOOK FOR THE INSPIRATION TO KEEP GOING IN THE FAITH.

The Son Superior to Angels

1 In the past God spoke to our forefathers through the prophets at many times and in various ways, ²but in these last days he has spoken to us by his Son, whom he appointed heir of all things, and through whom he made the universe. ³The Son is the radiance of God's glory and the exact representation of his being, sustaining all things by his powerful word. After he had provided purification for sins, he sat down at the right hand of the Majesty in heaven. ⁴So he became as much superior to the angels as the name he has inherited is superior to theirs.

⁵For to which of the angels did God ever say,

"You are my Son;
today I have become your
Father*ᵃ*"*ᵇ*?

Or again,

"I will be his Father,
and he will be my Son"*ᶜ*?

⁶And again, when God brings his firstborn into the world, he says,

"Let all God's angels worship him."*ᵈ*

⁷In speaking of the angels he says,

"He makes his angels winds,
his servants flames of fire."*ᵉ*

ᵃ 5 Or have begotten you   ᵇ 5 Psalm 2:7   ᶜ 5 2 Samuel 7:14; 1 Chron. 17:13   ᵈ 6 Deut. 32:43 (see Dead Sea Scrolls and Septuagint)   ᵉ 7 Psalm 104:4

8 But about the Son he says,

"Your throne, O God, will last for
      ever and ever,
    and righteousness will be the
      scepter of your kingdom.
9 You have loved righteousness and
      hated wickedness;
    therefore God, your God, has set
      you above your companions
    by anointing you with the oil of
      joy."[a]

10 He also says,

"In the beginning, O Lord, you laid
      the foundations of the earth,
    and the heavens are the work of
      your hands.
11 They will perish, but you remain;
    they will all wear out like a
      garment.
12 You will roll them up like a robe;
    like a garment they will be
      changed.
  But you remain the same,
    and your years will never end."[b]

13 To which of the angels did God ever
say,

"Sit at my right hand
    until I make your enemies
    a footstool for your feet"[c]?

14 Are not all angels ministering spirits
sent to serve those who will inherit salvation?

Warning to Pay Attention

2 We must pay more careful
attention, therefore, to what we
have heard, so that we do not drift away.
2 For if the message spoken by angels
was binding, and every violation and
disobedience received its just punishment, 3 how shall we escape if we ignore
such a great salvation? This salvation,
which was first announced by the Lord,
was confirmed to us by those who heard
him. 4 God also testified to it by signs,
wonders and various miracles, and gifts
of the Holy Spirit distributed according
to his will.

Jesus Made Like His Brothers

5 It is not to angels that he has subjected the world to come, about which we
are speaking. 6 But there is a place where
someone has testified:

"What is man that you are mindful of
      him,
    the son of man that you care for
      him?
7 You made him a little[d] lower than
      the angels;
    you crowned him with glory and
      honor
8   and put everything under his feet."[e]

In putting everything under him, God left
nothing that is not subject to him. Yet at
present we do not see everything subject
to him. 9 But we see Jesus, who was made
a little lower than the angels, now
crowned with glory and honor because he
suffered death, so that by the grace of
God he might taste death for everyone.

10 In bringing many sons to glory, it
was fitting that God, for whom and
through whom everything exists, should
make the author of their salvation perfect through suffering. 11 Both the one
who makes men holy and those who are
made holy are of the same family. So
Jesus is not ashamed to call them brothers. 12 He says,

"I will declare your name to my
      brothers;
    in the presence of the congregation
    I will sing your praises."[f]

13 And again,

"I will put my trust in him."[g]

And again he says,

"Here am I, and the children God has
      given me."[h]

14 Since the children have flesh and
blood, he too shared in their humanity
so that by his death he might destroy
him who holds the power of death—that
is, the devil— 15 and free those who all
their lives were held in slavery by their

---

a 9 Psalm 45:6,7   *b* 12 Psalm 102:25–27   *c* 13 Psalm 110:1   *d* 7 Or *him for a little while;* also in
verse 9   *e* 8 Psalm 8:4–6   *f* 12 Psalm 22:22   *g* 13 Isaiah 8:17   *h* 13 Isaiah 8:18

fear of death. ¹⁶For surely it is not angels he helps, but Abraham's descendants. ¹⁷For this reason he had to be made like his brothers in every way, in order that he might become a merciful and faithful high priest in service to God, and that he might make atonement for*a* the sins of the people. ¹⁸Because he himself suffered when he was tempted, he is able to help those who are being tempted.

Jesus Greater Than Moses

3 Therefore, holy brothers, who share in the heavenly calling, fix your thoughts on Jesus, the apostle and high priest whom we confess. ²He was faithful to the one who appointed him, just as Moses was faithful in all God's house. ³Jesus has been found worthy of greater honor than Moses, just as the builder of a house has greater honor than the house itself. ⁴For every house is built by someone, but God is the builder of everything. ⁵Moses was faithful as a servant in all God's house, testifying to what would be said in the future. ⁶But Christ is faithful as a son over God's house. And we are his house, if we hold on to our courage and the hope of which we boast.

Warning Against Unbelief

⁷So, as the Holy Spirit says:

"Today, if you hear his voice,
⁸ do not harden your hearts
as you did in the rebellion,
during the time of testing in the desert,
⁹where your fathers tested and tried me
and for forty years saw what I did.
¹⁰That is why I was angry with that generation,
and I said, 'Their hearts are always going astray,
and they have not known my ways.'
¹¹So I declared on oath in my anger,
'They shall never enter my rest.' "*b*

¹²See to it, brothers, that none of you has a sinful, unbelieving heart that turns away from the living God. ¹³But

encourage one another daily, as long as it is called Today, so that none of you may be hardened by sin's deceitfulness. ¹⁴We have come to share in Christ if we hold firmly till the end the confidence we had at first. ¹⁵As has just been said:

"Today, if you hear his voice,
do not harden your hearts
as you did in the rebellion."*c*

¹⁶Who were they who heard and rebelled? Were they not all those Moses led out of Egypt? ¹⁷And with whom was he angry for forty years? Was it not with those who sinned, whose bodies fell in the desert? ¹⁸And to whom did God swear that they would never enter his rest if not to those who disobeyed*d*? ¹⁹So we see that they were not able to enter, because of their unbelief.

A Sabbath-Rest for the People of God

4 Therefore, since the promise of entering his rest still stands, let us be careful that none of you be found to have fallen short of it. ²For we also have had the gospel preached to us, just as they did; but the message they heard was of no value to them, because those who heard did not combine it with faith.*e* ³Now we who have believed enter that rest, just as God has said,

"So I declared on oath in my anger,
'They shall never enter my rest.' "*f*

And yet his work has been finished since the creation of the world. ⁴For somewhere he has spoken about the seventh day in these words: "And on the seventh day God rested from all his work."*g* ⁵And again in the passage above he says, "They shall never enter my rest."

⁶It still remains that some will enter that rest, and those who formerly had the gospel preached to them did not go in, because of their disobedience. ⁷Therefore God again set a certain day, calling it Today, when a long time later he spoke through David, as was said before:

a 17 Or *and that he might turn aside God's wrath, taking away*   *b 11* Psalm 95:7–11
c 15 Psalm 95:7,8   *d 18* Or *disbelieved*   *e 2* Many manuscripts *because they did not share in the faith of those who obeyed*   *f 3* Psalm 95:11; also in verse 5   *g 4* Gen. 2:2

CONCERNING SAVING FAITH
Nikolaus Ludwig Count von Zinzendorf

VERSE: Hebrews 3:12   **PASSAGE:** Hebrews 3:12–15

n the Savior's affairs [Peter] was not just a natural, unconverted, unfamiliar man (which indeed is in itself sin enough), but rather he was a deliberate denier, what today is called a renegade. He would rather not know his Lord; he was ashamed of his Lord; he abjured his Lord three times. And a few days later his Lord came up and rose from the dead and was loved by those people who had followed him to death itself, by the women who had helped to place him into the grave and who came back at early dawn and looked for him out of love. "Ah," says the Savior to them, "you dear children, I absolutely beg of you not to delay here with me, but go and tell my Peter that I am here again" (see Mark 16:7).

This must have been an astonishing message to Peter. Was this all his punishment, to be notified that his Lord is risen again? And if so, should he have been the very first who was comforted, whose heart was revived? Thus, when the Savior said to him afterward, "Do you love me more than these do?" he said, "You know all things; you know how much I love you" (see John 21:15–17). And at that time he really did love him more than all the others. Before he had loved him in his imagination; he had honored him and out of esteem for him had rashly claimed to be ready to suffer death for him rather than forsake him. He did make a bold beginning, but he got stuck, because his love was dry and intellectual. But when the Savior forgave him everything, when he acquitted him of his sins, when he declared a renegade to be his apostle, then Peter could hold back no longer. If anyone said anything about his Lord to him, tears filled his eyes, and his body and soul were humbled. Already in the high priest's palace the bare presentiment of the character of his Lord had made his eyes fountains of tears.

ADDITIONAL SCRIPTURE READING:
Mark 16:7; John 21:15

Go to page 1437 for your next devotional reading.

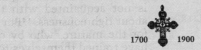

1700   1900

"Today, if you hear his voice,
do not harden your hearts."[a]

[8]For if Joshua had given them rest, God would not have spoken later about another day. [9]There remains, then, a Sabbath-rest for the people of God; [10]for anyone who enters God's rest also rests from his own work, just as God did from his. [11]Let us, therefore, make every effort to enter that rest, so that no one will fall by following their example of disobedience.

THE WORD OF GOD IS NOT A SOUNDING BUT A PIERCING WORD, NOT PRONOUNCEABLE BY THE TONGUE BUT EFFICACIOUS IN THE MIND, NOT SENSIBLE TO THE EAR BUT FASCINATING TO THE AFFECTION.   —Bernard of Clairvaux

---

[12]For the word of God is living and active. Sharper than any double-edged sword, it penetrates even to dividing soul and spirit, joints and marrow; it judges the thoughts and attitudes of the heart. [13]Nothing in all creation is hidden from God's sight. Everything is uncovered and laid bare before the eyes of him to whom we must give account.

Jesus the Great High Priest

[14]Therefore, since we have a great high priest who has gone through the heavens,[b] Jesus the Son of God, let us hold firmly to the faith we profess. [15]For we do not have a high priest who is unable to sympathize with our weaknesses, but we have one who has been tempted in every way, just as we are— yet was without sin. [16]Let us then approach the throne of grace with confidence, so that we may receive mercy and find grace to help us in our time of need.

PRAY, ALWAYS PRAY; THOUGH WEARY, FAINT, AND LONE,
PRAYER NESTLES BY THE FATHER'S SHELTERING THRONE.
                    —A. B. Simpson

---

[5] Every high priest is selected from among men and is appointed to represent them in matters related to God, to offer gifts and sacrifices for sins. [2]He is able to deal gently with those who are ignorant and are going astray, since he himself is subject to weakness. [3]This is why he has to offer sacrifices for his own sins, as well as for the sins of the people.

[4]No one takes this honor upon himself; he must be called by God, just as Aaron was. [5]So Christ also did not take upon himself the glory of becoming a high priest. But God said to him,

"You are my Son;
today I have become your
Father.[c] "[d]

[6]And he says in another place,

"You are a priest forever,
in the order of Melchizedek."[e]

[7]During the days of Jesus' life on earth, he offered up prayers and petitions with loud cries and tears to the one who could save him from death, and he was heard because of his reverent submission. [8]Although he was a son, he learned obedience from what he suffered [9]and, once made perfect, he became the source of eternal salvation for all who obey him [10]and was designated by God to be high priest in the order of Melchizedek.

Warning Against Falling Away

[11]We have much to say about this, but it is hard to explain because you are slow to learn. [12]In fact, though by this time you ought to be teachers, you need someone to teach you the elementary truths of God's word all over again. You need milk, not solid food! [13]Anyone who lives on milk, being still an infant, is not acquainted with the teaching about righteousness. [14]But solid food is for the mature, who by constant use have trained themselves to distinguish good from evil.

---

[a] 7 Psalm 95:7,8   [b] 14 Or gone into heaven   [c] 5 Or have begotten you   [d] 5 Psalm 2:7
[e] 6 Psalm 110:4

6 Therefore let us leave the elementary teachings about Christ and go on to maturity, not laying again the foundation of repentance from acts that lead to death,[a] and of faith in God, [2]instruction about baptisms, the laying on of hands, the resurrection of the dead, and eternal judgment. [3]And God permitting, we will do so.

[4]It is impossible for those who have once been enlightened, who have tasted the heavenly gift, who have shared in

[a] 1 Or *from useless rituals*

THURSDAY

THE PRIESTHOOD OF CHRIST

Jacobus Arminius

VERSE: Hebrews 4:15   **PASSAGE:** Hebrews 4:14–16

isdom was again desired in the Divine Council. She declared that [to resolve the conflict between Justice and Mercy] a man must be born from among men, who might have a nature in common with the rest of his brethren, that, being in all things tempted as they were, he might be able to sympathize with others in their suffering; and yet, that he should . . . not be under dominion of sin; that he should be one in whom Satan could find nothing worthy of condemnation, who should not be tormented by a consciousness of sin, and who should not even know sin, that is, one who should be "born in the likeness of sinful flesh, and yet without sin. For such a high priest became us, who is holy, harmless, undefiled, and separate from sinners" (Hebrews 7:26, KJV). But that he might have a community of nature with men, he ought to be born of a human being; and that he might have no participation in crime with them, but might be holy, he ought to be conceived by the Holy Ghost, because sanctification is his proper work . . . Therefore, the Word of God, who from the beginning was with God and by whom the worlds and all things visible and invisible were created, ought himself to be made flesh, to undertake the office of the priesthood, and to offer his own flesh to God as a sacrifice for the life of the world.

We now have the person who was entrusted with the priesthood and to whom the province was assigned of atoning for the common offense: it is Jesus Christ, the Son of God and of man.

ADDITIONAL SCRIPTURE READING:
John 1:1–5, 14; Hebrews 7:23–28

Go to page 1441 for your next devotional reading.

1500   1700

the Holy Spirit, [5]who have tasted the goodness of the word of God and the powers of the coming age, [6]if they fall away, to be brought back to repentance, because[a] to their loss they are crucifying the Son of God all over again and subjecting him to public disgrace.

[7]Land that drinks in the rain often falling on it and that produces a crop useful to those for whom it is farmed receives the blessing of God. [8]But land that produces thorns and thistles is worthless and is in danger of being cursed. In the end it will be burned.

[9]Even though we speak like this, dear friends, we are confident of better things in your case—things that accompany salvation. [10]God is not unjust; he will not forget your work and the love you have shown him as you have helped his people and continue to help them. [11]We want each of you to show this same diligence to the very end, in order to make your hope sure. [12]We do not want you to become lazy, but to imitate those who through faith and patience inherit what has been promised.

The Certainty of God's Promise

[13]When God made his promise to Abraham, since there was no one greater for him to swear by, he swore by himself, [14]saying, "I will surely bless you and give you many descendants."[b] [15]And so after waiting patiently, Abraham received what was promised.

[16]Men swear by someone greater than themselves, and the oath confirms what is said and puts an end to all argument. [17]Because God wanted to make the unchanging nature of his purpose very clear to the heirs of what was promised, he confirmed it with an oath. [18]God did this so that, by two unchangeable things in which it is impossible for God to lie, we who have fled to take hold of the hope offered to us may be greatly encouraged. [19]We have this hope as an anchor for the soul, firm and secure. It enters the inner sanctuary behind the curtain, [20]where Jesus, who went before us, has entered on our behalf. He has become a high priest forever, in the order of Melchizedek.

Melchizedek the Priest

7 This Melchizedek was king of Salem and priest of God Most High. He met Abraham returning from the defeat of the kings and blessed him, [2]and Abraham gave him a tenth of everything. First, his name means "king of righteousness"; then also, "king of Salem" means "king of peace." [3]Without father or mother, without genealogy, without beginning of days or end of life, like the Son of God he remains a priest forever.

[4]Just think how great he was: Even the patriarch Abraham gave him a tenth of the plunder! [5]Now the law requires the descendants of Levi who become priests to collect a tenth from the people—that is, their brothers—even though their brothers are descended from Abraham. [6]This man, however, did not trace his descent from Levi, yet he collected a tenth from Abraham and blessed him who had the promises. [7]And without doubt the lesser person is blessed by the greater. [8]In the one case, the tenth is collected by men who die; but in the other case, by him who is declared to be living. [9]One might even say that Levi, who collects the tenth, paid the tenth through Abraham, [10]because when Melchizedek met Abraham, Levi was still in the body of his ancestor.

Jesus Like Melchizedek

[11]If perfection could have been attained through the Levitical priesthood (for on the basis of it the law was given to the people), why was there still need for another priest to come—one in the order of Melchizedek, not in the order of Aaron? [12]For when there is a change of the priesthood, there must also be a change of the law. [13]He of whom these things are said belonged to a different tribe, and no one from that tribe has ever served at the altar. [14]For it is clear that our Lord descended from Judah, and in regard to that tribe Moses said nothing about priests. [15]And what we have said is even more clear if another priest like Melchizedek appears, [16]one who has become a priest not on the basis of a regulation as to his ancestry but on the

basis of the power of an indestructible life. **17**For it is declared:

"You are a priest forever,
    in the order of Melchizedek."*a*

18The former regulation is set aside because it was weak and useless **19**(for the law made nothing perfect), and a better hope is introduced, by which we draw near to God.

20And it was not without an oath! Others became priests without any oath, **21**but he became a priest with an oath when God said to him:

"The Lord has sworn
    and will not change his mind:
    'You are a priest forever.' "*a*

22Because of this oath, Jesus has become the guarantee of a better covenant.

23Now there have been many of those priests, since death prevented them from continuing in office; **24**but because Jesus lives forever, he has a permanent priesthood. **25**Therefore he is able to save completely*b* those who come to God through him, because he always lives to intercede for them.

26Such a high priest meets our need— one who is holy, blameless, pure, set apart from sinners, exalted above the heavens. **27**Unlike the other high priests, he does not need to offer sacrifices day after day, first for his own sins, and then for the sins of the people. He sacrificed for their sins once for all when he offered himself. **28**For the law appoints as high priests men who are weak; but the oath, which came after the law, appointed the Son, who has been made perfect forever.

The High Priest of a New Covenant

8 The point of what we are saying is this: We do have such a high priest, who sat down at the right hand of the throne of the Majesty in heaven, **2**and who serves in the sanctuary, the true tabernacle set up by the Lord, not by man.

3Every high priest is appointed to offer both gifts and sacrifices, and so it was necessary for this one also to have something to offer. **4**If he were on earth, he would not be a priest, for there are already men who offer the gifts prescribed by the law. **5**They serve at a sanctuary that is a copy and shadow of what is in heaven. This is why Moses was warned when he was about to build the tabernacle: "See to it that you make everything according to the pattern shown you on the mountain."*c* **6**But the ministry Jesus has received is as superior to theirs as the covenant of which he is mediator is superior to the old one, and it is founded on better promises.

7For if there had been nothing wrong with that first covenant, no place would have been sought for another. **8**But God found fault with the people and said*d*:

"The time is coming, declares the
        Lord,
    when I will make a new covenant
    with the house of Israel
    and with the house of Judah.
9It will not be like the covenant
    I made with their forefathers
    when I took them by the hand
    to lead them out of Egypt,
because they did not remain faithful
        to my covenant,
    and I turned away from them,
            declares the Lord.
10This is the covenant I will make with
        the house of Israel
    after that time, declares the Lord.
I will put my laws in their minds
    and write them on their hearts.
I will be their God,
    and they will be my people.
11No longer will a man teach his
        neighbor,
    or a man his brother, saying, 'Know
        the Lord,'
because they will all know me,
    from the least of them to the
        greatest.
12For I will forgive their wickedness
    and will remember their sins no
        more."*e*

13By calling this covenant "new," he has made the first one obsolete; and what is obsolete and aging will soon disappear.

a 17,21 Psalm 110:4   *b 25* Or *forever*   *c 5* Exodus 25:40   *d 8* Some manuscripts may be translated *fault and said to the people.*   *e 12* Jer. 31:31–34

Worship in the Earthly Tabernacle

9 Now the first covenant had regulations for worship and also an earthly sanctuary. ²A tabernacle was set up. In its first room were the lampstand, the table and the consecrated bread; this was called the Holy Place. ³Behind the second curtain was a room called the Most Holy Place, ⁴which had the golden altar of incense and the gold-covered ark of the covenant. This ark contained the gold jar of manna, Aaron's staff that had budded, and the stone tablets of the covenant. ⁵Above the ark were the cherubim of the Glory, overshadowing the atonement cover.ᵃ But we cannot discuss these things in detail now.

⁶When everything had been arranged like this, the priests entered regularly into the outer room to carry on their ministry. ⁷But only the high priest entered the inner room, and that only once a year, and never without blood, which he offered for himself and for the sins the people had committed in ignorance. ⁸The Holy Spirit was showing by this that the way into the Most Holy Place had not yet been disclosed as long as the first tabernacle was still standing. ⁹This is an illustration for the present time, indicating that the gifts and sacrifices being offered were not able to clear the conscience of the worshiper. ¹⁰They are only a matter of food and drink and various ceremonial washings—external regulations applying until the time of the new order.

The Blood of Christ

¹¹When Christ came as high priest of the good things that are already here,ᵇ he went through the greater and more perfect tabernacle that is not man-made, that is to say, not a part of this creation. ¹²He did not enter by means of the blood of goats and calves; but he entered the Most Holy Place once for all by his own blood, having obtained eternal redemption. ¹³The blood of goats and bulls and the ashes of a heifer sprinkled on those who are ceremonially unclean sanctify them so that they are outwardly clean. ¹⁴How much more, then, will the blood of Christ, who through the eternal Spirit offered himself unblemished to God, cleanse our consciences from acts that lead to death,ᶜ so that we may serve the living God!

¹⁵For this reason Christ is the mediator of a new covenant, that those who are called may receive the promised eternal inheritance—now that he has died as a ransom to set them free from the sins committed under the first covenant.

¹⁶In the case of a will,ᵈ it is necessary to prove the death of the one who made it, ¹⁷because a will is in force only when somebody has died; it never takes effect while the one who made it is living. ¹⁸This is why even the first covenant was not put into effect without blood. ¹⁹When Moses had proclaimed every commandment of the law to all the people, he took the blood of calves, together with water, scarlet wool and branches of hyssop, and sprinkled the scroll and all the people. ²⁰He said, "This is the blood of the covenant, which God has commanded you to keep."ᵉ ²¹In the same way, he sprinkled with the blood both the tabernacle and everything used in its ceremonies. ²²In fact, the law requires that nearly everything be cleansed with blood, and without the shedding of blood there is no forgiveness.

²³It was necessary, then, for the copies of the heavenly things to be purified with these sacrifices, but the heavenly things themselves with better sacrifices than these. ²⁴For Christ did not enter a man-made sanctuary that was only a copy of the true one; he entered heaven itself, now to appear for us in God's presence. ²⁵Nor did he enter heaven to offer himself again and again, the way the high priest enters the Most Holy Place every year with blood that is not his own. ²⁶Then Christ would have had to suffer many times since the creation of the world. But now he has appeared once for all at the end of the ages to do away with sin by the sacrifice of himself. ²⁷Just as man is destined to die once, and after that to face judgment, ²⁸so Christ was sacrificed once to take away the sins of many people; and he will appear a second time, not to bear

---

ᵃ 5 Traditionally *the mercy seat*   ᵇ 11 Some early manuscripts *are to come*   ᶜ 14 Or *from useless rituals*   ᵈ 16 Same Greek word as *covenant*; also in verse 17   ᵉ 20 Exodus 24:8

sin, but to bring salvation to those who are waiting for him.

Christ's Sacrifice Once for All

10 The law is only a shadow of the good things that are coming—not the realities themselves. For this reason it can never, by the same sacrifices repeated endlessly year after year, make perfect those who draw near to worship. ²If it could, would they not have stopped being offered? For the worshipers would have been cleansed once for all, and would no longer have felt guilty for their sins. ³But those sacrifices are an annual reminder of sins,

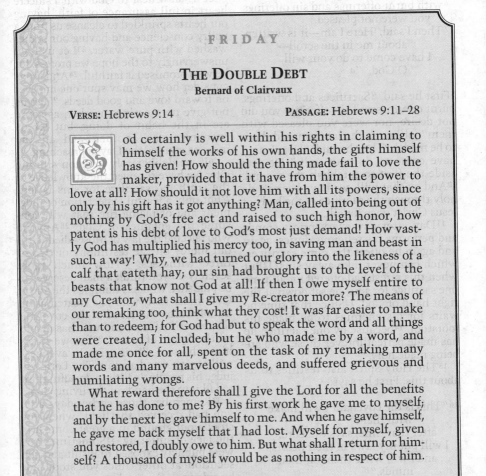

FRIDAY

THE DOUBLE DEBT

Bernard of Clairvaux

VERSE: Hebrews 9:14   **PASSAGE:** Hebrews 9:11–28

od certainly is well within his rights in claiming to himself the works of his own hands, the gifts himself has given! How should the thing made fail to love the maker, provided that it have from him the power to love at all? How should it not love him with all its powers, since only by his gift has it got anything? Man, called into being out of nothing by God's free act and raised to such high honor, how patent is his debt of love to God's most just demand! How vastly God has multiplied his mercy too, in saving man and beast in such a way! Why, we had turned our glory into the likeness of a calf that eateth hay; our sin had brought us to the level of the beasts that know not God at all! If then I owe myself entire to my Creator, what shall I give my Re-creator more? The means of our remaking too, think what they cost! It was far easier to make than to redeem; for God had but to speak the word and all things were created, I included; but he who made me by a word, and made me once for all, spent on the task of my remaking many words and many marvelous deeds, and suffered grievous and humiliating wrongs.

What reward therefore shall I give the Lord for all the benefits that he has done to me? By his first work he gave me to myself; and by the next he gave himself to me. And when he gave himself, he gave me back myself that I had lost. Myself for myself, given and restored, I doubly owe to him. But what shall I return for himself? A thousand of myself would be as nothing in respect of him.

ADDITIONAL SCRIPTURE READING:
Romans 12:1; Hebrews 13:15–16

Go to page 1444 for your next devotional reading.

500   1500

[4]because it is impossible for the blood of bulls and goats to take away sins.

[5]Therefore, when Christ came into the world, he said:

"Sacrifice and offering you did not desire,
    but a body you prepared for me;
[6]with burnt offerings and sin offerings you were not pleased.
[7]Then I said, 'Here I am—it is written about me in the scroll—
    I have come to do your will,
        O God.' "[a]

[8]First he said, "Sacrifices and offerings, burnt offerings and sin offerings you did not desire, nor were you pleased with them" (although the law required them to be made). [9]Then he said, "Here I am, I have come to do your will." He sets aside the first to establish the second. [10]And by that will, we have been made holy through the sacrifice of the body of Jesus Christ once for all.

[11]Day after day every priest stands and performs his religious duties; again and again he offers the same sacrifices, which can never take away sins. [12]But when this priest had offered for all time one sacrifice for sins, he sat down at the right hand of God. [13]Since that time he waits for his enemies to be made his footstool, [14]because by one sacrifice he has made perfect forever those who are being made holy.

[15]The Holy Spirit also testifies to us about this. First he says:

[16]"This is the covenant I will make with them
    after that time, says the Lord.
I will put my laws in their hearts,
    and I will write them on their minds."[b]

[17]Then he adds:

"Their sins and lawless acts
    I will remember no more."[c]

[18]And where these have been forgiven, there is no longer any sacrifice for sin.

A Call to Persevere

[19]Therefore, brothers, since we have confidence to enter the Most Holy Place by the blood of Jesus, [20]by a new and living way opened for us through the curtain, that is, his body, [21]and since we have a great priest over the house of God, [22]let us draw near to God with a sincere heart in full assurance of faith, having our hearts sprinkled to cleanse us from a guilty conscience and having our bodies washed with pure water. [23]Let us hold unswervingly to the hope we profess, for he who promised is faithful. [24]And let us consider how we may spur one another on toward love and good deeds. [25]Let us not give up meeting together, as some are in the habit of doing, but let us encourage one another—and all the more as you see the Day approaching.

[26]If we deliberately keep on sinning after we have received the knowledge of the truth, no sacrifice for sins is left, [27]but only a fearful expectation of judgment and of raging fire that will consume the enemies of God. [28]Anyone who rejected the law of Moses died without mercy on the testimony of two or three witnesses. [29]How much more severely do you think a man deserves to be punished who has trampled the Son of God under foot, who has treated as an unholy thing the blood of the covenant that sanctified him, and who has insulted the Spirit of grace? [30]For we know him who said, "It is mine to avenge; I will repay,"[d] and again, "The Lord will judge his people."[e] [31]It is a dreadful thing to fall into the hands of the living God.

[32]Remember those earlier days after you had received the light, when you stood your ground in a great contest in the face of suffering. [33]Sometimes you were publicly exposed to insult and persecution; at other times you stood side by side with those who were so treated. [34]You sympathized with those in prison and joyfully accepted the confiscation of your property, because you knew that you yourselves had better and lasting possessions.

[35]So do not throw away your confidence; it will be richly rewarded. [36]You need to persevere so that when you have

---

[a] 7 Psalm 40:6–8 (see Septuagint)   [b] 16 Jer. 31:33   [c] 17 Jer. 31:34   [d] 30 Deut. 32:35   [e] 30 Deut. 32:36; Psalm 135:14

done the will of God, you will receive what he has promised. ³⁷For in just a very little while,

"He who is coming will come and
      will not delay.
38   But my righteous one*a* will live by
         faith.
   And if he shrinks back,
      I will not be pleased with him."*b*

³⁹But we are not of those who shrink back and are destroyed, but of those who believe and are saved.

By Faith

11 Now faith is being sure of what we hope for and certain of what we do not see. ²This is what the ancients were commended for.

---

³By faith we understand that the universe was formed at God's command, so that what is seen was not made out of what was visible.

⁴By faith Abel offered God a better sacrifice than Cain did. By faith he was commended as a righteous man, when God spoke well of his offerings. And by faith he still speaks, even though he is dead.

⁵By faith Enoch was taken from this life, so that he did not experience death; he could not be found, because God had taken him away. For before he was taken, he was commended as one who pleased God. ⁶And without faith it is impossible to please God, because anyone who comes to him must believe that he exists and that he rewards those who earnestly seek him.

⁷By faith Noah, when warned about things not yet seen, in holy fear built an ark to save his family. By his faith he

condemned the world and became heir of the righteousness that comes by faith.

⁸By faith Abraham, when called to go to a place he would later receive as his inheritance, obeyed and went, even though he did not know where he was going. ⁹By faith he made his home in the promised land like a stranger in a foreign country; he lived in tents, as did Isaac and Jacob, who were heirs with him of the same promise. ¹⁰For he was looking forward to the city with foundations, whose architect and builder is God.

¹¹By faith Abraham, even though he was past age—and Sarah herself was barren—was enabled to become a father because he*c* considered him faithful who had made the promise. ¹²And so from this one man, and he as good as dead, came descendants as numerous as the stars in the sky and as countless as the sand on the seashore.

¹³All these people were still living by faith when they died. They did not receive the things promised; they only saw them and welcomed them from a distance. And they admitted that they were aliens and strangers on earth. ¹⁴People who say such things show that they are looking for a country of their own. ¹⁵If they had been thinking of the country they had left, they would have had opportunity to return. ¹⁶Instead, they were longing for a better country—a heavenly one. Therefore God is not ashamed to be called their God, for he has prepared a city for them.

¹⁷By faith Abraham, when God tested him, offered Isaac as a sacrifice. He who had received the promises was about to sacrifice his one and only son, ¹⁸even though God had said to him, "It is through Isaac that your offspring*d* will be reckoned."*e* ¹⁹Abraham reasoned that God could raise the dead, and figuratively speaking, he did receive Isaac back from death.

²⁰By faith Isaac blessed Jacob and Esau in regard to their future.

²¹By faith Jacob, when he was dying, blessed each of Joseph's sons, and worshiped as he leaned on the top of his staff.

²²By faith Joseph, when his end was near, spoke about the exodus of the

---

a 38 One early manuscript *But the righteous*   *b* 38 Hab. 2:3,4   *c* 11 Or *By faith even Sarah, who was*
past age, was enabled to bear children because she   *d* 18 Greek *seed*   *e* 18 Gen. 21:12

MY KING WILL SOON COME BACK AGAIN

Watchman Nee

VERSE: 2 Timothy 4:8   **PASSAGE:** 2 Timothy 4:6–8

y King will soon come back again,
The sky be filled with him;
The universe to be redeemed
Will see his light therein.
The Lord will soon fulfill his plan,
His footsteps now I hear;
His glorious frame I faintly see
Beginning to appear.

I'm longing for his presence blest
And dare not slothful be
While waiting for my Lord's return,
His own dear self to see.
My only hope—that he may come
And change my faith to sight;
There is no other joy on earth
Which gives my heart delight . . .

My Savior, all thy holy words
Can never doubted be;
With them encouraged day by day,
I'm faithful unto thee.
Oh, may thy glory soon appear,
The foe be overthrown;
Thy promises be realized,
And we brought to thy throne.

ADDITIONAL SCRIPTURE READING:
Matthew 25:31; Hebrews 9:28

Go to page 1446 for your next devotional reading.

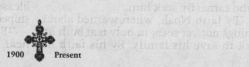

1900   Present

Israelites from Egypt and gave instructions about his bones.

23By faith Moses' parents hid him for three months after he was born, because they saw he was no ordinary child, and they were not afraid of the king's edict.

24By faith Moses, when he had grown up, refused to be known as the son of Pharaoh's daughter. 25He chose to be mistreated along with the people of God rather than to enjoy the pleasures of sin for a short time. 26He regarded disgrace for the sake of Christ as of greater value than the treasures of Egypt, because he was looking ahead to his reward. 27By faith he left Egypt, not fearing the king's anger; he persevered because he saw him who is invisible. 28By faith he kept the Passover and the sprinkling of blood, so that the destroyer of the firstborn would not touch the firstborn of Israel.

29By faith the people passed through the Red Sea*a* as on dry land; but when the Egyptians tried to do so, they were drowned.

30By faith the walls of Jericho fell, after the people had marched around them for seven days.

31By faith the prostitute Rahab, because she welcomed the spies, was not killed with those who were disobedient.*b*

32And what more shall I say? I do not have time to tell about Gideon, Barak, Samson, Jephthah, David, Samuel and the prophets, 33who through faith conquered kingdoms, administered justice, and gained what was promised; who shut the mouths of lions, 34quenched the fury of the flames, and escaped the edge of the sword; whose weakness was turned to strength; and who became powerful in battle and routed foreign armies. 35Women received back their dead, raised to life again. Others were tortured and refused to be released, so that they might gain a better resurrection. 36Some faced jeers and flogging, while still others were chained and put in prison. 37They were stoned*c*; they were sawed in two; they were put to death by the sword. They went about in sheepskins and goatskins, destitute, persecuted and mistreated— 38the world was not worthy of them. They wandered in deserts and mountains, and in caves and holes in the ground.

39These were all commended for their faith, yet none of them received what had been promised. 40God had planned something better for us so that only together with us would they be made perfect.

God Disciplines His Sons

12 Therefore, since we are surrounded by such a great cloud of witnesses, let us throw off everything that hinders and the sin that so easily entangles, and let us run with perseverance the race marked out for us. 2Let us fix our eyes on Jesus, the author and perfecter of our faith, who for the joy set before him endured the cross, scorning its shame, and sat down at the right hand of the throne of God. 3Consider him who endured such opposition from sinful men, so that you will not grow weary and lose heart.

4In your struggle against sin, you have not yet resisted to the point of shedding your blood. 5And you have forgotten that word of encouragement that addresses you as sons:

"My son, do not make light of the
    Lord's discipline,
  and do not lose heart when he
    rebukes you,
6because the Lord disciplines those he
    loves,
  and he punishes everyone he
    accepts as a son."*d*

7Endure hardship as discipline; God is treating you as sons. For what son is not disciplined by his father? 8If you are not disciplined (and everyone undergoes discipline), then you are illegitimate children and not true sons. 9Moreover, we have all had human fathers who disciplined us and we respected them for it. How much more should we submit to the Father of our spirits and live! 10Our fathers disciplined us for a little while as they thought best; but God disciplines us for our good, that we may share in his holiness. 11No discipline seems pleasant at the time, but painful. Later on, however, it produces a harvest of righteousness

a 29 That is, Sea of Reeds   *b 31* Or *unbelieving*   *c 37* Some early manuscripts *stoned; they were put*
to the test;   *d 6* Prov. 3:11,12

NOW IT IS OUR TURN
Cardinal John Henry Newman

VERSE: Hebrews 12:1   **PASSAGE:** Hebrews 12:1–3

nce it was the apostles' turn. It was St. Paul's turn once. He had all cares upon him all at once; covered from head to foot with cares, as Job with sores. And, as if all this were not enough, he had a thorn in the flesh added—some personal discomfort ever with him. Yet he did his part well—he was as a strong and bold wrestler in his day, and at the close of it was able to say, "I have fought a good fight, I have finished my course, I have kept the faith" (2 Timothy 4:7, KJV). And after him, the excellent of the earth, the white-robed army of martyrs, and the cheerful company of confessors, each in his turn, each in his day, have likewise played the man. And so down to this very time, when faith has well-nigh failed, first one and then another have been called out to exhibit before the Great King. It is as though all of us were allowed to stand round his throne at once, and he called on first this man, and then that, to take up the chant by himself, each in his turn having to repeat the melody which his brethren have before gone through. Or as if we held a solemn dance to his honor in the courts of heaven, and each had by himself to perform some one and the same solemn and graceful movement at a signal given. Or as if it were some trial of strength or of agility, and, while the ring of bystanders beheld and applauded, we in succession, one by one, were actors in the pageant. Such is our state; angels are looking on, Christ has gone before—Christ has given us an example, that we may follow in his steps. He went through far more, infinitely more, than we can be called to suffer. Our brethren have gone through much more; and they seem to encourage us by their success, and to sympathize in our essay. Now it is our turn; and all ministering spirits keep silence and look on. O let not your foot slip, or your eye be false, or your ear dull, or your attention flagging!

ADDITIONAL SCRIPTURE READING:
John 13:15; 1 Peter 2:20–21

Go to page 1451 for your next devotional reading.

1700   1900

and peace for those who have been trained by it.

12Therefore, strengthen your feeble arms and weak knees. 13"Make level paths for your feet,"a so that the lame may not be disabled, but rather healed.

Warning Against Refusing God

14Make every effort to live in peace with all men and to be holy; without holiness no one will see the Lord. 15See to it that no one misses the grace of God and that no bitter root grows up to cause trouble and defile many. 16See that no one is sexually immoral, or is godless like Esau, who for a single meal sold his inheritance rights as the oldest son. 17Afterward, as you know, when he wanted to inherit this blessing, he was rejected. He could bring about no change of mind, though he sought the blessing with tears.

18You have not come to a mountain that can be touched and that is burning with fire; to darkness, gloom and storm; 19to a trumpet blast or to such a voice speaking words that those who heard it begged that no further word be spoken to them, 20because they could not bear what was commanded: "If even an animal touches the mountain, it must be stoned."b 21The sight was so terrifying that Moses said, "I am trembling with fear."c

22But you have come to Mount Zion, to the heavenly Jerusalem, the city of the living God. You have come to thousands upon thousands of angels in joyful assembly, 23to the church of the firstborn, whose names are written in heaven. You have come to God, the judge of all men, to the spirits of righteous men made perfect, 24to Jesus the mediator of a new covenant, and to the sprinkled blood that speaks a better word than the blood of Abel.

25See to it that you do not refuse him who speaks. If they did not escape when they refused him who warned them on earth, how much less will we, if we turn away from him who warns us from heaven? 26At that time his voice shook the earth, but now he has promised, "Once more I will shake not only the earth but also the heavens."d 27The words "once more" indicate the removing of what can be shaken—that is, created things—so that what cannot be shaken may remain.

28Therefore, since we are receiving a kingdom that cannot be shaken, let us be thankful, and so worship God acceptably with reverence and awe, 29for our "God is a consuming fire."e

Concluding Exhortations

13 Keep on loving each other as brothers. 2Do not forget to entertain strangers, for by so doing some people have entertained angels without knowing it. 3Remember those in prison as if you were their fellow prisoners, and those who are mistreated as if you yourselves were suffering.

4Marriage should be honored by all, and the marriage bed kept pure, for God will judge the adulterer and all the sexually immoral. 5Keep your lives free from the love of money and be content with what you have, because God has said,

"Never will I leave you;
    never will I forsake you."f

6So we say with confidence,

"The Lord is my helper; I will not be
    afraid.
What can man do to me?"g

7Remember your leaders, who spoke the word of God to you. Consider the outcome of their way of life and imitate their faith. 8Jesus Christ is the same yesterday and today and forever.

9Do not be carried away by all kinds of strange teachings. It is good for our hearts to be strengthened by grace, not by ceremonial foods, which are of no value to those who eat them. 10We have an altar from which those who minister at the tabernacle have no right to eat.

11The high priest carries the blood of animals into the Most Holy Place as a sin offering, but the bodies are burned outside the camp. 12And so Jesus also suffered outside the city gate to make the people holy through his own blood. 13Let

a 13 Prov. 4:26   b 20 Exodus 19:12,13   c 21 Deut. 9:19   d 26 Haggai 2:6   e 29 Deut. 4:24
f 5 Deut. 31:6   g 6 Psalm 118:6,7

us, then, go to him outside the camp, bearing the disgrace he bore. ¹⁴For here we do not have an enduring city, but we are looking for the city that is to come.

¹⁵Through Jesus, therefore, let us continually offer to God a sacrifice of praise—the fruit of lips that confess his name. ¹⁶And do not forget to do good and to share with others, for with such sacrifices God is pleased.

¹⁷Obey your leaders and submit to their authority. They keep watch over you as men who must give an account. Obey them so that their work will be a joy, not a burden, for that would be of no advantage to you.

¹⁸Pray for us. We are sure that we have a clear conscience and desire to live honorably in every way. ¹⁹I particularly urge you to pray so that I may be restored to you soon.

²⁰May the God of peace, who through the blood of the eternal covenant brought back from the dead our Lord Jesus, that great Shepherd of the sheep, ²¹equip you with everything good for doing his will, and may he work in us what is pleasing to him, through Jesus Christ, to whom be glory for ever and ever. Amen.

²²Brothers, I urge you to bear with my word of exhortation, for I have written you only a short letter.

²³I want you to know that our brother Timothy has been released. If he arrives soon, I will come with him to see you.

²⁴Greet all your leaders and all God's people. Those from Italy send you their greetings.

²⁵Grace be with you all.

JAMES

HE AUTHOR OF THIS LETTER IDEN-
TIFIES HIMSELF AS JAMES, PROBABLY
THE BROTHER OF JESUS AND THE
LEADER OF THE JERUSALEM COUNCIL. THE
BOOK OF JAMES HAS A DISTINCTIVELY JEWISH
NATURE THAT SUGGESTS IT WAS COMPOSED
WHEN THE CHURCH WAS STILL PREDOMI-
NANTLY JEWISH. THE LETTER DEALS PRIMAR-
ILY WITH THE PRACTICAL ASPECTS OF THE
CHRISTIAN FAITH, CONSISTING OF HARD-
HITTING COUNSEL FOR EVERYDAY CONDUCT.

1 James, a servant of God and of the Lord Jesus Christ,

To the twelve tribes scattered among the nations:

Greetings.

Trials and Temptations

2Consider it pure joy, my brothers, whenever you face trials of many kinds,

---

ADVERSITIES DO NOT MAKE A MAN FRAIL; THEY
SHOW WHAT SORT OF MAN HE IS.

—*Thomas à Kempis*

3because you know that the testing of your faith develops perseverance. 4Perseverance must finish its work so that you may be mature and complete, not lacking anything. 5If any of you lacks wisdom, he should ask God, who gives generously to all without finding fault, and it will be given to him. 6But when he asks, he must believe and not doubt, because he who doubts is like a wave of the sea, blown and tossed by the wind. 7That man should not think he will receive anything from the Lord; 8he is a double-minded man, unstable in all he does.

9The brother in humble circumstances ought to take pride in his high position. 10But the one who is rich should take pride in his low position, because he will pass away like a wild flower. 11For the sun rises with scorching heat and withers the plant; its blossom falls and its beauty is destroyed. In the same way, the rich man will fade away even while he goes about his business.

¹²Blessed is the man who perseveres under trial, because when he has stood the test, he will receive the crown of life that God has promised to those who love him.

¹³When tempted, no one should say, "God is tempting me." For God cannot be tempted by evil, nor does he tempt anyone; ¹⁴but each one is tempted when, by his own evil desire, he is dragged away and enticed. ¹⁵Then, after desire has conceived, it gives birth to sin; and sin, when it is full-grown, gives birth to death.

¹⁶Don't be deceived, my dear brothers. ¹⁷Every good and perfect gift is from above, coming down from the Father of the heavenly lights, who does not change like shifting shadows. ¹⁸He chose to give us birth through the word of truth, that we might be a kind of firstfruits of all he created.

Listening and Doing

¹⁹My dear brothers, take note of this: Everyone should be quick to listen, slow to speak and slow to become angry, ²⁰for man's anger does not bring about the righteous life that God desires. ²¹Therefore, get rid of all moral filth and the evil that is so prevalent and humbly accept the word planted in you, which can save you.

ANGER IS A WEED; HATE IS THE TREE.
—*Augustine*

---

²²Do not merely listen to the word, and so deceive yourselves. Do what it says. ²³Anyone who listens to the word but does not do what it says is like a man who looks at his face in a mirror ²⁴and, after looking at himself, goes away and immediately forgets what he looks like. ²⁵But the man who looks intently into the perfect law that gives freedom, and continues to do this, not forgetting what he has heard, but doing it—he will be blessed in what he does.

²⁶If anyone considers himself religious and yet does not keep a tight rein on his tongue, he deceives himself and his religion is worthless. ²⁷Religion that God our Father accepts as pure and faultless is this: to look after orphans and widows in their distress and to keep oneself from being polluted by the world.

Favoritism Forbidden

2 My brothers, as believers in our glorious Lord Jesus Christ, don't show favoritism. ²Suppose a man comes into your meeting wearing a gold ring and fine clothes, and a poor man in shabby clothes also comes in. ³If you show special attention to the man wearing fine clothes and say, "Here's a good seat for you," but say to the poor man, "You stand there" or "Sit on the floor by my feet," ⁴have you not discriminated among yourselves and become judges with evil thoughts?

⁵Listen, my dear brothers: Has not God chosen those who are poor in the eyes of the world to be rich in faith and to inherit the kingdom he promised those who love him? ⁶But you have insulted the poor. Is it not the rich who are exploiting you? Are they not the ones who are dragging you into court? ⁷Are they not the ones who are slandering the noble name of him to whom you belong?

⁸If you really keep the royal law found in Scripture, "Love your neighbor as yourself,"ᵃ you are doing right. ⁹But if you show favoritism, you sin and are convicted by the law as lawbreakers. ¹⁰For whoever keeps the whole law and yet stumbles at just one point is guilty of breaking all of it. ¹¹For he who said, "Do not commit adultery,"ᵇ also said, "Do not murder."ᶜ If you do not commit adultery but do commit murder, you have become a lawbreaker.

¹²Speak and act as those who are going to be judged by the law that gives freedom, ¹³because judgment without mercy will be shown to anyone who has not been merciful. Mercy triumphs over judgment!

Faith and Deeds

¹⁴What good is it, my brothers, if a man claims to have faith but has no

---

ᵃ 8 Lev. 19:18   ᵇ 11 Exodus 20:14; Deut. 5:18   ᶜ 11 Exodus 20:13; Deut. 5:17

TUESDAY

GOD'S WORD IS TALKING TO ME
Søren Kierkegaard

VERSE: James 1:23–24   **PASSAGE:** James 1:22–25

 hat is required in order to look at oneself with true blessing in the mirror of the Word?

The first requirement is that you do not look at the mirror, in order to inspect it, but that you look at yourself in the mirror . . . If there were only a single passage in the Bible which you understood—well, that is your first concern. You need not sit down and ponder over the obscure passages. God's Word is given in order that you may act according to it, not in order that you may practice the interpretation of what you find obscure . . . The second requirement is that, in order to see yourself in the mirror when you read God's Word, you must remember to be constantly saying to yourself, "It is speaking to me; I am the one it is talking about" . . . If God's Word is only a doctrine to you, it is no mirror. It is just as impossible to be mirrored in a doctrine as in a wall . . . No, when you read God's Word, you must constantly be saying to yourself, "It is talking to me, and about me." Finally, if you desire to observe yourself in the mirror of the Word with real blessing, you must not at once begin to forget how you looked. You must not be the forgetful hearer (or reader) of whom the apostle says that he carefully looked at his own face in a mirror and straightway forgot what manner of man he was . . . The right thing to do is to say to yourself at once: "I shall begin now to prevent myself from forgetting. Now, this very moment, I make this promise to myself and to God, even if it be but for the next hour or for today. For that length of time it shall be certain that I do not forget" . . . Doing it this way is much better than taking too big a bite to begin with, and saying "I shall never forget." It is much better never to forget to remember immediately than immediately to say that you will never forget.

ADDITIONAL SCRIPTURE READING:
Hebrews 4:12; 2 Timothy 2:1–19

Go to page 1453 for your next devotional reading.

1900   Present

deeds? Can such faith save him? [15]Suppose a brother or sister is without clothes and daily food. [16]If one of you says to him, "Go, I wish you well; keep warm and well fed," but does nothing about his physical needs, what good is it? [17]In the same way, faith by itself, if it is not accompanied by action, is dead.

TEACH ME TO FEEL ANOTHER'S WOE,

   TO HIDE THE FAULT I SEE;

THAT MERCY I TO OTHERS SHOW,

   THAT MERCY SHOWN TO ME.

                    —*Alexander Pope*

---

[18]But someone will say, "You have faith; I have deeds."

Show me your faith without deeds, and I will show you my faith by what I do. [19]You believe that there is one God. Good! Even the demons believe that—and shudder.

[20]You foolish man, do you want evidence that faith without deeds is useless[a]? [21]Was not our ancestor Abraham considered righteous for what he did when he offered his son Isaac on the altar? [22]You see that his faith and his actions were working together, and his faith was made complete by what he did. [23]And the scripture was fulfilled that says, "Abraham believed God, and it was credited to him as righteousness,"[b] and he was called God's friend.

MANY CAN SPEAK WELL, BUT FEW CAN DO WELL.
WE ARE BETTER SCHOLARS IN THE THEORY THAN
THE PRACTICE PART, BUT HE IS A TRUE CHRISTIAN
THAT IS PROFICIENT IN BOTH.   —*Anne Bradstreet*

---

[24]You see that a person is justified by what he does and not by faith alone.

[25]In the same way, was not even Rahab the prostitute considered righteous for what she did when she gave lodging to the spies and sent them off in a different direction? [26]As the body without the spirit is dead, so faith without deeds is dead.

Taming the Tongue

3 Not many of you should presume to be teachers, my brothers, because you know that we who teach will be judged more strictly. [2]We all stumble in many ways. If anyone is never at fault in what he says, he is a perfect man, able to keep his whole body in check.

[3]When we put bits into the mouths of horses to make them obey us, we can turn the whole animal. [4]Or take ships as an example. Although they are so large and are driven by strong winds, they are steered by a very small rudder wherever the pilot wants to go. [5]Likewise the tongue is a small part of the body, but it makes great boasts. Consider what a great forest is set on fire by a small spark. [6]The tongue also is a fire, a world of evil among the parts of the body. It corrupts the whole person, sets the whole course of his life on fire, and is itself set on fire by hell.

[7]All kinds of animals, birds, reptiles and creatures of the sea are being tamed and have been tamed by man, [8]but no man can tame the tongue. It is a restless evil, full of deadly poison.

[9]With the tongue we praise our Lord and Father, and with it we curse men, who have been made in God's likeness. [10]Out of the same mouth come praise and cursing. My brothers, this should not be. [11]Can both fresh water and salt[c] water flow from the same spring? [12]My brothers, can a fig tree bear olives, or a grapevine bear figs? Neither can a salt spring produce fresh water.

Two Kinds of Wisdom

[13]Who is wise and understanding among you? Let him show it by his good life, by deeds done in the humility that comes from wisdom. [14]But if you harbor bitter envy and selfish ambition in your hearts, do not boast about it or deny the truth. [15]Such "wisdom" does not come down from heaven but is earthly, unspiritual, of the devil. [16]For where you have envy and selfish ambition, there you find disorder and every evil practice.

[17]But the wisdom that comes from

---

[a] 20 Some early manuscripts *dead*   [b] 23 Gen. 15:6   [c] 11 Greek *bitter* (see also verse 14)

WHO SHALL CONVERT ME?
John Wesley

VERSE: James 2:18   **PASSAGE:** James 2:14–19

 went to America, to convert the Indians; but O! who shall convert me? who, what is he that will deliver me from this evil heart of mischief? I have a fair summer religion. I can talk well; nay, and believe myself, while no danger is near; but let death look me in the face, and my spirit is troubled. Nor can I say, "To die is gain!" (see Philippians 1:21).

> I have a sin of fear, that when I've spun
> My last thread, I shall perish on the shore!

I think, verily, if the gospel be true, I am safe: for I not only have given, and do give, all my goods to feed the poor; I not only give my body to be burned, drowned, or whatever God shall appoint for me; but I follow after charity (though not as I ought, yet as I can), if haply I may attain it. I now believe the gospel is true. "I show my faith by my works," by staking my all upon it. I would do so again and again a thousand times, if the choice were still to make.

Whoever sees me, sees I would be a Christian. Therefore "are my ways not like other men's ways." Therefore I have been, I am, I am content to be, "a by-word, a proverb of reproach." But in a storm I think, "What, if the gospel be not true? Then thou art of all men most foolish. For what hast thou given thy goods, thy ease, thy friends, thy reputation, thy country, thy life? For what art thou wandering over the face of the earth?—A dream! a cunningly-devised fable!"

O! who will deliver me from this fear of death? What shall I do? Where shall I fly from it? Should I fight against it by thinking, or by not thinking of it? A wise man advised me some time since, "Be still and go on." Perhaps this is the best, to look upon it as my cross; when it comes, to let it humble me, and quicken all my good resolutions, especially that of praying without ceasing; and at other times, to take no thought about it, but quietly to go on "in the work of the Lord."

ADDITIONAL SCRIPTURE READING:
1 Corinthians 15:58; Ephesians 6:18

Go to page 1455 for your next devotional reading.

1700   1900

heaven is first of all pure; then peace-loving, considerate, submissive, full of mercy and good fruit, impartial and sincere. 18Peacemakers who sow in peace raise a harvest of righteousness.

Submit Yourselves to God

4 What causes fights and quarrels among you? Don't they come from your desires that battle within you? 2You want something but don't get it. You kill and covet, but you cannot have what you want. You quarrel and fight. You do not have, because you do not ask God. 3When you ask, you do not receive, because you ask with wrong motives, that you may spend what you get on your pleasures.

4You adulterous people, don't you know that friendship with the world is hatred toward God? Anyone who chooses to be a friend of the world becomes an enemy of God. 5Or do you think Scripture says without reason that the spirit he caused to live in us envies intensely?[a] 6But he gives us more grace. That is why Scripture says:

"God opposes the proud
    but gives grace to the humble."[b]

7Submit yourselves, then, to God. Resist the devil, and he will flee from you. 8Come near to God and he will come near to you. Wash your hands, you sinners, and purify your hearts, you double-minded. 9Grieve, mourn and wail. Change your laughter to mourning and your joy to gloom. 10Humble yourselves before the Lord, and he will lift you up.

11Brothers, do not slander one another. Anyone who speaks against his brother or judges him speaks against the law and judges it. When you judge the law, you are not keeping it, but sitting in judgment on it. 12There is only one Lawgiver and Judge, the one who is able to save and destroy. But you—who are you to judge your neighbor?

Boasting About Tomorrow

13Now listen, you who say, "Today or tomorrow we will go to this or that city, spend a year there, carry on business and make money." 14Why, you do not even know what will happen tomorrow. What is your life? You are a mist that appears for a little while and then vanishes. 15Instead, you ought to say, "If it is the Lord's will, we will live and do this or that." 16As it is, you boast and brag. All such boasting is evil. 17Anyone, then, who knows the good he ought to do and doesn't do it, sins.

Warning to Rich Oppressors

5 Now listen, you rich people, weep and wail because of the misery that is coming upon you. 2Your wealth has rotted, and moths have eaten your clothes. 3Your gold and silver are corroded. Their corrosion will testify against you and eat your flesh like fire. You have hoarded wealth in the last days. 4Look! The wages you failed to pay the workmen who mowed your fields are crying out against you. The cries of the harvesters have reached the ears of the Lord Almighty. 5You have lived on earth in luxury and self-indulgence. You have fattened yourselves in the day of slaughter.[c] 6You have condemned and murdered innocent men, who were not opposing you.

Patience in Suffering

7Be patient, then, brothers, until the Lord's coming. See how the farmer waits for the land to yield its valuable crop and how patient he is for the autumn and spring rains. 8You too, be patient and stand firm, because the Lord's coming is near. 9Don't grumble against each other, brothers, or you will be judged. The Judge is standing at the door!

10Brothers, as an example of patience in the face of suffering, take the prophets who spoke in the name of the Lord. 11As you know, we consider blessed those who have persevered. You have heard of Job's perseverance and have seen what the Lord finally brought about. The Lord is full of compassion and mercy.

---

a 5 Or *that God jealously longs for the spirit that he made to live in us; or that the Spirit he caused to live in us longs jealously*   *b 6* Prov. 3:34   *c 5* Or *yourselves as in a day of feasting*

WHERE, FOR WHOM, AND AT WHAT TIME WE OUGHT TO PRAY

John Knox

VERSE: James 5:16   **PASSAGE:** James 5:13–18

rivate prayer, such as men offer by themselves to God in secret, does not require any special place. Jesus Christ, indeed, commands us when we pray to enter into our chamber and close the door, and so to pray secretly unto our Father (see Matthew 6:6). By this he means that we should choose for our prayers such places as will offer least distraction; and also that in our times of prayer we should expel from our minds all vain thoughts. Otherwise, Jesus Christ himself observed no special place of prayer; for we find him sometimes praying on the Mount of Olives, sometimes in the desert, sometimes in the temple, and also in the Garden of Gethsemane. Peter prayed on a housetop; Paul prayed in prison and was heard of God; and he commands men to pray in all places, lifting up to God pure and clean hands, as we find that the prophets and other holy men did, whenever danger or necessity might require.

But public prayers should be made in places appointed for the assembling of Christians; and it is inexcusable willfully to absent oneself from these exercises of worship. I do not mean that to be absent from that particular place is sinful, because that place is more holy than any other; for the whole earth which God has created is equally holy. But the promise clearly made that, "For where two or three are gathered together in my name, there am I in the midst of them" (Matthew 18:20, KJV), condemns all those who neglect to join the congregation gathered in his name.

To be gathered in the name of Jesus Christ means this, to praise and magnify God, the Father, for the infinite blessings which he has given by his only Son, our Lord . . . Within such a congregation common prayers should be offered such as all men who hear may understand, that the hearts of all, joining with the voice of one, might unfeignedly and fervently say, "Amen!"

ADDITIONAL SCRIPTURE READING:
Matthew 6:6; Acts 4:31

Go to page 1459 for your next devotional reading.

1500   1700

12Above all, my brothers, do not swear—not by heaven or by earth or by anything else. Let your "Yes" be yes, and your "No," no, or you will be condemned.

The Prayer of Faith

13Is any one of you in trouble? He should pray. Is anyone happy? Let him sing songs of praise. 14Is any one of you sick? He should call the elders of the church to pray over him and anoint him with oil in the name of the Lord. 15And the prayer offered in faith will make the sick person well; the Lord will raise him up. If he has sinned, he will be forgiven. 16Therefore confess your sins to each other and pray for each other so that you may be healed. The prayer of a righteous man is powerful and effective.

17Elijah was a man just like us. He prayed earnestly that it would not rain, and it did not rain on the land for three and a half years. 18Again he prayed, and the heavens gave rain, and the earth produced its crops.

19My brothers, if one of you should wander from the truth and someone should bring him back, 20remember this: Whoever turns a sinner from the error of his way will save him from death and cover over a multitude of sins.

1 PETER

HE RECIPIENTS OF THIS LETTER HAD BEEN SUFFERING VARIOUS TRIALS AND AFFLICTIONS, WITH THE THREAT OF MORE SEVERE DIFFICULTIES BEING VERY REAL. PETER TOUCHES ON VARIOUS DOCTRINES AND HAS MUCH TO SAY ABOUT CHRISTIAN LIFE AND DUTIES. 1 PETER HAS BEEN CHARACTERIZED AS A LETTER OF SUFFERING AND PERSECUTION, OF SUFFERING AND GLORY, OF HOPE AND COURAGE. NO OTHER NEW TESTAMENT BOOK SO REFLECTS THE REAL NATURE AND EFFECT OF GOD'S LOVE IN JESUS CHRIST.

1 Peter, an apostle of Jesus Christ,

To God's elect, strangers in the world, scattered throughout Pontus, Galatia, Cappadocia, Asia and Bithynia, ²who have been chosen according to the foreknowledge of God the Father, through the sanctifying work of the Spirit, for obedience to Jesus Christ and sprinkling by his blood:

Grace and peace be yours in abundance.

Praise to God for a Living Hope

³Praise be to the God and Father of our Lord Jesus Christ! In his great mercy he has given us new birth into a living hope through the resurrection of Jesus Christ from the dead, ⁴and into an inheritance that can never perish, spoil or fade—kept in heaven for you, ⁵who through faith are shielded by God's power until the coming of the salvation that is ready to be revealed in the last time. ⁶In this you greatly rejoice, though now for a little while you may have had to suffer grief in all kinds of trials. ⁷These have come so that your faith—of greater worth than gold, which perishes even though refined by fire—may be proved genuine and may result in praise, glory and honor when Jesus Christ is revealed. ⁸Though you have not seen him, you love him; and even though you do not see him now, you believe in him and are filled with an inexpressible and glorious joy, ⁹for you are receiving the goal of your faith, the salvation of your souls.

[10]Concerning this salvation, the prophets, who spoke of the grace that was to come to you, searched intently and with the greatest care, [11]trying to find out the time and circumstances to

---

TRIALS ARE MEDICINES WHICH OUR GRACIOUS AND WISE PHYSICIAN PRESCRIBES BECAUSE WE NEED THEM; AND HE PROPORTIONS THE FREQUENCY AND WEIGHT OF THEM TO WHAT THE CASE REQUIRES. LET US TRUST IN HIS SKILL AND THANK HIM FOR HIS PRESCRIPTION.

—John Newton

---

which the Spirit of Christ in them was pointing when he predicted the sufferings of Christ and the glories that would follow. [12]It was revealed to them that they were not serving themselves but you, when they spoke of the things that have now been told you by those who have preached the gospel to you by the Holy Spirit sent from heaven. Even angels long to look into these things.

Be Holy

[13]Therefore, prepare your minds for action; be self-controlled; set your hope fully on the grace to be given you when Jesus Christ is revealed. [14]As obedient children, do not conform to the evil desires you had when you lived in ignorance. [15]But just as he who called you is holy, so be holy in all you do; [16]for it is written: "Be holy, because I am holy."[a]

AS MAN BECOMES HOLY, JUST, MERCIFUL, PATIENT, . . . BY THE COPY HE WILL KNOW THE ORIGINAL, AND BY THE WORKMANSHIP IN HIMSELF HE WILL BE ACQUAINTED WITH THE HOLY WORKMAN.

—William Penn

---

[17]Since you call on a Father who judges each man's work impartially, live your lives as strangers here in reverent fear. [18]For you know that it was not with perishable things such as silver or gold that you were redeemed from the empty way of life handed down to you from your forefathers, [19]but with the precious blood

of Christ, a lamb without blemish or defect. [20]He was chosen before the creation of the world, but was revealed in these last times for your sake. [21]Through him you believe in God, who raised him from the dead and glorified him, and so your faith and hope are in God.

[22]Now that you have purified yourselves by obeying the truth so that you have sincere love for your brothers, love one another deeply, from the heart.[b] [23]For you have been born again, not of perishable seed, but of imperishable, through the living and enduring word of God. [24]For,

"All men are like grass,
    and all their glory is like the
        flowers of the field;
the grass withers and the flowers fall,
25   but the word of the Lord stands
        forever."[c]

And this is the word that was preached to you.

2 Therefore, rid yourselves of all malice and all deceit, hypocrisy, envy, and slander of every kind. [2]Like newborn babies, crave pure spiritual milk, so that by it you may grow up in your salvation, [3]now that you have tasted that the Lord is good.

The Living Stone and a Chosen People

[4]As you come to him, the living Stone—rejected by men but chosen by God and precious to him— [5]you also, like living stones, are being built into a spiritual house to be a holy priesthood, offering spiritual sacrifices acceptable to God through Jesus Christ. [6]For in Scripture it says:

"See, I lay a stone in Zion,
    a chosen and precious cornerstone,
    and the one who trusts in him
        will never be put to shame."[d]

[7]Now to you who believe, this stone is precious. But to those who do not believe,

"The stone the builders rejected
    has become the capstone,[e] "[f]

---

[a] 16 Lev. 11:44,45; 19:2; 20:7   [b] 22 Some early manuscripts *from a pure heart*   [c] 25 Isaiah 40:6–8
[d] 6 Isaiah 28:16   [e] 7 Or *cornerstone*   [f] 7 Psalm 118:22

FROM THE AGONY OF CHRISTIANITY
Miguel de Unamuno

VERSE: 1 Peter 2:17   **PASSAGE:** 1 Peter 2:13–17

 hat is all this talk about social Christianity? What is all this noise about the social kingdom of Christ . . . and what about the much-heralded Christian democracy? . . .

Those who persecuted Christ in order to destroy him agreed among themselves to ask him whether it was lawful to pay tribute to Caesar, the invader, the enemy of the Jewish fatherland, who represented political authority. If he answered in the affirmative, they would then picture him to the people as a bad Jew, as a bad patriot; and if he answered in the negative, they would accuse him of sedition in the face of the imperial authorities. Once the question had been posed, Jesus asked for a piece of money, and, pointing to the image depicted on the coin, he inquired, "Whose picture is this?" "Caesar's," they replied. And then he said, "Very well: give to Caesar what is Caesar's, and to God what is God's." The meaning is clear: give to Caesar, to this world, to society, the money which belongs to Caesar, to the world, to society; and to God give the soul which is destined to rise with its body. Christ thus detached himself from every problem of social economy; the same Christ who said that it is more difficult for a rich man to enter into the kingdom of heaven than for a camel to pass through the eye of a needle (see Matthew 19:24); and he showed clearly that his glad tidings have nothing to do with socio-economical or national questions, nothing to do with democracy or international demagogy, nothing to do with nationalism.

ADDITIONAL SCRIPTURE READING:
Luke 20:25; John 18:36

Go to page 1461 for your next devotional reading.

1900   Present

8and,

> "A stone that causes men to stumble
> and a rock that makes them fall."[a]

They stumble because they disobey the message—which is also what they were destined for.

9But you are a chosen people, a royal priesthood, a holy nation, a people belonging to God, that you may declare the praises of him who called you out of darkness into his wonderful light. 10Once you were not a people, but now you are the people of God; once you had not received mercy, but now you have received mercy.

11Dear friends, I urge you, as aliens and strangers in the world, to abstain from sinful desires, which war against your soul. 12Live such good lives among the pagans that, though they accuse you of doing wrong, they may see your good deeds and glorify God on the day he visits us.

Submission to Rulers and Masters

13Submit yourselves for the Lord's sake to every authority instituted among men: whether to the king, as the supreme authority, 14or to governors, who are sent by him to punish those who do wrong and to commend those who do right. 15For it is God's will that by doing good you should silence the ignorant talk of foolish men. 16Live as free men, but do not use your freedom as a cover-up for evil; live as servants of God. 17Show proper respect to everyone: Love the brotherhood of believers, fear God, honor the king.

THE CHRISTIAN LIFE WAS NOT MEANT TO LIVE IN A SOLITUDE FOREVER, NOR IS IT SUITED TO IT. IT IS A SOCIAL LIFE. ALL ITS MOVEMENTS SUGGEST AND PROPHESY A BROTHERHOOD. THAT BROTHERHOOD OF BELIEVERS IS THE CHRISTIAN CHURCH.   —*Phillips Brooks*

18Slaves, submit yourselves to your masters with all respect, not only to those who are good and considerate, but also to those who are harsh. 19For it is commendable if a man bears up under the pain of unjust suffering because he is conscious of God. 20But how is it to your credit if you receive a beating for doing wrong and endure it? But if you suffer for doing good and you endure it, this is commendable before God. 21To this you were called, because Christ suffered for you, leaving you an example, that you should follow in his steps.

22 "He committed no sin,
> and no deceit was found in his
> mouth."[b]

23When they hurled their insults at him, he did not retaliate; when he suffered, he made no threats. Instead, he entrusted himself to him who judges justly. 24He himself bore our sins in his body on the tree, so that we might die to sins and live for righteousness; by his wounds you have been healed. 25For you were like sheep going astray, but now you have returned to the Shepherd and Overseer of your souls.

Wives and Husbands

3 Wives, in the same way be submissive to your husbands so that, if any of them do not believe the word, they may be won over without words by the behavior of their wives, 2when they see the purity and reverence of your lives. 3Your beauty should not come from outward adornment, such as braided hair and the wearing of gold jewelry and fine clothes. 4Instead, it should be that of your inner self, the unfading beauty of a gentle and quiet spirit, which is of great worth in God's sight. 5For this is the way the holy women of the past who put their hope in God used to make themselves beautiful. They were submissive to their own husbands, 6like Sarah, who obeyed Abraham and called him her master. You are her daughters if you do what is right and do not give way to fear.

7Husbands, in the same way be considerate as you live with your wives, and treat them with respect as the weaker partner and as heirs with you of the gracious gift of life, so that nothing will hinder your prayers.

---

a 8 Isaiah 8:14   *b 22* Isaiah 53:9

WEEKEND

STANDING BY THE SEA
Søren Kierkegaard

VERSE: Matthew 10:31   **PASSAGE:** Matthew 10:29–31

t has always been one of my favorite places. As I stood there one quiet evening as the sea struck up its song with a deep and calm solemnity, whilst my eye met not a single sail on the vast expanse of water, and the sea set bounds to the heavens, and the heavens to the sea; whilst on the other side the busy noise of life subsided and the birds sang their evening prayer . . . and the hoarse screech of the gulls reminded me that I stood alone, and everything vanished before my eyes, and I turned back with a heavy heart to mix in the busy world, yet without forgetting such blessed moments . . .

As I stood there alone and forsaken, and the power of the sea and the battle of the elements reminded me of my own nothingness, and on the other hand the sure flight of the birds recalled the words spoken by Christ: "Not a sparrow shall fall to the ground without your Father knowing" (see Matthew 10:29): then all at once I felt how great and how small I was; then did those two mighty forces, pride and humility, happily unite in friendship. Lucky is the man to whom *that* is possible at every moment of his life; in whose breast those two factors have not only come to an agreement but have joined hands and been wedded . . . His life will flow on peacefully and quietly and he will neither drain the intoxicating cup of pride nor the bitter chalice of despair. He has found what the great philosopher . . . desired, but did not find: that Archimedean point from which he could lift the whole world, the point which for that very reason must lie outside the world, outside the limitations of time and space.

ADDITIONAL SCRIPTURE READING:
Psalm 19:1–4; James 3:13

Go to page 1463 for your next devotional reading.

1700   1900

Suffering for Doing Good

⁸Finally, all of you, live in harmony with one another; be sympathetic, love as brothers, be compassionate and humble. ⁹Do not repay evil with evil or insult with insult, but with blessing, because to this you were called so that you may inherit a blessing. ¹⁰For,

"Whoever would love life
    and see good days
must keep his tongue from evil
    and his lips from deceitful speech.
¹¹He must turn from evil and do good;
    he must seek peace and pursue it.
¹²For the eyes of the Lord are on the
    righteous
    and his ears are attentive to their
      prayer,
but the face of the Lord is against
    those who do evil."ᵃ

¹³Who is going to harm you if you are eager to do good? ¹⁴But even if you should suffer for what is right, you are blessed. "Do not fear what they fearᵇ; do not be frightened."ᶜ ¹⁵But in your hearts set apart Christ as Lord. Always be prepared to give an answer to everyone who asks you to give the reason for the hope that you have. But do this with gentleness and respect, ¹⁶keeping a clear conscience, so that those who speak maliciously against your good behavior in Christ may be ashamed of their slander. ¹⁷It is better, if it is God's will, to suffer for doing good than for doing evil. ¹⁸For Christ died for sins once for all, the righteous for the unrighteous, to bring you to God. He was put to death in the body but made alive by the Spirit, ¹⁹through whomᵈ also he went and preached to the spirits in prison ²⁰who disobeyed long ago when God waited patiently in the days of Noah while the ark was being built. In it only a few people, eight in all, were saved through water, ²¹and this water symbolizes baptism that now saves you also—not the removal of dirt from the body but the pledgeᵉ of a good conscience toward God. It saves you by the resurrection of Jesus Christ, ²²who has gone into heaven and is at God's

right hand—with angels, authorities and powers in submission to him.

Living for God

4 Therefore, since Christ suffered in his body, arm yourselves also with the same attitude, because he who has suffered in his body is done with sin. ²As a result, he does not live the rest of his earthly life for evil human desires, but rather for the will of God. ³For you have spent enough time in the past doing what pagans choose to do—living in debauchery, lust, drunkenness, orgies, carousing and detestable idolatry. ⁴They think it strange that you do not plunge with them into the same flood of dissipation, and they heap abuse on you. ⁵But they will have to give account to him who is ready to judge the living and the dead. ⁶For this is the reason the gospel was preached even to those who are now dead, so that they might be judged according to men in regard to the body, but live according to God in regard to the spirit.

⁷The end of all things is near. Therefore be clear minded and self-controlled so that you can pray. ⁸Above all, love each other deeply, because love covers over a multitude of sins. ⁹Offer hospitality to one another without grumbling. ¹⁰Each one should use whatever gift he has received to serve others, faithfully administering God's grace in its various forms. ¹¹If anyone speaks, he should do it as one speaking the very words of God. If anyone serves, he should do it with the strength God provides, so that in all things God may be praised through Jesus Christ. To him be the glory and the power for ever and ever. Amen.

Suffering for Being a Christian

¹²Dear friends, do not be surprised at the painful trial you are suffering, as though something strange were happening to you. ¹³But rejoice that you participate in the sufferings of Christ, so that you may be overjoyed when his glory is revealed. ¹⁴If you are insulted because of the name of Christ, you are blessed, for the Spirit of glory and of God rests on you. ¹⁵If you suffer, it should not be as a

---

ᵃ 12 Psalm 34:12–16   ᵇ 14 Or *not fear their threats*   ᶜ 14 Isaiah 8:12   ᵈ 18,19 Or *alive in the spirit,* ¹⁹*through which*   ᵉ 21 Or *response*

murderer or thief or any other kind of criminal, or even as a meddler. [16]However, if you suffer as a Christian, do not be ashamed, but praise God that you bear that name. [17]For it is time for judgment to begin with the family of God;

and if it begins with us, what will the outcome be for those who do not obey the gospel of God? [18]And,

"If it is hard for the righteous to be saved,

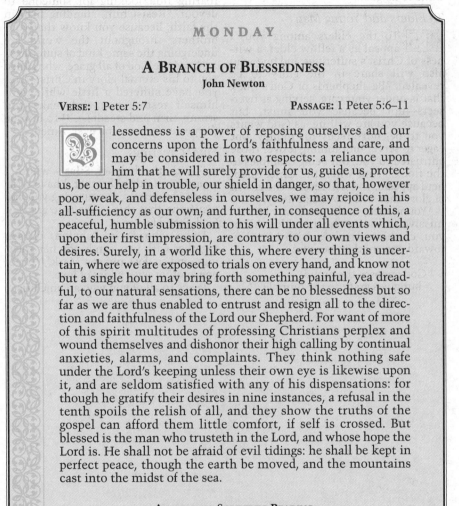

MONDAY

A BRANCH OF BLESSEDNESS
John Newton

VERSE: 1 Peter 5:7   **PASSAGE:** 1 Peter 5:6–11

lessedness is a power of reposing ourselves and our concerns upon the Lord's faithfulness and care, and may be considered in two respects: a reliance upon him that he will surely provide for us, guide us, protect us, be our help in trouble, our shield in danger, so that, however poor, weak, and defenseless in ourselves, we may rejoice in his all-sufficiency as our own; and further, in consequence of this, a peaceful, humble submission to his will under all events which, upon their first impression, are contrary to our own views and desires. Surely, in a world like this, where every thing is uncertain, where we are exposed to trials on every hand, and know not but a single hour may bring forth something painful, yea dreadful, to our natural sensations, there can be no blessedness but so far as we are thus enabled to entrust and resign all to the direction and faithfulness of the Lord our Shepherd. For want of more of this spirit multitudes of professing Christians perplex and wound themselves and dishonor their high calling by continual anxieties, alarms, and complaints. They think nothing safe under the Lord's keeping unless their own eye is likewise upon it, and are seldom satisfied with any of his dispensations: for though he gratify their desires in nine instances, a refusal in the tenth spoils the relish of all, and they show the truths of the gospel can afford them little comfort, if self is crossed. But blessed is the man who trusteth in the Lord, and whose hope the Lord is. He shall not be afraid of evil tidings: he shall be kept in perfect peace, though the earth be moved, and the mountains cast into the midst of the sea.

ADDITIONAL SCRIPTURE READING:
Psalm 55:22; 2 Timothy 4:5

Go to page 1467 for your next devotional reading.

1700   1900

what will become of the ungodly
and the sinner?"[a]

[19]So then, those who suffer according to God's will should commit themselves to their faithful Creator and continue to do good.

To Elders and Young Men

5 To the elders among you, I appeal as a fellow elder, a witness of Christ's sufferings and one who also will share in the glory to be revealed: [2]Be shepherds of God's flock that is under your care, serving as overseers—not because you must, but because you are willing, as God wants you to be; not greedy for money, but eager to serve; [3]not lording it over those entrusted to you, but being examples to the flock. [4]And when the Chief Shepherd appears, you will receive the crown of glory that will never fade away.

[5]Young men, in the same way be submissive to those who are older. All of you, clothe yourselves with humility toward one another, because,

"God opposes the proud
but gives grace to the humble."[b]

[6]Humble yourselves, therefore, under God's mighty hand, that he may lift you up in due time. [7]Cast all your anxiety on him because he cares for you.

[8]Be self-controlled and alert. Your enemy the devil prowls around like a roaring lion looking for someone to devour. [9]Resist him, standing firm in the faith, because you know that your brothers throughout the world are undergoing the same kind of sufferings.

[10]And the God of all grace, who called you to his eternal glory in Christ, after you have suffered a little while, will himself restore you and make you strong, firm and steadfast. [11]To him be the power for ever and ever. Amen.

Final Greetings

[12]With the help of Silas,[c] whom I regard as a faithful brother, I have written to you briefly, encouraging you and testifying that this is the true grace of God. Stand fast in it.

[13]She who is in Babylon, chosen together with you, sends you her greetings, and so does my son Mark. [14]Greet one another with a kiss of love.

Peace to all of you who are in Christ.

---

[a] 18 Prov. 11:31   [b] 5 Prov. 3:34   [c] 12 Greek *Silvanus*, a variant of *Silas*

2 PETER

HE SAME GROUP OF CHRISTIANS
ADDRESSED IN PETER'S FIRST LET-
TER WERE IN DANGER OF BEING
MISLED BY FALSE TEACHERS. PETER, AS A
"SHEPHERD" OF CHRIST'S SHEEP, TEACHES
THE CHURCH HOW TO DEAL WITH THESE
FALSE TEACHERS BUT ALSO SEEKS TO COM-
MEND TO HIS READERS A WHOLESOME COM-
BINATION OF CHRISTIAN FAITH AND PRAC-
TICE. LOOK FOR GUIDELINES ON DEVELOPING
CHRISTIAN CHARACTER AND ADMONITIONS
ON HOW TO LIVE IN VIEW OF THE LORD'S
COMING AGAIN.

1 Simon Peter, a servant and apostle of Jesus Christ,

To those who through the righteousness of our God and Savior Jesus Christ have received a faith as precious as ours:

²Grace and peace be yours in abundance through the knowledge of God and of Jesus our Lord.

Making One's Calling and Election Sure

³His divine power has given us everything we need for life and godliness through our knowledge of him who called us by his own glory and goodness. ⁴Through these he has given us his very great and precious promises, so that through them you may participate in the divine nature and escape the corruption in the world caused by evil desires.

⁵For this very reason, make every effort to add to your faith goodness; and to goodness, knowledge; ⁶and to knowledge, self-control; and to self-control, perseverance; and to perseverance, godliness; ⁷and to godliness, brotherly kindness; and to brotherly kindness, love. ⁸For if you possess these qualities in increasing measure, they will keep you from being ineffective and unproductive in your knowledge of our Lord Jesus Christ. ⁹But if anyone does not have them, he is nearsighted and blind, and has forgotten that he has been cleansed from his past sins.

¹⁰Therefore, my brothers, be all the more eager to make your calling and election sure. For if you do these things, you

will never fall, [11]and you will receive a rich welcome into the eternal kingdom of our Lord and Savior Jesus Christ.

Prophecy of Scripture

[12]So I will always remind you of these things, even though you know them and are firmly established in the truth you now have. [13]I think it is right to refresh your memory as long as I live in the tent of this body, [14]because I know that I will soon put it aside, as our Lord Jesus Christ has made clear to me. [15]And I will make every effort to see that after my departure you will always be able to remember these things.

[16]We did not follow cleverly invented stories when we told you about the power and coming of our Lord Jesus Christ, but we were eyewitnesses of his majesty. [17]For he received honor and glory from God the Father when the voice came to him from the Majestic Glory, saying, "This is my Son, whom I love; with him I am well pleased."[a] [18]We ourselves heard this voice that came from heaven when we were with him on the sacred mountain.

[19]And we have the word of the prophets made more certain, and you will do well to pay attention to it, as to a light shining in a dark place, until the day dawns and the morning star rises in your hearts. [20]Above all, you must understand that no prophecy of Scripture came about by the prophet's own interpretation. [21]For prophecy never had its origin in the will of man, but men spoke from God as they were carried along by the Holy Spirit.

False Teachers and Their Destruction

2 But there were also false prophets among the people, just as there will be false teachers among you. They will secretly introduce destructive heresies, even denying the sovereign Lord who bought them—bringing swift destruction on themselves. [2]Many will follow their shameful ways and will bring the way of truth into disrepute. [3]In their greed these teachers will exploit you with stories they have made up.

Their condemnation has long been hanging over them, and their destruction has not been sleeping.

[4]For if God did not spare angels when they sinned, but sent them to hell,[b] putting them into gloomy dungeons[c] to be held for judgment; [5]if he did not spare the ancient world when he brought the flood on its ungodly people, but protected Noah, a preacher of righteousness, and seven others; [6]if he condemned the cities of Sodom and Gomorrah by burning them to ashes, and made them an example of what is going to happen to the ungodly; [7]and if he rescued Lot, a righteous man, who was distressed by the filthy lives of lawless men [8](for that righteous man, living among them day after day, was tormented in his righteous soul by the lawless deeds he saw and heard)— [9]if this is so, then the Lord knows how to rescue godly men from trials and to hold the unrighteous for the day of judgment, while continuing their punishment.[d] [10]This is especially true of those who follow the corrupt desire of the sinful nature[e] and despise authority.

Bold and arrogant, these men are not afraid to slander celestial beings; [11]yet even angels, although they are stronger and more powerful, do not bring slanderous accusations against such beings in the presence of the Lord. [12]But these men blaspheme in matters they do not understand. They are like brute beasts, creatures of instinct, born only to be caught and destroyed, and like beasts they too will perish.

[13]They will be paid back with harm for the harm they have done. Their idea of pleasure is to carouse in broad daylight. They are blots and blemishes, reveling in their pleasures while they feast with you.[f] [14]With eyes full of adultery, they never stop sinning; they seduce the unstable; they are experts in greed—an accursed brood! [15]They have left the straight way and wandered off to follow the way of Balaam son of Beor, who loved the wages of wickedness. [16]But he was rebuked for his wrongdoing by a donkey—a beast without speech—who

---

[a] 17 Matt. 17:5; Mark 9:7; Luke 9:35   [b] 4 Greek *Tartarus*   [c] 4 Some manuscripts *into chains of darkness*   [d] 9 Or *unrighteous for punishment until the day of judgment*   [e] 10 Or *the flesh*   [f] 13 Some manuscripts *in their love feasts*

spoke with a man's voice and restrained the prophet's madness.

¹⁷These men are springs without water and mists driven by a storm. Blackest darkness is reserved for them. ¹⁸For they mouth empty, boastful words and, by appealing to the lustful desires of sinful human nature, they entice people who are just escaping from those who live in error. ¹⁹They promise them freedom, while they themselves are slaves of depravity—for a man is a slave to whatever has mastered him. ²⁰If they have escaped the corruption of the world by knowing our Lord and Savior Jesus Christ and are again entangled in it and overcome, they are worse off at the end than they were at the beginning. ²¹It

---

TUESDAY

GROW BY THE POWER OF AN INWARD LIFE
Hannah Whitall Smith

VERSE: 2 Peter 3:18   **PASSAGE:** 2 Peter 3:17–18

 o grow in grace is opposed to all growth in self-dependence or self-effort—to all legality, in fact, of every kind. It is to put our growing, as well as everything else, into the hands of the Lord and leave it with him. It is to be so satisfied with our husbandman, and with his skill and wisdom, that not a question will cross our minds as to his mode of treatment or his plan of cultivation. It is to grow as the lilies grow, or as the babies grow, without care and without anxiety; to grow by the power of an inward life-principle that cannot help but grow; to grow because we live, and therefore must grow; to grow because he who has planted us has planted a growing thing, and has made us on purpose to grow.

Surely this is what our Lord meant when he said, "Consider the lilies, how they grow: they toil not, neither do they spin: and yet I say unto you, that even Solomon in all his glory was not arrayed like one of these" (Matthew 6:28–29, KJV). Or, when he says again, "Which of you by taking thought can add one cubit unto his stature?" (Matthew 6:27). There is no effort in the growing of a babe or of a lily. The lily does not toil nor spin, it does not stretch nor strain, it does not make any effort of any kind to grow, it is not conscious even that it is growing; but by an inward life-principle, and through the nurturing care of God's providence and the fostering of caretaker or gardener, by the heat of the sun and the falling of the rain, it grows and buds and blossoms into the beautiful plant God meant it to be.

ADDITIONAL SCRIPTURE READING:
1 Kings 10:1–13; Luke 12:27

Go to page 1471 for your next devotional reading.

1700   1900

would have been better for them not to have known the way of righteousness, than to have known it and then to turn their backs on the sacred command that was passed on to them. ²²Of them the proverbs are true: "A dog returns to its vomit,"ᵃ and, "A sow that is washed goes back to her wallowing in the mud."

The Day of the Lord

3 Dear friends, this is now my second letter to you. I have written both of them as reminders to stimulate you to wholesome thinking. ²I want you to recall the words spoken in the past by the holy prophets and the command given by our Lord and Savior through your apostles.

³First of all, you must understand that in the last days scoffers will come, scoffing and following their own evil desires. ⁴They will say, "Where is this 'coming' he promised? Ever since our fathers died, everything goes on as it has since the beginning of creation." ⁵But they deliberately forget that long ago by God's word the heavens existed and the earth was formed out of water and by water. ⁶By these waters also the world of that time was deluged and destroyed. ⁷By the same word the present heavens and earth are reserved for fire, being kept for the day of judgment and destruction of ungodly men.

⁸But do not forget this one thing, dear friends: With the Lord a day is like a thousand years, and a thousand years are like a day. ⁹The Lord is not slow in keeping his promise, as some understand slowness. He is patient with you, not wanting anyone to perish, but everyone to come to repentance.

¹⁰But the day of the Lord will come like a thief. The heavens will disappear with a roar; the elements will be destroyed by fire, and the earth and everything in it will be laid bare.ᵇ

¹¹Since everything will be destroyed in this way, what kind of people ought you to be? You ought to live holy and godly lives ¹²as you look forward to the day of God and speed its coming.ᶜ That day will bring about the destruction of the heavens by fire, and the elements will melt in the heat. ¹³But in keeping with his promise we are looking forward to a new heaven and a new earth, the home of righteousness.

¹⁴So then, dear friends, since you are looking forward to this, make every effort to be found spotless, blameless and at peace with him. ¹⁵Bear in mind that our Lord's patience means salvation, just as our dear brother Paul also wrote you with the wisdom that God gave him. ¹⁶He writes the same way in all his letters, speaking in them of these matters. His letters contain some things that are hard to understand, which ignorant and unstable people distort, as they do the other Scriptures, to their own destruction.

¹⁷Therefore, dear friends, since you already know this, be on your guard so that you may not be carried away by the error of lawless men and fall from your secure position. ¹⁸But grow in the grace and knowledge of our Lord and Savior Jesus Christ. To him be glory both now and forever! Amen.

1 JOHN

HE AUTHOR OF THIS LETTER IS JOHN
THE SON OF ZEBEDEE—THE AUTHOR
OF THE GOSPEL OF JOHN AND THE
BOOK OF REVELATION. JOHN HAD TWO BASIC
PURPOSES IN MIND IN THIS LETTER: (1) TO
EXPOSE FALSE TEACHERS WHO DENIED, AMONG
OTHER THINGS, JESUS' HUMANITY, AND (2) TO
GIVE BELIEVERS ASSURANCE OF SALVATION. JOHN
STRESSES GOD'S LOVE AS AN EXAMPLE FOR US
TO FOLLOW IN OUR RELATIONSHIPS WITH EACH
OTHER. HE ENCOURAGES BELIEVERS TO LIVE
RIGHT AND TO MAINTAIN TRUTH BY MAINTAIN-
ING FELLOWSHIP WITH THE LORD.

The Word of Life

1 That which was from the beginning, which we have heard, which we have seen with our eyes, which we have looked at and our hands have touched—this we proclaim concerning the Word of life. ²The life appeared; we have seen it and testify to it, and we proclaim to you the eternal life, which was with the Father and has appeared to us. ³We proclaim to you what we have seen and heard, so that you also may have fellowship with us. And our fellowship is with the Father and with his Son, Jesus Christ. ⁴We write this to make our*a* joy complete.

Walking in the Light

⁵This is the message we have heard from him and declare to you: God is light; in him there is no darkness at all. ⁶If we claim to have fellowship with him yet walk in the darkness, we lie and do not live by the truth. ⁷But if we walk in the light, as he is in the light, we have

---

SIN WILL KEEP YOU FROM THIS BOOK. THIS BOOK
WILL KEEP YOU FROM SIN.   —*Dwight L. Moody*

---

fellowship with one another, and the blood of Jesus, his Son, purifies us from all*b* sin.

⁸If we claim to be without sin, we

deceive ourselves and the truth is not in us. ⁹If we confess our sins, he is faithful and just and will forgive us our sins and purify us from all unrighteousness. ¹⁰If we claim we have not sinned, we make him out to be a liar and his word has no place in our lives.

2 My dear children, I write this to you so that you will not sin. But if anybody does sin, we have one who speaks to the Father in our defense— Jesus Christ, the Righteous One. ²He is the atoning sacrifice for our sins, and not only for ours but also for*a* the sins of the whole world.

³We know that we have come to know him if we obey his commands. ⁴The man who says, "I know him," but does not do what he commands is a liar, and the truth is not in him. ⁵But if anyone obeys his word, God's love*b* is truly made complete in him. This is how we know we are in him: ⁶Whoever claims to live in him must walk as Jesus did.

⁷Dear friends, I am not writing you a new command but an old one, which you have had since the beginning. This old command is the message you have heard. ⁸Yet I am writing you a new command; its truth is seen in him and you, because the darkness is passing and the true light is already shining.

⁹Anyone who claims to be in the light but hates his brother is still in the darkness. ¹⁰Whoever loves his brother lives in the light, and there is nothing in him*c* to make him stumble. ¹¹But whoever hates his brother is in the darkness and walks around in the darkness; he does not know where he is going, because the darkness has blinded him.

¹²I write to you, dear children,
  because your sins have been
    forgiven on account of his
      name.
¹³I write to you, fathers,
  because you have known him who
    is from the beginning.
I write to you, young men,
  because you have overcome the
    evil one.
I write to you, dear children,
  because you have known the
    Father.
¹⁴I write to you, fathers,
  because you have known him who
    is from the beginning.
I write to you, young men,
  because you are strong,
    and the word of God lives in you,
    and you have overcome the evil
      one.

Do Not Love the World

¹⁵Do not love the world or anything in the world. If anyone loves the world, the love of the Father is not in him. ¹⁶For everything in the world—the cravings of sinful man, the lust of his eyes and the boasting of what he has and does— comes not from the Father but from the world. ¹⁷The world and its desires pass away, but the man who does the will of God lives forever.

Warning Against Antichrists

¹⁸Dear children, this is the last hour; and as you have heard that the antichrist is coming, even now many antichrists have come. This is how we know it is the last hour. ¹⁹They went out from us, but they did not really belong to us. For if they had belonged to us, they would have remained with us; but their going showed that none of them belonged to us.

²⁰But you have an anointing from the Holy One, and all of you know the truth.*d* ²¹I do not write to you because you do not know the truth, but because you do know it and because no lie comes from the truth. ²²Who is the liar? It is the man who denies that Jesus is the Christ. Such a man is the antichrist—he denies the Father and the Son. ²³No one who denies the Son has the Father; whoever acknowledges the Son has the Father also.

²⁴See that what you have heard from the beginning remains in you. If it does, you also will remain in the Son and in the Father. ²⁵And this is what he promised us—even eternal life.

²⁶I am writing these things to you about those who are trying to lead you astray. ²⁷As for you, the anointing

---

a 2 Or *He is the one who turns aside God's wrath, taking away our sins, and not only ours but also*
b 5 Or *word, love for God*   *c* 10 Or *it*   *d* 20 Some manuscripts *and you know all things*

you received from him remains in you, and you do not need anyone to teach you. But as his anointing teaches you about all things and as that anointing is real, not counterfeit—just as it has taught you, remain in him.

Children of God

28And now, dear children, continue in him, so that when he appears we may be confident and unashamed before him at his coming.

29If you know that he is righteous, you know that everyone who does what is right has been born of him.

3 How great is the love the Father has lavished on us, that we should be called children of God! And that is what we are! The reason the world does not know us is that it did not

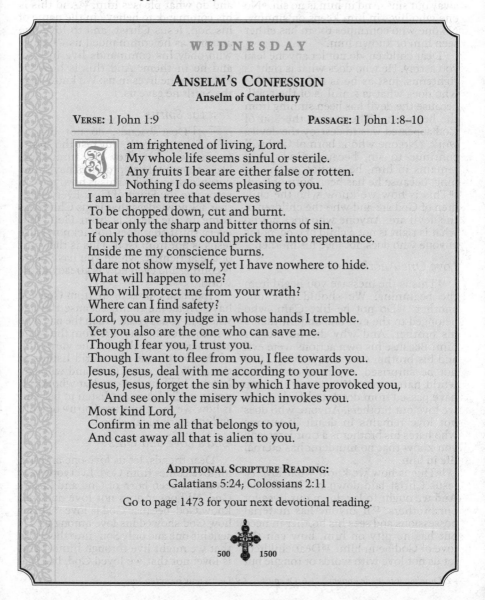

WEDNESDAY

ANSELM'S CONFESSION
Anselm of Canterbury

VERSE: 1 John 1:9   **PASSAGE:** 1 John 1:8–10

I am frightened of living, Lord.
My whole life seems sinful or sterile.
Any fruits I bear are either false or rotten.
Nothing I do seems pleasing to you.
I am a barren tree that deserves
To be chopped down, cut and burnt.
I bear only the sharp and bitter thorns of sin.
If only those thorns could prick me into repentance.
Inside me my conscience burns.
I dare not show myself, yet I have nowhere to hide.
What will happen to me?
Who will protect me from your wrath?
Where can I find safety?
Lord, you are my judge in whose hands I tremble.
Yet you also are the one who can save me.
Though I fear you, I trust you.
Though I want to flee from you, I flee towards you.
Jesus, Jesus, deal with me according to your love.
Jesus, Jesus, forget the sin by which I have provoked you,
    And see only the misery which invokes you.
Most kind Lord,
Confirm in me all that belongs to you,
And cast away all that is alien to you.

ADDITIONAL SCRIPTURE READING:
Galatians 5:24; Colossians 2:11

Go to page 1473 for your next devotional reading.

500   1500

know him. [2]Dear friends, now we are children of God, and what we will be has not yet been made known. But we know that when he appears,[a] we shall be like him, for we shall see him as he is. [3]Everyone who has this hope in him purifies himself, just as he is pure.

[4]Everyone who sins breaks the law; in fact, sin is lawlessness. [5]But you know that he appeared so that he might take away our sins. And in him is no sin. [6]No one who lives in him keeps on sinning. No one who continues to sin has either seen him or known him.

[7]Dear children, do not let anyone lead you astray. He who does what is right is righteous, just as he is righteous. [8]He who does what is sinful is of the devil, because the devil has been sinning from the beginning. The reason the Son of God appeared was to destroy the devil's work. [9]No one who is born of God will continue to sin, because God's seed remains in him; he cannot go on sinning, because he has been born of God. [10]This is how we know who the children of God are and who the children of the devil are: Anyone who does not do what is right is not a child of God; nor is anyone who does not love his brother.

Love One Another

[11]This is the message you heard from the beginning: We should love one another. [12]Do not be like Cain, who belonged to the evil one and murdered his brother. And why did he murder him? Because his own actions were evil and his brother's were righteous. [13]Do not be surprised, my brothers, if the world hates you. [14]We know that we have passed from death to life, because we love our brothers. Anyone who does not love remains in death. [15]Anyone who hates his brother is a murderer, and you know that no murderer has eternal life in him.

[16]This is how we know what love is: Jesus Christ laid down his life for us. And we ought to lay down our lives for our brothers. [17]If anyone has material possessions and sees his brother in need but has no pity on him, how can the love of God be in him? [18]Dear children, let us not love with words or tongue but

with actions and in truth. [19]This then is how we know that we belong to the truth, and how we set our hearts at rest in his presence [20]whenever our hearts condemn us. For God is greater than our hearts, and he knows everything.

[21]Dear friends, if our hearts do not condemn us, we have confidence before God [22]and receive from him anything we ask, because we obey his commands and do what pleases him. [23]And this is his command: to believe in the name of his Son, Jesus Christ, and to love one another as he commanded us. [24]Those who obey his commands live in him, and he in them. And this is how we know that he lives in us: We know it by the Spirit he gave us.

Test the Spirits

4 Dear friends, do not believe every spirit, but test the spirits to see whether they are from God, because many false prophets have gone out into the world. [2]This is how you can recognize the Spirit of God: Every spirit that acknowledges that Jesus Christ has come in the flesh is from God, [3]but every spirit that does not acknowledge Jesus is not from God. This is the spirit of the antichrist, which you have heard is coming and even now is already in the world.

[4]You, dear children, are from God and have overcome them, because the one who is in you is greater than the one who is in the world. [5]They are from the world and therefore speak from the viewpoint of the world, and the world listens to them. [6]We are from God, and whoever knows God listens to us; but whoever is not from God does not listen to us. This is how we recognize the Spirit[b] of truth and the spirit of falsehood.

God's Love and Ours

[7]Dear friends, let us love one another, for love comes from God. Everyone who loves has been born of God and knows God. [8]Whoever does not love does not know God, because God is love. [9]This is how God showed his love among us: He sent his one and only Son[c] into the world that we might live through him. [10]This is love: not that we loved God, but that

---

[a] 2 Or *when it is made known*   [b] 6 Or *spirit*   [c] 9 Or *his only begotten Son*

he loved us and sent his Son as an atoning sacrifice for[a] our sins. [11]Dear friends, since God so loved us, we also ought to love one another. [12]No one has ever seen God; but if we love one another, God lives in us and his love is made complete in us.

[13]We know that we live in him and he in us, because he has given us of his Spirit. [14]And we have seen and testify that the Father has sent his Son to be the Savior of the world. [15]If anyone acknowledges that Jesus is the Son of God, God lives in him and he in God. [16]And so we know and rely on the love God has for us.

God is love. Whoever lives in love lives in God, and God in him. [17]In this way, love is made complete among us so that we will have confidence on the day of judgment, because in this world we are like him. [18]There is no fear in love. But perfect love drives out fear, because fear has to do with punishment. The one who fears is not made perfect in love.

[19]We love because he first loved us. [20]If anyone says, "I love God," yet hates his brother, he is a liar. For anyone who

---

[a] 10 Or *as the one who would turn aside his wrath, taking away*

THURSDAY

THE MYSTERY OF THE SON
Athenagoras

VERSE: 1 John 4:15   PASSAGE: 1 John 4:13–16

et no one think it stupid for me to say that God has a Son. For we do not think of God the Father or of the Son in the way of the poets, who weave their myths by showing that gods are no better than men. But the Son of God is his Word in idea and in actuality; for by him and through him all things were made, the Father and the Son being one. And since the Son is in the Father and the Father in the Son by the unity and power of the Spirit, the Son of God is the mind and Word of the Father.

But if, owing to your sharp intelligence, it occurs to you to inquire further what is meant by the Son, I shall briefly explain. He is the first offspring of the Father. I do not mean that he was created, for, since God is eternal mind, he had his Word within himself from the beginning, being eternally wise. Rather did the Son come forth from God to give form and actuality to all material things, which essentially have a sort of formless nature and inert quality, the heavier particles being mixed up with the lighter.

ADDITIONAL SCRIPTURE READING:
Mark 14:61–62; John 9:35–39

Go to page 1476 for your next devotional reading.

100   500

does not love his brother, whom he has seen, cannot love God, whom he has not seen. [21]And he has given us this command: Whoever loves God must also love his brother.

Faith in the Son of God

[5] Everyone who believes that Jesus is the Christ is born of God, and everyone who loves the father loves his child as well. [2]This is how we know that we love the children of God: by loving God and carrying out his commands. [3]This is love for God: to obey his commands. And his commands are not burdensome, [4]for everyone born of God overcomes the world. This is the victory that has overcome the world, even our faith. [5]Who is it that overcomes the world? Only he who believes that Jesus is the Son of God.

[6]This is the one who came by water and blood—Jesus Christ. He did not come by water only, but by water and blood. And it is the Spirit who testifies, because the Spirit is the truth. [7]For there are three that testify: [8]the[a] Spirit, the water and the blood; and the three are in agreement. [9]We accept man's testimony, but God's testimony is greater because it is the testimony of God, which he has given about his Son. [10]Anyone who believes in the Son of God has this testimony in his heart. Anyone who does not believe God has made him out to be a liar, because he has not believed the testimony God has given about his Son. [11]And this is the testimony: God has

given us eternal life, and this life is in his Son. [12]He who has the Son has life; he who does not have the Son of God does not have life.

Concluding Remarks

[13]I write these things to you who believe in the name of the Son of God so that you may know that you have eternal life. [14]This is the confidence we have in approaching God: that if we ask anything according to his will, he hears us. [15]And if we know that he hears us— whatever we ask—we know that we have what we asked of him.

[16]If anyone sees his brother commit a sin that does not lead to death, he should pray and God will give him life. I refer to those whose sin does not lead to death. There is a sin that leads to death. I am not saying that he should pray about that. [17]All wrongdoing is sin, and there is sin that does not lead to death.

[18]We know that anyone born of God does not continue to sin; the one who was born of God keeps him safe, and the evil one cannot harm him. [19]We know that we are children of God, and that the whole world is under the control of the evil one. [20]We know also that the Son of God has come and has given us understanding, so that we may know him who is true. And we are in him who is true—even in his Son Jesus Christ. He is the true God and eternal life.

[21]Dear children, keep yourselves from idols.

---

[a] 7,8 Late manuscripts of the Vulgate *testify in heaven: the Father, the Word and the Holy Spirit, and these three are one.* [8]*And there are three that testify on earth: the* (not found in any Greek manuscript before the sixteenth century)

2 JOHN

URING THE FIRST TWO CENTURIES A.D. THE GOSPEL WAS TAKEN FROM PLACE TO PLACE BY TRAVELING EVANGELISTS. BELIEVERS CUSTOMARILY TOOK THESE MISSIONARIES INTO THEIR HOMES AND GAVE THEM PROVISIONS WHEN THEY LEFT. BECAUSE FALSE TEACHERS ALSO RELIED ON THIS PRACTICE, 2 JOHN WAS WRITTEN TO URGE DISCERNMENT IN SUPPORTING TRAVELING TEACHERS. LOOK FOR THE CHALLENGE TO BE CERTAIN ABOUT WHAT YOU BELIEVE AND HOW YOU LIVE.

¹The elder,

To the chosen lady and her children, whom I love in the truth—and not I only, but also all who know the truth— ²because of the truth, which lives in us and will be with us forever:

³Grace, mercy and peace from God the Father and from Jesus Christ, the Father's Son, will be with us in truth and love.

⁴It has given me great joy to find some of your children walking in the truth, just as the Father commanded us. ⁵And now, dear lady, I am not writing you a new command but one we have had from the beginning. I ask that we love one another. ⁶And this is love: that we walk in obedience to his commands. As you have heard from the beginning, his command is that you walk in love.

⁷Many deceivers, who do not acknowledge Jesus Christ as coming in the flesh, have gone out into the world. Any such person is the deceiver and the antichrist. ⁸Watch out that you do not lose what you have worked for, but that you may be rewarded fully. ⁹Anyone who runs ahead and does not continue in the teaching of Christ does not have God; whoever continues in the teaching has both the Father and the Son. ¹⁰If anyone comes to you and does not bring this teaching, do not take him into your house or welcome him. ¹¹Anyone who

welcomes him shares in his wicked work.

¹²I have much to write to you, but I do not want to use paper and ink. Instead, I hope to visit you and talk with you face to face, so that our joy may be complete.

¹³The children of your chosen sister send their greetings.

FRIDAY

ABIDING IN THE TEACHING OF CHRIST
John Calvin

VERSE: 2 John 9   **PASSAGE:** 2 John 7–11

All that Jesus Christ has done and suffered for our redemption, we veritably hold without any doubt, as it is contained in the Creed . . . that is to say, "I believe in God, the Father Almighty," and so on. Therefore we acknowledge the things which are consequently given to us by God in Jesus Christ: First, that being in our own nature enemies of God and subject to his wrath and judgment, we are reconciled with him and received again in grace through the intercession of Jesus Christ, so that by his righteousness and guiltlessness we have remission of our sins, and by the shedding of his blood we are cleansed and purified from all our stains.

Second, we acknowledge that by his spirit we are regenerated into a new spiritual nature. That is to say, the evil desires of our flesh are mortified by grace, so that they rule us no longer. On the contrary, our will is rendered conformable to God's will, to follow in his way and to seek what is pleasing to him. Therefore we are by him delivered from the servitude of sin, under whose power we were of ourselves held captive, and by this deliverance we are made capable and able to do good works.

Finally, we acknowledge that this regeneration is so effected in us that, until we slough off this mortal body, there remains always in us much imperfection and infirmity, so that we always remain poor and wretched sinners in the presence of God. And however much we ought day by day to increase and grow in God's righteousness, there will never be plenitude or perfection while we live here . . . And so we ought always to look for our righteousness in Jesus Christ, and not at all in ourselves, and in him be confident and assured, putting no faith in our works.

ADDITIONAL SCRIPTURE READING:
Psalm 14:1–3; Romans 3:9–24

Go to page 1477 for your next devotional reading.

1500   1700

WEEKEND

BE STILL, MY HEART!
John Newton

VERSE: Hebrews 10:22   **PASSAGE:** Hebrews 10:19–25

 e still, my heart! these anxious cares
To thee are burdens, thorns and snares;
They cast dishonor on the Lord,
And contradict his gracious word.

Brought safely by his hand thus far,
Why wilt thou now give place to fear?
How canst thou want if he provide,
Or lose thy way with such a guide?

When first before his mercy-seat
Thou didst to him thine all commit;
He gave thee warrant from that hour
To trust his wisdom, love, and power.

Did ever trouble yet befall,
And he refuse to hear thy call?
And has he not his promise passed,
That thou shalt overcome at last?

He who has helped me hitherto
Will help me all my journey through,
And give me daily cause to raise
New Ebenezers to his praise.

Though rough and thorny be the road,
It leads thee on, apace, to God;
Then count thy present trials small,
For God will make amends for all.

ADDITIONAL SCRIPTURE READING:
Psalm 91:1–2; James 5:7–8

Go to page 1479 for your next devotional reading.

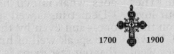

1700   1900

3 JOHN

ITINERANT TEACHERS SENT OUT BY JOHN WERE REJECTED IN ONE OF THE CHURCHES IN THE PROVINCE OF ASIA BY A DICTATORIAL LEADER, DIOTREPHES. JOHN WROTE TO GAIUS, HIS FRIEND AND A LEADER IN THE CHURCH, TO THANK GAIUS FOR HIS HELP AND TO ENCOURAGE HIM IN HIS SUPPORT OF LEGITIMATE TEACHERS. HE ALSO REPROVES DIOTREPHES FOR NOT COOPERATING AND FOR REBELLING AGAINST JOHN'S LEADERSHIP.

¹The elder,

To my dear friend Gaius, whom I love in the truth.

²Dear friend, I pray that you may enjoy good health and that all may go well with you, even as your soul is getting along well. ³It gave me great joy to have some brothers come and tell about your faithfulness to the truth and how you continue to walk in the truth. ⁴I have no greater joy than to hear that my children are walking in the truth.

⁵Dear friend, you are faithful in what you are doing for the brothers, even though they are strangers to you. ⁶They have told the church about your love. You will do well to send them on their way in a manner worthy of God. ⁷It was for the sake of the Name that they went out, receiving no help from the pagans.

⁸We ought therefore to show hospitality to such men so that we may work together for the truth.

⁹I wrote to the church, but Diotrephes, who loves to be first, will have nothing to do with us. ¹⁰So if I come, I will call attention to what he is doing, gossiping maliciously about us. Not satisfied with that, he refuses to welcome the brothers. He also stops those who want to do so and puts them out of the church.

¹¹Dear friend, do not imitate what is evil but what is good. Anyone who does what is good is from God. Anyone who does what is evil has not seen God. ¹²Demetrius is well spoken of by everyone—and even by the truth itself. We also speak well of him, and you know that our testimony is true.

¹³I have much to write you, but I do

not want to do so with pen and ink. 14I hope to see you soon, and we will talk face to face.

Peace to you. The friends here send their greetings. Greet the friends there by name.

MONDAY

FROM MARY MAGDALEN'S FUNERAL TEARS
Robert Southwell

VERSE: 3 John 11   **PASSAGE:** 3 John

 Christian soul, take Mary for your mirror; . . . learn, O sinful man, from this once-sinful woman, that sinners may find Christ if their sins be amended. Learn that those who are lost to sin may be recovered by love, that those who have been chased away by faintness of faith may be recalled by firmness of hope, and that which no mortal force, favor, or policy can grasp may be obtained by the continued tears of constant love.

Learn of Mary [to] rise early in the morning . . . Run with repentance to your sinful heart, which was meant to be a temple, but, through your own fault, was no better than a tomb for Christ, since, being unable to feel him living in you, he seems as if he were dead. Roll away the stone of your former hardness; remove all the heavy loads that oppress you in sin; and look into your soul to see if you can find the Lord. If he is not within you, then stand outside weeping . . .

Seek him only and nothing beside him. And if at first search he does not appear, then persevere in tears and continue your seeking. Stand upon the earth, treading upon all your earthly vanities, touching them with no more than the soles of your feet, that is, with the lowest and least part of your affection. To look better into the tomb, bow down your neck with the yoke of humility and stoop from lofty and proud conceits, so that with humbled and lowly looks you may find him whom your swelling and haughty thoughts had driven away . . .

And if he grants you the glorious sight of himself to your inward eyes, presume not to know him, but as his unworthy suppliant prostrate your petitions before him that you may truly discern him and faithfully serve him . . . If with Mary you crave no other solace from Jesus but Jesus himself, he will answer your tears with his presence and assure you of that presence with his own words, so that having seen him for yourself you may make him known to others, saying, with Mary, "I have seen our Lord, and these things he said to me" (see John 20:18).

ADDITIONAL SCRIPTURE READING:
Mark 16:9–10; Ephesians 1:3–10

Go to page 1481 for your next devotional reading.

1500   1700

JUDE

UDE ORIGINATED AS A PERSONAL LET-
TER TO ONE OR MORE OF THE CON-
GREGATIONS DISPERSED THROUGHOUT
THE ROMAN EMPIRE. THE DANGERS FACING
THE CHURCH AT THIS TIME WERE NOT THOSE OF
OUTRIGHT PERSECUTION BUT OF HERETICS AND
DISTORTERS OF THE FAITH. ALTHOUGH JUDE IS
EAGER TO WRITE TO HIS READERS ABOUT SALVA-
TION, HE MUST INSTEAD WARN THEM ABOUT
CERTAIN IMMORAL MEN WHO ARE PERVERTING
GOD'S GRACE. THE LETTER ADVISES BELIEVERS
TO STRENGTHEN THEIR RELATIONSHIP TO GOD
WITH PRAYER AND MUTUAL SUPPORT.

¹Jude, a servant of Jesus Christ and a brother of James,

To those who have been called, who are loved by God the Father and kept by^a Jesus Christ:

²Mercy, peace and love be yours in abundance.

The Sin and Doom of Godless Men

³Dear friends, although I was very eager to write to you about the salvation we share, I felt I had to write and urge you to contend for the faith that was once for all entrusted to the saints. ⁴For certain men whose condemnation was written about^b long ago have secretly slipped in among you. They are godless men, who change the grace of our God into a license for immorality and deny Jesus Christ our only Sovereign and Lord.

⁵Though you already know all this, I want to remind you that the Lord^c delivered his people out of Egypt, but later destroyed those who did not believe. ⁶And the angels who did not keep their positions of authority but abandoned their own home—these he has kept in darkness, bound with everlasting chains for judgment on the great Day. ⁷In a similar way, Sodom and Gomorrah and the surrounding towns gave themselves up to sexual immorality and perversion. They serve as an example of those who suffer the punishment of eternal fire.

^{a} 1 Or for; or in ^{b} 4 Or men who were marked out for condemnation ^{c} 5 Some early manuscripts Jesus

CHRISTIANITY AND

C. S. Lewis

VERSE: Jude 3   **PASSAGE:** Jude 3–4

[Satan writes to one of his minions:]

 y Dear Wormwood,

The real trouble about the set your patient is living in is that it is *merely* Christian. They all have individual interests, of course, but the bond remains mere Christianity. What we want, if men become Christians at all, is to keep them in the state of mind I call "Christianity And." You know—Christianity and the Crisis, Christianity and the New Psychology, Christianity and the New Order, Christianity and Faith Healing, Christianity and Psychical Research, Christianity and Vegetarianism, Christianity and Spelling Reform. If they must be Christians let them at least be Christians with a difference. Substitute for the faith itself some fashion with a Christian coloring. Work on their horror of the Same Old Thing.

The horror of the Same Old Thing is one of the most valuable passions we have produced in the human heart—an endless source of heresies in religion, folly in counsel, infidelity in marriage, and inconstancy in friendship. The humans live in time, and experience reality successively. To experience much of it, therefore, they must experience many different things; in other words, they must experience change . . .

Now just as we pick out and exaggerate the pleasure of eating to produce gluttony, so we pick out this natural pleasantness of change and twist it into a demand for absolute novelty. This demand is entirely our workmanship. If we neglect our duty, men will be not only contented but transported by the mixed novelty and familiarity of snowdrops *this* January, sunrise *this* morning, plum pudding *this* Christmas. Children, until we have taught them better, will be perfectly happy with a seasonal round of games in which conkers succeed hopscotch as regularly as autumn follows summer. Only by our incessant efforts is the demand for infinite, or unrhythmical, change kept up.

ADDITIONAL SCRIPTURE READING:
Psalm 17:3; Acts 1:7–8

Go to page 1484 for your next devotional reading.

1900   Present

8In the very same way, these dreamers pollute their own bodies, reject authority and slander celestial beings. 9But even the archangel Michael, when he was disputing with the devil about the body of Moses, did not dare to bring a slanderous accusation against him, but said, "The Lord rebuke you!" 10Yet these men speak abusively against whatever they do not understand; and what things they do understand by instinct, like unreasoning animals—these are the very things that destroy them.

11Woe to them! They have taken the way of Cain; they have rushed for profit into Balaam's error; they have been destroyed in Korah's rebellion.

12These men are blemishes at your love feasts, eating with you without the slightest qualm—shepherds who feed only themselves. They are clouds without rain, blown along by the wind; autumn trees, without fruit and uprooted—twice dead. 13They are wild waves of the sea, foaming up their shame; wandering stars, for whom blackest darkness has been reserved forever.

14Enoch, the seventh from Adam, prophesied about these men: "See, the Lord is coming with thousands upon thousands of his holy ones 15to judge everyone, and to convict all the ungodly of all the ungodly acts they have done in the ungodly way, and of all the harsh words ungodly sinners have spoken against him." 16These men are grumblers and faultfinders; they follow their own evil desires; they boast about themselves and flatter others for their own advantage.

A Call to Persevere

17But, dear friends, remember what the apostles of our Lord Jesus Christ foretold. 18They said to you, "In the last times there will be scoffers who will follow their own ungodly desires." 19These are the men who divide you, who follow mere natural instincts and do not have the Spirit.

20But you, dear friends, build yourselves up in your most holy faith and pray in the Holy Spirit. 21Keep yourselves in God's love as you wait for the mercy of our Lord Jesus Christ to bring you to eternal life.

22Be merciful to those who doubt; 23snatch others from the fire and save them; to others show mercy, mixed with fear—hating even the clothing stained by corrupted flesh.

AND NOW UNTO HIM WHO IS ABLE TO KEEP US FROM FALLING AND LIFT US FROM THE DARK VALLEY OF DESPAIR TO THE BRIGHT MOUNTAIN OF HOPE, FROM THE MIDNIGHT OF DESPERATION TO THE DAYBREAK OF JOY; TO HIM BE POWER AND AUTHORITY, FOR EVER AND EVER.

—*Martin Luther King, Jr.*

Doxology

24To him who is able to keep you from falling and to present you before his glorious presence without fault and with great joy— 25to the only God our Savior be glory, majesty, power and authority, through Jesus Christ our Lord, before all ages, now and forevermore! Amen.

REVELATION

OHN WRITES A MESSAGE THAT JESUS CHRIST REVEALS TO HIM. HE WRITES TO COMFORT BELIEVERS WHO ARE SUFFERING FOR THEIR FAITH. IT IS A BOOK OF HOPE, FOR ITS CENTRAL MESSAGE IS THAT GOD AND GOOD WILL TRIUMPH OVER EVIL. LOOK FOR A COMBINATION OF WARNINGS AND ENCOURAGEMENTS HERE— WARNINGS AGAINST FALLING AWAY FROM FAITH IN CHRIST AND ASSURANCES OF ULTI-MATE VICTORY FOR THOSE WHO ARE ON GOD'S SIDE.

Prologue

1 The revelation of Jesus Christ, which God gave him to show his servants what must soon take place. He made it known by sending his angel to his servant John, ²who testifies to everything he saw—that is, the word of God and the testimony of Jesus Christ. ³Blessed is the one who reads the words of this prophecy, and blessed are those who hear it and take to heart what is written in it, because the time is near.

Greetings and Doxology

⁴John,

To the seven churches in the province of Asia:

Grace and peace to you from him who is, and who was, and who is to come, and from the seven spirits*a* before his throne, ⁵and from Jesus Christ, who is the faithful witness, the firstborn from the dead, and the ruler of the kings of the earth.

To him who loves us and has freed us from our sins by his blood, ⁶and has made us to be a kingdom and priests to serve his God and Father—to him be glory and power for ever and ever! Amen.

⁷Look, he is coming with the clouds,
and every eye will see him,
even those who pierced him;
and all the peoples of the earth will
mourn because of him.
So shall it be! Amen.

a 4 Or the sevenfold Spirit

⁸"I am the Alpha and the Omega," says the Lord God, "who is, and who was, and who is to come, the Almighty."

One Like a Son of Man

⁹I, John, your brother and companion in the suffering and kingdom and patient endurance that are ours in Jesus, was on the island of Patmos because of the word of God and the testimony of Jesus. ¹⁰On the Lord's Day I was in the Spirit, and I heard behind me a loud

---

WEDNESDAY

LOVE BEFORE CLEANSING
Dwight L. Moody

VERSE: Revelation 1:5   **PASSAGE:** Revelation 1:4–6

 here was a boy, a great many years ago, who was kidnapped in London. Long months and years passed and the mother had prayed and prayed. All her efforts had failed, and they had given up all hope. But the mother did not quite give up her hope.

One day a boy was sent into the neighboring house to sweep the chimney, and by some mistake he got down through the wrong chimney. When he came down he came in by the sitting-room chimney.

His memory began at once to travel back through the years that had passed. He thought that things looked strangely familiar. The scenes of the early days of youth were dawning upon him; and as he stood there surveying the place, his mother came into the room.

He stood there, covered with rags and soot. Did she wait until she had sent him to be washed before she rushed and took him in her arms? No, indeed; it was her own boy. She took him to her arms, all black and sooty, hugged him to her bosom, and shed tears of joy on his head.

You have wandered very far from him, and there may not be a sound spot on you; but if you will just come to God he will forgive and receive you.

I think a good deal of Isaiah 38:17. It reads: "In your love you kept me from the pit of destruction; you have put all my sins behind your back." Notice, the love comes first. [God] did not say that he had taken away sins and cast them behind him. He loved us first, and then he took our sins away.

ADDITIONAL SCRIPTURE READING:
Isaiah 38:17; John 3:16

Go to page 1486 for your next devotional reading.

1900   Present

voice like a trumpet, ¹¹which said: "Write on a scroll what you see and send it to the seven churches: to Ephesus, Smyrna, Pergamum, Thyatira, Sardis, Philadelphia and Laodicea."

¹²I turned around to see the voice that was speaking to me. And when I turned I saw seven golden lampstands, ¹³and among the lampstands was someone "like a son of man,"ᵃ dressed in a robe reaching down to his feet and with a golden sash around his chest. ¹⁴His head and hair were white like wool, as white as snow, and his eyes were like blazing fire. ¹⁵His feet were like bronze glowing in a furnace, and his voice was like the sound of rushing waters. ¹⁶In his right hand he held seven stars, and out of his mouth came a sharp double-edged sword. His face was like the sun shining in all its brilliance.

¹⁷When I saw him, I fell at his feet as though dead. Then he placed his right hand on me and said: "Do not be afraid. I am the First and the Last. ¹⁸I am the Living One; I was dead, and behold I am alive for ever and ever! And I hold the keys of death and Hades.

¹⁹"Write, therefore, what you have seen, what is now and what will take place later. ²⁰The mystery of the seven stars that you saw in my right hand and of the seven golden lampstands is this: The seven stars are the angelsᵇ of the seven churches, and the seven lampstands are the seven churches.

To the Church in Ephesus

 "To the angelᶜ of the church in Ephesus write:

These are the words of him who holds the seven stars in his right hand and walks among the seven golden lampstands: ²I know your deeds, your hard work and your perseverance. I know that you cannot tolerate wicked men, that you have tested those who claim to be apostles but are not, and have found them false. ³You have persevered and have endured hardships for my name, and have not grown weary.

⁴Yet I hold this against you: You have forsaken your first love.

⁵Remember the height from which you have fallen! Repent and do the things you did at first. If you do not repent, I will come to you and remove your lampstand from its place. ⁶But you have this in your favor: You hate the practices of the Nicolaitans, which I also hate.

⁷He who has an ear, let him hear what the Spirit says to the churches. To him who overcomes, I will give the right to eat from the tree of life, which is in the paradise of God.

To the Church in Smyrna

⁸"To the angel of the church in Smyrna write:

These are the words of him who is the First and the Last, who died and came to life again. ⁹I know your afflictions and your poverty—yet you are rich! I know the slander of those who say they are Jews and are not, but are a synagogue of Satan. ¹⁰Do not be afraid of what you are about to suffer. I tell you, the devil will put some of you in prison to test you, and you will suffer persecution for ten days. Be faithful, even to the point of death, and I will give you the crown of life.

¹¹He who has an ear, let him hear what the Spirit says to the churches. He who overcomes will not be hurt at all by the second death.

To the Church in Pergamum

¹²"To the angel of the church in Pergamum write:

These are the words of him who has the sharp, double-edged sword. ¹³I know where you live—where Satan has his throne. Yet you remain true to my name. You did not renounce your faith in me, even in the days of Antipas, my faithful witness, who was put to death in your city—where Satan lives.

¹⁴Nevertheless, I have a few things against you: You have people there who hold to the teaching of Balaam, who taught Balak to entice the Israelites to sin by eating food sacrificed to idols and by committing sexual

ᵃ 13 Daniel 7:13   ᵇ 20 Or messengers   ᶜ 1 Or messenger; also in verses 8, 12 and 18

FOR THE RENEWAL OF GOD'S CHURCH
Isabella Graham

VERSE: Revelation 2:4   **PASSAGE:** Revelation 2:1–7

you who are Alpha and Omega, . . ." write with power, speak with power, in the heart of the angel of this church. Have you not in former days had your dwelling among them? In days of trouble did you not work in them the fruits of labor and patience, so that for your name's sake they labored and fainted not? You blessed them and gave them peace, and they rejoiced in the light of your countenance . . . Alas, Lord, we have . . . left our first love; we have not watched and prayed as you gave us command; . . . we have forsaken the counsel of our old men and given heed to flatterers; we have forgotten our dependence on you . . .

We are poor and blind and miserable and naked, rich in our fancied wisdom, seeing by our own light, compassing ourselves about with our own sparks, and flaunting our rags. "We feed on ashes . . ."

"Your covenant is well ordered in all things, and it is sure" (see 2 Samuel 23:5, KJV). Here, O Lord, I take my stand; here I lay my foundation, and on this your covenant I build; or rather here you yourself have laid my foundation, and on this rock you have set my soul and built my hopes, you subduing my enmity. I acquiesce. I will now "remember the years of your right hand" (see Psalm 77:10, KJV) . . .

O Lord, ever, ever, and again did you deliver [your people] and send provision for them by your own covenant: "chose David your servant and took him from the sheepfolds, from following the ewes great with young. You brought him to feed Jacob, your people, and Israel, your inheritance. So he fed them according to the integrity of his heart and guided them by the skillfulness of his hands . . ." (Psalm 78:70–71).

"This God is our God; we will make mention of his righteousness, and his only." By his own covenant, in his own time, and by means of his own providing, he will revive us. Amen.

ADDITIONAL SCRIPTURE READING:
Psalm 105:6–10; Isaiah 40:31

Go to page 1488 for your next devotional reading.

1700   1900

immorality. **15**Likewise you also have those who hold to the teaching of the Nicolaitans. **16**Repent therefore! Otherwise, I will soon come to you and will fight against them with the sword of my mouth.

17He who has an ear, let him hear what the Spirit says to the churches. To him who overcomes, I will give some of the hidden manna. I will also give him a white stone with a new name written on it, known only to him who receives it.

To the Church in Thyatira

18"To the angel of the church in Thyatira write:

These are the words of the Son of God, whose eyes are like blazing fire and whose feet are like burnished bronze. **19**I know your deeds, your love and faith, your service and perseverance, and that you are now doing more than you did at first.

20Nevertheless, I have this against you: You tolerate that woman Jezebel, who calls herself a prophetess. By her teaching she misleads my servants into sexual immorality and the eating of food sacrificed to idols. **21**I have given her time to repent of her immorality, but she is unwilling. **22**So I will cast her on a bed of suffering, and I will make those who commit adultery with her suffer intensely, unless they repent of her ways. **23**I will strike her children dead. Then all the churches will know that I am he who searches hearts and minds, and I will repay each of you according to your deeds. **24**Now I say to the rest of you in Thyatira, to you who do not hold to her teaching and have not learned Satan's so-called deep secrets (I will not impose any other burden on you): **25**Only hold on to what you have until I come.

26To him who overcomes and does my will to the end, I will give authority over the nations—

27'He will rule them with an iron
  scepter;

he will dash them to pieces
  like pottery'*a*—

just as I have received authority from my Father. **28**I will also give him the morning star. **29**He who has an ear, let him hear what the Spirit says to the churches.

To the Church in Sardis

3 "To the angel*b* of the church in Sardis write:

These are the words of him who holds the seven spirits*c* of God and the seven stars. I know your deeds; you have a reputation of being alive, but you are dead. **2**Wake up! Strengthen what remains and is about to die, for I have not found your deeds complete in the sight of my God. **3**Remember, therefore, what you have received and heard; obey it, and repent. But if you do not wake up, I will come like a thief, and you will not know at what time I will come to you.

4Yet you have a few people in Sardis who have not soiled their clothes. They will walk with me, dressed in white, for they are worthy. **5**He who overcomes will, like them, be dressed in white. I will never blot out his name from the book of life, but will acknowledge his name before my Father and his angels. **6**He who has an ear, let him hear what the Spirit says to the churches.

To the Church in Philadelphia

7"To the angel of the church in Philadelphia write:

These are the words of him who is holy and true, who holds the key of David. What he opens no one can shut, and what he shuts no one can open. **8**I know your deeds. See, I have placed before you an open door that no one can shut. I know that you have little strength, yet you have kept my word and have not denied my name. **9**I will make those who are of the synagogue of Satan, who claim to be Jews though they

---

a 27 Psalm 2:9   *b* 1 Or *messenger*; also in verses 7 and 14   *c* 1 Or *the sevenfold Spirit*

are not, but are liars—I will make them come and fall down at your feet and acknowledge that I have loved you. ¹⁰Since you have kept my command to endure patiently, I will also keep you from the hour of trial that is going to come upon the whole world to test those who live on the earth.

¹¹I am coming soon. Hold on to

FRIDAY

BE FAITHFUL, EVEN TO THE POINT OF DEATH
Ignatius of Antioch

VERSE: Revelation 3:12   **PASSAGE:** Revelation 3:10–13

rom Syria all the way to Rome I am fighting with wild beasts, on land and sea, by night and day, chained amidst ten leopards (that is, a company of soldiers) who only get worse when they are well treated. Yet because of their mistreatment I am becoming more of a disciple; nevertheless "I am not thereby justified" (see 1 Corinthians 4:4). May I have the pleasure of the wild beasts that have been prepared for me; and I pray that they prove to be prompt with me. I will even coax them to devour me promptly, not as they have done with some, whom they were too timid to touch. And if when I am willing and ready they are not, I will force them. Bear with me—I know what is best for me. Now at last I am beginning to be a disciple. May nothing visible or invisible envy me, so that I may reach Jesus Christ. Fire and cross and battles with wild beasts, mutilation, mangling, wrenching of bones, the hacking of limbs, the crushing of my whole body, cruel tortures of the devil—let these come upon me, only let me reach Jesus Christ!

Neither the ends of the earth nor the kingdoms of this age are of any use to me. It is better for me to die for Jesus Christ than to rule over the ends of the earth. Him I seek, who died on our behalf; him I long for, who rose again for our sake. The pains of birth are upon me. Bear with me, brothers: do not keep me from living; do not desire my death. Do not give to the world one who wants to belong to God, nor tempt him with material things. Let me receive the pure light, for when I arrive there I will be a man. Allow me to be an imitator of the suffering of my God. If anyone has him within himself, let him understand what I long for and sympathize with me, knowing what constrains me.

ADDITIONAL SCRIPTURE READING:
John 11:25–26; Philippians 1:20–21

Go to page 1491 for your next devotional reading.

100　500

what you have, so that no one will take your crown. [12]Him who overcomes I will make a pillar in the temple of my God. Never again will he leave it. I will write on him the name of my God and the name of the city of my God, the new Jerusalem, which is coming down out of heaven from my God; and I will also write on him my new name. [13]He who has an ear, let him hear what the Spirit says to the churches.

To the Church in Laodicea

[14]"To the angel of the church in Laodicea write:

These are the words of the Amen, the faithful and true witness, the ruler of God's creation. [15]I know your deeds, that you are neither cold nor hot. I wish you were either one or the other! [16]So, because you are lukewarm—neither hot nor cold—I am about to spit you out of my mouth. [17]You say, 'I am rich; I have acquired wealth and do not need a thing.' But you do not realize that you are wretched, pitiful, poor, blind and naked. [18]I counsel you to buy from me gold refined in the fire, so you can become rich; and white clothes to wear, so you can cover your shameful nakedness; and salve to put on your eyes, so you can see.

[19]Those whom I love I rebuke and discipline. So be earnest, and repent. [20]Here I am! I stand at the door and knock. If anyone hears my voice and opens the door, I will come in and eat with him, and he with me.

[21]To him who overcomes, I will give the right to sit with me on my throne, just as I overcame and sat down with my Father on his throne. [22]He who has an ear, let him hear what the Spirit says to the churches."

The Throne in Heaven

4 After this I looked, and there before me was a door standing open in heaven. And the voice I had first heard speaking to me like a trumpet said, "Come up here, and I will show you what must take place after this." [2]At once I was in the Spirit, and there before me was a throne in heaven with someone sitting on it. [3]And the one who sat there had the appearance of jasper and carnelian. A rainbow, resembling an emerald, encircled the throne. [4]Surrounding the throne were twenty-four other thrones, and seated on them were twenty-four elders. They were dressed in white and had crowns of gold on their heads. [5]From the throne came flashes of lightning, rumblings and peals of thunder. Before the throne, seven lamps were blazing. These are the seven spirits[a] of God. [6]Also before the throne there was what looked like a sea of glass, clear as crystal.

In the center, around the throne, were four living creatures, and they were covered with eyes, in front and in back. [7]The first living creature was like a lion, the second was like an ox, the third had a face like a man, the fourth was like a flying eagle. [8]Each of the four living creatures had six wings and was covered with eyes all around, even under his wings. Day and night they never stop saying:

"Holy, holy, holy
is the Lord God Almighty,
who was, and is, and is to come."

[9]Whenever the living creatures give glory, honor and thanks to him who sits on the throne and who lives for ever and ever, [10]the twenty-four elders fall down before him who sits on the throne, and worship him who lives for ever and ever. They lay their crowns before the throne and say:

[11]"You are worthy, our Lord and God,
to receive glory and honor and power,
for you created all things,
and by your will they were created
and have their being."

The Scroll and the Lamb

5 Then I saw in the right hand of him who sat on the throne a scroll with writing on both sides and

a 5 Or *the sevenfold Spirit*

sealed with seven seals. ²And I saw a mighty angel proclaiming in a loud voice, "Who is worthy to break the seals and open the scroll?" ³But no one in heaven or on earth or under the earth could open the scroll or even look inside it. ⁴I wept and wept because no one was found who was worthy to open the scroll or look inside. ⁵Then one of the elders said to me, "Do not weep! See, the Lion of the tribe of Judah, the Root of David, has triumphed. He is able to open the scroll and its seven seals."

⁶Then I saw a Lamb, looking as if it had been slain, standing in the center of the throne, encircled by the four living creatures and the elders. He had seven horns and seven eyes, which are the seven spirits*a* of God sent out into all the earth. ⁷He came and took the scroll from the right hand of him who sat on the throne. ⁸And when he had taken it, the four living creatures and the twenty-four elders fell down before the Lamb. Each one had a harp and they were holding golden bowls full of incense, which are the prayers of the saints. ⁹And they sang a new song:

"You are worthy to take the scroll
    and to open its seals,
because you were slain,
    and with your blood you purchased
      men for God
    from every tribe and language and
      people and nation.
¹⁰You have made them to be a
      kingdom and priests to serve
      our God,
    and they will reign on the earth."

¹¹Then I looked and heard the voice of many angels, numbering thousands upon thousands, and ten thousand times ten thousand. They encircled the throne and the living creatures and the elders. ¹²In a loud voice they sang:

"Worthy is the Lamb, who was slain,
    to receive power and wealth and
      wisdom and strength
    and honor and glory and praise!"

¹³Then I heard every creature in heaven and on earth and under the earth and

on the sea, and all that is in them, singing:

"To him who sits on the throne and
    to the Lamb
be praise and honor and glory and
    power,
      for ever and ever!"

¹⁴The four living creatures said, "Amen," and the elders fell down and worshiped.

The Seals

6 I watched as the Lamb opened the first of the seven seals. Then I heard one of the four living creatures say in a voice like thunder, "Come!" ²I looked, and there before me was a white horse! Its rider held a bow, and he was given a crown, and he rode out as a conqueror bent on conquest.

³When the Lamb opened the second seal, I heard the second living creature say, "Come!" ⁴Then another horse came out, a fiery red one. Its rider was given power to take peace from the earth and to make men slay each other. To him was given a large sword.

⁵When the Lamb opened the third seal, I heard the third living creature say, "Come!" I looked, and there before me was a black horse! Its rider was holding a pair of scales in his hand. ⁶Then I heard what sounded like a voice among the four living creatures, saying, "A quart*b* of wheat for a day's wages,*c* and three quarts of barley for a day's wages,*c* and do not damage the oil and the wine!"

⁷When the Lamb opened the fourth seal, I heard the voice of the fourth living creature say, "Come!" ⁸I looked, and there before me was a pale horse! Its rider was named Death, and Hades was following close behind him. They were given power over a fourth of the earth to kill by sword, famine and plague, and by the wild beasts of the earth.

⁹When he opened the fifth seal, I saw under the altar the souls of those who had been slain because of the word of God and the testimony they had maintained. ¹⁰They called out in a loud voice, "How long, Sovereign Lord, holy and true, until you judge the inhabitants of the earth and avenge our blood?" ¹¹Then

---

a 6 Or *the sevenfold Spirit*   *b* 6 Greek *a choinix* (probably about a liter)   *c* 6 Greek *a denarius*

WEEKEND

THE ENCOUNTER
John Newton

VERSE: Revelation 5:9   **PASSAGE:** Revelation 5:9–12

n evil long I took delight,
    Unawed by shame or fear,
Till a new object struck my sight,
    And stopped my wild career:
I saw One hanging on a tree
    In agonies and blood,
Who fixed his languid eyes on me,
    As near his cross I stood.

Sure never till my latest breath
    Can I forget that look:
It seemed to charge me with his death,
    Though not a word he spoke:
My conscience felt and owned the guilt,
    And plunged me in despair;
I saw my sins his blood had spilt
    And helped to nail him there.

Alas! I knew not what I did!
    But now my tears are vain:
Where shall my trembling soul be hid?
    For I the Lord have slain!
A second look he gave, which said,
    'I freely all forgive;
This blood is for thy ransom paid.
    I die, that thou mayst live.'

Thus, while his death my sin displays
    In all its blackest hue,
Such is the mystery of grace,
    It seals my pardon too . . .

ADDITIONAL SCRIPTURE READING:
Philippians 2:8; Colossians 2:13–15

Go to page 1494 for your next devotional reading.

1700   1900

each of them was given a white robe, and they were told to wait a little longer, until the number of their fellow servants and brothers who were to be killed as they had been was completed.

12I watched as he opened the sixth seal. There was a great earthquake. The sun turned black like sackcloth made of goat hair, the whole moon turned blood red, 13and the stars in the sky fell to earth, as late figs drop from a fig tree when shaken by a strong wind. 14The sky receded like a scroll, rolling up, and every mountain and island was removed from its place.

15Then the kings of the earth, the princes, the generals, the rich, the mighty, and every slave and every free man hid in caves and among the rocks of the mountains. 16They called to the mountains and the rocks, "Fall on us and hide us from the face of him who sits on the throne and from the wrath of the Lamb! 17For the great day of their wrath has come, and who can stand?"

144,000 Sealed

7 After this I saw four angels standing at the four corners of the earth, holding back the four winds of the earth to prevent any wind from blowing on the land or on the sea or on any tree. 2Then I saw another angel coming up from the east, having the seal of the living God. He called out in a loud voice to the four angels who had been given power to harm the land and the sea: 3"Do not harm the land or the sea or the trees until we put a seal on the foreheads of the servants of our God." 4Then I heard the number of those who were sealed: 144,000 from all the tribes of Israel.

5 From the tribe of Judah 12,000 were
   sealed,
   from the tribe of Reuben 12,000,
   from the tribe of Gad 12,000,
6from the tribe of Asher 12,000,
   from the tribe of Naphtali 12,000,
   from the tribe of Manasseh 12,000,
7from the tribe of Simeon 12,000,
   from the tribe of Levi 12,000,
   from the tribe of Issachar 12,000,
8from the tribe of Zebulun 12,000,
   from the tribe of Joseph 12,000,
   from the tribe of Benjamin 12,000.

The Great Multitude in White Robes

9After this I looked and there before me was a great multitude that no one could count, from every nation, tribe, people and language, standing before the throne and in front of the Lamb. They were wearing white robes and were holding palm branches in their hands. 10And they cried out in a loud voice:

"Salvation belongs to our God,
   who sits on the throne,
   and to the Lamb."

11All the angels were standing around the throne and around the elders and the four living creatures. They fell down on their faces before the throne and worshiped God, 12saying:

"Amen!
Praise and glory
and wisdom and thanks and honor
and power and strength
be to our God for ever and ever.
Amen!"

13Then one of the elders asked me, "These in white robes—who are they, and where did they come from?"
14I answered, "Sir, you know."
And he said, "These are they who have come out of the great tribulation; they have washed their robes and made them white in the blood of the Lamb. 15Therefore,

"they are before the throne of God
   and serve him day and night in his
      temple;
and he who sits on the throne will
      spread his tent over them.
16Never again will they hunger;
   never again will they thirst.
The sun will not beat upon them,
   nor any scorching heat.
17For the Lamb at the center of the
      throne will be their shepherd;
he will lead them to springs of
      living water.
And God will wipe away every tear
      from their eyes."

The Seventh Seal and the Golden Censer

8 When he opened the seventh seal, there was silence in heaven for about half an hour.

²And I saw the seven angels who stand before God, and to them were given seven trumpets.

³Another angel, who had a golden censer, came and stood at the altar. He was given much incense to offer, with the prayers of all the saints, on the golden altar before the throne. ⁴The smoke of the incense, together with the prayers of the saints, went up before God from the angel's hand. ⁵Then the angel took the censer, filled it with fire from the altar, and hurled it on the earth; and there came peals of thunder, rumblings, flashes of lightning and an earthquake.

PRAYER IS THE INCENSE OF A HOLY HEART

RISING TO GOD FROM BRUISED AND BROKEN

THINGS,

WHEN KINDLED BY THE SPIRIT'S BURNING

BREATH

AND UPWARD BORNE BY FAITH'S ASCENDING

WINGS.

—*A. B. Simpson*

The Trumpets

⁶Then the seven angels who had the seven trumpets prepared to sound them.

⁷The first angel sounded his trumpet, and there came hail and fire mixed with blood, and it was hurled down upon the earth. A third of the earth was burned up, a third of the trees were burned up, and all the green grass was burned up.

⁸The second angel sounded his trumpet, and something like a huge mountain, all ablaze, was thrown into the sea. A third of the sea turned into blood, ⁹a third of the living creatures in the sea died, and a third of the ships were destroyed.

¹⁰The third angel sounded his trumpet, and a great star, blazing like a torch, fell from the sky on a third of the rivers and on the springs of water— ¹¹the name of the star is Wormwood.ᵃ A third of the waters turned bitter, and many

people died from the waters that had become bitter.

¹²The fourth angel sounded his trumpet, and a third of the sun was struck, a third of the moon, and a third of the stars, so that a third of them turned dark. A third of the day was without light, and also a third of the night.

¹³As I watched, I heard an eagle that was flying in midair call out in a loud voice: "Woe! Woe! Woe to the inhabitants of the earth, because of the trumpet blasts about to be sounded by the other three angels!"

9 The fifth angel sounded his trumpet, and I saw a star that had fallen from the sky to the earth. The star was given the key to the shaft of the Abyss. ²When he opened the Abyss, smoke rose from it like the smoke from a gigantic furnace. The sun and sky were darkened by the smoke from the Abyss. ³And out of the smoke locusts came down upon the earth and were given power like that of scorpions of the earth. ⁴They were told not to harm the grass of the earth or any plant or tree, but only those people who did not have the seal of God on their foreheads. ⁵They were not given power to kill them, but only to torture them for five months. And the agony they suffered was like that of the sting of a scorpion when it strikes a man. ⁶During those days men will seek death, but will not find it; they will long to die, but death will elude them.

⁷The locusts looked like horses prepared for battle. On their heads they wore something like crowns of gold, and their faces resembled human faces. ⁸Their hair was like women's hair, and their teeth were like lions' teeth. ⁹They had breastplates like breastplates of iron, and the sound of their wings was like the thundering of many horses and chariots rushing into battle. ¹⁰They had tails and stings like scorpions, and in their tails they had power to torment people for five months. ¹¹They had as king over them the angel of the Abyss, whose name in Hebrew is Abaddon, and in Greek, Apollyon.ᵇ

¹²The first woe is past; two other woes are yet to come.

ᵃ 11 That is, Bitterness   ᵇ 11 *Abaddon* and *Apollyon* mean *Destroyer*.

EVENING PRAYER
Thomas Merton

VERSE: Revelation 8:4   **PASSAGE:** Revelation 8:3–5

ord, receive my prayer
Sweet as incense smoke
Rising from my heart
Full of care
I lift up my hands
In evening sacrifice
Lord, receive my prayer.

When I meet the man
On my way
When he starts to curse
And threatens me,
Lord, guard my lips
I will not reply
Guide my steps in the night
As I go my way.

Maybe he belongs
To some other Lord
Who is not so wise and good
Maybe that is why those bones
Lie scattered on his road.

When I look to right and left
No one cares to know
Who I am, where I go . . .

Lord, to you I raise
Wide and bright
Faith-filled eyes
In the night
You are my protection
Bring me home.

And receive my prayer
Sweet as incense smoke
Rising from my heart
Free of care.

ADDITIONAL SCRIPTURE READING:
Matthew 6:9–13; John 14:14

Go to page 1497 for your next devotional reading.

1900   Present

13The sixth angel sounded his trumpet, and I heard a voice coming from the horns[a] of the golden altar that is before God. 14It said to the sixth angel who had the trumpet, "Release the four angels who are bound at the great river Euphrates." 15And the four angels who had been kept ready for this very hour and day and month and year were released to kill a third of mankind. 16The number of the mounted troops was two hundred million. I heard their number.

17The horses and riders I saw in my vision looked like this: Their breastplates were fiery red, dark blue, and yellow as sulfur. The heads of the horses resembled the heads of lions, and out of their mouths came fire, smoke and sulfur. 18A third of mankind was killed by the three plagues of fire, smoke and sulfur that came out of their mouths. 19The power of the horses was in their mouths and in their tails; for their tails were like snakes, having heads with which they inflict injury.

20The rest of mankind that were not killed by these plagues still did not repent of the work of their hands; they did not stop worshiping demons, and idols of gold, silver, bronze, stone and wood—idols that cannot see or hear or walk. 21Nor did they repent of their murders, their magic arts, their sexual immorality or their thefts.

The Angel and the Little Scroll

10 Then I saw another mighty angel coming down from heaven. He was robed in a cloud, with a rainbow above his head; his face was like the sun, and his legs were like fiery pillars. 2He was holding a little scroll, which lay open in his hand. He planted his right foot on the sea and his left foot on the land, 3and he gave a loud shout like the roar of a lion. When he shouted, the voices of the seven thunders spoke. 4And when the seven thunders spoke, I was about to write; but I heard a voice from heaven say, "Seal up what the seven thunders have said and do not write it down."

5Then the angel I had seen standing on the sea and on the land raised his right hand to heaven. 6And he swore by him who lives for ever and ever, who created the heavens and all that is in them, the earth and all that is in it, and the sea and all that is in it, and said, "There will be no more delay! 7But in the days when the seventh angel is about to sound his trumpet, the mystery of God will be accomplished, just as he announced to his servants the prophets."

8Then the voice that I had heard from heaven spoke to me once more: "Go, take the scroll that lies open in the hand of the angel who is standing on the sea and on the land."

9So I went to the angel and asked him to give me the little scroll. He said to me, "Take it and eat it. It will turn your stomach sour, but in your mouth it will be as sweet as honey." 10I took the little scroll from the angel's hand and ate it. It tasted as sweet as honey in my mouth, but when I had eaten it, my stomach turned sour. 11Then I was told, "You must prophesy again about many peoples, nations, languages and kings."

The Two Witnesses

11 I was given a reed like a measuring rod and was told, "Go and measure the temple of God and the altar, and count the worshipers there. 2But exclude the outer court; do not measure it, because it has been given to the Gentiles. They will trample on the holy city for 42 months. 3And I will give power to my two witnesses, and they will prophesy for 1,260 days, clothed in sackcloth." 4These are the two olive trees and the two lampstands that stand before the Lord of the earth. 5If anyone tries to harm them, fire comes from their mouths and devours their enemies. This is how anyone who wants to harm them must die. 6These men have power to shut up the sky so that it will not rain during the time they are prophesying; and they have power to turn the waters into blood and to strike the earth with every kind of plague as often as they want.

7Now when they have finished their testimony, the beast that comes up from the Abyss will attack them, and overpower and kill them. 8Their bodies will lie in the street of the great city, which

---

[a] 13 That is, projections

is figuratively called Sodom and Egypt, where also their Lord was crucified. ⁹For three and a half days men from every people, tribe, language and nation will gaze on their bodies and refuse them burial. ¹⁰The inhabitants of the earth will gloat over them and will celebrate by sending each other gifts, because these two prophets had tormented those who live on the earth.

¹¹But after the three and a half days a breath of life from God entered them, and they stood on their feet, and terror struck those who saw them. ¹²Then they heard a loud voice from heaven saying to them, "Come up here." And they went up to heaven in a cloud, while their enemies looked on.

¹³At that very hour there was a severe earthquake and a tenth of the city collapsed. Seven thousand people were killed in the earthquake, and the survivors were terrified and gave glory to the God of heaven.

¹⁴The second woe has passed; the third woe is coming soon.

The Seventh Trumpet

¹⁵The seventh angel sounded his trumpet, and there were loud voices in heaven, which said:

"The kingdom of the world has
    become the kingdom of our
    Lord and of his Christ,
  and he will reign for ever and ever."

¹⁶And the twenty-four elders, who were seated on their thrones before God, fell on their faces and worshiped God, ¹⁷saying:

"We give thanks to you, Lord God
    Almighty,
  the One who is and who was,
  because you have taken your great
    power
  and have begun to reign.
¹⁸The nations were angry;
  and your wrath has come.
The time has come for judging the
    dead,
  and for rewarding your servants the
    prophets
  and your saints and those who
    reverence your name,

both small and great—
  and for destroying those who destroy
    the earth."

¹⁹Then God's temple in heaven was opened, and within his temple was seen the ark of his covenant. And there came flashes of lightning, rumblings, peals of thunder, an earthquake and a great hailstorm.

The Woman and the Dragon

12 A great and wondrous sign appeared in heaven: a woman clothed with the sun, with the moon under her feet and a crown of twelve stars on her head. ²She was pregnant and cried out in pain as she was about to give birth. ³Then another sign appeared in heaven: an enormous red dragon with seven heads and ten horns and seven crowns on his heads. ⁴His tail swept a third of the stars out of the sky and flung them to the earth. The dragon stood in front of the woman who was about to give birth, so that he might devour her child the moment it was born. ⁵She gave birth to a son, a male child, who will rule all the nations with an iron scepter. And her child was snatched up to God and to his throne. ⁶The woman fled into the desert to a place prepared for her by God, where she might be taken care of for 1,260 days.

⁷And there was war in heaven. Michael and his angels fought against the dragon, and the dragon and his angels fought back. ⁸But he was not strong enough, and they lost their place in heaven. ⁹The great dragon was hurled down—that ancient serpent called the devil, or Satan, who leads the whole world astray. He was hurled to the earth, and his angels with him.

¹⁰Then I heard a loud voice in heaven say:

"Now have come the salvation and
    the power and the kingdom of
    our God,
  and the authority of his Christ.
For the accuser of our brothers,
  who accuses them before our God
    day and night,
  has been hurled down.

11 They overcame him
by the blood of the Lamb
and by the word of their testimony;
they did not love their lives so much
as to shrink from death.
12 Therefore rejoice, you heavens
and you who dwell in them!
But woe to the earth and the sea,

because the devil has gone down to
you!
He is filled with fury,
because he knows that his time is
short."

13 When the dragon saw that he had
been hurled to the earth, he pursued the

TUESDAY

FROM LUCIFER
Joost van den Vondel

VERSE: Revelation 12:7   **PASSAGE:** Revelation 12:7–9

ICHAEL: Praise be to God! The state of things above
Has changed. Our Grand Foe has met his defeat;
And in our hands he leaves his standard, helm,
And morning-star, and shield and banners bold.
Which spoil, gained in pursuit, even now does hang,
'Mid joys triumphant, honors, songs of praise,
And sounds of trump, on Heaven's axis bright,
The mirror clear of all rebelliousness,
Of all ambition that would rear its crest
'Gainst God, the stem immovable—grand fount,
Prime source, and Father of all things that are,
Which from his hand their nature did receive,
And various attributes. No more shall we
Behold the glow of Majesty Supreme
Dimmed by the damp of base ingratitude.
There, deep beneath our sight and these high thrones,
They wander through the air and restlessly
Move to and fro, all blind and overcast
With shrouding clouds, and horribly deformed.
Thus is his fate, who would assail God's Throne.
CHORUS: Thus is his fate, who would assail God's Throne.
Thus his fate, who would, through envy, man,
In God's own image made, deprive of light.

ADDITIONAL SCRIPTURE READING:
Isaiah 14:12–15; Romans 16:20

Go to page 1501 for your next devotional reading.

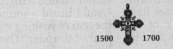

1500   1700

woman who had given birth to the male child. ¹⁴The woman was given the two wings of a great eagle, so that she might fly to the place prepared for her in the desert, where she would be taken care of for a time, times and half a time, out of the serpent's reach. ¹⁵Then from his mouth the serpent spewed water like a river, to overtake the woman and sweep her away with the torrent. ¹⁶But the earth helped the woman by opening its mouth and swallowing the river that the dragon had spewed out of his mouth. ¹⁷Then the dragon was enraged at the woman and went off to make war against the rest of her offspring—those who obey God's commandments and hold to the

13 testimony of Jesus. ¹And the dragon*a* stood on the shore of the sea.

The Beast out of the Sea

And I saw a beast coming out of the sea. He had ten horns and seven heads, with ten crowns on his horns, and on each head a blasphemous name. ²The beast I saw resembled a leopard, but had feet like those of a bear and a mouth like that of a lion. The dragon gave the beast his power and his throne and great authority. ³One of the heads of the beast seemed to have had a fatal wound, but the fatal wound had been healed. The whole world was astonished and followed the beast. ⁴Men worshiped the dragon because he had given authority to the beast, and they also worshiped the beast and asked, "Who is like the beast? Who can make war against him?"

⁵The beast was given a mouth to utter proud words and blasphemies and to exercise his authority for forty-two months. ⁶He opened his mouth to blaspheme God, and to slander his name and his dwelling place and those who live in heaven. ⁷He was given power to make war against the saints and to conquer them. And he was given authority over every tribe, people, language and nation. ⁸All inhabitants of the earth will worship the beast—all whose names have not been written in the book of life belonging to the Lamb that was slain from the creation of the world.*b*

⁹He who has an ear, let him hear.

¹⁰If anyone is to go into captivity,
  into captivity he will go.
If anyone is to be killed*c* with the
  sword,
  with the sword he will be killed.

This calls for patient endurance and faithfulness on the part of the saints.

The Beast out of the Earth

¹¹Then I saw another beast, coming out of the earth. He had two horns like a lamb, but he spoke like a dragon. ¹²He exercised all the authority of the first beast on his behalf, and made the earth and its inhabitants worship the first beast, whose fatal wound had been healed. ¹³And he performed great and miraculous signs, even causing fire to come down from heaven to earth in full view of men. ¹⁴Because of the signs he was given power to do on behalf of the first beast, he deceived the inhabitants of the earth. He ordered them to set up an image in honor of the beast who was wounded by the sword and yet lived. ¹⁵He was given power to give breath to the image of the first beast, so that it could speak and cause all who refused to worship the image to be killed. ¹⁶He also forced everyone, small and great, rich and poor, free and slave, to receive a mark on his right hand or on his forehead, ¹⁷so that no one could buy or sell unless he had the mark, which is the name of the beast or the number of his name.

¹⁸This calls for wisdom. If anyone has insight, let him calculate the number of the beast, for it is man's number. His number is 666.

The Lamb and the 144,000

14 Then I looked, and there before me was the Lamb, standing on Mount Zion, and with him 144,000 who had his name and his Father's name written on their foreheads. ²And I heard a sound from heaven like the roar of rushing waters and like a loud peal of thunder. The sound I heard was like that of harpists playing their harps.

---

a 1 Some late manuscripts *And I*   *b 8* Or *written from the creation of the world in the book of life belonging to the Lamb that was slain*   *c 10* Some manuscripts *anyone kills*

[3] And they sang a new song before the throne and before the four living creatures and the elders. No one could learn the song except the 144,000 who had been redeemed from the earth. [4] These are those who did not defile themselves with women, for they kept themselves pure. They follow the Lamb wherever he goes. They were purchased from among men and offered as firstfruits to God and the Lamb. [5] No lie was found in their mouths; they are blameless.

The Three Angels

[6] Then I saw another angel flying in midair, and he had the eternal gospel to proclaim to those who live on the earth—to every nation, tribe, language and people. [7] He said in a loud voice, "Fear God and give him glory, because the hour of his judgment has come. Worship him who made the heavens, the earth, the sea and the springs of water."

[8] A second angel followed and said, "Fallen! Fallen is Babylon the Great, which made all the nations drink the maddening wine of her adulteries."

[9] A third angel followed them and said in a loud voice: "If anyone worships the beast and his image and receives his mark on the forehead or on the hand, [10] he, too, will drink of the wine of God's fury, which has been poured full strength into the cup of his wrath. He will be tormented with burning sulfur in the presence of the holy angels and of the Lamb. [11] And the smoke of their torment rises for ever and ever. There is no rest day or night for those who worship the beast and his image, or for anyone who receives the mark of his name." [12] This calls for patient endurance on the part of the saints who obey God's commandments and remain faithful to Jesus.

[13] Then I heard a voice from heaven say, "Write: Blessed are the dead who die in the Lord from now on."

"Yes," says the Spirit, "they will rest from their labor, for their deeds will follow them."

The Harvest of the Earth

[14] I looked, and there before me was a white cloud, and seated on the cloud was one "like a son of man"[a] with a crown of gold on his head and a sharp sickle in his hand. [15] Then another angel came out of the temple and called in a loud voice to him who was sitting on the cloud, "Take your sickle and reap, because the time to reap has come, for the harvest of the earth is ripe." [16] So he who was seated on the cloud swung his sickle over the earth, and the earth was harvested.

[17] Another angel came out of the temple in heaven, and he too had a sharp sickle. [18] Still another angel, who had charge of the fire, came from the altar and called in a loud voice to him who had the sharp sickle, "Take your sharp sickle and gather the clusters of grapes from the earth's vine, because its grapes are ripe." [19] The angel swung his sickle on the earth, gathered its grapes and threw them into the great winepress of God's wrath. [20] They were trampled in the winepress outside the city, and blood flowed out of the press, rising as high as the horses' bridles for a distance of 1,600 stadia.[b]

Seven Angels With Seven Plagues

15 I saw in heaven another great and marvelous sign: seven angels with the seven last plagues—last, because with them God's wrath is completed. [2] And I saw what looked like a sea of glass mixed with fire and, standing beside the sea, those who had been victorious over the beast and his image and over the number of his name. They held harps given them by God [3] and sang the song of Moses the servant of God and the song of the Lamb:

"Great and marvelous are your deeds,
    Lord God Almighty.
Just and true are your ways,
    King of the ages.
[4] Who will not fear you, O Lord,
    and bring glory to your name?
For you alone are holy.
All nations will come
    and worship before you,
for your righteous acts have been
    revealed."

[5] After this I looked and in heaven the temple, that is, the tabernacle of the Testimony, was opened. [6] Out of the temple came the seven angels with the seven

a 14 Daniel 7:13   b 20 That is, about 180 miles (about 300 kilometers) plagues. They were dressed in clean, shining linen and wore golden sashes around their chests. 7Then one of the four living creatures gave to the seven angels seven golden bowls filled with the wrath of God, who lives for ever and ever. 8And the temple was filled with smoke from the glory of God and from his power, and no one could enter the temple until the seven plagues of the seven angels were completed.

The Seven Bowls of God's Wrath

16 Then I heard a loud voice from the temple saying to the seven angels, "Go, pour out the seven bowls of God's wrath on the earth."

2The first angel went and poured out his bowl on the land, and ugly and painful sores broke out on the people who had the mark of the beast and worshiped his image.

3The second angel poured out his bowl on the sea, and it turned into blood like that of a dead man, and every living thing in the sea died.

4The third angel poured out his bowl on the rivers and springs of water, and they became blood. 5Then I heard the angel in charge of the waters say:

"You are just in these judgments,
    you who are and who were, the
        Holy One,
    because you have so judged;
6for they have shed the blood of your
        saints and prophets,
    and you have given them blood to
        drink as they deserve."

7And I heard the altar respond:

"Yes, Lord God Almighty,
    true and just are your judgments."

8The fourth angel poured out his bowl on the sun, and the sun was given power to scorch people with fire. 9They were seared by the intense heat and they cursed the name of God, who had control over these plagues, but they refused to repent and glorify him.

10The fifth angel poured out his bowl on the throne of the beast, and his kingdom was plunged into darkness. Men gnawed their tongues in agony 11and cursed the God of heaven because of their pains and their sores, but they refused to repent of what they had done.

12The sixth angel poured out his bowl on the great river Euphrates, and its water was dried up to prepare the way for the kings from the East. 13Then I saw three evil*a* spirits that looked like frogs; they came out of the mouth of the dragon, out of the mouth of the beast and out of the mouth of the false prophet. 14They are spirits of demons performing miraculous signs, and they go out to the kings of the whole world, to gather them for the battle on the great day of God Almighty.

15"Behold, I come like a thief! Blessed is he who stays awake and keeps his clothes with him, so that he may not go naked and be shamefully exposed."

16Then they gathered the kings together to the place that in Hebrew is called Armageddon.

17The seventh angel poured out his bowl into the air, and out of the temple came a loud voice from the throne, saying, "It is done!" 18Then there came flashes of lightning, rumblings, peals of thunder and a severe earthquake. No earthquake like it has ever occurred since man has been on earth, so tremendous was the quake. 19The great city split into three parts, and the cities of the nations collapsed. God remembered Babylon the Great and gave her the cup filled with the wine of the fury of his wrath. 20Every island fled away and the mountains could not be found. 21From the sky huge hailstones of about a hundred pounds each fell upon men. And they cursed God on account of the plague of hail, because the plague was so terrible.

The Woman on the Beast

17 One of the seven angels who had the seven bowls came and said to me, "Come, I will show you the punishment of the great prostitute, who sits on many waters. 2With her the kings of the earth committed adultery and the inhabitants of the earth were intoxicated with the wine of her adulteries."

3Then the angel carried me away in the Spirit into a desert. There I saw a woman sitting on a scarlet beast that was

a 13 Greek *unclean*

covered with blasphemous names and had seven heads and ten horns. ⁴The woman was dressed in purple and scarlet, and was glittering with gold, precious stones and pearls. She held a golden cup in her hand, filled with abominable things and the filth of her adulteries. ⁵This title was written on her forehead:

MYSTERY
BABYLON THE GREAT
THE MOTHER OF PROSTITUTES
AND OF THE ABOMINATIONS OF THE EARTH.

⁶I saw that the woman was drunk with the blood of the saints, the blood of those who bore testimony to Jesus.

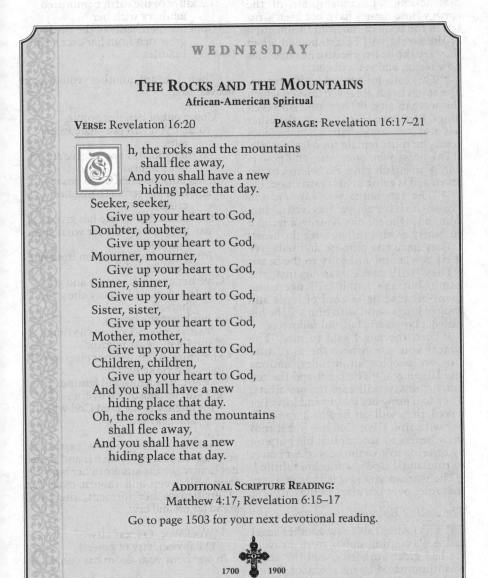

WEDNESDAY

THE ROCKS AND THE MOUNTAINS
African-American Spiritual

VERSE: Revelation 16:20   **PASSAGE:** Revelation 16:17–21

Oh, the rocks and the mountains
    shall flee away,
And you shall have a new
    hiding place that day.
Seeker, seeker,
    Give up your heart to God,
Doubter, doubter,
    Give up your heart to God,
Mourner, mourner,
    Give up your heart to God,
Sinner, sinner,
    Give up your heart to God,
Sister, sister,
    Give up your heart to God,
Mother, mother,
    Give up your heart to God,
Children, children,
    Give up your heart to God,
And you shall have a new
    hiding place that day.
Oh, the rocks and the mountains
    shall flee away,
And you shall have a new
    hiding place that day.

ADDITIONAL SCRIPTURE READING:
Matthew 4:17; Revelation 6:15–17

Go to page 1503 for your next devotional reading.

1700   1900

When I saw her, I was greatly astonished. [7]Then the angel said to me: "Why are you astonished? I will explain to you the mystery of the woman and of the beast she rides, which has the seven heads and ten horns. [8]The beast, which you saw, once was, now is not, and will come up out of the Abyss and go to his destruction. The inhabitants of the earth whose names have not been written in the book of life from the creation of the world will be astonished when they see the beast, because he once was, now is not, and yet will come.

[9]"This calls for a mind with wisdom. The seven heads are seven hills on which the woman sits. [10]They are also seven kings. Five have fallen, one is, the other has not yet come; but when he does come, he must remain for a little while. [11]The beast who once was, and now is not, is an eighth king. He belongs to the seven and is going to his destruction.

[12]"The ten horns you saw are ten kings who have not yet received a kingdom, but who for one hour will receive authority as kings along with the beast. [13]They have one purpose and will give their power and authority to the beast. [14]They will make war against the Lamb, but the Lamb will overcome them because he is Lord of lords and King of kings—and with him will be his called, chosen and faithful followers."

[15]Then the angel said to me, "The waters you saw, where the prostitute sits, are peoples, multitudes, nations and languages. [16]The beast and the ten horns you saw will hate the prostitute. They will bring her to ruin and leave her naked; they will eat her flesh and burn her with fire. [17]For God has put it into their hearts to accomplish his purpose by agreeing to give the beast their power to rule, until God's words are fulfilled. [18]The woman you saw is the great city that rules over the kings of the earth."

The Fall of Babylon

18 After this I saw another angel coming down from heaven. He had great authority, and the earth was illuminated by his splendor. [2]With a mighty voice he shouted:

"Fallen! Fallen is Babylon the Great!
    She has become a home for demons
and a haunt for every evil[a] spirit,
    a haunt for every unclean and
        detestable bird.
[3]For all the nations have drunk
    the maddening wine of her
        adulteries.
The kings of the earth committed
    adultery with her,
    and the merchants of the earth
        grew rich from her excessive
        luxuries."

[4]Then I heard another voice from heaven say:

"Come out of her, my people,
    so that you will not share in her
        sins,
    so that you will not receive any of
        her plagues;
[5]for her sins are piled up to heaven,
    and God has remembered her
        crimes.
[6]Give back to her as she has given;
    pay her back double for what she
        has done.
    Mix her a double portion from her
        own cup.
[7]Give her as much torture and grief
    as the glory and luxury she gave
        herself.
In her heart she boasts,
    'I sit as queen; I am not a widow,
    and I will never mourn.'
[8]Therefore in one day her plagues will
        overtake her:
    death, mourning and famine.
She will be consumed by fire,
    for mighty is the Lord God who
        judges her.

[9]"When the kings of the earth who committed adultery with her and shared her luxury see the smoke of her burning, they will weep and mourn over her. [10]Terrified at her torment, they will stand far off and cry:

" 'Woe! Woe, O great city,
    O Babylon, city of power!
In one hour your doom has come!'

[11]"The merchants of the earth will

---

[a] 2 Greek *unclean*

weep and mourn over her because no one buys their cargoes any more— [12]cargoes of gold, silver, precious stones and pearls; fine linen, purple, silk and scarlet cloth; every sort of citron wood, and articles of every kind made of ivory, costly wood, bronze, iron and marble; [13]cargoes of cinnamon and spice, of

THURSDAY

SONNET XIII & SONNET XIV
Edmund Spenser

VERSE: Revelation 17:3   **PASSAGE:** Revelation 17:1–18

I saw a woman sitting on a beast
Before mine eyes, of orange color hue:
Horror and dreadful name of blasphemy
Filled her with pride. And seven heads I saw,
Ten horns also the stately beast did bear.
She seemed with glory of the scarlet fair,
And with fine pearl and gold puffed up in heart.
The wine of whoredom in a cup she bare.
The name of Mystery writ in her face.
The blood of martyrs dear were her delight.
Most fierce and fell this woman seemed to me.
An angel then descending down from heaven,
With thundering voice cried out aloud, and said,
Now for a truth great Babylon is fallen.

Then might I see upon a white horse set
The faithful man with flaming countenance,
His head did shine with crowns set thereupon.
The word of God made him a noble name.
His precious robe I saw embrewed with blood.
Then saw I from the heaven on horses white,
A puissant army come the self-same way.
Then cried a shining angel as me thought,
That birds from air descending down on earth
Should war upon the kings, and eat their flesh.
Then did I see the beast and kings also
Joining their force to slay the faithful man.
But this fierce hateful beast and all her train,
Is pitiless thrown down in pit of fire.

ADDITIONAL SCRIPTURE READING:
Psalm 103:1–3; Revelation 19:11–16

Go to page 1507 for your next devotional reading.

1500   1700

incense, myrrh and frankincense, of wine and olive oil, of fine flour and wheat; cattle and sheep; horses and carriages; and bodies and souls of men.

14"They will say, 'The fruit you longed for is gone from you. All your riches and splendor have vanished, never to be recovered.' 15The merchants who sold these things and gained their wealth from her will stand far off, terrified at her torment. They will weep and mourn 16and cry out:

" 'Woe! Woe, O great city,
　　dressed in fine linen, purple and
　　　scarlet,
　　and glittering with gold, precious
　　　stones and pearls!
17 In one hour such great wealth has
　　been brought to ruin!'

"Every sea captain, and all who travel by ship, the sailors, and all who earn their living from the sea, will stand far off. 18When they see the smoke of her burning, they will exclaim, 'Was there ever a city like this great city?' 19They will throw dust on their heads, and with weeping and mourning cry out:

" 'Woe! Woe, O great city,
　　where all who had ships on the sea
　　　became rich through her wealth!
　　In one hour she has been brought to
　　　ruin!
20 Rejoice over her, O heaven!
　　Rejoice, saints and apostles and
　　　prophets!
　　God has judged her for the way she
　　　treated you.' "

21Then a mighty angel picked up a boulder the size of a large millstone and threw it into the sea, and said:

"With such violence
　　the great city of Babylon will be
　　　thrown down,
　　never to be found again.
22 The music of harpists and musicians,
　　　flute players and trumpeters,
　　will never be heard in you again.
　No workman of any trade
　　will ever be found in you again.
　The sound of a millstone
　　will never be heard in you again.

23 The light of a lamp
　　will never shine in you again.
　The voice of bridegroom and bride
　　will never be heard in you again.
　Your merchants were the world's
　　　great men.
　By your magic spell all the nations
　　　were led astray.
24 In her was found the blood of
　　　prophets and of the saints,
　　and of all who have been killed on
　　　the earth."

Hallelujah!

19 After this I heard what sounded like the roar of a great multitude in heaven shouting:

"Hallelujah!
Salvation and glory and power belong
　　to our God,
2 　for true and just are his judgments.
He has condemned the great
　　prostitute
　who corrupted the earth by her
　　adulteries.
He has avenged on her the blood of
　　his servants."

3And again they shouted:

"Hallelujah!
The smoke from her goes up for ever
　　and ever."

4The twenty-four elders and the four living creatures fell down and worshiped God, who was seated on the throne. And they cried:

"Amen, Hallelujah!"

5Then a voice came from the throne, saying:

"Praise our God,
　　all you his servants,
you who fear him,
　　both small and great!"

6Then I heard what sounded like a great multitude, like the roar of rushing waters and like loud peals of thunder, shouting:

"Hallelujah!
　For our Lord God Almighty reigns.

7 Let us rejoice and be glad
  and give him glory!
  For the wedding of the Lamb has
    come,
  and his bride has made herself
    ready.
8 Fine linen, bright and clean,
  was given her to wear."
(Fine linen stands for the righteous acts
of the saints.)

9 Then the angel said to me, "Write:
'Blessed are those who are invited to the
wedding supper of the Lamb!' " And he
added, "These are the true words of
God."
10 At this I fell at his feet to worship
him. But he said to me, "Do not do it! I
am a fellow servant with you and with
your brothers who hold to the testimony of Jesus. Worship God! For the testimony of Jesus is the spirit of prophecy."

The Rider on the White Horse

11 I saw heaven standing open and
there before me was a white horse,
whose rider is called Faithful and True.
With justice he judges and makes war.
12 His eyes are like blazing fire, and on
his head are many crowns. He has a
name written on him that no one knows
but he himself. 13 He is dressed in a robe
dipped in blood, and his name is the
Word of God. 14 The armies of heaven
were following him, riding on white
horses and dressed in fine linen, white
and clean. 15 Out of his mouth comes a
sharp sword with which to strike down
the nations. "He will rule them with an
iron scepter." [a] He treads the winepress
of the fury of the wrath of God
Almighty. 16 On his robe and on his
thigh he has this name written:

KING OF KINGS AND LORD OF LORDS.

17 And I saw an angel standing in the
sun, who cried in a loud voice to all the
birds flying in midair, "Come, gather
together for the great supper of God, 18 so
that you may eat the flesh of kings, generals, and mighty men, of horses and
their riders, and the flesh of all people,
free and slave, small and great."
19 Then I saw the beast and the kings
of the earth and their armies gathered

together to make war against the rider
on the horse and his army. 20 But the
beast was captured, and with him the
false prophet who had performed the
miraculous signs on his behalf. With
these signs he had deluded those who
had received the mark of the beast and
worshiped his image. The two of them
were thrown alive into the fiery lake of
burning sulfur. 21 The rest of them were
killed with the sword that came out of
the mouth of the rider on the horse, and
all the birds gorged themselves on their
flesh.

The Thousand Years

20 And I saw an angel coming
down out of heaven, having
the key to the Abyss and holding in his
hand a great chain. 2 He seized the dragon, that ancient serpent, who is the
devil, or Satan, and bound him for a
thousand years. 3 He threw him into the
Abyss, and locked and sealed it over
him, to keep him from deceiving the
nations anymore until the thousand
years were ended. After that, he must be
set free for a short time.
4 I saw thrones on which were seated
those who had been given authority to
judge. And I saw the souls of those who
had been beheaded because of their testimony for Jesus and because of the word
of God. They had not worshiped the
beast or his image and had not received
his mark on their foreheads or their
hands. They came to life and reigned
with Christ a thousand years. 5 (The rest
of the dead did not come to life until the
thousand years were ended.) This is the
first resurrection. 6 Blessed and holy are
those who have part in the first resurrection. The second death has no power
over them, but they will be priests of
God and of Christ and will reign with
him for a thousand years.

Satan's Doom

7 When the thousand years are over,
Satan will be released from his prison
8 and will go out to deceive the nations
in the four corners of the earth—Gog
and Magog—to gather them for battle.
In number they are like the sand on the
seashore. 9 They marched across the

a 15 Psalm 2:9

breadth of the earth and surrounded the camp of God's people, the city he loves. But fire came down from heaven and devoured them. 10And the devil, who deceived them, was thrown into the lake of burning sulfur, where the beast and the false prophet had been thrown. They will be tormented day and night for ever and ever.

The Dead Are Judged

11Then I saw a great white throne and him who was seated on it. Earth and sky fled from his presence, and there was no place for them. 12And I saw the dead, great and small, standing before the throne, and books were opened. Another book was opened, which is the book of life. The dead were judged according to what they had done as recorded in the books. 13The sea gave up the dead that were in it, and death and Hades gave up the dead that were in them, and each person was judged according to what he had done. 14Then death and Hades were thrown into the lake of fire. The lake of fire is the second death. 15If anyone's name was not found written in the book of life, he was thrown into the lake of fire.

The New Jerusalem

21 Then I saw a new heaven and a new earth, for the first heaven and the first earth had passed away, and there was no longer any sea. 2I saw the Holy City, the new Jerusalem, coming down out of heaven from God, prepared as a bride beautifully dressed for her husband. 3And I heard a loud voice from the throne saying, "Now the dwelling of God is with men, and he will live with them. They will be his people, and God himself will be with them and be their God. 4He will wipe every tear from their eyes. There will be no more death or mourning or crying or pain, for the old order of things has passed away."

5He who was seated on the throne said, "I am making everything new!" Then he said, "Write this down, for these words are trustworthy and true."

6He said to me: "It is done. I am the Alpha and the Omega, the Beginning and the End. To him who is thirsty I will give to drink without cost from the spring of the water of life. 7He who overcomes will inherit all this, and I will be his God and he will be my son. 8But the cowardly, the unbelieving, the vile, the murderers, the sexually immoral, those who practice magic arts, the idolaters and all liars—their place will be in the fiery lake of burning sulfur. This is the second death."

9One of the seven angels who had the seven bowls full of the seven last plagues came and said to me, "Come, I will show you the bride, the wife of the Lamb." 10And he carried me away in the Spirit to a mountain great and high, and showed me the Holy City, Jerusalem, coming down out of heaven from God. 11It shone with the glory of God, and its brilliance was like that of a very precious jewel, like a jasper, clear as crystal. 12It had a great, high wall with twelve gates, and with twelve angels at the gates. On the gates were written the names of the twelve tribes of Israel. 13There were three gates on the east, three on the north, three on the south and three on the west. 14The wall of the city had twelve foundations, and on them were the names of the twelve apostles of the Lamb.

15The angel who talked with me had a measuring rod of gold to measure the city, its gates and its walls. 16The city was laid out like a square, as long as it was wide. He measured the city with the rod and found it to be 12,000 stadia*a* in length, and as wide and high as it is long. 17He measured its wall and it was 144 cubits*b* thick,*c* by man's measurement, which the angel was using. 18The wall was made of jasper, and the city of pure gold, as pure as glass. 19The foundations of the city walls were decorated with every kind of precious stone. The first foundation was jasper, the second sapphire, the third chalcedony, the fourth emerald, 20the fifth sardonyx, the sixth carnelian, the seventh chrysolite, the eighth beryl, the ninth topaz, the tenth chrysoprase, the eleventh jacinth, and the twelfth amethyst.*d* 21The twelve

a 16 That is, about 1,400 miles (about 2,200 kilometers)   *b 17* That is, about 200 feet (about 65 meters)   *c 17* Or *high*   *d 20* The precise identification of some of these precious stones is uncertain.

WALK IN JERUSALEM JUST LIKE JOHN
African-American Spiritual

VERSE: Revelation 21:10   **PASSAGE:** Revelation 21:9–27

Version 1

 want to be ready,
I want to be ready,
I want to be ready,
To walk in Jerusalem just like John.

John said the city was just four square,
And he declared he'd meet me there;
John! Oh, John! what do you say?
That I'll be there in the coming day.
When Peter was preaching at Pentecost
He was endowed with the Holy Ghost.

I want to be ready,
I want to be ready,
I want to be ready,
To walk in Jerusalem just like John.

Version 2

Last Sunday morning, last Sunday morning,
    last Sunday morning,
Walk in Jerusalem, just like John.
Walk in Jerusalem, all God's people,
Walk in Jerusalem, tell the angels,
Walk in Jerusalem, just like John.

Train is a-coming, train is a-coming,
Walk in Jerusalem, just like John,
Walk in Jerusalem, all my brethren,
Walk in Jerusalem, all my sisters,
Walk in Jerusalem, just like John.
She is loaded down with angels,
    loaded down with angels,
Walk in Jerusalem, just like John,
Walk in Jerusalem, see my father,
Walk in Jerusalem, see my mother,
Walk in Jerusalem, just like John.

ADDITIONAL SCRIPTURE READING:
Matthew 24:42; John 14:2

Go to page 1509 for your next devotional reading.

1700   1900

gates were twelve pearls, each gate made of a single pearl. The great street of the city was of pure gold, like transparent glass.

22I did not see a temple in the city, because the Lord God Almighty and the Lamb are its temple. 23The city does not need the sun or the moon to shine on it, for the glory of God gives it light, and the Lamb is its lamp. 24The nations will walk by its light, and the kings of the earth will bring their splendor into it. 25On no day will its gates ever be shut, for there will be no night there. 26The glory and honor of the nations will be brought into it. 27Nothing impure will ever enter it, nor will anyone who does what is shameful or deceitful, but only those whose names are written in the Lamb's book of life.

The River of Life

22 Then the angel showed me the river of the water of life, as clear as crystal, flowing from the throne of God and of the Lamb 2down the middle of the great street of the city. On each side of the river stood the tree of life, bearing twelve crops of fruit, yielding its fruit every month. And the leaves of the tree are for the healing of the nations. 3No longer will there be any curse. The throne of God and of the Lamb will be in the city, and his servants will serve him. 4They will see his face, and his name will be on their foreheads. 5There will be no more night. They will not need the light of a lamp or the light of the sun, for the Lord God will give them light. And they will reign for ever and ever.

6The angel said to me, "These words are trustworthy and true. The Lord, the God of the spirits of the prophets, sent his angel to show his servants the things that must soon take place."

Jesus Is Coming

7"Behold, I am coming soon! Blessed is he who keeps the words of the prophecy in this book."

8I, John, am the one who heard and saw these things. And when I had heard and seen them, I fell down to worship at the feet of the angel who had been showing them to me. 9But he said to me, "Do not do it! I am a fellow servant with you and with your brothers the prophets and of all who keep the words of this book. Worship God!"

10Then he told me, "Do not seal up the words of the prophecy of this book, because the time is near. 11Let him who does wrong continue to do wrong; let him who is vile continue to be vile; let him who does right continue to do right; and let him who is holy continue to be holy."

12"Behold, I am coming soon! My reward is with me, and I will give to everyone according to what he has done. 13I am the Alpha and the Omega, the First and the Last, the Beginning and the End.

14"Blessed are those who wash their robes, that they may have the right to the tree of life and may go through the gates into the city. 15Outside are the dogs, those who practice magic arts, the sexually immoral, the murderers, the idolaters and everyone who loves and practices falsehood.

16"I, Jesus, have sent my angel to give you[a] this testimony for the churches. I am the Root and the Offspring of David, and the bright Morning Star."

17The Spirit and the bride say, "Come!" And let him who hears say, "Come!" Whoever is thirsty, let him come; and whoever wishes, let him take the free gift of the water of life.

18I warn everyone who hears the words of the prophecy of this book: If anyone adds anything to them, God will add to him the plagues described in this book. 19And if anyone takes words away from this book of prophecy, God will take away from him his share in the tree of life and in the holy city, which are described in this book.

20He who testifies to these things says, "Yes, I am coming soon."

Amen. Come, Lord Jesus.

21The grace of the Lord Jesus be with God's people. Amen.

a 16 The Greek is plural.

WEEKEND

CHRIST IS OUR REDEMPTION
George Whitefield

VERSE: Revelation 22:7   **PASSAGE:** Revelation 22:1–7

oes it not often dazzle your eyes, O ye children of God, to look at your own brightness, when the candle of the Lord shines out, and your Redeemer lifts up the light of his blessed countenance upon your souls? Are not you astonished, when you feel the love of God shed abroad in your hearts by the Holy Ghost, and God holds out the golden scepter of his mercy, and bids you ask what you will, and it shall be given you? Does not that peace of God, which keeps and rules your hearts, surpass the utmost limits of your understandings? And is not the joy you feel unspeakable? Is it not full of glory? I am persuaded it is; and in your secret communion, when the Lord's love flows in upon your souls, you are as it were swallowed up in, or, to use the apostle's phrase, "filled with all the fullness of God" (Ephesians 3:19, KJV). Are not you ready to cry out with Solomon, "And will the Lord, indeed, dwell thus with men!" (see 2 Chronicles 6:18). How is it that we should be thus thy sons and daughters, O Lord God Almighty!

If you are children of God, and know what it is to have fellowship with the Father and the Son; if you walk by faith, and not by sight; I am assured this is frequently the language of your hearts.

But look forward, and see an unbounded prospect of eternal happiness lying before thee, O believer! what thou hast already received are only the first-fruits, like the cluster of grapes brought out of the land of Canaan; only an earnest and pledge of yet infinitely better things to come: the harvest is to follow; thy grace is hereafter to be swallowed up in glory. Thy great Joshua, and merciful high priest, shall administer an abundant entrance to thee into the land of promise, that rest which awaits the children of God: for Christ is not only made to believers wisdom, righteousness, and sanctification, but also *redemption*.

ADDITIONAL SCRIPTURE READING:
John 12:35–36; Ephesians 1:13–14

1700   1900

WEIGHTS & MEASURES

THE figures of the table are calculated on the basis of a shekel equaling 11.5 grams, a cubit equaling 18 inches and an ephah equaling 22 liters. The quart referred to is either a dry quart (slightly smaller than a liter) or a liquid quart (slightly larger than a liter), whichever is applicable. The ton referred to in the footnotes is the American ton of 2,000 pounds.

This table is based upon the best available information, but it is not intended to be mathematically precise; like the measurement equivalents in the footnotes, it merely gives approximate amounts and distances. Weights and measures differed somewhat at various times and places in the ancient world. There is uncertainty particularly about the ephah and the bath; further discoveries may shed more light on these units of capacity.

		BIBLICAL UNIT	APPROXIMATE AMERICAN EQUIVALENT	APPROXIMATE METRIC EQUIVALENT
WEIGHTS	talent	*(60 minas)*	75 pounds	34 kilograms
	mina	*(50 shekels)*	1¼ pounds	0.6 kilogram
	shekel	*(2 bekas)*	²/₅ ounce	11.5 grams
	pim	*(²/₃) shekel)*	¹/₃ ounce	7.6 grams
	beka	*(10 gerahs)*	¹/₅ ounce	5.5 grams
	gerah		¹/₅₀ ounce	0.6 gram
LENGTH	cubit		18 inches	0.5 meter
	span		9 inches	23 centimeters
	handbreadth		3 inches	8 centimeters
CAPACITY				
Dry Measure	cor [homer]	*(10 ephahs)*	6 bushels	220 liters
	lethek	*(5 ephahs)*	3 bushels	110 liters
	ephah	*(10 omers)*	³/₅ bushels	22 liters
	seah	*(¹/₃ ephah)*	7 quarts	7.3 liters
	omer	*(¹/₁₀ ephah)*	2 quarts	2 liters
	cab	*(¹/₁₈ ephah)*	1 quart	1 liter
Liquid Measure	bath	*(1 ephah)*	6 gallons	22 liters
	hin	*(¹/₆ bath)*	4 quarts	4 liters
	log	*(¹/₇₂ bath)*	¹/₃ quart	0.3 liter

ACKNOWLEDGMENTS

SUBJECT GUIDE

AUTHOR BIOGRAPHIES

READING PLANS

ACKNOWLEDGMENTS

Page 2:   Taken from THE EVERLASTING MAN by G. K. Chesterton. Copyright © 1993 by Ignatius Press. Used by permission.

Page 15:   Taken from MY UTMOST FOR HIS HIGHEST by Oswald Chambers. Copyright © 1935 by Dodd Mead & Co., renewed (c) 1963 by the Oswald Chambers Publications Assn. Ltd., and is used by permission of Discovery House Publishers, Box 3566, Grand Rapids MI 49501. All rights reserved.

Page 17:   Taken from MY UTMOST FOR HIS HIGHEST by Oswald Chambers. Copyright © 1935 by Dodd Mead & Co., renewed (c) 1963 by the Oswald Chambers Publications Assn. Ltd., and is used by permission of Discovery House Publishers, Box 3566, Grand Rapids MI 49501. All rights reserved.

Page 26:   Taken from CLASSIC SERMONS ON THE ATTRIBUTES OF GOD by Warren W. Wiersbe, ed. Copyright © 1989 by Kregel Publications, a division of Kregel Inc., Grand Rapids, Michigan. Used by permission.

Page 64:   Taken from CAROLING DUSK by Countee Cullen. Copyright © 1993 by Carol Publishing Group. Used by permission of HarperCollins Publishers, Inc.

Page 75:   Taken from SEARCHLIGHTS FROM THE WORD by G. Campbell Morgan. Copyright © 1977 by Fleming H. Revell, Co., a division of Baker Book House, Grand Rapids, Michigan. Used by permission.

Page 76:   Taken from THE HYMNAL 1982 by Episcopal Church. Copyright © 1985 by The Church Pension Fund. Published by Church Hymnal Corporation. Used by permission.

Page 80:   Reprinted by arrangement with The Heirs to the Estate of Martin Luther King, Jr., c/o Writers House, Inc. as agent for the proprietor. Copyright 1963 by Martin Luther King, Jr., copyright renewed 1991 by Coretta Scott King.

Page 94:   Taken from CHRIST IN THE TABERNACLE by A. B. Simpson. Copyright © 1985 by Christian Publications, Inc., Camp Hill, Pennsylvania. Used by permission.

Page 99:   Taken from CHRIST IN THE TABERNACLE by A. B. Simpson. Copyright © 1985 by Christian Publications, Inc., Camp Hill, Pennsylvania. Used by permission.

Page 202:   Taken from KEYS TO THE DEEPER LIFE by A. W. Tozer. Copyright © 1984 by Zondervan Publishing House/Creation House. Used by permission.

Page 226:   Taken from A TESTAMENT OF DEVOTION. Copyright © 1941 by Harper & Row Publishers, Inc. Renewed 1969 by Lois Lael Kelly Statler. New introduction copyright © 1992 by HarperCollins Publishers, Inc. Reprinted by permission of HarperCollins Publishers, Inc.

Page 268:   Taken from A DIARY OF PRIVATE PRAYER by John Baillie. Copyright © 1977 by Ian Fowler Baillie. Published by Charles Scribner's Sons. Used by permission of Princeton University Press.

Page 270:   Taken from SEARCHLIGHTS FROM THE WORD by G. Campbell Morgan. Copyright © 1977 by Fleming H. Revell, a division of Baker Book House, Grand Rapids, Michigan. Used by permission.

Page 275:   Taken from THE PRAYERS OF PETER MARSHALL by Catherine Marshall, ed. Copyright © 1982 by Catherine Marshall. Published by Chosen Books, a division of Baker Book House, Grand Rapids, Michigan. Used by permission.

Page 302:   Taken from MY UTMOST FOR HIS HIGHEST by Oswald Chambers. Copyright © 1935 by Dodd Mead & Co., renewed (c) 1963 by the Oswald Chambers Publications Assn. Ltd., and is used by permission of Discovery House Publishers, Box 3566, Grand Rapids MI 49501. All rights reserved.

Page 310:   Taken from GREAT DEVOTIONAL CLASSICS by Douglas V. Steere, arr. and ed. Copyright © 1961 by Upper Room Books. Used by permission of Dutton, an imprint of Penguin USA.

1514 ACKNOWLEDGMENTS

Page 780: Taken from ABUNDANT LIVING by E. Stanley Jones. Copyright © 1942 by Whitmore & Stone. Published by Abingdon Press. Used by permission.

Page 798: Taken from MY UTMOST FOR HIS HIGHEST by Oswald Chambers. Copyright © 1935 by Dodd Mead & Co., renewed (c) 1963 by the Oswald Chambers Publications Assn. Ltd., and is used by permission of Discovery House Publishers, Box 3566, Grand Rapids MI 49501. All rights reserved.

Page 894: Taken from A DIARY OF PRIVATE PRAYER by John Baillie. Copyright © 1977 by Ian Fowler Baillie. Published by Charles Scribner's Sons. Used by permission.

Page 947: Taken from SEARCHLIGHTS FROM THE WORD by G. Campbell Morgan. Copyright © 1977 by Fleming H. Revell, a division of Baker Book House, Grand Rapids, Michigan. Used by permission.

Page 989: Taken from THEY WALKED WITH GOD by James S. Bell, Jr., comp. Copyright © 1993 by The Moody Bible Institute of Chicago. Published by Moody Press. Used by permission.

Page 1017: Taken from TRUE SPIRITUALITY by Francis Schaeffer. Copyright © 1979 by Tyndale House Publishers, Wheaton, Illinois. Used by permission.

Page 1019: Taken from CLASSIC SERMONS ON THE ATTRIBUTES OF GOD by Warren W. Wiersbe, ed. Copyright © 1989 by Kregel Publications, a division of Kregel, Inc., Grand Rapids, Michigan. Used by permission.

Page 1024: Taken from MERE CHRISTIANITY by C. S. Lewis. Copyright © 1952 by Macmillan Publishing. Reprinted by permission of HarperCollins Publishers Limited.

Page 1032: Reprinted by arrangement with The Heirs to the Estate of Martin Luther King, Jr., c/o Writers House, Inc. as agent for the proprietor. Copyright 1963 by Martin Luther King, Jr., copyright renewed 1991 by Coretta Scott King.

Page 1035: Reprinted by arrangement with The Heirs to the Estate of Martin Luther King, Jr., c/o Writers House, Inc. as agent for the proprietor. Copyright 1963 by Martin Luther King, Jr., copyright renewed 1991 by Coretta Scott King.

Page 1053: Taken from STREAMS IN THE DESERT, VOL. 2 by Mrs. Charles E. Cowman. Copyright © 1966 by Cowman Publishing Co. Published by Zondervan Publishing House. Used by permission.

Page 1065: Taken from HINDS' FEET ON HIGH PLACES by Hannah Hurnard. Copyright © 1977 by Tyndale House Publishers. Published by Barbour and Company. Used by permission.

Page 1069: Taken from A TREASURY OF CHRISTIAN VERSE by Hugh Martin, ed. Copyright © 1959 by SCM Press, Ltd. (UK). Published by Fortress Press/Augsburg Fortress Publications. Used by permission.

Page 1084: Taken from GREAT HYMNS OF THE FAITH by John W. Peterson, ed. Copyright © 1968 by Zondervan Publishing House/Singspiration Music. Used by permission.

Page 1104: Taken from COST OF DISCIPLESHIP by Dietrich Bonhoeffer. Copyright © 1948 by SCM Press, Ltd. Published by Macmillan Publishing. Used by permission.

Page 1110: Taken from COST OF DISCIPLESHIP by Dietrich Bonhoeffer. Copyright © 1948 by SCM Press, Ltd. Published by Macmillan Publishing. Used by permission.

Page 1114: Taken from MY UTMOST FOR HIS HIGHEST by Oswald Chambers. Copyright © 1935 by Dodd Mead & Co., renewed (c) 1963 by the Oswald Chambers Publications Assn. Ltd., and is used by permission of Discovery House Publishers, Box 3566, Grand Rapids MI 49501. All rights reserved.

Page 1119: Taken from THE NEW OXFORD BOOK OF CHRISTIAN VERSE by Donald Davie, ed. Copyright © 1981 by Donald Davie. Published by Oxford University Press. Used by permission.

Page 1123: Taken from SELECTED HYMNS AND SONG. Copyright © 1992 by Tree of Life Publishers. Used by permission.

Page 1159: Taken from THE PRAYERS OF PETER MARSHALL by Catherine Marshall, ed. Copyright © 1982 by Catherine Marshall. Published by Chosen Books, a division of Baker Book House, Grand Rapids, Michigan. Used by permission.

Page 1185: Reprinted by arrangement with The Heirs to the Estate of Martin Luther King, Jr., c/o Writers House, Inc. as agent for the proprietor. Copyright 1963 by Martin Luther King, Jr., copyright renewed 1991 by Coretta Scott King.

Page 1187: Taken from MERE CHRISTIANITY by C. S. Lewis. Copyright © 1952 by Macmillan Publishing. Reprinted by permission of HarperCollins Publishers Limited.

Page 1195: Taken from THOMAS MERTON READER by Thomas Merton. Copyright © 1974 by Trustees of the Merton Legacy Fund. Published by Bantam Doubleday Dell. Used by permission.

Page 1197: Taken from KEYS TO THE DEEPER LIFE by A. W. Tozer. Copyright © 1957 by Sunday Magazine. Copyright © 1987 by Zondervan Publishing House. Used by permission of Zondervan Publishing House.

Page 1217: Taken from THE GOSPEL OF JOHN by F. F. Bruce. Copyright © 1983 by F. F. Bruce. Published by Eerdmans Publishing Co. Used by permission.

Page 1226: Taken from THE GOSPEL OF JOHN by F. F. Bruce. Copyright © 1983 by F. F Bruce. Published by Eerdmans Publishing Co. Used by permission.

Page 1234: Taken from AN ANTHOLOGY OF DEVOTIONAL LITERATURE by Thomas S. Kepler, ed. Copyright © 1947 by Stone and Pierce. Published by Baker Book House, Grand Rapids, Michigan. Used by permission.

Page 1238: Taken from GREAT DEVOTIONAL CLASSICS by Douglas V. Steere, arr. and ed. Copyright © 1961 by Upper Room Books. Used by permission of Dutton, an imprint of Penguin USA.

Page 1240: Taken from NORMAL CHRISTIAN LIFE by Watchman Nee. Copyright © 1977 by Angus Kinnear. Published by Tyndale House Publishers, Wheaton, Illinois. Used by permission.

Page 1242: Taken from CHAPTERS INTO VERSE by Robert Atwan and Laurance Wieder. Copyright © 1993 by Robert Atwan and Laurance Wieder. Used by permission of Oxford University Press.

Page 1245: Taken from THE GOSPEL OF JOHN by F. F. Bruce. Copyright © 1983 by F. F. Bruce. Published by Eerdmans Publishing Company. Used by permission.

Page 1247: Taken from ABIDE IN CHRIST by Andrew Murray. Copyright © 1995 by Christian Literature Crusade. Used by permission.

Page 1275: Taken from A TESTAMENT OF DEVOTION. Copyright © 1941 by Harper & Row Publishers, Inc. Renewed 1969 by Lois Lael Kelly Statler. New introduction copyright © 1992 by HarperCollins Publishers, Inc. Reprinted by permission of HarperCollins Publishers, Inc.

Page 1287: Taken from TRUE SPIRITUALITY by Francis Schaeffer. Copyright © 1979 by Tyndale House Publishers, Wheaton, Illinois. Used by permission.

Page 1295: Taken from NATURE AND DESTINY OF MAN VOL. 2. by Niebuhr, © 1980. Reprinted by permission of Prentice-Hall, Inc., Upper Saddle River, NJ.

Page 1306: Taken from LETTERS TO YOUNG CHURCHES by J. B. Phillips. Copyright © 1958 by Macmillan Publishing. Used by permission.

Page 1308: Taken from COLLECTED POEMS OF THOMAS MERTON. Copyright © 1946 by New Directions, 1968, 1969, 1977 by the Trustees of the Merton Legacy Trust.

Page 1310: Taken from THE FRANCIS A. SCHAEFFER TRILOGY by Francis A. Schaeffer. Copyright © 1990. Used by permission of Good News Publishers/Crossway Books, Wheaton, Illinois 60187.

Page 1313: Taken from SELECTIONS FROM E. STANLEY JONES by E. Stanley Jones. Copyright © 1972 by Abingdon Press. Used by permission.

Page 1315: Taken from ASLEEP IN JESUS. Copyright © 1929 by Wm. B. Eerdmans Publishing Co. Used by permission of Wm. B. Eerdmans Publishing Co.

Page 1319: Taken from DELIVERANCE TO THE CAPTIVES. Translated by Marguerite Wieser. Copyright © 1978 by Harper & Row. Reprinted by permission of HarperCollins Publishers, Inc.

Page 1321: Reprinted by arrangement with The Heirs to the Estate of Martin Luther King, Jr., c/o Writers House, Inc. as agent for the proprietor. Copyright 1963 by Martin Luther King, Jr., copyright renewed 1991 by Coretta Scott King.

Page 1323: Taken from SCREWTAPE LETTERS by C. S. Lewis. Copyright © 1956 by Macmillan Publishing. Used by permission.

Page 1327: Taken from A DIARY OF READINGS by John Baillie. Copyright © 1955 by John Baillie. Published by Charles Scribner's Sons. Used by permission of Pilgrim Press.

Page 1345: Taken from LETTERS AND PAPERS FROM PRISON by Dietrich Bonhoeffer. Copyright © 1956 by SCM Press, Ltd. Published by Macmillan Publishing. Used by permission.

Page 1356: Taken from SELECTIONS FROM E. STANLEY JONES by E. Stanley Jones. Copyright © 1972 by Abingdon Press. Used by permission.

Page 1367: Taken from A KARL BARTH READER by Geoffrey W. Bromiley, ed. Copyright © 1986 by Eerdmans Publishing Co. Used by permission.

Page 1370: Taken from A KARL BARTH READER by Geoffrey W. Bromiley, ed. Copyright © 1986 by Eerdmans Publishing Co. Used by permission.

Page 1391: Taken from COST OF DISCIPLESHIP by Dietrich Bonhoeffer. Copyright © 1948 by SCM Press, Ltd. Published by Macmillan Publishing. Used by permission.

Page 1407: Taken from KEYS TO THE DEEPER LIFE by A. W. Tozer. Copyright © 1988 by Clarion Classics/Zondervan Publishing House. Used by permission.

Page 1408: Taken from LETTERS AND PAPERS FROM PRISON by Dietrich Bonhoeffer. Copyright © 1956 by SCM Press, Ltd. Published by Macmillan Publishing. Used by permission.

Page 1420: Taken from IN RETROSPECT by F. F. Bruce. Copyright © 1993 by F. F. Bruce. Published by Baker Book House Company. Used by permission.

Page 1444: Taken from SELECTED HYMNS AND SONGS. Copyright © 1992 by Tree of Life Publishers. Used by permission of Benson Music Group.

Page 1451: Taken from A DIARY OF READINGS by John Baillie. Copyright © 1955 by John Baillie. Published by Charles Scribner's Sons. Used by permission of Princeton University Press.

Page 1461: Taken from THE JOURNALS OF KIERKEGAARD. Translated by Alexander Dru. Copyright 1939 by Oxford University Press. Used by permission.

Page 1481: Taken from SCREWTAPE LETTERS by C. S. Lewis. Copyright © 1956 by Macmillan Publishing. Used by permission.

Page 1484: Taken from CLASSIC SERMONS ON THE ATTRIBUTES OF GOD by Warren W. Wiersbe, ed. Copyright © 1989 by Kregel Publications, a division of Kregel, Inc., Grand Rapids, Michigan. Used by permission.

Page 1494: Taken from COLLECTED POEMS OF THOMAS MERTON. Copyright © 1946 by New Directions, 1968, 1969, 1977 by the Trustees of the Merton Legacy Trust.

Every effort has been made to trace the ownership of copyright items in this collection and to obtain permission for their use. The publisher would appreciate notification of, and copyright details for, any instances where further acknowledgment is due, so that adjustments may be made in a future reprint.

SUBJECT GUIDE

AUTHOR BIOGRAPHIES

à Kempis, Thomas (c. 1380–1471). Born in Kempen near Kšln (Cologne), Germany, and educated in the school at Deventer run by the Brethren of the Common Life, he later entered the Augustinian Convent of Mt. Saint Agnes near Zwolle. Ordained as a priest in 1413, he became subprior in 1429. He worked as a copyist and purportedly copied the entire Bible at least four times. All of this German mystic's writings—letters, poems, homilies, etc.—are devotional in nature. He is known best for *The Imitation of Christ*, which is a manual of devotion to help the soul achieve communion with God. *A devotion by this author can be found on page 6.*

African-American Spirituals. *These devotions can be found on pages 73, 193, 865, 1501, 1507.*

Anselm of Canterbury (c. 1033–1109). Born in Aosta, Italy, Anselm was directed towards a political career but chose the life of a Benedictine monk at Bec, Normandy, where he became prior in 1063. After the Norman conquest in 1066, Anselm visited England and reluctantly accepted the appointment as Archbishop of Canterbury in 1089. As a scholar, Anselm reintroduced an Augustinian spirit into theology. He sought to demonstrate the existence and attributes of God by an appeal to reason alone. Anselm insisted, however, that faith must precede reason. "I do not seek to understand in order that I may believe," he said, "But I believe in order to understand." His most famous work is *Cur Deus homo?* *(Why Did God Become Man?)* completed in Italy in 1098. *Devotions by this author can be found on pages 1176, 1413, 1471.*

Aquinas, Thomas (1225–1274). Born in Italy, he studied at the University of Naples and became a Dominican in 1244. He had such a large physique that he was nicknamed "dumb ox." Later, his theological thought and Christian devotion grew so large that he was dubbed "angelic doctor." Maintaining that theology is the "queen of the sciences" and philosophy is its servant, he attempted to synthesize Aristotelian philosophy and Biblical theology. His theology has had a great stabilizing effect on Catholic thought through the centuries. Held in high regard as a philosopher both within and outside a Christian context, the prolific Aquinas left two major works: the *Summa Theologica* and *Summa contra Gentiles*. *Devotions by this author can be found on pages 1168, 1191.*

Arminius, Jacobus (1560–1609). This Dutch Reformation theologian's writings influenced the Wesleyans and Methodists and enraged the Calvinists, especially on the issue of predestination. The University of Leyden in Holland conferred upon Arminius the degree of Doctor of Divinity, and, by way of acceptance, he delivered an oration on the "Priesthood of Christ." Arminius vividly paints an imagined scene in heaven in which Justice and Mercy debate over the best way to deal with a sinful people. Justice demands a payment of a blood sacrifice for sin. Mercy cries out for forgiveness. That both might be satisfied, Wisdom steps in. *A devotion by this author can be found on page 1437.*

Athanasian Creed. This profession of faith, named after the great fourth-century defender of the faith Athanasius (see below), was probably written by Ambrose (339–97) and has been commonly used by liturgical churches of the West. Composed in two parts, the creed is devoted respectively to the doctrines of the Trinity and of the incarnation. Its preface and conclusion both assert that belief in the truths it declares is necessary for salvation. *A devotion from this creed can be found on page 1102.*

Athanasius (c. 295–373). Exiled five times, Athanasius devoted 45 years to the church's successful struggle against Arianism. A native of Alexandria, Egypt, Athanasius became an advisor there to Bishop Alexander, who condemned Arius for his heretical views in 319. Arius advocated that Christ was not eternal but was created by the Father. This view spread rapidly in the Eastern church and threatened to turn the faith into a philosophy mixed with pagan thought. Emperor Constantine called the Council of Nicea to settle this issue (325). Athanasius' main work, *The Three Orations against the Arians* (c. 335), emphasizes that it was necessary for the Word to be as eternal as God if he was to form the divine image in man. *A devotion by this author can be found on page 1334.*

Athenagoras (2d century). It is said that this philosopher and apologist from Athens became a Christian while reading the Scriptures in order to argue against them. In his *Apology* (177), addressed to Roman Emperor Marcus Aurelius and his son Commodus, Athenagoras refuted the allegations that Christians were atheists, that they practiced incestuous immorality, and that they ate human flesh as part of their ritual. He also wrote a pamphlet, *On the Resurrection of the Body.* *A devotion by this author can be found on page 1473.*

Augustine of Hippo (354–430). Born in North Africa as the son of a pagan father and a Christian mother, the brilliant Augustine began a quest for religious truth at age 19. From the dualistic system of Manicheism through Neo-Platonism he searched until his longing was satisfied in the Epistle to the Romans. Augustine was baptized in Milan in 387 and became bishop of Hippo, North Africa, in 395. He is a figure of major importance to the church. In his *Confessions* (c. 397) he gives a Biblical understanding of a person's life under grace. In his *City of God* (c. 413–26) he is the first to give a Biblical view of history, time, and the state. He established the doctrine of the church, gave a clear statement concerning the person of Christ, and made the grace of God the theme of theology in the West. *Devotions by this author can be found on pages 632, 764.*

Baillie, John (1886–1960). The devotional classic *A Diary of Private Prayer* (1936) is this Scottish theologian, educator, and ecumenical leader's enduring gift to the church. He served as a professor of divinity at Edinburgh University, moderator of the Church of Scotland General Assembly, and as a member of the central committee of the first assembly of the World Council of Churches (1948), which he later served as one of its six world presidents (1954). *Devotions by this author can be found on pages 268, 894.*

Barnabas, Epistle of. Although Clement of Alexandria attributed this treatise to the apostle Barnabas, this is quite improbable. Rather its author was most likely a Christian in Alexandria, Egypt, writing between A.D. 70 and 100. *The Epistle of Barnabas* attempts to show Christ in types and figures of the Old Testament. This approach is also used in the New Testament book of Hebrews and is a refreshing way to view the Scriptures. Unfortunately, *Barnabas* is stridently polemic in tone and contains a strong attack on Judaism. The author succeeds in finding in the Old Testament convincing testimonies for the Christian faith. However, because these are presented in the context of an denunciation of Judaism, it is likely that the author was sowing seeds of anti-Semitism. *A devotion from this epistle can be found on page 131.*

Barth, Karl (1886–1968). Born in Basel, this Swiss theologian's writings strengthened many European Christian leaders to stand under persecution. Ordained in the Swiss Reformed Church in 1909, he was driven to reconsider his liberal theological training when, in 1914, his teachers supported German militarism. In 1933, when Adolf Hitler's National Socialism gained power in Germany, Barth and his associate Eduard Thurneysen published a series of pamphlets entitled *Theological Existence Today.* These opposed Hitler's cultural perversion of the Christian faith. He fled Germany for Switzerland in 1935. Barth's theology emphasized God's sovereignty, placing him firmly in the Reformed tradition. Central among his major writings is his multivolume, systematic theology *Church Dogmatics* (1932–67), which runs nearly 7,500 pages. *Devotions by this author can be found on pages 1319, 1327, 1367, 1370.*

Baxter, Richard (1615–1691). A renowned Puritan divine and one of England's most prolific religious authors, Baxter wrote more than 100 books. Due to spending much time at home because of ill-health, he became a largely self-taught scholar and preacher. During one particularly severe illness, he wrote his most famous and influential work, *The Saints' Everlasting Rest.* In this lengthy and profound treatise, Baxter ponders the nature of life after death. *A devotion by this author can be found on page 1347.*

Beecher, Henry Ward (1813–1887). The brother of author Harriet Beecher Stowe, this Congregational clergyman, reformer, and political activist was one of the most popular and widely known preachers and lecturers in America. Beecher served in the pulpit of the Plymouth Congregational Church, Brooklyn, NY, for 40 years. Theologically he departed from Calvinism and radically reinterpreted the Bible in moralistic terms, stressing greatly the love of God. His sermons are published in several volumes entitled *The Plymouth Pulpit. Devotions by this author can be found on pages 851, 1092, 1100.*

Benedict of Nursia (c. 480–c. 547). Around 529 Benedict established a monastery at Monte Cassino, Italy, where he wrote the *Benedictine Rule,* which has been used until the present day as a pattern for monastic life. Through the *Rule* Benedict attempted to create an environment where ordinary men could pursue the service of God and their own spiritual improvement through a balanced life of manual labor, reading, prayer, and worship. *A devotion by this author can be found on page 1384.*

Bernard of Clairvaux (1090–1153). "Jesus the very thought of thee, with sweetness fills my soul." These words, written by this monk, mystic, leader, and spokesman for medieval Christianity, echo in churches even to this day. Bernard challenged all of Christendom, popes and princes, to examine their practice and develop lives of mystical devotion to God. His *Twelve Steps to Humility* describes a union of the divine and human wills that would not confuse the distinction between God and man. *Devotions by this author can be found on pages 712, 1164, 1342, 1441.*

Boehme, Jacob (1575–1624). An influential German Lutheran mystic, Jacob Boehme addressed diverse topics in his writing, including the person of God, the divine nature, the Fall, sin, death, and time and space. A modern reader may wish to refer to his *The Way to Christ.* He stated that his writings were based on divine revelation and spiritual experience. Boheme did not shy away from difficult and nontraditional concepts and language. This caused considerable controversy during his lifetime, yet Boheme's influence extended to William Law, John Milton, Issac Newton, and the Pietist movement. *Devotions by this author can be found on pages 480, 1217.*

Bonar, Horatius (1808–1889). Ira D. Sankey, musical associate of Dwight L. Moody acknowledged a debt of gratitude to this Scottish minister and hymn writer. Bonar published several volumes of hymns, which number about 600 songs. Bonar also wrote tracts and books, including significant contributions in the field of biography. His tract "Believe and Live," printed in more than a million copies, is said to have provided spiritual help to Queen Victoria. Bonar's hymns include "I Heard the Voice of Jesus Say," "Here, O My Lord, I See Thee Face to Face," "Upon a Life I Have Not Lived," and "For the Bread and For the Wine." *Devotions by this author can be found on pages 426, 1013, 1037, 1365.*

Bonaventura (1221–1274). Born in Italy and educated in France Bonaventura was a philosopher, theologian, and mystic whose ideas were akin to those of Augustine and the Protestant Reformers. The author of *The Journey of the Soul unto God*, he was one of the outstanding minds of the Middle Ages. More than a theologian, Bonaventura was also known for his piety and administrative ability. He has been called the second founder of the Franciscan order. *A devotion by this author can be found on page 1254.*

Bonhoeffer, Dietrich (1906–1945). This German theologian and modern Christian martyr refused to accept Hitler's interference in church affairs. So, with Karl Barth and others, Bonhoeffer helped found the Confessing Church in Germany. In 1935 he began an illegal seminary in Finkenwalde and early-on identified himself with the resistance against Nazism. After the arrest of 35,000 Jews on Krystalnacht (November 9, 1938), Bonhoeffer and others conspired to assassinate Hitler. When the plot failed, Bonhoeffer was arrested in April, 1943, and hung two years later. During his two-year prison stay, he wrote his two most widely read books: *The Cost of Discipleship* and *Letters and Papers from Prison. Devotions by this author can be found on pages 1104, 1110, 1345, 1391, 1408.*

Book of Common Prayer. The official prayer book of the Church of England and of Anglican churches in other countries, including the Episcopal church in the U.S., its full title is *The Book of Common Prayer and Administration of the Sacraments and Other Rites and Ceremonies of the Church.* It is the work of Thomas Cranmer and Nicholas Ridley and first appeared in 1549 during the reign of Edward VI. This book was a unified and simplified equivalent of Roman Catholic liturgical books yet in the common vernacular. It passed through suppression, restoration, amendments, and revisions until 1662. The Protestant Episcopal Church was formed in the U.S. in 1783 and a revised book for American use was produced and ratified in 1789. It was further revised in 1892, 1928, and 1979. *Devotions from this book can be found on pages 381, 751, 1381.*

Booth, William (1829–1912). The title of Booth's book *Darkest England and the Way Out* aptly describes the evangelist's view of conditions in his native land and his hope for its improvement. Booth was the founder and first general of the Salvation Army, which has been described as one of the most successful religious revivals of modern times. Converted in 1844, he became a Methodist minister only to resign in 1861. In 1865 he and his wife Catherine began a mission to slum-dwellers in Whitechapel, London, where he held open-air meetings accompanied by a lively band. He preached in taverns and jails, theaters and factories, and eventually built a network of agencies for social relief and rehabilitation. *A devotion by this author can be found on page 117.*

Bradstreet, Anne (1612–1672). "I have not studied in this you read to show my skill, but to declare the truth," wrote Anne Bradstreet to her children, "Not to set forth myself, but the glory of God." The Puritan poet arrived in the new world relatively early (1630) and lived in Massachusetts. Bradstreet's poetry was first published, unbeknownst to her, in London in 1650 (*The Tenth Muse, Lately Sprung Up in America*). Little direct information about America's first woman poet is recorded in historical sources. What is known can be amply found in Bradstreet's own poems, which are still in print through the Harvard University Press. *Devotions by this author can be found on pages 595, 1360, 1395.*

Brother Lawrence (c. 1605–1691). Nicholas Herman spent 18 years in the French army and later was an aide to the treasurer of France. In Paris when he was over 50 years old, he joined the

Carmelite order. There he became known as Brother Lawrence. He never sought to advance beyond the status of lay brother but served the community as a cook for 30 years. His sparse and simple writings were published after his death (1691). A portion of these have been published in English as *The Practice of the Presence of God*. Despite his life of Catholic religious service, the orthodox mystical spirituality of Brother Lawrence has been received more widely in Protestant churches than in the Roman Catholic Church. *Devotions by this author can be found on pages 716, 816.*

Bruce, F. F. (1910–1990). A Scotsman, Bruce was the preeminent evangelical scholar of the post-World War II era. Although a lifelong member of the Plymouth Brethren, he disliked partisan labels. Acclaimed across the Christian spectrum, Dr. Bruce was president of both the Society for Old Testament Studies and its New Testament complement. His works are quite numerous and include *The Books and the Parchments* (1950), *Paul: Apostle of the Soul Set Free* (1977), *History of the Bible in English* (1979), and *The Canon of Scripture* (1988). *Devotions by this author can be found on pages 1220, 1226, 1245, 1420.*

Bunyan, John (1628–1688). This son of a tinker was the author of *The Pilgrim's Progress*, one of the most famous religious allegories in the English language. After experiencing conversion through the influence of his wife, Margaret Bentley, Bunyan became one of the leaders of a congregation of Nonconformists (Puritans) in Bedford, giving sermons as a lay preacher. After the restoration of Charles II (1660), Puritans lost the freedom of worship. Bunyan persisted in his unlicensed preaching and was confined to Bedford county jail (1660–72). There he wrote religious tracts and pamphlets and the first of his major works, the spiritual autobiography *Grace Abounding to the Chief of Sinners* (1666). In 1675 Bunyan was imprisoned again for six months. During that time he probably wrote the major part of his masterpiece, *The Pilgrim's Progress from This World to That Which Is to Come*, a prose allegory of the pilgrimage of a soul in search of salvation. It became the most widely read book in English after the Bible. *Devotions by this author can be found on pages 230, 736, 1079.*

Burns, Robert (1759–1796). A Scottish poet, whose works are known and loved wherever the English language is read. Although the poet was unjustly represented after his death as a drunkard and a reprobate, Burns touched the traditional folk songs of Scotland with his genius, transforming them into great poetry. Thus he immortalized Scotland's countryside and humble farm life. He was a keen and discerning satirist who reserved his sharpest barbs for sham, hypocrisy, and cruelty. For example, "Holy Willie's Prayer" satirized local ecclesiastical squabbles and attacked Calvinist theology, bringing him into conflict with the church. Burns also wrote approximately 100 songs, including such favorites as "Auld Lang Syne," "Comin' Thro' the Rye," and "A Red, Red Rose." *A devotion by this author can be found on page 665.*

Calvin, John (1509–1564). Along with Martin Luther, this French Protestant Reformer is regarded as one of the key figures of the Protestant Reformation. Calvin's *Institutes of the Christian Religion* is considered one of the most influential works in world literature. In Strassburg and Geneva Calvin labored to organize evangelical churches and in so doing developed an adaptable model of church government. This earned him the appellation "organizer of Protestantism." As social institutions deteriorated in the sixteenth century, many new institutions developed under the influence of Calvin's model. From there his "presbyterian" example has extended to influence modern democratic political theory. Calvin expounded Biblical teaching on various issues of his day in light of particular controversies within the church. Theologically, in the Pauline-Augustinian tradition, he tried to navigate a middle course between an exclusive emphasis on either divine providence or human responsibility. *Devotions by this author can be found on pages 298, 522, 548, 596, 649, 1280, 1476.*

Catherine of Siena (1347–1380). Although nearly illiterate, Catherine of Siena was quite influential in the church of her day. Born in Florence she became a Dominican at age 16. She worked for ecclesiastical reform and exercised great authority over her followers through her dictated letters. She is prominent among the church's mystics. *The Dialogue* is her spiritual testament. *Devotions by this author can be found on pages 623, 1076, 1090.*

Chambers, Oswald (1874–1917). "I feel I shall be buried for a time, hidden away in obscurity; then suddenly I shall flame out, do my work and be gone." Oswald Chambers prophecy about his ministry was accurate. Converted through his father after a meeting directed by Charles Spurgeon, Chambers studied art in London and Edinburgh, but eventually responded to God's call to the ministry. After graduation from Dunoon College, Chambers traveled in America and Japan with the Japanese evangelist Juji Nakada. In 1911 he started the Bible Training College in London. But in 1915 he closed the college and sailed for Egypt to minister to the troops at the large YMCA encampment at Zeitoun, Egypt. There, until his death, Chambers ministered to the soldiers. His wife, Gertrude, took notes as he spoke and these have since been published in over 30 volumes, including the best-selling *My Utmost for His Highest* (1935). *Devotions by this author can be found on pages 15, 17, 302, 342, 363, 530, 534, 798, 1114.*

Chesterton, G. K. (1874–1936). Playwright, novelist, poet, literary commentator, pamphleteer, essayist, lectuer, apologist, and editor, the Englishman G. K Chesterton was phenomenally prolific. Of his 100 books, four are considered foremost—*Orthodoxy, The Everlasting Man, St. Thomas Aquinas,* and *St. Francis of Assisi.* With his typical brilliant wit, Chesterton describes *Orthodoxy* as his "elephantine adventures in pursuit of the obvious." Written in 1908, *Orthodoxy* is typical of the humor, crispness, and pace of Chesterton's best work. He is also the author of the well-known Father Brown series of detective stories. *A devotion by this author can be found on page 1242.*

Chrysostom, John (c. 344/354–407). A tax revolt in Antioch gave this gifted and popular preacher the opportunity to deliver his most famous series of sermons, *On the Statues* (387). Chrysostom's sound Biblical exposition combined with practical application calmly brought the city through its crisis. Chrysostom was an eloquent speaker (his name means "golden-mouthed") and his careful methods of Biblical exegesis—a grammatical examination of the exact literal meaning of each verse from the original languages—were revived by the Protestant Reformers. In 397 the patriarch of Constantinople died and Chrysostom was designated his replacement. But the unwilling appointee had to be arrested by imperial troops in order to be consecrated bishop in 398. He then vigorously attacked the vices of the church and even antagonized the empress. Exiled in 403, Chrysostom was soon recalled and resumed his offensive ways. He died in banishment three years later. *A devotion by this author can be found on page 720.*

Clement of Alexandria (c. 155–c. 220). This Athenian pagan became a Christian through his study of philosophy. As a Christian Clement studied with Pantaenus at his school in Alexandria and became the school's head in 190. (Pantaenus's school later became Alexandria's official church catechetical school under Origen.) During these years (190–202) Clement wrote most of his works. His approach to the Scriptures was influenced by the Jewish writer Philo who used Greek philosophy to interpret the Old Testament. Through Clement of Alexandria, Philo's allegorical method of scriptural interpretation became fashionable and is identified with Alexandria to this day. Counted among the church fathers, Clement was significant as the forerunner and teacher of Origen—a chief influence upon the theology of the East. *A devotion by this author can be found on page 1377.*

Clement of Rome (fl. c. 90–100). As bishop of Rome and perhaps the third bishop after Peter, he is assumed to be the presbyter and bishop who wrote a letter on behalf of the church in Rome to the church at Corinth (96). This is probably the earliest Christian writing outside the New Testament and provides important evidence that canonical New Testament books were in circulation among first-century churches. His letter quotes from the Old Testament, uses sayings found in Matthew, Mark, and Luke, and also quotes Romans, 1 Corinthians, and Hebrews. *Devotions by this author can be found on pages 171, 569, 1425, 1428.*

Conybeare, William John (1815–1857). Educated at Cambridge, he was principal of Liverpool Collegiate Institute (1842–48). Later his friend J. S. Howson joined him and they both began to write the two-volume work, *The Life and Epistles of St. Paul* (1852), an extensive treatment that incorporated theological, geographical, and historical studies on Paul and his writings. *A devotion by this author can be found on page 1362.*

Coverdale, Miles (1488–1569). Fleeing persecution, this Englishman translated and published the Bible in the safety of Europe. In 1534 he published a paraphrase of the Psalms and the first complete English Bible in 1535. Under the protection of the king's vice regent Thomas Cromwell, a friend of Coverdale, this Bible was published by English printers. Cromwell then convinced Henry VIII of the need of an official English Bible. Coverdale was commissioned to revise his translation for this purpose in 1538. Called the "Great Bible" (1539), it is Coverdale's greatest achievement. Together with the work of William Tyndale it had significant influence on the translators of the King James Version of the Bible (1611). *A devotion by this author can be found on page 1098.*

Cowman, Lettie B. (1870–1960). Better known as "Mrs. Cowman," she was one of the best-selling devotional writers and compilers of the twentieth century, second only to Oswald Chambers. She drew largely on other sources to compile her devotionals, the most famous of which is her *Streams in the Desert.* *A devotion by this author can be found on page 1053.*

Cowper, William (1731–1800). An English hymn writer and poet, whose mother, Anne Donne, belonged to the same family as John Donne, the seventeenth-century poet and preacher. William Cowper studied law, was called to the Bar in 1754, and nominated to administrative posts in the House of Lords. This turned into an ordeal that left him suicidal and mentally unbalanced. While hospitalized he began to read the Bible and was converted to Christianity. In time Cowper moved to Olney, Buckinghamshire. In 1779 he and his friend John Newton published *Olney Hymns,* "for the use of the plain people." Of the 348 hymns in this collection, Cowper wrote 68, including "O for a Closer Walk with God!," "There is a Fountain Filled with Blood," "Hark, My Soul! It is the Lord," "Jesus! Where'er Thy People Meet," and "God Moves in a Mysterious Way." *Devotions by this author can be found on pages 977, 1129.*

Cranmer, Thomas (1489–1556). This Archbishop of Canterbury and leader of the English Reformation became such by being embroiled in the marital maneuvers of Henry VIII. In an age when the English clergy was celibate, he married a niece of the Lutheran theologian Andreas Osiander (1532). When Cranmer renounced allegiance to the pope, he directed that the pope's name be erased from every prayer book in England. It was Cranmer who pronounced the king of England head of the English church. He also simplified distribution of Miles Coverdale's English translation of the Bible. The fruit of Cranmer's genius as an editor, translator, and composer of prayers and formulae was an English prayer book called *The Book of Common Prayer* (1548), which is used to this day in churches of the Anglican Communion. Political and religious shifts in England caused Cranmer to be condemned as a heretic and he was burned at the stake on March 21, 1556. *A devotion by this author can be found on page 830.*

Crosby, Fanny (1820–1915). Although she was 41 years old when she penned her first hymn, this beloved American hymn writer wrote over 2000 gospel songs. Blinded at the age of six weeks, Crosby attended the New York City Institution for the Blind and later taught there (1847–58). She was devoted to service in New York's Bowery missions and many of her hymns were written for their use. This explains why her songs emphasize conversion, hope, and new life in Christ. Most English language hymnals contain hymns by Fanny Crosby such as "Blessed Assurance, Jesus is Mine," "Rescue the Perishing," "All the Way My Savior Leads Me," "Sweet Hour of Prayer," and "To God Be the Glory." *A devotion by this author can be found on page 1397.*

Cushing, William O. (1823–1902). American writer of Christian hymns. *A devotion by this author can be found on page 1084.*

Cyprian (c. 200–258). The leader of the Christian church in Africa became a Christian late in life (c. 245) In 248 he was chosen bishop of Carthage. During persecution by Decius, Cyprian fled from there. When the persecution ended, the church was divided over the treatment of those who had left the faith under duress and also of those who had been baptized by heretics. Cyprian was inclined toward a middle road of leniency toward apostates. He was adamantly against accepting into the communion those baptized by heretics. Stephen of Rome disagreed with this view and for the first time a bishop of Rome used his reputation as successor to the apostle Peter to claim authority over the other bishops. During the persecution conducted by Emperor Valerian, Cyprian was tried and martyred by beheading. Cyprian's *On the Unity of the Catholic Church,* an exposition of the hierarchical organization of the church written in response to Stephen, seals his position as one of the most authoritative of church fathers. *A devotion by this author can be found on page 1234.*

Didache, The. The title of this ancient manual of instruction for Christian converts comes from a Greek term that means *teaching.* It is a summary of moral principles, instructions on the organization of Christian communities, and rules on worship. Probably written in Syria during the first century A.D., it is also known as the *Teaching of the Twelve Apostles.* Discovered in 1873, this document contains the oldest recorded eucharistic prayers and orders on baptism, fasting, prayer, and the treatment of bishops, deacons, and prophets. Many early Christians regarded *The Didache* as equal to the books of the New Testament. Today it is valuable as a resource about early Christian life and belief. *A devotion from this book can be found on page 1263.*

Diognetus, Epistle to. Both the author and recipient of this letter are unknown. It probably dates from the second or third century A.D. and provides information on three matters of import to the church of that day: (1) reflecting the defensive position the church held in the days before Constantine, *The Epistle to Diognetus* explains why paganism and Judaism cannot be tolerated; (2) describes Christians as the soul of the world; and (3) declares firmly that Christianity is the unique revelation of God and of his love. *A devotion from this letter can be found on page 1374.*

Donne, John (1572–1631). The seventeenth-century religious writers referred to as the metaphysical poets (including Richard Crashaw, George Herbert, and Henry Vaughan) drew inspiration from the religious poetry of John Donne. Thereafter his work was almost forgotten until the ninteenth century. Then, in the 1920s, Ezra Pound and T. S. Eliot cited the influence of this English poet, prose writer, and clergyman. Now Donne is considered the greatest of the metaphysical poets and a peerless writer of love poetry. Donne became a priest of the Anglican church in 1615 and was appointed royal chaplain later that year. He attained eminence as a preacher, delivering sermons regarded as the most brilliant and eloquent of his time. A modern edition of his sermons runs ten volumes. *Devotions by this author can be found on pages 573, 811, 1143, 1171, 1323.*

Dostoyevsky, Fyodor (1821–1881). A promising literary career seemed to await the young atheistic socialist, Fyodor Dostoyevsky. But in 1849 he and other Russian intellectuals were arrested for studying the forbidden subject of French socialist utopianism. Four years of Siberian exile and imprisonment left Dostoyevsky with psychological scars, epilepsy, and the Christian faith. His Siberian experiences are fictionalized in *The House of the Dead* (1861). Dostoyevsky's life was characterized by physical hardship, poverty, and great literary productivity. The novels *Crime and Punishment* (1866), *The Idiot* (1868–69), and *The Possessed* (1871–72) brought him world recognition by 1873. His last novel, *The Brothers Karamazov* was published in 1880. In it, four brothers struggle in their relationships with both a rancorous, degenerate earthly father and a distant, mysterious heavenly Father. Dostoyevsky was concerned with the justice of God and the idea that "if God does not exist, then everything is permitted." *Devotions by this author can be found on pages 593, 1062.*

Douglass, Frederick (1817–1895). This self-educated son of an American slave escaped his owners in 1838. A career as an abolitionist began in 1841 when an impromptu speech to an antislavery convention in Nantucket, Massachusetts, revealed Douglass' verbal eloquence. He referred to himself as "a recent graduate from the institution of slavery with his diploma on his back." Under threat of arrest under the fugitive slave laws, he escaped to England in 1845. There he aroused sympathy for the abolitionists' cause and admirers purchased his freedom. Back in the U.S. by 1847, Douglass was the "station-master and conductor" of the Underground Railroad in Rochester, New York, and established the abolitionist newspaper North Star. He campaigned for Abraham Lincoln in 1860 and helped raise the Massachusetts 54th and 55th regiments of African-American soldiers. The pro-slavery retinue refused to believe that Douglass had been a slave. They called him an impostor invented by abolitionists. In their opinion no slave could be so intelligent and articulate. In reply, Douglass wrote *Narrative of the Life of Frederick Douglass, an American Slave* (1845), later published as the *Life and Times of Frederick Douglass* (1882). *A devotion by this author can be found on page 1430.*

Du Bois, W. E. B. (1868–1963). William Edward Burghardt Du Bois was an American writer and sociologist. He was the first African-American to be awarded a Ph.D. degree from Harvard University (1895). As an advocate for complete racial equality, he helped found the National Association for the Advancement of Colored People (NAACP) in 1910 and served as its director of publications until 1932. After a visit to the Soviet Union, he was convinced that advancement of African-Americans could be achieved through socialism. Du Bois was awarded the Lenin Peace Prize (1959), joined the Communist party (1961) and settled in Ghana where he edited the *Encyclopedia Africana*. His books include *The Philadelphia Negro* (1899), *Black Reconstruction* (1935), and the trilogy, *Black Flame: The Ordeal of Mansart* (1957), *Mansart Builds a School* (1959), and *Worlds of Color* (1961). *A devotion by this author can be found on page 64.*

Edwards, Jonathan (1703–1758). It has been said that "the whole of [Jonathan Edwards] thought might be viewed as one magnificent answer to the question, 'What is true religion?' " At age 13 he entered the Collegiate School of Connecticut (now Yale University) and graduated valedictorian (1720). At age 26 Edwards, a firm believer in Calvinism and the doctrine of predestination, became pastor at Northampton, Massachusetts, where a religious revival occurred in 1734 as a result of Edwards preaching. The British evangelist George Whitefield visited Edwards in 1740 and together they started the revival known as the Great Awakening, which engulfed all New England. At that time Edward's sermon "Sinners in the Hands of an Angry God" caused the congregation of Enfield, Connecticut, to rise weeping and moaning from their seats. This was typical throughout the revival. Edwards was a stern religious disciplinarian. So much so that a council representing ten congregations in the region dismissed Edwards in 1750. After a time serving in Stockbridge, Massachusetts, Edwards accepted the presidency of the College of New Jersey (later Princeton University, 1757). There he died as the result of an inoculation against smallpox (1758). His works include *A Treatise Concerning Religious Affections* (1746), *Dissertation Concerning the End for Which God Created the World* (1754), and *The Great Christian Doctrine of Original Sin Defended* (1758). *Devotions by this author can be found on pages 233, 807.*

Eliot, T. S. (1888–1965). "Those who talk of the Bible as a 'monument of English prose' are merely admiring it as a monument over the grave of Christianity." So wrote the Nobel Laureate Thomas Stearns Eliot, arguably the most influential English writer in the twentieth century. American-born and a graduate of Harvard, Eliot settled in London and became a British citizen. His first notable poem, "The Love Song of J. Alfred Prufrock" (1911), offered the title character as a symbol of an age morally adrift. "The Waste Land" (1922), a landmark of modern poetry, concerns the sterility of modern societies. Eliot's Christian convictions are seen in "The Journey of the Magi" (1930), which traces the poet's spiritual journey; and "Ash Wednesday" (1930), which depicts the need for repentance. "The Four Quartets" (1934–43) is Eliot at the apex of his poetic strength. It deals with the relationship between time and eternity. Notable among his works is *Murder in the Cathedral* (1930), a drama about the martyrdom of Archbishop Thomas ö Becket in Canterbury Cathedral. Eliot received the Nobel Prize for literature in 1948 and the U.S. Presidential Medal of Freedom in 1964. *Devotions by this author can be found on pages 1069, 1119.*

Elliot, Charlotte (1789–1871). This discouraged invalid and minister's daughter was once visited by an evangelist who told her, "You must go to God just as you are." She did this and found the truth in God's loving acceptance. Later she wrote what may be the best known invitation in Christian hymnody—"Just As I Am Without One Plea." Over 100 of her hymns appeared first in The *Invalid's Hymn Book* (1854) and then in *Hymns for Public, Private and Social Worship*, edited by her brother Henry Elliot. *A devotion by this author can be found on page 76.*

Fénelon, François (1651–1715). An archbishop of Cambrai and ardent follower of Madame Jeannne Guyon in the French quietistic movement, Fénelon was condemned by Pope Innocent XII for Fénelon's book *Maxims of the Saints* (1697), a book that supported Guyon's mysticism. Fénelon's subsequent submission to the pope seemed to lack sincerity but was accepted nonetheless. He was known in his diocese as a diligent, benevolent, and autocratic administrator, an effective and influential preacher, and through his writings, deeply devotional. *Devotions by this author can be found on pages 135, 144, 1056.*

Finney, Charles P. (1792–1875). An American lawyer, Finney first began reading the Bible because he noticed how often his law books referred to it. Then he had a powerful conversion experience that redirected the entire course of his life. He eventually became one of the most renowned revivalists of the nineteenth century as well as a lecturer, minister, and educator. Later in his life, he wrote about his extremely mystical conversion experience. *A devotion by this author can be found on page 420.*

Fosdick, Harry Emerson (1878–1969). "I would rather live in a world where my life is surrounded by mystery than live in a world so small that my mind could comprehend it." So spoke this American clergyman in his *Riverside Sermons*. Born in Buffalo, New York, Fosdick was ordained in the Baptist ministry (1903) and was pastor in Montclair, New Jersey (1904–15). He then became professor of practical theology at Union Theological Seminary (1915–46) and pastor of New York City's Riverside Church (1926–46). Fosdick became a national figure partially through preaching on his "National Vespers" radio program. Among his books are *The Second Mile* (1908), *The Manhood of the Master* (1913), and *On Being a Real Person* (1943). *A devotion by this author can be found on page 776.*

Fox, George (1624–1691). At Derby in 1650 this English religious leader and founder of the Society of Friends was convicted on a trumped-up charge of blasphemy by Justice Gervase Bennet. The preacher warned the judge to "tremble at the word of the Lord." Bennet responded contemptuously, calling Fox and his followers "quakers." This, together with their agitated movements during times of revelation, caused them to be known by that name. Born to a Puritan family, Fox was 19 when he left home and traveled in search of religious enlightenment. Eventually he came to rely on the "Inner Light of the Living Christ." Fox stressed the priesthood of all believers and advocated a simple life-style. He objected to political and religious authority and opposed war and slavery. According to Fox, all human actions should be directed by inner contemplation and a social conscience inspired by God. His writings include the *Journal* (1694), which is a comprehensive account of the origins of Quakerism. *Devotions by this author can be found on pages 772, 1265.*

Foxe, John (1516–1587). It has been said that *Foxe's Book of Martyrs* helped to give to England a sense of being an "elect Protestant nation." This Protestant clergyman studied at the University of Oxford and was a fellow of Magdalen College. When the Roman Catholic Mary I ascended to the English throne, Foxe and his wife fled to the Continent. There he began to work on a history of Christian persecutions. After Elizabeth I became queen, Foxe returned and published his history of the Protestant martyrs (1559). In 1570 *Foxe's Book of Martyrs* was placed in every collegiate church in England. *A devotion by this author can be found on page 496.*

Francis of Assisi (1182–1226). As a reckless, materialistic young soldier, Francis began a spiritual struggle. In 1205 he performed charities among lepers and began working on the restoration of dilapidated churches. Francis' father was angered by this change of character and the expenditures for charity. So he legally disinherited his son. Thus Francis began his life as a preacher, mystic, and founder of monastic communities devoted to poverty and service to the poor known as *Franciscans*. However, by 1222 the Franciscan friars, who had formerly renounced wealth to find true freedom to serve God and the needy, were entering politics and the universities. Francis pleaded against this because he felt it would betray the simplicity of the gospel. Yet finding the direction of the order was beyond his control, Francis retired to Assisi in what is now northern Italy. *Devotions by this author can be found on pages 634, 767.*

Gordon, George Noel, Lord Byron (1788–1824). In literature there is something known as the Byronic hero. This is an emotional young man who eschews humankind wandering through life weighed down by a sense of guilt for mysterious past transgressions. The hero of Lord Byron's poem "Childe Harold" was the first example of such a character and is to some extent patterned after Byron himself. During his short life this English poet became one of the most important and versatile writers of the romantic movement. He died in Greece as commander in chief of forces fighting the Turks. *A devotion by this author can be found on page 239.*

Graham, Isabella (1742–1814). This Scottish church worker helped to found many charities for the disenfranchised of society: the poor, orphans and widows, the homeless, and prisoners. Published posthumously under the title *Devotional Exercises* (1819), her journal is a classic of prayer and devotional thought. *A devotion by this author can be found on page 1486.*

Gregory of Nazianzus (330–389). The son of the bishop of Nazianzus in Cappadocia, Gregory studied in the Middle East, Alexandria, and Athens. He wanted to be a hermit, but his father wanted him to be a leader of the church. As it turned out, Gregory did both. His eloquent preaching and scholarly writing earned him the title "the theologian." An active participant in the Council of Constantinople (381), Gregory defended the Nicene council's view of the Trinity, condemned the Apollinarian view that Christ's humanity was passive, and denounced the Emperor Julian for restricting the rights of Christians. *A devotion by this author can be found on page 644.*

Gregory of Nyssa (330–c. 395). This theological prodigy elaborated the doctrines of resurrection, divine grace, and Christology, wrote on ascetic piety and mystic communion with God, and served as bishop of Nyssa. He, his older brother Basil, and Gregory of Nazianzus—the "three Cappadocians"—greatly influenced the fourth-century Eastern church. *A devotion by this author can be found on page 1256.*

Hammarskjöld, Dag (1905–1961). This Swedish economist and diplomat helped to organize the European Recovery Program (1947) and was vice-chairman of the executive committee of the Organization for European Economic Cooperation (1948–49). Hammarskjöld was chief of the Swedish delegation to the United Nations, elected secretary-general of the UN in 1953, and died in this capacity in a plane crash while on a diplomatic mission in Africa. In 1961 he was posthumously awarded the Nobel Peace Prize. Hammarskjöld's deeply religious and ethical philosophy is expressed in his book of meditations, *Markings* (1964). *A devotion by this author can be found on page 598.*

Havergal, Frances R. (1836–79). An English woman, Havergal who wrote many remarkable religious poems and hymns, one of which is "Take My Life and Let It Be." Her most enduring collection is called *Ministry of Song*, published in 1870. *Devotions by this author can be found on pages 778, 929, 1058.*

Henry, Matthew (1662–1714). As a Biblical expositor, his multivolume *Commentary on the Bible* still enjoy popularity, even though they were written almost 300 years ago. Under the Act of Uniformity of 1662, Henry was expelled from the Church of England. He considered a career in law but instead studied for the ministry. Ordained as a Presbyterian, he served two English parishes until his early death. *Devotions by this author can be found on pages 315, 502.*

Herrick, Robert (1591–1674). The chief work of this English Cavalier poet is *Hesperides; or, the Works Both Human and Divine of Robert Herrick, Esq.* (1648). Within this book, though with a separate title page, is a group of religious poems, *His Noble Numbers* (1647). The collection includes more than 1200 short poems with pastoral themes concerning English country life and village customs. Educated at the University of Cambridge, Herrick became vicar of Dean Prior in Devonshire (1629), but the Great Rebellion did not tolerate his Royalist views and his position was taken away (1647). When Charles II was restored to the throne, Herrick returned to Dean Prior (1662) where he lived until his death. *Devotions by this author can be found on pages 1077, 1140.*

Hilary of Poitiers (c. 315–368). Born into a prominent pagan family France, Hilary was educated in philosophy and rhetoric, converted to Christianity about 350 and, although married, was elected bishop of Poitiers three years later. When the embattled Athanasius was banished for his orthodox opposition to Arianism in 355, Hilary rallied the leaders of the churches in Gaul to counter those who supported the Arian position, including the emperor. For this Hilary was exiled to Asia Minor where he wrote *On the Trinity* (356–59), a cogent defense of the divinity of Christ against those who did not hold the Son to be eternal but created by the Father (Arianism). Hilary understood that the Father and the Son have identity of substance yet are two. *A devotion by this author can be found on page 1291.*

Hippolytus (c. 160–236). This presbyter of the Roman church was the most important theologian in third-century Rome where a disagreement over the absolution of sins caused him to withdraw from the church, thus becoming the first anti-pope in history. Because of this schism and the fact that he wrote in Greek instead of Latin, Hippolytus was soon forgotten in the West. He is significant for upholding the Logos doctrine against modalism. This doctrine distinguishes the persons of the Trinity as opposed to the modalistic belief that the three of the Trinity are simply different manifestations of the same person. Hippollytus' *Refutation of All Heresies* is significant in that it makes evident that all Christian heresies find their source in pagan philosophies. *A devotion by this author can be found on page 1328.*

Holden, J. Stuart (1874–1934). This gifted and personable Anglican preacher served as the vicar of St. Paul's Church in London. For nearly 30 years, he also provided leadership for the Keswick movement. *A devotion by this author can be found on page 704.*

Hopkins, Gerard Manley (1844–1889). Born near London and educated at Oxford, this talented poet converted to Roman Catholicism in 1866. Two years later, upon becoming a Jesuit, he burned all his poetry and vowed only to write if instructed to do so by his superiors. But his talent compelled him instead and by 1875 he was writing once again. *A devotion by this author can be found on page 1349.*

Howson, John Saul (1816–1885). A New Testament scholar, he was educated at Cambridge, where he served as a teacher until becoming the headmaster of Liverpool Collegiate Institute. There he joined his friend W. J. Conybeare, with whom he worked together on *The Life and Epistles of St. Paul* (2 vols., 1852), an extensive treatment that incorporated theological, geographical, and historical studies on Paul and his writings. *A devotion by this author can be found on page 1362.*

Hurnard, Hannah (1905–1990). In 1929 she traveled to Palestine on what would be the first of many mission trips to the Middle East. Here she ministered both to Arab as well as Jewish settlements and spent several years seving in missionary hospitals in Jerusalem. From 1949 until her death, Hurnard devoted herself to writing and speaking on behalf of her mission work. Among her well-read inspirational titles are *Watchmen of the Walls, Hinds' Feet on High Places,* and *Thou Shalt Remember. A devotion by this author can be found on page 1065.*

Ignatius of Antioch (d. c. 116). During the reign of the Roman Emperor Trajan, Ignatius was condemned to be devoured by wild beasts. He wrote seven letters while en route under armed guard from Antioch to Rome for execution. Of these, five were addressed to the Christian communities of Ephesus, Magnesia, Tralles, Philadelphia, and Smyrna cities in Asia Minor that had sent representatives to greet him as he passed through. The sixth was addressed to Polycarp, bishop of Smyrna. In the seventh he wrote ahead to the Christian community of Rome to prevent their intervention with the authorities. He wanted nothing to stand in the way of his martyrdom. These letters show the early development of the episcopal structure in the early church. Except for the Old and New Testaments Ignatius was the first to speak of the virgin birth of Jesus. He emphasized that the disciples touched the body of the risen Christ and first described the church as *catholic* in reference to her universal quality. *Devotions by this author can be found on pages 1352, 1488.*

Jones, E. Stanley (1884–1973). Twice nominated for the Nobel Peace Prize, he received seven honorary doctorates and wrote 29 books, the first of which is entitled *The Christ of the Indian Road.* An evangelist to Indian intellectuals, Jones was acquainted with Mahatma Gandhi, Jawaharlal Nehru, and Rabindranath Tagore, and negotiated between President Franklin Roosevelt and Japanese envoys. The preaching of E. Stanley Jones in his numerous worldwide evangelistic crusades was marked by his advocacy of the uniqueness of Christ, the gospel, and church union. *Devotions by this author can be found on pages 555, 780, 1313, 1356.*

Jonson, Ben (1572–1637). An English dramatist, poet and great figure of English literature, his first original play, "Every Man in His Humour," was performed in 1598 by the Lord Chamberlain's Company with William Shakespeare in the cast. Jonson was the acknowledged leader of the men of letters of his time and his creative talents were many and varied. English literature of the Jacobean and Carolinian periods was formed in part by his critical theories which advanced English drama as a form of literature and conscious art through adherence to classical forms and rules. *Devotions by this author can be found on pages 1166, 1411.*

Jowett, John Henry (1864–1923). This Scotsman was a popular preacher and writer who served as minister in Newcastle, Birmingham, and other cities in England. In 1911 he came to the United States to assume the pulpit of the Fifth Avenue Presbyterian Church in New York City, a pastorate that lasted until 1918. He soon became one of the most colorful and popular preachers in New

York at the time. During his American stay he wrote and published a daily devotional book called *My Daily Meditation for the Circling Year. A devotion by this author can be found on page 786.*

Julian of Norwich (c. 1342–c. 1413). One of the greatest English mystics, Julian summarized her doctrine of God in this way: "I saw full surely that ere God made us he loved us; which love was never slacked nor ever shall be. And in this love he hath done all his works and in this love he hath made all things profitable to us and in this love our life is everlasting." Although very little is known with certainty about her, it is thought that Julian lived a solitary life of prayer and mediation near St. Julian's church, Norwich. In 1393 she wrote *The Sixteen Revelations of Divine Love*, the first book to be published by a female author in English. It sets forth the visions of Christ's suffering and the Trinity, which she claimed to have received in the course of two days in 1373. She spent the remainder of her life meditating on these ecstatic visions and her book expresses these insightful meditations with conviction, intelligence, and beauty. *Devotions by this author can be found on pages 1043, 1422.*

Kelly, Thomas R. (1893–1941). His *Testament of Devotion* is one of the most beloved devotional books of our time. Douglas V. Steere, a friend of his, compiled the book from Kelly's articles about the deeper life and published it three months after Kelly's death. In the most sublime terms Kelly describes the fellowship of true believers as those who live "at the Center." *A devotion by this author can be found on page 1275.*

Kierkegaard, Søren (1813–1855). Stressing that Christianity sees the incarnation as an actual historical event, this Danish Christian philosopher asserted that a Christian acquires salvation not through trying to live a moral life but through faith in the Jesus of history. The Danish edition of Kierkegaard's collected works runs 14 volumes, including essays, aphorisms, parables, fictional letters and diaries, and other literary forms. He applied the term *existential* to his philosophy because to him it was the expression of an intensely examined individual life, not the construction of a monolithic system. At the end of his life Kierkegaard attacked the Danish state church, which he claimed had reduced the Christian way of life to being a "nice person" conformed to acceptable manners. For Kierkegaard, being a Christian required a radical, courageous decision to follow Christ. It was this Christianity that he sought to reintroduce into Christendom. *Devotions by this author can be found on pages 1451, 1461.*

King, Martin Luther, Jr. (1929–1968). The eldest son of a prominent Baptist minister, he entered Morehouse College at the age of 15, was ordained a Baptist minister at the age of 17, graduated from Crozer Theological Seminary as class president in 1951, and received his Ph.D. from Boston University. The year the U.S. Supreme Court outlawed all segregated public education, King accepted an appointment as pastor in Montgomery, Alabama. There he organized a successful bus boycott (1955–56) to protest enforced racial segregation in public transportation. This catapulted King into national prominence as a leader for civil rights. In 1963 he led a massive civil rights campaign in Birmingham, Alabama, organized drives for black voter registration, desegregation, and better education and housing throughout the South. He led the historic March on Washington on August 28, 1963. There he delivered his famous "I Have a Dream" speech. In 1964 King was awarded the Nobel Peace Prize. In a speech in Memphis, Tennessee, on April 3, 1968, King said he had "been to the mountain top and seen the Promised Land." The following day he was assassinated. *Devotions by this author can be found on pages 80, 618, 1032, 1035, 1185, 1321.*

Kingsley, Charles (1819–1875). As an English minister, author, and social reformer, he was ferociously outspoken about the social ills of the day; as one man remarked, "Kingsley delivered sermons like a man wrestling with demons." In a message entitled "A Message of the Church to Laboring Men," he delivered a sermon at St. John's Church in London in which he denounced the social system that allowed the wealthy and educated to make money at the expense of the poor. *A devotion by this author can be found on page 729.*

Knox, John (1514–1572). This Scottish religious Reformer was the founder of Presbyterianism in Scotland. Originally a Roman Catholic priest, Knox became attracted to the preachings of the Scottish Protestant preacher George Wishart. When Wishart was executed in 1546, Knox preached in his place. Taken prisoner in 1547, Knox spent a year and a half in French galleys. When Edward VI, king of England interceded, he was released, joined the ministry of the Church of England, and was appointed a royal chaplain (1551). But the Roman Catholic Mary Tudor soon became Mary I, queen of England (1553) and the English Reformation came to a sudden halt. Knox then fled to Geneva where he studied under the French Protestant Reformer John Calvin. Knox returned to Scotland in 1559. When the Scottish parliment abolished papal authority and banned the Mass, it adopted a Reformed Confession of Faith that was largely written by Knox. Political and religious conflict continued for the remainder of his life. John Knox is still a figure who inspires controversy, yet none can deny his powerful influence on the Reformation. *A devotion by this author can be found on page 1455.*

Kuyper, Abraham (1837–1920). Kuyper was a famed Dutch Calvinist theologian and statesman, who, while spending an active life in politics, was able to write warm and compelling works of theology that proved popular among scholars and lay readers alike. *A devotion by this author can be found on page 1315.*

Law, William (1686–1761). When William Law refused to take an oath of allegiance to the Hanoverian English King George I, he was banned permanently from preaching in the Church of England. Through his writing on Christian ethics and mysticism, however, he influenced many, including John Wesley and George Whitefield. Law's best work is the still accessable *A Serious Call to a Devout and Holy Life* (1728). It delineates the Christian ideal of an ascetic life and sets a standard of honoring God in outward affairs. With simplicity and beauty Law asserts that such a life is realized through self-denial, humility, and self-control. Law's other important works are *A Practical Treatise upon Christian Perfection* (1726), *The Spirit of Prayer* (1749), and *The Spirit of Love* (1752). *Devotions by this author can be found on pages 599, 1400.*

Lewis, C. S. (1898–1963). *Surprised by Joy* is a title befitting the autobiography of Clive Staples Lewis. He was a tutor, lecturer, and classics scholar in the insular world of Oxford and Cambridge Universities. Slowly he realized that the Christian faith is the only way to understand the human existence and came to believe at the age of 30. The author of more than 25 Christian works, his books have sold many millions of copies. The best known of these may be *Mere Christianity* (1952) and *The Screwtape Letters* (1942). The latter consists of imaginative letters written from a major devil named Screwtape to his nephew, Wormwood, a lesser devil who is charged with undermining a young man's soul. *Mere Christianity* simply and eloquently portrays the Christian faith without directly quoting Scripture. A perennial favorite of children (and their parents) is the *Chronicles of Narnia* (1950–56). The title of this seven-volume set refers to a land watched over by a marvelous lion named Aslan where a group of children find amazing (and allegorical) adventures. *The Perelandra Trilogy* (1938–45) is an unique fusion of science fiction, fantasy, and allegory involving space flight, the temptation of Eve, and the second coming of Christ. *Devotions by this author can be found on pages 546, 1024, 1187, 1306, 1325, 1481.*

Luther, Martin (1483–1546). Arguably the most crucial figure in modern European history, this German theologian and religious Reformer not only initiated the Protestant Reformation, but he directly influenced politics, economics, education, and language as well. Although descended from peasants, Luther was a promising young law student when he suddenly abandoned his studies and entered an Augustinian monastery (1505). Ordained in 1507, he was assigned as a lecturer in moral philosophy at the University of Wittenburg (1508) where he received his doctorate and the chair of Biblical theology in 1512. Within the next five years Luther came to understand that God's free grace is the unique source of salvation. This seed of truth bore abundant fruit in his fertile heart and on October 31, 1517, he published his *Ninety-five Theses* opposing certain beliefs and practices of the Catholic Church. The Reformation had begun. As it proceeded Luther came into his own as a leader and innovator. While in hiding he translated the New Testament into the common German tongue. In all of its significance, this was also a seminal contribution to the development of a standard German language. In translation the collected works of Martin Luther runs 56 volumes. His most popular book, published in 1529, is the *Small Catechism*. Luther was preacher, professor, theologian, linguist, educator, political theorist, pastor, husband, and more. Although his faults were as visible as his virtues, Martin Luther was the gifted and versatile man of the hour chosen to usher in a truly new era in human history. *Devotions by this author can be found on pages 207, 327, 508, 576, 652, 804, 835, 1086, 1207, 1387.*

MacDonald, George (1824–1905). A Scotsman, MacDonald was among the great writers of his time and knew many of his contemporaries such as Dickens, Emerson, Longfellow, Tennyson, Thackeray, and Whittier. MacDonald's *Phantastes* (1858) is the mythopoetic novel that helped start C. S. Lewis on his journey to God. MacDonald's so-called fairy tales are still enjoyed at many a bedtime. They include *At the Back of the North Wind* (1871), *The Princess and the Goblin* (1872), *The Lost Princess* (1875), and *The Princess and Curdie* (1883). *Devotions by this author can be found on pages 103, 1250, 1358.*

Marshall, Peter (1902–1949). This Scottish emigrant to America served as chaplain to the United States Senate for two years until his untimely death in 1949. Prior to this he had graduated from Columbia Theological Seminary in Decatur, Georgia (1931), served churches in Georgia, and was called to the New York Avenue Presbyterian Church of Washington, D.C., in 1937. Some of Marshall's sermons and prayers were posthumously published under the title *Mr. Jones, Meet the Master* (1949). His widow, Catherine Marshall, made her husband's story known when she published his biography, *A Man Called Peter* (1951). This book was later produced as a popular film. *Devotions by this author can be found on pages 275, 1159.*

Merton, Thomas (1915–1968). Born in France, Merton's father was an English landscape painter and his mother an American Quaker. While teaching English at Columbia University, Merton also worked at a Roman Catholic center in the Harlem area of New York City. In his popular autobiography, *The Seven Storey Mountain* (1941), Merton tells of his dramatic conversion to Roman Catholicism (1938) while in the midst of living a full and worldly life. Two years later he entered the Trappist Monastery of Gethsemani in Kentucky. The autobiographical *The Waters of Siloe* (1949), and *The Sign of Jonas* (1952) are vivid descriptions of his life there. Merton was a poet of personal Christian mysticism. His volumes of verse include *Figures for an Apocalypse* (1947), *The Tears of the Blind Lions* (1949), and *The Strange Islands* (1957). His sensitivity to things contemporary such as the peace movement, the civil rights movement, and liturgical revival were remarkable. Merton died as a result of an accident while attending a Christian-Buddhist conference in Bangkok. *Devotions by this author can be found on pages 748, 1195, 1308, 1494.*

Meyer, F. B. (1847–1929). Born in London into a wealthy family, Frederick Brotherton Meyer was educated at London University and later studied theology at Regent's Park College. He held several successful pastorates and helped introduce churches to the then-unknown D. L. Moody. During much of Meyer's ministry he engaged in social work and temperance work. In 1904 he served as president of the Free Church Council and retired in 1921. For many years he was a popular convention speaker at Northfield, Keswick, and Portstewart. He also published a number of devotional studies on Biblical characters. *Devotions by this author can be found on pages 209, 257, 927, 1010.*

Milton, John (1608–1674). This extraordinary man, the greatest English poet after Shakespeare, spent the central years of his life writing prose tracts on religious, social, educational, and domestic responsibility. During the English Civil War (1640–60), Milton worked in government service. But he also wrote pamphlets on many pertinent topics: He attacked the institution of bishops, argued for divorce on the basis of incompatibility, for freedom of the press, for quality and balanced education, for constitutional rights of the people, for governmental reform, and for abolishment of the professional clergy. At the same time, he wrote some of the most notable sonnets in the English language and began the composition of *Paradise Lost*. He became totally blind in 1652. Milton's fields of study were extensive and he was fluent in, or familiar with, many ancient and modern languages, but the keystone of all his learning was the Bible. *Paradise Lost*, his masterpiece and one of the greatest poems in world literature, was completed in 1667. Milton himself said that with this work he aimed to "justify the ways of God to men." Composed of 12 cantos, the epic depicts the vast cosmic drama and focuses on God's acts in creation and Adam's fall. In it the reader soars to the apogee of John Milton's poetic imagination, intellect, and style. *Devotions by this author can be found on pages 4, 1135.*

Moody, Dwight L. (1837–1899). First a successful shoe salesman, Moody converted from Unitarianism to Congregationalism and became one of America's greatest evangelists. In 1860 he started missionary work in Chicago. There he did evangelistic work for the YMCA and started a Sunday school, which eventually became the Chicago Avenue Church. Later it was named the Moody Memorial Church. Joined by the American singer and hymn composer Ira Sankey (1840–1908), Moody mounted revival meetings. When his meetings met with great success in Britain, Moody and Sankey returned to America as heroes. Thereafter they were enthusiastically received in all quarters of the country. In 1879 Moody opened the Northfield Seminary for Young Women and in 1881 the Mount Hermon School for Boys in his hometown of Northfield, Massachusetts. In order to better train Christian workers, Moody founded a Bible school in Chicago, now known as the Moody Bible Institute (1889). *Devotions by this author can be found on pages 26, 409, 989, 1019, 1484.*

More, Thomas (1478–1535). A religious stance against King Henry VIII cost this English statesman and writer his life. As a young man More wrote comedies and studied Greek and Latin literature. In 1499 he became a Carthusian monk. Giving this up, he entered Parliament (1504). More ran afoul of King Henry VII because of his legislative activities, but upon the ascension of Henry VIII, he was appointed undersheriff of London. In 1518 he became a member of the Privy Council and was knighted in 1521. Two years later he was made speaker of the House of Commons, and became lord chancellor in 1529. When Henry VIII requested a divorce from Catherine of Aragon, More refused because he was not willing to sanction defiance of papal authority. Thus the king had his former friend imprisoned in 1534. After his trial the following year, More contended that Parliament did not have the right to usurp papal authority in favor of the king. Condemned for this stand, More was decapitated on July 7, 1535. *A devotion by this author can be found on page 1153.*

Morgan, G. Campbell (1863–1945). Born in England, this son of a Baptist preacher preached his first sermon at 13. As a famous Bible teacher and evangelist, George Campbell Morgan pastored various churches in England, including Westminster Chapel in London (1904–17; 1933–45). He also served as president of Cheshunt College, Cambridge (1911–14). His published works on Bible sermons and commentaries number approximately 50 books. *Devotions by this author can be found on pages 75, 270, 356, 709, 947.*

Mozarabic Sacramentary (3rd century). From the third through the eleventh century this liturgy was used by believers inhabitating parts of the Iberian peninsula comprising Spain and Portugal. *A devotion from this liturgy can be found on page 890.*

Müller, George (1805–1898). Of German birth, Müller was a naturalized British citizen and converted in 1825. He eventually became a successful preacher at Ebenezer Chapel, a Plymouth Brethren meeting place in Devon. He firmly believed that his material needs could be supplied through faith and prayer alone. Inspired by the work of A. H. Francke in Germany, Müller started an orphanage in Bristol. He was eventually providing for the physical, educational, and spiritual needs of over 2000 boys and girls. Müller's testimony of faith and prayer has caused the establishment of many orphanages and other Christian endeavors throughout the world. *A devotion by this author can be found on page 874.*

Murray, Andrew (1828–1917). Some titles among Andrew Murray's 240 publications are dear to the hearts of Christians who draw on devotional literature to enhance their spiritual life. Among these are *Abide in Christ, Absolute Surrender, With Christ in the School of Prayer,* and *The Spirit of Christ.* Murray was a leader of the South African Dutch Reformed Church with a strong ecumenical spirit. He promoted the call to missions in South Africa and helped to found the University College of the Orange Free State and the Stellenbosch Seminary. His abiding legacy, however, is his body of devotional writings that emphasize the need for a rich, personal devotional life and its outworking in a Christian's life. *Devotions by this author can be found on pages 133, 167, 1247.*

Nee, Watchman (1903–1972). The indigenous church movement formed and fostered by Watchman Nee in pre-World War II China helped lay the foundation for many of the house churches that today maintain Christ's testimony in Communist China. When still a promising student, the eighteen-year-old Nee began to devote himself entirely to Bible study and preaching. This bore fruit in what was to be known to outsiders as the "Little Flock" movement with many assemblies spread across China. Arrested and tried on false charges, Nee was imprisoned in 1952 and died in prison in 1972. Nee's many books continue to enrich the church. They include a book on Romans entitled *The Normal Christian Life,* and a book on Ephesians called *Sit, Walk, Stand. Devotions by this author can be found on pages 406, 1240, 1444.*

Newman, John Henry (1801–1890). Newman graduated from Oxford and was ordained an Anglican in 1824. Thereafter, he became leader of the Oxford movement. This opposed the growth of theological liberalism within the Church of England and advocated the return to the theology and ritual of the period following the Reformation. Newman was well-known and influential when in 1845 he converted to the Roman Catholicism. A year later in Rome he was ordained as a priest. On his return to England he retired to a monastic life outside Oxford. When the British novelist Charles Kingsley charged that Roman Catholicism was indifferent to the truth, In 1864 Newman published his masterpiece, *Apologia Pro Vita Sua,* to explain his spiritual development. This is acknowledged as a classic of both religious autobiography and English prose. Newman was elevated to cardinal in 1879. *Devotions by this author can be found on pages 138, 1446.*

Newton, John (1725–1807). As a young man Newton was forced to join the British navy where he attained the position of midshipman. But he deserted and spent ten years in the African slave trade, becoming the master of a slave ship. During a storm at sea he experienced conversion to Christ. Later, while a tide surveyor at Liverpool (1755–60), Newton met George Whitefield and later John Wesley. Their influence was so profound that he studied for the ministry. After some resistance from the Church of England, Newton became curate at Olney where at age 39 he was ordained (1764). There he became an intimate friend of the poet William Cowper and together they produced the *Olney Hymns* (1779), containing Newton's "Glorious Things of Thee Are Spoken" and "One There Is Above All Others." Newton is most remembered for these and other hymns, including "How Sweet the Name of Jesus Sounds in a Believer's Ear." His "Amazing Grace, How Sweet the Sound" may be one of the most frequently sung and best loved of all English songs. *Devotions by this author can be found on pages 1463, 1477, 1491.*

Niebuhr, Reinhold (1892–1971). Born in Wright City, Missouri, this Protestant theologian was educated at Elmhurst College, Illinois; Eden Theological Seminary, Missouri; and Yale Divinity School. After ordination into the ministry of the Evangelical Synod of North America (1915), he became pastor of the Bethel Evangelical Church of Detroit. This harsh industrial environment forced Neibuhr to examine the interrelationships between religion, individuals, and modern society. A concern with the nature of man as a contact point for religion and society has been called "theological anthropology." Niebuhr's social doctrines profoundly influenced American theological and political thought. In 1928 he joined the faculty of the Union Theological Seminary, New York City, where he taught for 30 years. Reinhold Niebuhr received the U.S. Presidential Medal of Freedom in 1964 and was made a member of the American Academy of Arts and Letters. His works include *Moral Man and Immoral Society* (1932), *Interpretation of Christian Ethics* (1935), and *The Nature and Destiny of Man* (2 vols., 1941, 1943). *A devotion by this author can be found on page 1295.*

Origen (c. 185–c. 254). Jerome called this writer, teacher, and theologian the second teacher of the church after Paul. Born in Alexandria, Egypt, Origen was a student of Clement of Alexandria and taught both Christians and pagans for about 28 years. When in 230 the bishop of Jerusalem and the bishop of Caesarea ordained him a presbyter without consulting Origen's own bishop, Origen was forbidden to teach in his home city and deprived of his priesthood. Thereafter Origen lived in Caesarea where he founded a school of literature, philosophy, and theology. During the persecutions under Emperor Decius (250), Origen was imprisoned and tortured. Although freed, it is thought that he died of complications from his injuries. Origen was an incredibly productive writer of letters, theological treatises, apologetics, exegeses, and textual criticism and is regarded as the father of the allegorical method of scriptural interpretation. *Devotions by this author can be found on pages 58, 588.*

Osler, Sir William (1849–1919). A renowned Canadian physician and teacher, Osler served at Johns Hopkins University and completed his career as a professor of medicine at Oxford University, England. *A devotion by this author can be found on page 1224.*

Owen, John (1616–1683). During the civil war in England, parliament was at war with the king and so had removed the bishops from the Church of England. At this time the English theologian John Owen had the opportunity to practice the Congregational form of church government at Coggeshall, Essex, and became its great advocate. He was chaplain to Oliver Cromwell (1649–51), vice chancellor of Oxford (1652–57), and dean of Christ Church Cathedral (1651–60), and thus prominent in the religious, political, and academic life of the nation. Owen refused invitations to the ministry in Boston (1663) and the presidency of Harvard (1670) and instead rebuked the Congregationalists of New England for their intolerance. *Devotions by this author can be found on pages 185, 1402.*

Parker, Joseph (1830–1902). Born in Hexham, Parker preached with authority and appeal and became one of England's most popular preachers. Largely self-educated, Parker had pulpit gifts that soon moved him into leadership among the Congregationalists. He was a fearless and imaginative preacher who attracted both common people and the aristocracy, and he was particularly a "man's preacher." His *People's Bible* is a collection of the short-hand reports of the sermons and prayers Parker delivered as he preached through the entire Bible in seven years (1884–92). *A devotion by this author can be found on page 821.*

Parkhurst, Charles Henry (1842–1933). Actively involved in mission work, this medical doctor wrote a variety of devotional pieces, some of which appear in the devotional classic, *Streams in the Desert*. *A devotion by this author can be found on page 319.*

Pascal, Blaise (1623–1662). "The last function of reason is to recognize that there are an infinity of things which surpass it," wrote Blaise Pascal in *Pens es* (1670), his posthumous classic of literature and Christian apologetics. This statement came from one of the great minds in Western intellectual history, an eminent mathematician and physicist who was at the same time one of the greatest mystical writers in Christian literature. By the age of 12 Pascal had worked out the equivalent of many of Euclid's geometrical theorems. At 19 he invented the first practical calculating machine. Later he verified the theory of atmospheric pressure and formulated the mathematical theory of probability, a fundamental element of modern theoretical physics. Pascal was an adherent of the Roman Catholic reform movement known as Jansenism. His *Provincial Letters* (1657) is at once a classic in the literature of irony and satire, and a demand for a reemphasis on Augustine's doctrine of grace within the Catholic church. *Devotions by this author can be found on pages 456, 637, 1389.*

Patrick of Ireland (c. 390–c. 461). Apart from what we know from his own writings (*The Confession* and *The Letter to the Christian Subjects of the Tyrant Coroticus*), little is known with certainty about Patrick. Despite various traditions, he probably had no connections with Rome but rather was born in Britain, the son of Calpurnius, a Roman magistrate living in Britain. After Patrick's conversion he managed to escape from bondage as a slave and traveled to Scotland. Shortly after this, however, he returned to Ireland about 432. For the next 30 years he ministered throughout Ireland where he successfully shared the Good News. *A devotion by this author can be found on page 848.*

Penn, William (1644–1718). The United States boasts a rich and varied heritage. One of its jewels is this founder of Pennsylvania (1681), which at the time was the most secure home for religious toleration in the world. While imprisoned in the tower of London for a tract attacking the doctrines of the Church of England, Penn wrote the devotional classic *No Cross, No Crown* (1669). This book vindicated its author while expounding on Christian suffering. In it Penn wrote, "No pain, no palm; no thorns, no throne; no gall, no glory; no cross, no crown." In 1671, imprisoned in Newgate prison, Penn wrote *The Great Cause of Liberty of Conscience*, a defense of the doctrine of toleration. Given the appellation "the Renaissance Quaker," modern historians have called Penn a "compassionate humanitarian, mystic, theologian, and profound political theorist." *A devotion by this author can be found on page 755.*

Polycarp of Smyrna (c. 70–155/160). This apostolic father of the church was bishop at Smyrna (now Izmir, Turkey). Ignatius of Antioch, another of the apostolic fathers, visited Polycarp and addressed an epistle to him just prior to Ignatius's martyrdom (c. 116). According to his pupil Irenaeus, Polycarp was a disciple of John the Evangelist and acquainted with the other disciples of Christ. He had a gift of preaching, a devout character, and a position of great authority among the Asian churches. Polycarp was martyred at Smyrna at the age of 86. *A devotion by this author can be found on page 1271.*

Pynson, Richard (c. 1470–1530). Norman printer Richard Pynson completed the printing of an anonymous treatise on the Ten Commandments called *Dives and Pauper* (1493). Written in the form of a dialogue, this entertaining book details the discussion between a rich man, Dives, and a poor man, Pauper. Pauper is the wise hero of this book; with his homespun humor and wisdom, he catechizes Dives on the true meaning of the Commandments, often using folk tales to illustrate his points. *A devotion by this author can be found on page 1127.*

Rossetti, Christina (1830–1894). This English lyric poet was a devout High Church Anglican. Her devotion to God is seen in the collections *Goblin Market and Other Poems* (1862), considered her finest poetry, and *The Prince's Progress and Other Poems* (1866). Sister to Dante Gabriel Rossetti, the pre-Raphaelite painter and poet, Christina also wrote delightful verse for children, such as the charming lyrics in *Sing-Song: A Nursery Rhyme Book* (1872). *Devotions by this author can be found on pages 675, 723, 759.*

Ryle, J. C. (1816–1900). Born in England and educated at Oxford, John Charles Ryle was the son of a wealthy banker. Converted at the age of 22, he was ordained four years later. He was a prolific writer, a strong leader of the evangelicals, and a capable administrator. At the age of 64, upon the recommendation of Disraeli, he was appointed bishop of Liverpool in 1880. *A devotion by this author can be found on page 996.*

Schaeffer, Francis (1912–1984). Ordained into the Presbyterian ministry, Francis Schaeffer had served various churches in Pennsylvania and St. Louis, Missouri when, in 1948, he was sent to Switzerland by the Presbyterian Board for Foreign Missions. Together with his wife Edith, Schaeffer founded an international study and ministry community in the Swiss Alps (1955). All were welcome at L'Abri (shelter), regardless of culture or beliefs, and thousands visited the Schaeffers to live, study, pray, and discuss secular culture. The work eventually spread to Milan, London, Amsterdam, and Rochester, Minnesota. Schaeffer wrote 23 books, of which he considered three to be essential to the understanding of his thought: *The God Who is There* (1968) shows how modern thought has forsaken the idea of truth and describes the tragic consequences of this abandonment; *Escape From Reason* (1968) explores and explains the sources of the disintegration of modern life; and *He Is There and He Is Not Silent* (1972) contrasts the despair of modern life with the Christian gospel of the knowable God. *Devotions by this author can be found on pages 470, 1017, 1287, 1310.*

Simpson, A. B. (1844–1919). The founder of the Christian and Missionary Alliance had his roots on the shores of Prince Edward Island, Canada. After serving various churches, A. B. Simpson built a congregation in New York City where he emphasized evangelism and pastoral visitation. He wrote some 70 books, numerous poems, and with his daughter Margaret composed a large number of songs featuring the sanctified life and confidence in divine healing. His books include *The Gospel of Healing, Holy Spirit, Christ in the Tabernacle,* and *The Life of Prayer. Devotions by this author can be found on pages 94, 99, 615, 1001, 1123.*

Smart, Christopher (1722–1771). After this English poet published his *Poems on Several Occasions,* including "The Hop Garden" (1752), and satirized the criticism of it in *Hilliad* (1753), his mental illness caused him to be confined to an asylum. There he produced the original and powerful poem, *A Song to David* (1763). Smart's other writings include *Hymns for Amusement of Children* (1775), and *Rejoice in the Lamb,* which was not published until 1939. *A devotion by this author can be found on page 685.*

Smith, Hannah Whitall (1832–1911). Raised in a strict Quaker home, this beloved author was married to Robert Piersall Smith (1851) and converted by the Plymouth Brethren (1858). An experience of faith caused this husband and wife team to embark on speaking tours in America and Europe. An outgrowth of their "Higher Christian Life" conferences in Great Britain were the ongoing Keswick Conventions (1874). Smith wrote the spiritual classic *The Christian's Secret of a Happy Life* (1875). *Devotions by this author can be found on pages 54, 241, 846, 1073, 1467.*

Smith, Robert (c. 1500–1555). Instead of directing recrimination toward his persecutors, this English clergyman and martyr left behind a poetic work entitled "The Exhortation of a Father to His Children." Written for his own children, he penned its gentle advice shortly before his execution. *A devotion by this author can be found on page 1338.*

Southwell, Robert (c. 1561–1595). Born in England and educated on the Continent, Southwell became a Jesuit and in 1586 returned to England where he served as a chaplain to the countess of Arundel. *St. Mary Magdalene's Funeral Tears* is the most famous sermon by this English Jesuit poet and martyr. It is a beautifully poetic exposition of John 20, in which Mary Magdalene comes to the empty tomb of Jesus. In the closing paragraphs, the author exhorts the reader to be more like Mary. Arrested in 1592, he was executed three years later. *A devotion by this author can be found on page 1479.*

Spenser, Edmund (1552–1599). This English poet spanned the divide between the medieval and Elizabethan periods and is most famous for his long allegorical romance, *The Faerie Queene* (1590). The poet, courtier, and explorer Sir Walter Raleigh brought Spenser and his poem to the attention of Queen Elizabeth I and *The Faerie Queene* received an enthusiastic reception. Gloriana, the poem's title character, queen of Fairyland, represents both glory and Queen Elizabeth I. In her honor, 12 knights engage in a series of adventures. Throughout the narrative, Arthur, the perfect knight, also appears. The six completed books (out of a planned twelve) relate the adventures of the knights who represent the qualities of holiness, temperance, chastity, friendship, justice, and courtesy. *Devotions by this author can be found on pages 1258, 1503.*

Spurgeon, Charles Haddon (1834–1892). The great English Baptist preacher and orator had difficulty finding a hall large enough to accommodate the crowds of people who desired to hear him. Although only 20 when he arrived at the New Park Street Chapel, London, he was soon preaching at the Surrey Gardens Music Hall while the Metropolitan Tabernacle was being built (1859–61). Seating 6000, this building provided a pulpit for Spurgeon until his death. A decided Calvinist, he could preach with power and humor while carefully expounding the Scriptures and presenting the gospel. Spurgeon's sermons, published weekly in his lifetime and eventually collected into 50 volumes, are still eminently readable today. *Devotions by this author can be found on pages 12, 105, 165, 253, 294, 345, 375, 585, 742, 876, 1005, 1040, 1148.*

Staley, W. W. (c. 1865–1940). In 1914 an American minister named W. W. Staley, pastor of Suffolk Christian Church in Virginia, delivered an address at a conference for ministers. Called "A Seaside Chautauqua and School of Methods," the conference was held in Virginia Beach. That address and four others by Staley that deal with ministerial life-style were later published in the book *The Minister.* Though meant for ministers, his talk on the subject of his love for books, "The Minister in His Study," is certainly true for many believers. *A devotion by this author can be found on page 1301.*

Taylor, James Hudson (1832–1905). This pioneer missionary and founder of the China Inland Mission is nearly the archetype of the ideal worker for God. At age five he indicated he wanted to be a missionary to China and was called by God to that work in 1849. Taylor prepared by studying medicine, theology, and Biblical languages, and practicing complete dependence on God for his material needs. After a short time in China, Taylor adopted native dress, a scandal to the other missionaries. Soon he had severed ties with his home mission and set off by faith to evangelize the interior—a task never before considered. Hudson Taylor proved to be one of the most profound pioneering spiritual influences in China and whatever Christian vitality exists there today is due in great part to his work. *Devotions by this author can be found on pages 395, 582, 1379, 1418.*

Temple, William (1881–1944). The son of Frederick Temple (archbishop of Canterbury, 1896–1902), William was ordained in 1908 by Randall Davidson (archbishop of Canterbury, 1903–28) and himself served as archbishop at Canterbury (1942–44). Temple's leadership of the Church of England had a threefold emphasis. First, in *Christian Faith and Life* (1931), *Nature, Man, and God* (1934), and *Reading in St. John's Gospel* (1939–40), he attempted to set forth a reasoned exposition of the

Christian faith. Second, he also labored for the union of the churches as president of the Edinburgh Ecumenical Conference (1937 and 1942) and had a hand in initiating the British Council of Churches. Third, Temple's *Christianity and the Social Order* (1942), which sold 139,000 copies during World War II, expressed his passionate concern for national and social righteousness. *Devotions by this author can be found on pages 121, 1137.*

Tennyson, Lord Alfred (1809–1892). The foremost poet of his day and a great representative figure of the Victorian Age, Tennyson produced acknowledged masterpieces in many different poetic genres. The sequence of elegies for his dear deceased friend Henry Hallam, titled *In Memoriam* and published in 1850, is considered to be Tennyson's finest work and portions of it have found their way into the church's hymnody. The year 1850 was a watershed in the poet's life when he was appointed Poet Laureate, successor to William Wordsworth. Tennyson's work is not particularly doctrinal, but his hope for the afterlife is quite evident. For example, the final lines of "Crossing the Bar" read, "I hope to see my pilot face to face/when I have crossed the bar." An oft-quoted poem by Tennyson is "The Charge of the Light Brigade" (1854) and the lyrics to the hymn "Strong Son of God, Immortal Love" (1850) come from his pen. *Devotions by this author can be found on pages 369, 1426.*

Teresa of Avila (1515–1582). The spiritual depth of this Spanish mystic was balanced by her extraordinary organizational skills. While the Reformation was transforming other parts of Europe, her labors to purify the Spanish religious life strengthened the forces that reformed the Spanish Roman Catholic church from within. In 1562 she helped found a convent at Avila under the original Carmelite Rule. Her writings include *The Way of Perfection* (after 1565), instruction for her nuns; *The Interior Castle* (1577), an eloquent description of the contemplative life; and *The Foundations* (1573–82), an account of the origins of the Discalced Carmelites. *Devotions by this author can be found on pages 601, 1340.*

Tolstoy, Leo (1828–1910). This orphaned son of a Russian nobleman left his university studies without a degree, fought in the Crimean War, wrote several acclaimed short novels, and experimented in the progressive education of children, all before he wed the eighteen-year-old Sofya Andreyevna Bers in 1862. While the couple raised their 19 children, Tolstoy successfully managed his considerable estate and wrote his two greatest novels, *War and Peace* (1865–99), considered one of the greatest novels ever written, and *Anna Karenina* (1875–77), which is among the foremost modern psychological novels. The epic *War and Peace* depicts the national catastrophe of the Napoleonic invasion of Russia. Set in the years 1805–15, it tells a vast story of war between the two halves of Europe using 559 characters. It tells of the struggle of human souls from war to peace and of love between men and women, love of country, and above all, Christian love. Late in his life Tolstoy was excommunicated by the Russian Orthodox Church. At that time he said, "I believe that the will of God is most intelligibly expressed in the teachings of the man Jesus." *A devotion by this author can be found on page 1215.*

Tozer, A. W. (1897–1963). A lifelong pastor in the Christian and Missionary Alliance with a rich pulpit ministry, A. W. Tozer was without any formal education beyond grade school. He was intensely devotional, mystical and well-read. He drew from the writings of others, including François Fénelon, Bernard of Clairvaux, Julian of Norwich, as well as Emerson and Shakespeare. Readers still feel the impact of Tozer's ministry through his books in which he encourages his readers to know God personally and experientially. They include *The Pursuit of God* (1948), *The Divine Conquest* (1950), and *The Knowledge of the Holy* (1961). *Devotions by this author can be found on pages 202, 629, 699, 725, 1197, 1407.*

Truth, Sojourner (c. 1797–1883). Born into slavery in Ulster County, New York, Truth (originally named Isabella) was freed when New York State emancipated slaves in 1828. A mystic, she immediately began to preach in the streets of New York City. In 1843 she took the name Sojourner Truth, started preaching along the eastern seaboard, and came into contact with the abolitionist movement. For the next few years she toured the country speaking on its behalf. Then in 1850 she encountered the women's rights movement. President Abraham Lincoln received her in the White House in 1864. Though illiterate, Truth was a charismatic speaker who often drew large crowds to her gatherings that continued until 1875. *A devotion by this author can be found on page 1045.*

Unamuno, Miguel de (1864–1936). This Spanish novelist and philosopher underwent a spiritual crisis while assisting in services at a Greek Orthodox church in Paris in 1924. At the time, he was exiled from Spain by an often tyrannical government that had the support of many Christians. The crisis Unamuno experienced led him to write his book *The Agony of Christianity*, in which he took exception with those who equate various "isms" (nationalism, socialism, capitalism, etc.) with Christianity. *A devotion by this author can be found on page 1459.*

Underhill, Evelyn (1875–1941). Underhill's classic evaluation of spirituality, *Mysticism: A Study in the Nature and Development of Man's Spiritual Consciousness* (1911), examines the church from the first through the nineteenth centuries. An Anglican educated at King's College for Women in London, she soon became noted lecturer on mysticism and religious life and from 1924 led regular retreats. Underhill authored prose and verse works on mystical religion, including *The Mystical Way* (1913), *Life of the Spirit and Life of Today* (1922), and *Worship* (1937), an acclaimed study in liturgical practices in various church traditions. *Devotions by this author can be found on pages 310, 474, 1238.*

Vondel, Joost van den (1587–1679). In 1653 a group of Dutch artists, known as the Guild of St. Luke, held a feast in honor of Dutch dramatist and poet Joost van den Vondel, one of the most renowned writers of the Dutch Renaissance. At that very moment, Vondel's crowning achievement, a poetic drama called *Lucifer*, was in the process of being printed. It appeared the next year and would soon influence another landmark of Christian literature, namely, Milton's *Paradise Lost* (1667). *A devotion by this author can be found on page 1497.*

Watts, Issac (1674–1748). Prior to the eighteenth century, a strong prejudice existed in England against singing hymns that were composed in modern times. But the English theologian and pastor Issac Watts succeeded in overcoming these objections. Educated at an academy for dissenters at Stoke Newington, he eventually became minister of a dissenting church in London (1702) and published *Hymns* in 1707. This collection included "When I Survey the Wondrous Cross," "O God, Our Help in Ages Past," "Joy to the World," "Jesus Shall Reign Where'er the Sun," and other hymns seldom omitted from hymnals to this day. Religious conservatives at the time called them "Watts' whims," but independent congregations sang no other songs for most of the century. Watts' books on theological subjects were well known, as, for example, his *Scripture History* (1732). Yet it is his more than 500 hymns that have made a lasting impact on the devotion and worship of the church. *A devotion by this author can be found on page 1336.*

Wesley, Charles (1707–1788). The spiritual awakening of Charles Wesley preceded that of his brother John by three days (1738) and together they lead the great Methodist revival that revolutionized English society. Charles wrote the hymns that objectified his rich faith in order to provide the church with sound teaching and material for praise and worship. He produced about three hymns per week for 57 years—more than 8000 hymns. Among the most widely known are "Jesus, Lover of My Soul" and "Love Divine, All Love Excelling." Hymns that celebrate important dates on the Christian include "Lo, He Comes" for the Advent season; "Hark! The Herald Angels Sing" for Christmas; "Christ the Lord is Risen Today" is for Easter; and "Hail the Day that Sees Him Rise" for Ascension. *Devotions by this author can be found on pages 532, 609.*

Wesley, John (1703–1791). The fifteenth child of a British clergyman, this theologian, evangelist, and founder of Methodism, did more than any single person of his era to transform English society and change the nature of its religion. Educated at Oxford, Wesley joined a group of students that adhered strictly and methodically to religious precepts and practices. They were derisively called "methodists" by their schoolmates. Disappointed by a failed attempt to be a missionary in Georgia, he returned to England where he experienced the "change which God works in the heart through faith in Christ," which would empower the remainder of his life. That power took him by horseback 250,000 miles on the roads of Great Britain to preach 42,000 sermons and write and publish 233 books. These included educational treatises, translations, histories, Biblical commentaries, an English dictionary, 23 collections of hymns, and a medical handbook, *Primitive Physick*, which went through 32 editions. By his own admission Wesley wanted to reform the nation. This he did through initiating or participating in legal and prison reform, the abolition of slavery, civil rights, and popular education. The last act of his life was the dictation of a letter to William Wilberforce to encourage him in the parliamentary fight over slavery. At John Wesley's death a popular secular magazine eulogized: "Instead of being 'an ornament to literature,' he was a blessing to his fellow creatures; instead of 'the genius of the age,' he was the servant of God!" *Devotions by this author can be found on pages 691, 892, 1453.*

Whitefield, George (1714–1770). The church in America is indebted to this great British evangelist and orator for participating with Jonathan Edwards in inaugurating the revival movement known as the Great Awakening (1739). In fact, Whitefield made seven trips to evangelize the American colonies and died in Newburyport, Massachusetts. Born in Gloucester, England, Whitefield became friends with John and Charles Wesley while a student at Oxford. Due to his unconventional manner of preaching and conducting services, many Church of England pulpits were closed to him. For this reason he preached in whatever venue was available, including open fields. Whitefield attracted vast crowds by his eloquence. People from every rank and station in life were held by the power of his preaching. Benjamin Franklin once estimated that Whitefield's voice could be heard by up to 30,000 people at one time. Because he believed that education was indispensable to a Christian, Whitefield helped found the American institutions that are now Princeton University, the University of Pennsylvania, and Dartmouth. *Devotions by this author can be found on pages 383, 1332, 1404, 1509.*

Woolman, John (1720–1772). One of the first abolitionist documents written in America, *Some Considerations on the Keeping of Negroes*(1754), came from the pen of John Woolman, the American Quaker leader, writer, and social reformer. Born near Mount Holly, New Jersey, self-educated, and deeply pious, Woolman worked as a tailor. He traveled through the colonies spreading the teachings of the Quakers and in time persuaded American Quakers to oppose slaveholding. John Woolman's *Journal* (1774), which gives an account of his spiritual life, greatly influenced abolitionists of the nineteenth century. Considered a classic of American literature, its 1871 edition was edited by the American poet John Greenleaf Whittier. While visiting the Society of Friends in England, Woolman died of smallpox and is buried in Kent. *A devotion by this author can be found on page 967.*

Wordsworth, William (1770–1850). This English poet collaborated with Samuel Taylor Coleridge on a slender book of poems entitled *Lyrical Ballads* (1798). It marked the beginning of the romantic movement in English poetry. The volume includes Wordsworth's memorable "Tintern Abbey" and Coleridge's famous "Rime of the Ancient Mariner." Most of the poems were written by Wordsworth. *Lyrical Ballads* was greeted with hostility by critics because it represented a revolt against the artificial classicism of contemporary English verse. But the theories and style of William Wordsworth created a new tradition in poetry. The greatest and most influential of England's romantic poets was born in Cockermouth, Cumberland, and educated at Cambridge. He developed a keen love of nature as a youth and the lyrical power and grace of his conversational blank verse is infused with an intense religious sense of the human relationship to nature. To Wordsworth, an orthodox member of the Church of England, God was manifest in the harmony of nature and his verse expresses the kinship between nature and the human soul. *A devotion by this author can be found on page 1284.*

Zinzendorf, Nicholaus Ludwig, Count Von (1700–1760). In 1722 this German-born member of Austrian nobility granted refuge on his estate in Bohemia to a group of persecuted Bohemian Brethren from Moravia. The community they formed there, called "Herrnhut," eventually became a refuge for Christians from other lands and religious backgrounds. In 1727 they formed a new denomination known as the Renewed Church of the Unity of the Brethren (known as the Moravian Brethren). Herrnhut missionaries were dispatched to many parts of the world. John Wesley encountered one such group of missionaries in passage to Georgia and was deeply moved by their faith. Zinzendorf himself visited the American colonies (1741–43) and worked among the Native Americans. Count Zinzendorf devoted his life, wealth, and labor to bring Christians of all persuasions together on the common ground of saving faith in Christ. He desired that this would be a visible expression of Christian love to the world. His writings include about 2000 hymns, many sermons, and various polemical treatises. An English volume entitled *Zinzendorf: Nine Public Lectures on Important Subjects in Religion* (1973) by George W. Forell provides a good introduction to Zinzendorf's views. *Devotions by this author can be found on pages 757, 1435.*

READING PLANS

GOD'S Word is his personal message of love to you today. The best way to grow as a Christian and get to know God in a more personal way is to spend time in his Word. Here are three ways for you to read through the Bible.

1. If you are reading the Bible for the first time:
   - Begin by reading the Gospel of Mark or the Gospel of John in the New Testament.
   - After reading one of these gospels, read the book of Acts or the book of Romans.
   - After reading Acts or Romans, pick an Old Testament book like Genesis or perhaps Psalms.

2. If you want to read through the entire Bible in one year:
   - Read three chapters each day, Monday through Saturday, and five chapters on Sunday.

3. If you want to read through the entire Bible in two years:
   - Read two chapters each day, Sunday through Saturday.

The following chart covers every book and chapter of the Bible. To keep track of what you have read, mark off each chapter as you complete it.

GENESIS

☐1 ☐2 ☐3 ☐4 ☐5 ☐6
☐7 ☐8 ☐9 ☐10 ☐11 ☐12
☐13 ☐14 ☐15 ☐16 ☐17 ☐18
☐19 ☐20 ☐21 ☐22 ☐23 ☐24
☐25 ☐26 ☐27 ☐28 ☐29 ☐30
☐31 ☐32 ☐33 ☐34 ☐35 ☐36
☐37 ☐38 ☐39 ☐40 ☐41 ☐42
☐43 ☐44 ☐45 ☐46 ☐47 ☐48
☐49 ☐50

EXODUS

☐1 ☐2 ☐3 ☐4 ☐5 ☐6
☐7 ☐8 ☐9 ☐10 ☐11 ☐12
☐13 ☐14 ☐15 ☐16 ☐17 ☐18
☐19 ☐20 ☐21 ☐22 ☐23 ☐24
☐25 ☐26 ☐27 ☐28 ☐29 ☐30
☐31 ☐32 ☐33 ☐34 ☐35 ☐36
☐37 ☐38 ☐39 ☐40

LEVITICUS

☐1 ☐2 ☐3 ☐4 ☐5 ☐6
☐7 ☐8 ☐9 ☐10 ☐11 ☐12
☐13 ☐14 ☐15 ☐16 ☐17 ☐18
☐19 ☐20 ☐21 ☐22 ☐23 ☐24
☐25 ☐26 ☐27

NUMBERS

☐1 ☐2 ☐3 ☐4 ☐5 ☐6
☐7 ☐8 ☐9 ☐10 ☐11 ☐12
☐13 ☐14 ☐15 ☐16 ☐17 ☐18
☐19 ☐20 ☐21 ☐22 ☐23 ☐24
☐25 ☐26 ☐27 ☐28 ☐29 ☐30
☐31 ☐32 ☐33 ☐34 ☐35 ☐36

DEUTERONOMY

☐1 ☐2 ☐3 ☐4 ☐5 ☐6
☐7 ☐8 ☐9 ☐10 ☐11 ☐12
☐13 ☐14 ☐15 ☐16 ☐17 ☐18
☐19 ☐20 ☐21 ☐22 ☐23 ☐24
☐25 ☐26 ☐27 ☐28 ☐29 ☐30
☐31 ☐32 ☐33 ☐34

JOSHUA

☐1 ☐2 ☐3 ☐4 ☐5 ☐6
☐7 ☐8 ☐9 ☐10 ☐11 ☐12
☐13 ☐14 ☐15 ☐16 ☐17 ☐18

☐19   ☐20   ☐21   ☐22   ☐23   ☐24   ☐31   ☐32   ☐33   ☐34   ☐35   ☐36

JUDGES

☐1   ☐2   ☐3   ☐4   ☐5   ☐6
☐7   ☐8   ☐9   ☐10   ☐11   ☐12
☐13   ☐14   ☐15   ☐16   ☐17   ☐18
☐19   ☐20   ☐21

RUTH

☐1   ☐2   ☐3   ☐4

1 SAMUEL

☐1   ☐2   ☐3   ☐4   ☐5   ☐6
☐7   ☐8   ☐9   ☐10   ☐11   ☐12
☐13   ☐14   ☐15   ☐16   ☐17   ☐18
☐19   ☐20   ☐21   ☐22   ☐23   ☐24
☐25   ☐26   ☐27   ☐28   ☐29   ☐30
☐31

2 SAMUEL

☐1   ☐2   ☐3   ☐4   ☐5   ☐6
☐7   ☐8   ☐9   ☐10   ☐11   ☐12
☐13   ☐14   ☐15   ☐16   ☐17   ☐18
☐19   ☐20   ☐21   ☐22   ☐23   ☐24

1 KINGS

☐1   ☐2   ☐3   ☐4   ☐5   ☐6
☐7   ☐8   ☐9   ☐10   ☐11   ☐12
☐13   ☐14   ☐15   ☐16   ☐17   ☐18
☐19   ☐20   ☐21   ☐22

2 KINGS

☐1   ☐2   ☐3   ☐4   ☐5   ☐6
☐7   ☐8   ☐9   ☐10   ☐11   ☐12
☐13   ☐14   ☐15   ☐16   ☐17   ☐18
☐19   ☐20   ☐21   ☐22   ☐23   ☐24
☐25

1 CHRONICLES

☐1   ☐2   ☐3   ☐4   ☐5   ☐6
☐7   ☐8   ☐9   ☐10   ☐11   ☐12
☐13   ☐14   ☐15   ☐16   ☐17   ☐18
☐19   ☐20   ☐21   ☐22   ☐23   ☐24
☐25   ☐26   ☐27   ☐28   ☐29

2 CHRONICLES

☐1   ☐2   ☐3   ☐4   ☐5   ☐6
☐7   ☐8   ☐9   ☐10   ☐11   ☐12
☐13   ☐14   ☐15   ☐16   ☐17   ☐18
☐19   ☐20   ☐21   ☐22   ☐23   ☐24
☐25   ☐26   ☐27   ☐28   ☐29   ☐30

EZRA

☐1   ☐2   ☐3   ☐4   ☐5   ☐6
☐7   ☐8   ☐9   ☐10

NEHEMIAH

☐1   ☐2   ☐3   ☐4   ☐5   ☐6
☐7   ☐8   ☐9   ☐10   ☐11   ☐12
☐13

ESTHER

☐1   ☐2   ☐3   ☐4   ☐5   ☐6
☐7   ☐8   ☐9   ☐10

JOB

☐1   ☐2   ☐3   ☐4   ☐5   ☐6
☐7   ☐8   ☐9   ☐10   ☐11   ☐12
☐13   ☐14   ☐15   ☐16   ☐17   ☐18
☐19   ☐20   ☐21   ☐22   ☐23   ☐24
☐25   ☐26   ☐27   ☐28   ☐29   ☐30
☐31   ☐32   ☐33   ☐34   ☐35   ☐36
☐37   ☐38   ☐39   ☐40   ☐41   ☐42

PSALMS

☐1   ☐2   ☐3   ☐4   ☐5   ☐6
☐7   ☐8   ☐9   ☐10   ☐11   ☐12
☐13   ☐14   ☐15   ☐16   ☐17   ☐18
☐19   ☐20   ☐21   ☐22   ☐23   ☐24
☐25   ☐26   ☐27   ☐28   ☐29   ☐30
☐31   ☐32   ☐33   ☐34   ☐35   ☐36
☐37   ☐38   ☐39   ☐40   ☐41   ☐42
☐43   ☐44   ☐45   ☐46   ☐47   ☐48
☐49   ☐50   ☐51   ☐52   ☐53   ☐54
☐55   ☐56   ☐57   ☐58   ☐59   ☐60
☐61   ☐62   ☐63   ☐64   ☐65   ☐66
☐67   ☐68   ☐69   ☐70   ☐71   ☐72
☐73   ☐74   ☐75   ☐76   ☐77   ☐78
☐79   ☐80   ☐81   ☐82   ☐83   ☐84
☐85   ☐86   ☐87   ☐88   ☐89   ☐90
☐91   ☐92   ☐93   ☐94   ☐95   ☐96
☐97   ☐98   ☐99   ☐100   ☐101   ☐102
☐103   ☐104   ☐105   ☐106   ☐107   ☐108
☐109   ☐110   ☐111   ☐112   ☐113   ☐114
☐115   ☐116   ☐117   ☐118   ☐119   ☐120
☐121   ☐122   ☐123   ☐124   ☐125   ☐126
☐127   ☐128   ☐129   ☐130   ☐131   ☐132
☐133   ☐134   ☐135   ☐136   ☐137   ☐138
☐139   ☐140   ☐141   ☐142   ☐143   ☐144

☐ 145 ☐ 146 ☐ 147 ☐ 148 ☐ 149 ☐ 150

PROVERBS

☐ 1 ☐ 2 ☐ 3 ☐ 4 ☐ 5 ☐ 6
☐ 7 ☐ 8 ☐ 9 ☐ 10 ☐ 11 ☐ 12
☐ 13 ☐ 14 ☐ 15 ☐ 16 ☐ 17 ☐ 18
☐ 19 ☐ 20 ☐ 21 ☐ 22 ☐ 23 ☐ 24
☐ 25 ☐ 26 ☐ 27 ☐ 28 ☐ 29 ☐ 30
☐ 31

ECCLESIASTES

☐ 1 ☐ 2 ☐ 3 ☐ 4 ☐ 5 ☐ 6
☐ 7 ☐ 8 ☐ 9 ☐ 10 ☐ 11 ☐ 12

SONG OF SONGS

☐ 1 ☐ 2 ☐ 3 ☐ 4 ☐ 5 ☐ 6
☐ 7 ☐ 8

ISAIAH

☐ 1 ☐ 2 ☐ 3 ☐ 4 ☐ 5 ☐ 6
☐ 7 ☐ 8 ☐ 9 ☐ 10 ☐ 11 ☐ 12
☐ 13 ☐ 14 ☐ 15 ☐ 16 ☐ 17 ☐ 18
☐ 19 ☐ 20 ☐ 21 ☐ 22 ☐ 23 ☐ 24
☐ 25 ☐ 26 ☐ 27 ☐ 28 ☐ 29 ☐ 30
☐ 31 ☐ 32 ☐ 33 ☐ 34 ☐ 35 ☐ 36
☐ 37 ☐ 38 ☐ 39 ☐ 40 ☐ 41 ☐ 42
☐ 43 ☐ 44 ☐ 45 ☐ 46 ☐ 47 ☐ 48
☐ 49 ☐ 50 ☐ 51 ☐ 52 ☐ 53 ☐ 54
☐ 55 ☐ 56 ☐ 57 ☐ 58 ☐ 59 ☐ 60
☐ 61 ☐ 62 ☐ 63 ☐ 64 ☐ 65 ☐ 66

JEREMIAH

☐ 1 ☐ 2 ☐ 3 ☐ 4 ☐ 5 ☐ 6
☐ 7 ☐ 8 ☐ 9 ☐ 10 ☐ 11 ☐ 12
☐ 13 ☐ 14 ☐ 15 ☐ 16 ☐ 17 ☐ 18
☐ 19 ☐ 20 ☐ 21 ☐ 22 ☐ 23 ☐ 24
☐ 25 ☐ 26 ☐ 27 ☐ 28 ☐ 29 ☐ 30
☐ 31 ☐ 32 ☐ 33 ☐ 34 ☐ 35 ☐ 36
☐ 37 ☐ 38 ☐ 39 ☐ 40 ☐ 41 ☐ 42
☐ 43 ☐ 44 ☐ 45 ☐ 46 ☐ 47 ☐ 48
☐ 49 ☐ 50 ☐ 51 ☐ 52

LAMENTATIONS

☐ 1 ☐ 2 ☐ 3 ☐ 4 ☐ 5

EZEKIEL

☐ 1 ☐ 2 ☐ 3 ☐ 4 ☐ 5 ☐ 6
☐ 7 ☐ 8 ☐ 9 ☐ 10 ☐ 11 ☐ 12
☐ 13 ☐ 14 ☐ 15 ☐ 16 ☐ 17 ☐ 18
☐ 19 ☐ 20 ☐ 21 ☐ 22 ☐ 23 ☐ 24

☐ 25 ☐ 26 ☐ 27 ☐ 28 ☐ 29 ☐ 30
☐ 31 ☐ 32 ☐ 33 ☐ 34 ☐ 35 ☐ 36
☐ 37 ☐ 38 ☐ 39 ☐ 40 ☐ 41 ☐ 42
☐ 43 ☐ 44 ☐ 45 ☐ 46 ☐ 47 ☐ 48

DANIEL

☐ 1 ☐ 2 ☐ 3 ☐ 4 ☐ 5 ☐ 6
☐ 7 ☐ 8 ☐ 9 ☐ 10 ☐ 11 ☐ 12

HOSEA

☐ 1 ☐ 2 ☐ 3 ☐ 4 ☐ 5 ☐ 6
☐ 7 ☐ 8 ☐ 9 ☐ 10 ☐ 11 ☐ 12
☐ 13 ☐ 14

JOEL

☐ 1 ☐ 2 ☐ 3

AMOS

☐ 1 ☐ 2 ☐ 3 ☐ 4 ☐ 5 ☐ 6
☐ 7 ☐ 8 ☐ 9

OBADIAH

☐ OBADIAH

JONAH

☐ 1 ☐ 2 ☐ 3 ☐ 4

MICAH

☐ 1 ☐ 2 ☐ 3 ☐ 4 ☐ 5 ☐ 6
☐ 7

NAHUM

☐ 1 ☐ 2 ☐ 3

HABAKKUK

☐ 1 ☐ 2 ☐ 3

ZEPHANIAH

☐ 1 ☐ 2 ☐ 3

HAGGAI

☐ 1 ☐ 2

ZECHARIAH

☐ 1 ☐ 2 ☐ 3 ☐ 4 ☐ 5 ☐ 6
☐ 7 ☐ 8 ☐ 9 ☐ 10 ☐ 11 ☐ 12
☐ 13 ☐ 14

MALACHI

☐ 1 ☐ 2 ☐ 3 ☐ 4

MATTHEW

☐ 1 ☐ 2 ☐ 3 ☐ 4 ☐ 5 ☐ 6
☐ 7 ☐ 8 ☐ 9 ☐ 10 ☐ 11 ☐ 12

☐13 ☐14 ☐15 ☐16 ☐17 ☐18
☐19 ☐20 ☐21 ☐22 ☐23 ☐24
☐25 ☐26 ☐27 ☐28

MARK

☐1 ☐2 ☐3 ☐4 ☐5 ☐6
☐7 ☐8 ☐9 ☐10 ☐11 ☐12
☐13 ☐14 ☐15 ☐16

LUKE

☐1 ☐2 ☐3 ☐4 ☐5 ☐6
☐7 ☐8 ☐9 ☐10 ☐11 ☐12
☐13 ☐14 ☐15 ☐16 ☐17 ☐18
☐19 ☐20 ☐21 ☐22 ☐23 ☐24

JOHN

☐1 ☐2 ☐3 ☐4 ☐5 ☐6
☐7 ☐8 ☐9 ☐10 ☐11 ☐12
☐13 ☐14 ☐15 ☐16 ☐17 ☐18
☐19 ☐20 ☐21

ACTS

☐1 ☐2 ☐3 ☐4 ☐5 ☐6
☐7 ☐8 ☐9 ☐10 ☐11 ☐12
☐13 ☐14 ☐15 ☐16 ☐17 ☐18
☐19 ☐20 ☐21 ☐22 ☐23 ☐24
☐25 ☐26 ☐27 ☐28

ROMANS

☐1 ☐2 ☐3 ☐4 ☐5 ☐6
☐7 ☐8 ☐9 ☐10 ☐11 ☐12
☐13 ☐14 ☐15 ☐16

1 CORINTHIANS

☐1 ☐2 ☐3 ☐4 ☐5 ☐6
☐7 ☐8 ☐9 ☐10 ☐11 ☐12
☐13 ☐14 ☐15 ☐16

2 CORINTHIANS

☐1 ☐2 ☐3 ☐4 ☐5 ☐6
☐7 ☐8 ☐9 ☐10 ☐11 ☐12
☐13

GALATIANS

☐1 ☐2 ☐3 ☐4 ☐5 ☐6

EPHESIANS

☐1 ☐2 ☐3 ☐4 ☐5 ☐6

PHILIPPIANS

☐1 ☐2 ☐3 ☐4

COLOSSIANS

☐1 ☐2 ☐3 ☐4

1 THESSALONIANS

☐1 ☐2 ☐3 ☐4 ☐5

2 THESSALONIANS

☐1 ☐2 ☐3

1 TIMOTHY

☐1 ☐2 ☐3 ☐4 ☐5 ☐6

2 TIMOTHY

☐1 ☐2 ☐3 ☐4

TITUS

☐1 ☐2 ☐3

PHILEMON

☐PHILEMON

HEBREWS

☐1 ☐2 ☐3 ☐4 ☐5 ☐6
☐7 ☐8 ☐9 ☐10 ☐11 ☐12
☐13

JAMES

☐1 ☐2 ☐3 ☐4 ☐5

1 PETER

☐1 ☐2 ☐3 ☐4 ☐5

2 PETER

☐1 ☐2 ☐3

1 JOHN

☐1 ☐2 ☐3 ☐4 ☐5

2 JOHN

☐2 JOHN

3 JOHN

☐3 JOHN

JUDE

☐JUDE

REVELATION

☐1 ☐2 ☐3 ☐4 ☐5 ☐6
☐7 ☐8 ☐9 ☐10 ☐11 ☐12
☐13 ☐14 ☐15 ☐16 ☐17 ☐18
☐19 ☐20 ☐21 ☐22

The Classics Devotional Bible

PROJECT MANAGEMENT AND EDITORIAL
BY GARY KNAPP

EDITORIAL ASSISTANCE BY SARAH HUPP
AND DANIEL PARTNER

INTERIOR DESIGN BY SHARON WRIGHT,
BELMONT, MI

INTERIOR TYPESETTING BY MULTOMAH GRAPHICS,
TROUTDALE, OR

INTERIOR PROOFREADNG BY PEACHTREE EDITORIAL
AND PROOFREADING SERVICE,
PEACHTREE CITY, GA

COVER DESIGN BY JAGER ASSOCIATES, INC.

PRINTED BY R.R. DONNELLEY & SONS COMPANY,
CRAWFORDSVILLE, IN